A DICTIONARY OF ROMAN COINS.

A

DICTIONARY OF ROMAN COINS,

REPUBLICAN AND IMPERIAL:

COMMENCED BY THE LATE

SETH WILLIAM STEVENSON, F.S.A.,

MEMBER OF THE NUMISMATIC SOCIETY OF LONDON;

REVISED, IN PART, BY

C. ROACH SMITH, F.S.A.,

MEMBER OF THE NUMISMATIC SOCIETY OF LONDON;

AND COMPLETED BY

FREDERIC W. MADDEN, M.R.A.S.

MEMBER OF THE NUMISMATIC SOCIETY OF LONDON; ASSOCIÉ ÉTRANGER DE LA SOCIÉTÉ
ROYALE DE LA NUMISMATIQUE BELGE; FOREIGN CORRESPONDING MEMBER OF
THE NUMISMATIC AND ANTIQUARIAN SOCIETY OF PHILADELPHIA;
FELLOW OF THE NUMISMATIC AND ARCHÆOLOGICAL
SOCIETY OF MONTREAL.

ILLUSTRATED BY UPWARDS OF SEVEN HUNDRED ENGRAVINGS ON
WOOD, CHIEFLY EXECUTED BY THE LATE

F. W. FAIRHOLT, F.S.A.

LONDON:

B. A. SEABY LTD., GREAT PORTLAND STREET

1964

First Published by George Bell and Sons, 1889

Reprinted by B. A. Seaby Ltd., 1964

Printed by ROBERT STOCKWELL LTD., London, S.E.1.

PREFACE.

—o—

This voluminous work, corresponding in size with Smith's " Dictionaries," was left incomplete, as to the last letters [UV—Z] at the time of Mr. SETH STEVENSON'S death, and its publication has been mainly delayed by the difficulty of finding anyone sufficiently versed in the subject and willing, as well as able, to devote the necessary time to the task. His son, the late Mr. Henry Stevenson, took a deep interest in the completion of the work, and with his assistance the proprietors obtained the valuable co-operation of Mr. F. W. MADDEN, M.R.A.S., formerly (1861-1868) one of the Editors of the " Numismatic Chronicle," and author of " The Handbook of Roman Numismatics " (1861), " Coins of the Jews " (8vo., 1864; 4to., 1881), &c., by whom the work has been brought to a satisfactory conclusion. The woodcuts necessary for this portion of the Dictionary have been effectively executed by Mr. Miller Smith, of Norwich.

Mr. F. W. Madden desires to record his best thanks to Mr. H. A. Grueber, F.S.A., Assistant in the Department of Coins and Medals, British Museum, and to Mr. Bernard Jackson, B.A., for much valuable assistance.

Amongst the Numismatic friends of the author who took a warm interest in this laborious undertaking during his life-time, may be mentioned the late Dr. Lee, F.R.S., F.S.A., President of the Numismatic Society, and the late Mr. J. Y. Akerman, F.S.A., Secretary to the Society of Antiquaries,

Lond.; and of those still surviving, Mr. John Evans, D.C.L., LL.D., F.R.S., F.S.A., now President of the Numismatic Society; and Mr. C. Roach Smith, F.S.A., &c., Temple Place, Strood. The latter, whose practical acquaintance with the Dictionary extended to a revision of the remaining MS., from letter L to letter T, and furthering, so far, the completion and printing of the volume, remarks, in a short memoir of Mr. Stevenson in his recently-published "Retrospections,"

The descriptions are lucid and comprehensive; and the style is easy and attractive. Altogether the Dictionary is just the work wanted, not merely for the young student but also for the more experienced numismatist. To both it is as indispensable as the dictionary of a language is to the most educated, as well as to the schoolboy.

The scope and object of the work itself will be best understood by a perusal of the Original Prospectus written by the Author, and issued at the time when the earlier portions were passing through the Press.

THE PUBLISHERS.

ORIGINAL PROSPECTUS.

———o———

It is admitted by all, who are really conversant with the subject, that no branch of Archæology offers greater intellectual advantages than that which leads to a correct knowledge of Ancient Coins in general, and of the *Moneta Romana* in particular. The last-named department of numismatic research opens, indeed, a field replete with instruction, no less valuable than varied, no less useful than interesting—a field which enables those who enter it, in the proper spirit of inquiry after truth, to share the benefits of that reciprocation, by which History so often throws its explanatory light on the hidden meaning and mysterious import of certain monetal devices and inscriptions—whilst those metallic monuments of antiquity serve, in their turn, to stamp on facts narrated in numerous passages of the old historians, otherwise left in doubt and uncertainty, the strongest and most striking impress of corroboration and support.—To facilitate and encourage the study of Roman coins, as well of the Republic as of the Empire, there already exist some excellent Manuals which may be regarded as the Grammars, and also some very complete Catalogues which equally well constitute the Nomenclatures and descriptive classifications of the science. With the exception, however, of the Spaniard Gusseme's work, and of that wonderful monument of human patience and laborious perseverance, the voluminous Lexicon of the German Rasche, both which professedly take a range through the *res universa* of antique medals, there is no Dictionary that treats of Roman Numismatics—certainly there is not as yet any publication exclusively devoted to them, in that form and in the English language.

A Dictionary, therefore, written in our vernacular tongue, and entirely limited in its aim at affording information, to those products of the Roman Mint, which bear Latin legends, seems still to be a desideratum. And the continued non-appearance of any such literary undertaking, by a more competent hand than his own, has at length induced the Author of this prospectus to do his best towards supplying the deficiency, by venturing, as he does with unaffected diffidence, to submit the result of what has been his leisure hours' occupation for the last ten years, to the indulgent consideration and patronage of the educated public.—In making this attempt, it has been the object of the compiler, if not to "popularise" the study of Roman Coins and Medallions, at least to assist in rendering it sufficiently attractive to the taste, and familiar to the acquaintance, even of the classical scholar. But the chief hope which influenced him to begin, and has incited him to pursue his task, is that by thus offering the gist of authentic observations, scattered over, and as to all general good intents and purposes, buried, in no small heap of Latin, French, Italian, and English tomes, his humble endeavours may prove acceptable to that numerous class of his countrymen, and countrywomen too, who do not come within the category of "learned" persons, but who, nevertheless, possessing intelligent and well-cultivated minds, may yet desire to initiate themselves in the above-named branch of the Medallic Science.

The volume, whose subject matter is briefly set forth in its title, will, when published, be found to contain, in alphabetical order of arrangement—

1. An explanation of the principal types, symbols. and devices, which appear on Coins with Latin legends and inscriptions, minted under the government of Ancient Rome, both consular and imperial, including those struck in the Colonies.

2. Biographical, Chronological, and Monetal References to the Emperors, Empresses, and Cæsars, from Julius (B.C. 44) to Mauricius (A.D. 602).

3. Mythological, Historical, and Geographical Notices, in elucidation of curious and rare obverses and reverses.

The whole has been compiled, with careful attention to the descriptions, and commentaries of the most eminent writers, from the times of Ursinus, Tristan, Vaillant, Patin, Seguin, Morell, Spanheim, Havercamp, of the elder and middle school ; Banduri, Liebe, Pellerin, Beauvais, Froelich, Khell, of a subsequent period ; down to ECKHEL (Facile princeps artis numariæ), Mionnet, Akerman, Hennin, and others, whose works have successively appeared during the last half century—works not of greater elaborateness, nor of profounder erudition, nor evincing more of zealous ardour in the cause of Numismatology than are displayed in the productions of their predecessors ; but whose respective authors, from superior advantages accruing to themselves, through greater experience and in a wider scope of investigation, have been enabled to secure more of that first essential, accuracy ; to exhibit clearer views, together with more judicious discrimination and less fanciful discursiveness, and consequently to impart to their labours a more decided character for practical utility, and for trustworthy reference.

The work will form one volume of about 1,000 pages, printed uniformly with the Dictionaries of "Greek and Roman Antiquities," and of "Greek and Roman Biography and Mythology." The illustrative wood-cuts, exceeding seven hundred in number, will, in every instance where an original specimen is accessible, be engraved either from the coins and medallions themselves, or after casts skilfully made from them in sulphur.

A DICTIONARY

OF

ROMAN COINS.

A, the first letter of the Latin Alphabet, which consists of 21 letters, very often occurs as a single letter on Roman coins. Sometimes it serves as the initial of a City, an Emperor, a Consul, &c. Sometimes it seems to be used as a mint-mark, and to have many other significations.

A. is written in various ways on Roman Consular coins.—See Eckhel, *Doct. num. vet.*, vol. v. p. 73.

A.—*Aulus*, a prenomen. A. VITELL. *Aulus Vitellius.*

A. *Ærarium.* AD. A. D. *Ad ærarium detulisset*: concluding letters of inscription on denarius of Augustus.—Rasche, *Lexicon rei num. vet.*—A. in the exergue denotes the first mint, as ANT. A. coined at Antioch, in the first mint. —Akerman, *Numis. Manual.*

A. A. A. F. F. *Auro, Argento, Aere, Flando, Feriundo.* This alludes to the monetal triumvirs, appointed for the coining and stamping of gold, silver, and brass money of the Romans. It was their office to take care that the public coinage should not be counterfeited, nor its material adulterated, nor its proper weight diminished.—On a consular denarius of Cossutius, one of Julius Cæsar's moneyers, we read, C. COSSVTIVS MARIDIANVS, followed by A.A.A.F.F. in the field. There is also a second brass of Augustus, which bears on its obverse, CAESAR AVGVSTVS TRIBUNI. POTES. (Tribunitiâ potestate); and on the reverse, C. PLOTIVS RVFVS IIIVIR. A.A.A.F.F, In the middle S. C. This

C. Plotius (or Plautius) was one of those trium-

virs of the mint, who, by the invariable inscription of the above characters, appear to have made themselves officially answerable, as it were, for the genuineness of the money, struck by their authority. There is also a second brass, on the obverse legend of which is CAESAR AVGVST. PONT. MAX. *(Pontifex Maximus)* TRIBVNI. POT. with head of Augustus, and on the reverse M. SALVIVS OTHO IIIVIR. A.A.A.F.F. Salvius Otho was another of those moneyers of the Republic, whose name is associated, in like manner, with the issues of gold, silver, and brass, in the early coinage of Augustus.—With regard to the expression *flando, feriundo*, the former word doubtless was intended to designate the process of preparing the globular lumps of metal forming the material for the coin; whilst the latter word shews that they were submitted to the stroke of the hammer, for the purpose of receiving the impress of the die. These were the two principal operations of the ancient mintage. For other specimens of this class of the Consular coinage in silver and brass, *see* PARENS PATRIÆ.—See also *Moneta.*

A. or AN. *Annus.*—See A. N. F. F.

ABBREVIATIONS.—The legends and inscriptions of Roman coins, as well imperial as consular, present many particularities, in the shape of abbreviations, monograms, and isolated letters, open to research, and susceptible of various explanations. The ancients, indeed, both Greeks and Romans, in order to bring their monetal inscriptions within the smallest space, adopted the use of *siglæ*, monogrammatic and conjoined letters. At first these were confined to proper names. Subsequently, they were employed to signify titles of authority and of dignity, and made to stand for certain words and for certain phrases. It is this objectionable custom of employing abbreviations in writing, which renders the explanation of legends, for the most part, so unsatisfactory, and at the same time, gives rise to so many false interpretations.

ABDERA.—A maritime town of Hispania Bœtica, founded according to Strabo, by the Carthaginians. It is now called *Adra*, in

Andalusia, on the shores of the Mediteranean, near the gulph of Almeria.

The coins of this place are Latin imperial, middle brass, and 1st brass. A second brass of

Abdera has the laureated head of Tiberius, and is inscribed TI. CAESAR. DIVI. AVG. F. AVGVSTVS; and on its reverse a tetrastyle temple, of which two of the columns have the forms of fish, between which we read the letters A B D E R A.—The characters inscribed in the pediment of the temple, form, according to competent interpreters, the Phœnician word for the city in question. An article, by the late M. Falbe, in a recent number of the *Numismatic Chronicle*, leaves scarcely a doubt of such being its signification. On this point reference may, with advantage, also be made to the authority of Mr. Akerman, who, in his scientific and accurate work on " Ancient Coins of Cities and Princes," has given a fac simile illustration of this remarkable coin, from the collection of the British Museum, whence the present wood-cut is faithfully copied. Referring to *Athenæus*, lib. vii. c. 17, he observes, that the two singularly formed columns are supposed to represent the tunny fish, which abounded on the shores of the Mediterranean, and were sacred to Neptune, to whom it was the practice of the fishermen to offer one as a propitiation.—*Abdera Bœticæ* seems to have been one of the few colonies established by Tiberius, although it does not, as Vaillant remarks, appear to have been honoured with the rank either of *Colonia* or of *Municipium*. Temples were erected (as Tacitus states, l. i.) after the apotheosis of Augustus, by imperial license, on the petition of the Spaniards, in honour of the deceased Emperor.

ABDICATION *of the Empire.*—This event, in the case of the Emperors Diocletian and of Maximinian Hercules, is marked on their coins.—See the respective legends of *Providentia Deorum. Quies Augg.—Requies Optimor. Merit.*

ABN. *Abnepos.*—A great grandson.

ABVNDANTIA.—Abundance: Plenty.—This allegorical divinity had neither temples nor altars erected to her honour; but she appears on several medals and monuments of the Romans.—On

these, whether represented by herself, or as personifying the liberality of the Emperor or Empress, she figures as a handsome woman, clothed in the stola, holding a cornucopiæ, the mouth of which she inclines towards the ground, and lets the contents fall in seemingly careless profusion.

In his illustration " of Roman medals by the ancient Poets," Addison says, " You see Abundance or Plenty makes the same figure in medals as in Horace.

—————— Tibi *Copia*
Manabit ad plenum benigno
Ruris honorum opulenta *cornu.*"

Spanheim, in his translation of the Cæsars of Julian, ascribes a silver coin, exhibiting ABVNDANTIA AVG. and a woman pouring money out of a horn of plenty, to Alexander Severus. And he goes on to observe, that " it serves to mark, amongst several others, the liberality exercised by that excellent Emperor towards his soldiers and subjects, in his distribution to them of portions of the *Ærarium publicum*, or public treasure.—Neither in Eckhel, nor in Mionnet, however, do we find an *Abundantia* of Alexander Severus; but both these authorities, together with Akerman, describe a similar reverse, on a silver coin of Julia Mamæa, the mother of Alexander, an ambitious woman, to whose avarice and intermeddling disposition he owed that unpopularity with the army which proved fatal to them both.

ABVNDANTIA AVG. (Abundantia Augusti) S. C.—In his equally pleasing and instructive work on the large brass coins of his own choice collection, Capt. W. H. Smyth, R.N., F.R.S., &c. thus describes, and comments on, a finely preserved specimen of the mint of Gordianus Pius, bearing the above legend.—The type presents " a female standing, who, habited in the stola and wearing a diadem, is emptying the Amalthæan horn, from which a shower of money descends. *Abundantia* was a profuse giver of all things, at all times; but *Copia* seems to have been applied to provisions, and *Annona* was restricted to the management of the supply for the current year.—This type of Abundantia illustrates Horace

—————— *Aurea fruges*
Italiam pleno diffudit copia cornu."

ABVNDANTIA AV*Gusti.* S. P. Q. R.—A billon denarius of Gallienus bears this legend, and the type of a recumbent river-god.

Baldini considers these to indicate the abundance of provisions obtained for the city of Rome, after Egypt (alluded to in the personification of the Nile), was rescued from the oppressions of the usurper Æmilianus—unless indeed the Tiber is meant by which the *annona* was conveyed.

ABVNDANTIA TEMPORVM.—A very rare brass medallion of Salonina, the wife of Gallienus, has for the type of its reverse, a woman seated, supporting a cornucopiæ, which she extends towards, and pours out before, five children, a woman on each side standing, one of them holding the *hasta pura.*

The epigraph of *Abundantia Temporum* is

here new to Roman coins. The Empress is represented under the attributes of Abundance, for

some noble act of characteristic munificence ascribed to her, as is seen on another coin bearing the legend ANNONA.—(Eckhel, vii. p. 18.)—The historians of the time, (from A. D. 253 to 268) apparently preferring to record stirring events rather than benevolent actions, offer no tribute to the retiring virtues of Salonina. It has been left for numismatic monuments to rescue from oblivion the modest merits of her, who has been called, and without flattery, "the Cornelia of the Lower Empire." Salonina not only caused distributions of corn to be made to the people; but she also took little children and young girls under her care and protection. And here, on this coin, we may probably recognize the attestation of a redeeming fact, that the Empress's goodness restored temporal abundance, and relieved social destitution, in a degenerate age, under a profligate prince and a disastrous reign.

The legend of ABVNDANTIA AVG., and the type of a woman standing with horn of plenty reversed, are found on gold of Trajanus Decius, on silver of his wife Etruscilla, and on third brass of both the elder and younger Tetricus. On a small brass of the latter, the *prefericulum*, or sacrificial vase, is the accompanying type.

ABURIA : a plebeian gens.—The family surnames, on coins, are *Caius* and *Marius*. The cognomen common to both is GEM., which Pighius, and others following him, read *Geminus*, but, as Eckhel thinks, on no certain authority. The pieces in bronze, ascribed to this family, are parts of the *As*. There are five varieties. Silver common.—The following type is the rarest : GEM. a helmed head; before it X. —*Rev.* C. ABVRI. Mars, with trophy in right, and spear and shield in left hand, stands in a quadriga, at full speed. Underneath, ROMA.— (*Thesaur.* Morell. p. 2, fig. iv.)—No satisfactory interpretation of this type of Mars ; nor of the derivation of the name *Aburius*, has yet been given.—See MARS.

AC. *Acceptæ.*—A. POP. FRVG. AC.

A. C.—*Absolvo. Condemno.*—These letters appear on a coin of the Cassia gens.—See *Tabellæ.*

ACCI, in Hispania Tarraconensis (now *Guadix el Viejo*), a colony founded by Julius Cæsar himself, or by his adopted son Augustus, partly for the veterans of LEGIO VI. *Ferrata,* and partly for those of LEG. VI. *Victrix,* from which twinship of two legions, this colony (says Vaillant) was called *Gemella.* Its coins are limited to the reigns of the three first Emperors, viz., Augustus, Tiberius, and Caligula. —On these, *Acci* is

entitled COL. GEM. ACCI. *Colonia Gemella Accitana;* or in abbreviation c. IVLIA G. A.— A first brass of this colony, bears on one side the head of Augustus ; and on the other, ACCI. C. I. G. L. II., which, with the type of two legionary eagles between two ensigns, shews that it was a military colony.—See Akerman's *Coins of Hispania,* p. 61, from pl. vii. of which work the above cut is copied.

ACILIA gens.—The Acilii had for their surnames *Aviola, Balbus,* and *Glabrio ;* the two first of whom would appear certainly to have been plebeian. But, says the author of Doctrina, with respect to the last name, we find Herodianus, in allusion to the *Glabrio* of his time, recording him as "omnium patriciorum nobilissimum ;" as being one who derived his ancestral origin from Æneas, son of Venus and Anchises. And Ausonius favours the same popular opinion :—

   Stemmate nobilium deductum nomen avorum,
     Glabrio Aquilini, Dardana progenies.
                 [Ecl. vi. 63.]

There are 18 varieties in the coins of this family, Silver common. The copper pieces are the As ; or parts of the As ; and are more or less rare. For the remarkable denarius, having on its obverse SALVTIS, and a female laureated head—on its reverse NV. ACILIVS, IIIVIR. VALETV., and a woman standing, with serpent held in her right hand, her left elbow resting on a small column.—See SALVS and VALETVDO, in Ursinus, *Fam. Rom. Numis.* p. 3.

ACCOLEIA gens.—This is classed among the plebeian families, of which no particulars are mentioned in history. One type only presents itself on the coins of this house, but for which (and, as Dr. Cardwell adds, one ancient incription in Gruter's collection) it would scarcely have been known at all.

P. ACCOLEIVS LARISCOLVS—A female head. *Rev.* Three females standing, their heads terminating in trees.—Silver R.

We have here an adumbration of the fable of Phaeton's sisters changed into *larices,* allusive to the name of Accoleius *Lariscolus,* a monetal triumvir, who caused this medal to be struck. According to the myth, Phaeton wishing to drive the chariot of the Sun, fell a victim to his temerity. His three sisters, inconsolable for his death, were metamorphosed into poplars or larches. Accoleius, in representing this fictitious incident on the medal, refers to the name of *Lariscolus*, which he derived from one of his ancestors, renowned no doubt for his zeal in cultivating the larch tree.—Eckhel, v., 118.

"It appears to me not improbable (says Dr. Cardwell) that Accoleius was of the Colony of Aquileia, which, as we learn from Livy, was founded on the Adriatic in the year B. C. 181, and afterwards became a place of considerable importance. The name of the family implies of itself some probable connection with it; but the supposition is much strengthened by the device which accompanies and elucidates it. The word Lariscolus shews still further the connection of the family, with that neighbourhood and with the shores of the Adriatic. Vitruvius says of the *larix*, that it is unknown, except to those citizens *(municipibus)* who inhabit the banks of the river Po, and the shores of the Adriatic sea. He also states that the wood is not easily ignited; so that we may doubt whether the word, which we commonly translate *larch*, does not really include a species of poplar."—Lecture viii. p. 164.

ACCUSATIVE CASE, rarely used on Roman coins, more frequently expressed on Greek money. We read GALLIENVM AVG. P. R. *(populus Romanus veneratur)*—and MARTEM PROPVGNATOREM, of Gordianus Pius.—*Rasche.*

ACCLAMATIONES, or customary words shouted out by the populace at public games, in the circus at Rome, and in other great cities, to express their aspirations for the success of their favourites in the contest: such as EVTIMI. VINCAS—OLYMPI. NIKA or NICAS—PLACEAS.

—These *formulæ acclamationum* are to be found inscribed on contorniate medals, and other *pseudo-monetæ.*—*Nika* is the Greek word corresponding in signification to *Vincas*. Acclamations of the same kind are exhibited on ancient gems, but of the period of the Lower Empire.—Eckhel, viii. 301.—They were also a species of benedictions, which consisted in wishing to the reigning Emperor, life, health, and victory: such as that which is seen on a coin of Constantine—*Plura natalitia feliciter;* and on that of Constans, *Felicia Decennalia* [see the words]. The respective legends on a large brass of Hadrian, and a denarius of Alexander Severus, may also be placed amongst these acclamations.—See A. N. F. F.; also AETERNITATIBVS.

Referring to a large brass in his own collection, having on the obverse "a laurelled head of HADRIANUS AUGUSTUS, and for legend of reverse *Consul Tertium Pater Patriæ* S. C.," Capt. Smyth says (p. 102), "This is an acclamation medal. The Emperor stands on a tribunal, decorated with rostra, before a temple. He is haranguing the public, and making a welcome announcement; the latter are represented by three togated citizens, who lift their hands in the fulness of admiration and applause." For a type similar to this very rare reverse, engraved from a coin in the British Museum, see COS. III. P. P. S. C. of Hadrian, in this Dictionary.

ACERRA.—The small box for holding perfumes held in the hand of the female figure represented on Roman coins, bearing on the reverse the legend PIETAS AVG. This box is of a cylindrical form on the coins of the earlier Emperors, but, at a lower period of the empire, the Acerra appears to have been of a different shape, as seen on coins of Faustina the Elder, of which an example, in the cabinet of Dr. John Lee, is here given:—

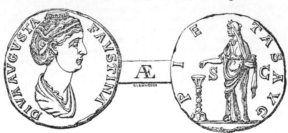

On the gold coins of this Empress the same object is represented of similar form. The celebrated vase discovered in one of the Bartlow tumuli is of copper, exquisitely enamelled, of precisely the same form, and was doubtless used to hold perfumes at the interment, when it was deposited with the remains. Festus (s. v. Acerra) gives us a passage having a two-fold illustration, shewing that it was the common practice to burn perfumes at the Roman burials, and that the term *Acerra* was also applied to the *altar* as well as to the vessel—"Acerra ara quæ ante mortuum poni solebant, in qua odores incendebantur;" and Pollux informs us, that the *altar* also was called

Acerra, This arose doubtless from the circumstance of a light or portable altar being used in such ceremonies exclusively for the burning of perfumes.—The above explanatory notice of the Acerra, its form and sacrificial use, is derived from the information contained in a letter, illustrative of an ancient enamelled vase, and addressed by John Yonge Akerman, Esq., Resident Secretary of the Society of Antiquaries, to Capt. Smyth, Director, through whose joint kindness the compiler of this dictionary has been allowed to use the wood-cut, employed in *Archæologia,* vol. xxxiii.

ACHAIA.—On this part of Greece, and especially at Athens, the most munificent public benefits, of almost every description, were bestowed by the Emperor Hadrian.—Eckhel, vi. p. 487. See RESTITVTORI ACHAIAE.

ACHILLIS, on a contorniate medal.—See PENTESILEA.

ACHILLEUS, an usurper in Egypt, in the reign of Diocletian, defeated and put to death by that Emperor. No certain coins are known of Achilleus.—Akerman, *Descr. Cat.*, vol. ii., 182.

ACISCULUS, an instrument like a hammer, used by workmen in stone quarries, the representation of one appears on a denarius of the Valeria family, allusive to its cognomen of Acisculus.—See *Valeria gens.*

ACROSTOLIUM (and *Acroterium*), a sort of ornament on the prow of an ancient galley.— " Vaillant (*in Coloniis*, ii. p. 245), publishes a coin of Salonina, struck at Berytus, on the reverse of which a female figure is described by him as standing on the *acrostolium.* This writer says, *acrostolia erant extremæ partes navis, quas Latini vocant rostra;*" or as he more clearly, though briefly, defines it in his index to vol. ii., "*Acrostolium, hoc est navis rostrum.*" Another coin of the same colony, struck under Gallienus, according to the engraving in Vaillant (vol. ii., p. 239), exhibits with the legend of COL. IVL. AVG. FEL. BER. the type of a half-naked woman (Astarte), with left foot planted on a ship's prow, holding in her right hand a banner, and in her left (what he denominates) the *acrostolium.* See *Aplustrum,* or *Aplustre;* see also *Berytus Colonia.*

A. C. I. V.—These letters appear on 3rd brass coins of the *Pacuvia,* or *Pacquia* gens, with the accompanying type of a boar lying down. Eckhel, in his numismatic notice of this family, (vol. v.) observes, that he had formerly interpreted the above initials as follows :— *Antonius Colonia Iulia Vienna.* But Sestini, he adds, interprets them *Colonia Veterana Invicta Apros;* and ascribes these coins to a city of that colony, which is placed by Pliny and Ptolemy, in Thrace, and called *Apros.*

ACT.—Actiacus or Actium.

ACT. IMP*erator* [X. or XII.]——Apollo, clothed in the stola, holds the lyre in his left hand and the plectrum in his right. On gold and silver of Augustus, struck v. c. 742, B. c. 12.—The

figure and abbreviated word ACT. bear allusion to the battle of Actium, which gave Augustus the empire of the world, and at which, according to the poetic flatterers of that Prince, Apollo flew to his support. The gratitude which Augustus professed towards Apollo is testified on many coins, and other monuments, as well as by ancient writers. But Suetonius states that, before the great game of *Actium* was played, Augustus had begun to manifest his devotion to the worship of Apollo.— There are those who suppose the figure on this reverse to be one of the Muses, substituted for that of Apollo; but this is a wrong conjecture;

because, on a coin of the *Antestia* family, a similar figure in the stola, is accompanied by the inscription APOLLINI ACTIO.—Eckhel (vi. p. 107) says, *Nota est Citharoedorum, et Apollinis citharoedi stola, sive palla cum ex monumentis, tum scriptoribus* (see coins of Nero inscribed PONT. MAX.) And Tibullus speaking of Apollo citharoedus (the harp-playing Apollo) says,

　Ima videbatur talis illudere palla,
　Namque hæc in nitido corpore vestis erat.

Actius Apollo was worshipped by the Romans after the time of Augustus, in memory of the battle of Actium.—See *Apollo.*

ACTIUM, a city of Epirus, on the coast of Acarnania (now Prevenza) in the Ambracian gulf. In the earliest period not a large town, it was celebrated for a temple of Apollo, also as a safe harbour, and for an adjacent promontory of the same name—afterwards rendered more splendid, on account of the decisive naval victory gained near it by Augustus over Antony.

ADFINIS (Affinis) cousin. By this term of relationship Constantius I. is called on 2nd and 3rd brass medals of consecration and dedication, struck under Maxentius, viz. IMP. MAXENTIVS DIVO CONSTANTIO ADFINI.—See *Affinity and Kindred.*

ADDITION OF A LETTER is observed in the legends of some family coins, as FEELIX, VAALA, VIIRTVS—for Felix, Vala, Virtus.

AD. FRV. EMV. EX. S.C.—*Two men habited in the toga and seated; on either side of them, an ear of corn.*—This denarius of the *Calpurnia* gens informs us, that Piso and Servilius Cœpio were sent as Quæstors, *ad frumentum emundum* EX. S. C. (to purchase corn, in obedience to a decree of the Senate). But in what year the event happened, and when the money was struck, are points apparently unascertained. A similar reverse is exhibited on silver coins of Critonius and of Fannius, ædiles of the people. The bearded head on the obverse, Eckhel (v. p. 159), considers to be in all probability that of Saturn; not only from the scythe placed near it; but also because, according to Plutarch, Saturn was regarded by the Romans as the deity presiding over Agriculture, and the productions of the earth; and in this view the obverse and reverse tally admirably. Saturn, armed with a similar instrument, may be seen on coins of the Memmia and Sentia families; but the most undoubted type of Saturn occurs on coins of the Neria *gens.*

ADI. Adjutrix: a Legion so surnamed, as aiding, or auxiliary to, another.—*See* LEGIO.

ADIAB.—Adiabenicus.

ADIABENI, a people of the east, on whom the Emperor Septimius Severus made successful war (A. D. 195).—*See* ARAB-ADIAB.

ADIUTRIX AVG.—Diana standing, at her feet a bow and quiver. On gold and silver of Victorinus senior, who invoked the aid of that goddess, in setting out on his expedition against Gallienus. Tanini gives a 3rd brass of Carausius, with the same legend, but for type the bust of Victory.

ADLOCUTIO.—Allocution.—The custom of haranguing the soldiers was frequent with the Emperors, as is evidenced by a variety of their coins. This ceremony was performed, either at the moment when an individual obtained the imperial purple, or when the reigning prince adopted some one with a view to the succession; or when he admitted another person into immediate participation of the empire, of which examples are often recorded by historians. Memorials of these military orations, which an emperor delivered before some expeditionary force, at the time of its going out on a campaign, or of its returning after a victory—in which the soldiers were to be reminded of their duty; or rewarded for their good conduct and success, with praises, and, "not *least* in their *dear* love," with donatives also—are preserved on many of the very finest coins of the *Augusti*.

On these reverses, a raised platform or tribune, more or less lofty, called by the Romans *suggestum*, is exhibited, on which the Emperor, habited either in the *toga*, or the *paludamentum*, is seen standing, with his right hand elevated, as if appealing to the sentiments of the troops, or beckoning for silence.

Frequently the Prætorian Prefect, in some cases *two* Prætorian Prefects, appear standing behind the Emperor. Below, is a group of the legionaries, from three to five or six generally in number, with their faces turned towards their prince; some holding the eagles, vexilla, and ensigns; others their bucklers and spears. With regard to the customary attitude and gesture of the speaker in addressing the troops, Cicero affords an illustrative passage, in his oration, against Gabinius—"When (says he) the general *(Imperator)*, openly, in the presence of the army, *stretched out his right hand*, not to incite the soldiers to glory, but to tell them that they might make their own market" *(Omnia sibi et empta et emenda esse.*—Provinc. cons. c. 4.)

ADLOCVT. COH.—(*Adlocutio Cohortium* —speech to the Cohorts). The Emperor Caius Cæsar (Caligula), habited in the toga, or

senatorial vestments, stands on a tribunal, before a curule chair, with right hand elevated, as if in the act of haranguing five military figures.—Touching this by no means rare, but extremely beautiful, reverse, in large brass, Schlegel is of opinion, that it refers to the oration delivered by Caligula, from a *suggestum*, raised in the midst of that bridge which, with foolishly applied skill, the architect Baulis built, in the sea at Puteoli. But Eckhel treats this supposition as erroneous, and considers the legend and type to indicate the allocution which that prince addressed to the Prætorian Cohorts, at the period of his accession to the supreme government; and that the same mode of recording the event was repeated on a later occasion, either for the sake of adding to his coinage, or because he had addressed other cohorts in a set, and indeed an eloquent, discourse; for Tacitus himself does not deny Caligula's talent for public speaking. While expressing, however, all due deference to the authority of Eckhel, Capt. Smyth does not think that it was struck in the first year of the tyrant's reign (A.D. 38) and points to the tribunitian date and the P. P. in the legend of the obverse, as rendering such a fact questionable. "An adlocution (he adds) was made to the Prætorian cohorts on Caligula's accession, but the coins which commemorate it, bear merely the legend C. CAESAR AUG. GERMANICVS PONT MAX. TR.P. The one just described, I am inclined to date A.D. 40, though the consulship is not marked, and the occasion may have been, the expedition to Britain." It is to be observed that the S. C. *(Senatus Consulto)* is omitted in all Roman brass coins, bearing the title and portrait of this Emperor. "Was it (Eckhel asks) because the senate, not authorising it, they were struck by order of the Prince himself, and distributed by him amongst the Prætorians?" Be this as it may, the military ceremony of the Allocution was first represented on the coins of Caligula. And it is to be noted that the one in question, though clearly of Roman die, has not the mark of Senatorial authority.—*Doct. num. vet.* vi., 221.

These military harangues occur many times afterwards in the mintage of the Imperial government, as will be seen by the following list, drawn out in chronological order :—

ADLOCVT. COH. S. C. Brass medallion and large brass of Nero.—Emperor, Prætorian Prefect, and three soldiers.—"Nero, attended by Burrhus, both togated, on a tribunal, standing near a circular edifice with columns, which may be emblematic of the prætorian camp. He is addressing three soldiers who stand before him, bearing military ensigns, and is probably promising the donative on which they proclaimed him Emperor; whence we may conclude the medal to have been struck A.D. 54."—Smyth, 41.

ADLOCVTIO. On the field S. C.—First brass of Galba.—The Emperor stands, with the chief of the Prætorian guards, on a raised platform, and harangues the Cohorts, who are generally represented by their standard bearer. In another Allocution, given by Havercamp, *(Mus. Christinæ)*, of the same Emperor, the cavalry of the guards are represented by a horse, the head of which is seen

amongst the foot soldiers. This coin (struck A. D. 68) is, by most numismatic antiquaries, thought to designate the occasion of Galba's speech to his legionaries in Spain, when he first revolted from Nero.

ADLOCVT. AVG. *(Adlocutio Augusti.)*—First brass of Nerva.—Emperor and two other figures on an estrade; four figures below.

ADLOCVTIO.—First and second brass of Hadrian.—Emperor addressing his soldiers: first brass, and ADLOCVTIO. COH. PRAETOR *(Cohortium Prætoriarum*—Allocution of the Body or Life Guards) with similar type.

ADLOCVTIO.—Brass medallion of Marcus Aurelius.—Emperor addressing soldiers, one of whom holds a horse by the bridle. *(Mus. de Camps.)*

ADLOCVT. AVG. COS. III.—First brass of Marcus Aurelius.—The Emperor, on a *suggestum*, accompanied by two prætorian prefects, is addressing three standard-bearers of the army. " This coin was struck A. D. 170, on Aurelius's waging war with the Marcomanni, a warlike people, who, leagued with the Quadi, the Sarmatians, the Roxolani, the Jazyges, and other barbarian nations, had invaded the Roman frontier. This opened one of the severest contests that ever Rome sustained."—Smyth, p. 136.

ADLOCVTIO.—Brass medallion, and first brass of L. Verus.—Emperor haranguing his soldiers.

ADLOCVTIO.—Brass medallion of Macrinus. —Emperor and his son (Diadumenianus), and four military figures.

ADLOCVTIO AVGVSTI.—Emperor and soldiers: on a first brass of Alexander Severus.

ADLOCVTIO AVGVSTI.—-Emperor and soldiers, on a brass medallion and a first brass of Gordianus Pius.

ADLOCVTIO AVGG. *(Augustorum.)*—The two Philips, addressing their troops—on a brass medallion and first brass of Philippus, sen.

ADLOCVTIO AVGVSTORVM.—Three figures in military habits, standing on a raised platform, under whom appear three soldiers with legionary standards. In reference to this legend and type, as found on a large-sized silver medallion, having on its obverse the head of Valerianus, Spanheim makes the following remark:—"Valerian before his captivity and imprisonment (by Sapor, King of Persia), asso-

ciated his son Gallienus, in the empire, as we see on medals their two heads and the words *Concordia Augustorum.* There is also another medal on which are three heads, viz., those of Valerian and his two sons Gallienus and Valerianus, jun., though the latter was then only Cæsar." The three figures standing on the *suggestum*, in the silver medallion above described, were therefore most probably designed to represent the same three imperial personages.

ADLOCVTIO AVG. and ADLOCVTIO TACITI AVG.—Brass medallions of Tacitus.— The Emperor, attended by the Prætorian prefect.

ADLOCVTIO AVG.—On a brass medallion of Probus.—Accompanying this legend, there is a remarkable type in which that Emperor and another personage are represented, standing together on an estrade; three soldiers on each side carry military ensigns; and before the estrade are four kneeling figures. *(Mus. De Camps*, p. 117.).—For an illustration of this reverse see *Probus.*

ADLOCVTIO.—Third brass of Maxentius.

Besides these reverses, in which the legend itself identifies the type with the occasion of an Emperor's speech to his troops, there are some splendid examples of Allocutional representations on brass medallions, such as the FIDES EXERCITVS of Commodus, and the FIDEI MILITVM of Sept. Severus—See the former illustrated.

In the foregoing examples the distinctive word ADLOCVTIO, or ADLOCVT is, for the most part, inscribed on the *exergue.* It can hardly fail to occasion some degree of surprise, that no Allocution should have been recorded on the coins of such eminently warlike and victorious princes of the earlier empire, as Vespasian, Titus, and Trajan,—[The ADLOCVTIO ascribed to the first named Emperor, engraved as a brass medallion, in *Numismata Cimelii Vindobonensis* (p. 15), being "*nonnihil suspectum.*"]

ADOPTIO : Adoption.—The act of a person adopting another as his son, was performed among the Romans, either in presence of the Prætor, or before an assembly of the people, in the times of the Republic; and under the Emperors by their sovereign authority.—An adopted Roman (says Eckhel, v., p. 59), was so completely translated into the *gens*, or race, of the party adopting him, that the name of his own family was put aside, and he received all the names of his parent by adoption—which names, however, were lengthened into the letters ANVS. —Thus, Æmilius Paullus, being adopted by Publius Cornelius Scipio, was called P. Cornelius Scipio Æmili*anus.*—C. Octavius, afterwards Augustus, adopted by the Dictator Cæsar, became C. Julius Cæsar Octavi*anus.*—So, on coins, we see A. LICINIVS NERVA SILI*anus*; and T. QVINCTIVS CRISPINVS SVLPICI*anus.*—This custom, nevertheless, was frequently departed from. For example, M. Junius Brutus, (he who killed Cæsar) after his adoption by Q. Servilius Coepio, was called Q. Coepio *Brutus*, the surname being still retained, for the sake of his own family; whereas he ought to have been called Q. Servilius Coepio *Junianus.* Thus again

Scipio, who took part against Julius Cæsar in Africa, adopted by Q. Cæcilius Metellus Pius, is termed on coins Q. Metellus Pius Scipio, not *Cornelianus.* Nor does it appear, that the adopted Romans were very particular in using the names to which they succeeded. M. Junius Brutus, notwithstanding his adoption, is called on several of his coins, only BRVTVS IMP.—And P. Clodius, adopted by Fonteius, continued to the end of his life, to be called P. Clodius. Also, by virtue of adoption, the surname was lengthened, as in the instance of Marcellus of the Cornelia family, afterwards called *Marcellinus.*

ADOPTIO.—Two figures, in the toga, joining hands: round the type PARTHIC. DIVI. TRAIAN. AVG. P.M. TR. P. COS. P.P.—This coin of Hadrian, in gold and silver, commemorates the adoption of Hadrian by Trajan. The former scattered abroad many monumental evidences of that fact, as there had been much doubt on the subject: for, says Spartian, "there are not wanting those who assert that, after the death of Trajan, Hadrian was, through the intrigues of Plotina, taken into adoption." For this reason, adds Vaillant *(Impp. Rom.*, ii., p. 136), who concurs in the sentiment of this quotation, was Hadrian so diligent, at first, in assuming the *cognomina* of his father by adoption.

Adoption self-assumed.—There is exhibited on first and second brass coins of Sept. Severus an evidence of that Emperor's adoption of himself into the family of M. Aurelius; the legend of the reverse reading DIVI. M. PII. F. &c., and the type representing Severus, in the imperial paludamentum, crowned by a helmeted figure holding a club in the left hand. This preposterous and unprecedented assumption, of which nearly all the old writers take notice, is thus numismatically confirmed. It was after so unwarrantable a use of the adoptive process, that the above named Emperor proceeded to trace his descent, in an uninterrupted line from Nerva, as is attested by many inscriptions on marble, more diffuse than those on coins—see Gruter, quoted by Eckhel vii., p. 173. See also DIVI. M. PII. F.

ADQ.—ADQVI.—*Adquisita,* added to (the Roman empire).—See ARABIA ADQUIS.

ADSERTORI LIBERTATIS PVBLICAE. S. P. Q. R. in an oaken or civic garland.—With this highly eulogistic title of "Maintainer of the Public Liberty," was Vespasian honoured by the Senate and People of Rome, on a large brass coin.—It is one of the rarest of that Emperor's mint. The inscription occurs solely in the instance of Vespasian. S. C. is omitted simply because S. P. Q. R. equally constitutes the impress of senatorial authority. See Spanheim, ii. 528—and Havercamp, in *Thesaur.* Morell. vol. iii., *Tab.* xiii.—see also Eckhel's comment, vi. p. 322. The obverse of this medal, on which appears the laureated head of the Emperor turned to the left, presents the legend of IMP. CAES.

VESPASIAN. AVG. P. M. TR. P. P. P. COS. III. which, "as well as all those struck in A. D. 71, proves Suetonius to be mistaken in stating that Vespasian was not invested with the tribunitian power, nor dignified with the title of Father of his country, till the latter part of his reign."—Smyth, p. 56, No. lxx.

ADV. or ADVENT.—AVG. or AVGG.—*Adventus Augusti,* or *Augustorum.*

ADVENTUS.—Inscriptions of this kind commemorate the imperial sovereign's arrival at Rome, either at the commencement of his reign, or on his return from a distance. They also refer to his advent in some city or province of the empire. At their accession to the throne, emperors were not conveyed in a chariot nor in any other vehicle, but went on horseback, and sometimes even on foot; and thus they made their first public entry into the capital of the Roman world. The fact of the equestrian procession of emperors into Rome, even if it were not authenticated from other sources, is abundantly established, by the type of an *Imperator eques,* accompanying the legend of ADVENTVS AVGVSTI, stamped on so numerous a series of coins. The other custom, viz., that of their arriving on horseback at the gates of the city, and then entering it on foot, is not, and indeed could not, with the same degree of clearness, be elucidated by means of monetal designs; but the fact is described by Dion Cassius, in his account of Septimius Severus's pedestrian entry into Rome.—That emperors occasionally *set out from* the city on foot is shewn on a large brass of Caracalla, the reverse type of which represents him marching, followed by a soldier.—See PROFECTIO AVG. The Emperor's departure.

The *Adventus* legend appears on coins of Nero, Trajan, Hadrian, M. Aurelius, Commodus, Sept. Severus, Caracalla, the Philips, Trebonianus Gallus, Volusianus, Valerianus, Gallienus, Carus, Claudius Gothius, Tacitus, Probus, Diocletianus, Maximianus Hercules, Carausius, Allectus, Constantine, Jovianus. The types (with the exception of those on Hadrian's inscribed *Adventui Augusti*) consist generally of the Emperor or Emperors on horseback, with their right hands elevated, sometimes preceded by a figure of Victory; in other instances, by soldiers bearing standards. These are all on 1st or 2nd brass. There is an *Adventus Aug.* of Elagabalus in silver; and an *Adventus Augusti* of the same Emperor in gold.

ADVENTUS AVGVSTI.—This memorial of an Emperor's progresses, is offered most frequently, as well as most interestingly, on the coins of Hadrian, always with the addition of the name of the province, or city, which that great prince had visited: viz., Africæ, Alexandriæ, Arabiæ, Asiæ, Bithyniæ, Britanniæ, Ciliciæ, Galliæ, Hispaniæ, Italiæ, Judaeæ, Macedoniæ, Mauretaniæ, Moesiæ, Phrygiæ, Siciliæ, Thraciæ.—These are all on first brass, but seven of them (see Akerman's *Descr. Cat.* vol. i.) are also to be found on second brass, and three on gold and silver.—The solicitude of Hadrian to become acquainted, by ocular observation and personal inquiry, with the customs, manners, laws, and condition of the various peoples, comprehended within the limits of his vast empire, induced him to be continually travelling through its different provinces, and colonies; to visit the chief cities, and to inspect the principal legionary masses of the Roman army. He made these excursions (of greater or less extent, and occupying more or less time) accompanied by only a few attendants, generally on foot and often bare-headed, seeing every thing, investigating every thing, and every where establishing the greatest order.—The accomplishment of numerous journies and visitations were, by his direction and with the sanction of the Senate, chronologically recorded, in a series of coins, which are remarkable for their fine style of workmanship. It comprises, as already noticed, all the Roman provinces, and confirms what History tells us of this emperor's voyages. The number of these geographical coins is considerable, and they are with good reason sought for. Some are very rare, others sufficiently common. The first class of them includes the names of the provinces and towns through which Hadrian passed. On these the countries, cities, and rivers, are represented by a figure and some attribute; as Egyptos, Alexandria, Nilus. The second expresses the satisfaction which the people experienced, or were supposed to have experienced, at his arrival among them: an event which is indicated by the legend of the reverse—AD-VENTVI AVG.; whilst the type (as in that of *Africa*, *Judæa*, Macedonia, &c.) exhibits the Emperor, and the Genius of the Province, standing opposite each other, and an altar (with its victim) between them, at which they are performing sacrifice.—The third class shows, through the medium of ingenious allegories, the benefits and reliefs which Hadrian bestowed on the oppressed provinces. In this branch of the series the Emperor is called RESTITUTOR, the restorer of the particular country, (as Achaia, Asia, Africa, Gallia, Hispania, &c.) and he raises up a kneeling figure. A fourth and last class refers to the military exercises, which he caused to be practiced, and to the discipline which he maintained amongst his legions, in their respective encampments and garrisons. The review of troops by the Emperor in person is usually figured by a type of allocution, with the name of the army, as in his EXERCITVS DACICVS, GERMANICVS, MAVRETANICVS, &c. on which are an equestrian figure, and four or five foot soldiers carrying military ensigns.

ADVENTVI AVG. AFRICAE.—On gold of Hadrian.

The Emperor, clothed in the toga, is seen holding his right hand elevated towards a female figure, who is distinguished by the trunk of an elephant covering her head as personifying the Roman province of Africa, and is in the act of sacrificing at a tripod. "We find (says Addison) on the several medals, struck in commemoration of Hadrian's progress through the empire, that on his arrival (adventus) they offered a sacrifice to the Gods, for the reception of so great a blessing. Horace mentions this custom, (Od. 2, lib. 4.)"

ADVENTVS AVGVSTI. G. P. *(Grœcia Peragrata.)*—A second brass of Nero, of colonial fabric, bearing this legend, and an ornamented praetorian galley, is considered to record the return of that prince from Greece.—Others with a similar type, and the abbreviation C. COR. in the field of the coin, designate his arrival at Corinth, for the purpose of celebrating the Isthmian games in that city.—(Vaillant *in coloniis*, vol. i.)

ADVENTVS AVG. PONT. MAX. TR. POT. COS. II., S. C.—Rome helmeted, seated on a heap of arms, joins right hands with the Emperor, who habited in the toga, stands opposite to her.—On a large brass of Hadrian, struck in the year of Our Lord 118.——Having arranged all things in Syria, (where he commanded when Trajan died), Hadrian proceeded through Illyria to Rome; and that this occurred in the year above mentioned, the present coin shows by the inscription COS. II.—Eckhel, vi. 477.

ADVENTVI AVG. IVDAEAE. S. C.—In this example amongst the *numi geographici* of Hadrian, the Emperor, with his right hand uplifted, stands opposite the province, which is personified under the figure of a female, robed and veiled: she holds a patera over an altar, at the foot of which is the victim: she carries a ball, or, as Mr. Akerman suggests, in reality the *Acerra* imperfectly represented, in her left hand, and beside her are two naked children, bearing each a palm branch—allusive to Judæa, of which, as part of Palestine, the palm tree is an emblem.

This type, struck between A. D. 130 and 135, is of historical interest. It represents the arrival of Hadrian in Judæa, not, as in the case of most of his visits elsewhere, on a mission of benevolence and mercy, but to confirm the stern imperial sentence, after a bloody war, of destruction to devoted Jerusalem, and of insult and humiliation to the rebellious Jews.—For a further numismatic reference to this fulfilment of Our Lord's prophecy, see *Aelia Capitolina Colonia.*

ADVENTVS AVG. BRITANNIAE.—In
the exergue s. c.—An altar with the fire kindled,
placed between the Emperor (who is clothed in
the toga), holding a patera, and a female figure
with a victim lying at her feet. On a large brass
of Hadrian, engraved in "Coins of the Romans
relating to Britain."—Pl. 2, No. 5.

Hadrian's arrival in Britain is commemorated
by this coin, struck in the year of Rome 874
A.D. 121. "In the reign of this prince," observes
Mr. Akerman (see his ably written, correctly
illustrated, and highly interesting work above-
named), "the Britons revolted; and Julius Severus was recalled to proceed against the Jews, who
had made an effort to regain their liberty. The
Caledonians also destroyed several forts, which
had been erected by Agricola. Hadrian, with
three legions, arrived in time to prevent the
Britons from throwing off the Roman yoke;
and, to protect the northern frontiers of the
province, built a wall which extended from
the Tyne in Northumberland to the Eden in
Cumberland. The war does not appear to have
been of long continuance, and the Southern
Britons, protected from the incursions of their
savage neighbours, were probably content to bear
the yoke." p. 22.

ADVENTVS AVG.—*M. Aurelius crossing a
bridge.*—On the reverse of a large brass the
Emperor is seen, followed by five soldiers, two
of whom bear standards; and the others have
their spears advanced as if to encounter resistance. They are passing over a bridge constructed on three boats, "precisely (says Capt.
Smyth) like the one over the Ister, represented
on the Trajan column. The bridge before us was
no doubt over the same river; since the Marcomanni, in abandoning Pannonia, sustained a
dreadful overthrow, whilst crossing it.—The
legend of this reverse is IMP. VI. COS. III., with
VIRTVS AVG. on the exergue. There is another
large brass of Aurelius, with the above reverse,
but inscribed *Adventus* instead of *Virtus*, and
recording IMP. VII. whence it affords a sure
testimony of the Emperor's return to Rome,
A. D. 174."—For an illustration of this reverse,
see IMP. VI. COS. III.

ADVENTVI AV*Gusti* FELICISSIMO. S.C.
—This legend appears on the reverse of a large
brass of Septimius Severus. The type represents
the emperor on horseback, either alone, or preceded by a soldier on foot.—After having re-

ing against Albinus, Severus returned to Rome,
where his entry was magnificent. That was the
same *Felicissimus Adventus*—"the most auspicious return"—which is alluded to here.

Capt. Smyth (p. 186) assigns the return
to Rome which this device commemorates,
to the year 196 of the Christian æra; and
adds—"The first public entry of Severus was
under every possible demonstration of joy:
yet he committed unheard of cruelties. After
commending the character of Commodus to the
Senators, who had declared his memory infamous, he executed a number of their body, without trial; and Rome was filled with bloodshed.
At the same time, however, he executed retributive justice on the insolent, venal, and treacherous Prætorians, whom he disarmed, degraded, and ignominiously banished to the distance of a hundred miles from Rome."

In describing an *Adventus* coin of the
elder Philip, whose equestrian figure is represented with the same "extraordinary disproportion between the steed and its rider," as is exhibited on the above reverse of Severus, the
intelligent writer above quoted, observes (p. 266)
—"the Emperor is probably mounted on the
Asturco, or ambling nag, as a more appropriate emblem of returning peace, than the
Equus bellator, or charger."—This is a shrewd
conjecture; but it does not fully account for the
under-sized horses on which we see emperors
mounted, in various types of the Roman mint.
These, indeed, are for the most part relatively
diminutive, whether the imperial rider is habited
in the pacific toga, or in the garb of war—
under the legend of ADVENTVS, or that of EX-
ERCITVS.

ADVENTVS AVGVSTI. S. C.—On a large
brass of Elagabalus, with this legend of reverse,
the type presents "an equestrian figure of
that emperor, with his right hand elevated, a
sceptre in his left, and the chlamys floating
behind his shoulders. Mœsa, well aware of what
Macrinus had lost by not proceeding to Rome
immediately after his election, urged her grandson, who was wallowing in brutal debauchery at
Nicomedia, to repair thither. She prevailed;
and he entered Rome A. D. 219, where he was
received with great demonstrations, largesses
being distributed to the populace, and public
shews exhibited."—Smyth, p. 214.

ADVENTVS AVGG. (*Adventus Augustorum*).
—Two military figures on horseback galloping.—

established peace in the east by the destruction of
Pescennius Niger, and with the design of march-

This legend and type appear on a brass medallion,

struck in honour of the Emperors Trebonianus Gallus, and Volusianus, jointly, about A. D. 252, the computed year of their arrival in Rome, after the death of Trajanus Decius, whose son Hostilianus had already been associated with Trebonianus as an *Augustus.*

On the obverse are the laurelled heads of both father and son, surrounded by the legend IMP. GALLVS. AVG. IMP. VOLVSIANVS. AVG.—The above cut is copied from the volume of Buonarotti (pl. xviii.), who praises this medallion as equal, in point both of design and workmanship, to the best examples of die-engraving, to be found in the mints of the earlier empire. Thus much for art and taste, as still occasionally found manifested even in the lower age of the imperial coinage. But the device of two equestrian warriors, one with couched lance, as if preparing to charge an enemy, is a more appropriate type for a *decursio,* or a *profectio militaris,* than for the peaceful approach of two newly-elected Emperors to the gates of "the eternal city." There is, moreover, something more than strange in the assumption of the imperial title by both Gallus and Volusianus—a circumstance which, as the learned and acute author of "*Osservazione Istoriche*" remarks (p. 312)—"*fa molto sospettare che Ostiliano, non vedendosi nominato, fosse già morto, o di peste, o di morte violenta, procuratagli da Gallo, per gelosia d' Imperio.*" The suspicion of foul play, in this case, is of the two, by far the more probable hypothesis.

ADVENTVS CARI. AVG.—The Emperor on horseback, with right hand raised, and a spear in his left.—This reverse appears on an aureus of Carus (struck A. D. 282-3.)—Some writers think it probable from this coin, that Carus actually went to Rome, from Pannonia, before he proceeded on his Persian expedition. But, at this period, to speak of the advent of the Emperor was not always intended to indicate his arrival at Rome. (Eckhel, vii. p. 588). This observation is also justified by the mint of the Emperor Tacitus.

ADVENTVS S. D. N. AVG.—-The Emperor, with the nimbus round his head, on horseback, in the garb of Peace.—[Akerman describes this equestrian figure as "wearing the diadem."]

This appears on a gold coin of Marcianus, published by Pellerin (Mel. 1. p. 163), who reads the legend—ADVENTVS S*ecundus* Domini N*ostri* AV*gusti,* meaning the second arrival of the Emperor. Eckhel, on the other hand, deems it more likely that the single S constitutes part of the imperial title of Marcianus, and should rather be read S*acratissimi.*—[The opinion of Eckhel is entitled to the greatest respect, and his interpretation is probably correct, but on Greek coins the second advent is recorded. See Mr. Akerman's remarks on the Coins of Ephesus, in *Num. Chron.* The S. preceding D. N. appears to sanction Eckhel's rendering.]

ADVENTVS AVGG.—There is a silver medallion, edited by Buonarotti, bearing on its obverse the head of Saloninus Valerianus Cæsar, without laurel crown, on the one side; and face

to face, with that of Gallienus, his father, laureated, on the other side—the legend being CONCORDIA AVGVSTORVM.—The reverse exhibits three galeated figures on horseback, their right hands raised. Victory preceding them, and five soldiers accompanying them, three of whom bear military ensigns. Near the horses' feet are two captives seated on the ground. See CONCORDIA AVGVSTORVM.

ADVERSA.—The obverse, or principal face of a coin; in contradistinction to the term *aversa,* or the reverse side.

ADYTUM, the most sacred place of a heathen temple in which stood the image of the principal deity to whom it was dedicated.—See *Templum.*

AEBUTIA gens.—It is uncertain to which order, patrician or plebeian, this family belongs. Its name is found on brass colonial coins of *Cæsar-Augusta* (Sarragozza) in Hispania Tarraconensis, and also of *Corinth.* There are four varieties.

AED.—*Aedes* or *Ædificia,* Edifices.—AED. S. *Ædibus Sacris.*

AED. P. or POT.—*Ædilitia Potestate.*

AED. DIVI. FAVSTINAE.—A temple of six columns, in which Faustina stands, or, as in others, is seated. Silver. To this may be joined the legend of another denarius of the same empress—viz., DEDICATIO AEDIS. The same building but no image within.

This represents the *aedes,* or *templum,* with which, after her death, the elder Faustina was honoured by Antoninus Pius. According to Capitolinus, it was situated in the *via sacra,* and was at first dedicated to Faustina alone. But, after the decease of the husband, religious rites were paid therein to him also. This temple, the ruins of which at Rome are still extant, bespeaks its original appropriation, for on its frontal the following dedication is still legible, viz., DIVO ANTONINO ET DIVAE FAVSTINAE. EX S. C. The same edifice is likewise represented on other coins of the same empress, inscribed AETERNITAS, or PIETAS.—Eckhel, vii. p. 39.— See TEMPLVM DIVI. AVG. REST. engraved in Caylus, No. 493.

AED. (in others AEDE) DIVI. AVG. REST. COS. IIII.—*Ædes Divi Augusti Restitutæ.*— On silver and large brass coins of Antoninus Pius (struck about A. D. 159) are the foregoing legend, and a temple of eight columns, with two seated figures in the intercolumniation. The pediment and entablature of the edifice are also adorned with statuary.

This temple of Augustus first appears on coins of Tiberius struck A.U.C. 787 (A.D. 34) ; also in the mint of Caligula of different years ; and here it is exhibited on coins of Antoninus, of the year above-mentioned (Eckhel, vii., 25). These, supplying what history has neglected to notice, teach us that such repairs and restorations, as either the decays of age, or the effects of casual injury, had rendered necessary, were made by the piety of Antoninus. The two statues in the temple are of Augustus and Julia, the latter placed there by the Emperor Claudius. Gold, silver, and brass of Antoninus, with the same type, but inscribed TEMPLVM. DIVI. AVG. also refer to this historical fact.—See *Templum.*

AED. Aedilis.—AED. PL. *Ædilis Plebis.*—AED. CVR. *Ædilis Curulis.*

ÆDILIS—A Roman magistrate, who exercised the Edileship, which was of three kinds: Plebeian, Curule, and Cereal.—See an able article, under this head, in "the Dictionary of Greek and Roman Antiquities, edited by Dr.W. Smith."

ÆDILIS PLEBIS.—The plebeian edileship was the most ancient of the offices above named. It embraced many functions, amongst which were the maintenance of the baths, aqueducts, common sewers, streets, and highways : also the preservation of the public records and archives, deposited in the temple *(ædes)* of Ceres. The plebeian ediles were, moreover, charged with the superintendence of commerce, and of what is now called the police ; together with the management of provisions.

Havercamp (in Morell, *Thesaur. Fam. Rom.*) gives two denarii referring to the office of Plebeian Ediles. One of these is of the Fannia, the other of the Critonia gens. Both these exhibit on their respective obverses, the head of *Ceres spicifera*, with the abbreviated words AED. PL. *Ædilium Plebis ;* on each of their reverses are two togated men, sitting upon common *sedilia.* Behind them is P.A. or *Publico Argento* (meaning coined with the public silver) ; below we read M. FAN. L. CRIT. *Marcius Fannius* and *Lucius Critonius ;* the two ediles employed on the occasion to which the coin refers.—Eckhel, v. p. 198.

ÆDILES CURULES.—Under the dictatorship of Furius Camillus (B.C. 368), the patricians obtained the nomination to the edileship of two of their own order, under the distinctive appellation of *Ædiles Curules ;* because they had the curule chair, the *prætexta*, or long white robe bordered with purple, the *jus imaginis*, or right of images, like the superior magistrates ; privileges never attained by the plebeian ediles. To the curule ediles were entrusted the care of the sacred edifices (especially the temple of Jupiter), the tribunals of justice, the city walls, and the theatres ; in short, all that was essential to the religion, defence, and embellishment of the city, came under their cognizance.—Pitiscus, *Lex. Ant. Rom.*

The symbols of the curule edileship, both in legend and in type, are found on denarii of the Livineia, Plætoria, Plancia, Plautia, and other families. In some of these, the curule chair presents itself on one side, and the dignity of AED. CVR. is stamped on the other, as in the above coin of the *Furia* gens. Others present the figures of the two ediles, sitting between two measures filled with ears of corn, as in a denarius of the Papiria family. Also a modius, or measure, between two ears of corn, as in silver of *L. Livineius Regulus*, one of which on the obverse has the head of Ceres adorned with a crown of corn ears, accompanied with the epigraph of AED. CVR. (See *Livineia* gens.) Likewise on a denarius of the Flaminia family, a head of Ceres with the letters, designating the Curule Edileship, appears on one side, whilst on the other are figures of two men, clothed in the toga, sitting together, having each a corn ear beside him, and below is inscribed T. FLAMIN. T.F.L. FLAC. P.F. EX. S. C. meaning *Titus Flaminius, Titi Filius, and L. Flaccus, Publii Filius, Ex Senatus Consulto.* (See Havercamp in Morell—*numi consulares.*) The addition of EX. S. C. denotes that those Curule Ediles purchased wheat for the supply of the Roman population, with the public money, by authority of the Senate. This purpose is more explicitly referred to, in the epigraph of AD. FRV. EMV. already given (p. 5).

Eckhel observes, that the curule edileship was not unfrequently attended with vast expense both to the state and to the individuals who held the office. That of M. Scaurus (which according to Pighius, took place in the year of Rome 696 B.C. 58) is reprobated by early Roman writers, for the excessive magnificence of the public shews, and the amount of largesses, almost beyond belief, which, with a prodigal ostentation of luxury and profusion, he lavished on his official year.

ÆDILES CEREALES.—This third class of Ediles was of much later appointment and of more questionable origin, clashing as they did in functional operations with the other two. Under the free republic, the number of Ediles had been limited to four ; viz., two plebeians and two patricians. But according to Dion, two Curators, with the like number of Cereal Ediles, were instituted by Julius Cæsar (when about to proceed on his expedition against Parthia), for the purpose of assisting in the conveyance of corn from foreign lands to Rome, and of distributing it among the people. (See *Annona*). This fact is confirmed by the inscriptions on two marbles, cited by Ursinus, bearing the words AEDILI PLEB. CERIAL.—A denarius of Critonius, who was a Cereal Edile, in the year of Rome 710 (B. C. 44), has for the type of its obverse (like *Fannia* above), the head of Ceres. "And appropriately too" says Eckhel, "for we learn from Cicero, that the care of providing *annona*, and of preparing the Cerealian games, belonged not less to the plebeian than to the curule ediles. The eminent author of *Doctrina num. vet.* then makes an apposite quotation from Livy, shewing expressly that on one of those occasions, when L. Valerius and M. Horatius were consuls (B. C. 449), the sacred ceremonies in the temple of Ceres were, by a *senatus consultum*, placed under the jurisdiction and management of the Plebeian Ediles."—See CEREALES.

The Edileship was continued under the Emperors, and it was not until the reign of Constantine the Great that the institution itself was abolished.—Pitiscus.

ÆGYPTVS: Egypt.—Augustus, having taken possession of Alexandria, the capital city of the Delta, in the 724th year of Rome (B. C. 30), formed the whole country into a Roman province, and entrusted the government to some individual member of the equestrian order; prohibiting all senators from going to Egypt, without special permission. Egypt is distinguished on coins by the crocodile, the sistrum, the ibis, the lotus, and ears of corn. The Nile, Jupiter, the Sun, the Moon, Apis, Osiris, Isis, Serapis, as objects of worship with the Egyptians, are also amongst the numismatic recognitions of that country. Egypt received no colony, after Julius Cæsar's time; but, as a province, was governed by an imperial prefect (*præfectus augustalis*) to whom, however, the privilege of the fasces was not assigned.

ÆGYPTOS.—Egypt personified under the image of a woman seated on the ground, holding in her right hand the sistrum, resting her left arm on the canistrum, or basket filled with fruits, and having on her right foot the Ibis standing.

This reverse which appears on coins of Hadrian, in all the three metals, was struck on the occasion of that Emperor's visit to Egypt, after having been in Judæa and Arabia, probably about the year U. C. 883, A. D. 130. (Eckhel, vi., 488.) The type is elegant, on gold and first brass, and is peculiarly appropriate to Egypt. The *sistrum* was a musical instrument sacred to Isis, in whose worship it was used, and national to Egypt. [See the word.] The *canistrum*, or basket of wheat, signifies the fruitfulness of the country, which is caused by the inundation of the Nile.

In reference to the sacred Ibis, a bird so peculiar to Egypt, that it was said to die, if taken to other countries, Cicero has observed, "the Egyptians, whom we are apt to ridicule so much, conferred honours upon animals only in proportion to the advantage derived from them. Thus their reason for worshipping the Ibis, was because it destroyed the serpent."

A large brass of Hadrian, the reverse without legend, but with s. c. in the field, "exhibits a majestic figure of the Emperor, with his left foot on a crocodile : he is in armour, with the paludamentum at his back, his right hand is supported by a spear, with the point peacefully downwards, and his left holds a parazonium. This was probably minted in remembrance of his visit to Egypt, and its date may therefore be nearly approximated—for Hadrian, having passed through Judæa and Arabia, arrived at Pelusium A. D. 130, where he repaired the tomb of Pompey."—Smyth, *Descr. Cat.* p. 103.

AEGYPTO CAPTA.—This historical legend appears on gold and silver of Augustus. The obverse presents the head of that emperor, without laurel, behind which is the augural lituus, and around is read CAESAR. COS. VI.—On the reverse are the foregoing words, accompanied with the figure of a crocodile, to the right.— The sixth consulate being inscribed on this denarius, shews it to have been struck in the year of Rome 726 (B. C. 28), under Augustus, to renew the memory of the capture of Alexandria, and thereby the conquest of Egypt, by his great uncle, and father by adoption, Julius Cæsar. [The original silver coin is neither rare nor high priced, but the same type restored by Trajan is valued by Mionnet at 100 francs.]

ÆGIS.—This, according to the Greek etymology of the word, was the skin of a *goat ;* some authors affirming it to be that of the goat Amalthæa, others pretending it to have been the skin of a destructive monster, Ægis, whom Minerva fought and slew—after which she is said to have placed its skin over her breast, partly to serve as a garment, partly as a protection against dangers, but also as a lasting evidence of her bravery : in the sequel she placed on it the snake-haired head of Medusa. Roman Emperors often appear, in their statues and on their coins, with their chests covered with the Ægis as with a cuirass; and several coins of Domitian and of Trajan exhibit those Emperors, with the head of Medusa affixed to the bust, as part of the body armour.—See *Lorica*—also *Domitianus*.

AEMILIA gens (originally *Aimilia*), a patrician family of great antiquity, as both writers and coins serve fully to attest. It was famous for the exploits and public services of its members, insomuch that they filled office, as chief pontiffs, dictators, governors, senators, consuls, masters of the horse, military tribunes with consular power, and triumvirs *reipublicæ constituendæ*, together with all the other magisterial and sacerdotal functions. Buca, Lepidus, Paulus, and Scaurus appear as surnames on the medals of this gens, and there are 43 numismatic varieties. Gold, of the highest rarity; Silver common, except scarce reverses. There are silver restored by Trajan. The brass are colonial. For the *cognomen* of *Buca*, see AIMILIA [*Basilica*] REFecit S. C.—For that of *Paulus* see TER PAVLVS.—For *Scaurus* see REX ARETAS.—The following relates to

Lepidus. The coins of the Lepidi are remarkable for their commemoration of warlike achievements performed by persons belonging to that branch of the Aemilia gens.—There is a denarius belonging to this family, which bears on its obverse, a female head with a diadem. On its reverse, an equestrian figure with a trophy on his shoulder; around the type AN. XV. PR. H. O. C. S.; on the exergue M. LEPIDVS.

The meaning of this abbreviated legend on a well known and interesting silver coin is—M. LEPIDVS ANnorum xv. PRætextatus. *Hostem Occidit Civem Servavit.*—Thus informing us that M. Lepidus at the age of fifteen, still *Prætextatus* (that is, wearing the robe peculiar to a patrician boy) killed an enemy [in battle] and saved [the life of] a Roman citizen.—Valerius Maximus (l. iii. c. i. n. i.) relates this fact in almost the same words:—*Aemilius Lepidus puer etiam tum progressus in aciem hostem interemit, civem servavit. Cujus tum memorabilis* (he adds) *operis index est, in Capitolio statua bullata et incincta prætexta S. C. posita.* —According to the above-named Roman historian, a statue of Lepidus, dressed in the costume appropriated to the male children of noblemen till 17 years of age, was placed in the Capitol, by order of the Senate, as an honourable record of this precocious act of valour and patriotism.— After further citing a passage from Macrobius, to shew that, in the times of the Kings, a similar deed, under similar circumstances as to age and bravery, had been performed, and had met with a like recompense—Eckhel calls to mind (vol. v. 123) that on the obverse of another of these

denarii, a crown of oak leaves, the honour conferred on him who saved a citizen, is added in the field of the coin behind the woman's head.

AEMILIA gens.—There is a denarius of this family engraved in Morell's *Thesaurus*, which bears on its obverse ROMA, and a female head. On its reverse M. AEMILIO, and an equestrian statue on a bridge; referring to the building of the *Pons Sublicius*, of stone, at Rome, between 660-688 U. C. (94-64 B. C.)

AEMILIANUS (Marcus or Caius Julius Æmilius), was born in Mauretania, of an obscure family, about the year of the Christian era 208. A good soldier, and of an enterprising character, he arrived at the highest dignities, and was honoured with the consulate. Appointed governor of Mæsia and Pannonia, he repulsed with great slaughter an invasion of the Goths, whom he also drove out of Illyria and Thrace. In admiration of his valour and firmness, as contrasted with the timid and yielding policy of Trebonianus Gallus, the Mæsian and Pannonian legions proclaimed him Emperor, A. D. 253, he being then forty-six years of age. Advancing, after his election, into Italy, he defeated Gallus and Volusianus in a pitched battle; and those two princes having been slain by their own troops, Æmilianus was acknowledged by the Senate, who confirmed him in all the imperial titles A. D. 254. Shortly after, being compelled to march against Valerianus, who had been elected Emperor by the legions of Rhetia and Noricum, he was killed by his own soldiers, near Spoletum, in Umbria, on a bridge afterwards called "the bloody bridge," in August of the same year. On his coins (which are of highest rarity in gold, rare in silver, and very rare in 1st and 2nd brass), he is styled IMP. M. AEM. AEMILIANVS AVG.—IMP. CAES. C. IVL. AEMILIANVS PIVS. FEL. AVG.

The above engraving is from a large brass coin, of the legends and types on which the following is descriptive:—

Obv. IMP. AEMILIANVS PIVS FEL. AVG.— (Imperator, Æmilianus, Pius, Felix, Augustus)— Laurelled head of Æmilian.

Rev. PACI. AVG.—(To the Peace of the Emperor.)—Peace holding the olive branch and the hasta, and leaning on a cippus, or short column.

AEMILIANVS *(Alexander)*, an usurper of the purple, in Ægypt, during the reign of Gallienus.—No authentic coins.—Akerman, vol. i. p. 81.

AELIA and ALLIA. Plebeian gens.—The surnames of this family, as they appear on its coins, are Bala, Lama, Pætus, Sejanus. Twenty-four varieties. Silver and first brass common. The brass were struck by the monetal triumvirs of Augustus, or are colonial of Bilbilis, in Spain. The following denarius is the least common :— *Obverse*, head of Pallas, behind it X. *Reverse*, F. PAETVS, below, ROMA. The dioscuri (Castor and Pollux) on horseback.—The word ROMA shows the coin to have been struck at Rome. The dioscuri on horseback, with spears in their hands, and the *pileus* on their heads, with stars over them, are frequent and accustomed types of the ancient denarii. It refers to *Publius Ælius Pætus*, who was consul with Cornelius Lentulus, A.U.C. 553 (B.C. 201).

AELIA CAPITOLINA.—Under this name was distinguished the colony established by the Emperor Aelius Hadrianus, in the very capital of Judæa, which, under its ancient and sacred appellation of Jerusalem *(Hierosolyma)*, was, A.D. 135, destroyed by Titus.——Ha-

drian having suppressed a great rebellion of the Jews against the Roman government, proceeded to expel them from Jerusalem; and, after destroying the once Holy City, which he prohibited the Jews from approaching on pain of death, he built on its site a new city, and called it after his family name AELIA. He afterwards sent a colony there to people it, having commanded a temple of Jupiter Capitolinus to be erected on the spot where the Temple dedicated to the worship of the True God had stood. Hence the colonial title of the place, COL. AEL. CAP. *Colonia Aelia Capitolina.*

The coins of this colony bear none but *Latin* legends, and are brass of the three modules.— Extending from Hadrian down to Hostilianus, they comprise the intermediate reigns of Antoninus Pius, M. Aurelius, L. Verus, S. Severus, Diadumenianus, Elagabalus, Trajanus Decius, and Herennius Etruscus.

Pellerin gives a middle brass of this colony, which is of material historic importance, inasmuch as its legend does what no other ancient monument appears to have done, viz. it corroborates the truth of the fact asserted by different writers, that Hadrian was the *founder* of the colony built on the ruins of Jerusalem. It is described as follows :—

Obv. IMP. CAES. TRAIANO. HADRIAN. Laureated head of Hadrian.

Rev. COL. AEL. CAPIT. COND. A priest driving two oxen at plough, to the right; in the field, a military ensign.—(See the engraving above.)

Here we see the title of founder given to Hadrian, by the term COND*itor*. " Probably (says Pellerin), it is one of the first of the medals that were struck at *Ælia Capitolina*, as it exhibits the type of a plough conducted by a minister of religion, who wears the sacerdotal dress. It also shews by the representation of a military ensign, that Hadrian began by forming this colony of veteran soldiers; but the

legion to which they belonged is not marked on the standard "—*Melange,* i. 242.

The total expulsion of the Jews, the desecration of their capital by the extinction of its ancient name, and the profanation of its Zion to heathen idolatries, are events shadowed forth in a rare middle brass, engraved in Vaillant's valuable work on the Colonies (vol. i. p. 152.—

On the obverse is IMP. CAES. TRAI. HADRIAN. with the laureated head of that emperor. The reverse exhibits the name of of his new colony, COL. AEL. CAP. and a temple of two columns, within which are three figures, viz. Jupiter seated, between Pallas and the Genius of the city, standing.

The types adopted by the moneyers of this imperial colony, besides the legionary eagle, the trophy, and the victory, comprise Romulus and Remus with the wolf, Bacchus with his thyrsus, the Dioscuri, Astarte, "the abomination of the Tyrians and Sidonians;" also Isis and Serapis, "the abomination of the Egyptians." A coin of *Ælia Capitolina*, struck under Antoninus Pius, has on its reverse a *hog* walking (" an *abomination" to* the Jews). Whilst Capitoline Jove figures predominantly, with the eagle at his feet, and in one instance (Hostilianus), with a human head in his hand. In short, it would seem to have been the study of the Roman government in Judæa to insult, and horrify, as well as to oppress, the once-favoured people of Jehovah.

ÆLIAN BRIDGE.—On the reverse of a first brass coin of Hadrian, without legend, is the type of a structure, which is designated by some as the Ælian Bridge, at Rome, built by that emperor over the Tiber, a structure which still remains, under the name of the *Ponte di San Angelo*, communicating with the castle of that name; the mausoleum of Hadrian, and one of his many great architectural works.— " The medallion with the *Pons Ælius* (observes Mr. Akerman), quoted by early numismatic writers, is a modern fabrication."

AELIANA PINCENSIA.—Within a garland of laurel.—This legend on a second and third brass of Hadrian, has been supposed by Fröelich and others to indicate certain public games celebrated at Pincum, in Moesia, to the honour of Ælius Hadrian. But Eckhel (vi. p. 445) regards it as one of the *numi metallorum*, or coins of the mines, which are found inscribed with the name of Trajan and of Hadrian. By supplying the omission of the word *metallum*, he considers the meaning to be clearly elucidated : METALLA AELIA. PINCENSIA. That is to say, *Æliana*, (so called, from its institutor, *Ælius* Hadrianus) and *Pincensia* from *Pincum*, near which city [on the Danube, in the neighbourhood of what is now the town of Gradisca] these mines, or *metalla* were worked.

AELIANUS (Quintus Valens); one of the so-called *tyranni,* or pretenders to imperial and augustal rank and authority, during the reign of Gallienus. The Museum Theupoli contains the following description of a 3rd brass coin, which Eckhel supposes to belong to this usurper, but its authenticity is doubted by Mionnet.—*Obv.* IMP. C. Q. VALENS AELIANVS. P. AVG. And on its reverse IOVI. CONSER. AVGG. with type of Jupiter, standing; the thunderbolt in the right and the hasta in the left hand. On the exergue S. M. I.

AELIUS CÆSAR—(Lucius Aurelius Cejonius Commodus Verus) was the son of Cejonius Commodus, a man of consular rank, descended from an illustrious Etrurian family. The date of his birth is unknown. On the death of Sabina, he was adopted by Hadrian, A. U. C. 888 or 889 (A. D. 135 or 36), and destined to the succession of the empire; declared Cæsar under the name of Lucius Ælius Verus, made Prætor and Tribune of the people; and appointed prefect of Pannonia, which province he governed with wisdom and courage; created, for the first time, Consul, A. D. 137, and elected to his second consulate the following year. He was brother of Annius Verus and of Faustina the elder; married Domitia Lucilla. Of a handsome figure, dignified in physiognomy, and stately in carriage, he possessed a highly cultivated understanding, was learned, eloquent, and wrote with elegance in both prose and verse. Refined in his tastes, but effeminate in his habits, he fell an early victim to the inroads made on a weak constitution by voluptuousness and dissipation. Ælius returned from Pannonia to Rome A. D. 138, and died on the very day appointed for him to deliver a florid eulogium in honour of Hadrian's kindness to him. His body was deposited in the tomb which Hadrian had built at Rome for his own mausoleum, now the castle of St. Angelo, and that emperor caused several temples and statues to be raised to his memory.

On his coins he is styled L. AELIVS. CAESAR. They are more or less scarce, in all the three metals. His brass medallions are of the highest degree of rarity.— Ælius is represented on all his coins with bare head, curly hair and beard, and a majestic countenance.

Havercamp (in *Museo Christinæ,* p. 69) has engraved, and Capt. Smyth cites from his own collection, a large brass of this prince, which with no other legend on its reverse than TR. POT COS. II. and S. C. on the exergue, typifies "Fortune with her rudder and cornucopiæ, meeting Hope, who advances in light vestments and bears the blossom before her. This elegant device alludes to the fortunate exaltation of Ælius, and the expectation of his becoming Emperor. But the hope was vain; and Hadrian, who had celebrated the adoption with magnificent games, a public largess, and a donative to the soldiers, could not conceal his chagrin on perceiving that Ælius was passing to a sepulchre rather than a

throne. Alluding to the approaching apotheosis of the sickening Cæsar, the Emperor exclaimed —'*Ego Divum adoptavi, non filium.*' And the event verified the prediction." *(Descr. Cat.* p. 114.)—The type above described is evidently taken from FORTUNA SPES on an aureus of Hadrian.—See Caylus, *Numis. Aurea Impp. Rom.,* No. 350.

ÆNEAS, a Trojan prince, the fabled son of Venus by Anchises.—Arrived at manhood, he accompanied Paris, the seducer of Helen, to Troy, where he married Creusa, daughter of Priam, by whom he had a son named Ascanius. After taking that city, the Greeks proclaimed that every free man might carry away some portion of his goods. Æneas, in consequence, bore off his household gods *(Penates.)* The Greeks were so touched by this action, that they gave him the same permission a second time. Æneas immediately took his father on his shoulders. They then liberated all his family, and left him to take whatever belonged to him; at the same time assisting him with means for quitting the country. After a variety of adventures, the incidents of which are immortalised by the Muse of Mantua, Æneas arrived in Italy, with the remnant of his Trojans; gained frequent victories over the native tribes and states, and at length, having killed Turnus in single combat, obtained of King Latinus his daughter Lavinia in marriage. It was in honour of that lady that, according to the Roman legend, he built a city called Lavinium : and the further result was the union of the aborigines with the Trojans, under the common appellation of *Latins.* It is added, that he died in battle with the *Rutuli,* on the banks of the Numicus. From Æneas Sylvius, his son by Lavinia, are said to have descended all the kings of Alba Longa; and lastly Romulus and Remus, founders of the city of Rome.— (Pitiscus, *Lexicon Antiq. Rom.*—Millin, *Dictionnaire de la Fable.)*

Æneæ Pietas : The filial piety of Æneas— This hero is represented, on many imperial coins, in the act of carrying the aged Anchises on his shoulders, and the Trojan palladium (image of Pallas) in his right hand, Ascanius following him. Sometimes the palladium is omitted, and the boy has hold of Æneas's hand. This son of Æneas was also called *Iulus,* and the members of the *Julia* family pretended to derive their origin from him; a claim which is frequently indicated on the coins of Julius Cæsar. Another allusion to so favourite a theme of national flattery, with the Romans, is seen on a very rare denarius of the Livineia gens, struck by Livineius Regulus, monetary triumvir under Augustus. Amongst the splendid and interesting series of bronze medallions, struck at Rome under Antoninus Pius, is one (of which the above is a copy after Mionnet's plate), with the legend P. M. TR. P. COS. III. and the type of Æneas bearing Anchises from Troy, and leading Ascanius by the hand. The old man, covered with a robe, holds a casket; the youth wears a Phrygian bonnet. The reference on this medallion to the piety of the Trojan chief (says Havercamp), is to be regarded as connecting itself with the surname of Pius, which Antoninus bore, and as conveying an eulogium on the filial virtues of that Emperor.—Capitolinus, speaking of the affection which Antoninus evinced towards his parents, states that the name of *Pius* had been conferred on him, because, in the presence of the assembled Senate, he had given his arm to his father-in-law, who was broken down by old age, and thus assisted him in walking.

There is a very rare first brass, with a similar type, minted between the third and fourth consulates of Antoninus (A. D. 140—45), and both were probably designed as a compliment to the good Emperor, whose dutiful attachments as a son were further shewn by the statues which he dedicated to the memory of his father and mother, as well as to others of his defunct relations.—See Havercamp, *Médailles de Christine*, pl. xvi. p. 77.

Amongst the contorniate medals, which have on their obverses the respective heads of Nero and Trajan, is one with AENEAS for legend of reverse, and for type the group of Æneas, Anchises, and Ascanius: that well-known subject having been copied from earlier coins, Greek as well as Latin.

Æneæ Adventus.—Arrival of Æneas in Italy.—In his celebrated work *"De la rareté des Médailles Romaines,"* Mionnet has given a beautiful engraving (whence the subjoined is carefully copied) of a brass medallion, which on its reverse, with remarkable minuteness of graphic illustration, typifies the description, given by Virgil, of this aboriginal legend of Rome.

On the obverse, we read ANTONINVS AVG. PIVS P.P. TR. P. COS. VI. and are presented with a re-

markably fine portrait of that Emperor. The reverse, which is without epigraph, depictures Æneas and Ascanius, disembarking from a vessel anchored close to shore, on the coast, as may be supposed, of Latium. Opposite to this group lies a sow suckling its young, under a tree: above which are to be discerned the walls of a city.

Here, in the first place, we are reminded of the Trojan's dream, in which, while "laid on Tiber's banks, oppress'd with grief," he was addressed by "the Father of the Roman flood," in these words:—

Jamque tibi, ne vana putes hæc fingere somnum,
Littoreis ingens inventa sub ilicibus sus,
Triginta capitum foetus enixa, jacebit,
Alba, solo recubans, albi circum ubera nati.
Hic locus urbis erit, requies ea certa laborum:
Ex quo ter denis urbem redeuntibus annis
Ascanius clari condet cognominis Albam.
                              Æneid, viii. 42.

And that this nightly vision may not seem
Th' effect of fancy, or an idle dream,
A sow beneath an oak shall lie along,
All white herself, and white her thirty young.
When thirty rolling years have run their race,
Thy son, Ascanius, on this empty space
Shall build a royal town, of lasting fame;
Which from this omen shall receive the name.
                    Dryden's translation.

Next, we have the fulfilment of the sign given to Æneas, according to the promise of Tiberinus, as described a little further on, in the same immortal poem:—

Ecce autem subitum, atque oculis mirabile monstrum.
Candide per silvam cum foetu concolor albo
Procubuit, viridique in littore conspicitur sus.

Now on the shore the fatal swine is found;
Wondrous to tell; she lay along the ground:
Her well-fed offspring at her udders hung;
She white herself, and white her thirty young.

The city delineated on the above medallion is clearly Lavinium.

AEQVI. or AEQVIT. AVG.—Æquitas Augusti.—(The Equity of the Emperor).

AEQVITAS.—The Equity, referred to on Roman coins, signifies that virtue so much to be desired in sovereign princes, which prompts them to administer the affairs of the public (especially *in re monetariâ*), with impartial devotedness to the interests of the people. *Aequitas* is almost always represented under the figure of a woman, clothed in the stola, generally standing, sometimes but not often seated, with a pair of scales, or (but very rarely) a patera, in the right hand, and in the left a cornucopiæ, or the *hasta pura*, or a sceptre.

"The scales, that natural emblem of Equity, are used by Persius to express the decision of right and wrong—the cornucopiæ signifies the good which results from examining into the real merits of cases."—Smyth.

The epigraph of AEQVITAS (or AEQVITATI) AVG. or AVGVSTI, belongs to the mints of Vitellius, Titus, Domitian, Antoninus Pius, Pertinax, S. Severus, Alex. Severus, Macrinus, Maximinus, Gordianus Pius, Volusianus, Macrianus, Quietus.

AEQVITAS PVBLICA, or AEQVITATI PVBLICAE presents itself on medals of S. Severus, Julia Domna, Caracalla, Geta, Elagabalus, Gallienus.

AEQVITAS AVG.—Equity with scales and horn of plenty.   Silver.—See VOLUSIANVS.

AEQVITAS AVGVSTI.—A woman holding in her right hand a pair of scales, in her left a cornucopiæ.   The inscription of *Aequitas*, inappropriately stamped on the medals of Vitellius, of Domitian, of Commodus, of Severus, of Caracalla, of Elagabalus, and such like tyrants, is with no more than strict justice engraven on coins, struck under the reigns of a Titus, a Nerva, and a Pertinax, by whom that quality appears to have been strictly and sincerely cherished.   It is indeed a virtue worthy of an emperor, as the bridle and rule of his sovereign power—a virtue which Ammianus calls the despised mother and the nurse of the Roman world; *Æquitate calcata parente nutriceque Orbis Romani*.—Spanheim.

AEQVITAS II.—A woman standing with balance and horn of plenty.   A silver medal of S. Severus (struck A. D. 194) with this unprecedented feature in the legend of its reverse, was first published by Eckhel in his *Sylloge*, i. p. 103.   He observes that in the mark II. it presents Equity and Liberality divided into numbers; a circumstance noticed neither by Mediobarbi, nor by Vaillant.   But the meaning of this *Equitas Duplicata* he cannot make out.   There is a coin of Julia Domna with the same reverse.   Vol. vii. 167–196.

AEQVITATI PVBLICAE. S. C.—The three *Monetæ* standing; each holds a balance in the right and a cornucopiæ in the left hand; at the foot of each is a vase.   On first brass of Sept. Severus.

The three female personifications of the Roman mint, each holding balances and cornucopiæ, with vases, or with conical heaps representing the three metals, at their feet, occur continually on coins of the imperial series, from Pertinax and S. Severus downwards, especially on medallions; but these are for the most part accompanied by the legend MONETAE AVG. or AVGG. and serve to shew, that the princes of the lower empire assumed to themselves the supreme power of coining money, in every metal, as signified by these *imagines monetarum*.—See MONETA.

There is a first brass coin of Aquilia Severa, with the legend of AEQVITAS PVBLICA. S. C. on its reverse, the type of which exhibits three females standing in full robes, with the attributes of Fortune (i. e. cornucopiæ and rudder).   "This (observes Capt. Smyth) is an uncommon device for medals in honour of females; and is only known upon this and one of Julia Paula—so that it may be taken for an allusion to the high fortune to which Elagabalus elevated those ladies. But in this sense the device has little relation to the legend."—Havercamp, in *Mus. Christinæ*, has given an engraving of this reverse.

ÆRA.—Era, or Epoch, is the point of commencement, from which years are reckoned, as taken from the date of some memorable event. Thus in Christendom, especially Christian Europe, we compute the number of years, from the era of Our Lord's incarnation.   The different cities and peoples of antiquity by whom the Greek language was used, began the year from the season of autumn, namely, about the autumnal equinox, or from the calends of September— although, after the correction of the calendar, promulgated under Julius Cæsar, the beginning of the year was taken from the calends of January, in some Greek cities influenced by Rome.——The commencement of numbering is expressed both in the Varronian years from the foundation of Rome, and in the vulgar era from the birth of Christ.   The year U. C. *(Urbis Conditæ)*, according to Terentius Varro, began 753 years before the Christian era.— According to Cato, Rome was founded in B. C. 751; according to Polybius in B. C. 750; according to Fabius Pictor in 747.—Visconti *(Iconographie Romaine*, i. p. 14, 8vo. edit.) says— " Je préfère, avec la plupart des chronologistes, le calcul de Varron, qui fut le plus suivi par les anciens, depuis le siècle d'Auguste."

From amongst the more illustrious epochs of cities, and those of more frequent occurrence, the following are selected, as bearing relation to Roman History:—

Æra Pompeiana—the period when Cn. Pompey, surnamed the Great, having made peace with Tigranes, King of Armenia, and driven Mithridates, King of Pontus, out of his dominions, assumes the government of affairs in Syria as a Roman province, subdues Phœnicia, and takes Jerusalem—began about the year of Rome 691 (B. C. 63.)

Æra Cæsariana, so called in honour of Julius Cæsar, the conqueror of Pompey, began with the battle of Pharsalia, A. U. C. 706 (B. C. 48). The murder of Cæsar took place B. C. 44, Mar. 15, in his 4th Dictatorship.

Æra Actiaca, derived from the defeat of Mark Antony and Cleopatra, by Octavianus (afterwards Cæsar Augustus), at the battle of Actium, dates from A. U. C. 723 (B. C. 31.)— [But this æra, in Egypt and in some cities, takes its commencement from the following year, viz. U. C. 724 (B. C. 30); in autumn amongst the Greeks.]

Æra Augustalis, in which Octavianus Cæsar accepted the title of *Augustus*, is taken from the year of Rome 727 (B. C. 30), or from the following year.

ÆRARIUM.——The Exchequer or Public

Treasury; the place where the annual revenues of the republic were deposited, and which derived its name from the metal of the money of the Romans, viz. *aes* (brass). It was in the temple of Saturn; and thence were drawn the funds to defray all needful expenses, as well in peace as in war. This *Ærarium* was generally filled with immense riches; and rarely, indeed, did it happen, that the state laboured under any want of money. The custody of it was confided to officers, selected from the people, and who were called *Tribuni Ærarii;* they were required to be men in high repute for great riches, probity, and disinterestedness. Besides this ordinary treasure, there was another, which bore the appellation of *Sanctius Ærarium,* because it was in the interior of the temple, or perhaps because it was not allowed to be resorted to except in pressing emergencies. Julius Cæsar, wanting money for his own purposes, during the civil war, took forcible possession of this deposit of public wealth, and carried away vast sums, as is acknowledged by all the historians, although they do not agree as to the quantity.—In addition to these two treasuries, there was likewise the *Ærarium Militare,* formed by Augustus, for the maintenance of the Roman troops, the ancient funds proving insufficient to furnish pay for all the legions.—See Pitiscus.

On gold and silver coins struck by L. VINI- CIVS. L. F. one of the moneyers of Augustus, we read the following inscription, which, as containing the initial letter of the word *Ærarium,* may, with propriety, be cited in this place: viz. S. P. Q. R. IMP. CAE. QVOD. V. M. S. EX. EA. P. Q. IS. AD. A. DE. *Senatus Populus- que Romanus, Imperatori Cæsari, Quod Viæ Munitæ Sint Ex Ea Pecunia, Quam Is Ad* AERA- RIUM *Detulisset.* A monument this of public gratitude to the Emperor above named, who by making and repairing great roads, had contributed to the public safety; and who did this so far at his own cost, that he had caused to be conveyed to the *Treasury of the State,* that money which was the fruit of his victories, and of the advantages he had gained over the foreign enemies of his country.—See Eckhel's remarks on a coin of the *Neria* family, corroborative of the fact that the *Ærarium,* or public treasury, at Rome, was in the temple of Saturn.—See also the word SATURNVS.

ÆRUGO.——Rust of a peculiar kind increases the price of *brass* coins, being an ornament imparted by nature alone, which the utmost rivalship of art has not yet been able successfully to imitate. There is, indeed, some particular earth that communicates to the metal in question a coating and a colour, which in its hue of blue jasper, or turquois, sometimes even excels the gem of that name. The crimson or ruby, which adheres to other coins, is a sign of genuineness. Others are covered with a natural *vernis,* or varnish, of shining and splendid violet or purple, leaving far behind, in point of brilliancy and of exquisite smoothness, that brass out of which statues are cast—a quality which never fails to be recognised by those possessing

the most ordinary acquaintance with numismatics, inasmuch as it greatly surpasses the colour so easily obtained from vinegar and ammoniac. The true *ærugo* is in general decidedly green, and at the same time forms a very thin covering, insinuating itself over the surface of the coin in the most delicate manner, without obliterating anything; somewhat in the way of an enamel. This, however, as already observed, solely applies to brass coins: for *viror* and rust corrode *silver* coins, and for that reason it is proper to rub it off from *them,* with juice of lemons.—Jobert, *Science de Med.* i. p. 335.

AERUGO NOBILIS; the perfection of *patina,* which is the smooth, coloured varnish of time.—Smyth.

AES.—Brass and copper were the metals first used as money by the Romans. Hence the word served afterwards, with them, to designate every kind of money, whether gold, silver, or brass. And even at that period when the wealth of the Republic was at its highest pitch, every species of current coin continued to be denominated *Aes.*—The *aes grave,* it is evident from the descriptions of their writers, was brass (or copper) in bars, of the weight of a pound *(pondus libralis)* used as money, before the introduction of a silver coinage. Eckhel, in support of this opinion, cites Festus, who says—*Grave aes dictum a pondere, quia deni asses, singuli pondo libræ, efficiebant denarium, ab hoc ipso numero dictum.* The collecting of such heavy masses, to any great amount of value, became so extremely inconvenient that, according to Livy, the *aes grave* was obliged to be conveyed to the treasury in waggons. Subsequently, in order to obviate this objection, pieces of copper, of less weight, but without any mark, were roughly cut; and these, on account of their uncouth form, were called *aes rude.* This improvement is by some ancient writers ascribed to Numa. But it was not until the reign of Servius Tullius, that the Romans are, with any due degree of authority, affirmed to have begun striking round coins of brass, with the type of a bull, &c. to which they gave the name (according to Pliny) of *Aes signatum.*—See *Brass*—also *As.*

AES CYPRIUM; the copper on which the Roman *dupondii* or second brass were minted.— See Smyth, xv.

ÆSCULAPIUS, in the more general opinion of mythographers, was regarded by the ancients, as the son of Apollo and of Coronis, daughter of Phlegius, King of Thessaly. According to the same fabulous authority, his reputed father confided his education to the centaur Chiron, who instructed him in medicine and other sciences, comprehending a thorough knowledge of plants. Conformably to the custom of those early ages, he combined the practice of surgery with the faculty of a physician; and with so high a degree of success was his career attended, that to him was superstitiously ascribed the power of curing, by words alone, all kinds of wounds, contusions, fevers, &c. It was even alleged that he had raised many persons from the dead. So great, in short, was the celebrity he acquired, that divine honours were paid to him after his decease; and he was venerated as the tutelary god of the healing art. Æsculapius had temples in many parts of Greece, Asia Minor, &c. He was especially the object of worship at Epidaurus (a city of Agria, in the Peloponnesus), the place of his birth.

This pagan divinity is usually portrayed, under the figure of a sedate-looking, middle-aged man, standing or (but rarely) sitting; wholly or partly covered with a cloak; and holding in his right hand a staff, round which a serpent is entwined.—A denarius of the Roman family *Acilia* exhibits, on its obverse, the head of Æsculapius laureated, and on its reverse a serpent coiled round a staff. (Morell).—On a 1st brass of Galba, the God of medicine is represented standing, naked, with right hand extended, and the left resting on his staff, round which the serpentine attribute is enfolded.—A brass medallion of L. Verus presents him on the same reverse with Hygeia, the goddess of health; and on other medals he is seen attended by the little *Telesphorus*, who appears to have his origin in Egyptian mythology, and to be identical with Harpocrates, the god of silence. In describing a middle brass of Caracalla, on which Æsculapius stands between Telesphorus and a small globe, Patin observes, that the Romans as well as the Greeks, worshipped him, as the author of the health of Augustus, and afterwards of every reigning emperor, for which reason he often appears on their coins; especially on those of Caracalla, Albinus, and Gallienus.

AESCVLAPIVS.—The only production of the Roman mint, on which the *name itself* of Æsculapius appears, is a fine medallion, in bronze, struck under Antoninus Pius—specimens of which very great numismatic rarity are contained in the cabinet of the *Bibliothéque Nationale*, at Paris, and in that of the Imperial Museum at Vienna.—The *obverse* exhibits a laureated bust of the emperor, wearing the paludamentum, around it is read ANTONINVS AVG. PIVS. P. P. TRP. COS. IIII.—The *reverse* has for its type a serpent darting from a galley, under a bridge of two arches. Before it is the Tiber personified, sitting in the midst of the water. The right hand of this river-god is ex-

tended towards the serpent; the left holds a reed, and rests on an urn, whence flows a co-

pious stream. Near it are several buildings and a tree, situate on a rock. The word AESCVLAPIVS is on the exergue.

The inscription and type of this reverse bear reference to the curious legendary narrative—one third probable fact and two thirds superstitious fable—concerning the arrival of Æsculapius at Rome; which Ovid describes in his *Metamorphoses* (lib. xv.); and which Valerius Maximus and other old writers have taken the pains to give, in substance as follows:—In the 463rd year from the foundation of the city (B.C. 291) the plague made great ravages within its walls. The pontiffs appointed to consult the Sybilline books, found that the only means of restoring health in Rome was to cause Æsculapius to visit it, from Epidaurus. Accordingly, a deputation of ten principal citizens was sent there, with Q. Ogulnius at their head. Whilst these persons, on entering the temple of the demi-god, were admiring the beauty of the statue, the serpent, which the inhabitants of Epidaurus seldom saw, and which they honoured as Æsculapius himself, made its appearance in the most frequented parts of the town, moving slowly about, and mildly looking around. After having thus shewn himself, during three days to the people, he proceeded to the harbour; entered the Roman galley, and ensconced himself snugly in Ogulnius's cabin, where he peaceably remained coiled up. The ambassadors having made themselves acquainted with the manner in which the serpent was to be honoured, immediately set sail and landed at Antium. There the serpent left the vessel, and entered the vestibule of the temple of Æsculapius. After remaining there three days, it re-entered the ship, in order to be conveyed to Rome; and whilst the deputation were disembarking on the banks of the Tiber, the serpent swam across to the island, where afterwards the temple of Æsculapius was built. His arrival, it is gravely added by the Roman historian, dispelled the contagious disease, for which his presence had been sought as the remedy.

"On the medallion of Antonine (observes Millin in his *Dictionnaire Mythologique*), the Tiber appears under the usual figure of personified rivers. Near him is the isle of the Tiber, called Mesopotamia, because it is in the middle of that river. It has the form of a galley, as indeed was the case; and to this day there still remain some fragments of it, which have escaped the injuries of time and the inundations. Upon the top of the prow of the ship, which the isle in question is made to resemble, is represented a serpent, in tortuous folds, advancing its head, in a contrary direction to the current of the water. The temple of Æsculapius built on the isle had a high reputation. The prætor Lucretius contributed greatly to its embellishment. It is now the Church of *S. Bartholomeo nel isola*, which is still one of the most celebrated churches in Rome."

On a denarius of Caracalla, bearing for its legend of reverse P. M. TR. P. XVIII. COS. IIII. P.P. (Sovereign Pontiff, invested with the tribunitian dignity for the 18th time, consul for the 4th

time), Æsculapius is designated by his inseparable attribute, and by his side,
or rather at his feet, we see
his dwarfish companion Telesphorus.——The fratricide
son and successor of the merciless Severus, who caused
this silver coin to be struck,
is said by Herodianus to have
visited Pergamos, about A. D. 215, "in order to
place himself under the tutelary care and healing influence of Æsculapius," to whom, amidst
combined tortures of mind and body, the ferocious tyrant was profuse in prayers and sacrifices. Under the frenzied illusions of a guilty
conscience, he saw his brother constantly before
him, brandishing a naked sword, and launching
the most terrible threats against him. Often
did he invoke the *manes* of the dead, and chiefly
those of his father, who appeared always accompanied by Geta. He had already implored
Apollo in vain to restore him; and now he
sought Æsculapius, who, having no respect for
murderers, was also deaf to his remorseful supplications.

On silver and second brass of Albinus (the
latter with COS. II. for legend of reverse), Æsculapius appears, upright, resting his right arm
on his *serpent twisted* staff. He also is found,
with his usual attributes, on silver and third
brass of Gallienus, sharing, as CONSERVATOR
AV*gusti* (the Emperor's preserver), those sacrificial honours which that rash and reckless
prince, amidst a world of calamities, physical,
social, and political, was at the same time in
the habit of paying to Apollo, to Hercules, to
Jupiter, to a whole Olympus of other false
gods, whom he vainly invoked to save him and
his distracted empire from impending destruction.

ÆSCULAPIUS and his DOG, on a brass medallion of Antoninus Pius.— See *Dog of Æsculapius.*

For a representation of Æsculapius, as a young
man, making his first essay in the healing art,
on the wounded foot of an ox, see DEO AESC.
SUB. or SUBVEN, on a coin of Parium.

Types of Æsculapius also appear on Latin
colonial coins of Babba, Corinth, Damascus,
Deultum, and Patræ. But it is on the Greek
imperial that we find the effigy and the various attributes of this demi-god, most fully developed. And on the medallions, in particular, this object is accomplished, with great
beauty of design and display of artistic skill :
the figure of Æsculapius being, in these instances, generally grouped with that of some
princely petitioner for his tutelary favours, and
also with the goddess Hygeia.

AET. *Æterna.*—VICT. AET. AVG. Victory
walking.—Billon of Gallienus.—Banduri, i. 180.

AET. *Æternitas.*—See AET. AVG. of Trajan.

AET. *Æternitas.*—See gold of Vespasian.

AETER. AVG. *Æternitas Augusti* of Hadrian.

AETER. *Æterno.*—D. N. DIOCLETIANO AE-
TER. AVG.—On second brass of Diocletian.—
Vaillant, Pr. i. 252.

AETERN. AVG. *Augustorum.*— Quadriga of
lions, with Cybele on a car.— Silver of Julia
Domna, mother of Caracalla and Geta, who is
here represented as Cybele, as though she had
brought forth *eternal sons.*—Vaillant, Pr. ii.
233.

AETERN. AVG. N. *Augusti Nostri.*—On
a coin of Maxentius.

AETERNA.—Rome is so called, either to
distinguish her from other cities, or on account
of the ancient opinion of the Romans that their
city would be eternal.—(Rasche.)—See ROMA.

AETERNA FELICITAS AVG.—Wolf with
the twins, on 2nd brass of Maxentius—Banduri,
ii. 157.

AETERNA MEMORIA.—A circular temple,
with front of six columns, resembling a mausoleum, one of the doors half open; an eagle
on the top of its dome; in the exergue, MOST P.
or MOST Q. or MOST S. The obverse has the
veiled head of Constantius Chlorus; with legend
IMP. MAXENTIVS DIVO CONSTANTIO ADFINI
(or COGN.)—Second brass, engraved in Banduri,
ii. p. 90.

This *immortal memory* (remarks Spanheim,
in reference to the above described coin of
Constantius I., father of Constantine the Great),
this *Æterna Memoria* was the great object, and
esteemed the most glorious recompense, of a
conqueror's exploits. From this strong sentiment of warlike ambition, and from the no less
strong desire to be remembered by posterity,
have proceeded not only the above inscription,
but also those of *Memoria Perpetua* and *Memoria Felix,* which are found on the coins of some
of the Roman Emperors, struck after their deaths,
and which clearly shew what must naturally
have been the true sense and meaning of their
consecration. For the same reason, such inscriptions are accompanied with representations
of temples, lighted altars, eagles, or of cars
destined for public processions, which constituted the ordinary marks of these *apotheoses.*—
(See Cæsars of Julian, 211.)—From the legend
of the obverse we learn that this coin was struck
by order of Maxentius, in honour of his deceased
relation Constantius.—See *Adfinis.*

AETERNA PIETAS.—A soldier standing, in
helmet, military dress, and cloak, a spear in his
right hand, and a globe in his left, surmounted
by a cross and monogram of Christ.—Eckhel
(viii. 92), authenticates this as a 3rd brass of
Constantinus Magnus, in the imperial cabinet;
and Beger gives a print of it in vol. ii. p. 805,
Thesaurus Brandenburgicus.

The obverse of this coin affixes, in its legend,
to the name of the Emperor, whose head is
veiled, the old mark of heathen consecration,
viz. DIVVS: consequently it must have been struck
after his death. The mixture, however, of
Christian emblems with Pagan observances, in
the inscriptions, is in perfect keeping with the
character and conduct of this able but most unscrupulous prince; a merciless conqueror, a cruel
father, and an unjust judge,—a man whose
"*piety,*" even after his openly professed conver-
sion to the religion of that Cross, through the

sign of which (in hoc signo) he boasted of having "overcome" his rivals, and attained the purple (A. D. 311), would seem from coins, and other monuments, to have been much more of the Pagan than of the Christian sort, and whose policy, in its whole tenor, shews that things, *not* "Eternal" but, temporal and secular, were those which *he* sought and prized.

AETERNAE MEMORIAE.—A round-formed temple, one of the doors of which is half opened. On the top of its dome stands an eagle, with expanded wings; on the exergue, POST.—This legend and type appear on the reverse of an *unique* gold medallion, which Maxentius, A. D. 309, caused to be struck to the *everlasting remembrance* of his son Romulus Cæsar, whose youthful bust, clothed in the toga, and with bare head, appears on the other side, with the legend DIVO ROMVLO NVBIS. CONS.—The above cut is accurately copied from the engraving in T. ii. p. 202, of the *Medailles Romaines* of Mionnet, by whom this fine medallic relic of the lower empire (15 lignes, French measure, in diameter), is valued at 1200 fr.—See some remarks on the words NVBIS. CONS. in their place.

A legend in the same dedicatory form appears on two second brass coins of Galerius Maximianus, one with the circular temple and eagle on its summit, and the other with a square altar lighted, and a branch placed in the middle, on which stands an eagle, with a crown in its beak. —Banduri, ii. p. 133.

AETERNITAS.—Eternity, to whom the Romans paid divine honours, although neither temples nor altars were dedicated by them to her worship, is represented on coins of the imperial series, under the personification of a matronly woman, clothed in the stola; sometimes veiled, at other times without a veil, sometimes seated, sometimes standing, in various attitudes and with various emblems and attributes. She makes her first monetal appearance, under the reign of Vespasian. It is on gold and silver of that emperor that she stands near an altar, supporting in one outstretched hand the radiated head of the Sun, and in the other the crescented head of the Moon. Next she is seen on one of those first brass coins, which were struck A. D. 141, and following year, by order of the Senate, in memory of the elder Faustina, whose supposed immortality, her "not wisely but too well" loving husband, the worthy Antoninus, delighted to honour with the title of DIVA, and with the symbols of AETERNITAS. The type is here a seated female, hold-

ing a sceptre, or the *hasta pura*, in her left hand, and a globe surmounted by the Phœnix (see that word) in her right.

Amongst the attributes (says Eckhel, viii. p. 457) borrowed by the emperors from the deities of their mythology, that of Eternity seems to have claimed the foremost place. The Romans called that *eternal* which had no end; which stood opposed to, because emancipated from, the conditions and restrictions inseparable from mortality—in a word, something divine. But the term *eternal* was also applied to that which from its nature might admit of comparison therewith—inasmuch as it was considered capable of long duration. For this reason the Phœnix (itself a fabulous bird) was a recognised symbol of eternity, because its life was, according to popular belief, circumscribed not by years but by whole centuries; on which account Claudian calls it *æterna avis*; and the elephant, from its reputed longevity, was likewise figured to signify eternity. There were other things which the law deemed eternal, as the fire of Vesta, the extinguishment of which demanded great atonement, and was viewed as a fearful omen.

Some derived this attribute from public opinion, as ROMA AETERNA, a common legend on coins; others from a vow, although an useless one, as AETERNITAS IMPERII, on a coin of Caracalla; and as AETERNITATIBVS, on a coin of Alexander Severus. The word eternity was appropriated not only to deceased and consecrated emperors, but also to living ones; and that not solely on coins and marbles, but likewise by the pens of ancient writers. Of this latter class of authorities, one instance may suffice to be adduced—namely, that of the younger Pliny, who, in his letters, frequently addresses Trajan as *æternitas tua*. But, in the case of living princes, the use of such an appellation might be allowable, because there was scarcely any other that could be employed with respect to them, except the *votum diuterni imperii;* at least it is thus only that one can understand and explain the following allusion of Horace to Augustus :—

> *Serus in coelum redeas, diuque*
> *Lætus intersis populo Quirini.*

"Oh! late return to heav'n, and may thy reign
"With lengthened blessings fill thy wide domain."

AETERNITAS.—This legend is commented upon by Eckhel as appearing on a brass medallion, in the Imperial collection at Vienna. Struck under Pertinax, about A. D. 193, it is described to have for the type of its reverse the statue of that emperor seated in a quadriga of elephants. The epigraph of the obverse is DIVVS. PERT. PIVS. PATER, with the bare head of the emperor.

A passage in the historian Victor explains the legend of the obverse, namely, that in which he says, that at the consecration of Pertinax by Sept. Severus, the people shouted till their voices failed—*imperante securi viximus neminem timuimus*; PATRI PIO, *Patri senatus, Patri omnium bonorum.*—In reference to the type of the reverse, Eckhel cites the following short but elucidatory passage from Dion: *Præcepit Severus, ut statua ejus aurea curru elephantorum veheretur in Circum.* It was it appears, therefore, by Severus's order, that the golden statue of the murdered Pertinax was carried round the *Circus Maximus* at Rome, in a chariot drawn by four elephants. [This coin is not described in either Mionnet's or Akerman's catalogues.]

AETERNITAS. P. R.—Victory approaching the Emperor (who is clothed in the paludamentum, and holds a spear in his left hand), offers him the Palladium.

A large brass coin of Vespasian, with this legend and type, was first published by Eckhel (in his *Sylloge* i.); and he observes that, although the expression *Æternitas Augusti* is common on medals from the time of Vespasian, yet that of Æternitas *Populi Romani* was till then unknown. Victory here holds out to the Emperor the palladium, or figure of Minerva armed; a superstition derived from Troy, the safety and eternity of which city was believed to be dependent on its possession of that symbol. The same palladium, by whatever means brought to Rome, was supposed to bestow the same protection and good fortune on the Trojan exiles and their descendants, wherever they went. This coin, Eckhel adds, was struck in the same year (U. c. 823, A. D. 70) that Vespasian (having just before received the empire, whilst at a distance from Rome) first entered the city. Accordingly Victory offers to him the above-named precious pledge of the stability of the Roman commonwealth.

AETERNITAS. S. C.—On a first brass, which bears on its obverse the veiled portrait of Faustina senior (DIVA AVGVSTA), we see the legend associated, on its reverse, with the image of Cybele, who, resting the right hand on her

customary attribute of the *tympanum*, is seated

on a car drawn by two lions; signifying (as Havercamp observes), that the Empress, thus compared to the *Magna Mater Deûm*, and placed amongst the divinities, is no longer subject to the accidents of mortality.—On another large brass coin, struck in memory of the same princess, the same legend accompanies the type of two, and even four, elephants (with their drivers), drawing a canopied chariot, in which is the seated statue of the consecrated Faustina.

AETERNITAS AVG.—AVGVST.—AVGVSTI.—AVGVSTA.—AVGVSTAE.—AVGG.—AVGVSTORVM.—(The Eternity of the Emperor, of the Empress, or of the Emperors.—When any of these inscriptions are combined with the title of the reigning prince, or with that of the wife, son, or other branch of the imperial family, the accompanying types represent, amongst other devices, sometimes a female veiled, seated on a stag, and holding a torch in her left hand, as on a brass medallion of Faustina, junior; sometimes a crescent and seven stars, as on gold of Pescennius Niger; sometimes an equestrian statue, as on first brass of Gordianus Pius; or an elephant, with driver on its back, as on silver and first brass of Philip, senior, and on brass of Val. Maximianus. Three radinted heads, the centre full-faced, accompany the same legend on gold of Postumus.—A temple with image in the adytum; or a woman resting one arm on a column, and holding a globe in the other hand, as on first brass of Faustina senior. Two hands joined, on billon of Gallienus.—A thensa, with the Empress's statue on it, drawn by two elephants, as in first brass of Faustina, the elder.—A female stands holding a globe, surmounted by a phœnix, on silver medallion of Trebonianus Gallus, and 1st brass of Æmilianus, and 2nd brass of Carinus.—The sun, with right hand raised, and holding a globe in the left, on small brass of Valerianus.—Romulus and Remus, suckled by the wolf, allusive to the eternity of Rome, on billon of Gallienus, and on second brass of Maxentius. The Emperor crowned by Victory, on second brass of Tacitus, &c. &c.

AETERNITAS, *symbolized by the images of the Sun and Moon.*—Allusion has already been made to gold and silver of Vespasian, on which a female figure, in the stola, holds in her hands the heads of the Sun and Moon. The same type appears on a middle brass of Domitian, as given in Morell. The reason why we see types

of these planets, exhibited on imperial coins, in association with the legend of Eternity, is that *Sol* and *Luna* were believed by the Romans, in common with the rest of the heathen world, to be eternal; and eternity was either feigned to be an attribute of, or prayed for *(vota)* as a blessing on, the Emperors. Thus, in the famous inscription, published by Gruter, is read SOLI AETERNO. LVNAE. PRO. AETERNITATE. IMPERII. ET. SALVTE. IMP. CA. ... SEPTIMII. SEVERI. &c.

And in another, LVNAE. AETER. SACR. PRO SALVTE. IMP. CAES. L. SEPTIMI. SEV. &c.—On these marbles we see eternity ascribed to the Sun and to the Moon, together with health promised, by vow, to the Emperors. These symbols were doubtless borrowed by the Romans from the Egyptians. According to the authority of Horus Apollinus, the two great lights constituted, in the glyphic language of Ancient Egypt, the element, which indicates *sæculum*, *ævum*, *æternitas*. This point of the subject is further illustrated by the author of *Doctrina, &c.* (vi. 23), in a coin of Trajan, which has for the legend of its reverse as follows :—

AET. AVG. *Aeternitas Augusti.*—A woman standing with the head of the Sun in her right hand. Eckhel thus describes, as from a specimen in the Vienna cabinet, under his own eye, a silver coin of Trajan, struck in that emperor's 7th consulate. It furnishes, in conjunction with a similar legend and type on gold of Vespasian, one of the earlier among numerous proofs, that the Romans assigned eternity to their Emperors, as a certain mark of divinity. The eternity of Trajan is here typified by those two "eternal stars" the Sun and Moon. That prince affords a particular example of this custom in allowing *His Eternity* to be recognised not only on his coins, but in his most confidential correspondence (see Pliny's Letters, l. x. epist. 87). Amongst the ancients, Eternity was symbolized by the Sun and the Moon; because, says Mamertinus, *Quidquid immortale est stare nescit, æternoque motu se servat æternitas.* (Whatever is immortal knows no rest; and eternity maintains itself by eternal motion). "His throne" (says the Royal Psalmist) "is as the Sun before me, and as the Moon eternally."—Eckhel also quotes Diodorus Siculus, to shew that the most ancient Egyptians, in contemplating with astonishment and admiration the universe above them, were led to think, that there were two eternal and principal deities, viz., the Sun and the Moon, of which they called the former *Osiris*, and the latter *Isis.*—Tristan (vol. i. 381) describes a coin of Trajan with this legend, and as having for its reverse type, the figure of a woman, who holds the effigies of the Sun and Moon—*qui en sont* (says he) *et comme il est assez cogneu, les vrais symboles.*—See *Doct. Num. vet.* vol. vii. p. 181, for a commentary on a coin of Sept. Severus, struck about A. D. 202, on the reverse of which is inscribed CONCORDIAE AETERNAE, wherein further light is thrown on the subject of the Solar and Lunar types, appropriated to their coins by the Roman emperors and empresses, as symbols of their own deified immortality.—It is to be observed, that no mention is made of the above coin in either Mionnet or Akerman.

AETERNITAS. S. C.—Among other coins, which M. Aurelius caused to be minted A. D. 140; whilst he was himself engaged in the infatuated employment of rendering "the divine honours" of the apotheosis to his, "and every man's," Faustina, viz. the younger of that name; there is one in large brass, on which the Empress, or rather her "deified spirit," is re-

presented, with a sceptre in her right hand, "like another Juno" (as Spanheim expresses it),

seated between two graceful young females, who, lightly treading, hold her chair uplifted from the ground, as if on the point of carrying her heaven-ward. Each of these nymphs holds a scarf of gossamer drapery, floating in an arch-like form above her head.—Eckhel describes this beautiful coin, from a specimen in the imperial cabinet, at Vienna.

AETERNITAS AVGG.—Apollo, or the Sun in a quadriga, elevating the right hand towards a globe, which appears in the air, and holding in the left a sceptre or a whip.—[This legend and type are exhibited on a large brass of Tetricus, jun. a fac-simile engraving of which is published by the author of *Leçons de Numismatique Romaine*, from that excellent writer's own collection. It is not noticed by, and most probably was not known, at the time, to Mionnet.—See *Tetricus, jun.*

AETERNITAS IMPER*ii.*—Figure of the Sun walking, his right hand lifted up, and a whip in the left; on silver of Philip senior.

For Eckhel's remarks respecting the Sun, as connected with the monetal legend of AETERNITAS, see the AET. AVG. of Trajan, in the left hand column of this page.

AETERNITAS AVG. N.—*(Augusti Nostri.)* Castor and Pollux standing, the former on the right side, the latter on the left. They hold spears in their right hands, and their horses' bridles in their left hands; between each are the wolf suckling Romulus and Remus. On silver and 2nd brass of Maxentius.—See Angeloni, p. 298, and Banduri, ii. 150, 151.

AETERNIT*as* IMPER*ii.*—Laureated heads of Sept. Severus and Caracalla face to face.—Silver. On another coin, in gold and silver, with the same legend, the heads of Caracalla and Geta face to face: the one laureated, the other bare.—Caylus, *Num. Aur. Impp.* No. 682.

The eternity of the Roman *Empire,* to propitiate the realization of which, according to Suetonius (c. xi.), games had been established by Nero, is here typified by the portraitures of the sons and successors of Severus, whose race became extinct in a single generation afterwards.

AETERNITAS. S. C.—The type which accompanies this legend, on the reverse of a large brass coin, struck under M. Aurelius to record the *consecration* of FAVSTINA PIA—represents her, "wafted through the skies," upborne on the shoulders of a winged female, who holds a

large torch in her hands.—The airy figure last described, from its light and flowing drapery, and the office it is performing, might be at once pronounced to represent a celestial genius, or *angel.* But Occo styles it *Victoria volans;* Agostini, a winged Eternity; Oiselius terms it simply a Victory; and it accords with that described in the dream of Alexander Severus. Tristan treats the typification with merited sarcasm :—" Here (says he) we behold the wife of Aurelius, carried aloft on the wings of Victory, or of Minerva, surnamed the Victorious. And this is done for her wise and virtuous conduct, and for her having been victorious over vice and incontinence, of which that goddess was the declared enemy." —Capt. Smyth.

AETERNITAS AVGG (Æternitas Augustorum).—On silver and first brass of Philip senior, the reverse presents a caparisoned elephant, with a naked rider, who holds a goad in his right hand, and sits on the animal's back. (For an engraving of the silver type see PHILIPPVS AVG).

AETERNITATI AVGG.—A bearded man, hooded, and in the toga, standing with a harpa or sickle in his left hand. (See *Harpa*).— Banduri gives an engraving of this from silver of Valerianus, vol. i. p. 103.—Eckhel (vol. vii. 383) observes, that the type, which also appears on silver of Gallienus, is a new one, and of recondite interpretation. After alluding to the conflicting opinions of Banduri and Tanini respecting it, he argues, with his usual ability, acuteness, and judicious discrimination, chiefly resting on the appearance of the *harpa* in the hand of the figure, that it must be that of Saturn. He then extends his inquiry, as to the connexion existing between the type of Saturn and the inscription of AETERNITAS. It has already been seen that the Sun was the most usual symbol of Eternity. Now, Macrobius affirms that Saturn was identical with the Sun, and he also shews, that Saturn was the same as Time. Euripides calls Time the Son of Saturn. " Therefore as Eternity consists of a perpetual succession of Time, so we see Saturn very properly serving to represent it. And truly the selection of such a type is the more appropriate in this instance, inasmuch as he, who is said to have established the Golden Age in Latium, was also best enabled to furnish forth a Golden Eternity."—See *Saturnus.*

AETERNITATIBUS.—A woman stands with a globe in her right hand, her left arm resting on a column. Silver of Alex. Severus.

The epigraph of this reverse is to be placed among those acclamations, which it was customary to make to the Emperors, and of which great plenty are to be found (some applicable to the present inscription), in the life of Alexander Severus, by Lampridius.—See ACCLAMATIONES.

AETERNITATIS AVGVSTAE CVTT.— *Colonia Victrix Togata Tarraco.*—See Aker-

man's " Ancient Coins of Cities and Princes," p. 108, No. 3, pl. xi. DEO. AVGVSTO. Hispania Tarraconensis.

ADFINIS or *Affinis.* Cousin.—By this term of relationship Constantius Chlorus is called, on second and third brass of Consecration and Remembrance, struck under Maxentius—viz. IMP. MAXENTIVS DIVO CONSTANTIO. ADFINI.—The term COGN. or COGNAT. *(Cognato),* is also used on other coins dedicated by Maxentius to the memory of his kinsman.—See *Aeterna Memoria.*

AFFINITY and Kindred.——The titles of father and mother; of grandmother, son, daughter, grandson, and great grandson; cousin and kinsman; are marked on Roman coins. Thus we find, Caius Cæsar, *Divi Julii Filius* (son of the Divine Julius.) Caius and Lucius Cæsares, *Augusti Filii* (sons of Augustus). Drusus Cæsar, *Tiberii Augusti Filius* (son of Tiberius Augustus). Germanicus Cæsar, *Tiberii Augusti Filius, Divi Augusti Nepos* (son of Tiberius Augustus, grandson of the Divine Augustus). Caius Cæsar, *D. Augusti Pro-nepos* (great grand child of the Divine Augustus). Divo Maximiniano *Patri* (to the Divine Maximinian, the *father).*—In another instance, the coin is dedicated Divo Maximiniano *socero* (father in law). Divo Romulo *Filio* (to the son of the Emperor Maxentius.) Divus Constantius *Adfinis or Cognatus* (cousin or kinsman perhaps) of *Maxentius.*— Agrippina *Mater Caii Cæsaris Augusti* (mother of Caius Cæsar [Caligula] Augustus). Agrippina *Aug. Divi Claudii Cæsaris Neronis Mater* (wife of the Divine Claudius, mother of Nero Cæsar). Domitella *Divi Vespasiani Filia* (daughter of the Divine Vespasian).—See Jobert, par Bimard, vol. i. p. 256.

AFR. *Africanus.* The African.—*Africani.* The two elder Gordians were thus surnamed.

AFRANIA gens plebeia.—There are eight varieties in its coins. The silver are rare. The brass are As, or some of its parts (see *As*).— The following is the rarest denarius of this family :—

Obv. Galeated head of Pallas, with X (mark of the denarius.)

Rev. Victory in a biga, at full speed; below, S. AFRA. ROMA.

The letter S. of the *prenomen* is generally read *Spurius,* but it also may be meant (says Eckhel, v. p. 132) for *Sextus;* as on marbles Sextus as well as Spurius is found prefixed to the family name of *Afranius.* Ursin, who confidently adopts the former, admits that of Spurius Afranio no mention is made on any ancient monument.

AFRICA.—The region, which the Roman geographers comprehended under this name, was limited to the northern part of that vast continent, extending along the shores of the Mediterranean, from about the present pashalic of Tunis, to the furthest extremity of the modern kingdom of Fez and Morocco. As a Roman province, it was one of great dignity and importance. It fell to Mark Antony's share, after the battle of Philippi.—The annexed wood cut, from a large brass of Hadrian, exhibits some of the numismatic symbols of Africa, all of which are well described by Addison : personified as a

woman, the province " is always quoifed with the head of an elephant, to shew that this animal is the breed of that country, as for the same reason she has a dragon [or serpent], lying at her feet. The lion on another medal, marks her out for the *Leonum arida nutrix*. The scorpion, on a third reverse, is another of her productions. Lucan mentions it in particular, in the long catalogue of her venomous animals.

—————— *quis fata putaret*
Scorpion, aut vires maturæ mortis habere ?
Ille minax nodis, et recto verbere sævus.
[Lib. 9.]

Who that the Scorpion's insect-form surveys,
Would think that ready death his call obeys,
As fierce he rears his knotty tail on high ?

This part of the world has always, on medals, something to denote her wonderful fruitfulness, as it was indeed the great granary of Italy. Hence we see the genius of Roman Africa holding a handful of corn ears, or a cornucopiæ, and resting her elbow on a basket of wheat, or fruits. These are all emblems of her great fertility, and signify what Horace alludes to in the words :

Frumenti quantum metit Africa.—[Sat. 3. lib. 2.]

Africa is personified, on a denarius struck under the republic, by the head of a woman, covered with the skin, tusks, and trunk of an elephant's head.—See engraving in *Cestia gens*.

AFRICA.—Gold, silver, and first and second brass coins, with this legend (the brass bearing S. C. in the exergue), struck under Hadrian, represent the Province seated, with attributes of elephant's head, scorpion, cornucopiæ, and *canistrum ;* in others with those of lion, and corn ears.—[Hadrian, according to Spartianus, bestowed many benefits on that province.—See RESTITVTORI AFRICAE.]

AFRICA. S.C.—A robed woman, whose headdress is distinguished by an elephant's proboscis, stands holding out corn ears in her tunic. At her feet is a lion.—First brass of Sept. Severus, engraved in Havercamp's *Médailles de Christine*, TAB. XXIV. Spartianus supplies the explanation of this coin (struck A. D. 194), when he relates that Severus, on his first arrival, as Emperor, at Rome, sent soldiers into Africa, lest, if Pescennius Niger should have invaded that province, there would have been a deficiency of corn-provision in Rome. Besides, as Africa was the birth-place of Severus, he doubtless bestowed many benefits upon it. That he treated Carthage

with great favour, coins of his (bearing the legend of INDVLGENTIA IN CARTH.) plainly testify. On which account (as Spartianus states), he was worshipped as a God by the Africans,—but then it was under Roman domination.—*Doct. Num. Vet.* vii. p. 171.]

AFRICA. S. C.—A woman standing, holds a cornucopiæ in the left hand, and in her extended right hand a large crown, or garland. First brass of Antoninus Pius ; struck A. D. 139. On other first brass, a dragon lies before the feet of the province, and behind her are three corn ears.—*(Médailles de Christine*, TAB. XV.)

As in the mint of Hadrian, so in that of Antoninus, personifications of various provinces of the empire are exhibited, of which this is one,—namely, that granary of Rome, *Africa*.— Eckhel considers the object which the female figure has in her stretched-out hand is meant for the *aurum coronarium*, or garland-like crown of gold, which it was a custom among the Greeks, afterwards copied by provinces, conquered by the Romans, to offer to those who were held in honour, or whose favour was sought. At first it was a voluntary gift ; but afterwards it became an oppressive exaction by tyrant emperors, on the more distant quarters of their dominions— vast sums of money being at length required instead of golden coronets.—In Bartoli's engraving of the coin *(Médailles de Christine*, TAB. XV.) the African province is eagerly stepping forward to present a crown of the largest size, as a grateful dedication to the really good Antoninus.—See *Aureum Coronarium*, in this Dictionary.

AFRICAE (ADVENTVI AVG.)—See p. 9.

AGIT. SPE. TESEVS.—The naked figure of Theseus, helmeted, standing with spear and shield, compels a Centaur, who holds a lyre, and on whose neck his hand is laid, to fall down on his knees. This type appears on a contorniate medal, given in Morell's Emperors, with the head of Nero on its obverse, bearing the above legend.—See *Thesaurus Impp. Rom.* T. ii. TAB. viii. fig. 15.

The group has evidently reference to Theseus at the nuptials of his friend Pirithous ; on which occasion, as Ovid's fable [*Metam.* xii. 227] relates, Eurytus offered violence to the bride Hippodamia, and with the rest of his fellow-centaurs, was severely punished for their insulting conduct, by the Lapithæ.—Of the words inscribed on the reverse no satisfactory attempt has yet been made to elucidate the meaning. By the lyre, in the hand of the Centaur, it would seem that, after the example of Chiron, this bi-membered race cultivated the musical art.—[Eckhel, viii. p. 288.]

AGNOMEN.—Pitiscus explains this word by saying, that it is the synonyme of the *cognomen* (or surname) conferred by the act of Adoption.—Eckhel appears to entertain a similar opinion. The adopted Roman took the name, the *pre-nomen*, and the surname of the adopting party, keeping only the name of his own family. P. Cornelius Scipio, for example, being adopted by Q. Cæcilius Metellus, quitted his *prenomen* and his name, calling himself Q. Metellus Scipio; thus he retained only the *agnomen*, the name he derived from his father, and was indebted to the adoption for the three other names.—See nomen, cognomen, prenomen *(in suis locis)*.—See also *Adoptio.*

AGRIGENTUM—a sea-port of Sicily, situate between the rivers Agraga and Camicus, formerly celebrated for its commercial importance, and ranking next to Syracuse. It is now called *Girgenti*. Its *Latin* coins consist of autonomes in silver and brass, and of colonial Imperial, struck under Augustus, who made it a Roman colony. The *colonial* exhibit on their obverse the *triquetra* and three corn ears; and on their reverse the *Latin* inscription AGRIGENTVM, on two lines, within a crown of laurel. Prince Torremuzza, amongst other coins of this city, has given the following *Colonial of Augustus*: AVGVSTO P. P. AGRIGENTI. Bare head of the Emperor.—*Rev.* L. CLODI*o* RVFO. PROCOS, in three lines, in the midst of a circular legend SALASSO. COMITIAE. SEX. REO. IIV*iri*.—See Mionnet, Suppl. T. i. 368.

AGRIPPA (MARCUS VIPSANIUS), a re-nowned commander both by sea and land, chosen by Augustus to be amongst the most familiar and inti-mate of his friends, and afterwards to become his son-in-law. Born in the year of Rome 691 (63 before Christ), of a family not highly distinguish-ed, Agrippa was raised, by his military talents and by his personal merits, to the first dignities of the State. A brave, sensible, honest, prudent, and labori-ously active man, he was made Prætor in his 23rd year; appointed to the government of Transalpine Gaul at 25; and next to the com-mand in chief of the Roman fleet. He filled these several posts with equal honour and suc-cess. He defeated Sextus Pompeius in a naval engagement, and compelled him to abandon Sicily. He shared in the Victory at Philippi; defeated Mark Antony at Actium, A. U. C .723 (B. C. 31); and afterwards effected the complete submission of Spain to the Roman arms, by vanquishing the Cantabrians and Asturians, so long the champions of national independence in

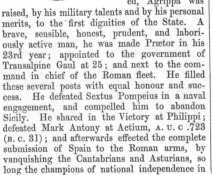

that country. Agrippa married Julia, daughter of Augustus, after the death of Marcellus, her first husband, 733 (B. C. 21)—was invested in 736, with the Tribunitian power, which was continued to him for five more consecutive years,—viz., to 741 (B. C. 13).—Being sent as governor into Syria, he reduced Judæa, and offered in the temple of Jerusalem a sacrifice of a hundred oxen.—This great general and con-summate statesman died in Campania, on his return from Pannonia, 742 (B. C. 12) aged 51 years, having been governor of Rome, three times consul, and destined by Augustus to succeed him in the empire. The remains of Agrippa were interred in the Mausoleum of Augustus. He adorned Rome with many magnificent edifices, amongst others the celebrated temple of the Pantheon, which still exists. His coins are, in gold (if genuine), of the highest rarity—in silver, very rare—in middle brass, common; ditto, restored by Titus and Domitian, rare.—On the obverses of the gold and silver appear his head, with the legend M. AGRIPPA COS. *(Consul)* and that of Augustus on the reverse. The following describes one of his second brass, a well-known historical coin; struck between the 30th and 28th year before the birth of Christ.

AGRIPPA (M) L. F. COS III *(Marcus Agrippa, son of Lucius, Consul for the third time)*. Head of Agrippa, ornamented with a rostral crown. *Reverse.* S. C. *(Senatus Consulto)*

Neptune stands holding in his right hand a dolphin, and in his left a trident. The majestic figure of the Sea-sove-reign is finely de-signed, and a pal-lium, or a paluda-mentum, is grace-fully thrown over the right arm and left shoulder. The types on each side of the above coin, bear allusion solely to the naval victories gained by Agrippa. The image of Neptune is appropriately introduced on the reverse, inasmuch as Agrippa, by his success at sea, had signally humbled the pride of Sextus Pompeius, who had passed himself off for the son of that god. The rostral crown (see *Corona*) on his manly but austere brows, points to his office of *Præfectus Classis*, or high admiral. It was a circlet of gold, relieved with figures of the prows and sterns of ships; and this mark of distinction was presented to him by Octavianus (afterwards Augustus) Cæsar, after the fight he won near Mylæ, together with the *cæruleum vexillum* (a *blue*, or sea-wave coloured flag), in-dicative of warlike triumphs on the domains of Neptune. "Agrippa, it would seem, like an-other Nelson, wore this identical naval crown, at the battle of Actium;" but unlike our own hero, escaping the fatal catastrophe to which so con-spicuous a decoration must have exposed him, the Roman commander survived many years, to receive fresh honours at the hands of the man, whom his prowess, wisdom, and strategic skill had raised to the sovereignty of the world.— Virgil alludes to this last decisive action, and the important share which Agrippa took in it, in the 8th Book of the Æneid, v. 678 :—

Hinc *Augustus* agens Italos in prælia *Cæsar,*
Cum patribus, populoque, Penatibus, et magnis Dîs,
Stans celsâ in puppi; geminas cui tempora flammas
Læta vomunt, patriumque aperitur vertice sidus.
Parte aliâ ventis et Dîs *Agrippa* secundis,
Arduus, agmen agens; cui, belli insigne superbum,
Tempora navali fulgent rostrata coronâ.

Young Cæsar, on the stern, in armour bright,
Here leads the Romans and their gods to fight :
His beamy temples shoot their flames afar,
And o'er his head is hung the Julian star.
Agrippa seconds him, with prosperous gales ;
And, with propitious gods, his foes assails.
A *naval crown,* that binds his manly brows,
The happy fortune of the fight fore-shews.
                                  Dryden's Translation.

AGRIPPA (M). PLATORINVS IIIVR.
    Bare head of Agrippa.
    Rev. CAESAR AVGVSTVS. Bare head of Augustus.—Silver.—See Akerman, 1, plate iv. No. 2, p. 142.
    AGRIPPA (M). COS TER. COSSVS LEN-TVLVS.—Head of Agrippa, with the mural and rostral crown.
    Rev. AVGVSTVS COS XI. Laureated head of Augustus.—Gold and silver. Also restored by Trajan.
    These effigies of Augustus and his son-in-law were struck on the same respective coins, by the monetal triumvir Platorinus, on the occasion of their serving the consulate together, in the year of Rome 727 (B.C. 27); the same year in which Octavianus Cæsar took the title of *Augustus.*— See PLATORINVS, and *Sulpicia* gens. See also *Corona muralis et rostrata.*
    AGRIPPA, *the younger,* surnamed *Postumus* —third and last son of M. Agrippa and Julia, born in the year of Rome 742 (B.C. 12), after the death of his father. Adopted by Augustus 757 (A.D. 4), he was styled AGRIPPA CAESAR, after the decease of his brothers Caius and Lucius. But, for subsequent misconduct. was banished to Sorentum, in Campania, A.U.C. 760 (A.D. 7), and put to death by order of Tiberius, at the age of 26. The only coin known of this young prince is a small brass of the colony of Corinth, bearing on its obverse the legend AGRIPPA CAE-SAR CORINTHI. with the bare head of Agrippa Postumus.—Engraved in Vaillant's *Coloniæ,* vol. i. p. 62.
    AGRIPPINA, *senior*—daughter of Marcus Agrippa and of Julia, grand daughter of Augustus, was born in the year of Rome 739 (B.C. 15). Married to Germanicus, nephew of Augustus, she proved, by her conjugal fidelity, by her feminine modesty, and by her more than feminine intrepidity of mind, how signally de-serving she was of that hero's choice. Beautiful as virtuous, a little too much haughtiness of temper and demeanour was the only reproach that the vindicatory and eulogistic pen of history

attaches to her character. In the year U.C. 770 (A.D. 17), she joined her husband in Syria, only to see him perish there by poison adminis-tered by the agents of Tiberius. Her fortitude rose superior to this calamity, though it was the source of almost all those other afflictions, which at length overwhelmed her. Accompanied by her child, she brought the ashes of Germanicus to Rome, at the gates of which they were re-ceived by the Senate, followed by the whole body of the population, and deposited in the tomb of Augustus, amidst the united lamenta-tions of the army and the people. Nevertheless, by the command of that cruel emperor, who was her chief calumniator and persecutor, she was sent in banishment to the island of Pandataria, where Tiberius suffered her, after three years' privation and misery, to die of hunger, in 786 (A.D. 33). Her son Caius (Caligula), at the commencement of his reign, brought back to Rome the ashes of his mother from the place of her exile ; paid her the honours of the *Circensis* and *Carpentum;* caused the remains to be laid in the magnificent tomb of Augustus; and coins of fine fabric to be struck to her memory. Those of Roman die are very rare in gold and silver; in large brass, common. The portraits of this princess, in gold and silver, are on the reverse of Caligula's coins, struck after her death, and of which the subjoined is an example.

    AGRIPPINA MATer caii CAESaris AVGusti GERManici.—The head of Agrippa.
    C. CAESAR AVG. GERM. P. M. TR. POT.—The head of Caligula, laureated.
    The large brass coins, minted by a decree of the Senate, in honour of Agrippina, present her head on their obverse, and have on the reverse the *carpentum,* or car drawn by mules, indicating her apotheosis. The legend is, S. P. Q. R. ME-MORIAE AGRIPPINAE. *(The Senate and the Ro-man People to the memory of Agrippina.)*
    On the obverse she is styled AGRIPPINA M. F. MAT. C. CAESARIS AVGVSTI (Agrippina, daughter of Marcus, mother of Caius Cæsar Augustus.) Her titles on other medals are AGRIPPINA M. F. GERMANICI CAESARIS (by implication, *uxor*—meaning wife of Germanicus.)—See MEMORIÆ AGRIPPINÆ.
    AGRIPPINA. DRVSILLA. IVLIA. S. C.—Three women standing, with a cornucopiæ, of whom the one on the right rests her right hand on a little pillar, and with her left touches the middle figure, who holds in her right hand a *patera,* while the woman on the left has the helm of a vessel in her right hand. First brass. —Patin has given a similar coin, but in middle brass.—Schlegel quotes coins with this type, and the legend TR. POT. III. IIII. (Morell, *Impp.*

vol. i. 622), but their genuineness is doubted by Eckhel.

On this coin are represented the three sisters of Caligula. At the commencement of his reign, when he was affecting a regard for the members of his own family, in order to gain popularity, Caligula advanced them to the highest posts of dignity. He went so far as to give orders, that in all oaths the names of his sisters should be joined with his own, and to assign them all the honours of Vestals; but ending by seducing them all three. When his passion was cooled, he banished them all to distant islands, with the exception of Drusilla, who escaped that fate by death. It was, then, during the ardour of his attachment to them, that the coins in question were struck, on which the three sisters are represented under the forms of *Securitas*, *Pietas*, and *Fortuna*.

AGRIPPINA, *junior* (Julia), the daughter of Germanicus and Agrippina the elder, born in a town on the Rhine, subsequently called after her *Colonia Agrippinensis*, now *Cologne*, in the year of Rome 769 (A. D. 16), was the grand daughter of Antonia, sister of Caligula, and the mother of Nero, by her first husband, Cn. Domitius Ahenobarbus, a senator, whom she married 781, (A. D. 28). After his death, she was espoused to her uncle, the Emperor Claudius, 802 (A. D. 49), and obtained the title of *Augusta*. She was a woman of great beauty, but of the most profligate disposition; of lofty and penetrating genius; of a proud imperious nature; of cruelly vindictive temper, and of insatiable ambition.— When her vile ungrateful son, for whose advancement she had acted most criminally, found himself unable to restrain her immoderate thirst for power, he caused her to be put to death, 812 (A. D. 59). She was the first of the *Augustæ*, who obtained brass medals from the Senate. One exhibits a female seated, another a triumphal arch. She is represented, as is shewn in the above cut, on a coin of Caligula, in company with her sisters Drusilla and Julia; the word AGRIPPINA being inscribed near her image. The head of this princess, ornamented with a wheaten crown, appears on the reverse of gold and silver coins of Claudius.

In the following denarius, we see, on one side, the words AGRIPPINAE AVGVSTAE, with her head; and on the other, TI. CLAVD*ius* CAESAR AVG. GERM. P. M. TRIB. POT. P. P. with the head of the Emperor Claudius.—On other coins, minted under Claudius and under Nero, she is also styled AGRIPPINA AVGVSTA MATER AVGVSTI.—

—There are silver medallions of hers struck in Asia, on one of which is a statue of the Ephesian Diana, within a temple. All her coins, in every metal, are rare; silver medallions in the highest degree.—Of the large brass, Capt. Smyth says—" I have never been able to procure a single specimen; nor is there one even in the British Museum. Vaillant has figured two of this magnitude, with reverses of Ceres and a triumphal arch; but there are no Latin brass of the other sizes. Agrippina was the first of the wives of the *Augusti* whose effigies appeared on gold and silver coins of the Roman mint."

AGRIPP. (or AGRIPPINA) AVG. DIVI. CLAVD. NERONIS. CAES. MATER. EX. S. C.—(Agrippina, wife [by implication] of the Divine Claudius, Mother of Nero Cæsar, by a decree of the Senate [this medal was ordered to be minted.])

Reverse type. Two figures, the one male the other female, both seated on a quadriga of elephants.—The obverse presents the jugated heads of Nero and Agrippina, around which is inscribed NERO CLAVD. DIVI. F. CAES. AVG. GERM. IMP. TR. P. COS.—See Akerman, *Descrip. Cat.* i. p. 159, plate iv. No. 6.—Gold.

Vaillant, in explanation of the reverse, cites the following passage from Suetonius (c. 11)— Claudius procured a decree of divine honours to his grandmother Livia, and of a car drawn by elephants, in a Circensian procession, similar to that of Augustus.—Nero and Agrippina caused this coin to be struck (in gold and silver), in order that the images of both Augustus and Livia should thereby be exhibited to the honour of their memories. Nero also dedicated statues to them, which are represented on one of his coins, with the epigraph of AVGVSTVS. AVGVSTA. —See the words.

AGRIPPINA, &c. Same legend as preceding.—The type of the *obverse* exhibits the heads of Agrippina and Nero, face to face.—The reverse is NERONI. CLAVD. DIVI. F. CAES. AVG. GERM. IMP. TR. P.—The letters EX. S. C. within an oaken garland.—See Caylus' plates of Roman *Gold* coins, in the *Cabinet de France*, fig. 102.

Of this coin, minted at Rome, in gold and silver, Agrippina occupies the most distinguished place, namely the obverse side. She styles herself (by implication) the wife of Claudius, and, in direct terms, the mother of Nero; as though the government of the empire had been in her hands, and her son only Cæsar. It is on this account that Tacitus (*Ann.* 23), asks—What help is there in him, who is governed by a woman? It is not to be wondered at therefore, adds Vaillant, if the oaken garland was decreed to this woman and to her son, as it had already been to Caligula and to Claudius, *ob cives servatos*, by the Senate, whom she assembled in the palace, where she sat discreetly veiled.—*Præst. Num. Impp.* ii. 60.

AGRIPPINA COLONIA, a city of Gallia Belgica, now Cologne on the Rhine. To this

oppidum Ubiorum, which, according to Tacitus *(Annal.* lib. xii. c. 27), was the birth-place of Agrippina junior, mother of Nero, and last wife of Claudius, that clever, assuming, and unscrupulous woman, sent a colony of veterans, in the tenth year of her imperial husband's reign, about u. c. 804 (A. D. 51), and gave it her own name. It was to this town, as Suetonius relates, that Vitellius sent the dagger with which Otho killed himself, for the purpose of its dedication to Mars.—Goltzius has recorded some medals of *Colonia Agrippina;* but they were suspected by later numismatists, and particularly by Vaillant, who has made no mention of them in his work on Colonial mintages. The annexed coin (in base silver or billon), registered by Banduri (i. 311) and of which an engraving as well as a description is given by Haym *(Thes. Brit.* ii. TAB. xxvi. p. 283, No. 5), as from the Duke of Devonshire's cabinet, is considered, however, to be indubitably genuine. Haym notes it as of good workmanship and well preserved. Mionnet also (in his *Médailles Romaines),* recognises the following legends and types, as those of a *Latin* imperial coin of Postumus, minted in the above named Roman colony, viz. :—

Obv. POSTVMVS P. F. AVG.   Radiated head of Postumus.

Rev. COL. CL. AGRIP. COS. IIII.   A woman standing, with balance and cornucopiæ.

Mionnet describes the type of the reverse as *L'Equité debout, avec ses attributs.* The letters CL. serve to shew that the place now so well known under the name of Cologne (formerly the City of the Ubii), *was* made a colony under *Claudius,* as Tacitus has affirmed.

A H A L A.——Accompanying this surname, which is that of the *Servilia* family, the bare head of C. Servilius Ahala appears on a denarius minted by Marcus Brutus, who assassinated Julius Cæsar. On the obverse of the same silver coin, is the bare head of L. Brutus, one of the first two Consuls of the Roman Republic.

The circumstance of these two portraits being included on the same medal, conclusively iden-

tifies it with the younger Brutus. For, as on the father's side, he was believed to be descended from Lucius Brutus, so on that of his mother, *Servilia,* it is certain that he had among his ancestors, *Servilius Ahala,* who, according to Plutarch, under the dictatorship of Cincinnatus, A. U. C. 315 (B. C. 439), slew with his own hand, Spurius Melius, for aiming at the sovereignty.—Eckhel, with his usual felicity of citation, quotes a passage from Cicero, as throwing light (which it does in a remarkable manner), on this denarius, in the following words : —*Brutos ego impellerem, quorum uterque* L. BRUTI *imaginem quotidie vderet, alter etiam,* AHALÆ ? [Should I (asks the great Orator) incite the *Bruti,* both of whom daily gaze on the portrait (or effigy) of L. Brutus, and one of them on that of Ahala also ?]—See *Junia gens.*

Visconti, who, in his *Iconographie Romaine* (8vo. edit. T. ii. No. 6), gives an engraving of this denarius, makes, *inter alia,* the following remarks (p. 51) :—" On the coins which Marcus Brutus, or his partisans, caused to be struck during the civil war, the head of Servilius Ahala was placed on the reverse of that of Lucius Brutus, whom the murderer of Cæsar affected to reckon among his ancestors. He doubtless thought, that those domestic examples would form an excuse for his homicidal outrage in the eyes of the Romans. This portrait of Servilius Ahala had probably been taken, like many others, from one of those images which the families of the nobility gloried in preserving.— The legend AHALA designates the personage represented on this side of the coin.—Cicero remarks that this surname of *Ahala* had been formed by the suppression of the *x,* and by pronouncing the word *axilla* (arm-pit), a nickname given to one of the ancestors of Servilius, in allusion to some particularities relative to this part of his bodily frame. The *Fasti Capitolini* exhibit the name of Servilius, sometimes with the surname of Ahala, sometimes with that of Axilla ; in consequence of which Pighius has attempted to distinguish one from the other, contrary to the opinion of Cicero, who, in conversation with Marcus Brutus, respecting this same Servilius, gives him both surnames, without distinction. The *Fasti Capitolini* prove that these surnames existed in the Servilia family before the time of the Ahala who was general of cavalry to Cincinnatus."

AHENOBARBVS.—This surname, which appears on a denarius of the *Domitia* gens, has reference to one of the most popular legends of early Rome.—The news of the important victory achieved by Postumius, over the Latins, near lake Regillus (B. C. 498) reached and spread through the city, with a rapidity, which, notwithstanding the short distance between the two places, was regarded by the credulous and over-joyed populace as a prodigy. Two young soldiers, as the story goes, had met Lucius Domitius, a distinguished citizen, who was on his return from the country. Announcing to him the news of the battle and the success of the Romans, they charged him to make it known to his fellow-citizens; and in order to win his confidence by a miracle, they touched his cheeks, the black beard of which instantly became red. (Suetonius, in *Nerone*, c. i. Plutarch, *Vita Pauli Æmilei*, § 25).—It is said to have been for this reason that Domitius was afterwards called *Ahenobarbus*, red beard, or beard of the colour of brass; a *sobriquet* which attached itself, for many ages, to one of the most illustrious families of the republic.— The Domitii, doubtless, were in the habit of exposing to view, in the vestibule of their house, the waxen image of that man, to whose eyes Castor and Pollux had condescended to make themselves visible, and whom they had chosen to be the bearer of such good news.—(Visconti, *Iconographie Romaine*, tome ii. p. 48.)—At the period of the civil war waged against Cassius and Brutus, a member of the family above named, Cneus Domitius Ahenobarbus, had allied himself to their party, and was placed in command of a formidable fleet, which, crossing the Ionian sea, blockaded the ports of Italy. This individual, to defray the expenses of his expedition, caused money to be minted, on which were stamped the head of his ancestor, the Lucius Domitius of the early republic, designated by his surname AHENOBARBVS. The reverse type is a trophy raised on the prow of a galley, allusive to the victory gained by *Cneus Domitius Imperator* (Emperor, that is to say Commander-in-Chief.—The battle alluded to was fought on the Ionian sea, between the port of Brundusium, whence the fleet of Octavius Cæsar (afterwards Augustus) had sailed, and Epirus, towards which it had steered. The event took place the same day that Cassius and Brutus were defeated at Philippi, in the year 42 before the Christian era. (Appian Alex. *de bello civili*, cited by Visconti in his work above-named.)

AHENOBAR.—The denarius on which this abbreviated word appears is a numismatic monument of the greatest rarity. Of this the erudite antiquary above-mentioned, has given an engraving in his *Roman Iconography* (TAB. V.*) and he presents it as preserving the portrait of Cneus Ahenobarbus. It is (says Visconti) a piece of gold money, which was probably struck at the period when this Roman admiral received intelligence of the death of Cassius and of Brutus, and regarded himself as the head of the republican party. The head, entirely shaved, is seen on one side of the coin, of which the surname AHENOBAR*bus* forms the legend. On the reverse we see his other names, and his title, CN. DOMITIVS. L. F. IMP. (Cneus Domitius, son of Lucius, imperator). The letters NEPT. stamped in the field of the reverse, point to the temple of

Neptune, which is the type, and in all probability was designed to represent, that edifice which Cneus Domitius Ahenobarbus, one of the ancestors of the personage in question, had built in the circus of Flaminius at Rome, in honour of the god of the sea, and which he had filled with sculptural *chefs d'œuvre* from the chisel of Scopas. Cneus Ahenobarbus seems thus to ascribe to the zeal of his progenitors for the worship of Neptune, the constant safety and success of his own vessels on the stormy waves of the Adriatic."—p. 221–22.—See also Morell *Thesaur. Fam. Domitia* gens.

AIMILIA (Basilica) REF*ecta*. S. C.—This legend, with the name of M. LEPIDVS below, appears on the reverse of a denarius of the Aemilia family, the accompanying type of which represents a building, with two stories of columns, and shields inserted between them, commonly called the *Basilica Aemilia*, or *Basilica Pauli*.— On the obverse of the same denarius is the veiled head of a woman; on one side of which is a garland, and on the other the simpulum. [By a graphic mistake the legend AIMILIA is not made to appear at the top of the reverse.]

It bears allusion to L. Æmilius Paulus, who served the consulship in the year of Rome 704 (B. C. 50), and to whom the merit is ascribed by old writers of having begun the reconstruction and adornment (B. C. 54) at his own expense, of the above-named public edifice, in the Forum at Rome. Being, however, left in an unfinished state by the founder, it was at length completed, and dedicated, by Paulus Aemilius Lepidus, in the year U. C. 720 (B. C. 34), according to Dion Cassius. The chief ornaments of the edifice were its columns of Phrygian marble, of which Pliny speaks in admiration. The Æmilian Basilica was twice repaired, after damage by fire. The first time in 740 (B. C. 14), when the temple of Vesta was also destroyed, and it was then restored *(refecta)* by Augustus and the friends of Paulus. The second time was during the reign of Tiberius, on which occasion Lepidus, with consent of the Senate, rebuilt and adorned it at his own cost.—Eckhel agrees with Havercamp in considering this denarius to have been coined under Augustus—*not* under Tiberius—and points to the head on the obverse as doubtless that of Vesta, allusive to the temple of that goddess, destroyed in the same conflagration, which consumed the Basilica, and was restored by Augustus. The archaism too of AIMILIA (the ancient spelling of AEMILIA), bespeaks it to be of the age of Augustus, rather than that of Tiberius. —*Doct. Num. Vet.* v. 127.

This coin is valued by Mionnet at 18 fr. The same, restored by Trajan, he prices at 100 fr.

ALACRITATI.—To Alacrity; with figure of Pegasus.—The foregoing legend occurs for the first, and indeed the only time, in the imperial series of coins, on a very rare middle brass of Gallienus. The type also is found on one of the billon pieces minted under the same emperor, but with a different legend [LEG. I. &c.]

Respecting this singular reverse, and its appropriate device of a winged horse (previously noticed and engraved by Angeloni and Banduri), Eckhel says, "I do not remember any altar, dedicated by the Romans to *Alacrity*. It seems probable that this virtue, or good quality, in a sovereign, to have been here commended in Gallienus, in consequence of his having, immediately on his accession to the empire, and during his first consulate, prepared an army in Germany, with great expedition, and sent it forth against the revolted Gauls."—See *Pegasns*.

ALAMANNI, or ALEMANNI.—Under this title are to be considered as included the Ubii, the Sicambri, the Tencteri, the Usipetes, the Catti, the Cherusces; that is to say, the inhabitants of the upper and lower Rhine, and those beyond that great river, such as the Westphalians, the Hessians, and the Saxons, as far as the Elbe and the Weser, on the banks of which, as well as on the Rhine and the Meuse, Drusus, in the time of Augustus, built forts and established garrisons, to hold the natives in check; at the same time that he opened a road for his troops through the Hyrcanian forest. The victories of Drusus (brother of Tiberius) over the Alamanni, are commemorated on medals, under the inscription DE GERMANIS (see the word.)—But those exploits were not followed by the entire subjugation of the Germanic nations, nor was their country reduced to the form of a province, in the same effectual manner as Augustus succeeded in doing with regard to Gaul, Spain, Illyria, Egypt, and other regions, over which the Roman arms had been victorious. At a later period, however, of the empire, the *Alamanni*, inhabiting that part of Germany, which is situated between the Danube, the Upper Rhine, and the Mayne, were subdued, first by Caracalla, and afterwards by Proculus, in the reign of Aurelian. Afterwards Constantius Chlorus, whilst Cæsar, overthrew them with great slaughter.—They continued, nevertheless, from time to time, to wage war against subsequent emperors, from Constantine the Great to Gratianus and downwards. Nor were they finally brought to subjection until A. D. 496, when they met with a decisive defeat by Clodovæus, king of the Franks.

ALAMANNIA.—The reverse of one of Constantine's gold coins has for its type, a woman seated at the foot of a trophy, supporting her head on her arm, as if lamenting her captivity. Round the field appears GAVDIVM ROMANORVM; and on the exergue is ALAMANNIA.—Engraved in Caylus, *Aurea Numis. Rom. Impp.* No. 108.

"This medal (says Spanheim, in his Cæsars of Julian), refers to the victories of Constantine over the *Alamanni*, and also over the *Franci*, a nation between the Rhine and the Weser.—With regard to *Alamannia*, Zozimus

relates that, after having defeated Maxentius, Constantine passed into Gaul, and directed his march against the Celtic tribes. With respect to *Francia*, other writers make mention of the bridge which he caused to be thrown over the Rhine, in the territory of the Ubians, now the diocese of Cologne, in order to attack the *Franci*, or people of Westphalia, and towards the Issel." There is also a similar legend and type on a gold coin of Crispus, to whose ill-requited valour his father was mainly indebted for this triumph.

ALA*Mannia* ET FRANC*ia*.—See FRANCIA.

ALAMANNIA DEVICTA.—Victory, at whose feet is a captive bound, holding a trophy and palm branch. This legend and type appear

on third brass of Crispus, natural son of Constantine the Great. They constitute another proof of the leading share taken by that heroic but ill-fated young prince, in vanquishing a most powerful coalition of enemies, and compelling them to acknowledge for awhile the ascendency of Rome.—"Placed (says Banduri, who publishes the coin) in command of the Legions in Gaul, Crispus fulfilled the hopes and objects of his imperial father, by suppressing a formidable rebellion of the *Franci* and *Alamanni*."—Spanheim has given this reverse to a coin of Constantinus, jun.; but it is not included in that emperor's mint by either Eckhel, Mionnet, or Akerman.

ALB. ALBINVS. *Albinus*—surname of the *Postumia* family.

ALBA.—On a brass medallion of Antoninus Pius, without legend of reverse, are represented the fortified walls of that city. Within are the sow and its young; above is Æneas carrying his father; behind him the fig tree, and before a circular temple stands an altar.—See *Scrofa*.

ALBOGALERUS, a sort of cap of white wool, which the *Flamen Dialis*, or priest of Jupiter, alone had the privilege of wearing. It was made from the fleece, or skin, of some white animal sacrificed to Jupiter, and was surmounted with a small sprig of olive. In the coins of Julius Cæsar, this albogalerus is seen to indicate the office of *pontifex maximus*.—See *Apex*.

ALBINUS (*Decimus Clodius Septimius*)—born at Hadrumetum, in Africa, had for his father Cejonius Postumus, and for his mother Aurelia Messalina. Highly educated, especially in geographical and strategical knowledge, he became, from a captain of Illyrian cavalry, one of the first and most successful generals of his time, in the chief charge and conduct of armies under Marcus Aurelius and Commodus, being at length placed in command of the legions in Bithynia, A. D. 175. Tall and portly in stature, with round visage, frizzled beard, large mouth, but with a very feeble voice, he was said to be retiring and melancholy in disposition, severe in matters of discipline, and of a repulsive humour; but his bravery and skill as a soldier, his love of justice, and his respect for senatorial rights and popular privileges, gained for him the attachment of all classes in the state. He was manly in his habits, free from enervating luxury, and, except his being a prodigious eater, without intemperance. Governor of Britain and Gaul, at the time of Pertinax's death, he made pretensions to the sovereignty, and was elected Emperor by the legions he commanded, in the year of Rome 946 (A. D. 193). He succeeded in causing himself to be declared Cæsar, by Septimius Severus, the same year : that merciless but artful man being at the time sufficiently occupied in subduing the eastern provinces of the empire. In the following year (194), Albinus served his second consulship with Severus himself for his colleague. But no sooner was Pescennius destroyed, than Severus led his army against his rival in the west. "The British legions under Albinus were opposed to those of Illyricum ; and the troops on each side combated with such bravery, that the result was long doubtful." But, after many sanguinary engagements, fought with alternate success, Albinus was defeated by his competitor in a decisive battle, on the plain of Tinurtium (now *Trevoux*), between the Rhone and Saone, near *Lugdunum* (Lyon), in France. And under circumstances of gratuitously brutal triumph on the part of the conqueror, Albinus lost his life, in the year U. c. 950 (A. D. 197). He was much looked up to by many ; and, indeed, was as much beloved by the Senate, as they hated Severus, on account of his fearfully vindictive cruelty. On his coins, which are found in the three metals, and of all sizes except small brass, this prince is styled D. CLODIVS ALBINVS CAESAR IMP.—also D. CLOD. SEPT. ALBIN. AVG.—and IMP. CAES. CL. SEPT. ALBIN. AVG. (on reverse P. P.)—His gold and brass medallions are of the highest rarity. Silver, and first and second brass, are also rare.

The large brass, from which the subjoined cut is engraved, was struck A. D. 194, as the mark of his second consulate attests.

Obv. D. CLOD. SEPT. ALBIN. CAES.—Bare head of Albinus.

Rev. FELICITAS COS. II. S. C.—Felicity standing with caduceus and *hasta pura*.—See *Felicitas*.

Khell, in his supplement to Vaillant (p. 106), has given an engraving of a most rare and elegant gold coin of Albinus, from the Vienna cabinet, with PROVID. AVG. COS. for legend, and Providentia, with her attributes, for type of its reverse.

Albinus (remarks the intelligent author of *Leçons de Numismatique Romaine*) hoping to keep on an amicable footing with Severus, paid him

all kinds of deferential attentions ; and the types on the reverses of his earlier coins bear testimony to his being influenced by this policy. But in the subsequent passages of his career, being forced to enter into an open struggle with his subtle rival, he declared himself *Augustus* as well as Cæsar. And from that period, the medals in which he takes this title, no longer evince the same character of caution and moderation. It is, however, necessary to observe, that the latter (with the titles of IMP. and AVG.) are not to be found in gold and silver ; whilst the bronze coins were still minted exclusively at Rome, and could not accord to him a title which the Emperor (Severus) and the Senate refused to grant him.

In reference to this question, Mr. Akerman also observes, that those coins of Albinus, which bear the title of "Cæsar" are considered to have been struck at Rome, Severus having consented to his assuming that title : and that those which have the styles "Imperator" and "Augustus," were struck in Gaul, after the entry of Albinus into that country.—A coin in the Vienna cabinet has *Pater Patriæ* on the reverse, the head side bearing the title of Cæsar. Another is described as having P. P. on it and AVG. on the obverse.—Hence Mionnet supposes that Albinus had a Council or Senate, in Gaul, who conferred on him the honourable title.—"However (adds the judicious compiler of the "Descriptive Catalogue of Roman Coins,") its assumption by Albinus without license, must not be wondered at in an age when Emperors aspired even to divine origin."

On the same point, Captain Smyth says, "such medals of Albinus as bear the title of Augustus, are without the S. C. and are probably from the officina of Lugdunum—since those minted by consent of Severus, were issued before Albinus had assumed that title."

ALCE, or *Alces*, an animal of the cervine species.—A representation of this remarkable quadruped is found on one of the SAECVLARES AVGG. 1st brass of Philippus senior.—See *Médailles de Christine*, TAB. XXXV. No. 18.

ALE.—*Alexandriæ cusus*—(struck at Alexandria.) It is read on the exergue of second brass coins of the lower empire, as in Diocletianus, Gal. Maximianus, &c.

ALEX.—*Alexander.*—IMP. CAES. M. AVR. SEV. ALEX. PIVS. AVG.—The Emperor and Cæsar, Marcus Aurelius Severus Alexander, the Pious, the August.

ALEXANDER SEVERUS (Bassianus Alexianus), born at Arca (Cæsarea Libani), in Phœnicia, A. D. 205, was the son of Gessius Marcianus and Julia Mamæa. The care which his mother bestowed on his education, amply compensated for his early loss of a father; and from his infancy he gave promise of those qualities and excellent abilities which distinguished him through life. He soon became a favourite with the best as well as noblest society in Rome. Through the sagacious policy and persuasion of Mæsa, his grandmother, he was adopted by Elagabalus.—Declared Cæsar A.D. 221, he took the names of Marcus Aurelius Alexander; served his first consulate the following year; and after the frightful reign of his execrable cousin, the Romans beheld a youth of scarcely fourteen years of age, on the throne of their emperors, possessed of talents, courage, correct morals—every human virtue and every personal accomplishment. His goodness as an individual, and his wisdom as a ruler, recalled to their remembrance the happier times of the empire, and formed a striking contrast to the hideous vices and misgovernment of his immediate predecessor.

On the death of Elagabalus, being saluted Augustus and Imperator (A.D. 222), by the enraptured Senate, he at the same time received the titles of Augustus, Pater Patriæ, with all the marks of imperial dignity; and from that period united to his other names that of Severus.—In 229, he proceeded consul for the 3rd time, having for his colleague that year Dion Cassius, the celebrated historian of Rome. It was during the reign of this emperor, that Artabanes IV. King of the Parthians, was killed by Artaxerxes, who re-established the Persian monarchy, and caused himself to be declared king. In consequence of the hostile progress of this prince against the Romans, Alexander Severus led a formidable army into the east, (about A.D. 231, according to Eckhel;) and having in a great battle defeated Artaxerxes, whom he drove back from the frontiers of the empire, returned to Rome, where he received triumphal honours for his victory over the Persians. The same year he accepted the title of PIVS. In 235, he engaged in another successful campaign. It was against the Germans, who had taken advantage of his absence in the East, to ravage the Gallic provinces. This was his last achievement. A band of factious soldiers (instigated by the Thracian savage, Maximinus, at that time advanced to be one of his generals), slew him and his mother (Mamæa), in the year of Our Lord 235, and the 27th of his age, after his having bravely commanded the Roman armies, with as consummate generalship and as much glory as any of his predecessors, for 13 years. His death was universally deplored, as that of the father of his country, the friend of his subjects, and one of the most just and generous of princes. The honours of *consecration* were awarded to him by the Senate, and a festival was instituted to his honour, which continued to be celebrated down to the reign of Constantine.—Alexander was the first Emperor who positively favoured the Christians, with whose moral precepts he seems to have been acquainted; for he caused to be inscribed over the palace gate, the golden rule of the Gospel—" Do as you would be done by."

(Quod tibi fieri non vis, alteri non feceris.)— Alexander Severus had three wives. The name of the first is not known; the second was called Memmia; the last *Barbia Orbiana*, of whom only there are coins. He does not appear to have left any children.—The monies of Alexander Severus are very numerous. Some pieces represent him with Julia Mamæa, and with Orbiana. His gold and silver coins (usual size) are common; first and second brass also common; gold, silver, and brass medallions, are of the highest rarity. On these he is styled M. AVR. ALEXANDER.—IMP. C. M. SEVERVS ALEXAND. PIVS AVGVSTVS (sometimes P. P.) The cut at the head of this biographical notice is from a silver coin. On the obverse, IMP. ALEXANDER PIVS AVG. Laureated head of the Emperor. The legend of the reverse, IOVI PROPVGNATORI (to Jupiter the defender, whose image stands brandishing a thunderbolt), frequently occurs in the mint of Alexander, which also has *Jupiter Conservator*, *Stator*, and *Ultor*, among its types.

Alexander occupied himself sedulously in reforming the abuses which prevailed in the state of the Roman mint. Hence the legend RESTITVTOR MONETAE on some of his medals, he being the only one of the *Augusti* who was styled on coins a restorer of money. He also used electrum. " About his time the sestertii (or large brass) diminish in magnitude, public events are given in less detail on the reverses; and the deities and moral virtues appear more frequently. The coins are however mostly common, and are retained in choice collections, only according to their perfection or individual interest."—See Captain Smyth's remarks on this prince's character and reign.—*Descr. Cat.* 226.

ALEXANDER (commonly surnamed *Tyrannus*) an usurper during the reign of Maxentius. Born of Pannonian peasants, or, according to some writers, sprung from an equally obscure origin in Phrygia, he entered the army, and though of no great military talent, nor of any very distinguished valour, became in his old age, pro-præfect of Africa. In consequence of the extreme severity of Maxentius towards him, he threw off his allegiance to that arbitrary prince, and drawing into his revolt the soldiers who had invested him with the purple, caused himself to be proclaimed emperor, A.D. 308. For three years Alexander maintained his usurped power at Carthage; but was at length defeated by the troops of Maxentius, taken prisoner, and put to death, A.D. 311. His coins, with Latin legends, in silver and brass, are of the highest rarity. They were minted in Africa; probably at Carthage. On these he is styled IMP. ALEXANDER P. F. AVG.—The above engraving from a second brass, presents the laureated head of this aged usurper, whilst the reverse bears the type of Victory, and the legend VICTORIA ALEXANDRI AVG. N.   Below P. K.—On the reverse of a third brass, given with his portrait, in Banduri, ii. p. 161, we read INVICTA ROMA. FELIX KARTHAGO—the type being a woman holding corn ears in each hand.

ALEXANDR*ia* AEGYPT*i*.—Alexandria, the capital of lower Egypt, an emporium of most opulent commerce. It was called *Rome*, by M. Antony, when he held his third consulship (B. C. 31) therein.—There is a coin of that triumvir, bearing the foregoing inscription, which has for its type a palm tree, with fruit pendent beneath its branches, and round it is the *corona hederacea*, or ivy crown. The palm abounded beyond all other trees in Egypt, and was the usual symbol of Alexandria. And perhaps, says Oiselius, who gives an engraving of this coin (TAB. xxxiv. No. 3, p. 149) the crown of ivy being a symbol of Bacchus, it is here conjoined with the palm tree, by M. Antony, who had already ordered himself to be called Bacchus.

ALEXANDRIA.—On the reverse of a silver Hadrian (engraved in Oiselius, TAB. xxxiv. p. 149), the type of a female standing, clothed in a tunic [supposed to represent the genius of Egypt]. She holds in her right hand the *sistrum*, in connexion with the worship of Isis [the movement of that instrument signifying the rise of the Nile.] In her left hand she holds a bucket or waterpot *(situla)* by which is indicated the flow of canals or watercourses.—Rasche.

The genius of Alexandria, or of Egypt in general, is figured on a brass medal of Hadrian (struck in Egypt), as a man, wearing on his own head the skin of an elephant's, and holding in his right hand a bundle of corn ears. He takes with the left hand that of the emperor, and lifts it to his lips, as if to kiss it, in acknowledgment of Hadrian's benefits to the city and country. Round the coin is engraved ALEXANDREA, and in the field LIE (year xv).—Zoega, *Num. Ægypt.* vii.—[Mr. Akerman, some time ago, referring to a specimen of this very interesting coin, then in his own possession, had remarked that the numeral 15 denotes the year of Hadrian's arrival at Alexandria.]

ALEXANDRIA. S. C.—On first and second brass of Hadrian, the city of Alexandria is personified by a woman seated on the ground, holding ears of corn in her right hand. Near her

left arm rises a vine branch, and her elbow rests on a vase, near which is a bunch of grapes. At

her feet also are three ears of wheat, indicative of the generally abundant harvests of Egypt.

On the reverse of another brass coin, with the same legend, and minted under the same emperor, Alexandria sits with corn-ears in her right hand and cornucopiæ in her left: her arm resting on the *canistrum*.—See Oiselius, TAB. xxxiv.

ALEXANDRIA TROAS *(Colonia)*.—A city so called from its being situated on that part of the coast of Mysia, called the Troad, or plain of Troy, eternized by the Iliad of Homer.—According to Strabo, it received the appellation of *Alexandria*, from Alexander the Great, who was the first to elevate it to the rank of a free city: from that period it continued increasing until the invasion and occupation of Asia Minor by the Romans, who unceasingly added to its splendour. Julius Cœsar greatly improved and ornamented it. His example was followed by Augustus, who made it *a Roman Colony;* and Hadrian (says Justin) adorned it with baths and aqueducts. It was from Augustus, that the city took the name of *Augusta*. But it was not called *Alexandria* on coins before the reign of Caracalla; and then it re-assumed the name, either to flatter that prince's affected fondness for the memory of Alexander the Great, or in acknowledgment of benefits conferred upon it by him as the eldest son and expectant successor of Septimius Severus. The era of Alexander Troas is fixed by Mionnet (Supplmt. T. v. 508) at 454 years from the foundation of Rome, 300 B. C. Its ruins still exist, and are called by the Turks *Eski-Stambul*, or *Old* Constantinople.

Among the *Latin* colonial autonomes (described by Mionnet, vol. ii. p. 639) is the following singular one, viz.:—*Obv.* CO. ALEX. TRO. Turreted head of a woman.— *Rev.* A peasant or shepherd, holding in his right hand the *pedum ;* he stands by the side of a cave, on which the Sybil *Herophile* rests herself: behind the shepherd is a ram.— The other types of this period of the colony's mint, are APOL. ZMINTHE. Apollo Sminthius (see Apollo) standing—a fawn —the vexillum—an eagle with a bull's head.

The colonial *imperial* coins extend in nearly an unbroken succession of reigns from Trajan to Gallienus and Salonina. They are numerous, and some few worthy of notice. On these we read COL. AVG. (TROA or TROAD.)—COL. AVG. TRO. ALEX. *Colonia Augusta Troas*, (or *Troadensis*) *Alexandria*, or COL. AVG. TRO. or TR.

There is, on a second brass dedicated by the city of Troas to Caracalla, the type of a horse depascent, behind which is a tree; and by its side is the figure of a rustic, who bears the *pedum* in his right hand.—Of this reverse the annexed cut is a copy, after a specimen in the British Museum.—Vaillant, who *(in Coloniis*, i. 46), describes the figure, as simply that of a shepherd holding the crook, usually employed in his pastoral vocation, considers this device of man, horse, and tree, to indicate the confirmation of privileges and immunities, granted to the Troadensians by Caracalla.

Among the imperial series, all with *Latin* legends, struck in this Roman colony, one, which is dedicated to the honour of Crispina, wife of Commodus, is of good design, and curious in its typification. *Obv.* CRISPINA AVGVSTA.—Head of the Empress.

Rev. COL. AVG. TROAD. (The August Colony of Troas.)—A figure standing in a military dress, sacrificing at a tripod, in front of the statue of Apollo, which stands on a cippus or pedestal. Above the tripod is an eagle with expanded wings, holding in its talons the head of a bull.—Vaillant, *in coloniis,* i. p. 223.

[Pellerin (in his *Mélange de Med.* T. i. pl. xvii. No. 15), gives a coin of this colony, dedicated to Commodus himself, from which the above wood-cut is taken. The type differs a little from that on Crispina's above described, inasmuch as, for the tripod is substituted a lighted altar; and the sacrificer wears a cloak over his military dress, and holds a sceptre, instead of a spear, in his left hand.]

"This medal (says Vaillant), refers to the augury which was taken when the foundations of New Troy *(Alexandria Troas)*, were about to be laid. Strabo relates (Lib. xiii.) that the city was built where it now is, from the ruins of ancient Troy, by command of the Oracle. Now all this appears to me very clearly expressed in the medal before us. For indeed, whilst the founder of New Troy is performing sacrifice at the tripod of Apollo (who was the guardian deity of Old Troy), with a view to learn what place he ought to fix upon for the city which he designed to build, an eagle is seen in the air, holding in his claws the head of an immolated bull; thereby signifying to him who sacrificed it, that he should lay the foundations of his new town on the spot, where the eagle is going to carry that portion of the victim. For this reason, the inhabitants of the colony, in remembrance of the foundation of their city, caused to be represented on their coins, sometimes a single eagle, which flies away with a bull's head; at other times the same bird and *caput bovis,* with their founder offering sacrifice to Apollo."

Mionnet gives a coin of this colony, dedicated to Commodus, having for its obverse legend, GEN. CON. COL. AVG. TROAD.—The genius of the colony is half naked, and stands holding in her right hand a small figure of Apollo, and in her left a cornucopiæ.—On the reverse of a coin of Crispina, the type is a mountain, on which is Apollo, clothed in the female habiliment of the *stola.* The bow and patera are in his hands. A herdsman, or shepherd, is before the god, holding the pedum, and in a suppliant posture; behind him is a ram.—A coin of Alexandria Troas, struck in honour of Trebonianus Gallus, exhibits as the type of its reverse, Apollo, naked,

who is carried to the skies between the wings of a griffin, holding his right hand on his head, and a lyre in his left. (Sestini.)—Another coin of the same emperor, with COL. AV. TROA. on its reverse, presents nine figures seated on a circular estrade. *(Cabinet de Rollin à Paris.)*

In the selection of ancient coins from the eminently rare and choice cabinet of M. Allier de Hauteroche, described and engraved by M. Du Mersan, is one (pl. xiii. fig. 3) dedicated by this colony to Caracalla.

On the obverse is M. AVREL. ANTONIN, and the laurelled head of that emperor.—The reverse (as will be seen by the annexed cut) bears for legend—COL. ALEXAND. D. AVG. and for type an equestrian figure, with right hand raised, riding at speed, before, what M. Du Mersan calls, the statue of *Minerva;* but which, by the turreted crown, and from other numismatic analogies, Mr. Akerman appears fully warranted in pronouncing to be *the Genius of the Colony.*

The other types of this colony consist of the head of a *turreted woman* and the *vexillum;* also Apollo *Sminthius* (see the word), as in Hadrian and in Commodus.—*Victory* marching; and *Eagle* with head of an ox; struck under Antoninus Pius.—A *satyr,* with wine-skin on his shoulder; a *horse* feeding, under M. Aurelius; a *tripod* and a *crow* beside it; a *turreted woman* carrying the palladium and vexillum; *Hercules* standing in repose like that (says Mionnet) of the *Palais Farnese;* minted under Commodus.—*Hercules* strangling Antæus; *Silenus,* supported by two Bacchants, and a satyr before him, minted under Caracalla.—*Remus* and *Romulus* with the wolf, struck under Elagabalus.—*Equestrian figure* before a statue of Apollo, as in Mæsa.—*Emperor* on horseback, with paludamentum, right hand raised, before him a statue of Apollo, placed on a cippus, dedicated to Alexander Severus.—*Bust of a woman,* behind which is the *vexillum,* on which is AV. CO.; struck under Gallienus.—*An eagle on a cippus,* as in Salonina, &c., &c.—See Mionnet, vol. ii. p. 653. Do. *Supplmt.* V. p. 508, et seq.

ALIM. ITAL. *Alimenta Italiæ.*—This legend, of which the general meaning is nourishment, food, provisions in corn, and other resources furnished by Trajan to Italy, has particular reference to the subsistence given by him to children of both sexes out of the public funds.

On a rare gold coin of the above-named emperor (in the *cabinet de France*), inscribed ALIM. ITAL.; on the exergue, the figure of Trajan, clothed in the toga, stands with his right hand extended over the heads of two children, who appear with uplifted hands before him. Around the field we read COS. V. P. S. P. Q. R. OPTIMO PRINC.—Another *aureus,* minted under the same reign, with the same legend, has for its type a woman standing.

This good emperor, desirous to favour the population of Italy, which had suffered much during the civil wars, assigned to his subjects certain landed estates, the produce of which was appropriated to the maintenance of a great number of children, otherwise destitute and unprovided for—an excellent trait of his, and worthy of great praise, although he owed the example of it to Nerva, his father by adoption.

The attention which Trajan bestowed, says the author of *Doctrina*, on the nurture of the young Italians, is attested as well by ancient authors as on marbles and coins. Dion alludes to this munificence, when he tells us, that on his return to Rome, U. C. 852 (A. D 99), the Emperor applied himself immediately to improve the condition of the commonwealth; and this he did with such extensive liberality, as to expend large sums on the provinces even for the education of children.—Pliny, too, in his panegyric, testifies that infants were diligently looked after and registered, in order to be brought up at the expense of the state. "There were very nearly 5000 free-born children, whom the liberality of our prince (says he), sought out and adopted. A reserve in case of war, and an ornament in peaceful times, they are nourished at the public cost; and learn to love their country, not as their country only, but also as their nursing mother. From the ranks of these will our camps, our tribes, be filled," &c.—This panegyric was spoken in the year U. C. 853 (A. D. 100), and it shews that from his first accession to the empire, Trajan applied his thoughts to these public plans of benevolence.

On a first brass of the same Emperor, a similar legend of reverse is to be found, accompanied with an allegorical type of elegantly simple design, as the subjoined engraving faithfully displays:—

In this we see the figure of a woman, clothed in a long robe. She bears a horn of plenty in her left hand; and in her right a bunch of corn ears, which she holds over the head of a small togated figure.

Between the years U. C. 854 and 856 (A. D. 101 and 103), a stone was erected, as is shewn by its having his 4th consulate inscribed on it, the language on which (as published by Muratori), extols the same example of Trajan's beneficence.

The monument next in the order of time, com-

memorative of Trajan's unceasing care for the wants of the people, is a brazen tablet, 10½ Italian feet wide, 5½ in height, and covered with an inscription in several columns, dug up in 1747, near Piacenza, and at a short distance from the Via Æmilia. This relic has been explained by Muratori, Maffei, and others, and copied *in extenso* by Eckhel (vol. vi. 424), who remarks, that the title *Dacici*, applied in it to the Emperor, shews that it was completed immediately after the year U. C. 856 (A.D. 103). It is by this inscription, contemporaneous with the date of the coin (to adopt the appropriate language of Dr. Cardwell), an inscription as remarkable as any one which has ever fallen under the notice of Antiquaries, that the case in question is strikingly illustrated. It records the bounty conferred by Trajan upon the obscure town of Veleia, a town almost unknown in ancient history: it specifies the monthly allowance granted to 281 children belonging to this town; and describes, with the greatest exactness, the proprietors in the neighbourhood, with the reports made by them of the value of their property, and the sums which they received on mortgage; binding themselves in return to pay the moderate interest of five per cent. for the support of the institution.—[Lecture ix. p. 222.]

Trajan's efforts directed towards the improvement of the condition of his subjects, are recorded also by Spartianus. Whilst the fact is proved by numerous coins, struck not only during his 5th consulship, but even later in his 6th, and which present elegant types allusive to that subject. We see, therefore, the liberality of Trajan designated and eulogised on public monuments, throughout his five last consulates, or from A.D. 99, to at least A. D. 112. Spanheim affords a variety of information respecting the *alimenta* distributed by Trajan; and Reinisius has collected, from inscribed marbles, a numerous list of *Quæstores* (paymasters) *alimentorum*, or as they are elsewhere called, *Quæstores pecuniæ alimentariæ*.—[Eckhel, vi. 424.]

It is pleasing to regard these monuments of Trajan's humane care of the families of the destitute poor; but it is not to be overlooked that the operation of this benevolent measure gave constant rise to fresh claims on the public treasury.—" By these and other prodigal largesses, frequently renewed, the Emperor is said to have supported nearly two millions of his people.— But in excuse for such wholesale pauperism, it must be remembered, that in Trajan's reign, most of the provinces suffered greatly by earthquakes; and many places were grievously afflicted with plague, famine, floods, and frequent conflagrations."—Smyth, *Cat.* 81.

ALIM. ITAL. S. C.—The following is engraved from another large brass medal of Trajan, bearing on its obverse, the legend which records his system of providing food for the inhabitants of Italy. The Emperor is here represented enthroned on a curule seat, with his feet on a footstool; he is crowned with laurel, attired in the toga, and supports his left arm on a spear. Before him is a matron, clothed in a long robe, presenting two of the Ulpian children, one of which she holds on her arm, whilst

the other stands beside her, and both of whom extend their little hands, in token of gratitude.

In commenting on this interesting type, Captain Smyth says—"This is struck upon an occasion similar to that described with reference to preceding coins; and corroborates history, by shewing that the public magazines were well filled; for instead of supplying the city by oppressing the Roman provinces, Trajan took off all restrictions, and laid the traffic in provisions open. This, and punctual payment, inspired confidence; and the provinces sent their corn to Italy in such abundance, that Rome was in a condition to relieve Egypt, the granary of the world, when distressed by famine. This fact is admirably detailed in the panegyric; and was so remarkable a return for former obligations, that the encomiast dwells upon it with manifest delight."—*Descr. Cat.* p. 82.

ALLECTUS, one of the Usurpers during the reigns of Diocletian and Maximian.—His family, country, and time of birth remain unknown.—Following the fortunes of CARAUSIUS, he became his Prætorian Præfect, and took part in the administration of Britain. Although skilled in war, and held in repute by the soldiers, yet whatever good qualities he possessed were darkened by his avarice, and sullied by his ambition. Many were the acts of injustice which he is said to have committed, under the influence of these two-fold vices; and fearing the resentment of Carausius, he came to the base and treacherous resolution of assassinating his benefactor and companion in arms.—Having perpetrated this foul crime, he employed his ill-gotten wealth in corrupting the legionaries as well as the sea forces. They declared him *Imperator* and *Augustus*, and he became the successor of Carausius, A. D. 293. Constantius Chlorus being then in Gaul, resolved to terminate the usurpation of Allectus: he prepared a fleet, which he divided into two squadrons, on board one of which he embarked himself, giving the command of the other to his prefect Asclepiodotus. That commander made, in a skilful manner, his descent upon the British shores; and instantly marched against Allectus, who had prepared for this expedition against him from the commencement of his reign. A battle ensued, which ended in favour of Constantius's general. The usurper was slain on the field of battle, after having held the sovereignty of Bri-

tain during three years. It was in consequence of this victory, gained by his lieutenant, that Constantius was enabled to re-establish the supremacy of Imperial Rome in Britain, A. D. 296, ten years after the government of that island had been separated from it.—On his coins he is styled IMP. (or IMP. C.) ALLECTVS P. F. AVG.—or only P. AVG. or ALLECTVS P. F. AVG.—or IMP. C. ALLECTVS P. F. I. AVG.: where the I. occurs, it is to be read *Invictus.*—The gold and silver (the latter generally of a very base quality), are of the highest rarity. The brass (small) are also many of them rare. They bear a well-executed bust, giving Allectus the appearance of a man of 50 or thereabouts. The head on the gold is laureated; on the silver and brass, radiated.—Altogether the portrait is of marked character, and may be regarded as a good likeness of the man.

The annexed cut is executed from a remarkably well-preserved third brass, covered with dark brown patina, stated to have been found within the area of the Roman camp at Caister (*Venta Icenorum*), near Norwich.—(The coin is now in the possession of Mr. W. Bensly).

Obv. IMP. C. ALLECTVS P. F. AVG. Radiated head of Allectus.

Rev. TEMPORVM FELICITAS. Felicity standing with caduceus and horn of plenty.

In the field S. A.—On the exergue M. S. L.

Eckhel observes, that whilst the coins of Carausius have their merit on account of the various legends and types which they exhibit, the coins of Allectus recommend themselves, in no other respect, than for their greater rarity. The same illustrious teacher in numismatics, also speaks of the reverses as common and trite, enumerating such only as Pax, Providentia, Oriens, Salus—but he could not have been aware of the numerous other varieties that exist, and which swell the catalogue in Mr. Akerman's work, such as the Adventus Aug.—Æquitas Aug.—Comes Aug.—Dianæ Reduci——Felicitas Seculi—Fides Militum–Hilaritas—Jovi Conservatori—Moneta Aug.—Pietas Aug.—Romæ Æternæ—Spes Publica—Temporum Felicitas—Victoria Aug. &c. Referring to the valuable treatise " on the Coins of the Romans relating to Britain," by the well-known and esteemed author above named, for an ampler monetal notice of Allectus, we shall take this occasion to quote one more new variety in the list of reverses on this usurper's coins, discovered (amongst others of Roman mintage), at Lillyhorn, near Oakridge common, and communicated, through Mr. Roach Smith, F.S.A. to the British Archæological Association, by Mr. T. Baker. It reads ..ICTORI. GER. *Victoria Germanica.* In the exergue C.; in the field, S. P. trophy and captives.

"This reverse (observes Mr. Smith), although common on coins of the period, had not been previously noticed on those of Allectus. Doubts have been thrown on the historical importance of some of the coins of Carausius and Allectus, from their close resemblance in type to those of their predecessors, of which it is therefore alleged, they are mere imitations. There are, however, many which certainly cannot be placed in this category, as they afford types both novel and appropriate." And Mr. Smith suggests that the coin now first published, may have been struck to record a victory gained by Allectus over some of the German or Saxon pirates, infesting the British coast.

ALLIANCE, or Concord, between different cities was a frequent usage in ancient times.— Alliances are found to have existed between neighbouring cities, and also between cities situated at a distance from each other, sometimes to the number of more than two. Under the power of the Romans, alliance with them is expressly noted on some coins. This state of political concord is itself recorded in the legend, and even personified in the type. In other instances, the citizens of a town declare themselves *allied* to each other. (Hennin, *Manuel*, vol. ii. p. 7.)— In connection with this subject, it may be noticed, that there is a rare family denarius (see *Veturia* gens), on the reverse of which is a *Fecialis*, or sacred herald, in a kneeling attitude, holding a sow, which is touched with their wands by a Roman soldier and by a man, who, from his dress, appears to belong to a foreign nation. —It was by such a ceremonial that the Roman people, in the earlier periods of their history, contracted alliances. When the two deputies touched the sow, the priest invoked Jupiter to treat the violators of the compact with the same degree of rigour as he was himself about to exercise upon that animal; and he forthwith killed it with a flint-stone. This solemnity, according to Livy, was as ancient as the reign of Tullus Hostilius, third king of Rome.

On a coin in silver of the Antistia gens, two figures are seen holding a victim over an altar, evidently in conclusion of some treaty of alliance and amity between the Romans and another state, as is indicated by the accompanying legend, FOEDVS, &c.—For instances of municipal alliances, see Akerman's "Ancient Coins of Cities and Princes"—Hispania; Gades, &c.—An article, headed FOEDERATÆ CIVITATES, in Dr. W. Smith's Dictionary of Greek and Roman Antiquities throws much historical light on this subject.

ALLIENUS.—This is doubtless a surname. Its name, as Ursinus thinks, is derived from Allius, in the same manner as from Nasidius, we have Nasidi*enus*, and from Satrius, Satri*enus*. But the name of the family to which the Allienus belonged, whose name appears on the following very rare denarius, is not known. It is the only type, viz.:—

Obv.—Caius CAES. IMP*erator* CO*n*sul ITER*um*. Head of Venus.

Rev.—Aulus ALLIENVS PROCO*n*sul.—A naked man, holding a small cloak folded round his left arm. In his right hand he holds the triquetra, or symbol of three cornered Sicily—his right foot on the prow of a vessel.—Morell *Thesaurus, Alliena*, TAB. iii. fig. 1, p. 15.

This Aulus Allienus (says Havercamp), was the lieutenant of Q. Cicero, in Asia, during the civil war. When he became Prætor, he attached himself to the party of Julius Cæsar, under whom he obtained the proconsulship of Sicily, which this coin attests, having been minted in the year of Rome 706 (B. C. 48).—See SICILIA —also TRIQVETRA.

ALPHABET.—It is not uncommon to see *single letters* of the alphabet in the field of Roman family coins.—Eckhel enumerates a few of them; observing that these letters sometimes appear on the obverse, at other times on the reverse; with this regulation, that whichever side the moneyer once fixes on, he constantly adheres to it. The denarii of Herennius, and of Antonius Balbus, present exceptions to this rule: they vary the stations of these letters. In some, when the letters are on the obverse, the same re-appear on the reverse. In others, Latin letters are mixed with Greek characters. Others again exhibit different letters occupying the obverse side, whilst arithmetical signs appear on the reverse.—Some of the richer cabinets have the whole alphabet in their series of family coins. In the imperial museum at Vienna, the number of letters is complete on denarii of Aelius Bala, Antonius Balbus, Cornelius Scipio Asiagenes— Herennius, Junius Silanus, and Thorius.—For further information on this subject, the reader is referred to *Doct. Num. Vet.* v. 75, et seq.

ALTAR.—See *Ara.*

ALTERED MEDALS.—The Italian fabricators of counterfeit coins, by ingeniously altering and retouching with their graving tools, the portraits, the reverses, and even the legends of ancient coins, have often succeeded in deceiving not only the tyro in numismatics, but also the most practised connoisseurs.—"Of a Claudius (says Pinkerton) struck at Antioch, they make an Otho; of a Faustina a Titiana; of a Julia Severi a Didia Clara; of a Macrinus a Pescennius; of an Orbiana an Annia Faustina; of a Mamæa a Tranquillina; of a Philip an Æmilian. Give them a Marcus Aurelius, he starts up a Pertinax, by thickening the beard a little and enlarging the nose. In short, wherever there is the least resemblance, an artist of this class can, from a trivial medal, generate a most scarce and valuable one."—*Essay on Medals*, ii. 218.

No one, however, who has a taste for the study of antique coins and medallions, ought to be deterred from collecting, under the apprehension of being imposed upon by counterfeits. Such deceptions are to be guarded against by ready access to cabinets of genuine specimens; and the judicious exercise of that discriminative faculty, which experience is sure to give the eye, when aided by "a little handling," and by attentively perusing a few standard works of modern numismatists—not omitting due reference to Beauvais's essay on this subject, especially through the late Mr. Brockett's annotated translation.

But after all, "the most shameless forgeries, (as Capt. Smyth observes), have been rather inventions than imitations, and would scarcely deceive a novice; such were medals bearing the heads of Priam, Plato, Aeneas, Hannibal, Scipio, Marius, Crassus, Cicero, and Virgil; giving new reverses to known heads; as *Veni, Vidi, Vici* to Cæsar; *Festina lente*, with an anchor and dolphin, or a terminus on a thunderbolt, expressive of stability to Augustus; the Pantheon; on a coin of Agrippa; and the *Pons Ælius*, and *Expeditio Judaica* on those of Hadrian. Yet gross as these attempts were, Paul IV. purchased several of them from Pietro Galileo at exorbitant prices."

AMALTHEA: the name of the goat, to which fable assigns the honour of having suckled Jupiter. Out of gratitude for this good office, the king of gods and of men placed her, with her two kids, as a constellation in the heavens; and gave one of her horns to the nymphs who had the care of his infancy, accompanied with the virtue of producing whatever they desired. This is what is called the horn of plenty (see *Cornucopiæ*), so often represented on Greek and Roman coins. Allusive to Amalthea, as *Nutrix Jovis infantis* (the nurse of the infant Jupiter), gold and silver coins of Domitian bear on their reverse the figure of a goat, within a laurel garland, and the legend *Princeps Juventutis*. On a second brass of Hadrian with s. c. the infant Jupiter is typified, under the goat Amalthea:—

Stat quoque capra simul (says Ovid)
Infanti lac dedit illa Jovi.

In the Farnese collection (v. 169), there is a brass medallion of Antoninus Pius, without legend of reverse, which exhibits the infant Jove sitting naked on the back of a goat, before an altar, with an eagle apparently sculptured on it, placed close to the trunk of a tree.

On the reverse of a billon coin of Gallienus, inscribed Jovi Con*servatori* Augusti, there is, instead of the usual majestic figure of the king of "gods and men," a goat, representing Amalthea. This piece of mythology is still more clearly alluded to, on a billon of Gallienus, and on gold and billon of his son Saloninus, which coins have, each for their type of reverse, a naked boy riding on a goat.—See IOVI CRESCENTI.

AMANDUS (Cneus Silvius), an usurper, in the joint reign of Diocletianus and Maximianus Hercules, assumed the title of Augustus, in colleagueship with Ælianus, a Gaulish chief, A. D. 285. But both were slain A. D. 207, in battle with the armies which had been sent against them by Maximianus.—Of Amandus no gold nor silver coins are extant. There is, however, a third brass assigned to him by Banduri (ii. p. 87), on which, with radiated head, he is styled IMP. C. C. AMANDVS; reverse legend SPES. PVBLICA; and type Minerva standing with spear and shield. Besides which, in the Pembroke collection is engraved, as a third brass, IMP. S. AMANDVS P. F AVG. and radiated head,

on the obverse; with VENVS AVG. and the goddess standing, on the reverse, clothed in the stola, holding an apple in the right hand, and the hasta in her left.—Both these are cited by Eckhel, without any doubt expressed by him as to their authenticity. But Mr. Akerman, as as well as Mionnet, states them to be strongly suspected. Indeed, from their discrepancy in the *prenomen*, one of them must be false.

AME *de la Médaille*.—This expression is ingeniously enough applied by some French numismatists, of the elder school, to the *Legend*, which they profess to regard as the "*soul* of the coin,", whilst they designate the type, or figures, as the *body*. "For example (says *Père* Jobert), we see on a (silver) medal of Augustus, two hands joined, holding a *caduceus*, between two horns of Amalthea—*this is the body.*—The word PAX, which is engraved on the medal, marks the peace which this prince had restored to the common-wealth of Rome, in reconciling himself with Mark Antony, which had brought back happiness and abundance to the people—*this is the soul*. And on a medal of Nerva, by means of the word CONCORDIA EXERCITVVM, the same two hands joined [holding a military ensign on the prow of a vessel], served to mark the fidelity of the soldiers, both by sea and land, to their new Emperor."— *Science des Médailles*, i. 216.

AMBIANI, now Amiens, in France.—AMB. Ducange and Bimard de la Bastie both conjecture that the coin of Magnentius, on the exergue of which they read the above letters, was struck at Amiens *(Ambianis)*. Whilst Vaillant *(Præst. Num.* i. 360), interprets it A. M. B. *Antiochiæ moneta officinæ secundæ* (money of the second mint of Antioch.)—See Rasche.

AMICTUS.—This word chiefly refers to the clothing or covering of the head, with crown, diadem, helmet, spoils of the lion, proboscis of the elephant, &c.

AMMON, a surname of Jupiter.—Alexander the Great styled himself the son of Jupiter Ammon; and his successors, the kings of Syria, and those of Cyrenaica have, on coins, their heads *adorned* with the horns of a ram, or of Ammon, the symbol of their dominion over Lybia. This deity appears on a great number of coins, and of engraved marbles. The Egyptians, whose popular divinity he was, regarded him as the author of fecundity and generation. The same superstition afterwards introduced itself among the Romans, who worshipped Ammon as the preserver of nature.—In the consular series of the Roman mint, the head of *Ammon* is found on coins of the *Cornuficia*, Lollia, Pinaria, Papia, and other families, and in the Imperial, on those of Augustus, Trajan, Hadrian, Aurelius, Severus, and Treb. Gallus.—The head of Jupiter *Ammon* exhibits itself on a denarius of Augustus, (see Pembroke Collection, p. iii. TAB. 9).—Eckhel (vi. p. 87) referring to this, observes, that it is a type of an unusual kind in the mint of that prince (then simply Octavianus), but he accounts for it from the circumstance of its having been struck in Africa, by

Pinarius Scarpus, one of his Lieutenants.—On a denarius of the *Antonia* family, given in Morell. *Thesaur.* we read M. ANTO. (Mark Antony) COS. III. IMP. IIII. The type is Jupiter Ammon, as designated by the attribute of a ram's horn, on the side of a bearded head.— For this device see *Cornificia* gens.

AMOR.—This legend is found inscribed above the figure of a horse, on a rare contorniate medal, published by Havercamp *(Num. Contorn.* fig. 10), and which he considers as either derived from the love, or attachment, which a master bears towards a horse that has carried off the palm of victory at the Circensian games; or is used to denote the noble nature of that animal.

AMORES. Two Loves, or Cupids, drawing Venus in a chariot, appear on a denarius of the *Julia* family—engraved in Morell. (TB. i. fig. 4.)

AMOR MVTVVS AVGG. *(Augustorum).*— Mutual affection of the Emperors.—Two right hands joined. This legend and type appear on large sized silver of Balbinus and of Pupienus, who were the first two emperors elected to reign with precisely equal rights.—For an example of two right hands joined, see *Mussidia* gens, and HERENNIVS ETRVSCVS.—See also *Hands joined.*

AMPHINOMUS and ANAPIS (or *Anapias*), two brothers, of Sicily, respecting whom it is related that they saved their parents, at the peril of their own lives, from the flames of Etna, at the moment when an eruption of that volcano threatened their immediate destruction. This was a favourite subject with the ancients, in symbolising filial piety; and is often represented on Greek coins of Catana (Catania), where this noble action is alleged to have been performed. Of these two Sicilian brothers, types of that devoted love, which is ever cherished by good children towards the earthly authors of their being, *Cornelius Severus,* alluding to Mount Etna, thus expresses himself:—

Amphinomus fraterque pares sub munere fortes,
Cum jam vicinis streperent incendia tectis,
Accipiunt pigrumque patrem, matremque senilem.

"Amphinomus and his brother, both equally courageous in the performance of a duty, whilst the flames murmured their threats against the neighbouring houses, rescue their decrepid father, and their aged mother."

On a well known denarius of Pompeius Magnus, struck in reference to his naval command, and to his victories over the pirates on the coasts of Sicily and of Italy, this popular legend is clearly alluded to, by a typification, in which Neptune forms the centre of a group; whilst on each side of him is a naked young man, carrying on his shoulders an aged figure, clothed. It is thus that on Roman coins, after the example of the Greek, Amphinomus and Anapis are seen rescuing their father and mother from the perils of the burning mountain.—See PRAEF. CLAS. ET ORAE. MARIT.—The above is engraved from the

silver coin restored by Trajan, valued by Mionnet at 300 fr. (£11 17s. 10d.)

AMPHITHEATRE.—This is a word which, even by its compound formation, designates an edifice consisting of two theatres facing each other, and leaving between a void space, called the *arena*, wherein different kinds of public games and spectacles were exhibited, especially combats of gladiators and wild beasts. The nature of these contests, which obliged the combatants alternately to pursue and be pursued, necessarily required an elongation of ground from the centre, and resulted in producing an oval instead of a circular form. Amphitheatres were peculiar to the Romans: they were unknown to the Greeks. These buildings were not covered in; but during grand displays, an awning was occasionally stretched across from the top to screen the spectators from the intense heat of the sun's rays. The arena was surrounded with dens *(carceres)*, in which were confined the ferocious animals destined for the different fights. Immediately above these dens, there was a gallery running round the whole arena, and in which the most distinguished persons took their respective places. Behind this gallery, the seats or steps rose in gradation to the summit. The lower tiers were for people of rank; the others were appropriated to the lower classes. The exterior of an amphitheatre was divided into stories, each ornamented with arcades, columns, and pilasters, in greater or less number, and sometimes with statues. Besides the circular rows of steps which served for seats, inside, there were also some which, in the form and for the purposes of staircases, intersected the others from the ground to the highest part of the structure. These formed the *baltei*, or belts. The portals of the vaulted avenues, through which the amphitheatre was entered, were called *vomitaria*. The successive rows, comprised within two staircases, bore the name of *cunei*; because the most elevated steps 'were broader than those which were nearer the arena, the whole presenting the form of a wedge.

AMPHITHEATRUM *Flavianum, vel Titi.* —Of the four amphitheatres of Rome, whose ruins are still to be seen, or whose memory is at all preserved, that of Titus, denominated in his days the Colossæum, now called the *Coliseum,* is the most remarkable. This building, of superb architectural design and of vast dimensions, was commenced A. D. 77, by Vespasian; and was finished and dedicated by his son and successor Titus, during A. U. C. 823 (A. D. 80). The same year a coin was minted, in large brass, having for the legend of its obverse—IMP*erator* T*itus* CAES*ar* VESP*asianus* AUG*ustus* P*ontifex* M*aximus* TRI*bunicia* Pote*state* P*ater* P*atriæ* CO*n*S*ul* VIII. (The Emperor Titus Cæsar Vespasian, the August, Sovereign Pontiff, enjoying the Tribunitian power, Father of the country, Consul for the eighth time.)— Head of Titus laureated.

On the reverse (without epigraph) is the Flavian *Amphitheatre,* originally so called in honour of Vespasian's family name.

The type is marked with its proper number of stories or arcades; and from the open top it is

seen to be filled with people, whose heads appear in the uppermost rows. On the right and left of the amphitheatre, as represented on this very rare coin, are what were meant for "the *Meta Sudens* and the *Domus Aurea*, as it was actually situated," observes Capt. Smyth, in some instructive remarks on his own specimen of this most interesting reverse. The edifice itself is of an elliptical form; covers nearly six acres of ground; and it was said to be capable of containing 70,000 spectators; but (adds the accurate writer above-named) "in a troublesome process of admeasurement, I could not make it contain more than 50,000."— Martial, who witnessed it in the integrity of its vast dimensions, thus encomiastically speaks of it.

Omnis Cæsareo cadat labor Amphitheatro,
Unum pro cunctis Fama loquatur opus.

["Let every laborious enterprize yield the palm to this Amphitheatre of Cæsar; and Fame, neglecting all others, blazon henceforth this one achievement."]

Of this colossal structure such is the solidity, that it would, even to this period, have remained almost entire, if the spoliative barbarism of more modern times had not, to a great extent, despoiled it of materials for the purpose of building therewith both public and private edifices. (Kolb, i. 133).—"In using the expression, that to build this work Titus 'turned from their course rivers of gold,' Cassiodorus (observes Eckhel) must not be considered to have spoken hyperbolically; for Barthélemy and P. Jacquier, after taking the admeasurement, and making their calculations, concluded that the walls of its enclosure alone would cost, in our days, nearly seventeen millions of francs (about £673,000 sterling.)

So important was it (adds the illustrious author of *Doctrina*) to lavish immense wealth, in order that a people, already athirst for monstrous pleasures, should be supplied with a fitting theatre, in which (as Arnobius complains) they might look on at human beings, delivered up to and torn in pieces by wild beasts; and killing each other for no other reason than the gratification of the spectators; and where they might spend in general dissipation, and festal hilarity, those very days on which such atrocities were perpetrated.—(vi. 358.)

To commemorate the building of this stupendous monument, the Senate, it appears, caused two coins to be struck, namely, the one above described, which was minted in Titus's life-time; and another first brass, a short time after his death (A. D. 81), with the following legend on the obverse: viz., DIVO. AVG. T. DIVI. VESPASIAN. S. C. on the exergue. Titus seated on spoils of war.—On the reverse, without epigraph, the amphitheatre, ornamented with statues.

The same reverse occurs again on a large brass of Domitian, with S. C.—The legend on the side of the head, is CAES. DIVI. VESP. F. DOMITIANVS. COS. VII.—Vespasian, indeed, as has already been observed, began the construction of this amphitheatre, but his eldest son Titus finished and dedicated it. It was on the opening of the Colossæum, that besides more than the usual display of gladiatorial homicides, he gave shews of wild beasts of every kind. Of these in one day 5000, according to Suetonius, (9000 according to Dion) were slaughtered to please the carnage-loving populace of Rome. After this a "*prælium* navale" was given in the old *naumachia* (or place for representing sea fights) where water was conducted into the interior of the building, and the extraordinary sight of (no *sham* but) a *real* engagement exhibited between opposing squadrons of gallies, took place, at great cost of human life and of the public money, this cruel and extravagant sacrifice having been allowed to occupy the protracted space of one hundred days!

"To say nothing of so demoralizing a loss of time, these unintellectual pleasures of a half-starved mob must have cost more than three millions sterling, including the structure. When (observes Capt. Smyth) I wandered over this scene of guilt, I could not but regard it as a costly monument of prodigal folly and savage sensuality. Moreover, from the haste with which it was run up, there are numerous architectural eye-sores, which with its cumbrous attic, render it very inferior in design to the elegant amphitheatre at Pola, in Istria."

Several other emperors were careful to bestow restorations on this most magnificent of all public structures. Antoninus repaired it. Elagabalus set about re-establishing it after the injuries which it had sustained from the violence of a tempest, in the reign of Macrinus. What Elagabalus began was completed by his successor, Alexander Severus; on which account the type of the same building appears on the reverse of a first brass (engraved in Havercamp, *Médailles de Christine*, TAB. xxxiii.), also a silver coin with the amphitheatre and five figures, all struck under the latter prince, with the epigraph of P. M. TR. P. II. COS. P. P.—One of the brass medallions of Gordianus Pius also bears a representation of the Colossæum, with columns and statues, and a legend apparently denoting that the edifice had undergone reparations under his reign. In the arena is seen a bull and an elephant fighting, the emperor being in the midst of the spectators.—See MUNIFICENTIA GORDIANI.

Many coins with Vespasian's name and portrait and this amphitheatre for the reverse type "are exposed for sale now a days (says Eckhel), but *they are all spurious.*"

AMPLIATORI CIVIVM. (To the augmentor [or enlarger] of citizens.) S. P. Q. R. within a laurel garland. Respecting this unique appellation, and the coin on which it appears, some difference of opinion has been expressed.—Spanheim, who was the first to publish it, in a note to his translation of the Cæsars of Julian, and who gives an engraving of it, pronounces it to be of genuine antiquity, and unhesitatingly ascribes it to Antoninus Pius. The legend of the head, it is to observed, is ANTONINVS AVG. PIVS. P. P. TR. P. COS. III.—It was found some years previous to 1683, with several other Roman coins, by workmen employed on the fortifications of Bonn, near Cologne ; and the eminent author of "*Dissertationes de usu numism.*" affirms that he "had seen it with his own eyes."— Spanheim moreover observes, that Antoninus Pius was worthy above all others to be denominated *Ampliator Civium*, inasmuch as he had granted the right of citizenship *(jus civitatis)* to all the inhabitants of the Roman empire.— Eckhel (vii. p. 12) on the other hand treats the argument of Spanheim as one more erudite than lucid, and remarks that "other writers, influenced doubtless by a passage from Dion, have with great semblance of truth, ascribed to Caracalla, the act of conferring this privilege on the whole Roman world, seeing that he also bore the appellation of Antoninus." Nevertheless, after referring to the compendium of Valesius and Fabricius, for a note on these words of Dion, Eckhel concludes with making the following admission : "But after all, Antoninus Pius might, on various accounts, have been styled *Ampliatori Civium*, especially since, after the munificent example of Trajan, he made provision for the children of Italy." (vii. 12.) —The coin being universally allowed to be genuine, it may indeed seem strange that any question should have been raised as to *which* Antoninus this singular epigraph belongs. Certainly, the mind revolts at the bare idea of transferring such an honourable designation from the mild and beneficent successor of Hadrian to the tyrant son of Severus. Still, it is not to be overlooked, that the same mendacious spirit of servile adulation, which pretended to recognise another *Antonine the Pious*, in the person of Caracalla the fratricide, was not likely to deem it too great a stretch of monetal flattery, if it complimented this truculent despot, on his having *enlarged* the number of Roman citizens.—It only remains to add, as sufficiently conclusive on the point of accurate appropriation, that Mionnet and Akerman concur in placing AMPLIATORI CIVIVM among the legends of brass medallions, minted under Antoninus Pius (*not* Caracalla.)

AN.— *Annus.*—The Latin letters AN. with the numeral letter or letters added, on certain colonial coins, denote the year in which the colony was planted or sent out *(deducta.)*— Thus in the coins of the *Dacian* province AN. I.

as far as X. occurs ; and in those of the colony of Viminacium, AN. I. to XVI. are read, &c.— See Rasche's Lexicon.

AN. XV. PR. H. O. C. S.—A horseman, or equestrian statue, with spear and trophy on his shoulder. On the exergue, M. LEPIDVS.—See ÆMILIA gens, p. 14 of this work.

ANADEMA, a fillet worn as part of the head-dress by Roman ladies. On coins of Sabina Hadriani, we see the portrait of that empress bound by an anadema, and hanging at the back of her neck. This club-fashioned coiffure also appears in the medallic portraitures of Antonia, and the Agrippinas.—Smyth.

ANASTASIUS I. Emperor of the East, was born at Dyrrhachium, in Illyria, of obscure parentage, (A.D. 430.) Simply an officer of the imperial household, he succeeded, after the Emperor Zeno's death, to the Byzantine throne ; and married Ariadne, the widow of his patron and predecessor, (A. D. 491). Anastasius died suddenly, having, as it was affirmed, been struck by lightning, A. D. 518.

On his coins, which are in general common in gold, brass medallions, and 1st, 2nd, and 3rd brass, he is styled D. N. ANASTASIVS P. P. AVG. or IMP. ANASTASIVS P. P. AVG.—His silver are rare, especially those in which his name is associated on the same coin with that of Theodoricus, King of the Ostrogoths, and with the name of Baduila, the king of some other barbarous nation.— See Akerman, ii. p. 386.

AN. B. or ANT. B.—*Antiochiæ officina secunda.*—Coinage of the second monetal office, or mint, at Antioch, in Syria—where there were very many offices belonging to the mint-masters, who superintended the striking of the money, or were otherwise employed in the public mint.

ANAGNIA, a city in Latium, now *Anagna*, in the States of the Church.—Mark Antony, during his triumvirate, had a mint for striking coins in his own name, at this place.—See Eckhel's remarks on coins of Roman die, minted *extra Urbem*, vol. v. 68.

ANCHISES, a Trojan prince, of the family of Priam, who, according to the poets and mythologists, secretly married Venus ; and she bore to him Æneas, on the banks of the Simois. After the siege of Troy, his escape from that devoted city is described to have been attended with great difficulty, on account of his extreme old age. The representation of Anchises carried on the shoulders of his son, appears on denarii of the *Cæcilia*, *Herennia*, and *Julia* families : also on coins of Julius Cæsar, when Dictator.—See *Æneæ Pietas*, p. 27 of this work.

ANCIENT COINS.—By the term *ancient* are meant all coins preceding the 9th century, or the age of Charlemagne ; and by *modern* all posterior to that period. (Pinkerton.)—The most ancient coins of the Romans are those stamped with the image of the ox, the sow, and the sheep ; the double-headed Janus, the *rostrum* or beak of a ship, or the foremost half of a ship, *ratis*. Hence the coin was called *ratitus.* —Rasche.

ANCHOR (Ancora).—This well-known nautical instrument, with which the personification of Hope is now-a-days painted, is not found to be amongst her attributes on ancient coins.—But the type of *Annona* has it on a medal of Alexander Severus.—The figure of *Asia* bears it on a large brass of Antoninus [see the engraving.]—A *river god*, seated on the ground, holds it in the right hand, on gold and silver of Hadrian.—*Lætitia* sustains it in the same manner, as probably indicating stability, on coins of Gallienus, Tetricus father and son, Florianus, Carausius, and others.—The goddess of health *(Salus)* also appears with it, as in the instance of Tetricus senior and junior.—The *anchor* is likewise seen behind the helmeted head of Rome, on denarii of the *Julia* and *Mussidia* families, as given in Morel; and these so united denote (says Havercamp) that such coins were struck at the expense of [the commander of] some expeditionary fleet.—There is a naval trophy, with *anchor* and trident, on a denarius of the *Pompeia* family, and on a coin of the *Sulpicia* family is another naval trophy, with oar, *anchor*, acrostolium, prow, and two captives. (See Morell. *Thesaur.*)—An *anchor* with a dolphin wound round it, forms the reverse type of a denarius of the Emperor Titus.—See *Dolphin*—also *Pompeia* gens.

ANCUS MARCIUS, fourth King of Rome; grandson of Numa Pompilius, and immediate successor to Tullus Hostilius. Ancus was the son of Marcius, chief pontiff under Numa, and of Pompilia, Numa's daughter. He was a brave and victorious warrior; revived the ceremonies for sacred worship which Numa instituted, but which had been neglected, and did much for the embellishment, the health, and the security of Rome. His reign is said to have lasted 24 years, during which the town of Ostia, at the mouth of the Tiber, was founded, and became the seaport of Rome.

ANCUS, and ANCUS MARCI.—See *Marcia* gens—also *Numa*.

ANDRISCUS, King of the Macedonians, conquered by Metellus.—See *Cæcilia*.

A. N. F. F.—*Annum Novum, Faustum Felicem.*—The wish of a happy and prosperous new year tendered for the Emperor.—On a large brass of Hadrian we read S. P. Q. R. A. N. F. F. OPTIMO PRINCIPI (or HADRIANO AVG. P. P.), within a laurel garland.—*Senatus Populusque Romanus, Annum Novum Faustum Felicem Optimo Principi* [i. e. *adprecatur.*]

This legend is the *acclamation*, by which the Roman Senate and people presaged for Hadrian a prosperous and happy new year. "But there was in the case of the Emperors a double new year annually. The first of these was the one common to all classes, viz., on the Calends of January, on which small presents called *strenæ* were usually sent from one house to another, often inscribed with these words in full—ANNVM. NOVVM. FAVSTVM. FELICEM. as we are told by Fabretti. And this form of inscription furnishes us with the manner in which the initial letters on the coins now under consider-

ation are to be interpreted. Good wishes for the well-being of a prince were customarily expressed at the beginning of the year, namely, on the third of the nones of January. [See the treatise *De Numis* VOTORUM, in *Doct. Num. Vet.* vol. viii.] The other new year was a day held sacred by the Emperors, as the one on which they commenced their reigns, being also called the natal day of the empire *(dies natalis imperii)*. And indeed, it is in this sense that Seneca, in his satirical work entitled *Apocolocyntosis*, calls the third of the ides of October, on which Claudius died, and Nero began to reign, "the new year, and the beginning of a most happy period" *(annum novum, initium seculi felicissimi)*. As, however, on the return of both these new years, prayers were offered for the welfare of the Emperor, it is difficult to decide which of the two should be understood on these coins; nor would the decision avail towards their illustration."

Thus leaving this point as much in doubt as he found it, Eckhel (vi. 509) next refers to Havercamp; but it is only to expose the absurdity of that writer's attempt to explain the legend of this coin, viz., S. P. Q. R. A*nno Natali* (i. e. U*rbis*) F*ieri* F*ecit* OPTIMO PRINCIPI.—Now what was the *natal day of the city?* Surely no other than that on which Romulus is said to have founded it. To accept the interpretation of Havercamp, therefore, would be to concur in supposing that these coins were dedicated by the Senate to Hadrian nearly nine hundred years before! "No doubt," adds the author of *Doctrina*, "this writer on many subjects—this *polygraph*—so learned on all other points, has in the present instance met the fate of those who eat of many dishes *(polyphagæ)*, and digest imperfectly."—It is with this sarcasm on the conjectural propensities of his erudite, but not always judicious, predecessor in the devious paths of numismatic criticism, that Eckhel concludes his own *in*conclusive remarks on the point in question—a point on which, from what Capt. Smyth aptly calls "the vexatious ambiguity of abbreviations," doubt is still left as to the new year in this instance meant—whether from the founding of the city, the birth-day of the Emperor or that of the kalends of January.—The S. C. is omitted from this large brass medal, the S. P. Q. R. being equally the stamp of senatorial authority.

ANNUS NOVUS.—The famous marble of Narbonne confirms the fact, that from at least the age of Augustus, the ceremony of benediction, or of well wishing *(bene precandi)*, took place on the commencement of a new year. And we learn, that during the kalends of January, there was the greatest eagerness, among the Romans, in proffering mutual good wishes for each other's health and prosperity, with the most studied forms of expression. Nothing was more the object of solicitude with them, than, on that good day, to say and do kind things, and to avoid all untoward speeches and actions. Accordingly Ovid (*Fastorum*, lib. i.) thus sings, as out of the mouth of Janus :—

Omina principiis, inquit, inesse solent,
Templa patent, auresque Deûm, nec lingua caduoas
Concipit ulla preces, dictaque pondus habent.

[Omens, says he, are wont to shew themselves at the beginning of a new year. The temples are open, and so are the ears of the gods; nor does any tongue utter prayers, which are likely to fail, but every thing uttered has its weight.]

Since, then (observes Rasche), at the beginning of a year, every one wished and endeavoured to promote happiness to himself and friends; it is surely not surprising to find the Roman people at large invoking prosperity and happiness for the reigning prince, on marble tablets and on medals.

ANCILIA—Bucklers, or shields, so denominated because they were cut sloping on each 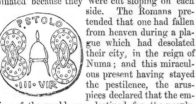 side. The Romans pretended that one had fallen from heaven during a plague which had desolated their city, in the reign of Numa; and this miraculous present having stayed the pestilence, the aruspices declared that the empire of the world was destined for the people, by whom this buckler should be preserved.—Numa, who so well knew the art of making superstition conduce to political advantages, ordered several other shields to be made in exact resemblance to this heaven-descended one, lest so precious a gift should be purloined; and he deposited the whole in the temple of Mars.—From that sanctuary they were taken when war was declared. And twelve priests, called *Salii*, to whose care they were confided, bore them, on stated days, in procession about the public places and streets of Rome. It is this which they called *movere ancilia*, and it was a bad augury to go into the country before they were replaced, as Suetonius explains by these words:—*Sed et motis, necdum conditis* ANCILIBVS.

On denarii of P. Stolo, of the *Licinia* family—one of the moneyers of Augustus, is a reverse type of the *ancilia*, between which is the apex, or cap, of one of the *Salii*, with the inscription P. STOLO. III. VIR. (an engraving of which is given above).—The obverse of this silver coin bears the legend of AVGVSTVS TR. POT. and an equestrian statue of that emperor, to whose honour (about A. D. 23), the statue was erected. It was in the month of March, when the twelve Salian priests celebrated their rites, which consisted chiefly in carrying the sacred bucklers in the left hand, leaping, and striking in cadence on them, with a javelin, or rod, which they held in their right. This ceremony always finished with superb banquets, called *Saliares Cænæ.*—See *Apex.*

ANCILIA. IMPERATOR. II. S. C.—On the reverse of a middle brass of Antoninus Pius, we see this legend, accompanied by a type, which represents two of the *Ancilian* shields. The legend and type of the obverse are ANTONINVS AVGVSTVS PIVS, and the laureated head of the emperor. Struck A. D. 140.

The forms of these "sacred bucklers," as represented on coins, and also on gems, do not exactly correspond either with each other, or with the descriptions which are given of them  in ancient writers. It will be observed that the *ancile*, delineated on the denarius of P. STOLO (see foregoing cut), is an oblong shield, divided into three smaller shields, the central an oval one, which has a thunder-bolt figured on it, and it is narrower than the other two: so that each of the ends projects beyond the middle compartment. An inspection of this type renders intelligible the expression of Festus (in Mamurius), that the buckler in question "was cut out on both sides, so that the top and bottom spread out from the centre; and also agrees with Plutarch's remark, that "it was partly cut out in a curved line like an escallop shell, and did not present a continuous circumference like the shield called *pelta*." On the other hand, the central bucklers of the two *ancilia* typified on the coin of Antoninus Pius, are nearly as broad as those at the upper and lower ends, each buckler appearing to resemble an oval shield in the centre, with very small rods, radiating at each extremity, and terminating in a semi-circular form.

It must not be omitted to be noticed, that there is a gem in the *Museum Florentinum*, which represents two of the Salii veiled in the Gabinian fashion, and bearing, on their shoulders, six bucklers suspended from a pole.—In the *Dictionary of Greek and Roman Antiquities*, edited by Dr. W. Smith, an engraving from this ancient relic is given (p. 47), to which the reader is referred. And, if the form of the shields, as copied from the antique gem, be compared with what appears on either of the two coins of Augustus and Antoninus (cuts of which are here respectively presented), it will be seen that, whilst a general resemblance to each other prevails in the shields on the coins, the shields represented on the gem, and described as six ancilia borne by Salii, are, in their contour and adornments, equally dissimilar to those associated with the word ANCILIA, and to those which form so conspicuous a feature in the reverse type of the denarius, struck by the monetary III. VIR. P. *(Licinius)* STOLO.—Yet, knowing the superior degree of attention paid by the Roman mint of the early and middle empire, to matters of delineative likeness, where is the numismatist, that would not, as evidence to accuracy, prefer the die-sinker's type to the lapidary's design?—See *Clipeus.*

Since the history of Antoninus supplies no information, it is left to be conjectured, that this type, from its connection with the word *ancilia*, was selected by the mint-masters, to gratify Aurelius Cæsar, his adopted son. On this point, Capitolinus says, "Hadrian caused him to be admitted of the Salian college in his eighth year. While enjoying this sacerdotal dignity, he was favoured with the omen of sovereignty. When the assembled people, as was customary, threw garlands upon the banquetting couches, some fell in one place, some in another; while, on the head of Aurelius, one was fixed as by the hand of Mars. In the Salian priesthood, he was president (præsul), seer (vates), and master (magister): he performed frequently the ceremony of inauguration into office, and also that of deprivation without a prompter, as he had himself learned by heart all the forms."

It was the duty of the Salii (as has already been stated), both to remove the *ancilia*, and to restore them to their place of safety. To account for this type, we may perhaps conclude, that some peculiar solemnity connected with the *ancilia*, was going forward about this time, the honour of which was directed to both the Antonines—to Marcus, as the President of the Order, and to Pius Augustus, as the Pontifex Maximus. Besides, another reason for placing, on the coin of Antoninus, the very name as well as the form of these sacred bucklers, is to be found in the well-known attachment and veneration of that emperor for the antiquities and traditions of the city.—See Eckhel, vii. p. 13.

ANIMA—the soul, or spirit.—On a large brass of Antoninus Pius, with reverse legend of CONSECRATIO. S. C., a cowering eagle is standing on a globe, emblematical of the *anima* of that prince soaring to take its seat in the celestial regions. Conformably to the professed belief, involved in the Roman ceremony of CONSECRATION, the spirit of Marcus Aurelius is typified on a coin (large brass) of that emperor, as carried on an eagle to its place amongst the stars.—An eagle is also seen on a consecration medal of the younger Faustina, conveying the soul of that empress to heaven.—"It was the custom of the Romans, says Spanheim (v. Cæsars de Julien, p. 17), to represent the emperors, and their wives, borne to the skies, on eagles, or on peacocks, or on the wings of Victory."

ANIMALS *figured on Military Ensigns.*—It was the practice of the Romans to distinguish the different Legions of their armies, not only by their number, but also by the representation of various animals, on their standards. Thus, on coins of Gallienus, besides the images of Neptune, Minerva, Mars, and other divinities, we see the figure of a *wild boar* appropriated to LEG. I. ITAL. VI. P. VI. F.—*The wolf and the two infants* to LEG. II.—*A crane* to LEG. III.—*A lion* to LEG. IIII.—*An eagle* to LEG. V. and VI.—*A bull or ox* to LEG. VII., VIII., and X.— Also, among other fabulous animals, *a Capricorn* (or sea goat) is the distinctive figure on the ensigns of the 1st, 14th, and 22nd Legions: *a Pegasus* and *a Centaur*, on those of the 2nd Legion, &c.—Rasche.

ANN. DCCCLXXIIII. NAT. VRB. P. CIR. CON.—This unique historical legend is found on the reverse of a gold coin, and also of a large brass, of Hadrian (the latter with S. C.) The type of both represents a female seated at the base of three obelisks, or *metæ*, (the gold coin exhibits only *one*) which she embraces with her left arm, whilst she holds a wheel resting on her right knee.—The legend of the obverse is IMP. CAES. HADRIANVS. AVG. COS. III.—The year 874 from the foundation of Rome agrees with the year 121 of the Christian æra.

Had it not been for the inconvenient practice, adopted by the Romans in the inscriptions of their marbles, as well as in the legends of their coins, of abbreviating a whole word into a single initial, there would be scarcely a pretence, and certainly no reasonable ground, for the conflicting interpretations so pertinaciously given to the legend, on this interesting coin, in consequence of the very opposite meanings attached, by different learned writers, to the letter P.—But on the contrary, what surrounds the device would have been as free from perplexity or doubt as is the device itself; which evidently serves to record a particular anniversary of Rome's foundation day, celebrated with more than usual splendour by the addition of circensian chariot-races.

Vaillant renders the P. by *populo;* and reads, *Anno* 874, *natali urbis Populo Circenses concessit.* That is to say, Hadrian had given *to the People* the spectacle of Games in the Circus at Rome, on the 874th anniversary of the City's foundation.—In this reading he is followed by Havercamp, who nevertheless, strange to say, has allowed Bartoli, in engraving from Queen Christina's specimen, to leave out the questionable letter, when copying the legend of the large brass.—*Plebei* is adopted by Hardouin. —Fogginus confidently suggests *Publici.*—On the other hand, rejecting these interpretations, Bimard de la Bastie, in his notes on Jobert, (vol. ii., p. 181), affirms the initial P. to stand for *Primum.* And, as usual with that truly judicious numismatist of the elder school, he supports his views on the point in dispute, with so much acuteness and force, that we are induced to subjoin the principal passage of his argument, clothed in an English dress :—

"To me it appears evident that by these medals of Hadrian, it was intended to preserve the remembrance of a new Institution formed during his reign, in honour of the *Birth* of the City of Rome, and to mark its precise epocha. Before this Emperor's time, the people had neglected to celebrate annually the foundation of Rome, with the solemnities which the day seemed to merit. It was honoured only as the festival of the Goddess *Pales*, and was known under no other name than *Parilia*, or *Palilia*.— Nothing distinguished it from the most common festivals. In an ancient calendar (published by Gruter, cxxxiii.) we read, on the 21st April, PAR. N.P. *Parilia Nefastus Primo;* that is to say, that it was only during the first part of the day, that the Tribunal of the Prætor was shut, and that he began again to administer justice in the afternoon. Ovid, in his *Fasti* (L. iv. v. 721 to 862), gives a long description of the sacrifices performed by the people in honour of *Pales*, on the day of her festival. He afterwards speaks of the anniversary of the foundation of Rome, which would occur on the same day; but he does not tell us that solemn sacrifices were made, and still less that public games were celebrated, on that occasion. In a word, up to the time of Hadrian, no monument, no author, is found to make mention of any games of the Circus, as celebrated to honour the anniversary of the foundation of Rome."—The Baron Bimard then undertakes to expose the false, and to shew the true, reading of a passage in Dion Cassius; and from the facts so corrected, combined with the negative evidence of Ovid, who wrote under Augustus, and of Gruter's calendar engraved in the time of Caligula and Claudius, he regards it as certain, that until the reign of Hadrian, the anniversary of Rome's foundation was marked, neither by a solemn festival, nor by public games. But this Prince, considering it to be a worthy and suitable act, to distinguish so remarkable a day, by public testimonies of veneration and rejoicing, caused a temple to be built in Rome itself, dedicated to the City of Rome, as had already been done in the provinces. He moreover changed the name of *Parilia*, which had been given to the foundation-day, to that of *Romana:* and ordered that, for the future, it should be accompanied by public feasts and entertainments [as one of the principal *Feriæ* or holidays of the Romans.] This fact, adds Bimard, we learn from Athenæus, who says, that on a subsequent celebration of this anniversary, whilst his Dipnosophists were at table, the whole city resounded on a sudden with the music of flutes and of cymbals, mingled with the voices of singers.

"It appears, therefore, that Hadrian created a new establishment for the better celebration of an event no less interesting than that of founding the capital of the world.—Buonarotti, whose notice the passage in Athenæus had not escaped, is of opinion, that the superb temple which the same emperor raised to the Genius of the City, and of which Spartianus makes mention, is represented on one of his medallions. (See *Osserv. Sopr. Medagl. Ant.* p. 17.)—Besides building this temple, Hadrian instituted public shews and banquets. Nor, as Juvenal concisely but expressly assures us, was there anything which the Roman people then more eagerly desired than (panem et circenses) the doles of bread and the courses of the circus. Hadrian took care to ordain that this spectacle should always make part of the festival annually celebrated in honour of the foundation of Rome. It has been shewn that there were no circensian games marked against the day of the city's foundation, in the Roman calendars anterior to the reign of Hadrian; but after him attention was paid to that point, and they are seen marked in that published by the Jesuit Fathers Petau and Bucher, under the designation of these abridged words N. VRB C. M. XXIIII. that is to say, *Natali urbis Circenses Missus*, 24. It is the epocha of the first institution of these annual games, or contests, the recollection of which the medals before us were designed to preserve." And for this reason (says Bimard, in conclusion), "I think that the legend ought to be read thus :—

ANN*o* DCCCLXXIIII NAT*ali* VRB*is. Primum.* CIR*censes.* CON*stituti. Senatus Consulto.* —[In the year eight hundred and seventy-four, the Games of the Circus were for the *first* time instituted (to be given or celebrated) on the anniversary day of the city's foundation—the day on which the festival of Parilia was held.]—The letter P. which I explain by *Primum,* can make no difficulty in this case; for the same letter is found standing by itself for *Prima,* on the [Latin] colonial medals of Cæsarea, in Palestine, struck under Hadrian, Marcus Aurelius, Diadumenianus, Elagabalus, Alex. Severus and Trajan Decius. (See Vaillant, *Colon.* i. and ii.)— And the sense in which this legend is to be taken, according to my explanation, seems to me sufficiently shewn, by every thing which I have adduced respecting the institution of the Games of the Circus by Hadrian."

Eckhel, in his commentary on this legend, observes, that Bimard's interpretation of it, if not clearly the correct one *(planè certa),* appears preferable to the others. But still, he observes, "the controversy cannot be pronounced as set at rest, until we shall become surer of the true signification of the letter P. which is susceptible of such various explanations."

Dr. Cardwell regards the interpretation of the word *Primum* as plausible; but adds, "to me it appears the best method to retain the word *Populo,* as suggested by Vaillant; a word which is constantly denoted on coins by the single letter P. and to make the inscription refer in the same restricted manner to the Circenses granted to the people, for the first time, on that occasion of holding the *Parilia.*" But the Learned Doctor's previously avowed impression seems to be the better founded of the two, viz., that in which he treats the conjecture of Vaillant *(populo circenses concessi)* as "opposed to the well-known fact, that the games of the circus had long been familiar to the Romans, and could not, without extreme absurdity, be said to have been established by Hadrian." Indeed, so frequent was the celebration of those games, that, as Bimard says, *on ne se persuadera pas aisément, que le souvenir d'un événement si ordinaire, ait mérité d'être conservé sur la Monnoye publique.*

These two coins *(Aur.* et *Æ.* I.) are, says Eckhel (vi. 511), the only ones on which is inscribed the epocha from the building of Rome, an epocha so sacred and so venerated throughout the empire, and which Latin writers frequently used in dating years. But neither, he adds, did it oftener appear on marbles. Only one is mentioned by Fabretti, viz, EXCESSIT. ANNO VRBIS. CONDITAE. DCCCXCVII.

ANN. P. M. TR. P. X. IMP. VII. COS. IIII. P. P.—A woman standing, with a little image in her right and a cornucopiæ in her left hand: at her feet on one side a *modius*, with corn ears, and on the other a ship, with two rowers. The ANN. in this legend is an abbreviation of *Annona*, the type personifying the Goddess, with her attributes of the galley and the corn measure. In giving this, as a silver coin of Commodus, Khell (p. 94) observes that, "though historians assign the great famine to the year of Rome 941 (A. D. 188), yet the ship represented on the present reverse, shews a similar calamity to have happened in 937 (184), that being a sign of *annonæ*, or importations of corn, from some quarter, for the relief of the population."— See below, *Annona*.

ANNI QUATUOR TEMPESTATES.—The four Seasons of the year.—See *Seasons*—also FELICIA TEMPORA.

ANNIA gens *plebeia*, known to be so from some of its members having held the tribuneship of the people. There are 28 varieties.— The silver rare. The brass coins of this family belong to the mint-masters of Augustus, and are common. The following is the rarest denarius :

Obv.—*Caius* ANNI*us*, *Titi Filius*, *Titi Nepos*, PRO. Con*Sule* EX *Senatus Consulto*.— Female head, with necklace, ear-rings, and head-dress, and accompanied sometimes with the balance.

Rev.—L. FABI. L. F. HISP. *Lucius* FA-BI*us Lucii Filius* HISP*ania*.—Victory in a quadriga, at speed, a long palm branch in her right hand.

On other reverses,—Q*uintus* TARQVIT*ius Publii Filius*. Victory, with palm, in a biga.— See *Tarquitia* gens.

Several numismatic antiquaries have expressed their opinion that the C. Annius named on this silver coin, was the same to whom Plutarch refers, as having been sent by Sulla into Spain against Sertorius ; and that L. Fabius and Q. Tarquitius, whose names appear on the reverses, were his quæstors. But Eckhel takes strong ground in regarding the above allegation as involved in much doubt. The female head, on the obverse, especially when designated by the balance, the same writer considers to be that of *Æquitas*, or of *Moneta*.—(v. 135.)

There is a colonial brass of Nero, struck at Corinth, which Morel classes with this family, and which exhibits on its reverse *Venus Marina*, in a car, drawn by a triton and a nereid.—It is noticed also by Vaillant.—See *Corinth*.

ANNIVERSARY—the 1000th of Rome.— See MILLIARIVM SAECVLVM.

ANNO I. II. &c.—It was under Justinus the First (A. D. 518), that the custom began of inscribing the years of an Emperor's reign on his brass coinage, especially those of the largest size. (See Eckhel's Treatise on Coins of the Lower Empire, vol. viii.)—On the reverse of a first brass of Justinus I. Emperor of the East, we read ANNO PRIMO, and in the midst of the field x. P.—(Banduri.)—On a brass medallion of Justinus II. (A. D. 565) the reverse presents—

A †
N X K
N
O M A
B.

On a second brass of the same Emperor we read—

A † V
N K
N
O S

On a second brass of Mauricius (declared Emperor A. D. 582), we read on the reverse ANNO *Quinto*. a large M in the middle, surmounted by a small cross, below the M is an E, and at the bottom RAVEN.

On the 1st and 2nd brass of Phocas (A. D. 602), the reverse bearing ANNO, with numbers added, mark the years of that usurping murderer's reign up to VIII. Heraclius I. and II. Constans II. Constantinus Pogonatus, and so downwards to Theophilus (A. D. 829), exhibit on their 1st and 2nd brass, as well as on their medallions of that metal, the same mode of noting that year of their respective reigns in which the coin was minted.

ANNO IIII.—A woman standing, holds ears of corn. In the field, A. In the exergue, a star between two palm branches.—Mionnet gives this from the Catalogue d'Ennery, as a silver quinarius of Honorius, and Mr. Akerman adopts it, with acknowledgment, into his Descriptive Catalogue (ii. 343). Eckhel does not notice the coin.

ANNONA, a provision of victuals for one year. This word particularly applies to corn. *Annona civilis*, the corn which was every year reserved, and put into magazines for the subsistence of the people. *Annona militaris*, the corn appropriated to the use of an army, during a campaign. This word also signifies the price which the Ediles put on marketable commodities ; for individuals, among the Romans, were not allowed to sell their merchandise, according to what each thought proper ; but the seller was obliged to abide by the value, which the magistrates assigned as the price of an article. *Annonam macelli*, says Tacitus, *Senatus arbitratu, quotannis temperari voluit*.—By the code *De Naviculariis*, the mariners appointed to carry corn from Egypt were capitally punished if they did not keep the proper course ; and if they did not sail in the proper season, the master of the vessel was banished.

"Annona was anciently worshipped as the goddess who prospered the year's increase. She was represented on an altar in the capitol, with the inscription "Annonæ Sanctæ Aelius Vitalio," &c. (Gruter, p. 8, n. 10), as a female, with the right arm and shoulder bare, and the rest of the body clothed, holding ears of corn in her right hand, and the cornucopiæ in her left."— *Dict. of Gr. and Rom. Antiquities*, p. 50.

The duty of the Ediles to secure for the people an abundance of provisions *(annonæ copiam)*, is plainly indicated on the coins of the Republic, in which the curule chair, ears of corn, and sometimes a cornucopiæ, are seen; as on denarii of the Flaminia, Lollia, Papiria, Quinctia, Rutilia, and Valeria families; some of which are inscribed with the abbreviated words AED. CVR. the mark of the Curule Ædileship: or with the *modius*, between two ears of corn, as on a denarius of the *Livineia* gens.—See *Ædilis*, p. 12 of this work.

Besides the Ediles, both curule and plebeian, there were sometimes *præfecti annonæ*, or extraordinary commissioners for affairs of provisions, appointed, who were furnished with the funds requisite to purchase and import wheat from those three principal granaries of Rome, the Sicilian, the Egyptian, and the African provinces, for the general consumption of the citizens. Memorials of this watchful care, taken by the Senate, to guard against, or at least to abate, the evils of scarcity, occur on denarii of the *Calpurnia* and *Servilia* families. The purchase and importation of provisions by the state, is also signified on certain consular coins. For example, we find in Morel, amongst the *incerta*, but supposed to be of the *Hostilia* family, a denarius, the obverse of which exhibits the head of Ceres, adorned with a crown of corn ears. On the reverse we read, C. MANCINus, *Auli Filius*— SEX*tus* ATIL*ius Marci Filius* SERRANVS.— The type figures two men seated, before the right hand of one of whom is a *modius*, filled with ears of wheat; and behind the other is an ear of corn.—It is clear, that this denarius was struck in honour of the Plebeian Ediles, Sextus Attilius Serranus, and C. Mancinus, through whose care and exertions a great plenty of corn and other provisions, at a cheap rate, were supplied to the inhabitants of Rome. Their edileship is referred to the year U. C. 609 (B. C. 145).—[See *Thesaurus Numi Consulares*, TAB. xviii. fig. 16.]

It is not, however, until we come to the imperial series, and then not before the 4th reign, that *Annona* appears on Roman coins personified as a divinity. Her traits, habiliments, and attributes are nearly the same as those of *Abundantia*, or to speak more in chronological order, *Abundantia* nearly resembles *Annona*. But there was this distinction between them, that the latter name was limited to express the supply for the current year, and like *Copia*, seems to have been applied to provisions, whereas *Abundantia* was a prodigal distributor of all kinds of things. Clothed in a long robe, and wear-

ing a veil, which she partly turns over her left arm, sometimes seated, sometimes standing, the goddess is seen holding ears of corn before a measure with the right hand, and a cornucopiæ in the left. The first emperor by whose mint *Annona* is represented under the appearance of a woman, is Nero. Previously, six corn ears tied together, served to symbolize, what Mangeart calls, " this deity of provisions for the mouth," and to indicate a supply of corn abundantly procured for the people, as on a coin of Augustus.— After Nero, she appears on reverses of Titus, Nerva, Ælius Cæsar, Commodus (see ANN. P. M. &c. p. 48), Sept. Severus, Caracalla, Macrinus, Alexander Severus, Mamæa, Gordianus Pius, Philip senior, Trebonianus Gallus, Gallienus, Salonina, Tacitus, down to Constantine. With one exception (viz. that of ANNONA AUGUSTA, coupled with CERES, and in that case, if genuine, referring to the two goddesses themselves), the legends are ANNONA AUG. or AUGUSTI, or AUGG. " to shew (says Mangeart), that it was through the care, and by the generosity of the Emperors, that this deity had become propitious; that she had spread her gifts, and shed her blessings on the subjects of those princes, and was therefore a fit object of adoration."

ANNONA AVGVSTI CERES. S. C.— Ceres veiled, sitting with corn ears in her right hand, and a torch in her left. Opposite to her stands the Goddess of Plenty, or *Annona*, holding a cornucopiæ in her left hand. Between the two figures is an altar or cippus, on which stands the *modius*. In the back ground is a ship's prow.—This legend and type appear on first and second brass of Nero; also on a brass medallion of the same emperor, in the imperial cabinet at Vienna.

Nero often ingratiated himself with the common people, by the profuse liberality of his largesses to them—a fact proved by the coins struck under that prince, bearing the legend CONGIAR. or CONGIARIVM. This trait of conduct looks fair enough; but the one recorded by Suetonius is most disgraceful, viz., that during a general scarcity at Rome, an Alexandrine ship brought a freight, *not* of wheat for the suffering inhabitants, but of *dust* for the Court wrestlers. It was at the critical time, when the revolt of Vindex in Gaul, had become openly known; and Nero was loaded with the most insulting reproaches from the populace (Eck. vi. 268.)— There is a second brass of S. Severus, and a contorniate medal of Constantine, with the same legend and a similar type.

ANNONA AVGVSTA CERES.—This legend, with a type similar to the above, is given, as from a brass medallion of Nero *(incuse)*, in *Thesaur. Morell. Impp.* TAB. vi. fig. 8, and as a contorniate, in the same work, TAB. vii. fig. 19. In the latter, an ear of corn is placed in the left hand of Ceres instead of the torch.

ANNONA AVG.—In Morel's *Thesaurus* (T. ii. TAB. v. figure 32), there is a gold, and in Mediobarbus a silver coin, given as struck under Vespasian, with this legend, and the type of a sedent female.—In the *Numism.'Musei Theupoli*, a silver coin of the same prince is described ANNONA AVG. Female figure seated, with corn ears in right hand and laurel branch in left.

It might indeed have been expected that the name and attributes of the goddess would appear on some generally recognized medal of that renowned emperor, were it only in grateful reference to the prompt and liberal supply of corn which by his provident care (as mentioned by Tacitus) was sent in ships to the port of Rome, during a period of great scarcity. But to judge from the silence of Eckhel, Mionnet, and Aker·man on this point, there is no ANNONA on any of the three metals, in the coinage of Vespasian.

ANNONA AUGUST*i.* S. C.—A similar type to that of Nero's coin.

This reference to the discharge of a most important duty in a Roman Emperor appears appropriately on a first brass of Nerva. That good prince, among other acts of provident attention to the welfare of his subjects, took care to furnish the city of Rome, and the whole of Italy, with victuals necessary for the subsistence of the people.

ANNONA AVG.—A modius, out* of which spring four ears of corn, on a denarius of Ælius Cæsar.

It seems strange and unaccountable, that whilst a coin with the above reverse should have been minted at Rome in honour of this indolent prince, who did not live long enough to become emperor, there appears to have been no similar legend struck on coins of such men as Antoninus Pius and M. Aurelius, of whom history attests their vigilant care for the public sustenance.

ANNONA AVG.—A robed female standing, holding a cornucopiæ; at her feet the modius; in her right hand a small figure; behind is the prow of a galley. On a first brass of Titus, in Capt. Smyth's cabinet.

Neither in Eckhel nor Mionnet, nor in the later work of Akerman, is any coin of the above-named emperor to be found with the legend of *Annona.* In the possession, and with the authority for its genuineness, of so intelligent a writer and so practised a numismatist, this acquisition therefore becomes doubly valuable: not only as an interesting specimen of the mint to which it belongs, but also as serving to supply a reverse, which it was natural to look for amongst the medals of a prince, who was distinguished beyond any of his predecessors for liberality, hu-

manity, and beneficence towards all classes of his subjects.

This first brass bears no mark of senatorial authority; but the same omission is to be noticed on the well-authenticated coin, which bears the type of the amphitheatre, struck under the same emperor.—See p. 42.

ANNONA AVG.—A female seated, holding ears of corn and a cornucopiæ, a modius at her feet. On silver of Macrinus.—There are also first and second brass of this brief reign, with the same legend and type.

It seems that Macrinus was sufficiently liberal; and although congiaria were not usually given unless the donor was in the city, we have medallic proof that this restriction was waived, that he might ingratiate himself with the people. But the indulgence of Severus, and the prodigality of Caracalla, to the army, shackled the means of their successors, and indeed debilitated the whole empire till the days of Diocletian. With a treasury at low water, and guards at least quadrupled since Cæsar's time, Macrinus was obliged, on proclaiming his son (Diadumenianus) Augustus, to promise the old donative of 5000 denarii per man, of which he gave them each 1000 in hand. While the soldiers—who had already pocketed the Emperor's first gift of 750 denarii—enjoyed these substantial pickings, the people of Rome were promised a congiary of 150 denarii each. Such was the state of the empire, A. D. 218.—Smyth.

ANNONA AVG.—A woman standing before a modius, with corn ears in her right hand and cornucopiæ in her left. On an elegant quinarius of Alexander Severus.—Other quinarii of the same reign give to *Annona* the appropriate attributes of the anchor, the rudder, and the prow.

These reverses are commemorative of the careful and vigorous attention, which characterised the proceedings of that excellent emperor, with respect to the purveyorship of wheat to the people, brought to Rome, at his own expense, from abroad; the frumentarian funds having been left exhausted by his infamous predecessor.—Vaillant, *Præst, Num. Impp. Rom.* p. 280.

ANNONA AUGG. (Augustorum).——With the usual type. On gold of Philip senior.

Roman emperors, *sub auspicia imperii,* were accustomed to seek popularity, by providing *annona.* To this Philip, as a matter of peculiarly urgent policy with him, was, it appears, promptly and abundantly attentive.

ANNONA AVG.—A woman with corn ears and cornucopiæ (on other coins an anchor), and a modius at her feet. On silver and third brass of Salonina, wife of Gallienus.

Banduri, who gives the above, remarks that it bears a reverse, which does not occur on the mintage of any other empress. But Khell, who published his Supplement to Vaillant nearly 50 years afterwards, has cited a silver coin of Julia Mamæa, from the Cabinet d'Ariosti, with the same legend and type. But perhaps it may be retorted that Mamæa was *not* an empress: she was, however, the mother of an emperor, and bore the title of *Augusta*, under which, on some of her numerous coins, she exhibits her portrait face to face with that of her son Alexander.— With respect to the Annona Aug. of Salonina, it is admitted that it may rightfully belong to this beneficent princess, since there are medals of her's dedicated to *Abundantia* and to *Dea Segetia*, a deity associated with *Annona*.—See *Abundantia Temporum*, p. 2 of this work.

ANNONA.—Besides this word, the meaning of which has already been explained, there are other legends of imperial coins, which refer nearly to the same thing—such as the *Providentia Aug.*, with galley and sail spread, of Commodus; the *Sæculo Frugifero* of Albinus, and *Opi Divin.* of Pertinax, with figures holding ears of corn; also the *Felicitas Temporum* of S. Severus, with cornucopiæ and *spicæ*. The legend ANNONA AETERNA, ascribed by Mediobarbue (p. 268) to the silver mint of S. Severus, is not noticed by Eckhel, nor is it to be found in either Mionnet or Akerman.

ANT. P. *Antiochiæ Percussa*, money struck at Antioch.

ANT. H. *Antiochiæ octava officina*—Money struck at Antioch, in the eighth office, or mint.

[Some of the principal cities of the empire, had the privilege of a Roman coinage. Antioch was one of these, and had in it several mint offices.]—See Rasche.

ANT. S. *Antiochiæ Signata.*—Coined at Antioch.

ANTÆUS, a famous, or rather infamous, giant of Lybia, son of Neptune and Terra, and king of Irasa. He murdered all strangers that came to his court. Hercules fought this giant, and "floored" him three times, but in vain; for *Mother Earth* restored to her child new strength whenever he touched her. Hercules therefore lifted him off the ground, and thus succeeded in squeezing to death this "prince of cut-throats." Many ancient monuments represent this combat; among others a gold coin of Postumus, with the type of a man holding up another in his arms, and rigidly compressing him. A *Latin* colonial of Antioch in Pisidia, struck under Caracalla, and a brass medal, with *Greek* inscription of Antoninus Pius, both exhibit in like manner the great Alcides in the act of hoisting up and stifling the African tyrant.— See Caylus, *Aurea Numismata*, fig 950—See also HERCVLI LYBICO.

ANTEON, son of Hercules.—There is a very rare gold coin of M. Antony, having on its reverse the name of one of his moneyers L. REGVLVS IIIIVIR. A. P. F. the type of which is supposed to represent this fabulous personage. The figure is sitting, his head covered with a lion's skin; a spear in his right hand, his left elbow resting on a shield, on which is a human countenance, conjectured to be that of Hercules. The flatterers of Antony and his own vanity encouraged him to claim descent from the demi-god. —See Morell. *Thesaur. Livineia* gens, TAB. ii. fig. 5.

ANTESTIA—-ANTISTIA.—Some writers consider these names to belong to two different families. But Eckhel unites them, as belonging to one and the same *gens*, which was of the plebeian order. The above named writer observes, however, that the name of *Antestia* is certainly older than that of *Antistia*, since the coins bearing the latter name were struck under Augustus: whereas the denarii, as well as the brass coins, bearing the word Antestia, argue from their type and their fabric, the mintage of a more remote age. The surnames of this gens are—*Reginus* and *Vetus*. There are twelve varieties in the types.—Gold, very rare—Silver, common. The brass coins of this family are the *As*, or some of its parts.

The subjoined is a rare denarius struck by *Reginus* Antistius, in his capacity of monetal triumvir, under Augustus. This Reginus had been one of Julius Cæsar's legates in Gaul: and appears, about 49 years B. C., to have had the command of the coast of the lower sea. (See Dr. Smith, *Dict. Rom. Biog.* iii. p. 642.)

Obv.—CAESAR AVGVSTVS. Bare head of Augustus.

Rev.—C. ANTISTIVS. REGINVS. III. VIR. Pontifical instruments.

This is one of those coins of the Antistia gens, which have given rise to much learned disputation, as to the date when they were minted; but from the reverse legends of two coins struck by Vetus Antistius, III. VIR., it may undoubtedly be inferred that this, as well as the two others, was placed under the hammer of the mint, during the viiith Tribunate and the xith Consulate of Augustus. (Eckhel, v. p. 137.)—The *instrumenta pontificalia*, which form, in this example, the type of the reverse, consist of the simpulum, lituus, tripod, and patera, an explanation of which words will be found in their respective places.—See Morell. *Antistia*, fig. 3 and fig. 4.

But among the types, with which the surnames of this family connect themselves on coins, there is one peculiarly deserving of attention, on account of its assisting graphically to illustrate certain ancient ceremonies performed at the ratification of international treaties. The denarius described as follows, was struck by *Vetus* Antistius, one of the moneyers of Augustus:—

Obv.—Head of Augustus.

Rev.—C. ANTISTIVS VETVS FOED. (or FOEDVS)
P. R. CVM GABINIS.—Two men standing, clothed
in the toga, and with heads veiled, hold, for
sacrifice, a pig over a lighted altar.

For an engraving and explanatory notice of
this denarius, see FOEDVS, &c.

ANTIA, gens plebeia. Its cognomen on
coins is *Restio.*—This family came from Antium.
It furnished, amongst others, C. Antius Restio,
who, in the time of Cicero, was a tribune of the
people, and the author of a sumptuary law.—
The coins of this *gens* appear only in silver:
they have three varieties, and are rare. For an
engraving of one of these, which though not the
rarest is, from its legend and type, the most interesting, see DEI PENATES. Also, see RESTIO.

ANTIGONUS, King of Judæa, beheaded by
order of Mark Antony.—See *Sosia* gens.

ANTIUM, a city of the Volscians, so called
from Anton or Anteon, son of Hercules.—
Ascanius, son of Æneas, is said to have founded
it. Its remains are still visible, situated on a
promontory bordering on the sea, in the *Campagna di Roma*, under the modern name of
Antio rovinato. Nero caused a fine port to be
built there, after having, according to Suetonius,
sent thither a colony of old Prætorians.—Antium
was celebrated for its temple of Fortune.—See
Anteon, p. 51.

ANTIAT.—*Antiatina*—See *Fortunæ Antiat.*
See also *Rustia.*

ANTICA, or *pars adversa.* That side of a
coin, which contains the portrait, or other principal figure. See *Obverse.*

ANTINOUS.—*Hadriani catamitus:* a young
Bithynian, who died about the 130th year of
our æra, having been drowned in the Nile.—
Hadrian, so wise and meritorious in his general public conduct, but in this wretched instance of personal criminality, one of the most
infatuated, as well as most depraved, of human
beings—had scarcely by this accident lost his
unhappy favourite, than he caused the most extravagant distinctions to be rendered to his memory. A temple and even a city were dedicated
to his name and *worship!* Nor were the Greeks,
always ready to flatter the most disgraceful
propensities of their imperial masters, ashamed
to stamp his image on their coins. To the
credit of, and in justice to, the *Roman* mint, be
it added, there exist no medals of Antinous
with *Latin* legends, nor any whatever with the
mark of Senatorial authority.

ANTIOCHIA.—Under this name, ancient
writers commemorate the existence, in their
times, of a great many cities in Asia. The following are the two most remarkable: viz.,
Antioch in Pisidia, and Antioch in Syria—both
being Roman colonies.

ANTIOCHIA *(Pisidiæ Colonia)*——situate
on the borders of Phrygia, not far from the
river Meander (and now called *Ak-Schehere*, in
Karaman, Asiatic Turkey.)—It was, for at least
270 years, the seat of a Roman *colony*, founded by
Augustus, and invested with the *jus Italicus*, under
the name of COLONIA ANTIOCHENSIS, or
COL. CAES*aria* ANTIOCHIA. The coins

of this city consist of
Latin autonomes (small
size), and of *Latin* im-
perial, both in brass.
The former have on their
obverse side, for legend,
ANT. and ANTIOCH, and
for type the head of the
God *Lunus*, with Phry-
gian cap, on a crescent.
—Their reverses are inscribed COLON. or COL.
ANT. ANTIO. or ANTIOCH, and the accompanying
types are a cock, and a buffalo, or wild ox.—
The *imperial* coins of this colony begin under
Tiberius, after whose reign a cessation of coinage
seems to have taken place, and continued until
Titus came to the throne; to whom, however,
the colonists appear to have dedicated only two
coins. Another gap then occurs in the series,
extending to the reigns of Antoninus Pius and
Marcus Aurelius. They thence, according to the
descriptive lists of Mionnet, proceed in more
regular succession, but still with occasional
omissions, as far as Gallienus and Valerianus
junior; the last recorded dedication of the
Antiochian mint of Pisidia being to Claudius
Gothicus. By far the more numerous portion was
struck under Caracalla and Gordianus III.—The
following are the various legends to be found on
reverses of the imperial colonial, viz. :

COL. ANT.—COLON. ANTIOCH.—COL. CAES.
ANTI. or ANTIOCH.—CO. ANTIOCHE, or ANTI-
ÓCHEN.——ANTIOCHENI COL.——ANTIOCHAEAE
COLONIAE.—GEN. or GENIVS COL. or COLONIAE
ANTIOCH.—COL. ANTIOCH MENSIS.—FORTVNA
COL. ANTIOCH.—ANTIOCHI.—ANTIOCHIA. S. R.
(Senatus Romanus).——ANTIO. CA. CL.—CAES.
ANTIOCH. COL.—ANTIOCHIA COLONIA. CAESARIA.
or CAESARI.—COL. ANTIOCHI.—AN. COLONI.

The types are as follows :—A *colonist*, or a
priest, at plough with two oxen, and with one
or two military ensigns behind them; also a
high priest, carrying a *vexillum*, tracing the
limits of the settlement with a plough and
two oxen—as in Tiberius, Titus, S. Severus,
Caracalla, Alex. Severus, Gordianus Pius, and
Gallienus. [These types are symbols of a colony
established.]

Cybele or *Rhea* seated between two lions; as
in M. Aurelius, Alex. Severus, and Gordianus III.

Diana, the huntress, taking with her right
hand an arrow from her quiver, and holding the
bow in her left; as in Caracalla.

Emperor standing veiled, sacrificing at a
lighted altar before three miltary ensigns—also
on horseback, with right hand elevated; and in a
triumphal quadriga; as in Gordianus III. and in
Philip sen.

Fortune of the colony, personified by the usual
type; as in M. Aurelius, and S. Severus.

Genius of Antioch, personified by a female
figure in the stola, standing with branch and
cornucopiæ. The colony is also represented by
a turreted woman, holding a caduceus; also by a
female figure standing near an altar, holding a
patera and horn of plenty—likewise by the type
of Fortune seated, holding a rudder and cornu-

copiæ, a wheel being under her chair. The legend to all these types is COLONIA CAESARIA.; as in Gordianus and in Julia Domna.

Hope walking; as in Saloninus. And *Hygeia*, standing, clothed in the stola, holding a serpent over a lighted altar, with the hasta pura in her left hand, as in Antoninus Pius.

Jupiter standing with an eagle in his right hand, and the hasta in his left, as in Caracalla.

Lunus (or *Mensis*) wearing the Phrygian cap, and with a crescent behind the back, holds the *hasta* and a small figure of Victory: a cock is at his feet; as in Antoninus Pius, S. Severus, Caracalla, Domna, and Philip senior. [See the word *Lunus* (in its place) for a further notice of this deity, who was worshipped with great veneration at *Antiochia Pisidiæ*.]

Mars walking; as in Gordianus III. *Military* ensigns, three together; as in Elagabalus.

Pallas, holding a small figure, and the hasta; a trophy and an altar, in the field, as in Volusianus.

River God. Pellerin gives the engraving of a second brass of Volusianus struck in this colony, on the reverse of which, with the legend ANTIOCH COL. is the figure of a man seated, symbolising a river (probably the Meander), who holds a reed in his right hand, and in his left a horn of plenty, resting his left arm on an urn whence water flows. In the exergue S. R.—[Melange, i. plate xxii. No. 1, from which the above cut is copied.]—Another river deity, with female countenance and dress, seated on the ground with a reed and cornucopiæ, appears on a coin of this colony, dedicated to Alexander Severus.

Victory. Two Victories holding a buckler attached to a palm tree, at the foot of which sit two captives; as in Gordianus Pius.

Vexillum between two military ensigns; as in Claudius Gothicus.

Wolf suckling the twins, under a tree; as in M. Aurelius, repeated in Caracalla, Alexander Severus, Gordian III., Philip senior, Gallienus. —[The Antiochians of Pisidia, says Vaillant, placed this type on their coins as Roman colonists, whose usual symbol it was to shew their national origin from Romulus and Remus.]

Faun, or *Satyr*, standing with a wine-skin on his shoulder; as in M. Aurelius.

Eagle with expanded wings, and legend of COLONIAE ANTIOCHIAE; as in M. Aurelius.

Eagle standing on a thunderbolt—*Two Eagles* —and Eagle with crown in its beak.

Legionary Eagle, on a banner between two ensigns, a crown above; with COLONIAE ANTIOCHIAE; as on coins struck under M. Aurelius, L. Verus, Gordian III., Philip jun., Volusianus, Valerianus, and Claudius Gothicus.—[The eagle with expanded wings was the indication of power. The legionary eagle above the vexillum, between two military standards, refers to the transmission of Roman veterans into Pisidia by Augustus.—(Vaillant, *in Col.* vol. i.)

The two following coins, struck at this Antioch, have, besides their rarity, an historical interest, as referring to the victories of Severus and his sons in *Britain*, viz.:

1. *Obv.* IMP. CAES. P. SEPT. GETA. AVG.— Laurelled head of Geta.

Rev. VIRT. AVG. COL. ANTIOCH. S. R.——A horseman riding at full speed, thrusts his lance at a prostrate enemy.

The Antiochians (says Vaillant), devoted to the family of Severus, dedicated this medal to Geta, (about A. D. 209), when, by his father's will, it was arranged for him to preside over the civil administration in that part of Britain subject to the Romans, whilst Caracalla was to accompany the old emperor in his expedition against the Caledonians. But Severus dying at York, the two brothers, in their joint imperial capacity, concluded a peace with those northern inhabitants of the island. Hence the name of *Britannicus* was conferred by the Roman Senate on both Caracalla and Geta; and the legend VIRTVS AVG*ustorum* (the valour of the Emperors) was placed on the coins minted to their honour, in this eastern colony.—(i. 53.)

2. *Obv.* Same legend and type as on preceding coin.

Rev. VICT. DD. NN. COL. ANTIOCH. S. R.— *Victoriæ Dominorum Nostrorum, Colonia Antiochensis (Senatus Romanus).*—Victory walking, carrying a trophy in both hands before her.

This (says Vaillant, i. p. 53), is a *Victoria Britannica*, recorded in honour of Caracalla and Geta, as joint *Augusti*, by the colonists of Antioch, after their father's death.

[The appellation of *Dominus*, employed in the present instance by the mint of this colony, instead of the usual word *Imperator*, is worthy of notice. The title of *Dominus*, first used by Caligula, who (as Spanheim says), endeavoured to make the people of Rome call him so, was revived by Domitian, although *he* never succeeded in obtaining that designation on the public money. It was at length fully recognised at Rome, under Aurelian, about A. D. 270.]

As the large brass coins of *Antioch in Pisidia* are esteemed rare, Pellerin has described no less than eight of that size, from his own collection, struck under Gordianus Pius, and which differ, for the most part, from the five which Vaillant published, as having been dedicated by the colony in question to that young prince. Five of these are engraved, in *Melange*, i. and to judge from their appearance on the plates, they present remarkably fine specimens of colonial mintage.—See pl. xx. Nos. 4, 5, 6, 7, and 8.

The following type on the reverse of a Gordian

III. struck by the colony of Pisidian Antioch, is unlike any other on the various coins of that city. It exhibits, as Mionnet describes it, *Un Guerrier assis sur un monçeau d'armes, soutenant de la main droite sa téte qui est penchée; devant lui, une trophée militaire: dans le champ* S. R.

ANTIOCHIA, *Syriæ*, or *ad Orontem ;* a celebrated town on the banks of that river, at the foot of Mount Silpius, and at one period ranking third in the world. It is recognised at the present day, only by the ruins of its walls, and by some inscriptions. Situate about 15 leagues from the Mediterranean, between Aleppo and Tarsus, it is now called by the Turks, *Antak,* or *Antakié.* This Antioch on the Orontes is said to have been built by Seleucus Nicator, founder of the empire of Syria, and was called after the name of his father Antiochus—a name which it preserves to this day. Under its kings it flourished for a long time as a capital: but after their expulsion by Pompeius Magnus, and the occupation of Syria as a Roman province (about 64 B. C.), it became *autonomos* (*i. e.* governed by laws of its own), and obtained from him the right of coining money. —Julius Cæsar and Augustus both bestowed benefits upon the city. And, under succeeding emperors, it arrived at the distinction of being acknowledged as *Metropolis totius Orientis,* still, however, subject to Roman domination; and was the seat and residence of the governor of Syria. It was here that the disciples of Our Lord were first called Christians.— After the death of Pertinax (A. D. 192), Syrian Antioch declared in favour of Pescennius Niger against Septimius Severus, who in the fury of his displeasure, stripped the city of all its privileges, and transferred them to Laodicea. At the intervention however of Caracalla, who made it a *Roman colony,* it was restored to its former rights and municipal consequence, in every respect but that of exemption from tribute, payment of which continued to be exacted from its inhabitants.

The coins of this city are very numerous, in brass, silver, and potin. The autonomes embrace not only the earlier æra of the Seleucidæ, and of Alex. Bala, king of Syria, but also the Actiac epocha (or of Augustus and Tiberius), and the immediately subsequent period, comprising Claudius, Nero, and Galba. But both Imperial, and Colonial Imperial, from Galba down to Volusianus and Valerianus senior, exhibit, with few exceptions, *only Greek* legends and inscriptions. —[See a full classification of them in Mionnet, vol. v. p. 148, et seq. and *Supplmt.* vol. vii. p. 139.]

The following brass colonial imperial, bearing *solely Latin* inscriptions, are selected as examples from among the only extant coins of this Antioch, that come within the plan of the present work to notice, viz. :—

Augustus—
AVGVST. TR. POT.—Laur. head of Augustus.
Rev. S. C. in crown of laurel.
IMP. AVGVST. TR. POT. Laureated.

Rev. S. C. and same type.—See Mionnet.
Vespasian—
IMP. CAESAR VESPASIAN AVG.

Head of the Emperor, laureated.—*Rev.* ANTIOCHIA, female head turreted. (Vaillant, *Col.* p. 131).—Similar reverses appear on coins of Titus and Domitian. The Antiocheans of Syria were the first to adhere to the cause of Vespasian, and were zealously attached to the Flavian family.

Caracalla—
M. AVR. ANTONINVS.—Head of Emperor.
Rev.—COL. MET. ANT. ANTINONIAN. (*Colonia Metropolis Antiochia Antoniniana*). A female head, turreted and veiled, before which is a cornucopiæ.

[Mionnet includes all the coins of *Antiochia ad Orontem,* dedicated to Caracalla, amongst those with *Greek* legends.—The above *Latin,* however, are published in the colonial series of the *Museum Theupoli.*—Eckhel also gives a third brass of Hadrian, of Roman mintage, on the reverse of which is the legend COS. III. S. C. and the figure of a woman, with turreted head, sitting on a rock, holding corn ears in her right hand; a river god is emerging at her feet. This he considers to be a type of Antioch on the Orontes.]

ANTIQVAE.—This appellation of a legion is found on a denarius of M. Antony.—LEG. XII. ANTIQVAE.

ANTONIA *gens.*—This family, says Vaillant, ranks amongst the noblest of those, who derive their origin from the first senators of the ancient stock, under the kings of Rome. According to Plutarch, it pretended to a descent from Anton, or Anteon (see the word, page 51) the son, or companion of Hercules. Such was the vanity of the Romans, that they ascribed the origin of their great men to their deities, or to the sons of their deities. The most celebrated personage of the Antonia family was Marcus Antonius, the Triumvir. Its surnames are *Balbus* and *Naso.* The minting of the subjoined denarius is referred by Vaillant and Havercamp, with whom Pigghius concurs, to Q. Antonius Balbus, who was Prætor in Sardinia, afterwards ejected thence by Sulla, and slain in the year of Rome, 672 (B. C. 82). But Eckhel, pointing to the circumstance that the medal is serrated, shews it to be likely to have been coined by a more ancient Q. Balbus, when he was Urban Prætor, although his name does not appear in the Roman annals.

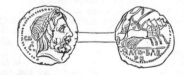

Obv. Head of Jupiter laureated, behind is S. C.
Rev. Q. A(N)TO. BA(L)B. PR*ætor.*—Victory

in a quadriga, at full speed, holds up the laurel in her right hand; and a long palm branch together with the reins in her left.

Morel gives a hundred and thirty-eight varieties in the coins of the Antonia family. This extraordinary number arises from the medals of M. Antonius, without his portrait, being classed under that head.—See AUGUR and LEGIO *(suis locis).*—The gold coins are rare in the highest degree. The silver are from common to the lowest degree of rarity.

ANTONIA *Augusta*, daughter of Marcus Antonius and of Octavia, married to Drusus senior, was the mother of Germanicus, Livilla, and (the afterwards emperor) Claudius. She was born in the year of Rome, 715 or 716 (B. C. 39 or 38), and died 791 (A. D. 38), being the second year of her grandson Caligula's reign, who according to Suetonius, was suspected to have caused her to be poisoned. She is spoken of, by historians, as a sensible, amiable woman; of a handsome countenance and of graceful manners; a noble exemplar of conjugal fidelity, and of honourable widowhood; a character which remains unsullied by the vague allegations of those who malevolently imputed a want of proper feeling to one, whose tenderness as a wife had proved itself too sincere to be associated, in the same breast, with maternal insensibility.

Her coins, in gold and silver, are very rare.—The subjoined cut is engraved from one of her denarii:—

Obv. ANTONIA AVGVSTA.   Laurelled head of Antonia.

Rev. CONSTANTIAE AVGVSTI.   (To the constancy of the emperor—meaning Claudius.)—See *Constantia.*

The second brass of Antonia are scarce. One of these presents on one side the head of Antonia, "with her hair twisted to the back of the neck, and a countenance expressive of sense and mildness," and with the legend ANTONIA AVGVSTA. The legend of the reverse is TI. CLAVDIVS AVG. P. M. TR. P. IMP. and the type a figure clothed in a long robe, and veiled, standing with a simpulum in the right hand.

Antonia was invested with the title of *Augusta* by her grandson (Caius) Caligula, who also caused the dignity of a Vestal to be granted to her. (See SACERDOS DIVI. AVGVSTI). But his filial attachment having been turned to hatred, no brass coins with her name and portraiture were struck during her life-time, though the coin above described, and another, were afterwards dedicated to her memory by her son Claudius.—Antonia was called *minor*, to distinguish her from her eldest sister, whose name was likewise Antonia, and who was married to

L. Domitius Ahenobarbus, the grandfather of Nero.

ANTONINUS PIUS *(Titus Aurelius Fulvius Bojonius Arrius)* whose paternal race came originally from Nismes, was born at Lanuvium (a city of Latium) in the year of Rome 839 (A. D. 86.) He was the son of Aurelius Fulvius—a man of consular rank—and of Arria Fadilla. Having passed through the offices of Quæstor and Prætor, with approved liberality, he served his first Consulship in the year U. C. 873, (A. D. 120) being then 33 years of age, in a magnificent style. The emperor Hadrian afterwards appointed him one of the four *ex-consuls*, to whom the administration of affairs in Italy, was committed. Sent next as Pro-consul to Asia, he governed that extensive and most important province, with great wisdom and integrity; insomuch as to have exceeded in repute all his predecessors. On his return, a seat was assigned to him in Hadrian's council of state; and, after the death of Aelius his brother-in-law, he was invested with the title of Cæsar, and with the Tribunitian Power, in 891, (A. D. 138.) Hadrian at the same time adopted him, on the condition, that he should himself adopt M. Aurelius, the son of his wife's (Faustina's) brother, and L. Verus, the son of Aelius Cæsar. It was then that he took the names of T. Aelius *Hadrianus Antoninus.* The same year, Hadrian dying, Antoninus received from the Senate the title of Augustus, and the surname of *Pius.* In the year U. C. 892 (A. D. 139) he accepted the title of *Pater Patriæ.* In 894 (A. D. 41) the third year of his reign, his wife Annia Galeria Faustina died. In A. D. 145, he served his 14th consulship, with Marcus Aurelius Cæsar for his colleague. Antoninus gave the *toga virilis* to L. Verus; dedicated a temple to his father by adoption, Hadrianus; and bestowed a *congiarium* on the people. A. U. C. 899 (A. D. 146) he celebrated with secular games, the 900th year of the city; and in 901 (A. D. 148) paid the vows due *(solvit vota)* for the first ten years of his reign *(Primi Decennales.)* From this period to the year of Rome 913 (A. D. 160,) ancient annals are either silent, or afford only vague and uncertain information, on the subject of events connected with the imperial government of Antoninus; although during that interval of 14 years, a great variety of coins, bearing reverses of geographical, historical, and mythologically religious interest, are extant; shewing, by their legends and types, that this emperor had restored several public edifices, and erected others, besides having concluded many important transactions, and given many public spectacles and largesses to the people. After a reign of 23 years, which the gratitude of his contemporaries has handed down to the veneration of mankind, he died in his palace at Lorium in Etruria, universally regretted, on the 7th of March, A. U. C. 914 (A. D. 161) in the 75th year of his age.

Antoninus richly merited the titles and distinctions conferred upon him, as well before as after his accession to the throne; not only by his many and rare virtues as an individual, but also because the welfare and happiness of his people were the constant objects of his care and occupation. Sagacious, learned, eloquent, benign, compassionate, and affable, he was peculiarly endowed with calmness and equanimity, well sustained, however, on all political occasions, by the requisite display of energy and firmness. Kindly disposed towards everybody, and free from vindictiveness, he anticipated, by acts of liberality and beneficence, the utmost wishes of his subjects. Distinguished for probity of character and for dignity of conduct, he delighted in rural retirement and innocent recreation. Well formed in person, mildly expressive in physiognomy, active in disposition, exhibiting an air which commanded respect, and a deportment which conciliated the most favourable opinion; he was plain in his dress, simple in his establishments, frugal at his table. Living within the limits of his patrimonial revenues, of which a portion was always spared for the relief and solace of the wretched; he treated his friends as if he had been their host or their guest rather than their sovereign master. His private habits were decorous and regular, though he was not altogether proof against the allurements of women. As a prince and a ruler, his maxim was to administer strict justice equally to rich and poor, to high and low, to the weak and humble, as well as to the proud and powerful. In attention to the sacred ceremonies and religious institutions of his country, his inclinations seem to have assimilated with the policy of Numa, whom he was said to resemble. He caused his adopted son, Marcus Aurelius, to serve all the state offices, and instructed him in the science of government, with a view to qualify him for the succession. Circumspect in his choice of ministers; vigilant, wise, and fortunate, in the management of public affairs, his sole aim was to rule the empire well, and to leave it in prosperity and peace to his successor. Chosen as an arbitrator by kings and peoples, at the most remote distances from Rome, he made a moral conquest of the world by his well-earned influence and pre-eminent reputation. Among other nations, the Hyrcanians, and the Bactrians, sent embassies of submission to him. Sovereign princes from Mesopotamia and from the further East, personally paid the homage of their admiration to the emperor at his own capital. Through his lieutenants and deputies, he subdued and kept in awe the Britons, the Mauretanians, the Dacians, and the different Germanic tribes; he also suppressed a revolt of the Jews, and put down rebellions in the provinces of Achaia and Egypt. Under this signally mild and tolerant prince, the Christians enjoyed comparative freedom from persecution, until about the 12th year of his reign (A. D. 151.) And even then he issued no edicts against them. But in consequence of his having been induced, rashly and unadvisedly, to withdraw his protection, many virtuous followers of Christianity were put to death under laws of former emperors. Afterwards, however, his own sense of humanity and justice again prevailed with him to grant certain indulgences to the Christians, who generally remained in peace and security throughout the remaining period of his life. In his matrimonial union he had been unfortunate, his consort being a woman of dissolute life. But judging from the honourable character of the man, there is every reason to believe, that he deeply felt the disgrace which his wife's misconduct had brought upon his family and court, although the impolicy of bringing her to public shame probably operated, with other motives, in inducing him to be lenient, and even affectionate towards her to the last. Still, nothing could justify the bestowal of "divine honours," by the Senate, at his own gratuitous solicitation, on the faithless Faustina.

The funeral of Antoninus was distinguished by all the imposing ceremonies of *Consecration;* and his ashes were deposited in the mausoleum of Hadrian. To shew how much he was beloved by those whom he governed, each Roman family was accustomed to have a statue of him in their houses. "No wonder, therefore, that," as Spanheim observes, "there should have come even to our days so many visible and durable monuments of his reign, some of which also *remain to us,* and *not* falsely, *on his coins.*"— These indeed are abundant, in each metal; and it is surprising, how many fine and interesting brass medallions there are of his mintage.— *Gold,* common (except some in the third degree of rarity)--*Silver,* common (except some in the sixth degree of rarity)—*Brass,* common (except some in the eighth degree of rarity).—He is thereon styled ANTONINVS AVG*ustus* PIVS. P. P. *(Pater Patriæ)*—also IMP*erator* CAES*ar* T. AELIVS. HADRIANVS. ANTONINVS PIVS. AVG.—The names of *Aelius Hadrianus* (as has been already mentioned) were those of his adoption.—Some rare pieces, struck under this emperor, represent him with *Hadrian, Faustina* senior, *Marcus Aurelius,* and *Lucius Verus.*

[The portrait at the head of this notice is engraved after the obverse type of a brass medallion, one of the finest in the *Cabinet de France*; for the reverse of which see *Bacchus and Ariadne.*]

ANTONINE Column at Rome. This monument is delineated on a large brass of Antoninus Pius.—See DIVO PIO.

ANTONIUS (MARCUS.)—The celebrated
Triumvir, born about the year of Rome 671
(B. C. 83), was the son of M. Antonius Creticus,
and grandson of Antonius the orator, killed

in the time of Marius; whence he is called,
on his coins, Marci Filius, Marci Nepos.—
Created Tribune of the people in the year U. C.
704 (B. C. 50) at the age of 34, he soon revealed his hostility to the Senate and Republic,
by leaving Rome for Gaul and joining Julius
Cæsar, whom he instigated to declare war against
Pompeius A. U. C. 705 (B. C. 49). It was as
Præfect that he commanded, with great distinction, the left wing of Cæsar's army at the battle of Pharsalia (B. C. 48). In the year following,
Julius made him General of his cavalry *(magister
equitum)*. He passed through the different
grades of office under the Commonwealth; but
these civil functions did not hinder him from
following the Dictator, to whose conquests he
lent his powerful aid in Egypt and in Asia.—
Consul in the year B. C. 44, he caused the
murdered Julius to be placed in the ranks of
the Gods, delivered Cæsar's funeral oration,
read his will, and exposed his dead body, to
the people. Antonius opposed, by every means
within his reach, though eventually without
success, the claim of Octavius to the heirship
of his uncle; and endeavoured to render himself
master of the government. In the year of Rome
711 (B. C. 43), the Senate, at the suggestion of
Cicero, declared him enemy of the country. He
thereupon assumed the government of Cisalpine
Gaul. Cæsar Octavianus (afterwards Augustus)
with the consuls Hirtius and Pansa, was sent
against him at the head of a great army, and defeated him in the neighbourhood of Bologna.
But both consuls were slain in the battle; and
Octavianus became commander in chief of the
victorious legions, at the early age of 21.—
Antonius now joined Lepidus in Gallia Narbonensis; and Octavianus seeing the policy of a
reconciliation, entered with those two men into
that infamous treaty of proscription, mis-called
Triumviratus causâ reipublicæ constituendæ,
by which, in reality, wholesale murder and con-
fiscation were organised, and the slavery of the
Romans was finally consummated. In the year
712 (B. C. 42), Antonius, united to Octavianus,
vanquished Brutus and Cassius at Philippi. In
713 (B. C. 41) at the head of his legions he
overran Greece, Cappadocia, and Cilicia, displaying a more than Asiatic pomp, whilst he arbi-
trated on the fate, or adjusted the differences,
of kings. It was during this luxurious expedition of his, that, Cleopatra having given him
the meeting at Tarsus, he became so enamoured

of that artful woman, as to take the fatal step of
following her to Alexandria, where he secretly
married her.—In 714 (B. C. 42) irritated by
his wife Fulvia against Octavianus, Antonius
returned to Italy, and affairs looked warlike;
but Fulvia dying, peace was restored between
the two rival triumvirs. A division of territorial
possessions took place (B. C. 40) Antonius
kept the east for his portion, whilst Octavianus
retained the west, and moreover gave his
sister Octavia in marriage to his colleague.
[See OCTAVIA.] Marcus then sent Ventidius
against the Parthians, who, under the refugee
Labienus (see the word), had been laying waste
the Roman province of Asia. In 715 (B. C.
39), Ventidius routed the Parthians with great
slaughter, and Labienus was slain. At the
close of the same year, Antonius set out with
his wife Octavia from Rome and wintered at
Athens. In 716 (B. C. 38) by his Legatus, C.
Sosius [the same who, as one of the triumvir's
moneyers, struck the coin engraved above], he
overcame Antigonus, King of Judæa, whom, after
scourging, he beheaded, and then bestowed the
kingdom on Herod the Great. At the close of
that year, Ventidius having again beaten the
Parthians, and Pacorus, son of King Orodes
being slain in battle, Antonius took his first Parthian triumph. In the year U. C. 717 (B. C. 37) he
returned to Rome, ostensibly to assist Octavianus
against Sextus Pompeius. [See Eckhel, vi. 45.]
The following year, after making a disgraceful
shew of going into Parthia and Media, he revi-
sited Egypt, and (to the great displeasure of the
Romans), distributed various cities and territories amongst the children borne to him by
Cleopatra.
  In 719 (B. C. 35), Sextus Pompeius, having, in
the preceding year, been defeated by Octavianus
Cæsar, and become a wanderer through Asia,
Antonius caused him to be decapitated on the
banks of the river Sangaris in Phrygia. Same
year, proceeding from Egypt to wage war against
the King of Armenia, he learnt that his wife
Octavia was on her way to join him. At the
importunate entreaties of the seductive Cleopatra,
he sent orders to Athens that she should go back
to Rome: soon after which, leaving the affairs
of his military expedition unaccomplished, he
returned to the embraces of the Egyptian Queen.
—A. U. C. 720 (B. C. 34). In the spring of
this year, being in Armenia, he, by a fraudulent
manœuvre, captured King Artavasdes, and carried
that unfortunate monarch, with his wife and
children, in triumph to Alexandria. He then
bestowed the finest provinces of Asia and Africa
on his own children by Cleopatra.—A. U. C. 721,
722 (B. C. 33–32). It was after returning from
his inglorious campaign in Parthia and Armenia,
that he divorced his wife Octavia, and insult-
ingly sent her to Rome. The following year
723 (B. C. 31), in contempt of the law, he
assumed the consulate (for the third time, as his
coins shew). The marriage of Antonius with
Cleopatra having drawn upon him the hatred of
his countrymen, Cæsar took advantage of it, not
less to serve his own ambitious designs, than to

avenge the wrongs of his sister. An open and deadly quarrel ensued between the brothers-in-law. And on the 2nd of September of that memorable year, at the naval fight off Actium, in Epirus, Antonius was totally defeated, and fled with Cleopatra to Egypt. In the year of Rome 724 (B.C. 30), Octavianus pursued and pressed Antonius, who, seeing that both his fleet and his land forces were gone over to the side of his victorious rival, lost all hope of retrieving his affairs, and died by his own sword.

Great qualities and great vices united to characterise this extraordinary man, whose gross misdeeds the eloquence of Cicero has stamped with the impress of a shameful celebrity: hence the implacable and vindictive hatred of Antonius against that illustrious orator, who he at length sacrificed by assassination. A brave and able general, he stood high in public estimation and confidence, at that critical period when the portentous honour of the Dictatorship was assumed by the great Julius, whose murder he professed to avenge, and whose place he aspired to fill. Yielding himself, however, to every excess of debauchery, he soon lost, amidst the enervating influences of voluptuousness, his former skill in the profession of arms, as well as in the art of civil government. After having in the plenitude of his power, and in the wantonness of his vain glory, distributed whole kingdoms at will, and been master of half the Roman world, he expired at the feet of the woman, who had been the cause of his disgrace and the source of his misfortunes. His remains and those of Queen Cleopatra were deposited in the same tomb.

The gold coins of Marcus Antonius are from the third to the eighth degree of rarity; the silver, from common to the fifth degree of rarity, and the brass (of which there are no large) from the first to the fourth degree of rarity.

On these with or without his portrait, he is styled, for the most part, ANTONI (or ANTONIVS).

ANTONIVS (M.) IMP. IIIVIR. R. P. C. [*Rei Publicæ Constituendæ*].—These words denote the second triumvirate of Rome, formed between Antonius, Lepidus, and Octavianus, under pretence of uniting to effect the re-establishment of the Republic.—See IIIVIR. and *Triumvirate*.

Some silver coins represent Mark Antony with Julius Cæsar, Lepidus, Octavius, Cleopatra, Marcus Antonius the son, and Lucius Antonius, a brother of the Triumvir.—The head of M. Antonius is not found on brass coins of the Roman mint; but it is frequently met with on those struck in different provinces by his lieutenants. · Such are those bearing the names of L. Sempronius Atratinus, M. Fonteius, and M. Oppius Capito, L. Calpurnius Bibulus, L. Pinarius Scarpus; also Sosius, Ventidius, and others his prefects and legates, minted in cities subject to his authority.—There are also silver medallions, struck in Asia, with the effigies of Antonius and of Cleopatra, either joined, or on separate sides.—On the reverse of one of these is the head of Cleopatra (or of Octavia) on a *cistus* between two serpents; on another the figure of Bacchus on

the same mystical chest, between two serpents; on a third a bow, quiver, and two serpents.—Gold and silver medals of the *Antonia* family give many of his legions, as designated by their *numbers* and the eagle standard on one side, and by *his* name as triumvir, with a galley, on the other.—The coins of Mark Antony typify his augurship, by the veiled head, the *lituus*, and the *præfericulum*; his pretensions to descent from Hercules, by the club; and his devotion to the worship of Bacchus by the crown of ivy leaves.—See AVGVR—see also *Cistophori*.

ANTONIUS (M.) M. F. M. N. IMP. ITER. —Antony, in a military dress, stands with his left foot planted on the prow of a ship; in his right hand is a spear, in his left the parazonium.

Rev.—IIIVR. R. P. C. COS. DESIG. ITER ET TERT.—A lion walking, a dagger held in his right fore paw; above is a star.

The foregoing is given in *Thesaur. Morell.* as from a rare gold coin of Mark Antony. The legend of the reverse assigns to him the title of *Consul Designatus Iterum et Tertium* (Consul Elect for the second and third time). It could not therefore have been struck earlier (says Eckhel) than the year U. C. 715 (B.C. 39). The type of the obverse represents Marcus Antonius, in his garb of war, as IMP*erator* or General of an army. His foot is placed on the prow of a vessel, to indicate his maritime power. It is to be observed, indeed, that the foot resting on any object imports the possession of that object, or a right over it; or it refers to a person's excelling, or being influential, in some particular. But the type of the reverse is still more appropriate to the biography of Antony. It presents the *Leo Gradiens*, previously marked on his coins in the year of Rome 711 (B.C. 43). Lions were in some way or other connected with the badge, or, as it were, heraldic device, of the proud triumvir. Nor ought this to be matter of surprise. "He certainly (as Dr. Cardwell observes) did claim to be descended from Hercules, and might therefore be expected to take a lion for his bearing. It was only five years previously [as attested by Pliny and Plutarch] on his return from the battle of Pharsalia, that he entered the city with lions yoked to his chariot; and you will remember the words of Cicero to Atticus [Epist. x. 13]. *Tu Antonii leones pertimescas cave*; where he speaks of lions as if they always suggested the recollection of Antony, and leads us to connect them with his well-known love of parade and ostentation."—(Lecture vii. 181.)

Plutarch informs us, that in the trimming of his beard, the breadth of forehead, and the aquiline nose, Antony resembled the statue of

Hercules; and a tradition existed that the Antonii derived their origin from that demi-god through his son Anton, or Anteon. According to Appian, Octavianus intimated to Antony, that Julius Cæsar had deliberated whether he should name him his successor, and that the sole obstacle in the way was the doubt, whether his pride would brook the change from the family of Hercules to that of Æneas. It was, doubtless, his exultation in this idea of high descent that led to his being exhibited, in the dress of Hercules, on Alexandrine coins, and on contorniate medals. That this lion of Antony should be represented clasping a dagger in his paw, does not appear susceptible of explanation; but it is remarkable, (says Eckhel, vi. 44), that there was precisely the same device, on a ring of Pompey the Great; for Plutarch says, that there was engraven on it "a lion holding a sword."

ANT. (M.) IMPER. COS. DESIGN. ITER. ET. TER. IIIVIR. R. P. C.—Two heads joined, viz., the bare head of Marcus Antonius, and a female head (that of Cleopatra, says Havercamp), adorned with the diadem.

Rev.—M. OPPIVS CAPITO. PROPR. PRAEF. CLASSI. F. C.—*(Pro Prætore Præfectus Classi Fieri Curavit.)*—Two clothed figures, standing on a quadriga of sea horses.

The above legends and types appear on what is given in Morel and Vaillant under the *Oppia* family, as a middle brass coin. Although, among the præfects of Antony, whose names are engraven on his coins, that of M. Oppius Capito occurs on no less than seven, yet ancient history supplies nothing respecting him.—See *Thesaur.* Oppia, fig. D. p. 305.

The two following pieces belong to a class of medals called *Cistophori* (see the word).

1.—ANTONIVS (M.) IMP. COS. DESIG. ITER. ET TERT. *(Marcus Antonius, Imperator, Consul Designatus, Iterum et Tertium).*—The head of Mark Antony jugated with that of a woman: the former is wreathed with ivy, the latter is bare.

Rev.—IIIVIR. R. P. C. *(Triumvir Reipublicæ Constituendæ.)*—Bacchus, clothed in the stola, holding in his right hand the *cantharus* (a flagon) and in his left the *thyrsus*, stands on the *cista mystica*, between two serpents.

The whole legend, that of the obverse followed by that of the reverse, reads—Mark Antony, Imperator (i. e. General in chief), Consul Elect for the second and third time, Triumvir to form (or reform) the Republic.—Engraved in Havercamp, *Médailles de Christine*, TAB. xlii. fig. 13.—Silver medallion, struck in Asia.

The woman's head jugated with that of the Triumvir on the above two coins, has given rise to much controversial argument; some learned numismatists regarding it as that of Queen Cleopatra, whilst others consider it to represent Octavia, sister of Octavianus, and the lawful wife of Antony.—For the *pros* and *cons* of this question, see Eckhel's commentary, vol. vi. p. 58, et seq.—For an explanation of the legends, see IMPER.—COS. DESIG.—and PROPR. PRAEF. &c. in their places.

2.—ANTONIUS (M.) IMP. COS. DESIG. ITER. ET. TERT.—Head of Mark Antony crowned with ivy.

Rev.—IIIVIR. R. P. C.—The mystic chest or basket of Bacchus, between two serpents, and surmounted by the bare head of a woman.—On a silver medallion of Antony, struck in Asia.

It will be borne in mind that the crown of ivy was one of the attributes of Bacchus. Antony, who as a Roman claimed lineage with Hercules, wishing to pass himself off for Bacchus, in his oriental expeditions, the Asiatics, with whom these *Cistophori* originated, sought to render themselves agreeable to him by restoring this Bacchanalian type on the coins which they minted in honour of the Triumvir. It was for the same reason that the types of the coins of the great Mithridates, King of Pontus, were included in similar crowns. The people of Asia Minor regarded that prince as a god sent from heaven to emancipate them from the Roman yoke, and they likened him to Bacchus, by a sort of superstitious adulation which was peculiar to them.

And now the same Antony, who on a coin of the year U. C. 715 (B. C. 39), is seen playing the part of Hercules, is here to be recognised as Bacchus by his crown of ivy, whilst abundant testimony of ancient writers goes to confirm the present record of his apotheosis. Dion Cassius and Seneca both relate, that Antony, on his return from Italy into Greece, in the year abovenamed, styled himself a second Bacchus, this title being even inscribed on his statues; and that he insisted on its being accorded to him by others. And when the Athenians went out to meet him, they saluted him as Bacchus (an honour which, according to Diogenes Laertius, they had already conferred on Alexander the Great), and begged that he would not disdain to accept their Minerva in marriage. To this he replied that he approved of the arrangement, but demanded as dowry 40,000 sestertii.—Seneca adds, that this appearing too hard a condition, one of the Greeks present said to Antony,—" My Lord, Jupiter took thy mother Semele without a dowry." Socrates, the Rhodian, in Athenæus, tells us that Antony himself, during a Bacchic procession, commanded that he should be proclaimed as Bacchus by the voice of the herald.— What Plutarch records to the same effect, occurred two years previously. For he says, that having gone into Asia after the defeat of Brutus, and entered Ephesus, he was received by the women attired as Bacchanals, and by the men and boys, as satyrs and pans, and was saluted openly as Bacchus, the benignant and genial, and that the whole city was filled with ivy, *thyrsi*, psalteries, pipes, and flutes. This record respecting Ephesus has the greater weight, because these coins, which present to us Antony in the character of Bacchus, were struck in the province of Asia, where it is ascertained beyond a doubt that all the *Cistophori* first saw the light. But it is also well-known, that Antony was not the first nor the only one upon whom the same Asiatics conferred all the honours due to Bacchus. (This is shewn in the instances of Alexander the Great, and Mithridates, already cited.)—Nor indeed did this infatuation of Mark Antony's give place to time; for Velleius informs us, that he, "with a crown of ivy and gold, and holding a thyrsus, and with buskins on his legs, was carried into Alexandria on a car, as *Liber Pater;*" and this piece of madness may be seen confirmed by an enduring monument, in the coinage of Balanca in Syria. That his favourite Cleopatra might not be wanting in her own celestial honours, he called himself, while in Egypt, Osiris and Liber Pater, and her Luna and Isis.—Of the date of both these coins nothing can be said, than they were struck before the year u. c. 720 (B. c. 34), as we learn from the consulate inscribed upon them.—See Eckhel, vi. 64, et seq.

ANTONIUS (Marcus the younger) son of the Triumvir, by Fulvia his second wife.—Invested

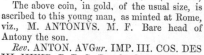

with the *toga virilis,* after the fatal day of Actium, he was, subsequently to his father's suicide, put to death, by order of Octavianus, at the foot of Cæsar's statue in Egypt, on the 30th of April, in the year of Rome 723 (B. c. 31.)

The above coin, in gold, of the usual size, is ascribed to this young man, as minted at Rome, viz., M. ANTONIVS. M. F. Bare head of Antony the son.

Rev. ANTON. AVG*ur.* IMP. III. COS. DES III. IIIVIR. R. P. C. Bare head of the Father.

Mionnet gives this aureus, as one of the first rarity, valuing it at 1000 francs.—According to Eckhel there are two specimens of it extant: the one is in the Imperial Cabinet at Vienna; the other, formerly in Peter Seguin's collection, is now in the French Cabinet at Paris.—See Seguin, *Selecta Numismata*, p. 112.

ANTONIUS (CAIUS) brother of the Triumvir. There are neither gold nor brass coins of this person, but a very rare silver coin of the Antonia gens, without portrait, is considered to bear his name and title, as the legend of its obverse:—viz.

C. ANTONIVS *Marci Filius.* PRO-CO*n*S*ul.* Bust of a woman with a broad shallow-hat.—*Rev.* PONTIFEX. The *securis* (or axe) and two *simpuvia* (or sacrificial vessels).—Engraved in Morell. Antonia gens, TAB. I. fig. v.

It has been made matter of controversy as to which of the two Antonii this denarius is rightly assignable to. One of them is C. Antonius, bro-

ther of Marcus. The other, the C. Antonius who was Cicero's colleague in the consulship, and who was the Triumvir's cousin-german.—Eckhel, who places the coin in question amongst those of Mark Antony's, struck in the year u. c. 718 (B. c. 42) gives some apparently good reasons for adhering himself to the opinion more generally prevailing amongst numismatic antiquaries, and which assigns the coin to the brother of Mark Antony. This Caius Antonius fought against Catiline. On the death of Julius Cæsar he was sent as *Pro-Consul* into Macedonia, and was there defeated by Brutus, who took him prisoner, and put him to death, 44 or 43 years before the Christian æra.—The *pileus* on the woman's head is, doubtless, the broad shallow hat, worn by the Macedonians, but whether it was meant (as Havercamp contests), to allude to Macedonia, of which C. Antonius had the government, is not so certain. He is called on this coin PONTIFEX—a dignity, which he seems to have obtained from Julius, when that ruler augmented the priesthood.—*Doctrina*, vi. 41.

ANTONIUS (LUCIUS) another brother of Mark Antony. The following coin, in gold and silver (unique in the former) is extant, and attributed to him :—viz.

L. ANTONIVS. COS. Bare head of Lucius Antonius.

Rev.—M. ANT. IMP. AVG. IIIVIR. R. P. C. M. NERVA PROQ. P. *(Marcus Antonius Imperator Augur Triumvir Reipublicæ Constituendæ. Marcus Nerva Proquæstor Provincialis* (by whom the coin was struck.)—Bare head of Mark Antony.

Declared in the year of Rome protector of the thirty tribes, he was appointed Consul in 713, (B. c. 41.)—During the absence of Mark Antony in Asia, Lucius originated what historians call the Perusinian war *(bellum Perusinum)* by exciting the people of Etruria against Octavianus Cæsar, who had divided their lands amongst his veteran legionaries. The Consul defended himself in Perusia against the besieging forces of Augustus and Agrippa, by whom he was taken prisoner; but he afterwards made his peace with Cæsar, who gave him the governorship of Spain. The time of his death, like that of his birth, remains unknown.

ANUBIS, one of the monster-gods of Egypt. —See his dog-headed figure on a brass coin of Julianus II. with legend VOTA PVBLICA.

ANXUR, a city of Latium, in the country of the Volscians, afterwards made a Roman colony; now *Terracina*, the episcopal see of the *Campagna di Roma.* Virgil makes mention of this ancient place as connected with the worship of Jupiter.—See AXUR.

APAMEA (Bithyniæ) *colonia*, now *Meda-niah-Mudagna*, in Asiatic Turkey. There were several Greek cities of this name (*Apameia*) but that situated in Bithynia, on the southern shores of the Propontis (Sea of Marmora) near the mouth of the river anciently called Rhyndacus, was the only Apamea, on which the Romans bestowed the rank and privileges of a *colony;* and as such it is mentioned by Pliny (L. V. c. 32.) It was at first called Myrlea, and afterwards received the appellation of Apamea from King Prusias, in honour of his wife *Apame*. In the civil wars, the Apameanians took the side of Julius Cæsar against Pompey; and it was under Augustus that their city became colonial. Its æra is 457 of the foundation of Rome (297 B. C.)

The *Latin* coins of Apamea (besides a few Autonomes) consist of *colonial imperial*, in brass. These commence with Julius Cæsar and Augustus: a cessation of coining then apparently occurred (with the exception of a Germanicus Cæsar and of an Agrippina, jun., struck under Caligula) till the reign of Nero—Then no more are to be found till we come to Titus, whence there is a skip to Trajan, and again to Antoninus Pius, and M. Aurelius; thence the list in Mionnet displays a dedicatory series of coins to consecutive emperors, with comparatively few omissions, as far down as Gallienus. The legends of their *reverses* are as follow:—

C. I. C. A. D. D.—and C. I. C. A. P. A. D. D. (Abbreviations for, *Colonia Julia Concordia Apamea, Decreto Decurionum.*)   CONC. APAM.—C. I. C. A. GENIO P. R. D. D.— APOLLINI CLAR*ius*. C. I. C. A.—I. A. A. P. A. COL. IVL. APAM.—COL. IVL. CONC. AV-*Gusta* APAM.—COL. APAM. AVG*usta*.— IVL. CONCORD. APAM. AVG. D. D.—CO-LONIA. IVL. CONC. AVG. APAM.

A second brass of this colony (given in Pellerin, *Melange*, i. pl. xxii. No. 4) presents on its obverse IMP. C. P. LIC. VALERIANUS. AVG. with the radiated head of Valerianus senior. On the reverse, (as on the annexed engraving) are for legend COL. IVL. CONC. AVG. APAM; and for type, the Indian Bacchus, naked to the waist; he stands holding the *cantharus* (or wine-pitcher) in his right hand, and supporting himself with his left hand resting on a pole, round which is entwined a vine-branch with grapes. At his feet a panther. In the field of the coin the letters D. D.

There are various other types of reverses, as the subjoined alphabetical classification of them serves to shew:—

Apollo Clarius (see the word) standing with patera, and bow, as in M. Aurelius.

Æneas, Anchises, and Ascanius; in the usual mode of representing that family group; as in Caracalla, (see Pellerin *Melange*, pl. xviii. No. 7, p. 290), Macrinus, and Alex. Severus.

Bacchus stands, presenting with one hand a bunch of grapes to a panther, and holding the *thyrsus* in the other; as in Geta, and Trajanus Decius.

On a coin of Volusianus, the Indian Bacchus, stands clothed in a long robe, and bearded, a *chlamys* falling from the top of his shoulders: he holds in his right hand the *cantharus*, and carries the left hand to his head: at his feet is a panther, (Mionnet, *Suppl*. T. V. p. 12, et seq.)

Colonist, or Priest, ploughing with two oxen; as in Nero, Antoninus, and Gallienus.

Diana Lucifera walking, with a torch in each hand; as in M. Aurelius, and J. Domna.

Fortune, with her usual attributes; as in Antoninus Pius, Philip sen., and Gallienus.

Galley, with three rowers; as in Commodus, Gordianus Pius, Tranquillina, Otacilia, Philip jun., Trebonianus Gallus, and Gallienus.

Genius Populi Romani, C. I. C. A. Half naked male figure, stands with rudder in right hand, and cornucopiæ in the left; as in Antoninus Pius.

Genius of Apamea, represented under the same personification and attributes as the preceding reverse, struck under Gallienus.

Jupiter, seated, holding the patera and the hasta, as in Caracalla; or standing, with the lower extremities covered with the *pallium*, the right hand raised, the *hasta pura* in the left.— A lighted altar, and the letters D. D. in the field, as in Gallienus.

Military Ensigns.—The legionary eagle between two standards; (or 3, 4, and 5 ensigns on a reverse), as in Nero and Caracalla.—[These says Vaillant, are insignia of the veteran legionaries originally placed in the colony either by Julius or Augustus, and doubtless intended to shew the antiquity of its establishment under the Romans; but none of the coins yet discovered exhibit the name of the legion, which was sent to Apamea.—*Col*. ii. 228.]

Romulus, Remus, and the Wolf; as in M. Aurelius, Caracalla, Maximus, and Philip the younger.

Soldier, standing on a trireme; as in Trajan, and in Antoninus.

Venus, seated on a dolphin, a rudder in her right hand and the aplustrum in her left; as in Commodus; or carrying a Cupid in her right hand; or standing as the goddess of beauty, on a coin of Julia Domna.—[The latter exhibits for the legend of its reverse VENVS. C. I. C. A. AVG. D. D. and for type the *Venus Pudica*—M. Du Mersan, in his description of select coins in the Allier de Hauteroche cabinet (pl. x. No. 19) has given, as usual with him, a beautiful engraving of this elegant colonial imperial.]   See VENVS PUDICA.

Victory, walking, with a buckler in one hand and an oar in the other, as in Julius Cæsar; or walking with laurel crown and palm branch, as in Gallienus.

Woman, turreted, with right hand raised, standing before a lighted altar, as in Gallienus; or helmeted, standing with patera and cornucopiæ, as in Titus; or seated on a dolphin, a small figure of Victory in the right, and the acrostolium in the left; as in Julia Domna.—Woman seated on a dolphin, which is swimming on the waves; she has her right hand extended over the head of the fish, and with her left hand she covers herself with a light drapery; as in Geta.—Vaillant.

Amongst the numerous instances in which Pellerin supplies descriptions and engravings of colonial coins, not given in Vaillant's work, is an elegant one minted in this colony, under M. Aurelius, having the young head of the emperor, and for legend and type of reverse DIANAE LVCIF, C. I. C. A. Diana walking, with a lighted torch in each hand.—*Melange*, i. pl. xvii. p. 279.

In a communication from Mr. Borrell, of Smyrna, addressed to the Editor of the *Numismatic Chronicle* (Mr. Akerman), and inserted in No. xix. (for Jan. 1843, p. 190) of that periodical, are given three (till then) unedited coins of this colony, viz., a Caligula with reverse of Germanicus, a Julia Domna, and a Caracalla.

A PARTH. RECVPER. *A Parthis Recuperatis.*—Recovered from the Parthians. This alludes to military ensigns, re-captured from, or restored by, those formidable enemies of both Consular and Imperial Rome. On gold and silver of Augustus.—See CIVIB. ET SIG. MILIT.

APER.—See *Boar.*

APEX, a covering for the head, somewhat resembling a bishop's mitre, for which its form probably in after ages furnished a pattern. On the top was a pointed piece of wood, the base of which was surrounded by a little woollen tuft. Two filaments of the same material, hanging from the bottom of it, served to fasten it under the chin. The derivation of this word is not satisfactorily explained by learned writers. But its sometimes round—sometimes conical shape—and the pointed tassel on the top *(Apex)* most probably gave the name to the cap itself. It seems to have been first used by the Salian priests, and was afterwards worn by the *Pontifex Maximus* and the *Flamines* generally. [The various forms of the *Apex*, and its appearance on the head of one of the Roman priests, are shewn and explained in the *Dictionary of G. and R. Antiquities*, edited by Dr. W. Smith.]

The *Apex* is found on a denarius of the Quinctia gens, as indicating the connection of Quinctius *Flaminius* with the priesthood of Jupiter. As a symbol of Valerius Flaccus being a Salian, or priest of Mars, it appears on a coin of the *Valeria* gens. The same is also seen between two ANCILIA, on a silver coin of P. STOLO, of the Licinia family, a monetary triumvir of Augustus. These *apices*, or head gear, worn by the members of the sacerdotal order, whilst performing religious ceremonies, are to be seen on other family and consular coins, especially on those of the *Julia* gens. On many of these it is also exhibited, in combination with the *securis* (or slaughtering axe), the *præfericulum* (vase for wine, &c.), and the *aspergillum* (water-sprinkler), all which sacrificial instruments serve to mark the Pontificate of Julius Cæsar.—See ANCILIA, p. 45 of this work.

A. P. F.   *Argento Publico Feriundo.*—On gold and silver of the Livineia and Mussidia families, the legend of the reverse reads L. REGVLVS IIIIVIR. A. P. F.—Referring to the Triumvir, or as in this case, Quatuorvir, one of the principal officers of the Roman mint, appointed to superintend the gold and silver coinage of the Republic.

APIS.—The sacred bull, which the ancient Egyptians worshipped under this name at Memphis, was consecrated to the moon (Isis); as another bull, at Heliopolis was, under the name of *Mnevis*, dedicated to the sun (Osiris). According to the belief which the Egyptian priests took care to inculcate, Apis was the offspring of a cow, rendered fertile by a ray of the moon coming over her in a supernatural manner. His appearance was that of a bull with black and white spots. When the animal died, search was made for another bull of the same pseudo-miraculous origin; and if perchance his life was terminated before the *appointed* time, all Egypt put on mourning until he was replaced. His successor was chosen with great care, as to the same bodily marks, being honoured with equal veneration in his sanctuary. He served as an oracle both to Egyptians and to foreigners. Julius Cæsar, Germanicus, Vespasian, and many other Romans of eminence, travelled to Memphis to see and adore this "divine" quadruped.

Several Alexandrine coins exhibit Apis with the attributes that characterise him, and a great number of other monuments likewise preserve his image—including certain coins of Julianus II. in second brass.—See SECVRITAS REIPVBLICAE and ISIS FARIA.

APLUSTRUM, or *Aplustre*, the ornament of the poop, or stern, of vessels, amongst the Romans, thus differing from the *acrostolium* (see the word, p. 5), which decorated the prow. It was composed of curved planks curiously carved, and painted with various colours. Probably some of the decorations of the *aplustrum* served the purpose of a vane, on board the ships of the ancients.

[From references, made by numismatic writers in general, it would appear to be one of the conventionalities of the science, to apply the term *acrostolium* to that object or symbol, which, whether seen in the hand of Neptune, or at the stern of a galley, seems, from its peculiar form and position, designed rather to represent the *Aplustrum*. For examples of this species of naval adornment, as agreeing with the descriptions given by ancient authors, the reader's attention may be directed to coins of the *Fonteia* and *Cassia* families—to the *Nep. Red.* of Vespasian, and to the Prætorian trireme *(Felicitati Aug.)* of Hadrian, &c. But a monetal specimen, on the larger scale, is to be found on a brass medallion of Agrippa, given by Vaillant *(Præst. Num. Impp. Rom.* iii. 104), who, having in his work on the Colonies, defined acrostolium to be "Navis Rostrum" (the beak of a ship), here designates the wing-like figure, on the reverse of the coin in question, not as acrostolium, but as "Navis Aplustrum."—See MVNICIPI. PARENS.]

APOLLO.—According to the mythology of the Greeks, from which the Romans almost exclusively borrowed their own objects of religious worship, Apollo was the son of Jupiter and of

Latona, and came into the world with his twin sister Diana, in the island of Delos. The god of health, of literature, and of the fine arts, it was chiefly under the youthful grace, the noble form, the handsome lineaments of Apollo, that manly beauty personified itself in the classic periods of antiquity. He it was, whom as "the god of all versemen," poets of old, in their "fine frenzy" invoked, to imbue them with his divine inspirations. As the patron of music, the instrument on which he delighted to exercise his heaven-born genius, was the lyre, or cithara, presented to him by Mercury. This most attractive and accomplished, but at the same time most cruel, licentious, and vindictive, of those *male* deities, who held superior rank in the celestial realms of ancient fable, was moreover regarded as a skilful charioteer, guiding steeds no less fleet and fiery than those of the Sun. An unerring archer, too, it was an arrow from his bow, that delivered the earth from the serpent Python;—which having sprung from the slimy mud of the deluge, spread its ravages around the sacred district of mount Parnassus. He afterwards covered with that monster's skin the tripod, on which the priestess of his temple seated herself when delivering her oracles. Allusion to all these incidents and attributes of Apollo are to be found on Roman coins. His votaries distinguished him by a confused and inconsistent variety of names, epithets, and assigned functions. Under the title of *Helios, Phœbus,* or *Sol,* as charged with the office of daily illuminating the world, he is represented on coins and other monuments, with his head radiated, and a whip in his hand, either standing on the ground, or riding in a car drawn by four horses. Numerous edifices were dedicated to his worship, throughout Greece. And one of the richest and most superb of his temples was that built at Rome, by Augustus. Various games were celebrated to his honour. The pythian, in many places; the deliquia in Delos; and at Nicea in Bithynia; the secular *(ludi sæculares Apollinares)* at Rome, &c. As presiding over the Muses, mount Helicon in Bœotia was held sacred to him; and numerous other places owned the superstitious influence of his godship. Among the animals consecrated to Apollo, were the wolf, the cock, the *raven*, the vulture, besides the fabulous Griffin.—Among plants and fruits were the laurel, the olive, and

the tamarind. At his altars were sacrificed lambs, black bulls, sheep, and horses. The hymns sung to his praise were *Pœans* and *Nomes;* and *Io Pean* is considered to be an acclamation of Victory referring to Python.

Apollo is depictured on ancient paintings, sculptures, and coins, in divers ways: with a juvenile countenance, a bare, a laureated, or a radiated head—the hair some times adjusted and turned up; at others, hanging down long and curled. Sometimes with bow and arrow as the archer and the dart-flinger; sometimes near a tripod as the *vates* or poet; with a serpent, either in allusion to Python, or as the inventor of medicine; with the lyre or the harp as the patron of music; with the *pedum*, or pastoral crook, as the tutelary god of shepherds; driving a quadriga and holding a whip in his right hand, as the charioteer of the Sun. On a large brass of Alexander Severus, struck A. D. 231, during that Emperor's campaigns in the East, Apollo stands in an easy attitude, his right hand pointing upwards, and his left holding a whip, indicative of his power to promote rapidity, in allusion to his horses. With the exception of a mantle on the shoulder, the figure is naked, and the head radiated. (Smyth, 232.) Most frequently he is represented naked or half-naked, but sometimes clothed in a woman's robe. Now, standing with elbow resting on a column, now seated on the tripod, or a conical vase, as if prepared for divination. On the generality of coins he appears as a beardless youth, and even with feminine features, though there are instances cited of a bearded Apollo.

Apollo's head laureated, with the lyre before it, the whole within a laurel crown, appears on a second brass of Augustus, as represented in the wood-cut at the head of this article.

Apollinis Vejovis Caput.—The head of *Apollo Ve-juppiter,* occurs on a denarius of the *Cæsia* gens—see the word.

Apollo's laureated head appears on denarii of the following Roman families, viz.: *Aquilia, Bæbia, Cæcilia, Carvilia,* Calpurnia, Cassia, Claudia, *Coponia* (diademed), Crepusia, Egnatuleia, Fonteia, Julia, Licinia, Lollia, *Marcia,* Memmia, Ogulnia, *Opeimia,* Papia, Pedania, Poblicia, Pomponia, Postumia, Servilia, Sulpicia, *Vibia,* &c.—[Those in italics are illustrated in their respective places.]

Apollo's head, adorned with curled hair, and with a star above, occurs on coins of the *Valeria* gens; with the diadem in the *Marcia;* encircled with the fillet and a sceptre behind, in the *Cassia, Claudia,* and Postumia families. [The sceptre so placed serves, according to Pigghius, to denote that the Romans, in their sacred rites, worshipped, as sovereign of all animated bodies, the deity, whom, after the example of the Greeks, they identified with the *Sun.*]

Apollo's head radiated is accordingly seen ornamented with the crown of rays, on coins of the Aquilia, Cæsia, Claudia, Lucretia, Mussidia, Valeria, and other families. The same head, forming the obverse type of so many denarii, refers to the Apollinarian games.

Apollo's head with the lyre, either before or behind it, is exhibited on family medals of the Claudii, Flavii, &c., and as that of a female, crowned with laurel on coins of the Voltcia gens.

Apollo's and Diana's heads present themselves together, on denarii of the Fonteia, and other families, allusive to the secular games.

Apollo and Diana, both standing, the one with laurel branch and lyre, the other, with bow and quiver, are found on the reverse of a silver coin of Valerianus, with legend of CONSERVAT. AVGG. contained in the imperial cabinet at Vienna. [Eckhel observes, that the association of Apollo with his sister Diana, under the title of joint preservers of the Emperor, occurs in this instance for the first time.—Khell remarks respecting this type, that as in the tragical case of Niobe and her children, the idolatrous illusions of pagan belief were prone to ascribe that dire continuance of the plague, which was destroying thousands on thousands, to the wrath of both those vengeful deities—Apollo and Diana.— vol. vii, 383.]

Apollo naked, with garland on his head, in a quadriga at full speed, holding a branch in the right hand, and a bow and arrow with the horses' reins in the left, appears on a coin of the *Bœbia* gens.—For engraved specimens of the above types see Morell. *Thesaurus*, and Vaillant's *Fam. Rom. Numis.*—See also *Bœbia*.

Apollo's name and image are also of continual recurrence throughout the imperial series, from Julius Cæsar to Julian the Apostate; among which the following are examples : viz.

Apollo, the favourite divinity of Augustus.— There is a silver coin of this emperor, the reverse of which displays Apollo, seated on a rock, playing on the lyre, and having behind his shoulders what Spanheim (in Julian's Cæsars, p. 304), calls a buckler, as a mark of security and peace after the battle of Actium, but which Mionnet terms the *pileus*. In the field of the coin is the inscription CAESAR. DIVI. F. (*Cæsaris Divi Filius*—son of the Divine Cæsar.)

This denarius, which Eckhel regards as having been minted at Rome between A. U. C. 719, (B. C. 35) and 726 (28) forms another of the many testimonies, afforded by coins and inscribed marbles, of the seemingly intense devotion paid by Augustus to Apollo, *before* as well as after the battle of Actium.—On this point Suetonius (c. 70) refers to letters from M. Antonius, who satirises the secret banquet, commonly called that of the "twelve" deities, at which the guests sat down, dressed in the habits of gods and goddesses, Octavianus (i. e. Augustus) himself personating Apollo. See *D. N. V.* vol. vi. 107-8.—The sister of the same deity, was also an object of worship with Augustus ; for he ascribed his good fortune to both, acknowledging the tutelary aid of the Sicilian Diana *(Diana Siculæ)* for his victory over Sextus Pompeius, as well as that of Apollo for his decisive success at Actium.—See SICIL. IMP.

Apollo seated, with his lyre, and the legend IMP. VII. COS. III. on a brass medallion of M. Aurelius.

Apollo and Bacchus, drawn by a goat and a panther, with Cupid riding on the goat, form the reverse type, without legend, of a brass medallion of Hadrian.—See *Bacchus*.

Apollini sacer Corvus.——Pedrusi gives, from the Farnese cabinet, the reverse type of a brass medallion of Antoninus Pius, which represents Apollo, nearly naked in front, a long cloak

hanging down his back—standing with a bow in his left hand, before a tripod, on which a dead serpent (Python) is suspended. On Apollo's right hand is a sort of table with a vase on it, behind which rises a tree, on one of whose branches a *crow* or raven is perched.—The learned Jesuit takes no little pains in citing the *reasons* given by old writers, both in poetry and prose, for consecrating the *corvus* to *Apollo*. But whether it has reference to the god's vindictive change of the crow's plumage from white to black, for betraying his secret amour with the nymph Coronis, or whether it relates to the croaking of this bird being more favourable than the singing of others to the pious frauds of augural divination, is by no means clearly decided.—See vol. v. p. 190.—[The legend TR. POT. IIII. COS. II. shews that this beautiful product of the Antoninian mint was struck about A. D. 139.]

APOLLINI. ACTIO, or *Actiacq*. (To the Actiac Apollo.)—In a female dress he stands, holding the lyre in his right hand and the plectrum in his left.—See ACT. IMP. p. 8, of this work.

On a denarius of Augustus, who, as his patron in the day of Actium, and afterwards as the reformer of his life and manners, affected (as Spanheim says) to resemble that god, at his festivals, in his statues, and on his medals.— Apollo Actius, striking the lyre with an *ivory plectrum*, is alluded to in the following line of the epic poet Albinovanus, a friend and contemporary of Ovid :—

" *Actius* ipse *lyram plectro* percussit *eburno*."

On another denarius of Augustus is the figure of Apollo, in the *stola*, standing on a substructure, ornamented with anchors and beaks of ships, before an altar, he holds a patera in the right, and the lyre in his left hand, round the upper part of which we read C. ANTISTI. VETVS. IIIVIR.

Struck A. U. C. 738, (B. C. 16), by one of his monetary triumvirs, Antistius Vetus, this coin adds another proof of the great devotion professed by Augustus towards Apollo, to whom, in fulfilment of his vow, he had built a temple at Actium, after his crowning victory over his competitor for the empire of the world. The legend of the head is IMP. CAESAR. AVGVS. TR. POT. IIX.—Eckhel assigns this and other coins with similar types and legends to the year of Rome 742 (B.C. 12), in the mint of Augustus.— See *Thesaur. Morell. Fam. Rom.* Antistia gens, fig. iii.—and *Impp. Rom.* vol. iii. TAB. xiv. fig. 36.

APOLLINI AVGVSTO. S. C.—Apollo *Lyristes* standing in a female dress, holding the lyre and a patera.—On a first brass of Antoninus Pius, struck A. U. C. 893, (A. D. 140).

It was in memory of the veneration rendered by Augustus to Apollo, that this coin was struck, in which the name itself of Augustus is given to. that deity, who is represented in the same costume and attitude, and with the same attributes as in the denarii minted by Augustus, and bearing the legend of ACT. IMP. X. and XII.— *Apollo Augustus,* says Eckhel, is the same as *Apollo Actius.*—See p. 8 of this work.

There is a silver coin of S. Severus, with a similar legend and type, which Rasche says was struck to commemorate the sacrifices which that emperor made to Apollo, on the occasion of Pescennius Niger's defeat and death. The same legend and type occur on silver and gold of Albinus.

APOL*lini* CONSERVATORI. S. C.— Apollo, naked, beardless, and with flowing hair, stands holding a laurel branch in the right hand, his left resting on the lyre, placed on a rock. On gold, silver, and first brass of Æmilianus.

The plague which raged through the length and breadth of the empire, at the period (about A D. 253) when these coins were struck, was the special occasion of this devotion to Apollo *medicus,* in other words to him as the god of health.—"Apollo (observes Capt. Smyth, describing this coin, in large brass) was a most popular deity, though Lucian stigmatised him as a vain and lying fortune-teller. He appears on the medals, of all sizes and metals, of this reign; not in the feminine apparel of the Palatine statue, but as a noble youth, delicate yet vigorous, with limbs free, and sometimes in an attitude not very dissimilar from that finest statue in the world, the Apollo Venator" (commonly called the Belvidere Apollo).—*Descr. Cat.* 292.

APOLLINI CONS. AVG. (To Apollo, preserver of the Emperor.)—On billon of Gallienus

—also APOLLINI CONSERVATORI, on a brass medallion, and APOLLINI CONSERVA. on first brass, of Valerianus and Gallienus.—Apollo standing, either with his right hand laid over his head, or [as in the preceding cut] holding a laurel branch; with his left resting on a lyre, placed on a pedestal.—(Struck between A. D. 254 and 266.)

Not only Augustus but his successors had always paid especial honours to Apollo, whose temple at Actium commanded a view of the bay where the combat took place. The name and image of the god had frequently figured on the coins of Rome. But at the period, when paganism was on the point of expiring, its divinities were more than ever invoked by the emperors, who endeavoured to stem the progress of its fall. Apollo, in particular, was the object of their homage, in those dreadful times, when the plague spread itself to depopulate the empire. —*Leçons Numismatiques,* p. 239.—The same legend and similar type appear on gold of Valerianus.

APOL. CONS.—Mionnet gives a gold Aurelian with this legend, and Apollo seated.— Vaillant publishes (*Pr.* i. 213) an aureus of the same emperor, on which a male figure, naked, stands with radiated head, right hand extended, and the left holding a globe—a captive on the ground sitting near his feet.

Here we find the name of *Apollo* identified, on the same coin, with the symbol of the *Sun,* and evidently referring to Aurelian's victories in the *East.*

APOLLINI CONSERVATORI.—This dedicatory legend at full length, with a temple, in which appears the statue of Apollo, is given in the *Museum Theupoli,* as from a brass medallion of Quintillus, Aurelian's immediate predecessor, who reigned after Claudius II. only during a few months of A. D. 270.

APOLLINI CONS. AVG.—A Centaur, holding a globe in one hand, and a rudder in the other; or a Centaur about to shoot an arrow.— On billon and 3rd brass of Gallienus.

Why the figure of a centaur is here employed in association with the legend of Apollo, "the Emperor's preserver," it is difficult if not impossible to discover; unless allusion be meant to the Centaur Chiron, to whom the myth assigns the tutorship of Apollo, and who was said to have been the first to teach the medicinal use of herbs. The signification of the globe and rudder is still more obscure.—There is a coin of Tetricus junior, with a centaur for its type, and the epigraph of SOLI CONSERV. On another base silver coin of Gallienus, with the same legend, the type is a gryphon, or griffin.—According to Philostratus, that monster was sacred to Apollo, or Sol; thus a fabulous animal is seen appositely consecrated to a fabulous deity.—On coins of Aureliopolis, in Lydia (says Eckhel), griffins are represented drawing the chariot of the Sun.

APOL. MONET. (on Silver.)—APOL. MONETAE P. M. TR. P. XV. IMP. VIII. COS. VI. S. C. (on 2nd Brass.)—Apollo naked, stands with his right hand lifted up to the top of his head, his left elbow resting on a column.

Respecting this singular legend, found on coins of Commodus, minted in his sixth consulate—viz., A. U. C. 943, (A. D. 190) Eckhel makes the following remarks:—"Although we find *Juno Moneta*, on coins of the *Carisia* family, and have the testimony of ancient authors to the appropriation of the title to that goddess, and even the reason why it was given, yet such is not the case with the inscription *Apollo Moneta*—a characteristic by which Apollo is distinguished only on the coins of Commodus. Unable to account for this circumstance, I will not spread my sails to the winds of conjecture; for in the same Emperor's mint, appellations are ascribed to deities, which were the offspring solely of the fertile brain of Commodus, who (as Lampridius says) made his alterations and additions in religious matters, rather from caprice than from a serious feeling." (vii. 123.)—Among the larger brass of the following year, we see the same Apollo Moneta repeated.

Apollo's Oracle is named on a coin of Philip the elder.—See EX ORACVLO APOLLINIS.

APOLLINI PROPVG*natori*. (To Apollo the Defender.)—Apollo in the act of discharging an arrow.

Apollo, "God of the silver bow," as the supposed inflicter of sudden death (especially if the deceased was "sun smitten"), as well as the stayer of pestilence, was at the period when this coin was struck regarded with more than usual veneration, on account of the increasing desolation of the plague. This malady seems to have travelled from Ethiopia, and is said to have raged 15 years, destroying incredible numbers of people. Mionnet gives this among the first brass of Valerianus (about A. D. 254); and Akerman among the billon coins of Gallienus; but Eckhel omits to notice it.

APOLLINI SANCTO.—Apollo naked, stands holding a branch in the right hand, and leaning on a column.

Eckhel and Mionnet both give this as from a silver coin of Pescennius Niger. The former pronounces it to have been struck at Antioch, referring as the ground of his opinion to a second brass of Julianus II. which exhibits on one side APOLLONI (sic) SANCTO. (type of Apollo in the stola, with patera and lyre), and on the other, GENIO ANTIOXENI. Apollo is known to have been ranked amongst the principal divinities worshipped by the people of *Antiochia in Syria*.

APOLLINI PAL. or APOL. PALATINO.—Apollo attired in the stola, (see ACT. IMP. p. 5), stands holding the *plectrum* in his right hand, and resting his left on the lyre, which surmounts a short column. On silver and first brass of Commodus.—A brass medallion of the same emperor, has for legend of reverse APOL. PALATINO. P. M. TR. P. XVI. IMP. VIII. COS. VI. P. P. and the type exhibits Apollo, in the same effeminate dress assigned to him in the Actiac denarii of Augustus, holding with his left hand a lyre conjointly with Victory, who stands by his side.——See *Selecta Numismata*, in *Mus. De Camps*, per D. Vaillant, p. 53.

These coins have reference to the temple, which Augustus, whilst as yet bearing no other name than that of Octavianus, erected at Rome, in honour of his guardian divinity in the Palatium, attaching to it, according to Suetonius, a public library. We have the testimony of Dion Cassius, that the date of this event was A. U. C. 718 (B. C. 36.) In alluding to this temple, Propertius describes the idol, its dress, and position, in these words:—

Deinde, inter matrem deus ipse, interque sororem
  Pythius in longâ carmina veste canit.

[And next, between his mother and twin sister, lo! the Pythian God himself, in flowing mantle, sings his lays.]

The fact of his building this temple (says Eckhel, vii. 124, 125,) is further confirmed by the statement of Augustus himself, on the marble of Ancyra. (TAB. iv. v. 1.) TEMPLVMQVE. APOLLINIS. IN. PALATIO – – FECI.—The renown of this *Apollo Palatinus* subsequently received augmentation, on the occasion of the victory gained A. U. C. 723 (B. C. 31), over Antony, at Actium, near the temple of Apollo Actius; Ovid himself ascribing that piece of good fortune to the intervention of this deity, in the following lines:—

"Visite laurigero sacrata Palatia Phœbo.
 "Ille Parætonias mersit in alta rates."
            Ovid. Art. amor. iii. v. 389.

["Go see the Palatia sacred to the laurel-bearing Phœbus.
He it was, who sank in the deep the Parætonian barks."]

The poet uses the word *Parætonias* for *Ægyptias*, from Parætorium a town of Marmarica, which had been added to the dominion of Egypt, and Cleopatra.—And this is the reason why Apollo Palatinus appears in the same garb, viz., the *stola*, as does Apollo Actius on numerous coins of Augustus, the mintage of which comes within the year U. C. 733 (B.C. 21), and also on denarii of the Antistia family, which are found with the legend, APOLLINI. ACTIO.—On a marble, published by Muratori, (p. 1119, i.) appears the following:—SACERDOS. DIANAE. VICTR. ET. APOLLINIS. PALAT*ini*. Zosimus also makes mention of the Palatine temple of Apollo; and Ammianus Marcellinus relates, that during the reign of Julian the Apostate it was destroyed by fire, when the Carmina Cumana had a narrow escape of sharing its fate.

APOL. SALVTARIS or APOLL*ini* SALVTARI. S. C.—Apollo, naked, stands holding in the right hand a branch of laurel, and in his left the lyre; or rests his left on a tripod. On large brass, and in other metal and forms, of Trebonianus Gallus, and Volusianus.

To the misfortunes of preceding reigns, to the internal convulsions of the empire, to the invasions of barbarians, was added the scourge of a terrible pestilence, which ravaged the Roman world, during the reigns of Trebonianus and some of his immediate successors. These princes, tottering on their thrones, invoked in vain, and in succession, those false deities to whom, under the illusions of paganism, they ascribed a power over the health of mortals. The epithet dedicatory to *Apollo*, on this reverse, evidently points to those prayers and vows.—*Leçons Numismatiques*, 231.

Referring to the above coins, Eckhel (vii. 356), also observes, that they were struck about A. D. 254, amidst the raging of that dreadful pestilence, which filled the world with mourning, and when Apollo, as the god presiding over health (*salutis præses*) was invoked by the emperors, and publicly implored by the whole community, for the removal of so universal and destructive a scourge. During this grievous mortality, as Victor expresses it, "Gallus and Volusianus won the favour of Apollo, by the anxious and sedulous attention which they paid to the burials of the most humble individuals."—Appropriately to the legend which propitiates the healing influences of Apollo, a branch of laurel, or of olive, is consecrated to this divinity; for both one and the other were used by the ancients in the ceremony of lustration. Thus Juvenal:

Cuperent lustrari ——— si foret humida laurus.
(Sat. ii. 157.)

And Virgil—
Idem ter socios purâ circumtulit undâ,
Spargens rore levi, et ramo felicis olivæ;
Lustravitque viros, dixitque novissima verba.
(Æneid, vi. v. 229.)

" Old Chorinæus compass'd thrice the crew,
And dipp'd an olive branch in holy dew;
Which thrice he sprinkled round, and thrice aloud
Invok'd the dead, and then dismiss'd the crowd."

Apollo Clarius.———Apollo had an oracle at Claros in Ionia; hence the name Clarius, under which he was worshipped by the people of Colophon, and by the inhabitants of Smyrna.—The image of this Apollo appears on a coin of Gordianus Pius, (in Patin's *col. Impp. Rom.* p.

475,) sitting with laurel in right hand, and the cithara in his left—see Rasche.—Also on an Apamean colonial, struck under M. Aurelius.—See *Apamea.*

Apollo Salutaris.—The healing or healthful Apollo.—On a denarius of Caracalla, having for the legend of its reverse, P. M. TR. P. XVIII.

COS. IIII. P. P. (i. e. Sovereign Pontiff, invested with tribunitian authority for the 18th time, Consul for the 4th time.) Apollo is seated, he holds up a branch of laurel in his right hand, and rests the left arm on his lyre, which is placed on a tripod.

This is one among several coins which were struck during the reign of Caracalla, and which bear direct allusion to the then precarious state of that execrable tyrant's health; racked as his guilty mind was with the pangs and terrors of remorse, at the remembrance of his fratricidal crime. Finding no repose for his affrighted conscience, after the murder of his brother Geta, he bethought himself of imploring the tutelary divinities of health, and accordingly addressed himself to Esculapius and to Apollo.—A similar type of Apollo on a third brass of the same emperor, the legend corresponds also, except in the TR. P. which is xvii.

Apollo Sminthius.——Amongst his various surnames, and distinctive appellations, that of Sminthius was assigned to Apollo, (according to some writers) from the *fact* of his having destroyed, or driven away, the *mice*, by which, before his benevolent interposition, the town of Sminthe, or Sminthium, on the coast of the Troad, had been over-run, and where, out of gratitude, a temple was built to his worship.—Types of the Sminthian Apollo appear on colonial imperial coins of Alexandria Troas, not far from which place Sminthium was situated.—For some notice *(quite* as much as the subject deserves) of what is conflictingly stated by ancient authors, respecting the origin of this epithet as applied to Apollo, by the inhabitants of Asia Minor, see *Doct. Num. Vet.* vol. ii. 480.

Apollo, standing with his lyre, his right hand holding ears of corn, appears on second brass of Claudius Gothicus, with legend SALVS AVG.

The following types of Apollo occur on colonial imperial coins, with *Latin* legends:—

Besides those of Alexandria Troas and Apamea, above noticed, Apollo appears on coins struck in the colony of Cæsarea Palestinæ, under Hadrian, Antonine, and Aurelius—of Corinth, under Commodus—of Patræ, under Nero, Domitian, M. Aurelius, and Commodus—of Deultum, under Maximus Cæsar, and under Gordianus Pius—of Tyre, under Trebonianus Gallus, and Gallienus.

On a third brass of Maximus (son of Maximinus) struck at Deultum, Apollo stands holding a laurel branch in the right hand, and placing with his left a lyre on a tripod. Before his feet is a lighted altar.—["Apollo (says Vaillant, ii. 145,) bears the *laurel*, as consecrated to him on account of his reputed gift of foretelling events—

the laurel tree, according to the Greeks, conferring the *afflatus*, or divine inspiration."]—The
tripod was the ordinary symbol of his oracular
power ; but Apollo's distinguishing tokens were
the *lyre* and the *laurel*.

"Whilst thus I sang, inflam'd with nobler fire,
I heard the great Apollo's tuneful lyre ;
His hand a branch of spreading laurel bore,
And on his head a laurel wreath he wore."

(Ovid, *Art of Love*. Yalden's translation.)

On a second brass of Antoninus Pius, minted
by the colonists of Patræ, Apollo is represented,
naked, standing ; in his right hand he holds a
patera, and rests his left on a lyre, placed on a
cippus.—[Apollo leaning on his lyre, embodies
the harmony of the celestial spheres, on which
account he was called *Musicus* and *Citharoedus*.
Vaillant, i, 72.]—In the last named character
(the lyre-striking Apollo) Nero appears on one
of his first brass coins, habited, as Suetonius
observes, like the statues of the God, with the
cithara in his left hand, and playing it with
his right.

On a second brass of Commodus, struck in
the colony of Patræ, Apollo stands in a female
dress, with his bow in the right hand, opposite
to him stands Venus, holding up a shield with
both hands. [Apollo and Venus were, in fabulous history, the offspring of Jupiter, the former
by Latona, the latter by the nymph Dione.—
Vaillant, i. 216.]

APOLLONIA ILLYRICI, one of the places,
extra urbem, where Roman coins were appointed
to be minted, under the government of the Republic.—See *D. N. V.* vol. v. p. 68.

APOLLODORUS of Damascus, the architect
of Trajan's bridge over the Danube, and of Trajan's Forum.—See FORVM. TRAIANI.—Eckhel,
vol vi, p. 432.

AP. N. *Appii Nepos*—APPIVS, the name of
a highly illustrious Roman race, of Sabine origin
—the stock of the Claudia family, whence sprang
the famous Censor, *Appius Claudius*, who constructed the celebrated public road, called, after
him, the Via Appia.

A. POST, *Aulus Postumius*—prenomen and
name of a man—see *Postumia*.

APOTHEOSIS, that grand ceremony of Paganism, by which its votaries pretended to place
a man, or a woman, amongst the number of their
deities. It was so named by the Greeks, who
first practised the rite, and from whom the Romans, especially under the Emperors, largely
borrowed it, as is testified by their coins.—Called
by the Latins *Consecratio*, it is symbolised on
coins under a triple variety of types, viz., either
by an eagle with expanded wings, or by a lighted
altar, or by the *rogus*, or funeral pile. It is
singular that an example of these three modes of
typifying an *Apotheosis* is exhibited on the coins
of an otherwise unknown young prince. The
funeral pile appears on gold struck in memory of
Nigrinianus, the eagle on his silver, and the
altar on his 3rd brass.

"The farce of the Apotheosis has been ascribed
(remarks Captain Smyth) to a taint of the Py-
thagorean doctrines ; but it obviously originated

in, what Tacitus termed 'the epidemic spirit of
adulation,' long before the Samian was born.—
* * * Neither the veil, nor the portrait, which
was the distinctive mark of deification among
the Romans, nor the other symbols of the Apotheosis, were done away from medals, till *after*
Constantine, when a hand from the clouds bestowing a crown, was substituted." (p. 297.)—
See CONSECRATIO.

APPELLATION (or Title).—In the most
flourishing times of the Empire, nothing was
esteemed more dignified, or more venerable, than
the titles of *Imperator*, *Cæsar*, and *Augustus*.
But as the power of the state decreased, the
power of names became augmented. Roman
princes wished to be called *Domini*, seeing that
the *Imperator* was head of the empire only, whereas the *Dominus* was head of the world. Hence in
the lower series, when, with less real strength of
government, they aimed at appearing to govern
all, they assumed the title of D. N. *Dominus
Noster*—or DD. NN. *Domini Nostri*.—There
was also a period in Rome's decline when, as
their coins shew, Emperors appropriated to
themselves titles or surnames borrowed from
those of heathen deities, and which, conceded
to them by the vile adulation of their contemporaries, have been handed down to modern ages.
Thus we read HERCVLIVS, IOVIVS, &c.—See
Rasche, vol. i., p. 75.

APPLE.—An attribute of Venus, allusive to
the prize obtained from the Trojan Paris. See
the VENERI GENETRICI, of Sabina.—Several
coins of Faustina, junior, also bear Venus with
the apple in her hand among other attributes,
on their reverses.

APPULEIA, or *Apuleia*, a family of the plebeian order, but of Consular rank, whence sprang
the turbulent L. Appuleius Saturninus. Its
(brass) coins, which are rare, present three varieties, and are the *as* or parts of the *as*.

A.P.R.—*A Populo Romano*—or *Auctoritate
Populi Romani*.—By authority of the Roman
People.

A POP. FRVG. AC.—These abbreviated
words, preceded by those of COS. XIIII. LVD.
SAEC. appear on the reverse of a first brass coin
of Domitian. The type represents the emperor
habited in the toga, seated on a *suggestum*.
Before him stand two (or, to speak after more
minuteness of inspection, three) togated figures,

one of whom holds in both hands, a sort of
small sack, out of which he is in the act of pour-

ing grain of fruits. Behind is a temple. On the exergue s. c.

This coin forms one of a set, minted under the prince above-named, A. U. C. 841 (A. D. 88), to commemorate his celebration of the Secular Games. The legend, chiefly owing to the ancient practice of verbal abbreviations, presents a difficulty of no ordinary kind.—Spanheim considers that it is to be explained thus:—A. POP*ulo* FRVG*es* AC*ceptæ*, and that these words are to be referred to the first offerings of fruit, wheat, barley, and beans, which it was customary for the entire people to dedicate, at the commencement of these (the Secular) Games, to the deities who presided over the solemnities, and which on their termination were, as Zosimus observes, distributed amongst the citizens. According, therefore, to the opinion of Spanheim and other writers, it was the *people*, who *received* the fruits, or, to adhere to the phraseology of the coins, by whom the fruits were received ("*fruges acceptæ* sunt.") An author of great learning, Steph. Antonius Morcellus has advanced another mode of explaining the abbreviations, viz., COS. XIIII. LVD*is* SAEC*ularibus* POP*ulo* FRVG*es* AC*cepit*, and expresses his surprise, that it should not have occurred to Spanheim, when that eminent writer, with his usual erudition, has pointed out the allusion to the offering of the first fruits by the Pontifex Maximus to the Gods.—" Perhaps (says Eckhel, vi. 387) Morcellus may have been induced to adopt his reading by the structure of the legend. For in it are expressed only the words—COS. XIIII. LVD. SAEC. without the FEC*it*, which invariably appears on other coins of this mintage. But it might possibly happen, that the word *fecit* was omitted to make room for the rest of the inscription, though it is still necessary to supply (or understand) it; just as on coins of Augustus, struck A. U. C. 737 (B. C. 17), and of the Sanquinia family, we read only AVGVST. DIVI. F. LVDOS. SAE. where *fecit*, though omitted, must nevertheless be supplied. A more probable reason [for Morcellus entertaining his opinion] may have been, that the natural law of the inscription seems to dictate its own proper interpretation. For, as it commences with the nominative case COS. XIIII. the sentence could not terminate with the word AC*ceptæ*, but AC*cepit*. I am (adds Eckhel) far from denying, that on Morcellus's plan of interpretation the legend presents greater elegance and terseness of expression, though I strongly doubt whether it be equally in accordance with truth and facts. For, if we so read it, the recipients of the fruits will be *not* the people, but Domitian himself, and at the hands of the people. Whereas, we have no ancient record of presents made by the people to their princes during the Games in question, but rather of the reverse. As, therefore, such a fact cannot be established, and the very author of the new reading does not attempt to prove it by the slightest argument, we may for the present adhere to the generally received interpretation of the legend, and conclude that the benefit

alluded to was conferred *upon*, and not *by*, the people."

[And yet it is worthy of notice, though seemingly overlooked by the great scrutinizer and critic of numismatic monuments, that in the very type which he has himself described and commented upon (and which is here faithfully copied from a well-preserved specimen in the British Museum) one of the figures personifying the *Populus Romanus* (the entire Roman people) is in the attitude of pouring out a contribution of FRVG*es*, at the base of the raised platform, on which the Emperor, with his right hand outstretched, is seated. Now, with all due willingness to acquiesce generally in what our illustrious guide and master himself defers to, as an *explicatio recepta*, let it nevertheless be permitted us in this instance to hazard a conjecture: viz. that the fruits here evidently offered, were possibly meant to represent those accepted by the emperor on such occasions, at the hands of togated citizens (i. e. men of substance), for the purpose of their being *first* dedicated to the gods, and afterwards distributed amongst the common people—that "*fruges* consumere nati" class, who were content to be the slaves of every imperial tyrant, so that they were allowed to enjoy the "circus and the dole." Be this, however, as it may, we have here, at any rate, on the reverse of a genuine and well-known coin, the typification of *fruges* brought *to* Domitian.]

A. PV. or ARG. PVB.—These abbreviations, found on coins of the Lucilia, Sentia, and Tituria families, are read by some *Argento Puro;* by others, *Aere Publico.*—Eckhel shews *Argento Publico* to be their right interpretation—signifying public money, and allusive to the monetal triumvir, or the edile, or other officer; to whom the money, or the expenditure of it, was entrusted.—See EX. A. PV.; also *Sentia gens.*

APRONIA gens.—Of plebeian origin, but of consular dignity, the third brass coins of this family, struck by the moneyers of Augustus, are common, having for their legend GALLVS MESSALA IIIVIR. SISENNA APRONIVS. A. A. A. F. F. or something similar. There is a first brass of colonial fabric, with the head of Drusus, son of Tiberius, which exhibits for legend PERMISSV. L. APRONII. PROCOS. III. and for type the *head of Mercury.*

AQ. O. B. F.—*Aquileiæ Officinæ Secundæ Fabrica.*—These abbreviations and the two subjoined are found chiefly on coins, in the age from Diocletian to the Constantines, and are interpreted as denoting them to have been struck at Aquileia, in the B or second mint; or struck (generally) in the city of *Aquileia.*—Rasche.

AQ. P. S. *Aquileiæ Pecunia Signata.*—AQ. P. Aquileiæ pecunia—or Aquileiæ percussa.

AQ. S. *Aquileiæ Signata.*—Money struck at Aquileia.

AQUÆ DUCTUS—Aqueduct or water conduit. It signifies a canal or channel, built of stone, or in brickwork, for the purpose of conveying across an uneven country a certain quantity of water, and of giving it a regulated declivity. This species of canal proceeds sometimes underground, sometimes along the surface of the soil, and occasionally upon one or more ranges of arcades. The latter even in their ruins exhibit the most striking features of picturesque grandeur; such as are seen in the *Campagna di Roma*, and in that noble remains of Roman architecture the *Pont du Gard*, at Nismes, in France.—The inhabitants of Rome, for a long time, contented themselves with the stream of the Tiber; but the remoteness of that river from considerable portions of the city, when it was so greatly increased in size, rendered the conveyance of water inconveniently difficult. In the year u. c. 441 (B.C. 313), conduits were planned for bringing a purer as well as a more plentiful supply of this indispensable element, from distant sources. Aqueducts of every kind, visible and subterraneous, were greatly multiplied, and constituted at length one of the wonders of "the Eternal City." In the emperor Nerva's time there were nine Aqueducts, which had 13,594 tunnels or pipes, of an inch in diameter. Subsequently there were 14 channels carried by 9 aqueducts. These structures served to convey water from places 30, 40, and even 60 miles distant from Rome.—Aqueducts were generally distinguished by the name of the place whence the water came, or by that of the person who caused them to be built, joined to the word *aqua*.—For many explanatory and instructive particulars on the subject of aqueducts, as well modern as ancient, see Millin, *Dictionnaire des Beaux Arts*.—Reference may also with advantage be had to an article on this subject, in Dr. W. Smith's *Dict. of Greek and Roman Antiquities*.

AQVA MAR.—Aqua *Marcia*.—This legend appears on a silver coin of the gens Marcia, and alludes to water conveyed to the city of Rome, by the care and liberality of the Prætor Quintus Marcius, a public-spirited citizen. This aqueduct, one of the noblest in Rome, both as to splendour and durability, was constructed under the authority of the Senate, in the time of the Republic. Some authors are disposed to regard the aqua *Marcia*, as the most ancient aqueduct, inasmuch as it was ascribed to *Ancus Marcius*. Whereas the honour is due to the above-named Quintus; or, according to Pliny, it was perfected by him, between A.U.C. 575 and 585 (B.C. 179 and 169), on the foundation of a work commenced by the reputed grandson of Numa. It was afterwards repaired, and enlarged, successively by M. Agrippa, Augustus, Titus, Trajan, and Caracalla. —There still exist remains of this great water course, both within and without the Esquiline gate.—See ANCVS and *Marcia* gens—(*suis locis*).

The aqua *Appia* is the oldest aqueduct, and owes its construction to the censor Appius Claudius. The aqua *Marcia* comes next. The other principal aqueducts at Rome were aqua *Tepula*, aqua *Julia*, aqua *Virgo*, Anio Vetus, aqua *Alsietina* (or Augusta), aqua *Cabra* (or Damnata), aqua *Trajana*, aqua *Alexandrina*, aqua *Antinoniana*. The finest of all was that called aqua *Claudia*, built under the Emperor Claudius. —See Millin's and Dr. Smith's *Dictionaries*, both above referred to.

AQVA. TRAIANA. S. P. Q. R. OPTIMO PRINCIPI. S. C.—The genius of a river reclined within a cavern, or arched vault, holding in his right hand an aquatic reed, and resting his left arm on an urn, whence there is a flow of waters.—On a first and middle brass of Trajan, struck about A.U.C. 864 [A.D. 111].

The rivulet to which this coin refers, after having been long lost, from want of care, was restored by Trajan, and conducted over Mount Aventine, not only for the use of his own baths, but also to supply the wants, to promote the salubrity, and to increase the embellishments of his capital.—Sextus Julius Frontinus, the Consul, who wrote a treatise on aqueducts, supplies abundant testimony of the sedulous attention bestowed by this emperor on the repair and improvement of those at Rome. "It was not (he says) the object of our Prince, merely to restore the volume of water most beneficially to the other streams; but he also was the person to perceive that the deleterious properties of the *Anio Novus* might be cut off." And after describing the plan by which the Emperor proposed to correct this fault, he concludes—This fortunate excellence of the water, bidding fair in quality to equal that of (aqua) *Marcia*, and in quantity to surpass it, supplied the place of that unseemly and turbid stream (the New Anio), under the auspices of the "Imperator, Cæsar Nerva Trajanus Augustus," as the title informs us.—This beneficial measure is recorded on coins, as early as Trajan's sixth consulate.— Eckhel, vi. 425-26.

Capt. Smyth, R.N., in describing a specimen of this medal, in his own collection, observes that the type "is opposed to the notion of Vaillant, that a recumbent *Fluvius* denotes a river which receives other streams, and that wading figures mean those which are tributary. Other antiquaries presume that river to be a navigable one, where the gods have beards—yet here at a mere spring, we have a regular long beard—whilst a reverse of the Emperor Philip shews the deity of the Meander without that appendage." p. 86.

AQUATIC ANIMALS *figured on coins.*— The crocodile or aligator; the dolphin; the hippopotamus, (or river horse); the palamys, (a fish of the tunny kind); the polypus (or many feet); the pompilos, (or nautilus); the sepia, (or cuttle fish); &c., respecting all which see Spanheim— *Dissert. de Præs. Num. Vet.*

AQUILA—and *Aquila legionaria.*—See Eagle.

AQUILEIA, a once famous city, near the Adriatic sea, and the barrier of Italy on that side. In the lower empire it was the capital of the Venetian territory, but was destroyed by the Huns, under Attila, in A.D. 453. It is now only a mass of ruins and hovels, the resort of fishermen.—It was at the siege of this town, by the ferocious Thracian, Maximinus, that the women of Aquileia afforded a memorable instance of courage and devotion; for the cordage belonging to the machines of war being worn out, they all cut off their tresses to supply the defect.—The initial letters of the name as a mint mark frequently occurs on the exergue of Roman coins from Diocletian downwards. See AQ. &c.

AQUILIA SEVERA, second wife of Elagabalus.—This princess, who is described to have possessed great personal attractions, was the daughter of Quintus Aquilius, who had been twice Consul, during the reign of Caracalla. Elagabalus, after repudiating Julia Paula, took Aquilia from the sacred community of the Vestals, and married her, in the year A. D, 220, to the great consternation of both priests and people at Rome.—In a few days, she also was divorced by that wretch of an Emperor, who then took Annia Faustina to wife, and afterwards two other ladies. Tired of the three last, Elagabalus expelled them, each in their turn, from his palace; and profaned afresh the rites of matrimony by again espousing Aquilia Severa. She continued with him till the termination of his monstrous life and most execrable reign, A. D. 222.—The prenomen of *Julia* is added on her coins, she being thereon styled IVLIA AQVILIA SEV. (or SEVERA) AVG.—The Senate enslaved to the imperial will, confirmed to this empress, the title of *Augusta*, which Elagabalus had given her.—All her coins, in each metal and size, are of more or less rarity: in gold of the highest degree.—Some pieces represent her with Elagabalus.

AQUILIA gens.—This Roman house had two branches, one Patrician, the other Plebeian. Amongst the 12 varieties given in Morel, there are some curious types on the denarii of this family; take the following reverse for example:—MAN. AQVIL. MAN. F. MAN. N. *(Manius Aquilius, Manii Filius, Manii Nepos.)* The type, a soldier standing, armed with a buckler, lifting up, or holding up, a kneeling woman: below is the word SICIL, (Siciliæ).—Eckhel, v. 142.

In this silver coin, and in another with the same type, reference is made to the historical fact, that Manius Aquilius (of the *patrician* stock) was consul in the year U.C. 654, (B.C. 101) and with his colleague C. Marius (COS. V.) was sent to Sicily, during the war of the Italian fugitives. That war he succeeded in bringing to a victorious termination, and having peacefully governed the province for two years, returned in triumph to Rome. See the word SICIL.

There are other types of the Aquilia family, struck by L. Aquilius Florus (who was of its *plebeian* stock) as a monetal triumvir of Augustus, about the year of Rome 734 (B.C. 20)—as for example the following

Obv.—CAESAR AVGVSTVS.—Bare head of Augustus.
Rev.—L. AQVILLIVS FLORVS IIIVIR.—A flower.

By this elegant type of an opened flower, (probably, from its form, the Cyanus), Lucius Aquillius alludes to the origin of the surname which he had derived from his ancestors.—Havercamp, in *Morell*.

Two other denarii, struck by the same Florus, possess historical interest; viz., such as bear the symbols of *Armenia Capta*, and of the *Military Ensigns recovered from the Parthians.*—See ARMENIA CAPT. and SIGNIS RECEP*tis*.

The coins of this family are in silver only, and of a low degree of rarity.

AQUILIFER—Eagle bearer. It was he, as the word imports, who carried the Eagle, in the midst of the *hastati*, in each Legion. The *aquiliferi* were different from those who were called *signiferi*, and who bore the other standards of the Roman army. (See *Signa Militaria*) Among other reverses, which, with the legends of *Adlocutio, Profectio, Imperator,* &c., frequently appear on coins of the Imperial series, chiefly in large brass, there is one of Trajan's described by Captain Smyth, p. 89, where "the Emperor, wearing a *lorica* (or breast plate) is seated on an X shaped curule chair, upon a high suggestum. He is addressing his army, which is represented by an officer, three *aquiliferi*, an infantry soldier, and one of cavalry—some of whom hold up their hands in applause.—The coin was struck A.D. 115."

ARA.—This word, and the word *Altare* (whence the French *autel*, and our English *Altar*), were used by the Romans, to signify respectively certain structures, elevated above the ground, at the former of which prayers, with libations, were offered up, and at the latter of which victims were immolated, to their Gods.

As regards pagan antiquity, the first inventor of Altars is unknown; but the custom of raising them for religious purposes evidently passed from the Greeks to the Romans. The Greeks had probably borrowed it from the Egyptians, to whom Herodotus ascribes the original adoption of Altars, and the dedication of images in honour of their deities. Holy Writ here steps in to the aid of historical truth; and teaches us that Noah, a worshipper of the Only True God, was the first who built an altar.

ARÆ—ALTARS, among the ancients, differed in their uses, their forms, their adornments, and the situations in which they were placed. They were sometimes round, but the square more generally prevailed. Their forms varied again according to their material. The metallic ones were for the most part of the triangular shape. The greater portion of those, however, which have escaped the ravages of time are of marble, or of other stone. Their height varied much; some did not exceed two feet; others were about as high again.—Those intended to receive the libations, as well as those designed to hold the blood of victims, were hollowed out at the top, and a moveable stove, or pan, served occasionally to contain the fire for burning incense.—On festivals, when prepared for sacrifice, they were dressed with festoons of flowers, fruits, and grasses, called *verbenæ;* also with the leaves, or branches of such trees or plants as were sacred to each of the different divinities.—Nor was the sculptor's art omitted to be employed in the more durable enrichment of Altars. We see on them basso relievos, representing the heads of sacrificed animals, figures of pateras, vases, and other sacrificial instruments, mingled with those of garlands *(coronæ)* that decorated the victim, and with woollen fillets, and other accessories of the same kind. Not a few are seen charged with inscriptions that mark the epocha and motives of their consecration, added to the names of those who caused them to be erected, and of the god, goddess, genius, or deified mortal, who happened to be the object of this devotional act. The finest of these are embellished with figures and attributes of the particular object of idolatrous worship. Indeed, from the sculptural ornaments of a Roman altar, may almost invariably be ascertained, what deity it had been intended to honour. For example, the eagle and the thunder bolt *(aquila et fulmen),* designated *Ara Jovis.* A trident and two dolphins marked an altar to Neptune. A Bacchante with the *thyrsus,* a panther, or a foliage of ivy leaves, shewed the *Bacchi Ara.* Olive leaves and sometimes the Owl were carved on those of Minerva. The raven, the stag, the lyre, or a tripod, indicated a consecration to Apollo, on whose altars laurel branches were also distinctive insignia. A serpent entwined round a staff, or a tripod, points to Esculapius, or Hygeia, or other divinities supposed to preside over health. Diana's altar is to be known by the goddess's own image, or by her attributes the bow, arrow, and quiver, sometimes with the accompaniments of the stag and the dog. A square altar, ornamented with the figures of two stags, and with festoons of ribbands, appears on a silver medallion of Augustus, bearing the legend of AVGVSTVS. [This medallion, says

Mionnet, was struck in Asia.] The myrtle and the dove revealed the Altar of Venus; the poplar, the club, or some representation connected with the story of his labours, are peculiar to altars at which Hercules was adored; the pinetree is given to Pan; and a bacchanal to Silenus. The altars of Ceres were known by their corncars and poppies, also by the image of the goddess, holding two torches, in a biga of dragons. The lotus bespake the devotee of Serapis; and the cypress tells us that Roman superstition dictated propitiatory sacrifices even to the *infernal* gods; whose altars, however, were assigned to subterraneous places.—See *Dictionaries* of Millin and Smith, article ARA.

Moreover, it was before Altars, that in touching and sacrificing upon them, both kings and peoples swore to keep treaties of peace, amity, and alliance; that magistrates took oaths of fidelity, and that individuals pledged themselves, in their reconciliations and their marriages.—See FOEDUS CVM. GABINIS—VOTA PUBLICA, &c.

Within the temples, the principal *Ara* was placed in the most sacred recess, at the foot of the statue of the deity worshipped there. This was the most elevated, and for that reason called *Altare:* on this incense and perfumes were burnt and libations made. The second was placed on the outside before the portal of the edifice, and was used for sacrifices in which blood was shed. The third was a portable altar, named *Anclabris,* on which were deposited the viscera of slaughtered animals for the Haruspices to inspect, together with the instruments of immolation. There was yet another class of altars, which stood by themselves, apart from any temple, and were distinguished by the name, and sometimes by the figure, of the *numen* or *genius* to whom it was consecrated.

On Roman coins, we find *Altars* dedicated to Æternity, *Bonus Eventus,* Concord, Fecundity, Fortune, (see FORT. RED. of Augustus,) *Genius,* Health, Liberty, *Piety,* Peace, (see PACI. PERP. of Tiberius,) Providence, Security, Tranquillity, Youth, (as in *Princeps Juventutis* of Domitian, (see No. 226 of Caylus).—They appear also on coins of the Antia, Cornelia, Oppia, Pomponia, Postumia, Rubria, and Vibia families. As for emperors and empresses, they are represented sacrificing at *Altars* throughout nearly the entire series, from Augustus to Licinius.

Aræ Consecrationis.—Altars of Consecration; some round, others square, with flame rising from the top, are seen on coins, round which we read CONSECRATIO. Also an altar over which is inscribed DIVO. PIO. &c., designating the apotheosis of Antoninus Pius. A consecration medal of Aurelius, in silver and large brass, exhibits an eagle with expanded wings, standing on a small square structure,—Capt. Smyth thinks this "probably represents the casket in which the ashes of Aurelius were transported from Germany to Rome. It is often, he adds, notwithstanding its shape, called an altar—but, as with the *Altare Viaticum* of Roman Catholic saints, it may have served both purposes."—On other consecration coins a branch is placed in the middle of the altar, on which an eagle sits with a garland in its beak; or, an eagle stands on a thunderbolt, accompanied by the words AETERNAE MEMORIAE, as on coins of Gal. Maximianus—or two eagles standing on each side of a lighted altar, with MEMORIA FELIX, as in Constantius Chlorus.—See *Memoriæ Felix.*

[The above wood-cut is from the reverse of a middle brass of Faustina senior, minted after her death and consecration; as is designated by the veiled portrait and the DIVA of the obverse legend.]

Aræ Ignitæ.—Lighted altars, some square, but more frequently round; some simply by themselves; others, before which the Emperor stands opposite the genius of a province or city, are found on coins of Hadrian.—See ADVENTVI AVG. ACHAIAE, BITHYNIAE, &c., &c.—Also, before which a female veiled, and in the stola, stands dropping incense into the flame, as on a gold coin of Sabina, and a PIETAS AVG. of Faustina senior, in first brass.—See *Acerra*, p. 4.

Ara Lugdunensis.—Altar of Lyon.—Numerous medals were struck, of which many varieties are extant, in large and middle brass, dedicated to the honour of Augustus, about the year of Rome 741 (B. C. 13), and afterwards to that of Tiberius, the reverses of which represent an altar, stated to have been raised to "Rome and to Augustus" by sixty Gaulish nations, at the confluence of the Rhone and the Saone.—This altar is

Ara Maxima Herculis. The great altar of Hercules.—A very rare denarius of the *Antia* gens has for the legend of its reverse, RESTIO, and for type, a lighted, or ignited, altar. Its obverse exhibits the name of C. ANTIUS, and the head of a bull, ornamented with the sacrificial *infulæ.* Comparing this coin with another of the same family, on which a naked Hercules is carrying his club uplifted in one hand, and a trophy in the other, Eckhel is of opinion, that the altar called *Maxima* at Rome, dedicated to the above-named demigod is here represented. The C. Antius Restio, whose appellations are inscribed on this coin, was, according to Eckhel, *not* the Restio, who carried a sumptuary law, before Sulla's death, A. U. C. 670 (B. C. 84), but the son of that legislator, who after his father's death took occasion, by this denarius, to honour the memory of a man so thoroughly attached to the spirit of the ancient commonwealth.—See *Antia* in Morell. *Thesaur.* fig 2 and 3.

Ara Providentiæ.—The altar of Providence is found on many coins of Augustus, and his successors in the empire, with the letters PROVIDENT. S. C.—The Romans dedicated temples to Providence as a divinity, and raised altars to her worship.—See PROVIDENTIA.

Ara Salutis Augusti—Altar for the Emperor's health and safety.—This type, seen on a very rare large brass of Tiberius, with the inscription SALUS AUGUSTI, was struck on the occasion of prayers being put up for the health of that emperor, especially at the commencement of his reign, when numerous altars smoked for the same purposes both at Rome and in the provinces.—See SALUTI AUGUSTI.

ARA PACIS. (or ARA PAC.) S. C.—On the reverse of a middle brass of Nero, is this inscription, with the type of a lighted altar, dedicated to *Peace*, which that emperor affected to cherish. Similar altars had been erected by a decree of the senate, in the reign of Augustus.

typified as standing between two columns, surmounted by Victories, and palm branches. On the face of the altar, two Genii support a crown placed between two pine-trees—or on other specimens of the same coin (as in the above cut), a laurel crown flanked with palm branches. Below is the inscription ROM*ae* ET AV*Gusto*. The columns of this altar have been sawn in two (says Millin in his *Gal. Mythologique*); and at this time form the pillars, which support the vaulting of the choir, in the church of Aisnay, near Lyon.—See ROM. ET AVG. in this Dictionary.

"It is (says Eckhel), a fact incontrovertible, that Nero preferred peace to the tumultuous scenes of war; from no love, on his part, however, of the blessings which peace bestows, but because it enabled him, with greater security, to pass his leisure in the amusements of the circus, and to have money in his treasury wherewith to join sea to sea, excavate mountains, and lay down monstrous foundations beneath the waters. We have accurate testimony, that, when hard pressed by the revolt of Vindex in Gaul, and at a time of the greatest necessity for levying troops, to be sent against the rebels, certain senators, after a hasty consultation, on the business for which he had summoned them, passed the rest of the day, in discussing the merits of some hydraulic engines of a novel construction, [the form of one of these is considered to be shown on a contorniate medal of Nero, having for legend of reverse LAVRENTI NIKA.] And that the Emperor declared his intention to introduce these novelties at the theatre, ' if Vindex would let him,' *(si per Vindicem liceret)*. The calendars of Amiternum and Præneste, as well as the poet Ovid, respectively allude to the ARA PACIS, as first raised, by senatorial authority, under Augustus, and dedicated four years afterwards."—vi. 268.

ARA PVDIC.—*(Ara Pudicitiæ*—The altar of Modesty or Chastity.)—This legend and type appear on gold and silver coins of the highest rarity, struck in Trajan's sixth consulate (about the beginning of A. D. 113), in honour of his wife Plotina.

Obv. PLOTINA. AVG. IMP. TRAIANI. *Plotina Augusta* (by implication *Uxor) Imperatoris Trajani.* Head of the Empress Plotina.

Rev. CAES. AVG. GERMA. DAC. COS. VI. P.P. (Trajan's Imperial and Consular titles.) An oblong square altar, on which is sculptured a stolated figure, standing on an oval base, which rests on three feet. At the bottom of the altar is inscribed ARA PVDIC.

In the earliest ages of Rome there stood in the city two shrines with an altar in each, one consecrated to *Pudicitia Patricia*, in the *Forum Boarium*, or ox market, the other to *Pudicitia Plebeia*, erected by Virginia, in the *Vicus Longus*, or high street. At these, it seems, none had the privilege of sacrificing, except a matron of thoroughly approved character for the peculiarly feminine qualities, and conjugal virtues, of chastity and modesty, and had been married but to one man. The name and antiquity of one of these altars are mentioned by Juvenal :—

Maura PUDICITIAE veterem cum præterit ARAM.
(*Sat.* vi.)

[When Maura passes the ancient *Altar* of *Pudicitia.*]

or, to give the purport of the allusion more amply from Gifford's free translation,

Flushed in her cups, "as Tullia homeward goes, With what contempt she tosses up her nose At Chastity's hoar fane! What impious jeers Collatia pours in Maura's tingling ears."

The altar dedicated to *Patrician* modesty was the more ancient of the two, and probably the scene of that nocturnal impurity, to which the Roman satirist adverts.

Of Plotina, whose name and portrait appear on the coins which bear this unique legend, Pliny the younger, addressing himself to her

husband, thus expresses himself:—"You have gained a wife, who will prove your ornament and glory. For what can be more sacred than her character ? What more of the old school ? How quiet is she in her attire ! How moderate in her retinue ! How homely in her deportment !" This eulogium, by such a writer, on the purity of her life, shews the appropriateness of the legend, *Ara Pudicitiæ*, joined to the name of Plotina. Yet it appears from Dion Cassius, that even this virtuous characteristic of the empress was subjected to aspersions, in consequence of her intimacy with Hadrian.

[It is to the kindness of its present possessor, the Rev. Wm. Grigson, rector of Whinburgh, Norfolk, that the compiler of this Dictionary is indebted for being enabled to exhibit here the *fac simile* engraving of a most rare and elegant denarius; found amongst a mass of about 300 other Roman Imperial coins, in silver and brass, ranging from Marcus Antonius to Marcus Aurelius. This discovery was made in the month of November, 1820, by some labourers who were employed in forming a clay pit, on an estate belonging to the Rev. B. Barker, in the village of Caston, three miles south-east of Watton, in the above named county. Full particulars relative to this "find" were communicated in March of the following year to the Society of Antiquaries; and the coins themselves at the same time submitted to the inspection of the then Director, Taylor Combe, Esq. for the information of that learned Body, by Goddard Johnson, Esq. now of Norwich, at that period residing at Little Dunham.—Mr. Combe, in his official report to the society, says : "The Plotina is perhaps the only denarius of that Empress, with the legend of ARA. PVDIC., which has been found in England. The coin is not indeed new; but it is one of considerable rarity, and has never, I believe, been accurately engraved."—See *Archæologia*, vol. 20, March 15, 1821, whence this account has been drawn up.

The only already published engraving of this denarius appears, in Vaillant, *Præst. Num. Impp.* (p. 135, Paris edition, 1694, and T. ii. 130, Rome edition, 1743). The reverse in these exhibits a square altar, without any figure, or ornament, on its face, and in other respects unlike the type in Mr. Grigson's specimen.]

ARABIA, one of the largest regions of Asia, between Egypt and India, divided nominally into three parts—*Felix, Deserta,* and *Petræa:* bounded by Syria and Mesopotamia on the north ; by the Persian Gulf on the east; by the Arabian Gulf or Red Sea on the west; and by the Indian Ocean *(Erythræum Mare),* on the south.—"Araby the Blest," the most extensive of the three divisions, derived its name from its great fertility.—Arabia *the desert,* the smallest and northernmost district, was inhabited by the Idumæans, the Moabites, the Midianites, and the Amalekites. It includes "that great and terrible wilderness," in which the Israelites held their wandering abode for a period of forty years after their *exodus* from Egypt. The Romans appear to have been unacquainted with that district.—Arabia the Rocky, which lies centrally, running from north-west to south-east, is towards its northern extremity sterile and scantily populated, but, in approaching the southern portion, plains are found to be fertile and cultivated. The Romans, under Augustus, sent troops into this last-named part of Arabia, but failed in their attempt to make a conquest of it, at that period; and the Arabs remained unsubdued till the time of Trajan.

Spanheim in his annotated translation of the Cæsars of Julian (pr. 88), cites and delineates a very rare first brass of Trajan, in the French king's cabinet, on the reverse of which the bust of a woman is represented, with towers on her head, and two infant children in her arms, which he considers to designate respectively Arabia Felix and Arabia Petræa. The legend gives the name and titles of Trajan in *Greek*, and below is the word ARABIA in *Latin* characters; "doubtless (adds Spanheim), to mark the fact, that this emperor, after having subdued the country, had made it a Roman province, as appears from other well-known medals."—See *Arab. Adquisita*, &c.

ARAB. ADQ. S. P. Q. R. OPTIMO PRINCIPI.—A woman standing, with a branch in the right hand, a reed in the left; at her feet a diminutive camel (on other coins an ostrich.) On a denarius of Trajan.

ARAB. ADQVIS. S. P. Q. R. OPTIMO PRINCIPI. S. C.—Same type—on first and second brass, of the same Emperor.

Coins with the above types and inscriptions, bear the date, on their obverse, of Trajan's fifth consulship, contemporaneous with A. U. C. 858 (A. D. 105.) It was up to that period, from the age of Augustus, who (B.C. 24), by his lieutenant Aelius Gallus, unsuccessfully attempted the conquest of Arabia, that it remained undisturbed by the Roman Arms. The same enterprize, however, was undertaken with a more fortunate result, by Trajan, who, according to Eutropius, reduced it to the state of a province.—It appears that A. Cornelius Palma, governor of Syria, was the commander of this expedition. Dion fixes the time: viz. that when the Emperor went out to the second Dacian war. And the Chronicle of Eusebius, as well as the Alexandrine Chronicle, more definitely teaches us, that the Petræan Arabs and the people of Bostra, computed their æra from the year of Rome 858. The coins in question, therefore, as records of *Arabia Adquisita*, are ascribed to the above-mentioned year, but without excluding the following one.—That part

of Arabia, however, which was occupied by the Romans, bore but a small proportion to the immense tract of territory above named. It was, in fact, that portion which bordered on Judæa, and called Petræa, as some say, from its principal city *Petra*.

With regard to the figure of an animal at the foot of the personified province, as in the above cut (from a first brass coin in the British Museum), it is evident from coins of the Aemilia and Plautia families, and also from Greek coins inscribed with the word APABIA, that it is the camel—an animal common in Arabia, and therefore an appropriate symbol of that region. The ostrich is no less evidently represented on another coin of Trajan, bearing the same legend, and is also a bird indigenous to the same country. Tristan conjectures that what the woman holds in her right hand is a branch of frankincense; and in her left a reed, or sweet cane, called *calamus odoratus* (or aromaticus), both which, according to ancient writers, were products of Arabia. In this opinion, Spanheim concurs, whose instructive remarks on this point deserve perusal by the students of natural history.—See also Eckhel, vi. 420.

ARAB. ADIAB.—*(Arabicus, Adiabenicus.)* COS. II. P.P.—Victory marching—appears on a gold coin of Septimius Severus.—ARAB. ADIABENIC. Same type, on a denarius of that Emperor.

The above inscriptions serve to record the reduction of the Arabs once more to the Roman yoke, by the warlike prince on whose coins they occur. In adding a new territory to Arabia, Severus rendered it a province of considerable extent, and thereon founded his pretensions to the surname of *Arabicus*. So says Ruffus, in his abridged History of the Roman Empire. "Septimius Severus, acerrimus Imperator, *Arabas interiores obtinuit, et Arabiam Provinciam fecit.*" In adverting to the titles of Arabicus and Adiabenicus, conferred on Severus, for his successes A.D. 195, and to their introduction also on his coins, Eckhel, (vii. 172) says—"As far as my information goes, they are found only on coins of the third Tribuneship (TR. P. III.) but ancient marbles blazon them later and more frequently; and in one inscription published by Muratori, they are joined with the words IMP. IIII." In reference to the two nations above-named, Spartianus affirms, that "he received the submission of the Arabians, and compelled the Adiabeni to become tributary."—See PART. ARAB. PART. ADIAB.

ARATRUM. The Plough. This well-known implement of agriculture appears on numerous Roman coins, as indicating the fertility and cultivation of the soil. Ceres being, as the ancients believed and as Ovid sang, the first *quæ unco terram demovit aratro*, is depicted with the plough and with similar instruments of husbandry. Thus the *aratrum Cereris* is seen on coins of the Vibia family; it also occurs over the head of Africa, in the *Cæcilia* and *Eppia* gentes. The plough was a distinguishing symbol of Roman colonies, in allusion to the ceremony of making therewith the circuit of a city, or settlement, about to be founded, in order that its locality or boundaries might be precisely marked out. Hence we see on colonial coins, the labourer, or the priest, guiding a plough, drawn by a yoke of oxen.

ARBORES.—Trees, peculiar to certain countries, serve on medals as the respective symbols, or *insignia*, of those countries. For example, the *palm*, of Judæa, Damascus, Tyre, Alexandria, and of the Phœnician colonies in Sicily and Spain. The *frankincense* and the *balsam* shrubs denoted Arabia.—On coins of the Pomponia family we see the *fig*-tree.—The *olive* " inter duos lapides Tyri" appears on colonial medals of Gordianus Pius and Valerianus. In like manner, a tree behind the figure of Diana signifies that she is the goddess of forests and groves. Three nymphs changed into *larch trees* are exhibited on a coin of the Accoleia gens. (See p. 3.)—For the type of a tree on which hang the spoils of the Nemæan lion—see HERC. COMMODIANO.—Two trees are seen on a medal of Vespasian.—And on many coins, chiefly colonial, of the emperors, from Nero to Gallienus, *trees* form in part, or wholly, the types of their reverses.—See Rasche, *Lex. Num.*

ARCADIUS (Flavius), son of Theodosius the Great, and of Flacilla, was born in Spain about A. D. 377—declared Augustus by his father (A. D. 383), whom he succeeded, as Emperor of the

East (395), he abandoning all claims to the empire of the West, in favour of his brother Honorius. Arcadius died at Constantinople A. D. 408. Himself of an equally weak and contemptible character, his government was quite as disgraceful, and nearly as calamitous, as that of his brother. An odious favourite of his father's named Rufinus, early exercised an absolute authority over the effeminate person and imbecile mind of Arcadius. It was under the administration of this avaricious traitor, that the provinces were oppressed with exactions, and laid waste by barbarian invaders. But he met his death (A. D. 395) under horrible circumstances, in the presence of the emperor, from the troops of Gainas the Goth, whom Stilico, the general of Honorius, had charged with the plan of his destruction. Eutropius and Eudoxia afterwards held divided sway over the indolent and feeble Arcadius; until the audacious eunuch fell a victim to the revenge of the empress. The unsuccessful revolt of Gainas, whose conspiracy cost him his life (A. D. 401) and Eudoxia's cruel persecution of the venerable Chrysostom, soon followed by her own decease, form the only remaining incidents of importance in the disastrous annals of this most incapable prince,—

" In the 31st year of his age, after a reign (if, says Gibbon, we may abuse that word) of thirteen years, three months, and fifteen days, Arcadius expired in the palace of Constantinople."

The name and titles of this Emperor on his coins (which in every metal, of the ordinary module, are common) always read, D. N. ARCADIVS. P. F. AVG. (very rarely AVGVSTVS)—his head encircled with a diadem of pearls.—The bust is also seen clothed in the paludamentum. On a medallion of pure gold, and of the largest size, published by Vaillant, from the French cabinet, Arcadius is so represented, holding in his left hand a globe surmounted by the small figure of Victory, extending a wreath towards the Emperor.—On the reverse of this splendid piece, Arcadius is represented full-faced, and adorned with the *nimbus*, standing with globe in his left hand, and the right hand elevated, in a triumphal car, drawn by six horses. The legend GLORIA ROMANORVM. In the field, the monogram of Christ. On the exergue CO. OB.—See *Præst. Impp. Rom.* III. 262.

ARCHITECTURE.—The Romans, who are considered to have imbibed from the Etruscans their first notions of the science of building, were in point of taste very inferior to the Greeks. They had however the merit of cultivating, with a high degree of success, the ornamental branch of the art, and also of realising plans for publicly useful structures, which were neglected by their more inventive contemporaries. Under the kings, especially the last two or three, several works of essential importance to the salubrity and convenience of their city, such as the *cloacæ* or common sewers, were begun and completed. During the republic, Rome was embellished with many temples, aqueducts, and other buildings, some of them on a large scale. And, at a later period of the commonwealth, Greek architects were employed there, in designing, and directing the progress of, magnificent edifices, both public and private.—Pompey raised the first Theatre of stone, at Rome, which was about the same time indebted to Julius Cæsar for some fine specimens of architectural skill.—Under the long and pacific reign of Augustus, great improvements took place. It was he who built the portico to which was given the name of his sister Octavia; the Forum Novum, and the temple of Mars Ultor ; the basilica in honour of Caius and Lucius ; the temple of Apollo ; the splendid mausoleum destined to receive his own ashes; and the theatre of Marcellus also, were successively reared by his direction. Augustus likewise caused several harbours to be formed in Italy and various other parts of the Roman dominions ; besides restoring the Flaminian way, and other public roads.—The edifices raised by relatives and friends of this celebrated Prince were, a temple of Hercules Musagetes, by Marcius Philippus [see MARCIA gens] ; a temple of Diana by L. Cornuficius [see CORNVFICIA gens] ; a temple of Saturn, by Munatius Plancus ; the Atrium Libertatis, by Asinius Pollio [see ASINIA gens] ; the temples of Concord, and Castor and Pollux, by Tiberius ; and an amphitheatre by

Statilius Taurus. Agrippa, the son-in-law of Augustus, adorned the city, with new aqueducts, fountains, basins, baths, and above all with the Pantheon.—After the great conflagration at Rome, Nero, in whose reign it took place, and to whose spirit of incendiarism it has been ascribed, engaged the services of the ablest architects, to rebuild many edifices ; and those of the Grecian School were principally employed in erecting his golden palace, described as an object of surpassing richness, both in materials and in decorations.   On a first brass of Nero we see a representation, not unworthy of that beautiful arch, adorned with statues and surmounted by a triumphal quadriga, accompanied with symbols of Victory, which Tacitus affirms to have been decreed A.U.C. 811 (A.D. 58) to that Emperor, and raised on the mount of the Capitol, in honour of the pretended successes, but real defeats, of Pætus, Nero's general in Armenia, employed

against the Parthians.   This was ordered by the Senate whilst the war was still pending ; nor, adds the Roman historian (Ann. xv. 18) was the work discontinued when the disastrous event became known.—The chief architectural undertaking of Vespasian, was his truly magnificent Amphitheatre, the first of that kind constructed of stone, but left for the elder and worthier of his sons to finish.—Amongst the works of his successors were—the triumphal arch of Titus; the naumachia and forum, commenced by Domitian, and finished by Nerva, who himself caused much to be accomplished in the department of aqueducts.—Trajan's reign was distinguished by the grandeur and elegance of the structures built under his auspices.   Of these the basilica, the forum, the column, and the triumphal arch, that bear his name, were the most remarkable, and they form types on his coins.

But of Hadrian it is, on all hands, admitted that no Emperor, more extensively or more munificently than he, devoted attention, authority, and means, to the construction of public buildings.   Not to speak of the restoration and embellishment of numerous cities in the provinces and colonies of the empire, the Mausoleum Hadriani and the Pons Aelius at Rome, (still extant under the names of the castle and the bridge of St. Angelo, though unrepresented on any coin of genuine antiquity,) together with the ruins of his extra-urban villa, are works that attest the splendid triumph of architecture in that prince's reign.

Under Antoninus Pius are to be noted his temple of Faustina, and also the column of that Em-peror.—Marcus Aurelius caused several temples and other public buildings to be erected in Rome, and many more in the provincial districts of his wide dominions.—After this period, namely that of the Antonines, " Architecture, (as Millin observes) like the empire, declined.   Of this we have proof in the triumphal arch of Septimius Severus, yet that prince loved and encouraged the art.   Under Alexander Severus, skilful builders—men of genius—met with patronage, and many edifices were constructed or restored.   But the science had deteriorated, and the increasing troubles of the empire prevented it from regaining any portion of its former purity.   At length, when Constantine established the seat of government at Byzantium, and when the hordes of the north poured themselves, in perpetual incursions, over the finest portions of the Roman territories, then architecture, properly so called, became extinct ; and instead of ornamenting and improving cities, nothing was thought of but the construction of fortresses."

Coins, both consular and imperial, have preserved to us the memory of many public edifices which existed, and some of which still exist, in Rome.—The *Basilica Aimilia* (see. p. 31) is represented on a denarius of that family.   The *Macellum*, or market-place, of Augustus, re-

built by Nero, forms the reverse of one type of that emperor's large brass coins, from which the annexed cut is copied.   The *colossæum*, or amphitheatre, begun by Vespasian, is figured on a large brass of Titus, and repeated on medals of succeeding emperors (see p. 42).—The *Basilica Ulpia*, the *Forum Trajani*, and the *Columna Trajana*, appear on gold, silver, and brass of that prince.   The temple dedicated to Faustina senior and Antoninus Pius, and the Antonine Pillar are also typified on contemporaneous coins.   (See DIVO PIO.)—It is, indeed, through the medium of numismatic monuments that we are made acquainted with the exterior forms of heathen temples; the princes, peoples, and cities of the ancient world, being accustomed frequently to adopt representations of these, their sacred, edifices, as types for their money.—See the words *Arcus, Aedes,* *Basilica, Columna, Forum, Templum,* and the woodcuts which respectively illustrate them.

Arcus, the bow, a weapon of the chase, and a symbol of Diana, which as the goddess of hunting, she sometimes holds in her right, at other times in her left hand.   This is shewn on coins of the Imperial series, as in Titus, Nerva, Crispina, Trebonianus Gallus, Aemilianus, Valerianus,

Postumus, &c. The bow and quiver behind the head of Diana appear on a medal of Antoninus Pius.

Arcus Apollinis.—The bow is frequently one of the insignia of Apollo, whence that deity was called by the poets [see Ovid, L. i. *Metem.*] *Arcitenens.* The bow as an attribute of Apollo is seen on coins of M. Aurelius, Gallus, Volusianus, Valerianus.

Arcus Herculis.—The bow of Hercules, with his club, and arrow, occurs on coins of the Curtia and Domitia families—also in the hands of the demigod, as in the Poblicia and Antonia families. It appears likewise on Imperial coins, as in Antoninus, L. Verus, Commodus, S. Severus, Aemilianus, Postumus, Diocletianus, Maximianus, Val. Severus.

Arcus Triumphalis. The triumphal arch.—This kind of monument consists of grand porticoes, erected at the entrance of cities, or across streets, or upon bridges, and public roads, either to the honour of a conqueror, or in remembrance of some important event. Most of these are charged with inscriptions dedicated to the individual who had been decreed to deserve the pre-eminently high distinctions of the Roman triumph. As an architectural invention—if indeed the appropriation of such isolated objects to the glory of individuals, may be termed an invention—the merit of designing and constructing triumphal arches belongs exclusively to the genius of ancient Rome. The first that were built, in the time of the Republic had, however, nothing of the magnificent or of the decorative about them. And for a long time they exhibited the simple form of the half circle, on the top of which were placed trophies and the statues of the victorious generals. Afterwards the dimensions of these arches were greatly increased; and they were more or less covered with ornaments of every description. The mass of their construction formed a square pierced with three arcades, which received not only inscriptions but bas reliefs, and which supported equestrian statues, chariots and horses, with other objects of a kind assimilated to the character and design of the memorial itself.

The *arch of Constantine* is the most considerable and the best preserved of all the existing monuments of that kind at Rome.—The *arch of Septimius Severus* resembles that of Constantine, or rather, it should be said, the latter resembles the former. The *arch of Titus*, much earlier in date, and more historically interesting, is of inferior architectural consideration compared with the two preceding ones. But though the three structures above named are still to be seen in a more or less satisfactory state of preservation, yet only one of them, namely that of Severus, is represented on any coin, whilst on the other hand, the types of many triumphal arches destroyed ages back, appear (like that of Nero above engraved) on genuine products of the Roman mint.

Arch of Septimius Severus.—The annexed cut is engraved from the cast of a very rare denarius, obligingly transmitted to the author

of this work, in 1851, by Mr. Doubleday, of the British Museum, soon after he had made a purchase of the original for the medal department of that Institution.

Obv.—SEVERVS PIVS. AVG. laureated head of the Emperor.

Rev.—COS. III. P.P.—Triumphal arch.

Arches of Augustus.—A silver coin of Augustus, the reverse of which bears the legend L. VINICIVS (one of his monetal triumvirs) has for its type a triumphal arch of a peculiar form. It consists of a grand arcade, flanked by two columns, which support an entablature, surmounted by an attic, on which is inscribed S. P. Q. R. IMP. CAES. and on the top is the imperial quadriga. On either side of the central arch are two square portals of smaller size, with a pediment, and a column at the two extremities, each surmounted by a statue.

In *Morell. Thesaur.* under the head of the Pomponia family, we see a second colonial brass struck at Corinth and dedicated to Augustus, on the reverse of which is a most elegant arch, with a large portal in the centre and two smaller ones on each side of it, surmounted by a triumphal quadriga and victories crowning the Emperor. Havercamp considers this to represent the arch erected at Corinth, either on the occasion of his entry into that city, or on account of the victory at Actium.

But amongst other triumphal arches represented on coins of Augustus, the most remarkable, perhaps, as well for its incription as its type, is that which was raised in memory of the victory gained over the Parthians, from whom he received back the military ensigns, which they had captured from Crassus and Mark Antony. The arch has three portals, and on its summit we see the emperor in a quadriga; one Parthian presenting to him a standard, and another a legionary eagle—See CIVIBVS, &c. A PARTHIS RECEP.

Claudius.—There are both silver and gold coins of Claudius, which exhibit the arch raised to commemorate the victories obtained in Britain, during the reign of Claudius.—See BRITAN. (DE)

Drusus, senior.—The arch of marble, which the Senate caused to be built in honour of Drusus senior, brother of Tiberius, as conqueror in an expedition against the Germans (in consequence of which he was called GERMANICVS), is typified on gold and silver coins, bearing the portrait of that hero on their obverse. The same subject is more architecturally displayed with Drusus on horseback, and with trophies surmounting it, on the reverse of a large brass, struck under Claudius.—See NERO CLAVDIVS DRVSVS, &c.

Trajanus.—A large brass of his (a copy of which follows this), presents an arch of stately proportions, rich in statuary and other ornaments, surmounted with trophies of Germanic arms, and on an *attique* (inscribed with the three letters, which shew it to have been dedicated to Jupiter—viz. I*ovi Optimo Maximo*,) we see the image of the emperor in a triumphal chariot, crowned by two figures of Victory.

This decorated structure was erected in honour of Trajan. "It was probably the vestibulum, or porch of the capitol, mentioned in the panegyric. Pedrusi following Xiphilinus, thinks it stood in the Forum. Aulus Gellius tells us that it was inscribed EX MANVBIIS. (Smyth, *Des. Cat.* 85.)

Galba.—There is on a large brass of Galba an arch formed of a single portal, to which there is an ascent by a flight of five small steps, and on the summit is the figure of the emperor in a quadriga. This, however, as Millin observes, is of the number of those, which ought to be excluded from the class of triumphal arches, properly so called, as may be perceived from the inscription.—See QVADRAGENS. REMISSAE.

Domitianus.—On a large brass is the arch of that emperor, which he, the most pusillanimous of tyrants, had the effrontery to claim from the Senate, for a victory, which he never obtained, over the Germans and Dacians. It is curiously represented, as formed of two stories, two arched portals occupying the lower one; the whole surmounted by two quadriga of elephants, with a triumpher in each, one facing to the right and the other to the left.—Engraved in King's Plates.

ARCUS AUGG. S. C.—A triumphal arch of three portals, decorated on the top with statues. On brass of Caracalla.

The period when, and the particular occasion on which, this ARCVS AVGVSTORVM was erected, is shewn by the inscription still remaining on its front. Eckhel (vii. 205) has given the words entire, as received by Barthelemy from the actual copyist. They teach us, that the arch was built in the year of Rome 956 (A. D. 203),

in honour of Severus and his sons, after their victories over the Parthians, the Arabs, and the Adiabeni. There is a remarkable circumstance connected with the inscription above alluded to, viz. that the name of *Geta* following those of *Severus* and *Caracalla* (ET P SEPTIMIO GETAE NOBILISSIMO CAESARI) was erased from the marble (the words P. P. *Optimis Fortissimisque Principibus* being inserted in their place.) This was done by his inhuman brother's orders; as indeed the same name and titles were also removed, in obedience to the same commands, from all other contemporaneous public edifices and memorials.

In reference to this interesting reverse, Capt. Smyth observes,—"One of the dupondii, inscribed ARCVS AVGG. represents the triumphal arch of Severus, at the foot of the Capitoline hill, exactly as it appears, now that the rubbish is removed in which it was half hidden" (p. 192.)

AREA, the field or surface of a coin.

ARELATE, a city in Gallia Narbonensis, now called *Arles*, and to this day a considerable town in Provence, being the see of an archbishopric. Ausonius calls it Gallula Roma.

Pande duplex, Arelate, tuos blanda hospita Portus
Gallula Roma ————
[Open wide, Arelate, thy ports with friendly welcome, thou little *Gallicised* Rome.]

It was one of the six cities, to which the right of coining money was conceded, in the lower empire; whence coins of Constantine and others have for their mint-mark ARL. P. Arclatensium Prima, &c.—See Pitiscus and Rasche, who call Arelate a Roman colony; it is, however, not included, as such, in the respective catalogues of Eckhel or Mionnet.

ARETAS, a King of Arabia, who, according to Josephus, gave 300 talents to Scaurus, to withdraw his army from that country. This prince is depicted, on a denarius of the *Aemilia* gens, kneeling, as if in the act of supplicating peace at the hands of the Romans.—See REX ARETAS.

ARGENTEI *Romanorum Numi*.—See *Silver* coins of the Romans.

ARGENTUM, Silver, was a word employed by the Latins to denote money in general, although silver money was not the first introduced into Rome (see *As*.)—"Argentum, Aurum, et Aes, signatum, factum, infectum." Isidorus cited by Eckhel (vol. v. 41) thus explains the signification of these words, as applied to the three metals—silver, gold, and brass, viz. *signatum* is that which has been coined into money; *factum* is that which has been converted into vases and images; *infectum*, that which is in the lump, or as we should now call it, ingots, or bullion.

ARGENTEUS, or the silver piece, is the name given to the large denarius of Caracalla and his successors, by the writers of the Augustan History, and in rescripts of the period. It was also called *Argenteus Philippus*, or the Silver Philip, the word Philip having, during the lower age of the imperial government, become a familiar appellation for any coin. The common denarii now first begin, adds Pinkerton, to be termed *minuti*, and *argentei philippi minuti*, to express their being smaller than the other. The first *argenteus* is worth one shilling sterling.——See *Essay*, vol. i. 167.

ARGUS, the name of the faithful dog of Ulysses, that alone knew his master returning home after twenty years' absence. [Homer. *Odyss.* l. xvii.] A family denarius represents Ulysses, disguised as a mendicant, and his dog in the attitude of fawning on him.—See *Mamilia* gens.

ARIADNE, or *Ariane*, is said to have been the daughter of Minos the second, and of Pasiphaé ; and to have become enamoured of Theseus, when that favourite hero of the Athenians arrived in her father's kingdom of Crete, with other youths to be delivered up to the Minotaur. Fable proceeds to relate that she shewed Theseus the way to vanquish that monster, and that she gave him a ball of thread, by the aid of which he was enabled to find his way out of the labyrinth.—The sequel of Ariadne's story, as generally adopted by poets, artists, and mythologists, is, that she was deserted, in the most faithless and ungrateful manner, by Theseus ; and had given herself up to despair, when Bacchus came and consoled her in the isle of Naxos.

Mionnet authenticates a medallion of Antoninus Pius, on the reverse of which appear Bacchus and Ariadne, in a car drawn by a Satyr and a Panther.

[The above is engraved after a cast from a genuine specimen in the *Cabinet de France.*— There is another in the Imperial Cabinet at Vienna.—On the obverse is a fine portrait of Antoninus. The inscription on the exergue P.M. TR. POT. COS. II. shews the date of its mintage to be A.D. 139]

Millin, in his *Dictionnaire Portatif de la Fable*, speaks of a fine medallion of Alexander Severus, in the Museum at Paris, and which he describes as representing Bacchus, naked, holding Ariadne, asleep, round him are three satyrs, whose gestures express astonishment, and near him is an old man dressed in a cloak, and leaning on a staff.—Of this medallion no mention is made either in Mionnet or in Akerman's descriptive notices of Roman coins.—See *Bacchus*.

ARIES.—See *Ram*.

ARM. *Armeniacus*——ARME. *Armenicus*— surnames derived from the conquest of Armenia by the Romans.

ARMENIA—a region of Asia, now forming part of the Diar Bekir and Kourdistan in the Turkish empire. It was anciently divided into two provinces, *Major* and *Minor*. Armenia Major was on the eastern bank of the Euphrates, bounded on the north by Colchis and Iberia ; on the south by Mesopotamia. Armenia Minor was on the western bank of the Euphrates, bounded on the west by Cappadocia, of which it originally formed part ; on the south by the chain of the Taurus. Armenia, as a country, was distinguished nationally by the bow, quiver of arrows, and oblong mitre in the shape of a hood (a covering for the head, which was common to its inhabitants of both sexes).—Lucullus was the first of the Roman generals, who, under the republic, invaded Armenia (B. C. 69). He vanquished its king, Tigranes II. son-in-law of Mithridates Eupator, and took Tigranocerta its capital (now *Sert* in Kourdistan). This king afterwards surrendered his crown to Pompey, the successor of Lucullus (B. C. 66), and who, after having despoiled him of Mesopotamia, permitted him to reign in Armenia.—Tigranes being dead, the Romans became almost the absolute masters of the kingdom.—M. Antonius filched its crown from Artavasdes the lawful sovereign, about the year U.C. 720 and 21 (B.C. 33).—Augustus gave a king to it, when at the death of Artaxias it was *recepta*, or taken into possession, by the Romans, A.U.C. 725 or 26, (B.C. 28,) and succeeding emperors continued to exercise an oppressive power over its government. At length Trajan united it as a province to the empire ; Antoninus (see REX. ARMENIS DATVS.) bestowed a king upon it ; and Armenia remained for ages afterwards the slave of Imperial Rome.

ARME. *or* ARMEN. *or* ARMENIA CAP.— *Cæsar Divi Filius, Armenia Capta.* Armenia taken or subdued.—This legend appears on a denarius of L. Aquillius Florus, one of Augustus's monetal triumvirs. The province is personified, under the figure of a female, in a long dress, wearing a tiara, or high cap, in the kneeling posture of a suppliant. The inscription ARMENIA RECEPT. &c. occurs on silver of Augustus, with upright figure of an Armenian, in the habit of his country, holding a spear and bow.—ARMENIA CAPTA at full length is seen on gold of that Emperor, having for type of reverse a capricorn, globe, and cornucopiæ. Another *aureus*, with the same words on its reverse, bears a sphinx. It was struck, on the occasion of a son of Tigranes having been made king of the greater Armenia, by Augustus.—A denarius of the same Emperor has also the epigraph of Armenia Capta, and for its type the royal tiara, together with a bow, and quiver full of arrows, the two latter illustrating what is said of Armenia, by the poet Lucan :—

> Armeniosque arcus Geticis intendite nervis.

[And bend Armenian bows with Getic strength.]

Nor must notice be omitted of the elegant reverse type on a gold coin, which was minted under the same reign, and which, as an accompaniment to ARMENIA CAPTA, represents a winged Victory holding down a bull by the horns—apt emblem of a conqueror reducing a formidable enemy to subjection by force of arms.—For engravings of these, see *Morell. Thesaur. Impp. Rom.* T. ii. TAB. xvii. fig. 4; and TAB.xi. figures 23, 25, 26.

ARME*nia* CAPT*a.* CAESAR*is Filius.*—Armenia on her knees lifts up her hands in supplication. On a denarius of Augustus.—Dion and Tacitus (cited by Eckhel, VI. 98) cursorily mention, that Tiberius was, A. U. C. 734 (B. C. 20), sent by Augustus from Syria, on an expedition into Armenia, in order that by defeating Artavasdes, he might confirm the possession of that country to his brother Tigranes. Velleius is more to the purpose of the coin in question, for he says, "Tiberius entering Armenia with his legions, and reducing it under the power of the Roman people, bestowed its government on Tigranes.

ARMENIA DEVICTA. (M ANTONI*us.*) Armenia vanquished or subdued.—A denarius of Mark Antony's has on its obverse the bare head of the Triumvir, with the tiara, or crown of the Armenian kings behind the neck, and the words ANTONI. ARMENIA DEVICTA.—On the reverse is to be read, CLEOPATRAE REGINAE REGVM. FILIORVM REGVM. (by implication *Matri.)* The type presents the head of Cleopatra, the *lituus* before it, in allusion to Antony's augurship.

This very rare coin serves, by what it exhibits on both sides of it, to commemorate events which took place in the year of Rome 720 (B. C. 34), confirmatory of the accounts given respecting them by historians. The obverse legend describes Armenia as subdued *(devicta)* and accordingly a tiara, symbolizing the Armenian monarchy, is placed on that side, behind the portrait of Antony, who, so far from having, in fair and open warfare, vanquished Artavasdes, had only succeeded, by a base stratagem, in drawing that unfortunate prince within his power, and then despoiling him of his dominions. The legend of the reverse is pompous in the extreme, though historically correct, calling Cleopatra the Queen of Kings, and (the word *matri* being understood) the Mother of Kings' Sons. The testimony of Dion supports the fact, that in a speech to the people of Alexandria, Mark Antony commanded that Cleopatra should be styled Queen of Kings, with right and title to Egypt and Cyprus. It is

also recorded that, of his own children by Cleopatra, he bestowed Syria, on Ptolemy, with all the territories bordering on the Hellespont; on Cleopatra the district of Cyrene; and on Alexander, Armenia and whatever countries he might subdue beyond the Euphrates.——See CLEOPATRA.

ARMENIAC.—On the reverse of a quinarius of Nero, is this legend, and a figure of Victory walking with garland elevated in the right hand, and a long palm branch carried on the left shoulder.—Engraved in Vaillant, *Præst. Impp. Rom.* p. 66, Paris edition, 1694.

That this coin was minted in the year of Rome 811 (A. D. 58), there appears to be no doubt; for, in his life of that Emperor, Tacitus informs us that Nero was declared *Imperator,* on account of great successes in Armenia; and that statues and arches were erected to his honour, &c. It cannot, however, with the same degree of confidence, be pronounced, whether the word ARMENIAC. stands for the title of *Armeniacus,* decreed perhaps to Nero, and temporarily assumed; or for *Victoria* ARMENIAC*a.*—The former supposition is favoured by similar coins of S. Severus, on the reverse of which are found the words ARAB. ADIABENIC. (with the type of Victory walking) which are certainly to be explained thus. ARAB*icus* ADIABENIC*us,* it being well known, that Severus had those titles conferred on him.—*Doct. Num. Vet.* vi. 263.

ARMENIA ET MESOPOTAMIA IN POTESTATEM *Populi Romani* REDACTAE.—In the field S. C.—On first brass of Trajan. The type exhibits the Emperor, attired in military vestments, with a spear in his right hand and the *parazonium* (see the word) in his left. He stands in the attitude of a conqueror, having his left foot planted on a vanquished foe. On each side is a river deity reclining on an urn, whence water flows.

Armenia is represented by the woman, on whose head is a mitre-formed covering, the national cap of that country; just as on coins of Augustus inscribed *Armenia Capta.*—Mesopotamia is indicated by the two personifications of rivers, as, bounded on one side by the Tigris, and on the other by the Euphrates, it took its name from its situation *between* those two mighty streams of the East, which almost at their confluence fall into the Persian Gulf.—Ovid, when predicting with unsuccessful augury, the victory over the Parthians by Caius Cæsar, son of Agrippa, and the consequent display of the symbols of vanquished nations and cities, introduces the following lines, which are singularly descriptive of the type above given :—

Hic est *Euphrates* precinctus arundine frontem,
  Cui coma dependet cærula, *Tigris* erit.
Hos facito Armenios, hæc est Danæia Persis,
  Urbs in Achæmeniis vallibus ista fuit.

[This is Euphrates, with his brow crowned with reeds ;
That form, with flowing blue hair, is Tigris ;
These suppose Armenians ; this is Danæian Persis ;
That, a city in the vallies of Achæmenia.]

Of this well-known historical reverse, in which so much design is comprehended within so narrow a space, little further requires to be said, than that the coin itself was struck A. U. C. 869 (A. D. 116), and that it relates to events of that and the preceding year.—Trajan, towards the close of his reign, actuated too much, for his own real glory and his empire's welfare, by a spirit of aggressive ambition, declared war against the Parthians, whom, after overrunning Syria, Mesopotamia and Armenia, he defeated in every encounter, nominating fresh kings, establishing several governments, and thereby gaining from the Roman Senate the title of *Parthicus.* This fine coin, and two others, form the respective numismatic records of these conquests.—See PARTHIA CAPTA, and REX PARTHIS DATVS.

ARMEN. *(Armenia).* TR. P. III. COS. II. &c.—The province personified, seated on the ground, amidst the arms of her country, supporting her head with the right hand, her left resting on the prow of a ship.

The legend and type appear on a denarius of L. Verus, minted A. D. 163.—There is also a brass medallion of the same emperor, the reverse of which has TR. VIII. IMP. III. COS. III. for its legend—the type representing Verus on horseback, followed by two soldiers ; beneath the horse a prostrate enemy. In the exergue ARMEN*ia.*——Engraved in Millin, *Galerie Mythologique,* T. i. pl. lxxxviii. No. 368—and in Oiselius, *Num. Sel.* xix. No. 7.

This voluptuous and indolent prince, without any personal risk or exertion of his own, but solely through the valour of the legions under his brave and able general Statius Priscus, had regained Armenia from the occupation of Vologaeses II. King of the Parthians ; who had himself ejected Soaemos, a prince sprung from the race of the Arsacidæ. On this account the title of *Armeniacus,* or the Armenian (originally conferred on Nero), was assumed as a cognomen by L. Verus, and also by his senior associate in the empire, M. Aurelius.

From these coins (says Eckhel, vii: 90) which attribute the title of *Armeniacus* to Verus as early as his third tribuneship, we learn that this emperor adopted the appellation sooner than M. Aurelius ; for the latter is not called Armeniacus, on coins, till his 18th tribuneship, which corresponds with the fourth of Verus. The vessel apparently refers to some naval victory gained over the Armenians on the Euphrates.

The type of Armenia, seated on the ground, is also seen on the coins of Aurelius.

"To the best of my knowledge (adds the author of *Doctrina*) these coins are the only ones which place the titles IMP. II. and Tribunatus III. in juxta-position."

ARMENIS. *To the Armenians.*—See REX ARMENIS DATVS. on coins of Antoninus Pius and Lucius Verus.

ARN. ASI. or ARN. AZI.—There is a brass medallion of Trebonianus Gallus, which on its reverse exhibits the figure of Apollo with radiated head, standing on rocks, raised into the form of a mountain, holding in one hand a large branch of olive or laurel, and in the other a bow unstrung. In the field of this coin is inscribed to the right ARN. and to the left ASI., or as it reads on a second brass of Volusianus ARN. AZI.— Vaillant, and after him Banduri, allude to a similar medallion, but neither of them seem to notice the type.

Mediobarbus, who appears to follow the author of the catalogue *Mus. Theupoli,* has, without mentioning the size, classed it amongst the colonial medals, as if ARN. and ASI. were the name of a colony.—Père Hardouin in endeavouring to explain it, wanders away, according to his usual manner.—Pellerin interprets these words as the abbreviated names of two towns in Umbria, namely *Arna* and *Asisum.* These were neighbours, and at their joint expense caused the figure of Apollo to be raised on an elevated spot, in order that it might be seen afar off, and invoked by all the people of the surrounding district, on account of a dreadful pestilence which raged in Italy during the reign of Trebonianus Gallus, between A. D. 252 and 254. That emperor had, in consequence, ordered propitiatory sacrifices to be offered to all the gods, in every province of the empire : and it is easily to be supposed that they would above all implore the aid of Apollo, who was particularly regarded as the healing and succouring deity, in cases of maladies. There are other medals of the same Emperor, bearing, on their reverses, the legend APOLLINI SALVTARI, and having for their type a representation of Apollo, with only this difference, that the health-restorer is placed in the above medallion, on the summit of a rocky hill, and seems to have been colossal. It was, adds Pellerin, most probably regarded as a monument of sufficient importance to merit being numismatically recorded, in honour of the cities *Arna* and *Asisum,* by whose inhabitants it had been jointly erected. These two places exist to this very day, the one under the name of *Civitella d'Arno,* and the other under that of *Assise.*— For an engraving of the coin, see *Recueil,* T. iii. p. 52.

Eckhel evidently inclines to treat Pellerin's conjecture as in all probability the right one ; but thinks the question still open, as to whether these coins were struck at Rome, or in the towns themselves. In the times of the Emperors there were no monetal offices (or mints) in Italy, out of Rome. "Now (he adds), had they been struck in the city I do not believe that the mark S. C. would have been left out, even on second brass coins. Nevertheless, easy as it may be to moot an opinion adverse to that of so eminent a man as Pellerin, it is very difficult to advance anything better, or of greater validity." (vii. 357). There are coins of Geta, of a similar description, bearing for legend STA. BOV.—See the word.

ARRIA, gens plebeia.—A family which, descended from Q. Arrius, tribune of the people, produced men serviceable to the republic, but it became still better known under the emperors. Its cognomen is *Secundus*, on coins, of which it presents seven varieties. Both gold and silver, very rare. The brass pieces are colonial (of Corinth) and rare.—The following legend and type appear on gold and silver minted by this family:

Obv.—M. ARRIVS SECVNDVS.—Male head, with youthful beard.

Rev.—Without legend. A spear between a garland, and an altar lighted.

There is another denarius with the same reverse, and the same family name on the obverse, but with a female head, and above it the letters F. P. R.

Much tedious and fruitless disputation has been held by certain monetal antiquaries, of the elder school, on the question as to who this *M. Arrius Secundus* was? With respect to the letters F. P. R. according to Havercamp's opinion, it signifies *Fortuna Populi Romani;* but Vaillant reads, *Fortitudo* Populi Romani; and Patin suggests, *Fecialis* Populi Romani. Eckhel (vol. v.) is decidedly in favour of the first interpretation, Fortitude not being recognised as a deity by the Romans, whilst they were peculiarly addicted to the worship of Fortune. In the *Sicinia* family there is a similar female head, round which we read FORT. P. R.

ARTAVASDES II. King of Armenia, whom Mark Antony took prisoner by stratagem, 34 years before the Christian æra, and led him away captive, with his children, in triumph to Alexandria. Hence, on a coin of Antony's, we see a trophy, allusive to the fate of Artavasdes; and on another, minted under the same Triumvir, appears the oriental Tiara, designed to symbolize the event of the Armenian crown falling into the hands of that Roman General.—See ARMENIA DEVICTA. See also *M. Antonius.*

ARTAXIAS, King of Armenia, by whose death the government of that country devolved to the Romans under Augustus.—See *Armenia.*

ASCANIUS, son of Æneas, by Creusa, daughter of Priam. He was afterwards called *Iulus,* allusive to the first down of the beard. (Virg. *Æn.* L. i.) Driven from Troy with his father, he after many wanderings, arrived with him in Latium. It was in memory of Ascanius that the *Trojan Games* (Troiæ *Ludi*) were cele-

brated at Rome. Of these gymnastic sports he was the reputed founder (*Æneid,* L. v.), and the youth of Italy took an exclusive part in them. The stripling who presided on these occasions was called *Princeps Juventutis* (Chief or Prince of Youth): whence that title came afterwards to be bestowed on the heirs and Cæsars of the empire, who are thus designated on a long succession of reverses, in the imperial series of Roman coins. Ascanius was the assumed progenitor of the *Julia* gens, to which Julius Cæsar belonged. Accordingly, the images of his father and grandfather (Æneas and Anchises), together with his own as a little boy, form a group on denarii, struck under Augustus, and on medallions of Antoninus Pius.—See *Aeneas,* pp. 16 and 17.

ARUSPICES.—See *Haruspices.*

AS, ASSIS, and ASSARIUS.—These were the words used by the Romans, in connection with the subject of money, to denominate an integer, or entire quantity of weight *(congeries ponderis,* as Eckhel expresses it), divided into twelve parts called *unciæ.* And as they commenced their coinage with brass, so the *as* was their most ancient money. The synonymes of *as* or *assis* were *libra, libella,* and *pondo;* the weight of the *as* money being the same as that of the pound of twelve ounces; and numerous coins are extant not only of the entire *as,* but also of the parts into which, for monetary purposes, it was divided.

Declining to touch upon numerous details of discussion, contained in the copious pages of controversial antiquaries; and simply referring, for further particulars, to what will be found given in this dictionary, under the head of *Brass Coinage,* it shall here suffice to assume as certain, that money consisting of *brass only* began to be fabricated at Rome, if not actually under Servius Tullius, at least soon after that king's death. The principal piece was the *as,* which constituted the primitive unit of the Roman mint. The earliest known specimens of it are of bulky dimensions; but they were nevertheless unquestionably money. That portion of them, however, which, from their form, size, and weight, come under our acceptation of the word *coin,* must evidently have been introduced at a much later period.—The brass coinage of Rome first established between the years 550 and 555 before the Christian æra, (or to take the computed duration of the reign of Servius Tullius, between 578 and 534 years B. C.), consisted, as above stated, of the *as,* the primary unit, weighing 12 *unciæ* (or ounces), and worth 12 unciæ in money. Its *multiples* and its *parts* were as follow:—

MULTIPLES.

Dupondius (two *as*).
Tripondius (three *as*).
Quadrussis (four *as*).
Decussis (ten *as*).

PARTS.

Semis (half of the *as,* or six unciæ).
Quincunx (five unciæ).
Triens (third of the *as,* or four unciæ).
Quadrans (fourth of the *as,* or three unciæ).

Sextans (sixth of the *as,* or two unciæ).

Uncia (twelfth of the *as,* or one ounce).

The quincussis (five *as,* or a quinarius); the Deunx (eleven unciæ); Dextans (nine unciæ); Bes (eight unciæ); Septunx (seven unciæ); were monetary fractions, (as M. Hennin observes), which were occasionally used in calculation, but which had no existence as real money.

Some of the above-named brass coins, of early Roman fabric, bear marks, and inscriptions, as well as types, from which a system has been formed for fixing their legal values and their denominations. The following is a descriptive list of them, compiled from Eckhel, Mionnet, Akerman, and Hennin:—

MARKS AND TYPES ON THE ROMAN As, ITS MULTIPLES AND PARTS.

1. The *Decussis,* marked X. has for the type of its obverse, the head of Minerva; on the reverse is the prow of a vessel.

2. The *Quadrussis* exhibits various types, the most common of which is a bull walking. [These pieces have the form of a long square. The specimens in the British Museum 6¾ inches by 3½ inches. The heaviest weighs 3 lbs. 12 oz.—See Akerman's *Descr. Cat.,* vol. 1.]

3. The *Tripondius,* marked III. bears on one side the head of Minerva; on the reverse a ship's prow.

4. The *Dupondius* is marked II. [Some of these pieces are of Italian origin, and bear the word FELATHRI, in retrograde Etruscan character.] The type of the obverse is Minerva's head, and of the reverse a ship's prow.

5. The *As* (primitive monetary unit).

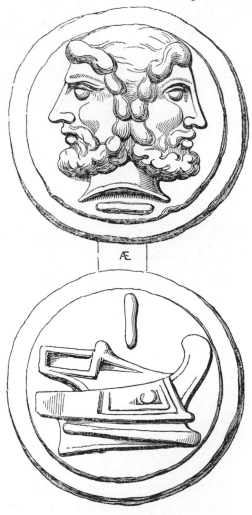

Æ.

Obv.—Head of Janus.

Rev.—Prow of a vessel.

The mark of this money is the sign | But it is not always found on it.—Such pieces mostly exhibit the word ROMA on the reverse side, and many of them bear the names of Roman families.

6. The *Semis*, exhibits several types; the larger sized ones have a hog, a vase, a Pegasus, a bull, or a wheel, on the obverse side. —The smaller sized and later Semis bears the head of Jupiter laureated. But its distinctive mark is the letter S, or six globules, thus . . . . . . See the word in S.

7. The *Quincunx*, has generally a cross on each side, the distinctive mark five globules . . . . and the letter V.—See the word in Q.

8. The *Triens*, bears the head of Minerva, and has four globules . . . . See the word in T.

9. The *Quadrans*, presents on its obverse the head of Hercules, and three globules . . . [Some of these pieces have for their obverse types, a dog, a bull and serpent, with the word ROMA, a man's hand, and a strigil.] See the word in Q.

10. The *Sextans* has the head of Mercury, and its mark is two globules . . See the word in S.

11. The *Uncia*, has the mark of a single globule . [Its type is a pentagon, in the centre of which the globule is placed, or a strigil, or a spear head.] See U.

The reverse type of all the above, *except* the Quincunx and the Uncia, is the prow of a ship.

But it appears that the *as*, or *libra*, among the Romans, was the principle, or basis, of calculation; not only in the matter of weight and of money, but also in measuring liquids, distances, and even in designating the claims of *hereditary succession*, with regard to those laws which regulated testamentary dispositions. (See Eckhel, *De Asse et ejus partibus*, v. p. 4, *et seq.* for examples of each.)

Assis diminutio.—It is under this head that the author of *Doctrina numorum veterum* has furnished a series of observations and arguments, at once interesting in themselves, and peculiarly valuable to the numismatic student, as the means of arriving at something like a right understanding, on the chief practical points of the difficult subject in question. Allusion is here had to the second chapter of Eckhel's treatise on Consular coins (vol v. p. 6, § ii.) wherein he has given the whole of that passage from Pliny, which forms the foundation of whatever is known respecting the diminution of the *as*, and its parts; a passage to which reference is always made by such of the learned as apply their attention to this branch of the Roman mint. It is hoped, therefore, that the subjoined attempt to present it in an English dress, will prove not unacceptable to those for whose use and information the present work is principally designed.

It is to be borne in mind, that, at the very earliest period, the Romans used unwrought brass [for money]; and that it was in the reign of Servius Tullius that brass was first stamped. So that the coined *as* [*as moneta*] would be of the same weight as the *as libralis*. But this law did not continue. We are made acquainted with the fact of its violation, in the following words of Pliny.—*(Natural History*, L. xxxiii. § 13.)

"The Roman people did not use even *silver* stamped, before the period when King Pyrrhus was vanquished. The *as* weighed a *libra*, whence the present term *libella*, and *dupondius* (two *libræ*). Thence also the penalty (or fine) called *aes grave* (heavy brass). . . . *Servius Rex primus signavit æs.* King Servius first stamped brass. Before him, as Timæus relates, the Romans used it in the rough state *(rude)*. It was stamped with the figures of cattle *(nota pecudum)* from which circumstance it was called *pecunia*. Silver was coined in the year of the city 485 (B.C. 269), during the consulship of Q. Fabius, and five years before the first Punic war. And a denarius passed for ten pounds of brass *(decem libris æris)*; a quinarius for five; a sestertius, for two pounds and a half *(pro dupondio et semisse)*. This pound weight of brass *(libra pondus aeris)* was, however, diminished during the first Punic war, when the resources of the Commonwealth were inadequate to meet its expenditure; and it was decreed that *asses* should be struck, of the weight of two ounces *(sextantario pondere)*. So five parts of it *(factæ lucri)* were thus gained, and the public debt was cancelled. The distinctive type *(nota)* on brass coins was on one side a double-headed Janus, on the other the beak of a ship; on the *triens* and *quadrans*, entire vessels. The Quadrans was originally called *Teruncius* from *tres unciæ.*—Subsequently, when the state was pressed upon by the war with Hannibal, and during the dictatorship of Q. Fabius Maximus, *asses* of an ounce weight *(unciales)* were minted: and a denarius was made exchangeable for sixteen *asses*, a quinarius for eight, a sestertius for four. Thus a profit of one half was realized by the republic. In military pay, however, a denarius was always given for ten *asses*.—The types of the silver were *bigæ* and *quadrigæ* (chariots drawn by two and four horses respectively) and were therefore called *bigati* and *quadrigati*. Soon afterwards by the Papirian law, half-ounce *asses* were struck. *(Mox, lege Papiriana Semunciales asses facti.)*"

From these words of Pliny, with whom may be conjoined Vitruvius, Mæcianus, and Pompeius Festus, it is clearly to be gathered, that the standard of the Roman brass money underwent many changes, even down to the age of the Emperors. And, of the *data* thus afforded by the celebrated old writer above quoted, Eckhel goes on to present the following analysis:

I. The *As Libralis*, was 12 unciæ (or ounces) in weight. This lasted from Servius Tullius, about the A. U. C. 107 (555 B.C.), as far as the time of the first Punic war, which commenced in the year of Rome 490 (B. C. 264).—The *Denarius*, a silver coin, began to be struck five years before this war, and was valued at 10 *asses librales*, whence its name.

II. The *As Sextantarius* was of the weight of two ounces. This standard began whilst the first Punic war was at its height, and continued till the dictatorship of Q. Fabius Maximus, upon which he entered A. U. C. 537 (B. C. 217, 2nd year 2nd Punic war.)

III. The *As Uncialis*, weighed one ounce; from the dictatorship of Q. Fabius until the introduction of the *Lex Papiria*; respecting which law, it is not precisely ascertained at what time or by which Papirius it was carried. The word *mox*, used by Pliny, shews that this form of the *as* did not last long. From that time the value of the *denarius* was authoritatively fixed at 16 *asses*.

IV. The *As Semiuncialis*, or of the half-ounce *(uncia)*. This commenced with the *Lex Papiria*.

Such are the sum and substance of the indications given by Pliny. But there are not a few circumstances which appear to be at variance with them. And these Eckhel proceeds to point out in the following manner :

"*Firstly*, they are contradicted by experience itself. For in many museums there are numerous specimens of the *as*, and those undoubtedly Roman, which weigh 11, 10, and 8 ounces, &c. Also *semisses* of 5, 4, &c.—And in the same ratio the *triens*, *quadrans*, *sextans*, and *uncialis*. Hence it is evident that the *as* could by no means have been (as Pliny appears to assert) reduced suddenly without any intermediate diminution, to the weight of 2 unciæ.

"*Secondly*, as the commonwealth, on the reduction of the *as* to 2 *unciæ*, gained a profit of 5-6ths for the liquidation of the public debt; so, to private individuals, the loss was proportionate. Then came the half of this ; when the *sextantarius* was diminished to one *uncia*. And lastly, the half of this again, on the introduction of the semiuncial *as*. Therefore he, who, in the year U. C. 490, had 60,000 *asses*, put out to interest, found himself suddenly reduced to 10,000 ; in forty-seven years afterwards to 5,000 ; and not long after that, by the Papirian law, to 2,500. Now, if as this money decreased in weight, the rich, by the concomitant rise in the price of articles, must have been reduced to poverty, and the poor to utter destitution, could any other result have happened than the entire ruin of the state ?

"*Thirdly*, since the denarius was worth 10 *asses librales*, and there were 34 denarii in the libra, (on Pliny's testimony concurred in by that of Celsus and Scribonius Largus,) it necessarily follows, that silver was to brass at that period, as 1 to 840, in value. Now, how much soever we may be inclined to regard the ancient Romans as poor, and deficient in the more precious metals, can such an extreme disproportion between silver and brass be considered probable ? But though to the great majority this opinion must appear repugnant to all truth, yet to many it was matter of belief that the *denarius*

struck at that time when the *as libralis* was still in use, was of greater weight. [After combatting with conclusive effect the visionary conjectures of Savot and others of the elder school of numismatists on this point, Eckhel next observes :]

"*Fourthly*, the most astonishing fact is this. The denarius, which at first was equivalent to 10 *asses librales*, or 120 *unciæ*, within a comparatively few years, was worth 16 *semi-uncial asses*, or 8 unciæ. I do not (adds our author) impugn this last proportion, which indeed does not exceed the bounds of moderation—namely that, for a *denarius*, which was one-seventh of an *uncia*, were exchanged 8 *unciæ* of brass money. But who can easily digest the notion, that in so short a space of time, silver, from being the most costly metal, was reduced to such cheapness ?"

So far the Author of "*Doctrina*," on Pliny's account of the early history of the Roman coinage, and of the diminution of the *as*.—Dr. Cardwell in one of his lectures, treating of the same subject, offers remarks, of which the tenor perfectly coincides with the above cited views and reasonings of the great Numismatist of Vienna, as to the doubtful correctness of Pliny's account. "But," adds the Learned Principal of St. Alban's Hall, "the strongest objection against the statement of Pliny still remains. If his account were correct, no *as* could ever have been minted of a weight between the *libralis* of the earliest period, and the *Sextantarius* of the Punic war ; nor, in like manner, any *Semissis* between the full weight of six ounces, and the reduction to one single ounce ; whereas the fact is, that we meet with both these coins, in all the several stages of degradation, proving incontestably that the change was gradual. That such changes were actually made, and that the common currency of Rome underwent repeated, and at last extreme variations in its standard, is a fact that might certainly be anticipated from the unscientific character of the times, from the demands of a constant state of warfare, and even from the universal prevalence of debt ; but this fact is fully established, as to the mode and extent of its operation, not by what we gather from history, but by what is clearly laid before us in a series of coins."—vi. p. 140.

[As to the voluminous opinions which have been founded on the statements of the old writers, by a host of modern ones, as well respecting the real weight of the ancient Roman *libra* (or p̊ound) as with regard to the reductions successively made in the weight of the *as*—neither are they clear enough in themselves, nor are they sufficiently accordant with each other, nor (what is most important) are they, with the requisite degree of correspondence, borne out by the coins themselves to which they refer, to furnish a clue by which any positive decision can be arrived at, on those respective points of discussion ; whilst they equally fall short of establishing any well-digested scale, by which to measure those sudden and extraordinary diminutions in the size and weight of the Roman brass coinage, that

Pliny and others affirm to have taken place. If indeed a Froëlich declared himself incompetent to the task of disentangling this question from its great ambiguities and difficulties—if even an Eckhel, with all his vigour of industrious research, but in the same spirit of modesty inseparable from true genius, has ventured to do little more, in this instance, than to adduce the varying opinions of others, and then "leave the reader to select that which appears to him most reasonable." And though last not least entitled to consideration, if, after the acquirements and exertions of such eminent antiquaries as Cardinal Zelada, and other Italian investigators of *Uncial* coins—men who had such superior advantages for evolving the truth, from the genuine pieces before them—if (we say) after all these advantages and efforts, so comparatively trifling an advance has been made in practical knowledge, on a question which has been most assiduously and obstinately disputed—we may well be excused for dwelling no longer upon it, than whilst summing-up the amount of the information furnished to us from the sources above-mentioned. And this cannot perhaps be better done than by here concentrating the remarks of M. Hennin, on this subject:—]

"The notices given by Pliny on the diminution of the *as*, and of weights, are neither free from the features of improbability, nor are they confirmed by the *data* furnished, on a comparison of the weights with the coins themselves. It is difficult indeed to believe that, in so short a space of time, the *as* should have been reduced from twelve to two ounces. The differences, which must have resulted from such large reductions, would have caused too great a destruction of property, to have admitted of such enormous changes.—On the other hand, there exist *as*, or parts of the *as*, whose size and weight indicate a still lower reduction than that to the *as semi-uncialis:* that is to say, a reduction from the half-ounce to the quarter-ounce *as;* whence it follows that the *as* was successively diminished to the forty-eighth part of its original weight. And whatever may have been these successive reductions, the fact remains that there exist *as* and fractions of the *as*, of different weights, and which may be classed according to their respective weights."

In conclusion, amidst much that is vague, confused, and improbable, thus much may be looked upon as matter of fact, devoid altogether of doubt and uncertainty, viz.—1. That the first Roman money was of *brass.*—2. That the first unit of the Roman mint was a value named *as*, which was likewise the unit of weight and measures.—3. That the first *as* money existed from the establishment of a coinage at Rome, under Servius Tullius, to the first Punic war.—4. That five years before that period, namely, A. U. C. 408 (B. C. 269), silver money was first struck at Rome.—5. That, at this epocha, an alteration took place in the monetal unit. The *as*, which had become of less and less value, ceased to serve the purpose of numbering sums, and the *Sestertius* took its place as the unit of money.—6. That the module and weight, and consequently the metallic value of the *as*, having experienced these successive reductions up to the æra of the imperial government of Rome, *brass* money then became fixed at a lower value, in the ratio of its weight; and this value preserved a greater degree of steadiness than it had previously possessed.—See *Manuel de Numismatique Ancienne*, T. i. *passim.*

[It has already been observed, that the *as* has for its types, on one side the head of Janus, called *bifrons*, having two faces, with an oblong sign ▐, placed at the top of the head, as the distinguishing *nota*, or mark; and on the other side, the prow of a ship, with a similar note or sign.

At the beginning of this article, on the subject of the *as*, is placed an engraving in wood, to the exact size, from a cast, of which the original is, with others of the same class, in the cabinet of the British Museum. It weighs 8 ozs. 4 dwts. 20 grains, and measures two inches and a half in diameter.

This well preserved and rare specimen of its circular brass coinage is assigned, by numismatic antiquaries, to a very early, though not the earliest, period of the Roman mint. Nevertheless, looking to its style of fabric—its free design—its high and bold relief—and particularly to the features of the *bifrons*, so decidedly analagous as they are with the characteristics of Etruscan art, it seems scarcely possible to avoid associating this noble relic of antiquity with an age of monetal workmanship anterior to that of Rome. But then there is the fact to encounter, that even this cast piece of rounded copper, from the die-sinker's matrix, with all its breadth, thickness, and weight, is itself an instance of great diminution from the original *as*, which from a pound of 12 ounces, gradually dwindled down to the weight of hardly half an ounce! So un-

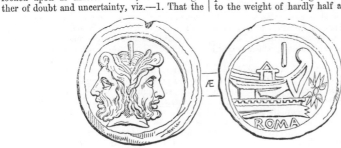

satisfactory, even to repulsiveness, are as yet the results of research and argument, on points of essential importance, connected with this particular branch of Roman Numismatics.

In the preceding example of the smaller sized *as*, without the names of families, the word ROMA on the reverse is certainly not required to indicate either the place, or the later date, of its mintage. The *archaics* of Etruria had clearly nothing to do with coins of this description, which are stamped, as to legend and fabric, with the indubitable impress of republican Rome.—This specimen is selected from a plate in Kolb's *Traité Elémentaire*, (T. i. pl. 1), chiefly on account of the winged thunderbolt accompanying the prow, a symbol rarely seen on this class of coins.

The two following are proofs of the still further reduction of the *as*, and each is inscribed with the name of a Roman family, viz.:—

The name of C. FABI. C. F. appears on the reverse of this second brass, struck by one (but there is no clue to ascertain which) of the members of this most ancient patrician house.—See *Fabia* gens.

Cornelia gens.—A second brass on which we read CINÆ, above the ship's prow, and ROMA. below it. It was Cn. Cornelius Magnus, grandson of Pompeius Magnus, whose name thus appears under the form of *Cina*.—See *Dict. of Greek and Roman Biography, &c.*, 1, 755.]

As libralis.—In reference to this appellation, given by Latin authors, to the most ancient brass money of Rome, and as also indicating a weight of twelve unciæ, Eckhel says, "Up to the present time, no Roman *as libralis* has ever been discovered; and of the parts of the *as*, Passeri cites but one instance of a *triens*, which weighed four *unciæ*."

As Italicus.—Several cities of *Magna Græcia*, and of other districts of Italy, adopted in the earlier times, for their monetary unit, the Roman *as*: their brass coinage was divided in conformity to that system and bore its marks. To these pieces have been given the name of the Italian *as*. And the explanations, which relate to the *as*, also apply to them.

It is to be observed, however, that by the elder school of numismatic antiquaries, sufficient distinction was not made, between the *as* minted at Rome, and that of the other Italian cities. More attention was paid to this subject by deeply learned men of a subsequent period; and the result of their recondite studies has established the fact, that certain nations of Italy (such as the Volaterrani, the Tudertes, the Iguvini, the Hadriani,) had each their own coinage of the *as*; and that these were of the proper weight, as is shewn by the name of the respective cities inscribed on their coins.—Livy, in more than one passage, relates, that the inhabitants of Italy, conquered at different periods by the Romans, were despoiled, by the victors, of their *brass* money. "Therefore," says Eckhel, "we must not reckon amongst the coinage of Rome, *all* pieces of that kind, which, being without inscriptions, do not declare the locality in which they were struck. *It is the* TYPES *which furnish the clearest evidence of the* ROMAN *die*. For the *as* presents on its obverse a head of Janus; the *semis*, of Jupiter; the *triens*, of Pallas; the *quadrans*, of Hercules; the *sextans*, of Mercury; the *uncia*, also of Pallas; whilst all of them exhibit the prow of a vessel on their reverse.—And that these types were peculiar to the Roman coins is proved by the *asses*, and their constituent parts, which, afterwards diminished in size, bear the names of Roman families, with ROMA inscribed near them; and which continued to be distinguished by the same types on both sides respectively, to the latest period of the Republic. For there are brass coins even of Sextus, which display on one side the head of Janus, and on the other the prow of a vessel."—The erudite and sagacious author of *Doctrina*, then goes on to caution his readers against considering, indiscriminately, coins which bear the very name of the Roman people to have been *all* of Roman fabric, many of them having been ascertained to belong to Panormus (Palermo, in Sicily), Pæstum (in Southern Italy), and other places.—Moreover there are extant, *brass* coins of the Clovia, Oppia, and other Roman families, which present every indication of a foreign mint.—If therefore all these are (and they ought to be) excluded, there would remain but an insignificantly small number of those which form exceptions to the rule, and respecting which any doubt could be entertained, as to whether they should be classed amongst the coins of Rome." Since then (adds Eckhel) "it may be regarded as a rule, failing only in a very few instances out of a vast number, that those are Roman coins, which are distinguished by the above-mentioned types, so I should scarcely hesitate to pronounce, that the exceptions belong, in almost every case, to a foreign people, though an unknown one."

For some further notices, incidental to this subject, see *Brass* coinage of the Romans.

ASI. *Asia.*—See COM. or COMM. ASI. *Communitas Asiæ.*

ASIA.—The name given, together with the title of *Oriens*, or the East, as a general term by the ancients, to one of the three parts of the world known to them, and which equalled, if not exceeded in extent, the other two. According to the old geographers, it was divided from Europe on the west, by the river Tanais (or Don) and by the Euxine and Egean seas. From Africa, its line of demarcation was the Nile, according to Pliny; the Arabian Gulph according to Ptolemy. Occupying the most fertile and delicious quarter of the habitable globe, its inhabitants have ever been noted for their indolent habits, their luxurious tastes, their voluptuous propensities, their effeminate manners; in other words, for dispositions and characteristics apparently rendering them fitter to obey than to command. Of Asia, Cicero says, that "for the productiveness of its soil, the variety of its fruits, the wide extent of its pasturages, and the multitude of its exports, it vastly exceeds all others."—It was from Asia, (both *Major* and *Minor*) that luxury, through the medium of the armies of the republic, introduced itself into Rome, where it exercised a fatal influence on the morals of the people, as it had done on the discipline of the soldiers.— In the year B.C. 191, Antiochus, king of Syria, declared war against the Romans, who sent against him the consul Glabrio, by whom he was vanquished, near Thermopylæ, and driven from Greece. The following year, the consul L. Scipio, brother of Scipio Africanus, also defeated the same monarch at the battle of Magnesia.— This victory put an end to the war, and Scipio enjoyed the honours of a triumph for Antiochus and for Asia. But peace was not ratified with Antiochus till the year B.C. 188.—After the death of King Eumenes, his son obtained "from the *generosity* of the Roman Senate," the throne of Syria, and that prince dying A.U.C. 621 (B.C. 133), appointed the Roman people his heirs. But Aristonicus, natural son of Eumenes, shortly afterwards invaded those Asiatic provinces which he claimed as his patrimony, and overcame the consul Crassus Mucianus, whom he made prisoner, and put to death, B.C. 130. Aristonicus, however, was in his turn defeated and captured by the consul Perpenna, whose successor the consul Aquillius, by overcoming and slaying Aristonicus, terminated the second Asiatic war. And thus was the Lesser Asia brought into subjection to Rome, and governed by pro-consuls. Of its riches, in Sulla's time, some idea may be formed from the tax of 20,000 talents which he imposed on it. Mark Antony, in one year of his government there, is said to have acquired an equal sum.

ASIA is symbolised on Roman coins by the serpent; (see the *cistophori* of M. Antonius) also by the ship's prow, and rudder—the latter "to shew (says Jobert) that it is a

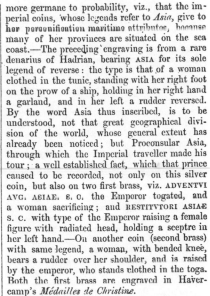

country which cannot be arrived at from Rome without going by sea"—an odd reason —"curious if true."—Eckhel alludes to, without discountenancing, the French Jesuit's conjecture; but at the same time assigns another reason,

more germane to probability, viz., that the imperial coins, whose legends refer to *Asia*, give to her personification maritime attributes, because many of her provinces are situated on the sea coast.—The preceding engraving is from a rare denarius of Hadrian, bearing ASIA for its sole legend of reverse : the type is that of a woman clothed in the tunic, standing with her right foot on the prow of a ship, holding in her right hand a garland, and in her left a rudder reversed. By the word Asia thus inscribed, is to be understood, not that great geographical division of the world, whose general extent has already been noticed; but Proconsular Asia, through which the Imperial traveller made his tour ; a well established fact, which that prince caused to be recorded, not only on this silver coin, but also on two first brass, viz. ADVENTVI AVG. ASIAE. S. C. the Emperor togated, and a woman sacrificing ; and RESTITVTORI ASIAE S. C. with type of the Emperor raising a female figure with radiated head, holding a sceptre in her left hand.—On another coin (second brass) with same legend, a woman, with bended kneè, bears a rudder over her shoulder, and is raised by the emperor, who stands clothed in the toga. Both the first brass are engraved in Havercamp's *Médailles de Christine*.

Spartian informs us, that while journeying through this region, Hadrian erected temples in his own name. And cities also are mentioned, which were so much enlarged by him, that their inhabitants hesitated not to proclaim him their second founder, and to appropriate his name. Amongst these were Cyzicus, Smyrna, Stratonica in Caria, and many others. What vast sums of money he expended on the embellishment of Smyrna alone, may be gathered from Philostratus. The services conferred by him upon Cyzicus, where a magnificent temple was erected to his honour, and games instituted, are indicated in the coinage of that city, whose inhabitants styled him the *thirteenth* god.—See Eckhel, vi. 492.

Asia Minor.——The region so named comprised the provinces between the Euxine and Mediterranean seas ; consequently it included Bithynia, Paphlagonia, Pontus, Galatia, Mysia (see Troas), Lydia, Caria, Æolia, Ionia, Lycia, Pamphilia, Phrygia, Cappadocia, Cilicia, and Lycaonia.—"The country (observes the late Bishop Butler in his admirable sketch of Ancient and Modern Geography) which we call Asia Minor (a term not in use among the ancients, who called it simply Asia) is now called Anatolia, or rather *Anadoli*, from ἀνατολὴ, the East."

ASIA RECEPTA.—Victory with expanded wings, and holding a crown, stands on a cylindrical basket between two serpents.—On a quinarius of Augustus (of which the subjoined cut is

an exact copy as to size and type, from the original in the British Museum).

The mystical *cista*, or basket, of Bacchus was the symbol of proconsular Asia, which this coin declares to be *recepta*, that is, taken possession of by Cæsar. All silver coins, which were struck in the same district of Asia, present a similar representation of the *cista*, and are for that reason called *cistophori*. (See the word.) Victory is placed on the *cista*, simply because, in the Roman mint, that figure was the perpetual type of the quinarius.—Augustus *received* Asia, within the sphere of his dominions when, in the year U. C. 724 (B. C. 30), either on his expedition into Egypt, or on his return to Asia, he tarried there, to arrange public affairs, and also wintered in the country, as Dion affirms. It is likewise stated, by Suetonius, that he went to Asia during his fourth consulate, and in his fifth left Samos for Rome. Looking, therefore, to the above epigraph, ASIA RECEPTA, as well as to the title IMP*erator* VII. inscribed on the obverse, we come (says Eckhel, vi. 82) pretty near at the age of this coin. Indeed, placing the event recorded, between the years U. C. 724 and 725, it is evident that in the latter year, when Augustus Cæsar proceeded to his fifth consulate, he was *Imperator* for the seventh time. This is shown by the famous marble published by Pighius, viz:

SENATVS POPVLVSQVE ROMANVS. IMP. CAE-SARI. DIVI IVLI. F. COS. QVINCT. COS. DESIG. SEX. IMP. SEPT. REPVBLICA. CONSERVATA.

From these dates it is clear, that this quinarius could not have been minted earlier than the year of Rome 724, nor later than 726 (B. C. 28); because in the following year Cæsar Octavianus began to use the name of Augustus.—See *Doct. Num.* vi. 82.

ASIA COS. II. S. C.—A woman, with turreted head, stands with a crown in her extended right hand, and her left hand is placed on an anchor. On a large brass of Antoninus Pius.

It would appear that this coin was struck (A.D. 139), in memory of those towns in Asia, which, having been overthrown by an earthquake, were restored by Antoninus—an act of beneficence recorded by Capitolinus, in his life of that prince. The crown in the right hand of the figure, is considered to represent an *aurum coronarium*.— And this refers to the circumstance, that the Roman governors of provinces, when they quitted their respective presidencies, demanded of the cities included under their administration a supply of pure gold, for the ostensible purpose

of making therewith a crown, to be afterwards consecrated at the shrine of Jupiter Capitolinus. —See *Aurum Coronarium.*

ASIAE.—See *Civitatibus Asiæ Restitutis.*

ASIAG.—*Asiagenes:* surname of L. Cornelius Scipio (brother of Scipio Africanus), who as the conqueror of Antiochus the Great, and for his Asiatic victories, was so called.—See *Cornelia.*

ASINA.—A contorniate medal of great rarity presents on its obverse D. N. HONORIVS. P. AVG. and a laureated head; on the reverse is inscribed the word ASINA, accompanied with the figure of an ass suckling a foal.

For an account of the attempts made by learned men to explain this medal—attempts as conflicting and inconclusive as the subject of them is curious and extraordinary—the reader is referred to vol. viii. p. 173, of *Doct. Num. Vet.* Suffice it here to notice, that the coin in question is allowed to be as old as the time of Honorius, during whose reign a great portion of the *contorniati* were struck—that Tanini, of whose collection it once formed a part, decidedly regarded it as one of a satirical character, and struck by the idolators in contempt of the Christians—that Eckhel, on the contrary, thinks that the legend and type of its reverse may have been one of the symbolical modes of expressing their faith in the Divine Author of their religion, "signifying something understood by themselves though hidden from us." After adverting in support of his opinion to the following contorniate, published by Victorius, viz. ALEXANDER and a head covered with lion's skin, on the obverse; and X. D. IV. I. H. S. X. P. S. DEI. FILIVS, and *an ass with head erect suckling a foal,* for the legend and type of its reverse—Eckhel adds, "But I am bestowing too much time upon a single coin, which no public authority will attempt to defend, and which any one will readily lay aside among the herd of *pseudo monetæ.*"

ASINI CAPUT—a symbol of Dacia.—The head of an ass, on the top of a walking staff, in the hand of a female figure, appears on coins of Trajanus Decius.—See DACIA.—DACIA FELIX. An ass, according to Clemens Alexandrinus, was sacrificed by the Scythians to Apollo.

ASINIA, a plebeian, but a consular family. Whether it derived its name from *Asinus*, as Porcia from *Porcus*, may be questioned. It was divided into many branches of which two surnames only are extant on coins, viz. the one *Gallus,* the other *Pollio.*—The name of Gallus as a monetary triumvir (thus: C. ASINIVS GALLVS IIIVIR. A. A. A. F. F.) is found on large and middle consular brass, with the head, or inscription, or symbol of Augustus. This Asinius Gallus, the son of C. Asinius Pollio, was a man eminent alike in the arts of war and of peace; and on that account a great favourite of Augustus. He wrote the history of the civil war between Cæsar and Pompey, and is said to have been the first to have opened his library to the public use at Rome. It was the same Gallus, who served the consulate in the year U. C. 746 (B. C. 8); and, what more redounded to his honour, when Tiberius divorced himself from Vipsania Agrippina, daughter of Agrippa, he took her to wife, and by that marriage became the father of a numerous progeny. The name of *Pollio* appears on a denarius published in Morel's *Thesaurus*, and in Vaillant's *Fam. Rom.* as follows:—

Obv.—POLLIO. Radiated head of Apollo.

Rev.—C. ASINI. C. N. F. (*Caius Asinius Cnei Filius.*) Crescent moon and seven stars.

For the above types see *Lucretia* gens.

A. SISC. Officina Prima Sisciæ.——Coin struck in the first mint-office at *Sisciæ*, in Pannonia.

ASPERGILLUM, or as otherwise called *Adspersorium*, a sprinkler or holy-water stick, having ends of long horse-hair, which the Romans made use of, to besprinkle those who assisted at the sacrifices, and also to throw the lustral water over the altar and the victims.— See *Pontifical Instruments*.

ASPIRATE.—This is wanting in the orthography of the more ancient Roman coins. Accordingly, we find written without the aspirate *(h)* the names CILO.—GRACCVS.—PILIPPVS.— TAMPILVS.—TRIVMPVS.—YPSAEVS.—for Chilo, Gracchus, Philippus, Tamphilus, Triumphus, Hypsæus.—See Rasche's *Lexicon*.

ASSERTOR.— See *Hercules*.

ASTA.—Bœticæ colonia (Hispania), now *Mesa d'Asta*, situated on the river Bœtis, opposite Gades (Cadiz, in Andalusia). Its coins are *bilingual* and *Latin* autonomes, in first and second brass. The former exhibit on their obverse ASTA. and the bare head of a man; on their reverse a Celtiberian inscription and a winged sphinx.—The latter have for obverse M. POPILLI. M. F. Laureated head of Apollo.—Reverse, P. COL. ASTA. RE. F. A bull standing.—See Mr. Akerman's *"Ancient Coins of Cities,"* &c. p. 22.

ASTARTE—called in Scripture "Ashtaroth" —was the favourite goddess of the Sidonians, Tyrians, Philistines, and Syro-Phœnicians generally. She appears to have been identical with the Greek *Aphrodite*, and the Roman *Venus Genetrix*, being believed by the ancients to be the goddess of generation, as well as of beauty. —By Milton, in his Paradise Regained, a place is assigned to her among the fallen angels :

> With these in troop
> Came Astoreth, whom the Phœnicians called
> *Astarte*, queen of Heaven, with crescent horns ;
> To whose bright image nightly by the moon
> Sidonian virgins paid their vows and songs.

Among the imperial colonies in the east, the cities of Berytus, Bostra, Sidon, and Tyre, are those in which *Astarte* was chiefly worshipped ; and on the respective coins of which she appears,

under the image of a young woman, wearing a tutulated, or tuft-like, head dress ; and clothed in a tunic, high in the neck—sometimes (as in the annexed engraving from a Tyrian coin), not reaching lower than the knees ; sometimes with a longer dress, but with the right knee exposed, and the foot planted on a ship's prow.

This object of gross idolatry had a fine temple at Bostra ; and on a large brass, struck there and dedicated to Julia Mamæa, the idol, as above described, stands within a portico of six columns, holding a cruciform staff in the right hand, and a cornucopiæ in the left.— Of Berytus also she was a great tutelary goddess ; for which reason Nonnus calls that city "the habitation of Venus."—The Tyrians also paid supreme adoration to Astarte, and their city contained a superb temple erected to her honour. The fact that this deity was the Venus of the Tyrians is corroborated by that passage of Cicero (lib. iii. *De Nat. Deor.)* in which he affirms, that the goddess, whom the Tyrians worshipped under the name of Astarte, was the Syrian Venus, who was said to have been married to Adonis.—Josephus records the building of a magnificent temple by Hiram, King of Tyre, in honour of Ashtaroth (Astarte). Coincident with which, we find a second brass of Elaga. balus, exhibiting the goddess, with her usual attributes, standing within a temple.—As the chief local deity of Tyre, she sometimes appears on Roman coins of that colony, standing together with the figure of *Angerona*, Goddess of Silence.—The Sidonians, like their Tyrian neighbours and rivals, were blind votaries to this "abomination" of Assyria ; and their city also had a fine temple of Astarte.—Amongst the numerous monetal dedications made by the Roman colonists at Sidon, to Elagabalus and the female members of his family, are first and second brass coins, which exhibit the effigy of *Astarte* standing (see the annexed woodcut) with her right hand placed on a trophy, whilst she carries in her left the *hasta* crosswise. At her left hand a figure of Victory, placed on a column, presents to her a crown. At her left foot is the *conchylium*, or shell fish, from whose blood the famous purple was said to have been made. The palm tree is a symbol common to Phœnicia and Palestine. This reverse is repeated on other colonial medals of Tyre and of Sidon, with the addition of representing the idol within its temple.

In Vaillant's *Colonies* are given a coin of Septimius Severus, and another of Diadumenianus, the former bearing the following legend and type on the reverse, viz. COL. AELIA CAPIT. (established by Hadrian on the ruins of *Jerusalem.)*—On this reverse *Astarte*, or Venus, holds, in one hand, the head of Serapis, and in the other the *hasta ;* her right foot being placed on the crouching figure of a river-god. In the coin dedicated to the youthful son of Macrinus, two winged Victories are added, standing at her feet on each side.—The same learned writer, in describing the well-known type which accompanies *Indulgentia Augg. in Carth.* on a denarius of the Emperor Severus, says of *Cybele vecta leone currente*—"This goddess is the Astarte of Carthage."—See *Aelia Capitolina—Bostra—Berytus—Sidon*, and *Tyrus*, in their respective places.

Astarte is also typified on many Greek coins of cities and people. Likewise on some *Greek* Imperial, struck under Caracalla, Geta, Elagabalus, Alexander Severus, Gordianus Pius, &c.

ASTRA.—Stars, either alone, or with other signs added to them, are exhibited on many family and consular coins.—On a denarius of the Asinia gens, the radiated head of Apollo (symbolising the Sun), appears on one side, and a crescent moon, surrounded by seven stars, on the other.—Stars appear over the caps of the *Dioscuri*, whom fable has placed amongst the heavenly host.—*Castor* and *Pollux* were, on this account, worshipped by navigators.—On a denarius of the *Rustia* family, a star is put before the head of Mars, because the year was reckoned to begin with the month *Martius*, (March) which takes its name from that god.— Stars above a curule chair, indicating the divinity of Julius Cæsar, appear on a silver coin of the *Aelia* family.—The *astrum crinitum*, or star with "tail of fire," on the reverse of gold and silver, struck under Augustus, in memory of Julius Cæsar, is regarded as allusive to the great comet, which, appearing soon after the Dictator's death, was looked on by the common people as denoting his immortality, and translation to the skies.—Of this popular credulity Augustus availed himself to honour his uncle with deification.—(See *Comet.)*—A star is sometimes placed, on coins, above or near the head of Julius Cæsar, "which (says Eckhel, vi. 11), perhaps indicates the star of Venus, mother of Æneas, or more likely the year when the calendar was brought, with greater exactness, to the course of the Sun. The figure of the crescent moon, also seen near the portrait of the same emperor, is of uncertain signification, unless *that* likewise has reference to the corrected year." (vi. 19.)—A star is found on many coins of Elagabalus, both those struck at Rome and those of colonial fabric. This symbol has reference to the Sun, in whose Syrian worship and priesthood he was initiated before his baneful accession to the empire.—A star over a ship's prow appears on the reverse of a denarius of Vespasian, with legend of COS. VIII. and the same figure occurs on some coin or other, throughout the greater part of the imperial series.

Two stars, under which Cupid sits bestriding a dolphin, with the inscription S. P. Q. R. appear on a rare silver coin of Augustus. Seguin understands it to mean, on one side the star of Venus, on the other the star of Julius, as indicating the assumed family origin of the first Cæsar.—See *Mionnet*, i. 105.

ASTROLOGICAL and ASTRONOMICAL symbols are found on Roman coins, as in the Capricorn, double and single, of Augustus and of Vespasian; the crescent moon and seven stars of Hadrian and of Faustina.—The Greek imperial series also present several fine medals, which

have for their reverse types the twelve signs of the Zodiac.—See *Capricorn.*

ASTURES, a people of Spain, subdued by P. Carisius, pro-prætor under Augustus. Their capital was Asturica, now *Astorga*, in the kingdom of Leon.—See Akerman's *Coins of Cities*, &c. p. 65.

ASTURICA.—Vaillant (*in Col.* i, p. 10) gives a second brass coin with the obverse legend of AVGVSTVS DIVI F. and bare head of Augustus, and which presents on its reverse a colonist ploughing with two oxen, with the legend COL. AST. AVGVSTA, which he renders *Colonia Asturica Augusta*, or colony of the Astures, a territory of Hispania Tarraconensis.—Eckhel, however, recognises in the abbreviation AST. the name of no colony but Asta of *Bætica*.—And Mionnet (S. I. 53) says, "cette médaille peut aussi bien appartenir à *Asta, ou Astapa, ou Astigi, villes de la Bætique.*"

ATHALARICUS, the grandson of Theodoricus, ascended the throne of the Goths, in Italy, on the death of his grandfather, A.D. 526. He died A.D. 534. He is styled on coins (which are rare) D. N. ATHALARICVS or ATALARICVS; also D. N. ATALARICVS REX. On silver quinarii of Justinus and Justinianus, emperors of the east, his name appears followed by that of REX or RIX. —Akerman, *Descr. Cat.* ii. 396.

Banduri (vol. ii. p. 643,) gives a third brass, with INVICTA ROMA, and the galeated head of a woman on the obverse, and on the reverse D. N. ATHALARICVS—with the type of that prince, standing, helmeted and paludated, face to the left, his right hand resting on a spear, and his left on a shield placed on the ground. In the field S. C. & X.

ATHENODORUS VABALATHUS.—See VABALATHUS.

ATHENÆ.—Athens, the most celebrated city of Greece, situate in that part of Achaia, called Attica.—There is a tetradrachm inscribed COS. III. with the figure of Minerva standing; with regard to which Vaillant (Pr. ii. 140) is of opinion, that the Athenians struck this coin, in memory of the benefits which Hadrian had liberally bestowed on their city, in which, according to Spartianus, he passed the winter of the year of Rome 875 (B. C. 122).

ATHLETÆ.—This appellation was given to those, who contended for the prizes at public games. And under this name, among the Greeks, were comprised the professors of five different kinds of gymnastics, or bodily exercises, viz. those of the race, and of the *discus*, leaping, wrestling, and pugilism.—The Romans, who took the Grecian model generally as the object of their imitation, appropriated the name of *Athletæ* almost exclusively to wrestlers, and to those who fought with their fists: whilst those who practised other feats of strength and activity had distinct and peculiar appellations.

Spanheim, in illustrating his translation of the Cæsars of Julian (p. 142), gives the figures of two naked wrestlers, or *Athletæ*, holding each other by the arms, as in the act of "trying a fall." They form the type of a coin struck at Laodicæa, in Syria, under Caracalla, on the occasion of some public games celebrated in that city, with the legend LAODICAEA, a Roman colony, and which, on another rare coin dedicated to the same emperor, exhibits, in abbreviation, all its titles, viz. COLonia SEPtimia AUrelia LAODicæa METRopolis.—Vaillant furnishes a similar reverse of Elagabalus. The same author (in *Col.* vol. ii. p. 105) makes the two following references to the contests of the *Athletæ* :—On the reverse of an *Annia Faustina*, colony of Sidon, CER. SAC. PER. OECVME. ISELA. *Certamina, Sacra, Periodonica, Oecumenica, Iselastica* ; within a laurel crown. —On the reverse of a colonial coin, struck at Tyre (COL. TYRO. METROP.) under Trebonianus Gallus, are two naked *Athletæ*, standing with a vase between them ; each holding in his hands a *discus*, out of which issues a palm branch. (Vaillant, *Col.* ii. 217)—See HELIOPOLIS and SIDON and TYRVS (*suis locis*). See also SAC. CAP. OEC. ISEL. and *Victors at Games.*—In connection with this subject, reference may be made to *Circus Maximus*—a representation of which is given on a brass medallion of Gordianus Pius, in which wrestlers and other *Athletæ* appear in the foreground.

ATIA, gens plebeia——which writers have divided into two families, whose respective surnames, as they appear on coins, were *Balbus* and *Labienus*. The *Atii*, or *Atti* take their fabulous origin from the Trojan Atys : Virgil says

    Alter Atys, genus unde Atti dixére Latini.

Perhaps, says Pitiscus, the poet spake thus, to flatter Augustus, whose mother was of the plebeian stock—a stock so obscure as never to have risen above the prætorship.—Atius *Balbus* is named on a rare second brass, for an accurate engraving of which see Visconti, *Iconographie Romaine*, part i. pl. v. fig. 1.

    Obv.—M. ATIVS BALBVS. PR.—Bare head of Balbus.

    Rev.—SARD. PATER.—Head of a man strangely attired.

The above coin shews that Atius Balbus was sent to Sardinia as Prætor, and that Augustus having already obtained submission to his rule from the Sardinians, this coin was struck with the head of Atius, in acknowledgment of their obligations to him.—"Its barbarous workmanship," adds Eckhel, "savours strongly of Sardinia, always inhospitable to the elegant arts."—Sard*us* Pater, whom the reverse exhibits, was said to be the son of Hercules, who having landed on the Sardinian coast, gave his name to that island.—For a coin and some account of a member of this family bearing its second surname, and who figures historically in the annals of the later republic, see *Labienus.*

ATILIA, gens patricia et plebeia.—On the coins of this family, one *Saranus* is commemorated. The obverse of the denarius has for legend SAR. or SARAN. and for type a winged and helmeted head of Pallas. The reverse bears M. ATIL. and the figures of the Dioscuri on horseback, with ROMA at the bottom—or Victory in

a biga.—The pieces, in bronze, of this gens, are by the mint-masters of Augustus.—See *Dioscuri.*

ATLAS, according to some mythographers, was chief of the Titans that made war against Jupiter, who, to punish, sentenced him to support the heavens. The account of him, divested of fable, is that Atlas was a philosopher of royal rank, whose territories lay in north-western Africa, and who, having been accustomed to make astronomical observations on a high mountain of Mauritania, gave his name to it, and also to the ocean (Atlantic), on which it borders.—Vaillant (Pr. iii. p. 124) gives a brass medallion of Antoninus Pius, the epigraph on the reverse of which is TR. POT. XX. COS. IIII.; and the type, Jupiter standing with *hasta* and *fulmen*, an eagle at his feet, and Atlas bearing a globe on his shoulders. There is in the French Cabinet another brass medallion, mounted in a large circle, struck under the above-named emperor, the reverse legend of which is the same as that already quoted; but the type differs from it. Jupiter, in the latter instance, stands before an altar; and this altar is ornamented with a bas-relief, representing Jupiter striking the Titans with his thunderbolts. On the altar is an eagle with expanded wings. Behind Jupiter is *Atlas* on his knees sustaining the globe.—See *Jupiter.*

ATTALUS PRISCUS, an usurper in the reign of Honorius, first in Italy, afterwards in Gaul. Born of an Ionian family, he was appointed Prefect of Rome. And King Alaric,

when he took that city (A. D. 409), proclaimed him emperor. Deprived of that title by the same gothic conqueror who had given it to him, he subsequently resumed it in Gaul, A. D. 410. Taken prisoner in 416, he had his right hand cut off, and was banished by Honorius to the island of Lipari, where he died. On his coins (which are very rare in gold, silver, and small brass) he is styled PRISC (or PRISCVS) ATTALVS P. P. AVG.—also IMP. PRISCVS ATTALVS P. F. AVG. These pieces were probably minted at Rome. There is a silver medallion with his diademed portrait, of extraordinary size and highest rarity, in the British Museum. Mr. Akerman has given an engraving of this coin, in vol. ii. p. 358 of his Descriptive Catalogue. Vaillant (Pr. iii. 264) had given a similar one from the Vatican collection. The legend and type of the reverse are INVICTA ROMA AETERNA; Rome helmeted and paludated, sits fronting, in a chair ornamented on each side with lions' heads; her right hand holds a *victoriola*, her left hand rests on the end of a spear reversed. In the exergue RMPS.

ATTILA, or *Atila*, or *Ateula*, King of the Huns, Goths, and Danes, was called the "dread of the world"—the "scourge of God." He succeeded to the government of these "Northmen," A. D. 434. After ravaging the provinces of the east, and compelling the Emperor Theodosius the Second to pay him tribute, he returned to his own dominions, having triumphed both in the Italian and in the Illyrian wars. He was contemplating the invasion of Asia and Africa, at the moment when, enslaved by lust and debauchery, he lost his reason, amidst feasting and concubinage, and died of a flow of blood from the nostrils, A. U. C. 1207 (B.C. 454). The pieces attributed to this extraordinary man, inscribed ATEVLA, or ATIVLA, and also ATIL. are said by Eckhel, Hennin, and others, not to be his, but coins of Gaulish chiefs.

ATYS, or *Attys.*—Except in association with types relating to Cybele, on many Roman as well as Greek coins, it would be scarcely worth while to notice the worse than absurd myths of Atys; who, according to one of several stories concerning him, was a handsome young shepherd of Phrygia, of whom the Mother of the Gods (Magna Mater Deûm), became greatly enamoured. She entrusted him with the care of her temple, having made him promise that he would always live in chaste celibacy. In violation of this vow, however, he fell in love with the nymph Sangaris, whom Cybele, in her jealous anger, caused to die. And Atys, in the frenzy of his grief, inflicted a nameless injury upon himself. But the goddess, who found this punishment too cruel, as well to her own feelings as to those of her beloved, physically restored him; and took him again into her service. The act of self-mutilation was, however, afterwards performed by the sacerdotal successors of Atys, as a condition attached to the priesthood of Cybele. On a contorniate medal of Vespasian, engraved in Morel's *Thesaurus*, this part of the subject is illustrated.—"*Atys, sive potius Gallus* (as the priest of Cybele was called) *se ipsum castrans.*"—See *Cybele*.

AV. and O. were indiscriminately used by the Romans, as is instanced in some denarii, whereon we read FOSTVLVS for FAVSTVLVS.—PLOTIVS for PLAVTIVS.

AV. *Augur.*—C. CALDVS. IMP. AV. X.—*Caius Caldus Imperator, Augur, Decemvir.*

AV. Augusta—or Augustus.

AV. *Aurelius.*—As AV. COMMODVS AVG. on coins of Commodus.—M. AV*relius* ANTONINVS PIVS AV*gustus*, on coins of Caracalla.—AV*relius* S. ALEXAND. AVG. of Severus Alexander.—AV. ANTONINVS, of Elagabalus.

AVCT. PIET. (on silver) and AVCTOR PIETAT. (on first brass) P. M. TR. P. XII. TR. P. VIII. COS. V. P. P.—A stolated woman standing

before an altar, holding a patera in her right hand, and the *acerra* in her left. Struck about A. D. 184.—See *Acerra*, p. 4.

Commodus, on whose coins this legend appears, may be supposed to have earned the title of *Auctor Pietatis*, whilst bestowing marked attention on religious matters. But in this, as in all other things, he conducted himself like a madman, and in a manner derogatory to the majesty of the empire. For, in celebrating the rites of Isis, he shaved his head, and carried the dog-headed god *Anubis*, during which ceremony he wantonly belaboured the heads of the worshippers with the face of the heavy image. He even attired himself as a sacrificer, and with his own hand immolated the victims. Nay, he went on so far as to supply fresh material for the *piety* of an enslaved and superstitious people, by assuming the titles DEVS and HERCVLES, during the year of Rome 944 (A. D. 191).—"Aeneas is styled by Ovid *pietatis idoneus auctor*, the true promoter of piety, doubtless on account of his attachment to the gods, and to his father, being in the mouths of all; therefore fitly *(idoneè)* so styled; whence, adds Eckhel, you may draw the distinction between that ancient *Auctor Pietatis*, and the one with whom we are here dealing."—vol. vii. p. 118.

AVCTA KART.—See *Salvis Augg.*

AVERSA.—The reverse side of a coin.—See *Reverse.*

AUFIDIA gens.—That this family was plebeian is shewn by the *tribuni plebis*, who were chosen from it. "Perhaps, says Vaillant, the river Aufidius, celebrated on account of the slaughter of the Romans at Cannæ, gave the original name to this family;" which however was not known until about the period of the republic's decline. Its coins consist of only two varieties, one of these, a rare denarius, has

Obv.—RVS. The winged head of Pallas, with XVI. behind it.

Rev.—M. AVF. Jupiter in a quadriga at full speed—below ROMA.

Vaillant considers RVS. to be meant for *Rusticus*, as a cognomen of the Aufidia family; Morel and Perizoni explain it *Ruso*. Eckhel prefers the former interpretation, because in the most perfect specimen in the Imperial Cabinet, RVS. alone is read, without a vestige of the o, which Morel thought was added.

AVG. *Augur.*—This abbreviation is of frequent occurrence on the coins of Mark Antony, accompanied by the augural symbols.

AVG.—On gold and silver coins of Vespasian, included by Eckhel (vi. 326) amongst those which bear testimony to the conquest of Judæa by that Emperor, and to his triumph on that account, in the year U. C. 824 (A. D. 71) the abbreviation AVG. appears on the reverse, within a crown of oak leaves, in others of olive, and in others inscribed on a shield, surrounded by an olive wreath. This AVG. is by some supposed to mean AVG*ur*. But Eckhel, who refers to one in the Vienna Cabinet, agrees with Liebe *(Goth Num.)* in thinking it more probable that, as there is no attribute of the augurship on these coins, the letters AVG. in this instance, should be read AVG*usto;* and that the crown, or shield, should be considered to typify the *corona,* or *clypeus,* offered and dedicated to Vespasian, as was customary on such triumphal occasions.

AVG. *Augurinus*—one of the three surnames of the Minucia gens, derived from the augural priesthood.

AVG. *Augustus*—or *Augusta.*—The usual designation of an Emperor or of an Empress.

AVG. *Augusta.*—The ordinary epithet of Roman colonies derived from Julius Cæsar and Augustus, as AVG. IVL. Augusta Julia, or IVL. AVG. Julia Augusta, on many of their colonial coins.

AVG. *Augusta.*—See CONCORDIA AVG.—FECVNDITAS AVG.—PIETAS AVG. &c. &c.

AVG. *Augusti.*—See APOLLO CONSERVATOR AVGVSTI, &c.

AVG. F. or FIL. *Augusti Filius,* or *Filia*—son or daughter of the August or Emperor.

AVG. D. F. or AVG. DIVI. F.—*Augustus Divi Filius.*—Augustus, son of the Divine, i. e. son of Julius Cæsar).

AVG. N. *Augusti Nepos.* Grandson of Augustus.—*e. g.* GERMANICVS CAESAR TI. F. DIVI. AVG. N.—*(Germanicus Cæsar Tiberii Augusti Filius, Divi Augusti Nepos.).*

AVG. N. *Augusti Nepos.*—Great grandchild of Augustus, as in Caius Caligula. C. CAESAR DIVI. AVG. PRON. AVG.

AVG. N. *Augusti Nostri.*—Of our Emperor. —See *Abundantia* AVG. N.—FELIX ADVENTVS AVG. N. &c.

AVG. *Duorum Augustorum.*—Two Gs after AV signify two *Augusti* or Emperors reigning together.—For examples of GG. see coins of Severus and Caracalla; also of Carus and Carinus, Carinus and Numerianus, Diocletianus and Maximianus Hercules, Constantius and Maximianus—also Philippus senior and junior, &c.

AVGGG. *Trium Augustorum.*—Where this abbreviation occurs it indicates that three *Augusti,* or Emperors, reigned together. For examples of this rare reading on Imperial coins see the VIRTVS AVGGG. of Carinus quoted by Eckhel, and the VICTORIA AVGGG. of Valentinianus I. cited by Mionnet.—Vaillant ascribes a VIRTVS AVGGG. to Numerian, but is not confirmed by either Eckhel or Mionnet.—See *Augusti.*

AVGV.—*Augusta, Augustæ, Augustus,* or *Augusti.*

AUGURES, Augurs.—This sacerdotal order was so called, because it professed to predict future events by signs and prodigies. Their discipline and religion were probably of Sabine origin, introduced into Rome at the earliest period of her foundation, but blended with the Etrurian rites and ceremonies of divination. In such high authority and reverence was this distinct branch of the priesthood held, that the early Romans never conducted anything, either within or beyond the walls of their city, until the auspices had been taken, in the observance of supernatural signs, which were publicly announced, by the Augurs. A mass of fraud and folly more puerile and absurd was never made the subject of scientific organization and of solemn practice. Yet it was this " vain mysterious art," which the Romans dignified with the highest privileges, next to those of the supreme pontificate. And patricians of the first rank—nay Emperors themselves,—deemed it an honour and an advantage to be received into membership by the Augural college. This *collegium,* at its institution, for which the policy of Romulus has the credit, was composed of three Augurs, taken from the three tribes, into which, as we are told, that Prince at first divided the subjects of his infant state. Numa is recorded to have added two more. These five were all patricians, till the year U.C. 454, (B. C. 300) when, by the Lex Ogulnia, it was enacted, that five of the Augurs should be plebeians. Up to this period, the college appears to have exercised the free and independent right of electing its own members, Sulla, when, in A. U. C. 672, (B.C. 82) created perpetual dictator, amongst other new laws and appointments, passed one to increase this number to fifteen. The first and oldest of the Augurs was called *Magister collegii.* They were originally chosen, as the other priests, by the patricians in their *comitia curiata.* Next, they were allowed to elect themselves. But after the introduction of plebeian members into the college, a somewhat more popular mode of filling up vacancies for a time prevailed. "The priests of the college of Augurs, for a long time arrogated to themselves the sole privilege of supplicating the gods for the health of every individual, and of the whole state,—as if any one could not ask it for himself. Yet nothing was more profitable. Pliny mentions several physicians who were pensioned at about £2000 per annum; and in the reign of Claudius, one *Doctor* Sterninus complaining of the smallness of his income, it was doubled for him." (Capt. Smyth, p. 195.) During the civil wars, the Augurs became ready instruments for furthering the designs of both the contending factions. In the reign of Augustus they underwent the same changes as the Pontiffs, namely election by the Plebs, subject however to the approval or veto of the prince. At length the Emperors reserved to themselves the right of nominating the Augurs, which continued to be exercised until the reign of Theodosius the Great (A.D. 379). Christianity being then fully established throughout both divisions of the empire, the augural, in common with every other, order of the heathen priesthood, was by law abolished. But the fire of this most ancient and most popular of Roman superstitions, smouldered amidst the ruins of paganism, long after the revenues which supported the augurship had been appropriated to the public treasury.

AUGURATION.—The augural function was to prognosticate good or evil, in observing the flight, the warbling, and the screams of birds; the avidity of fowls in eating, or their refusal to take food; also to note the various phenomena that appear in the heavens. The actual inspection of slaughtered animals devolved to an inferior order called Haruspices [see the word], who reported to the Augurs, whether the entrails of such animals were in a healthy or an unsound state. As the chief expounders and interpreters of all that related to the ceremonial law, and to the regulation of religious observances, the Augurs, under the kings, and afterwards during the early ages of the republic, were consulted always on the question of waging war, and on any other matter of great public importance. A striking proof of the peculiar consideration attached to this order of men, exhibits itself in what is stated respecting its priestly rank, which was not allowed to be taken away from any one on whom it had once been conferred, lest the secrets of the pagan system should be revealed to the multitude. Pliny the younger calls the augurship a priesthood *(sacerdotium)*, not only of ancient institution and holy character, but also evidently sacred and distinguished from the fact, that it is never taken away from a person during his life time *(quod non adimitur viventi)*. Accordingly, as we learn from Plutarch, whatever might be the crime committed by an Augur, he was secure of retaining his office for life, lest the pretended mysteries of an idolatrous worship might have become exposed to the ridicule of sensible persons.

The place for taking the augury lay on an elevated site, generally at a short distance beyond the walls of the city. The officiating priest proceeded to the spot, clothed in a long robe, which covered the head like a veil, and reached down to the feet, called *litea* or *trabea*. Then taking in his right hand the *lituus*, a short wand, curved at the upper end, he traced upon the ground the *templum* or *tabernaculum*. After this, he divided the heavens into four parts with the same *lituus*, marking on the earth, as well as in the air, the four quarters, east, west, north, and south. The Augur then examined with great attention, what birds appeared; in what manner they flew; and what sounds issued from their throats. Those signs which displayed themselves to the left passed for favourable ones, and those which were seen on the right side were pronounced to be of bad augury. In short, the whole was a combination of priestcraft with state policy, invested with extraordinary powers and privileges, and cultivated chiefly to increase the influence of the leading authorities over a credulous and ignorant people.

On a denarius of the *Cornuficia* gens, and on coins of Pompey the Great, Julius Cæsar, Mark Antony, Augustus, and others, the figure of an Augur, and the dignity of the office, are found represented and designated, not only by the sacerdotal robe and veil, but by the *lituus*, the *præfericulum*, and other symbols;

also by the word itself inscribed at full, or abridged; AVGVR. or AVG.—A denarius of Q. CASSIVS, has for the type of its reverse an eagle standing on a thunderbolt, between the *lituus* and the *præfericulum*. Jupiter was the tutelary god of the augural college.—On a silver coin of the Antonia family, the legends and types of which Havercamp considers to indicate the concord, subsisting when it was struck, between Mark Antony and Lepidus, we see on one

side (as in the annexed cut) *Marcus* ANTON*ius* IMP*erator*, with a raven, or as Du Choul describes it "one of the sacred chickens," relating to the pullispicium, or augury by fowls; the *præfericulum* and the *lituus*, are symbols of Antony's augurship. On the other side is M*arcus* LEPID*us* IMP*erator;* with the apex (or sacerdotal cap), the *securis* (or sacrificial axe), the *simpulum* (or chalice), and the *aspergillum* (or sprinkler), insignia of the office of Pontifex Maximus, which Lepidus had usurped.

AUGUR. PONT. MAX.—This designation of two distinct offices, with augural and pontifical instruments mingled together, namely, the *lituus* and the *præfericulum* with the *aspergillum*, *apex*, and *securis*, form the legend and type of denarii of Julius Cæsar, struck about A. U. C. 708 (B. C. 46). They serve to shew that the Dictator had at this time united the title of *Augur* to that of the chief pontificate and to his other titles. It was after his return from Egypt and Asia, that Julius caused his name to be inscribed in the college of Augurs, as well as is in the other sacerdotal corporations. The *lituus* marks the augural office, and the same instrument is sometimes placed on his coins behind his head.

Augurate of Mark Antony.—There are gold and silver of Mark Antony's on which the official title, accompanied by the robe and crook, of the augurship, is conspicuously represented. On the obverse (as in the annexed cut) we read M*arcus* ANTONIVS, M*arci* F*ilius*, M*arci* N*epos*,

AVGVR. IMP*erator* TER*tium*. A male figure, in the *trabea*, walking, holds the *lituus*. On the other side is the radiated head of the Sun, surrounded by the abridged inscription of Antony's other titles, viz. *Triumvir Reipublicæ Constituendæ, Consul Designatus, Iterum, et Tertium*. The veiled and robed figure, holding the *lituus*, represents M. Antony as Augur.

AUGUR. TRI. P. or TRI. POT.—This inscription appears on the reverse of a silver coin, minted by Vespasian, with sacerdotal instruments for its type. On the obverse of the denarius, struck A. U. C. 825 (A. D. 72), Vespasian calls himself Imperator, Augustus, and Pontifex Maximus, whilst on the reverse he takes the title of Augur, giving it precedence before the *Tribunitia Potestas*. This conjunction of the augural title and symbols with the highest marks of Imperial power, plainly indicates the consideration in which the dignity and functions of the former office continued down to this reign, and also that of Titus, to be held by the Romans. On a marble, transcribed from Muratori, Tiberius is not only termed PONT. MAX. but also AVGVR. XVVIR. S. F. VIIVIR. EPVLONVM; and so is Caligula, on his coins, called both PONT. MAX. and AVGVR.—Eckhel, vi. 332.

Amongst the denarii struck under the republic, and which Havercamp, in the *Thesaurus* of Morel, classes as *numi incerti* (the uncertainty being as to the particular *gens* to which they ought respectively to be assigned), there is one, which evidently bears allusion to the earliest traditions of Rome. The coin in question is a well-known one. It has for the

type of its obverse the usual head of Pallas, with the mark of the denarius X, and the word ROMA below. The reverse, without epigraph, exhibits a helmeted female, seated on a heap of shields, her right hand resting on her knee, whilst the left hand is supported by a spear. On each side of the figure is a bird flying towards her: at her feet is the common symbol of the wolf suckling the twins.

Here then we have before us, the personified genius of the Roman people, or the representation of deified Rome herself. She is seated on bucklers—it may perhaps be supposed—on those sacred bucklers (see *Ancilia*, p. 45), in the possession and custody of which, as of a heaven-descended gift, that people had gone forth from conquest to conquest. The genius, or goddess, is looking downwards, as if absorbed in reflection upon the rise of "the eternal city," from a humble origin, under its marvellously nurtured *first* king, to the palmy state of extended power and dominion, at which it had arrived as a consular common-wealth. The two birds were doubtless meant to adumbrate that part of the ancient legend, which describes the two intrepid brothers, become no longer mere leaders of pastoral comrades, but the acknowledged scions of royalty, and fierce rivals, the one against the other, for civic honours, and for supremacy of power. It was agreed that the question at issue between them, namely, where the city should be built, and after whose name it should be called as that of its founder, should be decided by augury. Remus was the first to see vultures, six in number. Romulus soon afterwards saw twelve. Each claimed the augury in his own favour. The sequel of the story requires not to be related in this place.

Considering the conspicuous part performed by those invested with the augural office, both during the time of the republic, and under the earlier succession of emperors, it seems calculated to excite surprise, that so few even of the family coins of the Romans exhibit any allusions to Augury, and that *after* the reigns of, what are called, the Twelve Cæsars (on whose mintages the symbols and name of an Augur but seldom

appear), neither legends nor types bear any reference to the institution or to its priesthood.

AUGUR NAVIUS. —See NAVIUS.

AVGVST.—*Augustæ* or *Augusti.*

AVGVSTA.—This epithet is of frequent occurrence on Roman coins of the Imperial series. It was a title decreed to the wives of Emperors; the quality of *Augusta*, as regarded the first empresses, being indeed the only distinctive appellation, which served (as it were) to consecrate their rank. These princesses, however, though declared *Augustæ*, were not on that account less subject to the laws which governed private individuals. Nor does it seem that they were admitted to the privilege of having their title and effigy borne on coins, except by degrees and under certain restrictions. At the commencement, these honours were dedicated to them only on coins struck in the provinces. Afterwards, when their portraits were engraved on those actually minted at Rome, it was done under the personifications, or symbols, of certain divinities, or of certain deified virtues. But the custom, once introduced by Augustus, perpetuated itself; and almost all his successors caused, or at least permitted, the likenesses of their wives (and occasionally other near relations, as well female as male), to be placed on a portion of their coinage. Accordingly, when not found on Roman coins, properly so called, they are usually seen on those of some provincial city of the empire.—"These medals of empresses, however (as the author of *Leçons Numismatiques* observes), are generally less abundant than those of the princes who really held the sceptre. And although for that reason much sought after by the curious, and also on account of their genealogical reference to imperial families, if the expression may be allowed; yet they are, for the most part, less interesting in point of chronology and of connection with national events, which they seldom trace in the same striking manner as do the coins of the emperors themselves."— This remark equally applies to medals struck in honour of young princes *(Cæsares)* who did not reign.

Pliny calls AVGVSTA the marriage name (L. XV. c. 30). And therein he is borne out by successive examples in the mintage of Imperial Rome. Thus on a gold coin, struck under Domitian, his wife is styled DOMITIA AVGVSTA IMP. DOMIT. (by implication *uxor*).—Faustina senior, wife of Antoninus Pius, is called FAVSTINA AVGVSTA, and FAVSTINA AVG. ANTONINI AVG. (by implication *uxor*). In like manner also, on coins of the younger Faustina, wife of M. Aurelius, we read FAVSTINA AVGVSTA AVG. ANTONINI PII. FIL. (Daughter of Antonine).—Livia, wife of Augustus, exchanging the name of Livia for that of Julia, on her adoption into that family, is styled on coins struck after her husband's death, IVLIA AVGVSTA—AVGVSTA MATER PATRIAE— and after her death, DIVA IVLIA AVGVSTA.— Lucilla, the wife of L. Verus, is designated on her medals as LVCILLA AVGVSTA, or LVCILLA AVG. M. ANTONINI AVG. F. (Daughter of M. Aurelius).— Messalina was not distinguished by this imperial title, till a late period of her infamous career, as the wife of Claudius. Indeed, according to Dion, that Emperor refused to allow her such an honour; but the Senate granted it, perhaps after the Britannic expedition. Some Greek medals, struck in Egypt exhibit, around her portrait, *Valeria Messalina Augusta.* And on some Latin colonial coins (for there were none of hers minted at Rome), she is called VALERIA MESSALINA AVG.—Sabina, wife of Hadrian, is entitled, on her coins, SABINA AVGVSTA IMP. HADRIANI AVG. (by implication *uxor*).

There are four imperial matrons of the lower empire, each of whom on her coins is denominated AVGVSTA. Yet ancient historians have made no mention of them. These are: Barbia Orbiana, third wife of Alexander Severus; Cornelia Supera, wife of Æmilianus; Severina, wife of Aurelianus; and Magnia Urbica, wife of Carinus. And it is only by the subsequent researches, discoveries, and assignments of Khell, Eckhel, and other eminently learned and sagacious numismatists, that the respective husbands of the ladies in question have become known at this period of time.

The title of *Augusta* was conferred, not only on the wives of emperors, and of the Cæsars, but also on their mothers, grand-mothers, sisters, daughters, grand-daughters, and other female relations. For example: Antonia, grandmother of Caligula; Julia Mæsa, grand-mother of Elagabalus; Julia Soaemias, mother of the same emperor; Julia Mamæa, mother of Alexander Severus; have on Roman coins the appendage of *Augusta* inscribed after their names.—The same honour was bestowed, though it but seldom occurs, on the daughters of emperors, simply as such—in proof of which see the instance of Julia Titi, daughter of Titus, and of Didia Clara, daughter of Didius Julianus. With respect to sisters of emperors, and other women of Augustal rank, but not married either to reigning princes or to heirs of those princes, we find (to say nothing of the revolting example of Drusilla and Julia, sisters of Caligula) the graceful compliment paid to Marciana, sister of Trajan, and to her daughter Matidia, consequently niece to that emperor, each decorated on their coins with the surname of *Augusta*.

The *Augustæ* or empresses and other princesses of the Roman empire (says Mangeart), manifested no less ambition than the potentates whom they espoused, or were related to. At first they had but one name, to which they soon added a prenomen and a cognomen, united with titles as vain as they were ostentatious. In the flattering assumption, that they resembled the goddesses, as the emperors did the gods, they wished to hold the same super-human rank; and therefore caused themselves to be portrayed like the images of those female divinities, whom they themselves respectively held in peculiar veneration. Accordingly after a time, we find them on their medals borrowing their very names and titles—their attributes, symbols, and statuary forms. One empress called herself Ceres; another Diana. This *Augusta* took the name of

Juno; that of Luna Lucifera. But not content with having robbed those goddesses of their appellations and qualities, some of the Roman princesses, such as the Faustinas, Crispina, Lucilla, Julia Domna, &c. elevated themselves at once into divinities, as is shewn by the legends on their coins, viz. Dea, Diva, Mater Deûm, Genetrix Orbis, Ceres Frugifera; Diana Augusta, Juno Regina. To some of them these titles were given during their life-time; to others after their death. There are, however, not a few who were honoured with these recognitions of divinity both while living and when dead.— (See *Introduction à la Science des Médailles*, p. 534 *et seq.*)

Augustæ, who were the wives of emperors (as will have been seen from preceding observations) are neither on their own coins nor on those of their husbands, ever called *uxores*, but always AVG. or AVGVSTAE. It is, therefore, from the title bestowed upon them in the imperial medals, that a valid argument may be drawn as to the fact of their having shared the augustal bed.

Vaillant (Pr. T. ii. 235), in alluding to the silver coin of Julia Domna, on which that ambitious woman is exhibited with the epigraph, and under the image, of Juno, observes, "that in order to surround the persons of empresses, with greater dignity and reverence, it had become the custom to assimilate them with the forms and attributes of goddesses, and to present them in their names to the people."—Empresses, in analogy with the examples of their consorts, were called *Matres Patriæ* (mothers of the country), *Matres Senatus* (mothers of the Senate), &c. On colonial coins the countenances of the *Augustæ* were, out of adulation, often represented, as *Genii Urbium*, apparently to indicate that such colonies held their cities under the protection and patronage of those empresses.

Augustæ had also the privilege of having their consecrated images carried in the *carpenta* (or covered chariots) on those public occasions, when the statues of the emperors were conveyed in the *thensæ*, or cars of state.—The inscriptions of PIETAS, PVDICITIA, VIRTVS, &c. followed by AVG. are often seen on the coins of *Augustæ*, accompanied by appropriate types. "Thus there is scarcely a female of the Augustal house, who, though she might not possess a true claim to character for being a. pious, modest, and good woman, yet failed to make an ostentation of her piety, chastity, and virtue. For this cause it was a favourite practice with them to have the figure of *Vesta* engraved on their coins, under whose image, as under the peculiar type of chastity, they thought fit to be represented before the public."

The series of *Augustæ*, whose names and portraits are found on Roman coins (though not of every metal), from the reign of Augustus, who died 14 years after the birth of our Saviour, to Basiliscus, brother-in-law of Leo I. who reigned A.D. 476, is as follows:—

Livia, wife of Augustus. Born 57 years before Christ; died A. D. 29.

Antonia, wife of Drusus senior. Born 39 years before Christ; died A.D. 38.

Agrippina senior, wife of Germanicus. Born 15 years before Christ; died A.D. 33.

Messalina, third wife of Claudius. Died A.D. 48.

Agrippina junior, fourth wife of Claudius, sister of Caligula. Born A.D. 16; died A.D. 50.

Octavia, first wife of Nero. Died A.D. 62.

Poppæa, second wife of Nero. Died A.D. 62.

Flavia Domitilla, wife of Vespasian. Died A.D. 68, the year previous to her husband's accession to the empire.

Julia, daughter of Titus. Died in the reign of Domitian, viz. between A.D. 81 and 96.

Domitia, wife of Domitian. Died in the reign of Antoninus Pius, viz. about A.D. 140.

Plotina, wife of Trajan. Died A.D. 129.

Marciana, sister of Trajan. Died about A.D. 114.

Matidia, daughter of Marciana. Died in the reign of Antoninus.

Sabina, wife of Hadrian. Died A.D. 137.

Faustina senior, wife of Antoninus Pius.— Born A.D. 105; died 141.

Faustina junior, wife and cousin german of M. Aurelius. Died A.D. 175.

Lucilla, daughter of M. Aurelius, and wife of L. Verus. Born A.D. 147; died about 183.

Crispina, wife of Commodus. Died A.D. 183.

Manlia Scantilla, wife of Didius Julianus, Emperor in A.D. 193.

Didia Clara, daughter of Didius Julianus and of Scantilla. Born A.D. 153.

Julia Domna, wife of Septimius Severus.— Died A.D. 217.

Plautilla (Fulvia), wife of Caracalla. Died A.D. 212.

Julia Paula, first wife of Elagabalus, to whom she was married about A.D. 219.

Julia Aquilia Severa, vestal, second wife of Elagabalus; survived her infamous husband, who was slain A.D. 222.

Annia Faustina, third wife of Elagabalus.

Julia Soaemias, mother of Elagabalus. Died A.D. 222.

Julia Mæsa, sister of Julia Domna, grandmother of Elagabalus. Died A.D. 223.

Julia Mamæa, daughter of Mæsa, sister of Soaemias, and mother of Alexander Severus.— Died A.D. 235.

Orbiana (Salustia Barbia), third wife of Alexander Severus, A.D. 226. Known only by her coins.

Paulina, wife of Maximinus, who reigned A.D. 235 to 238. Known only by her coins.

Tranquillina (Furia Sabina), third wife of Gordianus Pius; survived her husband, who died A.D. 244.

Marcia Otacilia Severa, wife of Philip senior, survived her husband, who died A.D. 249.

Herennia Etruscilla, known only by her coins and an inscription, was the wife of Trajanus Decius, who died A.D. 251.

Cornelia Supera, wife of Aemilianus, who usurped the purple A.D. 253. Known only by her coins.

Mariniana, supposed second wife of Valerianus senior, who was proclaimed Emperor A.D. 253.

Salonina, wife of Gallienus. Died A.D. 268.

Severina, wife of Aurelianus, Emperor A.D. 270.

Magnia Urbica, wife of Carinus, Emperor A.D. 283. Known only by her coins.

Helena, first wife of Constantius Chlorus.— Born A.D. 248; divorced by her husband; died 328.

Theodora, second wife of Chlorus, married to that prince A.D. 292.

Valeria (Galeria), second wife of Maximianus. Died A.D. 315.

Fausta, wife of Constantine the Great. Died A.D. 326.

Fausta, married to Constantius II. between A.D. 335 and 250.

Helena, supposed wife of Crispus Cæsar, A.D. 317, son of Constantine the Great.

Helena, wife of Julianus II. Died A.D. 360.

Flaccilla, wife of Theodosius the Great. Died A.D. 388.

Galla Placidia, wife of Constantius III.— Died A.D. 450.

Aelia Eudoxia, or Eudocia, wife of Theodosius the younger. Born A.D. 393; died 460.

Licinia Eudoxia, wife of Valentinian III.— Born A.D. 423.

Honoria, sister of Valentinian III. Born A.D. 417.

Pulcheria, sister of Theodosius II. wife of Marcianus. Born A.D. 399; Augusta 414; died 453.

Verina, wife of Leo I. Died A.D. 484.

Euphemia, wife of Anthemius, Emperor in A.D. 467.

Aelia, wife of Basiliscus, brother in law of Leo I. Died A.D. 477, the year after the dethronement of Romulus Augustus by Odoacer, which put an end to the Roman empire in the west.

[The above are further noticed under their respective heads.]

AVGVSTA. S. C.—This legend appears on a large brass of Faustina senior, struck after her death (A.D. 141). The obverse bears the legend DIVA FAVSTINA, with her portrait.—The reverse (as in the above cut), has for its type the deceased empress standing, under the figure and with the attributes of *Ceres*, namely: holding a torch, and ears of corn.—The same epigraph is repeated on the coins of Faustina senior, in every metal and size, and with types of this and other goddesses, with whom the flattery of the old superstition, ministering to a husband's fond weakness, was wont to assimilate the unworthy consort of Antoninus Pius.

AVGVSTA, S. C.—This legend appears on the reverse of a large brass of Galba, having for its type a veiled woman seated, with *patera* and *hasta pura*. Galba had received many favours from Livia Augusti, for which reason, according to Havercamp, he decorated the sitting statue of Livia.—The coin minted A. D. 68; is engraved in *Morell. Thesaur. Imp. Rom.*

AVGVSTA.—This epithet was applied to a colony, whose settlers had originally been sent thither by Augustus. That prince founded a great many colonies, both in and beyond Italy—plebeian or civil colonies, so long as he only shared the empire with his colleagues in the triumvirate; but afterwards military colonies, when, Pompey the son being driven from Sicily, Lepidus retiring into private life, Mark Antony dead, the wars in Spain, Dalmatia, and Germany finished, he sent legions of veteran soldiers to occupy them.—Accordingly we find the *municipium* Bilbilis, in Hispania Tarraconensis, called after its founder Augustus, MV. AVGVSTA BILBIL. or MV. AVG. BILBILIS. In the same province of Spain, the colony of CAESARAVGVSTA, or C. CA. AVGVSTA; and that of Ilici designated on its coins C. I. IL. A. Colonia Immunis Ilici Augusta. In like manner, COL. AVGVSTA EMERITA, or AVGVSTA EMERITA, in Lusitania; and COL. AVG. PATRENS. or C. A. A. P. Colonia Aroe Augusta Patrensis, &c. But when IVL. AVG. *Julia* and *Augusta*, occur as a joint name, it shews that the foundation of those colonies was the original act of Julius Cæsar, but that they were re-established by Augustus with fresh supplies of Roman settlers. As C. IVL. AVG. D. *Colonia Julia Augusta Dertosa.*—See *Coloniæ.*—Refer also to "Ancient Coins of Cities and Princes," by J. Y. Akerman, F. and Sec. S. A.

AVGVSTAE PACI.—On a denarius of Titus, with Victory walking, and at the bottom EPHE. in monogram.

It is, says Khell (Suppt. 39), very unusual thus to see the symbol of Victory joined to the above legend. The epigraph of *Pax Augusti* (the Peace of the Emperor), is of frequent occurrence; but that of *Augustæ Paci* (to August Peace), one reads on no other coin. Perhaps, it relates to the statue of Victory dedicated by Titus, in the temple of Peace, which his father built.—See PACI AVGVSTAE.

AVGVSTA MARCIANA.—See *Marciana.*

AVG. or AVGVST. IN PACE.—A woman sitting, with olive branch and transversed *hasta.* On silver and small brass of Salonina.—See Vaillant, Banduri, Mionnet, and Akerman.

Although this epigraph, says Eckhel, is unusual, I am not disposed to join with Vaillant in affirming that these coins of Salonina were struck by some usurper, to cast a slight on that empress—in the same way as another coin, inscribed VBIQVE PAX, is considered to have been designed to ridicule Gallienus. For whereas the

coin of Gallienus is *rarissimus*, that in question of Salonina is common. And it is quite possible for this legend of AVGVSTA IN PACE to admit of an interpretation not injurious to the honour of the wife of Gallienus. (vol. vii. 418.)—Capt. Smyth in still stronger and more decided terms scouts the absurd idea of this being a satyrical legend.

AVGVSTA MATER PATRIAE.—A woman veiled, seated with patera in her right hand, and the *hasta* in her left. Engraved in *Morell. Thes.*

This legend and type appear on a first brass, bearing the laurelled head of Augustus on its obverse (with IMP. CAES. AVG), and which, although the name of the colony is not recorded, must evidently be of colonial fabric (probably Spanish), and not, as Vaillant and Morel have thought, of Roman mintage. On this coin *Livia* (afterwards named Julia, second wife of Augustus) is called *Augusta Mater Patriæ.* Now, we learn from Dion Cassius, that the Senate had decreed the above adulatory title, together with the still more impiously fulsome one of *Genetrix orbis*, to this abandoned princess. But, according to Suetonius, her son Tiberius, from hatred to his family rather than from a better sense of propriety, refused his permission that she should be so named, or that she should be the object of any extraordinary public honour whatever. The titles however which Tiberius affected to deny his mother at Rome, he connived at being awarded her in the provinces; and this coin forms an example of the inconsistency—although the probability is, that it was not struck, even *extra urbem*, until after the death of Augustus. —The figure of the veiled woman, seated with *patera* and *hasta*, Eckhel shews to represent Livia in this instance under the form of Vesta, as on other coins she appears in the similitude of the Goddess *Pietas.* There is another first brass, given in *Mus. Theupoli*, with a similar reverse legend and type, but which bears on its obverse the image and superscription, not of Augustus, but of Tiberius himself.

AVGVSTA EMERITA.—See *Emerita.*

Augustarum Capitis Cultus.—The following remarks in reference to the head-dresses of the Roman Empresses, as represented on coins, are from vol. viii. p. 364 of *Doctrina Num. Vet.* "At the commencement of the empire, when as yet it would appear not to have been the usage to strike money with the names of women, it pleased the authorities to exhibit them, respectively under the figures of Vesta, Pietas, Justitia, Salus, Ceres, &c. It is in this way, that we see Livia Augusti, Antonia Drusi, Agrippina Claudii, personifying these divinities. This liberty is much more indulged on medals of foreign die, as may be seen on those of each of the above princesses. During a subsequent period, however, when the Flavia family occupied the imperial throne, and when monetary honours began to be fully extended to females of Augustal rank, the mint-masters returned to the representation of the *human* figure; and princesses are portrayed on coins, not with any indication of power or authority, but in the head-dress usually worn by ladies of their time, and which, as is the case in our own day, was open to the change and caprice of fashion, and susceptible of an infinite variety of form."

On their consecration medals, the heads of the *Augustæ* are covered with a veil : examples of which appear in both the Faustinæ ; also in Domna, Mæsa, Paulina, Mariniana. On coins of Roman die. Domna was the first whose head (placed over a crescent moon), was joined to the radiated head of Severus, her husband, as seen in the mint of that emperor (in the year U. C. 955 A. D. 202). The same custom was continued to the reign of Diocletian, and thence downwards to a much lower period of the empire.

Augustalia, holidays instituted by the Senate and People, to celebrate the return of Augustus to Rome.—See FORT*unæ* RED*uci* CAES. AVG.

Augustal laurels, or the Emperor's wreath.— See *Corona Laurea.*

AVGVSTI COS.—On gold, silver, and middle brass of Caracalla, this legend is accompanied by the type of that prince and the emperor Severus, sitting together on an estrade, both clothed in the toga ; on one side is a lictor with a rod ; on the other a togated figure. This coin (of which Khell, in his Supplement to Vaillant, has given an engraving), preserves the memory of the consulship, which Caracalla served as the colleague of his father, A. D. 202. Invested with this dignity, the two emperors went into Egypt, and thence returning to Rome, the son took Plautilla to wife. There is a similar legend and type, but on middle brass, in the mint of Severus.

AVGVSTI F. *Filia.*—Daughter of the Emperor.—See *Julia Titi.*

AVGVSTI F. *Filius.*—Son of the Emperor. —See *Tiberius, Caligula,* &c.

AVGVSTI PII FIL*ia.*—This appears on the silver and brass medals of Faustina junior, she being the daughter of Antoninus Pius.

AVGVSTI POR. OST. S, C.—On a first brass of Nero, bearing this legend, the reverse type represents a maritime port. The Emperor Claudius had caused some immense works to be constructed at Ostia, a town situate at the mouth of the Tiber ; but Nero appears, by this medal, to have assumed all the honour of having executed them.—See POR. OST.

AVGVSTI PROVINCIA.——By this title *Arabia*, as well as *Dacia*, is denominated on coins of Trajan.—Rasche.

AVGVSTO. OB. C. S. within a crown of oak leaves, on second brass of Augustus.—See *Ob. Cives Servatos.*

AVGVSTOR. *Augustorum.* Of the Emperors. As in *Adlocutio*, or *Adventus*, or *Concordia, Augustorum,* &c.

AUGUSTUS.—This was the surname which, in the year U. C. 727 (27 before the Christian æra), the Senate of Rome, in its own name and in that of the people, conferred on Octavius, or Octavianus, the adopted son and heir of Julius Cæsar, as an acknowledgment of the services

which he had rendered to his country. This epithet, which signifies " revered" or "worthy of veneration," and which, up to that time, had been appropriated solely to sacred persons and things, he ever afterwards bore, and it is that under which he is habitually designated.— After him it became the title of sovereignty, which all the other emperors took, as well out of respect for the memory of him on whom it was first bestowed, as for a mark of their right (whether valid or merely assumed), to succeed him. The appellation of Augustus was placed by his successors in the empire after their own name; and characterising, as it did, the supreme power of the state, it was invariably adopted, not only by legitimate princes, but even by those who in after times usurped the imperial purple. The title of Augustus was, however, at first confined to such as were actually invested with the sovereignty. The sons, or adopted sons, of emperors, previously to their being associated with them in the government, were each called simply *Cæsar ;* and this last, originally a proper name, became a dignity, which served to distinguish the heirs presumptive to the Augustal throne.

Having offered this general and brief explanation of the word *Augustus*, used as a title and a surname, we cannot, on a point which, from its constant recurrence, is so requisite to be fully understood by the student of Roman numismatics, do better (as it seems to us) than to subjoin the substance of Eckhel's learned citations and illustrative remarks on the subject, contained in the 8th volume of *Doctrina*, pp. 355, 356, *et seq.* :

1.—*Augustus, origin and occasion of the title.* Dion Cassius, in his history of the Roman Emperors (L. liii. § 16) remarks, that Cæsar Octavianus, "after the fulfilment of the promises he had made, assumed the name of *Augustus*, at the desire of the Senate and the People. For, as they had determined on distinguishing him by some peculiar appellation, and were comparing the merits of several, Cæsar, though himself very ambitious of the name of Romulus, still, on finding that he was from that circumstance suspected of aiming at *kingly* dignity, gave it up, and was styled *Augustus*, as if he were a being superior to the mortal race. For all things [among the Romans] which are considered most honourable and most sacred, are called *August* (Augusta) ; and on this account the Greeks rendered the word AUGUSTUS by ΣΕΒΑΣΤΟΣ, or *revered (quasi venerandum dicas).*" The same event is thus recorded by Suetonius : " He then assumed the name of C. Cæsar, and afterwards the cognomen of AU-GUSTUS ; the one in accordance with the will of his uncle ; the other at the suggestion of Munatius Plancus. For, whilst some were of opinion that he should be called *Romulus*, as though himself the founder of the city, it was determined that the title of AUGUSTUS should in preference be given him—a title not only novel, but also more dignified, inasmuch as places dedicated to religious purposes, and in which anything is

consecrated by divination, are called *Augusta.*
* * * Velleius also slightly alludes to the
subject: "The Roman standards were sent
back by the Parthian King to Augustus, a title
conferred on him by the universal consent of the
Senate and People of Rome, on the motion of
Plancus." And lastly Censorinus: "From
the day before the 16th of the calends of
February, *Cæsar Imperator Divi Filius* (i. e. son
of the Divine Julius), on the motion of L.
Munatius Plancus, was called Augustus by the
Senate and rest of the citizens, in his own
seventh consulate, and the third consulate of M.
Vipsanius Agrippa.—From these testimonies,
may be gathered the origin and cause of the
title of Augustus.

2.—*Augustus; signification and etymology
of the word.*—From the authors above quoted,
the explanation of the epithet is obtained, both
in the Latin form, AUGUSTUS, and in that of
the Greek ΣΕΒΑΣΤΟΣ. And to them may be
added the testimony of Ovid *(Fast* I. v. 609).

> Sancta vocant augusta patres, augusta vocantur
> Templa, sacerdotum ritè dicata manu.

[The Fathers (i. e. the Senate) call all sacred
things *August;* temples too, if duly consecrated
by sacerdotal hands, are styled *August.*
Also Pompeius Festus *(in Augusto).* Pausanias likewise (L. iii. c. 2), says, "His name
was Augustus, which in the Greek language
is equivalent to ΣΕΒΑΣΤΟΣ *(venerabilis).*—
At a later period it was erroneously supposed,
that the name Augustus was derived from
another root, namely, *augere, auctus,* to increase. As regards the character of this appellation, it is sufficiently evident from the testimonies adduced, that it was conferred upon
Octavianus for no other reason than that which
operated in giving the name *Torquatus* to Manlius, *Magnus* to Cn. Pompeius, *Pius* to Metellus,
&c. namely, on account of their eminent services."

3.—*Augustus the title of, transmitted to
descendants.*—As the posterity of Manlius and
others, adopted as of hereditary right, the same
respective appellations, so the family of Octavianus acquired a claim to the name of Augustus.
With propriety, therefore, not only did Tiberius
assume the name of Augustus after his adoptive
father's death; but his widow Livia, also adopted
by the will of her deceased husband, succeeded
to the titles *Julia* and *Augusta;* and Caius too
(called Caligula) being by adoption the grandson
of Tiberius. And it was for this reason, that
Suetonius has not hesitated to designate the title
of *Augustus* as *hereditary.*

Not long afterwards, this name was appropriated to those who had no hereditary right
to it: and Caligula was the first to set the
example, by giving the title of *Augusta* to his
grandmother Antonia, who was neither by blood
nor by adoption, connected with the Cæsarian
family. Claudius likewise, with as little pretension, on his elevation to the empire, after the
death of Caligula, assumed the title not only of
Cæsar, but of Augustus; and this example was

followed by all his successors. For not merely
did all, immediately on their accession, assume
the title (Vitellius alone shewing a temporary
disinclination to it), but they in like manner
dignified their wives. (See the article AUGUSTA,
p. 97). Claudius was the first (though tardily
and reluctantly), to allow of its being conferred
on Messalina. And a still more surprising circumstance subsequently occurred, viz. the bestowal of the title of *Augusta* on Domitilla,
wife of Vespasian, though she died before her
husband became Emperor (Vespasian himself, or
his son Titus, acting in the matter), in order
that neither the wife, nor the mother, of a
reigning prince might be compelled to pass her
time "among *the* manes *of private individuals.*"
Seeing then, even under Caligula, that the
quality of the title *Augustus* was changed, the
remark of Alexander Severus, quoted by Lampridius, is a just one: *Augustus primus, primus
est auctor imperii, et in ejus nomen omnes
VELVT quadam adoptione, aut jure hereditario
succedimus.*—"The first Augustus is the first
founder (or first increaser) of the empire; and
as if by a kind of adoption, or hereditary right,
we all succeed to his name."

4.—*Augustus, the title of, conferred honour
but no power.*—One of the other characteristics
of the above title was, that it imparted to him
on whom it was conferred, the most exalted
honour, but no accession of power. Dion (L.
iii. § 16), again learnedly explains this point:
"For the appellations *Cæsar* and *Augustus* added
nothing to the intrinsic power of the emperors.
It was by the former that their descent from a
certain race was indicated; by the latter, their
illustrious rank." And the reason of this circumstance is, that the offices of *Imperator* and
Pontifex Maximus, joined to, and merged in,
the Tribunate and the Proconsulate, gave them
possession, in effect, of universal power, while
the supreme title of *Augustus* shewed, that this
accumulated authority was vested in one individual. The consequence of this was, that looking to general estimation, and the majesty of
the empire, we find that the world itself had
not the title to exhibit, which could vie in grandeur and dignity with that of Augustus; and
that until it was bestowed, the pinnacle of greatness was yet unattained. There were emperors
who conferred the title of *Cæsar,* and also of
Imperator, on their sons; as did Vespasian on
Titus, and Hadrian on Antoninus. They were,
however, esteemed as of the second rank. But
in cases where princes conferred upon others the
title of *Augustus,* as M. Aurelius did on his
brother L. Verus, and afterwards on his son
Commodus, those persons were considered to
have attained the highest dignity, and to have become sharers and colleagues of the government,
in honour little inferior to those who thus elevated them; and that too in consequence of the
source whence the distinction was derived. Nevertheless, that the title of *Augustus* added dignity without power to its possessor, is plain
from the very fact, that the emperors hesitated
not to confer a similar nominal distinction on

their wives, and other females connected, or pretended to be connected, with the house of Cæsar, overlooking all those who enjoyed real power, because it was the policy of ancient Rome, at all times, to exclude women from any participation in the conduct of public affairs.

5.—*Augusti—the first example of* TWO *reigning together.*—From the earliest period of the empire, a single individual only had been distinguished at one and the same time, by the title of Augustus; but the middle of the second imperial age, saw *two* raised simultaneously to this eminence—viz. M. Aurelius and L. Verus; and shortly afterwards (on the death of Verus) M. Aurelius and his son Commodus. Not much later, Severus followed this precedent, associating with himself his son Antoninus, commonly called Caracalla; and towards the end of his life, his other son, Geta. So that, Rome had at that time (about A. D. 209) its *three* Augusti, a circumstance which had never before happened. At a subsequent period, many examples of this extension of the honour were witnessed. But it will be asked, what was the relative power or dignity of the respective bearers of the title? These (answers Eckhel), varied with circumstances. It is not to be doubted, that he, who attached to himself a colleague, whether his son, or his brother, or one not related to him, had the pre-eminence in rank, and in most instances in authority also. It is equally certain that in both these particulars, fathers were superior to sons; as Severus to Caracalla and Geta. Greater honour was also paid to Aurelius than to his adopted brother, L. Verus, whom he elevated to a share in the government; and for the like reason Diocletian held a higher rank than Maximian.—Caracalla enjoyed greater dignity than his younger brother Geta, notwithstanding the wish of their father, Severus, that they should reign with equal power. For Caracalla had the advantage in point of age, and likewise on account of the number of years, during which he had borne the title of Augustus: he was besides alone distingushed by the Pontificate. In the case of Balbinus and Pupienus none of these reasons prevailed; for they were both called to the head of affairs by the Senate, in consequence of the difficulties of the State. That body, therefore, conferred upon both equal dignity and authority, and, departing from the hitherto invariable custom, gave to both the office of Pontifex Maximus, lest the envy of either should be excited towards the other.

6.—*Of two or more Augusti, at the same time, which held the higher rank.*—From the reign of Diocletian there were constantly more than one Augustus at the same time. And the Cæsars, connected with each other by no ties of consanguinity, ruled, each over his own province, on such terms that neither depended on the other. Although they possessed equal power, yet in dignity they were distinct from each other, as this was imparted by the length of time during which each of those titles had been held by an individual. That individual Augustus, therefore, enjoyed the first position, who had

first received the title; and the like usage prevailed in the case of a Cæsar. It is on this principle, that Diocletian is styled, in Eusebius, "he who both in honour and in position held the first place." Constantine is stated, by the same author, to have stood superior to M. Licinius, "both in honour and in rank." Numerous instances may be found within that period of disputes arising from this mode of taking precedence. When Constantine the Great informed Maximianus, that, on the death of his father [Constantius Chlorus, A. D. 306] he had received the title of Augustus from the army, the latter felt aggrieved, and according to Lactantius *(de mont. perfec.* c. 25) "determined on naming (Fl. Val.) Severus, the elder by birth, Augustus; whilst he commanded that Constantine should not be styled *Imperator* (which he had been created) but *Cæsar*, in conjunction with Maximinus (Daza) in order to degrade Constantine from the second post of honour to the fourth." [For other instances of the jealousy and dissension caused by this clashing of claims to dignity and pre-eminence, reference may with great advantage be had to Eckhel's dissertation on the imperial coins of the lower empire, and also to the intelligent observations of Bimard de la Bastie on the same subject.]

7.—*A plurality of Augusti, how indicated.*—As already shewn in p. 95 of this dictionary—when there were two emperors at the same time, the fact was pointed out by the inscription AVGG.; a custom which, on coins at least, commenced under S. Severus, it being usual, in that emperor's mint, after he had associated Caracalla with himself in the supreme government, to use the legends ANNONAE AVGG.—VICT. AVGG. &c. And by a similar multiplication of the same letter, AVGGG. denoted a colleagueship of *three* Augusti.

8.—*Augusti, by association.*—It is to be observed, however, that even the son of an emperor, though only Cæsar, was by association with his father who was Augustus, also called by that title; as in the case of Maximus *Cæsar*, there is on a large brass coin, MAXIMINVS ET MAXIMVS AVGVSTI GERMANICI.—And this circumstance is still more clearly illustrated on a marble published by Spon, bearing the following inscription:—PRO SALVTE IMP. ET CAESAR. PHILIPPORUM AVGG. ET OTACILIAE SEVERAE AVG. MATRIS CAES. ET CASTROR. This marble was erected in the year U.C. 989 (A.D. 236), as appears from the addition of *Philippo Aug. et Titiano Cos.* (Philippus senior and Junius Titianus being consuls), in which year, however, the younger Philip was certainly not yet Augustus; and yet the monument exhibits the letters AVGG. That is to say there were *two* Augusti, *by association.* The prevalence of this custom is exemplified on the respective coins of Diadumenianus, Maximus, Tetricus the younger, Carinus, and others. It is much more surprising that the title of *Imperator* was in the same manner shared by the *wife* of a reigning prince. But *such* an extraordinary feature of the *ævum inferius* is given to us by Maffei, from an African marble inscribed thus—SALVIS DOMINIS NOSTRIS CHRISTIANISSIMIS IMPERATORIBVS IVSTINO ET SOFIA, &c.—On coins of the lower empire may frequently be seen AVGGGGG, imposing an arduous task in the identification of so many of the *Augusti.*

Augustus Perpetuus.—Not unfrequently some epithet is found united with the title of Augustus, as PERPETVVS AVGVSTVS.—Spanheim quotes a coin of Trajan, on which he is called AVG. PERP. to trace the first use of the addition to that emperor. But the genuineness of the coin in question rests solely on the statement of Mediobarbus; and Eckhel is not inclined, therefore, to adopt the opinion.—" The word *Perpetuus,* often written with only the letters PP. I find (says he) first added to the Emperors' titles under Probus: PERPETVO IMP. PROBO. AVG. From the time of the sons of Constantine the Great, the inscription PERP. AVG. is very frequent on coins. The origin of this piece of flattery belongs to a remote period, as on the coins of the earliest emperors their *eternity* was vauntingly put forward. But the legend PERPETVITATI. AVG. became more frequent from the time of Alexander Severus, in whose mint alone we read POTESTAS PERPETVA.—*Semper Augustus,* so frequently observed now-a-days, amongst the imperial titles, Spanheim could not find among ancient inscriptions, before Diocletian's time.—See PERP. AVG. and SEMPER AVGVSTVS.

AUGUSTUS CÆSAR, first Emperor of the Romans.—Caius Octavius Cœpius, afterwards surnamed Augustus, was the son of the Prætor C. Octavius Rufus and of Atia, niece of Julius Cæsar. He was born at Velitri Volscorum (now *Velletri,* in the *Campagna di Roma)* in October, in the year of Rome 691 (63 years before Christ), under the consulship of Cicero. When only four years old, he lost his father; but his education experienced no neglect on that account; for in his tenth year he proved himself capable of making an oration to the people. This prince united first-rate talents to striking advantages of person and address. His relationship, too, to the illustrious Dictator, of whom he was from the very first a great favourite, secured to him an early training for public life, and introduced him whilst as yet a mere stripling into the highest society. In the year of Julius Cæsar's second consulate, U. C. 706 (B. C. 48), he received the *toga virilis,* being then in his sixteenth year, and was soon afterwards ad-

mitted into the college of Pontiffs. In A. U. C. 709 (B. C. 45), returning to Rome with his grand uncle, whom he had joined in Spain, on a victorious expedition against the Pompeians, he was sent to Apollonia, in Illyricum, either to complete his civil education, or to receive practical instruction in the art of war amongst the legions there, or probably for both those purposes. The following year, being still at Apollonia, the tidings reached him of Julius Cæsar's murder; which caused him to return immediately from Illyricum to Rome. There, finding himself, by the will of Julius, adopted as the son of that celebrated man, he took the names of C. Julius Cæsar Octavianus. But on claiming the succession, he had to defend his rights as heir, against the opposition of M. Antonius, and succeeded only after a turbulent struggle.—Octavianus was but twenty years old, when he obtained the consulate A. U. C. 711 (B. C. 43), contrary to law, which required a much maturer age to be first reached. Then, pursuing with vengeance the assassins of his uncle, he was not long in uniting himself with Lepidus and M. Antonius, to form that triumvirate which, under pretence of re-constituting the republic *(Reipublicæ Constituendæ),* became a reign of wholesale cruelty and of proscriptive horrors. In A. U. C. 612 (B. C. 42) supported by M. Antonius, he defeated Brutus and Cassius on the Thessalian field of Philippi. The next year he vanquished Lucius Antonius at Perusia. In 714 (B. C. 40), he gained a decisive naval victory over Sextus Pompeius, whom he compelled to abandon Sicily. In 719 (B. C. 35), Octavianus quarrelled with M. Antonius, who had indeed given him cause, by divorcing his sister Octavia and marrying Cleopatra. The next three years were passed by Octavianus in concerting his measures against that infatuated triumvir. And having assembled around his own banner all the legions of the East, he attacked, and totally defeated his former colleague, and only formidable rival, in a sea fight near Actium, on the coast of Epirus, on the second of September, in the year of Rome 723 (B. C. 31.) In 724 (B. C. 30), he proceeded with an army to Egypt, and captured Alexandria.—Mark Antony and Cleopatra, deserted on all hands, brought their own hopeless affairs to a close, by each committing suicide; whilst Lepidus, indolently satisfied with descending again to a private station, left Octavianus sole master of the enslaved republic. Next year (B. C. 29) having rendered Egypt a tributary province, he returned to Rome, and enjoyed among other honours and distinctions, those of a three days' triumph—viz. for Dalmatia, for Actium, and for Alexandria. It was then, that this fortunate despot caused the temple of Janus to be shut, which had remained open for 205 years before; and having, by these crowning victories, brought the whole world under the power, or within the influence of Rome, he received from the Senate and People the designation of Imperator; not however in the former acceptation of the term as merely the general-in-chief of armies, but as a title indicative of supreme government—followed two years afterwards, from the same authority, by the surname of AVGVSTVS (see notice on that word, p. 101 of this dictionary).

In the year of Rome 726 (B. C. 28) he was Consul for the sixth time, with his son in law, Marcus Agrippa, for his colleague. A denarius which presents a fine head of Agrippa on its obverse, with the head of Augustus on the other side, was struck on that occasion, by Platorinus. The legend of the obverse is PLATORINVS IIIVIR. M. AGRIPPA. That of the reverse is CAESAR AVGVSTVS.—The above cut is copied from an unusually well-preserved specimen of a coin, no less valuable for its historical interest than as a numismatic rarity.—See Agrippa, p. 27.

The same year he caused the quinquennial ceremony of Lustral sacrifices and purgations to be performed; carried many laws; adorned the city with buildings; and repaired the public roads. This year also the Consuls took the census, at which the citizens numbered 4,164,000.

727 (B. C. 27).—Being the year of Augustus's expedition into Spain, against the Cantabrians and Asturians, the gates of the Temple of Janus were re-opened.

730 (B. C. 24).—From Spain he returned to Rome. And it is to the succeeding year that the coins are assigned, on which we read the date of the Tribunitian Power (TRIBVNITIA POTESTAS) awarded to him by the Senate—"a dignity," says Millin, "that recalled to mind the high consideration in which the Tribunes of the People (Tribuni Plebis) were formerly held, under the republic, and which, although not an honour of the first order, was also assumed by the successors of Augustus, because it would have given too much authority to simple citizens." This title serves, with certain exceptions, to mark the years of their reigns.—See Tribunitia Potestas.

733 (B. C. 21).—During the absence of Augustus in Sicily, frightful tumults arose on account of the elections of Consuls. He therefore sent for Agrippa from the east, and, requiring him to divorce his wife, gave him his own daughter Julia, the widow of Marcellus, in marriage. The presence of Agrippa quelled the disturbances at Rome. From Sicily, Augustus visited Greece; thence he proceeded to Samos, where he passed the winter.

734 (B. C. 20).—From Samos he went into the pro-consular province of Asia, and thence visited Syria; received from Phraates, king of Parthia, the military ensigns lost under Crassus, and the prisoners who had survived the slaughter of the legions in that fatal expedition; on which occasion, the following denarius was struck by one of his monetary triumvirs, Florus Aquil-

lius, bearing on one side a radiated head, which, if not that of Augustus (to whose physiognomy it has a palpable resemblance), was probably meant for that of the Sun, as allusive to the East; and on the other CAESAR AVGVSTVS SIGNis RECEptis. The type a Parthian on his knees, offering a military ensign.

The same year Tiberius was sent from Syria into Armenia, which, with its king Tigranes, he brought under the Roman yoke; and his successes are recorded on Augustus's coins of this date, which bear the epigraph of ARMENIA CAPTA.—See p. 80.

735 (B. C. 19).—Augustus returned from Asia to Rome, on which occasion the feasts called after him Augustalia, were celebrated in his honour. The same year, his son in law Agrippa suppressed rebellions in Gaul, Germany, and Spain.

737 (B. C. 17).—In this year he adopted Caius and Lucins, sons of Agrippa; and celebrated the Secular Games (Ludi Sæculares).

738. (B. C. 16).—The insurrectionary hostilities of the Germani, who had obtained some successes over detachments of the Roman army under Lollius, induced Augustus to make a journey into Gaul. And about the autumn of the same year, Agrippa set out for the East. The two following years saw the emperor occupied with the personal administration of affairs in Gaul; where, and in Spain, he founded several colonies; whilst Tiberius and Drusus brought the German and Rhætian tribes into subjection; and Agrippa quelled insurrections in the kingdom of the Bosphorus.

741 (B. C. 13).—Augustus returned from Gaul, and Agrippa from Asia, to Rome; and the Ara Pacis was erected in that city; but not dedicated till B. C. 9.—See p. 73.

742 (B. C. 12).—The title of Pontifex Maximus begins with this year to appear on the coins of Augustus, the death of Lepidus the preceding year having left that office vacant. He sustained a great and irreparable loss in the decease of the brave Agrippa.—The following year, on account of the disturbed state of affairs in territories bordering on the Gallic provinces, Augustus again took up his residence in them. But, in the year B. C. 10, peace being restored in Germania, Dalmatia, and Pannonia, he, with his lieutenants, Tiberius and Drusus, returned to Rome. The last named able and valiant commander was sent, B. C. 9, to renew war against the Germans.

746 (B. C. 8).—Augustus, who, the year preceding, in consequence of the death of Drusus on the banks of the Lower Rhine, followed by a fresh insurrection of the Germans in that quarter, had once more, and for the last time, quitted Rome for Gaul, still remained there. This year

the month *Sextilis* had its name changed to *Augustus*, in honour of the Emperor: And as the saviour of the citizens (OB CIVES SERVATOS) the oaken crown (corona quercea) was often after, as well as before, this period, decreed to him, and typified on his coins.

747 (B.C. 7)—Tiberius again sent to command in the German war. In his absence, Caius Cæsar celebrated the *ludi votivi* for the return of Augustus.

752 (B.C. 2).—Augustus, at Rome, exhibited a *naumachia*, or representation of a naval engagement, and other magnificent public spectacles. He dedicated the temple of Mars Ultor; whilst the Senate capped the climax of their adulatory homage, by bestowing on him the title of PATER PATRIAE.—Ovid, with the adroitness of a courtier, and with more than the usual tact of a poet, alludes to the event, and addresses the Sovereign as the *Sire* of the Romans :—

Sancte Pater Patriae, tibi Plebs, tibi Curia nomen
   Hoc dedit, &c.

753 (B.C. 1).—Eckhel, according to the calculation of Dionysius Exiguus, names this year of Rome as the one on which took place the most memorable and ever blessed event of OUR LORD AND SAVIOUR JESUS CHRIST'S NATIVITY, *in Bethlehem of Judæa.*

[*⁎* Usher and other eminent chronologists reckon it to have been in the 749th year of Rome.]

762. (A.D. 9).—The time for celebrating the triumphal honours decreed to Tiberius for his victories over the Dalmatians and Pannonians deferred, on account of tidings received that Quinctilius Varus, with three legions, had been slain by the Germans under their chief Arminius. The Romans, by this overwhelming misfortune, lost all their possessions in Germany east of the Rhine. The grief of Rome, and that of Augustus in particular, was very great indeed at this nationally humiliating disaster. A.D. 10, Tiberius and Germanicus, to avenge the slaughter, made an attack on the Germans, but returned to Rome the same year.

766 (A.D. 13).—Now sinking under the triple burthen of advanced years, bodily infirmities, and domestic infelicities, (his daughter Julia, convicted of manifold adulteries, had been banished to the island of Pandataria, B.C. 2), Augustus associated Tiberius with him in the Tribunitian power, in order that the latter, whom he had been so ill-advised as to adopt as his son and successor, might share with him the government of the provinces.

767 (A.D. 14).—Having attained his 76th year, Augustus caused the census to be again taken, when the citizens were 4,197,000. And notwithstanding his old age, he made a journey into Campania. But, at Nola, on his return towards Rome from Naples, he was seized with a disorder, which proved fatal. He died on the 19th day of August. His remains were interred in the mausoleum, which he had caused to be built in the Campus Martius at Rome, after his having (in conjunction with M. Antonius) ruled the republic for twelve, and governed alone as Emperor for 44 years.

An instrument in the hands of an over-ruling Providence, for laying the foundation of manifold and decisive changes in the religious as well as in the social condition of the human race—this extraordinary man, from the rank of a private citizen, had succeeded, by the soundness of his policy, taking advantage of every favourable opportunity, and without being a great military commander, in becoming the head and chief of an universal monarchy. No sooner placed in this unexampled position of supremacy, the world at peace, and his government firmly grounded, than he thought, or seemed to think, only of effacing the memory of his past crimes by reigning on the general principles of justice, wisdom, and clemency. Rome was increased and embellished by his munificence, and by that of the rich and illustrious citizens, who like Mæcenas and Agrippa, emulated his example, both in architectural improvements and in the establishment of useful institutions. It must be admitted that his adoption by Julius Cæsar; the spiritless temperament of Lepidus ; the mad folly of Antony, victim to his own profligate habits and the treachery of Cleopatra, were more than either manly courage, or true virtue of character on his part, the stepping stones and auxiliaries, by whose aid Augustus arrived at the highest summit of power. Yet favoured as he was by circumstances, and crowned by every species of terrestrial glory ; beloved by his subjects, endeared to his intimate friends, and prosperous in a reign of unprecedented duration, he was far from finding happiness in the bosom of his family. His wife Livia stood generally accused of having shortened the days of this great Prince, who having no posterity of his own, appointed Tiberius, his son in law, heir to the empire.

As Augustus was the founder of the imperial government of Rome, it may here be proper to recapitulate the epochas of the different dignities successively bestowed on him, and which constituted the united prerogatives of that monarchical sovereignty which was transmitted by him to his successors. These dates will serve to class the coins of this emperor, and are as follow :—As heir to the name of Cæsar in 710 (B.C. 44), he caused himself to be nominated Consul.—In 711 (B.C. 43), Triumvir [*Reipublicæ Constituendæ*] with Antony and Lepidus. (His effigy from that time appears on the gold and silver coinage of Rome, but later on that of brass.) This triumvirate, though it lasted no longer than U.C. 716 (B.C. 38), continued to be recorded on his coins till B.C. 35. After the defeat, followed by the death, of M. Antonius, B.C. 29, he took as a prenomen the title of *Imperator;* accepted the title of AUGUSTUS in 727 (B.C. 27); caused the *Tribunitia Potestas* to be inscribed on his money, and to be calculated from the date of June, 731 (B.C. 23); was invested with the *Chief Pontificate* in 742 (B.C. 12); and finally was honoured by the imposing appellation of *Pater Patriæ* (Father of the Country), by the Senate and people, in 752 (B.C. 2).

[It may be regarded as near the last mentioned date, that the rare first brass coin was struck, of which an engraving of the portrait side is placed at the head of this biographical notice.— The legend is CAESAR AVGVSTVS DIVI *Filius,* PATER PATRIAE. The type presents the laureated head of the Emperor. The altar of Lyon forms its type of reverse.—See *Ara Lugdunensis,* p. 73.]

The coins of Augustus are very numerous. On the earliest of them we read the title of IIIVIR. but on those of later date, its place is supplied by the names of *Caius Cæsar, Imperator, Augustus, Pontifex Maximus, Divi Filius, Pater Patriæ.*—Gold and silver of ordinary size (with exceptions) are common. A gold medallion (see SICIL.) found at Herculaneum, *unique.* Silver and brass medallions of foreign die, rare. First and second brass common (with reverse of Agrippa, rare in the 7th degree). Restored second brass by Emperors, from Claudius to Trajan, from 2nd to 6th degree of rarity.—See Akerman, who observes, "towards the end of this emperor's reign, the gold and silver coins are very beautiful, and the standard is of great purity."—*Numismatic Manual,* p. 179.

"The medals of this politic ruler (says Capt. Smyth), are easily obtainable, and at a moderate price. Large brass ones, indeed, with the portrait, are difficult to procure, and are high priced according to their condition; but those of middle brass and silver are extremely common; for of the latter metal alone I have seen at least two hundred different reverses."—p. 5.

Amongst the most curious types, in the fertile mint of Augustus, are those which represent the Temple of Janus shut (IAN. CLV.); the civic crown between the talons of the Roman eagle; the emperor himself in a quadriga on the top of a triumphal arch; the crocodile and legend of EGYPTO CAPTA, indicating the defeat of Antony and Cleopatra; Apollo Cytharoedus, and Diana, in memory of the battle of Actium, where those deities were worshipped; the Parthians restoring the legionary ensigns; the Zodiac sign of Capricorn, under which Augustus was born; the Apex between the Ancilia; the Roman eagles; the portrait of his daughter Livia between the heads of Lucius and Caius, his adopted sons; the inscriptive tribute to his construction of public roads; his equestrian statue, &c.—The medals struck after his death and apotheosis, bear the title of DIVVS AVGVSTVS, and of DIVVS AVGVSTVS PATER. The radiated head is the sign of his deification: it is sometimes accompanied with a thunderbolt and a

star. A middle brass, minted to his posthumous honour, by the Senate, exhibits on its reverse the figure of *Livia* as *Ceres,* with legend of DIVA AVGVSTA. We see him also holding a patera, and in a temple. His portrait was afterwards restored on coins struck by order of Caligula, Claudius, and other emperors. The colonial coins of Augustus, all bearing his "image and superscription," are numerous and generally common, but many of them very interesting.— See DIVVS AVGVSTVS—and DIVVS AVGVSTVS PATER.

AVGVST. CAESAR PONT. MAX. TRIBVNIC. POT. *Cæsar Augustus, Pontifex Maximus, Tribuniciâ Potestate.* (The August Cæsar, Sovereign Pontiff, invested with the Tribunitian Power). Laureated head of Augustus, crowned by Victory from behind.

Rev.—*Marcus* MAECILIVS IIIVIR *Auro Argento Aere Flando Feriundo.*—(See p. 1.)

These legends and types appear on large brass, struck by one of the monetary triumvirs of Octavianus Cæsar, *after* that prince had accepted the title of *Augustus,* A.U.C. 727 (B.C. 27), but *before* he received the appellation of *Pater Patriæ,* in 752 (B.C. 2.)

Lepidus having surrendered up his dignity as Triumvir, and M. Antonius not having long survived his ruinous defeat at Actium, Cæsar Octavianus remained in sole possession of the sovereign power. For this reason the goddess of Victory is here represented standing behind Augustus, with her right hand placing a crown of laurel on his head.—"In fact (says Havercamp), this man had then attained so high a degree of fortune and prosperity, that he seemed to be elevated above the common destiny of human nature. It was under these circumstances that the Senate decided that some mark of honour and pre-eminence should be awarded to him; and they chose the surname of AUGUSTUS, by which he was thenceforward called."

AVGV*stus* CAES*ar.*—An altar, with legend FORT. RED. This silver coin was struck in remembrance of an altar having been erected, on the return of the emperor to Rome, to *Fortuna Redux.*—(Vaillant, Pr. vol. ii. p. 27.)

AVGVSTVS.—A Sphinx (symbol of Egypt.) In memory of the seal of Augustus, on which the figure of that fabulous animal, according to Suetonius, was engraved.—This silver medallion, says Mionnet, was struck in Asia.—See *Sphinx.*

AVGVSTVS.—Capricorn and horn of plenty, some with globe and rudder, others without.— Silver medallion; also denarii. There is another denarius of this emperor, with same legend, the reverse type representing a Capricorn, above which is a female with floating drapery.—Augustus was born under the constellation Capricornus : hence the frequent occurrence of that sign on his coins. Akerman.—See *Capricornus*.

AVGVSTVS TR. POT.——An equestrian statue.

This sculptural honour was decreed by the Senate to Augustus, in commemoration of his munificence, in repairing the *Via Flaminia*, A. U. C. 731 (B. C. 23), when he also accepted the perpetual Tribunate. These events are recorded on silver coins bearing the above legend and type.

AVGVSTVS TR. POT. VIII.—Head of Augustus.

Rev.—A cippus, or milliary column, with this inscription: S. P. Q. R. IMP. CAES*ari*, QVOD. Vi*æ* M*unitæ* S*unt* EX. EA. P*ecunia Quam* IS. AD. Aerar*ium* DE*tulit*: L. VINICIVS, L. F. III. VIR. (The Senate and the Roman people to the Emperor, Cæsar, for his having caused the highways to be repaired with the money, with which he had replenished the public treasury.)

This coin (rare in silver, but of the highest rarity in gold) has reference to the repairs of the public roads throughout the empire, on which Augustus had bestowed great and continued care, in appropriating to that purpose the pecuniary contributions which he had levied on conquered nations. It has also particular allusion to his having restored the Flaminian way, at his own expense. The simplicity of this inscription is remarkably striking; whilst its meaning is perfectly clear, without being pompous or affected—a merit seldom to be ascribed to modern legends.

AVG*ustus* COMM. CONS.——There is an equally interesting specimen of Roman tact and simplicity in dedicatory inscriptions, exhibited on a denarius minted by L. Mescinius Rufus; the same individual who was Quæstor to Cicero in Cilicia B. C. 51; and who, from coins, appears to have held the office of monetal triumvir under Augustus, in the years B. C. 17 and 16.

On the obverse is a cippus with IMP. CAES. AVGV. COMM. CONS. that is, *Imperator Caesar Augustus communi consensu*, and round the cippus L. MESCINIVS RVFVS III. VIR. S. C.: on the reverse, inclosed in a chaplet of oak leaves, I. O. M. S. P. Q. R. V. S. PR. S. IMP. CAES. QVOD PER EV. R. P. IN AMP. ATQ. TRAN. S. E. that is, *Iovi Optimo Maximo S. P. Q. R. votum susceptum pro salute Imperatoris Caesaris, quod per eum res publica in ampliore atque tranquilliore statu est.* This interpretation is confirmed by the fact that, after the defeat of Varus some years afterwards, we read that games were vowed by Augustus to

Jupiter Optimus Maximus, *si respublica in meliorem statum vertisset* (Suet. *Aug.* 23.)—Eckhel, cited in *Dict. of Roman Biog.* &c. edited by Dr. W. Smith.

AVGVSTVS, within a rostral crown.—A brass medallion.

" Such were the advantages (observes (Havercamp) which Octavianus gained from his decisive naval victory at Actium, that the Senate caused a medal to be struck, which, by representing prows of galleys, interlaced with a crown of laurel, should present continually before the public eye, in every province of the empire, a monument recalling the remembrance of that great, and to him, glorious event. His new name of AVGVSTVS is also seen enclosed within the crown ; for the obverse of this coin bears simply the head of Augustus, bare, and without legend.—See *Corona Rostrata*.

AVGVSTVS. S. C.—An eagle holds in his talons an oaken crown, behind him are two branches of laurel. On the reverse of an *aureus* of Augustus, the obverse of which presents the bare head of that prince, with the following legend : CAESAR COS. VII. CIVIBVS SERVATIS.

Augustus having by his successes abroad, guaranteed the repose of the empire, and having protected the lives of the citizens of Rome by the re-establishment of internal peace and tranquillity, the Senate ordered that laurel trees should be planted in front of his palace, with a view to recall his victories to remembrance; and that in the midst a crown of oak leaves should be placed, as a symbol of the preservation which the emperor had secured to the Roman people. —See *Eagle*, for an engraving of this reverse.

AVGVSTVS AVGVSTA.—On gold and silver coins, minted by Nero, the type of reverse re-

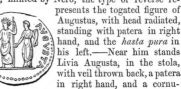

presents the togated figure of Augustus, with head radiated, standing with patera in right hand, and the *hasta pura* in his left.——Near him stands Livia Augusta, in the stola, with veil thrown back, a patera in right hand, and a cornucopiæ in her left.

Suetonius, in his life of Claudius (c. 11), relates of that Emperor, that having turned his attention to offices of Piety, he instituted an oath than which none was more binding upon, nor more frequently used by himself, viz. " by Augustus ;" and that he caused divine honours to be also decreed to his grandmother Livia (wife of Augustus).—This coin of Nero shews us, says Vaillant, (Pr. ii. p. 62), that he in emulation of Claudius, consecrated statues to Augustus and Livia, which *in rei memoriam*, he recorded on his gold and silver mintage.—Eckhel (vol. vi. 269) reminds his readers, on this point, that Augustus and Livia are figured on other coins of Nero, not very dissimilar in dress and attributes to the above example, but sitting in a quadriga of Elephants.—See Agrippina Claudii.

AVGVSTVS S. C.—An eagle with expanded wings, resting on a crown of oak leaves, on each side is a laurel branch.—Engraved in Caylus's *aurei* of Augustus.

In Dion Cassius (L. liii. § 16) there is a passage, which lucidly explains this reverse. A decree, says that historian, was made this year (U. C. 727, B. C. 27) " that laurels should be planted in front of Augustus's house on the Palatine, and a crown of oak suspended from the top of the house, as though he had been the ' perpetual conqueror of the enemies (of Rome)' and ' the preserver of citizens *(Civium Servator).' "* —The letters S. C. observes Eckhel (vol. vi. p. 88), were added on this gold coin to shew that Cæsar had, in the above mentioned year, been called *Augustus* by a decree of the Senate, and also that the oaken crown, and the laurels were voted to him by the same lawful authority. The expression of Pliny (L. xvi. § 3), likewise throws light on this legend and type, viz. that Augustus, after putting an end to the civil wars, accepted for himself a civic crown in recompense from the whole race of mankind— *(genere humano.)*—See *Eagle.*

AVG*ustus* DIVI. F.—A crescent with seven stars—IMP. X. in the field.

This rare denarius minted under Augustus relates to the war which Tiberius brought to a triumphant conclusion in Pannonia. On this Augustus is called Imperator X.—Vaillant submits whether it was not in that year that Augustus regulated the days of the year, to which these stars seem to allude.—Engraved in Morel and King.

AVG*ustus* SVF. *(Suffimenta Populo.)*—Gold of Augustus.—The emperor seated on an estrade, distributing the prizes of the secular games to two figures, standing before him. On the ground is a basket. On the estrade we read LVD. S. *(Ludi Seculares)* celebrated B. C. 17. See the SVF. P. D. *(Suffimentum Populo Datum)* of Domitian, minted on a like occasion.

Of this gold coin, struck by L. MESCINIVS, one of the mint masters of Augustus, Mionnet, who has valued it at 300 fr. has given a beautiful engraving.—See *Rareté des Médailles Romaines,* &c. T. i. p. 110.

AVGVSTVS DIVI F. Equestrian statue of Augustus.—*Rev.* P. STOLO. IIIVIR.—The apex between two bucklers.—See *Ancilia,* p. 45.

This rare and beautiful denarius refers (says Vaillant, *Pr. Impp. Rom.* ii. 25), to the statue erected in honour of Augustus, in the month of March, when the Salian solemnities were celebrated.

On various coins of Augustus, both silver and gold, he is styled CAESAR DIVI. F. (Cæsar son of the Divine Julius.) One of these reverses bears the type of an equestrian statue.—According to Dion (quoted by Vaillant) Augustus, after his return from Syria, in the year U. C. 735, (B. C. 19,) entered Rome on horseback, taking the honours of the ovation, for Roman successes. Another with the same legend, has for its device a triumphal quadriga. On his bringing to a termination the Sicilian war, arches, statues, and triumphal cars were, by universal and enthusiastic consent, decreed to Augustus Cæsar,

by the Senate and the Roman people. (Dion, quoted by Vaillant.) A gold coin of the same reign, with the same legend, and Victory in a biga, refers to the Circensian games given by Augustus.—See Morel's, King's, and Caylus's plates.

AVGVSTVS PATER PATRIAE.—See *Pater Patriæ.*

AVGVSTVS GERMANICVS.—On an *aureus* of Nero, bearing this legend on its reverse, the type represents a male figure standing, habited in the toga, his head surrounded with rays, holding in his right hand a branch, and in his left a small victory on a globe. The obverse exhibits NERO CAESAR, and a laureated head.

This gold coin has given rise to very opposite interpretations amongst numismatic antiquaries. Occo considers this figure to represent the Emperor Claudius, by whom, to the prejudice of Britannicus, Nero was adopted. Vaillant (Pr. ii. p. 63) concurs in this supposition, and points to the radiated head as indicating the apotheosis of Claudius.—Tristan (vol. i p. 211) who has copiously treated of this coin, differs from the above writers. After judiciously observing, that the legends on both sides of this aureus are to be taken in connection with each other viz. NERO CAESAR—AVGVSTVS GERMANICVS—and that the epithet, or surname of *Germanicus,* both in history and on coins, was given to Nero as well as Claudius, he decidedly pronounces that the radiated image is meant for that of Nero himself. Tristan is moreover of opinion that Nero was distinguished by the *corona radiata,* because he was ambitious to rival Apollo ; and indeed even Seneca, in his Apocolocyntosis, compares him to that deity, both in form, as of the rising sun, and in his vocal powers. After such gross flattery on the part of his preceptor, it seems but a natural consequence that this spoiled child of a prince should have appointed five thousand prætorian soldiers to accompany him to the theatre, and who used, when he sang, to shout—" *O beautiful Cæsar— O Apollo—O thou Pythius,* &c."

Eckhel (vi. p. 269), expresses his agreement with Tristan, as to the type in question being an indication that a statue of similar character had been erected in honour of Nero ; and he remarks, that it is the first instance of a radiated crown appearing on the head of a living emperor, though from that time it very frequently occurs on the obverses of Nero's coins, in *second brass.*—The learned author of *Doctrina* goes on, however, to say that he does not regard this distinction of crowning with rays, as conferred upon Nero, either from an admiration of his person, or through the extravagant language of the theatres.—" For why (he asks), does not the radiated crown appear on those coins, on which Nero is typified as moving in the full costume of Apollo the harp-player *(Citharoedus)* ? Are we to imagine that Vespasian also, and Antoninus Pius, and M. Aurelius, were desirous of being thought beautiful, and good musicians, because they too appear with radiated heads? or that those renowned, and honourable princes coveted for themselves an honour, which Nero, whose memory they abhorred, had acquired with so unworthy a motive? We must conclude then, that it was the pleasure of Nero, the vainest of men, to be considered as a deity—of which honour, or at any rate of a divine lineage, the radiated crown was the invariable symbol, as well amongst the Romans as the Greeks.—To Julius Cæsar, after his victory over the Pompeys in Spain, a radiated crown was (according to Flavus) decreed in the theatre, amongst other honours obviously of a divine character.—Augustus is represented, with radiated head, on many coins, struck after his death. And long before that period, Antiochus IV., king of Syria, was exhibited with this ornament; indeed he went so far as to cause himself to be reverenced as a deity, by the inscription, on his coins, of the word ΘΕΟΥ.—The emperors who succeeded Nero, cannot be said, so much to have sought divine honours, as to have shewn no repugnance, when any distinction, above the lot of man, was conferred upon them, by which they might inspire the people with veneration, and a kind of superstitious awe.—A convincing proof of this is to be found in the fact, that the heads of the *Augusti*, in the gold and silver coinage, (which was under the direction of the Emperors) are without exception destitute of the radiated crown, up to the time of Caracalla, who first introduced it, more frequently and promiscuously on his silver coins.— On the other hand, this radiated type constantly occurs on brass coins, especially of the *second* size; but, as it is well known, the care of this coinage devolved on the senate, whose flattery of the Emperors was thoroughly appreciated and acquiesced in by them.—Eckhel's remarks on the divinity ascribed to Nero are admirably illustrated from the following passage, which he cites from Tacitus (Ann. xv. 74):—"Cerealis Anicius, the consul elect, moved a resolution, that a temple be erected as soon as possible, at the public cost, in honour of DIVVS NERO." Although, as he afterwards adds, "the honours of the Gods are not bestowed on a prince, till he has ceased to live amongst mortals."—See *Corona radiata*.

Augustus Divus.—The emperor Augustus had divine honours paid him during his life time, in the provinces; but not at Rome, nor in any other part of Italy.—See DIVVS AVGVSTVS.

Augustus Iterum.—Hadrian is thus called on a coin of Mesembria in Thrace, preserved in the Imperial Museum at Vienna.—See *Doct. Num. Vet.* vol. viii. 359.

Augustus Semper.—Isidorus Hispalensis has remarked that "*Augustus*" was, among the Romans, a title designative of Empire, because the Emperors, in the earlier times, were accustomed to "increase the extent of the commonwealth." From this circumstance no doubt (adds Eckhel) arose the title of *Semper Augustus*.

Augustus Perpetuus.—See PERP. AVG.

AVIS.—A particular bird was assigned to certain gods and goddesses—as the eagle to Jupiter, the cock to Mars, the owl to Minerva, the peacock to Juno. Thus also the dove was the symbol of conjugal concord, as the stork was of filial piety.

AVES.—Birds appear on coins of Julius Cæsar, Augustus, Mark Antony, Titus, both the Faustinæ, Commodus, and Volusianus, &c. A bird, with the helmeted head of a woman, having a shield at its left side, and armed with two spears, is found on a denarius of the *Valeria gens*.

A. or AVL. VITELL.—*Aulus Vitellius.*

AVITUS *(Marcus Mæcilius).*—A native of that part of southern Gaul now called Aquitaine, descended from a noble family, and reckoning Patricians and Senators amongst his ancestors, he became, in consequence of his military exploits and high reputation, Prætorian prefect in Gaul under Valentinian III. (A. D. 425), and afterwards general of cavalry, under Petronius Maximus.—He was proclaimed Augustus at Arles, and his election confirmed by the senate and people of Rome, A.U.C. 1208 (A.D. 455).— His title of Emperor of the West was at the same time recognised by Marcianus, who became Emperor of the East, in marrying Pulcheria, sister of Theodosius II.—After a reign of 14 months he was taken prisoner by Ricimer, A.D. 436, one of his own generals; and being compelled to abdicate the government, he entered into ecclesiastical orders, and receiving consecration as Bishop of Placentia, died soon afterwards. His coins of each metal are very rare.

A gold coin of Avitus, in the British Museum, exhibits on the obverse the head of the emperor, wearing the diadem ornamented with pearls, and surrounded with the legend D. N. AVITVS PERP. F. AVG.—and on the reverse, VICTORIA AVGGG. A military figure, his left foot planted on a prostrate captive; a cross in his right hand, and a globe surmounted by a victoriola in his left. In the field A. R.—In the exergue COMOB.—Mionnet gives from the cabinet of M. Gosselin, another aureus of this prince, which as well as the one published by Banduri, has for the legend of reverse VRBIS *(sic)* RONA, the type Roma Victrix seated.—On other coins he is styled D.N. AVITHVS. P. F. AVG. and M. MAECIL AVITVS (or AVITHVS P. F. AVG.

AVR. *Aurelius.* name of the *Aurelia* family, and of several of the Emperors.

AVR. *Aureum,*—See SAEC. AVR. *Seculum Aureum,* on a gold coin of Hadrian.

AURELIA *gens plebeia;* of Sabine origin, noted for having produced very eminent men—

men on whom were conferred the highest offices of the State. According to Festus, this family was so called from the Sun: because the Roman people publicly granted it a place, in which sacrifices might be performed to the Sun. It was distinguished by the *prenomina* of *Caius, Lucius, Marcus;* and by the *cognomina* of *Cotta, Rufus, Scaurus,* both on coins and by ancient writers. The *Aurelia gens* often enjoyed the honours of the Consulate, of the Censorship, and of the Triumph, in the times of the Commonwealth, and was afterwards associated with monarchical dignity in the persons of several of the Emperors. Mionnet, out of 17 varieties (from Morel) gives the following as a rarity, in silver:

COTA. Winged head of Pallas: behind X (mark of the denarius.)

Rev.—M. AVRELI. Hercules in a car drawn by two centaurs, each holding a branch of a tree; below ROMA.

Eckhel says, "I prefer confessing my ignorance of the meaning of the singular type exhibited on the reverse of this coin, rather than avail myself of such irrelevant matter, as that with which some learned men have endeavoured to explain it; an instance of which may be found in Spanheim. One circumstance only, am I inclined to bring forward; viz. that a similar type exists on a Greek medal, with the inscription OPPE. (which I ascribe to Horreus of Epirus); on which we see on one side the head of Hercules, and on the other a centaur running, bearing a branch covered with berries. *Doct. Num. Vet.* vol. v. p. 147.)—See *Centaur*—also *Mars.*

AURELIANA, or Aurelianorum Civitas, now *Orleans* in France. A coin attributed to this colony is engraved in the Pembroke collection (iii. TAB. 91, fig. 5), with bare head of a woman, and METAL. AVRELIANVS, within a crown.—Rasche.

AURELIANUS *(Lucius Claudius Domitius),* born of an obscure family, at Sirmium, in Pannonia, or in Dacia Ripensis, about the year of Rome 960 (A.D. 207). A man of sagacity, valour, and talent, severe even to cruelty, he distinguished himself in Gaul, under Gordianus Pius (A.D. 241), against the Sarmatians. He rose to be general of the cavalry, in the army of Claudius Gothicus; and, with the consent of all the legions, was proclaimed Emperor in Pannonia, after the death of that prince 1023 (A.D. 270). He embellished Rome; and re-built the temple of the Sun, of which his wife was priestess. The Goths, Germans, and other northern tribes who assailed the empire, having deluged Italy with their myriads, defeated Aurelian at Placentia. But he avenged himself promptly by three victories, and the result was

peace with the vanquished barbarians. He also recovered Gaul and Spain out of the hands of the elder Tetricus. Scarcely, however, had he placed Rome in a state of security by repairing and fortifying the walls (one of which, commenced A.D. 271, bears his name and exists to this day), when the war against Zenobia called him into the East; and that ambitious and heroic Queen, widow of Odenathus, Prince of Palmyra, defended her dominions with a courage and conduct truly masculine. At length her magnificent capital, after a long siege, reduced to extremities by famine, surrendered to the Roman arms A. U. C. 1025 (A. D. 272). And Zenobia, after a fruitless attempt to escape, was brought as a prisoner to Rome, where she, together with Tetricus, graced the triumph of the victorious emperor, A. D. 273.—Palmyra destroyed and Egypt subdued, Aurelian endeavoured at Rome to gain the affections of a lazy and insolent populace, by his liberalities, which were of the most prodigal kind. But, in caressing the multitude, he still maintained order and justice, and was inexorable against crime, his punishment of which was sometimes carried to a dreadful extreme, as in the case of the monetal forgers, U. C. 1027 (A. D. 274.) His prudence dictated to him the abandonment of Dacia (the conquest of Trajan), situated beyond the Danube, which river then became the barrier of the empire. On his march against the Persians, whose King, Sapor, had begun the hostilities, he was assassinated between Byzantium and Heraclea, A.D. 275, by some of his generals (deceived by the treachery of his freedman and secretary Mnesteus), after reigning four years and nine months.

Aurelian is represented on his coins, sometimes laureated, sometimes radiated, after the usual manner of the Roman Emperors; at other times crowned with the diadem, according to the fashion of eastern kings.—Victor says of him, " *Primus apud Romanos diadematem capiti innexuit*"—and Jornandes (quoted by Oiselius), says, " *Is primus gemmas vestibus, calceamentisque inseruit, diadematemque in capite.*"

On the Latin coins of this emperor he is styled, AVRELIANVS AVG.—IMP. C. AVRELIANVS AVG.—IMP. C. L. DOM. AVRELIANVS AVG.—IMP. CAES. DOM. AVRELIANVS AVG.—IMP. C. AVRELIANVS INVICTVS AVG.—DEO ET DOMINO NATO AVRELIANO AVG.—DEO ET DOMINO NOSTRO, &c.

Thus we see, by the last of these titles, that " this humble Pannonian peasant was the first of the Roman princes who openly assumed the regal diadem, and now for the first time we read on medals struck [at Rome] during the life time of an emperor, the arrogant and impious titles of DOMINVS *et* DEVS."—See *Dictionary of Greek and Roman Biography and Mythology*, vol. i. 436.

Aurelian's money is numerous. The gold is of the second and fourth degree of rarity. Base silver also rare. The brass, with exceptional instances, is very common. Some pieces represent him with Ulpia Severina, his wife; and others with *Vabalathus Athenodorus*. On some of his medals, the entire bust appears, and shews this warlike prince with spear on right shoulder and shield on left arm.

Amongst the rarest types of reverse are the following:—

Gold Medallions. ADVENTVS AVG. Emperor on horseback, with lance reversed. [This, by far the rarest medallion of the Aurelian mint, and in extremely fine preservation, brought £26 at the sale of the Thomas collection, in 1844. The same type is engraved in Akerman, *Descr. Cat.* ii. pl. I. p. 91].—*Gold.* P. M. TR. P. VII. COS. II. PP. Mars carrying a trophy. [See the preceding cut. A well-preserved specimen of this fine type, at the Thomas sale, brought £5 7s. 6d.]—PROVIDENTIA DEORVM. Providence and the Sun.——*Third Brass.* PIETAS AVG. Two figures sacrificing.—RESTITVT ORBIS. The Emperor crowned by a female figure; with INVICTVS on the obverse.—DEO ET DOMINO NATO AVRELIANO AVG. Head of Aurelian.—*Rev.* RESTITVT. ORBIS.

AVRELIANVS AVG. CONS. *(Augusti Con-servator).*—A rare second brass. The Emperor in a military habit, before a lighted altar, holding a patera in his right, and a sceptre in his left hand.—There is a fine brass medallion, minted under the same *Augustus*, corresponding in legend and type with the above, except that the imperial sacrificer is habited in the toga.—See it engraved in the *Mus. Pisani*, TAB. lxxii.

Aurelian testified in various ways his particular devotion to the Sun, to whom on this medal he is represented in the act of sacrificing; and upon whose deityship he here bestows the title of *his preserver.*—See Spanheim's *Cæsars*, p. 189—see also SOL. DOMINVS IMPERI. ROMANI, and SOLI. INVICTO.—the rarest second brass of this Emperor.

AURELIUS—(MARCUS ANNIUS VERUS) son of Annius Verus, the prætor, and of Domitia Calvilla, born at Rome, in the year of the city 874 and of Christ 121. After the death of his father (who was brother to the wife of Antoninus Pius), he received from Hadrian the appellation of M. Annius Verissimus. At the early age of 15 years, he was permitted to assume the *toga virilis.* Adopted by Antoninus Pius at the time when Hadrian adopted Antoninus, he was named in the year U. C. 891 (A. D. 138), Cæsar and Consul; and from that period was called M. Ælius Aurelius. After having been declared Consul for the second time, he married (A. D. 145) Annia Faustina, daughter of Antoninus Pius and of Faustina senior, a woman infamous for her adulteries, but a skilful dissembler with her husband. In A. U. C. 900 (A. D. 147), he was invested with the Tribunitian power. At the death of Antoninus, U. C. 914 (A. D. 161), he succeeded to the empire, being proclaimed by the Senators, in conjunction with Verus, his adopted brother, whom he generously took for his colleague. And thus, for the first time, Rome saw herself governed by TWO *Augusti et Imperatores*, sharing with each other the supreme authority of the state, to exercise it in common. It was then (A. D. 161) that he took the names *M. Aurelius Antoninus*, thereby marking his transit from the Annia to the Aurelia family. From A. D. 162 to 165, he defeated and brought to submission the Parthians, the Medes, and the Armenians. In A. D. 166, he participated with Verus, in the honours of the triumph, at Rome, for these victories. From A. U C. 920 (A. D. 167), to 927 (A. D. 174), Aurelius was engaged in repelling the destructive inroads of the Marcomanni, the Quadi, the Sarmatians, and almost all the nations inhabiting the north of Europe, banded together during that period in a formidable league against the Romans. Making head against this furious storm, he saved the empire by the firmness of his character and the wisdom of his measures, by his indefatigable zeal and undaunted courage in the midst of dangers.— About A. D. 177, he received the title of P. P. *(Pater Patriæ.)* Meanwhile the whole of Italy and nearly all the provinces, were desolated by a most dreadful pestilence, which the troops of Verus had brought with them from the east.— That debauched young prince himself fell a victim to his excesses in A. D. 169. After subduing a rebellion in Germany, suppressing a revolt of the Britons, quelling the insurrection of Avidius Cassius in Italy, and triumphing over most of his enemies, this renowned emperor terminated his eventful career, in a renewed war with the Marcomanni and their barbaric allies; dying at Vindobona, in Pannonia (now Vienna, in Austria), according to some; or at Sirmium (now Sirmich, Austria), according to others, in the year of Rome 933 (A. D. 180), in the 59th of his age, and 19th of his reign.—He had by Faustina the younger, Commodus and Lucilla, also four sons and three daughters who died in their infancy.

Aurelius, no less celebrated for his literary accomplishments, than for his military exploits, is usually distinguished by the name of "the Philosopher," in consequence of his attachment to the system of the Stoics. But neither coins nor marbles hand down any inscriptions that assign to him this particular addition, however due to his learning and to his gravity of deportment. In public spirited disinterestedness and for irreproachable morals, he equalled, perhaps excelled, the best of his imperial predecessors, and successors too. When, in a calamitous struggle with invading myriads from the northern hive of nations, the public treasury became emptied, and fresh supplies of money were required to carry on the war, this illustrious prince brought to auction in the *Forum Trajani*, all the ornaments and furniture of his palace, generously parting with his private fortune rather than increase the pressure of provincial taxation. But Marcus Aurelius, wise and honest as he was, had nevertheless his weaknesses and his faults, amongst which must be noticed the dignities which he lavished on an openly abandoned wife, and the premature honours which he conferred on his monster of a son. The most grievous blot, however, which his just and merciful characteristics sustained, was in the cruelties, which, if he did not actually encourage, he too readily permitted, to be exercised against the Christians, and which were carried to such a height, that under his reign are chronologically placed the horrors of the fourth persecution. Yet "taking him for all in all"—looking to the correctness of his habits, the simplicity of his manners, the liberality of his natural disposition, as evinced in his written meditations, and practically exemplified in his conduct through life, it is not to be wondered at that his memory was long revered by posterity, or that more than a century after his death, many persons preserved his image amongst those of their tutelary deities.

[The wood cut, at the head of this notice, is from the obverse of a brass medallion in the French cabinet. With the legend M. ANTONINVS AVG. TR. P. XXVIII. it exhibits a striking portrait, of finished workmanship. In mature age, the emperor retains a full head of hair, to which the laurel crown is a conspicuous ornament; the beard is luxuriant, even to shagginess; his shoulders are covered with the imperial laticlavum, clasped with a fibula to the right shoulder.]

The coins of Aurelius are very numerous. The gold common, except some of second degree of rarity.—Silver common, except some of fifth degree of rarity.—Brass common, except some of eighth degree of rarity.—There are pieces which represent him with *Antoninus, Faustina junior, Lucius Verus,* and *Commodus.*—On these medals he is styled :—AVRELIVS CAESAR.—AVRELIVS CAESAR AVG*usti* PII FIL*ius* (with the young head).—M. AVRELIVS ANTONINVS.—IMP. CAES. M. AVREL. ANTONINVS.—M. ANTONINVS AVGVSTVS.—Also with the surnames of ARMENIACVS, PARTHICVS, MAXIMVS—MEDICVS (the *Median*); GERMANICVS, and SARMATICVS. —On his consecration medals appear, DIVVS M. ANTONINVS, and DIVVS M. ANTONI-

NVS PIVS.—Thus it appears that on several of his coins the name of *Aurelius* is omitted.

AVRELIVS CAESAR, ANTONINI AVG. PII F*ilius.* (Aurelius Caesar, son of Antoninus, the August and the Pius.)

On the obverse of a large brass, bearing the above legend, appears the bare head of the youthful Marcus Aurelius, with curly hair, adolescent beard, and a countenance of which the expression (as the above engraving testifies) is open and pleasing. This coin was struck a short time previous to the year A. D. 140, in which Antoninus, having given Aurelius his daughter Faustina in marriage, advanced the young Cæsar to the consulate.

Amongst the rarest and most remarkable legends and types, on reverses in the coinage of this emperor, are the following, viz. :—

Gold and Silver.—COMMODVS CÆSAR. Young head.—CONSECRATIO. Funeral pile.—COS. II. Emperor in a quadriga.—DE GERM. Heap of arms.—DE SARM. Do.—IMP. VI. COS. III. Emperor on horseback.—IMP. VII. COS. Do.— IMP. VI. COS. III. Emperor crowned by Victory. —PIETAS AVG. Sacrificial instruments.—RELIG. AVG. Mercury.—TR. POT. XV. COS. III. Emperor in a quadriga—(Cabinet de Gosselin).—VIC. PAR. Victory is inscribing on a buckler.—VOTA PUBLICA. Two figures standing with joined hands, Concord in the midst.

Brass Medallions.—ADLOCVTIO. One of the figures holds a horse by the bridle.—ADVENTVS AVG. Emperor walking towards a triumphal arch.—IMP. VII. COS. III. Jupiter Tonans and a Titan.—IMP. VIII. COS. III. Aurelius and Verus in a triumphal car.—PROFECTIO AVG. S. C. Two horsemen and two foot soldiers.—PROFECTIO AVG. COS. III. Emperor on horseback, and four foot soldiers.—TEMPORVM FELICITAS. Hercules in a car drawn by four centaurs.—TR. P. XXII. Jupiter, standing, between two small figures clothed in the toga.—VICT. PARTHICAE. On a shield supported by two Victories.—VOTA PVBLICA. A grand sacrificial group.—Without legend. Minerva and Vulcan.—Without legend. Neptune and Ceres.—Without legend. Imperator eques.

First Brass.—CONG. AVG. III. Aurelius and Verus distributing their third congiarium.— CONSECRATIO. Carpentum and four elephants.— DIVA FAVSTINA. Head of the Empress.—DIVVS VERVS. Bare head of Verus.—PROPVGNATORI IMP. VIII. COS. III. Jupiter hurling the fulmen at a prostrated figure.——PROVIDENTIA AVG. Type of an Allocution.—RELIG. AVG. A figure within a temple.—REX. ARMENIS DATVS. The Emperor and three other figures.—RESTITVTORI ITALIÆ. The Emperor raising up a kneeling woman.—TR. POT. XX. Aurelius and Verus in a triumphal car.—VIRTVS AVG. The Emperor on a bridge with soldiers.

Second Brass.——DIVO AVG. PARENTI. Emperor on horseback.—TR. P. XIII. Figure of a winged sphinx.

AURELIUS.—In the imperial series, the name of *Aurelius* occurs no less than 13 times, as will appear on consulting Mionnet's *Médailles Romaines*, or Akerman's *Descriptive Catalogue of Roman Coins*, viz.:—1. Marcus *Aurelius* Verus, successor of Antoninus Pius.—2. Commodus, his son, was called L. *Aurelius* and M. *Aurelius* Antoninus.—3. Caracalla, eldest son of Septimius Severus, when created Cæsar, took, or rather usurped, the name of M. *Aurelius Antoninus.*—4. Elagabalus, under pretence of being the son of Caracalla, assumed the names of M. *Aurelius* Antoninus.—5. Severus Alexander, successor of Elagabalus, took, by adoption, the name of Marcus *Aurelius* Alexander.—6. Marius, an usurper in the reign of Gallienus, bears on his coins the prenomina of *Marcus Aurelius.* [The coins described by Mediobarbus and Banduri, with the legends MARCVS AVRELIVS VICTORINVS (says Akerman) are doubted]—7. Claudius Gothicus, a great prince, though of an obscure family, is styled on his coins Marcus *Aurelius.*—8. His brother and successor Quintillus, had for his prenomina Marcus *Aurelius* Claudius.—9. Then we have Marcus *Aurelius* Probus.—10. Marcus *Aurelius* Carus. —11. Marcus *Aurelius* Valerianus Maximianus. —12. Marcus *Aurelius* Valerius Maxentius.— And 13. M. *Aurelius* Romulus, son of Maxentius. The first, however, of all these, MARCVS AURELIUS, surnamed the Philosopher, is the one who is usually, *par excellence*, designated by that name.

AUREOLUS (Marcus Acilius)—one of the many *tyranni* or usurpers, that sprang up in various parts of the empire, during the reign of Gallienus. A Dacian by birth, and (if Zonarus is to be credited) in his youthful days a shepherd, he rose in the army, and at length became governor of Illyria under Gallienus, whom he rescued out of the rebellious hands of Macrianus and his son, only, as it would seem, to revolt afterwards against his own sovereign.— He was proclaimed emperor by the legions in Illyria, or rather in Rhætia, about the year of Our Lord 267. Defeated by Gallienus, shortly afterwards, he shut himself up in Mediolanum (Milan); but was delivered from his besiegers by the assassination of Gallienus; to be slain by the troops of Claudius Gothicus, A. D. 268. On his coins, which consist of gold (if genuine) and small brass (no silver) of the highest rarity, he is styled, IMP. C. AVREOLVS AVG.—IMP. M. ACIL. AVREOLVS P. F. AVG.—Reverses are, PROVIDENTIA AVG. (Providence standing).—CONCORDIA EQVIT. (woman with rudder).—CONCORD. MIL. (two hands joined).—" These pieces, which are of Roman die, were (says Hennin), struck

in Rhætia, or in Upper Italy, or probably in Milan."

AURIGÆ—Charioteers—those who drove the cars at the games of the Circus, and contended for the prize in the races. It is the *auriga* whom we see, on coins, guiding so many *bigæ*, *trigæ*, and *quadrigæ*, under the form of Jupiter, of Victory, &c. or in the person of the Consul proceeding, or the Emperor triumphing. With regard to chariot racing on public occasions, at first, a Roman citizen disdained to exercise himself in such a competitorship; but afterwards, as corruption introduced itself into the manners of the people, persons of the first distinction, and some even of the *Augusti*, were not ashamed to practice the science of the *whip*. Nero and Domitian were passionately addicted to these sports; and the former frequently took a personal share in them.

The vanity of Nero (according to Dion Cassius) led him to attempt equalling the Sun in charioteering; and accordingly, with truly ridiculous acclamations (see AVGVSTVS GERMANICVS) the populace greeted him as victor at all the Circensian contests, with the titles of *Cæsar Apollo*, or *Nero Apollo*. Hence also on a Corinthian coin of that conceited tyrant, engraved by Vaillant (*in Col.* i. 117), we see the figure of the Sun (distinguished by the rays that adorn his head) standing in a quadriga, and holding a whip in his right hand.—Havercamp, in his dissertation on contorniate medals, furnishes many designs of charioteers, in the act of driving four horses, decorated with palm branches, &c.—See *Circus Maximus.*

AURORA.—The daughter of Titan, and harbinger of the Sun, appears as a winged figure, between four horses, whose reins she holds, on a coin of L. Plancus.—See *Plautia gens.*

There is also another image of "the rosy fingered" demi-goddess, on a brass medallion of

Trajan.—The obverse bears the head of that emperor, and is inscribed DIVO NERVAE TRAIANO AVG.—The legend of the reverse is S. P. Q. R. DIVO TRAIANO PARTHICO.—The type represents Aurora holding in her right hand a lighted torch, and in her left a palm branch. She stands in a chariot drawn conjointly by a lion and a wild boar. A Hercules precedes, holding a club on his right shoulder.—See Tristan, who gives an engraving of this reverse in T. i. p. 404 of his *Commentaires*, of which an accurate copy is furnished in the foregoing cut.

On this very remarkable relic of monetal antiquity, the author of *Doctrina* makes the following explanatory animadversions, in the 442nd page of his sixth volume, where he classes it amongst those, which were undoubtedly minted on the occasion of the triumphal honours decreed to Trajan after his decease :—

"This beautiful coin (vi. 442), on account of its singular type, I have determined by no means to overlook, although aware that by some it is reckoned amongst the *contorniati*. The appropriate management of the allegory, and the connexion between the obverse and the reverse, which is scarcely ever observable in the whole batch of contorniates, induce me without hesitation to concur with Havercamp, in rescuing it from that inferior class of medals. But I am not at all satisfied with the interpretations, far-fetched and beside the purpose, which have been applied to it, as well by Erizzo as by Tristan, and lastly by Havercamp himself. For, in the design of this precious medallion (says Eckhel) I recognize the triumph of Aurora, brought about under the auspices of Trajan, a second Hercules, with the vanquished barbarians reduced like wild beasts to her yoke. It is easy, indeed, to prove, that the figure in the chariot represents Aurora; and not, as others have thought, Victory, or a winged Diana. By common consent, the wings and the torch belong to Aurora alone. You see her winged on denarii of the *Plautia* family. She bears a torch on a famous Alexandrine coin, with a head of L. Verus. It was, in fact, a long established custom, to denote countries situate towards the east, by a figure of the Sun, or of Aurora. Thus on gold coins of Trajan, struck after he had set out on the Parthian campaign, you may frequently perceive a head of the Sun; and at the time that Lucius Verus was engaged in a war with the Parthians, a coin was struck at Alexandria, with the type of Aurora, and the inscription HΩ, the Greek word for *Aurora*.— And lastly, ORIENS AVG. with a type of the Sun, constantly occurs on coins from the time of Aurelian. So then, on all these monuments, either the Sun, or Aurora, indicates that quarter of the globe, which furnished the emperors with occasions both of war and of glory. On this principle too, Virgil calls the eastern countries *Auroræ populos*, or *vires Orientis*. With equal elegance of idea, the Nemæan lion and the boar of Erymanthus, yoked to a chariot, serve to signify the Parthians vanquished by the New Hercules, like monsters pernicious to the Roman world, and just brought to submission. Thus we read, that Sesostris was carried in public procession, on a triumphal car, drawn by the kings whom he had conquered in battle. The present coin, then, allegorizes, in a felicitous manner, the Roman provinces of the east delivered from the Parthians; the latter people reduced to the condition of servitude; and Trajan himself the avenger; it being for this reason that, omitting his other titles of *Germanicus*, and *Dacicus*, he is here styled only *Parthicus*."

AU. RUF.—Aurelius Rufus; name and surname of a man.—See *Aurelia gens*.

AURUM.—See *Gold*.

AURUM CORONARIUM.—This term is used in the code of Theodosius, as synonimous with extremely pure gold. It originally signified the very fine and brilliant gold of which crowns were made, or rather the precious metal itself, which was offered to the conqueror. For although, at first, it was customary to present him with golden crowns of honour, yet the more *convenient* practice of giving him a sum of money was afterwards introduced.—*Aurum Coronarium*, says Servius, *quòd hodie à victis gentibus datur*. But it was not the vanquished alone who paid this costly homage. Even the allies and friends of the Romans, when a consul or a pro-consul entered their territories, found it expedient to conciliate his favour with the tender of a large amount in gold. Under the imperial government, gifts of this sort soon began to be offered, on the occasion of some, so called, happy event; such as a birth or an adoption for example, or when a prince ascended the throne.—Speaking of Antoninus Pius, it is affirmed by Capitolinus—*Italicis totum, medium Provincialibus reddidit*. Thus it would appear that the *Aurum Coronarium* was in process of time a mere tribute in gold or in silver, which the Roman potentate received from those placed under his government. And although, during the republic, it might have been a voluntary act of grateful acknowledgment on the part of the different provinces and nations subjected to the sway of Rome; yet under the emperors it became an expected contribution, to replenish the coffers of a reigning prince.—See some further particulars on this subject, extracted from Eckhel's remarks (vii. pp. 6 and 7), under the legend SCYTHIA.——Also, for a symbolic allusion on an imperial coin to the *Coronarium* of gold, see the type of ASIA COS. II. of Antoninus Pius, p. 90.

AUREUS NUMUS.—See *Gold coinage of the Romans*.

AUSPICIUM.—This and *Augurium* are commonly used as convertible terms. But they are sometimes distinguished the one from the other. *Auspicium* was, strictly speaking, the foretelling of future events *(avem specere)* from *inspection of birds*, that is to say, from observing the flying, singing, and other actions of the feathered tribes. *Augurium* was the science of prediction, or of expounding the will of the gods from all kinds of omens and prodigies. One very prominent feature in the discipline of the Roman superstition, was, that nothing of importance was ever done either in public or in private life, without the auspices having first been taken. The presence of an aruspex, or of an augur, was not more necessary in deciding on peace to be preserved, or on war to be waged—the comitia to be held or broken off—a battle to be fought or shunned—than in determining the question whether a journey should be undertaken, and whether a marriage should be solemnized. *Quo ex more*, says Cicero, *nuptiis etiam nunc auspices interponuntur*. So fond, indeed, was the predilection entertained for such whimsical ceremonies, as those connected with these auspices and auguries, by the early Romans, that some of their generals are recorded to have quitted the army, in the most sudden and abrupt manner, for the purpose, or under the pretext, of performing them.—*Papirius Dictator*, says Livy, *à Pullario monitus, cum ad auspiciendum repetendum Romam proficeretur.* But on the other hand, individuals were to be found amongst them, who made no scruple of manifesting all the contempt they felt for such wretched absurdities. Take Claudius Pulcher, for example, who caused "the sacred chickens" that *would not* eat, to be thrown into the sea—add to which the instance of the Consul Flaminius, who fought the enemy, in spite of augury, and beat the foes of his country under the most *in*auspicious signs ever interpreted by grave soothsayers, in prognostication of defeat to the Roman arms.—See *Haruspex.*

AVSPIC. FEL. *(Auspici Felici—*To happy auspices).—Felicity standing, holds a tessera and a caduceus. At her feet is a small suppliant figure of a man, lifting up his hand.

This legend appears, for the first time on any Roman coin whatever, on a third brass of Diocletian. It belongs to the commencement of that Emperor's reign (about A. D. 284) which he was desirous to have welcomed by the praise of his subjects, for some act of liberality, and at the same time it indicates his wish to secure happiness to his government by the *vota suscepta.* —Eckhel, viii. p. 5.

AVSPICIB. *Auspicibus.*—See DIS AVSPICIBVS.

AUTONOMIA— *(αὐτονομία)* — Autonomy— the power, right, or liberty, possessed by any people, of living in their own accustomed way, and according to their own laws. It was a privilege of this kind which many cities, though tributary to Rome, still enjoyed, and by which they were authorised to elect their own magistrates, who administered justice to them, in exclusion of the Roman judges.—Antioch in Syria purchased this mark of honour from Pompeius Magnus.—Augustus granted the same permission to the inhabitants of Patrae; Nero, to all Achaia. The Arabians and Armenians, whom Trajan had subdued, recovered this token of independence, under Hadrian. The Athenians, the Lacedæmonians, even the Carthaginians, were thus allowed to preserve at least a shadow of ostensible self-government. It would appear, in short, that throughout the vast extent of territories comprised within the limits of the empire, there were few communities entirely subjected to the Roman form of laws. *Autonomia* was also identified with, and distinguished by, that right of *coining money*, the exercise of which every nation of antiquity considered to be an act of sovereignty. The different cities and states of Greece, who were the first to have a coinage, inscribed their respective names on their medals, to establish their autonomous privileges, and likewise to impart a legalised value to such money. The Romans followed this example, and some of their earliest coins bear the word

ROMA.—In later æras, the portraits of princes were placed on the money issued under their authority. Indeed, with those who acquired the supreme power, one of the first objects was to have coins stamped with their effigies. Even those ambitious aspirants to the purple, who, in different provinces, from time to time, raised the standard of revolt and usurpation against the reigning emperors, hastened, if they had sufficient time and means, to circulate some pieces bearing their likenesses, names, and assumed titles.—See the remarks of M. Hennin (i. 25), *sur le droit de frapper monnaie.*

AUTONOMI—(αὐτόνομοι)—Autonomous.— The name given to certain coins, minted by such Greek and other cities as were governed by their own laws. The right of coinage, as the criterion of an independent state, free from subjection to any foreign power, caused this appellation to be given generally to coins of such peoples and cities as possessed the character. That the monetal privilege was cherished with a high degree of appreciation and pride by those cities to whom it was granted, is sufficiently evident from the fact of its being recorded on their coins —as for example on the money of Antioch and of Halicarnassus, which after their own names as cities, bear the *autonomous* designation.— According as different countries (says M. Hennin), then in a state of civilization, were conquered by the Romans, or yielded themselves to the domination of that people, the authorities at Rome, in reconstituting those states under an apparently independent form, left to them nearly the whole of their political rights. The privilege of striking money was continued to those cities which had previously enjoyed it. But soon, when Rome became imperial, the Greek cities, whether out of adulation, or whether in consequence of ordinances formally made, adopted the custom of placing on their money the portraitures not only of the masters of the world, but also of their relations.— Autonomous coins were no longer fabricated. Rome also took away, from almost all the Greek cities, the right of issuing silver money, and confined the permission to exercise that right to a small number of the more considerable cities, such as Alexandria in Egypt, Antioch in Syria, Cæsarea in Cappadocia, Tarsus, &c. All coins minted by different cities and peoples, with imperial Roman effigies, take the generic name of *Imperial Greek.* The Roman colonies obtained the privilege of striking money, sometimes with their own local legends and types; but usually they placed on them imperial portraits, and inscribed the permission of the Emperor, or of the Pro-consul. These pieces take the name of *Colonial* money, and are divided into Colonial *autonomes*, and Colonial *Imperial* coins.—See *Manuel de Numismatique Ancienne*, vol. i. pp. 26–27.—See also *Coloniæ Romanæ.*

[It will not, it is presumed, be deemed irrelevant, in a work dedicated solely to Roman coins, that the two preceding articles should appear, in brief explanation of what is meant by autonomous mintages. For the word is perpetually used by Mionnet and others; and there are *Latin* as well as Greek *autonomes*.]

AUTRONIA.——A consular family, but of uncertain order. It has only one coin ascribed to it—(silver, rare) having the head of Pallas, and the mark of the denarius on the obverse. On the reverse is AVTRO in monogram, meaning Autronius, with the type of the Dioscuri on horseback; below ROMA.

AUTUMNUS.—On a brass medallion of Commodus inscribed FELICITAS TEMPORVM, and also on gold and silver coins of Caracalla and Geta, with legend of FELICIA TEMPORA, Autumn, in the group of the four seasons, is typified by the figure of a naked boy, carrying in his right hand a hare, and in his left a basket filled with fruit. —In Captain Smyth's *Descriptive Catalogue*, Autumn in this group on a first brass of Commodus, is described as "displaying a *cyathus* for wine in one hand, and placing his other upon a hound."—(p. 163.)

A. X.—*Augur, Decemvir.* C. CALDVS, IMP. A. X. Caius Caldus, Imperator, Augur, Decemvir.

AXIA or AXSIA, *gens plebeia.*—Received the surname of *Naso Appianus*, because the first of the name had a large nose. In its coins there are eight varieties. The silver *common*. The pieces in brass are *As*, or parts of the *As*.— Eckhel gives the following denarius of this family:—

Obv.—NASO. S. C. A female head covered with a helmet, which is adorned with two small sprigs of laurel or palm. In the field of the coin are arithmetical marks XVII.

Rev.—L. AXSIVS. L. F. *Diana,* in a short dress, as *Venatrix,* holding a spear in her right hand, stands in a car drawn by two stags— a dog runs before the goddess, and two others follow.—Eckhel treats the remarks of Vaillant, on the somewhat remarkable types of this coin, with a certain degree of ridicule; but omits to offer any explanations of his own.

AXVR. *Imberbis,* or Ve-Jupiter.—See the next word.

AXVR. IOVIS.—C. VIBIVS. C. F. C. N.— Jupiter Axur, or Anxur, seated, his right hand rests on the *hasta pura,* his left hand holds a *patera.*

On a denarius of the *Vibia* gens, bearing this legend on its reverse, is an elegant and unique type, as represented in the annexed engraving.——IOVIS is used for the nominative case, as on coins of Domitian inscribed IOVIS CVSTOS.—Virgil has made mention of Jupiter Anxur (*Æneid,* vii. 799.)

Circeumque jugum, queis *Juppiter Anxurus* arvis Præsidet:

[And the Circæan heights, the fields over which Jupiter Anxur holds sway.]

The denarius most probably presents to us a precise copy from the image of the Anxurian Jove, who from his radiated head and beardless face, seems to be identical with Apollo, or the *Sun,* like *Ve Juppiter* (see *Cæsia* gens), and Jupiter Heliopolitanus, whose figure appears on coins of Heliopolis, in Cœle Syria.—See Eckhel, v. p. 340.

AXE.—See *Securis,* and Pontifical Instruments, on a denarius of Marcus Antonius and Lepidus.

ANTHYLLUS, a surname given to Mark Antony, the younger, eldest of the Triumvir's children, by Fulvia his *third* wife [*not* his *second,* as inserted by mistake in p. 60].—Born in the year of Rome, 708, (B C. 46) he was, by his father's command, brought to Alexandria, "where (says Visconti) it is probable that the inhabitants, who were Greeks, designated him *Anthyllus,* or *little Antony.*" The noble and generous traits of his character, according to Plutarch, soon developed themselves at the Egyptian court. But the son, participating in the father's ruin, fell a victim to the vengeful policy of Octavianus Cæsar, in the sixteenth year of his age.

The erudite author of *Iconographie Romaine,* adds as follows:—"The coins which present to us the effigy of Anthyllus on the reverse of that of his father, are of gold, and extremely rare. They were struck 32 or 33 years before the vulgar æra, Anthyllus being then about thirteen years old. His father probably had just called the youth to his side. The legend which accompanies the head of Mark Antony, places this epocha beyond doubt: ANT. AVG. IMP. III. COS. III. IIIVIR. R.P.C. (Antonius, Augur, proclaimed imperator and elected consul, for the third time, triumvir for the arrangement of the republic).— Round the head of Anthyllus we read M. ANTON. M. F. (Marcus Antonius, son of Marcus).—It was in the year B.C. 34, that Mark Antony was consul for the second time; and in the year B.C. 31, he took his third consulate at Alexandria. This coin, therefore, must have been struck within the two intermediate years; and we know from Plutarch (loc. cit. § 57) that, in the year 32, Anthyllus was no longer at Rome."

Seguin was the first to publish this coin (*Num. Select.* p. 112, *edit.* 1684). And Morel afterwards gave it afresh in his *Thesaur. famil.* ANTONIA, pl. xi., No. 3.—Eckhel (vi. p. 68) had doubts respecting its authenticity, arising from, what he considered, circumstances of suspicion, affecting two similar coins in the Vienna Museum. Visconti, nevertheless, supports the genuineness of this numismatic monument, by referring to two specimens of it, in the *cabinet de la Bibliothèque du Roi* (now once more *Nationale),* at Paris, and out of which he selected, for his draughtsman to copy, that which is best preserved.—Mionnet includes this *aureus* in the mint of Mark Antony, confirming its rarity and value at a very high rate of appreciation. (T. i. p. 95.)

The inferiority of its workmanship, compared with that of the chief portion of Mark Antony's mintages, affords good reason to think, that the coin engraved in Visconti's work was struck at Alexandria, " where (as he observes) the monetary art was not very flourishing at the period in question. The coins of Antony and Cleopatra are a sufficient proof of that fact."—See *Iconographie Romaine*, Milan edit. 8vo. 1818, T. i. pl. vi.* No. 3, pp. 253 *et seq.*

[Our portrait of the younger Antonius (p. 60) was copied from Seguin's plate, which certainly bears no resemblance to Visconti's. It must however be admitted that the latter assimilates closely to the style and fabric of consular coins struck in Egypt. And if both refer to the same original, it serves as another instance amongst many, to shew how much more reliance is to be placed on medallic engravings of the present day, than on those of the artists who were employed to illustrate numismatic works of the elder school.]

ANTONINI PII *Moneta.*—A list of the most remarkable, as well as most rare, coins and medallions of this emperor's mint, not having been inserted in its proper place (viz. at the bottom of p. 56), the omission is supplied here :—

Gold.—AVRELIVS CAESAR. Head of Aurelius.—BRITAN. Victory on a globe.—COS. III. Emperor and his two children in a triumphal car.—PRIMI DECENNALES (within a garland)—TRIB. POT. COS. III. *Mars descending to (Rhea) Silvia.*—TEMPLVM DIVI. AVG. REST. COS. IIII. A temple.—TEMPORVM FELICITAS. Two cornuacopiæ, a child's head on each.—VOTA VIGENNALIA. The Emperor sacrificing.—LAETITIA COS. IIII. Two females (Ceres and Proserpine). LIBERALITAS AVG. II. or III. or IIII. The Emperor and several figures.

Silver.—AED. DIVI. AVG. REST. Two figures seated in a temple.—COS. III. Jupiter seated on arms.—DIVVS ANTONINVS ET DIVA FAVSTINA. Heads of Emperor and Empress.—LIB. VI. COS. IIII. Woman standing.—LIBERALITAS AVG. II. Emperor distributing gifts.——OPI. AVG. Ops seated.—PIETAS COS. IV. Piety at an altar.—PONT. MAX. Figure standing with a bow and an arrow.—TRANQ. TR. POT. XIII. &c. A female standing with a rudder and ears of corn.

Brass Medallions.——AESCVLAPIVS. (See p. 20.)——COCLES. Horatius Cocles swimming across the Tiber.—CONSECRATIO. Emperor on an Eagle.—COS. IIII. Hercules sacrificing before a temple.—COS. IIII. Emperor and the Goddess Rome.—NAVIVS. The Augur before Tarquin.—PM. TR. P. COS. III. Æneas, Anchises, and Ascanius. (See p. 16.)—PM. TR. P. COS. II. Bacchus and Ariadne drawn by Satyr and Panther. (See p. 80.)—TIBERIS. The Tiber recumbent.—TR. POT. XX. Jupiter Tonans and a Titan.—

Same legend. Jupiter, Juno, and Pallas.—*The following are without legend :*—The Sun preceded by Phosphorus.—Diana Lucifera seated on a horse at speed.—Prometheus and Minerva.—Vulcan and Minerva.—Æneas and Ascanius in Latium.—Hercules Bibax.—Hercules combatting the Centaurs.—Bacchus and Ariadne seated (see p. 121).—Bacchus in a temple, before which is a sacrificial group.—Hercules in the Garden of the Hesperides, &c. &c.

First Brass.——AFRICA—ALEXANDRIA—BRITANNIA—CAPPADOCIA. All with types of personified provinces.—CONCORDIA—CONGIARIVM. COS. III. Four children, representing the four Seasons.—DISCIPLINA. The Emperor and four soldiers.—FAVSTINA AVGVSTA. *Head of Faustina senior.*—HISPANIA.—LIBERALITAS TR. POT. II. Emperor and six figures.—REX ARMENIS DATVS. Two figures standing; at their feet a river-god.—REX QVADIS DATVS. The Emperor crowning a figure, in the toga.—ROMVLO AVGVSTO. Romulus, with trophy and spear.—S. C. *Rape of the Sabines.*—S. C. Emperor in a quadriga.—S. C. Do. two quadriga of Elephants.—S. C. Æneas carrying Anchises.—SCYTHIA—SICILIA. Both personifications of provinces.—SECVND DECENNALES. COS. III. within a crown.

Second Brass.—BRITANNIA COS. IIII. Female figure, seated on a rock.—CONSECRATIO. *Funeral pile.*—FAVSTINAE AVG. PII. AVG. FIL. Head of Faustina junior.—HADRIANVS AVGVSTVS. Bare head of Hadrian.—VICTORIA AVG. Victory in a quadriga.—VOTA. Three figures, in the toga, standing before a temple.—VERVS ET FAVSTINA. Heads of Verus and Faustina the younger.

A. Ω.—*Alpha—Omega.*—The reverse of a fine and rare silver medallion of Constans I. in the collection of the Imperial Museum at Vienna, exhibits for its legend VIRTVS EXERCITVM *(sic.),* and for its type four military ensigns, one of which is inscribed with the *first* letter, and another with the *last* letter, of the Greek alphabet. Above them is the monogram of Christ.

In these initial letters, we have an obvious reference to the declaration more than once repeated in the Apocalypse,

" I am *alpha* and *omega*, the beginning and the ending, the first and the last"—a symbol used on this occasion to indicate the Emperor's professed belief in the one true God, and " in Jesus Christ His only Son our Lord." From the time when the coin in question was struck, (viz. between A. D. 337 and 350), the same Greek initials are not unfrequently found together, both with and without the *monogram of Christ*, on money of the lower empire.—See Decentius, Magnentius, and Vetranio, in this Dictionary.—See also *Monogramma Christi.*

B.

B.—This letter is a numeral, and equivalent with the number 2.

B. *Bæbius.*—Q. B. Quæstor Bæbius.—See *Bæbia gens.*

B.—The mark of the second mint in any city —*ex. gr.* B. SIRM. Money struck *in secundâ officinâ monetariâ Sirmii* (in Pannonia, now Sirmich, in Sclavonia).—B. SIS. *In secundâ officinâ Sisciæ* (a city of Croatia, now Sisserc.)

BABBA *(Mauritaniæ) colonia.*—The city of Babba, in Mauritania Tingitana (now *Fez* and *Morocco*, North Africa), situate on the river Lixus *(El Haratel)*, was made a colony by Julius Cæsar, as its name Julia imports. It was also called *Campestris.* The decuriones of Babba caused coins to be minted, in middle and small brass, under Claudius, under Nero, and under Galba. Pellerin regards the short suite struck in this colony as commencing under Augustus; but Mionnet shews this to be a mistake. " It is, says Bimard (ad Jobert, if. p. 230), to M. Vaillant, that the honour belongs of having first pointed out the method of reading the [designative legend on the] coins of Babba."—viz. C. C. I, B, DD. PVBL. *Colonia Campestris Julia Babba—Decreto Decurionum Publicorae, ex conss.* D. *(Ex Consensu Decurionum.)*

The types are as follow :—

1. *Bull swimming*, represented on a coin of Nero.

By this device the colonists of Babba exhibit Jupiter, as under the figure of a Bull he carried away Europa, daughter of Agenor, King of the Phœnicians. Hence they indicated that the swimming Bull was an object of their idolatry, in like manner as the Bull Apis was worshipped by the Egyptians.—[The above woodcut is after a small brass in the British Museum.]

On another coin of the same Emperor, the type of reverse is a Bull butting with his horns. —Vaill. *in Col.* i. 106.

2. *Bearded head, with a serpent before it*, on a coin of Nero.

[This is a representation of Æsculapius, as shewn by the serpent, the symbol of health. And his effigy, placed on this coin, shews that divine honours were paid him at Babba.—Engraved in Vaill. *Col.* i. 115.]

3. *Livia Augusti.*—COL. I. BA. DD.—Livia represented under the image of a goddess, seated, with head veiled, holding in her right hand a patera, and supporting her left hand on a hasta. Engraved in Pellerin, *Mélange*, i. pl. xvi. fig. 2.

4. *Oaken crown*, with the abbreviated names of the colony within it.

5. *Palm tree.*—[The Roman colonists of Babba struck this and the preceding coin under Claudius, in congratulation of his victory over the revolted Mauritanians—a revolt against Roman cruelty and oppression, as exemplified in their king

Ptolemy, son of Juba, having been put to death by order of the execrable Caligula. The palm tree here denotes that the people of Babba derived their origin from the Phœnicians, who took their name, it is said, from the Greek word for a palm *(phoinix)*, with which species of tree that country abounds.—Vaillant, *Col.* i.]

6. *Victory*, marching with crown and palm branch, struck under Galba.—[The death of Nero, welcomed by all, excited the feelings of various minds in favour of Galba, especially among the legions. It was, indeed, an event which revealed a great state secret—namely, that an emperor might be made elsewhere than at Rome, thus furnishing an important principle for a new state of affairs. In Africa, Clodius Macer; in Germany, Fonteius Capito; had made some attempts to acquire the supreme power. At length both the Mauritanian provinces gave in their adhesion to the election of Galba. The colonists of Babba soon adopted the same course; and in testimony of their approval, they struck on coins dedicated to his honour, the figure of Victory, bearing the laurel crown, to commemorate the fall of Clodius Macer, slain in battle by the Procurator Garusianus.—Vaill. *Col.* i. p. 227.]

The remaining types are, a figure seated on a rock, holding an anchor and cornucopiæ, on a coin of Claudius. And a bridge of three arches, on coins struck under Nero.

BACCHIVS IVDAEVS.—This legend appears on a well-known consular denarius. The type is that of a man kneeling, who holds a camel by the bridle with his left hand, and in his right a branch of olive.—For an explanation of the event, which is typified on this rare silver coin, though left unrecorded by historians. See *Plautia gens.*

BACCHUS.—Of this fabled divinity, the poets differ much respecting the names of his parents; nor are they better agreed in relating the circumstances connected with his nativity. The more usual custom of mythologists, is to describe him as the son of Jupiter, by Semele, the daughter of Cadmus. And Ovid, in his *Metamorphoses*, details the wondrous incidents of his fiery birth. Bacchus is said to have been brought up by the daughters of Atlas, and to have afterwards had Silenus for his preceptor.— He became at length a celebrated warrior; fought valiantly for Jupiter, against the Titans; and made the conquest of India. It was on his return from that famous expedition, that he is related to have found Ariadne, whom Theseus had abandoned, in the isle of Naxos, and by the warmth of his attachment made her forget the ingratitude of her former lover.—See *Ariadne.*

Bacchus " ever fair and ever young," is generally represented in sculpture and on coins, without beard, crowned with vine leaves. He holds the *thyrsus* (see the word) in one hand, and a bunch of grapes in the other. Sometimes he is depicted naked; at others, and as the Indian Bacchus, he wears a long dress *(Apamea colonia*, p. 61).—The panther, as the nurse of Bacchus, was consecrated to him, and appears, on coins and bas-reliefs, as his almost inseparable companion. The image of this favourite deity of oriental paganism seldom appears on coins minted at Rome, especially those of the imperial series. There is indeed a large brass of Sept. Severus, with the legend of COS. III. LVD*os*. SAEC*ulares* FEC*it*, inscribed on a cippus, on each side of which Bacchus and Hercules stand with their respective attributes ; and to the legend DIS AVSPICIBVS reference may be made, as accompanied by another instance of those two deities being grouped together, on a large brass of the same emperor. But on medallions of Hadrian and Antoninus Pius, described below, the God of Wine, as the companion of Apollo, and as the lover of Ariadne, is elegantly depictured :—

The above cut is copied from an outline engraving in the *Galerie Mythologique*, vol. i. pl. lxxxviii. by Millin, who is himself indebted for it to a plate in Venuti, *Mus. Vaticanum*, xiii. —This reverse of Hadrian's medallion represents Bacchus seated on a *thensa* (or sacred car), drawn by a panther and a goat, on the latter of which sits a Cupid playing on a double flute. *Bacchus*, with graceful ease, rests his right arm on the side of the chariot, and holds the *thyrsus* in his left hand. *Apollo* sits by his side, playing on the lyre.—For another specimen of the grotesque fancy of ancient artists, in harnessing a sulky panther with some animal, real or fabulous, of a more lively and less ferocious disposition, see the wood-cut from a brass medallion of Antoninus Pius, under the head of *Ariadne* and *Bacchus*, p. 80.

Bacchus was called by the name of *Dionysus*, (from Nysa, the reputed place of his education) ; and often by that of LIBER PATER, whose young head crowned with ivy, is also seen on coins of the Titia and Volteia families.

In the list of coins struck under the republic, we find the head of Bacchus on a denarius of the Cassia gens, it is crowned with ivy leaves and berries. and behind it is the *thyrsus*. On a denarius of Blasio, of the patrician branch of the Cornelia family, the figure of Bacchus naked, appears standing, with the *thyrsus* in his right hand ; in his left the *strophium* (see the word), and a sheaf of arrows. Pallas stands on his left, and crowns him. On the right hand of Bacchus stands a woman, holding a wand, or the hasta pura. Engraved in *Morell. Thesaur. Fam. Rom.* TAB. i. fig 1—also under *Cornelia gens*, in this dictionary.

Bacchus is constantly to be recognised by his attribute of the *thyrsus*, but by no means so readily by the arrows. Nevertheless, by an apt citation from Nonnus, Eckhel shews, that the latter as well as the former were attributes of *Liber Pater*. Pallas addressing him, says

" Ubi tui validi *thyrsi*, et viteæ *sagittæ*."

He is crowned by the Goddess of Wisdom [Minerva] on account of his victory over the Titans, and of his warlike glory, spread forth to the ends of the world. That the associated worship of these two deities prevailed both at Rome and in Greece, is shewn by an onyx gem, in the imperial museum at Vienna, and which exhibits Bacchus armed in a similar manner, with *thyrsus* and arrow, Pallas, as on the coin minted by Blasio, crowning him. "Who the other female figure in this group may be," says Eckhel (v. 180), "*ignoro*."

Bacchus was worshipped, as amongst the superior deities, by Gallienus. This is indicated by a coin of that emperor's, in billon, exhibiting on its reverse the epigraph of LIBERO P. CONS. AVG. *(Libero Patri Conservatori Augusti)*, with a panther for its type.

Bacchus, with his attributes, is more frequently found on *colonial* imperial coins; especially on those struck in Syria and Phœnicia, by most cities of which regions he was worshipped, on account of his traditionary expeditions to the East. The following are amongst the colonies whose coins bear *Latin* legends; and on their reverses types of this deity :—

Besides *Apamea*, in whose mintages the *Indian* Bacchus appears (see p. 61), the God of Wine is seen on several coins of *Berytus*, mostly dedicated to Gordianus Pius. " It is a type (says Vaillant), which denotes the abundance and goodness of the grapes grown in the immediate neighbourhood of that city. On one of these, he stands unclothed, between two vine-shoots ; whilst with his right hand he places a garland on his own head, 'as the *first* discoverer of the *use* of the grape.' On his left hand is a satyr, whose love for wine was said to be very great. Squatting at his feet is a leopard, by ancient report equally fond of the inebriating juice."

On a second brass, dedicated at *Damascus*, to Trebonianus Gallus, *Bacchus*, under the figure of a young man, stands, naked, on a plinth, holding a vine tendril in each hand. His image on this coin shews that he was worshipped by the inhabitants of Damascus, in whose territory he was said to have originally planted the vine. (Engraved in Vaillant, *Col.* ii. 214.)

The colony of *Deultum*, on a second brass of Macrinus, honours this deity with an image, designated by his attributes of the *cantharus* (or wine vase), the thyrsus, and the panther—not an inappropriate reverse for the mint of a territory, whose abundance in vineyards is a circumstance noticed by Athenæus.—*(Ibid.* ii. 64.)

Olba, a colony in Pamphilia, also contributes a type of Bacchus—who likewise appears on a small brass coin, consecrated to Alexander Severus, by the pantheistic people of *Sidon*.

Bacchus and Ariadne.—There is, in the French Cabinet, a brass medallion of Antoninus Pius—the obverse of which presents a noble portrait of that emperor (see p. 55); and the reverse, without legend, is charged with a Bacchanalian group, not less classic in design than bold in relief, and beautiful in fabric.

To this numismatic gem, Seguin (in his *Selec. Num.* p. 127), has the merit of being one of the first—if not the very first—to call attention, by an engraving in outline, and also by verbal description; neither of which, however, have the requisite degree of accuracy to recommend them. With respect to the type, for example; in the principal figures in the foreground, to the left, he recognises *two* females, and in the centre *a woman holding an infant in swaddling clothes.* Under this false impression, he pronounces the subject represented, to be the *accouchement* of Rhea; in other words, the *birth* of Jupiter.— Eckhel points out the mistake thus made by the learned French antiquary of the elder school. But, whilst he justly remarks, that the surrounding chorus of nymphs and satyrs unquestionably indicates Bacchus, the great numismatist of Vienna himself falls into the same error of regarding the elevated figure in the background of the group, as "an infant wrapped in swaddling clothes, held aloft" by one of the nymphs— (vii. p. 10).

Mionnet rectifies, in great measure, the wrong views, and consequently fallacious descriptions, of both his eminent predecessors, by the following notice of this interesting reverse :— "*Bacchus and Ariadne seated;* at their feet a panther; opposite to them is an old man crouching, and several bacchants are carrying a terminus, and playing on divers instruments." But even Mionnet's description is faulty, as to the terminus being "*carried.*" Mr. Fairholt's engraving of this wonderfully fine antique exhibits these points in quite a different and a truer light.

The woman, supposed by Seguin, and by Eckhel, to be holding a swaddled infant, turns out to be a satyr, who raises his right arm above his head, and in his left holds a crook (the *pedum*). The terminal figure is *not* carried, but stands on a pillar, or base. The legs of the old man (who is doubtless meant for Silenus) are hidden by the panther. The terminus, like one in the Townley Gallery, British Museum, is wrapped up in a mantle, and holds something like a wine

cup. Silenus it will, on inspection, be seen, also holds a half-inverted wine cup. Besides these, there are a satyr behind Ariadne, a faun blowing a long flute; and to the right the figure of a young woman, clothed in long but light drapery, and with raised right arm striking the tympanum or tambour, as if dancing to its sound. The form and attitude of the principal female figure are symmetrical and graceful : she points with her left hand towards the terminus, whilst sitting close beside her lover, whom the *thyrsus* serves clearly to identify ; and the vine tendril on each side fills up every feature of the design needful to its appropriation, as a scene of revelry connected with the fable of Bacchus and Ariadne.

Two other brass medallions of the above mentioned emperor display on their respective reverses, without legend, typifications of Bacchus. They are noticed in Akerman, *Descr. Cat.* i. 265, as follows :—

1. Bacchus sleeping : before him is a female figure, standing near a statue, which is full faced and placed on a pedestal.

2. Bacchus standing in a temple, which has two circular galleries on the exterior ; before it is a man holding a goat.

Bacchanalia, on Contorniate medals.—On one of these *pseudo-monetæ,* bearing the head of Trajan, Bacchus stands holding a bunch of grapes to a panther with the right hand, and a thyrsus in the left ; near him on one side dance a flute player and a woman bearing a thyrsus ; on the other side is a boy with a crook in the right hand and a branch in the left. (This is in the Imperial cabinet.)—Havercamp gives a contorniate with the head of Caracalla, on the reverse of which is Bacchus drawn in a biga of panthers, preceded by a satyr, and accompanied by flute players.—For engravings of these and other medals of the same class, with bacchanalian types, having the heads of Nero, Trajan, and other emperors, on their obverses—see Havercamp and *Morell. Thesaur.*

Bacchi Cista.—The mystic basket of Bacchus —a numismatic symbol of pro-consular Asia.— See *Asia Recepta,* p. 89—also see *Cistophori.*

BÆBIA gens.—A plebeian but consular family. Tamphilus, or, as it is written *Tampilus,* (an *archaism,* or old way of spelling, in like manner as Triu*mpus* for Triu*mphus,*) is the only surname that appears on its coins. Nepos in his life of Atticus mentions the *Domus Tamphiliana,* which stood on the Quirinal, at Rome. Morel, in *Thesaur. Fam. Rom.* gives eight varieties. The brass pieces are *As,* or parts of the *As ;* or they are colonial. The two following are rare in silver—the latter much the rarer, though

not bearing so remarkable a reverse type as the former.

TAMPIL.—Winged head of Pallas; before it X.

Rev.—M. BAEBI. Q. F. ROMA. Apollo in a quadriga—(See *Apollo*.)

Obv.—Head of Jupiter.

Rev.—TAM in monogram. Victory crowning a trophy; below ROMA.

Q. Bæbius Tamphilus, about the year U. C. 535 (B. C. 219), was twice sent as Ambassador to the Carthaginians, for the purpose of expostulating with them on the subject of their attack on Saguntum; and at length declared war against them.—Cn. Bæbius Tamphilus was the first member of this family who served the office of Consul 572 (B. C. 182).——Marcus Bæbius Tamphilus, the son, by whom this denarius was struck, proceeded Consul in the year U. C. 573 (B. C. 181.)

BALAUSTIUM—the flower of the pomegranate tree—appears on a denarius of the *Cossutia gens;* also with the crab, and the *aplustrum,* on a coin of the *Servilia gens.*

BALISTA—one of the ephemeral usurpers in the reign of Gallienus; proclaimed Emperor in Syria, A. D. 262; slain 264. The coins, published as his, are false.

BASILISCUS—brother of Verina, wife of Leo I. proclaimed Emperor of the East, A. D. 476; dethroned by Zeno, and suffered to die of hunger A. D. 477.—His coins in each metal are rare. Some of them represent him with his son Marcus.

BALB.—Balbus.—C. Balbus of the *Antonia gens,* was duumvir of the Colony of Leptis in Africa—see *Morell. Thesaur. Fam. Rom.*

BALBUS.—A surname of the *Cornelia gens.*

BALBUS L. THORIUS.—See *Thoria gens.* Also see *Juno Sospita.*

BALBINUS *(Decimus Cœlius.)* Emperor with Pupienus, A. D. 238.—As soon as the tidings had reached Rome from Africa, that the two Gordians were dead, and that Maximinus was

approaching Italy, with a powerful army, the affrighted senate hastily assembled in the temple of Jupiter Capitolinus, and by a new institution created two *Augusti* (see p. 103) in the respective persons of the above-named Balbinus, and Maximus Pupienus, on the 9th of July, in the year above-named. And so equal was the degree of power entrusted to each, that it extended to a division between them of the supreme pontificate.—Balbinus, descended from a very noble family, was born A. D. 178. At the period of his elevation to Augustal rank and authority, he had attained 60 years of age; previously to which he had governed several provinces, with a high character for the justice and the mild-

ness of his administration. He had also been twice Consul. Although his great riches had given him a turn for pleasure, yet he had kept himself within the bounds of moderation, and acquired no common repute for forensic acquirements and for poetical talents. Pursuant to a senatorial decree, his colleague, a bold and experienced warrior, was sent to command the army levied to repel the invasion of Maximinus; whilst Balbinus, naturally timid, and holding in awe the very name of the Thracian savage, who had instigated the assassination of Alexander Severus, remained at Rome; his task, scarcely a less difficult one, being to keep down the spirit of sedition and tumult prevailing between the soldiery and the people, whose quarrels filled the capital with bloodshed.—Further to win the popular favour, the new emperors were obliged to name the younger Gordian as Cæsar, on the very day of their own election.—Pupienus who was at Ravenna when Maximinus and his son, Maximus, were slain before Aquileia (A. D. 238) returned to Rome; where he met with the most joyous reception from Balbinus, the Senators, and the people at large. Both emperors then devoted themselves to the duties of their joint government; and, notwithstanding mutual jealousies occasionally displayed by the one towards the other, they conducted public affairs together, upon the whole, in a wise, disinterested, and efficient manner. This state of things however did not last long. Balbinus was preparing to commence hostilities against the insurgent Goths, and Pupienus had already marched to repel an invasion of the Persians. At this critical juncture, the venal and sanguinary Prætorians, bearing a grudge against the two *Augusti* for having been chosen, not by themselves but by the Senate, and moreover not less displeased at their endeavours to restore military discipline—took advantage of the Capitoline games absorbing public attention, to assail the palace, and murder them both under circumstances of the most revolting and outrageous cruelty. Thus was the imperial career of Balbinus and his brave colleague terminated, after three months of state-service deserving of a better reward.

The style and titles of Balbinus on his coins (which are all rare, especially those in gold) are IMP. C. (or CAES.) D. CAEL. BALBINVS. AVG.— Some with radiated, others with laurelled heads. See *Pupienus.*

"The medals of Balbinus (says Capt. Smyth, p. 251), whether Latin, Greek, or Egyptian, are all rare and of a high price—the denarii and sestertii being the most common; nor are any colonial, or small brass, known. Although the arts were now on the decline, moneyers still possessed the power of executing accurate likenesses; for a comparison of the heads of Balbinus and Pupienus, throughout all the metals and sizes, affords internal evidence of the fidelity of their resemblance."

The large-sized silver of this emperor has the head with radiated crown—the smaller sized has the head laureated.—Akerman, i. 462.

The following are the rarest reverses under this short reign, viz. :—

Gold.—VOTIS DECENNALIBVS, within a garland (valued by Mionnet at 600 fr.)

Silver.—AMOR MVTVVS AVGG. Two hands joined (large size).

First Brass.—FIDES PVBLICA. Two hands holding caduceus.—LIBERALITAS AVGVSTORVM. Six figures.

Second Brass.—CONCORDIA AVGG.——IOVI CONSERVATORI. Jupiter standing.—VOTIS DECENNALIBVS.

BARBATIA.——This gens, whose name is given neither in Morel, nor Eckhel, nor Mionnet, is added to the list of plebeian families, by Riccio, who assigns to it two coins—one with head of M. Antonius on the obverse, and that of Octavianus Cæsar on the reverse. The other with the same obverse, but with the head of L. Antonius on the reverse. Both bear the name of C. *Marcus* BARBAT*ius (Philippus)*, who was *Quæstor Provincialis* and moneyer under the Triumvir, and who coined them between 713 (B. C. 41) and the following year.—See *Monete delle Famiglie di Roma*, &c. p. 35.

BARBARR. *Barbararum.*—See *Debellatori Gentium Barbararum.*—*Victor Gentium Barbararum*, &c. of Constantinus Magnus.

BARBA. The beard.—The Romans of the early ages were usually represented with a liberal garniture of beard. "That there were formerly (says Varro) no barbers among them, is to be inferred from the appearance of ancient statues, which, for the most part, have much hair on their heads, and a great beard." Even at the time of the capture of their city by the Gauls, they had not adopted the practice of shaving the beard: this is evident from the insult which Livy relates to have been offered, by one of the invading army, to Marcus Papirius (in the year of Rome 364, B.C. 390). It was not till A. U. C. 454 (B. C. 300) that barbers were employed at Rome; and these were at first sent for from Sicily. Pliny states that the first Roman who was shaved every day was Scipio Africanus. From the period last mentioned, young men began to remove their beards. They commenced the operation at 20 or 21 ; and this practice continued till the age of 49, after which no shaving was allowed. One reason for wearing a beard was extreme youth, which according to Roman custom did not admit of its being yet cut. Another reason was some occasion of mourning. An example of both kinds is furnished on the coins of Octavianus. On this point, Eckhel observes, (vi. 76,) that under his coinage of the year U.C. 717 (B.C. 37), the portraitures exhibit a beard of some growth. This appears to be at variance with the expression of Dion Cassius, who, speaking of the year 715, says—"Indeed, Cæsar, then for the first time shaving off his beard, not only spent that festal day sumptuously himself, but to all the rest gave a public banquet. From that time, he kept his cheeks smooth, as other people used to do." Nevertheless, coins of the period, all of which represent Cæsar, Triumvir for the 2nd time, with a beard, are testimonies that cannot deceive. To reconcile Dion's account, which refers that event to the year 715, with the fact of Octavian's wearing a beard in 717, as evidenced by the mintage of that year, Eckhel finds an explanation in the practice above alluded to, of the Roman youth wearing their beards up to a certain age, that is to say, to the 21st year; and considers it probable that having once laid his first beard aside, in accordance with the usual custom, Cæsar shortly afterwards allowed it to grow again on account of some occasion of public mourning. In support of this view of the subject in question, the author of *Doctrina* cites the expression of Suetonius respecting Julius Cæsar—"When news was brought of the *Titurian* slaughter, [a legion and five cohorts under Titurius Sabinus, destroyed by the Gauls under Ambiorix], he let his hair and beard grow till he had taken his revenge." And of Octavianus, but *after* his accession to the empire, Suetonius also remarks, "For they say, that he was so overwhelmed (by the news of the slaughter under Varus) that for months he allowed his beard and hair to grow, and sometimes used to dash his head against the doors." According to Plutarch, Mark Antony also let his beard grow after his entire defeat by Octavius Cæsar and the consuls Pansa and Hirtius in the year 711, (B.C. 43) at the battle of Mutina. There is a numismatic testimony of this fact, on the obverse of a very rare denarius, minted by that brave general, Ventidius Bassus, whose eminent services to the subsequent Triumvir met with no better requital from him than the privilege of stamping his name (P. VENTIDI*us)* and the titles of PONT*ifex* and IMP*erator*, on the reverse of a coin, the obverse of which presents a full *bearded* head of Mark Antony (with legend M. ANT. III. V. R. P. C.) as in the subjoined cut.

In addition to the cause above alluded to, scarcely a single reason can be adduced, why the head of Mark Antony should exhibit a beard on his early coins, except that he was mourning the death of Julius, whose life was of such importance to himself, and of whose murder he professed to be the avenger.

Cato likewise repudiated the use of the razor, on hearing of the discomfiture of his partizans at Thapsus, (B. C. 46.)—Eckhel thinks the reason for the public mourning in the case of Octavianus Cæsar, may have been the formidable system of hostilities pursued by Sextus Pompeius, (B. C. 38.)—not so much towards himself as towards the state ; supplies being, at that juncture, cut off, whilst famine extended its ravages:

then, when it came to a trial of arms, severe and repeated losses; and in addition to these public disasters, the disgrace attending them. When, however, on the defeat of Sextus, A. U. C. 718 (B. C. 36), this state of things was put an end to, he returned to the accustomed fashion.

Of Caligula, Suetonius tells us that, at the age of twenty, he assumed the *toga*, and laid aside his beard: and of Nero, that he did the same at a more advanced age, viz. 22, and when he was already Emperor, (A. D. 68), a fact conclusively proved by his coins, although on his early mint he is represented with a slight beard.—After that period his beard was laid aside, and thus all the Emperors are found to exhibit smooth chins, on their coins, from the time of Augustus to that of Hadrian.

Juvenal shews, that the day on which the first cutting off of the beard took place, was sacred to rejoicings:

Ille metit barbam, crinem hic deponit amati,
Plena domus libis venalibus.

[Here one reaps his crop of beard—there another lays aside the hair of his favourite; the house is filled with good cheer.]

The celebration of this event by princes was accompanied by various ceremonies and public solemnities. The same sort of feeling respecting the tender beard of the young heirs to empire was probably entertained, which is expressed in the words of Cicero—Nostri isti barbatuli *juvenes*—"those downy youths of ours."

It was Hadrian (Emperor A. D. 117), who, having publicly assumed the character of a *philosopher*, allowed his beard to grow as we see from his statues and coins. His example was followed by a long line of successors, who, whenever their age admitted of it, cherished this badge of manhood. According to Dion, indeed, Elagabalus adopted the shaving practice. An exception, this, however, unworthy to be quoted.— At length Constantine, A. D. 311, doubtless preferring a smooth chin, restored the fashion of the first Emperors, and eschewed the beard. His example was followed by his sons, and all the members of his family, with the exception of Julian called the apostate, "the greater part of whose wisdom (says Eckhel) for *he* was a philosopher, lay in his beard." It appears that this prince, whilst yet a private citizen, wore a beard; but having been ordered to remove it when called to the dignity of Cæsar, he does not exhibit that appendage, on the coins which give him that title. Those struck, after he had become Emperor, represent him, either without a beard, or, as is most frequently the case, liberally furnished with that article. There can be no doubt, but that the coins of the former kind are to be referred to the commencement of Julian's reign; when his fortunes being still in uncertainty, and all hope of reconciliation with Constantius II. not having been relinquished, he still adhered to the old custom. And this indeed was the reason why he at that time continued to take part in the religious rites of Christianity. Becoming gradually more secure, he resumed

the beard; which his uncle had been the first emperor to lay aside after an interval of more than 240 years. But Julian, it seems, did not make this innovation with impunity. He was openly ridiculed by the Antiochians, for wearing, as they said, the beard of a goat, with hairs so thick and coarse, that ropes might be spun of it. By way of retort, the emperor replied: 'you may do so, if you please, for aught I care; but I doubt, whether you would be able to pluck them out for the purpose, and am afraid their roughness will hurt your soft and delicate hands.'"

From the time of Jovianus, (Julian's successor A.D. 363) all the emperors again exhibited smooth faces. The usurper Phocas (A.D. 602) was the first, after this long interval, to revive the beard; and it continued in fashion till the fall of the empire.—"On the strength of coins (says Eckhel) I confidently pronounce that all Emperors, after Phocas, wore the beard. Nor is it surprising, that the emperors of that age, most of them of Greek extraction, should have gradually done away with the Latin practice of abstaining from beards, and returned to the custom of their own nation."—See D. N. V. vi. 36, 76.—Also the Treatise on Coins of the lower Empire, viii. § ii. 132.

BARBARUS NUMUS.—This term is applied to such ancient coins, whether of gold, silver, or brass, as, from their bad representations of the human countenance, and from the general obscurity of their legends, appear to be of barbaric origin.—Rasche.

BARBARI.—Barbarians.—It is thus that the Greeks called all other people; and the Romans afterwards used the same expression, to designate whomsoever were neither Greeks nor Latins. The Emperor Antoninus Pius, having, by an edict abolished all distinctions between citizens throughout the empire, the foreigner as well as the native of Rome and of Italy, took part in all civil and military employments. During the republic, and early in the imperial government, it was a very rare thing to see any one, except a Roman by birth, occupying any post of high importance. The case of Ventidius indeed, forms an exceptional instance. A native of Pisenum, and a manumitted prisoner, he became one of Mark Antony's best *legati*, during the civil wars, and served the office of consul. But after the Antonines, foreigners are found to have been, from time to time, appointed to the consulate. The famous Stilicho, son of a Vandal captain, governed the empire, in the nominal reign of Honorius, and was twice consul. The same change took place with regard to the troops. Auxiliaries were drafted into the Roman legions, and eventually formed legions of themselves.—See Pitiscus, *Lex. Ant. Rom.*

BARE HEAD.—The bare or naked head, as contradistinguished from the laureated or radiated head, on imperial coins, is generally indicative of a Cæsar, or son, either real or adopted, of an emperor or reigning prince.—See *Caput Nudum.*

BARBIA ORBIANA.—See *Orbiana.*

BASSIANUS, the father of Julia Domna, wife of Septimius Severus. It was also the name of Caracalla.—See Eckhel's pedigree of Elagabalus, viii. p. 202.

BASILICA.—This word, which properly signifies a *Royal House*, designated at Rome a sumptuous edifice, under the roof of which the magistrates administered justice; and so far it was distinguished from the *forum*, where the sessions were held in the open air. The form of these *basilicæ* was that of a long square, with a portico at each extremity. They had a lofty nave, with two side aisles, separated by two rows of pillars, and each formed a structure, which, adorned with columns, military ensigns, and trophies, administered to a taste for regal majesty and magnificence; and therefore might well be classed amongst the *ædes regiæ* of the State. The walls of the side aisles were furnished with shops, in which goods of all kinds were displayed for sale, and the centre hall served as a resort where merchants, and other men of business were wont to congregate. Thus were these buildings dedicated at once to the purposes of commerce and of judicature.

The simplicity of the early republic seems not to have indulged in the luxury of building. According to Livy (lxxvii. c. 27), there were no *basilicæ* in Rome till the year 544 (B. C. 210.) Subsequently to that period, the wealth of the city having greatly increased, Cato built the *Basilica* to which he himself gave the name of *Porcia*; others followed, amongst the most superb of which was that called by the name of *Æmilia*, or of *Paulus*, of which a representation is preserved on a denarius of the Æmilia gens. [See *Aimilia Refecta*, p. 31]—Plutarch states, that the tribunes of the *plebs* were accustomed to convoke public assemblies in the *Basilica Porcia*; and Seneca speaks of these *basilicæ* resounding with the roar of law verdicts and judgments *(fremitu judiciorum)*. For architectural details relative to edifices of this description, see Dr. Smith's *Dictionary of Greek and Roman Antiquities*, p. 130.

BASILICA ULPIA.—An elegant portico, with lofty steps, and adorned with statues.

This legend and type on gold and first brass of Trajan, designates and represents the remarkable edifice, which that emperor caused to be built at Rome, and to which he gave his family name. Its portico was supported by sixteen columns, adorned with numerous statues, and, according to the coins, crowned with tri-

umphal ornaments. In the area of the building was the equestrian statue of Trajan.—The large brass bears on its reverse the following legend: S. P. Q. R. OPTIMO PRINCIPI, on the exergue BASILICA VLPIA, S. C.—On the obverse we read IMP. CAES. NERVAE TRAIANO AVG. GER. DAC. P. M. T. R. P. COS. VI. P. P.

This magnificent and useful edifice, was by order of the Senate typified on the coins of Trajan, in the year of Rome 867 (B. C. 114), when the Basilica was dedicated.

Eckhel cites Lampridius as alluding to this sumptuous structure, in mentioning that Commodus, afterwards emperor, when he assumed the *toga virilis*, went to preside (as magistrate) in the *Basilica Trajani;* and Vaillant quotes Nicephorus, wherein he says, "the Senate, moreover, held a convocation in the Basilica called Ulpia."

BATHS of the Romans—see *Thermæ.*

BB. indicates a duplicate plural. Thus CRISPVS ET CONSTANT. IVN. are called NOBB. CAESS. *Nobilissimi Cæsares.*

BEATITUDO PUBLICA.—A woman sitting with right hand raised, and left hand holding the *hasta*. On a third brass of Magnentius, struck between A. D, 350 to 353.

A new reverse known to Banduri and later to Tanini. Besides this coin a marble dedicated to Constantius II. shews by the following that *Beatitudo*, or Happiness, was held at that period in the highest estimation:—PRO BEATI-TVDINE TEMPORVM D. D. CONSTANTII ET CONSTANTIS, &c.—*(D. N. V.* viii. p. 122.)

BEATA URBS ROMA.—On a large brass of Constans.—See *Urbs Roma Beata.*

BEATA TRANQUILLITAS.—*(Blessed or Happy Tranquillity.)* A celestial globe, placed on a cippus, inscribed VOTIS XX.—stars above.

Banduri gives this from a third brass of Licinius the younger, as struck between A. D. 317 and 323. It would seem to be the first occurrence of this legend, which afterwards appears in the mint of Crispus, and others of the Family of Constantine the Great, to whose government the tranquil state of the empire is ascribed.

BELLEROPHON.—The story of this favourite hero of the Corinthians is so mixed up with fable as to render the whole a matter of doubt amongst the writers of antiquity. On imperial colonial coins of Corinth, with *Latin* legends, (struck under Augustus. M. Aurelius, L. Verus, S. Severus, Geta, and Alex. Severus), *Bellerophon* appears, sometimes mounted on *Pegasus*, in the act of fighting with an enigmatical non-descript, y'clept *Chimæra*—sometimes on the same winged horse of Apollo, without the Chimæra being of the party. On other reverses of the fertile Corinthian mint, this intrepid horse-tamer is represented on foot holding Pegasus by the bridle. "The legendary conqueror of the triple monster (says Vaillant), seems introduced on these coins of Corinth under her Roman masters, to indicate the great antiquity of that city."—See *Corinthus Colonia.*

BELLONA.—A goddess created to share the fatigues and sanguinary glories of *Mars;* but whether as wife, sister, or companion, is not said. The figure of this female tutelary of warriors is considered, by some, to appear on a large brass of Gordianus Pius, bearing on its reverse the legend of VIRTVS AVGG. (*Virtus Augustorum);* standing with a spear in one hand, and resting the other on a shield upon the ground. The galeated Amazon is generally distinguished from Minerva, by holding a *parazonium ;* and from Roma, by not bearing an idol of Victory; and, excepting the right breast and the left foot, her limbs are covered with drapery.—Captain Smyth, p. 247.

BERYTUS *Phœniciæ colonia (Baruti, Bejrut, Beyrout,* Syria), one of the most ancient cities in Asia, situate on the sea coast.— The old geographers speak of Berytus as *terra amœna* (a pleasant land) ; and modern travellers confirm all that has been said, in former days, of the salubrity of its climate and the fertility of its soil; to which the latter add—what seldom employs the pen of either Greek or Roman prose writers—a warm panegyric on the mountain grandeurs and picturesque beauties of its favoured locality. By whom it was founded, as a Roman colony, has been matter of controversy, which seems to be thus settled—namely, that Berytus was colonized by Julius Cæsar, and thence derived its name of *Julia ;* that Augustus next sent to it a part of the veterans taken from two legions, viz. v. *Macedonica,* and viii. *Augusta,* as a reinforcement to the first military settlers; on which account the name *Augusta* was added. From Augustus also the city received the *Jus Italicum ;* and afterwards, according to Josephus (L. xix. c. 7), it was honoured with peculiar benefits from Agrippa, king of Judæa, at whose expense the Berytensian colony was embellished with a fine theatre, and a magnificent amphitheatre, besides baths, porticoes, and other architectural works, of equal utility and elegance. It is now called *Beyrout ;* and the gallant exploits of the British navy have, in our day, brought it again into European notice.

The coins of this city are numerous. They are classed by Mionnet into Phœnician autonomes in silver; Greek and bilingual in silver and brass; *Latin* colonial autonomes; and *Latin* imperial colonial, in small, middle, and large brass.

The *Latin* autonomous coins of Berytus, have for legend COL. BER. and for types Silenus walking—the prow of a ship—the turreted and veiled head of a woman—a galley—a partridge, cornucopiæ, and dolphin.

The *Latin* imperial colonial, commence under Julius Cæsar, and extend with scarcely a break, down to the reign of Gallienus. The legends of reverse are COL. BER.—COL. IVL. BER. as in Julius and Augustus ; COL. IVL. BER. and COL. IVL. AVG. BER. as in Augustus ; C. I. F. AVG.—COL. BER. —COL. IVL. ANT.—COL. IVL. AVG. FEL. BER. as in

Julia Domna and Caracalla.—Berytus is called *Felix,* because (says Vaillant) cities were accustomed to proclaim themselves happy, or fortunate, when they were admitted to the rank and privileges of Roman colonies. Amongst the types which present themselves on *Latin* imperial colonial of Berytensian mintage are the following :

1. *Æneas, Anchises, aud Ascanius.*—On a reverse of Elagabalus.

2. *Astarte.*—This object of oriental idolatry, which has already been noticed under its own name, was the chief tutelary goddess of Berytus. Accordingly we find her frequently and variously represented on its coinage. In p. 91, a Tyrian specimen of her image, clothed in a *short* dress has been given. The annexed cut shews Astarte with tutulated, or tufted headdress, and in a *long* robe, by which the entire person is covered, with the exception of the left knee, which is bare, whilst the foot is

planted on the prow of a vessel. In her left hand is the *aplustrum ;* and her right hand holds a staff as tall as the figure, and terminating in a cross, her peculiar symbol. A column close to her left hand is surmounted by a figure of Victory, which offers to her a garland or crown. Her left foot placed on the ship's prow.—On another reverse she appears with turreted head, standing in a temple of four columns, holding a trident in her right hand. The attributes are both allusive to the maritime locality of Berytus, which she was supposed to have under her guardianship. It is thus that this idol of the Berytensians appears, on coins struck under Trajan, Hadrian, Commodus, S. Severus, Julia Domna, Caracalla, Macrinus, &c.

Vaillant (ii. 142) has engraved the bust of *Astarte,* presenting a front face, between two legionary eagles, dedicated by this colony to Gordianus III.; and Eckhel describes the same type under Gallienus. There is also a temple of four columns, of which the frontispiece is adorned with statues, and before the steps of which is a lion, on coins of Berytus, struck with the portrait of the younger Gordianus. Sestini gives a coin of Hostilianus and another of Valerianus, on which Astarte, with the *modius* on her head, stands holding in the right hand her usual attribute of a cross-headed *hasta,* and in her left hand a cornucopiæ ; her right foot is on a prow, and a *victoriola* on a cippus extends a crown towards her head, [*as in the type above engraved.*]—Pellerin has given a beautiful little coin bearing the portrait of Sabinia Tranquillina, and on which Astarte is represented, with an infant Silenus dancing at her feet.—See *Mélange*, vol. i. plate xx. fig. 13.—Mionnet cites from the cabinet Cousinery, a Berytensian coin of Treb. Gallus, which exhibits this Syrian Venus, standing between two small Victories. each on a column. She holds up above her head a scarf filled by the wind.

On a second brass dedicated by this city to Salonina, as a mode of complimenting her husband Gallienus, Astarte under the figure of a woman, in a long dress, crowned with towers, stands on the *acrostolium* (or *beak* of a galley): she holds the cruciform attribute in her right hand, and gathers the skirt of her robe in her left. Behind her is a *victoriola*, on a column, with garland and palm branch.—See Vaillant *in Col.* ii. 245.

3. *Bacchus.*—The image of a god so popularly adored as *Liber Pater*, in the wine-producing district where Berytus flourished, could not fail to make its appearance on her coins. Accordingly, either unclothed, between two shoots of vine, holding in one hand the *rhyton*, and in the left the *thyrsus*—sometimes with a faun or satyr by his side—sometimes holding a bunch of grapes over the head of his inseparable friend the panther; or in a *long dress*, with the *cantharus*, and a staff entwined with foliage and fruit, as the Indian Bacchus; we see him represented on mintages of this colony, under Hadrian, Gordianus Pius, and other emperors.—[These types probably indicate that the people of Berytus worshipped him, as the reputed *first* planter of vineyards, in the regions of Phœnicia; and especially on the spurs of the mountainchain of Libanus, in the vicinity of which the more ancient *Beroes* was built.—*Vaill. in Col.* ii. 140.]

4. *Colonus.*—A colonist, or a priest veiled, guiding two oxen, or an ox and a cow, the common numismatic symbol of an established colony, is a very frequent type on the coins of Berytus. It successively appears under Julius Cæsar, Augustus, Tiberius, Caligula, Claudius, Nero, Vespasian, Titus, Domitian, Nerva, Trajan, Antoninus Pius, M. Aurelius.

5. *Circle of figures.*—On a coin of Berytus, struck under Elagabalus, are eight togated figures, seated in a round, forming a kind of circular group, in the centre of which is the abbreviated name of the city, BER. Below is a galley.

[The above cut is from a well preserved specimen in the British Museum, on comparing which with Pellerin's engraving of the same reverse, we have another instance among many of the fidelity with which the plates of coins in his *Recueil des Médailles*, are for the most part executed. See *Mélange*, i. pl. xix. fig. 4, p. 299, in which he contents himself with merely adding, " On ne rapporte cette Médaille précédente que par rapport à la singularité de sa type, qui ne se trouve point dans Vaillant."

To publish a coin from his own collection "qui ne se trouve point dans Vaillant," was (unfortunately for the cause of numismatic science) more often the aim of Pellerin than to exercise his great erudition and experienced sagacity, in assisting to interpret a puzzling type even of his own editing—as if it became one eminent antiquary to make somewhat of a parade in supplying the omissions, or exposing the deficiencies, of another equally eminent man, yet without either taking the same pains as his predecessor had done, to unravel a numismatic enigma, or having the candour to acknowledge his ignorance of its meaning.—On turning from writers of the elder school, to Mionnet, who, for years in charge of the grandest of cabinets, and surrounded by some of the best antiquaries in Europe, was himself a model of industry, we find his notice of the coin in question comprised in these words, "Huit figures assises, et formant un cercle." That is all. Not a word more, in the shape of note or comment respecting this very remarkable—perhaps *unique* reverse, which is worthy the attention of English numismatologists.—And, indeed, to elicit from *their* learning, research, and ingenuity, some clue, at least, to the solution of this riddle, is the principal motive which has led to its being included amongst the graphic illustrations of the present work, as a genuine, rare, and curious relic of the Roman colonial mint.—The figures are not those of the *Dii Majores*, for they are not sufficiently numerous, and are without distinctive attributes.—Appearing, as they do, to be all of the male sex, it may be no great piece of presumption to hazard a conjecture, that this circular group was intended to represent a council, not of *gods* but, of *men*—*quere* if of the duumviri, decuriones, and other governing authorities of the city of Berytus?]

6. *Hercules,* naked, standing between two serpents, upright on their tails.—Elagabalus. Engraved in Vaillant, ii. 76.

7. *Jupiter.*—His image within a tetrastyle temple, is represented on a first brass of Trajan, engraved in Havercamp's *Médailles de Christine*, p. 54.

8. *Lion* walking.—Valerianus.

9. *Legionary Eagles and Military Ensigns,* sometimes within a laurel crown, in other instances with COL. BER. and the numerals v. VIII. (meaning *Colonia Berytus, Quinta et Octava,* i. e. Legio.) These appear on coins struck at Berytus under the following Emperors, viz. Augustus, Tiberius, Claudius, Nerva, Hadrian, Commodus, Julia Domna, Caracalla, Gordianus Pius.

Such military symbols refer to the original formation of the colony by Julius Cæsar, or rather to the transmission of the two legions (fifth and eighth) above mentioned, to Berytus by Augustus. The exhibition of Legionary Eagles on colonial coins of Domna, alludes probably (as Vaillant observes) to the Senate having represented her, on their own mint at Rome, sacrificing before the Roman standards, in record of the title which they had conferred on that ambitious Princess, of *Mater Castrorum*, in imitation of a similar honour bestowed by Marcus Aurelius, with like impropriety, on his Empress Faustina.

10. *Neptune.*—Berytus, being maritime, built a temple to Neptune, whom its inhabitants worshiped as one of their tutelary deities. Local traditions, indeed, whilst naming Saturn as the founder of Berytus, add that he gave that city to the God of the Sea. It is not surprising, therefore, that his image frequently occurs on coins of this colony. These are found to have been minted under Augustus, Trajan, Hadrian, Antoninus Pius, Commodus, S. Severus, Caracalla, Macrinus, Elagabalus, Gordianus Pius.—See *Neptune.*

11. *Neptune and Beroë.*—A large brass, struck at Berytus, bears on its obverse the head of Elagabalus; and on the other side, COL. IVL. AVG. FEL. BER. with the remarkable type, which, from a specimen in the British Museum, is faithfully copied in the subjoined cut.

Vaillant (*in Coloniis*, ii. 75) was the first to give an engraving of this elegant reverse, which he describes and explains as follows : "Neptune, as distinguished by the trident in his left hand, lays hold, with his right, on a woman who is in a kneeling posture, and has a vase, or pitcher, in her right hand."—Berytus, if Nonnus is to be credited, took its first name of *Beroës* from the nymph Beroë, the fabled daughter of Venus and Adonis, whom Neptune demanded in marriage, but who was given to Bacchus. But here the nymph appears unwilling to be dragged away by Neptune ; "because (adds Vaillant's authority) the God of Wine was more pleasing to her than the God of the Sea."

12. *Silenus.*—A type of this "witty" preceptor of Bacchus, appears on coins of the Berytensians, minted under Elagabalus.—See *Silenus.*

13. *Temple.*—On a coin of this colony, dedicated to Julia Mæsa, is a tetrastyle temple, in which are the figures of three females, the middle one of whom is seated, the other two standing.—

Engraved by Pellerin, in *Mélange*, i. pl. xix. No. 12.

14. *Venus Marina*, naked, seated on a rock. —Hadrian.

15. *Victory*, marching, with right hand raised, and carrying a labarum on the left shoulder—before her is a galley with two sailors, each holding a labarum—large brass of Elagabalus.— Engraved in Pellerin, *Mélange*, i. pl. xix. fig 5, p. 299.

16. *Temple of Astarte.*—The subjoined is engraved from a first brass (in the British Museum), dedicated by this colony to Diadumenianus, son of the Emperor Macrinus. The legend COL. IVL. AVG. FEL. BER. identifies the coin with the mint of Berytus. As to the type, it is one of the most remarkable in the colonial series ; constituting, as it does, a *multum in parvo* of allusion to local traditions and ancient idolatries. Vaillant having published no coin of Diadumenianus, struck at Berytus, Pellerin has supplied the omission, by giving an exact delineation, accompanied with a minute description of the type, in his *Mélange*, i. pl. xix. No. 12, p. 303 :

A temple of four columns, in which Astarte is represented, clothed in a long dress, with face to the front, and tutulated head-gear, holding in the right hand the *hasta* terminated in form of a cross, and in her left a cornucopiæ. A Victory placed on a column close to the left side of Astarte offers to crown her. On each side of the goddess, a winged cupid, standing on a plinth, lifts its hands with a garland in them towards her. On the summit of the temple, Neptune with a trident in one hand, raises up with the other the nymph Beroë, (forming a similar group to that delineated in the wood-cut which illustrates reverse number 11.) On the entablature, on each side of the pediment, a Victory holds in both its hands a crown above its head. Below the temple to the right and left of the steps, two other cupids are seen, each seated on a dolphin, and holding a trident. Beneath both dolphins is a vase with a foot to it.

Mionnet adds a large brass coin of Macrinus minted at Berytus, similar in legend and type to those of Diadumenianus above described.

BETILIENUS.—This is the surname of a man, not the appellation of a Roman family. In this case, the name of the *gens* seems (says Eckhel, v. 150) to have become extinct ; and the surnames only to have been preserved. A third brass, struck under Augustus, has on its obverse P.

BETILIENVS BASSVS and S. C. in the middle of the field.—*Rev.* IIIVIR. A. A. A. F. F. *(incuse.)*

That Bassus Betilienus was one of Augustus's moneyers is shewn by this coin; but no further mention of the man is to be found. It is only conjectured that he may be the same person, to whom Seneca alludes as having been scourged to death, by order of Caligula, A.D. 40. On a very ancient marble, cited by Patin, in reference to this small brass coin is inscribed L. BETILIENVS L. F. VAARVS.

BIBULUS,—A cognomen of the *Calpurnia* family.

BICEPS, or double headed.—See *Janus.*

BICIPITES.—Coins are so called, which have heads on both sides; and they are highly prized by collectors. But many of these bicipitous rarities have been formed by the artifice of splitting a coin in two, and then joining the opposite parts of two coins together, so as to apply the reverse of one to the obverse of another. Thus Faustina senior's head has been impacted to an Antoninus Pius; her daughter's to that of Marcus Aurelius; Crispina to Commodus; and Otacilia to Philip—so that the unwary purchaser supposes that he has a man and his wife on the same piece.—" I had specimens of all these (adds Capt. Smyth, from the preface of whose valuable work the foregoing is extracted), so excellently finished as to require very minute inspection to detect the fraud; but the best forgery that has fallen in my way was an Alexander [Severus], with the rare legend 'Potestas perpetua' round a seated Security, which I purchased as a true coin, though it had a shade of *stiffness* about it; nor was its falsity quite manifest until the graver was applied."

BIFRONS.—See *Janus.*

BILLON.—This term is applied, by French numismatists, to coins of silver mixed with much alloy, or to copper with a small alloy of silver. From the reign of Gallienus to that of Claudius Gothicus (viz. from A. D. 253 to 270), scarcely any but these so named coins of *billon* are to be found. Some of them have been first struck on the copper alone, and afterwards covered with a thin silvery coating, and in that case they are called *saucées*, or washed coins; others have had a leaf of silver struck dexterously on the copper; and these bear the name of *fourrées*, or plated coins.

On this subject M. Hennin makes the following remarks:—*From and after* the reign of Claudius Gothicus, coinages of *billon* are no longer found. The standard of silver having been successively lowered, the money, which replaced that of this metal, proves under the above mentioned emperor, to be of silvered copper. In almost all such pieces, the effects of friction, and of time, have removed this covering, which appears only on those in the best state of preservation. The coins of Claudius Gothicus, and of the subsequent reigns, as far as Diocletian, which have been published as of *billon*, are but pieces of washed copper. Those of the same reigns described as being of *silver* are false.— *Manuel—Nomenclature,* ii. 440.—See the word *Potin.*

BIGÆ (from *bis jugum).*—A car or chariot, drawn by two horses, or other animals. On Roman coins, both consular and imperial, are seen *bigæ* of horses, elephants, mules, lions, bulls or oxen, stags (Diana), panthers (Bacchus), serpents (Ceres); besides centaurs, dragons, Griffins, &c.—See *Car.*

BIGATI.—A class of Roman silver coins, so called from their bearing on the reverse side, the type of a chariot drawn by two horses.— The subjoined cut, from a denarius of the Saufeia gens, serves as a specimen (otherwise without interest) of this common device :—

Pliny (L. xxxiii. § 13) says, "Notam argenti fuisse bigas atque quadrigas, et inde bigatos et quadrigatos dictos." And it is true, that Roman silver coins, with bigæ on their reverses, were called *bigati,* and with quadrigæ, were called *quadrigati;* but a great many denarii had other types. Tacitus incidentally alludes to these coins, saying, that the *Germani,* who generally traded in the way of barter, were still ready to take in payment old and well-known money; such as *bigati;* and Livy frequently uses the term when he enumerates the amount of Spanish and Cisalpine booty. It was a long period before the portraits of living personages were placed on Roman coins; and for centuries the denarii of the republic presented on one side only the head of the goddess ROMA, or of Pallas, and on the other a figure of Victory, with garland and palm branch, standing on a car drawn by two or by four horses. Hence they were called *bigati, quadrigati,* and *victoriati.* The type of the latter, however, combined itself with the other two appellations. The engraving above given, represents a Victoria *in bigis.*—For Victoria *in quadrigis,* see *Quadrigati.*

BILANX—the balance, or pair of scales.— A symbol of Justice and Equity. It is seen on several family coins; and in the imperial mintages from Galba far downwards. The balance, at the same time, formed one of the insignia of the Prætors, who administered justice at Rome. —On coins of the Flaminia, Fulvia, and Cæcilia families, engraved from, in *Morell. Thesaur.* it is seen over the *sella curulis,* indicating that Curule Ediles were likewise invested with magisterial power. On a denarius of the Annia gens, the balance placed before a female head, shews the latter to represent Æquitas or Moneta.

BILBILIS, *Tarraconensis* (Hispaniæ) *municipium;* now Calatayud, in Arragon.—On coins it is styled *Augusta,* from Augustus, by whom, and afterwards by Tiberius and Caligula, municipal and other privileges were conferred upon it. Hence the legend MV. AVGVSTA BILBILIS on its mintages, which are colonial imperial, in small and middle brass. Of the following obverse and reverse an engraving is given in Mr. Akerman's *Ancient Coins of Cities and Princes*, pl. viii. fig. 3, p. 68 :—

AVGVSTVS. Bare head of Augustus.

BILBILIS. A horseman bearing a lance and galloping. Æ 8½ R 2. *(British Museum)*.

On other coins of this Hispano-Roman city, with legends of MV. BILBILIS, and BILBILIS AVGVSTA, struck in honour of Augustus and of Tiberius, laurel as well as oaken garlands appear, (the names of Duumviri within). The laurels on account of victories; the oak leaves on pretence of "citizens preserved." To flatter even Caligula, the inhabitants of Bilbilis dedicated a reverse, with a crown of laurel, to that pusillanimous tyrant, with whose reign the coinage of this municipium appears to have ceased.—Vaillant (*in Col.* i. 12) has engraved a coin of Bilbilis and Italica in alliance. On the obverse is BILBILI. A beardless male head.—*Rev.* ITALICA. A horseman with couched lance, charging.—See Mionnet, *Supplt.* i. 55.—also Akerman (p. 66), who says, "Bilbilis, the capital of the Celtiberi, was celebrated for its waters, which were supposed to possess the quality of imparting an excellent temper to steel."

BIT. *Bithyniæ.*—COM. BIT. *Commune Bithyniæ.*

BITHYNIA, a region of Asia Minor (deriving its name from the river Bithya), *now* Natolia, Turkey in Asia. It was one of ten provinces established by Augustus. Hadrian shewed great favour to it. (It was the birth-place of Antinous).—On large brass of that emperor, we see ADVENTVI and RESTITVTORI BITHYNIAE, with the usual types of an imperial arrival at, and restoration of, a Roman province; in this instance marking the liberalities bestowed, by the above named prince, in re-establishing those Bithynian cities, which had been overthrown by earthquakes, principally Nicomedia and Nicea.—Bimard ad Jobert, i. 404.

BLUNDERED COINS.—This is a term used in reference to "those Roman medals in which mistakes have been made by the engraver. Some, for their rarity (Pinkerton observes), are undeservedly valued by certain connoisseurs." Froëlich and Monaldini have each treated of these instances of monetal fallibility. Thus on a reverse of Trajan the inscription is CONSENCAVTIO for CONSECRATIO. On a Gordian III. MLETARM PROPVGNATOREM for MARTEM. Of Alex. Severus DES. NOS. for COS. Of Nero IANVM CLVSTI for CLVSIT. &c. *(Essay, vol. ii. 190.)*

BOAR.—The figure of a wild boar transfixed by a spear, is exhibited on a denarius of Durmius, one of the monetal triumvirs of Augustus. On a coin of the Egnatia gens, is a lion seizing upon a stag.—Eckhel remarks, that these effigies of the boar and the lion, bear allusion to the splendid huntings, in which Augustus took such great delight, as narrated by Dion Cassius and by Suetonius. On a coin of the Volteia gens, the Erymanthian boar is represented. This

animal, amongst various other quadrupeds (such as the goat, bull, stag, lion, panther, &c.) are typified on the smaller coins of Gallienus. These were all sacred to the tutelary deities, at whose altars that eccentric prince offered up so many supplications, that he obtained the title of *Conservator Pietatis.*

BOCCHUS——a King of Mauritania and Gætulia, whose name occurs frequently in the most infamous transactions of the Jugurthine war. An obsequious ally of the Romans, and a treacherous friend to his Numidian neighbours, this unprincipled time-server, after various intrigues and manœuvres, with both the conflicting parties, basely delivered up to Sulla, then a quæstor of Marius, King Jugurtha, who had sought an asylum in the territories of Bocchus, after an unsuccessful contest with the Roman legions, B. C. 106. There are denarii of Faustus Cornelius Sulla, son of the Dictator, allusive to this historical incident.—See *Cornelia gens;* also the words FAVSTVS FELIX.

BAETICA (Hispania)—a Roman province of Spain—comprehending what is now Granada, and Andalusia.

BON. EVENT.   *Bonus Eventus.*——Good success was honoured at Rome with a peculiar worship. On a denarius of the Scribonia gens, occur these abbreviated words, owing no doubt (says Eckhel, v. 303) to the Roman practice of consecrating every thing capable of producing good or evil, as Fortune, Hope, Genius, &c. And thus with *Eventus;* just as Lucretius enumerates among events, Slavery, Liberty, Riches, Poverty, War, Peace (L. i. v. 456.)—*Eventus,* according to Cicero's definition (*De Invent. Rhet.* i. c. 28), is "the issue of any matter respecting which we generally inquire, what has resulted, or may result, or will ultimately result, from such circumstances." Thus if anything turned out well it was attributed to *Bonus Eventus:* that it was considered to be of the same nature as Felicitas, is proved by a denarius engraved in *Morell. Thesaur.* amongst the *incerti,* TAB. ii. A. on which near a female head is inscribed BON. EVENT ET FELICITAS.—Eckhel expresses his own opinion to be that "this Genius of the Romans is the same as the Ἀυτοματία of the Greeks; and he quotes what Plutarch says of Timoleon—"Having built in his house a shrine to Ἀυτοματία, he sacrificed to her; but the house itself he dedicated to the sacred Δαίμων (Genius.) And Nepos also, in his life, corroborates the fact of that great reverence, which Timoleon paid to the above named deification of *chance* or *fortunate events.* The reason for this conduct was, that whatever he undertook prospered. Consequently, Ἀυτοματία is neither more nor less than the spontaneous agency of Fortune, that is to say *Eventus,* and *Bonus Eventus,* because thanks were returned to it; and it was believed to be presided over by a good or sacred Genius, by the Greeks styled ἀγαθὸς, or ἴερος δαίμων."

Bonus Eventus, according to Publius Victor, had a temple in the ninth quarter of Rome; and Ammianus also mentions it.—On consular denarii the *female sex* is assigned to *Eventus*. (See Scribonia gens); as also on an autonomous, or family denarius of Galba. But on those of other emperors down to the time of Gallienus, this deity is represented as of the *male sex*. An example of this occurs on a second brass of Antoninus Pius, whence the subjoined cut is copied, and which bears on its reverse the full legend, in the dedicatory form.

BONO EVENTUI. S. C.—The naked figure of a man, standing beside an altar, and holding in his right hand a patera ; in his left, ears of corn. In the exergue COS. II. shewing the coin to have been struck A. D. 139.

This impersonation is graphically described by Pliny (xxxiv. p. 655) when he eulogizes "the statue of *Bonus Eventus*, holding a patera in its right hand, and an ear of corn and a poppy in its left"—the workmanship of Euphranor.—Varro, (de R. R. i. ch. 1.) has indeed reckoned *Bonus Eventus* among the rural deities, because "without success, and *Bonus Eventus*, there is but disappointment, and no produce."—And Festus also says "They used to fasten *rolls of bread* (Panes) round the head of a slaughtered horse, on the ides of October, in the Campus Martius, the sacrifice being offered for an abundant crop of fruit."

One of the pavements of the Roman villa, at Woodchester, is inscribed BONVM EVENTVM, whence it may be inferred, that the owner had invoked the protection of this deity for his building.—See Lysons' *Account of Roman Antiquities at Woodchester, in Gloucestershire*, pl. xix.

BONI EVENTUS.—This legend is accompanied by the type of a naked male figure, with patera in the right hand, and corn ears and a poppy flower in the left,—on silver of Galba. History sufficiently shows that the principal reason with Galba for worshipping this deification, was his happy escape from the dangers which impended over him, in the crisis between his revolt from Nero and his accession to the empire (A. D. 68).

BONUS EVENTUS AUGUSTUS.—Young naked male figure standing ; in his right hand three javelins.—Silver of Titus.—Akerman.

BONI EVENTUS, with type of a youthful figure, standing, appears on a denarius of Pescennius Niger (of course rare).—S. Severus, also dedicated a portion of his mint, in the first and most perturbed years of his reign, to acknowledge the salutary influence, and to propitiate the further protection, of *Bonus Eventus ;* which, on silver

of this emperor, and of his son Caracalla, is represented by a naked male figure standing at an altar, over which he holds with his right hand the sacrificial patera, and a bunch of corn-ears in his left, as in the engraved type of Antoninus Pius, above given.

On coins of Roman die, struck in honour of provinces, as in the instance of Illyricum, &c. under Trajanus Decius ; or by some colony dedicated to the reigning emperor, we see a male figure, unclothed, except his having the *chlamys* over his shoulders, standing with cornucopiæ and patera, and a modius on his head. "This represents the provincial or colonial genius, and was (says Capt. Smyth) equivalent to *Bonus Eventus*, or good success, a deity who presided over agriculture, and great actions ; and as such he was complimented on coins by Titus and other princes." (p. 276.)

BONAE FORTUNAE.——Fortune standing with rudder and cornucopiæ, on silver of Valerianus, given by Vaillant, *(Præst. Num. Impp. Rom.* ii. 343), and on a third brass, described by Eckhel from the Imperial Cabinet.

Bona Fortuna, the Αγαθη τυχη of the Greeks, worshipped by the Romans as the wife or sister of *Bonus Eventus*—had two temples at Rome ; one in the Forum Boarium, built (according to Dionysius Halicar.) by Servius Tullius ; the other in the *Curia Hostilia*, erected (as Dion affirms), by M. Lepidus, in honour of Julius Cæsar (Eckhel, vii. 383).—See *Fortuna*.

BONAE SPEI.—A female figure standing, holds a flower in the right hand, and lifts her robe with the left.—On silver of Pescennius Niger, published by Vaillant *(Præst. Num.* ii. 201) ; and, in correction of his own error, allowed by Eckhel (vii. 150) to be (and *not* BONA SPES) the true reading of the legend of a genuine and most rare coin. But, he adds, BONA SPES and BONAE SPEI are legends often occurring on coins struck under S. Severus at the same time, viz. A. D. 193–194).—It is indeed quite certain, that Severus and Niger frequently used the same type in their respective mints ; and this not by chance, but by design ; for they mutually adopted legends on their money, which are not to be found on the coins of other emperors. Each emulated the other :—the *spem* of Pescennius was met by the *spei* of Septimius ; *Eventus* competed with *Eventui*, in a manner difficult to account for.—Cicero opposed *bona spes* to despondency in all human affairs ; and at Rome there was an altar raised to Fortuna Bona Spes, as Plutarch records. Gruter has published a stone monument, dedicated BONAE SPEI AVG. (vii. 170).—See *Spes*.

BONO GENIO IMPERATORIS, or PII IMPERATORIS.—The genius stands, holding a patera and cornucopiæ—below is ALE.—On a second brass of Maximinus Daza ; struck between A. D. 308 and 313.

The *Good Genius*, called by the Greeks Αγαθος Δαιμων, and especially by those of Alexandria, where this and other coins of Daza were struck, received public worship there, under the form of a serpent, as appears from Alexandrine medals with the head of Nero.—

Banduri, who describes this coin, calls into grave examination, the right of *him* to proclaim himself "a *pious* emperor," who trampled on all laws, divine and human.   But Licinius afterwards dared to do the same thing, (as is proved by a second brass of his, in the Imperial Museum, unknown to Banduri) although the legend may more truly be ascribed to the base flattery of the Alexandrians.—*(D. N. V.* viii. p. 54.)

BONONIA, a maritime town of Gallia Belgica, now called by the French *Boulogne-sur-mer* (Picardy).   According to Peutinger's table or map, its more ancient name was *Gessoriacum*, by which, however, historians do not mention it, till after the time of Constantine.—Their testimonies are given by Cellarius.   But the most trustworthy record ¦(says Eckhel, viii. 110), is that adduced from some anonymous biographer of Constantius Magnus, by D'Anville. —" Hastening towards his father (Constantius Chlorus), he arrived at *Bononia*, which the Gauls used formerly to call *Gessoriacum.*"   It was a place of great importance in a military point of view, because the transit thence to Britain across the straits is very short.   According to Suetonius it was from this place that the Emperor Claudius passed over into Britain, A. D. 43.

BONONIA OCEANEN.—A brass medallion of Constans, bears the foregoing legend; and, for its type, presents a galley, with rowers; the emperor, in a military dress, and with a buckler and a lance, stands on the deck, in the attitude of hurling his missile weapon downwards, as if at a figure swimming in the sea.   On the prow of the galley is Victory, with garland and palm branch; at the stern are two ensigns.   On the shore is seen a light-house or some other edifice.

This extremely rare medallion relates to an expedition to Britain, undertaken by Constans, in the winter of A. D. 342–3, to repress the incursions of the Picts, who were desolating the Roman province.   The meaning of the type is well elucidated by Ducange, from Julius Firmicus, who, in a style of flattery sufficiently bombastic, thus addresses Constans—" In the season of winter thou hast trodden the swelling and raging waves of the ocean—a deed never before accomplished, nor ever again to happen :—under your oars hath trembled the flood of a sea almost unknown to us; and the Briton has gazed, appalled, at the unexpected sight of an emperor."—Libanius *(in Basilico)* has given a similar account.— Light is thrown on the date of this expedition

from the subscription of the Lex V. of the Codex Theodosius (lib. xi lit. 16), viz. " data viii. Kal. Febr. *Bononiæ,* Placido et Romulo Coss." These men having entered on their Consulship A. D. 343.—[Most of the above remarks, cited by Eckhel, are in Ducange, *Dissert. de Num. inf. ævi.* § 58].

In valuing this medallion at 200 fr. Mionnet observes, that it is the more remarkable, inasmuch as it appears to be the only ancient numismatic monument which has transmitted to us the memory of this historical event, and the name of *Bononia.*

[The cast from which the above cut has been engraved was taken from the original in the Cabinet de France.]

BONO REIPUBLICAE.—*Justa Grata Honoria,* daughter of Constantius III. and of Galla Placidia, born about the year 417, having cohabited with Eugenius the procurator, and become pregnant by him, was turned out of the palace by her brother Valentinian, and went to Theodosius II. at Constantinople, A. D. 434.— She soon after secretly stirred up Attila to invade the Western Empire; and was on the point of being married to him, when he died from vomiting blood.   The following is one of her coins :—

Obv.   D. N. IVST. GRAT. HONORIA, P. F. AVG. Head of Honoria, crowned by a hand appearing above it.

Rev.   BONO REIPVBLICAE.   A Victory standing with a long cross in the right hand; beneath, COMOB. (AV. Mus. Imp.)

And thus, she who was the pest and bane of the empire, ostentatiously boasts herself as born for the *good of the state.*   There is a similar legend on a coin of Fl. Victor, who was the son of Magnus Maximus.

BONO REIPUBLICE (sic.) NATI.—Two figures, seated, and clothed in the *paludamentum,* of which the one to the right is the taller; the left hand figure is that of a boy.   They together support a globe: above is a Victory.— On gold of Fl. Victor (Banduri), on silver (Tanini.)

This and other coins of Victor, however false in their declaration, are remarkable both for their legends and for their rarity.   Constantine, on one of his coins, is styled in abbreviation B. R. P. NAT. *(Bono Reipublicæ Natus.)*   Tanini, in illustration of his silver specimen of Flavius Victor's coin, cites the following inscription from Sigonius :—

D. D. N. N. MAG. CL. MAXIMO ET
FL. VICTORI. PIIS FELICIBVS
SEMPER AVGVSTIS
BONO R. P. NATIS.

This flattering compliment is often found in inscriptions to the Constantine family; and now and then it appears alone without any designation of the Emperor or Cæsar, to whom it was applied; as on the stone found at Wroxeter.

The above legend and inscription of *Bono Reipublicæ Nati,* together with the same, on a third brass of Priscus Attalus, serve to shew how true is the reading of B. R. P. N. instead of

B. A. P. N.; and to fortify, beyond all dispute, the interpretation of *Bono Reipublicæ Nato*, instead of BAP. NAT. or *Baptizatus Natus*, as erroneously assigned to the legend of a brass coin of Constantinus Magnus.

BOS.—Bull, Ox, or Heifer.—This animal is figured on numerous coins, in various postures, and with various indications: for example, sometimes standing, walking, butting with his horns, or rushing forward—sometimes adorned in preparation for the sacrifice; sometimes on his knees, about to be immolated at the altar of a deity. The Bull or Ox, the usual monetary type of colonies and municipal towns, bore reference to the culture of the soil, as well as to the security afforded by the protection of the emperor. The well-known type of a man ploughing with two oxen symbolizes the Roman ceremony of founding a city or a colony. Bulls' heads sometimes have an allusion to sacrifices, at other times to games.

The bull, like the horse Pegasus, was consecrated to the Sun. The figure of a bull forms the reverse type of silver, and third brass, of Gallienus; bearing the legend of SOLI CON-*Servatori* AVGusti.

Bos Vittatus—a Bull, whose head is ornamented with an *infula*, or flock of white and 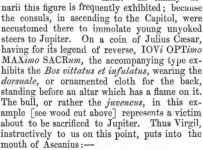 red wool, forming a kind of mitre or turban of triangular shape, and dressed with the *vitta*, (a sort of garland), between its horns, in honour of some religious ceremony, as the animal is led to the sacrificial altar. In family denarii this figure is frequently exhibited; because the consuls, in ascending to the Capitol, were accustomed there to immolate young unyoked steers to Jupiter. On a coin of Julius Cæsar, having for its legend of reverse, IOV*i* OPT*imo* MAX*imo* SACR*um*, the accompanying type exhibits the *Bos vittatus et infulatus*, wearing the *dorsuale*, or ornamented cloth for the back, standing before an altar which has a flame on it. The bull, or rather the *juvencus*, in this example [see wood cut above] represents a victim about to be sacrificed to Jupiter. Thus Virgil, instructively to us on this point, puts into the mouth of Ascanius:—

Jupiter omnipotens, audacibus annue cœptis.
Ipse tibi ad tua templa feram solennia dona,
Et statuam ante aras auratâ fronte juvencum
Candentem, pariterque caput cum matre ferentem.
Æneid, L. ix

My first attempt, great Jupiter, succeed;
An annual offering in thy grove shall bleed:
A *snow white steer* before thy altar led,
Who like his mother bears aloft his head.
Dryden's translation.

On a denarius of the Postumia gens, a bull stands as a victim, on a rock (supposed to be meant for Mount Aventine), close to a lighted altar; over the horns of the beast a priest extends his right hand.

The Romans were accustomed, at triumphal sacrifices, to adorn the horns of the victim with gold, whilst its back was clothed with the richest and most brilliant silks. Amidst such luxury and magnificence, the poor bedizened animals, (on some *grand* occasions paying the tribute of their blood at the shrines of superstition, by the hundred at a time), marched along in the procession, with gay "blindness to the future kindly given"—some so tame and quiet as perhaps to "lick the hand" of the *victimarius* who led them—all unconscious of being near the *securis*, so soon afterwards raised to fell them, and equally unaware of the *culter* just whetted to cut their decorated throats!

Bos et Stellæ.—A *bull*, standing with two stars over its head, is seen on middle brass of Julianus II. which has for legend of reverse SECVRITAS REIPVBLICÆ. It bears testimony to that emperor's relapse into Pagan idolatry, and denotes the restoration, made by the same satyrical and "philosophic" prince, of ruminating animals for victims on the altars of false gods, whereas all such sacrifices had been prohibited by his immediate predecessors, the professed Christian members of the Constantine family.—According to Ammianus (L. xxii.) Julian frequently offered up a hundred bulls, selecting *white ones in honour of Jupiter*. The stars over the head of the bull designate it to be Apis, which the Egyptians, and this Roman emperor in his "wisdom," worshipped as a god.

Bos Cornupeta.—This term (from *cornu petere*) is used by the elder numismatic writers to describe a bull, or steer, in the attitude of butting with its horns, and stamping with one of his fore feet, as on coins of Augustus and Vespasian.

 A denarius of the first named emperor, exhibits on its reverse, with legend of AVGVSTVS DIVI F. a specimen of the *Taurus* or *Bos Cornupeta*. The lowered horns and menacing posture of the animal at once correspond with, and illustrate, the line in Virgil, so spiritedly rendered by Dryden:

Jam cornu petat, et pedibus qui spargat arenam.

"Butts with his threatening brows, and bellowing stands,
"And dares the fight, and spurns the yellow sands."

The reason of its adoption as a type on this coin is doubtful. There can hardly, however, after what is adduced from ancient writers, in Morel (*Thesaur.* T. ii.) be much hesitation both in rejecting the idea of its mere allusion to the Zodiacal sign of that name, and in expressly referring it to some of those public shews, when horsemen combatted with bulls in the Circensian arena, and at which Augustus and the members of his family, often took their seats, as amongst the most ardent of the spectators.—See *Taurus*.

BOSTRA, *(Arabiæ) Colonia*—now Boszra, in the southern part of the Turkish pashalic of Damascus. The æra of this Arabian city dates from the 858th year of Rome (A. D. 105). Its coins are imperial, in brass, with *Greek* inscriptions, from the reign of Antoninus Pius to that of Elagabalus; and in the same metal, with *Latin* legends, from Alexander Severus to Trajanus Decius and Herennius Etruscus.—On imperial coins in large, middle, and small brass, the colony is called COL. BOSTR.—COLONIA BOSTRA.—Also on a large brass of Julia Mamæa, is read N. TR. ALEXANDRIANAE COL. BOSTR. *(Novæ Trajanæ Alexandrianæ Coloniæ Bostræ).* According to Vaillant, Bostra took the name of Trajan, on account of benefits (such as the building of bridges and other public structures,) received by it from that Emperor; and the appellation of Alexandrianæ was added in honour of Alexander Severus. On coins of Philip senior, and of Trajanus Decius, this city is styled COL. METROPOLIS BOSTRA, meaning the chief city of the Roman province, formed under the name of Arabia.—On a coin of Caracalla, in the *Museum San. Clem.* the legend of reverse is METRO. ANTONINIANA AVR. B. (that is, says Mionnet, *Supp.* viii. 384, *Aurelia Bostra.*)

The types of this colony are as follows:—

1. *Ammon* (Jupiter).—Head with ram's horn, surmounted by a globe, or by the *modius*—on small brass of Alex. Severus, engraved in Vaillant (*Col.* ii. 114)—and of Philip senior, engraved in Pellerin (*Mélange,* i.)

2. *Astarte.*—N. TR. ALEXANDRIANAE COL. BOSTR.—An upright figure of this divinity, in a four columned temple, holding an oval-headed staff, and a cornucopiæ. On each side at her feet is the figure of a centaur blowing a horn. This singular type appears on a large brass of Julia Mamæa.—Sestini, quoted by Mionnet, (*Supp.* viii. 284.—Engraved in Vaillant (*Col.* ii. 130.)

Astarte, or Venus, was worshipped, and had a fine temple, at Bostra. The fertility and plenteousness of whose territory is designated by the cornucopiæ. But why the two centaurs are introduced into the type is a question which remains unexplained.

Pellerin supplies an omission of Vaillant's, by giving an elegant little coin of this colony, struck under Trajanus Decius, with COL. METROPOL. BOSTRON, for its legend of reverse; and with the type of Astarte, who stands, in a long dress, presenting a front face, holding the cross-topped *hasta*; and having at her feet a figure

of the infant *Silenus,* dancing.—Engraved in *Mélange,* i. pl. xxi. fig. 7, p. 320.

3. *Colonus boves agens.*—Pellerin gives a coin with this type as struck under Elagabalus. "This medal (he observes) shews that the city of Bostra had been a colony *before* the reign of Severus Alexander, contrary to the opinion of Spanheim and of Vaillant."—See *Mélange,* i. 300.

On a coin dedicated to Alexander Severus, is the same type of a *Colonist* at plough; added to which well-known group is an edifice, with staircase of ascent to the upper part, where three vases are placed. [Described in Mionnet, *Médailles Romaines.*]

4. *Serapis,* head of, surmounted by the *modius,* or the *calathus,* on a coin of Alexander Severus, quoted by Mionnet, from the *Mus. San. Clem.* It is described and engraved in Vaillant (*Col.* ii. 129.) The bust of the principal deity of Egypt, on a coin struck at Bostra, shews that the god, whom Nonnus calls the Egyptian Jupiter, was amongst the objects of idolatrous worship in this Roman colony.

5. *Silenus,* standing, with right hand raised, and a wine skin on his left shoulder.—Engraved in Vaillant (Col. ii.)

In the second volume (p. 200) of *Collectanea Antiqua*—a work replete with the literary fruits of antiquarian research, and copiously adorned with etchings, illustrative of the habits, customs, and history of past ages—the names are given, of such heathen divinities as occur in dedicatory inscriptions, found on the line of that Roman wall which formerly extended from the Tyne to the Solway. Amongst these appears the name of *Astarte.*—This discovery is the more remarkable, because, whilst what is considered to be her image is so frequently and so variously typified on colonial coins of Phœnicia, Syria, Palestine, and Arabia—her *name* forms no part of the monetal legend: her effigy and attributes being the only clue to the identity of the goddess.

BRASS, the material of brass coins. In dividing coins according to metals, for the different series of a medallic collection, all copper comes under the classification of brass. This metal properly so called, is not malleable, and requires to be mixed with another metal before it can be applicable to the purposes of coinage. It is to be borne in mind, that what English numismatists call *brass* is by the French denominated *bronze.*

BRASS COINAGE *of the Romans.*—It has already been shewn (see p. 83 et seq. of this dictionary), that all the records left us by ancient writers, respecting the antiquity, or the original types of the Roman mint, tend to establish the same fact, viz. that the oldest money of that nation was *Brass,* and such testimony is confirmed by extant coins.—On the same evidence derived from ancient authors it has also been shewn, that brass coins were first struck of a pound weight. The words of Pliny are expressly to this effect (see *As).*—Aulus Gellius, speaking of the time when the Twelve Tables were instituted, says, "For at that period the Roman people used *Asses* of a pound weight."—So Festus "The heavy brass (*æs grave*) was so called from its weight; for *ten asses*, each weighing a pound, made up a *denarius*, which derived its name from that fact.—Also Dionysius of Halicarnassus:—" Now, the *as* was a brass coin weighing a pound."—Hence in ancient writers "the mulct, or forfeit of *heavy brass*," is an expression frequently met with.—Livy, speaking of Camillus, says, " In his absence he was fined in 15 thousands of *heavy brass;*" by which terms *asses* are always to be understood. From these facts, the inconvenient weight of the Roman money, even in moderate sums, may easily be conjectured. Not only was it needful to convey any considerable quantity of the *æs grave* in waggons to its place of public deposit; but, according to Livy, as from its bulk it could not be placed in a chest, it was stowed away (*stipabatur*) in some store-house, that it might not take up room less conveniently to be spared; from which circumstance it was called *stips*, whence the word *stipendia*.

From *Pondo* the synonyme of the *as* was derived the word *dupondium*. Varro says, "Dupondium is derived from *duo pondera* (two pounds weight); for one pound was called *assipondium*; and this again because the *as* was of a pound weight."—From the *as* were composed the *tressis*, or three asses; *octussis*, and *octas*, eight ditto; *decussis, vicessis, centussis*, 10, 20, and 100 asses respectively. From *decussis* was derived *decussare*, that is, according to Columella, to draw transverse lines in the form of the figure X; and Cicero speaks of planting trees in a *quincunx*, that is to say, in the form of the figure V. So long as the *as* maintained its pound weight, it follows that the parts of the *as* preserved a proportional weight; thus for example, the *semis* would weigh six solid *unciæ*; the *sextans* two, &c.—[Eckhel, v. p. 3, et seq.]—See *Libra*—and *Pecunia*.

In his observations on the distinctive marks (*characteres*) of the brass consular mint, Eckhel says, "It is an old doctrine, and one confirmed by both authority and experience, that *asses*, and their component parts, are the more ancient, in proportion as they are more weighty.—Guided by this rule, the learned Passeri, with great labour, framed his *Chronicon Numarium*, in which he has described the weight of Italian coins, from the heaviest to the lightest.—And, as by this criterion, it is readily understood, what coins (at least such as are of undoubted Roman origin) surpass others in antiquity ; so, concerning their actual age, nothing can be established with certainty, unless the diminutions of weight be referred to, as stated by Pliny [see p. 85 of this dictionary] ; in attending to which epoch, it will be perceived that the *Asses Sextantarii* cannot have made their appearance earlier than about the year u. c. 495 (b. c. 259) ; the *Unciales* before u. c. 539 (b. c. 217); and that the *Semi-unciales*, which were introduced by the Lex Papiria, took their date from some subsequent year, which cannot be accurately defined."

" It is a matter of inquiry (adds the author of *Doctrina*), whether some extant coins of heavy brass (*æs grave*) cannot with some semblance of truth, be referred even to the period of Servius Tullius. For were we to regard their remote antiquity only, this would not be repugnant to probability. The death of Servius is fixed at the year u. c. 218.—We have coins of Rhegium and Messana, minted about the year u. c. 276 (b. c. 478). And even these are surpassed in antiquity by coins inscribed with the name of Zancle ; not to mention the coins of *Caulonia Bruttiorum*, and others of neighbouring states, which coins have been known from the remotest antiquity. But the supposition is opposed to the authority of Pliny and other writers, who assert, that the first money of the Romans bore the figures of cattle ; notwithstanding, the oldest coins we possess, and those certainly of Roman origin, exhibit no such mark, with one exception, and that one (classified with the *as*) not of the most remote antiquity. Again, were any to be found of that period, they ought to be *librales*, if they are *asses;* or if parts of the *as*, of a weight bearing a certain proportion to the *as libralis*. But, up to the present time [as stated in p. 88], there is no extant specimen of a Roman *as libralis;* and with respect to parts of the *as*, only a *triens*, weighing four *unciæ*, has ever been cited."—See MONETA PRIMA ROMANA.

Brass coins of the Romans are so numerous, especially those of the Imperial series, that they have been divided into three classes—large, middle, and small—or first, second, and third sizes.

The class to which each brass piece belongs (says M. Hennin), is determined by reference to its volume, which at once includes the breadth and thickness of the coin, and the size and relief of the head. Thus a particular medal shall have the thickness of *large* brass; and yet shall be ranked with the middle brass, if it has only the portrait of the middle form. Whilst another, which shall not be so thick, will be classed with the large brass, on account of the size of the head. To the above must be added, as a separate arrangement—1st. Those pieces of the largest module, commonly called *brass medallions*, of which but an inconsiderable number is known, and which in all probability were not current coin.—2ndly. Pieces of various sizes called *Contorniati*, of which, like the preceding, but few are extant, and which certainly were not money.—*Manuel de Numismatique*, ii. 355.

This classification, though sanctioned and adopted by numismatic antiquaries, is yet somewhat arbitrary ; or at least may be termed a conventional arrangement rather than a perfectly exact plan. For the want of a better, however, it must be followed.

The imperial series of coins, struck in brass, at Rome, by order of the Senate, affords more positive and authentic evidence in illustration of historical facts, than those of silver or gold, which were fabricated under the exclusive authority of the sovereign. Both the latter coinages, indeed, were executed, sometimes when the prince was in the provinces, either making a journey or personally directing armies, consequently less care was taken in their mintage—and having moreover been counterfeited by forgers, they frequently exhibit types and legends, which no longer preserve the same historic accuracy.—*(Leçons de Numismatique Rom.* p. ix.)

The medallions, which for the most part do not bear the mark of the senate's authority (S. C.) and among which there is a material difference in the size and weight, seem to have been (as above observed), *not* common money, but pieces struck by the sole command of the emperors, for gratuitous distribution on state occasions, and in record of certain memorable circumstances and events. Such of these medallions, however, as constitute an exact multiple of the ordinary brass coin, and bear besides the senatorial authority, are regarded as current money, notwithstanding their being larger, and are called by Italian numismatists *double* coins, and not real medallions. As to the coins termed *large, middle,* and *small* brass, they were unquestionably the ordinary monied currency in that metal. Accordingly they are the more frequently found, whilst medallions are in general very rare.—*(Numismat. Rom.* ix.)

Of both the large and middle brass a nearly perfect series may be formed. Of the small brass a complete series cannot be made; and it is doubtful if any coins exist of some of the earlier emperors. On the disappearance of the large brass in the reign of Gallienus, the coinage of small brass re-commenced, and much of it is extremely common, as the extensive lists in the elaborate work of Bandurius testify. In the reign of Diocletian appeared a copper coin, termed the *Follis,* of the module of the middle brass of the first thirteen emperors, but much thinner. The coinage of these pieces appears to have been extensive, as they are at this day very common, both of Diocletian, and of his colleague Maximian, as also of Constantius-Chlorus, Severus Cæsar, and Maxentius.—Akerman, *Numismatic Manual,* p. 141.

It is generally admitted, and a thorough knowledge of the subject confirms the opinion, that Augustus reserved for himself and his successors the right of coining gold and silver, and left the brass and copper under the direction of the Senate, whose official signature, as it may be termed, is expressed by the well-known *siglæ* S. C. A further confirmation of this implied compact exists in an inscription found at Rome, and thus given by Gruter:—" *Officinatores monetæ aurariæ, argentariæ Cæsaris:*" Yet there are some who maintain that the Senate had power over the whole mintage of Rome; but though all the brass coins, with very few exceptions, have the "Senatûs Consulta" upon them, the gold and silver, with still rarer exceptions, are without it. Vespasian minted in the precious metals before his title was acknowledged in Rome, whereas the brass was only struck when the Senate received him. Albinus appears as *Augustus* on gold and silver coins, but on the brass series only as *Cæsar*; and it was for assuming the former title that he was

put to death. The soundest antiquaries, therefore, look upon the divided privilege of coinage to be satisfactorily established.—Capt. Smyth, R. N. on *Roman Brass Medals,* Preface, vi. and vii.

From the result of careful experiments, made in weighing a great number of *large brass medals* of the first emperors, in the best possible preservation, it has been satisfactorily ascertained, that the money now called by the above mentioned name passed in circulation for the *sestertius,* and had that value (about four *sols* French) under the first emperors—the *middle brass* must therefore have been worth the *half sestertius;* and the *small brass* must have passed for the *as.* This conjecture is confirmed by divers passages in ancient authors, who inform us that, under the emperors, the *nummus* or *sestertius* was the most common large copper coin. Lastly, the inspection of some bronze medals of Nero, which bear numeral marks, similar to those on the consular coins, and which agree with the weight of those pieces, appears further to sustain this opinion, and render it more and more probable.—*Numismatique Rom.* xxii.

In the *Discours de Savot* (p. 242), we find that early writer on numismatics, two centuries ago, expressing his opinion that the large Roman brass, posterior to the time of Pliny, were true *sestertii.* Pinkerton is of the same opinion.—Eckhel is afraid to decide.

See *Medallion* in this Dictionary: see also Capt. Smyth's Preface, p. xv.

BRITANNIA.—*Britain* (called also *Albion*), which, as Shakspeare says, " in the world's volume, seems as *of* it, *not* as *in* it : in a great pool a swan's nest," and whose inhabitants were " ultimi orbis" in ancient geography, remained unknown to the Romans, until Julius Cæsar, with characteristic boldness, ability, and foresight, crossed over from the Portus Iccius (situate on the coast, between Calais and Boulogne), to invade it. And this he did, in his 45th year, on the 26th of August, B. C. 55, landing on the Kentish shore, most probably at Lymne, with not more than two legions. But even the greatest commander of antiquity found it easier to defeat, than to subdue, the natives. The result of his first expedition appears to have been insignificant; and with regard to the victories so highly lauded afterwards by the Senate, the line of Lucan—

"Territa quæsitis ostendit terga Britannis,"
——— ——— Does he boast
His flight in Britain's new discovered coast ?
Rowe.

conveys no lofty notion of military success, as connected with that enterprise. In fact, from the day of his landing on the Kentish shore, near the South Foreland, where he met with a stout resistance, to that of his return with the invading force to Gaul, not more than three or four weeks were comprised. In the spring of the following year (B. C. 54), Cæsar undertook his second invasion of Britain: and he made good his landing at nearly the same spot as before, with five legions—an armament so vast both in its naval and military strength, as to defy all opposition. After a desultory and harassing warfare, carried on against Cassivellaunus, and other chiefs of tribes, or kings of nations, in the course of which the legionaries under their indomitable leader gained a footing in Essex and Middlesex, Cæsar compelled the Britons to sue for peace; himself only too glad to grant it to a brave and formidable, though undisciplined adversary. The conditions were, hostages to be delivered, and an annual tribute paid, to the Roman people, but without any concession of territory. And the *Imperator*, with chief portion of his mighty host, again returned to Gaul in September of the same year.—By his second invasion of Britain, Cæsar obtained no more solid advantages, as a conqueror, than had accrued to him from his first. He had indeed advanced further into the interior. But having established there no fortified chain of posts and encampments for his troops, the Roman name soon lost its influence, and the natives regained their warlike spirit of independence: thus justifying the opinion of Tacitus (*Vit. Agr.* c. 13), that the Great Julius "had only shewn Britain to the Romans, and did not make them masters of it."

The astute policy of Augustus, and the indolent apathy of Tiberius, being alike averse from the annexation to the empire, of Cæsar's *alius orbis terrarum*—"the last Western Isle" of Catullus, the Britons, during the period of 97 years, remained without molestation from any foreign attacks on their national freedom, "the island (says Dion Cassius) remaining subject to its own kings, and governed by its own laws." Caligula's mock invasion (A. D. 41), is too ridiculous to stand as an exception.

At length the Emperor Claudius, who aimed at popularity, and even shewed an ambition for military renown, undertook the task of subjecting Britain to the Roman yoke. His first step was to send thither Aulus Plautius, who, at the head of a numerous and well-appointed army, encountered and overthrew the Britons in several engagements. Stimulated to personal enterprise by these successes of his able lieutenant, the emperor (A. D. 43) went himself to the scene of action. And, though he stayed in the island only sixteen days, and made no extension

to the conquests of his officer, the obsequious Senate, on his return to Rome, six months after he had left the British shore, voted *him* a conqueror's most splendid triumph. Solemn processions also were formed ; trophied arches reared ; public games celebrated ; naval and provincial crowns of gold presented ; to perpetuate the memory of *his* victories ; and, whilst the surname of *Britannicus* was decreed to him and to his infant son, the real services of Plautius were rewarded with inferior honours, followed up by his dismissal from command. It is under Claudius that the appellation given by the Romans to the aborigines of our country, first appears on the coinage of Rome.—See [DE] BRITANNIS.

["Who were the oldest, and consequently the first, inhabitants of this island, and whence the name of Britain is derived, has given rise to a variety of opinions, with no ground of certainty to determine the question." It appears, however, that "the ancient Gauls and Britons used the same language, and by necessary consequence the origin of the Britons may be referred to the Gauls."—See Camden, edited by Gough, 1, p. lxiv.]

About A. D. 50, Claudius being still emperor, in consequence of continual conflicts carried on with the unsubdued natives, the southern part of the island was formed into a province by Ostorius, who defeated the Silures in a great battle, and taking their leader Caractacus (or Caradoc), sent him and his family prisoners to Rome. Neither the captivity, nor subsequent release, of this heroic chief, produced more than a brief suspension of hostilities between the legionaries and their harrassing antagonists. From A.D. 54 to A. D. 62, during which, Nero being emperor, Suetonius Paulinus commanded in Britain, battle after battle was fought, without producing any decisive effect on either of the belligerents. The capture of the isle of Anglesea, and the slaughter of the Druids, followed by a retributive and still more widely extended massacre of the Romans, by the insurgent Britons under their Queen Boadicea (A. D. 61); these sanguinary horrors succeeded by the terrible revenge, which the Romans took, when victory at length returned to their standards, and the British heroine fell a self-devoted victim to imperial cruelty and injustice—such are amongst the prominent features of atrocity and misery with which historians fill up that brief but eventful space of eleven years. Nor was this *bellum internecinum*—this "war to the knife" yet near the period of its termination.—When, however, Vespasian in A. D. 70, became emperor; he (who under Claudius had fought the Britons in many engagements, and consequently well knew the system of political as well as military tactics, best calculated to achieve success against the independent tribes of the island), adopted such a combination of bold and judicious measures, as, through his generals, Cerealis and Frontinus, before the end of the year 76, resulted in reducing the *Brigantes* wholly, and the *Silures* partly, to subjection.

A new æra of military glory, accompanied by a wiser and more humanised system of conduct towards the natives, began to be identified with the administration of Roman affairs in Britain, about the close of Vespasian's reign. This auspicious change continued throughout that of Titus. But it was totally blighted by the base ingratitude and vindictive tyranny of Domitian towards one of the ablest as well as most willing instruments of such public benefits, that Rome ever had the privilege to call her own. The pen of Tacitus, narrating events from A. D. 76 to 86, attests the splendid successes gained, and the solid advantages reaped, by Cneius Julius Agricola. That consummate warrior, and excellent governor, whilst he effectually kept down the refractory tribes by his vigilance and courage, no less advanced the cause of tranquility and civilization by his advice and assistance to those who faithfully adhered to their alliances with Rome—at the same time that he set an example of good order, by restoring the discipline of his army. It was the justly famed Agricola, who having, A. D. 78, accepted at the hands of his aged emperor, the post of command in this country, subdued the Ordovices and took the isle of Mona. It was Agricola who, after having reduced to submission the whole southern portion of Britain, augmented the superiority he had already acquired, by gradually securing a strong northern frontier to his conquests in his third campaign, A. D. 80, advancing as far as the Frith of Tay—not merely driving the Caledonians back into their inaccessible fastnesses among the Grampians, A. D. 83, but after defeating Galgacus, A. D. 84, being the first to ascertain, by means of his fleet, the geographical fact that Britain is an island.

All these substantial fruits, however, of dearly purchased victories in seven glorious campaigns—all these benefits of an enlightened energy—all these advantages of good government—were rendered null and void, by the worse than thankless conduct of Domitian to a *legatus*, of whom *such* a sovereign was not worthy.

After the recall of Agricola from his pro-prætorship, A. D. 85, the Roman province in Britain, which he had done so much to enlarge and improve, appears to have relapsed again into a state of commotion within, and of conflict pressed upon it from without. In this precarious and neglected condition, the power of Rome remained in this country till A. D. 117.—It is to be observed by the way, that no coins of Vespasian, Titus, and Domitian, any more than of their imperial predecessors, Nero, Galba, Otho, and Vitellius, bear, either in type or legend, the least reference to the Britons; although triumphs for Agricola's successes were assumed by both the sons of Vespasian.

At length, Hadrian being invested with the purple, that wise and active ruler, directing his attention to the subject of Britannic affairs, with a sagacious promptitude corresponding to its importance, began by sending large bodies of troops to reinforce the various garrisons and encampments which, under Agricola's plan, had been made to form a well-connected chain of military posts and stations over the country. And having by this means re-established comparative tranquillity, he next extended to Britain those administrative regulations for limiting the authority, and curbing the exactions, of prefects and subordinate magistrates, which he had already reduced to an uniform system in other provinces of the empire, and which had become equally indispensable to protect the Roman colonists themselves from flagrant injustice, and to rescue the native tribes from the most grinding tyranny.

Hadrian was the first emperor, subsequently to Claudius, who had set foot on British ground. The advent took place A. D. 121 ; and his presence in that island seems to have been owing to a far more important reason than that of mere curiosity. It is evident, from both coins and marbles, that marches were performed, battles fought, and victories gained by this prince, over the ever restless Caledonians. But there is one memorial of Hadrian's visit to Britain, which, though history makes but brief allusion to it, remains—*monumentum ære perennius*—an imperishable evidence of his directing mind, in the mural barrier which was constructed (not merely of turf but of stone), from the western to the eastern coast, for the purpose of resisting the incursions of the Caledonians (afterwards called Picts), and other unconquered inhabitants of North Britain.

During the reign of Antoninus Pius (comprising the period from A. D. 138 to 161), the *Meatæ* in the north, and the *Brigantes* in the south, revolted from the Roman sway ; and, after much bloodshed on both the conflicting sides, were reduced to submission by the proprætor Lollius.—Marcus Aurelius was, almost at his accession to the throne (A. D. 161), engaged in defending the northern and eastern frontiers of his vast empire, against the incursions of Germanic tribes, and the march of Parthian invaders. This fact may perhaps serve, in some measure, to account for his name and exploits not being recorded either by annalists or on coins, in relation to Britain : although for nearly the whole 28 years of his eventful life, as emperor, Britain was the arena of continuous hostilities between the uncivilized tribes of Caledonia and the legions stationed to defend the Roman province from their onslaughts.—Commodus (A. D. 184), aroused to make some effort for the safety of this part of his dominions, sent over Ulpius Marcellus. This general, a man of high reputation, after having defeated these freebooters, and driven them back into their sheltering highlands, proceeded to reform the legionaries themselves, by establishing better discipline and more effective regulations. For these, and other important public services, Ulpius was rewarded by Commodus, in the same manner that Agricola had been by Domitian—namely, by a recall from his prefecture ; and a narrow escape of his life from the jealous hatred of his execrable master.

The portentous insubordination of the Britannic army, at this period, was plainly shewn, in their clamorous accusations against Perennis (A. D. 185), and the base degradation of the imperial government became equally manifest, in the surrender, by the self-dubbed *Hercules Romanus*, of a favourite minister to the deadly revenge of a corrupt and seditious soldiery. In the fertile mint of this blood-thirsty profligate, one blushes to see the arts of design combined with the skill of the die-sinker, to furnish, in each metal and of almost every size, numismatic specimens of exquisite beauty, amongst other subjects, allusive, both in legend and in type, to that Britain, whose soil the degenerate son of Aurelius never trod, and about whose interests, as a province of the empire, he knew little and cared less. Albinus, on whom Severus, in A. D. 194, conferred the title of Cæsar in Britain, displayed great ability for civil government, and high talents for military command, whilst left awhile by his artful superior unmolested at the head of affairs in that island. He had, of course, no authority over the brass mint of Rome; and he struck no silver or gold money, on which there was any reference to Britain; although a mintage of silver, issued by him when he assumed the purple at Lyon (A. D. 197), exhibits a type of military ensigns, allusive probably to the British legions whom he had led into Gaul.

Septimius Severus, after he had put Albinus to death; and with the same merciless hand of power, restored tranquillity in the east, became closely associated, in bodily presence as well as in name, with the western provinces; and his military expeditions, together with the victories that crowned them, in Britain, are recorded on his coins. In the 207th year of our æra, and in the 15th year of his reign, this warlike prince divided the executive administration of the island into two prefectures, appointing able governors to each, and sending large reinforcements to assist one of them in waging war with the unconquered men of the north. Two years afterwards, accompanied by Caracalla and Geta, he went, an infirm old man, but still energetic and undaunted in spirit, to the assistance of his lieutenant Lupus, with a much more formidable armament. His invasion of Caledonia (A. D. 209); his dearly bought successes over, and his acceptance of a proffered but a feigned submission from the savage race of people, whose obstinate courage had inflicted such appalling losses on the Roman host—all these, added to his more permanent merit in repairing and strengthening the defences of the northern province, give an historical reality of interest to the VICTORIAE BRITANNICAE legends, and to the trophied types, which display themselves in the respective mints of Severus and his sons.

[Mr. Roach Smith, F. S. A. in his valuable and interesting Notes of an Archæological Tour performed by him, in 1851, along the Roman Wall, makes the following concluding remarks; which, coming as they do from one of the ablest, most indefatigable, and most faithfully correct writers of the present day, and offered by him as the result of his recent line of exploration, have a peculiar claim to the confidence and con-

sideration of the historical antiquary. Referring to the inscriptions which have strewed the ground from Bowness to Wallsend, he observes, that " these records very clearly explain the origin of the wall itself, and settle the questions which have so long been raised as to its date.—They prove that to Hadrian this honour is due; and that Severus, who has shared the credit with Hadrian, did nothing more than repair the fortresses and the public buildings, which had become dilapidated; that Hadrian brought together for this work the entire military force of the province, and that the British states, or communities, also contributed workmen."—See *Gentleman's Mag*. Oct. 1851. But more particularly see *Collectanea Antiqua*, by the same author, vol. ii. under the head of " The Roman Wall."]

From the death of Severus (at York), Feb. 4, 211, to the times of that fortunate usurper Carausius, and his perfidious murderer Allectus —(an interval of more than 70 years)—no notice, strange to say, of occurrences in Britain can be found in the old writers.

[The above historical summary, purposely closed here, is meant simply for an introductory tribute of attention, due to the subject of such monetal relics, as serve to associate the annals of ancient Rome with those of " the land we live in." And, as in framing the above outline, slight and circumscribed as it is, resort has been had to facts, dates, and authorities, to the pages of a Camden, a Henry, a Tyttler Frazer, a Francis Palgrave, a Lingard, an Eckhel—so has the scientific and intelligent pen of an Akerman been taken full advantage of in the *subjoined notices of coins and medallions*, which bear the names of our country and her native sons, as they were respectively designated by her earliest conquerors, and, for many centuries, ruling occupants. The more recent publication by the last named excellent writer, entitled " Coins of the Romans relating to Britain," is, indeed, regarded by all competent judges in England, as the best work extant, with reference to the nationally interesting points on which it treats. And European appreciation of its merits may fairly be recognised in the distinguished honour of the *Prix de Numismatique*, awarded to him, for the new edition, by the French Institute. From the accurately descriptive and elegantly illustrated contents of that volume, the student will derive every degree of useful information, which can be obtained or desired, in that particular branch of numismatic research, from the reign of Claudius down to the times of Constantine and his family.]

BRIT.—*Britanni.*—Pacatus, in his *Panegyr. Theodosii*, cited by Eckhel (vi. 247), calls the Britons by the strong term of *exules orbis* (exiles from the terrestrial globe). About the time of the Emperor Claudius (A. D. 41 to 54), it was customary to write BRITANNIA—BRITANNI —BRITANNICVS.—The name of the island and of its inhabitants was also spelled with only *one* т during the reigns of Hadrianus and Antoninus Pius, as will be seen on their respective coins.—Virgil had previously done the same, in the well known line, ending "*Britannos.*"—It was under Commodus (about A. D. 184), that the letter т began to be doubled, and only one N was used. (See next page).—Septimius Severus (A. D. 209), adopted the double т, but restored the N; and in legends of Geta and Caracalla (A. D. 198 to 217), we also read BRITTANNICAE. After that period of the empire, the word does not in any way appear on the coinage of Rome.

BRITAN. (DE) or *De Britann,* or *De Britanni,* or *De Britannis,* inscribed on a triumphal arch, above which is an equestrian statue, between two trophies.

This legend and type appear on gold and silver of Claudius, to whom as early as the year U. C. 796 (A. D. 43), honours were awarded by the Senate, for the conquest of Britain. No coins struck in preceding years, have yet been found, commemorative of this event. The above type (engraved from a specimen in the British Museum), exhibits the arch stated by Dion Cassius to have been decreed to Claudius, in addition to other marks of distinction.—Suetonius *(Claud.* ch. 17), adds that a naval crown was placed near the civic one, on the summit of the Palatine residence, as an emblem of the sea-traject, and, so to speak, a symbol of the Ocean subdued to the emperor's power.

BRITAN.——A first brass of Antoninus Pius presents a female figure helmeted, clothed, and seated on a rock : holding a javelin in the right hand, her left reposes on an ornamented shield by her side, and her right foot rests on a globe. Round the type we read IMPERATOR II.; and BRITAN is inscribed across the field.

This type differs materially from all the others of the Britannia series. "Instead of a female figure, with bare head, as on coins of Hadrian, we have here doubtless (says Mr. Akerman), a personification of Rome herself; her dominion being aptly enough portrayed by a globe beneath her right foot, whilst she grasps a javelin (a barbarian weapon) instead of a spear."—Engraved in "Coins relating to Britain," pl. iii. fig. 18.

BRITAN.—Inscribed in the exergue of another large brass of the same emperor, having the same legend of reverse. The type is a female figure seated on a globe, surrounded by waves; in her right hand a standard; in her left a javelin; her elbow resting upon the edge of a buckler by her side.

"This is perhaps the most interesting coin of the whole series." Every feature of the device serves to mark the insular and remote situation of Britain, which the Romans considered, and their poets (Virgil, Claudian, and Horace), alluded to, as a country divided, severed, and set apart from *their* world.—According to Dion Cassius, great difficulty was experienced by Plautius, in the time of Claudius, in inducing

his troops to embark for Britain : they complained that they were going to war in regions ' out of the world.'—The figure seated on the globe is unquestionably the typification of the Roman province."—See the work above named, in which the coin is engraved, pl. ii. fig. 16.

BRITAN. S. C. (across the field of the coin). —An elegant winged Victory, standing on a globe, holds a garland in her right hand, and

a palm branch in her left.—Round the type, IMPERATOR II. *(Imperator Iterum,* Emperor for the second time). On a first brass of Antoninus Pius.

According to Capitolinus, Antonine conquered a tribe of the Britons by his general, Lollius Urbicus, who kept back the barbarians by raising another turf wall still further to the northward (alio muro cespititio submotis barbaris ducto).

Pausanias also, in recording the victorious exploits performed in Britain by the above named imperial commander, calls the tribe whom he subdued by the name of *Brigantes,* and ascribes the war to their having attacked *Gerunia,* a territory subject to the Romans.

[The fine reverse above described and inserted, has been engraved from a specimen in the British Museum.]

The chronological value of the title *Imperator,* as inscribed on coins of Roman Emperors, is shewn by Eckhel (vii. p. 12) :—These coins prove what history has neglected to teach us, viz. that this war was carried on, or at least was finished by Urbicus, within the third quinquennial consulate of Antoninus Pius ; and thence was called after him *Imperator II.* being the first and last augmentation of his title.—Although, if Gruter's marble does not mislead, in which Antonine is styled TR. P. II. IMP. II. COS. II. DES. III. *that* title had already been conferred upon him at the expiration of the preceding year U. C. 892 (A. D. 140).—See the word *Imperator.*

There is a second brass of Antoninus Pius, with the same legend of reverse, of which the type is a Victory walking. She holds in her right hand a buckler, on which the abbreviated word BRITAN. is inscribed. This coin, bearing also IMPERATOR II. evidently refers to the same decisive victory gained over the Brigantes, which gave rise to the minting of the preceding coin. —Engraved in Akerman, "Roman Coins relating to Britain, pl. i. fig. 9.

BRITANNIA. S. C.—A first brass of Antoninus Pius with this legend, has for its reverse type, a male figure seated on a rock, his right hand holding a standard; his left hand resting on the upper edge of a shield placed by his side.

Mr. Akerman, in giving an engraving of it, says—"This curious coin is somewhat puzzling. It bears on the obverse the head and name of Antoninus Pius; but the seated figure is obviously a portrait of Hadrian. It is difficult to find a reason for this, unless we suppose that the die for the reverse was originally intended for a coin of Hadrian during the life of that emperor, but for some cause or other not used on his money. Or was it designed by the Senate as a tribute to the memory of Hadrian, who certainly performed more in Britain than his successor? In either case it is a very curious type." Referring to his engraved illustration of this reverse (pl. ii. fig. 15, of the work above quoted), Mr. A. adds, "That the figure is that of Hadrian, no one acquainted with the portraits of that emperor will deny."

BRITANNIA COS. IIII.—*Britannia Consul Quartum.*—A female figure seated on a rock, in an attitude of dejection; before her a large oval shield, and a military standard. On second brass of Antoninus Pius.

The legend of this reverse shews that the coin was struck in the 4th consulate of the emperor, A.D. 145.—"Of all the Roman coins relating to Britain, this is the most frequently discovered in England. They are generally found in very ordinary condition, and scarcely ever met with in fine preservation. It is somewhat singular, that among the numerous fine and interesting brass medallions of Antoninus, not one bears allusion to Britain."—Akerman, same work as above cited. Engraved in pl. ii. fig. 11 and 12.

BRITANNIA, P. M. TR. P. X. IMP. COS. IIII. P. P.—*Brittania, Pontifex Maximus Tribunitiâ Potestate decem, Imperator Septimum, Consul quartum, Pater Patriæ.*—A male figure seated on a rock, holding in his right hand a military standard, and in his left a javelin; his right arm rests on a shield, on which are inscribed the letters S. P. Q. R.—This legend and type appear on the reverse of a brass medallion, of large size and of the greatest rarity, struck under Commodus.—The obverse presents the laurelled head of that emperor, round which we read, M. COMMODVS ANTONINVS AVG. PIVS. BRIT.

Among other vain assumptions of unmerited honours, Commodus, from the date of his ninth tribunitian power, had taken the title of BRIT-*annicus*, on the occasion of some advantages gained in that country by his generals. And this medallion was struck to record the suppression of a rebellion in South Britain, and the defeat of a Caledonian incursion by Ulpius Marcellus. (See historical summary, p. 138). The figure thus representing a Roman province, displays as usual all the attributes of that province. —The form of the dress, bucklers, and lances used by a warlike race, are here plainly recognizable. Britannia also holds a Roman ensign, as the declared subject of the Emperor, Senate,

and People, who are indicated by the legend and type of the obverse, and by the S. P. Q. R. inscribed on the shield in the reverse.

[A graphic illustration of the above described medallion is placed at the head of article BRITANNIA (p. 136). The cut is executed after a cast taken from the interesting and very rare original in the French National collection.]

BRITTANIA.—The learned editor of the Thomas' sale catalogue (p. 33), thus describes the splendid Britannia medallion in, what, for comprehensive extent and extraordinary value, was appropriately termed, that "princely collection."

"*Obv.* a beautiful laureated and togated bust of Commodus looking to the right; *rev.* a military figure seated on a rock, with a standard in the right and a spear in the left hand; the latter rests on an ornamented oval shield (having the point of a lance in the centre) placed on a helmet.—Legend of the reverse, BRITANNIA, P. M. TR. P. X. IMP. VII. COS. IIII. P. P.—Legend of the obverse, M. COMMODVS ANTONINVS AVG. PIVS BRIT.; *extra fine and unique; size* 12 of Mionnet's scale.—A very correct engraving of this matchless Britannia adorns the title of Captain Smyth's valuable Catalogue; privately printed at Bedford, 1834."

[It will thus be seen that the medallion in question, forming part of the late Mr Thomas's collection, differed from that in the French cabinet, *only in not* having the initial letters S. P. Q. R. within the shield. Yet, whilst by that inscriptive addition instead of a mere lance point, the mintage of the latter becomes not less identified with senatorial than with imperial sanction, and in that respect has a superiority over the former—we find the medallion at Paris valued by Mionnet at 150 francs (£5 18s. 9d.), and that the celebrated acquisition of the English collector actually sold in 1848 for the sum of £75!]

In the Florentine museum there is a brass medallion of Commodus, bearing the same legends, and a similar type of reverse, except that the spear or lance in the hand of the province is armed at *both* ends.

BRITANNIA. S. C.—A second brass of Hadrian bears this inscription on the exergue of its reverse, with the legend PONT. MAX. TR. POT.

COS. III.——*Pontifex Maximus. Tribunitiâ Potestate, Consul tertium.*—The accompanying type is that of a female figure seated, her left foot planted on a rock; her head resting on her right hand —in her left hand is a spear, and by her side a shield, with a spike in the centre.

Spartian says—"Hadrian resorted to Britain, where he reformed many things, and was the first to raise a wall 72,000 paces in length, which served as a boundary between the *Barbari* and the Romans." And according to the same author, this journey of Hadrian's was made in the year u. c. 874 (a. d. 121).

[The above cut is from a satisfactorily preserved specimen which belongs to the compiler of this work, the gift of his friend W. C. Ewing, Esq. of Norwich.]

In a communication to the editor of the Numismatic Chronicle, in 1841, Mr. Roach Smith, alluding to this type of *Britannia*, on Hadrian's second brass, states that in some of the specimens which he possesses, "the development of the mammæ clearly decide the disputed point that the figure, under which the province of Britain is personified, is a female."

In the work on Roman Coins relating to Britain will be found two engravings of this type of Hadrian's. They differ in no material respect from each other, except that on one the legend BRITANNIA is carried round the margin of the coin, and the other (as in the present wood cut) is inscribed in the exergue.—See Mr. Akerman's remarks on this interesting type, in pp. 25 and 26.

BRITANNIAE *(Adventus Aug.)*—On a large brass of Hadrian there is for *obv.* HADRIANVS AVG. COS. III. P. P.   The laureated profile of that emperor, with the chlamys buckled on the right shoulder.—*Rev.* Legend as above; on the exergue S. C.—The figure of Hadrian in the toga stands in the left of the field, and a robed female on the right, who holds a patera over an altar, from which a flame rises.—" By this, and the victim at her side (observes Capt. Smyth), is expressed the sacrifice made by the Provincials in token of joy and cordiality at the august arrival; and the altar denotes mutual compact. He arrived A. D. 121, just in time, according to Camden, to prevent the Britons from throwing off the Roman yoke.   Here he made many regulations; and to secure his colonies from Caledonian incursions, caused a mighty wall to be built, extending from the river Eden in Cumberland, to the Tyne in Northumberland."—(p. 104).

BRIT. VICT.—See VICT. BRIT. and VICTORIAE BRITTANNICAE of Severus, Caracalla, and Geta.

BRIT*annicus*.—This appellation does not appear on any of the coins of Claudius, as part of his style and title, although on those which commemorate the expedition of that emperor into Britain, and some victories gained there by his *legati*, an inscription relating to that island *does* occur.--See BRITANNIS (DE).

It was by certain emperors of a lower age, that the surname of Britannicus was assumed.   Commodus first used it on his coins, A. D. 184.— And this he did in addition to another titular assumption—thus PIVS BRIT*annicus*, omitting the others which he had before obtained; such as Germanicus and Sarmaticus.   The same title of *Britannicus* is exhibited on the respective coins of S. Severus, Caracalla, and Geta.

BRITANNICUS *Cæsar.*—Tiberius Claudius Germanicus, afterwards called Britannicus, son of Claudius and of Messalina, was born A. D. 42. By the influence of Agrippina jun. the second

wife of Claudius, he was deprived of his hereditary right to succeed that emperor, and Nero was adopted in his stead, A. D. 50.   About five years afterwards, when he had scarcely reached his fourteenth year, this ill-fated prince was poisoned by Nero, partly out of envy of his fine voice, but more from fear that the youth should snatch the empire from him.

There are neither gold nor silver coins of Britannicus.   Brass, even of the Greek colonies, are exceedingly rare.—Eckhel ascribes to him as genuine, a large brass in the cabinet at Vienna, having on its obverse the bare head of Britannicus, with the legend of TI. CLAUDIVS CAESAR AVG. F. BRITANNICVS.—On the reverse S. C. Mars walking.—*(D. N. V.* T. vii. p. 155.)

Mionnet values this at 1000 francs, and pronounces it *unique.*

Captain Smyth says—" The only large brass of Britannicus which I know of is that with reverse of Mars, in the imperial cabinet of Vienna, which was purchased at Rome, in 1773, and has been pronounced to be genuine." (p. 36.)

The learned and accurate author of *Leçons de Numismatique Romaine,* after alluding to the extreme rarity even of colonial coins of Britannicus, expresses himself as follows (p. 95) :— " There has been cited but one medal of Roman die, or rather struck at Rome, bearing the name and effigy of this prince.   It is of large brass, and now in the collection of the Abbé Canova, brother of the celebrated sculptor.— But (adds this writer), although referred to as a true antique by several authors, we, who have seen and examined it; we who rest, in the first place, on the opinion of Eckhel, and in the second place, on that of the well-informed P. Caronni; believe it to be very suspicious.   It is of a larger module, and it is thicker than large brass of the ordinary size.   Its reverse presents the god Mars, an unusual type for a young prince invested with only the title of *Cæsar.*"

A second brass specimen was admitted into a collection by Morel, but Eckhel thinks it must be false.

Mionnet and Akerman both quote the following small brass, colonial, with *Latin* legends :— BRITANNICVS.   Bare infant head of Britannicus.

Rev. Legend effaced (within a garland). BRITANNICVS AVGV.   Bare head. *Rev.* TI. CLAVD....TR. POT. P. P. From Sestini.

The coins on which Britannicus is called Augustus are colonial; and to the ignorance of the moneyer, rather than to any particular motive, is to be attributed the above use of a title which was never conferred on that prince.—Mionnet.

B. R. P. NAT.—Bono Reipublicæ Nato (see p. 132), and not BAP. NAT. as interpreted by Occo and others after him, BAP*tismate* NAT*o.* In support of the former reading there is a paper in the Numismatic Journal, edited by J. Y. Akerman, F. S. A. (January, 1837, p. 260), which, entitled "Revival by Dr. Walsh of a refuted error," sets this question conclusively at rest.

BRUISE, in numismatic language, signifies

a break or injury in the patina of a brass or copper coin or medallion.

BRUNDUSIUM.—A city of Calabria (or rather of Apulia), on the coast of the Adriatic sea, now called *Brindisi*, in the *Terra di Otranto*, kingdom of Naples. In the time of the Romans, it was the chief resort of persons making the traject from Italy to Greece. Horace has described the road from Rome to this place, in the fifth satire of his first book.—Both Eckhel and Mionnet include Brundusium in their respective catalogues of *Roman colonies*.—Vaillant gives none of its coins, which according to Mionnet consist only of *Latin* Autonomes, in small and middle brass, almost exclusively bearing the legend BRUN*dusium ;* and the types consist of a laurelled and bearded head (of Neptune or Jupiter), or a naked male figure (Arion) riding on a dolphin, holding in the right hand a *victoriola* that crowns him, and in the left a lyre, with the mark of the *Semis*.

BRUTUS *(Marcus Junius)*, called by some the tyrannicide, was son of M. Junius Brutus, and of Servilia, who was half sister of Cato of Utica, by the mother's side. He came into the world in the 669th year of Rome (B. C. 85). At a very early age he lost his father; but his education, under the careful superintendence of his mother and uncles, was an excellent one; and, having imbibed an ardent love for learning, he studied literature and oratory at Rhodes.— It is not certain [see the point treated of further on] that he was descended from the celebrated Brutus, who drove the Tarquins from Rome, and served the first Consulate of the Republic: although the portraitures and inscriptions on his family coins shew that he laid pretensions to that origin.· Having, amidst the lamentable dissensions of the State, attached himself to the adherents of Pompeius Magnus, on the ground that it was that party which most favoured the cause of freedom, Marcus Brutus was in the army opposed to that of Julius Cæsar, at the battle of Pharsalia, A. U. C. 706 (B. C. 48). But he was afterwards not only pardoned by the victor in that decisive shock of arms, but was loaded by him with the highest distinctions.— Cæsar in fact gave Brutus the government of Cisalpine Gaul, and the prætorship of Rome— favours which he repaid, by becoming, in conjunction with C. Cassius, the foremost of his assassins.—It was doubtless the remembrance of these benefits conferred, that moved the mind of Cæsar in the very moment of the assault made upon him in full Senate (B. C. 44). So that seeing Brutus in the throng of his murderers, the exclamation burst from his. lips—"Tu ne etiam inter hos es, fili?" Art *thou*, too, amongst them, my son?—After the perpetration of the crime, compelled to quit Rome, Brutus fled with Cassius and others of the conspirators into the province of Macedonia. And when he learnt that ·war was declared, under the Lex Pedia, against him and his associates, he betook himself to defensive measures, not only for the support of the commonwealth, but for

his own personal safety. Being, however, defeated by Mark Antony and Octavian, at Philippi, he put an end to his existence in the year 712 (B. C. 42), and in the 37th year of his age.

"In private life (says Eckhel, vi. 20), M. Brutus was a man of unimpeachable morality—inaccessible to the allurements of pleasure and of avarice—the only individual of the conspirators, whom public opinion held to have joined in destroying Cæsar, under the impulse of a love of virtue and integrity; whilst the rest were looked upon as actuated by widely different motives.— These commendations, however, lose much of their foundation in truth; since in determining upon the death of Julius, he could not exhibit his patriotism except at the expense of ingratitude towards a second father—and moreover, since he ought to have reflected that his was a fruitless and inconsiderate zeal, so long as there existed in the corrupt commonwealth of Rome, so many Cæsars, ready to take the place of the departed one, and, as the event proved, to use their victory with infinitely greater pride and cruelty. But Brutus betrayed great inconsistency of principle and weakness of character, when, on the morrow after his defeat at Philippi, having resolved on self-destruction, he openly adopted the words which an ancient poet puts into the mouth of Hercules:—"Ah, wretched Virtue! thou wast, then, but a name! and yet I worshipped thee as a reality: but thou wast the slave of Fortune!"—From this closing incident, the inference is plain, that in his aspirations after Virtue, he had neglected the practical for the ideal."

1. BRUTUS.—Head of L. Junius Brutus. *Rev.* AHALA. Head of Ahala. On a denarius of the Servilia gens.—(See p. 30).

2. BRUTUS (M.) IMP. COSTA LEG.— (Brutus Imperator, Costa Legatus). Bare head of Marcus Brutus, within a crown of oak leaves. *Rev.* L. BRVTVS PRIM. COS. (Lucius Brutus, the First Consul). Bare head of Lucius Brutus, within a similar crown.

The two denarii above described exhibit the head of that Lucius Junius Brutus who expelled the kings from Rome, and was the first of the Consuls in the free commonwealth. Both were caused to be struck by M. Brutus, who murdered Julius Cæsar.

Before commenting on these truly precious coins, Eckhel (vi. 20 *et seq.*) enters into an inquiry whether the Marcus Brutus in question derived his lineage from the original L. Bratus above alluded to. He commences by observing that, even the ancient writers are at variance in their opinions on this subject. Foremost amongst these, Dionysius of Halicarnassus, citing the most distinguished writers on Roman history, affirms, that no issue, male or female, survived the Lucius who condemned his two sons for conspiracy with the Tarquin family, and who were executed by his orders, as consul. To this he adds the fact that Lucius was of patrician birth, whilst the Junii and Bruti, who boasted of their descent from him were, without exception, plebeians, and served plebeian offices in the state. Dion Cassius makes similar statements, borrowing them probably from Dionysius; and adds, that it was by many persons industriously rumoured, that Marcus ascribed his origin to Lucius, in order that such associations might stimulate him to the overthrow of the tyrant Cæsar.—Other authors take a different view of the question. For example, Plutarch, adducing the testimony of Poseidonius, asserts that though two of the sons of Lucius Brutus were put to death by his command, as traitors to the republic, yet a third, then an infant, was left, by whom the race was continued. Plutarch further asserts, on the same authority, that the features of several individuals of the Junia family resembled those of the statue of L. Junius Brutus.—But there is much weightier evidence in the words of Cicero, addressed to the Senate:— "Surely, it was that L. Brutus, who both in his own person liberated the commonwealth from kingly domination, and transmitted, to nearly the five hundredth year, a posterity of similar virtues and like exploits."—In another oration, alluding to Decimus Brutus, one of the most active originators of the conspiracy, he speaks yet more plainly. [See AHALA, p. 30 of this dictionary].—Further testimonies of the same orator, to the same point, may be seen in Havercamp's commentaries on the *Familiæ Romanæ* of Morel, p. 220.

Such is the conflicting language of the ancients on this subject. And from this diversity of opinion, Eckhel avows himself the more inclined to believe, that "*the genealogy was a fictitious one;* originating in the vanity so prevalent at that period, of hunting up a remote ancestry; abundant examples of which are furnished by the coins of the Calpurnii, the Marcii, and the Pomponii; not to mention the fabulous instances that occur in those of the Antonii, the Mamilii, and the Fabii.—In complaining of this very custom, Livy says—"In my opinion, history is vitiated by certain funereal eulogies, and by the false inscriptions on statues; whilst each family arrogates to itself, delusively, the renown of others' deeds and distinctions. The inevitable consequence has been the confounding of individual with national records."

[In his *Iconographie Romaine,* referring to the above observation of Eckhel in support of the opinion of those who deny that Marcus Brutus was descended from the ancient Brutus, Visconti intimates his non-concurrence on this point with Eckhel, and adduces the authority of Bayle for recognizing, as the more probable opinion, the validity of Brutus's genealogical pretensions—vol. i. 8vo. edit. p. 192.]

But wherever the truth may lie amongst these opposite statements and opinions, certain it is, that there were not wanting many, on the strength of this supposed relationship, to exhort Brutus to emulate the deeds of his ancestors, and this they did by distributing documents among the people. Even around the tribunal of M. Brutus (for he was Prætor Urbanus in the very year of Cæsar's murder), writing was discovered to this purport—"Thou sleepest, Brutus!"—and "Thou art *not* a Brutus."— *(Neque es, Brutus).*—Indeed the overthrow and destruction of kings were looked upon by the republicans as the peculiar province of the Bruti. Having made his general remarks as a requisite preliminary, the learned and judicious author of *Doctrina* proceeds to the task of considering the two coins separately, to the following effect:—

1. The first denarius presents on one side the head of L. Brutus; on the other that of Ahala. [See engraving in p. 30]. And this associating together of the two portraitures, in itself convincingly identifies the mintage with Marcus Brutus. For as on the father's side he was believed to trace his descent from Lucius Brutus, so on his mother Servilia's side, he undoubtedly reckoned among his progenitors Servilius Ahala, whose sole recorded claim to be remembered beyond his day, appears to rest on his having, as general of cavalry to the dictator Cincinnatus (B. C. 439), killed Sp. Mælius, on pretence that the latter was conspiring against the commonwealth.

2. The second coin, within a crown of oak leaves, presents what, from the legend, L. BRVTVS PRIM. COS. was evidently meant for the portrait of the *ancient* Brutus.—This type (observes Eckhel, vi. 22), bears reference to the state in which the republic was at the period of Cæsar's dictatorship (B. C. 44). For just as Lucius Brutus, after the expulsion of the kings, himself became PRIM*us* CO*n*S*ul,* so did Marcus Brutus, after the assassination of Julius, restore the ancient office of the Consulate, together with the liberties of the people, indicated by the *corona quernea.* The title of *Primus Consul,* in connection with the name of Lucius Junius Brutus, on this denarius, is amusingly as well as clearly illustrated by Suetonius, when (in *Cæsare,* ch. 80), he states that the following epigrammatic sentence was inscribed on the pedestal of Cæsar's statue :—

Brutus, quia reges ejecit, consnl primus factus est :
Hic (i. e. Cæsar) quia consules ejecit, rex postremo
   factus est.

Old Brutus, for causing all kings to be lacking
 At Rome, the first consulship gains :
Whilst Cæsar, because he sends consuls a-packing,
 Is, forthwith, made a king, for *his* pains.

The other side of this denarius exhibits the head of *Marcus* Brutus, representing him with a long and meagre visage. And that such was really his habit of body, may be gathered from an expression once used by Cæsar. For when M. Antonius and Dolabella were accused in his hearing of designs hostile to his person and government, he remarked, that he entertained no fears of those sleek and bushy men *(crinitos)*, but rather of the pale emaciated fellows, meaning Brutus and Cassius. (Plutarch, *in Cæs. M. Anton. et Bruto.*)—Shakspeare, in his play of Julius Cæsar, probably borrowing from this passage, turns the loan to good account, in making Cæsar thus address Mark Antony:—

" Let me have men about me that are fat ;
Sleek-headed men, and such as sleep a-nights.
Yon Cassius has a lean and hungry look :
He thinks too much ; such men are dangerous."
　　　　　　　　　　　Act 1, *Scene* 2.

It appears an extraordinary circumstance, that on coins should be introduced the portrait of of the very man who boasted of being the champion of freedom, when, in the independent days of the republic, such a distinction was never permitted; and first became included amongst the inordinate privileges heaped upon Cæsar himself. It might have been regarded as a flattering attention paid, without the knowledge of Brutus, by his lieutenants, whose names usually appear on his coins. But, if credit be given to Dion (xlvii. § 25), the type was struck with the consent, and by the direction, of Brutus himself.

On this same denarius Brutus is styled IMP*erator*, as he frequently is on others of his coins.—The time and occasion of his receiving the title are stated by Dion (as above), viz. that he made an expedition against the *Bessi*, a people of Thrace, " partly in order to chastise them for their hostility, and partly that he might gain for himself the title and dignity of *Imperator*, which would enable him the better to cope with Cæsar and Antony—and that he accomplished both those objects."—According to Plutarch *(in Brut.* c. 34), Brutus and Cassius together received each the title of IMP*erator*, by the acclamations of the army at Sardis.—*D. N. V.* vi. 22.

With regard to the epithet *primus*, employed in this instance, it is further to be observed, that Valerius Poplicola was also called *Consul primus*, because he was amongst the very first of those annually elected rulers of the early free republic.—The heads of both the Bruti—Lucius and Marcus—men chronologically separated from each others' times by an interval of more than 450 years—were conjoined on this denarius, clearly in order that he who slew Cæsar, might thereby shew forth his claim to kindred with the Brutus of ancient days, and his participation in like *glory* with his assumed ancestor.

" The civic (or oaken) crown which appears round each head of the two Bruti, alludes (says Riccio), to the victory won by the second Brutus over the adverse party, and to the rescue of Rome and her citizens out of the hands of those who usurped the sovereign power of the state."—See *Monete delle Ant. Fam. di Roma*, p. 120 et seq.

[A specimen of the above described denarius, in good condition, brought £26 at the sale of the Pembroke collection.]

BRUT*us* IMP*erator* L*ucius* PLAET*orius* CEST*ianus*. Head of Marcus Brutus.

Rev. EID*us* MAR*tiæ*. The pileus, or cap of

liberty, between two daggers. Silver of the Junia gens.

This rare and most remarkable silver coin, so important as a numismatic monument, Lucius Plætorius Cestianus, a *monetarius* as well as a *legatus* of Marcus Brutus, was the instrument of transmitting, as a record, to the most distant posterity. In describing it, Eckhel begins—*En pugiones*, &c.—" Observe the daggers employed in the perpetration of so fell a murder, brought before our eyes, on this coin—weapons, which, under the specious pretext of liberty, Brutus hesitated not to stain with the blood of that Cæsar, to whom personally he owed so much ; in the same deed a patriot and a cut-throat.—We have the testimony of Dion Cassius that the denarius [above engraved] was struck by order of Brutus himself; and since it graphically describes this numismatic gem, the author's words shall be given [See *D. N. V.* vi. p. 24, for both Greek and Latin :]—" And also on the coins, which he caused to be struck, he exhibited a likeness of himself, and a cap and two daggers; intimating by this type, and by the legend, that conjointly with Cassius, he had restored his country to liberty." The inscription EID. MAR. declares the fatal day, the ides of March, on which the bloody deed was done. The term *paricidium* was afterwards applied to these ides of March.

By way of counterpoise to the head of Julius Cæsar, struck on his coins, as Dictator, other coins, in opposition to his usurpation of absolute power at Rome, were minted in their turn by the partisans of the conspirators themselves, with the head of M. Brutus, and having on the other side, either the image of Brutus, the first Consul, or the two daggers, in allusion to the murder of Cæsar. "This (says Riccio) was for the purpose of shewing that as Lucius Brutus removed the ancient kings, so the poniards of Cassius and Brutus had, at a subsequent period of time, restored liberty to Rome, as symbolized by the cap."

Bimard de la Bastie (in his notes to Jobert), referring to this famous coin, observes that, though unquestionably genuine, both in gold and silver, yet that there is nothing in its appearance to justify the supposition that it was struck in Rome. The fact is that Brutus was at no time master of that city, nor was his party the strongest there. The above cited testimony of Dion decides the question as to who it was that caused this denarius to be minted ; and the time was that at which Brutus passed into Asia to join Cassius, after having rendered himself master of Macedonia and of a part of Greece.

[The foregoing cut is faithfully copied after the cast from a well-preserved specimen in the British Museum. There was another, forming part of the Pembroke collection, and described in the catalogue as "in very good condition, and which appeared to be a genuine specimen of this extremely rare and much falsified coin." This, in August 1848, brought £10 15s. The finest specimen that even the late Mr. Thomas could procure, obtained at the sale of his collection only £15 10s.—These sums, so disproportioned to the historical interest, as well as to the acknowledged rarity, and consequent high value of this denarius, would seem to indicate a prevalence of doubtfulness in the minds of connoisseurs present at the grand auctions in question. One is indeed almost ready to ask, whether there be such a thing as a genuine EID. MAR. of Marcus Brutus? so difficult is it to meet with one that embraces the triple requisites of being antique, *un*plated, and in good preservation.]

BRUTUS (Consularis Processus).—See Junia gens.

BRUTUS IMP.—*Obv.* Neptune.—*Rev.* Victoria.—See CASCA LONGUS.

BRUTUS (Q. CAEPIO) IMP.—*Rev.* Trophy.—See Servilia gens.

BRUTUS (CAEPIO) PRO. COS.—See LEIBERTAS.—Junia gens.

BRUTI. F. ALBINUS.—See Junia, Postumia, and Vibia families.

BRUTUS IMP.—Bare head of Marcus Junius Brutus, to the right, within a wreath of oak leaves.

Rev. CASCA LONGVS. A trophy between two prows: sometimes with, sometimes without, an insulated letter in the field.

In page 143, an engraving is given of a gold coin, which on one side presents the effigy of Brutus in the middle of a civic crown; and on the other that of Junius Brutus, from whom he claimed descent.—The above cut is from another coin, of the same metal, and which represents the head of this celebrated character within a similar crown. The trophy, raised upon the prows of ships, forming the type of the reverse, bears allusion to the success which attended the lieutenants of Brutus and Cassius, in a naval engagement, which they had with the fleet of the triumvirs, at the very time when the conspirators themselves were defeated by land.—The legend CASCA LONGVS points to Publius Servilius Casca; the man who struck the first blow at Cæsar, and who fought at Philippi. *Longus* is probably but the second surname of this same Casca.

It has already been remarked, with regard to coins stamped with the head of Brutus, that they were struck with his authority. They all combine to prove the immoderate ambition of Marcus Junius. The individuals of his party (observes Visconti), would not have dared, each independently of the other, to cause his effigy to be stamped on Roman money, in imitation of those abuses, which were found fault with in the government of Cæsar, if they had not been well assured of the consent and approbation of their chief. It is even matter of astonishment, that a like example should not have been followed by the lieutenants of Cassius, and that his head also should not have been struck on the money which he ordered to be coined.—*Icon. Rom.* i. 212.

We might have supposed (adds the same distinguished writer), that the portraits of Brutus, after his defeat and death, would have disappeared from the Roman world. But party spirit long survives the events that have decided its lot; and besides there is nothing so difficult to destroy as numismatic monuments.

The coin whence Visconti made his engraving, was at the time in the cabinet of the learned Abbé San Clemente, at Cremona. A similar one exists in the imperial cabinet of Vienna.—(Eckhel, *Catal. Mus. Cæs.* part ii. pl. i.)

[A very fine specimen of this consular aureus, weight 125 grs. brought at the Devonshire sale, in 1844, £17 17s., and at the sale of Mr. White's collection, in November, 1848, it obtained £37. The Pembroke specimen, lot 350, in the most perfect state of preservation, size 4½, 123 3-10 grs. brought £42.]

BUCA. L.—Head of Venus, with mitre, earrings, and necklace.

Rev. A man wrapped in a night-dress, lying asleep on the grass, with his head resting on a stone, to whom are present Diana and Victory.—A rare denarius of the Æmilia gens.

The figure in the recumbent posture is Sulla, to whom appeared in his sleep, Diana Tifatina, his protectress (according to the explanation of Borghesi), who with a rod came to awaken him, accompanied by Victory, who invited him to follow her and destroy his enemies, the partizans of Marius. It is moreover affirmed, that this took place in Sulla's consulate of the year U. C. 666 (B. C. 88), when returning from Campania, where he had been commanding at Nola the army destined for the Mithridatic war, he entered Rome; caused the tribune Sulpicius to be put to death; and drove away Marius from the city. Venus was the especial object of Sulla's adoration, in remembrance of whom he caused her effigy to be struck on the obverse of this coin. (See Riccio, p. 10.)—With regard to the name which appears on this denarius, it applies to L. Æmilius

Buca, the father of him who was one of the quatuorumviri of Julius Cæsar, and is supposed to have been quæstor under Sulla, in commemoration of whose alleged dream he struck this curious coin. (Eckhel, v. 121).—For a denarius struck by the son, L. BVCA, see CAESAR DICT. PERPETVVS.

BUCKLER, or Shield.—See *Clypeus*—also *Ancilia.*

BULLA, a small round ornament of gold, hollow in the inside, worn by Roman children of quality, together with the prætextal robe, and which hung pendant from their neck, until they attained the age of 17 years, when both that and the prætexta were exchanged for the toga virilis. Once arrived at adolescence, they consecrated the relinquished dress and decoration of childhood to the *Dii Lares*, household deities, as Persius thus indicates—

Bullaque succinctis Laribus donata pependit.

Macrobius relates the circumstance which led to the use of the *bulla* among the Romans. In the war which ended in the triumph of Tarquinius Priscus over the Sabines, that king's son, aged only 14 years, having distinguished himself by his valour, and killed an enemy with his own hand, his father publicly eulogized him, and conferred on him the honour of a golden bulla; (et pro concione laudavit et bulla aurea donavit). At first this ornamental privilege was granted only to patricians; but it was, in process of time, allowed to all children who wore the prætexta.—See the anecdote of young M. LEPIDVS in Æmilia gens, p. 14.

BUST.—This term, derived from the Italian *Busto* and the French *Buste*, is applied to such representations of the human figure as do not extend below the waist. One of the most ancient modes of representing gods and heroes, under human features, was that of giving only their heads. The invention of busts, properly so called, is one that dates from a much later epoch. These exhibit sometimes the head with the shoulders, and a small part of the chest— at other times the head with the whole chest; and sometimes, but very rarely, they include a full half of the body. The Romans called these representations of the head and part of the breast of the human figure, *imagines clypeorum*, or simply *clypei*. The *clypei imperatorum*, of which ancient authors often speak, were but portraits of a similar description. To the Roman custom of placing the busts of emperors and other great personages on their coins, is to be ascribed one of the most easy as well as certain modes of ascertaining the identity of a vast number of unknown sculptured heads, found from time to time amongst the ruins of ancient buildings, some with and others without the trunks. But though a comparison of busts with coins and medallions, in order to discover the person they represent, is the most likely to be successful, yet it is a method attended with some difficulties. On coins the same individual is often figured in many very different ways—either according to his appearance at different periods of life; or

because the portrait seen in profile often differs in aspect widely from that of the full face.— Besides which, the workmanship of coins, particularly those of the lower empire, was of an inferior kind, and executed probably after ill-designed portraits, especially such as were struck in the provinces.

The study of antique busts and heads cannot fail to be of great utility. To the antiquary and the historian they furnish matter for reflection on the form of vestments, or the ornaments of the person, or the head-dress and the changes which it underwent, also on the attributes of different deities, and on the lineaments of celebrated men. The artist, on the same subject of attention, finds his admiration excited by the perfection with which they are wrought, and the skill of the ancients in imparting to their portraiture something of the ideal, yet without impairing the likeness.—See Millin, *Dict. des Beaux Arts.*

Busts—Ornaments of.—The busts which appear on coins are accompanied by certain symbols peculiar to them, especially when the two arms are visible, as is generally the case on medallions; and even on the smallest coins of the *Lower* Empire. The princes represented on these monuments often hold a *globe* in their hand, to shew that they are the masters of the world. This globe is sometimes surmounted by a winged Victory, which holds a crown or wreath, designating that it is to Victory the reigning prince owes his imperial throne. The *sceptre* which they hold in their hand, when in the consular habit, is surmounted by a globe charged with an eagle, to shew by these marks of sovereign power that the prince governs by himself. From the time of Augustus the consular sceptre, to which reference is here made, appears constantly on the imperial series of Roman coins. When the persons represented are in arms, besides the *helmet* and *buckler*, they have generally a javelin in the hand or on the shoulder, as on brass medallions of Diocletian, S. Severus, Probus. (See the respective biographical notices of those emperors).

The *thunderbolt*, which is sometimes placed behind the head of a prince, as on a medal of Augustus, marks the sovereign authority, and indicates the assumption of a power equal to that of the gods.—The *crescent* is often employed as a support to the busts of empresses, who aspired to hold in the State, of which the emperor was assumed to be the sun, that place which was assigned to the moon in the heavens. (See Jobert edited by Bimard, vol. i. 370, et seq.)—On coins of the lower empire, the globe is seen surmounted by a *cross*, especially after the reign of Constantine, when the Christian Religion having been fully established as that of the State, emperors professed their wish to indicate thereby that they regarded themselves as holding the empire from Jesus Christ, whose bust the Byzantine emperors had the presumption to place on the reverse of their coins, and named for that ostensible reason, REX REGNANTIVM—the King of Kings.

BUTEO—the Latin name of a bird of the hawk genus, was a cognomen of the Fabii.—Pliny says (L. x. c. 8) Buteonem (accipitrem) hunc appellant Romani, familia etiam (Fabiorum) ex eo cognominata, cum prospero auspicio in ducis navi consedisset. On a common denarius of the Fabia gens, near the epigraph C. FABI. C. F. appears a bird which, says Eckhel, is doubtless the *Buteo.* v. p. 137.—*Morell. Thes.*

BUTHROTUM, a maritime city of Epirus (now *Butronto* or *Butrinto*, in Albania, opposite Corfu).—Pliny mentions Buthrotum (L. iv. c. i.) as a Roman colony; and Cellarius *(Not. Orb. Ant.* i. p. 876) so denominates it. Its coins consist of Latin colonial autonomes in brass, and of Latin colonial imperial, also in brass, all rare.—Vaillant gives the annexed, which, exhibiting the name of *Augusta*, warrants the inference that the colony of *Buthrotum* was founded by Augustus.

C. A. BVT. EX. D. D.—*Colonia Augusta, Buthrotum, ex decreto Decurionum.* Head of Augustus.

Rev. Q. NAEVI. SVRA. A. HIP. TVL. NICER. IIVIR. B.—*Quinto Nævio Sura, Aulo Hippio, Tullo Nicereo, Duumviris Bis.*—A figure standing in a military dress, his right hand hanging down, his left hand holds a rolled-up sheet, with something like strings attached.

The following also appears in Vaillant, as from the French King's cabinet, and of the highest rarity: BVTHR. AVGVSTVS. *Buthroti Augustus.* Head of the Emperor without laurel.

Rev. P. POMPON. *Publio Pomponio.* Bridge with three arches.—Engraved in *Morell. Thes. Impp. Rom.* T. iii. TAB. xxxiv. No. 16.

The reverse type alludes to a remarkably noble aqueduct, which, after having conferred upon Buthrotum the rank of a Roman colony, Augustus caused to be erected in the *Sinus Ambracius*, for the convenience of that city, and by which, according to Pliny, the waters of the river Acheron were conveyed from the lake *Thesprotiæ Acherucia*, on arches for many thousand yards. In grateful recollection of this work, and the benefit thereby provided for them, the inhabitants of Buthrotum placed the head of Augustus on this coin of the colony he had established.—See Vaillant, *in Col.* i. p. 14.

BYZANTIUM, a capital city of Thrace, founded by *Bysas*, a general of the Megarensians. Constantine the Great made it, about A. D. 330, the seat of empire, and after his name it was and is still called *Constantinopolis* or Constantinople. In 1453 it was captured by Mahomet II. (when Constantine Palæologus, the last Emperor of the East, was slain), and it remains to this day the seat of the Turkish government.

The coins of Byzantium were autonomous till the reign of Caligula, from which period they come into the Greek series, down to about the reign of Gallienus. Constantine and his family caused coins to be struck at Byzantium, with Latin legends and types, and with the inscription CONSTANTINOPOLIS.——(See Banduri, and the *Fam. Aug. Byzant.* of Ducange.]

Byzantium was one of the cities which de-

clared for Pescennius Niger, when he aspired to the empire on the death of Pertinax (A. D. 192). And "of all those who took part with this unfortunate warrior, none distinguished themselves so much as the Byzantines, who obstinately refused to submit till, after a three years' siege, they were reduced to the eating of human flesh : it is only to know that Severus, that stranger to mercy, was the conqueror, and the result may be anticipated—all the fortifications and public edifices were destroyed, the garrison massacred, and the inhabitants stripped and sold into slavery."—(Capt. Smyth, p. 177).

C.

C.—Caius, or Cæsar. The C. by itself signifies sometimes Caius, at other times Cæsar.

C.—*Cæcilius.*—See Cæcilia gens.

C.—This letter by itself may also signify—1. Carthage.—2. Censor.—3. Centum.—4. Civis.—5. Clypeus (a shield).—6. Cohors (a cohort).—7. Colonia.—8. Consultum (a decree).—9. Cornelius.

C. Condemno.—A. C. Absolvo-Condemno, on a coin of Cassia gens.

C. Consul.—P. C. Proconsul.—C. V. P. P. Consul Quintum, Pater Patriæ; on a brass medallion of Commodus.

C.—Constantinopolis.

C. Consulto.—S. C. Senatus Consulto.

C. Corona. C. CIV. *Corona Civica* (Colonial).

C. Cusus.—See C. A. P. R.

CA. CæsareaAugusta.—See *CaesareaPhilippi.*

CA. Capitolina.—CO. AE. CA.—See *Aelia Capitolina,* p. 15.

CAE. or CAES.—Cæsar or Cæsari.

CAE. or COE. or CAEL.—Cælius.

CAE.—Cæcina, Cæcilia.

CABELLIO (Galliæ Narbonensis) *colonia.*—This town, the *Caballio* of Strabo, is mentioned by Pliny (L. iii. c. 4), with Aquæ Sextiæ (Aix), Apta Julia (Apt), Nemausus (Nismes), and other *oppida Latina*, in the Narbonensian Gaul.—It is now called Cavaillon, in the Comtat Venaissin (department of Vaucluse), southern France. The coins of Cabellio are in silver and brass; and they prove the correctness of Ptolemy in stating it to have been a colony of the Romans. The following seven varieties are recognised by Mionnet and De la Saussaye :

Latin Autonomes.—1. The first exhibits on the obverse side, the head of a woman, and has for its legend CABE ; on the reverse are a cornucopiæ within a laurel crown, and the letters LEPI.—Small silver.——Engraved in Akerman, Coins of Gallia, p. 136, plate xiv. No. 12.

2. *Obv.* CABE. The same female head; and on the *rev.* COL. Helmeted head.—Small brass. Engraved in Akerman, pl. xiv. No. 14.

Consular.—3. *Obv.* CABE. Head of Janus. *Rev.* M. ANT. Bare head of M. Antony.

4. *Obv.* CABE. Head of Janus.—*Rev.* M. ANT. A lion walking.—Brass.—Engraved in Akerman, pl. xiv. No. 13.

Imperial.—5. *Obv.* CABE. Female head turreted.—*Rev.* IMP. CAESAR (Augustus) and cornucopiæ.—[This Morel *(in Thesaur.)* assigns to Æmilia gens; but Mionnet catalogues it as minted by the above named colony, under Augustus.]

Augustus.—6. *Obv.* CABE. Woman with turreted head.—*Rev.* IMP. CAESAR; a cornucopiæ. —[This Mionnet quotes from the cabinet of the Marquis De la Goy, and also ascribes it to the reign of Augustus.]

Augustus.—7. *Obv.* COL. CABE. Turreted female head.—*Rev.* IMP. CAES. AVGVST. COS. XI. A cornucopiæ.—Engraved in Akerman, pl. xiv. No. 15.

Vaillant describes a large brass, bearing on its obverse the helmeted head of a man, and the legend LEPIDVS; behind the head, in smaller characters, PON.—The legend of reverse is COL. CAB. and the type a head of Ceres crowned with corn ears. Of this, however, neither Mionnet, nor Akerman, takes any notice.

CABIRO.—See *Deo Cabiro.*

CABIRUS, son of Vulcan and Cabira, the daughter of Proteus, one of the tutelary gods of the Macedonians.—On a third brass of Claudius Gothicus, a coin of great rarity, is read DEO CABIRO; the type presents Cabirus, as a deity, standing with the *pileus* on his head, a hammer in his right hand, and nippers in his left, as if assuming the attributes of his reputed father.

CACUS, son of Vulcan, a gigantic monster, whose mouth vomited forth volumes of flame, and who, having stolen some of the cattle which Hercules had captured from Geryon, was attacked and strangled by that hero. In memory of the fabled victory, an annual fête was held in honour of Hercules, on mount Aventine.— On a bronze medallion of Antoninus Pius, Hercules is figured, with the spoils of the Nemæan lion on his left arm, the club in his right hand; and near him Cacus is extended on the ground, before the entrance of his cavern.—See engraving in Millin, *Gal. Mythol.* T. ii. pl. cv. 447.

CADUCEUS, or *Caduceum,* a wand or rod, entwined at one end by two serpents, each of whose bodies folds again in the form of two half circles, whilst the head passes above the wand. It was an attribute peculiar to Mercury. Prudence is generally supposed to be represented by these two serpents, and the wings which are sometimes added to the Caduceus, are the symbols of diligence, both needful qualities in the pursuit of trade and commerce, which Mercury patronized. It was also the symbol of peace and concord, which that deity is related to have received from Apollo in return for the lyre.

The Caduceus is found on the Roman family coins of Cestia, Claudia, Licinia, Plætoria, Sepullia—and in the imperial series, on the coins of Julius Cæsar, Augustus, M. Antony, Tiberius, Nero, Vespasian, Titus, Domitian, Nerva, Trajan, Postumus.

The Caduceus *in the hand of Mercury,* is seen on coins of the Emperors Tiberius (Colonial), Antoninus Pius, M. Aurelius, Herennius, Hostilianus, Gallienus, Postumus (MERCVRIO FELICI), Claudius Gothicus, Numerianus, &c.

The Caduceus *in the hand of a female figure,* such as the personifications of Felicity, Peace, Concord, Security—appears on coins of the Emperors, from Julius Cæsar, and Augustus to Constantine the Great.

The Caduceus *between two cornucopiæ,* indicates Concord, and is found on medals of Augustus, M. Antony, Vespasian, Titus, Domitian, Nerva, Anton. Pius, M. Aurelius, Albinus.—On a coin of Augustus we see three hands joined; with a caduceus, the fasces, the sacrificial axe, and globe—thus associating the caduceus with other symbols of power.

A Caduceus *and two corn-ears, held by two right hands joined,* is also seen on coins of the early empire; as on a large brass of Drusus jun. and in the instance of the FIDES PVBLICA, silver of Titus, and second brass of Domitian. —See a cut from the latter, in left hand column of this page.—See also *Mercury.*

CAECILIA gens.—At first patrician (there were nobles descended from the Metelli), afterwards plebeian, but of great antiquity, this family gave a host of illustrious citizens to the republic. It was divided into many surnames: the principal was Metellus, several members of which distinguished branch bore the names of conquered countries, as *Macedonicus, Numidicus, Balearicus,* and *Creticus.*—Its gold coins are extremely rare. The silver common; except pieces restored by Trajan, which are of very great rarity.—The name of the Cæcilia gens appears on Cistophori of Pergamus. The brass money are *asses* or parts of the *as.*—The following are among those denarii which possess a high historical interest, viz.:—

[1.]

1.—Head of Apollo, laureated, and with hair in ringlets; behind it ROMA; before it X.

Rev.—M. METELLVS. Q. F. written circularly. The type consists of an elephant's head in the centre of a Macedonian shield; the whole within a crown of laurel.

2.—ROMA. Galeated head of Rome; before it X.

Rev.—C. METELLVS. A male figure, perhaps of Jupiter, crowned by a flying Victory, in a biga of elephants.

[2.]

These, and many other coins with various types, were struck by Marcus and Caius Cecilius Metellus, sons of Quintus Metellus Macedonicus, in reference to the two principal glories of the family; that is to say, the overthrow of the Pseudo-Philippus (Andriscus) in Macedonia, defeated and taken prisoner by their father, the prætor, in 606 (B. c. 148), in the third Punic war; for which he enjoyed the honours of the triumph; and on which occasion shone a multiplicity of Macedonian shields, such as are found represented on coins; and also the great victory gained in 504 (B. c. 250) fifteenth year of the first Punic war, by the proconsul Lucius Metellus, their progenitor, over Hasdrubal, near Panormus (Palermo). Amongst the spoils were 120 elephants which he transported to Rome, and which formed the most astonishing feature of his magnificent triumph. This circumstance is modestly recorded by a simple biga of elephants on denarii, and by the head of an elephant, on brass pieces of this family.—See Riccio, p. 37.

3.—Female head; before it a stork.

Rev.—Q. C. M. P. I. Quintus Cæcilius Metellus Pius Imperator. An elephant walking.

This coin also alludes to the victory won by Quintus Metellus, over the Carthaginians, in Sicily, recorded on the preceding denarius.— [The same silver coin restored by Trajan, is of the highest degree of rarity—valued by Mionnet at 100 fr. and by Riccio at 25 *piastre.*—Engraved in Morel, and Riccio.]

4.—Q. METE. The winged head of Pallas, near it X.

Rev.—Jupiter, in a quadriga, holding his right hand a branch, in his left a thunderbolt.

Amongst the *Metelli* who bore the name of Quintus, by far the most celebrated was he who, as above adverted to, triumphed over Andriscus, pretender to the name of Philip, and to the kingdom of Macedonia, and who, on account of that victory, obtained the cognomen of Macedonicus. Velleius (cited by Havercamp) speaks of his singularly fortunate destiny. For besides his splendid triumphs, his ample honours, and his high position in the republic, he brought up four sons, at an advanced period of his life, beheld them arrive at maturity of age, and left them all occupying the most honourable situations. His funeral bier was carried to the *rostra*, by these four sons, one of whom was a censor and of consular rank, another also of consular rank, the third a consul, and the fourth a successful candidate for the consulship.—Eckhel agrees with Havercamp in ascribing this coin to the above-mentioned Q. Metellus; but considers it to have been struck before that prætorian personage achieved his great victory, and when he was in

the lower magistracy. Nor does he think that the type of " Jupiter in a quadriga " has reference to the Macedonian triumph of Metellus.—See *D. N. V.* vol. v. 151.

5.—L. METEL. A. ALB. S. F. Laureated head of Apollo, to the right; below a star.

Rev.—C. MAL. below ROMA. A male figure seated, to the left, upon shields, armed with hasta and parazonium, and crowned by Victory standing behind.

[5.]

This, not scarce but remarkable, coin, struck in honour, says Riccio, of Warrior-Rome *(di Roma guerriera)*, crowned by Victory, was so emblematical, that the conspirators of the Italian League imitated the type exactly, only substituting *Italia* for *Roma*, with the relative legends.

It seems indubitable that this denarius was struck by Aulus Postumius Albinus, son of Spurius, by *Lucius* Cæcilius Metellus, and by Caius Publicius Malleolus, contemporaneously monetal triumvirs; and the first of them, viz., Aulus Postumius Albinus, being consul in 655 (B. c. 99), it is the opinion of Cavedoni and of Eckhel also, that the mintage of this denarius is to be assigned to the 630th year of Rome (B. c. 124).—See *Monete delle Fam.* &c. p. 38.

6.—Q. METEL. PIVS. A laureated and bearded head, to the right, with hair in curls hanging behind.

Rev.—SCIPIO IMP. An elephant walking,

[6.]

7.—Q. METEL. PIVS SCIPIO IMP. A female figure, almost naked in front, with the head of a lion or panther, stands holding the nilometer (a measure of the increase of the Nile); above are the letters G. T. A. *(genius tutelaris Ægypti* or *Africæ.)*

Rev.—P. CRASSVS. JVN. LEG. PRO. PR. Victory holding the caduceus in the left hand, and a round shield in her right.

[This legend of reverse refers to Crassus Junianus, one of Scipio's lieutenants, who served with the title of legatus proprætor.—For an engraving of the coin, see *Morell. Fam. Rom. Cæcilia.*]

8.—Q. METEL. SCIPIO IMP. Female head covered with the skin of an elephant's head, before it an ear of corn, below it a plough.

Rev.—EPPIVS LEG. F. C. (*fieri curavit*). Hercules naked, in repose, resting on the club and lion's spoils.—See, in adjoining column, cut 8.

9.—METEL. PIVS. SCIP. IMP. Head of Jupiter, beneath it is the head of an eagle and a sceptre.

Rev.—CRASS. IVN. LEG. PROPR. Curule chair between a hand closed, and an ear of corn; above are the cornucopiæ and the balance.

[9.]

This in gold (see Pembroke and Eckhel) stands in the highest degree of rarity.

With these, and several other coins, honour was rendered to the warlike virtues of that Scipio, who was adopted by Q. Cæcilius Metellus Pius, pontifex maximus. He was the son of P. Cornelius Scipio Nasica, B. C. 94 but by Metellus's adoption of him, he passed from the Cornelia gens to that of the Cæcilia. They set forth the exploits of the same Metellus Scipio in his African campaign against Cæsar, after the tragic end of Pompey. These events are indicated by the elephants, by the ears of corn, by the tutelary genius of Egypt or of Africa, and by other African symbols and emblems, which indeed have reference to other historical facts connected with the ancient fame of the Cornelii and the Cæcilii; namely, the military enterprises of the first Scipio in Africa, already alluded to, and also those of Cæcilius Numidicus, and Cæcilius Macedonicus. They also call to remembrance the piety of Q. Cæcilius Metellus, son of Numidicus, who received, in B. C. 99, the surname of PIVS, for having obtained, by the affectionate earnestness of his appeal to the people, the recall of his father from banishment. They moreover refer to the Sicilian victories of the eldest of the Metelli (L. Cæcilius) over the Carthaginians, in his consulate; and likewise to the devoted courage displayed by the same person, in saving, but with the loss of his sight, the Palladium and other sacred objects from a fire which consumed the temple of Vesta, B. C. 241 : in acknowledgment of which service he was allowed thereafter, the till then forbidden privilege, of being conveyed to the senate-house, in a carriage. This is symbolised by the head of Piety and also by the stork.—Lastly, these coins bear record to his Pontificate, and to the title of IMP*erator*, conferred upon him by the soldiers —besides various appointments to the office of legatus, and of proprætor.—See Riccio, p. 39, plates ix. and x.

The following denarius, numbered 8, belongs to the Eppia gens; but as it distinctly refers to Metellus Scipio, it is inserted here, as illustrative of his connection with the Cæcilia family, whose worthies are named, and their public ser-

vices alluded to, on denarii, whence the preceding cuts have been engraved.

[8.]

CAECINA, a surname of a Roman : to what family it belongs is not ascertained. There are two varieties. The brass coins bearing the head of Janus, or the head of Pallas, on the obverse; and the abbreviation A. CAE. *Aulus Cæcina*, a ship's prow, and ROMA, on the reverse; are *asses*, or parts of the *as*.—See them engraved in Riccio, pp. 39, 40, pl. x. Nos. 1 and 2.

CAEDICIUS, a surname which, according to *Morell. Thesaur. Fam. Rom.* p. 526, belongs to the Cædicia family, plebeian but of consular rank. A denarius, engraved in TAB. xi. of *Numi Consulares*, has on one side a female head, and on the other, two togated figures standing, with hands joined, and behind one of them, the fasces with axes. The legend of the reverse is Q. CAEDICI Q. F. EX. S. C. Quintus Cædicius, Quinti Filius, Ex Senatus Consulto; at the bottom ROMA.

CAEPIO, surname allusive to the large size of the head.—See Servilia gens.

CAES. or CAESS. or CAESSS.—Cæsar or Cæsars. The double SS marks two Cæsars, and SSS denote three Cæsars.

CAES.—*Cæsarea*, surname of a colony founded by Augustus.—See *Antiochia, Pisidiæ*, p. 52.

CAES.—*Cæsarea*, surname of a colony.—See *Cæsarea Samaritis*, and *Cæsarea Philippi*.

CAES. DIC. QUAR. *Cæsar Dictator Quartum*. Cæsar Dictator for the fourth time. On a gold coin of Julius.

CAES. DIVI. F.——*Cæsar Divi Filius*.—Cæsar son of the Divine Julius. On coins of Augustus.

CAESAR PONT. MAX.—*Cæsar Pontifex Maximus*. Cæsar, Supreme Pontiff.

CAESAR DIC*tator* PERPET*uus*—Cæsar, Perpetual Dictator.

[1.]

CAESAR CAIUS JULIUS, one of the greatest men of whom history has handed down the deeds, or to whom coins have secured a perpetuity of remembrance, was of the Julia gens— a race who assumed to have derived their descent from Ascanius, otherwise called Iulus, son of

Æneas. Taking up the prevailing opinion, Virgil says—

Julius à magno demissum nomen Iulo.

According to Pliny, the surname of *Cæsar*, which his family bore, was derived from some ancestor, who had been taken, by incision, from the womb of his mother. Be this as it may, he was son of L. Julius Cæsar (prætor), and of Aurelia. The year of his birth, at Rome, was the 654th of the city (B. C. 100), in the consulship of C. Marius and L. Valerius Flaccus; which calculation (not undisputed) makes him six years younger than Pompeius Magnus and Marcus Tullius Cicero. His mother, who exercised a vigilant superintendence over her children's education, took the greatest interest in the advancement and welfare of her son; who on his part appears to have been affectionately and reverentially attached to her.

When as yet a mere boy, Julius was elected to the dignified office of *Flamen Dialis*, through the interest of Caius Marius, who had married his aunt Julia (B. C. 87). And after the death of that celebrated Roman, he took for his wife Cornelia, daughter of L. Cinna (B. C. 83), whom he refused to repudiate, although Sulla, greatly enraged against him for having joined the popular party, had commanded him to do so. This characteristic display of resolution, however, had the effect of placing his life in great danger, from the anger of the dictator, who at length, but with reluctance, was induced to pardon him; still meeting the plea of youth and insignificance urged in his favour by Cæsar's friends and intercessors, with the prophetic remark, that "in *that* boy there were many Mariuses (multos ei Marios), and that he would eventually be the ruin of the patrician order."

Quitting Rome for Asia (B. C. 81), after the conclusion of the Mithridatic war, he was sent by Minucius Thermus from Mytilene, on a mission to Nicomedes III. King of Bithynia, which having fulfilled, he returned to his general, by whom, for his conduct at the siege of Mytilene, he was rewarded with a civic crown. The death of Sulla occurring B. C. 78, whilst Cæsar was serving in Cilicia, under the command of P. Sulpicius, he instantly returned to Rome; and the following year, gained great credit and popularity for his ability and eloquence in accusing Dolabella of extortion in his government of Macedonia. He had then scarcely completed his 22nd year; and to perfect himself in oratory, in which ultimately he was considered second only to Cicero, he undertook a voyage to Rhodes. On this occasion, the young man displayed a fine example of promptitude and intrepidity; for being captured by pirates, and ransomed by a contribution of fifty talents raised for his liberation by a number of Greek maritime cities, he, with a hastily manned fleet of Milesian vessels, attacked the pirates, whom he captured and caused to be crucified.—In B. C. 74, he passed over from Rhodes into Asia, at the commencement of the second Mithridatic war. The same year he returned to Rome,

having in his absence been elected Pontiff, in the room of Aurelius Cotta, his uncle. Besides this appointment, through patrician interest, he was soon created Military Tribune against a powerful competitor, by dint of popular favour. Next he went as Quæstor to Spain, and at Gades (Cadiz), on seeing an effigy of Alexander the Great, he shed ambitious tears. Returned once more to Rome, and his first wife Cornelia being dead, Cæsar, in B. C. 67, married Pompeia, the daughter of Q. Pompeius Rufus and of Cornelia, daughter of Sulla. Having thus united himself to the house, Julius actively promoted the views, and efficiently aided the proceedings, of Pompey. In 688 (B. C. 66), he was elected one of the Curule Ediles; and the following year, having M. Bibulus for his colleague, served the office with unprecedented magnificence. Bibulus largely shared in the cost of the public games; but to Cæsar (immeasurably deep in debt) was awarded all the credit of the liberality, and all the applause of the people.

In the year U. C. 691 (B. C. 63), M. Tullius Cicero and C. Antony being consuls, on the death of Metellus Pius, Cæsar was declared Pontifex Maximus. On this occasion he caused munificent largesses to be distributed to the people; he having predicted to his mother, just before he went down to the *comitia*— "This day you will see your son either Pontifex Maximus, or an exile." (Plutarch, *in Cæs.*)— He had, however, already been enrolled in the Pontifical college, during his absence in Asia.

In 692 (B. C. 62), in the consulship of D. Junius Silanus and L. Licinius Murena, he was made *Prætor Urbanus*. After his prætorship (laden with debts and unable to face his creditors), he went as pro-consul into Lusitania; and there, in the following year, after vanquishing enemies, whom he did not find such, but rendered them so, through his ambition of a triumph and spoil, he was made *Imperator*.

[2.]

694 (B. C. 60), returning to Rome, and going to the *comitia*, he canvassed at the same time for a Triumph and for the Consulate; and being unable to attain both those objects (for he could not, without being personally present, be a candidate for the Consulate, and on the other hand, had he entered the city as a private individual, he could not afterwards, according to law, enjoy a Triumph)—he relinquished the latter, and was created for the year 695 (B. C. 59) Consul, with M. Bibulus. He carried his Agrarian law by force, against the protests and edicts of his colleague, and obtained from the Senate the government of Illyricum, and Gallia Citerior and Ulterior, as pro-consul, with three legions, for five years; at the expiration of

which, aided by Pompey and M. Crassus, he extorted another five years. His victories, during this period, over the Helveti, Germani, Galli, and Britanni, are well known. About this time, Cæsar gave his daughter in marriage to Pompey, and married himself Calpurnia, daughter of L. Piso, consul the following year.

After having been occupied, during the years 703 and 704 (B. c. 51 and 50), in completing the pacification of Gaul, Cæsar, in the spring of 705 (B. c. 49), began to approach nearer to Rome, and to bestow his attention on the affairs of the city, where circumstances were already occurring, which soon resulted in a total rupture of good understanding between Pompey and himself.

In 705 (B. c. 49), during the consulships of C. Claudius Marcellus and L. Cornelius Lentulus, the civil war with Pompey was commenced. Having passed the Rubicon, and driven Pompey, with the consuls, into Greece, he entered Rome, and broke into the treasury.—Going thence into Spain, that he might leave nothing unguarded in his rear, he reduced to submission, on the 2nd of August, Petreius and Afranius, generals of Pompey's legions, and having taken Massilia (Marseilles), returned to Rome; where he found that in his absence he had been appointed Dictator, for the purpose of holding *comitia* to elect the consuls; but he abdicated this office in eleven days after, with the view of pursuing Pompeius Magnus into Greece.

706 (B. c. 48). Consul for the second time, with P. Servilius Vatia Isauricus as colleague; having been first defeated at Dyrrhachium (Durazzo), he turned the tables at Pharsalia, in Thessaly, on the 5th of the ides of Sextilis, which day, *in the anticipatory Julian year*, fell in the month of June. (See Eckhel's remarks on the Cæsarian Æra, vol. iv. p. 400).—On the news of this victory reaching Rome, he was again created Dictator for a whole year; an honour which was subsequently renewed every year. Having followed the fugitive Pompey, he found him dead in Egypt; and there, ensnared by the charms of Cleopatra, he undertook a rash war with her brother Ptolemy, with the view of giving her the entire sovereignty of Egypt.

707 (B. c. 47), he took Alexandria on the 27th of March. Having put Ptolemy to death, he gave Egypt into the hands of Cleopatra. He then hurried his army against Pharnaces, the King of Bosphorus, and defeated him on the 2nd of August.—Returning to Rome, he put down the commotions that were going on there, and made preparations for the African war,—a war which took its rise out of the party feelings of animosity, engendered in the collision at Pharsalia; but owing to the accession of Juba to the throne of Numidia, one environed with danger, he passed over into Africa, prior to the winter solstice.

708 (B. c. 46.) Being Consul for the third time, with M. Æmilius Lepidus as his colleague, he defeated Scipio, Juba, and Petreius, at Thapsus, in Africa, on the 8th of the ides of April. Returning to the city, he celebrated during four days, four distinct triumphs, respectively referring to the Gauls, Egypt, Pharnaces, and Juba. He next prepared for a war in Spain with the sons of Pompey.

[3.]

709 (B. c. 45). Dictator for the third time (CAESAR DIC. TER.) and Consul for the fourth time, without colleague, he gained a difficult victory over the Pompeians at Munda, in the spring of the year, and at the time of the celebration of the festival of Bacchus (in March), the tidings of the victory reaching Rome on the day before the *Parilia*. On his return, he celebrated a triumph, such as had never occurred before, over vanquished *citizens*. By his ostentatious ambition of becoming a *king*, and by the assumption of honours too lofty for mortal man, he incurred the hatred of many individuals, and the envy of all classes.

710 (B. c. 44). Appointed Perpetual Dictator (CAESAR DIC. PERPETVVS) and Consul for the fifth time, with M. Antony as his colleague, whilst meditating a campaign against the Getæ and Parthians, he was poniarded in the senate-house, in the ides of March, by a conspiracy of haughty republicans, set on foot by Brutus and Cassius.—See BRVTVS EID. MAR. p. 145.

Cæsar was in his 56th year at the time of his assassination. A man, above all others, marvellously accomplished in the arts of both peace and war; one than whom antiquity cannot produce a more distinguished example. Noble and commanding in person, of lofty stature and fair complexion, his black eyes were piercing, and his whole countenance replete with expression. He seldom wore a beard (see BARBA), and towards the close of his career he had, what to him was said to have been a great annoyance, a bald head. Naturally of a delicate constitution, he strengthened and invigorated himself by a course of temperance in eating and drinking; and such was the firm state of his health, thus carefully sustained, that there was scarcely any degree of bodily fatigue or of mental exertion, which he was not able to encounter. Acute in intellect, he possessed an eloquence, both natural and cultivated by the study of literature—witness those inimitable "Commentaries" which have immortalized him as a writer. With a spirit prompt and daring, in peril collected and undaunted, he exhibited sagacity of the highest order, both in foreseeing difficulties, and in extricating himself therefrom, when most beset. Having energy for any enterprise, and patience to bring it to an issue, he proved himself at once wary and adventurous. Generally prudent in planning, always skilful in executing, with an unexcelled celerity in catching advantages, he was at the same time so resolute under reverses as never to lose his perfect self-possession.—When this bold leader of the Roman legions invaded Britain, though the wars in Gaul and Germany were unfinished, he, to ensure the passage, personally sounded the channel. Fifty pitched battles attested his military prowess; and, superior equally to the superstitions of augury, and to the contagious influence of despondency or of panic, he, on several occasions, by his individual bravery turned the tide of battle, when victory was declaring against him. His good fortune (greater perhaps than ever fell to the lot of any other mortal) never deserted him, notwithstanding his frequent rash and ill-considered plans and proceedings. To these qualities were in him added, a great and only too lavish disposition for liberality, an easy address and an affability of manners, most remarkable; above all a clemency towards the vanquished scarcely to be credited, and which prompted him to spare the lives of all who sued for quarter.—At the battle of Pharsalia, in order to save the citizens, he announced by the voice of the herald, that his animosity was laid aside with his arms; and not only did he return to terms of amity with his conquered foes, but he even granted them a share of wealth and honours. A man thus endowed with all the commanding and engaging qualities which give ascendancy in society, must have swayed the destinies of his contemporaries in any age and in any nation. But, besides his rapacity, prodigality, and scandalous incontinency, he had another vice of a more destructive character—*ambition*, which from his earliest years inspired him with the desire to attain the empire of the world. To appease this passion, many acts, from which his better nature would have shrunk, required to be done in defiance of justice; vast sums expended, to hasten or augment through the channel of popularity the honours which he coveted; nations, however peaceable and unoffending, were wantonly assailed and grievously outraged to furnish claims for fresh triumphs; well-disposed and amicable communities harrassed, temples thrown to the ground, public treasuries violated, and lastly his arms turned against his fellow-countrymen. By universal consent he would assuredly have been a prince most worthy of the eminence he gained, and preferable to all before or after him, had he either reached it by hereditary right, or at least not been compelled to win it at the point of the sword.—See Eckhel *(in Cæsare)*, vol. vi. pp. 2, 3, and 4—Capt. Smyth's *Descr. Catal.* pp. 1 and 2—see also a full and able sketch of Cæsar's life and character, in the *Dictionary of Greek and Roman Biography*, &c.

MINTAGES OF JULIUS CÆSAR.

Cæsar was the first Roman whose effigies were stamped on coins in his life-time; and, according to Dion, this compliment was amongst the profusion of honours lavished upon him by

the Senate, during the latter part of his eventful career. For his earliest denarii do not bear his portrait, but exhibit for the most part the head of Venus as their obverse type, and on their reverses there generally appears the word CAESAR, with types of cornucopiæ, trophies, elephant trampling on a serpent, pontifical and augural instruments, Æneas carrying Anchises and the palladium, &c.—For notices of these see Julia gens; also see *Palladium.*

To follow, as far as possible, the chronologico-numismatic order of arrangement, and at the same time to shew the progress of Cæsar's greatness, through the medium of his coins—Riccio has methodically classed such of them as bear his portrait, and either on one side or the other an indication of each office held by him, under five different heads, namely—1. Those with the head unaccompanied by a legend.—2. With title of Imperator.—3. Pontifex Maximus.—4. Dictator for the first, second, third, and fourth time.—5. Perpetual Dictator.—To these he adds the monetal records of Cæsar, as a man of the greatest clemency; as the father or parent of the country; lastly as raised, after death, to deification.—The following are among the most remarkable examples of each class :—

The Head without Legend.

Head of Julius Cæsar, laureated.

Rev.—VOCONIVS VITVLVS. Q. DESIGN. S. C.—A calf standing.

[See wood cut No. 1, at the head of the biographical notice, p. 151.]

Head of Julius Cæsar laureated. s. c.

Rev.—TI. SEMPRONIVS. GRACCVS. Q. DESIGN. s. c. Spear, plough, legionary eagle, and military ensign.

Head as above.

Rev.—L. FLAMINIVS IIII. VIR.—Venus standing, holding the hasta and the caduceus.

Head as above, with caduceus before it, and laurel branch behind it.

Rev.—L. LIVINEIVS REGVLVS.—A furious bull.

On his return from Africa, after having defeated the Pompeians, Cæsar obtained, by virtue of two Senatorial decrees, authority to cause his portrait to be struck on the coins of the republic; together with the privilege of wearing, as the highest honour of the triumph, the laurel crown, which served him both for ornament and to conceal his baldness.—Borghesi regards these and other coins of the foregoing class, as additional proofs that Cæsar did not commence striking his effigy on the Roman mint, before his fourth dictatorship, viz. until after the battle of Munda, in 709 (B. c. 45).

Altogether the above coins refer to the powers conferred upon Cæsar; to peace hoped for after such an effusion of fellow countrymen's blood; to Venus the Victorious, whose name was given as the signal-word to his legions in the battle days of Pharsalia and Munda; to his founding of colonies in many places, and to other objects peculiar either to himself or to the families of his moneyers.—See Riccio, p. 107.

WITH TITLE OF IMPERATOR.

CAESAR IMP.—Head of Cæsar laureated, behind it the simpulum and lituus.

Rev.—M. METTIVS.—Venus the Victorious, stands holding an image of Victory in the right hand, and with left arm resting on a buckler, and holding the *hasta* transversely in her left hand.

[A gold specimen of this, valued at 150 fr. is engraved in Mionnet, *Rareté des Médailles*, T. i. p. 81].

Same head and legend as above.

Rev.—SEPVLLIVS MACER.——Venus Victrix, standing as above.

[See wood cut No. 2, in biographical notice, p. 152].

Rev.—L. AEMILIVS BVCA, IIII. VIR.——Two hands joined.

C. CAESAR COS. ITER.—Female head.

Rev.—A. ALLIENVS PRO. COS.—Neptune, holding the *trinacria* in his right hand, and planting his foot on the prow of a ship.

As Cæsar won many battles; so for these victories he was as many times saluted Imperator by his soldiers. But he did not cause the number of times that he was thus proclaimed to be marked on his mint, as was the practice afterwards of Augustus and his successors.

The image of Venus Victrix refers as well to the pretended origin, as to the real victories, of Cæsar; the joined hands point to the concord established between Julius and the Senate.—Lastly, the Neptune bears allusion to Sicily, where the coin was struck by Allienus, the proconsul of Cæsar.

WITH TITLE OF PONTIFEX MAXIMUS.

CAESAR IMP. P. M.—Laurelled head of Cæsar, behind it a crescent.

Rev.—L. AEMILIVS BVCA.—Venus the Victorious, standing.

C. CAESAR DICT. PERP. PONT. MAX.—Laureated head of Cæsar.

Rev.—C. CAESAR COS. PONT. AVG.—Bare head of Octavian.

[Riccio values this RRRR. in gold at 50 piastres.—A fine specimen of this gold coin brought £14 10s. at the Thomas sale].

It has already been noted, that against all competition, Cæsar obtained the high pontificate in 691 (B. C. 63), on the death of Metellus Pius.—The half moon behind the head on the first of the coins above described has regard to the correction introduced by Cæsar, as pontifex maximus, into the keeping of annual festivals, and to the reformation of the calendar by adopting the solar instead of the lunar year.—In consequence of calculating from the lunar year, the calendar had been thrown into the greatest confusion, and the festivals at first appointed for the winter, had come to fall in the spring. Cæsar established the solar year of three hundred and sixty-five days, with a day of intercalation at the end of every four years.—For the first year (B. C. 46), however, it was needful, besides the intercalary month, to add sixty-seven days.

WITH TITLE OF DICTATOR.

CAESAR DIC. Laureated head of Cæsar; behind it the præfericulum.

Rev.—M. ANTO. IMP. R. P. C. Bare head of Antony—behind it the lituus.

[At the Thomas sale, a fine specimen of this gold coin brought £23 10s.]

The Rubicon passed; Pompey with his partizans driven in a panic out of Italy; and Afranius and Petreius, lieutenants of Pompey, afterwards defeated in Iberia, the Senate were obliged to raise Cæsar, in 705 (B. C. 49), to the office of Dictator, in order that he should be able thus to administer the affairs of the republic, with absolute and irresponsible power. But the great object of his thoughts being the overthrow of Pompey and his adherents, who, after eleven days, had made good their retreat into Macedonia and Thessaly, he resigned the appointment of Dictator at the end of eleven days, and causing himself to be elected consul for the second time, crossed over from Brundusium into Greece, B. C. 48.——The præfericulum of Cæsar is a pontifical symbol; as the lituus of Antony is an augural symbol.

SECOND DICTATORSHIP.

DICT. ITER. COS. TERT.—Head of Ceres crowned.

Rev.—AVGVR. PONT. MAX.—Sacrificial instruments with corn ears; symbols of Auguration and of the Supreme Pontificate; sometimes beside the lituus appears the insulated letter M. in others D.

CAESAR DICT.—The *securis* (axe) and the *simpulum.*

Rev.—ITER.—Vase and lituus, within a laurel crown.—[Riccio gives an engraving of this, in *Supplement*, pl. 58, No. 11, from the Mus. Bellini, RRRR. and values it, in gold, at 25 piastres.]

Cæsar having (B. C. 48) obtained from the Senate, with the consent of the consuls, the dictatorship for the second time, was himself consul for the third time in the year 708 (B. C. 46), with M. Emilius Lepidus as his colleague.—And, resolved not to abandon his assumption of absolute power, he exercised it sometimes as dictator, sometimes as consul.

The insulated letter M. or D. which presents itself on the reverse of the former of these two denarii admits, in the opinion of Borghesi, of being interpreted to mean *munus* or *donum*, thus indicating that they were struck to pay his soldiers or partisans. As to the head of Ceres, it may possibly allude to Africa vanquished, or to the defeat of King Juba.—Riccio, p. 100.

THIRD DICTATORSHIP.

CAESAR DIC. TER.—Bust of Victory, winged.
Rev.—CLOVI. PRAEF.—Minerva walking, with a trophy on her shoulder, and a serpent moving on the ground before her.—Middle brass.
[See wood cut, No. 3, in biographical notice, p. 153].
C. CAESAR DIC. TER.—Bust of a winged Victory.
Rev.—L. PLANC. PRAEF. VRB.—Sacrificial vase. In gold, RR.

In the following year, 709 (B. C. 45), after he had defeated the Pompeians in Africa, Cæsar was declared Dictator for the third time. And being obliged afterwards to repair to Spain for the purpose of carrying on the war there with Cneius Pompeius the younger, and the other remains of that party, he assigned over the government of Rome to Lepidus, as his master of the horse, with six, or as some writers have it, with eight prefects of the city, amongst whom appear, on the coins above described, the names of Caius Clovius and Lucius Plancus.—Riccio, p. 109.

FOURTH DICTATORSHIP.

CAESAR DICT. QUART.—Head of Julius Cæsar, laureated, behind it a lituus.
Rev.—M. METTIVS.—Juno Sospita in a rapid biga.
CAES. DIC. QVAR.—Head of Venus, well adorned.
Rev.—COS. QVINQ. within a crown of laurel. Gold, RRR.

Cæsar was made Dictator for the fourth time about the year 710 (B. C. 44), subsequently to young Cneius Pompey's defeat in Spain, for which success he triumphed with the greatest splendour, but also excited very great displeasure amongst the Romans.

During his fifth consulship, as indicated by the last described coin, on the ides of March of 710 (B. C. 44), Cæsar was assassinated in the senate house.

Now if, in that year, he was Dictator for the fourth time, and not yet Perpetual Dictator, it would seem that the last described coin offers a contradiction. But this vanishes, when it is considered that the consulate was an ordinary magistracy, which was conferred in the calends of January in each year; and that the dictature was an extraordinary magistracy, with which a man might be invested at any time whatsoever, and it also might be revoked, or laid aside, on the instant. Hence the fourth and the perpetual dictatorship might have been conjoined with the fourth and fifth consulate, during the year in which Cæsar ceased to live.—See Riccio, 110.

CÆSAR PERPETUAL DICTATOR.

CAESAR DIC. PERPETVO.—Head of Julius Cæsar, laureated.
Rev.—L. BVCA. Winged caduceus, laid across the consular fasces, an axe, two hands joined, and a globe.
The same legend and head.
Rev.—L. BVCA.—Venus standing.
Rev.—C. MARIDIANVS.—Venus standing.
Rev.—P. SEPVLLIVS MACER.—Venus the Victorious, standing, with buckler and hasta.

CAESAR [DICT.] PERPETVO.—Head of Julius laureated.
Rev.—L. BVCA.—Venus seated, holding the hasta pura in her left hand, and a Victoriola in her right.

In the last year of his life, Cæsar assumed, as a prominent token of sovereign power, the title of Perpetual Dictator; and the moneyers of that year, Buca, Cossutius, and Sepullius, transferred it to the coins above described.

These titles and distinctions, at no time in permanent use among the Romans, were so profusely lavished on Cæsar, that they drew down upon him the envy and hatred of no small portion of the citizens, and led to the fatal conspiracy of the pretors Brutus and Cassius, and of others, by whom he was in full senate slain with the mortal stabs of twenty daggers.—(See p. 143).

The indications on the above described denarii are allusive to Cæsar's victories; to his supreme and absolute power; and to the concord which he flattered himself to have established with the Senate.

WITH TITLE OF CONSUL.

Cæsar was five times Consul. This title is applied to him only three times on his coins; namely, the second, third, and fifth. But tho' there are no coins bearing the record of his first consulate, he is called consul for the second time, or for the third time, on coins engraved in Morel, *Imp. Rom.* T. iii. TAB. 3 and 4.
C. IVLIVS CAES. IMP. COS. III.
Rev.—Venus leaning on a pillar, with helmet, spear, and shield.—Restored by Trajan.
[This gold coin, in the highest state of preservation, brought £17 17s. 0d. at the Thomas sale].
Riccio describes and engraves the following,

in gold, RRR. which he values at ten ducats.—
(*Tav.* 23, No. 35).

C. CAESAR COS. TER.—Head of a woman,
veiled and laureated.

Rev.—A. HIRTIVS PR.—Lituus, vase, and axe.

Hirtius was one of the prefects, or pretors,
of the city, at the time (B. C. 46), when Cæsar's
frequent absences from Rome, rendered it expedient for him to appoint several lieutenants.—
For an engraving of this singular coin, which
on one side exhibits the record of Cæsar's third
consulship, and on the other associates the name
and office of the dictator's personal friend with
the symbols of the supreme pontificate, reference may be made to the word HIRTIVS.

No coins are known with the fourth consulship of Cæsar inscribed on them. A denarius,
of which the obverse exhibits, with his portrait,
the legend of his fourth dictatorship, has on the
reverse, COS. QVINQ. (Consul for the fifth time),
within a wreath of laurel.—Engraved in Riccio,
Julia gens, TAV. 23, No. 29.

WITH TITLE OF PARENT OF THE COUNTRY.

CAESAR PARENS PATRIAE.—Head of Cæsar
veiled and laureated; before it is an augural
lituus; behind is the pontifical apex.

Rev.—C. COSSVTIVS MARIDIANVS, inscribed
crosswise. A A A F.F. inside. (See p. 1.)

The fourth quatuorvir of Cæsar's mint, Cossutius Maridianus, has commemorated by this
silver coin, struck in the fatal year above alluded
to, 710 (B. C. 44), the honourable appellation
of *Parens Patriæ*, which Julius found conferred upon him after his victory in Spain, as is
recorded by Dion (xliv. § 4), Appian (*Bell. Civ.*
ii. ch. 106) and Suetonius (ch, 76). It was
continued even after his death, for Suetonius
informs us, that "where he had been assassinated, the people erected in the forum a solid
statue of Numidian marble, nearly twenty feet
high, and inscribed on it the words PARENTI.
PATRIAE."—The same fact is related by Cicero,
but attributed by him to *Antony*; "Your friend
(*Antony*) aggravates daily the popular fury; in
the first place, he has inscribed on the statue
which he erected in the *rostra*, PARENTI. OPTIME.
MERITO. (*Ad Familiares*, L. xii. ep. 3.) And
it was on account of this appellation, that his
murderers were always invidiously called *pari-
cidæ*, and the ides of March, the day on which
he was slain, *paricidium*.—Eckhel, vi. p. 17.

DIVVS.

Amongst the gold and brass coins struck in
memory of Julius Cæsar, with this legend of
consecration after his death, through the care and

direction of his grand nephew, heir, and adopted
son, the following are most rare:—

GOLD.—DIVVS IVLIVS DIVI F.—Heads of Julius and Augustus, face to face.

Rev.—M. AGRIPPA COS. DESIG. across the
field.—Engraved in Akerman, vol. i. pl. iii. No. 8.

DIVOS IVLIVS.—Head of Julius between the
apex and lituus.

Rev.—DIVI FILIVS.—Bare head of Augustus.
[A fine specimen of this rare coin brought at
the Thomas sale £6 2s. 6d.—Riccio marks it
RRRR, and values it at 30 piastres.]

DIVVS IVLIVS. Head of Julius laureated.

Rev.—IMP. CAES. TRAIAN. AVG. GER. DAC.
P. P. REST. A winged female (Victory) walking,
with right hand supports her vestment, and
holds a caduceus in her left hand.—RRRR. Engraved in Riccio, who values it at 50 piastres.
See *Supplt. Tav.* 58, No. 17.

BRASS.—Such as bear his portrait are rare,
but not in a high degree. Nor indeed does it
appear that any brass were minted at Rome
during his life time; although the head of Cæsar
is frequently found on colonial coins. But on
his apotheosis, some (and those not in a good
style either of design or of workmanship), were
struck at Rome, by order of Augustus.—For an
engraving of a well-preserved large brass specimen see DIVOS IVLIVS, p. 105 of Akerman,
Descr. Cat. pl. iv. No. 1.

Mionnet and Akerman concur in pronouncing
the coin, in gold and silver, having DIVVS IVLIVS
and his head on the obverse, and a comet without legend on the reverse, to be false.

The coin in gold, having DIVI IVLI, with
Cæsar's laurelled head and a comet behind it, on
the obverse; and DIVI FILIVS, with bare head
of Octavianus, on the reverse, and which Eckhel and Morel have placed amongst the Goltziani,
is found, says Riccio, to be *vera antica*, a genuine antique; and is marked in his *Monete
Famiglie*, RRRR. valued at 30 piastres.

CAESAR.—On the reverse of a silver coin of
Julius, is this word, with the type of Æneas,
walking; he holds in his right hand the image
of Minerva armed, and supports on his left
shoulder his aged father Anchises.—See *Palladium.* See also *Æneas*, p. 16 of this dictionary.

CAESAR.—An elephant, trampling with its
fore feet on a serpent, which is raising its head.
This legend and type appear on an early denarius of Julius Cæsar, for an explanation of
which see the word ELEPHANT.

CAESAR, *as a name and as a title.*—What
was originally the cognomen, or surname, of the
Julia gens, became, on the extinction of that
family, a title of honour and dignity. The
name of Cæsar was at first extended to individuals of other families, through *adoption*, in
the same manner as the title of Augustus. It
was in conformity to this practice, that Octavius, on his being adopted by the Dictator, was
first styled Cæsar, and afterwards Augustus.—
The three sons of Agrippa (Caius, Lucius, and
Agrippa), were the next to receive it from their
adoption by Augustus; and by the same emperor, it was afterwards conferred on his son-in-

law Tiberius, from whom it descended to his son Drusus. And lastly, by the adoption of Tiberius, it was borne by Germanicus and his sons.

The name of Cæsar, then, up to this point was simply hereditary; being transferred, in accordance with Roman custom, to those who were sons, either by birth or by adoption, and the last Cæsar, on this two-fold principle, was Caius, the son of Germanicus (commonly called Caligula). Nevertheless it is supposed by some that Claudius (who succeeded Caligula), and also his son Britannicus, together with Nero, the son of his adoption, should be reckoned in the list of genuine Cæsars; it being the almost unanimous verdict of ancient writers, as cited by Reimar on Dion (B. lxiii.), that the house of the Cæsars became extinct with Nero.

And yet Claudius did not bear the title of Cæsar before his accession to empire, in consequence of his not being the son of a Cæsar, by either birth or adoption; nor could he therefore transmit the title to his sons. By courtesy, however, he was acknowledged as a member of the Cæsarian house, being connected with it by affinity. (See *Adfinis*, p. 25). For he had two grandmothers of that family, viz. on his father Drusus's side, Livia, the wife of Augustus, and on his mother Antonia's side, Octavia, the sister of Augustus; to which circumstance may be added, that the Claudia gens at that time held the next rank to the Julia. There is therefore greater distinctness in the expression of Galba, given by Tacitus—"When the house of the Julii and the Claudii shall have been exhausted, *adoption* will discover worthy successors." But if acquiescence is to be yielded in the *courtesy* above mentioned, is the same claim to prevail even when truth is confounded with fictitious genealogies? Now, the pedigree of Nero is found, on several marbles, drawn as follows:—NERO CLAVDIVS DIVI CLAVDII *Filius*. GERMANICI. CAESARIS N*epos* TI. CAE-SARIS AVG. PRON*epos* DIVI AVG. ABN*e-pos*.—It is an established fact, that Nero was the adopted son of Claudius. But (asks Eckhel) is it so sure that he was the *nepos* of Germanicus? The word *nepos* has two significations; for it denotes either the son of one's son or daughter, or the son of a brother or sister. In the former sense, neither by birth nor by adoption could Nero be called the *nepos* of Germanicus; but in the latter sense, he had a right to the title, inasmuch as he was adopted by Claudius, who was the brother of Germanicus. Yet was it ever the custom to trace the descent from the uncle's family? Who does not at once perceive, that it was the aim of those who framed these inscriptions to play upon the double signification of the word *nepos*, in order, by a base adulation, to connect their idol Nero, with the house of the Cæsars. But there are amongst the marbles alluded to, some even bearing the stamp of public authority, and which are of so much the more audacious falsity, as they were published with impunity. Still more impudent in its pretensions is the tenour of an inscription

given by Gruter; wherein Nero is styled GER-MANICI. F. TI. AVGVSTI N. DIVI AVG. PRON. to the exclusion of his father, as having but little Cæsarian *préstige*, his place being fallaciously supplied by Germanicus Cæsar. It becomes, therefore, less a matter of astonishment that the emperor Septimius Severus should have forcibly intruded himself into the family of the Antonines.—(See *Adoption self-assumed*, p. 8 of this dictionary).

The shackles of the law having thus, even at that early period of the imperial government, been relaxed, it was no difficult task afterwards for princes, evidently alien to the Cæsarian race, to usurp the titles both of Cæsar and of Augustus—the latter having already begun to hold the foremost place in public opinion, as identified with the highest authority. (See AUGUSTUS, used as a title, p. 101 of this dictionary).—Thus, Galba, on receiving the news of Nero's death, and of the Senate's having espoused his own cause, hesitated not to fortify his position by assuming the title of Cæsar; and his example was immediately followed by Otho.—Less prone to adopt names to which he could lay no claim, Vitellius deferred accepting the title of Augustus, and rejected entirely that of Cæsar, as is shewn by his coins. But the general effect produced by the above cited examples, was that the custom strengthened into a fixed law, viz. that the holder of the supreme power in the empire, should be dignified with both titles. It is therefore manifest that the name of Cæsar was, at first, no more than the cognomen of the gens Julia, transmitted, according to Roman custom, to the sons; and that its importance was in the exact ratio of its possessor's prospects of obtaining supreme power—prospects which could not fail of realization, unless blighted by some violent occurrence.

2. CÆSAR, *a dignity of the second rank.*—As the title of Cæsar, like that of Augustus, implied in itself no power, but only dignity, and claiming as it did the reverence due to the anticipation of empire, it rested with the emperor or prince of the highest rank, to decide whether he would confine within the empty limits of this title, his Cæsar, or prince of the second grade; or whether he would add thereto a portion of real authority. Augustus denied to the three sons of Agrippa, who were Cæsars by adoption, the tribunitian power, whilst he bestowed it upon his son-in-law Tiberius, who had not at that time been created Cæsar. Domitian, likewise, who was Cæsar, so long as his father (Vespasian) and his brother (Titus) lived, had nothing to distinguish him from a private individual but the title of *Princeps Juventutis.*—Others died at too early an age to rise higher, and this was the fate of the above named three sons of Agrippa; of Drusus and Nero, the sons of Germanicus; of Britannicus, the son of Claudius; and of Piso, the son of Galba.—On the other hand, there were emperors who, by conferring upon their Cæsars the tribunitian power, or pro-consular government, or the title of Imperator, admitted them, as it were, into

colleagueship. A part of these honours, or several of them at the same time, were conferred upon the Cæsars—namely, Tiberius, Drusus junior, Nero, Titus, Trajan, Antoninus Pius, M. Aurelius, and others, as proved by the legends on their respective coins.—Diocletian and Maximinian, as *Augusti*, bestowed greater powers on their Cæsars, Constantius Chlorus, and Gal. Maximian, by entrusting them with provinces, which they were permitted to rule with an authority nearly equal to that exercised by the two emperors themselves over those which they more immediately governed. It was in reference to a similar instance, that Vopiscus observes, that Carinus was left by Carus in the west, to administer affairs in that portion of the empire—" with the authority of a *Cæsar*, and the permission to exercise all the functions pertaining to the *Augusti*."

3. *The dignity of* CÆSAR *varied in degree at different times.*—Ancient writers have recorded that there were various degrees of Cæsarian dignity.—Spartian, addressing Diocletian, after relating that Hadrian, under the pressure of disease, had adopted Ælius, says of the latter—" There is nothing in his life worthy of note, except the fact, that he was styled Cæsar, not as was formerly the case, in consequence of bequest, nor in the manner in which Trajan was adopted; but nearly in the same way as in our own time, through your (Diocletian's) favour, Maximianus and Constantius were called Cæsars, as being men of princely extraction, and presumptive heirs of imperial dignity."—Capitolinus, at the commencement of his life of L. Verus, says—" His real father was Ælius Verus, who, being adopted by Hadrian, was called Cæsar, and died holding that rank."—There were emperors who deferred the assumption of the title Cæsar in the case of their sons. Antoninus Pius, in adopting at the same time M. Aurelius and L. Verus, gave to the former, at once, the title of Cæsar, but not to Verus, whom throughout his reign he permitted to use no other distinction than *Augusti Filius*.——M. Aurelius again, did not bestow that title upon his sons Commodus and Annius Verus, till the sixth year of his reign.—Pertinax declined to assume the honour, notwithstanding the Senate decreed it to his son.—Septimius Severus bestowed it on Caracalla only in the third, and on Geta in the fifth, year of his reign. The practice followed by other emperors is to be ascertained by consulting their respective coins.

So long as the Julia family held sway, Cæsars were created neither by birth nor by adoption; CÆSAR, as has already been observed, being then nothing more than the cognomen of the Julia gens. On its extinction in Caligula, the same privilege was usurped by the Claudia family.— Thenceforth the right of conferring the title of Cæsar was, according to the various circumstances of time and place, possessed or arrogated by the Emperors themselves, or the Senate, or the Army; by the combined, or partial, votes of which three estates, it is well known that even the *Augusti* were chosen.

4. *Name of Nobilissimus added to that of* CÆSAR.—In progress of time, the Cæsars began to add the epithet *Nobilissimus* to their other titles, either to indicate an illustrious line of descent, or fictitiously to conceal a humble origin. This epithet is found to have been adopted even by Commodus on marbles. (See Spanheim).—On coins, Diadumenianus (son of Macrinus) is the first hitherto known to have had this title applied to him; these are of the colony of Laodicea, in Syria. In later times it travelled even into the Roman mint. The inscription on coins is NOB. CAES. or NOB. C. or still more briefly, N. C. It is extraordinary that Zeno and Leo III. should, on the coins of the East, be styled NOV. (for NOB.) CAES. and still more that both of them were Augusti. But there is no accounting for the anomalies of that period.

As the Cæsars were called *Nobilissimi*, so also were some females called Nobilissimæ; there being inscribed on their coins N. F. that is Nobilissima Femina: as for instance, HELENA N. F. perhaps the wife of Crispus; and FAVSTA N. F. perhaps the wife of Constantine II.; the value of which title is not sufficiently known.— In the later times of the empire, there arose a distinction between the *Cæsares* and the *Nobilissimi;* for Nicephorus, of Constantinople, at the conclusion of his history, relates that Constantine V. Copronymus created two of his sons, Christophorus and Nicephorus, Cæsars, and the third, Nicetas, was styled *Nobilissimus.* The title of Augustus was occasionally added to the Cæsars, but only through a *consortium*, or colleagueship, with their father, an *Augustus.*—See Eckhel, *De nomine et titulo Cæsaris*, vol. viii. p. 367, et seq.

CAES. AUG. CONS. S. OB. R. P. CONS.— *Cæsari Augusto Conservatori Senatus, ob rem publicam conservatam.*—Epigraph on a very rare denarius of the Mescinia family.—See *Morell. Thesaur. Fam. Rom.* p. 279.

[TITVS] CAESAR COS. DES. II. CAESAR DOMIT. COS. DES. II.—*Titus Cæsar Consul designatus iterum, Cæsar Domitianus Consul designatus iterum.*—In the field S. C.—On the reverse of a large brass of Vespasian, struck (A. D. 71) by that emperor in honour of his two sons, Titus and Domitian, on their both attaining a second consulship. The two Cæsars are in military habits, with the hasta pura, but bareheaded; Titus is the manlier of the two, and is further distinguished by the parazonium.—Capt. Smyth, p. 58.—The coin is engraved in *Morell. Thesau. Impp.* T. iii. TAB. xiii. But the type is more correctly given in the *Médailles de Christine*, TAB. vi.

CAIUS CAESAR and LUCIUS CAESAR, the sons of M. Vipsanius Agrippa, and of Julia; and the grandsons of Augustus.—Caius was born in the year of Rome 734 (B. C. 20), and Lucius in 737 (B. C. 17.) These two young princes had become by adoption the sons of Augustus, who carefully superintended the education of both, having designed them for his successors in the empire. Before they had laid aside the dress of boyhood, each was declared consul elect and *princeps juventutis* (see the word). Caius was nominated to the consulate B. C. 5, but the period for his entering upon it was deferred.

He was permitted to wear the *toga virilis* in the same year; and Lucius assumed it B. C. 2.— Honoured with the priesthood, and admitted into the senate, they seemed destined for a life of greatness and prosperity. But the younger of the two died suddenly at Marseilles, 755 (A. D. 2), when on his way to Spain; not without its being suspected that his step-mother Livia, who left no means, how foul soever, unemployed to advance her son Tiberius, had occasioned his sudden and untimely death. Caius, sent into Asia, where he passed his year of consulship, A. D. 1, had begun to shew talents for both civil government and military enterprise; but, after bringing the Parthian king Phraates IV. to terms of peace with the Romans, he was treacherously wounded on his return from an expedition into Armenia; and falling into a lingering illness, supposed to have been also nurtured by the secret arts of Livia, he died at Limyra, in Lycia, at the early age of 24, in the year U. C. 757 (A. D. 4).

On gold and silver coins of Augustus, the brothers are typified together both on foot and on horseback, and styled Cæsars, sons of Augustus, and *principes juventutis*. On some second brass *(colonial)* the heads of the brothers appear on the obverse, and that of Augustus on the reverse. (See engravings of these in Vaillant's *Coloniæ*, i. pp. 60, 61).—Other *colonial* second brass exhibit on their obverse the head of Caius or of Lucius only, and on their reverse the head of Augustus. The above cut presents a specimen of the last named coins.—See C. L. CAESARES, &c.

C. CAESAR AUGUST. F.—*Caius Cæsar Augusti Filius.*—This legend appears on the reverse of gold and silver of Augustus, accompanied by the type of a military figure on horseback, charging with lance elevated; behind him are a legionary eagle and two ensigns. This coin was struck when the emperor adopted Caius and his brother Lucius.—See above.

CAESAR-AUGUSTA, *colonia*, originally named Salduba, a city of Hispania Tarraconensis, and the capital of the Edetani, now Zaragoza, in Arragon, situate on the Ebro. At the close of his war with the Cantabri, Augustus invested it with colonial rights and privileges, for veteran soldiers from three legions. The coins of this colony are *Latin* imperial, in small middle and large brass, bearing on their re-spective obverses, portraits of Augustus, Agrippa, Livia, Caius and Lucius Cæsares, Tiberius, Julia and Tiberius, Germanicus, Tiberius and Germanicus, Nero and Drusus Cæsares, Agrippina senior, and Caligula; the legends being C. C. A. and COL. CAESAR-AVGVSTA.

[*Obs.*—The coins having C. A. within a laurel crown, given by Vaillant, and after him by Florez, to this Roman colony in Spain, and by Pellerin, to Cæsarea Augusta in Palestine, belong to Cæsarea Panias.—See *Cæsarea Philippi*]. Among other types the following claim notice for their historical interest and extreme rarity.

Augustus.—*Obv.*—AVGVSTO DIVI F. Three standards between the words LEG. IV. LEG. VI. LEG. X.

Rev.—C. C. A. TIB. FLAVO PRAEF. GERM. L. IVVENT. LVPERCO, IIVIR.—Colonia Cæsar-Augusta, Tiberio Flavo, Præfecto Germanici, Lucio Juventio Luperco, Duumviris.—Engraved in Vaillant, *Col.* i. p. 15.

This large brass, first edited by Seguin, was doubtless struck by the three legions stationed in the garrison town of Cæsar-Augusta. Whence these veterans derived their right of coinage is a question unresolved. According to Vaillant, "these military standards allude to the origin of the colony. The type of the cultivator and his oxen at plough, and that of the legionary ensigns are respectively symbols of the civil and of the military portion of the colonists. The names of the legions inscribed on the obverse indicate those whence the veterans sent to Cæsar-Augusta were drafted." The interpretation by Vaillant, and adopted also by Florez, of the abbreviation PRAEF. GERM. as *Præfectus Germanorum* (Prefect of a German Cohort) is scouted by Eckhel (iv. 475 et. seq.), who considers that the Tiberius Flavus, named on the obverse of this coin, is represented there as *Præfectus Germanici*, in allusion to Germanicus Cæsar, the son of Drusus.—See DUUMVIR.

Augustus.—*Obv.*—AVGVSTVS DIVI F. Laureated head of the emperor.

Rev.—Q. STATIO. M. FABRICIO IIVIR. CAESAR AVGVSTA. Priest guiding two oxen yoked to a plough.

[This large brass is engraved in Akerman. *Coins of Spain*, p. 72, pl. viii. No. 13].

Caius and Lucius Cæsares.—*Obv.*—AVG. C. CAES. COS. DESIG. L. CAES. COS. DES. Augustus holding the simpulum, stands between Caius and Lucius, his adopted grandsons; all three are clothed in the toga, and each stands on a cippus.

Rev.—(Names of duumvirs) CAESAR AVGVSTA. Vexillum placed on a cippus, between two military ensigns.

[This rare large brass is engraved in Vaillant's *Colonies*, i. p. 20].

Tiberius.—*Obv.*—TI. CAESAR DIVI AVG. F. AVGVSTVS PON. MAX. TR. POT. XXXIII. Tiberius wearing the toga, is seated on the curule chair, holding in his right hand a patera, and in his left the hasta.

Rev.—C. CA. L. VETTIACVS M. CATO IIVIR.— A vexillum and two military ensigns, between which we read LEG. IV. LEG. VI. LEG. X.

[Endeavours having proved fruitless to procure a cast from some authentic specimen of this very rare and remarkably interesting product of the Romano-Hispanian coinage, the subjoined cut has been copied from a print in the *Médailles de Christine*, engraved by Bartolo, whose drawings of numismatic types are usually accurate].

The vexillum, or cavalry standard, and the two other military ensigns, typified on the above reverse, refer to the veterans sent as a reinforcement to the colony, from the Fourth, Sixth, and Tenth Legions, whose respective designations stand on this coin as unmistakeably conspicuous, as do the names of the two duumvirs who caused it to be minted.

On the obverse of this large brass, the Roman authorities of Caesar-Augusta represent the emperor seated; and the record of the 33rd tribunitian power teaches us (says Vaillant, i. p. 70), that the people of this colony erected statues to Tiberius, on the occasion of Sejanus having been put to death. The Senate itself, indeed, according to Dion Cassius, set the example of public rejoicing when that event occurred; and the day of that bad minister's execution was celebrated as a *festus dies*, by all the magistrates and pontiffs, with unprecedented exultation, throughout all parts of the Roman world.—Amongst the Spanish colonies who congratulated Tiberius, and raised statues to his honour, on this occasion, Caesar-Augusta was the foremost.

The following is another proof in confirmation of the above mentioned fact:—On the obverse of a very rare large brass, dedicated by this colony to Tiberius, appear the name and titles of that emperor, accompanied by the same date of the tribunitian power (xxxiii.); the type is an equestrian figure of Tiberius, placed on a plinth. The reverse type is a legionary eagle and two standards, together with the colonial initials c. CA. (Colonia Caesar-Augusta); and the same names of M. Cato and L. Vettiacus, as duumvirs. The statue relates to the congratulatory honours paid to this unworthy emperor, who never thought of surrendering Sejanus to retributive justice, until his own personal safety was endangered by continuing that infamous minister in his service.—Engraved in p. 69 of Vaillant, *in Col*.

Obv.—TI. CAESAR DIVI AVG. F. AVGVSTVS.—Laureated head of Tiberius.

Rev.—C. CA. A bull, with infulated head, for sacrifice.—[See Akerman, *Coins of Hispania*, p. 74, plate viii. fig. 8].

Tiberius and Julia.—*Obv.*—TI. CAESAR DIVI AVGVSTI. F. AVGVSTVS. Laureated head of Tiberius.

Rev.—IVLIA AVGVSTA C. CA. Figure of Julia seated, as Piety, veiled and wearing the stola, holding a patera and the hasta.—Large brass, rare. Engraved in Akerman, *Coins of Hispania*, p. 75, plate viii. fig. 7.

Besides the types above described, the coins of Caesar-Augusta exhibit the winged lightning (*fulmen alatum*), as in Augustus. Also the figures of Nero and Drusus Caesares, sons of Germanicus, are represented in the toga; seated opposite each other and joining hands.

CAESAREA, *in Mauretania*, a maritime town (originally called Iol). During the period of Julius Caesar's dictatorship, it formed part of king Juba's dominions. The imperial coins struck in this city have bilingual legends, viz. Latin and African. A coin in the *Cabinet de France* is inscribed REX IVBA, with the head of Juba. On the reverse is CAESAREA R. XXXII. (which numerals denote the year of the reign); the type is a capricorn with cornucopiae and rudder.—See *Mus. Pembroke*, i. TB. 11, No. 5.—See also Spanheim, i. p. 543.—In enumerating the colonies founded by Claudius, Vaillant (i. p. 105), includes the Mauretanian Caesarea.—By some writers, and with no slight measure of topographical probability, the modern Algiers is considered to have been built on the site of this Roman settlement. Others assign it to the locality of *Chierchiel*, lying to the west of, but not far from, Algiers.

CAESAREA *ad Libanum* (Phoeniciae) *colonia*, formerly Arca, now Aresce, Archis, Arka.—The imperial coins of this city are in *Greek* brass of Antoninus Pius and M. Aurelius, and in *Latin* brass of Elagabalus, and Alexander Severus.—[Its era that of the Seleucidae, commencing in the year 442 of the foundation of Rome, 312 before the Christian era.]—Mionnet thus describes one of the *Latin* coins extant of this colony:—

Elagabalus.—.. ANTONINVS. Head laureated.

Rev.—COL. CESARIA (*sic*) LIB. ALPH.

A temple, of which the dome is supported by two Hermes. Below is the half-length figure of a female veiled, the head drooping towards the shoulder, on which is a crescent; on one side the Sun, on the other the Moon; to the right a sceptre.

Severus Alexander.—A coin dedicated to this emperor has the figure of Astarte in a temple.

CAESAREA PHILIPPI, or *Panites*, or ad *Panium*, so called from the pastoral deity *Pan* being a peculiar object of worship by the inhabitants of this Phoenician city. The tutelary god above named "is figured on many of its coins (observes Mr. Akerman), of which specimens exist from the time of Augustus to the days of Elagabalus. It was comprised in the tetrarchy of Iturea, and was anciently called *Dan*; but Philip, having enlarged and improved it, gave it the name of Caesarea, in honour of the emperor: and to distinguish it from other cities of the same name, it was called Cæsarea Philippi; though on the coins of Augustus, as in the specimen here given, the city is in-

dicated by the letters c. a. *Cæsarea Augusta*, within a fine specimen of the laurel crown."— See CORONA LAUREATA.

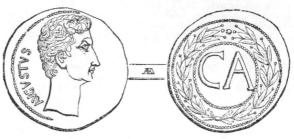

" These pieces of brass money must have been in circulation at the time of OUR LORD's visit to that district. This coin was erroneously ascribed to Cæsar-Augusta, in Spain, by the earlier numismatic writers."—See a brief but interesting and instructive work entitled *Numismatic Illustrations of the New Testament*, by John Yonge Akerman, Fellow and Secretary of the Society of Antiquaries, who has obligingly allowed the above cut to be used for this dictionary.

CÆSAREA *Samaritis* (or Palæstinæ) *colonia* (originally called Apollonia, and Turris Stratonis), a maritime town of Palestine, north-west of the ancient city of Samaria, in the plain of Megiddo.—King Herod augmented it into a magnificent port, calling it Cæsarea in honour of Augustus Cæsar. Its present name is *Kyserich*.—Vespasian, after subduing the Jews, made it a Roman colony, and gave it his family name of *Flavia*. His son and successor Titus conferred certain immunities on its territory; and hence this colony, in memory of the benefits bestowed, gave itself, on coins, the appellation of *Libera*. Afterwards it assumed the epithet of *Antoniniana*, in compliment to Caracalla; and was constituted a metropolis by Alexander Severus. Its title of *Prima* seems (says Vaillant, i. p. 138) to have originated from its being in the time of Vespasian the chief city of Palestine. The coins of Cæsarea Samaritis are numerous : consisting of imperial colonial, in small, middle, and large brass. Those with Latin legends begin with Trajan, and extend in an almost uninterrupted succession down to Gallienus. They bear for the most part for legend of reverse, COL*onia* CAESAREA LIB*era*, and COL. PRIM*a* FLAV*ia* AVGVSTA CAESAREN*sis*. There is c. p. f. AVG. CAESAR, of Hadrian, and c. p. f. AVG. CAE. METROPOLI. of Severus Alexander.

On a first brass of Trajanus Decius, the colonial legend reads COL. PR. F. AVG. CAES. METR. P. S. P. *(Colonia Prima Flavia Augusta Cæsarea Metropolis Provinciæ Syriæ Palæstinæ)* with the type of the emperor wearing a radiated crown; on horseback at speed, holding a spear couched in his right hand. A coin of great rarity.— Here we see the colony, designated by all the titles successively bestowed on it by various emperors from the period of its first establishment, under Vespasian. In the time of Decius,

Cæsarea Samaritis appears to have been recognised as the metropolis of that district of Syria-Palæstinæ, which included the cities of Ascalon, Gaza, and Julia. The figure of the imperial horseman on this coin alludes to some military expedition on which Trajan Decius had set out—perhaps against L. Priscus, in Syria, or against the Goths.—See Vaillant's *Colonies*, ii. p. 194, in which the type is engraved.

A second brass of Volusianus (son and successor of Trebonianus Gallus) struck in this colony, exhibits on its reverse the legend COL. P. F. CAES. MET. PR. S. PAL. *(Colonia Prima Flavia Cæsarea Metropolis Provinciæ Syriæ Palæstinæ)*, and the type of a male figure, with radiated head, recumbent on the back of a lion. The human figure elevates its right hand, and holds the *hasta pura*, or a long wand, in its left hand.—(From a coin in British Museum).

Under this type, the representation of Apollo or Sol seems intended. The *Sun* was the tutelary god of Cæsarea, and is here introduced, probably in flattery to young Volusianus, whose portrait on the obverse is also adorned with rays, as if he had been another Apollo, or Sol, to the colonists of this metropolitan city. The deity is depicted lying on the lion, as, according to Aratus (in phænom), *Hic notabilis et maximus inter signa sit*. Sol bears the *hasta pura*, a special attribute of pagan divinity.—Vaillant, *Col*. ii. p. 222.

[Mionnet ascribes to Trebonianus Gallus, as well as to Volusianus, a similar reverse, but mentions the type under both emperors as " BACCHUS *couché sur un lion*."—The justly-celebrated French numismatist had previously described a coin of this colony, dedicated to Trajanus Decius, as bearing the reverse type of *"Bacchus couché sur un panthére, et tenant le thyrse."* The thyrsus and the panther, indeed, clearly indicate the god of wine. But surely the radiated head, and the elevated right hand, are no less distinctive symbols of the Sun, as they are seen so often represented on coins of the lower empire.—See SOL INVICTVS COMES (AVGVSTI).]

Pellerin gives a coin of this colony, which Vaillant had missed. On the obverse is the laureated head of Trajan. On its reverse, C. AVG. CAESAR. (meaning *Cæsarea*). The type, Apollo standing, with his left arm resting on a tripod, and holding in his right hand a patera; before him is an altar, on the top of which a serpent rises. This (says Pellerin) is the first medal known to have been struck in this city, *subsequently* to its having been made a colony by Vespasian. (See *Mélange*, i. pl. XVII. No. 1.)—There are also coins of Antoninus Pius and M. Aurelius, which have types of Apollo standing, leaning on a tripod, and holding a laurel branch in the right hand, but without the altar.—On a Hadrian, Apollo holds a serpent.

The other types of this colony are—

Aesculapius— as in Annia Faustina.

Astarte, the worship of whom as Venus, this colony is said to have received from the people of Byblus, a maritime city of Phænicia, as in Hadrian, Faustina junior, and Trebonianus Gallus.—(See Pellerin, *Mélange*, pl. XVII. No. 4, for a curious Astarte type minted under Trajan)

Colonial Priest, driving oxen at plough, with a Victory flying towards and offering him a laurel crown. (Hadrian).—The same symbol of a colony, but without the Victory. (M. Aurelius, S. Severus, Caracalla, and Macrinus.)

Eagle, with expanded wings. (Alexander Severus and Trajanus Decius). A coin of Herennius, struck by the colony, bears METRO. P. S. P. with an eagle in a temple of two columns; engraved in Pellerin, *Mel.* pl. XXI. No. 8. Also of the same prince, COL. PR. ... AES. METR.—Pallas seated, Victory standing.—Ibid. No. 10.

Emperor, sacrificing to Rome. (Philip sen.)

Ditto, on horseback, charging over a prostrate enemy. (Trajanus Decius, Herennius, Etruscus, and Volusianus). Genius of the colony, seated with cornucopiæ. (Valerianus sen.)

Hercules, standing with club and lion's spoils. (On an elegant coin of M. Aurelius).

Jupiter Nicephorus, with eagle at his feet.—(Treb. Gallus).

Lion walking. (Hadrian).

Neptune, with trident and dolphin. (T. Gallus).

Serapis head of—as invariably distinguished by the calathus, or modius. (Hadrian, Antoninus Pius, L. Verus, Commodus, Macrinus, Diadumenianus, Elagabalus, and Trajan Decius).

[These are numismatic proofs of the continued idolatry paid at Cæsarea Samaritis, thro' so many reigns of Roman Emperors, to the principal deity of the Egyptians.—See *Serapis*].

Victory walking, holding a crown in the right, and a palm branch in the left hand.—(Trajan, in honour of whose successes in the East the coin was minted by the Cæsarienses).

Woman, whose head is adorned with towers, struck under Trajanus Decius and Hostilianus, denoting that Cæsarea was the chief city of the province of Palestine.——The same turreted female head, but with the addition of the *vexillum*, and the letters M. V. T. P. in the legend of reverse, appears on a coin of Gallienus, as quoted by Mionnet from Eckhel, *Anec. Cimel. Vindob.* xxiii. 7, p. 124.

CAESARVM N. N. or NOSTRORVM.—This perigraph is found only on coins of Licinius jun.; of Crispus; and of Constantius II. In the field, within a crown of laurel, VOTIS V. or X. On the exergue, PL. or QA. or SIS. Third brass. —See GENIO; also see VIRTUS.

CAESIA gens, plebeian, of which the name is one of little renown, and the cognomen unknown. There is but one coin assigned to it, viz. a denarius, on the obverse of which is the diademed bust of a young man, in the attitude of launching with his right hand, a triple-pointed dart. Behind the bust AP. in monogram. On the reverse, below are the words L. CAESI. and two juvenile figures, helmeted and half naked, seated; holding spears in their left hands; between them is a dog; above them a head of Vulcan, and the forceps. In the field of the coin are on one side what looks like an A, and on the other what seems simply an R, but which monogrammatologists pronounce to be respectively LA. and RE.

A passage from Gellius seems to warrant the belief that the head on the obverse of this silver coin is that of Apollo Ve-jupiter—"Simulacrum dei Vejovis ...... sagittas tenet, quæ sunt paratæ ad nocendum. Qua propter eum deûm plerique Apollinem esse dixerunt."—Eckhel, in quoting the above authority, refers to coins of the Fonteia and Licinia families for other instances in which the head of Apollo Vejupiter appears, with the letters AP. which are the first in the word Apollo, unless, indeed, it is more truly to be interpreted *Argentum Publicum.*—Fulvius Ursinus and other writers, with whom Eckhel agrees, consider the two sitting figures to be *Lares*, or Penates (household gods) —and that this is further proved by the appearance of the dog, as Plutarch as well as Ovid, explains. Then again, the head of Vulcan is regarded as another proof that the youthful figures represent Lares, by Ursinus, who cites a marble inscribed VOLCANO LARIBVS PVBLICIS SACRVM. Lastly, adds Eckhel, there are the two monograms, which joined together, form LARE, and thus bespeak them to be Lares. See Eckhel, v. 156, 7, 8.——Riccio (p. 40) says of this denarius, that "it was minted by the monetal triumvir Lucius Cæsius, perhaps the brother of that Marcus Cæsius who was pretor in 679 (B. C. 75), an acquaintance of Cicero. The workmanship displayed in this coin refers it to those times when Roman liberty was on the decline."

CALAGURRIS NASSICA, a city of Hispania Tarraconensis, now *Calahorra*, on the Ebro, in Old Castille, on the borders of Navarre, not far from Tudela. Its name of Calagurris associated itself, in Roman story, with the fearful miseries endured by the insurgent army of Sertorius, when Pompey and Metellus laid siege to it in that place, before 679 (B. C. 75.)— According to Pliny, it was first made a *municipium*, and afterwards a *colony ;* but on its coins, which bear the effigies and titles of no other emperors than Augustus and Tiberius, it is entitled a *municipium* only.—In the last days of the republic, Calagurris received the privileges of the *jus Latium ;* subsequently it was endowed with the *jus suffragii* by Julius Cæsar, after whom it was called *Julia.*—Cæsar indeed planted many colonies in Spain, and bestowed various benefits on their cities.—The numismatic type of the *Calaguritani*, whose coins (of a coarse, even barbarous fabric), are for the most part dedicated to Augustus, is a bull, or the head of a bull.—The first of the two following in middle brass exhibits its acquired surname of *Nassica.*

1. NASSICA.—The head (of Augustus) without laurel.

Rev.—MVN. CAL. IVL.—*(Municipium Calagurris Julia.)*—A bull or ox standing.—Engraved in Vaillant, *Col.* i. 25.

2. MVN. CAL. IVL.—Bare beardless head.

Rev.—L. GRANIO. C. VALERIO IIVIR.—A bull standing.—Engraved in Akerman's *Ancient Coins of Cities*, pl. viii. No. 6.

There is also a small brass of this colony, with the word *Nassica* before the head of Augustus on the obverse ; and the full-faced head of a bull on the reverse, which also bears, for inscription, C. VAL. C. SEX. AEDILES. *Caius Valerius, Caius Sextius, Aediles.*—(Valeria gens).

The word *Nassica* is the name, not of a man but, of the *municipium* itself. This clearly appears from Pliny (L. iii. c. 3), who expressly speaks of the people of Calagurris as being named *Nassici*—a statement confirmed by an ancient inscription given in the work of Ambrose Morales, MVN. CALAGVRRIS IVLIA NASSICA. And as Calagurris, on account of some immunities conferred upon it by Julius Cæsar, took the name of Julia, so (adds Vaillant) in like manner, by reason of certain benefits extended to it by Cornelius Scipio, it seems to have previously distinguished itself by his surname of *Nassica*, when he, with the rank of Pretor, administered the affairs of the republic in Spain, as Livy relates (L. v. *Dec.* 4.)—About the same period Calagurris was made a Roman *municipium ;* in remembrance of which boon, it assumed the name of Nassica ; and Scipio celebrated there those public games—called Ludi Megalenses—in honour of Cybele (Mater Idæa)—which he vowed to do amidst the perils of war, as Livy also shews.—*Coloniæ*, i. 25.

CALAGURRIS *Fibularia*—a town of Hispania Tarraconensis, in the country of the Illergetes, the site of which is occupied by Lahorre of the present day. The following coin is assigned to the *Fibularensian* Calagurris :

Obv.—L. Q. V. F. Q. ISC. F.—Bare head of a man.

Rev.—*Municipium.* C. F.——Female figure seated on a bull. She holds a veil inflated by the wind. Æ. 8, R. 1. *(British Museum).*—Engraved in plate viii. No. 9 of *Coins of Hispania*, by Mr. Akerman, who appositely reminds us, that "this figure of Europa on the bull occurs on many of the coins of Sidon."

CALENUS, surname of the Fufia gens, which came from Cales, a town of Campania. On coins of that family is read Q. CALENVS. COS.

CALIDIA gens plebeia. There is only one type to its coins, which are denarii of very antique form, exhibiting on one side the winged head of Minerva ; behind it ROMA.—On the reverse M. CAL. or CALID*ius*, in association with Q. MET*ellus*, and CN. FVLV*ius* or FOVL*vius*—on the exergue. The type is Victory with a crown raised in the right hand, in a biga.

These denarii (observes Riccio, p. 41), the ordinary specimens of the ancient *bigati*, bear evidence of their having been struck by the monetal triumvirs Marcus Calidius, Quintus Cæcilius Metellus, and Cneius Fulvius, about the beginning of the seventh century of Rome.

CALIGÆ. Military sandals used by the Romans.—"The *caliga* was a heavy sole, lashed with thongs to the leg, and armed with stout nails. The emperors gave largesses of nails to the soldiers, *donativum clavarium*, which perhaps meant also money to purchase them."— Capt. Smyth, p. 28.—See CALIGULA.

CALIGULA, the grand nephew and murderer of Tiberius, most worthy to succeed that emperor, because an equally infamous, though not so able a tyrant, reigned from A.U.C. 790 (A.D. 37) to 794 (A.D. 41).—His real appellation was CAIVS CAESAR, but, about the time of Augustus's death, he, still a child, being with the army of the Lower Rhine, the soldiers, with whom he was a great favourite, were accustomed, in the joking parlance of the camp, to give him the nickname of Caligula (from *Caligæ*) because he constantly appeared in the usual military leggings.—Hence Ausonius, in his poem, referring to this cruel wretch, says—

Post hunc castrensis *caliga* cognomine Cæsar
Successit, sævo sævior ingenio.

As emperor, however, he was always called Caius, and he considered himself insulted by the name of Caligula.

He was the youngest son of Germanicus the nephew of Tiberius, and of Agrippina; and in the year of Rome 765, (A. D. 12) on the day before the calends of September, at Antium, as Suetonius has proved at great length (in Caligula, ch. 8). In 770 (A. D. 17), he went into Syria with his father, at whose death, within two years afterwards, he returned to Rome with his mother; and on her being banished, he was transferred to his great grand-mother Julia, and when she died, to his grand-mother Antonia.— In 784 (A. D. 31) he was invested with the Pontificate; and, in consequence of the violent deaths of his brothers Nero and Drusus, and also of Sejanus, whose plots he alone had contrived to escape, being then the assured successor to the empire, he was nominated questor in 786 (A. D. 33)—invited by Tiberius to Capreæ, and on the same day assuming the *toga*, he laid aside his beard —Thenceforward he continued to live with Tiberius, feigning ignorance, or indifference, respecting the murder of his relations, as though it concerned him not; and so obsequiously obeying the behests of the tyrant, that it was a common expression, that "there never was a better servant, or a worse master." (Sueton, ch. 10.)

In 790 (A. D. 37), Tiberius having been attacked with severe illness, and scarcely recovering from it, Caligula, at the instigation of Macro, the pretorian prefect, put an end to his life, as it is affirmed, by smothering him *(injectu vestium oppressit)*. Dion states that this event took place on the 7th of the calends of April.

Having entered Rome, on the death of Tiberius, he compelled the Senate to join him, by a *Senatus Consultum*, in depriving of his right to the empire, Tiberius, the son of Drusus, jun., whom the elder Tiberius had, in his last will, nominated as his co-heir and colleague in the sovereignty. The funeral ceremonies of Tiberius were performed with due pomp by Caligula. In the eighth month of his reign he was attacked with severe sickness. On his recovery, he adopted his brother Tiberius, gave him the title of *Princeps Juventutis*, and afterwards put him to death. (Sueton.)—In the calends of July he entered upon the office of *Consul Suffectus*, as colleague to his uncle Claudius, and after two months resigned it.

791 (A.D. 38), he conceded to Soœmus, the kingdom of the Arabians of Ituræa; to Cotys, Armenia Minor; to Polemon, the son of Polemon, his father's dominions.—Relative to these events, Dion (L. lix. § 3) thus expresses himself: " In a short time he assumed so much the air of a *king*, that all those honours, which Augustus had accepted only when duly arrived at the sovereignty, and even then with hesitation and as they were decreed from time to time, and many of which Tiberius altogether declined, were by Caligula grasped in one day, with the exception only of the title *Pater Patriæ*, which, however, was not long deferred."

792 (A.D. 39).—In the calends of January, he entered upon his second Consulate, and resigned the office in thirty days. (Sueton ch. 17.) Having exhausted the treasury by his profuse expenditure on public spectacles and other extravagances, he endeavoured to repair the deficiency by the slaughter of the wealthy citizens; and then proceeded to Gaul, there to practice the like system of murder and spoliation.—The name of *Germanicus* does not appear on the coins of this year, nor ever subsequently.

793 (A. D. 40).—Caligula, without a colleague, entered upon his third consulate, at Lugdunum (Lyon), in Gaul; and resigned it on the ides of January. (Sueton. ch. 17).—Having invited over from Africa Ptolemy, the son of Juba, he put him to death, on pretence of the young prince's ostentatious bearing. (Dion, B. lix. 25).—Proceeding to the ocean, as if about to invade Britain, he ordered his soldiers to gather shell-fish, and returned as a conqueror, laden with the spoils of the sea. (Sueton. ch. 46).— L. Vitellius, prefect of Syria, the same year, gave such a lesson to Artabanus, the Persian, who was threatening an invasion of Armenia, that the latter abandoned his design, and paid his adorations to the statues of Augustus and of Caligula. (Dion, L. c.)—In 794 (A. D. 41), he began his fourth consulate, on the 7th of the ides of January. Shortly afterwards (viz. on the 9th of the calends of February), he was assassinated by the conspirators Cassius Chærea and Cornelius Sabinus.

Caligula's accession to the empire was hailed with joy by the Roman people; but their satisfaction was based on no solid foundation, being the result rather of their deep-rooted attachment to his father Germanicus. He seemingly, indeed, responded to the fond wishes of the nation, by many acts of piety, justice, and moderation. But it too soon became apparent, that these virtues were not of natural growth, but owed their exhibition to the policy of Tiberius, who wished through their influence to consolidate his own power in the empire. For there was no act of cruelty, folly, meanness, or infamy, which this monster and madman did not delight in perpetrating. He caused his horse, whom he called *Incitatus*, to be introduced at dinner time, setting before him gilded corn, and drinking his health in golden cups; and he would have created him consul, had he lived long enough. He imitated all the gods and goddesses, in the adoration which he caused to be paid to him, becoming by turns Jupiter, Bacchus, Hercules Juno, Diana, and Venus. He constructed a bridge of vessels joined together from Puteoli to Baiæ, and crossing over with his troops invaded Puteoli; and then recrossed it in a kind of triumph, delighting in hearing himself called Alexander the Great. By absurd and extravagant undertakings of this kind, before the year was fully expired, he had squandered the enormous sums of money left by Tiberius. (Vicies ac septies millies IIS.—See *Sestertium*).

He both claimed and received divine worship, and was the greatest blasphemer that ever lived; yet he quailed in the conviction of a deity, and crept under his bed whenever he heard thunder. With savage inhumanity he attended executions in person, and made parents behold the merciless torments inflicted on their unhappy children. He contracted and dissolved marriages with equal caprice and dishonesty. Besides his incestuous union with Drusilla, he seized and repudiated three wives, and was at last permanently attached to Cæsonia, a mother of children by another man, and without youth or beauty, but of depravity corresponding with his own.—The other instances of his incredible cruelty and lust, may be found in Suetonius, Philo, and Dion. Such infatuations are evident tokens not only of a brutal nature, but also of a distempered intellect: nor is it possible to entertain other than supreme contempt for the base servility of the Romans, who could offer solemn adoration to a wretch openly guilty of the most detestable and unnatural crimes; and whose adage was *oderint, dum metuant*.—See Eckhel, vi. pp. 215 to 218—See also Capt. Smyth's remarks on the character of Caligula.

The gold and silver coins of Caligula are of considerable rarity.—First brass also are rare, second brass common.—On these he is styled C. CAESAR. AVG.—C. CAESAR. DIVI. AVG. PRON, AVG. P.M. P.P. (sometimes GERM. *or* GERMANICVS). He assumed the name as the grandson of Drusus, who was so called for his victories over the Germans.

The coins of Caligula, minted at Rome, do not exhibit *Imperator* as a surname. This title is met with on colonial coins. But the only coin of Roman die struck under this emperor bearing the word IMP. is a denarius, in which it is joined to other titles.—See Mionnet's note i. 124, and Akerman's observation on that note, i. p. 151.

"When Caligula was destroyed, the dastardly senators, who had so recently sacrificed to him, ordered all his statues to be demolished, his acts abrogated, his money to be melted down, and his inscriptions defaced, in order that his memory might be extinguished for ever. Yet this sentence has not prevented a considerable number of his medals from reaching us, though consequently—except those of second brass— they are of considerable rarity when in good preservation." Captain Smyth, p. 30.

The following are amongst the rare and remarkable specimens of this emperor's coinage :—

GOLD.—AGRIPPINA. MAT. C. CAES.—Head of Agrippina. [See cut in p. 28.]—GERMANICVS CAES. &c.—Head of Germanicus.—TR. POT. IIII. Victory holding two palm branches.—OB. C. S. within an oaken garland.

SILVER.—*Obv.*—C. CAESAR AVG. GERM. P. M. TR. POT.—*Rev.*—DRVSVS. Head of Drusus.— (Valued by Mionnet at 100 fr.)

Obv.—C. CAESAR AVG. GERM. &c. Laureated head of Caligula.—*Rev.*—DIVVS AVG. PATER PATRIAE. Radiated head of Augustus.

FIRST BRASS.—The three sisters of Caligula (see engraving p. 29).—Three figures sacrificing before a temple. See DIVO AVG. PIETAS. Piety seated.—The commonest reverse is that which represents the emperor haranguing his guards; but it is a fine and interesting coin. See ADLOCVT. COH. engraved in p. 6, from a specimen in the compiler's possession, the portrait on the obverse of which will be found engraved at the head of the foregoing notice of Caligula.

SECOND BRASS.—These are common, but of good workmanship.

THIRD BRASS.—C. CAESAR DIVI. AVG. PRON. AVG.—Cap of liberty.—See R. C. C.

[The countenance of Caligula, as represented in profile on his coins, (*especially those in gold and silver*) somewhat resembles that of his grand-father, but is less noble, and has a malignant expression. He was at great pains to cherish this horrid index of his cruel disposition.]

CALLIOPE AVG.—Calliope stands as if singing to a lyre, which rests on a little pillar, on the base of which she places her left foot.— Tanini, in his supplement to Banduri, gives this as on a coin of Probus, in third brass.— Eckhel naming his authority, calls it *unique* (omnino singularis); observing, that although the group of Muses is found on coins of the Pomponia gens, yet not one of them announces Calliope's name. This type of the Epic Muse may have been selected, that she might *seem* to be sounding the praises due to the virtue of Probus. —(vii. 504.)

CALPURNIA gens.—This was a plebeian family, but one of great antiquity, tracing its origin to Calpus, the son of Numa.—Amongst the surnames of this family occurring on coins is *Piso*, the origin of which is stated by Saleius Bassus in the following lines of his Carmen ad Pisonem :—

Claraque Pisonis tulerit cognomina prima,
Humida callosâ cùm *pinseret* hordea dextrâ.

["And the illustrious surname of *Piso* he first derived from the fact of his *bruising* (or *kneading*) the moist barley in his horny palm."]

Frequently there is added to it the epithet *Frugi*, applied to L. Piso for his frugality, as Cicero testifies (pro Fonteio, ch. 13.) Valerius Maximus (iv. ch. 3) records a signal instance of abstinence in Calpurnius Piso. Another cognomen was *Bibulus*.—Eckhel, v. 158.

Morel (in his *Thesaurus Fam. Rom.*) gives no less than 150 varieties in the coins of this family; but those varieties consist chiefly of the different mintmarks. The gold *quinarius* is unique.—

Silver, some rare, but for the most part common.—The brass are by the moneyers of M. Antony and Augustus, or consist of the *as* and its divisions : some rare, others common.—The following, among others, claim notice and remark :—

Obv.—Radiated head of Apollo, with curls hanging behind ; before it, on other specimens, are different emblems, letters, or numerals.

Rev.—L. PISO FRVGI.—On other coins—C. PISO L. F. FRVGI. A horseman going at a rapid pace ; on some coins, he holds a palm branch, on others a trident, on others a torch, or a small sword or a whip. Beneath is frequently the word ROMA.—Silver.

The number of these denarii is incredible, and the greater part of them differ from each other, in some arithmetical mark, or some insulated symbol ; a variation which both Havercamp and Vaillant have devoted much learning, industry, and ingenuity to account for ; but which the less imaginative and more cautious Eckhel attributes simply to the caprice of the moneyer. The author of *Doctrina* (v. 158) allows that these denarii were struck by L. Piso Frugi and his son Caius, but at what period, he declines any attempt to decide.—Professor Cavedoni, however, and Riccio, who cites his authority (both writing after Eckhel's time), give cogent reasons, arising out of some recent monetal *trouvailles*, at Fiesole, in Italy—for the opinion which they pronounce, that the author of the above, and other coins of a similar kind, was *Lucius Piso Frugi*, son of *Lucius*, and a man of pretorian rank, in 684 (B. C. 70). This opinion, adds Riccio, " receives corroboration from a semi-uncial *asse* struck by this mint-master, and the date of which goes back to some year anterior to 680. Indeed, Borghesi himself refers coins, with insulated symbols and letters, to about the middle of the seventh century of Rome."—See *Monete delle Famiglie di Roma*—Calpurnia gens.

Leaving however the question of dates, on which the learned differ, there is one on which their opinions coincide, namely, that both sides of the above coin bear reference to the *Ludi Apollinares* ; " doubtless (says Eckhel) because those games were decreed to be perpetuated at the instance of Calpurnius, the Pretor, A. U. C. 543 (B. C. 211) whereas they had never before been sanctioned by a *Senatus Consultum* ; on which subject see Livy (xxv. 12, and xxvi. 23,) and Pighius (Ann. ii. p. 182), but especially Macrobius, who describes at length the origin of these games. (Sat. 1, ch. 17.)—That horse-races formed a part of their celebration has been well gathered by Spanheim from ancient writers (ii. p. 131).—

There is the same subject on coins of the Marcia family ; but it is further ascertained that a certain Marcius, famous for his skill in divination, whom Zonaras has erroneously called Μαρκος instead of Μαρκιος, was the individual who suggested to Calpurnius and the Senate the establishment of these games, as may be learned from the above mentioned passages of Livy and Macrobius. We have in these coins indubitable types of the *Ludi Apollinares*, which numismatists are too much inclined frequently to discover on the coins of families, with slight grounds for the supposition. Vaillant, Havercamp, and others, are considered by Eckhel to be incorrect in calling the horseman on these denarii the *desultor* ; for it was usual for the *desultores* to have at *least two* horses under their management, as is shewn under the coinage of the Marcia gens.—See *D. N. V.* vol. v. p. 158 et seq.

L. PISO. Bare head to the right.

Rev.—TER. in monogram. Victory standing before an altar ; on the other side a dagger.—Gold.—See PISO.

[" This unique coin was purchased at the sale of Lord Morton's cabinet for the British Museum, at eight guineas."—Akerman, *Descrip. Catal.* i. 33].

PISO CAEPIO Q. Laureated and bearded head of Saturn, behind it is an indented reaping hook.

Rev.—AD. FRV. EMV. EX. S. C. Two togated men, sitting on a subsellium, between corn ears.

On reference to p. 5 of this dictionary, it will be seen that, according to Eckhel, it is the head of Saturn which is represented on this denarius, because that deity presided over agriculture. But according to Professor Cavedoni (quoted by Riccio, p. 42), the head of that deity is referable to the office of the questors who presided over the public treasury, which was placed under the tutelary care of Saturn, and in the immediate vicinity of his temple. On the reverse are the two questors, who procured corn in abundance for the Roman people, namely, Piso and Cœpio, and who on that account were honoured by the Senate with this representation, as the legend felicitously explains. In opposition to Havercamp and Vaillant, who believed this rare silver coin to have been struck in the 508th year of Rome (B. C. 246), Riccio joins with Cavedoni in pronouncing its mintage to have taken place in 654 (B. C. 100), founding this opinion not only on certain monetal peculiarities ; but also on the fact that in that year, a great dearth of corn prevailed at Rome, in consequence of the continuance of the *Bellum Servile* in Sicily.—See AD. FRV. EMV.

CN. PISO PRO. Q. The bearded head of king

Numa Pompilius, whose name NVMA is inscribed on the diadem that encircles his forehead.

Rev.—MAGN. PRO. COS.　Prow of a ship.

This rare denarius was struck by Cneius Calpurnius Piso, son of Lucius, and nephew of Lucius, in his provincial pro-questorship of 681 (B. C. 73), following Pompeius Magnus then pro-consul with full powers to undertake his renowned expedition against the pirates, who infested the whole Mediterranean sea, and whom he entirely destroyed. It was this that obtained for Pompeius the title of *Magnus*, inscribed on the reverse of this coin; the ship's prow indicating the grand fleet placed at the disposal of the pro-consul. But the mint-master, wishing also to allude to the antiquity of his family, has struck to the right of his own name of PISO, the head of king Numa, from whom his family derived their origin.—Riccio, p. 43.

Rev.—BIBVLVS M. F. PRAEF. CLASS F. C.— The pretorian galley without sail.—On the obverse are the head of Mark Antony jugated with a female portrait, and, the legend M. ANT. IMP. TER. COS. DES. ITER. ET TER. IIIVIR. R.P.C.

Lucius Bibulus, to whose mintage belong this and another rare middle brass, coined in the east, was the son of M. Calpurnius Bibulus (colleague of Julius Cæsar in the consulate of 695 B. C. 59), and of the celebrated Porcia, daughter of Cato Uticensis, who espoused Marcus Brutus in her second marriage. As the son-in-law of that chief conspirator against Cæsar, he also was proscribed by the triumvirs: he followed his father-in-law into Macedonia and into Asia, during the war levied against them, and commanded the vanguard of their army on the day of Philippi. The conspirators being defeated, L. Bibulus surrendered to Antony, who, as we see on this piece of money, appointed him prefect of the fleet (PRAEF. CLASS). He is on another coin of the same mintage called Prætor Designatus (PR. DESIG.)—In 718 (B. C. 36), he gave in his adhesion to Octavian, after the death of the last of the Pompeys. The money, then, appertaining to Bibulus, cannot be beyond this epocha, because he attained afterwards to the pretorship, and, in 721 (B. C. 33), to the proconsulship of Syria, as successor to Munatius Plancus.

Rev.—M. PISO M. F. FRVGI.　Within a crown of laurel is a patera, close to which is a sacrificial knife (the handle only of which is shewn in the above cut).—The obverse of this rare denarius presents a terminal statue, between a garland and a *capeduncula* (the smaller sacrificial vase).

There is another equally rare denarius, with the same reverse in type and legend, but which on the obverse exhibits a juvenile bust, having a diademed head with wings, surrounded by capeduncula, crown, and star.

This Marcus Frugi, son of Marcus, must have been pretor in the third dictatorship of Julius Cæsar, 709 (B. C. 45), and therefore one of the moneyers some preceding year.

With respect to the terminal figure and the winged head, Cavedoni is induced, from their respective attributes, to regard both the one and the other as images of Mercury. The corona vittata seems sacerdotal, and the sacrificial vase, exhibited on both obverses, apparently belong to Mercury, regarded by the Romans as institutor of religious rites and ceremonies. And as Numa was the principal introducer of religion into Rome, as it were like another Mercury, so Marcus Piso, who, with the rest of the Calpurnii, must have been wont to boast of having this pacific king amongst his ancestors, may have aimed at a share of like glory, and to record the praise of Numa himself. "By this interpretation of mine (adds Cavedoni), it is not designed to exclude that of Ursinus, who sees in the figure in question a representation of the god *Terminus*, to whom Numa was the first to give temples and sacrifices. To Mercury the terminal stones were dedicated, and to him was also attributed the first invention of land-marks, and the boundaries of fields."—See Riccio on the Calpurnia gens, p. 43.

CALUMNIA.—See FISCI IVDAICI.

CAMALODUNUM—one of ₃the most important, and most ancient Roman towns, or stations, in Britain, within the present limits of that territorial division now called Essex.— Ptolemy, by a corrupt transposition of letters, denominates it *Camudolanum*. In the Itinerary of Antoninus, it is noted down as CAMVLODVNVM and CAMOLVDVNVM. But both by Tacitus (Annal.) and by Pliny (L. ii. sect. 77), it is more correctly written CAMALODV-NVM.—Camden (see Gough's edition, ii. 122), pronounces it to have been situated, where now stands the town of *Maldon*; observing, *inter alia*, "that the greatest part of the name is still remaining." This is the most plausible among the reasons which he assigns in support of his very positive opinion on this point, and for expressing his "wonder," that others should, "on the authority of Leland," seek it at Colchester. If, however, the venerable "Nourice of antiquity" (as Spenser justly terms him), could revisit the scenes of his chorographical researches, he would find in the clever and intelligent "History" by Mr. Thomas Cromwell, an accumulation of antiquarian facts, and of argumentative deductions, well calculated to shew that, those who have undertaken to identify the site of ancient Camalodunum with that of modern Colchester, are not such "blind observers," as he, whilst writing his immortal "Britannia," deemed them to be.

Camden's notion respecting Maldon has, indeed, been long abandoned. The *Itinera* all point to Colchester. Etymology has weight in the argument only when *existing* remains sup-

port it. At Maldon nothing ancient is found.—
Colchester, Mr. Roach Smith observes, " as the
source of discoveries of objects, which illustrate
the state of the arts, in Roman Britain, is, perhaps, second in interest to none of our ancient
towns and cities."—See a paper of his in the
Journal of the British Archæological Association, vol. ii. p. 29.

Thus much for the question of locality.—
With regard to the other branch of the subject—namely, the claim put forward to have
Camalodunum classed in the number of Roman
colonies, properly so called—it must be confessed, that the evidences on which such a claim
is founded, and those on which it is disallowed,
are almost equally unsatisfactory and inconclusive. On the one hand there are the passages
in Tacitus (Annal. L. xii. c. 32, and L. xiv. c.
31), according to which, *Camalodunum* was the
first colony of the Romans established in Britain, and was occupied by veteran soldiers,
drafted into it, when Claudius was emperor.—
There is also a marble, given in Gruter (p. 439,
No. 5), as found in Spain, the inscription of
which includes these words:—COLONIAE VICTRI-
CENSIS, QVAE EST IN BRITANNIA CAMALODVNI,
&c. On the other hand, the name of *Camalodunum* does *not* appear either in Eckhel's,
or in Mionnet's, or in any other lists of Roman colonies. Nor, with the sole exception of a
coin edited by Goltzius, and asserted by him to
have been struck under Claudius, but which no
collection can be referred to as containing, nor
any numismatist acknowledges to have recognised,
is there the least shadow of a monetal record (the
only safe corroboration on a point like this),
to prove that the *Camalodunum Britanniæ* of
Tacitus and of Pliny was more than a first class
oppidum of the Romans. It requires, in fact, to be
borne in mind, that Britain was a *province* of the
empire, governed (so far as, surrounded with
openly hostile or disaffected tribes, the Romans
could be said to govern the country), by prefects
and subordinate military officers. It is not improbable that, at the outset, an attempt was made
to establish colonies and municipia in this island;
but that the system, however successfully carried out in so many other parts of the world,
was soon abandoned here by Claudius, and for
cogent reasons not resumed by his imperial successors, seems scarcely to admit of a doubt.

CAMELUS (Camel).—This well-known and,
in its native countries of the East, most useful
animal, is represented on coins as the common
symbol of Arabia.——See the ARAB. ADQ. of
Trajan; the RESTITVTORI ARABIAE of Hadrian;
also REX ARETAS, in the Æmilia family; BAC-
CHIVS IVDAEVS, &c.

CANCELLI COMITIORUM.—Lattices, or
chancels, of the Comitia; in which the people,
when about to give their votes, were enclosed;
or perhaps barriers to prevent any one, except
the individual who was giving his vote, from
standing there. For within these inclosures it
was unlawful for any one to stand except the
voters, and the electoral officers (ministri comitiorum), whose business it was to call the names

and administer the oaths (ad appellandum, ro-
gandumque).—On a coin of Julius Cæsar we
see the *cancelli comitiorum*, in the form of a
galley, into which the ascent is by steps.—See
CLOACIN.

CANCER (the Crab) one of the twelve signs
of the Zodiac (see Zodiacus), thus called from
some similitude to the crab-fish : the sun entering that sign in the month of June, begins gradually to recede from us, and to take a retrograde course, as it were in a crab-like fashion.
On a coin struck by M. Durmius, one of the
moneyers of Augustus, is a crab, with a butterfly between its claws.—See Durmia gens.

The figure of a *Crab* holding an aplustrum in
its claws, there being under that shell-fish the
Rhodian rose, shews that the denarius of the
Servilia gens, on which it appears, was struck
at Rhodes.

CANDELABRUM—a candlestick. The use
of this instrument, in sustaining the kindled
light of the sacrificial altar, is considered to be
expressed by its appearance on a silver coin of
Augustus, with the inscription AVGVSTVS, within
a crown formed of the *crania* and *patellæ* (skulls
and kneepans) of oxen, which thus indicate the
sovereign pontificate of Augustus.—Engraved in
Morell. Thesaur. Impp. iii. TAB. xvi. No. 13.

CANIDIA gens, of plebeian origin, but of
consular rank, having for its surname *Crassus*.
The name of Canidius Crassus, an intimate friend
of Mark Antony, and by him appointed to the
government of Armenia, is read on a gold coin
of the Cæcilia gens, (p. 151, No. 9.) The following are legends and types on second brass of
this family :—

CRAS. Ship's prow to the right.
Rev.—Crocodilo on a pedestal. Second brass.
Obv.—Head of Apollo laureated.
Rev.—CRA. The fasces with axe. Second
brass.—Eckhel cites one of this family with the
head of Cleopatra, and the crocodile, but the
legend being *Greek*, excludes it from a work on
Latin coins.

These pieces of money are ascribed to the
Canidius Crassus above alluded to. They were
struck whilst Antony was trifling his time away
in Egypt, with the lascivious Cleopatra. Supporting to the last his infatuated and ruined commander, Crassus behaved bravely in administering the affairs of Armenia at this critical
period. But afterwards sharing in the defeat at
Actium, he returned with Antony to Egypt; and
on the conquest of that country by Octavian,
Canidius was put to death.—The ship's prow
indicates, perhaps, that he was admiral of Antony's fleet, or it was meant to shew the
maritime power of Egypt. The crocodile is the
usual emblem of that country, that species of
amphibious animal inhabiting the waters of the
Nile.—Riccio, pp. 44, 45.

CANINIA gens, a similarly plebeian but consular family. It had five branches, by which it
is named on ancient monuments; but on coins
it is known principally, if not solely, under the
reign of Augustus, and by the surname of *Gallus*. The *Thesaurus Morell.* furnishes eight

varieties. The silver are by moneyers of Augustus. The brass are colonial.

Obv.—AVGVSTVS. Bare head of the emperor. Silver.

Rev.—L. CONINIVS (sic) GALLVS IIIVIR.: on the side AVGVSTVS: above TR. POT. A four-legged table, with star and sceptre above. RR.

Obv.—Same legend and portrait. Silver.

Rev.—L. CANINIVS GALLVS III. A Parthian kneeling and presenting a military ensign.—[See an exactly similar type on the reverse of a denarius of Aquilius Florus, engraved in p. 105].

Obv.—AVGVSTVS. Bare head of Augustus. Gold.

Rev.—L. CANINIVS GALLVS IIIVIR.: above OB. C. S. An altar, over which is a crown, and on each side a branch of laurel. RRRR.—Pronounced *unique* by Riccio (*Tav.* 50), who values it at 30 piastres.

L. Caninius Gallus was a monetary triumvir of Augustus, in 734 (B.C. 20), in which year he struck these coins, which are all marks of homage rendered, in various ways, to the sovereign power and triumphant success of his lord and master. The last is a special piece of adulation, recording, as it does, the perpetual crown, and the branches of laurel, decreed by the Senate to Augustus, for having saved the citizens of Rome, according to the OB. CIVIS SERVATOS inscribed on the reverse.—*Monete delle Fam.* p. 45.

CANISTRUM—a basket, which, filled with flowers, was consecrated to the pagan deities, with religious rites. Hence on a gold coin of Antoninus Pius, with legend TR. POT. II. COS. II. a female figure (Piety) holding corn ears in her right hand, and in her left the *canistrum*, filled with flowers.—Engraved in Caylus, *Numis. Aurea Impp. Rom.* No. 531.

The canistrum generally appears on imperial coins bearing the legend and type of Annona.

CANTHARUS—a peculiar kind of cup or goblet, with one or two ears. On coins of the colonial imperial series, it is seen in the right hand of Bacchus.—See Apamea colonia, p. 61.

CAP. Capitolina.—COL. AEL. CAP. Colonia Aelia Capitolina.

CAP. *Capta.*—ARMEN. CAP. see *Armenia Capta.*——DAC. CAP. *Dacia Capta.*——IVD. CAP. *Judæa Capta.*

CAPEDUNCULA—a vase of smaller size than the capedo, or præfericulum, used in sacrifices. With other instruments employed by the Roman pontiffs and augurs in their religious ceremonies, it is of frequent occurrence on the coins of Julius Cæsar, M. Antonius, and others.

CAPIT. RESTIT. (*Capitolium Restituit*, or *Restitutum*).—This legend appears on the reverse of a silver medallion, struck under Domitian. It bears for type a temple of four columns.

Obv.—IMP. CAESAR DOMITIAN AVG. P. M. COS. VIII. Laureated head of Augustus.

The capitol, consumed by fire during the war of Vitellius, and afterwards restored by Vespasian, was again destroyed by the flames in the reign of Titus, A. U. C. 833 (A. D. 80). "That in that very year Titus took steps for its restor-

ation, we learn (says Eckhel), from an inscription of the *Fratres Arvales*, which has been illustrated in a treatise by Philippus-a-Turre

(*Monum. vet. Antii.*), and quoted by Muratori, p. 312; it informs us, that on the 7th of the ides of December, the priests assembled in the temple of Ops, to record their vows, AD. RESTITVTIONEM ET DEDICATIONEM CAPITOLI AB. IMP. T. CAESAR. VESPASIANO AVG. On the death of Titus, in the year following, the work was carried on by his brother Domitian, and completed by him, according to Suetonius (ch. 5), Silius Italicus, and other writers.—How great was the magnificence of this building, we have the abundant testimony of Plutarch (*in Poplicola*), who, after relating the fate of the capitol, thrice consumed and thrice restored, informs us, that on the gilding alone, Domitian expended twelve thousand talents; that the columns were of Pentelic marble, and that he had seen them himself at Athens, and admired their exquisite proportions; but that much of this beauty was diminished when they arrived at Rome, by the excess of polishing and chiselling which they there underwent. Historians have omitted to tell us the year in which the work was finished and dedicated; but this fine coin, by the 8th consulate of Domitian included in its obverse legend, assigns the year 835 (A. D. 82). The temple shewn on coins of Vespasian, struck in the year 824 (A. D. 71), exhibits six columns in front, but on the coin before us there are four. Consequently, either Domitian entirely altered the whole structure, or the moneyers were incorrect in their representation of it.

"I have frequently remarked (adds the Author of *Doctrina*), that silver medallions, struck during the earlier imperial period, appear to have first seen the light at a distance from Rome.—This opinion is confirmed by the present coin, unless we are disposed to treat lightly the evidences which it affords. The legend, which accompanies the portrait, bears no certain marks of Roman die. And even that of the reverse is not inscribed circularly, as on all other coins of Domitian, but is divided into lines. It is, however, a matter of uncertainty what city gave birth to this remarkable coin." vi. 377.

CAPITOLINUS, or CAPITOLIUM. The highest of Rome's seven hills was in a half circle and of an oval figure. It commanded the city, and was remarkable for the number of sacred buildings constructed upon it. It was at first called Saturnius, as the supposed habitation of Saturn; then Tarpeius, from the vestal Tarpcia; lastly, it was called the Capitoline mount, from a tradition that the *head* of one Olus had been discovered there in digging the foundations for the temple of Jupiter, to whom the Romans, in consequence, gave the surname of Capitolinus. It was in this temple of the capitol that solemn vows were made, that the citizens ratified the acts of government, and took the oaths of fidelity; also where the magistrates, and those who enjoyed the honours of the triumph, went to thank the gods for the victories they had gained, and to offer up their prayers for the prosperity of the country.—Pitiscus, *Lex. Ant. Rom.*

CAPITOLINUS——surname of the Petillia gens.—On a denarius of that family this word forms the obverse legend, accompanied by the head of Jupiter, with thick bushy hair and beard. The reverse legend is PETILLIVS, and the type exhibits a temple, with *façade* of six columns, and ornamented pediment.—Petillius Capitolinus, a friend of Augustus, struck, in his capacity of monetal triumvir, two denarii, of which the above was one; and which, amidst much uncertainty as to dates, serves at least to connect a Petillius in some sort of association with the temple of Jupiter Capitolinus.—See Petillia gens.—See also JUPITER.

CAPPADOCIA, an extensive country in Asia Minor, bordering northward on the Pontus Euxinus (Black Sea), eastward on Armenia, southward on Mount Taurus, which divided it from Cilicia, and westward on Galatia and Pamphilia. Its modern name is *Tocat*, it was famous, and is still noted, for horses, mules, and slaves. The ancient state of Cappadocia is very imperfectly known. It had its kings down to so late a period as the reign of Tiberius. And of those kings, coins are still extant. Germanicus Cæsar, after having vanquished the king of Armenia, made a Roman province of Cappadocia.

CAPPADOCIA, S. C.—On the reverse of a Hadrian, in large brass, this province is thus personified:—A young male figure, wearing a turreted crown, stands, with short tunic tightly girded. A lion's skin is thrown over his shoulders, and tied in a knot by the claws, over the breast. In his left hand he holds a vexillum; in the right, a mountain, or cluster of rocks, allusive to Mount Argæus, which is the common symbol of Cappadocia. On the obverse, HADRIANVS AVG. COS. III. P. P. with bare head of the emperor.—There is a second brass, with a similar reverse.

Hadrian, about 893 (A. D. 140), proceeding on his journey through pro-consular Asia, entered Cappadocia; and, as Spartian relates, "received from the inhabitants acts of submission and service, which would subsequently be advantageous to his military operations." The same writer adds, that the emperor had here an eye to the Parthian dominions, and to the maintenance of amicable relations with the neighbouring sovereigns.

The Abbé Greppo, in his valuable work, published at Paris, 1842, entitled "*Mémoire sur les Voyages de l'Empereur Hadrien*," &c. observes, that in the paucity of documents sufficiently precise on certain facts, it seems requisite to place the period of Hadrian's visit to Cappadocia, after that of his Syrian travels.— "All (says the learned vicar-general of Belley), that is told us positively by Spartian, is that Hadrian visited the province in question, and took thereout slaves for the service of the armies :—Deinde à Cappadocibus servitia castris profutura suscepit.—Cappadocia (the Abbé adds in a note), furnished Rome with numerous slaves, renowned for their lofty stature, their vigour, and their scantiness of intelligence." And he refers, for his authorities, to the Epistles of Horace, the Satires of Persius, the Epigrams of Martial, and to the oration *Post Reditum in Senatu* of Cicero. "As to the slaves attached to the Roman legions, frequent mention is made of them among the old writers; as Saumaise shews in a commentary on this passage of Spartian." p. 189.

There is also a first brass of Antoninus Pius; on the reverse of which is the legend CAPPADOCIA COS. II. The personified province stands with *Mons Argæus* at her foot; a frequent type on the numerous coins of Cæsarea, the metropolis of Cappadocia.—See Dr. King's *Plates*, TAB. XIV.

CAPPADOCIAE.—See *Restitutori* of Hadrian.

CAPPADOCICUS.—See *Exercitus* of Hadrian.

CAPRA.—See Goat.

CAPRICORNUS——a fabulous animal, of which the figure is that of a goat in the fore part, terminating in the tail of a fish. According to Hyginus (L. ii. *sign. cœl.*) this Capricornus is in reality Pan. For he says, the gods, on account of the terror with which the giant Typhon had inspired them, having changed themselves into all sorts of animals, Pan was not one of the last to adopt the expedient, and, throwing himself into a river, assumed the hybridous form above described. For this ingenious contrivance Jupiter enrolled him among the stars.

It is for this reason that Aratus (in *Phænom.*) calls him *Aegipan*.—See Pitiscus and Millin.

This type of Capricorn very frequently occurs on coins of AVGVSTVS, both Latin and Greek.

The reason assigned by Suetonius (ch. 61) for its appearance in the mint of this emperor is, that Theogenes, the mathematician of Apollonia, when informed by Augustus, then a youth, of the *time* of his nativity, leaped forward and paid him adoration. And he adds, " Augustus soon began to place such reliance on Fate, that he published his horoscope, and caused a silver coin to be struck, marked with the constellation Capricorn, under which he was born."—Schlegel adduces other testimonies, even from the poets, to the fact that Augustus was born under Capricorn *(Ad. Morell. Thesaur. Impp.* i. 194), and repeats the squabbles of the learned on this proof of Octavian Cæsar's superstitious or pretended belief in the prediction of astrologers, that he was born to attain the empire of the world.—Eckhel, vi. 109.

On these denarii we see frequently added to the figure of Capricorn, the cornucopiæ, and the rudder of a vessel, which Lactantius *(Institt.* B. iii. ch. 29) explains by saying—" they represent her (Fortune) with the horn of abundance, and a ship's helm, as though she both conferred wealth, and had the guidance of human affairs."—The globe too, as the symbol of the world, begins about the year of Rome 743 (A. D. 11) to make its appearance on Roman coins, as is shewn by a denarius of Augustus, with legend IMP. XI. beneath the figure of Capricorn.—See the word *Globe.*

Capricorn is also seen on coins of Vespasian, Titus, and Domitian, and on some of Hadrian and Antoninus Pius. A second brass of Domitian bears this type with a cornucopiæ, inscribed AVGVSTVS IMP. XX.

Two Capricorns, supporting a civic crown, a globe underneath them, appear on a large brass of Augustus, and also on one of Tiberius. A silver coin of Vespasian, from which the subjoined cut is taken, likewise presents the type of *two Capricorns,* supporting a shield, in which are the letters s. c. *(Senatus Consulto).* Under the shield is a globe.

There is a similar reverse on a denarius of Titus. This type is considered to denote that the felicity of the Roman empire, under these two princes, father and son, was equal to that which was enjoyed in the Augustan age.—See VESPASIAN.

Capricorn appears on a third brass of Gallienus.—See the legend NEPTVNO CONS. AVG.

Capricorn, as the symbol of Felicitas, borne on the standard of a Roman legion, appears on a billon coin of Gallienus, with the legend LEG. I. ADI. VII. P. VII. F. (Legio Prima Adjutrix, Septima Pia, Septima Fidelis).—Eckhel, *Cat. Mus. Imp.*

CAPTIVUS, captive, or prisoner of war.— The Romans were accustomed to place their military prisoners near the standards. They cut off the hair of the kings, and of the principal officers, and sent them to Rome, to grace their triumphs.

It was also the custom of the Romans to load the vanquished with fetters, and compel them in that state to precede the triumphal car of the conqueror. It was thus that the famous Zenobia, Queen of Palmyra, honoured the triumph of Aurelian. If death prevented captured princes and their families from being present at this, to them, most cruelly humiliating ceremony, their images were generally carried before the triumpher. Augustus caused this to be done in the case of Cleopatra, who had killed herself in order to escape so ignominious an exposure.—Statius *(Silva,* iii. v. 2), thus alludes to the fact—

Actias Ausonias fugit Cleopatra catenas.

" Cleopatra fled the chains of Italy at Actium."

Captives figures of, with their hands tied behind their backs, appear on coins of the Æmilia, Julia, Memmia, and Sulpicia families. And in like manner on coins of most of the emperors from Augustus to Constantine junior. See for examples, DEBELLATORI OMNIVM GENTIVM.—FRANCIA.—DE GERMANIS.—&c.

Captives, bound in chains, standing, or prostrate at the feet of deities, linked to the chariot wheels of emperors, trod upon by Victories, or seated beneath military ensigns and trophies, are also to be seen on imperial coins throughout almost the whole series.—See ALAMANNIA DEVICTA, p. 32—Triumphal reverses of Numerianus and L. Verus—PART. ARAB. PART. ADIAB. of Severus, &c.

Captive, or *Captives,* at the feet of the emperor, who is on foot or on horseback, are exhibited on coins from Vespasian and Titus to Constantine the Great and his family.—See IVDAEA CAPTA.—GERMANICO AVG. of M. Aurelius.—VIRTVS EXERCITVS ROMANORVM of Julianus II.

Captives, sitting under a trophy, or beneath a palm tree, in an attitude of grief and despondency, as on those coins of Vespasian and Titus which commemorate the overthrow of Jerusalem and the conquest of Judæa—also *captives* in a weeping posture, or sitting on a heap of arms, as in Domitian.—See captives at the foot of an imperial estrade, on a medallion of PROBVS.

CARACALLA, Emperor, was the eldest son of Septimius Severus. His mother was Julia Domna, erroneously stated by some writers to have been his step-mother. The surname of

Caracalla, by which he is commonly denominated by historians, does not appear on any coins or other public monuments. It was in fact only a nickname (like that of *Caligula* given to Caius

Cæsar (see p. 164), and derived from a kind of Gaulish vestment, which he, the spoiled child of his mother, had himself brought into fashion. He was born at Lugdunum, in Gaul (Lyon), whilst his father was governor of that province, in the year U. C. 941 (A. D. 188), on the 4th or 6th of April. At his birth the name of Bassianus was given him, derived, according to Victor, from his maternal grandfather. The mildness of disposition and lively temperament, which he displayed in early youth, and which rendered him the favourite alike of his parents and of the people, are mentioned by Spartian in terms of high commendation, and offer a striking contrast to the cruelty which disgraced his more advanced years, and rendered him the scourge of the world. During the first years of his father's reign, he remained in the position of a private citizen. But when, in 949 (A. D. 196), that emperor left Mesopotamia to conduct operations against Albinus, he stopped on his way at Viminacium (in Upper Mæsia, now Servia and Bulgaria), and there creating Caracalla a *Cæsar*, gave him the names of *M. Aurelius Antoninus*, in the place of that of Bassianus. He was in this year, on coins styled CAESAR and PRINCEPS IVVENTVTIS. In the following year (A. D. 197) he was elected member of the pontifical college, and the title PONTIFEX begins on his coins. In the same year, Albinus being overthrown, he was styled DESTINATVS IMPERATOR. (See the words).—In 951 (A. D. 198), having completed his 10th year, he was declared AVGVSTVS by his father and the army; and had the *Tribunitia Potestas* conferred upon him.

952 (A. D. 199). Caracalla was this year with his father in the East. The following year he was present at the Parthian campaign with Severus. The titles of PART. MAX. begin at this date to appear on his coins.

954 (A. D. 201). Returning with his father to Antioch, he assumed the toga virilis, and was nominated consul for the year ensuing. Accordingly in A. D. 202, he proceeded consul, in Syria, Severus himself being his colleague. He accompanied his father into Egypt, and thence returned with him to Rome, where he married Plautilla.—In the same year the title PIVS begins to appear on obverses.

956 (A. D. 203).—The titles of PART. MAX. now cease on his coins. For the occurrences of this and the four consecutive years, including the celebration of the Secular Games, 957 (A. D. 204), see biographical notice and coinage of Severus.

961 (A. D. 208). Caracalla, after having this year celebrated his *Decennales*, set out with his father for the campaign in Britain, where he was also present during the two following years of the war's continuance.

964 (A. D. 211).—In the preceding year he began to be styled BRIT. on his coins. On the death of his father, which took place this year at York, on the 4th of February, Caracalla, after duly solemnising the obsequies of Severus, hastened to conclude a peace with the Caledonians. At the same time, he endeavoured to induce the army to acknowledge him as sole emperor, to the exclusion of Geta. Failing in that attempt, he feigned amity towards his brother. A pretended reconciliation took place; and Geta and he returned to Rome together with the ashes of their parent. Yet even on their journey homeward, Caracalla indulged in frequent designs on his brother's life, but refrained to put them into execution, partly through fear of the soldiers, and partly through the watchful precautions of Geta, who was apprised of his own danger.

965 (A. D. 212). The two brothers entered the city together—together bestowed donatives on the troops, and distributed largesses to the people. But in the midst of negociations commenced for peaceably dividing the empire between them, Caracalla murdered Geta in the very arms of their mother. The soldiers, though at first exasperated by the atrocity of the act, were at length appeased by extravagant bribes, and thus enriched with the wealth accumulated during the reign of Severus, they unscrupulously pronounced Geta a public enemy. To the Senate he boldly justified his crime of fratricide, on the alleged plea that Geta had been engaged in plots against his life. He then put to death all those who were known, or suspected, to have favoured the cause of his brother, whose name was from that moment erased from the public monuments. (See a remarkable instance cited in p. 79). Many thousand persons are said to have fallen victims on this occasion to the cupidity and blood-thirstiness of the imperial despot: amongst these were Papinius, prefect of the pretorian guards, and a distinguished lawyer; together with other men, as well as women, of rank.

966 (A. D. 213).—Remorse at having committed these dreadful crimes pursued him every where; but abandoned to the torrent of his brutal passions, he never ceased to perpetrate cruelties and to inflict oppressions. In the vain endeavour to banish the terrors of an evil conscience, he addicted himself still more eagerly than ever to amusements which, measured by the Roman standard of public morals, might under other circumstances have found excuse in the desire to gratify the dissolute and inhuman

taste of a corrupt people. Chariot racing, combats of gladiators, and huntings of wild animals, at once served to divert the enslaved multitude, and to satiate his own savage nature. On a large brass, the reverse legend of which (P. M. TR. P. XVI. IMP. II. COS. IIII. P. P. S. C.) shews it to have been minted in this year—the type (as will be seen by the subjoined cut from a well preserved and genuine specimen), exhibits a grand edifice, composed of arcades, temples, walls, and portals, forming the outer enclosure; and of a lofty obelisk, with metæ, and statues, constituting the interior objects of the Circus Maximus, at Rome, as it existed in the beginning of the third century.

On comparing this type with that on a large brass coin of Trajan, it is evidently intended to represent the same magnificent building erected by that great emperor; and to the repairs of, or additions to, which Caracalla probably contributed some portion of those immense sums, he was in the habit of grinding out of the citizens in the shape of taxes, or of seizing as military plunder from the whole world besides.—See CIRCVS MAXIMVS.

The title of FELIX now begins to appear on coins of Caracalla, and BRITannicus ceases, being succeeded by that of GERManicus, which he had adopted on account of pretended victories over the Germans. This year, or perhaps at the close of the year preceding, he went into Gaul, and after cruelly despoiling that province, he returned to Rome.

In 967 (A. D. 214), he entered on an expedition against the Alamanni, over whom he gained a victory on the banks of the Mænus (river Mayne, in Germany). In this expedition it is stated, he made himself an object of ridicule even to the barbarians. Declared Imperator III. he proceeded into Dacia; thence into Thrace, and, crossing the Hellespont, wintered at Nicomedia.

968 (A. D. 215). After gladiatorial shews, on his birth-day, the 4th of April, at Nicomedia, he went to Pisidian Antioch, with the intention of invading the Parthians, on some far-fetched cause of quarrel. But they being seized with panic, and instantly complying with the demands of Caracalla, he proceeded to Alexandria, where he revenged himself for some railleries, by slaughtering twenty thousand of the inhabitants.

969 (A. D. 216).—Returning from Egypt to Antioch, Caracalla (who, four years before, had caused his wife Plautilla to be put to death), was "the meek and modest suitor" to ask in marriage the daughter of Artabanus, king of the Parthians. This request being refused, he crossed the Euphrates, invaded Media, took Arbela, and, after ravaging the whole region with fire and sword, returned to winter quarters in Edessa. Having inveigled Abagarus, king of the Osrhæni, into a conference, he loaded him with chains, and took possession of his kingdom.

970 (A. D. 217).—This year Caracalla prepared for war against the Parthians, who made their appearance with a large force, to avenge the aggression of the year preceding. On his way in Mesopotamia from Edessa to Carrhæ, where he intended to have visited the celebrated temple dedicated to the Syrian god Lunus, he was assassinated by a soldier of his own body guard, named Martialis, at the instigation of Macrinus, the pretorian prefect, on the 8th of April, in the 29th year of his age, during the celebration of the Megalensian games.

As, in boyhood he displayed so much moderation, affability, and averseness to even the most just severity, all, who had known him at that period of life, were lost in astonishment at the monstrous cruelties of Caracalla's riper years. Spartian is of opinion that his previous character was but the result of an artful dissimulation, or a desire of resembling Alexander the Great, of whose defects, rather than merits, both of mind and body, he shewed himself a servile imitator. Even during his father's life time, he was unable wholly to conceal the natural ferocity of his disposition; and to rid himself of the sense of restraint and fear which the old emperor's authority imposed, he made frequent attempts, during the campaign in Britain, by instigating plots and tumults, to put an end to the life of Severus. And when at length all apprehension of parental punishment was removed, he shewed at once his determination to kill his brother, which, as we have seen under the events of the year 965 (A. D. 212), he carried out with a cruelty that extended itself to every member of the unfortunate Geta's family. If to this we add the horrors of his massacre at Alexandria, perpetrated on the slightest possible provocation, we perceive clearly, that there were no relations, however sacred and religious, which he was not capable of violating by bloodshed. Finding the contents of the treasury insufficient to meet the demands of his cupidity, on account of his extravagant expenditure in public spectacles, and because it was matter of necessity to enrich his soldiers, both in order to reconcile them to the murder of Geta, and to retain their services as a defence against attempts on his own person,—he attacked with impunity the properties of the citizens, openly asserting, that the wealth of the world belonged to him alone, as the dispenser of it to his faithful soldiers; and it is said, that, when his mother remonstrated with him on the costliness and frequency of his donatives, adding, that shortly no means, fair or foul, of raising money would be left to him—his reply was, "Be of good courage, mother; for so long as we retain *this* (pointing to his sword), money will always be forthcoming." He exhibited so many instances of perfidy in the presence of the whole world, that at last no one believed him, even on his oath, and he became an object of hatred and contempt to foreign nations, as well as to his own. After death, his body was burned, and the bones brought to Rome, and deposited in the tomb of the Antonines.—See Eckhel, vii. 199, et seq.

MINTAGES OF CARACALLA.

On his coins Caracalla is styled M. AVRELIVS ANTONINVS, or M. AVR. ANTON. CAES.—IMP. M. AVR. ANTONIN.—IMP. C. or CAES. ANTONINVS—M. AVR. ANTONINVS PIVS AVG.—ANTONINVS PIVS AVG. BRIT*annicus.*—ANTONINVS PIVS FELIX AVG.—ANTONINVS PIVS AVG. GERM*anicus.*—DIVVS ANTONINVS MAGNVS.—On the reverses sometimes appear SEVERI AVG. PII. FIL*ius,* or PRINCEPS IVVENTVTIS, or DESTINATVS IMPERATOR. —On other reverses occur P. or PART*hicus*— MAX. or MAXIMVS—also RECTOR ORBIS.

The medallions and gold coins of this emperor are of considerable rarity; so are the small brass; but the denarii, together with the large and middle brass, are for the most part common. —His first brass, however, even with common reverses, when in very fine preservation, bring high prices. From the commencement of his reign the silver is found to be not pure but mixed with brass. His brass coinage of cities and colonies is abundant. That portion of the Roman mintages which give to Caracalla the name of "Great" are very rare, the epithet being found only on his consecrations—for, notwithstanding " his atrocious career of folly and barbarity (as Captain Smyth observes), this execrable ' Man of Blood' received the honours of deification, by command of the soldiers."

After Caracalla, another, and if possible still greater disgrace to the name of emperor, Elagabalus, profaned (by his own assumption of it) the title of M. AVRELIVS ANTONINVS. There is in consequence sometimes a difficulty to distinguish the coins of those two princes. It may not, therefore, be unacceptable, especially to the tyro, if the following rules are here cited for ascertaining the point, as concisely given by the learned and accurate author of *Leçons Elémentaires de Numismatique Romaine :*—

1st. The head without crown, and the title of *Caesar* alone, can belong only to *Caracalla,* since *Elagabalus* was at once created *Augustus.*

2nd. The dignity of PONTIFEX (without the epithet of MAX.) with which Caracalla was invested during the life time of his father, cannot be appropriated to *Elagabalus,* who was always *Pontifex Maximus.*

3rd. A very infantine head, or one strongly bearded; and the titles PART. MAX. BRIT. GERM. suit only with *Caracalla.* The same remark applies to the epithet AVGG. in the legends of certain reverses ; seeing that he reigned simultaneously during several years either with his father, or

with his brother; whilst we know that *Elagabalus* never had any colleague.

4th and lastly, *Caracalla,* in his 5th tribunate, was consul for the first time. *Elagabalus,* after his 5th tribunate (the epocha when he perished), was consul for the 4th time. Therefore every record of the tribunitian power marked by a number exceeding V. can apply only to the son of *Severus,* &c.

There is also a star, or small radiated sun, on many of the coins, especially the silver ones, of Elagabalus, which are not to be met with on those of Caracalla.

The following are amongst the rarest and most remarkable reverses :—

GOLD AND SILVER MEDALLIONS.—TR. P. XVIII. COS. IIII. The moon (or Diana) in a car drawn by two bulls. (gold, valued by Mionnet at 400 fr.)—VENVS VICTRIX, holding a victriola and hasta. (gold, valued by Mionnet at 400 fr.)—Young beardless head of Caracalla laureated, with reverse of VICTORIA AVGVSTA. (Silver, valued at 200 fr.)

GOLD *of common size.*—ADVENTVS. Three figures on horseback.—FELICITAS SAECVLI. Severus seated between his two sons. (Valued by Mionnet at 200 fr.)—LAETITIA TEMPORVM. Galley, cars, and animals.—PLAVTILLAE AVGVSTAE. Head of the empress.—TR. P. XIII. COS. IIII. Several figures sacrificing.—TR. P. XVII. COS. IIII. The circus, with chariots.—P. SEPT. GETA CAES. &c. Bare head of Geta.—*Obverse.* Bust of Caracalla. (A very fine specimen of this rare type, in a high state of preservation, brought £11 at the Pembroke sale).—AVGVSTI COS. Severus and Caracalla seated on an estrade, and two figures standing.—CONCORDIAE AETERNAE. Heads of Severus and Julia Domna.—CONCORDIA FELIX. Severus and Plautilla joining hands.—COS. LVDOS. SAECVL. FEC. Bacchus and Hercules.—FELICIA TEMPORA. The four Seasons.—P. M. TR. P. XVIII. &c. Esculapius in a temple; two figures sacrificing at an altar. (Brought £16 16s. at the Thomas sale).—VICTORIAE BRIT. Victory seated on bucklers, with palm and shield. (A very fine specimen brought £16 at the Thomas sale).

SILVER.—Head of Plautilla, as in gold.— AETERNIT. IMPERI. Heads of Severus and Caracalla.—ARCVS AVGG. Arch of Severus. (See engraving, p. 78).—CONCORDIAE. Heads of Severus and Julia.—DIVO. ANTONINO MAGNO. Consecration medal.—IMP. ET CAESAR. Three figures seated.—LIBERALITAS. Two emperors seated, two figures standing.—Heads of Caracalla and Geta.

BRASS MEDALLIONS.—CONCORDIAE AVG. Caracalla and Geta, each crowned by Victory. (Valued by Mionnet at 200 fr.)—IMP. II. COS. IIII. Emperor in a quadriga.—TR. P. XVI. IMP. II. COS. IIII. Grand circus, in which are an obelisk and chariot races.—SEVERI. AVG. PII. FIL. Sacrificial instruments. (Valued by Mionnet at 250 fr.)—TRAIECTVS. Emperor and soldiers crossing a river on a bridge of boats.

FIRST BRASS.—DIVO. ANTONINO MAGNO. Bare head.—*Rev.* CONSECRATIO. Funeral pile.

—COS. LVD. SAEC. FEC. A sacrifice : six figures. —PONTIF. &c. Caracalla and Geta, with three soldiers.—SAECVLARIA SACRA. Several figures sacrificing.—VIRTVS AVGG. The emperor standing near a trophy.—AEQVITATI PVBLICAE. The three Monetæ.—PONTIF. &c. Severus and Caracalla.—COS. III. Emperor addressing his soldiers. —COS. IIII. Circus. (See wood-cut p. 174).— COS. IIII. Lion with thunderbolt.—PROFECTVS AVG. Emperor and two soldiers.—VICTORIAE BRITTANNICAE.

SECOND BRASS.—ARCVS AVG. Arch of Severus. (See wood-cut, in p. 79).—AVGVSTI COS. —ANN. AVG. SAECVLI. FELICISSIMI.——LIBERALITAS, &c.

THIRD BRASS.—PRIM. DECE. S. C. A club within a garland.—PART. MAX. Trophy, on each side a captive.

CAR or CHARIOT. *(Currus).*——Ancient monuments, and coins amongst the rest, make us acquainted with such cars of the Romans as were used by them either for certain ceremonies of religion, for the pomp of triumphs, or for the courses of the Circus. They were of two kinds, on two wheels and on four. The former were smaller and more ancient than those on four wheels, which were at first reserved for the highest magistrates under the republic, and for the emperors afterwards. The cars of ceremony partook of the magnificence of the Romans; they were decorated profusely with silver, gold, ivory, and other costly materials. The imperial chariots, and those used by persons of the greatest distinction, were drawn by mules, or by white horses, which were most prized.

Cars of the Circus or Race course, served also on occasions of public festivals. This vehicle was a species of shell, mounted on two wheels; it was higher before than behind, and ornamented with painting and sculpture. When harnessed to two horses, these cars were called *bigæ* (see Axsia gens, p. 117—Saufeia gens, p. 129); and *quadrigæ* when drawn by four horses, which were always driven abreast.—See Annia gens, p. 48; Aufidia, 94; Bæbia, 121.—See also *Bigati* and *Quadrigati.*

Covered Cars (currus arcuati) were used by the Roman *flamines* for carrying the statues of their divinities. They differed from the others only in the arched roof placed above them, and under which those in the vehicle were protected from wind and bad weather.—See *Carpentum,* and *Thensa.*

Cars of Divinities, as seen on coins, are occasionally drawn by the animals which pagan mythology has consecrated to them. For example, that of Diana by stags; that of Cybele by lions; that of Bacchus by panthers; that of Hercules by centaurs; &c.—See Aurelia gens, p. 111.

Car of the proceeding Consul.—See *Consularis Processus.*

Car of Triumph (currus triumphalis).—This was at first harnessed to two horses, afterwards to four, and to two or four elephants (see Cæcilia gens, p. 111). It was of a circular form, had two wheels, and the triumpher stood in it, as is

shewn on various coins. After the example of the Greeks, the Romans ornamented these triumphal chariots with images designed to perpetuate the memory of their victories. The use of the *currus triumphalis* had been introduced, according to some, by Romulus, according to others, by Tarquin the Ancient, or Valerius Poplicola. Before the times of the empire, the *car of triumph* was generally gilt; under the emperors it was of gold—the triumpher himself held the reins of the horses. If he had young children, they were placed with him in the car; if they were adolescent, they accompanied it on horseback. On a great number of the imperial coins we see the *triumphator* in his chariot, as in Domitian, Antonine, &c. When he mounted into it, this prayer was said :—" Dii, nutu et imperio quorum nata et aucta est res Romana, eandem placati, propitiatique servate." The emperor triumphing was followed as well as preceded by soldiers, trumpeters, and others burning costly perfumes.—(Pitiscus—Millin—Rasche).

On a medallion in bronze of Gordianus Pius is a triumphal car, of which the emperor is the charioteer. It agrees with those of other cars of triumph exhibited on Roman coins—resembling as it does a short, compact, round tower, resting on only two wheels. The emperor stands guiding the vehicle, according to the old-established custom handed down from the consuls of the republic: hence Prudentius says—" Stantes que duces in curribus altis."—See *Triumph.* See also an excellent representation of the Roman car of triumph in the well-known coin of Germanicus Cæsar, with legend DEVICTIS GERM. SIGNIS RECEP.

CARAUSIUS *(Marcus Aurelius Valerius),* was born of obscure parents, in that part of Belgic Gaul called Menapia, a district between the Scheldt and the Meuse. Bred a pilot, he had recommended himself alike by his skill in nautical affairs, and by his bravery as a soldier, to the favour of Diocletian and Maximianus Hercules. It was the latter emperor that gave him the command of a naval force, which had been equipped for the purpose of putting a stop to the predatory expeditions of the Franks, who, cruising about in their light vessels, from place to place, were committing continual outrages on the coasts of what are now Holland, Belgium, France, and Spain. At first Carausius displayed zeal and activity in discharging the duties of his appointed service; but subsequently his equivocal movements, and increasing wealth, gave rise to strong suspicions that he allowed the sea-robbers whom he should have suppressed, to rove with impunity the narrow seas, in order afterwards to possess himself of the greater portion of their ill-acquired booty. Maximianus therefore ordered that he should be put to death. But with a vigilant eye to his own safety, Carausius instantly sailed across to Britain with the imperial fleet, which was devoted to his interests, and being well received by the Roman troops there, he assumed the purple with the title of Augustus, A. D. 287. His prudence and valour enabled him to maintain his independent government of the island. By the speedy construction of new galleys, and the formation of alliances with different tribes, whom he trained as sailors, the usurper made head against all the armaments sent against him by Maximianus, who, with the senior Augustus, Diocletian, was at length compelled (A. D. 289) to acknowledge him as their colleague, so far at least as Britain was concerned.

The sequel of this bold adventurer's history cannot be better related than in the terms employed by Mr. Akerman :—

"Carausius enjoyed his honours seven years, and, during that period, performed many acts which evinced his ability to rule, notwithstanding his defection from his masters. He defended the frontiers of his empire from the Caledonians, courted the friendship and alliance of the Franks (upon the confines of whose country he was born), and in reward for their services instructed them in naval and military affairs.— His fleets swept the seas, and commanding the mouths of the Rhine and the Seine, ravaged the coasts, and rendered the name of the once obscure Menapian pilot, as celebrated as those of the emperors. During this time, Carausius still kept possession of Boulogne; but in the year 292, the adoption of the two Cæsars, Constantius and Galerius, added strength to the Roman arms. Maximianus guarded the Rhine; and Constantius, taking command of the legions appointed for the British war, immediately laid siege to Boulogne, which, after an obstinate resistance, surrendered to the conqueror, who possessed himself of the naval stores of Carausius. Three years were consumed in the preparation of a fleet for the recovery of Britain: but ere it was launched, news arrived of the assassination of Carausius by his friend and prime minister Allectus, A. D. 293. The event was considered as a presage of victory to the Roman arms."—*Coins of the Romans relating to Britain*, 2nd edition.

MINTAGES OF CARAUSIUS.

The connection of this usurper with Britain has always rendered his coinage an object of peculiar curiosity and appreciation, with the numismatic antiquaries and collectors of our country. In Italy his coins are beyond comparison more rare than in England; and were almost equally scarce in France, until a recent *trouvaille* at Rouen brought a large hoard of them to light. Indeed they were for the far greater part struck in this island, during the six years (A. D. 286 to A. D. 293) in which its government was virtually separated from that of

the Roman empire.—"Of this eventful period (observes Mr. Roach Smith, in his *Antiquities of Richborough*, &c.) as far as regards Britain, no monumental inscriptions are extant; and the brief notices of historical writers, which have come down to us, are in the suspicious language of panegyrists and conquerors." p. 136.

In the last edition of Mr. Akerman's work above quoted, 53 varieties in gold and silver are enumerated, and no less than 233 in brass, which are of the third size only. And since 1844, others are now known, as scarcely a year passes without the discovery of some variety hitherto undescribed. "In the bed of the Thames, and in the neighbourhood of St. Alban's, and other Roman Stations (says Mr. Bergne), coins of Carausius are found in great numbers. Nor is it improbable that on examining any dozen coins picked up successively in the fields which occupy the site of the ancient Verulam, two or three would prove to be of Carausius. —(See *Numismatic Chronicle*, No. LV. Jan. 1852, p. 151).

The workmanship of the gold resembles that of the contemporary coins of Diocletian and his imperial colleague, being of a fine and bold, but peculiar fabric. With rare exceptions, the fabric of the silver is rough, and their quality of metal base. Of the brass, a great portion is of barbarous execution; "but (as Mr. Akerman remarks), all of them bear a portrait, which it is impossible to confound with any other in the Roman series."

Many of the types and legends of the money of this usurper obviously apply to Carausius only : among these may be noticed those of EX-PECTATE VENI. and CARAVSIVS ET FRATRES SVI ; whilst it is equally clear that such legends as PRINCIPI IVVENTVT(IS) and ORIENS AVG. can have no reference to the acts, or to the situation, of Carausius. In the latter case they must have been executed by ignorant, and probably illiterate, moneyers, without knowledge of their application or significance.

Carausius is styled on his coins—CARAVSIVS—CARAVSIVS AVG.—IMP. CARAVSIVS AVG.—IMP. CARAVSIVS P. F. AVG.—IMP. C. M. CARAVSIVS AVG.—IMP. C. M. AVR. V. CARAVSIVS P. AVG.—CARAVSIVS ET FRATRES SVI.—On his gold and silver coinage his effigy is adorned with a laurel wreath ; on the brass with a radiated diadem.

The following are amongst the rarest reverses :

GOLD.

CONSERVATORI AVGGG. Hercules standing, holding his club and a bow; behind is a quiver; on the exergue M. L.

Valued by Mionnet at 720 fr.

CONCORDIA MILITVM. Two women standing.—Valued by Mionnet at 600 fr.

LEG(IO) IIII. FL. Lion walking, with ears of corn in his mouth.—Valued by Mionnet at 600 fr.

Obv.—VIRTVS CARAVSI. Bust of Carausius to the left, with slight beard, and ornamented helmet ; spear in right hand; buckler over left shoulder, ornamented with griffin, to the left, and floral border.

Rev.—ROMANO RENOVA. Wolf to the right, with the twins ; in the exergue R. S. R.

Valued by Mionnet at 750 fr.

This coin, of the highest degree of rarity, and described to be in very good preservation, wt. 67 grs. brought £14 at the Thomas sale, lot 988.

SALVS AVGGG. In the exergue M. L.—This coin of Maximianus, certainly struck by Carausius, is in the cabinet of Mr. Roach Smith.

SILVER.

ADVENTVS AVG. The emperor on horseback, brandishing a spear over a fallen enemy.

This coin, well preserved, brought £8 at the Pembroke sale.

ADVENTVS AVG. Emperor on horseback, right hand elevated, &c. a captive at the fore feet of the horse; a thunderbolt in exergue. On the obverse, IMP. CARAVSIVS P. F. AV. laureated, togated, and bearded bust to right.

This fine and most rare, perhaps unique coin, brought £13 at the Brumell sale, in 1850.

CONSERVAT. AVG. Jupiter.—Engraved in Akerman, ii. p. 156, pl. xi. No. 5.

CONCORDIA AVGG. Two hands joined. (Haym. *Tesoro Britannico).*

CONCORDIA MILITVM. Same type. In the exergue, R. S. R.

This coin, of good silver, well preserved, brought £4 4s. at the Thomas sale.

FIDES MILITVM. A female to the left, holding two standards ; in the exergue R. S. R. Not in Mionnet or Akerman ; well preserved.—Curt.

This coin brought £5 17s. 6d. at the Brumell sale.

FELICITAS. Galley and four rowers; in exergue R. S. R.

This denarius, in perfect condition, brought £7 10s. at the Thomas and £8 15s. at the Pembroke sale.

FIDEM MILITVM N. N. A female standing, holding a pair of scales and a cornucopiæ.

This, of good silver, brought £8 at the Thomas sale.

IXPECTATE *(sic)* VENI. Emperor and a female figure.—See EXPECTATE.

LEG(IO) IIII. FL.—"A centauress (and not a centaur, says Mr. Curt), as in Etruscan Antiquities in the Naples Museum, &c." walking to the left, holding with both her hands a long club, which she rests on her shoulders. G. in exergue.

Of good silver, and fine as to preservation—see Catalogue, lot 1084, Brumell cabinet, at the sale of which it brought £22.—See engraving of it in Akerman ; see also his remarks, 124.

LEG. V. VII. VIII.—(Stukeley).

LIB(ERALITAS) III. Emperor on horseback. (British Museum).

MONETA AVG. The goddess Moneta standing, with scales and cornucopiæ. In the exergue X.—Engraved in plate vi. fig. 4, *Antiquities of Richborough,* &c.

ORIENS AVG. The Sun standing.

PRINCIPI IVVENT. A military figure stands resting on a spear, with olive twig in right hand.

This coin, of good silver, and one of the rarest of the Carausian types, obtained £8 at the Thomas sale.—See Akerman, No. 32 & 139.

ROMANO RENOV. Wolf suckling the founders of Rome ; in the exergue R. S. R.

A very fine specimen, and of good silver, pierced, went for £7 5s. 6d. at the Thomas sale.

VICTORIA AVG. The goddess marching.—VIRTVS IM. AVG. *(sic).* Military figure.

VIRTVS AVG. Lion with thunderbolt in its mouth.—This coin, in fine condition, brought £5 16s. at the Thomas sale.

VOTO PVBLICO, inscribed round a crown of laurel, in which is seen MVLTIS XX. R. S. R. On the obverse, IMP. CARAVSIVS P. F. AVG. Laureated bust of Carausius.

Mionnet attaches the value of 150 fr. to this coin ; an engraving of which is prefixed to the mintages of Carausius, p. 176 of this Dictionary.

VOTVM PVBLICVM. A square altar with fire, in the middle of which are MVLTIS XX. IMP.

Valued by Mionnet at 150 fr. A specimen of it, in good silver, fetched £5 17s. 6d. at the Thomas sale.

VBERVTA (blundered for *Ubertas)* AV. A female seated on a low stool, milking a cow. In the exergue R. S. R.

A silver coin of Carausius, with this legend and type on its reverse, brought £5 17s. 6d. at the above mentioned sale.—The letters on the exergue R. S. R. probably stand for RVTVPIAE or RVTVPIIS (Richborough) SIGNATA, as coins of Carausius are frequently found in the neighbourhood of that old Kentish town.—Akerman, 121.

THIRD BRASS.

ABVNDANTI. AVG. Abundance personified.

AEQVITAS MVNDI. Female with scales and cornucopiæ.

This third brass of Carausius, very fine and almost unique, only one other of this type being known to exist, was found at Rouen, where it formed part of M. Biliard's collection. It brought £2 15s. at the sale of " a well-known collector," 1851.

ADIVTRIX AVG. Half length bust of Victory, holding a garland and palm branch.

Coins of Victorinus occur in third brass with the same legend.—Akerman, 127.

ADVENTVS AVG. The emperor on horseback. In exergue R. S. R.—(In the cabinet of Mr. C. Roach Smith).

ADVENTVS CARAVSI. Emperor on horseback; his right hand raised, holding a globe. In the exergue of some R. S. P. (or M. L.)

AEQVITAS AVG. Equity with her attributes. (In the Hunter collection.)

APOLLINI CO. AVG. and APOLLINI CONS. and CONS. AVG. A Griffin.

These legends and types will be found on the abundant third brass of Gallienus. Akerman.

COH. PR.—*Cohors Pretoria.* Four military standards. (In Mr. Reader's collection.)

COHR. PRAET. Four standards. (In the Hunter collection.)

COMES AVG. Victory marching with garland and palm branch. On the obverse is the helmeted bust of Carausius, with javelin and shield ; legend CARAVSIVS AVG.

The coins of Carausius with these armed busts appear to be modelled on those of the Emperor

Probus, on whose money the imperial effigies are often thus represented. Akerman, p. 128.

COMES AVGG. Minerva standing, holding the hasta and an olive branch. In the field S. P. On the exergue MLXXI. (Tanini.)

CONCORDIA AVGG. A woman holding two standards, on others holding the hasta and cornucopiæ.

CONCORDIA MIL. or MILIT. or MILITVM. Two right hands joined; or the emperor joining hands with a female figure.

On one of this rare type, in the Roach Smith cabinet, we read on the obverse IMP. C. CARAVSIVS P. F. IN. AVG.

CONSERVAT. AVG. Neptune seated; in his right hand an anchor; in his left a trident reversed.

See remarks on this coin, in *Antiquities of Reculver*, &c. by Mr. Roach Smith, p. 136.

CONSTANT. (or CONSTAVNT. *(sic.)* AVG. Hercules. (Mionnet.)

DIANA.—Goddess seated. DIANAE. CONS. AVG. A stag.—DIANAE REDVCI. A stag.

EXPECTATE VENI. Two figures standing, with joined hands. In the exergue R. S. A.—See the words *suis locis*.

FELICITAS AVG. Woman with ensign and cornucopiæ.—Same legend. A galley on the sea, with rowers.

FELICITAS TEMP. Four children, representing the four seasons.—Engraved in Akerman, pl. v.

FIDES MILITVM—FIDES MILIT. Woman holding two military standards.

FIDEM MILITVM. Similar type.—(In the Douce collection, bequeathed to and deposited in the Bodleian Library.)

The last three types occur perpetually in the Roman series, but they are' very appropriate on the coins of one who owed so much to his military partisans.—Akerman, p. 130.

FORTVNA AVG. Fortune with rudder and cornucopiæ.—FORTVNA RED. Fortune seated.— *Obv.*—IMP. C. CARAVSIVS P. F. AVG.

A beautiful bust, in perfect preservation, and said to be unique, was purchased, at " a well-known collector's" sale, for £2 5s.

GENIO AVG. Woman holding globe and cornucopiæ.

GENIVS EXERCIT. Genius standing with patera and cornucopiæ.

This unique brass coin, of larger module than that of ordinary third brass, is engraved in *Roman Coins relating to Britain*, pl. v. No. 36.—" It was in the possession (observes Mr. Akerman) of the late Mr. R. F. Newman, City Solicitor, a relative of whom shewed it to Mr. C. Roach Smith, who made the drawing of which the engraving above referred to is given. It shews that the usurper was anxious to testify his gratitude to the army, which had enabled him to attain the sovereignty of Britain." p. 131.

GERMANICVS MAXV. A trophy and two captives. In exergue L.—(Mionnet.)

This legend and type occur both on the coins of Gallienus and of Postumus.—Akerman.

HERCVLI INVICT. Hercules standing, with his club.

HERCVLI PACIFERO. Hercules holding olive branch and club.—Engraved in Akerman, pl. v. No. 37.

HILARITAS AVG. and AVGGG. A woman standing, with branch and cornucopiæ.

INVICTVS and INVICTVS AVG. The Sun marching.—(Mionnet.)

I. O. X. The emperor in a military habit, on horseback; his right hand holding a spear, his left hand raised aloft.

The three letters on this coin have been supposed to indicate the acclamations of the multitude and to signify IO. *Decies*. Eckhel, after remarking on it adds, " Quisque pro se ænigma explicet!" Let every one solve the riddle for himself.

IOVI CONS. Jupiter and Carausius.

IOVI STATORI. Jupiter with hasta and thunderbolt.

LAETITIA AVG. A galley with rowers. In exergue M. C. Engraved in Akerman, pl. v. No. 38.

A specimen with the same legend and type of reverse: in exergue O. P. R.—of fine work, and as it came from the die, obtained £3 at a sale of coins 1851, the property of " a well-known collector."

Obv.—IMP. CARAVSIVS. P. AVG. Radiated head of Carausius.

Rev.—LAETITIA AVG. A galley; in exergue M. C.—A fine specimen, engraved in Akerman, on Romano British coins, pl. v. No. 38.

The galleys, with their masts and rowers, represented upon the coins of Carausius and Allectus, " furnish us with examples of the ships, which first obtained for Britain the sovereignty of the sea; and for the space of nine years, protected this island in an independent government. The Romans under Constantius, effected a landing on the southern coast, having evaded the fleet of Allectus (stationed off the Isle of Wight) which was enveloped in a thick fog. A land engagement reduced Britain once more to a province."—See *Antiquities of Richborough*, &c. (written by C. Roach Smith, F.S.A. and illustrated by F. W. Fairholt, F.S.A. who, in combining the spirit and industry of the typographical, historical, and numismatic antiquary, with the skill and accuracy of the archæological draughtsman and engraver, have together produced an elegant, interesting, and valuable little volume).

LAETITIA AVGGG. Woman holding garland and corn ears, or resting her hand on an anchor. *Obv.*—IMP. CARAVSIVS P. F. AVG. Radiated head of the Emperor to the right, the bust in the paludamentum.—*Rev.*—LEG. IIXX. PRIMIG. A figure of Capricorn. In the exergue M. L.— (Engraved in Akerman, pl. v. No. 40).—See *Capricorn*, p. 172.

This unique coin in small brass, was found, amongst others, in 1829, near Stroud, in Kent; and was communicated the same year to the Numismatic Society, by Mr. C. Roach Smith, (see *Num. Chron.* vol. ii., p. 114), who to the above description adds the following remarks:—

" The twenty-second legion, surnamed Primigenia, and bearing in common with at least six other legions, the badge of Capricorn, was probably formed not long prior to the time of Antoninus. By the Itinerary, it appears to have been composed of allied troops, and was quartered in Gaul and Belgium; six towns or places are named as stations in which were divisions of this legion. In several inscriptions given in Gruter and Ursinus, the title of Primigenia (or Primagenia) is affixed to the legion; but (adds Mr. S.) upon coins I can only find that it is expressed in one instance, and that is on a denarius of Severus. In the list of the legionary coins struck by Gallienus it does not occur, although such as have the LEG. XXII. merely, are not uncommon. This coin therefore must be allowed to possess the highest degree of interest, in recording a previously unknown, or unauthenticated fact, namely that the twenty-second legion, or at least one or more of its cohorts or battalions sided with Carausius in his successful assumption of the imperial power in the province of Britain. Its evidence on this point is strengthened by historical testimony, of this legion being composed of foreigners, that is to say, of Gauls and Britons; and thus constituted, it would naturally be presumed to be amongst the first to support a leader whose recent military conquests had enriched themselves, and readily to join their fellow countrymen in shaking off the yoke of foreign dominion."

LEG. II. PARTH. A centaur walking, &c.— Engraved in Akerman, *Descr. Cat.* ii. p. 164, No. 77.—Brumell cabinet, at the sale of which it brought £1 13s.

LEG. IIII. FLAVIA P. F. Two lions marching; above, a human head.—(Stukeley.)

LEG. VII. C. L. A bull.—(In the Rolfe cabinet).

MARS ...... Mars with spear in right hand, and with his left holding a horse.—(Douce).

MARS. VICTOR. Mars marching with a trophy. There are also legends and types of Mars Pacifer and Mars Ultor.

MERCVRIO CON. AVG. Mercury with his usual attributes, standing.

This unique and unpublished coin is in the cabinet of Mr. Roach Smith, and was presented to him by M. de Gerville, of Valognes, to whom it had been given, many years previously, by Mr. Reader, of Sandwich.

MONET(A) AVGGG. Moneta standing with her attributes. In the field S. P. In exergue C.

"This rare coin (says Mr. Akerman, who has given an engraving of it, p. 135, pl. v. fig. 39) is in the British Museum. It is remarkable on account of the title of IN*victus* on the obverse. The respect which Carausius seems here, and on many other pieces of money, to record for *Moneta*, the goddess of money, must have been sincere; since it doubtless was to his wealth that he owed the success of his rebellion. The three G's on this small brass, of course, denote the triple sovereignty. The C in the exergue denotes, in all probability, Clausentum (Bittern, near Southampton, in which neighbourhood coins of Carausius, with this mint-mark, are frequently found." *Roman Coins relating to Britain*, p. 135-6.

ORIENS AVG.—The Sun standing.—(Stukeley.)

ORIES *(sic)*. The Sun with extended right hand, and holding in the left a globe. In exergue R. S. R.

This coin was found at Stroud, in Kent.—See Mr. Akerman's remarks on a similar type in silver.

PACATOR ORBIS. Head of the Sun. (Hunter).

PAX. AVG. Peace standing, holds an olive branch in her right hand, her left hand grasping the hasta pura; in the field L.; in the exergue M. L. On the obverse IMP. CARAVSIVS P. F. AVG. Radiated bust.

A well spread and fine brass specimen is engraved in Mr. Smith's Richborough, fig. 5, pl. vi.

PAX AVGGG. Peace standing, and the hasta erect. In the field S. P. The obverses of some have the bust with paludamentum; on others a coat of mail.

It is generally believed that the coins of Carausius, with this legend, were struck in commemoration of the treaty between the usurper and the Emperors Diocletian and Maximianus; but which Mr. Akerman shews was never formally ratified, p. 115.

PIETAS AVGGG. Mercury, with attributes, standing. In the field L. P. In the exergue M. L. Unique, in Mr. Roach Smith's cabinet. It was found in the bed of the Thames. Engraved in Akerman, pl. v. fig. 41.

SALVS PVBLICA, of the Douce collection.

SALVS AVGGG. Hygeia stands to the right, feeding a serpent out of a patera; S. P. in the field.

See notice in Akerman, *Descr. Cat.* ii. p. 171, of this identical coin, which, being of singular beauty, brought £6 15s. 0d. at the Brumell sale. Three G's on this reverse, not only denote this united sovereignty of three emperors, but they also "refer (as Mr. Curt observes) to the title of Augustus, reluctantly given to the archpirate by Diocletian and Maximian."

TEMP. FELICITAS. The four Seasons. Found in the bed of the Thames, now in Mr. C. R. Smith's collection. Engraved in Akerman, pl. v. fig. 35. A specimen with this extremely rare legend and type, brought only £2 2s. at the Pembroke sale.

Obv.—VIRTVS CARA(VSI). Bust in armour, helmeted, and with radiated crown, to the left, buckler and spear.—*Rev.*—PROVID. AVG. Female standing, with cornucopiæ, and touching with a short wand a small globe at her feet. In the exergue C.

This very rare coin, well preserved, brought £3 10s. at the Brumell sale.

VICTORIA AVG. Victory with wreath and palm branch, standing on a globe between two sedent captives.

This coin was found in the bed of the Thames, near London bridge, and is now in the collection of Mr. Roach Smith.

VIRTV. AVG. Hercules arrayed in the lion's skin, joining hands over an altar with a female figure. In the exergue XX.

This unique coin, the property of Lord Londesborough, was found near Newbury. It is engraved in Mr. Akerman's work above quoted, pl. v. No. 43.

VBERITAS AVG. Figure standing with trident, facing the emperor with globe and javelin. Very rare; sold for £2 at the Pembroke sale.

VIRTVS SVI AVG. Carausius standing, holding in the right hand a Victory, in the left a spear and buckler.

One of the Rouen *trouvaille*, bearing this reverse, round, fine, and unpublished, sold in 1851, for £2 11s.

VITAVI. A woman standing, holding in each hand a serpent. (Formerly in the late Mr. Douce's cabinet, but unaccountably lost or purloined).

In his *Descriptive Catalogue*, (vol. ii. p. 174), Mr. Akerman, alluding to this extraordinary coin, makes the following remark:—" If it were not for the very singular legend EXPECTATE VENI. on the coins of Carausius, the authenticity of that with VITAVI. might be doubted, on the ground that its form is altogether unusual.— After all, the latter may have been one of those blundered, re-struck, or ill-struck, coins of Carausius, of which I have seen many examples. I have before me a brass coin of Carausius, struck on one of Victorinus, the ill-formed letters appearing not unlike this very word !"

The following additions to the above list of third brass, are described from an unique series of the coins of Carausius and Allectus, in the possession of Mr. Roach Smith; from whose writings relative to the mintages of those two usurpers, much information, useful to the numismatist, may be gleaned:—

PAX AVG. A female, with two military standards.

ROMAE AETERNAE. A temple. In the field S. A.

SALVS AVG. Female, with garland and anchor.

VIRTVS AVG. A military figure marching, at his feet a captive.

VIRTVTI AVG. Hercules, with bow and club. Unpublished.

CARAUSIUS, DIOCLETIANUS, AND MAXIMIANUS.

1. CARAVSIVS ET FRATRES SVI. The heads of Carausius, Diocletianus, and Maximianus, side by side; the first radiated, the other two bare.

Rev.—PAX AVGGG. Peace standing, holding an olive branch, and the hasta pura. In the field S. Q. (or probably S. P. the latter is indistinct). In the exergue C.

The above wood engraving, from a third brass of Carausius, in the British Museum, conveys the idea of a coin in better preservation, than that in which the original is. But in every other respect it presents a faithful copy.

The specimen of this interesting legend and type, which brought £8 10s. at the Thomas sale, and which was formerly in the Millingen collection, is thus described in the Catalogue, p. 90, lot 647 :—

2. " *Obv.*—Laureate busts, to the left, side by side, of the Emperors Carausius, Diocletian, and Maximinian Hercules.—CARAVSIVS ET FRATRES SVI.——*Rev.*—Peace standing, holds an olive branch in her right hand, and the hasta pura in her left.—PAX AVGGG. In the field S. P. In the exergue C. or G.; *well preserved.*"

" After several ineffectual attempts to crush the power of Carausius, the Emperors Diocletian and Maximian found it advisable, necessary, and most prudent, to acknowledge him as their colleague. The event is commemorated by the device, appropriate emblems, and legend of this coin."—*Note* by Mr. Burgon.

Eckhel (viii. 47) describes a third brass with the same remarkable legend on its obverse; but his description of the obverse type, as will be seen below, differs both from that in the British Museum and from that in the Thomas collection specimen :—

3. *Obv.*—CARAVSIVS ET FRATRES SVI. Three busts, jugated, the first of which is a radiated one of Carausius; the second, laureated, of Diocletian; and the third, with the lion's skin, of Maximianus Herculius.

Rev.—PAX AVGGG. A female standing, with olive branch in the right hand, and spear in the left. In the field the letters S. and Q.; at the bottom C.

This coin, which at the time of Eckhel's writing, was preserved in the cabinet of the Abbate Persico, at Genoa, was, we learn, brought to light by an individual of great attainments, Gaspar Oderic, in a letter addressed to Cajetano Marini, published in the year 1782, in the Italian Commentaries, entitled " *Giornali de' Letterati*, printed at Pisa (TOM. xlv. p. 205). The author above alluded to, subsequently published a separate notice of it at Genoa. The coin, however, could not properly be called an *unpublished* one, as it had previously been mentioned by Stukeley (vol. i. p. 106), "though I observe," adds Eckhel, " that his work was unknown to Oderic and Tanini. The value of this gem is owing, not only to its presenting the conjoined busts of the three Augusti, but also to the inscription which accompanies them, and which had never before been remarked on coins. There can be no doubt, that by the word *fratres* are to be understood Carausius, Diocletian, and Maximian, the two latter of whom, though at the first hostile to Carausius, afterwards entered into a partnership of dignity and power with him. This participation of the imperial title by three colleagues, is further confirmed by the inscription AVGGG. and it is also alluded to in legends found on other coins of his, such as LAETITIA AVGGG.; HILARITAS AVGGG; &c.— There are several instances of emperors, in colleagueship, styling each other *brothers.*"

The passage in the *Medallic History of Carausius*, published in 1757, to which Eckhel has alluded above. is cited by Mr. Akerman in his copious list of the Carausian coinage (p. 145) as follows :—

4. "A coin of this rare and interesting type is stated by Stukeley to have belonged to Mr. Wale, of Colne, in Lancashire, in whose custody it appears to have remained for some time unnoticed, in a mass of Roman coins found at Chesterford, until detected by the experienced eye of Mr. Charles Gray, F.R.S. and F.S.A.— Stukeley describes it " of excellent preservation, the faces of the three emperors distinct and easily known; Diocletian in the middle, Carausius on his right, Maximian uppermost, exactly according to the rule of manners."

Another specimen is in the collection of the Hon. R. C. Neville, F.S.A.

In the specimen whence the above inserted cut is taken, the bust of Carausius is placed to the *left* of the other two; a relative position, which surely agrees more exactly with "the rule of manners"—in other words, the order of precedence—than that, according to which Stukeley considered the busts to be arranged on the coin which *he* describes. But at any rate the force of assumption and arrogance can hardly go fur-

ther than Carausius has, in this instance, carried it, by placing a *radiated crown* on his own head, whilst he assigns the Cæsarian honours of the *caput nudum* to the two *Augusti—fratres sui!*

Lastly, supposing each respective description above quoted to be correct, it would appear that there are at least three, if not four specimens, and as many varieties in the obverse type, of this the most historically curious of our Anglo-Roman emperor's mint.

FULL-FACED BUST OF CARAUSIUS.

In consideration of the high esteem in which the mint of Carausius is justly held, for the light which it serves to throw on an otherwise un-illustrated, but far from unimportant, epoch in the annals of Britain, our notices of its most remarkable types and legends have thus been extended. Nor can a reference to such numismatic relics be brought, perhaps, to a more interesting close, than by here inserting a cut, which first appeared in the second volume of Mr. Roach Smith's *Collectanea Antiqua;* and which that distinguished antiquary has allowed to be used in this work.—Subjoined are citations from published remarks, to which so singular a monetal discovery has given rise.

" The coin here represented (says Mr. Smith) forms the unique example of a novel class, having a full-faced portrait of Carausius. For this valuable increase to my collection I am indebted to the kindness of the Rev. Edward Egremont, of Wroxeter, near Shrewsbury, a village which occupies the site of *Urioconium*, or *Viroconium*, one of the chief towns of Roman Britain, within the precincts of which the coin was found.— It is the portrait which gives the value to this remarkable piece. The gold, silver, and brass coins of this emperor have uniformly a profile, and in no instance, save in this specimen, is the head bare. It is either laureated, or helmeted, or radiated. Upon contemporary coins, moreover, it was not the practice to give a front face. This fact, coupled with that of the superior workmanship of our new specimen, suggests the belief, that the portrait is the result of a careful and successful attempt by the artist to produce a likeness. As such, we may contemplate the coin with additional interest.— Those who are familiar with the profile of Carausius, in the better executed specimens, will recognise in the front face the peculiar character of the former; with an expression of countenance indicative of decision and benignity, which the side face does not always convey. The por-

traits of historical personages are always interesting. This coin, which reveals to us in pleasing features what may probably be regarded as the most complete likeness we possess of so remarkable a man as Carausius, will be appreciated by all who have reflected on the conspicuous part he acted in the history of our country." pp. 153–54.

To these observations from the pen of the fortunate possessor of the brass coin, represented in the above engraving, may be most advantageously added the following extract from a paper of Mr. Bergne's, subsequently read by that gentleman before the Numismatic Society, Nov. 27, 1851; the coin itself, through the kindness of Mr. Roach Smith, being at the same time exhibited on the table of the Society.—(See *Numismatic Chronicle*, vol. xiv. No. 4) :—

" The obverse of this most valuable specimen presents the usual title of the emperor, but with the singular novelty of a bare and full-faced portrait. In both these respects it is unique; as all the coins of Carausius hitherto known, whether in gold, silver, or brass, present the portrait in profile, and either helmeted, laureated, or (as generally) with a radiated crown, but never bare. The work is good, and the condition fine: the portrait, as usual, bold and characteristic. The reverse is one of the most ordinary occurrence."

Obv.—IMP. CARAVSIVS P. F. AVG. The bare head of Carausius full-faced.

Rev.——SALVS AVG. An erect figure of a female (Hygeia) feeding, out of a patera, a serpent, which rises from the base of an altar.— In the exergue the letter C. probably for *Clausentum.*

"Among the coins of Maxentius (adds Mr. Bergne), struck from fifteen to twenty years after the death of Carausius, an instance occurs of a full-faced type in silver (No. 16, in Akerman's Catalogue); and there are also a few rare instances of the same sort of type among the gold coins of Licinius junior, and Constantine the Great. In brass of this period, however, the type is exceedingly rare, if not altogether unique. At a later period, in the Byzantine series, it becomes common. A full-faced bust appears also on some rare reverses of the gold and silver coins of Septimius Severus and his family, so represented for the sake of symetrical arrangement, between two other busts in profile, looking respectively to the right and left. But I think this coin of Carausius is the earliest example of that style of head, for the single bust on the principal side, or obverse, of a Roman imperial medal." p. 152.

Carausii Successoris ALLECTI *Moneta.*— Somewhat too brief a notice of the coins of Allectus having been given in page 38 of this volume, occasion is here taken, not only to describe the principal legends and types of money in each metal, minted under his reign, from A.D. 293 to A.D. 296; but also to mention the prices respectively obtained at almost all the great sales of recent occurrence, for the rarest specimens of this murderous usurper's coinage, as Carausius's successor in the government of Britain :—

GOLD.—ADVENTVS AVG. Allectus, wearing the radiated crown, on horseback.—In the cabinet of Count D'Erceville, communicated by M. De Longperier to Mr. Akerman, who has engraved it, pl. vi. No. 45.—Probably unique.

COMES AVG. Minerva.—ORIENS AVG. The Sun.—Both probably unique.

PAX AVG. Female standing, with branch in extended right hand: her left holds the hasta pura transversely. In exergue M. L.

Obv.—IMP. C. ALLECTVS P. F. AV (in mon.) G. His bust in armour, bearded and laureated.

See the above cut. A specimen of this, weighing, according to the Catalogue, " 67 7-10 grs. in very good preservation, and of the highest degree of rarity, but suspected," sold at the Pembroke auction for £8.

PA(X) AVG. Peace standing, her right hand holds aloft an olive branch, her left holds the hasta. In the exergue M. L.

This *aureus*, found at Reading, brought £37 10s. at the Brumell sale.

" From this identical coin, which is probably unique, there is an engraving in Akerman, ii. pl. 11, No. 6.

SALVS AVG. A woman standing.—(Valued by Mionnet at 600 fr.)

SPES AVG. Hope walking. In the exergue M. L.—(Valued by the French numismatist also at 600 fr.)

VIRTVS AVG. Emperor on horseback, armed with javelin, riding over a prostrate enemy.— In the Hunter collection, probably unique.

VIRTVS AVG. Mars standing. In the exergue M. S. L.

" This unique coin was purchased at the Trattle sale, by the Duke of Blacas, for £74 !"— Akerman, ii. 177.

SILVER.—*Rev.* LAETITIA AVG. Q. C. A galley. PAX AVG. S. P. C. Peace standing.

The above two coins, in the Brumell collection, both apparently plated, sold for £1 13s. each.—"The fine silver of Allectus (observes Mr. Akerman), is of extreme rarity: his denarii are generally of very base quality."

THIRD BRASS.—AEQVITAS. AVG. Equity.— COMES AVG. Minerva.—DIANAE REDVCI. Diana. —FELICITAS SAECVLI. Felicity.—ORIENS AVG. The Sun standing. (Hunter).—PAX AVG. On the obverse bust of Allectus, with radiated crown and coat of mail, holding javelin and buckler.— IMP. ALLECTVS P. F. AVG. (Hunter).—ROM. AETERN. Temple with eight columns, a sedent figure within. (Do.)—SAECVLI FELICITAS. Emperor standing, with spear and globe.——The above are probably unique.—See Akerman, *Descrip. Catalogue,* ii. p. 177, et seq.

CARINUS *(Marcus Aurelius),* the eldest son of the Emperor Carus; born A. D. 249; associated, during the reign of his father, in the government of the empire with his brother Numerianus, A. D. 282, with the titles of CAESAR and PRINC. IVVENT. The following year, whilst his father and brother were engaged in hostilities with Persia, he remained to govern the western provinces, with the title of *Imperator,* without having yet that of *Augustus.*— He made himself detested in Gaul and adjacent regions, by his excesses and cruelties. Carus dying A. D. 283, Carinus took the title of Augustus, whilst Numerianus assumed it in the East.—A good general and a brave warrior, he combated with success the barbarous nations of the North, who assailed the western empire

at different times. Returning to Rome, he conciliated the good will of her corrupt and degenerate inhabitants by the usual expedient of
celebrating public shews, which were of a superb
description. Compelled to quit the capital and
its luxuries, in order to march against the governor of Venetia, Sabinus Julianus, who, after
the death of Numerianus, had assumed the imperial purple, Carinus gained a victory, near
Verona, over that usurper, who lost his life in
the conflict. He was equally successful in Mæsia
against Diocletian, whom the legions of the
East, on the decease of Numerianus, had proclaimed Emperor. It was after having defeated
that able commander in different rencounters,
that Carinus gained the last battle he fought,
near the village of Murge, in Upper Mæsia.—
At the sequel of that action, he was assassinated by a tribune, whose wife he had violated,
and who had in consequence watched some time
for an opportunity of destroying him. He died
A. D. 285, aged thirty-six years, having reigned
alone one year.

In Carinus there was a *rendezvous* (so to
speak), a gathering—of all vices, natural and
acquired. He was a man who bore on his countenance the index of that pride and insolence
which reigned within him. Ferocious in disposition, the slave of brutal passions, he rendered
himself an object of execration and terror by
his avarice and his exactions, by his acts of
hateful violence, and his career of abandoned
licentiousness. He loaded his subjects with
taxes; drove from his presence the honest councillors assigned to him by his father, and in
their room filled his court with the associates of
his debaucheries, and the companions of his
crimes. According to Vopiscus, he had nine
wives, several of whom he is said to have
divorced, even whilst in a state of pregnancy
by him.

On his coins he is styled M. AVR. CARINVS
CAES.—CARINVS (or KARINVS) NOB. CAES.—
Also IMP. C. M. AVR. CARINVS P. F. AVG.—Carinus
and his brother Numerianus associated are called
CARINVS ET NVMERIANVS AVGG.

On a marble, quoted by Gruter, Carinus is
called *Victoriosissimus ;* because he overcame
the barbarous tribes on the Rhine, the Quadi,
the Sarmates; and slew the usurper Julianus in
battle with his own hand.

The bust of this emperor appears sometimes
laureated, at others radiated, exhibiting either
the *lorica* or the *paludamentum.* The medallions
and other gold coins, as well as the silver, of
Carinus, are extremely rare. His bronze medallions are also for the most part of the highest
rarity. The third brass are common.

The following are amongst the rarest and
most remarkable of this emperor's mint :—

GOLD MEDALLIONS.—*Rev.*—VIRTVS AVGVS-
TORVM. Carus and Carinus, standing opposite
each other, crowned by Hercules and the Sun.
Rev.—VICTORIAE AVGVSTI. Two Victories supporting a buckler.—See these respective legends.

PAX AETERNE. Peace standing with olive
branch and the hasta pura.-(See wood-cut above).

GOLD *of common size.*——FIDES MILITVM.
Woman and two standards.—P. M. TRI. P. COS.
The Emperor in a quadriga.——VICTORIA AVG.
The Emperor crowned by Victory.—PRINCIPI
IVVENTVT. Carinus in military habit, with
spear and globe.

SILVER.—It is supposed there are no coins of
Carinus in this metal. Mionnet alludes to a
quinarius, but only as " douteux."

BRASS MEDALLIONS.—TRAIECTVS AVG. Pretorian galley.—SAECVLI FELICITAS. The four
Seasons.—See Mionnet.

THIRD BRASS.—IMP. CARINVS. Helmeted
bust of Carinus, the right hand holding a horse
by the bridle, a buckler on the left arm.—*Rev.*
MAGNIA VRBICA. Head of Magnia Urbica, wife
of Carinus.

CARISIA, gens plebeia; a family little
known. Its coins belong to the last age of the
republic; and one of them is remarkable for
delineating, on its reverse, the instruments used
in the coining of money. There are some silver
pieces, struck by the mint-masters of Augustus,
and others by the colonists of EMERITA, in Hispania Bœtica (now Merida). The brass are all
colonial; and the whole, with one exception,
are common. The denarius of this family, with
MONETA for its legend, and the anvil, hammer,
forceps, and pileus for its type of reverse, restored by Trajan, is valued, for its very great
rarity, at 100 fr. by Mionnet.—See EMERITA ;
see also MONETA.

Obv.—Head of a woman, adorned with flowers.
Rev.—T. CARISIVS IIIVIR. A sphinx, sedent.
This denarius was, amongst various others,
coined by Titus Carisius, one of Julius Cæsar's
monetal triumvirs, in 710 (B. C. 44).–See *Sphinx.*

CARMO, an ancient city of Hispania Bœtica,
now *Carmona*, in Andalusia. Julius Cæsar
speaks of it, as " by far the strongest of the
whole province." The name of this place does
not appear in the list of the coloniæ or of the
municipia of the Romans in Spain. But its
coins, with CARMO on their reverses, are extant;
two of which in the British Museum, will be
found engraved from in Akerman, " *Coins of
Cities*," pl. iii. Nos. 5 and 6.

CARITAS MUTUA AUGG.——Two hands
joined. Silver coins of the larger size, with this
legend and type, are ascribed to Balbinus, by
Vaillant; but Mionnet (ii. 389), says he had
never seen one of them.

CARPENTUM, a car or chariot. There were
several kinds of these; some serving for rural
purposes; others for the public spectacles.—
Some had four wheels, others two. The Romans
at first used the carpentum for the ordinary purposes of travelling. Afterwards this appella-

tion was appropriated to those covered vehicles, which were used by ladies of illustrious rank, and even on certain occasions by the emperors themselves. At length the privilege of using the carpentum was included amongst the prerogatives exclusively enjoyed by members of the imperial family. The pontiffs and the *flamines* were however accustomed to convey to the Capitol, in this sort of tilted cart, those sacred objects, which it would have been deemed unbecoming to expose before the *profanum vulgus.*— Carriages of this description served to convey, at funereal solemnities, the images of deceased empresses; whilst the *currus* was employed to carry those of defunct *Augusti.* The carpentum moreover appeared in the *pompæ,* or solemn shews, of the Circus, and thence derived its name of *carpentum pompaticum.*——Caligula granted this distinction to the honour of his deceased mother's memory. Messalina and Agrippina junior obtained it during their lifetime

The *Carpentum* seems to have differed from the *Thensa* in this, that the former was covered over, and placed on two wheels; the latter was an open carriage, running on four wheels. Both were decreed by the Senate for the Circensian processions. But the *carpentum,* drawn by mules, was conceded to the imperial matrons; whilst the *thensa,* to which elephants were harnessed, was assigned to the gods and to the emperors. Some authors, indeed, regard *carpentum pompaticum* and *thensa* as convertible terms. It seems, however, that the former was not allowed to be used by women, how high soever their rank and station, except on public occasions of a religious or funereal kind. Several coins of consecrated empresses, or princesses, offer examples of this nature. On large brass dedicated respectively to Agrippina the wife of Germanicus, to Domitilla the wife of Vespasian, and to Julia the daughter of Titus, we find the *mulare carpentum* represented. The subjoined cut, engraved from a well-preserved specimen in the British Museum, is selected for an illustration of the richly-ornamented *carpentum :*—

MEMORIAE DOMITILLAE S. P. Q. R. The carpentum, ornamented with statues, covered in with an arched roof, and drawn by two mules. *Rev.*—IMP. T. CAES. DIVI. VESP. F. AVG. P. M. TR. P. P. P. COS. VIII. In the field S. C.
"This (says Capt. Smyth), may very safely

be pronounced to have been struck A. D. 80, by Titus, in honour of his mother Domitilla, who died before his father's elevation to the empire. Yet Occo, Dirugi, Mionnet, and other medallists, insist, that it commemorates Domitilla the sister of Titus, because the title Diva is omitted: but surely the sacred carpentum is sufficient to stamp the consecration."

On consecration coins of the two Faustinas, and of Marciana, the sister of Trajan, the carpentum in like manner appears.—See *Thensa.*

CARPI, a barbarous people of European Sarmatia, near the Danube. In the reigns of Maximinus, and of Balbinus and Pupienus, they gave rise to the Scythian war. They were subsequently repulsed by Gordianus Pius; and finally routed by his successor Philip, one of whose coins, allusive to the event, bears the legend VICTORIA CARPICA.

CARRHAE, the most ancient city of Mesopotamia, situate at no great distance from, and to the south-east of Edessa. It is the Haran, or (as St. Stephen calls it) Charran, mentioned in Holy writ (Gen. c. xi), as the place whence Abraham set out for the land of Canaan. More than eighteen centuries afterwards it was rendered memorable, in profane history, as the spot where the so-called triumvir Crassus and his army were destroyed by the Parthians, 701 (B. C. 53.) It was made a Roman *colony* under M. Aurelius and L. Verus, and from their reign down to that of Gordianus Pius, coins were struck at Charræ, on which it is called Metropolis, and Pellerin shews (*Mélange,* i. p. 348) that Carrhæ took on its medals the title of the *first* metropolis of Mesopotamia. All the legends of these imperial colonials, as given in Vaillant, Pellerin, the Museum Theupoli, and Haym, are (ΚΑΡΡΑΣ), and Mionnet's list coincides, being exclusively Greek. But M. Hennin, in the nomenclature of his *Manuel,* says, that "some of these pieces are found bearing *Latin* inscriptions."—The types consist of a star within a crescent moon, also a female head turreted, representing the genius of the city, with a small half-moon over it. The inhabitants of Carrhæ, in common with most other eastern nations, were greatly addicted to the worship of heavenly bodies, especially of the moon, both as *Luna* and *Lunus*—(see the words.)

CARTEIA, a maritime town of Hispania Bœtica, near the Straits, formerly of Hercules, now of Gibraltar. Originally called Heraclea, after its reputed founder, Carteia was created a Roman *colony* by the Senate, in the year 583 (B. C. 171). It now lies in ruins near Algeziras, Andalusia. The coins of this colony are *Latin* autonomes, in third brass. They are numerous, and identify themselves with the place by the legend CARTEIA on their reverses, many of which bear the names of the *quatuorviri,* who respectively caused them to be struck.—Mr. Akerman, in his *Coins of Ancient Cities* (see p. 26, et seq.) has given a descriptive list of these from Florez, and Mionnet, adding some from the British Museum; others from Dr. J. Lee's cabinet; and

has engraved the two following, viz. :—*Obv.*
CARTEIA. Turreted head.—*Rev.*—D. D. (Decreto
Decurionum). Neptune standing, with his right
foot placed on a rock, a dolphin in his right
hand, and in his left a trident.—The second
exhibits a singular type.   *Rev.*—C. MINIVS.
VIBI. IIIIVIR. A figure seated on a rock, holding an angle, from which depends a fish; by his
side, the basket with bait—(see No. 1 and No.
7, plate iii.)—Other types of reverse present
heads of Jupiter, Pallas, and Neptune, also the
dolphin, prow of galley, cupid on a dolphin, a
caduceus, a thunderbolt, club, and bow and
arrow.—See Mionnet, *Supplt.* T. i. 21.

CARTHAGO *(Antiqua,* or *Vetus,* Zeugitanæ,
Africæ), *colonia.*——Old Carthage : the most
celebrated city in all Africa, and for a long time
the formidable rival of Republican Rome. It
was a colony of the Tyrians, said to have been
founded by Dido, 72 years before the building
of Rome. The metropolis of the Punic nation,
and a great maritime power, Carthage waged
three terrible wars with the Romans ; and was
at length subdued by Scipio Africanus Minor,
A. U. C. 609 (B. C. 185) ; and the city itself, by
order of the Senate, was totally demolished.—
It was afterwards made the seat of a Roman
colony, by Julius Cæsar, 710 (B. C. 44), and
afterwards, being rebuilt and augmented by Augustus, in 725 (B. C. 29), it again became the
capital of Zeugitana, and continued to be the
principal of the African cities, until it was destroyed by the Arabs, towards the close of the
seventh century of the Christian era. Its ruins
are still to be distinguished near Tunis, the
ancient *Tunetum.*

The earlier coins of this African colony are
classed by Mionnet, in his *Descriptions des
Médailles Romaines,* as follows :—

1. *Latin Autonomes.*—KARTHAGO. Female
figure standing, holding the hasta.—*Rev.*—A
horse's head.—Another reverse has VENERIS
KAR. and a temple with four columns. In second
and third brass.

2. Coins of Clodius Macer, pro-pretor of
Africa; in silver.—See MACER.

3. Second brass coins of Augustus, Tiberius,
and Drusus junior ; assigned by different authors
to the colony of Carthage. (See Eckhel, *D. N.
Vet.* iv. 139).—The following is an example :

IMP. C. D. F. P. M. P. P.   Bare head of Augustus.—*Rev.*—C. I. C. (names of duumvirs) ; in
the middle of the field P. P. D. D. (Decreto Decurionum).

On the above cited coin the letters C. I. C. are
explained by Vaillant, with whom agrees Bimard,
to mean Colonia Julia Carthago.

The first of the later emperors, who revived
the name of ancient Carthage on coins of Roman
die, appears to have been Septimius Severus, who
was himself of African origin ; and on a coin
struck in each metal, during his reign, is the
legend INDVLGENTIA AVG. IN. CART. The type
being Cybele seated on a running lion, holding
in her right hand the tympanum, and in her
left a sceptre.—See INDVLGENTIA.

See also FELIX KART*hago* on coins of Severus, Caracalla, and Constantius Chlorus.—CON-
SERVATORES KART. SVAE. of Val. Maximianus,
and Maxentius.—SALVIS AVGG. AVCTA KART. of
Diocletian ; &c.

The last monetal record of *Carthago Vetus*
is preserved on two silver coins of Hilderic, king
of the Vandals, one of which is thus described in
the great work of Mionnet, above quoted :

D. N. HILDIRIX *(sic.)* REX. Beardless and
diademed head of Hilderic.

Rev.—FELIX KARTC. *(sic.)* Woman standing, with corn ears in each hand.

CARTHAGO NOVA, *colonia :* a city of
Hispania Tarraconensis, anciently the capital of
the Contestani, now the chief town of Murcia,
and an important port of Spain, well known by
the name of *Carthagena,* on the shore of the
Mediterranean. It was built by Hasdrubal,
" and probably (says Mr. Akerman) received its
name from the circumstance of its standing on a
peninsula like Old Carthage."—From the Carthaginians it was taken by Scipio.—Julius
Cæsar, when he restored the African Carthage,
peopled this new city with colonists, and gave to
each his name, and the right of striking money.
The coins of this early Roman settlement are
chiefly *Latin* imperial, in second and third brass,
beginning with the reign of Augustus and ending
with that of Caligula. Mionnet (*Supplt.* T. i. p.
70) gives an autonome, with the type of Pallas.
And also, from Florez, a second brass of Mark
Antony and Octavian. On some of the imperial
appear the initials, C. I. N. C. *Colonia Julia
Nova Carthago.* On others V. I. N. K. *Victrix
Julia Nova Karthago.* The surname of *Julia* re-
fers to its founder Julius, and with it the epithet
Victrix often companionizes on colonial coins.
The word *Nova* was added to distinguish it from
Carthago Vetus.—The reverse types of this
colony (engraved in Vaillant) are 1. A temple.
2. a labyrinth. 3. A togated figure, holding a
lustral vase, and an aspergillum, which Vaillant
supposes to represent the censor of the colony.—
The coin of Caius et Lucius Cæsares, ascribed by
Vaillant to Norba, in Spain, but assigned by
Pellerin and Florez to Carthago Nova, is queried
by Mionnet, but included with the rest by
Akerman (*Hispania,* p. 79-80).—The remaining
type given by Vaillant as connected with the imperial mint of New Carthage, is a second brass,
struck under Caligula, on which the portrait of
Cæsonia, wife of Caligula, has been (but as
Eckhel shews erroneously) supposed to be represented under the name of SAL*us* AUG*usti*—
(engraved in *Médailles de Christine,* TAB. XXV.)

CARVILIA gens.—Of the plebeian order, but of consular rank, this family distinguished itself as early as the Samnite wars. The first member of it, Sp. Carvilius, obtained the consulship 461 (B. C. 293), having L. Papirius Cursor as his colleague, and received the name of MAXIMUS, which was transmitted as a family cognomen to his descendants.——The above denarius, erroneously inserted by Morel amongst the coins of the Carisia gens, is rightly assigned to the Carvilii, by Perizoni.

Obv.—Head of Jupiter Anxur, beardless and laureated, beneath which is the *fulmen.*

Rev.——CAR*vilius*, OGVL*nius*, VER*gilius*, (triumvirs of the mint). The same young Jupiter, holding a thunderbolt in his right hand, stands guiding a rapid quadriga.

For some notices of Jupiter *Axur*, as inscribed on a coin of the Vibia gens, or Anxur, as for the better sound sake, the word is spelt by the old writers—see p. 117.

Perizoni, says Havercamp (in *Morell. Fam. Rom.* p. 76), ascribes the coinage of this denarius to Carvilius the Edile, son of Q. Maximus. But Vaillant refers it to Spurius, the son of Sp. Carvilius, whose age agrees with that of Q. Ogulnius, and T. Vergilius, about the year U. C. 509 and 510 (B. C. 245 and 244).

But to whatever year after the commencement of the silver mint of Rome the above coin is referable, it is a very fine one, probably the work of some Greek artist, for its style and fabric are strikingly Grecian; yet Riccio, who is enabled in his work to add new families to the old list, takes no notice of Carvilia gens. The brass money of this family are the *as*, or some of its divisions.

CARUS (*Marcus Aurelius*), born at Narbonne, in Illyricum (or, as some authorities represent, at Milan), about the year of Rome 983 (A. D. 230), of a family originally from Rome, in whose literature he was thoroughly versed. Having gone through various civil and military offices, he was created Pretorian Prefect by Probus, who held him in the highest respect for his talents and probity. And so much had he acquired the love of the soldiers, that at the death of that prince (by the hands of his own troops), he alone was thought worthy of the empire, both

by the army of Pannonia and by the Senate. He avenged the death of Probus; sent his son Carinus into Gaul (see p. 183); and having himself subdued the Sarmatians, he led his forces against Varanes II. King of Persia, whom having conquered A. D. 283, he assumed the surname of PERS*icus*, as his coins attest, some of which also bear the surname of PARTH*icus*. Carus was the first among the emperors who aspired, during his life-time, to be called and worshipped by the name of *God*. After a reign of scarcely more than two years, having besieged and taken Ctesiphon, a city of Assyria, he was killed by lightning, or died from a wound, or perished from disease, near that place (for writers differ on that point), the 20th December, A. D. 282.—Of his wife *Magnia Urbica*, and his sons *Numerianus* and *Carinus*, see the respective names.

The titles of Carus on his coins are IMP. C. M. AVR. CARVS.—also IMP. CARVS (or KARVS) P. F. AVG.—DEVS. ET DOMINVS CARVS.—*Carus* and his son Carinus are together called CARVS ET CARINVS AVGG. All the coins of Carus, gold, silver, and large brass, are rare; some of them most rare. The third brass, with certain exceptions, are common.

The following are the rarest and most remarkable legends and types minted during this short reign:—

GOLD.—DEO ET DOMINO CARO. Head of Carus.—*Rev.*—VICTORIA AVG. Victory on globe (valued by Mionnet at 150 fr.).—ADVENTVS AVG. Emperor on horseback (do. 100 fr.)—VICTORIA AVGG. FEL. Victory with garland and buckler (do. 100 fr.)—VIRTVS CARI. INVICTI. Hercules standing.——KARVS and KARINVS. Heads of Carus and his son (valued by Mionnet at 200 fr.)

BRASS MEDALLION.—*Obv.*—Laureated heads of Carus and Carinus.—*Rev.*—SAECVLI FELICITAS. Personification of the four seasons.

SECOND BRASS.—DEO ET DOMINO CARO. Two heads.—*Rev.*—Public Felicity (40 fr.)

THIRD BRASS.—Same legend, and with type of the Sun and Carus (30 fr.)

The numismatic head of *Carus* is either laureated, or radiated, with the *paludamentum* on the shoulders, or the *lorica* on the breast; or helmeted and radiated at the same time. The same emperor is likewise seen with laureated head, and bust as far as the breast, holding a sceptre in his right hand, a globe on which stands a *victoriola*, in his left. In other coins he carries a spear on his right shoulder, and on his left arm a shield of skilful workmanship.

CASCA LONGUS.—On the obverse of a denarius of the Servilia gens, bearing this legend, is the head of Neptune, laureated and bearded, behind which is a trident.—*Rev.*—BRVTVS IMP. A Victory, winged, and clothed in a long vestment, walking on a broken sceptre; holds a palm-branch resting on her left shoulder, and displays in both hands two pieces of fillet, or diademed ribband, opened wide.—See Servilia gens.

Caius Casca, surnamed Longus, soon after Julius Cæsar was murdered, left Rome for Asia, with the rest of the conspirators and assassins. From this coin he appears to have been the questor, or the *legatus*, of Brutus; in other words, one of the two chief commanders. The head of Neptune, and the Victory that spreads out the diadem, and treads upon a fractured sceptre, refer to some naval victory. These war-like emblems allude, possibly, to the particular circumstance of Brutus's success against the *Bessi* (see p. 145), which obtained for him the imperatorial salutation from his army, and which is indicated by the abbreviated word IMP. on all his coins. It is, however, more probable that the above described types bear allusion to the total defeat of the combined fleet of Octavian and Mark Antony—an event which, by an un-accountable fatality of misfortune, remaining for twenty days unknown to Brutus, led to the rout of Cassius, and subsequently to the total over-throw of both at Philippi. With regard to that battle, it appears, that although there was a Casca among the number of the slain, yet it was not this Caius Casca, but his brother Publius, as Plutarch expressly affirms.—See Riccio, pp. 119–20—see also BRVTVS IMP. and CASCA LONGVS, with Trophy, p. 146 of this dictionary.

CASCANTUM (Hispaniæ Tarraconensis, trans. Iberum) *municipium*, which the Itinerary of Antonine places between Cæsar-Augusta and Calagurris. It is now called *Cascante*, near Tudela, Spanish Navarre. The money of this city is *Latin* imperial, on small and middle brass, rare, and limited to one reign, viz. that of Tiberius; whose titles and laureate bust ap-pear on the obverse—the reverse exhibiting MVNICI CASCANTVM, and the type of a bull standing. There are four more specimens of coins, given in Mionnet *(Supplement*, T. i. p. 74), with the portrait of Tiberius on one side, and with MVN. CASCANT. and a bull, on the re-verse.—Engraved in *Médailles de Christine,* second brass, p. 306. See also Akerman, *Coins of Hispania,* p. 81.

Pliny (L. iii. c. 3) includes the *Cascantenses* among the old Latin colonists (inter populos Latinorum veterum) of Hispania ulterior (north-ern Spain). But the above cited coins give the title of *municipium* to the town of Cascantum. The bull on the reverse, observes Vaillant, is not intended to represent a victim sacrificed for the health of Tiberius, as Hardouin seems to think; but is typified there as the distinctive symbol of a municipium: bulls or oxen, referring to sacrifices, were adorned with the *infula*, or the *mitra* (see *Bos*, p. 133), which this is not.

CASSANDREA (Macedoniæ) *colonia.*—This city, situate on the eastern shore of the Egean sea, near the Sinus Thermaicus, now Gulf of Salonica, stood at the entrance of a lesser gulf called Sinus Toronaicus, now the Gulf of Cas-sandra, which name the town still bears, the Grecks of the present day calling it *Cassandra Capusi.* The coins of this colony are in second and third brass. The earliest have on its

Obv.—CASSANDRE, within a crown of laurel. *Rev.*—A vexillum, on which we read AVG.—above a crescent; in the field, on each side, a military ensign.

Other coins of Cassandrea bear on their ob-verses the respective effigies, names, and titles of Claudius, Nero, Vespasian, Nerva, Hadrian, M. Aurelius, Commodus, Caracalla, Geta, Gor-dianus Pius, Philippus senior, and the Empress Plotina. On the reverses of all these coins appears the name of the colony—COL. IVL. AVG. CASSANDR. or CASSANDREN. *(Colonia Julia Augusta Cassandrensis).*—And the type, with three exceptions, is uniformly the horned head of Ammon (see Cornuficia in this Dictionary), whose worship was borrowed by several of the Grecian states, from Libya, and adopted after-wards by the Romans. The three exceptions above alluded to, are Julia Domna, Gordianus Pius, and Philippus senior. In the first, with legend of COL. CASSA. a woman stands with right hand raised to her head, and holding the horn of plenty in her left. In the second the reverse reads COLONIA CASSANDREA, with simi-lar type. The third exhibits on its reverse COL. IVL. AVG. CASSAN. A man holding in his raised right hand a bunch of grapes; at his feet, on one side a serpent, on the other side an eagle, or some other bird.—See Pellerin, *Mélange,* I. pl. xviii.—xx. No. 9—and xxi. No. 1.

Of a very rare second brass, ascribed to this colony by Fröelich, and noticed also by Eckhel, *(Cat.* i. p. 84), the reverse exhibits the word CASSANDR.: type a turreted female, holding a bunch of grapes, and offering something to a seated child. On the obverse is IMP. PHILIPPS *(sic.)* and the radiated head of the elder Philip.

CASSIA gens.—This Roman house, whose coins exist in 37 varieties, was at first patrician, afterwards plebeian. Ancient, consular, and sur-named *Longinus,* this family figured eminently in the republic. Its name of CASSIA appears to have been assumed from *Cassis,* that is a helmet. The original silver coins of this family are com-mon—those restored by Trajan are very rare. The brass are *asses* or parts of the *as,* struck by the moneyers of Augustus, and by the Colonies. —Mionnet describes from *Morell. Thesau.* the following denarius of this family:—

Q. CASSIVS. A veiled head of Vesta, on the side VEST.

Rev.—A circular temple, in which is a curule chair; on the right is a vase, and there is on the left a little tablet with the letters A. C. being the initials of the words *absolvo* (I absolve); *con-demno* (I condemn.)

This bears reference, and is in conformity to the *Lex Tabellaria,* relative to certain judgments which Quintus Cassius, an ancestor of this family, had carried with great severity against two Vestals charged with misconduct whilst he was tribune, in the year of Rome 617 (B. C. 137). The vase is the urn destined to receive the tablets on which one of these two letters was written.— See Eckhel, v. 166—see also TABELLÆ.

On another denarius of this family, the temple, as in the preceding coin, appears on the reverse; but instead of the head of Vesta, that of Liberty (LIBERT.) is depictured on the obverse, as a young female.

C. CASSI. IMP. LEIBERTAS. Head of Liberty, with decorated hair, ear-rings, and necklace.— *Rev.*—LENTVLVS SPINTER. The lituus and the præfericulum.—Marked RRRR. by Riccio (p. 50) who values it, in gold, at 30 piastres.

This and several other coins were struck by Caius Cassius Longinus, commonly called *Cassius*—named on coins of the Cassia, Cornelia, and Servilia families, C. CASSI. IMP.—CASSI. LONGIN.—CASSI. PR. COS. (pro-consul). He was born in what was always regarded as one of the most distinguished families of Rome; it is not said in what year. Having joined Pompey against Cæsar, he fought under the orders of the former at the battle of Pharsalia, in the year of Rome 706 (B. C. 48).—See a notice of his further career below.

The lituus and sacrificial vase on the reverse of this denarius, refer to the augural priesthood of Lentulus Spinter, who, after the murder of the Dictator, openly declared himself a partizan of the conspirators; and when Brutus and Cassius took the field, he joined them, and in their name coined money, with the effigy and legend of Liberty, as is seen by the denarius above engraved. By the augural insignia on silver coins of Augustus, in which the name of Lentulus appears, it is also evident, not only that he escaped death after the civil conflict at Philippi, but that he was alive B. C. 27, when Octavian assumed the name of exclusive distinction and honour.—See *Dictionary of G. and R. Biog. and Mythol.* by Dr. Smith, ii. 731.

On a silver coin of this family, we see on one side the bare head of a young man with long hair, and behind it a sceptre. On the other side an eagle standing on a thunderbolt, between the lituus and the præfericulum, with legend of Q. CASSIVS.

In opposition to far-fetched and less probable opinions of the earlier antiquaries, Eckhel points to the *sceptrum*, the *fulmen*, and the *aquila*, as unquestionable and exclusive attributes of Jupiter; and shews other good reasons for concluding that this coin of Quintus Cassius was struck in honour of the young Jove.—v. p. 167.

On a rare denarius of this family, the name and military title of the same C. CASSIVS has for its obverse type a tripod, with its *cortina* (or cauldron), and a little net-work placed upon it. The reverse exhibits the lituus and præfericulum, with the legend LENTVLVS SPINT. as in the foregoing example.

These types have given rise to much imaginative speculation among numismatists of the elder school, but it does not appear that they refer to any other subject than the initiation of C. Cassius into some order of the Roman priesthood.

Obv.—Head of Vesta veiled; before it A, or some isolated letter of the alphabet.

Rev.—LONGINVS IIIVIR. A man, habited in the toga, holding in his left hand a sceptre or short staff, and in the right hand a *tabella*, or voting billet, on which is inscribed the letter V (as given in *Morell. Thesaur. Fam. Rom.* and in the following cut)—before the man is the *cista*, or basket for depositing the suffrage tablets.

Riccio considers the letter V on these ancient coins to mean *Veto*, which was the word uttered by the tribune of the *plebs*, in opposition to some law proposed by the nobles, or by the Senate, against the plebs, to prevent its taking effect. Lucius Cassius obtained this political privilege for the people of Rome, and in commemoration of the event, his descendants struck the present coin, which exhibits the tribune about to deposit the *tabella* of inhibition.—Cavedoni, on the other hand, is of opinion, that the said type has reference to the *lex tabularia*, whereby " the power and weight of votes was strengthened." He regards the letter V as the initial of *Volo*, which formal word stood for the rogations, *velitis jubeatis Quirites*, or at least of *Uti, Roges* being undertood. Or else it may refer to another law, viz. " the Lex Cassia, which confirmed the suffrages of the people on judicial questions."

This Cassius Longinus is unknown. The coins are contemporaneous with the last years of the free republic. Eckhel, looking to the head of Vesta on the obverse of this denarius, is disposed to assign its mintage to the Quintus Cassius already mentioned; but the style of the coin brings it to moneyers of a different age.

C. CASSI IMP. Female head laureated.— *Rev.*—M. SERVILIVS LEG. The aplustrum.— In gold RRRR. valued by Riccio at 20 piastres.

Same legend and type as the preceding.— *Rev.*—M. SERVILIVS LEG. A crab, which holds the aplustrum in its claws; below it are a flower and a diadem.

These and various other coins relate to Caius Cassius, the chief conspirator against, and foremost in the murder of, Julius Cæsar 710 (B. C. 44). He received the title of *Imperator* after the defeat of the Rhodians, friends of the triumvirs, when he was but just returned with his forces to Sardis. In combination with Brutus, he levied a formidable army, and equipped a fine fleet; but although he was conqueror by sea, the triumvirs totally defeated him by land; and Cassius slew himself, or was killed by his own freedman 712 (B. C. 42); notwithstanding the wing of the army, which Brutus commanded at Philippi, had gained possession of the enemy's camp.

The head of Liberty indicates that Cassius and the rest of the conspirators, had, from the time of the assassination, dated the accession of liberty to the people of Rome.

The aplustrum, that winged-like ornament of a ship's stern, is the cognizance, or mark of the people of Rhodes, and, placed on this denarius, it alludes to the overthrow of the maritime power of that island by Cassius.

CASTOR, the son of Tyndarus, king of Laconia, or, according to fable, of Jupiter by Leda, and twin brother of Pollux.—See Dioscuri.

CASTOR.—A male figure, half naked, stands holding a horse by a bridle, or halter, with his right hand, and in his left a spear.

This legend and type appear on silver, and first and second brass, coins of Geta, struck in commemoration of the Circensian games, celebrated under Severus.—CASTOR is a novel device in the imperial mint, though of very ancient date on Consular coins. On those in question the type alludes to the *Princeps Juventutis*, who, like Castor, presided over the equestrian sports called *Trojæ*, to which reference is elsewhere made. That the exercise of horsemanship was peculiar to Castor, as pugilism was to Pollux, is accredited by no less early an authority than that of Homer, who in the hymn to the Dioscuri, v. 3, says, "*Castor, the horse tamer,*" and more clearly in the *Odyssey*, book xi. v. 298—"Both Castor the tamer of steeds, and Pollux expert with his fists."

All the other poets have ascribed to Castor the characteristic of skilful equitation.—Theocritus, *Idyl*, xxvii. p. 138, thus expresses himself: "Thee, Castor, I will sing, son of Tyndarus, an adroit rider of horses, and most dexterous in handling the lance."—Horace (ii. SAT. i. v. 26) says : Castor gaudet equis, &c.

As Geta's coin of CASTOR presents but an unclassical and diminutive group of man and

horse, it has been deemed preferable to select for illustration of the subject the reverse of a brass medallion struck under M. Aurelius.

Obv.—AVRELIVS CAESAR AVG. PII. FIL. Bare head of Marcus Aurelius.

Rev.—[TR. POT.] VIIII. COS. II. Castor, with the chlamys thrown back from the front, stands resting his right hand on the neck of his horse, and holding a spear transversely in his left.

The preceding cut is copied from an engraving published by a celebrated continental antiquary and connoisseur, who states the original to have been in the possession of Onorato Caetano, an Italian nobleman, and it is shewn to represent Castor in an attitude perfectly similar to that exhibited on a remarkably fine *bas relief*, preserved in the Capitol, at Rome.—See *Monumens du Musée Chiaramonti*, par P. A. Visconti, Milan edition, 8vo. 1822, and compare TAB. a i. with TAB. ix. a p. 84 et seq.

Vaillant (in *Num. Impp. Rom. Præstant*, T. iii. p. 136) was the first to notice this grand and interesting coin; but he has inaccurately described it.

The head of *Castor*, with a star over it, appears on denarii of the Sanquinia and Valeria families.

CASTRA.—A camp or entrenchment, in which an army lodged.—From whomsoever they learnt, or perfectionated themselves in, the art of fortification, the Romans constructed their camp in a square form; and at each face there was a gate, so that there were only four, and each had a particular name. As soon as the army arrived on the ground where the camp had been marked out, the soldiers began by making an entrenchment; this precaution was invariably taken to guard against surprise. The entrenchment consisted of a fosse or ditch of five feet wide and three deep, from which they threw up the earth on the side of the camp, in order to form a kind of rampart, which they covered with turf, and planted with palisades, when the intention was to remain but a night or two, which they called a lodgement. But if they contemplated a longer stay, they dug a ditch of about twelve feet in width and proportionably deep, behind which a rampart was raised, made of earth, with fascines, and covered with turf, flanked with towers at regular intervals of eighty feet distance from each other, and accompanied with parapets, furnished with loop-holes, in the same way as the walls of a town. This was called *castra stativa*, or a pitched camp. Thence came the distinction of *castra hyberna*, or winter quarters, and *æstiva*, summer camps. Thence also the expressions *primis castris, secundis castris*, to signify the first or second day's march, which was understood of camps formed for the night; or of summer camps, which were much less fortified than those of winter, which were for residence. And as the conformation, dimensions, and interior arrangements of a summer camp, were always the same, so the soldiers knew at once in what part their tent was to be pitched, which was done under the inspection of the tribunes.

But, although the rules for forming the Roman *castra* were such, doubtless, as we learn from ancient writers, yet from examination of the remains of several which are yet traced, it is proved, that the regular system of fortification was often departed from, and that the encampments were adapted to the localities.

For notices and details, full and particular, at once curious and instructive, of all that relates to this interesting military subject, see Du Choul, *Discours sur la Castrametation, &c. des Romains.*—See also a learned and scientific illustration of the same subject, in the *Dictionary of Greek and Roman Antiquities*, edited by W. Smith, LL.D.

Castra Prætoria.—Pretorian Camp.—This was a large enclosure of buildings, which served as barracks for the soldiers of the imperial guard. It was quadrangular, fortified with walls, towers, and ditches—adorned with a temple, baths, and fountains. " In the conquered provinces (says Millin, *Dictionnaire des Beaux Arts)*, the Romans were accustomed to have considerable bodies of troops ; and the garrisons which were stationed in towns of importance, occupied buildings called *castrum*. Rome contained within its walls many edifices of this kind, the recollection of which is still preserved by their existing remains." The Emperor Tiberius was, it is said, the first who at the instigation of his minister Sejanus, caused these prætorian camps to be constructed.—Livy, in alluding to the permanent camps of the Romans, uses the expression *ædificare hyberna*, in allusion to the architectural strength and mural grandeur of these stations.

The noble remains at Richborough, Reculver, and Lymne, in Kent, also at Burgh, near Great Yarmouth, are fine examples of the *castra prætoria* or *hyberna*. These frequently assumed the appearance of fortified towns ; and a considerable space outside the walls was often covered with houses.

Accordingly we see on various coins of the lower empire (as on the above engraving from a denarius of Constantius I.) the pretorian camp typified as a castle with towers, and embattled curtain walls, before the gate of which, generally (though often the figures are wanting) stand a group of soldiers, two on each side of a tripod, sacrificing.

The *castra prætoria* is frequently represented on small brass coins of Constantinus Magnus and his family ; and the resemblance of its narrow gateway to a postern entrance, which Mr. Roach Smith discovered at Lymne, is shewn in p. 249 of his book on the Antiquities of that place.—For types of the *Porta castrorum* see Constantine the Great, with reverse of PROVI-

DENTIAE AVG. Also see VIRTVS MILITVM of Diocletian ; VICTORIAE SARMATICAE of Val. Maximianus, &c.—For the first representation of the pretorian gate on a coin see IMPER. RECEPT. of Claudius.

CASTROR, or CASTRORUM *Mater.*—Faustina, the wife of M. Aurelius, and Julia Domna, wife of S. Severus, are thus called on some rare specimens of their respective coins.—See MATER CASTRORVM.

CATO, surname of the Porcia gens.

CELEST.—See Venus.

CELSA (Tarraconensis) *colonia*, now called XELSA. It was a city of the Illergetes, whose inhabitants were called Celsenses. This very ancient place was situate near the Ebro. Its numismatic designation is C. or COL. V. I. CELSA *(Colonia Victrix Julia Celsa.)*—The coins of this colony consist of Celtiberian and bilingual autonomes in brass ; and of *Latin* imperial, in first, second, and third brass, of Augustus, Agrippa, and Tiberius. Its name of *Julia* indicates the founder to have been Julius Cæsar, in honour of whose victories, it probably (says Vaillant), received the additional appellation of *Victrix*. Of those struck under Augustus one (engraved in the *Médailles de Christine*) bears on its obverse the bare head of that emperor, within a crown of laurel, allusive (Vaillant supposes) to the signal successes, achieved by the adopted heir and successor of Julius over the *Cantabri* and *Asturi*, who then occupied that northern part of Hispania, now called the Asturias. The reverses of the Celsian imperials exhibit for the most part a bull standing, the usual sign of a Romano-Spanish colony, and are inscribed, according to custom, with the names of the Duumviri, who caused them to be struck. —There is, however, a reverse of Agrippa, with trophy and bucklers, and a Tiberius with the simpulum, securis, aspergillum, and apex.—Mr. Akerman, in his *Coins of Cities*, &c. has given an engraving of one of the autonomes, with a helmed horseman bearing a palm branch, (pl. ix. No. 3.)

CEN. or CENS.—*Censor*, as is frequently read in the imperial titles of Vespasian, Titus, and Domitian. In the case of Vespasian we see this censorship joined with his third and fourth consulship, viz. IMP. CAES. VESPASIAN AVG. P. M. P. P. COS. III. CENS(OR)—COS. IIII. CENS.

CENS. P. or PER. also PERP. also PERPET.—*Censor Perpetuus.*—It appears that Domitian was the first emperor on whose coins the perpetual assumption of the *Censorial* power is recorded. This unprecedented title he took 841 (A. .D 87).—Vespasian and Titus were indeed *Censores* of the Roman People, but not decreed to be *Censores Perpetui.*—CENS. P. P. P. *Censor Perpetuus Pater Patriæ*, is another numismatic title of Domitian.—CENS. POT. *Censoriá Potestáte.* This likewise appears on the coins of Domitian, in every metal, appended to the record of his 10th consulate ; whereas the power itself was given to Augustus himself for five years only.

CENSORES. Censors *(à censendo).*—These magistrates, two in number, were created in the year of Rome 311 (B. C. 443), when the consuls, distracted by continual wars, were unable to attend to the *census,* or numbering of the people. Their election was popular, and they had two principal functions. The first consisted of registering the citizens and their property. The second was to take care of the public buildings, for whose construction and repair they made terms with the contractors; also to levy taxes for the service of the republic. Besides which it was their peculiar province to censure and punish evil and indecent manners, such as the law took no cognizance of—by degrading the offenders, if senators and knights; and by disfranchising them, if common citizens. These magistrates had moreover other duties to perform, such as to order the distribution of water to the inhabitants of the city according to their necessities; to superintend the repairs of the public streets and highways; and to keep luxury within certain bounds.—See Pitiscus, *Lexicon Ant. Rom.*

A Censor is typified in his long robe of office, standing with vase in one hand and lustral branch in the other, on a coin of the Postumia gens, struck to commemorate the fact that Postumius Albinus and Camillus, were the first elected Censors of Rome.—See *Morell. Thesaur.* But the most important function exercised during the republican form of government at Rome, by the Censor, was that of causing the cavalry to pass in review before him, every year.— Allusive to this ceremony, there is a denarius which, with the reverse legend P. CRASSVS M. F. exhibits the figure of a soldier, standing with face to the front, clothed in the military sagum; he holds with the right hand his horse by the bridle, and a spear in the left; on the ground are a shield and a cuirass.

The most correct as well as the earliest interpretation csays Riccio, p. 124) given to the reverse of this silver (oin, is that it represents a Roman knight, furnished with all the equipments of war (un cavaliere Romano, fornito di tutti gli arnesi di guerra), in full preparation to be passed under the inspection of the Censor.—See Licinia gens.

The emperors at first abstained from taking the name of *Censor.* To Julius Cæsar, indeed, as he was *Dictator Perpetuus,* this honour was (as Dion informs us) decreed by the Senate, together, among others, with that of *Præfectus Morum.* Augustus declined from policy the preferred dignity of Perpetual Censor, but accepted it virtually under the name of *Censoria Potestas,* as the censorship was the summit of all honours. The ancient usage of investing two individuals of consular rank with this office was abolished under succeeding emperors, who either exercised its authority themselves, or delegated it to others.

Spanheim (Pr. T. ii. p. 101), without pro-

ducing the obverse, gives as the reverse of a gold coin of Claudius, a type which, if it could be received as genuine, would in a remarkable manner serve to attest the censorship of the Emperor Claudius, for it represents him seated on a curule chair, and before him is a male figure standing, who holds a horse by the bridle with the legend CENSOR. It is this perhaps which in the *Thesaur. Morell.* has been engraved and inserted amongst the mintages of Claudius. Eckhel (vi. 242) more than suspects this device to have been forged, especially after the account, which Suetonius and Tacitus respectively give, of things appertaining to the censorship, as, after many years, restored by Claudius. These were connected with the inspection and passing over of horsemen (ad equitum probationem et transvectionem), which was one of the functions of the censorship. The Roman *equites,* on some occasions, had their horses taken away from them by the Censors, or were compelled to sell them.—For an elucidation of this power, as originally exercised by the Censors of ancient Rome, see Spanheim and Le Beau.—See also Adams, *Rom. Antiq.*

But, although the numismatic testimony to Claudius's assumption of the Censorship may present itself in too questionable a shape to be implicitly accepted; yet the fact of his having associated Lucius Vitellius with himself, in the same dignity, is illustrated by three rare, and admittedly genuine coins, struck by order of the Emperor Vitellius, son of the above-mentioned Lucius, whom they bring before us, as Consul for the third time, and *Censor;* the latter the highest office to which a private individual among the Romans could attain ; and such as not only conferred distinction on himself, but also exercised an important influence on the fortunes of his son Aulus, as regarded his ambitious aspirations for sovereignty.—See biographical notice of (L.) VITELLIVS.

Their metals, legends, and types, are as follows :—

1. *Rev.*—L. VITELLIVS COS. III. CENSOR.— Head of Lucius Vitellius laureated, and before it a consular eagle.—*Obv.*—A. VITELLIVS GERM. IMP. AVG. TR. P. Head of Vitellius, the emperor.—In gold and silver.

On the reverse of this coin (engraved in Akerman, *Descript. Cat.* i. pl. v. No. 5, p. 177) appears the head of the above-named Lucius Vitellius, and what may appear an unusual occurrence, in the instance of a private individual, it is laureated after the manner of the emperors. (See Eckhel's Treatise on the Headdresses of the *Augusti*). Before the head is placed a sceptre, surmounted by an eagle, the badge of Consular authority.

2. *Rev.*—L. VITELLIVS COS. III. CENSOR. L. Vitellius, togated, sitting in a curule chair, with his right hand extended, and in his left a consular eagle—in the place of a foot-stool, the prow of a vessel. Gold and silver.—Engraved in *Morell. Thesau. Imp.* TOM. ii. TAB. 2, No. 2.

On this coin, Lucius Vitellius is sitting in the dress of a Censor. As regards that portion of a ship, on which the feet of the figure rest, and respecting which preceding commentators have given no explanation, Eckhel says, "My conjecture is, that it alludes to the *rostra*, in front of which the Senate erected a statue to this Lucius; and probably that statue represented him, in the same garb, as does the figure in the coin above described"—vi. p. 313.

3. *Rev.*—L. VITELLIVS CENSOR II. *(Lucius Vitellius Censor Iterum).* On the exergue s. c. —The *Magister Morum* is seen, on a curule chair, placed on a tribunal, in the exercise of his office. Opposite him is another sedent figure holding a roll in his hands. Before him, standing below, are three Romans, one of whom offers his hand to the Censor; the whole are togated.

In thus describing a specimen of this first brass in his own collection, Capt. Smyth (p. 53) observes, "This was struck to flatter the Emperor Vitellius, by recording the honours to which his father was advanced. Suetonius informs us of Lucius having been three times Consul, and once Censor; but the *iterum* which is here shewn, has never been properly accounted for." To shew, however, that the attempt at explanation has been made (whether successfully or not the reader will judge for himself), and that by no less eminent a writer than the shrewd, erudite, and searching Eckhel himself, reference has been made to a passage in the sixth volume of *Doctrina*—on *Censor Vitellius*; pp. 313–314. It is to the following effect:—

"The legend of this third reverse occasions difficulty on account of the numeral II. following the word CENSOR. It should be observed, that this addition is not found on the coin published by Patin (ad Sueton. in Vitell. ch. 2). And Spanheim also expressly testifies that such figures are absent on these coins (vol. ii. p. 475.) But among more recent writers, it is added by Vaillant (Num. Præst.), Pedrusi, Morel, Mezzabarba, *Theupoli,* and Pembroke, (part iii. TAB. 12.) If it be true that this mark exists on these coins, it was the duty of those who published them, to assign the reason for its addition.— Schlegel is the only one of those who briefly adverts to it. "Here the second Censorship of the same individual is brought to our notice," (in *Morell. Imp.* vol. ii. p. 236), but he omits to mention the authority, that establishes the fact of L. Vitellius having been twice Censor. And, moreover, in the same passage he intimates an opinion not much at variance with that of those writers, who consider this coin to belong to L. Vitellius, *the brother* of Aulus Vitellius, the emperor; for he too, Schlegel says, was Censor. But, upon whose authority does he make this assertion? And, even if we admit that he held that office, is it also ascertained that he was *twice* Censor, which, according to these writers, the coin testifies? Whatever may be the fact, thus much is certain, that L. Vitellius was Censor *only in conjunction with Claudius;* but the latter, on the marbles given by Gruter and Muratori, is called, indeed, Censor, yet with no figures added to shew that the office was held a second time; and, consequently, it is far from probable, that L. Vitellius could ever be described as Censor II. If, therefore, this numeral really occurs on the coin, some method must be discovered of explaining it with a semblance of probability.—Tacitus *(Annal.* xi. 25), expressly states, that Claudius closed the *lustrum* in the year U. C. 801 (A. D. 48). And yet the same author shortly before (ch. 13), and Dion (lx. 29), inform us that Claudius held the office of Censor in the year preceding, viz. 800 (A. D. 47). And it is to this year that Pliny also refers the censorship of Claudius. Since, then, all these writers agree in the statement that Claudius discharged the office of Censor in 800, and as Tacitus expressly records the closing of the *lustrum* in the year following, we must conclude that this censorship commenced in the year of Rome 800, but was either interrupted, or negligently discharged, and, resumed in earnest the year following, was closed with the solemnity above alluded to.—Suetonius appears to intimate the same explanation, when, mentioning the Censorship of Claudius, he says—" he also bore the office of Censor......but this, too, unequally; with inconstancy of mind and variableness of success (" sed hanc quoque inæqualiter, varioque et animo et eventu." In *Claud.* lib. v.) It must therefore have been ostentation which induced Aulus Vitellius, the son, thus to double the censorship of his father, L. Vitellius, whereas he really held the office but once."

It would seem from the tenour of his remarks, that Eckhel had not seen this remarkable first brass; and was in some doubt of its existence as a genuine antique. But besides the one quoted from Capt. Smyth's cabinet, the above wood-cut is from a specimen in the British Museum; and moreover both Mionnet and Akerman fully recognise its authenticity, in their respective descriptions of Roman Imperial Coins.

After the time of Vespasian and his sons, the title of *Censor* is not found in the imperial series. The *Censoria Potestas*, however, continued in the hands of the emperors. Thus, Valerianus, whilst as yet a private citizen, had that office delegated to him by Trajanus Decius. Theodosius the Great attempted to re-establish the Censorship, with its old functions of *Magister Morum;* but the Senate were opposed to its revival; and it remained tacitly merged in the Augustal dignity.

CENSO.—CENSOR.—CENSORIN.—CEN-

SORINVS.—This surname either abbreviated or written in full, appears on coins of the Marcia gens. It had originally been forbidden, for any one to fill the office of Censor more than once in his life, until the year of Rome 488 (B. C. 266), when a law abrogating the old restriction was carried by C. Martius Rutilus, whom the people wished to elect Censor a second time, and to whom in consequence was given the surname of Censorinus.

On a rare first brass of the same gens, the reverse has for legend C. MARCI CENSO. ROMA, with the type of two prows of ships, on the further one of which is a small column, surmounted by a Victory, with palm branch and crown. The obverse legend and type of the coin are NVMA POMPILI. ANCVS MARCI. and the jugated heads of Numa Pompilius, bearded and with diadem, and of Ancus Marcius, without beard.

This is classed with other coins, considered to have been struck by Marcius Censorinus, *quæstor urbanus et provincialis*, of the year 663 (B. C. 91), and a little before that time a monetal triumvir. The noble family of Marcia traced their descent from the two kings Numa and Ancus; and C. Marcius Censorinus thus takes occasion to perpetuate the remembrance of his ancestral greatness and antiquity.—See Marcia gens.

CENSUS—the numbering, which the Censors made of every Roman citizen, the valuation of his estate, together with the registering of himself, his years, tribe, family, profession, wife, children, and servants. This process, instituted by King Servius Tullius, was gone through every five years; and the interval of time was called *Lustrum*, on account of an expiatory sacrifice, denominated lustratio, which the Censors performed as a purification of the people. This took place after the registration was finished; and was termed *Lustrum Condere*, closing the Lustre. Such was the order of things during the existence of the republic. But, when Augustus attained the empire, and changed the form of government, he suppressed the ancient method of collecting tributes, which had become an instrument of avarice in the hands of Pretors and Pro-consuls, ruling in the provinces. For the old imposts, he substituted poll and land-taxes; and in order to secure their equal exaction, he ordered the numerical registration of the whole empire. It is this census of which mention is made in St. Luke's Gospel, c. ii. v. 1, "There went out a decree from Cæsar Augustus, that all the world should be taxed" [or enrolled],

or as the Vulgate expresses it, "ut describeretur universus orbis."—See Censor.

CENTAURI.—The Centaurs were inhabitants of Thessaly, famous for their great courage and address, in taming and training horses. The figment of the ancient poets ascribed to them a monstrous origin; and Greek artists sculptured them as combining, in their form, the upper part of the human figure, with the body and lower extremities of a horse.

On some coins, the centaur is figured as standing alone, armed with a bow and arrow, or with a staff; on others drawing the chariot of some pagan divinity. On a denarius of the Aurelia gens (see p. 111), Hercules standing in a car is drawn at full speed by two centaurs, each of whom uplifts a branch in his right hand.

The above is engraved from a fine brass medallion of Antoninus Pius, in the *Cabinet de France*. The subject is one of the combats of Hercules; and represents him in the act of avenging on the centaurs the rape of Halcyone, sister of Eurystheus, to whom the centaur Homadus had offered violence, and was in consequence killed by Hercules. In this classic design, the great Alcides has already slain one centaur, who is stretched on the ground. He presses his knee on a second whom he is about to crush with his club, although another centaur comes to his assistance, armed like his companion with a branch of a tree. Meanwhile, Homadus is seen carrying away Halcyone, whom Hercules afterwards rescued. It is related to have been at the sequel of a Bacchanalian festival, that these *horse*-men, under the excitement of intoxication, to which they had the character of being addicted, outraged hospitality, and ravished the women.—Diodorus Siculus describes the centaurs as having employed trunks of trees, as their weapons in the fight; and speaks of the contest as "worthy of the early renown of this hero." The temple in the back-ground is meant for that of Hercules Victor, built at Rome; as is indicated by an eagle in the pediment, which Antonine caused to be represented, as though Hercules, for this exploit alone, had deserved worship and a temple.—See D. Vaillant, *De Camps. Select. Numis.* p. 25—see also Millin, *Gal. Myth.* ii. 437.

There is a splendid brass medallion of M. Aurelius, bearing for its type of reverse, Hercules standing on a car, drawn by four centaurs, having each different attributes.—Engraved in Mionnet, *Rareté des Médailles*, and in Akerman, *Descriptive Catalogue*, vol. i.

Several coins of Gallienus exhibit a centaur holding a bow and arrow: some as the accompanying mark of a legion, as LEG. II. PART*hicæ*. On other coins of the same emperor, the same device appears in connection with the name of Apollo. APOLLINI CONS*ervatori* AVG*usti*. —Erastosthenes states, that the centaur Chiron was numbered amongst the stars, as the constellation called Sagittarius, or the archer; and according to Hyginus and Pliny, he was the first to introduce the art of healing by the use of herbs. Such are the reasons assigned for selecting the centaur, as in this instance, to personate Apollo, whether that god was regarded as presiding over the muses, or as the tutelary of the medical art. Why the centaur is made to hold a globe and a rudder in his hand, remains unexplained.—We find the bow-bearing centaur also on a coin of Tetricus the younger, with the legend SOLI CONSER*vatori;* for Chiron, the Sagittarius, was the tutor of Apollo and Diana.

CERBERUS—the canine guard of the infernal regions, whom Hercules dragged forth from his dread abode, and forced to see the light of day. The three heads of this monster were said to signify the power of Pluto over the three elements of water, earth, and air.—A silver medallion of Hadrian has the figure of Pluto, with Cerberus at his feet. But on a small brass of Postumus, "the dog of hell" is represented as conquered by Hercules. The legend of this rare coin is HERCVLI IMMORTALI, and the type shews the fabled son of Jupiter and Alcmene performing his twelfth and last labour, the enchainment of Cerberus.—See *Revue Numismatique,* T. vii. *Année* 1844, pl. viii.

CEREALIA.—Feasts instituted in honour of Ceres, at which the Roman matrons, holding torches in their hands, and hurrying about by night, represented the grief of Ceres seeking for Proserpine, whom Pluto had carried off.— They were celebrated in the month of April, and lasted eight days; during the ceremonies of which a rigorous silence was observed, especially at the sacrifices performed in honour of the goddess, at *Eleusis,* in Attica, whence the Romans had borrowed the mysteries of Ceres.— Memmius, a Curule Edile, was the first who established these feasts at Rome—feasts which were always accompanied with sports, as is shewn by a denarius of the Memmia family; on which appears Ceres with three ears of corn, and a torch (or distaff), a serpent at her feet, and the inscription——MEMMIVS AED*ilis* CEREALIA PREIMVS FECIT. Engraved in Akerman, ii. p. 63, pl. ii. No. 8.—See Memmia gens.

CERES, daughter of Saturn and Cybele, was the Goddess of Agriculture.—The abode usually assigned to her by the poets was in a delicious district of Sicily, denominated *Enna.* She was called *Legifera,* or the legislatrix, as being the instructress of mankind in the salutary art of tillage, which made it needful to enforce laws for the demarcation of fields. Ceres appears

generally, on coins and other ancient monuments' as a vigorous woman, crowned with corn ears, and holding in her hand a bunch of *poppies:* a circumstance allusive to her arrival in Greece, when some grains of that narcotic plant were given to procure her the repose, which she had not enjoyed since her daughter Proserpine had been carried away by Pluto; and because the poppy is extremely fertile. The first fruits of the earth were offered to this goddess: at her altars sheep were sacrificed, and above all the sow, because that animal is very destructive to seeds. Ceres appears on a great number both of consular and imperial coins. The empresses are often represented under the type of that divinity.—See p. 99 of this dictionary.

Ceres and a Colonist.—On a denarius of the Maria gens, the *obverse* legend, CAPIT*o* XXXXIII. has for its accompanying type the head of Ceres crowned with corn ears, and with ear-pendents. One of the various arbitrary mint-marks to these coins of Capito, being in this instance a trident before the face of Ceres. On the *reverse* we read *Caius* MARI*us Caii. Filius. Senatus Consulto.* The type is a man driving two oxen, with a goad in his hand.

It will readily be agreed by numismatists, that the head of Ceres alludes to abundance; and that the yoke of oxen, guided by a cultivator, indicates the planting of a colony. Perhaps, in praise of his ancestral house, the moneyer who struck this coin refers to some colony established in Gaul, or elsewhere, by the famous C. Marius.—See Riccio, on the Maria gens, p. 141.

Ceres, the symbol of fertility, is exhibited *standing,* sometimes before an altar, with corn ears, torch, serpent, poppies, cornucopiæ, or hasta, on coins of Nero, Julia Titi, Domitian, Trajan, Hadrian, &c.

Ceres appears *sitting* (sometimes on the *cista*), with the same attributes, on coins of Vespasian, Nerva, Trajan, Faustina senior and junior, and also Crispina, and Julia Severi.—She is also present with *Annona.*

Ceres walking, with a lighted torch in each hand, as if in the act of searching for her daughter Proserpine, and hence called *taedifera,* is seen on denarii of the Claudia and Manlia families, accompanied by a hog; or with a plough before her, in the Vibia gens.—See the respective notices of those families in this dictionary.

Ceres drawn in a biga by dragons or serpents, sometimes winged, at others not, in which the goddess stands with a lighted torch in each hand, or with corn ears and poppies, appears on denarii of the Vibia, Vipsania, and Volteia families.—See them *suis locis.*

The head of *Ceres*, crowned with corn ears, is also found on the family coins of those Ediles who had the care of *Annona*, or distribution of wheat and other grain amongst the people—such as Cassia, Critonia, Flaminia, Furia, Junia, Manlia, Memmia, Mussidia, &c. in which denarii, however, Ceres does not always designate the edileship, but occasionally some province fertile in produce, to which a pretor was appointed. (Spanheim).—See head of Ceres, adorned with corn ears, on a denarius of the Fannia gens, engraved in p. 12 of this dictionary.

CERES AVG. AVGVS. AVGVST. AVGVSTI, and AVGVSTA.—These several legends, with the different images and attributes of the goddess above described, appear on coins of the series from Claudius to Commodus.

An interesting example of an Empress represented under the type of this divinity, appears on a fine brass medallion of Galeria Faustina, in the *Cabinet de France*, from a cast of which the subjoined cut is engraved.

Faustina senior, the wife of Antoninus Pius, died in the third year of his reign; and by a decree of the Senate was numbered among the divinities. As during life she had been styled on her coins CERES AVGVSTA, so, after her decease, the same monuments shew that she was worshipped under the personification of that goddess. On the present medal we see a miniature image on a *cippus*, standing in a chariot drawn by two serpents, and holding a torch in each hand. In the field is a larger figure, stolated and veiled, also holding two lighted torches.

Two distinct representations appear to be here given of the search for Proserpine by Ceres—viz. 1. The lighting of the torches; and 2. The biga of snakes carrying Ceres with the torches.

D. Vaillant, in his commentary on this remarkable type, expresses an opinion that the figure of the veiled female, in the field of the coin, was intended to represent the Δαδοῦχος—the attendant or priestess—of Ceres, who with her right hand is lighting a torch at the sacred fire of the altar, whilst in her left she carries one already lighted, in preparation for the rites of the goddess. On this subject, Ovid *(Fast.* 4), thus speaks :—

" Illic accendit geminas pro lampade pinus ;
" Hinc Cereris sacris nunc quoque tæda datur :"

[There she lights two pine branches to serve as

a torch ; and hence, at the present day also, a torch is employed in the sacred rites of Ceres].

And this gave rise to the expression of Lactantius,—" On that account, during the celebration of her rites, torches are carried about."—And in memory of this practice, not only the attendant, but also the other officiating persons, shook torches as they ran, as Statius tells us, *(Silvar* 4) :—

" Tuque Actæa Ceres, cursu cui semper anhelo
" Votivam taciti quassamus lampada Mystæ :"

[And thou, Actæan Ceres, in whose honour we, your silent priests, ever brandish the votive torch, as we hurry on our panting course].

And Fulgentius says, that " on this account a *day of torches* was held sacred to Ceres."

By what ceremonial empresses were enrolled among the deities, we learn from the Commentaries of Panvinius on the second book of the Fasti ; to which account may be added, that the emperors at length adopted the practice of appropriating the names of other goddesses to their deified consorts, as Prudentius thus intimates (lib. i. *contra Symmach)* :—

" Adjicere sacrum, fieret quo Livia Juno."

Notwithstanding all the learning employed by the above quoted numismatist of the elder school, to fortify himself in his determination to regard the larger female figure, not as an image of the goddess herself but, as an officiating priestess at her altar, there really does not appear any sufficient reason to doubt that on this, as on other coins of Faustina senior, with similar types, struck after her death and consecration, it was designed to apply the ordinance by virtue of which that faithless wife could be made a *Ceres*, as Livia before her had become a *Juno*.

CERER. FRVGIF. *Cereri Frugiferæ.* (To the fruit-bearing Ceres).—The goddess, holding corn-ears and a torch.—On silver of S. Severus.

CERERI FRVGIF.—The goddess seated, holding ears of corn in the right hand, and the *hasta pura* in her left.—On silver of Julia Severi. See DOMNA.

CERERI AVG. *Cereri Augustæ.* (To the august Ceres).—The goddess seated, with her attributes.—On a silver coin of Salonina.—The above type and legend occur for the first time on this very rare coin.

CERERI REDVCI.—Silver of Julia Domna.

CERES.—The goddess sitting, with the usual attributes.—This epigraph and type appear on coins of Tiberius, Faustina senior and junior, Lucilla, Crispina, Severus, and Julia Domna.

CERES ANNONA AVG. or AVGVSTA.— See ANNONA, p. 49 of this dictionary.

CERERI FRVGIFERAE.—Ceres standing. Silver of Pescennius Niger.—Same legend, Ceres seated. Silver of S. Severus.—CERERI FRVGIF. Same type. Silver of Julia Domna.

CERES S. C.—A female figure seated, with two corn-ears in the right hand, and a torch resting on the left arm. On first brass of Tiberius. Valued by Mionnet at 150 fr.—Engraved in *Morell. Thesaur. Impp. Rom.* vol. iii. TAB. V. No. 5 ; and in Dr. King's Plates.

CERES AVGVSTA, with similar type, on second brass of Claudius.—Engraved in *Morell. Thesaur. Impp.* vol. iii. TAB. vi. No 9.

CERES AVGVSTA. S. C.—Female figure in the stola, standing, with corn-ears and the hasta pura. On second brass of Julia Titi.— Engraved in *Thesaur. Morell. Impp.* vol. iii. TAB. XV. No. 23.

CER. (CERTA. CERTAM) QUINQ. ROM. CO. (CON.) S. C.—A table, on which are an urn and a crown, and within (or *underneath)* the table a *discus,* and two griffins: in the field of some coins the letter S.— *Obv.*—NERO CAES. AVG. IMP. A laureated head.—Third brass of Nero.— (British Museum).

The *certamen quinquennale* was instituted at Rome in the year U. C. 813 (A. D. 60), in reference to which ancient writers have made many observations.—Suetonius thus mentions it :—" He (Nero) was the first to institute at Rome the *certamen quinquennale,* after the Greek fashion, a triple entertainment, consisting of music, gymnastics, and equestrianism ; to which he gave the appellation of NERONIA." (chap. 12).—Contests took place likewise, as the same author states, in oratory and ancient poetry.—Tacitus writes to the same purpose *(Ann.* xiv. 20). The motive of its establishment is declared by Dion (lxi. 21) to be " the safety and prolongation of his own reign;" and he adds, that Nero in this contest bore off the prize for harp-playing, all other competitors being adjudged unworthy of it. That this *certamen* was repeated after the interval of five years, we have the testimony of Tacitus *(Ann.* xvi. 2, 4). It is alluded to also by Victor Schotti, in the following notice of Gordian III. —" And in that year of the *lustrum,* after celebrating on a grander scale and re-establishing the *certamen,* which Nero introduced into Rome, he set out on his expedition against the Persians."—There are grounds of probability for supposing that it was continued to the age of Constantine.—See *Doct. Num. Vet.* vi. 264.

C. E. S.—These letters on a silver coin of Gallienus—IMP. C. E. S. inscribed on a pedestal on which Jupiter stands, are by Banduri, and also by Bimard, the annotator of Jobert, interpreted thus :—*Cum Exercito Suo.*

CEST.—*Cestianus,* a surname of adoption into the tribe Plætoria from the Cestia family.

CESTIA gens.—This was a plebeian family. Its coins comprise six varieties. The gold are of the highest degree of rarity. There are two remarkable specimens in that metal belonging to it :—

1. C. NORBANVS L. CESTIVS P. R. A woman's head, with the hair confined by a diadem.

Rev.—s. c. Cybele, with turreted head, in a biga of lions, her left hand resting on the *tympanum.* Gold.—Engraved in *Morell. Fam. Rom.*

2. A woman's head, covered with the skin of an elephant.

Rev.—L. CESTIVS C. NORBA. PR. S. C. A curule chair, on which is a helmet. Gold.

Vaillant, and some other writers of the elder school, have ascribed these coins to Lucius Cestius and C. Norbanus, whilst holding the office of Ediles, and when both were acting as Pretors, in 660 (B. C. 94). But Eckhel (see v. 169), and the more modern numismatists, seem disposed to adopt in preference the opinion of Havercamp, founded on the historical fact, that Julius Cæsar, in 708 (B. C. 46), meditating a campaign against the sons of Pompey in Spain, established, before his departure, a magistracy extraordinary, composed of six or eight lieutenants or *præfecti,* under Lepidus (as Dion relates, xliii. ch. 28). To these, Havercamp asserts *on the authority of coins,* was entrusted the privilege of striking money ; for Munatius Plancus, and Livineius Regulus, do actually inscribe themselves on coins PRAEF. VRB. ; Clovius, simply PRAEF. ; Hirtius, Cestius, Norbanus, and Oppius, only PR. which, accordingly, is to be expanded into PR*æfectus,* and not PR*ætor.* Consequently, the six individuals mentioned on the coins, will be those *præfecti* alluded to by Dion, and to whose names Havercamp (in Rubria gens) also adds that of L. Rubrius Dossenus. And it must be admitted, that the types go, with singular coincidence, to bear out this view of the case.

The head, on one coin, covered with the elephant's skin and proboscis, alludes to Cæsar's African victory ; whilst the head of Venus on the other, points indubitably to the reputed origin of the Julia family. The *sella curulis,* says Riccio (p. 51), denotes the power of the Dictator himself, and not of the prefects, who certainly usurped the *fasces,* and chair of curule office. (See Livineia gens). The helmet, which Havercamp looks upon as symbolising the valour of Cæsar, bears reference, as Cavedoni thinks, to Venus, whose name of *Victrix,* was given by the Dictator, as a countersign to the soldiers. The appearance of the S. C. is ascribed to the circumstance that these prefects of Cæsar had the power granted them of inscribing their names on the coinage ; "and lastly (concludes Eckhel), Cybele indicates the games called *Megalesia,*" celebrated in honour of that goddess.

C. F. *Caii Filius.*—C. F. C. N. *Caii Filius, Caii Nepos.*—C. F. Q. *Caii Filius Quæstor.*— C. F. Q. N. *Caii Filii Quinti Nepos.*

C. F. *Caius Fabius.*—Surname and name.

C. F. or C. FLAV. *Colonia Flavia.*

C. F. L. R. Q. M. *Caius Flavius Lucius Rupilius Quintus Marcius.*—Akerman, *Numismatic Manual.*

CHIMÆRA—a mountain of Lycia, in Asia Minor, the top of which abounded with lions, the sides with goats, and the bottom with serpents. Thence the Greek fable of the above named monster with a lion's head, a goat's head

and neck protruding out of its back, and a serpent for its tail. Others interpret it to mean the piratical ship taken by Bellerophon, the Corinthian hero, and which vessel had a lion at its prow, and a dragon at its stern. There are indeed various types on coins of the Corinthians which, in memory of his victory, bear the image of the Chimæra, as well as to shew the antiquity of their city. Thus also that enigmatical nondescript appears on colonial medals of Domitian, M. Aurelius, and L. Verus, struck at Corinth. —Sometimes the monster stands by itself; but more frequently appears as attacked by Bellerophon, mounted on the winged horse Pegasus, with legend COL. IVL. AVG. COR. *(Colonia Julia Augusta Corinthus)*, as in the above cut.—See BELLEROPHON (p. 125); also see PEGASUS.

[A superb tesselated pavement, found in France, bears this subject, wrought in the highest style of art].

CHLAMYS, a short military cloak, as worn by the Greeks. Amongst the Romans this was the same as the *paludamentum*. The latter was in fact a part of the military dress of the emperors, though sometimes worn by private individuals. Those who have undertaken to make a distinction between the two habiliments assert that the *paludamentum* was longer and larger than the *chlamys*. The Romans made it of coarse and thick woollen for the common soldiers, and of finer wool for the officers. The emperors wore it of purple silk, ornamented with gold and precious stones. This great coat, or pelisse, was put on over the cuirass, and fastened with a buckle on the right shoulder, so as to leave the movement of the arm perfectly free; and in fighting they wrapped the left arm in the folds of the chlamys, employing it as a defence to that part of the body.—See *Paludamentum.*

CHORTIUM PRAETORIARUM.—A legionary eagle, decorated with a necklace or collar, between two military ensigns.—*Obv.*— ANT. AVG. IIIVIR. R. P. C. A pretorian vessel. Gold and Silver. (Engraved in Pellerin, *Mel.* i. p. 165, plate v. No. 5.)

In reference to the pretorian cohort, Pomponius Festus remarks, "It was so named, from its being constantly attached to the person of the pretor. For Scipio Africanus was the first who made a selection of all the bravest soldiers, with orders never to leave his side in action, &c." And this custom was retained by the Roman commanders of armies who succeeded him. Julius Cæsar (according to Dion, xxxviii. § 47) made choice of the tenth legion as his pretorian cohort, a fact confirmed by himself in his commentaries *(Bell. Gall.* i. ch. 40), whilst rebuking the cowardice

of his troops in the following terms: "And that if no one else should follow him, he would go with only the tenth legion, of whose fidelity he had no fears, and that that legion should thenceforth be his pretorian cohort."— And in this sense Cicero (in *Catil.* ii. ch. 10) attributes to Catiline also a pretorian cohort, but one composed of the merest rabble *(ex scortis conflatum.)* To the pretorian cohort of Antony there is more than one allusion in Appian. In the year U. C. 710 (B. C. 44) when already meditating a civil war, he drafted every man distinguished for personal and other qualities to form a pretorian cohort, to which Cicero subsequently applied the invidious title of *cohors regia,* 'or σπεῖρα βασιλική.—Appian also elsewhere states, that Octavian and Antony enrolled the soldiers, who had served their time *(emeritos)*, in the pretorian cohort.—Octavia, in order to ingratiate herself with Antony, when setting out to join her husband, took with her " an escort of two thousand picked men, fully accoutred as a pretorian cohort."—(Plutarch in *Ant.* p. 940.)

The pretorian cohort of Antony, on the denarius above described, has the legionary eagle; but we have just seen that this cohort was also called a *legion* by Dion and Cæsar. The denarius exhibits the ancient mode of spelling the word, CHORTIVM instead of COHORTIVM, which is also employed on the marble published by Gruter (p. 538 8), where Marcianus is called a soldier of CHORT. XII.—And thus, on coins of the legions, struck under Gallienus, we find COHH. PRAET. VI. P. VI. F.— The collar, with which the eagle of the cohorts is decorated on this denarius, has not yet been explained. It is quite certain that the *legionary* eagles do not exhibit such an ornament.—See Eckhel, vi. 52, et seq.—See also ADLOCVT. COH. p. 6 of this dictionary.

CHORS.—See COHORS.

CHORTIS SPECULATORUM.—Three military ensigns (or, more properly speaking, spears), ornamented with crowns, and fixed in the prows of vessels.—On the obverse ANT*onius* AVG*ur* IIIVIR. *Rei Publicæ Constituendæ.* A pretorian vessel.—Gold.—*British Museum.*

These legends and types appear on gold and silver of the *Antonia* family, struck by order of Mark Antony, during his triumvirate.—On the subject of the ancient *Speculatores* Eckhel gives, in an abridged form, the result of Christian Schwart's industrious and admirable researches, to the following purport :—

" The functions of the *speculatores,* and the meanings of the term, were very various. They corresponded to *explorers,* called by the Greeks ὠτακουσταί and ἐπόπται (ear and eye-witnesses), and their services were in requisition, not only for military purposes in the discovery of an enemy's designs, but also in civil matters, when they differed in no respect from the *delatores*, or informers.—Varro says: "A *speculator* is one whom we send before us, to note such particulars as we wish to ascertain." For a similar reason, the word was applied to persons of a curious and prying disposition. In military affairs those also were called *speculatores*, who, stationed on towers or other elevated positions, watched the movements and approaches of an enemy, and kept a vigilant look out *(speculabantur)*, giving intelligence by beacon-fires. The Greeks termed them κατάσκοποι and διοπτηρες, and as it was part of their business to convey important information post haste, they were also called ημερόδρομοι, that is to say, runners over a certain distance in a day, as Livy informs us (xxxi. ch. 24.)—Again, to use the words of Festus (in *Explorare*) : "A *speculator* differs from an *explorator* (spy) in this respect, that the former *silently* observes the movements of an enemy in war, whilst the latter *loudly proclaims* the doings of others in time of peace." During the imperial government, the *speculatores* were a kind of apparitors and body-guard ; from which circumstance Tacitus joined together the two corps of pretorian cohorts and *speculatores* (*Hist.* ii. ch. 33) ; and Suidas explains Σπεκουλατωρ, by ὁ δορύφορος (the spearman or body-guard.) Hence we often observe, on marbles, the *speculatores* mixed up with the pretorian cohorts, as for example SPEC. COH. IIII. PR. See also SPEC. LEG. II. *Col. Antiqua*, i. p. 127.

Speculatores was also the name applied to those, whose office it was to execute capital punishment, a famous instance of which is afforded by Seneca *(de Irâ*, i. ch. 16). And thus, in the Græco-barbarian languages, the *speculator* is identical with *carnifex*, in Greek called ὁ δήμιος, ἀποκεφαλίστης, the public executioner, the headsman. Of this description, unless indeed he was a royal apparitor, must have been the individual whom Mark the Evangelist relates to have been sent to behead John the Baptist ; καί ἐυθέως ἀπόστειλας ὁ βασιλευς σπεκουλάτωρα κ. τ. λ. "And immediately the king sent an *executioner*, &c." (*Mark*, vi. 27.) The Latin Vulgate renders it *spiculator*, as though the word were to be derived from the *spiculum* or javelin, which this functionary bears. But this is incorrect, since as yet no difference of opinion (or reading) has been found in the *Codices* on the subject of the word σπεκουλάτωρα.

That the *Cohors Speculatorum*, which this denarius presents, was employed in naval affairs, is sufficiently indicated by the prows of ships. These marine *speculatores* exercised the same office at sea, which on land was performed by the *speculatores* posted on lofty situations, as look-outs, and *hemerodomi*, as already explained. —Vegetius (iv. ch. 37) furnishes a remarkable testimony on this point :—

"Exploring (or spying) boats accompany the larger Liburnian vessels. Their use is occasionally, to surprise an enemy, or to cut off

supplies from his ships, and, in the way of spies, to discover their approach or designs. Lest, however, these *exploring* vessels should betray themselves by their light colour, their sails and rigging are painted with Venetian blue, which resembles the colour of the sea, and the wax with which ships are usually smeared, is tinged with the same colour. The sailors also, or soldiers, are attired in blue clothes, that by day, as well as night, they may the more readily escape observation, when engaged in their work as spies." According to Polybius (iii. ch. 96), Scipio, when about to attack the Carthaginians in Spain, "sent forward two fast sailing vessels, belonging to the Massilienses (people of Marseilles), *on the look-out*."—Plutarch informs us, that Cn. Pompey collected vessels of this description for the civil war (in *Catone Nim.* ch. 54). "There were not less than five hundred ships of war, and of Liburnian, spying (κατασκόπικα speculatoriæ), and open-decked vessels, an immense number." To this branch of the service belonged M. Staberius, who on a marble given by Muratori is called a centurion COH*ortis* VI. SPECVLATor*um* CLAS*sis* MISEN*ensis*.

And thus, as Antony made a selection of all the best soldiers to form his *pretorian cohort*, so it is likewise probable, that he chose from the ablest naval soldiers *(milites classiarii)* a cohort, to attend him in his maritime expeditions, and perform the part of a marine pretorian cohort, as being calculated, from its experience in nautical matters, to be serviceable in the manifold perils of a life at sea. And as both these kinds of cohort, the *pretorian* and that of the *speculatores*, were held in high repute, from his having entrusted to their charge his own personal safety, he paid them the compliment of inscribing their names on this class of his coins. The three prows of ships, which are seen, on these *aurei*, affixed to spears, are without beaks, as we find from Livy was actually the case with the *naves speculatoriæ* (xxxvi. ch. 42.)—Livius crossed over to Delos, with eighty-one *beaked* vessels, and many others of smaller size, either open and beaked, or *speculatoriæ* without beaks."—See *Doctrina*, vol. v. pp. 53, 54, 55.

CHRISTI MONOGRAMMA.—See *Monogramma*.

C. I. C. A. P.   *Colonia Julia Carthago Augusta Pia.*—A galley with rowers. On a 3rd brass of Trebonianus Gallus.—Banduri.

CICERO.—See Tullia gens.

CIDARIS, a royal turban.—See *Tiara*.

CILICIA, now *Caramania*, or *Turcomania*, a country of Asia Minor, extending along the Mediterranean, opposite Cyprus. It was formerly one of the most opulent provinces of the Roman republic, and is memorable as the scene of Cicero's pro-consulship.

The large brass coins of Hadrian, bearing respectively the legends ADVENTVS AVG. CILICIAE, and RESTITVTORI CILICIAE, record the visit paid and allude to the benefits conferred, by that emperor on the province. Of the former (viz. *Adventui Augusti Ciliciæ)* the reverse type exhibits the emperor and a galeated female, who bears the labarum, standing with an altar between them, and a victim ready for sacrifice.—This typifies a general rejoicing on Hadrian's safe arrival in Cilicia. From the attire and attitude of this female, it is evident that the province was deemed warlike; but the Cilicians were despised by the Greeks as being prone to knavery, cruelty, and mendacity—whence the proverb, "Cilix haud facile verum dicit."—Capt. Smyth, *Descr. Cat.* p. 105—See RESTITVTORI CILICIAE.

CIPIA gens.—The same family as *Cispia,* was of plebeian rank, and figures little in history. There are four varieties, viz. :—

1. *Obv.*—M. CIP. M. F. *Marcus Cipius, Marci Filius,* who struck silver money with the usual types of Roman denarii, viz. the winged head of Minerva, and the mark X behind it; on the reverse Victory in a biga, and ROMA. Mint mark a rudder.

2. Same legend. Head of Jupiter laureated, behind it S.—*Rev.*—ROMA on the exergue. To the right S. Prow of a ship. A small brass *Semis.*—Engraved in *Morell. Thesaur.*—Rare.

3. Same legend and type.—*Rev.*—ROMA above, M. CIPI. M. F. below. Type simply a rudder in the middle of the coin, which is also a third brass *Semis.*

4. Head of young Hercules, with lion's skin. *Rev.*—ROMA above. M. CIPI. &c. below. Ship's rudder with its handle, in the field of the coin. "A very rare small brass *quadrans,* of magnificent preservation," says Riccio, "in my possession."

This Marcus Cipius was tribune of the plebs, afterwards questor in 691 (B. C. 63); and in previous year, a monetal triumvir.

The workmanship of the silver, and of the small brass of this family, carry them to the latest times of the republic.

CIPPUS, a raised stone, on which was placed an inscription to preserve the memory of some event. The cippus differed from the column, inasmuch as it was smaller, and of a square form, whilst the column was round, large, and lofty. These cippi served for many purposes, both religious and secular, sometimes marking a place of family sepulture, at others standing as *termini* or boundary stones. The form and ornaments of some of these, particularly as represented on coins, have caused them often to be mistaken for altars. They are placed sometimes alone in the field of a medal, charged with an inscription; in others they are placed near a deity, who generally rests him or herself against it. On the occasion of the civic crown having been voted by the Senate of Rome to be placed before the portal of Augustus's palace, in commemoration of his services as the great preserver and pacificator of the state, L. Mescinius

Rufus, one of the monetary triumvirs of that emperor, dedicated a coin to him with the vote from S. P. Q. R. inscribed on a cippus. In like manner we read on another coin of the same emperor, on a cippus, IMP. CAES. AVG. COMM. CONS. *Imperatori Caesari Augusto Conmuni Consensu.* —See p. 108 of this dictionary.

On another cippus, above which stands a helmeted Mars, with spear and *parazonium,* is inscribed S. P. Q. R. V. P. RED. CAES. *Senatus Populusque Romanus Votum Pro Reditu Caesaris.* On another, PRO SAL*ute* ET RED*itu* AUG*usti.* —A third reads, IMP. CAES. AVG. LVD. SAEC. *Imperator Caesar Augustus Ludos Saeculares.* The manner in which all these cippi were erected by Mescinius Rufus, to preserve the memory of events, under Augustus, is to be seen on the coins of that emperor, and of the Mescinia family.— So also those cippi which commemorate the Secular Games are observed, not only on Augustus's coins, but also on those of Domitian and of Severus. Thus an aureus of Domitian exhibits a cippus, with LVD. SAEC. FEC. COS. XIIII. within a laurel wreath. Silver and brass coins of the two Philips, and Otacilia Severa, have *cippi* with inscriptions allusive to the Games celebrated by the elder Philip, in the year of Rome 1000 (A. D. 248).—See SAECVLARES AVGG.

CIRCLE—a radiated ornament, or sacred symbol of distinction, to be seen on certain Roman coins, as surrounding the heads of Antoninus Pius, and some other emperors.—See NIMBUS.

CIRCUS.—This description of edifice, for the exhibition of horse, foot, and chariot racing, and for other popular sports, was peculiar to the Romans. Its form, like the stadion of the Greeks, was that of a long square, one of the extremities of which was rounded; the other end much less so. The principal parts of the circus were—the *area,* or space in which the sports took place; the seats for the spectators lining three sides of the area; the *carceres,* or starting posts, which formed the fourth side of the area; a wall called *spina,* from its similitude (says Buonarotti) to the spine or back-bone in fishes or other animals; and at each extremity a *meta,* or conical pillar, serving as a goal.

The *area* was the space appropriated to the games and races. It consisted of earth rendered perfectly hard, and covered with a layer of fine sand, to facilitate the career of the horses and cars. Hence this place also took the name of *arena.* The *area* was surrounded by a ditch called *euripus,* which terminated at a point where the *carceres* began. At the different entrances of the circus there was a bridge to cross this *euripus.*

The *spina* was a broad but not a lofty mass of masonry, which commenced at a sufficiently ample distance from the *carceres,* and finished at a less distance from the triumphal gate. This *spina,* dividing nearly the whole length of the area, served conveniently to separate those two portions of the circus in which the races took place, and to prevent the chariots from passing from one part to the other, without turning round the *metæ*. Before the race could be won, it was indispensably requisite to have gone round the *metæ* seven times: such a course was called *missus*.

The *area* was divided longitudinally by the *spina*, which however did not occupy the exact middle of that space, but ranged nearer the left than the right side. This right hand part of the area was thus wider than the left, so that the chariots, which at a given signal, started all at the same time from their *carceres*, had room enough to run abreast during the first part of the race. For the same reason, the wall of enclosure on the right side of the circus did not form a right line, but had an oblique direction. Neither was the *spina* parallel with the walls of enclosure, but was so planned and laid down as to give more width at the commencement of the right side of the *area*, near the first *metæ*, than at the other extremity of the same side; and, in like manner, more width at the extremity of the left side, placed close to that of which mention has just been made, than at that which was situated near the starting point.— The ground, appointed to be run over by the racing cars, was on the whole of a conical figure.

[The above engraving, from a contorniate medal, dedicated to Trajan, is here introduced for the purpose of shewing the idea of Circensian charioteering, meant to be conveyed by numismatic artists, who lived in times when such sights continued to be of frequent occurrence; when such diversions were as popular as ever; and when the buildings in which they were exhibited, before countless spectators, still retained their undiminished extensiveness, and their undilapidated grandeur. The *spina*, with *metæ*, at each extremity, and the obelisk in its centre, are here well defined. The "start" and the "coming in" are clearly marked; whilst the "break down" of one competitor, and the crowning of "the winner," are scarcely less recognizable in this curious and rare antique].

The *spina* was, so to speak, the sanctuary of the circus, it was decorated with altars, statues, and other consecrated objects. The middle of it was occupied not only by the grand obelisk, together with a small temple, but likewise by

images of Cybele, Victory, Fortune, &c. At each end of the *spina* were small structures, consisting of four columns, united by an architrave. One of these edifices supported seven dolphins consecrated to Neptune; the other, seven eggs consecrated to Castor and Pollux.— These referred to the seven courses of the chariots round the *metæ*, and served also to shew the number of races which had been run; for after the completion of each race, a dolphin and an egg were taken away. Each of the two *metæ* already alluded to, stood at a distance from each end of the *spina*. That which stood nearest the *carceres* was called the first; that which stood opposite the *portus triumphalis* was called the second. Each *meta* consisted of three cones, placed on a high pedestal, and surmounted by an egg. It was because the cars turned round the two goals, in describing different circles, that these races were latterly called *ludi circonses* (sports of the circus). And how passionately addicted the Roman people were to them, is sufficiently indicated by Juvenal's allusion to the *panem et circenses* (doles of bread and shews of the circus) as the only two things which they thought of or desired.

Three sides of the *area* were surrounded with a structure which supported the *sedilia* for the spectators: these seats were placed in receding rows, one above another, like those in the theatres. This building consisted of walls, in which there were passages or galleries, and of porticoes on the outside. Between the walls and the porticoes were staircases, which conducted to the spectators' seats. These staircases abutted upon a *podium* or walk, raised several feet above the level of the area. It was there that the seats were placed for the pontiffs, magistrates, and other distinguished personages. This *podium* was separated from the *area* by an iron railing, which served as a support to the persons who were placed there, and to guard them from wild beasts, when combats of such ferocious animals were given in the circus.

To see the games, the emperors occupied a particular place in the edifice, called the *pulvinar*, and from thence all that took place throughout the whole extent of the circus was completely visible. This was on the left side of the circus, in front of the first *meta*: a place better adapted than any other to observe the order of the course; to distinguish the fortunate *auriga* who first reached the goal; and to see the gymnastic, athletic, and other exercises, sometimes given in the area. This position was moreover the best suited for the imperial box, because it enabled the competitors for victory easily to see the signal which the emperor gave with the *mappa*, or napkin, for the start.— From this point too, could be viewed to the greatest advantage the *mêlée* of the chariots, and the dexterity with which the drivers rounded the second *meta*.

In the exterior walls of the circus were different entrances which led into the *area*. That situated in the semi-circular portion of the enclosure was termed the triumphal gate, because those who carried off the prizes proceeded in state, after the sports, through that outlet.—Two other portals were situated at the spot where the *carceres* began. One of these openings probably served as an entrance from the city into the circus, for the *pompa circensis*, that is to say, the procession which it was the custom to make in honour of the gods, previous to the commencement of the games; and it is equally probable that the other was used for the *exit* of the same procession, after sacrifice had been offered.—Circusses were principally dedicated to the god Consus or the equestrian Neptune. They were also consecrated to the Sun, to Castor and Pollux, and to other divinities.—See Millin's *Dictionnaire des Beaux Arts*, from which the foregoing account is abridged. See also an article, illustrated by ground plans, in Dr. Smith's *Dictionary of Roman Antiquities.*

CIRCUS MAXIMUS was the name of the place which Tarquin the Ancient, after his victory over the Latins, was the first to assign in Rome, as a fixed spot, for the celebration of those chariot races, of which the institution is dated so far back as the age of Romulus. The site chosen for that purpose was in the valley Marcia, between the Aventine and Palatine hills, in the 11th region of the city. And in process of years, it was known by no other name than that of *Maximus*, that is to say the *Greatest*, because it was in fact built on a scale of more grandeur and extent than the other *circi*, which were successively constructed at Rome.—In Tarquin's time and during the earlier ages of the republic, the length of this circus was 437 feet. The population of Rome having considerably augmented, Cæsar caused the Circus Maximus to be enlarged, and a deep and broad fossé to be dug quite round the area, separating it from the seats, in order that the spectators might no more be affrightened by the elephants employed in the games, as had repeatedly been the case before; on which occasions those stupendous animals exerted all their strength to throw down the gratings of iron with which the area was surrounded. After the new arrangement, the *area* of the circus was edged with three porticoes on the outside of the fossé.—The first portico served to support the stone seats; the second, which rose behind the first, sustained the wooden seats; the third surrounded the whole of the extensive edifice, not only serving for ornament, but containing also passages which led to the seats of the spectators. These porticoes were so disposed, that each division of seats had their respective entrances and outlets, with a view to prevent every kind of disorder which, without such architectural arrangements, would, necessarily have been liable to occur from the crowd of comers and goers.

Tiberius rebuilt a part of the circus which had been destroyed by fire. Claudius caused marble to be used in the construction of the *carceres*, which had before been built of sandstone; by his orders also the wooden *metæ* were gilt, and he appropriated particular seats for the senators. The Circus Maximus having been

consumed in the fatal Neronian conflagration of the city, it was restored either by Vespasian or by Domitian. In Trajan's time the Grand Circus had fallen into a very ruinous condition.—The population having however greatly increased, that emperor still further enlarged its dimensions; and so magnificent was the scale of his re-constructions as to establish for this Circus a claim to be ranked amongst the foremost of Rome's splendid public edifices. Under Antoninus Pius, the Circus Maximus underwent the repairs of which it again stood in need.—Some of the succeeding emperors likewise contributed to its maintenance and embellishment. But few relics even of its ruins at present remain.

The numbers which the Circus Maximus was capable of holding are computed at 150,000 by Dionysius, 260,000 by Pliny, and 385,000 by P. Victor; all of which are probably correct, but have reference to different periods of its history.

Besides the Great Circus, Rome contained eight edifices assigned to like purposes of popular entertainment.

The *Circus Maximus* is typified on Roman coins, in some instances with a variety of ornaments, and with a distinction of games celebrated, as we learn from different representations, which Havercamp and other writers have collected together.

Thus on two contorniate (not contemporaneous but still ancient) medals, bearing on their respective obverses the portraits of Augustus, with legend of DIVVS AVGVSTVS PATER, exterior views and internal decorations of the circus plainly offer themselves, exhibiting the portals and arcades of entrance; the spina, with an obelisk in the middle; and the metæ at each extremity; and the ascending rows of seats for the spectators.—See *Morell. Thesaur. Impp.* vol. iii. TAB. 23, Nos. 12 and 16.

On a contorniate with the laureated head of Nero for its obverse type, the reverse (without legend) exhibits the area of the Circus Maximus, with its great centre obelisk, on one side of which are two columns supporting an entablature, on which are statues, and on the other side is a small circular temple; the conical metæ standing on lofty pedestals at each end of the spina, round which six quadrigæ are running at full speed, some of them in opposite directions, as if their charioteers were reckless of collision.—See *Morell. Impp. Rom.* vol. iii. pl. vi. No 18.

Nerva's coinage includes a reference to this subject.—See NEPTUNO CIRCENS (in the Roach Smith cabinet).

On a large brass of Trajan we find the *Circus Maximus* minutely depictured:—

Obv.—IMP. CAES. NERVAE TRAIANO. Laureated head of Trajan.—*Rev.*—S. P. Q. R. OPTIMO. PRINCIPI. S. C. The Circus.

For an engraving of this reverse from a specimen in the British Museum, see preceding page.

It is recorded by Dion (lxviii. § 7) that Trajan expended large sums on the Circus Maximus:— " He inscribed on the Hippodrome, that he had made it perfect, for the gratification of the Roman people. For, after it had been partially destroyed, he repaired it on a larger scale, and with greater splendour."—Pausanias also numbers amongst the magnificent works of Trajan, the Hippodrome of two *stadia* (furlongs) in length (v. ch. 12). Dion, again, informs us, that this Prince delighted in a variety of spectacles. And Pliny says, that he was devoted to the sports of the chase.—It was in memory of what that emperor had done to enlarge, improve, and beautify so favourite a place of public resort at Rome, that this interesting and valuable coin was expressly struck, by order of the Senate. Nor is it to be imagined that, at a later age, so many of the medals, called *contorniati*, and on which the racing and hunting feats of the Circus are represented, would have been dedicated to him, unless it had been the universal belief of posterity, that for recreation sake, this emperor indulged the people, and even personally took part, in diversions of this kind.—[Respecting Trajan's victories (*merita*) in the Circus Maximus, Eckhel directs his readers to consult the brief notice of Morcellus, *de Stilo inscrip.* p. 69.]—A fine representation of this building, corresponding with the foregoing wood-cut, appears on a brass medallion of Trajan, engraved in the *Numismata* of the Imperial Museum at Vienna, p. 16.

That rare first brass of Hadrian, with the legend ANN. DCCCLXXIIII. NAT. VRB. P. CIR*censes* CON. (see page 46), and having for its reverse type a figure holding a wheel, recumbent at the base of three obelisks, has an obvious reference to the circus and chariot races.

On a gold coin, of beautiful workmanship, struck under S. Severus, COS. III. is a representation of the Circus.—See SEVERI MONETA.

A first brass of Caracalla, struck A. D. 213, presents a type of the Circus Maximus, exhibiting architectural details in every material point similar to those on the above reverse of Trajan (see an engraving of it in p. 174). This, among other coins of that emperor, attests his extravagant devotion to the sports of the circus, a passion which historians inform us took possession of him at a very early age.— According to Dion (lxxvii. § 10), he himself professed to emulate the Sun, in his chariot-driving. He is believed to have been the builder of a Circus, the vast ruins of which still exist in Rome, but with which no monetal delineation has yet been identified.

The most remarkable grouping of figures and other objects, illustrative of the *ludi circenses*, appears, however, on an elegant brass medallion of Gordianus III. from a specimen of which in the *Cabinet de France*, the subjoined cut has been executed:—

Here we have a representation of various diversions going on, in the area of the great structure in question. We see the metæ, whose conical terminations are surmounted by an egg-like form, symbolical of the *ovum Castoris* — Castor being patron of the *desultores*, or horse-riders of the circus. A lofty obelisk (one of those brought from Egypt, and dedicated to the Sun) rises in the centre of the *spina;* on the further side of which a biga and a quadriga are running. Still further in the distance, to the left, are three togated figures bearing palm branches, the foremost of which is holding up his right hand. On the right is a figure in imperial habiliments, crowned by a Victory from behind, and standing in a triumphal car drawn by six horses; whilst in the foreground a troop of gladiators, wrestlers, and other *athletæ*, are in divers ways contesting with each other. The whole number of figures crowded into the narrow round of the medallion is seventeen. The reverse legend of this most rare and interesting relic is P. M. TR. P. VII. COS. II. P. P.; shewing the coin to have been struck A. D. 244, the year of the young emperor's death.

The learned Buonarotti, among other historical and descriptive remarks on this unique reverse, of which he has given an accurate engraving, says: Gordian, who according to Eusebius reigned six entire years, was assassinated in Mesopotamia, in the spring of A. D. 244. Hence the festival here represented must have been given in honour of the victories gained over the Persians in 242 and 243. These victories are recorded by Capitolinus, who referring to the letters of Gordian to the Senate, adds—" His in Senatu lectis quadrigæ elephantorum Gordiano decretæ sunt, utpote qui Persas vicisset, ut triumpho Persico triumpharet."

Circumstances however occurred, not only to prevent the youthful prince from enjoying the honours due to his military successes, but soon after, thro' the wicked contrivances of the pretorian prefect Philip, to cause his death at a distance from the frontiers of the empire. Meanwhile in pursuance of the decree of the Senate, although there was little hope of his arrival at Rome, feasts and games were suddenly got up to treat the people with; and on this occasion of rejoicing, the image of the emperor was conveyed on a car, being attired in imperial robes and adorned with ornaments, similar to those destined for the celebration of a triumph, but on a scale of less magnificence, as is indicated in the above reverse, whereon is the statue of Gordian, drawn by six horses, not by elephants as decreed for the Persian triumph. And, as it is certain that the emperor was far away at the time, and returned no more to Rome, so by this medallion the manner is particularly shown of celebrating games, and feasts, on the news of victories, with the statues of emperors dressed in the same triumphal costume, in which those emperors assisted in person on occasions of public sports celebrated, and of triumphs enjoyed.

Respecting the biga and the quadriga, which are here represented racing, Buonarotti adds, (" credo, per esprimere le due sorte più principali de' cocchi, che adopravano,") these figures shew the two principal kinds of chariots made use of on the circensian course. Their direction, according to the statements of learned writers, and as we see by this medallion, was from the right to the left, that being the more natural movement. Amongst the little figures in the background, there is one who with its uplifted hand would seem to be giving the signal to start, perhaps by shewing or throwing the napkin or handkerchief (gettare la mappa). This function was customarily performed by the consul, pretor, emperor, or other person presiding at the games. As to the group of gladiators, wrestlers, &c., who were wont to exercise their vocations at triumphal as well as other fêtes, in the *Circus Maximus*, it appears from the words of a Greek author, cited by Buonarotti, that it was not until the aurigæ had finished their seven rounds, and the victors at the chariot races had been crowned, that what were regarded as a lower grade of combatants came forward to entertain the populace; and then "the higher class of spectators began to converse with each other, and to eat sugar plums *(Mangiare la treggea)*, because they took no pleasure in seeing contests of wrestlers and other *athletæ*."—See OSSERVAZIONI ISTORICHE *sopra alcuni Medaglioni*, p. 226 et seq.—[Mionnet values this medallion at only 300 fr.]

CISTOPHORI.—Coins were thus denominated, from the *cistæ*, or mystical baskets, used in the worship of Bacchus, and which were always found figured upon them. In its original sense the term of *cistophorus* and *cistophera* were applied to him or her who, in the mysteries of Bacchus, or of Ceres and of Proserpine, carried the *cista*, which enclosed the sacred serpent. Amongst the Greeks it was the custom for young girls of high rank to bear this mystic chest at public festivals. The medals called *cistophori* were coined by authority in reference to the feasts of Bacchus, and became the peculiar symbol of Asia.

Eckhel contends, that the cistophori, the number of which was very considerable, and which were in use throughout all Asia, were struck for the common welfare of the cities of that country, whose fruitful territory and extended commerce, rendered necessary the use of a coinage of known type, and uniform weight, which should inspire confidence and facilitate mercantile transactions. —M. Du Mersan adopts Eckhel's opinion, thinking with him that a coinage relating to the worship of Bacchus would naturally be adopted by a country in which that pagan divinity was peculiarly honoured.

The time when *cistophori* were first struck can hardly be determined with accuracy. Certain it is, however, that this kind of money was already known in Asia about the year of Rome 564 (B. C. 190.)—The number of *cistophori*, collected in the Asiatic wars of the Romans, and in countries subjected to Antiochus the Great, was prodigious; and it shews how enormously vast the whole aggregate quantity of the coinage must have been. Nevertheless *cistophori* are now amongst the number of rare coins.

The ordinary types of the *cistophori* are on the obverse a half-opened chest, or basket, with a serpent issuing from it, the whole surrounded by a crown of ivy and vine leaves.—The reverse presents a quiver, near which is seen a bow, surrounded by two serpents, with their tails interlaced.—See the word SERPENT.

The coinage of *cistophori* continued in the principal cities of the Asiatic provinces, after the Roman conquest. At a later period, the names of Roman magistrates are found on them, conjointly with those of Greek magistrates; and, according to all accounts, the districts under the authority of these tribunals, furnished each its proportion of silver for the coinage of the *cistophori*, and this was taken in payment of the tribute exacted of them in that coin by the Romans.

As serving further to prove the connection of Roman names and official titles under the republic, with the mintages of Asiatic *cistophori*, it will not be irrelevant here to note three remarkable coins of this class—one struck by Appius Clodius Pulcher, pro-consul of Cilicia, 699 (B. C. 55), and the two others by his successor in the government of that province, M. Tullius Cicero, the celebrated orator.

1. The first of these has on its obverse in Latin characters AP. PVLCHER AP. F. PRO-COS. *Appius Pulcher Appii Filius Pro-consule.* The rest of the legend is in Greek, shewing the *cistophorus* to have been coined at Laodicea, under the magistracy of Apollonius and Zosimus. The accompanying types are, as usual, two serpents and cista mystica, bow, quiver, and caduceus, within ivy and vine leaves. (Engraved in Seguin, p. 82, and in *Morell. Thesaur.* Claudia gens).—Pulcher was pro-consul in Asia about 700 (B. C. 54) : he is mentioned by Cicero, but only as pretor.

2. The second has on its reverse M. CICERO PRO COS. and APA(MEA), where it was struck, with the same type as the preceding. On the obverse the cista and serpent, without legend.

—Cicero here is styled pro-consul. But on the following (which is engraved in Seguin, p. 83, and in *Morell. Fam. Rom.* Tullia gens), he has that of *Imperator*, viz.:—

3. *Obv.*—M. TVLL. IMP.; the rest of the legend, in Greek, records it to have been struck at Laodicea, by Labas, son of Pyrrhus.

Rev.—Without legend. Serpent gliding out of the half-opened *cista*.

Marcus Tullius succeeded Pulcher as pro-consul of Cilicia, in 703 (B. C. 51). With regard to the title of IMP. the following is what he states of himself:—"Thus named *Imperator* after the victory near Issus; in the same place, where as I have often heard you say, Clitarchus relates, that Alexander vanquished Darius."—*Ad. Famil.* lib. ii. ep. 10.

4. There is a fourth Roman *cistophorus*, contemporaneous with and similar to the above.—It was struck at Apamea, in Syria, and records on its reverse, at full length, the name and title of P. LENTVLVS, IMPERATOR.—Engraved in *Morell. Fam. Rom.* Cornelia gens.

This Publius Cornelius Lentulus, surnamed Spinther, was a friend of Cicero's. He served the office of consul B. C. 57, and was the predecessor of Pulcher and Marcus Tullius in the pro-consulship of Cilicia, whither he went B. C. 56. He was saluted *Imperator* for a campaign in the Amanus; but did not obtain triumphal honours until B. C. 51, when Cicero was himself in Cilicia.

On the reverse of one of the *cistophori* of Pergamos, appears the name of the Cæcilia gens, as follows:—Q. METELLVS PIVS SCIPIO IMPER. The Roman eagle between two intertwined serpents. The legend betokens the son of Pro-consul Scipio Nasica, who was adopted by Q. Metellus Pius, and which son was afterwards pro-consul of Asia, about 705 (B. C. 49). —See Cæcilia gens, p. 151 of this dictionary.

Next in the Roman series of *cistophori* come those struck in Asia for Mark Antony, who, following the example of Mithridates, and other oriental princes, took the title of Bacchus.—See p. 59 of this dictionary—see also the *Familiæ Romanæ* of Morel, and of Riccio, Antonia gens.

On one of the coins of Augustus, which bears on the reverse the figures of two serpents, we read ASIA SVBACTA. On a quinarius of the same emperor, we find Victory standing on the mystical cista, on each side of which appear two serpents, and the legend ASIA RECEPTA (see p. 89.)—The same type is found on a gold coin of Vespasian.

The cistophori of all ages are uniform in type, except those of later times, when the Romans altered the primitive type. There was, however, no change but in those bearing the name of the Roman Magistrates.

"The ordinary weight of a *cistophorus*," according to M. Du Mersan, " is 12 grammes and two or three decigrammes, more or less. The drachm containing four grammes and five decigrammes, the cistophori must therefore be tridrachms."—According to the Abbé Belleye, as cited by Millin, the uniform weight of these medals, which are all of pure silver, is 240 grains, *poids de Paris*, intrinsic value two livres 14 sous.

See Eckhel, *De Cistophoris*—see generally Millin, *Dictionnaire des Beaux Arts*—see particularly " a memoir on coins called Cistophori," from the pen of M. Du Mersan, *premier Employé au Cabinet des Antiques de la Bibliothèque Nationale*, translated by the Editor of the Numismatic Chronicle, and inserted in that periodical, 1846.

CITHARA—the harp or lyre. The term is applied to designate the harp of Apollo, to whom its invention is ascribed: it was furnished with seven strings, in correspondence (say mythologists) with the number of the planets. The *cithara*, as a symbol of Apollo, on a gold coin of Augustus, struck by the monetary triumvir Turpilianus, on the occasion of that emperor's having erected on Mount Palatine a temple to the God of Music. (Vaillant, Pr. ii. p. 24).— Engraved in *Morell. Fam. Rom.* Petronia gens. —See the *Cithara*, supported by Victory and the Palatine Apollo, on a medallion of Commodus, engraved in p. 66 of this volume.

CITHAROEDVS APOLLO. The lyre-striking Apollo.—In this character Nero is represented on one of his first brass coins. " *Another Apollo* (as Suetonius observes), habited like the robed statues of the god, he appears walking, with the *cithara* in his left hand, and playing on it with his right.—Engraved in Dr. King's plates.

CIVIB. ET SIGN. MILIT. A. PART. RE-CVPER. sometimes RESTITVT. *Civibus et Signis Militaribus à Parthis recuperatis.*— (Citizens and military ensigns restored by the

 Parthians).——A triumphal arch, with three portals; on its summit is a figure in a quadriga; on each side of the quadriga stands a male figure, the one offering a military ensign, the other a legionary eagle.—Gold and silver medals of Augustus, bearing this legend and type, refer to a memorable blot on the military reputation of the Romans, namely, the defeat of M. Crassus, in Mesopotamia, in 701 (B. C. 53). See *Carrhæ.*——That rash and incapable commander had, to gratify his insatiate avarice, brought on a war with the Parthians; but the result proved disastrous in the extreme. It not only cost him his own worthless life, but the lives of thousands of his unfortunate soldiers, leaving in the power of the enemy a great number of prisoners, who, with their eagles and ensigns, remained in the hands of the Parthians for a space of thirty-three years, to the indelible shame of the Republic.— At length, however, Phraates, King of the Parthians, yielding to the threats of Augustus, and fearing that that prince would take measures to force a surrender of those captives and spoils of war, preferred sending them back to Rome; and the emperor received them, 734 (B. C. 20), with more joyous exultation than if he had vanquished the Parthians in a pitched battle. Augustus built in the capitol a temple which he dedicated to Mars Ultor (the Avenger), where the military ensigns were consecrated.

It was on this restoration of the captured standards by the Parthians, that Augustus, according to Dion, was honoured by the Senate and People with an ovation, he entering the city on horseback, and also with a triumphal arch. Moreover they paid him the homage of a votive shield, in commemoration of the same *glorious* event. There are coins in which this buckler is represented with a legend, recording the restitution of military ensigns.—See c. l. v. and signis receptis.

CIVIBVS SERVATIS CAESAR, COS. VII. Bare head of Augustus.—*Rev.*—AVGVSTVS. s. c. An eagle, with wings displayed, holds in its claws a crown of oak leaves, behind his wings are two laurel branches.—See *Eagle*.

Augustus having established the peace of the empire abroad, and secured protection to the lives of citizens by the restoration of internal order and peace, the Senate ordered that laurels should be planted before his palace, in order to recal the memory of his victories, and that a crown of oak leaves should be placed in the midst, as a symbol of the preservation of citizens.

CIVIS. A citizen.——At Rome they distinguished by the name of citizens *(Cives)*, those who not only had their abode in the city, but were incorporated in a tribe, or ward, and were eligible to the offices of the republic. The union of these three qualifications was necessary to constitute citizenship in full right, *pleno jure cives;* and neither strangers who had obtained residence, nor freedmen to whom the rights of the *tribus* had been granted, were ranked as citizens. Every Roman citizen was one of three orders in the state, either of the Senate, or of the Knights *(Equestres),* or of the people *(plebs).* A person did not deprive himself of the title of citizen, when his affairs required him to reside some time out of Rome; but he did forfeit it, when he caused himself to be enrolled amongst the citizens of another town. "Neque enim (says Cicero), jure Quiritium, idem duarum civitatum civis esse potuit."

During the existence of the republic, the rights of Roman citizenship were accorded to no other nation—to no other people. Under Augustus, however, and his imperial successors, this restriction was more and more relaxed. The privileges of this title, which kings themselves had not disdained to hold, consisted 1st, of being incorporated in a tribe and a century, exercising the electoral franchise, and filling public offices. 2nd, in exemption from the punishment by rods, from that of imprisonment, and even from that of death, at least in cases where sentence of condemnation was passed by the people. The first of these punishments was reserved for slaves; the *Porcian* and *Sempronian* laws having emancipated the citizens from it: 3rd, Roman citizens alone were enrolled in the legions; they alone shared in the rewards distributed among the beneficiary soldiers: 4th, they

had unlimited power over their children: 5th, they possessed the right of adoption, and that of wearing the *toga*, which was likewise a distinctive mark of the Roman citizen: 6th, they were the sole heir of a citizen, and foreigners were excluded from all succession.

Cives were divided into two sorts—old and new. The first were those who were born Roman citizens, and whose whole family enjoyed the right of the city. Under the distinction of *new*, were reckoned the allies of Latin name, and those who owed their citizenship to the favour of the emperor. The condition of the latter was inferior to that of the former class, inasmuch as they could not claim succession of relatives on the paternal side; a privilege which the old citizens possessed, by virtue of a Law of the Twelve Tables.

At the commencement of the Roman state, the people were composed but of *two* orders—the Patricians and the Plebeians. The first order included all the nobility. But after the Gracchi, become tribunes of the people, had carried the law which took away from the Senators the cognizance of certain causes, in order to give that privilege to the Knights, the latter formed a second order amongst the nobility, and thenceforth the Roman people became divided into *three* orders, the last of which comprised the Burgesses *(Municipes)*. This third order was itself composed of three sorts of persons; viz. of those who were born free, and who were called *Ingenui;* of the children of freemen, called *Libertini;* and of the freedmen themselves who from having been slaves were set at liberty by their masters: for so long as they remained slaves they could not be numbered among the people. Still, there was to be distinguished amongst the Roman citizens three different classes; viz. 1. Those who were of the city itself, and who enjoyed the following prerogatives: to be comprised in the census, to give their votes, to take office, to pay the capitation tax, to be enrolled in the legions, to sacrifice according to the custom of Rome; and these were called *Quirites, Populusque Romanus.*—2. The second class were municipals, who had in common, with the first mentioned kind, only to be included in the census, to give their suffrage, to take part in public situations, to pay tribute, whilst they were deprived of the other advantages. Finally, the third class was composed of those who possessed the *Jus Latii*, that is to say, those not natives of Rome, but, who having exercised some magistracy in their own country, had acquired the right of Roman burgessship, together with that of voting, and of eligibility to public office, as Pliny represents it—"His quoque quibus per Latium civitas Romana patuisset."— Thus Strabo remarks, that such of the inhabitants of Nismes, in Gaul, who had exercised the pretorship, or the edileship, became thenceforward Roman citizens.—See Pitiscus, *Lexicon Antiq. Rom.*

Soldiers also who had served a long time honourably, received a diploma admitting them to the rights of citizenship.

cIvIs as in the Augustan medal (OB cIvIs SERVATOS). *Civis* is often used for *Cives*, and the long syllable is mostly expressed by a taller character. The ancients terminated nominatives and accusatives in IS. [It was long that the veneration existed towards the memory of Augustus, of which the indication is to be found on the first brass coins of Tiberius, inscribed DIVO AVGVSTO S. P. Q. R. OB CIVIS (or CIVES) SERVATOS, and which display two capricorns, with a globe, sustaining an oaken crown].

Civica, or *quernea* corona.——The civic or oaken crown or wreath, was thus called, from the oak leaves and acorns of which it was composed, and from the custom of honouring with it those who protected the lives of the citizens. —See *Corona*.

CIVIVM.—See AMPLIATORI CIVIVM, on a coin of Antoninus Pius, noticed in p. 43.

CIVITAS.—This word, in its origin, signified, not what we call a city, but a nation; a society of men living in the same place, governed by the same magistrates, and under the power of the same laws. Thus *Civitas* had the same meaning as *Res Publica*. The Romans at first took the word in this sense. But afterwards it was made to designate the principal place, the capital of a nation, the centre of a republic, the seat of the laws, of the magistrates, and of all authority, and at length it was employed to signify every town—urbs—oppidum.

Civitas also signified the same thing as *Jus Quiritium*, the right of Roman citizenship.— No one was able to acquire that right, if he had not previously attained the second *Jus Latii*, which was very inferior to the other.— The *Jus Quiritium* necessarily implied the *Jus Civitatis*, but it was not all those who possessed the latter that enjoyed the former. For instance, freedmen had the *Civitas*, without having the *Jus Quiritium;* they were reckoned among the citizens, but not among the *Quirites*. From the moment they regained their liberty they, the former slaves, were regarded as citizens; but they had still to ask for the *Jus Quiritium*, which, once granted, gave them admission into the *Tribus* of the country, and facilitated their attainment of offices; and this right was reserved to the affranchised Romans; for as to the foreign freedmen, they were qualified for aspiring only to the right of citizenship, without any pretensions to enter into the country tribes, or to hold any offices. Those who quitted their native country to go and live at Rome, enjoyed all the privileges of Roman citizens.

After the city was burnt by the Gauls, measures were taken to induce individuals to establish themselves at Rome, by securing to them, as residents, the rights of citizenship. This condition was indispensable for enjoying the privileges of a Roman citizen to their fullest extent; but it was accorded also, with certain restrictions, to people who were not domiciliated at Rome, and this was called *Municipium*. At first the Latins alone were allowed to partake of this honour; then all Italy; afterwards some

nations beyond that region; and especially the principal cities throughout the whole extent of the empire. Lastly, a constitutional law, instituted by the Emperor Antoninus Pius, conferred that title on all freemen within the imperial dominions. This municipal franchise, or *Jus Suffragium*, was in the first instance granted by the people. In course of time the emperors rendered themselves masters of this, as of every other power of the state, and some of them made it a matter of pecuniary traffic. There were cities which received from the emperors a certain portion of land, the cultivation of which assisted them in paying the taxes, in defraying the expenses of sacrifices, and in repairing the public buildings; and when the prince had cause of displeasure against them, he took away their privileges.—See Pitiscus, *Lexicon Antiq. Rom.*

CIVITATIBVS ASIAE RESTITVTIS. (*The cities of Asia re-established.)*—A sedent figure, laureated and togated, its feet resting on a footstool; in the right hand a patera; in the left the *hasta pura.*—*Obv.*—TI. CAESAR DIVI AVG. F. AVGVST. P. M. TR. POT. XXIIII. (Tiberius Cæsar, Divi Augusti Filius, Augustus, Pontifex Maximus, Tribunitiæ Potestatis 24.)   In the field a large S. C.

The large brass of Tiberius, on the reverse of which this remarkable legend appears, was struck in the year of Rome 775 (A. D. 22), and records the munificence of this emperor, who had caused to be re-built, at his own expense, certain cities in Asia Minor, which in one night had been overthrown and ruined by an earthquake A. D. 17. The Senate, grateful for a benefit, thus bestowed on one of the most important provinces of the empire, raised a statue to his honour; and the coin above engraved from, serves still more lastingly to record an act of generous humanity, hardly to be credited of so selfish, avaricious, and cruel a man, had not the fact been so well authenticated as to leave no doubt or difficulty concerning it.—On this coin, equally deserving of notice as a remarkably fine specimen of monetal workmanship, and as an interesting historical monument, Eckhel (vi. 192–3) animadverts to the following effect :—

We learn from Tacitus, when treating of the year U. C. 770 (A. D. 17), that twelve cities of Asia, which had suffered severely from the effects of a violent earthquake, were re-built by the munificence of Tiberius. This liberal act is recorded by many other writers, whose expressions are quoted by Schlegel, in his explanation of this coin. *(Morell. Impp.* i. p. 578).— As regards the number of these cities, Pliny coincides with Tacitus *(Plin.* ii. § 86). He enumerates Sardis, Magnesia under Mount Sipylus, Temnos, Philadelphia, Ægea, Apollonia, the Mosteni, the Hyrcani, Hierocæsarea, Myrina, Cymen, and Tmolus. Others mention 13, 14, and 15 cities, including no doubt those, which, having at a subsequent period suffered the like calamity, experienced the beneficent care of Tiberius; and such we find from Tacitus to have been the case with Ægæ in Achia, and Cibyra in Phrygia, in the year 776 (A. D. 23). Indeed, the famous marble, dug up at Puteoli, at the end of the last century, which was dedicated to Tiberius Cæsar, exhibits fourteen female figures, having inscribed under them the names of the same number of Asiatic cities, identical with those, which are enumerated by Tacitus, with the addition of Ephesus and Cibyra.

In order to explain the type of the reverse, reference must be had to the account given by Phlegon Trallianus *(de reb. mirab.* c. 13), who, quoting Apollonius, states, that in the time of Tiberius many cities of renown were overthrown by an earthquake, and that the Emperor Tiberius afterwards restored them at his own cost; in consequence of which a colossal statue was dedicated to him at Rome, in the forum, near the temple of Venus, with other statues near it, representing the several cities. What Phlegon thus describes, the above-mentioned marble discovered at Puteoli brings before our eyes, having beyond doubt been sculptured in imitation of the Roman original, and dedicated at Puteoli to perpetuate the memory of Tiberius's liberality. There appears, however, to be no question, that the colossal figure alluded to by Phlegon, presented the same appearance as does Tiberius on the coin before us. The Puteolian marble does not contribute to our information on this point, as only its base remains, the *statue*, which in all probability surmounted it, having been destroyed by the effects of time.—Whoever wishes to obtain further particulars respecting this monument of Puteoli, its form, and inscription, will find them in the lengthy dissertation of Laurentius Gronovius, inserted in the 7th vol. of Antiquities, by Gronovius, and also Belleye (B. L. xxiv. p. 128.)

In the figure itself, as presented on the coin, nothing is wanting to express the present and actual deity. We see the *patera*, the spear, and the footstool. When, therefore, it is asserted by Tacitus and Suetonius, that Tiberius declined divine honours, such may really have been the case at the commencement of his reign, whilst his government was not firmly established; at a later period, however, he may have entertained loftier thoughts of his own dignity, or at least, though never exacting from his subjects the adoration due to a god, he may so faintly have opposed its tender, as to permit it; just as, without positively assuming the title of Augustus, he with complacency endured to hear it uttered or see it written. (Dion, lvii. § 8.)—

Certain it is, that in the year following he allowed a temple to be dedicated to himself and his mother Livia, at Smyrna: indeed, the latter is represented with all the attributes of a goddess on her coins.

This colossal statue of Tiberius appears to have been completed and dedicated in the year U. C. 775 (A. D. 21), and afterwards represented on coins.—In Belleye, Mediobarbus, and other catalogues, however, mention is made of his *Trib. potest.* xxi. inscribed on coins of similar subject; from which circumstance Eckhel infers, that the monument in question was dedicated two years after the calamity to which it alludes.

Dr. Cardwell makes this brass of Tiberius a subject of one of his lectures, and in his inquiry respecting the cause to which it was owing that the medal, clearly intended to commemorate the munificence of the emperor, was not minted till five years afterwards, observes, that such inquiry is the more necessary, "as we have another medal of similar inscription, which was minted only two years after the disaster had occurred, and when the bounty of Tiberius was fresh in every one's memory. Now (says the learned Lecturer), it might be a sufficient answer to observe, that some few years must necessarily have elapsed before these towns could be again inhabited; and that five years, as we learn from Tacitus, was the term actually allowed, in the cases in which the emperor granted a remission of their taxes. We may also observe that, in addition to the cities already noticed, Ephesus appears to have suffered severely in the following year, and the continuance of the danger would naturally retard the work of restoration. But this is not all."—The Rev. Doctor then refers to Phlegon, who probably lived in the days of Hadrian, and whom Eckhel had previously quoted as an authority; and after referring to the fragment of inscribed and sculptured marble above alluded to, and discovered in 1693, at Pozzuoli, he comes to a similar conclusion with the Author of *Doctrina*:—"Within two years after the great earthquake (observes Dr. Cardwell), it appears that the Senate had determined to erect a statue to Tiberius, and had issued a new mintage, as a memorial of his bounty; that within five years after the same event, the statue was completed, and a new die was cut from whence the medal in question was minted, and that finally in the year 783 (A. D. 30), when Tiberius had withdrawn himself from Rome, and was living in the neighbourhood of Puteoli, the inhabitants of that town erected another statue, after the model exhibited at Rome; thereby expressing their sorrow for a calamity, for which their own volcanic country would teach them to feel compassion, and honouring at the same time the emperor's repeated acts of generosity. We may infer, that the seated figure on the reverse of the medal was intended to resemble that colossal statue of Tiberius, which we have traced from the time when the plan of it was first adopted by the Senate, to the time when it was finally erected at Puteoli."— *Lecture*, viii. p. 195.

Capt. Smyth, after describing a specimen of this first brass in his own collection, says,—"Tiberius, to do him justice, behaved on this, as in other public calamities, with a generosity worthy of his high station—for he not only remitted the taxes of the ruined cities for five years; but also presented them with large sums for re-building. A few other such deeds faintly illume the dark picture of the tyrant's reign—his liberality, as Tacitus remarks, being retained after he had abandoned all other virtues. This medal countenances the historic record of Tiberius having been popular in the provinces, for he declined laying new taxes on them; saying that a good shepherd may shear, but not flay his flock."

The above is amongst the *Restitutiones*, or restored coins. That by Domitian is rarer than the one by Titus.

CLARA.—See DIDIA CLARA.

CLARITAS AV*Gusti.*—The brightness of the Emperor.—This legend, with heads of the Sun and the Moon, and also with an upright figure of the Sun, radiated, standing with right hand elevated, and globe in left hand, appears on gold and third brass coins of Postumus, Diocletian, and Val. Maximianus. CLARITAS REIPVBLICAE appears on silver and third brass of Constantinus jun., Constans, Licinius sen., and Crispus. The heads of the Sun and Moon indicate eternity (see p. 23). There is apparently some analogy between this *Claritas* of an Emperor and the name of *Clara Dea*, or the brilliant goddess, as applied to Isis.—See Akerman, vol. 1, p. 256, Constantinus jun.

CLASSICAE; of the Fleet.—Surname of the 17th Legion, inscribed on a denarius of M. Antony.—See LEG. XVII CLASSICAE.

CLAVD. *Claudius, Claudii.*—NERO. CLAVD. DIVI. CLAVD. F.—See the mintages of Nero, who styled himself *Filius Claudii*, by adoption, instead of using his family name of Domitius.

CLAUDIA gens—a duplex family, *i.e.* of patrician as well as plebeian rank, sprung from the Sabines.—Atta Clausus, the head of this house, a man of distinction, having been driven from Regillus by a seditious faction, came to Rome, followed by all his clients, to whom the republic granted the rights of citizenship. Clausus, who afterwards took the name of *Appius Claudius*, was admitted into the order of Patricians and to the rank of Senator. Afterwards, having been made consul, he left an illustrious name to his descendants, who sustained it with honour. The surnames of this family were *Centho, Crassus, Glicia, Marcellus, Nero, Pulcher.* The surname of Nero follows the prenomen of Drusus. The Patricians formed four branches, of whom coins are extant. The most distinguished members of the Plebeian branch were surnamed Marcellus. Each produced great men who rendered good service to the state. The Emperor Nero was the last and certainly the least worthy of its public characters. The prenomen of *Appius* was the one which the Claudia family appropriated to itself; whilst it repudiated that of *Lucius*. Amongst

the coins (comprising 43 varieties) which refer to this family are the three following:—

1. *Obv.*—MARCELLINVS. Male head, beardless, to the right. Behind it the *triquetra*.

Rev.—MARCELLVS. COS. QVINQ. *Marcellus consul quinquies.* A figure togated and veiled, bearing a warlike trophy, as if about to mount the steps of a temple.

The head on the obverse of this denarius is that of Marcus Claudius Marcellus, who, in his fifth consulate, 506 (B. C. 208), made the conquest of Syracuse, and, it may be said, of Sicily. This Roman was the contemporary of Fabius Maximus, and of Scipio. He was one of the Consular Generals who distinguished themselves in the second Punic war, and had already acquired a high reputation at the epoch of Hannibal's invasion. His active character and intrepid courage were conspicuouly displayed in single combats. Even in his first consulate the qualities of a daring valour made him triumph over *Virdomarus*, or *Viromarus*, a Gaulish chief, who, at the head of an army of his nation, had come to the succour of his fellow-countrymen, settled for some centuries, in the north of Italy, and then at war with the Romans. Virdomarus, who had advanced towards Clastidium (a city of Liguria, between Placentia and Tortona, now *Chiustezo*), with numerous troops, fell beneath the blows of the consul, who had darted forth from the ranks to fight him.

The portrait on this denarius is without beard, as usual with the Romans of that period, when they had attained a certain age. The *triquetra* (or three human legs united to each other by the hips), a well-known symbol of Sicily, was placed behind the head to designate its victor.—The legend *Marcellinus* refers to the magistrate who minted the coin—one Claudius Marcellus, who, being adopted into the family of the Cornelii Lentuli, had taken the surname of Marcellinus, and probably transmitted it to his descendants.—On the reverse we read the name of Marcellus, as having been five times consul. The type represents him bearing to the temple of Jupiter Feretrius, the *spolia opima* of Virdomarus. Jupiter was called *Feretrius*, because the triumpher went to his temple, carrying thither as a trophy the armour, offensive and defensive, of the general whom he had killed with his own hand in battle, and which were for that reason denominated *opima* (great or most honourable). To accomplish this religious observance, the conqueror covered his head with one of the lappets of his toga, according to the rites prescribed in the Roman worship. Romulus was the first to perform this ceremony, in consecrating the armour of *Acron*, King of the Ceninians; which act was repeated only by

A. Cornelius Cossus, and afterwards by M. Claudius Marcellus. Virgil thus celebrates this action in his *Æneid*:—

Aspice, ut insignis spoliis Marcellus opimis
Ingreditur, victorque viros supereminet omnes !
Hic rem Romanam, magno turbante tumultu,
Sistet eques ; sternet Pœnos, Gallumque rebellem ;
Tertia arma patri suspendet capta Quirino.
Lib. vi. v. 855 et seq.

See great Marcellus ! how, untir'd in toils,
He moves with mauly grace, how rich with regal
    spoils !
He, when his country (threaten'd with alarms)
Requires his courage, and his conquering arms,
Shall more than once the Punic bands affright:
Shall kill the Gaulish King in single fight:
Then to the capitol in triumph move,
And the third spoils shall grace Feretrian Jove.
Dryden's Translation.

This Marcellus was the very man who shewed the Romans that Hannibal was not only to be resisted, as Fabius had done before him, but also to be attacked and defeated. Indeed he beat the Carthaginian general near Nola, in a daring *sortie*. And after the conquest of Sicily, he assailed him several times with varied success. But his boldness, too often bordering on rashness, led him to expose himself near Venusia (*now* Venosa) to a snare which the sagacity of Hannibal had prepared for him. He fell into an ambuscade of the Carthaginians, and died defending himself with the greatest valour. The victor nobly rendered the funeral honours due to his heroic antagonist.—See Eckhel, v. p. 188 and 187—see also Visconti, *Iconographie Romaine*, T. i. p. 85, 8vo. edit.

2. *Obv.*—C. CLODIVS. C. F. (Caius Claudius, son of Caius.)—Head of Flora, crowned with flowers, and with a *corolla* behind her.—*Rev.*—VESTALIS, a female seated, holding a *simpulum*. Gold and silver.

This denarius was at first ascribed to Caius Claudius Pulcher, edile in 656 (B. c. 98), and consul in 662 (B. c. 92). But according to Borghesi, with whom Cavedoni agrees, it belongs to Caius Claudius, a *legatus* of Brutus and Hortensius, in Macedonia, 711 (B. c. 43) ; the same who caused Caius Antonius (brother of the triumvir), to be put to death, lest he should make his escape.

The female head on the obverse recalls to memory the splendid celebration of the *Floralia*, or feasts in honour of the goddess Flora, by C. Claudius Centho, consul in 514 (B. c. 240), in colleagueship with Sempronius Tuditanus.

With regard to the reverse type, it is matter of dispute amongst numismatists, whether the figure of the vestal be meant for the daughter of Appius Claudius Pulcher, consul in 611 (B. c. 143), who placed herself in front of her father, and defended him when a tribune of the *plebs* would have dragged him out of his triumphal car ; or whether it was intended to represent Quinta Claudia, niece of blind Appius ; that damsel, whom the Roman figment describes to have drawn, with her girdle, through the Tiber into Rome, the ship which bore from Pessinunta, the sacred image of Cybele. (See cut

in next page).—On this point Borghesi, cited by Riccio, says—"Observing that this figure, although holding the simpulum, is seated ; a posture in which sacrifice was not performed, there appears to me ground for suspecting, rather that it was intended, in this type, to represent a statue (che qui piùtosto, siesi voluto effigiare una statua). And supposing this to have been the case, a reason is further afforded for recognising in this image the statue erected to Quinta Claudia."—Engraved in *Morell. Fam. Rom.*—Riccio, p. 54, classes it amongst the RRRR in gold. A fine specimen of it brought £13 at the Thomas sale.— See VESTALIS.

Obv.—A juvenile head laureated, with hair tied in a knot, and with ringlets, and ear-pendants. Behind it a lyre.

Rev.—P. CLODIVS. M. F. Diana standing, with a bow and quiver on her shoulders, holding a long lighted torch in each hand.

If the head on the obverse of this coin be that of Apollo, as notwithstanding its entirely feminine appearance, is still to be inferred from the sister of that pagan deity, represented on the reverse, the whole together may be considered as referring to the Apollinarian games, which were splendidly celebrated in 715 (B. c. 39), in rejoicings at Rome, for the victory gained by Ventidius over the Parthians, P. Clodius being monetal triumvir 716. Riccio marks the above in gold RRRR, and values it at 30 piastres.

There are pieces of this family restored by Trajan. Its name appears on some of the *Cistophori*. The brass coins of this house were struck by the moneyers of Augustus.

CLAVA *Herculea*.—A long round club, headed with a knob ; it was one of the peculiar insignia of Hercules, as that which this hero used instead of a sword, spear, or other arms, and with which he conquered and slew monsters throughout the world. On coins, this knotty club of Hercules, sometimes upright, sometimes reversed, and at others in a transverse position, indicates that the worship of that deity prevailed amongst the people, by whom the coin was struck.

The club of Hercules is seen *alone* on a silver coin of Augustus, inscribed BALBVS PROPR(AETORE). The club erect bears reference to the origin of this Cornelius Balbus, who descended from a family of Cadiz, in Spain, where Hercules was worshipped with distinguished honours. The same massive weapon also appears *by itself*, on coins of Commodus, who ordered himself to be called Hercules the son of Jupiter, and to whom the coin is accordingly inscribed by its legend HERCVL. ROMANO.

The *Clava Herculea* appears on the field of other coins, in the imperial series, amongst those of Trajan, Gordianus Pius, Maximianus. It is seen in the *hand of Hercules* himself, sometimes the right, at others the left, or by his side, in coins of the Antia (see Restio), Æmilia, Cæcilia, Cornelia, Eppia, Poblicia, Pomponia, Vibia, &c., families; and on coins of the Emperors Trajan, Hadrian, Antonine, Aurelius, L. Verus, Commodus, Pertinax, Albinus, Severus, Caracalla, Geta, Gordianus Pius, Aemilian, Gallienus, Postumus, Victorinus, Claud. Gothicus, Tacitus, Probus, Carus, Carinus, Numerianus, Diocletianus, Maximianus, Constantinus Chlorus, Valerius, Severus, Galerius, Maxentius, Gal. Maximinus, Constantinus M.

The *Clava* at the head of Hercules appears on a denarius of M. Antony, who pretended to descend from the son of Alcmena; also on coins of Lepidus, Trajan, Probus, Maximianus.

The *Clava* and a Bow, with quiver, lion's skin, &c. is seen on a coin of Gallienus.

The *Clava* of Hercules, with bow and quiver, displays itself on the well-known coin of Commodus. The same symbols of the monster-killing hero are struck on a coin of Postumus. And the *Herculean Club*, with an *Eagle*, likewise exhibits itself on coins of Trajan, Maximianus, Constantine the Great, &c.—See HERCVLI ROMANO.

CLAUDIA, a vestal virgin, who, being suspected of unchastity, cleared herself from that imputation in the following extraordinary manner:—The image of Cybele or Vesta, being brought from Phrygia to Rome in a galley, and it happening to stick so fast in the shallows of the Tiber as not to be removable even by the strength of a thousand men, she tied her girdle to the vessel, and drew it along to the city, in triumph over her calumniators!—This story is illustrated by a brass medallion (in the French cabinet) above engraved from, struck in honour of the elder *Faustina:* of whom, though rumour had spread reports unfavourable to her matronly character, yet there were not wanting Roman flatterers to praise her as a wonderful pattern of correctness and modesty.—See CYBELE.

CLAUDIA, daughter of the emperor Nero, by Poppæa, born at Antium, in the year of Rome 816 (A. D. 64). She died an infant; and third brass coins (still extant and of extreme rarity) were struck in honour of her memory, under the style of CLAVD(IA) AVGVSTA—DIVA CLAVDIA NER. F. On the reverse of one is DIVA POPPAEA AVG. round a temple.—Mionnet.

CLAUDIUS I.—This emperor, the son of (Nero Claudius) Drusus the elder, and of Antonia, was the younger brother of Germanicus. Born at Lugdunum (Lyon), in Gaul, A. U. C. 744 (B. C. 10), on the kalends of August, he was named TIBERIUS CLAUDIUS DRUSUS. (Dion, lx. § 5.) Brought up from infancy amidst the baneful influences of a feeble constitution, terror, and the society of debased preceptors, he displayed so extraordinary an amount of obtuseness and stupidity, that his mother used to speak of him as a monster, a being only half-fashioned by nature, and when wishing to charge any person with senselessness, she said he was more dull than her son Claudius. (Sueton. ch. 3.) Being on this account neglected by Augustus himself, he received no distinction except that of the Augurship, and was left as heir only among those of the third class, and almost as an alien to the family. (Sueton, c. 4.) On the death of Augustus, he was nominated *Sodalis Augustalis* (Tacitus, *Ann.* i. 54); but, excluded by his uncle Tiberius from all the offices of state which he solicited, he abandoned every hope of acquiring dignity, and surrendered himself to ease, drunkenness, and companionship of the most degraded kind.

Caligula, who in the first year of his reign, lavished honours upon all the members of his family, alive or dead, raised his uncle Claudius also from his obscurity, and in 790 (B. C. 37), when he was himself *consul suffectus*, appointed him as his colleague for two months, from the kalends of July, and designated him *consul iterum* for the fourth year from that time. In 793, Caligula styled himself Jupiter Latialis, and gave Claudius the title of *his priest* (sacerdos). In spite of this, however, he was despised by the people even under Caligula for his dulness; but the low estimation in which he was held, in the long run, proved his safeguard. For, when almost all the males of his family were put to death, though he had a narrow escape for his own life, the mental deficiencies of his character stood him in great stead, and he was treated only as a laughing-stock. Caligula having been slain on the 9th kalends of February, 794 (B. C. 41), Claudius, terrified at the circumstance, concealed himself in the palace; but being discovered by a soldier passing that way, and recognised, he was saluted *Imperator*, and being led to the camp, he passed the night amidst the bivouacs of the soldiers. The Consuls and Conscript Fathers assembled in the capitol to deliberate on the means of re-establishing the government; and, coming to no agreement among themselves, on the following day the soldiers took the oaths in the name of Claudius, and compelled acquiescence by force of arms.

In this manner elevated to the throne in his 49th year, Claudius immediately received all the honours decreed to him, except the titles of *Imperator* and *Pater Patriæ*; but even the latter he soon after permitted to be applied to him. He ordered Cassius Chærea to be put to death, not from regret for the murder of Caligula, but for fear of a plot against his own safety. He restored to Antiochus, Commagene, which had been taken from him by Caligula.

He sent back to Spain Mithridates, who had been detained in chains by Caius; and on another Mithridates he bestowed the Bosporus, giving Polemon a part of Cilicia. For the benefit of the Jewish King Agrippa, who was then at Rome, and whose advice he had sought on entering upon his reign, he enlarged the kingdom of Judæa, and to his brother Herod he gave Chalcidene. In this the first year (A. D. 41) of Claudius's reign, the *Germani* were defeated by Galba and Gabinius.

In 795 (A. D. 42). He defeated the Mauritanians and the Numidians in various engagements. He divided Mauritania into Tingitanis and Cæsariensis. He constructed the port of Ostia at an immense cost. Furius Camillus Scribonianus, the prefect of Dalmatia, excited a seditious movement against Claudius, which was soon put down, its instigator being slain on the island of Issa.

796 (A. D. 43). He entered upon his third consulate, under novel circumstances for an emperor, viz., as substituted *(suffectus)* in the place of an individual deceased.—A. Plautius, having been sent forward into Britain, carried on the campaign there strenuously; but a still more serious disturbance arising, he was superseded by Claudius himself, who, aiming at military fame, passed over to the seat of war. Having excellent officers to do the fighting part, he vanquished the Britons, was declared *Imperator* over and over again, and after remaining in the island not more than seventeen days, he returned to the continent. During his absence a triumph had been decreed to him by the abject Senate, also an arch, and the prefix of Britannicus for himself and his son.—(See *Britannia* and *Britan*, pp. 137 and 140 of this dictionary.)

"Whilst speaking of British affairs it may be added, that he evinced generosity of heart, when, charmed with the noble boldness of the captive Caractacus, he ordered the liberation of that prince and his family; an act, the merit of which will be immediately felt, on calling to mind the horrid fate too often reserved for royal captives." Capt. Smyth, p. 33.]

797 (A. D. 44). Returning to Rome he celebrated his triumph over the Britons. He enlarged the patrimonial dominion of M. Julius Cottius, which he held in the district of the Alps, called by his name *(Cottian)*, and gave him the title of King.

798 and 799 (A. D. 45 and 46). No occurrence of note took place during these two years, with the exception of the vile intrigues of Messalina and the freedmen; not to omit mentioning the directions which he gave respecting the mode in which statues were to be erected.

800 (A. D. 47). He celebrated the 800th anniversary of the building of Rome with the exhibition of secular games, 64 years after their celebration by Augustus. He appointed as King over the Cherusci, Italicus, son of Flavius, the brother of Arminius. (Tacitus, *Ann*. xi. 16). Corbulo continued to command the Roman army in Lower Germania, and reduced the Frisii to submission—whilst Vespasian, with his son Titus, harrassed the Britons.

801 (A. D. 48). As Censor, having for his colleague L. Vitellius, the father of Aulus Vitellius, afterwards Emperor, he removed certain members of the Senate, and filled up their places with others. He conferred upon the inhabitants of Gallia Transalpina the privileges of Senators at Rome, and closed the *lustrum* this year. (Respecting the date of this censorship, see CENSOR II. p. 193, also the mint of VITELLIUS.)—During the absence of Claudius at Ostia, his wife Messalina publicly married C. Silius at Rome. Being informed of the circumstance on his return, he ordered her and her paramour to be put to death.—(Tac. *Ann*. xi.)

802 (A. D. 49). At the beginning of this year, he married his grand-daughter Agrippina. At the entreaty of the Parthians, he sent back Meherdates [one of the Arsacidæ, *i. e*. of the line of the kings of Parthia], who had been detained as a hostage at Rome, to become their king.—Mithridates of the Bosporus, making fresh attempts against Cotys, was taken prisoner to Rome. The Ituræi and Judæi, on the death of their kings Sohemius and Agrippa, were added to the province of Syria.

803 (A. D. 50). Claudius adopted L. Domitius Ahenobarbus (afterwards the emperor Nero) the son of Agrippina; who herself, the same year, received the title of *Augusta*. A colony was sent out to the town of the Ubii, her birthplace, and to which the name of Agrippina was given (now *Cologne)*.—L. Pomponius subdued the Catti.—Caractacus, king of Britain, after a war of nine years, was defeated and taken prisoner.

804 (A. D. 51). Nero prematurely assumed the *toga virilis*, before he completed his fourteenth year, and was designated consul, upon which office he would enter on reaching the age of twenty; a pro-consular jurisdiction without the walls of Rome was decreed to him, and he received the title of *Princeps Juventutis*.—Burrus was appointed prefect of the pretorians, through the influence of Agrippina.

805 (A. D. 52). The Clitæ, a wild race of people in Cilicia, having revolted against their Roman masters, were put down. The famous *naumachia*, or representation of a sea-fight, took place in the presence of the emperor, on the lake Fucinus, near Rome.—Claudius completed, with great magnificence, two aqueducts

of the purest water, one called *Aqua Claudia*, the other the New Anio, and dedicated them.— (See AQUA-DUCTUS, p. 69 et seq. of this dictionary).—In the succeeding year, Nero Cæsar, in his sixteenth year, married Octavia, the daughter of Claudius.

807 (A. D. 54). Whilst confined to his bed by illness, Claudius was put to death, on the 12th of October, by his wife Agrippina, who, through the instrumentality of Locusta, the sorceress, administered poison to him in a dish of mushrooms.

Thus perished in the 63rd year of his age, and 14th of his reign, the Emperor Claudius; one raised by a remarkable turn of fortune to a position, which he had neither expected nor coveted. The empire thus thrust upon him he administered much less at his own discretion than that of his wives and his freedmen, acting in all measures as best suited their convenience or pleasure. It was, therefore, wittily observed of him by Seneca, that he celebrated the month of Saturn the whole year through; the month, that is to say, in which slaves used to lord it over their masters. The most notorious among these freedmen were Narcissus, Pallas prefect of the exchequer, Callistus master of requests, Felix the eunuch, afterwards procurator of Judæa, Mnestor, the actor, a prime favourite of Messalina, Polybius, Posides, and Harpocras; all of whom, in influencing the conduct of the emperor, availed themselves less of his dulness, than of his timidity, which rendered him absurdly superstitious. Thus it was fear which induced him to put his signature to the deed of settlement, by which the marriage of his own wife Messalina with Silius was ratified; and again, a new terror caused him to order the execution of herself and her paramour. And hence it arose, that all who, during his reign, stood in the way of other's cupidity, on a hint from his wives or freedmen of some plot against himself, were forthwith put to death.—Of stupidity he gave numerous specimens, especially in the absurd laws which he introduced during his censorship, and in his habit of inviting to dinner, in a fit of forgetfulness, those whom the day before he had commanded to be destroyed. He had, moreover, plenty of cruelty in his disposition; for no spectacle gave him more delight than that of gladiators lacerated by each other's blows, or the attacks of beasts, and to gaze upon the agonies of their last moments.— But this passion extended itself only to gladiators, and the refuse of the people. Yet this man was a fair scholar, and was no mean writer of history; but even in this pursuit he could not refrain from trifling, by either introducing new letters into the alphabet, or by reviving antiquated ones, and thus interfering with the public convenience. Evidence of a loftier and more energetic spirit will be recognized in his presence during the campaign in Britain; the vast works of the port of Ostia; and the aqueducts completed by him. From these it may be concluded that he would have proved himself far from incapable of noble deeds, had his natural

abilities been cultivated by an education worthy of a sovereign; a post for which, however, he had never seemed to be destined till he had actually reached it.—See Eckhel, vi. p. 233 et seq.

The coins of Claudius are not numerous, yet for the most part easily to be procured. Gold rare. Silver, with certain exceptions, common. Those of the three sizes in brass also, with few exceptions, common. Some pieces representing him with Agrippina junior, and others restored by Titus and Trajan are very rare. On the products of his mint (as on the first brass *engraved* p. 212), he is styled TI. CLAVDIVS CAESAR AVG. P. M. TR. P. IMP.—On some obverses appears the surname of GERMANICUS, which he took in memory of his father and brother. But that of *Britannicus*, although awarded him, is not assumed amongst his numismatic appellations.

"This emperor (says Mionnet) constantly abstained from placing on any of his coins struck at Rome, the title of *Imperator* as a prenomen; but he used, and repeated frequently, that very title as a surname." In two instances only of *colonial* coins IMP. is found prefixed to the name CLAVDIVS. "It is a peculiarity (observes Capt. Smyth) of this reign that the tribunitian power is omitted in the legends."—Amongst the rarest and most remarkable reverses on this emperor's coinage are the following:—

SILVER MEDALLIONS.—COM. ASIA. Temple and two figures within.—DIANA EPHESIA, with portraits of Claudius and Agrippina—(valued by Mionnet at 80 fr.)

GOLD.—CONSTANTIAE AVGVSTI—(restored by Trajan, priced at 120 fr. by Mionnet.)—DE BRITAN. Triumphal arch—(40 fr.)—DE GERMANIS. Arch—(48 fr.)—DIVVS CLAVDIVS—(restored by Trajan, 120 fr.)—IMPER. RECEPT. Pretorian camp—(40 fr.)—Young portrait of Nero (72 fr.)—PRAETOR RECEPT.—(48 fr.)

SILVER.—SACERDOS DIVI. AVGVSTI—Two torches—(30 fr.)—Claudius in a quadriga— 34 fr.)—Peace preceded by a serpent.—See PACI. AVGVSTAE.

FIRST BRASS.—DE GERMANIS. Trophy— (valued by Mionnet at 60 fr.)

SECOND BRASS.—CONSTANTIAE AVGVSTI.— Helmeted figure.

There are no *Latin* coins in honour of any of the wives of Claudius, except of Agrippina. Those of Messalina are Greek and colonial.— This emperor established colonies in almost all parts of the Roman world.

CLAUDIUS II. (M. AURELIUS, surnamed GOTHICUS) was born in Illyria, on the 10th of May, A. D. 214 or 215. His family descent was so obscure that even the name of his father remains unknown. But indebted for distinction to his own talents both as a soldier and a states-man, he acquired the confidence of Trajanus Decius, by whom he was entrusted with the defence of Thermopylæ against the northern invaders of Greece.—Valerian gave him the rank of military tribune, and in A. D. 259, made him governor of Illyricum, and general in chief of all the provinces on the Lower Danube. The fame of Claudius in the wars, which the indolent Gallienus had to sustain against the usurpers who rose under his distracted reign, induced the Senate to honour him with a statue. Having been summoned to assist at the siege of Milan, where Gallienus was engaged in suppressing the revolt of Aureolus, it was believed, but not on any assured authority, that he gave his assent to the plot, which resulted in the assassination of the prince, whom he succeeded about the twentieth of March, A. D. 268. The choice of the army was enthusiastically confirmed by the Senate. Claudius fulfilled, with a character unchanged, and a reputation undiminished, the expectations and wishes of the Romans. He seemed to have only one wish, that of restoring to the republic its ancient liberty and its original splendour. After having destroyed Aureolus, and gained a decisive victory over a large body of the Alemanni, on the shores of the Lago di Garda, near Verona, he commenced the arduous task of re-establishing order and discipline. It was to this end that he decreed laws, which had they been followed out and obeyed, would have ensured the welfare and happiness of the empire. In A. D. 269, Claudius took the consulship, and the same year marched to the encounter of a more formidable enemy than had, up to that period, menaced the power of Rome. The different tribes of barbarians, known under the general appellation of Goths, having collected a fleet of more than two thousand vessels, at the mouth of the Dniester, embarked on board of it no less, it is said, than 320,000 men, who were landed on the shores of Macedonia; and thence advanced to meet Claudius, who after a terrible battle fought near Naissus, in Dardania, (A. D. 269), gained a great victory; 50,000 of them having been slain in one day. The following year the emperor succeeded in either destroying or dispersing the remainder: these achievements, gained for him the title of GOTHICUS. He then prepared to turn his arms against Queen Zenobia, and the usurper Tetricus; but at that moment, a pestilence which the Goths had brought with them into the confines of the empire, proved fatal to their conqueror. He was attacked by this widely spread epidemic at Sirmium (Sirmich), in Pannonia, and died there in the month of May, A. D. 270, aged 56, after a reign of about two years, recommending with his parting breath, his general Aurelianus as the worthiest candidate for the purple. This heroic prince is described to have had a tall and robust person, a broad countenance, and eye full of fire. He was dignified in his manners, calm in disposition, temperate in his habits. A foe to effeminacy, he delighted in warlike exercises; and set an example to his soldiers of a life subjected to the greatest fatigues and privations. To believe his panegyrists, he was of all the emperors the most beloved during his reign, and the most regretted after his death. There is no doubt, however, that he was a prince of great merit, and of splendid public qualities. The Senate heaped honours of every description on his memory; a golden buckler (see *clipeus votivus*) bearing his image, was placed in the *Curia Romana*; and a golden statue, six feet high, was erected to him in the capitol, at Rome.

This emperor is styled on coins, at first simply IMP. CLAVDIVS CAESAR AVG. or IMP. C. M. AVR. CLAVDIVS AVG.—After his victory over the Alemanni, and his still greater victory over the Goths, we read round his portrait IMP. C. M. AVR. CLAVDIVS GERM. GOTHICVS.—After his death DIVVS CLAVDIVS GOTHICVS and DIVVS CLAVD. OPT. IMP.

The following are amongst the rarest and most remarkable reverses in the coinage of Claudius Gothicus.

GOLD.—CONCORD EXERCI. A woman with two ensigns; one of which she holds erect in her right hand, and the other *under* her left arm—a singular feature in such a type.

INVICTVS AVG. Helmed head of Claudius.—MEMORIAE AETERNAE. Rome within a temple.

The above two are valued at 300 fr. each by Mionnet.

PAX EXERC. Peace. Brought £15 15s. at the Thomas sale.

VIRTVS CLAVDII. Emperor on horseback, riding over prostrate figures.

Engraved in Akerman. *Descr. Cat.* ii. pl. 10, No. 2. A finely preserved specimen of this very rare aureus brought £14 10s. at the Thomas sale.

VICTORIA AVG. A Victory standing; at her feet are two captives; one kneels, and is raising up his hands; the other is seated.—[This beautiful and extra rare coin brought £27 10s. at the Thomas sale. It is now in the British Museum. See an accurate engraving of it, prefixed to the foregoing biographical notice of this emperor].

BRASS MEDALLIONS.—ADVENTVS AVG. Emperor on horseback, with Victory and soldiers. Valued by Mionnet at 50 fr.

CONSECRATIO. Altar lighted.—MARS VLTOR. marching with trophy.—MARTI PACIF. With olive branch.—The above three are valued by Mionnet at 40 fr. each.

CONSECRATIO. Square altar.—Valued at 60 fr.

FIRST BRASS.—IOVI VICTORI. Jupiter standing.—60 fr.

SECOND BRASS.——VIRTVS AVG. Military figure.

THIRD BRASS.—DEO CABIRO. One of the Cabiri.

REGI ARTIS.   Vulcan standing.
VIR. AVG.   Minerva and one of the Cabiri.
REQVIES OPTIMORVM MERIT.   Figure veiled and seated.

CLAUDIUS TACITUS.—See TACITUS.

C. L. DOM.   *Cæsar Lucius Domitius.*—See AURELIANUS.

CLEMENTIAE.—Clemency—whom the Romans worshipped as a goddess, and for the most part set at naught as a virtue—had a temple erected to her honour, as in memory of the mercy which Julius Cæsar exercised towards his enemies after the victories he had gained. On a denarius of the Æmilia gens (engraved in *Morell. Thesaur. Fam. Rom.*) the obverse bears PAVLLVS LEPIDVS CONCORD. A veiled female head.—*Rev.*—CLEMENTIAE. S. C. Head of a female in the middle of an ornamented buckler.

L. Paulus is said to have given liberty, instead of servitude, to the Macedonians, whom he had fought with and subdued. The memory of this good action was handed down to posterity, through the durable medium of a coin, by a descendant of his.—See *Morell. Thesaur. Familiæ,* T. i. p. 644. Engraved in T. ii. TAB. 1, F.—Valued at 40 fr. by Mionnet.

A denarius of L. Buca, a moneyer of Julius Cæsar, exhibits on its reverse the legend CLEMENTIA, and the head of that goddess, with a laurel branch before it.

CLEMENTIAE CAESARIS. A tetrastyle temple.—On a silver coin of Julius Cæsar this legend and type appear. The latter represents the temple of Clemency which was erected at Rome, in memory of Julius, and in honour of that virtue, so rare in conquerors, yet which no one ever exercised more nobly than he, by the concurrent voice of all historic writers, is allowed to have done on every occasion.——Du Choul, in his quaint but honest style, says—" And as from piety come pity and clemency, in which Julius Cæsar surpassed all other princes, I have accompanied this medal with a sentence worthy to be engraved in letters of gold, taken from an antique marble, and which says—NIHIL EST QVOD MAGIS DECEAT PRINCIPEM QVAM LIBERALITAS ET CLEMENTIA—that is to say, there is nothing which more becomes a prince than clemency and liberality. And, in truth, there is nothing in this world more graceful than mercy."—See *La Religion des Romains,* p. 26.—See also *Thesaur. Morell. Impp.* T. iii. TAB. v. No. 8.

CLEMENTIA IMP. GERMAN. Clementia Imperatoris Germanici.—On coins of Vitellius  (rare in gold, but not so in silver), this legend accompanies a female figure, in the stola, seated, holding a small branch in one hand, and the *hasta pura* in the other.

On this and other imperial coins, the goddess is represented both standing and seated, sometimes holding a branch of olive, as marking peace and gentleness, or a laurel branch, because (says Jobert, citing Pliny's authority), " it was used to expiate the guilt of criminals."

Vaillant illustrates the signification of this coin, by adducing the historical fact, that Vitellius eagerly received the surname of *Germanicus* awarded to him by the army of Upper Germany. On the death of Otho, he spared the life of that emperor's brother Titianus, whom he excused on the ground of fraternal piety. He served the consulate with Marius Celsus, Otho's general, 822 (A. D. 69): nor did he act with severity either towards the persons or property of revolters against his government, which makes Tacitus say—" Vitellius victor *clementiæ* gloriam tulit."—*(Præstant.* vol. ii. p. 80).

CLEMENTIA AUG.—(Clemency of the Emperor). COS. II. also COS. III.—On silver and second brass of Albinus, who in this legend contrasts his own clemency with the cruel harshness of Severus, who had behaved with great barbarity towards such of the Senators as he suspected of being hostile to him, and especially towards those who followed the fortunes of Pescennius Niger.—(Eckhel, vii. 168).

CLEMENTIA TEMP. or TEMPORUM.—Two figures, representing Jupiter and the emperor, supporting a globe in their joined hands, or a woman standing by a column, accompany this legend on third brass of Florianus, Tacitus, Probus, and other *Augusti* of the lower empire.

CLEMENTIAE. To Clemency. S. C.—This dedicatory inscription occurs on a second brass of Tiberius, over a shield, of which the design is evidently borrowed from the *Clementia* of the Æmilia family already described. The full-faced bust in the centre is, in some specimens of this rare coin, that of a female (perhaps personifying Clemency); on others that of a man (probably meant for Tiberius himself)—immediately surrounded by a laurel crown, with double outer circle of a highly ornamented pattern.—See PATERA.

The praise of clemency, admitted by all ancient historians to have been justly bestowed on Julius Cæsar, was afterwards prostituted to the flattery of the most cruel emperors. Thus not only the *clemency* but the *moderation* of Tiberius is celebrated on his coins; and the Roman Senate commanded sacrifices to be made in acknowledgment of the same god-like quality in—Caligula!—The mark of Senatorial sanction on this coin seems by implication to indicate the wish of that obsequious body, that the emperor should *in future* be merciful, which for a long time previous he had *not* been.—The above reverse is engraved from a specimen, in the possession of Goddard Johnson, Esq. Norwich.

CLEOPATRA, the 7th (or 8th) and last Queen of Egypt, was born towards the end of 685 (B. C. 69).—This celebrated woman was the daughter of Ptolemy Auletes, and the sister and wife of Ptolemy (XII.) Dionysius Neoterus, who was slain at the battle of Alexandria, fighting against Julius Cæsar, in the year 797 (B. C. 47). Cæsar, being enamoured of Cleopatra, gave her Ptolemy XIII. (her brother), for a husband, to cover his own designs. But young Ptolemy was taken off by poison, or drowned in the Nile, and Cleopatra began to reign alone in the year 712 (B. C. 42). The next year Arsinoë, sister of Cleopatra, was assassinated by command of Mark Antony, who had in turn become, after Cæsar's death, the paramour of Cleopatra; and it was "for love" of her that this vain ambitious Roman acted as if he deemed "the world *well* lost." Antony having at length divorced his wife Octavia, the sister of Augustus, a quarrel and a war ensued between those two unscrupulous men of clashing interests.—In 723 (B. C. 31), Cleopatra accompanied her lover to Actium, with a fleet superbly equipped; and after his defeat fled to Alexandria, where she put an end to her life in 724 (B. C. 30), by the bite of an asp, in an unfinished Mausoleum (which had already served for the tomb of Antony), that she might not be led in triumph to Rome by the conqueror. Augustus, however, determined at least to chain her golden image to his car; and after his triumph, he deposited it in the temple of Venus, of which, according to Dion, it was a principal ornament.

Thus died one of the most captivating but most unprincipled of sovereign princesses, at the age of 39 years, of which she reigned seventeen. With her fell the dynasty of the Ptolemies in Egypt, and indeed the Egyptian monarchy.

Cleopatra had a son by Julius Cæsar, Cæsarion, called Ptolemy; and three children by Mark Antony, viz., a son called Alexander, a daughter named after herself, who was afterwards betrothed to Juba the younger (see IVBA REX), and Ptolemy, surnamed Philadelphus.

"The leading points of Cleopatra's character were ambition and voluptuousness. But in all the stories of her luxury and lavish expense, there is a splendour and a grandeur that somewhat refines them. In the days of her prosperity her arrogance was unbounded. She was avaricious to supply her extravagance, and cruel, or at least had no regard for human life, when her own objects were concerned. Her talents were great and varied: her knowledge of different languages was peculiarly remarkable; and in the midst of her most luxurious scenes, proofs are to be traced of a love for literature and for critical research. She added the library of Pergamos to that of Alexandria. Her ready and versatile wit; her knowledge of human nature, and power of using it; her attractive manners, and her exquisitely musical and flexible voice, compared by Plutarch to a many-stringed instrument, are also the subject of well-attested praise. The higher points in her character are admirably touched by Horace in the Ode (i. 37), on her defeat at Actium."—*Dictionary of Greek and Roman Biography*, edited by W. Smith, LL. D.

There are coins of this Queen, both silver and brass, with both *Latin* and Greek legends, exhibiting her head, either alone or jugated with that of Mark Antony. Amongst these are the two following:—

CLEOPATRAE, REGINAE REGVM, FILIORVM REGVM.—This legend appears on the reverse of a denarius of M. Antony, which also exhibits the head of Cleopatra, beside which is the prow of a ship, or a lituus. The obverse of this remarkable coin bears the head of Antony, behind which is the Armenian tiara, and round it M. ANTONI. ARMENIA DEVICTA.

Antony, having contrived to enveigle into his power Artavasdes, king of Armenia, deposed him and gave his crown and dominions to the son whom he (Antony) had by Cleopatra; to whom, in sacrifice of all justice and true policy, the infatuated triumvir stamped this reverse with her portrait, which has the appearance of neither youth nor beauty to recommend it. He also gave her the title of *(Regina regum, et filiorum regum,* the word *mater* being understood) the queen of kings and the mother of the sons of kings.—For an engraving of this coin (*not* of Roman die)—see page 81 of this dictionary.

The testimony of Dion Cassius supports the fact, that, in a speech to the people of Alexandria, Mark Antony commanded that Cleopatra should be styled Queen of Kings, with right and title to Egypt and Cyprus. It is also recorded that, of his sons by Cleopatra, he bestowed Syria on Ptolemy, with all the territories bordering on the Hellespont; on Alexander Armenia, and whatever countries he might subdue beyond the Euphrates; and on his daughter Cleopatra the district of Cyrene.

2. *Obv.*—M. ANTONIVS IMP. COS. DESIG. ITER ET TERT. Heads of a man and woman side by side.

Rev.—III. VIR. R. P. C. Bacchus standing on the cista between two serpents. Silver of Mark Antony.—See *Cistophori,* p. 204 of this volume.

After having conquered Brutus, Antony made his entry into Ephesus, with a procession of men, women, and children, clothed as bacchantes and satyrs; crowned with ivy and bearing thyrsi. Plutarch relates an account of these orgia, in which Mark Antony was honoured as a second Bacchus.—Antony repeated this folly till he came to the city of Alexandria, into which he made the same kind of entry, as Velleius Paterculus relates. Antony's cistophori struck in Asia, were probably coined at Ephesus, which, added to the others, this superior mark of adulation.

Eckhel has not pronounced on the doubt entertained by many numismatists, some of whom have attributed the female head to Octavia, and others to Cleopatra. However, he thinks that the latter would have been figured with a crowned head, if it had been meant for her.

It was in 720 (B. C. 34), that Antony united the finest provinces of Asia and Africa to his other conquests; and the coinage of Cleopatra could not be associated with his own till the year 722, when peace was broken between the triumviri. He was named consul for the third time, in 720. The woman's head on the cista may therefore be that of Octavia, and the diademed head joined to his, that of Cleopatra. (See *Doct. Num.* vol. iv. p. 66, et seq.)—See also Biographical Summary of M. Antonius, and notice of his mintages, pp. 57, 58, 59, of this Dictionary.

C. L. C AE SA R E S A V G V S T I F. COS. DESIG. PRINC. IVVENT. *(Caius et Lucius Cæsares Augusti Filii Consules Designati Principes Juventutis).* Two

figures veiled and togated, standing—each holds in his hand a spear, with a buckler resting on the ground; above is a *capeduncula* and *lituus*.

2. *Rev.*—C. L. CAESARES PRINC. IVVEN-

TVTIS.—Each Cæsar on horseback, going at a quick rate, lifts up his right hand.—These two silver coins of Roman die, each having a head of Augustus on its obverse, being, in the opinion of Eckhel, invaluable, as serving to illustrate the history of both Cæsars (see p. 159) he has given the following detailed account (it were superfluous to add, accurate explanation) of them :—

Consules Designati.—On this point Tacitus says—*(Annal.* i. ch. 3)—" For he had introduced the sons of Agrippa, Caius and Lucius, into the family of the Cæsars, before they had laid aside their youthful *prætexta*; and, under an affectation of declining those honours, had concealed a vehement desire that they should be entitled *Principes Juventutis*, and nominated *(designari)* Consuls."—Again, Suetonius (in *Aug.* ch. 64)—" And while still mere children he put them forward in offices of state, and as *consules designati* sent them forth among the provinces and the armies of the empire."—The year in which they became *consules designati* is fixed by an inscribed marble found at Ancyra, thus—" To do me honour, the Roman Senate and people designated them (Caius and Lucius) in their 15th year, consuls, that they might enter upon that office after a lapse of five years."—According to these words, Caius, who was born 734 (B. C. 20), and in 748 (B. C. 6) would be 15 years of age, was then made *consul designatus.* On a marble which Cardinal Noris quotes from Panvinius we read respecting the same Caius— " Whom the people created consul in his XIVth year; " and consequently on this latter marble the *completed* years only are reckoned. And, indeed, Caius did actually, as the marble of Ancyra has it, after the interval of five years, enter upon his consulship in the year U. C. 754 (A. D. 1); the year 748 not being taken into

account. As according to the record of the same marble, the same course was pursued with reference to his brother Lucius, and as he was born 737 (B. C. 17), it follows that he was designated consul A. U. C. 751 (B. C. 3), or as Cardinal Noris fixes it, 752; and in order that on the same analogy he might enter upon office in 757 (A. D. 4), but this was prevented by his death occurring in the interim.

Principes Juventutis.—That this distinction was conferred upon them, is abundantly testified by historians, coins, and marbles. In the case of Caius, the time is fixed by Zonaras, viz. in 749 (B. C. 5), and as he also records, that Lucius obtained the same honours in the year following, it appears that this title was shared by him also in the year U. C. 750 (B. C. 4).

On the first coin both Cæsars stand veiled and togated, no doubt a religious costume; above them, on one side, is a *lituus*, on the other a *capeduncula* (or ewer); though the position of these instruments varies, according to Pedrusi (Mus. Farnese), on different coins, so that some present the *lituus* on the right, others on the left side. The *capeduncula* certainly belongs to Caius, for Dion tells us that he entered the priesthood *(sacerdotium)* U. C. 748 (B. C. 6). The pontificate of Caius is further confirmed by a coin above quoted under his separate coinage, on which he is described as PONT. COS. and also by an inscription given by Gruter (p. 234.4).

C. CAESARI. AVGVSTI. F.
PONTIFICI. COS.
DESIGNATO.
PRINCIPI. IVVENTVTIS.

The *lituus* is the appropriate symbol of Lucius, as being that of an augur. That he held this office is proved by a marble published in the same place by Gruter :—

L. CAESARI. AVGVSTI. F.
AVGVRI. COS.
DESIGNATO.
PRINCIPI. IVVENTVTIS.

To which may be added other marbles, displayed in the same work, and exhibiting the same titles.

Both Cæsars hold the *hasta* and *clipeus.* Each of these arms they received from the Equestrian Order to which they belonged, as a gift on the occasion of being chosen *Principes Juventutis.*—Dion informs us (LV. § 12), that " the golden bucklers and spears of Caius and Lucius, which they received from the *equites* on assuming the *toga virilis*, were after their deaths suspended in the Senate-house."—But on the marble of Ancyra, which has greater claims to credit, they are said to have been of silver—" The Roman equites in a body gave them each the title of *Princeps Juventutis*, presenting them at the same time with bucklers and spears of *silver*."—A coin of Nero shews that he also was presented, as *Princeps Juventutis*, with a similar buckler by the equestrian order.—See EQVEST. ORD.

These coins were struck between the years U. C. 752 and 753 (B. C. 2 and 1) *not before;* for Augustus, who is styled on them *pater patriæ*, received this appellation for the first time in the year 752 (B. C. 2) *nor later ;* for in the year 754 (A.D. 1) Caius was no longer *consul designatus*, but *actually consul.* No imperial coins have been more frequently imitated by foreign moneyers (*barbaræ officinæ monetariorum*), than these we have been describing; so great is the number which has come down to us, of most unfinished, and, indeed, ludicrously bad workmanship.—*Doct. Num. Vet.* vi. 171–172.

Mionnet values No. 1, in gold, at 135 fr.; and No. 2, in silver, at 50 fr.

C. L. I. COR.—See CORINTHUS.

CLIO, one of the Muses, so called from κλεος, *Gloria,* because glory is derived to the poets from their verses.

On a denarius of Q. Pomponius the laureated head of a female appears as the obverse type. On the reverse is the legend Q. POMPONIVS MVSA, and the figure of a woman standing. This is supposed to represent Clio, and the lyre which she holds in her left hand, and on which she is in the attitude of playing, bears allusion to her reputed invention of that musical instrument, with which she sang the praises of heroes.

CLIPEUS—a buckler, or shield—one of the most ancient pieces of defensive armour. The Romans at first made use of the round shield of the Argæans, which they called *Clipeus.* After the union of the Sabines with the Romans, the latter adopted the *scutum* of the Sabines, which had the form of an oblong square, sometimes flat, concave inside, sometimes convex outside. And this at length became part of the defensive armour of the Roman infantry. The round buckler of the cavalry was called *parma.* The shields of the legionaries appear to have been ornamented with designs not unlike heraldic bearings—such as a thunderbolt, an anchor, a lion, a wild-boar, a serpent, or some other symbol. And these, being also painted of a particular colour, served to distinguish each legion, and each cohort, from others, and gave rise to the surnames, by which the legions were often designated.— Distinctive signs were also added to mark the buckler of each soldier, because in camp the bucklers were all deposited in a tent or magazine. A soldier was dishonoured, if he abandoned his shield. Warriors, frequently after having despoiled their enemy of his buckler, offered it in some temple to a deity : hence the appellation of votive shields (see C. L. V. below). They were soon fabricated of metals ; and were even made of marble, when placed on monuments ; but in these instances they enter into the composition of trophies. On coins, Victory is often seen inscribing the date of some great military exploit on these bucklers. There is a brass medallion of Antoninus, the reverse type of which forms a remarkably fine record of triumph over the Parthians, by inscription on a shield.—See VIC. PARTHICAE.

Clipeus Macedonicus—the Macedonian shield, of a round form, was manufactured of gold or silver, or both, with ingenious workmanship, conspicuous for its various embellishments.— The representation of such a shield is seen,

with the head of an elephant in it, on denarii of the Cæcilia family, struck by M. METEL-LVS, Q. F. in memory of his ancestor Cæcilius Metellus, who for his victory over the Carthaginians, was the first to enjoy the honours of a triumph in a chariot drawn by elephants. But it is on account of the triumph of his grandfather for Macedonia that the Macedonian shield was assumed in this coin.—See p. 149 of this Dictionary.

CL. V. *Clipeus Votivus.* The votive shield. Many of these appear on the gold and silver mintages of Augustus. Amongst the rest the two following :—

1. *Rev.*—CL. V. within a circular buckler, at each corner the initials S. P. Q. R. On one side of this round buckler is a legionary eagle, on the other a military ensign. Above and below the shield SIGNIS RECEPTIS. —2. *Rev.*—OB. CIVIS SER-VATOS. A buckler, on which is inscribed S. P. Q. R. C. L. V. encircled by an oaken crown.

These CL*ipei* V*otivi* (for so the abbreviation is to be expanded), are represented in various ways, which may be seen in Morel, or in the catalogue of the Imperial Museum, p. ii. p. 86. The custom of dedicating shields is a very ancient one. Thus, Virgil (*Æn.* v. 286) tells, that Æneas dedicated a shield to Apollo Actius (or at *Actium*) with the inscription, "Æneas hæc de Danais victoribus arma."—Pliny records the instances of the practice in Rome itself, and adds, that the ancient Trojans, and the Carthaginians, were in the habit of engraving their portraits on shields (xxxv. ch. 3.) As regards the Carthaginians, the statement is confirmed by Livy (xxv. 39), who says, that among the spoil was a silver shield 138 pounds in weight, with a likeness of Barcinus Hasdrubal. In like manner the Senate dedicated, in the curia, to Claudius Gothicus, a golden shield ; on which " was represented a likeness of his countenance as far as the throat," according to Trebellius Pollio ; and so there is on a coin of Mescinius, struck in the year 738 (B. C. 16), the head of Augustus in a shield ; and heads of *Clementia* and *Moderatio* are similarly exhibited on the coins of Tiberius. The joke of Cicero given by Macrobius is well-known : seeing in pro-consular Asia a likeness of his brother Quintus on a shield, painted in immense proportions as far as the chest (whereas Quintus was of small stature), he exclaimed, my brother's half length is greater than his whole.

The use, then, of these shields was, that by being suspended in public or private localities, they might either presesent a likeness of an individual, and that either in painting or alto-relievo, of which kind were the shields of Homer and Virgil, the work of Vulcan, and spoken of by Pliny (xxxv. ch. 2) ; or that, by means of an inscription, the remembrance of some illustrious exploit might be transmitted to posterity.— The latter mode is very frequently observed on the coins of Emperors. Philo Judæus has in one passage mentioned both kinds, where he says, that Pilate, the prefect of Judæa, "dedicated, in the palace of Herod which stands in the sacred city, gilded shields, exhibiting, indeed, no portrait or other device forbidden by the laws, but only the barely necessary inscription, by which two things might be understood, viz. the name of the person who dedicated them, and of the person to gratify whom the dedication was made." The shields of Domitian, which the Senate, on hearing of his death, caused to be pulled down from the walls of the curia, and thrown upon the ground, as Suetonius relates (in *Domit.* ch. 23), were doubtless distinguished with either the portrait or the names of that tyrant. To the foregoing may be added the information, which the learned interpreters of the Herculaneum Antiquities have lately gathered respecting these *clipei*.

CLIPEUS.—In p. 45 of this dictionary, article ANCILIA, reference has been made to the word *Clipeus*, with a view to some further remarks being offered, respecting the *form* of those *scuta sancta* of the Romans. Since that portion of the present work was committed to press, the compiler, through the kindness of Messrs. Taylor, Walton, and Mabberly, finds himself here enabled to insert a valuable illustration, employed in one of the most useful of their classical publications. By means of the subjoined cut, an opportunity is afforded for comparing the shape of an *Ancile*, as engraved on the antique gem in the Florentine Museum, with those representations of the same thing which appear on coins of Augustus and of Antoninus Pius. The two monetal specimens will be found to agree in most points with each other; but to differ materially from the delineation of the shields on the relic from which the subjoined is engraved. And now, it is left with the reader to judge, which corresponds the more closely with the description of those "sacred bucklers," given by Festus and by Plutarch :—

This group exhibits the figures of two Salian priests, with heads veiled, and wearing the *trabea*. On the short cloak of one a *hippocampus* (or sea-horse), is figured ; on that of the other a *triton*. They carry six ancilian bucklers on their shoulders, suspended from a pole. Above is inscribed ALLIVS, and below ALCE, in old

italiot characters, perhaps in allusion to the Salii of Aléso, a city which, in the ancient language of the country, was named *Alse*.—See LANZI, *Saggio* ii. cited by Millin, *Gal. Myth.* i. pl. xxxviii. No. 148.

It was the twelve priests of Mars Gradivus, who were appointed, under the denomination of Salii, to the office of preserving the twelve ancilia. The feast of the god was annually observed during several days ; when the Salii carried their shields about the city, singing songs in praise of Mars, Numa, and Mamurius Veturius (the armourer whom Numa ordered to make eleven other shields, exactly like the "heaven-descended" one). In performing their dance, the Salii struck the shields with rods (*virgæ*), so as to keep time with their voices, and with the movements of their dance. The above cut shews one of these rods, as represented on the tomb of a *pontifex salius*, or chief of the salii (Gruter, *Inscrip.*) Its form, as here exhibited, illustrates the manner of using it.—Virgil, describing the attire of Picus, a mythical king of Latium, says, he held the ancile in his left hand *(lævaque ancile gerebat, Æn.* vii. 187.) Other authors represent the salii as bearing the ancilia on their necks, or on their shoulders. These accounts may be reconciled on the supposition, that the shield was suspended by a leathern band (*lorum, Juv.* ii. 1 95), proceeding from the right shoulder, and passing round the neck. That the weight of the ancile (made of bronze) was considerable, and that the use of it, in the sacred dance, required no small exertion, is apparent from Juvenal's expression (ii. 126), "*sudavit clypeis ancilibus.*"—See *Dictionary of Greek and Roman Antiquities*, edited by Dr. W. Smith.

CLOACIN. *Cloacina.*—From some *cloaca*, or common-sewer, at Rome, in which a statue of Venus was found ; and, as all events contributed to furnish the Romans with occasions for giving new names to their divinities, so that of Cloacina was from this alleged circumstance assigned by them to Venus herself. On two denarii of the Mussidia gens, we see this abbreviated name at the bottom of the reverse, as follows :—

1. *Obv.*—Radiated head of the Sun, full-faced.—*Rev.* Q. MVSSIDIVS LONGVS. A structure in form like a galley ; upon it stand two figures. On the lower part of it we read the word CLOACIN.—2. *Obv.*—CONCORDIA. Veiled head of Concord, with sometimes a star, sometimes a crescent before it.—*Rev.*—Same legend and type.

The *Comitium*, or *Comitia*, one of two places, where assemblies of the people were held, is here represented, with its stair-case, and its *cancelli* or lattice work. The figures upon it are a distributor of electoral tickets, and a citizen in the act of giving his vote, for either the making of some law, or the election of a consul, or other public functionary. With regard to the legend CLOACIN, Eckhel says : this word denotes the Comitium itself; for T. Tatius, king of the Sabines, in consequence of a statue of Venus having been found in a *cloaca*, named it *Cloacina*, and dedicated it at a *Comitium*.

The *cloacæ*, or common sewers, at Rome, were begun by Tarquinius Priscus, and finished by Tarquinius Superbus. They extended under the whole area of the city. Their construction was so strong, and the stones with which they were built were so large and so firmly cemented, that though flushed perpetually by rapid torrents, they remained in a perfect state for 700 years and upwards.—See CANCELLI COMITIORUM (p. 69), also COMITIVM, and Mussidia gens.

CLODIUS MACER.—See MACER.

CLOVIA gens.—This Roman family (also called Cluvia for both modes of denomination are found on ancient monuments), derives its origin from the Cluvii Sexuli, brothers, who were tribunes of the *plebs* in 572 and 576 (B. C. 182 and 178) ; whence it is inferred, that it was plebeian. It was, however, of consular rank. The extant coins solely in brass (with the exception of one in lead), were struck by the moneyers of Julius Cæsar. Riccio gives six of these having on their obverse type the marks of the *as* and its divisions, with SAX. C. SAX. and ROM. for their legends of reverse. These coins are ascribed to Caius Clovius Saxula, pretor in 581 (B. C. 173), and a little while before one of the mint-masters —the same who in 586 (168) was the *legatus*, in Macedonia, of Emilius Paulus. For a cut of the following second brass, see p. 153 of this dictionary.

Obv.—CAESAR DIC. TER. Bust of a winged Victory.

Rev.—C. CLOVI PRAEF. Minerva helmeted and walking. The goddess carries in her right hand a trophy rested on her shoulder, and in her left an oval shield, on which is figured the head of Medusa. She is preceded by a serpent, erect on its tail.

Caius Clovius, entitled pretor on this coin, was one of the eight prefects of the city, left by Julius Cæsar for the government of Rome during his third dictatorship, when with a great army and fleet he went to Spain on his expedition against the sons of Pompey. It must therefore have been minted, in the year of Rome 708 (B. C. 46), in which recurred Cæsar's dictatorship for the third time; and his moneyer here prophecies, by the head of Victory and by Belligerent Minerva, typified on this coin, a prosperous result to Cæsar's enterprise.—Eckhel, with whom Cavedoni accords, expresses an opinion that this finely designed coin was not struck in Rome, and by the urban prefect; but by a prefect of the Dictator's fleet, stationed in the ports of Lycia, or of Rhodes, and who assuming the *jus cudendi*, engraved it in the same way as the prefects of Mark Antony's fleet afterwards did ; namely, to pay the troops and seamen with.

CLOULIA.—According to Festus, this gens had for its primogenitor, Cloelius, the companion of Æneas. It was one of the Alban families, whom Tullius Hostilius, after the ruin of Alba, attracted to Rome, and united to the patricians. Its coins present the two following types, in silver; engraved in *Morell. Fam. Rom.*

1. *Obv.*—ROMA. Galeated head of Rome : behind it a crown.
Rev.—T. CLOVLI. Victory in a biga of rearing horses. Below are two corn-ears.

2. *Obv.*—Head of Jupiter ; and K. or some varying letter of the alphabet.
Rev.—T. CLOVLI. Victory crowning a trophy, at the foot of which a naked captive is seated. In the exergue Q. A quinarius.

The numismatists of the elder school have attributed these coins to Titus Cloulius, *quæstor urbanus*, in 507 (B. C. 247), remarking, that they bear allusion to the victories gained in Sicily by the consuls, Lucius Cæcilius Metellus and N. Fabius Buteo, over the Carthaginians ; and that the corn ears in the first reverse refer to the fertility of that island. But numismatists of the present day, and Borghesi especially, maintain, that the circumstance of none of these denarii having been found amongst the *trouvailles* of Fiesole, forms a good reason for carrying them down to the date of 667 (B. C. 87), and thence to the times of C. Marius ; and he is inclined to believe that they may be assigned to the moneyership of T. Cloulius, of whom Cicero speaks (Pro Sex. Roscio Amerino, c. 23), previous to the year 674 (B. C. 80). He afterwards became one of Cæsar's Senators.—See Riccio, p. 57.

CLU. or CLUS. *Clusit*; the same as *Clausit.* —IAN. CLU. or CLUS. *Janum Clusit.*—The temple of Janus was opened in time of war, and shut during peace. Augustus shut this temple at Rome three times : the third time, indeed, was in 751 (B. C. 3), and in the 42nd year of his reign, peace being then established throughout the Roman world.—CLVSIT appears on brass coins of Nero.—See PACE P. R. &c.

CLUNIA—a town of Hispania Tarraconensis, now Corunna del Conte, in Old Castile, situate on the river Durius (Douro).—Clunia was a city of the Arevaci, according to Pliny. And by Ptolemy it is *called* a colony. Dion (L. 3, p. 115), mentions Clunia, "in an attack on which city (he states) Metellus overthrew the revolted Hispani." Clunia was also the city where Galba, pro-consul of Spain in the latter part of Nero's reign, commenced his proceedings for resisting the tyranny of that emperor, and for assuming himself the imperial title, power, and authority.

There is an autonomous small brass (see Akerman, *Coins of Hispania*, p. 85), which bears on its obverse a male head, with a dolphin before it ; and on its reverse CLOVNIOQ, with a horseman. The other coins of this place are second brass, having on their obverses the head of Tiberius, and on their reverses the legend CLVNIA, together with the names of the monetary *quatuorviri*, by whom they were struck, under that emperor. The type on all, with varieties, is a bull standing ; the usual symbol of Romano-Spanish colonies and *municipia*, although Clunia itself is not designated on any of them as either the one or the other.—See engraving in *Médailles de Christine*, p. 306, xlviii. also in *Morell. Impp.* vol. iii. TAB. iX.

Rasche (in *Lex. Num.* vol. i. part 2), places amongst the coinage of Clunia, the celebrated first brass of Galba, inscribed HISPANIA. CLVNIA SVL(PICIA). But *that* is of Roman die, struck *Senatus Consulto*, and belongs to the imperial series, properly so called.—See Hispania.

COCCEIA gens.—Respecting this family, it is uncertain whether it was patrician or plebeian. It gave consuls to Rome; but its chief title to distinction was that the Emperor Nerva belonged to it. Only two types are exhibited in its coinage: they are in silver, as follow:—

1. *Obv.*—M. ANT. IMP. AVG. IIIVIR. R. P. C. M. NERVA PRO. Q. P. Bare head of M. Antony.

Rev.—L. ANTONIVS COS. (Lucius Antonius [brother of the triumvir] Consul). Bare head of Lucius. This coin, rare in silver, is of the highest rarity in gold, and valued by Mionnet at 1200 fr. See a specimen of it engraved in p. 60 of this volume.

2. *Obv.*—Same legend and type as the foregoing.

Rev.—CAESAR IMP. PONT. IIIVIR. R. P. C.— Bare head of Octavianus Cæsar, behind it the *lituus.* Very rare in gold, valued by Mionnet at 150 fr.

Marcus Nerva, whose name appears on both the above denarii, was provincial pro-questor of the Antonii, in the Italian campaign of 713 (B. C. 41), that is to say in the war of Perusia (now Perugia), waged by that party against Octavian: this is manifest from the title of Consul given to Lucius Antonius. The second coin with the head of Octavian (possessed and published for the first time by Borghesi), "must have been minted in the beginning of the year, which followed the reconciliation of the two parties. But they having, from infringement made on the compact between them, come to blows, it is clear that the portrait of a foe must soon have ceased to appear on a coinage, which, as the sinews wherewith to carry on that renewed civil war, had been struck by the partizans of Lucius Antonius." Afterwards, this same pro-questor (Marcus Nerva) having obtained his pardon from Octavianus Cæsar, became twice the peace-maker between Mark Antony and his powerful rival.—See Riccio, p. 57.

COCLES, a word which signifies deprived of one eye. It was the surname of the Horatia gens; and Horatius Cocles was the name of that hero of Old Rome, who, according to the well-known legend or tradition, had the courage, either alone, or in conjunction with Spurius Lartius and Titus Herminius, to oppose the assault made by the army under Porsena, on the *Pons Sublicius*, defending it, whilst his comrades were employed in breaking it down behind him. When this work of demolition was nearly accomplished, Cocles, all armed as he was, threw himself into the Tiber, after invoking the god of that river; and notwithstanding he received a wound in the hip from the enemy's mis-

siles, he succeeded in his object, by swimming across the stream, and rejoining his countrymen.

As a testimony of admiration for his valour, and in grateful remembrance of the eminent service he had rendered the state, by thus preventing the Etrurian forces from entering Rome, as they had designed to do by a sudden and unexpected attack, the Senate and People raised a bronze statue to his honour in the Comitium; and allowed him as much land as he could plough round in one day. The citizens too, it is added, when a famine was raging, deprived themselves of food to support him.

Mr. Macauley, in his *Lays of Ancient Rome*, observes, "that among those parts of early Roman history, which had a poetical origin, was doubtless the legend of Horatius Cocles. There are several versions of the story, and these versions differ from each other in points of no small importance. According to Polybius, Horatius defended the bridge alone, and perished in the waters. Whilst according to the Chronicles which Livy and Dionysius followed, Horatius had two companions, swam safe to shore, and was loaded with honours and rewards."

The distinguished author of "The Lays," regards these discrepancies as capable of easy explanation; and points to the literature of our own country, as furnishing what he considers to be an exact parallel to what may have taken place in Rome. He thinks it highly probable that the memory of the war of Porsena was preserved by compositions much resembling the two ballads which relate to the fight at Otterborne, between the English under Percy and the Scots commanded by Douglas. They too differ in narrating several particulars of the bloody "fraye;" yet both relate to the same event.— And it is (adds Mr. Macauley), "by no means unlikely that there were two old Roman stories about the defence of the bridge; and that while the story which Livy has transmitted to us, was preferred by the multitude; the other, which ascribed the whole glory to Horatius alone, may have been the favourite with the Horatian house."

No one, however youthful or however aged, who has read (and who has not read?) the Roman story, will ever forget the impression made on his mind by the stirring incidents of this valiant deed of patriotic devotedness, to which, as well as to the gallant bearing of its reputed hero, Mr. Macauley, in his ingenious and beautiful work, has done the greatest poetical justice. The ballad is supposed to have been made about a hundred and twenty years after the war which it celebrates, and just before the taking of Rome by the Gauls. Nor is it difficult to enter into the nationally proud feelings of some honest citizen of the early republic, whilst reciting, with due solemnity of cadence and intonation, his staple of archaic verse, to an attentive group of domestic listeners :—

" When young and old in circle
  " Around the firebrands close ;
" When the girls are weaving baskets,
  " And the lads are shaping bows ;
" When the good man mends his armour,
  " And trims his helmet's plume ;
" When the good wife's shuttle merrily
  " Goes flashing through the loom ;
" With weeping and with laughter
  " Still is the story told,
" How well Horatius kept the bridge
  " In the brave days of old."

On a brass medallion of Antoninus Pius the reverse bears for its legend COCLES—and its type represents Horatius in the act of swimming, in his armour, across the Tiber. Five military figures are seen standing on the bridge, which is partly broken down. On one side a warrior, helmeted, is striking at the timbers of the bridge with an axe ; and on the other side, a soldier appears in the attitude of hurling a javelin at Cocles in the water.—See the woodcut at the head of this article, accurately engraved after a cast from the original coin in the *Cabinet de France.*

The name of COCLES, with the galeated head of Rome, (*not* the head of that valiant Roman, as erroneously described in the list of illustrations to the *Lays of Rome*, above quoted from, p. 207), appears on a denarius of the Horatia gens.—See the word.

COELESTIS—CAELESTIS—CELEST.— The Celestial; an epithet of Venus found on coins of Domna, Soæmias, Urbica, &c. The goddess in these stands, with an apple in the right and the *hasta* in her left hand. On a first brass of Soæmias, a small figure, most probably meant for Cupid, stands at the feet of Venus.

COELIA, or *Coilia* (for anciently the dipthong *oe* was written for *oi*) was a plebeian gens, but of consular rank. Some assert that the head of this family was Coelius Vibulo Etruscus, who came to the aid of Romulus against the Sabines, and gave his name to the Coelian Mount at Rome. There are twenty-one varieties. Silver common, Gold of the highest rarity.— The two following are its rarest coins, as described by Riccio, p. 58 and 59.

1. *Obv.*—C. COEL. CALDVS COS. A bare and beardless male head to the right, between a vexillum inscribed HIS(PANIA), and a boar.

Rev.—C. CALDVS IMP. A. X. (*Imperator augur Xvir agris dividendis*), written in two perpendicular lines. Two trophies, between which is a table, or altar, where a priest is preparing

the *lectisternium*, or banquet for the gods, in allusion to which, on the table, is inscribed L. CALDVS VII. VIR. EPVL(ONUM). Beneath is CALDVS IIIVIR.—See the word EPULONES, under which head an engraved specimen of this remarkable denarius is given.

This silver coin was minted by the monetary triumvir, Coelius Caldus, in 703 (B. C. 51), before the dictatorship of Julius Cæsar, when the moneyers of the republic were increased from three to four, though reduced again by Augustus to the old number.—Borghesi and Cavedoni (as cited by Riccio), believe C. Caldus to have been Cicero's quaestor in the year 703, and monetary triumvir about 696 (B. C. 58). This man, besides his own name, had evidently in view to recall on these coins the memory of the most famous members of his family, viz. :—

Caius Cœlius Caldus, tribune of the *plebs*, and consul in 660 (B. C. 94), whose striking physiognomy appears on the obverse of this denarius. After his consulship, he obtained Spain for his pro-consular province, as is usually inferred from the coins of this gens, bearing his name, the word HIS(PANIA), and the figure of a boar, which Eckhel refers to the town of Clunia.

To Caius Caldus, *imperator*, augur, and decemvir (viz., one of a commission appointed to superintend the distribution of lands), belong the two trophies represented on the reverse. The subject is known solely through this monetal remembrance of the grandson (or great nephew). As to whom he gained these warlike spoils from ; when and on what occasion he was proclaimed *imperator ;* at what time he filled the offices recorded on the coin, that coin alone shews, but in so laconic a manner, as to leave the meaning very obscure.

Lucius Coelius Caldus, perhaps the son of the consul, and the father of the mint-master ; here styled *Septemvir Epulonum*, is he, to whom appertains the veiled priest that sits or stands at the lectisternium. The *epulones* were members of the sacerdotal order, whose duty it was to assist the pontiffs in preparing all things necessary to rites and sacrifices. In the earlier times of the republic there were only three of them.—See SEPTEMVIR EPULONUM.

2. C. COEL. CALDVS COS. Head of the Consul Caius Caldus ; behind it L. D. in a *tabella.*

Rev.—CALDVS IIIVIR. Head of the sun radiated, to the right : before it is a round shield ornamented ; behind is an oblong shield, charged with the fulmen. Sometimes behind the head there appears an isolated S.—This in gold is RRRR. valued at 40 piastres by Riccio, and at 300 fr. by Mionnet.

On this coin, the same moneyer repeats the portrait of his grandfather or great grandfather, Caius Coelius Caldus, consul 670 (B. C. 84).— The two letters L. D. behind the head, signify *Libero—Damno.* I absolve—I condemn—bearing reference to the law which he carried during his year of office, 647 (B. C. 107), as tribune of the *plebs*, and by which the right of secret voting (by ballot) was conceded to the people ; this *lex tabellaria* was also extended to the courts of justice, in cases of high treason.—Cicero *(De leg.* iii. 16), states that Caldus regretted, throughout his life, having proposed this law, as it did injury to the republic.

The head of the sun has been considered by some numismatic writers to allude to the name of the *monetarius* himself—namely *Coelius*, because in the heaven, or firmament, that greater star holds his course; and *Caldus*, from the heat which the sun produces.—Borghesi, on the other hand, contends that the head of the sun, and the shields, are emblems of the East, and have reference to the victories won by the *Imperator* Coelius Caldus in the East, probably in the Mithridatic war, about the year 680 (B. C. 74), and not later than 696 (B. C. 58), the presumed date of the coin in question. Borghesi moreover recognizes in the consul of 660 (B. C. 94), the father of the *Septemvir Epulonum;* and this father or brother of the *Imperator*, from whom might have sprung the triumvir of 696, and questor in 703 (B. C. 51).

COELA or COILA : Chersonesi Thraciæ *municipium*—(now province of Rumilia, Turkey, in Europe). The following Latin imperial coins, in second and third brass, are regarded as correctly assigned to this place, viz. :

Antoninus Pius.—MVNICIPI COIL. Prow of a vessel, above which is a cornucopiæ.

Commodus.——AEL./MVNIC. COIL. *(Ælium Municipium Coila).*—Same type as preceding, with addition of a dolphin below.

Caracalla.—Same legend. Diana Venatrix walking.

Macrinus.—Same legend. Prow of a vessel.

Gordianus Pius.—AEL. MVNIC. COEL. AN.— Silenus walking, with the wine-skin on his left shoulder; and his right hand raised.

Trebonianus Gallus.—Same legend. Romulus and Remus suckled by the Wolf.

Vaillant, in his erudite work on the Colonies of Rome, had ascribed their mintage to a city in Numidia, at the mouth of the river Ampsagus, called *Cullu* by Pliny and Ptolemy, and *Chulli Municipium*, in the Itinerary of Antonine. And in this opinion he is supported by no less judicious a numismatist of the elder school than Bimard. On the other hand Pellerin, sustaining himself with the corresponding sentiments of the Abbé Belleye, confidently asserts *(Mélange*, i. p. 276), that the coins which bear on their reverses AEL. MVNICIP. COEL. and any other similar legend, and which are referred by Vaillant to *Cullu*, in Africa, "belong all of them to the city of (Coela, or) Coelum, in the Chersonesus of Thrace, which city was a port, and also called *Culla*." Moreover, it is to be observed, that neither Eckhel nor Mionnet has thought fit to include *Coellu Numidiæ*, in his respective lists of Roman Colonies, but they *do* enumerate *Coela Chersonesi Thraciæ* among the *municipia*.

On a coin of Volusianus, first published and engraved by Pellerin *(Mélange* i. p. 325, pl. xxii. No. 2), to supply an omission of Vaillant's, but which seems to have been overlooked

by Mionnet, the reverse legend is AELI. MVNICI. COEL. and the accompanying type a temple of four columns, in which a figure, in a short dress, stands, holding an idol in her right hand, and a cornucopiæ in her left.

If the figure be meant for that of Astarte, its appearance on this coin indicates, that the Syrian goddess had latterly its worshippers amongst the Roman inhabitants of the Thracian Chersonesus.

COGN. otherwise COGNAT. *Cognatus.*— A kinsman, properly by blood, a cousin.—DIVO CONSTANTIO COGN. MAXENTIVS AVG. on a coin of Constantius Chlorus.

COGNOMEN, or surname.—The third name of the three *(nomen*, and *prænomen*, being the two first) which the Romans were for the most part accustomed to bear.—In his brief but lucid exposition *" De cognomine et agnomine,"* the learned Eckhel (vol. v. p. 58) observes that, as the Roman families *(familiæ)* were distinguished by the *prænomina*, so were the races *(gentes)* by the *cognomina*. It of course occurred that the descendants, by marriage, of each house, founded separate families ; and these again it was necessary to distinguish by some particular name. Livy relates that in the year U. C. 442 (B. C. 312), there were in the Potitia gens, twelve families, and amongst these were branches to the number of 30.

On coins are to be found the names of many different families, springing from one race, whose root divided itself into extensive ramifications; as in the Æmilia gens (according to Vaillant), those of Buca, Lepidus, Paullus, Regillus, Scaurus.—In Cæcilia gens, the family of Metellus ; and these again are distinguished by seven or eight surnames on their respective denarii. As for example, those of Balearicus, Macedonicus, Creticus, Delmaticus, Numidicus, Calvus, Pius, Cornutus.—In Claudia gens, the Centhones, the Marcelli, and the Pulchri.—In Canidia and Licinia *gentes*, the Crassi.—In Cornelia gens, the Lentuli, and Scipiones ; and these with others hitherto used as surnames ; for instance the appellations Asina, Asiagenes, Africanus, &c. Moreover the Cethegi, in the same gens (Cornelia) with the Dolabellæ, the Sullæ, and others, indicate on their coins, not only individuals, but so many different stocks, or families of the same race. It likewise sometimes happened that names sprang from surnames, as the respective coins of Roman families serve to illustrate, in which Agrippa, Ahala, Atratinus, Brutus, Cæsar, Carbo, Cato, Crassus, Messalla, Metellus, Nerva, Scipio, Silanus, Sulla, Torquatus, and other illustrious *Quirites*, frequently occur, without the *nomen gentilicium*, or family name, and even without the first name. Besides which, some less commonly known, as Natta, in Pinaria gens ; Turdus, in Papiria ; Ascisculus, in Valeria ; without any prenomen to either, and without the family name of Pinaria, Papiria, or Valeria.

To these are to be added some surnames, scarcely known through any other than numismatic sources—at any rate by no means common—which, from the addition we find on coins, of the family name of Roman houses, at once indicate whereto they belong; as in Accoleia gens, Lariscolus; in Canidia, Crassus; in Luria Agrippa; in Antestia Reginus; in Claudia, Glicia; in Considia, Pætus; in Furia, Brocchus; in Julia, Bursio; in Maria, Capito and Trogus; in Nævia, Capella and Surdinus; in Sempronia, Pitio.

Some surnames are common to many families of different *gentes*, as appears from their coins, such as, amongst others, those of Balbus, Crassus, Flaccus, Gallus, Libo, Longus, Magnus, Maximus, Rufus, Varus. There are also extant on this class of Roman coins other surnames peculiar, as it were, to certain *gentes*, such as the Lepidi, to that of Æmilia; the Metelli, to Cæcilia; the Centhones, the Pulchri, the Marcelli, to Claudia; the Cethegi, Dolabellæ, Lentuli, Sullæ, to Cornelia; the Bruti and Silani, to Junia; the Scipiones, to Cæcilia; the Cæpiones, to Servilia; the Galbæ, to Sulpicia; the Messallæ, to Valeria—except in cases where the individuals who bore those surnames passed by adoption into another gens.—See Rasche, *Cognomina Romanorum*.

It has already been observed that some Roman families had evidently no surnames, the prænomen and ancestral appellation *(gentile nomen)* alone being designated on their coins. Thus, in the denarii extant of the gens Antonia, the surname of *Merenda* is omitted, though Livy teaches us that both were formerly borne by the *Antonii;* one, however, occurs with the cognomen of *Balbus,* viz. Q. ANTO. BALB. PR. *Quintus, Antonius, Balbus, Prætor.* But on their coins, the following families are found to want surnames, viz. Carisia, Cornuficia, Herennia, Hortensia, Numitoria, Rustia, Saufeia, Trebania, Vargunteia, Vatinia; also Plætoria (unless the last with the adopted name of Cestianus be an exception.)

As L. Sulla was surnamed *Felix,* and his son *Faustus;* so Sextus, the son of Pompeius Magnus, is distinguished on his coins, not only by the surnames of *Magnus,* but by that of *Pius* also. Some surnames are verbs, as *Caepio;* for on the coins of Brutus this verb stands for a name, as is shewn by the inscription—Q. CAEPIO BRVTVS.—Most Roman mint-masters gave their surnames only on their coins, as did historians to them in their books, because, during their life-time, they were known by other names in their capacity of magistrates: thus for example *Axsius,* on his coins is called simply NASO.

For an Index of the Names, Surnames, and Adopted Names, which occur on Consular coins, with the Families to which they belong.—See Eckhel, *Doct. Num.* vol. v.; Mionnet, *Rareté des Médailles Romaines;* and Akerman, *Descriptive Catalogue of Roman Coins;* also Rasche, *Lexicon Numismat.* T. i. part. ii.

Some surnames of men are feminine, as Asinia, Bestia, Caecina, Capella, Glicia, Murena, Musa, Sura, Vaala, Vatia, &c.

Cognomina (says Eckhel), "were derived from various causes, as well of a base as of a virtuous kind." Many of these may be traced and illustrated from the denarii of Roman families. Some of these surnames owe their origin to wisdom, as Sempronius *Sophus;* Lælius *Sapieus ,* or from the contrary quality, as Junius *Brutus.* From moral disposition, as Tarquinius *Superbus,* Fabius *Gurges,* (a riotous spendthrift), Aufidius *Lurco,* (a glutton.) From Art, as Fabius *Pictor.* From devotedness to rural pursuits, as Cornelius *Lentulus* (the lentil), Tullius *Cicero* (the vetch), Licinius *Stolo* (a scion or shoot) From a conquered kingdom, or a captured city, Servilius *Isauricus,* Marcius *Coriolanus.*

Some surnames are derived from parts of the human frame; from some corporeal deformity or infirmity, as is shewn on that silver coin of the Furia gens (see p. 12), where the human *foot,* placed behind a female head on the obverse, evidently alludes to the word CRASSIPES (splay-foot) inscribed on its reverse. So in the Pinaria gens we see the surname of SCARPUS, otherwise *carpus,* a wrist—the palm of a human hand appearing in the field of the coin. A singular circumstance is exhibited in these coins of Roman families, namely, that they exhibit not only honourable appellations, and those which allude to no vice or defect either of body or of mind; but also those which bespeak defects of each kind, yet without being intended to derogate in any respect from the signal reputation enjoyed by those families.

The surnames of the Strabones *(Volteia)* and of the Pæti *(Considia)* are expressly derived from terms signifying diseased or defective *eyes.* [*Strabo,* goggle-eyed—*Pætus,* squint or learing-eyed]. The *Coclites,* from *cocles,* one that is born with one eye only, are read on coins of the Pompeia, Aelia, and Horatia *gentes.* Moreover, from *natural* or other *marks* of the human *body,* the Romans took some of their family surnames, as appears by coins of the Albini, Atratini, Nigri, Rufi, Pulchri, Celsi, Longi, Longini, Gracchi, Macri, Crassi, Galbae. It was also from *similitudes* of no dignified kind, that the Scipiones (walking sticks), Lentuli Spintheres (from spinther a buckle), &c. took their appellatives.—From employments and offices of a low and sordid description, and even from vile animals, as we find as well from coins as from authors and from the calendars, the Catulli (from catulus, a whelp), &c. took their names: so likewise the Caprarii (goat-herds), the Cercones (marmosets), the Vespillones (bearers at burials). The name itself of the Fabia gens came, according to Pliny, from *faba* (a bean); that of the Pisones, from *pisendo* (pounding or stamping of corn in a mortar) — From habits and manners, or from the affections and virtues of the mind, denarii, in the Calpurnia, Cæcilia, Rubellia, Antonia families, take such inscriptions as the Frugi (thrifty), the Lepidi (witty or agreeable), the Blandi (kind and gentle), the Pii; nay they are even marked with the very name of PIETAS.

Taken from the names of brute animals, we find on consular coins the words Asinia, Bestia, Brutus, Capella, Lupus, Murena, Taurus, Vitulus, which were surnames of no less illustrious Roman houses, than those of Cornelia, Calpurnia, Caecilia, Fabia, Æmilia, Nævia, Rutilia, Licinia, Mamilia, Pomponia, Voconia, &c. So likewise, from the greatness of a man's actions, attended with good fortune, as indicated by the epithets Faustus, Felix, Magnus, Maximus; or from an extraordinary manifestation of zeal for the interests and liberties of the Roman people, as in the use of the surname *Poplicola* (Publicola, a popular person). Thus it is abundantly clear from the evidence of coins, that these were not only the true titles of the Memmii, the Scipiones, the Metelli, the Sullæ, the Pompeii, the Fabii, the Valerii, the Gelii, to whom they were ascribed; but also their *cognomina* or surnames; a fact moreover shewn in Roman authors, and by the *Fasti Capitolini.*—See Rasche, *Lex. Num.* T. i. pars. 2.

Old writers, observes Eckhel (vol. v. p. 56), have affirmed, that the *cognomen* was synonymous with the *agnomen.* Of this, he adds, we have an example in the case of L. Calpurnius Piso Frugi, respecting whom Cicero (pro M. Fonteio, c. 13), says, "But against what a man! in whom there was such virtue and integrity that even in those best of times (optimis temporibus), when you could scarcely find a dishonest man, he in particular should have been termed *Frugi.* For when Gracchus summoned him to attend an assembly of the people, and the messenger (viator) asked *which* Piso? there being more than one, he answered—you compel me to name my enemy, *Frugi.* It was this man to whom not even his enemy could give an appellation sufficiently distinguishing, without first praising him, whose single *cognomen* not only marked the identity, but also indicated the character of the individual," &c. This custom prevailed during the flourishing æra of the republic. It was different, however, both under the kings of Rome, and at the beginning of the republic. It was again different under the emperors; and the alteration began to be made even during the reign of Augustus himself.

For a similar purpose to that of the cognomen, the *agnomen* (says Eckhel) was invented, viz., to distinguish one family from another. And it was given without any design to convey thereby to the individual who bore it, either honour on the one hand, or reproach on the other; as Calpurnius Piso *Frugi;* Cornelius Scipio *Africanus;* Cornelius Lentulus *Spinther;* Cæcilius Metellus *Pius.*—See Agnomen.

The Emperors took surnames from *conquered nations* or from *victories,* as those of Germanicus, Britannicus, Dacicus, Sarmaticus, Adiabenicus, Parthicus, Armenicus, Gothicus, Persicus; and indeed now and then with the super-added title of Maximus. Lastly, they are found assuming not only the cognomen of *Victor,* but also that of *Invictus.* No one, however, aspired to be called *Judaicus,* in memory of the vanquished Jews. That surname appears, to have been repudiated by Vespasian, on account of the hatred in which the nation itself was held by the Romans, although on his and his son Titus's mintages we read the inscription—IVDAEA CAPTA.

COH. COHORT. *Cohortis, Cohortium*—of the Cohort, or of the Cohorts.—See ADLOCVT. COH. p. 6 of this dictionary.

COHORS, Cohort, a battalion of Roman foot soldiers, as *Turma,* was a squadron of cavalry. Each cohort was composed of three *manipuli,* or companies, and these of two centuries or of two hundred men; thus forming a body of six hundred men, of which under the emperors ten were required to compose the legion.—Equestrian cohorts *(Cohortes Equitatæ)* were bodies of foot and horse together. There were also cavalry to the number of 130, armed with cuirasses, in the first Cohort of the Legion.—The *Cohors Peditata* was wholly composed of infantry, in the beginning, and was so called in contra-distinction to the *Cohors Equitata.*—See LEGIO.

Cohors Prætoria.—The Pretorian cohort, was a *corps d'élite* of infantry and cavalry, which under the republic belonged to the Pretor, and never quitted him on service—in fact a portion of the Roman army whose duty it was to act as the body guard of the consul, or commander in chief. Julius Cæsar and Mark Antony successively employed many such cohorts. (See CHORTIVM PRAETORIARVM, p. 198.) Augustus established nine, each composed of a thousand men, and taught the people to regard them, under the above appellation, as a force similar to the old guard of Roman Generals. By succeeding emperors, these troops were rendered a powerful host. Galba augmented them to twelve, which number they are computed by Dion to have reached, in the reign of Severus. That emperor, in further augmenting them, added not only draughts from the Italian legions, but also the bravest soldiers from the provinces.

Destined exclusively to serve as guards to the emperor's person, they were, at his command, employed to escort and protect the members of the Imperial family. But it was not customary for the Pretorian guard to perform that duty for any but those of princely rank. They were commanded by the Pretorian Prefect, who had under him Tribunes and Centurions. Their pay was double. Instead of one denarius, worth ten *asses,* which was the ordinary pay of other soldiers, this select body of troops received two, and privileges not assigned to others. The ensigns of the Pretorian Cohorts had a crown or wreath on the top of the staff, and besides the usual military standards each of these "regiments" displayed its eagle.

In process of time the Pretorians, abusing the power which they had been suffered to usurp, carried their insolence to such a pitch as to elect and to dethrone, on their own authority, many emperors, in spite of the senate, whom they compelled to accept and confirm in the possession of the purple, those they had thus proclaimed.

Tiberius built them near Rome a walled-in camp, like a fortress, where they were constantly stationed. (See *castra prætoria*, p. 191). The Emperor Constantine destroyed this camp, after having entirely broken the military force of the pretorians, whose arrogance and excessive power had occasioned so many revolutions in the empire.—See Pitiscus, *Lexicon. Ant. Rom.*

COHORS SPECULATORUM.—For an explanation of this legend, see p. 198.

COHH. (*sic.*) PRAET. VI. (or VII.) P. VI. F. —On a billon of Gallienus, this legend, allusive to the pretorian cohorts of his time, is accompanied by the type of a lion walking. On another billon denarius, and also on a gold coin, together with a first brass of the same emperor, the respective legends FIDEI. PRAET; FID. PRAE-TORIANORVM, and COHORT. PRAET. PRINCIPI. svo. with military standards, legionary eagles, and a garland, combine to designate the confidence which he was *willing* to repose in the precarious loyalty of those formidable troops.

COIN MOULDS.—There have been discovered, from time to time, in England, as well as in France, clay moulds of circular form, bearing the impressions of Roman denarii, of a period contemporary with, and subsequent to, the Antonines. The last discovery in England was at Lingwell Gate, near Wakefield, Yorkshire. It is well known, that in the decline of the empire, the Roman silver was debased considerably; and this of course paved the way to the adoption of, or the occasional recurrence to, a different kind of mintage. Up to this time Roman coins were produced from dies struck with the hammer; but in the reign of Severus, casting in moulds, though not exclusively, was very generally resorted to. The thickness of the Roman denarii did not admit of the usual modern test of *ringing ;* and nothing but a very minute examination, or the more tedious process of assay, could have detected the spurious coin. Whether these cast coins were minted by imperial authority, or are the work of forgers, remain still questions for discussion ; but it appears highly probable that such a process was authorised by the despot whose effigies, and those of his sons Caracalla and Geta, they more frequently bear. There are, it is true, some cast coins of earlier reigns, but their number is comparatively few, and it is extremely probable that this was permitted in order that, in the event of detection, it might be cited as a precedent for such a practice.

In Mr. Akerman's "Coins of the Romans relating to Britain," as well as in the *Revue Numismatique,* are plates shewing the mode of casting these base coins, a process which often led to the fabrication of *blundered pieces* that have frequently perplexed numismatists. Thus a coin of Julia Soæmias has on the reverse PONT. TR. P. &c. titles which belong to some denarius of Severus or Caracalla. An explanation of the mode of casting will shew how this may be produced. The moulds being formed by pressing the coins between dies of plastic clay of large diameter, in order to form

ledges, were placed one upon the other, so that, with the exception of the first and last, they received on each face the impression of the obverse and reverse of a piece. The dies were then notched in order to form a passage for the fused metal; and after being hardened in the fire, were replaced one on another, notch over notch, and luted with clay, so as to form a cylinder, and thus three, or even four piles of moulds, might be filled with one jet. As regards the localities in which moulds of this description were prepared, it has been discovered by microscopic examination of the clay of which those found at Lingwell gate were formed, that it contains a species of fossil *infusoria* which abounds in the clay of that neighbourhood at this time. With regard to the debasement of the Roman silver, see the "ASSAY OF DENARII," prefixed to the *Descriptive Catalogue of Roman Coins,* vol. i. p. 14, by J. Y. Akerman, Esq. F.S.A. Secretary of the Society of Antiquaries.

COL. *Collegium.*—See COOP. IN OMN. COL. *Cooptatus in Omnia Collegia.* On a coin of Nero.

COLLEGIUM.—A name given to an assembly or body of many persons who have the same functions. The Romans had various communities who took the names of Colleges. The four principal ones were those of the Augurs, the Pontiffs, the Aruspices, and the Quindecemvirs. Besides these four colleges, which were those of the four great sacerdotal dignities, there were several other bodies known by the same name, as *Collegium Artificum* and *Opificum,* instituted by Numa, and each of which had a prefect at its head. These workmen, who at first exercised their skill and industry only at Rome, soon spread themselves over all Italy, and afterwards into the various provinces of the empire, which they furnished with every thing necessary for the armies, such as arrows, machines, armour, clothes, &c.—See Pitiscus.

COLISÆUM.—The Coliseum—a corruption of *colossæum,* the name given to the famous amphitheatre which Vespasian commenced at Rome, and which Titus finished. The building was so named on account of the colossal statue of Nero, that stood on the spot where was erected that magnificent edifice, whose stupendous ruins exist to this day. It is represented on coins of Titus, &c. See *Amphitheatrum,* p. 41.

COLONIA.—A colony, called by the Greeks ἀποικία, is a portion of a people, which, for various reasons leaving its native soil, has gone in search of a settlement and a home, in distant lands. Velleius Paterculus, at the commencement of his first book, enumerates many migrations of this nature, which took place in the earliest times of Greece, and states the causes which gave rise to them. But besides that they have been largely discussed both by ancient and modern authors, and are sufficiently familiar to all who are interested in the subject, it is beyond the purpose of the present work to take note of any other settlements than those of the Romans, whether called by the name of *coloniæ* or of *municipia.*

COLONIAE ROMANAE.—Colonies, in the Roman acceptation of the word, were towns or lands inhabited by citizens sent thither on the authority of the Senate and People, and allowed, on certain conditions, their respective portions of those territories, for the purposes of habitation and tillage.—It is a well established fact, that from the earliest period of their existence as a nation, the custom prevailed among the Romans of transplanting colonies into the country of their conquered enemies; and that it continued as long as their power lasted. The practice was productive of great benefits to Rome. For by its means, a check was provided against the undue increase of a poor population, prone to change; and the colonies of Roman citizens thus distributed over the world were so many outworks of the city; whilst the soldiery, in the apportionment of the land, received the reward of hard service. The colonies of the last mentioned kind, were called *military*.—It is further to be observed, that several cities acquired the rights of a colony, though still occupied by their original inhabitants, and without the intermixture of foreign colonists. It was in this manner that Julius Cæsar, after his victory over the Pompeys in Spain, bestowed upon the various towns, by whose fidelity and co-operation he had profited, either freedom, or the rights of citizenship, or the privileges of Roman colonies. Asconius, in allusion to Pompey, the father of Pompey the Great, and the colonies beyond the river Po *(Transpadanis)*, has the following expressions:—" For Pompey did not establish them with fresh colonists, but, allowing the original inhabitants to remain, conferred upon them the *Jus Latii.*" In other cases, new colonists were associated with the native occupants, as at Emporiæ, in Spain, or at Agrigentum, according to Cicero, and at Carteia.—Indeed it sometimes occurred, that a colony was composed partly of soldiers, and partly of a multitude drawn together from all sources and classes. Thus we learn, both from coins and from the authority of Strabo, that a military colony was planted by Augustus at Patræ, in Achaia. And Pausanias further tells us, that the inhabitants of the neighbouring towns were by the same emperor ordered to migrate to that colony.

According to the ancient law, it was held a profanation to introduce a new colony into any city already occupied by one. Cicero eloquently expresses his disapprobation of such a measure, when speaking against M. Antony, who settled a colony at Casilinum :—" I have asserted," he says, " that no new colony can legally be introduced into one already settled with the due ceremonies, provided the latter be in a prosperous condition; I deny that new colonists can be enrolled therein. You, however, carried away by your arrogance, have, in defiance of all the rules of auspices (or *augury)*, sent out a colony to Casilinum, a place already colonized but a few years ago."—But whatever the law on this subject might have been, in later times it became obsolete; for Augustus, and after him Nero, sent a fresh colony to Puteoli, which, according to Livy, was one in the year U. C. 560 (B. C. 194).—Hyginus has supplied the cause of this proceeding in an allusion to Augustus :—" He made colonists of the troops which had served under Antony or Lepidus, equally with the soldiers of his own legions, distributing them through Italy and the provinces; destroying certain cities of the enemy, he established new ones; some he planted in the old towns, and gave them the title of colonists. And moreover, to those cities, which had been settled by the kings or the dictators, but exhausted by the events of the civil wars, he again gave the name of a colony, and increased the numbers of their citizens; in some instances extending their boundaries."

The foregoing information furnishes us with the various causes which led to the planting of colonies, after the commonwealth had fallen into decay. But, what a difference between these and the colonies sent out during the flourishing period of the state! It is worth while to note how it is described in the severe language of Tacitus, when speaking of the times of Nero :—" For not, as in former times, were legions sent out, with their tribunes and centurions, and soldiers of every rank, that by their union and attachment they might form a community; but individuals, unknown to each other, in straggling bands, with no recognized leader, without the bond of mutual goodwill, gathered together suddenly, as it were, from a foreign race of beings; a motley crowd, rather than a colony."

The constitution of the colonies was not the same in all cases. For some were composed of Roman citizens; upon some the *Jus Latinum*, on others the *Jus Italicum* was conferred, doubtless according to the humour of the Senate and People, and afterwards of the Cæsars. " In what, however, consisted the distinction of these their various conditions; what greater advantages accrued to one over another; what was the stamp and character of each ;—has (adds Eckhel) continued to furnish the most eminent authors with a bone of contention, and the usual results, namely, that they differ even in essentials, and that we are left to this very day with the skein of the controversy still tangled."

CATALOGUE OF ROMAN COLONIES AND MUNICIPIA.
(According to Eckhel and Mionnet).

Abdera in Bœtica.
Acci in Tarraconensis.
Ælia Capitolina in Judæa.
Agrigentum in Sicily.
Agrippina in Germania Inferior.
Alexandria in Troas.
Antiochia in Pisidia.
Antiochia in Syria.
Apamea *(municipium)* in Bithynia.
Arva in Bœtica.
Asta in Bœtica.
Asturica in Tarraconensis.
Babba in Mauretania.
Berytus *(mun.)* in Phœnicia.
Bilbilis in Tarraconensis.
Bostra in Arabia.
Brundusium in Calabria.
Buthrotum in Epirus.
Cabellio in Narbonensis.
Cæsar-augusta in Tarraconensis.
Cæsarea ad Libanum in Phœnicia.
Cæsarea *(mun.)* in Samaria.
Calagurris *(mun.)* in Tarraconensis.
Carrhæ in Mesopotamia.
Carteia in Bœtica.
Carthago Nova in Tarraconensis.
Carthago Vetus *(mun.)* in Zeugitana.
Cascantum in Tarraconensis.
Cassandrea in Macedonia.
Celsa in Tarraconensis.
Clunia *(mun.)* in Tarraconensis.
Coela in the Thracian Chersonesus.
Comana in Pontus.
Copia in Lugdunensis.
Corduba Patricia in Bœtica.
Corinthus in Achaia.
Cremna in Pisidia.
Damascus in Cœle Syria.
Dertosa in Tarraconensis.
Deultum in Thracia.
Dium *(mun.)* in Macedonia.
Ebora in Lusitania.
Edessa in Mesopotamia.
Emerita in Lusitania.
Emisa *(mun.)* in Syria.
Emporiæ in Tarraconensis.
Enna in Sicilia.
Ercavica in Tarraconensis.
Gades *(mun.)* in Bœtica.
Germe *(mun.)* in Galatia.
Graccurris *(mun.)* in Tarraconensis.

Heliopolis in Cœle Syria.
Iconium in Lycaonia.
Ilercavonia *(mun.)* in Tarraconensis.
Ilerda *(mun.)* in Tarraconensis.
Ilici in Tarraconensis.
Italica *(mun.)* in Bœtica.
Julia in Bœtica.
Laodicea in Syria.
Leptis in Syrtica.
Neapolis in Samaria.
Nemausus in Narbonensis.
Nisibi in Mesopotamia.
Obulco in Bœtica.
Occa in Syrtica.
Olbasa *(mun.)* in Pisidia.
Osca in Tarraconensis.
Osicerda in Tarraconensis.
Pæstum in Lucania.
Panormus in Sicilia.
Parada in Zeugitana.
Parium in Mysia.
Parlais in Lycaonia.
Patræ in Achaia.
Pax Julia in Lusitania.
Pella in Macedonia.
Philippi in Macedonia.
Philippopolis in Thrace.
Ptolemais in Galilee.
Rhesæna in Mesopotamia.
Roma in Latium *(according to the Roman Coins of Commodus).*
Romula in Bœtica.
Ruscino *(mun.)* in Narbonensis.
Saguntum *(mun.)* in Tarraconensis.
Sebaste in Samaria.
Segobriga in Tarraconensis.
Sidon in Phœnicia.
Singara in Mesopotamia.
Sinope *(mun.)* in Paphlagonia.
Stobi *(mun.)* in Macedonia.
Tarraco in Tarraconensis.
Thessalonica in Macedonia.
Traducta *(mun.)* in Bœtica.
Turiaso *(mun.)* in Tarraconensis.
Tyana in Cappadocia.
Tyrus in Phœnicia.
Valentia of the Bruttii.
Vienna in Narbonensis.
Viminacium in Mæsia Superior.
Visontium *(mun.)* in Tarraconensis.
Utica in Zeugitana.

The following authentic and valuable information respecting the titles, magistracies, customary observances, peculiar privileges, and religious ceremonies, of Roman Colonies, as illustrated by the inscriptions and types found on their *Latin* coins, is compiled from Eckhel's Dissertation *De Coloniis Romanis,* in the fourth volume of his truly great work:—

1. *Colonial Coins, inscriptions on.*—Cities which were in the condition of colonies, added the word " Colonia;" and indeed those which were situated eastward, so invariably adhered to this practice, that scarcely one of their coins is to be found on which it is omitted. But, not unfrequently, it was rejected by the Spanish colonies, and came to be constantly so by the Italian and Sicilian, as may be learnt from the coins of the colonies of Agrigentum, Brundusium, Copia, Pæstum, Panormus, &c. In the *Latin* inscriptions, it is indicated by the initial letter c. or the abbreviation COL. rarely by the entire word COLONIA.—In the Greek, by ΚΟΛ. or ΚΟΛΩΝΙΑ, the word having been adopted into the Greek language; for the genuine Greek

term Ἀποικία is found on only a single coin of Panormus, and that regarded as a doubtful one.

As a general rule, the Roman colonies used the *Latin* tongue on their coins; as indeed did even Corinth, although situated in the very heart of Greece; and also the colonies planted in Phœnician or Arabian cities. But the Greek language was preferred by Phillipopolis of Thrace, and Thessalonica of Macedonia, in Europe; by Tyana of Cappadocia, Antioch of Syria, and the Mesopotamian colonies in Asia. Aelia Capitolina, in Judæa, used both tongues. The *municipia* used only the Latin, and they indicate their condition by the inscription M. or MVN. or MVNICIP. &c. On some appear the word VRBS.—See those words *suis locis*.

2. *Colonies, additional titles of.*—Besides the above mentioned words, expressive of the standing, or constitution, of a town, we find the addition of epithetical names on coins of colonies and of *municipia*, together with other notifications: which are to be explained as follows:—

In bestowing on any city the privileges of a colony, or of a *municipium*, it rarely occurred, that the Romans adopted the plan, so often pursued by other cities, viz. that of abolishing the old name of the place, and substituting a new one. Indeed they even went so far as to *restore* the ancient name to cities, which they had resuscitated from utter ruin, and peopled with their colonists—a circumstance which is known to have taken place in the cases of Carthage and Corinth.

Amongst the colonies that lost their ancient appellation, were Salduba, in Spain, which was named Cæsar-augusta; Hierosolymæ (Jerusalem), afterwards called Ælia Capitolina (see p. 15), and some others. Whilst the old names of the colonies (and *municipia*) were thus tenderly treated, the colonists were in the habit of adding various titles, or laudatory epithets, either on their own authority, or by permission of the Senate, or of the Emperors; and setting them forth on their public monuments.—So on a brass tablet published by Gruter, the *Hadrumetini Byzacenes* are styled colonies of "Concordia, Ulpia, Trajana, Augusta, Frugifera, and Hadrumetina."—Nor are coins free from this display of vanity. Among others the Apamenians of Bithynia used the legend COL. IVL. CONC. AVG. APAM. (See p. 61 of this dictionary). The opinion of Vaillant, that Apamea was called Concordia, in allusion to its alliance with the neighbouring Prusa, has been correctly refuted by Belleye, who asserts that the titles bestowed on colonies did not at all refer to their ancient but to their actual condition.— Eckhel, in citing the learned Abbé's authority on this point, adds, that he had, however, himself found in Fl. Josephus, a certain place on the borders of Galilee, which is really named 'Ομόνοια, i. e. *Concordia*.

3. *Colonial Magistrates.*—As the Grecian cities recorded on their coins their magistrates of various ranks, such as Archons, Pretors,

Scribes, &c. so likewise did the Roman colonies and *municipia*. Spartianus, whilst enumerating the different offices served by Hadrian in several cities, says, "throughout the Latin towns he was styled Dictator, and Edile, and Duumvir; in his own country, a Quinquennalis." On coins connected with the present subject appear the following as local magistrates, viz.: Ediles, Decuriones, Duumviri, Quinquennales, Prefecti, Quatuorviri, Triumviri. Of all these brief notices will be found under their respective alphabetical heads.

Colonial Ediles.—As at Rome, the Ediles (see p. 12) were reckoned among the magistrates of the highest rank, their office being to superintend the management of the commerce, provisions, and public games of the city, so also the colonies, which were, so to speak, small imitations of Rome, had *their* Ediles, subject to the authority of the chief magistrate. The coins of Calagurris, Celsa, Leptis, Parium, Saguntum, and Turiaso, shew that those colonies had their Duumviri; those of Carteia and Clunia, their Quatuorviri; and all of them their Ediles.— Cardinal Noris records further examples besides those on coins.—Moreover it is certain that there were some colonies and *municipia* in which Ediles acted as chief magistrates. A proof of this may be found on reference to an oft-quoted passage of Spartianus, according to which Hadrian "was Dictator, and *Edile*, and Duumvir, throughout the Latin towns:" nor is it by any means to be imagined that any honour would have been conferred by the colonies on an emperor, which was not held in the highest estimation by themselves. Another clear testimony is furnished from Cicero, speaking of Arpinum:—"For," he says, "in order to establish a *municipium* it has this year been my wish that my son, my brother's son, and M. Cæsius, should be elected Ediles; for that is the *only magistracy* which it is the custom to create in our *municipium*." This passage further shews, that there were colonies, and *municipia*, which were governed by *three* Ediles. Coins do not record more than *two*. There is frequent mention of the Ediles of *municipia*, on ancient marbles.

Calagurris, Celsa, and other colonies had their Duumviri, and yet these were not always exhibited on their coins, but in their stead sometimes the Ediles, a magistracy of an inferior grade. Eckhel's mode of accounting for this is, that "the Colonial Ediles had their names inscribed on coins, for the same, or a similar reason as that which led to the names of the *Curule* and *Plebeian* Ediles being inscribed on the Roman denarii. For, as at Rome, the business of striking money was entrusted to the Pretors, Questors, and Ediles, on which occasions their names were introduced on the coins, so, in the colonies likewise, whether the purpose might be to provide corn, or celebrate public games, unstamped brass was given to the Ediles, which they were then to mint for immediate use, with the insertion of their own names, for a similar reason."

Coloniarum Decurionatus.—Decurionate of

the Colonies.——See DECVRIONES——See also *Municipal Magistracies.*

Coloniarum Duumviratus.—See Duumvirate of the Colonies.

Coloniarum et Municipiorum Typi.—The coins of Colonies have either certain particular types, from which they rarely deviate, or such as vary without any fixed system. Of the former class, *e. g.* are a woman standing with military ensigns, peculiar to Viminacium; a head of (Jupiter) Ammon, to Cassandrea; a woman sitting on a rock, with a river flowing from beneath it, to Antioch in Syria, &c. Coins of the second class have types of a changeable and common character, throwing light on the period in which they were struck; or in some cases, more elaborate ones, founded doubtless on traditions preserved amongst themselves and traceable to a remote period of the history of the colony; though there might be nothing in them any longer applicable to the circumstances of the *foreign* settlers in those cities. To adduce some examples, a common type of the colony of Corinth, is the fable of Melicerta, also of Bellerophon, Chimæra, Pegasus, &c. On the coins of the Tyrians, and colonies founded by them, we see the *petræ ambrosiæ,* and the *murex,* a shell fish used for dying wool purple, &c.—See CORINTHUS and TYRUS.

The following are the types which only *Roman* colonies adopted, except in cases where independent cities assumed them :—

I. A MAN, DRESSED IN THE TOGA, AND VEILED, DRIVES *(sometimes with, sometimes without, a whip),* A PAIR OF OXEN YOKED TO A PLOUGH.

This type, of which an Antiochian specimen, in large brass (CAEsaria ANTIOCHia COLonia Senatus Romanus), will be found engraved in p. 227, is presented exclusively on coins of Roman Colonies, as the sacred rite alluded to by it, was not observed except on the occasion of founding a colony by the Romans. It is described everywhere by philologists, and among them by Heineccius in the following brief and clear manner : "Whenever either a new city was to be built, or a colony planted, the founder or Triumvir of the colony, attired in the Gabinian garb, fixed a brazen plough-share into a plough, and yoking to it a pair of oxen, male and female, in person turned up a deep furrow around the boundaries. The colonists followed and shovelled back into the furrow the clods raised by the plough. At the spot which they fixed upon for a gate, they took out the plough-share, lifted the plough, and left a space. The furrow completed, these oxen with other victims, were sacrificed to the *Dii medioxumi,* (Gods of the *earth,* as *middle* between heaven and the infernal regions?) and lastly they betook themselves to building the walls. Other ceremonies were added to these, for good omen's sake, as Festus shews under the word *Quadrata;* but of the nature of these we are as yet ignorant. From what has already been described, the fact can easily be accounted for, that the walls and not the gates of a city were held sacred. For

the latter did not receive the impression of the plough, because through them would be carried the bodies of the dead and other impurities."

Thus far Heineccius who quotes his authorities, with whom Florez may be compared—Eckhel adds a passage from Cato's "Origines," quoted by Servius, in which the type of similar coins is exactly described; "For the founders of a city used to yoke a bull on the off and a cow on the near side, and dressed in the Gabinian fashion, (i. e. using part of the toga as a veil for the head, and girding up the rest of it,) held in their hands the curved plough-tail," &c. To the same purport is the statement of Dion, that a golden statue of great weight, with figures of a bull and a cow, was erected in honour of Commodus, as founder of the Colony of Rome. (See COL. COMMODIANA.)—The coins of that emperor of about the date U. C. 943, (A. D. 190) serve to elucidate this point of the subject.

The religious obligation of tracing with a plough the boundaries of a colony was observed not only in the case of those, which were raised from the very foundation, but also of those, which, having already the external form of a city, obtained through the importation of foreign colonists, or even merely by the liberality of the Romans, the rights and privileges of a colony.

As a monetal illustration of the fact here asserted by Eckhel, the above reverse of a beautiful gold coin struck by C. MARIVS TROGVS, one of the moneyers of Augustus, has been engraved after Mionnet's fine plate, T. i. p. 109. The type of this very rare aureus (valued by the French Numismatist at 600 fr.) represents a colonist driving two oxen harnessed to a plough, *before the walls of a town.* On the obverse is the bare head of Augustus, with *simpulum* and *lituus* behind it, and the legend CAESAR AVGVST. Allusion is doubtless in this instance made to some colony planted by the first emperor, where a city already existed, but round which the sacred ceremonial peculiar to Roman colonization had still to be performed.

Casilinum was an example of a city of long standing, and already constituted a colony with the due rites; and yet when M. Antony sent thither a reinforcement of colonists, he did not neglect the ceremony of the plough, as Cicero informs us, in the following invective:—" You have led over a colony to Casilinum, ... that you might raise the standard (vexillum) and drive the plough round (the walls)." Hence, it is by no means surprising, that the figure of a plough should be found on the coins of colonies of remote foundation, such as Berytus, Sidon, Tyre, and Patræ. According to Cicero, however, the limits, not merely of the city, but of the land assigned to the colony, were traced out by the plough. For he thus continues the sentence above quoted · "With the coulter of which (*i. e.* Aratrum) you nearly grazed the gate of Capua, that the territory of that flourishing colony might be curtailed."

It ought further to be observed, that the type of a plough is not found on the coins of any *municipium*, and with good reason, for, those places were not under the same regulations as the colonies (see article MVNICIPIVM), the latter, as the off-shoots of Rome, using the laws and institutions of that people, and appearing to have been, as it were, imitations of Rome on a small scale. Hence, as Romulus, when founding Rome (to use Ovid's expression), grasping the ploughshare, marked out the walls with a furrow, a white bull and a white cow bearing the yoke; so, in planting colonies, a similar rite was practised. And this also, fully accounts for the fact, that, on the coins of *Greek* colonies, whose custom it was, by various types, to indicate their connexion with the metropolis, there never appears a priest ploughing, because this ceremony was peculiar to the Romans alone, and never extended to the Greeks.—*D. N. V.* vol. iv. 490.

II. MILITARY ENSIGNS, AND THE LEGIONS.

These frequently occur on colonial coins, but not on them alone. There are various modes in which they were represented, and the following is Eckhel's enumeration of them:—

Military Ensigns alone; as they are seen on coins of Acci, Cæsar-augusta, Emerita, Berytus, &c.

Military Ensigns, with the *names of the Legions* affixed. See Coins of Acci (p. 3), and Cæsar-augusta (p. 161 of this dictionary). See also Berytus, Patræ, &c.

Military Ensigns, with a Priest ploughing.— On coins of Ælia Capitolina, and Ptolemais; also on some of Antioch in Pisidia, and of Patræ, the priest is ploughing; but instead of his holding the customary whip, a *vexillum,* or *one or two military standards,* appear behind his oxen.—See p. 15 & p. 227 of this dictionary.

On a coin of Cæsar-augusta, military ensigns occupy the obverse; and a priest ploughing, the reverse.

On the coins of Viminacium, a woman standing, holding an ensign in each hand, is the common type.

Military ensigns on colonial coins, undoubtedly for the most part indicate military colonies. For soldiers were sent out into the colonies, partly because they had served their time, partly as a reward for eminent services (which was frequently the case under the Triumvirate), partly for the protection of the frontiers of the empire. That, however, may with much greater certainty be pronounced a military colony, whose coins exhibit the legions and their numbers added to the *vexilla,* as LEG. XI.—But the numbers are not unfrequently omitted. It is well known that soldiers, transferred to colonies, proceeded thither with their ensigns, and by troops. Tacitus, in a passage already quoted, says:

"For not at this period, as in a former one, were whole legions led forth, with their tribunes and centurions, and soldiers of every rank."—And also Hyginus—"It was the lot of many legions, after successful campaigns, to arrive, by the first act of their warlike apprenticeship, at the laborious ease of a farming life. For they were led out with their ensigns and eagle, their officers of rank and tribunes."— Sulla is said to have been the originator of military colonies, and his example was followed by the Cæsars.

Fabretti is of opinion, that by the help of the types already described, viz. of a priest ploughing, and of *vexilla,* a distinction might be established between plebeian and military colonies. For, he says, the plebeians were distinguished by the plough; the military, by the eagles and ensigns; whilst those, which on various coins exhibit the plough or the ensigns indiscriminately, and sometimes in combination, indicate a derivation in the first instance from the civilians, reinforced subsequently by veteran soldiers. Fabretti is entirely followed by Vaillant.

Eckhel, however, shows that this opinion is confuted by both authors and coins. He begins by comparing with it Velleius Paterculus, who says—"I could not easily recall to memory an instance of any colony sent out *after this period,* which was not a *military one.*" The period alluded to, he marks by the sixth consulate of Marius, which occurred U. C. 654 (B. C. 100). If, therefore, his testimony may be relied on, Berytus, Cæsar-augusta, Corinth, Emerita, Patræ, Sinope, were also *military* colonies, being all planted by Julius Cæsar, or Augustus, and consequently *after* the time mentioned by Velleius; and yet all these colonies exhibit on their coins a man ploughing. Nor could Fabretti defend his ploughman by the assertion, that the first planting by the civilians was denoted by this type; for it is certain, that none of the cities just enumerated were colonies *before* the colonization act on foot by the two Cæsars above named; and, therefore, that they were made at the same time colonies, and, according to Velleius, *military* colonies; as, indeed is proved by the name *Emerita* itself, which, according to authors, was applied to it from soldiers who had served their time (*emeriti*).— Again to adduce Cicero's declamation against M. Antony—"You have led forth a colony to Casilinum, that you might raise your standard (vexillum), and drive your plough round its walls."—That it was a *military* colony is clear from the expressions of Velleius, and yet the custom of ploughing was observed at its foundation. In like manner, the *vexillum,* though the symbol of *military* colonies, yet did not disprove them to be *plebeian.* For even when plebeian colonies were sent out, the colonists marched under military ensigns.—This we learn from Plutarch, when he says, that the principal *vexillum* was broken off by the wind, when a colony was led by C. Gracchus to Carthage.— But this colony was composed, not of soldiers, but of poor civilians.

The foregoing statements go to prove that the type of a plough is applicable equally to plebeian and to military colonies; and the same may be maintained respecting the *vexilla*; although, as far as the present purpose is concerned, it would appear an idle inquiry, how far military ensigns denote a military colony. For those colonies of which coins are extant, with one or two exceptions, were all military, doubtless planted by the Cæsars: so that it may, without hesitation, be pronounced that the *vexilla* typified on coins of Roman colonies have reference to the soldiers who settled in them, in the same manner as the *vexilla* on the coins of cities, which were *not* colonies, have reference to the cohorts stationed as a guard near them.— On coins of *Italica* a Spanish *municipium*, there appear *vexilla*; also on those of Nicæa and Juliopolis in Bithynia, and Hieropolis in Cyrhestica, none of which were colonies; and though Egypt had no colonies whatever, the coins of Alexandria, struck during the reigns of Numerianus and Carinus, bear the mark of *Legio. II. Trajana*, with the type of a legionary eagle.— *Doct. Num. Vet.* vol. iv. p. 492.

III. A SHE WOLF SUCKLING TWO CHILDREN.

The following colonies offer this type on their coins, viz.:—*Alexandria* in the Troad; *Antiochia* in Pisidia; *Apamea* in Bithynia; *Coela* (municipium) in the Thracian Chersonesus; *Damascus* in Coele Syriæ; *Deultum* in Thrace; *Germe* in Galatia; *Iconium* in Lycaonia; *Italica* (municipium) in Bœtica (Hispania); *Laodicea* in Syria; *Neapolis* in Samaria; *Parium* in Mysia; *Patræ* in Achaia; *Philippi* in Macedonia.

The above cut is after a cast from a coin of Laodicea, in the British Museum. The obverse bears the head and titles of Macrinus; the legend of the reverse is ROMAE FEL(ICI).

That the tradition of Romulus and Remus having been brought up by a she wolf, was the constant symbol of the origin of the Roman state, is evident from innumerable monuments. It was on this account that the colonies particularly affected the above described type, in order to declare themselves sprung as it were from a common parent; just as Probus struck coins, in third brass, with the legend ORIGINI. AVG. and the type of the wolf and twins; no doubt in order to proclaim himself a Roman by birth. *Municipia*, though but rarely, used this type, as they might, by a species of adoption, be considered the daughters of Rome. Motives

of attachment, or of adulation, appear also to have recommended this type to foreign cities, as it is found on a coin of Thyatira, in Lydia, given by Spon. Connected with the allusion to Rome as an original, is a type, in which Æneas is represented, carrying Anchises and accompanied by Ascanius, used by the colonies of Apamea in Bithynia, and Berytus, in Syria.—See Pellerin, *Mélange*, i. T. i. pl. 18.

IV. A BULL, STANDING.—On the coins of Calagurris, Celsa, in Hispania, and of other colonies, this type appears in allusion to Agriculture, to promote which colonists were sent from Rome, and of which a bull was the customary symbol.—Tacitus says, "therefore from the cattle market, where we see the brazen statue of a bull, because that species of animal is used in ploughing," &c.——See Akerman, *Ancient Coins of Cities*, p. 78, pl. viii. No. 6—also Havercamp, *Médailles de Christine*, p. 285, TAB. xliv.

V. SILENUS *standing, holds out his right hand, and with his left supports a wine-skin thrown over his shoulders.*—(COL. LAOD. METROPOLEOS.)

This device, copied from a first brass of Laodicea, occurs on coins of the following colonies, viz.:—*Alexandria* Troadis; *Berytus* Phœniciæ; *Bostra* Arabiæ; *Coela* (*mun.*) Thraciæ; *Damascus* Coelesyriæ; *Deultum* Thraciæ; *Laodicea* Syriæ; *Neapolis* Samariæ; *Parium*, Mysiæ; *Patræ* Achaiæ; *Sidon* Phœniciæ; *Tyrus* Phœniciæ.

That the above type is peculiar to coins of this class, is rendered probable by the fact, not only that it is found on the coinage of so many *colonies*, but also that it is found on them alone, for Silenus is not represented in the attitude above described on any coins of cities, which were *not* colonies.—Eckhel, without hesitation, pronounces this type to be strictly a colonial one; and as a sole exceptional instance, he refers to the Silenus which appears, in a similar attitude, on a denarius of the Censorini (see Marcia gens), although for what reason adopted thereon, is not known.

Vaillant regards this type, as having reference to abundant vintages, in which Silenus is understood to have delighted. And, in this opinion, that celebrated writer on Colonial Coins is followed by Belleye, in his dissertation on the coins of Bostra.—Eckhel, on the other hand, considers it to indicate the *jus Italicum;* and he asks "how is it that we do not also find the figure of Silenus on the coins of Greek cities—cities which were so fond of boasting the excellence of their wine, in so many various ways?" He then commences an inquiry into the reason why the Silenus in question appears almost exclusively on Roman coins, and to throw light on this enigma, quotes two passages from Servius. That ancient grammarian, in the first place, refers to Silenus under the name of Marsyas, as is to be inferred from his asserting that this Marsyas was under the guardianship of *Liber Pater* (Bacchus), and performed the part of his attendant, as is mythologically predicated of Silenus; and in the next place, Servius states, that the image of Marsyas (meaning Silenus), was customarily placed in the forum of the Italian cities, as the symbol of Liberty, with uplifted hand, proclaiming that the city was under the amplest protection (nihil urbi deesse); thus pointing out the very posture of the statue, resembling that of the figure on their coins.—The learned, acute, and judicious Author of *Doctrina* next observes, that no colonies appear to have used this type but those which had the *jus Italicum* granted to them by the emperors. This privilege (*jus*), the most ample of all those which the Romans were accustomed to confer on cities, involved immunity from capitation and land taxes; and it was termed *Italicum*, because Augustus wished that this advantage should extend to the whole of Italy.

Eckhel then proceeds to the following effect:—"It must be evident to every one, that the cities which were distinguished by this eminent privilege, could, without undue assumption, though not strictly in accordance with the Roman sense of the term, be called *free*, and make that boast, which Servius supposes to be intimated by the attitude of Silenus—namely that thenceforward they had no further privilege to wish for. If, then, as may reasonably be conjectured, it was in order to make a display of this their liberty, that the Italian cities so constantly represented Silenus as the symbol of freedom, Servius, himself a Roman, and one who had been an eye-witness of this custom of the Italian cities, could with propriety state the figure of this demi-god to denote the liberty of cities, notwithstanding his having, as a writer, made use of expressions not quite correct (as when he substitutes Marsyas for Silenus, and the term liberty for that of immunity, derived from the *jus Italicum*). Moreover, if the Italian cities declared their freedom, by the erection of a statue of Silenus in their forum, it is not surprising that the colonies abroad should have been fond of testifying, in a similar manner, that the same privileges had been extended to themselves. And, indeed, of the twelve cities which have employed the type of Silenus on their coins (see the list given above), there are five which it is certain enjoyed the *jus Italicum*, that is to say, Alexandria, Berytus, Laodicea, Parium, and Tyre. To these may safely be added Sidon, on which no doubt the *jus Italicum*, which Tyre possessed, was bestowed simultaneously with the transfer to it

of all the other privileges of Tyre, by order of Elagabalus."

By way of support to his conjecture, Eckhel adds, that out of all the numerous coins of Tyre, Silenus appears on those only which declare that city to be a colony. On the withdrawal of its colonial rights, by Elagabalus, it intimated its forlorn condition by the legend TYRIORVM, whilst Silenus was banished from its coinage. To this instance may be conjoined Patræ, in Achaia, on which, as Pausanias informs us, Augustus conferred *all* the advantages which were usually allowed to a colony; and if *all*, no doubt amongst them was included the *jus Italicum*. Consequently out of *twelve* cities, *seven* are seen to have enjoyed that right, and used the type of Silenus.

This view of the subject, taken by the acknowledged prince of numismatists, is materially confirmed by the fact, that on the coins of those colonies, to which the jurists Ulpian, Paulus, and other learned authors, deny the *jus Italicum*, viz. Ptolemais, Cæsarea in Samaria, Ælia Capitolina, and Antioch in Syria, not the least vestige of the Silenus type is to be found; although their coins are extant in abundance.—Of Ptolemais, Ulpian says, "It has nothing beyond the *name* of a colony;" and of Cæsarea and Aelia, the same writer says, "Neither of them possesses the *jus Italicum*." Antioch in Syria is not only passed over entirely by Ulpian; but Paulus has merely this brief notice of it—"Divus Antoninus constituted the Antiochians colonists, but *without exemption from tribute* (salvis tributis).—" From the circumstance however that the above named writers do not enumerate among the *Urbes Italicæ*, Bostra, Coela, Damascus, Denltum, Neapolis, Patræ, and Sidon, all of which exhibit the type of Silenus in their mintages, let it not (says Eckhel in conclusion) be supposed that I would have any one infer, that those cities did *not* possess the *jus Italicum;* for there is no doubt that some colonies were admitted to the privilege in question at a later period."—See *Doct. Num. Vet.* iv. 493, et seq.

Colonial Coins—metal employed in.—No colonial coin has yet been found in gold. Nemausus has given several in silver, with the inscription COL. Florez saw only one of Carthago Nova, and one of Ilicum, and has pronounced them to be the greatest rarities. There are very rare silver coins of Agrigentum, in Sicily, without the COL. and inscribed only AGRIGENTVM, but which, Eckhel has no doubt, were struck at Agrigentum, after the planting of a colony there. With these exceptions, the whole of the colonial coinage is in brass. It appears that the use of silver was not forbidden to the colonies planted under the republic; but that subsequently, brass alone was permitted, from the time that Augustus, and his successors, reserved to themselves the gold and silver mints.

Colonial mintages—cessation of.—The latest time of striking coins in the colonies of Hispania does not extend beyond the reign of Caligula. In the Gallic provinces they had ceased even under Augustus, and earlier still, on the continent of Italy; as there is no coin of an Italian colony, exhibiting a head of Cæsar, or of Augustus. The coins of the Sicilian colonies, Agrigentum and Panormus, furnish the portrait of Augustus alone. The colonies of old Africa gave up the minting-mallet, under Tiberius; and Babba alone, in New Africa, continued till the reign of Galba. But these limits apply not only to the coinage of the colonies, and *municipia* of those provinces, but also to that of their free cities. As regards the provinces situated eastward of the Adriatic, their colonies present examples of the same course, adopted in reference to money, by their free cities. For both equally abstained from striking money during the reign of Gallienus, with the exception of a very few, which exhibit the portraits of some of the emperors immediately succeeding him. And this cessation was owing, either to the universal feeling of satiety, or to the glut of Roman money, in the provinces; or to the fact, that about this time, mints were in the course of establishment, for the coining of money, which should be common to all the provinces of the empire.

Coloniarum cudendi permissio.—Permission to strike money in the colonies.—See PERM. AVGVSTI, and PERMISSV CAESARIS—*(suis locis.)*

COL. L. AN. COM. P. M. TR. P. XV. IMP. VIII. COS. VI. S. C.—A priest veiled, driving a plough, to which oxen are yoked.— First and second brass of Commodus.

On this reverse, we have the monetal proof of Rome having been called *Colonia Commodiana*, by command of Commodus. Lampridius (chap. 8) informs us that this emperor reached such a pitch of madness as to desire that the city of Rome should be called the Commodianian colony; an act of folly which is said to have been brought about, by the fascinations of Marcia, his Amazonian mistress. The same historian adds that, at the time when he introduced to the Senate his scheme for turning Rome into Commodiana, that degenerate body not only received it readily, but even gave itself the title of *(Senatus) Commodianus.* Thus the absurdity was fortified even by a *Senatus consultum*, as is shewn by the coin from which the above is an accurate cut, and which is marked with the s. c. To show how obstinately Commodus had set his mind on this object, it is stated by Dion (lxxii. § 15), that the people were commanded to call Rome itself *Commodiana*, and the armies *Commodiani.* And further, that Rome was styled by the emperor himself the "eternal

fortunate (*Felicem*) Colony of the world;" so intent was he on the city's being considered as his own colony. But this new "settlement" had a very narrow escape from destruction, by the hands of the very person who planted it: for he would have set fire to the city, says Lampridius (ch. 15), had he not been prevented by Lætus.

The type of a priest veiled, ploughing, with a yoke of oxen, admirably confirms the testimony of historians, for (as has been fully demonstrated in the preceding pages), it is a common one on coins of cities which were planted as colonies. The golden statue erected to him, with the figures of a bull and a cow, has reference to this foolish attempt of Commodus, in his pretended capacity of founder of a colony. The legend, also, perfectly agrees with the type of this remarkable coin, as it gives the word COL*onia.*

"The whole inscription (adds Eckhel) no doubt should be thus interpreted—COL*onia Lucia* AN*toniniana* COM*odiana*, just as Diospolis in Samaritis, and Eleutheropolis in Judæa, styled themselves on coins *Lucia Septimia Severiana.* Still, it is remarkable, that the prænomen of *Lucia* should have been given to Rome, at a time, when Commodus himself constantly used that of *Marcus*, unless, perhaps, he had in his mind the revival of the old and long disused name of *Lucius*, which he really adopted two years afterwards."—See vii. 122.

The same subject is alluded to on coins inscribed HERC. ROM. COND.—Among Vaillant's *Selectiora Numismata* from the De Camps collection, now in the *Cabinet de France*, there is one which exhibits this emperor indulging his insane fancy of guiding the colonial plough, but attired in the lion's skin like Hercules. And the impersonation is completed by a club which he carries in his right hand. For Lampridius records, that "He caused himself to be styled *Romanus Hercules*"—adding the reason for that designation, viz. "because he had slaughtered wild beasts in the amphitheatre at Lanuvium." It was in memory of his converting the eternal city" into a colony bearing his own name, and to his own *honour*, as "Hercules Romanus *Conditor*," that the medallion in question was struck, at the beginning of his 7th consulate, in colleagueship with Helvius Pertinax, 945 (A. D. 192), and during his 17th investiture with the tribunitian power.—See COMMODUS, biographical summary of (p. 240).—Engraved in Akerman, i. 312, pl. D.

COLONUS—a term obviously derived from *colo*, to till or cultivate the soil—means an inhabitant of a colony, who was nominally a citizen of Rome; because he had the rights of citizenship, though not in all their extent; nor did the *coloni* possess what was called *Optimum jus.* Cicero has given a detail of the privileges of which a colonist was deprived. Addressing himself to the Roman people, the great orator says,—Vos verò, Quirites, retinete istam possessionem gratiæ, libertatis, suffragiorum, dignitatis, Urbis, fori, ludorum, festorum, &c. Of whatever rank they were, the *coloni* were eligible to be enrolled among the rural tribes, so that they became equal, by the right of suffrages, to the richest and most distinguished citizens—Those who wished to become members of a new colony were accustomed to give in their names to the triumvirs charged as commissioners with the duty of forming such settlement. And thus persons burthened with the pressure of domestic circumstances, obtained with their families new and gratuitous means of support.— See Pitiscus, *Dictionnaire des Antiquités Romaines*.

Colonists were frequently sent out by the Romans into the *metropolis*, or capital city of a nation or a province. And this was done with a politic view, in order by the allegiance of one city the more easily to secure the adherence of the other towns in the same province or nation. Hence we find the united dignities of *Colonia* and *Metropolis* are marked on coins of *Charræ*, *Edessa*, &c. The legends being sometimes in the vernacular tongue of those places; at other times in the Latin language, as introduced by the colonists themselves.

COLOSSUS—a statue of prodigious grandeur, far beyond the size of life. At first they were made thus large and lofty only in honour of the gods, in order to indicate the extent of their power by the vastness of their stature. Afterwards, however, when human rulers affected divine honours, they readily allowed themselves to receive a homage which had till then been reserved to their deities. The Asiatics and Egyptians had a remarkable fondness for gigantic figures. The Greeks also possessed many Colossi, among which was the celebrated one of Rhodes, executed by Chares Lindius, a disciple of Lysippus, and which was 70 cubits high.— The Romans adorned their cities with similar monuments, which at first they brought thither from the countries they had conquered. At a later period the pride and ambition of the emperors added colossal magnitude to the other attributes of their power. Nero caused his colossal statue to be erected in the *via sacra* at Rome (near the spot afterwards occupied by Vespasian's amphitheatre); and on a large brass of that emperor there is a triumphal arch (see p. 77), in one of the sides of which we see a figure of extraordinary proportions, compared with the other statues that adorn it, and which, with probability, is regarded by Oiselius and others to represent Nero. See also a colossal figure of that emperor on the large brass of PORT. OSTIA. Domitian and Hadrian also erected colossal statues.—Haym has published a coin, on which is a colossus between two temples dedicated to Caracalla and Geta, or to Severus and Caracalla. Millingen has also given a colonial second brass dedicated to Antoninus Pius, on the reverse of which, in the middle of a harbour with ships in it (supposed to be meant for that of *Cenchrea)*, stands a colossal image of Neptune.—See CORINTHUS.

COLUMNA.—A column or pillar—round in form, and composed (in architectural language),

of a body called the *shaft*, of a head termed the *capital*, and of a foot denominated the *base*.— The Romans had epithets to designate different insulated columns, used for public purposes. Those noticeable on their coins were the *rostrated* and the *triumphal*.—The following are well-known examples of each:—

COLUMNA ANTONINIANA.—A magnificent pillar, which still "lifts its head" in one of the finest squares (or *piazze*) in Rome, is thus called, as having been raised, according to general belief, by the Senate and People to the memory of Antoninus Pius. And there are inscriptions on it which countenance and support this belief. But inasmuch as certain details of the war against the Marcomanni are recorded on this column—a war conducted by his successor Marcus Aurelius—it has been therefrom inferred that this famous monument was not finished till the reign of Commodus. It appears, however, more likely to have been erected during the reign of Marcus Aurelius. That prince having occasionally been called Divus Antoninus, or Marcus Antoninus, has perhaps given rise to the ambiguity. At any rate, the name of Antoninus remains attached to the column, which is 116 French feet in height, and 11 in diameter. It is entirely of marble, and is surrounded with *bassi relievi*, which form twenty spirals around the shaft.

Silver and large brass coins, bearing the portrait of Antoninus Pius, and judging from the legend of consecration, evidently struck *after* that emperor's death, exhibit a typification of the column, with a colossal statue of the *Imperator* standing on its summit, holding a spear in his right hand. The base of the pillar is surrounded with a railing. The above cut is engraved from a well-preserved large brass.— See DIVO PIO.

In describing a choice specimen of this interesting type in his own collection, Captain Smyth (p. 126) observes—" This celebrated column, erected by Marcus Aurelius, in the field of Mars, in imitation of that of Trajan, was inferior to it in all respects except that of height. The dimensions of this monument are thus given by Publius Victor :—' Templum Divi, cum coclide columnâ, quæ est alta pedes 175, habet intus gradus 206, et fenestellas (small windows) 56." It still exists *in situ*, although it has been greatly damaged by fire; and Pope Sixtus Vth having placed St. Peter on Trajan's pillar, set up St. Paul on this."

COLUMNA ROSTRATA.—This was a pillar which the Senate and the Roman People raised on the occasion of some naval successes, and adorned with the *rostra*, or prows of conquered squadrons. The first rostrated or beaked columns were erected in the forum, to commemorate a victory gained by the Roman fleet under the consul C. Duillius over that of the Carthaginians, B. c. 261. It was a marble pillar, found in 1560, and is to be seen in the capitol at Rome.—Engraved in Dr. W. Smith's *Dictionary of Roman Antiquities*, p. 267.

On a silver coin of Augustus, the reverse type presents a column, ornamented with beaks and anchors of ships, on which stands a figure of the emperor, in a military habit, with a spear in the right hand, and a short sword, or the *parazonium*, in the other. IMP. CAES. inscribed on the field of the coin.

This type bears reference to a circumstance recorded by Appian (B. c. lib. v. ch. 130), that on Octavianus Cæsar's return from the campaign in Sicily against Pompey, A. U. c. 718 (B. c. 36), amongst other honours decreed to Augustus was the following—that a gold statue of him, in the triumphal attire in which he entered the city, should be erected to him in the forum, on a column to which were affixed the beaks of ships, and inscribed, OB. PACEM. DIV. TVRBATAM. TERRA. MARIQVE. RESTITVTAM.— It is to this that Virgil also alludes, when amongst the famous monuments of Augustus, he mentions, " navali surgentes aere columnas," " columns soaring aloft, made of, or *adorned with*, naval brass." (*Georg.* iii. 29). To which Servius adds, " Augustus becoming the conqueror of all Egypt, part of which Cæsar had reduced, brought away from the naval engagement many beaks of ships, which he melted down and made into four columns, afterwards placed by Domitian in the capitol."—Eckhel, vi. 86.

A rostrated column, as represented in the annexed cut, surmounted by a male figure, with radiated head, holding the *hasta*, appears on gold and silver coins of Vespasian.— The statue on the top of the column seems (says Vaillant), to be that of Vespasian, and the coin which the legend of reverse, COS. VIII. TR. POT. X. shews to have been minted A. D. 77, refers to some victory; perhaps that naval engagement in which he defeated the Jews on the lake of Genesaret, as related by Josephus. There is a similar coin and type of Titus, struck in remembrance of his naval victories, and on which his image, with radiated head, surmounts the rostral column.

COLUMNA TRAJANA.—The superb monument bearing this appellation, and existing at this moment in the Eternal City, was erected by the Senate and the Roman People to the honour of Trajan, in the forum which that emperor had caused to be built at Rome (by Apollodorus of Athens), and which was called after his name. This noble pillar remained uninjured by the wear and tear of ages, except that the statue of the emperor had disappeared from its summit, and that a balustrade of brass, which originally surrounded the top, existed no longer. Pope Sixtus V. undertook to repair these losses, and employed the Cavaliere Fontana in supplying a balustrade of iron; but instead of raising another statue of Trajan, copied as it might have been from his coins, His Holiness preferred to see the vacant place filled up with a brazen figure of St. Peter, "who (as Eckhel says, with classical sarcasm on pontifical taste), " marvels no doubt what connection there can be between himself and the *relievos* of the column, which exhibit the horrors of war and the ceremonies of paganism—thus transforming this renowned work into a contemptible hybrid."

Several ancient historians have made allusion to this magnificent object, and state its dimensions, each after his own calculations.—Dion says, *inter alia*, "Trajan's column in the forum is of vast height."—Eutropius affirms, that it was 144 feet high.—Cassiodorus 140 feet.—P. Victor says, "It was 128 feet in height."—Modern writers, on more minute admeasurement, estimate its diameter at 12 feet and ⅓ (French), and its height at 100 feet, including the base and capital. The summit of the column is attained by means of an interior staircase, cut round in the marble. This staircase receives the light by 43 openings pierced in the shaft. The sculptured work with which the whole exterior of the column is decorated, makes a spiral ascent of 23 turns round the pillar like a shell (whence its appellation *cochlis*). It represents in a series of *tableaux* the exploits of Trajan, throughout both the Dacian campaigns. They are extremely curious as regards both art and history, exhibiting as they do, settings out on marches, forms of encampment, passages of rivers, sacrifices, battles, victories, and trophies. These pictures are all of fine workmanship, and deficient in a graphic sense only as to perspective, the rules of which the ancients seldom if ever appear to have understood. As a means, however, of retracing the most memorable incidents of the Dacian war, and of presenting many interesting details relative to military antiquities, such sculptured relics are of the greatest value.

Coins in gold and silver, also in first and second brass, minted A. D. 113, in memory of the time when this triumphal pillar was constructed, exhibit the statue (of brass gilt) by which it was originally surmounted. It represented Trajan in the garb of war, holding in one hand a spear, and in the other a globe. On the pedestal, close to the base of the column, stands an eagle on each side. The emperor, however, never beheld the column thus raised to record and perpetuate his military fame: for, returning from Persia, he died in the East on his way to Rome, A. D. 117. His ashes, inclosed in a golden urn, were interred under the column—being the first buried within the city.

The legend on the coin in each metal displaying this interesting type of reverse, is S. P. Q. R. OPTIMO PRINCIPI. (on the brass S. C. is added.)

The date (observes Eckhel) of the completion and dedication of this surprising monument is almost sufficiently defined by the inscription above the door of the column, viz.:—

SENATVS. POPVLVSQ. ROMANVS.
IMP. CAESARI. DIVI. NERVAE. F.
NERVAE. TRAIANO. AVG. GERM.
DACICO. PONTIF. MAXIMO. TRI.
POT. XVII. IMP. VI. COS. VI. P. P.
AD. DECLARANDVM. QVANTAE.
ALTITVDINIS. MONS. ET. LOCVS.
*TANT*is* operi*BVS SIT. EGE.
STVS.

* So Fabretti contends it should be read; others fill up the *lacunæ* differently: thus TANT*is ex colli*BVS SIT. EGESTVS.

According to this inscription, the column, among other purposes, answered that of a measure to indicate the depth (that is to say its height corresponding to the depth) of soil removed from the Quirinal Mount, to make room for the foundations of the immense *Forum Trajani*. The inscription also records the completion of the column to have been when Trajan had entered upon his XVIIth *Tribunitia Potestas*, which occurred in the autumn of the year V. C. 866 (A. D. 113). Its dedication, therefore, cannot be assigned to an earlier period, nor indeed to one much later than the beginning of the following year; for this emperor, in the year following (867) adopted, amongst his titles, that of OPTIMVS; and as the inscription above quoted does not give that title, it follows that the work was completed, and the inscription cut within the interval already pointed out.—See *D. N. V.* vol. vi. p. 429–30.

The *Columna Trajana* has been frequently engraved. An accurate series of plates from the original designs, with the observations of Gori, are to be found in *Morell. Thesau. Impp.* T. iii.

COM. *Communitas.*

COM. ASI. *Communitas Asiæ.*—Under the pro-consular province of Asia were comprised Lydia, Iconia, Caria, Mysia, Phrygia, and Hellespontus, which were in consequence called the Community of Asia.

COM. ASI. ROM. ET. AVG.—A silver medallion of Claudius has on its reverse the foregoing legend; and for the accompanying type,

a two-columned temple; within which is the figure of a man in a military habit, crowned by a female figure who holds a cornucopiæ.—The abbreviated words ROM. ET AVG. are inscribed on the frieze of the temple; whilst COM. ASI. appears on the field of the coin, the temple being between them. On the obverse is TI. CLAVDIVS CAESAR AVG. with the bare head of Claudius.—This medallion was struck at Pergamus, in Mysia, about 807 (A. D. 54).—Eckhel, vi. 245.

" It seems," says Tristan, *(Commentaires Historiques,* T. i. 183) " that the medal was minted in honour of Claudius, immediately after his accession to the empire; the Asiatics wishing to signify that Claudius was elevated to the Roman monarchy on account of the love borne him by the Romans, inspired thereto by the divine genius of the city of Rome." Havercamp, on the other hand (see *Moreli. Thesaur. Impp.* vol. ii. p. 15), expresses the more probable opinion that the temple thus typified is one which the Alabandenses of Caria, or some other province of the *Communitas Asiæ,* had built in honour of *Roma* and *Augustus,* and that the coin was struck simply in congratulation to Claudius, on his recent attainment of the supreme power formerly possessed by Augustus, whom they were then worshipping as a God.

Similar medallions, in silver, were coined under Nerva and Trajan. Vaillant, who gives the former (in *Num. Præst. Impp.* p. 113), does not consider that the temple refers to either of these emperors, as the AVG*ustus* of the inscription; although its type seems to have been considered worthy of being renewed in honour of each respectively, by the community of Asiatic provinces, comprised under the proconsular government of Rome.

Eckhel, whilst treating of the coinage of Augustus, under the year of Rome 735 (B. C. 19) proves, that these and similar coins of Claudius and Nerva were struck at Pergamus, in Mysia.

COM. ASIAE.—A temple of six columns, on the frieze of which is inscribed ROM. ET AVGVST.—On a silver medallion of Augustus, in the imperial museum at Vienna.

Eckhel, by the subjoined animadversions on this coin, shews how its legend and type combine to throw light on the meaning of those bearing similar inscriptions, struck under Claudius, and Nerva, as above described:—

Suetonius (cap. 52) says of Augustus,— " Though he was aware that temples used to be decreed even to pro-consuls, would permit none to be dedicated in any of the provinces, except jointly to himself and *Roma.* For in Rome itself he most resolutely abstained from the distinction of a *sole* dedication."—Schlegel is far from happy in his conjecture, that the temple on this coin represents that of Jupiter Olympicus, which stood in Athens, and was erected at the common cost of all the kings of Asia.—

From other sources we have indisputable evidence, that this is the temple at Pergamus, in Asia. The first testimony is that of Tacitus (*Annal.* vi. 37)—" Divus Augustus did not forbid the erection of a temple at Pergamus, in the joint names of himself and the city ROMA." —To the same purport also are certain Greek coins of Pergamus, which, struck not only after the decease of Augustus, but also during his life-time, exhibit that emperor standing within a temple, with a spear in his hand, and the inscription ΘΕΟΝ. ΣΕΒΑΣΤΟΝ. And again, on other coins, struck in the same city in the time of Augustus, we see a turreted head of Roma, with the legend ΘΕΑΝ. ΡΩΜΗΝ. And further, on a coin of Pergamus, in the imperial cabinet, struck in the reign of Trajan, is found the inscription ΡΩΜΗ. ΚΑΙ. ΣΕΒΑΣΤΩ. with the type of a temple, within which Augustus, standing and holding a spear in his right hand, is crowned by Roma, who stands beside him, with cornucopiæ in her left hand; and if with this we compare the silver medallions bearing heads of Claudius, Nerva, and Trajan, and inscribed COM. ASI. ROM. ET AVG. with a similar type, it will become sufficiently evident, that coins agreeing thus in legend and type, and differing only in *tongue*, must have been struck in one and the same city, viz. Pergamus.—Still more to the purpose of the coin before us, Dion Cassius (li. c. 20), after stating that Cæsar Augustus permitted temples to be erected at Ephesus and Nicæa, in honour of Rome and his father Julius, adds—" To foreigners, however, whom he used to term *Greeks*, he gave permission to erect temples to *himself* also, viz. to the Asiatics at Pergamus, and to the Bithynians at Nicomedia." These, therefore, were the same *Asiatics* who style themselves on this coin COM*munitas* ASIAE, thereby indicating, that the temple there represented was raised in honour of ROMA and AVGVSTus by their contributions.—*Doct. Num. Vet.* vi. 245.

COM. BIT. (*Commune Bithyniæ*).—A temple, on the frieze of which is inscribed ROM. S. P. AVG.—Silver medallion of Hadrian.

COM. BIT. S. P. R.—Inscribed on a silver medallion of the same emperor, on the reverse of which is a temple of four columns, with a military figure standing in it.—For an explanatory notice of both these coins, see ROM. ET AVG.

COM. *Commodus.*

COM. *Comes.*—COM. IMP. AVG. *Comes Imperatoris Augusti.*

COMANA in *Pontus, Colonia.*—This city (now Al Bostan) was, according to Vaillant, made a colony by Julius Cæsar, after the overthrow of Pharnaces, son of Mithridates ; hence its title of *Julia.* It was afterwards re-peopled with veterans by Augustus, and for that reason also called *Augusta.*—The imperial coins of this city are in large and small brass. They belong to only three reigns, viz. : Antoninus Pius and Caracalla, with *Latin* legends, and Alexander Severus, with a *Greek* legend. A first brass of this colony, dedicated to Caracalla, bears for its legend of reverse, COL. IVL. AVG. COMANORV.

(*Colonia Julia Augusta Comanorum.*) The type presents a temple of two columns, within which stands a woman, clothed in a tunic, and a large veil, which she spreads out with her extended arms.—Engraved in Vaillant, vol. ii. p. 32.

COMES, a word which means companion, in the proper and natural sense, was used under the princes of the lower empire, to designate those who were of the household, and in the train of the sovereign, and who had some peculiar functions. *Comes Imperii* signifies a colleague in government, and is, perhaps, in this sense to be taken, when the word is found on coins of the imperial series, whereon it serves as a species of flattery to the reigning emperor, with whose name are associated the names of certain deities, such as Hercules, Sol, Victoria, &c.

COMITI.—See HERCULI COMITI AUG.—SOLI INVICTO COMITI, &c.

COMITATUS AUGG.—(The train or retinue of the emperors.) Two horsemen with right hands raised, and a sceptre or spear in their left hands.

This legend and type, the latter of which is evidently borrowed from the *C. et L. Cæsares,* or the *Nero et Drusus Cæsares* of Augustus, are given by Banduri as those of a very rare gold coin of Constantius Chlorus, which he refers to the date of A. D. 292, when Constantius and Galerius were in colleagueship.—Khell (p. 215) gives an engraving of a gold coin, of the highest rarity, bearing on its obverse the head and legend of DIOCLETIANVS AVGVSTVS, with the same legend and type on its reverse as that above described, and which he assigns to about A. D. 286, when Diocletian and Maximinian Hercules were joint Augusti.—See Eckhel also relative to these coins, viii. 5.

COMITIUM.—This place of public assembly, to which reference has already been made under the head of CLOACIN (see p. 219), was situate in the *forum,* beginning, according to Martianus, from the gate of the palace, and finishing at the spot now occupied by the church of S. Maria Nova. Though surrounded by a wall, the comitium was without a roof in the early days of Rome. It was covered in during that year so memorable in Roman annals, when Hannibal entered Italy ; and it was afterwards ornamented with pictures and statues.—On a denarius of the Silia gens, two figures are seen ascending by steps to the bridge, or platform of the comitium, to cast their votes into baskets, having taken their tickets for that purpose from the *diribitores,* or scrutineers, below.—The *comitium* is likewise seen on coins of Hostilia, Licinia, and Mussidia families.—See *Morell. Thesaur. Fam. Rom.*

COMM. or COMMOD. *Commodus.*—COMM. ANT. AVG. BRIT.

COMMODUS (*Lucius Aurelius*) ANTONINUS, who on his coins is also called MARCUS, was the son of M. Aurelius and of Faustina junior ; and was born at Lanuvium, in Latium, 914 (A. D. 161), the year in which his father entered on his third consulate, and succeeded Antoninus in the sovereignty—viz. the day before the calends of September. His mother gave birth at the same time to another son, named *Antoninus,*

and, in reference to the event, *Geminus;* but that child died at the age of four years. Capitolinus, however, gives it as his opinion, that Commodus was the son, not of Aurelius, but of some gladiator. Whichever of the two may be the correct version, it is certain that Aurelius constantly acknowledged him as his own child; and was much attached to him, frequently carrying him in his arms, and shewing him to the soldiers; and not only endeavoured himself to instil virtuous principles into his mind, but also committed his education to the care of men remarkable for their moral and intellectual qualifications; with how little benefit was shewn throughout the whole of his atrocious career.

In 919 (A. D. 166), Commodus received the title of CAESAR, in conjunction with his brother Annius Verus, at the request of L. Verus, on the occasion of the triumph celebrated by both emperors, over the Parthians.

925 (A. D. 172). He was styled GERMANICVS.

928 (A. D. 175). Admitted as a priest into all the sacerdotal colleges, he went the same year from Rome into Germania, by order of his father, who there conferred on him the *toga virilis,* at the time of the revolt of Avidius Cassius, i. e. the 7th of July. On that occasion he was also styled PRINCEPS IVVENTVTIS, and before the customary time nominated consul. Same year, he set out with his father for the East, in order to put an end to the disturbances still resulting from the revolt of Cassius. The title of SARMATICVS, which Aurelius assumed this year, was also shared by Commodus.

929. (A. D. 176). Towards the close of this year, he returned with his father from the East, and received, in conjunction with Aurelius, the title of IMPERATOR, on the 27th of November. The honours of a triumph for victories over the Germani, and Sarmatæ, were conferred by a Senatus Consultum upon his father and himself on the 23rd of December. Shortly afterwards he was associated by Aurelius in the *Tribunitia Potestas;* on which occasion a *congiarium* was distributed to the people.

930 (A. D. 177). In January of this year, he *proceeded* Consul; about this time he married Crispina. The same year Aurelius conferred the title of AUGUSTUS and also that of PATER PATRIÆ on his unworthy son: and in consequence

of victories gained, associated him with himself as IMPERATOR II.

931 (A. D. 178). On the 5th of August, he set out with his father for the war in Germania.

932 (A. D. 179). Commodus was present in the German campaign. A bloody victory was gained over the Marcomanni, the Hermanduri, and the Sarmatæ, in consequence of which Aurelius was styled IMP. X. and Commodus IMP. III.

933 (A. D. 180). Marcus Aurelius dying on the 17th March, Commodus succeeded to the sole sovereignty. Leaving the war still unfinished, and concluding a peace with the barbarians, for which, as it would appear, he received the victorious title of IMP. IV. he returned to Rome, and celebrated a triumph.

935 (A. D. 182). Nothing of importance is recorded to have taken place, under this reign, during the preceding year. But in the latter part of this year, Commodus was declared IMPERATOR V. by acclamation, according to the testimony of coins, although in reward of what victory is not known; for historians record several wars, conducted by his lieutenants, without specifying dates.

936 (A. D. 183). Serving the consulate (IV.) with Aufidius Victorianus for his colleague, Commodus was styled IMP. VI. at the close of this year, though it is uncertain for what victory. Tillemont expresses his opinion that it was for one over the Britons. Commodus escaped a dangerous conspiracy set on foot by his sister Lucilla, whom, as well as his wife, he caused to be put to death. This year the agnomen of PIVS is added to his titles.

937 (A. D. 184). The title PONT. MAX. begins. This year the Caledonians having crossed the wall, an important war was waged with them by the Roman forces in Britain, under the generalship of Ulpius Marcellus, a man of the highest military renown; in consequence of whose victories, Commodus gained first the title of IMP. VII. and afterwards of BRIT*annicus.*

938 (A. D. 185). The soldiers demanded that Perennis, the pretorian prefect, should be given up to execution. Terrified by their threats, Commodus surrendered him to their fury; and they put him to death, with his whole family. After this, Commodus received the title of FELIX.

930 (A. D. 186). In his fifth consulate, Commodus was declared IMPERATOR VIII. by acclamation, but for what victory is doubtful. It is also uncertain what occurrences are to be assigned to the succeeding year.

941 (A. D. 188). On pretence of an expedition to Africa, he levied a vast sum of money. And in April VOTA were entered into for his success. Detained, however, at Rome, by his *faithful* Senate and People, he applied the cash to feasting and gaming.

942 (A. D. 189). To this year Tillemont assigns another cowardly abandonment of a public functionary to the vengeance of a mutinous soldiery. Cleander, the pretorian prefect, like his predecessor Perennis, was given up by this base emperor at the first summons, and with his whole family was slaughtered.

943 (A. D. 190). In his sixth consulship, M. Petronius Septimianus being his colleague, Commodus named Rome after himself, Colonia Commodiana, adding the *prenomina* of LUCIA ANTONINIANA.

944 (A. D. 191). In this, or the following year, the magnificent temple of PAX was destroyed by a terrible conflagration.

945 (A. D. 192). In his seventh consulate, Helvius Pertinax being his colleague, on the day before the calends of January, in the dead of night, Commodus perished by a violent death, aged 31 years and 4 months.—Eckhel, vii. 102.

For cruelty and profligacy he is to be classed with the worst of the many bad princes who swayed the affairs of Rome; and by the proficiency he displayed in gladiatorial exercises, he gave a colour to the prevalent rumour of his having owed his birth, not to Marcus Aurelius, but to the criminal intimacy of Faustina with some gladiator. Alike insensible to the influence of good example, and incapable of profiting from the advantages of education, he, soon after the death of his imperial predecessor, developed the whole wickedness of his disposition. He ordained himself to be worshipped as Jupiter and as Hercules, whose attributes he assumed. Abandoning himself to the grossest intemperance, and to the most odious vices, palaces and temples became, under his reign, the scenes of riot, debauchery, and crime. Pestilence, famine, and incendiary conflagrations, visited the widespread dominions of which he was at once the sovereign and the scourge.

That during his reign, the empire maintained its ascendency, in spite of the disaffection of so many provinces—the Mauritanians, the Dacians, the Pannonians, the Britons, and the Germans—is to be attributed solely to the valour and fidelity of his distinguished generals, Pertinax, Severus, Pescennius Niger, and Albinus. His own time was passed at Rome in cowardly inaction; if we except the fact of his there directing his arms not merely against brutes, both wild and tame, but also against human beings, provided they were wealthy, or ever so lightly suspected of designs against himself: nay, he declared war even against the months of the year, to which, instead of the old and received appellations, according to the testimony of Dion, his contemporary, he gave the following :—Amazonius, Invictus, Felix, Pius, Lucius, Ælius, Aurelius, Commodus, Augustus, Herculeus, Romanus, Exuperatorius. At length, having signalized his government by deeds of monstrous folly and of unspeakable infamy, of which many of his coins furnish the proof, and after having escaped from repeated attempts upon his life, this execrable tyrant perished at last by a conspiracy of his favourite concubine Marcia. This woman, seeing in the hands of a boy, to whom Commodus was much attached, a tablet which he had taken in play from his sleeping master, and on which she discovered her own name in a list of intended victims, on that very evening, which was the last in the year, first attempted to administer poison to Commodus, and when he offered resistance, called in the aid of a gladiator, by whom he was strangled. Thus Commodus, as he resembled Domitian in his life, met also a similar fate, the cruel designs of both becoming fatal to themselves, by being betrayed unwittingly by a boy. On the report of his death, the Senate and the People with one voice demanded that his corpse should be dragged thro' the streets with a hook, and thrown into the Tiber.—And here, without acquitting Commodus and other bad emperors, whose just doom for their crimes is in the hands of Eternal Justice—it may with truth be said, that it was the corrupt and pusillanimous conduct of the Senate, coupled with the wretched weakness of parents, and the blandishments of base and selfish flatterers, that mainly contributed to ruin them—by making them bad, and keeping them so.

MINTAGES OF COMMODUS.

The names and titles are infinitely varied on his coins. Sometimes he takes the prenomen of LUCIUS ; sometimes that of MARCUS. His other names were AELIUS AURELIUS ANTONINUS PIUS FELIX, to which he added BRIT*annicus*.

The legends on the coins of Commodus are thus classed by Mionnet, after arranging them as Eckhel has done, in chronological order, viz. : Those struck from the time that he was created Cæsar, to the year of Rome 933 (A. D. 180), bear the names of LVCIVS AVRELIVS COMMODVS. Those struck from the end of the year 933, to the year 944, bear the names of MARCVS COMMODVS ANTONINVS. And sometimes MARCVS AVRELIVS COMMODVS ANTONINVS.—From that period to his death, the name AELIVS is added to the others.

It is to be observed, that this prince obtained from his father only, in succession, though at short intervals, all the dignities which constituted the sovereignty. As to the tribunitian powers of Commodus, both their series and their chronology offer difficulties which have wearied the most learned.

COMMODO. CAES. AVG. FIL. GERM. SARM.— This legend round the young head (without a crown) of Commodus, on a large brass of that emperor, shews him to us as " Cæsar, son of Augustus" (meaning Marcus Aurelius), and already distinguished by the surnames of Germanicus and Sarmaticus.

On another large brass coin we see his young head crowned with laurel, and this legend IMP. L. AVREL. COMMODVS GER. SAR. Here the title *Imperator*, which (as shewn by TR. P. II.) had just been granted to him, is put before all his names. When Commodus had been named *Augustus*, and wished to designate the number of his " victories," or his " liberalities," the same title IMP. then followed by some number, appeared only at the end of, or rather amongst, the other titles: as for example, M. COMMODVS ANT. FELIX AVG. BRIT. P. M. TR. P. XI. IMP. VII. COS. V. P. P.—See *Numismatique Romaine*.

The Latin coins of this emperor—from his boyhood to his death—are found in every form and metal ; all the gold coins and most of the brass medallions, are of fine workmanship, and very rare ; the quinarii, and the small brass, are the rarest—and there is an abundance of them that were struck in Greece and the colonies.

The following are amongst the rarest and most remarkable reverses, minted under this reign :—
GOLD MEDALLIONS.—*Rev.*—FORT. FEL. Fortune standing.—PACI AETER. Peace seated.— (These are valued by Mionnet at 1000 fr. each).
GOLD.—*Rev.*—ADVENTVS AVG. Emperor on horseback.—CONC. MIL. Emperor and four soldiers.—DE GERM. (Brought £9 15s. at the Thomas sale).—DE SARMATIS.—FID. EXERC.— HERC. COM. Emperor sacrificing to Hercules. (Thomas, £7).—HERC. ROMANO. AVG. (Thomas, £6 17s. 6d.)—HERC. ROM. COND. Commodus as Hercules, and two oxen. (Mionnet, 150 fr.)— LIBERAL(ITAS) V. Emperor and 3 other figures. (Thomas, £10 15s.)

Rev.—MIN. AVG. P. M. TR. P. XVI. COS. VI.— Minerva helmeted, with branch in right hand, and spear and shield in left, walking and looking back.—*Obv.*—M. COMM. ANT. P. FEL. AVG. BRIT. Bust of Commodus, bearded, laureated, and paludated. (Pembroke sale, £7 10s. for British Museum).
NOBILI(TAS) AVG. (Mionnet, 120 fr.)—PRINC. IVVENT. Commodus and trophy. (Thomas, £5 6s.)—PROVIDENTIAE AVG. Commodus, as Hercules, and Africa. (Thomas, £10 8s.)—SECVRITAS PVBLICA. Female seated. (Thomas, £9). SERAPIDI CONSERV. AVG.—TR. P. VIIII. Jupiter Victor seated. (Thomas, £10 15s.)—VICTORIA AVG. Victory standing.—VIRT. AETER. Mars walking.—VOT. SVSC. DEC. Emperor sacrificing.
SILVER.—CONSECRATIO. Eagle and globe. (50 fr.)—LIBERALITAS. A congiarium of four figures.—MATRI. DEVM. Cybele on a lion.
BRASS MEDALLIONS.—*Rev.*—APOL. PALATINO. Apollo and Victory. (See p. 66).—BRITTANIA. (See p. 136).—FORTVNAE REDVCI. Fortune seated. (Thomas, £8 5s.)—FIDES EXERCIT. An allocution.—HERC. COMMODIANO. Hercules sacrificing.—HERC. ROM. CONDITORI. Hercules at plough. (Thomas, £5 7s. 6d.)—HERCVLI ROMANO AVG. Bow, club, and quiver. (Brought at the Thomas sale, £13.)
[The above seven, and three or four more, having on their obverses the bearded head of Commodus, covered with the lion's skin, in imitation of that of Hercules, are valued by Mionnet at from 200 to 120 fr. each.]
IOVI IVVENI. Commodus and Jupiter. (200 fr.)—M. AVREL. ANTONINVS and the infant Commodus. (400 fr.)—MINER. VICT. Minerva Victrix near a trophy. (Thomas, only £6 12s.)— MONETA—and PIETAS. (150 fr. each).—PRO.

IMP. OMNIA FELICIA. Neptune and Emperor.— TELLVS STABIL. The earth personified.—*Obv.* Janiform bust of Commodus. (Thomas, £19 5s.) —SALVS. (150 fr.) VOTA PVBLICA. Emperor and many figures sacrificing. (150 fr.)—VOTIS. FELICIBVS. Remarkable type. (150 fr.)
[Many other brass medallions of great value, without legend of reverse].
FIRST BRASS.—*Rev.*—ANNIVS VERVS.—*Obv.* COMMODVS. (600 fr.)—APOL. MONETA. (See p. 66).—COL. L. AN. COM. &c. Priest at plough. (See p. 234).—DINA DINA *(sic.)* PIA AVGVSTA. Emperor, Serapis, and Isis.—FAVSTINA AVG. PII FEL. AVG. Head of Faustina jun. (160 fr.) FELICIA TEMPORA. Four Seasons.—TEMPORVM FELICITAS.—VOTA. SOLV. PRO. SAL. Emperor and five figures sacrificing.
SECOND BRASS.—VOTA SVSCEPTA. Temple and eight sacrificial figures.
COMOB.—See OB.
COMPITALIA.—Feasts, in cross streets and ways, celebrated the second day of January, by the Romans, in honour of their rural gods, hence called *Lares,* or *Compitalitia.* They are alluded to in the reverse type of a family denarius.—See Cæsia gens, p. 163.
CON.—*Constantinopoli.*
CONC.—CONCO.—CONCOR.—*Concordia.*
CONCORDIA.—The Goddess of Concord was an object of religious faith and worship with the Romans, because through her authority and influence " small things were rendered great.''— As Sallust expresses it, " Concordiâ parvæ res crescunt, discordiâ verò dilabuntur.''

A magnificent temple was erected to her honour at Rome, which, having been consumed by a fire, was rebuilt by the Senate and People. Tiberius added some splendid embellishments to that edifice, and consecrated it to DIVVS AVGVSTVS. There were also temples of Concord in other quarters of the city. The feast of this deity was celebrated on the 16th of January, the day when her principal temple was dedicated.

Concord was worshipped under the form of a stork, either because that bird was held sacred to Concord, or because it was accustomed to shew much agreement with, and attachment towards, its parents. On other coins she is symbolised under the figure of a dove. See CONCORDIA of Faustina jun. On a silver coin of Julia Titi, " the Concord of the Empress'' is accompanied with a peacock.

Concord's more common types (particularly the CONCORDIA AVGVSTI, or AVGVSTORVM), are those in which she is represented under the figure of a woman, either seated or standing by herself, holding in one hand a patera, or a branch, and in the other a hasta, or a cornucopiæ. Two right hands joined is a frequent symbol of Concord. These sometimes hold a caduceus, to which are now and then united two horns of plenty.—Two right hands joined, holding a winged caduceus, may be seen on coins of Antonia and other families, either denoting concord and peace between the Triumviri Reipublicæ Constituendæ, or as indicating the concord and harmony of Cæsar with the Senate.

Concord holds forth her patera over the altar, that she may be strengthened and confirmed by religious rites. On these occasions she displays a double cornucopiæ, and sometimes a star is placed near her.

CONCORDIA. S. C.—Concord stands with patera and double cornucopiæ, near a lighted altar.—See AQVILIA SEVERA, p. 71.

CONCORDIA.——The head of the goddess veiled, appears on coins of the Æmilia and Scribonia families, to shew the concord subsisting between Paulus Lepidus and Scribonius Libo; or Paulus adopts this legend and type to denote his state of good understanding with his adopted brother M. Lepidus.—See TER. PAVLVS.

CONCORDIAE. S. C.—Antoninus, holding in his left hand a figure of Concordia, and Faustina, with a sceptre in her left hand, standing on a pedestal, join their right hands; below are two smaller figures, also joining their right hands; between them an altar. First brass of Antoninus Pius. (British Museum).

This coin elegantly typifies the concord subsisting between the imperial consorts, viz. Antoninus and Faustina senior; and at the same time, by means of the smaller figures, it alludes to the matrimonial alliance which had been recently formed between M. Aurelius and their daughter, Faustina junior.—Eckhel, vii. p. 14.

CONCORDIA.—On a gold coin of Faustina junior, a Dove is typified as the symbol of Concord. On other coins of the same empress, with the same legend, in gold, silver, and first brass, the type is a woman standing, who draws her cloak closer with her right hand, and in her left holds a cornucopiæ. On others, a woman is seated, with a flower in her right hand. Gold, and first and second brass.

Eckhel (vii. 77), noting all these from the imperial cabinet, observes, that a *Dove* is a novel type of Concordia, but one appropriately adopted in allusion to that bird's nature, the idea having been long ago expressed by Horace, where he says of himself and his friend Fuscus Aristius *(Epist.* x. v. 4) :—

Fraternis animis, quidquid negat alter, et alter :
Annuimus pariter, vetuli, notique columbi.

Like twin-born brothers, are our souls allied ;
And, as a pair of fondly constant *doves,*
What one dislikes the other disapproves.
                 FRANCIS.

Ancient historians have in more than one instance alluded to the concord which existed between Faustina and her husband (Aurelius) ; though, considering the opposite nature of their

dispositions, it must have been due to the philosophy and inherent forbearance of the latter.

In the Pembroke collection was a gold coin of Crispina, bearing for its reverse legend VENVS FELIX, and for type the Empress, as Venus, seated on a throne; a winged Cupid, with bow, on her extended right hand, and a sceptre in her left : a *dove* under the throne.

[This coin, in very good preservation, and of great rarity, sold for £7 7s. See Sale Catalogue, p. 157, lot 733].

Whilst touching on the *Columbus,* or *Columba,* as a bird consecrated in mythology to Venus, we may not irrelevantly refer to p. 72, in which, as illustrative of the article ARA, a wood-cut is introduced, which had been carefully copied from a first brass of Faustina senior. The reverse type of this coin, in perfect preservation (with legend PIETAS AVG.) is a high square altar, and flame in the centre : a device sufficiently common. But there are besides, at each end, two objects, similar to each other, yet both so different in conformation from the usual horns of a Roman altar, and so decidedly *bird*-like, as to induce the compiler (in whose possession the specimen remains), to class, in his own mind, their appearance there, with the foregoing examples of *doves* delineated on coins of empresses.—His friend Mr. Goddard Johnson has another good specimen of this first brass of the same empress, and is fully impressed with the belief that the two little objects alluded to, are the figures of birds, and probably meant for *doves.*—See FAUSTINA *junior.*

CONCORDIAE AVGG. S. C.—Caracalla and Geta, both in military dress, with spears, stand joining hands. Hercules from behind crowns Caracalla, and Bacchus, Geta.—On first brass of Geta.

This coin (above engraved from a well preserved specimen in the British Museum) is admirably explained by Dion (lxxvii. § 1.) It appears that, when the dissensions of the brothers, destined to be so fatal to the interests of Rome, became matter of observation, " it was decreed by the Senate, that for their mutual concord sacrifices should be offered up to the immortal gods, and especially to CONCORDIA. But even, at that very moment, *proof* was given that all such prayers were in vain ; for the worst of omens made its appearance, at the time of sacrifice, in the shape of two wolves, which were seen to ascend the capitol. The Greek cities followed the example of Rome, in celebrating everywhere games called Φιλαδελφεια, as their coins abundantly testify. Hercules and Bacchus are presented on the above coin, as the adopted deities of Severus the father, and the national gods of Caracalla and Geta, as though they were charged with bringing about that unanimity between the brothers, which was the first object of a nation's prayers.—Eckhel, vii. 231.

CONCORDIA AVGVSTORVM. S. C.—The Emperor Alexander Severus, and the Empress Barbia Orbiana, standing, and giving each the right hand to the other. First brass of Alexander Severus, and first and second brass of Orbiana. Other coins of Orbiana, in gold and silver, exhibit Concord seated.—See ORBIANA.

The state of domestic harmony subsisting between an emperor and his *Augusta*, or rather that which their subjects were supposed to wish them, was represented, sometimes by one, sometimes by the other, of these types.

CONCORDIAE AETERNAE.——Busts of Severus and Julia Domna, side by side. On gold of Caracalla.—[This very rare coin, in fine condition, brought £6 8s. 6d. at the Trattle, and £10 10s. at the Thomas sale].

CONCORD. AVGVSTOR. TR. P. COS. II. S. C.—M. Aurelius and L. Verus standing, habited in the toga, extend the right hand to each other. First brass of Verus—also in gold, with TR. P. XV. COS. III.

CONCORDIA. AVGVST. TR. P. XV. COS. III.—Aurelius and Verus standing, togated, join their right hands. Gold, and first and second brass of M. Aurelius.

These fine coins contribute to prove what historians affirm, that on the death of his father, Aurelius immediately associated L. Verus with himself in the sovereignty, assigning to him all the honours of an emperor, excepting only the title of *Pontifex Maximus;* though, as Capitolinus expressly informs us, the Senate, after Antonine's decease, had conferred the empire upon Aurelius alone. And thus, for the first time, the Romans beheld two *Augusti* at the head of the State, invested with equal authority; and as it accidentally happened that both of them were holding the office of consul for the third time in 914 (A. D. 161), the year itself was afterwards distinguished in the public records as the *Consulate of the two Augusti.* That the *Concord,* which this coin indicates, should at the commencement of their colleagueship have existed between the two princes, is by no means surprising; but that it should have remained unimpaired till the death of Verus, a period of nine years, in spite

of the great difference of their characters, is to be ascribed to the noble disposition and well regulated mind of Aurelius, who bore with equanimity the pretensions of a rival endeavoured to screen the faults of a brother, and above all by his influence and high example imposed a wholesome restraint on his excesses.—Eckhel, vii. 48.

CONCORD. AVGG. S. C.—Concord seated. Two hands joined. Both large brass of Balbinus.

Balbinus and Pupienus (of the latter there is an exactly similar medal) were the two first emperors elected with rights absolutely equal; even the grand pontificate was equally divided between the two. It was therefore still more necessary that the two princes should, in a manner, have but one heart and spirit, and it is to this that their coins make continual allusion.

Concordia Conjugalis.—Harmony in wedded life is marked on coins of the imperial series; but generally by the "rule of contraries;" as in Julia Cornelia Paula, first wife of Elagabalus, who repudiated her before she had been married to him a twelvemonth; on this (gold) medal, the goddess is seen joining the hands of the emperor and empress, with the words CONCORDIA AETERNA!—See JULIA PAULA.

Coins of Aquilia Severa, second and quickly divorced wife of the same fickle and infamous emperor, exhibit CONCORDIA, sacrificing at an altar.—See AQUILIA SEVERA, p. 71.

And Annia Faustina, his third and equally unfortunate spouse, appears on a very rare first brass, joining hands with him, in *Concord,* to be as speedily cast off with contempt and neglect.—See FAUSTINA ANNIA.

CONCORDIA EXERCITVVM.—Two right hands joined hold a legionary eagle, fixed into the prow of a vessel. Gold and silver, and with S. C. first brass, of Nerva.

The type of this reverse alludes to the concurrence and union of the forces, both on land and at sea, during the reign of this good prince.

CONCORDIA FELIX.—Caracalla, Plautilla, and Domna, standing. Gold of Caracalla.—(Brought £11 at the Thomas sale).

CONCORDIA AVG. Two hands joined.—Silver.—See HERENNIUS ETRUSCUS, who though only Cæsar, still shares on this coin the honours of his father, Trajan Decius.

CONCORDIA AVGG.——Tranquillina and Gordianus Pius, joining hands. Silver.—Engraved in Akerman, i. 476, pl. viii. No. 4.—

[Brought £25 at the Henderson sale].—There is the same legend and type in first brass.

CONCORDIA AVGG.   Concord seated.— Silver of Tranquillina; very rare.

CONCORDIA AVGG. D.D. NN.—*Concordia Augustorum Dominorum Nostrorum.*—On coins of Licinius senior and junior, and of Constantius Chlorus, we see two figures in military dress (representing the two emperors) each with spears in the left hand, and with the right sustaining a globe, on which is a Victoriola. With the same legends we see a galeated Rome, sitting with globe and hasta, or with the right foot placed on a ship's prow—or holding a banner with the monogram of Christ, as in Honorius, Valentinian, and others of the lower empire.

Concordia Militaris.—The Concord of the armies, or of the soldiers comprising those armies, is generally symbolised by legionary eagles and joined hands, or by a female figure holding two military ensigns, accompanied either by the legends CONCORDIA EXERCITVVM, as on the preceding coin of Nerva, or by the legends CONC. MIL. or CONCORD MILIT. or CONCORDIA MILIT. or by the words at full length—CONCORDIA MILITVM. On a gold coin of Didius Julianus (so rare that it brought £27 10s 0d. at the Thomas sale), we see the above described type and legend, also on a coin of Vetranio.—See JULIANUS I. and VETRANIO, in this dictionary.

CONCORDia MILITum FELICitas ROMANORum. Hercules stands holding his club, and joining hands with a veiled figure, who holds the hasta pura.—Gold of Maximianus Hercules, engraved in Akerman, *Descr. Cat.* ii. 141, pl. 11, No. 1. (£4 16s. Thomas).

CONCordia MILitum. P. M. TR. P. XI. IMP. VII. COS. V. P. P.— On a very rare gold coin of Commodus, from which the annexed cut is engraved, the legend is accompanied by the type of the Emperor, in the *paludamentum*, standing in an elevated position between four soldiers, two of whom join hands before him. This particular device, for a military concord, is to be found in the mint of no other emperor.

CONCORDIA PROVINCIARUM.— A female standing, with a branch in her right hand, and a cornucopiæ in her left. Gold and silver of Galba. [Engraved in *Morell. Thesaur. Impp.* TOM. iii. tab. iii. No. 11.]—A remarkable coin, from which we learn, that in the first instance, at the instigation of Vindex, and subsequently, with the sanction of the Senate, the provinces, one after another, gave in their allegiance to Galba.

COND. and CONDITORI.—See HER. ROM. CONDITORI of Commodus.

CON.—CONG.—CONGIAR.—*Congiarium.*

CONGIARIUM.—A gift made to the people by the emperors, and the presentation of which is often exhibited on Roman coins, accompanied by the legend above named, generally abbreviated, but sometimes inscribed at full. The word comes from *congius* (a measure of liquids, as *modius* was a measure of solids); because originally the gifts distributed to the people consisted of oil and wine, which was measured by *congii*. The imperial presents, on the other hand, consisted of silver, of spices, of corn, as things more suitable to the occasion; but the name remained the same.—On the reverse of coins recording these largesses, as a *Congiarium datum Populo*, the emperor is usually depictured, seated on a curule chair, which is placed on a *suggestum*, or raised platform, in the midst of several figures, several of whom appear in the act of delivering, others in that of receiving, the benefaction. When the reigning prince thought proper to grant a second, or a third, &c. we read on the coin *Congiarium Secundum, Tertium*, &c. Sometimes we see, standing on the same estrade with the emperor, the personification of *Liberalitas*, under the figure of a woman, having a *tessera*, or sort of square tablet, in her right hand; and, occasionally, a cornucopiæ resting on her left arm. It is further to be observed, that the *Congiarium* was a present from the emperor to the people. His gifts to the soldiery were called, not *congiaria* but, *donativa*.—Thus it was said—Congiarium populo dedit, militibus donativum addidit.—See Kolb, *Traité Elémentaire*, vol. i. p. 248.

Nero is the first emperor whose *congiaria* are recorded on coins; and he carried the practice itself of distributing gifts to the people, or rather the populace, to the most preposterous excess. He frequently established a species of lottery, for which the *tesseræ* served as tickets, and of which the numbers entitled the bearer to gifts of from the lowest to the highest value.—(See below).—After the reign of M. Aurelius, the word *congiarium* disappears from numismatic legends, and the term *Liberalitas* is alone employed. Indeed, considering the ancient simplicity of such distributions, the original phrase no longer corresponded with the munificence which the emperors afterwards displayed.

CONGIAR. PR.   *(Congiarium Primum).*— On a first brass of Nerva, the emperor togated, sits on a raised tribunal, the base of which is marked S. C.—Before him sits another togated figure, in the attitude of making distribution. The statue of Liberality stands near, holding a tessera; whilst a togated citizen is ascending the steps of the platform.—See wood-cut above.

This coin, an interesting product of the Roman imperial brass mint is sufficiently known; but there is no mention by the ancient historians of the largess to which it refers, and but for this coin, posterity would have been entirely ignorant of such an expensive act of liberality on the part of this prudent emperor.

CONG. DAT. POP. S. C.—The Emperor sitting on a raised seat or tribune; near him a statue of Minerva, holding in her extended right hand an owl, and in her left a spear; and *Liberalitas* standing with a *tessera* in her right hand; in front of the emperor sits a togated figure, which offers something to a citizen, or to a woman, who is ascending the steps, followed by the figure of a child. First brass of Nero. Imperial Museum.

CONG. II. DAT. POP. S. C.—The Emperor on a raised seat; near him a statue of Minerva; and above him another figure standing; below a man standing and holding out a *tessera* to a citizen, who receives the gift; behind is a building supported by columns. First brass of Nero, engraved in the *Cabinet de Christine*, TAB. iv.

Antiquaries have discovered that there are three donations (*congiaria*) made by Nero, commemorated on coins. The first is mentioned by the authors above cited (i. e. Morel and Havercamp); the second is frequently seen recorded on coins; and the third is alluded to only by Vaillant, and that quite *en passant*, without any statement of the legend or type, but with the remark that it is exceedingly rare (Vaill. *Num. Præst.* i. p. 22.) There is nothing satisfactory in the statements of antiquaries respecting the dates of these largesses. Suetonius (*Nero*, c. ii.) informs us that a *congiarium* was given by Nero at the games, which he exhibited *pro æternitate imperii*, when, he says, "there were scattered among the people, as long as the games lasted, every day a thousand *missiles* of all kinds of articles. A vast store of all species of birds, tickets for corn, clothing, gold, silver, jewels, pearls, painting, slaves, beasts of burden, and even tamed wild beasts, and last of all ships, islands, and fields." These games were the same as that which was denominated the *certamen quinquennale*. See the observations made by Eckhel on the mintage of Nero, under the year U. C. 813 (A. D. 60.)—Tacitus mentions another *congiarium* in the year 810 (A. D. 57)—He says, "And a congiarium was given to the people, of four hundred sesterces (*numi*) to each man." (*Ann.* xiii. 31.) But these writers do not record the number of the *congiarium*; and the other largesses, which they say Nero bestowed, bore reference only to the pretorian guards, and not to the people; so that we have only the vaguest conjecture to rest upon in assigning to certain years the *congiaria* mentioned on coins.—"I have not (adds Eckhel) as yet been able to discover the allusion intended by the statue of Minerva; for that it is *hers*, is proved by the owl in the right hand, presented by all the coins of this subject in the Imperial Museum."—*D. N. V.* vi. 271.

[This owl does not appear in the hand of Minerva in any of the *congiaria* of Nero, engraved in either the *Morell. Thesaur. Impp.* or the *Médailles de Christine*. The figure in both plates holds a victory in right hand and spear in the left].

CONGIAR. PRIMVM. P. R. DAT.—First brass of Titus.

This coin bears testimony to the first *congiarium* given to the Roman people by the emperor above named. At his side is the image of Minerva. Below the tribunal on which Titus is seated, stands an officer, holding in his hand the *tessera*, which authorised those who received it, to go for their assignment of corn to the public granaries. A Roman citizen approaches this man in the posture of an applicant for a share of these liberalities.—Engraved in the *Cabinet des Médailles de Christine*, TAB. vi. p. 40.

CONG. II. COS. II. S. C.—Domitian, togated, sitting on an estrade, with Liberalitas standing by his side, holding tessera and cornucopiæ; and below a figure holding up the dress to receive a *congiarium*. Second brass of Domitian.—Engraved in *Morell. Impp.* vol. iii. TAB. xiv. No. 16.

The above is a remarkable coin, and of the greatest rarity. Suetonius informs us (ch. 9), that whilst still in private rank, and during the first years of his reign, Domitian displayed excessive liberality: studying with great assiduity and expense by means of congiaries and largesses, as well as by military donatives, to conciliate the Roman public, and to render them well affected towards himself.—Eckhel, vi. 370.

CONG. PR. COS. II. P. P. S. C.—The emperor togated, sits intent on the distribution of a *congiarium*; other figures attending on him. First brass of Trajan. (Vaillant, *Imp. Mus.)*—Pliny expressly records, that on his return to the city, Trajan "enriched the tribes, and gave a *congiarium* to the people." (In *Paneg.* ch. 25), the same writer adds, that "the whole surplus was given to the people, after the soldiers had received their share" (et datum totum, cùm donativi partem milites accepissent.) —The letters PR. are doubtless explained by *Primum*, as they are not separated by a stop; otherwise they might be understood to mean *Populi Romani*. It is under the year 857 (A. D. 104) that we see the second *congiarium* (CONGIAR. SECVND.) of Trajan.—See *D. N. V.* vi. 413.

CONGIARIVM TERTIVM. S. C.—First brass of Trajan. The emperor, as on the preceding coin, is seated on a suggestum, super-intending one of the largesses to the people. The grouping and workmanship of this reverse render it one of the finest among the congiaria; and what claims remark, as something extraordinary in the type, is a high and singularly formed tripod placed near the emperor, instead, as on similar coins of Nero and Domitian, of the figure of Minerva with an owl. " Whether (says Haver· camp in his notes *sur les Médailles de Christine*) this refers to the place where the congiarium was given, as if one largess was distributed before the temple of Minerva, and another before the temple of Apollo; or whether some other mystery is concealed under these respective symbols,— *Lector judicet.*" The tripod may certainly be held to denote some sacerdotal office.—Eckhel (vi. 426) is unable to decide when this third congiary was bestowed by Trajan on the people.

From his own cabinet of large brass, Capt. Smyth quotes a *Consul quintum, Congiarium Secundum* of Trajan, with exactly the same type as the foregoing.—*Desc. Cat.* p. 81.

Mr. Roach Smith thinks it probable, that these distributions took place, for the most part, in or near the temple of Minerva, as the goddess of *justice* and fair dealing—an opinion with which our own coincides.

CONG. AVG. III. TR. POT. XX. IMP. III. COS. III.

CONG. AVG. IIII. TR. P. XXI. IMP. IIII. COS. III.

Two togated figures sitting together on an estrade, the impersonation of Liberality with *tessera* and cornucopiæ, standing before them; a male figure is ascending the stairs, spreading his garment for the reception of the imperial bounty.

The reverse types, on the two large brass coins of which the foregoing are the respective legends, represent two different congiaries given by M. Aurelius and L. Verus; being (says Havercamp) the third and fourth of this kind of presentations which the above-named princes jointly made to the Roman people; and they were distributed during the 20th and 21st years of their Tribunitian power, as is marked on the coins in question. The only difference in their types is that on the former the prefect, or commander, of the pretorian guard, stands behind the two emperors.—Engraved in the *Cabinet de Christine*, TAB. xviii. *Médailles de M. Aurelius.*

" These liberalities (says Eckhel, vii. 53) were the more acceptable and pleasing to the people, because about this time, they were afflicted with a grievous famine, as Capitolinus relates. The *congiaria* were therefore distributed at Rome, in the presence of the two emperors.

CONOB.—See OB.

CONS. S. *Conservatori suo.*—CAES. AVG. CONS. S. on a coin of Augustus.

CONS.—*Conservatrici;* on coins of Salonina. See Dianæ, Junoni, &c. For whilst Gallienus invoked the greater male deities, as *Conservatores,* his wife also invoked the principal goddesses, in that turbulent state of human affairs, in which she and her husband lived.—See Ant. Augustino, *Dialog.* p. 163.

CONS.—*Constantinopolis.*

CONSECRATION.—The custom in ancient times of paying divine honours to individuals, who had acquired renown from various circumstances, was of frequent occurrence amongst the Greeks, by whom it was called Aποθέωσις. It was their favourite superstition to include in the number of their gods, men whom they regarded as heroes, and as the founders of colonies and cities. Afterwards the name of *God* was assumed by living princes on coins and other monuments. This, however, is not the place even to touch upon the origin of this observance, or the ceremonies used on such occasions by various nations of antiquity. Information respecting these and other branches of the subject may be gathered from various treatises both by the old writers and in works of modern date. The object of the following notice is limited to the customs of the Romans, who during many years had contented themselves with rendering to Romulus alone the honours of the apotheosis, and who did not begin to imitate the Greeks, in this respect, until the extinction of the free republic. It was from the period of the Cæsars, whom universal flattery and their own ambition raised above the condition of mortality, that the practice was introduced and continued as long as Rome was governed by princes attached to paganism, and even by the first succession of so-called Christian Emperors.

Eckhel divides his masterly observations relative to this subject into two parts, the *first* of which treats of the consecration of individuals during their life-time; and the *second* of the consecration of the dead.

I.—CONSECRATION OF THE LIVING.

Ancient history records the names of many, who, either of their own accord aspired to divine honours, or on whom popular consent, actuated by motives of flattery or fear, conferred such distinction, even when there was no expectation of their death. This consecration of the living had its gradations, so to speak; but, to pass over that lowest grade which was confined to oral demonstrations and the impulse of enthusiasm, and of which numismatics furnish no examples—there is a middle rank, in which may be enumerated, the names, attributes, and marks, commonly appropriated by heathen votaries to their deities; but which sovereign princes assumed, or allowed to be conferred upon them, without, as they professed to think, irreverence to·· wards the gods, but so as to make it appear that they participated in certain of their qualities, which were denied to private individuals. Among the appellations, that of *Numen,* is the first to be observed, not only as a mark .of heavenly power, but one which was on all occasions permitted continuously to be given to the sovereign princes as well of the lower as of the earlier empire, much like that of *sacred majesty* to kings of the present day.

In the number of the divine *attributes* which the emperors borrowed from the gods, ÆTERNI-TAS claims the first place. For some of the most remarkable types, by which the Romans represented Eternity, the reader is referred to pp. 22, 23, 24, and 25 of this work; particularly those of coins struck under Trajan, during his fifth consulate, 856 (A. D. 103); and under Severus, of the year U. C. 955 (A. D. 202).

The GENIVS AVGVSTI, so frequent on imperial coins, was also a species of divinity, whether it be understood as the soul of the emperor, and his divine spirit, or some celestial being of an inferior order, such as in their superstition the ancients believed to have been attached to every mortal.—See the word GENIUS.

Other less direct indications of assumed divinity, on coins of the *Augusti*, were the *radiated crown*, an explanation of which will be found under the coinage of Nero, bearing the legend of AVGVSTVS GERMANICVS. (See p. 109). There is also the bright cloudy circlet on the heads of both emperors and empresses, found on coins of the lower empire. See *Nimbus.*— Likewise the chariot drawn by two mules. See coins of *Livia*.

The *highest* degree of Consecration during life is placed, by Eckhel (vi. p. 11), partly in divine appellations, partly in divine honours, which latter consist in solemn games, altars, temples, and sacrifices, all of which were conferred either at the instance of the emperors themselves, or were decreed to them in adulation, by their subjects. Examples of the custom were set, not only in the most remote period of Greece, but also in epochas of more recent date, such as the instance of Alexander the Great, styled at his own desire Jupiter Ammon. —Habituated to pay such honours to foreign princes, it was an easy matter for the Greeks, familiar with acts of servility, to transfer the same honours to the magistrates set over them by the Romans, and then to the emperors, who were the arbiters of the world. Even during the government of the republic, sacred and annual games, altars, temples, and the titles of divinity, were dedicated to pro-consuls, pro-pretors, and other individuals of high station, either in recompense of signal benefits conferred by them, or from motives of fear. In after times these honours were bestowed still more profusely upon the emperors and their families. It may suffice here to adduce the following few instances of divine appellations, invented by the fertile imagination, and prompted by the base sycophancy, of the Greeks ; on whose coins Livia, the wife of Augustus, is styled ΘΕΑ. ΛΙΒΙΑ, ΛΙΒΙΑΝ. ΗΡΑΝ. *(Liviam Junonem) ;* the daughter of Augustus, ΙΟΤΛΙΑΝ. ΑΦΡΟΔΙ-ΤΗΝ *(Juliam Venerem) ;* Drusus, the son of Tiberius, and Germanicus Cæsar, were called by the Greeks ΝΕΟΙ. ΘΕΟΙ. ΦΙΛΑΔΕΛΦΟΙ *(novi dei, fratres se mutuò amantes).*

The actual mint of Rome admitted these deifications of her living princes more sparingly, and at a much later period. For example, although it be well known that Caligula and Domitian desired to be called *gods,* yet the dignity of the *Moneta Romana* kept this disgrace at a distance. Nero was, on coins with *Greek* legends, styled Apollo ; yet this name of Apollo is not to be found on those very coins, struck at Rome, on which that emperor is represented in the garb of a harp-player (*citharoedus*). Commodus was the first who blazoned his impudence on the coinage of the city, when he vaunted himself as the *Roman Hercules,* indicated by the head covered with the lion's skin.—Not less memorable was the arrogance of Aurelian, who inscribed himself on his coins *deus, ac dominus noster ;* an example followed by Carus.

It was but consistent in the ancients to honour with altars, shrines, sacrifices, and every other superstitious device, the individual whom they declared to be a god. The commencement of this mania was, indeed, identical with that of the empire itself. This fact is attested by the well-known coins inscribed ROM*ae* ET AVG*usto,* minted throughout the various provinces, with the type of an altar or a temple; also the altar dedicated to Augustus, on coins of Tarraco. It is however to be observed, that no altar, or temple, was consecrated to Augustus, in Rome itself, during his life-time ; nor indeed to Cæsar, the Dictator, although the people overwhelmed him with honours almost divine. Some of his successors, however, were not so forbearing.—Suetonius informs us, that Caligula wished to be styled *Optimus Maximus,* the title of Jupiter ; and that he exhibited himself in the temple of Castor and Pollux, between the statues of those deities, to share the adoration of the worshippers. The same writer adds that " he (Caligula) erected a temple devoted to his own divinity, and instituted priests and elaborate sacrificial ceremonies. In the temple there stood a gold statue in his likeness, dressed in the fashion he was accustomed to adopt.— The wealthiest individuals eagerly canvassed, and outbid each other, for their turn in the higher offices of this priesthood ! The victims were parrots, peacocks, bustards, turkies, guinea fowls, pheasants, &c. The several species of which were sacrificed every day."—Domitian also desired to be styled *dominus et deus ;* and according to Pliny the orator, " the vile image of that most cruel prince was worshipped with as profuse an effusion of the blood of beasts, as he himself used to shed of man's." But these displays of impious presumption (with the exception of Commodus in the character of Hercules, and the *gods* Aurelianus and Carus), never disgraced the Roman coinage ; doubtless because, to the very perpetrators themselves, it appeared matter of reproach, that honours above the mortal condition, whether sought for or decreed to them, should be exhibited throughout the empire.

Seneca, in his satire on the death of Claudius, and Lucian, in his treatise on the assembly of the gods, both laugh (says Spanheim) pleasantly enough, at these pretended deifications, and at the *heap* of new gods to which this absurd custom gave rise.—Plutarch likewise, in the life of

Romulus, judiciously censures this practice.—
As to Augustus and other emperors (adds the
translator and annotator of *Julian's Cæsars*,
p. 275), it is well known, that policy and an
interested regard, not for the dead but, for the
living prince, or his destined successor, had most
to do with this multiplication of divinities.

II.—CONSECRATION OF THE DEAD.

It was at a comparatively late period, that
the mania for tranforming men into deities dishonoured the annals of Rome. In his peculiar
position as the founder of the nation, Romulus
had indeed been *apotheosised* under the name of
Quirinus. But neither L. Brutus, nor Camillus, nor the Scipios, though eminent benefactors
of their country, were distinguished with divine
honours. This contempt for the laws of mortality was reserved for the last days of the commonwealth and the beginning of the empire.

Cæsar the Dictator was the first, on whom the
suffrages of the people conferred both the title
and the honours of divinity. Dazzled no doubt
by the prodigies of his valour and the acquirements of his lofty intellect, and already won
by the attractions of the newly-risen superstition, they readily surrendered themselves to the
belief that in such a man a soul of more than
mortal nature had fixed its abode. The Senate
had already decreed to him during his life-time,
the *thensa*, the *ferculum*, a *pulvinar*, a *flamen*,
and *luperci;* all of them honours exclusively
attached to the ceremonial worship of a god.—
But after his death, during the shews which
Augustus gave in celebration of his memory,
there appeared a *comet*, which the people looked
upon as a sign that Cæsar had been admitted
into heaven. Augustus gave him the name of
Divus, and caused divine honours to be assigned
to him.

With this precedent before their eyes, the Romans found no difficulty in unanimously according the honours of consecration to Augustus, under whom they experienced not only a lengthened
reign, but one marked with moderation and
equity. And indeed, if in this rite of consecration regard had always been had to a real,
not a counterfeited, gratitude for services conferred on mankind, the institution might at least
have been productive of one beneficial result,
namely that of inducing princes to act virtu-
ously, by the prospect of such exaltation. " It

is the act of a god," says Pliny the elder, "when
one mortal *helps* or *does good* to another, and
this is the high road to immortal fame. By it
have passed the great ones of Rome; and by it
now, with heavenly tread, walks the greatest
sovereign of any age, Vespasian Augustus, advancing to the rescue of a tottering state. It is
the most ancient mode of recompensing a benefactor, to enrol his name among the deities."

The succeeding age, however, produced judges
unfairly biassed in their bestowal of such honours. Pliny the younger asserted, that "Tiberius promoted Augustus to heaven. Nero did
the same for Claudius, but merely to ridicule
him; Titus to Vespasian, and Domitian to Titus;
but the former that he might be regarded as the
son, the latter as the brother, of a god."—
What would have been Pliny's indignation had
he lived to see Faustina junior, Commodus, and
Caracalla thus raised to the skies? Pausanias,
after remarking that in former times men were
numbered among the gods on reasonable grounds,
as Hercules, the Dioscuri, &c. adds, that in his
own age, when fraud and audacity usurped the
place of worthy deeds, none were received into
the celestial ranks, but through the acclamations
and outrageous flattery of their fellow men.—
Pliny the elder lashes the absurdity of his contemporaries, "for paying adoration to the *manes*,
and making a god of one, who had ceased to be
even a man." Juvenal too, appropriately calls
the emperors "rivals of the gods," on account
of this same system of apotheosis.

The consecration of a deceased emperor was
usually urged by his successor, from motives
either of piety and gratitude, or of ambition, or
some other anticipated advantage. Thus piety
and gratitude may naturally be supposed to be
the feelings which induced Titus to transfer Vespasian to Olympus; which prompted Trajan to
pay the same honours to Nerva; Hadrian to
Trajan; Antoninus to Hadrian; M. Aurelius to
L. Verus; each, indeed, in the case of his own
father or brother. Different motives produced
the same result in different cases; as for instance, the wish to have a deity for a father or
a near relation, or to avoid the suspicion of foul
play, in the death of an individual, was the
reason for Domitian's deification of Titus. The
consecration of Commodus, whose real deserts
entitled him to the same quarter with Sysiphus
and Tantalus, took place under unwonted circumstances. Condemned to everlasting infamy
by the Senate, he was placed amongst the immortal gods by Sept. Severus; whose probable
reasons for so doing are attempted to be explained under the head of DIVVS COMMODVS.

If any during their life time had incurred
public hatred, like Tiberius, Caligula, and Domitian, they were left to pass an obscure existence amongst the *manes*. Others, as Caracalla,
were indebted to their popularity with the army.

There are instances of emperors to whom the
honours of divinity were accorded, not immediately after death but, at a subsequent period.
Accordingly, Livia was at length consecrated by
Claudius, Commodus by Severus, Domna by

Elagabalus. But it is remarkable, that the piety of some of the Augusti induced them to thrust into heaven their parents, though in a private station, and deceased before they were themselves elevated to the throne. Thus did Vespasian in the case of his mother Domitilla, and Trajan in that of his father Trajan; and the honour thus conferred they exhibited on their coins; nay, Vespasian, not content with this, bestowed on his mother the title of Augusta.

Eckhel has collected from coins the following names of persons consecrated after the Roman custom :—

Julius Cæsar.
Augustus.
Julia, wife of Augustus.
Claudius.
Poppæa, wife of Nero.
Claudia, daughter of Nero.
Vespasian.
Domitilla, wife of Vespasian.
Titus.
Julia, daughter of Titus.
Cæsar (anonymous), son of Domitian.
Nerva.
Trajan, the father.
Trajan, the emperor.
Plotina, wife of Trajan.
Marciana, sister of Trajan.
Matidia, grand daughter of Trajan.
Hadrian.
Sabina, wife of Hadrian.
Antoninus Pius.
Faustina, wife of Antoninus Pius.
M. Aurelius.
Faustina, wife of M. Aurelius.
L. Verus.
Commodus.
Pertinax.
Severus.
Julia Domna, wife of Severus.
Caracalla.
Julia Mæsa.
Alexander Severus.
Paulina, wife of Maximinus I.
Mariniana, wife of Valerian.
Gallienus (identity uncertain).
Saloninus.
Victorinus.
Tetricus (probably).
Claudius Gothicus.
Carus.
Numerianus.
Nigrinianus.
Maximianus Herculeus.
Constantius Chlorus.
Gal. Maximianus.
Romulus, son of Maxentius.
Constantine the Great.

Some particulars respecting the rites and ceremonies observed in the consecration of princes, as illustrating the types of coins, are given under the head of *Funeral Pile*, p. 251.

That the apotheosis of emperors was sanctioned by the authority of the Senate, and usually decreed by that body, is testified by ancient writers, as well as by coins and other monuments. Tertullian says—" It was an old established custom, that no emperor should be deified without the concurrence of the Senate"—a statement repeated by Orosius, and confirmed by Prudentius.

The Senate long opposed the petition of Antoninus Pius that they would decree the honours of consecration on his father by adoption, Hadrian. M. Aurelius earnestly besought the same distinction from the Senate for his wife Faustina. The fact is also clearly proved by the coins of Claudius and Vespasian, both gold and silver, bearing the type of consecration, and on which we read EX S. C. and more fully on a coin of Marciana, EX SENATVS CONSVLTO.— Nor does the rule appear at all disproved by the fact, that sometimes the emperors or the soldiers forcibly extorted a consecration from the Senate.—See MACRINUS and GORDIANUS PIUS.

Coins relating to Consecration.—These had their peculiar legends and types. By the expression, coins of consecration, however, are to be understood, only those which were struck on the occasion of the ceremony, and for the purpose of publishing it to the world; and such as exhibit, on the reverse, types which invariably represent this rite, and the soul received into heaven. For there are not a few coins, whose obverse, indeed, gives the title DIVVS to the emperor, but whose reverse offers nothing at all connected with consecration. Of this kind, for instance, is a coin of Divus Augustus, on the reverse of which we read SIGNIS RECEPTIS; and so, on the reverse of coins of Divus Vespasianus, CERES AVGVST.—VICTORIA AVGVSTI —to which may be added coins of Domitilla, the Faustinæ, &c. the execution of which was dictated by affection, to preserve the memory of ancestors, parents, and wives.

In bringing forward first the inscriptions, and then the types, of the coins which are properly to be connected with the subject of consecration, Eckhel (vol. vi.) observes that, "in the times of the first emperors, consecration was indicated more by types, than by verbal formulæ. The word CONSECRATIO (which an Alexandrine coin of Carus renders Αφιερωσις), was introduced at a later period. I do not find it (says he), inserted on any genuine coins before Plotina, Marciana, and Matidia. In after times, nothing was more common than the use of this word."

For some observations on DIVVS and DEVS as titles of consecration, and also with regard to the legend MEMORIAE, see those words, *suis locis*.

Consecration Types.——The various legends having thus been enumerated, the next subject for inquiry is into the types usually employed to indicate a Consecration.

The obverse exhibits the portrait of the person to whom the honour was decreed, but is variable in the style of the head-dress. On his coins Julius Cæsar appears with a *star* over his head, which denoted a comet, popularly believed to have been the soul of Cæsar after his reception into heaven. This type, therefore, as being peculiar to him alone, did not occur in the case of his successors. The *radiated head* of Augustus is a sure sign of consecration; for before Nero, no prince adopted the radiated crown during his life-time. On those coins, in which Trebonianus or some other emperor immediately preceding him, restored a consecration (i. e. *decreed divine honours which had been neglected before*), we always find a radiated head. Vespasian, Titus, Nerva, and Antoninus Pius, have the *laureated head* after their consecration, though they also exhibit the radiated crown.—— The *bare head* (caput nudum) was introduced by Nerva, and this fashion prevailed long afterwards. Divus Saloninus appears on most of his coins with a *radiated head*. Divus Claudius Gothicus exhibits sometimes the laurel crown, sometimes the radii; and he is, moreover, the first on whose coins the *veiled head* occurs, which afterwards appears in Constantius Chlorus, and Gal. Maximianus, though both these emperors have occasionally the *bare* or the *laureated* head. The head also of Divus Constantinus Magnus is *veiled*, and frequently *laureated*, on the same coin. The veil was generally regarded as a religious dress; the pontiffs were veiled when engaged in sacred functions; so were the augurs, and the vestals; and artists frequently represented the souls of men with veils, as when they were escorted by Mercury. In the case of consecrated Empresses, there is often no peculiar attire to distinguish them, as for instance, in those of Domitilla, Julia the daughter of Titus, Plotina, Marciana, Matidia, Sabina, and Faustina senior. But Sabina, and both the Faustinæ, not unfrequently added the veil to their ordinary head-dress. Afterwards, Mæsa and Mariniana used the veil. Diva Julia, the wife of Augustus, has a head crowned with ears of corn, after the manner of Ceres.

The reverse presents various types, as will be seen by the following list, from which, be it observed, are excluded those which are in reality unconnected with, and indeed irrelevant to, the subject of *consecration*.

1. *The Eagle* is common on coins of the early consecrated emperors and empresses; such as those of Plotina, Marciana, Matidia, Hadrianus, Sabina, M. Aurelius, L. Verus. (See preceding cut.) The reason for the introduction of this bird is, that in the ceremonies attending consecration, a funeral pile was lighted, and an *eagle* let loose from its summit, as if to bear the soul to heaven. This eagle is the more frequent

type of the consecrations *restored* (restitutæ) in the time of Trebonianus Gallus.

An Eagle, bearing aloft the soul of an Empress, appears on coins of Sabina, both the Faustinæ, and Julia Mæsa. On the celebrated base of the column of Antoninus Pius, on which is represented that emperor, and his wife Faustina, carried aloft by a winged Genius, an eagle accompanies both Antonine and Faustina.—— According to Artemidorus, "It is an ancient practice, to represent deceased princes as borne on high upon the wings of eagles."

2. *A Peacock*, on the coins of Empresses only; as for example, both the Faustinæ, Julia Domna, and Mariniana. In these are clearly to be recognised new rivals of Juno; the peacock being the bird of Juno, as the eagle was that of Jupiter.—See *Pavo*.

A Peacock, carrying aloft the soul of an Empress.—See MARINIANA.

3. *A Victory, bearing aloft the soul of an Empress*, appears on coins of both the Faustinæ. —see the AETERNITAS type of consecration engraved in p. 24 of this dictionary.

4. *A Funeral Pile* (Rogus).—From the time of Antoninus Pius this is the common type of consecration, on the coins of both emperors and empresses.—See next page.

5. *An Altar* is not an unfrequent type, and it is chiefly observable on coins recording the consecrations, awarded probably at the instance of Trebonianus. At any rate it is self-evident that the altar is that of a consecrated prince.

6. *A Chariot, drawn by two or four elephants.* This also is no unfrequent type. See the coins of Augustus, Vespasian, Julia the wife of Titus, Antoninus Pius, M. Aurelius, L. Verus, and Pertinax, and the explanation of the type there given.—See *Thensa*.

A Chariot and four horses.—Vespasian.

A Chariot (carpentum) *drawn by two or three female mules*, on coins of Julia, wife of Titus, a sacred type, and one not unfrequent on the coins of women. Examples of these appear on coins of Livia, Agrippina sen. and Domitilla—for the latter see p. 185.

7. *A Phœnix*, the symbol of Eternity. p. 22.

8. *A Lectisternium to Juno*, on coins of Faustina junior, now, as it were, another Juno.

9. *A Temple*, on coins of Divus Augustus, and Romulus Cæsar. Nevertheless, temples were privately erected in honour of illustrious persons, who had not been consecrated, as exemplified on coins of Domitianus Aug.

Other types of inferior note are passed over. —Those used by princes calling themselves Christians, at *their* consecration, may be learned from coins of Constantine the Great and his family.

The coins hitherto treated of are those which were struck soon after the consecration of the princes or princesses, whose portraits they bear, and for the purpose of giving publicity to the event. But there is another class of coins, which on the obverse present the effigy of some emperor; and on the reverse the legend CONSECRATIO, with the type of an eagle, on a lighted altar.—For a list of these, with observations thereupon, see the words DIVO and DIVUS.

With regard to the remaining subject of inquiry—namely, how long the custom of consecrating emperors prevailed amongst the Romans, Eckhel says—"So long as the worship of the gods was in force, it is by no means surprising that this absurd system should have continued. But it is extraordinary that Christian princes should have followed the example of the heathen. Besides Constantine the Great, Eutropius has told us that his son Constantius, and Jovianus, were deified; and that the same honour was paid to Valentinian by his son Gratian is recorded by Ausonius in these words: 'The most abundant testimony of his merit, is his father connected with divine honours.' Meanwhile, it cannot be doubted, that in these latter consecrations, the ceremonial differed greatly from that of former days, and was such as could easily [?] be blended with the Christian rites. For the ceremonies observed by the Christians at the funeral of Constantine the Great, were quite compatible with the regulations of the Christian religion [?] See a description of them by Eusebius. Nor is a different light thrown on the subject by the coins, which were dedicated to his honour after death. But they were the last which were struck in memory of a deceased emperor."

[On the two points against which a note of interrogation has been placed, the compiler of this dictionary is not disposed to acquiesce in the conclusion drawn by the transcendent author of *Doctrina*.——However the old ecclesiastical writers may *describe* the ceremonies which actually took place, the legends and types on the consecration coins of Constantine and his successors are far too clearly those of unmitigated paganism, to be "*easily*" blended" with any correct ideas of pure and scriptural Christianity.]

CONSECRATIO.—On the reverse of a first brass struck in honour of M. Aurelius, after his death, A.D. 180, the type is a funeral pile of four stories, the basement ornamented with festoons; the upper tiers adorned with statues, and at the summit an imperial quadriga. On the obverse the head of that emperor is represented under the features of an old man, with this legend,—DIVVS *Marcus* ANTONINVS PIVS.

The *Rogus*, or Funeral Pile, is described by Dion, as "a structure in the form of a turret, with three stories, of ivory and gold, and ornamented with statues." Herodian describes it as a mass of quadrangular shape, filled at the bot-

tom with combustibles, on which again a second tier was placed of similar form and appearance, but narrower and furnished with openings; to this a third and a fourth were added, each gradually diminishing in size, till the whole resembled a watch-tower."—The ceremony of consecration was very solemn and imposing. After the body had been clothed in the habiliments of death, it was placed on a bed of ivory; young men, chosen from the equestrian order, bore it on their shoulders to the pile. The corpse being then introduced into the second layer or story, it was surrounded with aromatics and precious balms. The usual ceremonies being completed, a torch was applied, and the mass was consumed. After this apotheosis, the deceased emperor or empress had temples, altars, and priests dedicated to his or her honour, and the same worship was paid to the defunct, as paganism rendered to its gods and goddesses; whilst the Augusti, or Augustæ, were thenceforth called DIVI and DIVAE. The form of the *rogus*, described as above by ancient writers, is brought to our view, with remarkable clearness, on numerous coins. "Amongst these," adds Eckhel, "there is one which I am told, stands conspicuous. This is a Julia Mæsa, discovered at Rome; respecting which its then possessor, Viscount Ennius, a renowned antiquary, wrote to Garampi, papal nuncio at Vienna, that it is so well executed, and in such high preservation, that in the second layer of the funeral pile, the corpse of the empress is seen recumbent on a bed; a minute particular, never before distinguished in the monetal representation of these funeral structures."

CONSECRATIO. S. C.—There are two other large brass consecrations, struck by authority of the Senate, in memory of Marcus Aurelius (DIVVS), which exhibit further examples of the types that represent the deification of this prince, and bear reference to its various ceremonies—namely: 1. An eagle, as if about to take flight from the top of an altar decorated with a festoon of ribbands.—2. A car, conveying the defunct emperor's statue, drawn by four elephants, each mounted by its driver—a device which serves to represent those preliminary displays of funeral pomp, in which the new emperor, or the surviving husband of an empress, made an ostentatious exhibition of costly magnificence.

CONSECRATIO.—The emperor seated on an eagle, holds a sceptre. Below, in a recumbent posture, is a female figure, personifying the Earth. This elegant, remarkable, and very rare type, appears on a brass medallion of Antoninus Pius, edited by Venuti, from the *Mus. Albani*, I. 26, i.—See an engraving of it p. 248.

CONSECRATIO.—An eagle, with expanded wings, standing on a globe, which is ornamented with stars.

This very finely executed large brass coin, of which the above described forms the legend and type of reverse, was struck to celebrate the consecration of Lucius Verus, associate in the empire with Marcus Aurelius, whose own benignity of disposition was so great (says the historian Capitolinus), that he always concealed and excused, so far as he was able, the vices of Verus, although they extremely displeased him; and that he caused him, after death, to be called *Divus*, and to be honoured with all the marks of worship usually decreed to consecrated emperors. See an engraving of this inserted in p. 249.

CONSECRATIO. S. C.—Eagle on a globe.—*Obv.*—DIVO. ANTONINO. MAGNO.—Bare head of Caracalla. On silver and large brass.

"These coins (observes the author of *Leçons de Numismatique Romaine*) may well excite astonishment. What! (he exclaims) were the honours of consecration and the title of "Great" conferred upon a monster, abhorred by all honest and good men? But it must be borne in mind, that his death was regretted by the soldiers; and to make friends of *them*, the Senate and Macrinus both stooped to this base flattery. Caracalla had foolishly presumed to compare himself with Alexander the Great."

CONSECRATIO.—Empress in a quadriga, a female guides the horses at full speed.—*Obv.*—DIVA AVGVSTA FAVSTINA.—For an engraving of this beautiful and rare gold coin, see *Faustina senior*.

CONSECRATIO.—Eagle standing with expanded wings, on a sceptre. Gold and first brass of Marciana. The former engraved in Akerman, i. 226, pl. vi. No. 1.

CONSECRATIO.—Eagle with expanded wings. Silver.—See Matidia.

CONSECRATIO. S. C.—A carpentum drawn by two mules; and the same legend, with the statue of the empress on a thensa drawn by two elephants—both first brass of Marciana; engraved in Havercamp, cabinet of Christina.

CONSECRATIO.—Hadrian holding a sceptre, borne by an eagle in full flight. Gold.—Engraved in Akerman, i. p. 231, pl. vi. No. 3.

CONSECRATIO.—Sabina on an eagle.—First brass. Engraved in p. 250.

CONSECRATIO. S. C.—Ceres seated on a modius, near a lighted altar, with patera and torch. First brass of Faustina senior.

CONSECRATIO, S. C.—Funeral pile. First brass of Pertinax.—Engraved in Mionnet, i. 269.

CONSECRATIO.—Empress on a peacock.—Silver.—See Mariniana.

CONSECRATIO.—Do. Silver. See Paulina.

CONSECRATIO.——Eagle with expanded wings. Small brass.—See Nigrinianus.

CONSESVS (*sic.*) EXERCIT.——Two military figures, joining right hands with each other, and holding in their left a legionary eagle. Gold and silver of Vespasian.—This very rare coin refers to the unanimity (*consesus* being a blunder of the moneyer for *consensus*) of the Roman armies of Judæa, Syria, and Egypt, in raising Vespasian to the empire. There is a similar legend in the mint of Vitellius, viz.:

CONSENSVS EXERCITVVM.—Mars helmeted, and marching, bears in his right hand a spear, and in his left a military ensign, or *labarum*, or trophy, resting on his shoulders.—Gold, silver, and second brass of Vitellius.

These coins, says Vaillant, were struck by Vitellius, before the death of Otho. They exhibit Mars, as *gradivus*, that is, in his attributed capacity of a warrior, to drive away the foe. This deity Vitellius invoked by a favourable omen, when some one brought to him the sword of Julius Cæsar, taken from the temple of Mars, according to Tacitus, after he had, by the consent and agreement of both armies of Germany, been elected emperor.

CONSENSV. SENAT*us* ET EQ*uestris* OR. DIN*is* *Populi* Q*ue* *Romani*. Statue of Augustus seated, holding in the right hand a branch, and a globe, or patera, in the left. On the obverse of this second brass coin is DIVVS AVGVSTVS, S. C. Bare head of the emperor.

Augustus during his life-time had, in the provinces, already been admitted to the rank of the gods; and this coin represents the statue which was decreed to him as *Divus Augustus*, by the unanimous votes of all the orders of the state. Many of these statues, Dion informs us, were erected in his honour after his decease. Such is the subject of the coin here described, respecting which Eckhel (vi. 126), observes, the three orders, into which the Romans were divided, are here inscribed according to their scale of rank, viz. Senate, Knights, and People. —Pliny has given the order differently (xxxiii. § 8)—From that period (i. e. the consulate of Cicero), this (i. e. the *equites*), was distinctly made a third body in the republic, and the *Equestrian Order* began to be added to the Senate and to the Roman People. Whence it arises, that even now-a-days it is inscribed *after* the People, as having been the most recently added." In the writings of the poets, this order of dignity has been either inverted or otherwise disturbed by the requirements of the metre, as for example in Martial (L. viii. Ep. 15):—

Dat populus, dat *gratus eques*, dat thura Senatus.

[The people, the grateful knights, the Senate, all give frankincense].—Also in Ovid, *Fasti*, ii. 123.

CONSER. CONSERV. *Conservator* or *Conservatrix*. *Conservatori* or *Conservatrici*.

CONSERVATOR. Preserver, Protector, or

Defender. This term frequently occurs on Roman coins; and has reference, in the first place, to those deities whom the emperors honoured as their favourite tutelaries, in professed acknowledgment either of their general protection, or of some particular favours. (Jobert, i. 231).

The attributes of a CONSERVATOR are annexed on coins, to the names of Jupiter, Apollo (or Sol), Neptune, Mars, Hercules, and also of Bacchus, under the appellation of *Liber Pater*.

In the next place, it refers to the Emperors themselves, some of whom were so called on their coins; as in the CONSERVATOR PIET*atis* of Gallienus. The emperor standing with spear in left hand, holds his right extended above the head of a kneeling figure. Also CONSERV*ator* SAL*utis*, PATRIAE, VRBIS SVAE *(Romæ)*, AFRICAE, KART*haginis*, EXERCITVVM, and MILITVM.

CONSERVATOR AVG.—A quadriga, conveying a conical-shaped stone, together with an eagle, spreading its wings. In the field a star. Gold of Elagabalus.

The stone fashioned in a cone-like form represents the Syrian deity whose worship Elagabalus introduced into Rome. See this remarkable reverse, engraved and annotated in Akerman, vol. i. 414, pl. vii. No. 7.—See also SANCT. DEO SOLI ELAGABAL. bearing allusion to the same object of that emperor's oriental idolatry.

CONSERVAT. AVGG.——A naked Apollo, standing with a branch in the right hand, and the left resting on a lyre. Diana stands beside him, in a dress closely girded, drawing an arrow from a quiver with her right hand, and holding a bow in her left. Silver of Valerianus.

Coins exhibiting Apollo *alone*, with this inscription, are well known, but till this instance, none have been discovered which associate with him his sister Diana. For the reason why both those deities were worshipped, especially during the period from the reign of Trebonianus Gallus to that of Valerianus, see *Apollo*, p. 65 et seq. of this dictionary. Khell, who, in his supplement to Vaillant (p. 175), has given an *engraving* of this elegant and extremely rare denarius, alludes to the plague which raged throughout the empire, from A.D. 251 to A.D. 260, both years inclusive; and pertinently remarks, in reference to this coin, that just as the sad bereavement of Niobe, so also any grievous pestilence was attributed by the superstition of those times to the wrath of both Apollo and Diana.

CONSERVATOR AFRICAE SVAE.——A woman standing, her head covered with an elephant's proboscis, at her feet a lion and a bull lying down. Second brass (Imperial Museum). Maximian Hercules.

An almost similar type appears on coins of Diocletian and Maximian, inscribed FELIX ADVENT AVGG. NN. The latter emperor defeated the Quinquegentiani in Africa, A.D. 297; and hence his popularity with the Africans and Carthaginians, which he now endeavoured to revive, in order to strengthen his hold on the empire.

The same reverse occurs on coins of Maxentius, and also on Constantine's.

CONSERVATORES KART. SVAE.——A temple of six columns, in which a woman stands, with a branch in each hand. Second brass of Maximian Hercules.

The same remarks apply to this as to the preceding coin. A like reverse is frequent on the coins of Maxentius and Constantine.

CONSERV. or CONSERVATORES VRB*is* SVAE.—A temple of six columns, in which is seated Rome, galeated, with a globe in her right hand, and a spear in her left hand. Second brass of Maximian Hercules.

Why the above specimen should be reckoned in this class of coins, notwithstanding the absence of the word SEN. (*Senior*) in the legend of the obverse—is a point which Eckhel regards as of easy explanation. That this distinctive title was not always added in the mintages of Maximian Hercules, is shewn by the fact, that coins inscribed CONSERV. VRB. SVAE, &c. are found only with the head of Maximian Hercules, Maxentius, or Constantine, who were contemporaneous emperors *(synchroni Augusti)*, and none with the head of Diocletian. And it would be very singular, whilst they are common in the case of Maximian, if, supposing any to have been struck during the colleagueship of Diocletian, none were forthcoming which bore his portrait, when it is well known, that they almost invariably used the same reverses. Similar reverses, which Banduri has connected with the heads of other emperors, Eckhel considers unworthy of notice, since they are derived solely from Mediobarbus. No doubt, after being harassed by the factions of Maxentius and Severus, Rome welcomed Maximianus, on his return from Lucania and re-assumption of the purple, as a regenerator, and, as the coins call him, a *conservator*; and his services to the city are oratorically lauded by the unknown author of a panegyric dedicated to Maximian and Constantine, chap. x. and xi.—See *Doct. Num. Vet.* viii. 25.

CONSERV. or CONSERVATORES VRB. SVAE.—A temple of four columns, in the pediment of which are the wolf and twins; and at each end of the entablature stand two victories holding crowns. Within the temple, Rome, galeated, sits on a buckler, resting her right hand on the hasta, and with her left hand offers a globe to a military figure, who stands before her, with spear in the right hand, and planting his right foot on a captive. In the exergue A. P. Q. On second brass of Maxentius, whence this reverse, so replete with interesting details of typification, is engraved as above. Pellerin has published an exactly similar coin of the same usurper of the purple, described to be of pure silver, and of the medallion size.—*Mel.* i. 191.

CONSERVATOR. AFRICAE SVAE.——A woman treading on a crocodile, in her right hand a military standard, in her left the tusk of an elephant. Maxentius. Second brass.

The coin (says Eckhel), must have been struck at the commencement of this man's assumption of imperial rank and authority, to conciliate the good will of so rich a province; on which subject see further remarks under the next coin,—CONSERVATORES KART. SVAE.— He barbarously harassed the same province at a later period, viz. about A. D. 308. Whether the animal, on which the woman treads, be really a crocodile, though Banduri affirms it, one may be pardoned for doubting. The crocodile was not a symbol of Africa, but of Egypt, which being under the dominion of Maximinus Daza, never had any connexion with Maxentius. On coins of Diocletian, inscribed FEL. ADVENT. AVG. a lion and a bull are represented at the feet of a figure of Africa. The author of the *Museum Theupoli Catalogue*, in describing a similar coin, has not ventured to determine the species of the animal represented.—viii. 57.

CONSERVATORES KART. SVAE.—A temple of six columns, in which a woman, standing, holds in each hand extended a branch or some kind of fruit. Second brass of Maxentius. (Imperial Museum).

Banduri asserts, that the two princes, whom Carthage acknowledges as her *conservatores*, appear to be Maxentius and Maximianus. But Eckhel considers it beyond a doubt, that this title pertained to *three* princes, Maximianus Herculius, Maxentius, and Constantinus, since it occurs on the coins of them all individually. From these coins, then (he adds), it is proved incontestably, that Africa and Carthage gave in their adhesion to Maximianus when he became emperor a second time, and to his son Maxentius, in gratitude, probably, for benefits conferred by him on that province during the reign of Diocletian (of which also coins inform us); and that Constantine was invited to a share of this honour, as they considered his friendship essential to their interests. Consequently, as is shewn by the coins of Maxentius, whilst still Cæsar, Africa soon attached herself to his side, and also espoused the cause of his father, on his recovery of the empire.—It is matter of certainty, that Maxentius did not *for the first time* receive the submission of Africa when his father died, and Alexander, the usurper of that province had been vanquished, as some have understood from the imperfect narrative of Zosimus, though the error has since been entirely confuted by Tillemont with arguments drawn from history.—*D. N. V.* viii. 58.

CONSERVAT. PIETAT.——The Emperor, standing, with his right hand extended, in his left a spear, and before him a small figure, on bended knee, raising its hands. Silver and 3rd brass of Gallienus. (Banduri. Imp. Mus.)

Commodus proclaimed himself on coins as

Auctor Pietatis, and Gallienus as her *Conservator*. From the type of a boy in a suppliant posture, it may be inferred, that by this reverse allusion is made to the piety (or *benevolence*) shewn towards the children maintained by the state (*pueris alimentariis*), many instances of which are recorded from the time of Trajan. The same reverse occurs on a coin of Claudius.—vii. 406.

CONSIDIA, an ancient gens of plebeian rank. Its surnames *Nonianus* and *Pætus*. Its coins have eight varieties. The following alone possesses interest :—

Obv.—C. CONSIDI. NONIANI. S. C.—Head of Venus, laureated and adorned with a mitre, necklace, and ear-rings. Before it S. C.

Rev.—ERVC. A small temple on the top of a steep rock, surrounded by walls : in the front of which, above the gate, is inscribed the above abbreviation for Erucina, or Erycina.

The head and the temple of this coin appertain to Venus Erycina, so called from Eryx, in Sicily. The moneyer who coined the denarius, named Caius Considius Nonianus, was a provincial quæstor, and a kinsman, if not the son, according to Borghesi, of M. Considius, pretor of the year 702 (B. C. 52), destined successor of Cæsar in the government of Gallia Citerior, and who was with Cicero at Capua, at the time of Pompey's flight. By a decree of the Senate, this Considius had the honour of exhibiting these types on his mintage, either because his family belonged to the city of Eryx, or from having by gifts and liberalities glorified the temple of Venus there—one of the most ancient and famous edifices raised in honour of the goddess, and which was accustomed to be visited and enriched by consuls, pretors, and every one entrusted by the Roman government with power and authority in Sicily.—See Riccio, *delle famiglie di Roma*, p. 59.

That mythical personage Dædalus, amongst numerous works of sculpture and architecture ascribed to him by the Greek writers, is said to have "enlarged the summit of mount Eryx by a wall, so as to make a firm foundation for the temple of Aphrodite. For this same temple he made a honeycomb of gold, which could scarcely be distinguished from a real honeycomb."—See Dr. Smith's *Dictionary of Greek and Roman Biog.* i. 927.

Riccio gives a silver sesterce, with C. CONSIDI. and the head of Cupid on its obverse; and a globe, surmounted by a cornucopiæ, with fillet, on its reverse. The Caius Considius by whom, as moneyer of the republic, this very rare monetal specimen of the gens was struck in 705 (B. C. 69), belonged to the Pompeian party.

CONS. PRINC. AVG.—Emperor standing, places his right hand on a trophy, at the foot of which are two captives. In his left he holds a spear. Billon of Aurelian. (Banduri).

The epigraph of this reverse is unusual.— The word *Princeps* is here used as an augmentation of that of Augustus. Ammian calls Aurelius "Marcus Princeps."

CONSTANS *(Flavius Julius)* Cæsar and Augustus; youngest son of Constantine the Great and Fausta; born about A. D. 320, he was declared Cæsar by his father in 333; and obtained two years afterwards the government of Italy, Illyria, and Africa. He shared in the partition of the empire, after the death of Constantine, A. D. 337. And his elder brother, Constantine 'the younger, being slain in 340, near Aquileia, whilst treacherously invading his territory, he became master of the whole West, as Constantius was of the East. In the following year he undertook an expedition against the Franks, who had passed the Rhine in order to ravage Gaul. He conducted this war in person with vigour; and having first defeated, he formed an alliance with, the invaders, whom he obliged to return in peace to their own country. Passing afterwards into Britain, he restored that important province of the empire to a degree of tranquillity, to which it had long been a stranger. Before he quitted the island on his return to Gaul, Constans established such laws there, as whilst they caused the Roman name to be respected, were a credit to his own judgment and policy. The remainder of his reign promised to be undisturbed and prosperous, but his passion for the chase, and his indulgence in a false security, afforded the opportunity to Marcellinus, his financial minister, and Chreste, one of his military officers, to form a conspiracy against his life. These two wretches came to a secret understanding with Magnentius, whom on the 18th January, 350, during the night, they invested with the purple, at the finish of a banquet in the city of Autun, where the Imperial Court then was. Magnentius, after having saluted emperor by the conspirators, sent Gaison, a Gaulish officer, with some soldiers, to murder Constans. But that prince apprised of what had just occurred, had taken horse to save himself in Spain. Gaison, with his band of assassins, followed and overtook him at Elne, in the Pyrenees, where, having dragged him out of a church into which he had fled for refuge, they put him to death with their daggers. Thus perished Constans, in the 30th year of his age, on the 27th of February, 350, after having reigned, from the period of his father's death, twelve years, nine months, and five days.

This prince protected the Christians, and was a good warrior; but cruel, debauched, and avaricious, he allowed his ministers to render his government, by their exactions, odious to the people, and disliked even by the soldiery. He had, however, courage and activity enough to preserve his dominions with a glory not inferior to any of his predecessors.

MINTAGES OF CONSTANS.

His brass coins are common: his gold and silver, rare. His style and titles as emperor are FL. CONSTANS *Pius Felix* AVG.—D. N. CONSTANS PERP. AVG.

The coins of Constans exhibit the head of that emperor with diadem ornamented with precious stones, and with the *paludamentum*, and sometimes the *lorica*, on the breast; in the right hand a javelin, in the left a buckler. On some of the coins the head is laureated, on others bound with a diadem of gems.

Amongst the more rare and curious reverses are the following:—

GOLD MEDALLIONS.—FELICIA DECENNALIA. Two cupids supporting a crown. (Valued by Mionnet at 400 fr.)

GLORIA REPVBLICAE. Two figures. (150 fr.)— TRIVMFATOR GENTIVM BARBARARVM. Emperor with labarum, and monogram of Christ. (500 fr.)

SILVER MEDALLIONS.—FELICITAS PERPETVA. Three figures seated. (Mionnet, 150 fr.)

TRIVMFATOR GENTIVM BARBARARVM (£6 12s. Pembroke sale.)

VIRTVS EXERCITVM *(sic)*. Four military ensigns, *Alpha* and *Omega*. (Engraved in p. 118.)

GOLD.—SECVRITAS PERPETVA. (Mt. 50 fr.)

VICTORIA AVGVSTORVM. Victory marching with garland and trophy.—*Obv.*—FL. IVL. CONSTANS. P. F. AVG. Diademed head of the emperor. (See engraving above.)

OB VICTORIAM TRIVMFALEM. Two victories and a buckler.—VICTORIA DD. NN. AVG. Two Victories. (£2 3s. Pembroke sale.)—VICTOR OMNIVM GENTIVM. Emperor with *labarum*. (50 fr.)—VIRTVS EXERCITVS GALL. Mars. (40 fr.)

BRASS MEDALLIONS. BONONIA OCEANEN. (Engraved in p. 132.)

DEBELLATORI GENTT. BARBARR. Emperor on horseback.—(Mionnet, 30 fr.)

GLORIA ROMANORVM. Emperor standing.

GAVDIVM POPVLI ROMANI, &c. &c.

SECOND BRASS.—TRIVMFVS *(sic.)* CAESARVM. Full-faced Victory in a quadriga.

CONSTANS, son of Constantinus Tyrannus, and styled on his very rare coin, in silver, D. N. CONSTANS P. F. AVG. was associated in the usurpation of government with his father, A. D. 408. He was assassinated at Vienne, in the Narbonnaise Gaul, by Gerontius, his father's general (who had quarrelled with his master), A. D. 411, a short time after the tragical end of Constantinus himself. The quinarii bear on their reverse VICTORIA AAAVGGG. A helmeted female seated, holding a Victory and the hasta pura. In the exergue CON. Small brass, SPES AVG. with the gate of a *castrum*.

CONSTANTIA.—Constancy, the symbol of the Emperor Claudius; though it was an attribute not always prominent in him. For his biographer Suetonius says of him, "In the faculties of reflection and discernment, his mind was remarkably variable and contrasted, he being sometimes circumspect and sagacious; at others inconsiderate and hasty, often frivolous and as though he were out of his wits."—The following three are examples of this legend :—

1. CONSTANTIAE AVGVSTI. A woman standing, with a long torch in her right hand, and a cornucopiæ in her left. On gold and silver of Antonia—Engraved in p. 55 of this dictionary.

The torch is to be referred to the ceremonial of the priesthood of Augustus (Antonia was called SACERDOS DIVI AVGVSTI), and that in the hand of the woman on the present coin, intended no doubt for Antonia, appears to have been added in allusion to the same office. But the difficulty is to reconcile the legend with the type. Havercamp thinks that the *constancy* of Antonia is alluded to, which she displayed in adhering to widowhood, and compelling her daughter Livilla to suffer death. But if such constancy really shewed itself in Antonia, why is the merit, according to the sense of the legend attributed to Augustus? For it should have been written AVGVSTAE, not AVGVSTI. To this may be added, that the legend is a common one on the coins of her son Claudius, and appears to be peculiar to him, as will be seen below. But if the legend refers to Claudius, and the type to Antonia, it is difficult to assign the reason for such an anomaly.— *D. N. V.* sixth vol. p. 179.

2. CONSTANTIAE AVGVSTI. A woman seated, touches her face with her right hand.—*Obv.* Laureated head of Claudius.—On gold and silver of that emperor; engraved in Caylus, *Num. Aur. Impp. Rom.* No. 92.

3. CONSTANTIAE AVGVSTI. S. C. A youth, wearing a helmet, and attired in a thin garment reaching to the knees, and with a cloke flowing behind him; holds up his right hand, and with the fore-finger touches his face; his left hand grasps a spear.—*Obv.* Bare head of Claudius. Second brass. Engraved in Havercamp, *Médailles de Christine.*, TAB. 49. Restored by Vespasian.

Respecting the second coin, Eckhel (vi. 236), makes the following observations :—" I find the type variously described by antiquaries. The one which I have here produced, is selected from five, in the most perfect state of preservation, in the imperial museum. The same legend (as above shewn), is found on coins of Antonia, mother of Claudius, struck during the reign of that emperor; but in these there is a difference in the type, which consists of a woman standing, with a long torch in her right hand, and a cornucopiæ in her left (see No. 1). It is difficult to reconcile the legend with the type, but that the legend undoubtedly refers to Claudius is an opinion confirmed by the coins now before us.— Yet even in these, there is the same difficulty, though there appears to be no doubt, that the moneyers had in view the life of Claudius, passed from infancy amidst contempt, ridicule, and fear; to all which disadvantages, by his invincible

constancy (or perseverance, or endurance), he proved himself superior. This opinion is supported by the gesture of both figures, female and male (2 & 3), which appear to be imposing silence on themselves, a quality which constitutes the main part of *constantia*. The Roman mythology contains two female deities who presided over silence, viz. Angerona and Tacita, respecting which I long ago treated copiously. *(Sylloge,* i. p. 71). I am not aware, whether the same source supplies a male being of the same character, such as Harpocrates was reckoned in Egypt."

CONSTANTINI AVG.—Two victories standing, hold together a crown, within which we read VOT. XXX. Gold medallion of Constantinus Magnus, engraved in Steinbüchel, *Notice sur les Médaillons en or du Musée Imperial,* No. 3.

The subjects of typification most frequent in this age of the empire were those which record vota decennalia, vicennalia, tricennalia (vows lasting ten, twenty, thirty years).

CONSTANTINIANA DAFNE.—A woman trampling on a captive, and holding in each hand a palm branch. On one side a trophy. In the exergue CONS. This epigraph occurs on a gold and a silver and on a third brass coin of Constantinus M. Various have been the opinions expressed by the learned respecting it.— Eckhel (viii. 81), in citing them all, considers that interpretation to be decidedly the most probable, which Gretser and Spanheim drew from Procopius, viz. that by *Constantiniana Dafne* is to be understood the castle or camp *(castrum) Dafne,* constructed by Constantine on the bank of the Danube.

CONSTANTINO P. AVG. B. R. P. NAT. —The Emperor in a military habit, stands holding a globe and spear. Second brass of Constantine the Great.

For a long time the inscription on this coin was read by antiquaries BAP. NAT. for BRP. NAT. and hence they were induced to regard it as a sure and genuine memorial of the *Baptism* of Constantine. Hardouin was the first to detect this inveterate error, which he felicitously removed by restoring (as Eckhel observes), the true reading *Bono Rei Publicæ Nato,* which is supported by inscriptions on marbles, cited in Gruter. Besides, Magnus Maximus and his son Fl. Victor are, on a coin of his, called BONO REIPVBLICE NATI. See p. 132.

CONSTANTINOPOLIS, formerly *Byzantium,* the most celebrated city of Thrace, derives its name from Constantine the Great, by whom it was enlarged with new buildings, and rendered almost equal to Old Rome; in order that Constantinople should be the capital of the empire in the east, as Rome was in the west. It was taken by the Turks in the year 1453, by whom it is now called *Stambul,* and in whose possession it still remains a great metropolitan and royal city. The coins which make mention of it, were struck either by Constantine or by his sons.

CONSTANTINOPOLIS.—This legend appears on the obverse of several brass medallions, accompanied by the helmeted bust of the city of Constantinople, personified; the hasta pura on her shoulders: on the reverses are the several legends of FEL. TEMP. REPARATIO—RESTITVTOR REIP.—VICTORIA AVGVSTI.—VICT. AVGG. &c. all allusive to the reparations, restorations, and military successes, claimed to have been achieved for the empire, by Constantine and the princes of his family.—Engraved in Havercamp, *Cabinet de Christine*, TAB. xl.

Constantinople, in a later age, was one amongst the number of those cities to which the right of coining money was granted. Hence on so many coins, we read, at the bottom, CON. CONST. &c.

CONSTANTINUS (*Flavius Galerius Valerianus*), surnamed *Magnus* or *Maximus*, was the son of Constantius Chlorus, and of Helena, first wife of that prince, son in law of Maximianus Herculeus, and brother in law of Licinius. He was born at Naissus, in Dardania, A. U. C. 1027 (A. D. 274). His birth-day is fixed by the calendar of Dionysius Philocalus, on the 3rd before the calends of March. When Diocletian, A. D. 292, sent his father with the title of Cæsar into Gaul, he detained Constantine as a kind of pledge, and became greatly attached to him on account of his amiability and integrity of disposition. On the abdication of Diocletian and Maximian, A. D. 305, Constantine, in the midst of his satisfaction at seeing his father raised from the Cæsarian to the Imperial dignity, still found himself placed in a most precarious position, since Gal. Maximianus, who succeeded to Diocletian, not only opposed his joining his father, but openly plotted against his life. He therefore made his escape from Nicomedia, after disabling the public horses in order to delay pursuit, and reached his father in Britain about the beginning of A. D. 306; and on the death of Constantius, which happened shortly afterwards at York, on the 25th of July, Constantine himself was on the same day proclaimed Augustus by the unanimous voice of the army. This choice, not daring openly to dispute, Gal. Maximianus (who in consequence of his being the successor of Diocletian, had arrogated to himself the supreme authority over the empire and even over its rulers), found himself compelled to acknowledge Constantine at least as Cæsar, though with reluctance; and

coins began forthwith to be struck with his name under that title.

A. D. 306. His father's provinces, Gaul and Britain, were assigned to Constantine. Galerius nominated Severus Cæsar as Augustus, in the room of Constantius I. deceased. Soon afterwards Maxentius also assumed the imperial title at Rome, and restored the purple to his father Maximianus Herculeus, recalling him from Lucania. Constantine gained a victory over the Franci and the Bructeri, and commenced the building of a bridge over the Rhine, near Agrippina (*Cologne*).

307. Constantine this year entered on his first consulate, according to the records of the Fasti, confused as they are at this period.— The same year Severus blockaded Maxentius in Rome, but being compelled to raise the siege, and taken prisoner at Ravenna, he was put to death by order of Herculeus Maximianus. Herculeus, dreading the vengeance of Galerius for this act, went into Gaul, and there, in order to win him over to his cause, gave Constantine the title of Augustus, and his daughter Fausta in marriage. Galerius attempted to take Rome, but being repulsed by Maxentius, and driven out of Italy, created Licinius emperor in the room of Severus. In the same year also Constantine and Maximinus Daza each received from Galerius the title of *Filius Augustorum* (FILIVS AVGG.)

308. Maximinus Daza assumed the title of Augustus, at first against the wishes of Galerius, but afterwards with his assent, Constantine being admitted to a participation of the same honour. In this year, accordingly, Constantine began to be acknowledged as emperor throughout the entire empire. And thus there were at the same time, in addition to Maximianus Herculeus, five Augusti, viz. Galerius Maximianus, Constantine, Maximinus, Licinius, and Maxentius.—Constantine, being informed of the plots organized against himself by Herculeus, besieged him in Massilia (*Marseilles*), and reduced him to a surrender, and the condition of a private citizen.

310. Maximianus Herculeus having been convicted of fresh plots, Constantine put him to death. The same year he proceeded with the war against the Alemanni.

311. Gal. Maximianus dying, Licinius and Maximinus took possession of his provinces. Constantine, on hearing that Maxentius had caused his statues to be thrown down at Rome, and was preparing hostilities against him in retaliation for his father's death, prepared for war. —Under these circumstances, from motives of policy, he betrothed his sister Constantia to Licinius. According to Eusebius, having seen in the heavens the figure of the cross, with the words, "In hoc signo victor eris," he openly adopted the Christian religion, and caused the sign of the cross to be displayed on the imperial standards and shields.

312. He defeated the Generals of Maxentius, first at Taurinus (*Turin*), and afterwards at Verona; and, in a final action at the Pons Milvius, near Rome, vanquished Maxentius himself, and

thus put an end to a bloody war. Immediately after this victory, Constantine entered Rome in triumph.—313. Licinius defeated Maximinus Daza, who died shortly after at Tarsus, and Licinius succeeded to the entire dominion of the East.

314. A war arose this year between Constantine and Licinius, on what grounds is uncertain. but probably on account of mutual envy and mistrust. After various engagements in Pannonia and Thrace, a peace was concluded with such a division of the empire between them, that the East, Thrace, and part of Mæsia fell to the share of Licinius, while Constantine held all the rest. On the calends of March, Crispus and Constantius, the sons of Constantine the Great, and Licinius, received the title of *Cæsar*. From A. D. 318 to A. D. 321, both inclusive, no record of any important transactions appears in the annals of this reign.—322. To this year is referred the war with the Sarmatæ, of which mention is made also on coins.

323. Another furious war with Licinius commenced, from no other cause, apparently, than rivalry. Constantine was victorious over him, first near Hadrianopolis, on the 3rd of July, then in a naval engagement under Crispus, and lastly near Chalcedon, on the 18th of September, Licinius having surrendered at Nicomedia, Constantine sent him to Thessalonica, but shortly afterwards (as some say contrary to his pledged word), ordered him to be put to death.

325. Having now got rid of all his rivals at home, subdued his foreign enemies, and attained a state of sole responsibility, Constantine directed his attention to the suppression of paganism; razed the temples, and erected in their stead places of Christian worship. He assisted at the Council of Nice; entered into a discussion with the Bishops on the subjects of the divinity of our Saviour, and the proper time for the celebration of Easter; and at the same time, according to Eusebius, solemnized his *Vicennalia*.

326. Constantine this year went to Rome, and remaining there a few months, proceeded into Pannonia, destined never again to re-visit the "eternal city." He ordered his son Crispus, and his wife Fausta, to be put to death, as is generally thought most unadvisedly, and much to his discredit. The same year he commenced the building of Constantinople.

A. D. 330. Constantine, with magnificent solemnities, dedicated the city of Constantinople, the building of which was begun four years before.—332. He conducted a campaign against the Goths, who were harrassing the Sarmatæ; and afterwards against the Sarmatæ themselves, whom he reduced to submission.

335. This year Constantine divided the empire amongst his sons and nephews *(nepotes ex fratre,* says Eckhel), so as to give his eldest son, Constantine, the territory held by Constantius Chlorus; to Constantius, the East; to Constans, Illyricum, Italy, and Africa; to his nephew Delmatius, whom he had this year created Cæsar, Thrace, Macedon, and Achaia; to his brother Hanniballianus, Armenia Minor, Cappadocia, and Pontus, with the title of king.

—The *Vota tricennalia* (of paganism) were discharged this year.

A. D. 337. In his eighth consulate, and amidst preparations for a war, into which he had been provoked, against Sapor the Persian, Constantine fell sick and died, near Nicomedia, in Bithynia, on the 22nd of May, in the 32nd year of his reign, and the 64th of his age.

In estimating the character and deeds of so great a prince (says the judicious Eckhel), much caution is requisite, lest, by relying wholly on the testimony of Christian writers, we should be led to regard Constantine less in the light of a mortal man than of a god; or by following, on the other hand, the aspersions of the enemies of the Christian faith, such as Zosimus and Julian, we should picture him to ourselves as a man disgraced by the foulest vices. It is sufficiently evident that the former class of writers were not in all instances unbiased judges of the quality of his life and morals, from a fear of admitting the imperfections of the champion of their faith. The preferable plan is to follow the accounts of Eutropius, who steers a middle course, giving way neither to partiality nor to hostility, and who has asserted that Constantine displayed surpassing excellencies of mind and body; that he was eager in the extreme for military distinction, and fortunate in his warlike enterprizes; that he was also devoted to the arts of peace and the pursuits of literature; and an ardent candidate for a well founded popularity, which he endeavoured to conciliate by his liberal acts and affable demeanour. Others, without denying him these merits say that he was, nevertheless, immoderate in his ambition, which brooked no rival, and embroiled him in civil war; that he paid too much attention to his personal adornment; that he was profuse in his expenditure on the building and decoration of the different cities, to meet which he was in the habit of recruiting his treasury by unjustifiable acts of spoliation. That prosperity had a deteriorating effect upon his character, Eutropius hesitates not to assert, comparing him in the earlier period of his reign with the best of his predecessors, and at its close with the worst: and Victor says, that had he but shewn more self-control in some particulars, he would, in the opinion of all who were wont to extol him to the skies, have been little less than a god. By taking the lives of his amiable son Crispus, and of his wife Fausta, though in her case at least he acted justifiably, yet it was not surprising that he gained a character for cruelty, or for hasty judgment, and that an unfavourable comparison was drawn between him and M. Aurelius, who bore with the profligacy of his son, and the conduct of an abandoned wife. With regard to his relinquishing the religion of his ancestors, and embracing Christianity, as it was a step intolerable to the adherents of the ancient superstition, so with the professors of the new faith it became matter of the highest encomium.— But he lost the credit thus acquired, when in the later years of his reign, he exhibited himself in the capacity rather of a theological disputant, than of a sovereign prince But Constantine struck a severe blow at the welfare of the empire, both in building a *New Rome* on the shores of the Propontis, and in dividing his dominions, unwarned by recent fatal examples, among his three sons and two nephews, destined thenceforth to be so many exasperated rivals, bent on each others destruction.—See *Doct. Num. Vet.* viii. 17, et seq.

Niebuhr makes the following just remarks on Constantine's *belief*:—" The religion which he had in his head must have been a strange compound indeed. The man who had on his coins the inscription *Sol invictus*, who worshipped pagan divinities, consulted haruspices, indulged in a number of pagan superstitions ; and on the other hand, built churches, shut up pagan temples, and interfered with the council of Nicæa, must have been a repulsive phœnomenon, and was certainly not a Christian. He did not allow himself to be baptized till the last moments of his life; and those who praise him for this, do not know what they are doing. To speak of him as a saint (which some oriental writers do), is a profanation of the word."— *History of Rome*, vol. v.

MINTAGES of CONSTANTINE the GREAT.

Constantine, on his coins, after A. D. 305, is styled *Cæsar* and *Princeps Juventutis*. FL. CL. CONSTANTINVS NOB. CAES.—CONSTANTINVS FIL. AVGGG. *Filius Augustorum*, a mere titular distinction received by Constantine from Galerius Maximianus, who refused him at first that of Augustus).—From and after A. D. 308, he is styled *Augustus*.—In A. D. 315, his coins record his fourth, and in 320, his sixth consulate. His full style and titles are IMP. C. FL. VAL. CONSTANTINVS. P. F. AVG.—The types of his obverses sometimes exhibit a galeated, at others a laureated, head. His monetal portraiture also appears as a bust, with helmet or laurel, and with either the *paludamentum*, or a coat of armour, on his shoulders and breast—holding in his right hand a spear, in his left a shield. On other coins a sceptre surmounted by an eagle in his right hand, also with a diademed head-dress, enriched with jewellery, a globe with Victory in his hand. On the coins struck after his death the head is veiled, and the legend DIVO CONSTANTINO.—There are coins of this emperor, in gold as well as silver, on which his head is encircled with the diadem, but without legend. In these the countenance is looking upward, as, according to Eusebius, it would seem, beholding the heavens.—See *Diadem*.

The coins of this emperor are rare in gold and in silver—the medallions in both these metals very rare. Second and third brass, with certain exceptions, common. Brass medallions rare ; some very rare.

The following are amongst the most rare and remarkable legends and types of reverse in each metal :—

GOLD MEDALLIONS.—ADVENTVS AVG. N.— Emperor on horseback, and Victory.

CONSTANTINI AVG. Two Victories supporting a crown.—FELICITAS PERPETVA. AVGEAT. REM. DD. NN.—GAVDIVM AVGVSTI. NOSTRI. Two winged Genii.—GLORIA ROMANORVM. Rome seated.—PIETAS AVGVSTI NOSTRI. The emperor between two figures.—[The above five valued by Mionnet at 150 francs each.]

SALVS ET SPES. REIPVBLICAE. The emperor seated between two military figures. (Mt. 600 fr.)

EQVIS (*sic.*) ROMANVS. (£4 12s. Thomas sale.) —GLORIA CONSTANTINI AVG. (£13 Thomas sale.)—SENATVS. Full length figure of Constantine (brought £38 at the Thomas sale.)

SILVER MEDALLIONS.—*Rev.*—CAESAR in a crown.—*Obv.*-Head of Constantine, with legend AVGVSTVS. (Mionnet, 60 fr.)—CONSTANTINVS AVG. Four military ensigns.—FELICITAS ROMANORVM. Three military figures under an arch.—MARTI. PATRI. CONSERVATORI. Mars standing.—PRINCIPI IVVENTVTIS. Figure and two ensigns.—VOTA ORBIS ET VRBIS. SEN. ET PR.

GOLD.—ADVENTVS AVGVSTI. (Mt. 120 fr.)— CONSTANTINIANA DAFNE. (£5 17s. 6d. Thomas). —CONSVL. DD. NN. Emperor standing in the toga. (Mt. 90 fr.)—CONSTANTINVS ET CRISPVS. (120 fr.)—CONSVL PP. PROCONSVL. Same type. —DEBELLATORI GENTIVM BARBARARVM. Several figures. GOTHIA.—FELICIA TEMPORA. The four Seasons. (Mt. 100 fr.)—FELICITAS REIPVBLICAE. (£4 12s. 6d. Thomas, £5 Pembroke).— FELIX PROCESSVS COS. IIII.—GAVDIVM ROMANORVM. (£3 16s. Thomas).—GLORIA EXERCITVS GALL. (£4 Thomas).—PIETAS AVGVSTI NOSTRI. Emperor crowned by Victory. (£6 2s. 6d. Thos.) RESTITVTORI LIBERTATIS.—SALVS REIP. DANVBIVS. Bridge of three arches. (Mt. 100 fr.) —SOLI. COMITI. AVG.—VDILVE VICTOR. (Pembroke, £3 6s.)—VBIQVE VICTORES. A quinarius. (£3 4s. Thomas).—VICTORIA CONSTANTINI AVG. (£7. Thomas).

VICTORIA AVGVSTORVM. Victory crowning the Emperor, who holds a globe in the right hand, and a spear reversed in the left ; on the exergue SM. TS.—On the obverse the laureated head of the Emperor, with legend of CONSTANTINVS. P. F. AVG.—(See cut, left-hand column).

VICTORIA CONSTANTINI AVG. (£3 1s. Thomas, £3 5s. Pembroke).—VIRTVS EXERCITVS GALL. (£4 4s. Thomas).—VICTORIAE LAETAE PRINC. PERP. (£4, Thomas ; £8, Pembroke).—VICTORIOSO SEMPER. (200 fr.)—VOTA PVBLICA.

SILVER.—DELMATIVS NOB. CAESAR. (60 fr. Mionnet.)—LIBERATOR ORBIS. (50 fr.)—VICTORIA DD. NN. AVGG.—VIRTVS MILITVM. (£1 6s. Thomas).

BRASS MEDALLIONS.—CONSTANTINVS MAX. AVG. Bust of Constantine, with diadem. For the reverse of this medallion (which brought £3 5s. at the Thomas sale), see GLORIA SECVLI VIRTVS CAESS.

CONSTANTINOPOLIS FEL. TEMP. REPARATIO.
DEBELLATORI GENT. BARBARR.—Emperor on horseback, charging an enemy.——*Obv.*—CONSTANTINVS MAX. AVG. Diademed head of Constantine.—See engraving at the head of the biographical summary, p. 257.

EXVPERATOR OMNIVM GENTIVM. Emperor seated between two captives. (100 fr. Mionnet.)

IN HOC. SIN. *(sic.)* VIC. Monogram of Christ. —SALVS ET SPES. REIPVBLICAE. Constantine between his two sons. (120 fr. each, Mionnet.)

SALVS REIP. DANVBIVS. Emperor and Victory on a bridge. (150 fr.—VICTORIA GOTHICA. Rome and Victory.—VRBS ROMA. *(Contorniate).*

SECOND BRASS.—GENIO FIL. AVGG.—VIRTVS PERPETVA AVG.

THIRD BRASS.—PLVRA. NATAL. FEL.—RECVPERATOR VRBIS SVAE.—SAPIENTIAE PRINCIPIS. Owl on cippus.—SPES PVBLICA. Labarum and monogram of Christ, on a serpent.—VIRT. EXERCIT. GALLIAE.—VOTA PVBLICA. Isis Pharia.

CONSTANTINUS (*Flavius Claudius Julius*). Constantine II. or junior, eldest son of Constantine the Great, and the first whom the emperor had by his second wife, Fausta, was born at Arelatum, now Arles, in France, the 14th May, or according to some authors the 7th of August, A.D. 316. As early as the following year he was named Cæsar, at Sardis, by his father and by Licinius, who at the same time gave him for colleagues in that dignity, Crispus and Licinius, jun.—Constantine declared him consul four times during his youth; and sent him at the age of sixteen years, on a campaign against the Goths, who had invaded Mæsia and Thrace, A.D. 332, In this war he greatly distinguished himself. defeating King Alaric, who, in the action, and in the retreat, according to contemporary writers, lost nearly a hundred thousand of his barbaric host. In 335, the government of Gaul, Britain, and Spain was entrusted to him. And, in conformity to the division of the Empire so fatally made by his father, he received after that emperor's death, the same provinces of which he had had the administration under Constantine, and also a part of Africa. In 337, this young prince was acknowledged *Augustus* by both Senate and Army. The death of Delmatius and of Hanniballianus caused a new division of territories between Constantine junior and his brothers; but impelled by a restless spirit, and besides being dissatisfied with the territorial treaty he had made, he demanded of Constans to be put in possession of the African provinces. —Constans, who reigned in Italy, refused. And the eldest son of Constantine declared war against his own brother. With a large military and naval force, he invaded Italy, and his army advanced as far as the city of Aquileia. There, however,

he was encountered by Constans, who had returned from Dacia to defend his Italian dominions. Constantine, proceeding in the confidence of victory, but without due precaution, fell into an ambuscade, where his army was cut to pieces; and he himself being mortally wounded, fell from his horse, and was dispatched on the spot. His body was thrown into the river Alsa (now Ansa); but was afterwards found, and interred at Constantinople with imperial honours. Thus perished, A.D. 340, Constantinus junior, in his 25th year, and the third of his reign, "regretted," (says Beauvais) "for his piety, his mildness of character, and his love for his subjects." It is not known whether he left children by the two Princesses whom he married, and whose names are not known.

MINTAGES of CONSTANTINE the Younger.

This prince from the year 317 to 337, is on his coins styled *Cæsar* and *Princeps Juventutis*; and from 337 to 340 *Augustus*. His style, as Cæsar, is DN. FL. IVL. CONSTANTINVS IVNIOR. NOB. or NOBILISS. CAESAR.—His style as Augustus, is FL. CL. CONSTANTINVS PIVS FELIX AVG.

That to him, as Augustus, coins were struck, even during the life time of his father appears not to be doubted. And many of these which are assigned to Constantine the Great most probably belonged to this prince, although destitute of the proper criterion. For this reason Eckhel (Cat. ii., p. 488), subscribes to the opinion of Banduri, who says (T. ii. p. 333.) "We are hitherto enabled to find no other coin, which we can refer to the younger Constantine, as Augustus, so like are all his to those of Constantinus Magnus."

Corroborative of the above observations, is the following note of Mionnet (ii. p. 244). "The coins which give to Constantine the younger, the title of Augustus are difficult to distinguish from those, which belong to Constantine the Great. They are therefore generally classed amongst those of the latter. We must, however, except from this arrangement, those coins on which we read the name of *Claudius*. These coins are to be assigned to the son, because the name of *Claudius* is not found on any genuine coin of the father's mint, whilst we find it on indubitable coins of the son."

The coins of this emperor are of high rarity in gold; medallions especially. Silver medallions are even more rare. Of pure silver scarcely any are to be found. *Potin* and *billon* are rare. Brass medallions very rare, and some few exceedingly so. Third brass very common.

The following are among the most remarkable reverses:—

GOLD MEDALLIONS.——FELICITAS PERPETVA. Emperor seated between two military figures.— SALVS ET SPES. (Valued by Mionnet at 500 francs each.)

PRINCIPI IVVENT. Emperor standing, with labarum. (200 fr.)--VIRTVS CONSTANTINI CAES. (100 fr.)

GOLD.—CLARITAS REIPVBLICAE.—CONSTAN-

TINVS CAESAR, or IVN. NOB. CAES.—FELIX PRO-
CESSVS. COS. II.—GAVDIVM ROM. SARMATIA.—
VICTORIA CAESAR. NN.—VICTORIA CONSTANTINI
CAES.—(The above six valued by Mionnet from
100 to 150 fr.)—PRINCIPI IVVENTVTIS. Emperor standing, with labarum, &c.—*Obv.*—IVNIOR
in the legend. (£4 1s. Thomas).

BRASS MEDALLIONS.—MONETA VRBIS VES-
TRAE.—SACRA MONETA VRBIS.—VICTORIA AVG.
Emperor in a galley.—VICTORIA BEATISSIMO-
RVM CAESS.

THIRD BRASS.—FELICITAS ROMANORVM.—
Constantine between his two sons.—VIRT. EXERC.
The Sun standing on the plan of a camp.—
VOTA VICENNALIOR *(sic.)* Emperor holding in
his hand a human head.

CONSTANTINUS *(Flavius Claudius)*,
usurper during the reign of Honorius (commonly called Constantine III.) A soldier from
the ranks, he was proclaimed Augustus by the
legions in Britain, A. D. 407. This man, who
owed his elevation to the venerated name which
he bore, rather than to his talents, passed over
into Gaul, at the head of the troops who had
elected him, and caused himself to be acknowledged as Emperor from Boulogne to the Alps.
On his march through the country, which for
the most part had been left undefended, he was
defeated by Sarus, general of Honorius, who
besieged him in Vienne (Dauphiné); but assisted
by Gerontius, an able commander but a treacherous ally, he compelled Sarus to fall back beyond
the Alps. Constantine then established his residence at Arles (Arelatum); and sent into
Spain his son Constans, who soon established his
father's authority there, for which he was recom-
pensed with the title of Augustus. Master of
Spain, of a large portion of Gaul, and of Britain, Constantine forced Honorius to send him
the purple, and to acknowledge him as emperor,
on condition that he should assist in defending
the empire against the Goths. A short time
afterwards Gerontius, his own general, revolted
against him in Spain, drove his son Constans
out of that country, and caused him to be assassinated in Gaul. The next step of Gerontius
was to besiege Constantine in Arles. But Constantius, the general of Honorius, compelled
Gerontius to raise the siege, and took the place
himself. Constantinus became a priest, in the
hope of saving his life. This, however, did not
deter Constantius from sending him and his
second son Julianus to Honorius, who, contrary
to the promise which had been made on their
surrender, caused them both to be decapitated,
near Ravenna.

"The revolt of Constantinus [Tyrannus] is of
great importance in the history of Britain (as is
justly observed by a writer in Dr. Smith's Dictionary of Roman Biography, i. 331), since, in
consequence of it, and the rebellion of the inhabitants against the officers of Constantine, the
Emperor Honorius gave up all hopes of restoring his authority over that country, and recognized its independence of Rome—a circumstance that led to the conquest of Britain by
the Saxons."

On a gold coin published by Banduri, the
only one which gives the *prenomina* of this
usurper, he is styled FL. CL. CONSTANTINVS AVG.
On others the legend round the head is D. N.
CONSTANTINVS P. F. AVG.

"The coins of this Constantine (says Mionnet, ii. 354), have often been confounded with
those of Constantine the Great, or with those
of Constantine junior. It is, however, easy to
distinguish them."

"It is now agreed (says Akerman, ii. 349),
that those coins which, with the name of Constantinus, bear AVGGG. or AVGGGG. belong to
this usurper, as legends of this description were
not used so early as the reigns of the two preceding emperors of the same name. Those,
therefore, which are assigned by Beger to Constantinus the younger, and others given by Banduri to Constantinus Magnus, are restored to
Constantinus III. Those also which are similar
to the denarius with VICTORIA AVGGGG. although
differing from it in the legend of the obverse,
and having on the reverse the same type of the
female sedent figure, are appropriated to this
usurper, as they resemble in fabric the coins of
Constans II. his son. Eckhel is of this opinion."

The following are reverses of the coins ascribed to the usurper called Constantine the
Third :

VICTORIA AAAVGGG.—The Emperor standing,
clothed in the *paludamentum*, holds the labarum in his right hand, and a globe surmounted
by a victory in his left. On the ground is a
prostrated captive, whom he treads under foot.
In the exergue COMOB.—*Obv.*—D. N. CONSTAN-
TINVS P. F. AVG. Diademed bust of Constantinus Tyrannus.—Engraved above from a gold coin.

VICTORIA AVGG. Same type. In the exergue
TROAS or TROBS. In gold.

VICTORIA AVGGGG. Same type. In gold.

VICTORIA AAAVGGG. or AAAVGGGG. A galeated female seated, bearing on the right hand a
small victory; in her left she holds the *hasta
pura*. In silver.

[Mionnet values the gold at 30 francs and the
silver at 6 francs each].

THIRD BRASS.—*Obv.*—D. N. CONSTANTINVS
P. F. AVG. Diademed head of the Emperor.—
Rev.—VICTORIA AVGGG. Same type as on the
gold and silver. See preceding cut.

[The coins struck by Constans, son of the
above (commonly called Constans II.) are sometimes confounded with those of Constans, the
son of Constantine the Great.—See p. 255.]

CONSTANTINUS.—-There were fourteen
princes of this name, from Constantine the
Great, A. D. 323, to Constantinus Palæologus,

the able and heroic defender of Constantinople against its Turkish besiegers, by whom, in the general assault on that unfortunate city, he was slain, A. D. 1453. With the exception of the three first Constantines already noticed, the coins of the Emperors, so called, belong to what is called the *Byzantine* series, with *Greek* legends. They consequently do not come within the notice of this dictionary, which is confined to such ancient coins as bear *Latin* legends.

CONSTANTIUS I. *(Flavius Valerianus),* surnamed *Chlorus,* from the alleged paleness of his countenance—the father of Constantine the Great—was son of Eutropius, a Dardanian nobleman, and of Claudia, niece of Claudius Gothicus, born in Upper Mæsia, about A. D. 282. Little enough addicted to literary pursuits, but decidedly inclined for a military life, he entered early into the service of the pretorian guards, and attained to the rank of tribune in that corps. He distinguished himself under Aurelianus and Probus, against the Sarmatians and Germans.— In 282, he was appointed governor of Dalmatia, under Carus, who held him in such high esteem, as to have intended to appoint Constantius as his successor, instead of his own unworthy son Carinus. But the death of Carus, unhappily for the empire, prevented this design from being carried into execution.—In 292, he was adopted, and declared Cæsar, by Maximian Hercules; Diocletian at the same time proclaiming Galerius Maximian as the first of the two. Both Cæsars received their appointment at Nicomedia. —In the apportionment of the empire between the four princes, Constantius had assigned to him the government of Gaul, Spain, and Britain. This island had been taken possession of by Carausius, who soon rendered himself independent of Diocletian and Maximian. Allectus, having murdered, succeeded, Carausius, in 293. But Constantius resolved that this usurpation should not much longer continue. After the re-establishment of tranquillity in Gaul, this energetic prince brought Britain into subjection, and re-united it to the empire. (See CARAUSIUS and ALLECTUS.)—In 298, he returned to Gaul, which the Alemanni had invaded, and into which they had advanced as far as Lingones, in Lugdunensis Prima, now Langres. There, after a great battle, in which the Romans were on the point of being utterly defeated, Constantius restored the fortune of the day, and the barbarians were slaughtered by tens of thousands. He was not less successful against the Helvetians, whom he is said not only to have driven out of Gaul, but, following up, to have vanquished them in the heart of their country.

On the 1st of May, 305, Diocletian and Maximian Hercules having abdicated, Constantius Chlorus and Galerius Maximianus were re-cognised as *Augusti,* and reigned as co-emperors with Maximinus Daza and Fl. Severus.— Another partition of the empire was then made between the four princes. Constantius remained in his old dominions of Gaul and Britain, where he governed with the title of senior Augustus during the space of fifteen months, at the expiration of which (July 25th, 306), he died at Eboracum, now York, aged 56. This event took place, just as he was returned from a successful expedition against the Picts in Caledonia, in which he was accompanied by his son Constantine. His remains were interred at York; and his memory continued long to be held in veneration by the Romans; who placed him by consecration in the rank of the gods.

This prince was worthy of being compared with the best sovereigns that ever held the imperial sceptre. It had been well for the Roman world had he been permitted to govern it alone. In person well made, of a majestic demeanor, and great benignity of countenance; calmness of temper, mildness of disposition, modesty and temperance, are described to have been amongst his most distinguishing characteristics. Humane, benevolent, true to his word of promise, just and equitable in his dealings, he entertained for his subjects a tenderness of regard, which made him always studious to promote their happiness. Although he never openly professed Christianity, he exhibited not only tolerance, but a pious sympathy towards the persecuted members of that religion. Convinced of their fidelity, he afforded them an asylum in his own palace, entrusted them with important affairs, and confided the safety of his person to their guardianship.

Constantius was twice married. His first wife was Helena, whom he repudiated at the requirement of Maximian Hercules, whose daughter Theodora became his second wife. By the former he had Constantine; by the second he had six children.

MINTAGES OF CONSTANTIUS I.

On coins of Constantius Chlorus, published by Banduri, with the inscription of NOB. C. or *Nobilissimi Cæsaris,* his head is for the most part seen adorned with a crown of laurel, except two coins in which the radiated crown appears.

A similar crown of laurel is usually found on some coins of Constantinus Magnus, and likewise of his sons, Crispus, Constantine, and Constantius, whilst as yet they were only Cæsars.

The coins of the emperor are common in *brass*; they are rare in *silver*; but in *gold* most rare. He is styled *Cæsar*, and *Princeps Juventutis*, from A. D. 292, as far as 305. And in the same year 305, and following, 306, he is designated *Augustus*; when the numismatic titles run—IMP. C. FL. VAL. CONSTANTIVS P. F. AVG.—DIVVS CONSTANTIVS PIVS PRINCEPS.— DIVVS CONSTANTIVS. ADFINIS. or COGN. (or COGNAT*us*), perhaps of Maxentius. (see p. 5.)

The subjoined are amongst the rarest reverses :

SILVER MEDALLIONS.—GENIO POPVLI. ROMANI. (Mt. 40 fr.)—MONETA AVGG. (20 fr.)

GOLD.—COMES AVG. Female with helmet and armed. (Unpublished type, brought £5 7s. 6d. at the Thomas sale).

COMITATVS AVG.—CONCORDIA AVGG. ET CAESS.—(£4 13s. Thomas).

CONSECRATIO. Funeral pile.—(Valued at 200 fr. by Mionnet).

CONSVL CAES.—CONSVL V. P. P. PROCOS.— HERCVLI. CONS. CAES. Hercules. Engraved in Akerman, ii. pl. 11, No. 3. (£5 5s. Thomas).

IOVI FVLGERATORI.—VIRTVS AVG. Hercules.— VIRTVS HERCVLI. CAESARIS. Emperor on horseback.—(The above six valued by Mionnet at 150 francs each).

MARTI. PROPVGNATORI. Mars combatting.— (200 fr. Mionnet).—VICT. CONSTANT. AVG.— (£4 4s. Pembroke sale).

SILVER.—FE. ADVENT. AVG. N. N.

VICTORIA SARMAT. Four soldiers. (80 fr.)

PROVIDENTIAE AVGG. Four figures sacrificing before a pretorian camp.——*Obv.*—CONSTANTIVS CAES. Laureated head of Constantius.—See engraving, p. 191.

BRASS MEDALLIONS.—*Rev.*—MEMORIA DIVI CONSTANTI. Round temple.—*Obv.*—DIVO CONSTANTIO AVG. Veiled head of the emperor.— SACRA MONETA AVGG. ET CAESS. NOSTR.—SALVIS AVGG. ET CAESS. AVCT. KART.—VICTORIA BEATISSIMORVM CAESS.—(The above four valued by Mionnet at 50 fr. each).

Obv.—CONSTANTIVS NOBIL. C. Head of Constantius.—*Rev.*—MAXIMIANVS NOB. C. Head of Gal. Maximianus.—(200 fr. Mionnet).

SECOND BRASS.—ADLOCVTIO AVG. N. Allocution type.—AETERNA MEMORIA. Round temple.—CONSTANTIVS ET MAXIMIANVS. Heads of Constantius Chlorus and Gal. Maximian.

MEMORIA FELIX. A lighted altar, between two eagles, with wings expanded. In the exergue P. TR. On the obverse is the veiled head of Constantius Chlorus, with this legend—DIVO CONSTANTIO PIO.

[A specimen of this not rare but interesting coin has been engraved from a well-preserved coin, and appears at the head of the foregoing biographical summary, p. 262].

THIRD BRASS.—PRAESIDIA REIPVBLIC.—REQVIES OPTIMORVM MERITORVM.—VBIQVE VIC.

CONSTANTIUS II. *(Flavius Julius)*, third son of Constantine the Great, and the second

whom that emperor had by his second wife Fausta, was born at Sirmium, capital of Pannonia (now *Sirmich*, in Sclavonia, between the Drave and the Suave), on the 7th or 13th

of August, A. D. 317. He was declared *Cæsar*, and *Princeps Juventutis* on the 8th of November, 323; and being created Consul in 326, he was entrusted by his father, at the age of 15 years, with the administration of affairs in Gaul. In the partition which that emperor made of his dominion 335, Asia, Syria, and Egypt were assigned to Constantius. At the death of his celebrated father in 337, he immediately quitted the eastern provinces of which he was holding the government, and hastening to Constantinople, was there acknowledged as Augustus, at the same time with his brothers (Constantine jun. and Constans). In the arrangements afterwards made, he kept the East for himself. The army had already proclaimed their determination, that none should reign but the sons of Constantine; thus excluding Delmatius and Hanniballianus from the sovereignty of those provinces which their uncle had assigned to them. So far from evincing any displeasure at this instance of military dictation, it was he who, according to general belief, instigated the soldiers to massacre the male descendants of his grand-father Constantius Chlorus, with the exception only of Gallus and Julianus. After implicating himself in this atrocious act of perfidy and bloodshed, Constantius met his brothers at Sirmium, in 337, for the purpose of dividing the empire anew; and three youths of twenty-one, twenty, and seventeen years of age, partitioned out between themselves the government of the Roman world. But scarcely had Constantius taken possession of his share of the spoil (which share comprised Thrace, Macedonia, Greece, the Asiatic provinces, and Egypt), when he found himself engaged in a war with Sapor the Second, King of Persia, a war chiefly waged in Mesopotamia and the Syrian frontier, and which, with brief intervals, continued during the whole of this prince's reign. He was accustomed to pass the winters at Antioch, and to employ the summers in ravaging the Persian territories. In these campaigns Constantius fought the enemy, sometimes with glory, but frequently with dishonour. Amongst the many battles which turned to his disadvantage, was that of Singara, in 343, when he commanded in person; and, after having been victorious during the day, he was defeated in the succeeding night, with immense loss to his army.

In 350, having left Persia to oppose Magnentius, who, after causing Constans to be murdered, had succeeded in his attempt to become master of the western empire, Constantius was for some time under the necessity of tolerating a colleagueship with Vetranio, who commanded the Illyrian legions, and who, like Magnentius, had assumed the purple, and the title of Augustus. Constantius at length, however, having compelled Vetranio to renounce his imperial rank and government, proceeded, A. D. 351, in search of Magnentius, whom he defeated at Mursa, now Essek, a town on the banks of the Drave, in Hungary.—Magnentius fled into Gaul, and being again routed in two consecutive engagements by the armies of the emperor, this usurper put an end to his own life at Lyon, A. D. 353; his brother Decentius following his tragical example. Constantius thus became master of the whole west. Meanwhile he had given the title of Cæsar to his cousin Gallus; but the crimes to which that young prince abandoned himself, were such that, by the emperor's order, he was beheaded, after a reign of about four years. (See CONSTANTIUS GALLUS.)—On the sixth of November, 355, Constantius conferred the title of Cæsar on Julian, the brother of Gallus, to whom he gave his sister Helena in marriage, investing him, at the same time, with the government of the Gauls, Spain, and Britain.

Having obtained peace for the empire, Constantius made preparations to visit Rome, which he had not yet seen. He made his entry there on the 28th of April, 357, in the habiliments of a Triumpher, although no captives followed his chariot, and he was surrounded by none but his courtiers and a detachment of his troops.— Astonished and enraptured at the magnificence of the city, he ordered the great obelisk, which his father had caused to be brought from Heliopolis, in Egypt, and which was remaining at Alexandria, to be transported to Rome, where it was erected in the Circus Maximus. Returned to Mesopotamia, in 359, to meet the invading armies of Sapor, he received the tidings that Julian had been proclaimed Emperor of the West. This event induced Constantius to retrace his steps: and in 360, having re-assembled nearly all the legions of the East, he marched with them to encounter his relation and rival. But agitation and excitement, added to the fatigue of the expedition, threw him into a fever. He halted at Mopsocrene, a small town situated at the foot of Mount Taurus; and after having declared Julian his successor and sole master of the empire, he died on the third of November, A. D. 361, in the 25th year of his reign, and 45th of his age.—Julian caused his remains to be conveyed to Constantinople; received the body at the gates of that city, amidst his soldiers under arms; and interred it in the tomb of Constantine the Great.

MINTAGES OF CONSTANTIUS II.

Many of his gold and silver medallions are of the highest rarity; gold of the usual size common; silver of usual size rare; brass medallions rare; second and third brass very common.—The style of this emperor, on the obverses of his coins, as Cæsar, is *Dominus* N*oster*

CONSTANTIVS.—As Augustus, it is IMP. FL*avius* IVL*ius* CONSTANTIVS MAX*imus* AVG*ustus*. Also D. N. FL. CONSTANTIVS P. F. PERP*etuus* AVG*ustus*.

GOLD MEDALLIONS.—CONSTANTINVS VICTOR SEMPER AVG. Emperor in triumphal car.— (Valued by Mionnet at 600 francs.)

GAVDIVM ROMANORVM. Constantine between Constantine jun. and Constans. (Mionnet, 600 fr.)

GAVDIVM ROMANORVM. Four figures. (Engraved in Steinbüchel, No. 4. Valued by Mionnet at 2000 francs.]

Same legend.—Female seated. (Mionnet, 600 francs). Engraved in Steinbüchel, L. c. No. 5.

GLORIA ROMANORVM. Unique medallion.— Engraved in Akerman, vol. ii. pl. G. No. 2. Brought £17 10s. at the Thomas sale. Lot 3006.

OB. VICTORIAM TRIVMPHALEM. (Mt. 100 fr.)

PRINCIPI IVVENTVTIS. Unique medallion. Engraved in Akerman, vol. ii. pl. G. No. 1. Brought £14 14s. at the Thomas sale, Lot 3007.

SALVS ET SPES REIPVBLICAE. (Mt. 600 fr.)

SECVRITAS PERPETVAE *(sic)*.—200 fr.

VIRTVS CONSTANTI AVG. Unique medallion. Engraved in Akerman, vol. ii. p. F. No. 5.— Brought £11 at the Thomas sale. Lot 3008.

SILVER MEDALLIONS.—GAVDIVM POPVLI ROMANI. (Mt. 100 fr.)—TRIVMFATOR GENTIVM BARBARARVM. (Mt. 100 fr.)—VIRTVS EXERCITVS. (Mt. 50 fr.)—VIRTVS D. N. AVG. (£1, Thomas.)—GLORIA REIPVBLICAE. (Pembroke, £1 15s.)—VICTORIA AVG. NOSTRI. (Valued by Mionnet at 50 fr.)

GOLD.——FELICITAS PERPETVA.——GAVDIVM POPVLI ROMANI.—SECVRITAS REIPVBLICAE.— VICTORIA CONSTANTI.–VIRTVS EXERCITVS GALL. —(The foregoing five valued by Mionnet at 30 francs each).

PRINCIPI IVVENTVTIS.—(Pembroke, £1 8s.)

SILVER.—CONSTANTIVS AVG.—GLORIA REIPVBLICAE. Two women seated.—PAX AVGVSTORVM.—(Valued by Mionnet at 20 fr. each).

BRASS MEDALLIONS.—DEBELLATORI GENTT. BARBARR. (Mionnet, 20 fr.)—FEL. TEMP. REPARATIO. (24 fr.)—LARGITIO. (50 fr.)—SABINAE. (50 fr.)—VIRTVS AVG. NOSTRI. (24 fr.)

SECOND BRASS.—HOC SIGNO VICTOR ERIS. Emperor with labarum, charged with the monogram of Christ.—MONETA AVG. The 3 Monetæ.

CONSTANTIUS GALLUS.—It is after this appellation that one of the nephews of Constantius II., and the eldest brother of Julianus, afterwards emperor, is commonly called by historians, although on coins he is named simply Constantius.—Gallus, born A.D. 325, was the son of Julius Constantius, youngest son of Constantius Chlorus, and of Galla. At the age of 12 years, he was, with Julian, spared from the sweeping massacre which their ambitious uncle Constantius perfidiously connived at, and which deprived their father of life. In 351, that very kinsman created him Cæsar; associated him in the imperial government; and caused him to add to his own the name of Constantius. Having also given him for wife his sister Constantina, the widow of Hannibalianus, the artful emperor assigned to Gallus the defence of the eastern provinces against the Persians, and sent him to reside at Antioch. The young prince was gifted with a well formed person, and a prepossessing countenance: he had also an imposing air of grandeur in his deportment. His brother Julian and himself had passed their youth together, in a kind of exile, and their education had been confined to the study of ecclesiastical literature, and to the practices of ascetic piety. This course of instruction had attached Gallus to the Christian Church, but it had not taught him to repress his passions, which were of such a haughty, insolent, and savage description, as to render him an object of dread and hatred during the whole period of his residence in Syria. It was there that he showed himself in the undisguised violence and brutality of his natural character. He perpetrated, both out of his own vicious disposition, and at the instigation of his wife who was not less guilty than himself, acts of the most flagrant injustice, and of the most revolting cruelty. At once the spy upon, and the accuser of, his subjects, he caused all, of whose wealth he was covetous, to be put to death without any form of legal procedure. The death of Theophilus, governor of Syria, whom he abandoned to the merciless fury of an Antiochian populace; and the atrocious barbarity with which he delivered numerous other personages of distinguished rank, into the hands of the public executioner, roused a general spirit of resistance to his tyranny; and he was denounced to the emperor.—Constantius II. sent Domitianus pretorian prefect of the East, and Montius questor of the palace, to his residence at Antioch, for the purpose of inquiring into his conduct. Justly charged with mal-administration, disobedience, and cruelty, in his government of the East, he enormously increased his guilt by putting the above-named imperial commissioners to death. It appears that these servants of Constantius, instead of ensnaring him with gentle persuasions, in conformity with their instructions, had the imprudence to adopt towards Gallus the language of menace and defiance; and the consequence was, they were torn to pieces by an infuriated multitude, whom Gallus had excited to destroy them. The emperor fearing that, after this, his nephew would, in desperation, be led to add open rebellion to his other offences, had recourse to new promises, with the view of drawing him away from Antioch; fully resolved to punish him afterwards. Accordingly he wrote to him letters full of professed affection, deceived by which Gallus set out to meet his uncle at Milan.—At Petovio (Pettau) in Pannonia, however, he was arrested, and sent to Pola, in Istria. Gallus there underwent a sort of trial for the crimes he had committed, and was convicted of them all. His judges, after receiving orders from Constantius, condemned him to death; and having been conducted to the place of execution, with his hands tied behind him, like a culprit of the lowest class, he was beheaded, at the close of the year 354, when he was in his second consulate. He was then only 29 years old, and had reigned, as Cæsar, but three years and eight months.—Most of those who had participated in his crimes were doomed by Constantius to share the same fate with him.

MINTAGES of CONSTANTIUS GALLUS.

On his coins, which are all very rare, in each metal, except second and third brass, he is styled CONSTANTIVS CAES.—FL. IVL. CONSTANTIVS NOB. CAES.——DN. CONSTANTIVS NOB. CAES.——DN. CONSTANTIVS IVN. NOB. C.

GOLD MEDALLIONS.—GLORIA ROMANORVM. Two types. (Valued by Mionnet at 200 fr. each.)

SILVER MEDALLIONS.—FELICITAS ROMANORVM.——GLORIA EXERCITVS.——VIRTVS EXERCITVS.—(200 francs each.)

GOLD.—FELICITAS ROMANORVM. (100 fr.) GLORIA REIPVBLICAE. (80 fr.)——VICTORIA AVGVSTORVM. (50 fr.)

SILVER.—PRINCIPIA IVVENTVTIS. The Cæsar stands between two military ensigns, to one of which he extends his left hand, whilst he holds a sceptre or baton in his right.—Obv.—FL. IVL. CONSTANTIVS NOB. CAES. Diademed head of Gallus.—Engraved in preceding page, from a finely preserved silver specimen in the British Museum.

BRASS MEDALLIONS.—GLORIA ROMANORVM. —VRBS ROMA.—VICTORIA AVGVSTORVM (Mionnet, 40 fr. each).—VIRTVS AVG.—VIRTVS AVGVSTORVM. (48 fr. each).

THIRD BRASS.—FELix TEMPorum REPARATIO. Military figure pierces with his spear a prostrate horse and its rider.—Obv.—D. N. CONSTANTIVS NOB. CAES. Diademed head of Constantius Gallus; as is seen in the above engraving.

CONSTANTIUS III. surnamed Patricius, was born at Naissus, in Illyria; his family unknown. He was the husband of the sister of Honorius, and A. D. 411 was appointed by that emperor to be the general of his armies. In 421, he was declared Augustus, and associated in the government of the western empire. He died the same year at Ravenna, having borne the title of Augustus only seven months. The coins of this last of the name stand in the highest degree of rarity. On these he is styled D. N. CONSTANTIVS P. F. AVG.—The reverses are as follow, viz. :—

GOLD.—VICTORIA AVGG. The emperor holding the labarum. (Valued by Mionnet at 400 fr.)—VICTORIA AVGVSTORVM. Victory marching. A quinarius. (300 fr.)

SILVER.—VICTORIA ROMANORVM.—VOTIS V. MVLTIS.—(100 fr. each.)

CONSULATUS, the consulate or office of CONSUL. This, the highest of the Roman magistracies conferred, as is well known, upon him who held it, the possession of sovereign authority during his term of office, which was for only one year. The consulate was established immediately after the abolition of royalty, in the year of Rome 244 (B. C. 510), at the first formation of the republic. It was then that the people, instead of any longer submitting to the rule of a king, began to confide their government to two persons, whom they called Consuls, Pitiscus says, à consulendo, from the act of consulting, because they gave their care and their counsel to their country.—J. W. D. in Smith's Dictionary, on the other hand says, "Without doubt the name consules means nothing more than simply colleagues." As these annually elected magistrates were substituted in the place of a monarch, so were they invested with all the prerogatives and powers of royalty, together with all the exterior marks of regal dignity. The consuls, so long as they remained in Rome, had under their controul every thing that related to public affairs. The other magistrates, with the exception of the tribunes, came under their cognizance. The consulate, however, even at an early period of the republic, began to descend from its high estate, when tribunes of the people were established with the right of opposing all the acts of the consuls. The only remedy in pressing times for the evils arising out of a factious exercise of the tribunitian veto, was one as dangerous as the disease to the state itself, viz., the dictatorship, So great, however, was the legal weight of the consulate—so prominent a place did its occupiers retain in the veneration and attachment of the people; and such were the external attributes of supreme grandeur with which the persons of the consuls themselves were gifted and surrounded, that the office never lost its political importance, nor its popular influence, so long as the republic lasted. Nor did this magistracy cease when the government fell into the hands of a single individual. The two consuls continued to be annually named; the consular fasti verified, as before, the chronological series of all the years; and these offices were solicited, from the favour of the prince, as they had before been asked at the suffrages of the citizens. The emperors distinguished their favourites and their relations with this title, already become purely of an honorary kind, and they likewise frequently took it for themselves.

To describe at large the origin, the dignity, and changes of the Roman consulate, does not come within the plan of this compilation. Such particulars are fully understood by those who are conversant with the history of Rome in her free state, whilst they contribute but little to the elucidation of the medallic science. But so far as the office of Consul, exercised under the Cæsars and Emperors, is referred to in monetal legends and types, the following analysis of Eckhel's learned dissertation on the subject will be found replete with useful information, and can hardly prove otherwise than acceptable to the numismatic student.

Since, from the time of Julius Cæsar, to the lower empire, the practice prevailed of princes inscribing on their coins their own consulates, and the repetitions of them, an acquaintance with the Cæsarian consulates is unquestionably of the greatest importance to a right understanding of the chronological history of the emperors and their times. After having, in opposition to the published opinions of certain learned authors, expressed his own firm conviction, that in the assumption of the consulate, the emperors observed no fixed rules, but, as in most other matters, followed their own inclination,—Eckhel proceeds to explain the conditions of the office in question, as established from the time of Julius Cæsar, and continuing in force through subsequent reigns, up to the period of its abolition, arranging under separate heads, the various branches of the subject, as follows:—

I.—CONSULES CONTINUI.—First on the list appear the continued consulates, which were either conferred upon princes or assumed by them.—It had been provided by a decree of the people (plebiscito) that no one should be re-elected consul till after an interval of ten years. But, at the close of the republic, when the laws no longer ruled, but were over-ruled, the ancient statute was infringed. The seven consulates of Marius are well known; and soon after, L. Sulla suffered only eight years to elapse before he was chosen consul for the second time, and also at the same moment dictator; and his example was followed by Julius Cæsar, who "received a renewed (continuum) consulate and a perpetual dictatorship;" and the fact of this renewal of office is confirmed also by his coins. When Artaxata was taken by Corbulo, in the year of Rome 811 (B. C. 58), the Senate decreed to Nero a continuous (or renewed) consulate. But the Fasti and coins prove that he did not accept the honour. Vitellius nominated himself a perpetual consul, but his intentions were frustrated. In the case of some of the Augusti, the assumed consulates differed little from the continuous. Vespasian, during a reign of ten years, renewed the consulate eight times; and Titus also was much inclined for this distinction; still more Domitian, whose consulates numbered seventeen. To these may be added Elagabalus. All preceding emperors were surpassed by Theodosius II. on whose Fasti (and perhaps his coins also), there appear eighteen consulates.

II.—CONSULS APPOINTED BY THE EMPERORS.—That, under the imperial government, the power of appointing consuls rested with the reigning princes, is shewn by the entire history of the augustal age; nor can the fact be called in question, considering the unlimited authority of the emperors. The *Augusti*, indeed, took upon themselves the office of consul, though they at all times combined the consular with the imperial authority ; either to throw in the teeth of the disaffected a certain resemblance to the old commonwealth, following, as Appian supposes, the example of Sulla ; or to render still more famous, by their consulate, a year in which some extraordinary festival was to occur ; or from vanity, or from the desire of outvying others, which Ausonius cleverly attacks in the case of Domitian ; or from some other motive. For, from the circumstance that there was not one even of the most rational and moderate amongst them, who did not several times renew to himself that distinction, it may be inferred that the consulship was a post most gratifying to the emperors.

III.—CONSULES SUFFECTI.—This term (from *sufficio* to put in the place of another) was used to denote substituted or added consuls. They were unknown in Free Rome, except in the case of one of them dying, during his year of office, when it became necessary that some person should be deputed to fill his place for the remainder of the period. Julius Cæsar set the first example of a *consul suffectus.*—In the year 709 (B. C. 45), according to Dion, "He entered upon the consulate immediately, and before his arrival in Rome. He did not, however, retain it for a whole year, but after his return to Rome, he resigned the office, and conferred it upon Q. Fabius and C. Trebonius. And as Fabius expired on the last day of his consulship, he (Cæsar) deputed to it C. Caninius for the few remaining hours."

Cicero, in recording this same fact, wittily adds—"So, you must know, that during the whole consulship of Caninius not a soul dined. Nevertheless, whilst he was consul, no mischief took place. For so marvellous was his vigilance, that he slept not once all the time he was consul." After the precedent thus established, it rarely happened that the individuals who entered upon office on the calends of January, retained it for the whole year ; as the emperors, in return for services performed, used to invite others to a participation in this honour. And there was a time, when this licence was carried beyond all bounds ; as Cleander, who from the position of a slave, had risen to be the all powerful chamberlain of Commodus, is related to have appointed twenty-five consuls in one year. There are also instances of emperors, but those only of a weak capacity, who deposed the legitimate consuls, and thrust themselves into their places. And in this manner Caligula and Elagabalus held their first consulates by substitution, *(suffectum consulatum)*, and Nero his last, as their respective coins attest.

The names of these substituted consuls were written on the consular *Fasti*, but the year was reckoned by the name of the *Consules ordinarii* (see next column). Now, as many princes, before their accession to the imperial throne, had been invested with this kind of honorary consulship,

or had not despised the office after their becoming emperors, this circumstance must be attended to, in order to reconcile apparent contradictions, which may sometimes present themselves on a comparison of the consulates with the tribunitian powers.

Consules ordinarii.—Those who entered upon office on the calends of January, were called *ordinarii ;* and it was they who gave a name to the year, and consequently enjoyed a higher authority than the *suffecti consules*, who were scarcely known beyond the bounds of Rome and Italy, and were therefore styled *consules minores*. Consuls by substitution, when they afterwards obtained the regular *(ordinarium)* consulship, were in the habit of reckoning the substituted one. Octavianus was chosen in the place of the consuls who fell in battle, A. U. C. 711 (B. C. 43) ; and when in the year 721 (B. C. 33), he again became consul, he was on all records styled *consul iterum*. Caligula being *consul suffectus* from the calends of July, 790 (A. D. 37), proceeded *consul iterum* (consul for the second time), on the calends of January, 792. —Domitian numbered five *suffecti consulatus*, which he had passed before his accession.— Many other instances are recorded in the annals of his reign. "Nevertheless (adds Eckhel), in the mintage of Domitian, under date of 832 (A. D. 79), there is a coin on which no mention is made of his five consulates by substitution."

IV.—CONSULES DESIGNATI.—Consuls elect (from *designare*), a term used to distinguish those who were appointed to fill that and other public offices. Magistrates were first *designati*, and some months after that formality, they entered upon the exercise of their authority.

During the times of the common-wealth, consuls were not considered as *elect*, except in relation to the year immediately following. But even that custom began very early to be disregarded. In the year 715 (B. C. 39), during the sovereignty of the Triumvirs *Rei Publicæ Constituendæ*, consuls were styled *elect* for eight years, of which A. U. C. 720 and 723 were assigned to Mark Antony. He is called, therefore, on his coins, simply COS. from the year 710, when he was first made consul, till the year 715 above mentioned. And from that date to 720 (B. C. 34), COS. DESIG. ITER. ET. TERT. From 720 to 723, COS. DESIG. III. From 723, when he actually entered upon his third consulate, COS. III. ; and this order is plainly to be recognised on his coins. The same regulation was observed by Octavianus, who was, in the same year 715, *designatus* consul for the years 721 and 723.—Augustus made his daughter's sons, Caius and Lucius, consuls elect, but on the condition of their taking office in five years' time (see p. 217 of this dictionary).—Nero was consul elect at the age of fourteen, intending to enter upon the consulate at twenty; whence he is styled on his coins COS. DESIGN.

And this pre-appointment the emperors were not backward in notifying on coins and other public monuments, when they felt a desire to enrol themselves as consuls. Whence it is usual to read on them, amongst other inscriptions, COS. III. DES. IIII.—Sometimes consulates simply promised, or designated, seem to have been confounded with consulates really acquired and held, or at least the word DES*ignatus* has been omitted. But instances of this sort are very rare; and it would even appear that the greater part of the medals cited as examples of the case, have been incorrectly read: the error being doubtless caused by the numbers expressed having been effaced by the lapse of time or by friction. It is, however, to be remarked that, although the consulate existed until the reign of Justinian, who united this dignity to the imperial crown, yet long before that epocha, and indeed from the commencement of what is called the lower empire, the emperors, for the most part, neglected to mention it on their money, where it appears only at very wide intervals.

V.—ORNAMENTA CONSULARIA.—By this term was meant those consular honours which, decreed to any individual by the emperors, were a kind of semblance of the consulate. Dion Cassius, indeed, tells us that, as early as the year of Rome 687 (B.C. 147), and consequently whilst the common-wealth was still in existence, C. Carbo, though as yet he had discharged only the tribuneship of the plebs, received the distinction of the *ornamenta consularia*. It is not, however, sufficiently understood in what these honours consisted. Their real origin is doubtless to be traced to Julius Cæsar, who, when in his endeavour to confer favours on a number of persons, he found himself unable to give to all either the regular (*ordinarium*) or the substituted (*suffectum*) consulate, invented this fictitious distinction. He admitted many, says Dion, into the patrician and consular ranks. And Suetonius also observes, "he bestowed consular honours on ten individuals who had been Pretors (*viris prætoriis*)."—When Octavianus, after the deaths of the consuls Hirtius and Pansa, was aiming at the consulate, the Senate, unwilling to confer so high a post upon a mere boy, nevertheless decreed to him, in its stead, consular honours. Several instances in which this dignity was awarded afterwards occur, and that too even to foreigners; as for example, Claudius procured it for Agrippa, the grandson of Herod the Great; the Senate having before, during the reign of Caligula, decreed him pretorian honours.

It is a question, whether those, who were thus distinguished, raised thereby the number of

their consulate, when they subsequently entered upon office in the regular way. Dion negatives this, in his life of Octavianus. For when this emperor first assumed consular honours, and shortly after, the consulate itself, he did not ambitiously call it his second. Indeed, the author above quoted, immediately adds, that the practice was observed from that period to his own times, in all similar cases, and that Severus was the first to alter it; inasmuch as, when he had first bestowed these honours, and afterwards the office of consul itself, upon Plautianus, he commanded him to be proclaimed as consul (*iterum*) for the second time; and that this example was followed by others. Nevertheless, he was averse to this rule being observed in his own case.

VI.—MOTIVES OF PRINCES FOR ASSUMING THE CONSULATE.—Having assigned some of the reasons which usually actuated the emperors in either undertaking or multiplying their consulships, Eckhel proceeds to explain with greater distinctness their various inducements to assume the office in some particular year.—Without denying, that many princes were in the habit of being inaugurated consuls on the first calends of January after their accession to empire, Eckhel shews that as a rule, it fails in the majority of instances. The custom appears to have been derived from Nero. At any rate, his immediate successors, Galba, Vespasian, Titus, Domitian, and Nerva, followed his example, by entering upon their consulate on the next calends of January after their accession.—When Trajan was averse to this practice, Pliny thus expressed himself—"You refused at the commencement of your reign the consulate, which all new emperors used to transfer to themselves, though it was destined for others." From these very words of Pliny, therefore, it is sufficiently evident, that the custom was, even at that time, observed by the emperors, and it is confirmed by Spartian, in speaking of Ælius Cæsar—"He was soon created consul, and having been deputed to hold the reins of government, he was styled consul for the second time."—After Trajan, not a few departed from the practice. They have been collected by Mazzoleni, and may be seen in the *Fasti*. It must therefore be concluded, that the custom was approved of by many of the emperors, but that the rule did not hold universally.

It also occurred, that the emperors assumed the consulate on account of public solemnities of various kinds. Suetonius has observed of Augustus, that he was desirous of entering upon his thirteenth and last consulate, in order that he might, in that high capacity, attend upon his sons Caius and Lucius, when they were introduced into the forum, on the occasion of their first public appearance (*tyrocinio*). The princes of the lower empire—at least those who were called consuls of the East—according to Themistius, always took great pains to prevent other individuals from holding this office on the recurrence of the quinquennial or decennial period, when it gave a name to the year.—

Whence, he says, it seemed a remarkable circumstance, that Theodosius Magnus should, at the quinquennalia, have ceded this honour to Saturninus, a private individual. In general terms it may be affirmed, that, as in most other matters, so in the assumption and repetition of the consulate, the will and pleasure of the emperors were their sole motive and guide.

VII.—CONSULSHIP UNDER THE EMPIRE ONLY HONORARY.—From the time when the emperors had brought every species of authority under their own control, it no longer came within the province of the consuls to conduct foreign wars, or to watch over the safety of the state; but, distinguished only by their robes of office, they were compelled to lead a life of ignoble ease at Rome, instead of attending to the weighty concerns of government. Truly, therefore, did Mamertinus speak of the consulates of the imperial age:—" In the administration of state affairs (in administrationibus), labour is conjoined with honour; but in the consulate honour only is involved, without the labour."—Cassiodorus is still more severe upon the slothfulness of consuls. The only advantage which this office conferred from that time forward, has been explained by the Emperor Julian:—" To private individuals (he says) it is a sort of recompense of virtue, or of fidelity and zeal in the service of the emperors, or for some deed of renown; whilst in the case of the princes themselves, it is a kind of decoration and embellishment, added to the advantage they already possess."

VIII.—CONSULATUS DIMIDIUS.——Amongst other particulars connected with the consulate previous to the final abolition of the office, the office of Consulatus Dimidius is to be briefly noticed. It seems that this "half consulship" consisted of but one consul; that is to say, a consul without a colleague. The first instance of this occurred in the year of Rome 702 (B.C. 52), in the third consulate of Pompey the Great, who was elected sole consul by the Comitia. As this case arose during the republic in consequence of dissensions among the citizens, so, at a much later period, namely, in the reign of Constantine the Great, it was occasioned by a disagreement among a plurality of reigning powers.—Several, indeed, of the ancient Fasti have marked the year A.D. 310 and 313, with the consulate of Maxentius alone.

IX.—CONSULATUS ORIENTALIS ET OCCIDENTALIS.—Constantine the Great, on the division of the Roman Empire into the Eastern and Western, determined that of the two annual consuls, the one should be appointed at Rome, the other at Constantinople. This practice came into operation A.D. 338, on the calends of January; in which year, Constantine having just before died; and the empire, according to his desire, being divided amongst his three sons, the first consuls under this new arrangement were elected; Ursus in the West, and Polemius in the East. In consequence of this, when it happened that there was any uncertainty respecting the consul of one or other portion of the em-

pire, the inscription on public records ran thus:—" The consuls being N. and whosoever shall be hereafter declared;" or, "The consuls, one of whom is Aristœnetus, for the name of his colleague is not known."

"Post Consulatum," formula.——Whenever, either from quarrels among the ruling powers, or from wars, or the assassination of emperors, or other causes, the year was deficient in its consuls, at least the regular and legitimate ones, it not unfrequently occurred, that this vacant year or years received its name from the regular consul of the preceding year, the inscription running thus, e. g. Basilio V. C. consule, Anno secundo post C. Basilii, Anno tertio post C. Basilii; such being the designation of the years A. D. 541, 542, and 543. This formula first appears A. D. 307, when the consuls of the preceding year had been Constantius Chlorus (VI.) and Gal. Maximianus (VI.); and it was more frequent in the latter periods of the emperors, when the regulations were various and often confused.

X.——CONSULARIA INSIGNIA.——The marks and badges of office by which the consuls were distinguished.—Florus says of Tarquinius Priscus—" By constant warfare, he subdued the twelve nations of Etruria, and from thence were derived the fasces, the trabea, the curule chairs, the rings, trappings, paludamenta, prætexta, the practice of being carried in triumph on a golden chariot, drawn by four horses, the embroidered toga, the tunic covered with broad golden ornaments (palmata), in short all the decorations and insignia for which the imperial dignity is conspicuous."—Dionysius of Halicarnassus, among the badges of sovereignty, which Priscus at that time transferred to Rome, mentions " the crown of gold, and the staff surmounted by the figure of an eagle, the purple tunic, ornamented with gold, and the purple embroidered toga (or that of many colours, toga picta)." He adds, that on the expulsion of the kings, these insignia were permitted to the consuls, with the exception of the crown and the embroidered toga, though, when they appeared in a triumph, they wore these also.

The Family Coins give us but little information as to the number of the badges that were allowed to the consuls whilst Rome remained free. On coins of the Junia gens we find represented the elder Brutus, who was also the first who held the office of consul, between two lictors formidable from their fasces and axes.—But it was already established from other sources, that the consuls used to be preceded by the twelve fasces.

On the denarii of Sulla (see Cornelia gens), which exhibit the names of two consuls, Sulla and Pompeius Rufus, as also on a denarius of Valerius Messala, inscribed PATRE COS. the sella curulis is attributed to the consuls; but this distinction was enjoyed by other officers of inferior rank to the consuls.

In a denarius of Augustus, struck in the year of Rome 752 (see PARENT. CONS. SVO.) there appear the staff with the eagle, the embroidered toga, and the laurel chaplet; all of which, however, may more probably be considered as triumphal rather than as consular decorations.

On this subject, the subsequent age, viz. that of the empire, supplies more abundant and trust-worthy information.—In Vopiscus, the Emperor Valerian thus addresses Aurelian:—"Take, therefore, in recompense for your exploits, ... the toga prætexta, the palmated tunic, the embroidered toga, the chair inlaid with ivory. For I this day nominate you consul, and am about to write directions to the Senate, that it confer upon you the staff, and the fasces."—Cassiodorus gives a similar account, inveighing bitterly against those whom the *Augusti*, for no adequate merits, decorated with the consular insignia—" But now you assume these distinctions under more fortunate auspices, whilst we sustain the toils of the consulate, and you enjoy the delights of dignity. —Picture to yourself, your broad shoulders adorned with the varied colours of the palmated tunic; your strong hand grasping the staff of victory; approach your own fire-side with even your shoes glittering with gold; ascend by many steps your lofty curule chair, that by lying at your ease, you may earn that which we assume by the severest labour in the administration of affairs."—And indeed, on the coins of the *Augusti*, from the time when the empire began to decline, there frequently occurs a half-length bust *(protome)* of the emperor, with the palmated robe, and carrying in his hand the staff surmounted by an eagle, from which is to be inferred an emperor serving the office of consul.

The following five examples are selected to shew the accordance of legend and type in connection with the consulate, on certain coins of the lower empire:—

1. On a gold coin of Maximinus Daza (see the annexed engraving, copied from Pellerin, *Mélange*, 1, pl. vi.) the reverse type represents the emperor, togated and laureated, standing with a globe, or an *aurum coronarium*, in his left hand, and a sceptre reversed in his right—surrounded by the legend CONSVL P. P. PRO-CONSVL.

2. On gold of Maximianus Herculeus, given in Banduri, the emperor stands in the toga, and laureated, holding a globe, the symbol of the Roman world, in his right hand, whilst with his left he gathers up his robe and holds a roll or volume. The legend of reverse is CONSVL IIII. P. P. PRO-COS.

3. On gold of Galerius Maximianus, with legend of CONSVL CAESS. the Cæsar stands with globe and sceptre.

4. On a gold medallion of Constantine the Great, the reverse presents a remarkably fine whole-length figure of an emperor, standing with laureated head, full-dressed in the consular insignia, consisting of the palmated tunic, and the embroidered toga—holding a globe in the right hand, and a sceptre in the left.—See SENATVS.

5. The reverse of a gold coin struck under Constantine the younger, exhibits the togated and laureated figure of the imperial consul, with globe and sceptre, accompanied with the explanatory legend of FELIX PROCESSVS COS. II. AVG.—[Numbers 2, 3, and 5, are engraved in Khell's Supplement to Vaillant.]

XI.—CONSULARIS PROCESSUS.—The consular procession, as it is represented on coins, still remains to be explained. Consuls were said *procedere* (to go in state) when, having been consuls elect in the year immediately preceding, they entered upon the office, on the calends of January, with the customary pomp and retinue; and this solemn occasion was commonly termed *processus consularis*, as coins prove.—See the legend FELIX PROCESS*us* CONSVL AVG. N.

But there are also examples which shew that ancient authors used the word *processus* alone, omitting all mention of the consul, to indicate the *consularis processus*.—When, however, the emperor is represented on coins in a quadriga, either of horses or elephants, and carrying the staff surmounted by an eagle, it is difficult at times to determine whether by this type is to be understood a triumph, or a consular procession; because from all that has hitherto been seen, this eagle is common both to those who enjoyed a triumph, and to those who proceeded as consuls. Still it not unfrequently happens, that the coin itself suggests a plan by which the one may be distinguished from the other solemnity.

When a similar type is found on a coin of that year in which it is certain that the emperor entered upon his consulate, and especially if history records no triumph performed during that year, there can be no doubt that a *consular procession* is intended, and that it is exhibited on the coins in the same way as all other events of importance were so handed down.

Amongst the first brass in Queen Christina's cabinet is one of Antoninus Pius (see the reverse engraved in p. 267), which Havercamp, with great probability, describes as recording one of the consular processions made by that good emperor. The prince is typified with the (ivory) sceptre in his left hand, and with his right hand stretched forth and open, standing in a chariot drawn by four horses. In the exergue of this reverse is the legend COS. IIII. S. C. (Consul for the 4th time by decree of the Senate), A. D. 145.

For further remarks and additional engravings illustrative of this branch of the subject, see PROCESSUS.

Some notice of the custom of scattering money amongst the people by consuls, during their procession, will be found affixed to the legend PETRONIUS MAXSIMUS U. C. CONS.

XII.—THE CONSULATE AFTER A TIME VERY SELDOM INSCRIBED ON COINS.—Though the consulates were recorded on monuments of various kinds, and in private chronicles, especially when the occurrence of some particular event was to be established, yet they at length ceased to be inscribed on coins. From the time of

Constantine the Great, and his sons, the Cæsars, a long interval elapsed till the time of Theodosius II. who inscribed on his coins his 17th and 18th consulates. The last were Heraclius II. (Constantinus) son of Heraclius I. on whose unique coin is inscribed ERACAIO CONSVA.

At length this venerable office, retaining now nothing of its ancient splendor, began to sink so low in general estimation, that Leo VIth, *Sapiens*, who came to the empire A. D. 886, ordered to be struck out of the catalogue of laws, with other useless matter, the *Novella* CV. of Justinian, which treats of the consulate, and contains the law, which no longer bore any reference to the existing state of things. And it became thenceforth the practice in the East, for the purpose of distinguishing the years, to use the epoch of the creation of the world (*epocha orbis conditi*), which by the calculation of the Septuagint translators, whether truly or falsely, was fixed on the first day of September, in the 5508th year, the third month, and 25th day before the birth of Christ.—On this subject consult the chronologists, and Gibbons' Compendium, chap. 40, at the end.

CONSULAR COINS.—See *Numi Consulares*.

CONTORNIATE COINS.—Both for abundance and for superiority of curious interest, the NUMI CONTORNIATI, as they are termed in Latin works, hold the foremost place amongst the *pseudo moneta* of ancient times. It is probable that this word is derived from the Italian *contorno*, or from the French *contour*, signifying the outline of anything; since most of these coins actually exhibit, on the outer edge of both obverse and reverse, a circular line deeply engraved. The subject is treated of, with his usual mastery and with his accustomed justice to the labours of others, by Eckhel, who (in *Doctrina*, viii. 277) has divided it into six heads, viz. the characteristics, the types, the date, the use, and the merit, of Contorniates. The following is a summary:—

I.—PECULIAR CHARACTERISTICS.—These are of a kind readily to strike the eye, and to distinguish this class of medals from the genuine coinage.

First.—The line on the edge of the coin, on both sides, marked circularly, and in the mode of a furrow; generally deep, in the place usually occupied, on the regular products of the Roman mint, by a ring of *globules*, which is rarely found on the coins now in the course of being described. This is the most certain token of a contorniate, and it is the circumstance, which, as already observed, probably gave rise to the term. There appears to be no doubt, that this line was made with a graving tool, *after* the coin was struck; for, on many specimens, the heads of the letters are divided by the instrument.

Secondly.—The next characteristic is the monogram, as exhibited on the foregoing cut, together with various small figures, placed beside the portrait of the obverse, among which the most frequent is the *palm branch*. When this, and the monogram are both present, the coin may assuredly be regarded as a contorniate. There are other figures, though more rarely to be seen, such as a star, an ivy leaf, a bow and quiver, and a flying *victory.*—There are contorniates, however, which display none of these marks. It is to be noted, that neither the monogram, nor the figures are in relief, but *cut into* the coin, and frequently filled up with silver. The monogram, which is resolved into EP. or PE. no one has yet been found to explain with any degree of probability. This identical EP. has, however, been seen inscribed on contorniates, near the monogram of Christ and the palm branch, on a brass plate, published by Pignori. Consequently, (adds Eckhel), as these letters EP. or PE. are on this monument found conjoined with the palm branch, and as on many contorniates they supply the place of that branch, it may fairly be conjectured, that they signify something connected with victory.

Thirdly.—All contorniates are of brass. Gold and silver of this class are unknown.

Fourthly.—Their size is the same as that of medallions, but not so their weight, for they are of thinner brass. There are some, however, though very rare, of smaller size, and somewhat thicker metal, like the coins called in Italian *medaglioncini*. Of this kind is a coin of Constantine the Great, in the imperial cabinet, but which is clearly proved to be a contorniate by the monogram EP. engraven on it.—Havercamp (Num. 56), has published one of unusual size, with the head of Placidius Valentinianus, from the cabinet of Queen Christina.

Fifthly.—Contorniates exhibit a workmanship peculiar to themselves, with the figures flat, and very little raised from the surface, no doubt because, as above stated, they are of thin metal. Occasionally the whole of the figures are engraved *into* the coin. Of this kind are those classed among the *decursiones*, under the heads of TOXXOTES, COSMVS, and SELEVCVS; silver being also run into the cavities, as before described. In these specimens the style of workmanship, at the best, does not surpass mediocrity. In many instances they afford evidence of a rough and unskilful hand.

II.—OF CONTORNIATE TYPES GENERALLY. —The obverses of this class of coins, as well as others, present for the most part some head or bust. The types of the reverses are generally borrowed from the Circensian games and other spectacles, though there are not wanting subjects derived from mythic and heroic tradition, whilst some are abstruse or altogether unintelligible.

Contorniate medals present this peculiarity, that there is scarcely ever any apparent connexion between the obverse and the reverse.— For no one will find it easy to reconcile the portrait of Alexander the Great with a representation of the Roman Circus, Scylla, or the Rape of the Sabines;—or again, Horace, Apollonius of Tyana, or Sallust, with the charioteers of the circus, wrestlers, and mountebanks;—or Nero with Faustina junior. The arbitrary principle, on which the obverses and reverses are joined, will appear the more strikingly, when it is observed, that the same types are presented with different portraits. Thus we have the fable of Scylla connected with the heads of Alexander the Great, of Nero, of Trajan, and of Roma; Cybele and her Atys, in company with the head of Homer, of Nero, of Vespasian, and of Trajan.—To how little purpose the learned Havercamp laboured, in the endeavour to reconcile, in every instance, the obverse and reverse of contorniates, is clearly proved in every page of the most laborious attempt ever made to describe and illustrate Contorniate Coins.—See *Dissertationes de Alexandri M. Numismat. &c.*

The portraits, which occupy the obverses, are those of men of various fortunes, ranks, and professions, both high and low. But no undoubted representation of deity has ever yet been discovered on these coins. On some, however, there appears the head, with the legend of ROMA, or INVICTA ROMA FELIX SENATVS. The majority of them present the portraits of Roman emperors, and frequently that of Alexander the Great, as also of such celebrated individuals as Homer, Terence, Horace, and others. And, lastly, not a few of them exhibit a figure, holding a whip in the right hand, and with the left leading a horse by the bridle, by which type some suppose is intended the portrait of various emperors, but Eckhel shews, in his remarks on the contorniate *decursiones*, that they are the figures of charioteers.

The following is a list of all the emperors and *Augustæ* whose names and portraits are found on contorniates, according to trust-worthy authorities, viz.:—Julius Cæsar, Mark Antony, Augustus, Agrippina senior, Caligula, Nero (whose contorniates are common), Galba, Vespasian, Domitian, Trajan (common), Antoninus Pius, Faustina senior, M. Aurelius, Faustina junior, Lucilla, Caracalla, Constantine the Great, Honorius, Theodosius II. Placidius Valentinianus, and Anthemius.

To some of the emperors no contorniates were dedicated; to others only a very few; but to Nero and Trajan a large number.—Eckhel expresses his decided opinion, that in their total neglect, or rare introduction of others, those who struck them were guided solely by caprice; and that the same cause may be assigned for their selection of Homer, Horace, &c. to the exclusion of individuals of equal renown among both Greeks and Romans.

III.—SPECIFIC EXAMPLES OF CONTORNIATE TYPES.—Havercamp, in his elaborate standard work on this peculiar class of medals, has given the heads of emperors and illustrious individuals; but in so doing has been under the necessity of frequently repeating the same reverses, in consequence of their being common to several princes. Eckhel (viii. p. 283 et seq.) properly regarding the reverses as of greater interest than the imperial portraits, already sufficiently known from other and better sources, has, in enumerating and describing these contorniates, confined himself principally to the reverses. His arrangement, as most to the purpose, has been adopted in the subjoined notices. And as these types are of various kinds, they will be found arranged according to Eckhel's classification, under distinct heads. The 1st embraces Mythology; 2nd History; 3rd Illustrious Persons, such as heroes and heroines, kings, and men renowned for their learning; 4th Spectacles, subdivided into *decursiones*, *venationes* (or huntings), pugilistic encounters, and dramatic exhibitions.

The different works which contain *engravings* of Contorniate types, and to which particular references will in each instance be found, are as follow:—*Morell. Thesaur. Familiarum Romanarum*, and *Imperatorum Romanorum; Numismata Cimelii Austriaci Vindobonensis* (Coins of the Imperial Cabinet at Vienna, by Fröelich); Havercamp, *de Numis Contorniatis;* Pedrusi, *Cabinet du Musée Farnese;* Coins of the Pembroke Collection, &c.

1.—MYTHOLOGICAL.

Rev.—Cybele and Atys in a quadriga of lions, going at a rapid pace.—*Obv.*—A head of Homer. (Engraved in Cabinet of Vienna.)

A head of Augustus. Do. of Nero. (Morell. Impp.)—Do. of Vespasian and Trajan.— (Pedrusi, Mus. Farnese, and Havercamp).—On a coin of Vespasian, above the quadriga, are two shields, on one of which appears a lion, on the other a crab; below, a woman seated on the ground. (Mus. Farnese).

Agrippina and Faustina senior.——MATRI. DEVM. SALVTARI.—A temple, before the entrance of which is seated Cybele between two lions, with the *tympanum* in her left hand; outside stands Atys, with the *pedum*, or sheephook, in the right hand, and touching a pine tree with the left.—(Morell. Thesaur. Impp. vol. iii. TAB. xiv. No. 12: also in Imperial Cabinet at Vienna.

Julius Cæsar.—Without legend. Jupiter sitting on a rock, with an eagle watching near him; a military figure stands close at hand holding-in a horse by the bridle.——(Morell. Impp. and in Fam. Juliæ).

Augustus.—Without legend. The emperor laureated, cuirassed, and paludated, is standing, with both hands raised, between two seated figures—one a veiled woman, holding a palm branch in her left hand—the other a man, seminude, holding the hasta pura in right and a globe in left hand—at the foot of the emperor stands an eagle with expanded wings, and a small figure of Victory offering a laurel crown to the emperor. Below are two recumbent females, as if river deities, one resting her left hand on a lion, and the other her right hand on a ship's prow, both with cornucopiæ. (Morell. Thesaur. Impp.)—A similar type of reverse appears also on a contorniate, with the name of Homer and his portrait on the obverse, in Pedrusi, Mus. Farnese, TAB. i.

Trajan.—A naked Bacchus stands, holding out a cluster of grapes to a panther, and with the thyrsus in the left hand; around him are dancing a female flute-player, and another female brandishing a thyrsus; also a boy with a sheephook, and another with a branch. (Imp. Mus.) Do. of Caracalla. (Imp. Mus. and Havercamp.)

Nero.—Bacchus riding in a biga of panthers, with a satyr going before him, and a flute-player in attendance. (Engraved in Havercamp and in Morel.)—Same type of reverse with head of Trajan. (In Havercamp, n. 20 and 70).

Nero.—A naked Mars, with his left foot on the prow of a ship, is hurrying onward with spear and scaling ladder.

Vespasian.—Same type. (In Morell. Impp.)

Vespasian.—Mars walking, with spear in right hand, and trophy in left, trampling on a prostrate foe. (Mus. Theupoli).

Nero.—Diana sitting opposite the sleeping Endymion, beside whom a dog is watching, whilst overhead a Cupid is hovering. (Pedrusi).

Trajan.—Same reverse. (Havercamp).

Hercules fighting with the centaur Nessus. Hercules head of, behind which is a club. Hercules struggling with a lion. (Imp. Mus.)

Obv.—ALEXANDER. Head covered with lion's skin. Before it the usual contorniate monogram (see engraving, p. 271).—*Rev.*—Ulysses, on board his vessel, passing before Scylla.

One of the most striking, though not the most rare, amongst the various subjects on this class of ancient medals, is that which, having the head of Alexander the Great, or the head of Trajan, for the type of its obverse, as indicated by the legend expressing his name, represents on its reverse, without legend, the fable of Scylla.——This formidable sea-monster, personifying a dangerous rock and whirlpool on the Italian side of the straits of Messina, is here typified, at the moment when, according to the Homeric narration, she made her tragical assault on the ship and companions of the son of Laertes The upper part of her body is that of a gigantic female, her waist is girdled with ravenous dogs; the lower extremity terminates in a fish's tail. In her right hand, she holds a rudder; with her left she has seized by the hair of his head one of the crew, as if about to drag him out of the vessel. A man standing close by, armed with a shield and javelin, is vainly attempting to defend his unfortunate comrade. A third holds up his hands, as if paralysed with fear and horror, at beholding such a spectacle. On one side of Scylla is a huge fish, with head downward, and tail broadly spread and erect. Two human figures are seen struggling in the troubled waves, the previous victims of the monster's resistless attack. Behind the whole group rises a tree, allusive probably to the immense fig tree, which grew over a rocky cavern, where another traditionary monster named Charybdis, whose whirlpool, on the Sicilian coast, was equally the dread of ancient mariners, held his or her dark abode.—See *Scylla.*

[The same type is found on reverses of contorniates, of which the respective obverses bear the heads of Alexander the Great, in the Vienna Cabinet, and Havercamp, No. 64; of Nero, in Morell. Impp.; and of Trajan, in the Imp. Museum, and Havercamp, and Museum Farnese.]

Bellerophon, on Pegasus, fighting with the Chimæra.—*Obv.*—Head of Alexander the Great. —See *Pegasus,* in this dictionary.

Trajan,—Amphion and Zethus, carrying off their stepmother Dirce, tied to a bull. (Mus. Com. Vitzai).

SOLI INVICTO.—The Sun, with his face turned towards you, in a quadriga.—*Obv.*—Head of Alexander the Great. (Havercamp, p. 38).

Honorius.—SAPIENTIA. Pallas standing, with branch of laurel or olive in the right hand.— (Tanini, Supplement to Banduri)

2.—HISTORICAL.

Eckhel remarks, that he has discovered only one example of this class, viz. :—

SABINAE. The Roman soldiers engaged in the rape of the Sabine women; behind, three obelisks, composing one of the Circensian metæ. *Obv.*—Head of Alexander the Great. (Havercamp, p. 1.)—Do. of Nero (Morell. Impp.)— Do. of Constantius II. (Banduri, T. ii. p. 378, Mus. Florent. TAB. c.)—Also head of Agrippina senior, with the legend AGRIPPINA M. F. MAT. CAESARIS AVGVSTI. (Mus. Prince de Waldeck).

3.—TYPES RELATING TO ILLUSTRIOUS PERSONS, HEROES, HEROINES, AND KINGS.

ACHILLIS PENTESILIA. Achilles armed, raises from the ground the prostrate Penthesilea; behind is a horse also lying on the ground.—*Obv.* Head of Divus Trajan. (Pedrusi, Mus. Farn.)

AENEAS. Æneas, bearing Anchises on his shoulder, and leading Ascanius by the hand.— *Obv.*—Head of Nero. (In Morell. Impp.)—Do. of Trajan. (Imperial Cabinet and Havercamp.)

Hero, watching from a tower the approach of Leander swimming in the sea; a cupid flying above. On another coin, Hero standing on a tower, holds out a torch in her right hand, whilst Leander is swimming below; on the shore is a fisherman casting a hook into the sea.— *Obv.*—Head of Vespasian.   (Morell. Impp. and Mus. Farnese.)

Laocoon and his two sons, entwined in the folds of serpents.—*Obv.*—Head of Nero. (Imp. Mus.)   Do. of Vespasian.   (Morell. Imp.)

PENTESILEA.—See above, *Achilles.*

AGIT. SPE. TESEVS.——Theseus, galeated and naked, standing with spear and shield, is forcing a centaur to kneel who holds a lyre, by placing his hand on his neck.—*Obv.*—Head of Nero. (Morell. Impp.)

STEFANAS.   A victor in the games, in a quadriga, with crown in right hand and palm branch in left.   (Mus. Theupoli.)

Without legend.   Head of Alexander the Great, diademed, looking up to heaven.

ALEXANDER MAG. MACEDON.—Alexander on horseback, hurling a spear at a prostrate barbarian.   (Imperial Cabinet.)

ALEXANDER MAGNVS MACEDON.   Diademed head, looking up to heaven.—*Rev.*—Rape of the Sabines, as above. (Havercamp, p. 1.)

Without legend.   Diademed head of Alexander the Great, with a ram's horn, looking up to heaven.—A naked man, standing, with a whip in his right hand, and with his left grasping a serpent about to spring.   (Imperial Cabinet.)

ALEXANDER.   Head of Alexander M. with lion's skin.   A circus.   (Havercamp, n. 48). Bellerophon fighting with the chimæra.   (Ibid. n. 49.)   Scylla, as before.   (Imp. Mus.)

ALEXANDER.   Head with lion's skin.—D. N. IHS. XPS. DEI. FILIVS.   An ass, with head erect, suckling her foal.

OLYMPIAS (on most specimens OLIMPIAS) REGINA.   Olympias veiled, and lying on a bed, stretches out her right hand towards a serpent raising itself; her left hand rests on a dolphin. Head of Nero. (Morell. Impp.)   Do. of Trajan. (Havercamp, num. 68.)

Without legend,   The same type, except that instead of the dolphin, there is simply the support (or leg) of the bed.—*Obv.*—Head of Nero. (Imp. Mus. and elsewhere.)

PETRONIVS MAXSIMVS *(sic.)* V. C. CONS.   Petronius sitting, clothed in the consular garb, with a roll in the right hand, in the left a dagger with an eagle; at the bottom are two bags stuffed with coins, one of which is open and exposes the money.

Head of Valentinian III.   (Banduri.)   See an engraving of this coin in Tanini, TAB. viii.

4.—TYPES RELATING TO MEN RENOWNED FOR THEIR LEARNING, OR ANY OTHER CAUSE.

ΩMHROC.   Bare head of Homer, with beard. A man leading a horse by the bridle.   (Imp. Mus.)   Cybele and Atys in a quadriga of lions. A man, galeated and paludated, standing, &c.— See Pembroke Museum, T. ii. pl. 234, and Havercamp, fig. 1. p. 148.

Socrates.—There are two contorniates of this philosopher.   One of them has been taken by Havercamp, from Ursinus: CΩKPATHC.   Bare head, with beard.   Reverse not given.   The other has been taken from the Farnese Cabinet, by Pedrusi, TAB. i. on which is a bearded head, without legend.   Eckhel does not understand why it should have been attributed to Socrates.

TERENTIVS.   Bare head, without beard.

- - - IVS.   A man leading a horse by the bridle.   (Morell. Fam. Rom. Terentia gens; also in Pembroke Museum, and in Liebe Gotha Numaria, p. 449.

SALVSTIVS AVTOR.   A bare head, bearded; on other coins beardless.—*Rev.*—PETRONI PLACEAS. Three men in the toga, standing, &c.   (Morell. *Fam. Rom.* Salustia gens.)   See the rest below, in dramatic types.

HORATIVS.   A bare head, beardless.

ALSAN.   A man leading a horse by the bridle. (Havercamp, p. 152); also Morell. Fam. Rom. Horatia gens—and in Pembroke, T. ii. 244–245.

APOLONIVS TYANEVS.   Laureated and bearded head.—STEFAN. NIKA. Stephanus the charioteer, in a quadriga.   (Havercamp, p. 152.)

APVLEIVS.   A juvenile head, with the hair bound backward with a ribbon.   (Morell. Fam. Rom. Apulcia gens.)—A bearded soldier, standing and looking up at a temple of two columns, on the summit of which are fixed three human heads.   (Morelli Specimen, p. 45).

5.—PUBLIC SPECTACLES.

1. *Decursiones, or Chariot and Horse Racing.*

Circus Maximus, with all its apparatus, and quadrigæ in motion.—Head of Alexander the Great, Nero, Trajan, Caracalla, &c.

ALSAN.   A man leading by the bridle a horse decorated with a palm branch.—Head of Horace. (Havercamp, Morel, and Pembroke).

ARTEMIVS VINCAS IMPERATOR PLENA.   A victor in a quadriga, with whip and crown in the right hand, and palm branch in the left.— Head of Honorius. (Theupoli, but not engraved).

AVRELIANVS.   A victor in the games standing in a chariot, which is drawn at a slow pace by four horses, ornamented with palm branches ; in the right hand is a crown and a whip, and in the left a palm branch; the figure is looking behind him.   Beneath is inserted PLACEAS.— Head of Nero. (Imperial Cabinet).   Do. of Trajan.   (Prince de Waldeck).

BABVLVS.   A victor in the games, with whip in right hand, and holding-in a horse by the bridle with the left; behind him is his cap.

BONIFATIVS.   A victor in the games, with crown and whip in the right hand, and palm branch in the left, is coming towards you in a quadriga, at a slow pace; the lower part of the coin is occupied by four monograms, each containing several letters.—Head of Placidius Valentinianus.   (Ducange, Banduri, Havercamp.)

CERVOMTIVS.   A victor in the games, borne in a chariot drawn by four horses at full speed, stands looking behind him ; in the right hand a crown and whip, in the left a palm branch.— Head of Caracalla.   (Havercamp).

CHRYSOPOLVS. Eckhel says, " I find a coin mentioning this name among the medallions of the Museum Theupoli, with the following description :"—C. CAESAR AVG. GERMANICVS PON. M. TR. P. A head of Caligula laureated ; before which is the name CHRYSOPOLVS.—Rev.—A victor in a quadriga, with crown in right hand, and palm branch in left.

COSMVS. A victor standing, with whip in right hand, and spear in left.

SERACVSVS. A winning horse, with palm branch on his head. (Theupoli.)

DESID. NC. The bust of a man, with bare head and bearded, in his left hand holding a horse by the rein, and in his right a whip.

MACCOMMO. A man sitting on a rock, leaning his head on his left hand, and looking behind him. (Havercamp, num. 72).

DOMNINVS. A victor in the games, holding the reins in his right hand, and palm branch in his left, is borne in a quadriga of horses, ornamented with palm, going at a slow pace. Head of Trajan. (Imperial Cabinet).

DOMNVS PHILOCOMVS. A victor in the games, with whip in right hand, and palm branch in left, advances towards you in a quadriga, at a slow pace.—Obv.—Head of Severus. (Havercamp, num. 63).

ELIANVS. A victor in the games standing in a chariot, drawn by four horses, with palm branches, and looking behind him, with whip in the right hand, and palm branch in the left. Bust of a man, with bare head, holding a whip in the right hand, and restraining a horse with the left; around are the letters MVP. R. cut in bas relief, and filled up with silver.— (Mus. Prince de Waldeck, and of C. Vitzai).

EVGENIVS. A victor in the games, with crown in right hand, and palm branch in left, is coming towards you in a slow-going quadriga of four palm-bearing horses, near which are inscribed their names, SPESCIOSVS DIGNVS. ACHILL. DESIDEREVS.—Obv.—Head of Honorius. (Havercamp, num. 54).

EVTHYMIVS, or EVTVMIVS, or EVTIMIVS. A victor, with whip and crown in right hand, and palm branch in left, is coming towards you in a slow-going quadriga of palm-bearing horses.— Head of Nero, or Trajan, or Honorius. (Havercamp, fig. 31, p. 55 ; Imperial Cabinet ; and Pedrusi, Mus. Farnese, TAV. iv.)

EVTIMI. VINCAS. Bust of a man with bare head and bearded, holds-in a horse with left hand, and carries a whip in the right; behind, a helmet.—Obv.—An emperor on horseback, going at speed, with right hand elevated; on the ground, a lion transfixed by a spear. (Imperial Museum).

EVTIMI. VINICAS (sic.) A charioteer coming towards you in a quadriga at a slow pace, with crown in right hand and palm branch in left; at the bottom MVSALLIGER. (sic.)—Obv.—Head and legend of Theodosius M. On another coin, a head of Honorius. (Tanini, Supplement ad Banduri).

EVTIMIVS—below, TYRIEI. CAT. - - -. A victor standing between two horses, decorated with

palm branches.—Obv.—Head of Trajan. (Havercamp, num. 30).

LISIFONVS. A victor with whip and crown in right hand, and palm branch in left, borne in a quadriga of palm-bearing horses going slowly. —Laureated head of Divus Augustus Pater.— (Morell. Impp. in Aug. TAB. xxiii.)

OLIMPIVS. Himself standing, in a coat of mail, with whip in right hand, and palm branch in left.—Galeated and beardless head of Constantine the Great, as Havercamp thinks, n. 51.

OLYMPI. NIKA. A victor standing naked in a biga going rapidly, and looking behind him with whip in right hand, and crown in left.— Obv.—Head of Nero. (Havercamp, num. 14.)

PANNONI. NIKA. A victor in a slow-going quadriga of palm-bearing horses, looking behind him, with whip and crown in right hand, and palm branch in the left.—A bust with bare and bearded head, with whip in right hand, and holding a horse by the rein with the left.. (Havercamp, num. 71).——Head of Honorius.— (Tanin. Suppl. ad Banduri.)

SELEVCVS. A victor standing, with whip in right hand, and palm branch in left ; at his feet on either side an altar, with palm branches rising out of it.—A victor in a biga going rapidly.— (Pembroke, p. iii. TAB. 118).

STEFANVS. A victor in a quadriga.—A head of Alexander M. (Theupoli.)—Do. of Nero. (Havercamp, Morell. Impp.)

STEFANVS. A victor naked, with whip in right hand, and palm branch in left, borne in a quadriga of palm-bearing horses.——Head of Divus Trajan. (Mus. Farnese).

STEFAN. NIKA. A victor in quadriga going slowly, is coming towards you, with whip in right hand, and palm branch in left.—Obv.— Head of Apollonius Tyanensis. (Havercamp).

VRSE VINCAS. A naked man standing, with whip in his elevated right hand, and a palm branch in the left, which hangs down.—Bust with bare head, spear (or more correctly, a whip) in the right hand, and holding-in a horse with the left ; behind, a palm branch. (Havercamp, num. 50).

ETERNIT. P. R. A victor with crown and whip in the right hand, and palm branch in the left, comes towards you in a chariot at a slow pace, drawn by four palm-bearing horses.—DIVO IVLIO. Head of Julius Cæsar laureated. (Morell. Impp.)

TOXXOTES. A horse walking, with a mark on the thigh ; in front of him a palm branch.— AMOR. A horse standing, with a similar mark, and a palm branch. Both horses are in bas-relief, and filled up with silver. (Morell. Specimen, p. 43).

2. Venationes (or Sports of the Chase).

A hunting of stags and hares in an amphitheatre.—A head of Divus Augustus. (Imperial Cabinet, and Morell. Impp.)—Do. of Nero. (Morell. Impp.)—Do. of Trajan. (Havercamp, num. 67).

COLENDVS. A hunter on horseback is pursuing a stag and a hare with drawn bow, in an amphitheatre.—Head of Trajan. (Farnese Col.)

A hunter attacking a boar with a hunting-spear, whilst a dog also leaps at it.—Head of Nero. (Havercamp, n. 5, Morell. Impp.)—Do. of Vespasian. (Imp. and Farnese Cabinets).

Two hunters, one of whom is on horseback, attacking a bear, the other a boar, on foot.—*Obv.*—Head of Nero. (Morell. Impp.)

A hunter is defending himself against the charge of a bear with some instrument, whilst above, five spectators are awaiting with alarm the issue of the combat.—*Obv.*—Head of Nero. (Morell. Impp. and Mus. Farnese).

A single man is holding two savage bulls by the horns.—Head of Nero. (Morell. Impp.)

An emperor on horseback, striking a lion with a javelin.—Head of Nero. (Morell. Impp.)—Do. of Trajan. (Havercamp, num. 21).—Bust of Eutimius the charioteer.

A man riding on a bull and combatting with a bear.—Head of Nero. (Morell. Impp.)

A *bestiarius* standing, with a spear in his right hand, and in his left something resembling a globe; at his feet a prostrate panther; on one side of the field three metæ, and on the other something that looks like a cave.—*Obv.*—Bust of a charioteer, with a whip in right hand, and with the left holding-in a horse. (Imp. Mus. and Pellerin, Suppl. ii. TAB. 7).

REPARATIO. MVNERIS. FELICITER. A hunter receiving the charge of a bear, with spear presented.—*Obv.*—INVICTA ROMA FELIX SENATVS. Galeated head of Rome. (Morell. num. fam. TAB. i. ROMA.)

3. *Pugilistic Encounters.*

FILINVS. A naked *athleta*, with a crown in his elevated right hand, and palm branch in his left, stands between two togated figures, of which the one on the right holds aloft a dagger, and the other a flute.—A head of Trajan. (Mus. Farnese, and Havercamp, num. 69).

IOHANNES NICAS. An athlete and an anointer (or trainer) standing. Head of Pla. Valentinian.

A naked pugilist seated on the ground, presses to the earth the head of an antagonist with his feet, and masters his head with his own. (Morell. Impp.) D. N. CONSTANTINVS MAX. AVG. Figure of an emperor as far as the middle, with a gemmed crown; a sceptre in the right hand, and a globe in the left. (Mus. Princ. de Waldeck).

4. *Dramatic Exhibitions.*

A naked man, carrying in either hand an immense theatrical mask; behind, a tree.—Head of Nero. (Mus. Farnese).

An hydraulic machine, with a figure on either side, of which the one to the right exhibits in his uplifted hand an instrument resembling a fan.—*Obv.*—Head of Nero. (Imperial Cabinet and Havercamp, num. 11).—Do. of Trajan. (Havercamp, num. 27).

LAVRENTI NICA. An hydraulic machine, on one side of which stands a figure with something resembling a fan; there are also two vases standing near; on the other side leaves scattered on the ground.—Head of Nero. (Imperial Cabinet).

[Havercamp, on a similar coin, reads, LAV-

RENTIN AVG.—Morell. LAVRENTINVS. (Impp. in Nerone).—Tristran, LAVRENTINVM.]

PETRONI. PLACEAS. Three togated figures standing, of which the middle one holds a very small hydraulic machine, another a flute, and the third is gesticulating like a person engaged in conversation.—Head and legend of Sallustius. (Mus. Imp.; Havercamp, p. 150; and others).

PLACEAS PETRI. An hydraulic machine, on either side of which stands a figure, apparently engaged in animating it; near it a terminus of the Sun.—*Obv.*—Head of Pla. Valentinian.—This is a coin of extraordinary size, originally in the collection of Queen Christina.

MARGARITA VINCAS. A woman standing, with crown in uplifted right hand, gathering up her dress with the left; a small Victory flying towards her, offers a crown; below are two palm branches.—Head of Pla. Valentinian. (Tanini Suppl. ad Band. TAB. xviii. Pembroke, p. 3, TAB. 102).

IV.——CONTORNIATES WITH WELL-KNOWN TYPES OF THE ROMAN MINT.—These consist of the MEMORIAE AGRIPPINAE, with a carpentum.—PACE P. R. &c. Temple of Janus, of Nero.—ROMA, Rome seated, of Nero.——DECVRSIO, Horsemen.—LIBERTAS PVBLICA, Liberty standing, of Galba.—ANNONA AVGVSTA CERES, Ceres and Annona, of Trajan.—DIVA FAVSTINA AVG. Faustina jun. standing at an altar, of Nero.—VICTORIA CONSTANTINI, Victory writing on a shield, of Constantine the Great.—These will be found engraved in Morell. Impp. and in the Imperial Cabinet at Vienna.—VOTA XX. A circus in which two quadrigæ are careering, and hunters are fighting with wild beasts.—*Obv.*—Head of Pla. Valentinianus.—Catalogue D'Ennery.

Eckhel devotes a concluding section to twelve Contorniates, " the explanation of which is doubtful." Engravings of most of them are given in Havercamp, Morel, and Pedrusi. But, as the author of *Doctrina* himself does not venture to do more than simply describe the respective types of these "inexplicable" coins, it would be useless to quote the list in question.—See viii. 305, *D. N. V.*

V.—DATE OF CONTORNIATES.—Respecting the age, in which the use of such coins began, various opinions have been held by the learned. Some have thought, that those contorniates, which bear the heads of emperors, are coeval with such emperors respectively. Among other writers of the elder numismatic school is that erudite and ingenious antiquary Spanheim, who explains a coin of Nero, as though it had been struck during the reign of that prince. Ducange and Pinkerton, in their respective works, entertain the same idea. But Eckhel refutes this notion, in the first place, by referring to the workmanship, which is of great assistance, in determining the date of other descriptions of coins.

"Experience (says he) teaches us, that each age of the emperors had its own style of art. And if in this respect alone there be a wide difference between the coins of Augustus and Trajan, how much wider must it be between those of Augustus and of Placidius Valentinianus ?. And yet we see that the same tone and style pervades all the contorniates—a convincing proof, that the times at which they were severally struck could not be far distant from each other ; and we are, therefore, certain, that the coins bearing portraits of Julius Cæsar, of Augustus, and the immediately succeeding princes, must, on account of this similarity to the coins of Honorius and Valentinian, be connected with them also in point of time; and consequently, that the contorniates of Julius Cæsar and Augustus are not contemporaneous with those emperors. For the same reason, antiquaries have long ago agreed, that certain imperial coins of Consecration, from their being all of the same workmanship, and with the same admixture of bad silver, were also struck at the same date. On this account, it is necessary to lay it down as a rule, that all contorniates are to be assigned to an age subsequent to the emperors, whose portraits they bear. We see, on these coins, many attributes appropriated to the earlier emperors, which were really either unknown or in disuse in their days. The head of Julius Cæsar, e. g. is adorned, not only with the laurel crown, but also with the diadem, which, for well-known reasons, does not appear on his contemporaneous coins.—Trajan, on a coin in the Imperial Cabinet at Vienna, is styled Pius Felix, which titles conjoined were unknown before the time of Commodus. On another, in the same collection, Trajan is called Pro-consul, a title never read except on coins of the lower empire. Doubtless, the persons who struck these coins, accommodated their style and legends to the times in which they lived.—Lastly, even that unique coin, bearing on its obverse the head of Nero, and on its reverse Faustina junior, of itself sufficiently proves, that it could not have been struck during the reign of Nero.—Jobert's opinion, that contorniates were struck as early as the reign of Gallienus, has been refuted by his annotator Bimard, and requires no further notice.—The sounder view is that of Morel and Mahudel, who pronounce this class of medals to have begun to be minted about the time of Constantine the Great, and to have been continued under his immediate successors down to Pla. Valentinian, when contorniates almost wholly cease."—D. N. V. viii. 310.

VI.—OF THE USE OF CONTORNIATES.—All writers on this branch of the subject appear to agree in considering, that contorniates were not of the nature and value of money, in consequence of their differing so entirely from the ordinary coinage. It is also universally admitted, that they were not struck by public authority, but by private individuals, and those of an uneducated class, since the types are generally borrowed from humble life, objects the most incongruous placed in juxta-position, and mistakes committed in orthography, which preclude the inference of their proceeding from public authority.

Eckhel informs us that, in the cabinet of the Prince of Waldeck, there is a contorniate,

on the reverse of which are two horsemen (eques) going at speed, spears in hand, with S. C. inscribed beneath. But it is not from these initials, he observes, for any one to suppose that the coin in question was minted by a Senatus Consultum, but rather that such types of the Decursiones were copied from coins of Nero, even to the insertion of the letters S. C.

Lastly, with respect to the opinion of several learned writers that contorniates were intended for the purposes of the circus and the arena— an opinion founded by them on the fact that athletic and Circensian exercises constituted the usual subjects of these types—Eckhel remarks as follows:—"Assuredly the games of the circus are pointed at in the figures of successful charioteers in their quadrigæ, frequently with their names inscribed, or their busts, "winning horses," pugilists, beast-fighters, venationes, and palms as the prizes of victory. Besides which, such formulæ as VRSE. VINCAS.—OLYMPI. NIKA.—PETRONI. PLACEAS.—and the like, are the very words of good omen and encouragement, which the spectators used to shout out to their favourites from the cunei. The fact, moreover, of Nero and Trajan being more frequently introduced on these coins than any other emperors, is a satisfactory evidence that they were struck for Circensian purposes. Not that I agree with the Frenchman Mahudel, that those princes were selected who were most addicted to the sports of the circus. For most writers say that the preference was given to Nero, on account of his well-known infatuation, in adorning victorious and worn-out steeds with the stola, and assigning them rations; whilst during his reign charioteers reached such a pitch of arrogance, as to oppose the authority of consuls and pretors. If this, however, were the correct view, why (to omit mention of others) did not Commodus come in for his share of such honour ? For his devotion to the circus was not a whit inferior, considering that he himself drove quadrigæ, and publicly slew beasts in the arena; and yet but one contorniate of this emperor has ever been discovered. And again, why load Trajan with such numbers of these medals, when no historian records of that emperor any violent attachment to the circensian scenes ? Some other reason, therefore, must be sought for the frequent appearance of Nero and Trajan on contorniates; and this is to be found in the fact, that the former instituted the quinquennale certamen at Rome, whilst in honour of the latter, after his decease, there were celebrated ludi Parthici, or triumphal games. Add to this, that Trajan expended vast sums on the embellishment and enlargement of the Circus Maximus. The directors, therefore, of similar spectacles, in after ages, would naturally revive the memory of those emperors more frequently, who had furnished them with such abundant material for victory and its rewards. That the memory of Nero, in consequence of this his predilection, was not only cherished for many succeeding centuries by the votaries of the Roman circus, but was also hailed with gratitude by the arena of Constantinople, is remarkably evidenced by a cameo, published by Caylus. *(Rec. d'Antiq.* T. i. TAB. 86). It represents Nero, with radiated head, borne in a quadriga, with the face turned towards you, as is usual on contorniates; in his right hand he holds a napkin (the *mappa*, see *Circus*, pp. 203–4), in the left a consular sceptre, with the legend NЄPꙊN. AΓOꙊCTЄ *(sic.)* The scene, and its accompaniments, together with the faulty inscription, clearly prove, that this gem was the work of a later age of the lower empire, and, from the Greek legend, not belonging to Italy, but doubtless to Constantinople, where it is well known that the rage for the sports of the Circus reached a greater height than even in the metropolis of Rome."

As to what was the actual use for which the Contorniates were designed, in connexion with the *ludi Circenses;* this is a question which, in the absence of historical, and in the paucity of numismatic, testimony, cannot be answered with confidence. The opinions of writers on the subject rest on the merest conjecture. Morel suspects that they were struck for the purpose of being given as prizes for the athletic games.— Havercamp (in his elaborate description of, and commentary on, Contorniates), supposes they were coined by the leaders and victors of the circus, who wished thus to celebrate the praises of their conquering steeds. But this can apply only to those coins on which horses appear.

Henry Cannegieter, one of the latest writers on the subject (in his *Misc. Observat. Crit. Novis,* T. i. anni 1740), takes a remarkable view: viz. that these medals were distributed among the spectators by the partizans of the charioteers, in order that their success might be favoured by the words of good omen with which they were inscribed, and the figures portrayed upon them. For it was the popular belief, that the speed of the horses could be increased or retarded by the arts of magic. And, to put in force or to counteract such influences, these contorniate medals were struck, bearing expressions of good omen; and the same virtue was believed to reside in the likenesses of Alexander the Great, of Olympias, Nero, Virgil, Apollonius of Tyana, Apuleius, Anchises, Æneas, &c. because it was matter of tradition that those worthies were either addicted to the practice of magic, or at any rate skilled in it. The same power also was attributed to the dragons often seen on these coins; and lastly, to the sign of the cross found inscribed on a quadriga in a coin given by Havercamp. But, as Eckhel observes, in citing the above opinion, it is deserving only of the praise which is due to a learned and ingenious conjecture. Of a later day, Pinkerton has supposed that they were used as *tesseræ,* or tickets, and were distributed among the people before the commencement of the games, entitling each individual to a "reserved seat" on the benches.

VII.—ON THE MERIT OF CONTORNIATES.— Whatever may be its real merits, this class of coins has its patrons, to whom it has appeared worthy of being diligently sought after, and to be useful in various respects. Others, however, have entertained a lower opinion of them; no doubt in consequence of the want of connection between the obverse and reverse; the unskilful grouping of the figures; and the subjects being for the most part derived from the feats of charioteers and wrestlers; and seldom affording any gratification to the mind or to the eye. The fastidious take alarm also at the errors in spelling, such as TESEVS, PENTESILIA, STEFANVS, OLIMPIAS, SALVSTIVS, APOLONIVS, ETERNITAS, and the like; together with the perpetual mistake of ΩMHROC for OMHPOC—the surest proof that these contorniates were put forth in an ignorant age, by people of an inferior class, and under no sanction of the state.

"It might be supposed (observes Eckhel) that they would be of service to portraiture, as professedly exhibiting the heads of various eminent individuals sought for in vain on other monuments of antiquity. But it is easy to imagine, what slight reliance can be placed on likenesses engraved many centuries after the death of the personages, in an age inimical to the arts, and for the most part by unskilful hands."

It is, however, in the face of this remark of the illustrious German, that a scarcely less illustrious Italian antiquary, professes to regard as authentic, up to a certain point, some portraits which are found only on contorniate medals.— "These heads (says M. Visconti), were struck at the epocha when the arts had declined—that is to say, in the fourth and fifth centuries of the Christian era. And although reproduced by the hand of art, after an interval of several centuries, are not to be considered as imaginary portraits. Collections of monuments of every kind, which exist at this day at Constantinople and at Rome, present models, from which the engravers of the *contorniates* had the opportunity of copying. And, in fact, they directed their entire attention to them, as may be proved by a comparison of the portraits in question with those which are preserved to us on monuments of greater antiquity. The only material difference to be remarked, is that which results from the unskilfulness of the contorniate die-sinkers. (See *Iconograph. Grec.* TAB. i. *Disc. preliminaire,* p. 15, 8vo. edition).

Pellerin confesses his aversion to this description of coins; and though some would include them, others would as resolutely exclude them from the list of true *medallions.*—"In this diversity of opinion (concludes the Author of *Doctrina*), the middle is the safer course. For although so little reliance can be placed on contorniates, they are still useful, as witnesses of their age, and its manners; and of the notorious fondness of the Roman people for public sports and spectacles. Some interest is also to be derived from their lively representations of the Circus and its equipages, the charioteering, the huntings, the dress and "turn-out" of the charioteers, the names of themselves and of their horses, together with the acclamations of applause and encouragement, with which they were greeted by the spectators.—Lastly, on certain specimens of them may be seen subjects by no means deficient in elegance and classicality; some of which cannot be found on other antique monuments; nay, in a very few instances, a workmanship worthy of a better age."

UNEDITED CONTORNIATES.—In vol. iii. of "*Revue Numismatique, année* 1840," there are three papers on Contorniate medals. Two are from the pen of the Abbé Greppo (author of a numismatic *Memoire sur les Voyages de l'Empereur Hadrien*), and the third is by that distinguished French antiquary M. Ch. Lenormant.

1. The former of these pieces is thus described (p. 89):—ANTONINVS PIVS. Bust of Antoninus Pius, to the right, bare head, the shoulders covered with the *paludamentum*.

Rev.—SALVS AVG. (as it would *seem*, for the deep circular furrow on the outer edge of the medal, peculiar to contorniates, has obliterated much of the lettering). Type, a ram, turned to the right, standing near a tree, feeding out of a crib standing on feet. Under the belly of the animal hangs a man, with the *pileus* on his head, holding on by his hands to the front of the ram's fleece, and throwing up his feet on the rump of the animal.

This curious reverse, in a learned and ingenious dissertation, the Abbé interprets, with great shew of probability, to adumbrate a passage in the *Odyssey* (ix. v. 434), where Ulysses, in order to effect his own and his companions' rescue from the sanguinary cruelties of Polyphemus, suspends himself, according to Homer's recital, under the belly of a large ram; and by this means, the King of Ithaca and all his men, who adopted the same stratagem with others of the cyclops' flock, succeeded in accomplishing their escape from the cavern of the giant, whom they had already deprived of sight.

The second medal is thus described:—*Obv.*—DIVO TRAIANO AVGVSTO. Bust of Trajan to the right, with the *paludamentum*, head laureated.

Rev.—Without legend. A bearded man, seated on a chair, to the right, clothed in a short garment, that leaves the breast and lower extremities bare: the muscles of the arms and legs strongly marked; hair bristled up on the top of the head. He seems occupied in contemplating a circular object placed on a tripod (much resembling the zodiacal type on an Alexandrine medallion of Antoninus Pius, in Zoega), placed before him. In the field of the coin, above, is a figure of Pallas helmeted, holding the hasta and resting on a buckler. Behind the principal figure is a *parazonium* with its baldrick.

There are, it seems, two specimens of this contorniate, one in the Cabinet National de France, the other in the possession of the Marquis de Pina. They are from different dies, and vary in some particulars, though they correspond in general. The Abbé Greppo writes his dissertation with M. de Pina's coin before him, and he inclines to the opinion that the type relates to judicial astrology, that the seated figure is "that of a charioteer of the circus, or at least of some other person employed at public spectacles, rather than of a judicial astrologer

by profession."—On the other hand, M. Ch. Lenormant, after comparing the Marquis's contorniate with that in the French National cabinet, proves by evidence derived from three medals of the Antoninian mint, that the seated figure, with bristled hair on end, above described, can be no other than the skilful and robust, but slovenly Vulcan. He further suggests that the circular object, having the twelve celestial signs round its outer compartment, and the sun and moon in the centre, is the shield of Achilles, on which the god of all artists who worked metals, is employed in the presence of Minerva, and that the tripod on which it is placed, is probably one of those famous tripods which Vulcan was occupied in fabricating when Thetis entered his dwelling.—See M. Lenormant's brief but judicious and classical remarks on this subject, p. 309, in the excellent French periodical above named.—See also, in this dictionary, the word VULCANVS.

COOP. *Cooptatus.*—Associated, elected.—See *Sacerdos*.

COPIA *(Lucaniæ)* colonia; an opulent town of Magna Græcia, originally called *Sybaris*, afterwards *Thurium;* and lastly by the Romans named *Copia* (now Sibari Rovinata, Southern Italy). Of this place, under the name of Sybaris and Thurium, there are, according to Mionnet and Hennin, autonomous coins, in small brass, of considerable rarity, with the legends COPIA and LCC. COPIA, and the types of Minerva, Hercules, and Mercury; but none to indicate that it was a colony under the emperors.

COPIA LUGDUNENSIS.—See *Lugdunum Copia*.

COPONIA gens—a plebeian family but of noble origin. There are two varieties of coins. The following silver is rare:—

Obv.—Q. SICINIVS. III. VIR. Head of Apollo, diademated; beneath it a star.

Rev.—C. COPONIVS. PR. S. C.—Spoils of the lion raised on a club. In the field a bow and an arrow.

"It is certain (says Borghesi), that the monetal triumvirs of 705 B. C. 49), although exiles, caused coins to be minted, there being a manifest proof of this fact, in the present example of Q. *Sicinius*, who was assuredly one of them. And these denarii were in all probability coined in some city recommended to the protection of the Pretor C. *Coponius*."—And Cavedoni adds, "We learn from Cicero, that C. Caponius commanded a fleet at Rhodes, *prætorio imperio*. And, considering that the very singular type of one of his denarii, *the club*, or *upright post, from the top of which is suspended the lion's skin*, appears to have been taken from one of the coins of *Alinda* in *Caria* (or some other city in that neighbourhood), it seems evident that the triumvir C. Sicinius struck part at least of his monies at or near Alinda, or some town nearer the Carian coast, opposite to the island of Rhodes, then under the government of the Pretor Coponius."—Cited by Riccio, p. 60.

Eckhel has no doubt but that the arms and attributes of Hercules, on the reverse of this silver coin, refer to the origin of Coponius, at Tibur (a town of the Sabines, about 20 miles from Rome), where great honours were paid to that demi-god. Whilst Riccio says—" The bow and arrow may refer as much to Hercules as to Apollo, whose diademated head is on the obverse; and this may possibly point to the government of the Pretor, in the island of Rhodes, where Apollo was peculiarly the object of worship."

CORDUBA, *Hispaniæ Bæticæ*, colonia (now Cordova, in Southern Spain). This city was founded by Marcellus; and made a colony in the time of the republic. But its colonists having been diminished by war, Augustus, as soon as he had pacificated Spain, gave it, according to Pliny, the name of *Patricia*, and granted it the privilege of striking money. (Vaillant).— The coins of this city, says Mionnet *(Supplt.* TAB. 1), consist of a *Latin* autonome in small brass, and of imperial *Latin* colonials in first and second brass, struck only under Augustus, whose portrait, without laurel, they bear on their obverses. The legends of their reverses are COLONIA PATRICIA, within a laurel wreath, or accompanied with types, some representing pontifical instruments, others military ensigns and the names of legions. The following three are specimens of the imperial class, viz. :—

1. PERMISSV CAESARIS AVGVSTI. Bare head of the Emperor.

Rev.—COL. PATR. LEG. V. X. *(Colonia Patricia Legiones quinta et decima).* A legionary eagle between two military ensigns.—Engraved in Vaillant, Colonies, T. i. p. 42. See that writer's learned remarks on this historical coin.

2. PER. CAES. AVGVSTI. Bare head of Augustus.—*Rev.*—COLONIA PATRICIA, within a civic garland.—Engraved in Akerman, *Ancient Coins of Cities*, p. 30, pl. iii. No. 11.

Rev.—COLON. PATR. Pontifical instruments. Ibid. pl. iv. No. 1.

3. *Latin Autonome.*—CN. IVLI. L. F. Q.— Head of Venus.

Rev.—CORDVBA. Cupid standing with torch and cornucopiæ.—Engraved in the same work, p. 29, plate iii. No. 10.

CORDIA gens, of Tuscan origin, and of plebeian rank; its surname *Rufus.*—This family has five varieties in its coins. The following are its two rarest denarii :—

1. RVFVS. An owl on a helmet.—*Rev.*—The Ægis of Minerva, with the words MAN*ius* CORDIVS around it.—Engraved in Morell. *Fam. Rom.*

2. RVFVS III. VIR. The conjoined heads of the *Dioscuri*, with diademed bonnets, and stars above each.—*Rev.*—MAN. CORDIVS. Venus standing, holding the balance in her right hand, and

the hasta pura in her left, with a cupid hung to her neck behind.

There is a denarius of this gens, on which a Cupid appears dancing, with crown and palm branch in his hands; and another with Cupid riding on a dolphin.

These coins are ascribed to Manius Cordius Rufus, monetary triumvir under Julius Cæsar, before or after the dictatorship. The type of Venus, with the balance, refers to the origin of Cæsar, and to his justice; that of the owl to his prudence and wisdom; the warlike helmet and the Egis to his valour; lastly, the palm and crown borne by the dancing Cupid, alludes to the triumphs of Julius.

The heads of the Dioscuri connect themselves with the worship paid to those demi-gods in Etruria, the native country of the moneyer, Cordius Rufus, who was pretor and pro-consul under Augustus, according to a marble discovered at Tusculum by the Abate Amati.—See further remarks on the types of the Cordia gens, cited from Cavedoni, by Riccio, p. 61.

CORINTHUS, colonia, now *Korito*, or *Corinto.*—Corinth was the most celebrated city of Achaia, situate at the end, and on the southern shore, of the Sinus Corinthiacus (Gulf of Lepanto), near the isthmus which bears its name. For its beauty and elegance, its riches and luxurious abundance, Cicero terms Corinth the light of all Greece *(totius Græciæ lumen).* Its more ancient appellation was *Ephyra.* From its local position, between the two seas, this place was called *Bimaris* by the poets : in reference to which, says Pellerin, it is also several times represented on coins, under the emblem of a naked figure—that is to say, the Genius of the City, who holds an oar in each hand, as in Elagabalus. Corinth had two ports, Lechæum on the Sinus Corinthiacus, and Cenchrea on the Sinus Saronicus (Gulf of Egina). It had also a citadel on a lofty rock, called Acrocorinthus. This far-famed city was taken and destroyed by the consul Mummius, general of the invading army of the Romans, A. U. C. 609 (B. C. 145), who made its territories tributary to the republic. It was restored by Julius Cæsar, who also in 710 (B. C. 44) made it a *colony*, and after whom it received the denomination of *Laus Julii*. In the civil war, Corinth sided with Mark Antony against Octavianus.

The coins of this city consist (besides *Greek* autonomes) of *Latin* colonial autonomes, and of *Latin* colonial imperial, in first, second, and third brass. Corinth struck money by permission, and to the honour, of the following personages, viz.:—Julius Cæsar, M. Antony, Augustus, Livia, M. Agrippa, Caius and Lucius, Agrippa junior, Tiberius, Antonia, Germanicus,

Drusus Cæsar, Caligula, Agrippina senior, Claudius, Domitian, Trajan, Plotina, Hadrian, Sabina, Antoninus Pius, Faustina senior, M. Aurelius, L. Verus, Lucilla, Commodus, S. Severus, Domna, Caracalla, Geta, Plautilla, Macrinus, Elagabalus, Gordianus Pius.

In fact, no colony struck more imperial coins than Corinth, especially from the commencement of Nero's reign. When, indeed, that prince visited Corinth, at the celebration of the Isthmian games, the citizens recorded his arrival on various coins, having already dedicated their monetal flattery to him, whilst he was yet but a youth, during the life-time of his father by adoption, the Emperor Claudius. It will be remarked, from the foregoing list, that no coins of the Corinthians were consecrated to either Vespasian or Titus. But the great number struck under Domitian seems to indicate a restitution of liberties, or a remission of taxation, by the last named prince to this colony, which it had not enjoyed during the reigns of his father and brother. The coins minted at Corinth with the respective effigies of Antoninus Pius, M. Aurelius, and L. Verus, are very numerous and varied in their types, particularly those of the latter emperor, who lingered a long time in that seat of abandoned voluptuousness, on his way to wage war against the Parthians. Very considerable issues from the *Latin* colonial mint of Corinth took place under Commodus and Septimius Severus.—See Mionnet, *Supplt.* T. iv.

The legends on the colonial imperial coins of Corinth are as follow, viz.:—C. COR. *Colonia Corinthus.*—C. L. I. COR. and COL. LAVS. IVL. COR. *Colonia Laus Julia Corinthus.*—COL. IVL. AVG. COR. *Colonia Julia Augusta Corinthus.*— It also, in flattery of Domitian, took the surname of his family: COL. FLAV. AVG. COR. *Colonia Flavia Augusta Corinthus;* thus leaving out the name of Julius, who founded the colony.—The legend of a coin struck at Corinth under the same emperor, is COR. PERM. IMP. *Corinthi Permissu Imperatoris;* alluding to the privilege of coining money, conceded by the emperors to this and other colonies.

The series of Corinthian money, both autonomous and imperial, are extremely interesting, from the great number of types which refer either to the history of their city, in its earlier ages, or which offer views of temples and other public edifices.—The Corinthians were great lovers of the fabulous; and whatever attached itself to their traditions and annals, whether true or false—probable or absurd, provided it served to augment their celebrity, was alluded to on their monuments. As Roman colonists, but in the servile spirit of Greek adulation, they sometimes represented the emperors in their mintages, under the form and with the attributes of gods. They were also accustomed to strike on their money the names of one of, or both, the *duumviri,* by whom as a colony they were governed.

Amongst the divinities worshipped, and to whom temples were dedicated and coins minted with their images, at Corinth, were Esculapius and Hygeia, Bacchus, Diana, Hercules, Jupiter, Mars, Mercury, Minerva, Neptune, and Venus.

The annexed wood-cut represents the type of a second brass, which Eckhel places among the *Latin* autonomes.

CORINTHVM.—Bellerophon taming Pegasus before one of the gates of Corinth.

Subjoined is an alphabetical notice of some of the principal types, which appear on the reverses of the *Latin* imperial coins of this colony:

Altar, with a tree upon it.—On coins of M. Aurelius and L. Verus this type appears. It is considered by Patin, with whom Vaillant agrees, to be the altar of Melicerta, whose body, according to that most foolish and confused of Greek myths, was found near a pine-tree, and an altar erected there.—See the word *Melicerta.*

Allocution.—The emperor addressing his soldiers, as in Nero.

Arch, with statues on it, as in Augustus, to whose honour as victor at Actium, a triumphal arch was erected at Corinth.—Engraved in Vaillant's *Coloniæ,* vol. i.

Adventus Augusti. C. COR.—This legend, referring to the arrival of Nero at Corinth, has for its accompanying types, the togated figure of the emperor, and the prætorian galley.

Of this journey made by Nero into Greece, Dion Cassius (lib. 63, p. 719) observes, that he went thither, "not as his warlike ancestors and predecessors (Flaminius Mummius, Agrippa, and Augustus) had done; but that he might drive the chariot, sing to his own playing on the harp, fill the office of herald at public games, and perform in tragedies."

Bellerophon.—This favourite hero of the Corinthians appears on their coins, sometimes mounted on the horse Pegasus and fighting the Chimæra, as in Julius Cæsar; sometimes on horseback without the Chimæra, as in Domitian, L. Verus, and S. Severus. The same destroyer of the triple monster appears on foot, holding Pegasus by the bridle (see the above cut). All these types were intended to indicate the remote antiquity of the city.—See p. 125, and p. 198 of this dictionary—see also COSSUTIA, and the word PEGASUS.

Caius and Lucius, Cæsares.—These two young princes (p. 217) are named together on coins of Augustus struck at Rome, but their portraits placed opposite to each other are found only on a few colonial pieces, amongst which are those of Corinth. On the obverse of these is the bare head of Augustus, with legend CAESAR CORINT. —Engraved in Vaillant, T. i.

Colonist driving oxen at plough.—The only

piece struck by the Roman colony of Corinth, which bears the common colonial symbol, is a second brass dedicated to Augustus, who reinforced, with his disbanded veterans, the too scanty population originally planted there by Julius.

Crown of Parsley (corona ex apio), within which is the word ISTHMIA, as in Nero, alluding to the Isthmian games (certamina Isthmiaca), celebrated near Corinth, on the isthmus, every fifth year.—Engraved in Vaillant, i. p. 118.

Chimæra (see p. 198).—The Corinthians struck this enigmatical object on their coins, in remembrance of their champion Bellerophon, as in Domitian, M. Aurelius, and L. Verus.

Emperors in triumphal quadrigæ, and on horseback, appear on first and second brass of this colony, dedicated to Domitian, and L. Verus. Engraved in Vaillant, i. p. 201.

Genius of the Colony of Corinth. (GEN. COL. COR.)—This appears under the form of a half-naked man, holding a patera and cornucopiæ, on a second brass of Nero, who in the characteristic spirit of adulation to that tyrant, is exhibited by the Corinthians, just as the *Genius Populi Romani* was customarily depicted on coins of Roman die.—Engraved in Vaillant, i. Pellerin, in *Mélange*, vol. i. pl. xvi. p. 264, gives a Corinthian coin of Agrippina Claudii, which, with GEN. COL. for its legend, exhibits a woman habited in the stola, standing with patera and cornucopiæ. There is a similar dedication of a second brass coin, by the Corinthians, to M. Aurelius.—See the word GENIUS.

Ino.—On a second brass, bearing on one side the head and titles of Sept. Severus, and on the other C. L. I. COR. The type is a woman standing, with one foot on a rock, and the other suspended, her right arm holds out an infant: at the bottom of the rock is a dolphin. This woman is Ino, daughter of Cadmus and Hermione, wife of Athamas, king of Thebes. She was the mother of Melicerta, and regarded as a goddess by the Greeks.—Engraved in Vaillant, ii. p. 9.

Melicerta.—Types connected with this legendary "nothing" about which, the Corinthians made so "much ado," upon their coins and other monuments, appears on second brass dedicated by this colony to Sabina, Antoninus Pius, M. Aurelius, L. Verus, Commodus, Sept. Severus, and Caracalla.

The son of Ino is represented under the figure of a naked boy on a dolphin, sometimes sitting astride the fish, on other reverses he stands upright on its back; in a third typification he lies stretched out at length, with his face downwards, on the dolphin which is placed on a table. On some of these there is a tree behind the boy and the dolphin. This alludes to a pine tree, near which was found the dead body of Melicerta, in memory of whom the victors at the Isthmian games were crowned with pine leaves.

On a well known and elegant coin of Corinth, struck in honour of M. Aurelius and L. Verus, the boy, the dolphin, and the pine tree, are exhibited within a round temple, having a dome

made of scales, allusive to the divine rites paid to Melicerta.—The same figure of a child is on another coin recumbent on a dolphin, near a tree, on the opposite side of which is *Sisyphus* under the figure of a naked man, holding in his right hand a *victoriola*, and in his left a palm branch. This type, which appears on a coin of M. Aurelius, is supposed by Vaillant to refer to the Isthmian games instituted in honour of Melicerta.

Neptune is a frequent type on the coins of the Roman colony, as being the tutelary deity of the Corinthians. He had a temple at Lechæum. And on coins of Augustus, Octavia Neronis, and Antoninus Pius, he is typified, holding the trident, and drawn in a shell-formed car by two sea-horses.—On a first brass of Domitian, the god appears sitting on a rock, on which his right hand rests, his left being extended towards a woman who stands before him, holding an infant in her arms.—[This refers to Ino, the unhappy wife of Athamas, imploring the assistance of Neptune to save her newly born son, Melicerta (in Ovid, *Metam.* 4.) The rock is that of Moluris, and the dolphin recals to recollection the fish on which the boy was carried. —See the word INO.

On coins of Domitian, Hadrian, and M. Aurelius, Neptune sits, or stands, with trident and dolphin; on some his left foot is planted on the prow of a vessel, as in Commodus; on a second brass of which last-named emperor, the god of the Sea stands holding his right hand over an altar, on the other side of which is a tree.—On a first brass dedicated to M. Aurelius, the Corinthians have figured Neptune, standing in a triumphal car, a trident in his right, and an image of Victory in his left hand, which obviously refers to the honours of the Triumph conferred on the Emperor by the Senate at Rome, for some signal success which he had just gained, and he is here displayed as Neptune himself.—The above are engraved in Vaillant's Colonial work, vol. i. pp. 140, 181.—Pellerin gives a coin of this colony, dedicated to Julia Domna, on which is Neptune with his right foot placed on the head of a bull, and holding in his right hand the *aplustrum*. (*Mel.* T. i. pl. xviii. No. 5, p. 289.)

Obelisk, on which is a naked image, with a spear in the left hand. On each side of the obelisk is an equestrian figure, in a military dress, as if galloping.

This appears on a coin of Corinth, dedicated to M. Aurelius, and which Vaillant thinks are intended to represent statues raised in honour of M. Aurelius and L. Verus; the obelisk itself being one on which were inscribed their warlike exploits respectively achieved against the Parthians and other enemies of Rome.—Engraved in Vaillant, i. 187.

Pegasus, the winged horse of Apollo, is represented flying, on Corinthian coins of Augustus, Caligula, and Domitian, he is figured standing on coins of M. Aurelius, L. Verus, and Commodus, also on the summit of the Acro-Corinthus in a medal of Claudius. For other types of this fabulous animal, in association with the traditions of Corinth, see wood-cuts in this article—see also the word PEGASUS.

Pirene.—On a third brass of Sept. Severus is the figure of a young woman, sitting on a rock, on which her left hand rests; with her right hand she supports a vase on her knee.— Vaillant (ii. 10) regards this to represent the nymph *Pirene*, who in consequence of Diana having rashly slain her son, is said to have shed tears so abundantly, that she was changed into the fountain which bears her name, and which is situate near the Acro-Corinthus.

In his "*Recueil de quelques Médailles Grecques Inédites*," the late M. Millingen (p. 46), has given the following second brass of L. Verus:

IMP. CAES. AVREL. VERVS AVG. Bare head of the Emperor Verus to the right.

Rev.—COL. I. COR. A woman seated, holding a vase on her knees, at the foot of the Acro-Corinthus; before her stands a winged horse, drinking.

This type, as the learned numismatist above named remarks, has evident allusion to the myth of Pegasus, captured whilst quenching his thirst at the fountain of Pirene, by Bellerophon, with the aid of Minerva.

Port of Cenchrea.—On a second brass of this colony, struck under Antoninus Pius, with the legend C. L. I. COR. the reverse type exhibits a port of semi-circular form, at each extremity of which is a temple, and in the centre of the harbour is a statue of Neptune. Before it are three vessels; and to the left is the trunk of a tree.

M. Millingen, in publishing an engraving of this perhaps unique coin, (an accurate copy of which appears in the right-hand column, observes, that "the port here represented must, according to the description of Pausanias, be that of *Cenchrea*. Its form was semi-circular, and at each extremity was a temple; that to the right was probably dedicated to Æsculapius and Isis; that on the opposite side, to Venus. A colossal bronze statue of Neptune was placed on a rock, or a massive foundation of masonry, raised in the midst of the current. The tree on the side

of the port is doubtless meant to signify th pine, near which Sisyphus found the body of Melicerta; and where Theseus compelled Sinis to undergo the same fate to which he had subjected those wretched people who fell into his hands. Although this tree was near Crommyon, and at a great distance from Cenchrea, yet by a license which ancient artists often allowed themselves, it is represented close to this port." On another rare Corinthian coin this same tree is found transported to the foot of the Acro-Corinthus; probably intended to indicate the Isthmian games, about which such great pains were taken to cause their frequent re-celebration. The head of the Emperor Antonine, which appears on the obverse of this remarkable specimen, may warrant the inference that the port of Cenchrea underwent certain reparations and embellishments, under the orders of that prince, of which history furnishes no record.—See *Recueil*, &c. p. 48.

This antique delineation of the port of Cenchrea derives additional interest from the circumstance of its local connection with the apostolic labours of St. Paul at Corinth, and of its having been the place of embarkation on his voyage to Ephesus, and thence to Cæsarea, in his way to Jerusalem. (Acts, c. xviii.)

Sol.—On a small brass of M. Aurelius, with the legend of *Colonia Laus Iulia Corinthus*, appears the head of the Sun, ornamented with rays.—A second brass of Nero exhibits the Sun, under the figure of a young man, with radiated head, and with a whip in his right hand, driving a quadriga at full speed.—Sol is also represented under the type of a male figure, clothed in a tunic, and crowned with rays, on coins dedicated by this colony to M. Aurelius and L. Verus.

Apollo, in quality of the god of day, was regarded, next to Neptunus, as the tutelary deity of the Corinthians. For, according to Pausanias, Neptunus and Sol competed with each other for the office of protector to their city; and Briareus being appointed to arbitrate between them, awarded the Isthmus to Neptune; and the promontory which commands the city, viz. the Acro-Corinthus, to the Sun's especial guardianship. In the case of L. Verus, it probably associates itself with the successful result of his eastern expedition, the flattery of the Achaians appropriating to imperial princes the form and fashion of the very gods they worshipped.—These types are engraved by Vaillant, *in Coloniis*, i. 199; and in Havercamp, *Cabinet de Christine*, second brass series.

Temples.—Types of this description, under several varieties, appear on many coins consecrated to the Roman Emperors and their *Augustæ* by this colony, such as Augustus, Octavia, Tiberius, Nero, Galba, L. Verus, &c.; some are of four, others of six, columns; some with, others without, flights of steps to them.

Temple of Venus.—A second brass, which offers on one side the name, titles, and portrait of the Emperor Lucius Verus, exhibits on its reverse the legend C. L. I. COR. and the type of the *Acro-Corinthus*, or citadel of Corinth, with the temple of Venus on its summit. From the extremity of the rock, the horse Pegasus takes his flight into the air, seemingly ascending towards the heavens, as if there to take a place amongst the constellations. At the foot of the mountain is an edifice and a grotto, on the left is a tree.

It is very difficult to determine what are the two architectural objects, in the lower part of the reverse. It is believed that the one on the right hand is meant for the temple of Neptune, and that on the opposite side is the grotto where Sisyphus deposited the body of Melicerta. The tree on the left hand side is probably the same of which mention has already been made.

This type of a temple on the top of a rock, with an edifice and a grotto at the base of the same perpendicular acclivity, is by no means rare; but the additional feature of Pegasus, springing up from the summit, has never displayed itself on a coin of Corinth, until published by Millingen, from whose "*Recueil,*" TAB. ii. No. 20, the above is copied.

On a second brass of this colony, struck under L. Verus, is the side view of a four-columned temple, with steps to its portico. This temple, namely that of Venus, on the summit of the Acro-Corinthian rock, Pausanias, confirmed by Strabo, stamps with an infamous celebrity, in the following terms, which Vaillant (i. 203), quoting from the Greek, gives in a Latin dress :—

"Et fanum Veneris Corinthi fuit locuples, ut plures quam CIƆ. habuerit sacrorum famulas meretrices, quas Deæ viri mulieresque dedicarunt. Ob hæc igitur et magna hominum multitudo ea in urbe et divitiæ fuerunt.

The Corinthians seem to have chosen this temple of Venus, as a fit type for a medal dedicated to L. Verus, because he was an especial worshipper of that goddess; for Capitolinus, his biographer, states him to have been so entire a slave to lust, that when in Syria, " non solum

licentiâ vitæ liberioris, sed etiam adulteriis et juventutis amoribus infamatus est."

Venus, standing undressed in a marine car, drawn by a triton and a nereid, with legend COR. and the names of the *duumviri* of Corinth at the time : a most elegant coin in second brass, struck in honour of Agrippina, wife of Claudius, and also another of the same type, dedicated to Nero.—Engraved in Vaillant, i. p. 113.—On a coin of Antoninus Pius, the same goddess is represented as a young woman clothed in the stola, and holding the apple awarded to her by Paris as the prize of beauty.—On a second brass of L. Verus she holds a shield in both hands, and Cupid stands before her feet.—On second brass of M. Aurelius, Lucilla, and Plautilla, the image of this grossly cherished deity of the Corinthians, stands within a temple placed on a high summit.—It was to Venus that the sensual people of this colony raised temples, under various names, and erected statues, not only on the summit of the Acro-Corinthus, but also in the suburbs and in the port of Cenchrea.—See the word VENUS.

Victory.—The Corinthians, like the inhabitants of the Greek cities, were accustomed to flatter their imperial masters, with this symbol of military success and triumph on their coins. Types of Victory, with palm branch and laurel wreath, standing on the ground, or in a galloping quadriga, appear on coins dedicated to Commodus, Sept. Severus, Julia Domna, and Caracalla.—Pellerin gives us an engraving *(Mélange,* i. pl. xvi.) of a Corinthian small brass of Galba, whose coins struck in the colonies are rare, on the reverse of which is *Victory* standing with garland and palm branch. Also another of the same emperor, with type of two hands joined, not given in Vaillant.

CORNELIA gens.—This was of plebeian as well as patrician rank; Sabine in origin, and divided into various branches. In its patrician stem, the highest and most noble of all the Roman families, it gave many remarkable and illustrious subjects to the republic. Amongst its numerous surnames, those which appear on coins are Balbus, Blasio, Cethegus, Cinna, Cossus, Faustus, Lentulus, Scipio, Sisenna, Spinther, Sulla, &c.—No less than 121 varieties are ascribed by Morel, confirmed by Mionnet, to the coins of Cornelia gens, whose name is also read on the *cistophori.* The brass pieces are the *As,* or some of its parts, or they were struck by the moneyers of Augustus.

The following are some of the rarest and most interesting of the Cornelian mintages :—

1. BLASIO. CN. F. Helmeted head of a soldier, without beard.——*Rev.*—A male figure,

naked, with hasta in the right, and arrows or the fulmen in the left hand, stands between two clothed female figures, one of them galeated, and who holds a crown over the central figure. In the exergue ROMA.

The head on the obverse of this denarius has all the appearance of being a portrait. Visconti and Borghesi agree in attributing it to the first Scipio Africanus, as struck by the moneyer Cneus Cornelius Blasio, in honour and praise of his own family. Its likeness to the bust of that great man, preserved in the capitol, seems to warrant the supposition.

Eckhel (v. p. 180), treats the reverse of this coin as representing Dionysus (Bacchus), with Pallas on his left hand, in the act of crowning him ; the other female figure he leaves unidentified.—See his remarks on the group as quoted in p. 120 of this dictionary.—Mionnet gives a similar description of the reverse, viz. :—" Bacchus debout entre Pallas et une femme."

Riccio, on the other hand, pronounces the three figures to be " Jove standing with *hasta* and *fulmen*, Juno on his right, and Pallas on his left hand," adding that " the type is consecrated to the three principal deities of paganism, to which the Romans paid the highest worship, and which were the objects of peculiar adoration in the interior recess of the Capitoline temple, where Scipio paid his devotions (*facendosi supporre figlio di Giove*), affecting to be the son of Jupiter.

2. BALBVS PRO PR. A club.—*Rev.*—Head of Octavian. C. CAESARE III. VIR. R. P. C.— Engraved in Morell. *Fam. Rom.* Cornelia.

This coin belongs to Lucius Balbus, provincial pro-prætor in 712 (B. C. 42), and afterwards consul, although of Spanish origin. He was one of the early adherents of Octavianus, whose head he has stamped on this coin ; and the club on the reverse may perhaps refer to the worship of Hercules by the Gaditani (people of Cadiz), of whom he was a fellow countryman.—Riccio, p. 67, who gives an engraving.—See also Morell.

3. L. LENTVLVS FLAMEN. MARTIALIS.—See *Flamen.*

4. COSSVS CN. F. LENTVLVS.—An equestrian statue, holds on his left shoulder a trophy, and has for pedestal the prow of a ship.—*Obv.* AVGVSTVS DIVI. F. Laureated head of Augustus.

A rare denarius from the original mintage under Augustus, but of the highest rarity, as restored by Trajan.—Engraved in Caylus, and in Morel.

M. AGRIPPA COS. TERT. COSSVS LENTVLVS.— Head of Agrippa, with the mural and rostrated crown.—*Obv.*—AVGVSTVS COS. XI. Laureated head of Augustus.

This is of great rarity, as contemporaneous with the mintages of Augustus, but the restitution by Trajan, especially in gold, is rare in the highest degree.—See an engraving from a well preserved specimen of this coin, under the head of CORONA ROSTRATA et MURALIS.

The above two coins were struck by Cneus Cornelius Lentulus, called Cossus, one of the moneyers of Augustus, son of the consul of the same name, and consul himself in 753 (B. C. 1). They were both minted about the year 731 (B. C. 23), certainly not beyond 742 (B. C. 12), in which year Agrippa died.—Riccio, 67.

In the former of the two most probably is represented the statue of Augustus, erected on the occasion of his victory at Actium, to which the ship's prow refers that adorns the base of the statue.

On the second reverse is the head of Agrippa, general and afterwards son-in-law of Augustus, who greatly contributed by his counsels and by his military valour to advance the fortunes and to embellish the life of the first Roman emperor. (See p. 27 of this dictionary.) —The rostral crown was awarded to victors in naval engagements, and that which is seen on the head of Agrippa is referable to the abovementioned battle of Actium, gained by him whilst in command of Octavian's fleet against that of Mark Antony and Cleopatra.

5. EX. S. C. Female head with a helmet, terminated with the head of a griffin.—*Rev.*— CETHEGVS or CETEGVS *(sic.)* A naked man, with Phrygian bonnet, riding on a goat at full speed. Below ROMA, all within a crown of ivy. —Valued by Mionnet at 200 fr.—Engraved in Morell. *Fam. Rom.* Cornelia.

In the mintages of the Fonteia family Eckhel recognises the genius of Apollo Vejovis riding on the goat, which was held sacred to him.— By the same rule, Cavedoni is disposed to view, in the above reverse, the genius of Juno Lanuvina, and to suppose that it alludes to a passage in the life of Caius Cornelius Cethegus, consul in 557 (B. C. 197) who, at a battle with the *Insubres* (people of Lombardy), made the vow of a temple to the goddess ; and that the goat and ivy crown refers to the cognomen of *Cethegus*, which in the Greek language corresponds with *edera* and *capra*. The workmanship of this denarius, of classic rarity, carries it to the latest age of the republic.—Riccio, p. 63.

6. L. SCIP. ASIAG. Jupiter in a quadriga at full speed, holding a sceptre and the reins in his right hand.—*Obv.*—Head of Jupiter Capitolinus.

This denarius, Eckhel, agreeing with preceding numismatists, considers to have been coined in reference to Lucius Cornelius Scipio, consul in the year of Rome 564 (B. C. 190), to whom the people then and not before, decreed the government of Greece, and the carrying on of the war with Antiochus the Great. He was the eldest brother of Publius Scipio. And as Publius Scipio took the name of *Africanus*, for his conquests in Africa, so Lucius Scipio, having subdued the Syrian monarch and restored peace in Asia, received the name of *Asiagenes*, or *Asiaticus*.

On the other hand, Borghesi contends that this denarius does not belong to the consul of 564, but to another Lucius posterior to 600 (B. C. 154), and Cavedoni refers it to the consul of 671, viz. L. Cornelius Scipio Asiaticus (B. C. 83). The head of Jupiter on the obverse, and the same deity in the quadriga of the reverse, appears to allude to the protection extended by that deity to the Romans.—See Riccio, p. 68.

7. Laureated and bearded head of Jupiter.—*Rev.*—C. N. LENTVL*us.* Eagle on a thunderbolt. In gold.—Valued by Mionnet at 150 fr. by Riccio at 30 piastres.

Borghesi ascribes this to Cn. Lentulus Clodianus consul in 682 (B. C. 72), probably questor in 670 (B. C. 84), and two or three years previously one of the monetal triumvirs.

8. NERI. Q. VRB. Bearded male head.—*Rev.* L. LENT. C. MARC. COS. A legionary eagle between two standards. On one H. on the other P.—See NERIA family.

9. L. LENTVLVS C. MARC. COS. Statue of Diana of Ephesus, with a prop, or support in each hand.—*Obv.*—Head with bushy hair and beard.

The obverse type represents Jupiter Pluvius; and the Ephesian Diana, *mammifera*, on the reverse, designates the place where this rare denarius was coined. In fact towards the close of 705 (B. C. 49), Lucius Cornelius Lentulus, and his colleague in the consulate, Caius Claudius Marcellus were residing at Ephesus.—Riccio, p. 65.

10. SISENA. ROMA. Galeated head of Rome, before it X.—*Rev.*—CN. CORNEL. L. F. Jupiter in a rapid quadriga strikes Titan with a thunderbolt, whilst his horses gallop over the rebellious giant. Above are the heads of the sun and moon, and two stars.

Almost every one is acquainted with the myth of the Titans, who attempted to invade the throne of Jove, and were all destroyed by the Thunderer, in punishment of their impious audacity. What object the moneyer may have contemplated in borrowing such a fabulous incident, is not to be deciphered by any help that history supplies. But an endeavour may be made to interpret the meaning, by resorting to the assistance of proximate and contemporaneous events.

Cneus Cornelius Sisenna, son of Lucius, was *quæstor urbanus*, some year previous to 623 (B. C. 131), in which year he occupied the pretorship. At that time the consul Perpenna having defeated and taken prisoner Aristonicus (who in Asia attempted to throw off the Roman yoke), was rewarded in consequence with triumphal honours. Sisenna wished perhaps to indicate,

in the above reverse, that it was not with impunity that the power of the Roman people could be disparaged or insulted; and that as the daring Titans were destroyed by the exterminating thunderbolts of Jupiter, so the enemies of Rome were pulverised and dispersed by the Roman sword.—Eckhel himself regards it as a symbolical representation :—qui ceterum simbolicus totus videtur, et notare seditionem aliquam Romæ feliciter sopitam. (v. p. 189).

Cavedoni, cited by Riccio (p. 68), says, " I am inclined to think that the busts of the Sun and the crescent Moon are introduced here by way of allusion to the name of Cornelius, composed of *Cornu* and *Ælius*." A far-fetched and unsatisfactory conjecture. The appearance of these two planets is more likely to connect itself with some incident relating to the giants' war.

11. C. CASSI IMP. LEIBERTAS. Head of Liberty diademed.—*Rev.*—LENTVLVS SPINT.— The *prefericulum* and the *lituus.*—See this coin, rare in gold, engraved in p. 189 of this volume.

12. BRVTVS. The *simpulum,* axe, and the *secespita.*—*Rev.*—LENTVLVS SPINT.—Riccio values this in gold at 30 piastre.

13. C. CASSI IMP. Tripod with *cortina.*—*Rev.*—LENTVLVS SPINTER. Prefericulum and lituus.—See TRIPOS.

These coins were struck in Asia by Publius Cornelius Lentulus Spinther, son of P. Cornelius Lentulus Spinther, consul in 697 (B. C. 57).— He was augur, and opposed to Cæsar in the civil war, in which he lost his father. After the battle of Pharsalia he fled to Alexandria, and was pardoned by Julius. On the death of the Dictator, he followed the party of the conspirators, and held military command under them, with rank of pro-pretor and pro-questor.—After the battle of Philippi he was put to death by order of Mark Antony and Octavian. It was in 711 or 712 (B. C. 43 or 42), that as proquestor of Brutus and Cassius, in Asia, he caused these coins to be struck, the types of which shew him to have been appointed to the augurate and also to the priesthood.—See Riccio, p. 65.

14. L. SVLLA.—Head of Venus Victrix, much ornamented; before it stands Cupid, with a bow and long palm branch in his hands.—*Rev.*— IMPER. ITERVM. Prefericulum and lituus between two trophies.—In gold, brought £7 7s. at the sale of the Pembroke collection.

This coin bears on its obverse the head of Venus, because, according to Plutarch, Sulla inscribed Mars, Fortuna, Venus, on a trophy.— Cupid with a palm branch obviously denotes *Venus Victrix.* The two trophies on the reverse allude to two victories which, in the year 667

(B. C. 87), he gained over Archelaüs, the general of Mithridates, on Mount Thurius, and in the field of Chæronea, on which account two trophies were erected. And for this twofold measure of success he was called IMP*erator* ITERVM (General in Chief for the second time).— According to universal admission, this coin, in gold and silver, was struck in Sulla's life-time. The *guttus* and *lituus*, sure signs of the augural office, shew Sulla to have been Augur, as was also Faustus his son.—Appian affirms that the former was also invested with the Priesthood.— See *Doctrina*, vol. v. p. 190.

15. L. MANLI. PROQ*uæstor*. Head of Pallas, with winged helmet.—*Rev.*—L. SVLLA IMP. Sulla in a triumphal quadriga, a flying Victory holding out a crown over him.

A highly-preserved specimen of this very rare coin, in gold, brought £22 10s. at the Thomas sale; and a somewhat less perfect specimen of the same obtained £15 10s. at the Pembroke sale.

This type of reverse seems to shadow forth one or more of the signal triumphs which the Dictator achieved, and enjoyed the honours of, over Mithridates, King of Pontus.—For an engraving of this denarius see the word SVLLA.

Lucius Manlius, who caused the above coin to be minted, was pro-questor in 673 (B. C. 81). He was allied to the family of the *Torquati*, according to Cavedoni.

16. The head of Pallas helmeted, on which a small figure of Victory behind is placing a garland.—*Rev.*—Sulla in military dress, standing with parazonium in his left hand, joining his right to that of another military figure, who holds a short javelin. Behind is a ship, whence Sulla appears to have disembarked.—See this extremely rare coin engraved under the head of SVLLA.

17. SVLLA COS. Beardless head of a man.— *Rev.*—Q. POM. RVFI. RVFVS COS. Another bare and beardless head.—See the word SVLLA.

18. SVLLA COS. Q. POMPEI. RVF. A curule chair, between a lituus and a crown.—*Rev.*—Q. POMPEI. Q. F. RVFVS COS. A curule chair, between an arrow and a branch of laurel.

Lucius Cornelius Sulla (Felix), and Quintus Pompeius Rufus were both consuls contemporaneously in 666 (B. C. 88). It is contended by the old numismatists, that Faustus, son of the consul and dictator Sulla, born of Cecilia Metella, his fourth wife, wished to celebrate such consulate on this medal by typifying the symbols of two consuls. But this, says Riccio, is contrary to the reading of the legend both on the obverse and reverse, which shews it to have been minted by a certain Quintus Pompeius

Rufus, son of Quintus, that is to say, a nephew descendant of the consul, and maternal nephew of Sulla, because born of Fausta his daughter; and thus he re-commemorated his ancestors both paternal and maternal. The curule chairs recal to mind the insignia of the two consuls. The branch and the crown of laurel allude to the triumphs of Sulla; or, according to Cavedoni, they are introduced here, perhaps, to indicate that Sulla was one of the *Decemviri sacris faciundis*. The lituus attests the fact of his augurate. The arrow refers to the Apollinarian games, the celebration of which belonged to the pretor, an office certainly held by those two consuls. Sulla effectively obtained the pro-pretorship in 660 (B. C. 94), prior to his being sent on his Asiatic expedition against Mithridates and Ariobarzanes.

19. FEELIX. A heroic head diademed, with small beard, and the skin of a lion tied to the shoulders.—*Rev.*—FAVSTVS. Diana in a biga at full speed, with whip or lituus in her right hand, and three stars in the field of the coin.

20. FAVSTVS. Head of Diana, surmounted by a half moon, behind it the lituus.—*Rev.* FELIX. Sulla in the toga, seated on an elevated platform; behind him, below, is an old man kneeling on one knee, with his hands tied behind him. Before him kneels another figure, who presents to Sulla a branch of laurel.—For an engraving of this coin see the words FAVSTVS— FELIX.

The above and other money with these legends, were coined by Faustus the son of Sulla, in the time of Pompey the Great, of whom he was the son in law, and in the year 700 (B. C. 54), when he was urban questor.

21. L. SVLLA IMP. Figure on horseback, in the garb of pacificator, or ambassador.—*Obv.* —A. MANLI. A. F. Q. Head of Rome or of Minerva.—In gold, valued by Mionnet at 200 fr.

22. L. SVLLA FE(LIX). Same type of reverse. —*Obv.*—Same legend and type.—[Valued by Mionnet at 300 fr.—A specimen of this almost unique gold coin brought £19 10s. at the Pembroke sale].

These two *aurei* seem to borrow light from a passage in Cicero, wherein he mentions a gilt equestrian statue raised to the honour of Sulla. Eckhel considers either that the equestrian figure represents a statue which was dedicated to Sulla, or that it refers to the peace obtained for the republic by means of his famous victories.

A. Manlius, whose name is inscribed on these coins, appears to be the same person who was lieutenant to C. Marius, in the war against Jugurtha, and was sent, together with Sulla, to the Numidian, Bocchus, when that artful king was desirous of peace with the Romans. Afterwards, 'Manlius appears to have adhered to Sulla. Eckhel further remarks, that the two gold coins above mentioned, much exceed the usual and prescribed weight of the *aurei*. And Barthelemy regards them as being of that kind which was struck in the Peloponnessus, during Sulla's government in Greece, through the instrumentality of Lucullus ; for which reason they were called *pecunia Lucullea.*—See *Num. Vet.* v. 191.

23. Head of Venus, and a globe.—*Rev.*—A figure reclining between Diana and Victory.—In silver, valued by Mionnet at 30 fr.—See an engraving of this rare reverse from a denarius of the Æmilia gens, L. BUCA, p. 146 of this dictionary.—See also the word SULLA.

24. Head of Venus, behind it a sceptre and S. C.—*Rev.*—FAVST. in monogram. Three trophies, between the *præfericulum* and the *lituus.* —See the word SULLA.

25. FAVST. Beardless head of the young Hercules, covered with the spoils of the lion ; behind it S. C.—*Rev.*—A globe in the midst of four crowns ; below it an *acrostolium* and a corn-ear.

The trophies on No. 24 allude to those of Sulla, that is to say, two gained against Archelaus and Dorilaus, the generals in chief of Mithridates ; and the third against Fimbria, general of the Marian faction. Eckhel believes that they refer to the entire successes of Sulla in the Mithridatic war ; that is to say, the battles of Cheronea, Thurius, and Orcomenes.

The last, with the crowns, alludes, according to the general opinion of numismatic antiquaries, rather to the victorious achievements of Pompeius Magnus than to those of Sulla. The *acrostolium* refers to the destruction of the pirates, and the ear of corn to the victualling of Rome through commerce promoted by the restored freedom of the seas.—See Riccio, p. 74.

26. The triuacria ; in the centre Medusa's head ; three ears of corn, one in each angle.— *Rev.*—LENT*ulus* MARC. COS. Jupiter standing ; in his left hand an eagle, in his right the *fulmen.*—Engraved in Morell. *Fam. Rom.* and in Riccio.

The trinacria or triquetra, well known as a symbol of Sicily, obviously refers to the place where this and other denarii classed to the Cornelia family, were minted, by Lucius Lentulus and Caius Marcellus, consuls in 705 (B. C. 49), but exiles from Rome, in consequence of the civil war between Cæsar and Pompey having then commenced. Moreover the head of Medusa in the centre of the trinacria, sufficiently indicates the mint of Syracuse. The Syracusans, colonists of Sicily from Corinth, were fond of allusions to the Corinthian fable of Perseus, who cut the throat of the snake-haired Gorgon, from whose blood sprang Pegasus, of whom Bellerophon availed himself to combat and vanquish the Chimæra. This winged horse is common to the money of Corinth and its colonies, amongst which was Syracuse.—See Riccio, p. 65.

CORNELIA SUPERA, wife of the Emperor Æmilius.—See SUPERA.

CORNELIA SALONINA, wife of Gallienus. —See SALONINA.

CORNU. A horn.—This was the symbol of power and strength, by which men in ancient times sought to imitate that " glory of the forehead," which nature has given to certain animals. The ram's horn decorates the head of Alexander the Great and his successors. But *that* token most frequently designates *Jupiter Ammon* himself, on coins of Alexandria, Bostra, Cassandrea, Laodicæa, and other Egyptian and Greek cities. Moreover it appears on denarii and aurei of the Cornuficia and Pinaria families. Lastly on imperial coins of Augustus, M. Antonius, Trajanus, Hadrianus, M. Aurelius, and S. Severus. (See Ammon, p. 40).—*Serapis* with horns is seen on coins of Trajanus, Hadrianus, Antoninus, M. Aurelius, struck in Egypt.— *Juno* having her head covered with horns of the goat, appears on coins of the Papia, Procilia, Roscia, and Tituria families, and of the Emperors Antoninus and Commodus.

Cornua Fluviorum.—Horns on the heads of river-gods are metaphorically exhibited from bulls, whose chief strength is in their horns.— The ancients depicted the heads of personified rivers as adorned with horns, to indicate the violence of waters, with which the earth was torn up as with the horns of a bull.—Spanheim, *Pr.* i. 394.—See *Fluvius.*

Cornu Amalthea.—See *Amalthea*, p. 40.

CORNUCOPIAE.—This well-known, and, on coins, often recurring symbol of abundance, fecundity, fertility, and happiness, is by some mythological writers identified with the horn of *Amalthea*, the nurse of Jupiter, and from which horn fruits and flowers, and all the riches of nature and of art, are represented as issuing.— Others pretend that it was the horn which Hercules tore from the head of Archeloüs, in his encounter with that protean monster, and which the nymphs picked up and converted into the *horn of plenty.*—This ornament appears on a variety of antique monuments, both sculptural and numismatical. " It is (says Millin, *Dictionnaire des Beaux Arts),* the characteristic attribute of *Euthemia*, a goddess of the Greeks ; *Abundantia* of the Romans ; to mark the fertility which they produce."

Cornucopiæ, filled with fruits, or inclosed within a wreath, formed of corn-ears and flowers, appear either as the symbol of the monetal triumvirs, denoting the abundance of all things, to be supplied by means of money, or as the symbol of the curule ediles, and are found on coins of the Æmilia, Annia, Carisia, Claudia, Fabia, Livineia, Mussidia, Julia, and Statilia families. It is also displayed on coins of Lepidus, Domitian, Hadrian, and others. It is likewise seen on a denarius of Augustus, placed on the back of a Capricorn, which holds between its fore feet a globe and rudder (see p. 172).— Also on a little pillar, as in M. Aurelius. The horn is filled with money, which a woman is pouring out, as in *Abundantia, Liberalitas,* &c.

Cornucopiæ and balance appear on a coin of Hadrian. It is seen on the *curule chair*, as in Julius Cæsar, Augustus, and Titus : also with the caduceus, rudder, globe, and apex, as on silver of Julius Cæsar.—For a *cornucopiæ*, with thunderbolt at the back of it, see Fabia gens.— The horn of plenty in the hands of *Abundantia* appears on coins of Julia Mamæa, Trajanus Decius, Gallienus, Salonina, Tetricus senior and junior (see pp. 2, 3, of this dictionary).

Cornucopiæ is seen in the hands of *Æquitas*, or of *Moneta*, on coins of the imperial series, from Vitellius to Honorius. In those of *Æternitas* on a coin of Titus—of *Africa*, as in Hadrian and Constantine the Great—of *Annona*, as in Nero, Titus, Nerva, Trajan, Hadrian, Antonine, M. Aurelius, Commodus, Severus, Caracalla, Alexander Severus, &c. It is an attribute of *Asia*, as in Claudius—of *Ceres*, as in Faustina jun. and Domna—in those of *Concordia*, as in denarii of the Æmilia family, and of Mark Antony, Caligula, Nero, Galba, Vitellius, Titus, Domitian, Trajan, Sabina, and many others of the *Augusti* and *Augustæ*, as far down as the age of Constantine and his family.

Two Cornucopiæ, with a caduceus between them, form a symbolical type on a coin of Drusus junior, elegantly allusive to the fecundity, and consequent happiness, of the imperial family. The heads of the two infants—represented on the large brass from which the above cut is engraved, and which, instead of the usual issue of corn-ears, fruits, and flowers, surmount each horn typified on this coin—are those of the twin children, to whom young Livia, wife of Drusus, son of Tiberius, gave birth in the year of Rome 776 (A. D. 23), to the exceeding great joy of that emperor, who notified the auspicious event, in rapturous terms, to the Senate; and by their ordinance the piece was struck, Drusus Cæsar then exercising the tribunitian power for the second time, as the legend of reverse sets forth.

Double Cornucopiæ fastened together, most commonly brimful of fruits, exhibit themselves on Latin coins of Julius Cæsar, Livia, Tiberius, Domitian, Antonine.

Two Cornucopiæ, with a winged caduceus between them, appear on medals of Augustus, M. Antony, Tiberius, Claudius, Titus, Domitian, &c.—A duplex horn of plenty, on which a woman is seated, presents itself on a coin of Trajan, and on another of Antoninus Pius.

The *Cornucopiæ* held by *Constantia* is found on coins of Caligula, Antonia minor, and Claudius—in the hands of *Fecunditas*, on medals of the Empresses Julia Mæsa, Orbiana, Mamæa, Etruscilla, Salonina, and Severina—of *Felicitas*,

as in Galba, Vespasian, and many of the succeeding Emperors to Constantine the Great—of *Fides Publica*, on coins of Vespasian, Volusianus, Carausius—of a recumbent *River God*, as in Domitian, Trajan, Hadrian, Ælius Cæsar, Commodus, &c.—of the goddess *Fortune*, on imperial medals from Augustus to Constantius Chlorus.

The *cornucopiæ* appears in the left hand of the personified Genii of the Roman People, Emperors, and Colonies, on numerous coins, as well consular as imperial—such as those of Cornelia gens; and of Nero, Hadrian, Antoninus Pius, Commodus, Albinus, Severus, Licinius senior, Domitius Domitianus, Constantinus Magnus, &c. &c.—See GENIO POPVLI ROMANI.—GENIO AVGVSTI, &c. in this volume.

The *Cornucopiæ* appears in the hands of *Gallia*, personified on coins of Gallienus and Postumus—of *Honos* (the God of Honour), as in Galba, Vitellius, Vespasian, Titus, Antonine, and M. Aurelius—of *Italia*, as in the Fusia and Mucia families, and on the imperials of Vespasian, Titus, Hadrian, Antonine, &c.—of *Lætitia*, as in Hadrian, M. Aurelius, Faustina jun. Lucilla, Commodus, &c.—of *Liberalitas*, as in Hadrian, Antonine, M. Aurelius, L. Verus, &c.—of *Felicitas Temporum* and of *Libertas*, as in Vespasian, Antoninus, Severus, &c.—of *Pax*, as in Augustus, Galba, Vespasian, &c. of *Pietas*, as in Mark Antony, Trajan, the Faustinæ, &c.—of *Providentia*, as in M. Aurelius, and other emperors as far as Constantine M.—of *Roma*, as in Hadrian, Commodus, Probus, &c.—of *Salus*, as in M. Aurelius, Valerian, &c.—of *Securitas*, as in Trajan, Hadrian, Decius, Gallienus—of *Utilitas Publica*, on a coin of Constantine the Great.

CORNUFICIA gens, of the plebeian order, but of consular rank.—Morel assigns five varieties to the coins of this family: and Mionnet gives a fine engraving from the gold specimen of one described as follows:—

1. Head of Jupiter Ammon, horned and crowned. Without legend.—*Rev.*—Q. CORNVFICI. AVGVR IMP. A figure, in the augural habit, holding in the right hand the *lituus*, is crowned by Juno Sispita, who stands behind him, and who holds on her left arm a shield.

2. Head of Ceres, crowned with corn-ears.—Same reverse and legend as the first.

3. Head of Africa, personified as that of a woman covered with an elephant's proboscis.

All these are of the highest rarity both in silver and gold, especially No. 2, restored by Trajan.

Quintus Cornificius, to whom these coins belong, was an adherent of Julius Cæsar, under whom he served as pro-pretor in Illyria 706

(B. C. 48), and perhaps, says Eckhel, through that cause obtained the title of IMP*erator*, stamped on the reverse of coin No. 1; or according to others, he acquired it at a later date in Africa. —After Cæsar's death, and disliking the sanguinary government of the triumvirate, he seceded to the opposite party, at the time when the proscribed conspirators made their retreat into Asia, under the leadership of Brutus and Cassius, and he went as their appointed lieutenant into old Africa. These coins, it appears probable, were struck in Africa in 711 (B. C. 43). For African Ceres, Jupiter Ammon, and the head itself of Africa, covered with the elephant's skin, allude to the place, and its principal deities, where Cornificius held for a short period the chief command.

From the type of Juno Sispita (see the word), it is inferred that this Quintus Cornificius was a native of Lanuvium, where the worship of the goddess was specially observed.—The inscription AVGVR shews not only that he was an augur, whilst the type represents him in his augural dress, but also designates one whom Cicero, himself an augur, salutes in many letters, as a colleague (conlega), and speaks of (B. C. 45) as a man of literary judgment, habits, and tastes.

COROLLA, a diminutive from *corona*—a little crown, or garland, either composed of flowers, or formed of thin plates of brass lightly gilt. This ornament appears on coins of Faustina jun. Commodus, Crispina, Pertinax, and several others of the imperial series. It also surrounds the *Puteal Libonis* on a denarius of the Æmilia and Scribonia family; and is seen in the hand of *Lætitia*.

CORONAE.—Crowns were employed from a remote period of antiquity, either to ornament the statues of deities, in reference to their attributes, or to decorate the heads of great men in recompense of their ascribed virtues. They also came into use amongst the people at spectacles during days of public rejoicing, and amongst private individuals at banquets and festivals; in the one case they were regarded as rewards of valour and as proofs of merit, in the other as sources of amusement and as pledges of conviviality.—See Pitiscus.

Crowns were not indiscriminately bestowed by the ancients; each god and each hero had his distinctive embellishment of this kind. Olympian Jupiter appears crowned with laurel; Dodonian Jove with oak; Jupiter Olivarius with olive; Ceres has a crown of corn-ears; Apollo a crown of laurel; Cybele and the deified personifications of cities wear turreted coronets; Venus wears the golden crown given to her by the Hours, or a crown of myrtle; Minerva a crown of olive leaves; that of Flora is of roses; that of Bacchus and his followers is composed of vine leaves, or of ivy; the crown of Hercules is of poplar, because he carried that tree into Greece; Sylvanus and the woodland gods were crowned with pine; whilst Arethusa, and the divinities of the water, bound their brows with reeds.—Millin, *Dic. des Beaux Arts*.

Crowns were made of different materials, according to the purpose for which they were intended. Thus the crown of gold, *corona aurea*, was an extraordinary recompense of bravery as well amongst the Romans as the Greeks. Those who obtained it, were privileged to wear it at theatres and other public places.— Crowns of gold were also consecrated to various deities, especially to Jupiter.—Crowns of the same precious metal were likewise presented to different provinces of the empire to the reigning prince.—See *Aurum Coronarium*, p. 115.

The Romans gave *Crowns* to those whose military exploits and civil services entitled them to distinction and reward.——The subjoined notices on the subject are exclusively limited to such *coronæ* as are represented on coins :—

1. CORONA CIVICA (or *Corona Querna* or *Quercea*). The civic crown.—This was, with the Romans, the greatest military recompense, the most distinguished personal ornament. It was awarded to him who had saved the life of a citizen in battle. The emperors themselves distributed this high reward of valour and merit, and even decked their own heads therewith.— It was formed, or after the appearance, of oak leaves with the acorns. For this reason it was called *quercus civilis*, or oak of citizenship.— And the decoration was esteemed so honourable that, at Rome, when he who had received it went to the public shews, the spectators rose at his entrance; and a conspicuous place was assigned to him near that of the Senators. He was also exempted from the obligation of serving public offices.—In the case of Augustus, the Senate granted to him the peculiar and unprecedented honour of a civic crown suspended from the summit of his palace.—See the word *Eagle*.

During the calends of March, 727 (B. C. 27), and yearly thereafter, a gold crown formed of leaves in imitation of oak, was tendered by the Senate to Augustus. Accordingly we see on these coins the oaken crown *(corona quercea)*, and read O. C. S. or OB. CIVES SERVATOS, with, or without, S. C. for having saved the lives of citizens, being an allusion to the peace which that prince had restored to the empire (see p. 106). In like manner, the silver and large brass coins of Claudius exhibit on their reverses S. P. Q. R. OB. C. S. or EX. S. C. OB. CIVES SERVATOS, within a crown of oak leaves.—(See the above engraving from a well-preserved first brass specimen of Claudius).

The civic crown of oak leaves, with inscrip·tions or figures, appears on coins of the Aelia, Aquilia, Durmia, Licinia, and other families; and (besides those above mentioned) on coins of Tiberius, Caligula, Nero, Galba, Vespasian, Titus, Domitian, Nerva, Trajan, and several others.

2. CORONA LAVREA.—The laureated crown was the most ancient head-dress of the emperors, as it began to be used as early as the time of Julius Cæsar. This honour was publicly decreed, and was moreover particularly gratifying to him, as a means of concealing, on public occasions, that baldness of the head, which some time before his death had come on to his great annoyance. This *laurea* of Julius Cæsar, as plainly appears from his coins (see pp. 152, 154, 155, 156), was a simple one, whereas that, which Octavianus and his successors wore, was bound with a diadem, or fillet, which was tied in a knot at the back of the head, the two ends descending to the shoulders.

Eckhel, in an inquiry which he enters into (viii. 360—61, et seq.), as to whether the *corona laurea* was a badge of sovereignty, makes the following instructive remarks:—

Here is an involved question, since the signification of this crown, as of many other things, no doubt varied at different periods. That which was at the first decreed to Julius Cæsar, and afterwards to Octavianus, was but a part of those distinctions so liberally showered by flattery upon both those individuals; though it, nevertheless, by the manner in which it was conferred, carried with it a peculiar mark of dignity and superiority. It is now a well-established fact, that neither Julius Cæsar, nor Octavianus (afterwards Augustus), bore any honours but such as were publicly decreed to them. And M. Agrippa, accordingly, does not appear on coins with a laureated head, because the laurel was never decreed to him. For the same reason Tiberius also abstained from its use, being always represented with bare head, as long as Augustus was alive, and he himself was only Cæsar. On the death of Augustus he immediately assumed it, and indeed all the other honours and privileges of his father by adoption, as his own by right. In like manner, Nero, till he became emperor, declined the laurel crown. From all which instances we might infer, that this badge belonged properly to the emperors only, unless the cases of Drusus Senior, Titus and Domitian, be considered as invalidating such a rule. And yet the elder Drusus was not even Cæsar, though he is generally seen on coins with a laureated head; and notwithstanding it is well-known that his coins were not struck till after his death, yet the laurel could not have been given to him, had it been the proper and peculiar mark of sovereignty. To this instance may be added that of L. Vitellius, the father of the Emperor Aulus Vitellius, who, though he died in a private rank of life, yet appears with a laureated head on the coins struck by his son. I would not be severe upon Titus, though he was at the same time Cæsar, yet endowed with the *Tribunitia Potestas*, and associated with his father in the empire; but what right to the laurel crown could Domitian possess, when yet only Cæsar, and deficient in all these other titles?

It is evident, therefore, that the *laurea* did not, at that period, denote the highest post in the realm. Was it then an arbitrary distinction? Far from it. For it could be conferred as a reward for great exploits in war, of which species of merit the laurel has at all times been the symbol. Victory always carries it in her hand, and letters bearing news of a victory were always bound with laurel. We know, that Drusus, on account of his tried valour in battle, not only received the title of *Imperator*, but also statues and a triumphal arch. L. Vitellius too, for bringing back to his allegiance the Parthian Artabanus, gained no small credit.—And as for the warlike deeds of Titus, and the honours heaped upon him in consequence, who does not remember them? It is, indeed, more difficult to associate with such men Domitian. Yet it is highly probable, that, by the indulgence of Vespasian and Titus, when they enjoyed their Jewish triumph, some of the outward distinctions of military renown were permitted to Domitian. Indeed, it is well known, that he was present at that triumph on horseback, and on the coins of that year, viz. 824 (A. D. 71), he appears, habited in the *paludamentum*, and holding a short sword in his left hand, and that it is only from that time that he is represented with a laurel crown, having always before been given bare headed.

That in after times it passed into a law, that no one but an emperor should be crowned with laurel, is distinctly proved by coins. In the case of Commodus alone this honour was anticipated, and even there only under the circumstances of his being associated with his father in the empire, as Titus was, though the title of emperor had not been actually conferred. From that period, then, all the Cæsars, at least on coins struck in Rome, were represented with bare heads; the radiated crown being afterwards permitted, but *never the laurel*. The laurel, however, was considered one of the insignia of sovereignty in other parts of the world, as well as at Rome. According to Herodian (vii. ch. 6), when Gordianus Africanus senior entered Carthage, on the occasion of the Africans declaring him, who was their pro-consul, emperor, out of hatred to Maximinus, "laureated fasces were borne before him, which was the sign to distinguish the fasces of sovereigns from those of private individuals." From the time of Diocletian, all the Cæsars admitted as associates of the Augusti *(Cæsares collegæ)*, in opposition to long received custom, assumed the laurel, viz. Constantius Chlorus, Gal. Maximianus, Maximinus Daza, Fl. Severus, and Constantine the Great. The reason for this may have been, that each of them ruled his own province with almost plenary powers. Their example was afterwards followed by the Cæsars Crispus, Delmatius, and the sons of Constantine the Great. But the *king* Hannibalianus, Decentius, Constantius Gallus, and Julianus, as Cæsars, being held in less repute, appear with bare head. After the sons of Constantine the Great, the laurel began to fall into disuse, and the preference was given to the diadem.

The crown of laurel appears on the reverse of many coins of families, and on numberless coins of emperors, either by itself, or held by some figure over the head of another figure.

For a fine engraved specimen of the *laurel crown*, see *Cæsarea Philippi*, p. 162.

Representations of the laurel crown on the heads of emperors, engraved from well-preserved specimens in large brass and medallions, are given in pages 104, 112, 155, 168, 173, 187, 207, 212, 239, &c. of this dictionary.

3. CORONA LAUREATA ET ROSTRATA.—A crown composed of laurel leaves and berries, interlaced with the prows and sterns of gallies, placed alternately, in the centre of which is inscribed the word AVGVSTVS, appears on a brass medallion and on a large brass of that emperor. The above engraving of this reverse is from a specimen in the British Museum. It was struck in commemoration of the decisive naval victory gained by Octavian over Mark Antony at Actium.

4. CORONA MVRALIS.—The mural crown was of gold or of silver, made in the form of a wall with towers and curtains. It was given by the general to him who had been the first to scale the ramparts of an enemy's town, or who had entered by the breach. These turreted crowns are frequently seen on Roman coins ornamenting the heads of Genii, and of Divinities, to whom the guardianship of cities was supposed to be committed. Hence Cybele, goddess of the earth, and the rest of those tutelary deities who presided over provinces and colonies, are represented on coins, with mural crowns on their heads.—See p. 12 (Furia gens) ; p. 171 (Cappadocia) ; also see *Corona Rostrata et Muralis*, in the next page.

5. CORONA PAMPINEA.—On a silver medallion of Mark Antony, the triumvir's head appears, within a crown of mingled vine and ivy leaves.

6. CORONA RADIATA.—The radiated crown, that is to say, a crown composed of rays, is of frequent occurrence on coins. It owes its origin to the *nimbus* (see the word), with which the ancients decorated the heads of their gods. The statues of the Sun were thus crowned, as repre-

senting the vivid irradiations of his light. An illustration of this presents itself on a silver coin of the Mussidia gens (engraved in Morell. *Fam. Rom.*), the obverse of which exhibits a youthful male head, from around which sharp-pointed rays diverge as from the centre, personifying Apollo, in his quality of the God of Day.— In like manner are some of Jupiter's statues adorned. (See p. 117).—Serapis also has the head radiated. The Sun of the Egyptian pantheon, he was regarded as the eternal benefactor of mankind, and his attribute of the rays became the symbol of eternity and beneficence.

Amongst the Romans, Julius Cæsar was the first who obtained the radiated crown. It is, however, only on coins which were struck after his death, that the head of Cæsar appears with this decoration.—Augustus is represented with a radiated head on several coins, struck after his decease.—The radiated crown, as the ornament of an emperor's head during his life-time, was introduced in the first instance by Nero. (See *Augustus Augusta*, p. 108; and *Augustus Germanicus*, p. 109).—Vespasian afterwards adopted it. But for a long period it made its appearance only on second brass.

As exemplified on coins of S. Severus, struck in 955 (A. D. 202), the radiated portraits of emperors, and a head of the moon placed on the coins of their wives, denote the Sun and the Moon ; and by such devices is shadowed forth the Eternity attributed to Princes by the ancients. (See p. 23—24).—Under Caracalla the radiated crown is seen on brass coins of the second size ; and also on the silver, but only on those, which as a novelty, he caused to be struck of a larger size ; an example followed by his immediate successors. In later times the use of it was various and fluctuating, as may be observed on reference to the coins themselves. Though the laureated crown was for a long time withheld from those who were only Cæsars, yet the radiated one began to be permitted them as early as the time of Diadumenianus. On the other hand, coins give the laureated crown to Domitian, whilst still Cæsar ; but never the radiated, though his brother Titus, in the same station, wears both indiscriminately. The radiated crown was afterwards in less esteem than the laureated. This is proved by a silver coin, exhibiting the heads of Balbinus and Pupienus Augg, and Gordianus Cæsar, the two former laureated, the latter radiated. The crown of rays was also a symbol of consecration. And that it was the peculiarly appropriated badge of the emperors, or at least of those of the lower empire, is clearly shewn, by the panegyric of Mamertinus on Maximianus Augustus (chap. iii.) ; where, besides "the triumphal robes, the consular fasces, the curule chairs, the retinue of courtiers, and the glittering pageant," which he says were the usual accompaniments of an emperor's presence; he also mentions—"that light which encircled his god-like head with a bright halo ;" by which expression was doubtless meant the radiated crown, as illustrated by certain types of coins, minted under Constantine the Great.—See Eckhel, vi. 270, and viii. 362.

For representations of the *radiated* crown on the head of an emperor, see pages 39, 105, 109, 181, 187.—See also DIVVS AVGVSTVS PATER, and NERO.

7. CORONA ROSTRATA, MURALIS.—The rostral crown, so called from its ornaments, which imitated the prows and sterns of ships, was the peculiar mark of honour conferred upon the maritime prefect (or naval commander in chief), who had gained some great victory at sea; in contra-distinction to the naval crown *(corona navalis)*, which was given to him who had first boarded an enemy's vessel. Illustrative of this point, there is extant a gold coin of the highest rarity, which bears on it

AVGVSTVS COS. XI. and the head of Augustus, laureated.——*Rev.*——M. AGRIPPA COS. TERT. COSSVS. LENTVLVS. Head of Agrippa, encircled with a crown, on which the turreted peculiarities of the *mural*, are commingled with the naval attributes of the *rostral* crown.

The first particular to be noted (says Eckhel, vi. 164) in the above coin, is the crown in part composed of the beaks of ships, which the ancients used to term the (corona) *navalis, classica,* or *rostrata.*—Octavianus conferred this on Agrippa after his naval victory over Sextus Pompeius; and that he was the only Roman who was so honoured, we have the testimony of various writers—among whom are Velleius (ii. ch. 81), Livy (*in epitome* cxxxix), Seneca *(de benefic.* ch. 32), and Dion Cassius (xlix. § 3), who further states that the crown was of gold. Pliny, however, (xvi. § 3), says, that a *corona rostrata* was given to M. Varro, by Pompey the Great, after the piratic war. This crown of Agrippa is celebrated by Virgil (see pp. 27 and 28).—And Ovid also speaks allusively to the same valiant and successful commander *(in arte,* iii. 392.)

" Navalique gener cinctus honore caput."

[And (his) son-in-law, having his brows adorned with the naval decoration.]

The author of *Doctrina* next briefly directs attention to the *mural* or *turreted* crown; observing, however, that he had not been able to discover, from ancient writers, at what time Agrippa earned this distinction.—For the name of Lentulus, the moneyer who struck the above engraved coin, see *Cornelia* gens, p. 285 of this dictionary.

8. CORONA SPICEA, from *Spicæ,* ears of corn, the token of *Annona,* or of provisions (chiefly corn) procured for the public use by the Curule Ediles, to whom that care appertained, as is shewn on their family coins. The head of *Ceres*

is also distinguished by the same ornament.—See p. 12.

On a coin, having for its obverse legend AGRIPPINAE AVGVSTAE, there is a female head crowned with corn ears. Agrippina was the first of the wives of Claudius, whose portrait that emperor permitted to be stamped on coins, in the same manner as his own; from which very fact it is evident, how much influence she assumed in public affairs. The *corona spicea,* is seen also on the heads of Livia and Antonia, in imitation of Ceres.—On a very rare coin, with obverse legend SABINA AVGVSTA, we see Sabina's head crowned with ears of corn, as representing Ceres.—See Eckhel, vi. 257 and 522.

9. CORONA TRIUMPHALIS.——The triumphal crown was of two kinds. One was given by the army to its general, and he wore it during the triumphal procession. It was composed of laurel branches, or of gold fashioned after the form of laurel leaves. The other was that presented by foreign cities, or conquered provinces, to a Roman general, to grace the triumphs which he was about to celebrate at Rome, and in which they were carried before them, with great parade, as Livy frequently records. Festus on this subject says—" *Triumphal* crowns are those which are carried before a victorious general, and made of gold; though in earlier times, for lack of means, they used to be of laurel."—Julius Cæsar is stated, by Appianus, to have had carried before him, in his triumphs, 2822 of these crowns. —See *Aurum Coronarium,* or crown-gold, p. 115—also a symbol of it in the hands of ASIA, on a first brass of Antoninus Pius, p. 90.

CORVUS.—The crow was sacred to Apollo (see p. 64), because, as Ovid writes, the god changed himself into that bird. The crow appears standing on a branch of laurel, in a coin of Domitian, and beneath a tripod on a denarius of Vitellius.—See XVVIR. SAC. FAC.

COS. *Consul.*—PATRE COS. *Patre Consule,* on a denarius of Valerius Messala.

COS. DES. or DESIG. *Consul Designatus.* —Consul Elect, that is to say, before he entered upon his first consulate.—See CONSULATUS, p. 267.

COS. DESIG. ITER. ET. TERT. *Consul Designatus, Iterum et Tertium.*—Consul Elect for the second and third time. On a coin of Mark Antony.

COS. ITER. DESIG. TERT.—Consul a second time, elected for a third time. On a denarius of Augustus.

COS. II. *Consul Secundum.*—DESIGN. III. *Designatus Tertium,* as in Nerva.

COS. III. *Consul Tertium.*—Consul for the third time.

COS. IIII. *Consul Quartum.*—Consul for the fourth time.

COS. LUD. SAEC. FEC. *Consul, Ludos Sæculares Fecit.*—See Ludi Sæculares.

COS. PREIVER. CAPTU.—*Caius Plautius Hypsæus in suo Consulatu.*—Privernum taken in the consulate of C. P. Hypsæus. On a denarius of the Plautia gens.—See HYPSAE (P) AED. CVR.

COS. V. or QUINQ.—*Consul Quinquies.*

COS. TER. DICT. ITER. *Consul Tertium, Dictator Iterum.*—Julius Cæsar, contrary to ancient usage and law, was both consul and dictator; for, before him no one was consul and dictator, at the same time.

COS. VI. VII. *Consul Sextum* and *Septimum.* —Consul for the sixth and 7th time, as on coins of Vespasian, Titus, and Commodus.

COS. OCTAVO DESIG. IX. Consul elect for the eighth time.—Augustus.—(See Eckhel, vi. 89).

COS. XIII. and XIIII. Consul for the 13th and 14th time.—Domitian.

COSS. *Consules* or *Consulibus.*—Consuls.

COS. ITERO.—Hadrian.

AVG. GER. DAC. PAR. P. M. TR. P. COS. ITERO. *(sic.)* S. P. Q. R.—A military figure, standing, with a spear in the right hand, and a short sword in the left. (Imperial Museum.)—" I published this coin (says Eckhel), some time ago *(Sylloge,* i. p. 101), not only because in many respects it differs from all the coins of Hadrian hitherto discovered, but also on account of the singular substitution of ITERO for the customary ITERVM. The coin, however, is of elegant workmanship, as is most of this emperor's coinage, and its genuineness is indisputable." vi. 477.

COSCONIA appears to have been *gens plebeia;* for a member of it is recorded as having held the tribuneship of the people. There is only one coin of this family, a denarius, on which is read L. COSCO. M. F. Lucius Cosconius, Marci Filius. Winged head of Minerva.—*Rev.*—L. LIC. CN. DOM. Lucius Licinius, Cneus Domitius. Mars standing in a biga at full speed, brandishes a spear in the right hand, and holds a shield and a military lituus in the left.—See *Lituus Militaris.*

The reverse of this silver coin is uniform in type with that of one belonging to the Aurelia gens (Scaurus), hereto subjoined:—

A similar type presents itself on denarii of the Domitia, Pomponia, Poblicia, and Porcia gentes.—The denarii in question were each of them struck in commemoration of the monetal triumvirs, in the four years of the censorship of Lucius Licinius Crassus, and Cneus Domitius Ahenobarbus.——Lucius Cosconius struck his, from 658 (B. C. 96) to 662, according to Eckhel's opinion. It seems that he never figured in more conspicuous employments.—Riccio, 75.

COSSUTIA.—An opulent gens of the equestrian order. The surnames are *Maridianus* and *Sabula.* Its coins are contemporaneous with the dictatorship of Julius Cæsar, when the republic was extinct. There are three varieties.

—The two following have historical references, viz.:—

1. CAESAR DICT. PERPETVO. Head of Julius Cæsar, veiled and laureated.—*Rev.*—C. MARIDIANVS. Venus Victrix, holding a Victory in her right hand, and in her left a buckler resting on a globe. Of the highest rarity in gold.

2. CAESAR PARENS. PATRIAE. The head of Cæsar.——*Rev.* C. COSSVTIVS MARIDIANVS, in two lines crosswise, round it A. A. A. F. F.—Engraved in p. 157.

3. SABVLA. Head of Medusa, winged and hair braided with serpents.—*Rev.*—L. COSSVTI. C. F. Bellerophon on Pegasus, brandishing a spear in his raised right hand.

It seems, from the respective legends and types of the above coins, that the two first were struck by Caius Cossutius Maridianus, one of Julius Cæsar's moneyers, just before the dictator's death, viz. in 710 (B. C. 44); and that the same Caius Cossutius Maridianus continued for some time to take part in the direction of the public mint, under the *Triumviri Reipublicæ Constituendæ;* and that the coin of L. Cossutius, the son perhaps of the preceding, might be dated 711, because it commemorates the foundation of the Roman colony at Corinth, with the emblems of Medusa, and of Pegasus mounted by Bellerophon—the planting of that colony having been accomplished by Julius Cæsar in the before mentioned year 710.

Venus the victorious is well known to have been the favourite symbol of Julius, allusive to the assumed origin of his family. The position of the legend in No. 2, crosswise and roundabout combined, is unique amongst the family class of Roman coins.

COSTA, surname of the Pedania family.— COSTA LEG. Costa was one of Brutus's *Legati,* or lieutenant-generals.

COUNTERFEIT COINS.—These are of two distinct kinds, namely:—

I. Those which are of unquestionable antiquity, fabricated to impose as the current money of the country or district, and those which are the productions of forgers in modern times, to deceive the amateur and collector. Of the former, examples are known which are almost coeval with the coinage of stamped money.— In the Roman series ancient forgeries are of very common occurrence, both in the consular and the imperial money. They consist of casts, apparently from the true coins, in copper, most ingeniously plated with silver, so that they are only to be detected by an experienced eye. In many specimens this coating of silver has been worn away in circulation, and the copper or *anima* of the ancient forgery is easily perceived; but in those which have not been subjected to wear, the deception is only to be detected by very close examination. Pliny mentions that in his time these false pieces were prized for the ingenuity of their fabrication, and states that many true denarii were often exchanged for a forged example; an assertion which it is difficult to reconcile with the fact, that ancient forgeries of both consular and imperial denarii are constantly to be met with in our times, and that some types,—the denarius of Claudius with DE BRITANN. for example,—are almost invariably found to be plated.

II. The forgeries of ancient coins, in modern times, date probably from the latter half of the 16th century, when the productions of ancient medallic art had begun to excite attention and invite the study of the learned, who, destitute of *practical* knowledge, were doubtless easily deceived in those days; hence we find spurious coins of Julius Cæsar with VENI. VIDI. VICI. and ÆGYPTO CAPTA.—Also the effigies of Priam, Dido, Æneas, Plato, Artemisia, Alcibiades, and other personages of antiquity, specimens of a nefarious art, which would not in our times deceive the merest tyro in numismatics.—Modern counterfeit coins have been arranged under several classes, viz :—

1. Coins well-known to be modern imitations, chiefly in large brass, the work of the Paduan artists, perhaps not originally designed to impose upon the ignorant or unwary, but simply executed in rivalry of the ancient examples. Of these many specimens still exist, and are now little valued.

2. Coins cast from the former.

3. Coins, or rather casts, taken from moulds formed from ancient specimens.

4. Retouched ancient coins which have been expertly altered with the graving tool.

5. Spurious pieces formed by the union of two faces of different coins, namely by placing the head of Ælius as the reverse of a coin of Hadrian, or a head of Aurelius to a reverse of Antoninus Pius. The last type occurs as a true coin, and has been often imitated in this way.

The above described fraud, when dexterously executed, is difficult to detect. Beauvais, who has written an elaborate treatise on this subject, enters into many details which may be perused with advantage; but it is very obvious that no written instructions can be sufficient to guard the collector against an ingenious forgery, and that nothing but the constant examination of well-authenticated coins, of which there are abundant examples, can afford him the means of judging of the integrity of any rare specimen that may be offered to him.

On this subject the reader is referred to that section of Mr. Akerman's "Introduction to the Study of Ancient and Modern Coins," which treats of "*Forgeries of Public Money*"—an essay, which like the other contents of that instructive little volume, will amply repay perusal.

See also ALTERED MEDALS, p. 39.

CREMNA (Pisidiæ—Asia Minor) *colonia*, now called *Kebrinaz*, in Anatolia.—The coins of this city are *Latin* imperial in brass, dedicated to Caracalla, Geta, Elagabalus, Etruscilla, and Tranquillina. Their legends are COL. CR. PRO. P. *(Colonia Cremna Provinciæ Pisidiæ)*—COL. IVL. AVG. FE. CREMNA. *(Colonia Julia Augusta Felix Cremna).*—The accompanying types are a Cupid standing, drawing a bow—and a legionary eagle between two military ensigns—also Bacchus and Mercury, with their respective attributes.—There is a first brass of great rarity and elegance, struck at Cremna, in honour of Etruscilla, wife of Trajan Decius, which has for its reverse type the radiated head of Decius between that of Herennius and Hostilianus, his two sons, above which is an eagle with wings spread.—Engraved in Vaillant, ii. 202.

CREPEREIA gens.—A family of the equestrian order, respecting whom little, if anything, is known. Its surname on coins is Rocus.—There are six varieties. The rarest denarius is inscribed Q. CREPER. M. F. ROCVS, and has for the type of its reverse, Neptunus or Portunus, standing in a car drawn by two sea-horses, and brandishing the trident in his right hand. On the obverse is a female bust, probably intended to represent some marine deity; behind it is a fish. Eckhel regards this coin as referring to the colony of Corinth, founded by Julius Cæsar. —This Quintus Crepereius is not known.

CREPUSIA gens.—Ancient but little known —even its order is uncertain. There are only two types, but many varieties, on its coins :—

1. CENSORIN. Female bust, well adorned, with veiled head.—*Rev.*—L. LIMETA. P. CREPVSI. Woman seated in a biga, with left shoulder towards the horses; guides them at full speed, with both hands holding the reins.

2. A young head, probably that of Apollo, with a shell before and a sceptre behind.—*Rev.* P. CREPVSI. A man on horseback, galloping, brandishing a javelin in his right hand—in the round of the coin various numerals or symbols.

The former of these denarii informs us that Publius Crepusius was monetal triumvir with Lucius Censorinus. Beyond the record of this fact nothing can be positively affirmed respecting them. Cavedoni is of opinion that the year 660 (B. C. 94), is to be assigned as the date of these silver coins.

CRISPINA *(Bruttia)*, daughter of Bruttius Præsens, a man of consular rank.—She was a woman of great beauty, and was married to the Emperor Commodus, in the year of Rome 930 (A. D. 177). On account of adultery she was divorced, a few years after his accession to the throne, by her infinitely more profligate and abandoned husband; and, having been exiled to Capreæ, was there, by his orders, put to death by strangulation, at an early age (A. D. 183).— Her coins in brass and silver are common; gold and brass medallions very rare. On *Latin* coins she is styled CRISPINA AVG(VSTA) IMP. COMMODI. AVG. Some pieces represent her with Commodus.

The rarest reverses amongst the coins struck in honour of this empress are—

GOLD.—CERES.—DIS. GENITALIBVS. (Value 150 and 300 fr. according to Mionnet).—DIS. CONIVGALIBVS. (Brought £10 10s. 0d. at the Thomas sale).—PVDICITIA. (£11 at the same). —VENVS FELIX. (£16 at do.)

BRASS MEDALLIONS.—Diana standing, holding a bow and an arrow (see DIANA.)—COMMODVS and CRISPINA, with reverse of CONCORDIA. —VOTA PVBLICA. (300 fr. each).

LARGE BRASS.—ROMAE AETERNAE. (24 fr.)

CRISPUS *(Flavius Julius)*, eldest of the sons of Constantine the Great, by Minervina, born, some say, in the East, others, at Arles, about A. D. 300. He derived his name from his great grandfather Crispus, brother of Claudius Gothicus. According to St. Jerome he received his education under Lactantius. Be that as it may, certain it is his father made him Cæsar on the 1st of March, A. D. 317, together with his brother Constantinus, and Licinius junior; and he was nominated consul the following year. A prince of great talents and virtues, Crispus distinguished himself at an early age by his military skill and valour. In the war carried on by his imperial father in Gaul, he turned the tide of victory against the incursive Franks, A. D. 320. The following year he served the office of consul for the second time, with Constantinus Cæsar for his colleague. In 323 he destroyed the fleet of the Emperor Licinius at Gallipoli.— By a rash and cruel order of his father, in 326, Crispus was put to death, before he had completed his thirtieth year, on a false accusation brought against him by his mother-in-law Fausta, whose criminal love, it is said, he had repelled; and to whose revenge or jealousy he fell a victim. His numismatic style is D. N. FL. IVL. CRISPVS NOB. CAES.—Crispus and his brother Constantine the younger, associated on coins, are called CRISPVS ET CONSTANTINVS NOBB. CAESS.

MINTAGES OF CRISPUS.

The gold are of great, some of extreme, rarity. There are no silver. Small brass mostly common.

The following are amongst the rarest reverses: GOLD.—CONCORDIA AVGG.—CRISPVS NOB. CAES.—GLORIA ROMANORVM. (Valued by Mionnet at 120 fr. each).—GAVDIVM ROMANORVM. —ALAMANNIA. (130 fr. each).—VBIQVE VICTORES.—VICTOR OMNIVM GENT. (150 fr. each).

—PRINCIPI IVVENTVTIS. (Brought £14 10s. at the Thomas sale).

BRASS MEDALLIONS.—IVVENTVS.—MONETA CAESARVM.—SALVS ET SPES XRPVBLICAE. *(sic.* 150 fr.)

SMALL BRASS.—ALAMANNIA DEVICTA (see p. 32).—BEATA TRANQVILLITAS VOTIS XX. P. T. R. (see p. 125).

CRITONIA, gens plebeia, of which the following is the only coin:—

AED. PL. Head of Ceres, crowned with corn-ears.—*Rev.*—M. FAN. L. CRIT. Two togated men, seated. To their right are the letters P. A. and to their left a corn-ear. Silver, rare. —See a cut of this denarius in p. 12.

That Lucius Critonius was AED*ilis* PL*ebis* is (observes Eckhel, v. 199) sufficiently evidenced by the obverse legend and the reverse type of this denarius; for the latter represents him seated, with his colleague Marcus Fannius, each on a common *sedile;* whereas the curule ediles used a curule chair, from which circumstance of honour they derived their name of office—a distinction exhibited with the greatest clearness, on the denarii of Furius Crassipes, curule edile (see p. 12). The two ediles are here represented, in the act of distributing corn among the Roman people, as is indicated by the *spica* before them; and by the head of Ceres, on the obverse, symbolising the divinity who presided over the culture of wheat. The letters P. A. on the reverse, have been variously interpreted. Eckhel believes them, and with apparent probability, to signify the same thing that, in a greater number of letters—viz. ARG. PVB.—is inscribed on coins of the Sentia family. And he considers it to shew, that the cost of providing corn for the population of Rome was defrayed out of the public money *(ex argento publico).*— See ANNONA, p. 48, et seq.

According to Riccio (p. 77) referring to the authority of Cavedoni, it seems that to the father of that Critonius, stated by Appianus to have been edile in 710 (B. C. 44), this coin should be ascribed.

CROCODILE, the usual symbol of Egypt and the Nile, especially on coins; because that amphibious quadruped is indigenous to the Egyptian soil, and to the other regions which are watered by the Nile. The Romans placed this formidable animal amongst the number of those wild beasts, about which they were so curious in their triumphal pageants and theatric exhibitions.—Pitiscus.

On the medals of the Nemausensian colony (Nismes) struck under Augustus, a crocodile chained to a palm tree is the sign of Egypt subdued to the power of Rome. It is also conspicuous, with open mouth, on silver and gold medals of Augustus, accompanied by the historical legend of *Egypt captured.*—On gold and silver coins of Hadrian, and on first brass of M. Aurelius, we also see the *crocodile* and hippopotamus at the feet of the recumbent personification of the Nile.—Mionnet.—See AEGYPTO CAPTA (p. 13), NILVS, and NEM. COL.

The crocodile was worshipped in many cities

of ancient Egypt, amongst others in Thebes, at Arsinoe, called on that account Crocodilopolis, at Coptos, &c. whilst in other countries it was regarded as a noxious animal, and treated as such by the inhabitants.—Millin, *de Beaux Arts.*

CROTALUM.—This instrument, which is seen on coins, in the left hand, or by the side, of the goddess Cybèle, was a species of castanets made of thin brass plates, which were struck one against the other with different movements of the fingers, and from which was produced a sound like that which a stork makes with its beak. Players on this rude music were admitted to feasts, to regale the ears and eyes of the guests, with the tone of their *crotala,* and with their gestures, not always the most decent.—Pitiscus.—See CYBELE.

CRUMENA.—The purse was one of the insignia of Mercury, who (says Suidas) was the author of trade, and presided over commerce: for which reason in statues and on coins he is seen holding the money-bag. Mercury appears with the *crumena* in his hand, in the mintages of M. Aurelius, Trajanus Decius, Herennius, Hostilianus, Valerianus, father and son, Gallienus, Postumus, Claudius Gothicus, Numerianus, and Carinus.—See also a medal of Colonia Heliopolitana, inscribed to Philip senior.—Mercury has the purse in his right hand, on a coin of Sinope colonia, in Pellerin, *Mélange,* i. pl. xix. No. 3.—Also see the word MERCURIUS in this volume.

The *Crumena* is likewise the symbol of Abundance, and appears in the right hand of a female figure, who has the cornucopiæ in her left, with the epigraph VBERITAS or VBERTAS, on coins of Decius, Gallus, Gallienus, Postumus, Claudius II. Tacitus, &c. By which monetal type is indicated that Plenty holds a full purse, because all things are obtainable by money.—Rasche.

The *Crumena* is likewise an attribute of *Lætitia,* and of *Securitas,* as is seen on coins of S. Severus and of Trajanus Decius.

CRUX.—The Cross, an instrument of punishment amongst the Romans and several other nations of antiquity. Cicero calls it *crudelissimum, teterimumque.* In fact none but slaves, and malefactors of the lowest description, were subjected to it. The word *crux* was applied by the Romans to every species of punishment, whether it was a tree, or simply a stake, to which the criminal was bound or nailed. Hence it was designated under the names of *arbor infelix, infame lignum, cruciatus servilis.*—Generally speaking, however, it is usual to understand by the appellation Cross, a long beam traversed at its upper end by a much shorter piece of wood, whereon to fasten the arms of the sufferer, whilst the body is placed on the beam. Such was the "accursed tree" on which the Jews, in the reign of Tiberius (786, A. D. 33), "hanged" the living Body of OUR DIVINE AND EVER-BLESSED SAVIOUR—and the instrument of HIS death has become the revered sign of Christianity. From the establishment of the Religion of Jesus of Nazareth, that sacred symbol is found on all Christian monuments, especially from the period when Constantine the Great issued his commands for putting it on the *labarum* and other military ensigns. Thenceforward he also prohibited the punishment of death by crucifixion, throughout the whole extent of the Roman empire.—And from the time of that prince, it does not appear ever to have been inflicted again. But from having been an instrument of horror and of ignominy, the Cross was converted into a mark of reverence and honour, which figured not only on imperial coins and sculptures, but on the standards, and even on the arms of the soldiers.—Pitiscus.—Millin.

Crucis signum.—Cross on a globe; frequent on coins of the lower empire.—A globe was considered as the type of dominion over the world, from as early a date as the reign of Augustus. Afterwards a figure of Victory was placed upon the globe, inasmuch as to her was ascribed not only the conquest, but the retention, of such dominion. And when, in later times, Christian emperors were inclined to attribute their successes to the sign of the cross, they substituted it in the place of Victory.—A globe and cross appear, first, on coins of Jovianus, in the hand of Victory: subsequently, it is often seen in the emperor's hand.—See VICTORIA AVGVSTORVM, gold of Jovianus (Banduri), and VICTORIA ROMANORVM, brass medallion and second brass of Jovianus (Tanini).

On a second brass of Constantius II. with legend HOC. SIGNO. VICTOR ERIS, Victory is seen crowning the emperor, who stands habited in the *paludamentum,* and holds in his right hand the *labarum,* on which is the monogram of Christ.—See DECENTIVS for this monogram.

Some account of the "Holy Cross," as figured by order of Constantine the Great on the imperial standard, when about to engage with Maxentius, will be found under the legend SPES. PVBLICA. It was borne on that occasion amidst the ranks of his army, where the conflict appeared to be sharpest; and, according to Eusebius and his transcribers, this new ensign was invariably accompanied by decisive victory. Hence it began to be looked upon as alone sufficient to ensure success; and hence also the force of the legend *Hoc Signo Victor eris,* which no doubt was also inscribed on the standard. By some writers this reverse is referred to the cross, which Constantine boldly asserted that he beheld in the heavens, accompanied by the words EN. TOVTωI. NIKA. *in hoc (signo) vince* —See Eckhel. viii. 117—and 505.

Crux.—The cross by itself, or within a laurel crown, appears on coins of Valentinian I. Victor, Arcadius, Theodosius, Honorius, Justinianus, Leo I. and other emperors, professing Christianity.—See JULIUS NEPOS in this dictionary for a specimen of the type.

A *cross,* with one or two stars, is found on coins of Eudocia, wife of Arcadius, Eudocia, wife of Theodosius II. and others.

A *cross* in the hand of an emperor, or of Victory, or placed on a globe, appears on coins of Valentinian, Valens, Theodosius I. and II.

Flacilla, Maximus, *Marcianus* and *Mauricius*
(see the names), also Zeno, Leo, *Majorianus*
(see the name), and other princes, to almost
the end of the Byzantine age.—The same sign
appears either by itself, or with a globe, in the
hand of Victory, on coins of Valentinian I.
Theodosius, Arcadius, Honorius, and Zeno, down
to Phocas and Leontius II. It is also exhibited on
gold coins of Galla Placidia, and Ælia Flacilla, a
female figure with wings, holding the cross in her
right hand. Likewise, with or without a globe,
in the hands of a female, seated, as in the
instances of the Valentiniani, the Theodosii, &c.

The *cross* upon a graduated pedestal is seen on
medals of Justinian I. Justin II. and other
Byzantine Emperors.

A *cross*, surmounting a globe placed on a graduated pedestal, with the legend of DEVS ADIVTA
ROMANIS is stamped on the reverse of a silver
medallion of Heraclius I. who undertook an
expedition against Cosraes, King of the Persians,
"ut crucis signum ab eo Hierosolymis auctum
repeteret.–Spanheim, *Pr.* ii. 638.–Mion. ii. 434.

CUDENDAE *æreæ monetæ jus, vel permissio.*
—The privilege, or permission, of coining brass
money. That this was granted to, and exercised
by, the Roman *colonies,* may be gathered, in
most instances, from the coins themselves,
especially from the Hispanian and Corinthian, on
which the duplex D. or DD. explained as *Decreto
Decurionum,* is usually understood to indicate
the right of stamping coins. Nay, even the
special permission of Augustus appears on certain products of the colonial mint.—See COLO-
NIAE ROMANAE, p. 233—see also PERM. AVG.
and INDVLGENTIAE AVG. MONETA.

C. V. *Consul Quintum.*—C. V. P. P. Consul for the fifth time, Father of the Country, on
a silver coin of Commodus.

C. V. *Clipeus Votivus.*—A votive buckler.—
See p. 218.—See also *Dedication of Bucklers.*

CULLA or CULLU.—See COELA, p. 223.

CULTER *Victimarius* or *Sacrificus,* also
called SECESPITA *(à seco).* The appellation
given to the knife which the flamines, flaminian
virgins, and pontiffs, used at sacrifices. This
instrument had a long blade, with a round solid
handle, of either ivory or bronze, bound at the
hilt with gold or silver. It was with this that
the assistant cut the throat of the victim, and
the *sacerdos* afterwards examined its entrails.—
This sacrificial knife is seen, by itself, on a coin
of Julius Cæsar (engraved in Morell. *Impp.* p.
72).—It appears, with the *securis* or axe, and
the *simpulum,* on a denarius of the Cornelia
gens, with the word BRVTVS below it.—Engraved in Morel and Riccio.

CUM EXER. SUO. *Cum Exercito suo.*—
See coinage of Gallienus.

CUNICULUS—rabbit. A symbol of Hispania.—See coinage of Hadrian.

CUPID, god of love and pleasure.—It is
difficult to trace the true mythological origin of
him whom the Greeks called *Eros,* and the
Latins *Cupido.* The opinion most generally
followed is that he was the son of Mars and of
Venus. He is represented as a boy with wings;

jumping, dancing, toying, playing, climbing
trees, or plunging into water; sometimes seated
on animals; at others riding in a chariot. In
short he is made to perform all sorts of parts;
and he is most frequently depictured gambolling
with his beautiful mother.—Millin, *Dictionnaire de la Fable.*

On a denarius of the Egnatia gens, as in the
above cut, the naked bust of Cupid, with bow
and arrow on his shoulders, appears as the obverse type.—On another silver coin of the same
family, a winged Cupid is seen clinging to the
back of a bust of Venus.—On a denarius of the
Julia family, two Cupids are drawing the chariot of Venus.

On coins of the Cordia and Lucretia families,
he is seen sitting on a dolphin, which he guides
with reins; an elegant type.—See Lucretia gens.

On a coin of the Julia family, Cupid appears
protruding from the breast of Venus.

In the imperial series, he stands on the hand
of Venus, as in Faustina junior. And there is
a brass medallion of Lucilla, with VENVS for its
reverse legend, in which he is represented of
adolescent stature, standing opposite the figure
of the goddess.—This type is finely engraved in
Iconographie des Empereurs Romains, by M.
Ch. Lenormant.

Cupid also appears on coins of Julia Domna
(Venus Genetrix), Julia Mamæa, and Salonina.

On a colonial imperial of Cremna, struck
under Geta, he stands with bended bow ready to
discharge an arrow. On a small brass colonial
of Corduba, he stands, winged, holding a torch
and a cornucopiæ, a diademed head of Venus
being the obverse type.—See Akerman, *Coins of
Hispania,* pl. iii. No. 10, p. 29.

CUPIENNIA.—Of this family, whose very
order is uncertain, Eckhel laconically says "gens
parum cognita." Its coins consist of three different types, which have nothing in them to interest. The brass pieces are divisions of the *As.*
The silver has the galeated head of Rome, with
the mark X before, and a cornucopiæ behind,
it.—*Rev.*—L. CVP. The dioscuri on horseback.
Below ROMA.

CUR. *Curulis,* as AED. CUR. *Aedilis Curulis.*—See AEDILES, p. 12.

CURIATIA, a very ancient gens of the plebeian order. It was originally from Alba, and
admitted, with others of its inhabitants, into
citizenship at Rome, after the destruction of the
former city, under Tullus Hostilius (B. C. 673
to 641). The family is famous chiefly for the
association of its name with that of the three
brothers who fought with the three Horatii;
the well-known result of which particular combat was the annexation and subjection of the
Alban to the Roman people. Its coins have

four varieties. The brass pieces are parts of the *As.* The following is the only one in silver :—

TRIG. or TRIGE. Galeated head of Rome.— *Rev.*—C. CVR. F. A woman, habited in the tunic, guides a quadriga at full speed, holding in the left hand a long sceptre, and crowned by Victory standing behind her.

Eckhel observes, that to Caius Curiatius [who was tribune of the *plebs* in 616 (B C. 138), under the consuls Decius Brutus and Scipio Nasica], or to a son of his, this denarius probably belongs ; and that, in adopting the surname of *Trigeminus*, and causing it to be inscribed on this and other coins of the family, he doubtless wished to appear as having descended from the Curiatii of Alba. "Tergeminos (says Pliny, l. vii. § 2), nosci certum est Horatiorum, Curiatiorumque exemplo."—Who the female deity is, with the long sceptre or *hasta pura*, in the quadriga, or to what the type refers, does not appear to have met with any satisfactory explanation from numismatic antiquaries, either of the elder or of the modern school.—See Riccio's remarks, p. 78.

CURRUS.—See *Car*, p. 176.——Also see QUADRIGA, and TRIUMPH.

CURSUS PUBLICUS.—Public conveyance, or posting.—See VEHICULATIO.

CURTIA gens, known only by its name agreeing with that of the Roman knight who, for his country's sake, precipitated himself into a gulf in the Forum. That it was of the plebeian order is shewn by the tribuneship of a *Quintus* CURT*ius*, whose coins, as connected with that family, are still extant, in four varieties of type, none of which, however, make the least allusion to the self-devoting patriot of the Roman legend.—The brass pieces are Trientes and Semisses. The following is the only denarius ; but it is common :—

Q. CVRT. Galeated head of Rome.—*Rev.*—M. SILA. Jupiter Tonans in a quadriga at speed, holding the sceptre in his left hand. Above is the *lituus*, below ROMA.

This silver coin records the name of Quintus Curtius and of Marcus Junius Silanus, monetal triumvirs.—Riccio (p. 79), from its fabric, considers it to have been struck about the middle of the seventh century of Rome.

CURULE EDILES.—See AEDILES CURULES, p. 12. See also ANNONA, p. 48.

CUSTODES DII, or DEAE, with the type of Fortune.—See DIS CUSTODIBUS.

CUSTOS, an epithet of Jupiter.—IOVIS CVS-TOS is read on coins of Titus and Caracalla.— In like manner IVPITER (or IVPPITER) CVSTOS appears on coins of Nero and Hadrian.

CYBELE.—The myth of this goddess, whose worship was adopted from the oriental regions of ancient superstition into the pantheistic system of the Romans, is replete with contradiction, obscurity, and confusion.—Nevertheless, "It would," as M. Lenormant observes, "be to call in question the universal testimonies of antiquity, to refuse a recognition of the primitive affinities which have united the religion of *Cybèle* to that of *Rhea* (the wife of Saturn), in Crete and in Arcadia ; of *Ops* and of *Maïa*, in the Italian peninsula. But, without speaking of the differences which may have existed between Cybèle, Ops, and Rhea, the continued worship of the first-named of these goddesses, its more and more flourishing state in Asia Minor, must have contributed to throw back the worship of the two other remaining divinities, in Greece and in Italy, among religious recollections, rather than add it to the number of deities of whom the worship had been maintained with fervour. From this last fact it results that the monuments of Ops and of Rhea must be rare, whilst the number of those which relate to Cybèle must have increased in a large proportion, and that to an epoch comparatively recent."

Admitting the almost insurmountable difficulties which oppose themselves to affording anything like a satisfactory explanation of the mysterious attributes of Cybèle, through the medium of graphic illustrations, the distinguished French writer refers the reader to his work, *sur la Religion Phrygienne de Cybèle*, whilst in *La Nouvelle Galerie Mythologique* (p. 10 et seq.) he directs his sole attention to the exterior and to the *matériel* of the Phrygian worship.

With regard to the parents of Cybèle we are in reality left ignorant of them ; unless she may be considered as the daughter of Uranus (Heaven), and of Gæa (Earth). Amongst the surnames of this goddess there are some which refer to localities of Asia Minor, such as those of the *Idæan*, of *Dindymène*, of *goddess of Pessinus*, or of *Berecynthia*, &c. Other surnames of the Phrygian goddess are drawn from qualifications simply titular, which have often, however, the isolated and independent quality of a proper name. Such are the names of *Magna Mater*, of *Mater Deûm*, &c. For the more perspicuous but less becoming incidents of the great and god-bearing Mother's history, reference may be had to ATYS (p. 94), her youthful priest and lover. (See also MATRI DEVM SALV-TARI).—Numerous coins are extant which prove how extensively the worship of Cybèle prevailed among the cities of Asia Minor.

Cybèle is uniformly represented on Roman, as well as on Greek coins, as a dignified matron, robed and veiled, having her head ornamented with a crown of towers. She holds sometimes the *crotalum*, but more usually the *tympanum*, in one hand, and a sceptre, or sometimes a branch of pine, in the other. Her chariot is drawn by lions, or lions couch by her side, or she herself is seated on a lion (see p. 186).— More rarely she carries ears of corn as designating the fertility and abundance with which the earth brings forth all things.

The *turreted crown*, such as coins display on the head of Cybèle, forms the most common attribute of personified cities.

The *pine* was the tree of Cybèle, being that into which Atys was changed (Ovid, *Metam.* x. 104). The oak was also sacred to the mother of the gods.

The *tympanum*, as the attribute of Cybèle, is not designed solely to retrace the furious running of the *Galli* (priests of Cybèle), and the noise which they made with their drums. The *tympanum*, from its round form, and the manner in which the sound was obtained (by sliding the finger, and by pressing it on the exterior surface of the skin, which was stretched at the bottom of the tambourine), belonged to all the mysteries of antiquity. It is found to have been regarded as a sacred object at Eleusis—that mystical centre from which the excesses, similar to those practised by the Galli, had been carefully excluded. To the idea of the circle already expressed by the crenelated crown, and the modius, the *tympanum* joined that of the circular movement equally expressed by the *rhombus* of Eleusis. It is this circular movement, and this perpetual course round the same which, according to Plato (in the Dialogue of the Cratylus) constitute the essence of the gods. p. 12, *Nouvelle Galerie Mythologique.*

The *lion* consecrated to Cybèle has not yet received a satisfactory elucidation. The respective explanations which Lucretius, Fulgentius, Servius, &c. have given in reference to the lions of that goddess, savour, more or less, of the spirit of the allegorical school, which it is necessary to avoid confounding with the symbolic school.— At any rate these explanations belong to that epoch, when, under the name of *natural theology,* the aim was to open a way to the progress of the sciences, in a religion based on a complete ignorance of the laws of physics and of astronomy.—*Ibid,* p. 13.

Cybèle is, in the Roman mint, for the most part typified on coins of Empresses :—

On a brass medallion of the younger Faustina, Cybèle is represented seated on a throne with a foot-stool, holding with one hand the *tympanum* and in the other a branch of pine. On each side of the throne is a lion. *Crotala* are suspended near her from a pine tree. On the left is Atys,

standing with his face towards the goddess; his head covered with the Phrygian cap. He holds in his left hand the *pedum,* or crooked stick, and in his right the *syrinx,* or flute of reeds.

This fine medallion presents to us the united personifications of Cybèle and Atys, under the most frequently recurring form in the domain of figured antiquity.—"The resinous pine, consecrated to Atys, reminds us," says M. Lenormant, "of the myrrh tree, into which the mother of Adonis was transformed, and of the bark, from which the young god was drawn by the women of Arabia, when the moment of his birth was come (Ovid, *Metam.* x. 490, seq. 512, et seq.) * * * * The pine of Atys, and the tree of Adonis, are forms of the same idea appropriated to the productions of two different climates."—These approximations, M. Lenormant considers to be, in the Phrygian religion, representations of the doctrine of the λόγος, from which, conformably to the genius of the the reform of Zoroaster, every anthropomorphique appearance had been banished."—See *Nouvelle Galerie Mythol.* p. 14.

On a first brass of Faustina senior, the mother of the gods *(Cybèle),* with a crown of towers, seated on a throne, holds the *tympanum* on her knee—on each side the throne is a lion. —See MATRI DEVM SALVTARI.

On a large brass of Faustina junior, there is a similar type of Cybèle.—See MATRI MAGNAE.

On a brass medallion of the elder Faustina, with veiled portrait, the great Pessinuntian goddess, of whom King Attalus had made a present to the Romans, is represented as brought to Rome, in a ship drawn by the vestal Claudia Quinta, who gives a proof of her virtue by causing the vessel to advance by means of her girdle which she attaches to it. Many matrons, with torches in their hands, are near the vestal. —See CLAVDIA, p. 211.

On a brass medallion of Hadrian, Cybèle holding the tympanum, is seated on a car drawn by four lions. Cybèle also appears on medallions and first brass coins of Sabina, Antoninus Pius, Lucilla, Commodus, Julia Domna, &c.

On a brass medallion of Hadrian, Cybèle, holding the *tympanum* in her left hand, rested on her knees, is seated on a car drawn by four lions. On the exergue of this reverse is COn-*Sul* III.

The figure of Cybèle, in the quadriga, recalls in a striking manner the verse of Lucretius *(De Nat. Rer.* ii. 600–604):—

Hanc veteres Graiûm docti cecinere poetæ
Sublimem in curru bijugos agitare leones :
Aeris in spatio magnam pendere docentes
Tellurem ; neque posse in terra sistere terram.

[She it is, whom the ancient and skilled bards of Greece have sung, as guiding aloft two lions yoked to her car ; maintaining, that this vast world hangs poised in mid air ; and that earth cannot rest on earth.]

"There is," says M. Lenormant, in aptly citing this illustrative passage from the Latin poet, "no other difference offered by Lucretius, and the type of the medal in question, than the number of lions, which is two in Lucretius and four on the coin. The last verse of the poet is remarkable; inasmuch as it seems to unite a knowledge proceeding from a physical science (d'une physique) already sufficiently advanced, that of the rotatory movement of the earth on itself, and the application of this notion to the primitive belief already quoted, following which the gods, or the world (which is the same thing with the ancients), would have been drawn into a perpetual movement of concentric rotation.— This movement, by its constancy and regularity, explains the apparently contrary idea of a perfect stability. Accordingly, we have no hesitation in comparing this medallion of Hadrian with another of the same prince, on which we read, TELLVS STABILITA, and medals in gold and silver, also of Hadrian, with the same legend. The meaning of these last mentioned pieces has been very justly considered by Eckhel (*D. N.* vi. 509), as an allegory of order and of peace, re-established by Hadrian throughout the Roman world. In following the indication of Lucretius, the medallion above described would express the same idea in a more indirect manner. In each case, this concentration of the person of Cybèle in the personification of the Earth, appears to us conformable to the principles of natural theology, and consequently to agree with a learned period like that of Hadrian." * * * " As to the rest," adds the learned and ingenious author of *La Nouvelle Galerie* (p. 13), " it is possible that this reverse alludes only to the translation of the BONA DEA from one temple to another, which, according to Spartian, took place at Rome, during Hadrian's reign."

A contorniate, bearing on its obverse the head of Nero, typifies Cybèle and Atys together in a car drawn by four running lions. The goddess has a crown of towers, and holds a sceptre.— Atys wears the Phrygian cap, and bears the pastoral crook in his left hand.—[The contorniates belong to the lower empire. They were pieces distributed at the Circensian games.—See p. 271 et seq. of this dictionary.]

On a denarius of the Cestia gens (p. 197), Cybèle is seated in a biga of lions. For a type of that goddess, as an emblem of *Eternity*, or rather Faustina senior represented, after death, under Cybèle's image, see p. 23, left hand col.

D.

D. fourth letter in the alphabet of the Romans. —Amongst numerals it signifies five hundred (*quingenti*.)

D. as an initial letter indicates *Dacia*, D. F. *Dacia Felix*, occurs on the *vexillum*, or standard, on coins of the province of Dacia.

D. *Dacicus.*—G. D. PARTH. Germanicus, Dacicus, Parthicus, on coins of Trajan, whose surnames as Emperor, are derived from the names of conquered nations.

D. *Damno.* I condemn.—See Coelia gens, p. 222.

D. *Decreto.*—D. D. *Decreto Decurionum.*

D. *Decimus, Divus, Designatus.*

D. *Dictator.*—CAESAR D. PERPETVO, on a silver coin of Julius Cæsar.

DAC. *Dacicus.*

DAT. *Datum.*—See Congiarium, p. 244.

DACIA, a region of European Scythia, now comprehending the modern countries of Hungary, Transylvania, Wallachia, and Moldavia.—Under Augustus, the Dacians first came into warlike collision with the Romans, and were driven back beyond the Danube by Lentulus. A hundred years afterwards, Trajan, at the head of his cohorts, penetrated into the interior of Dacia, difficult as it was of access, being closed up and fortified by narrow gorges of mountains. That prince, in two successive wars, met with a vigorous resistance; but at length, having conquered Decebalus, whose death shortly followed, he converted the Dacian king's dominions into a Roman province.—Hadrian at first, it is said, was inclined to abandon these hard-earned conquests of his great predecessor; but continued to occupy the province with a powerful army.— Decius (Trajanus), about A. D. 249 struggled successfully, but with great difficulty, to defend the province against repeated incursions of the Goths. But at his death, it soon became an object of assault, and a scene of devastation, for fresh hordes of northern barbarians.—Dacia, at length lost to Rome under Gallienus, was recovered by Aurelianus; but he, despairing of being able to retain it permanently as a possession of the empire, transported the inhabitants into Mæsia, which (according to Vopiscus) then took the name of *Dacia Cis-Istrensis*, or Dacia on this side the Danube. Although eventually compelled to give way before the strategic skill and superior discipline of the imperial legionaries, the Dacian people, both before and after their subjection to the Romans, shewed themselves to be

Prodiga gens animæ, studiisque asperrima belli.

DACIA. S. C.—On a first brass of Hadrian, bearing on the exergue this simple legend, with the mark of senatorial authority in the field of the reverse, the province is personified under the figure of a young man, bareheaded, habited in a short dress, a military cloak thrown across his shoulders, and half-boots with ornamented tops. This figure is seated on a rock, with a legionary eagle in the right hand, and a palm branch in the left: his right foot rests on an oval-formed stone.

The above is engraved from a well-preserved specimen in the British Museum. It is thus

also that the coin is delineated in Queen Christina's and the Farnese cabinets; and Captain
Smyth notes a similar type of Hadrian in his
own collection. It is however to be observed,
that Eckhel describes the first and second brass
Dacia of Hadrian's mint, as personified by a
woman, who holds in her left hand a curved
sword *(gladium incurvum).* But all numismatic
descriptions agree as to the military ensigns being put into the right hand of the conquered
province, seated on a rock—the last feature of
typification denoting the peculiar situation and
national habitudes of the Dacians, allusive to
which L. Florianus (lib. 4), says, the Dacians
cleave to their mountains *(Daci montibus inhæ-
rent).*—It appears from Spartian, that, before he
ascended the throne, Hadrian was twice in
Dacia, and took part as an officer in Trajan's
two expeditions against that country. At the
period of the second war he commanded the 1st
legion, surnamed *Minervia.*

We learn distinctly from Eutropius (lib. 8),
that as Hadrian, on at best a doubtful policy,
had given up possession of Syria, Mesopotamia,
Armenia, and other conquests of Trajan in the
East, so if left to himself, he would have renounced even Dacia; but that he was otherwise
persuaded by his friends, who remonstrated with
him against such a withdrawal of the legions,
ne multi cives Romani barbaris traderentur.—
For, immediately after the annexation of Dacia
to the empire by Trajan, many Roman colonies
were established there, which would all have
been immediately exposed to, and in subsequent
reigns were actually ravaged by, the inroads of
fierce enemies, without the means of defending
themselves. He was therefore induced to make
no change in this quarter, except the dis-
creditable one of causing Trajan's celebrated
bridge over the Danube to be thrown down;
lest (according to Dion, 68, s. 16), the barbarians should overpower the guard of the bridge,
and enter Mæsia. Historians make no mention
of any journey by Hadrian in that country when
emperor.—But from his geographical coins it is
to be inferred that he visited the Dacian province
also. One of these, inscribed solely with the name
DACIA, presents its type of personification, as
given in the above and other examples. Others,
purely military, repeat the usual type of an
emperor addressing his soldiers, with a corresponding legend.—See EXERCITVS DACICVS.

The Abbé Greppo, in his work, *" sur les Voyages d' Hadrien,"* observes, that there are several inscriptions of Dacia which connect themselves with the history of Hadrian. One deserves to be cited in this place. Although it be
of a date posterior to the probable period of that
prince's advent in the province, yet the public
works which it mentions may be regarded as a
result of that journey. It relates to water conveyed (AQVA INDVCTA) into the ancient capital
of Decebalus, which, having become a Roman
colony, is recorded on ancient marbles—COLO-
Nia VLPia TRAIANA AVGusta DACICA
SARMIZ.—The inscription is given in Gruter,
Corpus Inscrip. Antiq. vol. 1, clxxvii. 3 M.

DACIA. S. C.—A woman, clothed in the
stola, stands, holding in her right hand a staff

surmounted by an ass's head. This legend, and
very singular type, present themselves on gold
and silver, as well as on first and second brass, of
Trajanus Decius.

On coins of Trajan (with legend of *Provincia
Dacia Augusti),* the genius of the Dacian province, is seated on a rock, holding a military
standard; and on coins struck in the province
itself, under Philip senior (with *Provincia Dacia*
for their reverse legend) the same personification of the province carries the bent sword of
her country. On the present second brass of
Trajanus Decius, both the above mentioned
attributes are omitted; and in their place is
clearly displayed the veritable head of an ass.

" What may be the meaning of this symbol,
I shall not (says Eckhel) in the absence of any
ancient testimony, attempt to pronounce. For
if, as some suppose, an allegory is concealed
under it, the risk of error is in the ratio of the
vagueness of all allegory, and I have an aversion
to the troubled sea of conjecture. Instead of
the ass's head, Engelius sees on these coins the
head of the Dacian dragon, fixed on a pole, the
body and tail being left out, either by the carelessness of the moneyer, or to shorten his
labour, or for want of space in the coin. *(En-
gel. Comment. de Exped. Traj.* p. 201). We
know, indeed, from the relievos on Trajan's
column, that dragons supported on spears,
served the Dacians as military standards. I
would readily give in my adhesion to this view
of the subject, as we should then have a tangible
point to start from, without being reduced to
the uncertainties of allegory. But, on the most
perfect of these coins, so long are the ears of
the animal, as to leave no doubt on the mind
that they represent those of an ass."

Among the mintages of Philip senior there is
a coin inscribed TRANQVILLITAS AVGG. on which
is a woman standing, with a dragon in her right
hand, by which type is probably intended one
of the dragons, which, among the Romans, quite
as much as among the barbarian nations, used to
be carried, suspended from a pole, in the front
ranks of an army.—" If this head (observes
Eckhel), be compared with that which appears
on the coin before us, the difference between the
two instantly strikes the eye. Whoever is inclined to refer this type to the religion of the
Dacians, may suppose that it alludes to the ass,
which, among the Scythians, is one of Apollo's
victims, according to Clemens Alexandrinus

(Protrepticos, p. 25, Edit. Oxon.)—" Phœbus is worshipped with the Hyperborean sacrifice of asses."

DAC*ia* CAP*ta* (conquest of Dacia).—On a silver coin of Trajan, having for the legend of

its reverse DAC. CAP. COS. .V. P.P. S.P.Q.R. OPTIMO PRINC. appears a captive, with his hands tied behind him, seated on three bucklers; behind him are two swords, bent in the Dacian fashion, and before him are two javelins.

Obv.—IMP. TRAIANO AVG. GER. DAC. P.M. TR.P. Laureated head of Trajan.

Trajan having finished the construction of that stupendous work, his bridge over the Danube, entered Dacia a second time (A. D. 105), and again attacked Decebalus its king, who had been the terror of the Romans under Domitian. That emperor declared war against the Dacians, but the result proving seriously unfavourable to the Roman arms, he soon gave up the enterprise, and settled affairs by submitting to pay an annual tribute. Trajan, incapable of any longer enduring such a national humiliation, marched his army into the territories of Decebalus, and compelled him to sue for peace, which, however, was granted only on very hard conditions. But the king not having fulfilled his promise, it became necessary for Trajan to recommence hostilities. Having sustained a total defeat, and being deprived of every thing, Decebalus slew himself. The emperor found the treasures of the unfortunate monarch either in the river Sargetia, or buried in caves. This took place in the year of Rome 859 (A. D. 106). It was then that Dacia became a Roman province; and Trajan, returning to Rome, triumphed for thus ending the Dacian wars. Other coins of this prince relate to this important event.

Eckhel remarks that " the coins struck after Trajan's first war with the Dacians, do not bear the inscriptive record of DAC(IA) CAP(TA) ; because Decebalus was still permitted to retain possession of his kingdom, though on very disadvantageous and degrading terms: But now we read *capta*, as, according to Dion and others, it was a conquest in reality (capta revera)."

The above reverse is copied from pl. iv. fig. 12, of Kolb's *Traité de Numismatique Ancienne*, the illustrative engravings of which elementary work are remarkable for their artistic fidelity to the originals; and have evidently been selected from genuine specimens. It is also engraved in M. Lenormant's *Iconographie des Empereurs*. This explanation seems the more requisite, because neither Mionnet, nor Akerman, includes that important historical legend DAC. CAP. in their respective Catalogues.

DACIA FELIX. S. C.—A woman standing, with a military ensign in her right hand. On gold, silver, and first and second brass of Trajanus Decius.

The frequency with which Dacia is alluded to, on the coins of Decius, is attributable to the activity he displayed in protecting it from the incursions of the barbarians, by whom that tract of country was, during his reign, most grievously harrassed. And hence, in an inscription preserved by Muratori (page 1101, 3), he is styled RESTITVTOR DACIARVM.—The legend DACIA FELIX explains the letters D. F. found on so many of the coins of Dacia, inscribed on a standard.

DACIA PROVINCIA.—See PROVINCIA DACIA.

DACIA PROVINCIA AVGVST.—See PROVINCIA DACIA AVGVST.

DACICVS.—It was not without having fairly earned it, as a victorious commander, that Trajan was honoured with this surname, after his first contest with the Dacians. At almost the beginning of his reign, when that warlike people again invaded the Roman provinces, he immediately took the field against them with a powerful force, and compelled Decebalus, who was feared at the time like another Hannibal, to supplicate peace, by his ambassadors, at the hands of the Roman Senate. Thereupon the title of Dacicus was conferred upon Trajan, together with the most signal honours of the triumph. Hence we find him styled on his coins IMP. NERVA TRAIANVS AVG. GER. DACICVS, &c. This distinguished appellation was not given to him, however, till about the autumn of the year U. C. 856 (A. D. 103), and the end of the sixth year of his tribunitian power, to which date it is sufficiently agreed upon, amongst historical antiquaries, that this Dacian victory is to be referred; and the fact is confirmed by the non-appearance of the word *Dacicus* on the coins of this emperor until the year above-mentioned. It is in the following year, namely A. D. 104, that the title of *Optimus Princeps* begins to appear on the mintages of Trajan. See DAC. CAP.

Dacicus gladius.—The curved sword of the Dacians, on Roman coins, is held in the right hand of the personified province. It was called ἄρπη, falx (a falchion, or short crooked sword), such as the Thracians first used.—[It may not be irrelevant to remark, that the descendants of those who inhabited a part of ancient Dacia—namely, *Hungary that now is*,—have long been famous for military prowess, and for skill in the use of their favourite weapon, the *sabre*.]

In his *Collectanea Antiqua*, vol. ii. Mr. Roach Smith fully describes, and by etchings illustrates, several specimens of Saxon and Frankish short, knife-shaped swords, amongst which is a very remarkable example of one, found in the bed of the Thames, and now in his own possession. On this subject, our observant and discriminating Archæologist makes the following observations :—

" In ancient representations of the arms of the Germans, swords slightly curved are almost always introduced. It would be easy to cite numerous instances; but the sculptures on Trajan's column, of scenes in the Dacian wars, and the coins of that emperor, afford types which, allowing for a certain conventionality in the artistic treatment, are not very unlike some of these knife-swords.—The Dacians on the column of Trajan are almost always armed with this single-edged weapon, which curves slightly, sometimes inwards, sometimes outwards, but in one or two instances the weapon is straight like those under consideration. And until we discover ancient swords which are curved, we must, as in the case of the double axe, and barbed javelin, consider the representations referred to, as having been influenced by the fancy of the artist." p. 46–47.

DAC. PARTHICO P. M. T. R. P. COS. P. P.—Two figures, clothed in the toga, supporting a globe. First brass of Hadrian.

The above appears on the reverse of one of those coins, which, alike interesting from the beauty of their types, and from their connection with historical facts, exhibit all the various titles of honour bestowed, together with the imperial purple, by the Emperor Trajan on the fortunate Hadrian, his adopted successor.—The obverse of this coin bears the laureated head of Hadrian, and the following legend : IMPeratori CAESari DIVI TRAIANI AVGusti Filio TRAIANO HADRIANO OPTimo AVG. GER. to which, in reading, is to be joined the legend of the reverse, namely, DACico PARTHICO Pontifici Maximo TRibunitiâ Potestate COnSuli Patri Patriæ. S. C. And the whole expresses itself as follows :—To the Emperor, Cæsar, son of the Divine Trajanus Augustus, Trajanus Hadrianus the most excellent Augustus—the German—the Dacian, the Parthian, Sovereign Pontiff, exercising the Tribunitian Power, Consul, Father of the Country. By decree of the Senate.

In his annotations on this coin (p. 56 Cabinet de Christine) Havercamp, after giving an accurate copy of its inscription on both sides, states the type of the reverse to represent " the adoption of Ælius Cæsar made by Hadrian, in like manner as he had himself been adopted by Trajan." Having given this strange interpretation of what he admits to be a very curious coin, Havercamp professes to recollect no author who had spoken of it, unless it was Angeloni ; to the 125th page of whose work he expressly refers—and where indeed a delineation of the coin is to be found. But, so far from bearing out the dictum of Havercamp, Angeloni adduces it as an additional testimony of the clearest kind to the truth of history, as to the fact of Trajan's adoption of Hadrian :—" Every author (says he) concurs in stating that Hadrian was cousin to Trajan, who, through the influence of the

Empress Plotina, adopted him as his imperial successor. This is rendered still more clear by the coin of Hadrian himself."—The Italian antiquary then describes the portrait of Hadrian on the coin in question as that of a young man (which it is), and quotes the legend of the obverse, as given in the preceding column.—Angeloni concludes as follows :—" This coin represents, in my opinion, the above-mentioned adoption, and also Trajan's admission of Hadrian to share with him the government of the empire, together with a concession, to his adopted son, of the titles usually borne by the Emperors, and especially those which the Senate and People conferred on himself."—Eckhel evidently takes the same view ; for in noticing a specimen, from the Vienna collection (vi. 475), he describes the type as " Trajanus et Hadrianus [not Ælius] togati stantes, globum una tenent." But at the same time observes, that this coin, and some others of the same date (A. D. 117), in assigning to Hadrian the appellation of Pater Patriæ is opposed to the oracle of historians (oraculo historicorum).—See what the Author of Doctrina says on this point, in vii. p. 515 et seq. Also consult his animadversions on the names which Hadrian assumed by right of his adoption. (vii. 518.)

DAMASCUS, colonia, now Damisk, or Damasco, as Europeans call it ; Sciam or Chiam, as it is named by the Turks.—The most ancient city of Coele-Syria (the Hollow Syria), it is situated in a beautiful and fertile valley, at the foot of Mount Hermon, from which flow two rivers, the Abana and the Pharpar. Of these mountain streams mention is made in Holy Writ (Kings, bk. 2, ch. 5, v. 12)—" Are not Abana and Pharpar, rivers of Damascus, better than all the waters of Israel ?" The former passes through the middle of the city ; the other rolls its waters amidst gardens and orchards beyond the walls ; both afterwards unite, and form one river named the Chrysorrhoas, or golden river (now the Barrada). In more remote antiquity, the metropolis of Phœnicia, and in later ages, comprehended in the patriarchate of Antioch, Damascus is still, according to description, the most agreeable, city in the East, as it was once the most celebrated, city in the East, on account of the grandeur of its public edifices, and the elegance of its private habitations. Conflicting opinions are entertained respecting the origin of the word Damascus ; amongst which Vaillant (in Coloniis, i. 232) suggests, on the strength of a frequent type on its coins, the derivation to be " à Dama nutrice et Asco puero" (from the boy Ascus nourished by a Doe). This city had at an early period from the foundation its own kings. Josephus (Antiq. 7, cap. 6), speaks of Adadus, in the time of David, as king of Damascus, and whose posterity retained that royal title and authority to the tenth generation.— Overthrown by the Assyrians, it became subject to the Seleucidæ, whose æra dates from the year of Rome 442, 312 years before Christ.— The Arabians subsequently gained possession of it ; and at length Pompey annexed it to the Roman republic. It was not made a colony until the reign of the emperor Philippus senior. And, although on coins its title of *colonia* takes precedence of its dignity of metropolis, viz. COL. DAMAS METRO. &c. yet it had enjoyed the latter prerogative long before it obtained its colonial character. On many coins, with Greek legends, from Hadrian to Alexander Severus, is read *Metropoleos*, given to it as an honorary distinction, on account of the amplitude and importance of the place.

Besides Greek autonomes, and Greek imperials in brass, there are bilingual (viz. Greek and *Latin)* brass coins of this colony, dedicated consecutively to Philip senior, and to Otacilia, Philip junior, Herennius Etruscus, Trajanus Decius, Trebonianus Gallus, Volusianus, Aemilianus, Valerianus senior, Gallienus, and Salonina. These coins are inscribed COL. DAMAS. METRO. or DAMASCO COLONIA, or COL. DAMA. METR. or MET.

Bacchus and Silenus were the two tutelary deities of Damascus. Temples were erected to their worship in that city; and they are typified on coins of Trebonianus Gallus and Philip sen.

The following are amongst the principal types which appear on the reverses of coins struck in this city, with bilingual legends:—

1. *Bacchus.*—On second brass of Trebonianus Gallus.—See type described in p. 120.

2. *Cypress tree.*—On a rare second brass, struck in honour of Volusianus, with the legend of *Colonia Damascus Metropolis*, this tree stands between a horse and a bull.—[The meaning of this singular type is far from having been satisfactorily explained. Vaillant, who seems to reject the idea of any local allusion in the case, puts it interrogatively whether this combined group of the tree and the two quadrupeds may not have a mystic signification?—For an ingenious conjecture see that author, *in Coloniis,* ii. 222].

On second and third brass of Philip senior, Silenus stands before a cypress, which tree was held in veneration by the Phœnicians, being, according to Plutarch, dedicated to the Sun.—Vaillant, ii. p. 161.

3. *Doe* (DAMA) *giving suck to a little boy.*— On first and second brass coins of this colony, minted under Philip senior, Otacilia his wife, and Trebonianus Gallus.

This type, accompanied by the legend of reverse COL. DAMAS. METR. occurs on coins of this colony, during the above reigns; and has given rise among the learned to a variety of conjectures. It is generally regarded as bearing reference to the name of the city, and to the

origin of its reputed founder.—Vaillant quotes some of the interpretations put upon it; but does not argue in favour of any of them. He simply remarks, that these, and other coins of similar type, seem intended to preserve in remembrance the tradition of Ascus, who having been exposed in infancy, was suckled by a *Dama,* or female deer, and afterwards, rising to eminence, laid the foundations of Damascus.

But here let this eminent numismatist of the seventeenth century, speak his own sentiments on this point, in his own way, if not indeed in his native tongue:—

"Should we venture (says Vaillant, *in Col.* ii. p. 271), to regard this type of a boy sucking a doe, as referring to the origin of the city of Damascus; and should we further assert, that the name itself of that city is derived from the words *dama* (the doe) and *Ascus* (the boy), the whole host of the learned would be ready to cry out against us: let us, notwithstanding, propound our own conjectures. What is the import of the boy suckled by a doe, who so frequently appears on the coins of Damascus?— Does not that type illustrate the history of some boy nourished by a doe, just as that of the wolf suckling Romulus and Remus, depicts the first mode in which those infants were nourished; and was not another boy, similarly brought up by a deer (ἀπό τινος ἐλάφου) named, accordingly, *Telephus?* The animal *dama,* however, derives its name from δαμάζω (*to tame*), by the figure antiphrasis. Stephens, in his *Thesaurus,* v. Δαμασκός, states, that Damascus was so called from *Ascus,* a giant. Now, this giant might have been brought up by a deer; and it is a reasonable conjecture, that the name of the city, Δαμασκός, was compounded of the two words Δάμα and 'Ασκός;—but if this etymology does not meet with approbation, we take refuge in another founder of the city, by name *Damascus,* after whom Damascus, the noblest city in Syria, was called, as Justin thus relates, xxxvi. 2—'The name was given to the city by its king *Damascus,* in whose honour the Syrians reverenced the sepulchre of his wife Arathis as a temple, and paid her the highest adoration as a deity.'—Perhaps this king had been exposed, and tended by a deer, and so by the act of sucking that animal, he points to the memory of the founder, and the origin of the city."

In a learned Dissertation on certain coins of Damascus, inserted in the *Revue Numismatique* (vol. vii. year 1844, p. 1. et seq.) M. J. De Witte, who has illustrated his subject with appropriate engravings, enters at great length into the traditions, often as contradictory as they are various, which have been furnished by mythographers, but which (he observes), result in shewing only that the name of the city owes its origin to one of those *jeux de mots* in which the ancients, especially the Greeks, took delight.

"Mythological legends (says in substance this living French numismatist), relate that a personage of the family of the earth-born Giants, bearing the name of *Ascus* (who, from a numismatic type, is supposed to have been deserted in his infancy, and suckled by a doe), pursued in his manhood a heroic and successful career; until, having cut down the vineyards which Dionysus (Bacchus) had planted in Syria, that god, in his wrath, flayed the offender; and of his skin was made a leathern bottle or sack, which served to contain wine."

Vaillant, it will have been seen, in explaining the type of the above reverse, recognises in the infant suckled by an animal resembling a female deer (*Dama*) the *young Ascus*; and suggests that the word *Dama* being prefixed to that of *Ascus*, which assimilates with ασκος, signifying in Greek a wine skin, Δαμα Ασκος, abbreviated to *Damascus*, became the name of the city.

Eckhel (*D. N. V.* iii. p. 332), refuses to admit the explanation given, in this instance, by Vaillant, first of all, because the word Δαμα, as used to designate a doe, is not Greek; and secondly, because the doe appears by itself on pieces struck whilst Damascus enjoyed a government and laws of its own, long before the epoch when that city was declared a Roman colony.— M. De Witte combats both these objections, first by pointing to the bilingual feature of the legends on the colonial imperial coins of Damascus, and next by a series of arguments founded on philological, historical, and mythological data, to which, as well as to the entire dissertation, the numismatic student will be advantaged by referring; for they throw light on other types of the Damascene colonial mintages, with both Greek and Latin inscriptions. The following are his concluding remarks on this disputed point :—

"Vaillant, confining himself to the study of an isolated numismatic type, has not pushed his investigations far enough. But his explanation perfectly elucidates the *play upon words* concealed in the type of the infant *Ascus* suckled by the doe (*dama*). The animal, however, which nourishes Ascus does not figure in the traditionary legends of Damascus, at least in those with which we are acquainted. On what ground has a doe been given as a nurse for Ascus? Would this animal have been chosen for any other reason than to complete the *jeu de mots?* These are questions which we should wish to clear up.

"The legends we have drawn from ancient sources teach us that Ascus was a *giant*, γίγας. Now, all the giants appear to us in mythology as sons of the Earth. *Dama* then would here represent the *Earth nourishing* the children, Γῆ κουροτρόφος (Pausanias, i. 22–3). In effect, we discover again in the word δάμα the primitive *Ma*, whence comes *Meter*, *Mater*; as a consequence of this comparison, we arrive at Δαματηρ, Ceres, the nutritive Earth, the mother of the giant Ascus. Demeter is besides the same as *Damia*, honoured with Auxésia, at Egina, at Epidaurus, at Trezen. The legend thus completes itself, and in the pun (*jeu de mots*), we find again the mythological beings put on the stage by the mythographers." pp. 22–23.

M. De Witte, moreover, regards the commentary of Vaillant on another coin of Damascus, as serving to sustain what he has himself above advanced. The reverse of the piece, which belongs to the reign of Philip the younger, is described (*in Col.* ii. p. 271) as follows :—

Rev.—COL. DAMA. METROP. A naked infant standing, crowns a woman whose head is turreted.

Vaillant recognises in this type *Ascus* offering a crown to the city which he had founded. —But this jumbling together of boyhood and manhood, at one time and in one action, offers a much more difficult subject for interpretation than the foregoing. And we must leave both the text of the elder, and the coinciding animadversions of the modern, commentator, to the criticism of the *Revue Numismatique* (T. vii. p. 22), and to the judgment of its readers.

4. *Genius of the City and River Gods.*— There is a first brass, inscribed to Herennius, which Pellerin assigns to this colony, and which is remarkable not only for its size and for the manner in which the first characters of its reverse legend are formed, but also for the type which it presents, viz. :—

Rev.—ΛΛΑSCO. COLONIA.—The genius of the city, under the figure of a woman, having towers on her head, and holding corn-ears in her right hand, is seated on rocks, between two rivers, which are represented, at her feet, by two men who seem to throw themselves partly out of the water, as if in the act of swimming. Besides these two aquatic deities, there is also, on each side of the seated female figure, a military ensign, on one of which is the letter S. and on the other the letter T. (See *Recueil des Médailles D'Asie*, tom. ii. title page of second part, p. vii.)

[Such is the description which Pellerin gives of this singular reverse, and with which the engraving he has furnished of it, from a specimen in his own collection, perfectly corresponds. He pronounces the coin in question to belong to *Damas*, in Syria, and shews that the legend, of which the first four letters are in Greek monogram, ought to be read ΔΑΜΑSCO COLONIA. The type (says he) marks the situation of Damascus at the foot of Mount Hermon, whence the two rivers *Abana* and *Pharpar* flowing, passed round the city, and are on this coin symbolised under the figures of the two men emerging from the water. —The same practised numismatist of the elder school adds, that this particular coin differs from every other which had, up to his time, been published, inasmuch as thereon Damascus takes the title of *colony* only, instead, as in all other instances, of assuming the additional title of *metropolis*. With respect to the S. and the T. on the ensigns, Pellerin observes that "those letters hold there the place of cyphers or numerals, which are commonly inscribed on such representations of military standards, in order to designate the legions, from which the veteran soldiers were sent into the different Roman colonies. Those legions, in their origin were distinguished solely by the name respectively of *first, second, third,* and so on with the rest. As it happened, however, in the sequel, that there were many which were called first, second, third, &c. so surnames, for their further designation, and distinction one from another, were given them, either of deities, or of emperors, or of provinces, or other surnames, which circumstances and events caused the Romans to adopt. Conformably to this idea, he considers it is the more probable interpretation, that the letter S. denotes the IIIIth Legion, surnamed *Scythica*, and the letter T. points to the IInd Legion, surnamed *Trajana;* since ancient authors, in speaking of legions,· sometimes call them by their surnames."]

5. *Ram* (Aries) on a second brass, inscribed to Philip senior.—[This type which refers to the Zodiacal sign of that name, frequently occurs on Syrian, Phœnician, and Coele-Syrian coins. The ancients differed, not only as to the number and arrangement of the months composing the solar year, but also as to its beginning. For with some nations it commenced under the vernal equinox, when the Sun enters Aries. Others made the year begin under the autumnal equinox, because they believed that the world was at that season created, with its fruits ripe.—Vaillant, ii. p. 162.—See M. De Witte's observations in *Revue Numismatique*, T. vii. 11, on this type of the *Ram*].

6. *River God*, in a recumbent posture, naked to the waist, holding a small image on his right hand, a cornucopiæ in his left, and his left elbow resting on an urn, out of which issues water—on a first brass dedicated to Philip sen.

[The figure denotes the site of Damascus, washed by two streams, whose confluence as has already been noticed forms the Chrysorrhoas (Barrada or Bardinés), which the river deity seems to represent.—Vaill. ii. p. 162.—" The little figure doubtless is an image of the young Ascus."—De Witte; see *Dissert.* above quoted].

7. *Silenus*—see Cypress, No. 3.

8. *Temple.*—On a first brass, struck in Damascus to the honour of Otacilia, wife of the emperor who made that city a Roman colony.—Besides the usual *Latin* legend COL. DAMAS. METRO. the Greek word ΠΗΓΑΙ, *Fountains*, appears at the bottom of the reverse. The type is a temple of four columns, in which stands the image of Silenus. Below the base of the temple is an arch, beneath which reclines a river deity, without beard, holding in his right hand a branch, his left arm resting on an urn; in his left hand is a horn of plenty. On one side a star, on the other the moon; on the right side a small altar.

[The temple is that of Silenus, who was an object of especial worship with the inhabitants of Damascus, in common with all the people of Phœnicia and Syria. The personified river under the arch refers to Damascus. It represents the plain where the stream of the Abana was distributed in fountains through the whole city (see River-god above described). The river bears a cornucopiæ in indication of the abundance that springs from the irrigation of its waters. The altar belongs to Silenus's temple.—The star and the crescent designate Sol and Luna, to whom, as to presiding deities, the

Syrian superstition referred all things.—See engraving in Vaillant, ii. p. 100].

9. *Vexillum.*—A second brass, dedicated by Damascus to Trebonianus Gallus, exhibits on its reverse the above-named military standard, on which is LEG. III. GAL. *Legio Tertia Gallica:* on each side is an eagle.

[Evidence is here adduced that the veterans of the Third Gallic Legion, which at the time of Philip's assumption of the imperial power was in winter quarters in Phœnicia, were transplanted as colonists to Damascus, by that emperor—a fact confirmed by the two eagles at the foot of the *vexillum*].

10. *Wolf and Twins.*—On first and second brass of Otacilia, this well known type appears, with the addition of the *labarum*, on which is inscribed LEG. VI. F.—See Genius of the City, No. 4.

[The coins of Damascus, dedicated to Philip senior, shew, it was not until his murderous usurpation of the empire, that this celebrated city became a Roman colony. And this medal, struck with others, in honour of his wife, points out from which legion, after the assassination of Gordian III. the veterans were sent by Philip to Damascus—namely, *Legio Sexta Ferrata.*—Vaillant, ii. p. 179].

11. *Woman, with turreted head,* sitting on a mount; before her stands Silenus, bearing the goat-skin on his shoulder. At the top of the coin is Pegasus. Below the seated female are five other women, with turreted heads, who stand sacrificing at an altar. This curious type appears on a rare brass coin, dedicated by the citizens of Damascus to Otacilia, in compliment to her husband Philip.

[The female figure seated represents the city; she is turreted as being a metropolis; she sits on a ·mountain, as indicating the situation of Damascus, whose territory embraced the spurs of Mount Hermon; she bears a cornucopiæ to denote the plenty which reigned within her borders. Above her is the flying horse Pegasus, the city's sign or token; before her stands Silenus, whom the Damascenes worshipped, as has already been noticed. The five women at the bottom of the medal, in the act of performing sacrifice, personify the principal cities of Cœle-Syria, of which Damascus was the chief.—Vaillant, ii. p. 178–9].

DANUVIUS and DANUBIUS, *Donau* or *Danube;* the grandest river in Europe. A part of it was called *Ister,* but the differences of ancient writers render it uncertain through which regions of its course the name of Danubius, and which that of Ister, was appropriated to it.—Xiphilinus affirms that Trajan's bridge was built over the Ister. The Danube was worshipped as a divinity by the Getæ, the Dacians, Thracians, &c.

The Danube rises at Donauschingen, in the mountains of the Black Forest, territory of Baden, in Suabia (" Mons Abnoba', of Tacitus) ; and after receiving more than 100 fine tributaries in its course of 2,100 miles, discharges its waters into the Black Sea (Pontus Euxinus), in Bessarabia.

In Mæsia Superior (now Servia), east of Viminiacum (near whose site is the small town of Alt Golnubac), on the river's bank was Taliatis, or Taliata. Near this place was a ridge of rocks, remarkable as thought to be the spot where the Danube changes its name, the eastern part of it being called Ister by the ancients, as the western was termed Danubius. A little east of this place was Pons Trajani (now called Trajan's Rock), the bridge built by the Emperor Trajan to pass into *his* province of Dacia.—See Bp. ·Butler, *Geog.* pp. 106—189—195, whose account corroborates the assertion of Xiphilinus above cited, that Trajan's bridge was built over that part of the river anciently called the Ister.

DANUVIUS CO*n*S*uli* P*atriæ* OPTIMO PRINC*ipi* (Consul for the fifth time, Father of

the Country, ExcellentPrince). The Danube, under the form of a bearded man, crowned with reeds, in a recumbent posture. The right hand of the personified river is extended to a galley, the left rests upon his urn: a drapery is placed under the arms of the god, a portion of which, filled by the wind, floats semi-circularly above his head.

This reverse, which appears on gold as well as silver of Trajan, was struck in the 858th year of Rome (A. D. 105), after the passage of the Danube by the legionary troops. The famous river whose name occupies the exergue, was indeed well worthy a place on coins, both on account of its close proximity to the scene of conflict in the Dacian wars, and also because it had to be crossed by the imperial forces, in order to reach the enemy's territory. But the highest glory was gained by Trajan on the river itself, when he adorned it with a stone bridge—a work, which, if credit may be given to Dion's description (lxviii. § 13), far surpassed all others accomplished by that prince, and which furnished proof that scarcely any enterprise is too vast for the genius, hardihood, and perseverance of man. [It was 3325 English feet in length].—Learned writers have imagined that they recognised the architectural features on the column of Trajan, still seen at Rome (and indeed it is so given in Table E, segment lxxiv. No. 260, of a series of engravings placed at the end of *Morell. Thesaurus Impp. Rom. Numismata*).

Among other passages in Dion's detailed account of this gigantic structure, is the following :—"Trajan caused that stone bridge to be built on the Danube, of which I cannot sufficiently express my admiration. For although there are many other magnificent works of his, yet this bridge far surpasses them all."—The same author enters into copious particulars on the subject, stating for example, how many piles it was supported by, their heighth and breadth; adding what distance those piles, conjoined by arches, were from each other. It may be imagined how many and how great were the obstacles to be overcome, in order to erect such a bridge over a river so broad and so deep as the

Danube. Apollodorus Damascenus is named as the architect.

Writers, however (Marsilius and Reimar among others), are not wanting, who have rigorously examined that passage of Dion, in which he describes the bridge; and these deny the possibility of reconciling the measurements there given with the rules of architecture. They say that, so far as can be gathered from the remains which are extant at the present day, at the " Iron Gate" *(porta ferrea)*, between Servia and Wallachia, the entire work could not have been so large as is represented; and that the piles only of the bridge were of stone, whilst the arches were of wood. According to Procopius, at each end of this bridge stood a castle (or fort).—See Eckhel's Commentary, vi. 418, et seq.

The obverse of the coin exhibits the laureated head of Trajan to the right, bearing the Ægis; with the following legend :—IMP. TRAIANO AVG. GER. DAC. P. M. TR. P. To the Emperor Trajanus, Augustus, the Germanicus, the Dacicus, Sovereign Pontiff (invested) with the tribunitian power. The silver alone (from a specimen of which the above cut is copied), is catalogued by Mionnet and Akerman. The gold is beautifully engraved in *Iconographie des Empereurs, par* M. Ch. Lenormant, p. 47, No. 13.

It was not to be expected that Hadrian would have struck a coin allusive to that mighty stream whose name was associated with his predecessor's conquests; for Hadrian caused the Roman bridge over it to be destroyed. But it is singular that, with the exception of the coin above described and commented upon, there should not, in the fertile mints of Trajan, be any instance in which the word DANVVIVS or DANVBIVS forms part of the legend on a contemporaneous coin of his. There is indeed, a first brass of that emperor, bearing the date of his fifth consulate, on which the most intelligent numismatists, as well of the present day as of the elder school, recognise one arch of the bridge in question (see *Pons*), but it is only probable conjecture, not positive identification. Another first brass of Trajan (common, but of good design and workmanship), is generally regarded as having been meant to symbolize the Danube, and to refer to the first victories of imperial Rome over her brave Dacian foe, viz.:

Rev.—S. P. Q. R. OPTIMO PRINCIPI. S. C. A river-god, holding a reed in the left hand, presses with the right knee on the thigh, and with the right hand on the neck, of a recumbent male figure, clothed in the Dacian habit.

But this is allegory, of which the meaning may be shrewdly guessed at, not the open record and typification which might have been expected, relative to an event so important as Trajan's first successes on the Danube.—See RIVER-GOD.

" The personification (says Eckhel, in his notice of this coin, vi. 418), as displayed on the above coin, appears by the gesture of laying violent hands on the prostrate Dacian, to intimate that the river also had some share in the merit of reducing that nation. That a fleet really had its station in Mæsia, and consequently on the Danube to repress the incursions of the barbarians, is proved by an inscription published by Gruter (p. 575, i.), in which mention is made of a *classis Flavia Mœsica*."

The following notice of a brass medallion, relates to another bridge over the Danube, said to be the work of Constantine the Great :—

CONSTANTINVS MAX*imus* AVG*ustus*.— Bust of Constantine the Great, to the right, diademed.

Rev.—SALVS REIP*ublicæ*. A stone bridge of three arches, over which Victory walking, carries in her left hand a trophy resting on her shoulder, and with her right hand points out the way to the emperor, who follows with spear and buckler. At the extremity of the bridge, a barbarian kneeling holds up his hands in an attitude of supplication to both. Below is the figure of a river-god in a recumbent posture, with right hand uplifted. On the exergue the word DANVBIVS.

A brass medallion corresponding in legends and types with the one above described, is in the Cabinet of the Bibliothèque Nationale at Paris. Our wood-cut is after a cast from that original. Pellerin *(Mélange*, 1, pl. xii. No. 3, p. 215), published a specimen of it, which closely agrees with that in the French Cabinet, to which grand repertory it was probably, after his death, transferred with numerous other medals, from his own collection.

In referring his readers to this medallion, Pellerin says—" It shews by its type that Constantine had passed the Danube on a bridge, and gained a victory in the country through which it flows, either over the Sarmatians, or over the Goths, or other barbarians with whom he was at war. It is stated in the Chronicle of Alexandria, and in the histories of both the Victors, that this emperor built on the Danube a stone bridge of three arches only, as that seems to be which is represented on the medallion here given. Learned men have judged it scarcely possible, from the width and depth of the river, in that country, that a bridge of such a kind should have been erected there, and hence they have looked upon the medallion as suspicious *(comme suspect)*. Nevertheless historians and coins of Trajan leave no room to doubt but that that emperor built on the same river a bridge, which Dion has described, and even given

the dimensions of its various parts. It is very possible, that the bridge built by Constantine had more than three arches. There was no occasion to represent them all in order to impart an idea of its construction, and to convey a knowledge of the military exploit, which it was intended to designate by the same type." (p. 215–16).

Eckhel, who treats with doubtless well-merited condemnation another medallion of the largest size, in the Vienna cabinet, which bears the same legend of reverse, but not the same, though in some respects a similar, type, has handled the claims of the present one to be regarded as authentic, with very little more indulgence. He observes, that " the shape of the letters upon it, *provided the copy be true to the original*, savours of the time of Nero or thereabouts, and that it does not belong to the age of Constantine." We should not venture to dissent from the great master and highest authority in numismatic science, did he not himself plainly intimate that he had never seen the original piece of which Pellerin's work had furnished him with a copy. Neither has it fallen to our lot to have seen the medallion itself ; but we now write with a skilfully-taken cast from it before us ; and after comparing the lettering, on both obverse and reverse, with that of other medallions of the same reign—(for example, the EXVPERATOR OMNIVM GENTIVM), we, with deference, but without hesitation, affirm, that the conformation of the letters exhibited on the DANVBIVS medallion of the French museum, perfectly assimilates, on both sides, with that of the one just cited, as a well-known specimen.— And with respect to Pellerin's print of his own coin, they who are most familiar with the style of numismatic engraving adopted by the artists employed to illustrate that eminent antiquary's numerous volumes, will, we believe, be amongst the most ready to acknowledge that though the *types* of his coins are delineated with comparative truthfulness, yet no regard is paid in them to those peculiarities of lettering which distinguish the respective ages of the Roman coinage ; but that on the contrary, all his legends and inscriptions, whether Greek or Latin, exhibit a uniform sameness of character.

Having thus endeavoured to meet those arguments against the recognition of this coin as a genuine antique, which are derived, by the learned Author of *Doctrina*, according to his supposition, from its workmanship, it might suffice for us here to close with simply adding, that Mionnet, in his *Recueil des Médailles Romaines* (T. ii. p. 230), describes the legend and type of this remarkable reverse, nearly in the terms above quoted, and gives his attestation to the genuineness of the medallion, by affixing to it the value of 150 francs.—But in justice to such arguments as the illustrious numismatist of Vienna employs from historical sources to support his suspicions of Pellerin's coin, a luminous passage from Eckhel's commentary (see viii. 86–87), is hereto subjoined ; and the reader left to form his own judgment on the subject :—

" The vastness of such an undertaking as a

stone bridge over the Danube, where its stream is so wide as it is in Mæsia, prevents our according any credence to the Chronicon of Alexandria, filled as it is with so many old woman's tales. And, indeed, had it been constructed of cemented materials, there would of necessity have remained some vestiges of it even to the present day, as is the case with the bridge of Trajan, nearly two centuries older, though even these are not found to extend completely across the bed of the river. I am aware, that Constantine, A. D. 310, planned a stone bridge over the Rhine, at Agrippina (Cologne), of which fact there can be no doubt, since Eumenius asserts it in the panegyric which he delivered in the presence of Constantine (Panegyr. vii. ch. 13). But at the time when Eumenius used those expressions, the bridge was only just begun; and that the work was interrupted, is inferred by learned writers from the fact, that no remains of so vast a work are to be found on the spot in the river-bed. And, that the design of a stone bridge over the Danube was liable to greater obstacles than a like work over the Rhine, is evident from the superiority of the former river, in Mæsia, to the latter, in the volume of its waters.— The testimonies of both the Victors, which many quote on this subject, lead to no practical decision, as the one, in his Constantine, says—'A bridge was built over the Danube;' and the other —' He (i. e. Constantine) constructed a bridge over the Danube;' but neither of them tell us that it was of *stone*. It is more probable, therefore, that it was a bridge of boats, which, supposing it to have been put together at the point where the river hastens to its outlet, and is swelled to an immense volume by the combined waters of central Europe, it must have been a work not inferior in magnitude to that of Xerxes over the Hellespont, described at large by so many writers. It was at about the same spot that Darius, the son of Hystaspes, in the invasion of Scythia, crossed the Danube with his forces, by a bridge, as recorded by Herodotus, Strabo (vii. p. 409), and Trogus; but this also was composed only of boats. Marsilius, speaking of this vaunted bridge of Constantine— (Danub. ii. p. 37), says, that having searched the whole stream throughout this tract of country, without discovering the remains of so great a work, he was informed by the inhabitants, that when the river subsides below a certain level, there appear above the surface some wooden piles, a little higher up than the place where the Aluta mingles with the Danube. I can scarcely credit the fact of the remains of a wooden bridge being extant after a lapse of thirteen centuries and more; but let others inquire into the truth of this statement. It is sufficient for my present purpose, to know, that Marsilius, after a diligent investigation of the whole neighbourhood, and the course of the river, discovered no vestiges of a *stone* bridge built by Constantine. And, consequently, till I find such a coin as the one in question, approved by several numismatists of acknowledged eminence, I must be allowed to doubt the fact of a stone bridge over

the Danube. If, however, we allow these coins to be authentic, Eumenius (vii. p. 409), has used most graphic language in accordance with their type:—'And above all, by building the bridge at Agrippina, you trample upon the remnant of a wretched people, preventing their ever laying aside their terrors, but keeping them ever in alarm, *ever stretching out their hands in supplication*.'"

DARDANICI.—This word, on a third brass of Trajan, is accompanied by a type in which a woman stands, with corn-ears in one hand, and gathering her robe with the other.

Eckhel classes this, not with the coins of Roman fabric and of Senatorial authority, but amongst what he terms *Numi Metallorum*.— He observes—" Dardania was a region situated in Upper Mæsia, over against Macedonia, and often mentioned by ancient historians as well as geographers; and on a marble of the age of Trajan, L. Befius is called PRAEF. ALAE. DARDANORVM. This appellation of its district continued as long as the reign of Diocletian; for Trebellius Pollio states, that Dardania was the birth-place of Claudius Gothicus. Now it is certain that in this tract of country there were mines, which having taken their name from that region, supplied metal; wherewith, like those of Dalmatia and Pannonia, coins were struck with the epigraph simply of DARDANICI, suppressing the word METALLI, by which PANNONICI, DELM(ATICI), and VLPIANI, are preceded, on other medals of a similar nature, which the industry and avarice of the Romans established and circulated in various provinces, and of which there exist several inscribed with the name of Trajan and of Hadrian."—See *D. N. V.* vol. vi. p. 446.

DCCCLXXIIII.—The year of Rome 874 (A. D. 121), appears on a coin of Hadrian, which, struck in the fifth year of his reign, remarkably illustrates the year of the city's foundation, by the following inscription :—ANN. DCCCLXXIIII. NAT. VRB. &c. (Natali Urbis).—See ANN. p. 46.

D. C. A.—*Divus Cæsar Augustus.*

D. D.—*Decreto Decurionum.*—This is usually understood as referring to the liberty of striking coins in colonies, as S. C. *Senatus Consulto*, denoted coins struck at Rome by authority of the Senate.

DD.—*Domini*, speaking of two, and DDD. of three.

DD. NN.—*Domini Nostri*, or *Dominorum Nostrorum*—Our Lords, two Ns signify two, and NNN. three Lords or Emperors.—See DOMINUS NOSTER.

DE GER.—*De Germanis.*—See GERMANIS

DE IVD.—*De Judæis.*—See IUDAEIS.

DE SARM.—*De Sarmatis.*—See SARMATIS.

DEAE. or DII. are for the most part represented on coins, with the body, or at least as far as the breast, naked. For nudity, in ancient sculpture and painting, denoted beatitude and immortality.—Rasche.

Dearum simulacra.—The images of goddesses are distinguished on ancient coins by the following attributes :——*Bellona*, by spear and buckler.—*Ceres*, by crown of corn ears, torch, and car drawn by serpents.—*Cybèle*, by turreted crown and lions.——*Diana*, by hunting dress, bow, arrow, and quiver; also car drawn by stags, and by a small horned moon.——*Diana Ephesia*, by her many breasts, stags at her feet, and small basket filled with fruit on her head.—*Flora*, by flowers.—*Isis*, the Egyptian goddess, by star, sistrum, and flower on her head.—*Juno*, by veiled head and peacock.— *Juno Moneta*, by the balance, because coins were minted in the temple of Juno at Rome.— *Juno Sospita* or *Sispita*, by the goat-skin and horns.—*Minerva*, by the owl, olive branch, serpent, helmet, buckler, spear, and thunderbolt. *Venus*, by the apple, Cupid, rudder, and dove. —*Venus Paphia*, by the terminal or conical stone.—*Vesta*, by veiled head, simpulum, palladium, and torch.—Rasche.

Dearum templa.—The temples of goddesses, as exhibited on coins, are not of the common square-formed structure, but round; either as on the medallion of Faustina senior, inscribed *Matri Deum Salutari* (Cybèle); or on the coin of Trebonianus Gallus, with legend of *Junoni Martiali;* or the temple of *Vesta*, as on the coin of Lucilla, and on a denarius of the Cassia gens, with the letters A. C.—See *Templum.*

DEAE. SEGETIAE.—On the reverse of gold and billon of Salonina, wife of Gallienus, are this epigraph, and a temple supported by four columns, within which the deity, wearing a crescent on her head, appears with uplifted hands.

It would seem by the testimony of this coin (see SALONINA), that the empress had erected a temple to the goddess *Segetia*, who before that had only an altar in the Circus Maximus. She was called *Segetia*, as being *(præfecta segetibus)* a presiding divinity over the harvests when they were sprung up from the soil. (See Eckhel, vii. 399—419).—Mr. Akerman, in a note on this legend, observes—" Some authors are of opinion, that Segetia was the same as Fortune, called also Sejana, to whom, as Pliny informs us, Nero built a temple of transparent marble."—*Descr. Cat.* ii. 42.

DEBELLATOR GENTIUM BARBARARUM. The Vanquisher of Barbarian Nations. Constantine, called the Great, was rewarded with

this title, when in the year 322 of the Christian era, he gained repeated victories over the Goths and Sarmatians, in Illyria and in Mæsia,

pursuing his successes beyond the Danube, until the fugitive remains of both these tribes were almost exterminated by the Roman sword.— Banduri, ii. p. 244, obs. 3.

On a brass medallion of Constantius II. in the Cabinet de France, after a cast from which the above reverse has been engraved, the following legends and types appear :—

CONSTANTIUS *Pius Felix* AUG*ustus.*— Bust, to the right, of Constantius the Second, diademed.

Rev.—DEBELLATORI GENTI*um* BARBAR*um.* The emperor, bare-headed, wearing the *paludamentum*, mounted on a horse, which gallops to the right, strikes with the point of his lance a warrior, who meets the blow on one knee; whilst another enemy lies under the horse.

Flattery here awards to the second son of Constantine the Great a title which his father had acquired for successive triumphs in many a slaughterous battle, fought with " barbarians." For the younger Constantius was heir, neither to the valour nor to the good fortune of the First Constantine, being oftener vanquished than victorious, except in the civil wars with his brothers and cousins.—See Eckhel, viii. 83– 116.—See also Biog. Notice, in p. 263 of this dictionary.

DEC.—Decius, Decennalia, &c.

DEC. ANN.—(Decem. Annus) Decennalis, of ten years: Decennial.

Decem.—The usual mark of the denarius was thus stamped X.—See DENARIVS.

DECEN. DECENNAL.—*Decennales ludi,* or *Decennalia Festa.*—Festivals celebrated under the Emperors, at Rome, every *ten years.* Their origin was as follows :—Augustus, after having tranquillised the empire, and enjoyed ten years of peaceful sovereignty, wearied with state fatigues, and failing in health, affected to be desirous of abdicating the government. Accordingly he assembled the Senate, to whom he rendered an account of his administration, and communicated his wish to resign. But the Senators pressed upon him a continuance of his reign for four years longer, and he was not so obdurate as to decline compliance with their importunities. At the expiration of this period, they *obliged* him to load himself with five years more of imperial care; and at the end of that term ten more were required of him : insomuch that from one ten years' end to another this *un*-ambitious but yielding prince held sway for life. (cf. Dion Cass. 53, 13). Some of his successors made similar tenders every ten years; and after the refusal to accept, which they were sure enough to meet with from those to whom the offer was made, they gave a public feast on such renewal of power. The celebration consisted of sacrifices to the gods, of donatives to the soldiers, and of largesses to the people, accompanied with shows and games on the most magnificent and costly scale.

DECENNALES PRIMI.—On gold and silver, and with S. C. on second brass of Antoninus Pius, we see PRIMI DECENNALES within an oaken crown—with the addition, on some specimens, of COS. IIII.

The *Decennales*, and *Vota* (vows), either undertaken or accomplished, that is to say, for the safety of the prince, make their appearance for the first time on coins of Antoninus Pius; although from the commencement of the empire, certain public vows were sometimes recorded on them, and though destined thereafter, and especially during the age of Constantine, to form the constant subject of coins.

DECEM. ANNALES SECVND. COS. IIII. S. C.—On a very rare first brass, the legend of reverse reads as above, inscribed in a garland of oak leaves.

The first *Decennales* of Antonine closed on the 10th of July, A. D. 148; and the second began, in which vows were fulfilled for the prosperous issue of the past ten years, and fresh ones undertaken for the like period to come.— That first-rate numismatist, the author of *Leçons de Numismatique Romaine* (p. 127), who cites the above legend from a very rare first brass in his own collection, observes—"The Romans (a people essentially of a religious disposition), often addressed solemn vows to their deities: in other words, prayers, accompanied with sacrifices. It was thus that Augustus celebrated his pretended re-acceptances of sovereign authority. And it was with equally feigned, but not always equally credited, modesty, that his successors imitated him, in these *decennial sacrifices*, offered up principally for the preservation of the prince, and the welfare of the empire."

DECENNALIA.—A gold medallion of Constans presents on its reverse the legend FELICIA DECENNALIA; and the elegant type of two young genii, or winged boys, supporting between them, in their hands, a crown, in which are inscribed VOTIS X. MVLTIS XX. that is to say, *Votis Decennalibus, Multis Vicennalibus.* In the exergue TES. signifying that it was minted at TESsalonica (so spelt for THESsalonica).—The above cut is from a remarkably well preserved specimen of this fine and very rare coin in the *Cabinet de France.*—For some of Tristan's remarks on it (iii. 615) see FELICIA DECENNALIA.

The fact that *decennial* vows were reckoned as accomplished, not at the beginning but at the termination of the tenth year of an emperor's reign, is shown by numismatic inscriptions, concurrently with the voice of antiquity. Amongst

the examples to this effect, are VOT. COS. IIII. S. C. on first and second brass of Antoninus Pius—the emperor sacrificing before a tripod— VOTA SVSCEPTA X. COS. IIII. same reign and type, in silver.—VOT. or VOTIS X. ET XX. in a crown, of Gallienus.—VOT. X. ET XV. in a crown of laurel, of Constantius II.

In like manner the *Vicennalia*, or VOT. XX. were accomplished at the expiration of the twentieth year of a reign; and after each had, in a happy manner, come to pass, it was usual to record them thus:—VOTIS VICENNALIBVS (in a laurel crown), as on gold and silver of Alexander Severus; and VOT. X. SIC. XX. (in a crown). as on silver of Constantius Chlorus.

On coins of Commodus, Severus, and Caracalla, we read VOT. SVSC. DEC. (*Vota Suscepta Decennalia*), also VOTA SVSCEPTA X. and XX. with figures sacrificing.—These *decennial* vows being SOLVTA (redeemed) by the fulfilment of the term, others for another ten years were undertaken (*suscepta*).

See PRIMI DECENNALES ; see also the system of VOTA explained, in Eckhel's treatise dedicated to the subject, in vol. viii. of *D. N. V.* p. 475 et seq.

DECENTIUS (*Magnus*), brother or cousin of Magnentius, by whom, after the death of Constans, he was named Cæsar, at Milan, A. D. 351, and raised to the consulship the following year. Magnentius appointed him to command in Gaul, for the purpose of keeping in check the German tribes; but he was defeated by Chnodomarius, leader of the Allemanni, and other barbarians. On this, on some previous occasion, the people of Treves revolting, closed the gates of their city against him. On being apprised of the death of Magnentius, to whose assistance he was hastening; apprehensive of falling into the hands of Constantius Chlorus, who had already defeated his brother; and surrounded by foes without hope of escape, Decentius strangled himself at Sens, A. D. 353.—His brass coins are common, except medallions, which are rare—silver very rare, especially medallions—gold still rarer, one medallion in gold is of extreme rarity. He is styled on these *Dominus Noster* DECENTIVS FORT*issimus* CAES*ar ;* also D. N. MAG*nus* DECENTIVS NOB*ilissimus* CAES*ar.*—D. N. DECENTIVS NOB. CAES. The head always bare. The reverse of second brass, bears generally the monogram of Christ, with the letters A. and ω.

It has been pretended (says Mionnet), that Decentius had also the title of Augustus; but no historian makes any mention of such a fact; and the medal on which the assertion founded itself is suspicious.

MINTAGES OF DECENTIUS.

GOLD MEDALLION.—GLORIA ROMANORVM. Roma Nicephorus seated. (Valued by Mionnet at 200 fr.)—VICTORIA AVG. LIBERTAS ROMAN-OR(VM.) Published for the first time in Lenormant's *Iconographie des Empereurs*, 126, No. 5.

SILVER MEDALLION.—PRINCIPI IVVENTVTIS. Mionnet 150 fr.)

GOLD.—VICTORIA AVG. LIB. ROM.—(Brought at the Pembroke sale £4 2s.)—VIRTVS EXERCITI. (Mionnet 72 fr.)

BRASS MEDALLIONS.—VICTORIA AVGG. and VIRTVS AVG. (30 fr. each).

SMALL BRASS.—D. N. DECENTIVS NOB. CAES. Bust of Decentius.—*Rev.*—SALVS. DD. NN. AVG. ET CAES. The monogram of Christ, between A. and ω. In the exergue DIC.—See the cut in preceding page.

DECIUS (*Caius*, or Cnæus, *Messius, Quintus, Trajanus*).—This Emperor was born at Bubalia, a town of the Sirmienses, in Lower Pannonia (near what is now Micowitz, in Hungary), A. D. 201. Descended from an Illyrian family of rank, he proved himself an able statesman and a great captain. But by what means he acquired his earliest promotion is not recorded. Whilst the Mæsian and Pannonian legions were in revolt, he was at Rome; in favour with Philip, and free from all suspicion on the score of his loyalty. Accordingly he was selected by that prince for the task of settling the seditious tumult of the insurgent soldiers, who had proclaimed Marinus. But no sooner did he appear in their sight, than, in order to avoid the threatened chastisement, they, without his consent, proclaimed him *Imperator*. Yielding, therefore, to the necessity of the moment, he struck his tents, and hastened into Italy; where in an engagement with Philip, near Verona, he gained the victory, A. D. 249. On the defeat and death of Philip, Decius was acknowledged as Emperor at Rome, and declared Augustus by the Senate at least as early as the beginning of autumn. In the year 250 he conferred the dignity of Cæsar, and the office of Consul, on his son Herennius Etruscus, and sent him against the Illyrians, who routed the son, but were energetically repulsed by the father. In a battle with the Goths, fought near Abricium, in Thrace, A. D. 251, he was, thro' the treachery of Trebonianus Gallus, lost in a morass, his body never having been recovered for burial. In the same engagement the young Herennius also perished. This occurred after the month of October.

The historian, Victor (II.) bears testimony to the eminent virtues and great accomplishments of Decius; to his quiet demeanor as a man, and to his promptness and energy as a soldier. In all these characteristics he is represented by Zosimus, as being greatly the superior of Philip. The most remarkable event by which the records of his life and government are distinguished, was his revival and restoration to the Senate, of the office of Censor, so many years disused, and, till this time, discharged almost universally by the Emperor. Eutropius, ever liberal in awarding divine honours to princes, states, that Decius and his son were numbered among the gods. —By ecclesiastical historians, however, he is accused of having, in a spirit of injustice and persecution, exercised great cruelty towards the Christians during his reign. He perished in the 55th year of his age, after holding the imperial sceptre somewhat more than two years. He married Herennia Etruscilla, who bore to him two sons, namely, Herennius above named, and Hostilianus.—See *D. N. Vet.* viii. 342–43.

The coins of this Emperor are common in brass, except two or three medallions. In silver they are also common, except a medallion. The gold are all of very great rarity. On these he is styled IMP. TRAIANVS AVG.—IMP. *Caesar* M. Q. TRAIANVS DECIVS AVG. or *Pius Felix Aug.*—[The last two titles are confined to colonial coins].

MINTAGES OF TRAJANUS DECIUS.

SILVER MEDALLION.—CONCORDIA AVGG.— Etruscilla and her two sons.—(Valued by Mionnet at 300 fr.]

GOLD.—ABVNDANTIA.—ADVENTVS.—AEQVITAS.—DACIA.—DACIA FELIX. (Mionnet 150 fr. each),—GENIVS EXERC. ILLYRICIANI. (Brought £9 5s. at the Thomas sale).—GENIVS ILLYRICI. (Mionnet 200 fr.)—PANNONIAE.—VICTORIA AVG. (200 fr. each).—VBERITAS. AVG. (Fine, brought £6 at the Thomas sale).

SILVER.—VICTORIA GERMANICA. Emperor and Victory.

BRASS MEDALLIONS.—CONCORDIA AVGVSTI. Heads of Decius and Etruscilla.—*Rev.*—DACIA. (200 fr.)—CONCORDIA AVGVSTORVM. Heads of Decius and Etruscilla.—*Rev.*—PIETAS AVGVSTORVM. Heads of Hostilianus and Herennius. —(250 fr.)

SECOND BRASS.—IMP. C. M. Q. TRAIANVS IMP. AVG. Radiated head of the Emperor.—*Rev.* PANNONIAE. Two women, one of whom holds a military ensign.—See the engraving above.

DECURIONES. Decurions.—Officers who, in the colonies, corresponded to the Senators of Rome. They were denominated Decuriones, because, at the time when Roman citizens and soldiers were sent as colonists to occupy the conquered countries; ten men were chosen to compose a Senate, or a Court of Councillors, who were charged with the administration of justice, and were intitled *Curia Decurionum*, and *Minor Senatus.*—Pitiscus.

It was requisite that they should possess an income of 100,000 *sestertii*; and from their ranks were chosen the magistrates, just as, by the votes of the latter, the *Duumviri*, the Prefects for enforcing obedience to the laws, and other functionaries, were respectively created.— The enrolled Decurions *(decuriones conscripti),* were called (after the appellation given to the Senate) ORDO, with the addition of the epithets AMPLISSIMVS, SPLENDIDISSIMVS, &c. They were also, sometimes, in imitation of Rome, styled *Senatores,* and *Patres,* chiefly during the decline of the empire; whilst the rest of the inhabitants were called *plebs, populus, cives,* and *coloni.* The names of the *Decuriones* are never found inscribed on the coins of colonies; but in their stead, are frequently read (not only on those of Europe, but of Asia and Africa), the abbreviations D. D. or EX. D. D. that is, EX. *Decreto Decurionum,* which is equivalent to the EX. S. C. of the Roman Senate.—The abbreviations D. D. or EX. D. D. are exhibited on the coins of Abdera, Apamea, Babba, Buthrotum, Carteia, Carthago Nova, Parium, and Sinope. They are remarkable on the coins of Babba, in Mauretania; D. D. PVBL. that is *Decreto Decurionum* PVBL*ico*; and EX. CONSENSV. D.D.

That there were *decuriones* in the *municipia* also is rendered certain, both by coins of Osca, given in Florez, and of Utica, on which D. D. is found; and also by ancient authors, among whom is Suetonius:—" The *decuriones* of the *municipia* and colonies conveyed the body [of Augustus] from Nola (a city in Campania), as far as Bovillæ" (a town in Latium).—The same letters occur also on coins of the *municipia* Calagurris, Emporiæ, Ercavica, and Saguntum —" but with such an appearance (adds Eckhel), that they cannot have been engraved on the die, or *matrix,* but were added afterwards, like marks cut into the metal; a fact which has never been observed on coins of *colonies.* And from this I infer, that *Traducta,* in Boetica, of which there is a coin exhibiting the same mark, enjoyed the privileges only of a *municipium.*"

It is highly probable that the *Decuriones* were indicated on coins, in consequence of their being charged with the direction of the mint; a position which they had been permitted to occupy either by the *Augusti,* or by the Senate of Rome, and involving the superintendance of the weight, types, and number of the money. As then the Roman Senate, to whom pertained the care of striking brass money, had their S. C. engraved upon it, so the *Decuriones,* who were the representatives of Senators in the colonies, took care to stamp on their coins their own D*ecretum* D*ecurionum.*—See *D. N. V. De Numis Coloniarum,* vol. iv. p. 481, et seq.

Speaking of the functions of the Decuriones, Pitiscus observes, that they were as onerous as they were honourable, for, besides the exercise of the monetal privilege, the care devolved to them of making every arrangement for the shews of the circus, and for the spectacles of the theatre; in addition to which it was their duty to furnish the means of defraying all expenses. They had also to levy imposts, and, what was more serious to themselves, they were compelled to supply, out of their own resources, what was deficient.

DECURSIO.—A manœuvre, evolution, hostile incursion.—This word appears on the ex-

ergue of two large brass coins, struck by the Senate, during the reign of Nero.

There were three kinds of Decursio, viz. :— 1. That of military evolution, and mock combats.— 2. The decursio circensis, or manœuvres of the circus, in which, at public spectacles, feats of dexterity and swiftness were performed, as well by horse-riders as by charioteers. (See *Contorniate Coins,* p. 274–75).—3. Cavalcades setting out on hostile incursions.—See EXPEDITIO and PROFECTIO *(suis locis).*

The above type represents the Emperor Nero on horseback, with lance couched in his right hand, as if ready to engage in some combat; a soldier on foot precedes him, with a *vexillum* on his shoulder, and another closely follows. This is taken from a remarkably well-preserved specimen in the British Museum. It is almost of medallion size, and wants the *Senatus Consulto.*

Suetonius states, that whilst Nero was yet only Cæsar, the *decursio* was instituted at the same time as the pretorian guards *(cum prætorianis).* That youths of noble birth were trained to these martial exercises is evident from the observations of learned authors on the coins alluding to the *Princeps Juventutis.* And hence the Emperor Julian, speaking of Constantius II. mentions with approbation, that he was early instructed in "the practice of leaping and running, in full armour, and in the art of horsemanship." *(Orat.* i. p. 11).—In like manner Livy has used the expression "exercitum *decurrere,*" and applied those of " decursum, et simulacrum ludicrum pugnæ," on the occasion of Perseus and Demetrius, sons of Philip V. king of Macedon, tilting with each other in a mock fight. (xl. ch. 6, 9).—According to the same author, Gracchus, when in Spain, ordered all his troops, infantry and cavalry, to run in full armour, in order to display their strength to the Celtiberian ambassadors. (ch. 48).— According to Dion, Nero was so delighted with the running of horses (ἱπποδρομία), that when the animals engaged in the contest distinguished themselves, on their growing old, he used to adorn them, like men, with the *stola forensis* (out-of-door dress of the Romans), and appropriated to their use a sum of money for their maintenance.

See Eckhel, vi. 271, who for some learned remarks on the three kinds of decursio refers to the letters of Cuper, p. 259, and to an anonymous writer in the *Mémoires de Trevaux*, April, 1709.

DECVRSIO. S. C.—Nero, bare-headed, holding a spear on the rest, and mounted on a horse galloping to the right. He is followed by another warrior, also on horseback, and who carries a *vexillum*.

In describing the spirited group on his engraved specimen of this finely fabricated large brass, M. Lenormant observes, that it refers to Nero's institution of cavalry manœuvres for the pretorian soldiers; or perhaps to the presence of the emperor at some equestrian evolutions performed in their armour, offensive and defensive, by the young patricians, in the Campus Martius, at Rome. But notwithstanding the very decided taste of Nero for running horses, there is nothing in the above type to correspond with the legend, in that acceptation of the word *Decursio*. The speed of the horses is not sufficiently rapid; nor is the attitude of the equestrians that of men either charging an enemy or riding a race. In order to be convinced of the difference, it is only needful to look at the coins of the Calpurnia gens, which represent the horses actually racing. The horsemen in those types are absolutely in the attitude of the *jockies* of our own times."—*Iconographie des Empereurs Romains*, p. 31.

There is a very rare silver coin of Nero, bearing on its reverse the exergal legend DECVR. and the type of a horseman attended by a foot soldier, and riding down an enemy. No such type in silver has been catalogued by either Mionnet or Akerman; but there is a well-preserved specimen of it in the British Museum. See DENARIUS, p. 317, in which an engraving of it is inserted.

DECUSSIS.—The name of an early Roman brass coin, a multiple of the *as*. The value of ten *asses* was assigned to the decussis, at the time when the *as libralis* was established. But the *as* was changed under the dictatorship of Q. Fabius, and continued in a course of diminution until the passing of the *Lex Papiria*, which authoritatively fixed the decussis of brass, and the denarius of silver, at 16 semi-uncial *asses*. (See *Assis diminutio*, p. 85, et seq. of this dictionary).—These pieces, which are of the highest rarity, bear on one side the galeated head of Minerva; on the other the prow of a vessel; and are marked with the sign X. One of them

is stamped ROMA, and has the type of Victory in a biga.—Hennin—Mionnet.—See DENARIUS.

DEDICATIO AEDIS. A temple of six columns.—This inscription and type appear on silver and gold coins of Faustina senior; and refer to the temple erected in memory of that empress by her husband Antoninus Pius. It was built in the *Via Sacra* at Rome, and its remains exist to this day. At first it was dedicated to Faustina alone, but after the death of Antonine, worship was paid in it to both, as its front bespeaks, on which is read DIVO ANTONINO ET DIVAE FAVSTINAE EX. S. C. The same temple is seen on the coins of Faustina, with AED. DIV. FAVSTINAE. and between the two centre columns of the building stands or sits the image of the empress.—See *Templum*.

DEDICATION *of Shields*.—On a silver coin of Augustus are the following legend and type: CAESAR AVGVSTVS S. P. Q. R. Buckler between two olive branches. C. L. V.

The custom of dedicating shields (says Eckhel, vi. 121), is of a very ancient date. Ac-

cordingly, even Virgil represents Æneas as dedicating his shield to *Apollo Actius*, with the epigraph—"Æneas hæc de Danais victoribus arma."—On a coin struck by Mescinius, one of the moneyers of Augustus, we find the portrait of that emperor in the centre of a shield; and the heads of *Clemency* and *Moderation* are similarly exhibited on coins of Tiberius.—See C. L. *Clipeus Votivus*, p. 218, and CLEMENTIA, p. 215, of this dictionary.

DEI PENATES.—On a coin of the Antia gens appears this legend, with the type of two young heads, jugated and diademed, of household gods; indicating that Roman family to have originally come from Lavinium.——See PENATES.

DELMATIUS *(Flavius Julius)* or Dalmatius, for the name is spelt in both ways on coins and by authors, was the son of Delmatius, brother of Constantine the Great, who was elevated to the office of Censor. He was born at Toulouse, or, as some say, at Arles. His mother's name is unknown. Being a favourite with his uncle Constantine, whom he resembled in character, he was elected Consul U. C. 1086 (A. D. 333), and two years afterwards (335) was created Cæsar. Whilst yet in a private capacity, he defeated Calocerus, who had revolted in Cyprus, and brought him prisoner to his uncle, who consigned him to the flames. In the memorable partition of the empire, which Constantine made in this latter year, Delmatius received as his share Thrace, Macedonia, and Achaia; but shortly after the decease of Constantine, he was put to death by the soldiers, A. D. 337, under the pretence of desiring to be governed only by the children of Constantine; and this was done with the connivance of Constantius II. who was envious of him.

On his coins, which are rare even in brass, and of the highest rarity in gold and silver, he is styled DELMATIVS CAESAR—DELMATIVS NOB(ILISSIMVS) CAESAR—and FL. IVL. DELMATIVS (or DALMATIVS) NOB. C.

The following are the rarest reverses of coins minted by, or struck in honour of, this young prince :—

GOLD.—DELMATIVS CAESAR. Victory walking.—PRINCIPI IVVENTVTIS. Delmatius stands holding a spear and military ensign.—(Valued by Mionnet at 200 fr. each).

SILVER.—DELMATIVS NOB. CAE. Laureated head of Constantine the Great.—(60 fr.)

SMALL BRASS.—GLORIA EXERCITVS. Two military figures, armed with spear and buckler, standing one on each side a tripod, on others a *labarum*, with the monogram of Christ. On the exergue SIS. or SMKA.—*Obv.*—FL. IVL. DELMATIVS NOB. C. Diademed head of Delmatius. —See the preceding cut (p. 315).

DENARIUS.—This well-known coin of the Romans derived its appellation *à denis assibus* (from ten *asses),* for which it used to be exchanged, weighing a pound each, as they did at the time when silver first began to be coined at Rome, namely, A. U. C. 485 (B. C. 269).— According to Pliny, it was established that the *denarius* should be given in exchange for ten pounds of brass, the *quinarius* for five pounds, and the *sestertius* for two pounds and a half.— But when the *as,* about the year U. C. 537 (B.C. 217), was reduced in weight to one ounce, it was established, that the denarius should be given in exchange for sixteen *asses,* the quinarius for eight, and the sestertius for four. And though the reason for its being so called no longer existed, yet the denarius retained its original name. The difficulties which embarrass this theory of Pliny are adverted to in the citations made from Eckhel, under the head of *Assis Diminutio* (p. 85 et seq. of this dictionary), but which he leaves without solving them. There are specimens of the early minted denarius, bearing on the obverse a double beardless head; and on the reverse Jupiter in a quadriga, and the word ROMA in indented letters.

With respect to the weight of the denarius, it appears, according to Pliny, and other writers, that there were, in the ancient *libra,* 84 denarii. The author of *Doctrina* (v. p. 18), denies that there is any well-grounded argument to prove that ancient denarii were heavier than those of

subsequent date, and adduces proofs to shew, that those, which exceed the weight just specified, must be regarded as belonging to a foreign mint.

As to the statement of those who assert that the ancient denarius was equivalent to the Attic drachma, Eckhel (vol. v. page 18, et seq.), in quoting from Eisenschmid, their names and testimonies, observes :—"You may constantly remark, that writers, when comparing the Greek and Roman coinages, use the denarius, or, what comes to the same thing, four sestertii, for the attic drachma. Of the promiscuous employment of the words innumerable instances are to be found, and this accounts for the fact, that several Latin authors, though most incorrectly, give the name of denarius to the drachma of the Greeks. But, though public opinion and the usage of commerce have assigned the same weight to the denarius and the drachma, it is nevertheless ascertained by the accurate researches of Eisenschmid and Barré, that the attic drachma is somewhat heavier than the denarius, and stands in relation to it as 112 to 100, or to come still nearer, as 9 to 8. And, indeed, the same proportion is arrived at on a comparison of the respective weights of some attic tetra-drachmæ (pieces of four drachmæ), and some denarii of Augustus; so that not only the authorities quoted by learned writers, but also experience founded on the coinages of the two nations, serve to establish the true proportion of the drachma to the denarius. But this proportion applies only to those denarii which were struck under the republic, or at least as early as the reign of Augustus.

[A specimen of that emperor's silver coinage, as struck about U. C. 735 (B. C. 19), by Durmius, one of his moneyers, is hereto subjoined.]

"Under the successors of Augustus, and especially from the time of Nero, they were reduced to nearly an eighth part of their original weight; though even these lighter coins were by the tyrant custom, who always prefers the old-fashioned to the true, still held equivalent to the drachma."

The mark of the consular denarius was X or one or two variations in the form of that letter. A similar mark was used on the brass coinage (see p. 135) to indicate the weight of X *asses;* but on denarii also it denotes the value of X *asses,* for which, as already stated, the denarius was given in exchange. Instead of this mark, however, on coins of the Atilia, Aufidia, Julia, Titinia, and Valeria families, appears the numeral XVI. by which doubtless is indicated the value of a denarius of 16 *asses,* to which it was reduced when the second Punic war was at its

height, under the dictatorship of Q. Fabius
Maximus, U. C. 537 (B. C. 217). "Hence
(adds Eckhel), it has been thought by not a few
antiquaries, that denarii marked XVI. were
struck during that war, when the regulation was
introduced, and that shortly afterwards, the old
mark X. was resumed; an opinion which I shall
not venture either to confirm or to deny, tho'
I consider it more probable, that it was left to
the discretion of the moneyer to use whichever
mark he preferred. For as the mark X. refers
to the name of denarius given to the coin, so
does the mark XVI. to its value. Indeed, denarii of Valerius Flaccus, of the ancient form,
which are proved incontestably to have been all
struck at one and the same time, are marked
some X. and others XVI.:"—See Aufidia gens,
p. 94 in this dictionary.

With respect to the types of denarii, Pliny
simply states (xxxiii. 13), that "the type of
silver was *bigæ* and *quadrigæ*."—This is the fact
with reference to a large portion, but many
bear other types. Tacitus *(De Morib. Germ.)*
has mentioned the *bigati*, and so has Livy frequently, whilst describing the booty taken in
Hispania and Gallia Cisalpina. On denarii struck
during the later periods of the republic, the
types varied in many ways, conformably to the
will of consular magistrates, and finally of the
monetal triumvirs. The obverses of these silver
coins were stamped with the galeated head of
Rome, whilst their reverses exhibit representations of the *Dioscuri* on horseback (as on the
fine denarius of the Horatia family, inserted
as a specimen in p. 316, left-hand column); also
figures drawing *bigæ* and *quadrigæ* (see those
words); from which circumstance the pieces
were termed *bigati* and *quadrigati* (p. 129).—
They were also called *Victoriati*, when their
types displayed a figure of Victory, as in the
subjoined cut, from a denarius of Fannia gens,
in which the goddess is driving her chariot and
four horses at full speed.

This was the case with the half denarius, denominated *quinarius* (see EGNATIA and EGNA-
TULEIA), or piece of five *asses*. Of this and of
the small silver coin called *sestertius*, but few
specimens are extant.

Engraved examples of the consular denarius
will be found in this volume, under the respective heads of Atilia *(Dioscuri*, p. 93)—Annia (Victory in a quadriga, p. 48)——Bæbia,
(Quadriga, p. 121)—Cæcilia *(Biga* of elephants,
p. 150)—Cipia (Victory *in Bigis citis*, p. 200)
—Cornelia (Jupiter *in Quadrigis*, p. 286)—
Curiatia *(Quadriga*, p. 299)—Saufeia (Victoria
in citis Bigis, p. 129), &c. &c.

For specimens of the imperial denarius see
Cæsar Augustus (p. 13)—Agrippa and Augustus

(p. 105)—Caligula and Agrippina (p. 28)—Antonia (p. 55)—Balbinus (p. 122)—Alexander
Severus (p. 33)—Plotina (p. 74)—For a quinarius of Augustus (p. 89). To these we add the
subjoined cut from a rare *Decursio* in silver, as
a specimen of the denarius under Nero's reign :

Frequent mention is made of the denarius or
(Roman) penny, in Holy Writ, wherein it is
spoken of as the daily wages of a labourer, and
also as the tribute money. "Whose is this
image and superscription?"

In his "Numismatic Illustrations of the Narrative Portions of the New Testament," Mr.
Akerman, quoting from St. Matthew, xx. v. 2,
the words "a penny a day," makes the following
observations :—

"The penny here mentioned was the denarius which, at the time of Our Lord's ministry,
was equivalent in value to about sevenpence
halfpenny of our money. With the decline of
the Roman empire, the denarius was by degrees
debased; and before the time of Diocletian had
entirely disappeared, or rather had ceased to be
struck in the imperial mints; but that emperor
restored the coinage of silver; and denarii were
again minted, though reduced in weight. This
reduction went on, after the division of the empire, until the denarius, once a very beautiful
medalet, became a coin of very inferior execution, low relief, and reduced thickness and
weight. * * * The term 'denarius' is yet preserved in our notation of pounds, shillings, and
pence, by £. s. d. * * * It is worthy of remark, that, in this country, a penny a day appears to have been the pay of a field labourer,
in the middle ages; whilst, among the Romans
(see Tacitus, *Ann.* lib. i. c. 17) the daily pay
of a soldier was a denarius," pp. 7 and 8.

From the 6th section of the same work (pp.
10 and 11), another passage referring to the imperial denarius, as circulated during the latter
period of Our Saviour's appearance on earth,
will be found cited in this dictionary, amongst
the mintages of TIBERIUS.

Respecting *base* denarii, see the words MA-
JORINA PECUNIA.

DEO. AESC. SVB.—On a colonial coin of
Parium, in Mysia, as identified by the usual
initials C. G. I. H. P. *Colonia Gemella Julia
Hadriana Pariana*, noticed by the Abbé Belley,

from the collection of
Pellerin, there appears
on one side the head of
Commodus, and on the
other the figure of a man,
with naked head, and
without beard, sitting,
to whom an ox, which is
before him, presents its

foot, as if to have it examined. Above this group is inscribed DEO. AESC. SVB.—Belley has given to the word SVB. the interpretation of *Subvenienti*——Pellerin that of *Suburbano.*—Each, however, regards the type as referring to Æsculapius. Pellerin (in his Additions *aux Recueils*, p. 29), in support of his own reading, observes, that " Æsculapius on this medal is represented young, without crown and without beard. This gives occasion to presume that he is thus figured in his youth, as allusive to the time when he began to practice medicine, in which he had received instructions, not only from his father Apollo, but also from the Centaur Chiron, and that the first essays of his art were exercised on animals."—Æsculapius is always represented old and bearded, on medals of cities within whose walls temples were erected to him as a divinity. But, Pellerin goes on to shew, on the authority of many ancient authors, that almost all the cities had temples of Esculapius in their *suburbs*, which seems to him to prove that the sense which he gives to the word SVB. is the true one—viz. a *suburban* edifice, where the inhabitants of *Parium* and its neighbourhood went to offer gifts to the god, in supplication for the blessing of health.—The above cut is from a second brass coin in the British Museum. It will be found closely to correspond with the reverse engraved in *Mélange* I. plate xvii. of Pellerin.—See also *Parium.*

DEO AVGVSTO.—Statue of Augustus, who sits in the manner of Jupiter, with radiated head, and having a spear in his left hand, and a figure of Victory in his right. C. V. T. T. *Colonia Victrix Togata Tarraco.*—On the reverse AETERNITATIS AVGVSTAE. A magnificent temple of eight columns.—Large brass colonial.—The colonists of Tarragona, in Spain, after the apotheosis of Augustus, sent an embassy to Rome, petitioning for leave to erect a temple to him; a privilege which they were the first to obtain. (Vaillant, *in Col.* i. p. 45).—See Akerman, *Coins of Cities*, &c. No. 3, pl. ix. p. 188.—See also in this dictionary TARRACO.

DEO AVGVSTO.—This epigraph round the head of Augustus, appears on the obverse of a gold coin, having on its reverse the head of Gallienus.

Most of the *Consecration* medals of his imperial predecessors were restored by Gallienus, and round the effigy of each is commonly read DIVO. But on this gold coin Gallienus conjoins with the effigy of the founder of the empire, the epigraph of DEO AVGVSTO. Thus substituting for DIVVS or divine, the unusual and still more outrageous assumption of DEVS, God! Servius thus draws the distinction between *Deos* and *Divos*—viz. that the eternals are called by the former name; but *Divi* were those who, from being mere mortal men, were placed by the ceremony of *apotheosis* amongst the gods. The title of *Divi* was at first conferred after death on those Roman princes who in their lifetime had performed some illustrious service for the republic or state. Afterwards, however, as the spirit and love of adulation daily increased,

many living emperors did not refuse to accept that fulsome and presumptuous honour. Nay they even courted the appellation of *Deus;* as Eutropius writes of Domitian, who commanded to have himself called *Dominus* and *Deus*, but after death did not either merit or obtain even the less obnoxious title of *Divus.*"

DEO CABIRO.—Cabirus, or rather one of the Cabiri, with cap on his head, and a band round the body, standing, a hammer in his right and a pair of nippers or tongs in his left hand. Third brass of Claudius Gothicus.—(See Banduri, ii. p. 340, who describes, but does not give, an engraving of the coin).

The Cabiri were sons of Vulcan and of Cabira, daughter of Proteus, who taught men the use of fire, and the manufacture of iron. The advantages thence derived to the human race established a claim for them to divine honours, and they were adored as gods in different places.—Their mysteries were celebrated with profound secrecy, and the most remarkable feature, according to what has been related of them, is that those who had the good fortune to be initiated, were protected from all dangers, as well by land as by sea.—See below, DEO VOLKANO.

Eckhel says that " this is the only coin of Roman die *(commatis Romani),* itself of the greatest rarity, upon which [the name and type of] Cabirus is found; but of whom frequent mention is made on the coins of the Thessalonians, whose tutelary deity he was. Banduri therefore imputes the impress of the deity's image on this coin to a grateful feeling on the part of Claudius, inasmuch as the Goths, attempting the siege of Thessalonica, as Zosimus and Trebellius relate, were repulsed by the tutelary deity of that place."—*Doct. Num. Vet.* vol. vii. p. 472.

DEO VOLKANO.—A temple of four columns, in which Vulcan stands before an anvil, holding in his right hand a hammer, and in his left a pair of fire-tongs *(forceps).*——The above appears on a billon coin of Valerianus senior, who, according to Tristan, "built," or according to Vaillant, "restored," the temple of Vulcan, at Rome, in order to render that god propitious to him and his arms, for which he had at the time great employment against so many barbarous nations as then assailed the empire.—See VULCANUS.

DEO ET DOMINO CARO. AVG.——The heads opposite to each other of the Sun radiated, and of Carus also radiated.—This appears on a third brass of Carus, "who desired (says Banduri) while still living, to be worshipped as and called a god—a fact indicated by the poets of that age, by whom, when yet reigning, he is honoured as a deity."—There is also a gold coin of Carus bearing the same legend and the head of that emperor on its obverse, and VICTORIA AVG. with the type of a Victory standing on a globe, on its reverse.

DEO ET DOMINO NATO. AVRELIANO AVG. A radiated head.—*Rev.*—RESTITVT. OR- BIS. A woman standing, offers a crown to the emperor, dressed in the paludamentum. Second brass.—(Spanheim, vol. ii. p. 491.—Banduri).

DEO ET DOMINO NOSTRO AVRELIANO AVG. A radiated head.—*Rev.*—RESTITVT. OR- BIS. A woman offering a crown to the emperor, who stands beside her in the paludamentum.— Third brass.—(Mus. Genov. TAB. xxi. No. 11).

Spanheim, in his comments on the former of these coins, cleverly remarks, that Aurelian is on this coin styled *Deus et Dominus* NATVS, to distinguish him from Sol, who was one of the *unbegotten* and eternal deities, and who, on some coins of not much later date, is styled *Dominus Imperii Romani*. And this opinion appears to Eckhel (vol. vii. p. 482), much more probable than that of Banduri, who considers this coin to have been struck after the death of Aurelian. We have here, says he, a memorable instance of the greatest arrogance of which a mortal can be guilty. Up to this time the title of *dominus* had been thought too proud a one, and had accordingly been excluded from the coinage of Rome, though in the salutations and common conversation of courtiers it was applied to the emperors. But now we find Aurelian openly introducing it on his coins, and not content with monopolizing, by this invidious appel- lation, the empire of the whole world, he rashly invades the honours of heaven, and even during his life-time, insignificant mortal as he is, allows himself to be described on public monuments as *a god;* so that our surprise is greatly dimi- nished at finding Carus afterwards glorying in both those titles.—In the case of Domitian, not only has Passeri (Lucern. vol. i. TAB. 74, vol. iii. TAB. 26, 28), seen the titles *deus* and *do- minus* ascribed to him on works of pottery, but Suetonius (Domit. ch. 13), also has recorded that they were eagerly desired by that infatu- ated emperor; and hence, in allusion to him, Martial uses the words—

"Edictum domini deique nostri."—(Epig. v. 8.)

DEO MARTI.—Mars naked, except the head, which is galeated, stands with a spear in one hand,

and resting his other hand on a buckler; in a temple of four columns. This le- gend and type appear on a silver coin of P. L. COR- NELIVS SALONINVS VALE- RIANVS CAES. son of Gal- lienus & Salonina, struck in memory of the temple of Mars, which his father Valerianus had re- stored in the Flaminian way; for says Banduri, as Gallienus styled Jupiter Victor the educator (nutritor) of his son, so it was likewise his wish to shew that by his example, his son had become a worshipper of the god of war.—See MARS.

DEO SANCTO NILO.—On a third brass of Julianus II.—See a lengthened commentary on this and other coins of the same description, struck under Julian, viii. p. 137 of Eckhel.— See also NILO.

DEO SANCTO SERAPIDI.—The radiated head of Serapis, with the *modius*, and with the paludamentum on his shoulders.—Engraved in Spanheim's *Cæsars of Julian*, p. 67.

This is one of four brass coins which, bearing the inscription DEO SERAPIDI or DEO SARAPIDI, are assigned by antiquaries to Julian II. sur- named the Apostate. They are regarded as evi- dences of his singular and superstitious defer- ence towards that Egyptian deity, who, on coins and inscriptions, is called *Sarapis* or *Serapis.*— These types are the more exclusively attributed to him, because having embraced, he endea- voured to restore, paganism and all its idola- trous rites, in prejudice to the Christian reli- gion, to which Constantine the Great, having made public profession of his faith, had given the chief place.—See SERAPIS.

DEOR. Deorum.—See FELICITAS, and PRO- VIDENTIA.

DERTOSA, a city of Hispania Tarraconensis, now *Tortosa*, in South Catalonia, situate near the mouth of the Ebro. Pliny says the people of Dertosa were comprised in the juridical con- vention of Tarragona; and Strabo speaks of it as a colony planted by Julius Cæsar. Coins confirm this statement, there being second brass struck in honour of Augustus, and of Tiberius, bearing on their respective obverses C. I. A. D. AVG. *Colonia Julia Augusta Dertosa Augusta,* with radiated head of Augustus; and on their reverse C. I. A. D. TI. CAES. with laureated head of Tiberius—which shews that they were struck after the death and consecration of Augustus.— (Engraved in Vaillant, i. p. 23; also in the *Cabinet de Christine,* p. 305).—In Akerman, *Coins of Hispania,* &c. the following small brass of Dertosa is quoted from Sestini, viz.:—*Obv.* C. IVL. TANC. C. ARRI. AF. C. I. D, Laureated head of Julius Cæsar.—*Rev.*—A plough; which type, together with the letters C. I. D. seems to confirm the asserted claim of this city to be ranked amongst the Roman colonies.—There are coins of the same place which, with the type of a galley, also exhibit the name of *Ilercavonia,* demonstrating that the two towns were in alli- ance with each other.

DES. *alias* DESIG.—*Designatus.* Elected, appointed.—COS. DES. *Consul Designatus.* Consul Elect; that is to say, before he entered his first consulate. (See CONSULATUS, p. 267). The term *Designatus,* or *Designati,* applied to those who, in the *comitia,* were for the ensuing year elected consuls, questors, ediles, &c.

DESTINATO IMPERAT*ore.* Designation to the Empire.—On a silver coin of Caracalla, with accompanying type of pontifical instruments (viz. lituus, apex, tripus, simpulum); behind them the skeleton head of an ox (allusive to the sacrificial victim).

Spanheim explains this coin, when he says that the Emperor Severus "demanded of the Senate that his eldest son, Bassianus Antoninus (Caracalla), should be proclaimed Cæsar, and invested with the usual imperial insignia."— This was done at that period in which, after subduing and putting to death his rival Albinus, in Gaul, Severus returned to Rome, and before he proceeded to wage war in person against the Parthians. Many inscriptive marbles (in Gruter and Muratori) also call Caracalla *destinatus imperator*. In the same manner, the cenotaph at · Pisa describes Caius Cæsar, the son of Agrippa, as "already *designated* prince, of the most just character, and perfectly resembling his parent in all virtues," i. e. Augustus, who adopted him ; and, on coins of the year U. C. 824 (A. D. 71), Titus is called *imperator designatus*.—See Eckhel, vii. 200.

The pontifical instruments refer to the sovereign priesthood conferred upon Caracalla by his father, and they supply the place of the titular initials P. M. *(Pontifex Maximus)*, omitted in the legend of this coin.

DESULTOR, a leaper, a vaulter; the technical appellation of a sort of riders, whose practice it was, in the circus games, to urge two horses to their utmost speed, leaping from one to the other with surprising agility, without stopping. The term was also applied to those young Romans, some of them of the highest rank, who, not content with driving bigæ and quadrigæ in the circus, carried the reigning taste for these exercises to the utmost excess. They, too, mounted bare-backed horses, riding one of them and leading another in hand. On these they alternately vaulted whilst gallopping, and thus changed their position many times, with wonderful celerity, after the manner of a troop of horse in the Numidian army, as described by Livy (xxiii. 29). The Roman desultor wore a *pileus*, or cap of felt, and his horse was without a saddle, but he had the use of both whip and bridle.

From these volatile feats of horsemanship the term *desultor* was, by a metaphor, applied to the fickle and inconstant, and to those who were prone to betray a cause. And so, Ovid says of himself (Amor. i. eleg. 3, v. 15) :—

Non mihi mille placent, non sum *desultor* amoris.

that is, " I am not a fickle lover."

The remarkable type exhibited on the reverse of the above engraved denarius (the obverse bears the heads of Numa and Ancus), is described by Hyginus (TAB. 80), when speaking of the *Dioscuri*—" Whence also the Romans keep up the custom, when they exhibit a *desultor ;* for one individual manages two horses, with a cap on his head, and leaps from one horse to the other, in memory of his (i. e. Pollux) representing his brother (Castor) as well as himself."—In conformity with this account, the *desultor* is represented wearing a cap of a conical form, doubtless the more closely to imitate the Dioscuri, whose caps were of this kind, as is testified by numerous monuments, and also by

Lucian *(Dial. deor.* 36), who calls them τοῦ ᾦου ἡμίτομον—" the half segment of an egg," by which was indicated the myth which affirms their being sprung from an egg.—Eckhel then quotes the verses of Homer *(Iliad,* O. v. 679), so graphically descriptive of the exploits of a *desultor,* to the following effect :—

" As when a man, well-skilled in the management of race horses, who, after selecting from a multitude four steeds, hurrying them from the plain, drives them to the city by the much-frequented road ; and crowds gaze on him with admiration, both men and women; whilst he, with firm seat and in security, leaps alternately from one to another; they flying the while."

Manilius also well illustrates this type *(Astron.* v. 85) :—

Necnon alterno *desultor* sidere dorso
Quadrupedum, et stabiles poterit defigere plantas ,
Perque volabit equos, ludens per terga volantum.

[The *vaulter,* too, may alight alternately on the back of each quadruped, and plant his firm feet, flying amidst the horses, and playing his pranks over their backs, as they go at full speed.]

This type was selected by Censorinus in memory of a celebrated seer *(vates)* of the Marcia family, named Marcius, who suggested to the Senate the establishment of the *Ludi Apollinares*—Equestrian games in honour of Apollo.

As a numismatic illustration, the foregoing cut is inserted from a coin of the Marcia gens, which exhibits one of the *desultores*, with conical cap, and with whip in right hand, urging to their fullest speed two horses, one of which he is riding, the wreath and palm, as symbols of victory, accompany the equestrian group, on the Sepullia and other family coins. See Calpurnia gens (p. 167), on a coin of which is a figure of a man, with a palm branch on his shoulder, riding a horse at a rapid rate—but which Eckhel does not consider to typify the *desultor*, who he observes had at least *two horses* in hand, as exemplified in the denarius engraved in left-hand column.—For three other illustrations of the subject, see Dr. Smith's *Dictionary of Greek and Roman Antiquities*, p. 327, article DESULTOR.

DEVICT. Devictis.

DEVICTÆ PROVINCIÆ.—Conquered countries, or provinces, are indicated on Roman coins, very frequently, by figures seated and weeping : for not only amongst the Jews, and people of the East generally, the sitting posture signified grief; but also amongst the Greeks, the Etruscans, and others, as Gori shews in his *Museum Etruscum*.

DEVICTA.—See ALAMANNIA DEVICTA (p. 32)—ARMENIA DEVICTA (p. 81)—JUDÆA DEVICTA—SARMATIA DEVICTA.

DEVICTIS GERMANIS.——SIGNIS RECeptis.——See GERMANICUS CAESAR—see also SIGNIS.

DEULTUM (Thracia) *Colonia,* now Derkon, in Rumilia, European Turkey. Ancient Deultum was situated on the Parysus, near the outflow of. that river into the Euxine, between Mesembria and Apollonia.—According to Poly·

bius, Thrace was colonised, not only by the Romans, but also long before, by the Greeks, and this city is said to have been originally founded by Milesian emigrants. Its name is differently spelt by different authors. Ptolemy calls it *Develtus;* Ammianus, *Debultus;* and in the "Acta Conciliorum," it is denominated *Debeltus,*—Vaillant (*in Coloniis*) adopts the appellation given to it by Pliny, namely Deultum; where a colony of veterans was planted by Vespasian. This Roman settlement assumed his family name, *Flavia;* and on account of his remarkable tokens of devotion to the goddess of Peace (to whom that emperor built a temple at Rome); it was called *Pacensis,* or *Pacifica.*— The place was once surrounded with strong walls, and still exhibits the remains of its ramparts. The coins of Deultum are *Latin* imperial, in small, middle, and first brass. They commence A. D. 97 and end A. D. 249, and are inscribed either with the initial letters C. F. P. D. or with the abbreviated words COL. FL. PAC. DEVLT. (Colonia Flavia Pacensis [or Pacifica] *Deultum*).

The Emperors, Cæsars, and Empresses to whom this colony dedicated the products of her mint were—Trajanus, Macrinus, Diadumenianus, Alexander Severus, Mamæa, Maximinus, Maximus, Gordianus Pius, Tranquillina, Philippus senior, Otacilia, and Philippus junior.

The deities worshipped at Deultum, and whose images with their respective attributes appear on her coins, are as follow :—Apollo (the tutelary god of the city) Æsculapius, Bacchus, Ceres, Cybèle, Diana, Fortuna, Hygeia, Jupiter, Minerva, Nemesis, Silenus, and Serapis.

Besides the above types there are others on the colonial coinage of this Thracian city; such as a bull's head on a third brass of Trajan ; the *Genius Urbis,* under Alexander Severus ; a lion, with Philip senior and junior on its obverse ; legionary eagles and other Roman military standards, referring to the original peopling of the colony with veteran soldiers (engraved in Vaillant, ii. p. 155) ; the Wolf and twins, on second brass of Caracalla and Macrinus ; the dolphin, in small brass, dedicated to Maximus Cæsar ; the three Graces, inscribed to Alexander Severus, &c. &c. Only two subjects have any direct allusion to the locality of Deultum. An engraving of one of them is hereto subjoined :—

River-deities.—Two of these fluvial personifications, one bearded, holds a reed in the right hand, in the left a cornucopiæ, resting on an urn, whence water flows. The other a female figure, in long drapery, also holds a reed in one hand, and resting in like manner to the other on an urn. Above the female figure is a ship with sail. This appears on a second brass of Gordianus III. with legend of COL. FL. PAC. DEVLT. *Colonia Flavia Pacensis Deultana.*

[There is another reverse of this coin, varying in the grouping of the objects from the above, also given in Vaillant (ii. 144), who observes, that "Rivers emptying themselves into the sea, are depicted on ancient medals under the figures of old men, with flowing beards, as though they were the fathers of other streams. But the personifications of those rivers which discharge their waters into other rivers, are represented without beards. The name of the river which issues into the Parysus (near the banks of which Deultum appears to have been situated), is not found in the geographies of antiquity. The sailing vessel denotes that the Parysus was navigable. The cornucopiæ indicates the affluence derived to the city from its navigation. According to Pliny, Deultum was situated on a lake."]

DEUS.—If Plutarch is to be credited on the subject, Numa Pompilius had given to the Romans so sublime an idea of the Supreme Being, that, convinced of the impossibility of arriving at a knowledge of Him, except through the understanding, they regarded it as a sacrilege to represent the Deity under any human form. And accordingly, for a time, it is affirmed, neither figure nor painting of the gods was seen at Rome, although temples were erected to them, in which they were worshipped.— The use of idols was derived to the Romans from the Tuscans, and from the Greeks. It was mainly from those two sources that they drew their superstitions ; and they afterwards improved upon their models. For when Rome became mistress of a great part of the world, she allowed almost every foreign religion to be introduced within her walls ; and there might be seen in that city as many divinities as worshippers. So great, in fact, was the number of statues raised in honour of these gods, as to give rise to the saying, that the inanimate portion of the people in Rome was larger than that which was living, although, the latter amounted to millions. The Romans divided all these deities into different classes ; viz. those of the first order, which depended, like the rest, on Fate.— Those of an inferior order, and all the other minor gods and goddesses. Those who presided over each place or each nation. Those which were assigned to each individual being, and even to most human actions. The last named were, indeed, so many *genii,* whom they made sometimes masculine, sometimes feminine; and to these they paid a particular worship, following the bent of their supposed wants, and conforming to the caprice of their devotions.

For all such classes of deities as are found alluded to in the legends or types of Roman Coins, see DII, &c. (p. 328).

DEVS ADIVTA ROMANIS.—A cross standing on steps.—This legend and type appear on a large silver medallion of Heraclius I. Eckhel says of it—"This pious medal appears with others, to have been coined from that silver which, on the eve of a war with the Persians, the emperor, to supply a deficient treasury, took for this purpose, out of the sacred edifices."—vol. viii. 223.

DEUSO or DEUSONA.—See HERCULI DEUSONIENSI.

DEXTRAE DUÆ JUNCTÆ.——See *Right Hands joined.*

D. F. *Divi Filius.*—AVG. D. F. LVD. SAEC. FEC.—See *Ludi Sæculares.*

DIADEMA.—It was by this name that the white fillet, or band, was called, which bound the temples of kings in the earliest ages. The head of Bacchus (to whom fable has ascribed the invention of that head-dress), also the heads of Neptune, of Hercules, of Victory, and some other divinities, appear on coins encircled with the diadem. Considering it certain, therefore, that this ornament was distinguished, from a remote antiquity, as an essentially royal badge, it is not surprising that amongst a free people, such as the Romans were after the expulsion of the Tarquins, and the abolition of monarchical government, the diadem should have been held in universal abhorrence. For this reason both Augustus and Tiberius had the wisdom to abstain from wearing it. Nevertheless, certain vain emperors entertained a great desire to assume the diadem, although they wanted the courage to do so.—According to Suetonius, Caligula was much inclined to try the experiment on the popular feeling, but refrained.—Lampridius states, that Elagabalus wished to use the gemmed diadem, as a means of making himself more attractive, and because it was more adapted to the female countenance; and this he wore within doors *(domi).*—Aurelian is said to have been the first among the Romans who decked his brows with the diadem; but coins do not confirm this statement. It was by Constantine the Great that the example was *publicly* set of a Roman Emperor wearing this royal badge, either in its simple form, or adorned with clasps or jewels, and that too divested of both the laurel and the radiated crown.—Victor alludes to the fact of Constantine "decking his royal robes with gems, and his head with the invariable diadem." And its introduction is clearly shewn on his numismatic portraitures.

"It is (observes Eckhel) to this fashion, in part, that Julian must have referred, when he so bitterly commented on the voluptuousness and extravagance of that emperor, his effeminate mode of head-dress, and all the other topics of reproach, which he spitefully heaps upon him, as on a second Sardanapalus. These accounts are confirmed by the *Chronicon Alexandrinum*, which informs us, that ' he first adopted the diadem enriched with pearls,' and other gems.—Synesius, whilst lashing with more than Grecian license, in his oration περὶ βασιλείας *(concerning the kingdom)*, the luxury of Arcadius and the princes of that period, speaks as follows, according to the translation of Petavius:—' At what time, think you, were the affairs of Rome in better plight? Is it since you have covered yourselves from head to foot with purple and gold, and fetching from the mountains of the barbarii (lands beyond sea),

precious stones, you wear them in your crowns, and in your shoes, fasten your girdles with them, make of them your bracelets and your brooches, nay, even adorn your seats with them?' And, that he might not appear to express himself too violently, he has softened down the offensiveness of his remarks, with this prelude:—' Not that this has arisen from your fault, but from theirs, who were the originators of this morbid passion, and who transmitted to after times this highly prized infection.'—That these words were intended as a *hit* at Constantine, may be inferred from what is stated above."—See *Doct. Num. Vet.* viii. pp. 79–360–502.

Diademed head of Constantine in coelum spectans.—It is to be observed, that the head turned upwards to the heavens, which occurs on the gold and silver coins of this emperor, has

no parallel in former or in subsequent times.—Eckhel, in consulting the opinions of writers upon this peculiarity of posture, first quotes Eusebius as follows:—' Indeed, the fervent faith which had taken possession of his mind, may be recognized in the fact of his causing his portrait to be so represented on his gold coins, as to give him the appearance of gazing upwards, like one engaged in prayer to the Deity. Instances of this coin were common throughout the Roman dominions.'—Thus far the ecclesiastical historian. "But (continues Eckhel), I am much mistaken if Julian has not held up to derision this position of the head as well as every thing else connected with Constantine. For it is at this he appears to aim his shaft when he relates that Constantine, when summoned to the council of the gods, remained fixed at the threshold of Luna—For, to use his own words, ' he was desperately enamoured of her, and, occupied solely with gazing upon her, he paid no heed to Victory.' Certainly, the attitude, which the coin represents, is that of a man looking at the moon or the stars; whence the joke.—In an inquiry like the present, I think that implicit reliance should not be placed on either of these writers; the former of whom can see in Constantine nothing but what is holy and divine, whilst the latter treats every thing with sarcasm and abuse. Perhaps the main ambition of Constantine was to resemble Alexander the Great, whom not only ancient authors, but extant monuments, prove to have been represented in a very similar manner; as may be seen under the coinage of that king."—*D. N. V.* vol. viii. 80.

[The above cut is from a highly preserved specimen in the British Museum, for the reverse of which see GLORIA CONSTANTINI AVG.]

According to Ammianus, and the testimony of coins, Julian the Apostate, notwithstanding all he has said (in his satire on the Cæsars) to disparage and ridicule his predecessor and uncle, wore a diadem of the same form, and with the same embellishments, as Constantine's. Another proof of the inconsistency of that pagan prince. This royal decoration of the head prevailed long afterwards, though it occasionally gave place to the helmet.—On this subject, see the word *Head-dresses.*

On a coin of the Terentia family, the bearded head of Quirinus (Romulus) appears bound with the diadem, after the example of other kings, both European and Asiatic. On a denarius of the Calpurnia gens, the bearded head of NVMA exhibits itself with the diadem. On a coin of Coponia is the diademed head of Apollo. On a coin of Marcia is the head of ANCVS, also with the diadem. One of the constant symbols of the imperial dignity, the *diadem,* in modern times, though its form is very different, has in name become synonimous with the word *crown.*

For a fine example of an imperial diadem, see Constantine the Great (p. 257).

GOLD.—PRINC. IVVENTVTIS (valued by Mionnet at 400 & 600 fr.)—SPES. PVBLICA (600 fr.)

SILVER.—FIDES MILITVM. (60 fr.)

BRASS MEDALLION.—PRINC. IVVENTVTIS.

FIRST BRASS.—M. OPEL. ANTONINVS DIADVMENIANVS. Bust of Diadumenian, to the right, bare head, habited in the paludamentum.

Rev.—PRINC(EPS) IVVENTVTIS. *Prince of the Youth.*—The young Cæsar, wearing the paludamentum, stands bare-headed, holding in the right hand an ensign, and in the left a spear; on his left are two other ensigns planted on the ground. In the field S. C.

[A fine specimen of this large brass brought £3 at the Devonshire sale.—From another, in the highest state of preservation, the preceding type of the obverse has been faithfully engraved; and an accurate cut from its reverse, equally remarkable for its fine workmanship as the portrait, will be found under PRINC. IVVENTVTIS].

DIADUMENIANUS *(Marcus Opelius),* son of Macrinus, and of Nonia Celsa, was born in the year of Rome 961 (A. D. 208), on the 19th of December, the anniversary day of the birth of Antoninus Pius. Macrinus, become emperor A. D. 217, gave to his son the name of Antoninus, and the titles of Cæsar and of Prince of the Youth; and in 218 named him Augustus, although he was then only ten years of age.— The fall of Macrinus followed so closely on the elevation of his son to the dignity of Augustus, that no coins struck in the name of this young prince are known to have this title. Macrinus having been defeated, sent Diadumenianus to Artabanes, King of the Parthians; but the soldiers entrusted with the charge of conducting him to the territories of that eastern monarch, delivered him over to the partisans of Elagabalus, and he was slain. From his maternal grandfather he inherited the name of Diadumenus, which, on his pretended adoption into the family of the Antonines, was changed into Diadumenianus. His portrait on coins does not answer to the description which Lampridius gives of the extreme beauty of this child. He is, on numismatic monuments, styled M. OPEL. ANTONINVS DIADVMENIANVS CAES(AR), or M. OP. DIADVMEN.—The silver coins of Diadumenian are rare; the gold, of the highest rarity. Second brass are rare; first brass very rare.—Notwithstanding the shortness of his life and reign, the number of coins minted in his name, particularly out of Rome, is considerable. The following are among the rarest reverses :—

DIANA, an Italian Divinity, afterwards regarded as identical with the goddess whom the Greeks called Ἀρτεμις.—According to Cicero *(Nat. Deor.)* there were three of this name, of whom that most commonly celebrated among mythologists was the daughter of Jupiter and Latona, and twin sister of Apollo. Diana was worshipped in various ways, and under various figures, by divers ancient nations. In rivalship with the similar claims of Delos, the Ephesians assumed the honour of their city having witnessed the birth of Diana, and the most famous of her temples was that in their city. Skilful, like Apollo, in the use of the bow, her employment on earth was the chase; and if her brother were the god of day, she under the name of *Luna,* the moon, enlightened mortals during the night. She was the patroness of virginity, and the presiding deity over child-birth, on which account she was called *Lucina,* or *Juno Pronuba,* when invoked by women in parturition; and *Trivia,* when worshipped in the cross-ways, where her statues were generally erected. The earliest trace of her worship at Rome occurs in the tradition, that Servius Tullius dedicated to her a temple on the Aventine mount. Diana was protectress of the slaves; and the day, on which that temple had been dedicated, is said to have been afterwards celebrated every year by slaves of both sexes, and was called the day of the slaves. (See Dr. Smith's *Dictionary of Roman Mythology).*—On coins, gems, and other monuments of antiquity, Diana, as the *Ephesian* goddess, is represented by an image with many breasts, indicating the plenteousness of nature. As *Lucifera*, she stands either dressed in the stola, holding a lighted torch transversely, in both hands, or she wears the lunar crescent on her head, and drives a chariot drawn by two stags, holding the reins in one hand, and a burning torch in the other.—As *Diana Pergensis* (or of Perga), her symbol is either a stone, or some cylinder-shaped vase, marked with celestial signs and figures.—As *Diana Venatrix* (the huntress), she appears with bow and arrow, as on a coin of Gallienus.—On a consecration medal of Faustina senior, the figure of Diana in a biga, is the type of the Empress's eternity.—When she performs the part of *Luna*, she wears a crescent on her head, and her chariot is a biga of bulls, as on a first brass of Julia Domna.

[On a brass medallion of Crispina, without legend of reverse, is the graceful figure of a female, dressed in the *stola*, or long flowing robe of Roman matrons; recognizable as Diana by the bow she holds in her left, and the arrow in her right hand.—See preceding cut from a cast after a rare specimen in the *Cabinet de France*].

The goddess also appears, with attributes of either bow, dog, or torch, on coins of Augustus, Plotina, Faustina jun. Lucilla, Plautilla, Gordianus Pius, Valerianus, Salonina, Postumus, Claudius Gothicus, Quintillus. It is, however, a comparatively rare type on Roman coins.

On a denarius of a consular family, having for its legend of reverse *Lucius Hostilius Saserna*, Diana stands, with face to the front, holding in the left hand a lance, and in the right the horns of a stag rearing by her side.—See Hostilia gens.

On a denarius of the Axsia gens (see p. 117), the reverse presents Diana standing, armed with a javelin, in a car drawn by two stags; she is preceded by a dog, and followed by two others. —This denarius is attributed to Lucius Axius Naso, who was proscribed in the last civil war of the republic.

On a silver coin of the Cornelia gens, Diana appears standing in the Ephesian attitude and dress.—(Engraved in *Morell. Fam. Rom.* TAB. ii. No. 6).

The following are among the most remarkable reverses on which Diana is typified in the imperial series of Roman coins:—

DIANAE CONS. AVG. *Diana Conservatrix Augusti.* A stag.—This legend and type, with variations, frequently appears on coins of Gallienus, whose 'father Valerianus was singularly attached to the worship of Diana the Preserver, insomuch that he dedicated a temple to her honour at Rome, called *Ædes Valerianæ*.—A similar epigraph—DIANA CONS.—with the same symbol of the goddess of the chase, appears on a third brass of Carausius, who also professed greatly to honour the sylvan deity.

DIAN. EPHE. *Diana Ephesia.*—Diana of Ephesus.—This appears on a silver medallion of Claudius, struck in Asia. The goddess is represented in an elegant temple of four columns, not with tucked-up dress *(veste succinctâ)*, as the agile huntress, but with her Asiatic attributes of heavy head-dress, many-breasted bust *(poly-mammia)*, swaddling-clothed body, supported on each side with props, resembling tridents reversed, on which she rests each hand, just as she was worshipped by the Ephesians in St. Paul's time. The temple here delineated was obviously intended to associate the honour of Diana, with that once celebrated edifice at Ephesus, which took all Asia 220 years to build, and cost Herostratus, the incendiary, but a moment to fire and destroy.—See M. Dumersan's beautiful engraving of this medal, in the Allier d'Hauteroche collection, Pl. xiv. No. 18.

"The authors of antiquity are not agreed as to the order of the temple of Diana: Pliny asserting that it was *Attic*, whilst Vitruvius says it was *Ionic*. Again, the image of the goddess is said by Vitruvius to have been formed of cedar; and Xenophon describes it as of gold—discrepancies which may be reconciled by a reference to the description which Pausanias gives of many gilded statues. The words of Pliny shew that there was some doubt as to the material of which it was formed; but whatever that may have been, the figure was never changed, though the temple was restored seven times."—See *Numismatic Illustrations of the New Testament*, by J. Y. Akerman, F.S.A. p. 48.

DIANA EPHESIA.—Another silver medallion bears on its obverse TIberius CLAVDius CAESar AVGustus AGRIPPina AVGVSTA, and the jugated heads of Claudius and Agrippina.—On its reverse are the above legend, and the type of Diana of Ephesus.

The above engraving (for the loan of which the compiler is indebted to the kindness of Mr. Akerman), renders it unnecessary to give a minute description of the form under which Diana Ephesia was worshipped.

"The above medallion (says our eminent numismatic authority) appears to offer the best representation of this remarkable image, and is the more curious, as, in bearing the heads of Claudius and Agrippina, it proves itself to be nearly contemporaneous with the period of St. Paul's visit to Ephesus. These pieces were doubtless in circulation throughout all Asia Minor, and could be obtained by devotees at the shrine of the Ephesian goddess.

" It seems probable that the vulgar were not allowed to approach too near to this grotesque but time-honoured figure; and that the artists of antiquity sometimes drew on their fancies in their representations of her; for even in the coins of Ephesus the goddess is not always represented in precisely the same manner. The idol was preserved from decay by resinous gums, which were inserted in cavities made for that purpose."—*Ibid.* p. 49.

In commenting on that passage in Acts, xix. 27, wherein " the town clerk" speaks of " the temple of the great goddess Diana, whom all Asia and the world worshippeth," the writer above quoted observes, that " the singular archaic figure under which *Diana Ephesia* was worshipped, is not to be confounded with that of Diana the huntress, but is distinguished by her characteristic attributes as *nutrix* of all living things." *Ibid.* p. 47.

DIANA EPHESIA.—On a coin of Hadrian, struck at Ephesus, having the foregoing appellation on its reverse, the statue of the goddess stands between two stags. On another silver coin of the same emperor, having CONSVL III. for its legend of reverse, a similar type appears. Both these are engraved in *Nouvelle Galerie Mythol.* par M. Lenormant, p. 143, pl. xlix. Nos. 10 and 11.

DIANA LAPHRIA. C. P. *Colonia Patrensis.*—On colonial coins of Patræ, respectively dedicated to Nero and to Domitian, bearing the above legend, and of which Vaillant *(in Col.* i. 24), gives an engraving, Diana stands, clothed in a short dress, with a quiver at her shoulder, her right hand placed on the hip, and her left hand resting on a bow.—On small brass of M. Aurelius and of L. Verus, struck in the same colony, is the image of Diana Laphria, as *Venatrix,* in the attitude of walking quick, with a lighted torch in her right hand, a spear in her left, and a hound running before her. (Engraved in Vaillant, i. 199).—Laphria was a name given to Diana, in consequence of Laphrius, a Phœnician, having erected a statue to her honour in Calydon (Ætolia). With the name of this city is associated the legend of the wild boar, which was sent by Diana to ravage the surrounding district, and which Meleager killed, giving the head to Atalanta, of whom he was enamoured.—With the Patrenses she was an object of supreme adoration. According to Pausanias, when Ætolia was laid waste by Augustus, her image was removed from Calydon, and placed in a shrine at Patræ.

DIANA LUCIFERA. *Diana the bringer of light.*—On first and second brass of Faustina, and on gold of Julia Domna, bearing this legend of reverse, the image of the goddess stands, holding transversely, with both hands, a lighted torch.——Engraved in Spanheim's *Cæsars of Julian,* p. 45.

In exchanging the bow and arrow for the torch, allusion is here made to her other titles and qualities, as *Lucifera,* or as *Luna,* whose light being borrowed from the Sun, she was styled his sister.

On a denarius of the Claudia gens, Diana, in long clothing, but designated by the quiver at her back, stands holding in each hand a long torch planted on the ground.—See p. 210 of this dictionary.

On a bronze medallion of Antoninus Pius, Diana Lucifera is represented sitting with a torch in her hands, on a horse galloping to the right. And on a bronze medallion of Faustina junior, the *light-bringing* goddess appears veiled, holding a torch in the left hand, and sitting on a stag, accompanying the legend of AETERNITAS AVGVSTA.—Both these medallions are engraved in *Nouvelle Gal. Mythol.* p. 142, pl. xlix. Nos. 4 and 5.

DIANA PERG. *Diana Pergensis.*—A rare silver medallion of Nerva, bearing the date of COS. III. exhibits the foregoing legend on the front of a temple, in which stands an image of Diana of Perga.—" The inscription itself, as well as the form of this medal, show that it first saw light among the Pergenses of Pamphylia."—Eckhel, vi. 410.

The same legend and type appear on a silver medallion of Trajan (COS. II.) The city of Perga was a place peculiarly addicted to the worship of the *multi-mammian* Diana.

DIANAE REDUCI.—To the return of Diana—who, in appropriate dress as the huntress, leads a stag in her right hand, and holds a bow in her left.—Of this inscription and type, which appears on a silver coin of Postumus senior, Eckhel laconically remarks—" Novelty recommends it, but its cause is unknown."

Diana Venatrix.—This title is not used as a legend on any Roman coins; but it serves with numismatists to designate those types, in which Diana, in quality of huntress, appears with short habit, and the usual weapons and dogs of the chase, together with her favourite attribute, the stag. Of this class is the DIANA FELIX of Gallienus (in first brass), the accompanying type of which, as the annexed cut serves to shew, typifies the goddess in her *sport-*

ing dress, with bow in left hand, and right hand raised to head, as having just discharged an arrow. She is attended by a small stag.

On denarii of Augustus, the hunting Diana also appears.—See SICIL.

The reverse of a brass medallion of Antoninus exhibits the goddess in this character, and at the same time, with quiver on shoulder; behind her is a tree; before her a hind or stag.—Engraved in *Nouv. Gal. Mythol.* pl. 48, No. 10.

On another brass medallion of the same emperor, *Diana Venatrix*, leaving the bath, stands already re-clothed with a short tunic, and is covering herself with other drapery. Actæon, already metamorphosed into a stag, is in front of her, and a dog is rushing upon the indiscreet hunter.—Engraved in *Nouvelle Gal. Mythol.* pl. xlix. No. 4, p. 143.

On a second brass, struck by the Roman colony of Corinth, the goddess stands with a bow in her extended left hand, whilst the right is raised in the attitude of drawing an arrow from her quiver. At her side is a stag.—Engraved in Vaillant, ii.—*Corinth, Geta.*

DIANAE VICTRICI.—*To Diana the Victorious.*—Diana standing with bow and arrow. This legend, which first occurs on silver of Trebonianus Gallus, is also seen on coins (gold as well as silver) of Aemilianus.—"It is probable (says Eckhel), that in the common calamities of those times, it was out of respect to Apollo that his sister was joined with him. Otherwise, it would appear (from a coin of Trebonianus, dedicated APOL*lini* CONSERVAT*ori*), that in the celebration of the secular games, for the safety of the empire, the principal honours were customarily paid to Apollo and Diana." vii. 372.

DIC. Dictator.—DIC. III. Dictator for the third time.

DICT. ITER*um.* Dictator for the second time.—DIC. QVART. for the fourth time.

DICT. PERP. *Dictator Perpetuus.*—Perpetual Dictator.

DICTATOR. A magistrate extraordinary, appointed by the Romans only under circumstances of alleged public and pressing necessity. He was originally called *Magister Populi,* and also *Prætor Maximus;* afterwards Dictator, because (Dictus) named by the consul for the time, or because the people implicitly obeyed his commands. The first Dictator created at Rome was T. Lartius Flavus, in the year U.C. 253 (B.C. 501). He, being then one of the consuls, was nominated to this office, under an expectation of war with the Sabines and Latins. The consuls, at that time of emergency, being found unable to make levies among the plebeians, who had refused to enlist without a remission of their debts by the patricians, the Senate elected this officer, whom they invested with absolute and unbounded authority. The dictature was for a time confined to the patricians, but the plebeians were afterwards admitted to share in it. The dictator remained in power for six months, after which he was again elected, if the state of affairs seemed desperate; otherwise he generally resigned before the allotted period had expired.

The dictatorship was on a par with even regal dignity, and armed with more than regal power, yet, unlike royalty, it was not held in hatred by the people. Amongst the insignia which distinguished this supreme and unusual

functionary, were the purple robe, the curule chair, caparisoned horses, and 20 lictors, bearing the fasces with axes. The decision of peace and war resided with him; and the fortunes and lives of soldiers, citizens, and magistrates were alike subject to his absolute government. During the dictature, the authority of all the other magistrates ceased, except that of the tribunes of the *plebs;* nor was any appeal allowed from the sentence, or judgment, of the dictator, until U. C. 303 (B. C. 451), when the *lex Duillia* was passed, which provided that, thenceforward, no magistrate should be appointed, without his public acts being open to be appealed against before the people. This office so potent, so dignified, in the earlier periods of the republic, became at length odious to the Romans, from the despotic usurpations of Sulla, and of Julius Cæsar; the former to glut the cruelty of his personal vengeance; and the latter to compass the schemes of his own boundless ambition.

When Cæsar, therefore, not daring to assume the titles of *Rex,* and *Dominus,* accepted that of *Imperator* (see p. 155), he was not long in becoming *Dictator;* and in a short time afterwards *Perpetual Dictator.* That is to say, he received the dictature U. C. 705 (B. C. 49), M. Æmilius Lepidus (afterwards the triumvir) being pretor at the time, convened the people, and procured that all-superseding power for Cæsar, then absent from Rome, but who, quickly arriving there, entered upon the office; and having accomplished his object in taking it, laid down the name of dictator, retaining, however, not an atom less than all the authority of one. From that period we read on a chronological series of his coins—CAES. DIC.—next DIC. ITER. then DIC. TER.—But why *Dictator Tertium ?*—"Without doubt (says Schlegel, *ad Morell.)* he was named for the third time by the consul Lepidus, U. C. 709 (B. C. 45), after he had entered Rome in triumph, as conqueror from Africa." In like manner we read DIC. QVART. *Dictator Quartum,* because for the fourth time that office was offered to him, about 710 (B. C. 44), in which year he entered the city from Mount Albano, with the honours of an ovation. And it was during the same fourth dictatorship, that Cæsar obtained from the Senate the right in perpetuity of wearing the laurel crown, according to Appianus and Dion; the latter of whom thus pursues the subject:—"In this year, the fourth dictatorship (*quarta dictatura)* was decreed to him, not merely for so long as the state of public affairs required, but for the term of his natural life, to govern and administer with dictatorial power." Thus on gold and silver coins, struck by his moneyers, L. Buca, and C. Maridianus, we find him called DIC. PERPETVO CAESAR, and DICT. IN PERPETVO CAESAR, on others, DICT. IN PERPETVVM.—See Mintages of Cæsar, pp. 155, 156, and 157 of this dictionary.

And this office the Great Julius held to the day of his death; after which Mark Antony, as consul, obtained the passing of a law, which expressly and permanently abolished both the name and functions of this powerful, but at length, to the public liberties, fatally dangerous, magistracy.

DECIMIA.—A plebeian family, of which there is only the following denarius :—

Obv.—Galeated head of Rome, to the right; behind it X.—*Rev.*—FLAVVS. Diana with the crescent moon on her head, driving a biga at full speed ; below ROMA.

"This coin (says Riccio, p. 79), has for a long time been ascribed to the Flavia family; but the learned Borghesi has assigned it to the Decimia gens, and properly to Caius Decimius Flavus, pretor in U. c. 570 (B. c. 184), coeval with P. Cornelius Silla, who was in the magistracy, a little after the government of Sillanus. Modern lovers of antiquity have concurred in opinion with Borghesi."—[Neither by Morel nor by Mionnet is this name included among the Roman families].

DIDIA gens, of the plebeian order.—Three varieties in silver, rare.—The following denarius has given rise to a controversy amongst the learned, which, as Eckhel observes, " is of long standing, and, as it seems, continues undecided."

1. *Obv.*—Head of Rome, to the right, below X, behind ROMA.—*Rev.*—T. DEIDI. A soldier with a spear (or sword) is feebly contending against another military man, who has a sword girded to his right side, but is brandishing a whip, or vine switch, upraised in his right hand. Each is armed with a buckler on the left arm.

[This silver coin was, according to Eckhel, restored by Trajan, and is of the highest degree of rarity].

Some writers have supposed that the infliction of military punishment, or at least the castigation of some deserter from his post in the day of battle, is meant to be indicated in the above type. Others treat it only as a combat between two men, whose offensive weapons, however, are very different from each other. In the latter case, *he* of the *flagellum* has evidently the advantage over *him* of the *hasta.*

Riccio, in his remarks on the Didia gens, says (p. 80)—" Most antiquaries join in attributing this coin to Titus Didius, son of Titus, and nephew of Sprenius, who having been sent as pretor into Illyrium, in the year of Rome 640 (B. c. 114), found the affairs of that Roman province in a most perilous state; for the Thracians, and a ferocious people called *Scordisci,* had put the consul Porcius Cato to flight. On investigating the causes of this disaster, Didius discovered that the army had conducted itself in a base and cowardly manner, and no longer sustained the rigor of military discipline with becoming endurance or obedience. Wishing therefore to correct such great disorders, he

caused an allusion to be made to the circumstance on this coin, which represents a centurion inflicting corporal punishment on an undisciplined soldier.—Among modern Archæologists of eminence, P. Cavedoni, concurring with the the above explanation, says—" It is clear, that in the type of this medal, it is the centurion who punishes a soldier with the vine twig divided into two twists, or lashes. In fact, the army having been re-organised by Didius, and brought again under the regulations of true military subordination and exactitude, he attacked the enemy, defeated them, and obtained for his victory the honours of a triumph. Perhaps he caused these denarii to be minted, and distributed as donatives, that should remind the Roman army, that the foe was to be beaten only by the observance of perfect discipline, and by threats of punishment carried into effect against unbridled and refractory soldiers. If in that epoch, and under those circumstances, this coin was struck, its date is to be carried back to the 640th year of Rome (B. c. 114), the year in which Didius triumphed for his successes over the Scordisci." *Le Monete delle Famiglie di Roma,* p. 80.

2. Another and a much rarer denarius of the Didia family has on the obverse P. FONTEIVS CAPITO. IIIVIR. CONCORDIA ; with the veiled head of Concord. Whilst the reverse is inscribed T. DIDI. IMP. VIL. PVB. the type exhibiting a grand portico formed of two tiers of columns.

Of the VIL*la* PVB*lica* alluded to in the above legend, Varro explains the use, by comparing it with the *Villa Reatina* (so called from *Reate,* a very ancient town of the Sabines, *now* Ricti). " The former (viz. the *publica*) was the place into which the citizens went from the field (*à campo*) ; the latter that into which were put horses and asses (of which latter animal Reate was famous for a valuable breed). The villa publica was moreover useful for purposes of public business ; as a place where the cohorts might take up their quarters, when called together by the consul, where the show of arms was made; also where the censors might admit the people to citizenship by the census. Another use for these *villæ publicæ,* erected *extra urbem,* was to receive such ambassadors from hostile states as it was not deemed expedient to introduce into the city. This is referred to by Livy (lxxxiii. c. 9)—' The Macedonians were conducted out of the city to the villa publica, where accommodation and provisions were afforded them.' "—Eckhel, v. 201.

The reason of this type of the portico being struck is uncertain. " Perhaps (says Riccio, p. 80), on the occasion of some civic office held by Didius subsequent to 660 (B. C. 94), he caused to be built, or restored, the above mentioned edifice. He is called on this numismatic monument IMP*erator*, a title which he obtained after his mission into Northern Spain, which ascends to that epocha, and in which he defeated the Celtiberians, and received triumphal honours on that account."

Sallust, quoted by Gellius (L. 11, c. 27), thus alludes to T*itus* DIDI*us* IMP*erator* :—" *Magna gloria tribunus militum in Hispania T. Didio imperatore.*"—He [Sertorius] gained great credit as military tribune, T. Didius being general in chief.

DIDIA CLARA, daughter of the Emperor Didius Julianus, and of Manlia Scantilla. She is described to have been the most beautiful of the young women of her age; in which case her medallic portraits, especially those in brass, do her no justice.—She was born about the year of Rome 906 (A. D. 153). Married to Cornelius Repentinus, who was appointed Prefectus Urbis, in the room of Flavius Sulpicianus, she was, at the accession of her father, named *Augusta*, together with her mother, by the Senate; and was deprived of both title and rank after Julian's death. Coins were struck as a record of the high but short-lived honours conferred upon her. They are all of the highest rarity.— A gold specimen, of the usual module, brought £13 5s. at the Thomas sale.—Silver (see the above cut), antique but plated, brought £5 7s. 6d. at the same sale. Mionnet values a solid silver specimen at 210 fr.—First brass, £2 at the Thomas sale.—On the obverse of each she is styled DIDIA CLARA AVG.—The reverse has for legend HILAR. TEMP. *(Hilaritas Temporum)*. A woman standing, holds a palm branch, &c.

DII. *Divinitie*s. (See DEUS).—The Romans, generally speaking, reckoned two classes of the gods, the *dii majorum gentium*, or *dii consentes*, and the *dii minorum gentium*, or *dii selecti*.— The names and typifications of the following appear on Roman coins :—

Dii Consentes—These formed the council of the gods, and especially of Jupiter, under whose supremacy, *quasi erant consentientes.* They were also called celestial and great divinities.-- They were twelve in number, comprised in the following distich of Ennius :—

Juno, Vesta, Minerva, Ceres, Diana, Venus, Mars, Mercurius, Jovis, Neptunus, Vulcanus, Apollo.

Dii Selecti.—These were eight in number, associated with the *Consentes*, and classed with the great divinities. They were also called *Populares*, and their respective names were Janus, Saturnus, Cybèle, Rhea, Pluto, Sol (or Apollo), Liber Pater (or Bacchus), Luna.

Dii Indigetes.—These were the heroes whose rare merit had raised them, after death, in pagan credence to the rank of gods, and who were regarded as the patron deities of their country. See DII PATRII.

Dii Genitales. (See DIS GENITALIBUS).—The same, according to some, as the *Indigetes*; or, according to others, they were those who were believed to be the parents and procreators of all things, both animate and inanimate. To these deities of universal production Ausonius alludes (in *Periochæ*, L. iv.) :—

Juppiter in terra cum *Dis Genitalibus* una
Concilium cogit superum de rebus Achivis.

Dii Marini. Sea Deities.—These were subordinate to the *Consentes* and *Selecti.* Some were represented under the figure of old men with white beards, in allusion to the froth of the sea; others as young men, and as females, but terminaitng in the form of a fish.—See TRITON, NEREID, &c.

Dii Nuptiales.—Plutarch counts three of these, viz. Juno, Diana (or Lucina), and Venus. Vows were made to these nuptial goddesses to propitiate their favours, in rendering marriages happy.—See DIS CONJUGALIBUS.

Dii Penates. Household gods.—These divinities were brought to Rome from Lanuvium, and were also worshipped in Sicily. They are seen with their heads jugated, on coins of Roman families.—See PENATES.

Dii Semones or *Semi Dii.*—Half gods and half men. These were a class of divinities to whom, says Lipsius, the heavens were not given for a dwelling-place, because they were not found sufficiently deserving of it, and who were yet too much the objects of veneration to be left on earth amongst the number of mortals. Some of these demi-gods, however, are found to have inhabited the earth, and to have differed from mankind only in their being immortal.—See DIOSCURI (Castor and Pollux)—also see HERCULES—AESCULAPIUS, &c.

Dii Superi and *Dii Inferi.*—The gods of the celestial differed from those of the infernal regions, in the number of their altars, and in the manner of their sacrifices. The *Consentes* and *Selecti* above named, belonged to the celestial deities or *Dii Superi*—Pluto and Proserpine were *Inferi*, inhabiting the *shades*, and regarded as implacable; death being as " a necessary end" imposed on all men.

Dii Custodes, the preservers—amongst whom the goddess *Fortuna* was a particular object of ancient worship.—See DIS CUSTODIBUS.

There was a kind of solemn flattery amongst the Roman people, whereby they assigned to the emperors and their wives the figures and titles peculiar to the deities whom they worshipped. Hence on coins and other monuments, relating to Augustus, Antoninus Pius, Commodus, and others, it is common to see such inscriptions as the following:—APOLLINI AVGVSTO—IOVI AVGVSTO—HERCVLI ROMANO AVGVSTO—HERCVLI COMMODIANO.—In like manner, IOVIVS DIOCLETIANVS, in the case of Diocletian; and HERCVLIVS MAXIMIANVS, in that of Maximianus.—On coins of the imperial series we also frequently see the words IVNO, or CERES, or VENVS AVGVSTA, with the dress and attributes of those goddesses, but with the respective effigies of the *Augustæ* themselves.

DII NVTRITORES.—Jupiter standing, holds in his left hand the hasta, and with his right extended offers a Victory to the emperor.—For an engraving of this reverse see SALONINVS.

Respecting the above legend, which appears on silver and small brass coins of Saloninus Cæsar, son of Gallienus and of Salonina, the following remarks are made by Eckhel:—"We see *Deos Genitales*, in Crispina; *Auspices*, in S. Severus; *Patrios*, in Caracalla and Geta. But until this time (A. D. 253 to 259), of Saloninus, we meet with no mention of DII NVTRITORES (the fostering, rearing, educating gods). Libanus calls them δεους κουροτροφους.—Tristan makes out the figure standing opposite Jupiter to be intended for Gallienus himself, and affirms that the latter, together with Jove, is the god and bringer up (*nutritor*) of his son. This I believe to be the meaning, because the epigraph proclaims more deities than one, and therefore would not be correct, unless it had also embraced within the scope of its meaning the other figure. There is no doubt of this being the true interpretation; for from the head of the figure joining hands with Jupiter, being crowned with laurel, which Saloninus never wore so long as he was Cæsar, it clearly must be the Emperor Gallienus."—*D. N. Vet.* vii. p. 421.

DII or DI PATRI.—This epigraph, with the type of Hercules and Bacchus standing, each with their respective attributes, appears on a rare gold coin of Caracalla (engraved in Caylus, No. 740), and on second brass of Geta.

The *Dii Patrii* were the gods of a man's ancestors, family, and country. They presided over the pious affections of parents towards their children, and of children towards their parents. "Dii Patrii servate domum, servate nepotem," as Virgil expresses it.—Eckhel (vii. 205–220), observes, that the same deities, standing thus together, on coins of S. Severus, are called DII AVSPICES; but in Caracalla and Geta they are designated as DII PATRII; whence it is evident, that the two princes professed this worship (of Hercules and Bacchus) hereditarily from their father."—See the same type engraved in DIS AVSPICIBVS.

DIOCLETIANUS (*Caius Valerianus*), at first named *Dioclès*, a native of Dioclea, in Dalmatia, the town from which he took his surname.—Born A. D 254, of an obscure family, that circumstance did not, when he had obtained the empire, deter him from pretending to have descended from Claudius Gothicus. He had become an able general, and commanded the legions in Mæsia, under Probus. Having risen to the highest military dignities, he followed Carus, in that emperor's Persian campaign, A.D. 283; and was made *consul suffectus*, the same year. After the death of Carus, he was of the number of those who attached themselves to

Numerianus. In 284 he was declared Augustus, at Chalcedon, by the army of the East, after the assassination of Numerianus; and he slew with his own hand Arrius Aper, prefect of the pretorians, who had taken part in the murder of that good young prince, which happened the following year. In possession of the purple, he immediately created Maximianus Cæsar; and towards the close of the year, set out for the East. [Here commences the celebrated æra of Diocletian, also called the *æra of Martyrs*].—The same year he prepared to wage war against Carinus.—A. D. 285, Diocletian was consul for the second time; same year he gave battle to Carinus, near Widdin, in Bulgaria (Viminacium, in Upper Mæsia). At the first encounter, Diocletian had the worst of it; but Carinus having been killed by his own people, Diocletian gained a victory, thus become easy, and found himself sole master of the Roman world.—In 286 of our æra, being at Nicomedia, in Bythinia, he proclaimed as Augustus, and associated with himself in the empire, Maximianus, afterwards surnamed Herculius, to whom he assigned the government of the Western provinces, reserving for himself the administration of affairs in the East. The new Augustus entered actively upon his duties, by proceeding into Gaul, and suppressing an insurrection raised there by Ælianus and Amandus.—Diocletian served the consulate for the third time, 287. Maximianus defeated the Germans, who had invaded Gaul, and drove them back beyond the Danube (288).

After vain efforts made against Carausius, who had proclaimed himself Emperor in Britain, the two Augusti gave up that island to the successful usurper. In 290, Diocletian served his fourth consulship. In 291, he regulated affairs in those provinces of the empire which he had retained to himself. In addition to the old dangers of barbarian incursions, new perils had begun to manifest themselves—namely, in the East, on the part of the Persians; in Africa, on the part of the Mauritanians, called *Quinquegentani*; in Egypt, from a pretender to the purple named Achilleus: Diocletian, therefore, being at Nicomedia, March 1, A. D. 292, declared Cæsars Constantius Chlorus and Galerius Maximianus, and decided that he, *Diocletianus Jovius*, should govern the East, and that his colleague *Maximianus Herculius* should govern Italy, Africa, and the Isles, whilst Thrace and Illyria were assigned to Galerius, and the Gallic provinces, together with Britain, Spain, and Mauritania, to Constantius Chlorus. In 293, Diocletian was consul for the fifth time, and the following year served his sixth consulate.— Carausius assassinated, A. D. 296, and Allectus slain, the province of Britain returned under the yoke of the emperors. In 297, Diocletian sent Galerius against Narses, King of the Persians, who was at first victorious, but the war ended triumphantly for Galerius. The seventh and eighth consulates of Diocletian took place in 298 and 303. At the commencement of the latter year, at the instigation of Galerius, Diocletian ordered at Nicomedia a persecution against the Christians. Soon afterwards he departed for Rome, where he and Maximianus Herculius jointly enjoyed the honours of a triumph for victories over the enemy gained since their accession to the empire.—A. D. 304, Diocletian, consul for the ninth time, returned to Nicomedia, disordered in body and wretched in mind. In 305, advised or compelled by Galerius Maximian, Diocletian, enfeebled perhaps by sickness, and tired of power and its increasing anxieties, abdicated the government, at Nicomedia. The same day, following his senior colleague's example, Maximianus Herculius laid down the purple at Milan. Galerius and Constantius Chlorus were declared *Augusti;* Severus and Maximinus Daza, Cæsars. Diocletian retired as a private individual to Salona, in Dalmatia, the province in which he was born. He retained the title of Augustus, and the honours attached to that title. But, solely to distinguish him from the emperors in actual government, he was thenceforward called on coins *Beatissimus,* or *Felicissimus senior Augustus.*—Diocletian died A. D. 313, during the reign of Constantine the Great. He had been married, but his wife's name remains unknown; whoever she was, he had by her a daughter, Galeria Valeria, the wife of Galerius Maximianus.

As emperor, Diocletian exhibited in his administrative capacity the skill and courage of a great commander, combined with abilities of the highest order for civil government. Introducing as he did a most comprehensive and important change in the political system of the empire, his object was evidently not so much to gratify his own love of imperial splendour, as to "hedge round" his person, and the persons of his associates and successors in power, with a barrier of superstitious as well as of real protection against insurrectionary violence and pretorian treachery. But his plans, however well concerted, and energetically carried into effect, being founded on the necessity of pressing emergencies, scarcely remained in effective operation during his own life-time, and at his death fell to pieces amidst the sanguinary struggles of rival Emperors and Cæsars. Still, to his statesmanlike sagacity and military talent, the events of his reign pay this tribute, as expressed in the language of a living biographer [Smith's *Dictionary,* i. 1014]:—" He found the empire weak and shattered, threatened with immediate dissolution from intestine discord and external

violence. He left it strong and compact, at peace within, and triumphant abroad, stretching from the Tigris to the Nile, from the shores of Holland to the Euxine."—But these great qualities of a wise and usually discreet prince, were obscured by great defects, and tarnished by enormous wickedness. From the rank of a private soldier, arrived at the summit of worldly dignity, Diocletian, either following the bent of his own injustice and inhumanity, or yielding with equal culpability to the influence of his colleagues, after a twenty years reign of glory, and only two years before his abdication, committed himself to the promulgation of decrees against the Christians, which long continued to arm the hands of the blood-thirsty against the lives of the innocent, and have associated his memory ignominiously with all the atrocities of a most cruel persecution.

MINTAGES OF DIOCLETIANUS.

On his coins Diocletian is styled IMP. CAIVS VALERIVS DIOCLETIANVS P. F. AVG.— Also D*ominus* N*oster* DIOCLETIANVS P. F. SEN*ior* AVG.—The silver of this emperor are rare; the gold very rare; the brass (second and third) common, except some medallions, which are very rare.—Diocletian was surnamed *Jovius,* as his colleague Maximian was called *Herculius;* either on account of a peculiar worship, in which Diocletian invoked Jupiter, and Maximian the powerful Hercules, against the poor defenceless Christians; or because it was meant to be expressed that Diocletian by his wisdom in council, and Maximian by his valour in the field, had preserved the state.

The following are amongst the rarest reverses in each metal:—

GOLD MEDALLIONS.—The two Emperors, crowned by Victory, standing in a car drawn by four elephants. (Valued by Mionnet at 600 fr.) *Obv.*—Busts of Diocletian and Maximian holding the eagle.—*Rev.*—IOVI ET HERCVLIO.—Diocletian and Maximian standing, are in the act of performing sacrifice; above them, on a small platform, stand Jupiter and Hercules.—The obverse presents the laureated heads of the two emperors facing each other.—This beautiful coin is engraved in Mionnet (ii. p. 141), by whom it is valued at 480 fr.

SILVER MEDALLIONS.—With laureated head and cuirassed bust of Diocletian on one side, and the laureated head of Maximian on the other.

GOLD.—COMITATVS AVGG.—FATIS VICTRICIBVS.—VIRTVS ILLYRICI. (Valued by Mionnet at 150 fr. each).—ADVENTVS AVGVSTORVM. (200 fr.)—CONCORDIAE AVGG. N. N.—PRIMIS X. MVLTIS XX.—PROVIDENTIA AVG. Pretorian camp. —VOTIS ROMANORVM.—XX. DIOCLETIANI AVG. (80 fr. each).—IOVI FVLGERATORI. Jupiter striking a Titan. (£2 2s. Borrell—£2 12s. 6d. Trattle).—CONSVL VI. P. P. PROCOS. The Emperor holding globe and parazonium. (An extremely fine specimen brought £14 14s. at the Borrell sale).—ROMAE AETERNAE. (£4 4s. at the Campana sale).

SILVER.—VICTORIA AVG. Pretorian camp.

(80 fr.)—*Obv.*—DIOCLETIANVS AVG. Laureated head of Diocletian.——*Rev.*—VIRTVS MILITVM. Four soldiers sacrificing before the gate of the pretorian camp (as in the cut subjoined) :—

BRASS MEDALLIONS.—Diocletian and Maximian. Busts facing each other.—*Rev.*—The two Emperors in a triumphal car drawn by four elephants; behind is a Victory crowning them; eight pretorian soldiers accompany them carrying palms.—[This medallion is finely engraved in *Iconographie des Empereurs*, par M. Lenormant].—MONETA IOVI ET HERCVLI AVGG. The goddess Moneta standing between Jupiter and Hercules.—[The obverse of this medallion has for its legend IMP. C. C. VAL. DIOCLETIANVS AVG. and for its type the Emperor laureated, and richly cuirassed, carrying a barbed javelin on his shoulder. For an accurate engraving of this fine bust, from a specimen in the highest state of preservation, see the head of our biographical notice. An engraving of the reverse will be found under the head of MONETA, &c.—Mionnet values the above at 120 fr.; another with the same reverse, but with the heads of both emperors on the obverse, he values at 200 fr.]—IOVI CONSERVATORI AVG. Jupiter in a six columned temple.—HERCVLIO MAXIMIANO AVG. ROM. (150 fr. each).—PROVIDENTIA DEOR(VM) QVIES AVG.—VOTA PVBLICA. Serapis. (120 fr. each).

SECOND BRASS.—CONSERVATORES AVGG.—Jupiter and Hercules; with the heads, face to face, of Diocletian and Maximian on the obverse. (Mionnet, 50 fr.)

DIOSCURI.—A name which signifies *sons of Jupiter*, and which was given in common to Castor and Pollux, who were also sometimes called *Tyndarides*, because their mother, Leda, was the wife of Tyndarus, King of Sparta.—There were festivals in their honour, celebrated by the people of Corcyra (Corfu), and chiefly by the Lacedemonians.—In Rome, their festival was celebrated on the 28th of January (Ovid, *Fasti,* i. 705), on which day Tiberius consecrated to them a temple, near the *lacus Juturnæ.*—According to Morel *(Fam. Rom.)* the worship of the *Dioscuri,* as divinities, had its origin at Rome, from the victory which the consul Postumius gained, near the Lake Regillus, over the Latins and the sons of Tarquinius Superbus (B.C. 493 or 496.)

It was said that, after that engagement, the *Dioscuri* appeared in the forum of Rome, wearing conical bonnets, over each of which was a star. They stood resting upon their lances, beside their horses, which were drinking at a fountain. These twin heroes disappeared as soon as they had announced the news of the battle,

at a moment when, on account of the distance of that city from the scene of slaughter, no one could as yet have become acquainted with the event. It is also related that, during the action, two young men, mounted on two white horses, were seen fighting valiantly for the Romans.—This legend is alluded to in the type of a consular denarius.—See POSTUMIA gens.

It also forms the subject of one of the most spirit-stirring poems in Mr. Macaulay's "Lays of Ancient Rome," under the title of "*the Battle of the Lake Regillus,* as sung at the Feast of Castor and Pollux, on the ides of Quintilis, in the year of the city CCCCLI." (B. C. 303).—This characteristic tradition of supernatural powers crowning with victory the arms of the yet young republic, is, by the author's genius and his conversance with classic lore, filled to overflowing with warlike incident, and with patriotic animation. After proclaiming to a great throng of people,

> This day by lake Regillus,
>   Under the Porcian height,
> All in the lands of Tusculum,
>   Was fought a glorious fight,

the two strange horsemen, recognised by their pointed caps, and the stars above them, as the "Great Twin Brethren, to whom the Dorians pray,"

> When they drew nigh to Vesta,
>   They vaulted down amain,
> And wash'd their horses in the well
>   That springs by Vesta's fane.
> And straight again they mounted,
>   And rode to Vesta's door,
> Then like a blast, away they past,
>   And no man saw them more.   (p. 137.)

On a denarius of the Sulpicia gens, struck in memory of L. SERVIVS RVFVS (son of Servius Sulpicius Rufus, a friend of Cicero's), the Dioscuri are represented as two naked men, galeated, standing together, front faced, armed with spears, which they hold transversely, as in the above engraving. On another denarius, they stand holding their spears, with a horse on each side of them, and a star over each of their heads.—See MEMMIA gens.

The Dioscuri most frequently appear, on family coins, as horsemen galloping, with couched lances, and stars above their *pilei.*—See Atilia (p. 93); Horatia (p. 316); Cordia, conjoined heads of twin brothers (p. 280); the same in Fonteia; Servilia (on horseback, proceeding in opposite directions), and many other consular denarii.

In the imperial series, this type (which was meant to denote brotherly concord), is of rare occurrence. On a brass medallion of M. Aurelius, and a second brass of Geta, one of the

Dioscuri, holding a spear, stands beside his horse.—See CASTOR (p. 190).

On a brass medallion of Maxentius (valued by Mionnet at 100 fr.) they stand each with the *pileus* on his head, and the *pallium* hanging behind his back, holding his spear with one hand and his horse's bridle with the other. There is a second brass of the same reign and type, the legend being on both AETERNITAS AVG. N.

Dioscurorum stellæ.—The stars placed over the caps of Leda's sons, have, on ancient coins, a symbolical reference to maritime cities— (Wilde, *num. sel.* 50), and also to the constellation of Castor and Pollux; those twin stars (Gemini) serving as a guide to mariners.— (Horat. Ep. ii. 1–5).—See *Pilei:* also *Stella.*

DIRIBITOR (so called *à diribendo*, to distribute), an officer who, at the Roman elections, marshalled the tribes into their several classes, and distributed the tablets *(tabellæ)* among the people when they voted. Such a functionary of the republic is represented on a family denarius inscribed P. NERVA, the type of which also exhibits the inclosure of the *Comitia.*—See SILIA gens; also CLOACIN (p. 220).

DIS AVSPICIBus TRibunicia Potestate II. COnSul II. Pater Patriæ.—Two male figures stand together undraped. The one is that of Hercules, with the spoils of the Nemæan lion hanging on his left arm, and his right hand resting on the club. The other is that of Bacchus, who holds the *cantharus* in his right hand, and rests his left on the *thyrsus:* a panther sits at his feet.—On gold, silver, and brass of S. Severus, struck about A. D. 194.

The title of *Dii Auspices* (the gods-protectors), was given to the deities in general, and to each of them in particular, thus indicating acknowledgment of their special protection; and sacrifices were offered to them accordingly.— This legend and type "serve (says Eckhel, vii. 171) completely to prove what Dion states, that Severus caused a grand temple to be built in honour of Bacchus and Hercules, and they also shew the peculiar name by which those deities were called by that emperor;" and whose respective images frequently occur on his coins.

The author of *Leçons Numismatiques Romaines*, describes as in his collection a very rare brass medallion, having on the obverse L. SEPTIMIVS SEVERVS PERTINAX AVG. IMP. III. with the laurelled bust of Severus. The emperor, he remarks, in carrying the war into the East against Pescennius Niger, affected to choose for

his *patrons*, Bacchus and Hercules, whom ancient traditions had designated as the first conquerors of that region. The same divinities, on coins of his sons Caracalla and Geta, are called DII PATRII.—(See p. 329).

DIS CONIVGALIBVS.—A round altar, ornamented with a festoon, and lighted.—On gold of Crispina.

Mionnet appears to have been the first to describe this remarkable and extremely rare *aureus;* and he has given an engraving of it in his *Rareté des Médailles Romaines* (T. i. p. 267). The legend of reverse occurs only in this instance throughout the imperial series.— Tacitus alludes to deities presiding over the state of marriage *(hos conjugales deos arbitrantur).* And it may be presumed that they were identified with the *Dii Nuptiales* (see p. 328), to whom vows were made to propitiate their favour towards the matrimonial relations of their votaries. That the beautiful Crispina, "more sinned against than sinning," as the wife of Commodus, was, before that profligate tyrant divorced her, a worshipper of one at least of the nuptial tutelaries, is shewn by her adoption of VENVS, and VENVS FELIX, on the reverses of her coins. It is no less evident, that she had dedicated an altar to the *dii conjugales*, as well as, in broader terms, to the *dii genitales*, in the hope that her union in wedlock to the emperor might be blessed with fecundity.—Mionnet values this coin at 300 fr.

DIS CVSTODIBVS.—A woman standing, with the helm of a ship in her right hand, and a cornucopiæ in her left.—On silver and first brass of Pertinax.—The latter engraved from in Dr. King's plates, and in Spanheim's Cæsars of Julian, p. 91.

This reverse presents the figure of *Fortuna;* and as there were many different forms of worship paid by the Romans to Fortune, and under various appellations of that deity, which are copiously detailed by Plutarch *(de Fort. Rom.)* so on this coin they are all indicated under the title of *dii custodes* (the guardian gods), to whom, on his accession to the empire, Pertinax here commends his safety. *(D. N. V.* vol. vii. 141).* With the ancients, Fortune had the chief place amongst those genii, who watched over and preserved mankind. The *Fortuna aurea*, or golden image of Fortune, was worshipped in the bed-chamber of the emperor; and, together with the empire itself, was handed down to his successor.

DIS GENITALIBVS.—A square altar, on which appears a flame.—Silver of Crispina. Engraved in Vaillant, *Num. Præst.* ii. 192.

From this imperial denarius it would seem, that the empress had dedicated an altar to the *dii genitales*, either for having had children, or that she might obtain fertility from them, or that she might commend the child, with which she was pregnant, to their care and protection. "Genitalis (says Eckhel, vii. 139), or in the neuter gender, *genitale*, is that which possesses, or imparts, the faculty of generating."

DIS GENITORIBVS.—Cybèle standing before a tripod ; on the other side of which is a small figure seated on a globe.—On a rare first brass of Pertinax.

This good old man who, at the commencement of his brief reign, A. D. 193, had commended himself to his guardian deities (DIS CVSTODIBVS), now dedicates a coin, DIS GENITORIBVS, that is, to the generative or creative divinities, from whom he selects one for his type, viz. Cybèle, the most ancient of them, commonly called MATER DEVM, the mother of the gods.——" The youth (Eckhel slyly observes), standing by her side, will no doubt be of the number of those, in relation to whom she had acquired the title of *Genetrix*." (vii. 141.)

DISCIPLINA AVG. S. C.   The discipline of the Emperor.—On a first brass (and also on gold) of Hadrian, whom the type represents marching, bare-headed, with his military cloak drawn round him, and a baton, or a *volumen*, held in his left hand, followed by the pretorian prefect, and by three soldiers, bearing a legionary eagle and two military ensigns.—On other coins (see Vaillant) the legend is DISCIPVLINA AVG.

Although Hadrian carried on no wars in person, and was desirous of peace rather than of war, yet he exercised his troops as though hostilities were immediately impending. For the proper explanation of this reverse, reference should be had to Spartianus (Hadrian, ch. 10), who says—" This prince trained the soldier as regularly as if on actual service, with lessons of patience, ... accustoming him to the food of the camp, in the open air, that is to say, cheese, bacon, and weak sour wine, in imitation of the practice of Æmilianus, Metellus, and his own model, Trajan ; rewarding many with money, and some with honours, to enable them to bear the more willingly his rigorous commands ; indeed, he restored the discipline, which through carelessness of preceding emperors had become relaxed from the time of Cæsar Octavius. ...... Encouraging, by the example of his own energies, the conduct of others, he used to march twenty miles [a day] on foot, in full armour ; banished from the camp all such luxuries as the *triclinia*, the porticoes, the cloisters, and the arbours ; frequently wore the commonest attire, a sword-belt unadorned with gold ; removed everything of an enervating tendency, and reformed the arms and baggage of the soldiers, &c."—Dion also speaks in the same strain (lxix. § 9), adding, that all the soldiers were so thoroughly drilled and instructed by Hadrian, that

the regulations then introduced remained to his own day, as an integral part of Roman military discipline.—Victor, too, says (in *Epit.)*—" He reduced the offices of state, of the household, and also of the army, to the form in which they remain to the present day, with the exception of a few alterations made by Constantine."— See Eckhel, vi. 503.

Among the inscriptions found on the line of Hadrian's wall, in Britain, is one reading DISCIPVLINAE AVG. *(sic.)*, which Mr. Roach Smith, comparing with coins, considers to refer to Hadrian.—*Collect. Antiq.* vol. ii. p. 175.

DIVA.—With this title a deceased Augusta, or Empress, was distinguished on Roman coins, after the ceremony of consecration. On medals struck in memory of Empresses, or ladies of the imperial family, received into the rank of female deities *(inter divas relata)*, the back part of the head is found covered with a drapery, as tho' in token of divinity.—See *Consecratio.*

DIVA AUGUSTA.—A woman dressed in the stola or long robe, holding a *patera* and *hasta*. The above appears on gold, silver, and brass of Galba, who was greatly indebted to Livia, the wife of Augustus ; on which account he held her memory in gratitude, and caused her image to be struck on his coins. The gold is engraved in Caylus, No. 115.

DIVA FAUSTINA and DIVA AUGUSTA FAUSTINA.—After the death of Faustina sen. in the third year of her husband's reign, Antoninus Pius caused several coins, in each metal, to be struck, on which, by the title DIVA, which precedes her name, the ceremony of her *apotheosis* is more or less directly recalled to mind. In the same spirit of flattery this princess was successively compared to almost all the goddesses, and typified on coins accordingly.—See FAUSTINA ANTONINI.

DIVA FAUSTINA PIA.—Head of Faustina junior, who after her death, was, in spite of her great and notorious immoralities, mourned for, and placed in the rank of divinities, by Marcus Aurelius, her husband, whilst coins were struck in gold, silver, and bronze, which offer various new types of consecration.—See SIDERIBUS RECEPTA, &c.

DIVAE MATIDIAE SOCRUI. S. C.—*To the divine Matidia, mother in law* [of the Emperor Hadrian].—A temple in which is a sedent female figure, clothed in the stola, and having on each side of it a female figure, standing on a pedestal. From each flank of the temple an elegant portico of two tiers extends itself to the front.—On the obverse, IMP. CAESAR TRAIAN. HADRIANVS AVG. P. M. TR. P. COS. III. A laureated head of Hadrian.—Engraved, as a brass medallion, in Cabinet of Vienna, pl. 21, p. 5.

Eckhel makes the following observations relative to this remarkable coin, on which both Baldini (in his Roman edition of Vaillant's *Impp.* iii. 118), and Froelich (in the work above referred to), have pronounced a verdict of genuine :—

" Conspicuous from its large size ; for not only does it exceed the dimensions of first brass coins, but it is also thicker than usual; this medal has been transferred from the museum of the Carthusians at Rome to Vienna. Its obverse appears to be free from all suspicion of fraud; but the workmanship of the reverse is not equally pure. The reader will pardon me, if I am severe in my judgment of coins, on whose acknowledged genuineness the truth of history is made to depend. If this coin be really genuine, we may be certain, that Matidia died and was consecrated during the reign of Hadrian, a fact which is rendered doubtful by other circumstances. I cannot imagine what blindness can have induced Casaubon to represent Marciana, instead of Matidia, as the mother-in-law of Hadrian." vi. 472.

DIVI CAES. MATER. S. C.—A veiled female, stands with hasta pura in left hand, and patera in right hand, sacrificing at a lighted altar.—*Obv.*—DOMITIA AVG. CAES. DIVI. F. DOMITIAN AVG. Head of Domitian.—On second brass of Domitia, engraved in Havercamp's *Cabinet de Christine*, TAB. liv.

DIVI CAESAR*is* MATRI. S. C.—A female seated, her right hand extended towards a child, standing at her knees, her left hand holding the hasta. On first brass of Domitia.—The obverse is inscribed DOMITIAE AVG. IMP. CAES. DIVI F. DOMITIAN AVG. and exhibits a striking portrait of the empress, with an elaborately dressed *chevelure.* An engraving of it is given in Akerman, vol. i. forming the vignette to title-page.

On both the above coins we find the legends styling the wife of Domitian *the mother of the divine Cæsar.* The child typified on the large brass specimen, standing near the sedent figure, is clothed in the gown called *prætexta,* and is supposed to represent that anonymous son whom the empress bore to Domitian in his second consulate, but who died in his infancy, and was afterwards *apotheosised.* This coin was minted to commemorate his birth; a circumstance which accounts for Domitia's being styled DIVI CAESARIS MATER.—Eckhel, in placing it with others struck under Domitian, says—This coin is "*rarissimus,* si modo certæ fidei." Mionnet and Akerman unqualifiedly recognise its authenticity.

Capt. Smyth, R. N. in describing a well-conditioned specimen of this rare coin, in his own cabinet of large brass, says—" I cannot entirely omit my doubts as to its being really genuine. As Eckhel says, it has not the look of antiquity, a vexatious *pativinity* interferes with its apparent purity of legend, edge, and other usual tests, and recals to mind the fraudulent brothers, who headed the *falsarii* of the sixteenth century.— It is unquestionably a fine and correct likeness of the empress, but from the objection advanced, it was knocked down for only five guineas at Mr. Henderson's sale, in 1830. It is singular (adds our distinguished antiquary), that the head-dress of this specimen and that of Vaillant's are identical, while those in the cabinet of Queen Christina and the British Museum have the hair braided round the head; the legends and reverses being alike in all the four.

The legitimacy of the last was long in question, although Ennery had bought a whole collection to secure it; but my friend Mr. Hawkins, in whose charge it is, informed me that the erudite Steinbüchel of Vienna, after repeated examinations, pronounced it to be a genuine medal."— *Descr. Cat.* p. 74.

For an engraving of that interesting gold coin which represents the empress on one side, and on the other her deified son, sitting naked on a globe, in the midst of seven stars, see DOMITIA.

DIVI F. *Divi Filius.*—Son of the divine [Julius.]—Augustus was thus named, having been adopted by Cæsar as his son, and constituted his heir by will.

DIVI M. PII. F. P. M. TR. P. III. COS. II. P. P. S. C.—The emperor, with laurelled head, and in the *paludamentum,* standing with a small Victory in his right hand, and a spear in the left, is crowned by a military figure, holding a club in the left hand.—On first and second brass of Sept. Severus.

The occasion, which these coins serve to commemorate, has already been briefly noticed under the head of *Adoption self-assumed* (p. 8). The legend of reverse above quoted confirms nearly all the augustal historians in recording not only that Severus, at the commencement of his reign, promised to emulate in his future government the example of Marcus Aurelius; but also that the same bold ambitious man offered himself to adoption by that renowned emperor, who had been dead fifteen years!

On this extraordinary circumstance, which occurred in the year of Rome 948 (A. D. 195), Dion, his contemporary, remarks—" But he inspired us (the Senators) with the greatest terror, when he called himself the *son of Marcus* [DIVI M*arci* PII *Filius*], and the brother of Commodus." (lxxv. § 7). And Spartian states, that he was desirous of being numbered among the family of Marcus. (ch. 10). Victor tells us that Commodus was reckoned among the gods by Severus, and called his brother. And thus, by this absurd species of adoption, he traced his descent through an uninterrupted series to Nerva, as is testified by numerous marbles, more explicit than coins.

This conduct of Severus, observes Eckhel (vii. 173–174), appeared to the ancients themselves most ludicrous, as it was natural it should; indeed, Dion informs us of a witty expression of a certain Aspax (or Aspaces), a sarcastic individual, whose racy speeches were then in every one's mouth, and who, on hearing that Severus had enrolled himself of the family of

Marcus, thus addressed him—" I congratulate you, O Cæsar, on having found a father ;" as though he had till then been without a father, so obscure and unknown was his parentage. (lxxvi. 9). This proceeding, however, in the case of Severus, was no evidence of folly or madness, from which he was perfectly free, but rather of the qualities for which he was remarkable : acuteness and tact. For, by this false assumption of an illustrious genealogy, he rendered himself particularly acceptable to the soldiers and to the uneducated classes of the people ; and it was from this circumstance that he acquired the power of conferring upon his son Bassianus (Caracalla) the name of *Antoninus*, and by its *prestige* making him an object of universal veneration. It may be said that Severus was, in this act, guilty of falsehood. He was so ; but with him it was unusual to refrain from any thing which furthered his interests.— Similar motives were professed by Alexander the Great, when desirous of being called the son of Ammon :—" Would that (said he), the Indians also could believe me to be a god ! For the success of war depends on reputation ; and frequently has a false belief answered all the purpose of the real truth." *(Curt.* viii. ch. 8).— And in the same terms does he excuse himself in Lucian *(Dial. mort.* 14). Nero furnishes a still older example of the ambition of a noble genealogy, in preferring to be considered as a scion of the Julian family, though belonging by adoption to the Claudian.

[Eckhel describes this historical coin from a specimen in the imperial cabinet at Vienna. Neither Mionnet, nor Akerman, includes it in his respective catalogue.—The preceding cut is engraved after a cast from a specimen formerly belonging to an Italian collection].

DIVI NERVA ET TRAIANVS PATER.

A laureated head of Nerva, and a bare head of Trajanus Pater, facing each other.

This reverse appears on a rare gold coin of Trajan ; who, in order to manifest his piety towards his relations, placed by consecration his own father, and his parent by adoption, in the rank of deities ; " and to preserve the memory of this double *apotheosis* (adds Vaillant), he consigned the event to the perpetuation, which medals, more durable than written history, are calculated to ensure it." Engraved in Pembroke, T. 16, fig. 12 ; also in Caylus, No. 276. —See TRAIANVS PATER.

DIVI NERVA P. ET PLOTINA IMPeratoris TRAIANi.

Heads of the Emperor Nerva, and Plotina, the wife of Trajan, face to face.

This gold coin was struck in the time of Hadrian, although its obverse bears the head of Trajan ; for Plotina survived her husband's reign, and could not, therefore, until after his and her own decease, have the appellation of DIVA prefixed to her name.—See Morell. *Specimen rei Numar.* lib. 5, p. 58.—Vaillant, in noticing the above singularly elegant and rare coin *(Pr.* ii. p. 119), says—" This *aureus*, struck by Hadrian, is another exemplification of a grateful mind cherished towards parents ; for he here continues the mint of Trajan, and recommends the consecration of Nerva and of Plotina."— Engraved in Caylus ; gold of the French cabinet, No. 277.

DIVI TITI F. or at full length FILIA

(daughter of the divine Titus).—This appears on gold and silver of IVLIA AVGVSTA, the handsome but unworthy daughter of the conqueror of Judæa. They were struck after her father's death, and when she was incestuously connected with Domitian.—See IVLIA TITI.

DIVIS PARENTIBVS.

The heads face to face of Trajan and Plotina, each surmounted by a star.—On gold of Hadrian.—Engraved in Akerman, i. plate vi. No. 5.

Hadrian obtained the ceremony of deification not only for Trajan but also for Plotina. Grateful towards both the father and the mother by whom he had been adopted, and resolved to hand down the record of the event to posterity, he caused their effigies, with the astral tokens of consecration, to be represented on one of his coins, accompanied by the inscription *Divis Parentibus*. (To his parent deities).—Vaillant, *Pr.* ii. p. 242.

The above coin is further elucidated by a marble, which Donati has cited on the authority of Maffei, viz. DIVO NERVAE TRAIANO ET DIVAE PLOTINAE, &c. IMP. HADRIANVS, &c. PARENTIBVS SVIS.—(Eckhel).

DIUM

(Macedoniæ) *colonia,* now Standia, in European Turkey.—A maritime city of Macedonia, situate between the mouths of the rivers Haliacmon (the Mauro) and Bapbyrus (the Mauronero), on the shores of the Thermæus Sinus (Gulf of Salonica), in the Pierian region, according to Ptolemy, beyond it, according to Strabo. It was made a colony by Julius Cæsar, and replenished afterwards by settlers under Augustus ; consequently the titles assumed on its coins are COLonia IVLia AUGusta DIENSIS, or COL. DIENSIS, or COL. CLAudia DIVM.—The mintages of this city are imperial *Latin,* in small and middle brass ; and were struck under the following emperors :—

Tiberius, Nero (COL. CLA. DIVM), Domitianus, Trajanus, Hadrianus, Antoninus Pius, Faustina junior, Septimius Severus, Caracalla, Geta, Macrinus, Elagabalus, Soemias Elagabali Mater, Severus Alexander, Maximinus, Maximus, Gordianus Pius, Philippus senior, Philippus junior, Æmilianus, Gallienus, Salonina.—See Mionnet, *Supplt.* T. iii. p. 61.

The types indicative of the deities worshipped by the colonists of Dium, are—

Jupiter, Minerva, Neptune, Æsculapius, and Cupid, in honour of which last-named god, the Diensians erected a temple, celebrated festivals, and, according to both Pausanias and Plutarch, instituted splendid games, called *Thespienses Erotidia,* that is to say, sacred to Love, which took place every five years.—On a very rare second brass, *Decreto Decurionum* of *Colonia Julia Diensis,* dedicated to Alexander Severus, a winged Cupid stands within a temple of two columns.—See Vaillant *(in Col.)* ii. p. 120.

DIVO.—On most of those Roman coins which

were struck to attest the ceremony of placing an emperor, or some member of his family, after death, amongst the gods, it was usual to omit those multiplied and various names and titles which such personages, when living, were accustomed to have inscribed on their coins.— Hence we read DIVO AVGVSTO—DIVO ANTONINO PIO—DIVO ALEXANDRO—on the respective consecration medals of Augustus, Antoninus Pius, Alexander Severus, &c. minted after their death.

DIVO AVGVSTO. S. P. Q. R. (To the divine Augustus, the ·Senate, and the Roman People).—The image of Augustus, clothed, the head radiated, holding a branch of olive in his extended right hand, and resting his left on a sceptre, is seated on a four-wheeled car of honour, drawn by four elephants, each of which has a conductor sitting on its back. On the reverse we read TI. CAESAR DIVI AVG. F. AVGVST. P. M. TR. P. XXXVII. (Tiberius Cæsar, son of the divine Augustus, sovereign pontiff [invested] for the 37th time with the Tribunitian power).— In the field of the coin the initials S. C. (by decree of the Senate).

This type and accompanying legends appear on a large brass, which, struck towards the close of Tiberius's reign (A. D. 35), alludes to some display of funereal pomp, in honour of the memory of Augustus, which the policy of his immediate successor induced him frequently to renew. That Augustus was thus honoured after his death is a fact particularised by Suetonius, who, in the *Life of Claudius*, ch. xi. says—" He decreed divine honours to Livia, his grandmother; and ordered that, on the grand days of the Circus, her statue should be borne, *like that of Augustus*, on a car drawn by elephants." Dion also makes mention of the elephants, which drew the car of Augustus.

DIVO AUG*usto* VESP*asiano*, S. P. Q. R.— A quadriga of elephants, with their *rectores*, as in the coin above described, drawing the statue of Vespasian on a car.—The legend of reverse is IMP*erator* T*itus* CAES*ar* DIVI VES-P*asiani* F*ilius* AVG*ustus* P. M. TRP. P. P. COS. VIII.—Large brass. (S. P. Q. R. equivalent to S. C. as a mark of Senatorial authority). Engraved from a specimen in the British Museum.

This type represents one striking feature of the pompous ceremonies attendant upon the *apotheosis* of Vespasian. It was minted by order of his son Titus, between A. D. 79 and 80, in

imitation (as will be seen on reference to the preceding notice), of the same monetal honour paid by Tiberius to Augustus. The only material points in which the two examples differ from each other is, that the statue of the deified Vespasian is bare-headed instead of radiated, and holds a small figure of Victory instead of an olive branch. Also that one of the four elephant-drivers has a staff, and another holds out a wreath. In workmanship and relief it is far superior to Augustus's consecration medal.

DIVO AVG. T. DIVI. VESP. F. VESPASIAN. (To the divine Augustus, Titus Vespasian, son of the divine Vespasian). S. C.—The statue of Titus, with bare head, sits clothed in the toga, on a curule chair, surrounded by warlike spoils won from the enemy, ' holding a branch in his right and a scroll in his left hand.

On the reverse of a large brass, struck by order of the Senate, after the death of Titus, in honour of that emperor's memory, A. U. C. 834 (A. D. 81). The Flavian amphitheatre forms the type on the other side.—Engraved in Havercamp, *Cabinet de Christine*, pl. vii. p. 41.— The type of reverse is almost an exact copy of that on a large brass of Nero Claudius Drusus, son of Tiberius.—See DRUSUS JUNIOR.

DIVO COMMODO.—Head of Commodus, with radiated crown.—*Rev.*—An eagle, or (on others) an altar, with the fire kindled.—On one of the coins in billon, restored by Gallienus.— See Akerman, ii. 33.

Respecting the title *Divus*, as applied to *Commodus*, Eckhel makes the following instructive observations:—

" This monster, disgraced by every vice, was nevertheless enrolled by Severus among the immortal gods.—Lampridius, who records the circumstance *(in Comm.* c. 17), is of opinion that Severus took this step through motives of hostility to the Senate; and in this view Spartian coincides, where he states (c. 11) that Severus, in order to gratify his feelings of revenge towards the Senate, determined to consecrate Commodus, and was the first to bestow upon him the title of *Divus Commodus*, in the hearing of the soldiers, after the defeat of Albinus, notifying the fact in the letter he addressed to the Senate announcing his victory.— Another reason for this consecration may have been the ambition of Severus to be regarded as the son of Marcus, and the brother of Commodus. And thus, in bestowing divine honours upon his brother, he appeared to be actuated by affectionate feelings, and so procured a more ready credence for the impression he wished to produce amongst the people at large, so universally under the influence of superstition. It should, however, be remarked, that hitherto no coin has been discovered which bears allusion to the consecration of Commodus, struck in the reign of Severus. All that we possess, are of that class, which were struck at a later period in memory of emperors who had been consecrated." (vii. p. 132).

DIVO CONSTANTINO.—The veiled head of Constantine the Great.——*Rev.*—AETERNA

PIETAS. A military figure, wearing helmet and paludamentum, stands with spear in the right hand; in his left is a globe, on which is fixed the monogram of Christ's name.—On third brass, Banduri, ii. p. 267.

DV. CONSTANTINVS, &c. (*Divus Constantinus*). Veiled head of Constantine.—*Rev.* Without legend. The emperor, with a star over his head, in a quadriga, carried upwards; a hand stretched forth from above to receive him.—Below, S. M. N. T. Fourth brass.—*Cat. Mus. Cæs. Num. Vet.* ii. 479.—Engraved in Banduri, ii. 219.

"That Constantine received the honours of consecration, we learn expressly from Eutropius; and coins as plainly teach us that he was called DIVVS (divine). It is most probable, however, that this posthumous distinction was bestowed, with accompanying ceremonies differing from those in which hitherto we see emperors translated to the skies, and in a way not repugnant to the laws of Christianity. Indeed, there are coins still extant, as above, which in reference to this subject, exhibit nothing which is profane, or which can offend *our* religion (quod *nostra* possit stomachari *religio*)."

[Such are the terms in which the learned Eckhel animadverts on the legend "Divus Constantinus." (See *D. N. Vet.* viii. 92).—We here find him expressing his opinion that there is nothing in these coins—not even in the appellation of *Divus*, as applied to a created being, which can possibly be offensive to *his* "religion." Now, to *our* religion, nothing can be more offensive than this portentous medley of Christian symbols and pagan superstitions—these titles of polytheism and false worship conjoined with the name in monogram of GOD's *true* and *only* SON. But Constantine was, indeed, no Christian, except politically.—See his coins, SOLI INVICTO COMITI, and others.

DIVO.——On most monetal monuments of Consecration, that is to say, such as were struck to record the pagan ceremony of placing a Roman Emperor, after death, amongst the gods, it was usual to omit those multiplied and various names and titles, by which, when living, he was accustomed to be styled. Hence we read simply DIVO AVGVSTO, DIVO ANTONINO PIO, DIVO VESPASIANO, DIVO ALEXANDRO, &c. on the respective consecration coins of Augustus, Antoninus Pius, Vespasian, Alexander Severus, &c.

DIVO PIO.—A column inclosed by palisades, on the top of which is placed a statue of the emperor, with a spear in his left hand.—*Obv.* DIVVS ANTONINVS. A bare head.—On silver, and on first and second brass of Antoninus Pius. For an engraving of this reverse see COLUMNA, p. 235.

The following is the tenour of Eckhel's comments on the legend and type (vii. 28):—

This is the famous column of solid marble, variegated with red spots (or veins), extant in Rome at the present day, but unfortunately fallen to the ground, and which is to be seen at the back of the magnificent senate-house (*curia*), which derives its name from the Mons Cytorius:

its height is 50 Roman feet. And no less remarkable is its pedestal of solid Parian marble, all the sides of which are 12 feet in breadth, and 11 in heighth, and on one of which is inscribed DIVO ANTONINO AVG. PIO. ANTONINVS AVGVSTVS ET VERVS AVGVSTVS FILII; on another side is a beautiful work in relief, representing Antoninus Pius and Faustina carried aloft by a winged genius, whilst beneath are seen in a sitting posture a figure of Rome, in the usual garb, and of Eternity, clasping an obelisk with her left arm. The other two sides exhibit equestrian processions (*decursiones*) such as usually formed part of the ceremonial at great funerals.

DIVO PIO AVG.—First brass of Caligula.—See *Sacrificia*.

DIVOS instead of DIVVS.—This substitution, made for no other known reason than that the letters V and O were in the earlier ages of Rome frequently used the one for the other, is exemplified on marbles and on coins—*ex. gr.* IVLIOS, AEGYPTOS, VOLTEIA, VOLCANO, CONSOLES, HERCOLI, for *Julius, Aegyptus, Vulteia, Vulcano, Consules, Herculi.*

DIVOS IVLIVS DIVI F*ilius*.—The heads facing each other of Julius Cæsar and Augustus, the one laureated the other bare.—On gold and silver.—Engraved in Dr. King's Plates.

That this coin was struck after the assassination of Julius Cæsar is shewn not only in the flattery of DIVVS, but also in his successor and adopted son's appearing with him on the same coin—an union which, at the same time, Augustus knew how to turn to his own advantage, and to conciliate thence to himself greater honour and authority with the Roman people.—Augustus called himself DIVI FILIVS, because, according to Suetonius, he was testamentarily appointed Cæsar's heir.

DIVUS, the mark of consecration.——This word *Divus* given to any one on a coin, indicates that the same was struck after his or her apotheosis. A question has been raised among the learned, whether there be any distinction between *deum* and *divum*. Vaillant for instance (*in Col.* i. 45), on the authority of Servius, thus distinguishes between *dei* and *divi*, viz.—"Dii dicantur æterni, Divi autem ex hominibus fiunt." The former are gods from eternity, but the latter have been made deities from human beings.—On this point Eckhel, also consulting the old writers, seems to be of opinion, that there is no difference in the meaning of the two names, as used on coins. He observes that the word DIVUS was always turned by the Greeks into ΘΕΟΣ, which certainly is the *Deus* of the Latins. Thus, where the latter inscribed DIVVS AVGVSTVS—DIVO CARO, &c. the former wrote ΘΕΟΣ ΣΕΒΑΣΤΟΣ—ΘΕΩ ΚΑΡΩ, &c.——See vol. viii. 465–6.

DIVVS IVLIVS. A comet.—This legend and type occur on silver of Augustus, whose laureated head appears on the obverse of the coin.—See *Stella*.

In his supplement to Vaillant (p. 1), Khell gives from the *Cabinet de France*, the engraving of a gold coin having on the obverse the legend DIVI IVLI, and for type a comet. This also it is to be observed, was struck *after* Cæsar's death, by order of Augustus.—See ASTRA, p. 92.

DIVUS AUGUSTUS.—That Augustus, during his life-time, was treated as a deity, is manifest on good authority; and Tacitus relates, that he was commonly reproached with this—" Nihil deorum honoribus relictum, cum se templis, et effigie numinum per Flamines, et sacerdotes coli vellet." Moreover Appianus states that, after the defeat of Sextus Pompey, and the abdication of Lepidus, " he was in every town *(oppidatim)* consecrated among the tutelary gods."— The Pisanian cenotaph, illustrated by Cardinal Noris, shews that, whilst living, he had, besides altars and temples, his *flamen* also and priests. Other marbles and monuments also attest the fact that divine honours were paid to the living Augustus—take, for example, the coins inscribed ROM. ET AVG. But it is no less true that Augustus did not permit those divine honours to be paid him at Rome, which he allowed the provinces to confer on him. At length, on the death of Augustus, it became necessary for the Senate to decree to him the honours of consecration, as that body had already committed the same insane act in the case of his father Julius, and thus established an absurd example which found imitators in plenty during succeeding ages of the empire. Dion and Tacitus both affirm that Augustus was received among the immortal gods, and that *flamines*, and a priesthood with sacred rites, were instituted to his honour.

On coins of the Roman mint he is invariably styled DIVVS, but on consecration medals, struck out of Rome, the word DEVS is used. Thus we find on coins of Tarraco (Tarragona, in Spain), DEO AVGVSTO. On an unique coin of Gallienus of Roman die, Augustus is called DEVS.—Connected also with the consecration of Augustus were the groves *(luci)* dedicated to him in the provinces, to which allusion is made on a medal of Juba II. King of Mauretania, inscribed LVCV. AVG. That is to say, according to Servius (a commentator on the Mantuan bard)—" Ubicunque Virgilius lucum ponit, sequitur etiam consecratio."

Numerous coins attest the fact of Augustus's consecration, struck not only by his successor Tiberius, but afterwards under many other emperors.—See Eckhel, vi. pp. 124–125.

DIVVS AVGVSTVS. S. C. (Head radiated). —On a middle brass coin, struck after the death of Augustus, the foregoing legend appears on the obverse. The legend of the reverse is CONSENSV. SENAT. ET EQ. ORDIN. P. Q. R. The type is a statue of Augustus seated, holding in his right hand a branch, and in his left a globe.— Engraved in the *Cabinet de Christine*, p. 285, TAB. xliv. No. 2.

Augustus, already admitted in the provinces to the rank of deity, had this last homage paid him at Rome after his death; statues were also raised to him. Such is the subject of this medal, the epigraph of which is particular in ex-

plaining that all these honours were decreed to him by the concurrence of the three orders of the state; the Senate, the Equestrian order, and the Roman People.—See CONSENSV, &c. p. 252.

DIVVS AVGVSTVS PATER.——Augustus, with radiated head, and in the toga, seated near an altar, on which fire is kindled, holds a branch in his extended right hand, and rests his left on the *hasta pura.*—The legend of the obverse is TI. CAESAR DIVI AVG. F. AVGVST. P. M. TR. POT. XXIIII. in the middle S. C.—On first brass of Tiberius.

Tacitus, amongst the events of the year of Rome 775 (A. D. 22), records the following:— " About the same time, the severe indisposition of Julia Augusta (widow of Augustus), rendered necessary the immediate return of the emperor (Tiberius, her son by adoption), to Rome; the good understanding between the mother and son being up to this moment undisturbed, or at least their animosity was disguised; for it was not long before this that, when Julia dedicated a statue to *Divus Augustus*, near the theatre of Marcellus, she placed the name of Tiberius *after* her own." (Tac. *Ann.* iii. 64).

Here (says Eckhel) we find the year of the coin, as expressed by the 24th tribunate, perfectly coinciding with the year assigned by Tacitus; and we cannot, therefore, doubt, that the figure on the coin is intended to represent the statue to which Tacitus refers. But there is still stronger testimony to adduce. In the Fasti of Verrius, at the date of the 24th of April, we find—SIG. DIVO AVGVSTO PATRI AD THEATRVM MAR - - - IVLIA AVGVSTA ET TI. AVGVSTVS DEDICARVNT. Thus, from the coin, and from Tacitus, we learn the year in which this dedication took place, and the record in the Fasti just quoted, gives the very day of the month, viz. the 24th of April; in addition to which, it exhibits the same verbal formula as the coin, and confirms the statement of Tacitus, that Julia had the courage to inscribe the name of Tiberius *after* her own; and lastly, it is conclusive on the point, that the severe indisposition of Julia could not have shewn itself till *after* the day in question. (vi. 193–4).

DIVVS PATER TRAIANVS, also DIVVS TRAIAN. PARTH. PATER.—See TRAIANVS PATER.

DOG *of Æsculapius.*—See *Hygeia* and *Æsculapius.*

DOLPHIN. *(Delphinus).*—The representation of this fish offers itself on ancient coins in more than one fashion; sometimes in a quiet and fixed position, at others in a state of movement. The dolphin was consecrated to Apollo, who, according to Homer, had transformed himself into one. Hence we see a Delphic tripod with a dolphin upon it, on a silver coin of Vitellius, that emperor having, as the inscription teaches us, been one of the XV. *viri* appointed to the care of sacrificial ceremonies. A similar type appears on a denarius of Titus, but not with the same legend.—See XV. VIR. SACR*is* FAC*iundis.*

The *Dolphin* was also sacred to Neptune, the deity who presided over the sea and affairs of navigation; hence we find the dolphin in the hand of that god, on coins of Agrippa, Augustus, Caligula, Vespasian, Hadrian, and other Roman Emperors.

The *Dolphin* was likewise sacred to Venus.

On early Roman money the figure of a dolphin occurs on the *triens*, the *quadrans*, and *sextans*. Thus the dolphin, with four globules under it, is a mark of the *triens*.

The *Dolphin*, with Cupid on its back, appears on coins of the Cordia and Lucretia families; and, bearing Melicerta, is frequently repeated on the colonial mintages of Corinth.

The *Dolphin* and an eagle, with a sceptre between them, form the reverse of a denarius of the Terentia gens, struck in honour of Pompey the Great, with legend MAGN. PRO. COS.— In this instance, the sceptre indicates supreme power, and undivided command; the fish referring to the sea, and the bird to the land.—See *Eagle*.

The *Dolphin*, entwined round an *anchor*, was at one time a symbol of Augustus.—It is also seen on coins struck by princes of the Flavia family, sons of Vespasian.

In *Morell. Thesaur. Impp. Rom.* T. iii. TAB. vi. No. 64, there is an engraving of this type, from gold of Titus (TR. P. IX. IMP. XV. COS. VIII.) also one from silver of the same emperor, and with the same legend of reverse (TAB. viii. No. 84). Moreover, amongst the silver coinage of Domitian, engraved in the same standard work, we find two examples of the dolphin and anchor (COS. VII. DESIGN. VIII.) see T. iii. TAB. viii. Nos. 36 and 39. The subjoined cut is from a first brass of Domitian, having on its obverse—

IMP*erator* CAES*ar* DIVI VESP*asiani Filius* DOMITIAN*us* AV*Gustus* P*ontifex Maximus.* Laureated head of Domitian to the right.—The

legend is continued on the reverse, viz. IM*perator* VIIII. TR. P. CO*n*Sul VIII.——Below, *Senatus Consulto.* The type—Delphinus anchoræ implicitus.

[The cast, after which this cut is engraved, was purchased of Mr. Doubleday. The impressions of both obverse and reverse vouch for the original being in good condition. And although in none of the numismatic books, either by old or modern writers, to which the compiler has access, does this type appear as a *brass* coin, yet there seems to be no reason whatever to doubt the authenticity of the specimen in question. This not inelegant device has, down to our own times, been constantly adopted as a naval emblem; and, to say nothing as to the conformation of the *fish*, it presents, doubtless, a correct delineation of the Roman ship-*anchor*].

D. N. *Domina Nostra.* Our Lady.—This title, thus abbreviated, appears on coins of the Empresses Ælia Flacilla, Galla Placidia, Honoria, &c. Spanheim observes, that wives were called *Dominæ* by the Romans.

D. N. *Dominus Noster.*—A title conferred, in the declining ages of the empire, on the *Augusti* and the *Cæsars.*—The following are among the remarks which Eckhel makes on this subject:

Dominus, a word so repugnant to liberty (as it generally implied the authority over *slaves*), was not adopted by the first emperors, nor afterwards by those who preferred to rule rather through the affection than the fears of their subjects; and at any rate they did not approve of it. Augustus declined it, and, to use the words of Tertullian, 'Though the founder of the empire, he would not allow himself to be styled *Dominus*; and, indeed, it is an appellation applicable only to the deity.' And, further on, he adds, 'How can he, who is the father of his country, be also its Lord (*Dominus*)?' Even Tiberius also avoided it, openly declaring, 'that he was lord (*dominus*) over the slaves, general (*imperator*) of the soldiers, and sovereign (*princeps*) of the rest of his people:'— nay, according to Suetonius, he went so far as to address the Senators by that very invidious title, which in his own case he refused to accept, saying, 'I have ever esteemed you, and still do so, as my good, and just, and kind Lords (*Dominos*).'—Caligula was the first whose arrogant ears could endure the appellation *dominus*, and his example was followed by that rival of his vices, Domitian.—Victor, whilst satirizing the character of Diocletian, remarks, 'He was the first, after Caligula and Domitian, who allowed himself to be called openly *Dominus*.' This was the less remarkable in Domitian, as he wished to be called not only *dominus* but *deus*, of both which appellations Martial furnishes many instances. By degrees, however, the offensiveness of this title became softened from use and familiarity, so that by the time of Ti. Claudius it was regarded merely as a term of courtesy.—Seneca says, 'You have called him *friend*, just in the same way as we call all candidates *good men*, or as we salute persons whom we meet, should we not remember their names, as *Domini*.'—It is not surprising that Trajan himself should have permitted Pliny to address him constantly in his epistles as *Dominus*.

Antoninus Pius was the first to whom the title of *Dominus* was applied on coins; but it was Greece and Asia—conquered Greece and captured Asia—which furnished the instances, as usual, of extreme adulation. The word Κύριος (Lord) is found on a coin of Antioch ad Hippum, in Decapolis—thus ΑΥΤΟΚΡ. ΚΥΡ. ΑΝΤΩΝΕΙΝΟϹ. Shortly afterwards, on coins of M. Aurelius and his family, struck in Mesopotamia, a similar use is made of the word Κύριος. On coins of the colony of Antioch, in Pisidia, with the heads of Caracalla and Geta, we read VICT. DD. NN. And on a coin of Gordianus Pius, minted in the same colony, appears VICTORIA DOMINI.

The foregoing examples, however, belong only to the foreign coinage. It was the Emperor Aurelian who first introduced the title *Dominus* upon coins of Roman die, when he allowed the following inscription to appear:—DEO ET DOMINO NATO (on others NOSTRO) AVRELIANO AVG. (see p, 319 of this dictionary). Next to the above, in point of time, Diocletianus and Maximianus, received the distinction of D. N. but not until their abdication of the empire (A. D. 305). Afterwards, it was conferred more frequently on the Cæsars than on the Emperors, though for what reason is uncertain. Lastly, from the the times of the sons of Constantine the Great, it became a common prenomen, that of IMP*erator* being gradually abolished. And at length it was rendered so much a matter of course, that if any one in the reign of Justinian, had used the word *Imperator* instead of *Dominus*, and of *Augusta* instead of *Domina*, he would have been considered guilty of an insult, or at least of great ignorance.—See *Doct. Num. Vet.* viii. p. 364–5–6.

DOMITIA gens—at first plebeian, afterwards patrician; bearing the respective surnames of *Ahenobarbus* and *Calvinus*.—The gold coins of this family are very rare; the silver, with a few exceptions, common. The brass are *semi-asses*, and other parts of the *as*.—Among other varieties of legends and types are the following :—

1. AHENOBAR*bus*.—A head, nearly bald, and with beard closely cropped.——*Rev.* CN. DOMITIVS L. F. IMP*erator*. A temple of four columns, represented in perspective, near the pediment of which we read NEPT. (*Neptunus*).

[Mionnet quotes this extremely rare gold coin, from the cabinet of the Duke de Blacas, and values it at 600 fr.—A fine specimen brought

£22 10s. at the Pembroke sale.—The above cut is after a cast from a beautiful specimen in the British Museum. The head on the obverse is evidently a portraiture, and Visconti at once ascribes it to Cneus Domitius Ahenobarbus].

2. AHENOBAR.—A bare head, slightly bearded.—*Rev.*—C. N. DOMITIVS IMP. Prow of a ship on which is a trophy.—[This silver coin, valued by Mionnet at 40 fr. brought 19s. at the Brunell sale].

The cognomen *Ahenobarbus* was derived to this family from an event said to have occurred to the Consul Lucius Domitius. As the fable goes, it was to him that the Dioscuri announced the Roman victory at Regillus; and in consequence of this unexpected encounter with Castor and Pollux, or through the exultation which the good news excited in him, the Consul's beard became red.

For a more ample notice of this popular tradition, together with an explanation of the ship and trophy type on the former of these two reverses, and of the temple (dedicated to Neptune) on the latter—both coins being struck in the year of Rome 713 (A. D. 41), the reader is referred to p. 31 and 32, article AHENOBARBUS. Also to *Dioscuri*, p. 331.

3. CN. DOMITIVS AHENOBARBVS IMP. Ship's prow, above which is a star.—*Obv.*—ANT. IMP. IIIVIR. R. P. C. Bare head of Mark Antony, behind it the *lituus*.

Cneus Domitius, who minted this coin out of Rome, was son of Lucius Domitius, and nephew of the consul and censor Cneius Domitius, grandfather of Nero, nephew on the sister's side to Cato of Utica, and fifth cousin of M. Brutus. Attaching himself at the commencement of the civil war to the conspirators' party, he afterwards became Antony's naval commander against Octavian; but after the death of the former triumvir, he became reconciled to Augustus, and in 722 (B. C. 32), served the office of consul at Rome.—See Riccio, p. 82.

[Mionnet values this coin in gold at 200 fr.]

4. M. AVRELI. ROMA. Galeated head of Rome, with mark of the denarius.—*Rev.*—L. LIC. CN. DOM*itius*. Mars, undraped, stands in a biga going at full speed; he brandishes a spear in his right hand, and holds a buckler and a military lituus on his left arm. Under the horses is the word SCAVRI.—See an engraving of the same coin in COSCONIA gens, p. 294.

5. Same obverse.——*Rev.*—CN. DOM. below ROMA. Victory in a biga; beneath the horses of which, a gladiator, armed with a spear, is seen fighting with a lion.—See *Morell. Fam. Rom.* plate 1, No. vi.

The Domitius of this and the preceding denarius appears to Eckhel uncertain. Older numismatists ascribe it to Domitius, son of another Cneus, and nephew of Lucius, grand-father of Domitius the censor. It was coined perhaps on the occasion of his filling a municipal office, different from that of moneyer; or rather it might have been minted by some descendant of his, who desired to commemorate the municipal honours of his family. Gladiatorial spectacles, indeed, and the care of supplying an abundant *annona*, belonged to the ediles, and these public shews and responsibilities are plainly indicated in the symbols of the last described coin. (Riccio, p. 81).

6. OSCA.—Head of a bearded man.—*Rev.* DOM. COS. ITER. IMP. with the type of pontifical instruments.

This denarius is considered by Eckhel to belong to Cneus Domitius *Calvinus*, who served his first consulate in the year u. c. 701 (b. c. 53), in colleagueship with M. Valerius Messala, and was consul for the second time, with C. Asinius Pollio, in 714 (b. c. 40). He followed Cæsar's party through various circumstances, and was the rival and enemy of the above mentioned Domitius Ahenobarbus. The present coin was struck at Osca, a city of the Ilergeti, in Hispania Tarraconensis, Calvinus having, after his second consulship, triumphed over the rebellious Ceretani, of the Pyrenees.

Eckhel believes the head to be that of some native hero of Spain. Cavedoni thinks it meant for that of *Iberus*, son of Hercules, reputed founder of that nation. The emblems of the reverse all allude to the Sovereign Pontificate.

DOMITIA *Longina*, daughter of Domitius Corbulo, and wife of the Emperor Domitian, who took her away by force from her first husband, L. Lamia Aemilianus, in the year of Rome 823 (A. D. 70). She bore the tyrant one son in A. D. 82, whose name is not handed down, but who died in his infancy, and was consecrated, as appears by one of her coins. In 83, on account of her adultery with Paris, an actor, Domitian divorced her, put her paramour to death, and thenceforth lived with Julia, his brother's daughter. Shortly after, the imperial profligate restored Domitilla to his bed, but continued his incestuous intercourse with Julia. At length, informed that her own life was in danger from her husband, she encouraged the conspiracy which she knew was on foot against him, and to which he fell a merited victim in A. D. 96.— She died under the reign of Trajan.

The coins of Domitia are, of all the Empresses, amongst the most rare. On these she is styled DOMITIA AVGVSTA—DOMITIA AVGVSTA IMP*eratoris* DOMIT*iani* (by implication VXOR)—DOMITIA AVG. IMP. CAES. DIVI F. DOMITIAN*i* AVG*usti* (that is VXOR). The following is an account of their estimated value, and of the prices at which some of them have been sold:—

SILVER MEDALLIONS.—With the laureated head of Domitian on one side, and her own on the other. (Valued by Mionnet at 100 fr.)— VENVS AVG. (Brought £3 at the Devonshire sale).

GOLD.—DOMITIA AVG. IMP. DOMITIAN AVG. GERM. Head of the empress.—*Rev.* CONCORDIA AVGVST. A peacock.—[A specimen of this imperial *aureus* brought £8 15s. at the Devonshire sale; another, £6 6s. at the Pembroke, and a third, £16 15s. at the Thomas, from the Trattle sale, where it was bought for £14 5s. 0d.; and afterwards another specimen obtained £9 7s. 6d. at the Brumell auction.]— These coins are considered to have been struck on the occasion of Domitian becoming "reconciled" to Domitia, after he had repudiated her on a charge of adultery, as above mentioned.

Obv.—DOMITIA AVGVSTA IMP. DOMIT. Head of the empress.—*Rev.*—IMP. CAES. DOMITIANVS AVG. P. M. Head of Domitian.—[A fine specimen of this the rarest coin of Domitia, brought £27 at the Campana sale].

Obv.—DOMITIA AVGVSTA IMP. DOMIT. Head of the empress.—*Rev.*—DIVVS CAESAR IMP. DOMITIANI. A child on a globe, surrounded by seven stars.—[Mionnet values the gold at 150 fr. and the silver at 50 fr. A specimen of the latter sold for about £2 at the Devonshire sale].

These coins record the consecration of that nameless son of Domitia and Domitian, who was born, as it would appear, A. D. 82, and who died very young.—See the preceding engraving, from a specimen in the British Museum.

SILVER.—CONCORDIA AVG. A Peacock.— [Brought £4 18s. at the Devonshire and £4 3s. at the Thomas sale].—PIETAS AVGVST. Domitia seated, holds in her left hand the *hasta pura*, and extends the right hand towards a young child standing before her, clothed in the toga. [A specimen brought £3 12s. at the Devonshire and another obtained £1 15s. at the Thomas sale]. The young child represented on this reverse, can be no other than the son of Domitian already alluded to. See PIETAS AUG. for an engraving of it.

LARGE BRASS.—DIVI CAESARIS MATER.—See this reverse described in p. 334. It serves, with preceding coins, to recal the birth and premature death of Domitian's son.—Same legend. A woman standing, sacrifices at an altar.

[Mionnet values the above two at 550 fr. each].

MIDDLE BRASS.—Same legend. A veiled woman stands holding a patera, and the *hasta pura*. (Mt. 150 fr.)— DIVI CAESARIS MATER. The empress sacrificing, as in the large brass specimen.—Engraved in the *Cabinet de Christine*, plate liv. No. 4, p. 345.

DOMITIANUS (*Flavius*), the younger of the two sons of Vespasian, by Flavia Domitilla, was born at Rome, the 24th of October, in the year u. c. 804 (A. D. 51), when his father was consul *designatus*, and about entering upon office in the following month. This was the first consulate of Vespasian, still a private citizen; and it was a *consulatus suffectus*, held during the two last months of the above named year. Vespasian, having been proclaimed *imperator* by the legions of the east, Domitian, who was left at Rome, finding himself exposed to the vengeance of the partizans of Vitellius, took refuge in the capitol, with his uncle Sabinus, at the end of December. And, after that building had been besieged and set fire to, eventually made his escape, disguised as a priest of Isis, his hiding-place being sought for in every other direction. (Suetonius, chap. i. Tacitus Hist. iv.)—Vitellius having been put to death, about the 20th of December, 822 (A. D. 69), Domitian issued from his retreat, and was hailed as Cæsar by the army. The choice of the soldiers was confirmed by the Senate, who, in addition, decreed to Domitian the pretorship of the city, and the consular dignity. In January,

823 (A. D. 70), he entered upon the government of the city, and discharged its functions in an unprincipled manner, distributing capriciously the public offices; insomuch as to cause the absent Vespasian to express his surprise, that his son did not send out some one to supersede himself. He set out with Mucianus against the Galli, Batavi, and Germani, who were in revolt; but, hearing by the way that success had attended the operations of Petilius Cerealis, he stopped at Lugdunum (Lyon). Same year, he married Domitia Longina, whom he took away by force from her husband Æmilianus.

824 (A. D. 71).—This year, *consul suffectus*, and afterwards *consul designatus* for the second time, he assisted at the triumph of his father and brother, for the capture of Jerusalem—an object of notice on that occasion from being mounted on a white horse.

825 (A. D. 72).—During this and the six following years, no particulars of Domitian's life are furnished by public records. But coins had begun to be abundant.—"It is very probable (observes Eckhel), that suspicions being entertained of his revolutionary designs, he now assumed a modesty and simplicity of demeanour, and affected especially a passion for literature, in order to conceal the real bent of his mind." Volagases I. King of Parthia, in 828 (A. D. 75), requesting succours from Vespasian against the Alani, and another general from among his sons, Domitian used every effort to procure the appointment for himself. But Vespasian refused the required aid altogether.

832 (A. D. 79).—His father dying on the 9th kalends of July, his elder brother Titus succeeded to the empire. Domitian complained, that tho' left a share in the sovereignty, the will of his father had been tampered with. His brother endeavoured to console him with the assurance, that he should be not only the sharer of the empire, but should also be his successor.

833 (A. D. 80).——He unceasingly, both in secret and openly, engaged in plots against his brother, attempting to seduce the army, and meditated flight. Titus, all the while, bearing those annoyances with patience; and sometimes with tears entreating his brother to return to terms of affection.

834 (A. D. 81).—This year Domitian was proclaimed emperor, on the death of Titus his brother.

835 (A. D. 82).—Domitian signalised his ac-

cession to the throne by the introduction of salutary laws. He restored the Capitol magnificently. A son was born to him, respecting whom see DOMITIA.

836 (A. D. 83).—Agricola defeated the Caledonians. Under that able, brave, and active commander, it was then for the first time ascertained that Britain is entirely surrounded by water. Domitian undertook this year an expedition against the *Catti* (people of Hesse).

837 (A. D. 84).—The war with the Catti was put an end to by Domitian without coming to blows with the enemy. The title of *Germanicus* appeared for the first time on coins of this year. By the valour of Agricola, Britain was for a time reduced to a state of peaceful subjection.

838 (A. D. 85).—Foreign wars, relative to which there is no certain information; and at home atrocious acts of cruelty on the part of Domitian.

839 (A. D. 86).—The first Capitoline games were celebrated this year, intended, like the Olympic, to recur every fifth year. The Dacian war commenced, being set on foot by Decebalus, king of that nation, and was carried on for many years with varied success, but with great discredit to the Roman arms.

841 (A. D. 88).—*Celebration of the Secular Games.*—To this year (though the matter is in great uncertainty), Tillemont refers the revolt of L. Antonius, governor of Upper Germany, who made an attempt to invade the empire.— Domitian went out to repel his advance, but returned on learning that Antonius had been defeated and slain by L. Maximus.

842–843 (A. D. 89 and 90).—There are no certain records of the events of these two years.

344 (A. D. 91).—Eusebius refers the triumph over the Dacians to this year, as recorded also by Suetonius, but without a date.

846 (A. D. 93).—It is probable that the war with the Sarmatæ by Domitian was undertaken this year, when a whole legion, with its general, was destroyed, as Suetonius states.

848 (A. D. 95).—Domitian ordered Flavius Clemens, his cousin-german, and the then consul, to be put to death for his attachment to the Christian religion, or as it was then termed, the superstition of the Jews, and this occasion is treated of by ecclesiastical writers as the second persecution of the Church.

849 (A. D. 96).—On the 18th of September, at the instigation of his wife, whom with other friends he, in his insupportable tyranny, had doomed to be slaughtered, Domitian was assassinated by his freedman Stephanus, in the 45th year of his age, after a reign of 15 years and six days.

The character of this most execrable prince is thus ably summed up and commented upon by the pen of Eckhel (vi. 391-2) :—

There could not have appeared anything premature in the death of a ruler, who, for so long a space in the life-time of man, displayed the greatest cruelty towards all worthy men ; appropriated the property of the citizens, as if it had been his own ; and who detested as crimes the virtues and noble deeds of the illustrious, punishing them as such with death and exile. His inhuman disposition is thus severely touched on by Tacitus (in vitâ Agricolæ, ch. 2), whilst speaking of this reign of oppression and impiety : " We have, indeed, afforded a notable example of patience ; and, as the olden times witnessed the ne plus ultra of liberty, so have we that of servitude, when the very intercourse of speaking and listening has been taken from us by an inquisitorial superintendence. We should have lost our memory too with our voices, had it been equally within the power of our volition to forget, as to be silent." And this cruelty of disposition was the less endurable from its being conjoined with incredible arrogance and vanity. The same individual, who, on entering upon a campaign, would suddenly retrace his steps without even seeing his enemy, and who was satisfied with such a triumph over the Dacians, that he was not ashamed to pay them a yearly tribute—could, nevertheless, erect so many arches, surmounted by quadrigæ, and other triumphal insignia (as even coins testify), that they were equalled by no preceding emperor. According to Suetonius, he called the months of September and October after his own names of Germanicus and Domitianus, because in the one he had succeeded to the empire, and in the other was born (ch. 13). He built a temple in honour of the gens Flavia (his own family), and at length styling himself Dominus and Deus, desired those titles to be applied to him by others ; and though they never appear on his coins, they are still to be found on the works of pottery, given by Passeri, not to mention the flatteries of contemporary writers, especially the poets. And this Lord and God was wont to devote an hour in each day to the catching and transfixing of flies ! Nothing was ever more absurd than the funereal

banquet which he set before the most dignified personages of Rome, and which Dion has so minutely described (lxvii. § 9).—No wonder, then, that the Senate should have shewn their satisfaction at his death, by ordering ladders to be immediately brought, and his shields and busts to be pulled down and scattered on the ground, his titles erased, and every memorial of his existence banished from their sight. (Suet. ch. 23). This, indeed, is the chief reason why Procopius asserts, that in his time but one statue of this emperor remained ; though there is reason to suspect some egregious falsehood to be mixed up with his account.—The army, however, were much incensed at the murder of Domitian, and instantly endeavoured to procure him the title of Divus, demanding that the perpetrators of the crime should be given up to punishment. (Suet. ch. 23). The motive for this display of affection on their parts, was his having increased their pay one fourth ; the result of which inconsiderate liberality was, that the treasury being inadequate to meet the additional expense, he was compelled to reduce the numbers of the army ; and the provinces, thus deprived of their necessary garrisons, became more open to the incursions of barbarian tribes.

Domitian died without any progeny surviving him. By his wife he had one son, who died at nine years of age.—See DOMITIA.

MINTAGES OF DOMITIAN.

" The medals of this emperor (as Capt. Smyth observes), are abundant and cheap, and are prized according to their preservation, and the degree of interest attached to their reverses.— Many of them were struck in the life-time of his father."—With the exception of medallions in gold, silver, and brass, and some reverses, in each metal, of the usual size, all are common. On these he is styled IMPerator CAESAR DOMITIANVS GERManicus AVGusti Filius (viz. the son of Vespasian) Pater Patriæ. On a silver coin, struck A. D. 69, when Vespasian was reigning, and Titus and Domitian were both only Cæsars, we see the respective bare heads of the two brothers facing each other, as in token of that fraternal concord which the latter never sincerely manifested a desire to maintain.— Other denarii, for a like purpose, exhibit them both seated on a curule chair, holding olive branches, and with the legend TITVS ET DOMITianus CAESares PRINcipes IVVENtutis. (Morell. Impp. Roman. TAB. vii. figs. 17 & 18). Among the rarest reverses are the following :

GOLD MEDALLIONS.—Obv.—IMP. CAES. DOMIT. AVG. GER. P. M. TR. P. VII. Laurelled bust of the emperor, with amulet (Medusa's head) on the throat.—Rev.—IMP. XIIII. COS. XIIII. CENS. PP. P. Minerva standing on a ship's prow, holding a spear in the right hand, and a buckler on the left arm ; at her feet is an owl. On the prow E. A.—There is nothing rare in the reverse of this medallion, its type being similar to that of the commonest denarius of Domitian.—[Mionnet values this at 1200 fr. in gold, and 600 fr. in silver].

See cut at the head of the foregoing biographical notice, engraved after a cast from the original in the *Cabinet de France*.

SILVER MEDALLIONS.—CAPIT. RESTIT. Jupiter Capitolinus, seated in a temple, between two standing figures. See an engraving of the coin in p. 170 of this dictionary.—PRINCIP. IVVENTVT. Emperor on horseback. (Mionnet values the above two at 80 fr. each).

GOLD.—GERMANICVS COS. XIIII. A German captive seated, with broken spear. (Two of this subject brought £3 16s. at the Devonshire, and another [COS. XV.] £4 3s. at the Thomas sale). —DOMITIANVS AVGVSTVS.—*Rev.* GERMANICVS COS. XIIII. Minerva. (Pembroke sale, £4 8s.) —LVD. SAEC. FEC. Salian priest. (Mt. 60 fr.) —DOMITIA AVGVSTA IMP. DOMITI. Head of Domitia. (Mt. 200 fr.)—LVD. SAEC. FEC. COS. XIIII. On a cippus. (Mt. 60 fr.)—PRINCEPS IVVENTVTIS. Helmet on a curule chair. (£2 12s. Devonshire).——Same legend. Goat within a crown of laurel. (Mt. 40 fr.)—VESTA. Temple and 3 figures. (48 fr.)—Cornucopiæ, a beautiful *aureus*, with this type of reverse, brought £3 at the Thomas sale.

SILVER.—CONCORDIA AVG. Woman seated. (Mt. 25 fr.)—DIVVS CAESAR IMP. DOMITIANI F. Infant on a globe. (Devonshire, £2 10s.)—DOMITIA AVGVSTA. Head of Domitia. (90 fr.)—DOMITIANV CAES. AVG. Bare head of Domitian, with the bust cuirassed.—*Rev.*-PACI. AVG. (Mt. 25 fr.)

BRASS MEDALLIONS.—S. C. The Emperor, with a river-god at his feet.—S. C. The Emperor crowned by Victory. (Mionnet values these two medallions, which are surrounded with a large circle, at 150 fr. each).

LARGE BRASS.—LVD. SAEC. FEC. The Emperor and several figures. (Mionnet, 40 fr. Sold for £1 19s. at the Pembroke sale).—FIDES EXERCIT. Emperor and soldiers sacrificing. (20 fr.) —S. C. Flavian Amphitheatre. (60 fr.)—S. C. Emperor in a temple, a soldier on each side. (50 fr.)—S. C. Two quadrigæ of elephants on an arch. (24 fr.)—S. C. Woman in a temple, soldier on each side. (80 fr.)

DOMITILLA (*Flavia*), wife of Vespasian, by whom he had three children, Titus, Domitian, and a daughter Domitilla. She was of obscure birth, being the daughter of Flavius Liberalis, a questorian scribe. She was originally a bond woman, or slave, to Statilius Capella, a Roman *eques*. Subsequently, however, she was manumitted, and Vespasian married her A. D. 40. She as well as her daughter died before Vespasian became emperor. And her name was scarcely known in Rome until it was drawn from oblivion by divine honours paid,

and consecration coins struck, during the reign of her son Titus.—" This public deification (remarks Capt. Smyth, p. 59), though unnoticed by either Tacitus, Dion, or Suetonius, is recorded on gold and silver medals of extreme rarity ; and we learn from an inscription preserved by Gruter, the excellent philologist, that an order of priests was instituted for her altars : *Sacerdos Divæ Domitillæ.*"

Although Flavia Domitilla, wife of Vespasian, was dead before the accession of her husband to the empire, she was not on that account deemed less worthy to be declared Augusta. It is unknown whether it was her husband or her son who caused this posthumous honour to be rendered to her. It is the first example of an emperor's wife declared *Augusta* and *Diva*, having died without having occupied the supreme rank of empress.

The following are the coins dedicated to her memory by her eldest son ; and on the obverses of which she is styled DIVA DOMITILLA AVGVSTA, and the legend is accompanied by her portrait.

SILVER MEDALLION.—PIETAS AVGVSTA. A woman seated. (Valued by Mionnet at 300 fr.)

GOLD.—*Rev.* DIVVS AVGVSTVS VESPASIANVS. Head of Vespasian. (Valued by Mionnet at 600 fr. Brought at the Trattle sale £29 10s.)

SILVER.——*Obv.* DIVA DOMITILLA AVGVSTA. Bust of the wife of Vespasian.—*Rev.* FORTVNA AVGVSTA. Fortune standing with her usual attributes.—(See the above engraving ; it is also figured in Akerman, i. plate 5, No. 8.—Mionnet values this excessively rare denarius at 125 fr. A specimen of it, in extremely fine condition, brought £20 10s. 0d. at the Tovey sale.)— PACI AVGVSTAE. The type of Peace.—PIETAS AVGVST. A woman seated to the right, having near her a young child, whom she seems to protect. Allusion is doubtless here made to the virtues of Vespasian's deceased wife. The child is most probably meant for Titus, elder son of Vespasian. [The legend and type of reverse are the same as appear on a denarius of Domitia, the latter obviously borrowed from Domitilla's coin. Mionnet values the *Paci* and the *Pietas* at 125 fr. each.]

DOMITILLAE MEMORIAE.—It is matter of dispute amongst numismatic antiquaries, whether a large brass, which, minted by Titus, bears the foregoing legend and the type of a *carpentum* drawn by two mules, is to be referred to Domitilla, the *mother* of that emperor, or to his *sister*, of the same name. As an investigation of the principal arguments, adduced on both sides of this question, so far from being profitless, is calculated to afford some useful information, a summary will be found given of them under the head of MEMORIAE DOMITILLAE.

DOMITIUS DOMITIANUS.—These names appear only on coins, and are supposed to be those of one of Diocletian's generals, who declared himself emperor at Alexandria, whilst in command of the imperial legions in Egypt ; in which year is not known ; but it is supposed to have been about the time of Diocletian's abdication. The subjoined engraving is from one of the only coins with *Latin* legends ascribed to this usurper; and although no doubt whatever exists as to its authenticity, yet the subject itself presents difficulties which are far from being resolved satisfactorily, by either preceding or present numismatists.

Obv.—IMP*erator* CAESAR *Lucius* DOMI-TIVS DOMITIANVS AVG*ustus*. Bust, to the right, of Domitius Domitianus, laureated.—*Rev.* GENIO POPVLI ROMANI. The Genius of the Roman People unclothed, except with the *pallium* on his shoulders; the face beardless, holding in the right hand a *patera*, and in the other

a *cornucopiæ*. At his feet is an eagle. In the field I'. (mark of the year iii.) On the exergue ALE. (for Alexandria).—This coin, in middle brass, was considered almost unique in D'Ennery's time.—The above cut is after a cast from a specimen in the British Museum.

Without pretending to unravel a skein of historical uncertainties, which environs the researches and baffles the conjectures of learned and ingenious antiquaries, we may cite the following passages in reference to this still unsettled question of identity and date, from two of the most celebrated of modern numismatists:—

" Of this Domitius Domitianus (says Mionnet) the name, career, and fate are equally unknown. But on the reverse of these *Latin* medals, the exergue presents the letters ALE. which shews that they were struck at Alexandria. Now, at the period when Latin coins began to be struck in that city, Greek ones had ceased to appear. The latest Greek medals of Alexandria, of which we have any knowledge, are Diocletian's, and bear the date ιε (15), which answers to the year of Rome 1051 (A. D. 298). The Latin medals of Domit. Domitianus cannot, therefore, be anterior to that epocha. Neither are they greatly posterior to that time; because the type, the workmanship, and the value of these medals unite in proving that they are of Diocletian's age."—(*Rareté*, &c. ii. 171).

The above piece is not an isolated one.—There exist *Greek* coins of Alexandria equally indubitable, and which also belong to a Domitianus. M. Ch. Lenormant, in his splendid work, *Iconographie des Empereurs*, gives a wood-cut of one of these. The following is a description of it:—

DOMITIANOC CEB*αστος*. (*Domitianus Augustus*). Radiated head of Domitian, turned to the right.

Rev.—Serapis, walking to the right, the right hand raised, and holding a long sceptre in the left. In the field a palm branch, and L. B. (Λυκαβάντος δευτέρου) the year II. Æ. 4.

" When we compare (says M. Lenormant), the Latin coin with the Greek one, it is impossible to doubt but that they both belong to one and the same personage. Eckhel, indeed, attri-butes the Greek medal to a Domitianus, contemporary of Gallienus, and conqueror of the two Macriani, whilst he makes the Latin piece descend down as far as the epocha of Diocletian. This opinion I consider to be unstable at its very foundation. As to the opinion of numismatists, who have recognised in the Latin medal the style and workmanship of the æra of Diocletian, it appears to be well warranted; and we do not hesitate to regard the personage, whose portrait it represents, as a contemporary of that emperor. The two pieces were minted at Alexandria. The one belongs to the monetary series of that city, which was verging upon its close; the other is a *Latin* middle brass, but bearing the same distinction (*différent*) as the great gold medal of Diocletian (see *Iconographie Romaine*, No. 7, plate lv.) ALE. mark of the money of Alexandria.—The *Greek* medal indicates the second year of this Domitianus; the Latin middle brass has in the field a Γ, which it is by no means rash to consider as a mark of the *third year*. The pretender, represented on these pieces, is not one of those ephemeral usurpers, whose trace can have disappeared from history. Although the texts relative to the reign of Diocletian be extremely succinct, it would be far too extraordinary that no literary record should have been preserved of a prince who wore the purple in Egypt for three, or at least for two, years. These texts, nevertheless, say nothing of Domitius Domitianus; but they enter into some details in connection with the usurpation of an Achilleus, who was, during a sufficiently long time, master of Alexandria." (p. 114).

The learned and accomplished Author of the work above quoted, then submits to his readers whether it would not be " possible to ascribe to this *Achilleus* the coins which bear the name of Domitius Domitianus?" and he proceeds to employ some ingenious arguments by analogy drawn from the early empire, and backed by references to the events during the reign of Diocletian, to shew, that such might have been the case. At the same time however he confesses, that to justify his suspicion (*soupçon*) it was needful to have some inscription [at present undiscovered] which should give in a manner more complete than coins do, the names of this usurping emperor.

[My esteemed friend, Mr. Matthew Young, the late eminent medallist, once sent down for my inspection, a specimen of this usurper's *Latin* coin, which, as to both legends and types, was in the most beautifully perfect preservation, covered with a smooth, dark brown-coloured patina; and in every respect accordant with the above cited description of Mionnet: who (be it observed), places this second brass in the fourth degree of rarity, and he values it at only 15 fr. Mr. Young's price for his *flower of the die* was £2, the exact sum which it afterwards brought at the Thomas sale.—Mr. Roach Smith informs me, that one of these was lately found in Germany, with a large number of Diocletian's and Maximian's coins.—Note by the compiler.]

DOMNA *(Julia)*, second wife of Septimius Severus, was the offspring of a plebeian family, of Emesa, in Syria. Her father was Julius Bassianus (a name which was given to Caracalla, and which he bore till Severus made him exchange it for that of Antoninus). Her mother's name was Soemias. What Julia wanted in nobility of birth was supplied by the planet of her nativity. Her horoscope was of such a kind, that she professed a perfect assurance of being, at some time or other, the wife of a king.— Severus hearing of this circumstance, whilst yet in a private station, and being addicted himself to astrology, through a strong ambition of sovereignty, married her after the death of his wife Marcia. That this event cannot be fixed later than the year U.C. 928 (A.D. 175), is proved by the express assertion of Dion (lxxiv. § 3), that Faustina, the wife of Marcus Aurelius, prepared for this marriage, a nuptial couch, in the temple of Venus, which was situated near the palace. For it was in this year that Faustina junior set out for the East, in company with her husband, and died on the journey. Domna possessed beauty, wit, learning, eloquence. Her talents and her ambition were alike remarkable; and notwithstanding her notoriously loose character, and the treasonable attempts of which she was suspected, continued always to be a favourite with Severus. After his death, Julia had the grief to see her sons despise her entreaties, and remain enemies. Although treated with some degree of deference by her son Caracalla, she was forced to witness the murder of Geta by his own brother, in her very arms, and to see herself covered with the blood of one of her own sons. And, when her lamentations for Geta's death became too bitter for his liking, Caracalla nearly went the length of doubling his crime in her person. Afterwards, she suc-

ceeded in dissembling her grief, to secure the good will of her surviving son, who in recompense for this condescension, bestowed upon her abundant honours, and even conferred upon her a portion of his imperial authority.—Spartianus, Eutropius, and Aurelius Victor, relate an odious scandal against this celebrated but licentious woman, in reference to Caracalla. It is not mentioned, however, by contemporaneous writers; and, for the honour of womanhood, and especially of maternity, it is to be hoped there was no truth in the accusation, even though alluded to in the severe jests of the Alexandrians.— After the death of Caracalla, she stayed at Antioch; and not being able to reconcile herself to private life, she determined to put an end to her existence by starvation, overwhelming Macrinus with reproaches and maledictions. But soon laying aside her assumed grief for the death of Caracalla, she took heart at finding herself courteously addressed, in the letters of the new emperor; who, however, when he discovered that she had obvious designs on the sovereignty, ordered her to quit Antioch, and go whither soever she pleased. Driven to desperation by this affront, Julia refused all nourishment, and died A.D. 217. Her remains were transported to Rome; and deposited, at first, in the tomb of Caius and Lucius. Afterwards, her sister Mæsa caused them to be placed, together with the bones of Geta, in the mausoleum of Antoninus Pius (according to Dion, lxxviii. § 23, 24).— The children of Domna were Caracalla and Geta, and some daughters of no celebrity.

She is surnamed *Felix* and *Domna;* the latter is her own family appellation, and, according to Spanheim, a Syrian word; inscribed with which her coins are more prized than when they have Pia, a name given to Julia at Rome, in honour of Fulvia Pia, the mother of Severus.—Her numismatic style is IVLIA AVGVSTA (with Mater Castrorum or Augustorum often on the reverse). Also IVLIA PIA FELIX DOMNA AVG. (with Mater Patriæ on the reverse).— The brass coins minted in honour of this empress (except medallions and some others with the word *Domna*), are very common; the gold are rare; the silver of usual size, for the most part common.

The following are amongst the rarest reverses, in each metal:—

GOLD MEDALLION.—VENVS GENETRIX. Venus seated.—(Small size; brought £11 5s. at the Trattle sale).

GOLD.—AETERNIT. IMPERI. Busts of Severus and Caracalla. (Mt. 150 fr.)—Same epigraph, with heads of Caracalla and Geta. (£9 9s. 0d. Thomas; Trattle, £11 10s.)—DIANA LVCIFERA standing. (£7 7s. 6d. at the Thomas sale).— FECVNDITAS. Female seated, and four children near a globe. (£11 Thomas).—HILARITAS. A female, with cornucopiæ and palm branch. (£8 at the Thomas).—IVNO REGINA. (£7 15s. at the Devonshire).—LAETITIA.—LVNA LVCIFERA. —MATER AVG. (Mt. 80 fr. each).—MATER AVGG. Cybèle in quadriga of lions. (£7 15s. at Devonshire; £9 at the Thomas).—MATER DEVM. (£3

10s. at the Thomas; £5 Trattle.)—MAT. AVGG. MAT. SEN. M. PATR. (£9 Thomas).—MATRI CASTRORVM. The Empress standing, sacrificing before two military ensigns. Engraved in Mionnet (i. 303), who values that, and another with the Empress seated, at 100 fr. each.—SEVERVS PIVS AVG. Bust of Severus. (Mt. 100 fr.)—VESTA MATER. Sacrifice by six females before a temple. (£5 10s. Trattle; £8 15s. Thomas).—VENER. VICTR. Venus resting on a column. (Highly preserved, obtained £8 at Thomas sale; bought at the Trattle for £5 7s. 6d.)—VENVS GENETRIX. (A specimen of this extremely rare *aureus*, in perfect condition, £5 7s. at the Brumell, brought £6 6s. at the Pembroke sale).—PIETATI. Figure and altar. (£12 10s. Trattle).

SILVER MEDALLION.—AEQVITAS PVBLICA. The three monetæ. (Mionnet, 30 fr.)

SILVER.—ANTONINVS PIVS AVG. BRIT. Head of Caracalla. (Mt. 50 fr.)—CERERI FRVGIF. [See wood-cut at head of biographical notice.]—CONCORDIA FELIX. Two figures. Engraved in Khell, page 114. (24 fr.)—P. SEPT. GETA. Head of Geta. (45 fr.)—SEVERVS AVG. PARTH. MAX. Head of Severus. (60 fr.)—VESTA MATER. Sacrifice before a temple. (40 fr.)

BRASS MEDALLIONS.—CERES, standing near an altar. (150 fr.)—FECVNDITATI AVG. Woman seated with children. (Mionnet, 300 fr.)

LARGE BRASS.—AEQVITATI PVBLICAE. (Mt. 72 fr.)—IVNONEM. (Beautiful specimen, £2 9s. Thomas).—LVNA LVCIF.—MATER AVG.—PIETATI AVG.—PRIMI DECENNALES. (24 fr. each).—SEPTIMIVS SEVERVS. Head of Severus. (72 fr.)—VESTA MATER & VOTA PVBLICA. (30 fr. each).—VESTA. The goddess seated.—*Obv.* IVLIA DOMNA AVG. (£8 8s. at the Thomas sale).

DOMNUS.—DOMNUS PHILOCOMUS.—These epigraphs appear, the former on a *contorniate* of Trajan, the latter on a *contorniate* of Sept. Severus. The type of both represents *hieronicus*, or victor at the Circensian games, holding a whip in his right hand, a palm branch in his left, and carried in a triumphal quadriga. It is known that palms were amongst the rewards distributed to the successful charioteers on those occasions.

DONA. AVG.—This legend, which Vaillant and Banduri quote as inscribed on the reverse of a silver coin of Gallienus, has for its type Mercury standing, with the *crumena* in one hand, and the *caduceus* in the other, and a dog at his feet.—See *Mercury*.

All antiquaries (says Eckhel) who have commented on this coin, explain its reverse in the words of Trebellius, who says, that Gallienus was renowned for his accomplishments in oratory, in poetry, and in all arts, of which [according to the popular superstition of his day], Mercury was the author and giver. Hence we learn the cause why Gallienus, in this coin, is exhibited under the form of that god.

DONATIVA, donatives, or presents in money, which the emperors made to the soldiers, either after a victory, by way of recompence to them, or at the beginning of a reign, to gain their friendship, or on other occasions. The confer-

ring of donatives on the soldiery, or on the people, is sometimes alluded to on Roman coins, as appears from those on which the pretorian guards stand before the imperial tribune.—Sometimes CONG. is read, with the addition of II. or some other number (Spanheim, *Pr.* ii. p. 533, et seq.) Of all monarchs the Roman emperors alone returned their superfluous wealth to the people: a system doubtless founded on the best policy; since the usefulness of money lies more in giving it circulation, than in locking it up in a treasury; especially since, on any emergency, they had the power of recalling it again. Nor was it otherwise than a free gift to the people, inasmuch as it consisted of the spoils of conquered nations. (Rasche, T. ii. part 1, p. 434.)—See *Congiaria—Largitio—Liberalitas.*

D. P.—*Dii Penates,* or *Dis Penatibus.*—This abbreviation appears on coins of the Sulpicia family, accompanied with the type of two jugated and laureated heads of the *Dii Penates* or household gods.

DR. *Drusus.*—DR. CAE. Q. PR. *Druso Cæsare Quæstore Provinciali.*-(Angeloni, p. 28.)

DRACO, dragon, so called from a Greek word which signifies to *see clearly,* was distinguished from the serpent *(serpens),* by its magnitude, crest, and beard; also sometimes by the addition of wings and feet, and was considered as tutelary genius and guardian in many ancient nations. On a consecration coin of Faustina, two of them draw a car. On denarii of the Vibia, Vipsania, and Volteia families, we see bigæ of dragons, driven by Ceres.

The *Dragon* served as a Roman ensign under the emperors. They borrowed the custom, most probably, from the Dacians and Parthians, who themselves adopted it from the people of India. (Pitiscus). And the Romans having once brought these figures of a fabulous animal into military use, dragons became common to all the cohorts, as is expressly stated by Vegetius:—Primum signum totius legionis est Aquila, quam aquilifer portat; Dracones etiam per singulas cohortes à draconariis feruntur ad prælium.—That the officer who bore the image itself of a dragon, or an ensign, on which the figure was woven into the *vexillum,* had the appellation of *Draconarius,* we learn from Ammianus, in describing the solemn entry of Constantius II. into Rome.

On a large brass of Philip senior, a woman stands holding a two-footed dragon in her right hand, and a spear in her left.—For Eckhel's explanation of this enigmatical type, see TRANQUILLITAS AUG.

Draco Lanuvius, or symbolical serpent of *Juno Sospita,* winding its folds round, and erecting its head above, an altar, is a frequent type on the denarii of Roman families.

The mystical *dragon,* lying prostrate, is represented on some coins of the Christian Emperors. Thus the dragon is seen under the feet of Theodosius, and in like manner of Valentinian junior, of Libius Severus, of Heraclius, and others.—See *Serpens.*

DRUSILLA.—The appellation of this woman is thus read, unaccompanied by the title of *Augusta*, on a large brass of Caligula, in association with the names of her two sisters, AGRIPPINA and IVLIA, both objects, with herself, of that tyrant's incestuous love. Julia Drusilla, the daughter of Agrippina senior and of Germanicus, was born 768 (A. D. 15), at Treves; married by Tiberius to L. Cassius Longinus, grandson of Cassius, and taken from her husband by her own execrable brother to cohabit with him. Drusilla died A. D. 38.—See the reverse engraved in p. 29.

DRUSUS *senior*.——Nero Claudius Drusus Germanicus, commonly called Drusus senior, was the son of Ti. Claudius Nero and of Livia. He came into the world in the year of Rome 716 (B. C. 38), not however at his father's house, but in that of Octavianus (afterwards Augustus), three months after he had, with the permission of her husband, married Livia, then *enceinte* with Drusus; a circumstance which gave rise to the line—Beatis trimestres liberos nasci—"To the fortunate, children of three months are born." (Sueton. in Claud. c. 1).—His prenomen was at first *Decimus*, and after-

wards *Nero*, by which he is invariably designated on coins, thus—NERO CLAVDIVS DRVSVS, so as to indicate by the names *Nero*, and *Claudius* his paternal, and by that of Drusus his maternal, genealogy, through the gens Livia. For, according to Suetonius (in Tiber. c. 3), he was enrolled also in the family of the Livii, by the adoption into it of his maternal grandfather. Being promoted, by the influence of Augustus, to an earlier share in public honours than the strict letter of the law would have permitted, he was enabled to devote himself to the campaigns in Germany, from the year U. C. 739 (B. C. 15), for six years till his death; during which period he partly kept in check the Suevi, Sicambri, Cherusci, and Frisii, and partly reduced them to the Roman allegiance. He completed with vast labour a dam, or dyke, across the Rhine, to moderate the force of the stream, and which, as late as the time of Suetonius, was called the *(Fossa) Drusina*, and is to this day an object of wonder. At the beginning of his consulate, in the year U. C. 745 (B. C. 9), he proceeded into Germany, and was the first Roman who penetrated as far as the Albis (now the *Elbe*).—Eckhel, vi. 175–76.

Drusus senior died the same year, thirty days after a fall from his horse, caused doubtless by a frightful apparition, under the superstitious influence of which he was deterred from pursuing the Germans beyond the Elbe. He was so distinguished a favourite of Augustus, on account of his valour and integrity, that, in the oration which that emperor delivered at his burial, he prayed "the gods to make his own Cæsars like the deceased, and grant to himself as honourable an end as his had been."—Valerius Maximus speaks in high terms of his moral qualities, and of his conjugal fidelity. The foreign victories of Drusus, and the regrets

which he publicly expressed on the loss of the free republic, rendered his name popular; and his premature death, which took place during his journey homewards, before he reached the Rhine, contributed to render his memory still more dear to the Romans. His remains were conveyed to Rome, and placed, with the highest honours, in the family mausoleum of Augustus.

His brass coins (only those of the large size are extant), struck under Claudius, are not rare; with the exception of those restored by Titus and by Domitian. On these he is styled

1. NERO CLAVDIVS DRVSVS GERMANICVS IMP*erator*. Bare head of Drusus senior to the left.—*Rev.*-TI*berius* CLAVDIVS CAESAR AVG*ustus* Pontifex Maximus TR*ibunitiæ* Potestatis IMP*erator*. (Tiberius Claudius Cæsar Augustus, Sovereign Pontiff, invested with the tribunitian power). Statue of the elder Drusus, clothed in the toga, turned to the right, seated on a heap of arms, and holding a branch in the right hand. Below is the mark of Senatorial authority for striking the coin.—Engraved as above from a specimen in the compiler's possession.

This brass coin, and the two following *aurei*, were minted by order of the Emperor Claudius, and in honour of his father's memory. They renew the memory of the statues, both equestrian and pedestrian, which, with other honours, were dedicated to him after his decease. The surname of *Germanicus*, attached here to the legend of Drusus, was not decreed to him until after his death—the Senate at the same time authorising all his descendants to bear a name which recalled the glory of their ancestor.

2. *Obv.*—Same legend, with laureated head of Drusus senior.—*Rev.*-DE GERM. (Victory over the Germans). Equestrian statue to the

right, on a triumphal arch, between two trophies. Silver.

The arch of Drusus here represented still exists almost entire near the Appian Gate, now called the Gate of St. Sebastian, at Rome. The group of sculptures which crowned the arch have disappeared.—(Lenormant).

3. *Obv.*—Same legend, with the laureated head of Drusus.—*Rev.*—DE GERMANIS.—Trophy composed of German arms.

DRUSUS junior.—Drusus called the younger, to distinguish him from his uncle *Nero Claudius Drusus*, was born during the marriage of Tiberius and of Vipsania Agrippina, probably about the year of Rome 740 (B. C. 14). Being early advanced to public honours, he was Questor in 764 (A. D. 11), and *Consul Designatus* in 767 (A. D. 14), when he was sent by his father Tiberius into Pannonia, and there recalled to its allegiance the army of that region, which on the death of Augustus had betrayed symptoms of revolt. Consul for the first time in 768 (A. D. 15), he entered Rome in an Ovation decreed to him in 773 (A. D. 20), on account of his settlement of the affairs of Germany, and establishment of Vannius as king of the Suevi.—In 774 he became consul for the second time, and in 775 (A. D. 22), received from his father the *Tribunitia Potestas.* Nor did he long survive this period, being cut off in the flower of his age. For, incensed at the influence of Sejanus, he went the length of striking him in a quarrel. Sejanus, burning for revenge, and already meditating his death, communicated his designs to Livia or Livilla, the wife of Drusus, whose co-operation he had secured by the criminal intimacy subsisting between them, and poisoned him in the midst of his security, in the year U. C. 776 (A. D. 23). The crime was hushed up for a time through fear of Sejanus; but on his death in 784 (A. D. 31), it was brought to light by the declaration of Apicata, the wife of Sejanus; who, finding that her children were involved in her husband's fate, and losing her reason in her grief, sent a letter to Tiberius, in which she betrayed the perpetrators of the murder of Drusus, and then put an end to her own existence. This Drusus was considered an able soldier; but a man of no stability of character, and dissolute in his habits. He delighted in bloodshed, even of the vilest of mankind; and so marked was this trait, that sharp swords used to be called *Drusiani* (gladii). He was thought inferior to his father in every respect, except his passion for drinking. Cassiodorus says, that he was honoured with a public burial.—*D. N. Vet.* vi. 202.

His first brass coins, with his portrait on one side, and Tiberius on the other, are rare; 2nd brass common, except with the reverse of Tiberius, which are very rare. The silver are all extremely rare.—The following is a description of legends and types, in each metal:—

1. *Rev.*—DRVSVS - - - AVG. COC. II. TR. P. Bare head of Drusus the younger.—*Obv.* TI. CAES. AVG. P. M. TR. P. XXXV. Laureated head of Tiberius. Silver.—Engraved in Khell, p. 16.

This medal of Drusus the younger belongs to a suite of pieces struck out of Rome, and probably at Cæsaræa, in Cappadocia, a short time after the union of that province to the Roman empire. The unusual titles which Tiberius bears on these pieces confirm this conjecture. Eckhel, who was the first to hazard it, thinks also that the epocha of the medals in question answers to that in which Tiberius having become acquainted with the part which Sejanus and Livilla had taken in the death of Drusus junior, the provinces of the empire eagerly seized the occasion to flatter the emperor by dedicating money to his son's memory.

2. DRVSVS CAESAR TI*berii* AVG*usti* Filius DIVI AVG*usti* Nepos. Bare head of Drusus the younger to the left.—*Rev.*—PONTIF*ex* TRIBVN*itiæ* POTEST*atis* ITER*um.*—In the field, the initials S. C. (struck by authority of the Senate.) Middle brass.

The first tribunitian power of Drusus the younger dates from the year of Rome 776 (A. D. 23), one year before his death.

3. *Rev.*—DRVSVS CAESAR TI. AVG. F. DIVI AVG. N. PONT. TR. POT. II. In the field, S. C.—*Obv.*—A caduceus, at the foot of which two cornucopiæ cross themselves, supporting two children's heads, facing each other. Large brass.—See an engraving of it, p. 289.

The two infants represented on this obverse are the two twins born of the marriage of Drusus junior and Livilla. One of these sons, whose name is unknown, died at about four years of age; the other added to his name of Tiberius the surname of *Gemellus.* This latter youth, whom Tiberius designed to have shared his heritage with Caligula, died suddenly in the year 790 (A. D. 37), at the age of nineteen, victim of Caligula's jealousy. Amongst other evidences of the great joy with which the birth of these twin brothers filled the heart of Tiberius, that old emperor made it a matter of boast, in full Senate, that until then, no Roman of a rank as elevated as his own had had the happiness of seeing twin children born in his family:—Nulli ante Romanorum ejusdem fastigii viro geminam stirpem editam. (Tac. *Ann.* ii. 84).—

"The ancients had particular reasons—connected with the most profound branch of their religious beliefs—for attaching a superstitious importance to the birth of twins." M. Lenormant, in making the above remark in his *Iconographie* (p. 20), refers his readers for an exposition of those reasons to his *Nouvelle Gal. Mythologique.*

DRUSUS *Cæsar*, second son of Germanicus and of Agrippina senior, was born about the year 761 (A. D. 8); assumed the *toga virilis* in 776 (A. D. 23); and being the same year recommended by Tiberius to the Senate, together with his brother Nero, is said by Tacitus (*Ann.* iv. 36), to have been appointed prefect of the city, 778 (A. D. 25). He was a youth of an extremely cruel disposition, and through ambition of power conspired with Sejanus against his own brother Nero. But he very early paid the penalty; for after his brother had been got rid of, becoming himself the next obstacle to the projects of Sejanus, he fell a victim to the same machinations, and was closely confined in the dungeons of the *Palatium.* His death was deferred, not from motives of mercy, but in order that Tiberius might have some one to take part against Sejanus, then destined to destruction, in the event of his resorting to violent measures; as the inclinations of the people were strongly biassed in favour of the son of Germanicus. But when Sejanus had been put to death, the imperial tyrant, feeling secure of his safety, had the cruelty to deprive Drusus of food. And, thus reduced to gnaw the very wool of his bed, the wretched young prince protracted an agonizing existence till the ninth day, when he expired, 786 (A. D. 33). Tiberius ordered his ashes to be scattered, that he might never receive the honours of burial.—Eckhel, vi. 217.

The equestrian effigies of Drusus and his brother Nero appear on second brass of Caligula. —See NERO ET DRUSUS CAESARES.

DUCENTISSIMA.—See R. CC. *Remissa Ducentissima.*

DUILLIA—a plebeian gens, little known.— The coins ascribed to it are brass, consisting solely of the *as*, and some of its divisions, viz. the semis, the triens, and the sextans. Under the head of Duillia, Riccio (p. 83, plate xix. No. 1), gives engravings of two pieces; one with double-headed Janus, the second with the head of Mercury on one side, and on the reverse of both a ship's prow, on the top of which stands a small figure of a bull; at the bottom ROMA. In the upper part of the field are the letters MD, being the only mark that distinguishes them from common specimens of the *as* coinage, without names of families. With this slight clue, however, Borghesi reads *M. Dullius,* and assigns them both to the Duillia family.

DUPLEX *Cornucopiæ*——a double horn of plenty.—This conjunction, which appears on some Roman coins, served to predict a future abundance of all things to the government of the prince.

DUPLICATION *of Letters*, a mark of the plural number. Thus we find AVGG. written to signify two Emperors. Or it is written AVGGG. as on a coin of Licinius, and on some of Carausius, to denote *three* Augusti. In like manner CAESS. for *two* Cæsars; and CAESSS. for *three* Cæsars. By the same rule, on coins of a lower age, are observed DD. NN. or more rarely DDD. NNN. *Domini Nostri.* On medals also of Sept. Severus and Caracalla is read, IMPP. INVICTI PII AVGG. *Imperatores Invicti Pii Augusti.*—See p. 95.

Besides these titles of Emperors, the *reduplication of letters* is a mark of the plural when it occurs as follows :—DD. *Decuriones.* DPP. *Dii Penates.*——DEBELLATORI GENTT. BARBARR. *Gentium Barbararum.*—COHH. PRAET. *Cohortes Prætorianæ*, &c.

DUPONDIUS, a weight of two pounds ;— also a piece of Roman money, valued at two *asses*, and which preserved the same name, notwithstanding the diminution of the *as*, which was reduced below the pound.—See AS and its parts.

DURMIA gens.—A family of uncertain rank, and scarcely known till the age of Augustus.— There are six varieties of its coins. Gold rare; silver common. Marcus Durmius was Augustus's moneyer in 735 (B. C. 19), conjointly with Marcus Aquilius Florus, and Publius Petronius Turpilianus. Four of his coins have on their obverses the head of *Honour*, and on their reverses types which regard the exploits and the honours ascribed to Augustus Cæsar. Four others have each on their obverses the head of Augustus, and on their reverses four different types as singular as any in the series of family coins; and which have, more or less, employed the pens of the most eminent numismatologists for a series of years.

1. [CAESAR] AVGVSTVS. Bare head of Augustus.—*Rev.*—M. DVRMIVS III. VIR. (Monetal Triumvir). A wild boar transfixed with a hunting spear. Silver.

2. CAESAR AVGVSTVS.——Same type as above.—*Rev.*—M. DVRMIVS III. VIR. A lion devouring a stag. Silver.—See engraving, p. 316, article DENARIUS.

[The above devices of the wild boar and the lion evidently refer to those sumptuous hunting parties, in which, according to both Dion and Suetonius, Augustus took very great delight].

3 HONORI. M. DVRMIVS IIIVIR. The bare juvenile head of Honour.—*Rev.*—CAESAR AVGVSTVS. Augustus standing in a biga of elephants, holds in the right hand a branch of laurel, and in the left the sceptre. Silver.

4. Same legend and young head.—*Rev.*—CAESAR AVGVSTVS, S. C. A basket with a flower, on a quadriga. Silver.—See *Flos.*

5. Same legend, and young head between two stars.—*Rev.*—AVGVSTO OB. C. S. in a crown of oak leaves. Gold.—Eckhel marks it RRRR. Mionnet values it at 48 fr.

6. M. DVRMIVS IIIVIR. HONORI.— Same juvenile head.—*Rev.*-CAESAR AVGVS-TVS SIGN*is* RECEP*tis*. A male figure kneeling, offers up an ensign with his right hand.

With respect to those denarii of Durmius, whose obverses bear the name and head of HONOS, Eckhel recalls to the recollection of numismatists, that on similar coins, struck about the same time by Aquilius Florus, is seen the head of VIRTVS. Dion acquaints us that in the year of Rome 727 (B. C. 17), Augustus made some alteration in the games dedicated to Virtue and Honour; for which reason, Durmius and his monetary colleagues, in the years immediately following 734 (B. C. 20), appear to have caused the head of each to be stamped on their respective denarii.—See HONOS ET VIRTVS; also see MUCIA GENS.

The epocha in which medals 3, 4, 5, and 6 were struck, is, by consent of all writers on the subject, referred to the last war waged by Augustus against the Parthians, which ended in the submission of Phraates their king, and with the voluntary restitution of prisoners, ensigns, and spoils taken from the Romans B. C. 20.— Hence, for Augustus's having saved the blood of his fellow citizens, the Senate decreed to him quadrigæ and bigæ, with golden crowns, and all the military and civic honours of the triumph. Borghesi considers that Honour and Virtue refer to the *Clipeus Votivus* dedicated to Augustus on the termination of the Parthian war, and deposited in the temple of those two Roman divinities.

7. CAESAR AVGVSTVS. Laureated head. *Rev.*—M. DVRMIVS III. VIR. A sea-crab, holding a butterfly in its claws. Gold.—(Valued by Mionnet at 60 fr.)

["The crab grasping the butterfly (says Eckhel), is an enigma, which no one appears, as yet, to have satisfactorily solved." It is, however, like many other types to be found among the mintages of Augustus, a fantastic design, elegantly executed. The above cut of it is after a cast from a beautiful specimen in the British Museum].

8. CAESAR AVGVSTVS. Bare head of Augustus.—*Rev.*—M. DVRMIVS III. VIR.— Bull with human face, walking to the right, crowned by a flying genius, like the type of the Campanian money. This coin is not given in Mionnet. But Riccio describes and engraves it in his *Famiglie di Roma, Suppl.* pl. 56, No. 2.

[This bull with a human countenance is regarded by Eckhel as an emblem involved in utter obscurity. Riccio remarks, that "it is a type peculiar to almost all the cities of Campania, as the wild boar transfixed, or not transfixed, belongs to Capua and Pæstum; and as to Velia belongs the type of the lion devouring a stag].

DUUMVIRI, so called from their number, were magistrates inferior in rank to the Pretors, and who presided as judges at a court *(curia)* in Rome, where cognizance was taken only of criminal cases. The office was held in much consideration during the Republic, as well for the power it conferred, as on account of its antiquity, the creation of duumviri being referred to a period so far back as the reign of Tullus Hostillius.

Duumviri Municipales were also two men appointed to perform the functions of the ordinary magistracy, in Roman colonies and municipal towns. This fact is attested not by coins only, but likewise by marbles, and by various writers.—"Doubtless (says Eckhel), as, according to the expressions of Aulus Gellius, the colonies were a sort of miniature imitation of Rome, their mother-city, so these Duumvirs resembled, in a certain degree, the two Consuls of Rome. And, similarly, what in the latter was the Senate, in the colonies and *municipia* was the *Curia*; whilst in the place of Senators stood the *Decuriones*. (See the word, p. 313). Moreover, as the Consuls were, at Rome, not only the ordinary but the highest magistrates, so also in the colonies were the *Duumviri*. This is evident from the well-known fact, that an honorary duumvirate in the colonies was frequently passed through by Cæsars, Emperors, and Kings. And since the colonies were thus in the practice of conferring a local office on such distinguished personages, it cannot be supposed, that it was any other than the highest in their power to bestow. And this also explains the expression of Apuleius—"In which colony (says he), I had a father in the highest position, a duumvir."

On the cited authority of marbles, there are learned writers who have asserted, that the *Duumviri* sometimes styled themselves *Consuls* of their colonies, on the plea of the resemblance of their own office to that of the true Roman Consul. The Author of *Doctrina*, who considers those citations to be of doubtful accuracy, and consequently entitled to but little credit, contends that, even if the *Duumviri* were sometimes styled *Consuls*, it was in a manner resembling that in which the *Decuriones* were occasionally called Senators. Nor is there any doubt but that, if the law, or the permission of the higher powers, did not allow them these titles, they were at least tacitly accorded by virtue of the similarity of the office.—iv. 475.

The *Duumviri* are indicated on coins by the letters IIV. or IIVIR. On those of Osca, in Spain, the two units are joined together by a transverse line, thus HVIR. in the same way as for IIS. which is the mark denoting a sestertius.—HS. is often seen on marbles. Not unfrequently, the *names* only of the *Duumviri* are stated on colonial money, without the mark IIVIR.—*Duumviri* are mentioned on coins of the following places :—

Accium, in Tarraconensis.
Agrigentum, in Sicily.
Bilbilis, in Tarraconensis.
Buthrotum, in Epirus.
Cæsar-Augusta, in Tarraconensis.
Calagurris, in do.
Carthago Nova, in do.
Carthago Vetus, in Africa.
Celsa, in Tarraconensis.
Corinth, in Achaia.
Dertosa, in Tarraconensis.
Enna, in Sicily.
Ercavica, in Tarraconensis.
Ilicum, in do.
Julia, in Bœtica.
Leptis, in Syrtica.
Onuba, in Bœtica.
Osca, in Tarraconensis.
Pæstum, in Lucania.
Panormus, in Sicily.
Parium, in Mysia.
Saguntum, in Tarraconensis.
Turiaso, in do.
Utica, in Zeugitana.

That the Duumvirate was an office lasting for a year, is gathered not only from the fact, that it was a function of the same character as the Consulate of the Romans, but also because the II*viri* (in the same way as the Archons, Pretors, and Scribes of the Greek cities) are found to repeat the record of their magistracy on their coins, expressed by IIVIR. ITER*um*; as, for example, on the money of Corinth, and other places. But from certain coins it is evident, that this custom did not obtain everywhere, or not invariably, and that in several cities the Duumvirate was prolonged for five years.

The mark of the IIVIR. is seen on coins of the Pomponia and Quintillia families.

Duumviri Quinquennales.——See Quinquennales.

Duumviri Honorarii.—The Cæsars and *Augusti* frequently bore the honorary offices of government in the various cities of the empire. This is a fact assured to us by the often quoted testimony of Spartian, accepted, in a question like the present, as paramount authority by Eckhel himself, who furnishes a list of these personages, and states the circumstances connected with their respective appointments.—Amongst them are, Augustus, M. Agrippa, and Tiberius Cæsar, Quinquennales of Celsa—Tiberius, IIVIR of Corinth—Germanicus and Drusus, sons of Tiberius, II*viri* of Accium, and IIIIVIR*i* of Carteia—Nero and Drusus, sons of Germanicus, II*viri* of Cæsar-Augusta and Carthago Nova—Juba II. and Ptolemy, Kings of Mauretania, II*viri* (perhaps) of Carthago Nova. —Hadrian, in Etruria, served the Pretorship; and throughout the *Latin* towns he was Dictator, Edile, and Duumvir; at Neapolis he was ΔHMAPX (invested with Tribunitian power) in his native place (Italica, in Spain), he was Quinquennalis; as also at Adria, his

adopted country; whilst at Athens he was Archon. The same procedure, therefore, was observed in the colonies, as occasionally in the free cities. Coins of Trajan testify that he discharged the highest office of the magistracy at Byzantium, a free city. And historical writers concur with ancient marbles to confirm the evidence of coins. On a marble found in the *municipium* of Consabrum, in Hispania Tarraconensis, published by Gruter (p. 421), we read EO. ANNO QVO. ET OPTIMVS IMP. HADRIANVS ETIAM DVVMVIRATVS HONOREM SVSCEPIT.—On a tablet found at Præneste, given by Peter Foggini, appears the inscription GERMANICVS CAESAR DRVSVS CAESAR, QVIN*Quennales Præneste.*——Under the commonwealth, eminent Romans bore the office of II*viri* in the colonies near home, as *e. g.* Piso, and Pompey the Great at Capua.—See Eckhel, (iv. 487), who adds that at the subsequent periods of Augustus and Tiberius, the *quinquennial* magistracy was held in the colonies by the *Præfecti* II*viri*, as representatives of the Cæsars.

E.

E.—Fifth letter, and the second vowel, of the *Latin* alphabet.

E long is sometimes found inscribed on the earlier coins of Rome with two Es; as for example, FEELIX instead of FELIX, on a denarius of Sulla's.

E single, in the place of AE dipthong, now and then occurs. Thus EQVITAS for AEQVITAS, as in Nerva; REIPVBLICE for REIPVBLICAE, as in Constantine jun. Julian, and Jovian. CESAR for CAESAR; IVDEA for IVDAEA; MAMEA for MAMAEA.

E, by a false change of vowels, is sometimes found used for AE, as BAETISSIMORVM, on coins of Diocletian, Maximian, and Constantius Chlorus; FAELICITAS, as in Trajanus Decius, and SAECVRITAS, as in Diocletian.

E displaced by A or by I, as SARAPIDI instead of SERAPIDI, in Julian II.; GENITRIX instead of GENETRIX.—[But these, and the other literal alterations and substitutions above mentioned, are of rare occurrence].

E serves on Roman coins to mark the *fifth* monetary office, or mint.

EAGLE *(Aquila),* which is still called "the King of Birds," and which fable consecrated to Jupiter, as the minister of his lightnings, is the type under which, standing on a thunderbolt, a globe, a laurel wreath, a palm branch, an altar, or a ship's prow, the Roman empire is most frequently designated on coins of Augustus, Antoninus, L. Verus (p. 249), Sabina, &c.

On a denarius of the Terentia gens, struck by Varro, naval pro-questor of Pompeius Magnus, the reverse exhibits the emblems of Pompey's power by sea and by land, consisting of a sceptre in the midst of a dolphin and an *eagle*.

At the consecration of Emperors, an *eagle* was let forth from amidst the flames of the funeral pile; and, flying into the air, it was supposed to bear to heaven the soul of the deified personage. It is for this reason that, on imperial coins, the bare head of the Prince, or the veiled head of the *Augusta*, is impressed on one side, and on the other an eagle in full flight, with the emperor or empress on its back.—See CONSECRATIO, pp. 248 and 250.

The *Eagle* stands in the middle between an owl and a peacock, on coins of Antoninus Pius and Marcus Aurelius. It is thus that Jupiter, Minerva, and Juno are designated by their respective attributes. And, as if to shew more clearly the meaning of this remarkable group, there is a brass medallion of Antoninus Pius in the *Cabinet de France*, on the reverse of which, without legend, Jupiter is seated, with Minerva, also seated, on his right, and Juno on his left. A coin of Vespasian exhibits a similar type of the three shrines in the temple of Jupiter Capitolinus, in which the statues of those three deities stood, each with its attendant bird occupying the same relative position as on the first coin above described.

Legionary EAGLE.—It is an established fact, that the *Eagle* was the principal standard of the Legion, and continued to be used as such so long as that body existed. These legionary eagles, not great in size, were affixed to spears, the lower ends of which were sharp-pointed, for the purpose of their being more easily planted in the ground. They are exhibited on coins, as holding in their talons a thunderbolt. Nor has this peculiarity escaped the observation of ancient writers. Dion states that, among the portents which presented themselves to Cn. Pompey the younger, when in Spain, was the following:—"That his *legionary eagles*, shaking their wings, and casting from them the golden thunderbolts which some of them grasped in their claws, openly denounced an evil fate against him, and flew off to Cæsar."—Silver was preferred for the material of the eagle itself, and the reason, according to Pliny, was that it is a metal which is seen at the greatest distance.—(Du Choul, *Castrametation Romaine,*

p. 12).—Respecting the Eagle-bearer, see AQUILIFER, p. 71.

On the legionary coins of M. Antony we see the *Eagle*, placed between two ensigns, distinguished with three circular appendages, and terminating above in a spear-point.—*Eagles* between simple ensigns, of a similar form and the same number, appear on denarii of Clodius Macer and of S. Severus; also on the well-known coins which record the recovery of the ensigns from the Parthians, and are inscribed SIGNA P. R. several of which are published in *Morell. Thesaur. Fam. Rom.* under the head of *Incerta*, plate ii. They are also to be found amongst the colonial mintages, such as in Acci (see p. 3), and in Cæsar-Augusta, Patræ, Emerita, &c. (see Vaillant). On coins of Augustus commemorating the restitution of the standards, Mars Ultor appears, with a legionary eagle in his right hand, and in his left an ensign—also a votive shield between a legionary eagle and a simple ensign (C. L. V. SIGNIS RECEPTIS, engraved in p. 218).—See LEGIO.

The legionary *eagle* appears fixed to a ship's prow, and held by two right hands, on a first brass of Nerva, with legend of CONCORDIA EX·ERCITVVM (p. 243). It is also seen in the hands of the emperor, on coins of M. Aurelius, Commodus, Alex. Severus, Philip, jun. Probus, &c.

Eagle and Infant Jove.—In the Farnese cabinet there is a brass medallion of Antoninus Pius, the reverse of which (without legend) exhibits Jupiter Crescens, seated, naked, on the back of a goat, before an altar, with an *Eagle* sculptured on it, placed close to the trunk of a tree.—See Pedrusi, vol. v. p. 174.

Eagle and Oaken Crown.—On a beautiful coin of Augustus, an eagle, with wings expanded, is seen perched (as in the subjoined cut) on a crown of oak leaves; behind which are two branches of laurel.—See CIVIBVS SERVATIS CAESAR, p. 206.

The legends and types of this historical *aureus* are well elucidated by the statement of Dion (liii. ch. 16), that it was decreed A. U. C. 727 (B. C. 27), that laurels should be planted before the house of Augustus, in the *Palatium*, and a crown of oak leaves should be suspended from the summit of the roof, to indicate that he was "the perpetual vanquisher of his foes," and "preserver of the citizens."—See coins of the gens Caninia, one of which, though struck many years later, exhibits the same design.—The S. C. on this coin indicates, both that Augustus was styled Cæsar by a *Senatus Consultum,* and that by the same sanction, the oak crown and the laurels were decreed. The expression of Pliny is memorable—"That Augustus, after

quelling the civil wars, received a civic crown
from the whole human race."——See *Corona
Querna*, p. 290.

EBOR.–*Ebora*, in Lusitania, between the Anas
(Guadiana) and the Tagus rivers; by Pliny
classed among the *Oppida Veteris Latii.* It was
not strictly a colony of the Romans, but is said
to have been invested by them with great privileges as a *municipium.* The present name is
Evora, an episcopal city of Portugal, in the
province of Alentejo. Coins struck at *Ebora*,
under Augustus, give it the title of LIBERALI-
TAS IVLIA EBOR. whence Vaillant infers it to
have derived its establishment as a Roman station from Julius Cæsar. A second brass, published by Ant. Augustino, in his dialogues, and
described below, does not exhibit the epigraph
either of a colony or a municipium, but simply
the *Latin* inscription usually adopted by cities
possessing the *jus Latii*—

PERM. CAES. AVG. P. M *(Permissu Cæsaris
Augusti, Pontificis Maximi).* Bare head of
Augustus.—*Rev.*—LIBERALITATIS IVLIAE EBOR.
In four lines, within a garland.—Engraved in
Akerman, *Coins of Hispania*, p. 11, pl. ii. No. 3.

EBORACUM or EBURACUM, now York;
the chief city of Northern Britain, or Valentia,
and the station of the sixth legion, surnamed
Victrix. Aurelius Victor terms it a *municipium;*
and the sculptures, pavements, inscriptions, and
other remains discovered on and about its site,
prove that it was a large and flourishing city,
second, probably, to Londinium only. It was
the residence, during their expeditionary visits
to Britain, of the emperors Septimius Severus
and Constantius Chlorus, both of whom died
there, the former in A. D. 211, and the latter
A. D. 306. Coins have been cited as inscribed
COL. EBOR. but if any such exist, they were
issued from the workshops of the *falsarii*, and
not from any mint at Eburacum. It is to be
noted, that while we have coins of the Constantine family inscribed PLON. *Pecunia Londinensis*, we have none recording York; neither
does it appear to be indicated by the exergual
letters on any of the coins of Carausius and
Allectus.—For the Antiquities of York see the
Rev. C. Wellbèloved's "Eburacum."

EDIFICES.—Public buildings and structures
are represented on numerous Roman coins,
in many instances so artistically, that their original forms may clearly be traced, on a comparison of existing ruins with the monetal types.
Amongst the grandest of these are—*Temples*,
with their peristyles and pediments; some
simply raised on flights of steps, others flanked
with porticoes and adorned with statues.

As a very striking specimen of this sacred
class of types, and at the same time one the
least faulty in perspective design, to be found
on coins of Roman die, the following engraving
is given from a large brass of Trajan.

Rev.–S. P. Q. R. OPTIMO PRINCIPI. A superbly
decorated temple of eight columns, through the
central intercolumniation of which is seen an
image seated. At each extremity a portico is
advanced at right angles with the *façade.*

[In this peculiar feature of its construction,
the edifice, or the above type of it, would seem
to have served as a model of imitation for that
much larger-sized and more floridly designed
coin which, if genuine, was dedicated to the
deified memory of Trajan's sister, whom Hadrian
had consecrated.—See DIVAE MATIDIAE SOCRVI.
(p. 333].

Consular and family coins are by no means
deficient in architectural delineations. The old
Rostra, that ancient seat of Roman eloquence, is
adumbrated on a denarius of the Lollia gens,
inscribed with the word PALIKANVS. There
is also a representation of the *Rostra* erected by
Julius Cæsar, extant on silver of the Sulpicia
family, bearing the surname of PLATORI*Nus.*
In like manner, the *Basilica Aemilia*, a court
of justice, on denarii of that family (p. 31)—
the VIL*la* PVB*lica*, on a coin of the Didia
gens (p. 327)—and the temple of Jupiter Capitolinus, on a denarius, struck by Petillius
(page 171), serve respectively to hand down
some resemblance of those buildings. Whilst
the type of the *Comitium* meets the eye in
association with the legend of CLOACIN*a*
(p. 219).

But it is in the imperial series, and especially
in the early and middle periods, that testimonies to the architectural splendour of Rome, her
provinces, and her colonies, most abound. The
coinages of Tiberius and Claudius, of Nero,
Vespasian, Titus, and Domitian, of Trajan, Hadrian, the Antonines, S. Severus, Caracalla, &c.
are more or less rich in types of this interesting
kind, executed with consummate skill. Take
for examples, the *Macellum* (p. 77); the Flavian Amphitheatre (p. 42); the *Basilica Ulpia*
(p. 125); the *Forum Trajani* (see the words);
the *Circus Maximus*, with its spina, metæ, and
sculptural decorations (pp. 174, 201, and 202.)
Other coins exhibit harbours (see *Port. Ostia*
and *Portum Trajani*); triumphal arches (pp. 77,
78, 79, 358); altars (pp. 72, 73, 74). Besides
these we see rostral, triumphal, and other isolated
pillars (pp. 235, 236); together with obelisks,
bridges (p. 309), either thrown over rivers, or used
as viaducts, in the construction and reparation of
public roads. As to the minor and less durable
objects, such as funeral piles (p. 251); curule
chairs (p. 12); chariots, gallies, &c.—so many
and so various are these representations on products of the Roman mint, that they almost set
description at defiance.

EGNATIA gens—of the plebeian order. Its surname on coins is *Maximus*, or *Maxsumus.*—There are three principal varieties in the types. Gold rare; silver common.

1. MAXSVMVS. Bust of Venus, well adorned, with a winged Cupid hanging to her neck behind.—*Rev.*—C. EGNATIVS CN. F. CN. N. A woman in a biga, moving slowly to the left, crowned by a victory flying towards her; behind the car a cap of liberty.

2. MAXSVMVS. Naked winged bust of Cupid, with bow and quiver on his shoulder.—*Rev.*—C. EGNATIVS CN. F. CN. N. Two columns of a temple, between which stand a man in the toga, with *hasta* in right hand, and a woman clothed in the tunic.—See engraving, p. 208—CUPID.

Eckhel, after some comments on the conjectures of preceding numismatists, dismisses them by saying, that the types (exhibited on the above two denarii, and on that described and engraved below), are precisely of a kind to excite a curiosity to learn their true meaning, but for which neither Vaillant nor Havercamp had done aught to rescue them from the obscurity in which they found them involved.

Undeterred by the great author of *Doctrina's* tone of discouragement, Riccio devotes some attention to the subject. After citing the attempt made in *Morell. Thesaur. Fam. Rom.* to prove that this Caius Egnatius, son of Cneus, and nephew of Cneus, had been a provincial quæstor of Sulla, in the time of the first Mithridatic war (B. C. 87–86), he admits that the head and other emblems of Liberty are not usually, if ever, found on the coinages of Sulla, and that they seem rather to belong to Cassius and Brutus, and their adherents, in Asia and Africa, after the murder of Julius Cæsar (B. C. 44).—He then proceeds to observe, that Venus may possibly allude to the birth-place of the moneyer, or to the place where the denarius was struck. But the repetition of the caps of liberty; the woman in a triumphal chariot, who may be the goddess of Rome; the prows and oars of ships, which were amongst such means as the conspirators would have had to employ, in order to arrive again in Italy, pursuant to their intended enterprise for the destruction of the Triumvirs—these and other symbols seem allusive to the last civil war, and to manifest in the Egnatius who minted the coins a decided maintainer of Roman liberty. And this opinion of ours (adds Riccio), is concurred in by Cavedoni, who recognizes as the author of this denarius, the son of Cneus Egnatius, son of that Cneus, who was left behind with the Senators, when his father was expelled from Rome, about the year 683 (B. C. 71), in Pompey the Great's time, at the commencement of the second Mithridatic war.—See *Monete delle Fam. di Roma.* pp. 85, 86.

3. MAXSVMVS. Female head, perhaps of Liberty, with mitre: behind it the cap of Liberty.—*Rev.*-CN. EGNATIVS CN. F. CN. N. Two women clothed in the stola, and galeated, standing full-faced, and each holding spears; one of them plants her naked left foot on the head of some animal. On each side is an oar or rudder set upright on a ship's prow. In some reverses of this type, a figure of Cupid is flying between the two females.

EGNATULEIA gens. Little known. Its coins, which are in silver (quinarii) only, have but one type, as follows, and are common. The surname *Egnatuleius* :—

C. EGNATVLEI. C. F. Laureated head of Apollo.—*Rev.* ROMA in the exergue. Victory stands writing on a shield attached to a trophy; in the field Q.

This Caius Egnatuleius is unknown as an historical personage; but according to a recent opinion of Borghesi, must have been mint master towards the 667th year of Rome (B. C. 87).

EI dipthong appears on the earlier, that is to say, the consular and family coins of the Romans, written for I. Thus, PREIVER*num*, in Plautia; DEIDI*us*, in Didia; PREIMVS, in Memmia; OPEIMI*us*, SERVEILI*us*, LEIBERTAS in Cassia, and elsewhere.

EID. MAR.—*Idibus Martii*, the dipthong EI being put for I. This inscription appears on the reverse of a most rare denarius, the type of which is the *pileus*, or cap of liberty, between two daggers.—See M. BRUTUS, p. 145.

ELAGABALUS, Emperor.—Varius Avitus Bassianus, surnamed Elagabalus, from the name of the divinity, whose worship he had introduced into Rome, was born at Emesa, in Syria, A. V. C. 958 (A. D. 205). He was son of Sextus Varius Marcellus and of Julia Soæmias, daughter of Julia Mæsa, and niece of Julia Domna; consequently he was cousin-german to Caracalla. The wealth of his grandmother, added to his relationship with the imperial family of Severus, obtained for him the advantage of being appointed Priest of Elagabalus, or Heliogabalus, a deity the object of particular adoration at Emesa. The same honour was conferred on his cousin.

german Alexander Severus, son of Mamæa, second daughter of Julia Mæsa. In 971 (A. D. 218), Mæsa, having in view to obtain the empire for her grandson, changed his names into those of Marcus Aurelius Antoninus, and pretended that he was not the son of his mother's husband, but the fruit of Caracalla's intimacy with Soæmias. The soldiers encamped near Emesa, gained over by the riches of Julia Mæsa ; and perhaps giving credence to this adulterous parentage, which besides had nothing of unlikelihood in it, proclaimed the new Antoninus emperor. The troops of Macrinus having been defeated, Elagabalus, at thirteen years of age, became sole master of the Roman world. After having entered Antioch as conqueror, he addressed to the Senate letters in which, without waiting for the decree of that body, he assumed the titles of " Cæsar, son of Antoninus, grandson of Severus, Pius, Felix, Augustus, Pro-consul, and invested with the Tribunitian power." At the same time, he named himself consul in the place of Macrinus. He afterwards took the road to Rome, but on his way thither passed the winter at Nicomedia. In 972 (A. D. 219), Elagabalus was consul for the second time at Nicomedia. On his arrival at Rome, he gave there some magnificent spectacles, and caused a temple to be built in honour of his Syrian god. A. D. 220 is the date of his third consulate. In 221 he was consul for the fourth time. Julia Mæsa, perceiving that the manners of Elagabalus were displeasing to the Romans, persuaded him to adopt his cousin Alexander Severus, above named. To this Elagabalus consented, and designated him consul with himself for the following year. A short time after, repenting of his compliance with his mother's suggestion, he sought to make away with Severus Alexander; whose life, however, was protected by the vigilant care of Mæsa, and still better defended by the affection which the soldiers began to entertain for him. In A. D. 222, the pretorians having discovered that Elagabalus was fully bent on the destruction of his cousin, raised a tumult, and required that Alexander, who had been shut up in the palace some days, should be immediately shewn to them. Elagabalus, yielding to necessity, repaired to the camp of the pretorians, on a car, with the youthful Alexander. The next day, as Elagabalus had given orders to arrest those who had taken a leading part in the insurrectionary movement of the day before—the rest of the soldiers took advantage of that occasion to get rid of a prince they detested ; and they killed Elagabalus, together with his mother Soæmias, and his principal confidants. His body, after having been dragged through the city, was thrown into the Tibur. Thus perished, on the 11th of March, one of the most cruel, debauched, and shameless wretches, that ever disgraced humanity, or polluted a throne, after a reign of three years and nine months, disfigured with every feature of hideous criminality and extravagant folly, not having attained more than the eighteenth year of his age.

Elagabalus celebrated (or rather desecrated) several nuptials. His first wife was Julia Cornelia Paula ; but her he soon divorced, for some alleged personal blemish. He next stole away from the sacred college of Vestals, and married, Aquilia Severa, whom he also repudiated, and afterwards took her again. His third wife was Annia Faustina, whom he forcibly possessed himself of (after causing her husband Pomponius Bassus to be slain), but whom he quickly dismissed, to re-unite himself to Aquilia Severa. Some of his Latin coins represent him with Aquilia Severa, and his mother Soæmias ; also, a doubtful one, with Annia Faustina. The coins of this emperor are numerous. His gold and first brass are rare ; his silver, and second and small brass for the most part common.— Style—IMP. ANTONINVS PIVS AVG.— also IMP. CAES. M: AVR. ANTONINVS PIVS AVG.—also ANTONINVS V. PIVS FEL. AVG.

It is a work of some tact and discrimination to distinguish the coins of Elagabalus from those of Caracalla, both of whom assumed the title of M. AVR. ANTONINVS. Those, indeed, who are conversant with coins, are enabled from the peculiar countenances of each, to recognise Elagabalus by his thick lips, and Caracalla by his harsh and angry features. It behoves the tyro, however, to look on the one hand for the *star* of Elagabalus, whilst on the other hand he will remember that the surname GERMANICVS is added to the titles of Caracalla alone.—The following remarks on points needful to be regarded with a view to ascertain the medals of the two princes, are condensed from those of the able author of *Leçons de Numismatique Romaine :* 1st. Elagabalus, raised to the imperial throne, at 14 years of age, perished at eighteen.—2nd. On attaining his fifth and last Tribunitian power, he was invested with the consulate for the fourth time ; whilst *Caracalla*, at the time of *his* fifth Tribunate, was consul only for the first time.—3rd. From the third consulate of *Elagabalus*, his medals have almost always a *star* on the field of the reverse. This *star*, conjoined to various types, refers doubtless to his favourite divinity, analagous with the *Sun*, and is also found on the medals of his three wives.—4th and lastly, in the combination of names and titles, we again discover some further indications. For example (but only on the brass coins) the titles IMP. CAES. appear at the beginning of the legend of the obverse, in the case of *Elagabalus*, but not in that of *Caracalla*.

MINTAGES OF ELAGABALUS.

The following are the rarest types of reverse :

GOLD.—ADVENTVS AVGVSTI. Emperor on horseback. (Brought £4 at the Trattle sale).—CONSERVATOR AVG. Conical-shaped stone, ornamented with stars, standing before which is an eagle—the whole placed in a quadriga: a star in the field.—*Obv.*—IMP. ANTONINVS PIVS AVG. Laureated head of the Emperor. [This stone was the idol which Elagabalus brought with him from Syria, and to which he raised altars at Rome, stripping the ancient temples to enrich that of his foreign divinity (Heliogabalus).—Engraved in vol. i. pl. vii. No. 7, of Akerman, who elucidates the subject in a note, p. 214.—A most highly preserved specimen of this extra rare coin brought £8 10s. at the Thomas sale.]—CONSVL II. P. P. The emperor standing in a quadriga. (Valued by Mionnet at 80 fr.—sold for £4 11s. at the Trattle auction). —FIDES MILITVM. Emperor and two soldiers. (Mt. 120 fr.)—INVICTVS SACERDOS. AVG. Emperor sacrificing. (Valued by Mionnet at 50 fr. See the preceding wood-cut).—IVLIA AQVILIA SEVERA AVG. Head of the Empress Aquilia. (Mt. 600 fr.)—LIB. AVG. II. P. M. COS. II. (£4 3s. at the Brumell sale).—LIB. AVG. &c. Emperor and three figures. (Mt. 120 fr.)—PONTIF. MAX. &c. Roma Victrix seated. (£6 12s. 6d. Thomas).—TR. P. IIII. COS. III. The Sun radiated, standing with whip in right hand (£2 13s. at the White sale).—TRIB. POT. COS. II. Emperor in quadriga. (£4 17s. Trattle.)—SANCT. DEO. SOLI. ELAGABAL. Quadriga, with conical-stone, eagle, and four ensigns. (Mt. 63 fr.)—P. M. TR. P. V. COS. IIII. Emperor in quadriga. (£7 7s. 6d. Thomas).—VICTOR. ANTONINI AVG. (£5 5s. ditto).

SILVER.—COS. III. P. P.—Stone of conical form, ornamented with stars, and an eagle before it. (*Cabinet de Gosselin*) engraved in Mionnet, T. i. 343, by whom it is valued at 30 fr.)—FIDES MILITVM. (Mt. 60 fr.)—IVLIA SOAEMIAS. (100 fr.)—TR. P. III. COS. Emperor in a quadriga, crowned by Victory. (60 fr.)

BRASS MEDALLIONS.—AEQVITAS AVGVSTI. The three Monetæ. (Mt. 50 fr.)—CONSERVATOR AVGVSTI COS. IIII. Conical stone in a quadriga. (Mt. 150 fr.)—TR. P. III. COS. III. Emperor in a triumphal car, and four horses. (Mt. 200 fr.) SPES PVBLICA. Hope walking.—*Obv.*-Heads of Elagabalus and Aquilia Severa. (Mt. 300 fr.)

LARGE BRASS.—LIBERAL. AVG. II. P. M. TR. P. II. COS. II. Emperor and two figures.—LIBERALITAS AVGVSTI III. Three figures on an estrade. (Mt. 24 fr. each).—PAX. AVGVSTI. Peace walking. (Mt. 40 fr.)

ELEPHANT. (*Elephantus*).-The representation of this animal frequently occurs on Roman coins. The head, and sometimes the proboscis only, of an Elephant is a symbol of Africa.—Lybia was accounted *Elephantorum nutrix*.—On denarii of the Cæcilia gens, elephants walking, both singly and in bigæ, are typified to attest victories gained by the Metelli, in Sicily and in Macedonia, during the 504th (B.C. 250), and 606th years of Rome (B.C. 148). The skull and trunk also cover a female head, and appear in the centre of a shield, on other coins of the same family, allusive to the successes of its celebrated members over the Carthaginians and Macedonians.—See pp. 149, 150, 151.

An Elephant trampling on a serpent with its fore feet, is the well-known type on a common denarius of Julius Cæsar. But it has given rise

to various opinions among the learned. Some refer it to the victory of Juba over Scipio, in Africa. Others to the fact, that the grandfather of Julius Cæsar, according to Servius and Spartian, killed an elephant in that region; and the animal being called in the Punic language *Caesar*, this name became appropriated to the family.

"But" says Eckhel (vi. pp. 5 and 6), in noticing these conflicting opinions, "prior to this grandfather of Julius, we find in Livy the cognomen of Cæsar. Now, if that be true, which is stated by Constantinus Manasses, that 'elephants are called *Cæsares* by the Phœnicians,' and which, as we have just observed, is confirmed by Servius and Spartian, the present elephant would be an allusion to the name; as, moreover, it is represented as trampling on a serpent, with which reptile, according to Pliny, the elephant is at perpetual feud; and as it is established by Artemidorus, that the elephant in Italy denotes δεσποτης, βασιλευς, και ανηρ μεγιστος—a lord, a king, or a man in high authority; we shall then recognize a type flattering to the ambition of Cæsar, and by which he was desirous to intimate his victory over the barbarians, and all who were envious of his glory. Whatever may be the decision on this point, the type may be considered as a *presage* of future dominion. For the elephant, independently of its uses in war and the amphitheatre, was an undoubted symbol of honour or of arrogance. According to Suetonius (*in Nerone*, chap. 2), Cn. Domitius, the ancestor of Nero, after his victory, during his consulate, over the Allobroges, was carried through the province on an elephant, preceded by a large body of troops, as in the solemnity of a triumph. Cornuficius, on account of having carried his soldiers off safely in Sicily, assumed such airs, that whenever he dined out at Rome, he used to ride home on an elephant. Julius Cæsar himself, when his military toils were over, ascended the Capitol, lighted by forty elephants, bearing torches, on either side of him. Lastly, there was no special use for elephants, except to draw the imperial *thensæ* at funerals, or the chariots of the Cæsars, either in a triumph, or in their consular processions. Correctly, therefore, has Juvenal styled these natives of a torrid clime,

Cæsaris armentum, nulli servire paratum Privato.

[Cæsar's beast of burden, that deigns not to serve a private individual.]

Elephants are represented on coins as an emblem of Eternity, it being among the vulgar errors of the ancients to believe that those stupendous creatures lived two or even three hun-

dred years. It was, however, on the known longevity of the elephant (exceeding, as Pliny, quoting
Aristotle, says, that of all other animals), that
they were employed in the funeral processions
of emperors and empresses, on the occasion of
their *apotheosis.*

On consecration medals, the elephant appears,
either singly, with or without the driver, or as
bigæ and quadrigæ, there being placed on the
vehicle to which they are attached the image of
the deceased personage.   On a large brass,
struck by order of the Senate, in honour of
Faustina senior's consecration, she is figured
sitting on a canopied biga of elephants, with the
accompanying legend of AETERNITAS.

Elephantus loricatus, or *reticulatus.*—The elephant in armour, or some defensive covering of
iron, resembling net-work, employed to protect
them (as well as horses), from the spears and
darts of an enemy in battle.   Representations
of this kind appear on consular money—as for
example, a denarius of the Metelli (see Cæcilia),
a coin restored by Trajan.   They are also seen,
from time to time, in the imperial series, as on
gold of Titus.   The subjoined engraving is from
a consecration first brass of Faustina Antonini:

Here the sedent statue of the deceased empress, holding the sceptrum in her left hand,
and a branch in her right, is placed, in token
of deification,   on a four-wheeled car (the
thensa), drawn by two elephants, whose bodies
are loricated, and whose necks are mounted each
by its conductor.   The EX S. C. on the exergue,
stamps this fine reverse with the impress of
Senatorial authority.

Elephantorum quadrigæ.—A first brass of Augustus, coined in pursuance of a decree of the
Senate, after his death, represents him in the
guise of a divinity, seated on the thensa of consecration, drawn by four elephants, on each of
which sits a driver.—That Augustus was honoured, after his decease, with the exhibition of
such *quadrigæ,* we have the testimony of Suetonius and Dion.

On a large brass of Titus, struck in honour
of his father's consecration (see p. 336), as well
as the well-known coin of Augustus, from the
reverse of which the type was borrowed, *four*
elephants draw the *thensa* of the deified prince,
but in neither instance are the bodies of those
animals loricated.   It is not uncommon to find
them harnessed with the ornamental panoply in
which they bore a part at the public shews, on

coins of several emperors, from Domitian to
Gordianus Pius.—See MVNIFICENTIA AVG.

Elephantorum duplices quadrigæ.—On a large
brass bearing on its obverse IMP. CAES. DOMIT.
AVG. GERM. COS. XVII. CENS. &c. and the laurelled head of Domitian ; but with no other
legend of reverse than the *Senatus Consultum,*
we see a triumphal arch, surmounted by two
cars, to each of which four elephants are harnessed.   In each car stands a togated figure,
holding a whip, or branch.

The above and other coins attest, that
triumphal arches, adorned with two quadrigæ of
elephants, were erected by Domitian, in which
were placed (golden or brass gilt) statues of that
vain-glorious tyrant.—Tristan has well illustrated the remarkable subject of this piece in the
following observations :—

This triumphal arch was raised in honour of
Domitian during the last year of his reign, and
under his last consulate, namely, the 17th, 849
(A.D. 96).   For he was so malicious, and so
covetous of another's glory, that he caused himself to be elected such a number of times consul,
in order to monopolize the authority of that
office (pour en occuper toujours la qualité).   It
is this which Ausonius refers to, in censuring
his rapacity, his ambition, and his envious
malignity, whilst pronouncing himself the panegyric of Gratian, in the presence of that emperor, whom he was thanking for promoting
him to the Consulate—" Scis inquam (says he)
septem et decem Domitiani Consulatus, quos
illa invidia alteros provehendi, continuando con-
servit ; ita ejus aviditate derisos, ut hoc eum
pagina fastorum suorum, imo fastidiorum, fecerit
insolentem, nec potuerit præstare felicem."   See
also the poem which Statius has written respecting the seventeenth Consulship of Domitian.
As to the triumphal arch here represented, so
superbly charged with two cars drawn by elephants, it clearly relates to the two victories
which he wished to have credit for having
achieved over the Gauls, Germans, Sarmatians,
Dacians, and Quadi; and for which he triumphed.
This arch, erected to perpetuate the memory of
those alleged facts, has been honoured with
an allusion by Martial (see lib. viii. *Epigr.* 65.)
From the poet's verses it would appear that this
triumphal gate, enriched with two magnificent
quadrigæ (Hic gemini currus numerant Ele-
phanta) was constructed in a place, which served
as a *parvis* to temples dedicated to *Fortuna
Redux,* in favour of Vespasian, of Titus, and of

Domitian; and which was the place (as Tristan supposes), where the Senate and the people went to receive and salute the emperor last named, on his return from his expeditions.—See *Commentaires Historiques*, T. i. p. 333.

In *Morell. Imp. Rom.* T. ii. TAB. xiii. the portal on the summit of which the two quadrigæ of elephants stand, has a tier of columns with entablatnre *above* the arch-ways.

EMERITA *Colonia.*—A city of great importance, during the early empire, situate on the banks of the *Anas* (Guadiana), in Hispania Lusitania (Spanish Estremadura). Some relics of it remain to this day, and *Merida* is now the name of the place. In the year of Rome 729 (B. C. 25), Augustus, having concluded the Cantabrian war, placed there, as colonists, by way of reward, certain soldiers whose term of service had expired *(emeritos)*, and who accordingly called the new settlement AVGVSTA EMERITA; and by his permission (PERM. or PERMISSV. AVG.) struck numerous coins in honour of their founder.—The *Emeritenses* also consecrated a temple to the Eternity of Augustus (AETERNITATIS AVGVSTAE); after whose death they paid the same monetal distinctions to Julia. And being very desirous to secure for their city, as the seat of the Lusitanian legation, the patronage of his successor Tiberius, they dedicated coins to him also. It was for these reasons, that, as a new town, and built by Roman veterans, a representation of its fortified gate and mural enclosure was struck on the coins of this colony, and the name of EMERITA (or IMERITA) inscribed over its gateway. Nor was this distinctive token confined to colonial brass (as C. A. E. or COL. AVGVSTA EMERITA); but the name of Augustus was also identified with the foundation of *Merida* by one of his own moneyers, on denarii which bear a similar type and inscription. For description and plates of the colonial mintages, in first and second brass, the reader is referred to Mr. Akerman's *Coins of Ancient Cities, &c.* p. 11, pl. i. Nos. 4 and 5. The following cut is from silver of the Carisia gens :—

IMP. CAESAR AVGVST.—Bare head of Augustus.—*Rev.*—P. CARISIVS LEG. PRO. PR. Gate of the fortified city of Merida, above which is written IMERTIA.

This denarius, struck by Publius Carisius, *legatus propraetor* of Augustus, alludes to the Spanish campaign, in which that officer defeated the Astures, and captured from them the city of Lancia. This led to the foundation of the city of *Emerita*, which afterwards became the capital of Lusitania. The monetal issues of this colony do not appear to have extended beyond Tiberius.

EMESA or EMISA, Syriæ, *Colonia;* near the region of Mount Lebanon, situate on the Orontes, and now called *Hams*. It was the native place of Julia Domna, wife of Severus, and mother of Caracalla. The latter emperor conferred upon it the rank of a Roman colony. Emesa contained a temple of the Sun, in which Elagabalus officiated as a priest before he was made emperor. The coins of this city are imperial in brass (except one small medallion in *potin*.) The legends are exclusively *Greek*, from Domna to Alexander Severus, including the unique coin of Sulpicius Antoninus (Tanini, *Supp.* p. 116). The types of reverse are mostly —Head of the Sun; Eagle on a cone-formed stone; turreted woman; basilicæ, and temples. —Mionnet, v. 227, and *Suppt.* viii. 156.

EMPORIAE Tarraconensis (Hispaniæ), *municipium*, now Ampurias.—The coins of this town are *Greek* autonomes in silver; and brass, with Celtiberian and *Latin* inscriptions. The obverses have for the most part a galeated head, and the Latin legends of reverse are EMPOR. or EMPORI, with the type of a Pegasus, sometimes the head of Minerva, a lion walking, a hippocampus, a bull, a bust of Diana.—See Mionnet, *Suppt.* i. 82 : see also Akerman, *Coins of Hispania*, p. 86.

No imperial or colonial money was struck by this Spanish municipium.

ENNA (Siciliæ), *municipium*, now Castro Giovanni.—A very ancient city, where Ceres was worshipped in a magnificent temple.— The coins of this place are autonomous; all brass (with one exception, unique, in silver)— a few Latin, but chiefly Greek legends; the types are—Proserpine, head of Ceres, head of Apollo. There are no imperial coins. On a large brass, which is classed in *Morell. Fam. Rom.* with coins of the Cestia gens, is a veiled head of Ceres, with a torch before it, alluding to the torches with which, as the poets feigned, that goddess sought her lost daughter, on Mount Etna; and on the reverse, Pluto, the ravisher, is carrying away the virgin in a quadriga. The obverse legend is M. CESTIVS and L. MVNATIVS (Duumviri). The legend of reverse is MVN. HENN. (municipium Henna). There is also a middle brass, bearing the names of the same duumvirs, with the type of Venus. And a third autonomous brass, with M. CESTIVS and the head of Ceres, on its obverse, and MVN. HENNA, with two female figures in a quadriga, on the reverse, is cited by Mionnet *(Suppt.* i. 384) from E. Harwood, *pop. et urb. sel. num.* p. 56.

EPIGRAPHE, Epigraph—Inscription.

EPPIA gens—A noble family, but not much known. Cicero calls Eppius a man of his order. It has two varieties; the undermentioned *silver* coin is the rarest :—

EPPIVS LEG*atus*. F. C. Hercules standing, with front face, naked, and in repose, with club and lion's skin.—*Rev.*—Q. METEL*lus* SCIPIO IMP. Female head, covered with the elephant's skin; underneath it a plough; before it an ear of corn (page 151).——"From this coin we learn that Eppius was the Lieutenant of Scipio in the African war against Julius Cæsar, and had the office of coining *denarii* for the purposes of that war, as is confirmed by the F. C. *Faciendum* or *Feriundum Curavit;* unless it be more correctly interpreted F*landum Curavit*, as on coins of Lentulus, in Cornelia gens: CVR. X. FL." The brass coins of this family are *as*, or parts of the *as*.

See an engraving of this coin, inserted amongst the Metelli of the Cæcilia gens, p. 151, right hand column.

EPULONES.—Subsequently to the first war with Hannibal, the Roman pontiffs being overwhelmed with the multitude of sacrifices, and of ceremonies attendant thereon, were allowed in the year of the city 557 (B. C. 197), to appoint three men to whom was given the name of *Triumviri Epulones*. These presided as priests at the public feasts which took place at the conclusion of each sacrifice offered to Jupiter and others of their deities, whom they professed to propitiate, by placing their statues, laid on couches (hence called *lectisternia),* in the temples, and inviting them to partake of a banquet prepared with all possible magnificence and sumptuousness; and if *they* were not able to eat, drink, and be merry, there were doubtless *other* guests present who could. Sulla augmented the number of these ministers of the sacred banquets in honour of the gods to seven. Julius Cæsar added three more; but after his time, the number appears again to have been limited to seven. The subjoined wood-cut is faithfully executed from an extremely well-preserved denarius in the British Museum, the reverse type of which represents an *Epulo* preparing a lectisternium for Jupiter, conformably to custom, in the Epulum Jovis.

C. COEL. CALDVS COS. Bare male head to the right, between a vexillum, inscribed HIS and a boar.—*Rev.*—C. CALDVS IMP. A. X. A table or lectisternium, with a robed and veiled figure behind it. The inscription is L. CALDVS VII VIR. EPVL. On each side is a trophy; below CALDVS III VIR.—For an explanation of this coin see p. 222.

The Epulones were next to the Augurs in dignity, and were privileged to wear the toga prætexta. They also formed a college, and were one of the four great sacerdotal corporations at Rome, the Pontifices, Augures, and Quindecemviri, being the other three.

EQ. Equestris.—EQ. COH. *Equestris Cohortis.*—EQ. ORD. *Equestris Ordinis.*

EQUES. A horseman.—Typically speaking, a man on horseback, appears on many consular coins (see Sulla, p. 287), and is of still more frequent occurrence in the imperial series. *Imperator Eques,* the equestrian figure of the

emperor, either in the garb of Peace, or in military habiliments, with right hand raised, moving at a slow pace; or galloping with spear at the charge; or in the attitude of hurling his javelin at a barbarian foe, who is down on one knee in a defensive posture, or is fallen prostrate before him, appears on coins, in each metal, from Augustus to Nero; thence to Domitian, Trajan, Hadrian, M. Aurelius, Commodus, Severus, Caracalla, &c. &c.—See ADVENTVS AVG. and ADVENTVI AVG. (p. 10)—DEBELLATORI GENT. BARBAR (p.311)—DECVRSIO (pp. 314–315)—EXPEDITIO AUG. *(suo loco)*—PROFECTIO AUG. (ditto)—PRINCIPES JUVENTUTIS (p. 217)—VIRTUS AUGG. (p. 53.)

Equestrian figures of Castor and Pollux are seen on the most ancient coins of the Aelia, Antestia, Atilia (p. 93), Cupiennia, Domitia, Horatia (Denarius, p. 316), Itia, Junia, Lucretia, Marcia, Minucia, Plautia, Quinctia, Scribonia, Sempronia, and Terentia families.—See *Dioscuri.*

EQUESTER ORDO.—The Equestrian Order: one of the degrees of rank, or estates of Rome. It derived its name at an early period of the commonwealth from the legionary *Equites;* and became subsequently the middle grade between the Senate and the people. They were called *juventus,* because that word was used by the Romans in speaking of their soldiers collectively; and *principes juventutis,* because king Servius, when he divided the entire people into six classes, enrolled, according to Livy, " twelve centuries of *equites,* chosen from the first men of the nation;" or as Dionysius of Halicarnassus states, " he made a selection of *equites* from amongst those citizens who were wealthiest and of noble birth.'—And this, observes Eckhel (see his *Dissert. de Principe Juventutis*), accounts for the *equites* being so frequently styled *primores, principes,* or *proceres juventutis.* A remarkable example of this occurs in the speech which Livy has put into the mouth of Perseus, King of the Macedonians, whom he addresses after the defeat of the Roman cavalry, in these words—" You have turned to flight the more important part of your enemies' forces, the Roman cavalry, in which they boasted themselves invincible. For with them the *equites* are their *principes juventutis;* with them the *equites* are the nursery of their Senate; from them are chosen into the ranks of the *patres,* the men whom they create consuls and emperors (imperatores.)" And much earlier, the same author has said of L. Brutus—" He raised to the number of three hundred the ranks of the *patres,* (thinned by the assassinations of Tarquinius Superbus), by electing into them the *primores* of the Equestrian Order." With propriety, therefore, might the *equites* be called the *principes* of the entire *juventus* of Rome; and, without doubt, they obtained, by their superiority of fortune and birth, the pre-eminence among the people, along with whom they were still reckoned, there being as yet no Equestrian Order instituted. The *equites* afterwards received an important accession of authority and honour, namely when the brothers Ti. et C. Gracchus introduced a law for the transfer of the judicial courts, from the Senate to the *Equites.* Thereby they also gained an opportunity of accumulating wealth. For, as in consequence of their hereditary possessions, they enjoyed almost a monopoly in the farming of the taxes, under the title of *publicani*, it was an easy matter, with such aids, to increase their store. Thus, therefore, in the course of time was the renowned *Equester Ordo* instituted ; and so called and distinguished from the other two Orders of Senate and People. These facts are confirmed by the testimony of Pliny, who says—" The distinction of this Order, under the appellation of *judices* was first introduced by the Gracchi, through a factious desire of popularity, and to bring the Senate into disrepute. And this authority, having soon afterwards been weakened by the vicissitudes of civil dissension, became vested in the *publicani*, who for a considerable period constituted the third Estate of the Republic. It was M. Cicero, who at length during his consulate, and having overthrown Catiline, firmly established the equestrian title, boasting his own origin from that Order, and maintaining its authority with peculiar zeal. From that time it became distinctly a third portion of the commonwealth ; and the *Equester Ordo*, properly so called, began to be added to those of the Senate and the People. And this is the reason (adds Pliny) why, even at the present day, it is specified *after* the *Populus*, as being the more recently established Order."—(See CONSENSU. SENAT. ET EQ. ORDIN. &c. p. 252.)

The *equites*, elated by this accession of dignity and wealth, became less eager to rally round the standards of their legions, partly because they could, without peril or inconvenience, attain at home the highest honours ; and also because they felt ashamed to follow a military service, to which the lowest and meanest of the populace, following in the steps of Marius, were beginning to give a corresponding character. And yet, when the Equestrian Order was once instituted, the rank of an *eques*, like that of a patrician, descended by inheritance to the sons, provided that the requisite income were forthcoming. But although this Order might have been obtained by heirdom from a man's ancestors (as Ovid states to have been his case), yet it also (as he admits) might have been the result of distinguished conduct in the field of battle ; just as L. Aconius is stated by Fabretti, " to have been raised by Trajan from the condition of a soldier to that of an *eques*, for services performed in the German and the Sarmatian wars." But that an income of the legal amount was even then necessary, is clearly hinted by the same poet, when, with the usual pride of noble birth, as towards the *parvenu*, he complains of his mistress preferring a knight, lately elevated to that rank for military services, to himself, who held the distinction by inheritance :—

Ecce recens dives, parto per vulnera censu,
Præfertur nobis, sanguine, factus, eques.

[For lo ! a newly-rich man, a *knight* created by an income acquired by wounds, is preferred to *me* (who am a knight created) by *blood* (i. e. descent.)]

According, however, to Suetonius, the law respecting a deficiency of income was modified by Augustus, who added a condition to it. It may thence be concluded, that the *equites*, who in former times were properly styled *principes juventutis*, and destined to the profession of arms, after the establishment of the Equestrian Order, gradually withdrew from military service, and betook themselves with impunity to the profitable business of the law-courts, or to the ease and pleasures of a town life, notwithstanding that, even at a later period, a horse was provided for them at the public cost. This Equestrian Order, to whose knights Cicero gives the title of *Homines amplissimi et honestissimi*, and of whom he speaks as the flower of the Roman chivalry *(flos equitum Romanorum)* ; the ornament of the City, and the strength of the Republic , this body, whence occasionally persons were chosen to fill vacant places in the Senate, became extremely numerous under the emperors, many of whom admitted their freedmen, or whomsoever they pleased, to the estate and dignity of *Eques*.

EQVESTER ORDO. PRINCIPI. IVVENT. (The Equestrian Order to the Prince of the Youth.)— This legend, within a buckler, appears on the reverse of gold and silver of Nero.—The obverse bears an epigraph in the dedicatory form— NERONI CLAVDIO DRVSO GERM. COS. DESIGN. and the young bust, bare headed, of Nero, as Cæsar.

It was customary (remarks M. Lenormant), for the Order of Roman Knights to give the Princes of the Youth a silver spear and buckler. Caius and Lucius, sons of Agrippa, received a similar present, being Principes Juventutis.— It is also, in this quality, that Nero is here recorded to have been complimented with a buckler by the Equestrian Order. The following inscription on a marble, published by Gruter, records the same fact—NERONI CLAVDIO DRVSO GER*manico* CO*n*Suli DES*ignato*.— EQVESTER ORDO PRINCIPI IVVENTVTIS.—Nero was made Prince of the Youth in the year of Rome 804 (A. D. 51).—See *Iconographie Romaine.*

Eckhel (viii. p. 371, et seq.) cites similar monuments which tend to prove the connection of the *Principes Juventutis* with the Equestrian Order. A second brass of Commodus, as Cæsar, bears within a laurel crown the same dedicatory legend. Tacitus, among the honours decreed to the memory of Germanicus, who was a Prince of the Youth, records the following :—" The Equestrian Order

gave the name of Germanicus to the battalion
(*cuneus*) which used to be called that of the
"juniors;" and ordained that on the ides of
March the troops (of knights) should follow his
image in procession. For some additional particulars relative to the *Equester Ordo*, see PRIN-
CIPES JUVENTUTIS, in this dictionary.

EQVIS (*sic.*) ROMANVS. The emperor on
horseback in the garb of peace. In the exergue
SMN.—*Obv.*—DN. CONSTANTINVS MAX.
AVG. Bust of Constantine the Great diadem-
ated. Small gold medallion. Engraved in
Numism. Cimelii. Vindobon. Aurei, TAB. 1.

Eckhel observes, "the attempt of Khell to
explain this singular coin, has produced nothing
valid by which the enigma of its legend can be
unravelled, nor can I hope to be more fortunate
than my master : unless perhaps it alludes to
the *Princeps Juventutis*, by which title, as Augustus was before him, Constantine is designated
frequently on coins ; and he himself κατ εξοχην,
is here called EQVIS ROMANVS, as he was also
prince of the youth and prince of the equestrian order. It is to be noted, that on this
medallion the unusual word EQVIS stands for
EQVES, a horseman or knight." viii. 83.

ERCAVICA (Tarraconensis) *municipium.*—
A city of the Celtiberi, enumerated by Pliny
among the towns attached to the convention
of Cæsar-Augusta (Saragozza), and classed by
Livy among the nobler and more powerful
class of *civitates* in the part of northern
Spain. "It was situated near the river Gau-
diela, in the neighbourhood of the modern
Santaver." The coins of this place are imperial *Latin*, in second and third brass, struck
under the respective reigns of Augustus, Tiberius, and Caligula. On one of these (Tiberius)
the name ERCAVICA alone is inscribed ; on those
of Augustus and Caligula it is accompanied with
the title of MVNicipium. It seems (says Vaillant, *in Coloniis*), to have been made one about
the year of Rome 574 (B. C. 180). Under
Tiberius and Caligula its coins bear the names
of the Duumvirs. The only types are an oaken
crown encircling the name of the city ; and a
a bull standing, the latter the usual symbol of
a *municipium.*—See Mionnet, *Supplt.* T. i. and
Akerman, *Coins of Hispania,* p. 86.

ERVC. *Erycis*—a name given to Venus, in
memory of her son Eryx, who, relying on his
strength, challenged all strangers to fight with
him. Killed by Hercules in the combat of the
cestus, he was buried on a mountain (now called
Giuliano), near Drepanum, in Sicily, where he
had built a temple to Venus, to which he had
given his name. The temple of Venus Erycina,
with the inscription ERVC. appears on a denarius
struck by C. CONSIDIus NONIANus.—See
CONSIDIA gens, p. 254.

ETRV. *Etruscus.*—See HERENNIUS.

ETRUSCILLA *(Herennia).*—Coins bearing
on their obverses the legend HERENNIA
ETRVSCILLA AVGusta, shew that there was
an empress of that name ; but of themselves
leave us only to *infer* that she might be the
wife of Trajanus Decius. An inscription pub-

lished by Muratori (p. 1036, 4), has put an end
however to the discussions amongst antiquaries
on this point. That inscription calls her Herennia Cupressenia Etruscilla, wife of *our lord*

(domini nostri) *Decius*, &c. Nothing is known
of her life. She had two children, Herennius
Etruscus and Hostillianus. Her coins are common in silver ; tolerably common in large brass ;
very rare in brass medallions ; and of extreme
rarity in gold. The principal reverses are :—

GOLD.—PVDICITIA AVG. A woman standing, or seated. (Valued by Mionnet at 200 fr.)

BRASS MEDALLION.——VESTA. Six women
veiled, sacrificing before a temple. (Mt. 150 fr.)
[The obverse of this fine and very rare coin
(not an extra-sized large brass, but a real brass
medallion), presents the striking portraiture
above engraved from the original in the *Cabinet
de France.* For the reverse type see VESTA].

MIDDLE BRASS.—PVDICITIA AVGVSTA. The
empress seated between two other female figures
standing.—*(Médaille de deux cuivres, sans le
sénatus-consulto.* 40 fr. Mionnet).

EUDOCIA (or *Eudoxia*), married to the
emperor Arcadius A. D. 395, and died A D. 404.
There are no authenticated coins of this empress.

EUDOXIA *(Aelia)* or Eudocia, daughter of
Leontius, an Athenian, born about A. D. 393,
married to the emperor Theodosius the younger
A. D. 421. Being separated from her husband,
she took up her abode at Jerusalem, where she
died A. D. 460.—The coins assigned to this Augusta are rare in small brass ; in gold and silver
very rare indeed. On these she is styled AEL.
EVDOXIA FE. AVG.
[For an explanatory note in reference to the
above and preceding empress, see Akerman,
Descript. Cat. ii. 357.]

EUDOXIA *(Licinia)* daughter of Theodosius
II. and Aelia Eudoxia, wife of Valentinian III.
born at Constantinople, A. D. 423 ; a widow in
455. She called Genseric to Rome to avenge
herself of Petronius Maximus, who forced her
to a marriage with him, after assassinating Valentinian ; Rome was pillaged ; Eudoxia carried
away to Carthage, but afterwards returned to
Rome, 462, and died there. Her coins (in gold
only) are of the greatest rarity. Style—LICINIA
EVDOXIA P. F. AVG.

EUGENIUS, an usurper of the imperial purple, in the age of Theodosius the Great. Of
obscure birth, he began by teaching grammar
and rhetoric ; and afterwards rose to the situation of master of the palace to Valentinian II.

He was proclaimed Augustus at Vienne, in Dauphiny, by Count Arbogastes, who murdered Valentinian the younger, in A. D. 392, and who kept the authority in his own hands. Eugenius, acknowledged as emperor throughout Gaul and in the other provinces of the West, allied himself to the Germans and Franks. Attacked by Theodosius near Aquileia, in Cisalpine Gaul, he was defeated, taken prisoner, and put to death, A. D. 394. Arbogastes killed himself. Style, D. N. EVGENIVS P. F. AVG. His brass (small) coins are of the highest rarity; silver rare; gold very rare.

MINTAGES OF EUGENIUS.

GOLD MEDALLIONS (small size).——GLORIA ROMANORVM. Rome and Constantinople personified, seated together. (Valued by Mionnet at 200 fr.)

GOLD.—VICTORIA AVGG. Two emperors, each adorned with the nimbus, seated on one throne, and holding a globe together. (Valued by Mionnet at 60 fr. Engraved in Akerman, ii. plate xii. No. 5, p. 338).—VICTORIA AVGVSTORVM. Victory walking. (Quinarius. Mt. 50 fr.)

THIRD BRASS.—VICTORIA AVGGG. Victory with wreath and palm branch, marching to the left.—Obv.—D. N. EVGENIVS P. F. AVG. Diademed bust.—[This is unique. It forms part of Mr. Rolfe's collection; was published for the first time by Mr. Roach Smith, in his "Antiquities of Richborough (Kent);" and engraved by Mr Fairholt, among other coins discovered at that Roman station. See fig. 15, pl. vi.]——VIRTVS ROMANORVM. Same type as the preceding reverse. (Valued by Mionnet at 40 fr.)

EX. A. PV. or A. P.—These letters appear (in the field of the coins) on denarii of the Fabia, Fonteia, and other Roman families.—Eckhel (v. 210), observes that they are to be interpreted, not as some have done, EX. Argento PVblico, but, EX. Auctoritate PVblicâ—meaning that the silver or gold money thus inscribed had been struck by public authority.—See Fabia gens.

EXAGIVM SOLIDI.—An inscription stamped on certain quadrangular pieces of brass, used during the lower empire, by the exactores auri, who were specially charged with preserving the weight, as well as the purity, of that metal in the Roman mint.—"By the word exagium (says Eckhel, viii. 513, et seq.) especially in the times of Arcadius, Honorius, Theodosius junior, and Valentinian III. was meant a weight, or a weighing, intended to test the legitimate weight of the Solidus."—See that word.

EX. S. C.—Ex. Senatus Consulto. (By a Decree of the Senate; or, by a Senatus Consultum). When these letters occur on Roman gold and silver coins, they signify, not that the Senate caused them to be struck, but that the coinage of them had the senatus consultum, or senatorial sanction, when struck. The mark EX. S. C. also denotes certain disbursements made from the public treasury to defray expenses of public games. And in some instances the form was added to the title of pro-consul and of pro-pretor, when those officers, without popular elec-

tion, were chosen from among the men of consular and pretorian rank, and sent EX. S. C. into the provinces. Thus we read PR. COS. or PROCOS EX. S. C, on coins of the Annia, Cæcilia, Julia, Manlia, and Scribonia families; and in like manner PROPR. Proprætor, with the same stamp of Senatorial authority.—Spanheim, vol. ii. p. 177.

EX. S. C. appears on a great many family coins; but in the imperial series the mark is observable only on those of Augustus, M. Agrippa, Claudius, Nero, Vespasian, Titus, Faustina, sen. Marciana, Hadrian, Sept. Severus, &c.—On coins of Emperors and Augustæ, this mark of EX. S. C. is generally found associated with the legend, or at least with the types, of Consecration, as in Claudius, Marciana, Faustina sen.

EX. S. C. S. P. Q. R.—A temple of ten columns, adorned with various statues; on a brass medallion of Hadrian.—See Temple.

EXER.——Exercitus, or Exercituum.——See CONCORDIA, FIDES, GENIUS, VIRTUS.

EXERCITUS.—The Romans, in order that a soldier should not be allowed to waste his strength or enervate his courage in sloth and idleness, employed him in various exercises, which, even in the midst of peace, kept before his view the representation, the fatigue, and the dangers of war. Thus from the word Exercitatio, exercise, came that of Exercitus, army, because the more troops are exercised, the better training they are in for war. On those days when the soldiers were not on guard in the camp, they were drilled to the use of their weapons; they practised in archery, slinging, and raced with each other in full armour. By this means they were always in good breathing, and their ardour was preserved at the highest pitch. During peace they had to make roads, form encampments, build houses, and even construct entire towns, if Dion Cassius is to be credited, who affirms that the city of Lugdunum (Lyon, in France), was one of the fruits of this system.—The same is said of Augusta Vindelicorum (Augsbourg, in Germany). And in North Britain the wall of Hadrian and that of Antoninus Pius, attest by their remains, how magnificently extensive were the military works of the Romans. It was this custom which moreover served to increase the docility of the soldier, at once divesting him of both inclination and time for entering into plans of desertion or of revolt. And neglect of this active discipline mainly caused the ruin of the Roman armies.

The names of the different bodies of Roman troops employed in various parts of Europe, Asia, and Africa, are recorded on coins; principally on those of Hadrian for example, bearing the inscriptions Exercitus Britannicus, Cappadocicus, Dacicus, Germanicus, Hispanicus, Judaicus, Mauretanicus, Noricus, Parthicus, Raeticus, Syriacus, &c. as will be seen in the immediately following pages. For the Romans were accustomed to call their legions and expeditionary forces after the names of those places, or countries, in which they were stationed, or were carrying on war. On other coins a commemoration is made not only of the local habitations of Roman armies, but also of their valour, fortitude, and renown. Thus we read on some, VIRTVS MILITVM, or VIRTVS EXERCITVS ROMAN-

ORVM: on others, VIRTVS or GLORIA EXERCITVS GALLI(CANI), &c.

EXER*citus* AUGUSTORUM.—*The Army of the Emperors.*—See LICINIUS junior.

EXER*citus* BRITANN*icus*. S. C.—The emperor Hadrian, bare headed, habited in the paludamentum, on horseback, with right hand raised, as haranguing his army, represented by one soldier bearing a vexillum, and three ensign bearers, a fourth (indistinctly) appearing behind them.— *Obv.*—HADRIANVS AV*gustus* CO*n*S*ul* III. *Pater Patriæ.* Bare head of Hadrian, to the right.

This is one of that class of *geographical* coins (as Eckhel calls them), which respectively bear the *name* of the army that happened to be stationed in the province visited by the emperor; and it derives in the English eye a great additional degree of interest, from the circumstance of its exhibiting the collective appellation of the Roman soldiers who occupied camps and garrisons in Britain, at the time of Hadrian's advent and stay there, A. D. 121.

Spartian's account of Hadrian's visit to Britain (see it quoted in p. 141), is as verbally brief and yet as intrinsically important, as were the incidents of that visit itself; for it records much good to have resulted therefrom in a short space of time.—See BRITANNIA, p. 141.

" Four provinces of Europe (says the Abbé Greppo) were visited consecutively by Hadrian, in the first years of his reign, as it would appear; namely, the Gauls, Germany, Britain, and Spain. * * * * It is from *Germania* that Spartian passes Hadrian into the isle of the Britons, but without entering into any detail, even without making known to us the port whence he embarked. The biographer limits himself to say—Ergo conversis regio more militibus Britanniam petit. * * * * History is equally far from satisfying our curiosity respecting the sojourn which Hadrian made in that island. He corrected there numerous abuses (in qua multa correxit) a very vague statement, and common to all the *tours* of Hadrian. But the historian adds a fact of greater interest, when he speaks of the wall raised, by order of that prince, to separate the lands of the barbarian inhabitants from those which were subject to the Romans, and that upon an extent of eighty miles. Murumque per octoginta millia passuum PRIMUS duxit, qui Barbaros Romanosque divideret."—After expressing his opinion that the word *primus* is not used in this passage,

without intention, seeing that other similar works had been executed in Britain, between the epocha of Hadrian and that in which Spartian wrote—the learned Abbé proceeds to give a summary of what is communicated by other ancient authors; and this he does by way of commentary on the text of Spartian.—See that valuable contribution in aid of the study of geographical and historical numismatology, *Mémoire sur les Voyages d'Hadrien*, p. 72, et seq.

The large brass engraved above is not described in the Catalogues of Mionnet and Akerman, nor is it included amongst those which illustrate "Coins of the Romans relating to Britain." But the author of that standard publication has made the following descriptive allusion to the subject in p. 24:—

" In the Museum Theupolum, a work, to the general accuracy of which Eckhel bears testimony, a large brass coin of Hadrian is thus described :

"*Reverse.*—EXERC. BRITAN. The emperor on a tribune or estrade, haranguing his troops.

" Although this coin is not known to our English numismatists, it is by no means a proof that it does not exist. Vaillant notices a type and legend very similar, viz.:

" EXERC. BRITANNICUS. Imperator paludatus, stans in suggestu, adloquitur cohortes.—In aliis, Imperator eques.

" To this he (Vaillant) appends the following remark—' Hic nummus primæ formæ inter rariores numerandus (imo inter rarissimos).' Nevertheless some artful rogue may have formed this coin from another of a similar type, by altering the letters of the legend."

Eckhel takes Vaillant for his authority in citing and describing this coin, making only this remark, that " scarcely any other information than that afforded by the few lines in Spartian, is recorded respecting Britain during Hadrian's time; nor do the types of coins furnish any hints on which we can dwell."

[A well-preserved and finely patinated specimen of the coin in question was purchased, about four years ago, for the British Museum, at the Campana sale (where it brought £14 14s), by Mr. Doubleday, who recently furnished the compiler with a cast. And this having been submitted to the practised eye and acute discernment of Mr.

Akerman, that gentleman in reply says—" To what I have stated regarding the large brass *Exercitus Britannicus* of Hadrian, I have nothing to add, except that I had not seen the coin, of which you send me a cast—but, looking to the appearance of that cast, I see no reason to doubt the genuineness of the original." It is under these circumstances, and with these sanctions, that an engraving of it is here published *for the first time*.

EXERCITVS CAPPADOCIVS. S. C.—The emperor on horseback, addressing the soldiers. First brass of Hadrian, who travelled in Asia A. D. 124. The legend and type of this reverse are explained, under the head of CAPPADOCIA, p. 171.

EXERC. DACICVS. S. C.—The emperor, with laurelled head, wearing the paludamentum over his military dress, and standing on a *suggestus*, raises his right hand aloft, as addressing the Roman army in Dacia, represented by three soldiers, one of whom bears a legionary eagle, another holds a military ensign surmounted by a right hand (see LEGIO), and the third figure carries a spear transversely. Below the *suggestus*, between the empéror and the soldiers, stands the prætorian prefect. On first brass of Hadrian. On others, the emperor is on horseback.

In quoting an example of the equestrian type, from the Imperial Cabinet, Eckhel (vi. 494) alludes to the marble (published by Gruter, page 249-4), which, erected to the honour of Hadrian, is inscribed "cujus virtute Dacia imperio addita felix est," an inscription which, as applied to him who *would* have abandoned Dacia altogether, and who *did* destroy Trajan's bridge of intercommunication with that hard-earned conquest, "must be considered either not genuine, or chargeable with base adulation. —See DACIA, p. 302.

EXERCITVS GALL*icus*.——Gold of Constantine.—See VIRTVS EXERC. GALL.

EXERCITVS HISPANICVS.—Mionnet leaves this legend out of the list of Hadrian's military medals, and Mr. Akerman does the same. But Havercamp, in the *Cabinet de Christine*, gives an engraving of a middle brass, inscribed with the above legend, and exhibiting the type of the emperor on horseback, with soldiers before him, indicating probably the assembling of an army in Spain destined to keep in awe some unsubdued portion of the population.

EXERCITVS IVDAICUS. S. C.—The emperor standing on a *suggestus*, delivers an allocution to his soldiers. On a first brass of Hadrian.

This coin finds no place in the respective catalogues of Mionnet and Akerman, consequently it may be inferred that certainly the French Cabinet, and perhaps, the British Museum do not possess a specimen of it; nor does it appear amongst the *Exercitus* series in the Imperial collection at Vienna. The Museum Theupolum moreover affords no testimony to its existence.—It is described in Mediobarbus, p. 178, and given by Patin, in his numismatic commentary on Suetonius, p. 377.—To this last named work Eckhel himself resorts, as to his sole named authority for including the Roman army of Judæa in the number of those military bodies, to whom "the Great Traveller" dedicated so many types of Allocution, after visiting the different countries, which their presence served either to defend, or to keep quiet. Taking it for granted, however, that the author of *Doctrina*, of all authors in the world, would not be at the pains of animadverting historically, on any other than what he believed an extant and a genuine monument of antiquity, we subjoin what he says under the head of EXERCITVS IVDAICVS.

The arrival of Hadrian in Judæa is recorded by Dion (lxix. § 11.) There are no coins to be seen, which celebrate Hadrian as *Restitutor Judææ*, though the type of ADVENTVI AVG. IVDAEAE (p. 9), really bears allusion to that restoration. During his reign, however, this nation was undeserving of such a princely act of benevolence. It is well known, with what fury, exceeding belief, this fanatic people, during the time of Trajan, stung as it were to frenzy, devastated with sword, fire, and rapine, the region of Cyrenaica, nursery of crime, and then Alexandria and Cyprus. Reduced to submission by force of arms, they remained quiet for a time. But subsequently, either in consequence of Hadrian's founding a Roman colony at Jerusalem, or because they were forbidden to practice circumcision, as Spartian imagines, they again threw off their allegiance, and the whole of Palestine rose in savage warfare under their leader Barchocebas. Though, on account of the contemptibility of the people in revolt, the commencement of this war might have been regarded as unimportant, yet Hadrian viewing it in a more serious light, recalled from Britain, Julius Severus, one of the most renowned generals of the age, and gave him the command-in-chief. But it was not without considerable difficulty, and many reverses, that he at length, for the second time, took and destroyed Jerusalem, rased her fortresses, slew all who offered resistance, and sold the remainder to slavery, and thus put an end to the war.

The precise year in which Hadrian visited Judæa is a controverted point. It has been asserted by some that this event took place in 872 (A. D. 119). Eckhel however shews, that the fact of Hadrian having made so early a journey into Judæa and its neighbourhood, not only rests on insecure authority, but is irreconcileable with the programme of the route, which he himself drew up, previously to commencing his tour of the provinces of the empire. But that Hadrian visited Judæa in the year 883 (A. D. 130), and thence passed into Egypt is proved from coins.—See *D. N.* vi. 496.

Reference may here be advantageously had to the comments of Abbé Greppo, on the *Exercitus Judaicus* of Hadrian—a coin which points to Judæa, as the station of a Roman army, under circumstances the most calamitous to that unhappy country.—*Voyages d' Hadrien*, p. 182, et seq.

EXERCITVS GERMANICVS.—The emperor, laurelled and paludated, on horseback, addressing the Germanic army, represented by three military figures, the foremost of which holds a staff surmounted by a superb eagle standing on a labarum, the next soldier holds a simple ensign, the hindmost carries a standard, surmounted by a right hand.—(See the article LEGIO). On first brass.

The Roman legionaries of the province, in memory of Hadrian's visit to which this beautiful coin was struck, came under his disciplinarian inspection immediately after his visit to Gaul, and before he went into Britain, it is believed about 872 (A. D. 119).

" Other than the name of Germany (observes the Abbé Greppo, adverting to the above legend), Spartian furnishes us with no geographical indications. His data are indeed very vague, and enable us to gain too little acquaintance with the extent of the districts occupied by the Romans in that country, or with the state of divers tribes of people, either in subjection, alliance, or hostility, that would justify us to hazard, as at all probable, any conjectures on the subject of those portions of Germany which Hadrian had then to visit. The fact, however, which Spartian alludes to, of a king given by Hadrian to the Germans—*Germanis regem constituit*—goes at least to prove that under his reign, Rome still enjoyed some consideration amongst that people. The coins struck to consecrate the remembrance of this part of Hadrian's travels, have all a military character.— In none of the types do we see the symbolising of a happy province, celebrating by sacrifices the advent of the sovereign, and recognizing him as the restorer of its prosperity. The legends ADVENTVI AVG. or RESTITVTORI AVG. are not found here. Germany appears on its coins in silver, with its name alone for legend,

GERMANIA; but she is personified by a figure standing, armed with the lance, and resting on a buckler. On others, in large brass, we read EXERCITVS GERMANICVS, and we see the emperor on horseback, haranguing soldiers." p. 70.

As Spartian, in his notice of Hadrian in Germany, has alluded with more than usual amplitude of details to the attentive care of that prince for military discipline, the Abbé ingeniously associates the well-known legend and type of DISCIPLINA AVG. (p. 333) with the probable though uucertain events connected with this epocha of the emperor's history.—See p. 70.

EXERCITVS MAVRETANICVS. S. C.— Large brass of Hadrian.—" The emperor on horseback, paludated, harangues three soldiers bearing military ensigns. This device alludes to a review of the army stationed in Mauretania, for Hadrian sagaciously maintained peace, by being always prepared for war."—Captain Smyth, *Descriptive Cat.* p. 107.

Hadrian's visit to the Roman military forces occupying the Mauretanian region of Africa, took place after his sojourn in Egypt, and immediately prior to his going into Syria, consequently between 883 (A. D. 130) and 884 (A. D. 131).—See MAVRETANIA.

EXER*citus* NORICVS. S. C.—The emperor, bare-headed, habited in the paludamentum, and standing on a raised place, addresses his army, personified by ensign-bearers; to the left is a soldier, who holds the emperor's horse. Behind the prince, on the same platform, is another military personage.

On the exergue of the present reverse we read the name of the army which occupied that part of Southern Germany, called *Noricum*, a country lying between the Danube and the Alps, now forming the territory of Nuremberg, and a portion of Bavaria.

Ancient writers are silent as to the journey of Hadrian into Noricum, but it is clearly recorded by those coins of his, which display the above legend and type.—Besides this device, sufficiently common to such analogous coins, Mionnet, in his *Rareté des Med. Rom.* (i. 198), has described a rarer and more interesting type, viz. one which represents Hadrian standing on an estrade, and behind him another figure, which is doubtless meant for the pretorian prefect.

Abbé Greppo, in citing this type from Mionnet, remarks that *Noricum* was essentially a military country, and that inscriptions mention divers legionary bodies called after its name.— For another presumed object of Hadrian's visit to this otherwise unattractive station, see ME-*Tallum* NOR*icum*.

For the probable date about which Hadrian presented himself in person to his Norican army, see EXERCITVS GERMANICVS.

EXERCITVS PARTHICVS.—The emperor standing on a *suggestus* with two other military figures, makes an oration to the soldiers. On a brass medallion of Hadrian, described in Vaillant, *Num. Max. Mod.* p. 116.

By this coin it is shewn that Hadrian, altho' he had given up Parthia with the other oriental conquests of his predecessor, still continued vigilantly to keep up an army of observation on the frontiers of that country, and which, no doubt, was stationed near the Euphrates.

Spartian states that Hadrian, who was desirous to establish amicable relations with all the princes of the East, proffered an invitation of friendship to Chosroes, king of the Parthians, sending back to him his daughter whom Trajan had taken, and promising the restoration of his royal throne (which was of gold, but which was *not* given up by Hadrian). The same historian also says, that this emperor was always on terms of good understanding with the Parthians. Nevertheless, a war with that people would inevitably have broken out, had it not been averted by a conference between Hadrian and (as it would seem) their king. It is perhaps by this passage of the Roman historian that the brass medallion may be explained, which exhibits on its reverse the legend and typification of EXERCITVS PARTHICVS.

EXERCITVS RAETICVS (or RHAETICVS) S. C.—" The emperor, on horseback, is addressing a party of soldiers, bearing military standards. The foremost of these men holds an unusually large square shield before him, which may allude to Rhætia's being deemed a buckler against the depredations of the Gauls and Germans."—Capt. Smyth, *Descr. Cat.* p. 109.

This first brass of Hadrian is engraved in the *Cabinet de Christine*, TAB. xii.

We should be absolutely ignorant of the fact that this prince visited Rhætia, but for these brass coins, which attest it. This country [now comprehending the Voralberg and the Tyrol] had given its name to different bodies of troops, mentioned on ancient marbles.

EXERC. SYRIACVS. S. C.—The emperor on horseback, clothed in the toga, before him are four soldiers bearing legionary eagles and simple ensigns.

Among the geographical coins of Hadrian, Syria is named only on those struck in large brass, having the above legend and accompanying type of the *Syrian army*. But others of his mintages bear the names of several countries in the East.

Arrived in the province of Syria, Hadrian made Judæa the object of a special visit. There are large and middle brass on which, for example, we read ADVENTVI AVG. IVDAEAE (engraved in p. 9.) Their type offers this particularity, that the two figures sacrificing, are accompanied, sometimes by two, sometimes by three smaller figures, bearing palm branches.

In reference to such geographical coins of Hadrian as specially relate to his voyages and travels, M. Charles Lenormant observes, "that at least a good portion of them were not struck in the same year of the journey, which they serve to record. In fact on several of them the emperor is called *Pater Patriæ*. Now, he did not accept that title until the year of Rome 881 (A.D. 128), whilst the series of his visits to the different parts of his dominions, commenced in 873 (A.D. 120). It is certain, therefore, that, at a

little later period the Senate caused the collection of these medals to be completed, for the purpose of handing down to posterity a memorial of each of his voyages."—*(Iconographie des Empereurs*, p. 54.)

EXERCITVS VSC. or ISC.—The Emperor Postumus, on horseback, with several military figures standing before him.

EXERCITVS VAC.—Same emperor and type.

Hadrian's mint has obviously furnished the arch-type of these two large brass coins. Some learned men, among others Havercamp, who has given engravings of both in his *Cabinet de Christine*, pronounce the added names of VSC. or ISC. and VAC. to mean, the former *Ysca* or *Isch*, the river *Ex* [see Gough's Camden, Devonshire, river *Ex*, vol. i. p. 42]; and the latter the *Vaccæi*, a people of Spain.—As to *Isca*, Eckhel (vii. 442) laconically but conclusively says, "To some the above reading appeared suspicious, and to have originated in an error of the moneyer, and I prefer *their* opinion to the *first* mentioned authorities." But after all, are these coins *true?*

EXERGUE, or EXERGUM—the lowest part of a coin, divided from the rest by a horizontal line. The word signifies an outwork (or, as the French numismatists interpret it, *hors d'œuvre*) in relation to the type and to the legend. It is usually found on the reverse; seldom on the side of the head. In coins of families and those of the higher empire, the exergual inscription marks either Consular dates, or Senatorial authority, or frequently, what is of more importance, it directly applies to the subject typified on the reverse. In the mintages of the lower empire, letters occupy the exergue which generally serve to indicate the cities in which they were struck, and in both instances these words or letters form a straight line, whilst the rest of the legend is placed circularly. For examples of the exergue and its various uses, see pages 5, 7, 9, 11, 20, 37, 41, 70, 163, 217, 301, 307, 308, 317, 333, &c. in this dictionary.

EXPECTATE VENI. *(Come, O expected one!)*—Figure in military dress, his left hand resting on the *hasta*, stands joining hands with a robed female, also standing, and who holds a trident. In the exergue RSR. (probably meant for *Rutupiæ*, now Richborough, in Kent).—*Obv.* IMP. CARAVSIVS P. F. AVG. Laurelled bust of Carausius.

This unique legend, with its hardly less rare and remarkable type, appears on the reverse of a silver Carausius, of which Mr. Akerman was the first to publish an engraving. (See his *Descriptive Catalogue*, vol. ii. vignette in wood,

p. 154), from "a specimen in unusually good condition." It formed part of the late Mr. Thomas's "princely collection," at the sale of which this precious monetal relic of the usurping but independent sovereign of Britain, brought the sum of £10 5s. The learned editor of the auction catalogue (Mr. Burgon, p. 285), observes, that the coin in question "is of far better silver than Carausius's generally are."

The preceding cut is after a cast, furnished to the compiler by Mr. Doubleday, apparently from the Thomas specimen. The same type also occurs in gold, according to Mionnet (*Rareté*, &c. ii. 166), who values it at 600 fr. whilst he prices the silver type at 150 fr.—See Mintages of Carausius, p. 178, et seq.

"Both type and legend seem to imply, that Carausius had sounded the Britons before he ran off with the fleet from Boulogne. Genèbrier, describing, probably, from an ill-preserved coin, takes the female figure for Felicity, and supposes the trident to be the long caduceus, with which that Roman goddess is generally represented. But that it is a trident which she holds is quite evident, and that the figure is the Genius of Britain will be acknowledged even by the unimaginative."—See Akerman.

Eckhel (viii. 45), who formed his opinion apparently, not from having seen the coin, but from an engraving in Haym's *Tesoro Britannico* still considers the female figure to be the Genius of Britain. His words are—"Figuram muliebrem esse genium Britanniæ, verisimile existimo, qui Carausium ad se, et capessendum imperium invitare videtur." And he aptly cites Virgil, who makes Æneas speak to Hector in like phraseology—"Quibus Hector ab oris expectate venis?"

EX. ORACVLO APOLLINIS. A round temple, on whose summit is an eagle; within is an idol, or three idols.

On the subject of this singular epigraph, which Mionnet and Akerman do not either of them notice, but which Eckhel recognises, as being on the reverse of a brass coin of Philip senior—the last named numismatist says— "Whether he received the empire in accordance with the response of Apollo's oracle, or procured the building of the temple, exhibited on the reverse, or benefitted it in any other way, is matter of uncertainty; and *(to solve the question)* we have need of another oracle of Apollo. But whatever it may be, this coin offers a sinister omen to the opinion of those who assert Philip to have professed the Christian religion. Venuti, in his coin of the Museo Albano, sees three idols, which he supposes to be Capitoline—viz. of Jupiter, Minerva, and Juno." vol. vii.

EXPEDITIO.—Whenever the memorial of an emperor's *expedition* against *the enemy* is struck on a coin, he is made to appear in haste. Thus we see Sept. Severus represented on horseback, galloping with couched spear, on a silver coin, which is referred by Vaillant to that emperor's Britannic campaign. But the departure of the emperor on a pacific journey (according to the same author) is depicted on coins by a horseman going at a moderate pace. The subjoined type of Hadrian would, with the aid of the legend, signify a *setting out ;* but the slow pace of the horse rather denotes the *adventus*, or arrival.

EXPED. AVG. S. C. *Expeditio Augusti.*— The expedition of the Emperor. Hadrian, bareheaded, on horseback (COS. III). The obverse of this coin represents Hadrian laureated, and in the paludamentum, or military cloak. The legend is IMP*erator* CAES*ar* TRAIANVS AVG*ustus*.

This is a finely-designed coin in first brass. The equestrian group is in a spirited style of workmanship, both horse and man. The Augustus raises aloft his right hand, and with his left holds the bridle of his generous steed, as setting out on him on some journey, about that vague period, his third consulate.

The Abbé Greppo notices the legend EXPE-D*itio*, and its accompanying type, in a passage of his work to the following effect (p. 28) :—

In addition to those geographical coins which, by exhibiting the very *name* of the country visited, leave no doubt whatever as to their signification, there are some others, which, though in a manner less precise, unquestionably bear reference also to the journeyings of this prince. These cease to present to us the names of divers provinces, or to bear the symbols which characterise them. They simply indicate the departure of the emperor, going to visit some one or other of them, yet without enabling us to ascribe them to this or to that voyage, more than to the rest. Thus, on large brass coins, which represent Hadrian on horseback, we read EXPED. AVG. P. M. TR. P. COS. III.—Others in gold and in large brass, presenting the same type, but without legend, seem to have been struck with the same intention. The expeditions of this emperor in Gaul and in Syria are designated in an interesting inscription, forming the epitaph of a freedman, who had accompanied his master, a secretary and personal attendant of Hadrian in the Gaulish and Syrian expeditions, as the inscription itself (p. 198) sets forth (IN EXPEDITIONIBVS DVABVS GALLIAE ET SYRIAE).—There are, as the Abbé observes, more varieties in the reverses which recall the sea-trajects of the same emperor, and which are seen on silver, brass, and some medallions. For a description and engraving of one of these obvious emblems of good wishes for a happy voyage to the emperor. —See FELICITATI AVG.

EX. SENATVS CONSVLTO. *Diva Marciana.*—That Marciana was enrolled among the divinities is proved by marbles, as well as by several coins. In Gruter's work is given a stone erected at Cetrania Severina, in memory of her priestess (SACERDOTI DIVAE MARCIANÆ.) We are not informed as to the year in which she acquired these honours. We only know that she was entitled to the epithet *diva* about the year 867, (B. C. 114); as on the arch of the Portus Anconitanus (Ancona), which records the xviiith Tribunicia Potestas of Trajan (unless, indeed, we should there read xviiii), there is found the inscription DIVAE MARCIANAE AVG. SORORI AVG. (cited by Eckhel, vi. 468, from Gruter, 247, 6).

Obv.—DIVA AVGVSTA MARCIANA. A head of Marciana.—*Rev.*—EX. SENATVS CONSVLTO. A chariot drawn by two elephants with riders, and a veiled figure seated in it. Silver and first brass.—See exactly same type engraved in p. 358.

EXVPERATOR OMNIVM GENTIVM.— (The Conqueror of all Nations).—The emperor, with laurelled head, is seated on a cuirass, between two captives crouching on the ground. He rests his left hand on the hasta (or rather staff with foliaged head), and holds in his right a globe surmounted by a victoriola with a garland.—Brass medallion of Constantine the Great. *Obv.*—CONSTANTINVS MAX. AVG. Bust of the Emperor, with the diadem.—[The above reverse is engraved after a cast from a fine specimen in the *Cabinet de France.*]

"The word *Exuperator* (says Rasche) I have hitherto no where found on coins, except in this instance, but besides the word *Exupero* (to surpass, to be predominant), there occur also *Exuperantia* (pre-eminence, superiority), *Exuperatio,* (an exceeding or surpassing), *Exuperabilis,* or more properly *Exsuperabilis* (what may be exceeded)."

The coinage of Constantine (observes Eckhel), is full of novel and extravagant titles, too proud and presumptuous, even when they are true.— On the coins of Commodus, we see Jupiter *Exuperantissimus* (the most excellent, the supreme); but then Commodus applied to himself the epithet *Exuperatorius* (conquering), and caused the month of November to be called *mensis exuperatorius,* after him as conqueror! viii. 83.

F, the sixth letter of the Latin alphabet, stands for PH on some coins of the lower empire; as in Numerianus, TRIVMFVS QVAD; and in Honorius, TRIVMFATOR GENT. BARBAR. There is also a coin of Constans, which reads OB. VICTORIAM TRIVMFALEM.

F. or FAB. *Fabius.*—C. F. *Caius Fabius,* name and surname of the Fabia family.

F.—FAC. *Faciundum, Faciundis.*—CVR. X. F. *Curavit Denarium Faciundum;* or Curator Denariorum flandorum.—SACR. FAC. *Sacris Faciundis.*

F. *Fecit.*—LVD. SAEC. F.—*Ludos Sæculares Fecit.*

F. *Felicitas.*—F. B. *Felicitas Beata.*

F. *Felix.*—P. F. or PIVS F. frequent on Roman imperial coins.

F. *Fidelis.*—P. F. LEG. *Pia Fidelis Legio.*

F. *Fieri.*—F. C. *Fieri Curavit.*

F. *Filia* or *Filiæ.*—ANTONINI AVG. F. (Lucilla), &c.

F. *Filii.*—C. L. CAESARES AVGVSTI F. *Caius and Lucius Filii Augusti* (that is to say, *ab Augusto Adoptati)*

F. *Filius.*—Frequent on coins of Roman families (in like manner as N. *Nepos); e. g.* A. F. *Auli Filius.*—BRVTI. F. *Bruti Filius.*

F stands for the same on a great number of imperial coins, as AVG. D. F. *Augustus Divi [Julii] Filius.*—AVG. F. AVG. *Augusti Filius Augustus.*

F. *Flando.*—See marks of the Monetal Triumvirs, A. A. A. F. F. *Auro, Argento, Aere, Flando, Feriundo.*—(See p. 1.)

F. *Flavia.*—C. F. *Colonia Flavia.*

F. *Fortuna.*—F. P. R. *Fortuna Populi Romani.*

FABIA gens.—An ancient, noble, and powerful family, that gave many great men to the republic of Rome. It extended itself into six branches, five of which (viz. Buteo, Labeo, Pictor, Hispaniensis, Maximus), exhibit their respective surnames on coins. Discarding the fable of Silius Italicus, who carries its origin to Fabius, the son of Hercules, and giving scarcely more credit to historians who kill off all the males of the family save one, in a general engagement, which they entered 306 strong, near the Cremera, against the Veientes, B. C. 447; the celebrated characters who are supposed to have sprung from the sole survivor of that fatal day, amounted to thirty-six individuals, and who in the space of 250 years, were invested with forty-eight Consulates, eight Censorships, and ten Tribunates of the Plebs, five Principes Senatus, together with the honours of thirteen triumphs, and of two ovations. From Fabius Maximus, surnamed Cunctator, the famous dictator in the second Punic war, down to the reign of Tiberius, the Fabii sustained the splendour of their race at Rome.

There are eleven or twelve distinctly different types, and many more unimportant varieties in the coins of this gens; but they offer few subjects of interest, even on the most select and rare of their reverses. To make amends, however, for historical and mythological deficiencies, the initial letters and abbreviated words, on some of them, have supplied ample themes for exercising the ingenuity, and for displaying the erudition, of numismatic antiquaries.

The brass pieces belonging to this gens are *asses*, or parts of the *as*, and Imperial Greek.

The following are among the denarii most open to historical illustration :—

1.—EX. A. PV. Bust of a veiled and turreted woman, to the right.—*Rev.*—C. FABI. C. F. Victory in a rapid biga; beneath the fore feet of the horses is a vulture, or other bird of prey. In the field of the coin some letter or other of the Latin alphabet. Silver. [The obverse type is probably the head of Juno, in whose temple the public money was kept.— For an interpretation of the obverse legend, see p. 69.]

There is a large brass *as* with the name of this family, published by Liebe, bearing on the reverse side the usual ship's prow, but with a vulture, or a buteo (see p. 148) standing on the lower part of it.

With respect to peculiar, yet constant symbols, Borghesi is of opinion, that when they appear on single denarii of Roman families, and especially when they are repeated on their brass coins, they bear allusion to the surnames of that particular family. Hence he is induced to regard the vulture, or whatever bird it may be, which is represented on the two coins above described, as having relation to the cognomen of the family of C. Fabius Buteo.—Ursin and Eckhel appear to have viewed it in the same light. The earliest numismatic writers, in general, believe the silver coin to have been the first in that metal struck by the Romans, and attribute it to a C. Fabius Pictor, consul with Q. Ogulnius Gallus in 484 (B. c. 270); and that the EX A. PV. indicates the authority of the Roman people, who in that year caused it to be minted. But its workmanship, and its style of representing objects, preclude the acceptance of this opinion. Borghesi, looking to the symbols above mentioned, considers them to belong to the time of Marius. And with him others concur, that they were coined in Africa by Caius Fabius Adrianus, pretor and pro-pretor of the consuls L. Cornelius Cinna and Cn. Papirius Carbo, in 669 and 670 (B. c. 85 and 84), partizans of Marius, (who died the previous year 668).—Cavedoni thinks it probable that it was C. Fabius, who being in 670 pretor in Africa, expelled thence Q. Metellus; and two years

afterwards, he himself, on account of his cruelty and avarice, whilst pretor, was burnt alive.— (Liv. *Epit.* 84-86.)—See Riccio, p. 89.

2.—LABEO. ROMA. Galeated head of Rome, before the neck X.—*Rev.*—Q. FABI. Jupiter Tonans, in a rapid quadriga, brandishing the thunderbolt, and holding the sceptre. Beneath the horses a ship's head.

The learned refer this silver coin to Quintus Fabius Labeo, who, in the year of Rome 565 (B. c. 189), under the consulship of M. Fulvius Nobilior and Cneus Manlius Vulso, and during the war with King Antiochus Major, was appointed as pretor, to the command of the fleet. But peace with Syria, having in the meanwhile been made, he landed at Crete, and rescued from captivity the Roman citizens, who were dispersed through the greater part of that island, on which account (according to Livy) he claimed and enjoyed the honours of a naval triumph. It was for this reason also, as is believed, that the ship's prow displays itself on his coins.—Eckhel, v. p. 208.

3.—N. FABI. N. PICTOR. A galeated figure, seated to the left, holds in the right hand the pontifical apex; in the left the *hasta pura*; near her, resting on the ground, is a shield, inscribed QVIRIN.—In the exergue ROMA.— *Obv.*—Head of Rome, with mark of the denarius.

Differing from Ursin, Vaillant, and Spanheim, who have all three interpreted the abbreviation on the shield QVIRIN*us*, and who have even yielded to the strange supposition that Quirinus (or Romulus) himself is represented in the seated figure.—Eckhel (v. 209) affirms, that an accurate inspection of all the specimens of this silver coin proves it to be the type of a woman, and observes that Quirinus is usually depicted with a long beard.—[In the above cut, the galeated figure on the reverse has *not* a womanly countenance; but in other respects it agrees with the martial character in which deified Rome usually appears on coins]. For these reasons Eckhel coincides with Havercamp, both in pronouncing the image to personify Rome, and in reading the inscription QVIRIN*alis*, that is to say *Flamen Quirinalis*, an office hereditary in the Fabia family. Of the Fabii who were *Flamines Quirinales* frequent mention is made in Livy and in Val. Maximus. The surname of *Pictor* is stated to have been derived to this family from C. Fabius, who in 450 (B. c. 394) gratuitously painted the temple of the Goddess of Health (Ædes Salutis), erected after the Samnite war, by Caius Junius Brutus Bubulcus —which painting was, it seems, in existence until the time of Claudius, during whose reign that sacred edifice was destroyed by fire, as is testified by Pliny, who considers that effort of art to have been creditable to the Fabia family— an opinion, however, widely dissented from by Val. Maximus, who, in narrating the same fact, denounces painting as an occupation too mean for a citizen of the noblest rank to pursue, and treats the performance of Pictor with corresponding disdain.

Riccio (p. 88) says—"Numerius Flavius Pictor, great grandson to the famous C. Fabius above mentioned, was the author of this silver coin, but the precise time when he exercised his monetal triumvirate is not known.—See QUIRINUS—see also *Flamen Quirinalis*.

4.—L. FABI. L. F. HISP. Victory in a fast-going quadriga, holding a palm branch ; under the horses' feet Q.—*Obverse.*—C. ANNI. T. F. T. N. PRO. COS. EX. S. C. Head of a woman, adorned with small mitre, ear-rings, and necklace ; behind it a caduceus : sometimes within a crown, sometimes not.

Lucius Fabius, son of Lucius, was pro-questor in Spain to the pro-consul C. Annius, sent thither by Sulla in 671 (B. C. 83), to subdue Sertorius, of the Marian party.

5.—Q. MAX. ROMA. Galeated head of Rome : before it X.—*Rev.*—Cornucopiæ with fruit, and with which a thunderbolt is put crosswise ; the whole within a crown formed of poppies and corn-ears.

Cavedoni says that this denarius, with the initial Q, belongs to Quintus Fabius Maximus Servilianus, consul [with Cecilius Metellus] in 612 (B. C. 142) ; and that the cornucopiæ traversed with the *fulmen*, still the symbol of the city of Valentia, in Spain, alludes to the exploits of the father, and of the brother, against Viriatus, in that country. It is to be observed, that the crown which encompasses the field of the above silver coin, is composed of leaves tied together with heads of poppies, and finishes with corn-ears.—May not these (asks Riccio) point to the corona *obsidionalis*, the honour of which was earned by Quintus Fabius Maximus, the *delayer*, as he was called ?— page 88.

FABRICIA gens plebeia.—Morel gives two coins of this family, which, according to Vaillant, has *Paternus* for its surname.

FABRINIA gens.—Unrecorded (says Eckhel) by history or by any ancient monument, coins excepted. The name of M. FABRINI (*Fabrinus*) appears on the triens, quadrans, and semis of the early brass coinage.—See one of each engraved in Riccio, TAV. XX.

FACE of a Coin.—Every perfect coin has two faces or sides ; one called the obverse, the

other the reverse ; and the figure, and legend, or inscription, on each are alike subjects for consideration.

FADIA gens plebeia ; not noticed in Morel, Mionnet, Akerman, nor in Riccio ; but of which Eckhel states that some small brass coins are extant. L. FAD*ius*, a contemporary of Julius Cæsar and Augustus, appears to have been one of their mint-masters.

FALX, a sickle : the sign of Saturn, the reputed inventor of agriculture, whence he was called *falcifer* by the poets. The figure of this instrument of husbandry, indented, appears on coins of the Calpurnia, Memmia, and Servilia families.—See SATURN.

FAMILY COINS.—See NUMI FAMILIARUM ROMANARUM.

FANNIA gens—of the plebeian order, but of consular rank.—The silver coins of this family have two varieties, and the brass one type, as follow :—

1. AED. PL. (Ædilis Plebis). Head of Ceres crowned with corn ears.—*Rev.*—M. FAN. L. CRIT. Marcus Fannius and Lucius Critonius togated, occupying their respective *sedilia*, and presiding over the public distribution of wheat. On some specimens this is additionally indicated by a corn-ear placed upright before them. Behind, in the field, are the letters P. A. *(Publico Argento).*—See ÆDILIS, p. 12—see also Critonia gens, p. 296.

2. Head of Rome, helmeted : before it X.— *Rev.*—M. FAN. C. F. Victory in a quadriga at full speed, holding a branch, sometimes a crown, in her right hand.—For a wood-cut of it see DENARIUS, p. 317, left hand column.

3. M. FAN. C. F. above ; ROMA below.— *Rev.*—S. (Semis). Ship's prow.—Middle brass.

The author of these two last coins is unknown. It is thought that possibly they may have been struck by M. Fannius, pretor in 672 (B. C. 82), during his monetal triumvirate.—See Riccio, 90.

The name of Fannius (C. FAN. PONT. PR.) is read on the cistophori of Tralles (Asia) coined in 705 (B. C. 49).

FARSULEIA gens, an obscure family of the plebeian order, known only by its coins, which are silver, and have but one type, with some unimportant varieties. It has *Farsuleius* for its name, and *Mensor* for its surname. The following is the least common :—

S. C. MENSOR. Bust of a woman, with small tiara, or mitella, on her head ; behind is the *pileus* of liberty.—*Rev.*—L. FARSVLEI. A galeated and paludated figure, in a biga to the right, extends the right hand to another figure, clothed in the toga, to assist him in ascending the car. Under the horses are letters, and in some specimens, a·scorpion.

As is the family's origin so is the type's meaning—obscure. Learned men (observes Eckhel, v. 212), suppose this to be symbolically allusive to the *lex Julia*, enacted 664 (B. C. 90), conferring the right of citizenship on the Italians, which privilege is further conjectured to be here shadowed forth by the armed figure, personifying the Roman people, who is receiving his new associate of Italy into the same vehicle with himself. The head of Liberty, exhibited on the obverse, also seems to favour this attempt at an interpretation.—Cavedoni is of opinion, that to this subject of Italians admitted into Roman privileges the type of Mucia gens [in which, as also in that of Furia gens, the heads of Honour and Virtue are conjoined] more applies than does this type of Farsuleia, because the heroic car, and the excited action of the horses, do not correspond with the workmanship of the times in question; nor with the supposed signification, but rather with the style of a later age; that is to say, the decay of the republic.—See Riccio, p. 91.

FASCES—bundles of birchen rods, carried by the lictors before the highest class of Roman magistrates, with an axe bound up in the middle of them, as for the punishment of wicked doers. The rods to shew the more lenient infliction for faults capable of correction; the axe *(securis)* to indicate that the perpetrators of heinous and unatonable crimes were to be cut off from society. These *fasces* and *secures*, on coins, denote the supreme authority of the consuls and other principal magistrates, as having the right and power of life and death. The figure of a curule chair (symbolical of the consular office), placed between two *fasces* (sometimes with, sometimes without, the *axes*) is a frequent type on coins of Roman families. (See FUFIA and LIVINEIA.)—The *fasces*, and a *caduceus*, placed crosswise, with an axe below and a globe above them, and on one side two right hands joined, appear on silver coins of Aemilius Buca and Julius Cæsar. (See p. 156.)—The fasces with *the axe* appear on coins of the Licinia (Morell. TAB. 3) and Norbana families.

FASTI—a name given to the tables of marble, on which the Romans dedicated to posterity the names, achievements, and triumphs of their great men, and made known to the people the *dies fasti et nefasti*—the days when they *were*, and were *not*, to offer sacrifices to their gods, and discharge the duties imposed on them by the *Pontifices*, as those of religion. These annual records were subdivided into several kinds, of which the principal were—

1. *Fasti Kalendares.*—These were so called, because the days of each month, from kalends to kalends, were marked in them; and because they also noted all the religious ceremonies from the beginning to the end of each month. Towards the close of the republic, and afterwards under the imperial government, insensate pride in the governors, and adulatory baseness in the governed, occasioned the prostitution of these tables, and rendered them ultimately subservient to the extravagance of princes and the degeneracy of the people. For a *man* to have his name *adscriptum* on the *Fasti*, had always been reckoned an object of legitimate ambition, as it was indeed one of the highest honour; but then it was confined to the consular and triumphal *Fasti*. The emperors, not content with ruling the world, affected Divinity, and obtruded themselves on the calendar as objects of every kind of religious adoration.

2. *Fasti Consulares,* in which were annually marked the names of magistrates, particularly consuls, and dictators, (when these latter were appointed); also the wars, victories, and political changes of the republic, together with memorials of secular games and other remarkable events. And this was done, as well to preserve the dates of successive years, as to hand down the remembrance of important transactions.——See Pitiscus and Adams.

A most important specimen of *Fasti*, belonging to the class of *Consulares*, supposed to have been executed at the beginning of the reign of Tiberius, has been partially preserved. " In the year 1547, several fragments of marble tablets were discovered, in excavating the Roman forum, and were found to contain a list of consuls, dictators, and their masters of horse, censors with the lustra which they closed, triumphs and ovations, all arranged in regular succession, according to the years of the Catonian æra. These had evidently extended from the expulsion of the kings to the death of Augustus; and, although defective in many places, have proved of the greatest value in chronology. The different pieces were collected and arranged under the inspection of Cardinal Alexander Farnese, and deposited in the Capitol, where they still remain. From this circumstance they are generally distinguished as the *Fasti Capitolini.*—In the years 1817 and 1818, two other fragments of the same marble tablets were discovered in the course of a new excavation in the forum. A fac-simile of them was published at Milan, by Borghesi, in 1818."— [The foregoing passage is extracted from an able article, embracing notices of all points needful to be known on the subject, contained in the *Dictionary of Greek and Roman Antiquities,* edited by Dr. Smith, at the end of which work the *Fasti Consulares* themselves are given.]

FATA, the same three fabulous deities as the *Parcæ,* daughters of Erebus: they inhabited a gloomy cave in Tartarus, symbolical of the obscurity which envelopes the future, whose course they were able at once to predict and determine, according to the Pagan system of Theology. These awful sisters constituted Destiny, or at least were the mistresses of Destiny. The Romans, following the example of the Greeks in all superstitious practices, paid great honours to the *Fata;* and invoked them generally after Apollo, because they, like that god, presided over the future.

FATIS VICTRICIBVS. (To the Victorious Fates).--This remarkable legend appears on the reverse of a very rare gold coin of Diocletian. —The type, which accompanies it, represent

three women clothed in the stola, standing together—and it is regarded as referring to the
Tria Fata, in whose name, and for the worship
of whom, a temple was dedicated at Rome.—
For an explanation by Opanlicini, and observations thereon by Eckhel, see the word
PARCAE.

FAUSTA *(Flavia Maxima)* was daughter of
Maximianus Hercules and of Eutropia, sister of
Maxentius, and second wife of Constantine the
Great. She was married to that emperor in the
year of Rome 1060 (A. D. 307). She gave
birth to Constantine the younger, to Constantius the younger, and to Constans. She died
in 1079 (A. D. 326), from suffocation in a hot
bath, by order of her husband, for having
caused the death of Crispus, in falsely accusing
him of incestuous designs upon her chastity, or
of rebellious projects against his father's imperial authority.

The coins of this empress in gold, silver, and
brass (with the exception of the following very
rare reverses) are common :—

GOLD MEDALLION.—PIETAS AVGVSTA. The
empress, seated between two women, carrying a
child in her arms ; the one on the right hand
supports a long caduceus. Below are two genii,
holding a garland. In the exergue P.T.R. *(Morellii Specimen*, p. 53).—[This, if authentic, is
unique. Mionnet values it at 1000 francs].

GOLD.—SALVS REIPVBLICAE. A woman standing, robed and veiled, suckling two infants. On
the exergue P. T. *(Percussum Thessalonicæ*, struck
at Thessalonica): a crescent or some other symbol, between the two letters. (Mionnet, 500 fr.
gold, 50 fr. silver). Engraved in Lenormant,
Iconographie des Empereurs.——SPES REIPVB-
LICAE. The same type. On the exergue P. T.
(Mt. 500 fr. in gold, 50 fr. in silver).—*Obv.*
FLAV. MAX. FAVSTA. AVG. Head of the empress, young and handsome. (Mt. 500 fr. in
gold, 50 fr. in silver).—See the above wood-cut
from a small brass specimen of the same legend
and type.

BRASS MEDALLION.—PIETAS AVGVSTE *(sic.)*
Fausta standing, carrying an infant on the left
arm, and extending the right hand to another
child, who, standing at her feet, presents some-
thing to her.—*Obv.*—FLAV. MAX. FAVSTA AVG.
Diademed head of the empress. (Valued by
Mionnet at 72 fr.) Engraved in *Iconographie
Romaine*, p. 121.

For the purport of some observations made
by M. Le Baron Marchant, in his xviith *Lettre
Numismatique* (and to which M. Charles Lenormant yields his support) in a new attribution of coins to *this* Fausta, see NOBILISSIMA
FAEMINA.

FAUSTINA *(Annia Galeria)* designated by
numismatists sometimes by the name of Faustina
the mother, sometimes by that of Faustina the
elder, was born in the year of Rome 858 (A. D.
105), under the reign of Trajan. She was
daughter of Marcus Annius Verus, a man of
consular rank, prefect of Rome, paternal grandfather of Marcus Aurelius Having married
Antoninus Pius whilst he was still a private
citizen, she received from the Senate the title of
Augusta shortly after the death of Hadrian, as
her husband did that of *Pius*. She did not,
however, long enjoy her honours, dying in the
third year of the reign of Antonine, U. C. 894
(B. C. 141), according to Capitolinus ; whose
record is confirmed by a marble published by
Muratori, which speaks of Faustina as already
Diva in the fourth tribunate of Antonine. According to a marble of Gruter's, she was 36
years, three months, and eleven days old, when
she died. Capitolinus is severe upon the levity of
her conduct ; but he also states that Antonine did
his utmost to conceal her irregularities, though
at the expense of great disquietude to himself.
Thus much is certain, that, as is testified by
the legends and types of her coins, Antonine
lavished every honour upon her, both during
life and after her decease. Faustina gave her
husband two sons : Marcus Galerius Antoninus,
whose name is known to us only through the
medium of a Greek imperial coin, engraved in the
Iconographie Romaine, p. 63 ; and Marcus Aurelius Fulvius Antoninus, known solely from
the inscription published by Pagi (v. *Crit.
Baron.* ad U. C. 914 A. D. 161) ; also two
daughters, Aurelia Fadilla, married to Lamia
Syllanus, who was already dead when her father
set out for his government of Asia, under
Hadrian. The other daughter was Faustina,
called junior, who was married to Marcus
Aurelius, her cousin-german.

The coins of this empress in gold and silver
(with exceptions subjoined) are common; brass
medallions rare ; first and second brass, for the
most part, very common. On these she is styled
FAVSTINA AVGVSTA—FAVSTINA AVG.
ANTONINI AVG. (by implication, *uxor*.)—
FAVSTINA AVG. ANTONINI AVG. PII.
P. P.—DIVA AVGVSTA FAVSTINA.

The greater part of these coins were struck,
after her decease, with the usual legends and
symbols of Consecration, and especially with the
various types of Eternity.

RAREST REVERSES of FAUSTINA.

GOLD.—CONSECRATIO. A quadriga, in which a woman stands, veiled and in the stola, holding the *hasta pura*, whilst another female guides the horses.—On the obverse of this beautiful coin is the bust of Faustina, not veiled, but with the head-dress of a living Augusta.— (Mionnet values it at 72 fr. A fine specimen went for £2 14s. at the Thomas sale).

AETERNITAS. Four-wheeled car, in which, under canopy, is placed the *image* of Faustina seated, drawn by two elephants, each mounted by a conductor.—*Obv.*—DIVA FAVSTINA. (The divine Faustina). Bust of the deceased empress.— (Mionnet values it at 72 fr. A fine specimen brought £3 17s. at the Thomas sale. Engraved in Caylus, *Num. Aur. Impp. Rom.* No. 522.)— Another *aureus* has for legend of reverse, AETERNITAS, with type of a six-columned temple, in the middle of which is placed the sedent statue of Faustina, as Juno, holding the sceptre. The *fronton* of the temple is adorned with a bas-relief. On the summit is a quadriga; at the two extremities a Victory, front-faced, carrying a buckler on its head. The steps are fenced in by a railing. (Mt. 36 fr.)—AETERNITAS. Empress standing with rudder and patera. (£3 7s. at the Brumell sale).—AVGVSTA. Empress holding a lighted torch in each hand, (obtained £7 10s. at the Thomas sale. A flower of the die reverse went for only £3 at the Pembroke).—CONCORDIA AVG. Female seated. (Pembroke Cat. lot 272, brought at sale £3 4s.)—EX. SENATVS CONSVLTO. Car drawn by two elephants. (Mt. 100 fr.)—IVNONI REGINAE. Throne, sceptre, peacock, and cista. (£4 1s. Thomas).—Same legend. Throne, with a sceptre, between a peacock and a crow. (Mionnet, 60 fr.)—FORTUNA OBSEQVENS. The Empress standing with the attributes of Fortune.

[Nearly all the above are engraved in the imperial gold coins of the *Cabinet de France* by Count Caylus.]

PVELLAE FAVSTINIANAE. *(The young Faustinians).* Faustina seated on a tribunal. Opposite to her the emperor stands holding out his hands and receiving an infant, which is presented to him by a woman. At the foot of the tribunal is a man bringing also an infant.—*Obv.*—DIVA FAVSTINA. Bust of Faustina, to the right. (Mt. 200 fr. *Cabinet de France).*—Without legend; a hexastyle temple, still extant at Rome. (£2 10s. Thomas sale).

SILVER.——PVELLAE FAVSTINIANAE. Same type as in gold.—*Obv.*—DIVA AVG. FAVSTINA. (Mt. 100 fr.)—[See the following engraving.— Capitolinus states, that Antoninus founded a college of young girls, who were maintained at his

own expense, whom he called *Puellæ Faustinianæ,* in honour of Faustina. Eckhel (vii. p. 7), cites several inscriptions dedicated to the PVELLAE FAVSTINIANAE].—PIETAS AVG. The empress sacrificing. (Brought £4 10s. at the Pembroke).

BRASS MEDALLIONS.—MATRI DEVM SALVTARI. *(Contorniate;* valued by Mionnet at 100 fr. See the words *suis locis).*—TRI. POT. Combat of Romulus and Tatius. (Mt. 300 fr. see ROMULUS.)—VESTA. (Mt. 100 fr.)—Without legend. Cybèle and the vestal Claudia. (Mt. 300 fr. It is engraved in p. 311).—Without legend. Cybèle and Atys. (Mt. 300 fr. Engraved in p. 300). [The foregoing five medallions are in the *Cabinet de France*].—The following types, also without legend, are valued by Mionnet at from 100 to 150 francs each, viz. : —Faustina, with the attributes of Ceres, lighting an altar [see an engraving of it in p. 196]. —Faustina seated on a globe; the emperor standing, presents her with a Victory.—Diana Lucifera walking.—Faustina, as Vesta, holding the *palladium,* a Vestal standing before her.— *Obv.*—DIVA AVGVSTA FAVSTINA. Bust of Faustina.—*Rev.*—The empress in a biga, going to the left. (Mionnet's valuation 120 fr. An extra fine specimen of this medallion was bought for £10 for the British Museum at the Campana sale).

LARGE BRASS.—AETERNITAS. A woman seated. (Engraved in p. 22).—ÆTERNITAS.— Cybèle, in a chariot drawn by two lions. (Mt. 20 fr. See engraving of this reverse p. 22).— CONCORDIA. The emperor and Faustina, and two smaller figures. (Mt. 24 fr. Engraved in p. 242).—CONSECRATIO. Victory bearing away Faustina. (Mt. 48 fr. Brought about £3 at the Devonshire sale. See engraving, p. 25).— MATRI DEVM SALVTARI. (£1 at the Devonshire sale).—A draped female stands holding a phœnix, (brought £2 2s. at the Pembroke sale).

FAUSTINA the Younger.—Annia Faustina was the daughter of Antoninus Pius Aug. and Galeria Faustina Aug. The year of her birth is uncertain. By desire of Hadrian she was destined to be the wife of L. Verus, but after Hadrian's death, Antonine, on account of the extreme youth of Verus, gave her in marriage to M. Aurelius; the nuptials being consummated a few years later. That she was decorated with the title of *Augusta*, whilst her husband was merely Cæsar, is a fact proved from coins.— She died in the year U. c. 928 (A. D. 175) at the village of Halale, on the skirts of Mount Taurus, whilst on her way to join her husband in Syria.

To the beauty of this woman the Antonine mint bears constant testimony in all the three metals, and perhaps in no example more strikingly than on the brass medallion whence the above portrait is copied. But her character was, by all historical accounts, unworthy of her father and her husband, whose virtues have been the theme of eulogy in every age. Faustina is accused of having led a life still more dissolute than that of her mother. It was even believed that the sudden death of L. Verus was due to her agency; and that she took a secret part in the conspiracy of Avidius Cassius against her husband. The most notorious instances of her licentiousness and criminality produced so little effect on the mind of Marcus Aurelius that, when urged, if unwilling to put her to death, that at least he would divorce her, his reply was, " If we dismiss the wife, let us also restore the dowry," *i. e.* the empire. This ill-judged forbearance (as Eckhel observes) "might perhaps be excused, had he not gone the length of publicly lamenting her death, and, polluted as she was with crime, enrolling her in the assembly of Roman deities." Faustina gave to her husband a great number of children, among others Lucilla (see the word), married to Lucius Verus; Commodus and Antoninus, twins, the former destined to become emperor, and the latter dying at the age of four years; also Annius Verus, who died young (see VERUS ANNIUS).

Lampridius states, that three of Faustina's daughters were living after the period when Commodus was assassinated, and Herodian has observed, speaking generally, that M. Aurelius had several daughters born to him.—See *D. N. Vet* vii. 76.

Her coins, in gold and silver (certain examples of great rarity excepted), are common. Her bronze medallions are almost all of high rarity; large and middle brass for the most part common, rising in price only according to the workmanship and the type. On these she is styled FAVSTINA AVGVSTA.—DIVA FAVSTINA PIA—(with sometimes AVGVSTI PII. FIL*ia*, or MATER CASTRORUM on reverse).

RAREST REVERSES of FAUSTINA the YOUNGER.

GOLD.—AVGVSTI PII. FILIA. The empress as Diana. (£2 10s. at the Thomas sale).—CONCORDIA. *(Quinarius)*. A bird, which Eckhel describes to be a dove, and Lenormant pronounces a pea-hen, attribute of Juno. (£2 7s. at the Thomas sale, £2 18s. at the Devonshire; £3 4s. at the Campana).—FECVNDITATI AVGVSTAE. (Mt. 40 fr.)—FORTVNAE MVLIEBRI. (Mt.

48 fr.)—IVNO. The goddess seated, and two children. (£2 3s. Thomas).—MATRI CASTRORVM. (Mt. 200 fr.)—-LAETITIAE PVBLICAE. (£1 18s. Thomas).—MATRI MAGNAE. Cybèle. (Thomas, £3 3s.; Devonshire, £1 15s.)—VENERI GENETRICI. (£3 8s. Thomas).—VENERI AVGVSTAE. Venus seated. (Mt. 100 fr.)—VENERI FELICI. A dove. (£2 4s. Thomas).—VENVS standing, diademed, clothed, holding the sceptre and apple. *Quinarius*. (£1 19s. Thomas).

SILVER.—CONSECRATIO. Funeral pile, surmounted by a biga.—Same legend. Funeral pile, with MATRI CASTRORVM on the side of the head.

IVNONI REGINAE. The empress seated as Juno, with peacock at her feet.—*Obv.*—FAVSTINA AVGVSTA. Bust of the empress.

BRASS MEDALLIONS.—-AETERNITAS AVGVSTAS. Woman holding a torch, seated on a stag. (Engraved in *Icon. Romaine*, Lenormant.— TELLVS STABILIS.—VENVS FELIX. (Mt. 150 fr. each).—Without legend. Fortune seated.— (Mt. 100 fr.)—Without do. Six female figures. (Mt. 150 fr.)—Without do. Isis Pharia. (Mt. 100 fr.)—Cybèle and Atys. (Mt. 200 fr. Engraved in p. 300 of this dictionary).

LARGE BRASS.—AETERNITAS. Woman seated, carried by two others.—CONSECRATIO. Funeral pile.—Without legend. Peacock carrying Faustina to the skies.—Without do. Throne of Juno, sceptre and peacock. (Mt. 18 fr.)—MATRI CASTRORVM. Female sacrificing before 3 standards. —PIETAS. Faustina as Piety, a young girl at her feet. (Lenormant).—SAECVLI FELICITAS. Two children on a seat with a back.—SIDERIBVS RECEPTA. Diana in a biga. S. P. Q. R. Car drawn by two mules.—VENVS. Female figure draped to the feet, with apple and sceptre. (£1 18s. at the Pembroke sale).

MIDDLE BRASS.—VENERI VICTRICI. Mars and Venus standing.

FAUSTINA *(Annia)*, daughter of Claudius Severus and of Vibia Aurelia Sabina (daughter of Marcus Aurelius and of the younger Faustina), was third wife of Elagabalus, who, as a preliminary to his marriage with her, caused her husband to be put to death, and then the wretch forbade her to weep for him. These new nuptials took place in the year of Rome 974 (A. D. 221). Like the preceding ones, this worse than mockery of a matrimonial union was dissolved at the expiration of a very short space of time. She was repudiated to give place to others.

"Annia Faustina (remarks M. Lenormant), did not follow the custom, adopted by all the women who had the title of Augusta at that period, of adding the name of Julia to their own. Her birth was so illustrious, that she had no need to borrow a foreign *éclât*. The name of Annia Faustina is known only from coins.— Dion Cassius speaks only of a wife [of Elagabalus] who descended from Marcus Aurelius.— In fact the names of *Annia* and of *Faustina* belong to the family of that emperor."

Her coins, in silver and first brass, are few in number, and all of the highest rarity; on these she is styled ANNIA FAVSTINA AVG. or AVGVSTA. The reverses are as follow :—

SILVER.—1. CONCORDIA. Elagabalus and Annia Faustina standing, give each the right hand to the other. In the field is a star.

2. PIETAS AVG. A woman stands before an altar. (Mionnet values these two coins at 1000 francs each.)

LARGE BRASS.—CONCORDIA. Same subject as No. 1.—The obverse bears the legend ANNIA FAVSTINA AVGVSTA, and the bust of the empress for its type. (Priced by Mionnet at 600 fr.)— From a finely preserved specimen of this, one of the rarest of Roman coins, the foregoing cut has been executed. For a fine engraving of the same reverse, as well as of the obverse, see Mionnet, *Rareté des Med. Rom.* i. p, 354.

FAUSTULUS.—For a type of the royal shepherd of the Roman legend, the bringer-up of Quirinus, with the wolf-suckled twins, under the Ruminal fig tree, see FOSTULUS, Pompeia gens.

FAUSTUS —FELIX.—The above wood-cut, carefully engraved from a finely preserved specimen of that elegant denarius, is the one referred to in p. 287, under the head of Cornelia gens, No. 20.

On the obverse we see the bust of Diana, distinguished by a crescent surmounting the mitella of her elaborately arranged head-dress. Behind is the lituus. The legend FAVSTVS (literally meaning fortunate, auspicious), is a surname of L. Cornelius Sulla, son of the celebrated Dictator, also called Faustus Sulla. On the reverse of the same coin, with FELIX for legend, the type groups together a man clothed in the toga, on an elevated seat, and two kneeling male figures below him. One of these offers up to the seated figure a branch with three stems; the other has his arms tied behind him.

Sulla, the Dictator, was surnamed *Felix*, the happy or the lucky, from having been successful in all his enterprises. Jugurtha, king of the Numidians, in a long war which he sustained against the Romans, was in A. U. C. 648 (B. C. 106) defeated by Marius, and compelled to take refuge in the territories of king Bocchus, of Mauretania. Sulla, though then only second in command, had influence enough with this sordid and treacherous man, to procure from him the surrender of Jugurtha into his own hands. This historical incident forms the subject of the above described and illustrated coin.—The *lituus* symbolizes the Augurate of Sulla.—See Cornelia gens, p. 287.

F. B. *Felicitas Beata ;* an abbreviation which appears on coins of the Constantinian age.

F. C. These letters appear not only on coins of the triumvirs M. Antony and Octavius, but also on denarii of the Cæcilia, Eppia, Memmia, Sempronia, and Vibia families.—For the meaning of the abbreviation see EPPIA gens, p. 360.

FE. *Felix.*—FE. AUG. *Felix Augustus.*

FEC. *Fecit.*—COS. LUDOS. SAECUL*ares.* FEC. on coins of Caracalla.

FECIALES.—These were sacred heralds, who proclaimed truces, treaties of peace, and declarations of war. Numa, or, according to others, Ancus Martius, instituted a college of them to the number of twelve. The chief of this order of priesthood was called *Pater Patratus,* accomplished father. Their functions were originally intended to cause treaties to be observed, and to prevent the Romans from undertaking an unjust war. It seems probable that the Romans took from the ancient people of Latium the idea of establishing the college of the *Feciales.* On a silver coin of the Veturia gens we see a Fecial priest, on his knees, holding a sow, which a Roman on one side, and on the other side a man who by his dress appears to be of a different nation, both touch with their wands. It was thus that alliances were made by the Roman people with other states. And when the two deputies touched the sow, the *Fecialis* invoked Jupiter to deal as severely with those who might violate the treaty, as he, the priest himself, was about to do towards that animal : he then knocked it on the head with a flint stone. On a denarius of the Antestia gens a similar sacrifice of a pig is seen, to record the ratification of a treaty.—See FOED. P. R. CVM. GABINIS.

FECUNDITAS.—Nero erected a temple to *Fecundity,* on the occasion of a daughter being borne to him by Poppæa (Tacit. xv. 23). And the adoration of this divinity, once established at Rome, became a frequent subject of allusion and typification on the coins of succeeding empresses.

It has been thought that, under this name, worship was paid to Juno. The priest of Fecundity was called *Lupercus ;* and to him one of the artful and indecent superstitions of paganism ascribed the power of rendering women fertile, by *strapping* them, while in a state of nudity, with thongs made of oat-skin !—On coins of the *Augustæ*, Fecundity appears as a matron, clothed in the stola, sometimes standing with the *hasta pura* in her right hand, and supporting an infant in her left; sometimes with a cornucopiæ in her left hand, and before her a child, to which she extends her right hand.—On others she is seated, with children in her lap, or standing at each side of her; sometimes with one on each arm.

FECVNDITAS. S. C.—A woman seated, with three infants. On first brass of Lucilla. There are gold, silver, and second brass of this empress, with similar legend and type.

From this reverse (observes Eckhel, vii. 99) Mediobarbus has attempted to prove, that coins bearing the legend LVCILLA AVGVSTA are to be referred, not to the Lucilla, who married Lucius Verus, but, to one who, as that numismatist himself admits, had no claim to the epithet *fecunda*. That Lucilla, the daughter of M. Aurelius and of Faustina junior, bore children to Verus is a reasonable conclusion; but there is nothing reasonable in supposing that coins celebrate likewise her fecundity by Claudius Pompeianus, to whom she was afterwards married, since it is known that though having for her second husband a private citizen, she was treated with all the honours due to an Augusta.—See biographical notice of LUCILLA.

FECVNDITAS.—A woman seated on the ground with a cluster of grapes in her left hand, and resting her elbow on a basket or vase, is touching with her right hand a globe adorned with stars, over which four small figures are walking. Gold of *Julia Domna*.

On coins of Hadrian, and also of Commodus of the year U. C. 940 (A. D. 187), in connection with a very similar type, we read the legend TELLVS STABIL. Consequently, by this application of the two different inscriptions to one of the same type, is indicated that "the earth was strengthened *(tellus stabilita)* by the *fecundity* of women consequent on marriages."—*D. N. Vet.* vii. 196.

"The flatterers of Domna pretended that all things were owing to her. The star-besprinkled globe represents the Roman world, which with her husband Severus she governed; and to the empire of which she destines her two sons, Caracalla and Geta, who, together with as many daughters, are the proofs of her fecundity."—Rasche, T. ii. pl. 1. p. 932.

FECVNDITAS AVG.—A woman standing, extends her right hand over a small figure stand-

ing beside her; in her left hand a cornucopiæ. Third brass of Gallienus. (Banduri).

Fecundity used to be ascribed on coins to females only. It is surprising to find her on the coin of an emperor—even of so eccentric an one as Gallienus. In the Imperial Cabinet at Vienna there are two denarii of Alexander Severus, with the legend FECVND. AVGVSTAE, but there can be no doubt, that this reverse was erroneously transferred from the coinage of Mamæa to that of her son. And from this circumstance it becomes probable that the reverse now before us ought to be restored to the coinage of Salonina, the wife of Gallienus.—(Eckhel, vii. 407.)

FECVNDITAS AVG.—A woman standing, with rudder in her right hand, and cornucopiæ in her left. Gold of Sulpicius Uranius Antoninus.

"The reverse of this coin (observes Eckhel, vii. 289) might lead to a suspicion of its genuineness, since (as above remarked) FECVNDITAS is a legend, with one exception, not found on the coins of emperors, and the type represents *Fortuna*, and not *Fecunditas*. But, as Bimard, whose copious observations on this coin it will be an advantage to consult, vouches for its undoubted antiquity, and I, not having seen the coin, being therefore unable to offer any arguments on the other side, am well content to acquiesce in the judgment of so eminent a writer." [This *unique* coin is valued by Mionnet at 1500 francs.]

FECVND*itas* AVGVSTAE. (Fecundity of the Empress.)—This legend on silver, and on first and second brass of Faustina the younger, with the type, in which a woman is represented, as in the above engraving, with four children, is the first indisputably genuine coin, which boasts of female fertility.

"Faustina (observes Eckhel, vii. 78) proved her fecundity beyond question by the number of her children; would that her fidelity to her husband rested on as clear evidence!" On the above coin she is accompanied by four children, but on coins inscribed TEMPOR. FELIC. their number is increased to six. That she had more than six children, may be gathered from what has been already stated in her biography. On coins bearing the legend IVNONI LVCINAE there are three infants.

FECVNDITAS TEMPORVM.——A woman, seated on the ground, holds out a branch towards two little boys standing near her; in her left hand is a cornucopiæ. Silver of Otacilia.—Engraved in Pellerin, *Mélange*, i. p. 193.

FEELIX (thus, with double E) appears on a coin of the Cornelia family, struck in honour of Sulla the dictator, by order of the Senate, who also caused an equestrian statue to be raised to him with the same attributes inscribed thereon. (see p. 207). This epithet, which flattery bestowed on that " bold bad" man, was after-wards adopted as his surname, and the fortuitous and unforeseen prosperity to which it referred became his boast. [see SULLA.]—Cicero *(pro lege Manilia)* has bestowed extraordinary com-pliments on the good fortune *(felicitatem)* which so invariably attended Pompey the Great.— Commodus was the first emperor who used the word, in consequence of his safely escaping the resentment of the soldiers, who were demanding the death of Perennis, prefect of the pretorians, as is shewn on his coins minted A. D. 185 (see p. 239). His example met with the approval and imitation of his successors, but with this modification, that they almost always joined the title *Felix* with that of *Pius*, placing Pius first and Felix last.—The first, after Commodus, who used both titles, though rarely, was Cara-calla; afterwards Elagabalus, frequently; and then most of the emperors down to the period of the lower empire And, indeed, so great was the importance attached to the two epithets used conjointly, that they were considered as much the distinctive badge of an emperor as the title of *Augustus* itself, and were constantly assumed by them on their accession to empire, or were decreed to them by the Senate; as in the case of Macrinus and Elagabalus, a fact proved by their respective coins.—From none of the writers of Augustal history does it appear that any indi-vidual holding the rank only of Cæsar was ever permitted to use them, with the exception of Carinus, some of whose coins appear with the inscription—M. AVR. CARINVS P. F. NOB. CAES. But Carinus exhibited, in conjunction with the simple title of Cæsar, the prenomen of *Imperator*, as is shewn on his coins.

The epithets *Pia Felix* were also shared by the empresses. Julia Domna is the first, who was so honoured on coins, thus, IVLIA PIA. FELIX AVG. It is stated by Bimard (ad Jobert, i. p. 282) that Severina, the wife of Aurelian, also enjoyed the same distinction, but he omits to mention where the coin is to be seen. It becomes common, however, on the coins of empresses, from the time of Honorius. Jobert (i. p. 254) is therefore incorrect, in stating that Domna alone used these words, and is properly corrected by Bimard.—Banduri (ii. p. 563 and 566) fell into the opposite error, and states that Eudoxia, the wife of Theodosius II. was the first who adopted the titles *Pia Felix*, thus passing over Domna.—See Eckhel, viii. 454.

Many cities likewise received the epithet *Felix*, and particularly colonies.—See Berytus, p. 126; Cremna, p. 295; Heliopolis; Laodicæa (Coloniæ Romanæ), p. 232, &c.

In allusion to the coin of Sulla (Cornelia

gens), inscribed FEELIX, Eckhel says—" Haver-camp considers FEELIX to have been put for FELIX by an error of the moneyer, whereas it is most certainly an archaism. For if it be a mis-take of the moneyer's, so also must be the sub-stitution of VAALA for VALA on coins of the Numonia gens."—v. 194.

FEL.   *Felix, Felicia, Felicitas,* &c.

FEL. ADVENT. AVGG. NN.—See FELIX ADVENTVS.

FEL. AVG.   *Felicitas Augusti.*

FEL. KART.—See FELIX KART.

FEL. P. R.   *Felicitas Populi Romani.*

FEL. PROCESS.—See FELIX PROCESSVS.

FEL. TEMP. REPARATIO.—This reverse legend is found constantly recurring on silver, and on second and third brass coins from the time of Constans and Constantius jun. to that of Gratian (A. D. 337 to A. D. 375); they are common.—The following is a description of the various types :—

1. The phœnix standing on a pyramid of steps, with a wreath in its beak, or attaching a branch of laurel to the prow of a ship.

2. A galley, on which the emperor paludated stands with a phœnix in his right hand.

3. On another specimen the emperor, in military habiliments, stands on the prow of a galley, holding in his right hand a globe, sur-mounted by a Victoriola, and resting his left hand on a labarum, bearing the monogram of Christ, whilst Victory is sitting at the helm.

4. A soldier dragging a barbarian, by the hair of his head, from a hut, or wooded retreat.

5. A soldier, dispatching a prostrate horseman with a spear.—(Engraved in Constantius Gallus. p. 265.)

6. The emperor standing, with a banner in his right hand, and two prisoners sitting on the ground beside him.

7. The emperor, on horseback, charging with levelled lance, a prostrate and suppliant enemy.

That these coins (says Eckhel, viii. p. 111) saw the light after the death of Constantine the Great, and Constantine jun., father and son, is rendered certain by the fact, that no authen-ticated coin of this kind has been seen, which exhibits the portrait of either.   They require no explanation, as they present well known, or at least intelligible, symbols of a *felix temporum reparatio ;* especially in the *phœnix*, a figure exhibited on the reverse of a coin of Divus Trajanus, and also on one of Hadrian with the legend SAEC. AVR.; and on no occasion with a happier application of the type, than when the intention was to indicate a *restoration of the times*, in accordance with the accounts, which ancient writers have given of this marvellous bird.—See Tacitus, Pliny, and others, as also a long-winded poem about the phœnix, attributed to Lactantius.

FELICIA DECENNALIA.—Two young genii, or winged loves, snpporting each with both hands a crown, within which we read VOTIS X MVLTIS XX (that is to say *Votis Decennalibus Multis Vicennalibus.*—On the obverse, FL. IVL. CONSTANS PIVS FELIX AVG. Bust of Constans, with diademed head.—In the exergue TES. *(Thessalonica).*

This splendid medallion of Constans I. was found with a number of other gold coins, at Thessalonica, in 1526.—"You see (says Tristan, iii. 616) that it was struck in that city, where the decennial vows of Constans were celebrated, as the quinquennial had been in the same capital of Macedonia. And by the present legend of "Happy Decennalia," the wish was expressed, that Constans might live to see them celebrated as he witnessed those of the quinquennalia. * * * —With less regard to truth in eulogizing an emperor than generally characterises the historical commentaries of the old French antiquary, he adds—"The little angels carrying loftily and stoutly, with both hands, the laurel crown, as the posture in which they are placed so well shews, serve to intimate, that this *virtuous* prince, continuing *always* to reign *piously,* would, by the grace of heaven, be enabled many times more, to solemnize in a *holy* manner the *Vicennalia* reiterated, after having happily passed the first ten years of his reign in an uninterrupted career of victories."—See T. iii. p. 615–16.

See the type of the above-described reverse, engraved in p. 312, under the head of DECENNALIA.

FELICIA TEMPORA.—Four little boys, with attributes allusive to the four seasons of the year.　Silver of Caracalla.—See TEMPORUM FELICITAS.

FELICITAS—a symbolical divinity of the Romans, to whom, according to Pliny, Licinius Lucullus, about the year of Rome 680 (B.C. 74), on his return from the war against Mithridates, wished to raise a statue, of which Archesilas was to have been the sculptor; but both the artist and his employer died before the work was completed. A temple erected to this deified protectress, in one of the public places of Rome, fell a prey to the flames during the reign of the emperor Claudius. Felicity is represented on coins of the imperial series (particularly those of Hadrian, Antonine, and Philip), under the figure of a woman, clothed in the stola, and exhibiting different figures and postures; sometimes standing, sometimes seated, generally she holds the caduceus in one hand, and the cornucopiæ in the other—the former as the sign of peace, the latter as signifying that true felicity consists in possessing the most precious gifts of providence; for what is greater happiness in this world than to enjoy peace and to possess plenty. At other times Felicitas stands holding the caduceus on a staff in her right hand, and a patera in her left, at a lighted altar, as in Mæsa. Again we see her with a rudder, a globe, or a ship's prow in her hand, in allusion to the naval victories gained by those princes whose coins display this allegorical type; and also in reference to the abundance which navigation procures to the state. With respect to the caduceus, Millin, in his *Dictionaire des Beaux Arts*, observes that in the hymn to Mercury, ascribed to Homer, Apollo designates that instrument as the rod or staff of Felicity and of Riches. On a medallion of Commodus FELICITAS TEMPORVM (the happiness of the times or of the age), is figured under the form of a woman sitting under a tree surrounded by children, who personify the four seasons.—For other typifications of this deity on Roman coins, see SAECVLI—or TEMPORVM FELICITAS.

Felicity's image occurs on almost all the imperial coins; because the Senate professed to wish that all princes should consider it their duty to promote public happiness, and also because those princes themselves were peculiarly desirous of having it regarded as a blessing attached to their own reign. This however was ascribed to various causes, and shadowed forth under various tokens.

Jobert, in his sixth instruction, observes, that when (as is most frequently the case on imperial coins) to the names of *Felicitas*, Securitas, Spes, Providentia, Aequitas, and other virtues, the word AVG. is added, there is no doubt but that the virtue or good quality in question, is applied to the prince himself, as residing and shining in him, and should then be read FELICITAS AVGVSTI or FELICITATI AVGVSTI, &c.— But on the other hand, when it is read AVGVSTA, it is the opinion of most numismatic antiquaries, although not as yet reduced to a certainty, that by this form of expression, the virtue or divinity itself (as *Augusta,* that is to say, sacred), rather than the emperor, was the intended object of inscription and honour. According to this opinion, therefore, FELICITAS AVGVSTA would not be an eulogy of the prince, for rendering the state happy, but simply the proper epithet attached to the name of the goddess. Havercamp also, adverting to this point, remarks that, when the figure of a woman occurs on a coin, holding a rudder resting on a globe, whether she be called Fortune or Felicity, it would seem to represent the golden fortune *(aurea fortuna)* of the imperial house, which the emperors worshipped in their bed-chamber, and which, when at the point of death, they transmitted to their successors.

FELICITAS AVG. S. C.—A woman draped in the stola, stands holding a branch in her right, and the long caduceus in her left hand. First brass of Hadrian, engraved in preceding page, from a fine and well-preserved specimen of the type.

FELICITAS DEORVM.—This remarkable legend appears only on a silver coin of Mariniana, wife of Valerianus senior. Its accompanying type is a woman standing, who holds in her right hand a caduceus, and in her left a cornucopiæ, in token of universal peace, and the abundance of all things, at an epocha when the empire was one world-wide scene of war, pestilence, and famine! Eckhel's observation respecting the coin is—"Numus etiam propter epigraphem adhuc inusitatam singularis." vii. 388.

FELICITAS AVG*usta*. S. C.—August Felicity. Hadrian, bare headed, stands clothed in the toga, holding a globe in the left hand, and joining his right hand with that of the goddess, who holds a short caduceus in her left hand.— The wood-cut has been executed after one of the finest and best preserved specimens in first brass of Hadrian's mint. As another variety of the Felicitas type, some fruitless pains have also been taken to ascertain the particular time and occasion when it was struck; for it evidently typifies the emperor's arrival in a city, or a province, to which Felicity welcomes him.

FELICITAS PERPETVA.——The emperor, with his face turned towards you, and in the consular dress, is seated on a lofty frame-work, (*pegma*—see the word), with head surrounded by a nimbus, and the right hand elevated. On the footstool is inscribed VOT. V. whilst on a lower platform is seated a youthful figure, in the same dress, with a book in the right hand. Below are the letters SIS. Gold. (Formerly in the French Cabinet). Silver medallion. (Banduri). —On another specimen; Victory walking, with laurel branch in her right hand, and trophy in her left. Below, AQ. Silver of Constans I. in the Imperial Cabinet at Vienna.

"The subject of the former of these types is very difficult to explain, by reason of the obscurity which envelopes the history of that period. Consult the far from probable conjec-

tures of Banduri and Khell on the type of the latter coin."—This is all that Eckhel says respecting these two reverses.—See vii. 83.

FELICITAS ROMANORVM.—An arch supported by two spiral columns; within are two paludated figures, holding spears. In the exergue SIRM. Engraved in Cim. Vind. (Cabinet of Vienna), p, xlv. Silver of Constans.

FELICITAS SAECVLI.—FELICITAS TEMPORVM.—The felicity of their age, or of their times, was a characteristic, which a great many emperors, solicitous to have at least the repute of it handed down in association with their names and reigns, have caused to be inscribed on some of their finest coins. Amongst various other instances are the legend AETERNA FELICITAS AVG. on a coin of Maxentius, and that of ANN. AVG. SAECVLI FELICISSIMI, on a coin of Caracalla. In like manner we find FELICITAS AVGG. NN. (*Augustorum Nostrorum*) as in Maximian and Constans.—FELICITAS IMPERII or IMPERATORVM as in Philip.—FELICITAS PERPETVA as in Constans (cited in the preceding notice), also in Magnentius, &c.—FELICITAS PVBLICA is to be found on coins of numerous other princes, from Vespasian and Titus downwards to Valerianus senior, &c.—FELICITATI AVGVSTAE, as on the gold and large brass of Hadrian.—All these different epigraphs are illustrated respectively on each reverse by various symbols, viz. by a galley, to denote the course of prosperous navigation, or a good voyage; by four boys, signifying the happy abundance of the four seasons of the year (see VERUS ANNIUS); by the olive branch and the caduceus, as symbolizing the messengers of peace and amity; lastly, and not unfrequently, by figures of Victories, as attesting the fact of a war brought to a successful conclusion.

FELICITAS SAECVLI.—Full-faced bust of Domna, between profile heads of Caracalla and Geta. Gold of S. Severus. (See Eckhel, vii. 179. Engraved in Akerman, I. pl. vii. No. 6). A middle brass of the same emperor, exhibiting the same legend, has for its type three togated figures seated, and a fourth standing on an estrade.—Engraved in Havercamp, *Cabinet de Christine*.

FELICITAS TEMPORVM.—The emperor, in the toga, seated in a curule chair, and holding a globe, Victory from behind placing a laurel crown on his head. On the opposite side are two female figures draped, and standing; one of them holds the *hasta pura*.

Obv.—IMP. SEV. ALEXAND. AVG. IVLIA MAMAEA AVG. MATER AVG. Busts face to face of Severus Alexander and of his mother Mamæa. Gold medallion. Engraved in Mionnet, i. 359. [A beautiful work of art, but in which Alexander looks more like an emp*ress* than an emp*eror*.]

There is a second brass of the same reign, having the reverse type above described, but with the head of Alexander alone on the obverse.

FELICIT. TEMPORVM.—A basket full of

fruit. Silver of Pescennius Niger. Engraved in Kolb, *Traité Numismatique.*

FELICITAS TEMPORVM.——The goddess standing with caduceus and cornucopiæ. On large brass of Sabinia Tranquillina. Engraved in Mionnet, i. 402.

FELICITATEM ITALICAM.——A woman standing, with caduceus and cornucopiæ. Silver of Caracalla. (Mus. d'Ennery).

FELICITATEM PO. R. (Populi Romani.)— A woman standing, with caduceus in her right hand, and a cornucopiæ in her left. First brass of Gordianus III. (Vaillant).

[On this and the preceding coin will be remarked a singular use of the accusative case in the legend.]

FELICITATI AVG. (*Felicitati Augusti*).— To the happiness of the Emperor. In the exergue COS. III. P. P. S. C. (*Consulis tertium, Patris Patriæ, Senatus Consulto*).—First brass.

[So finely designed, so perfectly preserved, and so peculiarly interesting a specimen of one of Hadrian's nautical coins, having had ample justice done to it in the above engraving, it only remains to furnish the type with the accompaniment of a correspondingly good description. Nor can this surely be better accomplished than by borrowing the following equally classical and seamanlike passage, from the work of a gallant officer, the advantages of whose numismatic *lessons* on the large brass coinage of imperial Rome, the compiler has been proud already to acknowledge, in the course of his present attempt] :—

"A pretorian galley, full of men, impelled along both by oars and a large square sail, across which the inscription is written, in the taste then prevalent; for we are assured, that, in the time of Trajan, it was not uncommon to have the name of the emperor embroidered on the sails, in gold and silver. Besides being the type of felicity, this medal is supposed to allude to the prudent government of Hadrian; for as in a ship—though the officers and crew are liable to the same hazard, the success of the voyage will chiefly depend on the skill and judgment of the commander—so in the management of the State, the happiness and prosperity of the community depend upon the wisdom and prudence of the sovereign at the helm of affairs.— The sail to this ship—this 'navis velis ventique' —is stretched to a yard supported by lifts; it is deep roached, with both sheets aft, in token of auspicious winds; the emblem of happiness :

"En ego non paucis quondam munitus amicis, Dum flavit velis aura secunda meis."

"And the oars being put out, at the same time, illustrate another passage of Ovid—

"Sive opus est, minimam velis bene currit ad auram, Sive opus est remo remige carpit iter."

[In the highly interesting, because doubtless accurate, delineation of a Roman admiral's flag ship, thus associated with the dedicatory epigraph, which invokes a happy voyage for the emperor, we see Hadrian himself represented on the poop, seated under a sort of tent, over which curve the wing-like filaments of the *aplustre,* and near which are a vexillum and a legionary eagle. At the extreme end of the prow we see the figure of Neptune, with his trident in one hand and a conch shell in the other].

This reverse seems to have had for its object to record the vows made by the Senate for the success of one of Hadrian's sea-voyages, but which in particular is not known.

On a brass medallion of the same emperor, Minerva fills the place here occupied by Neptune, whilst dolphins disport themselves in the waves around this magnificent sea-boat as it glides along. This coin is in the Vatican cabinet, and is described by Vaillant, *Num. Impp. Rom.* т. iii. p. 118.

Three other first brass of Hadrian, with trireme types, are with instructive technicality, described from specimens in his own cabinet by Capt. Smyth, R. N. as follows :—

2. FELICITATI AVG. S. C. COS. III. P.P. —"A pretorian galley, with the gubernator and five sitters, but with ten oars, or rather sweeps, over the sides : as these appear to have no communication with the persons in view, but carry their looms through the upper works, the sitters are rather passengers than rowers, and they wear hats, as if to protect them against the heat upon deck. The prow is armed with three spikes, the *rostrisque tridentibus* of Virgil. The tutela is highly decorated, and the poop shews the bend, mentioned by that author and Ovid— *puppique recurvæ,* upon the bow appears the parasemon, and over that the labarum, or banner, on a staff which steeves like a bowsprit.— Both this, and the streamer from the corymbus, by blowing forwards, shew that the vessel has a fair wind, an ancient symbol of Felicity, which will be readily understood by the moderns.— *Descript. Catal.* p. 100, No. clvii.

3. The same legend.—"A pretorian galley, rowing swiftly over the waves. The poop is high and curved, like that of a Chinese sampan, and the post occupied by the pilot recalls the idea of his liability to be washed overboard,

Ipse gubernator puppi Palinurus ab altâ.

Over the aplustre appear two military standards, which are considered as a testimony that an important personage is embarked. A colossal sea-god—half man and half fish—is placed on the prow; on some medals this is a triton, blowing a conch shell, but here he is in the act of darting a spear. This is equivalent to the modern figure-head, and represented the tutelary protector to whom, as with the modern Mediterranean sailors, the ship was dedicated. There are six sitters in a line below the pilot, and the rudder is projected through the upper works of the quarter." *Ibid*, p. 101, No. clvii.

4. FELIC. AVG. TR. P. III. COS. II. S. C. (*Felicitati Augusti, Tribunitiâ Potestate tertium, Consul Iterum.*—First brass of Lucius Verus.

"A large pretorian galley, with the emperor reclining under the *aplustre* [or ornament] of the stern. There are six rowers; and on the forecastle is a mast raking forwards, with a sail upon it, shewing that the vessel is going with the wind aft.—In the work of Bayfius, ' *De Re Navali*,' the sail is represented as a banner; but here it is unusually large, roached, bent to one yard, and sheeted home to another, and certainly assists in propelling the vessel.—This medal (adds Capt. Smyth), was struck A. D. 163, for the safe navigation, and happy deliverance of Verus from the perils of sea and war. But, instead of being at the head of his army, the luxurious prince took that opportunity of visiting Greece, in a vessel magnificently adorned, and freighted with mimes and musicians. 'He made his voyages to Corinth and to Athens (says the Roman historian), amidst songs and symphonies, and at each of the most celebrated cities of Asia, Pamphylia, and Cilicia, he suffered himself to be detained by his passions as a voluptuary.' "—*Descr. Cat.* p. 150, No. cclxxv.

FELICITATI AVG. IMP. VIII. COS. III. S. C. A ship, with many rowers; on some specimens Neptune stands on the prow. 2nd brass of M. Aurelius.

This coin serves admirably to illustrate the expressions of Capitolinus (ch. 27 Aurel.) in reference to the return of Aurelius by sea from Athens to Rome; "Returning to Italy in a vessel, he met with a violent storm." His escape from this danger is, therefore, attributed on these coins *felicitati Augusti*. The same type is also to be seen on coins of Commodus of the year A. D. 177, with the legend FELICITATI CAES.; but it is also an established fact, that Commodus was the companion of Aurelius in this voyage and peril.—Eckhel, vii. 64.

The galley was the type of the Roman Republic.

For some remarks on the subject of naval architecture and equipment under the Romans, see TRIREMIS.

FELICITAS REIPVBLICAE.—The emperor, seated on a curule chair, placed on a *suggestus*, two other figures standing on each side of him. At the foot of the tribunal are two kneeling figures, holding up their hands. On the exergue P. T. R. Gold of Constantine the Great.

Constantine, assisted by the two Cæsars his sons, Constantine junior and Crispus, is here sitting on the judgment seat, and appears as about to decide, with his usual severity towards conquered nations, on the fate of the *Franci* and the *Alamanni*, over whom Crispus gained the victory A. D. 320, and who are personified as kneeling supplicants, imploring the emperor's pardon and mercy.—This elegant coin is engraved in Vaillant, *Impp. Rom.* Pr. iii. p. 84.

FELICITAS AVG. The busts of Victory and Peace, side by side.—*Obv.*—IMP. C. POSTVMVS P. F. AVG. The busts of Postumus and Hercules, side by side, both laureated. Gold medallion of Postumus. (Valued at 1200 francs, by Mionnet, in whose *Rareté*, &c. T. ii. 59, it is exquisitely engraved.

Jean Tristan, in giving a fairly accurate delineation of this very beautiful medallion, describes it as exhibiting "les Effigies du Postume, père, *et fils*"—in other words, the heads of Postumus senior and *Postumus junior !*—That any writer like himself, who, with a proneness indeed to indulge in the fanciful, the conjectural, and the discursive, displays nevertheless a profound knowledge of mythology and of ancient history, combined with unequivocal proofs of capability to form just conclusions from numismatic monuments—that such a writer should have fallen into an error of this sort, is not a little extraordinary. He has done so, however, not only in the present instance, but also in two others. (See *Commentaires*, &c. T. iii. 138, plates No. 1, and 147, pl. No. 10). What adds to the apparent strangeness of the hallucination is, that his animadversions on events connected with the reign of Postumus, bear immediate reference to many of that emperor's coins, on which the whole-length figure of Hercules is represented, either isolatedly, or in association with his own. These the worthy "*Escuyer Sieur de St. Amant*" has illustrated with well-designed engravings by the burin of Picart; and from these it is evident that, great prince and conqueror as he was—Emperor and Augustus in all but senatorial recognition—Postumus, like other successful soldiers of fortune and of obscure birth, inflated with the pride of his victories, was in the vain-glorious habit of comparing himself with Hercules. And perhaps his features were not without some slight analogy to those which the sculptor of classic antiquity bestows on that hero. But, to judge from the general examples of his monetal portraitures, the likeness of Postumus, on the above medallion, would appear to be but an *ideal* one, flatteringly assimilated with the Grecian lineaments of the face to which it is joined, in the same way as it is on other medallions with the helmed bust of Mars.—Tristan has himself given an engraving of POSTVMVS AVGVSTVS, with radiated head, on the obverse, and with *Jupiter Stator* for legend and type of reverse (see *Commentaires*, iii. 158), an example which may be accepted as *vera effigies*—a true portrait of the celebrated usurper of the western provinces, and of which abundance are to be found in every good collection; but, except in bushiness of beard and roughness of aspect, it is scarcely to be called a resemblance of the visage assigned to the demi-god of Fable. And yet the face is a good face too, in its *Gaulish* fashion, indicating as it does the indomitable courage, the resolute bearing, the politic sagacity, of a man equally distinguished both in the arts of civil government, and by his talents for warlike commandership.

But in Tristan's time, not to speak of a subsequent age, there was, amongst numismatic collectors and writers, a fond and not unnatural belief, that Postumus, the son, who had reigned for nine years over the Gauls with his father, must have left some monetary records behind him. But no authentic specimens of such a mintage having, up to the middle of the 17th century, been found to exist, the learned author of "History of the Emperors," writing about that period, allowed his zeal for the publication of medallic rarities so far to overstep his judgment and discrimination, as to make him pronounce the bearded head of a man, whether jugated or face to face with that of Postumus, on a coin, to be meant for a profile of the son, although looking as aged as the father's.

Tristan is happier in his observations on the reverse type of this interesting and most valuable coin. "I do not doubt (says he) that the two heads are those of Victory and Peace. The two goddesses, thus united, serve to intimate that Postumus had the power to conquer, whenever his enemies obliged him to act, whether on the offensive or the defensive, Victory always coming to his aid, and enabling him to make peace when he pleased; and the goddess PAX inspiring him with desire for the restoration of tranquillity, and facilitating its execution. These two divinities thus continually united to render him happy, and whether he made war, or remained at peace, he was ever victorious."—See T. iii. p. 152, et seq.

In an article by Mons. J. De Witte, relating to certain unpublished coins of Postumus, in the *Revue Numismatique* (vol. vii. p. 330, et seq.) that intelligent numismatist has ably discussed the probable motives which induced Postumus to place himself under the protection of Hercules, and to assimilate himself to that god. This dissertation not only throws light on the above described medallion, and other mintages of the same usurper, but also refers back to the origin of a custom early adopted by Roman emperors, namely, that of having their portraits represented with the attributes of Hercules, as emblematical of force and power. The whole, though long, has strong claims to perusal.—Some extracts from its most instructive passages will be found annexed to the biographical notice of POSTUMUS.

FELICITER NVBTIIS.—This epigraph (thus spelt) appears on an almost *unique* gold coin of Marcianus, the equally singular type of which represents that emperor and Pulcheria (sister of Theodosius II.) joining hands: whilst Anatolus, the patriarch of Constantinople, stands between them. Each figure has the nimbus round the head. On the exergue CONOB.

Eckhel observes respecting this extremely rare and very remarkable coin, that "the nuptials of Pulcheria with Marcianus were of a nature which Vestals themselves might regard without a blush. Indeed the husband engaged himself by a solemn pledge to leave her pure and untouched to the day of her death."—FELICITER NVBTIIS was a form of popular acclamation on various joyful occasions, and was also accustomed to be used at marriages.

A similar type appears on coins of Cornelia Paula, wife of Elagabalus, where the emperor and empress are joining hands in testimony of connubial fidelity, a veiled pontiff standing between them.—An engraving of this coin will be found in Khell's Supplement to Vaillant, p. 291.

FELIX ADVENT. AVG. *Felix Adventus Augusti*—the happy arrival of the Emperor.— FELIX ADVENT. AVGG. NN. *Augustorum Nostrorum*—of both our Emperors.—These epigraphs, with the types of the reigning princes on horseback, figures holding the *labarum*, or Victories planting their feet on prostrate captives, appear on coins of Diocletianus, Gal. Maximianus, Constantius Chlorus, &c.—See ADVENTUS.

FELIX INGRESSVS SEN. AVG. *Senioris Augusti*—the happy entry of the elder Emperor. —A gold coin of Maximianus Herculeus, bearing the foregoing legend, has for the type of its reverse the galeated Genius of Rome, seated on a shield, resting her left hand on the *hasta pura*, and holding on her knees with her right hand a buckler, on which is inscribed VOT. XXX. On the exergue PR.

This unique coin is extolled by Khell (p. 220), and recognized by Eckhel (viii. 26), as one of the most precious gems of the Vienna cabinet; for it serves to prove that Maximianus, having again resumed the purple, made his entry into Rome. But says the author of *Doctrina*, " it does not appear that the learned writer first named, draws an equally just inference from the words VOT(IS) XXX. namely, that they fix the date of the event on the year U. C. 1059 (A. D. 307); when, and not before, these vows of thirty years (*vota tricennalia*) could have commenced. Maximianus reached the twentieth year of his reign before his abdication took place, including the period during which he was only Cæsar; for the author of his panegyric expressly addresses him in the following terms :—' Thee, again, as Emperor for *twenty years*, and Consul for the eighth time, &c.' And, further on—' Thou hast betaken thyself afresh to the empire, it is impossible, of which already thou hadst had a *twenty years'* experience.' But it is established by many other coins, that, at the beginning of the tenth year of his reign, XX. *vota* were already undertaken (*concepta*), and at the beginning of the twentieth year of his reign, XXX. *vota*. As, therefore, Maximian's XXX. *vota* had commenced before he resigned the empire, it is impossible, from the inscribed VOT. XXX. to draw a conclusion respecting the exact year in which he resumed the purple."—See MAXIMIANUS HERCULEUS; also an engraving of the coin, in *Num. Cimelii Vindobonensis, Aur.* TAB. V. No. 14.

FELIX PROCESS. CONSVLAT. AVG. N. —The emperor, togated, standing, with a globe in the right hand, and a sceptre reversed, or a parazonium, in the left. In the exergue P. R.— On gold and silver of Maxentius. The silver specimen of this extremely rare coin is engraved in Vaillant, *Num. Impp. Rom.* iii. 72.

Maxentius proceeded consul A. D. 308, which consulate he assumed in the month of April, there having been no consuls during the year preceding.—See CONSULATUS, p. 270.

FELIX PROCESSVS COS. VI. AVG. N.— Same type as on the preceding reverse. In the exergue A. Q. Gold of Constantinus Magnus.

The date of A. D. 320 is assigned to this coin, in which year Constantine the father, for the sixth, and Constantine the son, for the first time proceeded consuls. (Vaillant.)—There is another *aureus* of the same emperor, with the same type and legend, except as to the consulate, which is IV. and this Eckhel (viii. 74) places under A. D. 315.—See *Processus Consularis*.

FELIX KARTHAGO—on others KARTAGO —on others CARTAGO.—In every example the type is a woman clothed in the stola. She stands holding in each hand a branch or corn-ears. In the exergue P. K. Gold coin of Maxentius.

Maxentius, on this very rare *aureus*, calls Carthage *Felix*, because she abounded in corn and fruits. For when, in consequence of a deficient inundation of the Nile, Egypt suffered scarcity, the Roman ships employed in the importation of wheat, steered for Carthage, whence they brought back a sufficient supply to the Eternal City.—Vaillant, *Impp. Rom.* iii. p. 72. Engraved in Banduri; and in Spanheim's *Cæsars of Julian, Pr.* 74.—See also INDULGENTIA IN CARTH. p. 186.—There is a coin of Commodus, (see *Providentia Augusti*), in which Neptune accepts a handful of corn-ears from a woman whose head is adorned with an elephant's proboscis ; a figure which personifies Africa, or perhaps Carthage herself.

FELIX KART.—See SALVIS AVGG. ET CAESS. &c. First and third brass of Maxentius.

FERETRIUS, a surname given by the Romans to Jupiter, and under which they consecrated to him the *opima spolia* (warlike spoils of the most honourable kind), that is to say, such as a Roman general had won in battle from an enemy's general. A denarius exhibits the consul Marcellus ascending the steps of the temple dedicated to Feretrian Jove, to present there as a trophy the armour of a Gaulish chieftain.— See CLAUDIA gens, p. 209.

FERONIA, a goddess, whom Dionysius of Halicarnassus has recorded to have been worshipped by the Sabines, and called by the Greeks Ανθηφορος, Φιλοστεφανος, Φερσεφονη (iii. p. 173).—According to Strabo, there stood, at the foot of Mount Soracte, a city called *Feronia*, where a goddess of the same name was worshipped with peculiar veneration. (Eckhel, v. 270). Enfranchised slaves received in her temple the *pileus*, or cap, which was the sign of Liberty. By some mythographers, *Feronia* is regarded as a surname of Juno. Be this as it may, her head appears on a denarius of the Petronia gens, struck by a monetal triumvir of Augustus, as subjoined :—

FERO. or FERON. TVRPILIANVS III. VIR.—The bust of a woman, on whose head is a crown of peculiar pattern, and whose neck is adorned with a string of pearls. The abbreviated word FERON. shews it to be the effigy of the *Dea Feronia*, whose worship was transplanted from Latium into Rome. And the name of TVRPILIANVS refers to Publius Petronius Turpillianus, who as a moneyer in 734 or 735 (B. C. 20), in colleagueship with Aquillius and Durmius (see their respective families, pp. 71 and 350), struck these and other denarii.—The reverse is inscribed CAESAR AVGVSTVS SIGN(IS) RECE(PTIS). A man kneeling, and in the posture of surrendering up a military ensign. This well-known legend and type form that favourite record of Augustus, which attests the voluntary restitution of ensigns and prisoners captured by Phraates, king of the Parthians, but sent back to the Romans again on the approach alone of Augustus and his army ; although that oriental sovereign esteemed himself invincible, and bore the title of King of Kings, and Brother of the Sun and Moon.—See PETRONIA gens.

F. F. *Faustum Felicem.* Prosperous and happy ; it is prayed that an emperor may be so. —See A. N. F. F. (p. 44.)

F. F. *Flando, Feriundo.*—See A. A. A. F. F. (p. 1) symbol of the monetal triumvirs.—*Flare*, is to found or cast metal; because brass was first melted in a furnace, and the fused material afterwards coined into money.

FIDES (Good Faith, Fidelity, Loyalty) was

adored as a goddess by the Romans, according to Cicero, Lactantius, and others. Attilius Calatinus dedicated to *Fides* a temple, near that of Jupiter, where she had priests and sacrifices peculiar to her worship. On denarii of the Licinia and other Roman families, her head appears, sometimes crowned with olive, as the preserver of peace; at others adorned with laurel, as the guarantee of victory. The type of the same divinity exhibits itself in various ways on imperial coins. As FIDES (the goddess herself), the figure on a coin of Claudius Gothicus is that of a woman, with a spear in her left hand.— As FIDES AVGVSTA, she appears on a large brass of Plotina.—As FIDES AVGVSTORVM, she stands holding a cornucopiæ, on silver of Maximianus. Sometimes the type consists of two right hands joined; or with a caduceus and two corn-ears, held by two right hands; or with a military standard, held by two right hands; but then we read FIDES PVBLICA, as in Titus (p. 149), or FIDES EXERCITVVM, as in large brass of Vitellius, and also as in Nerva. And in that case the two united hands were meant to symbolize the good faith and fidelity of soldiers and people to the reigning prince; and not to represent *Fides* in her quality of goddess. Examples of the latter kind are also to be found on coins of Balbinus, and Pupienus.

The type of a draped female, holding in her right hand one military ensign planted upright on the ground, and carrying another transversely under her left arm, accompanies the legend CONCORD EXERCI. on gold of Claudius II. (see p. 214.)

FIDES AVGVST*a*. *August Fidelity.*—Good Faith standing, holds in the left hand a basket with fruit, and in the right, ears of corn. In the field, *Senatus Consulto.*—*Obv.* PLOTINA AVG*usta* IMP*eratoris* TRAIANI. (Plotina Augusta [wife] of the Emperor Trajan). Bust of the empress. First brass.—The above engraving is after a cast from a remarkably fine specimen in the British Museum.

This coin is one among other convincing proofs of the high esteem with which Trajan honoured the empress, with whose name, as his wife, he here associates the personification and attributes of Fidelity. That emperor, indeed, always manifested the greatest respect for the virtues, and the utmost confidence in the talents, of Plotina, to whom he entrusted the reins of government, whenever he set out for distant expeditions. On the journey, however, during which her husband

was attacked by the malady of which he died, at Selinus, in Cilicia, she accompanied him; and brought his ashes to Rome.—See PLOTINA.

FIDES EXERCIT. P. M. TR. P. XI. IMP. VII. COS. V. P. P. The emperor Commodus, and his pretorian prefect, standing together on a *suggestus*, in front of several soldiers, wearing shields and carrying military ensigns. A brass medallion of excellent design and fabric, engraved in Vaillant, *Mus. de Descamps*, p. 260, now in the *Cabinet de France*.

FIDES EXERCITVS.—The emperor (Gordianus Pius) in a military habit, and upright posture, is crowned by Victory from behind, at the same time that he joins his right hand with that of a soldier. In the lower part of this silver medallion are the personifications of two rivers, seated.

These rivers signify Mesopotamia (as may be seen in the well-known coin of Trajan, inscribed *Armenia et Mesopotamia in potestatem P. R. redactæ*) where laurels were gained by the Roman forces, during the reign of the third Gordian; on other coins of that emperor the Sun appears in a quadriga, by which is to be understood that the East had yielded to the imperial legions (Eckhel, vii. 314).—A similar type to the above, with the addition of two military ensigns, is struck on a silver medallion of Gallienus, on whose coins the epigraphs of *Fides Exerc. Fidei Equitum, Fid. Prætorianorum*, are also to be found, together with a numerous series of LEG*iones*.

FIDES MAXIMA.—A woman standing, who, holding in her left hand a rudder reversed, presents a globe to the emperor. This epigraph, quoted by Banduri, as from a brass medallion of Probus, is unusual, and till this instance (says Eckhel, vii. 504), unknown on coins.— Henceforward, Fortune, in delivering the empire to Probus, shews that she had reposed in him (*fidem maximam*) the greatest confidence.

FIDES MIL. or MILIT. or MILITVM.— (*Fides Militum*—the fidelity of the soldiers).— This epigraph, which first appears in the mint of Macrinus, continuing to Gallienus (see above cut from a gold specimen), is found occurring under nearly each successive reign down to Constantius Chlorus and Maxentius. To this military legend is sometimes added AVG. or AVGG. or AVGG. ET CAESS. Its accompanying type is generally the draped figure of a woman, sometimes standing, sometimes seated, but always holding one, and usually two, military ensigns, or some other representation of the standards and eagles of the Roman armies, as in Caracalla, Elagabalus, Gordianus Pius, Postumus, Maximianus, &c. &c.

Addison (see his Dialogues on Ancient Medals) considers a great light to be thrown on the inscriptions of *Fides Militum*, and *Fides Exercitus*, from the following verses of Silius Italicus (lib. 2) :—

———————— ad limina sanctæ
Tendebat *Fidei*, secretaque pectora tentat.
Ante Jovem generata, decus divumque hominumque,
Quâ sine non tellus pacem, non æquora norunt ;
Justitiæ consors.

" He to the shrines of *Faith* his steps addrest.
" Ere Jove was born *she* grac'd the bright abodes,
" Consort of *Justice*, boast of men and gods ;
" Without whose heavenly aid no peace below
" The steadfast earth, and rolling ocean know."

The goddess of Fidelity (says the author of the celebrated treatise), is posted between two military ensigns, for the good quality that the poet ascribes to her, of preserving the public peace, by keeping the army true to its allegiance. (p. 43).

As the legends FIDES EXERCITVS and FIDES MILITVM are of very frequent occurrence on coins of the imperial series, it may suffice here to observe that " by means of successive adoptions the empire had become in some measure hereditary from Augustus to Nero. After the death of the latter named emperor, it was the armies that furnished the first examples of those violent elections which so cruelly tore the state in pieces. Vitellius, like his competitors, being indebted to the soldiers for his seat on the imperial throne, took care to record on his coins their sentiments and their promises in his favour"—symbolized by *Fides Exercituum* and two right hands joined.—" In proportion (adds an able French writer) as they recede to a distance from the higher empire, the medals of the Romans [with certain exceptions] become less and less historically interesting. In fact even before the reign of Valerian, their reverses (as in the employment of the words FELICITAS, PAX, FIDES, &c.) offer scarcely any thing except hacknied subjects of vows, and of flatteries which flagrantly contrast themselves with the misfortunes, the wars, the treasons, and the miseries of every description, which in those times desolated the Roman world."—*Leçons Numismat.*

FIDES MILITVM. S. C.—Gordianus Pius on horseback, between two military ensigns.— Large brass, engraved in Havercamp, *Cabinet de Christine.*

Same legend and type, on gold of Probus.

How very little these soldiers were to be confided in, is shewn by the tragical end of that brave and able emperor ; for by those same military subjects, who had ostentatiously sworn allegiance to him, ere he had reigned seven years, Probus was slain.

FIDES MILITVM AVGG. NN. *Augustorum Nostrorum.*—A woman seated, holding two standards.

On a very rare second brass of Maxentius, struck at the time when a treaty was entered into between Maximinus Daza and Maxentius against Constantine the Great.

FIDES or FIDEI LEG. TR. P. COS.—A

female figure standing, holds a small image of Victory in the right hand, and in her left a vexillum or banner. Large brass of Severus. Engraved in the *Cabinet de Christine.*—See LEGIO.

FIDES MVTVA AVGG.—Two right hands joined. On silver of Balbinus and Pupienus.— This epigraph, together with that of PIETAS MVTVA AVGG. with a similar type, is common to each of the above emperors. But *Amor* and *Caritas* are as rare in Balbinus, as *Fides* and *Pietas* are in Pupienus. It was greatly to have been wished, that " mutual Love" could have perpetually existed between these two joint possessors of the Roman empire. The sentiment at first was doubtless sincere, but afterwards, the fear of Maximinus being removed, mutual suspicion tainted mutual love, to an extreme that proved fatal to them both.

FIDES—also FIDEI MILIT. P. M. TR. P. II. COS. II. P. P.—The emperor paludated, a sceptre in his left hand, and his right hand extended, with two figures accompanying him (doubtless meant to represent his sons Caracalla and Geta), on a *suggestus*, addressing six soldiers, who have oblong bucklers on their left arms, and of whom three carry a vexillum, and two bear ensigns.—*Obv.*-L. SEPTIMIVS SEVERVS PERTINAX AVG. IMP. III. Bust of Severus, laurelled and cuirassed.

The original of this splendid brass medallion, from a cast of which the above cut has been engraved, is in the *Cabinet de France.* It forms one among other remarkable specimens of the still flourishing state of the arts of design, in the age of Septimius Severus. That fierce ambitious man hereby records his obligations to those legionaries who, first against Didius Julianus, afterwards in opposition to Pescennius Niger in the East, and to Albinus in the West, had proved their devotedness to his cause. Nor did his commemoration of their ready services to him confine itself to a general acknowledgment, but he specially inscribed the respective names of those legions on other coins.

FIL. *Filia.*—Faustina junior and Lucilla were the only empresses whose fathers were emperors : hence the name of the parent was assumed by each respectively on their coins.

FIL. *Filius.*—ANNIVS VERVS CAES. ANTONINI AVG. FIL*ius.* This Annius Verus and Commodus were sons of M. Aurelius and

Faustina; hence Commodus is also read CAES. ANTONINI AVG. FIL*ius*. So Caracalla and Geta are noted on their coins each as FIL*ius*, meaning the son of Septimius Severus.

FIL. AVGG. *Filius* or *Filii Augustorum*.— As, according to constant usage, the double G signifies two Emperors or *Augusti*, so Maximinus Daza and Constantinus M. are thus called on certain coins. They are denominated neither *Cæsares*, nor *Imperatores*, nor *Augusti*; but *Filii Augustorum*. This new title was impressed on the mintages of those two princes, A. D. 307 (as it appears), under the following circumstances:—Maximinus Daza, indignant at finding the title of Augustus conferred by Galerius Maximianus on Licinius, his junior in rank, while he himself was denied the honour, endeavoured to obtain the same distinction by some compact or other, avowing himself tired of the name of Cæsar, and complaining of being wronged in having only the third rank in the empire assigned to him. Galerius Maximianus in vain urged him to acquiesce in the arrangements he had made. At length Galerius, yielding to the obstinate importunities of Maximinus, but at the same time unwilling to retract what he had done in favour of Licinius, suspended the title of Cæsar, and, reserving that of Augustus exclusively for himself and for Licinius, gave to Maximinus and to Constantinus the name of *Sons of the Emperors* (Augustorum).—The concluding words of Lactantius, in relating the event are—" Victus contumaciâ tollit Cæsarum nomen se Liciniumque Augustos appellat, Maximinum et Constantinum Filios Augustorum."—By supplying as the nominative to *tollit* the word *Galerius* (as has been done by Baluze, whose reading is supported by Bimard, and approved of by Eckhel), all difficulty in interpreting the passage is removed, and the meaning, thus rendered clear, is fully confirmed by coins that have come to light.—A second brass, which bears on one side the laureated head of Maximinus, with the legend MAXIMINVS FIL. AVGG. exhibits on its reverse the standing 'figure of the emperor's genius, holding in one hand a patera, and in the other a cornucopiæ; round it is read GENIO AVGVSTI; on another middle brass of Maximinus it is CAESARIS.—There is also with the same type, a coin of Constantine's, around whose head, crowned with laurel, is CONSTANTINVS FIL. AVG. and on the reverse GENIO CAESARIS, with other similarities, so as to leave no doubt but that these coins were struck at the same time and place. "Now (says Bimard, in his annotations on Jobert), since, on the reverses of the coins whereon Maximin and Constantine are called *Sons of the Augusti*, we find indifferently *Genio Cæsaris* and *Genio Augusti*, it is natural thence to conclude that the new title created by Galerius Maximianus, partook equally of the title of Cæsar and of that of Augustus, the only ones which up to that period had been known in the empire." There was indeed a time when the appellation of *Filii Augusti* was inferior to the appellation of *Cæsar*. Augustus took, on his coins the name of Son of Julius. Caius and

Lucius, sons of Agrippa had by their grandfather Augustus the title conferred upon them of Filii Augusti, in order that his adoption of them might be made known to the whole world. Tiberius called himself "Augusti Filius."— Titus and Domitian were allowed the appellation of "Sons of Vespasianus Augustus."—Lucius Verus, during the life of Antoninus Pius, had no other distinction than to be called *Augusti Filius*. Faustina junior also and Lucilla were called *Filiæ Augustorum*. But (as Bimard observes) "in all these cases the name of *Son of Augustus* marks simply the birth or adoption of those princes. It was not a title of dignity; it gave the rank of Cæsar neither to Lucius Verus nor to Annius Verus. In the case of Maximin and Constantine, on the contrary, the title of FIL*ii* AVGVSTORVM was a new dignity, and a rank superior to that of the Cæsars."

To complete the proofs on which this opinion is founded, the same acute and profound numismatist has annexed to his remarks, the engraving of a medal, which certainly throws great light upon the subject in question. It is a middle brass, on which Constantine unites the name of *Son of the Augustus*, which he derived from his birth alone, to the title of *Son of the Augusti*, which Galerius Maximianus had conferred upon him. Around the head of Constantine, crowned with laurel, we read FL. VAL. CONSTAN-TINVS FIL. AVG. On the reverse, which exhibits the ordinary type of the genius of an emperor, are the words GENIO FIL. AVGG. (To the Genius of the Son of the *Augusti*) : a title not inappropriately given to, and accepted by, Constantine (afterwards emperor, and called the Great), whose father Constantius Chlorus, and whose grandfather by adoption Maximianus Herculeus, had been *Augusti*; and the Emperor Claudius, surnamed Gothicus, was one of his ancestors.—(Bimard ad Jobert, T. ii. 366 to 382, No. v. *Nouvelles Découvertes*.—See the whole of this luminous annotation).

FILIA.—Amongst the Romans a daughter was not always called after the *prenomen* of her father : for example, Herennia Etruscilla, daughter of (the emperor) Q. Messius Trajanus Decius, no paternal name having been taken for her, was called after that of her mother. The daughters of emperors are on some coins styled *Augustæ* : on others that appellation is omitted. Thus Faustina junior is sometimes read AVGVSTI PII FILIA; at other times, FAVSTINA AVG. PII AVG. FILIA.—In like manner, Julia, the daughter of Titus, is numismatically styled either IVLIA AVGVSTA TITI AVGVSTI F.—or IVLIA IMP. T. AVG. F. AVGVSTA, and also DIVI TITI FILIA.

FISCI IVDAICI CALVMNIA SVBLATA. S. C. A palm tree.—First brass of Nerva.— See IVDAICI.

FLACCILLA *(Aelia)*, the first wife of Theodosius the Great; born in Spain, daughter of Antonius, prefect of Gaul, she was celebrated for her piety, and for her benevolence to the poor. Arcadius and Honorius were her sons by the above named emperor, who married her before his accession to the imperial throne. She

died in Thrace, A. D. 388. Her brass coins are
of the lowest degree of rarity, her gold and
silver most rare. A half aureus of this em-

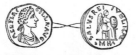

press's, on which she is styled AEL. FLACCILLA
AVG. bears her head crowned with a diadem
enriched with precious stones.—SALVS REIPVB-
LICAE is the legend, and a Victory inscribing on
a shield the monogram of Christ, is the type, of
the reverse.

[This gold coin is valued by Mionnet at 80 fr.
and 50 fr. in silver.—See wood-cut above.]

GOLD.—Without legend.—The monogram of
Christ within a laurel garland. In the exergue
CONOB. P. or CONS. (A *quinarius*, valued by
Mionnet at 72 fr. Engraved in Akerman, ii.
pl. xii. No. 4).

FLAMINES. Roman priests of particular
gods.—These occupied the first rank after the
Pontifex Maximus. The following three principal *Flamines* were held in high consideration,
and enjoyed great privileges. They were also
called *Filamines*, from the fillet which each wore
around his head.

Flamen DIALIS, the priest of Jupiter, and
the most distinguished of the flamines, was constantly on duty, nor could he quit the city for
a single night. He was distinguished by an attendant lictor, by the curule chair, and the *toga
prætexta*. The *flamen dialis* was not forbidden
the use either of wine or flour.

There is a gold coin of the Cornelia gens, on
which the heads of Bacchus and Ceres are joined,
and a cornucopiæ placed beside them, to shew,
as some have conjectured, that the *Flamen
Dialis* greatly venerated those deities. The coin
referred to bears on its reverse the name of
SER*vius* LENTVL*us*, and a representation of
the *Ancilia*, or sacred shields (see p. 45), which
were entrusted to the special custody of the
Flamen Dialis. And this gold piece, which is
engraved amongst the *nummi consulares*, in
Morell. Thesaur. (TAB. xv. No. 2), appears to
be the only one, in the whole range of Roman
numismatic monuments, which alludes, and that
by implication only, to the highly-privileged
priest of Jupiter.

Flamen MARTIALIS, a priest of Mars, whose
dignity was the most exalted, after that of the
Flamen Dialis, and was required to be held by
a patrician.—A denarius of the Cornelia gens,
struck under Augustus, distinctly names this
office, and represents the sacerdotal fanctionary

himself; for L. LENTVLVS is there called FLA-
MEN MARTIALIS.

In the preceding engraving of this illustrative
coin, we see a figure, naked except round the
middle, holding a small Victory in his right hand,
and a spear transversely in his left. He is crowned
by a togated figure, who stands beside him, and
resting the left hand on a shield inscribed with
the letters C. V. *(Clipeus Votivus)*. The crown
held by the togated figure over the head of the
smaller one is like a star.

Havercamp is of opinion, that this type represents one Lentulus, a priest, who in the name
of Augustus, is dedicating a statue of Julius
Cæsar, over the head of which was placed the
Julium Sidus, in the temple of Mars Ultor,
whilst the shield which he holds in his right
hand is a *votive* one. This explanation, which
rests on no conclusive evidence, Eckhel (v. 182),
leaves to the adoption of those who approve of
it. At the same time he acknowledges his inability to improve upon it. Cicero (ad Quintum fratrem, iii. ep. 1, § 5), mentions a L.
Lentulus, the son of a priest, prior to the one
in question.

Riccio (in his *Monete delle Famiglie*, p. 67),
takes the same view of the subject with Havercamp. He says, " Lucius Lentulus, Flamen Martialis, that is, priest of Mars, is represented on
this coin of the Cornelia gens, in the act of
dedicating, in the name of Augustus, the statue
of his father by adoption, Julius Cæsar, in the
temple of Mars Ultor, after the voluntary submission of the conflicting parties in the Roman
state, which took place in 732 (B. C. 22). The
above mentioned dedication, however, was not
performed till 752 (B. C. 2), in other words, until
20 years afterwards; the emperor thus absolving
himself of the vow he had made to shew posterity that he had completely avenged the murder of Cæsar, and that he had accomplished his
design of subduing that supposed invincible
party, whose project for defeating him was fatal
to themselves."

Flamen QVIRINALIS, a priest of Quirinus (*i.
e.* Romulus, after his deification).—This *Flamen*
was the third in rank, and is supposed to be designated on a silver coin of the Fabia family,
on the reverse of which we see (p. 371) the inscription of N. FABI PICTOR. And, for the type,
a galeated figure seated; with the pontifical apex
in the right hand, in the left a spear, and a
shield, on which is inscribed QVIRIN. On the
exergue ROMA.

Havercamp (says Eckhel, v. 208) justly remarks, that the seated figure personifies Rome,
and that the QVIRIN. should be expanded into
QVIRIN*alis*, that is, *Flamen Quirinalis*; just
as on coins of the Cornelia family we find inscribed in full, L. LENTVLVS FLAMEN MARTIALIS
(as engraved in left hand column).

FLAMINIA gens.—Of the plebeian order,
having *Flaminius* for its name (from *Flamen*),
and *Cilo* or *Chilo* for its surname. It offers,
for its record, the following three coins, of no
particular rarity :—

ROMA. Galeated head of Rome.—*Rev.*—L

FLAMINI. below CILO. Victory, holding a crown, in a biga at full speed.

Lucius Flaminius Cilo must have been questor of the republic in the time of Sulla, or at the beginning of Cæsar's domination; and although the more ancient types are preserved, yet the Sullian or Cæsarian coins are allusive to the respective achievements of those two despotic rulers over the affairs of Rome.

2. IIII. VIR. PRI. FL. Adorned head of Venus. —Rev.—L. FLAMIN. Below, CHILO. Victory in a rapid biga, as in the above engraving.

3. Laureated head of Julius Cæsar.—Rev.— L. FLAMINIVS IIII. VIR. A woman draped in the stola, stands holding in the right hand a caduceus, and in the left the *hasta pura*.

Lucius Flaminius Chilo, nephew perhaps of the preceding, was moneyer to Julius Cæsar, during his dictatorship, when the number of those magistrates was increased from three to four.

What PRI. FL. means has given rise to discussion among numismatists. First, it is believed by some that it should be read *primus flando*, as designating the first monetal *quatuorvir* added to the other colleagues by Cæsar. Next, Borghesi and Cavedoni concur with Ursin, that it ought to be interpreted *primus flamen*, there being a corresponding example in the coeval medal of Ti. Sempronius Gracchus, who besides the title of IIII. V(IR.) took that of *quæstor designatus ;* and in this instance the first priest *(primus flamen)*, has placed the head of the new divinity on a coin struck during his own monetal magistrature, the date of which is to be referred to 711 (B. C. 43), according to the calculation of Cavedoni, in the course of his examination of discovered repositories *(repostigli)*. The head of Venus on coin No. 2 is allusive to the assumed origin of Cæsar; and the woman on the reverse of No. 3 is thought to represent *Felicitas.*—See Borghesi's reasons for entertaining this opinion, cited by Riccio, p. 91.

FLAVIA, gens plebeia, has but the following coin (with three unimportant varieties), which is common :—

C. FLAV. HEMIC. LEG. PRO. PR. Head of Apollo, before it a lyre.—Rev.—Q. C. BRVT. IMP. Victory on foot, crowning with her right hand a trophy, and holding in her left hand a palm branch resting on her shoulder.

The letters HEMIC. at the bottom of this denarius, are an abbreviation not as yet satisfactorily explained; but in what way soever they ought to be read, they indubitably stand as the surname of Flavius. "There is no record (says Eckhel) among the ancient writers to shew that Flavius was the lieutenant or deputy of Brutus."

Yet here we see the name of Brutus—the same who assisted at the murder of Julius Cæsar, in A. U. C. 710, on a family coin of the Flavii.

Riccio speaks more confidently. He says— " Caius Flavius, who caused the above described denarius to be minted, was *legatus pro-prætor* to Brutus, when, united to Cassius, that conspirator fled into Asia from the fury of the triumvirs, who had raised an armament against him. The *legatus,* according to Borghesi, was one of the brothers *Flavii*, to whom Plutarch and Appian bear testimony, and who, properly named Caius, took part against Octavianus, and was put to death at the capture of Perugia.— The other brother, who perished at the battle of Philippi, was not called Caius, and moreover he occupied the office of prefect of the Fabri (la carica di prefetto de' Fabri), a charge inferior to that of *legatus.*"—For the reverse, referring to Brutus, see Junia gens.

FLAVIA.—The legion which was raised by Vespasian received this appellation in allusion to the family name of the emperor. It is inscribed on a silver coin of Gallienus, in the epigraph LEG. IIII. FL. VI. F. with the type of a lion.—On a gold coin of Victorinus senior this legion is symbolized by the type of two lions and a helmeted head. The inscription LEG. IIII. FLAVIA P. F.

FLORA, a goddess of Sabine origin, who presided over flowers and gardens. The poets, in order to ennoble her history, represented Flora as a nymph under the name of Chloris, and married her to Zephyr, the son of Aurora. The worship dedicated, in the earlier times, to this divinity, took place some days before the beginning of May; as Ovid sings *(Fast.* iv. 947) :—

" Incipis Aprili, transis in tempora Maii."

[You commence in April, and are adjourned to May].

During the beautiful days of the latter month women and maidens are said to have assembled by themselves to enjoy the gay and probably the then harmless pleasures of such a springtide celebration. The festivals of Flora received additional splendour, but lost their modest and inoffensive character, when a courtezan named Acca Laurentia, dying during the reign of Ancus Martius, left immense riches, amassed during a life of prostitution, to the Roman people, as her heir. From that period, the Floral games were renewed in her especial honour, and it was to this meretricious benefactress, that the people affected to apply the name of the goddess, to defray the expenses of whose yearly feasts, she had bequeathed her ill-gotten wealth.

In Flora, no longer regarded as a presiding deity over the most lovely and innocent of natural objects, the profligate multitude saw only the patroness of harlots; and seizing on this pretext for authorising excesses, they at length converted her worship into a source of public scandal. It was not however until the year of Rome 580 (B. C. 174), that the *Floralia* were celebrated regularly every year. In these popular sports, obscenity and libertinism were (according to Lactantius and other writers) carried to the highest pitch. "Nam præter verborum licentiam, nudabantur flagitante populo meretrices quæ spectatores impudicis motibus detinerent." This festival was frequently kept up by torch-light, when Night lent to indecency of gestures, her aid to consummate its provocatives by deeds of debauchery.

FLORAL. PRIMVS.—This epigraph appears on a denarius of the Servilia gens, with the type of a woman's head, having necklace and ear-rings, the hair being adorned with flowers.— There is a *lituus* behind the head. On the reverse we read C. SERVEIL. C. F. And the type represents two warriors, in short military dress, with brimmed caps. They stand opposite each other, holding shields on their left arms, and joining their drawn swords, hilt and blade together, as in token of confederacy or alliance.

This fine silver coin has presented not a few difficulties in the way of correctly explaining its legends and types. The difference of opinion amongst numismatists is, or rather has been, as to the first institution of the *Floralia*. According to Velleius Paterculus, they commenced in the year of Rome 514 (B. C. 240), C. Servilius being the reputed originator of those festivals. Eckhel quotes as a clue to ascertain the date of the event above alluded to, the following passage from Ovid *(Fasti,* v. 327):—

Convenêre patres, et, si bene floreat annus,
　Numinibus nostris (Floræ) annua festa vovent.
Adnuimus voto.　Consul cum consule ludos
　Postumio Lænas persoluêre mihi.

[The Fathers are assembled, and, if the year has proved abundant in flowers, they vote an annual festival to my goddess-ship. I nod my acquiescence. Postumius and Lænas, the consuls, have carried it into effect by celebrating games for me (*i. e.* for my satisfaction, or honour)].

The Author of *Doctrina* goes on to observe, that the foregoing quotation from Ovid seems to be at variance with the statement of Velleius; since the consulate of L. Postumius Albinus and M. Popilius Lænas took place in 581 (B. C. 173). But the same poet has elsewhere said, that these *Florales ludi* had fallen into neglect, which the goddess had resented by allowing her productions to be blighted; and in consequence of that calamity, by a decree of the Senate *(patres)* in 581, annual and perpetual celebrations of the *Floralia* were voted.

The infamies committed at them became, however, so revolting, that Cato, the censor, being one day present in the theatre, a friend remarked to him that the people, embarrassed at seeing him there, dared not call, according to custom, for the public display of meretricious depravity.

And this great Roman, so grave and so severe, had the complaisance to retire, that he might not interrupt the unbridled license of the people, nor on the other hand pollute his eyes with the sight of disorders committed at such spectacles. The people, it is added, appreciating this as a concession to their vicious tastes, bestowed a thousand plaudits upon Cato. This fact Martial (i. *Epigr.* 3) humorously glances at :—

　Nosses jocosæ dulce cùm sacrum Floræ,
　Festosque lusus, et licentiam vulgi,
　Cur in theatrum, Cato severe, venisti ?
　An ideo tantum veneras, ut exires.

["As you must have been well acquainted with the rites of the mirthful Flora, the holiday entertainments, and the broad licentiousness of the rabble, why, O strait-laced Cato, did you shew your face in the theatre ? Did you really come in, *only* to walk out again ?]

But, indeed, the same satirist had previously said, that some of the frequenters of Flora's Festival, in epigrammatic language, contended that Cato ought not to have entered their theatre, or, having entered, should have remained to witness the *scena joci.* To this Ausonius in all probability alludes (says Eckhel) when (in *Carmin.* 385, v. 25), he thus writes:—

　Necnon lascivi Floralia læta theatri,
　Quæ spectare volunt, qui voluisse negant.

["Also, the joyous Floralia of the licentious theatre, which they who most deprecate them, still desire to see."]

By the lituus behind the head on the obverse of the coin engraved at the top of this article, the moneyer who caused it to be struck proclaims himself a descendant of C. Servilius, the augur, who was pretor in 659 (B. C. 95). But the workmanship of the denarius, brings it down to the Cæsarian age; and hence Riccio (p. 210), agrees with Eckhel and with Morel, that it was struck in the last period of the republic, and by the questor of Brutus and Cassius, in 711 (B. C. 43). In placing on the obverse of his coin the bust of Flora, with a gay head-dress of flowers, the moneyer pays honour to his celebrated ancestor, that *Floralia primus fecisset.*

Next, as to the type of the reverse, which indicates either the alliance of Romulus and Tatius; or the conspiracy of the two brothers Casca against the life of Cæsar. It is, says Riccio, such a type of alliance as is seen uniformly represented on coins of two Italian cities, Atella and Capua, but to which it is to be specially referred is not known. "Sine dubio (observes Eckhel, v. 310) vetus aliquod, illustrisusque foedus, a quopiam ex gente Servilia procuratum, in his C. Servilii denariis renovatur."

Flora is also supposed to be typified by the head of a woman, crowned with a chaplet of flowers, and with a flower behind it, on the obverse of a denarius of the Claudia gens, having for legend C. CLODIVS, C. F. The portrait sufficiently corresponds with that which Ovid draws (L. iv. *Fastor*):—

　Mille venit variis florum dea nexa coronis.

[The goddess comes, crowned with garlands of a thousand varied flowers].

But the reverse, which bears the title of VES-TALIS, and a seated image of one of those chaste priestesses, is but ill-assorted with any record of the Floreal celebration.—See CLAVDIA gens, p. 210.

FLORENTE FORTVNA. P. R.—A woman standing, with branch in the right hand, and cornucopiæ in the left.—*Obv.*—HERCVLES AD-SERTOR. A laureated and bearded head of Hercules.

Bimard de la Bastie, in his annotations to Jobert (i. 299) was the first to describe the above, as being the legends and types of a silver coin in the *De Rothelin* cabinet of his time (1739). Eckhel, who quotes Bimard, calls it "silver of Galba," and, referring to it, as one of several coins that allude to the successes of that emperor, makes the following remark:—"If coins, bearing the legend MARS ADSERTOR (see *Incerta, Morell. Fam. Rom.* TAB. 4), were struck during the reign of Galba, there appears to be no doubt that the present one, inscribed HERCVLES ADSERTOR is to be associated with them; especially as its types furnish an admirable allegory in allusion to those times. For, as Hercules on his return from Spain, after slaying Cacus, the robber, restored the seven hills to freedom, so Galba, returning from the same country, after the overthrow of Nero, gave liberty to Rome, planted on those self-same seven hills, and brought it to pass, that the fortune of the Roman people should once more begin to flourish." (vi. 298).

FLORIANUS (*Marcus Annius*), brother of Tacitus, whom he had followed into the East, and on whose death he was acknowledged emperor by the Senate and by all the provinces, except Syria, whose army supported the cause of Probus. A civil war was on the point of ensuing from the rivalship of these two competitors, when Florianus was killed by his own soldiers, near Tarsus, only three months after he had assumed the purple, A. D. 276.—Style: IMP. C. M. ANNIVS FLORIANVS AVG.—Short as was his reign, the reverses of his coins have sufficient variety to shew that at least the Roman mint was active with his name and effigy, which appear, among others, on a brass medallion, having the epigraph of MONETA AVG. and the three monetæ standing, with their attributes. His silver of base metal are of the second degree of rarity; second brass rare; third brass common.

The following gold, of the usual size, are valued by Mionnet at 120 francs each, viz. CON-

CORD MILIT. Two soldiers joining hands.—CONSERVATOR AVG. Sun in quadriga.—PER-PETVITATE (*sic*.) AVG. Woman holding a globe.

The following, at 100 francs each, viz. IOVI VICTORI. Jupiter Nicephorus standing.—ROMAE AETERNAE. Roma Nicephorus seated.—VIRTVS AVGVSTI. Mars walking.—MARTI VICTORI. Mars with spear and trophy. (Brought £3 at the Campana sale).

[A gold coin of Florian, found at Deddington, was bought by Mr. Cove Jones for £12. —There were no gold coins of this emperor either in the Thomas, the Pembroke, or the Devonshire cabinets].

FLOS, a flower, appears on coins of Aquillius Florus, a monetary triumvir of Augustus.—The type of that reverse bears allusion to the cognomen. Vaillant gives it as his opinion that the flower represented on the denarius alluded to (see Aquillia gens, p. 71) is unknown to botanists. Havercamp (in *Morell. Thesaur.*) contends that it is the *cyanus* [κύανος—the blue corn flower]. Eckhel (v. 143) bluntly says—"Let those look to it, who are conversant with the study."

A denarius of the Durmia family, with legend HONORI, and the head of Honour for its obverse type, exhibits on the reverse the legend CAESAR AVGVSTVS, and a slow quadriga, on which is a basket, with a *flower* in it (see above). An exactly similar type of reverse appears on gold and silver coins of Titus.—Vaillant's explanation (ii. p. 97) of this device is its reference to a triumph of that emperor's; and that this *flower*, or rather *bud*, similar to what the goddess SPES carries in her hand, denotes the hope reposed by the Senate and people of Rome in the victorious arms of Judæa's conqueror.

A *flower*, according to Pliny, was the symbol of Spring; and in confirmation of this, on the coins of the four Seasons (by Antoninus Pius, Commodus, and others), we see the boy who personifies the vernal quarter of the year, bearing a basket laden with flowers.—See SAECULI, and TEMPORUM FELICITAS.

FOCAS, or PHOCAS (Flavius), a low-born Bithynian, who atrociously assuming the imperial purple, caused the deposition of his sovereign Mauricius, and the murder of that emperor and his family, A. D. 602. In eight years afetrwards he was himself taken prisoner in Constantinople, and decapitated. On some of this villain's brass coins, where his style is DN. FO-CAS AVG. he and his wife Leontia appear, profaning Christian symbols with their usurped and blood-stained dignities.

FOEDUS.—A treaty of alliance made by one people with another people. Amongst the Romans, in early times, alliances were always made

by order of the People, by authority of the Senate, and through the ministration of the *Feciales* (see p. 376).—The *foedera*, or treaties of Rome with foreign nations, are recorded on some of her consular and family coins. There is in particular a denarius which, bearing on the obverse the effigy and titles of Augustus, places before us, with beautiful distinctness, in the legend and type of its reverse, the ordained rite of forming alliances solemnised by the Romans, from which rare coin an engraving is subjoined.

FOED. P. R. CVM. GA-BINIS C. ANTIS. VETVS. (on another coin, FOEDVS P. R. QVM. *(sic.)* GABINIS). Two men togated & veiled, stand opposite each other, holding a sow over a light-ed altar.—*Obv.*—CAESAR AVGVSTVS. Head of Augustus. Silver of Antistia gens.—(See p. 51).

This reverse offers a type peculiar to the Antistii, and one chosen by Antistius, a moneyer of Augustus, to indicate his connexion by descent with Gabii, that ancient city of Latium. Indeed, Dionysius of Halicarnassus, calls " Antistius Petro by far the most renowned of the Gabini-ans ;" on whose death, caused by the treachery of Sextus Tarquinius, the city in question was brought under the dominion of his father the king. (Dionys. *Hal.* iii. p. m. 255). Shortly after this event, peace having been restored, a treaty was entered into between the two people, accompanied with sacrifices and oaths ; the terms of which Dionysius relates to have been preserved to his own day, inscribed in ancient characters, in the temple of Jupiter Pistius.—The same writer informs us, that it was an ox which was offered as a victim on the occasion ; whereas the coins exhibit a pig or a sow, which assuredly was the animal usually immolated at the ratification of treaties, as Livy has expressly stated (i. c. 24), in whose work the entire rite and formularies are specified ; and Virgil, too, elegantly bears out the testimony of coins, in the passage where he records the treaty entered into between Romulus and Tatius, after the rape of the Sabines (*Æn.* viii. 638) :

Tum iidem inter se, posito certamine, reges,
Armati Jovis ante aras, paterasque tenentes
Stabant, et *cæsâ* jungebant fœdera *porcâ.*

["Then, these two princes, laying aside their strife, took their stand, completely armed, be-side the altar of Jupiter, each holding a patera, and having sacrificed a sow, ratified a solemn treaty."]

And Varro says (*de R. R. L.* ii. 4)—" When a treaty is ratified at the commencement of a peace, it is customary to sacrifice a pig." The lighted altar, therefore, on this coin, is that of Jupiter ; for the name of *Diespiter* occurs also in the formulary used on the occasion, and this practice too was derived from the Greeks ; for in Theocritus, Tiresias is found enjoining Alc-mena " to sacrifice to the supreme Jupiter a male pig. *(Idyll.* xxiv. v. 97).—Homer, how-

ever, has recorded a much more ancient usage of sacrificing a pig to Jupiter, where he says, that Agamemnon swore that he restored Briseis to Achilles inviolate. *(Iliad,* T. 250). But Talthybius " stood (the while) beside the pastor of the people, holding in his arms a pig."—The athletes in the Olympic games used, with a similar rite, to call Jupiter 'Ορκιος to witness, that they would resort to no fraud in their con-tests. The sacrifice of a sow, and the ceremo-nial of ratifying a treaty, are expressed in nearly the same manner on coins of Acerra, in Cam-pania, and on those of the Samnites. See coins of the Veturia gens.—See also Eckhel, v. 137 and 138.

FONTEIA gens, of the highest antiquity ; but plebeian, for Clodius caused himself to be adopted by P. Fonteius, in order that he might be a tribune of the plebs. The surname is Ca-pito.—There are nine distinct mintages in its coins, besides a great many minor varieties.—The silver are, with few exceptions, common. The brass pieces are the *as*, or its parts, struck by the moneyers of M. Antony.—The following are amongst the most rare, or curious, denarii of this family :—

1. A double head, of youthful appearance, before it the mark of the denarius, behind it some isolated alphabetic character.—*Rev.* C. FONT.; below ROMA. A galley with helmsman, or captain, and rowers at their oars, and the stern adorned with the *aplustre* and streamers.

In these types Vaillant recognises an indica-tion of the origin of the *Fonteii*, who, accord-ing to Arnobius, assumed to have descended from *Fontus*, the son of Janus. Eckhel cha-racterises this, as " præclara conjectura," and points to several examples presenting analogous selections of reputed ancestors, which fully con-firm its correctness.–See *Doctrina,* v. 214, et seq.

The ship with rowers is regarded by Riccio (p. 92) as allusive to some maritime expeditions of the ancient members of the family, not re-corded in history, or perhaps to the arrival by by sea, in Italy, of Janus, the father of Fontus above named. The same modern writer on family coins observes, that Caius Fonteius, who caused this denarius to be minted, probably lived about the year 641 (B. C. 113). And, ap-parently to Cavedoni, he might be the Fonteius slain by the Ascolani, together with the pro-consul Servilius, at the breaking-out of the social war, in 663 (B. C. 91).

2. Two juvenile heads, coupled together, lau-reated, with a star over each. Before them the mark of the denarius, and in some the letters P. P.—*Rev.* MAN. FONTEI. A trireme, with pilot sitting at the helm. In the field three globules.

The two heads on the obverse are those of the *Dioscuri*, who are the *Penates of the capital.* On a specimen of the above denarius, engraved in Riccio *(Tav.* 20, No. 2), the letters P. P. appear before the heads. This is made still more clear in similar types of the Antia and Sulpicia families. For some explanatory remarks on these domestic deities, the reader is referred to the word *Penates.*—"The mint of Fonteius (says Eckhel) adopts these types, because, as we learn in the case of the Sulpicia family, the Penates were held in the highest honour at Tusculum, from which town the Fonteii originally came." See *Doct. Num.* v. 218.

Cavedoni (cited by Riccio, p. 93), says, that the Manius Fonteius of the silver coins and also of large brass, classed with the mintages of the Fonteia gens, must be the same person who was defended by Cicero; since, in the newly-discovered fragment of the oration delivered by him, M. Fonteius is expressly mentioned as his monetal triumvir, and his questor. He was pretor in 675 (B.C. 79), and thence it is to be inferred that a little while before he was moneyer.

3. M. FONTEI. C. F. The head of a young man laureated, beneath which is the *fulmen.*—*Rev.* A winged boy riding on a goat. In the field of the coin are two *pilei,* with a star over each. Below is the thyrsus. All within a myrtle garland.

The portrait on the obverse of this denarius is, in the opinion of Eckhel himself, not incorrectly believed to be that of Apollo Vejovis, to whom the thunderbolt under the head bears allusion. As to the winged boy sitting on a goat, the same commentator says, that it seems to be rather the "*Genius of Vejovis*," than, as to others it has appeared, the figure of Cupid, in which opinion (says he), I follow Passeri, who regards such figures of winged children, except when they hold a bow or an arrow, as *genii.* The bonnets of the Dioscuri belong to the *Dei Penates.* As to why the thyrsus and the myrtle crown form part of the type, and also as to who was Manius Fonteius, the author of these denarii, the numismatist of Vienna, with his usual repudiation of conjecture, simply adds "*ignoro.*"

Riccio, in describing the above denarius, says "This Manius Fonteius must have been moneyer about 670 (B.C. 84), and son of that Caius

Fonteius, who was *legatus* to Manius Fonteius, pretor in Gaul, posterior to 675 (B.C. 79), and reckoned among the *primarii viri* by Cicero.

Cavedoni believes the infant figure on the goat to be meant for the genius of *Jupiter Crescens,* seated on the back of his own goat [Amalthæa], and is of opinion that the reiterated appearance of the caps of the Dioscuri bears allusion to the original country of the monetal functionary who caused the coin to be struck.

4. P. FONTEIVS P. F. CAPITO III. VIR. The helmed bust of Mars, with but little beard. Behind it a trophy.—*Rev.* An armed horseman, riding at full speed. Under him are two military figures.

This is one among many family coins, in which both legends and types are involved in uncertainty, and the expectations raised by either a full inscription, or an interesting device, are more or less disappointed. Eckhel (v. p. 220), does not regard it as satisfactorily made out why *Mars Tropæophorus* appears on the obverse, nor who the horseman is on the reverse, nor to whom the inscription MAN*ius* FONT*eius* TR*ibunus* MIL*itum* should be assigned. He describes the two armed figures beneath the horse's feet as engaged in single combat, whilst Mionnet sees in them two enemies, whom the cavalier has laid prostrate.

Riccio endeavours to supply some of these desiderata. He pronounces this Publius Fonteius Capito to have been moneyer in the 660th year of Rome (B.C. 94) if not later. He regards the types of the above engraved coin as alluding to certain exploits performed by a member of this family, that is to say, to the military tribune Manius Fonteius, who, under the command, and in presence of, Titus Didius (p. 327), in Celtiberia, displayed his prowess by slaying the enemy's general.

Some think that the tribune above mentioned was brother of the Fonteius Capito who struck this denarius, but its fine workmanship carries it down to a later period.—[Mr. Akerman thinks that the head of trophy-bearing Mars, together with the reverse type, refers either to that successful Spanish expedition, or to some other specific victory.]

P. FONTEIVS III. VIR. CONCORDIA.— Veiled head of Concord.—*Rev.*—T. DIDI. IMP. VIL. PVB. Grand portico of two stories.

This coin commemorates the *Imperator* (General in command of an army) Titus Didius, under whom the tribune P. Fonteius fought, and respecting whom see coin No. 2, in Didia gens (p. 327).

FORGERIES *of Public Money.*—On this subject, so important to the numismatist, and so interesting in an historical point of view, some general observations will be found in pp. 294

and 295 of this volume, under the head of *Counterfeit Coins.* But for further information respecting the works of *falsarii* amongst the Romans, the reader is especially referred to a valuable essay by the Editor of the *Numismatic. Chronicle* for July, 1846, including a masterly letter to Mr. Akerman from Mr. Burgon, with regard to the practices of the Greek forgers.— The whole dissertation merits attention; for, commencing with early epochs of antiquity, it pursues the history of monetal frauds through the middle ages down to the times of our own Tudors and Stuarts.

FORT. *Fortissimus.*—One of the titular epithets given on coins to Decentius.

FORT. CAESAR. *Fortissimus Cæsar.*

FOR. RE.——*Fortuna Redux* appears frequently on coins of Augustus.

FORT. FEL. *Fortunæ Felici.*—On silver and brass of Commodus, and silver of Domna.

FORT. P. R.—For an explanation of this abbreviated legend see ARRIA gens, p. 83.

FORTUNA.—Fortune; a goddess, to whose worship the Romans were devoutly attached.— The common people regarded her as a divinity who distributed good and evil amongst mankind, according to her caprice, and without having any regard to merit. But the more sensible portion of the ancients either denied the existence of this deity, or understood by Fortune no other than Divine Providence, whose decrees being unknown to mortals, human events appear to happen by chance. The Romans, who were, at the earliest period of their history, content to consult *Sors et Fortuna* at Antium, afterwards adopted the goddess into the number of their tutelaries, and consecrated nearly thirty temples to her, in the different districts of the city. Servius Tullius set the first example, which was followed by Ancus Martius, and it was largely adopted in the time of the republic.— The Emperor Nero built a temple to Fortune of transparent stones. The Romans pretended that Fortune, having deserted the Persians and Assyrians, and after having flown lightly over Macedonia, and seen Alexander perish, passed over into Egypt and Syria, and, at last arriving on Mount Palatine, threw aside her wings, cast away her wheel, and entered Rome, there to take up her abode for ever.—*Fortune* was Sulla's favourite divinity : to her, not to himself, or to his own wisdom, he was accustomed to ascribe all the glory of his many successful achievements, and, in allusion to this, assumed the name of *Felix.*—The Romans gave many different names to this versatile goddess. The following are those which appear on coins, viz.: Antiatina, Bona, Felix, Fors, Mala, Muliebris, Manens, Obsequens, Primigenia, Redux; lastly, Fortuna Augusta, or Augusti, and Fortuna Populi Romani (see those names, *suis locis*).

FORTUNE appears on a great number of imperial coins, in each metal and size, from Augustus to Diocletian, with the legend FORTVNA, but more frequently FORTVNA AVG. and AVGVSTI, under the figure of a young woman, habited in the stola, standing (as in the following en-

graved example of Hadrian, first brass), or seated, holding in the right hand a rudder, resting on the prow of a ship, and in the left hand a cornucopiæ. In some types a wheel appears at her feet, or under her chair, as in Albinus, Gordianus III. &c. On other specimens we see her with the rudder planted on a globe, as in Verus, Commodus, &c. but the cornucopiæ is her invariable attribute.

Fortune is seated with a young boy before her, on a coin of Julia Domna; standing with a caduceus, in L. Aelius; with her arm resting on a column, as in Hadrian; in a temple of six columns, on a coin of Treb. Gallus.

Fortune also appears with *Hope* on first brass of Hadrian and of Aelius Cæsar. She is seen in a chair, opposite to the emperor, who is sacrificing, as in Sept. Severus.—[The sedent goddess is said to denote the emperor's fortune to be firm and stable. Sometimes *Fortuna sedens* holds with her right hand a short staff, or tiller, at the top of the rudder, as in Antoninus Pius, Albinus, &c. And on a well-known coin of Commodus (see further on) she sits holding a horse by the bridle. On a coin of Geta she is recumbent on the ground, with a wheel and cornucopiæ by her side].

Fortuna Mala, and Fortuna Bona, were both worshipped in their respective temples at Rome. Vaillant is of opinion that the two busts on a coin of the Rustia gens (Fortunæ Antiates) were intended to personify *Good* and *Ill Fortune.* —See GENIUS.

FORTVNAE ANTIAT*es Quintus* RVSTIVS.

Two beardless busts, side by side, one of which wears a helmet, and is naked as far as the breast, and holds a patera; the other has a mitella on her head-dress, and a tunic close to the neck; both placed on a flattened cippus, each extremity of which is ornamented with a ram's head.—*Rev.* CAESARI AVGVSTO EX. S. C. An altar, on which is inscribed FOR*tunæ* RE*duci.*—On silver of the Rustia gens, struck under Augustus, in the year of Rome 736 (B. C. 18).

Fortune was called by this title of locality on account of a celebrated temple erected to her honour at Antium, a town in Latium, not far from the sea coast (now *Anzio*), the birth-place of Nero. At this place she was doubtless in high repute for oracles; Suetonius says—"Monuerunt et Fortunæ *Antiatinæ*, ut à Cassio caveret."—Perhaps, says Eckhel (v. 298), what I have called a *cippus*, is the vehicle, by which, as Macrobius informs us, the images of the two Fortunes *(simulacra Fortunarum)*, were conveyed in Antium to utter the (oracular) responses.

Addison, in mentioning his visit to the ruins of Antium, makes the following observations:—"All agree there were two *Fortunes* worshipped here. Suetonius calls them *Fortunæ Antiates*, and Martial the *Sorores Antii.* * * *—Fabretti and others are apt to believe that by the two Fortunes were only meant in general the goddess who sent prosperity, and she who sent affliction, to mankind; and [these Italian antiquaries] produce in their behalf, an ancient monument found in this very place, and superscribed FORTVNAE FELICI. SACRVM; and also another with the words FORTI. FORTVNAE SACRVM. [See *Morell. Thesaur. Fam. Rom.* T. i. p. 369].—This double function of the goddess, adds our own illustrious countryman, gives a considerable light and beauty to the ode, L. i. 35, which Horace has addressed to her. The whole poem is a prayer to *Fortune*, that she would prosper Augustus Cæsar's arms, and confound his enemies; so that each of the goddesses has her task assigned in the poet's prayer; and we may observe, the invocation is divided between the two deities, the first line relating indifferently to either. That printed in Italic type speaks to the goddess of Prosperity, or to the *Nemesis* of the Good, and the other to the goddess of Adversity, or to the *Nemesis* of the Wicked:—

> O Diva, gratum quæ regis Antium,
> Præsens vel imo tollere de gradu
> 　　Mortale corpus, *vel superbos*
> 　　Vertere funeribus triumphos, &c.

Great Goddess, *Antium's* Guardian Power,
Whose force is strong, and quick to raise
The lowest to the highest place,
　Or with a wondrous fall
　To bring the haughty lower,
And turn proud triumphs to a funeral, &c.
　　　　　　　　　　　　CREECH.

"If we take the first interpretation of the two Fortunes for the double *Nemesis*, the compliment to Cæsar is the greater, and the fifth stanza clearer than the commentators usually make it."—See *Remarks on Italy*, p. 169.

FORTI FORTVNAE, or FORS FORTVNA.—Fortune standing, with a rudder in her right hand, a cornucopiæ in her left, and a wheel before her feet.

This epigraph is not given in either Mionnet or Akerman. But Eckhel, and before him Spanheim, recognize it as borne on a second brass coin of Gal. Maximianus, in the imperial cabinet at Vienna. The remarks of the great German numismatist on this recondite subject are of the following tenour:—

Fors was the same with *Fortuna*, as may be abundantly proved from Latin writers; and Cicero *(de Divin.* ii. c. 6), makes no distinction between *Fors, Fortuna, Casus,* and *Eventus.*—Apuleius also (in *Hermet. Trismeg. sub fin.*) says, "*Eventus* or *Fors* is intermingled with all things earthly."—*Fors Fortuna* was, according to Varro *(de L. L.)* a deity among the Romans; "a certain day was styled by Servius Tullius the king, *dies Fortis Fortunæ*, because in the month of June he dedicated a temple to *Fors Fortuna* near the Tiber, outside the walls of Rome."—Consult also Ovid *(Fast.* vi. 773), who records besides, that honours were paid to *Fors Fortuna* on the viiith of the kalends of July. In later times the Romans erected another temple to this goddess in the gardens, which Julius Cæsar bequeathed to the people. Plutarch, who relates the circumstance *(de Fort. Rom.* p. 319, A.) describes her in these words—"*Fortuna*, whom they call *Fors*, that is to say, powerful, over-ruling, masculine, and possessing as it were a force which prevails over all things." And the same author had just before said, that *Fortuna* had been adopted by the Romans "as a kind of cognomen of *Fortitudo* (ἀνδρεια)," as though *fortuna* were to be derived from *fortis.*—It was the prevailing belief of the ancients, that all things were under the direction and control of Fortune. And hence Plautus called her *hera*, or mistress (in *Mercatore)*; and Ennius, as quoted by Cicero *(de Officiis,* i. 12), says—"Whether he would prefer you or me (*i. e.* Fortune) to reign as mistress *(hera)*." There is a remarkable passage of Pliny, illustrative of this subject *(Hist. Nat.* ii. p. 73)—"Throughout the world, and in all places, and at all hours, Fortune alone is invoked by the voices of all mankind; her name alone is heard; she alone bears the blame; she only is convicted as the culprit; she, the sole object of men's thoughts, praises, and abuse, yet still of their universal homage; considered by all to be mutable, and even blind; roving, inconstant, unstable, changeable, and the friend of the unworthy. To her are referred all events, and she it is who fills both pages in the life of mortals."—No wonder then that Momus should complain, in Lucian *(Concil. Deorum),* that no one is any longer inclined to offer sacrifices to the gods, from the conviction, that tho' endless hecatombs smoked upon their altars, it would still be Fortune that would execute the decrees of Fate. In Horace (b. i. *Carm.* 35), we have a striking picture of her power:—

> "Te semper anteit sæva Necessitas,
> "Clavos trabales et cuneos manu
> "Gestans ahenâ: nec severus
> "Uncus abest, liquidumque plumbum."

With solemn pace and firm, in awful state,
Before thee stalks inexorable Fate,
And grasps empaling nails, and wedges dread,
The hook tormentous, and the melted lead.
　　　　　　　　　　　　FRANCIS.

What may have been the intention in introducing *Fors Fortuna* on the present coin ,(adds Eckhel) it is not easy to discern. A wheel is seen at her feet, to indicate that Fortune is *volubilis;* a characteristic also elegantly described by Horace (iii. *Carm.* 29), in the well-known

passage, beginning—"Fortuna sævo læta ne-
gotio," &c.

Tomyris, Queen of the Massagetæ (Scythia),
having learnt by experience the nature of Fortune, thus addresses Cyrus, when indulging his
dream of happiness—"Above all things learn
this truth, that there is a cycle of human affairs,
which in its revolution permits not the same
individuals to be always happy." (Herodotus,
i. c. 207). The *wheel* was a symbol of *Nemesis*,
who had many attributes in common with Fortune. Terence constantly alludes to *Fors Fortuna*, when matters have turned out prosperously.—(viii. 38 and 39).

FORTVNAE MANENTI. To abiding For-
tune—is the epigraph of a silver and brass coin
of Commodus, of which the type is a woman
seated, with a cornucopiæ in her left hand, and
holding with her right a horse by the bridle.

This shews that Commodus paid his vows to
Fortune under the surname of *Manens;* a superstition of which, however, there are other and
abundant instances to be found amongst Roman
writers. *Fortuna manens* is praised by Horace
(L. iii. Ode 29), as opposed to *Fortuna mobilis.*
But the reason why the goddess, as in this coin,
should be holding in the horse, seems obscure.
Perhaps it was because Fortune, who is here
called *manens*, might have been the same as
Fortuna *equestris*, to whom Fulvius Flaccus,
after having by the strength of his cavalry forces
defeated the Celtiberians, vowed to erect a temple, which Tacitus alludes to as standing near
Antium.—See Eckhel, vii. 15.

FORTVNAE MVLIEBRI. (To womanly
Fortune).—A female figure seated, with a rudder in her right hand, and a cornucopiæ in her
left. Gold and silver of Faustina the younger.
Engraved in Kolb. *Traité Elémentaire.*

As *Fortuna virilis* was an object of adoration
at Rome, and that as early as the times of Servius Tullius, so the statue of *Fortuna muliebris*
was, with her temple, consecrated at the time,
when (as the legend relates) the entreaties of
his mother deterred Coriolanus from destroying
the city. To this deity reference is made in
the following passage of Festus:—"Also, the
statue of *Fortuna Muliebris*, at the fourth mile-
stone of the Via Latina, is forbidden to be
touched *(nefas erat attingi)* save by her who
had been but once married." Faustina the
younger (observes Vaillant, p. 175), owed a great
debt to that divinity, as she was the daughter

of an emperor—indeed the eldest daughter—
and was married to an emperor.

FORTVNA OPSEQVENS (*sic.*) COS. IIII.
S. C.—A woman standing, with a patera, or a
rudder, in the right hand, and a cornucopiæ in
the left. Second brass of Antoninus Pius.—
Engraved in the *Cabinet de Christine.*

This reverse first appears on the coinage of
A. U. C. 911 (A. D. 158), though destined to be
frequently employed during Antonine's twenty-
second investiture with the tribunician power, in
both gold and silver. A singular change, from
one consonant to another of similar sound, is
exemplified in this instance of OPSEQVENS.—
But on all the specimens which came under
Eckhel's notice, it is inscribed exactly as above
given; whereas, according to the usual method
of spelling, it should have been OBSEQVENS.—
(See the philological remarks on this feature
of the coin, offered by the author of *Doctrina*, vii. 24).--According to Victor, there
were at Rome *two* temples of *Fortuna Obsequens*, one of which is conjectured by Vaillant
to have been restored by Antonine. This *Fortuna* was acknowledged at Rome in the days of
Plautus ; for the slave Leonida (Plaut. Asin. A.
iii. sc. 3), when asked by what deity's name
she would prefer to be addressed, replies, by that
of *Fortuna Obsequens.*

On another coin of the same emperor, with
FORTVNA OBSEQVENS for its epigraph, Fortune
places her rudder on the prow of a ship. " This
denotes, says Patin, that the goddess had shewn
herself condescending *(obsequentem)* in all things
to the emperor : the rudder and stern of a galley appear to signify the achievement of great
victories, and the happy return of the legions."

FORTVNA REDVX.—Fortune that brings
back [the Emperor in safety].

FORT*una* RED*ux* CAES. AVG. S. P. Q. R.
—A silver and a gold coin of Augustus, struck
A. U. C. 735 (B. C. 19), bear the foregoing
inscribed on an altar ; and it was frequently
adopted by his successors, as if emperors brought
with them the *Fortune* of the city, of the province, or of the world.—Augustus, when many
and various honours were decreed to him in his
absence, " would accept nothing except permission to consecrate an altar to *Fortuna Redux*,
and that the day of his return should be included amongst the holidays, and called *Augustalia.*" This event took place in the year above
mentioned, and the numismatic monument cor-
roborating the historian (Dion), is fully illustrated by the calendar, which records that the
emperor EX. TRANS-MARIN. PROVINC. VRBEM.
INTRAVIT. ARAQ. FORT. REDVCI. CONSTIT.

FORT. RED. in others, FORTVNAE RE-
DVCI COS. III. S. C.—Fortune seated, veiled
and robed, holding in the right hand a rudder,
which rests on a globe, in the left a cornucopiæ.
First brass of Hadrian.

The Romans were accustomed to render
thanks, and perform sacrifices, to *Fortuna Redux*, whilst celebrating the return of the reigning prince from his visit to distant provinces.—
This is shewn on coins, beginning as above

stated, with Augustus, and occurring afterwards under Vespasian, Trajan, Hadrian, Antoninus Pius, M. Aurelius, L. Verus, Commodus, &c.

Fortune was said to distribute wealth by her cornucopiæ, and to wield by her rudder the government of human affairs.

Fortune seated, as in the above engraving, was meant to denote that the fortune of the emperor was firm and stable; whereas she is almost always depicted as upright and moving on. All these are equally appropriate to Hadrian's return after frequent absences abroad, and to the general strength and security of his government at home.

FORTVNAE REDVCI.—This epigraph appears on small brass coins, with the titles of CAESarum Nostrorum, common alike to Diocletian and his colleague Maximianus Herculeus.

The goddess stands with a wheel at her feet. On this particular Eckhel remarks that, "the Rota, which was an attribute of Nemesis, should here be appropriated to Fortune, will surprise no one who knows that the two goddesses partook of almost the same nature."—(viii. p. 8).

FORTVNA—SPES.—Fortune and Hope; on a gold and a brass coin of Hadrian, engraved after the adoption of L. Ælius, and struck by order of the Senate to designate the Fortune and the Hope which Hadrian anticipated and entertained from that adoption; for the personification of Fortune occurs as often on the coins of the Augusti, as that of Hope does on those of the Cæsars.—Vaillant, Impp. Rom. T. ii. p. 143.

FORUM. Market, public place.—In ancient times there was no city or town so small, but it had its public place, where the inhabitants, together with the population of the neighbouring country, might assemble. Those of the Romans, distinguished by the appellation of Forum, whether at Rome, or in the other capitals of Italy, were of an oblong square in form, of which the width was equal to two-thirds of the length. There were at Rome seventeen of these public places or markets, fourteen of which were appropriated to the purposes of trade in provisions and other merchandise. These were called fora venalia. The others, where assemblies of the people were held, and where justice was administered, were named fora civilia and judiciaria. Among the most noted were those marked by the epithets of Romanum, Julium, Augustum. The first of these was the grandest and the most celebrated, now the Campo Vaccino: it occupied the space between the Capi-

toline Mount and Mount Palatine, surrounded by porticoes (basilicæ), and the shops of money changers (argentariæ), and being the most ancient, was sometimes called forum vetus or Latinum, or simply forum.—Julius Cæsar built that which bears his name. And the increase of inhabitants still requiring more accommodation of this kind, Augustus built a third. Several succeeding emperors established new fora at Rome; such as Vespasian and Domitian, whose work, though only finished by Nerva, was called forum Nervæ. Lastly, Trajan and Antoninus Pius equally contributed to the embellishment and convenience of the great metropolis by similar constructions.—Pitiscus—Millin.

FORVM TRAIANi. S. P. Q. R. OPTIMO PRINCIPI. S. C. View of one of the entrances of the celebrated Forum of Trajan. The summit of the edifice is occupied by a triumphal car, to which four horses are harnessed, and in which the figure of the emperor may be distinguished. To the right and left of the quadriga are trophies and statues.—Obv. IMPeratori TRAIANO AVGusto GERmanico DACico Pontifici Maximo TRibunitiæ Potestatis COnsuli VI. Patri Patriæ. (To the Emperor Trajan, Augustus, the German, the Dacian, Sovereign Pontiff; [invested] with the tribunitian power, consul for the sixth time, father of the country). —First brass.

The Forum of Trajan, built by command of that emperor, and so called by himself, was situated in the 8th district of the city, as P. Victor testifies. Dion names as its architect Apollodorus of Damascus, the same who constructed the wonderful bridge over the Danube.

It was to find a level and a suitable situation for this renowned Forum, that Trajan ordered the Mons Quirinalis to be reduced in height exactly so many feet as the spiral column numbers. This fact has been expressly stated by Dion, and is confirmed by the inscription on the pillar itself. (See COLUMNA, pp. 236–237).—That it was embellished, in every part, with statues of men and horses, and with military ensigns, is shewn not only by the admirably executed coin (from a finely preserved specimen of which the above cut has been engraved), but has also been recorded in history by Pausanias and Aulus Gellius; the latter of whom adds, that there was inscribed on its walls EX. MANVBIEIS (sic.) that is, out of the spoils; namely, those which were taken in the Dacian campaigns. Ammianus Marcellinus speaks of "its construction" as "marvellous from the concurrence of the deities themselves" *(etiam numinum assensione mirabilem).* And he states "its gigantic proportions to have been such as surpassed description, and could never again be produced by the agency of man." (L. xiv.)—Among other pieces of sculpture with which it was decorated, the same writer mentions the statue of Trajan:—"the very one (observes Eckhel) which, in my opinion, appears on his coins struck during his sixth consulate." But the splendour of this edifice has been alluded to, at a much later date, by Cassiodorus, where he says—*Trajani forum vel sub assiduitate videre miraculum est.* Nay, even at the close of the eighth century of the Christian æra, its remains were still so remarkable, that Pope Gregory the Great, passing that way, was seized with such admiration for the genius of the prince who had raised so magnificent a monument, that he had the hardihood to supplicate the Supreme Being for Trajan's exemption from the eternal pains of hell; a prayer which, as the story goes, was granted; though it is matter of astonishment, how Paul the deacon (in *Vitâ S. Greg. M.*) could have countenanced and published such a fable.—*D. N. Vet.* vi. 432.

The excavations, executed by order of the French government in 1812, resulted in discovering the traces of divers edifices which formerly ornamented the Forum, and afforded to an able architect, Antonio di Romanis, the opportunity of laying out a plan of the Forum. This plan is given in the 3rd edition of Nardini's *Roma Antica,* published at Rome, in 1818, with notes and additions by Antonio Nebby, member of the Roman Academy of Archæology.—Lenormant, *Iconographie Romaine,* p. 50.

The Forum contained within its spacious enclosure, besides the edifice represented in the gold as well as brass mint of Trajan, other architectural objects of great elegance of design, and richness of ornament. On one side was a temple; on the other, the Basilica Ulpia (see p. 175), in which stood an equestrian statue of Trajan, in bronze; also near it a library. And in the centre rose the beautiful pillar, which exists in good preservation to this day.

In giving an engraving of the first brass coin, which represents a temple with lateral porticoes (and two figures sacrificing at an altar before the *façade),* M. Ch. Lenormant, in his *Iconographie,* says—"This *is the temple of Trajan.* It was thought that Trajan had caused it to be erected in honour of some divinity; and that it was Hadrian who, after having deified his adoptive father, consecrated this temple to him. It is more probable, and it is what the legends of two medals give us to understand, that the temple in question (see an engraving of it, p. 354 of this dictionary), was dedicated to Trajan during his life-time, by a Senatus Consultum."

FRANCIA—GAVDIVM ROMANORVM.— A trophy, near which is a woman, in the attitude of grief, seated on the ground.—On the obverse, CONSTANTINVS P. F. AVG. Laurelled head of Constantine the Great. Gold.— Engraved from a specimen in British Museum.

Respecting the Franci and the Alamanni, so frequently and on various occasions vanquished by Constantine, the ecclesiastical and secular historians of the period furnish abundant information, as do also the authors of the panegyrics. It agreeably tickles the ear of a people to hear of their enemies' defeat, and therefore the expression *Gaudium Romanorum* was no inappropriate synonyme for the Alamanni and Franci, in the estimation of a people so inveterately attached as the Romans were to the cruel spectacles of the circus. For Constantine, according to Eutropius (X.) "after the slaughter of the Franci and Alamanni, took their kings and exposed them to the fury of wild beasts, by way of public shews of more than ordinary magnificence." And from that time the *Ludi Franci* took their commencement, which are noticed in the calendar of Philocalus, which Lambecius has published from the imperial library.—Eckhel, viii. 84.

FRANCIA, on other coins ALAMANNIA GAVDIVM ROMANORVM. The type same as on the above coin. Gold of Crispus.—(Banduri—Pellerin, *Mel.* i. p. 168).

The author of *Doctrina* says—"From this coin we clearly perceive, that the exploits of the father are recorded on the mintage of the son." But this surely is not very extraordinary, since it was Crispus who gained more than one of the victories alluded to in the foregoing legend, acting in his quality of Cæsar, and as general in command of an expeditionary army, under his father, against these two nations, whose united revolt from the Roman yoke, he effectually suppressed in A. D. 320.

Francia.—The country thus named was Francia Orientalis, lying between the Maine and the Rhine, antecedently forming part of Germania. *Alamannia* was a region chiefly lying between the Danube and the Atmuhl, one of the northern tributaries of the Danube. At present all that was called Alamannia is included in Germany.

Franci.—The people so named in Constantine's time are not to be confounded with the Gauls. And according to Spartianus and Victor, the *Alamanni* were a distinct nation from the Franks and Germans.—See ALAMANNIA DEVICTA, p. 32.

FRV. *Frumentum.*—See AD FRV. EMV. p. 5.

FRVG. *Fruges.*—See A. POP. FRVG. AC. p. 68.

FRVGIF. *Frugiferæ.*—CERERI FRVGIFeræ. (To the fruit-bearing Ceres). See p. 196.

FRUMENTARIAE LARGITIONES.–Grants of Corn to the Plebs, instituted by Nerva.—

See LARGITIO.——See also PLEBEI VRBANAE FRVMENTO CONSTITVTO.

FUFIA gens, plebeian, but of consular rank. It took its surname from the town of Cales, in Campania Felix, whence *Kalenus* is derived.——The coins of this family consist of only one type, serrated denarii, and rare. The following is a description of it :—

KALENI. Two conjoined youthful heads, the former laureated, the latter galeated. Before the one VIRT. behind the other IIO.

Rev.—CORDI. Two female figures, one holding a cornucopiæ, and having a caduceus and ITAL. behind her ; the other paludated, and holding a sceptre, with right foot on a globe, behind which is inscribed RO.

Respecting the heads of *Honos* and *Virtus* a notice of the Mucia gens may be referred to.—The type on the reverse, in which Italy and Rome stand joining hands, is regarded by the learned as allusive to the restoration of peace and amity between the Romans and the people of the different Italian states, when at length those rights of citizenship were conceded to the latter, which by a general revolt and resort to arms, they had sought to acquire.—Barthelemy refers this coin to the treaty entered into by Sulla, with the nations of Italy, but only as among other conjectures.

Eckhel (v. 220), considers it difficult to divine, with what magistracy the Lucius Fufius Calenus referred to on this denarius was invested, and who was the Mucius Cordus with whom this reverse unites him in colleagueship.—Riccio (p. 94), states, that the first named was moneyer of the republic about 664 (B. C. 90) ; and according to Dion, the same person was pretor in conjunction with Mucius Cordus.——Cavedoni concurs in the opinion that, on this medal, in highly expressive characters, is represented the famous act of reconciliation accomplished between Rome and Italy, after the murderous social wars. He adds, that the remembrance here perpetuated ·of that event, must have been an especial subject of pride to Mucius Cordus ; because Italy pacified shewed his attachment (*attinenza*) to the side of Papius Mutilus, first general of the Romans in the Italian war. On this denarius we see Rome belligerent and Italy fertile, as distinguished by their respective attributes, reciprocally offer right hands to each other. And, because such reconciliation had been effected, not by force of arms but, through the virtue and honour of Italy, of which Rome was the capital, so we see here the heads of these two divinities, who had each their temple, but so united together, that no one could enter that of Honour, without first passing through that of Virtue.—See *Monete delle Famiglie*, &c. p. 94.

FULMEN. *A thunder-bolt.*—Lightning, the weapon of Jove, forged by Vulcan, is commonly delineated on ancient sculptures, paintings, and coins, as cloven into three, and sometimes more, points or forks, like the subjoined figure :—

" Virgil (observes Addison) insists on the number *three* in its description, and seems to hint at the wings we see on it. He has worked up such a noise and terror in the composition of his Thunder-bolt, as cannot be expressed by a pencil or graving tool" :—

Tres imbris torti radios, tres nubis aquosæ
Addiderant, rutili tres ignis, et Alitis Austri.
Fulgores nunc terrificos sonitumque metumque
Miscebant operi, flammisque sequacibus iras.
                 Æneid, lib. 8.

Three rays of writhen rain, of fire three more,
Of winged southern winds, and cloudy store
As many parts, the dreadful mixture frame,
And fears are added, and avenging flame.
                 DRYDEN.

Amongst other examples of the *fulmen* appearing on Roman coins, are the following :—Vulcan is seen forging it in the presence of the goddess Minerva, on a brass medallion of Antoninus Pius.—First brass coins, struck under Tiberius, to the memory of Augustus, bearing for obverse legend DIVVS AVGVSTVS and DIVVS AVGVSTVS PATER, typify his portrait with a thunderbolt before it, as if he were become, through his apotheosis, *Jupiter Latii*, and, invested with the fulminating power, reigned in heaven with the king of gods and men. And as Jupiter is represented bearing the thunder-bolt, so the figure of Augustus, with radiated head, and holding the *fulmen*, appears on a brass medallion of Tiberius, minted by the *municipium* of Turiaso, *now* Tarazona, Spain, (engraved in Vaillant, *Sel. Num. Descamps*).—On a coin of another Hispanian colony, viz. Cæsar-Augusta (*Zaragoza*), struck in honour of Augustus, during his life-time, is a winged thunderbolt, similar to that on the above engraving. One of the earliest examples of a Roman coin with an eagle standing on the *fulmen*, is to be seen on a denarius of M. Antonius (see p. 52 of this dictionary). The same symbol appears frequently on coins of Augustus, restored by Titus and by Domitian, either isolatedly, or with an eagle standing on it. On a large brass, dedicated to Caligula by the Spanish colony of Cæsar-Augusta (C. C. A.) the Roman eagle is placed on a thunder-bolt between two standards. The same type occurs on coins COL. A. A. PATR*ensis*, struck under Claudius and under Nero.—There is a large brass of Galba, on which Rome stands holding transversely the legionary standard, which is distinguished by an eagle, with the *fulmen* in his talons *(Morell. Thesaur. Impp.* TAB. V.) The FIDES EXERCITVVM of Vitellius has the eagle and the thunder-bolt for its accompanying type.—Vespasian's CONCORDIA EXERCITVVM exhibits also the thunder-bolt beneath the claws of the legionary eagle.—On silver of Vespasian, and on gold and silver of Titus, appears a thunder-bolt, placed horizontally on a throne (see wood-cut below).—Although peculiarly assigned to Jove, there are instances of this attribute being appropriated to another divinity, viz. Jove's daughter.—On silver and middle brass of Titus, and more frequently of Domitian, Minerva stands holding the *hasta* in her left hand, and the *fulmen* in her right.—A large brass of Domitian exhibits the sedent image of IVPPITER CVSTOS, with the thunder-bolt and spear. *(Morell. Impp.* TAB. xiv.)—Another large brass of Domitian represents the emperor *himself* holding Jove's thunder in his right hand, and the *hasta* of divinity in his left, crowned by Victory from behind. *(Morell.* TAB. XV. No. 24).—IVPPITER CONSERVATOR. Eagle with expanded wings, standing on the *fulmen.* Silver and middle brass of Domitian. *(Ibid,* TAB. vi. No. 14).—PRINCEPS IVVENTVTIS. Thunder-bolt surmounted by an eagle. *(Ibid.* TAB. xvii. No. 14).—Before quitting the examples furnished from the Flavian mintages, a specimen of Vespasian's silver is subjoined:—

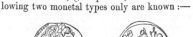

Rev.–TR. P. IX, IMP. XV. COS. VIII. P. P. The *fulmen* placed on a throne (viz. that of Jupiter). The lightning was regarded as symbolical of warlike power (Wilde)—a power also conjoined (according to Beger) with public utility, as indicated on a denarius of the Fabia gens. (See p. 371 of this volume). In the CONSERVATORI PATRIS PATRIAE, brass medallion of Trajan, we see the figure of Jupiter holding his protecting hand, armed with a thunder-bolt, over the head of the emperor, standing at his feet.—A similar type is described by Mionnet, from a large brass of Hadrian.—A two-fold representation of this tutelary object of imperial invocation is finely displayed on a brass medallion of L. Verus, in which he and M. Aurelius stand beneath the towering figure of "the Thunderer."—On a gold coin of Antoninus Pius, the image of Jupiter is seated, with the *fulmen* and *hasta*; the legend IMPERATOR II. (Spanheim, *Pr.* i. 429).—The lightning was emblematical of Divine Providence, as is clearly shewn on those coins which represent the *fulmen,* conjoined to the legend PROVIDENTIA DEORVM, to be seen on gold, silver, and large brass of Antoninus. (See above). —Coins struck under Caracalla, and also under Maximianus, respectively bear for their type of

reverse a lion, with radiated head, carrying a thunder-bolt in its mouth.—On a brass medallion of Diocletianus, Jupiter seated holds the *fulmen* and *hasta,* and an eagle stands at his feet.—For a finely designed type of JUPITER PROPUGNATOR, brandishing the *fulmen,* see Alexander Severus, p. 33 of this dictionary.

Augustus, when in Spain, narrowly escaped being killed by lightning, and held a thunderstorm in great dread ever afterwards.—See IOVIS TON(ANTIS).

FULVIA gens, plebeian but consular.——A family distinguished for the high offices occupied, and the talents displayed, by several of its members. It has only the two following coins of Roman die :—

1. ROMA. Galeated head of Rome; before it X.—*Rev.*—CN. FOVL. Below M. CAL. Victory, naked to the waist, guiding a biga at speed.

2. M. CALID. Q. MET. CN. FVL. Same type as the preceding.

It is not known who were the authors of these denarii.

FUNDANIA, gens plebeia, of which the following two monetal types only are known :—

1. Bearded and laureated head of Jupiter.— *Rev.*—C. FVNDA. Victory holding a palm branch, and crowning a trophy, supported on the shoulders of a kneeling captive. *Quinarius.*

In reference to coin No. 1, Eckhel says "Here again the anticipation of historical interest, raised by the nature of the above type, and which, if found on an imperial coin, would scarcely fail to be realised, is in this case of a family *quinarius,* disappointed. It is on no well authenticated grounds that antiquaries make out this Fundanius to have been a *quæstor* of Scipio's in the Numantine war, and that they associate the types of Victory and the trophy with the capture of that renowned Spanish city Numantia, after its twenty years of resistance to the Roman power." (v. 221.)

2. Galeated head of Rome.—*Rev.*—C. FVNDAN. on the exergue. Above is Q. (interpreted *quæstor*). A triumphal figure with sceptre, or small wand, in his hand, stands in a slow quadriga, guided by a naked child, who is seated on one of the horses, and carries a branch of laurel.

Cavedoni and Borghesi, cited by Riccio, think that the little figure which conducts the quadriga, represented on this denarius, was meant for the *filius prætextatus,* or son of some patrician triumpher, *insidens funali equo* (sitting on the horse next to that yoked to the pole of the car) to whom it would well belong to bear the branch of laurel—that this coin recalls to remembrance the triumph of Caius Marius for his victories over the Cimbri, in 653 (B. C. 101)—that the boy on the horse would therefore be the young C. Marius—that lastly, the moneyer in this case, would be Caius Fundanius, father of the father-in-law of the most learned Varro, recorded by Tully (ad Q. Fr. lib. i. ep. 2, § 3).

[This is all very clever, and gives an historical interest to the type far more attractive than a merely allegorical one could impart, but, after what Eckhel, coinciding with Passeri, says of such figures of children, it seems best to regard the infant cavalier on the above reverse, as one of those vague and fanciful creations of Roman superstition called a *winged genius*.—See *Fonteia*, p. 393, cut No. 3].

The denarius of this family having been found amongst the deposit (nel ripostiglio) of Fiesole, it positively results, that it was struck before 667 (B. C. 87).—Riccio, p. 95).

FUNDATOR PACIS. (The founder or establisher of peace).—This magnificent title, accompanying the type of the emperor standing, togated and veiled, with an olive branch in his right hand, appears on the reverse of a coin of Sept. Severus (both gold and silver), struck probably after his expedition against, and victory over, the Parthians. Not only his cruel son Caracalla, but even Julia Domna his wife was allowed, by the flattery of the same mint, which called her *Mater Castrorum*, to share the honour of founding peace (as usual, on the wilderness-making principle of Roman policy.)

FUNERAL PILE.—See CONSECRATIO—also ROGVS.

FURIA, gens patricia; amongst whose members was the great Camillus; but he is not noticed on its coins. It also included other great men, who filled high employments under the republic. This gens branched into families whose respective surnames, as they appear on denarii, are *Brocchus, Crassipes, Philus*, and *Purpureo*. It is uncertain whether the Brocchi were of patrician rank or not. Ten numismatic varieties are given in Morel, and eight in Riccio, who observes—" si hanno di essa molte monete, et la terra ne dà spesso delle nuove."

Gold very rare; silver common. Its brass are the *as* and its parts. The following are among its principal denarii:—

1. BROCCHI III. VIR. Bust of Ceres, crowned with corn-ears, behind the head is an ear of wheat, and before it a grain of barley.—*Rev.*— L. FVRI. CN. F. A curule chair between two fasces, with axes.

The triumvir, L. Furius Brocchus, son of Cerus, must have been moneyer about the year 640 (B. C. 114). The *sella curulis* with the fasces, and the head of Ceres, doubtless allude to some glory of the Furia gens, and perhaps to the first pretor of Rome, A. U. C. 388 (B.C. 366), and who in that age of the republic was *collega consulibus, atque iisdem auspiciis creatus ;* but it is more reasonable to regard the head of Ceres, as referable to some distinguished curule edileship in this family, than to the achievements of the first pretor ; the chair with the axed-fasces still more strongly points to the dictatorship of M. Furius Camillus.

These elegant denarii, through the discovery of monetal deposits, are shewn to belong to a time anterior to 686 (B. C. 68). We here see accents employed in the abbreviation of words, and also an example of refinement in pronunciation ; this very word FVRI being used instead of FOVRI.—Riccio, 96-97.

2. AED. CVR. Head of a turreted woman ; behind it is a human foot.—*Rev.*—P. FOVRIVS, inscribed on the front of a curule chair.—On the exergue CRASSIPES.—See an engraving of this fine denarius in p. 12.

By the last word it is clear, that from the thickness of the foot this branch of the Furia gens derived its peculiar surname. P. Furius, of the thick foot *(Crassipes)*, curule edile, must have been contemporary with Fannius and Cretonius (plebeian ediles, see p. 12), and consequently magistrate in 709 (B. C. 45). By the head of Cybèle, and the chair of office, reference is made to the Megalesian games, celebrated with extraordinary pomp in the year above-named.—Riccio, p. 97.

3. M. FOVRI. L. F. Head of Janus bifrons, bearded and laureated.—*Rev.*—PHILI. ROMA. Rome, stolated and galeated, stands holding a sceptre and the hasta in the left hand, and crowning a trophy with the right.—Engraved in *Morell. Thesau. Fam.* TAB. Furia gens, No. iii.

M. Furius Philus, son of Lucius, is considered by Ursin, followed by Vaillant and Havercamp, to have been nephew of P. Furius Philus, consul, who together with Caius Flaminius, enjoyed the honours of the triumph for victories gained over the Ligurian Gauls, in 531 (B. c. 223), father of the pretor of 583 (B c. 171). In his monetal triumvirate, which occurred about the middle of the century afterwards, M. Furius, in honour of his family, was pleased to represent the triumph in question.—See further remarks by Riccio on this denarius.

4. Head of Rome, galeated, behind it X— *Rev.*—PVR*pureo*. Diana with the crescent on her forehead, in a biga at speed ; above is the *murex*, or purple-shell—allusive to the surname of *Purpureo* assumed by this branch of the Furia gens.

This coin is assigned by Eckhel to Lucius Furius Purpureo, who was pretor under the consul C. Aurelius Cotta, in 554 (B. C. 200).—Borghesi believes that the moneyer of the denarius above described was the Lucius Furius Purpureo, who in the year above-mentioned, whilst his father served as pretor in Gaul, was *legatus* of the consul P. Sulpicius Galba, in Ætolia, as is stated by Livy (l. 31, c. 29.)—See Riccio, p. 95-96.

G.

G.—Respecting this letter Rasche observes, that amongst the ancient Romans C filled the place of the later adopted G.

G.—Accordingly, in a very ancient inscription, LECIONES is found occurring for LE-GIONES.—On a coin of the Ogulnia gens OCVLNIVS is written for OGVLNIVS.

G. as an alphabetical mark of the die is observable on many family coins.

G. *Galerius.*—G. MAXIMIANVS. *Gal. Maximianus.*

G. *Germanica.*—VICTORIA G. M.— *Germanica Maxima*, on coins of Valerianus senior, and Gallienus.—Khell, Supplt. to Vaillant, p. 184.

G. A. *Gemella Accitana*, colony of Hispania Tarraconensis. (See p. 3.)

GG. is constantly used to signify the plural : for example, the word AVGG. is employed when speaking of two *Augusti*, as VIRTVS AVGG. in Carus and Numerianus.

GGG. in AVGGG. is a compendious mode of expressing *three* Augusti or Emperors, as VICTORIA AVGGG. in Arcadius, Honorius, Valentinian III. &c.

GABII, a city of Latium, nearly equi-distant between Rome and Præneste. Frequent mention is made of the *Gabini* in the history of Tarquinius Superbus, and his contests with the Volscians.

GABIN. *Gabinis.*—See FOEDVS. P. R. CVM. GABIN. (p. 392).

GADES (Bœticæ Hispaniæ) *municipium*, now Cadiz. The coins of this city consist of autonomes, and imperial municipals (with a single *silver* exception) in small and middle brass. The autonomes are with phœnician inscriptions, and for types bear heads of the Sun, and of Hercules, dolphins, tridents, and fishes. Father Florez gives one autonome with Latin legends, viz.—*Obv.*—MVN. inscribed in two lines and a corn-ear above.—*Rev.*—GADES and a fish.—No. 109 of Mionnet has for obverse type the head of Hercules covered with the lion's skin, and with the club near the neck. The legend of reverse is BALBVS PONT. and in the field are a *simpulum* and a *lituus.*

In reference to the antiquity of this city, Mr. Akerman observes, "Both Strabo and Stephanus call it Gadeira." Alluding to the autonomes, the same writer adds as follows : "The larger brass coins of Gades are extremely common, and attest its importance as a commercial city, before the subjugation of Spain by the Romans. They remain to this day remarkable evidences of the imperishable nature of a national coinage. * * * * Hercules was the chief deity in *Gades;* and Hannibal sacrificed to him previously to his expedition against the Romans.— Philostratus mentions the temple, but says it was of the Egyptian Hercules—Ηρακλέους Αιγυπ·

τιου."—See *Ancient Coins of Cities,* &c., p. 31, et seq. Plates iii. and iv.

The *imperial Latin* coins struck by this *municipium* are of Augustus, Caius and Lucius, Agrippa, and Nero. The reverse types consist of winged lightning ; pontifical instruments ; a four-columned temple within a crown of laurel ; the *simpulum;* and the *aplustre.* For the latter symbol, see MVNICIPII PARENS, and MVNICIP. GA. PATRONVS—see also HERCVLES GADITANVS.

GALBA *(Servius Sulpicius).*—According to Suetonius, this aged depository of short-lived imperial power was born on the 9th of the kalends of January, in the year 751 (A. D. 3.) He belonged to the ancient and renowned family of the Sulpicii, whose founder, on the father's side, if we may give credence to Galba himself, was Jupiter ; and on the mother's Pasiphae the wife of Minos ; and this account is confirmed by Silius Italicus. The mother of Galba was Mummia Achaica, great grand-daughter of the L. Mummius, who destroyed Corinth. (Sueton. c. 3.) When arrived at the fitting age for taking part in state affairs, he made his appearance in public ; and after a time was appointed governor of the Galliæ. Subsequently being removed to a similar position in Africa, he obtained no ordinary credit by his justice, and by the valour and discipline he displayed in a military capacity. Later still he received from Nero the jurisdiction of Hispania Tarraconensis, which he administered with fluctuating success. When urged by Vindex, governor of the Galliæ, to supplant Nero in the empire, he for some time repudiated the proposition, but at length consented, on hearing that Nero was plotting his destruction. (Sueton. c. 3). Being then saluted emperor by the acclamations of the army, he declared himself to be but the lieutenant (or deputy) of the Senate and People. Tidings having reached him that Vindex, after being defeated by the troops of Verginius Rufus, *legatus* in Germania, had put an end to his own existence, Galba had serious thoughts of embracing the same fate; but intelligence of Nero's death, and the Senate's unanimous declaration in his own favour, arriving shortly after, he accepted the title of Cæsar (Sueton. c. 11), and proceeded on his journey to present himself at Rome. The massacre, however, which he caused of certain soldiers of the fleet on his arrival at Ponte-Molle, augured ill for his reign.

Galba, then about 72 years of age, was of a

good heigth and advantageous figure. His forehead was wrinkled; his nose aquiline, and his head bald in front, although on many of his coins (especially those in large brass), that defect is more or less concealed. The employments through which he passed had given him much experience, and he appeared to be worthy of commanding Romans; but his harsh inexorable character, and the sordid avarice of his disposition, which displayed itself in endeavours by untimely parsimony to replenish an exhausted treasury; these, together with his neglect of public affairs, which he left to functionaries who committed infinite acts of injustice under his name, rendered him so much the more odious, as he had caused Nero's ministers to be put to death. The affections of the pretorian guard, and of the rest of the army, he utterly estranged by the refusal of a *donative*, to which they considered themselves entitled. The consequence of this was, that the army of Germania Superior took the lead in throwing off its allegiance. When this event was announced to the emperor, he imagined that he had incurred contempt, not by his faults, but on account of his advanced and childless age, and accordingly he adopted Piso Frugi Licinianus (Tacit. Hist. i. 18), a noble and distinguished young man, on the 10th of January, 822 (A.D. 69). But he marred the effect of a proceeding in itself laudable and acceptable to the people, by a fresh instance of his innate avarice. For when, on the introduction of his adopted son Piso, to the soldiery, he still omitted all mention of the donative, at a time which so peculiarly demanded it—Otho, chagrined at seeing another preferred to himself as the adopted son of Galba, availed himself of the recently excited feelings of the army, and took possession of the camp six days after the adoption. The general feeling being thus transferred to the new chief, Galba was deserted by his adherents, and together with Piso, was assassinated on the 15th of January of the same year.—See Eckhel, vi. 299—Beauvais, T. i. 148.

His style on coins is IMP. GALBA—IMP. SER. SVLP. GALBA CAES. AVG. TR. P.—SER. GALBA IMP. CAESAR AVG. *Pater Patriæ.*—The brass and silver (with some distinguished exceptions) are common; the gold are rare (restitutions by Trajan very rare); and notwithstanding his very brief reign, the whole exhibit several curious reverses.

For a specimen of his portraiture in silver, see OB. C. S.—*Obv.*-IMP. SER. GALBA AVG. Bare head of the emperor.

MINTAGES OF GALBA.

GOLD.—CONCORDIA PROVINCIARVM. (Valued by Mionnet at 72 fr.)—DIVA AVGVSTA. (Brought at the Thomas sale £3 9s.)—FORTVNA AVG. (Mt. 60 fr.)—HISPANIA. Female holding ears of corn. (Devonshire sale, £1 12s.)—IMP. Emperor on horseback. (Trattle sale, £2 2s.)—IMP. AVG. Female with ears of corn. (Brought £12 15s. at the Thomas sale).—Liberty standing. (Restored by Trajan. Valued by Mionnet at 200 fr.)—LIBERTAS RESTITVTA. (Mt. 50 fr.)

—PAX. AVG. (120 fr.)—ROMA RENASC. Military figure. (Thomas sale, £9 10s.)—ROMA VICTRIX. (Mt. 72 fr.)—SALVS GEN. HVMANI. (Thomas, £4 16s.)—TIBERIS. (Trattle, £2 16s.)—VICTORIA P. R. (Trattle, £1 16s.)—Victory writing on a buckler. (Mt. 80 fr.)

SILVER.—GALLIA—HISPANIA. (Mt. 30 fr.)—LIBERTAS RESTITVTA. (72 fr.)—REST. NVM. (72 fr.)—S. P. Q. R. OB. C. S. (Thomas, £4 1s.)—SER. SVL. GALBAE. Head of Spain. (20 fr.)

LARGE BRASS.—ADLOCVTIO. The emperor haranguing his soldiers. (Mt. 30 fr. See woodcut in p. 7.)—CONCORDIA. (Trattle sale, £7. 2s. 6d.)—EX. S. C. OB. CIVES SER. (£2 6s. at the Brumell sale).—HISPANIA CLVNIA. SVL. (Trattle, £2 2s.)—HONOS ET VIRTVS. (Campana sale, £1 9s.)—LIBERTAS PVBLICA. (Thomas sale, £1 6s.)—LIBERTAS RESTIT. (Mt. 30 fr.)—QVADRAGENS REMISSAE. Arch. (Devonshire sale, £2 2s.)—REMISSAE XXXX. (Mt. 60 fr.)—ROMAE RESTIT. (30 fr.)—SENATVS PIETATI AVGVSTI. (48 fr.)—ROMA. The city personified, seated on armour. (A highly preserved finely patinated specimen brought £7 7s. 6d. at the Campana sale).

GALEATVM CAPVT.—The galeated or helmed head of an emperor is not unfrequent from the time of Probus; and it is still more common on gold coins of the lower empire, especially when the emperor is represented in full panoply. The helmet is sometimes encircled with the laurel crown, or with rays.—*Doctrina*, viii. 361.

GALERIA VALERIA.—See VALERIA.

GALERUS, or *pileus*, a cap; the mark of Liberty. See LIBERTAS.—It is also the attribute of Mercury. See *Petasus.*

GALLA PLACIDIA.—See PLACIDIA.

GALLIA, a plebeian family, belonging to which are the following three coins in large and middle brass, all common:—

1. C. GALLVS C. F. LVPERCVS IIIVIR. A. A. A. F. F. (see p. 1) S. C.—*Rev.*—OB. CIVIS SERVATOS, within a crown of laurel, between two branches of the same.

2. Obverse uniform with the preceding.—*Rev.* AVGVSTVS TRIBVNIC. POTEST. in a laurel crown.

3. CAESAR AVGVSTVS TRIBVNIC. POTEST.—Bare head of Augustus.—*Rev.*—C. GALLVS LVPERCVS IIIVIR. A. A. A. F.F. In the field S. C.

Caius Gallus Lupercus was monetal triumvir under the government of Octavianus Augustus, not before 727 (B. C. 27), in which year the latter assumed the title of Cæsar. The crowns of laurel are those voted to the Emperor by the Senate and the Roman People; and the S. C. is allusive to the prerogative of the Senate to strike brass coins, whilst to the emperor belonged the privileges of the gold and silver mints.

GALLIA.—Gaul anciently comprised the territories which are now called France and Lombardy. The former, being beyond the mountains as regards Rome, had the name of *Gallia Transalpina*, and the latter *Cisalpina.*—Transalpine Gaul again was subdivided into three parts, namely, *Togata, Comata,* and *Braccata.* Togata, which lay on the side of Italy, was so called because its inhabitants had adopted the Roman toga. Comata derived its name from the large heads of hair in which its people were accustomed to luxuriate, and included all Trans-alpine Gaul, except the *Narbonensis*, that is to say, the whole extent of the country from the Alps to the ocean. Gallia Comata is that which Cæsar subdued, and which, submitting to the Romans, was divided into Aquitannica, Belgica, and Celtica. The third, Braccata, so termed from the trousers or breeches made of a shaggy frieze, or other very coarse material, which the male inhabitants of that district wore, was situate between Italy and Spain.-See TRES GALLIAE.

GALLIA.—A female head, before which are two ears of corn; behind are two small spears, and beneath is a small round shield.—*Obv.* SER. GALBA IMP. Galba on horseback, galloping. Silver of Galba.—Engraved in *Morell. Imp.* vol. iii. TAB. iii. No. 30.

The head personifies Gallia; and the corn-ears before her denote the abundance of that grain, which her fields produce. The arms represent those used by the Gauls, designating their warlike character, and their eminence in the military art. The equestrian figure of Galba seemingly bears reference to the statue which the Gauls had decreed to him. (Vaillant, *Impp.* ii. p. 71).—Gallia, owing to the instigations of Vindex, had the first and main share in procuring the empire for Galba; and even after the death of Vindex, it was amongst the foremost provinces which declared for him. Grateful for such zealous services, Galba rewarded the *Galli* with the rights of citizenship, and with exemption thenceforward from payment of tribute; and this is the reason for the occurrence of GALLIA as legend and type on his coins.

GALLIA—HISPANIA.—A male genius of Gallia, holding an inverted spear in the left hand, joins the right hand with that of a male genius of Hispania, in whose left hand is a round shield and an inverted spear.——*Obv.* IMP. GALBA.—Laureated head of the emperor. Silver of Galba.—Engraved in Akerman, vol. i. pl. v. No. 2.

On the above denarius we find mentioned in conjunction with each other, the two provinces which were so favourable to Galba's claims. And as in Gaul, under Julius Vindex, the revolt against Nero began, so it was in Spain that Galba was first saluted with the title of IMP*erator*. Indeed, according to Suetonius, almost all the cities of Spain and the three Gauls simultaneously gave in their adhesion to his government. It is to be regretted that the heads of Gallia and Hispania should have been represented, by the moneyers, with the self-same attributes, so that, but for the legend, either of them might be mistaken for the other.

For other denarii of Galba referring to events immediately concomitant with, and instrumental to, his accession to the empire, see HISPANIA.

GALLIENAE AVGVSTAE.—See VBIQVE PAX.

GALLIENVM AVG. P. R.   *Gallienum Augustum Populus Romanus* (*colit* understood).

The Roman people (*worships*) Gallienus the August.—This inscription appears on the obverse of a second brass of Gallienus, with the bust of that emperor laureated, and with spear and shield.—*Rev.*—OB CONSERVATIONEM SALVTIS. Hygeia standing.

GALLIENVM AVG. SENATVS (that is to say *veneratur*). The Senate (*adores*) the Emperor Gallienus.—Another second brass, with OB LIBERT*atem* REC*eptam*, and a woman standing with palm branch and spear.

"This and the foregoing coin (observes Eckhel) are remarkable for the heavy grandeur and the novel style (*molem et novam legem*) of their inscription. For the rest, the base and lying adulation, as well of the Senate as of the Roman people, must be glaringly obvious to any one."—vii. 408.

"The emperor's name in the *accusative case* on these coins (Mr. Akerman remarks) is curious. It had long been a practice with the degenerate Greeks."

GALLIENUS (*Publius Licinius*), the son of Valerianus, by that emperor's first wife, whose name is not recorded; but probably his mother's name was Galliena. Born in the year of Rome 971 (A. D. 218) he owed his own fortunes to his father, by whom, when, on the death of Trebonianus and of Æmilianus, he had obtained the sovereignty, Gallienus was chosen as his colleague in the empire. Victor asserts that he was created Cæsar by the Senate.—"On the truth of this statement, says Eckhel (vii. 389), I will not decide. At any rate, no coins have yet been discovered with the title of *Cæsar* only; but all pronounce him *Augustus*."

In the year of Rome 1006 (A. D. 253), his father Valerian, assumed the title of Augustus, and the Tribunicia Potestas, and nominated himself consul for the following year.—He made his son Gallienus *particeps imperii*.

1007 (A.D. 254).—Gallienus proceeded consul, in colleagueship with his father (Consul II). Æmilianus dying at Spoletum, Valerian and Gallienus were acknowledged as *Augusti*, and as consuls for the year.

1008 (A.D. 255).—Gallienus proceeded consul for the second, with his father consul for the third, time. Valerian, intent on his operations in the East, entrusted to Gallienus the European armies; and the conduct of the campaigns against the Franci, the Alamanni, and various other rebellious tribes.

1009 (A. D. 256).—It is probable that, in this

year, Gallienus was engaged in the war with the *Germani,* from which he derived his military honours.

1010 (A. D. 257).—Consul for the third time. His repeated victories in Germania obtained for him, as well as for his father, the surname of Germanicus.

1011 (A. D. 258).—Postumus invaded and took possession of the Gallic portion of the empire.

1012 (A. D. 259).—Postumus having got possession of Saloninus, and, to his own inexpiable dishonour, put him to death, Gallienus contented himself with placing his murdered son in the rank of the gods!

1013 (A. D. 260).—This year, it is believed, Valerian was made prisoner by the Persians.— Gallienus proceeded consul for the fourth time.

1014 (A. D. 261).—During the captivity of Valerian, several military governors in different provinces usurped the sovereign authority.— Amongst them was Ingenuus in Mœsia, who, however, was taken and decapitated by Gallienus. Also Regalianus in Illyricum; Macrianus and his sons in the East; and other pretenders of less importance.

Balista, prefect of the pretorians under Valerian, in conjunction with Odenathus, King of Palmyra, drove Sapor from Syria into Persia, and re-established, or at least sustained for a time, the Roman power in the East.

1015 (A. D. 262).—Gallienus, consul for the fifth time, celebrated a triumph over the Persians conquered by Odenathus. As one set of usurpers fell, others rose to assume the purple.

1016 (A. D. 263).—Returning to Rome, Gallienus fulfilled the *vota decennalia.* Trebellius relates that this emperor, having taken Byzantium, and in spite of his promise to the contrary, put its garrison to the sword, returned in all haste to Rome, as though he had accomplished a great and laudable work, and there celebrated the *decennalia.*

1017 (A. D. 264).—Gallienus, consul for the sixth time, invested Odenathus, for his victories over the Persians, with all the honours of an Augustus.

1018 (A. D. 265).—Valerianus junior, brother of Gallienus, proceeded consul, in colleagueship with Macro Lucullus Rufinianus.

1019 (A. D. 266).—Gallienus consul for the seventh time. To this year Tillemont refers the destructive invasion of Bithynia, and a large portion of Asia Minor, by the Scythians.

1020 (A. D. 267).—The Goths this year again laid waste Mæsia, and the Heruli ravaged Greece and Asia. Gallienus set out for Greece, to fight these barbarians.

1021 (A. D. 268).—Recalled into Italy by the sedition of Aureolus, who had declared himself emperor, and whilst besieging in Milan the new competitor, Gallienus was assassinated by conspirators, in the month of March, in the 50th year of his age. He had married Cornelia Salonina, by whom he had Saloninus.

Such, observes the judicious Eckhel— such was the end of Gallienus, an emperor, to whom historians have ascribed every vice imaginable, and whose proper vocation seemed to be, not the government of a State, but the indulgence of sloth and unbounded licentiousness; and this at a juncture when an empire divided among so many usurpers; the incursions of barbarian hordes from every side; the renewed ravages of the plague which commenced in the reign of Trebonianus—demanded a prince endowed with moral [he was not deficient in physical] courage, magnanimity, and decision. Of the cruelty and vindictiveness of his character, we may gather some notion from the epistle, in which he enjoins Celer Verianus to destroy the partizans of the usurper Ingenuus; 'mutilate them,' he says, 'kill and exterminate them; you understand my mind respecting them; make your own the rage of him who writes these orders with his own hand.' With such perverted feelings, it is no matter of surprise that to his other delinquencies he should have added the almost incredible impiety of looking on unmoved at the captivity and ignominious treatment of his father by the Persians; and that this was the only injury which remained unavenged by one, who in every other case behaved with implacable severity. There is, however, the best reason for supposing that he preferred his father's captivity to his freedom, inasmuch as Valerian's strict morals were a perpetual reproach to his own enormities. Consequently, it is not so much to be wondered at, that this unworthy prince was cut off at last by his own subjects, as that so long a time elapsed before a Hercules appeared to suppress such a monster.—*D. N. V.* vii. 394.

The brass coins of Gallienus are for the most part common; so are those in billon; gold and pure silver very rare. On these he is styled IMP. C. LICIN. GALLIENVS PIVS FELIX AVG. and sometimes GERMANICVS MAX.

Gallienus appears on some of his coins with Valerianus, Salonina, and Saloninus. Amongst the money struck by this emperor are to be noted the pieces which he caused to be restored, in honour of many of his predecessors, who had been placed, by consecration, in the rank of the gods, from Augustus down to Alexander Severus.

It deserves here to be remarked that from the reign of Sept. Severus to Gallienus the standard of the silver coinage was successively reduced. These pieces are customarily designated as being of silver, although that metal had progressively been alloyed into billon of a very low standard. From the age of Gallienus, silver money becoming more and more debased, and yet some coins of pure silver having occasionally been struck, the billon pieces are classed separately. To take the date from Claudius Gothicus, these coins were no better than copper washed with silver. Under Diocletian a coinage of fine silver was re-established.—See Hennin, *Manuel,* vol. ii. p. 432, *Nomenclature.*

MINTAGES OF GALLIENUS.

No pagan prince, perhaps, testified his devotion to so many divinities as Gallienus did on his coins. There are reverses in his mint which respectively exhibit the images of Jupiter, Neptune, Mars, Mercury, Diana, Minerva, the Sun, Vulcan, Bacchus, Victoria, Hercules, Deus Augustus, and above all the rest, Apollo, whom the coins of this emperor depicture in various attire. It would seem indeed that, amidst the surrounding perils and calamities of his time, from pestilence, from earthquakes, and from the slaughter of wars threatening him and the empire itself with destruction, Gallienus was accustomed to invoke almost all the *dii majores* for his *conservation.*

The following are among the rarest reverses:
GOLD MEDALLIONS.—CHORS. *(sic.)* TERTIA PRETORIA. Emperor standing in military habit, holding the hasta pura, in the midst of four military ensigns. (Valued by Mionnet at 300 francs).——FIDEI EQVITVM. (Small medallion, brought £3 9s. 0d. at the Brumell sale).—FIDES MILITVM. Woman and two ensigns. Double aureus. (Valued by Mionnet at 200 fr. Brought £14 at the Thomas sale).—IMP. VI. COS. V. Emperor on horseback, holding a lance, preceded by a soldier, and followed by a Victory that crowns him.—(Mt. 400 fr.)—VIRTVS GALLIENI AVGVSTI. Emperor, holding in each hand a labarum. (Mt. 200 fr.)

SILVER MEDALLIONS.—OB. CONSERVATOREM PATRIAE—OB. CONSERVATOREM SALVTIS—OB. REDDIT. LIBERT. (Mt. 72 fr. each).—MONETA AVG. (Mt. 100 fr. A specimen at the Campana sale brought £1 3s.)—PIETAS FALERI. (Mt. 300 fr.)—ADVENTVS AVGG. Three emperors on horseback, preceded by Victory, and followed by several soldiers. (Mt. 300 fr.)

GOLD.—ADVENTVS AVG.—*Obv.* Gallienus and Salonina. (Mt. 100 fr.)——CONCORDIA AVGG. (100 fr. Brought £8 15s. at the Trattle sale).

CONCORDIA EXERCIT.—DEO AVGVSTO—FELICITAS SAECVLI—FIDEI PRAET. (Mt. 100 fr. each).

FELICITAS AVGG. Half aureus. (Brumell sale, £1 13s.)—FIDES MILIT. (Brought at the Campana sale £3 3s.)—FORTVNA REDVX—IOVI VLTORI—PIETAS AVG.—ORIENS AVG.—LIBERTAS AVGG.—VBERITAS AVG.—and VENVS VICTRIX. (Mt. 48 fr. each).—IANO PATRI. (Mt. 120 fr.) INDVLGENT. AVG. Quinarius. (£2 9s. Thomas). —IOVI CONSERVA. (£5 7s. 6d. Trattle).— IOVIS STATOR. (£1 9s. Trattle).——LAETITIA AVGG. (£4 2s. Thomas).——LIB. AVG. T.— LIBERALITAS AVG.—MARTI PROPVGNATORI— and SECVRITAS ORBIS. (60 fr. each).—LIBERAL. AVG. (£1 9s. Trattle).—OB. LIBERTAT. REC. A half aureus. (Mt. 120 fr. Brought at the Thomas £2 5s.)—PAX. AVGG. Quinarius. (£1 5s. Trattle).—TR. P. VII. COS. IIII. The emperor and two rivers. (Mt. 150 fr. £1 10s. Trattle).—PROVIDENTIA AVGG. (72 fr.)—SECVRIT. PERPET. Lion within a crown. (100 fr.)— S. P. Q. R. Lion with eagle. (150 fr.)—TRIB. POT. Mars and Venus. (150 fr.)—VBIQVE PAX. —*Obv.* GALLIAENAE AVGVSTAE. (200 fr.)—VICTORIA AVG. Emperor crowned by Victory. Engraved in Akerman, ii. pl. ix. No. 5, p. 31. (£3 18s. Thomas sale).—VICTORIA GALL. AVG. (72 fr.)—VIRT. GALLIENI AVG. (Mt. 100 fr. £1

3s. Trattle).—VIRTVS AVG. (100 fr. A doubtful specimen brought £2 19s. at the Devonshire sale).—VOTIS DECENNALIBVS. (100 fr.)

BILLON.—ABVNDANTIA AVG. (Mt. 20 fr.)— INVICTVS. The Sun. (60 fr.)——LIBERALITAS AVG. (60 fr.)—SISCIA AVG. (20 fr.)

Amongst the restitutions under Gallienus in billon are—
Augustus.—IVNONI MARTIALI. (100 fr.)
Trajan.—VIA TRAIANA. (150 fr.)

BRASS MEDALLIONS.—ADVENTVS AVGG. Two emperors on horseback, Victory and a soldier.— ADLOCVTIO AVGG. Fine portrait and allocution. Engraved in *Iconographie,* pl. lii. (Mt. 72 fr). —SALONINA head of. (72 fr.)—FIDES EXERCITVS. (100 fr.)—VICTORIA GERMANICA. (50 fr.) —Gallienus and Salonina—LIBERALITAS AVGVSTORVM—ADVENTVS AVGG.—CONCORDIA AVGG. with reverse of Liberalitas. (150 fr. each.)— MONETA AVG. (72 fr.)—VICTORIA AVGVSTORVM. (100 fr.)

LARGE BRASS.—COHORT. PRAEF. PRINCIPI. SVO.—RESTITVTOR ORBIS—and S. P. Q. R. OPTIMO PRINCIPI, within a crown. (Mt. 24 fr. each).—ADVENTVS AVGG. Gallienus and Saloninus. (50 fr.)

GALLIENVS CVM. EXERC. SVO.——A cippus, or pedestal, with the legend IOVI VICTORI, on which is seated Jupiter, holding the thunder-bolt in his right hand, and spear in his left. Silver of Valerianus. Engraved in Banduri.

Valerianus, when himself intent on the affairs of the East, committed to Gallienus the charge of the western armies. The latter, therefore, on the occasion of any victory being gained (over the Germans, for example, who had made irruptions into Gaul), and which he was desirous of ascribing to the interposition of Jupiter, was accustomed, in gra'itude, to erect a statue to that god, under the epithet of *Victor,* the army also joining in the religious act.

The above serves, in a remarkable manner, to interpret another coin of Gallienus, bearing on its obverse the legend IMP. C. E. S. namely, IMP*erator* (Gallienus) *Cum Exercitu Suo,* as Banduri, confirming Hardouin, remarks. Thus by joining, on the coin of Valerian, the two legends of the head and the reverse, a perfect inscription is made :——Imperator (Gallienus) cum Exercitu suo Jovi Victori (*statuam ponit*).

GARCILIA, gens plebeia.—Count Borghesi treats this as a new family, and assigns to it the following types, supposed to have been struck about 670 (B. C. 84) :—

1. Head of Apollo Vejovis, beneath it is the *fulmen.*—*Rev.*—GAR. OGVL. VER. Jupiter in a quadriga. A very rare denarius.

2. Head of Janus, above it **|**.—*Rev.*-GAR. OGVL*nius* VER*gilius* or *Verginius.* A ship's prow. Semi-uncial brass. Rare.

The eminent Italian antiquary above named gives his reasons for attributing to one Garcilius the name of the first monetal triumvir, concealed in the monogram GAR. of these two coins, and rejects the reading *C*AR. under which Perizoni, and other numismatists, have ascribed it to the Carvilii (see p. 187 of this dictionary).

Riccio cites and adopts this transferred attribution, which accounts for the exclusion of CARVILIA gens from his *Monete delle Famiglie*, &c.

GAVDETE ROMANI.—Two Victories holding a tablet, on which is inscribed SIC XX. SIC XXX. that is, " *sic* ad annum imperii vicessimum *sic* ad tricessimum usque victorias suas contineat" *—even as* to the twentieth *so* also to the thirtieth year of the emperor's reign may he pursue his victories.

This small gold coin of Maximianus Herculius contains on its reverse a joyous acclamation (faustam acclamationem)—that is to say, the *Romans rejoiced* for vows acquitted XX. and again made XXX.—See Eckhel, viii. p. 18.

GAVDIVM POPVLI ROMANI.—This legend, which occurs only on gold and silver medallions of Constantius and Constans his brother, indicates a public rejoicing. It may be conjectured, that such coins as that on which this epigraph appears, were distributed among the people at the festive celebration of solemn vows, that all so advised might join in the general gladness.—(Morel, *rei numaria*, p. 80).

GAVDIVM ROMANORVM.—A paludated man, taller than the rest of the group, stands resting his right hand on the hasta, whilst a hand protruded from a cloud above him places a crown upon his head. On his left stands another man similarly attired, but of shorter stature, whom a victory by his side is in the act of crowning; and on his right a third male figure, of the same appearance, but shorter even than the last described, upon whose head a personification of Rome, standing beside him, is placing a crown. At the bottom, MCONS. Struck at Constantinople.

Obv.—FL. IVL. CONSTANTIVS. NOB. CAES. A laureated bust, holding in the right hand the hasta, and in the left a buckler, on which is represented the emperor on horseback, charging with levelled spear some suppliant barbarians, whilst he is crowned by a Victory flying towards him, and followed by a band of soldiers.

[The grand and interesting medallion, of which the above represents the reverse, formed one of a large deposit of Roman medallions in gold, several of them of unusual size, found with chains and other objects of antiquity in the same precious metal, in Hungary, during the year 1797.

M. Steinbüchel, in his valuable " NOTICE" of these and other gold medallions preserved in the Imperial Cabinet, has given what he vouches for as being " a faithful engraving," and of which Mr. Fairholt's cut is an equally faithful copy. Respecting monetal rarities, of such scarcely appreciable value, so suddenly brought to light, it appears to have been Eckhel's intention at the time to have contributed a dissertation, worthy of his zeal, erudition, and judgment; but his premature death in 1798, left him time only to sketch a few notes, which remained in manuscript until M. Steinbüchel, his friend and successor in the directorship of the Vienna Museum, published them in 1826.

In elucidation of this splendid monument, the subjoined extract from the manuscript in question will scarcely fail to prove acceptable to the numismatic student] :—

After having, with characteristic minuteness of accuracy, described the piece, our illustrious author says—" It stands pre-eminent among the most remarkable hitherto discovered, not only on account of its great weight [nearly 74 Hungarian ducats —*aurei*] but also for the design as well as for the workmanship of the types, its obverse and reverse exhibiting the highest degree of elegance and finish, of which the state of the arts at that period admitted. The head is that of Constantius II. second of the three sons of Constantine the Great; and as he is here styled Cæsar only, not having yet attained the title of Augustus, this coin must have been struck between A. D. 323 and 337; for in the former year he received the appellation of Cæsar, and in the latter, in consequence of his father's death, that of Augustus. As, however, the countenance of Constantius on the obverse displays a fulness and maturity of contour, I am inclined to consider that the coin before us was struck a very short time before the death of Constantine the Great, when he (Constantius) was at least in the twentieth year of his age. The supposition is corroborated by the military garb in which he is depicted, for it was at that very time that his father entrusted to him the conduct of the war in Persia. To which may be added, that the presence of the abbreviation CONS. (sure sign of the mintage of Constantinople) sufficiently proves, that this coin could not have been struck before A. D. 330, since we know that it was not till that year that the city was dedicated, and received from its founder the name of Constantinople."

With regard to the reverse, adds Eckhel, "I do not hesitate to pronounce that the central and tallest figure of the group is Constantine the father, whose venerable age and piety are thus early acknowledged by a heaven-sent crown; that the figure on his left is the eldest son, Constantine; and that on his right, the youngest, Constans. Constantius, already pourtrayed on the obverse, does not appear in this group. Portraits of the reigning family, similarly distributed between the two faces of a medal have already occurred to our notice on coins of Septimius Severus, which I have brought forward in my *Doctrina*, under the date 954 (A. D. 201). Constantine the brother is represented as crowned by a Victory, because at the exact time when I imagine this coin to have been struck, he was in reality a conqueror, as is testified by his coin inscribed, VICTORIA CONSTANTINI CAES. and this type is also common on the coinages of preceding emperors. * * * The galeated figure standing by the side of Constans, being female in dress, must be that of Rome, rendering the same complimentary office to Constans, which Victory does to Constantine jun. or, if you will, a figure of *Virtus* (Force), which frequently appears on ancient coins in a shape not very dissimilar. Observe, that thus early the gradations of rank and dignity in the imperial family, are denoted by a greater or lesser bodily stature, a circumstance constantly to be remarked on Byzantine coins of later date."

GAVDIVM ROMANORVM, with FRANC. ET ALAM. *(Francia et Alamannia).*—A gold coin of Constantine the Great, struck on the occasion of his having defeated those two nations, and brought them into subjection to the Roman arms.—See ALAMANNIA, p. 32, and FRANCIA, p. 398.

GAVDIVM ROMANORVM, below which is SARMATIA.—A trophy, and woman near it weeping. On silver and gold of Constantinus II.

Coins with the same legend, but inscribed *Alamannia* or *Francia*, were struck under Constantine jun. and Crispus; but in no instance with the SARMATIA.—"It is probable (says Eckhel) that coins of the father (Constantinus M.) were struck with this reverse; for whether the father himself carried on the war in person with the Goths and Sarmatians, or whether he entrusted the expedition against these people to his son Constantine (A. D. 332), certain it is that warlike honours and distinctions were shared in common between father and son."—(viii. i. 107).—See SARMATIA.

GAVDIVM ROMANORVM.—A female captive sitting near a trophy, offers her breast to a little child.—This legend and type, which first appears on a gold coin of Maximianus Herculius, and which are common on the money of succeeding emperors, shew the *joy of the Romans*, not only in having conquered the barbarians, and driven them back from the confines of the empire, but also in having made slaves of them and their wives. (*D. N.* viii. 19).—Thus likewise we find

GAVDIVM REIPVBLICAE on a very rare gold coin of Constantine the Great; and see a trophy erected between an *Alamannian* woman and a male *Frank*, both captives, and sitting in a weeping posture on the ground.

GELLIA gens.—Whether of the patrician or plebeian order is uncertain. There are three varieties in its denarii, on each of which appears the name of GEL*lius*. The following two are coins belonging to this family:—

1. Galeated head of Rome; behind it X; within a crown of laurel.—*Rev.* A galeated soldier, in a rapid quadriga, embracing with his right arm a woman, as if to retain her with him in the car; on his left arm is a shield.— CN. GEL. below the horses. ROMA on the exergue.

Every attempt to interpret with certainty the type of the above reverse (pregnant with meaning, either mythological or historical, as it would appear to be), has hitherto signally failed; and it is even doubtful who was the Cn. Gellius, whose name is stamped on this denarius.—See Vaillant on the one hand, and Havercamp, *in Morell.* on the other, and compare with Cavedoni, cited by Riccio, p. 99.

2. M. ANT. IMP. AVG(VR) IIIVIR. R. P. C. C. L. GEL(LIVS) Q. P. Bare head of Mark Antony, behind which is the præfericulum.—*Rev.*—CAESAR IMP. PONT. IIIVIR. R. P. C. Bare head of Octa-

vianus, behind which is the lituus. This is a denarius of some rarity.

The letters Q. P. affixed to GEL. on the obverse, are considered by Eckhel to signify *Quæstor Proprætore*, rather than, as by others it is thought to mean *Quæstor Provinciæ*.—Riccio, however, adopting the latter opinion, says—Lucius Gellius (Poplicola) was provincial questor of Mark Antony, at the time which that famous Triumvir Reipublicæ Constituendæ was amicably colleagued with Octavianus, and coined the medal above described. He was also consul with M. Cocceius Nerva, in 718 (B. c. 36).—This same Gellius, however, was one of the most inconsistent and faithless of men, passing over, in a treacherous manner, from the friendship of Brutus and Cassius to that of Antony, and from the party of Antony to that of Augustus.

GEM. *Gemella.*—The cause why certain legions were called *Gemellæ* (or twins) is derived by the accurate Bimard from the Commentaries of Cæsar *(Bell. Civ.* iii. c. 4), where, in speaking of the legions which Pompey had assembled, he says, unam (LEGIONEM) ex Siciliâ veteranam, quam factam ex duabus GEMELLAM appellabat, (ad Jobert, ii. 273.)

Gemella, surnamed Acci, a colony of Hispania Tarraconensis, to which colonists were sent from the third and fourth legion, as coins of Augustus and Tiberius testify, on which it is called COL. GEM. ACCI.—See p. 3.

Gemellæ cum Lupâ.——The twin children (Romulus and Remus) with the wolf is a frequent mark of Roman colonies, as on coins of Corinth, Alexandria Troadis, Neapolis, Damascus, and others. (Spanheim, *Pr.* i. p. 571).—See COLONIAE ROMANAE, p. 232.

Gemmæ. Gems or precious stones.—The use of these as ornaments for the head is said to have begun under Aurelian. Other emperors neither unwillingly nor unfreely followed the same example; and thenceforward pearls and other jewels are seen on the diadems of the *Augusti* and *Augustæ.*

Gems and rings find in most instances their sources of explanation on coins.—See Rasche's citations from Spanheim and Beger.

GEN. *Generis.*—SAL*us* HVMANI GENERIS of Galba and Caracalla.

GEN. *Genius or Genio.*—GENIO AVGVSTI. To the Genius of the Emperor.

GENIUS.—It was the opinion of the ancients that every man from the moment of his birth had his *genius,* or according to others two *genii,* a good and a bad one; and that as the one or the other of these personal tutelaries was the stronger of the two, that individual became good or bad. In process of time each house and each town had its *genius;* the former were called *Lares,* the latter were named *Penates.* Rome had her Genius-goddess, to whom a statue was erected in the eighth region of the city. The influential presence of these unseen beings was held by the Romans in such high veneration, that when they entered for the first time into any place, they invariably paid a salutation to the *genius loci.* During the republic, they

swore by the Genius of the Roman people, and afterwards by that of the Emperor. At both periods, the violation of the oath was treated as the most heinous of perjuries, and was punished with the greatest severity.

Genii are represented on Roman coins, under different forms, as well in the consular as in the imperial series.

In his observations on *Genii,* as they are typified on family coins, Eckhel says that these come next in order of dignity to the gods and goddesses, meaning by the term—1. Certain images (or figures) appropriated to some country, city, or people, whether they were nothing more than allegories intended to represent a province or a city by some peculiarity of their habits or circumstances; or whether some celestial powers, though of a subordinate rank, were actually supposed to preside over them.— 2. The Virtues; such as clemency, faith, piety, &c. or those adjuncts which are always reckoned among the good things of life, but which are not always under our own control, such as fortune, honour, liberty, safety, victory, and health.— 3. The vices and the ills of life; as *pallor, pavor, febris,* &c. These and similar subjects, the emblematical representations of which we see on ancient monuments, were not regarded as mere idealities, but as actual beings of a divine nature, as is proved by the fact, that temples were erected to their honour, equally with the gods themselves. Some of these, such as Virtus, Honor, Mens, Fortuna, under various titles, have been enumerated by Cicero, Plutarch, Juvenal; and many other examples may be found in P. Victor's work on the districts of Rome.

The subject receives illustration from a letter of Cicero to his brother Quintus (I. *Epist.* i. § 10)—" Wherefore, since you are passing your time, in a position of the highest authority, in those very cities, where you see your own virtues consecrated, and reckoned among the divinities, &c." And thus, not only the Romans, but the Greeks also, crowded Olympus with fresh colonists. (See *Fors,* p. 395). No one any longer cared to offer sacrifices to the greater and elder gods, whilst they lavished whole hecatombs on *Virtus, Natura, Fatum,* and *Fortuna,* who had but as yesterday found their way into heaven; whilst a *sextarius* of ambrosia and nectar could not be bought for less than a *mina,* so vast was the assemblage of celestial guests. And yet one could have tolerated a superstition which conceded divine honours to the virtues; but what could surpass the infatuation of placing on a level with the gods, the vices, the diseases, and the bugbears of mankind? Indeed, this fanaticism was estimated at its true value, and detested accordingly, by all the ancients themselves who were possessed of superior intellects. A proof of this is to be found in the law introduced by the wisest of the Romans; " But those qualities, which entitle a man to admission into heaven, mind, valour, piety, faith,— for their glorification let there be shrines. But let no sacred solemnities be performed in honour of the vices." (Cic. *de Legib*. ii. ch. 8.) These expressions Cicero explains a little further on; "It is well done, that *Mens, Pietas, Virtus,* and *Fides,* are consecrated, to all of which temples are publicly dedicated in Rome, in order that the possessors of such qualities (and all good men do possess them), may reflect that the gods themselves are the occupants of their own bosoms. For that, on the contrary, was a disgraceful circumstance in the history of Athens, that after the crime of Cylon had been expiated, they followed the suggestion of Epimenides, and erected a temple to Contumely and Impudence. For it is the virtues, and not the vices, which should be made the subject of consecration. Now, there is standing in the Palatium an ancient altar to *Febris* (Fever), and another on the Esquiliæ to *Mala Fortuna ;* all of which anomalies should be abolished." He then refers in terms of commendation to the honours paid to *Salus, Honor, Ops, Victoria, Spes* (consecrated by Calatinus), *Fortuna* of the present time, and retrospective, and to *Fors Primigenia.* He might have added some foreign examples, such as the altars of *Impietas* and *Nequitia,* erected by one Dicæarchus, and the shrine of *Voracitas* in Sicily. The ancients, however, were not at a loss to find excuses for the folly of this custom.—Plutarch informs us *(in Agide et Cleomene,* p. m. 808), that there were among the Lacedæmonians, "temples sacred not only to Fear, but also to Death, and to Laughter, and other affections of the like kind. To Fear, however, they pay this adoration, not as they do to other objects of detestation, because they consider it hurtful, but because in their estimation it is a passion which mainly contributes to the safety of a State." Valerius Maximus, when remarking that there were in Rome three temples erected in honour of *Febris* (fever), adds that she was worshipped in order that she might cause less destruction. Pliny also affords similar information.—See *Doctrina,* v. 85, 86, where will also be found a list of Genii, selected from the coins of families under three heads, viz. :—

1. Genii of Countries, Cities, and Peoples.— 2. Good Genii, under which virtues, honours, and other attributes of good qualities are symbolized.—3. *Mali Genii*; such as *Pallor* and *Pavor* in Hostilia gens. No others of this absurd description are found on Roman coins. The Imperial mintages furnish a host of *Genii.* A few examples from each series are subjoined hereto.

GENIO AVGVSTI.—On a third brass of Nero, revealing Greek art in its high relief, its fine design and finished workmanship, this dedicatory legend accompanies a male figure, typifying the *Genius of the Emperor,* sacrificing at an altar with fire kindled. That this cruel tyrant was held in universal abhorrence, except amongst the vilest of the populace, and the most venal of the soldiery, whom his spectacles and largesses had seduced, is a fact proved by the burst of joy and gladnesss, which spread throughout the empire at the news of his death. Nevertheless

such was the baseness of the Senate, and such the dread of his vengeance, which prevailed during his lifetime, that every mark, even of divine honours, was paid to that fearful personification of mingled crime and folly. Hence we see *his* genius (evil as it was) immortalised by the obsequious mint of Rome.

Eckhel observes, "*the Genius Augusti*" so frequent on coins was some species of divinity, or it was designed to embody the intellectual spirit of the Cæsar himself, and his deity, such as the superstition of the ancients taught the common people to regard as an attendant on men."—viii. 458.

GENIVS POPVLI ROMANI. (Genius of the Roman People).—Upright figure of a young man, bare headed, clothed in the toga, bearing on his left arm a cornucopiæ, and holding a patera in his right hand, which he extends over a lighted altar, as in the act of sacrificing.

Although not the first in either chronological or alphabetical order of notice, yet as the largest and most boldly developed specimen of the type, a wood-cut is above inserted, engraved after a cast from a large brass medallion of Hadrian, in the *Cabinet de France,* valued by Mionnet at 150 francs. The type has evidently been borrowed from Nero's beautiful little coin *Genio Augusti,* but is of equally fine fabric, and from its superior magnitude forms a noble reverse.

On a second brass of Antoninus Pius, with the same legend of reverse, the Genius holds the hasta, instead of a patera in the right hand.

"The pagan religion, complicated and contradictory in its dogmas, admitted besides the gods the existence of beings, who were supposed to have peculiar influence over states, and peoples, and even to inspire, for good or evil, the minds of illustrious men."—*Leçons Numismatiques,* p. 136.

G. P. R.—A bearded and diademed head. Behind it a sceptre, with the letters G. P. R. *Genius Populi Romani* on a denarius of the Cornelia gens, struck by Cn. Cornelius Lentulus. It is also found on autonomes minted under the emperors (see *Incerti* in Morel. TAB. ii.) with the addition of GENIVS P. R. When, however, flattery had insinuated itself into the operations of the mint, the Genius of the people of Rome assumed the features of the emperor for the time being. According to Dion, there were at

Rome temples consecrated to this Genius as a deity. Examples of this occur amongst the coins of Augustus, under the year 734 (B. C. 20), and also in Galba—see below.

A beardless figure, representing the *Genius of the Roman People*, appears on the reverse of another denarius of the Cornelia family, in the act of crowning a warrior, alluding to the victories of Pompey in the East, 693 (B. C. 61), struck by CN. LENTVLVS MARCELLINVS, between 695 (B. C. 59) and 698 (B. C. 56).—Engraved in Morel and Riccio, *Fam. Rom.*

On another silver coin of the same family, the reverse exhibits the sedent figure of a man naked to the waist, holding in the right hand the cornucopiæ, and in the left the hasta; the right foot is planted on a globe; his face is directed towards a flying victory that crowns him. The legend on one side is P. LENTVLVS P. F. (Publius Lentulus, son of Publius), and on the other SPIN. *(Spinther)*. The seated figure is considered to personify the *Genius of Rome*, a device repeatedly associated with the affairs of the Lentuli, and thence most probably allusive to some glory of the Cornelia family.—Engraved in *Morell. Fam. Rom.* ii. 5, and in Riccio, *Tav.* xvi. 32.

GENIO P. R.—On a silver coin bearing on one side this epigraph, and on the other the legend and type of *Mars Ultor*, the head of Galba is figured, with a cornucopiæ behind it. The forepart of the head is bald, as that emperor's is described to have been. In their general hatred of Nero and exultation at his death, the people of Rome, ever prone to excess, paid the veteran governor of the Gauls and of Spain, now their deliverer from domestic tyranny, more than mortal honours, by hailing him as their tutelary demigod. The reign of Galba was at first regarded as an epoch of happiness and liberty; and frequent allusion is made on his coins to these favourable anticipations.

GENIVS EXERCITVS ILLYRICIANI. S.C.
—The Genius naked, except that the pallium hangs from his shoulders on his left arm, on which rests a cornucopiæ, and close to which is a military ensign. In the right hand is a patera. On other coins there is an altar in addition.—Gold, silver, and first and second brass of Trajan Decius. The above is engraved from a specimen in the British Museum.

GEN. or GENIVS ILLYRICI.—Male figure standing, with patera and cornucopiæ. Silver

of the same emperor. The first brass is engraved in the *Cabinet de Christine.*

On coins of this emperor there are reverses implying his acknowledgment of obligations to DACIA, as well as to both the PANNONIAE, superior and inferior, and here we have a still more pointed record of his gratitude to the army of Illyria.

The reason why such a distinction was conferred upon these provinces is sufficiently obvious; for it was in them that Decius was first declared *Imperator* by acclamation; and to the fidelity of these legions he owed his victory over Philip; while in turn he protected and freed them from the incursions of barbarian tribes, and so again obtained distinction for himself. A similar reverse is to be found on coins of Julian the Usurper.

Thus the *Exercitus Illyricianus* had too many claims upon the immediate successor of the elder Philip, to make it difficult to account for this imperial compliment to its *Genius.*

GENIVS EXERCITI. The Genius of the Army.—Du Choul, in his observations on this and the various other numismatic dedications to *Genius*, says—" The ancients esteemed it to be the God of Nature. And such was the religion of the Romans that it assigned to every man his genius and his presiding spirit. Thus we find inscriptions to the Genius of the Emperor, of the Senate, of the Roman People, and (as in Aurelian and others) of the Army. This last named legend is accompanied by a type pourtraying the image of *Genius*, with a cloak half covering the shoulders, and leaving the rest of the body naked, holding a cornucopiæ in one hand, and a simpulum or a patera in the other. Censorinus, in his treatise *De Die Natali*, says, that the moment we are born, we live under the guard and tutelage of Genius. Other writers assert that the *Lares* and *Genius* were the same thing. (pp. 148, 149).

GEN. LVG. (The Genius of Lugdunum).— This legend appears on the reverse of a rare silver coin of Clodius Albinus, accompanied by the type of a naked *Genius*, with turreted head, standing : he holds a spear in his right hand, a cornucopiæ in his left; and there is an eagle at his feet. The above cut is after a cast from a specimen in the British Museum.

" That Albinus, when he came over from Britain, took up his quarters at Lugdunum (now Lyon, in France), in the vicinity of which he was afterwards defeated and slain, is a fact distinctly related to us by Herodian. In that city, therefore, the above described denarius, exhibiting GEN*ium* LVG*duni*, was doubtless struck; and it is very probable that in the same place several other coins of Albinus, already named Augustus, were minted. The mint of Lyon (Officina Lugdunensis) is mentioned as early as on coins of Antony the triumvir, but much more frequently on those of a lower age. The eagle placed at the feet of the Genius indicates, perhaps, that Lugdunum was under the supreme protection of Jupiter; indeed Albinus ascribed the first victories which he gained to that deity, as is proved by a silver coin quoted by Vaillant, with the epigraph IOVI VICTORI."—Eckhel, viii. 164.

Obv.—GENIO ANTIOXENI. A female figure, with turreted and veiled head, sitting on a rock; a river issuing from beneath her feet. Third brass of Julian II. (Imp. Mus.)

Obv.—GENIO CIVITATIS. Female head, veiled and turreted. Third brass of do. (Tanini, p. 318).

These coins were struck at Antioch, in Syria. It is probable that they first saw the light during the reign of Julian (between A. D. 360 and 363). The obverse exhibits the *Genius Antiocheni*, i. e. *populi*, under the figure of a woman with turreted head, sitting on a rock, from which flows a river. The species of legend is found more fully expressed on coins of Diocletian's age, thus—GENIO POPVLI ROMANI. Respecting the *Genii* of peoples, cities, and localities, &c. to whose guardianship they were respectively committed, abundant information will be found in the works of various learned writers. (viii. 141.)

GENIO SENATVS. S. C.—The Genius of the Roman Senate, under the figure and features of a man, clothed in the toga, standing; he holds in his right hand an *olive branch*, the sign of peace; and in his left the *ivory sceptre*, distinctive mark of the consuls. Silver and first brass of Antoninus Pius. The above engraving is from a specimen in the compilers possession.

On a first brass of Galba, bearing for its legend of reverse, SENATVS PIETATI AVGVSTI, the accompanying type represents the *Father*, or the *Genius* of the *Senate* crowning the emperor.

Although *Genii* were usually represented by young men, yet the *Genius* of the Senate is impersonated by a man of mature years, habited in the *toga*, very probably for the purpose of making a more complimentary allusion (quite in character with that excellent prince Antoninus Pius) to the dignity and to the gravity of an ancient and once illustrious, but long before its

extinction, most degenerate, corrupt, and degraded body.

When indeed it is remembered that an assembly formerly so jealous of its independence, and so haughty in the exercise of its power, at length became the subservient tool—the fulsome panegyrist—of the weakest as well as the worst of beings that ever wore the human form, of madmen and monsters permitted for the punishment of a wicked world to be its plagues in the shape of its rulers; the fall of the Roman Senate into a state of slavery and thence through yet lower grades of humiliation, can be regarded in no other light than that of a judgment as just as it was inevitable. Nor is there, perhaps, a more striking lesson, it might be added, a more awful warning, to be derived from the records of past ages, than is handed down to us in the flagrant examples of base and impious adulation—of venal flattery committing open outrage upon decency by the most palpable falsehoods, which, with such fulsome frequency, present themselves on Roman coins of the Imperial series, bearing the well-known impress of a *Senatus Consultum*.

GENIO POPVLI ROMANI.—The Genius, having a *modius* on his head, on his left arm holding a horn of abundance, and in the act of making a libation from a patera on an altar, appears on the reverse of a middle brass of Constantine the Great. Engraved in Banduri, ii. 2. There is an exactly similar type on the reverse of a second brass of Licinius senior, with the legend GENIO IMPERATORIS.

Baudelot De Dairval observes, that "all the medals which have on the reverse *Genio Augusti*, *Genio Imperatoris*, *Genio Senatus*, *Genio Populi Romani*, with other symbols of *Lares*, bear reference in their legends and types, either to the princes themselves whom flattery caused to be thus represented; or otherwise to the guardian deities of those magistrates, or of those cities, that struck the coins."—See *De l'Utilité des Voyages*.

Genius of Alexandria.—Our references to the subject of Genii, so far as it receives illustration from coins, shall be concluded with the description of a large brass of Hadrian, struck in Egypt. The reverse of this piece exhibits a female figure in a short dress (somewhat resembling that assigned to *Diana Venatrix*), wearing as a head-gear the skull and proboscis of an elephant, and holding in the left hand a couple of corn-ears. Standing opposite to her is a male figure of mature age, whose right hand she lifts up with her own, and kisses it. This male figure, laureated and togated, holds in the left hand a sceptre surmounted by an eagle. In the field of the coin is I. E. (marking the xvth year of a reign).

This unique, elegant, and remarkable type, is recognised by Eckhel *(Doctr.* vi. 489), and by Millin *(Gal. Mythol.* i. 378), as representing the Genius of Alexandria, hastening to meet Hadrian on one of his arrivals in that city, and to welcome him as her guest, which she does in the most expressive mode of shewing grateful acknowledgment for benefits already conferred.

[For the cast (in gutta percha) after which the above cut has been executed, the compiler is indebted to his friend Mr. Akerman, who was in possession of the original].

In Zoega *(Num. Ægypt.* vii.) is a similar type with the addition of ALEXANDRIA for its accompanying legend. But it places a simple wand, or the hasta pura, in the emperor's left hand, instead of the eagle-topped sceptre of empire.

GENS.—A clan, embracing several families, united together by a common name. This word has a different meaning from that of *Familia* and also from that of *Stirps.* Amongst the Romans there were *Gentes* and *Familiæ,* so indeed that the *familiæ* might be said to be comprehended as a species under the *gens,* or race.

Gens seems to belong to the *nomen* or name ; *familia* to the *cognomen* or surname of a house : the former included the whole ; the latter only a part. For example, all the *Valerii* were of the same *gens* or race, because they were all comprised under the same name. But this *gens* had several branches which were distinguished by the respective *cognomina,* and these branches were called *Familiæ,* Families. Thus in the *Gens Valeria* there was the Maximi, the Messalæ, the Flacci, the Lacuni, the Poplicolæ, who formed so many families of the same house. Festus therefore gives a good definition of this word *Gens,* in saying—Gens appellatur, quæ ex multis familiis conficitur. Accordingly, again, if we take the *Gens Cornelia,* we have for its *familiæ* the Blasiones, Cethegi, Dolabellæ, Lentuli, Scipiones, Sisennæ, &c. These examples are confirmed by the testimonies of ancient writers ; amongst whom may be cited Suetonius and Livy. The former says—Imagines et elogia universi generis (Sulpicii) exsequi longum est, familiæ (Galbæ) breviter attingam.—Livy says, P. Scipio Nasica tribunos appellavit, orationemque habuit plenam veris decoribus, non communiter modo Corneliæ gentis, sed proprie familiæ suæ."—Eckhel v. 54.

There were patrician houses, and there were houses of the plebeian order, and sometimes in the same *gens* there were some families of patrician rank and others of plebeian.

Gens, says Rasche, means all the offspring, who, from one ancestor and as it were first parent, always by blood relationship (traduce sanguine) had descended in a right line. *Familia* was a branch growing out of the trunk or middle

nearest to the side (ad latus proxime). *Stirps* in the last place may rightly be denominated a branch of the branch (ramus rami).

For a descriptive list of the *Gentes* and *Familiæ Romanæ,* as found on Consular coins—see Mionnet, *Rareté des Med.*—Akerman, *Descr. Cat.*—Riccio, *Monete delle Famiglie di Roma.*

GENTILES.—Those of the same gens were called *gentiles,* and those of the same family, *agnati.* The term gentiles, says Eckhel, was applied not only to those who belonged to the same gens, but also to those who bore only the same name. Cicero tells us—" They are called gentiles who share the same name." He was, therefore, justified in saying on another occasion, " Pherecydes the Syrian was the first to make the observation, that the minds of men were immortal ; and he was one of a very remote age, as he lived during the reign of my *gentilis (namesake)"*—i. e. Servius *Tullius ;* between whom, however, and Cicero there was no point of connexion besides the similarity of name. Festus too gives the same account—" The term *gentilis* is applied, both to him who is descended from the same stock, and to him who is called by the same name ; witness the expression of Cincius—" They are my *gentiles* who bear my name." Consequently, he who was connected with a certain lineage by name, might easily appear, in the eyes of the interested, to be allied also by blood. They who oppose their own conjectures to the authority of Dionysius, tell us, for example, that the later *Junii* passed over from the patrician to the plebeian ranks. It is not uninteresting to call to mind, that in the earliest period of the commonwealth the same impositon was practised by a certain L. Junius of plebeian origin and ignoble station, who, when the people retired to the Mons Sacer, in order the more effectually to direct their vengeance against the *Patres,* assumed the cognomen of *Brutus,* and was thereupon chosen the first tribune of the people.—See *Doctr.* vi. 20.

GENT. *Gentium.*—Of Nations.—See DE-BELLATORI GENT. BARBAR. and TRIUMFATOR GENT. BARB.

GENTES *captæ, subactæ, devictæ, receptæ,* &c.—Nations or territories captured, subdued, vanquished, regained, &c. are recorded by name on the coins of Roman emperors.—See ÆGYPTUS, ALAMANNIA, ARABIA, ARMENIA, DACIA, FRANCIA, GERMANIA, JUDÆA, PARTHIA, SARMATIA, &c. Similar reference is made to nations and countries subdued and taken possession of by the Romans, on coins of the *Emperors* and *Cæsars,* bearing the inscription DE PARTHIS, as in Augustus ; DE BRITANNIS, as in Claudius ; DE GERM. or GERMANIS, as in Augustus, Nero Drusus, Claudius, Domitian, M. Aurelius, and others ; and in Sept. Severus, the legend of GERM. VOTA SUSCEPTA ; also the DE IVDAEIS of Vespasian ; and the DE SARM(ATIS) of M. Aurelius and of Commodus. The same token of conquest and victory is conveyed under the name alone of a particular tribe or region, as BRITANN. and BRITANNIA, on coins of Claudius,

Antoninus Pius, Commodus, Severus; DACIA, as in Trajan; FRANCIA & GOTHIA, as in Constantinus M.—GOTHI on coins of Probus and Tacitus. The accompanying types to these are for the most part a woman veiled and weeping, or a captive sitting bound at the foot of a trophy of arms. On some of the imperial series, we also find the highest terms of eulogy employed, not as for the conquest of a single nation merely, but for many simultaneously vanquished, as in the DEBELLATORI GENTIVM BARBARARVM of Constantine the Great; the VNDIQVE or VBIQVE VICTOR, first in Numerianus, and afterwards in Constantine and his sons Crispus and Constantius; and to crown the foolery of extravagant boasting peculiar to the lower empire, VICTOR OMNIVM GENTIVM appears on coins of Maxentius, Constantine, and Constantinus junior.

GENUS HUMANUM. The human race or mankind.—This term inscribed on some coins, signifies the world as it was comprehended under the imperial sway of Rome.—See SALVS GENERIS HVMANI of Galba; also the RESTITVTOR GENER. HVMANI of Valerian and Gordianus Pius.

GEOGRAPHY.—How greatly the study of Ancient Geography is benefitted and assisted by a knowledge of the numismatic science is copiously shewn by Froëlich (in 4 *Tentamina*, p. 45 et seq.) The utility of such authentic monuments for that purpose had also been previously acknowledged by the father of revived geography Abraham Ortelius, who availed himself of the aid which coins afforded him to rescue from obscurity and doubt the names of many cities and places. The learned work of Cellarius would neither have reflected so much credit on its author, nor proved of so much use to literary men, unless many things read there had previously been confirmed as true by the evidence of medals.—Rasche, *Lexicon Num.*

GER. GERM. *Germania.*—GER. CAP. *Germania Capta.*

GER. *Germanici.*—PAX. GER*manici*, not *Germanica*, on first brass of Vitellius.—See PAX. GER. ROMA.

GER. Germanicus.

GERMANIA.—This legend, and its type, a woman standing, with spear and German shield, on a denarius of Hadrian, are considered allusive to the circumstance of that emperor's passing over from Gaul into Germania, as Spartian relates in the year 877 (A. D. 120); and on which occasion, according to the same authority, he imposed a king on the Germans. In reference to this subject see EXERCITVS GERMANICVS, p. 366.

GERMANIA CAPTA. (Germania conquered). —A female figure, personifying Germania weeping, seated on a buckler, at the foot of a trophy composed of German arms. On the right stands a German captive, his hands bound behind him, his shield at his feet. In the exergue S. C.— *Obv.*—IMP*erator* CAES*ar* DOMIT*ianus* AV-G*ustus* GERM*anicus* C0n*Sul* XI. CENS*oriæ* POT*estatis* P*ater* P*atriæ.* Bust of Domitian laureated, adorned with the Ægis.

This rare first brass is of the year 837 of Rome (A. D. 84). Domitian was no sooner seated on the throne, than it pleased him to undertake an expedition against the Catti, a German tribe, and though so far from coming to action with them, he had not once even seen the enemy, yet repassing the Rhine, this cowardly tyrant had the arrogance to take the honours of the triumph for his foolish campaign against this people, and to assume the surname of Germanicus. He caused slaves to be bought, who were dressed after the manner of the Germans, and whose hair was suffered to grow, in order that they might pass for Germans in the eyes of the Roman citizens.

On the reverse of another large brass, struck the same year as the preceding coin, and having reference to the same ridiculous pretensions of Domitian to the honour of having beaten the Germans, represents some king or chieftain of that people holding a buckler, and on his knee before the emperor, who stands habited in the *paludamentum*, holding in his right hand the *parazonium*, and in his left the hasta. In the field S. C.

[Passing gladly from the *sham* victories of a cowardly tyrant to the *real* triumphs of a brave defender of his empire, we proceed to notice the two following monuments of important successes gained by M. Aurelius in battle with the Germans :—]

GERMANICO AV*Gusto* IMP*eratori* VI. C0n*Suli* III. S. C. The accompanying type of this reverse represents a very fine trophy, on one side of which sits a weeping female, on the other stands a tall half-naked man, whose upright posture and manly air are characteristic of the unsubdued spirit of the German tribes.— *Obv.* M. ANTONINVS AVG*ustus.* Laurelled head of Aurelius, to whom the legend of reverse ascribes the glory of having terminated the *Germanic* war.

GERMANIA SVBACTA. IMP*erator* VI. C0n*Sul* VI. A female figure is seated at the foot of a trophy, in an attitude of extreme dejection and grief—her head bent down and her hands joined upon her left knee; she seems to deplore her lot as a vanquished province. The legend of reverse is couched in prouder terms than those which usually record the victories of Marcus Aurelius—viz. *Germania subjugated.*

These and other epigraphs, accompanied by types representing captive Germans, standing or sitting with their hands tied behind them,

near a trophy, are amongst the coins, in large and middle bronze, which record the reduction of Germany, by repeated victories, to the power of Rome, by the arms of Marcus Aurelius, about the years u. c. 926 and 927 (A. D. 173 and 174).

The latter part of that emperor's reign was disturbed by wars, which he conducted in person. The discipline and valour of the legions under his immediate command, proved as usual irresistible by the barbarous tribes whom they encountered, and gave rise to new triumphs, and to the surnames of GERMANICVS and of SARM*aticus*, which are found on coins of that celebrated prince.

GERMANICUS is a name, or rather a surname, which, having at first been justly acquired by the courageous and active Drusus, and deservedly continued to his son Germanicus Cæsar, was afterwards assumed by many of the emperors ; by some as the due acknowledgment of their valour and success against the German tribes, as in the instances of Tiberius, Galba, Vitellius, Vespasian, Titus, Nerva, Trajan, Marcus Aurelius, Postumus, Claudius Gothicus, &c. ; by others on the most groundless and disgraceful pretensions, as in the respective cases of Caligula, Nero, Domitian, Commodus, &c.— Amongst other surnames derived from conquered countries, Valerianus and Gallienus were called not only *Germanici* but even *Maximi ;* and so likewise was Postumus ; but the latter with better reason, for he gained victory on victory over the Germans, and built fortresses for the Roman garrisons on the banks of the Rhine.

GERMANICUS *Cæsar*, the son of Drusus sen. and of Antonia junior, was born in the year of Rome 739 (B. c. 15), for he was thirty-two years of age when he died in 772 (A. D. 19). He derived the name *Germanicus* from his father Drusus. Being adopted by Tiberius, at the in-

stance of Augustus, in the year 757 (A. D. 4), he began to be styled *Cæsar Tiberii filius,* and *Augusti nepos.* In 760 (A. D. 7), he held the questorship, and was sent with succours to Tiberius for the war in Dalmatia. For successes gained in this campaign, he earned triumphal and pretorian honours, 763 (A. D. 10). In the year following, vested with pro-consular authority, he, in conjunction with Tiberius, made an expedition into Germany, to avenge the slaughter under Varus. In 765 (A. D. 12), he was elected consul, and in 767 (A. D. 14), about the time of Augustus' death, being appointed to the legions on the Rhine, he quelled a revolt of both armies, occasioned by their repugnance to Tiberius, and their desire to have him as a successor to the empire ; threatening them, in case of their persisting, that he would put an end to his own life. And such was the effect of his firmness, that they very shortly gave in their adhesion to Tiberius. For his other exploits during the war in Germany, and the honours which he thence acquired, from 767 to 770, see the biographical notice of Tiberius. In 771 (A. D. 18), he was made consul for the second time at Nicopolis, in Achaia, with Tiberius for his colleague, and being sent into the East, he established Artaxias on the throne of Armenia (see p. 416), and reduced Cappadocia and Commagene to the condition of a Roman province. In 772 (A. D. 19), having gone into Egypt for the purpose of studying its antiquities *(cognoscendæ antiquitatis causá),* and thence passed into Syria, he became the victim of the indignities and evil practices of Piso, prefect of Syria, and his wife Plancina ; unable to escape their snares, he fell into ill health, which was aggravated by the apprehension that poison had been administered to him by Piso ; and he died at Epidaphne, near Antioch, on the 9th of October of the same year. When the tidings of his death spread abroad, it is scarcely credible what grief and consternation it caused throughout the empire, and in Rome itself ; no one refraining from the most liberal abuse of Tiberius, whom the popular voice condemned as the instigator of Piso's crime. Nor was this suspicion without foundation. For it is very improbable, that Piso and Plancina would have openly acted with hostility towards a Cæsar sent with plenary powers into the East, had they not been assured of the approval of Tiberius and Julia. Besides, it was a sufficiently well-known fact, that Tiberius hated Germanicus, inasmuch as he feared in him a successor to the empire, on account of his popularity and the public animosity against himself. The indignation of the people knew no bounds ; for even the altars of the gods were pulled down, as though they had neglected their charge, the temples were dismantled, and the *Lares* thrown into the streets. Even barbarian tribes were affected with pity, and there was a universal mourning, not only throughout the Roman empire, but the entire world. Assuredly, the history of ages does not record a single instance, from the time of Alexander the Great, of any individual's decease being so bitterly and sincerely deplored: nor was this the feeling of the moment only, but it continued for many years afterwards, insomuch that the Romans used to rejoice in the prosperity, and sympathise with the misfortunes, of the children whom he left behind him. His praises became the theme of all the writers of Roman annals, who have extolled in the highest terms his advantages of person and mind, his bravery, his wisdom, his eloquence and learning, his courteous demeanour to his friends, and his clemency towards his enemies. His ashes were transported by his wife Agrippina from Syria to Rome, and deposited in the tomb of Augustus. —*(Doctr.* vi. 208).

He married Agrippina, by whom he had nine children, six of whom survived him,—viz. Nero, Drusus, and Caius, called Caligula; Agrippina (who married Claudius), Drusilla, and Julia Livilla.

The coins struck in honour of Germanicus are very rare in gold; of the highest rarity in first brass; common in second brass; colonial rare. Those of Roman die, bearing his portrait, were minted after his death, under Caligula and Claudius. Some of them were restored by Vespasian. On these he is styled GERMANICVS CAESAR TI. AVGVST. F. DIVI. AVG. N. (as on the foregoing cut)—also GERM. CAESAR; GERMANICVS CAES. C. CAESARIS (Caligulæ) PATER.

GERMANICVS CAESAR.—A warrior stands with a sceptre in his left hand, guiding a triumphal quadriga.

Rev.—SIGNIS RECE*ptis* DEVICTIS GER-M*anis.* A warrior, clothed in a complete suit of armour, stands with his right hand extended, and in his left holds a legionary eagle. In the field are the initials S. C. (struck by authority of the Senate).

This middle brass, coined during the life-time of Germanicus, is a monument of the honours which were decreed to that prince, when he had retaken from the Germans, and brought back to Rome, the military ensigns lost by Varus, in the reign of Augustus. And, although common, these coins are of remarkable interest, as commemorative of so important an historical event.

GERMANICVS CAESAR TI*berii* AV-GVS*ti* F*ilius* DIVI. AV*Gusti* N*epos.* (Germanicus Cæsar, son of Tiberius Augustus, grandson of the divine Augustus.) Bare head of Germanicus. (Engraved in preceding page, from a second brass).

Rev.—*Caius* CAESAR AV*Gustus* GERMA-NICVS PON*tifex* M*aximus* TR*ibuniciæ* PO-

T*estatis.* In the middle of the coin S. C. *(Senatus Consulto).*

The before described coin is, as the legend shews, a mark of Caligula's professed veneration for the memory of his illustrious father.

In the *Revue Numismatique* for 1838, a gold coin of *Germanicus* is for the first time published. It had recently been brought from Asia Minor, where it is considered to have been struck. The legends and types are of surpassing interest, inasmuch as they constitute an historical monument, confirmatory of the fact, that during the fatal sojourn of that heroic Roman in the East, he conferred royal powers on an Armenian prince named Artaxias. From the able commentary on the subject, inserted in vol. i. p. 338 et seq. of the above-named French periodical; and also from a letter, replete with learning and intelligence, from the pen of the late Mr. Borrell, of Smyrna, addressed to Mr. Akerman, and published in the *Numismatic Chronicle* for July, 1839, an article has been compiled, which, together with a graphic illustration (unavoidably omitted here), will be found in letter R of this dictionary, under the head of *Rex* AR-TAXIAS—*Caesar* GERMANICVS.

[At the sale of the Sabatier collection, in April, 1853, this unique denarius brought £30 10s. It is now in Lord Londesborough's cabinet].

GERMANICVS COS. X.—A woman half naked, sitting in a sorrowful attitude on a Germanic shield; below is a broken spear.—Gold of Domitian.—With the tenth consulate of this emperor 837 (A. D. 84), the title of *Germanicus* occurs on his coins for the first time; derived, as he wished it to be understood, from his *conquest* of the *Germani*; whereas he actually returned from that absurd expedition without even seeing the enemy, as Dion has testified. (lxvii. § 4). Nor did he hesitate to celebrate a triumph, which, however, as Tacitus informs us (Agricola, c. 39), furnished matter for ridicule, from the fact that individuals were paid to personate prisoners of war. The title thus conceded to a contemptible vanity, he made so much part and parcel of his designation, that not only on all coins struck thenceforth up to the day of his death did he insist on its being added to the rest of his distinctions, but even Martial, Silius Italicus, and Statius, invariably style him *par excellence* Germanicus. Now this may be tolerated as a poetical license, inasmuch as the poets would naturally adopt a word, which offended less against the laws of metre than that of Domitianus. But even that base flatterer Quinctilian, though unconstrained by any such metrical difficulty, can find no other appellation for him, than that of *Germanicus Augustus.* (Just. x. c. 1.) There are numerous coins of succeeding years, which bear this unfounded assumption of victory over a valiant people in the legend of their reverse: viz. GER-MANICVS, or GERMANIA CAPTA, or IMP. with the addition of various numerals; and of which the types are, like the coin before us, Germania, as a woman sitting on a shield in an attitude of grief; the shield from its oblong shape being a Germanic one, and distinctive of that people; or a trophy erected between a woman sitting and a German, with his hands bound behind him, standing by his arms.—Eckhel, vi. 379.

GERMANICVS MAX. TER.—A trophy between two captives seated on the ground. This silver coin of Valerianus is, on account of the addition TER. treated with great distinction by Banduri, who affirms that there is no coin of any other emperor bearing such an inscription. Nevertheless, the same reverse is plainly to be seen on a coin of Gallienus, in the cabinet of Vienna. Each emperor, on account of the victories won by Gallienus over the Germans, calls himself *Germanicus Maximus*, and the *Ter.* is affixed in record of three victories gained. Gallienus, indeed, supplies several examples, shewing that in that age, victories were enumerated, in like manner as at an earlier period the title of IMP*erator* was exalted according to the number of victories.—See GERMANICVS MAX. v. of Gallienus.—*D. N.* vii. 385 and 401.

GERMANIS (DE). Victory over the Germans.-A trophy composed of German arms.—*Obv.* NERO CLAVDIVS DRVSVS GERMANICVS IMP(ERATOR). Laurelled head of Drusus senior. Gold.— Engraved from a specimen in the British Museum.

GERMANIS (DE). An equestrian statue on a triumphal arch, between two trophies.—*Obv.* Same legend and type as the preceding.—See p. 349 for a wood-cut of this gold coin.

The two subjects above described serve, with other numismatic monuments to recal the honours decreed to Drusus after his death; including the statues, both equestrian and pedestrian, which were raised to his memory, and the triumphal arch built on the Appian way in honour of this celebrated general of Augustus.

Of *Germania*, now, under the general designation of Germany, the most extensive country in modern Europe, the derivation of the name is not clearly ascertained. By some it is supposed to have been so called from the nation that passed the Rhine and expelled those Gauls who, in the time of Tacitus, were called the Tungri (inhabiting the present territory of Juliers and Treves). Afterwards, the whole vast region from the shores of the Baltic to the Rhætian and Norican Alps, was included under that appellation. It was divided by the Romans into Germania Prima, Superior or Upper; and Germania Secunda, Inferior or Lower. The former so called as being more inland, lay along the western bank of the Rhine, and contained several German nations. On the eastern bank of that river, were the Frisii (in part of Holland, Friesland, and Groningen), whose country was intersected by a canal, made

by the elder Drusus, whose victories our coin here commemorates. North-east of the Frisii were the Chauci, distinguished by Tacitus as the most noble and just of all the German nations. South-east of the Chauci were the Cherusci (inhabiting the country now comprehending Luneburg, Brunswick, and part of Brandenburg). It was by this nation, in league with neighbouring tribes, under the conduct of Arminius, that the three legions commanded by Quintilius Varus, 762 (A. D. 9), were defeated and slain, in the Saltus Teutobergiensis *(Bishopric of Paderborn)*. And it was on this very scene of his countrymen's slaughter, and of disgrace to the Roman arms, that, about seven years afterwards, Germanicus terminated his campaigns in Germany by a crowning victory, the triumphal result of which was the recapture, by that hero, of the lost ensigns from a brave but thoroughly vanquished, and for a long time humbled foe; as recorded on his well known coin; SIGNIS RECEPTIS DEVICTIS GERM.—For an account of the different nations comprised within the division of Germania Inferior (now Southern Germany), the principal seat of war in the reign of M. Aurelius, see *Ancient and Modern Geography*, by the late Bp. Butler, edit. 1846.

GERMANIS (DE.)—IMP. VIII. COS. III. P. P.—A heap of arms and armour.—*Obv. Marcus* ANTONINVS AVG*ustus* GER*Manicus* SARM*aticus* TR. P. XXX. P. P.—DE GERM. TR. P. XXXI. IMP. VIII. COS. III. P. P.— Gold, silver, and large brass of M. Aurelius.

It is remarkable that in the graves in Germany, no example of oblong shields are found, but all are round.—See Roach Smith, *Collectanea Antiqua*.

There is something not a little refreshing and satisfactory in the tokens of victory displayed on these military coins of the "philosophic prince;" because, unlike the vain conceited lies of Domitian's prostituted mint, they truly attest that series of arduous but eventually successful campaigns, his personal share in which as *Imperator* and *Augustus*, obtained for Aurelius the surname of *Germanicus*. What renders them of peculiar interest is, that the coins in question were struck at a period so calamitous and full of difficulties, that historians compare the perils which then environed Rome to those of the Punic wars. In 920 (A. D. 167), with which the third consulate in the legend corresponds, the empire was ravaged by a pestilence, believed to have been brought from the East by the legions of L. Verus. The Marcomanni, the Quadi, and almost all the barbarian tribes of the North, rose in one wide circle of revolt against the empire. It was at the commencement of that year, that the two emperors, M. Aurelius and L. Verus set out for Germania. On their arrival there, the barbarians asked for and obtained peace. In 921 (A. D. 168), the emperors returned to Rome. The following year saw the *Germani* in renewed and formidable insurrection, and the two *Augusti* made instant preparations for another campaign. The sudden death of Verus, from apoplexy, left Aurelius sole emperor, but after bringing back the remains of his colleague to Rome, and causing the honours of consecration to be decreed to him, Marcus, mindful of his duty to the State, resumed his march on rebellious Germania. In 923 (A. D. 170), pressing vigorously the war against the Marcomanni, he established his head quarters in Pannonia. Thence he pursued the course of his victories over the Germans. And in 925 (A. D. 172), the title of *Germanicus* was conferred as a well-earned distinction upon Marcus Aurelius. The interval from 926 (A. D. 173) to 928 (A. D. 175) was occupied, however, with an almost ceaseless struggle on the part of the barbarians in arms against the military power of the Romans; but the enemy being beaten on all sides, and forced to sue for peace, the brave and victorious emperor added the title of *Sarmaticus* to that of Germanicus, and returned in triumph to Rome. In less than four years afterwards the Germans were again leagued against the empire; and although they were defeated in many bloody battles, and the Marcomanni in particular nearly exterminated by his legions, M. Aurelius was not destined to revisit his capital, but died 933 (A. D. 180), at Vindobona, (Vienna), in Pannonia, the base of his warlike operations and scene of his proudest achievements.

GERME, Galatiæ, *colonia*, to the south of Pessinus now *Ghermesti* in Asiatic Turkey.—The coins of this colony are *Latin* imperial, in first and second brass, from Domitian to Etruscilla, including Commodus, Diadumenianus, and Otacilia Severa. One of the types consists of an eagle with wings spread, on a pedestal between two ensigns, allusive to the veterans of some legion whose name is not known, but who from the legend COL*onia* AVG*usta* GER-MEN*orum* would appear to have been sent in the time of its founder Augustus to people that colony. It took the title of *Felix* out of ill-bestowed compliment to Commodus. The other types are the wolf and twins; a priest guiding two oxen at plough. And the Etruscilla exhibits on its reverse, COL. GERMEN*orum* ACTIA Δ VSARIA *(sic)*. A table raised on three steps, and on which is a globe between two urns. Above the globe is the *torcular* (wine or oil press); the whole within a crown of laurel.—[Tanini, cited by Mionnet.]

GETA *(Lucius* or Publius), the younger son of Severus and Domna, brother of Caracalla, was born at Mediolanum (Milan), about the year of Rome 942 (A. D. 189.) He was called Lucius

from his father, and took the name of Publius from his uncle, a Roman knight. In 951 (A. D. 197), Severus having assumed the sole authority on the removal of his rivals, Geta followed his father to join the Parthian campaign in the East, where he declined to accept the title of Cæsar, though pressed upon him by the army, approved by the Senate and the Emperor, and though at the same time his brother Caracalla was already styled *Augustus*. But he received the titles of *Princeps Juventutis* and of *Pontifex*.

951 to 957 (A. D. 198 to 204.)—Being as yet too young to participate in affairs of state, no events worthy of record occurred during these years.

958 (A. D. 205).—The name of *Lucius* was dropped, but that of *Publius* retained. Geta proceeded consul for the first time, as colleague to his brother, who was then in his second consulate.

961 (A. D. 208).—Consul for the second time, with his brother (Consul III.) he accompanied his father and Caracalla to the war in Britain.

962 (A. D. 209).—He received from his father the title of *Augustus*, and was invested with the tribunician power. The following year he began to be styled BRIT*anicus*.

964 (A. D. 211).—His father dying this year, he began to be styled P*ater* P*atriæ*; and the PONT*ifex* was discontinued. On the death of Severus at Eboracum, on the 4th February, their father's funeral being solemnized, and peace being concluded with the Caledonians, the two brothers returned to Rome. Serious apprehensions were excited throughout the empire by their disagreements. Caracalla, both on the journey, and when arrived at Rome, was constantly engaged in plots for Geta's destruction.

965 (A. D. 212).—No hopes being entertained of a reconciliation between these two young princes; and the disturbances which arose in every quarter from their dissensions, increasing day by day, a division of the empire was contemplated; but given up at the instance of their mother. At length, having long in vain attempted to put an end to Geta's life, Caracalla inveigled him by a show of affection into security, and killed him in the arms of his mother, at the age of 22 years and nine months.

"Never (observes the author of *Doctrina*) since the days of the Theban brothers (Eteocles and Polynices), had the world beheld a more cruel and disastrous feud between men related to each other by the nearest ties of consanguinity.

That one of them would eventually perish by the other's hand, had long before been anticipated, from the animosity so openly manifested between them, and from the obvious intentions of Caracalla. Yet all joined in the prayer that a fate, which could not be averted, might at last befall Caracalla, rather than Geta. The ferocious and ungovernable disposition of the former was well known; whilst Geta, on the other hand, maintained a character for integrity and moderation; he was courteous in his intercourse with the world, particularly fond of the society of eminent men, and devoted to refined pursuits; though Spartian attributes to him a roughness of manners, unaccompanied however with profligacy. The cruelty exercised by Caracalla towards the friends of his murdered brother, is recorded by historians. And, indeed, that implacable hatred, which usually subsides on the death of its object, even if one not connected by blood, yet in this case of a brother, continued so unappeased, that all who even wrote or pronounced the name of Geta were put to death; so that the very poets dared not thenceforth use that customary and familiar name for a slave. His fury extended itself to the statues and coins of the deceased, which he destroyed. But he was foiled in his attempts to obliterate all memorials of his brother; for not only are numerous coins of Geta extant at this moment, but some also of his statues escaped, at sight of which, if we may credit Spartian, Caracalla was wont to weep. This emotion, however, was no proof of repentance, but only of unavoidable remorse. The erasure of Geta's name from public monuments is testified by numerous marbles, and particularly by the arch of Severus, still standing at Rome. (See pp. 78–79). Notwithstanding this relentless conduct, Caracalla bestowed greater attention than could have been expected upon his brother's funeral, and deposited his remains in the tomb of Severus, on the Via Appia."—(vii. 227–230–233.)

It is not known whether this unfortunate prince was married or not.

MINTAGES OF GETA.

On his coins which are numerous (very rare in gold, for the most part common in silver, rare in first but common in second brass), he is styled P. SEPT. GETA—GETA CAES*ar*—IMP. CAES. P. SEPT. GETA AVG.—or P. SEPT. GETA PIVS. AVG. BRIT. Sometimes the prenomen of Lucius, sometimes that of Publius is seen on the *Latin* coins of Geta; but on some *Greek* coins both names are found together. There are pieces which represent him with Sept. Severus, Julia Domna, and Caracalla.

The following are amongst the rarest reverses: GOLD.—ANTONINVS AVGVSTVS. Young head of Caracalla. (Valued by Mionnet at 200 fr. and 55 fr. in silver).—CASTOR. (Mt. 150 fr).—CONCORDIAE AVGG. Caracalla and Geta. (160 fr.)—COS. Geta in a quadriga. (160 fr.)—FELICITAS PVBLICA. (150 fr).——FELICITAS TEMPOR. (100 fr.)—FORT. RED. (120 fr.)

LIB. AVGG. VI. ET V. Caracalla and Geta seated together on an estrade; *Liberalitas* with her *tessera* stands near them. Below is a recipient of their bounty.

Obv.—P. SEPT. GETA PIVS AVG. BRIT. Laurelled and bearded head of Geta. (Mionnet values the *aureus*, from which the above is engraved, at 200 fr.)

MINERV. SANCT. Pallas standing.—MINER. VICTRIX. (Mt. 120 fr. each).—PONTIF. COS. II. Minerva seated. (150 fr.)—Same epigraph. Woman and two children.—Same epigraph. Woman holding fruits. (120 fr. each.)—PRINC. IVVENT. COS. (A well preserved specimen of this very rare coin brought £14 5s. at the Thomas sale).—PRINC. IVVENT. Geta near a trophy. (100 fr.)—SEVERI INVICTI AVG. PII. FIL. Radiated bust of Geta. (£14, Thomas).—SPES. PVBLICA. (Mt. 110 fr.)—TRP. III. COS. II. Emperor trampling on a captive.—Same epigraph. Geta stands before Rome seated. (Mt. 150 fr. each.)—VOTA PVBLICA. A sacrificial group. (An extremely well preserved specimen, £16 16. Thomas; £18 5s. Brumell).—Same legend. Sacrifice.—*Obv.*—GETA CAES. PONT. COS. (£13, Brumell).

SILVER.—AETERNIT. IMPERI. Heads of Severus and Caracalla. (Mt. 55 fr.)—IVLIA AVGVSTA. Head of Domna.—L. SEPT. SEVERVS. Head of Severus. (45 fr. each).——PONTIF. COS. II. The three emperors seated.—ROMAE AETERNAE. Rome seated in a temple. (40 fr. each).

BRASS MEDALLIONS.—AEQVITATI PVBLICAE. (See p. 18. Mt. 100 fr.)—CONCORDIA MILITVM. Emperor between five military standards. *Obv.* P. SEPTIMIVS GETA CAESAR. Bust of Geta. (Brought £13 at the Campana sale).—PRINC. IVVENT. Three horsemen galloping.—IOVI SOSPITATORI. Temple. (A specimen formed with parts of two different medals, joined together, and assisted by the graver, sold for £3 4s. at the Campana auction).

FIRST BRASS.—CASTOR.—CONCORDIA AVGG. Caracalla and Geta crowned by two figures. See p. 248.—IOVI SOSPITATORI.——PONTIF. TR. P. Three figures at a sacrifice. (£3 3s. Trattle).

PRINC. IVVENTVTIS. Three horsemen riding at full speed. For an explanation of the *decursion* type see pp. 314–315.

Obv.—GETA CAES*ar* PONTIFEX CON*sul*. S. C. Bust of Geta, the head bare, and the shoulders clothed with the *paludamentum*. See wood-cut at the head of biographical notice, p. 418.

This coin, bearing the youngest portraiture of the prince, was minted between A. D. 197 and 207, in which interval, Geta, then about ten years old, was proclaimed Cæsar by the Senate and the Army, but consented to receive only the titles of Prince of the Youth, and of Pontifex.—See PRINCEPS IVVENTVTIS.

SAECVLARIA SACRA. Temple and four figures. (Two specimens of this type sold together for £15 15s. at the Trattle sale).—VICT. BRIT. (£2 8s. Trattle)—VICTORIAE BRITANNICAE (Mt. 30 fr.) VICTORIA AVGVSTORVM. (50 fr.)

SECOND BRASS.—PONTIF. COS. II. Minerva *Medica* seated, feeding a serpent.--See Lenormant, *Iconographie Rom.* p. 82, pl. xi. No. 11.

GETA III VIR.—See HOSIDIA gens.

GIGAS. A giant.—One of these fabled rebels against the king of gods and men, is represented as struck with lightning by Jupiter, who stands in a quadriga. See a denarius of the Cornelia gens, engraved in p. 286. The monster beneath the quadriga is pronounced by certain antiquaries to be *Triton*, whereas (says Eckhel, v. 189) it is certainly meant for one of the giants, whose lower parts are described to have terminated in two serpents. There is no account of enmity subsisting between Jupiter and Triton; but every one is familiar with the expression—Jupiter "*clarus Gigantum triumpho.*" Vain, therefore, are the conjectures of the learned, to support which they have wrested the interpretation of this type, which appears to be wholly symbolical, in allusion to some sedition, quelled at Rome as effectually as Jupiter put down the revolted giants. A similar combat of Jupiter with a snake-legged Titan is exhibited on a brass medallion of Antoninus Pius.—See *Jupiter.*

GLOBULI.—Globules, or pellets, marked on ancient coins, shew their weight and value. For example . or a single globule is the sign of the *uncia.*—*Two globules* on small brass coins are the mark of the *sextans* in value, although it became less in weight on account of the diminution of the coinage during the first and second Punic war. It is thus on coins of the Aburia, Afraria, and other families.—*Three globules* on Roman *brass* denote the fourth part of the *as*, three *quadrans* being three *uncia* in value. They are seen on coins of the Aburia and Domitia families.—*Four globules* are the mark of the *triens*, as on the brass of the Cornelia gens.—*Five globules*, the *quincunx.*—*Six globules*, the *semis.*—See *as* and its parts (p. 83).

GLOBUS.—A Globe is the symbol of the world *(orbis terrarum)*, or rather of dominion in the world; hence it forms the sign of the Roman empire. The same spherical figure is the type of eternity, because (according to Pierius on Hieroglyphics) it hath neither beginning nor end.—Rasche.

The symbolical *globe* first makes its appearance on coins of Augustus. "On this subject, Isidorus makes the following assertion *(Orig.* b. xviii. ch. 3):—'Augustus is said to have used a ball as a military ensign (pilam in signo constituisse), to indicate the nations which he had subdued, in a perfect circle around him, and the more vividly to display the figure of the world.' With the same intention, it is often subsequently borne in the hand of emperors."—Eckhel.

A *globe* appears on a great many different coins of the imperial series, in the hand of *Hercules*, of *Jupiter*, of the *Sun*, and of *Oriens*, an appellation of the sun. Also in the hand (surmounted by a phœnix) of Eternity, of Felicity, of Fortune, of Providence, of the Genus Humanum, of Indulgentia, of Nobilitas, of Perpetuitas, of Securitas, and of Virtus.—Rome seated, likewise holds the *globe* in her right hand, whilst resting her left on the hasta.— Italy is seated on a *globe.*—The same emblem repeatedly appears under the feet of Victory, of Honour, and of several emperors.

A *globe* supported by two capricorns refers to the horoscope of Augustus, on large brass of that prince.

A *globe*, on the face of which a rudder is placed, on a second brass of Augustus (restored by Nerva), represents the earth, as the rudder does the sea, over both which the government of Rome had extended itself. A second brass of Tiberius bears the same type as in the above engraving. On a gold coin of the last named emperor, Victory seated on a globe holds a crown. The same emblem of power is held by the *Princeps Juventutis*, or *Cæsar*, as the designated successor to the empire.

A *globe* surmounted by an *eagle* with expanded wings, serves to shew the supreme power of imperial Rome, and the subjection of the world to its government; and is a type which may be seen on coins of Augustus, Vespasian, Titus, Hadrian, M. Aurelius, L. Verus, Pertinax, &c. Or it is used for a symbol of *Consecration*, as on coins of M. Aurelius, Verus, Pertinax, S. Severus, Caracalla, Alex. Severus, Carus and others. See CONSECRATIO, p. 249.— There is a coin of Antoninus Pius, on the reverse of which an eagle, with its wings shut, holds a crown in its beak.

A *globe* is held jointly by Vespasian and Titus, by Nerva and a Senator, by Diocletian and Maximianus. It frequently displays itself in the hand of an emperor, as in the *Rector Orbis* of Didius Julianus, the *Victoria Aug.* of Gallienus; the *Sarmatia* of Constantinus jun. It was by this figure, as symbolical of the whole earth, that the *Augusti* proclaimed themselves invested with imperial power. A *victoriola*, or small image of victory, standing on a *globe* and held by the emperor generally signifies that this dominion over the world was the fruit of successful wars.

A *globe*, surmounted by a victoriola, is on coins seen delivered by Jupiter to Alexander Severus and to Carinus; by Hercules to Maximian; by Jupiter to Diocletian; by Carus to Numerianus; as if the gods and demi-gods united in bestowing upon emperors the government of the whole earth. Thus we likewise see the Genius of Rome giving the same symbol, respectively, to Tacitus, Probus, Maxentius, &c.

A *globe*, surmounted by a *phœnix*, appears in the hands of Emperors and Cæsars of the Constantine family.—See *Fel. Temp. Rep.* (p. 378) *Gloria Sæculi*, &c.

A *globe*, surmounted by the sign of the *cross*, either held by Victory, or placed, instead of a *victoriola*, in the hand of the *Augustus* himself, appears on coins of Christian emperors, from Valentinian I. Theodosius II. Justinus, Justinianus, through the entire Byzantine series to the last of the Palæologi, A. D. 1453.

The two symbols thus combined were received amongst the insignia of the lower empire, whence they have been uninterruptedly handed down to the present time. The meaning of this cross-surmounted globe being adopted is explained as follows by *Suidas*, in his life of Justinian, "it signifies (says he), that through Faith in the Cross, he (the Emperor) is made Lord of the earth; for the globe represents the earth by the rotundity of its form; whilst faith is designated by the cross on account of the Incarnate Deity who was fixed to it."

The cross is not placed on the globe, in the mint of Julian II. His hatred of Christianity and love of idolatrous worship again supplied, in its stead, the small image of Victory used by other heathen emperors.

GLORIA. Glory.—This word, which appears for the first time on a coin of Probus, in conjunction with Orbis (see below), and is repeated with wearisome frequency on coins of the lower empire, is interpreted by Vaillant to mean—"manifestatio virtutis et rectè factorum per ora hominum divulgatio"—(the manifestation of valour, and the publication of worthy exploits, by the tongues of men.) For example, the Glory of the Army—the Glory of the Roman people—the Glory of the Romans—the Glory of the world. Yet never was glory more boasted of by those Romans than when the once proud empire of the Cæsars was with the greatest rapidity hastening to decay and ruin.

GLORIA CONSTANTINI AV*Gusti.*—The emperor, helmed and paludated, stands with a

trophy on his left shoulder: he drags by the hair of his head a captive with bound hands; and treads with his left foot on another.—*Obv.* Without legend. The head of Constantine the Great, adorned with a gemmed fillet, face looking up to heaven: on the exergue SIS.

Of this rare, elegant, and largest sized *aureus*, the above reverse is engraved, after a *flower-of-the-die* specimen in the British Museum.—For the obverse type see *Diadem*, p. 322.

If, says Vaillant *(Num. Impp.* ii. 89), the authority of Nazarius is to be received, the captive figures may be looked upon as representing those two kings of the *Franci*, of whom the writer above named says in his panegyric—"Tu ferocissimis regibus Ascarico, et comite suo, tanta laude res bellicas auspicatus es, ut jam inauditæ magnitudinis obsidem teneremus."

From the mint-mark SIS. the initials of *Siscia*, a city of Pannonia, it may be inferred, that this coin was struck about 1079 (A. D. 326), when Constantine visited Rome, and, after a short stay quitted the capital of the empire, never to see it again. As to the epithet *ferocissimi*, applied to the poor Francian kings, Ascaricus and Ragaiscus, his panegyrist with less of the courtier but more of the man of truth, might have addressed the emperor himself with—"*Tu ferocissime princeps,*" &c. No sooner, indeed, had Constantine become sole master of the empire, than he abandoned himself to wrath and cruelty,—"The punishment inflicted (observes the impartial Beauvais) on two kings, his prisoners, whom he caused to be devoured by wild beasts at a public spectacle; the death of the two Licinii, with whom he broke faith; and that of his eldest son Crispus, who had won battles for him, and whom, nevertheless, he unjustly doomed to perish;—these and other barbarous actions of this nature are indelible stains on his character."

GLORIA ET REPARATIO TEMPORVM. The emperor standing in a military habit, holding a Victory and the labarum.—*Obv.* D. N. MAGNENTIVS P. F. AVG. Laurelled bust of the usurper, with the paludamentum.

This gold coin was probably struck about 1103 (A. D. 350), whilst Magnentius, his hands just imbrued in the blood of the Emperor Constans, was endeavouring, but in vain, to effect terms of accommodation with the brother of his murdered prince, Constantius the Second. To a man of his perfidious and most cruel disposition, whose usurped reign was one dark tissue of avarice and tyranny, unrelieved by a single feature of distinction but what ability and valour imparted to it—such titles as are recorded in the above legend, and also that of Restitutor Libertatis, were flagrantly unsuited. But such perverted *eulogia* had only too many precedents in the earlier mintages of Rome; and the later the period of her empire, the more numerous are the examples of monetal flattery and mendacity.—See *Magnentius*.

GLORIA EXERCITVS, with soldiers armed with spears and shields, standing on each side a labarum, or two military ensigns. On coins of Christian emperors the labarum bears the monogram of Christ. This legend and type are common on the coins of Constantine the Great, Delmatius, Constantine jun. Constans, and Constantius. They are regarded as bearing reference to the bravery and fortitude of the soldiers in subduing the barbarous tribes, especially those of Francia and Alamannia.

GLORIA EXERCITVS.—Two soldiers with a tripod between them.—See DELMATIUS, p. 315.—Amongst the Romans, the soldiers were allowed to participate with their general in the honours of the triumph, and with that view, according to Plutarch, Marius on one occasion refused a triumph, that he might not by accepting it prevent his then absent troops from sharing in it. The soldiers were accustomed to march before the triumphal car, with branches of laurel in their hands, as we see it on a medallion of the younger Gordian. And in the various Roman coins, especially of the Constantinian age, it is clearly shewn by the trophies with captives attached, and by the inscriptions to the valour and to the glory ·of particular corps, as well as of the whole Roman army, that the emperors hesitated not to ascribe to their troops the honour of victory, and to decree the monuments which handed their exploits down to posterity.—Spanheim's *Cæsars of Julian*, pp. 226–241.

GLORIA EXERCITVS GALL*icani.*—An equestrian figure, bare-headed and paludated, with right hand raised. On the exergue PTR. —Gold of Constantine the Great.

Whether by *Exercitus Gallicanus* is to be understood all the legions which served in Gallia under Constantius Chlorus and under his son Constantine; or whether by the term was meant the cavalry of the Gaulish nobility, fighting under the Roman standards; this legend has at least the merit (rare enough on imperial coins) of recording a complimentary truth; for it appears on gold and silver of Constantine the Great, who mainly owed his repeated successes over the Alamanni on the banks of the Rhine, and his signal victory over Maxentius near the Tibur, to the aid and prowess of that army, whose glory is predicated on these rare and fine coins.—Vaillant, *Impp. Rom.* iii. 89.

GLORIA EXERCITVS KART. (or KARTH).—An equestrian figure, in a pacific dress. In the exergue TPR.

Pellerin, in the first volume, pl. xii. No. 2 of his *Mélange*, gives the engraving of a second brass, which (from the legend of its obverse IMP. ALEXANDER P. F. AVG.) is ascribed to Alexander, who in 1061 (A. D. 308), revolting against Maxentius, was proclaimed emperor by the soldiers at Carthage. (See p. 34). Of this usurper's coins very few are extant; and the one above cited is the more remarkable, inasmuch as no other has been seen with the legend inscribed on this reverse. Eckhel moreover points out another remarkable feature on this coin, viz. that instead of an elderly and bearded head, like that on other coins of the African Alexander, the obverse type of Pellerin's second brass exhibits the profile of a young man, without beard, which, from the narrative of Zosimus, he thinks it not improbable to be that of Alexander's son—the same whom Maxentius demanded of the usurper as a hostage, and who was then in the flower of his age.

GLORIA NOVI SAECVLI.—The emperor, in the paludamentum, stands with an image of Victory in his right hand, and in his left the labarum. On silver and third brass of Gratian.

A new style of legend, which, says Eckhel (in condemnation of the distorted fancies of Harduin respecting its meaning), signifies neither more nor less than predicting glory to a new government of the empire under Gratian.— (viii. 159.)

GLORIA ORBIS.—On the exergue COS. V. In a triumphal car, drawn by six horses abreast, the emperor Probus stands with his right hand extended, holding a *volumen* or a short *baton*, whilst victory crowns him from behind. About the car are four figures on foot with palm branches. Two soldiers, armed with spears, lead the outermost horses.—*Obv.*—INVICTVS PROBVS P. F. AVG. Bust of Probus laureated and paludated, holding in his left hand a globe surmounted by a victoriola.

Of this large silver medallion, both Khell and Buonarotti have given engravings. The former (p. 206), justly characterises it, not only for weight and purity of metal, but also for superlative elegance of device, and vividness of historical interest, as one of the most valuable relics of monetal antiquity.

The legends and types appear to have immediate reference to that brilliant period of his brief career, between 1032 (A. D. 279) and 1034 (A. D. 281), when, after having driven the *Franci* and *Alamanni* out of Gaul; relieved the Illyrian and Thracian provinces from the barbarian hordes that infested them; concluded a treaty of peace, on honourable terms, with the Persians; and lastly, caused no less than three competitors to pay the forfeit of their lives for their assumption of the purple,—this great prince and successful commander, at length enabled the empire to enjoy a general peace, and himself to celebrate a series of magnificent triumphs at Rome, for his victories gained over many nations. This sudden lull, however, in the constant storm of invasions from without, and of interior conflicts, by which the State had alternately been assailed and lacerated—this abrupt transition from world-wide war to universal tranquillity—proved fatal to " Unconquered Probus." The legions, tired of planting vines in Hungary, rose mutinously against their brave sovereign; whom, in their military licentiousness regarding him rather as their taskmaster than their general, they killed at Sirmium, in the year U. C. 1035 (A. D. 282), whilst he was preparing for another expedition against the Persians, and had proceeded consul for the *fifth* time, as is indicated on the lower part of the preceding reverse.—*Sic transivit Gloria* ORBIS!

GLORIA REIPVBLICAE.—Two sedent female figures, each holding a *hasta*. The figure to the right is galeated; that on the left wears a

turreted crown, and places her right foot on the prow of a ship. Together they support with their right hands a shield, on which is inscribed VOT. XXX. MVLT. XXXX. *(For the vows of thirty years multiplied for forty years)*.

Obv. DN. CONSTANTIVS MAX. AVGVSTVS. Diademed head of Constantius II. On the exergue TES. (money of Thessalonica) between two stars, or CON.—Other coins of this reign exhibit the same legend and type of reverse, but with VOT. XXXV. MVLT. XXXX. and on the exergue SIRM(IUM). The obverse legend is FL*avius* IVL*ius* CONSTANTIVS PERP*etuus* AVG*ustus*. The type exhibits the bust of Constantius II. face to the front, the head covered with a helmet, ornamented with a diadem of precious stones, and an aigrette, the shoulders clothed with the *paludamentum*, holding in the right hand a javelin, and carrying on the left arm a buckler, on which is represented a horseman (the emperor himself) charging an enemy.

These elegant and peculiarly interesting gold coins would appear to have been minted in 1114 (A. D. 364), when Constantius, having driven back Sapor II. king of Persia, found himself free for a war against Julianus as Cæsar, who had already established his authority in Italy and Illyria.—It was in the midst of preparations for this formidable struggle that he was attacked with sickness at Mopsucrène, in Cilicia, and died there.

Alluding to the respective coverings to the heads of the two personifications on the above described reverse, Eckhel says——" By these marks the *two* Romes are distinguished. The *old*, which sits on the right, wears a helmet; the *new*, with towers around her brows, as appears on those coins first issued from Constantine the Great's mint, and which are inscribed CONSTANTINOPOLIS. The VOTA XXXV. are rare; the renewal of vows for the emperors being usually not quinquennial but, from ten years to ten years.—See *Doctr.* viii. 116. Also Khell, supplement to Vaillant, p. 157.

GLORIA ROMANORUM.—This legend was first used, as a new title of personal honour, under Constantine the Great, who certainly did perform so many remarkable achievements, that in his case, the emperor was the whole *Glory of the Romans*. The same epigraph also appears on coins, not only of his sons Constantine jun. Constans, and Constantius; but likewise of Nepotianus, Vetranio, Magnentius, Constantius Gallus, Julianus II. Valentinianus, *Valens* (see p. 424), Procopius, Gratianus, Valentinianus II. Theodosius the Great, Arcadius, Honorius, &c.

The types assigned to the epigraph of *Gloria*

Romanorum are generally either Rome seated; or the emperor on horseback, javelin in hand, trampling on a kneeling or a prostrate captive. Sometimes it is a woman turret-crowned, or an altar inscribed with votive numerals. On gold of Eugenius, Rome and Constantinople are personified seated together (as in Gloria Reipublicæ of Constantius above engraved). On a gold medallion of Arcadius, that emperor nimbated, right hand held up, the left holding a globe, stands in a chariot drawn by six horses, fullfaced; and in the field is the monogram of Christ. It is engraved in Vaillant, *Impp. Rom.* iii. 262.

There are, however, examples of types accompanying GLORIA ROMANORUM shewing that legend not always to identify itself with the person of the emperor on whose coin the legend appears. One of these is a gold medallion of Constantius the Second, the reverse of which exhibits a woman seated on a throne, holding in her right hand a globe surmounted by a *victoriola*, and in her left the *hasta*, or a sceptre with oval-formed top. Her right foot rests on the prow of a vessel.—When a highly-preserved specimen of this extra rare piece formed part of the Thomas cabinet, Mr. Akerman caused it to be engraved, for his *Descriptive Catalogue of Roman Coins*. See vol. ii. pl. G. and also a note on the subject by the same writer, who suggests that the female figure may, from her imperial robe and embroidered shoes, probably be a portrait of the empress Fausta (p. 271), he further remarks, that the symbol which she supports in her left hand resembles the thyrsus of Bacchus.

There is a gold medallion of Valens, with the same legend and a reverse similar to the one above described, but with ROMA on the exergue, engraved in Steinbüchel, p. 21, pl. i. No. 6, but not in so fine a state of preservation as the one above described.

GLORIA ROMANORUM.—The Emperor (Valens) on horseback, with the nimbus, and togated. Before him is the figure of a woman habited in the stola, and wearing a turreted crown, holding in the left hand a lighted torch, and with the right hand lifting a portion of her girdle, which falls to her feet. She bends herself as if to receive the emperor with the greater degree of respect. Below is another female figure, recumbent, holding apples or other fruits in the folds of her tunic, whilst on her left arm, as far as can be discerned, rests a cornucopiæ. Near the recumbent figure are the letters A. N. shewing that the medallion was struck at Antioch, in Syria.

Obv.—D. N. VALENS P. F. AVG. Bust of the emperor, the head crowned with a diadem of pearls. The right hand held up, and in the left a globe. Gold, weighing 63 (Hungarian *aurei*) ducats.

There is another gold piece of the same emperor, part of the *Trèsor trouvé en Hongrie*, 1797, since preserved in the Imperial Museum. It bears exactly the same legends and types as the one above described, and surpasses in weight

all of ancient date yet discovered; being equal to 118 ducats.

The following is an extract from the manuscript of Eckhel, as published by Steinbüchel, relative to these two medallions, the smaller of which is represented in the above wood-cut:—

"The type of this reverse, as it is evidently a novel one, and such as the numismatic soil has never before produced, so for various reasons it presents several particulars deserving of remark. I shall not greatly err in pronouncing that by this type is indicated the visit of Valens to some city of note. To cite one out of the many instances confirmatory of this opinion, on a coin of Commodus, struck in 933 (A. D. 80), that emperor is represented mounted on a horse, proceeding at a gentle pace, the accompanying legend ADVENTVS AVG. And, what points with still greater certainty to an *arrival* at some place, is the figure of the genius of a city, shewn to be such by the turreted head, in the act of meeting the emperor, and paying him reverence by a slight bending of the body. Of this kind of meeting there are other examples. On some imperial coins, struck in Egypt, a female figure of the *Genius of Alexandria* (see p. 412 of this dictionary) meets Hadrian, and takes in her hand, and kisses, the right hand of her imperial visitor; or the same Genius, bearing a vexillum and corn-ears, joins right hands with the emperor on his arrival; or, holding out an olive branch, hastens to meet the emperor, who approaches in a quadriga.—If more proofs were needed, I might add, that on another coin of Hadrian, with the legend ADVENTVI AVG. ALEXANDRIAE, even the presiding deities of that city, Serapis and Isis themselves, have deigned to honour with their presence the advent of the emperor. With regard to the torch in the left hand, since it cannot be considered as the distin-

guishing symbol of any particular city, its appearance, no doubt, indicates a compliment paid to Valens. For by numerous testimonies of ancient writers, and especially of Herodian, we are assured, that it was the custom to bear lights before the emperors, as a mark of the highest respect; and we may venture also to say, as a kind of attribution of divinity. Dion Cassius is the first to supply an instance of this practice, when, speaking of the modesty of M. Aurelius, he says of him, that whenever he appeared in public unaccompanied by his father, he wore a cloak of a sombre colour, and never, when alone, permitted lights to be carried before him. We have a confirmation of the truth of Dion's statement in the Commentaries of M. Aurelius himself, where he remarks, that he had learnt from his father the possibility of living even at court without a crowd of attendants, or an ostentatious display of dress, or *flambeaux* and statues. According to Herodian, when Pertinax, at a perilous juncture, was hailed *imperator* by acclamation, and made his appearance in the Senate-house, he suffered neither lights to be borne before him, nor any other insignia of sovereignty to be displayed. And the same author informs us that Pescennius Niger, on being proclaimed Augustus in opposition to Didius Julianus, immediately arrayed himself in the purple and all the imperial paraphernalia that could be procured at short notice, and, with lights preceding him, visited in procession the temples at Antioch. The same distinction was accorded to Quartinus, whom the Osrhænian soldiers set up in opposition to Maximinus, who had incurred their enmity on account of the murder of Alexander Severus; and not long afterwards the like compliment was paid at Carthage to Gordianus Africanus. Nor did the *Augusti* withhold this honour from the empresses. The same Herodian informs us, that Commodus, even after the death of L. Verus, and her subsequent marriage with Pompeianus, a private citizen, preserved to his sister Lucilla all the insignia of imperial dignity; for he permitted her to view the public games from an imperial throne, and to have lights carried before her. Indeed, that this "fiery" distinction was by far the most exalted of the honours paid to sovereignty, we learn again from the statement of Herodian, that Commodus carried his infatuated attachment for Marcia to such a length, that her position differed in no respect from that of a legitimate wife, all the privileges of an empress being showered upon her, except that of having lights borne before her. I think the foregoing testimonies from ancient writers are sufficient to prove the existence of the custom in question. But there are monuments also extant, which corroborate their statements. Count Caylus has published a marble in bas-relief, which presents the emperor delivering an *adlocutio* from a *suggestus*. By his side stand soldiers with military ensigns, one of which exhibits a lighted fire fixed on the end of a spear *(Rec. d' Ant.* iii. pl. 66), intended doubtless to indicate the custom of which we are now speaking. Who was the originator of the practice, or what the country from which it was first derived, are questions about which I do not much trouble myself. It very likely came from the East, where fire is held in such peculiar veneration. And Ammianus, in reciting the customs of the Persian magi, says, that a small quantity of celestial fire was carried before the kings of Asia; and generally we may remark, that antiquity was in the habit of connecting every bright and fiery object with its princes, witness, on the coins of emperors, the radiated crown, the nimbus, the emperors and empresses compared with the Sun and the Moon, &c. &c.

"As I have said that the type of this reverse alludes to some imperial *arrival*, I must endeavour to discover some probable conjecture, by which the name of the very city may be elicited. My belief is, that it refers to the city of Antioch, the most renowned in the East, and where history informs us that Valens resided for many years, whilst engaged in the war with Sapor the Persian; where, too, he built baths. This opinion is confirmed by the letters AN. the initials of Antioch. There can be no doubt that the female figure lying on the ground is *Mater Tellus*, so frequently observed in this posture on ancient monuments. * * * * * By the open fold of the tunic, with apples appearing therein, and by the cornucopiæ, she boasts her own peculiar gifts, and seems to prognosticate increased abundance and fertility from the arrival of the emperor. Nor was such hope without foundation, for it was to Hadrian's visit that the Africans attributed the grateful fall of rain after a five years' drought. Indeed some of the ancients believed that fate itself was controlled, or executed, by the power of princes. On the obverse of the first described medallion, Valens is typified raising his right hand, which was the customary gesture of emperors, when proclaiming peace and their own supremacy."

[Such is the light which, with his peculiar tact and ability, the Prince of the Science we study after his system, has thrown on the subject of these monetal prodigies. In fulfilling the duty which had devolved to him, of giving publicity to Eckhel's manuscript, M. Steinbüchel admits that nothing can be more clear than the *ensemble* of the elucidation—that it is the arrival of the emperor—that the female figure must be the genius of the city, or of the province, which receives him with all due submission—and that the symbolical figure of the earth, below, indicates an imperial journey into distant countries. Having thus unhesitatingly adopted the general views expressed in the preceding observations, Steinbüchel proceeds to animadvert on some points of detail, the meaning of which is less apparent, and the arguments adduced in support of which are less convincing, to him, than the other parts of Eckhel's explanation.]

" The whole difficulty (says the learned *Ex-Directeur du Musée* I. R.) consists in the female figure before the emperor. Eckhel, guided by history and the expedition of Valens to Antioch, coupled with that prince's long residence in the rich capital of Syria, has taken it for the Genius of that city. His erudition furnished him with the explanation of the lighted torch; he derives its signification from the custom which prevailed in ancient times of carrying the sacred fire before kings and emperors. * * * But it is needful to observe, that this fire which was borne before princes is not proved to have been of lighted torches, as Eckhel has supposed. We are on the contrary persuaded that on these occasions portable altars were used, such as we see actually represented in the bacchanalian processions on some antique bas-reliefs. It is generally allowed that this custom came from the East; and we find these altars even distinctly named by Curtius, lib. iii. and by Xenoph, Cyropœd, lib. iii. c. 3.

" Again, it is necessary to observe, that on so many coins and other monuments which represent the arrival of emperors in different provinces and cities, we in no instance find an allusion to the usage in question, that is to say, of carrying the sacred fire; or, as Eckhel says, lighted torches before them. If sometimes we find on these coins an altar placed in the centre between the figure of the emperor and that of the province, it is evidently to indicate thanksgivings rendered to the gods for the happiness which the presence of the emperor had afforded them. On most of these reverses the victim there seen offered on the occasion, is a bull extended on the ground, in such a way as to lead to the conclusion, that the ancients did not employ the symbol of the lighted torch to represent the arrival of emperors. Why then should it have been adopted on these medals of Antioch ?

"The torch, without any reference to the action of the emperor, seems to us a distinctive and characteristic mark of the female figure. Our reason for believing it is this:—In the *Museum Theupolum*, which the Emperor of Austria caused to be purchased for the Imperial Museum at Vienna—[an acquisition made subsequently to Eckhel's death]—there is a small Greek coin in brass which exhibits on the obverse the bust of the Sun, with radiated crown, and a torch; on the reverse the bust of Diana, with the crescent and likewise a lighted torch. What constitute the merit of this little monument are the inscriptions ΑΝΑΤολη and ΔΥΣΙΣ, that is to say East and West. Are we to suppose that these types represent to us only the two stars of day and of night? Without entering into detail respecting the times of M. Aurelius, to whose reign the coin belongs, it is nevertheless certain that the signification of it will prove altogether symbolical. There is no doubt but that these same figures of the sun and moon have already been made use of on the triumphal arch of Constantine the Great at Rome, for the purpose of indicating the two great divisions of our world *(Oriens et Occidens)*, East and West. Now, the spirit of Christianity no longer permitted it under Valens, to avail itself too faithfully of pagan symbols. This accounts for our no longer seeing the crescent on the forehead of the woman on our medallion; but we have there the torch and the turreted crown to replace them. There is nothing, therefore, opposed to our recognising the image of the West in this figure, which seems to enter into the presence of the emperor, and to receive him. In that case it would be the grand expedition against the Goths which was meant to be pointed to—an expedition whence a very different issue was assuredly hoped for than a defeat, destined to cost Valens both throne and life.

"But it will be said that, as on the coins of Valerianus and Gallienus, with *Restitutori Orientis* (Banduri, i. 110 and 124), the East is represented by a similar figure of a woman, with the same radiated crown, although without torch, why should she not be the East, on the medallions of Valens, coming to meet him, and why should not these medallions have actually been struck for his journey into Syria, and for the expedition which he was contemplating against the Persians? To speak frankly (concludes M. Steinbüchel), we have nothing to oppose to such an assertion, provided that the female figure remains the symbolical figure of the East, and not that of the city of Antioch, and that the torch be then a *flambeau du soleil*, the great tutelary of the East, and not an indication of ceremonies for the entry of the emperor into Antioch."—See *Notice sur les Médaillons Romains en Or, du Musée de Vienne*, p. 22 et seq.

[Here then the opinions of two such high authorities as those above quoted are placed in juxta-position, as well where they conflict as where they agree with each other, on a matter of more than ordinary numismatic interest.— In having done so, the compiler grudges not the space thus occupied in his pages, but he leaves the respective points, on which a Steinbüchel and an Eckhel differ and coincide, to the reader's consideration and judgment].

GLORIA ROMANORVM.—Rome seated, holding a *victoriola* in the right hand and resting left hand on the hasta. In the exergue SMN.— *Obv.* without legend, Head looking upwards, diadem with pearls, &c. (see p. 322). Gold medallion of Constantine the Great. Size 8.

[An unpublished specimen in the highest preservation, brought £11 at the Sabatier sale, engraved in pl. ii. No. 3, annexed to the catalogue, lot 532].

GLORIA ROMANORVM. Personified Rome seated.—In the exergue TR.—*Obv.*—FL. IVL. CONSTANTIVS NOB. C. Bust diademed with pearls, and wearing the paludamentum. Gold medallion of Constantius II. size 7.

[A fine specimen, brought £9 at the sale of the Sabatier collection, the catalogue of which contains an engraving of it in pl. ii. No. 4, lot 538].

GLORIA SAECVLI VIRTVS CAESS. (Cæsarum). *The valour of the Cæsars is the glory of the age.*—The emperor, naked to the waist, seated on a cuirass, and resting his left hand on a long sceptre. In front of him stands a young warrior, wearing the *paludamentum*, he bears a trophy on his left shoulder, and with his right hand offers a globe surmounted by a *phœnix*, to the emperor. At his feet is a panther. On the exergue, P. R. *(Percussum Romæ*—struck at Rome.)

Obv.—CONSTANTINVS MAX*imus* AV-*Gustus*. Bust of Constantine the Great, wearing the paludamentum, and a diadem ornamented with precious stones and laurel leaves. (See this portrait engraved in p. 257.)

Vaillant, in his series of brass medallions, *(Impp. Rom.* T. iii. 237), has given a print of this fine historical monument. Buonarotti also *(Medagl Ant.* p. 390), has engraved it, and moreover made it the subject of a learned commentary, without however resolving all the difficulties to which the reverse has given rise. Eckhel makes no mention of it. Nor, indeed, has Vaillant contributed anything to its elucidation, but he at once pronounces Crispus to be represented in the figure of the warrior.

M. Ch. Lenormant, on the other hand, and with greater shew of reason, says—"The Cæsar who presents the globe appears to us indubitably Constantius the Second. The trophy which he carries, surmounted by a Phrygian cap, points to a victory gained over the peoples of the East; and Constantius is the only one of Constantine the Great's sons, who had been charged, two years before the death of his father, with an expedition against the Parthians. The plural CAESARVM indicates, it is true, several Cæsars; but according to a custom, already become old at the epoch of Constantine, it is probable that the achievements of one Cæsar were intercommunicated with the others. A more precise explanation of this plural is also capable of being furnished. Constantine junior, five years before the expedition of Constantius, had obtained a great victory over the Goths; probably it is that prince whom the legend here associates with his brother. The panther doubtless alludes to the public shews celebrated with the animals which Constantius had brought to Rome from his eastern campaign. It will be perceived, that the young prince has his right foot placed on the tail of the panther, whose mouth is half open as if crying out. It is indeed by acting on the tail *(en agissant sur la queue)* that the most ferocious beasts are tamed. As to the *phœnix*, Buonarotti, on good ground, affirms, that this symbol of renovation had been adopted by the first Christians, which serves to explain to us why it is met with on a monument of the last years of Constantine's reign. The same Italian antiquary even cites a passage from John of Salisbury, a writer of the 13th century, according to whom the symbol of the *phœnix* shewed itself from the foundation of Constantinople. To what more ancient author John of Salisbury was indebted for this piece of information, we have not been able to verify."— *Iconographie des Empereurs Romains*, p. 121, pl. lvii. No. 13.

There are gold and silver coins of the same emperor, but of the ordinary size, having for legend of reverse GLORIA SAECVLI VIRTVS CAES. with simply two figures standing, the one presenting a globe to the other.

GL. P. R. *Gloria Populi Romani.*—Rasche.

GL. R. *Gloria Romanorum.*—Vaillant, *Pr.* i. p. 300.

GL. E. R. *Gloria Exercitus Romani.*— Akerman—Rasche.

G. P. R. *Genius Populi Romani.*—Denarius of Cornelia gens. 2 B. Hadrian and Antoninus.

GRA. and GRAC. *Gracchus.*—Surname of Sempronia gens.

G. T. A. *Genius Tutelaris Ægypti*, or *Africæ.* —See silver of Cæcilia gens.

GLYCERIUS *(Flavius)* usurped the empire after the death of Olybrius (the son in law of Valentinian III.) A. D. 470, and the next year he was forced to abdicate, and content himself with the bishopric of Salona, in Dalmatia.— Died about the year 480. On his coins, which are in gold and silver, of very great rarity, he is styled D. N. GLYCERIVS P. F. AVG.

G. M. *Germanicus Maximus.*—It thus appears on a coin of Gallienus—IMP. GALLIENVS P. F. AVG. G. M.—Banduri, i.

G. M. Q. or C. MESS. Q. &c.—*Gneus Messius Quintus. These are prenomina of Trajan Decius.*—See DECIUS, p. 313.

G. M. V. *Gemina Minervia Victrix.*—Name of a Roman legion.

GOLD COINAGE *of the Romans.*—At the period when silver money was introduced into Rome, namely in the year U. C. 485 (B. C. 269), Roman power had already gained a great increase. It extended itself still more and more as riches and the mass of the circulating medium augmented. According to Pliny, gold was first coined at Rome in the year of that city 547 (B. C. 206). It has been supposed, that amongst the money issued from that epoch to the time of the first Triumvirate, some coins were minted, not in Rome but, in one or other of the Italian cities subject to Rome. But on this point sufficiently positive data do not exist whence satisfactory inferences can be drawn.

When gold was first employed by the moneyers of Rome—namely, at the date above mentioned, when the war with Hannibal was at its height, coins in that metal, which, to abide by the statement of Pliny, "were struck like the silver ones, in such a manner, that the scruple [twenty grains of gold] was equivalent to twenty sestertii [of silver], which, conformably to the standard of sestertii then prevailing, gave 900 sestertii to the pound.— Subsequently it became the custom to strike 40 denarii to the pound of gold; and gradually the weight was diminished by successive emperors; by Nero so low as 45 to the pound." And these coins are frequently called by Pliny *denarii*, as their half were called *quinarii*, a misapplication of the term, as they were neither of the weight, nor of the relative value, of the silver coins, though nearly the same in dimensions.—Arrian, too, mentions 'a gold and a silver *denarius;*' and Petronius says —'instead of black and white counters, he used gold and silver denarii.'

It is thus that the weight of the gold denarius has been calculated from the ascertained weight of the silver one. From Pliny we know that 84 denarii were struck to the pound of silver. Since each of these weighed 75 Parisian grains, the number of grains required to make up the monetary pound would be 6,300. But as we have already learned from the same authority, that 40 denarii were struck to the pound of *gold*, you will, by dividing 6300 by 40, arrive at the number of grains which each gold piece weighed, viz. 157½.—Hence it is clear that the *gold denarius* weighed more than two silver ones by 7½ grains. And thus it follows, that from Nero's time, when 45 denarii were first struck to the pound of gold, the weight of the *gold denarius* was 140 grains.

The Roman *aureus* held the invariable value of 25 denarii, under such regulations, that any increase, or diminution, of weight in the *aureus*, should be attended by a corresponding alteration in the weight of the *denarius.*—The above mentioned weight of the aureus is confirmed by abundant testimony. Zonaras speaks clearly on this point—" Among the Romans twenty-five drachmæ [drachm, 8th part of an ounce Troy weight] make one gold coin."—Xiphilinus says the same.—According to Lucian, 30 *aurei* are equivalent to 750 drachmæ, and consequently one *aureus* to 25 drachmæ, or denarii.—Suetonius relates, that Otho gave an aureus to each of the soldiers composing his outlying cohort; and Plutarch, who records the same fact, says, in Greek—χρυσοῦν ἑκάστῳ διανέμων—distributing to each an *aureus.* What these authors call an *aureus,* Tacitus describes as a *sestertius* —" that he might distribute 100 *numi* to each man of the cohort, which was keeping watch and ward." But 100 sestertii are equal to 25 denarii. Suetonius says of Domitian—" He added a fourth *aureus* to the pay of the soldier, which was three aurei." Zonaras gives the same sum in drachmæ—" Whereas 75 drachmæ were usually paid to each soldier, he ordered 100 to be paid to them." This will enable us to understand the expression of Martial, when he desires that, to the 57 years which he had already lived, should be added twice nine more, that he might complete his *tres aurei* of life. He would then have lived 75 years, the number of denarii contained in three aurei.

Most authors of modern times state the proportion of gold to silver, among the ancient Romans, as nearly 1 to 12, so that 12 pounds of silver were exchanged for one of gold. Nor does investigation materially contradict this statement; since for the aureus, which was rather more than double the weight of the denarius, 25 denarii were given in exchange. To compare it, for example, with the modern coinage, an aureus of Julius Cæsar, or Augustus, is worth $2 \frac{1}{2} \frac{1}{3} \frac{1}{4}$ Hungarian or Dutch gold pieces [viz. ducats, 2 dwts. 5 $\frac{3}{4}$ grs. 9s. 5$\frac{1}{4}$d. English value], the weight decreasing gradually, in successive periods.

The proportion or relation borne by *Gold* to *Silver* in the coinage of Rome, is a subject, with the abstruse difficulties of which Eckhel has powerfully grappled, in his dissertation *De Monetâ Aureâ Romanorum* (v. c. iv. p. 28), whence the foregoing passages have been taken. Referring the reader to that portion of his *Doctrina,* for other details too copious to be even alluded to within our limits, we hereto subjoin an extract from M. Hennin's *Manuel* (T. i. ix. p. 183, on *" The Value and Weight of Ancient Money"*), in which that scientific French numismatist has given an analysis of the opinions respectively entertained by Savot, Nauze, Barthèlemy, Letronne, and Eckhel, on the matter in question :—

The proportion of gold to silver is more easy to establish by proofs, in the case of the Romans than of the Greeks, and we have, in that respect, certain aids, which fail us in investigating the monetary systems of other nations. The passages in ancient authors which connect themselves with this subject, are not entirely satisfactory; but in comparing these data with what we know respecting the value of the gold denarius, fixed at 25 silver denarii, and in making the calculation of weights, results are arrived at. Moreover we find in the coins themselves sources of important information, which ought to serve us by way of guide, although they relate to only one epoch.

Three very rare pieces of gold money, which were in all probability struck in Campania, under Roman authority during the republic, are considered to have been issued, about the time when gold coins of Roman die began to be struck. These three coins bear the following numeral marks : $\bigvee$ x. (sixty *sestertii) ;* xxxx. (forty *sestertii) ;* xx. (twenty *sestertii).* There is no doubt as to the accuracy of these interpretations. After the examinations to which the weight of these pieces were submitted, with as much exactness as circumstances would allow, the coins being very rare, and few specimens of them extant, there appeared the following results, which nevertheless ought to be regarded only as approximations, for they were not exactly in agreement with each other :
Piece of 60 *sestertii,* weighing three
  scruples of the Roman pound...... 64 grains.
Piece of 40 *sestertii,* weighing two
  scruples of the Roman pound...... 43 „
Piece of 20 *sestertii,* weighing one
  scruple of the Roman pound ...... 21$\frac{1}{3}$ „
The following calculations were subsequently made :—

The scruple of gold being the twenty-fourth part of the ounce, an ancient pound contained 288 scruples. In multiplying 288 by 21$\frac{1}{3}$ grains weight of the gold piece of 20 sestertii, which weighed a scruple, we have for the weight of the ancient pound 6,144 grains. The gold scruple being worth 20 silver sestertii, or five denarii, the pound of gold, containing 288 scruples, was worth 1,440 silver denarii.

We know from Pliny, already quoted, that 84 silver denarii were made out of one pound of that metal. Dividing 1440 by 84, leaves 17$\frac{1}{7}$. Therefore the proportion of gold to silver was then that of 1 to 17$\frac{1}{7}$ pounds of silver, that is to say, one pound of gold was worth 17$\frac{1}{7}$ pounds of silver.

It is necessary, however, to observe, that these calculations, and the bases on which they are founded, have not been generally accepted, and that the results have been given by divers authors, in somewhat different ways.—The following are the principal of these valuations :—

Savot fixed the weight of the Roman scruple at 21 grains, and that of the Roman pound at 6,048 grains.

Nauze carries them to 21 grains $\frac{1}{2}$, and to 6,144 grains.

Romè de l'Isle the same as Savot.

Eckhel the same as Nauze.

M. Letronne fixed these weights at 21$\frac{868}{1000}$ grains, and 6,160 grains.

Be it as it may with regard to these differences, and some others which are not of much importance, the proportion of gold to silver was, under the adoption of this system, that of 1 to about 17, when gold was for the first time employed in coining by the Romans.

At this epoch, gold existed only in a small quantity. It became by degrees less rare. It has been sought to fix the divers æras to which the relation of this metal with silver was progressively reduced. The details on this subject would be too numerous for us to enter into them. It must suffice here to point out what is the opinion most generally entertained on this point. We subjoin therefore the indication of these proportions, according to the most universally adopted system :—

1. From the year of Rome 547 (B.C. 206) to 560 (B.C. 193) .... 1 to $17\frac{1}{7}$
2. From the above epoch to the year 620 (B.C. 133) .... 1 to $14\frac{2}{7}$
3. From that epoch to 635 (B.C. 118) 1 to 13
4. From that epoch to 650 (B.C. 103) 1 to $12\frac{1}{2}$
5. From that epoch to 717 (B.C. 36) 1 to $11\frac{19}{21}$
6. From that epoch to 767 (A.D. 14) 1 to $11\frac{63}{86}$
7. From that epoch to 821 (A.D. 68) viz. from the death of Augustus to the last years of Nero .... ,, ,,

["A reference to the scales (says Eckhel), proves the truth of Pliny's statement, that the emperors gradually diminished the weight of the aureus, 42, 43, and 44 aurei being now struck to the pound."]

8. From 821 (A.D. 60) to 970 (A.D. 217) viz. from the last years of Nero to the last of Caracalla, 45 aurei to the pound, each weighing $136\frac{8}{15}$ grains .... 1 to 12

["The coins themselves (says Eckhel) serve to confirm this rule; not, however, without exceptions. For the coins of Domitian, Nerva, and Trajan (in the first two years of his reign) weigh 140 grains and more, up to 145. From the period when 45 aurei were struck to the pound, 96 denarii were struck to the pound of silver. If, therefore, 45 be multiplied by 25 (the number of denarii equivalent to one aureus), the result will be 1125, and this divided by 96, will give a quotient of $11\frac{23}{32}$, the proportion of gold to silver, i. e. nearly 1 to 12."]—*D. N. Vet.* v. 33.

This scale of variations in the proportion of gold to silver is shewn by Eckhel to be far from certain. He contends that the doctrine of Barthèlemy and Nauze, which refers to the three aurei, exhibiting the arithmetical marks LX. XXXX. and XX. is at once refuted, if that be true which is now supposed by the majority of writers, viz. that those celebrated coins, which served as the basis of Barthèlemy's calculations, are not to be reckoned as belonging to the Roman mint, but are rather to be regarded as the productions of Magna Græcia or Sicily. In other respects he also differs from his learned contemporaries above-named, whose calculations on this matter he criticises with great freedom and at considerable length, pronouncing them not to have been established in a clear and authentic manner, and viewing the experiments made on the coins

themselves as having been neither sufficiently numerous nor sufficiently exact.

On the other hand, some passages of ancient writers (Livy, l. 38, c. 11—Sueton. J. Cæsar, c. 54), point to data of a different kind. It would seem, according to those passages, that the proportion in question would have been, at first, that of 1 to 15, afterwards 1 to 10, 1 to 9, and even less. It is obvious then that these important points have not yet been cleared up in a satisfactory manner. From the reign of S. Severus the disorder which had introduced itself into the coinage, with regard to standards, renders the ideas relative to the connection of gold with silver still more obscure and more intricate; and almost goes to set at defiance any further endeavours to establish reasonable suppositions.— In the times of the lower empire this obscurity is still greater.

At the epoch of commencing a gold mint at Rome, there were, as we have seen, two effective gold coins introduced, viz. a gold denarius (worth 25 silver denarii), and a quinarius of gold (worth half the gold denarius), the gold denarius was also called an *aureus*. In the third century of the Christian era, this money took the name of *solidus*. Under the lower empire the weights and dimensions of these coins varied greatly, in consequence of the disorder which then prevailed.

2.—GOLD COINAGE OF ROME—*Was it, during the commonwealth, struck under the ordinary regulations* (ex lege ordinariâ)? This subject is discussed by Eckhel (vol. v. pp. 37–42), in a way so well calculated to assist in rescuing from obscurity, and even to render generally interesting, that recondite but still, from historical associations, important branch of monetary research—the origin and progress of a gold currency in Free Rome—that, omitting those personal allusions with which his animadversions on the main question are mixed up in controversy by our great preceptor and guide, we shall not be prevented, merely on account of the extent to which they run, from inserting the principal passages of so fine a display of learned research, and acute argumentation. They are to the following effect :—

The remarkable paucity of coins struck in gold during the republic serves to suggest doubts. And to render the fact more evident, Eckhel has brought together, at one view, those pieces which are attributed to the time of the commonwealth down to the government of Julius Cæsar. Of these there are two kinds, viz. :—

First.—Those which belong to Epoch I. (547 to 560), inscribed with only the word ROMA, and bearing certain arithmetical marks (see p. 428), the type being a head of Mars. And also those which belong to Epoch II. (560 to 620), also with the sole inscription ROMA ; the types being—head of Janus ; soldiers touching a sow with their spears ; and the Dioscuri.

Second.—Those inscribed with the name of a family—ex. gr. Cornelius, Blasio, C. Servilius, Nerva, Furius Philus, and Cn. Lentulus ; which are said to have been struck between the years

547 and 650. After that time till the reign of
Julius Cæsar, the following:—Cl. Clodius,
Numonius, Arrius, Cestius, Metellus, Sulla,
and Fufius Calenus.

The above is the entire list of gold *consular*
coins hitherto discovered. Nor is even this perfect; for from it must be taken two, namely, the
first cited, as inscribed with the word ROMA only;
and which more correctly are to be ascribed to a
foreign mint, as stated in Section I. on this subject of the Gold Coinage. Also *two*, the date of
which should be fixed at the time of Julius Cæsar,
or the Triumvirs; for that which Nauze assigns
to them is often arbitrary, and founded merely on
conjecture. If then, all these be deducted from
the scanty number of gold *consular* coins,
scarcely a tenth part will remain of such as by
universal consent are attributed to the age of the
commonwealth. Since, therefore, gold coins of
this class (acknowledged to have been certainly
struck from the years 547 to the reign of Julius
Cæsar), are so rare, can these furnish any valid
argument, that gold coins were struck, under
the consuls, by the law ordinarily in force *(lege
ordinariâ?)* The point might readily be conceded, if abundant specimens were extant of the
few coins of this class, as is the case in the
silver coinage; but the fact is, that all the gold
coins, properly assigned to the times of the consuls, are either exceedingly rare, or unique; a
paucity which so little favours the notion of
their being regulated by the same laws as the
ordinary coinage, especially under so vast an
empire, that it would seem rather to be totally
at variance with it."

The question then, as to whether there was
no gold struck, under the Commonwealth, by
any fixed law? the author of *Doctrina* meets by
demanding, that a probable reason be first adduced, why during the glorious period of a
mighty empire, extending over so long a time,
scarcely even a few should have been left to us?

"It will be conjectured, that they have perished
through the injuries of Time. But why should
Time have directed his wrath so specially against
this species of coins, when he has been so lenient
to the gold coins of Philip II. of Macedon,
which preceded by 150 years the alleged date of
the introduction of a gold coinage into Rome—
and again those of Alexander the Great and Lysi-
machus—that they have not even yet ceased to
annoy us by their abundance and worthlessness?
But to pass over these more important kingdoms;
there still remain numerous gold coins of Syracuse, Tarentum, and the remote Cyrene, all
struck long prior to the period of the *golden age*
in Rome; and yet how insignificant the territory of all these states together compared with
the Roman Empire! And so, forsooth, the gold
coins of Julius Cæsar, Sextus Pompeius, Brutus,
Cassius, the Triumvirs, all could escape destruction, but those which immediately preceded
them could not! What more reasonable or appropriate juncture could there have been for
striking gold coins, than when L. Scipio, after
he conquered Antiochus the Great, or Cn. Pompey, victorious over Mithridates and Tigranes,

poured into Rome the treasures of all Asia?
—But silver coins of both those individuals
are extant in abundance, while of gold not one
has been discovered. If any one is inclined to
wonder, that, in a city of such power and wealth
as Rome, gold was not employed in its coinage,
let him extend his surprise to the fact, that so
far as our present knowledge goes, the same
custom prevailed among the Athenians, whose
power and resources are well known, but of
whom not a single gold coin has yet been found;
and that it prevails at the present day in the
powerful Empire of the Chinese.

With regard to the statement of Pliny, Eckhel
asks, "if this illustrious writer had bestowed so
much pains on determining the date of the introduction of a gold coinage into Rome, why did
he abstain, in the gold coins alone, from noticing
the types by which they were distinguished, or
their division into parts, and the names of those
parts, when he has not failed to describe all
these particulars in the silver and brass coinage? How is it that Livy, who so learnedly
recorded the first striking of silver at Rome, did
not introduce the slightest allusion to stamped
gold, when he arrived at that period of his
history, when, according to Pliny, a gold coinage was introduced? Why did no one of the
ancient writers, whilst narrating the events of
that age, make mention of Roman gold money?
Though, even if any testimony for it existed, it
would prove nothing more than that the author
might have spoken *by anticipation*, and thought
only of an equivalent value?—Indeed, according
to the accounts of ancient writers, and especially
of Livy, the highest authority of all on this
subject, it appears that, before the era stated by
Pliny, or A. U. C. 547, the Romans, in making
payments, used gold by weight instead of by the
number of pieces—(i. e. *weighed instead of
counting it.)* Every one is aware, how they redeemed the capitol from the Gauls, viz. by gold
weighed out. In the year U. C. 544 (B. C. 210),
when Hannibal was pressing them hard, and
the treasury was bankrupt, wrought gold was
liberally brought forward by the senators to defray the expenses of the war. In the following
year, U. C. 545, when the want of money was
still more harassing, 'it was determined to appropriate the *gold raised by the tax of the twentieth part (aurum vicesimarium)*, which was
reserved for emergencies in a more sacred treasury.' That, therefore, which supplied the *place
of money*, would very naturally be called *money*,
even subsequently to the period at which Pliny
has fixed the introduction of *coined* gold into
Rome.

"Lastly, it may be inquired, why we have not
a single gold *Consular* coin restored by Trajan,
when we possess several *Imperial* gold coins restored by that Emperor, who was in the habit
of adhering not merely to the types but to the
metal also of his restitutions. From this fact a
suspicion arises, that at the same time that many
other privileges were conferred on Julius Cæsar,
there was granted to him also that of striking
gold coins in the ordinary course of things *(lege*

ordinariâ), a privilege retained through the licence of that age by those who immediately succeeded him, i. e. Sextus Pompeius, Brutus, the Triumvirs, and others; and that those few gold coins, which we have a right to reckon as consular, owe their existence to *extraordinary occasions*, which like many other points in history have escaped us; though we may readily account for the appearance of Sulla's *aurei* (and even *they* are extremely rare), when we reflect on that Dictator's power and extravagance. It is needless to insist on the evidence afforded of the fact in question by the law which this very Sulla introduced. 'By the *Lex Cornelia*,' says Ulpian, 'it is enacted, that whosoever shall mix any foreign ingredient with the gold, or stamp coins of adulterated silver, shall be convicted of fraud.' Now, if it was then struck in the ordinary course, why does this law use the word *aurum* simply, and not *aureos numos*, just as, afterwards, *numos argenteos?* If, however, any one should consider such a practice to be incredible under the commonwealth, and wish to have some more tangible reason assigned for it, he would be acting in the same manner as if he were to require to be informed why, on the other hand, from the time of Claudius Gothicus to that of Diocletian, the *silver* coinage was almost entirely stopped, whilst the gold money continued to be struck under its usual regulations and in abundance. There are many knotty points in antiquarian research worthy enough of an elucidator, but no deity has as yet appeared to solve them. And for myself, I undertook the discussion of these matters, not with a view to convict Pliny of falsehood or a hasty conclusion, but to challenge those who espouse the side of Pliny, to produce in greater abundance coins, which by indisputable signs are to be referred to consular times.

"I will not conceal the existence of other authorities favourable to the upholders of the *consular* gold coinage, namely, those of Pomponius and Cicero himself. According to Pomponius. 'the Monetal Triumvirs' were constituted 'strikers (coiners) of brass, silver, and *gold*,' about the year 465 (B. C. 189). Cicero, in his epistle to Trebatius, about the year 700 (B. C. 54), says :—' I advise you to keep out of the way of the Treviri [the men of Treves—a play on the words *Triumviri* Monetales]. I hear that they are sharp fellows (capitales). I would rather that they were charged with the striking of *gold*, silver, and brass.' And again, in his third book *De Legibus*, chap. 3, a work which appears to have seen the light two years after Fabricius, he enunciates this law : ' Let them publicly coin brass, silver, and *gold*.' The passage from Pomponius claims but little attention. That writer's statement, even if its truth be admitted, may certainly be modified in the interpretation. But there is a weightier authority in both the passages of Cicero ; for though the former of them be spoken in joke, and in the latter he be laying down a rule of his own, it is nevertheless evident that the writer is alluding to a recognized institution of his country. This

conflicting testimony, however, does not give me much trouble ; since I am not denying that gold was stamped under the consuls, but simply denying that it was stamped in the *ordinary procedure of the mint.*—Livy himself may give rise to a doubt on the question, when he tells us that M. Valerius Lævinus, consul, A. U. C. 544, on the failing of the treasury in consequence of the protracted war with Hannibal, thus addressed the Senators : 'Let us Senators bring forward to-morrow, for the public benefit, all our gold, silver, and stamped brass,'—words which may appear to indicate, that even at that time the Romans were using *stamped gold*. But I can easily prove, that in this passage of Livy the word *signatum* by no means refers to the *gold*, but only to the brass, or perhaps also to the silver. I have two reasons for saying this— First, if the word *signatum* refers also to the gold, it will follow, that so early as the year 544, the Romans used a gold coinage universally ; but on this supposition, we must throw over the authority of Pliny, who states that gold was not stamped at Rome till the year U. C. 547. And secondly, that the sense of Livy's words is such as I have stated it to be, will clearly appear from the succeeding context. For, when Lævinus defines how much of these three metals might be reserved for the use of each of the Senators themselves, he specifies the *brass* only as *stamped (signatum)*, and sums up the rest of the fund in *wrought (factum)* gold and silver : to each Senator he allows an ounce of gold for rings for himself and his wife, and a *bulla* for his son ; a pound of silver for his horses' caparison, his salt cellar, and the *patella* of the gods ; but of *stamped brass five thousand pieces (sestertii.)* In another part of his writings, Livy explains his meaning more clearly, where, describing the same period of the war with Hannibal, he introduces L. Valerius, the tribune of the people, thus speaking—' Care was taken that we should have no more *wrought* gold and silver, no more *stamped* silver and brass, in our houses.' The purport of which words has been well rendered by Isidorus— ' There are,' he says, ' three kinds of silver, gold, and brass, the *stamped*, the *wrought*, and the *unwrought*. The *stamped* is that which is *coined ;* the *wrought* appears in vases and statues ; the *unwrought* in masses.' * * *

" Though, however we may come to the conclusion, that the Romans at the period in question almost wholly abstained from coining gold, there was, notwithstanding, no deficiency of gold money in Rome, when we consider the abundance of it which flowed in from foreign countries. I refer to the *Philippei*, or coins bearing the names of Philip II. king of Macedon, the extraordinary number of which that found their way to Rome may be seen stated in Livy. Quinctius, returning in triumph from Greece, brought with him 14,515 *Philippei ;* Scipio Asiaticus, after the conquest of Antiochus the Great, 140,000 ; M. Fulvius, on his triumph over the Ætolians, 12,422 ; Cn. Manlius, having reduced the Gallogræci, 16,320.—If so enormous a sum was thus transferred to the treasury of Rome by the rapine of war, as stated by Livy alone, and that in a part of his writings wretchedly mutilated, what must have been the amount produced by private speculation, and by the commercial intercourse between the Romans and the Greeks? What I have advanced respecting this employment of foreign money in Rome, receives remarkable confirmation from the expressions of Pompeius Festus—' For the Romans were in the habit, even from the time of Romulus, of using foreign *(ultramarinis)* coins of stamped gold and silver; a fact proved both by public and private memoranda.' Lactantius relates, that the Sibyl demanded of Tarquinius Priscus three hundred *Philippei* for her Nine Books of Prophecy.—I shall not stop to consider the absurd anachronism by which Tarquin and Philip are made contemporaneous.— Thus much the author, who in other matters was well enough informed, intended to convey, that when the Romans had no gold coinage of their own, they availed themselves of that of a foreign nation. Consequently, if at so remote a period of their history, the Romans were well supplied with foreign money, how much greater an abundance of it must they have had at their command in after times, when the treasures of so many vanquished kingdoms rolled into their city!"—*D. N. V.* v. 37–42.

GOLTZIANI *numi.*–A term given to the coins engraved in the Fasti; the Historia Impp. Julii, Augusti, et Tiberii; the Thesaurus; the Græciæ et Siciliæ numismata; and other works, by Hubert Goltz, or Goltzius. Of this extraordinary man's proceedings, much has been written by numismatists both of the elder and the more modern school; on the one hand to support his character; and on the other to impugn not only his accuracy but his veracity and good faith. The most unqualified panegyrist of the learned and industrious Antwerpian's labours, and least scrupulous defender of his literary conduct, is Mediobarbus. Next in the rank of admirers and supporters are antiquarian critics of no less eminence than Noris, Pagi, Tillemont, and Dodwell: to these must be added the name of Pinkerton, who, without hesitation, "recommends Goltzius, tho' all his works have many coins not found in cabinets. Yet, adds our English Essayist on Medals, it is certain that he was often imposed upon, and his works must be used with great caution." —Similar language had previously been used by Vaillant, Morel, Havercamp, and others who profess general deference to Goltzius as a numismatic authority, but who finish by exhibiting particular examples of his dealings with legends and types on both Greek and Roman coins, that destroy the very foundation of confidence in what he has written and engraved respecting them. The sentiments of Bimard de la Bastie and of Eckhel, are most decidedly Anti-Goltzian. The former in his notes on Jobert, (т. i. p. 99), intimates that it was his intention to have published a dissertation on the subject of a MS. volume left by Goltzius on Imperial Medals, in which he would have shewn what kind of con-

fidence it is reasonable to place in Goltzius with reference to medals, which that antiquary had professed to have drawn from the originals with his own hand, yet which, on examination, are not to be found at the present day."—It seems that this dissertation never saw the light : a circumstance to be regretted; inasmuch as such a work, emanating from a man of Bimard's erudition, integrity, and judicious application of numismatic knowledge, to every branch of the science, would have been a great aid to simple truth and justice in a case like the one in question.

Eckhel, who had entered early into the Goltzian controversy, and with characteristic energy encountered the arguments employed by the partisans of Goltzius to exonerate him from suspicion of fraud—avails himself of his *Bibliotheca Numismatica*, to repeat his charges, the correctness of which further and more deliberate investigation had only served to confirm in his own mind. Rendering a free tribute of praise and appreciation to the singular diligence and industry of the celebrated author, in acquiring numerous coins, and obtaining access to others, and allowing him the merit that belongs to an indefatigable spirit of research amongst ancient monuments, and of great learning, particularly in Roman History, displayed in the explanation of those relics of antiquity; Eckhel nevertheless contends, that the greater part of the coins contained in the plates of Goltzius are counterfeit—that scattered up and down his volumes many coins are to be found, genuine of their kind, but which the author has dishonestly falsified—that he frequently states a coin to be gold, which in the original is only silver. That whilst he delineates an abundance of consular coins which no one ever saw, or is likely to see, he gives many which have no pretensions to rarity, and includes in his copious engravings none of the restitutions of Trajan.—Alluding to his work on Sicilian coins, the Prince of Torremuzza, speaking of the medals of Drepane, says, "the good faith of Goltzius is to be suspected." Florez, the devoted collector, and profound critic, of the Hispanian mint, refers in terms of ridicule to that cornucopiæ of coins assigned to Spanish cities, as struck *after* the reign of Caligula, and published by Goltzius.—Spanheim, mentioning a coin adduced from the same fertile source, observes—" it has hitherto remained elsewhere unseen, and is therefore justly to be held in suspicion."

Andrew Morel, in a letter to Perizoni, says, " Numi consulares Goltzii, ordine alphabetico, ad finem operis adjecti sunt, sicut libri apocryphi canonicis, quia dubiæ sunt fidei, et major pars haud incertas notas falsitatis præ se fert."— [The consular coins of Goltzius are subjoined, in alphabetical order, at the end of the work, just as the Apocrypha is added to the canonical books of Scripture, because their genuineness is suspected, and the majority of them present unequivocal indications of fraud.]

Havercamp subjoins to the foregoing, "Tantus Goltzianorum numorum est numerus, qui nusquam observantur, quorundam quoque non injusta velut subditorum suspicio, ut a Morellii sententia nequaquam discedam."—[So large a proportion of the Goltzian coins have never come under observation, whilst to some of them attaches a justifiable suspicion of spuriousness, that I find it impossible to differ from the opinion of Morel.]

Entertaining such opinions as these, is it not to be lamented that they should have copied so many of the *Goltzians* into the *Thesaurus*, both consular and imperial, which one of these learned men collected materials for, and the other contributed his explanatory comments upon? It has doubtless tended much to mislead and confuse the student, and was an inconsistent step to take in a work of such standard value.

"That Goltzius (says Eckhel) has in his works presented an incredible number of coins, of which the like were never again seen from that time—is a fact not only not denied, but even extolled by the writers who patronise his cause. I refer my reader however to testimonies of the most learned men, which shew that it is not only extremely suspicious but positively beyond belief, that one man should have been able to obtain, or even to have inspected in museums then known in Europe, coins of such a nature, and in such overflowing abundance, as neither the extensive means of princes, nor the stubborn cupidity of wealthy individuals, nor the eager competition of those who all their lives have been occupied in poring into the bowels of their native soil, for the purpose of extracting therefrom the relics of antiquity—have since succeeded in discovering or procuring. In this respect the Kings of France, as well as Pellerin, Hunter, Ennery, &c. were nothing as compared to Goltzius."

Now, it often happens in numismatic pursuits, that by the effect of time and other causes operating injuriously on the legends of ancient coins, the eyes of the most skilful may be deceived, and false opinions may be based thereon, without the least infringement on the principles of honesty. It is not, however, on any such grounds that Eckhel accuses Goltzius of imposture. He combats offences of quite another description. By examples taken from Goltzius' own works, tested by coins in the Imperial Museum, Eckhel proves that the celebrated Flemish antiquary, not from error or inadvertency, but with a deliberate attempt at deception, has affixed to really genuine coins inscriptions of a different and a spurious kind. —See *Doctrina Num. Vet.* v. c. xxii. p. cxl. et seq.—*Prolegomena Generalia.*

GORDIANUS I. *(Marcus Antonius)* Africanus senior, was the issue of an illustrious family. His father was Metius Marulus, his mother Ulpia Gordiana. He was born about the year of Rome 940 (A. D. 157). Of a mild, just, and munificent disposition, correct in morals and dignified in manners; well versed in the higher branches of literature, loving and cultivating both eloquence and poetry, he soon obtained public offices, and displayed his virtues and moderation in a remarkable manner. His edileship was a splendid one; for the riches of his family enabled him to serve that ruinously expensive magistrature with great brilliancy. In 966 (A. D. 213), he was consul for the first time. In 982 (A. D. 229), his second consulate was in colleagueship with the Emperor Alexander Severus, replacing in the middle of the year Dion Cassius, the historian. The emperor sent Gordian into Africa, as proconsul, and appointed his son to be his lieutenant. In that province he won, as governor, the affection of the governed—and this popularity proved at once glorious and fatal to him.

991 (A. D. 238).—A *procurator* (commissioner) of Maximinus arriving in Africa, and having by his exactions exasperated the people, was killed by some young nobles. These rash men, to escape the anger of the Thracian savage, who would have been sure to avenge the death of his officers in a cruel manner, compelled Gordian, then 80 years of age, and who was at the moment at Thysdras, to accept the empire, which they also decreed to his son. This choice of the army and province was approved by the Senate and by the whole city of Rome, who detested Maximinus on account of his ferocious tyranny. A senatus consultum proclaimed the deposition of Maximinus, and the accession of the two Gordians. The new *Augusti* did not long enjoy the honours of imperial sovereignty. Capellianus, governor of Mauretania, enraged against Gordian, the father, who had superseded him in that lieutenancy, marched upon Carthage with a numerous army. On receiving this intelligence, the elder Gordian, under the desponding impression, that he should not be able to resist so vast a multitude of assailants, put an end to his life by strangulation. His son was slain in the conflict which took place when the partizans of Capellianus entered Carthage. Thus perished both father and son, after having jointly held the supreme power about forty-five days. The Senate in token of its regrets placed the two *Augusti* in the rank of the gods. Gordian senior had married Fabia Orestilla, great grand-daughter of Antoninus Pius, by whom he had Gordian, afterwards his associate in the empire, and Metia Faustina, wife of Junius Balbus, a consular personage.

His style is IMP. C. (or CAES.) M. ANT. GORDIANVS AFR. AVG. His coins consist of silver and brass, and are of extreme rarity. The Latin pieces are considered (by Hennin) to have been struck at Carthage. If so, they are a credit from their workmanship to the mint of the African province. But it is much more probable they were minted at Rome.

MINTAGES of GORDIANUS AFR. PATER.

SILVER.—CONCORDIA AVG. Woman seated. (Valued by Mionnet at 110 fr.)—P. M. TR. P. COS. P. P. Figure standing, in the toga, with laurel twig. (£3 15s. Pembroke; £7 5s. Thomas; £3 6s. Brumell; £4 4s. Tovey.)—SECVRITAS AVG. or AVGG. Woman seated. (£3 3s. Brumell; £3 19s. Sabatier).—VICTORIA AVGG. (£3 8s. Thomas).—VIRTVS AVGG. (£4 5s. Thomas; £4 0s. Campana).

ROMAE AETERNAE. Rome the victory-bearer seated.—*Obv.* IMP. M. ANT. GORDIANVS. AFR. AVG. Head of the elder Gordian. (£3 3s. Brumell; £3 6s. Sabatier sale. Engraved at the head of this article.

FIRST BRASS.—P. M. TR. P. COS. P. P. Figure standing, habited in the toga, holding in the right hand an olive branch, and a truncheon in the left. (Mt. 45 fr.) Engraved in the *Cabinet de Christine.*—PROVIDENT. AVGG. S. A woman stands with cornucopiæ pointing to a globe. (£4 1s. Devonshire). Engraved in Akerman, i. p. 461, pl. 8, No. 1.—SECVRITAS AVGG. A woman seated. (£3 1s. 0d. Thomas).—ROMAE AETERNAE. Rome seated. (Mt. 45 fr.)—VICTORIA AVGG. Victory walking. (£3 11s. 0d. Thomas; £2 12s. Campana).

** The easiest method, according to M. Rollin, of Paris, for classifying the rare medals of the two first Gordians, is to remember that on the father's hair is fuller on the forehead, and the cheek is rather sunk in through age, whilst the son is bald in front, but has a much fuller face.—*Note in p. 126 of the Campana Sale Catalogue.*

GORDIANUS II. *(Marcus Antoninus),* son of Gordianus Africanus I. and of Fabia Orestilla, was born under the reign of Commodus, A. D. 191. He was instructed in the highest and most elegant branches of literature by Serenus Sammonicus the younger, who left him his library composed of 62,000 volumes, and he profited from the instructions he had received from his friend and preceptor to render himself accomplished in the study of the law, and moreover gained a high reputation amongst the writers of his time, in publishing several works both in prose and verse, which reflected honour on his talents and attainments. Capitolinus, in praising him for these high qualities, adverts to his handsome figure, courteous demeanour, and mildness of character; but at the same time remarks that he was too fond of women. He was questor under Elagabalus; pretor and consul under Alexander Severus, by whom (A. D. 229) he was appointed the *legatus* of his father in Africa, and was acknowledged emperor with him at the end of eight years' residence in that

province (A. D. 238). He was killed a few weeks afterwards, fighting valiantly at the head of the troops which his father and he had levied to oppose the advance from Mauretania of Capellianus, a ready instrument of Maximin's cruelty. He was forty-six years old when he died; having occupied the rank of Augustus for only the short space of forty days. The name of his wife is unknown. His son was Gordianus III. called *Pius.*

The *Gordiani,* father and son, having adopted the same legend, it is difficult to distinguish, amongst the coins of those emperors, what belong to the one and what to the other.—Eckhel (vii. 31) has treated this question in a satisfactory manner. He agrees with Vaillant, that the pieces which bear the legend P. M. TR. P. COS. P. P. are the only ones which can with certainty be attributed to Gordian the father. As to the other pieces, the iconographic indications are our only guide. Frequently the leanness of the father, the good condition and more marked features of the son, lead to distinctions nearly indubitable. In other respects, the uncertainty remains complete; and above all, one is indisposed to ask how an octogenarian in age, and a man of forty-six years, could have been represented in a manner almost identical? It is even possible that at Rome, where these coins were struck in great haste, the artists had at their disposal only the portraits of the elder Gordian, already old, and which remounted to the epoch of his maturity of manhood.—M. Lenormant, *Iconographie Romaine,* p. 91.

If we apply these remarks to the denarii, we shall unquestionably recognize each Gordian as prefixed to the notices of their respective reigns. The large brass are more embarrassing: and in general it is to be observed, that these monies, struck at Rome by authority of the Senate, are those of which the iconographic characters are less distinct. Some of them would appear to belong to the son; from their appearance more assimilating with the meridian of life; others would be assigned to the father, to judge from the strongly indicated signs of old age, which they present.

The two Gordians, proclaimed in Africa, had neither time nor opportunity to arrive at Rome: a fact which shows that the Senate did not always wait for the actual entry of the new emperor into the capital, before they caused brass money to be minted bearing his image and superscription. The abbreviation on some reverses AVGG. for AVGVSTORVM, recalls to mind that there were then two *Augusti.*

MINTAGES OF GORDIANUS AFRICANUS JUNIOR.

On coins he is styled IMP. C. (or CAES.) M. ANT. GORDIANVS. AFR. AVG.—The following list of reverses in silver and large brass shews, that like those of the father their rarity constitutes their greatest merit.

SILVER.—CONCORDIA AVGG. Concord seated. (Valued by Mionnet at 100 fr.)—PROVIDENTIA

AVGG. Providence stands leaning on a column, a globe at her feet. (Brought £5 10s. at the Devonshire; £4 1s. at the Thomas; £5 at the Tovey, sales.)——VICTORIA AVGG. (£4 5s. Thomas), VIRTVS AVGG. A military figure (£6 10s. Devonshire; £3 15s. Pembroke; £3 14s. Thomas; £4 Campana; £4 2s. Brumell).

LARGE BRASS.—PROVIDENTIA AVGG. (Mt. 50 fr.)—ROMAE AETERNAE. Rome seated. (£4 7s. Thomas; £4 18s. Campana.)—VICTORIA AVGG. Victory walking. (Mt. 50 fr.).—VIRTVS. AVGG. Military figure. S. C. in the field. (£2 12s. Pembroke; £4 2s. Brumell; £4 10s. Tovey.)— Same legend. Mars carrying a trophy and a lance (*Cat. d' Ennery*; valued by Mionnet at 60 fr.)

GORDIANUS PIUS (or III.)—The year of this young prince's birth is not ascertained.— All that appears certain is that his anniversary fell on the 13th of the calends of February (20th January). He was the grandson of Gordianus I. but whether by his son Gordianus II. or by his daughter, is still unknown. In the year of Rome 991 (A.D. 238), the youngest Gordian, who was at Rome when the two African Gordians were massacred, was named Prince of the Youth by the Senate. The people who loved him, in remembrance of his relations, had never ceased to besiege the capitol until the dignity of Cæsar had been conferred on him. He was then thirteen or sixteen years of age. Pupienus and Balbinus were elected *Augusti*. The same year Pupienus proceeded to the war against Maximinus, whilst Balbinus and Gordianus acted on the defensive at Rome. A serious tumult arising between the pretorian guards and the people, the young Cæsar was lifted up and shewn to the contending parties, which had the effect of allaying their excited feelings, and bringing about a reconciliation. The authority of the new emperors was re-established by the death of Maximinus and of his son Maximus. At the end of the month of July, in the same year, Balbinus and Pupienus being put to death by the pretorians, Gordianus was formally declared *Augustus* by the unanimous voice of the pretorians and the Senate.—In 992 (A.D. 239), Gordianus III. proceeded consul for the first time. History records nothing certain respecting the events of this year.

993 (A.D. 240), or the following year, Sabinianus usurped the imperial government in Africa, but was defeated and taken prisoner by the governor of Mauretania, through the treachery of his own party. The young emperor planted at Viminacium (see the word), a city of Upper Mæsia (now *Widdin*), a colony which dates its foundation from this year.

994 (A.D. 241).—This year, which was that of Gordian's second consulate, Sapor I. king of the Persians, invaded Mesopotamia, then subject to the Romans; and the terror which his arms inspired, spread not only in the East, but through Italy itself. The Sapor in question was son of that Artaxerxes who, after overthrowing the Arsacidæ, brought Parthia again under Persian rule, as it is said, during the reign of Alexander Severus. Gordianus III. made immense preparations to meet this powerful foe. The same year he married Sabinia Tranquillina.

995 (A.D. 242).—Gordian left Rome and proceeded through Mæsia and Thrace into Asia, and thence into Syria. He defeated Sapor in several battles; and, recapturing from him many cities which the latter had taken from the Romans, drove the Persian monarch out of Mesopotamia.

996 (A.D. 243).—In consequence of his brilliant successes in war, a triumph in a biga of elephants was decreed to Gordianus III. (see the monetal record of this fact in p. 203).— Misitheus, prefect of the pretorian guard, father-in-law of the emperor, and who had greatly contributed to his successes, on the same occasion triumphed in a quadriga of horses. That wise and true friend of the emperor died the same year, poisoned, as it was believed, by Philippus, an Arabian, who fatally succeeded him in the dignity of pretorian prefect.

997 (A.D. 244).—This artful and ambitious man, having an eye upon empire, intercepted the supplies for the campaign, and thus irritated the army against their prince. Gordian was assassinated at Zeila, on the Euphrates, in the month of February, in the 22nd year of his age, after he had reigned about six years.

"Thus terminated the life of Gordianus III. in whom nothing was wanting to establish the character of a first-rate prince, except a longer life. The love of the people, founded on the merits of his grandfather and father, conferred upon him first the title of Cæsar, and then that of Augustus; and so adored was he for the beauty of his person, and the suavity of his manners, that the Senate and army called him their son, and the people their darling. A remarkable proof of the excellence of his disposition was shewn in the docility with which, at an age exposed to every temptation, he listened not to the voice of passion, but to the sage counsels of Misitheus, than whom the empire could boast no one more learned, eloquent, or distinguished in the arts of peace and war; and whom he had chosen, not only as his prefect of the pretorian guard, but as his father-in-law, by marrying his daughter Tranquillina. As he was happy, so long as he had the advantage of such a man's assistance, so was he most unfortunate in his selection of a successor. For by appointing Philippus, thro' whose nefarious arts it was supposed that Misitheus himself met his death, he fell a victim to his ingratitude and hostility, in the atrocious manner above described. The soldiers afterwards erected his tomb at the Circesian camp on the borders of Persia, and Ammianus Marcellinus affirms, that as late as the time of Julianus II. it was seen by himself, and that it was a conspicuous object from a considerable distance. The life of Gordian III. has been given at great length by Capitolinus."—*D. N. V.* vol. vii. 309, 310, 313.

The Latin coins of Gordianus Pius are rare in gold; but for the most part common in silver and brass, except those with the title of Cæsar.

Before his accession to the empire, the youngest Gordian is styled M. ANT. GORDIANVS CAES. (the head bare) A. D. 238. The same year, ascending the throne on the death of Balbinus and Pupienus, his coins exhibit the titles of IMP. CAES. M. ANT. GORDIANVS AVG. and these he bore during the two first years of his reign.—In A. D. 239, the title of PIVS was added; in 240, the further addition was made of FELIX; and to the end of his life he preserved the style of IMP. GORDIANVS PIVS FEL*ix* AVG.

MINTAGES OF GORDIANUS III.

GOLD MEDALLION.——MLETHRM *(sic.)* PROPVGNATOREN *(sic.)* Mars armed with buckler and lance.—*Obv.* IMP. GORDIANVS PIVS FELT. *(sic.)* AVG. Radiated head of Gordianus Pius. (Mionnet values this piece, which is of barbarous workmanship, at 200 fr. See *De la Rareté des Med.* T. i. p. 394).

SILVER MEDALLIONS.—AEQVITAS AVGVSTI. The three monetæ. (Mionnet, 200 fr.)—VIRTVS AVGVSTI. Emperor and the Sun supporting a globe, with trophy, standards, captives, and soldiers. (Brought £12 at the sale of Mr. Sabatier's collection, lot 433).—MONETA AVGVSTI. The monetæ type. (Mt. 250 fr.)—PROFECTIO AVG. Emperor on horseback and other figures). Mt. 300 fr.)—VICTORIA AVG. Emperor and several attendants sacrificing before a round temple, on the front of which is read NEIKH ΟΠΛΟΦΟΡΟC. (Mt. 300 fr.)

GOLD.—AETERNITATI AVG. Sun standing. (£3 3s. Brumell sale).—AEQVITAS AVG. (£2. 2s. Pembroke; £2 12s. Sabatier).—CONCORDIA AVG.—FELICIT! TEMP.—FIDES MILITVM. (48 fr. each.)—IOVI STATORI. (£4 5s. Trattle; Sabatier, £2 12s.)—DIANA LVCIFERA. (£2 3s. Trattle).—LAETITIA AVG. N. (Trattle, £5 12s. 6d.) —LIBERALITAS AVG. II. (£4 5s. Trattle).—PIETAS AVGVSTI. (£5 12s. Trattle).—P. M. TR. P. II. and III. COS. II. P. P. Sacrificial group. (£3 10s. Brumell).—P. M. TR. P. II. Soldier standing (a finely-preserved specimen bought at the Thomas sale for £4 10s.)—PROVIDENTIA AVG. Providence with globe. (£3 10s. Thomas).–SECVRITAS AVG. (£2 Trattle; £1 8s. Sabatier).—SECVRIT. PERP. Security leaning on a column. (Mt. 48 fr.)—VICTORIA AVG. A Victory holding a wreath and palm branch. (£3 1s. Trattle; £3 10s. Thomas; £2 12s. Pembroke; £3 7s. De-

vonshire; £2 2s. Campana.——P. M. TR. P. II. Jupiter the protector and a little figure. (Mt. 50 fr.)—P. M. TR. P. IIII. COS. II. Figure seated with olive twig. (£3 6s. Sabatier sale).—P. M. TR. P. VI. COS. II. Emperor with lance and globe. (£2 5s. Trattle).—VIRTVTI AVGVSTI. Hercules (Farnese) resting on his club. (£3 10s. Thomas; £3 4s. Brumell).

SILVER.—P. M. TR. P. IIII. COS. II. Emperor in a quadriga, crowned by Victory.—PRINCIPI IVVENT. Emperor with globe and hasta. (Mt. 24 fr. each).

BRASS MEDALLIONS.—ADLOCVTIO AVGVSTI. Emperor and four other military figures.— (Brought £7 10s. at the Thomas sale. In Mionnet it is valued at 120 fr.)—MVNIFICENTIA GORDIANI AVG.—Amphitheatre, bull and elephant combatting.—See *Munificentia.* (Mionnet 300 fr.)—P. M. TR. P. V. COS. II. The great circus, with wrestling, chariot racing, &c. (Mt. 300 fr.)

P. M. TR. P. V. COS. II. Rome presenting a globe to the emperor, in presence of two pretorians.—TRAIECTVS. Trireme, with several figures.—VICTORIA AVGVSTI. Emperor and attendants, sacrificing before a round temple, as in the silver medallion described above.— (Mionnet values these three medallions at 200 fr. each).—LIBERALITAS AVGVSTI II. The emperor and several other figures. (Mt. 150 fr.) —PAX AETERNA. Sun in a quadriga, the emperor sacrificing, &c. (A specimen, partially injured, obtained £4 19s. at the Thomas sale.)— PONTIFEX MAX. TR. P. IIII. COS. II. Emperor in a quadriga, full-faced, crowned by a victory, a foot soldier on each side of the horses. (£7 5s. Thomas.)

FELICITAS AVGVSTI.—VICT. GORDIANI. Pretorian galley.—PONTIFEX MAX. TR. P. II. COS. II. Emperor in a quadriga, holding a Roman eagle.—PONT. MAX. TR. P. III. Rome presenting a globe to the emperor, accompanied by two soldiers.—PONT. MAX. TR. P. IIII. COS. II. Emperor in a quadriga crowned by Victory; Rome leads the horses, preceded by soldiers holding palms.—VICTORIA AVG. Emperor seated, Victory crowning him; in the group are captives with military ensigns.—VICTORIA AVGVSTI. Emperor on horseback, preceded by a Victory, and escorted by soldiers bearing trophies and eagles. This alludes to Gordian's successes over the Persians. (The foregoing seven are valued by Mionnet at 120 fr. each.)

VIRTVS AVGVSTI. Emperor crowned by Victory; and three other figures. (Mt. 150 fr.)— FIDES EXERCITVS. Two military figures joining hands—P. M. TR. P. VI. COS. II. Imperator eques, Victory, and soldiers. (The two foregoing 100 frs. each, Mionnet).

P. M. TR. P. VII. COS. II. P. P.—The interior of a circus. In the centre of the *spina* is an obelisk; at each of the two extremities are three *metæ* of a conic form. In the fore-ground, several groups; the first, to the right, exhibits two gladiators fighting; the second, two wrestlers; the third, two *athletæ*, exercising themselves in the use of the *halteres* (the dumbbells of modern gymnastics); the fourth, two other *athletæ* combatting with the cestus; the fifth, a wounded gladiator, led out of the circus by an apparitor. Behind the *spina* are two quadrigæ driven at a racing pace by their respective *aurigæ*. And lastly, quite in the back-ground, a car drawn by six horses, in which stands the emperor, holding a branch of laurel, accompanied by Victory, and preceded by three pretorians carrying palms.—*Obv.* IMP*erator* GORDIANVS PIVS FELIX AV-*Gustus*. Bust of Gordianus III. laureated, clothed in the *paludamentum*, the lance resting on his right shoulder. On the front of his cuirass, the emperor is figured on horseback, overthrowing two barbarians.

This fine monument belongs to the last year of Gordian's reign. For an engraving of the reverse, see p. 203. That of the obverse is placed at the head of the biographical summary, (p. 435). The original is in the *Cabinet de France*. Mionnet values it at 300 francs.

LARGE BRASS.—ADLOCVTIO AVGVSTI. (Mt. 40 fr.)—AETERNITAS AVGVSTI. Equestrian statue. (Mt. 30 fr.)

LIBERALITAS AVGVSTI IIII. Three figures seated, and several others standing.—P. M. TR. P. II. COS. Emperor in a quadriga.—VIRTVS AVGVSTI. Emperor on horseback. (Mt. 20 fr. each.)

MIDDLE BRASS.—MART. VICTOR. Sacrifice before a round temple, on the frieze is inscribed ΘΕΟΥ ΟΠΛΟΦΟΡΟΥ. (Mt. 48 fr.)—PONTIF. MAXIM. TR. P. Rome seated, three figures standing. (20 fr.)—PONTIF. MAX. COS. II. Emperor in a quadriga, crowned by Victory, preceded by a soldier. (40 fr.)

P. M. TR. P. VI. COS. II. Apollo seated on a throne, resting on the lyre, holding a laurel branch. Engraved in Lenormant, *Iconog. Rom.* p. 92, pl. vi. No. 8.—SECVRIT(AS) PERPET(VA). Security stands resting herself on a column.— Engraved in *Iconog. Rom.* p. 92, pl. vi. No. 8.

GOTHI—The Goths; ancient tribes of northern Europe, who inhabited the borders of the Vistula to its mouth in the Baltic Sea, where at the present stands the city of Dantzic. This barbarous people spreading themselves as far as the Oder, combined with the Heruli, and during the reign of Marcus Aurelius passed the Vistula, and proceeding south eastward as far as the *Palus Mæotis* (now sea of Asof), took possession of Dacia after having crossed the Borysthenes (now the Dnieper). Afterwards those who inhabited the more eastern parts towards the Black Sea (Pontus Euxinus), were called Ostrogoths, or Eastern Goths; the others who dwelt towards the west were called Visi-goths, or Western Goths. These two nations ravaged at different times many provinces of the Roman empire. In the time of Gallienus, the whole of Thrace was depopulated by them. (Vaillant.)—Claudius II. Tacitus, Probus, Constantine and his sons, Julian II. Valentinian, and other emperors respectively defeated them, and succeeded in confining those desolating hordes within their own natural confines. But during the government of Valens, the Huns, having passed the *Palus Mæotis*, came like an impetuous torrent upon the Goths, subdued the Ostrogoths, and driving the Visigoths from their new country established themselves there in their room. The Visigoths thus compelled to emigrate across the Danube, applied for support to Valens, and that emperor, without any treaty, and even without disarming them, gave up to their possession a portion of Thrace, whence they soon afterwards began to make war upon other provinces of the empire. Valens proceeded to attack them near Hadrianopolis, but his army having been cut to pieces, and himself wounded by an arrow, he took refuge in a cabin, where he was burnt alive A. D. 278. The Visigoths, intoxicated with this success, went on carrying fire and sword everywhere, and set about besieging Constantinople. Theodosius the Great, Valens' successor, from A. D. 379 to 382, gained several victories over them, forcing them and their king Athanaricus to submit to his laws. After the death of that emperor (A. D. 395), the Visigoths elected for their monarch Alaric; who, after the death of Stilicho, the intriguing and ambitious minister of Honorius, invaded Italy, and besieged Rome, which was obliged to pay a heavy ransom (A. D. 408). The following year Rome, again besieged by the Visigothic king, was taken by him; and Priscus Attalus was proclaimed emperor under his protection. In A. D. 410, Attalus was deposed by Alaric, who was then on the point of concluding a treaty with Honorius. But in a fit of irritation and caprice, the Visigoth broke off his negociations with the emperor, and restored to Attalus the imperial title; but almost immediately again deprived him of it. He then marched to Rome, which he took and pillaged. Alaric died A. D. 410; and was succeeded by his brother-in-law Ataulphus, who after a time retired with his army into Gaul, where he instituted the kingdom of the Visigoths in Aquitania and Gallia Narbonnensis (since called Languedoc), and Italy was once more left free from invaders.

In A. D. 476, Odoacer, king of the Heruli, being invited by the party of Junius Nepos to enter Italy with a vast army of barbarians, compelled the then reigning and last Emperor of the West, ROMULUS AUGUSTUS, to abdicate his throne, and retire as an exile into Campania. In 477, the Eastern, or Ostrogoths, were called in to the assistance of Zeno, Emperor of the East, against Odoacer, and the result, after many battles, was their amalgamation in Italy with the Heruli, and the foundation of a kingdom there under Theodoricus, who died 526. The Gothic monarchy in Italy lasted from that period till the year 553—77 years; and the series of its kings is—Theodoricus, Athalaricus, Theodahatus, Witiges, Hildibaldus, Araricus, Baduela, Theias. It was these diademed chiefs of the hardy northern warriors, who under the successive reigns of Anastasius, Justinus, and Justinianus, occupied the western seat of the Roman empire, its "Eternal City;" whilst INVICTA [sometimes blundered into INVITA] ROMA, and the name of some Gothic REX.

figured in strange companionship on coins of the imperial series!—See Mionnet and Akerman.

GOTHIA, that is to say *Gothia subacta* (subdued), is read on the exergue of a very rare gold coin of Constantine the Great, the epigraph of which is DEBELLATORI GENTIVM BARBARARVM; and the type, two military figures standing, the hand of one (representing the emperor) resting on the head of a youth by his side.

This singular coin relates to the year 322, when Constantine overcame the Goths and Sarmatians in repeated battles, both in Illyria and in Mæsia—the remnants of whom, fleeing beyond the Danube, he pursued across that river, again overthrew, and punished with an almost exterminating slaughter. (Vaillant, iii. p. 87).—On this signal success the emperor was congratulated by a coin struck at Treves, whence the words GOTHIA TR*everis*, by the mint of which colony the exploits of emperors were sometimes commemorated.—Banduri.

GOTHIC. *Gothicus*—on coins of Claudius, surnamed Gothicus, not only as a distinction from the former emperor of that name, but also on account of a signal victory gained by him over the Goths.

GOTHICO.—The surname, in the dative case, conferred on the above mentioned Claudius, who reigned two centuries and more after the first Claudius, and before Aurelianus. Several of his coins bear this titular cognomen, and these were struck as well during his life-time as after his death; viz. :—GERMANICO GOTHICO OPTIMO PRINCIPI—and DIVO CLAVDIO GOTHICO.—Banduri, i. pp. 353–354.

GOTHICUS.—This appellation (says Banduri) was fitly given to that *Claudius* who recovered Dacia to the empire, and conquered the Scythians and the *Quadi*, having first of all repelled from the Roman territory an irruption of Goths and Sarmatians, whose cupidity of plunder he punished by a signal slaughter, to the amount (according to historians) of three hundred and twenty thousand men. Hence we read on his coins IMP. CAESAR CLAVDIVS GER. GOTHICVS.—The same surname of Gothicus was assigned by the Senate to Probus, but it no where occurs on that emperor's coins.

GRAC.—GRACC.—*Gracchus.*—Surname of the Sempronia gens.

GRACES *(Gratiæ*, a translation of the Greek χάριτες). The three goddesses of favour, loveliness, and benevolence. They were respectively named, the first, Aglaia, (which means *Venustas*, or Beauty) ; the second, Euphrosyne (that is *Hilaritas) ;* and the third, Thalia *(Festivitas).* But the ancients were not more agreed respecting the number of the Graces than as to their parentage ; some making them the daughters of Jupiter, others assigning to Bacchus the honour of their paternity. Homer describes them as employed in attendance on Venus and the other most beautiful of the goddesses. In various parts of Greece there were temples dedicated to their worship, as the acknowledged patronesses of refinement, gentleness, and moderation, in social intercourse. The most perfect works of art were therefore called the works of the Graces. —They are represented on many ancient bas-reliefs, and in two or more numismatic monuments, as beautiful women, standing together, entirely undraped, the central figure having an arm placed each on a shoulder of the other two. They thus display, as if in a dancing attitude, symmetry of person, combining with elegance of movement, unadorned beauty, unconscious of offence to modesty, designed to indicate the constant reciprocation of kindness and friendship, without concealment or reserve, but untainted by any mixture of voluptuous familiarity. Such was the sentimental gloss put by the imaginative Greeks on the questionable exhibition of three young virgins in a state of nudity.—It is, says Spanheim (in his *Cæsars de Julien)* not disagreeable to see the figures of the Graces, as they are found on ancient coins, conformable to those which the poets describe to us. The one (see foregoing wood-cut), was dedicated to Alexander Severus by a city of Thrace, called COLONIA FLAVIA PACIFICA [or Pacensis], DEULTUM [or *Deultana*] ; and the other, bearing a Greek legend, struck by the inhabitants of *Hadrianopolis*, in the same country.—See *Deultum*, p. 320.—See also Vaillant, *in Coloniis*, ii. 118.

GRACCURRIS, a Roman *municipium* of Hispania Tarraconensis, now *Agreda*, near Turiaso, in Arragon. It was anciently called *Illuricis*, but changed its name in honour of Titus Sempronius Gracchus, who repaired it after his victories over the Celtiberians. It preserved the memory of his name by a second brass coin, on the obverse of which is TI. CAESAR DIVI. AVGVSTVS, and the laureated head of Tiberius. On the reverse MVNICIP(IVM) GRACCVRRIS. The type is an ox standing, adorned with the *infula* or veil, as a victim.—Engraved in Vaillant, *Col.* i. p. 76 ; and in the *Cabinet de Christine.*—See Akerman, *Coins of Cities and Princes*, p. 89.

GRAECIA, *Greece*, formerly the most renowned for polity and civilization, and still the most classically interesting, country in Europe. The vast region to which this name, and that of Hellas, were generally given, comprehended to the south, below the Sinus Corinthiacus (Gulf of Lepanto), and Sinus Saronicus (Gulf of Egina), a great peninsula called the Peloponessus (Morea) —and this contained to the west the several states of Achaia, Elis, and Arcadia ; to the south-west Messenia ; to the east Corinth, Megaris, Attica, (including the city of Athens), and Argolis ; to the south-east Laconica. The northern great division of *Græcia Antiqua* comprised, from west to east, Acarnania, Ætolia, Locriozolæ, Doris, Phocis, Bœotia—and stretching much further in the same northward direction, the more extensive kingdoms and territories of Epirus, Thessalia, and Macedonia. Of the Græcian islands in the Ionian Sea, along the north and south-western coasts—and in the Ægæan Sea, to the east and south-east, opposite the coast of Asia Minor, the principal were Corcyra (Corfu), Leucadia (St. Maura), Cephalenia (Cephalonia), Ithaca, Zacynthus (Zante), Eubœa (Negropont), Lemnos, Naxos, Crete, Carpathos, Ceos, Cythera, and the smaller islands of the Archipelago, the names of which, as also of the larger, are well known to every scholar.—"It is remarkable (says Dr. Butler, *Ancient Geog.* p. 198), that the word Græcia was not *legally* recognized by the Romans. The name of Græcia, however, was sufficiently familiar among them, in writing and conversation."

GRAECI. The *Grecians, Greeks.*—Historical references to Greece, and the coins struck by the respective kings and cities of its various distinct and independent states, high as are the peculiar claims of both to the attentive study of the artist and the antiquary, form no part of the compiler's design to touch upon in this volume, except from and after the epoch at which those peoples were finally subjugated by the Romans; and then solely with a view to a brief numismatic notice of the few colonies planted by their conquerors, in Macedonia, Achaia, and Epirus, whose mintages bear *Latin* legends. Not only must the *fabulous,* and the *first* historic, age of Greece be here passed by, but also the *second* historic æra, commencing with the reign of Darius I. and finishing with the death of Alexander the Great—a period in which, besides the military glory which they acquired by their victories over the Persians, the Greeks carried (particularly the Athenians) their philosophy and their oratory, their sentiments and tastes, their knowledge in science, and their skill in art, to the highest pitch of contemporaneous refinement and pre-eminence. Little more, therefore, remains for us to observe on this subject, than that after the war between Macedonia and Rome, which, after seven years' duration, terminated A. U. C. 586 (B. C. 168), in the defeat and capture of king Perseus, by the town-destroying consul Paulus Æmilius, when one thousand of the principal Achæans (Polybius amongst the rest) were sent prisoners to Rome. In the year U. C. 607 (B. C. 147), Macedonia was reduced to the form of a Roman province. The following year, war having been resumed between Rome and the Achæans, the latter were defeated, and Corinth was taken and pillaged by L. Mummius, consul, A. U. C. 609 (B. C. 145). The Romans, after having thus established their power over all Greece *(Græcia Universa),* divided it into two provinces, the one called Macedonia, and the other Achaia, which they respectively assigned to the government of a pretor, or a pro-consul.

It was then and thenceforward that this highly polished but degenerate people began to vie with each other in flattering their conquerors—in literally deifying the Emperors, the Senate, and the City of Rome—in ostentatiously dedicating to Princes and Empresses, their *Neocoria,* a worship till then exclusively appropri-

ated to their gods—and in impressing upon their coins figures and inscriptions never before used, but indicative of voluntary subjection on their part to the meanest slavery. An exception, perhaps, is to be made in favour of the Athenians, who appear to have been free from this black spot of servile adulation; nor did they, before the time of Vespasian, allow either the name or the effigy of any Roman personage to be struck on their medals.

Mr. Akerman, in his learned and instructive "Remarks on the Coins of Ephesus, struck under the dominion of the Romans," makes the following observations respecting a coin minted at Ephesus, on which Hadrian is styled KAICAP OΛΥΜΠΙΟC, *Cæsar Olympius*—"Long before the days of Hadrian, the Greeks had been in the habit of paying divine honours to the worst of princes. Magnificent temples were built in honour of, and the most fulsome adulation was offered to, men who practised every species of vice that can debase human nature. Hadrian was unquestionably possessed of qualities which if rightly exercised, might have rendered him without a parallel in the history of the Roman empire, but these were obscured by vices which will bear neither description nor comment.— Why and on what occasion, the people of Ephesus gave to Hadrian the title of *Olympius* is, I believe, unknown. That odious system of polytheism which associated Jupiter with Ganymede, might have suggested the epithet. Whilst the Ephesians were bestowing a surname of the king of the gods upon their emperor, other cities of Greece were erecting temples to Antinous!"—*Numismatic Chronicle,* vol. iv. p. 89.

"The practice of paying divine honours to their rulers was, as already noticed, a very common one with the degenerate and degraded Greeks. Every one acquainted with ancient history will remember the account which Plutarch gives of Antony and Cleopatra, at Alexandria, when the triumvir was styled Νεος Διονυσος (the *New Bacchus*), and his paramour, Νεα Ισις (the *New Isis*), which latter title, or rather that of Θεα Νεα or Νεωτερα, is found on a coin of Cleopatra, doubtless struck at the very time of that insane mummery.—Buonarotti cites many examples of this practice, quoting a marble from Spon, on which Sabina the empress is styled the New Ceres, and another from the same author, inscribed to Julia Domna as the New Vesta." Ibid, p. 109.—See also DIANA EPHESIA, p. 324 of this dictionary.

Greek coins, whether they were struck by states, or cities, or by colonies, are deserving of particular attention, not only on the ground of their remoter antiquity, but also chiefly because they are of a kind totally different from what were issued from the mints of Greece, after that country had fallen under the sway of Rome. Indeed, that the people of Free Greece, and even after the loss of their independence, were greatly superior to the Romans in the art of engraving money is a fact, to be convinced of which we need only to examine those of the former which remain to us, and compare them with the mintages of Roman die, coined under the empire, with the exception of such from Nero to Commodus, as are evidently the work of Greek artists.

GRADIVUS.—See *Mars*.

GRATIANUS, the son of Valentinian I. and Val. Severa, was born at Sirmium, in Pannonia, A. D. 359, whilst his father was still a private citizen. In A. D. 367, when eight years old, he was declared Augustus at Ambianum (Amiens), having for colleagues his father Valentinian I. and his uncle Valens. Gratianus was sixteen years of age when his father died, A. D. 375.— He immediately acknowledged as his colleague Valentinianus, his natural brother, whom on the death of his father the legions had proclaimed Augustus, though he was scarcely five years old. The empire was then so divided between them, that Gratianus had for his share Hispania, the Galliæ and Britain, and Valentinian Italy, Illyricum, and Africa, but under the regency of his brother, while Valens retained the East. He was victorious over the Lentiani Alamanni, a people inhabiting Rhætia (the Tyrol), in a memorable battle fought at Argentovaria, or Argentaria (at or near Colmar, in Alsace). He went to reinforce Valens, who was hard pressed by the Goths in Thrace, but arrived only in time to find him overpowered and slain, A. D. 378. The barbarians completely over-running and devastating this region, he recalled Theodosius from his exile in Hispania, and for his services against those tribes on the Ister, gave him the title of Augustus, at the beginning of the year 379, and appointed him governor of the eastern provinces held by Valens. Having set out on an expedition against Magnus Maximus, a man of energy and reputation (who, elected by the legions in Britain, had assumed the purple in that island, and invaded Gallia), he found himself abandoned by his troops near Paris, at the moment of his being about to attack the usurper's army, who put him to death in his flight near Lugdunum (Lyon), A. D. 383, in the 24th year of his age.

"Historians, Pagan and Christian (says an able writer in Dr. Smith's Biographical Dictionary, ii. p. 302), are agreed as to the character of Gratian. In person he was well made and good looking; in his disposition gentle and and docile—possessed of a cultivated understanding and of a ready and pleasing eloquence, he was chaste and temperate, but too yielding and pliant, the influence of others leading him to severities foreign to his own character. His piety and his reverence for ecclesiastics, especially Ambrose of Milan, rendered him too willing a party to the persecutions, which the Christians, now gaining the ascendancy, were too ready to exercise, whether against the heathen, or against heretics [the Arians especially] of their own body. Whilst by these excesses of religious zeal, he cooled the attachment of those of his subjects who were exposed to his severity, his constant engagement in archery, field sports, and other amusements, to the neglect of more serious matters, incurred contempt, and rendered him unpopular with both the army and the people."

Eckhel says of him—"He was a prince of many good qualities, by which he distinguished himself at the commencement of his reign, though towards the close of his career, he was deficient in the discretion and energy so indispensably requisite for managing the affairs of an empire, vast in extent, and involved in such difficulties and dangers as pressed upon it at the critical epoch, in which his lot was cast among the rulers of the Roman world. With regard to his attachment to the Christian religion, as he was detested by the pagans, so was he regretted by the orthodox."—*D. N. V.* viii. 137.

Gratian, in A. D. 378, married Constantia, daughter of Constantius II. and Maxima Faustina, who was born A. D. 362, and died some years before her husband.

The coins of this emperor in second and third brass are common; nor are his gold and silver of the usual size very rare. But the few medallions extant in gold, are of extreme rarity. On these he is styled D. N. GRATIANVS AVG.— D. N. GRATIANVS P. F. AVG.—One of his coins bears round the head D. N. GRATIANVS AVGG. AVG. Of this singular legend various interpretations have been given, which may be seen in the "Remarques" of Bimard (see Jobert's *Science des Médailles*, edit. 1739, T. ii. p. 324).—See also the observations of Eckhel, *Doctr. Num. Vet.* viii. 158.

MINTAGES OF GRATIANUS.

GOLD MEDALLIONS.—-GLORIA ROMANORVM. Rome seated. Engraved in Steinbüchel's notice of the Vienna Medallions. (Mionnet values this at 600 fr. and another, with the same legend and type, at 800 fr.)—Same legend, Rome and a turreted woman seated (at 200 fr.)

SILVER MEDALLIONS.—GLORIA ROMANORVM. Emperor with globe and hasta. (Mt. 30 fr.)— VICTORIA AVGG. Gratian and Valentinian jun. seated. (Tovey sale, £1 6s. Mt. 50 fr.)—VIRTVS EXERCITVS. (15s. Thomas. Engraved in Akerman, ii. p. 324).—VOTIS V. MVLTIS X.— VOTIS XV. MVLTIS XX. (Mt. 30 fr. each).

GOLD.—-CONCORDIA AVGGGE. *(sic.)* Rome helmed and seated. In exergue CONOB. (Mt. 24 fr. (Brumell, 13s.)—VICTORIA AVGVSTORVM. Victory seated and writing VOT. V. MVLT. X. (Mt. 24 fr.)—VICTORIA AVGG. The emperor and his father Valentinian I. seated. Struck A. D. 367. (Brought only 17s. at Campana sale). —GLORIA NOVIS *(sic.)* or NOVI SAECVLI. Emperor stands in a military dress, supporting a *victoriola* on a globe, and holding the *labarum*, adorned with the monogram of Christ. ☧ (Mt. 30 fr.)— PRINCIPIVM IVVENTVTIS. ☧ RESTITVTOR REIPVBLICAE.—VOTA PVBLICA. (Mt. 30 fr. each.)

SILVER.—GLORIA NOVI SAECLI. *(sic.)* The emperor holding the Christian *labarum*.—VOTA PVBLICA. Hercules stands with right hand upon the mouth. (Mt. 24 fr.)

VRBS ROMA. Rome seated, holding the hasta and a victoriola.—*Obv.* D. N. GRATIANVS P. F. AVG. Diademed head of the emperor.—(See wood-cut at the head of this article).

BRASS MEDALLION.—VRBS ROMA. (20 fr.)

SMALL BRASS.—VOTA PVBLICA. Isis holding the sistrum.—Same legend. Isis in a car drawn by two mules.—Same legend. Anubis standing, with caduceus and branch.

[It is curious, as an evidence either of imperial inconsistency, or of monetal carelessness, that whilst the sacred symbol of Christianity adorns so many of Gratian's gold and silver coins, his small brass are paganised not only with Greek but with Egyptian mythology —Hercules with club and lion's spoils; Isis with her sistrum, and Anubis with dog's head!]

GRYPHI. *Griffins* or *Griffons*.—Fabulous animals, having the body of a lion, and the head of an eagle or hawk, with a crest and wings.— They were sacred to Apollo or the Sun, and are often figured near him. On coins of Aureliopolis, griffins are represented drawing his chariot. A third brass of Gallienus exhibits a griffin walking, the accompanying legend being APOLLINI CONS*ervatori* AVG*usti*. On a brass medallion of Antoninus Pius, this monster appears flying, with a young man on his back, wearing a Phrygian cap. A woman seated on a griffin forms the reverse type of a brass medallion of Hadrian. It is also seen on denarii of the Aelia, Junia, and Papia families. Vaillant considers the griffin to indicate the Apollinarian games. There is a griffin sitting, on a small brass coin of Domitian (engraved in *Morell. Thesaurus*, TAB. 25).

GUBERNACULUM.—The rudder of a ship appears on numerous Roman coins, generally in the hand of Fortune; sometimes at the feet of Victory. This nautical instrument is delineated in types of the Pretorian gallies, on consular as well as on imperial coins.—See Fonteia gens. p. 392—*Felicitat. Aug.* of Hadrian, p. 381, and *Fortuna*, pp. 394–396–397.

GUTTUS, an oblong vase, designating the augural priesthood. It is seen on coins of Pompeius Magnus, Julius Cæsar, and M. Antonius, &c. accompanied by the *lituus*.—See *Præfericulum*.

H.

H. This letter, the eighth of the Latin alphabet, has two general uses. The former before vowels at the beginning of syllables, as in *Honos*; and the second after consonants, as in *thronus*. According to Quintilian, the ancient Romans did not use the H. after consonants. "Diu deinde reservatum ne consonantibus adspiraretur, ut in *Graccis* and *Triumpis*." Cicero has also remarked, "Quin ergo ipse, cum scirem, ita majores locutos esse, ut nusquam nisi in vocali, adspiratione uterentur, loquebar sic, ut *pulcros* et *Cetegos, triumpos, Cartaginem* dicerem." And on coins, for the most part, the words *Graccus* and *Triumpus*, are found without this letter. In the Latinity of the early age, as chewn on the more ancient marbles, as well as on denarii of the Marcia family, PILIPPVS—PILIPPI is read for *Philippus, Philippi*.—YPSAEVS also instead of *Hypsæus*.—Nor, to quote the authority of Quintilian and of other old grammarians, is it to be ascribed to an error of the engraver, when we find on the coins of M. Antony, CHORTIS SPECVLATORVM and CHORTIVM PRAETORIARVM. On coins moreover of Gallienus we find COOR. PRAET. VI. P. VI, F. *Cohors Prætoria Sextum Pia, Sextum Felix,* or *Fidelis.* The H is sometimes omitted as in ERCVLI, and sometimes doubled as in the COHH. PRAET. *Cohortes Pretorianæ,* of Gallienus.—See Eckhel, vol. v. 75 and 171.

H. This letter served to mark the standard of the Hastati, who were accustomed to be placed in the front of the Roman legionaries, when in battle array, armed with spears. And H. P. signified *Hastati. Principes.* These letters inscribed on standards appear on coins of the Neria and Valeria families.—See Rasche, *Lex. Num.* T. ii. p. 2, et seq.

H. *Heliopolis.*—Also *Herennius.*

H. Hispaniæ.—P. H. C. Provincia Hispaniæ Citerioris.

HAD. *Hadrianus.*—Also HADR. also HADRI and HADRIAN.—See below.

HADRIANUS *(Publius Ælius)*, born at Rome, according to some; according to others, at Italica, a colonial city of Spain, where his family, originally of Hadria in Italy, was established from the time of the Scipios—that is to say, from about two centuries before Christ.— His father was Ælius Hadrianus Afer, his mother Domitia Paulina; and he was born on the

9th of the calends of February, A. U. C. 829
(A. D. 76). Losing his father at the age of ten,
he was placed under the guardianship of Trajan,
his cousin and fellow countryman (afterwards
emperor), at that time holding the office of pretor. After discharging the first offices usually
conferred upon a youth, he was sent into Mæsia;
and having subsequently set out to greet Trajan,
as the new Cæsar by adoption, and to convey
to him the congratulations of the army, he was
ordered to remain in Germania Superior. Being
from the first a great favourite with Trajan, on
account of his handsome person and captivating
manners, he afterwards drew closer the bonds
of friendship by marrying (it is not known in
what year) the emperor's niece Sabina, daughter
of Marciana; and thus opened the path to his
future greatness. In 854 (A. D. 101), he became questor, and at the expiration of that
office, followed Trajan to the Dacian war.—In
858 (105) he was tribune of the plebs; and
having, about the same epoch, entered upon another campaign in Dacia, he was appointed to
the command of Legio I. Minervia; and gave
signal proofs of his valour. At the termination
of this war, he celebrated games at Rome, with
great magnificence, as pretor. After this he
was sent as pro-pretor into Pannonia Inferior, where he defeated the Sarmatians, and
earned his consulate; which, however, was not
of the ordinary kind, but by *substitution* (suffectus). This consulate took place in 862 (A. D.
109). Growing more and more in favour with
Trajan, he was appointed, as *legatus*, to conduct the war then impending with Parthia.—
In 870 (117), when Trajan was preparing to return from the East, in consequence of ill-health,
he left to Hadrian the command of the army
in Syria, after the latter had been nominated,
through the agency of Plotina, as consul for the
year ensuing. Shortly afterwards, Trajan died
at Selinus (now *Selenti*), Cilicia. And Hadrian,
in virtue of letters of adoption, signed by Plotina, and forwarded to Rome, took at Antioch
the title of emperor, without waiting for the
Senatorial confirmation. It was on the 5th day
before the ides of August, that Hadrian received his letters of adoption, and thenceforth
kept that day as his *birth-day by adoption.*—
On the 3rd day before the ides of August, the
death of Trajan was publicly announced; and
this was afterwards reckoned as the *natal day
of his reign.*—The same year, he withdrew the
legions from Armenia, Mesopotamia, and Assyria, assigning as his reason for so doing, the
difficulty of keeping those regions in subjection;
and fixed on the Euphrates for the eastern
boundary of the empire. He sent to Rome the
ashes of Trajan; and the same year was elected
consul for the first time, from the month of
August to the month of January.

A. U. C. 871 (A. D. 118.—Hadrian made his
public entry into Rome. And soon paid divine
honours to Trajan. Proceeding consul for the
second time, he remitted to the people all debts
on account of taxation.

872 (119).—Consul for the third and last

time, he was victorious over the Sarmatæ,
through the instrumentality of his lieutenants.

873 (120).—It is conjectured by the learned,
that Hadrian this year commenced his tour
through the different provinces of the empire.
He first visited the Galliæ, and then Germania.

874 (121).—He passed over into Britain,
where he constructed a wall from one sea to the
other, to keep the Caledonian tribes within
bounds. Returning to Gaul, he proceeded to
Spain.

876 (123).—It is considered uncertain in
which direction he went on leaving Spain. But
it is not improbable that he passed a portion of
the year at Athens.

877 (124).—Hadrian is believed to have
journied this year into Asia, and made the inspection of its provinces.

878 (125).—After having visited the islands
of the Archipelago, he returned to Athens, and
it is thought that he then made a voyage to
Sicily.

880 (127).—It is uncertain where he went
this year, but he is supposed to have returned
from Sicily to Rome.

881 (128).—Hadrian accepted the title of
Pater Patriæ, and conferred that of Augusta on
his wife Sabina.

882 (129).—It is inferred from the proceedings of the following year, when he visited
Egypt, that at the end of this the emperor was
in Arabia. That he went thither from Syria,
Eckhel (vi. 481) gathers from Dion and from
the coins of Gaza, which town established (A. D.
130) a fresh æra in honour of his visit. A
temple of Rome, and another of Venus, were
built there in memory of the same event. The
succeeding year Hadrian returned from Egypt
into Syria.

885 (132).—Eckhel thinks it probable that
in this year began the Jewish war, set on foot
by Barchocebas, though Tillemont dates it two
years later. The events of the two following
years are uncertain.

888 (135).—Hadrian returned to Athens, and
was initiated into the mysteries of Eleusis. He
also completed a temple of Jupiter Olympius, at
Athens, which had been commenced many ages
before. Finding himself in a declining state of
health, he adopted L. Ælius. It is probable
that the Jewish war was this year brought to a
conclusion by the valour of Julius Severus.

889 (136).—His strength being exhausted
by repeated bleeding at the nose, and his temper
in consequence becoming morose, he caused
several individuals to be put to death, on charges
of attempted usurpation.

891 (138).—L. Ælius, whom Hadrian had
adopted, being dead, Antoninus, on the 25th of
February, was adopted in his stead; Antoninus
at the same time having adopted Marcus Aurelius and L. Verus. After protracted suffering,
and having lost Sabina, he died of dropsy, at
Baiæ, on the 10th of July, at the age of 62
years and nearly six months, after a reign of 20
years and 11 months.

The subjoined character of this celebrated

prince is by a master-hand for fidelity, discrimination, and judgment in the province of biographical writing:—

"Hadrian's name deserves to be handed down to posterity among those of the greatest benefactors of the Roman empire; though his merits were tarnished by crimes of great magnitude, and by vices of the worst description.—If we credit the accounts of his life, furnished by his biographer Spartianus, and by Dion Cassius, we shall find that there was no emperor who entered more into the most minute details, as well as into the highest concerns, of government. How indefatigable he was in visiting all the provinces of the empire, and investigating in person their respective grievances; how severe an exactor of military discipline, and how ready to share the duties, not only of a general, but of a private soldier, a reference to his coins affords frequent opportunities of proving, [as has already been shewn, and will continue to be shewn, in this dictionary.] Courteous in his demeanour to all persons, he was in the constant habit of joining the social meetings of his friends; the sick, though of much lower rank, he used to visit two or three times a day, and cheer them with encouragement; in short, conducted himself in all respects as a private individual. As in social life, so in public, his liberality was displayed in his remitting to the nation, A. U. C. 871 (A. D. 118), an enormous debt to the treasury, and relieving the provinces which had suffered loss, by money supplied from his private resources; also in the erection of temples of the greatest splendour, especially at Athens, of which city he was very fond, and in the construction of aqueducts and ports, by which he consulted both the ornament and the utility of the different cities.—There is still to be seen at Rome a mausoleum of vast proportions, built by him near the Tiber, accurately described by Procopius (now well-known under the name of the castle of St. Angelo); also the remains of the town of Tibur, a lasting monument of his magnificence, where, as Spartian relates, he built himself a villa, and introduced the novelty of inscribing on its several parts the names of the most celebrated provinces and localities, such as the Lyceum, the Academia, the Prytaneum, Canopus, Pæcile, and Tempe. Although, from the moment of his accession to empire, he devoted his whole attention to the preservation of peace throughout the world, in pursuance of which policy he voluntarily ceded Armenia and the other regions beyond the Euphrates, as being a perpetual hot-bed of war, yet he did not permit the soldiers to become enervated by inaction, but kept them ever on the alert and in the practice of arms; a circumstance which rendered him constantly formidable to foreign powers, and the more ready to suppress aggression, that he never himself took the initiative.

"Amidst these weighty cares of state, he still found time to bestow on his bodily exercise and intellectual pursuits. His coins bear witness to his untiring love of the chace. To Grecian literature he was, from his boyhood, so devoted, that he was called by many *Græculus*. He was a proficient not only in arithmetic, geometry, painting, and music, but even in the arts of moulding in brass and chiselling in marble; whether, indeed, in such a manner as to rival the Polycleti and Euphranors, we have only the testimony of Victor to assure us. He was so fond of travelling, that he wished to verify, by personal inspection, all the accounts which he had read of different parts of the world. His extreme addiction to sensual pleasures to the extent of indulgence in propensities not to be named, nor, even to be alluded to, was a foul and detestable blot upon his character. The infatuated attachment which he manifested for Antinous, and his ill-treatment of an amiable wife, cannot be too severely reprobated. It is a matter of history, that his love of peace carried him beyond bounds at all consistent with the honour of the empire. For, that he was in the habit of bribing foreign powers to forego their offensive designs, is stated not only by Dion, but Victor also more openly charges him with boasting, after purchasing pacific relations from many kings, that he had gained more without stirring foot, than others had by their campaigns. But, much more fatal in its effects was the spirit of envy, in which he persecuted those who excelled in any of the arts, going even so far as to put some of them to death; among whom were Euphrates, a celebrated philosopher of the period, and Apollodorus Damascenus, the architect of the Forum of Trajan, and the bridge over the Danube; nay many have supposed that a desire of peace and public tranquillity was but an ostensible reason for the relinquishment of Armenia and other provinces, and the dismantling of the famous bridge over the Danube, the actual one being his envy of Trajan's renown. His character, as drawn by Spartian, is full of contradictions, shewing him at one time cheerful, liberal, and merciful; at another severe, obstinate, perfidious, and cruel. The sanguinary disposition, indeed, which at the commencement of his reign he displayed in putting several eminent men to death, broke out with still greater violence in the later years of his life, when sourness of temper supervened upon the sufferings of disease, and a morbid suspicion took possession of his mind, which prompted him to take the lives of the most distinguished men in the state, and many of consular rank, on the charge of cherishing designs upon the sovereignty."—See *Doctrina*, vi. 473 to 484.

He was buried first at Puteoli, in the villa of Cicero; and subsequently his ashes were transferred to Rome, and deposited in the tomb, which he had built for himself on the banks of the Tiber.

Hadrian, in the first instance, not only took the name of Trajan [HADRIANVS TRAIANVS CAESAR]; but he also called himself *Filius Optimi Trajani*; and also the grandson of Nerva [IMP. CAES. HADRIANVS DIVI NER. TRAIAN. OPT. FIL.] Afterwards the style and title of this prince, as struck on his money, were for the most part HADRIANVS

AVGVSTVS P. P. with the addition, towards the close of his reign, of P*ater* P*atriæ*.

On *Hadrian's* coins, after A. D. 117, we read P. M. TR. P. COS. And from A. D. 119 to 138, TR. P. II. to XXI. COS. III. P. P. IMP. II. For from COS. III. A. D. 119, the number of the consulates is no longer repeated, nor are the successive investitures of the tribunitian power any longer recorded, a circumstance which renders it so difficult to mark the date of his mintages. The subjoined observations on the *obverses* of Hadrian's coins are from Eckhel, vi. 484 et seq.:

Firstly.—That Hadrian appears on them, for the most part, with *bare head*, which is of less frequent occurrence in the emperors immediately preceding and following him. Some suppose that this arises from the fact that, according to his biographer Spartianus, "he was so indifferent to cold and weather, that he never covered his head." And this testimony is confirmed by Dion; "he could not be induced by any extremity of heat or cold, to go with his head covered; for even amidst the Celtic snows, and the burning suns of Egypt, he always travelled with his head bare." This practice, however, was eventually fatal to him; for, according to the same writer, "after travelling in every direction with no covering to his head, and generally amidst storms of wet and cold, he at length fell a victim to disease."

Secondly.—The beard is also a novelty; as we gather not only from coins, but from the express statement of Dion—" For Hadrian," he says, "was the first emperor who allowed his beard to grow." We see, indeed, that on coins, both Augustus and Nero display a small beard, but in their cases, as we have before remarked, the reason for its appearance was either some occasion of public mourning, or that their age was not sufficient to admit of their laying aside their beard, in accordance with ancient custom. Spartian says, that the motive in Hadrian's case was "that he might conceal some natural blemishes on the face." But I suspect, that another motive was at the bottom of this fashion, viz. that he was more constant in his devotion to the study of philosophy, than its professors were to the cultivation of their beards. And that such was the view of the subject taken by the Emperor Julian is evident from the fling he has at him in his *Cæsars*—"After him (Trajan) appears a venerable old man, with a long beard. * * * Silenus, observing him frequently lifting up his eyes to heaven, and anxiously enquiring after abstruse subjects, exclaims, what think you of this Sophist?" Certainly, it is well known, that Hadrian greatly encouraged the Sophists, with the exception of those against whom he entertained feelings of envy; and Spartian informs us, that at the museum in Alexandria, he proposed many questions to the professors, which he answered himself, and that the sole reason for his attachment to Athens was its long established reputation for the encouragement of philosophy. His immediate successors in the empire, devoting their attention with equal ardour to these pursuits, also

allowed their beards to grow; unless Spartian would have us believe, that they too were desirous of hiding personal defects. The fashion, thus introduced in connexion with philosophical habits, became in subsequent emperors a mere custom, so that for a long period, all the emperors, however little addicted to learning, still persisted in wearing the beard.—See BARBA, pp. 123, 124.

Thirdly.—Whoever will inspect attentively the coins of Hadrian, cannot fail to remark, that on those struck in his first and second consulates, there appears rather a *bust* than a head of the emperor; in other words, a portrait, including the greater portion of the breast and the back; also a considerable thinness in the face, and sharpness of the chin; and further, that the inscription accompanying such busts continues to give the name of TRAIANI, in reference to his adoption, whereas, subsequently where the head, and not the bust, is displayed, and that too with fuller features, the name is invariably absent. And this peculiarity, both of the portrait and the legend, is observed also on some coins of the third consulate. Whence it follows, that during the first year of his third consulate, the original mode of pourtraying and inscribing was retained, and consequently that all such coins must be referred to the beginning of Consulate III.

Fourthly.—Again, the custom of using the *dative case* in the legend, borrowed from the coinage of Trajan, is observed still in force during the first consulate of Hadrian, or the year U. C. 870 (A. D. 117). Nevertheless, at the end of the year, in which he is styled, COS. DES. II. the *nominative case* begins to take its place. There are a very few coins of the second consulate, which retain the *dative case*.

Hadrian carried his display of reverence and affection for his parents, by adoption, to so high a pitch, as to cause a gold coin to be struck with the epigraph of DIVIS PARENTIBVS, and the heads of Trajan and Plotina on the reverse; and others with the head of Trajan and the inscription DIVO TRAIANO PATRI or PATRI AVG. or DIVVS TRAIANVS AVG. (See p. 335.)

Hadrian's various and continual journeyings amongst the provinces of the Roman world—as for example into Gaul, Germany, Britain, Spain, Africa, Mauretania, Asia, Achaia, Egypt, &c. are narrated by Spartianus and by Aurelius Victor. No mention, however, is made on his coins of the word *profectio*, as we find it (PRO-FECTIO AVG.) on the coins of succeeding emperors. But on the other hand we find the commemoration of arrivals (ADVENTVS) no where more numerously or more curiously exhibited on any of the imperial series than on the coins of Hadrian. This geographical class of medals present on their obverse the laureated head of Hadrian, and on the reverse the emperor and another figure, generally a woman, in the act of performing sacrifice, and sometimes a victim before the altar, bearing for inscription the words *Adventus* or *Adventui*, prefixed to the name of each province or city, viz. :—AFRICAE—ALEXANDRIAE——ARABIAE—ASIAE—BITHYNIAE—BRITANNIAE—CILICIAE—GALLIAE—HISPANIAE—ITALIAE—IVDEAE——MACEDONIAE——MAVRETANIAE—MOESIAE-PHRYGIAE—SICILIAE THRACIAE.

And as no journeyings or progresses from the capital into the different provinces of the Roman empire were more numerous than those of Hadrian, so neither were there any in which the arrival of an emperor in a provincial city was attended with greater benefit or advantage to that city, either in privileges granted or in embellishments bestowed. These are indicated on those of his coins which bear the inscriptions, RESTITVTORI ACHAIAE——AFRICAE——ASIAE—ARABIAE——BITHYNIAE——GALLIAE—HISPANIAE——MACEDONIAE——MAVRETANIAE—PHRYGIAE—SICILIAE.—We find also on the coinage of this great prince memorials of his visit to, or favours conferred on, AEGYPTOS, and CAPPADOCIA, inscribed on coins without the addition of either *adventus* or *restitutor*. Whilst first brass of the same Emperor, bearing, in comprehensive magnificence of terms, the epigraph RESTITVTORI ORBIS TERRARVM, will be found described and illustrated in its proper place.—See also ADVENTVS AVGVSTI, pp. 8 and 9.

It is stated by Spartian, that many cities called themselves after him by the name of *Hadriana*, or *Hadrianopolis;* but that he does not remember any colonies to have been planted by him; although Eusebius, in his *Chronicles,* affirms that the emperor sent many into Lybia, in the fifth year of his reign.

With certain exceptions, arising from the rarity, historical interest, workmanship, or preservation of the specimens, *Hadrian's* coins, of every metal and size, as well Greek as Latin, are common; especially those in first, second, and third brass. First brass colonial are rare, the others common.

MINTAGES OF HADRIANUS.

The following are among the rarest reverses :

SILVER MEDALLIONS.——COS. III. Jupiter Æthophorus standing.—COS. III. Minerva—Pluto & Cerberus—Apollo—Æsculapius—Ephesian Diana.—COM. BIT. Octostyle temple ; on its frieze ROM. S. P. AVG. (Brought only £1 4s. at the Thomas sale).—[The above seven Mionnet values at 40 fr. each.]—COS. III. Neptune—Two Furies—Cybèle. (Mt. 48 fr. each).—PONT. MAX. TR. POT. COS. III. Jupiter Victor seated. [This splendid medallion (engraved in Mionnet, who values it at 600 fr.) nearly the size of large brass, is of Roman die. The preceding ones were struck in Asia].

GOLD.——ANN. D. CCC. LXXIIII. NAT. VRB. P. CIR. CONC.——[This, one of the rarest of Hadrian's *aurei,* and of high historical interest, (see p. 46), brought £7 15s. at the sale of the Thomas collection. A specimen, at the Pembroke auction brought £4 3s.]

ADVENTVI AVG. ITALIAE. (£1 14s. Thomas

sale; Brumell, £2 2s.)—AEGYPTOS. (£4 5s. Thomas).—AFRICA. (£3 18s. 0d. same collection.)—CONSECRATIO. Emperor on an eagle. (Brought at the Thomas sale £12 10s.)—COS. III. Jupiter, Hadrian, and Rome. (£4 0s. Thomas). —DISCIPLINA AVG. (Mt. 72 fr.; Pembroke, £6 10s.; Thomas sale, £3 5s.; see same in brass, engraved in p. 333).—DIVIS PARENTIBVS. Busts of Trajanus and Plotina. (Mt. 100 fr.; Thomas sale, £13; Brumell, £11 15s.)—DIVO TRAIANO PATRI AVG. Head of Trajan. (Mt. 120 fr.; brought £9 15s. at the Thomas sale). Engraved in Akerman, pl. vi. No. 4.——HERC. GADIT. Hercules standing. (Mt. 60 fr.——HISPANIA. (£5 10s. Thomas).—IMP. HADRIAN DIVI NER. TRAIAN OPT. FIL. REST. The emperor sacrificing. (Mt. 150 fr.)—P. M. TR. P. COS. III. Mars. (£3 1s. Pembroke).—P. M. TR. P. COS. III. Hercules and two figures in a temple. (Mt. 60 fr.; Thomas, £4. Engraved in p. 456). —P. M. TR. P. COS. III. £3 11s. Thomas.—Same legend. Hercules in a temple. (£3 19s. Thomas).—Same legend. Hercules seated on armour. (£2 10s. 0d. Thomas).——ADVENTVI AFRICAE. (Mt. 50 fr. Engraved in p. 9).—RESTITVTORI HISPANIAE. (Mt. 60 fr.)—RESTITVTORI ITALIAE.—TELLVS STABIL. A woman seated on the ground. (Mt. 72 fr. each).—ROMVLO CONDITORI. (£2 Thomas.)—SAEC. AVR. P. M. &c. (Mt. 72 fr.; Pembroke, £5 15s. 6d. Thomas, £1 14s.)— SECVRITAS AVG. (£2 9s. Brumell).—VOTA PVBLICA. Emperor and four figures sacrificing. (Estimated by Mionnet at 120 fr.; brought £6 2s. 6d. at the Thomas sale). —Without legend. Wolf and Roman twins. (£6 12s. 6d. Pembroke; £4 10s. Thomas).—Without legend. The Nile seated, sphinx and hippopotamus. (£3 10s. Thomas).—Without legend. Trophy with shields. *(Half aureus,* (£4 1s. Thomas).—COS. III. The emperor on horseback. (This very fine *aureus* sold for £16 at the Thomas auction).

SILVER.——ITALIA FELIX. (Mt. 20 fr.)—MARTI. (30 fr.)—RESTITVTORI ACHAIAE. (24 fr.)—SABINA AVGVSTA. Head of the empress. (48 fr.)

BRASS MEDALLIONS.——CONCORDIA PARTH. &c. Female sacrificing. (£2 14s. Thomas).—COS. III. P. P. Man dragging a ram towards an altar. Engraved in Akerman, i. plate A. No. 1. (Mt. 200 fr.; £2 14s. Thomas).—[A beautifully patinated specimen of this rare and fine medallion brought the sum of thirty pounds at the sale of Signor Campana's collection].—COS. II. P. P. Cybèle drawn by four lions.—COS. III. P. P. Victory in a biga.—DECVRSIO. Two horsemen and one on foot.—Diana carrying two torches. (Mt. 100 fr. each).—COS. III. P. P. S. C. A galley, on the sail of which FELICITATI AVG. (Mt. 40 fr. Engraved in p. 383). —COS. III. FORT. RED. Fortune seated.—COS. III. Romulus and Remus and the wolf.—VOTA SVSCEPTA. Two figures sacrificing. (Mt. 50 fr. each)—FELICITATI AVG. COS. III. P. P. S. C. Pretorian galley, with eight rowers, gubernator, &c. (£1 5s. Thomas.)—GENIVS POPVLI ROMANI. Mt. 150 fr. Engraved in p. 410).—-P. M. TR. P.

Roma Nicephorus seated.——Without legend. Apollo and Bacchus drawn by a goat and a panther. See p. 120. (Mt. 150 fr. each).—P. M. TR. P. IIII. Jupiter standing between two galeated females. Without legend. Jupiter seated between Juno and Minerva. (Mt. 200 fr. each). —VIRTVTI AVGVSTI. Emperor on horseback, chasing a lion. (£5 15s. Campana sale).—P. M. TR. P. COS. III. Sow and numerous piglets. (£4 16s. Campana).

[The medallion with the Pons Ælius, ornamented with statues, quoted by the early numismatic writers, is a modern fabrication.—Mionnet—Akerman.]

LARGE BRASS.—ADLOCVTIO COH. PRAETOR. —ADVENTVI AVG. ALEXANDRIAE. Serapis, Isis, Hadrian and Sabina.—Without legend. Eagle, peacock, and owl. (Mt. 24 fr. each).—ADVEN- TVI AVG. BRITANNIAE.—ADVENTVI AVG. MOE- SIAE.—DO. PHRYGIAE. (30 fr. each).—COS. III. Emperor fully armed. (£2 5s. Pembroke sale. —COS. III. Emperor in the toga, addressing six personages from the steps of a portico.—[See this reverse engraved under the head of TEM- PLVM.]—EXERCITVS SYRIACVS. (£2 15s. 0d. Campana).——EXERCITVS DACICVS. (£2 same sale).—EXERCITVS CAPPADOCICVS. (Mt. 30 fr.) —GERMANICVS.--MAVRETANICVS.—RHAETICVS. (20 fr. each).—MOESIACVS.—NORICVS. (40 fr. each).—FORTVNA REDVCI. Rome and the emperor. (Not in Mionnet : brought £4 2s. at the Brumell sale).—LOCVPLETATORI ORBIS TERRA- RVM.—RELIQ. VETERA, &c. (30 fr. each).— ROMVLO CONDITORI. Emperor carrying trophy. (24 fr.)—SABINA. Head of empress. (Mt. 40 fr.) —SICILIA. Head of Medusa.—VIRTVS AVGVSTI. Emperor on horseback, pursuing a lion.—VOT. PVB. Emperor and several figures at a sacrifice. —Without legend. Pons Ælius. (72 fr.)— Without legend. Jupiter, Juno, and Minerva seated. (30 fr.)

MIDDLE BRASS.—S. C. Four children representing the four seasons. (20 fr.)

SMALL BRASS.—AELIA PINCENSIA, within a crown of laurel. (18 fr.) See p. 15.

HADR.—*Hadrumetum*, the capital of a particular country in Africa, called *Byzacena*, between the Syrtis and Zeugitana.—"All authors who speak of Africa (says Pellerin) make mention of this city as one of considerable importance, and as the metropolis of the province in which it was situated. Pliny includes it in the list of free cities. But Gruter has given an inscription by which it appears that it was made a colony by the Emperor Trajan ; and Ptolemy in effect assigns to it the title of a colony."— Vaillant does not appear to have been aware of the existence of any coins belonging to this colony. But Pellerin has published two. One of these he shews by an engraving to be of a module, which approaches the size of a medallion, and which he describes to be in perfect preservation ; the other is about the dimensions of first brass. Both have on their obverse HADR*umetum* AVGVSTVS, and the naked head of Augustus ; and for their reverse the bare head of Julius, with lituus and star, and

the legend CAESAR.—See vol. iv. pl. lxxxviii. page 17 ; also *Mélange*, i. vignette title-page.

It is only by these two medals that the city of Hadrumetum (although a considerable city in the most fertile and corn-growing district of Africa Propria), is numismatically identified with the imperial series of Roman colonies and *municipia*. It is not, however, included in Eckhel's or Mionnet's list of either.

HANDS *joined*.—See *Manus humana*.

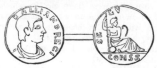

HANNIBALLIANUS *(Flavius Claudius)*, nephew of Constantine the Great, and brother to Delmatius, born at Toulouse, in what year is uncertain. He was called *Nobilissimus* by his uncle Constantine, who appointed him prefect of Cappadocia and Armenia, which provinces he governed with the title of king, A. D. 335. He and his brother Delmatius were killed by the soldiers, A. D. 337. (See DELMATIVS, p. 315). Of this prince there are no gold or silver coins. His third brass are very rare. They bear on their obverse FL. HANNIBALLIANO REGI, with the bare head, and the *paludamentum ;* and on the reverse SECVRITAS PVBLICA, and also REIPVBLICAE, with a river god.—The former valued by Mionnet at 50 fr. the latter at 72 fr.

HARPA, a very ancient kind of instrument, in the form of a denticulated sickle, of which Saturn, according to a horrid myth, made use to mutilate his father Uranus, and is therefore one of the symbols of that god.— The harpa is seen on a coin of the Neria gens, behind the head of Saturn, and on a denarius of the Sentia family, in the hands of the same deity ; also on a silver coin of Valerianus, accompanying the epigraph of Eternitas. (Eckhel).— Mercury is also said to have used it to kill Argus, and Perseus employed it as a weapon to cut off the head of Medusa.—See SATURNUS.

HARUSPICES.—See ARUSPICES.

HASTA, a spear, lance, or pike—a weapon derived by the Romans from the Etrurians, who called it *Corim*. By the Sabines it was named *Quiris*, whence Romulus received the designation of Quirinus, as Ovid affirms—

Sive quod hasta Quiris priscis est dicta Sabinis,
  Bellicus à telo venit in astra Deus.

The Sabines called their kings *Coritos*, that is to say *Joves hastatos*, because the spear was with them the attribute of royalty. Per ea tempora (says Justin), Reges hastas pro diademate habebant, quas Græci sceptra dixère.

The *Hasta* was the symbol not only of power, fortitude, and valour, but also of majesty and even of divinity. Inverted or reversed it denoted tranquillity.——Havercamp, *ad Morell. Thesaur. Fam.* p. 458.

Hasta Pura was a spear staff, without an iron head—as in Virgil,

Ille, vides, purâ juvenis qui nititur hastâ.

Whereupon Servius remarks, that the ancient Romans presented a spear, without an iron point, to him who had conquered for the first time.— Spanheim (Pr i p 455), says the hasta pura, as a kind of sceptre, is an indication of power both divine and human. It is one of the insignia of the Gods, and of the Emperors and *Augustæ* after their apotheosis, implying that they had become objects of worship. It is generally found in the hands of female divinities and personifications; as the war-spear is in those of warriors and heroes.

Hasta.——We see this weapon on Roman coins in the hands of various deities, amongst the rest those of Apollo, Bacchus, Castor and Pollux, Ceres, Cybèle, Diana, Hercules, Juno, Jupiter, Mars, Pallas, Sol, Venus, Vesta, and (as a demigod) Romulus. In like manner it is an attribute of qualities, such as Æquitas, Æternitas, Annona, Clementia, Concordia, Fecunditas, Felicitas, Fides, Fortune, Hilaritas, Honos, Indulgentia, Justitia, Liberalitas, Munificentia, Nobilitas, Patientia, Pax, Perennitas, Perpetuitas, Pietas, Providentia, Pudicitia, Quies, Salus, Securitas, Tranquillitas, Virtus, &c. A man on horseback with the hasta in his hand, on imperial coins, betokens an emperor hastening to the wars. The type of an emperor shaking his spear over an enemy lying prostrate on the ground, denotes that his heroism in battle against the " barbarians" shone like that of another Mars, and such like flattery. The genius of a city carries a hasta in the right hand for the defence of the citizens against the barbarians. Rome, when personified on coins, is almost always represented holding the hasta, that particular mark of dominion and sovereignty.

Hastæ, placed crosswise behind a shield, are marks of the equestrian dignity. See EQVESTER ORDO PRINCIPI IVVENT. on a coin of Commodus. For the Romans under the empire were accustomed to offer such spears, as well as a shield, to young princes.

Hastati, infantry of the Roman legions, so called because at the commencement of their institution, they were armed with spears.— Hastati (says Varro), quòd primo Hastis pugnabant. And though afterwards armed in a different manner, they always preserved the name; for in Polybius's time they fought with swords, and a dart called *Pilum;* the *Velites*, or light troops, alone continued to use the javelin termed *Hasta*. (Pitiscus).——*Hastati* and *Principes* are expressed on family coins by the letters H. and P. (See Neria gens).— The *Principes*, like the *Hastati*, were the most distinguished of the Roman soldiers: their post was at the head of an army, the first in rank, and as it were, the princes; it also meant the first cohorts and the first legions.—(Kolb.)

HEDERA.—See *Ivy*.

HELENA (*Flavia Julia*), born at Drepanum, in Bithynia (A. D. 248), was the first wife of Constantius Chlorus, to whom she was married several years previously to his being invested with the rank of Cæsar, and by whom she was divorced after his elevation to that high dignity, A. D. 292, Constantius immediately afterwards took Theodora, daughter-in-law of Maximianus Hercules, for his second wife; and Helena retired into private life; but was subsequently honoured with the title of Augusta by her son Constantine the Great. She died A. D. 328. There are brass medallions (rare) of this empress, and third brass which are common; on these she is styled FLavia IVLia HELENA AVGusta.

Mionnet values SECVRITAS AVGVSTA, and PIETAS AVGVSTAE, two brass medallions of this empress, at 100 fr. each.

HELENA (*Flavia*), wife of Julian the Apostate, to whom she was united in marriage when that emperor was declared Cæsar, A. D. 355. She was the daughter of Constantine the Great by the empress Fausta. Her death took place in 360, a short time after Julian had been proclaimed Augustus. The coins of this lady have been by mistake assigned to Helena, wife of Constantine I. The gold are of extreme rarity, but the third brass are common: on these she is styled FL. HELENA AVGVSTA.

An *aureus*, with legend SECVRITAS REIPVBLICAE. Female standing; S. M. T. (Valued by Mionnet at 1000 fr.)

[This coin Eckhel (see his observations, *D. N. V.* vol. viii. p. 143), confidently assigns to Helena, wife of Julian.——Mionnet (*De la Rareté des Med.* vol. ii. p. 303), follows on this point the opinion of Eckhel.—M. Le Baron Marchant (in his xviith *Lettre Numismatique)*, at once repudiates the distinctions previously established between the coins of the three different Helenas, and ascribes all the pieces which bear that name to the mother of Constantine. —In this absolute revolt against a part of the system of appropriation, laid down by the illustrious German, and for some time acquiesced in without further contest by the numismatic world, M. Ch. Lenormant has joined. And in vol. vi. p. 88 et seq. of *Revue Numismatique*, the latter has given his reasons in full for undertaking to corroborate and carry out the ideas of Baron Marchant. To this luminous dissertation the attention of the student is particularly directed.]

HELENA N. F. (*Nobilissima Femina*).—A third brass, bearing this legend and the undecorated head of a female.—*Rev.* without legend. A large star within a garland.—" This princess is not alluded to in history, but from the mention of her name together with that of Crispus, in the Theodosian code, she is supposed to have been the wife of that Cæsar, the son of Constantine, although it does not clearly state that she was. The supposition is strengthened by the style of the coin (engraved in preceding page), which bears a strong resemblance to that of Fausta, the supposed wife of Constantius the Second.—Akerman, *Descript. Cat.* ii. 25.

[According to the new distribution by Baron Marchant and M. Ch. Lenormant, this is, amongst others, rendered up, as a coin struck under her son, to the mother of Constantine.— See *Nobilissima Femina*].

HEL.—*Heliopolis*, or city of the Sun.

HELIOPOLIS.—There were more cities than one of this name. That however, which is distinguished numismatically, was situated near Mount Lebanon; and having received from the Egyptian Heliopolis an idol of the Sun, adopted the same appellation. It became a Roman *colony* under Julius Cæsar's foundation, and therefore called *Julia*. Augustus sent many veterans to it; and the name of *Augusta* was consequently added to its colonial titles.

The *jus Italicum* was moreover conferred upon it by Sept. Severus, for its attachment to his interest during his struggle for empire with Pescennius Niger. The ancient *Heliopolis* is now called *Balbec* or *Baalbeck*; and the ruins of its once celebrated temple still exist. It is marked by some geographers a city of Phœnicia, by others a city of Cœle-syria. Those, however, who place it in Phœnicia, make a double Phœnicia, one proper or by the sea shore, the other Lybanisia or Damascan (Damascena—Plin. l. v. c. 18). That old soldiers were sent by Augustus to Heliopolis as a recruitment to the colony, drafted from the Fifth or Macedonica, and the Eighth or Augustan Legions, is shewn by its coins under Philip senior. This city inscribed money to Nerva, Hadrian, Antoninus Pius, M. Aurelius, Commodus, Pertinax, S. Severus, Julia Domna, Caracalla, Plautilla, Geta, Macrinus, Alexander Severus, Gordianus Pius, Philip sen. Philip jun. Valerianus, Gallienus; and styled COL. H. or HEL. *Colonia Heliopolis*. On one of Caracalla's it bears the title of COL. IVL. AVG. FEL. HEL. *Colonia Julia Augusta Felix Heliopolis*, or *Heliopolitani*.—The epigraph of this colony on a coin of the elder Philip is COL. HEL. LEG. V. MACED. AVG. *Colonia Heliopolis Legionum Quintæ Macedonicæ et Octavæ Augustæ*.—Spanheim, ii. p. 602—Vaillant, *in Col.* i. and ii.

The coins of this colony are *Latin* imperial, in small, middle, and large brass (see Mionnet, *Supplt.* T. viii. 208). Amongst the types which occur on their reverses are the following, viz.:

Astarte.—On large brass of Philip sen. A woman, with tutulated head, standing, and clothed in the stola, holds a rudder in the right hand, and a cornucopiæ in the left. At her feet are two small figures, each supporting a *vex-*

illum. On either side, elevated on a cippus, is a young draped female, each holding the ends of a veil, floating in the air above the head of the goddess, whom Vaillant calls the *genius* of Heliopolis, and Mionnet describes as *Astarte*.— It is at any rate as remarkable a type as any engraved on a colonial coin.

Athleta (wrestler).—On a second brass struck by the Heliopolitans, in honour of the emperor Valerianus, a male figure naked, stands with his right hand placed on a vase (or is in the act of

receiving it as a prize). He holds in his left hand a palm-branch, the symbol of victory.— [Coins were minted at Heliopolis to record the arrival of Valerianus in Syria, on his way to undertake against the Persians (A. D. 258), an expedition, to the catastrophe of which he fell a miserable victim].

The abbreviated legend COL. CER. SAC. CAP. OEC. ISEL. HEL. Vaillant, supported by Bimard, interprets *Colonia Certamen Sacrum Capitolinum, Oecumenicum, Iselasticum, Heliopolitanum*, and considers that it alludes to the public games which were celebrated at Heliopolis in the above named emperor's presence, the same year. In these games the objects of competition and contest were of a three-fold kind, namely equestrian, gymnastic, and musical. The certamen was called Oecumenicum; because not only Syrian athletæ, but other champions, from all parts, were admitted as candidates for the prizes.— *Iselasticum*, because the victors were said εἰσελαυνειν, to be carried in quadrigæ through the country. The shews were called sacred (sacrum) because they were celebrated in honour of some deity; and at Heliopolis they were dedicated to Jupiter, surnamed *Capitolinus* by the Romans. —*Colonia*, ii. 37.

The above figure is that of an *Athleta*, who seems to have triumphed in the gymnastic branch of the *certamen*, which itself comprised five different kinds of bodily exercises, viz. running, leaping, wrestling, pugilism, and throwing the discus, in all which they contended naked.— The vase or discus was the prize, the palm-branch the symbol, of victory.—(ii. 231–233).

Colonist driving Oxen at plough, behind which are two military ensigns.—See COLONIAE ROMANAE, p. 227.

Cornucopiæ (double, with caduceus between them). On third brass of Gallienus.

Eagles.—Two legionary eagles within a wreath of laurel appear on third brass coins of Heliopolis, dedicated to Sept. Severus, and to his second son Geta; also to his wife Julia Domna, who was a native of the province in which this colony was situated. The same type likewise occurs on a medal of Philip jun.—[The eagle-standard of the legionaries, exhibited on coins of Roman colonies, indicates (as has already been observed), the origin of such colonies from the veterans of a legion; and when *two* eagles are represented, they argue that the colonists had been selected and sent from the soldiers of two legions. The two here alluded to were the 5th and 8th. See *Philip sen.*—Vaillant, ii. p. 20.]

Fortunæ Duæ.—On a coin of this colony, inscribed to Hadrian, two draped females stand arm in arm. One holds a rudder in the right hand, the other a similar attribute in the left.

[The legend is LEG. H. COL. H. which Vaillant (i. 158), interprets *Legio Heliopolis— Colonia Heliopolis;* adding that, "under the effigies of *two* Fortunes, which often stand for *genii loci,* the people of this city, mindful of their Roman origin, dedicated the genius of the legion and that of the colony to Hadrian, then tarrying within the borders of Syria."—Bimard, in noticing the same coin, whilst admitting that it is properly assigned to Heliopolis, in Cœle-syria, expresses his opinion that LEG. H. should be explained by *Legio Octava;* the 8th legion (*Macedonica*) belonging to this colony, and the letter H being employed, after the fashion of the Greeks, for a numeral sign. This eminent numismatist supports himself in this hypothesis on the precedent of a coin struck in the same colony, also under Philip, and which exhibits the union of a *Greek* legend with a *Latin* legend. (*ad Jobert,* ii. 187).—Pellerin, commenting on these two opinions, says "there is no apparent likelihood that the city which coined the medals here quoted by Bimard, should have used numeral letters purely *Latin* on the one, and *Greek* numerals on the other, for the purpose of designating the Roman legions which were stationed in this colony." He therefore infers, as Vaillant does, that it was a legion bearing the name of Heliopolis, the initial of which follows the abbreviated word LEG. in the reverse legend of this coin, and he adds that it was, beyond doubt, struck at the Cœle-syrian Heliopolis.— *Mélange,* i. 273].

Mercury.—On small brass of Philip senior and junior, this deity, standing clothed in a short dress, holds the *crumena* in his right hand, and the caduceus in his left.. From this and other numismatic evidences, it appears that Mercury was, as well as Jupiter, worshipped in the Heliopolitan colony.—See Vaill. ii. 166.

Temples.—There are two specimens of this type on second brass of Sept. Severus, one presenting the front of a temple, with a portico of ten columns. The other exhibits a side view of the whole building, which has steps leading up to it. The legend is COL. HEL. I. O. M. H.— *Colonia Heliopolis Jovi Optimo Maximo Heliopolitano.*

[Both these types are intended to represent the temple dedicated at Heliopolis to Jupiter, who, as he was called *Capitolinus* at Rome, so is he here surnamed *Heliopolitanus;* and at both places he was termed *Optimus Maximus.* The people of this Cœle-syrian colony, in return for their obligations to Severus, who had conferred on them the *jus Italicum,* inscribed the above described coins to that emperor, adding the type and the name of the temple which they had erected to Jupiter Heliopolitanus. Coins with similar legends and types were dedicated to Caracalla.—Vaillant, ii. pp. 13 and 37.]

Temple, upon a foundation of rock, with a flight of many stairs up to it. Before the temple is an *arula* (or small altar), and near that a sacrificial urn. In the field of the coin, which is a first brass of Philip senior, near the top of the stair-case is a caduceus. Legend COL. IVL. AVG. FEL. HEL.

[Judging from the caduceus, Vaillant (ii. 167) adopts the opinion that this reverse typifies the temple of Mercury, to whom another coin of the same colony, struck under the same emperor, and already noticed in this list, points as to a favourite object of religious worship at Heliopolis. The situation of that city being on one of the spurs of Mount Lebanon, is supposed to account for the temple being delineated as built on a rock].

Pellerin (in *Mélange,* i. pl. xxii. Nó. 5, p. 328), has engraved a coin of Valerianus, which, with legend COL. HEL. typifies two temples, placed sideways opposite each other. Above are three urns or vases, with palm branches in each.

Victors at Games.—On a second brass of the same emperor, having for the legend of its reverse SAC. CAP. OEC. ISE. but without the COL. HEL. engraved on the preceding coin, the type consists of two seated male figures, facing one another, each wearing the pallium, and placing with his left hand a crown on his own head.— These two figures sustain between them with the right hand a *discus,* or broad round vase, in which are two palm branches. Between the two men is an altar.

[The two figures above described are evidently designed to represent victors at the *certamen sacrum,* celebrated at Heliopolis, although the epigraph does not give the name of that city.— At such public trials of skill, all the conquerors were crowned. But the question is, which kind of crown was given as a prize at these Capitoline games? Vaillant thinks it probable that it was the olive leaf, as at the Olympic. The seated figures both supporting the same vase, which has two branches in it, serve to indicate that they had both come off victors at one of the three exercises (viz. gymnastics, equitation, and music). In this case there is room for conjecture that it was for music, because the two figures are seated, and invested with the *pallium* or cloak. In wrestling and in horsemanship the candidates exercised naked. In music they performed clothed. The altar is placed between them on the coin, to denote that sacred rites had been paid to the gods before and after the games were celebrated.—Vaillant, ii. 231].

The other types, occurring on coins of this colony consist of a turreted woman, represented both as a whole figure and as a bust, portraying the genius of Heliopolis. Also urns *(disci)*, from one to three in number, in each of which are from one to three palm branches, struck on the occasion of the Capitoline games, celebrated there, in honour of Jupiter, as already mentioned under the head of *Athletæ* in this article.

HERCULES.—This celebrated hero of mythological romance was at first called Alcides, but received the name of Hercules, or Heracles, from the Pythia of Delphos. Feigned by the poets of antiquity to have been a son of "the Thunderer," but born of an earthly mother, he was exposed, through Juno's implacable hatred to him as the offspring of Alcmena, to a course of perils, which commenced whilst he was yet in his cradle, and under each of which he seemed ready to perish, but as constantly proved victorious. At length finishing his allotted career with native valour and generosity, though too frequently the submissive agent of the meanness and injustice of others, he perished self-devotedly on the funeral pile, which was lighted on Mount Oeta. Jupiter raised his heroic progeny to the skies; and Hercules was honoured by the pagan world, as the most illustrious of deified mortals. The extraordinary enterprises cruelly imposed upon, but gloriously achieved by, this famous demigod, are to be found depictured, not only on Greek coins, but also on the Roman series both consular and imperial. The first, and one of the most dangerous, of undertakings, well-known under the name of the twelve labours of Hercules, was that of killing the huge lion of Nemæa; on which account the intrepid warrior is represented, clothed in the skin of that forest monarch; he also bears uniformly a massive club, sometimes without any other arms, but at others with a bow and quiver of arrows. On a denarius of the Antia gens he is represented walking with trophy and club. (See RESTIO.)—When his head alone is typified, as in Mucia gens, it is covered with the lion's spoils, in which distinctive decoration he was imitated by many princes, and especially by those who claimed descent from him—as for example, the kings of Macedonia, and the successors of Alexander the Great. Among the Roman emperors Trajan is the first whose coins exhibit the figure and attributes of Hercules. On a dena-

rius of this prince (P. M. TR. P. COS. III. P. P.) his image standing on a *basis*, has a club in the right hand, and an apple in the left (allusive to the Hesperides); the skin of the Nemæan lion being thrown, like the *pallium*, over his shoulders, and falling on his left arm.—On a first brass of the same emperor (S. P. Q. R. OPT. PRIN.) appears a club resting perpendicularly on the head of a lion placed on a pedestal. But it was left for Commodus to shew his folly in affecting "the Herc'les vein." And not only does the effigy of the demi-god appear on numerous coins of that pest of society, but his own head is covered with the leonine attribute, and he assumes the appellation of "the Roman Hercules."—Gallienus, Postumus, Probus, Maximianus Hercules, and other emperors, also selected this deity as the peculiar object of their worship.

Hercules and the Centaurs.—On a silver coin of the Aurelia gens (see p. 111), Hercules stands in a car drawn by two centaurs, holding branches in their hands. His victory over these quadrupedal monsters is referred to on several coins; amongst others a beautiful medallion of Antoninus Pius. (See the subject described and engraved in p. 194).—On a highly-relieved brass medallion of M. Aurelius, Hercules bearing a trophy on his left shoulder, and holding the club in his right hand, stands in a car drawn by four centaurs. (See *Temporum Felicitas.*) Engraved in Mionnet and in Akerman.

HERCULIS LABORES.

M. De Witte, an eminent numismatist, resident at Cologne, in an elaborate and ably written paper, addressed to the Editor of the *Revue Numismatique* (vol. vii. p. 330 to 369), respecting the veneration which Postumus manifested towards Hercules, gives a description of a set of coins, struck under that prince, the reverses of which present a complete series of the labours of Hercules. It is from the engravings (plate vii.) which illustrate the dissertation in question, that the subjoined cuts have been copied; whilst advantage has also been taken of M. De Witte's commentary on the different types, to throw fresh light on the numismatic as well as mythological bearings of the subject:—

1.　　　　　　　　　2.

No. 1.—HERCVLI NEMAEO. Hercules suffocating a lion, that tremendous beast, which ravaged the country near the Nemæan forest, in the neighbourhood of Cleonas, and which he had in vain endeavoured to kill, with the sword, the club, and the stone; and the skin of which he afterwards wore as a trophy of his victory.

Mythographers speak of two or three lions

slain by Hercules. That of Mount Cithera, or rather that of Mount Helicon, that of Lesbos, and that of Nemæa. His combats with the "king of beasts" have often been represented by ancient artists; this group offering favourable combinations, as well for sculpture as for painting; numberless and very varied repetitions are also found of it, especially on Greek coins. It is the lion of Nemæa, the slaying of which was the first of the hero's twelve labours, that is shewn by the inscription on the denarius of Postumus, No. 1.

Mionnet has described an *aureus* similar to the above, with the legend HERCVLI INVICTO; which accompanies the group of Alcides and the lion on a reverse of Postumus. Lastly, Banduri cites a brass coin of Postumus, which bears on its reverse the legend VIRTVS POSTVMI AVG. s. c. with the same type.

No. 2.—*Rev.*—HERCVLI ARGIVO. Hercules armed with the club, the skin of the lion wrapped round the left arm, attacking the Hydra, or many-headed serpent of Lerna.

Obv.—POSTVMVS PIVS FELIX AVG. Jugated heads of Postumus and Hercules, both crowned with laurel, to the right. (See obverse of a silver medallion of Postumus, p. 382).

From an unpublished denarius of billon, belonging to the collection of M. Dupré. This piece (says M. De Witte) formed part of a depôt of medals found in the environs of Cologne.—Compare with Banduri, *Num. Imp. Rom.* vol. i. p. 286.

Hercules and the Hydra are represented on a tolerably large number of monuments in marble and on painted vases. With regard to coins, this type is found on some Greek money, and upon imperial Latin coins of Maximianus Hercules, bearing the legends HERCVLI DEBELLATORI (brass medallion, and gold and silver)—HERCVLI VICTORI (gold)—and HERCVLI INVICTO—and on those of Constantius Chlorus, VIRTVTI AVGG. (also gold). It has been conjectured that the extermination of the Hydra, which is often repeated on coins of Maximianus Hercules, bear reference to the persecution exercised against the Christians.

The marshes of Lerna were situated in Argolis, whence came the epithet *Argivus*, which Hercules bears on the denarius of Postumus, engraved in preceding page. "Of all the reverses of the labours of Hercules, says M. Dupré, that with the legend HERCVLI ARGIVO is the most rare. Published solely by Goltzius, and not being found in the greatest collections, its existence has been doubted. But we are acquainted with an indubitable specimen of it, discovered amongst a deposit found near Treves."

3.

No. 3.—POSTVMVS P. F. AVG. COS. Radiated head of Postumus to the left.

Rev.—VIRTV POSTVMI AVG.—Hercules seizing by the antlers, the hind or stag *Ceryquita.*—Middle brass, in the *Cabinet de France.*—Mionnet, *Rareté des Med.* ii. 68.

The hind, with golden horns and brazen hoofs, furnished to Hercules his third labour. This is a rare subject on ancient monuments, except on the bas-reliefs dedicated to this series of representations. A few paintings on vases refer to the capture of this wild stag so famous for its swiftness. Sometimes also Hercules and Apollo are seen contending for this fleet animal, a struggle figured on a magnificent medal of bronze, in the collection of M. le Duc de Luynes, and on two painted vases. The type of the hind tamed by Hercules, although not of frequent occurrence, is not unknown in Greek numismatics; and it is found on the gold and small brass of Diocletian, and of Maximian Hercules; VIRTVS AVGG. or VIRTVTI AVGG. The brass coin of Postumus (engraved above) is unique.—De Witte, *Revue Num.* vol. vii.

No. 4.—HERCVLI ERYMANTINO *(sic.)*—Hercules carrying on his shoulders the wild boar of Erymanthus. The lion's skin is hung on the left arm. At his feet is a *pithos* or wine-jar. Denarius of billon in the *Cabinet de France.*—Mionnet, ii. 61. Banduri i. 285 and 291, in whose work it is engraved.

4.　　　　5.

Hercules, carrying the huge wild boar alive on his shoulders, is often depictured on painted vases as well as on marbles, on one of which Eurystheus is seen hiding himself in the *pithos.* The king of Mycénæ, affrighted at the sight of the enormous victim to heroic strength and courage, lifts up both his arms, and seems to conjure Hercules to take himself away with his dreadful burthen.—On coin No. 4, neither the head nor the arms of Eurystheus are visible.—On other coins the *pithos* is seen, and Eurystheus concealing himself therein, in the same manner as on the painted urns—as for example, on a brass coin struck at Alexandria, in Egypt, under Antoninus Pius; on another brass coin, struck at Hadrianopolis of Thrace, under Caracalla; and lastly, on three brass medallions of Perinthus, struck under Caracalla, Geta, and Gordianus Pius.

No. 5.—HERC...... PISAEO. Hercules naked, carrying on his right shoulder what M. De Witte calls a kind of *hoyau pioche* (but what in the engraving looks more like a club), proceeding to the task of cleansing the Augean stables.— A denarius of Postumus in billon, unpublished, from the Treves Museum.

The myth of the stable of Augias is represented only on a small number of ancient monuments; for instance, on the celebrated cup Albani; on the Borgia marble; and on the altar of the Giustiniani gallery. The representation which corresponds most closely with the type of this rare denarius (No. 5), is the bas relief on the altar last named, and on which Hercules is seen walking to the left, armed with a σκαπανη (hoe or mattock), by means of which he prepares to split rocks, and open a passage for the waters of the Alpheus and the Peneus. The club is placed against the rock.

The coin (No. 5) is unfortunately defective in point of preservation. "In the type of the reverse (remarks M. De Witte) may without hesitation be recognized the fifth labour of Hercules—that in which the hero cleansed the Elide. But there remain difficulties attached to the task of reading the legend, in which it might have been supposed that more than one surname would have been connected with the operation—such as those of *Herculi Alpheo, Eleo,* or *Peneo.* The first letter especially is of an uncertain form.—M. Chassot de Florencourt, to whom I had communicated my doubts, shewed in the most convincing manner, that it was a a P, and that it ought to be read HERCVLI PISAEO."

Pisæus is a new surname for Hercules. This epithet alludes to the territory of Elis, within the confines of which once stood the city of Pisa, of which no vestiges are now discoverable, although known to have been situated near the plain of Olympia, where the Olympic games in honour of Jupiter were celebrated.

"Pisa was regarded as the residence of king Augias, and the capital of the country called *Pisatis.* Some authors seem to make a distinction between Olympia and Pisa; others say that it was the same city. Seneca the tragedian gives the epithet of Pisæus to Jupiter *(Agamemnon,* 930):—

"Et ista donum palma Pisæi Jovis."

M. De Witte concludes his learned commentary on coin No. 5, by observing, that on a bas-relief in the Vatican, and on a brass coin of Egyptian Alexandria, struck under Antoninus Pius, Hercules, after having finished his labour (of opening a passage through a rock for the waters of two rivers—symbolized under the figure of stable-cleansing), is seen *washing his hands.*

6.   7.

No. 6.—*Rev.*—HERCVLI AV(G). Hercules standing, the lion's skin on his shoulders, shoots with his arrows two of the *Stymphalides.* On an aureus of Postumus in the *Cabinet de France.*—Tanini, *Num. Imp. Rom.* TAB. ii.

Hercules killing with shafts discharged from his unerring bow the birds of Stymphalus, is a subject found on ancient monuments of every kind, and on many Greek coins. This aureus, which bears on its obverse the jugated heads of Postumus and Hercules, both crowned with laurel, is a fine one, and may be considered to have been unpublished until engraved in the *Revue Numismatique* to illustrate with others M. De Witte's dissertation. Mionnet has not described it. Tanini has given a very bad copy of it, the only one heretofore known. Nor are the birds of Stymphalus represented on any other *Latin* coin.

[These birds were so called from the lake Stymphalus, in Arcadia, the neighbourhood of which they infested. They were said to have been of prodigious size, of insatiable voracity, and to have fed on human flesh. With the assistance of Minerva, they were partly destroyed by the arrows of Hercules, and the rest driven away by the sound of brass timbrels. A specimen of these winged monsters (which differed from the Syren and the Harpy), is supposed by certain numismatists of the elder school to be exhibited on a well-known denarius of the Valeria gens. That type, however, does not agree with Pausanias's description of the *Stymphales Aves,* which the Greek writer compares to a crane in size, and with a head and beak somewhat like those of an Ibis. It were, however, worse than trifling to criticise the form and dimensions of creatures about which even fable contradicts itself, and the existence of which probably had no place but in the imagination of the ancient poets].

No. 7.—HERCVLI CRETENSI.—Hercules, naked (turned to the right), seizes a bull by the horns. *Obv.*—POSTVMVS PIVS FELIX AVG. Jugated heads of Postumus and Hercules (as in p. 382). On gold, in the Museum of Berlin.—Mionnet, *Rareté des Med.* v. ii. 61—Banduri, *Num. Impp.* i. 287.—For a cast of this unique *aureus,* M. De Witte acknowledges himself indebted to M. Th. Panofka and to M. Pinder, keepers of the Berlin Cabinet.

The type of Hercules, struggling with a bull, also appears on a middle brass of Postumus, with the legend HERCVLI INVICTO.—Engraved in Patin, *Imp. Num. Rom.* p. 335, edit. 1696.

On other monuments, Hercules is sometimes seen endeavouring to bind a bull with cords :— viz. on an amphora with black figures, in the

Musée Gregorien, at Rome; and on another (unpublished) amphora, also with black figures, in the collection Panckoucke.

[Diodorus designates Hercules by the surname of *Cretensis*. And the reverse of this coin typifies a great success which the hero achieved in taming a wild bull. The scene of the exploit is assigned to Crete; and it is enumerated as the seventh of the labours awarded by his tyrant brother to this never-daunted, ever-victorious, undertaker of apparently impracticable enterprises.]

8.

No. 8.—POSTVMVS AVG.—Bust of Postumus, with face to the front, and head encircled with a radiated crown.

Rev.—HERCVLI THRACIO. Hercules taming a horse. On gold, in the *Cabinet de France.* Lenormant, *Iconographie des Empereurs Romains*, pl. lii. No. 14.—Mionnet, *Rareté*, &c. ii. 62.—On a denarius of billon the same type of reverse occurs.

[*Hercules Thracius* was the conqueror of Diomede, king of Thrace, son of Mars and Cyrene, who fed his horses with human flesh. It was one of the formidable tasks imposed on Hercules to destroy Diomede. And accordingly the hero, accompanied by some of his friends, attacked the cruel monarch, forcibly took possession of his horses, and gave him up to be devoured by the same savage animals which he had employed to destroy the unfortunate dupes of his barbarous treachery].

The subject of Hercules taking the horses of Diomede is rarely represented on monuments of antiquity. Independently of a group in marble preserved at the Vatican, it is recognised on a painted cup in the second collection of Sir Wm. Hamilton. Several Greek medals bear the type of the horses taken away by Hercules.—Eckhel quotes, after Tanini, a billon of Postumus, which on the reverse of a galeated head of that emperor, exhibits Hercules accomplishing his 8th labour.

9.   10.

No. 9.—*Rev.*—HERCVLI INVICTO.—Hercules standing, presses with his right foot on the body of a draped female, stretched on the ground beneath him, and from whose waist he is preparing to detach the girdle. The club is in his left hand, and the lion's spoils are wrapped round his left arm.—*Obv.*—POSTVMVS PIVS FELIX AVG. Têtes accolées de Postume et d'Hercule.—"This denarius of billon, unpublished, from the collection of M. Dupré, was found near Rennes, in Britanny."

[The type alludes to the combat of Hercules with *Hyppolita*, whom, having overcome (in scarcely to *him* very creditable fight) he forthwith dispossessed of the baldrick or sword-belt of *Mars*, which this queen of the Amazons carried at her girdle, as the mark of her royalty; and which Admeta, daughter of Eurystheus, and a priestess of Juno at Argos, had ordered the Theban hero to bring to her.—In Millin, *Galerie Mythologique*, ii. pl. cxxii. No. 443, the subject, copied from a Greek vase, is artistically dealt with, at an earlier stage of the encounter; when the beautiful equestrian is about to hurl her ineffectual lance at the man of the ponderous club].

"Hercules fighting with the Amazons (says M. De Witte), a frequent subject on painted vases, is of very rare occurrence on monetary types. Hercules is seen pursuing an Amazon on horseback, on brass money of Heraclea, in Bithynia. There is also a specimen of the same type in the *Cabinet de France*, of *médiocre* preservation; but there is in the imperial and royal cabinet at Vienna a third example, as well preserved as that in M. Dupré's collection."

No. 10.——HERCVLI GADITANO.——Hercules standing, with the lion's skin suspended on the left arm, and the right arm raised as in the attitude of fighting against armed men. On a denarius of billon, from the collection of M. Dupré, unpublished till engraved in the *Revue Numismatique* for the dissertation of M. De Witte, who says "this unique piece was found in the neighbourhood of Cologne, at the same time as denarius No. 2.

[In type No. 10 is to be recognised the fabled conflict between Hercules and the triple Geryon, represented in this instance by three heavy-armed soldiers), in the garb of Roman warriors.— The passage in question, like several others connected with the labours of Hercules, is very confused and contradictory. Geryon is described, by the poets, as a giant with three bodies, three heads, six arms, and six legs.— This monster, who lived in the island of Gadira or Gades, kept numerous herds of oxen; Eurystheus, the hard and malignant task-master of Hercules, believing that it was impossible to take away these cattle, charged Hercules with the consummation of this exploit. The hero nevertheless went to Gades, destroyed Geryon, although the giant was succoured by Juno, and carried away all the cattle to Tirynthus.—According to Servius, Geryon was king of the three Balearic islands, Majorca, Minorca, and Ivica; from which circumstance the ancients have made him with a three-fold set of bodies and limbs. —In later ages, the people of Gades (now *Cadiz)*, reverencing the valour of Hercules, dedicated a temple to his memory under the name of *Hercules Gaditanus.*—See GADES].

" The combat of Hercules with Geryon (observes M. De Witte) is figured on only one brass coin of oriental fabric, and of which there are but two specimens extant. The following is a description of the piece :—*Obv.* Hercules armed with the club, and wearing the lion's spoils, in a fighting attitude.—*Rev.* Geryon with three heads, each covered with a Phrygian cap, and armed with a round buckler, in the act of combatting. Æ. 3.

" The above was not long ago the only medal known, as offering the type of Hercules fighting with the triple king of Iberia. But Mr. Samuel Birch has recently published a rare brass medallion of Caracalla, struck at Blandos, in Lydia. This medallion is preserved in the British Museum. Its reverse type exhibits Hercules, armed with the club, seizing the heads of Geryon, figured under the form of a little man, entirely naked, having three heads. On the left arm the triple giant carries a buckler, which resembles a wheel. In the field of the coin are two oxen. Æ. 1, 2."

M. De Witte contends for the Asiatic origin of the myth of Geryon, remarking that " a tradition, preserved by Pausanias, places the tomb of Geryon in Lydia." The coin of Blandos alludes to that local myth—a circumstance which he regards as corroborative of his own views on the subject.

The legend HERC. GADIT. appears on an *aureus* of Hadrian ; but the type of that coin does not represent Hercules fighting with Geryon : but the unconquered hero holds the apples of the Hesperides, whilst at his feet is the recumbent figure of Oceanus.

11.   12.

No. 11.—HERCVLI LIBYCO.—Hercules, wrestling with Antæus, suffocates him in his arms.— Gold of Postumus, formerly of the *Cabinet de France*, disappeared at the time of the robbery in 1831. Mionnet, T. ii. p. 61.—This piece, which will be found in Banduri's work (T. i. 287), was engraved after a cast preserved at the French Institute.

[Fable tells us that when, in the course of his peregrinations, Hercules arrived in Lybia, his progress was opposed by a mighty giant named Antæus, son of Neptunus and Terra, whose strength as a wrestler was invincible, so long as he remained in contact with his mother earth. Boasting that he would raise a temple to his father's honour with the skulls of those whom he conquered *in certamine luctationis*, he compelled the strangers who came to the country of Irasa, of which he was king, to engage in athletic combat with him, and slew his antagonists, when he had exhausted them with fatigue.

Having challenged Hercules, the cruel savage was three times prostrated by the intrepid hero, but in vain. Hercules, perceiving at length the source of the giant's force and security, lifted him up from the ground, and caused him to expire by violently compressing him in his arms].

" In the series of the twelve labours (observes M. De Witte), the wrestling of Antæus is substituted, on the reverse of Postumus, for the taking away of the apples of the Hesperides.— Sometimes in the succession of the labours the order is changed. At other times, some subjects are omitted, or one of the twelve great labours is replaced by one of the other exploits of Hercules. It is thus that Pausanias, in describing the pediment of the temple of Hercules Promachos at Thebes, makes a remark, that Praxitéles, instead of the combat against the birds of Stymphalus, and the cleansing of the Augean stables, in other words, the draining of the country of Elis, had introduced the contest with Antæus. Moreover, the scene of this wrestling with the giant, as well as the garden of the Hesperides, was placed in Lybia; thence the epithet Lybicus, which Hercules bears on the *aureus* of Postumus; and Servius gives it to be understood, that it was in pursuing his course towards the abode of the Hesperides, that Hercules vanquished Antæus.—" Item ad Hesperides perrexit, et Anthæum, filium Terræ victum luctatione necavit." Some painted vases, and several Greek coins, exhibit the conflict of Hercules with the Libyan athlete. This group is also found on a small brass of Maximianus Hercules, with the legend VIRTVTI AVGG."

No. 12.—HERCVLI INMORTALI. (*sic.*) Hercules, with the club and lion's skin on his shoulder, drags Cerberus enchained. Billon of Postumus, in the imperial and royal cabinet of Vienna.—Spanheim, i. 265 ; Mionnet, ii. 61 ; Banduri, i. 291.

[The twelfth and last labour of Hercules was that in which, conducted by Minerva and by Mercury, he descended into the kingdom of Pluto, whence he delivered Theseus; and dragged forth into the light of day the watch-dog of the infernal regions. Eurystheus, however, after having seen that triple-headed monster, ordered Hercules to lead him back again. Of this crowning and closing trial Ausonius sings—

Cerberus extremi suprema est meta laboris.

The myth of Cerberus describes him as born of Typhon and Echidna ; huge in size, extremely cruel, with a terrible voice, and of extraordinary strength. Guard of the gates of hell, and of the dismal palace of its sovereign, this fearful dog was not less cunning than ferocious ; he fawned upon and gave a deceitful welcome to those who entered ; but he never permitted them to go out again, and devoured those who attempted to escape from the dark realms of " gloomy *Dis*."—See Millin, *Dictionnaire de la Fable*, for an article on Cerberus, full of well-condensed mythological information].

The subject is typified on a great many painted vases, engraved stones, and Greek coins;— also on an *aureus* of Maximianus Hercules, in which the dragging forth of Cerberus is accompanied by the legend HERCVLI INMORTALI, exactly the same as is read on the denarius of billon engraved in No. 12.

All the labours of Hercules being then accomplished, his submission to Eurystheus no longer continued, and the hero reposed. This repose, like his labours, was a favourite and a noble subject of composition for artists; a fine example of which, though prostituted to the flattery of an execrable prince, will, for its monetary excellence, be given in another page.—See HERCVLI ROMANO.

Then commenced a series of exploits, performed, so to speak, from his own will and on his own account. Amongst other desperate enterprises, he descended again into the regions below, and rescued theretrom Alceste, who had devoted herself to death for her husband.— "These descents into the subterranean world of paganism (says Millin, *Gal. Mythol.* ii. 181), are allegories of the mysteries of Eleusis, into which he gained initiation."—Unable, after suffering horrible tortures, longer to endure the effects of wearing a tunic tainted with the empoisoned blood of Nessus, which that centaur had deceitfully persuaded Dejanira to send her husband, he, to terminate his miseries, caused an immense funeral pile to be raised on Mount Oeta; and Philoctetes lighted the fire in which the hero was consumed. The *idole* of the great Alcides descended to the infernal regions, but he was himself conducted by Iris and by Mercury into the presence of the celestial deities; Jupiter reconciled him to Juno; he received the honours of the *apotheosis*, and obtained the hand of Hebe.

And here, in direct reference to the tradition of his deification, this coin presents the type of his concluding work, and conformably to pagan assumptions, the legend records the title of his immortality. Tacitus says—"Hercules and Bacchus among the Greeks, and Quirinus (Romulus) amongst the Romans, are placed in the ranks of the gods." And thus by comparing the reign of Postumus with the career of Hercules, the people of Gaul sought to honour an emperor who had long prosperously governed, and against all opponents gloriously defended them.

Hercules Alexiacus.——Among other attributes this apotheosised hero had a medicinal influence assigned to him, and for that reason was surnamed Alexiacus (one who drives away illness). He was likewise regarded as the presiding divinity over baths of health supplied from hot springs. This serves to explain the meaning of one of two medals struck during the last years of Caracalla's reign, and which bear reference to the precarious state of the health of that emperor, which the remembrance of his crime, as the murderer of his brother, was secretly undermining. The silver coin in question has for the legend of its reverse P. M. TR. P. XVIII. COS. IIII. P. P. (Sovereign Pontiff, in-

vested with the Tribunitian dignity for the eighteenth time, Consul for the fourth time, Father of the Country). The type represents Hercules holding a branch in his right hand, and in his left his club and the spoils of the Nemæan lion.—See AESCULAPIUS, p. 21.

Hercules, the destroyer of Cacus.—The myth of Cacus, son of Vulcan and Medusa, represents him as a monster of enormous size, half-man half-snake, and as vomiting flames. He resided in Italy; and the paths to his cavern, dug in Mount Aventine, were covered with human bones. Setting, as usual with these legends, geographical and other probabilities at defiance, the story brings Hercules, the conqueror of Geryon (see *Herc. Gadit.*) to the immediate vicinity of what afterwards formed one of the seven hills of Rome.—Cacus stole some of the oxen of which Hercules had forcibly dispossessed the triple-giant of Cadiz, and which the hero was driving along the banks of the Tiber. The lowing of the cattle of Hercules was answered by the stolen ones shut up in the den of Cacus, and the robbery was thus revealed to Hercules, who attacked the horrid monster and strangled him in his blood-stained cavern. Hercules is said to have erected an altar to Jupiter Conservator, in commemoration of his victory, and the inhabitants of the surrounding country every year celebrated a festival in honour of the occasion.

It is to this that allusion is made, on a brass medallion of Antoninus Pius, published by Venuti, from the Museum Albani: the valiant and all-conquering Alcides has just slain the giant robber, half of whose dead body is still within the cavern, the upper extremities alone being visible. The inhabitants of Mount Aventine are returning thanks to the hero for having delivered them from the tyrant of their fields, and they kiss the hand of the brave champion to whom they owe the blessing.

Hercules Bibax.—On another brass medallion of the same emperor (published by Vaillant from the Decamps collection), without epigraph on the reverse, Hercules is represented sitting before a table, with club in left hand, and patera in right. Opposite to him sit several figures holding pateras: around are urns and vases of various sizes; and on each side are vine-trees spreading their branches.—Vaillant considers this unique type to be one of the attempts of Antoninus to restore an old local tradition—namely, the sacrifice performed by Hercules before the great altar *(ara maxima)* at Rome ; and he describes the piece as exhibiting the demi-god *sitting* with Pinarius and Potitius on bundles of grass. The vines and vases, and especially the huge bowl above the great altar, he considers to indicate a libation poured out by the hard-drinking hero *(Heros bibax)*.—Eckhel, on the other hand, explains the type as allusive to the banquet instituted by Hercules himself, after he had put Cacus to death. This feast was afterwards made an annual one ; the Pinaria and Potitia families being the superintendents of the sacred ceremonies, to which Virgil rather copiously alludes *(Æn.* т. viii. 268). The guests at these banquets did not assume the recumbent posture, but *sat* at table. This would seem to be a peculiarity of the feast ; for says Macrobius (cited by Eckhel, vii. 30), " It is a distinguishing custom connected with the worship of Hercules, that the guests are *seated* at the banquet. Cornelius Balbus, in his 18th book, says that, in the ceremonies of the *Ara Maxima* it was customary to have no *triclinia*."—See LECTISTERNIUM.

Herculis Ara Maxima. The great altar of Hercules.—A denarius of the Antia gens has for its obverse legend RESTIO, and for type an altar with flame kindled. Its reverse exhibits the name of c. ANTIVS, and the head of a bull, ornamented with the *infulæ.* Comparing this coin with another of the same family, on which a naked Hercules is carrying his club uplifted in one hand, and a trophy in the other, Eckhel is of opinion, that the altar called *maxima* at Rome, dedicated to the above-named demi-god, is here represented.

Hercules in the Garden of the Hesperides.—This subject is so vague in itself, and treated even as a myth in so unsatisfactory a manner, by poets and scholiasts, that it would scarcely claim notice amongst the exploits of Hercules, but for the fine bas-reliefs, and other monuments of antiquity, on which it is grouped, especially on that noble brass medallion of Antoninus Pius, in the *Cabinet de France*, from a cast after which the above wood-cut is executed.

[The Hesperides are described to have been three (some say four) young women, celebrated for their beauty, daughters of Hesperus. They

were appointed to guard the golden apples of a tree planted in a delightful garden, situated near Mount Atlas, in Africa. But the nymphs, instead of preserving their splendid charge from depredation, were always gathering for their own eating ; Juno therefore confided the care both of the fruit and of the Hesperides themselves to a terrible serpent, which never slept. It was imposed by Eurystheus, as an extra labour, on Hercules, to procure some of the golden apples from the garden above named. This he effected, after having killed the watchful monster, whose dreadful folds were always coiled around the tree which bore those precious fruits].

On this medallion, the hero, personifying manly strength and symmetry in perfection, after having slain the serpent, which remains entwined about the tree, elevates his right hand, as if about to pluck one of the apples. He holds in the other hand the club and the lion's skin. On the other side, standing close to the tree, are the three nymphs, whose neglect of duty, according to the fable, led to an undertaking full of danger to Hercules ; but who succeeded in bringing away the golden produce of the tree, and in releasing the Hesperides.

Hercules between Virtus and Voluptas.—P. M. TR. P. COS. III.—A temple with two columns,

within which a naked male figure stands with a club in his right hand, whilst a draped female on his right, and another on his left, appear endeavouring to attract him each to her side. Gold of Hadrian.

This coin involves in itself a moral subject. The remarkable type is explained in the words of Cicero himself *(De Officiis,* i. c. 32). According to Xenophon, " Hercules Prodicius, as soon as he arrived at years of puberty, a time assigned by Nature for every individual to choose his path in life, went forth into some desert spot ; and, sitting there a long time by himself, was much perplexed with doubts, whilst he reflected that there were two ways, the one of Pleasure the other of Virtue." Respecting this Hercules Prodicius, Eckhel refers to Xenophon, Quinctilian, and others enumerated by Potter" *(ad Clementis Alexand. Pedagog.* ii. ch. 10).

The fable was afterwards elegantly applied by Silius Italicus *(Punic,* xv. v. 20) to the elder Africanus ; and in later times, as we here see, the moneyer compares Hadrian with Hercules. For, as that demi-god, with a disposition averse to pleasure, chose a life of severe discipline, and by exterminating, with vast exertions, the monsters that infested it, restored tranquillity to the world,—so Hadrian also, eschewing the allurements of a luxurious life, preferred, with a remarkable endurance of fatigue, to travel over the Roman world, and by chastising the extortions of the governors of its provinces, by settling legal disputes, and by alleviating the condition of the destitute, to leave behind him imperishable monuments of his benevolence.—We have already seen, that Hadrian is compared with Hercules repeatedly throughout the types of his coins; "whether, however (adds the Author of *Doctrina)*, there be really such coins in existence as the one which Casaubon declares that he has seen *apud præsidem Thuanum (ad Spartiani Hadr.* ch. 13), inscribed AYT. K. AΔ-PIANOC. CEBACTOC. HPAKLHC. PΩMAIOC. and representing the emperor with the attributes of Hercules, I am much inclined to doubt. It is probable that this is a coin of Commodus, who was often styled *Hercules Romanus* both on Roman and Greek coins; though there is actually quoted, among the medallions of the Museum Theupoli, page 778, one on which the head of Hadrian is said to be covered with the skin of a lion; provided, indeed, that this coin is considered to be genuine. What is meant by the aged and reclining figure, I am at a loss to discover. If it either held a reed, or were leaning on the customary urn, I should pronounce it a *river;* but even then I could not account for its appearance."

Hercules, his attributes and arms.—On a denarius of C. COPONIVS PR. S. C. is a club erect, with the skin of a lion; on one side a dart or arrow, on the other a bow. The arms of Hercules undoubtedly bear allusion to Coponius deriving his origin from Tibur, in which city great honours were paid to Hercules, whence Propertius calls it *Herculeum* (ii. *Eleg.* 32); and Strabo states that there was a temple of Hercules at Tibur.—See COPONIA gens, p. 279.

A second brass of the Curtia gens (engraved in *Morell. Thesaur. Fam. Rom.* vol. ii.) exhibits on its obverse the beardless head of Hercules, covered with the lion's skin; and on its reverse a bow, club, and arrow are typified.

On a brass medallion of Commodus, with legend of reverse P. M. TR. P. X. IMP. VII. COS. IIII. Hercules is represented naked, standing with the club and lion's skin, lifting up with his right hand a crown to his own head. To the right are a bow and a quiver of arrows, suspended from a branch of a tree; to his left is an altar with the fire kindled.—See a cut of this reverse, engraved after a cast from the original in the *Cabinet de France,* at the head of the article HERCVLES, p. 450.

The same vile caricature of an emperor, to whose fertile mints, nevertheless, our numismatic treasuries are indebted for many a fine and interesting coin, caused, in his Herculean frenzy, the above legend to be struck, with the type of the club, bow, and quiver full of arrows,

which symbolize the hero, with whose world-wide fame his own contemptible notoriety dared to compare itself.—See HERCVLI ROMANO.

HERCVLES ADSERTOR. *(Hercules the Assister or Liberator).*—See FLORENTE FOR-TVNA P. R. p. 391.

HERCVLI. COMITI. AVG. COS. III. A naked Hercules, standing with club and lion's skin; near him the emperor veiled, sacrificing over a tripod; the *victimarius* stands beside him holding an ox. Brass medallion of Postumus. *(Morelli. Specimen.* p. 41).

On this coin, which Morel states to be in the highest state of preservation, and of the most elegant workmanship, not only do the portraits of the obverse correspond in every feature, but the countenances of Hercules and Postumus, given on the reverse, also bear the closest resemblance to those on the obverse. And from this circumstance, it is evident that the *jugated* heads, which so commonly appear on the obverses of Postumus' coins, are not those of *two* Postumi, but those of Postumus and Hercules (see p. 382.)—To the worship of that deity the Gauls were much devoted, and to the sculptured lineaments of his countenance Postumus studiously conformed his own, in the hope of rendering himself personally more sacred, by this conciliatory homage to the popular superstition of the provinces he governed.—*Doctrina,* vii. 448.

This title given to Hercules as *Comes Augusti* (companion of the emperor), was in compliment to Postumus, who, bravest in war, faithful in peace, grave in character and counsels, was regarded as accompanied every where by the courageous genius of Hercules himself,—and this brave prince is on the above medal rendering thanks to his tutelary divinity for being present with him as his companion in the triumph he had just achieved over his enemies the Germans. On a gold coin of Maximinus Daza appears the inscription of *Hercules Comès Cæsarum Nostrorum,* as indicating the companionship of the same deity with himself and Constantine.

HERC. COMM. or COMMODIANO. P. M. TR. P. XVI. COS. VI. Hercules, standing before an altar, with patera in his right hand, and cornucopiæ in his left, near him a tree, from which is suspended the skin of a lion. Gold of Commodus (engraved in Caylus)—Brass medallion of do. (in Mus. Albani).—First brass, engraved in the Cabinet de Christine.—See HERCVLI.

HERCVLI CONS*ervatori* AVGVS*ti.* (To Hercules the Preserver of the Emperor).—On a very rare gold coin of Gallienus, having for the type of its reverse the Calydonian boar running, a symbol of Hercules.

HERCVLI CRETENSI. See *Herculis Labores,* p. 452.

HERCVLI DEBELLATORI. (To Hercules the Vanquisher).—This legend, with the killing of the Hydra as its type, appears on a coin of Maximianus Herculius, respecting which Eckhel observes as follows:—"As his colleague Diocletian made an ostentatious display on his coins of his attachment to the worship and name of

Jupiter, so Maximianus, in like manner, boasted of Hercules. Thus we find on the medals of the latter emperor, Hercules the *Preserver*, the *Conqueror*, the *Unvanquished*, the *Peace-bearing*, the *Victorious*, with various accompanying types, which exhibit different labours of the god, and many others occur on those coins of Maxentius which are inscribed VIRTVS AVGG.— This was the reason why sometimes he appears on his coins in the worship of his favourite deity, his head covered with the skin of the lion, as though he made his son Maxentius heir of the glory symbolized in this reverse. And if we consider the barbarians every where vanquished and subdued by him, as monsters dangerous to the empire, Maximianus may be esteemed, if not Hercules, at least his most sedulous and warlike imitator." viii. p. 19.

1.   2.

1. HERC. DEVSONIENSI.—Hercules, with the club in his right hand, and the lion's spoils on his left arm, stands in a temple of four columns. On a denarius in billon of Postumus, whence cut No. 1 is engraved.—On another billon coin, engraved in Banduri, Hercules stands (not within a temple), but with the usual attributes of club and lion's skin.

This appellation was given to Hercules from a place where he was worshipped, though it is not as yet sufficiently ascertained where *Deuso* or *Deuson* was situated.—Tristan, following other writers, considered it not improbable that this place was the same as that of which Hieronymus thus speaks in the Chronicon of Eusebius—"The Saxons were slaughtered at Deuso, in the district of the Franci." Tristan conjectures that Deuso may possibly have been what is now called *Duyz*, on the Rhine, opposite to Colonia Agrippinæ (Cologn). If resemblance of name be the object, it is not necessary to look for the site of Deuso, on the other side of the Rhine; for there are on this bank at the present day several towns called *Duisburg*, which may have derived their name from Deuso. It is the opinion of the authors of a work entitled *La Religion des Gaulois*, b. iii. ch. 8, that this Hercules was identical with the Hercules Magusanus mentioned below.

2. HERCVLI MAGVSANO.—Hercules stands, in repose, the right hand placed on the right hip; whilst his left hand, on which hangs the lion's skin, rests on the club.—Silver and first and second brass of Postumus.

As in the case of Hercules Deusoniensis, so in this of Hercules Magusanus, there is a dispute as to the locality. It is probable, that Macusa, or Magusa, was a town celebrated for the worship of Hercules. Muratori cites (p. 64,

Nos. 1 and 2), two marbles dedicated to this Hercules, and states that they were discovered in Belgium.—See various conjectures on this subject in Tristan, Muratori, and the authors of the work entitled *De la Religion des Gaulois*.— An anonymous writer of Ravenna enumerates, among the towns situated on the river Moselle, *Macusa (Geogr.* iv. c. 26), from which perhaps this Hercules derived his appellation. Few will imagine, with Harduin *(ad Plin.* vi. p. 344), that he was so called from Magusa, in Æthiopia. Keysler has published a marble found at Westchapel *(Westcapellæ)*, on which is inscribed— HERCVLI MAGVSANO - - - TERTIVS. V. S. L. M. with a figure of the deity, representing him as standing naked, and holding in his right hand a dolphin, in his left the trunk of a tree cleft in two, and at his feet a scorpion *(Antiq. Septembr.* p. 200); "though (adds Eckhel) I am not aware how these attributes can appertain to Hercules, such as through classical myths we are made acquainted with him. The types of the coins in question differ in no respect from the Hercules of the Greeks." vii. 444.

HERCVLI ERYMANTHINO.—See Labours of Hercules, p. 451.

HERC. GADIT. P. M. TR. P. COS. III. Hercules standing, rests his right hand on the club; in his left hand are three apples. On one side of him is a man reclining on the ground; on the other is the half of a ship. Coinage of Hadrian. Engraved in Caylus (No. 379), gold imperial series, in the *Cabinet de France.*

"Transported from the metropolis Tyre to the colony Gades, *Hercules Gaditanus* became celebrated, not only in Spain, but at Rome itself; insomuch that, according to the Roman law, the Hercules of Gades acquired a privilege, denied to most other foreign deities, of inheriting property by bequest. *(Vlpian Fragm.* xxv.)—This deity appears on the coinage of Hadrian; firstly, because the town of Gades, from its proximity to Italica, his native place, easily communicated to it the worship of Hercules, Domitia Paulina, his mother, also deriving her origin from Gades; and in the next place, because Hadrian, by visiting all the provinces of the empire, and conferring benefits on each of them, in a certain sense earned the name and honours of Hercules. The ship doubtless alludes to the maritime power of the Gaditani; but the reclining figure, which most other writers have pronounced a river, Eckhel agrees with Florez in considering to be still a matter of dispute. It is not, perhaps, a very rash conjecture to say, that it is a figure of Oceanus. At any rate, on coins of Tyre the metropolis, we see Oceanus represented under the same figure of a man reclining, and inscribed near it, to prevent misinterpretation, the word ΩΚΕΑΝΟC; and it is known to every one, that Gades was situated on the sea coast."—*Doctrina*, vol. vi. 504.

A similar figure of a man reclining appears on a coin of Hadrian, referring to the anecdote of Hercules *(Prodicius)* standing between *Virtus* and *Voluptas*, accompanied by the legend P. M. TR. P. COS. III. described and engraved in

p. 456. To the same subject may be referred the gold and silver coins of the same emperor inscribed COS. III. or ,P. M. TR. P. COS. III. and the type of which is a naked Hercules, sitting by his armour, with the club in his right hand, and a thunder-bolt in his left. Engraved in Caylus, gold, No. 380.

HERCVLI INVICTO.—See Labours of Hercules, No. 9, p. 453.

HERCVLI NEMAEO.—See Labour of Hercules, No. 1, p. 450.

HERCVLES MVSARVM.——See Pomponia gens.

HERC. PAC.—Hercules naked, stands holding a branch. Gold of L. Verus.—" No mention (says Vaillant) is made except on ancient coins of Hercules Pacifer (the pacific Hercules). In ancient times strong men were called Hercules, and many Roman princes were exhibited under the name and image of that hero. Verus also, after having performed *his* labours in the Parthian war, *condescended* to give peace to the enemy, and was called *Hercules the Peace-bearer*."

HERCVLI PACIFERO.——Hercules naked, stands with the face turned to the right, holding up a branch in his left hand, whilst he bears the club and lion's skin in his right.—Postumus.

Banduri is of opinion that this rare silver coin is most correctly to be referred to the year A. D. 266, in which Gallienus, despairing of an opportunity to avenge the murder of his son Cornelius Saloninus, left off carrying on the war which up to that period had, with mutual loss, been waged in Gaul between him and Postumus, in order that he might, with the universal strength of the empire, resist and repel the Scythian nations, who had for nearly fifteen years been ravaging both the European and the Asiatic provinces ; for such was then the condition of the Roman government, that it was unable to sustain against one sufficiently formidable enemy two wars at the same time. But

this coin shews that Postumus chose to ascribe the accepted peace to his own valour, rather than to the calamities of the state. There are similar pieces in brass. vol. i. p. 292.

HERCVLI ROMANO AVGVSTO.——This legend appears on a silver coin of Commodus, which has for its type Hercules standing ; he holds his club and lion's spoils, and is crowning a trophy. On first and second brass of the above emperor, with the same legend, we see, in the place of Hercules, only his attribute of the club, either by itself placed upright within a laurel crown ; or accompanied by a bow and quiver.

HERCVLI ROM*æ* COND*itori* COS. VII. P. P.—Hercules driving a plough with oxen.—On the other side of a gold medal is the head of Commodus covered with the lion's skin.

Commodus carried his ridiculous vanity and presumption so far as to cause himself to be called the young Jupiter, and the Roman Hercules (Hercules Augustus, or Commodianus).—The above three coins furnish additional proofs of this fact, as regards the latter assumption. It appears that in order the better to accomplish his preposterous design, he laid down the laurel crown which emperors were accustomed to wear, affecting to cover himself with the lion's skin, and to carry a club like Hercules. He appeared in public in this costume, and with these accoutrements. His statues and his medals often represent him in this new dress. Indeed, having given multiplied proofs of his prodigious strength, and even of physical courage, in vanquishing divers ferocious animals in the Circus, he might well, on that account, be compared to Hercules.

The last quoted coin, bearing the extraordinary inscription of—" To Hercules the Founder of Rome," has reference to the insanity of Commodus, in decreeing to change the city of Rome into a *Colony*, bearing his name !—See COL*onia Lucia* A N*toniniana* COM*modiana*, p. 234.

Æ

HERCVLI ROMANO AVG. P. M. TR. P. XVIII. COS. VII. P. P.—Hercules stands leaning with his left arm on the club, which is placed on a rock. His left hand grasps a bow, behind which hang the lion's spoils. His right hand rests on the hip. An attitude which the artists of antiquity were fond of assigning to their statues of this hero.

Obv.—L. AELIVS AVRELIVS COMMODVS AVG. PIVS FELIX. Laureated head, exhibiting the likeness of the emperor, but covered with a lion's skin, being intended to represent Commodus as Hercules.

[Brass medallion, engraved after a cast from the original in the *Cabinet de France*. Besides the very fine preservation and high relief of this

particular specimen, the compiler has been induced to select it for the classic example which
its reverse presents of *Hercules in repose;* and
also because the obverse serves, as a striking
type, to illustrate those portraitures of Roman
emperors who successively adopted the titles and
attributes of the demi-god.]

To such a pitch of madness did Commodus
arrive, as not only to give himself out as
a god, which indeed he would have done in
common with several of his predecessors, but
throwing aside even the laurel crown, the customary badge of sovereignty, he caused his portrait to be exhibited on his coins with the attributes of divinity. Up to this time, such an
indulgence had been conceded to Grecian vanity,
which was wont to liken its kings to various
deities, as it also did some of the Augusti, of
which we have seen instances in the coins of
Nero of foreign die. But till this moment the
mint of Rome was guiltless of so base an adulation; and though its reverses sometimes clothed
an emperor in the attributes of a god, it was
still done with some shew of reverence; for the
legend invariably abstained from the name of a
deity, nor was any change made in the attire of
the head, inconsistent with the majesty of the
empire. Those barriers, however, were broken
down by the shamelessness of Commodus; and
from that year to the end of his life, both the
legends and types of his coins speak of him as a
present deity,—on the same principle that he insisted, as Lampridius observes (ch. 15), on having
recorded in the annals of Rome, all the base, foul,
cruel, butcherly, and profligate acts of his life.
Having the power to assume what character he
would, he chose that of Hercules, because he
wished it to be thought, that in the slaughter
of savage beasts he had rivalled that personage.
This folly of the sometime man, but now, forsooth, divinity! is proved not merely by numerous coins, but by a host of ancient writers, the
most remarkable of whose testimonies are here
subjoined:—

Commodus was first called *Hercules Romanus*
on account of his having slain wild beasts in the
amphitheatre of Lanuvium. If we may credit
the accounts of historians, his personal strength
entitled him to the name, for he transfixed an
elephant with a spear; and in one day killed a
hundred bears with darts; fatigued with which
exploits, he drained at a draught a cup brought
to him by a girl,—faithful to the character of
Hercules even in his drinking and amours.—
These particulars are related by Dion, an eye-
witness, and by Lampridius. That a hundred
lions were killed by him in one day, is stated by
Herodianus and Ammianus. Being regarded,
on account of these doings, as a second Alcides,
and wishing to be so called, a crowd of statues
were instantly executed, representing Commodus
in the attributes of that deity, and soon after,
sacrifice was offered to him. So persuaded was
he that he was indeed Hercules, that when he
went abroad, he ordered the lion's skin and club
to be carried before him. And to carry on his
imitation of Hercules in the slaying of mon-

sters, which were universally believed to be
fabulous, he had men sewn up alive in sacks,
and made into the form of giants, and then
killed them with darts. A report having been
spread that the emperor intended to put several
persons to death by shooting arrows at them, as
Hercules had done in one of his encounters, few
had the courage even to appear in the amphitheatre. And all this took place before the eyes
of the people and the Senate. To such a depth
of infamy had sunk the son of Marcus, and to
such a degree of degradation was that venerable
assembly of the Fathers reduced by fear. The
people, indeed, as far as they could, took their
revenge in lampoons, of which the following
example from Lampridius is not without merit.

Commodus Herculeum nomen habere cupit,
Antoninorum non putat esse bonum,
Expers humani juris et imperii,
Sperans quinetiam clarius esse deum,
Quàm si sit princeps nominis egregii,
Non erit iste deus, nec tamen ullus homo.
          (Lamp. in Diadumen.)

[Commodus covets the name of Hercules, nor
thinks that of the Antonines good enough for
him. Setting at defiance all human law and
control, and imagining it a more glorious lot to
be a god than a prince of noble fame, he will
not after all be a god, nor in any sense a man].

One writer, however, has been found somewhat to mitigate the sentence of condemnation
on this emperor's follies. "Why then (says
Athenæus, xii. p. 537), should we feel so much
surprize, that the Emperor Commodus, when
riding in his chariot, should have had placed
beside him the club of Hercules, and the lion's
skin spread beneath him, and desire to be called
Hercules, when Alexander, though imbued with
the precepts of Aristotle, could liken himself to
the deities, nay even to Diana."—Eckhel, vii.
pp. 125, 126.

HERCVLI THRACIO.—See *Herculis Labores,* No. 8, p. 453.

HERCVLES VICTOR.—See RESTIO.

HERCVLI VICTORI.—Hercules naked,
stands with club reversed in his right hand resting on the ground, and holding a bow in his
left: the spoils of the lion hang from his left
arm.—This appears on a silver coin of Æmilianus, struck on the occasion of a victory gained
by that emperor over the Scythians. (Banduri).
The temple of Hercules the Victorious was built
at Rome, by Octavius Herennius. (Havercamp).
—This surname of Victor, amongst the many
appropriated to Hercules on Roman coins, agrees
with the epithet *Callinicus,* given to him by the
Greeks, and which was borne by the successors
of Alexander the Great, who pretended like himself to have descended in a right line from Hercules. (Spanheim's *Cæsars of Julian).*

HERCVLI VICTORI.—A naked Hercules,
standing with a club in his right hand, and an
apple and lion's skin in his left; in the field the
letter Z, and at the bottom S. M. S. D. Gold of
Fl. Severus, in the imperial museum of Vienna.

"This fine coin (says Eckhel), which came
into my possession many years ago, I published

at the time with the greater satisfaction, that it was then an unique specimen of a gold coin of Severus, bearing the title of Augustus. Tanin has since added two more, one of which is of medallion size." vii. 444.

HERCVLI VICTORI.—This legend also accompanies the type of *Hercules Requiescens*, which represents the demi-god reposing after his victorious labours, either standing with his right hand resting on his club, and his left holding the apples of the Hesperides, as is seen on a second brass of Val. Maximianus, or sitting on a rock, with his bow and other attributes, as on coins of Constantius Chlorus, Valer. Severus, Maximinus Daza. There is also a most rare brass coin of Constantine the Great, with the same legend and type, quoted by Banduri from Mediobarbus and Spanheim.

HERCVLIO MAXIMIANO AVG.—Maximianus in the *paludamentum*, seated with a globe in his left hand, on which side sits Hercules. Victory flying behind crowns them both; at the bottom ROM. Brass medallion of Diocletian. The above cut engraved after a cast from the original in the French Cabinet.

In illustration of the meaning of this coin, as well as of a gold medallion of the same emperor (see IOVIO ET HERCVLIO), the author of *Doctrina* (viii. p. 9), quotes a passage from Victor (*in Cæsaribus*); "He (Maximianus) afterwards acquired the surname of *Herculius* from the circumstance of his worshipping that deity, just as Valerius (Diocletian) did that of *Jovius*; whence the name was also applied to such portions of the army as had evidently distinguished themselves."—The first part of this passage receives confirmation from the coin before us: and the second, as Banduri observes, from the fact, that in the *Notitia imperii*, there occur repeatedly the expressions—*ala Jovia, legio Jovia, ala Herculia, auxilia Herculia, Herculiana, Herculensia*, &c.—Claudian (*de bello Gild.* v. 418) makes allusion to them as late as the reign of Honorius :—

Herculeam suns Alcides, Joviam que cohortem
Rex ducit superûm.

[The Herculean cohort is led by its own Alcides, and the Jovian by the king of the gods.]

That these Jovian and Herculean bands held the most exalted position in the Roman army,

and acted as body guard to the emperor, we learn from Sozomen, speaking of the reign of Julian (vi. ch. 6).—Respecting this absurd vanity of Diocletian and Maximian, in their adoption, respectively, of the titles *Jovius* and *Herculius*, see further remarks in Spanheim (vol. ii. p. 494), and Banduri (p. 13, note 4); also the inscription VIRTVS HERCVLI CAESARIS, and Eckhel's comments on a coin of Constantius I.

HERENNIA gens.—A plebeian family, but of consular rank. It has many varieties on its coins. The only one of any interest, and that not rare, bears on its obverse PIETAS, with a female head; on the reverse M. HERENNI, and the group of a young man carrying his father on his shoulders.—Who this Herennius was, and what occasion led to the adoption of this type, is uncertain. But it evidently alludes to the story of the two pious brothers of Catana, who rescued their parents from the flames of Etna, during an eruption which endangered their lives. —See Amphinomus and Anapis, p. 41.

HERENNIA ETRUSCILLA.—See ETRUS-CILLA.

HERENNIUS ETRUSCUS (*Q. Messius Decius*), eldest son of Trajanus Decius and Etruscilla, was named Cæsar by his father, A. D. 249. He gained the following year the battle of Nicopolis against the Goths; but was afterwards surprised and defeated at Beréa. In A.D. 251, he was named Augustus; served the consulate, fully associated with his father in the empire. He perished with Trajan Decius at the battle of Abrittium, a town of Mæsia, the same year.—On his coins, which, with the exception of the silver (some of which are common), are of more or less rarity, he is styled HEREN. ETRV. MES. QV. DECIVS CAESAR or AVG.

The following are the rarest reverses :—

GOLD.——PRINC. IVVENT. A seated figure. (Valued by Mionnet at 600 fr.)—PRINCIPI IV-VENTVTIS. A military figure standing. (Mt. 600 fr.

SILVER.—Same epigraph and type. (Quinarius. Mionnet, 24 fr.)—CONCORDIA AVGG. Right hands joined.—*Obv.* Q. HER. ETR. MES. DECIVS NOB. CAES. Radiated head of Herennius.—SECVRITAS AVGG. Woman standing, resting on a column. (Mt. 24 fr.)—VICTORIA GER-

MANICA. Victory passing. (Mt. 10 fr.)—VOTIS DECENNALIBVS within a crown. (Mt. 30 fr.)

LARGE BRASS.—PACI. Temple of six cols. (Mt. 20 fr.)—PRINCIPI IVVENTVTIS. Prince in military habit, holding a sceptre and the hasta. (Large size, Mt. 24 fr.)—PIETAS AVGVSTORVM. Sacrificial instruments. (Mt. 20 fr.; brought at Thomas sale 10s.)

HESPERIDES.—See Hercules in the garden of, p. 456.

HILARITAS (Gaiety or Joy personified).— On most Roman coins this legend has for its accompanying type the figure of a matron, standing with a long foliaged branch of palm in her right hand, which she plants in the ground.— Green branches are the signs of gladness; and thence amongst almost all nations, on occasions of joy both public and private, it was the custom to ornament streets, temples, gates, houses, and even entire cities, with branches and leaves of trees. In her left hand Hilarity holds the cornucopiæ; sometimes a patera supplies the place of a branch; sometimes a hasta; at other times a flower; but the palm is the most frequent and peculiar attribute.

HILARITAS P. Romani (Joy of the Roman People), S. C. COS. III.—On a first brass of Hadrian, Hilarity, figured as above, appears between two draped children. According to Artemidorus, the children of princes are themselves designated by palm branches. In Scriptural language, the olive emblematically designates the products of conjugal union.

Referring to this reverse, old Angeloni (p. 112) in substance says—"To fill up the emperor's cup of glory many coins were continually decreed to him by the Senate. And amongst these, none held a superior place to those which represented the provinces he had visited, or which, having been first conquered and then lost by others, he had recovered back again; or which he had enriched with his favours, embellished with buildings, furnished with laws, loaded moreover with gifts, and afterwards restored to the Roman Republic; one remarkable instance of which was that of Egypt."

HILAR. TEMPORVM. (Joy of the Times). By the same type of a woman holding a palm branch and cornucopiæ, was the delight of the Romans intended to be signified, at the period which gave birth to children by Didia Clara, only daughter of the emperor Didius Julianus.

The same legend and type of Hilaritas, with the addition of AVGVSTI AVG. AVGG. (Hilarity of the Emperor, Empress, or Emperors) are found on coins of M. Aurelius, Faustina jun. Lucilla, Commodus, Crispina, Julia Domna, Plautilla, Caracalla, Tetricus senior, Claudius Gothicus, &c.—See LAETITIA.

HIPPOPOTAMUS (river horse).—A huge amphibious animal, inhabiting the Nile, and also found on the Ganges. On coins which serves to symbolize Egypt (see the word NILVS). The figure of this remarkable beast occurs on several coins of the two Philips, and also on those of Otacilia Severa, with the legend of SAECVLARES AVGG.—Spanheim (Pr. i. p. 175) shews when this fluvial monster was first exhibited at Rome in the public spectacles.

HIRCO (a goat).—The figure of this animal is seen on some consular coins. A family denarius exhibits a naked man, riding on a goat, at full speed, and holding a branch in his right hand.—See CORNELIA gens, Cethegus, p. 285, No. 5.—On a silver coin of Fonteius, a winged boy is typified riding on a goat.—See FONTEIA gens, p. 393.—On a denarius of the Renia family, a woman, in a biga of goats, is going at a rapid pace.—See RENIA.

HIRTIA, gens plebeia.—Its coins, rare and in gold only, have but one type, as follows :— Obv.—C. CAESAR COS. III. A veiled female head.—Rev.—A. HIRTIVS P. R. Pontifical instruments, viz. lituus (the augural crook), urceus (the pitcher), and secespita (the axe).

Eckhel reads the legend of reverse thus:— Aulus Hirtius Prefectus and not Pretor, as some have done. (See his explanatory reasons, in Cestia gens, vol. v. 269.) A. Hirtius was a great favourite of the Dictator Cæsar, to whose commentaries he is believed to have put the last finishing touches. Consul in the year of Rome 711 (B. C. 43), he perished, together with his colleague, Vibius Pansa, at the battle of Mutina.

HIS.—This abbreviation of Hispania appears on a vexillum behind the head of Coelius Caldus, who, having, subsequently to A. U. C. 660, been sent as proconsul to Spain, gained in that country much military renown.—See COELIA gens, p. 223—also EPULONES, p. 360.

HISPAN. Hispania.—See POSTUMIA gens.

Hispania (Spain).—The Romans under this name comprehended all that extent of territory, which is bounded by the Pyrenées on the east, by the Mediterranean to the south and east, and by the ocean to the north and west.—The same motive which carried them into Sicily, led them into Spain; that is to say, the political necessity of opposing the Carthaginians who occupied the larger portion of the country. After a long and bloody struggle the Romans succeeded in driving the Carthaginians entirely out of Spain. It was Publius Scipio, afterwards surnamed *Africanus,* under whose command the legions triumphed over the troops of Hannibal. And Hispania being thus subjected to the power of the republic, was divided into two provinces. Augustus afterwards made three of it, Bœtica, Lusitania, and Tarraconensis. He left the last named to the Roman people, who sent a Pretor there; and he reserved the two other portions, which were governed by his Lieutenants. Bœtica comprised the kingdoms of Grenada and Andalusia, Estremadura, and some places in New Castille. Lusitania included the kingdoms of Portugal, the Algarves, and some parts of the two Castilles. Tarraconensis comprehended the kingdoms of Valentia, Murcia, Arragon, Navarre, Galicia, and Leon, a large part of the two Castilles, the principality of the Asturias, Biscay, and Catalonia.—(See *Pitiscus).*

HISPANIA.—On several imperial coins Hispania *in genere* is personified by a female figure, clothed sometimes in the stola, at others in the lighter folds of the tunic; holding in one hand corn-ears, poppies, or (more frequently) an olive branch, emblems of the fertility of that country; and in the other hand a garland, or some warlike weapon. The rabbit too, a well-known symbol of Hispania, appears on coins of Hadrian and Antoninus Pius. On a first brass of the last-named emperor (engraved above from a cast after the original in the British Museum), with the legend of reverse HISPANIA S. C. COS. II. The province represented by a turreted woman, stands holding in her right hand a crown of laurel, and in her left a spreading branch of olive. At her feet is a rabbit. The quantity of rabbits in Spain was such, that, according to Pliny, they undermined a whole town with their burrows; and Strabo affirms, that a portion of the inhabitants entreated the Romans to give them a settlement elsewhere, because they were no longer able to prevent the increase of this race of animals.

Hispania was greatly replenished with numerous colonies by Julius Cæsar and by Augustus, under whom, as well as under Galba, Vespasian, Hadrian, Antonine, and other emperors, coins were struck referring in legend and in type to Roman domination in the provinces of Spain.

The types of the autonomous coins of the Spanish cities make the same kind of reference to the fertility of the country, to its productions, and to the warlike spirit of its natives. Coins bearing the inscription HISPANORVM, exhibit horses, cavaliers armed and crowned,

branches of olive, corn-ears, and fish.—See Akerman, *Ancient Coins of Cities and Princes,* p. 9 to 120.

HISPANIA.—A woman, clothed in a long dress, stands holding in her right hand some corn-ears; and in her left she bears two short javelins, and the small round Spanish shield. This reverse legend and accompanying type appear on gold and silver coins of Galba, *(Obv.—*GALBA IMP. Laureated head of that emperor), under whom Spain and the provinces of Gaul were highly favoured, because they had been the first to declare themselves against Nero. The corn-ears indicate the fertility of Spain; the buckler and the two spears represent the weapons in use amongst her warriors.—(Kolb. vol. i. p. 124.)

An elegant silver coin with the same epigraph, exhibits the head of a woman, with two javelins. On the obverse is the figure of Galba on horseback.

This female bust represents Spain; her head of hair flows curling upon her neck; the small shield behind her is what Livy calls the *cetra.*—Hispania is struck on the coins of the emperor, not only because it was in Spain that he was first proclaimed, but also on account of the equestrian statue which the *exercitus Hispanicus* decreed should be erected to his honour.—(Vaillant, *Pr.* vol. ii.)

HISPANIA.—A woman standing, with ears of corn in her extended right hand, and two spears in her left; a Spanish buckler hanging behind her.

On a *gold* coin of Vespasian, the reverse type of which so closely resembles the preceding silver coin of Galba, Eckhel gives the following description and commentary, as from a specimen in the Imperial Cabinet at Vienna,

"This beautiful coin (says the author of *Doctrina,* vi. 338) I formerly published in my *Sylloge* i. where I remarked, that it was intended to commend the attachment shewn by Hispania towards Vespasian; it being a well-known circumstance, that at a very early period, and at the instigation of Primus Antonius, that country favoured the pretensions of Vespasian, at the expense of Vitellius, as Tacitus has recorded. *(Hist.* iii. ch. 53, 70.) It is probable, that it was on this very account that, as Pliny expresses it (iii. p. 144), "Vespasian, Imperator and Augustus, when tossed by the storms of civil commotion, conferred upon the whole of Hispania the *Jus Latii.*—Indeed, in such a position of affairs. Hispania might have been a formidable auxiliary being, as Tacitus says, considered in conjunction with Gaul, "the most powerful portion of the earth."—Juvenal, too *(Sat.* viii. 116), cautions the governors of those provinces against harassing and provoking such robust and hardy tribes, as though they were so many effeminate Asiatics. Perhaps, also, this type was intended to intimate the transfer to Vespasian of the affections of the *Legio Hispanica,* which formerly accompanied

Galba, and kept guard in Rome. (*Tacit. Hist.* i. ch. 6.) All these circumstances may have combined to induce a repetition, on Vespasian's coins, of a type frequently observed on those of Galba. This coin appears to have been struck at Rome immediately on the accession of Vespasian, and whilst he was still absent abroad; for, though it is of undoubted antiquity, yet the likeness of the portrait is not very striking, and we do not find on his later coins the AVG. placed before the *Vespasianus.*"—The coin in question is not included in the catalogue of either Mionnet or Akerman.

HISPANIA. S. C.—Spain personified on coins of Hadrian. Capt. Smyth, R.N. thus describes and animadverts upon the reverse of a large brass of Hadrian, with this legend, in his own cabinet of first brass:—"A robed female reclining against a rock, holds in her right hand a branch of olive—which, according to Pliny, flourished luxuriantly in Bœtica. Her head is encircled by a sort of wreath, which some medallists have also pronounced to be of olive, from recollecting the '*Bœtis olivifera crinem redimite corona,*' of Martial, and the description of Claudian, '*glaucis tum primó Minervæ, Nexa comam soliis.*'" (p. 105).

The same type appears on other reverses of Hadrian, in gold, silver, and second brass.

HISPANICVS EXERCITVS. S. C.—The emperor on horseback, addressing his soldiers. First brass, engraved in the *Cabinet de Christine.*

HISPANIAE RESTITVTORI.——Hadrian togated, raises a kneeling woman, who holds a branch in her left hand, at her feet is a rabbit—an altar between the two figures. Silver and first brass. See p. 365. Engraved in *Cabinet de Christine.*

In respect of his ancestors, Hadrian's native country was Hispania, and the place of his birth was Italica, a *municipium* of Bœtica; though Hadrian himself first saw the light at Rome. When a boy he spent some time in Spain, till he was called away to Germany, and subsequently to Rome, as has already been observed. After his accession he went to Hispania, on leaving Gaul, and having held a congress of all the *Hispani* at Tarraco, he wintered in that place, and at his own cost restored the temple of *Divus Augustus.* Though then within so short a distance, he did not visit Italica; nevertheless, he lavished upon it many honours and munificent presents. Spartian positively informs us, that he there celebrated *quinquennalia*, to do honour to the place. *D. N. Vet.* vi. 495.

See Eckhel's remarks on the rabbit as a symbol of Hispania, in his *prolegomena* to the coins of Hispania, vol. i. p. 8.

HISPANIA CLVNIA SVL. S. C.—A large brass coin of Galba, bearing this remarkable inscription, is equally remarkable for its finely-designed type, engraved above. The emperor is there seen, seated, armed with a cuirass, the head crowned with laurel. He holds the *parazonium* in his left hand, and extends his right to a woman who stands opposite to him. She is clothed in a long flowing robe, and holds in her left hand a horn of plenty, whilst with her right she presents the figure of a Victory, or some trophy, to the emperor. Round it we read *Hispania: Clunia: Sul*(picia).

The explanation of the subject rests entirely on the following statement of Suetonius (ch. 9), that Galba, when hesitating whether he should accept the sovereignty, "was encouraged to do so both by the most favourable auspices and omens, and also by the prediction of a virgin of good birth, to which was added the circumstance that the priest of Jupiter at *Clunia*, instructed by a dream, had discovered in the *penetrale* of the temple, the self-same verses, similarly pronounced by a young prophetess two hundred years before; the purport of which verses was that at some future time a prince or *Lord of the world* would arise in Hispania."— We must not (says Eckhel. vi. 294) omit, what Plutarch (*in Galba*, p. 1055) relates, viz. that Galba, on hearing of the death of Vindex, retired to Colunia, and actuated by repentance for his past conduct, and a longing for his former life of ease, took no decided steps on his own account, but remained at that place till the *Senatus Consultum* was brought, by which the empire was decreed to him. There is no doubt, that the Κολουνια of Plutarch is identical with the *Clunia* mentioned on the coin; and that this city was an especial favourite with Galba, both on account of the prediction above alluded to, and as being the place where he was first assured of his accession to empire; in consequence of which he loaded it with honours and benefits, as is proved by his conferring upon it even the distinguished name of SVL*picia*, as testified by the coin before us."

HOC. SIGNO. VICTOR ERIS.—Victory crowning the emperor, who stands in a military dress, holding in his right hand a *labarum*, on which appears the monogram of Christ, and in his left a spear. Second brass.—See VETRANIO.

This is a coin, common in Constantius II. and Vetranio, though rare in Gallus. The monogram of Christ (see the word) was introduced by order of Constantine the Great on a standard, when setting out on his campaign against Maxentius. This standard being carried into the middle of the ranks, where the danger appeared to be greatest, and invariably bringing victory with it, according to Eusebius, it at length became the belief, that success was to be attributed to the standard alone; and hence is gathered the sense of the legend, HOC SIGNO VICTOR ERIS, which, in all probability, was inscribed upon the actual standard. Some have referred this reverse to the cross seen by Constantine in the heavens, accompanied with the words—EN. TOYTΩI. NIKA. *in hoc* (signo) *vince.*—See Eckhel's remarks on the legend SPES PVBLICA. viii. 117.

HONOR and HONOS. Honour. The Romans, not satisfied with receiving amongst the objects of their worship, the gods of Greece, of Egypt, and even of Persia, thought fit to deify the *virtues*, the *qualities*, the *affections* of the mind, and to represent them by various attributes, on their monuments, principally those of a monetal kind. Such divinities were called *allegorical*, but had not, like the others, a mythological history.

HONOS. S. C. A young man togated, stands, with a branch in his right hand, and the cornucopiæ in his left. On gold, silver, and first brass of M. Aurelius.

The above is not the only occasion on which HONOS occurs on the coins of this prince—"Rare proofs (says Eckhel), vii. 4), in the mintages of a youthful Cæsar, of his bias towards honour and virtue, even in such times."

HONORI.—*Obv.*—HONORI M. DVRMIVS III. VIR. A youthful head on the denarii of the DURMIA gens.—See p. 350.

The obverse of these denarii constantly presents a head of *Honos*, just as on similar coins of Aquillius Florus, the triumvir, struck at the same period there appears the head of *Virtus.*—Dion Cassius states, that in the year U. C. 737 (B. C. 20), Augustus made some alteration in the games consecrated to Virtus and Honos, in consequence of which it appears, that Aquillius and Durmius, who in the years immediately following 734 were Triumviri Monetales in conjunction with Caninius and Petronius, introduced the personified head of each of those qualities on their coins. (v. 236.)

The laureated head of Honour also appears on coins of the Lollia *(Morell. Fam. Rom.* p. 249), the Memmia (p. 277), and Sulpicia families (p. 405).

Honour is generally depictured on the mintages of Republican Rome, with a long robe, or toga, as though the Roman Magistrates derived their dignity from that divinity. The jugated heads of Honour and of Virtue (or Valour); the former designated by a laurel crown, the latter by a helmet, appears on denarii of the Fufia and Mucia families.—See FUFIA gens, pp. 399.

HONOS ET VIRTVS. S. C.—*Honos*, naked to the waist, stands with spear in right hand, and cornucopiæ in the left; whilst *Virtus* stands opposite, with galeated head, a *parazonium* in the right hand, and a spear in the left, and with the right foot planted on a stone. First brass of Galba. The above engraving is after a cast from a specimen in the British Museum.

We have already seen on coins of the Fufia family the head of HONOS joined with that of VIRTVS. And here both those divinities are represented on the coinage of Galba; but why they should have found a place there, Eckhel says he has no reason to assign, any more than their appearance on a similar reverse of Vitellius. Respecting the temple erected at Rome to Honour and Virtue, see Livy, xxvii. c. 25.

Honour, says Gesner, is occasionally exhibited on coins as the associate of Virtue, in which case he bears a spear as well as a cornucopiæ. Virtue stands face to face with Honour, indicating that through the temple of Virtue that of Honour was to be entered.

Du Choul in his ingenious book *De la Religion des Romains*, cites the fact of Marius having been the first to erect a temple to Honour and Virtue—and observes, that "the temple of Virtue was anciently placed before the temple of Honour, which had only one gate, shewing that the path which leads to honour was inaccessible but by means of virtue. This (he adds) is what Marcus Marcellus designated to impress on the understanding of the people of Rome, when he built two square temples joined together, one consecrated to Virtue, and the other to Honour. And unquestionably great honours spring from the pure and beautiful root of Virtue, whence it happens that they are rendered more illustrious, more glorious, and full of immortal recollections." (p. 34).

HONORIA *(Justa Grata)*, daughter of Constantius III. and of Placidia, was born at Ravenna, in Cisalpine Gaul, A. D. 417. Brought up at the court of her brother Valentinian III. under the eyes of her mother, who kept her under great restraint, she received the title of *Augusta*, about A. D. 433, being then sixteen years of age.

It is conjectured that this elevation was conferred upon her, in order to prevent her from entering into any matrimonial engagement, by raising her above the rank of a subject. Thus debarred from marriage, however, she secretly communicated, by one of her eunuchs whom she sent, with Attila, who had lately become king of the Huns, inviting him to come into Italy, and to marry her. It is most probable that at the time of this mission (exact period unknown) she conveyed her ring to Attila, as a pledge of her faith. But the barbaric chief treated her invitation with apparent inattention. And she afterwards dishonoured herself and the imperial dignity she held, by an illicit connection with a man named Eugenius, her own household steward, by whom she became pregnant. On the discovery of her condition, she was expelled from the palace; and sent (A. D. 434) to Constantinople, where Theodosius II. and Pulcheria received her with kindness. It appears that she remained in the East, until the death of Theodosius, which occurred A. D. 450. In that year, Attila, desirous of some pretext for quarrelling with the Emperor of the West, sent an embassy to Valentinian, setting forth the wrongs of Honoria, and claiming her as having engaged herself to him; furthermore he said, that he regarded her as his wife, and was entitled to have half of the empire as the dowry of the princess. The answer of Valentinian was, that Honoria was already married (supposed to be a forced alliance with some obscure person); that women had no part in the succession of the empire, and that consequently his sister had no claim. The fatal war which followed this refusal, and which brought so many calamities upon the Romans, having been terminated, Honoria passed the remainder of her days in Italy, where there is reason to believe she died, though at what time, or in what place, is doubtful, but later than A. D. 454.

The coins of this princess are in gold and silver, and of the highest rarity. On these she is styled D. N. IVST. (or IVSTA) GRAT. (or GRATA) HONORIA P. F. AVG.

GOLD.—The *a reus* described below is valued by Mionnet at 20 francs, and brought at the sale of the Pembr le collection £7.

D. N. IVST. GRAT HONORIA. Bust *stolata* to the right, a cross on the right shoulder, double necklace, ear-rings, and helmet-like head-dress, formed of double diadem of laurel and pearls,

with round jewel in front: above the head a hand holding a wreath.—*Rev.*—BONO REIPVBLICAE. . Victory standing, holding a long staff surmounted by a broad cross, near which is a star. On the exergue CONOB.

The above is engraved after a cast from the original, in the finest preservation, in the British Museum.

Rev.—SALVS REIPVBLICAE. Crown of laurel, in the middle of which is the monogram of Christ. On the exergue COMOB. (*Quinarius*. Mionnet, 150 fr.)

Rev.—VOT. XX. MVLT. XXX. Victory standing, holding a cross. (Mt. 200 ft.)

SILVER.—*Rev.*—Without legend. Cross within a crown of laurel; on exergue COMOB. (*Quinarius*. Mt. 100 fr.)

HONORIUS, the son of Theodosius the Great, and Æl. Flaccilla, was born in the year of our Lord 384. When ten years old, he received from his father the title of Augustus; and at his death in 395, he presided over the Western Empire, under the guardianship of Stilicho. Being at the first much favoured by fortune, he quelled the revolt of Gildo in Africa, and of others in different parts of the empire. Alaric, king of the Goths, and Radagaisus, king of the Huns, elated with their occupation of the very centre of Italy, were checked in some memorable engagements by Stilicho, who, even then, however, revolving in his mind plans for securing the sovereignty, invited Alaric into Italy, and other barbarians into Gaul, but was put to death with his son Eucherius, by his own soldiers, at Ravenna. Alaric, finding no opposition, besieged Rome, which he took and sacked A. D. 410; but died shortly after in Lucania, whilst preparing to pass over into Africa. His successor Ataulphus, leaving Italy, turned his steps towards Gaul, where he had married Galla Placidia, whom he had forcibly taken away from her brother Honorius; and proceeding thence into Hispania, he died at Barcinone (Barcelona). —Amidst these disturbances in Italy, the Alamanni occupied the part of Germany adjoining the Alps, and the Franci, under Pharamond, Gallia Belgica; whilst the Alani and Vandals, coming down from the shores of the Baltic, and scouring the Galliæ, made an incursion into Hispania; and the Burgundiones retained forcible possession of that part of Gaul bordering on the Upper Rhine.—Pressed on all sides by so many dangers, Honorius, in the year 421, conferred the title of Augustus upon Constantius, a man of distinguished military reputation, with whom he had already allied himself, by giving him in marriage his sister Placidia, the widow of Ataulphus; and in 423 he died, leaving no issue by either of his two wives; a prince of a slothful disposition, to whom, if Procopius has told truth *(Bell. Vand.* i. c. 2), the safety of his wife Gallina, whom he used to nickname *Roma*, was matter of much greater solicitude than that of the city itself.—See viii. 171 and 172.

His coins in each metal are common, with the exception of medallions, which in gold and silver, are of the highest rarity. On these he is styled—HONORIVS AVGVSTVS—D. N. HONORIVS AVG.—D. N. HONORIVS P. F. AVG.

The following are the rarest reverses :—

GOLD MEDALLIONS.——GLORIA ROMANORVM. Rome seated. COMOB. Front face. (Valued by Mionnet at 300 francs.)—GLORIA ROMANORVM. Similar type. (Mt. 600 fr.)——Same legend. Emperor drawn in car and six. (Mt. 200 fr.)

SILVER MEDALLION.——TRIVMFATOR GENT. BARB. Emperor holding Christian labarum.

SILVER.–IVSSV. RICHIARI. REGES *(sic.)* round a crown, within which is X between B. and R. (Mionnet, 250 fr.)

EXAGIVM SOLIDI.—D. N. HONORIVS P. F. AVG. Bearded head of Honorius.——*Rev.*—EXAGIVM SOLIDI. Equity standing. (Mt. 18 fr.)

Rev.—EXAG. SOL. SVB. V. INL. IOANNI *(sic.)* COM. S. L. In exergue CONS. (24 fr.)

HORATIA *gens*—a most ancient and noble family, of consular rank, bearing the surname of *Cocles.* The following denarius is of the highest rarity, inscribed COCLES. Galeated head of Rome; behind it X.—*Rev.*—ROMA. In the exergue. The dioscuri on horseback, galloping with levelled lances, and with their caps laureated, and stars above.

Mionnet values at 150 francs this elegant denarius (of which an engraving will be found in p. 316 of this dictionary, under the head of DENARIUS.—The same restored by Trajan he prices at 300 fr. There is a modern fabrication of this coin, which must be guarded against.

The name of Horatius Cocles recalls the memory of transcendant benefits derived from members of that family to the primitive Romans. Two are most remarkable. The former was the successful resistance offered by the first Cocles, on the Pons Sublicius, to the troops of Porsenna, king of Etruria, who attempted to take Rome by a *coup-de-main.*—For a medallion of Antoninus Pius, representing this exploit, see p. 221.

On account of this valuable service the Romans erected a statue to his honour in the Comitium, and gave him as much land as he could plough round in a day. The other benefit rendered to Rome by the *Horatii,* was their combat with the Curiatii, who to the number of three, remained slain by the last of the Horatii. The cognomen of *Cocles* was attached to the first Horatius, from the circumstance of his having lost an eye on the occasion of some fight with the enemy.

HOSIDIA gens.—It is not known whether this family was patrician or plebeian. The following is its sole type.

GETA IIIVIR. Bust of Diana with jewels, mitella, and ear-rings. On her shoulder the bow and quiver.

Rev.—C. HOSIDI. C. F. A wild boar transfixed with a dart, and followed by a dog. There is one variety of no importance.

The precise period when Caius Hosidius Geta was monetal triumvir is not known. The type of reverse is supposed by Havercamp to refer to the great hunting parties with which in 734 (B. C. 20), the birth-day of Augustus was so magnificently celebrated. Eckhel gives his reasons for regarding this coin as older than the age of Augustus, and considers the wounded boar only as an apt accompaniment to *Diana Venatrix,* whose bust Hosidius has, for some reason, chosen to place on the obverse of his denarius.

HOSTILIA gens patricia; an ancient and illustrious family, which claimed descent from Tullus Hostilius. Saserna and Tubulus are the two surnames, attached to it on coins. There are five varieties. The silver are rare. Two denarii of Hostilius Saserna (whom Cicero mentions as among the most eminent senators living in his time), are remarkable for bearing, one the head of *Pallor,* the other that of *Pavor.*

1.—Head of Pavor (Fear or Dread), typified by the bearded head of a man, with hair on end; behind it a feather, or leaf; in some, a buckler.

Rev.—HOSTILIVS SASERNA. A naked man, in a rapid biga, turns himself to the rear, and fights with spear and shield, perhaps against enemies who assail him, and the biga is driven by an auriga also naked, who whips the horses.

2.—Head of Pallor (Paleness), behind whose head, as a follower of Mars, is the military lituus, or trumpet.

Rev.—L. HOSTILIVS SASERNA. Diana standing, with the radiated crown, and dressed after the Ephesian fashion of that goddess. The right hand holds a stag by its horns, and the left carries a spear.

The image of φοβος (Terror) ornaments the breastplate of Ptolemy Philadelphos, on a splendid *Cameo*, which formerly belonged to Madame Buonaparte. The Romans worshipped Terror under the name of *Pavor*, and they also addressed their invocations to *Pallor*, which is at once the result and evidence of terror.

The story on this point is that Victory having, through the treachery of the *Albani*, threatened to turn against the Romans, in a battle they fought with the *Veii*, King Tullius Hostilius made a vow to consecrate a temple to Paleness and to Terror. The enemy were finally routed; and from that epocha Pallor and Pavor were honoured as divinities at Rome. One is represented to the full as spectrally woe-begone as he that " drew back Priam's curtains in the dead of night"—the other, with every particular hair on end, "like quills upon the fretful porcupine." Hostilius Saserna, as one of the monetal trium virs of the republic, caused these two imaginary personifications to be engraved on his family denarii, with the view to have it believed by posterity, that he was descended from Tullius Hostillius. "The trick of an insignificant person *(homuncio)* remarks Eckhel, whose only pretence for so vain an assumption was a community of name."

3.—Head of Venus, richly adorned with laurel, flowers, mitella, ear-rings, and necklace. *Rev.*—L. HOSTILIVS SASERNA. A winged Victory in a long light dress, walking, carries a trophy on her left shoulder, and a caduceus in her left hand.

The head of Venus bears, on other coins, allusion to the origin of Cæsar. Victory refers to Cæsarian prosperity, given by signal *(per tessera)* to his legions. The head of Diana on the denarius No. 2, bears reference to that divinity, whether worshipped in the place where the coin was struck, or more peculiarly the object of devotion with the family of the moneyer.

4.—There is another denarius of the Hostilia gens, on the obverse of which are the word SASERNA, and the bust of *Pallor*, with the right hand raised up to the chin, as in a thoughtful attitude; behind the head is a military lituus. On the reverse L. HOSTIL. A bridge, on which three togated figures stand, as on the *Cancelli* of the Comitia to give their votes.

This very rare coin constitutes an honorary representation of the *Comitia* at Rome, in which the Hostilii allude to the election of Tullus Hostilius, which the Romans carried by popular suffrage, according to Havercamp, in which opinion Eckhel concurs.——Cavedoni adds,—"Cicero points to the true and sole nature of the Cancelli of the Comitia, as exhibited on a de-

narius of Hostilius Saserna, where he says, King Tullus Hostilius *(de Rep.* ii. 17*)* " fecitque idem et septis de manibus *Comitium et Curiam*. Come la Curia dal nome lui fu detta *Ostilia*, il simile può credersi avvenisse ancora del *Comizio*."—Borghesi throws some doubt on the genuine existence, of this medal, on account of his never having seen it. But Riccio (p. 102) confirms its authenticity from his own possession of the coin.—There is no specimen of it in the British Museum.

All these denarii would appear to have been struck, in from the 704 to 712th year of Rome (B. C. 50 to 42), and, according to Eckhel, with whom Cavedoni agrees, belong to the brother of P. Saserna, whose surname is not known; or to L. Hostilius Saserna, son of the one or of the other, who had fought in 708, with Cæsar in Africa, against Scipio and the other adherents of Pompey the Great.

Obv.—Head of Pallas, to the right.—*Rev.*—L. H. TVB. *(Lucius Hostilius Tubulus)* in the field of the coin, and within an oaken crown; below ROMA. On an uncia of brass.

Patin first published this very small and very rare coin, and afterwards Perizoni gave the attribution of it, in which he was followed by all the numismatists. The subject of the coin, and the precise time when it was struck, are equally unknown, according to Eckhel and the other later writers; although some of the elder school have ascribed it to a certain Hostilius Tubulus, who was pretor in 611 (B. C. 143).

HOSTILIANUS *(Carus Valens Messius Quintus)*, second son of Trajanus Decius, was created Cæsar at the same time with his brother Herennius Etruscus, A. D. 249, and on the death of his father, being proclaimed Emperor by the Senate, reigned in association with Trebonianus Gallus, whom the soldiers elected A. D. 251. In order to the proper understanding of this prince's history and coins, the following requisite particulars are premised by Eckhel:—

" That, during the reign of Decius, there was one third person of the male sex distinguished with the title of Cæsar, we have already seen from coins of Decius, inscribed CONCORDIA AVGG. or PIETAS AVGVSTORVM, on which, in addition to the heads of Decius,

Etruscilla, and Herennius, there appears another joined with that of Herennius. That this belongs to the individual, whom several coins describe as *C. Valens Hostilianus Messius Quintus*, is a point upon which all antiquaries are agreed. For, not only is Herennius joined with Hostilianus in express words on a coin, which Spanheim has given from the Barberini collection (ii. p. 256), inscribed Q. HER. ETR. DECIVS C. VAL. HOSTILIANVS, but also on a marble, which Muratori cites from Gori. But, there is an old dispute among the learned, some stoutly affirming Hostilianus to be the *son*, others the *son-in-law* of Decius. Those who consider him the son, and their opinion Eckhel himself embraces, rest on the authority of Zosimus, who expressly mentions a second son of Decius, though without giving his name, who, after the miserable end of his father and his brother Herennius, was associated by Trebonianus as his colleague in the empire. And, moreover, the custom which was retained even up to this period, of considering as sons of an emperor, those individuals who are represented on coins in juxta-position with him, accompanied with the appellation and dress of Cæsars, unless where some special reason demands a different account of the matter, and such has not as yet been adduced by the partizans of the opposite theory,—this very custom will go far to prove, that Hostilianus was the *son* of Decius, from his being in the same manner associated on coins with Decius, Etruscilla, and Herennius. To this may be added the fact of the name *Messius Quintus* being assigned to Hostilianus, which he certainly could have derived only from his *father* Messius Quintus Decius. Those who consider Hostilianus to have been the *son-in-law* of Decius among whom (after Panvini, Tristan, Spanheim, and others), is Liebe *(Goth. Num.* p. 429), endeavour to support their case by the authority of historians, and by the very names of Hostilianus.

"I pay no regard (continues the Author of *Doctrina)* to the historians who have recorded the events of this period, as it is well known that they have contradicted themselves in so barefaced a manner, that you find yourself in the end utterly at a loss for a true conclusion. As regards the names *Valens Hostilianus*, these, they say, belong neither to Decius nor to Etruscilla, and thence argue, that he was transferred from some other family into that of Decius.— They, therefore, think it probable that Decius gave some daughter to this stranger in marriage, and thus made him his son-in-law, with the rank of Cæsar. To strengthen the credibility of their views, it occurred to them, that Zonaras and Cedrenus mention a certain Severus Hostilianus, who, they say, was amongst the successors of Gordian III. and whose son was the Hostilianus of the present memoir; and thus he received the names *Messius Quintus* from his adoptative father Decius, and those of *Valens Hostilianus* from his natural parent.—But after all, this argument founded on the names, is a weak one. For sons have derived their appel-

lations, not only from their fathers and mothers, but even from their grandfathers and grandmothers. Many years earlier, M. Aurelius was called Annius Verus from his grandfather; Catilius Severus, from his great grandfather on his mother's side; Geta, the son of Severus, took his name from his paternal grandfather, or from his uncle. *(Spartian in Getâ,* c. 2). Caracalla was named Bassianus from his maternal grandfather. Elagabalus, before his accession, was called Varius Avitus, from his father and grandfather. Consequently, as Herennius, the son of Decius, derived his names from both his father and mother, it is most probable, that the second son Hostilianus, took his from his father and his grandfather, either paternal or maternal. Neither am I much disturbed by the testimonies of Zonaras and Cedrenus respecting one Severus Hostilianus Aug. as their credibility has already been called in question by Tillemont *(Nota* ii. *in Philipp.) ;* nor do I suppose that such insignificant writers would have had much weight with the eminent numismatists above mentioned, who are in favour of the *son in law* theory, had not their judgments been warped by the authority of Goltzius, from whose dictum it is thought a crime to differ, and who has put forward a coin inscribed IMP. CAES. L. AVR. SEV. HOSTILIANVS AVG. P. M. TR. P. *(Thes.* p. 105), which we had better look upon as *coined* by Goltzius himself out of the words of Zonaras.

"Hostilianus, then, the second son of Decius, as he most probably was, remained at Rome, when his father and brother set out on their campaign. Both of them being killed in battle, Trebonianus Gallus, the successor of Decius, adopted him, in order to pay a public compliment to the late emperor's reign; but shortly afterwards, through apprehension of revolutionary designs, he plotted against him, with a total disregard both of honour and of the relationship existing between them by adoption. Eutropius also records his elevation to the sovereignty, διαδεχεται την βασιλειαν Γαλλος, 'Οστιλιανος, και ω τουτου παις Βουλουσιανος; which passage Pæanius renders, more agreeably to fact, thus— ' The emperors then appointed were Gallus, Hostilianus, and Volusianus, the son of Gallus.'— The former Victor says—' When these things came to the knowledge of the Senate, they decreed the rank of Augusti to Gallus and Hostilianus, and that of Cæsar to Volusianus, the son of Gallus.' And Victor II.—' In their time (viz. that of Gallus and Volusianus), Hostilianus Perpenna was created Imperator by the Senate.' "—See *Doctr. Num. Vet.* vii. 350, 351, 352.

From the foregoing observations it is plain, that the coins of Hostilianus will be found to belong to two reigns, viz. those on which he is styled Cæsar, to the reign of his father, and those which bear the title of Augustus, to that of Trebonianus.

Hostilianus received the title of Augustus from the Senate and Trebonianus A. D. 251, and not long after either fell a victim to a pestilence which was then committing great ravages, or he had met his end through the machinations of Gallus.

On his coins, which are rare in each metal, and of the highest rarity in gold, he is styled C. VAL. HOST. M. QVINTVS NOB. CAE.— IMP. C. VAL. HOSTIL. MES. QVINTVS AVG.

MINTAGES OF HOSTILIANUS.

The following are the rarest reverses:—

GOLD.—PIETAS AVG. Sacrificial instruments. —PIETAS AVGG. Mercury standing.—PRINC. IVVENTVTIS. Emperor with baton and lance, by the side of two ensigns.—Same legend, with slight typical variety.——ROMAE AETERNAE. Rome seated. (These five *aurei* are valued by Mionnet at 600 fr. each.)

SILVER.—AEQVITAS AVGG. Equity standing. The obverse legend of this denarius is CO. VAL. M. QVINTVS AVG. (Mt. 12 fr.)——SAECVLVM NOVVM, & VICTORIA GERMANICA. (15 fr. each).

BRASS MEDALLIONS.—PRINCIPI IVVENTVTIS. (Mionnet, 200 fr.)—VICTORIA AVGG. Victory. --Same epigraph. Apollo. (100 fr. each.)

LARGE BRASS.—SALVS AVGVS. Hygeia and a serpent.—VICTORIA AVGVSTORVM. (24 fr. each).—VOTIS DECENNALIBVS. (30 fr.)

H. S.—See *Sestertius.*

HUM. *Humani.*——See SAL. GEN. HVM.— *Salus Generis Humani.*

HYDRA.—See *Herculis Labores*, p. 451.

HYPSAE AED. CVR.—See *Plautia gens.*

HYGIA, the daughter of Æsculapius Medicus, called by the Greeks Ύγεια, and inscribed on Roman coins SALVS. The Gentiles are supposed to have adopted the serpent as the symbol of health, from the brazen one of Moses. The patera in Hygia's hand indicates that health is to be sought through religion. On coins of Deultum, struck under Alexander Severus, Hygia stands with serpent and patera. Of Alexander himself Lampridius says—" He visited the sick soldiers in their tents, even those the most distant, causing them to be conveyed in waggons, and assisted them with all things needful.

When mention of Hygia, or of Æsculapius, as deities of health, is made on the imperial mint of Rome, it always indicates that those emperors are at the time themselves labouring under disease; or that sacrifices have been performed for their recovery.—See SALVS.—SALVS AVGVSTA.—SALVS AVGVSTORVM.

Hygia et Æsculapius cum cane suo.—Pausanias alludes to the magnificent works which Antoninus Pius dedicated to the honour of Æsculapius. The veneration of that emperor for the god of medicine has been evidenced by a brass medallion (see p. 20 of this dictionary), bearing on its reverse the name of AESCVLAPIVS, and a type allusive to the legend of that divinity's arrival in the form of a serpent at Rome from Epidaurus. Another brass medallion of the same emperor exhibits Æsculapius, seated on a throne, with a dog at his feet. In his left hand he holds a staff, round which coils a serpent; in his right is a patera, attesting his as-

signed divinity. The other figure represents his daughter Hygia, clothed in the stola ; she stands near an altar, and in the act of sacrificing.— Behind the goddess is a tree.

Pedrusi having thus described the reverse type of this unique and remarkable medallion, and caused it to be engraved in the 5th volume of the *Museum Farnese* (TAV. ix. fig. 6), a faithful copy of it is inserted below, together with the purport of some of the learned Italian's animadversions on the subject :—

This pious but mistaken display of personified deification has for its object to promote the health of a beloved monarch. All united in putting up vows for its restoration, for every one enjoyed the results of the imperial beneficence. Punctiliously courteous to his subjects, " Imperatorium fastigium ad summam civilitatem deduxit :"—Kind and considerate with the Senate, to which " tantum detulit Imperator, quantum, cum privatus esset, deferri sibi ab alio Principe optavit :"—Most benignant towards the people, among other examples—" Balneum, quo usus fuisset, sine mercede, populo exhibuit."—Provident, and always attentive to the good of the conquered provinces, it was under Antoninus that all the provinces flourished.— Most honest in his opinions, he was resorted to by nations even as distant from Rome as the Bactrians and the Indians, when they had differences to settle, soliciting his decision as that of an oracle. A monarch adorned, then, with so many estimable qualities, might well lay claim to the public vows in favour of his own health.

But the true Æsculapius, who watched over the health of Antoninus, was the celebrated Galen, to whose consummate knowledge this prince, in one of his dangerous sicknesses, was indebted for the preservation of his life. * .* * The ancients frequently associated Hygia with Æsculapius, and in Achaia and other districts of Greece, their statues stood together in the temples erected to their united honour. And at Rome the same union took place in the worship of father and daughter, with this sole difference, that the goddess whom the Greeks called Hygeia, was by the Latins termed *Salus* or *Bona Valetudo.*

Eckhel (vi. 33) remarks, that frequently as the image of Æsculapius appears on ancient coins, the dog is rarely seen as his companion. Pausanias, however, affirms a figure of that animal to have been placed at the feet of the celebrated statue of Æsculapius at Epidaurus.— The reason, as explained by the same writer, was that having soon after his birth been left exposed, he was suckled by a goat and guarded by a dog. "Canes adhibebantur ejus (Æsculapii) templo, quod is uberibus canis sit nutribus."—"Cane ad pedes (simulacri Æsculapii) decumbente." (Pausan. ii. 61).

The appearance of the tree rising in the field of the reverse, is supposed to bear reference to another superstitious belief of the ancients respecting Æsculapius, that the god of medicine took no satisfaction in the worship of his votaries unless paid to him in his own grove. On this point Pausanias (ii. 60) says—"Æsculapii lucum, circumquaque, montes incingunt, intra cujus ambitum mori quenquam, aut nasci, religio est."

I.

I a Latin vowel, which Cicero *(Orat.* iii.) calls *Iota*. Sometimes it is made a consonant, either simple as in IVNO, IVPITER, &c. or double as in EIVS, MAIOR, &c. The ancients sometimes changed it into V, and wrote MAXVMO for MAXIMO, of which there are not only examples from Pliny, Livy, and Cicero, but the proofs appear also on coins. Rasche.

I is the customary mark of the *As.* See the word (p. 83).

I. This letter, by itself, signifies *Jovi*, or Julius, or Juno.

I. This Latin letter served, as a numeral sign in the products of the Roman mint. Thus I. II. III. IIII. &c. as may be seen within a laurel crown on brass of Augustus. COS. II. III. IIII. Consul for the second, third, fourth time.— LEG. I. II. III. IIII. First, second, third, fourth Legion. II VIR. *Duumvir,* III VIR. *Triumvir,* IIII VIR. *Quatuorvir.*

JANUS, the fabled offspring of Coelus and Hecate, or of Apollo and Creusa, reigned, says Arnobius *(Adv. Gentes,* iiii. p. m. 69), in early times over Italy, and was the founder of the town Janiculum, the boasted father of Fontus.

[For a learned dissertation on the myth of Janus, see *Nouvelle Gallerie Mythologique,* par M. Ch. Lenormant, p. 5].

Representations of Janus occur, as well on the early Roman *As* (see p. 83, et seq.) as on those of much later date, marked by the names of families, to which are to be added the following specimen, which forms the obverse type of a denarius of the Furia gens, described in p. 401.

All these coins present a double head, which procured for Janus, among the ancients, the appellation of *Bifrons.* Both faces exhibit a long beard, while the head itself is variously ornamented. Generally it is wreathed with a crown of laurel. Sometimes he has a half moon (lunulam) intercepted by both heads. On other asses, as in the Cæsia gens, the double head is covered with a sort of cap. The same representation of Janus, just described from Roman coins, undoubtedly found its way into several coins of foreign die; as on coins struck at Panormus (Palermo). The same double head also appears on coins of Amphipolis and Thessalonica, in Macedonia. We have not, says Eckhel in describing them (vol. i. p. 234), to pronounce them portraits of Janus. No doubt the different peoples of Greece often had come under Roman dominion, by representing on their coins the figure of Janus, who, from the very infancy of Rome, was worshipped among her principal divinities, testified that they paid to the Roman gods the same adoration, which in private they did to their own; just as several other Greek cities exhibited on their coins Jupiter Capitolinus. See v. 216.

From the above examples, and others that might be adduced, it is shewn that the Janus of the Romans invariably appeared with a beard. Nor are monuments of a later age at variance with this rule. For he appears bearded on brass coins of Hadrian, Antoninus Pius, Commodus, and Pertinax.

The Author of *Doctrina* then alludes to opinions entertained by other men of great learning, who have pronounced certain *beardless* heads, joined in the same manner, to be those of Janus; and confesses that before he had sufficiently considered the subject, his own opinion was the same. (See his observations, p. 94).— "One reason for their supposition (says he), is the resemblance of the mode of joining the heads, being such as Janus exhibits. But it is found that this mode was in vogue with foreign nations, who certainly employed it with no reference whatever either to the religion or customs of the Romans. From such evidence it is clearly shewn, that this unnatural device was in use both among the Greeks, the Etrurians, and the Romans."—Passing over the conjectures of those who have attempted to ascertain to which people's imagination the invention of such a monster is to be attributed, Eckhel prefers rather to consider the question, what the ancients understood by those two-headed figures? That some allegory lay beneath them is evident, even from the accounts which Roman writers have given of their Janus. Some have said, that he was represented with two faces, because he had been endowed by Saturn with the knowledge of past and future events (Cedrenus ex Dione). Others, in order that, by being placed between them, he might seem to be looking upon the commencing and the retiring year.— Servius says, in one place *(ad Virg. Æn.)* I. v. 291)—"It is stated by some that, Tatius and Romulus built a temple, after entering into a treaty with each other, whence Janus himself has two faces, as if in allusion to the coalition of the two kings." And, in another passage (ad Æneid, I. v. 198)—"It is with propriety that he invokes him (Janus) as he presides at the ratification of treaties; for after Romulus and Titus Tatias had entered into a compact, a statue was erected to Janus, with two faces, as if to represent the two nations." And lastly, Pliny (xxxiv. § 16)—"The double Janus was consecrated by king Numa, and is worshipped in matters both of peace and war." The double heads of Janus, as well as those of the man and woman on the coinage of Tenedos, have been explained by ancient writers allegorically. The devotion of Caracalla to the memory of Alexander the Great becoming the subject of general remark, a circumstance occurred which is recorded by Herodian (iv. in Caracall.)—"We have also seen figures absurdly represented, with one body and one head, but two half faces, of Alexander and Antoninus (i. e. Caracalla)."— These instances of allegory may suffice; altho' it is not necessary, at all times, to suppose an allegorical allusion. For it might happen, that an artist would represent some deity with two heads; because, perhaps, the statue was intended to be so placed, that every one, whether within or without the building, might have a view of his countenance; such as was the case, according to Lucian, with some of the Hermæ —"two-headed, and alike both ways, in whichever direction you turn yourself." "I have seen (says Schultze, in his Introduzione alla scienza della Monete Antiche), a four-faced Janus on a coin of Hadrian, in the rich and noble collection of the illustrious Antonio Guntler."

When, therefore, you see double heads on coins, either of the Etrurians or the Syracusans, or the Athenians. You may be sure, that they convey some allegory, though it may often be beyond our power to discover its meaning.— And, when we see on Roman coins the two heads in question, sometimes with beards, at others without, we need be in no doubt, that if they are bearded, Janus is intended; and if beardless, some other account, and without much difficulty, can be given of them. Thus, in the case of the gold coin, on the reverse of which is a double head without beard; and on the reverse ROMA, and the sacrificing of a sow, since this type of the reverse, undoubtedly signifies the rite of ratifying a treaty; and the coin was unquestionably struck without the walls of Rome, it is not necessary to suppose that the double head on the obverse belongs to Janus, but that after the fashion of the Greeks, some reconciliation between themselves and the Romans is thereby allegorically signified.——See Doct. N. Vet. v. 216 to 333.

Janus' Head on the Monetal As.—The *head of Janus* on one side, and the *prow of a ship* on the other, is an almost perpetual type on the Roman As. Several ancient writers have alluded to this fact, and the reason for it.—Macrobius says—"This Janus having hospitably received Saturnus, who had come with a fleet to Italy, and after having been instructed by him in agriculture, had improved the rude and savage mode of living which had prevailed before fruits were known, he bestowed upon him (Saturnus) a share in the kingdom. He was the first also who stamped brass; and in this, too, he displayed his respect for Saturnus; for, as he had arrived in a ship, on one side was expressed a likeness of his own head, and on the other a ship, to perpetuate the memory of Saturnus.— That the money was so stamped, may be gathered from the game of 'pitch and toss' at the present day, in which boys, throwing up their denarii, cry out ' *heads or ships?* '"—Aurelius Victor gives the same information. And Ovid, having made the following enquiry of Janus— (Fast. i. 229):—

"Multa quidem didici; sed cur navalis in aere
   "Altera signata est, altera forma biceps?"

["I have learned a thing or two in my life; but, why is the figure of a ship stamped on one side of money, and a double head on the other?"]

—receives from that deity this answer:—

"Causa ratis superest; Tuscum rate venit in amnem
   "Ante pererrato falcifer orbe deus. - - -
"At bona posteritas puppim servavit in ære,
   "Hospitis adventum testificata dei."

["The reason for the appearance of the ship remains to be explained. The scythe-bearing god (i. e. Saturn) entered with his vessel a river of Etruria, after traversing the earth. Now, worthy posterity has preserved the ship on money, in commemoration of the arrival of their divine visitant."]

Plutarch speaks to the same effect. (Quæst. Rom.)—Draco of Corcyra has the following in allusion to Janus (apud Athenæum, xv. p. m. 692), that "he first invented crowns, ships, and boats, and first stamped brass money. On which account, many Greek, Italian, and Sicilian cities engraved on their coins a double head, and on the other side either a boat, or a crown, or a ship."—The same also is to be found in Eustathius (ad Odyss. E. v. 251). We have no coin of any Greek or Sicilian city with these types on both sides. All that are extant are undoubtedly Roman. According to Pliny (xxxiii. § 13), when the as fell as low as the sextantarius, "the mark of brass (i. e. of the as) was, on one side a double Janus, on the other the beak of a ship, and on the triens and quadrans, boats."—Eckhel, v. p. 14.

The half-naked figure of *Janus Bifrons* standing, with spear in right hand, cos. III. s. c. belongs to the second brass of Hadrian.

I. A.—*Imperator Augustus*, or *Indulgentia Augusti*.

IAN. *Janum.*—IAN. CLV. *Janum Clusit* or *Clausit*, the temple of Janus closed.

Janus, the fabled son of Uranus, is believed to have been the most ancient King of Italy, who hospitably received Saturn, when, as a fugitive from Crete, the father of Jupiter, banished by his son, arrived in a ship on the shores of *Latium*.—According to the account of Aurelius Victor, Janus was the master-mind of the age in which he lived; he was the founder of a city called *Janiculum*, taught his people the divisions of the year, the use of shipping, and of money, the rules of justice, and the mode of living happily under the authority of the laws; he also instructed them how to build temples and to honour the Gods with sacrificial worship; to surround the cities with walls, to grow corn and to plant the vine. It was out of gratitude for these alleged benefits that Janus was placed by the Romans in the rank of the Gods, and regarded as presiding over treaties. On the first of January, or in the calends of that month, they celebrated the Janualia. At that festival they offered to Janus a mixture of flour and salt, with incense and with wine. The temple of Janus was said to have been built by Romulus, after he had made peace with the Sabines; and in this temple was a statue with two faces. King Numa ordained that it should be opened during war and shut during peace. In the seventh book of the Æneid, Virgil has described, in some fine verses, this imposing ceremony. The figure of this temple is preserved on medals. It was shut only twice from the foundation of Rome to the year 725; namely, under the reign of Numa, year 38, and after the second Punic war, in 519, under the consulate of Titus Manlius. It was shut three times under Augustus, first in 725, after the Actiac war, and subsequently in 729 and 752. Therefore it became an important event to *shut the Janus*, an allegorical expression signifying the restoration of peace to the empire. The poets celebrated these memorable *closings*.— From the first book of Ovid's Tristia, it appears that the temple of Janus was shut under the reign of Tiberius. On a brass coin of Nero we read PACE. P. R. TERRA MARIQ. PARTA IANUM CLVSIT. (after having procured peace for the Roman people, on land and on the sea, he, the Emperor, has shut the Janus,) because this temple was called *the Janus*.—Lucan makes mention of the closing of this temple under Nero, to which the coin referred to above refers. Other princes afterwards performed the same ceremony, on a similar consummation of general peace. Trajan not only shut the Janus but embellished its site with an enlarged area. The last epocha when the fane of this deity was closed was under the Emperor Constantius (Gallus), about A. D. 353 or 4.

Janus Bifrons.—This was an appellation assigned to Janus, because he was represented with two faces, in consideration, as *Servius*

states, of the alliance made between the Romans and the Sabines. Also, perhaps, according to other writers, to signify that he knew both the past and the future.—The *as*, the most ancient coin of the Romans, bears on one side the head of *Janus* with two faces, bearded, and above it a crescent, symbol of eternity; on the reverse, we see the *prow of the ship* which brought Saturn to Italy: a type which has caused this coinage of brass money to be called *ratiti*, from the Latin word *ratis*, a ship or galley. These pieces are common in numismatic cabinets.—The half naked figure of two-headed Janus, standing with a spear in his right hand, on a first brass medal of Antoninus Pius, indicates either some sacred honours paid to Janus by that Emperor; or that the security of the age was established by the providential care of Antoninus, as formerly under the reign of Janus. The legend of this coin is TR. POT. COS. III., which Eckhel gives to v. c. 893.—There is a brass medallion of Commodus, which exhibits on its reverse the head of *Janus*, one of the faces having the likeness of that Emperor: the epigraph which accompanies it is—P.M. TR. P. XII. IMP. VIII. COS. V. P.P.—See also the TELLVS. STABIL. of COMMODVS. on a brass medallion.

There are other medallions of Commodus, which all present the figure of the double Janus, and are remarkable for their elegance and rarity though the reason for the selection of such a type remains unknown.—This adoration of Janus on the part of Commodus, appears to have been an exemplification of that *Pietas* of which we see him styled the *Auctor*. The excess of his predilection for Janus is manifested by a coin of the *Medicean* collection, on the obverse of which the head of Commodus is represented with double face, like that of the god.—*D. N. Vet.* vii., 119.

The head of *Janus*, with its beardless faces, after the likeness of Cnæius Pompeius (Pompey the Great) appears on the obverse of Pompey's first brass, and the prow of a ship on the reverse.

Janus is said to have had a son, named Fontus, from whom the *Fonteii* assumed to derive their origin, and their right to place the head of Janus on their coins.—See Fonteia.

Janus Quadrifrons.—Janus with *four* faces (three of which only are seen), is found on a second brass coin of Hadrian.

IAN. CLV.—On a silver coin of Augustus, and either relates to the second time of that Emperor's closing the temple of Janus, viz., in the year of Rome 729 (A.D. 25), after the conquest of the *Cantabri* (of northern Spain); or it was struck to renew the memory of the year 725, when the temple was closed on the occasion of terminating the *Bellum Actiacum*, or the war ending with the battle of Actium, which ruined Marc Antony, and made Augustus master of the Roman world.

For the most detailed architectural representation of the temple of Janus closed, to be found on the imperial mintages, is the first brass of Nero, in which this celebrated fane is typified with one gate, and a double door. Its form is

square, and its walls are ornamented with laurel
garlands, which the Romans placed on it after
a victory. The doors are shut.—See the
legend PACE P.R. TERRA MARIQ. PARTA IANVM
CLVSIT.

IANO CONSERVAT, Janus with two faces,
standing with a spear in the right hand.—Silver
of Pertinax.

"Pertinax here styles Janus his preserver,
and with some reason; for at the very time that
Janus begins the new year, he commenced his
reign; and this appears beyond question to be
the motive for the adoption of the type."—
Eckhel vii., 141.

IANO PATRI.—Two head Janus, with one
face bearded, the other without a beard: the
whole figure stands clothed in the toga, holding
a patera in the right and a sceptre in his
left hand.—See gold mintages of Gallienus,
p. 406.

Pellerin, in his Mélange i. p. 166, gives an
engraving of the above, and merely says "the
legend IANO PATRI which one sees on this silver
piece of Gallienus, is singular. It is found on no
other known coin."—But Eckhel, animadverting
on the still more singular circumstance of its
exhibiting a bearded head joined to a head without a beard, enters at some length into a research
into all previous numismatic examples which
show that the two faces must be *bearded* in
order to be characteristic of Janus, and concludes
with saying, "I think, therefore, it may be
allowed one to suppose either that the portraiture
of Pellerin is fallacious, which depictures Janus
with one head only bearded, the other without
beard; or that in the age (of Gallienus—A.D.
253 to 268), there was something in the mode
of representing this deity which deviated from
the old immutible imagery."—Vol. vii., p. 397.

Ibex.—A figure of this animal, walking
towards the right, with the epigraph SAECVLARES
AVGG, and the note VI. (perhaps because on the
sixth day of the games this alpine animal was
exhibited) appears on a silver coin of Philip
senior.—*Angeloni* calls it the *Gazelle.*

Ibis, a bird held sacred by the Egyptians,
similar to a stork, except that its beak is somewhat thicker and more crooked.—The Ibis is the
peculiar symbol of Egypt, on account of the
benefit which it rendered to that country in
constantly waging a destructive war with serpents

and insects, in which Egypt abounds, and which
it pursues and kills.

The *Ibis* is seen at the feet of a female figure,
lying on the ground, with the epigraph AEGYPTOS,
on gold, silver, and brass of Hadrian.—See
p. 13.

ICONIVM, (now *Konich,* or *Cogni,*) the
ancient capital of Lycaonia, (now *Karamania,*
Asiatic Turkey). This city is mentioned in the
Acts of the Apostles, c. xiii., v. 51.—A Roman
colony, its coins (besides autonomes in sm. brass
and imperial *Greek* in brass) consist of brass
of the three modules, with *Latin* legends. The
pieces with *Greek* inscriptions are respectively
of Nero, Hadrian, and Faustina, jun. The
following are its *Latin* brass:—

Gordianus Pius.—*Rev.* COL AEL. ICONIEN.
S. R—A veiled priest tracing the limits of a
colony with plough and two oxen. In the field
two military ensigns.—*Rev.* ICONIENSI. COLO.
S.R. Fortune seated.

Valerianus, sen.—Same legend. Fortune
seated, a wheel under her chair.

Gallienus.—*Rev.* ICONIENSIVM CO. S.R.—
The twins and the wolf—*same legend,* Hercules
standing—*same legend,* Minerva seated.

Icuncula (from icon) a small image of frequent occurrence on Roman coins, sometimes in
the right, sometimes in the left-hand of the
principal figure.

Idus, the Ides, from *Iduus,* an Etruscan
verb, *iduare,* to divide, because the Ides
divide the month into two almost equal parts.—
They were (says Vaillant) sacred to Jupiter.—
The Ides of March are marked on a denarius
of Junius Brutus—EID. MAR.—See Marcus
Brutus, p. 145 of this Dictionary.

Jerusalem, the most illustrious and most
celebrated city of Palestine, besieged and destroyed by Titus; restored by Hadrian at his
own expense. For further allusions to this
place, in its state of subjection to the Romans,
see AELIA CAPITOLINA. p. 15.

II. *Secundus.*—COS. II. *Consul Secundum.*
Consul for the second time.—IMP. II. *Imperator
Secundum.*—LEG. II. *Legio Secunda,* &c.

IIS. or HS. *Sestertius.*—See the word.

II. *Iterum.* TR. P. II. *Tribunitia Potestate
Iterum.*

IIVIR. *Duumvir.*—A dignity in place of
Consul, in the Roman colonies.

IIVIR. QVINQ. *Duumvir Quinquenalis.*—
The dignity of the Quinquenniel Duumvir in the
Colonies rivalled that of the Censorship at Rome.

II. VICT. *Duæ Victoriæ.* VICTORIAE AVGG.
II. GERM.—Two Germanic Victories of the
Emperors—on a coin of Gallienus.

III. VIR. A.A.A.F.F. *Triumvir* or *Triumviri*
(monetales), *Auro, Argento, Aere, Flando,
Feriundo.*—One of, or all, the three Roman
Magistrates appointed to superintend the coinage of money.—See p. 1.—Also *Moneta Romana,*
and *Saturnus.*

III. VIR. R.P.C. Triumvir Reipublicæ
Constituendæ—*Triumvir for the establishing of
the Republic.*

IIII. VIR. *Quatuorviri* A. P. E.—See p. 62.

ILERCAVONIA, or Ilergavonia; a Roman *municipium* in Hispania Tarraconensis (now *Amposta* in Catalonia, near Tortosa.) It was the capital city of the Ilercaonenses, situated on the coast near the mouth of the Ebro. Its coins struck, in alliance with Dertosa, under Augustus, Agrippa, and Tiberius, bear on their reverses the legend M. HI. ILERCAVONIA DERT. The type is a galley, with sail set.—See Akerman, "Ancient Coins of Cities and Princes." p. 91.

ILERDA, a city of Hispania Tarraconensis, the capital of the Ilergetes, which by a slight transposition of letters, is now called *Lerida*, in Catalonia.—Under the Roman sway it became a *municipium*, as is proved by a small brass coin of Augustus, inscribed MVN. ILERDA. with the type of a wolf walking.—See Akerman, "Coins of Ancient Cities, &c." p. 92. Pl. x., No. 1, 2, 3, 4, and 5, for specimens of the Celtiberian and *Latin* brass of this municipium.

ILICI, a city of Hispania Tarraconensis. It was situated in the country of the Contestani. It is now called *Elche*, and gave the name to the port called *Alicant*—portus Ilicitanus.— It appears from the legends of its coins C. I. IL. A. struck under Augustus and Tiberius, that it was a colony, and the second letter is considered the initial of *Immunis.—Colonia Immunis Illici Augusta.*—See Akerman, same work, p. 94. The Imperial Latin coins of this Colony are engraved in Vaillant, vol. i. p. 37., p. 73—78.

ILLVRICVS or ILLYRIANVS.—See Genius Exercitus Illyriciani, p. 411.

Illyricum, or as it is otherwise called Illyris, is a region lying on the shores of the Adriatic, opposite to those of Italy, and extending inwards from the Alps and the sea, to the Danube. By some writers this tract of country is considered to be what is now called *Dalmatia.*

IMP. *Imperator.*—CAESAR. IMP. P.M.

IMPERATOR.—The title of Emperor *(Imperator)* was, at first, only used as a surname, and placed after all the names of the individual on whom it was conferred. But at the establishment of the empire, this appellation took another nature. The prince being generalissimo of the Roman legions, appropriated to himself the merit of all the victories achieved, whether he commanded the army in person, or whether he merely carried on the war by his lieutenants. When the Senate in the year 29 before Christ (725 of Rome) bestowed on Augustus the title of *Imperator*, it was placed after his name. Subsequently we see it borne by Emperors from the first days of their reign; and without any victory, even without any war to give occasion for it. In fact the word, from that time, became one of the attributes of sovereignty; but, in this latter case, it is found preceding all the other names and dignities, even that of *Cæsar*, and is not followed by any *number* as I. II. III. &c., on medals. But when, on the contrary, the word IMP. or IMPERATOR was designed to enumerate victories, it is usually placed after the name, and often at the end of all the other titles. Thus we

sometimes see the prince declaring himself *Emperor* for the fifteenth or twentieth time, and giving himself for surnames, titles formed out of the names of the vanquished nations. To such a pitch of mad presumption was this imperial vanity carried, that we sometimes see an emperor assuming the marks of triumph, and impudently pretending to be the conqueror of people who had actually defeated his armies.— After the extinction of the consular government, the name of IMPERATOR was very seldom conferred upon private individuals, either on account of military command, or of victories gained; and it soon became the exclusive appendage of Imperial rank and power.—This title is expressed in Greek by the word ΑΥΤΟΚΡΑΤΩΡ, which is often abridged.

After the death of Caligula, the title of Emperor became elective, and it was the soldiers of the Prætorian Guard who proclaimed the Emperor Claudius. The children, however, of the deceased Prince, or he whom the Emperor had adopted, pretty generally succeeded to the empire, not by right of succession, but because the reigning sovereign had, during his life-time, associated them in the government, or had created them Cæsars, that is to say, appointed them his successors, with the concurrence of the armies, who, having the strength to enforce their wishes, had wrested from the Senate the right of election. The choice of the soldiery almost always fell on some one of their own chiefs, whose bravery was well known; and held higher in their appreciation than either birth or political abilities. It was thus that the empire frequently devolved into the hands of mere soldiers of fortune, whose only merit was their ferocious valour. On the other hand, when the Senate could influence the choice of an Emperor, that body, with all its faults, consulted with more judgment the qualities most suitable in the master of so mighty an empire. Immediately after their election, the Emperors sent their image to Rome and to the armies, in order that it might be placed on the military standards. This was the customary mode of acknowledging the new Princes. Their accession thus announced, they failed not to distribute largesses amongst the troops, each soldier receiving his share as he marched past the emperor, to mark their joy at whose election they carried crowns of laurel on their heads. The first who introduced the system of giving money to the soldiers was Claudius, who, in gratitude for their choice of him, promised them fifteen sesterces a head. Soon after the election of the Emperor, the Senate conferred the name of *Augusta* on his wife and daughters.

That the Imperial title, or appellative of the Roman general was augmented according to the number of victories, so that on coins it should be found marked by the inscription of IMP. ITERVM or III., IV., &c., there are frequent proofs, in the series of the *Augusti;* nor are like examples wanting, during the existence of the republic, or at least before it was utterly abolished, though these however are more rare.

Sylla is numismatically called IMPER. ITERVM; whilst Cn. Pompey M., after having gained the greatest victories and those of the most varied description, is styled on his coins only IMP.— Cæsar the Dictator, only IMP. ITER.—Nor is Sextus Pompey, son of Pompey the Great, mentioned as having oftener enjoyed the title. But Antony the IIIVIR is recorded as IMP. IIII. —And it is certain that after Blæsus, who was the last private individual (by Tiberius's permission) to be called *Imperator*, the important honour, although obtained by the Lieutenants of the Augusti, belonged to the Prince alone, because wars were carried on under his sole auspices; thus a prætor of former times derived the title of *Imperator* from a victory achieved by his quæstor, of which Varro records one example. If Dio is to be relied on, it was the Roman custom to assume the name of *Imperator* not oftener than once, for one war; and this practice was abused by Claudius Aug., who allowed himself to be called by that title several times on account of victories over the Britons. —It is very questionable, however, whether this usage was, even in the earlier age, religiously observed, for from the coins of Sylla it is probable that he was called Imperator for the second time, during the same war.

It is abundantly clear on inspection, that the greater part of the Imperial coins exhibit a numeral addition to this inscription of IMPERATOR on account of fresh victories gained. But it is observable, that Caracalla was the last who stamped this illustrious title on his coinage, as now by degrees the ancient institutions of the Roman empire had begun to be neglected or corrupted. Nevertheless, in the mint of Postumus, singular to say, there occur IMP. V. and IMP. X. —But Ducange adduces from marbles, some examples of *adding* numbers to the title continued to a later period, although of rarer occurrence.—The gold *solidi* of Theodosius II. are common, bearing amongst his titles even IMP. XXXXII., which Ducange considers to import the old acclamation of the soldiers. But Eckhel is of opinion that on the coins of this emperor the years of his reign are indicated by that number.—Gallienus, for the reiterated title of *Imp.* called himself Germanicus Maximus III. or V., or inscribed on his coins VICTORIA AVG. VI. VII. VIII.; and similar examples occur on the medals of Postumus, as before observed; especially on one bearing the legend of P.M. TR. P. IMP. V. &c.—Other evidences which verify the derivation of the title from Victories, are to be found in the *Doct. Num. Vet.* of Eckhel. *De Nomine Imperatoris.* vol. viii. p. 346.

IMP.—Imperator. Cassius, the assassin of Cæsar, is so called: C. CASSI. IMP. *Caio Cassio Imperatori.*—In like manner, *Brutus*, BRVT. IMP. otherwise Q. CAEP. BRVT. IMP.—see the *Junia* family.—M. LEPIDVS obtained the title of IMP. in Spain, and received triumphal honours for his victories there.—In imitation also of M. Antonius IMP. the title of Imperator is given on coins to Caius Cæsar.—Moreover Pompey is

styled MAG. or MAGN. PIVS. IMP.—See the Pompeia family.

IMP. BRVTVS.—See BRVTVS IMP.

IMP. or IMPER.—*Imperator* is frequently read on coins of Julius Cæsar, (he being already dead) on which this single title of honour is assigned to him, in place of the *prenomen*; not for any victory obtained, but by that signification which refers to the heighth of power conferred upon him, he is called CÆSAR. IMP. or IMPER. and afterwards with the Julian star.— For as in others, struck before his death, he is, after the ancient manner of the republic, called IMP. QVINT., on others IMP. SEX. and besides DICT. QVART., or DICTATOR PERPETVO, so this one title IMP. on only two coins, and a few struck after his death, can hardly be understood otherwise than as that highest title of *Imperator*, then for the first time granted to him by the Senate, not long before he was slain; because, as occurs on many other coins of Roman Emperors, that name of supreme power does not occupy the place of a *prenomen* but rather that of a surname. Such is the opinion of *Vaillant* and of *Spanheim* on these coins of Julius.

IMP.—On a silver and a gold coin of Galba, bearing this word on its reverse, that Emperor, in the *paludamentum*, appears on horseback, extending his right hand.—The figure of Galba appears to refer to the statues erected to his honour in Gaul and in Spain, as he does not sit on horseback in the garb of peace, as emperors were accustomed to do when approaching Rome, but he is represented as they are depictured when setting out on a military expedition.—See HISPANIA.

IMP. AVG.—*Imperator Augustus.* On another silver coin of Galba, a female figure, clothed in a robe, holds an olive branch in her right hand, whilst her left rests on a shield placed on the ground.

This figure of a woman personifies *Peace*, bearing the olive branch which was peculiarly dedicated to that goddess, and was also worn on the head at pacific celebrations.

Galba, through the concord of the two provinces, Spain and Gaul, by whom he was elected Emperor, declared his conciliatory feelings to the Roman people.

IMP. CAES AVG. LVD. SAEC.—On a coin of Augustus, in memory of the Secular games, which that Emperor restored and celebrated afresh.

IMP. CAES.—A naval trophy fixed on the prow of a ship, with spoils of arms also appended, and a rudder and anchor added.

This appears on a silver coin of Augustus, by whom, after the defeat of Antony at Actium, this trophy seems to have been erected. Others think the coin was struck in memory of the naval victory gained by Augustus's lieutenant over Sextus Pompey, near Sicily.

IMP. CAESAR AVG. FILI. COS.—Severus seated on a *suggestum* (or raised platform) between Caracalla and Geta.—On a *silver* coin of Caracalla. The epigraph of the reverse (says

Eckhel) is thus to be read:—*Imperator* (Antoninus—meaning Caracalla) *et Cæsar (Geta) Augusti* (Severi) *filii consules*, who doubtless made their consular procession together in the year when the coin was struck, viz., A.D. 205.

The type represents Severus distributing the *congiarium* to the people, after his return from the East.

IMP. NERVA CAESAR AVGVSTVS REST. —This legend appears on a brass medallion, by which the Emperor Nerva restored the memory of Augustus and of his consecration.—*Vaill.* Pr. III. p. 101.

IMP. PERP.—*Imperator Perpetuus*, is read on coins of Alexander and of Probus.

IMP. QVART. *Imperator Quartum.*—Julius Cæsar was styled Emperor for the fourth time.

IMP. INVICTI PII AVGG.—Laureated heads of Severus and Caracalla, side by side, each with the paludamentum.

Rev.—VICTORIA PARTHICA MAXIMA. Victory marching with a garland and palm branch. Silver and gold.

IMPER*atore* RECEPT*o.*—This inscription is found on a gold coin of Claudius, placed above the gateway of a structure, designed to represent

the camp of the Prætorian guard.—It serves to shew in what manner Claudius was presented to the Prætorians, recognised by them as Emperor, and taken under their protection.—As Eckhel observes this rare *aureus* together with the equally remarkable one of *Prætorianis Receptis*, confirms history with wonderful precision, both in legend and in type. Suetonius relates that "he was received within the entrenchments [of the Prætorian camp] and passed the night amongst the sentinels of the army; where also on the following day, according to the account of Dion Cassius, the empire was offered to him with the unanimous consent of the soldiers, as the descendant of an imperial line, and as a man of good reputation."—See PRAETOR RECEP., which has for its type the Emperor and one of his guards joining hands, allusive to the protection which Claudius extended in his turn to the Prætorians, who took an oath of fidelity to him, on the same day that he received the imperial power.

IMP. TER *Imperator Tertium.*—Emperor for the third time.—This inscription with a trophy, and two bucklers and spears, appears on a silver coin of M. Antony, who, having captured Artavasde, King of Armenia, triumphed at Alexandria.—*Gessner. Impp. Rom.*

IMP. P.V. COS. II. P.P. *Imperator, Tribunitia Potestate Quinta, Consul Secundum, Pater Patriæ.*—Oiselius in his Select. Numis. gives a coin with the foregoing legend, and for its type, a most elegant and sumptuous building, with trophies and victories about its upper ranges, and a quadriga on the top of it.

IMPERATOR VII. *Septimum.*—The Emperor sitting on an estrade, haranguing the soldiers.

This legend and type, on a very rare *gold coin of Trajan*, refer to an anecdote of that Emperor, who assumed the title of *Imperator for the seventh time*, on the occasion of his overcoming the *Adiabeni* and Assyrians, A.V.C. 867. Being about to wage war against the Parthians, Trajan made an oration to his assembled troops. —(Cimel. Vindob. Eckhel.)

IMPERATOR VIII. (or VIIII.) S. C.— The Emperor seated on a *suggestum*, attended by two figures: below and before him stand four or five soldiers with standards and a horse.— This legend and type appear on a first brass of Trajan.

IMP. X.—Augustus was called *Imperator Decimum*, in honour of a victory gained by the Roman legions in Pannonia.

IMP. X —A military figure presents a branch to the Emperor, seated.—This silver coin of Augustus refers to the signal victory gained by Tiberius, as that Emperor's lieutenant, over the Pannonians.

IMP. X.—Two male figures, or Tiberius and his brother Drusus, offer a laurel to Augustus, sitting on a curule chair; the former for the Pannonian, the latter for the German conquest; or they are two ambassadors, with olive branches, asking terms of peace with the Emperor.

IMP. X. SICIL. *Imperator Decimum Sicilia.* —See SICIL.

IMP. XI. ACT. *Imperator Undecimum, Actiacus.*—See ACT.

IMP. XIII.—Sow and pigs. Vespasian.— See Rasche.

IMP. XIIII. *Imperator Decimum Quartum.* —The Emperor, seated on an *estrade*, receives into his hands a child offered to him by a man wearing a chlamys.—*Gold* and *Silver* of Augustus.

The learned widely differ in their explanations of this type, which is the more to be regretted, because it obviously refers to some rather interesting point in the history of Augustus. Some think it represents Germanicus presenting Caius to the Emperor; but this idea is not probable.— *Vaillant* pronounces it to be Tiridates, who, driven from Parthia by Phraates, fled with his infant son to Augustus.—*Eckhel*, however, adduces chronological objections to this otherwise likely supposition; but suggests no opinion in its place. " It is certain, however (he says), that the dress of the person offering the child, on this denarius is foreign, and, as it seems to me, is that of a German."—(Vol. vi. 111)

IMP. XXXXII. COS. XVII. P.P.—On a gold coin of Theodosius II.—The number of forty-two, hitherto unusual, and almost without precedent, doubtless indicates the years of Theodosius's reign, when this coin was struck, Therefore, as he was proclaimed Augustus A.D. 402, the year XXXXII. began in the year of Christ 443; and he was the Consul for the seventeenth time, as the *fasti* testify; and about to enter into the eighteenth consulate the following year. Why this particular year should thus ostentatiously be stamped on the gold coinage of Theodosius II., adds Eckhel, I do not inquire, because I may judge rashly. It is, however, extraordinary that the same reverse should appear on coins of his wife Eudoxia, of his sister Pulcheria, of Galla Placidia, Valentinianus III. and Leo I., although to them belongs neither the year nor the consulate.—Vol. viii. p. 182.

Imperator.—This title is not found attached to the names of the Roman Emperors much beyond the time of *Constantine.* For the sons of that great prince, instead of *Imperator,* caused themselves to be called D. N. *Domini Nostri.*

Imperatores.—After Nero, the Emperors for the most part ceased to govern by hereditary right. (Spanh. Pr. ii. p. 238). Writing to the governors of provinces they called themselves, *not Augusti,* but *Imperatores (ibid.* p. 374)—nay, sometimes they even mentioned themselves as of the *number of the Senators (ibid.* p. 413).— Emperors were called Patres, after the example of Jupiter, as *Patres Ausonii, Patres Latii,* &c. *(ibid.* p. 450).—Appellations peculiar to the *Imperatores Romanorum,* and observable on their coins, are *Pater Castrorum, Pater Exercituum,* which as words denoting the highest rank were accustomed to be exclusively applied to the *Augusti,* or to their appointed heirs. Moreover a new surname was invented in honour of the Emperors, viz., that of *Pater Senatus,* which was first received by Commodus, called on his silver coin PATER SENATVS; and afterwards by Pupienus and Balbinus, as appears on their coins, inscribed PATRES SENATVS.— (Vaillant).—Some Emperors were called *Optimi,* some *Maximi,* and others *Optimi Maximi,* the two being joined as if equalling them with Jupiter himself. (Spanh. Pr. 500-501).—*Pii* and *Felices* were also among the titles of honour. And in like manner some of them were called *Orbis Rectores, Restitutores, Locupletatores orbis terrarum*—also *Pacatores Orbis, Ubique Victores,* &c., &c.

The *Imperatores Romani* had by right no other power in sacerdotal and sacred affairs than that which they derived from holding the highest pontificate *(maximus pontificatus),* and the Emperors themselves exhibited their testimonies of piety to the Gods, in discharging the offices of pontiffs. For after Tiberius they were admitted to all the functions of the priesthood; and from the very moment of their accession to the empire, they sacrificed bare-headed and covered, and in quality of pontiffs performed sacred rites. The Emperors, on their coins, are represented in the act of sacrificing. We see the contents of the *patera* poured out by them on the lighted altar; the *popa,* or priest whose province it was to slay the victim, standing near it, and ready to perform his office. Amongst the numerous representations of this kind to be found on the Latin Cæsarian medals may be mentioned— Caligula sacrificing in front of a temple (see PIETAS.) Alexander Severus sacrificing before Jupiter. On coins also of Trajan, M. Aurelius, L. Verus, Commodus, Severus, Alexander, Maximinus, Gordianus Pius, we see some fine sacrificial groups, in which the Emperors are the prominent figures.—See *Sacrifices.*

Some of the *Imperial* series bear legends and types which testify the piety or religion of the reigning prince towards the gods, as in the RELIGIO AVG. of M. Aurelius and Valerianus; and in the PIETAS AVG. of Trajan, Hadrian, Antoninus, M. Aurelius, and others, with an altar, or with the Emperors sacrificing; or with pontifical instruments, or with a temple, or with Piety personified under the figure of a woman, standing with a patera in her hand before an altar; also with the image of Mercury holding his caduceus, and crumena, or purse.— Even the truculent monster Commodus is on one of his coins called AVCTOR PIETATis.—In token of Piety, the temples of the Gods were frequently either erected, or repaired, or dedicated by the Emperors as well at Rome as in the provinces; a custom which explains why on so many of their coins, we read, AEDES AVG. or AED DIVI AVG. REST; DEDICATIO AEDIS, and similar inscriptions.

IMPERI, instead of IMPERII.—See *Aeternitas Imperii.*

IMPERII FELICITAS.—A female standing, holding an infant.

On a silver coin of Marcus Aurelius, which appears to have been struck on the birth of a son of that Emperor, through which event the *Happiness of the Empire* was predestined, an heir having at length been born after so many adoptions. The goddess of Felicity, therefore, holds in her hand the child Annius Verus, who, however, died in his seventh year, after Aurelius had proclaimed him Cæsar.—(Vaill., Pr. ii. 171.)

IMPERATORI.—See DESTINATO IMPERATORI.

Imperium Romanum.—The Roman Empire was sometimes governed by two *Augusti,* at first as a compact and undivided territory as in the case of M. Aurelius and L. Verus, and also of Diocletian and Val. Maximian; but afterwards divided into two parts, the Eastern and the Western.—The Imperial coins are distinguished by their chronological order, as belonging either to the earlier, which is called the Higher Empire, or to the age of its decline, which is called the Lower Empire.

CATALOGUE OF THE IMPERIAL SERIES.

Strictly speaking the *Imperial Series* commences with Augustus; but many of his coins properly come under the Consular or Family Series, in which department all prior to Augustus may, with propriety, be ranged. But the following catalogue is drawn up in accordance with the usual sequence in which the coins are arranged in cabinets and described by numismatic writers:—

Cnaeius Pompeius.	Marciana.	Herennius Etruscus.	Romulus.
Caius Julius Caesar.	Matidia.	Hostillianus.	Alexander II.
Cnaeius Pompeius, the son.	Hadrianus.	Trebonianus Gallus.	Licinius, the Father.
	Sabina.	Volusianus.	Licinius, the Son.
Sextus Pompeius.	Lucius Aelius,	Aemilianus.	Martinianus.
Marcus Junius Brutus.	Antoninus Pius.	Cornelia Supera.	Constantinus I.—
Caius Cassius Longinus.	Faustina the Elder.	Valerianus.	(Maximus).
	Galerius Antoninus.	Mariniana.	Fausta.
Marcus Aemilius Lepidus.	Marcus Aurelius.	Gallienus.	Crispus.
	Faustina the Younger.	Salonina.	Delmatius.
Marcus Antonius.	Annius Verus.	Saloninus.	Hanniballianus.
Octavia.	Lucius Verus.	Postumus.	Constantinus II.
Marcus Antonius, the son.	Lucilla.	Postumus, the Son?	Constans.
	Commodus.	Laelianus.	Constantius II.
Cleopatra.	Crispina.	Victorinus.	Nepotianus.
Caius Antonius.	Pertinax.	Victorina?	Vetranio.
Lucius Antonius.	Titiana.	Marius.	Magnentius.
Augustus.	Didius Julianus.	Tetricus, the Father.	Decentius.
Livia.	Manlia Scantilla.	Tetricus, the Son.	Constantius III.—
Marcus Vipsanius Agrippa.	Didia Clara.	Macrianus, the Father.	(Gallus).
	Pescennius Niger.	Macrianus, the Son.	Julianus II.
Julia.	Fulvia Plautiana.	Quietus.	Jovianus.
Caius and Lucius.	Clodius Albinus.	Alexander Aemilianus.	Valentinianus I.
Postumus Agrippa.	Septimius Severus.	Regalianus.	Valens.
Tiberius.	Julia Domna.	Dryantilla?	Procopius.
Nero Claudius Drusus, son of Tiberius.	Caracalla.	Aureolus?	Gratianus.
	Geta.	Claudius Gothicus.	Valentinianus II.
Nero Claudius Drusus, brother of Tiberius.	Plautilla.	Quintillus.	Theodosius I.
	Julia Maesa.	Aurelianus.	Aelia Flaccilla.
Antonia.	Macrinus.	Severiana.	Magnus Maximus.
Germanicus.	Diadumenianus.	Odenathus.	Victor.
Agrippina, senior.	Elagabalus.	Zenobia.	Eugenius.
Nero and Drusus.	Julia Paula.	Vabalathus.	Arcadius.
Caius (Caligula).	Aquilia Severa.	Athenodorus.	Aelia Eudoxia?
Agrippina, junior.	Annia Faustina.	Tacitus.	Honorius.
Drusilla.	Julia Soaemias.	Florianus.	Constantinus IV.
Julia.	Severus Alexander.	Probus.	Galla Placidia.
Claudius.	Barbia Orbiana.	Bonosus?	Constantinus III.
Messalina.	Julia Mammaea.	Carus.	Constans II.
Claudia Antonia.	Uranius Antoninus.	Carinus.	Maximus?
Britannicus.	Maximinus I.	Magnia Urbica.	Jovinus.
Nero.	Paulina.	Nigrinianus.	Sebastianus.
Octavia.	Maximus.	Numerianus.	Priscus Attalus.
Poppaea.	Gordianus Africanus, the Father.	Julianus II.	Theodosius II.
Messalina.		Diocletianus.	Aelia Eudoxia.
Claudia.	Gordianus Africanus, the Son.	Maximianus I. (Herculeus).	Johannes.
Clodius Macer.			Valentinianus III.
Galba.	Balbinus.	Carausius.	Licinia Eudoxia.
Otho.	Pupienus.	Allectus.	Honoria.
Vitellius.	Gordianus Pius.	Domitius Domitianus.	Petronius Maximus.
Vespasianus.	Tranquillina.	Constantius I.—	Marcianus.
Flavia Domitilla.	Philippus, the Father.	(Chlorus).	Pulcheria.
Domitilla, junior.	Otacilia Severa.	Helena.	Avitus.
Titus.	Philippus, the Son.	Theodora.	Leo I.
Julia.	Marinus.	Maximianus II. (Galerius Valerius).	Verina.
Domitianus.	Iotapianus.		Majorianus.
Domitia.	Pacatianus.	Galeria Valeria.	Severus III.
Nerva.	Sponsianus.	Severus II.	Anthemius.
Trajanus.	Trajanus Decius.	Maximinus II. (Daza).	Euphemia.
Plotina.	Etruscilla.	Maxentius.	Olybrius.

Placidia.

Glycerius.

Leo II.

Zeno.

Basiliscus.

Aelia Zenonis.

Leontius.

Julius Nepos.

Romulus Augustus.

Anastasius.

Justinus.

Vitalianus.

Justinianus.

Justinus II.

Sophia.

Tiberius II.

Mauricius.

The Incus, in the field of a coin, is a mark of the monetal triumvirs, designed to shew either the instrument or office of the mint, or the power of striking money. It is seen on coins of the Annia, Apronia, Claudia, Livineia, Nævia, Rubellia, Silia, Statilia, Valeria, and other families. So on denarii of Claudia, Livineia, and Statilia families, the *incus*, as a mint mark, is seen opposite the letters III. VIR. A.A.A. F.F. added to their surnames PVLCHER. TAVRVS. REGVLVS.—On a denarius of the *Carisia* family we see all the tools used in the Roman process of coinage, namely, the *incus*, or anvil; the *forceps*, or tongs; and the *malleus*, or hammer.

Incuse.—This epithet is applied to coins, which exhibit the same image, concave on one side, convex on the other. Some of these, from the rudeness of the workmanship, are obviously of the most ancient date; others, it is no less evident, were thus stamped through the carelessness of the moneyers, in putting the metal to be struck on a coin already struck.

Accordingly incuse coins (numi incusi) are found to bear neither a new figure nor a new inscription on the opposite face. The example here given is a second brass coin of Diocletian.

IND. *Indictio.*—This form of IND. II. began for the first time to be struck on small brass of Mauricius, about A.D. 582.

Indictio. Indiction.—Indiction, a mode of reckoning, which contained a revolution of 15 years. Under Augustus, the indiction, according to some authors, signified the year when tributes were paid to the Roman Treasury. Most writers, however, insist that the indiction was not known till long after the reign of that Emperor, and that under Constantine the Great it was introduced, not for the payment of tributes, but simply to obviate errors in the mode of counting years. It would, however, be difficult to fix the year in which they began to reckon by indiction, as indeed it would be to explain the reason why the indiction is comprised within the space of fifteen years, or why this appellation was given to it.

Indulgentia. Clemency, lenity, grace, favour. —This word is used on Roman coins to denote either some permission given, some privilege bestowed, or some tribute remitted.—In inscriptions of a very early date, princes are called *indulgentissimi.*

INDVLGENTIA. AVGG. IN. CARTH.— Silver and middle brass coins of Septim. Severus bearing this inscription on the reverse, have for accompanying type, Cybele with a turreted crown on her head, seated on a lion; she holds a thunderbolt in her right and a spear in her left hand. The mother of the Gods was the favourite deity of the Carthagenians; here the lion, which Virgil tells us (*Æneid* lib. 3) was tamed by Cybele, may be taken as an emblem of Africa.—Severus was of African origin, and, attached to the land of his birth, conferred benefits (among others the *jus Italicum*) on Carthage and Utica, according to Ulpianus.—A medal of Caracalla exhibits the same reverse.

INDVLG. AVG. *Indulgentia Augusti.*— On a medal of Gallienus, *Indulgence* is represented under the form of a woman seated, holding out the right hand, and grasping *hasta pura* in the left. On another of the same reign, she appears in the act of walking, with a flower held in the right hand and spreading her robe with her left, "as if (says Millin, fancifully enough,) for the purpose of skreening the guilty."

INDVLGENTIA AVG.—On a first brass of Antoninus Pius, the virtue is personified by a woman seated, having in the left hand a wand, and the other open, or holding a patera.

Eckhel observes that "by this coin the words of Capitolinus are confirmed, where he asserts that Antoninus Pius was eminently disposed to acts of indulgence and favour." (*Ad indulgentias pronissimum.*)

INDVLGENTIA AVGG. IN ITALIAM.—
A female figure with turreted crown, sitting on
a globe, bears a trophy in her right hand, and
a cornucopia in her left.—Silver of O. Oovorum.
In memory of this Emperor's indulgences towards
Italy. *Vaillant* connects this with a passage in
Spartianus, and supposes it to relate to some
remission of the *vehiculatio* (or posting impost)
of Italy, by which, as in the case of Nerva, the
burthen was taken off individuals and transferred
to the public treasury.

INDVLGENTIAE AVG MONETA IMPE-
TRATA. (The privilege of coining money
obtained by permission of Augustus.)—This
legend appears on the reverse of a large brass
struck by the colony of Patræ in honour of Julia
(or Livia) wife of Augustus.—See *Patræ* colonia.

INDVLG. PIA. POSTVMI AVG.—The
Emperor seated, extends his right hand to a
woman bending the knee before him.—This
legend on a gold coin of Postumus, is to be
remarked for its novelty; and also for its reference
to the *indulgence* of that powerful usurper both
in remitting tribute at the supplication of the
Gauls, and in showing mercy to condemned
criminals.

IN. HOC. SIGNO VICTOR ERIS.—On a
coin of Constantius.—See HOC SIGNO, &c.

Ino, daughter of Cadmus and Hermione, and
the unhappy wife of Athamas, King of Thebes.
She was mother of Melicerta, and regarded as a
goddess by the Greeks. On a first brass coin
struck at Corinth, under Domitian, and on another
minted in the same colony under Lucius Verus,
a female is holding an infant in her arms towards
a male figure, seated on a rock by the sea side.
A fish appears at his feet.—Above this group the
legend is PERM. IMP. (with the permission of the
Emperor). This, says Vaillant (in col. I. 140),
refers to Ino presenting her newly born son to
Neptune, and imploring his assistance and pro
tection (see *Ovid* Metam. 4). The rock is that
of Moluris; and the fish bears allusion to the
dolphin, on the back of which Melicerta was
carried away and saved from the unnatural
persecutions of Athamas.—See *Melicerta*, also
Corinthus colonia.

Inscription.—A brief statement, or sentence,
by which a memorable event is recorded on some
monument. The Latin word *inscriptio* is derived
from two words, *in*, above, and *scribere*, to
write; as the Greek word, for the same thing,
is derived from *epi*, above, and *graphein*, to
write.—Properly and distinctively speaking, the
inscriptions are engraved on the field of the coin;
the legend, *epigraphe*, is placed around it. (See
Legend).—On many Greek and Latin medals,
no other inscription is found than a few initial
letters, such as S. C., that is to say, by a *Senatus
Consultum*—or A. E. letters which indicate the
Tribunitian Power, mostly enclosed in a crown.
On others the inscriptions form a species of
epochas, as in Marcus Aurelius *(Primi Decennales, Cos. III.)* Sometimes great events
are marked on them, such as the victory gained
over the Germans in the third consulate of
Marcus Aurelius *(Victoria Germanica, Imp. VI.*

Cos. III.) : the military standards re-taken from
the Parthians, an event commemorated on
coins of Augustus *(Signis Parthicis Receptis,
S. P. Q. R.)* : the victory gained over the Parthians under Sept. Severus *(Victoria Parthicu
Maxima.)*—Other inscriptions express titles of
honour given to the prince, as *S. P. Q. R.
Optimo Principi*, in Trajan, and in Antoninus
Pius; and the *Adsertori Publicæ Libertatis* of
Vespasian. Others are marks of grateful acknowledgment from the Senate and the People;
as in Vespasian, *Libertate P. R. Restituta
ex S. C.* In Galba *S. P. Q. R. Ob Cives Servatos.*
In Augustus, Galba, and Caracalla, *Salus Generis
Humani.* Some of these inscriptions have reference only to particular benefits granted on
certain occasions and to certain places, or to the
vows *(vota)* addressed to the Gods for the re-
establishment, or for the preservation of the
health of Princes, as objects of importance to
the state and of interest to the people.

The ancients seem to have been of opinion
that medals should be charged with none but
very short and expressive inscriptions; the
longer ones they reserved for public edifices,
for columns, for triumphal arches, and for
tombs.—Sometimes monetary inscriptions simply
comprise the names of magistrates, as in a coin
of Julius Cæsar, *L. Æmilius, Q. F. Buca
IIIIvir. A. A. A. F. F.*; and in Agrippa, *M.
Agrippa Cos. Designatus.*

It is well and truly observed by the learned
Charles Patin, that how justly soever we may
prize the different reverses of medals, as deserving to be ranked among the most precious remains
of antiquity, it would ill become us to neglect
the *inscriptions* which we read around the portraits of those whom they represent. "We
behold there (says he) all the dignities with
which the Romans honoured their Emperors,
and indeed they often serve to authenticate
chronology by the number of years of their
reign, which is marked upon them. The style
of these two kind of inscriptions (that of the
obverse and that of the reverse) is as simple as
it is grand; and I believe that with all the
rhetoric of our moderns, the thought cannot be
more nobly expressed, although it may be with
greater delicacy. The ancients despised all
affectation, and dwelt more on the grandeur of
the subject they described than on the cadence
and the pomp of words, which they deemed
unworthy of their attention. Demosthenes and
Cicero give us the first proof of this, in their
writings, which are altogether of a grand and
natural style, a style of which the magnificence
has nothing of the affected. And I take the
second from medals, wherein we see histories
perfectly described in two or three words, as
may be seen in the following examples :—

ADLOCVTIO COHORTIVM.
SALVS GENERIS HVMANI.
PAX ORBIS TERRARVM.
VICTORIA AVGVSTI.
DECVRSIO.
CONCORDIA EXERCITVVM.
VIRTVS EXERCITVS.

IVDAEA CAPTA.
ADSERTORI LIBERTATIS PVBLICAE,
LIBERTAS RESTITVTA.
REX PARTHIS DATVS.
REGNA ADSIGNATA.
AMOR MVTVVS AVGVSTORVM.
PAX FVNDATA CVM PERSIS.
RESTITVTOR VRBIS.
PACATOR ORBIS.
SECVRITAS ORBIS.
LOCLVPLETATORI ORBIS TERRARVM.
VICTOR OMNIVM GENTIVM.
AMPLIATORI CIVIVM. &c.

Eckhel, with his usual sagacity, remarks that
the brevity of inscriptions on medals is the
character of a flourishing empire; whilst their
loquacity, consequent upon flattery, vanity, and
ambition, is, on the contrary, the sign of a state
tottering to its fall.

Instruments of sacrifice, and relating to the
priesthood, designate Piety; and it was customary to stamp the figure of such instruments on the coins of a new emperor or
of a recently proclaimed Cæsar, as if to shew
that the business of empire began with the care
of divine things. (See the word *Augur*.)—The
tripos, patera, capeduncula, and lituus, all
appear on a coin of Nero. (See SACERDOS
COOPTATVS, &c.—The lituus, capeduncula, and
aspergillum, on a first brass of Maximus Cæsar,
&c.—See PIETAS AVG.

INT. VRB—This appears on a coin commonly assigned to Gallienus. *Patin* thinks it
was dedicated to that Emperor INT*ranti* VRB*em*,
on the occasion of his re-entry into Rome. The
legend of this obverse GENIVS *Populi Romani*,
connected with that of the reverse INT*ra* VRBEM,
seems to explain it flatteringly to the Prince.
Eckhel quotes Patin's opinion, and refers to
Banduri, but declines adding, "in so doubtful
a case," any conjecture of his own.

INV. and INVIC. *Invictus.*—MAXENTIVS.
P. F. AVG. INV. AVG. according to Khell.

IMP. C. PROBVS INVIC.—Probus took this
grand surname, as having been the conqueror
of all the barbarous nations, and also victor over
the usurpers.—INV. also, occasionally, appears
on the coins of Carausius.

INVICTA ROMA AETERNA.——Rome
seated.—This ridiculous and insolent *epigraph*
appears on a third brass of Priscus Attalus.—
The epithets of Unconquered and Eternal are
here applied to a city which had already been
three times besieged, whose impending destruction was delayed only by its submission to the
commands of the barbarians, and by the almost
total exhaustion of its wealth; yet such was
the inscription invented at the period of her
ruin; for it does not occur before.

INVICTA ROMA. FELIX SENATVS.—
This sounding legend belongs to no part of the
regular coinage of either Rome or her colonies;
but appears on one of those *Contorniates*, which
relate to amphitheatric shews *(munera)* of gladiators and wild beasts; which were struck in
the times of the Christian Emperors. The
obverse exhibits the bust of the Genius of

Rome helmeted; and the reverse is inscribed
REPARATIO MVNERIS, FELICITER, with the type
of a hunter killing a bear; another represents a gladiator victorious and his antagonist
slain, referring to the same barbarous and cruel
sports with which princes calling themselves
Christian entertained the people of Constantinople.—(See Morell, Num. Contorn.)

INVICTA VIRTVS.—The Emperor on
horseback trampling on a captive. This legend,
of which the accompanying type renders the
meaning sufficiently clear, as a compliment to
Imperial valour, appears for the first time on a
silver coin of Sept. Severus. There is a similar
reverse on one of Caracalla's medals.—The
warlike *virtus* may be said in the case of
Severus to have been *unconquered*, if what
Spartianus asserts be true, that he was victorious
in every action with the enemy, and no less distinguished for science in the military art than
for courage in the field.—(Vaillant.)

INVICTI.—Those military commanders were
thus called who gained a glorious victory over
the enemy. On some coins, Severus together
with his sons Caracalla and Geta, took this surname on account of their united successes in
warlike expeditions.

INVICTVS. AV.—The Sun holding up his
right hand and bearing a globe in the left. On
a small *brass* of Carausius.—There are numerous
coins in the Roman Imperial series which refer
to the worship of the *Sun*—in the same manner
as ORIENS. AVG. with a similar type, or PACATOR
ORBIS, with the radiated bust of the same deity,
which name and types are frequently found on
the coinage of Aurelian, Probus, and those Emperors to whom the disturbed condition of the
Eastern provinces gave much employment.—
But to Carausius (says Eckhel), who governed
in the furthest (then known) regions of the
West, the affairs of the East do not belong.
It must therefore be understood to be one of
those types which his mint-masters restored,
without attention to appropriate circumstances.—
Vol. viii. 45.

INVICTVS. PROBVS. P. F. AVG.—Bust of
the Emperor laureated, in his right hand a globe
surmounted by a Victoriola.—For the reverse
type of this fine silver medallion of Probus, see
GLORIA ROMANORVM, in Khell, p. 206.

INVICTVS SACERDOS AVG.—The Em-
peror togated, stands before a lighted altar,
with a palm branch in his left hand; on the
ground is a bull ready to serve as the victim: in
the field of the coin is a star. Silver.—This
is one of the coins which serve to attest the
insane passion of Elagabalus for the worship of
that Syriac divinity, whose priest he was at
Emesa, when, under the name of *Varius Avitus
Bassianus*, he was, through the intrigues of
his female relations, called to the empire. The
mad adoration which this young monster paid to
his idol, is referred to on the coin which is
inscribed SANCT. DEO. SOLI. commemorative of
his introduction of it into Rome, and of his
performing the part of Chief Pontiff to his
favourite ELAGABALVS, who, from the star on

his coins, is believed to be the Sun, although the idol for which he built a temple was only a large black stone of conical form. See SACERDO DEI SOLIS; see also SVMMVS SACERDOS.

JOVE, or JUPITER, the king of Gods and men, was the son of Saturn and of Rhea. The Greeks called him Zeus, and he was their principal deity as well as of the Romans. Fable has been more than usually whimsical and obscure in describing the circumstances alleged to have been connected with his birth and education. We find him, however, at length arrived at adolescence, and making no ceremony of dethroning and mutilating his very unnatural father; he then divided the empire of the world with his brothers; to Pluto he assigned the infernal regions, to Neptune the seas; for himself he reserved the whole of *terra firma*, with the air and the heaven. But before he was allowed to remain in peaceable possession of his new government, Jupiter, having already dispatched the Titans to Tartarus, had to encounter the Giants,

[Medallion of Antoninus Pius, in brass.]

his memorable victory over whom is represented on a great number of monuments. We see him on marbles, on engraved gems, and on medals represented in the act of hurling the thunder with destructive aim at his gigantic foes. —Jupiter was worshipped in all the states of Greece, and throughout the whole Roman empire. At Rome, his principal temple was in the Capitol, with those of Juno and Minerva; for which reason they are often called the three divinities of the Capitol.

On a brass medallion of Antoninus Pius, in the French cabinet, Jupiter is represented with

hasta and *fulmen* standing between Atlas and an altar surmounted by an eagle. The altar is oranamented with a bas-relief, the subject of which is Jupiter overcoming the Titans.

On a medallion of Hadrian, Jupiter, full face, is seated between two female figures also seated: the one on his right hand, Minerva, wears a helmet and holds the hasta; the figure on his left, Juno, holds the patera and hasta.

Jupiter was venerated as the supreme deity, and received the name, therefore, of OPTIMVS MAXIMVS. The attribute of his majestic power was the lightning. On coins he appears sometimes with naked head; on others crowned with laurel or olive; and often bound with a small band, his form and aspect being that of a venerable man in vigorous old age, with a handsome beard, and generally an eagle near him; when seated he is naked to the waist, and the lower half of his body clothed. On most Roman Imperial medals he holds a figure of Victory in his right hand.

The Greeks and Romans, but more particularly the former, gave Jupiter many surnames, taken or derived from some quality ascribed or some action performed, otherwise from some province, city, or temple, where he was worshipped. On Roman coins we find this deity distinguished by the following names :—

IVPITER AVGVSTVS.—Jupiter the August is seated, and holds in his right hand a globe with victory, as may be seen on coins of Diocletian.

IVPPITER CVSTOS. Jupiter the Preserver. —Under this title, on the coins of Nero and

others, he is generally represented seated, holding in his right hand something intended to resemble the thunderbolt, and in his left a spear.—IVPPITER LIBERATOR of Nero has a similar type.—Vaillant observes that Nero caused a coin to be struck, on which the effigy of Jupiter is seen sitting, with the epigraph of *Jupiter Liberator*, on the occasion of the Pisonian plot having been discovered, in acknowledgment that the deity had rescued him from so great a danger, as in the former medal of IVPPITER he recognised Jove as his keeper and guardian.

This execrable tyrant was, however, not content with honouring Jupiter as his *liberator* from the poniards of his enemies; but he made a bloody libation at the shrine of his tutelary divinity, by putting Seneca and Thraseas Paetus to death, with a hecatomb of other victims, (IOVI VINDICI) to the avenging Jove of the Capitol, or rather to the sanguinary impulse of his own vindictive and cruel nature.

IVPITER CONSERVATOR.—Jupiter the Protector is depicted either sitting or standing with the *fulmen* in his right hand, and a hasta in the other; or to the same attributes are generally added the eagle; and a figure of Victory which he holds in his right hand.

On a *large brass* of Commodus, (edited by *Pedrusi*, in Mus. Farnese vii. xxi. 2) Jupiter the Conservator holds the *sceptre*, extends his mantle and raises, his thunderbolt over the head of a small figure representing the emperor, who has also in his hands the *sceptrum* and the *fulmen*: around it we read IVPITER CONSERVATOR TR. P. III. IMP. IIII. COS. III. P.P.

The annexed cut represents Jupiter standing

between two togated figures, Antoninus and Marcus Aurelius. It is engraved from a fine medallion in the British Museum.

IVPITER PROPVGNATOR.—Jupiter the Defender is represented on foot, or walking in the attitude of attacking an enemy, and for the most part he is naked, having only a mantle hanging from the arm.

IOVI PROPVGNATORI.—On a silver coin of Alexander Severus this legend appears with the type of the god standing with thunderbolt and spear.

Jupiter is often exhibited in the Imperial Series with the surname of *Propugnator*, to denote that the emperors in their contest with the barbarians were defended in battle, as it were, by Jove himself; hence they made sacrifices of congratulation on their own safety, in the temple of the god, according to Gruter.—(Vaillant.)

IVPITER STATOR, or IOVIS STATOR.—Jupiter Stator appears also on foot, naked, resting himself on his spear, and sometimes holding the thunderbolt in his left hand—on silver coins of Gallienus.

Jupiter was denominated *Stator*, either because he restored stability and firmness to an army of the Romans which was fleeing before the Sabines,

or because (as Cicero appears to indicate) all things exist and are established by his beneficence.—Romulus dedicated a temple to Jupiter Stator on the Palatine hill after he had overcome the Sabines. The example here given is from a large brass coin of Antoninus Pius.

IOVI TVTATORI.—This word Tutator, which is derived from *tutari*, to defend or keep safe, Banduri observes :—*Minus Latinum esse plerique volunt*: certain it is that except on the coins of Diocletian and Val. Maximian, it is not easily to be found. Besides which we find him named in coins of Commodus DEFENSOR SALVTISAVG. and SPONSOR SECVRITATIS AVGVSTI.

Amongst the Consular coins, on which the figure or the head of Jupiter is often seen, there is one which has for its type the temple of Jupiter Feretrius (Jovis Feretrius.), in which stands a triumphant warrior, who bears the *spolia opimá*. This figure may be found in *Morell* on the coins of the *Claudia* family, in which Marcellus is represented in the act of carrying into the above-named temple the spoils which he had just captured from the slain king of the Gauls, Viridomarus.—*Jupiter Ammon*, with the horns of a ram on his head, is seen on coins of the Cornuficia, Pinaria, and Papia families, and on medals of Augustus, M. Antony, Trajan, and M. Aurelius.—*Jupiter Serapis*, the Jove of the Egyptians, with the *modius* on his head, appears on a medallion of Antoninus Pius, surrounded by Zodiacal signs, struck at Alexandria.

IVPITER VICTOR.—Jupiter the Victorious —sitting with the image of *Victory* in his right hand, and an eagle near him—is found on coins of Vitellius, of Domitian, of Numerian, of Claudius Gothicus, &c.

Jupiter is named *Victor*, as being regarded the conqueror of all things, according to Livy. His temple was on Mount Palatine. He appears on the coins of Vitellius, in commemoration of that emperor's army having vanquished the forces of Otho at Bebriacum, on the feast day of Jupiter, celebrated at Rome in the Ides of April. (Vaillant, p. 81.)

IOVI VICTORI.—When the emperors represent Jupiter the Victorious on their coins, they either intend to ascribe the glory of their victories to him, or rather to designate themselves under the form and attributes of Jupiter Victor, as though they had conquered the enemy under his auspices.—This legend appears first on a coin of Commodus, and afterwards on those of many other emperors.—Eckhel vii. 108.

On the coins of Gallienus and of Saloninus,

we see Jupiter represented as a child riding on a goat with the inscription IOVI CRESCENTI.—[See Eckhel vii. 33 medallion of Antonine.]—This reverse bears relation to the fable of Jove having been suckled by the goat Amalthæa.

IO. CANTAB.—Jupiter standing with thunbolt and spear. Silver and small brass of Gallienus. Here we have a foreign Jupiter; this medal being dedicated IO*vi* CANTAB*riorum*—to the Jove of the Cantabri, a people of Hispania Tarraconensis.

IOVI CONSERVATORI.—Jupiter sitting or standing, holds a Victory in his right and the hasta in his left. This appears on a first brass of Domitian, and on a silver coin of S. Severus, &c.—And (as Vaillant remarks) it is not to be wondered at, if that Emperor, after so many wars conducted on his part with surpassing valour and military skill, should have performed sacrifice *Jovi Conservatori*, as ascribing his own preservation and success to the help and assistance of the *Optimus Maximus* of the Roman Pantheon; and it is in memory of so many victories that Jupiter himself bears the image of Victory."—(p. 219.)

IOVI EXSVPER.—This legend, with Jupiter

seated, holding a branch in his right hand and a spear in his left, appears on a *large brass* of Commodus.

That this abbreviated word EXSVPER is to be filled up thus—EXSVPER*antissimo*, is shown by that celebrated marble which Spon has published, and on which is read I. O. M. SVMMO. EXSVPERANTISSIMO (to Jupiter the most beneficent, the greatest, the highest, the *all surpassing.*) —Of this Jove the Vienna marble published by Scipio Maffeus speaks more copiously as follows:

SVMMO
SVPERANTISSIMO
DIVINARVM HV
MANARVMQVE
RERVM RECTORI
FATORVMQVE AR
BITRO.

Commodus himself added the title of *Exsuperatorius* to his own, as if he had excelled all other mortals in all things, (according to the explanation of Dio).—See EXVPERATOR.

IOVI FVLGERATORI.—Jupiter hurling a thunderbolt at a Titan: in the exergue PR. upon

a gold coin of Diocletian. The same legend occurs on coins of Claudius Gothicus.

IOVI IVVENI.—Commodus represented as Jupiter with his attributes. At his feet are an

eagle, and an altar with a bas relief, the subject of which is Jupiter launching a thunderbolt against the Titans. Brass medallion of Commodus.

IOVI. OLYM. To Olympian Jove.—A temple of six columns, surmounted by a pediment.

This is considered to represent the temple of Jupiter Olympius, the building of which was commenced at Athens at a very early period, and the completion of which was effected at the common expense of the kings in alliance with the Roman people, by whom it was dedicated to the genius of Augustus.

IOVI PACATORI ORBIS. To Jove the Appeaser of the world.—On a silver coin of Valerianus (given in Banduri) this epigraph appears with Jupiter seated, and an eagle at his feet.

Eckhel observes, "This is a rare inscription, and it is remarkable that the title of the Appeaser of the world (*pacator orbis*) should be assigned to Jupiter at a time (from A.D. 253 to 260 and afterwards) when the whole earth was shaken by a vast movement of all people. But, indeed, it is sufficiently evident elsewhere that the types of coins were often ordered to be struck in conformity with the public desire."

IOVI PRAE. ORBIS.—This inscription appears for the first time on a silver coin of

Pescennius Niger, (edited by Vaillant). Severus, however, immediately afterwards adopted the same dedication in his own coinage. The ancients always believed *Jupiter* to be *Præses Orbis*—the governor of the world—and on this occasion (of contest for the empire between Pescennius and Septimius) the deity was equally acknowledged by each of the two competitors, when the one refused to yield superiority to the other.—[Eckhel v. vii. 155.]

IOVI. TON. To *Jupiter Tonans.*—The

image of the thunderer stands in a temple of six columns, bearing the usual attributes. Augustus, on the occasion of his escape from imminent danger during a storm of thunder and lightning, encountered in his Cantabrian (Spanish) expedition, dedicated a temple in the Capitol of Rome *Jovi Tonanti*, in the year 732.—[Dio. lib. 53.]—The engraving is from a denarius of Augustus.

IOVI VLTORI.—On first and second brass of Alexander Severus, (P.M. TR. P. III. COS. P.P.) statue of Jupiter seated within a temple standing

in a spacious enclosure.—Also on coins of Gallienus this dedication appears with Jupiter and his fulminating attributes. The name of *Ultor* was given to Jove because he was considered to be the avenger of wicked men's impieties.— According to Pliny, the temple, called also the Pantheon, was erected to his honour by Agrippa the kinsman of Augustus. Another temple was also built and consecrated—*Jovi Ultori*—by Alexander Severus, and the type of one of that emperor's large brass is regarded by *Vaillant* as confirmatory of the fact.

IOVI VOT. SVSC. PRO. SAL. CAES. AVG. S.P.Q.R., with a crown of oak leaves.— *Jovi Votis Susceptis Pro Salute Cæsaris Augusti Senatus Populusque Romanus.—Gold* of Augustus.

This and the coin inscribed PRO VALETVDINE. CAESARIS are considered to bear reference to the dangerous illness with which Augustus was

attacked when at Tarragona, in Spain, and when public vows were made for his restoration and safe return.

IOVIS CVSTOS.— Jupiter standing and holding the *hasta pura* and a patera : at his feet is a small lighted altar. On a denarius of Titus.

I. O. M.—*Jovi Optimo Maximo*, under which name *Jupiter Capitolinus* is always understood.

I. O. M. D. *Jovi Optimo Maximo Dicatum.*— Dedicated to Jupiter the most excellent and the greatest of deities.

I. O. MAX. CAPITO- LINUS. Statue of Jupiter seated in a temple.—*Silver of Vitellius.*—See Eckhel v. 6 p. 312.

I. O. M. ET VICT. CONSER. DD. NN.— On second brass of Licinius and his son appears this legend, with the type of Jupiter standing crowned by Victory.

I. O. M. SPONSOR*ori* SEC*uritatis* AVG*usti.* —IOVI. DEFENS. SALVTIS. AVG.—On silver coins of Commodus these inscriptions respectively appear, in which Jupiter is recognised as the *sponsor or watching over the security*, and as the *defender of the health* of the emperor.

I. O. M. S. P. Q. R. V. S. PR. S. IMP. CAES. QVOD. PER. EV. R. P. IN. AMP. ATQ. TRAN. S. E.—*Jovi Optimo Maximo, Senatus Populusque Romanus vota suscepta pro salute Imperatoris Caesaris quod per eum Res Publica in ampliore atque tranquilliore statu est.* [struck about 738 v.c.]—The Senate and the Roman people have addressed vows to the best and greatest Jupiter for the preservation of the Emperor Cæsar, in acknowledgment of his having re-established the republic in a better, richer, happier, and more tranquil condition.— The above long and remarkable inscription, within an oaken or civic crown, is stamped on the reverse of gold and silver coins of Augustus, in relation to which Suetonius (vita c. 23) says,—" *Vovit et magnos ludos Jovi Optimo Maximo, si res-publica in meliorem statum vertisset, quod factum Cimbrico Marsicoque bello erat."*

Jupiter Feretrius.—See FERETRIUS—CLAVDIA family.

Jupiter Axur.—See AXVR, or Vijovis.

Jupiter Capitolinus.—A large brass of Vespasian exhibits the *façade* of a temple of six columns, the exterior and pediment of which are ornamented with statues.—In the inside the figure of Jupiter is seated, having Minerva on his right and Juno on his left hand. In the exergue is s.c.

The temple of Jupiter in the Capitol at Rome, burnt during the disorders which prevailed in that city at the close of Vitellius' reign, was rebuilt with costly magnificence by Vespasian.—It was the Jews who contributed the most largely towards the expenses of this grand undertaking; for whereas being by their own laws obliged to furnish each two drachmas towards the maintenance of the temple at Jerusalem, they received the emperor's order to surrender this money to the proposed purpose of rebuilding the temple of Jupiter. The statues of the three divinities were placed in the same manner that they are represented on the medal, in which we see Minerva occupying the place of precedence to Juno. It was certainly the custom at Rome to render to Pallas the first honours after Jupiter. Thus Horace, speaking of the god, says—*" Proximos illi tamen occupavit Pallas honores."* On a brass medallion of Trajan, the three divinities of

the Capitol are represented standing, Minerva being on the right of Jupiter.

For the same reason there appear on a medal of Antoninus Pius the birds consecrated to these three deities, in the order above described, viz., the eagle in the middle, the owl of Minerva on the right, and the peacock of Juno on the left.

IOVIO ET HERCVLIO.—On a gold medal-

lion of Diocletian, edited by Banduri, that emperor appears, with his colleague Maximianus, sacrificing at a tripod to Jupiter and Hercules.

Jupiter was the favourite deity of, and his name was assumed by, Diocletian, as *Hercules* was, in like manner, by Maximian.—See HERCVLIO.

IO. IO. TRIVMP. IO. SAT. IO.—Eckhel in his Section II. on Pseudo-Moneta, notices two small brass *tesseræ*, one with the former, the other with the latter inscription.—The *Io Triumphe* doubtless relates to the joyous acclamation which welcomed the victorious charioteer at the circus.—The other epigraph is explained by Seguin, who reads it IO. SAT*urnalia* IO.—(See Eckhel, vol. 8, p. 316.)

Jovianus (Flavius Claudius), born in Pannonia (A.D. 331) son of Varronianus, an illustrious nobleman of that province. He distinguished himself in the war against the Persians, during the reign of Julian the Apostate, at whose death he was elected emperor by the army. Compelled by necessity, he agreed to conditions of peace with Sapor, far from honourable to the Romans. Though luxurious and even dissolute in his manners, Jovian possessed many excellent qualities; he was watchful over the tranquillity and zealous for the happiness of his subjects. He recalled the bishops and priests whom Julian had banished, and was judiciously promoting the restoration of Christianity through the empire, when he died suddenly in Bithynia, A.D. 364, after reigning little more than four months.—His style is D.N. FL. C. IOVIANVS. P. F. AVG.; or D.N. IOVIANVS P.F. AVG.

His *brass* coins, of which an example is here given, are scarce; silver rare; gold very rare.

Jovinus, the most noble of the Gallic chiefs, in the reign of Honorius, assumed the imperial purple in the Gaulish provinces, A.D. 411. He was, however, taken prisoner by Adolphus, King of the Goths, and put to death A.D. 413. On his coins, which are all of extreme rarity, he is styled D.N. IOVINVS P. F. AVG.

I. S. *Juno Sispita.*—I. S. *Jussu Senatus.*

ISIS, the most ancient and most celebrated of the Egyptian divinities. Her husband was Osiris, the symbol of the sun and of the source of all fertility. Amongst the various foreign deities whose worship became in time introduced among the Romans, *Isis* appears to have been one of the greatest favourites of that superstitious people. In Rome itself she had several temples, the ceremonies in which, whatever might be their mystic meaning, real or pretended, teemed with abominations. The festivals of this goddess were indeed so frequently marked by indecencies that decrees were passed for their abolition, but they were as often re-established. In the year of Rome 711, Augustus and Antony pandered to the depraved and dissolute taste of their age by dedicating to Isis a temple in the centre of the city. Even Tiberius, however, found it needful to close it. But the prohibition of her worship was not of long duration. Domitian, Commodus, and Caracalla became her priests. And some of the empresses are represented under the figure of Isis.—On a coin of the *Cæcilia* family, edited by Morell, (p. 52 tab. iii.) Isis appears standing: she has the head of a lion, ornamented with the *lotus flower*; she is clothed in the Egyptian fashion, and holds in her right hand the sistrum, and her left hand is in the act of pressing the right breast. The legend to this type is METEL*lus*. PIVS. SCIPIO IMP*erator*. Near the head of this figure are the letters G. T. A. which are interpreted by some to mean *Genius Tutelaris Africæ*, (by others *Aegypti*), Isis being called the tutelary genius of Africa.—We also see the figure of this goddess on coins of Commodus and Caracalla, with the sistrum and situla (or bucket) and sometimes carried by a dog.—See *Osiris*.

ISIS FARIA.—These words, inscribed round the beardless head of Julian II., on third brass of that emperor, have reference to *Isis* as protectress of the *Pharos* islet at Alexandria. Banduri quotes *Statius* to show that Isis was the "*regina Phari, numenque Orientis anheli.*" Respecting the *sistrum* and the *situla* in the hands of Isis, Servius, as quoted by Eckhel, says, "Isis is the genius of Egypt, who by the movement of her *sistrum*, which she carries in her right hand, signifies the access and recess (or the rising and falling) of the Nile; and by the *situla*, or bucket, which she holds in her left hand, she shows the filling of all *lacunæ*, that is of all ditches and furrows into which the stagnant water of the Nile is received."—See *Pharia Isis*.

Isis and Serapis.—Busts of Isis and Serapis, face to face: *her* head ornamented with the *lotus*: *his*, with the modius. DEVS SARA.—*Rev.* VOTA PVBLICA. Isis suckling Horus. Small brass struck under Julian the Apostate.

Isis suckling Horus.—This Egyptian goddess seated in a chair before an altar, with the lotus flower upon her head; in her lap a naked infant whom she is suckling, and who has also a flower upon his head: in the field L. B.

Large brass of Antoninus Pius, struck in Egypt.

I. S. M. R. (*Juno Sispita*, or *Sospita*, *Magna Regina.*)—On a coin of the Thoria family, we find these abbreviations, accompanied with the head of the Lanuvinian Juno, covered with the goatskin, and even the leg and hoof of the goat are seen below the neck of the bust.—See *Juno*.

IT. *Iterum*. COS. DES. IT. *Consul Designatus Iterum*.—Consul Elect for the second time.

ITALIA. Italy.—This most noble and most interesting of European countries was thus called, from Italus, ancient King of the Œnotrians, or, as Thucydides says, of the Sicilians, previous to which it bore the name of *Hesperia*, from Hesperius, brother of Atlas, King of Mauritania.—*Latium* and *Ausonia* are also names of certain parts of the same celebrated and beautiful region, which has for its natural boundaries the Alps and the Mediterranean Sea.

ITALIA.—*Italy's* fertility and power over the rest of the world are expressed—the one by the cornucopiæ and the ears of corn, the other by the sceptre, on coins of Vespasian, Titus, Hadrian, &c. First brass medals of Antoninus Pius and also of Commodus represent ITALIA under the figure of a matronly female (the latter with head turrited) sitting on a globe and holding the *hasta pura* and *cornucopiæ*.

ITALIA.—A woman standing with spear in her right and cornucopiæ in the left hand. It is thus that Italy and its personified genius are stamped on silver coins of Hadrian, whose arrival in that country (ADVENTVS AVG. ITALIAE) is also marked on others of his medals.—A woman with cornucopiæ, holding a patera on a lighted altar, on the other side of which stands the emperor: ADVENTVI AVG. ITALIAE: on the gold, silver, and brass of Hadrian.

Hadrian's first coming to Italy is dated in the year of Rome 871, and this advent was often commemorated; as often, indeed, as he returned to the capital of his empire from his accustomed peregrinations. But it also appears that the mistress of the world received many benefits and embellishments from him. He remitted her fiscal debt; an indulgence which greatly relieved Italy.—In an increased spirit of liberality he remitted to her moreover the *aurum coronarium* (see the words); and he augmented the funds which Trajan had destined for the maintenance (alimenta) of a certain number of the Italian youth of both sexes. He likewise bore annual honorary office in the magistracy of many cities of Italy; thus establishing, beyond the mere claim of imperial flattery, his pretension to be called RESTITVTOR ITALIAE, as he is styled on a fine large brass medal, the reverse of which exhibits the emperor who, standing, raises with his hand a woman bending the knee to him, and holding the cornucopiæ.

ITALIA REST*ituta*. S. P. Q. R. OPTIMO PRINCIPI.—The Emperor, in the toga, with sceptre surmounted by an eagle in his left hand, stands holding out his right hand to a female wearing a turreted crown, who kneels before him, accompanied by several children, who hold up their hands to "the best of princes."—On second brass of Trajan.

ITALIC. *Italicum. Italica.*

Italica was a city of Hispania Bætica (Andalusia), and a Roman *municipium*, situate on the river Bætis (Guadalquiver): it is now called *Sevilla la Vieja* (Old Seville). An inscription of Gruter's refers to this place under the title of COLONIA ITALICENSIS IN PROV. BAETICA. It was in the neighbourhood of Hispalis, the native country of Trajan, Hadrian, and Theodosius senior.—In the year V.C. 654, when Scipio Africanus, after bringing the affairs of Rome with the Carthaginians in Spain to a pacific settlement, contemplated his return to Italy, he allocated all the Italian soldiers, disabled by wounds and fatigue, in one town, which, from their native country, he called *Italica*. This is what *Appianus Alexandrinus* states in his *Bellum Hispan.* p. 463.—The town had afterwards the title of *municipium* bestowed upon it; but as the number of its citizens became greatly diminished by the wars, it seems to have been re-peopled with legionary veterans sent thither by Augustus. Hence its coins, dedicated to Augustus, Livia, Drusus, and Germanicus, bear the inscription MVN. ITAL. or MVNIC. or MVNICIP. ITALIC.
—It here deserves remark that the privilege of coinage granted to the Spanish municipium by Augustus, is noted on all its coins by the abbreviated word PER. or PERM. AVG. *Permissu Augusti.*

The following are among the types of this Roman *municipium*:—

Altar.—On a second brass struck by the *Italicenses*, in memory of Augustus, (whose radiated head appears on its obverse with legend of DIVVS AVGVSTVS PATER.) an altar is represented on which is the word PROVIDENT. The rest of the legend is MVN. ITAL. PERM. AVG.—*Municipium Italica, or Italicense, Permissu Augusti.*

After the example of many cities who, after the apotheosis of Augustus, built temples to his honour, the people of this *municipium* placed on their coins a representation of the altar, which they erected to the Providence of their benefactor—as if in his deified capacity he still, as whilst living, happily administered the affairs and watched over the interests of the Roman world.

A similar reverse appears on a second brass of the same colony, struck in honour of Tiberius, with the sole difference of the words PROVIDENTIAE AUGUSTI being engraved on the side, instead of at the foot, of the altar. The Providence which the coin is meant to commemorate is, in the opinion of Vaillant, *not* that of Tiberius, but of his imperial predecessor DIVVS AVGVSTVS PATER—the august Father, whom by the ceremony of *consecration* Rome had placed among her Gods!

Woman seated, holding in her right hand a patera, in her left the *hasta*. This type appears on the reverse of a rare and elegant coin dedicated to Julia (Livia), called in the legend AVGVSTA.—The obverse presents a female head (that of Livia herself) surrounded by the inscription of MVNIC. ITALICA. PERM. AVG.— [The seated female figure seems to be the statue of Livia, which is often found represented on coins struck by order of the Senate, in reference to statues raised to her honour.—The colony of Italica, mindful of the privileges bestowed on them by Augustus, and amongst others the right of coinage, placed the statue here depicted, in token of their congratulation, that Livia his wife had been adopted into the Julia family.] —Vaillant, i. 51.

Legionary Eagle and Vexillum, a second brass, noticed as elegant and very rare, by Vaillant (i. 92), bears on its obverse DRVSVS CAESAR TI. AVG. F. with the bare head of Drusus. And on its reverse appear the *aquila et vexillum* of a legion.—[The Duumviri who struck the above coin in honour of Drusus obviously designed by this type to indicate the military origin of the municipium.—There is the same reverse and the same legend (MVNIC. ITALIC. PER. AVG.) on a second brass of Germanicus. Thus the veterans of Italica pay a compliment to each of the two young Cæsars: to Drusus, indeed, because, as the son of Tiberius by natural right, he stood apparent heir to the empire; and to Germanicus, because being adopted by Tiberius at the desire of Augustus, he became the associate of Drusus.]

There are pieces which on one side bear the name of *Italica,* and on the other that of *Bilbilis.* This circumstance is noticed in Hardouin's Oper. Selec.—M. Hennin also mentions it, in the nomenclature of his Manuel, as indicating that an alliance subsisted between the two cities.

Itia, a family of unknown rank; its denarii of a single type; rare, but devoid of both numismatic and historical interest. Winged head of Minerva: X.—*Rev.* L. IT*ius.* The Dioscuri on horseback.—In the exergue ROMA.

Itinera Hadriani. Hadrian's travels.—See Rasche. IT.—1016.

IV. *Juventutis.*—Titus and Domitianus are called PRIN*cipes* IV*ventutis*.

Juba I., son of Hiempsalis, and King of Numidia, in the time of Sylla and Pompey, died in the year of Rome 708, 46 years before Christ, A silver coin of this prince bears on one side the *Latin* legend of REX IVBA, with the head of the king, bearded, and curiously curled hair on his head ; on his shoulder a sceptre, the sign of royal majesty. On the reverse are unknown characters, supposed to be Numidian, and a temple of eight columns, with a flight of steps to the portal.

IVD. Judaea.—*Judaea*, a region of Syria, comprising the whole country of Palestine, but more strictly speaking that part inhabited by the two tribes of Judah and Benjamin. It was conquered by Pompey, and given at first to Herod, then to Antiochus, next to Philip, and to a second Herod, and after their time it became a province of the Roman empire. But, revolting against the tyranny and exactions of Gessius Florus, the people of Judaea waged a long and bloody war with the Romans. Flavius Vespasianus was, however, at length sent by Nero against them with a vast army, and brought them again into complete subjection to the Roman power. He took and entirely destroyed Jerusalem, and since that time the Jews, driven from their country, have been scattered as wanderers over the face of the earth.

It was under Vespasian that those medals were first struck which record the victories gained by the Romans over the Jews. They bear the inscription of IVDAEA, IVDAEA CAPTA, IVDAEA DEVICTA, DE IVDAEIS, and their types are most interestingly allusive to the conquest of Judaea, and to that awfully destructive war which ended in making "Jerusalem a heap of stones."—There are coins of Titus, bearing the same character.— On a large brass of Hadrian (in the Farnese Museum), with the legend IVDAEA, the vanquished country is personified by a woman bending the knee before that Emperor. She is accompanied by three children bearing palms, and who, according to Winkleman, are intended to represent the three divisions of the province, namely, Judæa, Galilæa, and Petræa. Another coin of the same emperor represents a togated

figure (Hadrian himself), standing opposite a

female clothed in the stola, and holding a patera over an altar, by the side of which is a victim for sacrifice. By the side of the woman stands a child ; and two children, bearing palms, approach the emperor : in the exergue is inscribed IVDAEA.

On a very rare first brass of Vespasian, bearing the usual mark of Senatorial authority, but without legend, the Emperor, with radiated head, is represented standing, with his right foot placed on a ship's prow, or on a helmet ; he holds the hasta in his left, and a *victoriola* in his right hand ; before his feet an old man is kneeling, behind whom, under a palm tree, stands a woman in a tunic, raising her hands towards the Prince, in the act of supplication.—

There is a large bronze coin, which Vaillant gives as struck under Titus, and which agrees with it in type except that the head of the Emperor is helmeted. This medal is described to bear the legend of IVDAEA.

IVDAEA CAPTA. S C.—On the well-known coin of Vespasian, in large *brass*, Judaea appears under the figure of a woman, clothed in a tunic, with short sleeves : she sits, in the attitude of

extreme sorrow, at the foot of a palm, which tree is peculiarly the growth of Palestine : behind her stands the Emperor habited in military vestments, holding a spear in his right and the parazonium in his left hand ; and with a buckler or a helmet under his left foot.—A medal in the same metal, and of the same module, struck under Titus, exhibits the same legend and a similar type.

This coin presents the emblem of Judaea, whose inhabitants, not easily to be ruled over, were compelled at length to crouch under the Roman yoke, in consequence of the wise and skilful measures taken by Vespasian, and especially after the taking of Jerusalem by Titus, in the 70th year of the Christian era.

IVDAEA CAPTA.—On another first brass of Vespasian a female sits weeping beside a palm, close to which tree a man stands with his hands tied behind him.—Havercamp gives a first brass of Titus, with a slight variation in the grouping of the figures, and with a helmet and buckler on the ground before the captive.— The legend of this fine medal is inscribed IVD. CAP. S. C. in the field.

IVDEA DEVICTA.—This legend is read on coins of Vespasian and Titus. The type is a woman standing in a sorrowful posture under a palm tree.—Mionnet and Akerman give examples of this in all the three metals.

DE IVDAEIS. A Trophy.—On gold coins of Vespasian.

FISCI. IVDAICI. CALVMNIA. SVBLATA. S. C. A Palm Tree.—First brass of Nerva.

The type of this historically interesting reverse is, as well on ancient Jewish as on Roman coins, symbolical of Judæa, the palm being indigenous to the country.—It is engraved in Akerman's *Descr. Catalogue;* in Havercamp's *Cabinet de Christine;* in Kolb's *Traité Elémentaire.*

In explanation of the unique and very remarkable legend attached to this reverse, the observations made by the author of *Doctrina* are hereto subjoined as worthy of the coin's historical interest, and of his own learned sagacity:—From the earliest period of the Jewish Commonwealth, the Jews were enjoined to pay the half of a *ficlus*, or two drachmæ, for the service of the altar, as may be seen from the Book of Exodus (ch. xxx. 12, 13.) This money, in after times, went towards the expenses of the Temple, being collected, not only from the inhabitants of Judæa, but from all Jews, in whatever part of the world residing: and this private system of taxation was sometimes prohibited by the Romans, of which I have given instances, under the coins of Vespasian (p. 327), and sometimes sanctioned by an edict, an example of which, issued in the name of Augustus, has been given by Philo Judæus (*de Legat. ad Caium*, p. 592); and several by Josephus (*Antiq.* xvi. c. 6.) The same Philo frequently throughout his treatise calls this money ἀπαρχαι, *first-fruits (or offerings);* and, consequently, it was of the same nature as those gifts, which colonies were formerly in the habit of presenting every year to their mother-countries, to support the worship of the national deities; just as Polybius has applied the term ἀπαρχαι to the contribution which the Carthaginians used to send to their mother-country Tyre. Now it is certain, that the Holy City was regarded by the Jews of every clime, as their mother-country. But the *half ficlus* alluded to above was the well-known didrachm, which our Saviour paid for himself and Peter with the *stater* miraculously found in the mouth of the fish, as recorded in the Gospel of St. Matthew (ch. xvii. 24.) When Jerusalem and its Temple were overthrown by Vespasian in the year v.c. 823 (A.D. 69), the Jews, wheresoever residing, were ordered to continue the payment of this didrachm, not, however, to be applied to their own religious uses, but to the worship of Jupiter Capitolinus, as is expressly stated by Josephus (*de Bell. Jud.* vii. c. 6, § 6) and Dio (lxvi. § 7.)—Suetonius relates (*Domit.* c. 12) that Domitian "rigorously exacted the Jewish tax, under which were charged all, who either clandestinely lived after the Jewish fashion within the walls of Rome, or who, concealing their origin, had evaded the payment of the tribute imposed upon their nation."—Spanheim, who has proved his learning and eloquence in his explanation of this coin (vol. ii. p 500), argues from the terms of the legend itself, that it was not intended to convey the notion, that the Jewish tax or didrachm, as many have supposed, was abolished by Nerva, but simply that the *calumnia (system of false accusation)* was done away *(sublata);* that is to say, exemption from the tax in question was thenceforth secured to all who did not admit themselves to be Jews, and their names no longer entered on the fiscal lists as belonging to that nation. For the iniquitous inquisitorial system pursued by Domitian towards those who were suspected of Judaism, is circumstantially recorded by Suetonius in the passage above referred to.

In confirmation of this mode of interpreting the legend in question, Eckhel adduces an admirable example:—According to Eusebius *(in vitâ Const.* ii. c. 45), Constantine the Great, with a view to repress the excesses of idolatry, drew up two laws, one of which was called "a law to suppress the abominations so long perpetrated by idolatry throughout the cities and districts."—Not a few individuals have taken these words to mean that Constantine wished, by this law, to put a stop to all the rites of Paganism; a notion entirely at variance with history.—Eusebius merely says that such *abominations* (τὰ μύσαρα) were forbidden by the Emperor, as the ancient superstition cherished, especially beyond the walls of the city. That the Jews were not afterwards exempt from the payment of the didrachm, is shewn from an epistle of Origen to Africanus, in which the expression occurs:—" Since even at the present time the Jews still pay the didrachm to them (the Romans.")—It is sufficiently evident that the affair of the Jews had become one of considerable moment *(rem Judaicum magni fuisse momenti)* even within the walls of Rome; and that the people generally suffered so much indiscriminate severity, on account of suspected Judaism, that, when at last the evil was removed, the Senate considered the event of sufficient importance to be perpetuated on coins. —Eckhel, vi. 405.

IVDAICVS.—Although it was a frequent custom with Roman conquerors to assume the appellation of a vanquished people as a surname of honour, as *Dacicus, Parthicus, Britannicus,* &c., yet neither Vespasian nor Titus was called *Judaicus,* so greatly were the name and the religion of the Jews held in detestation.

Jugurtha, a King of Numidia, grandson of Masinissa, delivered by his father-in-law *Bocchus,* King of Gætulia to Sylla, when the latter was lieutenant to Marius.—See *Cornelia* family.

IVL. *Julia.*—A colony is thus called as having been planted by Julius Cæsar, as the name indicates, or as having received benefits from him. Such for the most part relates to Africa.—The epigraph COL. IVL*iæ*, or in reversed order AVG*ustæ* IVL, when it occurs on colonial coins is considered to signify a colony established in the first instance by Julius Cæsar, and after augmented by Augustus.

IVLI. *Julii.*—DIVI IVLI. The customary epigraph on coins of Julius Cæsar struck after his death.

Julia Augusta.—From an ancient inscription, edited by Mark Velserus, *Julia Augusta,* it appears, is the *Augusta Vindelicorum,* now Augsburg, in Germany. To this splendid colony of the Rhætian province, reference is made on coins of Augustus, Nerva, and Gordianus Pius, under the name of COL. IVL. AVG.

Julia (Traducta), a colony of Hispania Bætica (now Algesiras).—See *Traducta.*

Julia.—This illustrious family is that of Julius Cæsar.—The name *Julius* is derived from *Iulus,* whom some believe to be Ascanius, the son of Æneas; and others, the son of that Ascanius. In claiming to be descended from this stock, Julius Cæsar prided himself on his origin from the Goddess of Beauty, and hence the images of Venus, and of Æneas carrying Anchises, which are often found on his denarii. Be the question of pedigree decided as it may, it appears that after the destruction of Alba, the family came to Rome, and eventually furnished twelve personages, honoured as *Imperatores,* with the highest offices and dignities of the Roman Commonwealth. According to Eckhel it is patrician in the *Cæsarian* branch, and uncertain in that of *Bursio,* the only two surnames which occur on its coins.—There are seventy-five varieties, of which the rarest type is a silver one, bearing on its obverse a youthful head, ornamented with wings, and having hair hanging down in ringlets, behind which is a trident and two arrows (in others, a scorpion),—the reverse is inscribed L. IVLI. BVRSIO (in another EX A. P.), with Victory in a quadriga holding a crown. The head which presents itself on the obverse of this denarius is of an unusual kind, and there has been much ado amongst antiquarians to find out its meaning. Ursin and Vaillant take it to be that of Mercury, whilst Havercamp boldly calls it the head of "Triumph." But it is evidently not a male but a female head, and, as the judicious Eckhel observes, it is scarcely worth while to enter into a new field of conjectures about what nymph or goddess (of the sea or sky) it is meant to depicture. And, even after the prolix guessings of Vaillant and Havercamp, it is perhaps better openly to confess ignorance as to who *Bursio* is, to whom these medals belong.

Those denarii of the Julia family with the elephant trampling on a serpent, and Pontifical instruments on the reverse; also with the head of Venus, and Æneas bearing the palladium in his hand and his father on his shoulders, are common enough. The name of this family is also found on coins struck by the mint masters of the great Julius.—See CAESAR—DICT.

Julia is a name frequently found given on coins to the wives of Emperors, and in several instances to their daughters and mothers.— *Livia,* fourth wife of Augustus, assumed it when by adoption she had passed into the *Julia* family. We find also medals of *Julia Agrippina, senior,* mother of Caligula; *Julia,* mother of Caius and Lucius, by Agrippa; *Julia,* sister of Caligula; *Julia,* daughter of Titus; *Julia Agrippina, junior,* second wife of Claudius, and mother of Nero; *Julia Aquilia Severa,* second wife of Elagabalus; *Julia Paula,* first wife of Elagabalus; *Julia Domna,* second wife of Severus; *Julia Maesa,* grandmother of Elagabalus and Alexander Severus; *Julia Mamaea,* mother of Alexander Severus; *Julia Paulina,* wife of Maximinus.

IVL (or IVLIA) AQVIL. (or AQVILIA)
SEV. (or SEVERA.) AVGusta. Julia Aquilia
Severa.—See *Aquilia Severa.*

IVLIA AVGVSTA GENETRIX ORBIS.—
See *Livia.*

Julia Augusta, the wife of Severus, is styled
Julia Augusta, or *Julia Domna Aug.*; or *Julia
Pia Augusta*; or *Julia Pia Felix Aug.* as upon
the large brass of which an example is subjoined.—See *Domna.*

Julia Cornelia Paula, said to be the
daughter of Paulus, prætorian prefect, was the
first wife of Elagabalus having been married
to that odious miscreant A.D. 219.—Divorced
shortly after her nuptials, on some pretence of
bodily defect, she died in retirement.—Her gold
coins are of the highest rarity, *silver* by no
means scarce, first and second *brass* very rare.—
Her name of *Cornelia,* to which illustrious
family she belonged, is omitted on her Latin
medals, on which she is styled only IVLIA PAVLA
AVGVSTA.

Julia Maesa, the grandmother of two Emperors, Elagabalus and Alexander Severus, is
honoured on medals with the title of *Augusta.*
—See *Maesa.*

Julia Mamaea, daughter of the *Julia Maesa*
and mother of Alexander Severus, bears the title
of *Augusta* on her coins.—See *Mamaea.*

Julia Soaemias, mother of Elagabalus.—See
Soaemias.

Julia, the daughter of *Titus,* by Furnilla,
his second wife; she was a woman of great
beauty, at first refused the infamous addresses
of her uncle Domitian, married Sabinus her
cousin german, afterwards became the mistress
of her father's brother and successor, who
caused her husband to be put to death, and
lived in open concubinage with her. Julia
abandoning herself to debauchery, died in the
attempt to destroy the fruits of her incestuous
connection. She was nevertheless placed by
apotheosis amongst the deities, and is called
DIVA on her coins, which in *brass* and *silver*
are rare, and in *gold* of the highest rarity.
On medals struck during her life-time, she is
styled IVLIA AVGVSTA TITI AVGVSTI
Filia; also IVLIA IMP. T. AVG. F. AVGVSTA.
(The August Julia, daughter of the August
Titus). The reverse of one of her gold coins bears
the legend of DIVI TITI FILIA, with a peacock; and on a silver coin of hers appears the
word VESTA, and that Goddess seated, whence
it would seem that she wished at least to be
thought chaste; and this incident agrees with
the attempt to conceal her pregnancy, to which
she fell a victim.

On a large brass of this princess, who died
in Domitian's reign, we see her consecration

recorded, and the honours of deification paid to
her memory at the will of her profligate uncle,
by an obsequious senate, in the following dedicatory inscription, DIVAE IVLIAE AVG. DIV. TITI
F., accompanied with the type of the carpentum,
or funeral car, drawn by mules. There is no
portrait; but the emperor's titles, and the mark
of COS. XVI., shew the direct influence under
which the coin was struck *Senatus Consultu;*
and in the name of that body and of the Roman
people (S.P.Q.R.) On a silver medal the image
of DIVA IVLIA appears on a car, drawn by
elephants.

IVLIANVS. *(Didius Severus.)*—The father
of this emperor was Petronius Didius Severus,
his mother Clara Aemilia, and his paternal
grandfather Insuber Mediolanensis. *(Spartian.)*—
According to the calculation of Dio, whom, in
the disagreement of other writers, we prefer to
follow, as he lived at Rome at that period,
Didius Julianus was born A.V.C. 886, at the end
of January. Being advanced in due time to a
share in public business, he defeated, in the
reign of Marcus, the Cauci, a people living on
the river Albis, and gained his Consulate; after
which he succeeded Pertinax in the government
of Africa. *(Spartian.)*—Pertinax, having been
put to death by the Prætorian guards, and those
soldiers having fortified their camp, and from
its walls proclaimed the empire open to the
highest bidder, though all men of standing and
integrity strove to avert such a disgrace, Julian
listened to the instigation of his party, and
taking his stand outside the trenches, blushed
not to bid against Flavius Sulpicianus, the
father-in-law of Pertinax, who within the camp

offered his own price for the empire.—Julian, however, made the most liberal offers, scaling ladders were let down from the walls, and he was received into the camp, acknowledged Emperor, and, escorted by a guard of Prætorians, was conducted to the Senate-house. But the people, irritated no less by the undeserved fate of Pertinax, than by the recent disgraceful sale of the empire, attacked the newly-created Emperor first with abuse, and then with a shower of stones; nor would they be satisfied without demanding as their Emperor, Pescennius Niger, the newly appointed Governor of Syria. On learning this position of affairs, Pescennius allowed himself to be declared Emperor by his friends, but neglecting to follow up his advantage, Severus, the Præfect of Pannonia, in obedience to the wish of a party, put in his claim to the honours of the sovereignty, and taking all his measures, made a hasty journey to Italy. (Eckhel, vii. 148, *Didius Julian.*)—Intelligence of this movement being received at Rome, Julianus gave orders that Severus should be declared by the Senate as the enemy of his country; but he found the army less prepared than he expected to act on the defensive; and in a state of disaffection, partly because he was dilatory in the liquidation of the sum he had agreed upon in the purchase of the empire, and partly because, from being long habituated to sloth and inactivity, they wanted the courage to cope with the hardy soldiers of Severus.—Severus meanwhile threatening the city, Julian is driven to adopt milder counsels, and induces the Senate to allow him a participation in the sovereignty; but a universal turn of feeling in favour of Severus having taken place, he is deserted by all, and put to death. His body was restored by Severus to his wife Scantilla for burial, and deposited in the tomb of his great-grandfather on the Via Lavicana.—According to Dio, he lived sixty years, four months, and four days, and reigned sixty-six days. It is generally admitted that he was a distinguished lawyer. Spartian speaks of his economical habits, his gentle manners, and other virtues; but Dio, his contemporary, and also Herodian, assert that his vices were numerous.—Eckhel, vii. 147.

Julianus (Flavius Claudius), usually called *Julian the Apostate,* because he, at an early age, abandoned the Christian faith, and, as soon as he had the power, restored the worship of idols, which he pretended to reform, but which he in fact enforced in all the

bigoted extravagance and blind absurdity of Pagan superstition. He was the son of Julius Constantius, nephew of Constantine the Great, and brother of Constantius Gallus, born at Constantinople A.D. 331. He was created Cæsar

A.D. 355, and married Helena, sister of Constantius II. The government of Gaul, Spain, and Britain was committed to his charge. He repulsed the Germans from Gaul, and established himself at *Lutetiæ,* now Paris, in 358. Proclaimed Emperor by the troops in 360; the death of Constantius soon after left him sole master of the empire.—Julian was a great general —a man of learning—a fine writer—possessing many qualities of a wise, energetic, and excellent prince; but in matters of religion one of the weakest, most fantastic, and mischievous of mankind. This declared and inveterate enemy of Christianity made war upon Persia, with decided success; but was slain in an engagement on the banks of the Tigris, at the age of thirty-one, A.D. 362, in the fourth year of his reign. His second and third *brass* coins are, with certain exceptions, common; his silver of the usual size, are by no means scarce; but his *gold* are rare.—On these he is styled D. N. IVLIANVS NOB. CAES.—IMP. FL. CL. JVLIANVS PERP. or P.F. AVG.

"The Cæsars" of Julian, a work which that Emperor wrote in Greek, is a remarkable proof no less of his scholarship than of his talent for raillery and satire. The translation of that extraordinary production by *Ezech. Spanheim,* illustrated by the most learned remarks, mythological, historical, and numismatical, enriched by a profusion of medals and other ancient monuments, is one of the most interesting as well as instructive volumes which can be perused by the student of the medallic science.

Julian is noted, by *Ammianus* his pagan admirer, but by no means indiscriminate panegyrist, for having made himself very conspicuous in wearing a long and bushy beard, which amongst the courtiers of Constantius procured for him the derisive appellation of a goat *(capellam non hominem).* In confirmation of this alleged peculiarity we find him on many of his coins "bearded like a pard :" as Cæsar he appears with naked head; but as Emperor he wears a diadem ornamented with precious stones.

Under the reign of Julian coins were struck, which Banduri exhibits, and which Eckhel comments upon, inscribed DEO SERAPIDI (see the words), and VOTA PUBLICA, shewing that this philosophic contemner of the Christian mysteries was not ashamed to stamp his imperial coinage with representations of Serapis, Isis, and Anubis, and to revive the monstrous Egyptian idolatry.

Julianus (Marcus Aurelianus), an usurper of the imperial purple at the period of Numerianus's death, from which time (A.D. 284) Pannonia acknowledged his claim and submitted to his government, until defeated and slain in a battle with Carinus, near Verona, in the following year.—There are gold and brass coins of this "tyrant," all of extreme rarity, and on which he is styled IMP. C. M. AVR. IVLIANVS P. F. AVG.

Julius (C.) Cæsar.—See Caius Julius Cæsar.

IVN. *Junior.*—*Augusti* reigning together, but with unequal authority, were called *majores* and *seniores*, or *minores* and *juniores.* Thus *Commodus*, advanced by his father, M. Aurelius, from the Cæsarship to the title of *Augustus*, is called on one of his coins IVN. AVG., or *Junior Augustus.*—In like manner *Galerius Maximianus*, in contradistinction to his father-in-law, Diocletian, is called IVN. AVG.—We find also Constantinus IVN., and Constantius IVN., &c.

IVNI. *Junianus.*—P. CRAS. IVNI. LEG. PROPR. *Publius Crassus Junianus Legatus Propraetor*, that is to say, of Metellus Scipio in Africa.— See *Cæcilia* family.

Junia, this celebrated Roman family was patrician under the kings, but, as it appears from coins, was regarded as plebeian under the consular government. The surnames are *Brutus*, *Silanus*, and perhaps *Libo*. It took its name from Junius, the companion of Æneas, from whom, as *Dion Halic.* writes, this family derived its origin. It took the cognomen of *Brutus* on account of the idiotic folly which, through fear of Tarquin, was feigned by *Lucius Junius*, previous to the overthrow of the monarchy, as Plutarch informs us.—Of this renowned avenger of his country's liberty upon a proud tyrant and his licentious sons, there are no coins extant of contemporaneous date; but in honour of the man who was the first consul, with his colleague Collatinus, after the expulsion of the Tarquins, the head of Lucius Junius, with the inscription BRVTVS, has been placed on the obverse of a denarius belonging to the *Servilia* family, which bears on its obverse the naked head of Servilius AHALA.

Of the name of *Brutus* there are also two individuals recorded on the coins of the *Junia* family—viz., *M. Junius Brutus*, likewise called *Caepio*, the assassin of Cæsar the Dictator, and *Decimus Junius Brutus*, an orator and lawyer, who each of them gained a very conspicuous place in the history of their age.—The coins of M. Brutus Caepio are ranged with the Imperial series. (See BRVTVS.)

The coinage of this family, which Morell states to consist of more than seventy varieties, exhibits an interesting type on a denarius, of which the following is a description:—

LIBERTAS.—Head of Liberty.

Rev. BRVTVS.—The march of the Consul (*Consulis Processus*) between two lictors, carrying the *fasces*, and preceded by a verger or usher (*accensus.*)

Some of the silver pieces are restored by Trajan, and are rarer than the original coins.—

The brass of this family are the *As*, or parts of the *As.*

Juno, daughter of Saturn, and at once the sister and the spouse of Jove, the goddess of kingdoms and of riches, was believed to preside over marriages, and thence received her appellation of *Pronuba*; and from her supposed obstetrical tutelage over women, was likewise called *Lucina.*—The Romans, as well as the Greeks, assigned to her the highest rank amongst the goddesses, and the poets relate many fables respecting her jealous and imperious disposition, which she carried sometimes to the length of attempting to put even Jupiter himself (who gave but too much cause of offence) under her feet.—The figures of Juno differ from each other, inasmuch as we find this deity on the most ancient coins of the Romans, as *Juno Lanuvina*, or Sispita (Sospita), and *Juno Moneta.* She is most frequently represented with her head veiled, and when, as *Juno Pronuba*, the goddess patronises a solemnization of nuptials, she is covered with a veil that conceals half the body. Whilst, on the other hand, as *Juno Sospita*, her head is adorned with the skin and two horns of a goat. The distinctive symbol and *protégé* of this goddess is the peacock, into which bird she had changed her faithful Argus, after he had, as the guard of Io, fallen a victim to the pandering artfulness of Mercury, and the intriguing revenge of Jupiter.

On the imperial coins Juno appears under various aspects—viz., sometimes standing, sometimes sitting, as in Faustina, jun., at others in a walking attitude, with a serpent at her feet, holding a flower, a sceptre, a patera, the *hasta*, or a child, as *Juno Augusta*, *Juno Regina*, *Juno Conservatrix*, &c.

On a first brass of Faustina the Younger, the reverse, without legend, is charged with a female figure, clothed in the stola, standing between a peacock and a lion.

IVNO.—On silver and second brass coins of Julia Domna with this inscription, the goddess stands veiled, holding a patera in the right, a hasta in her left hand; and a peacock stands at her feet.

The Empress herself is exhibited under this image, for, in order to conciliate greater dignity and reverence towards women, the Empresses were fond of assimilating themselves to the goddesses, and were accustomed to represent their own forms, under the names of female divinities, to the people.

IVNO AVGVSTAE.—Silver and brass coins of Julia Mamæa, with this legend, exhibit the goddess sitting, holding in her right hand a flower, and in her left an infant in swathing bands. This *Juno of the Empress* is obviously *Juno Lucina*, and the coin is struck in acknowledgment of the favour of the goddess at the birth of an imperial heir.

IVNONEM (in the accusative case), occurs on silver and brass coins of Julia Domna.— See p. 493.

IVNO CONSERVATRIX.—Juno, the protectress or preserver, is another surname given on medals of the *Augustæ* to the great Queen of the Goddesses. Her figure on *silver, gold,* and *brass,* of Julia Mamæa, Otacilia Severa, and Salonina, is that of a female stolated and veiled, holding a patera and the hasta pura, and generally with a peacock at her feet.

Juno Lanuvina, or with the title in full, *Juno Sispita,* or *Sospita Maxima Regina,* as it is expressed on denarii of Thorius Balbus; see the initial letters I.S.M.R., p. 488 of this Dict.—The goddess bearing this surname is found on the silver coins of those Roman families who drew their origin from the town or *municipium* of Lanuvina, to which the Cornuficii, the Mettii, the Papii, the Procillii, the Roscii, and the Thorii belonged. Her appearance on these coins nearly corresponds with the description given by Cicero, in lib. i. *de nat. Deor.* cap. 23, viz., *cum pelle caprina, cum hasta, cum scutulo, cum calceolis repandis* (shoes turned up at the points), to which it only· remains to be added that her head is covered with a goat's skin, as Hercules's head is with that of a lion, having, moreover, two horns, and her entire vestment is composed of this skin, with the fur outwards. On a denarius of the *Cornuficia* family is an eagle on the top of her shield (probably intended for a legionary one); at other times she is depictured in a biga, as on some medals of the *Mettia* and *Procilia* families, a great serpent preceding her, and in the act of raising itself. On a denarius of the *Roscia* family we see opposite to the serpent a woman offering food to it, the meaning of which may be learnt in Elianus and Propertius. Cicero teaches us in his Oration *pro Muræna,* in what high estimation this goddess was with the Romans, to which may be joined the testimony of Livy, who says that she was worshipped *(majoribus hostiis)* with sacrifices of the highest order, shewing that the Romans granted to the Lanuvians the right of citizenship, on condition that they themselves (the people of Rome) should have a share in the Temple, and in the sacred grove of the Goddess.

In the Imperial series, *Juno Lanuvina,* or *Sispita,* is seldom to be seen. Mediobarba, however, notes two medals of Antoninus Pius (A.D. 140), and one of Commodus (A.D. 177), with the inscription IVNONI SOSPITAE: after which period it again disappears.—See *Juno Sospita.*

Juno Lucina.—It was under this name, as has been already observed, that Juno presided over parturition; and accordingly on medals of those Empresses, who either had brought forth a child, or who had invoked the aid of the goddess in their approaching *accouchement,* we see her represented seated, holding an infant and a flower. On coins of Faustina, wife of M. Aurelius, she appears with two children near her.—There are some writers, indeed, who think this *Juno Lucina* to be the same as *Diana;* and with *Luna,* one deity.

IVNONI LVCINAE.—The Goddess sits with a flower in her extended right hand; in her left an infant in swathing bands.—Silver and brass coins of Lucilla, with the above legend and type, present that tutelary goddess presiding over child-birth, whom the Greeks called *Ilithyia,* and the Romans denominated *Juno Lucina.*—It is in reference to the custom of parturient women to addréss their prayers to to her that Terence, in his Andria, puts these words into the mouth of Glycerium:—

Juno Lucina, fer opem, serva me, obsecro.

For this reason, therefore, she holds a child in her left hand, whilst her right is extended with a flower in it, because this is the symbol of hope, and she delights in hoping well of the safety and growth of the child; or rather, says Eckhel, she herself displays her attribute manifestly as indicated by Ovid. In the specimen here selected from the first brass of Lucilla, the right hand is extended empty.

Juno was called *Magna Regina.*—See I. S. M. R.

IVNONI MARTIALI.—*Juno Martialis,* or the warlike Juno, is seen seated with globe in left hand and corn ears in right. She is also seated in a round temple, with a shield or

[Large brass of Volusian.]

other attributes, on silver and first brass coins of Trebonianus Gallus, and also of Volusianus, by the latter of whom the legend and type appear to have been restored. The legend originated with Trebonian, and was struck about the period when a dreadful pestilence excited the then reigning princes of the empire to "weary" all the gods, of every name in Olympus, with victims and with prayers. Juno might appear at that juncture a deity whose aid ought to be propitiated, because, according to Tully, "The air which floats between the skies and the ocean is consecrated to the name of Juno; and it was this region (or element) which, having contracted some taint, brought destruction on men." And the same author says shortly afterwards—"But I believe the name *Juno* to be derived *a juvendo*, from rendering aid."

"But why *Juno* is in this instance called *Martialis*, I have not (says Eckhel) been as yet able satisfactorily to ascertain." Yet by that title the goddess was commemorated not only on medals, but in a temple erected to her honour as the *Martial* Juno, in the Roman Forum.

Juno Moneta.—According to Suidas, Juno was surnamed *Moneta* by the Romans, *a monendo*, because this goddess is said to have counselled that *very docile* and *scrupulous* people to undertake none but just wars, promising them, that, in that case, they should never want for money. A pretty story; but it would be much more to the purpose to suppose that she was honoured with this cognomen, as denoting her presidency over the *Roman mint*, which was established in the precincts of the temple.

The (supposed) effigy of Juno, with the title of *Moneta*, appears on a denarius of the *Carisia* family; the reverse of the coin exhibits a hammer, a pair of tongs, and an anvil, above which is the bonnet of Vulcan, with the circumscription of T. CARISIVS, and on some coins SALVTARIS, the whole surmounted by a laurel.—See *Carisia*—*Moneta*.

Juno Regina.—This surname of REGINA was given to IVNO, because she was the wife of Jupiter, who was the King of Gods and Men. The type, which generally accompanies this legend on coins of the Imperial series, is that of a woman standing or sitting, veiled, who holds in the right hand a patera, and in the left a hasta pura, or rather, perhaps, a sceptre; and frequently at her side the peacock, a bird consecrated to her, either because it is so beautiful in plumage, or because all the colours in its tail are comparable to the rainbow, or Iris, who was the messenger of Juno, as Mercury was of Jupiter.

IVNONI REGINAE.—A throne and a peacock with tail spread beneath it; on some a sceptre is placed transversely upon the throne.—On large brass of Faustina, senior.

IVNO REGINA and IVNONI REGINAE. —This legend is never seen on coins of the Emperors, except one of Claudius Gothicus. But as the venerated *Queen* of Deities, Juno was

a favourite patroness of the Empresses, and thus she appears on coins of Sabina, Lucilla, Faustina, junior, Manlia Scantilla, Julia, Soaemias, Etruscilla, Cornelia Supera, and others. With some of the Augustæ, the inscription (in the dative case) was simply a dedication of the medal to the honour of the goddess; with others it was a positive appropriation of the name in flattery to the Emperor's wife, who was herself in a concealed manner represented under the figure of Juno.

Juno Sospita, or according to the more ancient mode of writing it Sispita, Juno the preserver; also called *Lanuvina* (see above), because she had a temple and statue at *Lanuvium*. On a coin of the *Procilia* family she has on her tunic a goat-skin, which also serves as the covering of her head. The points of her shoes are turned up, after a fashion which was renewed in the twelfth century of the Christian era. She is armed with a buckler and a lance to defend the people under her protection. The serpent which is at her feet is a symbol of the health and safety which they owe to her, and also serves to typify the serpent to which a young girl of *Lanuvium* went every year to offer it nourishment in its cavern. This denarius was struck by *L. Procilius* whilst he was monetary triumvir. He chose this type because his family was originally of *Lanuvium*, where he perhaps possessed the estate called *Prociliana*, and by corruption Porcilien, which has become celebrated for the great number of monuments discovered there.—See *Procilia*.

Juno Sospita crowning an Augur, is seen on a denarius of the *Cornuficia* family, bearing the inscription of Q. CORNVFICI. AVGVR. IMP.—For by an institution of Numa, perpetuating a most ancient ceremony of the Aborigines, a goat was sacrificed at the altar of Juno, in the presence of an Augur, as appears from a denarius of Licinius Varus; whence Juno Sospita herself is made to place a crown on the head of Quintus Cornuficius, standing in his augural robes and with his *lituus* of office. The Emperor Trajan restored this numismatic monument, relating to the religion and to the history of times long antecedent to his own.

IVNONI SOSPITAE—and SISPITAE.— On first brass of Antoninus Pius and of Commodus, the former legend spelt Sospitæ, the

latter Sispitae, the Goddess appears with goat-skin and horns on her head, and casting a javelin, having a serpent before her.

Juno Samia.—The Samian Juno, so called
from the island of Samos, where she was (also
as *Pronuba)* worshiped with great devotion. A
figure of the Goddess in question, standing with
an ear of corn at her feet, appears on a silver
medallion of Hadrian, with the legend COS. III.
a legend very common on that Emperor's silver
coins.

Juppiter and Jupiter.—On coins this name is
spelt both *without* and *with* the double P.

IVPPITER CVSTOS—IVPPITER LIBE-
RATOR.—Jupiter seated, holds the thunderbolt in his right hand and a spear in his left.

The above two legends (with the *double* P),
accompanied by the same type, appear on gold
and silver of Nero.—" It is very probable (says
Eckhel) what Vaillant thinks, that these coins
were struck on the occasion of the tyrant's
escape from the conspiracy of Piso, about the
year of Rome 818, under the peril of which he
acknowledges the interposing guardianship of
Jupiter the *Protector* and the *Liberator*. It
appears that Nero, after the defeat of that plot
against his life, consecrated in the Capitol the
dagger which had been aimed at him, and inscribed it IOVI VINDICI.—The Greek colonies of
Patras and of Corinth, were also induced, in
consequence of this danger, to inscribe on their
coins under Nero, IVPPITER LIBERATOR.—See
Patræ col. in which he is represented standing
with Eagle in right and hasta in left hand.—
And not only with Nero, but also with others,
at the same period, was *Jupiter the Liberator*
held in honour, though from different causes.
For Seneca and Thraseas Pætus, doomed by that
sanguinary monster to suffer death, sprinkling
around the blood from their opened veins, exclaimed *libemus Jovi Liberatori.*—See *Jupiter.*

Jus appellandi or *provocandi*—The exercise
of this privilege is well represented on a coin of
the Porcia family, on the obverse of which there
is the head of Rome helmeted, with the inscription *Publius* LAECA ROMA : on the reverse
is a figure in a military dress between two
others, of whom the one on the right hand is
togated, or in the habit of a Roman citizen,
over the head of which the other extends his
hand; on the left is a Lictor with rods : in the
exergue we read PROVOCO.—See PORCIA family.
—This medal is a monument of a law carried by
a Tribune of the People, called the *Lex Porcia,*
that no citizen of Rome should be beaten with
rods. The advantages of this law have been
attested by many writers ; and especially by
Cicero.—On another coin of the same family
is found a monument of this Tribune in the
safety of the main liberty of Roman citizens.
The obverse of this is nearly like the one above
described; but on the reverse appears the
Goddess of Liberty with the *pileus* or bonnet in
her right hand, and with a spear in her left,
standing in a quadriga, and crowned by a figure
of Victory. The legend is *Marcus* PORC*ius*
ROMA.

IVSSV. RICHIARI. REGES. *(sic.)*—This
memorial of Richiarus, King of the Suevi,
appears on the reverse of a silver medal of

Honorius. It is inscribed round a garland,
within which is a cross, between the letters
B. R.

This singular coin was first published in the
Catalogue of the D'Ennery Cabinet (p. 393), the
author of which adds that it was found at
Tolosa (Toulouse), where reigned Theodoricus,
King of the Goths, who, about the year 449,
gave his daughter in marriage to Rechiarius,
son of Rechila, King of the Suevi.—Tanini,
who republishes the same coin, merely adds :
*Richiarius Suevorum rex in monumentum pacis
hunc singularem nummum percutere jussit.*—
" That celebrated collection (says Eckhel in his
note on this subject), well deserved to have been
more thoroughly examined, nor ought it to have
been so loosely asserted that the medal in question
was struck by Rechiarius, the son-in-law of
Theodoric. The former, according to Idacius
and the Chronicle of Isidorus, became King of
the Suevi, in Spain, in the year 447 ; but
Honorius, to whom the coin is inscribed, had
already paid the debt of nature (423). This
coin, therefore, must necessarily belong to some
King of the Suevi of the same name, who,
during the reign of Honorius, might have
obtained kingly power over his countrymen, or
a portion of them, and to whom it may have
seemed fit thus publicly to honour this emperor.
In the same manner at a later period, the
Gothic Kings of Italy adopted the practice of
placing the heads of the Emperors of the East
on their coinage."

Mionnet gives the above coin, as from the
cabinet of M. Gosselin, and observes—*Cette
médaille unique paroit être le seul monument
que l'on ait des Suèves.*

IVST. *Justa.*—IVST. VENER. MEMOR.
—*Justa Venerandæ Memoriæ (Soluta* being
understood).—Legend on a coin of Constantine,
mentioned by Bimard in his notes on *Joubert,*
vol. i. p. 283.—See also Eckhel, vol. viii.
p. 93.

Justinianus I. (Flavius Anicius), born in the
district of Bederiana, or in the town of Tauresium,
near Bederiana, in Illyria, A.D. 483, was the
nephew of Justinus the First, by his sister
Vigilantia, the divorced wife of Sebatius, and
adopted by his uncle in 527, succeeded to
the empire a few months afterwards. He was a
prince of weak, ungenerous, vain, and heartless character ; whose reign, though marked
by events of honour to the Roman name, was
no less stained by the Emperor's meanness
under adversity, overbearing arrogance in more
prosperous circumstances ; and, worst of all, by
his ingratitude to Belisarius, the most illustrious
of his many able generals. Of a studious disposition, his talents for jurisprudence have
served more than his princely virtues to hand
down his name to posterity. For, by his
command, all the laws, as well as edicts of
sovereigns, and the opinions of jurisconsults,
were collected into one body, afterwards digested
into those celebrated volumes called the *codex,*
pandects, institutions, &c. Before his death
(A.D. 565), he made a fifty years' truce with

Chosroes, King of the Persians, which, however, that scourge of the Romans broke under Justinian's imprudent successor, Justinus the Second.

Justinianus is styled on his coins D. N. IVSTINIANVS. P.P. AVG. and appears, after the manner of Constantinopolitan Emperors, crowned with a gemmed diadem. His brass coins are common; silver and gold less so. An *unique* gold medallion exhibits his full-faced bust on one side; and his equestrian figure with SALVS and GLORIA ROMANORVM, on the reverse.—See Mionnet.

Justinus I. born of a peasant family at Bederiana, in Thrace, in the year 450, and employed during his earliest years in the lowest occupations. He travelled to Constantinople in his sixteenth year, and there exchanged his ragged garments for the dress and arms of a soldier. His striking figure recommended him to one Emperor, and his military qualities to another, till at length, by dint of cunning and courage united, the poor cottager's half-starved son contrived to mount the first throne of the east.—On the death of Anastasius, whose Prætorian prefect he had become, A.D. 518, he was proclaimed emperor at Constantinople.—Considering his origin, it is not surprising if his natural abilities proved greater than his educational acquirements. In fact, he could neither write nor read. But, says Beauvais, "The mildness of his character, the affability of his deportment towards his subjects, the justice with which he governed them, his zeal (carried, however, to a rigorous excess against the Arians) for the purity of the Christian faith, marked the course of his reign, and have entitled him to a place in the rank of good princes."—In 526, Cabades, king of Persia, having broken the peace which subsisted between the two empires, Justin sent against him an army commanded by the celebrated Belisarius, who marched victoriously into the heart of Persia; but the Emperor did not see the end of that war, for he died on the first of August, 527, having a few months before associated his nephew Justinianus in the government. He had no children by his wife, named Eufemia.—On his coins (which are *common* in gold, with his head only, and in brass of every size; but *rare* in silver, and *very rare* with his figure and that of Justinian) he is styled D.N. IVSTINVS P.P. AVG.—On the reverses of some, appear the monograms of Theodoricus and of Athalaricus, kings of the Ostrogoths.

Justinus II. (Flavius Anicius), who had held the office of master of the palace to his uncle Justinianus, was the son of Dulcissimus and Vigilantia, and became, by succession, Emperor of the East, A.D. 565. A weak and imprudent prince, addicted to pleasure, and selfish in policy, he re-called and ill-treated Narses, his predecessor's wise general, and conqueror of the Goths in Italy; who, in revenge, invited the Lombards *(Longobardi)* into Italy, which that Scandinavian people overran, with 200,000 fighting men, making themselves masters of the greatest portion of that country, A.D. 568.—Italy lost, Justin had to struggle with the increasing difficulties of a Persian war, and died in the midst of it, a Pelagian heretic, in the year of Christ 578, and the thirteenth of his reign, having appointed Tiberius as his successor.—He is numismatically styled D.N. IVSTINVS. INN. PP. AVG. His coins in *gold* are common, except those with title of *junior,* and with the legend of *Gabalorum;* silver are very rare; brass are common, except those on which his name is conjoined to that of his truculent and imperious wife SOPHIA.—"The coins, however (says Akerman), of Justinus the Second are difficult to distinguish from those of the elder Justinus; but those which are supposed to belong to the latter are more common than the others."

Justitia, the virtue that renders to everyone his own *(suum cuique).* On coins of the Roman mint, struck under the Emperors Tiberius, Nerva, Hadrian, Antoninus Pius, Pescennius Niger, Sept. Severus, and Alexander Severus, *Justitia,* or *Justitia Augusti,* is represented under the type of a woman, standing with patera, sceptre, hasta, or rudder, in her hands; or, like AEQVITAS, sitting with balance in one hand, and holding the *hasta pura* in the other, or a cornucopiæ.

IVSTITIA.—On a gold coin of Hadrian's, Justice is seated on the curule chair, as on a tribunal: with the insignia of the *hasta pura* and the extended *patera* she displays her care for religion.—The head of this goddess, whose other name is *Themis,* appears adorned with the diadem on a coin of the *Mamilia* family, in memory of a law made respecting boundaries or land marks.

IVSTITIA.—On a second brass, *Livia,* or Julia, appears with the name, and after the form of *Justitia.* It is one of three medals on which the mother of Tiberius is represented under the figure, or attributes of different Divinities. She is called on the first, SALVS AVGVSTA; on the second, IVSTITIA; on the third, PIETAS. These medals were struck under Tiberius; the two latter were afterwards restored by Titus.

IVV. *Juventutis.*—PRINceps IVVentvtis.—See the words.

IVVENTAS—IVVENTA—IVVENTVS.—The Goddess *Juventas,* or of Youth, the same with her who was called *Hebe* by the Greeks, is thus made by Ovid to perform the office of cup bearer at the feasts of the Gods:—

Nectar, et ambrosiam, latices, epulasque, deorum
Det mihi formosa nava *Juventa* manu.
Pontic. Epist. I. x. 11.

There was a temple of *Juventas* at Rome, where, by a very ancient custom, money was deposited by those who assumed the *toga virilis.*

After Antoninus Pius, adopting M. Aurelius, had nominated him as his successor, a medal was struck, on the obverse of which we see M. Aurelius having the down merely on his cheeks, and with the inscription AVR. CAE. AVG. PII. F., and on the reverse a crown, within which is the word IVVENTVS, or in some coins IVVENTAS; and, below, s. c.—Antonio Agostini believes that this medal was struck in remembrance of that *important* day when the beard of Aurelius was first submitted to the tonsor's operation, and the downy fruits were, according to established usage, consecrated to this same goddess.—Allusive to the same event, there are the coins in which *Juventas* stands under the figure of a woman placing frankincense on a candelabrum, with her right hand, and holding

a patera in her left, as here shown from a second brass coin of Marcus Aurelius.

IVVENTAS. S. C.—On a first brass of M. Aurelius, bearing this legend, the type, instead of the goddess above described, presents the figure of a young man, in a short dress, standing with a branch in one hand, and a *hasta* in the other, near a trophy.

The type of a young man standing with a spear near a trophy is frequently seen on coins of subsequent reigns, with the accompanying legend of PRINCEPS IVVENTVTIS; and this, perhaps, was intended to represent the statue dedicated to M. Aurelius as Prince of the Roman youth.

IVVENTA IMPERII.—This legend appears on a denarius of Caracalla, on the reverse of which the Emperor stands, in military garb, holding a globe surmounted by Victory, and a spear; a captive crouching at his feet.

Caracalla, says Vaillant, when his father Severus had already become an old man, was called *Juventa Imperii*, the youth of the empire, because great hope was entertained of him in his early years. Thus we see him represented on this coin with a Victory in his hands, having, in conjunction with his father, conquered the Parthians, as the captive at his feet serves to testify. Hence also on another silver coin of this ferocious prince, struck during the reign of his scarcely less truculent sire, he is fondly called *Imperii Felicitas*.

Juventia; this family is scarcely to be classed amongst those of the Romans. The colony of *Cæsar-Augusta* exhibits on its coins the names of magistrates who bear the surname of *Juventius*. For example the *Luperci*: IVVENT LVPERCO IIVIR. *Juventio Luperco Duumviro*.

Juventus.—See PRINCEPS IVVENTVTIS.

IX. Numeral marks—as IMP. IX. &c., on coins of Augustus—*Imperator Nonum* for the ninth time.

K, the *Kappa* of the Greeks, and the tenth letter of their alphabet, very seldom appears amongst Latin letters, and then only in small words. On Roman coins, with Latin inscriptions, the K is used only in the instance of *Karthago*, as FELIX KART., and that not always; for on the well-known coins of Severus we read INDVLGENTIA IN CART.—See the legend.

K and C were formerly, from similarity of sound, employed indiscriminately the one for the other, as in the above-named example—KARTHAGO, KALENDAE, &c. But though this was the most ancient custom, yet in inscriptions of a subsequent date the K was relinquished and those words remained written with the letter C. In later times the K resumed its ascendancy.

K is found in use on Latin coins of the lower empire, viz.: KAA. and BKA., on medals of Tacitus, Florianus, Probus, Carus, Numerianus, Carinus, as *subsignationes* (or monetary under-signings.)—Tristan, in his, remarks on the Carthaginian state, has attempted an interpretation of these letters.

L.

L.—The eleventh letter of the Roman alphabet.—A single L is sometimes put for a double one, as APOLINI for APOLLINI. Banduri i. p. 157. AQVILIVS for AQVILLIVS. See the *Aquilia* family.—This letter is used as a mint mark on many family coins.

L.—This letter signifies the colony called *Laus*, or *Julia Laus*. It also signifies *Legio* (Legion), or *Lucius*, or *Ludi*, the public games.

L. on a tablet means *Libero*. See the denarius of the *Coelia* family, on which are the letters L. D., *Libero, Damno*, struck in memory of C. Coelius Caldus.

L., *Lugdunum*, or *Lugduni*, the city of Lyon.—L. P., *Lugduni Percussa* (money) struck at Lyons; or *Lugdunensis Pecunia*, money of Lyons.—L., on coins of Carausius and Allectus, *Londinium*.

L. is a Latin sign for the number fifty.

LA., *Latienus*, as in *Postumus*.

Labarum, a Roman military ensign, which is described to have been a more distinguished species of *vexillum*, or cavalry standard, and, like the rest, was an object of religious veneration amongst the soldiers, who paid it divine honours. That the *Labarum* dated its designation as the imperial standard from an early period of the empire, is a supposition confirmed by a colonial medal of Tiberius (dedicated to that Prince by *Cæsarea Augusta*—Saragozza), on which may be remarked the form of that ensign. It was originally a kind of square banner of purple bordered with gold fringe, attached to the upper end of a long pike or spear; on the drapery of this banner an eagle was painted, or embroidered, in gold tissue, and it was hoisted only when the Emperor was with the army. But Constantine, after having abandoned paganism, caused a decided change to be made in the ornaments of the labarum. The staff of the pike was crossed at a certain height by a piece of wood, forming a cross. At the upper part, above this cross-piece, was fastened a brilliant crown of gold and precious stones, in the middle of which appeared the monogram of Christ, formed by two Greek initials, X. P., joined together thus ☧ and often accompanied by two other letters, ☧ A. and Ω., placed on each side, indicating the belief of Our Saviour's divinity, in the words of St. John's Apocalypse, as noted in Eusebius's Life of Constantine. From the two arms of the cross-piece, hung the purple banner, richly ornamented with jewels and with gold embroidery. And, instead of the Roman Eagle, the former object of the soldiers' idolatry, Constantine caused the monogram of Christ to be placed on the banner also. In the space between the crown and the flag, the Emperor placed his bust in gold, or those of his children. But this feature is not engraved on the medals.—Fifty chosen men were charged by him with the appointment of carrying and defending this sacred standard at the head of the army, when commanded by the Emperor in person, and were thence called *Labariferi*.

The *Labarum* marked with the monogram of Christ is seen on coins of Constantine the Great, also of Constans, of Jovianus, of Valentinianus, &c. A *vexillum*, or cavalry standard, resembling the *Labarum*, appears on several colonial coins, such as Acci, Antiochia Pisidiæ, Cæsar-Augusta, &c.—It is also found in the left hand of emperors, on some military figures, on coins of Nero, Domitian, Trajan, Hadrian, Antoninus Pius, M. Aurelius, Commodus, Severus, and other princes anterior to Constantine, with whose family and successors it appears on coins with the Christian symbols to the end of the imperial series.

The *Labarum*, or at least the *vexillum*, is an attribute which accompanies the numismatic personification of many of the Roman provinces, viz., *Africa*, under Diocletian, Maximian, Galerius, Constantius Chlorus.—*Armenia*, under Marcus Aurelius, and Lucius Verus.—*Britannia*, under Antoninus Pius, and Sept. Severus.—*Cappadocia*, under Hadrian, and Antonine.—*Dacia*, under Antonine, Philip sen., Trajanus Decius.—*Ilium*, under Caracalla.—*Pannonia*, under Aelius Cæsar.

LABIENVS, a Roman General under the Republic, surnamed *Parthicus*, for his having conquered the Parthians, is thus recorded on a denarius of the *Atia* family :—Q. LABIENVS PARTHICVS IMP*erator.—Rev.* A horse saddled and bridled.—This coin is of the first rarity : in gold *unique.—See Atia.*

Laelianus (Ulpius Cornelius), one of the usurpers in the time of Gallienus.—He appears to have been of Spanish origin, and when Postumus was slain by his soldiers, he seized upon the government at Maguntiacum, (Mayence, in Germany), about A.D. 267. An active and very courageous man, he was distinguished for his military knowledge and skill, and made head

against the Germans on the Rhine, where he fortified several towns ; but after a few months, in the midst of his labours, he was treacherously slain by his troops, at the instigation of Victorinus.—He is styled IMP. C. VLP. COR. LAELIANVS. P. F. AVG.—His gold and base silver are the rarest of all the coins struck by the usurpers in the time of Gallienus. Those in third brass are also rare.

Mr. Akerman, in his "Descriptive Catalogue" (vol. ii. p. 63), observes :—"The names of Laelianus, Lollianus, and Aelianus, are used indiscriminately by historians, who appear to apply them to the same personage, namely, the usurper who assumed the purple in Gaul, during the reign of Postumus in that country ; but, according to some coins, upon which the prenomen is different, the above names belong to three different persons. The coins of Laelianus are fully authenticated ; not so those ascribed to Lollianus and Aelianus."

L. AELIVS CAESAR.—*Lucius Aelius Cæsar*, son of Annius, created Cæsar by Hadrian, and adopted as his successor.—See AELIVS.

Laetitia, Joy, or *Rejoicing,* is personified on many Roman medals, and characterised by different attributes. This *Lætitia* first occurs on a gold coin of Antoninus Pius, struck in his fourth consulate (V.C. 902), under the figure of a woman, having corn-ears in her right hand and an apple in her left ; and the same type is frequently found, in subsequent reigns, engraved on Imperial coins, with various additions to the name, viz., *Lætitia, Aug., Temporum, Publica, Fundata,* &c. Nor (says Eckhel), is there any room for doubt but that sacred rites were publicly dedicated to her, the same as, on an ancient marble we read, were paid to *Jucunditas:*—

GENIO IVCVNDITATI MVSIS FLORAEQ. S.

On other coins she appears, sometimes holding a sceptre or wand in one hand, and in the other a *crown*, because in public festal rejoicings the people were accustomed to wear crowns. Sometimes she holds a *branch* of a tree, because the verdure of boughs and branches delight the mind ; on which account, during public occasions of rejoicing, the houses and streets of a city were ornamented with them.—On some medals Lætitia holds an *anchor*, to shew that the cause of hilarity was of a solid and lasting kind. It is thus that we see her represented on coins of Gordianus Pius, Philip senior, Valerian, Gallienus, Victorinus, Quintillus, Aurelian and Severina, Tetricus, Florianus, Probus, Carausius, Allectus, Galerius.—Sometimes Lætitia is depictured standing, with a garland and a rudder, as on coins of Crispina, Lucilla, Severus, Domna, Caracalla, Elagabalus, Aquilia, Alexander Severus, Mæsa, Philip senior, Tacitus, and Carinus.—On other medals she is seated with the same attributes, as we see in the case of Philip senior. —See *Hilaritas.*

LAET*itia* FVNDAT*a*—Well founded rejoicing.—On coins of Crispina and also of Philip senior, with this inscription, a woman with a garland in her right hand ; and in her left the rudder of a ship placed on a globe ; because, says Oiselius *(Sel. Num.),* "the pilots of vessels direct their course firmly through the waves of the ocean to the place of their destination."

LAETITIAE PVBLICAE—*To Public Joy.*

—Lætitia stands with corn-ears in her right hand and the hasta pura in her left: on first brass of Faustina jun.

LAETITIA AVG.—On coins of Gallienus, in all the three metals, this legend appears with type of a woman holding a garland and an anchor, struck by order of that voluptuous, heartless, and eccentric emperor, when his father Valerian was actually groaning under the cruel and ignominious captivity of the Persians.—According to Pollio, "Gallienus, aware that Macrianus and his children had been slain, and that his father was still a prisoner to Sapor, in fancied security against consequences, abandoned himself to lewd pleasures, gave public games, and invited the people as if in days of victory to festivity and rejoicing."—Sometimes the legend of *Lætitia Augusti* (Joy of the Emperor) has for its accompanying type a galley at sea, with rowers propelling it, and the Emperor standing at the helm : as on gold, silver, and brass coins of Postumus.

LAETITIA COS. IIII. Two female figures standing together ; one holding corn-ears, the other a globe. On a gold coin of Antoninus Pius.

LAETITIA TEMPORVM.—A galley with sail spread, about which *quadrigæ* are running ; and many animals.—This unusual type, on the reverse of a gold coin of Sept. Severus, serves to illustrate a passage in *Dio,* wherein that writer referring to various spectacles, exhibited by the above Emperor on his return from the East, and in which a great many wild beasts were killed, says—" A receptacle was built for them in the amphitheatre, constructed in the form of a ship, so that 150 (C. D.) wild beasts

might be received into it, and at the same time be at once sent forth from it. The ship suddenly falling to pieces, there issued out of it bears, lionesses, panthers, lions, &c."—A gold coin of Caracalla here engraved has also the same reverse.

LAETITIAE C. V. S. P. Q. R.—*Laetitiæ Clipeum Vovit Senatus Populusq. Romanus.*—This appears on a first and second brass of Commodus.

Lanuvina.—Juno with head covered with the goat-skin, carrying spear and small shield, and wearing shoes turned up at the toes.—See *Juno Sospita* or *Sispita.*

Lanuvina, the virgin who, according to the ancient Campania fable, was yearly sent to offer a serpent food in its cave, represented on a denarius of L. Papius Celsus, to shew his origin from the city of Lanuvium.—The same virgin is seen on coins of the *Papia* and *Roscia* families, offering food to a serpent, which is raising itself in coils before her.—A bronze medallion of Antoninus Pius, in the *Mus. Pisan.* exhibits a girl standing near a tree and feeding a serpent folded round the trunk.

The *Lanuvinian* serpent, or dragon, coiled in folds, appears on coins of Pomponia and Papia families, with the figure of a woman near it.

Lanuvinium, or *Lanuvium,* also *Lavinium,* a municipal and colonial city of Campania, whose temples were restored by Antoninus Pius.

LAOCOON, with his two sons, entwined in the folds of serpents, appears on the reverse of a *contorniate* medal (in the Imperial Museum at Vienna), having on the obverse the head of Nero, and the legend IMP. NERO CAESAR AVG.

Laodicea Syriæ (now called *Ladkeyah* or *Latakia*), a maritime city situated on a peninsula towards Phœnicia, and possessed of one of the finest harbours. It was founded by Seleucus Nicator (one of the most powerful of Alexander's generals, and the first of the Seleucidæ, Kings of Syria). It afterwards received many favours from Cæsar, and in consequence took the name of *Julia,* about A. V. C. 707, from which time it dates its new epocha (before Christ 48).—It struck both *Autonomous* and Greek Imperial coins. The former offer the head of Alexander I., *Bala,* King of Syria.—An Imperial Greek of Hadrian bears the name of *Aradus,* in token of its alliance with that island ; but it was not till the reign of Sept. Severus that this Laodicea became a Roman Colony. By the same Emperor it was constituted a Metropolis, and invested with the privilege of striking coins with *Latin* legends, which it exercised under his reign, (including his Empress Julia Domna), and continued to do so in considerable numbers, under the succeeding reigns of Caracalla, Geta, Macrinus, Diadumenianus, Elagabalus, Philip senior, Trebonianus Gallus, and Valerian senior ; on which were inscribed COL. SEP. AUR. LAOD. METRO. *Colonia Septimia Aurelia Laodicea Metropolis.* The name of *Septimia* being adopted in memory of its benefactor Severus, and the former name of *Julia* abandoned.

Vaillant has not enumerated any colonial medals of *Laodicea in Syria ad mare,* struck under S. Severus. But Pellerin has supplied that omission by giving engravings of three fine large brass of this colony dedicated to that emperor, viz. :—

1.—IMP. CAES. L. SP. SEVERO AVG.

T. IVL. AVG. M.C.—Radiated head of Severus, joined with that of Julia Domna.—It is judged that this legend should be read IMP*eratori* CAES*ari Lucio De*P*timio* SEVERO AVG*usto* e T. IVL*iæ* AVG*ustæ* M*atri* C*astrorum*.

Reverse.—SEP. LAOD., that is to say, SEP*timia* LAOD*icea*.—Jupiter seated, holds a Victory in one hand, and rests his other hand on a spear. Under his chair is an eagle. Before him is a table, on which is a large urn.

2.—On the second medal are the same legend and portraits on the obverse; and on the reverse a figure of Silenus standing.

3.—The third coin has the single head of Severus on its obverse; and on the reverse ANT. AVG. GET. CAE.—Caracalla and Geta joining hands.

The following are also amongst the types of this colony, as given in Vaillant :—

Temple.—On a second brass of Caracalla, which bears the legend of COL. LAODICEAS METROPOLEOS, and the initials Δ. E.; in the field of the coin an eagle, with its wings spread, stands within a temple of two columns surmounted by a dome.—The same reverse appears on a coin of Elagabalus.—[The eagle in the temple is considered by Vaillant as referring to Jupiter rather than to the Roman empire.—ii. 38.]

In Vaillant's work there is only one medal of this colony inscribed to Caracalla.—Pellerin, however, speaks of no less than ten others struck under the same emperor. Among the more remarkable of these he mentions those that have for their legend AETERNVM BENEFICIVM, and for their type a measure full of corn-ears; also those attributed to this city which represent the wolf suckling Romulus and Remus, with the legend ROMAE FEL.

Laurel Crown.—A small brass, inscribed to Geta as Cæsar, bears for legend SEPT. COL. LAOD. METRO. *Septimia Colonia*, &c., within a laurel wreath.

[Laodicea, as has been already remarked, computed a new era from the times of Severus, to whom, deserting the cause of Pescennius, this city adhered, during the brief but bloody struggle of those two ambitious men for the imperial throne. The consequence was that Pescennius treated her with the greatest oppression and cruelty. But as soon as he was slain, Laodicea was invested with the colonial privileges of which Severus had instantly stripped the people of Antioch, who had sided with his rival. As Antioch, however, was afterwards pardoned by Severus, he, as if by way of compensation, made Laodicea a colony, and amongst other great privileges allowed it to assume *Metropolis* for its second title.—The laurel wreath alludes to the victory gained by Severus over the Parthians, and on which account the title of Cæsar was conferred upon Geta by his father—ii. p. 57.]

Diana.—On a middle brass of Elagabalus (ii. 82), this goddess in her character and costume of huntress stands in the attitude of drawing with her right hand an arrow from the quiver which hangs at her back, and holding the bow in her left.

[The Laodiceans of Syria, from the variety of coins which they dedicated to Elagabalus, a native of that country, seem to have been among the first who proclaimed him Emperor. They selected Diana as the type of this reverse, doubtless, on account of her being the object of supreme worship in their city, as Lampridius records, in noticing her image placed in the *adytum*, a most secret and sacred place of her temple there.]

Diana also appears on a small brass of Philip senior, standing with bow and arrow in her hands, and with two stags at her feet, one on each side; those animals being sacred to her, as Apollodius affirms.—In this medal the goddess appears with the *tutulus* on her head, and clothed in a long tunic.—ii. p. 162.

Turreted head.—On a small brass of Elagabalus is the turreted head of a female, with the legend LAODICEON.—On another of the same size, is the same head, placed within a temple of two columns : in each are the letters Δ. E.

[Vaillant gives what appear to be sufficient reasons for regarding this type as representing the Genius of the City, and not one of the *Dii majorum gentium*, such as Pallas and Diana, as Patin seems to consider it.—ii. 82.]

Wrestlers.—On a small coin of the same Emperor are two naked *Athletæ* wrestling.—Legend LAODECEON.

[These male figures indicate certain *certamina* or public sports celebrated at Laodicea. On such occasions the competitors for the prize were stripped of every particle of clothing, and being previously annointed with ceroma (oil mixed with wax), they contended together with mutual grappling and lifting, whilst each endeavoured to give the other "a flooring."—Hercules was, according to Pausanias, the reputed institutor of the olympic games.—There are colonial medals of Caracalla which inform us that the *certamina olympia* were performed at Tyre; and this coin shews the probability of the same contests having been celebrated at Laodicea.—ii. 83.]

Woman, with a tutulated or turreted head, stands holding in her right hand an eagle, and in her left a rudder, on a small brass of Philip senior; on another the same female figure extends her hand but without the eagle; and on a third she appears sitting on the rudder, holding the handle of it in her right hand.—The legend of the reverse, on all three coins, is COL. LAOD. or LAODICEON METROPOLEOS.

[The woman delineated in these different ways represents the city of Laodicea, and is the *Genius loci*, adorned with towers as if strongly fortified; bears a ship's rudder, to indicate its maritime site, and its possession of a directing influence. As a Roman colony, the Genius of Laodicea holds an eagle, the symbol of Rome. (The port of the city appears, from the description given of its ruins by Shaw, to have been spacious and well sheltered.)

The Genius being seated on the rudder (an unusual mode of representation) argues the tranquil state of the colony ; for Laodicea reposed awhile after peace had been entered into by Philip with the Persians, who, occupying part of Mesopotamia, threatened Syria herself, and therefore the city, in congratulation, inscribed these coins to the Emperor.—ii 168.]

Woman standing with *tutulus* on her head and clothed in the tunic, places her right hand on the tiller of a ship's rudder, and in her extended left hand holds two small images.

[The personification of Laodicea here supports the small statues of Trebonianus Gallus and his son Volusianus, as if those two princes were the Genii of the city, in like manner as on coins of Phillipopolis, Rome seated is seen bearing in her hand the images of the Philips, father and son.—ii. 214.]

Silenus.—On a first brass of Trebonianus Gallus, struck by the Laodiceans, Silenus appears in his usual posture and with his usual attributes, the right hand uplifted, and the goat-skin bag on his left shoulder.

[This type shews that the deified tutor and associate of Bacchus was worshipped at Laodicea.—ii. 215.]

Wolf suckling Romulus and Remus.—This type appears on a second brass of this colony struck under Macrinus, omitted in Vaillant, but engraved in Pellerin (*Mél.* i. pl. xviii. No. 11), with legend of reverse ROMAE FEL—also on a very fine first brass of Diadumenianus, not noticed in Vaillant, but given in Planch. xix. of the *Mélange*, TOM. i. No. 2.

Women with turreted heads.—On a large brass of Elagabalus struck in this colony, the reverse presents for legend COL. LAOD. METROPOLEOS, and for type a group of six figures, the centre one of which represents a woman with towers on her head, seated, having the figure of a river god at her feet. Four other females standing, two on each side of the middle one, have the like turreted ornaments on their heads, and have their faces turned towards the woman who is seated. In the field of the coin are the letters Δ E.—This remarkable and elegant medal is described in Pellerin's *Mélange*, T. i. pl. xix. No. 7.

Quadriga.—On a second brass of Laodicea struck under the same emperor, is another remarkable reverse, allusive to the stone worship introduced by that Syrian priest of the Sun into the city of Rome. The reverse COL*onia* SEP*timia* Laodicea; and the type, a car drawn by four horses, on which is the image of the God *Elagabalus*, represented under the symbol of a round conical formed stone.—This also is engraved in Pellerin's *Mélange*, pl. xix. No. 8.—For further explanation of the type see CONSERVATOR. AVG. of Elagabalus.

Table, with urn and palms.—On a second brass of Gordianus Pius, with legend COL. HELIOP. is a table on which is placed a large urn, containing three palm branches.—Pellerin, *Mél.* i. pl xx. No. 11.

Colonist at plough.—This type appears on a second brass of Philip junior, inscribed to him by the Laodiceans.

Lapis, a stone, was with certain oriental nations of antiquity a symbol of divinity. (Jobert, i. p. 394—423.)—A stone shaped in the form of a cone, or of a pyramid, and placed in a temple, was the type of *Venus.* And under this *lapidary* form Jupiter himself appears to have been worshipped, and was hence called *Jupiter Lapis.* (Bimard, i. p. 423.)—A huge stone in the form of a mount, and placed in a car, was the representative of the *Sun,* whom Elagabalus worshipped, and by whom this type was impressed on silver coins, with the legend of CONSERVATOR AVG. and SANCT. DEI. SOLI. ELAGABAL.—See those inscriptions.

Lares, household gods, who were supposed to take care of both house and land ; and hence the *Latins* called them *Dii familiares.* Each tutelary deity, chosen by a family, received this appellation. They were at first worshipped on the domestic hearth *(focus),* but afterwards in a particular chapel or oratory named the *Lararium.* The *Lares* were commonly represented under the figure of twins in the age of adolescence ; still oftener as young men, between whom was placed a dog, the usual house-guard.—There was a more than ordinary display of superstition among the Romans with regard to the *Lares.* They were crowned with flowers, and at each meal a portion of the victuals was served to them, no one daring to touch it ; but it was burnt in honour of them. Slaves on their emancipation consecrated their chains to the *Lares ;* and youths arrived at manhood, dedicated to these household gods the symbols of their minority ; that is to say, the golden *bullæ* as children they had worn on their breast. Young women did the same when they married.—The *Lares* were considered to be the guardians of the cross-ways. And Augustus, according to Ovid in the *Fasti,* decreed that, at the commencement of spring, the cross-ways *(compita)* should be adorned with chaplets of flowers.

A denarius of the *Cæsia* family (see the word, p. 197), on one side of which appears the image of the God *Vejovis,* represented in the manner in which Aulus Gellius describes it at Rome near the capitol ; with the letters AP. (Argentum Publicum) in monogram.—On the reverse of this rare silver coin, we see the legend of L. CAESI ; and the type consists of two juvenile figures with spears, seated together, each with helmets on, the upper part of their bodies naked ; the lower part clothed ; with a dog between them, and above them the bust of Vulcan, with forceps. In the field on one side is LA. on the other RE., both in monogram—which put together makes LARE ; and which fully warrants the supposition that the Vejovis on the obverse was a god chosen as *Lar* or special protector of *L. Caesius,* who caused the medal to be struck.

This reverse exhibits in the seated youths two of the *Lares,* whose domestic and familiar guardianship has just been adverted to ; and to these household gods the head of Vulcan is appropriately conjoined, because the *focus* or hearth, whose protection was religiously assigned to the *Lares*, was moreover sacred to the God of Fire *(Volcanus,)* The figure of a dog seated between them refers to the fidelity and domestic habits of that animal. The composition and union of such objects as these was not of rare occurrence among the Romans, as the following words of Ovid very illustratively shew :—

Præstitibus Maiae *Laribus* videre Kalendæ
　Aram constitui, *signaque parva deum.....*
At *canis ante pedes* saxo fabricatus eodem
　Stabat. Quæ standi cum Lare causa fuit?
Servat uterque domum, domino quoque, fidus uterque,
　Compita grata deo, compita grata cani.
Exagitant et Lar, et turba Diania fures,
　Pervigilantque Lares, pervigilantque canes.
Bina gemellorum quærebam *signa deorum...*
　　　　　　　　　　　　Fasti. Lib. v. l. 129.

In *Bandelot de Dairval's* curious work entitled *De l'utilité des Voyages*, vol. i. p. 171, the medal in question is given, with some learned remarks on the *Lares* and *Penates* of the Romans.

LARGITIO, a bountiful largess.—This word, indicative of the *Liberalitas Imperatorum*, occurs on a brass medallion of Constantius II. (son of Constantinus Magnus), on the obverse of which is D. N. CONSTANTIVS P. F. AVG. ; and on the reverse, the Emperor, crowned with a tiara, sitting between two figures standing, the one helmeted and in a military dress, the other wearing a radiated crown, and extending the right hand to Constantius, from whom it appears to be receiving something—with the epigraph of LARGITIO.

The learned differ in their explanations of this very rare medallion.—Eckhel, however, adopts, and apparently on the better grounds, the opinion of Gori, the Florentine numismatist, that Constantinople is personified by the type of the woman with radiated head : that the female with a helmet is intended to represent Ancient Rome ; and that the whole relates to *donations* on an extensive scale distributed to the troops and people by Constantius. The word LARGITIO is introduced in this instance for the first time on coins, instead of the *Liberalitas*, and the *Congiarium*, previously in use. " In fact (adds Eckhel) this was the term peculiar to the period in question, whence the expression *Comites privatarum*, or *sacrarum largitionum*, &c." [vol. viii. p. 117.]—See ABVNDANTIA—LIBERALITAS.

Larices, larch trees.—For the fable of three nymphs, sisters of Phaeton, changed into these trees, see *Accoleia.*

LARISCOLVS, surname of the Accoleii, from the abundance of the larch tree. P. ACCOLEIVS LARISCOLVS, whose name appears on a denarius of the *Accoleia* family, is believed to have been appointed monetal triumvir by Julius Cæsar.

LAT. otherwise LATI. *Latienus :* one of the *prenomina* of *Postumus senior.*

Latii jus.—To what regions, states, and cities, the privilege of this *Latin law* was con-

ceded, and of what rights it consisted, *Bimard de la Bastie*, in his notes on Jobert, has shewn in a very able and diffuse inquiry.

Latium, or the country of the Latins ; a region of Italy, between the Tiber and the plains of Circe, a city of the Volscian territory.

Lavinium, a city of Latium, built, according to Servius, by Lavinius, brother to Latinus, King of the Latins, under whose reign Æneas landed in Italy.—For an interesting illustration of the story of the arrival of Æneas on the shore of Latium, see *Æneas.*

Laurea corona, the laurel crown, among the Romans, was rightly conferred only on those who had acquired pro-consular dignity ; nor was it granted even to the *Cæsars*, unless they had been invested with the title of Emperor.— Respecting the laurel crown of *Julius Cæsar*, Suetonius (in his " Life" of him, c. 45) says : " He manifested much impatience under the blemish of baldness, which often exposed him to the jest of malicious detractors. It was on this account that he was desirous to remedy the deficiency of hair on his head ; and of all the honours decreed to him by the Senate and people, there was none which he more readily received or more freely availed himself of, than the *jus laureæ perpetuo gestandæ*—the privilege of perpetually wearing the laurel.—This statement is confirmed by Dion Cassius (L. xliii.) who observes, speaking of Julius—" Always and everywhere he wore the laurel crown, with which he covered his head, because he was bald."—The *laurel crown*, as the principal ornament of *Augusti*, is seen for the most part on Roman coins, tied with a kind of ribband, which they employed in place of a diadem, although that specially royal emblem was itself not placed on the head of an Emperor.

Augustus, after the example of Julius, by whom he was adopted, frequently allowed the *laurea corona* to be assigned him. Referring to this point Dion (L. xlix.) says—" By unanimous consent, at Rome, among other honours, this also was decreed to him *ut semper lauro coronaretur.*"—Hence, on many of his coins we see the *laurel* encircling his head. And the same author affirms (L. liii.) that, in addition to numerous honours already conferred on Augustus, it was ordained by the Senate and people that *laurel* trees should be planted in front of his palace, and *oaken crowns* suspended on them, as though he were the perpetual conqueror of the enemies, and saviour of the citizens of the republic."

In memory of this Senatorial decree, a gold coin was struck, having on the obverse the naked head of Augustus, with the legend of CAESAR COS. VII. CIVIBVS SERVATEIS, and on the reverse the words AVGVSTVS S. C. with the type of an Eagle, whose wings are expanded, and who stands on an oaken crown, behind which are two branches of *laurel.*—A denarius of the Caninia family bears a type which alludes to the same event.

The s. c. observes Eckhel, in this coin, " shews both Cæsar called Augustus, *Senatus*

Consulto, and by the same law decreed the oaken wreath and the laurels. Illustrating the voice of Pliny, that Augustus having put an end to the civil wars of Rome, accepted a civic crown from the human race."—vol. vi. p. 58.

Dion further mentions that after the death of *Drusus*, Augustus carried the *laurel* into the temple of *Jupiter Feretrius, præter consuetudinem Romanam*, and that ascending to the capital, he took off the laurel from the fasces and placed it on the lap of Jupiter.—L. liv.

The head of *Tiberius* likewise occurs, on coins, adorned with a crown formed of laurel, which sign of the highest rank is known to have devolved to him from Julius Cæsar himself, although it is also known that he wore it as a preservative against danger from lightning, conformably to "a vulgar error" of the ancients, which even Pliny adopts, and which encouraged the belief that the electric fluid never struck the laurel. His predecessor and relative Augustus is said to have had the same dread of thunder, and to have worn the laurel for the same reason. The numismatic portraits of succeeding emperors are crowned with laurel, generally tied round the head with a *fascia* or fillet, of which the ends hang down behind.

The *laureated* ornament of the Imperial head does not appear beyond the reign of Constantine. It is indeed found as far down as on coins of his son, accompanied with the title of Cæsar; but afterwards the *Augusti* assumed the *diadem*, the use of which Constantine had already introduced, as may be seen on the chief portion of their coins.—See *Diadem*.

Upon a medal of Probus we see the laurel between two Victories. The laurel appears in the hands of *Pietas*, of *Securitas*, of *Clementia*, on medals of Tiberius, of Helena, wife of Constantius Chlorus, &c. Two laurels before the palace of the Emperor Augustus are given amongst others by Oiselius, plate 92.—The laurel is also to be remarked on coins of the *Axia, Caninia, Claudia, Cornelia,* and *Junia* families; and the Emperors *Augustus, Nero, Vespasian, Domitian, Nerva,* &c. The same type also exhibits itself on coins of Trajan, Caracalla, Trebonianus Gallus, Volusianus, Æmilianus, Valerianus, Gallienus, and Quintillus, The branch of laurel is sometimes in the hand of another figure, but often in the hands of the Emperor.

The *laurel* crown is observable on coins of colonies, families, and emperors, from Julius Cæsar to Honorius, sometimes by itself, sometimes containing an inscription within it; at others with the addition of emblems; or placed on the head of a figure.—The *laurel in the hand of* Victory, or of Jove, of Minerva, and other figures appears on coins of the Cordia, Julia, and Sallustia families; and in the Imperial series on those of Claudius, Nero, Vespasian, Trajan, Hadrian, Antoninus, Caracalla, &c.—The *laurel in the beak of an eagle* appears on coins of the Emperors Geta, Macrinus, Gallienus,

Probus, Licinius, and Julian the Apostate.—The *laurel branch in the hand of Apollo* is a frequent type on coins of Trajan, Caracalla, Trebonianus Gallus, Volusianus, Æmilianus, Valerianus, Gallienus, Quintillus.

L. AVREL. *Lucius Aurelius.*—See *Commodus.*

L. AVREL. COMMOD. GERM. SARM. *Lucius Aurelius Commodus Germanicus Sarmaticus.*

LAVRENTIA NICA.—Amongst the Contorniate medals described by Eckhel from the Imperial Cabinet at Vienna, is one bearing on its obverse the head and superscription of Nero; and on its reverse the above legend. The type represents an instrument, composed of pipes

ranged in regular order, joined together, and descending in size, as the pipes of Pan are represented. Near it stands the figure of a man holding out something similar to a fan. The legend expresses a wish that Laurentius (the organ player) may succeed or conquer.

All the learned, in explaining this and similar medals (of which Havercamp has given engravings in his *Dissertatio de Nummis Contorniatis)*, agree in pronouncing the type in question to be that of a *musical organ*, thus exhibiting the image of a machine already known to the ancients, and which serves also in our age for various uses. This organ was also of two kinds, the *hydraulic*, which was worked by water, and the *pneumatic*, in which bellows, or a ball filled with wind (follis) was employed. Of the former more frequent mention is made by ancient authors.—"Nero," says Suetonius (in allusion to the eccentric manner in which that prince trifled away time which ought to have been devoted to state affairs), "Nero, at the suggestion of those who were now really his greatest enemies, spent the principal part of the day in shewing the first men of the city certain hydraulic instruments *(organa)* of a novel and hitherto unknown description."—Testimony of a more definite kind, adds Eckhel, is to be found on this subject in Theodoretus *(de Provident. Orat.* 3.) For it was, says that writer, "of the same construction as the *organ* composed of brass tubes (or trumpets), and blown into by bellows, which when put in motion by the fingers of the player produces those harmonic modulations."

It would seem that the *hydraulic* were on

a small, what the *pneumatic* organs were on a larger scale.—" Athenæus (observes Millin) in the chapter wherein he treats of musical instruments, speaks of an hydraulic organ, and in a way which proves that it was sufficiently small to be capable of being transported from place to place like the hand organs of our Savoyards. The same passage informs us that the people were in extacy when at a fair they heard unexpectedly an instrument of this description."

L. CAN. *Lucius Caninius.*—Name and prenomen of a man.

L. D.—Letters inscribed on tablets, exhibited in a denarius of the *Coelia* family, to signify the words *Libero Damno*, in giving votes at elections.—LD, a mint-mark, *Lugdunum.*

LE. *Lepidus,*

Lectisternium, a species of sacrifice, at which, in times of great public calamity, the Gods themselves were invited to a solemn feast. Their statues were taken from their pedestals, and they were laid on *pulvinaria*, or *lecti.*, that is to say, on beds prepared purposely for their reception in the temples, with pillows under their heads, and in this posture they were each day of the festival served with a magnificent banquet, which the priests never failed to clear away in the evening. There were tables set out in all the different quarters of the city, to which every one, without distinction, was admitted. The festival, whilst it lasted, was a signal for reconciliation, and an occasion of universal good-will, in which enemies were treated as friends, and liberty was given to all prisoners and captives. This ceremony was appointed by the order of magistrates called *Quindecemviri sacris faciendis,* and the feast was prepared by those who went under the appellation of *Septemviri epulones,* or *Epulones.* The first celebration of the kind was held by *Duumvirs,* in the year 356, after the foundation of Rome.—Livy (in his xxii. book, cap. x.) gives an account of the most splendid *lectisternia,* reckoning in them the twelve principal cities. *Tum lectisternium,* says he, *per triduum habitum decemviris sacrorum curantibus; sex pulvinaria in conspectu fuere: Jovi et Junoni unum; alterum Neptuno ac Minervæ; tertium Marti et Veneri, quartum Apollini ac Dianæ; quintum Vulcano et Vestæ; sextum Mercurio et Cereri.*—The word *lectisternium* signifies the act of making or preparing beds. It is derived from *lectus,* a bed, and *sternere,* to raise, prepare, spread. The word also designates sometimes the bed itself, on which was placed the statue of the divinity in honour of whom the above-mentioned ceremony of the lectistern was celebrated.—A true representation of a *lectisternium,* with the recumbent figure of Jupiter upon it, is seen on a denarius of the *Coelia* family, with the inscription L. CALDVS VIIVIR EPVL. *Septemvir Epulonum.*—In further numismatic illustration of this subject, it may be mentioned that a medal of Caracalla's, struck by the colony of *Sinope* (C. I. A. V. SINOP.) exhibits in the attitude of lying on a *lectisternium,* Jupiter, who has *a calathus* on his head, an

eagle on his right hand and a *hasta* in his left.—The same deity is in like manner figured on a coin of Pergamus. By Jupiter's side a woman is seated, and there is also a young man who seems to wait at table.

Lectisternium.—We also see this represented on medals of Marcus Aurelius, Lucilla, Alexander Severus, and Philip senior, whereon Fortune, Isis, or some other female figure is seated.—On a coin of Nero, there is upon this *prepared bed of honour* a woman who offers food out of a small vase to a serpent.—Some authors consider this figure to be meant for Hygæa; others refer the type to Agrippina, mother of Nero, who was desirous of passing with the Roman people for Hygeia Salutaris—the health-giving Goddess.— On the medals of Vespasian, Titus, Domitian, &c., there are lectisterns on which a thunderbolt is placed. Several coins of the Elder Faustina present a lectistern, with a peacock having its tail spread, and the *hasta pura,* or sceptre of divinity. These medals evidently refer to the apotheosis of that Empress, the wife of Antoninus, indicated sometimes by the word IVNONI REGINAE, in others by that of CONSECRATIO.— A coin of Faustina the younger, in first brass, SAECVLI FELICIT. S. C., has for its type a lectistern, on which are seated two young

children, viz., Commodus and Annius Verus, who were twins. The same legend *Saeculi Felicitas* (the happiness of the age) occurs also in silver.—On a coin of Septimius Severus appear the lectisternium and the *corona laurea,* both of them insignia of the Emperor's consecration.

LEG. *Legatus,* a Lieutenant or Deputy.— LEG. AVG. PR. R. LEG*atus* AVG*usti* Pro-*Prætore.* Lieutenant of the Emperor for the Prætor.

LEG. *Legio,* the Roman Legion.

Legend.—By this appellation numismatists distinguish the words engraved on coins around heads and types, from the *inscription* which, on the contrary, is an assemblage of words that hold, in the area, or middle, of the medal, the place of a type. After this distinction, it may be said that each medal bears two legends, that of the head and that of the reverse. The former generally serves no other purpose than to make known the personage represented, by his proper name, by his offices, or by certain surnames which his alleged good qualities have assigned for him. The second is destined to publish, whether justly or unjustly, his virtues and his fine actions; or to perpetuate the remembrance of advantages derived through his means to the empire; and also of the glorious monuments which serve to dedicate his name to immortality. Sometimes great actions are expressed on medals, either in a natural manner, or by symbols, which the *legend* explains. It is thus that on a medal of Trajan, which shews that prince putting the crown on the head of the Parthian King, we find the legend to be REX PARTHIS DATVS. (a King given to the Parthians). On the other hand, by a symbol, the victories of Julius and of Augustus in Egypt are represented by a crocodile chained to a palm-tree, with the words :—AEGYPTO CAPTA.

A considerable number of legends are only the explanations of symbols which form the types of medals, intended to proclaim the virtues of princes, together with certain events of their life, the honours decreed to them, the services rendered by them to the state, the monuments of their glory, the deities they professed in an especial manner to worship, and from whom they believed, or pretended to believe, that they had received particular protection. The legend of a medal, therefore, is (so to speak) the key to its type, which without it would sometimes be with difficulty explained. Amongst Roman medals, the types of those of the first Emperors are always studiously chosen, and applied from some motive which the legend reveals to us. In the lower empire, on the contrary, the same types and the same legends are continually and without discrimination recurring under all the Emperors. The legends which express the benefits conferred on the cities, and spread over the provinces of the empire, are generally very short and simple; without being on that account the less magnificent; such as CONSERVATOR VRBIS SVAE (the saviour of his city); RESTITVTOR VRBIS—HISPANIAE—GALLIAE, &c. (the Prince who has re-established the City, Spain, Gaul, &c.); SALVS GENERIS HUMANI (the safety of the human race); EXVPERATOR OMNIVM GENTIVM (the conqueror of all the nations); ROMA RENASCENS (Rome reviving), &c. The particular acts of public benefit conferred by the reigning prince are sometimes more distinctly expressed in the legends of Imperial medals, as REMISSA DVCENTESIMA.—Legends also occasionally point to events peculiar to a province, when they are represented only by ordinary symbols, such as a military trophy, a figure of Victory, &c. At other times the legend specifically indicates the victory and over whom it was gained. Thus on a medal of Claudius the legend tells us of the glorious reception which the soldiers of his army gave to that Emperor. In the same manner, the unusual mark of favour shewn to Nero, whilst he was as yet only *Princeps Juventutis* (Prince of the Roman Youth), in admitting him a member of all the sacerdotal colleges is a fact which has been preserved by the legend *Sacerdos co-optatus in omnia collegia supra numerum.*—In a coin of

Philip senior, there is this legend, PAX FVNDATA CVM PERSIS (Peace concluded with the Persians); by which that Emperor has left us a monument of the pacific treaty which he made with the people of that powerful monarchy.—The legends of some coins shew, as has already been hinted, the professed attachment of certain princes for particular deities. For example, we become acquainted with the marked veneration of Numerianus for Mercury, from the circumstance of several medals of that Emperor exhibiting on their reverse the legend PIETAS AVG*usti*, round a figure of Mercury.—Jupiter was the tutelary deity of Diocletian; and we see on medals of that prince the legends of IOVI CONSERVATORI; IOVI PROPVGNATORI (to Jupiter the Preserver; to Jupiter the Defender). This Emperor also took the surname of Jovius. —Gordianus Pius, having gained a battle by the firmness of his soldiers, who would not abandon their position, caused a medal to be struck which has for its legend IOVI STATORI. The good fortune of the Roman Emperors is often recorded, in a dedicatory form, on their coins.

The names of particular legions are also recorded in the legends of medals which likewise make known the names of public games, the vows for the Emperors; their titles, alliances, adoptions, &c. It is by means of these legends that we also ascertain how long *their* gratitude lasted, who, having received the empire from their father, or from their predecessor who had adopted them, soon afterwards quitted the name and quality of son, which they had at first most eagerly assumed.—Trajan began his reign by joining to his own name that of Nerva, whose successor he was by adoption. Sometimes, however, either ambition or vanity prompted certain emperors to retain and even to assume the names of princes, whose memory was cherished by the people. Accordingly we find that of Antoninus used by six Emperors down to Elagabalus. The circumstance of this name having become common to several princes, has indeed occasioned much difficulty in numismatic researches. The natural position of the legend is along the round of the medal, within the engrailed ring, commencing from left to right; there are instances also in which it is read from right to left; and even where it is partly to the left, partly to the right. Some legends appear only on the *exergue* (see the word); or upon two parallel lines, one above the type, the other at the bottom; sometimes they are placed across; at other times *saltier*-wise.

LEG. *Legio.*—Legion, the body of soldiers thus named by the Romans, was composed of cavalry and infantry, but the number of which it consisted differed considerably at different epochas. Under the republic, the legions were commanded by one of the consuls, and by their lieutenants. Under the emperors they were commanded by a *præfectus exercituum*. In the earliest ages of Rome, when the number of the legion did not exceed three thousand foot-soldiers, there were only three tribunes in each. But when afterwards the legion was augmented to four thousand and five thousand, that of the tribunes was carried to six; and on a further increase to six thousand infantry, the number of tribunes was increased again, even to sixteen. Each *manipulus* or division of two hundred men, had for its chief an officer named *ducenarius;* and he who commanded a century, or one hundred men, was called a *centurion.* Each legion had for its general ensign an eagle with stretched-out wings.— The cavalry which belonged to each legion bore the name of *alæ,* because usually placed on its flanks it formed its wings. It was divided into ten parts, called *turmæ,* as many as there were cohorts. The cavalry of the Roman armies were heavily armed; but made no use of spears, and had only flat saddles.—Among the Roman legionaries under the republic there was no light cavalry; it was a species of force known only among the auxiliary troops. But the Emperors established troops of light horse under the name of *sagittarii,* or archers, armed only with sword, bow, and quiver of arrows. When the legions had gained a victory, the Roman eagles were adorned with laurels, and so were the standards of the cavalry, and the ensigns on which the portrait of the Emperor was placed, and before which perfumes were burnt, as a religious ceremony.

The *Legions* were distinguished by the order in which they were respectively raised, as *prima, secunda, tria,* (LEG. I. II. III.) &c.—Previous to the time of Mark Antony, no mention is made of the Legions on Roman coins. The thirtieth (LEG. XXX.) is the last noted on the *denarii* of that Triumvir. The series up to XX. is perfect. From that to the thirtieth there are several gaps. The twenty-fifth, the twenty-eighth, and the twenty-ninth are not to be found on coins. The twenty-seventh appears, indeed, on one medal, but its genuineness is not authenticated. The twenty-second, surnamed *Primigenia,* is found on coins of Carausius.—Besides the denarii of Antony, of which an example is here intro-

duced, we find the number of the legions marked on coins struck under the Emperors Severus, Gallienus, Victorinus, Carausius, &c., as well as upon many colonial medals.—It is to be remarked, that upon the coins, not only of Mark Antony, but also of many emperors, the indication of legions, between the numbers twenty and thirty were incomplete. Their number, which had too much increased during the civil wars of the republic, was diminished by Augustus.—Dion Cassius relates that in the year of Rome, 758, the number of legions of Roman citizens was, according to some, twenty-three; according to others, twenty-five. Under Alexander Severus, there yet remain nineteen. As to the legions not composed of Roman citizens, the same author says that they had been either totally disbanded, or amalgamated with the other legions under different emperors. The imperial series of

Roman coins exhibit the number of the legions no further than the twenty-second: the seven following are not mentioned on them. But the *thirtieth* is again found on medals of Severus, of Galhenus, of Victorinus, and Carausius. Some of these intermediate legions are, however, recorded in lapidary inscriptions.

Legions were, after Augustus's time, sometimes designated by the same number. Thus there were *three* "third legions," distinguished from each other by the surnames of *Gallica, Cyrenaica,* and *Augusta;* also two "sixth legions," the one called *Victrix,* and the other *Ferrata.* The Emperor *Galba* raised a *Legio Prima,* surnamed *Adjutrix,* although *Nero* had already formed a first legion, called *Italica.*

With regard to the probable motives which led to the inscription of legions on Roman medals, it may be observed that not only Mark Antony and Clodius Macer; but in later times Septimius Severus and other Emperors were, in certain periods of their career, dependent in a great measure for their very existence on the favour of the troops, whom they thus sought to conciliate.—On colonial coins, the legions were numerically cited, either in consequence of certain veterans belonging to these legions having been sent by some of the emperors into those cities; or because the particular legions so marked happened to be stationed there. Accordingly, on coins of *Emerita* (now Merida in Portugal), we see LEG. V. and LEG. X., corresponding with the fact adduced by Dion Cassius, that a colony of old Legionaries was established in that Lusitanian city by Augustus. The coins of *Viminiacum* record the Fourth and Seventh Legions (LEG*iones* IV. and VII.) as having been placed there.—From the same cause the coins of the Dacian province present to us Legions V. and XIII.; and those of Egypt LEG*io* II. Traiana—(the Second Trajanian Legion.)

Legions derived their peculiar appellations from various causes.—Whilst the republic existed, they were almost wholly distinguished by their number alone, as Legio I. II. &c.—Some, however, even at this period, received their names from those of their commanders. The *Legiones Valerianæ,* or Valerian legions, were thus denominated, because they were raised by Caius Valerius Flaccus, the same chief who gave the name of *Valeria* to the Twentieth legion. On the denarii of Mark Antony we have the legions called *Antiqua, Classica, Lybica.* Under the Emperors, the legions received titles derived from the names or families of the reigning princes, as *Augusta, Flavia, Trajana, Ulpia,* &c. Also from deities, as *Minervia;* or from regions, as *Italica, Parthica, Macedonica,* &c.; or from some event, as *Victrix, Adjutrix, Liberatrix,* &c. Sometimes the legions bear the name of GEMELLA or GEMINA. But of all the surnames assigned to the Roman legions, none are so common as those of *Pia* and *Fidelis.*—Dion fully explains these names, and shews that Ti. Claudius caused the Seventh and Eleventh Legions, who in the sedition of Camillus had preserved their fidelity to him, to be named *Claudiæ et Fideles et Piæ*, by a *senatus consultum*.—To this may be added the celebrated marble, adduced by Gruter and Fabretti, inscribed under the reign of Commodus, on which C. Vesnius Vindex is called TRIB. MIL. LEG. VIII. AVG. QVO. MILITANTE. CVM. LIBERATA. ESSET. NOVIA. OBSIDIONE. LEGIO. PIA. FIDELIS. CONSTANS. COMMODA. COGNO-MINATA. EST. Monumental inscriptions should be studied conjointly with coins for the location of the legions : much information of importance will be found in Horsley's *Britannia Romana*, a standard work on the Roman inscriptions relating to Britain up to 1732. Gough, Lysons, and others, including Wellbeloved's *Eburacum*, J. E. Lee's *Caerleon*, and the *Collectanea Antiqua*, may be consulted for the more recent discoveries in Great Britain.

Legionum Insignia.—Most of the insignia of the Legions may be seen on the silver coins of Gallienus. As the legion was composed of *hastati, principes*, and *legionarii*, even after the form of the *Militia Romana* was changed by C. Marius, so there are to be observed on denarii of the Claudia family, and others, three military ensigns; the first of which may denote the Hastati, that is to say, those who formed the first line of the army, carrying spears; another, the *Principes*, who formed the second line of battle array, and were of a more robust age; and the third the eagle of the legionarii placed in the middle, between the two above mentioned. Upon a second brass of Galba

are three military standards, which, from being mounted on prows of galleys, denote the two services, the army and the navy. The eagle is the especial symbol of the legions. The legions were divided into cohorts, maniples, and centuries. To the second of these the hand, *manus*, which is often seen upon some of the standards, may apply.

Legionarii.—This is the name given to the foot soldiers of the Roman legions. The horsemen were distinguished by the appellation of *Equites*. Amongst the Legionarii the *Velites*, the *Hastati*, the *Principes*, and the *Triarii* (see these words), held a conspicuous place, as has above been alluded to. The term of sixteen years was the period fixed for the service of the Legionarii. Before the reign of S. Severus they were not permitted to marry, or at least to have their wives with them in the camp. The military discipline of these troops was very severe. They led a life of great hardship, and made long marches, laden with heavy burthens.

During peace they were employed in working on the fortifications of towns and of camps, as well as in repairing the high roads.

LEG*io* IV.—The legionary eagle, between two military ensigns.

Rev.—The Prætorian galley, with the legend of ANT*onius* AVG*ur* III. VIR. *Rei Publicæ Constituendæ*.

Many legions are found on the denarii of Antony, which he caused to be struck with ensigns and numbers, in order to ingratiate himself with the soldiers, and to display his resources both by sea and land.

LEG. VIII.—See *Pinaria gens*.

LEG. M. XX.—*Legio Macedonica*, or *Minervia Vicesima*, on a silver coin of Gallienus.—V. Banduri.

LEG. PRI.—*Legio Prima*, with the eagle and ensigns of the *First* Legion, on a silver coin of M. Antony.

LEG. PRO. COS.—*Legatus Pro-consule*, Legate for the Consul.—See *Sempronia* family.

LEG. PRO. PR.—*Legatus Pro Prætore.*—On a denarius belonging to the *Cæcilia* family we see on the obverse METEL. PIVS. SCIP. IMP., a male head, with curled beard and a fillet; below, an eagle's head and sceptre.—On the reverse, CRASS. IVN. LEG. PRO. PR., a curule chair, on the right of which is the head of an eagle, and above it are a cornucopiæ and a pair of scales.

On another silver coin of the same family, the legend METEL. PIVS. SCIP. IMP., and the type of a trophy between the lituus and prefericulum occupies the obverse; and the reverse exhibits a female head, with turreted crown, between an ear of corn and a caduceus, the legend being the same as above, shewing that Crassus jun., whilst LEGATVS PRO PRAETORE, caused these denarii to be struck in honour of his celebrated ancestor Metellus.

The Legate, or Deputy of the Prætor, was an officer who, according to the institution of Augustus, held the chief authority in the province of the Emperor, at the discretion of the Pro-consuls, who governed the provinces of the Roman people, and at the same time were accustomed to coin money for the use of the army, especially when war broke out in the province where they administered the government.—Hence P. CARISIVS LEG*atus* PRO PR*ætore*, under Augustus, for the public convenience, ordered a coinage of *denarii* for ten asses, and for the daily pay of the soldiers; also *quinarii*, the half of the *denarius*—viz., five asses—These denarii bear on their obverse the portrait of the above named Emperor, and on their reverses trophies of victory.

LEIBERTAS, instead of LIBERTAS, according to the ancient mode of spelling with the dipthong EI for the single letter I.—It is thus that it appears, with his head, on the denarius of M. Brutus, to show that he was the asserter of Liberty.—See *Junia*.

LEIBERTAS, with the head of the Goddess of Liberty veiled, appears on a coin of C. Cassius, in memory of the event in which he and Marcus Brutus, with the other conspirators, killed Julius Cæsar, and asserted what they, who "called" it freedom when themselves were free, termed the Liberty of the Republic.

LEN.—*Lentulus*, a surname of the *Cornelia* family.

LENTVLVS SPINT*er*.—This inscription appears on a silver coin of Augustus, having for its type the *Lituus* and the *Praefericulum* (see those words) which instruments of augury *Lentulus*, surnamed *Spinter*, caused to be engraved on the said coin, to shew his sacerdotal functions.

L. LENTVLVS FLAMEN. MARTIALIS, of whom and of whose sumptuous supper see Macrobius.—The name appears on a denarius of Augustus.

The *Lion* appears in the attitude of walking on coins of Mark Antony, of Antonine, Caracalla, Philip, Gallienus, Aurelian, Probus, and other emperors.—In this attitude he is also the symbol of Imperial *Consecration*, see MEMORIAE AETERNAE ; likewise of *Munificence*, see MVNIFICENTIA—SAECVLARES AVG.

A *Lion* with a thunderbolt in his mouth is

seen on coins of Caracalla, of Aurelian, of Postumus, Probus, and Diocletian.—He stands at the feet of Hercules in a brass medallion of Hadrian, and at the feet of Cybele (see MATRI DEVM), who also is seen seated on a lion.—On account of the abundance of these animals in that quarter of the globe, Africa is personified, having likewise a lion at her feet on coins of Hadrian, Commodus, and Diocletian.—A biga of lions, with the legend of AETERNITAS, is the type of Consecration.

A *Lion* pierced with a lance, which the Emperor on horseback holds in his hand, is seen on a coin of Commodus, with the legend VIRTVTI AVGVSTI.—On a first brass of Hadrian, the emperor on horseback is striking his dart at a lion running before him, with the legend VIRTVS AVGVST.—On a silver medal of Constantine is the same type ; see LIBERATOR ORBIS.

A *Lion* fighting with a stag, which it is tearing to pieces, appears on a coin of Augustus, struck in memory of a grand hunting of wild beasts, instituted in celebration of that emperor's birthday.—See *Durmia gens*,

A *Lion* and a boar yoked together to a chariot in which Victory is seated, and before which Hercules marches, is given by *Havercamp* among the Contorniate medals of Trajan.—On a coin

of the same emperor, four lions draw a car in which are Trajan and Plotina.

The *Lion* is the sign of Fortitude. Hence we see him on a coin of Gallienus as the accompanying type of LEG*io* IIII. FL*avia*.—By the same rule the *Lion* is the symbol of Hercules, and of Herculean labour and fortitude.—Represented with radiated head, and with the thunderbolt between his teeth, as on coins of Caracalla, Alex. Severus, Probus, Val. Maximianus, and other emperors, the *Lion* is the acknowledged symbol of *Empire* and of *Providence*.

On an elegant gold coin of Gallienus in the Imperial Cabinet at Vienna, the type of a lion with an eagle on its back appears within a crown of laurel, and below are the initial letters S. P. Q. R.—The lion's skin is seen on the head of some Roman Emperors, such as Commodus, Alexander Severus, and others ; also, though more rarely, on the head of Gallienus.

Leo (Flavius Valerius), surnamed the Great, of Thracian origin, was raised to the Empire of the East, A.D. 457, on the death of Marcianus. A prince of high character for clemency, generosity, and piety. He died A.D. 474.—His style on coins is D. N. LEO. PERP*etuus* F. AVG.—Gold and silver, common ; third brass, rare.

Leo II., the son of Zeno and of Ariadne, daughter of Leo I., was born at Rome A.D. 459, and created Cæsar while as yet a youth, by his grandfather. The following year, Leo the First dying, he was proclaimed Augustus, but soon after he himself died, having reigned only six months.—His style, as associated with his father, is on coins D. N. LEO ET. ZENO P.P. AVG. —Akerman observes that "if any coins exist on which the style of this Emperor is found alone, they are confounded with those of Leo I."— Gold and Quinarii very rare.

Leo III., surnamed *Isaurus*, from an Isaurian family of ignoble rank to which he belonged, was proclaimed Emperor by the soldiers near Nicomedia, and crowned in that royal city A.D. 717, when Theodosius III. abdicated the throne. He was a prince of some military talent, but of tyrannical disposition, and stands condemned by ecclesiastical writers of that period as impious, having been a great hater and destroyer of sacred images. Leo died A.D. 741.—His style is D. N. LEON. P. AV.—His gold coins are common ; silver and brass more or less rare.

Leo IV., surnamed *Chazarus*, because his mother Irene was the daughter of a Khan of the Chozars, was the son of Constantinus Copronymus. He was born at Constantinople A.D. 750, and proclaimed Emperor in the following year, in association with his father, whom he succeeded A.D. 775. He died A.D. 780, in the fourth year of his reign, and the thirtieth of his age.—His coins, on which he is styled LEO, are very rare in gold, and equally rare in third brass, if indeed there be any of his authentic in that metal.

Leo V., surnamed *Armenus*, son of the patrician Bardus, of Armenian origin, on the expulsion of Michael I., whose general he was,

was proclaimed Emperor by the army, A.D. 813. He was, however, assassinated in about seven years after he had ascended the throne.—There are only third brass extant of this insignificant Emperor of the East, coins equally rare and barbarous.

Leo VI., surnamed *Sapiens*, or *Philosopher*, the son of Basilius, succeeded his father as Emperor of the East, A.D. 886.—A learned man, but an indifferent soldier, he was first beaten by the Bulgarians, and afterwards by the Saracens. He died A.D. 911.—His style on his coins is LEON. BASILEVS. ROM.—The brass of this prince are rare, the silver still rarer, the gold most rare.

Leontius, an usurper in the reign of Zeno, who having assumed the purple in Syria, when he was soon afterwards taken prisoner by the Imperial army, and beheaded at Constantinople A.D. 488.—There are gold coins of Leontius, on which he is styled D. N. LEONTIVS. P. F. AVG. They are very rare.

Leontius, surnamed *Isaurus* from the birthplace of his family, was the *second* usurper of that name, and belonged to the patrician order. He employed the armies of Justinianus II. to overthrow that emperor, and to obtain his throne, A.D. 695.—Absimarus, however, defeated him in Dalmatia, and, cutting off his nose and ears, imprisoned him in a monastery, where he was put to death, together with Absimarus himself, on the restoration of Justinian the Second, A.D. 705.—On his coins which are *gold*, of the highest rarity, Leontius II. is styled D. LEONTI. A.—The unique third brass, published by Mionnet, is supposed to belong to Leontius I.

LEPI.—*Lepidus*, the surname of a Roman Patrician family, in which are found seventeen of the greater Magistracies.

Lepidus (Marcus), the most celebrated of his name and race, is that Triumvir whose weakness was as fatal to the Republic as the sanguinary disposition of his colleagues, Octavius and Antony. The year of his birth is unknown, but in the civil wars he is found following Cæsar's party, and his colleague in the Consulate, V.C. 708. The year following he was appointed Master of the Horse to the Dictator, at whose death he contrived to obtain the vacant high dignity of *Pontifex Maximus.*—Entrusted by the Senate with the government of Transalpine Gaul, he, through perfidy or the most inconsiderate fear, soon after gave up his legions to Mark Antony and Octavius, by whom he was at the same time admitted into that political association on which the second Triumvirate was formed, in the year of Rome 711 (43 A.C.), and took the honours of a triumph for his previous successes in Spain.—In recompense of his nefarious share in the proscriptive horrors that ensued, Lepidus had Spain and Gallia Narbonensis assigned to him in the division of provinces; elected consul for the second time *(iterum)* V.C. 712, he had the care of Italy whilst his brother-triumvirs were engaged in war with Brutus.—Having answered the purposes

of his more astute colleagues, the legions he commanded were seduced from him by the blandishments of Octavius, who, depriving him of his triumvirship (V.C. 718), still allowed him to pass the remainder of his life in tranquil obscurity at Circæum, on the shores of Latium, where he died (V.C. 741, B.C. 13) despised for his indolence of character, and total want of the talents necessary to sustain that leading part in the tragic drama of the times to which the selfishness of his ambition had induced him to aspire.

The gold coins of this Triumvir are of the highest rarity; the silver also are rare, especially those with the head of Octavius, and those without the head of Mark Antony, on the reverse.—On these he is styled M. LEP. IMP. IIIVIR. R.P.C.   *Marcus Lepidus Imperator Triumvir. Rei Publicæ Constituendæ.*

M. LEPIDVS. IIIVIR. R.P.C. Head of Lepidus to the left.—*Rev.* IIIVIR. A. P. F. L. MVSSIDIVS. T. F. LONGVS. A nude warrior standing with his left foot upon a shield, holding a spear and parazonium. In gold and silver.

Though the head of Lepidus appears on silver and gold coins of the Roman mint, yet it is never seen on those of brass of the same fabric. But on some very rare brass medals of certain Greek cities, and also of some *colonial* of Gallia Narbonensis, his portrait is found.

LEPIDVS. PONT. MAX. IIIVIR. R.P.C. (Lepidus, Sovereign Pontiff, Triumvir of the Republic.)—On a silver medal, the naked head of Lepidus has this legend around it.—On the reverse CAES. IMP. IIIVIR. R.P.C. The naked head of Octavius, general of the armies, triumvir of the republic.

Mongez, in his *Encyclopédie Méthodique, recueil d'antiquités*, observes, pointedly, "Lepidus was a man without talents, without energy; whom whimsical fortune took pleasure in elevating; who was twice consul, sovereign pontiff, triumpher without having fought an enemy, commanding thirty legions without knowing the art of war, triumvir and master of the fate of his two colleagues (Octavius and M. Antony) without being able to profit by it; and who finally dragged on a long old age in shame and contempt."

(M.) LEPIDVS. COS. IMP.—Sacrificial instruments (viz.: *Capeduncula, aspergillum, secespita, apex*),—Reverse: M. ANTON. COS. IMP. Augural symbols (viz.: *Lituus, præfericulum, corivus*).

On this denarius we see the title of IMP*erator* given to Lepidus, who, before medals of that kind were struck, had been already called *Imperator iterum*, according to Cicero. And not only had he legions under him, but he twice enjoyed triumphal honours, although from no personal claim to military merit.—On this coin Lepidus, as sovereign pontiff, exhibits the instruments of the priesthood, just as Antony's quality of augur is designated by the augural insignia.—See *Aemilia*.

Leptis Magna, a city (says Pellerin, *Recuil*, vol. iv. p. 15), situate at some distance from the river Cynipas (Wad-Quaham) in the *Syrtica*, by which is understood the entire space between the Syrtis Major (Gulf of Sidra) and the Syrtis Minor (Gulf of Cabes), the shores of which form at this time the greater part of the territory called the kingdom of Tripoli. It was called Magna to distinguish it from another Leptis, which was in Byzacium or Emporiæ, and which was called *Leptis Parva*, below Hadrumetum, now called *Lemta*.—Leptis Magna is now called *Lebda*, not far from Tripoli. It is marked as a Roman colony in the Itinerary of Antoninus.—Vaillant states it to have been invested with the *Jus Italicum*, by Sept. Severus; but gives no description or engraving of any of its money.—Havercamp, in his notes on the Queen of Sweden's medals, has given a second brass, which bears on its obverse DRVSO CAESARI with the head of Drusus, son of Tiberius, and on the reverse a head of Mercury, with the following legend:—PERMISSV *Lucii* APRONI*i* PROCO*n*S*ulis* III. This medal he attributes to Leptis; but on no other apparent ground than that the said Apronius was the successor of M. Camillus in the Pro-consulate of Africa. The coins of this city consist of Colonial Autonomes, with Latin legends, and Imperial of Augustus and Tiberius, with Latin or Greek legends.—Autonomous and Imperial coins, with Punic legends, are also assigned to Leptis Major, (which is said to have been founded by the Phœnicians). But, says M. Hennin, *ces attributions sont douteuses.*—Pellerin has given three medals, which he inclines to assign to the greater Leptis—1. Has the helmeted head of Rome, and COL. VIC. IVL. LEP. Reverse: a bull, with names of Duumvirs. —2. Female head with same legend on obverse, and same type on reverse.—3. A female head, with palm branch. Over the head is PR. II. VIR., and below it C. V. I. L. *Colonia Victrix Julia Leptis*, shewing its origin under Julius Cæsar.

Lex, a Law.—This word in its peculiar sense, as applied to the Romans, signifies that order or command, which was decided upon by the Roman people in their assemblies by centuries; *Lex est quam Populus Centuriatis comitiis sciverit*. The laws were proposed by certain high magistrates, most frequently in the *Forum*, or in the *Campus Martius*; under stated preliminary forms, which being gone through, every one was permitted to speak for or against them. And if a law passed, it was engraved on a table of brass; and being thus received, it remained in force until it pleased the people to abolish, or, as it was called, abrogate it *(abrogare legem)*. During the republic a very great number of laws were published, either by the Decemvirs under the name of the Twelve Tables, or by the Consuls, or the Dictators, or the Tribunes of the people.—The following are those few laws to which allusion is made on coins of the Romans :—

Lex Didia, de Pœnis Militum.—Traces of this law, in reference to military punishments, are found, or said to be found, on a silver coin of the *Didia* family; on the obverse of which appears the head of Minerva, and behind it ROMA, in monogram. On the reverse are two men engaged in combat, one of them armed with a whip, the other with a sword, and both bearing shields. The legend on the exergue is T. DEIDI*us*.—Opinions amongst the learned respecting this representation are various enough, and the question seems still undecided.—Havercamp has given a long account of them in his Commentary on Morell's *Thesaurus*. Some refer it to the castigation of slaves, during the servile war; others to the restoration of military discipline by a law proposed by T. Didius *(Lex Didii)*, and to the punishment of the soldier with the centurion's rod *(centurionis vitis)*; others think otherwise. But none of their explanations carry conviction of the truth, nor even of that which is probable, to our minds, respecting the meaning of this very curious and *unique* type.— See *Didia*.

Lex Julia, de Maritandis Ordinibus.—History bears testimony to the good intention of Augustus in renewing by this enactment, the provisions of an ancient law *(Lex Papia Poppæa)*, compelling and encouraging men of a proper age to take to themselves wives, giving rewards to those who had children born to them in wedlock, and on the other hand inflicting penalties on *bachelors.*—Amongst the coins of Augustus, there is one on the reverse of which appears the Emperor seated on a small *estrade*, and before him a figure standing, in the act of presenting to him a naked child; on the exergue we read IMP. XIII.—Schulze, in the introduction to his Science of Ancient Coins, expresses an opinion that "the type of this medal seems to be explained by those words of Suetonius *(In Aug.* cap. 34), in which he says:—*Sic quoque abolitionem ejus (Legis Juliæ) publico spectaculo pertinaciter postulante Equite, adcitos Germanici liberos, receptosque partim ad se, partim in patris gremium, ostentavit : manu vultuque significans, ne gravarentur imitari juvenis exemplum.*"

Lex Papia.—A law carried in the time of the republic by C. Papius, a Tribune of the people, for excluding foreigners from Rome.— There is a denarius of the *Papia* family, edited by Morell, which close to the head of Juno Sispita exhibits a tablet *(tabella)*, on which is inscribed the word PAPI. and which is supposed to allude to this *Lex Papia*, which in the opinion of Cicero was equally unjust and inhuman.

Lex Porcia.—The law so called was made by Porcius Laeca, Tribune of the people in 453, in favour of Roman citizens, whom it exempted from being subjected to the ignominious punishment of the scourge.—*Porcia Lex*, says Cicero, *virgas ab omnium civium Romanorum corpore amovit.* [*Pro C. Rabir.* c. iv.].—This example took place only in the cities, and was not allowed to prevail in the camp on behalf of the soldiers, who were entirely dependent on their general.—An allusion to the law of appeal *(Provocatio)* offers itself on a coin of the *Porcia* family; on the obverse of which is the winged head of Minerva, with the legend P. LAECA and ROMA.—On the reverse is a figure in a military dress; a Lictor behind crowning a citizen: on the exergue we read the word PROVOCO.—See *Porcia*.

Lex Tabellaria.—A law carried by L. Cassius Longinus, a Tribune of the people, and which prohibited the Roman citizen from giving his suffrage *viva voce*, and required him to write down on a tablet (see *tabella*), the first letters of the name of the candidate for whom he voted.—The *tabella* was also used in public judgments *(in judiciis publicis)*, and the Prætor distributed to the Judges three tablets; viz.: that of *absolution*, marked with a letter A.; that of *condemnation*, on which was written the letter C.; and the third tablet, demanding more ample information, was marked with the letters N. and L., signifying *Non liquet.*—The memory of L. Cassius Longinus, and his *Lex tabellaria* are recalled by a denarius of the *Cassia* family,

on the obverse of which is the head of VESTA; and on the reverse a round temple, within which is a curule chair *(sella curulis).* In the field of the coin is on one side an urn, and on the other a *tabella*, inscribed A. C., that is to say *Absolvo.* —*Condemno.* This Cassius, having, in the year of Rome 641, been appointed, under the Peduceian law, Commissioner with prætorian power to investigate cases of violation of chastity in Vestals, summoned again to trial, and condemned (to death) Licinia and Marcia, who had been acquitted by L. Metellus P.M., according to Asconius Pædianus on *Cic. pro Milone.*—Cassius was so great an exemplar of severity, that he was commonly called *reorum scopulus*, and *Cassiana judicia* became a proverb. [See Morell.] —The curule chair within the temple denotes the Prætorian power. The urn (or cista) is that into which the *tabellæ* were cast.—There is also another silver coin of the same family, which bearing the same reverse, but having on its obverse the head and name of LIBERTAS, belongs to the history of the same Cassius. In these designs the ballot law concerning trials is alluded to, by which, in all cases except that of treason, the people were allowed to vote by tablets *(i. e.* the *ballot)*, "a regulation (adds the unsuspecting Eckhel, who had not lived to see the shameful example of the United States as to the abuses, corruptions, and intimidations practised under it), eminently adapted for the preservation of *Liberty.*"

LIBER.—This appellation was given to Bacchus, for various reasons noticed by historians. Not from a license of expression, says Seneca, is the inventor of wine called *Liber*, but because he rescues the free mind from the thraldom of cares, and impels it with more quickness and greater boldness into all enterprises. His feasts were called *Liberalia.*—Macrobius affirms that *Liber* and *Mars* were one and the same deity. And it was under that notion that the Romans worshipped both by the appellation of *Pater*.

LIBERO PATRI.—This legend appears on a rare gold and on an equally rare silver coin of Sept. Severus, having for its type the

god Bacchus, under the image of a young man who holds in his left hand the thyrsus, and in his right a dish or cup; at his feet is a panther or tiger.— It may be supposed, says Pedrusi, who gives an engraving of this medal *(Mus. Farnes.* vol. iii. p. 291), that the vain devotion which Severus professed towards this divinity might occasion him to believe himself indebted to the high patronage of Father Bacchus for the favourable issue of his military enterprises in Asia— " *Nella stolta credenza di quei tempi veneravasi Bacco come Signore e Conquestatore dell' Oriente ; e in consequenza pregiavasi molto in quelle regioni la di lui protezione.*"

The alleged reason for giving the appellation of *Liber* to Bacchus has already been stated.— The thyrsus, observes Pedrusi, is the appropriate sceptre of Bacchus, but in the present instance he holds instead of it a spear in his left hand; and in that peculiarity the type conforms to Macrobius's description of the image of *Liber Pater* worshipped with peculiar attachment by the Lacedemonians, and which bore (says the writer) " *Hasta insigne, non Thyrso.*"

Bacchus is attended by a tiger or panther, as an animal consecrated to him, and which is often seen on medals and bas reliefs drawing the chariot of the god.—Alluding to this Seneca *(in Hyppolit.)* is thus descriptive in his poetry :—

Et tu thyrsigerâ Liber ab India
Intonsi juvenis perpetuum comâ
Tigres pampinea cuspide territans, &c.

And thus also sings Martial (lib. 8, epig. 26):—
Nam cum captivos ageret sub curribus Indos
Contentus geminâ tigride Bacchus erat.

The head of *Liber*, crowned with ivy, appears on coins of the *Cassia, Petronia, Porcia, Vibia, Vipsania,* and *Volteia* families.

LIBERO. P. CONS. AVG. *Libero Patri Conservatori Augusti.*—With a panther or tiger, sacred to Bacchus, who is the same with *Liber pater.* Gallienus on a silver and a third brass coin calls him his *Conservator*, as indeed he was in the habit of calling Jupiter, Mars, Mercury, Neptune, and other members of the Heathen Pantheon—all were Preservers of Emperors.

Liberalitas.—Liberality, being one of the princely virtues and at the same time a most popular quality, appears both as a legend and as a type on a great many Roman Imperial medals. These attest the occasions when the Emperors made a display of their generosity towards the people by all kinds of distributions amongst them, in money and provisions. In the earlier age this was called *Congiarium (Munus)*, because they distributed *congios oleo plenos.*—In the time of the free republic, the Ediles were specially entrusted with these distributions, as a means of acquiring the good-will of the people. The same practice was followed under the Emperors; and we occasionally find on their coins the word CONGIARIVM, but the more common term is LIBERALITAS, to which is frequently added the number of times, I. II. III. up to VII. and VIII. that such liberality has been exercised by each Emperor.—On these occasions of Imperial munificence, a certain sum of money was for the most part given to each person, and when grain was distributed, or bread, to prevent the evils of dearness and famine from affecting the Roman populace, it was called *Annona;* (see the word.) But when something beyond their ordinary pay was bestowed upon the soldiers, it was denominated *Donativum,* a word, however, not found on coins, but comprised under that of *Liberalitas,* or of *Congiarium;* and after the reign of Marcus Aurelius, CONGIARIVM is no longer found, and the expression LIBERALITAS is alone employed.

Liberality is personified under the image of a woman, holding in one hand a *tessera,* or square tablet, furnished with a handle, and on which is a certain number of points, shewing that the prince had given to the people money, corn, and other articles of consumption. In the other hand she holds a *cornucopiæ,* to indicate the abundance of wheat contained in the public granaries.—*Liberalitas* is represented as presiding at all *congiaria* (see the word). The liberalities of the *Augusti,* by which the distribution of their bounties to the people is signified, were of two kinds, ordinary and extraordinary.—The first mention of *Liberalitas* occurs on coins of Hadrian; on those of succeeding Emperors it is frequently reiterated. Indeed these instances of imperial generosity are more carefully recorded on medals than they are by history.—On a coin of Hadrian, struck under his second consulate, in the year of Rome 870, we see two figures seated on a *suggestum,* or raised platform. The genius of Liberality, with the attributes above described, stands beside or behind them; and another figure is ascending a small flight of steps, which leads to the raised platform, where the gift of the Emperor is received.—On a gold coin of Antoninus Pius, and also on one of Philippus senior, the Emperor sits in a curule chair, placed on a raised platform; before him stands the image of *Liberalitas,* pouring out from a cornucopiæ money into the bosom of a man, who is ascending by steps on the opposite side.—On a silver coin of Antonine we see the figure of a woman

standing by herself, holding a horn of plenty in her left hand, and in her right hand a *tessera,* or a tablet, which specifies the quantity of wheat delivered to each person at a low price through the *liberality* of the Emperor, or on which was inscribed what was given to each citizen.—A gold coin of Elagabalus exhibits that Emperor sitting on a *suggestum,* with Liberality standing on one side, and the Prætorian Prefect, or a Lictor, on the other—distributing the *congiarium* to the Roman citizens.—In that emphatic tribute of eulogy to Hadrian's unexampled munificence, the celebrated coin which bears the legend of LOCVPLETATORI ORBIS TERRARVM, we see that the type refers to the *Liberalitates* of that emperor, who, under the auspices of the Goddess, is distributing his bounties with an outstretched hand.—Many medals consecrated to the liberality of the emperors shew by a numeral cipher how many times that liberality has been repeated by the same prince.—Thus, a coin of Antoninu Pius, struck a short time before his death, under his fourth consulate, in the year of Rome 914, bears the epigraph LIBERALITAS AVG. IX., that is to say, *the ninth Liberality or distribution made by the Emperor.*—The medals of Commodus and of Caracalla present to us eight liberalities or donations; those of Hadrian and M. Aurelius record seven. On the coins of Sept. Severus and of Geta, we find indications of six liberalities; there are five recorded on a medal of Alexander Severus; four on coins of Elagabalus, of Gordianus Pius, and of Gallienus; three on some of Verus; and of the two Philips (in these the Emperors, father and son, are represented sitting together, without attendants or recipients). It is, however, to be borne in mind as to the emperors of whom some medals offer us a more considerable number of liberalities, that some others give us also most of the preceding liberalities.—The greater part of these coins refer to the times when it was the custom to bestow on each citizen a quantity of corn from out of the public granaries.—One of the most remarkable of Hadrian's liberalities was that of his having remitted to the people their arrears of taxes accumulated during the space of sixteen years, and of his having caused the vouchers, by which the Imperial Treasury could have made good its claim to fiscal dues, to be burnt in the Forum at Rome.—See RELIQVA VETERA, &c.

LIB. AVG. TR. P. COS. II. S. C.—The Emperor, on an estrade, distributes a *liberality.*

Behind him is the prætorian prefect; on the right, a little in advance, stands the Goddess Liberalitas ; a recipient of the bounty is ascending the steps.—Large brass of Pertinax.

LIB. AVGG. VI. ET V.—*Liberalitas Augustorum Sexta et Quinta.*—This, which appears on first brass coins of Caracalla and of Geta, means the sixth liberality of the former, and the fifth of his brother Geta.—The two princes are sitting together on an estrade, and a figure stands at the bottom of the steps.

LIBERALITAS AVG. TR. P. II. COS. S.C—On a first brass of Septimius Severus we see that Emperor sitting on the same estrade with his two sons, Caracalla and Geta, and Liberality, with another figure standing near them : a fifth figure appears in the act of ascending the steps.—Herodianus says of Severus that he made the most profuse and costly distributions.—There is a gold coin of the same Emperor inscribed LIBERALITAS VI., with the above type.

LIBERALITAS AVG., in others with II. III. IIII.—On a gold coin of Gordianus Pius the personification of Liberality stands holding up the *tessera* in her right hand, and *two* horns of abundance in her left, as designating a *double* gift made at that time ; or, as was usual to be done, a donative to the soldiery, a congiarium to the people.—A great many " Liberalities" of Gordianus Pius appear on the coins of that prince, of which no notice is taken by historians.

LIBERALITAS VII. IMP. VIII. COS. III. S. C.—This legend appears on a first brass of Marcus Aurelius, which has on its reverse the usual type of Liberality standing alone. Noris pronounces this seventh *Liberalitas* to have been the donative given by that emperor to the Legions in Germany.

LIBERALITAS AVGVSTORVM.—The Liberality of the Emperors.—On a large brass of Balbinus and Pupienus, with this legend on the reverse, we see an *estrade*, on which are seated those two emperors and the young Gordian, then only Cæsar, between two figures standing, one of whom holds a tablet; and at the foot of the estrade is a *sixth* figure.—Here, then, we have three imperial personages, attended by the prætorian prefect, and in the supposed presence of the Liberal Goddess, presenting a gift to a Roman citizen.—On a coin of Valerianus, with the above legend, that Emperor and his son Gallienus appear, both clothed in the toga and laureated, sitting on raised curule chairs ; another figure stands near them, extending the right hand, and holding a wand or sceptre in the left.

LIBERALITAS. AVG. II (or III).—The type of a Congiarium, in which the Emperor, seated on an estrade, is distributing presents.— On gold of Antoninus Pius; also with legend of LIBERALITAS. AVG. VII. IMP. VIII. COS. II.; on first brass of the same Emperor.

We perceive from his coins that the first Liberality exercised by this Emperor took place in his second Consulate. The third Consulate offers two following each other. Capitolinus in

many passages of his history notices the *congiaria* and the donatives bestowed by Antonine, and *vini, olei, et tritici, penuriam per aerarii sui damna emendo, et gratis populo dando, sedavit.* But he mentions these generally without making mention of the time. Of these liberalities, however, which the coins in question extol, one doubtless seems to have been that of which Capitolinus speaks thus—*Nuptias filiæ suæ Faustinæ usque ad donativum militum celeberrimas fecit.*

LIBERALITAS COS. IIII. AVG. IIII. or V.—LIBERALITAS AVG. V.—On first brass of Antoninus Pius. Similar type to the preceding medals, except that here the prætorian prefect stands behind the *Augustus.*

LIB. IIII. COS. IIII.—A woman stands with the *labarum* in her right hand and a cornucopiæ in her left.—Silver coin of Antonine. According to Capitolinus, on the day when Verus took the *toga virilis,* Antoninus Pius dedicated the temple of his father and was *liberal* to the people. This silver coin, in which *Liberalitas* is represented as holding the splendid *labarum* instead of the accustomed *tessera,* teaches us that the liberality of the Emperor was also extended to the soldiers, as indeed is testified by Capitolinus, who, however, takes no notice of the time : *Congiarium populo dedit, militibus donativum addidit.*

LIBERALI (tas Aug. Cos. IIII.)—A woman standing, holding in her right hand a tessera, and in her left a labarum, in which is VI.— First brass of Antoninus Pius.

LIBERAL*itas* AVG. II.; in others III.; in others IIII.—Liberality is standing (in the field of the coin a star).—Elagabalus. Silver and second brass.—On a first brass medal of the same Emperor he is figured seated on an estrade distributing gifts.

This vile youth profaned and degraded the name of Liberality by having two about the year A.D. 220 ; but the cause of them is not assigned.—Thus much is known on the authority of Lampridius that the mad-brained monster caused a species of lottery tickets to be distributed amongst the people, which assigned to " the fortunate holders" ten camels, or ten pounds (libræ) of gold, or as many pounds of lead, &c.; whilst other lots appropriated to those who drew them ten bears, ten dormice, ten lettuces, &c., whereby the populace, whether desirous of gain or of amusement, were abundantly delighted.

LIBERAL. AVG. TR. P. COS. II. SC.—
The Emperor seated on an estrade; in advance
of him, on the right hand, is the personification
of Liberality; behind him stands the prœtorian
prefect; a figure is ascending the staves of the
raised platform.—On a first brass of Pertinax
this legend and type appear, and with apparent
fidelity and truth, for Capitolinus observes that
the donatives and *congiaria* which Commodus
had promised Pertinax distributed.—[There is
also a second brass of Pertinax with the same
legend, but the type is simply that of Liberality
standing.]

LIBERALITAS AVGVSTI. III. S.C.—The
Emperor seated on a *suggestum*, two figures
standing behind him, the statue of the goddess
at his right hand, and a figure ascending from
below.—On a first brass of Alexander Severus,
under whom were struck other coins in each
metal, recording a *fourth* act of similar munificence, and on which seven, and even eight
figures are seen at the foot of the estrade.—The

illustration selected is taken from a medallion of
this Emperor.

LIBERALITAS AVG. or AVGVSTI.—On
a first brass of Maximinus the emperor is represented sitting on a curule chair surmounting a
platform on which are three other figures; and
there are several small ones at the foot of the
suggestum.

LIB. *Libertas.*—LIB. AVG. *Libertas Augusti,* or *Augustæ.*

LIBERATIS CIVIBVS.—To Citizens restored
to Liberty.—This inscription, which appears on
a rare silver coin of Pertinax, is new to the
Roman mint; but its meaning is obvious, as
struck by the virtuous prince who restored
Rome to liberty, after the tyranny of Commodus
had been abolished. It is, however, more
difficult to find any agreement between the
epigraph and the type of this medal, which is
simply the usual one of Liberality (a woman
with *tessera* and *cornucopiæ*). It appears that
by this reverse only the liberality of Pertinax is
indicated, which has been noticed on a preceding
medal, but which was the more agreeable to the
Roman people, because it was a liberality no
longer bestowed on citizens oppressed with
tyranny, but granted at length *liberatis civibus*—
to freemen.

LIBERATOR ORBIS.—The Liberator of
the World.—This new title, and sufficiently

assumptive, appears on a third brass of Constantine the Great, the type which it accompanies
being that of the Emperor on horseback with
his right hand raised, and a lion crouching
under his horse's feet.—Eckhel refers it to the
successes of Constantine over either his rivals or
the barbarians whose incursions were pernicious
to the whole Roman world, and who therefore on this medal are shadowed forth under
the image of a lion trampled upon by a horseman.

LIBERATOR REIPVBLICAE.—This legend
is found on a gold coin of Magnentius, who is
typified on the reverse as on horseback, offering
his right hand to a woman turret-crowned, holding a palm branch and cornucopiæ.—It forms
one amongst several medals struck under this
usurper, in which, prematurely enough, he
boasts of himself as the liberator of the republic,
the renovator of the Imperial City, and the
restorer of the liberties of the Roman world,
chiefly grounded on his victory over Nepotianus,
who only imitated him in assuming the purple,
and in acting with great cruelty during a short
career.

LIBERI IMP. GERM. AVG. *Liberi Imperatoris Germanici Augusti.*—This legend
appears on an elegant gold coin of Vitellius,
which has for the type of its reverse the naked
heads of that Emperor's two sons, looking
towards each other. The names of these children are not known. Of one of them Tacitus
speaks (Hist. ii.) in reference to the time
when reports were sent to Vitellius respecting
the death of Nero:—"*Mox universum exercitum occurrere infanti filio jubet: perlatum,
et paludamento opertum, sinu retinens, Ger-
manicum appellavit.*"—According to Suetonius,
he perished at the same time with his father
and uncle.

LIBERI IMP. AVG. VESPAS*ianus.*—The
heads of Titus and Domitian, on a silver coin
of Vespasian.

This reverse is taken from the above cited
coin of Vitellius, except that the faces in
the latter look towards, and these look from,
each other. Titus and Domitian are here
called the children of the Emperor Vespasian;
their mother was Flavia Domitilla; and each in
his turn reigned after the father, but both died
without male issue.

There is another rare and elegant silver coin
of Vespasian, with the same legend, but of
which the type consists of two veiled figures
standing, each holding in his right hand a
patera. These represent Titus and Domitian,
on whom their father conferred the honours of
the priesthood, in the anticipation of their
future succession to the empire. This custom
was borrowed from the example of Augustus,
in his adoption of Caius and Lucius, on
which occasion that Emperor placed the one
amongst the Pontiffs and the other amongst the
Augurs.

LIBERIS AVG*usti* COL. A. A. P.—The
Colonia Augusta Aroë Patrensis (in *Achaia)*
is pronounced by Vaillant, and confirmed by

Eckhel, to have struck a second brass coin, which throws a light on the domestic history of Claudius. On the obverse is that Emperor's image and superscription; on the reverse is the uncovered head of Britannicus between the heads of his sisters Antonia and Octavia, placed on a cornucopiæ—a proof of the fecundity of the Imperial house.—See *Patrae Col.*

LIBERT. *Libertas.*—This word appears behind the head of the Goddess of Liberty, on a silver coin of the *Cassia* family.

LIBERTAS.—Liberty is represented in two ways on coins: the one as a woman with a naked head, which is the image of Roman Liberty; the other having her head covered with a veil, and adorned with a diadem, is the effigy of the Goddess of Liberty, whose temple was on Mount Aventine. The veil is in this case the token of divinity, as indeed the diadem is the ornament of a goddess.—Liberty is represented not only on Consular medals, but also with considerable frequency on those of the Imperial series.

The head of Liberty is the type of many medals of Roman families; she is crowned with an olive garland in Licinia; with laurel in Junia, Pedania, Servilia, Vibia; and her head-dress in different styles on coins of the Cæcilia, Cassia, Considia, Junia, Petillia, Porcia, Postumia, Sempronia, Silia, and Valeria families; she appears veiled on the denarii of the Æmilia, Calpurnia, Crepusia, Lollia, Lutatia, Mamilia, Marcia, and Sulpicia families; and she is both veiled and laureated on a medal of the Sestia family.—On the greater part of the denarii, struck by the conspirators against Cæsar, we see the *head of Liberty*, sometimes ornamented, at other times veiled. "By this symbol (says Millin) they intended to shew that they had taken up arms only to deliver Rome from the tyranny of Julius; whilst on the other hand even Cæsar himself pretended also that to avenge the liberty of the Roman people was his sole object."—On a celebrated silver coin the head of M. Brutus appears on one side; and on the other a cap between two daggers, with this historically interesting inscription EID*ibus* MAR*tiis;* "to the Ides of March," the day of Cæsar's murder.—Dion Cassius (in the 25th chap. of his 47th book) also acquaints us that Brutus caused coins to be struck, of which the type was similar to the one above described. The same writer adds that by this type and by a medal bearing the legend of LIRERTAS P.R. REST. (Liberty restored to the Roman people), Brutus wished to shew that, conjointly with Cassius, he had restored the liberty of his country.—See EID. MAR.—M. BRVTVS—and *Junia* family.

Liberty is often depicted under the figure of a woman standing, with a hat or cap (pileus) in her right hand, and holding in her left a hasta, or perhaps that particular wand which the Romans called *rudis* or *vindicta*, with which slaves were slightly struck, at the moment of their emancipation. Under this form and with such attributes she is seen on medals of Claudius,

Vitellius, Galba, Vespasian, Nerva, Trajan, Marciana, Hadrian, Antonine, Commodus, Severus, Caracalla, Geta, Elagabalus, Alexander Severus, Mamæa, Gordianus Pius, Trajanus Decius, Trebonianus Gallus, and Claudius Gothicus.—On a medal of Hadrian we see Liberty seated, holding in the left hand a branch, and in the right a spear.—A coin of Galba shews us this Goddess standing, with a horn of plenty in the left hand, holding in her right the *pileus* or cap of liberty.—On a coin of Antoninus Pius she holds a *patera* in her right hand.—On a medal of Clodius Macer, and on a gold coin of Galba, restored by Trajan, she holds a cap in the right and the *patera* in the left hand.—The pileus held in the right and the cornucopiæ in the left are the attributes of Liberty on coins of Antoninus, Elagabalus, Volusianus, Gallienus, Quintillus, Aurelianus, Julianus the usurper, and Julianus II.

LIBERTAS AVG*usta* (August Liberty), or LIBERTAS AVG*ustorum* (the Liberty of the Emperors), "who called it freedom when *themselves* were free." We find the title of LIB. P. R. (the Liberty of the Roman *people*), indiscriminately expressed on coins of Galba, Vitellius, Vespasian, Nerva, Hadrian, Antonine, Commodus, Gordianus Pius, Treb. Gallus, and Gallienus, as if LIBERTAS PVBLICA and LIBERTAS RESTITVTA were epigraphs applicable to the political state of the Roman Commonwealth under the best and mildest of those princes, even a Nerva, or an Antonine.

Liberty is a type especially repeated on the medals of Galba; a circumstance not surprising, when it is considered that after the death of Nero the people testified so lively a joy, and so fully believed that the republic was re-established, that according to the testimony of Suetonius, they ran through the streets, their heads covered with the cap of liberty.

Liberty, in a biga, appears on coins of the Crepusia, Mamilia, and Marcia families; and in a quadriga on a denarius of the family Cassia; she sometimes holds a cap with one hand and the reins of the horses in the other, or otherwise she holds the reins with both hands.—On a silver coin of L. Dolabella, in the Cornelia family, a figure of Victory flying through the air offers a crown to Liberty.

LIBERTAS. *Head of Liberty.—Reverse.* BRVTVS.—Procession of the Consul, between two lictors, preceded by the *accensus*, a public officer of Rome, appointed to call courts and assemblies.—On a silver coin of M. BRVTVS.—See the name.

LIBERTAS. *Head of Liberty.—Reverse. Populo Romano* REST*ituta.*—The pileus or cap of Liberty, between two daggers.—On another denarius of M. BRVTVS.—See the name.

LEIBERTAS for LIBERTAS.—The head of a female crowned with a *nimbus* or glory; on others veiled besides —On a denarius of C. Cassius Longinus, the colleague of Brutus, who here places the head of Liberty on his medals, because he had taken up arms in her cause.

LIBERTATIS.—See *Lollia* gens.

LIBERTAS AVGVSTA S. C.—The goddess standing, holds the *pileus* in her right hand, and extends her left.—This legend and type appear on a second brass of Claudius, as if *he* had restored liberty to the Republic after Caligula's tyranny and oppression.

LIBERTATIS P. R. VINDEX.—This flattering title—*Vindicator of the Liberty of the Roman People*—appears on the obverse of a silver medallion of that *Liberticide*, Augustus! So much for Roman flattery. It is, however, the only instance in which the adopted son of the great Julius received such adulation on a coin, and none of the succeeding emperors offer on their respective coins a similar example.—The reverse of this coin exhibits a female figure, holding a caduceus; near to which is an altar with a serpent on it. The word PAX is in the field of the coin, and the whole is within a laurel garland.

LIBERTAS P. R.—The Liberty of the Roman People.—This legend appears on a denarius of Galba, which presents the image of *Liberty* in an unusual attitude. She is depicted under the form of a woman standing between two corn ears, and raising her hands towards heaven.—"It seems (says Eckhel) that this type involves a fine allegory, namely, that Liberty exhorts the people to devote themselves anew to the pursuits of agriculture, after the extinction of that execrable tyranny with which Nero had desolated the empire—as if in joyful accents she exclaimed to the Roman husbandmen, with Maro:—

"*Pascite ut ante boves, pueri, submittite tauros.*"

LIBERTAS RESTITVTA. S. C.—The restoration of liberty is for the first time typified on a first brass of Galba, by a group representing that Emperor standing, in the toga, and raising up

a kneeling female figure, whilst a soldier stands behind him, allusive to the freedom of the Roman people rescued from destruction by the death of Nero, and the accession of Galba.

This coin of Galba evidently formed the prototype from which Hadrian afterwards took his types in reference to restored provinces.

On a first brass of Hadrian, with the same legend, we see the Emperor seated on an estrade, below which stands a woman, who offers in her left hand a child to the Emperor.—Eckhel expresses himself at a loss to know what this type signifies, unless it be to what Spartianus mentions: *Liberis proscriptorum duodecimas bonorum concessit.*

LICI. *Licinius.*—LICIN. *Licinianus.*

Licinia.—A plebeian family. Its surnames on coins are *Crassus, Macer, Murena, Nerva, Stolo.* From this stock many illustrious branches, adorned by men of consular and pontifical dignity, have sprung, as the above appellations serve to impart.—There are silver medals bearing the name of this family amongst those struck by the moneyers of Augustus.—The brass pieces are the *As*, or its parts, and some are also by the moneyers of Augustus.—There are thirty-one varieties. *Silver* and *first brass* rare; the rest common.

The following denarius of this family, bearing the surname of *Crassus*, is rare:—

The head of Venus: behind which is S. C.

Rev. P. CRASSVS M. F.—A soldier standing, holds in his left hand a spear and buckler, with his right he holds a horse by the bridle.

⁕This silver coin appears to have been struck by P. Crassus, the son of Marcus Crassus, killed by the Parthians, and who himself lost his life in the same war; but who, previously to the Parthian war, followed the camp of Cæsar in the Gallic war, as the latter often testifies in his Commentaries. Whether this denarius, as some have supposed, was struck by him whilst he was quæstor in Gaul, or at another time, is uncertain.—The type of the reverse is believed to allude to the ceremony of the *transvectio equi*, or parading of the horse, accustomed to be performed before the Censor, thus recalling to remembrance an ancestral honour, for both his father and grandfather were censors.—See Spanheim, TOM. ii. p. 99.

The following denarius of the same family, under the surname of *Stolo*, is also rare:—

AVGVSTVS TR. POT.—Augustus on horseback, holding a garland in his right hand.

Rev. The pontifical *Apex* between two *ancilia*, with P. STOLO IIIVIR.—On first and second brass of Augustus we read P. LICINIVS STOLO IIIVIR.

This Licinius, who, as tribune of the people, caused a law to be passed, prohibiting any Roman citizen from possessing more than five hundred acres of land, was, according to Varro, called *Stolo*, because he bestowed so much care in cultivating his land, that no one could find a *stolo*, or off-shoot of a plant, on his farm.— One of this man's descendants was Stolo, whom these coins shew to have been a monetal triumvir of Augustus —Vaillant is of opinion that on these denarii Augustus is exhibited on his return from Syria, entering the city with the honours of an ovation, because without bloodshed he had recovered Roman citizens and standards from the Parthians, as Dion relates; to which event the reverse type is also thought to bear reference, for these military standards were hung up in the temple of Mars Ultor, whose *flamen*, or priest, wore the *apex*, and whose duty it was to preserve the *ancilia.*—See the word.

Licinius (Publius Flavius Claudius Galerius Valerius Licinianus) was born of an obscure family in Dacia, A.D 263 : distinguished himself against the Persians.—Upon the death of Severus II., he was named Cæsar and Augustus by Galerius Maximianus, who associated him in the empire, A.D. 307, and assigned Pannonia and Rhœtia to his government.—Covetous, and of infamous habits, he cruelly persecuted the Christians. In 313 he espoused Constantia, the sister of Constantine the Great, and daughter of Constantius Chlorus. The same year he defeated Maximinus Daza, and reigned with Constantine; caused the deaths of Valeria and Prisca; made war upon Constantine; was beaten at Cibalis in 314, and was offered terms by the victor; declared his son Licinius, Cæsar; and again appealed to arms against Constantine, by whose generals he was defeated at Adrianople, in 323, and at Chalcedon; shortly afterwards he surrendered himself at Thessalonica, where, by order of Constantine, he was strangled A.D. 324 —The style of this prince on his coins (which are very rare in all metals except second and third brass) is IMP. C. GAL. VAL. LICIN. LICINIVS P. F. AVG.—The coins published by Banduri, on which Licinius is styled Cæsar only, when it would appear that Galerius had first given him that title alone, are regarded by Eckhel to be either false or to belong to Licinius jun.

Licinius (Fl. Val. Licinian.) the younger, son of the elder Licinius, by Constantia, was born A.D. 315, and declared Cæsar A.D. 317; a prince of great promise; but the victim of Constantine's policy, he was stripped of his title on the death of his father in 323, and put to death in 326. His style is LICINIVS IVN. NOB *Cæsar*—also FL. VAL. LICINIANVS LICINIVS NOB. CAES.—On the same coin with his father it is DD. NN. IOVII LICINII. INVICT. AVG. ET. CAES.—His *gold* and *silver* are very rare; *brass medallions* still rarer; *third brass* very common.

Lictores.—Lictors, officers established by Romulus, after the example of the Etruscans.

They were usually taken from the dregs of the people, but were nevertheless free, and sometimes emancipated by the magistrates they served. Their functions were various :—1st. They walked in procession before the magistrates with *fasces*, composed of axes and rods. 2nd. They gave notice to the people to render to the magistrates the honour due to them. 3rd. They walked before the magistrates, not two and two, nor confusedly, but ranged one after the other in single file. 4th. When the magistrates pronounced these words :—*I, Lictor, adde virgas reo, et in eum lege age*, they struck the guilty person with rods, and cut off his head. The Dictator had twenty-four of these officers in attendance on him; the Master of the Horse six; the Consul twelve; the Prætor six.

A denarius of the *Junia* family, bearing on its reverse the head of Liberty, exhibits on its obverse a group of four figures, considered to represent the sons of Junius Brutus, guarded by the lictors.—See BRVTVS.

A *Lictor* standing with the *virga* or rod is seen on a brass coin of Antoninus—also on a second brass *Liberalitas* of Alexander Severus.— See likewise the denarius inscribed PROVOCO.

L. I. MIN. RESTITVTA. *Legio Prima Minervia Restituta.*—On a brass coin of Aureolus, who is figured joining hands with Minerva, a palm branch being between them both.— Banduri, i. p. 328.

Lituus Augurum, the augural staff, like a Bishop's crosier, but shorter, which the augur held in his hand, whilst describing and measuring off the different regions of the sky, is found on a denarius of the Licinia family, bearing the portrait of Numa Pompilius—and also is seen behind the head of King Ancus, on a denarius of the Marcia family, inscribed ANCVS. Ancus Martius being the king who restored from their neglected state the institutions of religion which Numa had formed.—The same augural instrument appears on coins of Julius Cæsar, M. Antony, Lepidus, Augustus, Caius Lucius, and Caligula,—frequently accompanied with other religious utensils, such as the præfericulum, secespita, &c.

The *Lituus Auguralis*, or pontifical symbol, also appears on coins of Vespasian, Nerva, Hadrian, Antonine, M. Aurelius, Commodus, Elagabalus, Gordianus Pius, Maximus Cæsar, Philippus junior, Herennius, Hostilianus, Volusianus, and other Emperors.—The *Lituus* is likewise observed on medals of the Annia, Cassia, Cornelia, Domitia, and other Roman families.

Lituus Militaris, a military instrument, so called from its resemblance to the augural *lituus*,

 was a species of curved trumpet, which served in camps to mark, by its sounding, the day and night watches of the soldiers. In the Junia family, a denarius exhibits on its reverse two of these military *litui*, placed crosswise, with bucklers at top and bottom. A silver coin of the same family bears for type Jupiter in a quadriga, holding a military *lituus*; as does Mars, on a coin of the Domitia family.—Two military *litui* appear placed with shields and spears, on a coin of Marcus Aurelius.

Livia Drusilla, also called *Julia*, was the daughter of Livius Calidianus of the Claudia family, and the fourth wife of Augustus. She first was espoused to Tiberius Claudius Nero, by whom she was yielded up to Augustus, who divorced his third wife Scribonia in order to marry her; she being already mother of Tiberius, and pregnant with Nero Drusus. Handsome, and of great abilities, yet proud, cruel, and unprincipled, she compassed the deaths of Augustus's heirs, Marcellus, Agrippa junior, and Germanicus, in order to raise her son Tiberius to the imperial throne.

The coins of this princess, of Roman mintage, do not bear her portrait. She is represented as JVSTITIA, as PIETAS, and as SALVS, on second brass (which are scarce) struck under Tiberius: the two latter restored by Titus. A first brass with the head of Justice is very rare. (See IVSTITIA) It was after the death of Augustus that she took the name of *Julia*, and these pieces are of that epocha.—On Latin coins she is always styled IVLIA AVGVSTA.—On some Greek medals she is called LIVIA.—The legend AVGVSTA MATER PATRIAE is found on a coin struck in her honour by some unknown colony.

LIVIAN. *Livianus*, surname of the Æmilia family.

Livineia, a plebeian family, whose surnames on coins are *Regulus* and *Gallus*. Its medals present thirteen varieties, extremely rare in gold; somewhat common in silver, except those pieces restored by Trajan: the third brass of this family are by the moneyers of Augustus, and are common.

The following are among the few interesting denarii of the *Livineia* family :—

L. REGVLVS. PR.—The bare head of a young man, without beard.

Rev. REGVLVS. F. PRAEF. VR.—A curule chair, upon which is a crown; on each side are the *fasces* without axes.

Same head.—*Rev*. Two men, with spears, fighting with a lion, a tiger, and a bull.—In the exergue L. REGVLVS.

The portrait on the obverse of these coins is certainly intended to represent some one of the more ancient *Reguli*, but which of them in particular does not seem to be known.—Havercamp thinks that the letters PR. following the word REGVLVS should be read P*ater* R*eguli*, because on the reverse of the first coin we read REGVLVS F*ilius*.—Eckhel clearly proves, however, that there should be no point between the P and the R, as erroneously engraved in Morell, but that it should be read PR*ætor*. He, moreover, entertains no doubt of the epigraph of the reverse reading REGVLVS F*ilius*, meaning the son of the Prætor Regulus. It is thus also on coins of the Valeria family that we read MESSAL. F.—These coins, in the opinion of Havercamp, were struck by that L. Regulus,

who, as may be implied from the addition PRAEF. VR., was one of the Præfects of the City, whom Julius Cæsar, when he went to Spain, left at Rome (as Dion relates), and who assumed to themselves the *jus lictorum et sellæ curulis*, as the coins of this Regulus seem to shew, unless perhaps the type in the above described denarii more correctly belongs to the Prætorship of Regulus the father, especially as there are no axes *(secures)* to the fasces; and we learn from Spanheim that such was the case with the fasces of the *prætores urbani*.—By the type of the combat of men with wild beasts, the magnificent gladiatorial shews, given by Julius Cæsar, are probably indicated.

LN., as a mint-mark, *Lugdunum*.

Lollia, a plebeian family, having for its surname PALIKANVS. Its coins offer twelve varieties, two of which deserve note, viz., one a denarius with legend LIBERTATIS and head of Liberty, and the other inscribed HONORIS, with laureated head of Honour.

LIBERTATIS.—The head of Liberty.

Rev. PALIKANVS.—A portico, to the columns of which are affixed the beaks of ships, and on the top of which is placed a table.—The foregoing is Eckhel's description of the type. By Mionnet it is described as a bridge with several arches; a table above, and three galleys below.

The brass pieces of this family were struck in Cyrenaica, by L. Lollius, one of the lieutenants of Augustus.

HONORIS.—A juvenile head laureated.

Rev. PALIKANVS.—A curule chair between two ears of corn.

The reverse of the first denarius exhibits the *rostra Populi Romani*, an appellation given to the *suggestum*, or elevated platform, constructed in the forum, and adorned with the beaks of galleys captured from the Antiates. The type is regarded as referring to M. Lollius Palikanus, who, being tribune of the people in the year of Rome 684, succeeded, with the assistance of Pompey the Consul, in restoring to the tribuneship its ancient power, of which Sylla had left the shadow without the substance. [See Tribunitia Potestas.] By the head of Liberty, therefore, the restoration of liberty to the Roman people is clearly indicated : whilst the *rostra* point to the place where the *tribuni plebis* were accustomed to speak on behalf of the assemblies of the people.

LOCVPLETATORI ORBIS TERRARVM. S.C. (To him who enriches the world).—The Emperor Hadrian, seated on an *estrade*, has

Liberalitas beside him, who, from a horn of plenty, pours forth gifts into the bosoms of two figures standing beneath.

The generosity and munificent largesses of Hadrian, after having been recorded many times on various coins and in divers ways, are on the reverse of a first brass medal of great rarity, glorified altogether by the above splendid title—"The Benefactor of the World"—a superlative the more remarkable, inasmuch as, neither before nor afterwards, is it found conferred on any other Emperor.—Dion Cassius at once illustrates and countenances the otherwise hyperbolical character of this legend—*locupletator orbis terrarum*, in a passage wherein he says of this prince that he was accustomed to enrich whole provinces with his gifts, which were bestowed on a crowd of citizens of all ranks and classes, and that he never waited to be asked, but bestowed his beneficence wherever the necessity of the case required it.—See *Hadrian*.

Lollianus.—See *Laelianus.*

LON. *Longus.*—Surname of a man.

LONGVS is a surname common to many families of different races. It is an addition to the *Casca* branch of the *Servilia family*—CASCA LONGVS.

Lorica, the cuirass of the Romans. This piece of defensive armour, which the ancients at first made of leather, was afterwards formed of iron rings, and lastly of steel, brass, silver, and even gold scales. The *loricæ squameæ* of the Emperors is frequently seen on their coins. —See *Domitian, Severus,* &c.

L. P. D. AE. P. *Lucius Papirius Designatus Ædilis Plebis.*—Plebeian Edile elect.—Vaillant in his coins of Families gives this as inscribed on a remarkable brass coin, having on one side Janus, and on the other the prow.

L. R. *Lucius Rubrius* or *Roscius.*

L. S. DEN. *Lucius Sicinius Dentatus.*—Prenomen, name, and surname of a man.

L. VAL. *Lucius Valerius.*—Prenomen and name.

LVCIF. *Lucifera.*—See DIANA LVCIFERA.—LVNA LVCIFERA.

Lucilia, a plebeian family, whose cognomen is *Rufus.* It has only one type, winged head of Minerva, behind it A. PV., the whole within a laurel crown.—*Rev.* Victory in a biga, inscribed M. LVCILI. RVF. Silver common.

Lucilla (Annia), daughter of Marcus Aurelius

and of Faustina the younger. Handsome, and at first virtuous, she was married to Lucius Verus. Forsaken by him, she gave herself up to lewdness and excess. After Verus's death, to which Lucilla is accused of having been an accessory, she espoused Claudius Pompeianus, a Roman senator; lived with Commodus as his mistress; abandoned by him she conspired against that tyrant, by whom she was exiled to Capreæ, where she was shortly after put to death.

She is styled on her coins (which in every metal are more or less common), LVCILLA AVGVSTA—and as the daughter of Marcus Aurelius, LVCILLA AVG. M. ANTONINI AVG. *Filia.* The types of some of her brass medallions are of great beauty and rarity. She had children by her two husbands, and her medals often make allusion to her fecundity.

LVCINA.—See IVNO LVCINA.

LVCIO.—See CAIO ET LVCIO.

Lucius, born seventeen years before Christ, was one of the sons of Agrippa, by Julia, daughter of Augustus, and with his elder brother *Caius* was adopted into the *Julia gens,* and at the same time into the family of the Cæsars, by his grandfather Augustus, and was called *Princeps Juventutis*—Prince of the Roman youth. His portrait appears on second brass colonial of Augustus (L. AVG. or L. CAES AVG. F. PRINC. IVVEN.) Sent to the army of Spain, he died on his way, at Marseilles (Massilia), A.D. 2; supposed to have fallen a victim to the *poisoning* arts of Livia.

LVC. or LVG. P.S. *Lucduni,* or *Lugduni, pecunia signata.*—Money struck at Lugdunum, now Lyons.

LVCR.—LVCRETI.—The name of *Lucretius.* —See *Lucretia gens,* a family extinct in its patrician branch; but its plebeian cognomen of TRIO is preserved on eleven varieties of coins; none, however, of any remarkable interest.

The following is a rare denarius; but as restored by Trajan it is trebly rare :—

I. Head of the Sun radiated.—*Rev.* The crescent Moon between the *Triones,* or constellation of seven stars—L. LVCRETI TRIO.

There is an elegant though by no means a scarce silver coin :—

II. Head of Neptune, behind it a trident and XXXI.—*Rev.* Cupid riding on the back of a dolphin, which he guides with a bridle—L. LVCRETI TRIO.

It is evident that the seven stars, or Triones, are placed on this family coin in allusion to its name.—Eckhel adds, "The symbols of the sun and moon were, moreover, engraved on it, because those planets diffusing, as they do above all others, an abundant light, have a reference, in my opinion, to the name of *Lucretius.*"

Cupid mounted on a dolphin is a doubtful subject on this second denarius of Lucretius.— Vaillant refers to the naval victory of Aemilius, Prætor of Sicily; but that eminent writer carries his perspicuity so far as, from the numerals XXXI. which he sees near the head of Neptune, to gather the very number of ships captured! _Quis hæc refutabit?_ drily asks the unimaginative but sagacious Eckhel.

LVD. _Ludi, Ludis, Ludos._

Ludi. Games.—Public sports or spectacles exhibited for the amusement of the people. These celebrations formed part of the religion of the ancients; the games themselves were solemnized for the professed purpose either of appeasing the wrath of the gods, and meriting their favour; or of invoking the blessing of health for the people, whose good graces were also sought to be conciliated by those who instituted and arranged them.—The Grecian states, in the ages of their independence, carried the system of holding public games to the highest point of national distinction. Afterwards when Greece submitted to the Roman yoke, her conquerors encouraged this extravagant taste, which better suited their ambitious policy than to leave her to the galling thoughts of lost liberty. And from numismatic evidence, it would even appear that the provinces increased the number of their public games in the very ratio of their decreasing prosperity.—From the time of Septimius Severus, medals are found to indicate many new institutions of this sort, of which no preceding record had been made. But their number was never so great as under Valerianus and Gallienus—that is to say, during reigns in which the Greek provinces of the empire were in the most neglected and ruinous state. Passing over (by no means as uninteresting but simply as exceeding the limits of a work expressly confined to _Roman_ numismatics) those notices of Grecian games which Millin has so nobly given in his _Dictionaire des Beaux Arts_, we proceed to enumerate and shall attempt concisely to explain the _Ludi Romani_. These received their respective appellations from the places where they were celebrated, as _circensian_ and as _scenic_ games; or by the name of the deity to whom they were consecrated; and these latter were divided into _sacred games_, and _votive games, funeral games,_ and _games_ of _amusement._ The Plebeian Ediles had the management of the plebeian games. The Prætor, or the Curule Edile, took the direction of the games dedicated to Ceres, to Apollo, to Jupiter, to Cybele, and to the other principal deities, under the name of Ludi Megalenses. Amongst this variety of public spectacles, there were some which were _specially_ denominated _Ludi Romani,_ and which were themselves divided into _magni,_ and _maximi._

Ludi Publici, the public games which the Roman Emperors dedicated to the amusement of the people, were a species of feasts or holidays; but it was not every public festivity that was accompanied by public games. On coins these _ludi_ are very frequently noticed.—Besides being indicated by vases, whence spring palm branches, or over which appear crowns, they are distinguished by legends, which for the most part exhibit either the name of the author, or that of the deity to whose honour they were instituted.—Thus Nero is shewn to be the author of certain contests celebrated every five years by a coin bearing the inscription CER. QVINQ. ROM. CO. _Certamen Quinquennale Romæ Constitutum._—See CER. QVINQ. ROM. CO.—And from a legend on a Greek coin of Caracalla, it is ascertained that at Ancyra in Galatia games had been celebrated in honour of Esculapius, in like manner with those already dedicated in the Isthmus of Corinth to Apollo.

Ludorum Præmia, the prizes or symbols of public games, were the caduceus, the corona or garland, the laurel, the palm, vases, &c.

The following are the only Roman games alluded to on medals with _Latin_ inscriptions :—

Ludi Apollinares, which were instituted in Rome to the honour of Apollo by a _Senatus consultum,_ and celebrated for the first time in 543. These annual games consisted of horse-racing in the circus. Several coins of the _Calpurnia_ family offer types which, in the head of Apollo, the laurel crown, the vase, and a horse at full gallop with its rider, are considered as having reference to the Apollinarian games, which were identical with the Pythian games of the Greeks.

Ludi Cereales.—These games, common to Ceres and to Bacchus, were under the direction of the Curule Ediles.

Ludi Circenses.—The games of this name, borrowed from the Greek, were first celebrated at Rome, when the Elder Tarquin built a circus between Mounts Aventine and Palatine. They commenced on the 23rd September, lasted five days, and five sorts of exercises, called _Gymnici,_ were performed at them—viz., racing, pugilism, wrestling, the discus, and the dance. The procession from the Capitol to the Circus, on the opening day, was of the most imposing description.—A coin of Nerva records the games of the Circus in connection with their reputed founder, Neptune; and an equally interesting allusion to them is found on coins of Roman mintage, that which is inscribed on a coin of Hadrian, inscribed ANNo DCCCLXXIII NATali VRBis Primum CIRcenses CONstituti, recording the revival and re-establishment, after long disuse, of the Circensian games, in celebration of the 874th anniversary of Rome's natal or foundation day (see the words ANNO, &c).—Havercamp, in his remarks on Contorniate medals, shews to what an insane pitch the love of these games was carried, even under the Christian Emperors.

Ludi Decennales.—Games which the Emperors gave to the people on the tenth year of their reign. The custom of celebrating the decennial games derived its origin from Augustus, after whose example other Emperors adopted it, as Dion Cassius teaches us (L. iii.)—See PRIMI DECENNALES and DECENNALIA.

Ludi Florales.—Floral games which were celebrated at Rome in honour of the Goddess Flora, under the direction of the Curule Ediles, on the 29th of April, to invoke the seasonable appearance of the Flowers.—A record of one of these celebrations is seen on a denarius of the _Servilia_ family.—See _Flora._

Ludi Funebres.—Funeral games given in

honour of persons of distinction after their death, under the superstitious idea of satisfying their *manes*, and of appeasing the wrath of the infernal gods. They included combats of gladiators; and this cruel spectacle was called *munus*, that is to say a gift.—The Romans forbade women being present at these murderous exhibitions. The games lasted three or four days, and the people attended them in mourning habits.

The *ludi funebres* in honour of *Divus Augustus*, instituted by the *Col. Victr. Jul. Carth.*, are referred to on coins of Roman families, edited by Havercamp and Morell.

Ludi Francici.—In the *calendarium* of Philocalus, published by Lambecius, mention is made of games bearing the name of *Francici*, and which are supposed to have been instituted on the occasion of the victory gained over the Franks and Alemanni by Constantine the Great, who, according to Eutropius—"*Cæsis Francis atque Alemannis reges eorum cepit, et bestiis, cum magnificum spectaculum muneris parasset, objecit.*"—If this horrible act of ungenerous bloodthirstiness was really committed by this first *professed* imperial convert from Paganism to the religion of the Cross, the GAVDIVM which stands on the numismatic record of his achievement, as the vanquisher FRAN*Corum et* ALAM*annorum*, should have been written CRVDELITAS ROMANORVM. The man, indeed, who could deliver up the chiefs of his no longer resisting foes to wild beasts at the games which he exhibited for the *amusement* of the people, was *not* a monarch but a monster—*not* a *Christian* Emperor, but an incarnate fiend.—Eumenius, in his panegyrics, lauds Constantine in giving his Frankish prisoners in such numbers to the wild beasts that they at last stood still, satiated with slaughter.—See a notice of the amphitheatre at Treves, the site of the carnage, in Mr. Roach Smith's *Col. Ant.* vol. ii.

Ludi Magni, or *Romani,* were instituted under the Kings of Rome, and were called *magni,* because they were given on a grand scale and at a great expense. They were dedicated to Jove, Juno, and Minerva. The curule chair, with the thunderbolt and face of Jupiter above it, on the obverse of denarii, shew that it was the Ediles who celebrated these grand or Roman games.

Ludi Megalenses, or *Megalesii,* in honour of Mater Magna, the Idæan Goddess (Cybele), were held in April, with great religious pomp. The early coinage of Rome shews that the above-named goddess was a principal deity, whose favour it was sought to invoke, and whose wrath to appease, by these games. Their types are found on certain denarii of Roman families (see Havercamp; and Morell, *Fam.* p. 298). These public games were celebrated by Scipio at Nassica, in Spain.—See *Calagurris.*

Ludi Parthici.—The Parthian games were celebrated at Rome in remembrance of the victories gained by Trajan over the Parthians.— "It would seem (says Millin) that the commemorations occasioned a great number of Con-

torniate medals, with the head of Trajan on them, to be distributed amongst the people."

Ludi Sæculares.—Secular games, so called, because they were celebrated only once in a century or age, or perhaps because it was scarcely given to a man to see them more than once in his life. They constituted one of the most solemn of the Roman festivals. Their actual origin is thus related. In the same year when the kingly government was abolished, Rome became afflicted with a dreadful pestilence; and Publius Valerius Publicola, then one of the two consuls, sought to stay the vengeance of the offended deities, by causing sacrifices to be offered on the same altars to Pluto and Proserpine; and, as we are told, the plague ceased.— Sixty years afterwards, the same rites were repeated by order of the priests of the Sybilline Oracle, and certain ceremonies were added, as pretended to be prescribed in the sacred books of the Sybills; and then it was ordained that these feasts should take place at the end of each century. The preparation for and arrangements of these games were extremely imposing, especially during the period of the empire, with whose preservation they were, in popular opinion, identified. When the time arrived for holding these secular sports, the Quindecemvirs sent heralds throughout all Italy, for the express purpose of inviting the people to assist at a festival "which they had never seen, and which they would never see again."—When everybody was assembled, the solemnities began with a procession, consisting of the Priesthood, the Senate, and the Magistrates, accompanied by a multitude of citizens clothed in white, crowned with flowers, and each holding a palm-branch. For the three days and nights that the festival lasted, three different hymns were sung in the temples, and various shows were exhibited to the people. The scene of action was changed each day. The first was in the Campus Martius; the second at the Capitol; the third on the Palatine Hill. After a preparatory form of devotion, called *Pervigilium,* when lustral ceremonies were gone through, and black victims offered up to the Infernal Gods, the multitude assembled in the Field of Mars, and sacrificed to Jupiter, Juno, Apollo, Diana, Ceres, and other divinities. The first night of the games, the Emperor himself, at the head of fifteen Pontiffs, proceeded to the banks of the Tiber, and there at three altars erected for the occasion, and sprinkled with the blood of three lambs, they dedicated victims and other burnt-offerings. A certain space of ground was afterwards marked out, and converted into an illuminated scene. During the first two days appropriate hymns were chanted in chorus; different kinds of games were performed; scenic pieces were exhibited at the theatre; and at the circus there were foot, horse, and chariot races. The third day, which concluded the festival, seventeen young men and as many young women of condition, and having their fathers and mothers living, entered the temple of Apollo Palatinus, and sang hymns in Greek and Latin, invoking upon Rome the protection of the gods, who had just been honoured by the most solemn sacrifices. At length the Sibylline Priests who had opened the *ludi sæculares* with prayers to the deities, closed them in the same manner.

In giving an account of the various epochas when the Secular games were celebrated under the Emperors, M. Millin observes that after an interruption which lasted for a long series of years, these festivities took place for the sixth time from their original institution during the reign of Augustus, and in the year of Rome 737.—The Emperor Claudius, indeed, when he was but a private individual, had borne testimony to the fact that Augustus's calculation of the year for performing the secular games was carefully and correctly made. But when Claudius became emperor he found fault with this calculation, which he said had anticipated the time; and he pretended that the celebration ought to have been reserved to the end of the century in which he was living. In conformity with this his professed opinion, Claudius repeated these games in the 800th year after the foundation of Rome. It is in reference to that occasion Suetonius remarks that the proclamation of the herald, about "what people had never seen and would not see again," failed in its application to this particular instance; because many persons who had witnessed the secular games under Augustus, were then still living; and because there were even actors that had been employed on the former occasion, who took part in the spectacle of this Claudian celebration.—Forty-one years afterwards, Domitian renewed the secular games, not according to the calculation established by Claudius, but agreeably to that of Augustus, by which it had been laid down that the games in question were to be celebrated every hundred and ten years.—Tacitus was then prætor, and actively assisted at this celebration of Domitian, in his office of *quindecemvir*, or sibylline pontiff, as he calls himself, says in his Annals (Lib xi. c. 11).— Antoninus Pius, as Aurelius Victor informs us, celebrated the 900th year of Rome, with great magnificence; it is not said that the secular games were then exhibited, but that they were is the more probable, inasmuch as the writer above-mentioned does not even use that expression when speaking of the secular games celebrated in the reign of Philip.—Septimius Severus adopted the computation of Augustus, in giving the secular games at Rome, in the year 957. It is well-known that Philip repeated them with unexampled magnificence and splendour, in the year of the city 1001. The types of several medals of Gallienus shew that, under his reign, there was a performance of these games. And Eckhel, *Syllog.* i. *Num. Vet.* has published (plate 10, No. 11) a coin of Maximianus, which goes to prove that under that prince also the same games were celebrated. Nevertheless, according to the two modes of calculating the epochas of the secular games, which we have seen were adopted by preceding emperors, viz., a period of one hundred and

ten years, in taking for a base the 737th year of Rome, when Augustus re-established them; or else the period of one hundred years adopted by Claudius, Antoninus Pius, and Philip—in taking for a base the secular games celebrated in 957 under Severus, according to the computation of Augustus, they ought to have been celebrated one hundred and ten years after, that is to say, in 1067; but Maximianus was dead in 1063. The same reasoning may be employed in order to prove that during the reign of Gallienus, which comes in the series between that of Philip and that of Maximian, there should not have been any secular games. It is this circumstance which induced Eckhel to suppose that, having found the period of a whole century too long, the Emperors determined upon celebrating these splendid feasts at the end of half a century. This hypothesis acquires great weight, when it is considered, in the first place, that at this epocha, the Roman empire was afflicted with pestilence and ravaged with wars, and that it was expressly with the view of removing these scourges that the celebration of the secular games was instituted; in the next place, according to the newer computation, the time for performing them coincides with the reign of Gallienus, and with that of Maximianus, under whom the testimony of medals shews that they took place.—Severus celebrated the games in 957, on the computation of Augustus. In adding thereto 55 years, the half of 110, according to Augustus, composing the period required to elapse between one celebration and another, we arrive at the year 1012, which corresponds with the seventh year of the tribunitian power of Gallienus, a period at which his father Valerianus was taken prisoner by the Persians—an event which perhaps induced Gallienus to give the secular games as a supposed means of appeasing the anger of the gods.— With respect to Maximianus, it must be concluded that he took for the basis of his calculation the games celebrated in 1001 under Philip, adding thereto fifty years, as the half century, according to the computation followed by Claudius, in which case the secular games would have been celebrated under Maximianus, in the year 1051 of Rome—the thirteenth year of his tribunitian power.—Constantine did not celebrate them in the year when he was consul, with Licinius for the third time, in the 1066th year of Rome, or A.D. 313.—But the Emperor Honorius, having received intelligence of the victory gained by his general Stilico over Alaric, permitted all the Pagans again to celebrate the secular games; and these were the last of which history makes mention.

Ludi Votivi.—Games which Roman Generals caused to be celebrated when they were about to depart for the wars, or which they made a vow to celebrate in the event of their escaping some imminent danger.—The *ludi votivi* were performed on various occasions, being of a *private* as well as *public* kind. Mention is made of them on a coin of the *Nonia* family, the reverse of which has for its circumscription SEX*tus* NONI*ius* PR*imus* (or as some read it PR*ætor*) *Ludus* V*otivus* P*ublicos* F*ecit*.—To this may be added a medal of the *Maria* family, in tab. i. no. 5 of Morell's *Thesaurus*.

LVD. SAEC.—On a rare silver coin of Augustus is a cippus on which are inscribed the words IMP. CAES. AVG. LVD. SAEC. In the field, on one side, is XV., on the other, S. F., which means *Cæsar Augustus ludos sæculares, (subanditur fecit,) Quindecemvir sacris faciundis.* (The Emperor Cæsar Augustus instituted the Secular games as Quindecemvir having the care of sacred things.)

Augustus, as has been stated, restored the secular games in the year of Rome 737, when he was one of the *Quindecemviri*, or officers appointed to superintend the sacrifices. Hence we find it recorded on the *cippus*, as on the coins of Domitian and of Philip.

LVD. SAEC. FEC. COS. XIIII.—*Ludos*

sæculares fecit Consul XIIII.—The Emperor (Domitian) caused to be celebrated—or rather under the reign of Domitian, and during his 14th Consulate, the secular games were celebrated, about the year of Rome 841; 104 years after those of Augustus, and 41 after those of Claudius. The coin above, in second brass, commemorates this event.

Of all the medals struck under different Emperors in commemoration of the secular games, none are more curious, none are more replete with antiquarian interest, than those of Domitian, representing the solemn ceremonies of these games.—On one of these (a denarius) we see a man habited in the toga, standing near

a cippus inscribed as above, and wearing on his head a helmet, whence spring two wings; in his right hand he holds a small staff, and in his left a round buckler.— This figure, it is conjectured, is that of the herald whose duty it was to announce the celebration of the games; or perhaps one of the *quindecemvirs* who presided at them. The same figure (says Millin) is found on coins of the *Sanquinia* family, of which the type recalls the memory of those secular games which Augustus re-established (737), and when one of the members of the above named family was monetary triumvir.

On a first brass of the same Emperor, bearing the same legend, we see his figure standing, clothed in the toga, holding a patera in his right hand, and performing sacrifice before an altar.

Near the Emperor, a woman holding a cornucopiæ is seated on the ground; whilst on the other side we see a harper, a flute player, and a *popa* (or priest who slew the victims) with a sow.— The woman whom we see on the ground, says Eckhel, is *Tellus*, or Mother Earth—the fertile nurse of all living creatures, characterised as such by the horn of plenty. The sow which we see brought to the altar is destined to be sacrificed to her, as the verses of the Sibylls, quoted in Zosimus, indicate, by mentioning the *hog* and the *black sow* as fit immolations to the Goddess of the Fertile Earth. Hence also Horace, amongst other deities, to whom vows were accustomed to be made, invokes Tellus, in the *Carmen Sæculare* :—

> *Fertilis frugum, pecorisque Tellus*
> *Spicea donet Cererem corona.*

On another first brass of Domitian, bearing the same legend of LVD. SAEC. FEC. COS. XIIII. S. C., the Emperor stands in front of a Temple, holding a patera over a lighted altar; opposite him is a man seated on the ground with a harp in his hand; behind are two flute players. On a second brass of Domitian, the Emperor is seen in the act of sacrificing at a lighted altar,

whilst one *popa* holds down an ox, the second *popa* strikes him with his axe. This type refers to the custom which prevailed at the Secular games of offering up *white* bulls to Jupiter and Juno, and *black* ones to Pluto and Proserpine, as Horace says—*Quæque vos bobus veneratur albis.*—

Sheep and goats were also sacrificed on these occasions, as may be remarked on other second brass coins of Domitian, which bear equally specific reference to the *Secular games*.

On a first and second brass of the same

Emperor we see a river personified in a recumbent posture, and holding a cornucopiæ.—This river, says Eckhel, is the Tiber; for, according to the laws of these games, as Zosimus instructs us, the victims were immolated on the bank of the Tiber, near the *Campus Martius*, at the spot called Terentum.

On a first brass of Domitian the Emperor appears clothed in the toga, and holding a

volumen, or roll of papyrus, in his left hand; behind him is another togated man; whilst near him is a procession of three young persons, whose hands are raised, and who hold palm branches.— This type has relation to the twenty-seven boys and the twenty-seven girls, who *(ambos parentes adhuc superstites habent)* had both parents still surviving, and who chanted hymns in Latin and Greek.—Horace illustrates this custom thus in his *Carm. Sæc.*:—

> *Condito mitis, placidusque telo*
> *Supplices audi pueros, Apollo;*
> *Siderum regina bicornis audi*
>   *Luna, puellas.*

And Catullus still more pointedly:—

> *Dianæ sumus in fide*
> *Puellæ, et pueri integri,*
> *Dianam pueri integri,*
> *Puellæque canamus.*

On a first brass also of Domitian, which on its obverse bears his laureated head, with the newly assumed title of CEN*sor* PER*petuus*, and which on the reverse is notified as having been struck in the 14th Consulate (COS. XIIII). We read as on all the foregoing:—

LVD. SAEC. FEC. S. C.; and we see the Emperor clothed in the toga, sitting in front of a temple on the *suggestum*, or raised platform,

on which is written SVFPD; and, unattended by the usual assistants, he is making a distribution to a man and a child.—This type, according to the concurrent opinion of the learned, refers to certain functions performed by the Emperor as *quindecemvir sacris faciundis*. The letters SVFPD being explained to mean SVF*fimenta* Populo Data LVD*os* SAEC*ulares* FEC*it*, that is to say, *perfumes* (for the purpose of *lustrations*) *given to the people*, some days before the commencement of the Sæcular games.

A large brass of the same Emperor, which has for the legend of its reverse COS. XIIII. LVD. SAEC. A. POP., and on the base of a suggestum FRVG. AC.—Here we see Domitian seated; before him stand two figures, in front of a temple. This last legend gives rise to two interpretations. Some read: COS. XIIII. *Ludi Sæcularibus a Populo fruges accepit;* which alludes to the first fruits of the harvests offered to the Gods by the people. But the greater number of numismatists, holding opinion with Spanheim, think it should be interpreted *Cos.* XIIII. *Ludos Sæculares,* (the word *fecit* being understood) *a Populo fruges acceptæ,* it being remembered that after the games an abundance of distributions were made to the multitude.— Another first brass, with the same legend (but without the abbreviated words FRVG. AC.), represents Domitian near a temple, having before him several figures kneeling, with their hands raised towards the Emperor.

LVDOS. SAECVL. FECIT. COS. III.— *Bacchus with panther, and Hercules with club standing*; and between them a cippus bearing this legend constitute the reverse of a second brass of Severus in the Queen of Sweden's cabinet. A gold coin is given by Mionnet, which he values at 150 francs, bearing the same legend and type, but apparently without the cippus.— These medals record the renewal, by this warlike Emperor, of the Secular games celebrated by Domitian; but not till after a lapse of 116 years, as perhaps on account of the civil wars he was unable to give them at the prescribed time. Herodianus (as quoted by Vaillant) thus alludes to them—"We see also under him (Severus) certain games of every kind produced at all the theatres, and at the same time public festivities celebrated, and vigils after the manner of the initiated in the rites of Ceres; these are now called the Secular games."—Dion Cassius states that Severus built a large temple to Bacchus and Hercules.

COS. III. LVD. SAEC. FEC. S. C.—The

Emperor sacrificing before an altar, attended by Hercules and Bacchus. In the back ground a flute player. In the front, on the left, is Tellus ; on the right, a boy holding the victim.—First brass of Severus.

Thus we see from the above cited instances of Augustus, Claudius, Domitian, and Severus, that in spite of their name (SAECVLARES), these solemnities had no decidedly fixed epochas ; the will of the reigning prince, and the circumstances of the empire, uniting to alter the era from which their return was computed.

LVG.   *Lugdunensis.*—C. C. COL. LVG. *Claudius Copia Colonia Lugdunensis.*—The Roman colony of *Lugdunum.*

Lugdunum, a city and colony of Gaul; according to *Herodianus* a large and opulent city, now called *Lyon,* in central France.— Havercamp *(ad Morell Fam.* p. 26*)* states that Lugdunum was made a Roman *municipium* under the provincial quæstorship of *M. Antonius Creticus,* the father of Mark Antony the triumvir. It was furthermore invested with the *jus civitatis Romanæ* by the Emperor Claudius, who, by his mother Antonia, was related to the Antonii.—An ancient copy of the decree of Claudius, upon brass plates, is preserved at Lyon. They were discovered in 1528.

LVGDVNI A. XL.—*A Lion walking.*—This inscription and type appear on a quinarius of M. Antonius, and shew it to have been struck at Lugdunum in Gaul, now Lyon.

Lugduni Genius.—The Genius of Lyon, personified by a male figure, turret-crowned, standing with a spear in his right, and a cornucopiæ in his left hand, with an eagle at his feet, appears on a silver coin of Clodius Albinus.—See GEN. LVG.

Luna, the Moon.—This deity was by the Romans, who borrowed their worship of her from the Greeks, generally identified with *Diana,* from which chaste goddess she is, however, to be distinguished, inasmuch as to *Luna,* or *Selena,* were attributed certain amorous adventures, amongst others that with Endymion, of which the fable is depicted on one of the *Contorniates* in Havercamp's collection.

The symbols of *Luna* are various on Roman coins ; on those of Vespasian, Titus, Domitian, Trajan, and Hadrian (second brass), the figure of *Eternity* holds in her hands the heads of the Sun and *Moon.*—The moon mingled with stars is a type of *Consecration,* and serves on a second brass of Faustina senior to designate the reception of that Empress amongst the celestial divinities.—On a second brass of the younger Faustina *Luna* is seen standing with a torch in each hand, symbolically pointing to that princess as SIDERIBVS RECEPTA.—See that legend; also see AETERNITAS and CONSECRATIO.

Luna is represented in different designs on coins of the Empresses, amongst others in those which exhibit Julia Domna, whether in allusion to the fecundity of that princess, or as flattering her with the fond idea of being another light to the world. She appears in a biga of bulls on coins of Caracalla.—The crescent, or two-horned

moon, over or under the head of the Emperor or Empress, on coins of Augustus, Nero, Commodus, Mamæa, Otacilia, Etruscilla, Salonina, Saloninus, Postumus, &c.

The *Luna Crescens,* with seven stars, appears on a silver coin of Hadrian.

LVNA LVCIFERA.—A female figure in a car drawn by two horses, and having a crescent moon on her head.—This epigraph and type appear on silver, gold, and second brass coins of Julia Domna. The ambitious wife of Severus

is exhibited on her coins now as Cybele, then as Venus, but here as Diana, or *Luna.* Just as her imperial husband is styled numismatically *Pacator Orbis* under the figure of the *Sun,* so Julia on account of her fertility in bearing sons, is called *Luna Lucifera,* for as Cicero says, (Lib. ii. *De Nat. Deor.*) Diana was invoked by women at the time of child-birth.

It is singular to find such a legend as this, with the type of the Goddess (her head adorned with a crescent, walking and holding a torch in her hand), on a coin (third brass) of Gallienus; but that Emperor was a complete pantheist in his mint, and has dedicated his coins to all the *Goddesses* as well as Gods of Heaven, Earth, and Hell !

Lunus, a deity; that, by the testimony of many coins, and also according to Spartianus *(Anton. Caracallus,* c. vii.), was a peculiar object of Pagan worship throughout almost all Asia Minor and Syria. It was in fact Luna, or the Moon, adored by several nations under the figure of a man, because, as the above-mentioned author affirms, they persuaded themselves that he alone would obtain obedience from his wife who worshiped *Lunus* as a male divinity ; but that he who adored the moon as *Luna* that is to say, as a female divinity, could not assure himself that his wife would obey him. The Romans called him *Mensis* as well as Lunus.— On medals of Antioch in Pisidia (see Vaillant, *Col.* i. p. 180), struck under Antoninus Pius, we see this deity standing, clothed in the long dress of a woman, wearing a phrygian *pileus,* or cap ; holding the hasta in his right hand, and extending his left with a Victory in it. At his feet is what looks like an eagle, but which is described to represent the *gallus gallinaceus,* or cock. At his back is a crescent, the characteristic attribute of Lunus. The legend of the reverse is MENSIS COL. CAES. ANTIOCH.— "The Antiochians of Pisidia by this medal (says Havercamp in *Mus. Christ.* 396), appear to have designed the congratulation of Antonine on some victory gained by his lieutenants under his fourth consulate (COS. IIII. as recorded on the side of the portrait)."—It is not without a cause that mention is made of Mensis (or Month) in the inscription of the reverse, for the people of Pisidian Antioch rendered a religious worship to the month, called *Ascens*, as we learn by a passage from Strabo (L. xii. p. 557), quoted by Vaillant, in *Col.* TOM. i. p. 240.—*Lunus*, as distinguished by the above noted attributes, appears on the reverse of a first brass of Sept. Severus, in the *Colonies* of Vaillant (TOM. II. p. 4), who shews that the worship of this god was particularly observed in Pamphylia, and that the Antiochians had consecrated this medal to Severus after his victory over Pescennius Niger.—In the coin of Severus, the legend of the reverse is COL. CAES. ANTIOCH. *Colonia Cæsarea Antiochensis.* In the field are the letters S. R., which Vaillant interprets *Senatus Romanus;* but without assigning his reasons for so doing.—On the medal in question, as engraved in his "Colonies," the god Lunus is represented in male attire; a similar medal of Severus and of Julia Domna (*in Mus. Christinæ*) gives him the long robe of a female.—See *Antiochia Pisidiæ*.

Lupa.—The she wolf suckling Romulus and Remus. On one of the coins (struck in each metal) of Antoninus Pius, we see the fabled cohabitation of Mars with Rhea Sylvia, the *Vestal* daughter of Numitor; and on another we see the fruits of that alleged connection in the birth of the twin brothers, and in their preservation by the popularly credited miracle of a savage animal performing the office of a mother to the exposed and deserted babes.—We see on a second brass of M. Aurelius the wolf in the cave on the banks of the Tiber, with the two sturdy infants imbibing nourishment at her *pendent* dugs—a representation consecrated on innumerable monuments, and held as a symbol indicating the origin of the Roman Commonwealth, especially of the Colonies: the whole is singularly illustrated by the following verses of Virgil:—

Fecerat et viridi fetam Mavortis in antro
Procubuisse lupam : geminos huic ubera circum
Ludere pendentes pueros, et lambere matrem
Impavidos; illam tereti cervice reflexam
Mulcere alternos, et corpora fingere lingua.
　　　　　　　　　　Æn. viii. 630.

The illustration, taken from a large brass of Antoninus Pius, exhibits above the cave a bird,

which has been usually considered to be an eagle. It may be so ; but Ovid describes the woodpecker as officiating at the nursing of the infants.

Besides those of Antoninus Pius, the well-known type of the *Lupa cum puerulis*, occurs on coins of that Emperor's *predecessors* Tiberius, Vespasian, Titus, Domitian, Trajan, and Hadrian; and of his *successors* M. Aurelius, Commodus, Severus, Caracalla, Macrinus, Elagabalus, Alex. Severus, Gordianus Pius, Philippus, Trebonianus Gallus, Valerianus, Gallienus, Aurelianus, Probus, Carausius, Maxentius, and Constantine the Great. The last-named exhibits the wolf suckling the twins ; and, on some, two stars appear above the wolf, an emblem under which Castor and Pollux are generally represented. With the mint-masters of the Roman colonies this is a frequently recurring type.—See *Deultum*.—On a coin of Maxentius quoted by Vaillant, the same type is united to a singular epigraph, viz., AETERNA FELICITAS.—On a family coin of Sextus Pompeius (having the helmeted head of Rome on its obverse, and for the legend of its reverse SEX. POMP. FOSTVLVS.) we see the wolf standing before the fig-tree quietly devoting her teats to the mouths of Romulus and Remus.

LVP. *Luperous.*—The name of a man.— On a coin of the Gallia family is read G. GALLIVS LVPERCVS III. VIR. A.A.A.F.F.

L. V. P. F. *Ludos Votivos Publicos Fecit.*— In the collection of Ursinus, p. 188, and in Vaillant's *Fam. Rom.* ii. p. 172, a coin is given, in which a togated figure, sitting on spoils, is crowned by a victory; with the inscription of SEX*tus* NONI*us* PR. and the above letters — The *Ludi Votivi* in this instance are considered to relate to the celebration of a victory gained by Sulla, the uncle of this Nonius, over Mithridates.

LVPO PR. C. CAESAR. *Lupo Præfecto Cohortis Caesareæ.*—On a coin of Livia in Vaillant's *Colonies*, i. p. 50.

Lupus.—The wolf was sacred to Mars.—On a coin of the *Satriena* family, we see a she-wolf walking, and above it the word ROMA.— A wolf is also the distinctive sign of the Roman colonial town of Ilerda, now *Lerida*, in Spain.— See *Ilerda*.

On a coin of the *Papia* family, we see a wolf holding a log in his mouth, whilst an eagle stands by it with expanded wings, near a fire. This coin was struck to shew the origin of the Papii in the town of Lanuvium, of whose "wonderful wolf" Dionysius Halicarnassus relates a strange story.—See *Papia.*

LVRIA, a family little known. Its cognomen *Agrippa :*—P. LVRIVS AGRIPPA IIIVIR. &c., on first and second brass of Augustus.

Lusitania, part of *Hispania ulterior,* which Pliny (L. iv. c. 12) bounds by the river Durius (or Douro), calling the other and by far the larger portion by the name of *Hispania citerior.* But Strabo and Mela ascribe to it much ampler boundaries. It is now called *Portugal.*—Vaillant in his *Colonies* (L. p. 35) shews it to have been a province under Augustus. —The *Lusitani* offered a resistance of some duration to the Romans, but were conquered by D. Brutus.

Lustratio. Lustration.—A ceremony by which things both animate and inanimate were purified. The Romans regarded it as so solemn a rite, that on certain occasions not only the army but also the city itself was lustrated, crimes being then expiated, and the polluted citizens purgated with pure water.—The manner of purifying the armies was by dividing a sacrificial victim in two, and causing the soldiers to march between the two portions, in pronouncing some form of prayer.—The rite of Lustration is shadowed forth on a coin of the *Postumia* family (see the word).—A large *brass medallion* of *Lucilla,* without legend, is also considered to be a monument of the lustral ceremony performed on infants—viz., a female shaking a tree, from which an infant is falling; another female bathing an infant in the sea; three winged genii; one on an estrade, the other on an altar, the third on a garden wall.

Lupercal, a place thus named, was situated under the Palatine Hill at Rome. It was sacred to the God *Lupercus* whom the Romans otherwise called *Pan Lycæus.* There were yearly feasts termed *Lupercalia,* on the days of which the *Luperci* or Priests of Pan, ran naked through the streets, and with the whips they carried struck the hands of women, who held them out to receive the lash that they might conceive and bear children.—As bearing allusion to this piece of indecent superstition, Du Choul, in his *Religion des Anciens Romains,* professes to copy a large brass of Lucilla, exhibiting *Juno Lucina* sitting with a sceptre in one hand and a whip in the other.

LVTATIA, a plebeian family, whose surname on its coins is *Cerco.*—It has three varieties. The following is a rare denarius, viz., CERCO ROMA. Helmeted head of Minerva.—On the reverse Q. LVTATI. Q. A galley within an oaken garland.

The type of the reverse is supposed to indicate the celebrated naval victory, which Lutatius Catulus gained at Ægates over the Carthagenians, in the year of Rome 512, and which at a later period this Q. Lutatius Cerco has in this manner alluded to in honour of his family.

LVX MVNDI.—Banduri gives this epigraph, on a silver coin of Tiberius Constantinus (Emperor of the East in A.D. 578), with a cross in the middle.

Lyra.—The lyre was generally regarded as the instrument of Apollo, although artists have given it also to other divinities. It was distinguished by many names such as *lyra, chelys, barbiton, cithara.* It seems that the grand lyre of the Apollo Citharoede and Palatine was the barbiton. The number of strings to this instrument varied much; that of seven strings was the most used, it was that appropriated to Apollo, and was the most perfect. The lyre was played with the fingers, or with a small ivory instrument, or a reed, called *pecten,* or *plectrum,* which was employed to save the fingers; but it was deemed more skilful to touch the lyre without the *plectrum.* The lyre was also performed upon with both hands, which was called touching or nipping it *inside and outside.* The great lyre was considered to be the invention of the God of Music, the divine Apollo, whilst the smaller or *cithara* was reputed to have been invented by Mercury.

The *Lyre* is figured on various coins both Roman and Greek. One or two of these instruments appear on medals which have been struck in those cities where Apollo Actius, or the God of the Muses, was worshipped.—A single lyre is found on coins of Aemilia, Papia, and Petronia families; and in the Imperial series on medals of Augustus, Hadrian, and Domitian.

The *Lyre,* as displaying the image of celestial harmony, is represented in the hand of Apollo, or the arm of that deity is seen resting upon it, on coins of Augustus, Nero, Domitian, Hadrian, Antonine, Commodus, Severus, Caracalla, Trebonianus Gallus, Valerian, Gallienus, Probus, &c.—In the hand of Calliope, or the Muse Clio, and of Hercules Musagetes, in the *Pomponia* family.—In the hand of a *citharoedus,* or harper, it is a frequent type in sacrificial solemnities; likewise in the secular festivals— see LVD. SAEC. FEC.—On Nero's coins, we see it in more than one instance in the hands of that imperial *"fiddler."*

The *Lyre* and laurel branch is exhibited on a coin of Domitian.

Two *Lyres* suspended, one on each side of an altar, on a coin of the *Scribonia* family—and the same number with a caduceus in the middle, on a silver coin of Domitian.—Havercamp on Morell *(Fam.* p. 204) gives the type of two *Lyres,* on which an owl is standing, designating as he interprets it, Concord assisted by prudent counsel, or indicating simply the worship of Apollo and Minerva.—See *Cithara.*

M.

M, The twelfth letter of the Latin alphabet. A capital M appears on coins of Anastasius, Justinus I., Justinus II., Tiberius Constantinus, Mauricius, Phocas, Heraclius, and other Emperors of the East.

M. as a letter of the alphabet is observed on many coins of Roman families.

M. *Magister.*—EQ. M. Equitum Magister. Master of the Horse.

M. *Magna.*—I. S. M. R. Juno Sospita Magna Regina.

M. *Marci.*—M. F. Marci Filius. In like manner as M. N. *Marci Nepos.*

M. or MA. *Marcia.*—AQVA. M. on a denarius of the Marcia family.

M. *Marcia,* a prenomen and name of a woman.

M. *Marcius.*—Q. M. *Quintus Marcius.*

M. or MA. *Marcus,* a prenomen, frequently found on coins of Roman families, and likewise on those of the Imperial series, where we see IMP. C. M. (or MA.) AVREL. ANTONINVS; on a coin of Caracalla.

M. A. *Marcus Antonius,* also *Marcus Aurelius.*

M. AVR. *Marcus Aurelius.*

M. *Martia.*—LEG. XIIII. GEMINA. M. V. *Legio* XIIII. *Gemina Martia Victrix.*—This epigraph, with the legionary eagle between two standards, appears on a very rare silver coin of Sept. Severus, as edited in Khell's *Suppl.* p. 108.

M. *Mater.*—M, C. *Mater Cæsaris;* or *Mater Castrorum.*—M. PATR. *Mater Patriæ.*

M. *Maxima.*—VICTORIA G. M. *Germanica Maxima,* on a coin of· Gallienus, in Khell's *Suppl.* p. 184.

M. *Maximo.*—See I. O. M. *Jovi Optimo Maximo.*

M. *Maximus.*—P. M. *Pontifex Maximus.*

M. *Messius,* prenomen of *Trajanus Decius.* M. Q. TRAIANVS.

M. *Metropolis.*—COL. SEP. AVR. LAOD. M. *Colonia Septimia Aurelia Metropolis.*

M. *Militaris.*—R. M. *Rei Militaris.*

M. *Minervia.*—LEG. M. XX. *Legio Minervia Vicesima.*

M. *Moesiæ.*—P. M. S. COL. VIM. *Provincia Moesiæ Superioris Colonia Viminiacum.*

M. *Moneta.*—M. SACRA AVGG. ET CAESS. NN. *Moneta Sacra Augustorum Et Cæsarum Nostrorum.*

M. *Multis.*—See VOTIS X. M. XX. on coins of Galerius.

M. *Munitæ.*—QVOD. V. M. S. &c. *Quod Viæ Munitæ Sunt.*

M. *Municipes.*—M. IVL. VTICEN. *Municipes Julii Uticensis.*

M. *Municipium.*—M. R.—*Municipium Ravennatum.*—Vaillant, *Pr.* i. 300.

M. at the end of Roman words was now and then formerly omitted; for example we find it wanting on *denarii* of the *Aemilia* family, as PRIVER. CAPTV.—It is also sometimes observed to be left out in the word AVGVSTORVM, as VICTORIA AVGVSTORV.

M. as a numeral signifies *Mille,* a thousand.

MAC. or MACED. *Macedonica.*—LEG. V. MAC. *Legio Macedonica Quinta, Sexta, &c.*

MAC. AVG. *Macellum Augusti.*—On the reverse of a large and a middle brass of Nero we find this inscription, and for its accompanying type an ,elegant edifice, with many columns, into which the ascent is by a flight of steps, ornamented with a statue in its portico. These rare coins were struck in memory of the Market-place, which, as Dion relates, was constructed by order of Nero.—See a view of the building, p. 77.

The *Macellum* was a place where meat and other eatables were sold. It appears that at Rome the place appropriated to the slaughtering of beasts was not the same as that destined to the sale of meat, but that each had its particular locality. Hence the word *macellum,* which is commonly translated *butchery,* properly means a market for meat, fish, and other eatables; and in this sense the word as used by Varro, Plautus, and other writers, must be understood. On the above quoted medal of Nero, we see a building equal in exterior magnificence of architecture to the public baths, to the circuses, and to the amphitheatres. This Market-place is perfectly characteristic of the Roman empire, which lavished the utmost grandeur of design and splendour of art, on the simplest monuments of public utility.—The word *macellum* (adds Millin), written on the map of the capitol, in front of an edifice adorned with columns, leaves no doubt as to its destination; but it does not appear to be the same with that represented on the medal in question.

Therefore by this epigraph of MAC. AVG. and the type above described the *macellum* is recorded, respecting which Xiphilinus from Dion thus speaks:—"Then also Nero dedicated the forum of provisions, which is called the *macellum.*"—The name is derived from Macellus, formerly a noted robber in Rome, on whose condemnation the censors ordained that in his house victuals should be sold. Suetonius also mentions *annona macelli.* This coin of Nero clearly then confirms the words of Dion, and at the same time shews the form of the building, with which that emperor embellished the *forum obsoniorum.* The ever visionary Harduin interprets the epigraph M*Ausoleum Cæsaris* A V*Gusti !*

MACED. *Macedonica.*—LEG. V. MACED. VIII. AVG. *Legionis Quintæ Macedonicæ Octavæ Augustæ.* On a colonial coin of Philip senior.

Macedonia, an ancient Greek monarchy, in the south of Europe; the kingdom of Philip and of Alexander the Great. After royalty became extinct in Macedonia, the people governed themselves by their own laws. Conquered by Æmilius, it was at first left free, but was at length made a Roman province by Cecilius Metellus, and was divided into four parts.— During the empire it struck *Greek* medals in honour of Augustus, Claudius, Nero, Vitellius, Vespasian, Domitian, Hadrian, Antonine, Marcus Aurelius, Faustina, Commodus, Severus, Gordianus Pius, and Diadumenianus.—The four Roman colonies in Macedonia, of Cassandra, Dium, Pella, and Philippi, indicate their establishment by Julius Cæsar, or Augustus, on their coins which bear the inscription COL. IVL. AVG. *Colonia Julia Augusta.*—Macedonia, as a province under Imperial Rome, is personified on two distinct coins of Hadrian, viz., the ADVENTVS and the RESTITVTOR MACEDONIAE of his large brass geographical series: the latter exhibits in its type the pointed cap and the round buckler of the Macedonians.

MACEDONIC. *Macedonicus,* a surname of Metellus. Q. METE. MACEDONIC. *Quintus Metellus Macedonicus,* appears on the denarius which records the triumphal honours decreed to Metellus on the conquest of Macedonia.

MACER *(Lucius Clodius),* Proprætor of Africa under Nero, and afterwards for a short interval invested with the title of Augustus, until he was deposed and put to death by order of Galba. His coins, struck in Africa, are in silver, and very rare, those without the head being, perhaps, somewhat more common than those with the portrait. They present several varieties of type, one of the most interesting of which is here engraved:—*Obv.* L. CLODIVS

MACER S.C. Bare head of Clodius Macer.— *Rev.* PRO PRAE. AFRICAE. A galley upon which is a military standard.—Valued by Mionnet at 300 francs.

M. ACILIVS.—Prenomen and name of the *Acilia* family.

MACRIANVS *(Marcus Fulvius)* the elder, one of the many usurpers who took advantage of the distracted state of the empire, during the reign of Gallienus. The friend of Valerianus, he excited him against the Christians, and then betrayed his cause. Elected Emperor A.D. 261, he appointed Balista his general, and defeated the Persians. But soon afterwards marching into Illyria against Aureolus, another tyrant, he was himself defeated, and fell a victim to the treachery of his own soldiers A.D. 262.— Beauvais, in his History, quotes coins of the elder Macrianus; but according to the opinion of Vaillant, confirmed by later writers, there are no Latin coins of his extant; but those which remain belong to the younger Macrianus. Those, in potin, struck at Alexandria, are of extreme rarity.

MACRIANVS junior *(Marcus, or Titus, Fulvius),* proclaimed Augustus at the same time with his father, by the legions of the eastern provinces A.D. 261. He was a good soldier; acted as a tribune under Valerianus; associated in government with his father, whose fate he shared after their just defeat by Aureolus.—There are no gold coins of Macrianus jun., and those called

silver are of base metal (often described as third brass). On these he is styled MACRIANVS, NOBIL. CAES., or IMP. C. FVLVIVS. MACRIANVS P.F. AVG.

"It would appear (says Mr. Akerman) from the first of these titles that, contrary to the testimony of historians, Macrianus the younger was first declared Cæsar, and that the title of Augustus was conferrred upon him subsequently. The Latin coins of the young Macrianus do not bear the prenomen. His Greek coins differ in the name; some have MARCVS, others TITVS. If any of the coins with these names bore an old head, instead of the youthful portrait always found on them, it might reasonably be supposed that either Titus or Marcus belonged to the elder Macrianus. Nevertheless, it is certain that many of the Imperial Greek coins have portraits but little resembling those on the Latin coins of the same emperor."—*Descript. Catal.* vol. ii. p. 77, 78.

MACRINUS *(Marcus Opelius Severus),* the successor of Caracalla, who was assassinated in Mesopotamia at his instigation. He was born in Africa, of an obscure family (A.D. 164). At first an advocate, he came to Rome and was favourably received by Septimius Severus; afterwards appointed Prætorian Prefect by Caracalla, but having ascertained the intention of that ferocious tyrant to destroy him, he took the above-mentioned effectual but treacherous step to prevent it, and was proclaimed Emperor A.D. 217. He was a prince well skilled in the laws, and just in their administration; a protector of literature, and a great disciplinarian, but somewhat cruel and voluptuous. Although confirmed in the government by the Senate, he did not proceed to Rome, having immediately entered into a war with the Parthians, by whom he was defeated, and at length was constrained to make a peace with their King Artabanes on terms disgraceful to the Roman arms. Having by his parsimony and severity indisposed the troops towards him, and being attacked by the generals of Elagabalus, he was defeated, pursued, and slain, in Bythinia, A.D. 218, in the 54th year of his age, not having completed the second year of his reign.—The coins of Macrinus are of extreme rarity in gold; not scarce in silver; but rare in first and second brass, and his brass medallions are very rare. On these he is styled IMP. CAES. M. OPEL. SEV. MACRINVS AVG.

On the obverse of a first brass medal, with the above names and titles for its legend, is the laureated head of the Emperor.—On the reverse, the epigraph is SECVRITAS TEMPORVM, and the type a woman holding the hasta in her left hand, and resting her right hand on a column.

The more frequently revolutions multiplied themselves under the Emperors, the more the throne tottered on its base; and the princes who were called to the government of the empire affected to invoke a *security* of which they would hardly have been otherwise than doubtful.

For the portrait of Macrinus, see *Annona Aug.*

M. ÆM. *Marcus Æmilius.*—Prenomen and name of a man.

MÆCILIA, a plebeian family; surname *Tullus*. Four varieties of coins, all common.— M. MAECILIVS. TVLLVS. IIIVIR. A. A. A. F. F. This inscription is found on first and second brass of Augustus.

MÆNIA, a plebeian family, which extended itself from the two *Mænii*, tribunes of the people. Its surname is said to be *Antiaticus*. There are four varieties on its coins, which are rare in silver, and much rarer in third brass.— The types of the silver (Mænia) are the common ones of Minerva's head on the obverse; and Victory in a quadriga, or the Dioscuri on horse-back, on the reverse, with the legend P. MAE. or P. MAE. ANT.—A small brass of this family bears on one side the head of Hercules, and on the other the prow of a galley, with the inscrip-tion P. MAE. ANT. ME.

Aloysius Odericus thus signally explains the above coins in the dissertation which he has given in *Saggi di Cortona*. Havercamp, says he, from these contracted epigraphs, *(epigraphes siglæ,* for the letters are tied together) *(colligatæ)* has made out three persons, viz., P. Mænius, Antonius (or Antronius), and Metellus, when nevertheless only one individual is named, that is to say, P. *Mænius Antiaticus*, *Meyellus*, or *Medullinus*, or what other surname soever begins with the syllable ME. The first surname rightly belongs to the *Mænia* race, of which was C. Mænius, who, in the year of Rome 416, triumphed over the Antiates, according to Livy's history, and the Fasti Capitolini, in which latter appears as follows:—C. MAENIVS P. F. P. N. COnSul DE ANTIATIBVS.—The second cognomen, whatever it was, distinguishes this Mænius from other *Antiatici*, just as the cognomen *Spinther* serves to distinguish the *Cornelii Lentuli* from the *Marcellini*.

MAESA (*Julia*), born at Emesa in Syria, daughter of Julius Bassianus, priest of the Sun, sister of Julia Domna, and grandmother of Elagabalus. She married Julius Avitus, by whom she had Julia Soæmias and Julia Mamæa, the mother of Alexander Severus. She was a woman of great sagacity and courage, possessed of vast wealth. Retiring to Emesa, at the period of Caracalla's death, she gained over the soldiery by her largesses ; proclaimed Elagabalus emperor ; fought at the head of his troops against Macrinus ; proceeded to Rome, took her seat in the Senate, though contrary to the laws ; gave good counsels, but in vain, to her infamous grandson ; and died regretted in the reign of Alexander Severus, A.D. 223, whom she had

adroitly induced Elagabalus to adopt for his successor, and by whom she was honoured with the ceremonies of *consecration.*—Her coins are of extreme rarity in gold; but common in silver and first and second brass. On these she is styled IVLIA MAESA AVGVSTA, and, after death, DIVA MAESA AVG.

On a large brass medal, with the head of Mæsa, we read IVLIA MAESA AVG. ; and on the reverse SAECVLI FELICITAS S. C. A woman standing, with a caduceus in her hand ; at her feet a *modius*, or bushel, out of which issue ears of coins ; in the field of the medal is a star.—The greater part of Mæsa's coins probably belong to the reign of Elagabalus.

MAG. *Magister.*—MAG. IVVENT. *Magister Juventutis.*

MAG. PIVS. *Magnus Pius.*—Great and Pious, names and titles of Cneius Pompey.— See *Pompeia fam.*

Magister Juventutis. One of the coins on which this title is read, according to Morell, is of the *Mitreia* family, thus—on the obverse C. MITREIVS L. F. MAG*ister* IVVENT*utis*, with the naked head of a man.—On the reverse the number XII. within a laurel crown.—In the Pembroke coins this is placed amongst the *Spintriæ.*—The office of the *Magister Juventutis* seems to have been that of instructing in military discipline and equestrian exercises the Roman youth—*i.e.*, the young nobility, and, in the first place, Caius and Lucius, on whom Augustus had conferred the title of *principes juventutis.*—On one of the ancient inscriptions by *Gruter* is read M. PVERORVM DOM. AVGVST. *Magister puerorum domus Augustæ.*—The word *Magister* properly signifies a man invested with some authority—a master, one who has more power than another.

Magistratus.—Magistracy or the dignity of Magistrate.—This name was at Rome given only to those offices, which were discharged in that city, and the functions of those who governed in the provinces were simply denomi-nated *Potestates.*—*Magistratus* also (derived from *Magister*) signifies the Magistrate, of whom there were several sorts among the Romans. 1. The ordinary magistrates, and the extraordinary magistrates. 2. Patrician, Plebeian, and mixed magistrates. 3. And these were again distinguished as the great and the lesser magistrates. There were, moreover, *Curules* and *Non Curules*, Magistrates of the City, or Capital, and Provincial Magistrates.—The *Magis-tratus Curules* were those who had a right to the curule chair, as the Dictator, the Consul, the Prætor, and the Curule Edile, and these alone possessed the *jus imaginis*, or right to have the images of their ancestors in their houses, &c.—The *Magistratus Majores*, or superior magistrates, were so called because they had the grand auspices, the right to have lictors and messuages, and were chosen in the *comitia* by centuries, such were the Consuls, the Prætors, and the Censors.—The *Magistratus Minores* were those who were appointed in the comitia by tribes—viz., the Curule and Plebeian Ediles, the Tribunes of the people, the Questors, the Monetary Triumvirs, and the Provincial Magistrates, both ordinary and extraordinary.—*Magistratus Patricii*: At the commencement of the republic the magistrates were all patricians, but in the end the people acquired a share in all these dignities, except that of the *interrex*.—*Magistratus Plebeii*: The plebeian magistrates were the Tribunes and Ediles of the people; all the others were mixt.—*Magistratus Provinciales* were those the exercise of whose functions was limited within the provinces to which the republic sent them, as governors, in quality either of Proconsul, of Prætor, of Proprætor, and for the purpose of administering justice according to the Roman laws.

The insignia of Roman Magistrates, represented on the reverses of Consular medals, are *sellæ curules, fasces, secures, gubernacula, tripodes*, &c.—See those words.

MAGN. *Magnentia.*—SALVS D. N. MAGN. ET. CAES.—*Salus Domini Nostri Magnentii et Cæsaris—(Decentii* understood.)

MAGNENTIVS *(Fl. Magnus)*, born in Gaul, of obscure British or German parents, about A.D. 303, was brought up by Constans, with whom he was so great a favourite, on account of his skill in military affairs, that in a tumult when the soldiers were on the point of putting him as captain of the guard to death, his imperial master threw his *paludamentum* as a protection over him, and thus saved his life. This kindness Magnentius most ungratefully requited with treachery, and the basest machinations, through which the Emperor fell a victim, and this usurper obtained the empire, after having assumed the purple at *Autun* (Augustodunum), A.D. 350. He was a man of studious habits, powerful in conversation, but hard-hearted and cruel. He named as Cæsar his brother Decentius whom he sent with an army to defend Gaul beyond the Alps; and he himself marched against

Constantius, brother of Constans, whose terms of peace he had rashly rejected, and by whom he was defeated in two engagements, one in Italy, the other in Gaul. Fleeing to Lyons, and unable to retrieve his affairs, he then slew himself A.D. 353, in the 50th year of his age.—The second and third brass of Magnentius are very common; his gold are rare; his silver rarer. On these he is styled IMP. CAE. MAGNENTIVS AVG.—DN MAGNENTIVS P.F. AVG —IMP. FL. MAGNENTIVS P.F. AVG.—Also MAGNENTIVS P.F. AVG. The signification of the letters TR. has not been explained.

MAGNIA VRBICA, whose coins in every metal are extremely rare, has by some been ascribed as the wife of Maxentius, by others of Magnentius or Decentius, by others again of Carus and Numerianus; but Khell and Eckhel assign her to Carinus.—See *Urbica.*

MAGNIFICENTIA AVG.—The magnificence, or as it is generally expressed *munificence* (MVNIFICENTIA) of the Emperors, is a legend which has relation to public games, through the attractive medium of which the Roman Emperors strove to gain the affections of the people. The usual type is the figure of an elephant standing, as we see it on coins of Antoninus Pius, of Commodus, of Sept. Severus, and of Elagabalus.

MAGNIFICENTIAE AVG. COS. VI. P. P. within a crown.—Second brass of Commodus.— This coin is wanting in Mediobarbus, but appears in Vaillant, and in Havercamps's *Cabinet of Queen Christina*, and is recognised by Mionnet and Akerman. It is an unique example of *Magnificentia* (says Eckhel) inscribed on coins; an epigraph the adoption of which any occasion or motive, how trifling and absurd soever, might suggest to so very vain a man.

MAGNVS, a surname or title of gods, heroes, kings, and emperors. The deities were generally called *Magni*, and the term was particularly applied to Jupiter, Diana. &c.—*Magnus* and *Maximus* are titles often found assigned to Roman Emperors. The inscription DIVO ANTONINO MAGNO appears on coins of Caracalla struck after his death; for that bad prince, as vain as he was ferocious, loved to be saluted with the distinctive appellation of *Magnus*, after the example of Alexander the Great, whom he affected to imitate.

MAGNVS is a cognomen ascribed on certain consular coins to *Pompey* and to his sons, *Cnaeus* and *Sextus*; to the father on account of his victorious exploits, and to his posterity as an hereditary distinction —See *Pompeia* family.

The name of *Magnus* was assumed by the usurper *Magnentius*, and also by his brother *Decentius.*—*Maximus*, another pretender to the imperial throne, during the reign of Theodosius I., took the prenomen of *Magnus.*

Magusano, or *Macusano*, on coins of Postumus.—See *Herculi Magusano.*

MAIANIA, a family of uncertain rank, and respecting which no mention is made by ancient writers. Its coins bearing on the reverse C. MAIANI. present three varieties; are rare in silver; common in first brass, being parts of the *as*; but very rare in third brass, which are by the moneyers of Augustus.

The denarius of this family bears on its obverse the head of Minerva, with winged helmet.—*Rev.* C. MAIANI. A winged figure, with a whip guiding a biga at full speed. In the exergue ROMA.

Vaillant assigns this silver coin to the Mænia family, and Havercamp leans to this opinion; but Ursin and Morell place it under the head of *Maiania*, and in doing so appear to have the sanction of Eckhel.

MAJORIANVS *(Flavius Julius)*, appointed by Leo, Emperor of the East, to be his general in chief, and sent by him to occupy the government of the western empire; assumed the title of Imperator, at Ravenna, after the deposition of Avitus A.D. 457. He had proved himself a good general under Aetius, and possessed great and excellent qualities. He inflicted severe injury on the barbarian tribes both in Italy and in Gaul: whilst his friend and general, Ricimer, defeated Genseric, 458; Majorian beat the Goths under Theodoric; but he had scarcely made peace with Genseric, when Ricimer conspired against and deposed him at Dertona, now *Tortona*, in Liguria; and he died by his own hand A.D. 461.—The gold coins of Majorianus are esteemed rare; the brass still rarer; on these he is styled D. N. IVLIVS. MAIORIANVS. FELIX. AVG. P.

M. or MAM. *Mamercus;* a prenomen, and afterwards a name of the *Aemilia* family :— MAM. LEPIDVS. *Mamercus Lepidus.*

MAMAEA *(Julia)*, daughter of Julia Mæsa, sister of Julia Soaemias, and mother of Alexander Severus. She took the name of the Julia family from her father, whom some call Julius Avitus, but her surname of Mamea, like that of her sister Soaemias, is believed to be Syriac.—

Julia Mamaca was married to Genesius Marcianus, by whom she had Theoclia and Alexander Severus. On Roman coins she is honoured with the title of *Augusta* (A.D. 222). By her sagacity she conciliated the good-will of the soldiery in favour of her son Alexander, of whom by education she made a perfect prince; by her assiduity with her mother Mæsa she promoted his adoption to the empire, whilst by her prudence she extricated him from the snares laid for him by Elagabalus. She ruled under her son with talent and courage; was his companion even in the Persian war; but ambitious, haughty, and covetous, she committed some acts of injustice from the love of money. It is said, on historical authority, that she had embraced the Christian faith. This princess was murdered at the same time with her imperial son A.D. 235.

The silver coins of *Mamaea* are common; the brass, *first* and *second*, very common; *third* brass rare; her *gold* are of the highest rarity. On these she is styled IVLIA MAMAEA AVG*usta* MAT*er* AVG*usta*. On the reverse is sometimes MATER CASTRORVM.

MAMILIA, although a most noble and most ancient family, emigrating, it is said, from Tusculum, or from Tibur, yet it became plebeian

at Rome. It derived its surname *Limetanus,* it is believed, from its being given at first to C. Mamilius, tribune of the people, because he (V.C. 589) carried the *lex de limitibus* or boundary law. In its coins which are for the most part common, there are eighteen varieties; the silver pieces restored by Trajan are extremely rare, amongst these is the following interesting type:—

C. MAMIL. LIMETAN.—A man in a short habit, wearing on his head the *pileus*, or hemispherical bonnet, and holding a long knotted

stick, and a dog at his feet fawning on him.— The *obverse* of this denarius bears the head of Mercury, as designated by his attributes, the winged cap and the *caduceus*. This coin has been explained as representing Ulysses recognised by his dog.—According to the Homeric recital, that Grecian hero, after an absence of twenty years, resolved to repair once more to his kingdom of Ithaca without making himself known. Accordingly he disguised himself, as a pilgrim, or traveller, and effectually escaped discovery by any man, when his faithful dog Argus, knew again his long lost master, and by wagging his tail, and other canine blandishments, testified his dying joy at the sudden recognition—

" *Et moriens reminiscitur Argos.*"

The affecting incident is most graphically recorded on this elegant denarius. The *Mamilia* family pretended to derive its origin from Mamilia, the daughter of Telegonus, the reputed son of Ulysses and Circe; and C. Mamilius, as a monetal triumvir, caused this subject to be adopted on one of his medals.

There is another denarius, with same reverse, but, instead of the bust of Mercury, its obverse exhibits that of *Diana Venatrix*, below which is S. C.

MAN. *Manius;* a prenomen, which, in linked monogrammated letters (MN), appears on coins of *Fonteia* family.

M. AN. *Marcus Annius.*—See *Florianus*.

Manens, an epithet of Fortune, on a coin of Commodus.—See FORTVNAE MANENTI.

MANLIA, a plebeian family. The coins said to belong to it are passed over by Eckhel as " numi Goltziani," and not noticed by Mionnet or Akerman.

Manipulus, a band or company of Roman soldiers, whose military ensign was an extended hand placed on the top of a spear.

MANL. or MANLI. *Manlius.*

MANLIA, a patrician family, of the most noble descent. Its principal surname is *Torquatus,* celebrated in its association with *Manlius* in Roman story.—The gold coins are very rare;

the silver common.—This family took the surname of *Torquatus* from the valour of T. Manlius, who, in the year of Rome 393, slew in single combat a Gaul of superior strength to himself, and took away his collar (torques). Thenceforward the *Manlii* adopted the honourable addition, and stamped it on their coins. —Thus on the reverse of a silver medal of this family we see L. TORQVA. Q. EX. S. C.

A man, armed with helmet, spear, and buckler, galloping on horseback.—The obverse presents the winged head of Pallas, the word ROMA and X., all within a *torques.*—On the reverse of another denarius of the *Manlia* family we read the words L. SVLLA. IMP., and the type represents Sylla in a triumphal quadriga, holding in his right hand a caduceus, and crowned by a flying Victory.—The obverse of this coin bears the legend L. MANLI. PRO. Q., and for its type has the winged head of Minerva.—We learn from Plutarch that Manlius Torquatus, who on the above is called *Proquæstor*, was one of Sylla's generals.—Another coin of the *Manlia* family exhibits the same reverse of Sylla triumphing, and bears on its obverse ROM. and the mark X., together with the head of Pallas, all within a *torques,* or ornamental *collar,* allusive to their intrepid and victorious ancestor.

Besides the silver coins above described, there is an elegant one inscribed SER. (*Serranus,* or more probably *Sergius*), with the head of Minerva for the type of its obverse, and ROMA before it; on the reverse of which is A. MANLI. Q. F., and Apollo, or the Sun, in a chariot drawn by four horses, on his left X., on his right a crescent, and on each side a star.—See SOL.

Also another denarius, with female head, and inscribed SIBVLLA.—*Rev.:* L. TORQVAT*us* III. VIR. A tripod, above which are two stars, the whole within an ornamental circle.— See *Sibylla.*

MANLIA SCANTILLA, the wife of *Didius Julianus,* by whom she had the beautiful *Didia Clara,* she being herself the most deformed of women. On the same day that her husband became Emperor (A.D. 193), she was proclaimed *Augusta,* by a decree of the Senate, but her happiness was of brief duration, for Julianus having in a few weeks been put to death, the imperial titles were taken away both from her and her daughter by Severus, and Manlia Scantilla died in obscurity.—She is numismatically styled MANL. (or MANLIA) SCANTILLA. AVG.—All her coins are

of extreme rarity, the gold, silver, and **second** brass particularly so.—The silver and bronze have on their reverse IVNO REGINA, and a veiled female, or deity, standing with a patera in her right hand, a *hasta* in her left, and a peacock at her feet.—The illustration has been selected from a gold coin in the British Museum.

M. ANN. *Marcus Annius;* prenomen and name of a man.

Manus Humana, the human hand, is sometimes the numismatic index of Liberality; at other times two hands joined together serve to symbolize the concord of individuals, and to designate the confirmation of friendship and of treaties.—We see a human hand, intended to represent "the hand divine," put forth from clouds on a coin of Constantine the Great; another holding the cross or a crown, on coins of Arcadius, and of Eudoxia his wife.

Manus duæ junctæ.—Two hands joined, holding a caduceus, or corn-ears, with poppies, or other fruits, in indication of the happy consequences of concord, appears on coins of the Junia family; also on medals of Julius Cæsar, M. Antony, Lepidus, Augustus, Vespasian, Titus, Domitian (see *Caduceus*), Antoninus, M. Aurelius, Albinus.

Manus duæ junctæ.—Two hands joined, holding a military ensign placed on the prow of a galley, symbolical of the concord of the army, is a type found on coins of M. Antony, Vespasian, Domitian, Nerva, M. Aurelius, Commodus.—See *Concordia Exercituum.*

Two hands joined, occur on silver of Balbinus and Pupienus, with AMOR MVTVVS AVGG.; and PIETAS MVTVA AVGG.; and on silver of Carausius with the legend CONCORDIA MILITVM.

Three hands joined, appear on coins of Antoninus, Salonina, and Valerian, jun., and the same holding a caduceus on a coin of Augustus.

MAQ. *Moneta Aquileiæ Percussa.*—SMAQP. *Secra Moneta Aquileiæ Percussa.*—These letters appear on the exergue of a coin of Gratianus; also on one of Theodosius M.—[Aquileia, formerly a rich town, near the Gulf of Venice, is now a small village.]

MAR. *Marcellinus.*—LENT. MAR. F. *Lentulus Marcellini Filius.*

MAR. *Marcellus.*—MAR. CL.—*Marcellus Clodius.*

MAR. *Marcus.*—MAR. AVRELIVS PROBVS.— Banduri, i. p. 456.

MAR. *Mars, Marti.*

MAR. The month of March.—EID. MAR. *Idus Martii.* The Ides of March.—See *Junia* family.

MARCELLINVS.—On a denarius of the *Claudia* family appears the name of MARCELLINVS., and the head of Claudius Marcellus, behind which is the *triquetra* (or three mens' legs), allusive to his conquest of Sicily. On the reverse of the same denarius appears the word.

MARCELLVS, the surname of the abovementioned plebeian family. MARCELLVS COS. QVINQ. (*Consul Quinquies,* five times Consul.)— The type represents this valiant commander, clothed in the toga, carrying into a temple of four columns, a trophy formed of armour which he had himself taken from the person of Viridomarus, a Gaulish chief.—See *Claudia*.

MARCI. *Marcius*

MARCIA, a family originally patrician, but afterwards plebeian. Its surnames are *Censorinus, Libo, Philippus.*—Morell gives forty-two varieties of type, of which the silver are common, the brass rare. Many of the latter pieces are *asses* or parts of the *as*, or struck by the moneyers of Augustus. —The *Marcia* family claimed to derive its origin from Ancus Marcius, King of the Romans—a claim which is plainly indicated on a silver coin of that house, on which are exhibited the name and portrait of ANCVS, with the lituus behind the head.—On the reverse are the word PHILIPPVS, and an equestrian statue on a

bridge, underneath the arches of which we read AQVA MAR*cia*. This is allusive to the famous Marcian aqueduct at Rome, whence flowed another honour to the family. Respecting it Pliny expresses himself in the following emphatic terms : "The most renowned of all waters (conveyed by aqueducts) for the merit of coolness and wholesome qualities is, by the city's testimony, that of MARCIA. Ancus Marcius, one of the Kings of Rome, was the first to introduce it into the city. In after times .Q. Marcius restored it, during his prætorship, and the same thing was done subsequently by M. Agrippa."—With respect to the figure of the horseman placed on the arches of the aqueduct, Eckhel observes that as the same recurs on several coins of the *Philippi*, it is probable that it may allude to the surname *Philippus*, although he would not deny that it may probably refer besides to the domestic praise of the family, since both Livy and Pliny bear witness to an equestrian statue publicly erected to Q. Marcius Tremulus, on his victory over the Samnites.—See *Ancus Marcius*, p. 44.

MARCIA, the prenomen of a woman, taken from *Marcus*—as MARCIA OTACILIA SEVERA, wife of Philip senior.—See *Otacilia*.

MARCIA, a concubine of Commodus, to whom (according to Lampridius and other historians) above all others that profligate emperor was the most passionately attached, appears depicted on his coins under the form of an Amazon. (Spanheim, *Pr.* ii. p. 292.)—On the obverse of a fine bronze medallion of this prince (having for the type of its reverse a sacrificial group) are the joined heads of Commodus and Marcia; that of the former is laureated; that of the other helmeted. The bust of this woman is sometimes clothed in a cuirass; at other times it is accompanied by the Amazonian *pelta*. This

medallion is valued by Mionnet at 200 fr.; and there are others, of equal value, which he describes in his *Recueil des Médailles Romaines*, and on which, in the opinion of Vaillant, the head of this Amazonian female is to be recognised.

MARCIANA, sister of the Emperor Trajan, and mother of Matidia, an accomplished woman. She lost her husband previous to the accession of her brother to the empire, and lived as a widow with the Emperor's wife, Plotina, to whom she was united by the tenderest and most uninterrupted friendship. She died about A.D. 114, and received the honours of Consecration (see that word).—She is styled MARCIANA AVG. SOROR. IMP. TRAIANI—DIVA AVGVSTA MARCIANA. The coins of this princess are, in every metal, exceedingly rare. The brass which form a monument of her consecration are all of the first size.—The annexed cut is from a specimen in the British Museum.

In commenting on the medals of Plotina, Marciana, and Matidia, the intelligent and accurate author of *Leçons de Numismatique Romaine* observes, in reference to the types of Consecration, which appear on the coins of these three princesses, that "although the Roman mintage retraces, from the earliest reigns and in divers manners, the apotheosis of Emperors and Empresses, yet the word CONSECRATIO appears only for the first time on the medals of *Marciana;* and with that legend a funeral pile, an altar, chariots of various forms, &c., serve to represent the apotheosis, without its being possible to determine the rules by which one type was employed in preference to another. Nevertheless the eagle taking its flight, a type at first common to both sexes (as is shewn in a large brass medal of Marciana), was afterwards reserved for the *Augusti* alone; whilst the peacock (a bird consecrated to Juno), and the covered car drawn by two mules, known by antiquaries under the name of *carpentum*, became types exclusively appropriated to the Empresses and other *Augustæ.*

MARCIANVS *(Flavius Valerius)*, born of humble parentage in Thrace, or in Illyria, but an accomplished soldier, he was honoured in marriage with the hand of Pulcheria, sister of Theodosius the Second, who proclaimed him Emperor of the East, A.D. 450. From that time to the end of his reign, seven years after, he preserved the peace and integrity of the empire; refused to pay tribute to Attila; destroyed paganism; favoured the Christians;

and died regretted, at Constantinople A.D. 457, supposed to have been poisoned, in the 65th year of his age.—All his coins are of the highest rarity, and on them he is called D. N. MARCIANVS P. F. AVG.

MARCVS, a frequently recurring prenomen, which on silver coins of the Æmilia, Antonia, and Aquilia families, is commonly found joined with the *prenomina* of relations and ancestors, for we read M. AEMILI. M. F. M. N. *Marcus Aemilius, Marci Filius, Marci Nepos.* In like manner M. AQVILIVS M. F. M. N.—The Emperor Commodus used the same prenomen of *Marcus*, which, as well as that of *Lucius*, by the initials M. and L. is designated on his coins.

Marcus Agrippa.—See *Vipsania* family.

Marcus Antonius.—See *Antonia* fam.

Marcus Aurelius.—See *Aurelius.*

MARI. *Marius.*—See *Maria* fam.

MARIA, a plebeian family. Its surnames, on coins, are *Capito* and *Trogus.*—The varieties are forty-six—most of them rare. Connected with its surname of Marcus, is a denarius, on the obverse of which we read C. MARI. C. F. *(Caius Marius, Caii Filius)* CAPIT. XXVIII., with head of Ceres.—*Rev.:* A man driving two oxen.

Trogus.—C. Marius Trogus was one of the moneyers of Augustus, as is shewn by his denarii, which are all honoured with the portrait of that prince. It is probable that they were struck about the year v.c. 741. As these denarii, with the exception of the name, offer nothing that relates to Trogus, but refer in all their types to Augustus and his family, and they are also of doubtful explanation, it will suffice to notice a few, and those briefly :—

Epigraph.—C. MARIVS. TRO. IIIVIR., or C. MARIVS. C. F. TRO.

Types.—On the obverse, as has been stated, the head of Augustus.—On the reverse, the head of Julia, daughter of Augustus, between the heads of Caius and Lucius, her sons by Agrippa.—This coin was struck under Augustus, about the year 737.—See AVGVSTVS DIVI. F., in which the type is explained.

Two men, clothed in the toga, standing, one of whom has his head laureated, the other wears a turreted crown; they both hold a roll in their left hands, and at the feet of each is something that resembles an altar, or pedestal; or, as Havercamp thinks, the *scrinium* (or casket), such as it was customary to place at the feet of senatorial statues. The same writer recognises in these two figures, Augustus and Agrippa, and the latter especially from his turreted crown.

A priest veiled stands, holding in his right hand the *simpulum* (or small chalice used in sacrifice). This is perhaps intended for Augustus, promoted to be *pontifex maximus*, in the year of Rome 741.

Some pieces in gold and silver of this family are by the moneyers of Augustus; and there are denarii restored by Trajan.

MARIDIANVS.—Caius Cossutius, a very rich man, seems to have adopted *Maridius*, who, according to the custom of those who were adopted, lengthened out the name, and was called *Maridianus.*—C. MARIDIANVS, who is read on the denarii of Julius Cæsar, was of the Cossutia family, that is of the equestrian order.— As one of the monetary triumvirs, he placed the figure of Venus Victrix on Julius's coins, to indicate the latter's pretensions to divine origin.

MARINIANA, the second wife, as it is believed, of Valerianus, and the mother of Valerianus jun.—This princess is known only through the medals on which her name as DIVA MARINIANA appears, and from which it is inferred that she died at the beginning of Valerian's reign. It is still a matter of doubt whether she was the wife of Valerianus; but she certainly was of his family. Her silver coins, or rather *billon*, are very rare, on the reverse of which we see a peacock, the symbol of her *consecration.* The brass are still rarer.—See Akerman's note on *Mariniana.*

MARIQVE.—See PACE P. R. TERRA MARIQVE on a coin of Nero.

MARIT. *Maritimæ.*—PRAEF. CLAS. ET OR. MARIT. *Præfectus Classis Et Oræ Maritimæ.*— See *Pompeia.*

Maritime, or naval power, is denoted on Roman coins by the prow of a ship, as on a denarius of Pompey the Great (with legend MAGN. PRO. COS.), or by the Roman Eagle and two standards, the latter resting on the prows of vessels, on a second brass of Sergius Galba.— The prætorian galley, with rowers, also serves to mark the *prefecture* and command of the sea, as on medals of Hadrian and other emperors.— See *Prætoria Navis* and *Felicitati Augusti.*

MARIVS *(Caius.)*—It is observed by Plutarch in the beginning of his life of this man, ennobled by so many consulates and by two triumphs, that he had no *cognomen* or third name. That this, however, is not to be referred to the entire family called amongst the Romans by the name of *Maria*, but only to the branch of the house whence *Marius* descended, the surname of *Capilo* and of *Trogus* struck on other coins of the same family serve abundantly to shew.

MARIVS *(Marcus Aurelius)*, called also *Manurius* and *Vecturius*, from being an artificer in iron and an armourer, became a Roman General, and proclaimed himself Emperor A.D. 267, by favour of the Gaulish legions, after the death of Victorinus. He was a bold and active man, conspicuous for prodigious powers of body, and of especial strength in the use of his hands and fingers. According to *Pollio* he reigned only three days, having been killed by one of his ancient comrades with a sword which he had himself fabricated. The mode of his death may have been authentically described; but that the career of his usurpation should have been so extremely short is scarcely credible, when regard is had to the abundance of coins (of limited variety) struck with the name and portrait of

Marius, and which though exceedingly rare in gold; are scarce in potin or base silver, and in third brass, but less so in the latter. He is styled IMP. C.M. AVR. MARIVS. P.F. AVG.— The cut is taken from a gold coin in the British Museum.

MARS, the god of war, was, according to the common belief of the ancients, the son of Jupiter and of Juno; or as some of the later poets have pretended, the son of Juno, by whom solely he was generated, as the goddess Minerva was brought forth of Jupiter alone. Mars was regarded as a great leader in battle; as presiding over discord and contest, everywhere exciting slaughter and war. Although this divinity had numerous adorers in Greece and in many other countries, there was no place where his worship became more popular than at Rome.—On a gold coin and also on a middle brass of Antoninus Pius, appears a type which recals to mind the legendary origin of Rome. It represents Mars armed with helmet, spear, and shield, descending to Ilia or Rhea, the Vestal mother of Romulus and Remus, who is depicted half naked in a recumbent posture, and buried in a profound sleep. It was to support the fable which made Romulus pass for the son of Mars, that the Romans gave to their first king, in his apotheosis, the name of *Quirinus,* and afterwards to Mars himself many temples, amongst which that built by Augustus after the battle of Philippi, under the name of MARS VICTOR, was the most celebrated. The priests of this deity, called Salians, had the custody of the *ancilia,* or sacred shields. The Latins derived his name from *Mares* (males), because it is men who are employed in wars. They also called him *Gradivus* and sometimes *Quirinus;* and established this difference between the two appellations, that the former indicated this god during war, and the latter during peace. The Romans likewise denominated him PATER, on several of their imperial coins, in allusion to his being father of Romulus and Remus.—On medals and other ancient monuments Mars is represented under the figure of a man armed with a helmet, a lance, and a shield, sometimes naked, at others in a military habit, or with a soldier's mantle over the shoulders; in some instances bearded, but more frequently without a beard. *Mars Victor* appears bearing a trophy, and *Mars Gradivus* is depictured in the attitude of a man who is walking with great strides. The wolf was sacred to Mars, and the Romans sacrificed a horse to him on the 12th of October. His familiarity with Venus is shadowed forth on coins of Marcus Aurelius and Faustina jun., in which we see the goddess of beauty, as VENVS VICTRIX, embracing him in her arms, and retaining him by her blandishments.

The unbearded head of *Mars* appears on a denarius of the *Cornelia* family, with inscription

of CN. BLASIO C. IV. F.—See Visconti and Riccio on this point.

The *temple* of Mars, with the epigraph of MAR. VLT., *Marti Ultori,* appears on coins of Augustus. On medals of Caracalla, Gordianus III. and other emperors, he has the name of PROPVGNATOR (the defender); and Constantine, previous to his profession of Christianity, dedicated a coin to his honour, with the circumscription of MARTI PATRI PROPVGNATORI.— The legend of MARS VICTOR is found on medals of Domitian, Antoninus, Numerianus, Claudius Gothicus, Probus, &c. MARS VLTOR (the avenger) on those of Alexander Severus, and others; MARS PACIFER (the peace-bearer) on those of Gallienus, &c.; MARS CONSERVATOR (the preserver) on those of Licinius, Constantine, &c. We see, moreover, on other products of the Imperial mint, that this favourite deity of warlike Rome was distinguished, according to the occasion on which the medal was struck, by titles of ADSERTOR, STATOR, and PACATOR.

MARS ADSERTOR. (Mars the Assister.)— On a silver coin of Galba this legend appears, with the type of Mars in the *paludamentum,* standing with trophy and shield. Like that which bears the inscription of MARS VLTOR, with the same type, it was clearly intended as a memorial of acknowledgment on the part of the veteran general of Nero's Legions in Spain, that he owed the success of his enterprise against the tyrant, and his own elevation to the empire, to the assistance and tutelary favour of the god of war.

MARTI AVGVSTO.—Mars helmeted, marching with spear in right hand and trophy on his left shoulder. On silver of Pescennius Niger.— See *Pescennius.*

Khell, in recording this coin from the Imperial Cabinet at Vienna, says—" *Unicum hunc, atque pretii non æstimandi pronunciare confidenter audeo.*"—Vaillant notes two coins of Niger as *rarissimi,* with the epigraph of *Marti Victori;* and with the exception of the *parazonium* instead of the *spear,* the type of one of them is the same as that above described. The legend of *Mars Augustus* appears on no other Roman Imperial medals as yet discovered.

MARTI DEO.—See DEO MARTI.—On a silver coin of Gallienus we see this rare inscription, with a figure of Mars, supporting his left hand on his spear and his right hand on his shield, standing helmeted in a temple of four columns.

MARTI.—The figure of Mars stands helmeted and in a military dress, his right hand grasping the *hasta ferrata* or iron-headed lance, and his left placed on a shield resting on the ground. On this rare silver medal Hadrian is depictured under the form of Mars.—" A similar image, says Vaillant, may be seen in Parian marble at the Capitol in Rome, with this sole difference, that in the statue Hadrian is represented naked; while on the coin he appears in the costume of a warrior."

MARTI CONSERVATORI.—Respecting this dedicatory inscription which appears on coins of

Maxentius, Licinius, and Constantine,—Spanheim, in his "Cæsars of Julian," observes—"Ancient medals present to us this son of Jupiter, not only under the images of an avenging, a victorious, and a fighting god—*Martis Ultoris, Victoris, Propugnatoris*—in a word, he who takes delight in nothing but war and combats ; but they also designate him to us under the appearance of a peaceable and peace-making, a preserving, and fatherly deity—*Martis Pacifici, Pacatoris, Conservatoris, Statoris, Patris,* in order to teach us what are the duties of conquerors, and even what ought to be the aim of their conquests."—Banduri gives a second brass of *Maxentius,* with an armed Mars walking, and the legend MARTI. CONSERVAT*ori* AVG*usti* N*ostri.* (To Mars the Preserver of our Emperor.)

MARS PACATOR.—A half-naked figure of a man, with helmet, a branch in the right and a hasta in the left hand. On silver of S. Severus. Mars here carries the olive branch, a symbol of peace.—As the supposed father of their city's founder, the Romans (observes Vaillant) paid the highest honours of their religious worship to Mars, whom they denominated *Gradivus,* and offered sacrifices to, when on the point of war ; but whom they called *Pacator* when they entered into pacific treaties with the enemy. To this Ovid alludes in the 3rd book of his *Fasti* :—

Nunc primum studiis pacis, deus utilis armis, Advocor.

MARTI PACIFERO.—This dedication, with the image of the god holding the olive branch, appears on a silver coin of Volusianus, who thus assumes to be Mars the Pacificator, or Peace-bearer, on account of the peace made, under his father, with the Vandals. The same legend appears on coins of Florianus, &c.

MARTI PATRI CONSERVATORI.—This new title on a second brass of Constantine has for its accompanying type an armed and helmeted effigy of Mars, under whose lineaments Beger thinks the features and helmet of Constantine himself are plainly to be recognised. Hence he observes we may understand that it was the emperor himself rather than the heathen deity who is on this medal represented. Constantine is called Mars on the occasion of his great slaughter of the *Franci* and *Alemanni,* and his capture of their kings, thus *preserving* Gaul to the empire.

The surname of *Conservator* is found assigned to *Mars,* not only on coins, but on an ancient inscription, given in Gruter—(p. lvii.)

Mars is called Pater, as Liber (or Bacchus) was called Pater, and as Janus was called Pater, because, as Lactantius writes, it was "the custom to invoke by that name every god when offering to him solemn rites and prayers ;" besides, who does not know that Mars was commonly held to be the parent of the Romans?

MARTI PATRI SEMP. VICTORI. (To the ever victorious Father Mars).—On another second brass of Constantine the Great appears this epigraph ; and it occurs only in the case of this emperor.

MARTI PROPAG. IMP. AVG. N.—Mars, in military garments, stands with spear in left hand, and joins his right hand to that of a woman standing before him, between both is the wolf suckling the twins.—Respecting this epigraph and type on a silver coin of Maxentius, Eckhel observes that *Mars Propagator imperii,* like *Princeps imperii Romani,* on a gold coin of the same *Augustus,* is a new title, contrived by the ingenuity of Maxentius, to be conferred upon this deity.

Vaillant says, " At a time when Constantine was in possession of great part of the empire, and Galerius with Licinius governed a still larger portion, Maxentius invokes Mars as the author of the City of Rome, praying him that he would amplify and propagate the boundaries of his empire."

MARS PROPVG*nator,* and MARS PROPVGNAT*ori.* (Mars the Champion or Defender.)—A helmeted figure, clothed in armour, walking, with spear and buckler. The former legend appears on a silver piece of Gordianus Pius, and the latter on a denarius of Gallienus, who, as his coins teach us, paid particular adoration to Mars. Indeed he is known to have raised a temple to the worship of that divinity in the Circus Flaminius, and to have called the god *Propugnator.* See *Hostilianus.*—Well indeed he might, being at that period sore pressed in every quarter of his government by both civil and foreign wars. (Vaillant.)—There is a second brass of Constantine which presents on its reverse the naked figure of Mars, with spear and buckler, marching, and the inscription MARTI PATRI PROPVGNATORI.

MARS VICTOR.—A helmeted figure walking, holding a spear transversed, and in his left hand a trophy resting on the shoulder.—A very rare gold coin of Probus bears this legend and inscription, by which this warlike emperor is compared to Mars—no inappropriate or unmeaning compliment to a prince, of whom it has been recorded that every part of the Roman world was rendered celebrated by his victories.

[From a large brass of Caracalla.]

MARTI VICTORI.—In noticing this legend of Pescennius Niger, Vaillant *(Pr.* ii. 204) observes that Mars, in his quality of presiding over war seems to have had the cognomen of *Victor* assigned to him ; and that, as the coins bearing that epigraph denote, it is probable that Pescennius performed sacrifices to the God of

Battles, propitiating his aid to gain the hoped-for victory over Severus—a rival who, however, proved to be his conqueror.—See MARTI AVGVSTO.

MART VLTO.—On a denarius of Augustus we see a round temple, in which is a figure of *Mars Ultor*, whose temple Augustus caused to be built in the capital.

There is another silver coin of the same Emperor, with the same epigraph, and a similarly formed edifice, in which is a military ensign. This represents the temple of *Mars the Avenger*, which Augustus ordered to be built at Rome, in imitation of that of Jupiter Feretrius, in which the military standards restored by the Parthians were suspended.

MARS VLTOR.—Mars walking with spear in hand, and trophy on his shoulder; on coins of Alex. Severus, Claudius Gothicus, Quintillus, Tacitus, and Probus.—With the ancient Romans, as well as Greeks, it was one of the principal marks of worship paid to their gods, to honour them as *Avengers* of injuries received; hence originated, amongst others, the titles of *Jupiter Ultor*, of *Mars Ultor*, and the like, which medals so frequently exhibit to us.

MARTI VLTORI.—On a silver coin of Galba edited in Morell's *Impp. Rom.* we see this legend accompanied by the type of Mars, naked, except the helmet, walking: he brandishes aloft a dart in his right hand, and holds out a small round shield on his left arm.

MARTI COMITI AVG*usti Nostri*. (To Mars, the companion of our Emperor.)—A second brass of Maxentius bears this sufficiently presumptuous inscription. The Emperor who thus makes a colleague of his deity is represented on horseback, with right hand uplifted, and a soldier with spoils preceding him.—The epigraph and type occur only on the money of Maxentius, who on other coins treats Hercules with the same familiarity *(Herculi Comiti)*.

MARTIALI.—See IVNONI MARTIALI.

MARTINIANVS *(Marcus)*, general of Licinius, in whose palace he held the post of *Magister Officinorum*.—He was created Cæsar by that prince, after the latter had declared against Constantine, A.D. 324.—Martinianus usurped the style and title of Augustus, as appears by his coins, which are in third brass, and most rare, D. N. M. MARTIANVS P. F. AVG.—Two years afterwards he shared the fate of his master, both he and Licinius, after the two disastrous battles of Adrianopolis and Chalcedon, having been put to death by order of Constantine.

Martius, formerly the first month of the year with the Romans, it being named by Romulus after his reputed father.—It appears on certain celebrated coins.—See EID. MAR.

MASSO, a surname of the patrician family of *Papiria*.

MAT. *Mater.*—Thus *Julia Mamæa* is styled MAT. AVGVSTI. (Mother of the Emperor.)

MATER AVGG.—*Cybele in a quadriga of lions*, holding a branch. This appears on gold and silver of Julia Domna, wife of Severus; and, as Eckhel observes, there does not exist on coins a weightier proof of servile adulation. Here we behold Domna held out as the object of the high worship paid to Cybele, and that, too, when this "Mother of the Gods" was really the parent of Caracalla, and of Geta; see also by how subtle a device these two young *Augusti* are placed on an equality with the gods themselves!—This coin was struck when Geta, as well as his elder brother, had attained to Augustal honours.

MAT. AVGG. MAT. SEN. M. PATR. *Mater Augustorum, Mater Senatus, Mater Patriæ.*—A female figure representing Julia, sitting or standing, with corn ears in one hand, and the *hasta* in the other.—Gold, silver, and large brass of Domna exhibit this unique and remarkable inscription.

On this medal we see not only new titles, but such as no other princess ever before assumed. For one Domna to call herself, on her coins, the *Mother of the Senate*, and the *Mother of the Country*, was bold indeed. It was the result of that insensate veneration which her son *Caracalla* affected to entertain for her, it being also under his reign that the surnames of PIA, FELIX, were conferred on the imperial widow of Severus.

MATER AVGVSTI ET CASTRORVM.—The Mother of the Emperor and of Camps are the titles assumed (on large and second brass coins) by Mamæa, mother of Alexander Severus, who in all things acted under her counsels, and who, with her, was assassinated by the troops of the ferocious Maximinus.

MATER CASTRORVM.—A woman seated, having before her three military ensigns. This reverse of a large brass of Faustina the younger, is remarkable. The title of *Mother of Camps*, which no empress *previous* to her had borne, though others afterwards received it, was given to Faustina, on the occasion of her having followed her husband, M. Aurelius, in his victorious expedition against the *Quadi*, A.D. 174, a campaign memorable for the victory regarded as miraculous, and ascribed to the prayers of the Theban legion, called *Legio fulminans*.—Julia Domna, and Julia Mamæa, successively exhibit the same title on their coins, the latter (as above observed) prefixing to it that of MATER AVGVSTI, as the mother of Alexander Severus.—The type in Julia Domna's first and second brass, with this legend, is a female figure, sacrificing before three military ensigns.

MATRES AVGUSTORVM.—The following are nearly all the mothers of emperors of whom there are authentic coins:—

1.—*Livia*, of Tiberius.
2.—*Antonia*, of Claudius.
3.—*Agrippina*, of Caligula.
4.—*Agrippina*, of Nero.
5.—*Domitilla*, of Titus.
6.—*Julia Domna*, of Caracalla and of Geta.
7.—*Julia Soaemias*, of Elagabalus.
8.—*Julia Mamaea*, of Alexander Severus.

9.—*Marcia Otacilia Severa*, of Philip jun.
10.—*Mariniana*, of Valerianus jun.
11.—*Flavia Helena*, of Constantine the Great.

To no living mother was there by any son, being emperor, any coin struck representing two portraits, except to those who either had mingled in the affairs of state, or had sons under their guardianship who were afterwards advanced to the empire. Of these there were six, viz., *Livia* with Tiberius. 2. *Agrippina* with Caius (Caligula). 3. *Agrippina*, jun., with Nero. 4. *Domna* with Caracalla and Geta, whose coins, however, were struck with the heads of the sons upon them during the lifetime of their father Severus. 5. *Julia Soæmias* with Elagabalus. 6. *Julia Mamaea* with Alexander.

MATER DEVM. See *Cybele*.—Numerous coins of pro-consular cities in Asia attest the worship of this Phrygian deity, by the exhibition of her image. The same *Magna Deum Mater*, or Great Mother of the Gods, celebrated under so many names, was worshiped in her inmost sanctuary under the form of nothing more than a black stone *(lapis niger)*, as Arnobius, L. vii., from personal observation describes.—Her temple was repaired by Augustus.—As identified with *Tellus*, Cybele carries the *tympanum*, by which the terrestrial globe was signified; and the towers on her head bespeak her influence over towns.

MATER DEVM. and MATRI DEVM.— Cybele seated between two lions, or Cybele

standing, with a lion at her feet.—On gold, silver, and brass of *Julia Domna*, called on the obverse IVLIA AVGVSTA.—The ambitious wife of Severus is not more fully exhibited by the title of *Mater Augustorum* than she is as Cybele; but on the above coin, with the epigraph of *Mater Deum*, she is represented as though Cybele and Julia were the same.

MATRI CASTRORVM.—On her coins, in

gold, silver, and brass, Julia Domna stands

veiled before a small altar, and two, or three military ensigns, performing sacrifice, as though partaking the councils of her husband, in his warlike expeditions, she invoked success on his enterprises, and made herself a consort in his victories.—This title of *Mater Castrorum* conferred for the first time on the unworthy wife of M. Aurelius, was afterwards, in the same spirit of congratulation to the husband, bestowed on the masculine and ambitious empress of Septimius Severus.—We see the same inscription and a similar type on a medal of *Julia Soæmias;* whose claim to this martial appellation of honour, as an imperial *camp mistress*, is in like manner substantiated by her historical character as a courageous princess and a leader of armies.

MATIDIA, the daughter of Marciana and niece of Trajan; she was the mother of Sabina, who became the wife of Hadrian. She was declared *Augusta* along with Plotina, by a decree of the

Senate about the year of Christ, 113; possessing all the virtues of her mother, she equally received with her the honours of the apotheosis, under the reign of Hadrian, some say of Antoninus Pius. The medals of Matidia, like those of Plotina and Marciana, are in each metal of the highest degree of rarity, especially the first brass. On these she is styled MATIDIA. AVG. F.—MATIDIA AVG. DIVAE MARCIANAE *Filia.*—also DIVA MATIDIA SOCRVS.—The annexed cut is from a denarius in the British Museum.

MATRI DEVM CONSERV. AVG. *(Conservatrici Augusti.)*—This legend, with Cybele riding on a lion, appears on first and second brass and on silver of Commodus; who with his characteristic audacity, whilst he was violating every law, divine and human, calls the Mother of the Gods his preserver; in like manner as on other medals he selects Jupiter himself as the sponsor for his security *(sponsor securitatis)*, and as the defender of his health and safety *(defensor salutis.)*

MATRI DEVM SALVTARI.—A temple in which Cybele is seated: on the outside stands Atys near a tree, which he touches with his left hand.—Bronze medallion of Faustina, senior.

The type of Cybele, or mother of the gods, is common on the coinage of Faustina the elder; but on this exceedingly rare medallion we see also introduced, Atys both the priest and the lover of Cybele. He stands near a tree, and touches it; either because he was detected by the goddess in a forbidden amour, and being sought after to receive punishment, hid himself under a pine tree, or because he was changed into a pine tree by Cybele (which are the several opinions of certain mythologists), or because this was the very tree on whose existence depended the life of the nymph *Sangaris*, with whom Atys had fallen desperately in love, and which tree the goddess, in wrath at her lover's infidelity, had cut down and destroyed.—See *Cybele*—and *Atys*.

Matrix (Matrice).—This word is used by some numismatic writers to signify the *die*, *square*, or *punch*, that is to say, the mass of hardened medal, on which is engraved or sunk, the inverse way, the type of the medal, in order to impress it, the right way, on the blank which is exposed to its stroke. The word by which the Romans designated the die, or as the French call it the *coin* of the medal, is not known.

MAVRETANIA—spelt with an E as well on inscribed marbles, edited by Gruter, as on coins of Hadrian, Antonine, and Commodus—a region of Africa, separated from Spain by the straits of Gibraltar *(fretum Gaditanum)*, and from Numidia by the river Ampsaga. It now forms the kingdoms of Fez and Morocco.—Mauretania was made a conquest of by Julius Cæsar, who having vanquished its king, Juba, reduced the country to a Roman province, giving the government of it to the Pro-consul Crispus Sallustius.—Augustus afterwards exchanged it with Juba, the son, for Numidia.—This region remained under subjection to the Romans till about A.D. 441, when Genseric, King of the Vandals, gained possession of it. The Emperor Valentinian disputed with him its retention, sword in hand, for three years, with various success; and at length peace was established between these two potentates, who divided Northern Africa between them. At the death of Valentinian, Genscric not only recovered all which he had ceded, but again overthrew the Empire of the West. Justinian re-conquered this territory ninety-five years after the Vandals had permanently occupied it.

Spanheim *(Pr.* ii. p. 583) affirms that the ensigns of royalty were accustomed to be sent to the Mauretanian Kings by the Roman Emperors, and in no other way were they confirmed in their regal dignity.

MAVRETANIA.—An inhabitant of this province stands with a spear in his left hand, and holds with the other a horse by the bridle.— This name and appropriate type of the Moorish race, appears on a large brass of Hadrian, of which an illustration is here given. The

cavalry of the *Mauri* was renowned of old both for the excellence of the horses and the skill of the riders.—Accordingly we find the figures of horses stamped even on the earliest coins of the Mauretanian Kings. That this equestrian people were employed, under their

leader Lusius Quintus, in the various wars of Trajan, is attested in several passages of Dion; and the Trajan column itself affords a lasting testimony to this fact, in that compartment of its sculptured shaft, on which the Moorish horsemen are represented making a furious charge upon the Dacians.

The Mauretanian is depictured on the coin, walking with bridle and lance in his hand, because that people, according to Strabo, generally fought with spears and on horseback.

MAVRETANIA. COS. II. S.C.—A man, with garment tucked-up, standing with basket in right hand, and spear in left. First brass of Antoninus Pius.—Eckhel.

For other numismatic memorials connecting the same province with the Emperor Hadrian, see ADVENTVI AVG. MAVRETANIAE.—EXERCITVS MAVRETANICVS.—RESTITVTORI MAVRETANIAE.

MAVRICIVS TIBERIVS, as on coins he is styled, was born in Cappadocia, but of a family of Roman extraction, A.D. 539. Adopted by his father-in-law Tiberius, he succeeded to the empire in 582. An energetic prince, skilled in war and not less conversant with peaceful arts, but avaricious and wrathful. He conquered the Persians, by his generals Philippicus and Germanns: he also fought many battles, with different degrees of success, against Chosroes, king of Persia, and also against the Avars, who had invaded the eastern provinces. His soldiers revolting, under the leadership of Focas, either because they had not received their pay, or because the emperor had refused to ransom, at a small price, many thousand captives taken by the Avars, paid the forfeit of his outrageous covetousness; the emperor himself, with his whole family, having been murdered by the traitorous usurper Focas, A.D. 602, in his 63rd year and 20th of his reign.—The *gold* of Mauricius are common; *silver* rare; *brass* common, except *quinarii*. His name and titles are D. N. MAVRIC. TIBER. P. P. AVG.—The legends of his medals are in the *Latin* character, but like nearly all the rest of the Byzantine series, the types are uninteresting and the execution barbarous.

MAX. *Maxima.*—See VICT PART. MAX. *Victoria Parthica Maxima* on coins of Caracalla.

MAX. *Maximo.*—I. O. MAX.—*Jovi Optimo Maximo.*

MAX. *Maximus.*—A title of the chief pontiff. Thus, P. MAX. *Pontifex Maximus*, in Nero; PON. MAX. in Domitian.

MAX. *Maximus.*—A masculine surname derived from illustrious exploits.

MAX. *Maximus.*—An epithet of honour applied to several emperors, as referring to some conquest or victory. Thus M. Aurelius, L. Verus, Sept. Severus, Caracalla, were distinguished by the title of *Parthicus Maximus;* Commodus with that of *Britannicus Maximus.* Constantine the Great, after overcoming Maxentius, assumed this superlative MAX., which was afterwards conferred on Constans and Valens.

MAXENTIVS *(Marc. Aurel. Valerius)*, son of Maximianus Hercules and of Eutropia, was born A.D. 282.—Diocletian wished to have named him Cæsar; Galerius was opposed to it. This neglect, and the promotion of Severus, Maximinus Daza, and, later, of Constantine to that rank, made him a mal-content; and he caused himself to be declared Emperor at Rome by the Pretorian soldiers; the Senate assented, and proclaimed his assumption of the purple, according to history, in 306. But "the medals, which assign to Maxentius the title of Cæsar only, lead (as Mionnet observes) to the belief that this prince was at first content with that honour, and that he did not receive the title of Augustus until some time afterwards. In that case the coins are at variance with the historians, who make him Cæsar and Augustus at once, by the united voice of the soldiers and the senate."— Maxentius was a monster of cruelty and lust; he compelled his father to re-ascend the throne in order to maintain him in the government of the empire; he ruled Rome like a sanguinary tyrant, resembling his parent in harshness of disposition; pillaged Italy by his confiscations of private property and by fiscal extortions to increase his revenues, till he became the object of universal hatred. After having sustained his authority against Severus II., and against Galerius Maximianus, by whom he was successively attacked; he drove Maximianus Hercules, his father, from Rome; defeated the usurper Alexander in Egypt, which he ravaged; burnt Carthage in 311; and having quarrelled with Constantine, his former ally, he proceeded horribly to persecute the Christians. Constantine, however, secretly invited by the Senate, marched from Gaul, and arriving near Rome, gave battle at the Milvian bridge to Maxentius, who being totally defeated, threw himself as a fugitive into the Tiber and was drowned, on the 28th December, 312, in the 30th year of his age and sixth of his reign, leaving his victorious rival Constantine undisputed master of the Roman empire.—Maxentius had a son, named Romulus, who died before his father, in the fourth year of his age, to whose AETERNA MEMORIA medals were struck, and are extant in each metal. (See ROMVLVS.)——The style of Maxentius on his coins is MAXENTIVS NOB. CAESAR.—IMP. MAXENTIVS. P. F. AVG.——MAXENTIVS. P. F. AVG.—MAXENTIVS PRINCeps INVICTus.—Several of the reverses are of historical interest.

MAXIMIANVS.—Two Emperors rejoiced in the common name of Maximianus; and of these *Galerius Maximianus* was called *junior*, to distinguish him from the elder by birth, and who in respect to the other was called *senior*. This distinction, however, we do not always see observed in either case. For the coins of Maximianus the elder born, called by the other name of *Herculeus*, do not all present the name SEN. or *senior;* and it is very seldom

that the appellative of IVN. or *junior* is found on the coins of *Galerius*. For as Herculeus Maximianus alone had hitherto borne the title of Augustus, it was the less necessary by the word SENior to distinguish him from Galerius, who was at that time only Cæsar. Nor was there any risk of Galerius being confounded with Herculeus Maximianus, because the title of Cæsar sufficiently distinguished his coins from those of the elder one, who is said never to have received the dignity of Cæsar, but was declared at once Augustus by Diocletian. Hence it is that the title of IVNior is never found conjoined to NOBilissimus CAESar on the medals of Galerius; nor is the prenomen of *Galerius* by any means common on them, as for example by MAXIMIANVS NOB. CAES. Galerius is indicated, although no mark of the prenomen GAL. should be found, the title NOBilissimus CAESar sufficiently distinguishing him from Herculeus. But when Galerius became Augustus, the prenomen of each might be left out, and the title alone of IVNior and of SENior might be placed on their respective medals. And we find this done on their coins which are inscribed— MAXIMIANVS *SEN.* P.F. AVG. when *Valerius Maximianus* is indicated, or IMP. MAXIMIANVS *IVN.* P.F. AVG. when *Galerius Maximianus* is intended to be designated.—The following are the observations of the perspicuous and accurate Bimard (in his notes on Jobert), with reference to this point, than which nothing is better calculated completely to remove the difficulty which some learned writers have started thereupon:—"History, both ecclesiastic and profane, teaches us that there were two, and only two Emperors, of the name of Maximianus; one of whom called himself *M. Aurelius Valerius Maximianus*, and the other *C. Galerius Valerius Maximianus*. The former was, on the medals struck after his abdication (as Diocletian's colleague), called *Maximianus Senior Augustus*; the latter to distinguish himself took at the same time the appellation of *Maximianus Junior Augustus.* It is, however, needful to observe, that *Junior* is never found except on medals whence we see only the name of *Maximianus*, and which we have not yet remarked on those which bear the family name of Galerius Maximianus, because then the name of *Galerius* suffices to distinguish him from Maximianus Aurelius. Nor do we find *Maximianus Junior Nobilissimus. Cæsar*, because the quality of *Cæsar* sufficiently distinguished Galerius Maximianus from Maximianus Hercules, who always bore the title of Augustus."—(vol. ii. p. 309.)

MAXIMIANVS *(Marcus Aurelius Valerius),* surnamed *Herculeus*, on the ground of his pretended descent from Hercules, was born at Sirmium (Sirmich), in Pannonia, in the year of our Lord 250. Entering the army he served with distinction under Aurelian and Probus. It was on account of his valour and military talents, and in spite of his unpolished mind and harsh temper, that he was associated in the empire with the title of Augustus, by Diocletian,

A.D. 286, having previously been created Cæsar by the same emperor.—Maximianus was an outrageous tyrant, covetous, violent, and cruel; an abominable persecutor of Christians, against whom he further instigated his sufficiently prejudiced colleague. He conquered and kept down the Bagaudæ, the Persians, and the Germans.—In 292, whilst Diocletian adopted *Galerius* Maximianus, he on his part conferred the title of Cæsar on Constantius Chlorus, and besides adopting the two emperors joined them by the closer bond of relationship. After becoming Augustus, he defeated and dispersed the *Mauri* of Africa (296).—On the day of Diocletian's abdication (305), Maximianus renounced the empire also, the former retiring to Nicomedia, the latter into Lucania, having named Severus in his place. At the solicitation of his son Maxentius, or as some say for the lust of power, he resumed the quality of Emperor at Rome (307); but driven from that city, he fled (308) into Gaul, and received protection from Constantine, afterwards the Great, who had married his daughter Fausta, and to whom he had given the title of Augustus. Lodged in the palace of Constantine at Arles, he, in the absence of that prince, once more attempted to regain the imperial dignity A.D. 309. But Constantine having retraced his steps back into Gaul, soon compelled Maximianus to make his escape to the city of Marseilles, where he was made prisoner, and for the third time forced to abdicate his pretentions to empire. Having, however, entered into a plot against his son-in-law, he was detected, through the disclosures of his wife, who preferred, in this case, her husband to her father, and Constantine ordered him to be strangled, at Marseilles, in the 60th year of his age, and in the year of Christ 310. He is numismatically styled VAL. MAXIMIANVS NO*Bilissimus* CAES.—IMP. M. AVR. VAL. MAXIMIANVS P. F. AVG.—HERCVLEVS MAXIMIANVS AVG. &c.—The same as in the instance of Diocletian, the medals which give to Maximian the epithets of SEN*ior*, BEATIS-SIMUS, FELIC*issimus*, and the title of *Dominus* N*oster*, are posterior to his first abdication, as above noticed. Maximianus the elder boasted of celestial origin; hence on his coins is read HERCVLI DEBELLATORI, with the figure of Hercules striking the hydra; then HERCVLI PACIFERO; and also HERCVLI VICTORI. His head not unfrequently appears covered with the lion's skin. (See IOVI ET HERCVLI AVGG.)—Eutropia, a Syrian woman, was the wife of this Maximianus. His silver medals are rare; his gold still rarer; second and third brass for the most part very common. —See *Herculio Maximiano.*

MAXIMIANVS *(Galerius Valerius)*, the son of a peasant, was born near Sardica, in Dacia; he distinguished himself by his ability and valour under Aurelian and Probus; in the year of the Christian era, 292, he was declared Cæsar, by Diocletian, who adopted him, and gave him his own daughter Valeria in marriage. A man of lofty stature and robust frame, his look, voice, and gesture inspired terror by their savage rudeness. Ignorant, arrogant, brutal, and cruel, his lust for power was equalled only by his ingratitude to his benefactors; he persecuted the Christians with unexampled barbarity; constrained Diocletian and Maximian to abdicate, and reigned in their place with the assumed dignity of Augustus, A.D. 305. This prince founded the colony of *Valeria*, in Illyria; defeated Narses, King of Persia, and forced him to conclude a peace favourable to the empire; declared Constantine Cæsar, and Severus Augustus, A.D. 306; died in 311 of a most horrible disease, nineteen years after being nominated Cæsar, and the seventh from Diocletian's abdication. He was buried in the place of his birth, and placed in the rank of the gods by Maxentius.

The second and third brass coins of this Maximianus are common; his silver are rare, and gold rarer. On them he is styled GAL. MAXIMIANVS CAES.——IMP. GAL. VAL. MAXIMIANVS P.F. AVG.— DIVVS MAXIMIANVS SOCER (that is to say SOCER *Maxentii.*)

MAXIMINVS *(Caius Julius Verus)*, born in Thrace, A.D. 173, of an obscure and barbarous family, the son of Micca, a Goth, and of Ababa, an Alanian. This herdsman, by

original occupation, entering into the Roman cavalry, attracted by his extraordinary size and strength the notice of Septimius Severus, who eventually raised him to military dignities.—Alexander Severus caused him to be elected a senator, and appointed him to different governments. In the war against Persia he shewed his courage and capacity. Accompanying that excellent Emperor into Germany, he basely procured his assassination; and then usurped the empire A.D. 235. The army having proclaimed him Augustus, he associated with himself his son Maximus, as Cæsar, and the Senate confirmed their election. A harsh and distrustful tyrant, pride, insolence, avarice, and bloodthirtiness governed all his actions. Of gigantic stature and of prodigious muscular powers, the wondrous proofs of his bodily form obtained for him the names of Hercules and Milo. His ferocity was equally manifested in his devastations of Germany by fire and sword; and in letting loose his fury against the Christians as well as his other subjects. At length, justly abhorred for his cruelty, and declared the enemy of the country, this sanguinary despot was massacred by his own soldiers, at Aquileia, (together with his son.) in the 65th year of his age, A.D. 238.—Maximinus married *Paulina,* by whom he had *Maximus.*—This Emperor's brass and silver coins are common, but the gold extremely rare. His numismatic titles are IMP. MAXIMINVS PIVS AVG. (for this most impious usurper assumed the honoured surname of the good Antoninus!)—MAXIMINVS PIVS AVG. GERM.—IMP. C. IVL. MAXIMINVS AVG.—The reverses of the large brass medals are common enough, such as LIBERALITAS AVG.—FIDES MILITVM.—VICTORIA GERMANICA.

There is a large brass medal of Maximinus, which exhibits the laureated head of that emperor, and which has for the legend of its reverse P.M. TR. P. IIII. COS. P.P. S.C. (Sovereign Pontiff, possessing the tribuneship for the fourth time; Consul; Father of the Country; struck under the authority of the Senate.) The type is the Emperor standing, holding his spear, in the midst of three military ensigns.

The above medal has an interest in reference to chronology. Historians were not agreed respecting the duration of Maximinus's reign. Several assign to him only two years, whilst others suppose it to be five or six. But we here see by the fourth tribunitian power, which this coin records, that the third year of his reign was at least begun when it was struck. On the other hand, the fifth tribunitian power for *Maximinus,* is found on no public monument whatever: and since chronologers determine the commencement of his reign to have been the month of March, in the year of Rome 988; the fourth tribunate of Maximinus must be referred to the year of Rome 991, the more probable epocha of the death of this barbarian, as well as of the ephemeral reigns of the two *African* Gordians, immediately followed by those of *Balbinus* and *Pupienus.*

MAXIMINVS II. *(Galerius Valerius),* surnamed Daza, born in Illyria, was the son of the sister of Galerius Maximianus, and like his paternal ancestor, rude and uneducated.—Importuned by Galerius, Diocletian reluctantly confers upon him the dignity of Cæsar, A.D. 305. He governed Syria and other provinces of the East. Timid, superstitious, addicted to drunkenness, cruelty with him went hand in hand with debauchery. This savage tyrant persecuted the Christians in the most horrible manner. In the year 307, Maximinus received the title of *Filius Augusti,* at the same time with Constantine, conferred by Galerius Maximianus. The year following he caused himself to be proclaimed Augustus, by his army. In 313, he having imprudently allied himself to Maxentius, the enemy of Constantine and Licinius, the latter marched against him into Thrace, and defeated him in a decisive battle. Pursued and besieged by Licinius, he poisoned himself at Tarsus, in Cilicia, A.D. 313, **eight years** after being named Cæsar, and five

and a half after assuming the purple.—Adverting to the dreadful tortures both of mind and body which marked the end of Maximinus Daza, Beauvais observes—"This destroyer of the faithful exclaimed in the paroxysm of his torment ;—*It is the blood of the Christians which I have caused to be shed that has reduced me to this state.* His memory was stigmatised as that of a brutal ruffian; his children were put to death; and his wife was thrown (at Antioch) alive into the river Orontes, where by her orders a great number of Christian women had been drowned "

The coins of this emperor are extremely rare in gold: of still greater rarity in silver; but for the most part common in third brass, and very common in second brass. On them he is styled MAXIMINVS NOB. CAESAR.—GAL. VAL. MAXIMINVS NOB. C.—MAXIMINVS FIL. AVGG.— IMP. GAL. VAL. MAXIMINVS. P.F. INV. AVG.

MAXIMVS, a surname of the *Fabia* family.— The title of *Maximus* appears on Imperial coins, as ascribed to some few princes, not as a family name, but as an adjunct to the surnames of conquest. Thus we find *Parthicus Maximus* borne by S. Severus, who subdued the Parthians; *Armeniacus Maximus* is included in the style of Lucius Verus, for his successes, or rather for those of his colleague M. Aurelius, over the Armenians.—We read on the coins of Valerianus, Gallienus, and Postumus, *Germanicus Maximus,* a title which these princes assumed on account of victories gained by them respectively over the Germans.—Constantine the Great is called, on his coins, MAXIMVS, as a title of the greatest distinction.—The idea of Harduin, concurred in by Jobert, that *Maximus* was a name belonging to Constantine's family is clearly shewn by Bimard, in every point of view, to be unsustainable.

MAXIMVS.—See GERMANICVS.

MAXIMVS.—See *Petronius,* on whose coins the circumscription of the head is PETRONIVS MAXIMVS.

MAXIMVS.—See *Pupienus,* whose coins bear PVPIENVS MAXIMVS. AVG.

MAXIMVS *(Caius Julius Verus),* son of Maximinus I. and (as is supposed) of Paulina, came into the world about A.D. 216. He passed for one of the finest and handsomest young men of the empire; but early abandoned himself to pleasure and luxury. After the elevation of his father, who declared him Cæsar (235), he became so proud, insolent, and vicious, as to render himself as much detested by the Romans as Maximinus himself was. This beautiful and accomplished but ill-mannered prince, who was eighteen years of age when clothed with the purple, enjoyed his honours but a short time, for being obliged to join his father in Germany, he was assassinated with him by his soldiers near Aquileia (238), just as he was on the point of uniting his barbarian blood to that of the illustrious family of Antoninus Pius, by a marriage with Junia Fadilla.— His silver coins are rare; the gold exceedingly so; the brass scarce. He is styled C. IVL. VERVS. MAXIMVS CAES.—MAXIMVS CAES. GERM.

MAXIMVS *(Flavius Magnus)*, born in a family of little distinction in Spain, he rose, from serving in the army of Britain, to be a general under Theodosius. Profiting by the hatred entertained by the legions in that island towards Gratian, who neglected them, he corrupted their fidelity, and was proclaimed by them Emperor. This usurper then passed over from England into Gaul, A.D. 383, and assembling around him a' large force, marched against Gratian, who was encamped near Paris, seduced that emperor's army from their allegiance, and caused him to be assassinated at Lyon the same year. Thus become master of Gaul, Spain, and Britain, with all the legions of the west under his orders, Maximus sought alliance with Theodosius, who, on certain conditions made in favour of Valentinian the Second, conferred on him the title of Augustus. He subsequently established his residence at Treves, rendering himself formidable to the nations surrounding him, especially to the Germans, whom he laid under tribute. His ambition leading him to drive Justina and Valentinian II. from Milan, he was attacked by Theodosius, defeated on the Save, near Siscia, and being taken prisoner at Aquileia, was put to death by the soldiers of Theodosius, in spite of the wish of that emperor to spare the life of a man who had borne with glory the title of Augustus for more than five years.— " Brave, skilled in war, active and vigorous, this tyrant (says Beauvais) would have appeared worthy of the throne if he had not ascended it by means of a crime."—His coins are rare in gold and in second brass; common in silver of the usual size; but extremely rare in large silver or medallions; and scarce in third brass. On these he is styled D.N. MAG. MAXIMVS. P.F. AVG.

The annexed cut is from a fine silver medallion in the British Museum.

The portrait of Magnus Maximus on some of the brass coins is very different from the above, as is shewn by an example found at Richborough, in Kent, and published in Mr. Roach Smith's "Antiquities of Richborough, Reculver, and Lymne." It appears to exhibit much individuality of features.

MAXIMVS *(Tyrannus)*, on the death of Constans II., was proclaimed Emperor in Spain by Gerontius, one of the generals of the usurper Constantinus, A.D. 409. But divesting himself of the purple, he returned into private life, and might have died in peace.—" The caprice (however, says Gibbon,) of the barbarians who ravaged Spain, once more seated this imperial phantom on the throne: but they soon resigned him to the justice of Honorius; and the tyrant Maximus, after he had been shewn to the people of Ravenna and Rome, was publicly executed A.D. 411.—There are two varieties of *silver* coins of this Maximus, bearing his portrait, and the legend D.N. MAXIMVS P.F. AVG. The reverse of one is inscribed VICTORIA AAVGGG., a helmeted woman holding a globe, surmounted by a Victory; and that of the other VICTORIA ROMANORVM, a similar type.

M. C. I. or IV. *Municipium Calagurris Julia.*—The Municipality of Calagurris Julia, (now Lahorre, in Spain.)

M. COMMODVS ANTONINVS AVG. BRIT. *Marcus Commodus Antoninus Augustus Britannicus.*

M. D. M. I. *Magna Deum Matri Ideæ.*— To Idæan Cybele, the great mother of the gods.

MEDAGLIONI. Medallions.—Everybody in the least acquainted with the Italian language knows that the augmentations end in *one*; thus of *medaglia*, medal, they have made *medaglione*. The French have borrowed from the Italians the word *médaillon*, grand médaille; and we have taken from the French our word medallion, to express a large medal.

MEDALET, an appellation given by Pinkerton to a curious though not uncommon class of Roman pieces not intended for currency, which consists of small coins, or *missilia*, scattered among the people on solemn occasions; those struck for the slaves in the Saturnalia; private counters for gaming; tickets for baths and feasts; tokens in copper and lead, and remains of a like kind.

MEDAL, from the French word *médaille*, which takes its derivation from the Latin, *metallum.* The appellation of medal is given to every piece of gold, of silver, or of brass, which bears an impression designed to preserve the remembrance of a great man, of a sovereign, or of a remarkable event. Medals or coins in the *monetary* sense of the term may also be defined as pieces of metal on which public authority has stamped different signs to indicate their weight and their value, in order that they might serve for the acquisition of things necessary to human existence, and that they might facilitate commerce, which, without that means of exchange, would be too difficult.

The Greeks called money or coins νόμισμα, the Latins *nummus* or *numus.* The science of medals has been called by modern French archæologists *Numismatique.*

MEDALLION.—Under this term are, without distinction, comprised all monetary productions of the ancients, whether in gold, silver, or brass, the volume and weight of which materially exceed the usual size of coins struck in those respective metals.—There is, however, a difference of opinion amongst numismatic antiquaries as to whether what are called medallions were or were not used for money.—Patin observes that they were made for no other original purpose than that of satisfying the curiosity of princes, as is done to this day with fancy pieces (pièce de plaiser).—Jobert, in his *Science des Médailles*, remarks that their workmanship was too exquisite, and their size too unwieldy for common currency.—Bimard, in his historical and critical notes on the work of the last named writer, agrees that it is most probable not to have been the intention of those, who in ancient times caused medallions to be struck, that they should serve for money; but with his usual cautious and discriminative judgment adds—" I think, nevertheless, that when those pieces had fulfilled their first destination, and were dispersed abroad (distribuées), a free currency was given them in commerce, by regulating their value in proportion to their weight and to their standard of purity. At least I have thought myself warranted in coming to this conclusion, from the *countermarks* which I have seen on several Greek medallions of the Imperial series, and it is certain that the Greek medallions were real money. It was doubtless after the example of the Greeks, that the Romans put also their medallions into circulation as current coin."—Mahudal, to whose dissertation on the same subject Bimard refers, supports the opinion, " that medallions were pieces distinguished from money, as they were with us from medals."—But, says Millin, "there are *other* writers, who far from entertaining this opinion, maintain against the system of Mahudal, that we are to recognise money in those medallions which are multiplied from a piece generally acknowledged to be money, such

as the *tetradrachms* and the *cistophori*, the only pieces with which the province of Asia payed its tributes to the Roman republic; and by analogy, all the Greek medallions of the same weight and form. Millin himself goes on to instance the fine gold medallion of the Emperor Augustus, found at Herculaneum, which "ought, he says, to be regarded as a piece of money, so likewise those of Domitian and Commodus, all these quadruples of the *aurei* of Augustus, which weigh nearly two *gros*. Whatever might have been the weight of their monies, the Romans neither knew, nor employed, more than the two synonyms *numi* and *numismata* to designate them all. Marcus Aurelius caused a great number of medallions of the largest volume to be struck, *numos maximos*, says Julius Capitolinus. A particular word would have been invented to name these extraordinary pieces, if they had been anything else than extra sized money. An inference favourable to this opinion (adds Millin) is derived from types which adorn the Roman medals in each metal; these types and their legends are absolutely the same with those of the ordinary sized medals. We find, indeed, on the medallions, especially from the reign of Gallienus to that of the Constantines, the figure of *Moneta*, sometimes alone, at others under the emblem of three women, bearing each a balance. These symbols are accompanied with legends used, in a similar case; MONETA AVG.; AEQVITAS AVG.; MONETA AVGG.; and upon a *medallion* of Crispus, MONETA VRBIS VESTRAE. Some *medallions*, few however in number, bear the two letters S. C., that is to say, *Senatus Consultus*, which are generally placed on the bronze medals of the three modules (first, second, and third brass), and announce the authority of the Senate.—As it is nowhere read that the Senate made largesses or liberalities, the pieces which have the mark of the *Senatus Consultus*, large and heavy as they may be, were therefore struck by order of that body, only to be used as money.— As to the rest it is generally to be observed on medallions of all the three metals, that they are worn just like the coins. This wearing of the coin is certainly attributable to the same cause, namely the continual rubbing to which circulation exposes all monies. The medallions, therefore, (proceeds Millin,) served for the same purpose, although they were much more rare. They moreover often exhibit a characteristic which only belongs to money, and which is the *countermark*. Their fabrication, therefore, has always had a commercial object, into which they entered, after having originally been presentation pieces *(pièces de largesses)*.—Such (concludes Millin) was doubtless their first destination. The Emperors caused them to be struck for the purpose of distributing them on solemn days, and on occasions of state pomp. Those who came afterwards into possession of them, were competent to supply with them the wants of life and the demands of commerce."

Amongst the number of writers opposed to this theory is our own Addison, who, in his "Dialogues upon the usefulness of Ancient Medals," makes Philander tell his numismatic pupils that "formerly there was no difference between money and medals. An old Roman had his purse full of the same pieces that we now preserve in cabinets. As soon as an Emperor had done anything remarkable, it was immediately stamped on a coin, and became current through the whole dominions." (p. 147). And a little further on, in answer to Cynthio's question, "were all the ancient coins that are now in cabinets once current money?" our illustrious countryman, through the mouth of his imaginary representative, replies, "It is the most probable opinion that they were all of them such, *excepting those we call medallions.* These in respect of the other coins were the same as modern medals in respect of modern money. They were exempted from all commerce, and had no other value but what was set upon them by the fancy of the owner. They are supposed to have been struck by Emperors for presents to their friends, foreign princes, or ambassadors. However, that the smallness of their number might not endanger the loss of the devices they bore, the Romans took care generally to stamp the subject of their medallions on their ordinary coins that were the running cash of the nation. As if in England, we should see on our half-penny and farthing pieces, the several designs that shew themselves in their perfection on our medals."—(p. 148.)

A later and perhaps more practised English numismatist, the dogmatical but still scientific and sagacious Pinkerton, in his "Essay on Medals," says—"Under the term of *medallions* are included all the pieces produced by the ancient mints, which, from their superior size, were evidently not intended for circulation as coins, but for other occasions. Medallions were presented by the emperor to his friends, and by the mint-masters to the emperor, as specimens of fine workmanship. They were struck upon the commencement of the reign of a new emperor, and other solemn occasions, as monuments of gratitude or of flattery. Sometimes they were merely what we would call trial, or pattern pieces, *testimonia probatæ monetæ;* and such abound after the reign of Maximian, with the *tres monetæ* on the reverse."—(vol. i. p. 273.)

The most recently published observations on the subject in question are from the pen of M. Hennin, a very acute and accomplished French numismatist, who in his "Manuel" of the Science, devotes a chapter to the purpose of *defining* the difference between coins and medals," *(différence des monnaies aux médailles),* words which are continually confounded with each other, particularly in reference to the mintages of ancient times.

"*Coins*" *(les monnaies),* says the above-named writer, "are pieces of metal which, uniformly and very numerously multiplied, and bearing similar impressions in evidence of their value, whether real or fictitious, serve for an universal medium of exchange against all other objects of value.—Coins, or *money,* ought necessarily to unite these three determinate, uniform, and known characters—standard, weight, and types.

"*Medals (médailles)* are pieces of metal which, multiplied in an uniform manner, without having any precise value, and without uniting the known and determinate characters for standard, weight, and types, are designed to serve in commemoration of events or of personages."

M. Hennin proceeds to remark that, in giving the name of *medals* to the money of the ancients, three inconveniences are incurred—the first is that of calling these pieces by what is not their real name ; the second, that of giving a false idea of what they were in the ages of antiquity ; the third, that of confounding thereby antique coins with antique medals, for the ancients themselves knew the difference between one and the other.

So much for the question, whether any of the pieces called medallions passed as coins with the ancients, a matter of no intrinsic importance. It is of much greater moment to notice the different articles belonging to the class of medallions. There were a great number of medallions struck in the Greek cities, subject to the Roman empire, and they are of considerable importance on account of the extent of their inscriptions, which elucidate many extremely curious points connected with antiquity. Pellerin has published and explained many of these medallions, and the Royal Library at Paris possesses a large collection of them. They are particularly useful to beginners, because their legends are more easily read than those on coins of a smaller *module,* and because they exhibit themselves in a great variety of form.—But passing by the Greek, both *Autonomous* and Imperial, which though highly interesting in each metal, from the general excellence of their workmanship and the diversity of their types, do not come within the province of this work, we proceed to that more truly Roman branch of the Imperial series, commonly called *Latin Medallions.* All gold and silver pieces larger than the diameter ordinarily assigned to imperial money may be regarded as comprised in this category, and are all of greater or less rarity.

Medallions are indeed generally more adapted to facilitate the study of antiquity than common medals, because their types present more curious and interesting subjects in reference to mythology, and to ceremonies and customs religious, civil, military, &c., representing as they generally do, on their reverses, triumphs, games, edifices, and other monuments, which are the most particular objects of an antiquary's research. Nor is the information to be derived from medallions less important with regard to the history of art. Their superior size has enabled those who executed them to charge their reverses with more complex designs ; and accordingly we find amongst the medallions of the Roman Emperors, many specimens of workmanship almost equal in point of exquisiteness to that of the finest engraved stones.

Millin places at the head of these antique pieces of metal the gold medallion of Justinian, in the French King's Cabinet. This magnificent product of coinage, not for money purposes, is more than three inches (French) in diameter, and in proportionably high relief. Its extraordinary volume, equal to that of the gold medallion of *Tetricus*, shews it to have been appropriated to the same use. The perforated rams-horns (*bélières*, as the French call them), which are attached to the former, clearly point out that it was originally destined to serve as an ornament, principally for suspension from the neck.

With these medallions should be classed those pieces, which are surrounded with borders, encircled with ornamental mountings, and which are double the size of coins, to which, however, their types are common. Sometimes the circles are of the same metal as that of those extraordinary pieces, and in that case they are continuous with the field of the coin; at other times they are found composed of a metal, or rather of a mixture of metals (*alliage*), different from that of the medallion with which they have been soldered after being placed between the dies. These sorts of medallions do not commence until the reign of Commodus. Sometimes even the circle made of a different metal, or alloy, is itself enclosed in a rim, the material of which still differs from its own. In these singularities is seen a marked intention to place them out of currency. It was the custom to use these extraordinary medallions as ornaments for the decoration of military ensigns, whether they were suspended to them with *bélières*, or fixed to the standards by means of holes pierced in the centre of their diameter, or whether they were inlaid on them from space to space. Perhaps the medallions which were composed of two different metals were employed for the same purpose.

Medallions from the time of Julius to that of Hadrian, are very uncommon, and of enormous price; from Hadrian to the close of the western empire they are generally speaking less rare.

The largeness of medallions is not to be understood merely in comparison with that of common coins, of which the greater have some advantage over the others. The size of medallions is so considerable, that it sometimes exceeds the ordinary weight of medals by one or two proportions. The thickness, the height of relief, and the extent of surface are the qualities which are held by numismatists in the higher esteem.

A remarkable distinction between tho Greek and Roman medallions lies in their different thickness, the Roman being often three or four lines thick, whilst the other seldom exceed one.

M. Mionnet, in some observations which he makes (in the preface to his celebrated work *De la rareté et du prix des Médailles Romaines,*) on the module of the coins, says,—"Silver medals of the larger size, as they are called,

ought not to bo confounded with medallions; they are distinguishable by the head of the Prince, which is always radiated, whilst it is laureated on coins of the common size. These medals were not struck till the period from Caracalla's reign to that of the elder Philip inclusive.—As to medallions of gold and of silver, it is very easy to recognise them; it suffices that they are found to exceed the usual module by their weight, or their diameter; when however of extraordinary dimensions they are of extreme rarity, and should not be mixed up with the smaller size, which in general are less estimated.—Brass medallions and large brass medals have for the most part been frequently the object of mistaken notions with authors and connoisseurs. Some, for the reign of Postumus especially, have given us for medallions the coins which belong only to large brass; whilst others, for the Lower Empire, have passed off for large brass what can be regarded as no more than middle brass."

The following remarks concerning the *Roman medallions* are chiefly drawn from Pinkerton and Millin:—Many of these have s. c. as being struck by order of the Senate; others have not, as being by order of the Emperor. Of Augustus a noble gold medallion was found in Herculaneum. There are many of Tiberius and Claudius. Some of Agrippina, Nero, Galba, Vespasian, and Domitian, are also extant. Those of Trajan and Hadrian have generally a broad rim beyond the legend with indented circles. Above all it was under the reign of Antoninus Pius, and some of his first successors, that very fine medallions were struck. That emperor had a religious respect for all which recalled the history of Rome's foundation and that of her first ages. Thus we find on these medallions Hercules, whom the inhabitants of Mount Aventine thanked, for having delivered them from the giant Cacus; likewise we see Horatius Cocles defending the Sublician bridge; the arrival of Æsculapius at Rome, under the form of a serpent, &c., &c. These medallions, moreover, retrace many ancient and important features of mythological and heroic history. A medallion of Lucilla represents the combat of the Romans and the Sabines, and Hersilia throwing herself between Tatius her father and Romulus her husband.—A fine one of the same empress has for the type of its reverse that lady walking in a garden and several cupids overturning each other—"A meet emblem (says Pinkerton) of her various amours; and which calls to mind Anacreon's description of his heart, as a nest in which old loves begot young ones." There are medallions of Commodus remarkable for their superior workmanship: one of them in bronze, Patin has engraved in his "*Histoire des Médailles,*" of which the reverse is enriched with one of the finest sacrificial groups, a master-piece of ancient art.—On another of this emperor we see him and his concubine Marcia; their heads joined, and she wearing a helmet.— One of Pertinax has for reverse that emperor sacrificing, with VOTIS' DECENNALIBVS. Of

Septimius Severus there are many. The mints of Gordian III. and of Philip contribute to the number. Numerous varieties subsequently appear of Trebonianus Gallus, Valerian, Gallienus, Aurelian, Probus, Diocletian, Maximian I., Constantius I., Constantinus I. and II., Constans and Constantius II.—For a notice of the curious brass medallion of Constans, which represents him standing in a ship, and a human figure in the waves,—see the legend BONONIA OCEANEN.

It has been asserted that no ·medallions were ever struck in the colonies. Nevertheless, Vaillant has published one of Cordova and another of Saragossa. The medallions called *Contorniate*, from an Italian word, indicating the manner in which they are struck, are quite a distinct class of pieces.—See the word.

It is very difficult to form a numerous suite of medallions; those extant do not furnish all the Emperors, and thus the series remains always imperfect.—The first who collected any considerable number of these pieces was Gothifredi, a Roman gentleman, who possessed nearly two hundred of them about the middle of the seventeenth century. These he augmented from time to time, and in 1672, when they became the property of Christina, Queen of Sweden, they amounted to more than three hundred.—Cardinal Gaspard Carpegna was also one of the earliest who attached themselves to the task of forming a suite of medallions. He caused one hundred and ninety-five of them to be engraved, and they were accompanied with observations by Buonarotti.—Vaillant has described about four hundred and fifty from Julius Cæsar to Constans, which he had seen in different cabinets of France and Italy.—According to a catalogue published at Venice, there were two hundred and twenty-nine medallions in the Museum Pisani.—The Carthusians at Rome had a very fine collection of medallions, which was afterwards sold to the Emperor of Germany; the engravings from it are now extremely rare.—In the seventeenth century more than four hundred medallions in the French King's Cabinet were engraved. Their number had been much increased since the acquisition made of all that belonged to Marshal D'Estrées. This suite comprised all the medallions which had enriched the collection of the Abbé de Camps, besides those which appeared with the explanations of Vaillant, and which did not exceed one hundred and forty. The Abbé de Rothelin also possessed a very considerable series of them.— Above all, Cardinal Albani's fine series of medallions ought to be mentioned. These afterwards passed to the Vatican; *Venuti* engraved and described them. This collection and those of Cardinal Carpegna were, in Buonaparte's time, united to that in the cabinet of antiques in the national Library at Paris, which even before that period was one of the most numerous in Europe. [Restored to the Vatican at the peace of 1815.] In 1806, when M. Millin was *Conservateur des Médailles* in that magnificent establishment, the number of antique medallions there accumulated was not less than 1,500.

Medals and *Monies*, or *Coins*, difference between.—See *Medallion*.

The following are among the terms used by French numismatists to denominate and distinguish the different pecularities of ancient medals and coins :—

Médailles non frappées.—Pieces of metal of a certain weight, which served wherewith to make exchanges against merchandize and commodities, before the art was discovered of impressing figures or characters upon them, by means of dies and of the hammer.

Médailles affrontées, &c.—A medal sometimes offers several heads. The French call them *affrontées*, or *opposées*, according as they look towards each other, or as they are placed in a contrary direction. They are *conjugées*, or conjoined, when there are more than one on the same side.

Médailles enchassées. Enchased medals,— A small number of pieces in bronze, are of two metals, that is to say, of two different qualities of copper, the centre being, as the French calls it, *enchassé*, or surrounded by a circle of another quality. The plates *(plans)* thus prepared were afterwards struck, and of this there can be no doubt (says Hennin) since the letters of the legends are often found imprinted on the two metals at one time. These pieces are all Imperial of the Roman die, and they appear under the reign of various Emperors up to the end of the third century. They ought, without doubt, to be considered as true medals, contradistinguished from current coins, and to be ranged amongst the *medallions*—(see the word). They are generally of fine workmanship, and remarkable for the pains bestowed on their fabrication.

MEDUSA, one of the three Gorgonides, who, according to Ovid's amplification of the fable, was a most beautiful nymph, both in form and feature; but of all the charms with which she was gifted, none were more lovely than her luxuriant locks of golden hue. Neptune declared to her his passion in the temple of Minerva, who was so offended that she changed the hair of Medusa into serpents; and gave to this horrible image of deformity the power of turning into stone all who looked upon it. The beauty thus become a monster, fatal to all beholders, was at length encountered by Perseus, who cut off her head with the sword of Minerva; and that goddess placed the viper-tresses and the hideous countenance on her own redoubtable Ægis.—The head of Medusa appears on a first brass of Hadrian, bearing the legend of SICILIA.—Also on *gold* and *silver* of Septimius Severus, with the epigraph PROVIDENTIA, where the winged head of the ·Gorgon, bristling with serpents, is exhibited as the symbol of Providence.

MELICERTA or Melicertes, called by the Latins *Portumnus*, and by the Corinthians *Palæmon*, was the son of Athamus, King of Thebes, and of Ino. It was with Melicerta that Ino is said to have cast herself into the sea, from the summit of the Moluris rock, to avoid the persecutions of Athamas. Melicerta then became a marine deity, and was worshipped under the name of Palæmon. Sisyphus instituted the Isthmian games to his honour. He was regarded as the god who came to the succour of the shipwrecked. The Romans have confounded Palæmon with their tutelary divinity of the sea-ports, Portumnus.—See *Corinthus Colonia* for the following types :—

Melicerta is represented on a first brass struck at Corinth under Domitian. Ino presents him as a child to Neptune, who is seated on a rock by the sea-side; a dolphin is at his feet; above we read PERM. IMP. (by permission of the Emperor), referring solely to the mintage of the coin.

Melicerta, lying on the dolphin who saved his life; behind him is the pine-tree near to which he had fallen, when Sisyphus took care of him. This type with the legend CLICOR, *(Colonia Julia Corinthus,)* appears on a coin struck at Corinth.

The same subject is alluded to on another Colonial medal of the Romano-Corinthian mint, struck under Aurelius. In the round temple of Neptune, of which the dome is formed of fish scales, and where a dolphin is placed on each side of the roof, we see the same recumbent figure of a boy on a dolphin, and read the same inscription of CLI COR.

A third medal of Corinth exhibits its acropolis, or citadel, with the temple of Neptune on the top, and a grotto at the bottom, in which the body of *Melicerta* had been deposited. On the right is the pine where Sisyphus found him. Same inscription.

On a fourth medal struck by the Roman colony of Corinth, *Melicerta* is seen on a dolphin. By his side is Sisyphus, conqueror at the Isthmian games, which he had instituted in honour of Melicerta. He bears away the *vase* and the *palm-branch*, symbols of the prizes he had won.

MEMMIA, a plebeian family. Its surnames are uncertain. Its coins which in silver are common exhibit fifteen varieties. Some were restored by Trajan and are very rare. The bronze pieces of this family are parts of the *as*. One of the scarce types refers to the *Cerialia*, or festival of Ceres; it bears on its obverse a laureated head, with curled beard, and the inscription C. MEMMI. C. F. QVIRINVS.—On the reverse Ceres sitting; a serpent at her feet; in her right hand three ears of corn; in her left a distaff, and MEMMIVS. AED. CERIALIA. PREIMVS. FECIT.

Whether the word *Quirinus* may be considered as a cognomen of the Memmia family, or whether it refers to the head as that of Quirinus or Romulus, or both together, is a point in dispute among the learned. But the reverse of this rare denarius teaches us that Memmius, in his edileship, was the *first* who celebrated at Rome the *Cerialia*, or feasts, in honour of the Goddess of Harvests, a ceremony held in much consideration by the Romans, but of the time of first celebrating it no mention

is made by ancient writers.—We see Ceres with serpent, torch, and corn-ears, things dedicated to that divinity on account of the earth's fertility. The *colus* or distaff seems to point her out as presiding over the domestic care of matrons.—See *Ceres*. and *Cerialia*.

The same type, as restored by Trajan, bears on its exterior circle IMP. CAES. TRAIAN. AVG. GERM. DAC. P. P. REST. *Imperator Cæsar Traianus Augustus Germanicus Dacicus Pater Patriæ Restituit.*

MEMOR. *Memoriæ.*—On a coin of Maximianus.

MEMORIA.—See AETERNAE MEMORIAE, on a gold medallion of Maxentius, having for type a temple with an eagle seated on the summit of its dome.

MEMORIAE AETERNAE.—There are two third brass coins of Claudius Gothicus (both struck after that Emperor's death, as the inscription of DIVO CLAVDIO OPT. IMP. on the obverse clearly shew), but the type of one is an eagle with expanded wings, and of the other a lion standing.

MEMORIA DIVI CONSTANTI.—On a medallion of second brass of Constantius Chlorus, the type of which is a round temple surmounted by an eagle.

Spanheim, in his commentaries on the Cæsars of Julian, observes that "*Immortal remembrance*" was esteemed the most glorious reward of conquerors in ancient times. Hence proceeded the choice of such inscriptions as those of *Aeterna Memoria*, of *Memoria Perpetua*, and of *Memoria Felix*, which are found on the coins of some Roman Emperors, struck after their death, and which clearly mark that this was the end and true meaning of their consecration.— Moreover we find these inscriptions accompanied either with temples, or with lighted altars, or eagles (generally with expanded wings), or with cars destined for public processions, the usual symbols of *Apotheosis*, as (amongst others) on two medals of Constantius I., the father of Constantine, both of them struck at Treves—one with the words *Memoria Divi Constantii*, the other *Æterna Memoria.*

MEMORIA FELIX.—An eagle with expanded wings, within a temple, on the frieze of which is another eagle.—The obverse has the *veiled head* of Constantius I.—See *Constantius I.,—Aræ,—Consecratio.*

MEMORIAE AGRIPPINAE. S.P.Q.R.—A funeral *carpentum* drawn by two mules.—This medal, in large brass, and also a bronze medallion cited by Morell, bear on the obverse the portrait of Agrippina senior, struck after her death, in exile under the cruel and unjust Tiberius, and remind us of the translation of her ashes from the island of Pandataria, and of all the funeral honours which were decreed to her by the filial piety of Caligula her son, at the seemingly auspicious commencement of his reign.—Suetonius, whose account is confirmed by Dion, adds that the above-named emperor caused annual sacrifices to be instituted to the manes of his mother, together with Circensian celebrations, in which the *carpentum* was drawn in state procession.

MEMORIAE DOMITILLAE S.P.Q.R.— Funeral car as in the foregoing. On a rare large brass, struck under Titus; the reverse of which has s. c. in the middle of the field, surrounded with the inscription IMP. T. CAES. DIVI. VESP. F. AVG. P.M. TR. P. P.P.—See *Carpentum*, with illustration.

"Antiquaries (says the author of *Leçons de Numismatique Romaine)* are divided on the question whether the medal belongs to the wife or to the daughter of Vespasian, for each of them bore the same name. It seems with more probability assignable to the daughter, who never received the title of *Augusta,* nor the honours of the apotheosis, whilst those high distinctions were decreed to *Domitilla* the mother, who was consequently called DIVA. AVG*usta* on the gold and silver coins which incontestably belong to her, and who would undoubtedly have been in like manner honoured on those of brass.—The car with two mules was not exclusively appropriated to consecrations; and the type of the above medal, struck by order of *Titus,* is copied after that of *Agrippina*" above noticed.

MENS, the mind, was worshipped as a goddess by the Romans, who erected an altar and a temple to its honour. Ovid bears witness to this fact when (in L. vi. *Fastor.* l. 241) he sings—

Mens quoque numen habet. Menti delubra videmus.
(See MENTI LAVDANDAE below.)

MENSA, a table on three feet—*Tripus.*—See the word *Table.*

MENSIS, the name of the god *Lunus,* which is read on coins of Antioch in Pisidia, dedicated to Antoninus Pius. COL. CAES. ANTIOCH. MENSIS, according to Patin, Havercamp, and Vaillant.—See *Lunus.*

MENSOR, one who measures fields or camps; the surname of the *Farsuleia* family.—L. FAR-SVLEI MENSOR.

MENTI LAVDANDAE.—A woman standing, holds in her right hand a crown and in her left a lance. The coin, which bears on its reverse this singular legend, is a Pertinax in silver, treasured in the Imperial Cabinet at Vienna, and for a long time unknown to other museums, till afterwards produced in the collection of M. D'Ennery.—By the words *mens* was understood human reason, sense, or judgment, which are in themselves susceptible of good or (: evil influences. Taken in a favourable acceptation, such for instance as *bona mens,* a temple was erected and worship paid to "the divine intelligence."

But the reign of Commodus having been one continuous outbreak of *dementedness,* or *mala mens;* it was of great consequence to Pertinax to restore the sanity of public sentiment and ideas *(mentem bonam vel laudandam.)* He made a virtuous and bold attempt to re-establish good morals and military discipline, but in vain. The goddess of the praiseworthy mind was not a match for the *malus animus* which caused the wise and honest Pertinax to be butchered at the shrine of Prætorian avarice.

MER., *Meritorum.*—See REQVIES OPTi-*morum* MER*itorum ;* on third brass of Claudius Gothicus.

MERC. *Mercurio.*

MERCVRIVS.—The God Mercury, son of Jupiter, and Maia one of the daughters of Atlas: so called by the Latins (according to *Festus)* from *merces* or the gains of trade, because he was supposed to preside over mercantile affairs. The Greeks called him *Hermes.* By the poets he was honoured under various surnames; and the offices and occupations assigned to him by mythologists were still more numerous and diversified. His principal characteristic was that of being the faithful and intimate attendant upon Jupiter, and his ordinary messenger. Next in importance was his dignity of chief herald and minister of the gods, as well infernal as celestial.—*Diodorus Siculus* says of Mercury that he was the first amongst the deities who instituted religious worship and sacrifices; hence we see him on coins imaged with caduceus and purse, and the inscription around his effigy of PIETAS AVG., or AVGG.—There is a coin of Gallienus which illustrates his attributes of rewarding acts of religion to the gods with gifts, and on which Mercury is represented with *caduceus* and *crumena,* the inscription being DONA AVG.—He is distinguished on all ancient monuments by his head being covered with a winged cap (in latin *petasus),* and his feet are also furnished with wings. He wears a hat, as the reputed god of merchants, because (says Vaillant in his *Colonies)* all business negociations should be kept hidden; and wings are appended to it, because the bargaining between sellers and buyers should be speedily dispatched like a bird through the air.—The rod with serpents entwined on it, called *caduceus,* signifies the regal power which is sometimes given to merchants, or it is the symbol of contentions removed and peace promoted. Sometimes we see a ram, a tortoise, a dog, or a cock at his feet.

Mercury, the worship of whom was borrowed (so early, it is said, as the time of Romulus) from the Etruscans, has his bust impressed (with or without the *petasus* covering his head) on the ancient brass coins of the Romans.—See the *Sextantes* or parts of the *As.*—On a quinarius of the *Papia* family appears the head of Mercury, and a lyre on the reverse, an association which corroborates the pretensions made for him by Horace and other poets, to be considered as the inventor of that instrument.—We also see the head of Mercury, with the caduceus behind it, on denarii of the Aburia, Apronia, Pomponia, and other families.

Mercury's image at full length is not often found on coins of the republic or of the upper empire. His head is, however, to be discerned on some denarii of the *Mamilia* family ; and on one of the *Rubria* family it exhibits itself united

to that of Hercules, like the head of Janus.—
Mercury seated is the most rare to be met with.
His posture is almost uniformly upright.—
Beger, however, gives a very rare medal of
Tiberius, on the obverse of which is that
Emperor's head laureated, with the circumscription TI. CAES. DIVI. AVG. F. AVG. IMP.—On
the reverse appears Mercury sitting on a rock,
with a caduceus in his right hand, and with the
inscription PERMIS. P. CORNELI. DOLABELLAE.
PROCOS. C.P. CAS. D.D.—Spanheim (in his
Cæsars of Julian) gives us, on two Greek
Imperial medals, Mercury with all his adornments, his hat with two wings, his caduceus in
one hand, his purse in the other; and his two
winged buskins, which he put on when he performed the part of Jupiter's messenger.

Mercury, with his attributes, is depictured
on a rare third brass of Claudius Gothicus, with
the epigraph FIDES. AVG.—A half-naked male
figure, with radiated head, holding the winged
caduceus of *Mercury* in his right and an instrument like a trident in his left hand, appears
on a first brass of Albinus, with legend of
SAECVLO FRVGIFERO.—A similar figure, and the
same legend is seen on first brass of Sept.
Severus.

Mercury standing, with the *crumena* in his
right hand, forms the reverse type of a very rare
gold coin of Gallienus, inscribed FORTUNA
REDVX.—An image of the same deity appears
on coins of Herennius, Hostilianus, Valerianus,
Postumus, Carinus, and Numerianus: the epigraph to most of these is PIETAS AVG*usti*.—
On a gold coin of Gallienus Mercury accompanies
the legend of PROVIDENTIA AVG.—On a first
brass of Marcus Aurelius, he appears in a
temple; and also without the temple. See
REGLIG*io* AVGVSTI.—On a silver coin of
Gallienus, Mercury with his attributes accompanies the legend of DONA AVG.

Mercury dragging a ram to the altar is the
type, without legend, of one of the beautiful
medallions of Antoninus Pius.

Mercury, though not unfrequently typified
on coins of Roman die, is represented with his
various attributes of the petasus, caduceus, and
crumena, on many colonial medals, bearing
Latin legends.—See *Heliopolis* (Philip, sen.),
Patræ (Caracalla and Elagabalus), and *Tyrus*
(Valerianus and Salonina).

MERCVRIO CONS. AVG.—The Egyptian
sea-ram, with horns turned backwards like
those of *Capricornus.*—Silver and third brass
of Gallienus.

The ram is here united with Mercury, because
as Pausanias affirms, this deity was esteemed
above others as the protector of flocks; and as
the shepherds chose him for their patron he is
found on ancient monuments associated with the
ram. It is also stated that near Tanagra, in
Bœotia, a temple was erected to him under the
name of *Chriophorus.*—The Chriophorian Mercury has his hand on a ram; but on some gems,
and on a Corinthian coin of L. Verus, the *he goat*
is substituted for the *he sheep*. It is not so easy
to assign the reason, from ancient monuments

or ancient writers, why in this instance the ram
should have a fish's tail, except from the fancy
of poets and painters to change almost every
animal which the earth produces into fishes.—
Eckhel—Millin.

MERCVRIO FELICI.—This circumscription appears on gold, silver, and small brass
coins of Postumus, with the effigy of Mer-

cury standing naked, with
the pallium thrown back
on the left shoulder,
the purse in his right
hand, as the tutelary of
merchants, and in his left
a caduceus.—The Gauls
(according to Cæsar) wor-
shipped Mercury as the
inventor of arts, as the
guide of journeyings, and also as the favourer
of merchants. Allusion in this coin is made to
the civic virtues in which Postumus was acknowledged to excel; and for encouraging, as well
as enforcing, the practice of which he was
esteemed *vir dignissimus* by the Gauls, whom
he governed.

On a small brass of Diadumenianus, struck
by the Roman colonists of Sinope, Mercury is
represented holding the purse in his right hand
and caduceus in left.—See *Crumena.*

MERCVRIO PACIFERO.—Mercury standing, the *caduceus* in his right hand, the
petasus on his head. This legend, on small
brass coins of Postumus, is quoted by Banduri.
It is not included in either the catalogues or the
Doctrina Num. of Eckhel; but both Mionnet
and Akerman give it as authentic.—The epithet
of Pacifer would well apply to Postumus, who restored peace to Gallia, by defeating and coercing
her German invaders.

MERIT. *Meritorum.*—REQVIES OPTI-
MOR*um* MERIT*orum* on third brass of Claudius Gothicus; also Val. Maximianus and Constantius Chlorus.

MESCINIA, a plebeian family; surname
Rufus.—L. MESCINIVS RVFVS was monetary
triumvir under Augustus. Many coins inscribed
with his name are extant, (both in gold and
silver, the former of extreme rarity,) because
they proclaim the deeds of that Emperor, as
occurring in the years v.c. 737 and 738, when
he was moneyer.—Morell gives six varieties.

MESOPOTAMIA, so called, because it lay
between the Tigris and Euphrates. It is now
denominated *Diarbec.*—According to Spartianus,
Mesopotamia was brought under the power of
Rome as a province of the empire by Trajan;
declared free of tribute by Hadrian, and afterwards relinquished to the Parthians by that
Emperor; received into the empire again by
Verus; lost by Commodus; recovered again by
Sept. Severus; ceded to the Persians together
with Armenia by Philip.—See on a large brass
coin of Trajan, the fine group composed of that
Emperor standing, armed and sceptred, amidst
the prostrate personifications of the Armenian
province, and of the two celebrated rivers above-
mentioned—with the inscription ARMENIA ET

MESOPOTAMIA IN POTESTATEM P.R. REDACTAE.
s.c.—See *Armenia*.

MESS. *Messius.*—A family Roman name, occupying the place of a prænomen, on coins of *Trajanus Decius, Herennius Etruscus,* and *Hostilianus.*

MESSAL. *Messala.*—A surname of the Valeria family.

MESSALINA *(Valeria)*, fourth wife of the Emperor Claudius, was daughter of Val. Messala Barbatus and Domitia Lepida (daughter of Domitius Lepidus and of Antonia, daughter of M. Antony and Octavia, sister of Augustus.) Though thus high in birth and rank, and the mother of Octavia and Britannicus, the name of this woman has descended with horror to posterity, as a monster of shameless lust, avarice, and cruelty. She caused Julia Livilla, Julia, daughter of the younger Drusus, Silanus, Vinucius, Poppæa senior, and many others, to be put to death ; and was herself subjected to the same fate, from her adulteries and prostitutions, by order of Claudius, A.D. 48.—There are no Latin coins of this *Augusta*, except colonial.

MESSALINA *(Statilia)*, third wife of Nero, who put to death *her* fourth husband, Atticus Vestinus. She was distinguished for her taste in the sciences, and for her perfect eloquence. After Nero's death, Otho would have married her, if he had survived his defeat.—Of this Empress no Latin coins are extant.

MET. otherwise **METAL.** *Metallum.*—There are coins extant which serve as memorials of mines, which the industry and cupidity of the Romans established in different provinces of the empire. Of this kind are some inscribed with the name of Trajan, and of Hadrian ; and perhaps also of their immediate successors ; they are all of third brass, although it is certain that the mines commemorated on these coins also yielded more noble metals. From thence it may be reasonably supposed that this description of money was struck to pay the wages of those who were employed in the occupation of making the metals. Eckhel has (in the sixth volume of his Doct. Num. Vet. p. 445 *et seq.*) brought together the various specimens of these *numi metallorum.* Thus we see, among others in small brass, bearing the head and titles of Trajan, the following reverses :—

METALLI VLPIANI DELM*atici* (Ulpian and Dalmatian metals) ; a woman with balance and cornucopia.

METAL. PANNONICI (Metals of Pannonia), in the field of the coin.

Third brass of Hadrian bear the inscriptions of MET. NOR. (*Metallum Noricum,* Metal of Noricum), within a crown of oak leaves; and METAL. DELM. (*Metallum Delmaticum,* metal of Dalmatia) ; a coat of mail ; shewing that the mines of Noricum and Dalmatia contributed their treasures to the mint of Hadrian.

MET.—METR.—METRO.—METROP.— *Metropolis.*

METROPOLIS *(Mater Urbium)*, the mother city.—The Greeks called a chief city Μητρόπολις, the Latins *civitas.* Afterwards the term was applied to the larger or more ancient city, in which deputies from other cities *(civitates)* assembled on provincial affairs.

The more distinguished *metropoles* of the Roman empire were designated on their respective coins, both Greek and Latin.

Thus on medals of Cæsarea, in Palestine, is read COL. PR. FL. AVG. CAES. METRO. P. S. P. *Colonia Prima Flavia Augusta Cæsarea Metropolis Provinciæ Syriæ Palæstinæ.*—Also on coins of Damascus, Laodicea, Sidon, and Tyre, the dignity of each of those cities as the METRO*polis* of Roman colonies is in like manner recorded.

META, a pillar, or boundary mark placed in the circus. It consisted of three columns, or pyramidal figures, round which the racing chariots turned. Horace alludes to them in his ode to Mæcenas—*Metaque fervidis evitata rotis.* The rule was to turn seven times round these bounds ; and in doing so it was necessary to avoid approaching too near to them, lest in driving against them the chariots should be broken ; whilst, on the other hand, if the charioteer kept too far distant from them, he ran the risk of being cut off by a competitor, who should have taken advantage of the interval. These *metæ circensium* were of wood ; and the Emperor Claudius, according to Suetonius, caused them to be gilt. They are shewn with great clearness on several medallions and coins of Augustus, Nero, Vespasian, Titus, Trajan, Hadrian, Caracalla, Alexander Severus, and Gordianus Pius.—See *Circus.*

META SUDANS, a fountain so called, situate at Rome, near the amphitheatre of Titus, and from whose waters the people drank who came to the public spectacles exhibited in that vast structure.—It is thought to be represented on a large brass of *Vespasian,* and a middle brass of *Titus.*

METELL. *Metellus.*—Surname of the *Cæcilia* family, from which descended many very great personages. Of these, nineteen obtained four Chief Pontificates, two Dictatorships, three the titles of Princes of the Senate, seven Censorships, twenty Consulates, and nine Triumphs, in the space of 290 years.—Q. METELL. SCIPIO IMP*erator,* on a denarius of the *Cæcilia* family.

METTI. *Mettius.*—Name of the Mettia family.

METTIA, a family of uncertain rank, and little known in Roman history.—There are coins inscribed with the name of *M. Mettius,* of which the greater part present on their obverse the head of Julius Cæsar, one of whose moneyers he appears to have been. Indeed, Cæsar, in two passages of his Commentaries, mentions M. Mettius as having been bound in chains, and afterwards liberated by Ariovistus. Mettius is also named by Cicero.—Two very rare *quinarii,* each bearing (the first on its obverse, the second on its reverse) the type of

Juno Sispita, would warrant the inference that the *Mettii* were of Lanuvian origin; "unless perhaps (says Eckhel) it may rather be supposed that this goddess and her attributes were engraved on these coins, in consequence of Lanuvium having, from a *municipium*, been made a colony, and surrounded by a wall, by J. Cæsar, as is affirmed by Frontinus *(de coloniis)*."—Eight varieties are given by Morell.

M. F.   *Manii Filius.*—M. N.   *Manii Nepos.*

M. F.   *Marci Filia.*—AGRIPPINA M. F. GERMANICI CAESARIS.

MGN.   *Magnus.*—MGN. PIVS. IMP. *Magnus Pius Imperator*, and two-headed Janus, on coins of Pompey the Great.

M. H. ILLERGAVONIA DERT. *Municipium Ibera Illergavonia Dertora.*—Municipality of Hibera, Illergavonia Dertora (*Tortosa* in Catalonia, Spain).

Michael I., Michael II., Michael III., Michael IV., Michael V,, Michael VI., Michael VII., Michael VIII., Michael IX.—The coins of these Byzantine Emperors, whose reigns took place between A.D. 811 and A.D. 1320, present no *Latin* inscriptions, except the *mixed* one of IHS. XIS. REX. REGNANTIVM on the reverse of a gold coin belonging to the *second* of that name.—See Akerman's *Descriptive Catalogue*, vol. ii.

MIL. *Militum.*—CONCORD. MIL. *Concordia Militum.*—Concord of the Soldiers.— FIDES MIL*itum.* Fidelity of the Soldiers.— TR. MIL. *Tribunus Militum.*—Military Tribune; the last on a coin of the Fonteia family.

MILIARIVM SAECVLVM.—On the reverse of a large brass of Philip, senior, we read this legend, which is accompanied by a *cippus*, whereon is incribed COS. III. It forms the first of a series of five medals, struck under that emperor, in record of his having, with extraordinary magnificence, celebrated the secular games (they were the ninth and last); for the purpose of consecrating the completion of the year 1000 from the foundation of Rome. This memorable period, appropriately called the *millenary age*, might well seem to authorise the commencement of a new era; and the appropriation of the term *sæculum novum*, or a new age, to that which was about to begin.—See *Ludi Sæculares*.

Miliarium is on these coins almost invariably spelt with only one L, it is scarcely ever written MILLIARIVM; not, however, from any error of the mint-masters, for both *mile* and *mille* are written by the ancients, as Papinianus (in Cassiodorus) has it, and as not a few antique monuments also shew; but it is never read MILLENARIVM on these coins, although in Occo and the Arschot collection it is thus written.

MILITARY ENSIGNS.—The image of an *eagle* (aquila) was the ensign of the whole legion. One of these, either in gold or in silver, was placed on the top of a spear, with wings expanded, and frequently holding a thunderbolt (fulmen) in its talons.—In the first period of Rome, the standards of her armies were but a bundle of hay tied to the end of a

pole, called in Latin *Manipulus foeni*, which caused the name of *Munipulus* to be given to the companies which are ranged under those ensigns. Two such may be seen represented on a first brass of Augustus, given in Seguin's *Sel. Num. Ant.*, p. 110. But these *standards of poverty* soon assumed a new and more imposing form. The Roman troops placed either a cross piece of wood at the top of a lance, whence hung a *velum*, or banner, as may be seen on the same coin of Augustus between the two *manipuli;* or they surmounted the ensign staff with the figure of a *hand*, as may be observed on two military ensigns which appear on a large brass of Tiberius, given in Seguin *(l. c.* 109); perhaps as the word *manus* bore allusion to the word *manipulus*. Below this hand, covering the whole shaft of the spear, were little round plates of gold or silver *(orbiculi)*, on which are portraits at first of the Gods, and subsequently of the Emperors, and other persons of princely distinction. The names of Emperors were also inscribed on the *vexilla*, or cavalry standards of the army.—On a denarius of the *Valeria* family is seen the name of C. VAL*erius* FLA*vius* IMPERAT*or*, and a legionary eagle, between two military ensigns.—On a silver coin of the *Neria* family is a legionary eagle, between two *vexilla*, one of which has on it H*(astati)*, the other P*(rincipes)*. A similar type appears on a denarius of the Cornelia.—It is to be observed, as a reason why these military ensigns appear in an upright position on Roman coins and other monuments, that the lower end of the spears on which the ensigns were placed had sharp points, in order that they might be planted into the ground, and be made to stand perpendicularly whether in the camp or in the field of battle. —See *Signa Militaria ;* also *Aquila,—Labarum,—Vexillum.*

Military Standards, on Roman coins, near a colonist ploughing with oxen, shew that the colony had been peopled by veteran soldiers.

Military Lituus.—See *Lituus.*

MIN. *Minerva.*—MIN. *Minervia.*—The name of a legion, so denominated by Domitian, on account of the particular devotedness of that emperor to the worship of Minerva, as appears from his coins.—There is on a gold coin of Sept. Severus, in Banduri, which exhibits two military standards and a legionary eagle between them, with this inscription, LEG. I. MIN. *Legio Prima Minervia.*

MINAT. *Minatius.*—Family name of the *gens Minatia.*

MINATIA, a plebeian family; its surname *Sabinus.*—There are three varieties, all very rare.—The following silver pieces, which bear the name of this family, were struck in Spain by Cnaeius Pompey the younger, after his father's death, or by the other son, Sextus, in Sicily:—

1st.—CN*eus* MAGNVS IMP. F.—The bare head of Cnaeius Pompey.

Rev.—Marcus MINAT*ius* SABIN*us* PR*o* Q*uæstor.*—Pompey landing from a ship joins his right hand with that of a woman, wearing

a turreted crown, and holding a spear in her left hand, before whose feet is a heap of Spanish arms.

On this denarius (says Vaillant) is represented the entry of Pompeius Magnus into Spain (for the purpose of assisting Metellus against Sertorius), respecting which event great expectations had been entertained both by the Romans themselves and by their Spanish allies.— Plutarch in his life of Pompey, narratest hat when he "first reached Spain, the reputation of the new commander inspired, as is usual, new hopes in the minds of men, that such of the Spanish nations as had not taken a decisive part with Sertorius, began to change their opinions and go over to the Romans."—Therefore we here see *Hispania* meeting Pompey with congratulations on his happy arrival.—The above cut is engraved from a denarius in the British Museum.

2nd.—CN. MAGN. IMP.—The same head.

Rev. M. MINAT. SABIN. PR. Q.—Pompey the Great, in a military habit, stands with a spear in the right hand. On one side stands a woman, with turreted head and short dress, and who, holding two spears in her left hand, offers her right to Pompey. On the other side, a woman carrying a trophy on her left shoulder, places with her right hand a crown on the head of the middle figure.

Havercamp, in Morell (differing from Vaillant, who considers the middle figure to represent not Pompey, but Metellus), shews on good historical grounds that on this coin Minatius had in view to display the honours not of Metellus but of Pompey. Indeed, referring to the authority of Plutarch for the results of the sanguinary struggle engaged in by the latter, first with the brave, skilful, and active Sertorius, and afterwards with that formidable chieftain's assassin and successor, Perpenna, Havercamp appears warranted in his opinion that the type of this rare denarius alludes to the two closing victories, by which the Sertorian revolt was subdued, and Spain restored to the Roman empire. Nor is there, perhaps, anything erroneous in the conjecture of the same antiquary, that the trophy-bearing figure personifies Rome herself, crowning the victor; Hispania, as a Roman province, standing by, and with extended hand bearing testimony to the merits of the all powerful *imperator.*

3rd.—On another very rare denarius, with the same head (that of the elder Pompey), and stamped with the name of M. Minatius Sabinus, Proquæstor, the type of the reverse is a military figure standing between two women, both *turreted*; one of whom, bending on one knee. offers a crown of laurel to him.

In Morell's *Thesaurus* (under the head of the *Minatia* family), Havercamp, who characterises Vaillant's reference of this denarius to Pompey's successes in Spain as *interpretatio infelicissima,* after describing the standing female figure as having her head *radiated,* proceeds to give his own opinion, that the above type alludes to the Mithridatic war.—It shows (according to the learned but often fanciful commentator) that the long-continued war with the great barbaric king could be brought to a termination by no other Roman General than Pompey, "and therefore (says he) I understand the figure wearing the *pallium,* and having her head *radiated,* to mean the East (Oriens), who beckons and seems to call Pompey to her; whilst he himself displays his expectation of a sure victory over Mithridates, by pointing with hand stretched forth and finger extended to the garland *(corolla),* which Spain (the kneeling figure) gratefully offers to him, as to the conqueror of the republic's foes."—After quoting a passage from *Florus,* lib. iii., cap. 5, as the *quasi interpres* of this very coin, Havercamp concludes by exclaiming—"Behold here the honours and titles of Pompey, especially those gained in Spain, about to be augmented in the East."

By the above cited observations, it will be seen that Havercamp lays some stress on the fact which he asserts, that the figure of the woman, standing before Pompey, is *palliata et radiata,* whereas in Morell's engraving of this denarius, (and Dr. King's is the same,) the female in question, though wearing the *pallium* or cloak, falling from the shoulders, has a turreted, *not* a radiated, head-dress.—And Eckhel describes both women as *turretæ.*—Mr. Akerman, in his *Descriptive Catalogue of Roman Coins,* has given (see plate 3, No. 9,) the design of a silver coin amongst those struck by Cnæius Pompey the son, which with the head of the father for its obverse, exhibits on the reverse a type resembling in most particulars, though not in all, the denarius of Morell and King.—The able secretary of the Numismatic Society states that the kneeling figure is presenting not a crown but "a petition, or written instrument, as appears *very plain* from this denarius, which shews four minute, but distinct lines, drawn across the object called by Morell a crown."—But, unfortunately for those who have only the engraving in Mr. Akerman's catalogue to form their opinions by, the type of the reverse is so *indistinctly* delineated as to make the "*kneeling*" figure look as if she was *seated,* and what she holds in her *lap* resembles a shield more than a petition.— Be this as it may, the difference in the represented type has suggested a different interpretation to Mr. Brumell, in whose cabinet the coin is, which Mr. Akerman has caused to be copied.—"I should describe the reverse (says Mr. Brumell) as bearing the personification of the East, inviting Pompey to relieve that region, oppressed by Mithridates,—an invitation which he appears to decline; and points to the kneeling figure, whose *petition* claims priority of attention."—That kneeling figure, Mr. Brumell thinks it probable, is the personification, not of Spain as Morell conjectures, but of " Cilicia, who implores the aid of Pompey, that country being ravaged by pirates, whose power was crushed by the Roman general, immediately before he obtained the command in the Mithridatic war."—Who shall decide when the learned, the scientific, and the ingenious disagree?

MINEIA, a family of uncertain rank, to which Morell assigns some small brass coins; one has on its obverse MINEIA. M. F. and a female head, and an edifice on the reverse;—rare; the others equally uninteresting.

MINERVA, the goddess whom fable describes to have come forth fully armed and of mature age from the brain of Jupiter—in other words, an emanation from the intellect of Jove himself.—She was the tutelary divinity of the Athenians, and was called in Greek *Athené*. Her head is the type of the medals of Athens; and, under the name of *Pallas*, she was worshipped in that city and throughout Greece, as the protectress of heroes.—By the Romans she was regarded as the first in rank after Jupiter and Juno, and, with the statues of those deities, was placed in the principal temple of the capitol at Rome. As the goddess of reason, wisdom, and prudence, she was considered to preside over literature and the sciences. The invention of weaving and embroidery, together with the honour of having first taught mankind the use of the olive, was ascribed to her.—On consular coins Minerva but seldom appears. Morell has given her image or attributes on coins of the Clovia, Cordia, Cornelia, and Vibia families. During the period of the empire, she occupies somewhat more frequently a place on Roman medals, particularly those of Domitian (see *Domitianus*), Commodus, Albinus, Severus, Caracalla, Geta, as far as Gallienus and Postumus. —On these generally she is figured in a walking attitude, clothed in a long tunic, with sometimes the ægis on her breast, a helmet on her head, holding in her right hand by turns—as the deity both of war and of peace—a spear, the thunderbolt, an image of Victory, a branch of olive, and in her left hand a buckler.—On one silver coin of the Vibia family she stands as Minerva the Vanquisher, with victory and spear; on another her bust is represented, and on a third she stands in a quadriga.—Amongst the rare medallions in brass, struck under Antoninus Pius, without legend, the image of this goddess is three times introduced—viz., 1. Where she is placed on the right hand of Jupiter, whilst Juno is on his left, and all three are seated, full faced, on curule chairs. 2. Minerva leaning against a tree, around which a serpent is entwined, and looking at Prometheus, who is in the act of forming a man. 3. Minerva standing before Vulcan, who is forging a thunderbolt: on another coin a helmet. 4. Vulcan standing before a statue of Minerva placed on a cippus.—On a coin of Clodius Albinus the surname of *Pacifera*

is assigned to this goddess.—See *Oleæ Ramus,* the *olive branch*.

Minerva was the object of especial adoration with that vain, profligate, and murderous tyrant Domitian; on coins of each metal struck under this Emperor, we see a well executed figure of the goddess, holding in one hand her buckler, and in the other the *fulmen* or thunderbolt, which she is going to launch, intended, says *Oiselius,* " as the symbol of Domitian's authority," with the circumscription IMP. XIX. COS. XVI. CENS. P. P. (emperor for the nineteenth time, consul for the sixteenth, censor, father of the country.)—On a first brass of this emperor, without legend on its reverse, but bearing the authorisation of the Senate, he stands between Minerva and Victory, the latter of whom is placing a laurel crown on his head.

MINER*va* VICT*rix*. Minerva the Victorious. —On a large brass of Commodus, with this legend, we see the victory-bringing Minerva *(Nicephora)* helmeted, having in one hand an image of Victory, which holds a palm branch, and in the other hand a spear; behind her is a trophy.—Minerva the Victorious was called by the Greeks Aθηνη Νικηφόρος, as is shewn on the coinage of the Athenians.

Eckhel dedicates a short chapter of his Prolegomena on Family Coins (vol, v., 84-5) to shew that, when on the silver coin of the Roman, as well as of the Athenian mint, we see a *winged* Pallas, or Minerva, it is to be understood as representing Pallas Νικηφόρος, or Minerva Victrix.

A brass medallion of Trajan exhibits Minerva standing on the right, and Juno on the left of Jupiter.—See *Jupiter*.

MINERVAE VICTRICI.—*Vaillant,* in describing a silver coin of *Pescennius Niger* having a similar figure, but without the trophy, and inscribed to the Victorious Minerva, observes that Minerva, like Mars, was said to preside in war; thus as the surname of *Victor* was applied to Mars, so also the appellation of *Victrix* was given to Minerva; and that the title was dedicated to that goddess by Pescennius for a victory *about to be* obtained over Severus, is indicated by this coin, on which, as if certain *success* had been assured him, she bears the sign in her right hand.

MINERVA SANCT.—The goddess stands with spear and shield.—On a silver coin of Sept. Severus this legend of *Minerva Sancta* appears for the first time, and afterwards occurs on coins of Geta Cæsar.

That the ancients put *sanctus* (sacred) for *propitius* (favourable or propitious) we learn from Tibullus respecting Juno, whom he addresses *At tu sancta fave;* and from Catullus, speaking of Venus, *Quem neque sancta Venus.* Moreover, Minerva was accounted the Goddess of Arts, and Geta, according to Herodianus, *Disciplinarum laude celebres circà se frequentes habebat,* instructed by his mother Julia, who daily disputed with philosophers.—(Vaillant, ii. p. 260.)

MINER FAVTR. *Minerva Fautrix.*—The favouring Minerva.—This legend, accompanying the usual type of the goddess, appears only on a silver coin of Postumus, who was so renowned for valour and for wisdom, that Gallienus assigned to him the education of his young son, Cornelius Saloninus, choosing him, according to Pollio, *quasi custodi vitæ, et morum et actuum imperialium institutori.* Besides, Minerva was, in the estimation of the heathen world, the goddess of wisdom and fortitude.

Mint Marks.—See *Notæ Monetales.*

MINVCIA, a plebeian family, whose surnames, as they appear on coins, are *Augurinus, Rufus, Thermus.*—The gold are very rare; the silver common. Some of the latter, restored by Trajan, are of high price. The brass pieces of this family are parts of the *As.*—Amongst the same types is one in silver, having on its obverse a female head helmeted, and on the reverse the legend Q. THERMus M. F. Two soldiers, armed with sword and buckler, engaged in combat; another soldier similarly armed, on his knees between them.

This type clearly points to the honour of having saved a Roman citizen's life in battle; but leaves it in doubt to whom the glory of this distinguished exploit belongs.

Morell gives his reasons at some length for believing that this denarius was struck by Quintus Minucius Thermus, the son of Marcus (as the inscription indicates), a monetal triumvir perhaps, or quatuorvir, under Julius Cæsar, who had just attained the direction of affairs in that public department, and that he had particularly fixed on this type, in order at once to compliment Cæsar, and to recall his own father's prowess to remembrance.—For we have the testimony of Suetonius that Cæsar made the first payments to the legions in Asia, in the tent of Marcus Thermus, and that Cæsar was by the same Thermus presented with a civic crown at the taking of Mitylene.

The head of Pallas, or of Rome, winged; behind it X.

Rev.—c. MINVCI C. F. AVGVRINI.—A fluted or chamfered column, on which a statue is placed; on the left of the column stands a man in the augural habit, and holding the lituus; to the right stands another togated figure, holding in each hand something uncertain, and planting his left foot on something equally doubtful; from the base of the column on each side springs a corn-ear; above, ROMA.

These denarii revive the memory of Lucius Minucius, who is also by Pliny called Augurinus, and who, being *Præfectus Annonæ* at a time of dearth, when Spurius Mælius was attempting to corrupt the populace with largesses of corn, detected his pernicious designs, reported him to the senate, and then at a low price distributed the corn to the common people. On this account, according to Pliny, a statue was erected to him outside the *Porta Trigemina* (at Rome) at the public expense. The statue in question is here represented mounted on a column, as Vaillant says *striata*, fluted; perhaps, says Havercamp,

with more ingenuity than judgment, consisting of *modii* (or bushel measures) placed one on the top of another; and, in connection with the subject which the medal was struck to commemorate, there are ears of corn rising up from the base of this pillar.—(*Doct. num. vet.* vol. v. p. 255.)

MISSILIA, now called by the Italians *Medaglioni*, is a term applied generally to the medals which the Emperors caused to be struck for their own especial use, with a view to distribute them as presents among their friends.—The term *Missilia* was also applied to those gifts which princes scattered amongst the people on festival days, and which, like money, were in no danger of being spoiled by their being flung, as they were generally, from some lofty spot. Thus, according to Suetonius Caligula ascended to the top of Basilica *Julia,* in order to throw money to the people. *Quim et nummos non mediocris summæ è fastigio Basilicæ Juliæ per aliquot dies sparsit in plebem.*—"Caligula," cap. xxxvii.

MITREIA, a family of uncertain rank, and known only from its name of MITREIVS appearing on two third brass coins struck by the moneyers of Augustus.

M. K. V. *Moneta Carthaginensis Urbis.*—Money of the city of Carthage.

M. L. *Moneta Lugdunensis.*—Money of Lyons, in France.

M. MARC. *Marcus Marcellus.*—Prenomen and name of a man.

M. M. I. V. *Municipes Municipii Julii Uticensis.*—The citizens of the municipality of Julius, of Utica (now Biserta in Africa).

M. N. *Moneta Narbonensis.*—Money of Narbonne.

MO. *Moneta.*

MODERATIONI. A richly decorated shield, in the centre of which is the full front-faced head of Moderation.—On a second brass of Tiberius.—See *Clementia.*

MODIVS, a bushel measure—of wheat for instance, or any dry or solid commodity. It contained the third part of an *amphora,* and four of these measures per month was the ordinary allowance given to slaves.

On Roman coins we see the *modius* represented with corn-ears, and sometimes a poppy hanging or rising from it—and having reference to distributions of wheat to the people, by various Emperors, such as Nerva, Vespasian, M. Aurelius, and Domitian. On a denarius of Nerva, with the legend cos. iiii., there is a *modius* with six ears of corn. The *modius* is also the sign of the Ædileship on coins of the *Papia* and other families, and is represented full of wheat, between two ears of corn, as the symbol and attribute of *Abundantia* and of *Annona* (see the words). The coins of Nero, and from that Emperor down to Gallienus, furnish frequent examples of this figure as indicating the fruits of fertility, whether domestic or foreign; and the Imperial liberality and providence in procuring, and in bestowing them on the people.—See *Spica.*

MOESIA, a country of Europe, between Mount Hemus and the Danube, joining to Pannonia. There were two provinces of Mœsia, now called *Servia* and *Bulgaria*. The latter (or Upper Mœsia) lying towards the Black Sea, and which was subdued by the Romans under L. Piso, during the reign of Augustus, the former (or Lower Mœsia) was inhabited by the *Getæ*. See P. M. S. COL. VIM. *Provinciæ Mœsiæ Superioris Colonia Viminacium.*—The Roman legions stationed in the Upper Province are honoured by one of the large brass of Hadrian, on which, with the legend EXERCITVS MOESIACVS, that Emperor stands on an estrade addressing four soldiers. A visit paid by the same Prince to the province itself is also commemorated on another large bronze medal, inscribed ADVENTVI AVG. MOESIAE, and exhibiting the Emperor and the Province sacrificing at an altar.

MON. *Moneta* (the Goddess.)

MONET. AVG. *Moneta Angusti.*—The mint of the Emperor.

MO. S. T. *Moneta Signata Treveris.*

M. S. TR. Money struck at Treves.

M. S. AVGG. ET CAESS. NOSTR. *Moneta Sacra Augustorum et Cæsarum Nostrorum.*— The sacred mint of our Emperors and of our Cæsars. Inscription on coins of Diocletian, Val. Maximian, Constantius Chlorus, and Gal. Maximian.

MONETA.—This term was used by the Romans to designate their public mint, in consequence of money having originally been struck at Rome, in the temple of *Juno Moneta*—a surname given to the consort of Jupiter, because she was said to have counselled the Romans to undertake none but just wars, in which case she promised that they should never be in want of money.—The name of *Moneta* was afterwards used alike to signify pieces of money, and the *officinæ* or workshops in which they were fabricated.—There are some consular denarii of the *Carisia* family, which on their obverse represent the head of a woman, with the legend MONETA; and on the reverse a pair of pincers,

an anvil, and a hammer—instruments used by the ancients in the coinage of money—these are surmounted by the cap of Vulcan, and circumscribed by the word T. CARISIVS.—Upon another silver coin of the same family, similar monetal instruments are figured, the accompanying legend being SALVTARIS.—See *Carisia*.

The epithet SALVTARIS refers to Juno Moneta having afforded relief to the Romans when their affairs were straightened by the events of war. The head of the Goddess is also found with but slight difference on coins of the *Plætoria* family. The legend MONETA is indeed, as has

already been remarked, very frequently seen on medals of the Emperors, and particularly on medals of the lower empire.

MONETA, typified as a woman holding the balance and cornucopiæ, occurs on coins of nearly all the Emperors, from Vitellius to Constantine the Great, both inclusive, with the epigraph of AEQVITAS—AEQVITAS AVG. &c.; or with the inscription MON, AVG.—MONETA AVGG. &c.—The head of the Goddess, with MONETA round it, appears on a silver coin of the *Plætoria* and (as above-mentioned) of the *Carisia* family.

MONETÆ—the *three* standing with their accustomed attributes, sometimes with and other times without the mass of metal at the feet of each female, make their first appearance on a brass medallion of Commodus.—Under the reign of Septimius Severus they begin frequently to display themselves; and they are also found on coins of the following princes:—Caracalla, Geta, Elagabalus, Alexander, Maximinus, Gordianus III., the Philips, Trajan Decius, Herennius, Trebonianus Gallus, Claudius Gothicus, Tetricus, Tacitus, Florianus, Probus, Carus, Carinus, Numerianus, Diocletianus, Val. Maximianus, Constantius Chlorus, Gal. Maximianus, Maxentius, Maximinus Daza, Constantine and Family, Jovian, Valentinian, and down to Valens.—The illustration given above is from a brass medallion of Diocletian.

MONETA AVGVSTA. *(The mint of the Emperor.)*—A woman standing with balance and cornucopiæ, (or as in Alexander Severus,) dropping coins from her right hand into a measure.—Coins bearing the image of the Goddess *Moneta*, with the above epigraph, occur for the first time in the reign of Domitian, in whose honour they were struck for his imputed care in restoring purity, exact weight, and good workmanship, to the coinage of the empire. Certain it is that the medals of this otherwise worthless prince, are in every metal finely designed and boldly executed. The recurrence of this legend and type on so many imperial medals of divers reigns is in itself one of the clearest and most direct proofs that these medals were real money.

MONETA AVG.—A female figure, with the usual attributes of Moneta. On a most rare silver coin of Pescennius Niger, edited by Vaillant, who says—" Moneta is exhibited on the coins of Pescennius to denote the supreme right which he asserted over the imperial mint.

The woman holds the balance to shew that the quantity of metal was to be weighed, and a just portion assigned to each piece."

MONET. AVG. COS. II.—Moneta, with her accustomed attributes. On a very rare coin of Albinus.

The coining of gold and silver money was a right which Augustus and his imperial successors reserved to themselves exclusively, leaving to the Senate the privilege of striking brass money.— Albinus, whom Severus had made his associate in the empire, had the same right as the latter to coin money, and he exercised it throughout his short, but eventful, career of power.

MONETA AVG.—Moneta personified in the usual form.—This legend and type occur on a silver coin of Julia Domna, the wife of Severus, and indicate the supreme authority which that ambitious woman was allowed to share with her husband, who had yielded to her the privilege of the Roman mint. There is a medallion of Julia with the three Monetæ, and the epigraph *Aequitas Publica;* the same may be observed on coins of Julia Paula, Julia Aquilia, and Julia Mæsa, struck under Elagabalus; also on coins of Salonina, wife of Gallienus, and other *Augustæ.*

MONETA AVGG.—The three *Monetæ* standing.—This type and legend occur (says Vaillant) on coins of Volusianus, not because he was the restorer of purity to the Roman mint, for his silver was not better than that of his predecessors; but simply to shew a new coinage struck with his image. This coin, in gold, is of the utmost rarity.

MON*eta* RESTITVTA. S. C.—Moneta standing, with balance and cornucopiæ; at her feet a heap of metal.—This epigraph and figure appear on a second *brass* of Alexander Severus. Another brass coin of the same Emperor, and the same module, bears the legend of RESTITVTOR MON. S. C., and represents Alexander wearing the paludamentum, extending his right arm, and a spear in his left hand.

Alexander is the only Emperor who boasts of being the *restorer of the mint* (restitutor Monetæ and Moneta *restituta).*—Eckhel, in his annotation on these two coins, after quoting a long passage from Lampridius, whom he shews to be no safe authority to guide the opinion of a practical numismatist, appeals to the fact that the silver coinage of Alexander is not purer than that of preceding reigns, but rather more adulterated, "so that (he adds) were it not for the testimony of the above-named author, and the legends of the medals in question, we should not know that this Emperor had made any improvement whatever in the state of monetary affairs."

MONETA IOVI ET HERCVLI AVGG.— Moneta with her attributes, standing between Jupiter and Hercules, standing in like manner with their respective attributes.—Brass medallion of Diocletian.

The brass medallions of Diocletian are rare, but this is amongst the rarest of them, and forms a curious deviation from the common types under which the *Moneta Augustorum* is represented.—We here see depicted, as supporters on each hand of the Monetary Goddess, the tutelary divinities of those two cruel persecutors of the Christians—Diocletianus, who called himself *Jovius,* after Jupiter, and Maximianus, who assumed the name of *Herculius,* after Hercules.

MONETA VRBIS VESTRAE. The mint of your city.—This unusual expression of *Vestræ* in this legend, which (accompanied by the three *Monetæ)* is found on brass medallions of Crispus, and Constantinus, jun., indicates (according to the opinion of Du Cange,) that the right of coinage was conceded to other cities besides Rome, from the period when Claudius is supposed to have taken away from the Senate the power of striking money.

MONETA SACRA.; in others SACRA MONET. AVGG. ET CAESS. NOSTR.; in others SACRA MON. VRB. AVGG. ET CAESS. NN.—Woman standing, with balance and cornucopiæ. On second brass of Diocletian. The above are common under the reign of this Emperor.

The *divinity* whom the avarice of individuals in every age had made an object of private adoration, has at length a public expression of honour consecrated to her; and "we now (says Eckhel) find *Moneta* called SACRA." This appellation was assigned to the public mint, doubtless, on account of the vast advantages which it confers on mankind, whom in return it behoves to guard that institution from being violated, either by adulteration of metal or diminution in weight. Accordingly, to preserve its sacred character, the penalties of sacrilege were denounced against offenders of this description, similar to those enacted for the punishment of such as had dared to assault the *Tribuni Plebis.*—The inscription *Sacra Moneta urbis,* which from Diocletian's time becomes more and more frequent, is recorded on the marble, cited by Muratorius, and at the conclusion of which, as appears from the correct emendation of Marini, is read—CVRANTE VAL. PELAGIO *Viro Egregio* PROC*uratore Sacrae Monetæ* V*rbis* VNA. CVM. P.P. *(præpositis)* ET. OFFICINATORIBVS. Lastly, it may be observed that long before this, the Antiochians used the inscription MON*eta* VRB*is* on their coins.

MONETAL TRIUMVIRS.—From the commencement of the republican form of government at Rome, the coinage of money was entrusted to three officers, who bore the title of IIIVIR., A.A.A. F.F., which signifies *Triumviri Auro, Argento, Aere, Flando, Feriundo.* The supposed date of their institution is about the year of Rome 465 (289 before Christ).—Julius Cæsar added one more person to this Monetary Triumvirate, who thus became IIIIVIRI. But the number was again reduced to three by Augustus.—From their first institution under the republic, these Monetal Magistrates were invested with a supreme degree of authority in all things that related to the fabrication of money; a striking proof of which is exhibited in the privilege which belonged to them of recording, by means of types and legends, facts connected with the history of their ancestors or of other branches of their families.—On money struck during the existence of the republic, and even afterwards, the names of those who formed the potent triumvirate of the mint, together with the initial letters which indicate their office, were inscribed on medals of Roman die. But it is to the ancient marbles that we are obliged to resort for information as to the different appellations given to the workmen employed in the various processes of the coinage. We there find the following denominations :—*Monetarii; Officinatores monetæ aurariæ, argentariæ, Cæsaris; Numularii officinarum argentareum; Familiæ monetariæ; Numularii officinatores monetæ; Exactores auri, argenti, aeris; Signatores; Suppostores; Malleatores; Flatores.* But though the officers and even the mere artizans of the mint are thus noticed, yet neither the coins themselves, nor any writers on monuments of antiquity, furnish the slightest particulars respecting the artists who engraved the dies for the mint of Rome. There is, however, an antique inscription, (edited by Marini), which bears these words— NOVELLIVS AVG. LIB. ATIVTOR PRAE- POS*itus* SCALPTORVM SACRAE MONE- TAE,—See *Triumviri Monetales.*

MONETARII, coiners, or workmen of the mint.—Amonst the Romans they formed, with their wives and their children, an immense body, exclusively employed in the fabrication of specie, and, doubtless paid from the public treasury, were under the orders of particular magistrates. It is not to be supposed, however, that there would have been so vast a number of them, if in ancient times the process of striking coins had been as simple as it is become in our days.—The *monetarii* were, moreover, of the lowest order, and classed so much as a matter of course amongst those who follow menial occupations, that the path to honours was closed to them, and their position in society differed little from that of slaves.—On coins of the Cornelia family, edited in the Pembroke collection, we read CVR. ✠ FL. CVR*ator Denariorum* FL*andorum.* And as in the age of Julius and of Augustus, *Triumviri* or *Quatuorviri* were appointed as mint-masters, so in the reign of Diocletian and his successors, the superintendents of those who coined the money of the empire were called *Procuratores Monetæ,* or *Præpositi Monetæ.*

The *monetarii* not unfrequently made blunders, especially in the case of plated coins, where the type was least accordant with the legend.—Frœlich and Morell notice many instances of monetal errors committed by the workmen, and amongst others that of producing a duplicate impression of the type when the medal was turned on the die. Of these *lapsi monetariorum* several examples are given in the *Mus. Pembroch.*

MONOGRAMMA. Monogram.—This name is given to a figure which joins together several letters, so that they seem to make but one.— Monograms are thus characters composed of many united letters, and therefore differ from the ligature which is only a connecting stroke which unites several letters. Monograms, which are very frequent on Greek money, are seldom found on Latin medals, except on those of Roman families.—Millin, in his *Dictionnaire des beaux Arts,* after acknowledging the great learning and research displayed by Montfaucon, Frœlich, Combe, Torremuzza, Pellerin, Rasche, and other distinguished numismatists, in their endeavours to explain the meaning of monograms, observes that "the pains thus taken can hardly be regarded as otherwise than useless, since these abbreviations are for the most part incapable of being deciphered, and to be considered in no other light than as conventional signs, whose signification was known perhaps only to a few persons. Possibly (he adds) these monograms were adopted for the purpose of throwing difficulties in the way of forgers. It may be as well to know what letters are represented by such and such monograms, but with the exception of some, it is lost labour to attempt to discover their meaning."

Monograms appear on coins of the *Calpurnia, Didia, Papiria,* and other Roman families.

MONOGRAMMA CHRISTI.—The monogram of Christ ☧ is observed on coins of Constantine the Great, Licinius, jun., Constantine, jun., Constans, Constantius II., Vetranio, Magnentius, Decentius, Constantius Gallus, Jovianus, Valentinianus I., Valens, Procopius, Gratianus, Valentinianus II., Theodosius, Magnus Maximus, Arcadius, Honorius, and most of the Emperors of the East down to Heraclius.—See *Decentius.*

MOS. *Moneta Ostiæ Signata.*—These initials are found under the exergue of coins struck under Maxentius and others.—See Banduri, who also gives MOSP. MOST. MOSTA. MOSTB., &c.

MOS. S. T. or TR. *Moneta Signata Treveris.* —Money struck at Treves.

M. POP. *Marcus Popilius.*—Mark Popilius, prænomen and name of a man.

M. R. P. *Moneta Romæ Percussa.*

M. S. *Mæsia Superior.*—P. M. S. COL. VIM. *Provinciæ Mæsiæ Superioris Colonia Viminacium.*

M. S. or MVN. S. *Munitæ sunt.*—See QVOD. V. M. S. *Quod Viæ Munitæ sunt;* on coins of Augustus.

M. S. AVGG. NOSTR. *Moneta Sacra Augustorum Nostrorum.*—The sacred mint of our Emperors.

MV. *Municipium.*—MV. AVGVSTA BILBILIS, in Hispania Tarraconensis.

MVCIVS; name of the Mucia family.—C. Mucius was a distinguished architect in the time of Marius, about v.c. 653.

MVCIA. A plebeian family. The surname *Cordus.*—The only coin attributed to it is one, respecting which it holds a contested claim for, with the *Fufia* family. The denarius in question has on its obverse KALENI, with two jugated heads, one juvenile and laureated, near which are the letters HO; and the other juvenile and helmeted, near which is the word VIRT — Eckhel remarks that the Mucia family was equally worthy with the Fufia to claim the distinction of *Honor* and *Virtus*, by adorning their medal with the heads of those favourite Roman divinities. This silver coin is rare. That in gold is pronounced by Mionnet to be false.

MVL. *Multa.*—MVL. FEL. *Multa Felicia.*— Vows made for the Emperors, and wishing them prosperity and happiness.

MVL. X. MVL. XX. MVLT. XXX.— *Multis Decennalibus. Multis Vicennalibus. Multis Tricennalibus.*—Other kinds of vows and acclamations, by which the Emperors were wished long life, as of many tens or scores of years, or many thirties of years, &c.—See VOTA.

MVLT. XXXX. *Multis,* or *Multiplicatis Quadricennalibus,*—On a gold coin of Constantius jun.—Eckhel, *Catal.*

Mules.—Vehicles drawn by these animals were amongst the accustomed shews of funeral pomp connected with the interment of womens' remains. It was a custom borrowed by the Romans from eastern nations.

The *Carpentum Mulare,* or covered chariot, with two mules, is a type of consecration. [See *Carpentum—Consecratio—Thensa.*] One of these with the epigraph S.P.Q.R. IVLIAE AVGVST., in honour of Livia, appears on a first brass of Tiberius.—A funeral biga of mules appears on large brass of *Agrippina,* wife of Germanicus; and of *Domitilla,* wife of Vespasian, with the word MEMORIAE preceding their respective names.—The same type appears on a silver coin of *Marciana,* Trajan's sister, with the epigraph CONSECRATIO; and also on a first brass of *Faustina* senior.—A carpentum, drawn by two mules, appears on a rare first brass of *Julia Titi,* struck after her death, under the 15th consulate of Domitian, and which by the sacred title of DIVA prefixed to her name, proves that that princess had been placed by her "incestuous uncle" in the rank of divinities.—But we see other instances, as the intelligent author of *Leçons de Numismatique Romaine* says, that "the car and pair of mules were not exclusively appropriated to designate consecrations."

MVMMIA, a plebeian family, but of consular rank.—Goltzius alone, and on his authority Morell assign coins to it, which, however, are not recognised either by Eckhel, Mionnet, or Akerman.

MVN. or MVNI. *Municipium.*—MVN. AVG. BILBILIS. *Municipium Augusta Bilbilis.*—The municipality of Augusta Bilbilis.

MVN. CAL. IVL. *Municipium Calaguris Julia.*—See *Calaguris.*

MVN. CLVN. *Municipium Clunia.*—Municipium of Clunia, an ancient city of Spain (now Corunna.)

MVN. FANE. AEL. *Municipium Fanestre Ælium.*

MVNICIP. STOB. or STOBENS.—*Muni-* *cipium Stobensium.*—Municipium of the Stobians, in Macedonia.

MVNIC. ITAL. PER. AVG.—*Municipium Italicense Permissu Augusti.*—The Italian Municipality (of Hispania Bœtica, now Andalusia), by permission of the Emperor.

MVN. IVL. VTICEN. D. D. P. P.—*Municipii Julii Uticensis Decuriones Posuere.*— The Decurions of the Municipality of Utica; (or, of Julius, of Utica), have placed, &c.

MVNICIPI PARENS.—See Vaillant *(Præst. Num. Impp,* iii. 104).

MVN. TVR. or MV. TV.—*Municipium Turiaso,* in *Hispania Tarraconensis.*

MVNAT. *Munatius.*

MVNATIA, a plebeian family, surnamed *Plancus.*—L. Munatius Plancus joined Cæsar the Dictator, and in the beginning of the civil war in Spain took up arms against L. Afranius; was appointed by Cæsar Prefect of Rome, and next governed in Gaul as Pro-consul. Afterwards, in V.C. 714, Mark Antony promoted him to the government of Asia; and he served his second Consulship in 718.—Morell notes three varieties in the coins of the Munatia family.— Its gold and silver pieces were struck under Mark Antony, and are rare, particularly the latter; one of which is inscribed L. PLANCVS PRAEF*ectus* VRB*is*—and another bears the same surname followed by PRO CO*n*S*ul.*

The following rare coin, struck in gold and silver by the monetal triumvir, by order of his patron and chief Mark Antony, is curious from its exhibition of sacrificial instruments and religious symbols:—

M. ANTON. IMP. AVG*ur* IIIVIR. R. P. C. —The lituus and the præfericulum.

Rev—L. PLANCVS IMP. ITER.—The præfericulum between a thunderbolt and a caduceus.

For a further account of Munatius Plancus, and some remarks on a brass medal of extreme rarity, bearing the head of that consular personage, see the word *Plancus.*

MVNICIPIA.—This name was given to towns in the Roman provinces, whose inhabitants had obtained from the Senate, with the consent of the people, some or all of the civic rights and privileges of Rome, and were allowed to govern themselves by their own laws.—Sometimes the *coloniæ Romanorum* are called *municipia*; but this appears to arise from writers being in the habit of indiscriminately using one word for the other. That there was, however, a marked distinction between the *coloniæ* and the *municipia,* and that the superiority of condition rested with the latter, is shewn by a passage in Aulus Gellius, wherein he relates that the Emperor Hadrian expressed his indignant surprise that the inhabitants of *Italica,* (in Spain,) the place whence he himself derived his origin, and which had been elevated to the rank of a *municipium,* should have petitioned him to bestow on them the rights of a colony.

Among the privileges granted by Rome, under her Emperors, to these *municipal* cities, was the right of coinage; and taking as their inhabitants did the title of Roman citizens, they were subject to no burthens or offices but such as were imposed on the Romans themselves. It is not precisely known what were the nature and extent of power yielded in this instance; but the towns on whom these peculiar privileges were conferred did not fail to stamp on their money the name of *Municipium.*—On those of the Spanish provinces a bull appears to be the customary symbol; as may be seen on coins of Cascantum, Ercavica, Graccurris, Osicerda, &c.— For a review of the *Municipia* of Imperial medals, see Vaillant's learned and *unique* work on the *Colonies of Rome;* of the principal points of information contained in which an analysis has been attempted in this Dictionary.

MVNIFICENTIA.   Munificence.—Another term for expressing the magnificent liberality of the reigning prince to the Roman people, in giving them public shews, or spectacles, with the accustomed exhibition of games.   We find it commonly represented on coins of Antoninus Pius, Commodus, Severus, and Elagabalus, by the symbol of a lion or of an elephant.   On a brass medallion of Gordianus Pius, which presents the figure of a man sitting on an elephant, and fighting with a bull in the Flavian amphitheatre, the inscription added is MVNIFICENTIA GORDIANI AVG.—The incomparable munificence of Hadrian is most elegantly complimented on that most rare coin, in first brass, which bears the epigraph LOCVPLETATORI ORBIS TERRARVM. —The munificence displayed by different Emperors, at stated times, in the distribution of largesses to the Roman people is frequently recorded on their coins, nuder the designation of CONGIARIA DATA POP. R., or LIBERALITAS AVG.— Other examples of imperial *munificence*, either in the remission of taxes *(centesimæ, ducentesimæ, quadragesimæ)*, or in the abolition of outstanding claims on state-debtors are to be found in the same series of Roman coins.

MVNIFICENTIA AVG. COS. IIII.—An elephant harnessed in armour.   The types of two coins (the former a brass medallion, the latter a second brass,) of Antoninus Pius, most clearly explain what Capitolinus relates of that Emperor.   " He gave public spectacles, *(munera)* in which were exhibited ELEPHANTS, and *crocutæ* (a mongrel beast of Ethiopia), and bouquetins (strepsicerotæ) with *tigers*, and all rare animals from every part of the world. He also shewed a hundred LIONS at one display."—It is under this prince that the epigraph MVNIFICENTIA first appeared on coins (to which Eckhel assigns the date v.c. 902), though it became of frequent occurrence in subsequent reigns, with the accompanying type of some wild or foreign animal destined to be hunted in the arena of the amphitheatre.   For the word *munus* was used by the old writers to signify a shew of wild beasts, or a combat of gladiators, as Cicero says—*Magnificentissima vero nostri Pompeii munera secundo consulatu.*—(See Eckhel, vol. vii. p. 19.)

It is also to be observed that on the second coin the elephant is represented in a covering of armour (loricatus).   The first type of this kind is seen on medals of Titus, about the year of Rome 833.   That it alludes to the games then celebrated by that Emperor is more fully proved, because of Titus it is said by Suetonius—*et tamen nemine ante se* MVNIFICENTIA *minor. Amphitheatro dedicato, thermisque juxta celeriter exstructis, munus edidit adparatissimum, largissimumque.*—The same type of a loricated elephant, with the legend MVNIFICENTIA AVG. recurs on coins of Commodus, in the year v.c. 936 (when he shewed his wondrous skill in archery at a public spectacle), and also on coins of Severus in 950 (before he set out on his Parthian expedition), and is therefore to be regarded like that of Gordianus Pius above quoted, as indicating some grand display of Roman prodigality and cruelty in the sports and combats of the amphitheatre.—See *Elephant.*

MVNIFICENTIA GORDIANI AVG.—The Flavian Amphitheatre, in which a bull and an

elephant (the latter with a man sitting on it) are opposed to each other.   On each side of the amphitheatre is an edifice; by the side of that on the left stands a colossal figure of Hercules.

To a description of this remarkable type, which appears on a brass medallion of Gordianus III., Eckhel appends the following illustrative note.   After adverting to the word *Munificentia*, accompanied with the figure of an elephant on coins of Antoninus Pius (see preceding column of this work), he says—"Livy has recorded that elephants first appeared in the games of the circus, in the year v.c. 586. Extravagance keeping pace with the increase of wealth, they were frequently introduced into the spectacle, and afforded a sight, not only extraordinary, but in many instances pitiable. Pompey the Great, in his second Consulate, exhibited altogether eighteen of these animals, which, wounded and mutilated as they were during the progress of the performances, met with the commiseration even of the people, when, on feeling their wounds they desisted from the combat, and moving round the circus, with their trunks lifted into the air, they appeared to entreat the interference of the spectators, and to call their lords to witness, reminding them, as it were, of the oath by which they had been induced to allow themselves to be allured from Africa.   This is Dion's account; to which Pliny, writing on the same subject, adds that the people were so excited with indignation at this spectacle, that disregarding the general in chief *(imperator)*, and the signal munificence displayed by him in their honour, they rose as one man, with tears in their eyes, and showered on Pompey imprecations, the weight of which he soon afterwards experienced.—Cicero, also, who was a spectator on the occasion, has related, that great as was the astonishment of the people, they felt no gratification at the sight, but rather that a feeling of pity followed the exhibition, and an opinion that there was a kind of affinity between that animal and the human race.—" For myself," adds Eckhel, "I would willingly bestow my praise on the feeling displayed by the people, who suffered themselves to be touched by the toils and pains even of beasts. But I am reluctantly compelled to withhold my commendations, when I reflect on the inconsistent sympathies of this same populace, which, desiring that the blood of brutes should be spared, could feed its eyes and thoughts with the slaughter of human beings in the arena.—I now recur to the coin itself, which represents the Amphitheatre of the Flavii (at Rome), and within it, in addition to the elephant, a bull also; for these animals used anciently to be pitted against each other; Martial having described such a combat."—*Doct. Num. Vet.* vol. vii. p. 315.

MURAL CROWN.—The *Corona Muralis* was given by the Emperor to him who first scaled the wall or fortifications of an enemy's town or camp.—M. Agrippa was decorated with both the mural and the rostral crown; with the former for having suppressed an insurrection in Rome; and he bore the latter also on account of his victory over Sextus Pompey.—The mural crown is an attribute of Cybele; and its turreted circlet is found adorning the head of those images which serve as the personifications of cities and provinces.—See *Corona*.

M. VRB. *Moneta Urbis.*—The mint or money of the City.—See M. VRB. AVGG. ET. CAESS. N.N. *Sacra Moneta Urbis Augustorum Et Cæsarum Nostrorum.*—On a coin of Constantius Chlorus.

MVRCVS, surname of L. Statius, as it is read on a coin of the *Statia* family.

MVRENA, surname of the *Licinia* family.

MVREX, a shell-fish, of the liquor whereof was made the celebrated purple of the Tyrians; accordingly it forms the numismatic symbol of Tyre.—It is said that the inventor of this purple dye made the discovery by accidentally observing the jaws of his dog tinctured with the liquor of the *murex*.—A colonial medal of Tyre, struck under Elagabalus, and another under Gallienus, are given by Vaillant as exhibiting the murex, or *conchylium*.—See *Tyrus*.

MVS—a mouse or rat—the figure of one is seen under a horse on a coin of the *Quinctia* family, on which are the letters TI. Q.—Havercamp not improbably conjectures that this medal refers to some TI*berius Quinctius*, who perhaps had the surname (like Decius) of *Mus*.

MVSÆ *(Muses)*, the goddesses of song, of verse, and of civilization, given to mankind through the medium of music and poesy.—The daughters of Jupiter and of *Mnemosyne* (Memory), their usual abode were the heights of Parnassus, except when they assisted at the banquets of the gods. At first there were only three of them, but the poets successively increased their number to *nine*, and artists represented them sometimes together, at others in separate figures, in a great variety of compositions. Amongst the rest, the *muses* are found on the denarii of the *Pomponia* family, on account of the analogy between the name of *Pomponius Musa* (who caused their images to be thus exhibited), and the generic designation of these "Heavenly maids." They are ordinarily depictured in long dresses and the neck covered. Sometimes, however, the shoulder and the arm are naked, to facilitate their performance on the *cithara* or harp.—At Rome one temple of worship was common to them and to *Hercules Musagetes*.

In Morell's *Thesaurus Fam. Rom.*, amongst the coins of the *Pomponia* family, are given the types of denarii, on which Ursin, Vaillant, and Havercamp have, each in their turn, exercised their spirit of research and ingenuity, to distinguish successively by their habiliments and attributes the respective personifications of the whole choral troup. The same difficulty has, however, opposed itself to the success of this attempt at discriminating the different demigoddesses, which is experienced with regard to the sculptures of the celebrated sarcophagus published by Spon; because, unlike the case of the Herculaneum pictures, no names of muses are inscribed, but the inquirer is left to identify each member of the "tuneful choir," merely from the accompanying insignia, which are not in all instances either clearly delineated, or exclusively appropriated.—Of each of this series, the obverse bears the head of a young female, laureated, (representing the muse,) with a *volumen*, or a star, or a garland, or some other distinctive mark, behind it.—On the reverse we see a female figure, and the words MVSA. Q. POMPONI.—The types and substance of the explanations are as follow, viz. :—

Calliope, the inventor of the heroic poem *(carmen heroicum)* stands holding in her right hand a rolled volume, her left arm resting on a column, with the epigraph Q. POMPONIVS MVSA.

Clio, inventress of the lyre *(cithara)*, stands holding against her side with the left hand that musical instrument, the strings of which she touches with her right, as if playing on it, not with the *plectrum*, but (what was more highly esteemed) with the fingers.

Erato, who invented hymns to the Gods, is represented as if singing; with dishevelled locks she stands, clothed in the stola, quietly holding her right hand thrust into her vest; the *graphium*, or iron pen, is in her left hand, which hangs down.

Euterpe, the inventor of Tragedy, stands

resting her right hand on a club, and holding a mask in her left.—The *sceptrum* (says Havercamp in Morell) which appears behind the head of the female on the obverse of this denarius shews to what muse the image on its reverse is to be assigned, viz., to Euterpe, to whom, as above stated, the invention of Tragedy was imputed by the Greeks.

In describing *Tragedia* herself, Ovid says—

Læva manus sceptrum late regale tenebat.

The costume and attributes of the muse on this coin are singular: she not only holds a massy club, but she wears the lion's skin for a head-dress. The *carmen tragicum* seems to have been regarded by Ovid as robust, violent, immortal, and therefore truly Herculean. Thus he sings (in his Amor. iii. 1. 68) :—

Exiguum vati concede, Tragœdia, tempus.
Tu, labor œternus, quod petit illa, breve est.

Melpomene, to whom Horace ascribes the epigram, stands playing on a *barbiton* resting on a pillar before her; the right hand, with extended fingers, strikes the strings, and the left supports the instrument. She seems to be accompanying her voice on this harp.

Polymnia, to whom the invention of the *barbiton* is attributed by Horace (L. i. Od. i.), stands with right hand hanging down, holding the *plectrum* : she supports the lyre in her left hand, and her right foot is slightly uplifted. This last named attitude alone (as we are told) proclaims this type to be that of "*Polymnia mater chorea;*" for it was by the silent movement of the foot that regular time was given to the song. And thus on this denarius the goddess (as Havercamp quotes from Virgil (in *Catalectis,)*

Carmina vultu
Signat cuncta, manu, loquitur Polyhymnia gestu.

Terpsichore, who taught the act of playing on the pipes *(calamos inflare)* is recognised by Morell in the female figure, clothed in the *stola,* who stands supporting her head on her left hand, which she rests on a column, whilst she holds two flutes *(tibiæ)* in her right hand.—Others, however, refer this type to Euterpe.

Thalia, the inventress of comedy, and delineator of the manners of society, stands with her left elbow resting on a column, and holding a theatric mask in her right hand.

Urania, the muse of astronomy, stands before a globe placed on a tripod, which she touches with a wand held in her right hand.—According to the old Greek epigram, Urania discovered the pole, or point of the axis, on which the ancients supposed the heavens to be turned, and also the mystic dance of the stars *(chorus celestium astrorum).*—For this reason a star is placed behind the head of this muse on the obverse of the medal.

MVSARVM.—See *Hercules Musarum.*

MVSSIDI. *Mussidius.*

MVSSIDIA, a family little known, except on the coins of Rome struck during the latest days of her republic. Its surname is *Longus.*—The silver are rare. There are pieces of this family, in gold and silver, struck by the moneyers of Julius Cæsar and of the triumvirate (Antony, Lepidus, and Octavius).—The brass coins of the Mussidia family are by the moneyers of Augustus, and are common.

Among twenty varieties given in Morell, there is a denarius of this family, bearing on one side either a portrait of Julius Cæsar, or the radiated head of the Sun, or the head of *Concordia*; and, on the reverse, a representation of the *Comitium,* in which is seen a distributer *(diribitor)* of voting tablets, and a citizen giving his suffrage. On the base of the *comitium* is inscribed CLOACIN, and above it is read L. MVSSIDIVS LONGVS.—See *Cloacina,* and *Comitium.*

MVTVA.—Mutual, reciprocated, equal on both sides.—See CARITAS MVTVA AVGG.—AMOR MVTVVS.—PIETAS MVTVA.—On coins of Balbinus and Pupienus.

Mysteries of Bacchus.—See *Cista Mystica*; also ASIA RECEPTA.

N.

N. the thirteenth letter of the Latins, is to be observed as a mint mark *(ad matrices discernendas)* on coins of the Antonia, Calpurnia, Cornelia, Fabia, Herennia, Julia, Junia, Mamilia, Poblicia, Servilia, Sulpicia, and other Roman families.

N. is also seen on the exergue, and in the field of coins of Gallienus, Claudius Gothicus, Quintillus, Probus, Diocletian, and of a subsequent age.

N. This letter signifies Natalis (birth), or Nepos (nephew), or Nobilis (noble), or Noster (ours), or Novus—Nova (new), or Numen (divinity), or Numus (money).

NN. *Nostri.*—The double N, like the double D and double G, denotes the plural, thus DD. NN. AVGG. *Dominorum Nostrorum Augustorum.* This letter is three times repeated on a coin of Constans, and on another of Valens, to express three *Augusti*—AVGGG. NNN.—and four times repeated on medals of Constantius Chlorus, Diocletian, and Val. Maximianus, to acknowledge the authority of two emperors and two Cæsars—as for example, AVGG. ET. CAESS. NNNN.

NAEVIA, a plebeian family—its name NAEVIVS —its surnames BALBUS, CAPELLA, SURDINUS.— The silver coins, of which there are many varieties, are common. Its brass pieces are by the moneyers of Augustus. None of them are interesting; very few rare.

Head of Venus, with S. C. in the field.

Rev.—C. NAE*vius* BALB*us.* Victory in a car drawn by three horses, at full speed.

The denarii of this type are all serrated.

Names on coins of Roman families.—See *Nomina Romanorum.*

NARBONENSIS. The Narbonnaise; part of Gaul, which, under the Romans, comprised Savoy, Dauphiny, Provence, the Cevennes, the county of Foix, and the rest of Languedoc.

NASIDIA, a family whose name comes forward late, and whose rank is plebeian. Some silver coins, however, bearing the name of this family, are by Sextus Pompey; and the following is both rare and interesting :—

NEPTVNI. The head of Pompey the Great, in front of which is a trident.

Rev.—Q. NASIDIVS. A ship with sails spread.
—This Nasidius was the præfect (or admiral) of Sextus Pompey's fleet in Sicily, and afterwards served in the same capacity under the appointment of Mark Antony.—See NEPTVNI.

NASO, surname of the *Axia* family, the first man of which had perhaps a large nose. L. AXIVS L. F. NASO.—It was the cognomen of Ovid, OVIDIVS NASO.

NAT. *Natalis.* Relating to birth.—ANN. DCCCLXXIIII. NAT. VRB. CIRC. CON. Anno 874. *Natalis Urbis Circenses Constituit,* on a coin of Hadrian, allusive to certain games of the circus, or combats, instituted on the anniversary day of the foundation of Rome, noticed in pp. 202 and 203 of this Dictionary.

NAT. *Nato.*—See CONSTANTINO P. AVG.
B.R.P. NAT. *Bono Rei Publicæ Nato.*

NAVALIS CORONA.—The naval crown was given to him who was the first to board an enemy's ship.—See *Corona.*

NAVIS—a ship or galley.—See the former word.

The representation of a ship's prow is the customary symbol of the Roman *As* and its parts.—See Eckhel's explanation as to its cause.—vol. v. p. 14.

NAVIS PRÆTORIA—or admiral's ship.—See *Prætoria Navis.*

NAVIVS.—The Augur Nævius, with head veiled, and holding the *lituus* in his left hand, kneels before Tarquinius Priscus, who stands clothed in the toga, and sees with astonishment the miracle performed of cutting a whetstone in two with a razor.

This inscription and type on a brass medallion of Antoninus Pius, assist in handing down, from the mass of Roman traditions that notable prodigy performed by Accius Navius for the *timely* and *effectual* removal of all doubts in the King's mind as to the veritable powers of augury !—See *Augur.*

N. C. *Nero Cæsar*—or *Nobilissimus Cæsar*—or *Nostri Cæsaris.*

N. CAPR.—Letters struck on some coins of Augustus, Germanicus, Drusus, Antonia Drusi, Claudius, and Agrippina. Some numismatists think that it signifies N*ota* C*usa* or N*ummus* C*usus,* A P*opulo* R*omano.*

NEAPOLIS, the name of many ancient cities; that which, on account of its *Latin* coins alone, comes within our province to notice, is *Neapolis,* in Samaria, situate at the base of Mount Garizim, and called *Sichem* in our Saviour's time. Its modern name is *Naplouse* or *Napulosa.*

It was near "Sichem, in the plain of Moreh," that (Genesis 12) the Patriarch Abraham dwelt, and built an altar to the Lord, as did also his descendant Jacob (Genesis 33). Of this place there are Imperial coins, with *Greek* legends, from Titus and Domitian to Antoninus Pius, M. Aurelius, Commodus, Caracalla, Elagabalus, and Maximinus. It was, as is believed, made a Roman *colony* by Philip senior, for the first coins struck by the Samarian Neapolis, in its colonial quality, have the head of that Emperor, and from his reign to that of Volusianus, its coins bear *Latin* as well as Greek inscriptions. The former run—COL. NEAPOL.; or COL. SERG. NEAPOL.; or COL. NEAPOL. NEOCORO.

The following are the types which appear on coins of this colony, on every one of which (besides the particular subject) appears a mount with a temple upon it, pointing to the site of Neapolis Samariæ, in the immediate vicinity of Mount Garizim :—

Colonist ploughing with oxen.—On a middle brass of Neapolis Samariæ dedicated to Otacilia, wife of Philip, appears this customary symbol of a Roman colony, above which is a temple on a mountain.

Cybele, seated between two lions, a patera in her right hand, a *cymbalum* in her left; above her is a mount with a temple upon it, with legend of COL. NEAPOL. *Colonia Neapolis,* or Neapolitana. On second brass of Philip senior. The goddess is represented on this medal as having been worshipped at Neapolis.

Æsculapius and Hygeia.—On a second brass of the same Emperor, the God of Medicine, seated, extends his right hand towards the Goddess of Health, who is standing opposite him ; both are respectively distinguished by their usual attributes.—The legend of this coin is COL. SERG. NEAPOL. *Colonia Sergia Neapolis.* At the upper part of this medal is a temple on a rock.

SERG*ia,* or *Sergiana,* or *Sergiapolitana,* is placed on this coin instead of its former appellation of *Flavia,* which it bore in honour of Vespasian and his family, under whom it first began to strike money. But why Neapolis should have adopted this word, after Philip had made it a colony, is difficult to comprehend. Vaillant ingeniously conjectures that the colonists selected and sent by the last named Emperor belonged to the tribe called *Sergia* at Rome, and hence the appellation on Philip's coin. Esculapius and Hygeia were deities of the colony, and their images were perhaps engraven on the above medal, in commemoration of sacrifices performed by the Neapolitans of Samaria for Philip the founder.

Silenus.—On two medals of this colony, inscribed to the same Emperor, Silenus stands in the usual manner; before him is a temple on a rock. On one of these medals (of which the rarity is very great) an eagle stands at the foot of Silenus, with legend COL. SERG. NEAPO.—On the obverse of the same coin appear the laureated heads of the two Philips, father and son, with the inscription D.D. N.N. PHILIPPIS AVGG. *Dominis Nostris Philippis Augustis.*

The example selected for illustration is taken from a brass coin in the British Museum. It is explained by the description given of the preceding varieties.

The image of the associate of Bacchus warrants the inference that as one of the minor deities the Pagan conquerors of Samaria worshipped him. On Mount Garizim (figured on this and all other coins of Neapolis), a temple had been built in honour of Jupiter, as is shewn by a passage in Josephus (lib. 12, cap. 7), stating that the Garizitanean temple was formerly dedicated to the Most High (and only true) God; but that the Samaritans sent ambassadors to Antiochus Epiphanes, petitioning him that as the temple had not hitherto the title of any God, it might thenceforth be called that of *Jupiter Græcanicus,* which request was granted. —The eagle with wings spread is regarded by some as an ensign of the Romans, whilst others think it refers to Jupiter, to whom the temple on Mount Garizim was dedicated.

Triumphal Quadriga.—The following singular type, on a first brass of this colony, struck under Philippus senior, is given in Pellerin's *Mélange,* i. pl. xxi. No. 2, p. 316:—

Rev.—NEAPOLI. NEOCOR. On a car drawn by four horses, abreast, the figure of a man is represented standing, facing to the front, having the right hand extended, and holding a spear in his left. Two other male figures, one at his right, the other at his left hand, hold each a spear in the left hand; he on the right side extends his right hand; and he on the left side raises his right hand over the centre figure, as if in the act of crowning him. In the upper part of the medal is seen Mount Garizim and a temple on its summit.

Wolf, with Twin Children.—This type (the accustomed symbol of Roman colonies) also appears on first and second brass of Philip senior, with a temple on Mount Garizim at the top of the coin. The legend of the reverse is COL. NEAPOLI NEOKORO. *Colonia Neapolitana Neocoros.*

The Neapolitan colony of Syria Palastina,

after the manner of the Greek cities in Asia Minor, adopted the inscription of *Neocoros.* The coins indeed exhibit the letter K for C, but the Romans used both letters, as in the instance of Calend and Kalend. The Neocori (Νεωκόροι) seem to have been the curators of sacred edifices, and managers of public games, or as in Latin they would be called *Aediles.*—See *Neocoros.*

Venus and Hercules.—On a first brass of Philip senior are the following legends and type, which Pellerin adds to those of Neapolis, edited by Vaillant:—

NEAPOL. NEOCORO. COL.—Venus, clothed, is standing before Hercules, who extends his hand towards her. Above is Mount Garizim with a temple, on one side of which is the sign of the sun, and on the other the sign of the moon.—*Mélange,* i. pl. xxi. No. 2, p. 317.

Eagle with expanded wings, beneath a temple on a rock, appears on a coin of Trebonianus Gallus, struck at Neapolis Samariæ, with *Greek* legends on both sides.

Legionary Eagle and Serapis.—On a second brass of Volusianus, struck by the colonists at the Samaritan Neapolis, Serapis stands opposite a cippus, on which is placed a legionary eagle with a military ensign; between them is a ram on one side and three corn-ears on the other; above them is a temple on a rock—legend COL. NEAPOL.

[The legionary eagle and military ensign on this coin shew that not only togated citizens from the *Sergia* gens (whence Neapolis is called Sergia) were transmitted to it (in Vespasian's time), but also that this colony was reinforced with legionary veterans. Serapis was worshipped at Neapolis as coins of M. Aurelius and Caracalla (Greek) serve to prove. The ears of corn signify their abundance in the territory of Neapolis. The ram (aries) seems to designate the season of spring, with which under the above-mentioned sign of the Zodiac the Neapolitans, like the Antiochians and Damascenes, were accustomed to begin this year, whilst some cities in these regions calculated theirs from autumn.]

Nebrus, an animal represented on coins of Gallienus, sacred on account of the chase, to Diana.

NE. CA. Q. PR. *Nerone Cæsare, Quæstore Provinciali.*—See *Utica.*

NE. CAES. *Nerone Cæsare.*

NEM. *Nemausus,* or *Nemauseniorum.*

Nemausus, a celebrated city in Gallia Narbonensis, so called from its founder of that name, was established as a *colony* of the Romans during the reign of Augustus. It is now called *Nismes,* in Languedoc (France). A large number of its coins, gold, silver, and brass, have been found at various times.—The *autonomous* medals of this colony, in second and third brass, have the head of Mars or of Rome for their type, and are inscribed NEM. COL., *Nemausus Colonia,* within a crown of laurel —The *imperial* medals struck at Nismes are of middle brass, and present on their obverse the heads of Augustus

and Agrippa placed back to back, with the inscription IMP. DIVI. F., *Imperator Divi Filius;* and, on the obverse, a crocodile attached by a chain to a palm-tree, with the epigraph COL. NEM.—The type refers to the conquest of Egypt, and its reduction into the form of a province.—Strabo speaks of *Nomausus* as of a colony invested with great privileges, among the rest that of the *jus Latii*; and an ancient inscription found at Nismes calls it COL*onia* AVG*usta*. Thus derived and constituted, the *Nemausenses* invariably struck the associated effigies of Agrippa with Augustus, and the image of the crocodile tied to a palm-tree, on their coins, as pointing to the origin and date of their colonial foundation. After Mark Antony's overthrow, a great many veterans from various Legions were, as a matter of necessity, sent to defend different colonies, partly in Italy, partly in other provinces. And those who were passed over to Nismes, having perhaps been themselves present in the Alexandrine war, were pleased to commemorate that occurrence by stamping on their coins also that symbol of vanquished Egypt which has just been described.

Nemesis, avenger of crimes and punisher of wicked doers. The divinity thus named and adored by the Greeks was also by the Romans held in high respect for the equitable and impartial severity of her chastisements; an altar was consecrated to her in the capitol; and there before setting out for battle, warriors resorted to immolate victims and to make her the offering of a sword. In a philosophic sense, Nemesis was the symbol of Providence, and of the care which the supreme power takes of what happens in this world.—On a medallion of Macrinus, struck at Cyzicus, Nemesis is crowned with towers, because it is the Fortune of Cyzicus.— *Nemesis* is recognised as having a sister goddess of the same name, though sometimes called *Adrastia*. The two avenging goddesses appear on Greek medallions of Marcus Aurelius, Antoninus, Severus, and others.—Millin says that these *Nemeses* are the two *Fortunæ Antiates*, which are seen on a denarius of the *Rustia* family, (see *Fortuna* and *Rustia)*. Both divinities, principally invoked in treaties of peace, were guarantees for the fidelity of oaths.—On Roman coins Nemesis has accordingly the same attributes with the Goddess of Peace *(Pax)*. The *Nemeses* of Smyrna, where they had a temple, appear on a brass medallion of Hadrian, standing, the one holding a wheel, the other a sword:

each has her right hand lifted to her mouth, with the inscription COS. III.—The Nemeses have often a finger placed on the mouth, to shew that it is necessary to be discreet.—On a very rare gold coin of the *Vibia* family, a winged woman stands, holding her robe. This figure Eckhel pronounces to be that of Nemesis, and gives examples of similar types on gold and silver coins of Claudius, in which the same winged figure of a female is walking, lifting her robe from the bosom towards the face with one hand, and holding a caduceus in the other, a serpent on the ground before her, with the inscription PACI AVGVSTAE.—Also on a silver coin of Hadrian there appears the same type of a woman, only that she holds a branch in her left hand, with VICTORIA AVG.—The former of these Eckhel calls the Nemesis of *Peace*, the latter the Nemesis of *Victory.*—[See vol. vi. pp. 237 and 511.]

NEP. *Nepos*, or *Nepoti*—Grandson.—DIVI NER. NEP. *Divi Nervæ Nepos.*—By this appellation Hadrian is frequently called in inscriptions, and sometimes, rarely, on coins (second brass.)

NEP. *Nepotianus.*—FL. NEP. CONSTANTINVS AVG.—See *Nepotianus*.

NEPOS *(Julius)*, born in Dalmatia, was son of Nepotianus, a general officer, and of a sister of Marcellinus, who had been made sovereign of that province under the reign of Severus III.

The Emperor Leo I. gave him the niece of his wife in marriage, and having first deposed Glycerius, declared him Emperor of the West and Augustus A.D. 474. Victorious, humane, courageous, he was both worthy to hold the sceptre and capable of re-establishing by his wisdom and justice the glory of that more truly Roman portion of the empire over which he had been placed. But his desire to preserve peace and tranquillity for his war-worn and exhausted people was frustrated by the revolt of Orestes, commander of the Gallic legions, an ambitious and intelligent usurper, who compelled Nepos to abandon Italy; and this unfortunate prince was, about four years after his dethronement, assassinated at Salona in Dalmatia, by two members of his own household, at the instigation of Glycerius, who had there afforded him an asylum, A.D. 480, having reigned in Italy one year and two months.

—His coins are all very rare. He is styled
D.N. IVLIVS NEPOS. P.F. AVG.; or D.N. IVLIVS
NEPOS. PERP. P.F. AVG. The example given
is from an aureus in the British Museum.

NEPOTIANUS *(Constantinus Flavius
Popilius)* was the son of a senator of that name,
and of Eutropia, sister to Constantine the Great.
He was consul in A.D. 336. In imitation of

Magnentius, he aspired
to the empire, assumed
the purple in June, A.D.
350; took the title of
Augustus, which his
gladiatorial mercenaries
pretended to confirm to
him; and after repulsing
Anicetus, prefect of the
Prætorians at Rome,
obtained easy possession of the capital of the
West. But this usurper had not the genius to
preserve to himself what his good fortune had
acquired. Instead of conciliating the Romans
who, from hatred to Magnentius, had received
him with pleasure, he struck terror through the
city with his proscriptions, and irritated the
inhabitants by his murderous cruelties. Within
a month the tyrant was killed, desperately defending himself, in a battle with Marcellianus,
one of the generals of Magnentius, who punished
Rome for her revolt by the most ferocious
execution of military vengeance on the wretched
people.—The only coins of Nepotianus probably
struck at Rome are in second brass, and of
the highest rarity. He is styled FL. POP.
NEPOTIANVS P. F. AVG.; and FL. NEP. CONSTAN-
TINVS AVG.—The example given above is taken
from a coin in the British Museum

Neptes Augustorum.—The grand-daughters
and grand-nieces of emperors were called
Augustæ, as Matidia, daughter of Trajan's
sister.

NEP. S. or SACR. *Neptuno Sacrum.*

NEPT. RED. *Neptuno Reduci,* as if Rome
was about to render thanks to Neptune, who
had been propitious to the Emperor's invocation,
and guarded him safely over the sea.

NEPT. *Neptunus.*—Neptune, son of Saturn
and Rhea, was one of the twelve greater
divinities of Greek and Roman worship. In the
partition of the world with his brothers Jupiter
and Pluto, the empire of the waters fell to his
share. Statues, medals, and engraved stones,
present to us the peculiar incidents of his fabled
history. His image differs but little from that
of Jupiter; there is a great conformity in the
arrangement of the hair of the head, and in the
form of the beard, but the expression of power
and majesty is comparatively feeble in the figure
of the Sea-King. He is usually pourtrayed
naked, or with a very light *chlamys.*—On some
medals, coins of Corinth and of Berytus, he is
seen drawn by sea-horses, which have the upper
portion of that animal, whilst the lower
extremities terminate in a fish's tail. This
imaginative creature is the *hippocampus.* Neptune carries a sceptre with three points or teeth,
called the trident.—Mythologists give many

reasons for this attribute, amongst others to
mark the triple authority of the God over the
sea, which he was supposed to have the power
of troubling and of calming, and which he also
preserves.—*Millin* suggests whether it may not
be regarded "as an instrument for catching
fish," and he instances the Greek fishermen, who,
to this day, make use of a similar instrument
for that purpose.—See *Berytus—Hippocampus.*

The poets have ascribed a prodigious number
of amatory adventures to Neptune, and made
him the father of various enterprising heroes
and warriors, the founders of cities. In Greece
and in Italy, especially in maritime places, a
great many temples were raised to his worship.
The Romans held him in such veneration that
festivals and games of the circus, at Rome,
were celebrated in his honour on the first of
July, and which were marked for that day in
their calendar by the words *D. Neptuni Ludi.*
What is most singular, as they believed that
Neptune formed the first horse, so all horses
and mules remained without working during the
feasts of this deity, and enjoyed a repose which
no one dared interrupt.—Neptune crowned by
Victory signifies the gratitude of him who
ascribed to that divinity the means of his gaining a naval victory.—The great number of
children assigned to this god arose from the
circumstance of those being generally called the
sons of Neptune who had distinguished themselves in sea fights, or by their skill in navigation. *Sextus Pompey,* puffed up with his naval
successes, chose to be so denominated; and we
find this title on his medals.—The temple of
Neptune is seen represented on a coin of the
Domitia family. The god himself placing his
foot on a globe, in a medal of Augustus
(inscribed CAESAR DIVI. F.), and in another of
Titus, indicates that the Emperors assumed
equally to be masters of land and sea. Besides
the trident, the dolphin, the rudder, and the
acrostolium were attributes of Neptune, and
bear reference on medals to maritime power.—
Neptune was held to be the author of earthquakes, which he produced by pressing the
earth with his feet; hence we often see him on
coins with sometimes the right, sometimes the
left foot on a globe.—See *Trident—Dolphin—
Acrostolium.*

Neptune, lying down, is seen on a coin of Nero,
representing the port of *Ostia.* He is figured
in a *sitting* posture, with a dolphin in the right
hand and trident in the left, on colonial coins
of Corinth, struck during the reigns of Domitian,
Antoninus Pius, M. Aurelius, and Commodus.
He *stands* naked on colonial coins of Augustus,
Trajan, Antonine. and Commodus.—See PORT.
OST.—and CORINTHVS.

Neptune standing, with dolphin and trident,
appears on a second brass medal of Agrippa,
with the epigraph of M. AGRIPPA. L. F. COS. III.,
his head bearing the rostrated crown.—See
Agrippa.

Neptune standing, to the right, his left hand
grasping a trident; behind him the Tiber;
NEPTVNO CIRCENS. REST. or CONSTIT.—On a

rare second brass of Nerva.—See Mr. R. Smith's "Catalogue of London Antiquities;" and "Num. Chron." vol iv. p. 150.

Neptune appears, on a brass medallion of Commodus, *standing*, with the trident in his right hand, a dolphin in his left, and his right foot on the prow of a vessel; the Emperor, full-faced and in the toga, sacrificing before him. The accompanying epigraph is PIO. IMP. OMNIA FELICIA, &c. *(see the words)*, which shews that Neptune was a type of Felicity and of Congratulation.

Neptune's head, with long beard, and crowned with laurel, appears on a coin of the *Proculeia* family. Medals of other Roman families exhibit similar busts of this deity.

NEPT*unus.*—This inscription accompanies the type of a temple of four columns, on a very rare gold coin of the *Domitia* family, struck by *Cn. Domitius Ahenobarbus*, son of L. Domitius, who in the year of Rome, 705, dared to resist Julius Cæsar's passage of the Rubicon, but afterwards became reconciled to Antony and Octavian's party. The temple of Neptune indicated by the abbreviated word NEPT., shews maritime power, which Domitius retained under the Triumvirate, as commander of a fleet of triremes, on the Italian coasts.

NEPT. COMITI.—Neptune standing, holding the trident; his right foot upon the prow of a vessel: on gold of Postumus.—*Tanini.*

NEP. RED.—Neptune stamping with his right foot on a globe, holds the *acrostolium* in his right hand, and a spear in the left. This type appears on gold and silver of Vespasian, and also recurs on coins of Titus.—Vespasian had, indeed, in the year of Rome 823 (A.D. 70), and Titus in the following year had safely returned to Rome, by a sea voyage; in consequence of which honours were rendered to Neptune under the name of *Redux.*

NEPTVNI.—On the obverse of one of Sextus Pompey's silver coins, this verbal dedication accompanies the head of his father, Pompey the Great, below which is a dolphin, and before it a trident.—The reverse presents a galley with swelling sail, and star near it. Another denarius, with the same portrait, has on the reverse side four galleys with their rowers. See *Nasidia* family.

Neptuni, inscribed over the head of *Pompeius Magnus*, was doubtless intended to be read *Neptuni filius*, "the son of Neptune," whom Sextus himself pretended to be! Hence the typical allusions on his medals are all maritime.

NEPTVNO REDVCI.—Neptune standing.

holding a dolphin, and the trident; at the feet, in some instances, an anchor: on coins of Postumus. In the example here engraved (from the cabinet of Mr. Roach Smith), Neptune holds what, no doubt, was intended for a dolphin, though it more resembles *an eel.*

NEPTVNO AVG.—Neptune standing, holds a dolphin in one hand, a trident in the other.—On a third brass of Claudius Gothicus.

NEPTVNO CIRCENS. (RESTIT. or CONSTIT.)—See "Num. Chron." vol. iv. p. 150; and "Eckhel," vol. vi. p. 406.

NEPTVNO CONS. AVG. *Neptuno Conservatori Augusti.*—This dedicatory inscription, with the accompanying type of a sea-horse, is quoted by Banduri as occurring on *silver* and *third brass* of Gallienus: on other third brass coins of the same Emperor the type is *Capricornus*, or the sea-goat. On these Eckhel remarks—"That the horse was held sacred to Neptune is generally known."

This compound animal is conjoined with Neptune, either because it terminates in the form of a fish; and according to Hyginus formerly inhabited the Nile; [this doubtless is an allusion to the *Hippopotamus* or River Horse]; or because it assailed the Titans with sea-shells.—"Banduri thinks that this coin was struck on occasion of the naval victory gained over the Scythians in the Euxine, of which Trebellius speaks, and confirms this opinion by a coin inscribed VICTORIA NEPT. But his reading is erroneous: it should be VICTORIA AET."—There is the same inscription to *Neptune the Preserver*, and the same type of a *sea-horse* on a third brass of *Tetricus Pater.*—The other coin, with the type of Capricorn, was unknown to Banduri.

NER. *Nero;* or *Nerva.*

NER. I. Q. VRB., as some interpret it *Nerva Primus Quæstor Urbis.*

Nereides.—Nereids were sea-nymphs, to whom the poets of antiquity ascribed the human form, and whom artists represented under the form of women as far as the waist, but terminating in two tails of fishes—in short the *mermaid* of the *middle ages.*—There is a figure exactly answering to this description on a silver coin of the *Valeria* family.

Neria, a plebeian family.—The following in silver is its only type:—NERI*us Quæstor* VRB*is* or *Urbanus.*—The head of Saturn, with the *Harpa* projecting behind.—*Rev. Lucius* LENT*ulus Caius* MAR*Cellus* CO*nSules.* A legionary eagle between two military standards, on one of which is incribed H.; on the other P. The former is by some numismatists considered to signify *Hastati*, the latter *Principes*, as referring to certain *corps* of the legion. But Eckhel regards the interpretation as doubtful.—See the family *Cornelia.*—See *Saturnus.*

NERO, a surname common to the *Claudia* family, as appears from writers on Roman affairs, and from inscriptions in the *fasti*, as well as from the ancient denarii of that family; thus we see C. CLAVDIVS NERO, or TI. CLAVDIVS TI. F. NERO, and NERO CLAVDIVS DRVSVS GERM*anicus* IMP*erator.*

Nero Claudius Drusus, commonly called *Drusus* senior, brother of Tiberius, second son of Tiberius Claudius Nero and of Livia, was born in the year of Rome 716, three months after his father had yielded up Livia to Augustus. Realizing the anticipations of that Emperor, he became the most accomplished hero of his time. Sent at the age of twenty-three into Rhaetia (the Tyrol) to quell a revolt, he conquered the insurgents at Trent in a pitched battle. Afterwards named General of the armies in Germany, his successes were so great that he extended the dominion of the Romans to the banks of the Elbe. This fine character conceived the design of reestablishing the Republic, and entrusted his secret to his brother Tiberius, who it is said betrayed him to Augustus.—He died in the year 745 (A.D. 9), before he had repassed the Rhine, in the 30th year of his age, deeply regretted by the whole empire for the great and virtuous qualities with which his name was so gloriously associated. After his death the Senate surnamed him GERMANICVS, which was transmitted to his children. Statues and triumphal arches were also erected to his honour and figured on his medals. This Prince had married Antonia, by whom he had *Germanicus* and Livilla. On his coins which, in each metal, are all more or less rare, he is styled DRVSVS—NERO CLAVDIVS DRVSVS GERMAN*icus* IMP.

NERO ET DRVSVS CAESARES QVINQ. C. V. I. N .C.—*Nero et Drusus Cæsares Quinquennales, Coloniæ Victricis Juliæ Nova, Carthaginis.*—Nero and Drusus, Cæsars, Quinquennial (Duumvirs) of the Victorious Colony Julia Nova Carthago—now Carthage.

Nero, son of Germanicus and of Agrippina, brother of Drusus, with whom he was carefully educated and trained by his mother. He was born 760 (A.D. 7), an accomplished character and of excellent qualities. The monster Tiberius, who had married him at 15 years old to his grand-daughter Julia, soon after employed the infamous minister Sejanus to entangle him in the snares of his cruelty, and becoming himself his accuser, caused his exile in 784 to the Ponza isles (Pontia), where he was left to die of hunger, in the course of the following year. Caligula his brother, at the beginning of his reign, brought back his ashes with those of their mother, Agrippina, and deposited them in the same tomb. (See *Drusus*).—The coins of

these two young princes (in second brass) are common—they are represented together on horseback, with the style, NERO ET DRVSVS CAESARES.—See *Drusus Cæsar.*

NERO *(Claudius Domitius)*, son of Cneius Domitius Ahenobarbus and of Agrippina the younger, was born at Antium, in the 37th year

of the Christian era. He was adopted (A.D 50)

and created Cæsar by Claudius, whose daughter, Octavia, he married, and whom he eventually succeeded, although he had no family claim or birth-right to the imperial throne. But Claudius having espoused Agrippina, that unscrupulously ambitious princess persuaded him to adopt her son by Domitius, and consequently to exclude *Britannicus*, whom the Emperor had by Messalina. From this time he took the name of *Claudius Nero*; received the title of *Princeps Juventutis* in 51 ; and, Claudius being removed by poison, Nero succeeded him A.D. 54, being then 17 years of age. It is said that he naturally possessed great and even good qualities. His preceptor Seneca certainly neglected nothing to ennoble his mind and to accomplish his education. He was fond of the fine arts, of poetry, and above all of music, his passion for which led him to commit a multitude of extravagances. In the first year he seemed to give promise of a happy reign. But in this he evidently was disguising the atrocity of his disposition. Nero soon dropped the mask of virtue ; and abandoned himself to his vicious and cruel propensities. He successively put to death Britannicus his half-brother (55), Agrippina his mother (59), Domitia his aunt, Octavia his wife, Claudia his sister-in-law, Seneca and Burrhus, who had been his tutors, and Corbulo his victorious general ; Lucan and Petronius, and his second wife Poppæa, also became the victims of his murderous fury, which extended to a multitude of other persons. In the year 64 he caused ten districts of Rome to be burnt, at the same time falsely accusing the Christians as the incendiaries ; and this crime being imputed to them, gave rise to the first persecution. Among the works which he caused to be constructed in Rome after this horrible conflagration, was a palace for himself, called the *golden house*, on which he lavished prodigious expenses. Meanwhile he amused himself publicly in contesting for the prize with musicians, with actors, and with charioteers of the circus, both in Italy and in Greece. In social life he gave himself up to such excesses of cruelty and infamy that his name afterwards became synonymous with that of monster and of tyrant. At length his detestable conduct having rendered him an object of universal execration, the Gallic and Spanish provinces revolted in 68. Galba was proclaimed Emperor, the Senate confirming the election, declared Nero enemy of the Republic ;

and this odious prince, abandoned by everyone, found himself compelled to plunge a dagger into his own throat. His death, to the joy of all, took place in the 60th year of the Christian era, in the 31st year of his age, and in the 14th of his reign. He left no children by his three wives— Octavia, Poppæa, and Statilia Messalina. His name on coins is NERO. CLAVD. CAESAR. AVG. GERMANICVS. P.M.—NERO CLAVDIVS DRVSVS, &c.—IMP. NERO CAESAR, &c —On medals struck after Christ 51 to 53, Nero is styled CAESAR PRINC. IVVENT. COS. DES.—In 54, his titles are AVGVSTVS TR. P. COS. DES. P.M. IMP. The name of Drusus is dropped, which he bore during the lifetime of Claudius.—In 66 he is styled IMP. NERO CLAVD. CAES. AVG. GERM*anicus*.

Nero established in Italy the colonies of Antium and Atina in Latium; Beneventum in the Herpini; and reinforced with fresh veterans Capua and Nuceria in Campania: the city of Puteoli in Campania received from him the right and title of a colony.—Vaillant, *Col.* i. p. 115.

Nero's first wife was *Octavia*, daughter of Claudius by adoption, whom, however, he soon got rid of after that Emperor's death.—*Poppæa* was his second, whose nuptials are celebrated on an Ephesian medal.—*Statilia Messalina* was his third.—See their *names*.

Nero's coins are numerous, and for the most part common in each metal. Some of them represent the Emperor with his mother Agrippina the younger.—"The silver pieces," says Akerman, "are generally ill struck, or are in bad condition. A really fine round denarius is seldom met with, and will consequently bring a high price.—The bronze on the other hand afford many specimens of high relief and fine workmanship.—Havercamp on Morell gives numerous illustrations and descriptions of the *Contorniate* medals of Nero. But as the pieces so denominated are well understood not to have been struck under the princes whose portraits they bear, it is unnecessary to say more respecting them than that the most interesting of the inscriptions and types on their reverses will be found noticed in this Dictionary under their proper heads.

Neronia, an appellation given to the quinquennial meetings, for contests *(certamina)* in music, poetry, and gymnastic exercises, founded at Rome by the Emperor Nero, in the 60th year of our era. An evidence of this institution of Nero's, so far as relates to his favourite science of music, is given on a brass coin of that Emperor's, the reverse of which, inscribed PONT. MAX. TR. POT. and S.C., exhibits his whole length figure, in a walking attitude, clothed in a long flowing tunic, and holding a lyre, on which he seems to be in the act of playing.

Neroniana.—The city of *Patrae*, in Achaia, was so called, as Vaillant (i. *Col.* 179) proves from Pausanias; and the same is shewn also by a coin, bearing for its inscription GEN. COL. NER. PAT. *Genius, vel Genio, Coloniæ Neronianæ Patrensis.*—See *Patrae*.

NERVA *(Marcus Cocceius)*, born at Narni (Narnia), in Umbria, A.D. 32. He was the son of M. C. Nerva, of a family not particularly illustrious, though eminent from its consular

honours; of Cretan origin. His mother was Sergia Plautilla, daughter of Lænas. For his warlike virtues, or, as some have said, for his poetic talents, he was on good terms with Nero, who accorded to him triumphal ornaments in the year of Rome 818; placed his statue in the imperial palace, and the following year appointed him Prætor.—In 824 (A.D. 71) he was consul with Vespasian; and in 843 (A.D. 90) consul for the second time, with Domitian for his colleague. On the day of that tyrant's death, Nerva was elected Emperor by the Senate and the Prætorians (A.D. 96). Upright, moderate, merciful, wise, generous, and of a sweet disposition, this prince sought no other object than to restore happiness to the empire. Substituting for the horrors of his predecessor's reign a government of justice and equity, he re-established the laws, reduced the taxes, protected and encouraged literature, and taking for his motto that *a good conscience is worth a kingdom*, displayed his humanity, fortitude, clemency, and munificence, less as the master than as the father of his subjects. Nevertheless being advanced in years, and under the impression that on that account the Prætorian guard failed to treat him with the consideration due to the exalted rank which he held, he completed his noble and virtuous administration of public affairs by adopting Trajan, A.D. 97, whom he created Cæsar and made his colleague and successor.— Nerva died three months afterwards, in the 66th year of his age, having reigned sixteen months, leaving a name venerated by all good men.—The inscriptions borne on his medals are IMP. NERVA CAES. AVG. GERM., and after his death DIVVS NERVA.

Nerva's coins in the year of Christ 96 (the year of his accession), bear P.M. TR. P. COS. II.—Those struck in 97 read COS. III. DES. IV. In the same year commences the title of GERMAN*icus*.—On those of 98 he is called TR. P. II. COS. IV. IMP. II. GERM.

Notwithstanding the shortness of his reign, the coins of this prince are numerous. Some of them represent him with Trajan.—The gold, especially those restored by Trajan, are very rare; so are the silver medallions.—Silver of the ordinary size, common, except some reverses.—The brass are for the most part common; but there are some rare reverses, and of great historical interest, as illustrative of the mild and equitable character of his government.

N. F.—N. N. *Numerii filius*, or *Numerii Nepos*.—Son or Nephew of Numerius.

NICEPH. *Nicephorium*,—A city of Mesopotamia, situate near Edessa, according to Pliny, who states it to have been founded in the neighbourhood of the Euphrates, by order of Alexander the Great, on account of the advantages of its locality. In it was the temple of Jupiter Nicephorus, whence, as Spartianus relates, an oracle announced the destination of Hadrian to the empire.—Banduri (i. p. 205), in a note on a *Greek* second brass of Gallienus, quotes, on the authority of Mediobarbus, a *colonial* coin of that prince as bearing on its reverse COLONIA NICEPH. CONS. or COND.—But no such coin is to be found in Vaillant.—And *Greek* imperial of Gordianus Pius and Gallienus are all that M. Hennin, under the head of Nicephorium, recognizes in the nomenclature of his Manual.—vol. 2. p. 293.

NICOMEDIAE.—See RESTITVTORI NICOMEDIAE, on a first brass of Hadrian, with the the accustomed type on coins of restored cities and provinces, viz., the figure of the Emperor, clothed in the toga, standing, and lifting up with the right hand a woman, who bends the knee before him.

Nicomedia, a city of Bithynia (in Asia Minor, on the Black Sea). It is described by ancient writers as a place of superior size and magnificence, ranking next to Rome, Alexandria, and Antioch in the splendour and beauty of its buildings; and was one which Diocletian studied to make the equal of Rome itself. But notwithstanding the great consequence of Nicomedia among the provincial cities of the empire, and though its Greek medals present a numerous and almost uninterrupted series from Augustus down to the age of Gallienus, there appears to be no coin, with *Latin* inscription, which refers to Nicomedia, except the *Restitutori* of Hadrian above-named; and *that* was evidently *not* struck in Asia, but is of Roman die.— Eckhel gives and describes it from the Imperial Museum at Vienna, but Mionnet does not include it in his catalogue.

NIG. *Niger*.—Surname of the Emperor Pescennius Niger —See *Pescennius*.

NIGRINIANVS.—This name, accompanied by a youthful radiated head, appears on certain gold coins of the *greatest* degree of rarity, and on third brass also of great rarity—coupled with the appellation of DIVVS. ; and on the reverse is CONSECRATIO. The type of the *gold* is a funeral pile with a biga placed on the summit. The type of the *third brass*, (which are sometimes found *washed* with gold or with silver,) is an eagle having its wings expanded. The annexed portrait is from a brass coin in the British Museum.

History makes no mention of this *Nigrinianus*, who is known only by the coins above alluded to. —Tristan supposes him to have been son of the tyrant Alexander, who reigned in Africa during the time of Maxentius.—Beauvais and other subsequent writers, on the other hand, furnish more conclusive reasons for giving him Carinus for his father, and with much probability Arria Nigrina for his mother.—It would further appear that this prince died in his early youth, and that Carinus, after the example of Domitian, ambitiously gave Nigrinianus the honours of the *apotheosis*.—Both Eckhel and Mionnet quote the gold coin from the museum of Saxe Gotha.

Nilus, the Nile, after traversing a large portion of Northern Africa, enters Egypt, which it passes through in its course towards the Mediterranean sea. This most celebrated river, formerly more than at present abounding with crocodiles and *hippopotami*, is by its inundations the principal cause of the fertility of Egypt; hence the ancient inhabitants of that country paid divine honours to it.

NILVS.—The river personified, recumbent, holding in his right hand the cornucopiæ, in his left a reed; sometimes with a female figure in the stola, standing at his feet: below him a crocodile.—On large brass of M. Aurelius (struck in Egypt), without legend.

NILVS. S.C.—The Nile lying down, with a cornucopiæ in his right hand; a hippopotamus

at his feet; a crocodile below. In other coins a child is seated on the hippopotamus; several children also are either standing round the old long-bearded man, or are creeping over his body.—On first and second brass of the same Emperor (Hadrian).

The above coins, struck during the reign of Hadrian, have reference to Antinous, who was drowned whilst navigating this illustrious river. —Hence (as Eckhel observes,) on these most elegant medals, we have the Nile pourtrayed with all his attributes; the reed, the *sphinx* (who had two natures, as indicated by her woman's bust and lion's body); the *crocodile* and the hippopotamus (amphibious animals), and the children, being symbols frequently found on coins of Alexandria, which present a similar personification of the river in the same recumbent posture.

The Nile was considered and adored as a god by the Egyptians, among other reasons, as possessing the property of spreading its waters and of fertilizing the country by its periodical risings. And perhaps the most ingenious allegory under which this famous stream has been represented, is that of the sixteen children which are grouped around the fine half-colossal statue of the Nile, preserved in the Vatican at Rome, and which allude to the sixteen cubits to which the river required to rise in order to make Egypt fertile. The degree of actual elevation was ascertained by an instrument called *nilometer.*—This subject is admirably illustrated by Pliny, (N.H. lib. v.,) who thus expresses himself *Justum incrementum est cubitorum xvi.—In xii. cubitis famem sentit ; in xiii. etiamnum esurit ; xiv. cubita hilaritatem afferunt ; xv. securitatem ; xvi. delicias.* The proper increase of the Nile is sixteen cubits. At twelve, Egypt experiences famine ; at thirteen, it feels want ; fourteen, restores gaiety ; fifteen, security ; and sixteen, the pleasures of abundance. This last-named number is designated on coins by the mark *is*, which signifies sixteen, and serves to shew that in that year the Nile attained the height so much desired by the Egyptians.

NILO.—DEO. SANCTO. SERAPIDI. The head of Serapis.—*Rev.* DEO. SANCTO NILO. A River, bearded, sitting on the ground, with reed in right hand and cornucopiæ in left ; and leaning upon an urn ; below ALE. Third brass of Julian.—(Banduri.)

On the obverse of a third brass of the same prince, published by Tanini, we read *Deo Sancto Serapidi*, and on the reverse DEO SANCTO NILO, its accompanying type being the personified Nile holding a reed and a sceptre, sitting upon a hippopotamus : in the exergue ALE.

It is stated by Eusebius, amongst other authors, that the Nile was religiously worshipped by the natives of those regions through which it flowed. Sozomenus also expressly testifies that, conformably to the established custom of the ancients, sacrifices were offered up to it, that its overflowings might be plentiful. To this coin, which exhibits the God Serapis on one side and the God Nile on the other, applies what Sozomenus relates as having been ordered by Julian, that according to the custom of the ancients, the *cubitus Nili* should be carried to the temple of Serapis, as in previous years by command of Constantine the Great, it had been carried to the church.—Moreover, Serapis and Nilus were appropriately conjoined on these coins, because the former was believed by the Egyptians to bring the latter through their country for its irrigation, and to regulate the river's increase and decrease.

Nimbus, a circlet, or disc, which on Roman coins, almost exclusively of the lower empire, appears around the head of Deities and of Emperors similar to that lucid nebulous ring with which the hands of Christian artists were afterwards accustomed to adorn the Saviour, the Virgin Mary, the Angels, Apostles, and at length all the Saints in the calendar. The word *nimbus* was formerly used in a varied sense. It originally signified the veil or band which women wore round their foreheads. As a small

forehead was a mark of beauty, those women who possessed that feature on too large a scale, diminished its extent by means of this *bandeau,* and they effected it with so much art as to render it difficult of detection. This frontal decoration is seen on the head of goddesses, and principally of Juno.—Of the coins which exhibit specimens of the *nimbus,* the most ancient is that in large brass of Antoninus Pius, on the reverse of which is the figure of that Emperor, who stands with this circlet surrounding his head, which is radiated also : in his right hand

he holds a branch, and in his left a spear. The Emperor is here represented with the emblems of Apollo.

Nimbus purus, that is to say, without rays, simply the form of a circle, after a long series of years from the age of the Antonines, presents itself as ornamenting the bust of Constantine the Great, on a gold coin published by Morell, inscribed GAVDIVM ROMANORVM.—The same ornament appears on an aureus of Flavia Maxima Fausta, wife of Constantine. Then it occurs on coins of Constans and Constantius. From that period it became frequent on the Eastern Imperial medals ; and especially on those of Valens. Lastly, among the Byzantine Emperors, we see the head of Our Saviour, and of the Virgin, crowned with the *nimbus,* as on the coins of Iohn Zimisces, a medal of whose reign bears a cross enclosed in the *nimbus.*—Eckhel remarks that the Romans conferred the honour of the nimbus on the phœnix, regarding that fabulous bird as the symbol of immortality and of eternity.

Nisibis, or *Nesibis,* a city of Mesopotamia, at the foot of Mount Masius, erected into a Roman Colony by S. Severus, and made metropolis of the province by Philip senior.—There are Imperial *Greek* coins of this colony (struck in honour of Julia Paula, wife of Elagabalus, Alexander Severus, Gordianus Pius, and Philip) ; but none with *Latin* inscriptions.

NOB. C. NOB*ilis* or NOB*ilissimus Cæsar.*—Noble or Most Noble Cæsar.

Nobilis Cæsar, Philip the younger, before he was declared Augustus, and admitted by his father to all the honours of the sovereign power, enjoyed the title of *Nobilis Cæsar ;* a distinction which was afterwards continued to princes who were not associated in the government of the empire, as well as to those on whom the Emperors devolved the administration of their State affairs. For example, Diocletian gave the title of *Nobilis* or *Nobilissimus*

Cæsar, to Constantius, Maximinus, Severus, and Maximianus, as we perceive by their medals (Bimard and Jobert, vol. i. 248).—The style of NOB. C. occurs on Imperial coins from Herennius, A.D. 249, to Julianus II., A.D. 355.—Some women also, were, in like manner distinguished—for example *Nobilissima Fausta*.

Noctua—the image of Wisdom.—See *Owl*.

Nobility, both as a privilege and as a quality, was always held in the highest consideration with the Romans. Those were called Nobles who could shew a long series of ancestral portraits. For in the times when the Republic was free, the *Jus imaginum* or right of images was but another term to express the right of Nobility, and the one is often used for the other. Thus it was not the circumstance of birth which conferred nobility, but the public offices, which entitling their possessors to the right of images, consequently rendered them noble. At first none were accounted Nobles but the Patricians, they alone being invested with functions that gave nobility. Afterwards, however, the appellation of *Nobles* was extended to those, who without belonging to the mere ancient families of Rome, could point to their ancestors or themselves as having occupied the chair and fulfilled the office of a Curule Magistrate.—*Nobilitas* is personified on medals of Commodus, Geta, Elagabalus, Philip the elder, and Tetricus the elder.

NOBILIT*as* AV*Gusti*.—A woman clothed in the stola, standing, with the hasta pura in her right hand, and the palladium in her left. On gold, silver, and first brass of Commodus.— On this coin a degenerate Emperor boasts to his own shame of his own nobility. It would appear that although Roman respect for the nobility of families was from the earliest date of their history intimately associated with their patriotism, yet the type of *nobleness* as a virtue, does not occur on coins of the empire before the reign of Commodus. His example was, however, followed by several of his successors. The figure, with varieties, is seen principally on coins struck in honour of those young Imperial heirs, to whom was subsequently given the title of *Nobilissimus Cæsar*.

NOBILITAS.—A female figure standing, with a lance in one hand and the palladium in the other. This type, on a silver medal of Geta, indicates by the attribute of the spear, and the image of Minerva, the two means (valour in war, wisdom in council,) by which nobility was or ought to be acquired.— Commodus, the descendant of Emperors, might rightly lay claim to the highest distinctions of hereditary rank, though he disgraced his illustrious birth by every vice; but the nobility of Geta's father was that of a *novus homo*, the first great man of his family, and therefore not fit matter for self glorification on the part of a younger son.

Nomina Romanorum. The proper names of the Romans.—Cicero thus defines the word *nomen*; it is, says he, *quod unicuique personæ datur quo suo quæque proprio et certo vocabulo appellatur*. Amongst the Romans there were *gentes* and *familiæ*. The latter, as a species, were comprehended under the former. The *gens* or race was made up of many families, or branches. Thus the *gens Cornelia* had for its families the Blasiones, Cethegi, Dolabellæ, Lentuli, Scipiones, &c. Whilst the Greeks assigned to each individual but one name, the Romans, who allowed only one name to their slaves, gave each citizen three and even four, especially when he was adopted, viz., prænomen, nomen, and cognomen—as *Publius Cornelius Scipio*. The prænomen served to distinguish each person such as that of *Publius*; the *nomen* designated the race whence he sprang, such as that of *Cornelius*; and the surname marked the family to which he immediately belonged, such as that of *Scipio*. To these sometimes was added a fourth, called *agnomen*, which was given, either on account of adoption, or in reward of some great exploit, and even for some personal defect or peculiarity. Thus, on Publius Cornelius Scipio, for his conquests and services to the republic, was conferred the *agnomen*, or additional appellative, of *Africanus*. An ancient grammarian, whose authority Eckhel quotes from Sigonius, thus succinctly defines the appellative words by which the heads of Roman families were distinguished, and which were of four kinds—viz., the *Prænomen*, which was prefixed to mark the difference in the ancestral name (*Nomini gentilitio*): the *Nomen*, which was designed to shew the origin of the *gens* or race: the *Cognomen*, which was subjoined to the ancestral names: and the *Agnomen*, which was an extrinsic designation constantly added, for some particular reason, or on account of some public incident. Valerius expresses himself of a similar opinion on these points.—By some writers even the *agnomen* was recognised as the *cognomen* or surname. "Of this an example," observes Eckhel, "is furnished to us in the case of L. Calpurnius Piso *Frugi*, by Cicero, who distinctly points to, and comments on, *Frugi* as the surname of *Calpurnius Piso*.—See *Doct. Num. Vet.* vol v. p. 56.—See also *Cognomen*.

It has been remarked that, during the existence of the Republic, it was the sedulous care of the Romans to preserve and hand down their *nomen gentilitium*, or name which came to them by descent from their ancestors. The eldest son usually took the proper name of his father, as in the Claudia, Fabia, and Cornelia families. With respect to the younger sons, they, it appears, assumed indifferently other names. But under the Imperial Government of Rome the people gradually relaxed in attention to this rule, till at length, when the Emperor Caracalla made it a law to bestow the name of Citizen indiscriminately on all the subjects of the Roman empire, the ancient custom with regard to names was entirely forgotten, and everyone called himself what he pleased.

Nomina gentilicia.—The ancestral names ended in IVS. "This rule of termination," observes Eckhel, "*seems*, but only seems, to fail in some cases. For we have in this very class of families, Norbanus, Cæcina, Betilienus, Allienus, Setrienus, which end otherwise. Nevertheless, it is almost beyond a doubt that these were not *nomina gentilicia*, but *cognomena*, or *agnomena*, the real *nomina* being unknown, in consequence of the practice which prevailed among the Romans of calling some individuals by the name of their *gens* and others by their *cognomen*. Thus Cicero, in his orations and elsewhere, always speaks of *Cæsar*, never of *Julius;* on the other hand he always names *Pompeius*, never *Strabo.*—Moreover there were those who in speaking of themselves always omitted the *nomen gentis*, or name of their original race. *Agrippa* at no time either called or wrote himself *Vipsanius*, but *M. Agrippa.* And hence historians, as the established custom leant one way or the other, designated them by their surnames only. For which reason, when we read the name of a Roman personage ending otherwise than in IVS, it is to be considered as the *cognomen*, and unless we have other means of ascertaining the *nomen gentis*, we may be certain that the *nomen gentilicium* was, not indeed wanting, but unknown. But this rule also applies only to the times when the republic flourished, and was deviated from at a subsequent period."

Nomina per adoptionem. Names by adoption. —The adopted Romans passed into the family of him who adopted them, so that having received all his names they placed the name of their own family last, but lengthened out to ANVS. Thus Aemilius Paulus, adopted by P. Cornelius Scipio, was thenceforward called P. Cornelius Scipio *Aemilianus.* C. Octavius, afterwards Augustus, adopted by Cæsar the Dictator, became C. Julius Cæsar *Octavianus;* and in like manner on coins we see A. LICINIVS. NERVA SILIAN*us;* and T. QVINCTIVS CRISPINVS SVLPICIANVS.—This rule, however, was often departed from. M. Junius Brutus, he who slew Cæsar, being the adopted son of Q. Servilius Cæpio, was called Q. Cæpio *Brutus*, that is to say, his family surname was retained, whereas he ought to have been called Q. Servilius Cæpio *Junianus.*—So also Scipio, who opposed himself to Cæsar in Africa, being adopted by Q. Cæcilius Metellus Pius, is called on coins, Q. Metellus Pius *Scipio*, not *Cornelianus.*—It does not appear, however, that about the assumption of names, to which they *succeeded*, they were particularly scrupulous. The same adopted Brutus is often on coins styled only: BRVTVS IMP.; and P. Clodius, adopted by Fonteius, to the end of his life continued to be called P. Clodius. Moreover the surname was elongated by adoption, as from Marcellus, *Marcellinus*, of which an example may be seen on coins of Lentulus Marcellinus, in the Cornelia family.

Nomen patris et avi.—The name of a father and even of a grandfather will sometimes be found alluded to on the family coins of the Romans; as, P. CRASSVS M. F., or C. ANNI. T. F. T. N., that is to say *Titi Filius Titi Nepos.* Another way of mentioning the name of a father, but a somewhat ambiguous one, is that exemplified by REGVLVS. F., that is *Filius*, as may be observed on coins of the Curiatia family.

Nomina foeminina.—Names of females as given to men, are to be found on the family medals of ancient Rome. For example, ASINA, BESTIA, CAECINA, CAPELLA, FIMBRIA, GLVCIA, MVRENA, MVSA, SVRA, VAALA, &c.—Harduin says "the names of the Romans were derived to them partly from the fathers', partly from the mothers' side."—But this was not always the case; for Spanheim *(Pr.* ii. p. 309), among other instances to the contrary, quotes that of *Herennia Etruscilla*, daughter of Trajanus Decius, who took no part of the paternal name, but was called after her mother.

Nomina gentilicia mulierum.—The family name of the woman frequently received the addition of the husband's. In the earliest ages of Rome women had but one name; afterwards, following the men's example, the names of women were multiplied.

Nomina Augustorum.—The names commonly assigned to some Roman Emperors are not to be found on their coins, Thus we never read *Caligula*, but *Caius;* never *Caracalla*, but *Marcus Aurelius Antoninus.* The word *Elagabalus* is not placed as a *name* round the head of that Emperor, but forms part of a legend to the reverse, as *Sancto Deo Elagabulo;* whilst on the obverse he also *pirates*, or rather pollutes, the name of *M. A. Antoninus.*

We find Emperors, on their accession to the throne, assuming the names of their immediate predecessors, in cases where those predecessors were their parents by nature or by adoption. Thus Trajan, adopted by Nerva, called himself NERVA TRAIANVS; Hadrian wishing to appear in the same relationship to Trajan, at first took the style of TRAIANVS HADRIANVS.—Hadrian, adopted by Hadrian, is called on his earliest mintages HADRIANVS ANTONINVS. *His* successor, Marcus Aurelius, took, not his *prenomen*, but his surname, and is styled on medals M. AVRELIVS ANTONINVS.—Commodus bears the name sometimes of his natural parent, sometimes that of his family—and his coins accordingly are inscribed either L. or M. ANTONINVS COMMODVS, or M. COMMODVS ANTONINVS. —Spanheim explains the reason *(Pr.* ii. p. 508) why *Severus*, who was not the son of *Pertinax*, either by nature or by adoption, nor assumed the government either in association with, or as succeeding him, yet, being made Emperor, added the name of Pertinax to his own.

NONIA, a plebeian family, but of consular rank. Its surnames are *Sufenas* and *Quinctilianus.* There are three varieties of type. The *silver* are scarce: the *brass* pieces are by the moneyers of Augustus and common. The following is a rare type:—

SVFENAS S.C.—The head of Saturn as Eckhel considers and shews it to be.

Rev.—SEX. NONI. PR. L. V. P. F., which some learned antiquaries read *Sextus Nonius Primus Ludos Votivos Publicas Fecit;* or as others interpret it, *Sextus Nonius Prætor Ludos Publicos Fecit.*—The type is a female figure, considered to personify Rome, sitting on spoils, holding in her right hand a spear and in her left a *parazonium* : a Victory stands behind and crowns her with a garland.—Spanheim decidedly gives preference to the reading, which records Nonius as having celebrated the *Ludi Votivi* during his prætorship; not as being the author of those games.

NOR. *Noricum.*—See MET. NOR. *Metellum Noricum,* on third brass of Hadrian.—The ancient Noricum was part of Illyria.—See EXERC. NORIC., on first and second brass of Hadrian.

Norba, a city situate on the river Tagus, formerly part of Lusitania, supposed to be the modern Alcantara, in Old Castille, in Spain.— Rasche, on the authority of Hardouin, Patin, and Liebe, quotes coins as struck there, not only under Augustus, but also under Tiberius and Caligula.—The assignment of this coin to what Pellerin calls "the pretended colony" of Norba, is shewn to be erroneous by that writer, who on the contrary agrees with Florez in reading the four letters in question, as *Colonia Cæsarea Nova Carthago* (New Carthage now Carthagena, in Spain.)—M. Hennin, in the nomenclature of his Manual, under the head of Lusitania (ii. p. 37), makes Norba to be now *Brozas;* and he limits its coinage to imperial autonomes, and even these he appears to treat as of doubtful attribution.

NORBANA.—The name of this family is lost, and the surname NORBANVS substituted in its room. It appears to have been plebeian, but consular. There are many varieties in the coins, but none of any interest, although some of the silver were restored by Trajan. The latter denarii are very rare—the rest common. It is not ascertained to which C. Norbanus they belong.—There are gold of high rarity inscribed C. NORBANVS L. CESTIVS. PR., which come under the *Cestia* family.—See *Cestia.*

NOST. NOSTR. *Nostrorum.*—See AVGG. ET CAESS. NOST. *Augustorum et Cæsarum Nostrorum,* on coins of Diocletian, Constantius Chlorus, &c.

Notæ Monetales.—The family coins of the Romans exhibit an infinite number of marks peculiar to the moneyers, placed there to distinguish their workmanship. These consist of characters and of small figures; and are found also in great abundance on coins of the lower empire, particularly from the time of Trebonianus Gallus and Volusianus, to denote (Jobert, vol. i. 186) the place where they were struck; but often in so obscure a manner as to baffle the conjectural skill of the most erudite numismatists.

NOVA SPES REIPVBLICAE.—Victory seated on spoils of the enemy, inscribes on a

buckler xx. xxx. ; in the field is a star : below CONOB.—This legend and type appear on a very rare gold coin of Arcadius, one of which is now in the Hunterian Museum.—Banduri is (naturally enough) at a loss to know in what manner Arcadius could at the time when the vows for xx. (years) were already discharged for him, be called *Nova Spes Reipublicæ*; he offers therefore various conjectures on the point—the trouble of settling which Eckhel, in his quiet easy way, freely leaves to those who are fond of exercising their critical skill on coins struck in "times" so much "out of joint," as the age of Arcadius.

NOVI.—See GLORIA NOVI SAECVLI. On coins of Gratian.

Novia, a plebeian family, as may be inferred from the fact of L. Nonius having been a tribune of the people.—But the coins struck at Corinth by the colonial Duumvir *Novius,* belong not to the family class.

NOVIES MILL*ies* ABOLITA.—See RE-LIQVA VETERA, &c. On a coin of Hadrian.

NVBIS CONS.—The signification of these letters, on the coins of young Romulus, the

son of Maxentius, notwithstanding all the attempts made by the learned to explain it, still remains not fully ascertained.—The Baron Bimard, in his commentary on Jobert's work, decides that the *Nostræ Vrbis* CON*servatori* of *Tristan;* the *Nostræ Vrbis Bis* CON*suli* of *Harduin;* and the *Nobilissimo Consuli* of *Cardinal Noris,* are interpretations all of them respectively beyond the bounds of probable conjecture.—Eckhel confesses himself destitute of

patience sufficient either to record or refute the conflicting opinions on these still ambiguous words. And Mionnet pleads absolute ignorance of their import.—E. C. B., in the "Numismatic Journal," vol. i., thinks that Jobert is correct in reading N. V. as *Nostræ Urbis.* He adds that "it would of course be absurd to expect to find DIVVS and CONSVL in the same legend;" but it does not appear evident to us why they should be so inconsistent; and

BIS CONSVL. (twice Consul), seems at least not objectionable; and as upon one of his earlier coins Romulus is styled NOBILIS CAES., the previous letters may be considered rather as something equivalent, in preference to *Nostræ Vrbis.*—See *Romulus.*

N. T.—*Numini Tutelari.*

N. TR. ALEXANDRIANAE COL. BOSTR. *Nerviæ Trajanæ Alexandrianæ Coloniæ Bostrensis.*—To the Nervian, Trajan, Alexandrian Colony of Bostra (a city of Palestine).

NVM. *Numa.*—NVM. POMPILI.—*Numa Pompilius.*—NVM. *Numerus.*

Numa Pompilius, of a Sabine family, was, after the death of Romulus, elected to fill the throne of Rome, and is calculated to have commenced his reign in the third year of the sixteenth Olympiad. Conspicuous for justice and piety, he entered into treaties of peace and amity with the neighbouring nations, whose minds hitherto brutalized by long and cruel wars, he led to cultivate the arts of peace. He shewed particular attachment to the ceremonies of religion; reformed the manners, and improved the legislation of the people; and of a mere band of warriors, undertook to make a nation of men civilized, just, and fearing the Gods. To Numa is ascribed the honour of having first founded a temple to Janus, and also of having been the original author of the Roman coinage. He created the pontifical order of the *Flamines (Dialis, Martialis,* and *Quirialis.)* Twelve Salian Priests were also assigned by him to the worship of Mars. He instituted the Vestals, as a body of virgins, to preserve the sacred fire; established on the calendar the *dies fasti et nefasti;* and divided the year into twelve months. To Numa is likewise attributed the foundation of the *Feciales,* heralds who decided on the justice, and made the declaration of war, and who watched over the observance of pacific treaties.

NVMA.—The head of this king, with his name inscribed on the diadem (see the word), appears on a rare silver coin of the *Calpurnia* family, whose boast it was that they were descended from Calpus, the son of Numa Pompilius, as both Plutarch and Festus expressly affirm.—The head of Numa also occurs on a denarius of the *Pompeia* family, with the legend CN. PISO PRO Q.—Likewise on a brass coin of the same monetary triumvir, on the reverse of which is the head of Augustus, as may be seen in Morell.—A denarius of the *Marcia* family also presents a portrait of this royal lawgiver; and on a scarce denarius of the *Pomponia* family, the reverse exhibits the following:—

NVM. POMPIL.—A figure representing Numa in his quality of Augur, holding the lituus, stands before a lighted altar, to which a man is leading a goat.—See *Pomponia.*

That the Pomponia family referred its origin to Numa we have the positive testimony of Plutarch. And to his account of the four sons of Numa, being Pompo, Pinus, Calpus, and Mamercus, he subjoins "for from Pompo are

descended the Pomponia." On the reverse of this coin Numa is represented employed in that sacred office, of which he was the chief author.

NVMA POMPILI ANCVS MARCI.—Heads of Numa Pompilius and Ancus Marcius. *Rev.* C. CENSO*rinus:* below ROMA. Two sterns of galleys, on one of which is a figure of Victory placed on a column. This appears on a second brass of the Marcia family, of which Censorinus is one of the surnames.—See *Ancus Marcius* for another coin of the same family. Both types appear to refer to the Port of Ostia, built by Ancus Marcius.

NVMERIANVS *(Marcus Aurelius),* second son of Carus, was born about A.D. 254. Declared Cæsar at the beginning of his father's reign, he accompanied him in the war against the Sarmatians, and afterwards against the Persians. On the death of Carus, A.D. 283, he was recognised Emperor of the army in Persia, conjointly with his elder brother Carinus, who resided in the West.—Unlike that brother, however, he was an excellent prince, endowed with the most amiable virtues, governed by the most honourable principles, eloquent, a good poet, a man of tried courage and sound wisdom, a decided supporter of the laws and promoter of the public interests. Attacked by illness, and obliged to be conveyed in a litter, on his return into Europe, he was basely assassinated by his father-in-law Arrius Aper, near Heraclea, in Thrace, A.D. 284, to the great grief of his subjects, in the thirtieth year of his age, having reigned only nine months.—The honours of consecration were paid to his memory by Carinus or by Diocletian.

The coins of this prince in third brass are common—silver doubtful, if any—brass medallions very rare—gold most rare. Some pieces represent him with his brother Carinus.

Numerianus is styled M. AVR. NVMERIANVS. C. (On reverse, sometimes PRINCEPS IVVENT.) —NVMERIANVS NOB. CAES.—IMP. C. M. AVR. NVMERIANVS NOB. C.—IMP. NVMERIANVS. P.F. AVG.—IMP. NVMERIANVS INVICT. AVG.—DIVVS. NVMERIANVS.—The illustration is taken from a fine brass medallion.

Numerius, a surname peculiar to the *Fabia* family, and which the Latins designated by the single letter N.—Valerius Maximus informs us that the only one of the Fabii who escaped the massacre of Cremera, where 306 of them perished, married the wife of Numerius Otacilius, on condition that the son whom he might have should bear the name of Numerius. The denarii of this family bear witness to the alleged fact that the Fabian race used the *prænomen* of Numerius, and expressed it solely by the letter N., as N. FABI. PICTOR. *Numerius Fabius Pictor.*—Sigonius, however, states that two other ancient and patrician families, *Furia* and *Quinctia*, also used the surname of *Numerius.*

Numidia, a part of Africa between Mauretania Cæsariensis and the Carthaginian region, whose inhabitants were called Numidæ by the Romans. —Jugurtha, King of Numidia, waged a long and bloody war against the Roman republic. Twice subdued by the Consul Quintus Metellus, he again took up arms against the power of Rome; but, though at first occasionally successful, he was finally vanquished by Marius, with Bocchus, King of Mauritania, whom he had drawn over to his party. That traitor betrayed him to Marius, who conveyed him to Rome, dragged him in the train of his triumphal procession, and caused him to perish in prison. Numidia, in the year of Rome, became a province of the republic, and, after the death of Lepidus, was ceded to Augustus.—For the kings of Numidia, on Roman coins, see *Juba.*

NVMITORIA, a plebeian family, as appears from its having furnished to the republic tribunes of the people; but it was also a family of the greatest antiquity, and seems to have referred for its origin to Numitor, brother of Aurelius, grandfather of Romulus and Remus.—There are five varieties. Silver very rare. The brass, which are common, form parts of the *As.*—A denarius of this family has on one side the winged head of Pallas, and ROMA; on the other, C. NVMITORI, a man in a triumphal quadriga, crowned by a flying victory.

NVMONIA, a family of but little celebrity in Roman annals. Whether it was plebeian or patrician is uncertain.—Its surname on coins is *Vala*, or *Vaala.*—Velleius alludes to Numonius Vala, who basely deserted Varus in Germany; and Horace writes an epistle to Numonius Vala (Lib. i. 15).—There are three varieties. Both the gold and silver coins of this family are extremely rare; of the latter, some were restored by Trajan, and these are of the highest degree of rarity.

One of the gold medals bears on its reverse the name of NVMONIVS VAALA, and for its type a soldier attacking the rampart of a camp, which two others inside are defending, The same type occurs in silver, of which an example is here given.

"From this," says Eckhel, "we learn, what besides is attested by ancient writers, that a

certain C. Numonius gained renown by assaulting an enemy's entrenchment *(vallum)*; and, moreover, that on account of such exploit the surname of *Vala* was conferred on him, which, handed down as usual, is in this instance made matter of boast by one of his descendants, who places the image of his distinguished ancestor on this coin.—VAALA for VALA is an archaism, as on coins of Sylla we read FEELIX for FELIX.— An archaism also leaves out an H. Thus PILIPVS, for PHILIPPVS, in the Marcia family.—On the above denarius you have also a representation of the form of the Roman *vallum.*"

Numus, or *Nummus*, the name by which the Romans denoted a coined piece of metal. The word seems to be derived from the Greek νόμος, although among the Greeks the word νόμισμα was more in use, whence the Latins wrote *Numisma*, which signifies what (from the French *monnoie*) we call money—namely, pieces of metal bearing the impress of different signs, indicative of their weight and value, which, for the public accommodation and benefit, are ordained by law to circulate in exchange for the necessaries and the luxuries of life, and to facilitate the otherwise too difficult means of conducting commercial transactions, but the liberty of fabricating which was denied to private individuals.

Numi bigati.—Roman coins so called, from their bearing the representation of cars drawn by two horses.

Numi bracteati. Plated coins.—This name was given to a species of fraudulent coinage practised by the ancients, which consisted in covering with leaves of gold or of silver pieces of metal of inferior value.

Numi cistophori, medals so denominated from their presenting the mystical *cista* or basket, with a serpent issuing from or coiled round it, allusive to the worship of Bacchus.— See *Cistophori.*

Numi contorniati.—See *Contorniate Coins.*

Numi contrasignati. Countermarked coins. —Numerous instances of medals stamped with some particular mark occur, in the ancient mints of *Greece*, especially those of kings and cities. Coins struck with a similar countersign are to be found in the *Roman* Imperial series, under Claudius and also under Vespasian.

Numi frustati.—The Latin word *frustatus*, derived from *frustum*, a bit, a fragment, is applied by numismatic antiquaries to a medal which is so much defaced that its inscription is illegible.—The French call it *une medaille fruste.*

Numi incusi.—Incuse medals are those which are stamped only on one side, and which represent the same type on both sides, one in relief and the other hollow. The process was employed by some cities of Magna Græcia in striking their silver money. But they must not be confounded with those which are incuse through the neglect or participation of the moneyers, and which are found as well among the Consular coins as among the brass and silver of the Imperial series.

Numi pelliculati.—The same as *subærati.* —See below.

Numi quadrigati.—So called from the *qnadrigæ,* or chariots with four horses, which form the type of their reverses.

Numi ratiti.—A name given to the most ancient pieces of the Roman mint, which bear on the reverse a galley *(ratis),* or rather the rostrum or beak of a galley.

Numi restituti. Restored medals.—These are pieces, both Consular and Imperial, on which, besides the type and legend which belonged to their original fabric, exhibit the name of the Emperor, by whose order they were struck a second time.—See REST.

Numi serrati.—By this term are distinguished certain Greek and Roman medals, of which the rim is indented, or garnished with teeth.— Authors have conjectured various reasons for this process having been adopted in the mints of antiquity, but none which appear to solve the mystery.—Eckhel is of opinion that the earliest of these *médailles dentelées* (as the French call them) mount to as remote a date as the year of Rome, 564. Under the Emperors none of these serrated coins are found, but they frequently occur amongst the Consular medals.

Numi subærati. Another term for plated coins.—Rink (in his work *De Vet. Numism.*) describes this species of money in the following terms :—" It should be understood that the *numus subæratus* is a brass (or copper) coin, which has been overlaid with a coating of silver, in such a manner that the silver can easily be removed from the brass, by merely loosening it at the edge."

Numi tincti.—These are what the French call *médailles saucées,* namely, struck on copper and afterwards covered with a leaf of tin— numbers of which are found amongst those struck in the declining periods of the empire.

Numi victoriati.—On the Consular coins the figure of Victory in a *biga* or a *quadriga* is frequently seen ; and hence this kind of money took the name of *victoriatus.*

Numi metallorum.—See MET. or METAL ; also *Trajan.*

Numi pro moneta habiti (says Vaillant) *marmore perenniores, ac monumentis veteribus sunt accuratiores.*—Coins are more durable than marble, and more accurate than ancient monuments. For (he adds) they were struck by authority of magistrates after mature deliberation ; therefore, all things respecting them must have been carefully weighed, rendered clear and perspicuous, and freed from obscurity and doubt. The same writer admits, however, that in some cases medals are of less value than monuments.

Numismatique.—By this word, used substantively, the French designate that science which has for its object the study of medals, principally those struck by the ancient Greeks and by the ancient Romans.—See *Numus.*

Numismatiste.—Hennin, in the introduction to "his Manual," observes that the word *numismate* has been for some years replaced by that of *numismatiste,* which is now adopted to signify a person who studies, explains, and collects antique coins and medals ; in short who cultivates the *numismatic science,* or *la numismatique.*

Nymphæ.—The ancients were accustomed to place under the protection of beings whom they called *nymphs,* those productions of nature which, as in the vegetable world, seem to possess certain attributes of life. Neither goddesses nor mortals, but partaking to a degree of the quality of both, they lived a long time, for *ambrosia* was their food ; but their life at length yielded to the fatal axe of the woodman, or to the scissors of the inexorable Fates.

The *nymphs* of Roman fable were of divers kinds. For some of them presided over mountains, others over fountains and fields, whilst others again found their element in the sea and other places.—Some writers appear to regard them in no other light than as celebrated women of the most remote antiquity. For example, *Egeria,* the familiar spirit of Numa ; *Acca Laurentia,* the nurse of Romulus ; *Anna Perenna,* the sister of Dido ; *Flora* is said to have been a most noted courtezan.—Figures of *nymphs* are often found on Roman monuments and vases ; they also appear on a few Greek Imperial and Colonial coins. But the only Latin coins which present them, as a type, are that denarius of the *Accoleia* family, on which the *three* sisters of Phaeton appear, as changed into larch trees ; and the bronze medallion of Antoninus Pius, which exhibits two *nymphs* of the *Hesperides* standing close to a tree bearing apples, round the trunk of which a serpent is entwined.—See *Hercules.*

O.

O. Fourteenth letter of the Latin alphabet.

O. a globule or circle, is generally accepted as denoting the *uncia,* as the sign of weight and value—viz., o, *uncia ;* thence oooo, *triens ;* ooo, *quadrans ;* oo, *sextans.*

O. and AV. were used promiscuously by the more ancient Romans.—Thus in the Claudia family CLODIVS and CLAVDIVS ; in like manner in the Plautia family PLOTIVS and PLAVTIVS appear on consular denarii. By the same custom the foster-father of Quirinus (Romulus), whose name among Latin writers, spelt *Faustulus,* is inscribed FOSTVLVS on the denarius of the Pompeia family.

O. was often substituted by the ancient Latins for V.—Of this we have examples in the words AEGYPTOS instead of AEGYPTVS ; DIVOS for DIVVS ; VOLCANO for VVLCANO, &c.

O. is adjoined sometimes to V., forming the diphthong OV., in place of the single letter V. Thus on family denarii FOVLVIVS, is written in the room of *Fulvius,* FOVRI, or FOVRIVS, for *Furius.*

O. This letter by itself signifies *Ob,* on account of ; or *officina,* office of the mint ; or *Ogulnius,* the name of a man ; or *optimo,* an epithet often given to Jupiter.

OB. C. S., or OB. CIV. SER., or O. C. S. *Ob Cives Servatos*.—Money struck in honour of, or an oaken crown dedicated and given to, some one for having been the preserver or saviour of citizens.

OB CIVIS SERVATOS.—Many coins, in gold, silver, and brass, struck by the moneyers of *Augustus*, exhibit this commendatory legend (the letter ɪ being usually elongated), within a crown of oak leaves, or around a votive shield (ᴄʟ. ᴠ.), inscribed ѕ. ᴘ. ǫ. ʀ.—This more frequently occurs after the Emperor above-named had caused the Roman citizens made prisoners in Parthia to be restored to liberty in the year of Rome 734, as may be seen on coins of Aquilius, Caninius Durmius, and Petronius, who about that period were monetal III *Viri* at Rome. (See *Caninia* family.) —"This reverse (observes Eckhel), which makes its first appearance under Augustus, was frequently revived by succeeding Cæsars, not often careful about whether such praise could truly be bestowed upon them."—For example, the words ᴇx ѕ. ᴄ. ᴏʙ ᴄɪᴠᴇѕ ѕᴇʀᴠᴀᴛᴏѕ inscribed with a laurel crown, forms the legend of the reverse on a first brass coin of Claudius, as if that most indolent and apathetic, if not most stupid, of Emperors, ever did an heroic or humane action to merit the eulogy conveyed in this *senatus consultum*.

OB. C.S. S.P.Q.R. P.P. Within an oaken crown.—On gold, silver (and first brass, with addition of ᴘ.ᴘ.) of Caligula.—According to Dion, Caligula accepted the honours (such as *Augustus, Pater Patriæ*, &c.), some of which his predecessor Tiberius uniformly refused. On these coins we see not only the title of Pater Patriæ, but also the civic crown, neither of which are found in the mintage of Tiberius, and rightly so, for Suetonius tells us of Tiberius *cognomenque Patris Patriæ, et civicam in vestibulo coronam recusavit*. By these coins, therefore, it is (says Eckhel) revealed to us, that this commendatory distinction meritoriously earned by Augustus; afterwards decreed to, but rejected by, Tiberius, was seized upon quite early enough by Caligula, and subsequently intruded into the public coinage, by one so utterly unworthy as the man, who far from deserving rewards for saving his fellow-citizens, had openly wished that all had but one neck that he might dispatch them at one blow.—(Vol. vi. 223.)

OB. C.S. S.P.Q.R. P.P. Within a laurel wreath.—Silver of Albinus.—On this coin as given in Vaillant, *Num. Præst.* ᴛ. ii. edit. Rom. p. 208,—Eckhel makes the following remarks : "As Albinus, from the moment of his usurping the honours of an Augustus, in defiance of Severus, was declared the enemy of Rome, this medal could not have been struck in the city, "nor could the honour, which the coin indicates, have been conferred upon him by the Senate, devoted as that body might be to his service. If, therefore, it be ˏgenuine, the above quoted coin teaches us what all historians have passed over without notice, that Albinus in Gaul formed a Senate of his own, from whom

he obtained the appellation of *Pater Patriæ*, and the distinctive *ob cives servatos*, with͡the laurel crown. For the same reason, in an earlier age, Pompey the Great in Greece, Scipio in Spain, had each his Senate, although Cæsar had at the same time the city, which was the seat of the Senate, in his power. And at a later period of the empire, the same thing was done by Postumus, as is shewn on his coinage."— (Vol. vii. p. 164.)

OB CONSERVATIONEM PATRIAE. —GALLIENVM AVGVSTVM POPVLVS ROMANVS.—Hygeia feeding a serpent.—By this epigraph, which appears on a large and very rare silver coin of Gallienus, the Roman people are made to *worship* that Emperor for his having saved the country *(ob conservationem patriæ)*, after the model of the servile Greek inscriptions. "The goddess of health, and the word *Salutis* in the next coin (says Vaillant), shews that the merit of having effectually exerted himself to drive away the pestilence from Rome was claimed by Gallienus," and awarded by the obsequious Senate.

OB CONSERVATIONEM SALVTIS.— Same type as above.—Here *Gallienus Augustus* receives the religious veneration of the Roman people, as the preserver of the public health.— On this legend and type, Vaillant observes— "The praise, though flatteringly, was not altogether falsely bestowed by the people on their prince; for that general plague, or pestilence, which had raged throughout the empire, under Decius, Gallus, and Æmilianus, after fifteen years' duration, ceased under Gallienus, who seems thus to have fulfilled his vow to the goddess *Salus*.—Tristan, therefore, is of opinion, from the epigraph of this coin, that a statue was erected to him in honour of the event."

OB CONSERVATOREM SALVTIS.—A similar type on a silver medallion of Gallienus.

OB LIBERTATEM RECEPTAM.—GAL-LIENVM AVG. P.P.—With the laureated head of the same Emperor on one side, and the figure of Liberty on the other; a gold medal records the veneration of the Roman people towards *Gallienus Augustus* for their "recovered liberty."—That was indeed a vain and false display of popular praise, which could openly affirm ͡the existence of Liberty, under the son, whilst the Emperor Valerianus, his father, was languishing in ignominious and cruel captivity amongst the Persians, to the great disgrace of the whole Roman empire.

In adding a second brass of the same emperor, bearing a similar type, and having for its epigraph ᴏʙ. ʀᴇᴅᴅɪᴛᴀᴍ ʟɪʙᴇʀᴛᴀᴛᴇᴍ, Eckhel justly observes that "the above coins are remarkable for the ostentatious grandeur and novel terms of their respective inscriptions. But the base adulation, as well of the Senate as of the people, which they betray, must be obvious to everyone."

OB VICTORIAM TRIVMFALEM *(sic.)*— Two victories holding a crown, on which is inscribed ᴠᴏᴛ. x. ᴍᴠʟᴛ. xᴠ. or ᴍᴠʟᴛ. xx.—This occurs on gold and silver coins of Constans I.

(son of Constantine the Great), who it appears had waged war with the Franks, and afterwards with the Caledonians, which procured for him this distinction of a *triumphal victory.*

OB. DV. FILII SVI.—A legend of uncertain signification on a coin of Licinius senior.— Noris has made it the subject of a dissertation, in which he expresses his opinion that the letters OB. DV. mean *Oblationem Devotam,* and endeavours to shew that gifts were accustomed to be offered to princes on account of the performance of vows. But other writers of equal erudition prefer reading the DV. as *Decennalia Vota,* that is to say *suscepta,* accepted or received.

Obeliscus, an obelisk, formed of the hardest stone, rising from a square base, becoming " fine by degrees and beautifully less" to generally a commanding altitude.—This figure may be observed, as situate in the *circus maximus,* on medals of Augustus, Nero, Trajan, Caracalla, Alexander Severus, Gordianus Pius, and elsewhere.—See *Circus.*

An *obelisk,* placed on a round foundation, adorned with statues, appears on a second brass of Titus.—Vaillant in his *Colonies* (i. p. 137) gives on a coin of Corinth, struck under M. Aurelius, an *obelisk,* on which stands a little naked image, and on each side an equestrian figure as if in the act of running.—See *Corinthus Colonia.*

Obices Castrorum.—The gates of a camp, with a spear, and below it the *pileus* (or cap of liberty), appear on a denarius of Cæpio Brutus, to shew that he was in arms for the defence of liberty, and that his camps were for such Roman soldiers as were friends to liberty.

OBSEQVENS.—See *Fortuna Obsequens.*— On silver and brass of Antoninus Pius. It is also written OPSEQVENS from interchange of the consonants B and P.

Obsidionalis Corona.—See *Corona.*

Obulco, a Roman *municipium,* of Hispania Bætica (Andalusia), now called *Porcuna,* a town of some note between Cordova and Gienna.—Its coins, which are autonomous, bear for their types generally a female head, sometimes a horseman, at others a bull, and the word OBVLCO, with the names of Roman duumvirs, and Celtiberian inscriptions.

OCEANVS, on a coin of Constans.—See BONONIA.

Octavia, one of the most ancient families of Rome.—Elected into the Senate by Tarquinius Priscus, and introduced amongst the patricians by Servius Tullius, it in aftertimes united itself to the plebeian order, and then returned again with great influence into the patrician ranks through Julius Cæsar. It was principally noted from Cæsar Octavianus Augustus.—Mionnet and Akerman do not include the reputed coins of this family in their catalogues.—Eckhel mentions them only as *numi Goltziani, aut IIvirorum Corinthi.*

Octavia, the sister of Augustus, the third wife of Mark Antony, whom she married in the year of Rome 714 (B.C. 40), and by whom she was divorced in 722. She is said to have died of grief for the loss of the young Marcellus, her son by a former husband. There are coins of this Octavia, but, according to Mionnet, none are known in either metal of Roman die bearing her likeness, except a gold one of the highest degree of rarity, thus described by that eminent medallist, COS. DESIGN. ITER ET TER. IIIVIR. R.P.C. Naked head of *Octavia.*

Rev.—M. ANTONIVS M.F. M.N AVG. IMP. TER. Naked head of M. Antony. But the portrait and even the name of Octavia, adds Mionnet, is also found on a *Latin* brass medallion of Tiberius, struck out of Rome (in what province is not known). On the reverse of this coin appears the head of the princess, fronting that of her brother Augustus; and the legend is DIVVS AVG. IMP. OCTAVIA.

Octavia, the daughter of the Emperor Claudius, by Messalina. Born at Rome in 795-6 (A.D. 42 or 43); given in marriage to Nero (806), by whom soon after her father's death she was put away and banished to Campania, and afterwards to the island of Pandataria, where the ungrateful tyrant caused her death by suffocation in a bath, under pretext of her being an adulteress, A.D. 62, in the 20th year of her age. Her successful rival Poppæa, at whose instigation she was murdered, had the bleeding head of the victim brought to her; and little perhaps anticipating the fatal *kick* of her brutal paramour, fed her own monstrous barbarity with the sight of it. The Romans were dismayed at her death, and preserved her memory as that of a virtuous as well as a most unfortunate empress.

The only coins of this empress which are known are of Colonial and of Greek fabric. From one of the former in the British Museum,

in potin, the portrait annexed has been engraved. They are all of great rarity. One in third brass with her head is mentioned by Beauvais, as contained in his time in the cabinet of Pellerin, having for its legend OCTAVIAE AVG. C. I. F. *Colonia Julia Felix.*—On the reverse is the head of Nero, crowned with laurel, and inscribed NERO CLAVD. CAES. AVG. ANN. C. IIII. A medal, adds Beauvais, which may be regarded as unique.—Eckhel has since edited from the cabinet of Count Festitic, a remarkable coin of an uncertain colony, with the following:—OCTAVIA AVGVSTA. Octavia veiled, standing before an altar: patera in her right hand.—*Rev.* AGRIPPINA AVG. Agrippina seated.

Octavianus, a name elongated from *Octavius,* who was afterwards called Augústus. (See *Nomina Romanorum).*—But Augustus, after his adoption by Julius Cæsar, is never styled on coins either *Octavianus* or *Octavius.*

Odenathus Septimius, Prince of the Palmyrenians, a warlike man, the saviour of the

Roman empire in the East. When Valerian became the captive of Sapor, Odenathus took the Persian Generals prisoners; and commanded himself to be styled in the first place King, and then Emperor. He married the famous Zenobia, Queen of Palmyra, and died A.D. 267.

"The coins of Odenathus (says Eckhel) are known only to Goltzius; and if any one will put faith in their existence, let him go to the fountain head (i.e. Goltzius).—According to Trebellius, Gallienus caused a coin to be struck in honour of Odenathus, on which he was represented leading the Persians captive; but a coin of this kind has met, as yet, no one's eye—not even that of Goltzius."

Oea, or *Ocea*, a maritime city of Africa, situate on the Sertice, and according to Pliny (L. v. c. 4), a Roman colony.—The city of Oea *(Civitas Oeensis* or *Oecensis)* was one of three, which from their number gave the title to the African Tripolis, according to *Solinus*, quoted by Rasche. To this city Vaillant attributes a coin of Antoninus Pius, on the obverse of which appear the titles and portrait of that Emperor; and on the reverse C. A. O. A. F., which he has rendered *Colonia Aelia Oea* (or *Ocensis*), *Augusta Felix*, with the turreted head of the *Genius loci*. But Pellerin, by the production of a better preserved but exactly similar medal, has shewn it to belong to Hadrian's colony of *Ælia Capitolina* (Jerusalem).— Pellerin adds that no coins of the city of Oea were known in his time..

O EC. *Oecumenicum*, or *Oecumenica*.— Public games or combats of *athletæ*, so called because competitors from every part of the world were allowed to enter the lists, in contra-distinction to the Επιχωρια, which were only provincial games *(certamina provincialia)*. On colonial coins of Heliopolis in Cælo Syria, among other epigraphs allusive to these *wrestling matches*, is one of Valerianus senior, given by Banduri (I. p. 120), CER. SAC. CAP. OEC. ISEL. HEL. *Certamen Sacrum Capitolinum Oecumenicum Iselasticum Heliopolitanum.*— See *Heliopolis Colonia*.

OFF. III. CONST. *Officinæ Tertiæ Constantinopoli.*—Struck in the third office of the mint of Constantinople.

Officina monetæ, a monetary workshop or mint.—*Officinatores monetæ*, inspectors of the mint.—Inscriptions on ancient marbles collected by Gruter and others have preserved the appellations given to the respective workmen employed in different parts of the coinage. Among these are found the following denominations :— *Monetarii; Officinatores monetæ aurariæ, argentariæ, Cæsaris; Numularii officinarum argentiarum; Familiæ monetariæ; Numularii; Officinatores monetæ; Exactores auri, argento, aeris; Signatores; Suppostores; Malleatores; Flatores.*

The learned are of opinion that under the reign of Probus, or thereabouts, those cities of the empire which enjoyed the right of coinage designated their names, and the *officinæ*, in which their money was struck. This was done

by certain initial letters and numerals, as well Greek as Latin, engraved either in the field of the coin or on the *exergue*. Of this sort are the following :—

ANTP. *Antiochiæ Percussa.*—Struck at Antioch.

ANTS. *Antiochiæ Signata.*—Coined at Antioch.

AQPS. *Aquileiæ Pecunia Signata.*—Coined at Aquileia.

COMOB. otherwise CONOB.—*Constantinopoli Obsignata,* or *Constantinopoli officina Secunda.*

LVGPS. *Lugduni Pecunia Signata.*—Money coined at Lyons.

PTR. *Percussa Treveris—(Treves.)*

SISCPZ. *Sciscæ Percussa in officina Septima.*

SMA. *Signata Moneta Antiochiæ*—or SMAB. *Signata Moneta Antiochiæ in officina Secunda.*

SMSISE. *Sacra Moneta Sisciæ in officina Quinta.*

The following inscription on a coin of Mauricius, edited by Banduri and Ducange, in which the debated syllables are drawn out at length, favours the above interpretations—viz., VIENNA DE OFFICINA LAVRENTI.

Officinæ Monetariæ.—The monetary offices are frequently recorded on coins of Valentinianus II., as well as on those of Valens and Gratianus, thus—OF. II. III. &c., or R. PRIMA, R. SECVNDA, R. TERTIA, R. QVARTA.

OGVLNIA *gens.*—Q. and Cn. Ogulnius, being recorded as *tribuni plebis*, teach us that this family was plebeian. They had the cognomen of *Gallus*.—Five varieties of its coins are given in Morell; one of which in silver, bears on one side a juvenile head laureated, under it a thunderbolt; and on the other, OGVL. VER. CAR.—The bronze pieces are the *as* or some of its parts.—Coins of the *Carvilia* family exhibit the same name and cognomen, but not the same types.

Olba, and not *Olbia*, according to Vaillant, quoting Ptolemy, was a city of Pamphylia, which territory borders on Cilicia. It was also a Roman *colony*, as its coins testify, bearing the legend COL. IVL. AVG. OLBANEN, with the equestrian figure of the God Lunus. It has one autonomous coin, one Greek Imperial, struck in honour of M. Aurelius, and two Colonial Imperial, inscribed to Julia Mæsa and Gordianus Pius.

Olbasa, Pisidia, Colonia.—The Latin Imperial medal *ascribed* to this colony, is following in middle brass, namely, with the style and portrait of Gordianus Pius on the obverse—and with COL. OLBA on the reverse, and the type of Bacchus standing, holding the cartherus and thyrsus: a leopard squatting at his feet. But Mionnet marks it "*questionable.*"

Olea, the Olive, of which Minerva is (by Virgil) styled the inventress; or, according to Ovid *(Metam.* lib. vi., v. 80), Pallas produced out of the earth the olive tree, during her contest with Neptune for the possession and name of Athens. Hence, on coins, this goddess has her helmet adorned with an olive branch, as sacred to her, or she carries the same in her right hand. And when *Minerva* bears this symbol of peace, she is called *Pacifera;* an example of which appellation and type is found on a brass coin of Albinus. Minerva is also seen with similar attributes on coins of Antoninus, Commodus, Postumus, and Tetricus junior.

Oleæ Ramus.—The olive branch in the hand of Peace is to be seen on nearly all the medals of the Imperial series, from Augustus to Gallienus, and further downwards to Gal. Maximianus.—The same as a symbol of peace, appears in the hand of *Mars Pacifer,* on coins of Commodus, Sept. Severus, Caracalla, Alex. Severus, Maximianus I., Gordianus III., Gallus, Volusianus, Æmilianus, Gallienus, and other emperors.—The *olive* branch appears in the hand of *Emperors,* as the preservers of peace, on coins of Augustus, Tiberius, Vespasian, Titus, Trajan, Commodus, Sept. Severus, Balbinus, Pupienus, Æmilianus, Diocletian, and Maximianus.

The *olive* branch appears on divers of the Imperial medals, in the hand of *Concord,* of *Felicity,* of *Security,* of *Providentia.* It is the symbol of Hispania, on account of the abundance of olive trees in that country.

OLV. for OLY. Olympico.—See IOVI OLYM.; and a temple on a coin of Augustus.

OLYBRIVS *(Anicius),* descended from the ancient family of the Anicii, who held a high senatorial rank, married (A.D. 462) Placidia, daughter of Valentinian III. and of Eudoxia.

The Emperor Leo nominated him Consul 464, and sent him against Ricimer, who proclaimed him Augustus in 472, in the place of the Emperor Anthemius, whom Ricimer caused to be assassinated. Olybrius is described as a man of distinguished merit, estimable for his morals, piety, and patriotism. A good general, but an ambitious subject, he had not the time allowed him to perform any memorable action, as he terminated his days in the year of his accession, possessing the empire only three months from the death of his predecessor. His daughter Juliana married, during the reign of Anastasius, the patrician Areobindus. His style is D. N. ANICIVS OLYBRIVS AVG.—D. N. ANIC. (or ANICIVS.) OLYBRIVS, P.F. AVG. His coins both in gold and silver are very rare.—Tanini gives a piece in lead with a reverse similar to that on the aureus represented above; but the obverse bears full-faced heads of Olybrius and Placidia.

OLYMPIAS (or sometimes OLIMPIAS) REGINA.—A female veiled, reposing on a richly adorned bed, extends her right hand towards a serpent which is rearing itself before her.—This legend and type appear on a Roman Contorniate medal, bearing the head of Nero; and, according to Havercamp, the recumbent female is no other than Queen Olympias herself, the faithless wife of Philip, King of Macedon, and the courageous mother of Alexander the Great. Of this lady it is related, by Plutarch, among other writers, that becoming pregnant during the absence of Philip, she, for the purpose of concealing her shame, devised a story about her having had intercourse with Lybian Jove, or Jupiter Ammon, who had assumed the form of a serpent.

Olympias, an olympiad, the space of four years, sometimes used as equivalent to the Roman *Lustrum,* which included five years. From the period when the Greeks began to reckon dates of time by olympiads, they enumerated them as, the first, or second, or third, &c., olympiad.

Olympicus, Olympic, or what is of or belonging to Olympus.—*Jupiter* was called *Olympicus,* either from Mount Olympus, in Thessaly, the reputed place of his education, or from heaven itself, which the Greeks denominated Olympus, and in which he was said to reign.—The title of *Olympicus* was also assigned to *Hercules,* who instituted the *certamen olympicum,* and won at those games the victory in wrestling.

Olympius.—This appellation (says Eckhel, vi. 518), peculiarly appropriated to the king of heathen divinities, was, by an unusual stretch of even Grecian flattery, assigned in common to the Emperor Hadrian and to Jove himself, as appears from a variety of inscriptions both on marbles and on coins, especially Athenian. The cause or pretext for this adulation was the finishing and dedication by the above Emperor, of the great temple of Olympian Jupiter at Athens. Connected with this fact was the institution of games, called *Hadriana Olympia,* by various Greek cities.—This application of a celestial cognomen to Hadrian finds no example on any *Latin* coins; and we find on contorniate coins, the epithet of *Olympius* degraded so low as to be the designation of an *auriga* or an *athleta.*

Olympiodorus, Olympius.—These names occur on the reverses of contorniates, the obverses of which bear the portrait of Nero. The types are naked men standing in quadrigæ, and the names are doubtless those of victorious charioteers or wrestlers.

O. M. *Optimus Maximus.*—I. O. M. *Jovi Optimo Maximo.*—To the name of *Jupiter,* the tutelary Deity of Rome, these letters are added, in recognition of his goodness and his power.

OMN. *Omnia.*—SACERDos COOPTatus IN OMNia CONLegia SVPRA NVMerum. On a coin of Nero.

Omnipotens.—Jupiter is thus called on a colonial coin quoted by Vaillant.

O. M. T. *Optimo Maximo Tonanti—i.e.* (Jovi) (to Jupiter) the best, the greatest, the thunderer.

OP. or OPT. or OPTIM. PRIN. or PR. *Optimo Principi.*—To the best of Princes. An epithet given to Trajan.

Opeimia, as written on coins, otherwise *Opimia*, a plebeian family; but it was distinguished nevertheless by several consulships, especially that of L. Opimius, by whom C. Gracchus was put down.—Among seven varieties of coins is a rare denarius with a winged head of Minerva on one side; and on the other M. OPEIMI. and Apollo in a biga, holding his bow: below it ROMA. The bronze pieces of this family are the *as*, or some of its parts.

OPEL. *Opelius.*—We learn from coins that Macrinus and his son Diadumenianus should be called *Opelius*, and not *Opilius*, as it is commonly written by historians.

OPI. DIVIN. *Opi Divinæ.*—A female seated, holding ears of corn. On a very rare large brass of Pertinax.

This reverse will admit of a two-fold interpretation. It may be taken for the *Divine Ops*, wife of Saturn, who had a temple dedicated to her at Rome. Or it may be supposed to mean the power of producing in abundance all things generally useful. The abundance, personified on this medal, holding in her right hand ears of corn, that truly divine gift of nature to mankind, apparently refers to the great pains which *Pertinax* took for the subsistence and advantage of his subjects.—Capitolinus says of this virtuous Emperor, *Annonæ consultissime providit;* and Dion also in like manner speaks of his provident care. In dedicating this medal to *Ops*, who is the same as Rhea, or *Terra*, which brings forth corn, *Pertinax* shews his disposition to ascribe to divine assistance that universal plenty which he had secured for his people.—With this legend and type, therefore, may be appropriately conjoined the inscription which Gruter has published, and which reads: OPI. DIVINAE. ET FORTVNAE. PRIMIGENIAE. SACR. IMP. SACR. IMP. CAESAR. HELVII PERTINACIS AVGVSTI. V. D. D.

There are coins of Antoninus Pius in *silver* and first *brass*, struck in the year of Rome 893, on which is the epigraph OPI. AVG*ustæ ;* and the type a woman sitting with the *hasta* in her right hand, and her left hand lifted to her head.—The *Ops Augusta* whom this coin was intended to honour, is considered by Spanheim (in his notes on Julian's Cæsars), as only another name for the Goddess *Cybele*, to whom the Romans assigned a feast of two days duration, under the name of *Opalia.*—See *Templum Opis.*

Opima Spolia.—See *Spolia.*

(M) OPPIVS CAPIT. PROPR. PRAEF. CLAS. *(Marcus) Oppius Capito Proprætor Præfectus Classis.*—Propretor and Commandant of the Fleet.

OPPIA.—This family is known to have been of the plebeian order, from the tribunes and ediles of the people, who belonged to it. Its surnames were *Capito* and *Salinator.*—The former appears on brass coins of Mark Antony, struck during his triumvirate. The latter may be considered as belonging to two families, viz., Livia and Oppia.—In the whole there are nine varieties, all of second brass. The rarest of which bears on its obverse the double head of Janus, and on the reverse C. CASSI. L. SALIN. The prow of a galley, with the doubtful epigraph of DSS.—Livy affirms that L. Oppius Salinator was sent in the year of Rome, 561, with a fleet to guard the coast of Sicily, and to bring back a supply of corn. And this *frumentatio* is regarded by Havercamp as here commemorated. Eckhel, however, shews that such an inference is not to be drawn merely from a ship's prow, which is in fact a perpetual and almost exclusive type on the brass coinage of Republican Rome. There are bronze pieces of this family struck in Cyreniaca. The following second brass is probably one of them:—The head of Venus, with a capricorn behind it.— *Rev.* Q. OPPIVS PR. Victory walking, holds on her right shoulder a long palm branch, and in her left hand a *patera* containing fruit.

According to Havercamp, the letters PR. are to be read *Præfectus*, and Oppius was one of eight prefects, whom Julius Cæsar, on setting out for Spain, appointed to act for him at Rome.—"This opinion (says Eckhel) I have enlarged upon in commenting on the medals of the *Cestia* family; and as I have there noticed its vagueness and uncertainty, so I hesitate not to assert that respecting these coins of Oppius he is greatly mistaken. For the *capricorn* which in some of them is placed beside the head of Venus, points to a later period; in all probability the time when Augustus was at the head of Roman affairs, and in honour of whom alone that fabulous animal was engraved on medals. Moreover, the fabric of the coins themselves, bears evidence of their not having proceeded from the mint of Rome, insomuch that in all likelihood they were struck in some province."

OPT. *Optimo*, in other instances OPTIM., or at full length OPTIMO.

OPT. IMP. *Optimo Imperatori*, on coins of Claudius Gothicus, and also (as given by Banduri) of Constantius Chlorus.

OPT. *Optimorum.*—OPT. MER. *Optimorum Meritorum,*—See *Requies.*

OPTIME MAXIME.—Jupiter stands holding the thunderbolt in his right, and a spear in his left hand; on some an eagle is at his feet.— *Silver* and second *brass* of Commodus.

Jupiter (observes Vaillant) was called *Optimus* for his beneficence and *Maximus* for his power. But this epigraph of OPTIME MAXIME seems placed on the above coin on account of the

acclamation made to Commodus by the Senate.
—Eckhel, in noticing this legend, alludes to
the opinion of Spanheim, that on this coin
Commodus is addressed (proponi) with the
worship of Jupiter, and that to him also were
applied the names *Optimus Maximus*. But he
does not see sufficient cause for coming to such
a conclusion. Each of these epithets (he adds)
is ascribed to Commodus on the marble of
Muratori; but several emperors before him
were called by titles sacred to Jupiter, as is
shewn by inscriptions.

OPTIMO. PRINCIPI. S.P.Q.R.—This legend, either in abbreviation or at full length,
is most frequently to be read on coins of Trajan,
of whom *Dion Cassius* observes that he seemed
to take much greater pride in the surname of
Optimus (as combined with *Princeps)*, than in
all the rest of his titles, from which trait of
character might be recognised his mild nature
and his courteous manner, which predominated
over his love for military renown..—See *Trajanus.*

The same legend also appears on coins of
S. Severus, Gallienus, Daza, Licinius Sen., and
Constantine the Great.

OPTIMO. PRINCIPI. S.P.Q.R. S.C.—This
same legend also appears within laurel, on a
second brass of Antoninus Pius, in the Imperial
Cabinet of Vienna. That the title of *Optimus
Princeps* was decreed to Antonine, as it had
been to Trajan, by the Senate, is not affirmed
by history. But the right to this title devolved
to him from Trajan by adoption.—Eckhel, vol.
vii., 18.

OPTIMVS.—This laudatory cognomen, first
conferred on Trajan, was regarded by the
Roman people as exclusively suitable to that
Emperor, insomuch that after him (according to
Pliny) it was a solemn custom in public acclama-
tions thus to address each succeeding Augustus :
" May you be better than Trajan :" *(Sis melior
Trajano).* We learn from coins that Trajan did
not accept this, by him most highly prized,
title of *Optimus* before his sixth consulate.
There are extant some coins of Hadrian, who
was adopted by Trajan and succeeded him in the
empire, on which not only the name *Trajanus,*
but that of *Optimus* is retained—viz., IMP.
CAES. TRAIAN. HADRIANVS. OPT. AVG, GER.
DAC.—The appellation of *Optimus* conjoined to
Maximus has already been noticed as occurring
on a coin of Commodus.—And the same title
appears on a consecration medal of Claudius
Gothicus : DIVO CLAVDIO OPT. or OPTIMO.

Optimus Princeps.—Patin in his work on
Imperial coins (p. 455) remarks that not only
Trajan, Antonine, Aurelius, and other good
Emperors were honoured with this high compliment, but it is mendaciously applied (amongst
others undeserving of it) to Sept. Severus,
whose conduct, at least during the first years of
his reign, was atrociously cruel and inhumanly
vindictive. Nay even the Thracian Maximinus
was so styled by the *Senatus Populusque
Romanus,* at the very worst period of his bad
reign, and at a time when he was not in Rome.

The most probable supposition is that this barbarian was so called by his own creatures
(terming themselves a Senate) out of sheer
adulation.

OR. *Oræ.*—PRAEF. CLAS. ET. OR. MARIT.
Præfectus Classis et Oræ Maritimæ.

ORB. *Orbis.*—ORB. TERR. *Orbis Terrarum.*
—The world; the universe.—See *Gloria Orbis.*

ORBIANA *(Gneia, Seia, Herennia, Sallustia,
Barbia.)* This princess is not mentioned even
by name in the writings
of any historian. It
is to modern research
alone, amongst antique
medals, that we owe
the knowledge of her
having existed, and the
proofs that she was the
last wife of Alexander
Severus. Her first three
prenomina are only on Greek coins. Antiquaries
had long been of opinion that SALLVSTIA BARBIA
ORBIANA was the Empress of Trajanus Decius.
But medals of Alexander Severus having been
found which bear her portrait on their reverse,
the lot of this lady has been fixed and a true
place in the Imperial series assigned to her.—
Orbiana is represented on medals (especially on
large brass where her features are more developed) as possessing an agreeable physiognomy.
—The author of *Leçons de Numismatique
Romaine* describes a coin of this princess in his
collection, which, on its reverse, with the
legend CONCORDIA AVGVSTORVM, typifies the
Emperor and the Empress standing hand in hand.
And this intelligent numismatist remarks, that
" small as are the two figures they are so clearly
engraved (when the medal is in perfect preservation) that in the lineaments of the emperor
the likeness may plainly be traced of the true
husband, and *not* the totally different countenance of Trajanus Decius" (p. 200.)—It
appears by a coin struck at Alexandria, that she
was married to Alexander, A.D. 226. Her gold
medals and brass medallions are of the highest
degree of rarity—the silver and first brass are
very rare. On these she is styled SAL. or (SALL.)
BARB. (or BARBIA) ORBIANA. AVG. Some pieces
represent her with *Julia Mamæa* as well as with
Severus Alexander.

Orbis.—An orb, or circle, on coins denote the
Roman empire. We see it united sometimes
to the rudder a symbol of government; at other
times to the sacrificial axes, the fasces, the
joined right hands, and the caduceus on a gold
medal of Julius Cæsar; and placed on a tripod,
in a coin of Augustus. It is also the symbol of
the terraqueous globe. In the hand of the
Emperor it signifies his accession to the supreme
power.

Orbis terrarum.—The world, which the
ancients divided into three parts, and to which
one of the most ephemeral of the Roman
Emperors assumed to have given *Peace.*—See
PAX ORBIS TERRARVM on gold and silver of Otho.

ORBIS.—This word forms a component part
of several different epigraphs on medals of the

Imperial series.—See FELICITAS; GENETRIX; GLORIA; IOVI CONSERVATORI; LOCVPLETATORI; PACATOR; RECTOR; RESTITVTOR; SECVRITAS; VOTA DECENNALIA, ORBIS.

ORD. or ORDIN, *Ordini.*—EQ. ORD. *Equestri Ordini.*—See *Equester Ord.*

Organum hydraulicum.—A representation of one of these (supposed) musical instruments—a water·organ of a triangular form—appears on a large contorniate brass of Nero, which Havercamp has given an engraving and description of in his work on that peculiar class of medals.—See LAVRENTI NIKA.

Oriens. The East.—This word was used by the Romans to designate either that part of the world where the sun appears to rise, or some province of the empire situate towards the East; or the Sun itself. The East is figured by a young head crowned with rays; and *Oriens* often is the accompanying legend.

ORIENS.—Vaillant, in noticing a coin struck under Trajan, referring to a similar one of Hadrian, observes: *Oriens,* personified by a radiated head, represents the provinces of Armenia and Mesopotamia, which Trajan had just added to the Roman territories in that quarter of the globe where the sun seemed to rise.—*Oriens,* as meaning the Sun, is pourtrayed under the form of a naked man, generally standing with the right hand raised, and the left holding a globe, or a whip, on coins of Gordianus Pius, Valerianus, senior and junior, Gallienus, Postumus, Claudius Gothicus, Aurelianus, Probus, Numerianus, Diocletian, Constantius Chlorus, Allectus, &c.—A medal of Diocletian places a branch in one hand and a bow in the other; and on a reverse of Gallienus, Oriens is represented under the figure of a woman, wearing a turreed crown, who, offering a figure of Victory to the Emperor, gives him assurance of success against the barbarians who have over-run the Asiatic provinces.

ORIENS AVGG.—Sol standing, naked, except a cloak thrown back from his shoulders, lifts up the right hand, and holds a whip or scourge in his left. On third brass of Valerian.

On a *quinarius* of Valerian the elder, exhibiting this epigraph and type, the Editor of the Roman edition of Vaillant makes the following historical remark:—" When the empire of Rome was on all sides assailed by barbarian arms, Valerianus declared his son Gallienus Emperor, and leaving him to the defence of Gaul and Germany, he himself, having assembled together the legions from the neighbouring provinces, resolved to march and give battle in the East to the Scythians who were peopling Asia, and to the Persians who had already taken possession of Mesopotamia and of Syria. For this reason *Oriens Augustorum*—(the rising Sun of the Emperors)—was struck on their coins;" already anticipating—alas! how fallaciously—the *Victories* of Valerian.

ORIENS.—Valerian the younger, in a military garb, places a crown on a trophy. A very rare silver coin bearing this legend and type, is given both in Banduri and Vaillant, the latter of whom makes the following annotation:—" Valerianus junior is on his coins called *Oriens,* as though a new sun had risen on the empire, when he was associated in the government with Gallienus."

ORIGINI AVG.—The wolf suckling the twins,—On a very rare third brass of Probus, whose origin is veiled in obscurity. This is a new reverse (says Eckhel), and known only from the coins of Probus. It seems to intimate that Probus was descended from Roman blood, which might be true, although he was affirmed to have been born in Pannonia.

Origin of the *Surnames* belonging to *Roman Families* and races. This is derived either from brute animals, as ASINA, CAPELLA, VITVLVS, &c.; or from some mark or member of the human body, and especially from the head, as CAPITO, CHILO, LABEO, &c.; or from some corporeal affection or peculiarity, as NIGER, PVLCHER, RVFVS, &c.; or from the manners and disposition of men, BLANDVS, FRVGI, LEPIDVS, &c.; or from occupations and offices, as CAPRARIVS, FIGVLVS, VESPILLO, &c.; or from deeds and achievements, as ACHAICVS, AFRICANVS, NUMIDICVS, &c.; nay, even from garden herbs or pulse, as CICERO, FABIVS, PISO, &c.—See *Familiæ Romanæ.*

Orontes, the largest river of Syria, which has its source not far from the ancient Seleucia, Pieria, and Mount Lebanon, and flows past Antioch, into the Mediterranean sea.—On a Greek colonial coin of Trajan, a figure personifying the *Orontes,* is seen emerging, with extended arms as if swimming, at the feet of the Genius of Antioch, who is sitting on a hill, the rocky features of which indicate the lofty site of that city.—"The Antiochians (says Vaillant) commemorated by this medal the visit of Trajan to their town."—See *Antioch.*

Orus, or *Horus,* the son of Osiris and of Isis, by which the Egyptians, according to Plutarch, understood the subjection of this world to birth and to death—to decay and to revival. By Isis and Osiris all those effects were said to be designated, which by Solar and Lunar influences are produced in the world.—On a third brass of Julianus II., among other types of the monstrous superstitions of Egypt, which that philosophic repudiator of Christianity "delighted to honour," is Isis seated, in the act of suckling Orus: the legend, VOTA PVBLICA.

Osca, a very ancient and noble city of Hispania Tarraconensis, formerly a Roman *municipium,* now called *Huesca,* in Arragon.—According to Morell, it is denominated on coins v. v. OSCA, or Osca was called *Urbs,* as the city *par excellence,* and took its name of *Victrix* from Julius Cæsar.

VRB. VIC. OSCA. *Urbs Victrix Osca.*—The monetary triumvirs of Osca are almost always designated by the surnames only; hence it is impossible from their coins to ascertain their respective families.   The Oscenses uniformly stamped their medals with the figure of a man on horseback, wearing a helmet, holding a lance, and riding at full speed.   That Osca was a place of great riches is shewn by the *argentum oscense* (its silver bullion), to which Livy more than once alludes.   But the *argentum oscense* differs from the *bigati*, in this respect, that the latter signify silver coined by the Romans, either at Rome, or in the provinces; whereas *argentum oscense* is a term applied to money struck in Spain and in the city of Osca, having, moreover, Spanish types.   Accordingly Livy afterwards distinguishes those particular coins from Roman denarii.

There are five varieties of *autonomous* coins belonging to this once celebrated town: one of these bears a beardless head of a man, and in the field URBS. VICT.; on the reverse is a horseman, with couched spear, galloping.—The *Imperial* coins of OSCA extend from Augustus to Tiberius, Germanicus, and Caligula; all with the equestrian figure on the reverse—"either," says Vaillant, "because the country abounded in good horses, or because the inhabitants were pre-eminently warlike.   Julius Cæsar himself praises the Spanish Cavalry."

On a first brass, bearing on its reverse the same horseman galloping, with spear couched in his right hand, is the following legend:— V. V. OSCA. C. TARRACINA. P. PRISCO. II. VIR. *Urbs Victrix Osca, Caio Tarracina (et) Publio Prisco, Duumviris.*—[This is a coin which Vaillant gives as of the highest rarity, struck by the municipium of Osca, in congratulation to Caius Cæsar (Caligula) Augustus, whom it calls by the name of his father *Germanicus*, but by whom its privilege of coining money was, in common with the other Roman cities in Spain, taken away, never afterwards to be renewed, it appears, by any subsequent Emperors.]

OSCA.—On a silver coin of the Cornelia family is the head of a man, bare and bearded. Behind it is the word OSCA.   On the reverse is a male figure, seated on a curule chair, holding a cornucopia and a spear, over whom a Victory floats with a crown, with the legend P. LENT. P. F.

SPINT.
Eckhel points to the bare head, bearded, such as occurs on common denarii of Hispania, and also to OSCA, as that of the noted Tarraconensian city, and as sufficiently warranting the belief that these denarii were coined in Spain. A similar head, and the same inscription of OSCA, appear on a denarius of the Domitia family.

Osicerda, a city of Hispania Tarraconensis, whose people are called by Pliny *Ossigerdenses;* it was admitted to the rank of a *municipium* under the Romans.   But the only imperial coin extant is one struck under Tiberius, on the reverse of which is inscribed MVN. OSICERDA,

with a bull for its type, the common symbol of a *Roman Municipium.*—Its autonomous coins bear celtiberian and latino-celtiberian legends. There are coins of this city which also bear the name of *Sesaraca*, as in alliance.

Osiris, the principal deity of the Egyptians, who attributed to him their original laws, their instruction in agriculture, and all useful inventions.   According to the recitals which compose his mythological history, he married Isis, his sister, and lived with her in uninterrupted harmony; both applying themselves to the civilization and instruction of their subjects. He was the founder of Thebes, and extended his conquests far and wide.   From the most remote periods of antiquity, the Nile, which is the centre of the whole religion of the Egyptian people, was represented under the image of Osiris, and worshipped as such in that country. Osiris was also regarded by the same superstitious nation as a symbol of the sun, and figured sometimes with the head of a man, at others with that of a hawk.   Sometimes he has the horns of an ox, allusive to his union with the earth, which owed to him the blessings of fertilization.   His living representative was the bull *Apis*, and he often appears with the *lotus* flower on his head.—Osiris was afterwards replaced by *Serapis*.   The Roman Emperors placed his statue among the images of their own pantheon.—There is in *Pedrusi's* "Museum Farnese," a brass medallion of Commodus, which bears a very elegant group allusive to *Osiris*, who stands with the *modius* on his head, whilst the Emperor holds out his hand to him, over a lighted altar.   Behind the togated figure of Commodus is Victory holding a garland over his head; and by the side of Osiris is the Goddess Isis, with the *sistrum* in her right hand.—The legend of this fine reverse is P.M. TR. P. XVII. IMP. VIII. COS. VII. P.P.

OST. *Ostiæ.*—M. OST. P.—*Moneta Ostiæ Percussa.*—Money struck at Ostia—on the exergue of coins of Val. Maximianus, Maxentius, Romulus, and Licinius Senior.

Ostiensis.—See PORT. OST. AVGVSTI. *Portus Ostiensis Augusti.*   On large brass of Nero.

Ostia, a Latian city, built by Ancus Martius at the mouth of the Tiber; it was afterwards made a colony and a sea-port by that enterprising king.   This commodious haven afforded to Rome the easy means of enjoying all the riches of foreign lands.   Its excellent baths, its good cheer, and its healthy site, fanned by the breezes of the Mediterranean, rendered Ostia a favourite resort with the pleasure-loving Romans.

Ostiensis Portus.—The port of Ostia, according to Suetonius, was with difficulty constructed by the Emperor Claudius, although thirty thousand men were unintermittingly employed on the work for eleven years in succession—a quay being carried round the harbour right and left, and a mole carried out at the entrance of it into deep water.   Moreover, in order to strengthen its foundation, he caused, before this mole, a ship to be sunk, on board of which a large obelisk from Egypt had been brought, and placed a very lofty tower on a basis of piles, in imitation of the Alexandrian pharos, for the purpose of directing the course of navigators by fires at night. The same author (in his Life of Nero, c. 9 and 31,) relates that when Claudius had resolved upon building the port, he questioned the architects what they estimated the cost of his work would be. They answered by naming such a sum as he might be unwilling to incur, hoping that when he heard the magnitude of the charge, he would abandon the design altogether. Nothing discouraged, however, the Emperor bent his mind upon pursuing his plan, which he accomplished in a manner worthy of Roman powers.—Nevertheless, there

are no coins of Claudius extant which exhibit types of this port, though many of Nero's appear with a representation of it, (as the large brass here introduced) a circumstance which shews either that the latter named prince put the finishing stroke to this grand work, or that he was so ungrateful and vain as not to acknowledge even that a share of the merit belonged to his Imperial predecessor.— See POR. OSTIA. AVGVSTI.

Ostro Gothi.—Those tribes of the Goths were so called whose original country lay towards the East. See *Gothici numi.*—For the Ostro Gothic Kings in Italy—see *Athalaricus—Baduila—Theodahatus—Witiges.*

OT. or OTACIL. *Otacilia*, or *Otacilius.*—Otacilia, the name of an Empress, or Otacilius, the name of a man.

OTACILIA *(Marcia) Severa*, daughter of Severus, Governor of Pannonia, married Philip senior, about A.D. 234, by whom she had Philip the younger, seven years before the elevation of her husband to the Imperial throne. Of an engaging person, and in private conduct without reproach, she was culpably ambitious, and participated with Philip in the murder of the Third Gordian. This princess professed Christianity, and is said to have been subjected to ecclesiastical penance by the Bishop of Antioch, Saint Babylas, for her criminal share in the death of the virtuous young emperor. It was, however, by Otacilia's protection that the Christians breathed in peace, during the reign of her husband, and by her instruction that her son, a youth of great promise, was brought up in the piety and wisdom of their holy faith. But the death of Philip precipitated this woman into the obscure condition in which she was born, and, after sustaining the

horror of having her son slain in her arms by the Pretorians, in whose camp they jointly sought a refuge on the approach of Trajan Dacius to Rome, Otacilia passed the remainder of her days in retirement. The inscriptions on her coins are OTACILIA. SEVERA. AVG., and MARCIA. OTACILIA. SEVERA. AVG. Some pieces represent her with Philip the father and Philip the younger—and many of her coins retrace the celebrated epocha, and the festal solemnities which occcupy so large a portion of the types struck in honour of her husband and her son. On the large brass of this Empress we read

CONCORDIA AVG. S.C.; PVDICITIA. AVG. S.C.; and on another SAECVLARES AVG. S.C., with the figure of a hippopotamus.—Pellerin also gives in his *Mélange* a silver coin of Otacilia, with FECVNDITAS TEMPORVM., and a woman seated on the ground, holding a cornucopiæ in her left hand, and extending a branch in her right towards two children. She is said to have had a daughter as well as a son. Her gold coins and brass medallions are very rare: silver of the usual size, and first and second brass, very common.

OTHO, surname of the Salvia family. M. SALVIVS OTHO IIIVIR. A. A. A. F. F. on a large brass struck by Salvius Otho, one of the moneyers of Augustus, and the maternal uncle of the Emperor Otho.—See *Salvia.*

OTHO *(Marcus Salvius)*, born A.D. 32, was son of Lucius Salvius Otho, a man of consular rank, and of an illustrious Etrurian family. His mother's name was Albia Terentia, also of an illustrious house.—Handsome, brave, and possessed of talents, his youth gave promise of high distinction. As one of the favourites of Nero, he soon, however, became voluptuous and prodigal, abandoning himself, like his infamous master, to the most shameful excesses of debauchery. He had scarcely served the Prætorship, when that tyrant libertine, wishing to possess himself of Poppæa, his wife, sent him, in the year 58, as Governor to Lusitania. After ten years' absence from Rome, he took part in the revolt which led to Nero's death. He was at first faithful to Galba; but, in 69, displeased and disappointed at Piso's adoption, Otho basely instigated the Prætorian soldiers to assassinate this veteran Emperor; and, by their audacious aid, succeeded in mounting the throne. But his reign was short. Having to contest the crown with his competitor Vitellius, whom he three times defeated, Otho was vanquished in his turn at the battle of Bedriacum; and, rather than be the occasion of further bloodshed in civil war, he preferred making the sacrifice of his life, and with a firmness wholly unlooked for from so effeminately luxurious a character, deliberately slew himself with his own hand. He died on the 16th of April, v.c. 822 (A.D. 69), in the 37th year of his age, having reigned only ninety-five days.

The inscriptions on the medals of this Prince style him—IMP. OTHO CAESAR AVG., or M. OTHO CAES. AVG*ust*. IMP. P. P.—All Otho's medals of Roman die are in gold or in silver.—No *Latin* brass coin, properly so called, is known or acknowledged as truly authentic.—The medal on which Otho is styled P. P. (Father of the Country) is of brass, " but (says Mionnet) *elle est suspecte. C'est une médaille de restitution.*"—All the brass medals of Otho were struck at Antioch, in Syria, or at Alexandria, in Egypt. His genuine gold and silver medals present nothing very remarkable, except that which bears the legend of VICTORIA OTHONIS.

It has been alleged, as a reason for the total absence of authentic coins of Otho in brass of Roman fabric, that the senate did not declare itself in that prince's favour, being desirous, before it recognised his imperial title and caused brass money to be struck in his name, to see a termination put to the civil war which had arisen between his party and that of Vitellius. Still (as Mr. Akerman observes) it is singular that " no medal by order of the conscript fathers would appear to have been struck in honour of the new prince; for Tacitus informs us that, when Otho was elected, the senate assembled, and voted him the title of Augustus and the Tribunicia Potestas. Some antiquaries indulge the fond hope that, at a future time, a deposit of the (Roman) brass coins of the Emperor may be discovered."

M. Hennin, a scientific and highly intelligent numismatist of the present day, in his " Manuel," referring to those ancient writings and historical facts which support the opinion that the brass coinage alone was under the jurisdiction of the senate, says—" Gold and silver money of Otho is found in large quantities; but of this prince not a brass coin exists of Roman die. If the senate had been invested with the right of striking money in all three metals, why should it have exercised that right with respect to the two precious metals, and not have done the same with the brass, since the latter was the most common money? The division of the right of coinage between the Emperor and the senate explains this circumstance. Otho caused money with his effigy to be struck in gold and in silver, therein exercising his privilege; and yet the senate did not order any brass money to be struck for that Emperor, although it had yielded to him, and he was master of Italy. The

reason of this is unknown. It might be because he was the first Emperor proclaimed by the Praetorians, and as such not likely to conciliate the good will of the senators. The short duration of his reign might also be alleged as a cause. But these reasons are not entirely satisfactory. There must have been for this conduct of the senate motives of which we are ignorant."

See on this subject Eckhel, *Doctrina Num. Vet.* vol. vi. p. 302 *et seq.*

Otho's Coin of the Colony of Antioch.— The obverse of this middle *brass* coin bears on its obverse IMP. M. OTHO CAES. AVG. round the head of this Emperor. The reverse exhibits simply S. C. in a crown of laurel.

This medal is described to be of coarser workmanship than that of the Roman mint, but by no means of a barbarous fabric. Although marked with the two letters S. C. *(Senatus Consulto)*, it could not have been struck at Rome, where the senate never, *by any formal act*, acknowledged the authority of Otho. Many circumstances, such as its workmanship, its resemblance to other coins bearing Greek legends round the heads, and peculiar to *Antioch in Syria*, seem to shew that it must have been struck in the last mentioned city, to which the right of coinage had been continued from the time of Pompey, by senatorial decree, which is what is meant by the letters S. C.

The desire to fill up the void left in the Roman brass series of imperial medals, causes this *Antiochian* piece to be sought after with an eagerness that renders it extremely dear. But, as before observed, all other brass medals with the head of *Otho*, and with Latin legends, are known to be false.

Otho (M. Salvius). This name appears on brass of Augustus, struck S. C. Obverse: CAESAR AVGVST. PONT. MAX. TRIBVNIC. POT., with laureated head of the Emperor, behind which is a winged Victory. Reverse: M. SALVIVS OTHO IIIVIR. (See A. A. A. F. F., p. 1 of this Dict.) This coin, and two others by monetal triumvirs, are the only ones which, in *large brass* of the real Roman mint, were coined during the life-time of Augustus, and present to us the head of that prince. They are rare; whilst the *large brass* of the same reign, without the head of Augustus, are common; and those in middle brass, with the head, are extremely common. With reference to the moneyer OTHO, above-named, it may be observed that certain persons, curious, but not well-informed, in these matters, have sometimes confounded him, from close similarity of appellation, with the Emperor Otho. Hence so many popular tales respecting *Othos* in brass found in such and such a place. (See *Leçons de Num. Rom.* p. 71.)

Ovatio, the lesser triumph. This was distinguished from the triumph, by its being conducted with less pomp and magnificence than the greater ceremony, for (as Dionysius, of Helicarnassus relates) the successful general on whom the honours of an ovation were conferred made his entry into the city commonly on foot, never in a chariot, seldom even on horseback; to the sound of flutes not of trumpets; neither did he bear the triumphal insignia, the *toga picta*, the sceptre, &c. Preceded by warriors, he held a branch of olive in his hand, was clothed in a white robe bordered with purple, and wore a crown of myrtle on his head, to indicate that the action had not been sanguinary. The Senate, the members of the Equestrian Order, and the principal inhabitants attended the procession, which terminated at the capitol, where a sacrifice of rams was performed. The ovation was awarded to those who had gained over the enemy some advantage which had cost but few lives, and which had not been sufficiently decisive to finish the war; or in which the foe defeated was of no reputation and unworthy of the Roman arms, or even when a war had not been declared with all the accustomed forms.—The term *ovatio* is derived from *Ovis*, a sheep being the animal sacrificed by the *ovantes*, or those honoured with an ovation.

After the servile war, an ovation was conceded to M. Licinius Crassus; to have vanquished slaves being deemed unworthy of the full honours of the triumph. Augustus, after the recovery of the captured standards from Parthia, returning from the East, entered Rome in an ovation; and Vaillant thinks this event expressed on a coin of the *Licinia* family, in which that Emperor on horseback is holding a crown; but Spanheim is not of that opinion.

The *ovation* of M. Aurelius, who, after an eight years' war carried on against numerous nations of Germany, returned victorious to Rome, is, according to Vaillant, typified on a brass medallion, on which that Emperor marches on foot, adorned neither with the *trabea* nor with the *toga picta*, but in a military garb, holding a spear in his right hand. He appears to have been sacrificing at an altar in front of the temple of Jupiter Capitolinus, which is seen behind him, and to be about to pass through a triumphal arch as if on his way back to the Imperial palace. A prætorian standard bearer, as was the custom, precedes him, and Victory follows him, holding a laurel crown over his head.—The xxviiith Tribunitian power, with the title of IMP*erator* VI. COS. III. round

the medallion, shews, says Vaillant, the time when the ovation was decreed. At the bottom

of the coin the epigraph of ADVENTVS AVG*usti* also points to the period when it took place, namely, after the return of the Emperor.

P.

P. the fifteenth letter of the Latins.—On some very early coins of the Romans its form is somewhat like the Γ of the Greeks, the semicircular part not being complete, as on coins of the *Minucia* and of the *Furia* families.

P. is found serving as a mint-mark on the denarii of several Roman families, and appears also on the field and in the exergue of many coins of the Lower Empire. It is sometimes doubled as in *Jupiter*, written JVPPITER.

P. was occasionally used by the Latins for B, and this not only in the more ancient times but also in later ages, probably from similarity of sound. An instance occurs, so far in the Imperial series of Roman coins, as Antoninus Pius, on a second brass of whose reign is to be observed the word O*P*SEQVENS, as an epithet to FORTVNA, when, according to the ordinary rule of writing, it should be O*B*SEQVENS.

P. This letter by itself signifies *Pater;* or *Patriæ;* or *Per;* or *Percussa;* or *Perpetuus;* or *Pius;* or *Pontifex;* or *Populus;* or *Posuit;* or *Præfectus;* or *Primus;* or *Princeps;* or *Provinciæ;* or *Publius;* or *Publico;* &c.

P. *Pecunia,* or *Percussa moneta.*—AQVIL. P. *Aquiliensis Pecunia,* or *Aquileiæ Percussa;* on a coin of Julianus II.

P. *Penates.*—D. P. *Dii Penates.*—(Baudelot, i. p. 180.)

P. *Peragrata.*—ADVENTVS AVGVSTI. G. P., that is to say, Romam in urbem *Adventus Augusti Græcia Peragrata;* on a medal of Nero.

P. *Pia.*—LEG*io* V. P. C. *Pia Constans.*—P. for *Pia* is also an epithet frequently applied to Roman colonies.

P. *Plebis.*—TR. P. *Tribunus Plebis.* A Tribune of the people.

P. *Pondus—Pondera.*—PNR. On the field of a second brass of Claudius; *Pondus Numi Restitutum,* as it has been interpreted.

P. *Populi.*—P. R. *Populi Romani.*—CAPR. *Cusus Auctoritate Populi Romani.* Money struck by the authority of the Roman people.

P. *Populo.*—P. CIR. CON. *Populo Circenses Concessit.*—P. D. *Populo Datum.*

P. *Potestate.*—T. P. or TR. P. *Tribunicia Potestate.*

P. *Prætor.*—PRO P. *Pro Prætore.*

P. in the *vexillum,* or cavalry standard, means *Principes,* or that corps of Roman soldiers which formed their second line in battle array. Thus on certain denarii of the *Valeria* family the letters H. and P. on the legionary standards signify *Principes* and *Hastati.*

P. *Pro.*—P. C. *Pro Consul* or *Pro Consule.*—P. Q. *Pro Quæstore.*

P. *Pronepos.*—C. OCTAVIVS. C. P. *Caii Pronepos.*

P. *Provincia.*—A. P. *Armenia Provincia.*
P. *Publicæ.*—R. P. C. *Rei Publicæ Constituendæ.*
P. *Publius*, a frequent Roman prænomen, both on Family and Imperial coins.
P. A. *Pietas Augusti*, or *Augustæ*; also *Perpetuus Augustus.*
PAC. *Paci.*—PAC. ORBIS. TERRARVM. *Paci Orbis Terrarum*; also *Pacator, Pacifer, Pacifero*, as MARS. PAC. *Mars Pacifer.*—HERC. PACI. *Herculi Pacifero.*—[To the Pacific Hercules, or the Pacific Mars.]
PAC. *Pacis.*—ARA PAC*is.*
PACATIANVS, an usurper whose existence has not been alluded to by any historian, and whose memory is preserved by medals alone.—Even on coins the names of TIBERIVS CLAVDIVS MARIVS, or MARCIVS, PACATIANVS were unknown to antiquaries "until (says Beauvais) for the first time a medal of him was discovered by *Chamillart*, during his travels in the Pyrenees. This was at first regarded as spurious; but several others, and all of them in silver, were afterwards found."—Of the medal brought home and engraved by Chamillart, the antiquity is on all hands allowed to be incontestable. The obverse exhibits the radiated head of this tyrant with the inscription, not as Jobert gives it IMP. *T. IVL.* MAR.; but, according to Eckhel, with the coin before his eyes, IMP. *TI. CL.* MAR. PACATIANVS. P.F. AVG.—The reverse represents a woman standing clothed in the robe called *stola*, holding in her right hand an olive branch; and in her left, which is also employed in lifting the skirt of her gown, is a *hasta pura;* the legend reads PAX AETERNA.—From the workmanship of this coin and others, the *Tyrannus* whom it represents is supposed to have lived during the reign of Philip or of Trajan Decius; and to have been recognised as Emperor at the same time that *Marinus* and *Jotapianus* assumed the purple.—There is another silver medal engraved in Akerman from the one in the French King's cabinet, which has for its legend round the radiated head, IMP. TI. CL. PACATIANVS AVG., and on the reverse ROMAE. AETER. AN. MIL. ET. PRIMO. Roma-Victrix, seated.—Eckhel, in correcting the egregious error into which both Frœlich and Khell, as well as some other writers had fallen, quotes a letter of M. D'Ennery to Khell in 1772, in which the learned French numismatist says—"The legend of this tyrant (Pacatianus) does *not* bear the *prenomina* of T. IVL., but those of TI. CL., as I have ascertained from all the medals of that prince, which are esteemed to be indubitably genuine; and you may rely upon it that those, on which you do not find the aforesaid *prenomina* of *Tiberius Claudius*, are of modern fabrication. It is an error which I have corrected in several works."
With respect to the theatre of Pacatian's revolt, observes Mionnet, "opinions are divided. Some place it in the south of Gaul, where his medals were first found; others, on the contrary, believe that there are reasons for placing it in

the same country (Mœsia), where Marinus took the title of Augustus. There are even antiquaries, he adds, who suspect that Marinus and Pacatianus are the same person, and that the prenomen MAR. in the legend ought to be read *Marinus*, instead of *Marius* or of *Marcius*."—The latter conjecture may or may not be well founded; but the former suspicion appears totally devoid of any valid support; and after the description above given of the medals themselves may surely be dismissed without hesitation. There is ground to suppose that, falling into the power of Trajanus Decius, (who in that age of usurpers "passed for no better than one himself," as Beauvais says, "before he had vanquished Philip,") *Pacatianus* was deprived of life in the district where he commanded, shortly after his assumption of the purple. His medals, which present five different reverses, and which give him the physiognomy of a man of about thirty, are of the highest degree of

rarity. They were evidently struck at the seat of his usurped authority, whether that were in Gaul, which is most probable, or in Mœsia, or in Pannonia, or elsewhere.—The illustration of the coins of Pacatianus which appears above is taken from a denarius in the cabinet of Thomas Faulkner, Esq., F.S.A., who purchased it at the sale of the Sabatier collection for £19 10s.
PACATOR.—Sometimes by this cognomen, at others by that of *Bellator*, Mars, as the reputed father of Romulus, was distinguished by his most ardent worshippers the Romans. A bronze medallion of Gordianus Pius, in the *Des Camps* Collection, and exhibiting a fine sacrificial group, is considered by Vaillant to shew the devotion of that young prince to the God of Armies, in his two-fold character of *pacific* and *warlike.*
PACATOR ORBIS.—The radiated head of the Sun. This appears on the reverse of a gold and a silver coin of Sept. Severus; and alludes to the restoration of peace to the world by the conquest of Parthia, lying as regards Rome, to the *East.*—Of *Oriens* or the East, the ancient symbol was the Sun, as represented by a young man's head adorned with rays.—It was after having subdued the Parthians that Severus took the name of *Parthicus Maximus;* and now, on his making peace with them, he is called *Pacator Orbis.*—This Emperor is also designated on a marble in Gruter, as *Pacator Orbis* and *Fundator Imperii.*—Besides its appropriation to Severus, the title of *Pacator Orbis* is bestowed, in the inscription of their coins, on Caracalla, Gallienus, Postumus, Marius, Aurelianus, Florianus, and after them on other

Roman Emperors, but more out of hope than from reality, for the world was never at peace under any of these princes.

PACE. P.R. TERRA. MARIQ. PARTA. IANVM. CLVSIT.—The first and second brass medals of Nero, on which this interesting legend appears, represent in their type the temple of Janus shut—a circumstance limited to the very rare epochas of an universal peace.—It is only on his coins that Nero is recorded to have closed the sacred fane of old BIFRONS, *after having procured peace for the Roman people by land and by sea.* But possibly the infatuation of that vain tyrant prompted him to boast of a peace which seems denied as a fact by some historians—and though the coins themselves are common, it is uncertain to what year the reverse alludes.—On others we read *Pace populi Romani ubique* (instead of *Terra Marique) parta Janum clusit.*—It will be remarked that CLVSIT is here read for CLAVSIT. That "this was a mode of writing the word in Nero's time is proved (observes Eckhel), not only by these coins, but by the contemporaneous authority of Seneca, who in various passages of his work employs the term *cludere* for *claudere.*"— See *Janus.*

According to Livy, the temple of Janus, which remained always open when Rome was at war, was shut only once, from the foundation of the city to the battle of Actium. Under Augustus it was closed three times; and one of the occasions was about the period of our Blessed Saviour's Nativity, when, as the writings of the Fathers attest, the whole world enjoyed peace.

PACI. AETER*nae.*—A female figure seated, holding the *hasta pura* and an olive branch.— This inscription and type appear on a very rare gold medallion of Commodus, accompanied with the following record of the date when it was struck, namely :—TR. P. XIIII. IMP. VIII. COS. V., to mark, as Vaillant observes, victories over the Mauritanians and Dacians, and the pacification of the Pannonians; in Britain, in Germany, and in Dacia, the revolted provinces being quieted by the government of this emperor, as though *pax æterna* was *about to be (esset futura).*—(vol. ii. p. 188.)

PACI AVGVSTAE.—The Goddess of Peace, in the form of a winged victory walking, lifts with her right hand the border of her robe to her face, and holds in her left a winged caduceus, before her feet a serpent is moving forwards."— "This elegant type, on a gold coin of Claudius (says Eckhel in his *Catalogue,* ii.), expresses the manifold virtues of the Emperor and the public happiness enjoyed under his government. For in one single image are represented the symbols of Victory, Peace, Felicity, Prudence, and Modesty, qualities which indeed were *not all* wanting in the character of Claudius."

PACI AVGVSTI.—To the Peace of the Emperor.—Victory walking, in the dress and with the attributes above described. This appears on a silver coin of Vespasianus, who, evidently borrowing the legend and type from Claudius,

caused it to be struck on the occasion of his having brought to completion the structure of a splendid temple dedicated to the Goddess of Peace.—The reverse of a silver medal of Domitilla, wife of Vespasian, bears a similar type.— See PACI AVGVSTAE —Vaillant. ii. p. 94.

PACI ORBIS TERR*arum* AVG.—The head of a woman, adorned with a crown, on which are two towers.- -On a silver coin of Vespasian, with whose mint this deity appears to be a frequent type, as the goddess herself was a favourite object of the Emperor's worship.· It was in the year of Christ 75, when he and Titus were consuls together, that he dedicated the temple, begun under Claudius, and described by ancient writers as the most beautiful in Rome, to *Peace.* In that building, if Hieronymus is to be relied upon, were deposited the vases and other spoils of the Holy Temple of Jerusalem, brought in triumph by Titus to Rome.

PACI PERP*etuæ.*—A temple of six columns, in the middle of which is an altar, on a silver coin of Augustus. The temple of Janus was twice shut by Augustus; hence the occasion of this silver coin being struck, with the legend to *Perpetual Peace.*—Suetonius says Augustus shut the temple of Janus three times.

PACIS EVENT.—The Genius *Eventus* stands naked, holding in the right hand a *patera,* and corn-ears and poppies in his left.—Silver of Vespasian.

Bonus Eventus (the God of good Success) was worshipped by the Romans among the other *Dei Consentes,* as a deity especially presiding over agriculture. His statue is said to have been sculptured by Praxiteles, in a form similar to the figure on this medal, and which is designated by the epigraph as *Pacis Eventus,* as if Vespasian wished to have it inferred that through the prosperous event of peace, a greater disposition had been promoted for agricultural pursuits.—[Vaillant, ii., p. 88.]

Pacuvia or *Paquia,* a family of uncertain rank, indeed scarcely if at all mentioned by old writers, although sometimes its name occurs on ancient marbles.—Gruter gives an inscription which reads C. PAQVIVS ; and Muratori another, OSSA PAQVVIAE. PAQVVI RVFI., an example probably of Q. used for C., thus rendering it likely that PAQVIVVIVS is the same as PACVVIVS, and consequently that the Paquius Rufus of the following coin was of the same family as the Pecuvius Rufus of the inscribed marble :—

A. C. L. V. Bare head of M. Antony.

Q. PAQVIVS. RVF. LEG. A togated figure seated in a curule chair, holding a charta or sheet of parchment in his right hand, into which he is looking; on the ground is a vase or globe.—*Small brass. rare.*

Paduan.—By this name are designated the false medals executed with much care and with surpassing skill, by *Giovanni del Cavino,* surnamed *il paduano,* and by *Bassiano.*—These fabricators of counterfeits, who are equally distinguished by the appellation of the *Paduans,* copied medals from the *antique,* or according to the antique method, or they composed designs for reverses, with a profound knowledge of history.

These medals, which belong to the sixteenth century, were held in great repute, and are still much in request on account of their beautiful workmanship. It is to the Paduans, and also to the Dutchman *Carteron* that the greatest portion of the false coins are to be ascribed, which find a place in almost all cabinets. The French King's Collection, at Paris, contains a fine *suite* of these mock antiques.

PAETVS, surname of the *Aelia* family ; on a denarius of which is P. PAETVS. ROMA. with the Dioscuri on horseback.

PAL. *Palæstinæ.*—PR. S. PAL. *Provinciæ Syriæ Palæstinæ.*

PAL. *Palatino.*—APOL. PAL. or PALAT. *Apollini Palatino.*—IMP. VIII. TR. P. XIII. COS. v. On a first brass of Commodus, which represents Apollo holding a lyre. *Apollo Actius* is meant in this case. The god was called *Palatinus*, because a dedication was made to him by Augustus in the *Palatium* at Rome, after the battle of Actium. The coins of Commodus, struck with this epigraph, refer to the *ludi Apollinares*, or *Apollinarian* games, which were celebrated at Rome, in supplication to Apollo as the God of Medicine, that he would stay a dreadful pestilence raging in that city in the year 943, during the height of which, by the testimony of Dion, it often happened that two thousand persons died of it in one day.

Palaeographia, Paleography—the science which serves to make us acquainted with the writing used on ancient marbles, coins, manuscripts, &c.—The coins of some cities shew that they bore a succession of different names." These variations (says Hennin, ii. p. 12) are useful to geography and history, and also to (numismatic) Paleography, inasmuch as they serve to establish the epochas of coinage.—Under the Roman power, many Greek cities added to their own names imperial denominations, particularly those of *Augusta;* or otherwise changed their names for those of the Emperors, *Trajanopolis, Hadrianotheræ,* &c. Other epithets of divers kinds are useful in a geographical point of view."
—[See *Inscription.*—Millin, *Dict. Des Beaux Arts.*]

Pæstum, a city of Lucania (now a province of Naples), called by the Greeks *Posidonia*, situate on the shore of the Mediterranean.— "This city," says Eckhel, "when under the government of its own laws, struck many coins with its Greek name of *Posidonia.* But once established as a Roman colony it was called on its coins *Pæstum*, in the old Latin form of letters and orthography. And from the time of its receiving the rights of a colony, no coins of *Pæstum* exist, except brass ones, and those with Latin inscriptions, whence it appears that to their colonies no privilege was given by the Romans for the coinage of gold and silver, but solely of brass."—[*Num. Vet.* p. 39.]

Palatium, Mount Palatine, one of the seven hills of Rome, on which the Kings first, then the Consuls, afterwards the Emperors, from Augustus downwards, in a long succession, fixed their residence. Hence the word *Palace*, as designating the house of a royal or imperial personage.—The term PALATIVM does not occur on any ancient Roman medals, that ascribed to *Nerva* being pronounced spurious.—[See Eckhel, vi. 411.]

PALIKANVS, the surname of the *Lollia* family, on whose denarii we see it sometimes accompanying the head of *Felicitas;* sometimes the head of *Libertas*, and a bridge of five arches ; at others, the laureated head of *Honos*, with a curule chair between corn-ears, the symbols of the edileship.—See *Lollia.*

Palladium, an image of *Pallas*, or Minerva, to which were attached the destinies of Troy. This statue, three cubits in height, held a lance in the right hand, a shield on the left arm. Dionysius of Halicarnassus, who follows the Grecian figment that it was the gift of heaven to the Trojans, adds that Æneas possessed himself of it, and conveyed it to Italy, with his household gods *(Penates).* It was said to have long been preserved in the Temple of Vesta, at Rome, and many medals represent that goddess seated, with the Palladium in her hand.

That the *Palladium* was preserved in the Temple of Vesta, at Rome, is a fact considered by Eckhel to be typified on a brass medallion of Lucilla, Empress of Lucius Verus, on which, without epigraph, appears a temple, in which is an idol, and before which six female figures are sacrificing, at a lighted altar. It is narrated by Val. Maximus that, at the burning of the temple of Vesta, Metellus preserved the *Palladium*, which was snatched unharmed from out of the midst of the conflagration. Lucan, Herodian, and Livy, confirm this statement; the last named writer says—" *Quid do æternis Vestæ ignibus signoque, quod imperii pignus custodia ejus templi tenetur, loquar ?"*— ["Why need I speak of the eternal fire of Vesta, and of the statue (i.e. *Palladium*) which is preserved, as a pledge of the empire's safety, in the sanctuary of her temple ?"]

The *Palladium* borne by Æneas in his right hand, whilst he carries Anchises on his shoulders, appears on coins of the Cecilia and Julia families, and on denarii of Julius Cæsar.— Minerva also holds it on some imperial medals. —It appears in the hand of *Juno*, on a coin of Julia Soemias. In the hands of *Vesta* it is placed, on coins of Vespasian, Titus, Domitian, Trajan, and Antonine ; and also on medals of the Faustinas and other Empresses.—Also in the hand of Venus, on a coin of Faustina, jun.

The *Palladium* also is seen in the right hand of the Genius of *Rome*, on coins of Vespasian, Domitian, Antoninus Pius, and Constantius Chlorus.—It also appears in the right hand of *Annona*, on a silver medal of Titus, as indicating the popular belief that so long as that image was preserved the Roman empire would flourish.

Pallas, the daughter of Jupiter, from whose brain she is said to have sprung, is the same deity whom the Latins called *Minerva.*—Pallas is represented on numberless coins as a young virgin wearing a helmet. In a variety of types she is depictured armed with javelin, or with thunderbolt, or with spear and shield.

Pallas Bellatrix, as the presiding divinity of wars, appears in Roman medals armed with the hasta and the buckler.

Pallas Fulminatrix. Minerva armed with the irresistible bolts of *Jupiter Tonans* is most frequently exhibited on gold and silver coins of Domitian, who, by this image of the *thunderess,* aimed to shew himself born to be a terror to the enemies of the Roman name.

Pallas Jaculatrix. The dart-throwing Pallas, armed with the ægis and shield, and in the act of casting a javelin, standing on a ship's prow, and with her symbol, an owl, at her feet, occurs on a great many, gold, silver, and brass coins of Domitian, who paid a peculiarly zealous worship to this goddess. That vain and cruel Emperor is said to have preserved her image in his bed-chamber, to have devoted the most solemn adoration to her shrine, and to have boasted that he governed himself in all things by her auspicious will and pleasure.

Pallas (or Minerva) *Nicephora,* the tutelary deity of the Athenians, appears on a second brass of the *Clovia* family.—The goddess walks with a trophy on her right shoulder, and in her left a shield charged with the head of Medusa. C. CLOVI*us* PRAEF*ectus.*—Her attributes: the owl standing on a helmet, are seen on denarii of the *Cordia* family.—All her attributes are collected in one type on a coin of the *Valeria* family, under the figure of a bird, with the helmeted head of a virgin, and a shield and two spears attached to its left side.

Pallas Victrix, depicted with small figure of victory in the right, and a spear in the left hand, with a shield at her feet, appears on silver of Domitian; also with a trophy by her side on a brass medallion of Commodus.—See MINER*va.*

The helmeted head of *Pallas* appears frequently on the early brass coinage of the Romans; and also on denarii of the *Claudia, Valeria, Vibia,* and other families.

Pallium, an open vestment, used by the Greeks and Romans as a cloke, or exterior garment. Some writers say it was of a round, others of a semi-circular form. It was so worn (and much nicety was displayed in its proper adjustment), as to be capable of covering the other habiliments, and even to envelop the whole person of a man. On coins the figures of Emperors and Gods sometimes appear clothed in the pallium.

Pallor, the Goddess of *Paleness,* as indicative of *Fear,* is represented by the countenance of a woman, with long dishevelled hair, on a denarius of the *Hostilia* family. This type, and the head of *Pavor,* on another silver coin of L. *Hostilius Saserna,* were adopted by that monetary triumvir to denote his claimed descent from King Tullus Hostilius, who (Livy tells us) being in the heat of battle with the Veïans, in danger of defeat, vowed twelve Salian priests and a temple each to *Pallor* and *Pavor;*

which vows, after victory, he performed, and afterwards worshipped these "white-faced" personifications of the very opposites to martial courage. This seems preposterously absurd; but as heathen superstition scrupled not to consecrate altars to impiety, to worship obscenity, and even to place some diseases in the number of her divinities, there is nothing very surprising in the folly of her having deifyed the attributes of pusillanimity and panic!

Palma, the palm-tree, or a branch of it, may be remarked on an infinity of ancient medals and other monuments. It is the numismatic symbol of Phœnicia; and also offers itself as the token of fecundity, because the palm constantly fructifies as long as it lives. It was, moreover, the symbol of *Judæa,* as is shewn (says Spanheim) not only on coins struck by the Roman mint, after the conquest of that country, under Vespasian, Titus, and Domitian, but likewise on much older medals, formerly coined by the Jews themselves. The palm-tree forms the type of a consular coin, struck under M. Antony, with legend ALEXANDR. AEGYPT.

The *Palm* sometimes serves as the symbol of victory, because, on the days of triumph, the conqueror, besides the crown, bore a palm-branch; at other times it signified the duration and permanence of the empire, because the palm lives a long time. Palm-branches were borne before a victor on his reception at the gate of a city. The palm sometimes denotes joy *(hilaritas),* abundance, equity, piety, health, and felicity. We also see it on coins in the hand of Hercules, of Jupiter, of Juno, of Mars, of Mercury, of Venus, and especially of *Pallas* (or Minerva). It is given to Rome, to Victory, to Fortune, to Liberty, and to Peace.— The Emperors Julius Cæsar, Augustus, Trajan, Elagabalus, Alexander Severus, Probus, are represented with a palm-branch in their hand.—A long branch of it appears in the right hand of a woman, with the epigraph of HILARITAS TEMPORVM, on a coin of *Didia Clara.*

Palm-branches in the hands of wrestlers *(athletæ)* appear on *Contorniate* medals of Nero, Trajan, Sept. Severus, Caracalla, Honorius, Julianus II., &c.

Palmyra, a region of Syria, in which was a once celebrated metropolis of that name. The city called by the Romans Palmyra, was more anciently named *Thadmor,* that is to say, *City of Palms,* whence it derived its appellation of Palmyra. This magnificent capital was situated to the north-east of Damascus, between that city and the Euphrates, within a fertile territory, watered with springs, but surrounded by sandy deserts. After the destruction of the kingdom of Israel, it fell into the possession of independent princes, who formed a state, centrally situated between the Roman empire and the kingdom of Parthia; and they succeeded in aggrandising it at the expense of both.— *Odenathus,* the last powerful prince of Palmyra, was associated in the Imperial government by Gallienus, and conjointly with that emperor made conquests of territory from the Persians.

Septimia Zenobia, his widow, succeeded her husband, who had been assassinated by his nephew. That woman had the repute of being the most heroic and the wisest princess of her age. In 270, after a brave and long resistance to the progress of her Roman invaders, she was vanquished by Aurelian, who barbarously *graced* his triumph with her presence as a captive at Rome.—The effigy of *Vabalathus*, a Palmyrenian Prince, appears on the reverse of a small brass coin of Aurelian.—See VABALATHVS.

Paludamentum, a military cloke, like that which the Greeks called *chlamys*. It was fastened with a *fibula* or clasp upon the right shoulder, in such a manner as to leave that side uncovered in order to give freedom to the right arm. This peculiarity gave rise to the occasional application of the term *Paludati* to warriors in general, although it properly belonged only to the chiefs who won the *paludamentum*. This mantle, not so large as the *pallium*, was easily put on and off, and adapted itself conveniently to service in the field. When a Roman Emperor or General was on the point of setting out to take the command of his army, he went first to the capital, and was there invested with the *paludamentum*. On his return from the expedition, he threw off his war-cloke at the gates, and entered Rome clothed in the *toga*. This custom, it appears, was so well established, that (according to Suetonius) Vitellius was looked upon as having committed, not only a novel but a tyrannical act, because he entered the city *paludatus*.—Septimius Severus, on the other hand, had the policy always to doff his soldier-like habiliments, and to assume the civil garb on such occasions. On the coins of this Emperor and his son Caracalla we see him with the fibulated *paludamentum*. Indeed, we are told by Spartianus, that he wore such scanty clothing that he scarcely had any purple vestment over his tunic, but covered his shoulders with a shaggy *chlamys*.—The cuirass and the *paludamentum* often appear together. Some medals, however, present the figures of Emperors in the cuirass without the military cloke; yet the *paludamentum* over the tucked-up tunic is more rarely to be seen without the cuirass.

Paludatus.—An Emperor, or General, was thus called, when dressed in the warlike habit, which consisted of *paludamentum* or short mantle, *lorica* or breast-plate, with other military armour and ornaments.—When Roman authors, such as Suetonius (in his Life of Galba), make mention of an Emperor's going out with his army *(faciens profectionem ad bellum)*, they almost invariably say that he departed *paludatus*.—On a large brass of Domitian we see the Emperor standing, in the dress of a warrior, holding a lance in his left hand, and the *paludamentum* on his shoulder; a captive at his feet.

Pampinea corona.—The crown of vine leaves adorns the head of Bacchus, on many coins of cities; and, in imitation of that deity, appears on the head of the vain and presumptuous

Mark Antony, in more than one of his medals, struck during the period of his Asiatic campaigns.

Pan, the fabled son of Mercury and Penelope, and one of the companions of Bacchus. The infancy of this god of shepherds and husbandmen, was entrusted to the nymphs of Arcadia; and in reference to the worship paid to him as the guardian of flocks and herds, Virgil thus sings of him:—

Pan primus calamos cera conjungere plures
Instituit: Pan curat oves oviumque magistros.
　　　　　　　　　　　　Ecl. ii. l. 31.

And not of shepherds only, but of all nature he was the reputed divinity, his name being, according to some writers, derived from the similar word in Greek, πὰν, by which *omne* or *totum* (everything or all) is signified.—Pan is usually represented in the form of a satyr, with goat's horns, and a cloak of goat's skin, playing the *Syrinx*, or flute of seven pipes, and holding the pedum or pastoral staff. It was in his honour, as presiding over an important branch of rural affairs, that the festivals called *Lupercalia* (from *Lupercus*, the wolf hunter, as Pan was also called) were instituted, at first by Evander, and afterwards introduced into Rome by Romulus. They were celebrated on the 15th of February, with ceremonies so absurd and disgusting, that, after they had for a time fallen into disuetude, it seems strange that so decorous a prince as Augustus affected to be, on his accession to imperial power, should have revived and patronised them.

Panis persona. The mask of Pan, with the attribute of the *pedum*, appears on a *denarius* of the *Vibia* family, in allusion, as Havercamp says, to the name of C. Vibias *Pansa*, who was consul in the year of Rome 711. Another silver coin of the same family, bearing the cognomen of PANSA, exhibits the mask of Pan, encircled with ivy leaves and berries.—The only other *Latin* medal which represents this rustic deity is one struck by the *Colonia Laus Iulia* COR*inthus*, under Marcus Aurelius, on which his entire figure, with horns and hoofs, appears, holding on his left arm the head of a goat, and in his hand a crook. Another coin, with Greek inscription, bearing the names of two cities of Cappadocia, *Cerasus* and *Tiana*, exhibits this same goat-footed god, with the pastoral staff in his left hand, and a lighted torch in his right; allusive (as Spanheim observes) to his having been one of those divinities whose feasts were celebrated with burning *flambeaux;* and, according to Pausanias, a fire was perpetually kept up in his temple in Arcadia.—PANSA, says Pitiscus, is the surname of a Roman, given him on account of the large size of his feet.

Panis civilis was bread which the authorities at Rome distributed among the people.—*Panis gradilis* was a distribution of bread made in a public place, at the *liberalities* of the Emperors. We see on various coins a representation of the *suggestum*, or, as the French term it, an *estrade*, meaning a raised platform, to which those appointed to receive the *congiarium* or bounty, of the imperial donor, were accustomed to ascend by steps *(gradibus)*; hence the term *gradilis panis,*—See CONGIARIVM and LIBERALITAS.

PANN.—PANNON. *Pannoniæ.* The Pannonian provinces.—METALL. VLPIAN PANN. *Metalli Ulpiani Pannonici.*—Coins in third brass struck of metal dug from the mines of Pannonia, and which were called *Ulpiani,* after the family name of Trajan, in whose reign, it is said, the Romans first discovered them.

Pannonia, a country of Eastern Europe, which the ancients divided into Upper Pannonia, now Austria and Hungary; and Lower Pannonia, which at this time of day comprehends Bulgaria, Bosnia, and Servia.—Tiberius, during the reign of Augustus, conquered this country in two years. Its name and personified genius appear on coins of Aelius Verus, Trajanus Decius, Hostilianus, and Aurelianus.

Pannonia is designated on medals by two figures of women clothed, "because that country (says Jobert) is cold. They also hold military ensigns in their hands, as betokening the valour of its inhabitants."

PANNONIA.—Pannonia personified under the form of a woman, stands covered with the pileus or bonnet of the country, holding a pike in her right hand, on which is a small standard. This legend and type appear on first and second brass of L. Aelius, who, adopted as successor and proclaimed Cæsar by Hadrian, was (according to Spartianus) soon afterwards sent by that Emperor as Governor into Pannonia; and these coins were struck in commemoration of the event.—"The figure representing this province is distinguished by a kind of cap, which ancient authors assert to have been the covering for the head, worn by people inhabiting the western shores of the Black Sea.—The square standard at the top of the lance which *Pannonia* holds in her hand, called at first *vexillum,* and peculiar to the cavalry, was in a later age denominated *labarum,* and became, in the Lower Empire, the principal ensign of the Roman armies."—[*Leçons de Num. Rom.* 133.]

PANNONIAE.—The division of this region into two parts is characterised by two female figures, on gold, silver, and brass of Trajanus Decius. [See *Decius Trajanus.*]—The cause of this Emperor's attachment to these provinces is sufficiently obvious; for they were the first to proclaim his election to the purple, and it was to the fidelity and bravery of the Pannonian legions that he owed his victory over Philip. Hence it was the peculiar care and pride of Decius to rescue or defend Pannonia from the incursions of the barbarians.—There is a similar reverse on a coin of Julianus the usurper.—[Eckhel, vol. vii. p. 345.]

Pannonia, according to *Lampridius,* was brought into a state of pacification with the Romans, during the reign of Commodus.—Vaillant, in his selections from the cabinet of *Descamps,* interprets a medallion of that Emperor's, inscribed VIRTVS AVG., &c., and exhibiting for its type Rome sitting on a heap of spoils, as referring to that event having been accomplished by the lieutenants of Commodus.

Panormus, a maritime and very celebrated city of Sicily, now called *Palermo.* It was founded by the Carthaginians; and the whole island having become a conquest of the Romans, *Panormus* was in process of time established into a *colony* by Augustus.—Vespasian afterwards assigned its territory to the veterans of his army and to the members of his family. The number of coins of this city is very considerable, especially the autonomous pieces both *Punic* and *Greek.* There are brass Imperial of Augustus, and his family, and of Tiberius.—Among the *Latin* coins some are found bearing the name HISPANORVM.—Vaillant, in his *Colonies* (vol. i. p. 52), gives one *Latin* Imperial second brass with the head of Augustus, and the epigraph PANORMITANORVM. On the reverse is CN. DOMITI*VS* PRO*Con*S*ul,* and the type of the three human legs, the triquetral symbol of Sicily, over which is placed capricorn, the sign of Augustus.

Pantheon, a temple in honour of all the gods, as the Greek word signifies. The most celebrated edifice of this description is the one at Rome, which, built by Agrippa, the son-in-law of Augustus, exists to this day, under the well-known appellation of the *Rotunda,* its interior being circular. It also still retains the name of the Pantheon, and constitutes, with its surperb portico, one of the most perfect as well as majestic remains of Roman antiquity.

The term *Pantheon* or *Panthea* was also applied to statues or images, which bear the signs or symbols of several divinities united together. Of those represented by medals the most remarkable is that on a coin of Antoninus Pius, and of the younger Faustina, where at once are to be recognised Serapis by his *modius* or bushel; the Sun by his rays; Jupiter Ammon by his ram's horns; Pluto by his large beard; Neptune as indicated by the trident; and Esculapius distinguished by the serpent twined around his staff.—Another medal, quoted by *Tristan,* exhibits a man with head veiled and body naked, who bears the weapons and attributes of Sol, Mercury, and Neptune.—Vaillant calls this kind of medals *pantheon;* and there is little doubt but that the spirit of Pagan superstition encouraged the design of rendering such figures portable, as representations of the *Dei Lares,* as Baudelot learnedly and forcibly contends.—These pantheons, or their symbols, are conjectured to be represented by certain types on coins of the *Julia* and *Plætoria* families.—[See Eckhel.]

Panther, an animal sacred to Bacchus (LIBER PATER as in Gallienus); and its image forms on coins and other monuments at once the attribute of, and the attendant upon, that deity. Bacchus and his followers, indeed, appear on ancient monuments covered with the skin of this animal, which is also symbolical of Pan. This ferocious beast, which is still very common in Asia, was in the time of the Romans to be found in considerable numbers in Caria, Pamphylia, and

Syria. It was often brought from the East, and also from Africa, to figure at Rome in the sports of the circus, where sometimes it was harnessed to chariots; at others made to fight. —Scaurus, during his edileship, was the first to furnish a public shew of panthers to the number of one hundred and fifty. Pompey produced five hundred and ten; and Augustus four hundred and twenty, according to Pliny.

Panthers appear on coins as the companions of Bacchus, because the natural history of the ancients ascribed to these animals a peculiar fondness for wine; and this liquor was one of the means said to have been employed to take them; the hunters using it to make the panthers intoxicated. The round spots on the hide forbid our confounding either the *panther* or the *pard* with the tiger, and the distinction is observable on coins.

A *panther*, on which Cybele or Isis is seated, occurs on a coin of Hadrian. It appears at the feet of Bacchus on colonial coins of Antoninus Pius, M. Aurelius, Sept. Severus, Caracalla, and Geta.—On a medallion of Hadrian a panther and a goat draw a chariot, in which are seated Bacchus and Apollo.—And on a coin of Antoninus a *panther* is similarly employed, with a satyr for his yoke-fellow, in a car where the God of Wine is recognised by his thyrsus, and the fair Ariadne sits beside him.—Vaillant, in his *Latin Colonies*, gives us a coin of Corinth, struck under M. Aurelius, on the reverse of which is C. L. I. COR. *Colonia Laus Julia Corinthus;* and *Liber Pater* standing with the cup or flagon in his right hand and the thyrsus in his left. A panther sits at his feet looking up as if at the goblet which contains "the liquor that he loves."

A *panther* appears on a brass coin of Galllenus, with legend of LIBERO *Patri* CON*servatori* AV*Gusti*.

PAP. *Papius.* The name of a family.— L. PAP. AVIT. *Lucius Papius Avitus*, prænomen, name, and surname.

Papaver.—The poppy was, with the ancients, the symbol of fertility, on account of the large quantity of seeds which this plant produces, and therefore consecrated to Ceres. Hence Virgil *(Georg.* L. i.) calls it *Cereale Papaver;* and amongst the corn-ears given to that goddess the poppy is generally intermingled.—The *poppy* between two corn-ears, held by Ceres, occurs on a second brass of Vitellius, with the epigraph of CERES AVGVSTA. The same goddess, with the same attributes, seated, and a female standing by her, appears on a first brass of Nerva, with the legend of ANNONA AVGVST.—It also is seen on coins of Nero, Julia Titi, and Caracalla; and the poppy, ears of corn, and *modius* are found on medals of Trajan, Hadrian, and M. Aurelius.—On a coin of Domitian the poppy is represented in conjunction with corn-ears, whilst two right hands united sustain a caduceus; the epigraph is FIDES PVBL*ica*. [Eckhel, *Cat.* ii. p. 156.]—See PLEBEI VRBANAE, &c.

PAPI. *Papia.*—This abbreviated word appears on a tablet behind the head of Juno Sospita on a coin of the Papia family, struck in commemoration of a law, carried by C. Papius, against permitting foreigners to reside in Rome. —See *Papia.*

PAPI. also stands for *Papirius*, the name of a man.

PAPIA, a plebeian family of consular rank, and originally belonging to *Lanuvium;* its surname on coins is *Celsus.* The *Papii* were tribunes of the people, who passed the laws named *Papiæ* respecting vestals and strangers.— Morell enumerates no less than 63 varieties. The silver are common. Among the scarce types is that on a denarius, the obverse of which bears the word TRIVMPVS, a young laureated head, with a trophy behind it (others have the head of *Juno Sospita* without legend). The reverse presents L. PAPIVS CELSVS IIIVIR. A wolf holding in his mouth a lighted stick, and setting fire to a heap of wood placed before an eagle with its wings spread.—For some remarks on the legend and type of the obverse, see TRIVMPVS.—With respect to the singular type on the reverse, it is considered by numismatists (Eckhel among the rest) to be explained by a passage in Dionysius Halicarnassus, who says—when Lavinium was about to be built, some prodigies offered themselves to the (superstitious) apprehensions of the Trojans. In a wood they observed that a fire lighted spontaneously was fed by a wolf bringing to it a dry stick or faggot, as fuel, in its mouth; and an eagle which had flown to the same spot was fanning the flame with its wings. On the other hand a fox having dipped his tail in the river was seen sprinkling water over the conflagration; and sometimes those who had raised, at other times the fox who endeavoured to extinguish the flame, prevailed; but at length the latter failed of success, and the wolf with his aquiline ally triumphed. The historian adds to this evidently allegorical statement, what was possibly the literal fact, that the brazen images of the wolf and an eagle were preserved in the forum at Lavinium, to the day in which he wrote, in record of the event, which, as Mr. Akerman observes, was the mode adopted by Æneas to predict the destiny of "the infant colony, which, although exposed to the enmity of surrounding states, would finally subdue them."—For other denarii of this family, bearing on their reverse a griffin, see Eckhel, vol. v. 268.—For Juno Sispita see the word; also see *Roscia* family.—On each of the many silver coins of this family, and others, we see a small stamp, or mark (such as an apex, an owl, a lion's head, a foot, a sistrum, &c., &c., prettily engraved), of which the infinite variety impresses one with a most forcible idea of the stupendous quantity of different *matrices* employed in the mint of Rome, under the republic.

Papilio.—The butterfly held in the claws of the sea-crab *(pagurus)* appears on a gold coin of M. DVRMIVS, one of the monetal triumvirs of Augustus.—The application of this type to the Durmia family is unascertained.

By the image of the *Papilio* the ancients understood the power and origin of the soul to be designated. And the mind, or *Psyche*, itself is no otherwise attempted to be expressed than by this figure of a butterfly.—Thus, on the reverse of a brass medallion of Antoninus Pius (without epigraph), the fable of Prometheus occurs, in which *Minerva* places a butterfly on the head of the man whom the Promethean touch has just formed, as if intended to symbolise " the breath of life"—" the living soul" of a human being under the winged form of that volant and ephemeral insect.—On the obverse of this curious coin, which Vaillant notices as being in the Vatican collection, is read ANTONINVS AVG. PIVS. P.P. TR. P. COS. III., and we see the portrait of that most wise and prudent Emperor, with head laureated, and the *chlamys* on his breast.—See *Prometheus*.

PAPIRIA, a family of double order, the one *patrician* of the junior race *(minorum gentium)*, called in the earlier ages *Papisia ;* the other was *plebeian*, according to Cicero, whose words of the *epistola ad Pætum*, both Ursinus and Havercamp quote in illustration of *Papiria gens*.—The surnames of the plebeian branch, which was of consular rank, and to which alone the coins of this family belong, are *Carbo* and *Turdus*. There are sixteen varieties : *silver* common. On one of the denarii of this family appears the head of Pallas, winged : behind which is a branch.—*Rev.* Jupiter in a quadriga at full speed. The *brass* pieces of this family, less common than the silver, are the *as* and parts of the *as*.

P. AQ. *Percussa Aquileiæ*.—Money struck at Aquileia. Mint-marks on the lower part of coins.

P. AR. *Percussa Arelate*.—Money struck at Arles, on the exergue of a coin of Magnentius.

PAR. *Parium*, a colony in Mysia.

PAR. *Parthica*.—LEG. III. PAR. *Legio Tertia Parthica*.—VIC. PAR. *Victoria Parthica*.

PAR. *Parthicus*.—PAR. AR. AD. *Parthicus Arabicus Adiabenicus*.—The Parthian, the Arabian, the Adiabenican titles given to Sept. Severus for having conquered those countries; and which appear on a silver coin of that Emperor, exhibiting a trophy between two captives sitting on the ground, struck in his sixth consulate ; and also on other medals of his.

Parazonium.—Numismatic antiquaries are not agreed as to the proper signification of the word, when applied to an object seen on several Roman coins of the Imperial series. Patin, also referring to its Greek etymology, says the *parazonium* was a weapon so called because it was worn suspended by a belt or chain from the *zona*, or girdle ; but that it had no point, because a general ought not to be cruel towards his own people. Spanheim speaks of *parazonia* as swords attached to the thigh, or hanging from a girdle. " But," says Jobert, " Its very form, and the manner in which it is held, is opposed to this opinion." And then he alludes to the medal of *Honos et Virtus*, struck

under Galba, in which Virtus holds what is called the *parazonium* upright, one end resting on his knee. He also adduces instances, on coins of Titus and Domitian, in both which it rests on the side, not attached to the girdle. And he quotes a reverse of Antoninus Pius, in which this *parazonium*, which Patin calls *scipio*, is across both shoulders in the form of a quiver. These exceptional cases of the manner in which it appears upon coins to have been carried, do not, however, interfere with the more usual acceptation of the word as signifying a short sheathed sword, worn at the girdle. The circular termination does not shew that the sword had no point, for it is merely the metallic end of the sheath.

The *Parazonium*, as a symbol of virtue, or rather of valour *(Virtus)*, appears in the right hand of that Roman deification, on coins of the Licinia family, in Morell's *Num. Consular ;* and Vaillant shews it on coins of the *Volteia* family. —It appears in the left hand of the Emperor on Trajan's well-known large brass, ARMENIA REDACTA ; also on coins of Vespasian, Titus, Domitian, M. Aurelius, L. Verus, Commodus, Caracalla, Alexander Severus, and other *Augusti*.

Parcæ, the three sisters, *Clotho, Lachesis, Atropos*, the same as the *Fates* in Pagan theology, according to which they were the daughters of Night, and employed together in dispensing the thread of human life ; the first holding the distaff ; the second spinning the length of each mortal's existence to its destined termination ; the third cutting the thread ; that is to say, awarding death at the appointed time. Procopius mentions a temple erected to the *Parcæ* at Rome ; and that it was erected in the reign of Diocletian seems probable from the gold coins of that Emperor and his colleague Val. Maximianus, inscribed FATIS VICTRICIBVS, and on which three *Parcæ* stand, each holding a torch on a ・rudder in their right hands joined together ; for the Romans were accustomed to call the *Parcæ* by the name of *Fata*, and to give them the title of *Dominæ* and *Victrices ;* as they spoke of Venus Victrix, and Diana Victrix.

PAREN*ti* CONSER*vatori* SVO.—This, preceded by S. P. Q. R., appears on the reverse of a denarius of Augustus, the type being the *toga picta* between a sceptre surmounted by an eagle and a garland of laurel.—[The obverse of this coin presents a car drawn by four horses, with CAESARI. AVGVST.]—The reverse of this silver coin exhibits the principal personal ornaments of the triumpher, according to Livy (viz., the *aurea corona*, the *scipio eburneus*, the *toga picta*, to which were added the *tunica palmata*, and the *sella curulis*).—And, by the inscription S. P. Q. R., it appears that the senate and the Roman people had decreed these honours to Augustus.—Eckhel assigns the coinage of this piece to A. V. C. 752 (B. C. 2), because Augustus is thereon called *Parens*, by which name, not by senatorial decree, but from affection, he was at that period distinguished.—On the same medal he is called *Conservator*, although it does not appear that this name was given to him *Ex Senatus Consulto.*

PARENS.—As Augustus was at first surnamed PATER PATRIAE, so also (according to Spon) he is entitled on medals PARENS COLONIAE. —M. Agrippa is also denominated MVNICIP. PARENS. on a coin of the Gaditani (people of Cadiz.)

PARENS. PATRIAE. (CAESAR.) EX. S.C. —A circular temple of six columns, in which is a statue on a pedestal.—This honourable title Julius Cæsar saw conferred upon him after his victory in Spain, according to the concurrent evidences of Dion, Appianus, and Suetonius. It was also continued after his death, for it is related by the writer last named—that "after he had been put to death, the people erected in the forum a solid column, nearly twenty feet high, of Numidian marble, and inscribed on it the words PARENTI. PATRIAE." Cicero states the same fact, but transfers the cause to Antony—"Your friend (Antony) adds fuel to the flame daily; especially by inscribing on the statue, which he erected in the rostra, the words PARENTI. OPTIME. MERITO.—For this reason the assassins of Cæsar were everywhere, out of hatred, called *parricides*, and even the ides of March, in which he was slain, received the name of *parricidium.*—See CAESAR PARENS PATRIAE, on coins, in gold and silver, of Julius Cæsar, which confirm this title, the monetary record of which is supposed to date about the year of Rome 710.—See Eckhel vol. vi. p. 17.

PARENTIBVS.—See *Divis Parentibus,* on a gold coin of Hadrian.

Parium, a city of Mysia, on the Propontis, built by the Parians, inhabitants of an island in the Egean Sea, afterwards a Roman colony, founded by Julius Cæsar, whence its name of Julia; it also took the name of *Augusta,* from its having been re-peopled with veteran colonists by Augustus. This city possessed the privileges of the Jus Italica. Its ruins are still to be seen near a place now called *Kamares,* or *Porto Camera.* Its coins, which are numerous, consist of autonomes, colonial autonomes, and colonial imperials: the last-named include the reigns of Nerva? Trajan, Antoninus, M. Aurelius, Commodus, Plautilla, wife of Caracalla, Geta, Macrinus, Severus Alexander, Valerianus, Gallienus, and Salonina. These colonial imperial coins, some of which are very rare, have *Latin* legends. In the time of Trajan, and antecedent to his reign, it appears the only initial letters inscribed on the reverse of the Parian medals were C. G. I. P. *Colonia Gemella Julia Pariana;* but after Hadrian, who was a great benefactor to, and embellisher of, this colony, the city of Parium, as if to perpetuate the memory of those benefits, always added the letter *H* to the others already enumerated, and thenceforth they read C. G. I. H. P. Colonia Gemella Julia *Hadriana* Pariana. This is an observation of the Abbé Belley, quoted by Pellerin, and supported by the authority of the two following medals, the one being dedicated to Trajan, the other to Antoninus Pius :—

1.—IMP. CAESARI. TRAIANO. AVG. GER. DA.—Laureated head of the Emperor.

Rev.—OPTIMO PRINCIPI. C. G. I. P. D.D,—A capricorn, having on the top of its back a cornucopiæ.

Pellerin, in referring to this example, says— This medal in particular serves to prove that Vaillant (who has edited no medals of Parium under Trajan,) and other antiquaries have been wrong in attributing certain medals [viz., those with the initial letters separate, C. G. I. *H.* P.] to the city of Hippo, in Africa, and he asserts that all such, as well as the above, belong to Parium, in Mysia. *(Mélange,* i. 270.)—See *Hippo.*

2.—ANTONINVS AVG.—Head of Antoninus crowned with laurel.

Rev.—C. G. I. H. P. A colonist driving two oxen.

Vaillant furnishes no coins of Parium under Antonine; but here Belley gives one dedicated to the immediate successor of Hadrian, and we see *H.* added to the other letters (C. G. I. P.) inscribed on the coin of Trajan above described.

On coins of M. Aurelius, Commodus, and Caracalla, is the type of Ceres walking with a lighted torch in each hand, accompanied by the separated initial letters C. G. I. H. P. A. All these Vaillant assigns to the city of *Hippo.* But Pellerin, with greater shew of probability, affirms them to be of Parium, adding " *on n'en connoit point de la colonie d'Hippo.*"

The only coin which Vaillant assigns to Parium is a second brass of M. Aurelius, which has for the type of its reverse a woman, clothed in the stola, standing with a military ensign in the right hand, and a horn of plenty in the left. The legend is one respecting which there can be no mistake, viz., COL. PARIA. IVL. AVG. Doubtless to be read *Colonia Pariana Julia Augusta.*

Among the colonial coins of Commodus apparently unknown to Vaillant, but given by Pellerin, who for the reasons above alluded to attributes them all to Parium, are the following:—A youthful and beardless male figure is seated, and before him is an ox, which seems to be holding up one of his fore feet to him, as if it were wounded, and the animal was praying the man to cure him.

This coin, and some others of Commodus and Gallienus, bearing a similar type, were edited by the Abbé Belley in one of his dissertations, and the interpretation of the legend, as offered by him, is DEO AES*culapio* SV*B*venienti.—Pellerin, on the other hand, reads it DEO AES*culapio* SV*B*urbano.

The other types of this colony given by Pellerin to supply the omissions in Vaillant are

1. The colonist at plough, as in Commodus and in Geta.

2. *Hygeia,* with her attributes of patera and serpent.

3. *Capricorn* and cornucopiæ, as in Commodus and Æmilianus.

4. The wolf suckling the twins, as in Commodus, Alexander Severus, and Gallienus; and

the *Genius of the City* standing at an altar, as in Macrinus and in Salonina.

These different coins are inscribed C. G. I. H. PA., or PAR., or PARIA.—And it deserves remark that there are points between the *first four* letters of the legend, but none between PA. and PAR., which are at the end. "This circumstance (says Pellerin) serves to show that each of them belongs to the colony of *Parium*, and the more convincingly so as, in their form and workmanship, they resemble other medals, whose legend is terminated by the entire word PARIANA.

M. Dumersan gives from the Allier de Hauteroche cabinet the following inedited brass coin of this colony (in Pl. xii. No. 15).

Obv.—M. BARBATO. MAN. ACILIO II VIR. C. G. I. P.   Naked head to the right.

Rev.—P. VIBIO. SAC.CAES. Q. BARB. PRAEF. PRO. II VIR.   Colonist at plough.

Vaillant appears to have been unaware that there were coins of Cornelia Supera struck in the colonies, but Pellerin has edited one, which he assigns to Parium, in his *Recueil*, tom. 1, p. xxi., and gives an engraving of it, on account of its singularity, in p. 207—as follows : *Gnea* CORNE*lia* SVPER*a* AVG.   Head of the Empress.—*Rev.* :   C. G. H. I. P.   A capricorn with globe between its feet, and a cornucopiæ on its back.

The letters (says Pellerin) C. G. H. I. P. signify *Colonia Gemella Hadriana Julia Pariana*.

Parlais, a city of Lycaonia, and a Roman colony. As its coins are very rare, Eckhel has arranged them according to the age in which they were first issued. The colonial imperial are from M. Aurelius to Maximinus : the imperial from Gallienus. The colonial have *Latin* legends, viz., IVL. AVG. COL. PARLAIS.—Vaillant not only gives no coins of *Parlais*, but seems to deny the existence of such a city in ancient Lycaonia, and considers a coin which Hardouin ascribes to Parlais to belong to Parium.—Haym, in his *Thesaurus Britannicus* [ii. t. 6. 39. fig. 8] gives a medal of Julia Domna, with the legend IVL. AVG. COL. PARLAIS. and type of the god *Mensis* wearing the Phrygian cap ; and Gessner and Eckhel repeat it in their catalogues.—The editor of the *Museum Pembroc.* published a second, bearing the head of L. Verus ; and on the reverse, Fortune standing, with the legend above quoted.— Pelerin *(Rec.* i. p xvii. and p. 1.) produces another of this colony, struck in honour of this Empress. Pellerin's coin on its obverse bears the legend IVLIA DOMNA and the head of that Empress.— Its reverse has for legend IVL. AVG. COL. PARLAIS., with the type of Fortune standing with her usual attributes.

PART. or PARTHIC. *Parthicus.*—A surname adopted by several Roman Emperors, amongst others by Trajan, Hadrian, Marcus Aurelius, and his imperial associate L. Verus : *Profligato bello* (says Capitolinus) *uterque Parthicus appellatus est.*

PART. ARAB. PART. ADIAB. *Parthicus Arabicus, Parthicus Adiabenicus.*—On silver and brass coins of Septimius Severus, accom-panied with the type of two seated captives, on each side a trophy, on that of Victory walking. —See ARAB. ADIAB.

After the defeat and death of his rival Pescennius Niger, Severus, crossing the Euphrates, attacked and conquered the Arabs, the Osrhoeni, and the Adiabenians. It is to these victories that the above quoted medal relates.—There is an inscription still legible on t'ie arch of Severus at Rome, where the same titles are given without abbreviation. And with this for guide we may read here PART*hicus* ARAB*icus*, PART*hicus* ADIAB*enicus ;* but without being able to explain why the word Parthicus is thus repeated. —Capt. Smyth adverts to this circumstance in describing a specimen of this large brass in his own select cabinet—"Severus obtained some success over the Parthians, but, apparently not in open warfare, since he would not assume the title of Parthicus (which here, oddly enough, is twice repeated), lest he should give umbrage to that still powerful nation :—*Tela fugacis equi, et braccati militis arcus.*"—Respecting the Arabians and the Adiabenians, Spartianus says, in reference to the Emperor's expedition against those two nations, *Arabas in deditionem accepit. Adiabenos in tributarios coegit.*—Eckkel assigns the striking of these medals to A.D. 195.

Parthamasiris, son of Pacorus, King of the Parthians, grandson of Artabanus, on the death of his father, was appointed King of Armenia, by Chosroes, King of the Parthians, on the expulsion of Exedares, but was despoiled of his kingdom by the Emperor Trajan.—See REX PARTHIS DATVS.

Parthamaspates, the king whom Trajan gave to the Parthians, and who, after having been expelled by them, accepted from the Emperor Hadrian his native kingdom of Armenia. Achaemenides, son of this Parthamaspates, succeeded his father in the kingdom of Armenia, Antoninus Pius having placed the diadem on his head, as we learn from coins.—See REX PARTHIS DATVS.

Parthenope, one of the Syrens, half virgin, half bird. Her image playing on a double flute appears on a gold coin struck by *Petronius Turpilianus*, one of the moneyers of Augustus. —The same appears on a coin of the *Petronia* family,—See *Sirenes.*

Parthia, a region of Asia, whose inhabitants were called *Parthi*, originally the most inveterate enemies of the Roman name, and who, under their King Orodes, having laid a snare for Crassus, into which that unfortunate general fell, destroyed him and his whole army in one general slaughter. This disaster to the Romans was soon after avenged by Cassius, the Questor of Crassus, who cut the Parthian army to pieces. The Parthians sided with Pompey against Cæsar, and also with the party of Cæsar's murderers, to whose aid they sent troops. After the defeat of Brutus and his friends at Philippi, Pacorus, son of Orodes, put himself at the head of the Parthian auxiliaries, but perished in a battle which he gave to Ventidius Bassus, the Roman General, in Syria.

Sometime afterwards Orodes was murdered by his son Phraates, who took possession of the kingdom, and gained a decisive victory over Antony the triumvir; but having treated his subjects with great cruelty and oppression, they drove him from the throne, and elected one Tyridates for their sovereign. Phraates, however, by the aid of the Scythians, defeated Tyridates; regained the Parthian sceptre, and to conciliate the favour of Augustus, sent back to Rome the prisoners and the standards which had been taken from Crassus and from Antony; an event commemorated with no little ostentation on coins bearing the following inscriptions: CAESAR AVGVSTVS. SIGNIS RECE.— CIVIB*us* ET SIGN*is* MILIT*aribus* A PARTHIS RECVPERATIS—and A PARTHIS RESTITVTIS.—On the death of Phraates, one of his sons succeeded him under the same name, and was followed by Orodes, who, being assassinated, Vonones, eldest son of the first Phraates, whom the Parthians had invited from Rome (where he had resided as a hostage to Augustus), became king, but was soon dethroned; and Artabanus, assuming the diadem of Parthia, declared war against the Romans, and was conquered by Vitellius, then Governor of Syria, who raised to the throne Tiridates, a prince of the blood royal of the Arsacides.— After several ephemeral sovereigns had appeared and disappeared, the kingdom devolved to Vologeses, a prince of some celebrity, who had a long war to sustain against the Romans, in which he not only proved himself their equal, but often achieved victories over them. Under the reign of Nero, Vologeses took Armenia from the empire, and caused two legions to pass under the yoke. In Trajan's time, Parthia was governed by Chosroes, on whom that emperor made war; and after taking from him Armenia, Mesopotamia, and Assyria, drove him from the throne, and placed thereon Parthamaspates—(see the name above). Sometime afterwards Chosroes again became king, and left his dominions to his son Vologeses, who had to fight for his crown against the Emperors Marcus Aurelius and Lucius Verus. At length Artabanus succeeded Vologeses, and was the last king of the race of the Arsacides. He carried on a fierce war against the empire of Rome, during the reigns of Severus, Caracalla, and Macrinus; and having, whilst Alexander Severus was emperor, been attacked by Artabanus, King of Persia, he was defeated in three battles, and lost both his kingdom and his life. Thus, four hundred and seventy-three years after the reign of its founder Arsaces, the Parthian monarchy was again transferred to the Persians.

Parthians offering branches of laurel to the emperors are seen on gold and silver coins of Augustus. The numismatic record of their restoring the captured standards to that prince is already noticed above.—A *Parthian* holding up with both his hands a little boy to Augustus, sitting on a curule chair, occurs on silver coins of that prince.—On the medal REX PARTHIS DATVS a Parthian appears kneeling; and on the first brass of L. Verus, a captive of the same nation sits on the ground with his hands tied behind him.

PARTHIA, with COS. II. S.C. at the bottom. —A Parthian soldier standing, holding in his right hand a radiated crown, in the left his weapons, consisting of a bow and quiver of arrows.—On a *first brass* of Antoninus Pius.— The medal, with this legend and type, forms one of a series struck under the above-named Emperor in his *second* consulate, and in which those inscribed ASIA, CAPPADOCIA, HISPANIA, SCYTHIA, SICILIA, SYRIA, are also to be included. They all present to us the Genius of each province holding a crown, or a vase, or a small chest *(canistrum)*. These symbols involve an interesting subject. It was customary in Greece to offer crowns of gold to princes and other great men, on occasions when the object was to testify the loyal devotedness of their subjects, or to give them proofs of popular attachment. This custom, being profitable to those in whose honour it was observed, did not fail to meet with favour from the Romans. History makes frequent mention of similar presentations of crowns by cities and provinces to Roman generals as soon as the latter entered their territories. Under the Emperors, every extraordinary event served to multiply the occasions for their reception of such valuable gifts. When, for example, they had just gained a victory, or been raised to the throne, or even when they assumed a new title, the provinces never missed such an opportunity of uniting, as a token of their joy and congratulation, in the tender of a golden crown; and, although, at first, the donation had been purely voluntary, it afterwards degenerated into a forced presentation, and at length became a species of tribute, differing from that exaction only in the name assigned to it. It was, in fact, what we now understand by the appellation of a *free gift*. This system quietly sank into complete abuse; and this description of presents became very burthensome to the provinces, especially when it was made compulsory upon them, as was the case under *Caracalla*, who extorted these *donaria* in the most arbitrary manner, and for the most trivial occurrences.— It is necessary to explain that these *offerings* did not always consist of actual crowns of gold, but often were given in coined gold, or in gold bullion, which thence derived the name of crown gold, *aurum coronarium*. At the accession of Antoninus Pius to the imperial throne, the envoys from the provinces came to him for the purpose of presenting their golden crowns, and the names of those very provinces are recorded on his medals. They are usually represented on the reverses under the figure of a woman, who holds either a crown, or a small coffer, enclosing the value of a real crown. Writers affirm that Antoninus had the generosity to relieve all Italy and half the exterior provinces from the pressure of this tribute.—It may on this point be objected that *Parthia* and *Scythia* are here ranged amongst the friendly provinces, whereas during the greater part of the time they were active enemies of the Romans. But it is necessary to bear in mind that foreign nations often rendered these honours to princes who governed the empire, in order to conciliate their good will, or secure their protection, which necessity sometimes obliged them to implore. Josephus, in his History of the Jews, relates that the King of the Parthians had sent a crown of gold to Titus, in commemoration of his conquests in Judæa.

Attention ought, moreover, to be paid to the characteristic symbols of the provinces. *Asia* has beside her an anchor and a vessel, because to visit Rome from that province it was needful to perform a sea voyage.—*Cappadocia* has mount *Argaeus* at her feet, that mountain having been worshipped by the Cappadocians as a deity, on account of its sometimes appearing on fire during the night.—*Parthia* is seen armed with bow and quiver, in consequence of its inhabitants being celebrated as the best *archers* or bowmen.

PARTHIA CAPTA (Conquest of Parthia), with the date of cos. vi., and the type of a trophy, on each side of which a captive is seated, appears on a gold coin of Trajan.

The subject and device of this coin, together with those inscribed PARTHICO.—ORIENS AVG.—REGNA ADSIGNATA—REX PARTHIS DATVS, &c., refer to events alike glorious to the Roman name, and to Trajan himself.—We learn from Dion, Eutropius, and other historians, that this illustrious Emperor, during his stay in the East, after the conquest of Armenia, gave kings not only to the *Parthians*, but also to other nations; that he accepted the allegiance of some, and adjusted the disputes of others.

Parthica tiara.—An ornament for the head, worn by the kings of Parthia, and other oriental sovereigns, is seen conjoined with bow and quiver full of arrows, which were also amongst the insignia of the monarchs of the east.

PARTHICA.—See VIC*toria* PARTHICA on coins of S. Severus.

PARTHICO or PARTHICVS.—This word, as a title of honour, is read on coins of Trajan, Hadrian, M. Aurelius, L. Verus, Commodus, S. Severus, Caracalla, and Carus.

PARTHICVS IMP.—*Obv.* Q. LABIENVS. PARTHICVS. IMP. Bare head, with beard of moderate size.—*Rev.* No legend. A horse with bridle and housings. Silver.—This appears on a denarius of the *Atia* family, as the surname of Q. LABIENVS. (see the name), who was the son of T. LABIENVS, of whose assistance Julius Cæsar availed himself much in his Gallic wars; but who, at the beginning of the civil war, went over to Pompey, and shared the common flight and dispersion of that party. The son, whose portrait is supposed to be represented on the obverse of this silver coin, proved himself to be the heir of his father's hatred against Cæsar, and having followed the army of Brutus, was sent by him to Orodes, the Parthian King, for the purpose of seeking his assistance; but presently hearing of the disaster to his friends at Philippi, and despairing of pardon from the victors, when he heard that Antony was revelling in base indolence in Egypt,

he incited the Parthians against the Romans, and with the assistance he obtained from Orodes and his son Pacorus, crossed the Euphrates, and occupied Palestine, Phœnicia, Syria, and Caria, calling himself *Parthicus Imperator*, because that appellation, as Dion observes, was the more alien from Roman custom; since the Romans had affected titles from nations subdued, he from one which was victorious. Having at length sought a battle with P. Ventidius, the lieutenant of Antony, he was routed and captured; and he closed his scenic empire v.c. 715.

PARTHI. MAX. *Parthicus Maximus.*—This honorary surname was assumed in the first instance by M. Aurelius, and L. Verus, and afterwards by Sept. Severus and his son Caracalla.

PARTHICA MAXIMA.—See VICTORIA PART. MAX.

PARTHICVS TRIVMPHVS.—See TRIVMPHVS.

Julian in his "Cæsars" makes it a matter of reproach that, after a war of more than three hundred years' duration, the Romans had not been able to bring under their dominion a single portion of territory beyond the Tigris, which is under the power of the Parthians.—In reference to this remark, Spanheim says—"Nevertheless there were Roman generals, such, for instance, as Lucullus, Ventidius, Corbulo; and also emperors, as Trajan, Verus, Severus, Caracalla, Carus, and Galerius, who carried the war into Parthia, or into its neighbourhood; conquered their country; took their cities, and even Ctesiphon, their capital; who, moreover, saw these kings of kings either driven from their thrones, or made prisoners, or prostrated before the legions of Rome, and compelled to receive on their knees, as they did from Trajan, their tiara and the empire of the Parthians. It is of these events, amongst others, that the medals of some of the Emperors, particularly of Trajan, are to this day the glorious monuments, with such fine inscriptions as *Rex Parthis Datus*; *Parthia Capta*; or *Victoria Parthica Maxima*, on a medal of Severus; and, lastly, the surnames of *Parthicus* and *Adiabenicus*, which we find on their coins."

The same learned translator of, and able commentator on, the "Cæsars" of Julian (which he has numismatically illustrated, in so authentic and interesting a manner), observes that "it was in the eastern portion of Assyria, *beyond the Tigris*, that the seat of the Parthian empire was situated. This was their nearest province to the Roman boundaries: *citra omnes propinqua est nobis Assyria*, says Ammianus; and consequently the most exposed to the Roman arms. Whence also it happens that the Parthians are sometimes designated by the name of *Assyrians*, as in Lucan—*Assyriæ paci finem fortuna precamur*, to express the existence of peace with the Parthians."

PAT. *Pater.*—PAT. PA. *Pater Patriæ*, on coins of Augustus. Father of his country.

PAT. *Patræ, Patrensis*, in Achaia.

PATER.—The appellation of *Pater* is sometimes given alone (that is to say without the addition of the name *Patriæ*) to the Emperors, after their deaths, and when their deification or consecration had taken place. Thus we find DIVVS AVGVSTVS PATER inscribed on some of that Emperor's coins, with the various symbols of the apotheosis.—In like manner, after they were dead, medals, with the addition of that word, were struck in honour of the memory of Trajan, and of Pertinax—viz., DIVVS TRAIANVS. PARTH. PATER.—DIVVS PERT. PATER.

The title of *Pater* appears on a gold coin struck by order of Trajan in memory of his own father, Marcus Ulpius Trajanus, who is thereon styled DIVVS PATER TRAIANVS, and represented seated on a curule chair. And in like manner some coins of Hadrian (who was, through the intervention of Plotina, the adopted son and appointed successor of Trajan), present the heads of Trajan and Plotina face to face, with the inscription DIVIS PARENTIBVS.— Another medal with the head of Trajan bears DIVVS TRAIANVS PATER AVGVSTVS. Besides which there is another of Hadrian, on which we read DIVVS TRAIANVS AVG. PARTH*icus* PATER. To the same class of medals, on which sons, natural or adopted, of deceased emperors, pay filial honour to their memory, are to be referred these coins of Maximianus Hercules, inscribed DIVVS MAXI-MIANVS PATER; and on another DIVVS MAXIMIANVS SOCER (perhaps, as Akerman says, MAXENTII), probably struck after his death by his son Maxentius.

Pater; almost every Pagan God was so called; as *Neptunus Pater, Janus Pater*, &c. (Vaillant, Pr. ii. p. 223).—Thus also on coins of Commodus and of Severus, *Bacchus Pater*. See LIBERO PATRI.—See also LIBERO P. CONS. AVG. on a medal of Gallienus.—In like manner *Mars* is surnamed Pater, as the founder (through Romulus) of the city and the empire of Rome. See MARS PATER; to which are added the titles of CONSERVATOR and PROPVGNATOR on medals of Constantinus M.

Pater, as already observed, is also an appellation given on coins to Augustus, as seated in the likeness of Jupiter himself, that Emperor is depictured as one of the celestial deities. DIVVS AVGVSTVS PATER appears not only with radiated head, but also with naked and with laureate head, and with various symbols of consecration.

Pater Patratus was one of the Fecial priests, and, indeed, according to Spanheim and Pitiscus, the chief of the sacerdotal college so called.— On a denarius of the *Veturia* family, two men armed with spears are touching with their daggers a sow, which is held by a man on his knees.—"This (says Schulze, in his *Introduzione*, &c.) is the *Pater Patratus*, whose office it was to preside on occasions when treaties were to be ratified, and to kill a sow or hog with a stone." —"*Pater Patratus*, says Festus, *adjusjurandum Patrandum, id est, jusjurandum sit*; because he took the oath for the whole people."

Pater Patriæ.—The man who first of all obtained this glorious title was Cicero, on whom it was conferred by the Senate of Rome, in acknowledgment of his paternal guardianship of the republic, as the detector of Catiline's conspiracy. It is a phrase purely of honour, unconnected with power.—Nor indeed was it (says Oiselius) bestowed immediately on all the Roman Emperors.—It was from *Julius Cæsar* that the custom of conferring this cognomen passed to his successors; and this is shewn by coins struck during his lifetime, on which he is called CAESAR PARENS PATRIAE.—To *Augustus*, on account of his clemency (as Aurelius Victor affirms), the cognomen of *Pater Patriæ* was given in the year of Rome 752, and in the twenty-first renewal of his tribunitian power, in consequence of which medals were forthwith struck, charged with the inscription of CAESAR AVGVSTVS DIVI F. PATER PATRIAE.— And on some large brass, struck out of Rome, supposed to be of the mint of *Lyons*, we moreover read the same inscription round the Emperor's head—the reverse exhibiting the altar, dedicated by the Gaulish tribes to ROM. ET AVG*ustus*.—*Tiberius* constantly refused this title, and his coins omit it.—*Nero* also, at the beginning of his reign, rejected the honourable surname, but soon after accepted it, as appears from his coins.—The same distinction was borne by Vespasian, according to Suetonius, and is recorded on medals of his, struck in the second year of his reign.—We likewise read the well-deserved compliment of *Pater Patriæ* on the coins of *Nerva*.—Of *Trajan* it is related by the younger Pliny, that he declined the offer of this title, upon his accession to the throne, assigning as a reason that he did not esteem himself worthy of being denominated the Father of his Country. Nevertheless, we find coins struck in his second year, and frequently afterwards inscribed, among the rest, with *Pater Patriæ*.—Hadrian's coins, bearing the senatorial mark S.C., and struck in the first year of his Imperatorship and tribunitian power, present numerous examples in which he is styled P.P.—And the same initial letters are frequently found appended to the names of other Emperors.

Pater Senatus.—The flattering title of Father of the Senate, bestowed in the first instance out of fear on the monster Commodus, was afterwards conferred on Balbinus and Pupienus, whose extraordinary merit as mild and prudent rulers of the empire gave them some claim to this new and honourable surname.—Julia Domna, under a succeeding reign, had the daring boldness to assume on her coins the appellation of *Mother* of the Senate (MAT*er* SENAT*us.)* She had (in imitation of Faustina, jun.) already dubbed herself MAT*er* CASTRORVM.

PATER SENAT. or SENATVS.—A togated figure stands with a branch in the right hand, and in his left a wand surmounted by an eagle, held crosswise. On *silver* of Commodus.

Vaillant aptly observes, in noticing this medal, that Commodus had more rightly earned the distinction of being called *Senatus car-nifex*—the *executioner* rather than the Father of the Roman Senate. He had thinned the ranks of that once powerful body by the slaughter of its most illustrious members; and was especially infuriated against them after the discovery of his sister Lucilla's conspiracy. But in proportion to his cruelties were the flatteries lavished on this gladiatorial cut-throat by the degenerate people and abject Senate of Rome.

Patera, a round shallow dish or vase used by the Romans, (who adopted it from the Etrurians,) at their religious ceremonies, either in making libations of wine to the gods, or in receiving the blood of sacrificial victims. On Roman coins and other monuments the patera is placed in the hands of all the deities, whether of the first or of the second rank, as a symbol of the divine honours rendered to them, or in that of their ministers as an attribute of their functions. It also appears often in the hands of princes, to mark the union of the sacerdotal with the imperial power, effected through the office of *Pontifex Maximus*. For this reason the figure of the deity, priest, or emperor is frequently seen beside an altar, upon which he seems to be pouring the contents of the patera. In the more ancient periods, these utensils, always consecrated to religious purposes, were made of baked earth: afterwards of brass, a metal peculiarly dedicated to the gods; still later they were also fabricated of gold and silver, and sometimes ornamented with fine compositions in high relief; as in the case of that magnificent gold one in the Royal Library at Paris.

A serpent feeding out of a patera is the symbol of the Goddess of Health *(Salus)*.—A patera appears in the right hand of Cybele, of Clementia, of Concordia.—And the *Genius* of a city holding in his right hand a patera, as in the act of performing sacrifice for the health of the Emperor is a frequent type. We see this in the GENIVS EXERC. ILLYRICIANI of Trajanus Decius; and the GENIVS AV*Gusti* of Gallienus and Claudius Gothicus.

The *patera* is to be observed in the right hand of IVPITER CONSERVATOR, of Hercules, Juno Conservatrix, Mercury, Patientia, Pietas, &c.; also in the hand of the Emperor sitting, as in Tiberius; and of the Emperor standing, as in Elagabalus.—See INVICTVS SACERDOS.

PATIENTIA AVGVSTI.—A woman seated, holding a patera in the right hand, and the hasta in her left.—On a silver coin of Hadrian, struck in his third consulate—and, singular to say, on the coin of no other; and as Hadrian in his conduct shewed himself to have, in one sense of the word, possessed very little patience—this legend has been suspected as a false quotation, or a forgery, for CLEMENTIA AVGVSTI. But Eckhel admits its genuineness, and alludes to two specimens of it in the Royal Cabinet. —Vaillant, in reference to this reverse, observes that Patience does not appear to have been regarded by the heathen world in the same light as that in which it was viewed among Christians.

According to the acceptation of the latter it consists in enduring contumely and misfortune with submissive resignation; according to the ideas of the former, it is the voluntary and daily struggle with difficult circumstances, and likewise the endurance of personal hardships, as in the case of Hadrian, who *patiently* bore the vicissitudes of heat and cold, and never covered his head; thus corresponding to the definition of Cicero—"*Patientia est honestatis, aut utilitatis causa, rerum arduarum, ac difficilium voluntaria, ac diuturna ac perpessio.*—See Eckhel, vol. vi. p. 506.

Patina is that beautiful and brilliant kind of time-created varnish, of a green or brownish colour, which covers the surface of some ancient brass medals. It prevents them from deteriorating, and is regarded as an evidence of antiquity. The patina does not, however, readily attach itself to brass and copper: this depends much on the state of the soil in which the medals have lain for ages. The fabricators of false coins have endeavoured to imitate it with sal ammoniac, vinegar, and other artificial compounds; but a coating of this kind is easily removed, and it is by no means difficult to detect the fraud: whilst on the other hand the genuine patina becomes so inherent to the metal that it would be impossible to scrape it off without injuring the medal which it covers.— False varnish (says Beauvais) may be discovered with the greater facility, as it is in general black, coarse, and glossy, or the colour of verdigris, *empâté* and tender to the point of any sharp instrument, instead of which the *patina* (or antique encrustation) is extremely brilliant and as hard as the metal itself. The agreeable appearance of this splendid rust having rendered it particularly acceptable to the taste of the Italians, they gave it the name of *Patina verde*, as counterfeiting the emerald; and the French numismatists introduced the expression into their own language by calling it *Patine*. It should be observed, however, that the natural *ærugo*, or rust, which adds so much beauty to bronze medals, is injurious and even destructive to siver coins.

PATR. *Patrensis*.—COL. PATR. *Colonia Patrensis*.—The colony of *Patræ*.

Patræ (now Patra-Patrasso), a principal city of Achaia, situated on the longest promontory of the Peloponnessus. Under Augustus it became a Roman Colony (in the year of Rome 725), the veterans of the xxii. Primigenian Legion having been sent thither, as is shewn by the name of that legion, and its military standards being a frequent type on the coins of the colony.— Augustus is said to have given liberty of self-government to Patræ, in memory of which and of other benefits which that prince heaped upon the city, the inhabitants called themselves on their coins COL. A. A. P. *Colonia, Augusta, Aroe, Patrensis*. Thus recording the name of its three founders and restorers, Eumelus, Patræus, and Augustus. It was also called *Neroniana*, after Nero.—A coin of this colony, struck under Commodus, a prospect of the city is *attempted* to be given, with three temples above, and two gallies in the sea below.— Besides the Autonomous, and Colonial Autonomous coins struck at the mint of Patræ, there are extant Colonial Imperial medals of this celebrated colony from Augustus to Gordianus Pius, with but few breaks in the series, as will be seen by the following list :—Augustus, Tiberius, Claudius, Nero, Galba, Domitian, Nerva, Hadrian, Antoninus, M. Aurelius, L. Verus, Commodus, Sept. Severus, Caracalla, Elagabalus, Gordianus Pius.—The legends of the Colonial Autonomes and of the Imperial are *Latin*. Some few are Greek.

The following are among the types of this Roman colony :—

Æsculapius, standing, with right hand placed on his side, and the usual attribute of staff and serpent in his left. On second brass of Commodus.

Apollo, standing, naked, holds in his right hand a patera, and rests his left on a lyre placed on a cippus. Second brass of Antoninus Pius.

[The people of Patræ dedicated but few coins to this good emperor, how ready soever they were to exercise their monetary privileges for the purpose of flattering any tyrant master. There was indeed a rebellion excited during Antonine's reign, in Achaia (as well as in Egypt), which Capitolinus records, and which may possibly account for the fact above-stated. From the figure of Apollo it may be inferred that he was adored at Patræ; and Pausanias warrants such a supposition, by speaking of an image of this deity placed in the Odeum of that city.—Apollo bears the patera to indicate that sacrifices had been performed for the Emperor. —Apollo leaning on his lyre embodies the harmony of the celestial spheres, whence he was called Musicus and Citharœdus.]

Apollo and Venus.—On a second brass of Commodus, struck at Patræ, Apollo appears standing in a female dress; he holds a bow in his right hand. Opposite him stands also *Venus Victrix*, half unclothed, holding up a shield with both hands.

[In thus associating together the above-mentioned god and goddess, the colony evidently sought to flatter Commodus and his wife Crispina; for *he* was fond of being called, not only Hercules, but Apollo (Apollo *Palatinus* and *Monetalis*). And *she* was often on medals pointed to and even represented as Venus. The temples of these two divinities were (according to Pausanias's description) erected in Patræ on the same spot.]

Colonus agens boves.—The colonist with his right hand on the plough appears on two Patræan coins of Augustus, one struck during his lifetime, and the other after his apotheosis. —Same type also appears on coins of Domitian and of Commodus, in which the colonist holds the plough with his right hand, and in his left bears the *vexillum*; with legend PATR. C. A. A. P. and COL. A. A. PATR. *Colonia Augusta Aroe Patrensis.*

[Vaillant says (i. 40) the *colonus* at plough is the type of citizens (or civilians), as military ensigns are the insignia of veterans sent to reinforce the population of a Roman colony. But a colonist carrying the *vexillum* in his left hand, and in his right holding the plough, shews the coin to have been struck by colonial *Duumviri*, one of whom had been selected from the citizens, and the other from the old soldiers.]

Cornucopiæ (double.)—On a second brass struck under Claudius, are two horns of plenty, over which is the head of a boy between two female heads. Legend : COL. A. A. P. LIBERIS AVG. *Colonia Augusta Aroe Patrensis Liberis Augusti.*

[The colony of Patræ here dedicates a coin to Claudius and his children. The boy's head is meant for that of the unfortunate young prince Britannicus. On the left is that of Octavia his sister, whom Claudius had by *Messalina;* on the right is Antonia, whom he before had by *Ælia Petina.*]

Diana, standing, in her dress as a huntress, rests her left hand on a bow. Legend : DIANA LAPHRIA. On coins of Nero and of Domitian.

[Although the above does not present the name of the city, yet the word *Laphria* justifies the belief that it belongs to the colony of Patræ. It was a name given to her, in consequence of L. Laphrius, a Phocian, having erected a statue to her honour in Calydon (Ætolia).—Diana Laphria had a shrine in the citadel of Patræ.—Vaillant, i. 124.]

On a small brass coin of M. Aurelius and of L. Verus, bearing for the legend of its reverse COL. A. A. PATRÆ. *(Colonia Augusta Aroe Patrensis)* is Diana Venatrix, with a torch in her right, a spear in her left hand, and a hound at her feet.

[This Diana (says Vaillant, i. 199) is the *Laphria* recorded above, and whom the Patrenses adored with a supreme shew of devotion. Her image, when Ætolia was laid waste by Augustus, was removed from Calydon to Patræ, as Pausanias narrates.—Diana is most frequently figured in a hunting dress; the spear and dog are her attributes, as president over the chase, or, as some say, because she was the tamer of ferocious dogs. She carried a torch in her right hand, as being identified with Luna, whose lucid orb illumes the circumambient air at night; whence in like manner, on coins inscribed DIANA LVCIFERA, she is represented carrying a lighted torch.]

On a third brass inscribed to Caracalla by this colony, Diana stands with quiver at her back, carrying an arrow in her right hand, and resting her left on a bow.

On a second brass of the same colony and reign, the same goddess stands leaning on her bow. In both types a hunting dog is at Diana's feet.

[According to Pausanias, a variety of Dianas were worshipped at Patræ—viz., Laphria, Limnatis, and Triclaria. The above two coins represent her like the Diana Laphria of Nero and Domitian, namely as a huntress.]

On a very rare second brass of this city, dedicated to M. Aurelius, there is a female figure seated in a chariot drawn by two stags.

[Patin and other numismatists regard this figure as Diana herself; but she is adorned neither with the crescent moon nor with the quiver, nor does she indeed exhibit any attribute of that goddess.—Vaillant therefore discards that idea, and pronounces it to be the Virgin, who, on an anniversary when, conformably to the custom of the country, the sacred rites of *Diana Laphria* were celebrated, was, as the officiating priestess of the goddess, carried about in a chariot drawn by two stags, as Pausanias describes it.]

A similar type exhibits itself on a Patræan coin of Elagabalus. Cities and colonies (says Vaillant) never caused anything to be engraved on their coins without some reason or mysterious object in view.

Emperor in a quadriga.—On a large brass dedicated to Livia (by the name of *Julia Augusta*), Augustus is depictured in a chariot drawn by four horses; he holds in his right hand a sceptre, on the top of which is an eagle. Legend: COL. A. A. P. CAESARI. AVG. *Colonia Augusta Aroe Patrensis Cæsari Augusto.*

[The Patrenses, in acknowledgment of their obligation to Augustus, who had been a great benefactor to them, exhibit on one side of this coin the head of his wife, with inscription INDVLGENTIAE AVG. MONETA IMPETRATA; and on the reverse his own effigy in a triumphal chariot, principally on account of the naval victory at Actium. For the Roman colony, newly established at Patræ, had been depopulated, during the civil war between Augustus and Antony, and was afterwards re-established through the clemency and care of Augustus, the inhabitants of the neighbouring towns being introduced into the city, and the veterans of the twenty-second legion having also been allocated there, were made colonists of Patræ. The word *Indulgentia* is used on this coin for *Permissio.*]

Emperor and Genius.—On a second brass of Sept. Severus, with the usual legend of the *Colonia Patrensis*, a military figure standing, and a female figure seated, hold each in their right hands a patera over an altar.

[Vaillant observes, respecting this type, that it represents Severus on one side, and the Genius of the city on the other. *He* as a mortal is standing. *She* as a deity is sitting. *He* holds a patera as sacrificing to himself. *She* also holds a patera, as denoting the sacrifice to be acceptable to herself. Severus performs the sacred rite, habited as an *Imperator*, on the point of setting out on a warlike expedition; for it was competent to him to sacrifice both as Emperor and as *Pontifex Maximus.*

Euripylus.—On a small brass of Patræ, dedicated to L. Verus, appears a male figure, naked, holding in his right hand a patera over an altar, and placing his left on the head of some image terminating in a square form.

[This figure is supposed, by Vaillant, to re-present a favourite legendary hero of the Patrenses, namely Euripylus. He is said to have been the son of Telephus and Astyoche, who was the daughter of Laomedon, and sister of Priam. He was King of the Cetæans, a people of Mysia, and came to the aid of the Trojans towards the close of the war. A man of the greatest bravery, he was regarded as the noblest prince of his time, and is said to have proved a most formidable enemy to the besiegers of Troy, several of whose leaders he killed with his own hand, but was at length slain by Pyrrhus or Neoptolemus. The history of Euripylus is so mixed up with fable and so confused an incident, that but for the episode of his being driven by adverse winds into the port of Patræ, in time to prevent the superstitious horrors of a human sacrifice to Diana Triclaria, it would not deserve adverting to here.]

Genius of the Port.—On a rare second brass coin of Nero, Genius stands with cornucopiæ, his right hand resting upon what is probably intended for an anchor: around, PORTVS FRVGIFERA: in the field C. P.—From the cabinet of Mr. Roach Smith.

Genius.—On a second brass of Nero, with the legend GEN. COL. NER. PATREN., meaning the Genius of the Colony of *Neronia Patrensis*, the Genius stands half clothed, with the pallium on his arm, holding in his right hand a patera over an altar, and in his left hand a cornucopiæ.

[The type and legend of the above medal constitute a monument of the gross flattery paid to Nero by this colony, yet only following in that respect the example of Rome herself. The Senate had already decreed coins to the Genius of the Emperor *(Genio Augusti).* The colonists of Patræ called Nero *Coloniæ Genius.* And to *Genius* the ancients gave the appellation of a tutelary or local Deity *(tutelaris seu topicus Deus);* thus the emperor was worshipped as a god.—Accordingly Suetonius (in *Neron. Vita* cap. 60) relates that a temple was dedicated to Nero's Genius at Athens. And although Augustus himself had already bestowed many immunities and some exclusive privileges on Patræ, yet, as if forgetful of all these peculiar favours, they dropped the name of *Augusta* and called their colony after Nero's name, thus professing to be more indebted to Nero, who had extended freedom indiscriminately to the whole province of Greece, than to Augustus, who had bestowed his boon of liberty on their own city alone.

A similar type, but with legend of GEN. COL. A. A. PATREN. presents itself on a coin dedicated to Domitian by this colony, evidently in the same spirit of adulation to the reigning monarch, although the unworthy successor of Vespasian and Titus; he who carried his impious arrogance so far as (according to Suetonius) to require his ministers to call him a God; and a letter of one of his procurators begins thus—"*Dominus et Deus noster sic fieri jubet.*"

Hercules stands, with his right hand resting on his club. In his left he holds the spoils of the Nemæan lion. Legend: C. P. HERCVLI AVGVSTO.

[A second brass of Nero bears this reverse. On coins struck at Rome, *senatus consulto*, Nero is represented as Apollo striking the lyre. On this medal of Patræ he appears under the effigy of Hercules, as if victor at all the public games of Greece.]

On second and small brass of M. Aurelius and L. Verus, Hercules stands leaning with his left arm on his massive club, in the attitude of the Farnese statue. The accompanying legend is COL. A. A. PATR. *Colonia Augusta Aroe Patrensis.*

[This is rather a frequent type of the Patrenses, who, to flatter M. Aurelius and his colleague Verus, simultaneously inscribed coins to each. The image of the demi-god on these medals shews that he was adored at Patræ.— Hercules bears the club as his favourite weapon. He is decorated with the lion's skin, because the slaying of one in the Nemæan forest was his first and one of his most glorious achievements, hence Ausonius sings *(Edyll.* 19):—

Prima Cleonæi tolerata ærumna leonis.

Jupiter standing, naked, holds an eagle in his right and the hasta in his left hand. Legend: C. P. IVPITER LIBERATOR. Second brass of Nero.

[This colony erected a statue to Jupiter the Liberator, on account of the freedom restored to the province (of Achaia) by Nero; and this statue, therefore, they delineated on their coins. —Jupiter is variously depicted; sometimes naked, sometimes adorned rather than clothed with the *pallium;* at other times he is clothed in a robe: nearly as various were his attributes and names.]

On a second brass of Hadrian, with legend of COL. A. A. PATRENS., Jupiter is seated within a temple of six columns.

[Struck by the *colonia Patrensis* in congratulation to Hadrian on his arrival in the Roman province of Achaia.—Pausanias alludes to the temple of Jupiter Olympius at Patræ, as a most superb structure, situate in the forum of that city, and describes the image of that god as seated on a throne, within that temple. From inscriptions on coins of Laodicea and Smyrna, and on a statue at Smyrna, we learn that Greek flattery pointed to the *living* deification of Hadrian, under the surname of OLYMPIOC (Hadrianus Olympius).]

On a Patræan coin of Commodus, Jupiter is seated with a Victory in his right hand, but not within a temple.

[The Victory placed in the hand of Jove alludes to some battle gained by the Emperor's lieutenants over the enemy in one or more of the provinces of the empire.]

Legionary Eagles.—These military symbols appear on second and small brass of Claudius, Nero, Galba, Domitian, M. Aurelius, L. Verus, and Commodus, struck by this colony. The eagles are placed between two ordinary ensigns of the Roman army; and the accompanying legend is COL. A. A. PATR. XXII. *(Colonia Augusta Aroe Patrensis vicesima secunda*— the word *Legio* being understood).

[The colonists of Patræ having dedicated coins to Claudius on his having adopted Nero as his son, congratulated Nero in like manner on his adoption by Claudius.—Vaillant says that the Patrenses chose this type to indicate the origin of their colony as derived from the veterans of the Twenty-second Legion, surnamed *Primigenia.* Augustus had sent those old soldiers as colonists to Patræ, from Egypt, where the legion itself was stationed, and where it remained until the time of Vespasian, who employed it in the Judaic war. In Hadrian's time the Twenty-second Legion seems to have been quartered in Germany.—Livy states that there was a temple to *Fortuna primigenia* on the Quirinal Hill at Rome.]

Mercury, seated (sometimes in a temple of two columns); he extends his right hand (which sometimes has the *crumena),* whilst holding the caduceus in his left. A ram stands at his feet. On second brass of this colony, dedicated to Antoninus Pius, Commodus, Caracalla, and Elagabalus.

Mercury, seated, is a frequent type of the Patræan coins, and as in the case of Antonine and Commodus, his image is exhibited in a temple, it may be inferred that this deity was also included in the polytheistic worship of the colony, though Pausanias, in his detailed descriptions of Patræ, makes no mention of Mercury having a temple there.—A ram is here made the companion of Mercury, as on the Corinthian coins, because that god was regarded as peculiarly watchful over the protection and increase of sheep flocks, on which account he was called the God of Shepherds. Mercury carries in his hand the caduceus (namely, a wand, round which two serpents are entwined), as a symbol of peace: hence ambassadors *(Legati)* sent on pacific negociations were denominated *caduceatores.*]

Minerva.—On a small brass of this colony, inscribed to Marcus Aurelius, Minerva, helmeted, stands within a two-columned temple, with right hand extended, and holding a spear in the other. At her feet, on one side, is an owl, and on the other a shield.

[This coin shews, and Pausanias confirms, that Minerva had a temple at Patræ. She was called Panachæis, because her temple was common to all the Achaians.]

Neptune, standing, naked, his right foot placed on a rock, holds in his right hand a dolphin, and in his left the trident. Second brass of Domitian.

[The maritime cities of antiquity made Neptune an especial and pre-eminent object of their superstitious adoration. The Patrenses (as Pausanias affirms) called him *Pelagius* and *Asphalion*, or the Guardian, and erected a temple to his honour near the harbour. The people in Pagan times were accustomed to exhibit on their coins the divinities whom they principally worshipped; accordingly we find the colonists of Patræ placing on theirs the figure of the God of the Sea.]

On a second brass of S. Severus, Neptune stands with his right foot planted on a pedestal; he holds an image of Victory in his right hand, and the trident in his left.

[Struck by the Patrenses in honour of this victorious emperor, for Neptune bears this *victoriola* in record of Severus's successes over the Parthians. There was, according to Pausanias, a temple at Patras dedicated to the monarch of the waves.

Nero's Statue.—This is represented on a small brass coin, having for legend C. P. CLEANDRO. *Colonia Patrensis Cleandro.* The Emperor's effigy, clothed in the toga, stands on a pedestal, with the right hand extended, and the left holding a roll of papyrus.

[The statue here delineated seems to have been one erected by the people of Patræ, in commemoration of the liberties conceded (according to Suetonius) by Nero to all Greece. Who this Cleander was does not appear to be known. Nor is it discernible from the coin what magisterial office was held by him, in consequence of some letters being effaced.]

Roma, helmeted, sitting on a shield, and holding a *victoriola* in her right hand, and a spear in her left, is crowned by the Emperor, who stands behind her, dressed in a military habit. On a second brass of M. Aurelius, having for legend COL. A. A. PATR.

[The colony congratulates M. Aurelius, by striking this coin, which forms indeed a monument of his victory, but in such a way as to make the emperor ascribe to the republic the whole merit of his great warlike exploits. For here he crowns Rome personified, as though he acknowledged himself wholly indebted to the assistance of the Goddess Roma (ΘΕΑ ΡΩΜΑ as the Greeks phrased it), for his victories over the foes and invaders of the empire. But in thus giving the glory to the republic, Marcus was far from loading the state with all the onerous consequences of war. On the contrary, his conduct towards the provinces was marked by wonderful moderation and benignity. And to prevent any extraordinary expenses from falling on them on account of the war with the Marcomanni, he caused the imperial ornaments to be sold by auction in the *forum Trajani*, thus ruling the state, amidst the love and veneration of all.]

There is a similar type to the above on a second brass of L. Verus, in honour of his successes over the Parthians.

On a second brass of this colony, inscribed to Commodus, appears a female figure seated on a heap of arms, holding a spear in her right hand, and having a shield near her left side. She is crowned by Hercules, who holds his club in his left hand.

[To flatter this vain and frenzied tyrant of an emperor, and at the same time to identify themselves as Romans, the colonists of Patræ have here represented Commodus under the image of Hercules, by whose name (as Herodianus relates) he had expressly commanded himself to be called. In this madly assumed character, which the mint of Rome herself had already been submitted to the degradation of recognising, he places a crown on the head of that "goddess," to whom his ancestor by adoption, Antoninus Pius, had raised a temple under the title of ROMA AETERNA.]

Statue on a Column.—A second brass of Patræ, inscribed to Domitian, exhibits a column on which stands a colossal figure in a military garb, with sceptre in right hand, and spear in left.

[Vaillant considers this to have been meant for an honorary reference to the restoration of liberty to the Achaians by Domitian, whose father and brother had taken away and withheld their previously enjoyed immunities and privileges—a circumstance which accounts for there being no coins of the Patrenses found bearing the heads and inscriptions either of Vespasian or of Titus.]

There is a similar type on a very rare second brass of this colony struck under Commodus.

Victory.—On a small brass of Gordianus III., struck at Patræ, a figure of Victory stands on a globe, bearing a laurel crown in her right, and a palm branch in her left hand.

[The Patrenses, to compliment the youthful emperor on his victory over the Persians, dedicate to him this medal, on which the personification of Victory is placed on a globe; because Gordian, by that last successful exploit, is supposed to have overcome all the enemies of the Roman world. For at Rome, solely through his timely election to the empire, a sedition of the veteran legionaries with the people was quelled. In Africa the Carthaginians rebelled, but Gordianus Pius succeeded in suppressing the insurrection. In Europe, he drove back the barbarian invaders of Mœsia and Thrace; lastly he defeated the Persians, and expelled them from the Roman provinces.]

View of Patræ.—On coins of Commodus and of Gordianus III. a city is attempted to be delineated by a structure composed of columns, in two tiers, above which are three temples. At the bottom are three galleys in the water. In front of the whole, below, is a statue placed on a pedestal.

[Vaillant (I. 219) calls this *prospectus urbis*, meaning a view of Patræ, but it fails to convey any distinct idea of either the local features or the architectural character of a place once so celebrated for its magnificence amongst the cities of the Peloponnesus. The most recognisable objects are the temples at the top of the coin, and the triremes, which plainly designate a seaport. The Patrenses, in remembrance of Augustus, as the founder and benefactor of their colony, seem to have placed his colossal statue on the shore, for the figure is in the military dress of an emperor.]

Wolf and the Twin Children appear on a small coin of Patræ, inscribed to M. Aurelius.

[Most of the Roman colonies engraved this well-known group amongst the types of their coins, by way of reference to their origin, and to show that they possessed, or assumed to possess, the same rights as the resident citizens of Rome, to whom the fable of Romulus and Remus nourished by a wolf was, from its national associations, a fondly endeared subject.

Woman's Head, turreted, appears on a second brass of the *Colonia Patrensis*, struck under M. Aurelius; also with a cornucopiæ behind it, on coins inscribed to Commodus and to S. Severus.

[This is a typo, says Vaillant, which, besides denoting Cybele, is also a symbol of cities. For Cybele was believed to be the earth itself, and therefore her image was crowned with towers, in reference to great walled cities. All cities, however, were not represented by a turreted female head, but only the principal ones, and particularly the metropolis. Now, the colony of Patræ, founded by Augustus, increased by his command from the population of neighbouring towns, and distinguished by the benefits he conferred upon it, was in effect the metropolis of Achaia; and it was to the Patrenses alone that Augustus granted those privileges and immunities, which Nero and other succeeding princes extended to the whole province.]

Woman with Turreted Head, standing with patera in right hand and cornucopiæ in left, on a second brass of Commodus.

[This type, like the preceding, represents the *Genius* of the colonial city performing sacrifices for the health of the emperor, on the occasion of that terrible plague which in the reign of Commodus raged with depopulating fury throughout all Italy, and especially at Rome. It was from fear of falling a victim to that dreadful scourge that Commodus retired to Laurentum. The cornucopiæ was the customary symbol of a *Genius*, who was supposed to possess the procreative and productive power. It also by analogy signified the fertility of the soil.]

Pellerin supplies an omission of Vaillant's by giving a coin of this colony dedicated to Faustina the younger, the obverse of which bears the legend FAVSTINA AVG. C. A. A. PA. *Colonia Augusta Aroe Patrensis*. Head of the Empress. —*Rev.* IMP. C. ANTONINVS AV. Head of M. Aurelius crowned with laurel.—(*Mélange* i. pl. xvii. No. 8 p. 281.)

Patraus or *Patreus*, the son of Preugenes, grandson of Agenor, the conqueror and general of the Iones, occupied, with his companions in arms, Aroe in Achaia, and gave his name to the city afterwards colony of *Patræ*, but so that the more ancient appellation of Aroe was not altogether abolished, but was often united to the more recent name.—See *Patræ*.

Patres Augustorum.—The fathers of Emperors, although they might have held only a private station, had their names and portraits struck on the coins of their sons, and were placed in the rank of divinities—for example, DIVVS PATER TRAIANVS, head of Trajan the Father; and DIVI NERVA ET TRAIANVS PAT., heads of Nerva and Trajan the Father, on coins of Trajan.

Patres Castrorum.—This title of Fathers of Camps was appropriated to Emperors alone, or to their appointed heirs.

PATRES SENATVS.—It was by this title that Balbinus and Pupienus were designated on their coins, accompanied by two hands joined; which appellation of *Pater Senatus* was adopted instead of that of *Princeps Senatus* as under the old republic.—On coins of Commodus PATER SENATVS had already appeared.

PATRIAE.—See PATER PATRIAE.

PATRIC. *Patricia.*—COL. PATRIC. *Colonia Patricia.*

Patricia, a city in *Hispania Bætica* (Andalusia), and the first *colony* planted by the Romans in Spain; its original name was Corduba—now Cordova.—Pliny speaks of *Corduba* as taking the name of *Colonia Patricia*, when it became a Roman colony; and Antonio Augustino describes it as a colony of veterans and worthy men, to whom honour was due, as to Fathers *(Patribus)*.—Mention is made of *Patricia* on an inscription in *Gruter*, where it is called COLONIA PATRICIA CORDVBENSIS.—The autonomous coins of this city bear the name of CORDVBA.—The colonial imperial are, according to Vaillant, confined to the reign of Augustus, and the same writer gives *five* specimens of their types, all of which bear on their obverse the head of Augustus without laurel, with the legend PERM. CAES. AVG. *Permissu Cæsaris Augusti;* and on their reverses the inscription COLONIA PATRICIA, whilst the types vary—some representing sacerdotal insignia, others sacrificial instruments, or legionary eagles between other military standards.

Types of the *Spanish Colony of Patricia*, from Vaillant, vol. i. pp. 40, 41, 42.

COLONIA PATRICIA, within an oaken crown. The obverse of this coin in second brass bears the bare head of Augustus, and has for inscription PERM. CAES. AVG. *Permissa Cæsaris Augusti.*

[The colonists placed an oaken crown on this coin of Augustus, on account of citizens preserved by him in the war, which he brought to a termination favourable to Roman interests in Spain.]—See a fac simile of this in Akerman's *Coins of Hispania*, pl. iii. No. 11, p. 30.

The same legend.—*Apex* and *Simpulum.*—See those words.

[On the death of Lepidus, Augustus having been created Pontifex Maximus, the people of Corduba (or Patricia), in congratulating him, placed the appropriate type of sacerdotal or pontifical instruments on this small and also on larger brass coins.]

A very large brass inscribed by this colony to

Augustus, on the same occasion, bears a still more ample display of sacrificial instruments, symbolic of the chief priesthood, viz., the *aspergillum*, the *præfericulum*, the *lituus*, and the *patera.*—See those words.

[The dignity of Pontifex Maximus, which comprised all things appertaining to the priestly functions, was transmitted, as it were hereditarily, from Augustus to his imperial successors.]

On a large brass of extreme rarity, dedicated to Augustus and struck " by his permission," appears a legionary eagle between two military ensigns, and on a second brass this type is accompanied with the legend COL. PATR. LEG. V. X.   *Colonia Patricia Legiones quinta decima.*

[Military ensigns, as has been noticed respecting coins of Roman colonies, serve to denote towns originally peopled by veterans transmitted to them. This was the case with Patricia, founded by Augustus. And on the very rare second brass of the same colony, dedicated to that emperor, the *eagle* is accompanied with the *names* of the Legions ; viz., the Fifth and Tenth, from which the veterans destined to occupy the city now called Cordova were drafted.]

PATRON.—See MVNICIPI*um* GAD*itanum* PATRONO. " The municipium of the Gaditani to its patron ;" on a coin of M. Agrippa ; " which teaches us (says Bimard) that under the reign of Augustus the Municipium of Cadiz had chosen Agrippa for its protector."

P. AV.   *Perpetuus* or *Pius* Augustus.

PAVLA *(Julia Cornelia)*, daughter of Julius Paulus, of an illustrious family, was the first wife of the Emperor Elagabalus, whose Prætorian Prefect her father had become. Handsome, graceful, agreeable, well regulated in her conduct, but seduced by the ambition of being mistress of the empire, she gave her hand (A.D. 219) to the most cruel and infamous wretch that ever disgraced humanity and polluted a throne, only to be the victim of his brutal inconstancy.—At the end of a year from the day of her marriage, which had been celebrated at Rome with unprecedented magnificence, she was repudiated by her husband, stripped of the title of *Augusta*, bestowed on her by the senate, and, without being allowed to retain a single honour connected with her short-lived dignity of Empress, Paula returned into private life, and died in retirement.

She is styled on coins of Roman die IVLIA PAVLA AVG. The name of *Cornelia* is given to this lady only on Greek medals.—In all metals her coins are rare : those in *gold* extremely so.

PAVLINA.—Beyond the fact, of which there appears no doubt, that the DIVA PAVLINA of the Roman Imperial series was the wife of Maximinus the Thracian, nothing is authentically known of her, history being silent on the subject of that gigantic barbarian's marriage. The medals, bearing the name of Paulina, present the portraiture of a comely woman, whose regular features are set off with an air of dignity ; on some the features are those of a woman in more advanced life.—There are no gold coins of her : the first brass are rare, the silver still rarer.—The legend of the reverse is CONSECRATIO, and the usual symbol of a peacock bearing the Empress to the skies ; or, standing, with its tail spread ; but a coin in large brass presents Paulina in a biga.

PAVLLVS, thus written with the double L, as it is seen on Roman coins and other monuments, was at first (says Pitiscus) the name of the family of the *Aemilii*, and towards the decline of the republic became the prenomen of that family. Thus the (adopted) brother of the Triumvir Lepidus assumed the name of Paulus Aemilius Lepidus.

PAVLVS LEPIDVS CONCORDIA.—A veiled head of a female, wearing a diadem.— *Rev.* TER PAVLLVS. Three captives standing opposite a figure erecting a trophy. On gold and silver coins of the *Aemilia* family.

This legend and type " evidently refer (as Akerman observes) to the victory of Lepidus over Perseus, King of Macedon, to whom and to his two children the three captives probably allude."—*Descriptive Catalogue*, vol. i., p. 21.

The word TER (according to Morell) points to the fact of *Aemilius* (who, adopted by the father of Lepidus, the Triumvir, was called *Paulus Lepidus)*, having *three times* enjoyed the honours of the triumph.

Pavor——consternation——dread——was, with *Pallor*, deified by the Greeks, who in war sought to appease these two terrible goddesses by sacrifices. The Corinthians consecrated a statue to *Pavor*, who was also worshipped by the Spartans. Tullus Hostilius in a battle, in which his soldiers had begun to give way, vowed a temple to Fear and Paleness (*Pavor* and *Pallor*), and he won the victory. This tradition is commemorated on medals of the *Hostilia* family. On one of them is a head, with hair standing on end, the face raised, the mouth open, and the countenance troubled. The other has a long and lean visage, the hair lank and flat, and a fixed look. It is the true picture of that peculiar ghastliness of expression which great fear produces on the human countenance.—See *Pallor* in Hostilia family.

PAX. Peace.—This word is of very frequent occurrence on Roman coins, nor is it always possible to decide as to which particular pacification it is to be referred.

Pax, regarded by the ancients as a goddess, was worshipped not only at Rome but also at Athens. Her altar could not be stained with blood. The Emperor Claudius began the construction of a magnificent temple to her honour, which Vespasian finished, in the *Via Sacra*. The attributes of Peace, as exhibited on medals, are the *hasta pura*, the olive branch, the cornucopiæ; and often the caduceus. Sometimes (as on coins of Vespasian, Domitian, and M. Aurelius) she is represented setting fire to a pile of arms.

Peace was considered to be in the power of him, to whom belonged the auspices (*auspicia*); whence, according to Dion, the Cæsars were called the Lords of Peace and War (*Pacis et Belli Domini*). Accordingly we find coins of the Emperors proclaiming *Pax* AVGusta, or AVGusti; *Pax Aeterna*; *Pax Perpetua*; *Pax Fundata*; *Pax Publica*; *Pax Ubique Parta*; and these inscriptions are accompanied by various symbols such as the Temple of Peace, as on medals of Augustus, or the Temple of Janus shut, as on those of Nero; or a woman holding a cornucopiæ in her left hand as in Augustus, Hadrian, &c. The symbol of *Eternal Peace*, as manifested in the figure of the goddess setting fire to a heap of armour both offensive and defensive, is seen on coins of Galba, Vitellius, Vespasian, Antoninus Pius, and Aurelius.—See *Pax Augusti*.

Singular to say, no representation of the superb Temple of Peace, built by Vespasian, appears on coins of that Emperor, nor of his son Titus.—See *Templum Pacis*.

The head of *Pax* is seen on *denarii* of Julius Cæsar and of Augustus.

Pax.—The effigy of this goddess (whose blessings the Romans were never more prone to boast of than when their proud empire, hastening to decay, was least in a condition to enjoy them), is seen with caduceus and olive branch on coins of Titus, Galba, and Otho; with cornucopiæ and torch, as in Galba, Vitellius, and Vespasian; with cornucopiæ and olive branch, as in Vespasian, M. Aurelius, L. Verus; bearing the olive branch and hasta, as in Alex. Severus; standing by an altar with patera in right hand, as in Vespasian and Titus; walking with laurel crown, as in Claudius Gothicus;

adorned with the sceptre, as in Gordianus Pius, Maximinus, Philip senior, Æmilianus, Numerianus, Trajanus Decius, Volusianus, Gallienus, Postumus, Victorinus sen., Gal. Maximianus, &c.; carrying a trophy, as on a coin of Claudius Gothicus: also with olive branch and military ensign, as in Constantine the Great, and Carus.—On coins of Augustus (says Woltereck) we see the Goddess of Peace not only with the caduceus, the olive crown, and other ornaments usually appropriated to her, but with attributes belonging to the Goddess of Health, as if with a view to represent under one type all the emblems of felicity which Rome was supposed to enjoy beneath the paternal sway of that Emperor.

Peace is signified by two right hands joined as in M. Antony, Augustus, Antoninus Pius. She is also figured under the form of a bull, on a coin of Vespasian.

The *images of Peace* appear in an unbroken series on the coins of the Roman Emperors, several of the *Augustæ*, and most of the usurpers, from Julius Cæsar to Justinian.—See PACE and PACI; PACATOR, &c.; also ARA PACIS.

PAX.—A female standing, holding a caduceus and ears of corn. On a denarius of Augustus.—See also the medallion, p. 519.

The inscription of COS. VI. shews that this coin was struck in the year of Rome 726.—The title which flattery has given on the obverse to this Emperor, of LIBERTATIS P. R. VINDEX, (the champion of the Roman people's liberties) appears on no other medal of this prince, nor of succeeding *Augusti*. It was designed to commemorate the peace which was established, on the death of Antony, whose removal put an end to the civil war. Hence the expression of Paterculus:—*Finita vicesimo anno bella civilia, sepulta externa, revocata Pax*. L. ii. cap. 89.

PAX. AVG. *Pax Augusta*.—August Peace.

PAX AVGusti.—A female standing, dressed in the stola, holds in her left hand an olive branch; in her right a torch, the flame of which she applies to a heap of armour, placed by the side of an altar. Behind the female is a column, at the foot of which is a shield, and the capital is surmounted by a statue.—This legend and type, with varieties as below, appear on first brass of Vespasian.

PAX AETERNA AVGusti.—A woman stands holding a branch raised in her right hand, and a spear in her left. On silver and brass of Alexander Severus.

This "eternal peace" of the emperor was the one which followed his splendidly victorious campaign against the Persians,—*Artaxerxes*, after having conquered *Artabanus*, the last King of the Parthians, and re-established the Persian empire, proceeded to contend with the Romans. This led to Alexander's departure (*profectio*) from Rome to his victories, to his triumphs. and finally to the treaty which concluded the war by a peace highly honourable to the Emperor and advantageous to the Roman interests, or rather to Roman ambition.

PAX FVNDATA CVM PERSIS.—A woman standing, with olive branch and spear. On silver of Philip senior.

This coin confirms, what Zosimus relates, that Philip, soon after the murder of Gordian III., established relations of peace and friendship with Sapor, King of the Persians, about A.D. 244.

PAX GERM*anicus* ROMA. S. C.—Rome, the Emperor and a female standing ; the latter presenting an olive branch to Vitellius.

This (on a first brass) does not appear to have been struck in record of any particular peace, but merely offers, with others of the same short reign, subjects of flattery, and pledges of hope and good wishes, with which it was customary to greet the event of a new accession to the imperial throne.

PAX ORBIS TERRARVM.—The figure of a woman standing, clothed in the stola ; a caduceus in her right hand, a branch in her left.—AVR. and AR. of Otho.

This appears but an inappropriate legend on the coin of a prince who had raised the banner of insurrection, and directed the dagger of assassination against a rightful possessor of the empire. But, according to Tacitus, Otho, notwithstanding the civil war then waging between his party and that of Vitellius, disposed of public offices, and engrossed the administration of government as if it had been in a time of profound peace; and because, in consequence of the Sarmatians being quieted, there were no external hostilities, this strange compound of personal effeminacy and physical courage, caused a medal to be struck with the above epigraph—boasting of "Peace all over the world!"—Spanheim (in his *Césars de Julien*) justly observes, that to have been accessory to the death of his master and benefactor Galba, added to the effeminacy of his life, to say nothing of his suicide which to some seems so glorious, renders Otho worthy enough of the name of *Brutal*, rather than gives him the least claim to assume on his medals, as he has done, and in times so disastrous and so full of confusion, to be the security of the Roman people, and to vaunt about having restored the peace of the whole universe !"

PAX PERPETVA.—This legend is found on a gold coin (a *quinarius*) of Valentinianus I., which has for its type Victory seated on a coat of mail, holding a buckler, supported by a winged Genius, inscribed VOT. V. MVLT. X.—On another gold *quinarius* of the same Emperor, is Victory standing, full-faced, waving in each hand a laurel garland.—Eckhel (vol. viii. p. 150) observes that these two coins are known to exist in no other cabinet than the Imperial at Vienna.

The only two of Valentinian's predecessors who ventured to assert that they had established *perpetual* peace (even by implication in dedicating a medal PACI PERPET.) were Augustus, and Constantine the Great, who might each be said to have some claim to the honour. Vespasian himself, who re-built the Temple of Peace at Rome, abstained from such self-flattery, and inscribed his beautiful coin, representing the portico of that temple, to the Senate and the people.—But Valentinian, though an able, brave, and generally victorious prince, was, during the latter part of his reign, so constantly engaged in repelling the incursions and punishing the chieftains of the barbarian tribes, that BELLO PERPETVO would have been *his* more appropriate and more veracious legend.

PAXS anciently written for PAX appears on a silver coin struck by AEMILIVS BVCA, one of Julius Cæsar's moneyers.

PAXS. AVGVSTI.—This old-fashioned mode of writing the word PAX, which presents itself on a second brass of Galba, is quite unusual as respects the period of that Emperor's reign.—The accompanying type, viz., a woman applying a lighted torch to a pile of arms, occurs for the first time on this coin ; but is found repeated afterwards in the Imperial series, on medals of Vitellius, Vespasian, Domitian, etc.

PAX*s* AVG*usti* also appears on a coin of Aemilianus.

Pax Julia, a city of Lusitanian Spain, and according to Pliny a Roman colony *(Colonia Pacensis)*.—Vaillant, in describing the coins of the municipium *Ebora*, quotes the above authority for including *Pax Julia* amongst the colonies of Lusitania (i. p. 33), but he gives none of its medals.—Hennin, however, in the nomenclature of his *Manuel*, mentions it as the modern *Badajoz*, and assigns to it colonial imperial coins, as of great rarity, and inscribed to its founder Augustus.—See Akerman's Coins of Hispania, pl. 1, No. 7, p. 15.

P. BARCIN.—*Pia Barcino.*—See Bimard on *Jobert*, ii. p. 232.

P. B. G. MAX. *Parthicus, Britanicus, Germanicus, Maximus.*—Caracalla is thus surnamed on a first brass of Laodicea in Syria, viz., M. AVREL. ANTONINVS PIVS AVG. P. B. G. MAX.

P. B. M. V. N. R. P. on coins of Constantine the Great, of which letters a doubtful explanation is given by Bimard in his notes on *Jobert*, vol. ii. p. 192.

P. BRIT. *Pius Britannicus.*—Commodus is thus surnamed on a coin struck A.D. 184.

P. C. *Pro Consul.*—M. AVR. COT. P. C. *Marcus Aurelius Cotta Pro Consul.*

P. C. CAES. or CAESAR. *Pater Caii Cæsaris.*—Germanicus was thus called as the father of Caligula.

P. CIR. CON. *Plebei Circenses Constituit,* or *Populo Circenses Concessit.*

P. C. L. VALERIANVS, &c. *Publius Cornelius Licinius Valerianus.*—See *Saloninus.*

P. CONS. AVG. *Patri Conservatori Augusti.* —On a coin of Gallienus.—See LIBERO, &c.

P. D.—These initials appear on a second brass of Commodus, forming the first letters of the legend on the reverse of the coins thus :—P. D. S. P. Q. R. LAETITIAE. C. V. (within laurel).

Patin and other numismatists have supposed that P. D. was falsely engraved for P. P., and that therefore the reading should be *Pater Patriæ*; but Eckhel has shewn, from other coins with a similar reverse in the Imperial cabinet, that P. D. is the right reading; and that, meaning PRIMI DECENNALES, it serves to recall to mind the *vota primi decennales*, or vows for the first ten years of the Emperor's reign, which were solved or accomplished in the year (A.D.) 186 when the medal was struck.—See Eckhel, vol. vii. p. 116).

P. D. *Populo Dedit*, or *Populo Datum*.

Peacock.—A bird originally brought into Europe from the further East, and which the ancients held in great estimation. It is related of Alexander the Great, that having seen peacocks for the first time in India, he was so much struck with the variety and beauty of their plumage, that he forbade killing them under the heaviest penalties.—The Romans, however, were not so scrupulous, but made them an article of food on solemn festivals, and gave great prices for the eggs of these birds.—With Pagan mythology, the *peacock* is connected by the well-known story of Argus, to whom Juno confided the faithful keeping of Jupiter's favourite Io, under the form of a cow. Mercury having first lulled to sleep, and then slain, *him* of the hundred eyes, Juno metamorphosed her *panoptical* watchman into a *peacock*, and took that bird under her especial protection.

Hence the peacock was called *Junonia Avis*, by the Romans; and we see its image on their coins, sometimes as the symbol or attendant of Juno Regina, at others as the attribute of an Empress's consecration.—See AETERNITAS.—CONSECRATIO.

Pavo.—The peacock at the feet of Juno is seen on coins of Trajan, Antoninus, the two Faustinas, Lucilla, Crispina, Scantilla, Julia Domna, and others of the Imperial series down to Severina.—See IVNO.

The peacock is also the type of conjugal concord, because Juno was feigned to preside over marriages; for which reason it appears on coins of *Julia*, the daughter of Titus, who, having abandoned herself to marriage with her uncle Domitian, that incestuous tyrant caused a *silver* coin to be struck with her portrait on one side, and a peacock, with expanded tail, on the other. The legend of the reverse is CONCORDIA AVGVST.; also a *gold* medal with DIVI TITI FILIA, and a peacock.

The *peacock* marks the consecration of princesses. It is never the symbol of the consecration of princes; though the eagle, as well as the peacock, sometimes serves to designate the consecration of princesses, as may be seen on medals of Plotina, Marciana, Sabina, and Faustina senior.

As the eagle, Jove's bird, was appropriated to the Emperors as the sign of their consecration after death, so the *peacock*, Juno's bird, was dedicated to the apotheosis of their wives. Hence it forms the type of a reverse, on various coins of the *Augustæ* above-mentioned, sometimes with tail spread, at others with the tail compressed; and sometimes flying, with the figure of a woman (or the spirit of the Empress), seated on its back, as on coins of Faustina senior and junior, Julia Domna, Julia Mæsa, Paulina, Mariniana.

Pecunia.—Money was by the Latins called *pecunia*, either because it was in the course of commercial exchanges employed in lieu of *pecudes* (cattle); or because the images on the earliest coins chiefly related to some sort of *pecus*, as a bull, a sheep, a ram, a horse, a goat, a sow, or other animals.

A writer in the French *Transactions philosophiques* (tom. i. 2nde partie, p. 299) observes—"The first riches of mankind were their flocks and herds, especially their oxen. The first money in Italy was called *pecunia* or *pecus*, and the most ancient pieces of money had the figure of an ox stamped on one of its sides. The Greeks, from the time of Homer, calculated their wealth by the number of oxen to which it was equivalent, as we learn from that celebrated poet; for he tells us that the armour of King Glaucus was worth a hundred oxen, whilst that of Diomede, for which it was exchanged, was not valued at more than nine. The figure of the ox, which appears on the earliest money, seems in Etruria to have been converted into the symbol of the head of that animal, united with that of *Janus*, who, it is said, was the first who introduced money into Italy."

PEDANIA, a plebeian family, as it seems, for its origin is veiled in obscurity. It has *Costa* for its surname.—Of two varieties, in silver, the rarer bears on one side COSTA. LEG. A laureated female head.—*Rev.* BRVTVS IMP. A trophy.—From this denarius nothing else is to be gleaned but that a person named Costa adhered to Brutus in the civil war.

Pedum, the pastoral staff of Apollo, with which he tended the flocks of Admetus. This implement was of knotted wood, crooked at the end, in order to entangle the legs of the cattle and sheep that endeavoured to escape, and to throw after them occasionally. Hence the word *pedum*, which is derived from *pes*, the foot. As the symbol of pastoral life, the pedum appears on Roman coins in the hands of Atys, of Pan, and of deities reduced to the station of shepherds, as Apollo, the Fauns, Satyrs, Bacchants, also the muse Thalia, considered as the Goddess of Agriculture. The shepherd Faustulus, who, according to the Roman legend, found Romulus and Remus suckled by the wolf, is represented on ancient monuments carrying the *pedum*, which in after times was dedicated to sacred uses, and served the purpose of taking the auguries. In the religious ceremonies of Pagan Rome it bore the name of *lituus*, by which appellation was also distinguished a military wind instrument which was crooked in like manner at its further extremity. It is indeed said to have been a questionable point, even in ancient times, which of the two, the augural staff or the wind instrument, had given its name to the other. Subsequently the *lituus* became the sign of augural functions, as the *pedum* was that of pastoral life. Its figure is found on the most ancient medals struck at Rome, not only as a mark of the angurship, but likewise as an ornament of the *Pontifex Maximus*. It is on this account that it appears on coins of many of the

Emperors, because, amongst other offices, they appropriated to themselves the sovereign pontificate. The pedum once converted into the *lituus*, and used as an instrument of divination, was employed, as before observed, for the purpose of taking the auguries. The priest invested with this office divided the heavens into as many regions as Romulus had partitioned his city, and drew presages of signs which he had observed there. The custom of carrying the lituus continued till the total extinction of paganism, and it is seen on monuments coeval with the period when Christianity was greatly extended. Indeed, there is no doubt but that the crosier of bishops was either borrowed from the lituus of the augurs, or was derived from the form of the *pedum*, which is of greater antiquity.

Pegasus, the celebrated winged horse, sprung from the blood of Medusa. Flying to Helicon he struck the earth with his hoof, and caused the fountain of Hippocrene to flow. Bellerophon afterwards rode him in his combat with the Chimæra.

Pegasus, either alone or with his rider Bellerophon—who is sometimes fighting with a lion, or with the Chimæra, at other times performing the part of *breaker* to this winged horse, appears on the Latin coins of Corinth, with the inscription CORINTHVS, or COL. L. IVL. COR.—or it is found with the words AVG. and FLAV. added—namely, COL*onia* L*aus* IVL*ia* AVG*usta* FLAV*ia* COR*inthus*.— See *Corinthus Colonia*.

Pegasus, as the symbol of Apollo, because he gave rise to the Heliconian fountain, sacred to the nine muses, over whom the God of Poetry and Song presided, occurs on coins of Valerianus and Gallienus, with the inscriptions APOLLINI CONS. AVG.—SOLI CONS. AVG.—and ALACRITATI.

Pegasus, sometimes flying, at other times walking, occurs on coins of the Aemilia, Cæcilia, Maria, Petronia, Popilia, Titia, and other Roman families.—Also on coins of Augustus, Claudius, Nero, Domitian, Trajan, Hadrian, L. Verus, Commodus, Sept. Severus.

Pegasus flying, with Faustina senior on his back, appears on a consecration medallion in brass struck in honour of that Empress, under her husband Antoninus Pius.—Vaillant and Spanheim both recognise the coin of which this fine and remarkable design forms the type of the reverse. The latter, in his notes on the *Césars of Julian*, speaks of it as belonging to the French King's Cabinet, and gives an engraving of it (p. 82) with the following descriptive remarks:—" This beautiful medallion represents on one side the Emperor Antoninus, and on the other the consecration of his wife Faustina, symbolised under a type of great rarity, representing this new goddess half veiled, and borne to heaven, not on an eagle, but on a *Pegasus*. And this medallion (adds Spanheim) has relation to another placed at the head of the medallions published by Cardinal Carpegna, where this same Faustina is represented as carried to the skies on a horse, with two lighted

torches in her hands: that is to say, under the usual figure of Diana, or Luna Lucifera."

PELAG. *Pelagia.*—Title given to Venus.

PELL. *Pella* in Macedonia.—COL. IVL. AVG. PELL. *Colonia Julia Augusta Pella.*—On a colonial coin (3rd brass) of Macrinus.

Pella, formerly the capital and metropolis of the third region of Macedonia, situate (according to Livy, l. xliv. c. 6) on a mount on the shore of the Ægean sea, near the confluence of the rivers Erigonus and Axius.—Pella was the birthplace of Philip, King of Macedon, who greatly augmented, and strongly fortified it. As a place of importance it was so much regarded by Julius Cæsar that he formed it into a colony; and for the security of the province in which it was situated, Augustus preserved its rights and increased its population with discharged veterans. To this circumstance Lucan (happily quoted by Spanheim) alludes:—

Exiguæ secura fuit Provincia Pellæ.

On the Imperial coins Pella, in reference to its founders, is called IVL*ia* and AVG*usta*.— The coins of this once important place consist of *Autonomes* (Greek), and of Colonial Imperial, with *Latin* legends, beginning with Hadrian and finishing with Philip the younger, including Caracalla, Macrinus, Elagabalus, Alexander Severus, Julia Mamæa, Maximinus, Maximus, and Gordianus Pius.

The following are the types of this colony, as given in Vaillant:—

On second and small brass of this colony, inscribed to Hadrian, to Macrinus, and to Gordianus III., the reverse exhibits the figure of a young man, sitting naked on a rock, having his right hand lifted over his head, and his left elbow resting on musical reeds, or Pan's pipes.— Pellerin supplies a coin of Pella, dedicated to Maximus Cæsar, which Vaillant omits, and which exhibits the same type on its reverse.— See *Mélange*, i. pl. xx. No. 2.

A second brass of Pella, struck under Alex. Severus, presents the same figure of a naked man, sitting on a rock, with his right hand over his head; but in this instance he holds the *pedum* (or shepherd's crook) in his left hand, and the fistula or pipe of reeds appears before him in the field of the coin.

Pellerin supplies a coin of this colony, struck under Maximus, of whom, as well as of his son Maximus, Vaillant has failed to give any medals. —COL. IVL. AVG. PELLA. A *female* figure seated on a rock, on which she rests her left hand; she lifts her right hand to her mouth.

[Spanheim, in his notes on the *Cæsars of Julian* (p. 160), cites this colonial medal of Pella, and refers to the figure sitting on a rock, as allusive to the fact of its being a city built on a hill.—Seguin regards it as a wrestler, the victor at some athletic games, who is placing the crown he has won on his own head.—Others, amongst whom is Eckhel himself, seem to consider the figure to be intended for Pan, and Mionnet adopts that designation.—On the other hand, Vaillant, throughout his various notices of the same type, as it occurs successively under Hadrian, Macrinus, Alex. Severus, and Gordian III., argues that it is meant for Apollo, in his pastoral capacity (as God of Shepherds), crowning himself after his victory over the unfortunate Marsyas, who had daringly provoked this vindictive and merciless deity to a trial of musical skill, and that his left arm is resting on the pipe of the satyr, as the trophy of his triumph.— In confirmation of this opinion, Vaillant adds that according to Goltzius *(in Græciæ nummis)*, the inhabitants of Pella represented Apollo on their coins, with the tripod and a crown of laurel, whence it is inferred that he was worshipped there.]

On coins of Caracalla, and also on one dedicated to Julia Mamæa, appears a woman clothed in a tunic, sitting; she seems to be lifting her right hand up to her face, whilst her left hand falls at ease beside her chair. The legend of this reverse is C. IV. ; in others COL. IVL. AVG. PELLA. *Colonia Julia Augusta Pella.*

[This is the *Genius Urbis*, seated in the attitude which *Security* is made to assume on coins of Roman die ; a security that belongs to a city built upon a hill.]

On a small brass of Macrinus, bearing the legend of that colony, Victory seated on the spoils of war, holds a *stylus* in her right hand, and with her left supports a shield, which rests on her knee.

[This type refers to the Parthian war : that war having been brought to an end, and peace made with the Parthians by Macrinus, we see Victory seated.—The Roman Senate had decreed sacrifices to Macrinus on account of the alleged victory, and offered him the surname of *Parthicus*, which, however, he did not accept. The Pellenses have here intimated the compliment to the short-lived and intrusive emperor.]

There was another city called Pella, situate on the *Decapolis* of Syria, which is said to have struck some coins with *Greek* inscriptions, under Commodus and Elagabulus.]

Pelliculati Numi.—See *Numi Pelliculati.*

Pellis Caprina.—The goat's skin covers the head of *Juno Sospita.*—See the word.

Pellis Leonina.—The lion's skin, which appears so often on ancient coins, not only indicates the valour and strength of Hercules, as he is supposed to be going forth invested with the skin, but it was also the distinguishing mark of the Heraclidæ, and of other Kings; such, for example, as those of Macedonia, who, like Amyntas, Philip, and Alexander the Great, arrogating to themselves the honour of being descendants of the renowned Alcides, imitated his attribute by placing the spoils of the Nemæan lion on their coins.

In the same spirit of imitation, but with infinitely less pretension, that gladiatorial ruffian of the empire, Commodus, calling himself the *Roman Hercules*, caused his numismatic portraits to be decorated with the *exuviæ leonis.*

Peloponnesus, a fertile peninsula, plenteously flowing with all things needful to man's subsistence and convenience; its most ancient name was *Aegialea*, which, derived from Aegialus, it retained till the time of *Pelops*, a Phygian by birth, who having ascended the throne of this country, called this celebrated part of Greece after his own name. It is united to the northern regions of Greece by the Isthmus of Corinth, and is washed by five seas—viz., the Ionian, the Siculan, the Cretan, the Ægaean, and the Myrtoan, which from the advantages they offer for navigation, give it a local superiority over the other Greek provinces. For coins struck in the Peloponnesus, by Roman colonists, under the Emperors, see CORINTHVS and PATRAE.

Pelta, a short buckler or shield, the use of which is traditionally ascribed to the Amazons, and also, with more authenticity, to the warriors of Thrace ; but the latter differs from the former in having two sloping indentations. On medals and monuments the *Pelta* of the Amazons is in the form of a half-moon.

Penates.—What these were is perspicuously shown by *Millin* in his *Dictionaire de la Fable.* —According to Servius, it was a title given to all deities who were worshipped privately and at home *(qui domi coluntur).* Cicero *(de Nat. Deor.* ii.) says the *Penates* are so called *sive a penu ducto nomine, est enim omne, quo vescuntur homines, penus;* or because, *penitus insident,* they rest in the inmost and most secure part of the family dwelling.

These domestic gods are sometimes confounded with the *Lares* and *Genii*, but they are still more frequently distinguished the one from the other. It was permitted by the religion of the Romans for each individual to choose his Penates ; thus sometimes Jupiter, and oftener Vesta, with other deities of the heavens, the earth, the water, and the infernal regions, were selected for household worship. Even living Emperors, and a man's own ancestors were allowed to be amongst the number of these *Penates*, and the last-mentioned case was the most common of all.—The origin, indeed, of this species of devotion was founded on the opinion entertained by that most superstitious people, that the *manes* of their forefathers delighted, after their removal from this life, still to dwell in their former habitations, where not unfrequently their ashes were deposited, and where their portraits were usually preserved in the most honourable situations. For, after having been praised whilst living as illustrious persons, they became gradually the object of homage and respect when dead, and at length their assistance was implored, and religious rights were assigned to be paid to them. The statues of the Penates were consecrated in the Penetralia, or most secret apartment, and on certain occasions were covered with festoons of garlic and poppies ; wine and incense likewise were offered, and sometimes sheep and lambs were sacrificed to them. It was during the *Saturnalia* that the festivals of the Lares and Penates were celebrated ; besides which a day in each month was dedicated to the honour of these domestic gods. The zeal for this species of worship sometimes went so far that they were *fêted* every day. Nero is recorded to have forsaken all the other divinities for the sake of favourite Penates. The figure of these deities was at times the simple representation of some god, genius, hero, or demi-god, or in short of some celebrated ancestor. They were often represented by *Panthean* figures; that is to say, such as bore the symbols of many divinities.—Eckhel considers them to be identical with the *Dioscuri* and the *Cabiri*.

DEI PENATES.—On a coin of the *Antia* family, quoted and figured by Morell, appear two juvenile heads jugated, and close to which is the foregoing inscription, clearly shewing that the images are those of *Penates*.—See *Antia*.

On a gold coin of the *Sulpicia* family, with the inscription L. SERVIVS RVFVS, occur two juvenile heads laureated, wearing the pileus, and with each a star over him.—The type on the reverse of this denarius exhibits the walls of a city, whose gate is inscribed TVSCVL.—A silver coin of the same family has two young heads on the obverse, and the letters D. P. P., that is to say *Dei Penates*.—On the reverse of this silver coin, which is inscribed C. SVLPICI C.F., appear two men, in military habits, standing with spears in their hands, they point to one kneeling between them holding a sow.—See *Scrofa*.

Eckhel, in commenting on the reverse of the first coin inscribed L. SERVIVS RVFVS, pronounces the two juvenile heads to be those of the Dioscuri, as plainly bespoken by their appearance and attributes. And the type bears reference to the following historical fact—viz., that "Servius Sulpicius, a military tribune, being invested with consular power, in the year V.C. 378, proceeded to the relief of Tusculum with an army from Rome, and obliged the Latins to raise the siege of that place. Now it appears from Cicero that the temple of Castor and Pollux stood in Tusculum, and Festus also states that Castor was worshipped in that town.—Therefore (adds Eckhel), not only the two deities who were anciently honoured with especial worship by the inhabitants of Tusculum, but the walls of the town itself are exhibited on this superlatively rare and curious gold coin."

PENTESILEÆ ACHILLIS, on a contorniate medal of Trajan.—See Eckhel, vol. viii. p. 287; and Havercamp, *De Num. Contor.* p. 145.

Penetrale.—The ancient Romans called by this name a small apartment in their houses, which they dedicated as a private chapel, to the *Penates;* it was a sacred and retired spot, in which they deposited, as in a secret and sure asylum, whatever they held most precious.

Peplus, a long robe, clothed in which Minerva appears on coins: it is a garment much celebrated by poets and mythologists; and was worn by honourable matrons at Rome whenever they went into public.

PER. *Periodicum*.—CER. PER. *Certamen Periodicum*.—Rejecting as incorrect interpretations both the *Certamen Periodicum* of Vaillant, and the *Certamen Perpetuum* of Harduin, followed by Jobert, the Baron Bimard adopts the opinion of his contemporary Iselin, of the French Academy, who, in a dissertation on this point, has shewn that by CER. PER. is to be understood CER*tamen* PER*iodicum*, that is to say, games at which were united all the different kinds of combats and gymnastic exercises practised in the four grand spectacles of Greece. To these were given the name of *certamen periodicum*, because to conquer at the Pythian, Isthmian, Nemæan, and Olympic games was denominated νικᾶν τὴν περίοδον.

PER. or PERM. *Permissu*, by the Permission.—This marks the privilege of striking coins granted by Augustus to any *municipium* or colony.—PER. AVG. *Permissu Augusti* (by permission of the Emperor), occurs on medals of the municipium *Italica*, in Hispania Bætica (Southern Spain).—IMP. CAESARIS AVG. PER. On a coin of Patricia (Cordova) in the same province.

PER. A. or PERPET. *Perpetuus Augustus*. Perpetual Emperor.—Also *Perpetuo*—as CAESAR DIC*tator* PER*petuo*, on coins of Julius Cæsar.

PER. *Persicus*.—EXERCITVS PER. on a coin of Probus.

PER. *Pertinax*.—SEVERVS PER AVG.—See *Sept. Severus*.

PER. or PERP. AVG. *Perpetuus Augustus*, as on coins of Gal. Maximianus, Constantinus jun., and Julian the Apostate ; also Zeno and Focas.

PERG. *Pergaea*.—Diana was thus called, from the city of Perga, in Pamphylia, where there existed a temple of that goddess, to which the privileges of a sanctuary were attached.— A silver medallion of Trajan bears on its reverse the date of COS. II., and has for its type a statue of Diana, of Perga, within a temple : on the frieze of which is inscribed DIANA PERG.

PERM. IMP. *Permissu Imperatoris*, on coins of the Corinthians, to whom the privilege of coining money together, with the liberty of the province *(libertas provinciæ)*, seems to have been extended by Vespasian, inasmuch as there are coins which signify that this privilege had been restored to the colony of Corinth, by Domitian his son. Hence, in Morell, we read on their coins COR. PERM. IMP.

PERMISSV.—After Augustus had given up the brass mint to the Senate—a shadow as it were of Roman liberty, that body granted the power of coining to certain cities in those provinces which remained under its authority, as Augustus did to those whose government he still retained. Some coins are inscribed as having been struck by permission of the pro-ccnsul (Morell, *Fam.* p. 32)—an instance of this is found on a coin bearing the head of Tiberius, and inscribed PERMISSV DOLABELLAE PROCOS.— And on another, bearing the head of Drusus, son of Tiberius, with the inscription PERMISSV L. APRONI. PROCOS III.—Thus we see that even a simple magistrate, governing one of the provinces, of which the Emperor had left the administration to the Senate and to the Roman people, sometimes gave these sorts of permissions : examples of the kind are to be found on medals struck in the cities of Achaia, and of Africa.—Bimard, i. 210,

PERP. *Perpetuus.*—CENS. PERP. *Censor Perpetuus.* This abbreviation appears frequently on the medals of Domitian.—IMP. PERP. *Imperator Perpetuus* occurs on coins of Alexander Severus, and of Probus.

PERPETVETAS *(sic).*—This epigraph occurs for the first time on a silver coin of Valentinian II. But though the legend is new, the accompanying type, which is a phœnix radiated, standing on a globe, is by no means an unusual mark of eternity, or symbol of ages. Still there is this novelty as respects the type itself, that it forms the sole instance in which *Perpetuitas* unites itself on the same medal with the phœnix.

PERPETVITAS AVG. or **AVGG.** (the immortality of the Emperors) appears on coins of Gallienus, Fl. Severus, Florianus, Probus, Carus, and others; but the type is, on all these, a woman, who stands holding a globe and spear, and resting her elbow on a column.

PERPETVA CONCORDIA. On a silver coin of S. Severus, bearing the portraits of Caracalla and Geta.—This epigraph also appears on the reverse of a most rare and elegant gold coin of Sept. Severus, which exhibits all the heads of himself and family; viz., the Emperor and his wife Julia on one side, and their two sons, Caracalla and Geta, on the other. There seems no doubt but that this, and three other gold and silver medals offering a similar union of portraits of the reigning house, were struck in that period of S. Severus's life (about A.D. 201), when he was in Syria, occupied with the affairs of the East, and when he gave the *toga virilis* to his ferocious first-born, Caracalla.—With respect to the legend, unless " the wish" rather than the *fact* be taken as "father" to the phrase, nothing could be less veracious; for perpetual *dis*cord, mutual hatred, and sanguinary dissention were the real characteristics of that ambitious and ill-governed house—the Imperial family of Severus.

PERPETVA VIRTVS.—A military figure, with spear and buckler, marching.—In the exergue, S. T. On second brass of Constantinus Magnus.

PERPETVA VIRTVS AVG.—The Emperor on horseback, preceded by a foot-soldier. On gold of Licinius.

PERPETVO! was a form of acclamation addressed by the soldiers and people to their Emperors.—According to Lampridius, in his Life of Alex. Severus, on the inauguration of a new *Augustus*, the multitude shouted not only *Dii te servent*, but also *Dii te perpetuent!*

Perpetuus Augustus.—Spanheim alludes to Trajan and Bimard to Nerva, as the first who added this emphatic word *perpetuus* to the Imperial titles. But Eckhel rejects both these authorities, and assigns the primary assumption of it to Probus.—PERPETVO IMP. PROBO. AVG., with the helmeted or radiated bust of Probus appears on third brass coins of that Emperor; [on the reverse RESTITVTOR ORBIS.]—Harduin, with a degree of judgment which that learned Jesuit but seldom displays, observes, "that the

appellation *Perpetui Imperatoris*, thus assigned to Probus as the highest title of honour, clearly teaches us that not all the Roman Emperors were perpetual Emperors, but only temporarily appointed by the Senate."

Afterwards, we find PERP. AVG. inscribed on their coins by the sons of Constantine the Great. The origin of this epithet, *perpetuus*, dates itself from a remote period, as on coins of the earliest princes a boast is made of their eternity, but PERPETVITATI AVG. occurs frequently from the period of Alexander Severus, on a single coin of whom is also read POTESTAS PERPETVA.

PERS.—On a consecration medal of Carus is read the surname of *Persicus*, which the biographer of that Emperor says he merited.—DIVO CARO PERSICO.

Persia, a region of Asia, so called (according to Stephanus) from Perse, son of Medeas.—The people of this country—the Persians—were noted as the most corruptly addicted to luxury and pleasures. Ptolemy describes the geography of Persia, as bounded on the north by Media, on the west of Susiana, on the east by the two Carmaniæ, on the south by the Persian Gulf.—As the empire of the Persians was in ancient times celebrated, so to this day it is an important state, and includes several extensive provinces, which are governed in our age by the *Sophis*, Kings of Persia.—Except on a coin of Philip senior, no mention is made of the Persians on Roman Imperial medals.—See PAX FVNDATA CVM PERSIS.

Perruques, or Wigs.—From a learned, elaborate, and comprehensive historical dissertation on *Perruques*, contained in M. Millin's *Dictionaire des Beaux Arts*, the following extracts are made, as applicable to the connection of the subject with Roman numismatics :—

"The custom of covering the head with false hair (or more correctly speaking with hair of its own growth), fixed in whatever manner it might be, is traceable to a very remote antiquity—it is a custom which prevailed especially amongst the Greeks and the Romans. The usage is to be ascribed not less to necessity than to luxury and to the love of dress. The Romans designated the adornment of the head with false hair by such expressions as the following :—*Coma adulterina, coma apposita, positi capilli, galerus, capillamentum, reticulum.* They had also adopted the Greek term *corymbus.*—Martial uses the word *persona capitis*, when speaking of what the French call perruques and we call wigs.—The commonest denomination of perruques, with the Romans, was *galerus*, a word which originally meant a bonnet which went circularly round the head. We learn from Suetonius that Domitian was entirely bald; and yet upon all his medals he is represented with hair. Now, we see on the other hand, Julius Cæsar figured on many medals with the head bald, but having a crown of laurel, under which this defect is concealed. It is therefore probable that Domitian covered his baldness with a species of perruque, which had already become common enough to be represented on medals as if it were the natural head of hair. This is the more probable, as the biographer of that emperor says, he was vexed at being bald, and never liked to have it mentioned to him.—Domitian's head of hair, as we observe it on his medals, has the form of a *galerus*, rounded and curled with so much care and art, as leaves it necessarily to be inferred that it is represented as he wore it, because it is not handsome enough to be taken for an ideal head of hair, and it is an undisputed fact that Domitian had a bald head.—Suetonius and Plutarch both affirm that Galba had but little hair. Upon some of his coins he is bald, upon others he is figured with hair. It seems probable, therefore, that sometimes this prince wore a wig.—The Emperor Otho constantly wore one, which, according to Suetonius, was so well made, that it was impossible to distinguish it from natural locks.

"The Roman women especially took great pains with the *coiffure*, and generally wore veritable wigs.—A passage of the 7th chapter of Tertullian's treatise, *de cultu feminarum*, seems to indicate that in his time, that is to say, in the third century of the Christian æra, the art of wig-making had already arrived at perfection. By the same passage it is also shewn that the name of *galerus* was given only to those round perruques which covered the top of the head, or which surrounded the head, and that they differed from the *corymbus*, which formed a point, or cone.—Julia, the daughter of Titus, on her medals has a similar corymbus. The coins struck in honour of the Roman Empresses, together with the statues, busts, intaglios, and other works of antiquity, which have been preserved to us, in the various museums of Europe, serve to make us acquainted with the various ways of dressing the hair in use amongst the Roman ladies. But it is scarcely possible to distinguish with precision the natural *chevelure* from that which represents the false hair. Some marble busts of Roman ladies, which have a moveable *coiffure*, prove evidently the use of perruques by the women of Rome. There is one of this kind, representing the Empress Lucilla, and greatly resembling her image on medals.—The *coiffure* of Plautilla, wife of Caracalla, is clearly a perruque, and the same may be said of a bust of Julia Pia."—See *Galerus*.

PERT. *Pertinax.*—According to Orosius, Septimius Severus was desirous of being called by this name, after that of the Emperor, whose death he affected to avenge. Hence on his coins we read IMP. SEV. PERT. AVG. &c.

PERTIN. *Pertinax.*—IMP*erator* CAES*ar* P*ublius* HELV*ius* PERTIN*ax* AVG*ustus*.

PERTINAX *(Publius Helvius)*, the son of a freedman and timbermerchant, named Helvius Successus, was born, according to Capitolinus, in Villa Martis, in the Appennines; according to Dion, at Alba Pompeia,

A.D. 126.—Quitting his father's business, he first applied himself to literary pursuits, and soon afterwards adopting the military profession, he distinguished himself in Parthia, Britain, and Noricum (part of Illyria). For his good conduct he was placed among the Senators by Marcus Aurelius, then the prætorship, and lastly the consulate, was conferred upon him.—Recalled from a distant command, under Commodus, he was appointed Prefect of Rome, and although he discharged the duties of the office with the strictest integrity, he yet succeeded in securing the approval of that worst of Emperors, who even chose him as colleague in his seventh and last consulate, and last year of his life.—In the year of Rome 945 (A.D. 192), on the night when Commodus was slain, the conspirators, looking round for an able, honest, sober-minded man to fill the vacant thone, fixed upon Pertinax, and at their earnest and repeated persuasions, he reluctantly accepted the fatal gift of supreme power. The soldiers elected him by acclamation in their camp, and the Senate confirmed their choice with sincere felicitations. To restore the ancient discipline, to reform the morals of the city, to banish informers, to replenish an exhausted treasury, and in his own person to set the first example of frugality—were objects to which the sexagenarian Emperor was intent in commencing his unwilling career of government. But it was these very measures for the public good that brought upon Pertinax the furious displeasure of the Prætorians, whom the intemperate liberalities of Commodus had rendered impatient of all restraint. A hastily assembled troop of these military debauchees, rushed into the palace, and seizing upon the virtuous and unsuspecting prince, slew him after a reign of only 87 days, in the 66th year of his age. He was a venerable looking old man, with flowing beard and thick hair turned back—a character honest, just, and virtuous. The people and senate lamented his death, and distinguished his funeral with the deifying rites of consecration.—Severus also, after Didius Julianus had been also removed by a violent death, paid a tribute to the virtues, in assuming the name, of Pertinax, and by dedicating other honours to his memory.

The coins of *Pertinax*, in each metal, are very rare. The large brass are especially so, and the gold and silver hardly otherwise. As this Emperor reigned only four months, Vaillant finds no medals struck by the colonies to his honour.—The head of Pertinax on his Latin coins is circumscribed—IMP. CAES. P. HELV. PERT. (or PERTIN. or PERTINAX.) AVG.—Also, struck after his death, DIVVS PERT. PIVS PATER., with the usual symbols of consecration.

PES. or PESV. *Pesuvius*—A prenomen of Tetricus senior.—IMP. C. C. PESV. TETRICVS.

PESC. NIG. *Pescennius Niger.*

PE. S. C. on a denarius of Lentulus, which letters *Manutius* has, from ancient inscriptions interpreted—*Publico Aere, Senatus Consulto.*

Pescennius Niger (Caius) was descended from a family that originally belonged to

Aquinum (now *Aquino*). His parents, Annius Fuscus and Lampridia, were of the middle class. After discharging in a laudable manner various military offices, he was declared Consul by Commodus, and at length was appointed to the command of the Syrian army.—On the death of Pertinax, and the execrable purchase of the empire by Didius Julianus, the troops of Niger immediately invested him with the purple, in the year of Rome 946 (A.D. 193). He was a man conversant with every important branch of public affairs, eminently skilled in the art of war, and a great disciplinarian; but ferocious in his manners, and given to the unbridled indulgence of a libidinous disposition. —Septimius Severus made war upon him, as against a public enemy, and routed his forces in several engagements. Pescennius finally took refuge at Antioch, where, whilst endeavouring to conceal himself, he was discovered by some of Severus's soldiers, and put to death in the 58th year of his age, A.D. 195.

The extreme rarity of *Pescennius Niger's* coins is a fact known to all numismatists.— Eckhel, in his *animadversio* on the *Latin* coins of this brief reign, says:—

"All the medals of *Pescennius*, even those wrought after the manner of the Roman mint, are certainly of foreign fabric, and were doubtless struck at Antioch, that being the capital city of the region, in which he fixed the seat of his temporary government. For at the time when he usurped the purple in the East, Didius Julianus, and, presently after, Severus held possession of Rome, by whom, although the senate and people might have been well affected to his cause, either he was not acknowledged as an associate in the empire, or what happened at a later period, he was denounced as an enemy. This is the reason why no brass coins of Pescennius struck (ex s. c.) by order of the Senate are extant; and if you happen to light upon any pretending to be such, you may condemn them at once as unworthy of credit. As, however, the gold and silver coinage belonged of right to the Emperors, and as, in whatever part of the world they seized upon the imperial sceptre, it was their practice to coin money instantly in token of their power (a palpable instance of which we see in the case of Vespasian), so following the same example Pescennius issued gold and silver coins stamped with his image." After remarking that a gold medal of Pescennius hitherto *unique* had been found, with the inscription of CONCORDIA, and that all the rest bearing *Latin* legends are silver, and of the greatest rarity, and consequently of the highest price, the illustrious numismatist above quoted, concludes his animadversion by saying—" Be it observed that all these coins are of very inferior workmanship, the letters of the inscription often vilely distorted and disjointed, whence their foreign origin

may at once be inferred; a circumstance to be borne in mind, lest on account of the ill-favouredness of their appearance, we should undeservedly impute a spurious origin to the medal itself."

Style:—IMP. CAES. PESC. NIGER. IVST. or IVSTVS.—IMP. CAES. C. PESCEN. NIG. IVS. AVG.

"His brass coins (says Akerman) have Greek legends; and although there are many types, are all very rare. The unique gold coin (alluded to by Eckhel) was formerly in the cabinet of the French King. It has been considered dubious by most medallists, on account of the title "Pater Patriæ," which it bears on the reverse; and which Niger could not have received from the Senate of Rome. This coin unfortunately formed part of the recent plunder of the French cabinet, and has, in all probability, been consigned to the crucible."— *(Descriptive Cat.* vol. i. p. 333.)

The illustration selected above is from a fine denarius in the British Museum.

The only colonial coins struck in honour of Pescennius, during his reign of a year and a half, were those of *Cæsarea* and *Aelia Capitolina*, which indicate that his authority did not extend beyond Syria and Palestine.

Petasus, Mercury's cap, with two wings.— See *Mercury*.

PETILLIA, a plebeian family—surname *Capitolinus*. Its coins (which are rare) consist of two varieties; one denarius bears on its obverse CAPITOLINVS, with the head of Jupiter, and on its reverse PETILLIVS, with a temple of five columns. [See engraving p. 171.] The other has on one side PETILLIVS CAPITOLINVS. An eagle standing on a thunderbolt. *Rev.* A temple of six columns richly adorned with statues.

"Whatever might have been the reason why the *Petillii* took the cognomen of Capitolinus, certain it is (says Eckhel) that the type as well of Jupiter Capitolinus, as of the temple, refers to that cognomen.—At a subsequent period, some individual of the same family, being curator of the Capitoline temple, is said by Horace to have pilfered various precious things therefrom:—

> *Mentio si qua*
> *De Capitolini furtis injecta Petilli*
> *Te coram fuerit.*
>
> Lib. i. Sat. iv. l. 93.

PETRONIA, a Roman family, which although of the plebeian order, was of consular rank, and of the most ancient date, for it was noted as early as the reigns of the Tarquins, and had a Sabine origin. Its only surname on coins is *Turpilianus*. P. Petronius Turpilianus was monetary triumvir under Augustus, whose head or epigraph appears on all the coins of this family, which are rare both in silver and gold, and present nineteen varieties. The types allude to Petronius himself, or they are occupied in celebrating certain deeds of Augustus; as in those which represent *Armenia kneeling—a Parthian restoring standards—the Emperor borne in a biga of elephants—and other similar events of the year of Rome 734.—Petronius was the name of a pro-consul of Asia under Tiberius, and after-wards of Syria under Claudius.

FERON. TVRPILLIANVS IIIVIR. Head of the Goddess Feronia.—*Rev.* CAESAR AVGVSTVS. SIGN*is* RECEPT*is.* A Parthian kneeling, offers a military ensign. AV. R.

From this type it may be inferred that Petronius was master of the Imperial mint when the Parthians restored to Augustus the Roman eagles they had formerly taken from Crassus. Feronia, whose head appears on the obverse of this denarius, was worshipped as a goddess by the Sabines, in a city of the same name, situate at the foot of Mount Soracte.—See *Feronia.*

Another denarius of this family bears on its reverse the surname of TVRPILLIANVS IIIVIR. (one of Augustus's moneyers), and the figure of a woman half-buried in a heap of shields.—Here we have a fresh instance of a Sabine type adopted by Petronius, which indeed from the birth-place of his remote ancestors he had a right to make choice of. The subject shadowed forth in the above denarius, is the well-known legend of *Tarpeia,* the virgin daughter of Sp. Tarpeius, who, during the war which arose out of the famous rape of the Sabine women, com-manded the citadel of Rome. The Roman maiden, as Livy relates, being allured by the desire of possessing the bracelets of gold which the Sabine soldiers wore on their arms, engaged to admit them into the fortress, on condition that they gave her what they had on their left wrists (meaning the bracelets). And the Sabines were as good as their word; only, instead of their bracelets (armillæ), they threw upon her the shields which also they carried on their left arms, until she was crushed to death by their overwhelming weight.

For a medal of Petronius, exhibiting a Siren on its reverse, see the word *Sirenes.*

PETRONIVS MAXIMVS *(Flavius Anicius),* a wealthy senator of the Anician family, who by the favour of Valentinian III., had risen to be patrician, twice consul, and three times prætorian præfect; but, enraged at his imperial benefactor's having dishonoured his wife, he em-ployed assassins to destroy him A.D. 455. He afterwards seized upon the empire, and com-pelled Licinia Eudoxia, widow of his sovereign prince, to marry him. She, however, to avenge the death of Valentinian, and in resentment of this forced union with her husband's murderer, invited Genseric from Africa into Italy; and on the approach of that Gothic chieftain to Rome, Petronius was torn to pieces in an insurrection of the people, in the third month of his usurpation.—There are no brass coins of this tyrant, and both his gold and silver ones are of extreme rarity. On these he is styled D. N. PETRONIVS MAXIMVS. P.F. AVG. A beardless head, crowned with an impearled diadem.—On the reverse VICTORIA AVG. The Emperor hold-ing an oblong cross and treading on a dragon's head. The coins resemble in character those of Honorius and his time.

P. F.   *Pia Felix.*—Pious, happy, a feminine title of honour given to none of the Roman Empresses before the time of Theodosius jun. Thus *Aelia Eudoxia,* wife of that Emperor, Licinia Eudoxia, wife of Valentinian III., Galla Placidia, and Honoria, are styled P. F. AV*Gusta.*

P. F.   *Pia Fidelis.*—Pious, faithful : epithets applied on coins to certain Roman colonies and legions.

P. F.   *Pius Felix,* a frequent abbreviation on Imperial medals.—Everyone is aware that the Emperor Antoninus was distinguished by the surname of PIVS; but why it was thus formally appropriated to him is a point on which opinions vary; whether it was on account of his signal devotion to the gods of his religion, as Pau-sanias hands it down, or rather for his virtue of clemency.

P. F.   *Primus Fecit.*—He did such and such a thing the first. SEX. NONI. PR. L. V. P. F.—See *Nonia* fam.

P. F.   *Publii Filius,* son of Publius; or *Pii Filia,* daughter of Pius (viz., of Antoninus Pius.)

P. H. C.   *Provinciæ Hispaniæ Citerioris.*—Of the province of hither Spain (*i.e.* nearer to Italy.)

Phaëton, son of Apollo (or the Sun), drawn in a quadriga, appears on a Corinthian coin of M. Aurelius.—See Vaillant, *in Col.* vol. i. p 181.

Phaëton's sisters changed into larch-trees.—This subject is found constantly and exclusively repeated on the denarii of the *Accoleia* family; on one side of which is the effigy of Clymene, with the epigraph P. ACCOLEIVS LARISCOLVS; on the other, the three sisters metamorphosed, according to the ancient myth, as a consequence of their grief for the loss of their rash brother.

Pharetra, the quiver or case for arrows and darts, is a frequent type on coins of kings, cities, and people, with *Greek* inscriptions. It is by no means common on Roman medals. Conjoined with the bow and a tiara, it occurs on coins of Augustus, with the inscriptions ARMENIA CAPTA, and DE PARTHIS; also on a brass medallion of Hadrian, without legend, appears a quiver pendant from the branch of a tree, near which stands Hercules, holding his club and lion's skin.—The quiver, according to Vaillant, was dedicated to that demi-god. It appears as a mint-mark on coins of the *Julia* and other Roman families; and as an emblem of Hercules, on coins of Postumus.

Pharia Isis, or as on coins of Julian the Apostate it is written FARIA, was so called according to Pliny, from Pharus, in Egypt, an island joined by a bridge to the Roman colony of Alexandria. *Isis* here means the protectress of the Pharus, on which a light-house was built.—Isis is fabled to have been the daughter of Inachus, King of the Argives, and to have been trans-formed by Jupiter into a cow; and having afterwards been restored to her pristine form was made a goddess, and adored as such by the Egyptians above all other divinities. On coins she holds in her right hand the *sistrum*, a musical instrument used in the sacred rites of this favourite divinity of Egypt; whose worse than absurd—whose grossly indecent—worship, the above-named imperial *philosopher* preferred to the pure and holy religion of Christ!—One or two of the Roman Empresses appear on medals under the figure of Isis.—See *Isis Faria*.

Philippi, in Macedonia, named in the Acts of the Apostles (c. xvi. v. 12) as "a chief city and a colony," and to the Christian converts in which the epistle of St. Paul was addressed. Situate at the foot of Mount Pangæus, it was originally a part of Thrace, under the name of *Crenides*; but afterwards became annexed to Macedonia, and was then called after his own name by King Philip. Subsequently it was made a Roman colony, and invested with the *Jus Italica*. Near this town two celebrated battles in the civil wars of Rome were fought, namely, first that memorable *campus Philippicus*, where Pompey was defeated by Julius Cæsar, and afterwards that when Brutus and Cassius were vanquished by Octavius and Mark Antony, memorable events to which Lucan in his *Pharsalia* alludes repeatedly; and which are recorded by other poets and historians.

It was Philip, the son of Amyntas, who enlarged the city, and from whom it derived its name of Philippi. By this appellation it is also designated on its imperial coins, with the addition of surnames, which shew it to have been made a colony by *Julius*, and to have been re-peopled with veterans by *Augustus*. COL. IVL. AVG. PHILIP.—The series (a very much broken one) of these coins extends as far (says Rasche) as Caracalla. Hennin carries it to Gallienus. The modern name of the city is written *Filippi*.

In the *types* there is but little variety.—The first colonial imperial medal of this colony appears to be a second brass inscribed to Claudius, and bearing on its reverse COL. IVL. AVG. PHILIPP. *Colonia Augusta Julia Philippensis*. Two figures standing on a pedestal, one that of a man clothed in military habiliments, with right hand elevated, and left hand placed against his side. The other that of a woman having in her right hand a crown, which she from behind holds over the head of the male figure. On the pedestal is engraved DIVVS AVG.

Patin, in his engraving of this type, has caused both figures to be represented in the dress of warriors *(paludata)*, lifting up each his right hand; and that learned numismatist has pronounced his opinion from the inscription on the pedestal, that the images of Julius Cæsar and Augustus are therein delineated.—Spanheim, in his *Cæsars of Julian*, has given a similar representation (p. 221), and although at first of opinion that the hinder figure was that of a woman, afterwards adopted Patin's sentiments. —But Vaillant affirms that on the above coin of Claudius, as well as on others inscribed by the Philippians to several succeeding emperors, it is constantly a woman who holds the crown over the head of the foremost figure, which alone is in military garments. And then, observing that the title DIVVS AVG. belonged solely to Augustus, as indeed an honour of deification awarded to him after death, the last-named writer goes on to express his decided opinion that the type in question represents the Genius of the city crowning the image of Augustus, whose statue had been erected in the public forum of Philippi, in gratitude for his having re-established and greatly favoured that colony. —[The type of a Genius placing a crown on the head of an Emperor is often met with on Greek coins.]—Hardouin, Havercamp, and several others take the same view of the subject.

Pellerin, on the other hand, publishes a second brass medal of *Philippi*, which he observes was unknown to any of the above-mentioned numismatists (tom. i *Recueil des Médailles*, p. xiv.) On the obverse of this coin appears the laureated head of Augustus, with PHIL. IVSSV. AVG. COL AVG. IVL.—*Rev.* DIVO. IVLIO. AVG. DIVI. F. Two figures standing on a pedestal, the foremost young and in a military dress; the one behind, older, and in the toga, who holds his right hand extended over the head of the other. Respecting the figure last-described, Pellerin says—"*Il est indubitable que cette figure est celle de Jules César désigné par son nom* DIVO IVLIO, *inscrit derrière lui; comme Auguste est pareillement désigné par son nom* AVG. DIVI. F. *inscrit au-devant*."—The same judicious author adds, however, that this medal is not to be regarded as laying down any rule for the explanation of those other coins which have on the pedestal DIVVS AVG., but on those of this kind in his collection, whereon the above described type appears; he concludes by pronouncing the hinder one of the two figures to be that of *Julius Cæsar deified*, holding the right hand stretched out and elevated, with the body naked to the waist. [This is not so clearly discernible in the engraving.] The same as Jupiter and the other pagan deities are most generally represented on medals and other ancient monuments. —Havercamp gives the engraving of a small brass of Philippi as struck under Vespasian, very like Pellerin's, except that the hindermost figure is not naked to the waist, but clothed in the toga from the shoulders to the feet.

It appears, moreover, from a second brass of Claudius and Nero, which are described in Eckhel's *Catalogue* (i. p. 86, n. 5 and 6), and the figures on which he identifies with Augustus and Julius Cæsar, that the interpretation of Patin and of Spanheim is supported by that of the great German numismatist, but it is no less evident that their interpretation refers to another coin of Claudius quite distinct from that commented upon in Vaillant's work on the colonies, but of which the type corresponds with that delineated in Patin and Spanheim. Thus both opinions may be reconciled in almost every material point, or at any rate need no longer to be regarded as conflicting with each other.

Second brass dedicated by the Philippians successively to Galba, Vespasian, Domitian, Hadrian, M. Aurelius, and Caracalla, how different soever the precise occasion might be for striking such medals, still continue to exhibit (with the exception of the wolf and children on a coin of Commodus) the type of the military figure crowned by a female figure, together with the DIVVS AVG. on the pedestal, as if to perpetuate the remembrance of their great benefactor, Augustus.

Philippopolis.—There were two cities of this name : one in Thrace, dignified with the title of metropolis ; the other in Arabia, which was included amongst the number of the Roman *colonies.*—The Thracian *Philippopolis* (now *Filibé*), situate in that province of European Turkey at this day called *Romelia*, derived its original name from the Philips of Macedon. It does not appear to have been a Roman colony ; but its Imperial coins are very numerous, beginning with Domitian, and extending to Salonina, wife of Gallienus.—The pieces of Domitian have *Latin* legends on the side of the head—namely, IMP. CAES. DOMIT. AVG. GERM. COS. XIIII. CENS PER. P. P. *Imperator Cæsar Domitianus Augustus Germanicus Consul* (for the fourteenth time) *Censor Perpetuus Pater Patriæ.*—On the reverse in Greek characters ΦΙΛΙΠΠΟΠΟΛΕΙΤΩΝ *Philippopolitarum.* A woman with turreted crown stands holding patera and branch ; at her feet is the recumbent personification of a river.—This large brass *bilingual* coin is published in Eckhel's *Doct. Num. Vet.*, and is also noted in his Catalogue of the Imperial Museum at Vienna.—The Arabian Philippopolis was founded by Philip senior, in honour of his native country. One coin of this Philippopolis, edited by Vaillant (ii. p. 173), has its legend, both of the obverse and reverse, in *Greek*. It is a first brass of elegant design, inscribed to Philip, who colonised as well as built the city ; and the type is Rome seated, holding in her hand an eagle, on which are placed the images of the Emperor and his son.

PHILIPPVS *(Marcus Julius)*, commonly called the Arab, or *Senior*, or the Father, was, according to Zonarus, born in the Arabian colony of Bostra, his father being, it is said, a captain of robbers. Rising through the various grades of office in the Roman army, on the death of Misitheus (in which he is supposed to have had a secret hand), he became Prætorian Prefect under Gordian III. And when that young prince was (at his instigation) slain in Mesopotamia, Philip was proclaimed Emperor

by the soldiers, A.D. 244. He is said, by

historians, to have been a man of wonderful craftiness, and of the greatest military skill. He won the mercenary hearts of the troops with ample largesses, whilst he sent the discharged veterans into colonies which he had himself established, viz., *Damascus* in Coelesyria, *Neapolis* in Samaria, *Philippolis* in Arabia, which latter city he himself founded. Immediately on his accession to the throne, he made an inglorious peace with Sapor, King of the Persians, and returned to Rome. He marched afterwards against the Carpi, a Scythian or Gothic people, who had given trouble (during the reign of Balbinus and Pupienus and the younger Gordian), to the Roman provinces bordering on the Danube, and compelled them to be peaceable. And that *Dacia* should owe its preservation to him, he declared it to be a free province. He was the first *ipse primus* alien foreigner presented with the rights of a Roman citizen. He celebrated the *saecularia* or secular games on the thousandth anniversary of the foundation of Rome. He took to wife *Marcia Otacilia Severa*, who is believed to have been a Christian. By this marriage he had a son and a daughter, the former bore his own name of Philip, and was declared Cæsar and Augustus. Marching against Trajanus Decius, who had been saluted Emperor by the army in Pannonia, Philip was killed at Verona by his own troops, about the sixth year of his reign, A.D. 249.

The monies of this Emperor are very numerous ; the gold very rare ; the silver and brass, with certain exceptions, common. Some pieces represent him with *Otacilia* and with Philip jun. His numismatic titles are IMP. M. IVL. FILIPPVS. *(sic.)*—IMP. PHILIPPVS AVG. or P. F. AVG.

PHILIPPVS *(Marcus Julius)*, junior, the son of Philip and Otacilia, appears to have been seven years old when his father usurped the empire, and immediately proclaimed him Cæsar, A.D. 244. The Roman Senate granted to him the title of *Nobilissimus*, as if to conceal the ignobleness of his Arab sire ; although Philip is said to have boasted of his origin from Anchises, and consequent connection with the *Julia* family.—In 247 the son was associated, as *imperii consors*, with Philip, who bestowed on this mere child the title of *Augustus*. The unhappy youth shared the fate of his clever but unprincipled father; and when the latter was, under a just retribution, slain at Verona by his own soldiers his innocent son was murdered by the same prætorian banditti, in the very arms of his mother, A.D. 249, in the 12th year of his age.— From the period when the younger Philip was declared *Augustus*, and admitted to all the honours of the sovereign power, the reverses of most of the coins both of father and son exhibit similar types.—The coins of Philip junior are numerous, and for the most part common in *brass*, and also in *silver*, but are very rare in *gold*. On them he is styled M. IVL. PHILIP. CAES. —PRINCEPS IVVENTVTIS.—M. IVL. PHILIPPVS. NOBIL. CAES.—IMP. PHILIPPVS. P. F. AVG.— Some pieces represent him with *Philip* senior and *Otacilia*.

Philosophus.—The Emperor *M. Aurelius Antoninus* was commonly called the philosopher, because he was enthusiastically addicted to philosophical pursuits, and had that sentiment of Plato constantly on his lips, which expresses an opinion that "The state would flourish if either philosophers governed or Emperors were philosophised." It is to be observed, however, that neither monetal legends nor lapidary inscriptions of any kind take the least notice of this imputed denomination of Aurelius, though some writers have mistaken the epithet for his surname.

PHILVS, surname of the *Furia* family.— M. FOVRI. L.F. round the head of Janus.—*Rev.* PHILI. Minerva crowning a trophy.

Phoenice, part of Syria.—All ancient and the most accurate modern writers write the word *Phœnice*, not *Phoenicia*—witness the coins of Antoninus Pius and of Caracalla, inscribed PHOENICE.—Vaillant, in his Colonies (l. p. 106), derives the name of this country from the Greek word *Phoinix*, a Palm. Nor is it to be denied that the Palm is a type of Syria, Judæa, Egypt, and of other countries remarkable for Palms; but it is more probable that the tree received its name from the country than the country from the tree. Above all other regions belonging to the ancient Phœnicians, that of Tyre was celebrated, hence the Palm occurs on a coin quoted by Spanheim, and which is inscribed TYRVS METROPOLIS COLONIA. According to *Strabo*, the Phœnicians were distinguished for their knowledge of arithmetic and astronomy, and equally so for their skill in the arts of navigation and of war—insomuch that they became the sovereigns of the Mediterranean Sea, and everywhere established colonies on its coasts.

The imperial coins of the Phœnicians were struck at Tyre; they comprise only four reigns. Those of Nero and Trajan bear Greek inscriptions; those of Antoninus Pius and of Caracalla are in Latin.

PHOENICE. COS II. S. C.—A figure stands holding a vase, or basket, in the right hand, a wand in the left—behind is a palm tree. Respecting a large brass, with the head of Antoninus Pius on its obverse (in the imperial cabinet at Vienna), bearing the above legend and type on its reverse, Eckhel remarks to the following brief purport:—"Cellarius, in his Geographia Antiqua, says this region is properly written in Latin *Phoenice*, not *Phoenicia*, which opinion, indeed, this medal confirms."—*(D.N.V.,* vii. 5.)

A similar medal is ascribed in Mediobarbus (Occo) to Caracalla, but it is not acknowledged either in Mionnet or Akerman; nor is the Antoninus Pius, above quoted, in *their* catalogues.

Phœnix.—This name was given by the Egyptians to a bird, which some writers have professed to regard as a reality, or at least as possible; whilst others have treated its existence and history as equally fabulous. Many Christian ecclesiastics of the early ages have followed (strange to say) the traditions of paganism respecting the Phœnix, and adopted it as a symbol of the resurrection.—On imperial medals we find it with its head surrounded by rays, symbolizing eternity.

The radiated head of the Phœnix (says Addison) gives us the meaning of a passage in Claudian, who must have had his eye on the figure of this bird, in ancient sculpture and painting, as indeed it was impossible to take it from the life:—

Arcanum radiant oculi jubar: igneus ora
Cingit honos: rutilo cognatum vertice sidus
Attollit cristatus apex, tenebrasque serenâ
Luce secat.

His fiery eyes shoot forth a glittering ray,
And round his head ten thousand glories play:
High on his crest, a star celestial bright
Divides the darkness with its piercing light.

The *Phœnix* occurs on medals of Constantine the Great, and of his children, after the example of the Princes and Princesses of the early empire, in order to designate, by this bird of reputed immortality, either the eternity of the empire, or the eternity of happiness supposed to be enjoyed by those princes who already were placed in the ranks of the immortal gods.— Bimard, confirming this observation of Jobert, says, "the phœnix appears on coins of the upper empire. We see it in Trajan and in many other emperors. On a first brass of Faustina senior, a female seated, holds a phœnix on her right hand."—See AETERNITAS.

[Amongst the medals which have birds on their reverses, scarcely any are more curious than those of Hadrian and of Antoninus Pius. The type represents an Eagle, a Peacock, and an Owl, placed on the same line, with the simple legend COS III. for Hadrian, and COS IIII. for Antoninus Pius. These medals have their meaning easily explained by means of a medallion of Antoninus, which represents Jupiter, Juno, and Minerva on its reverse. It is to these three divinities that the type of the three birds refers, the Eagle being consecrated to Jupiter, the Peacock to Juno, and the Owl to Minerva.]—See *Birds.*

The *Phœnix*, on medals, signifies not only eternity, but also the hope of better times, because this bird was formerly believed to rise again into existence from its ashes. Sometimes it is seen by itself perched on a globe; but

more frequently on the hand of the emperor.—
The fable of the Phœnix, and its revival from
extreme old age to a new youth (on a funeral
pile of its own construction), probably led to its
adoption as a symbol of restoration, on the
reverse of medals (with the legend FEL. TEMP.
REPARATIO), struck in honour of the Emperor
Constans, under whom the city of Smyrna was
restored.—On a coin of Constantius jun. a figure
in military garb holds a *Phœnix* instead of the
more usual figure of a Victory.—Sometimes this
"wondrous" bird is seen standing on a rock;
at others, placed on the funeral pile.—See FEL.
TEMP. REPARATIO; also CONSECRATIO.

Phrygia, a region of Asia Minor, adjoining
to Caria, Lydia, Mysia, and Bithynia, "of all
which (says Strabo) the boundaries so intermix
as to be with difficulty distinguished."

PHRYGIAE.—See ADVENTVI PHRYGIAE on
a coin of Hadrian, who performs sacrifice with
the Genius of the Province, personified by a
figure wearing the Phrygian bonnet.—Also see
RESTITVTORI PHRYGIAE, on a first brass of
Hadrian, on which the Emperor is seen lifting
up a figure clothed in the Phrygian habit, and
bearing a branch or garland.

Physiognomia, or more correctly (in accordance with its Greek derivation) *Physiognomonia.*
On the utility of medals for prosecuting the study
of this science (the object of which is to teach
the mode of discerning the dispositions and
qualities of men, from their eyes, countenances,
forehead, and personal appearance), the celebrated Swiss antiquary Spon published a Dissertation.

PI. or PIAV. *Piauvonius,* the prenomen of
Victorinus, both senior and junior. IMP. C. PI.
(or PIAV.) VICTORINVS AVG.

PI. *Pius;* as in Commodus. AVG. PI. MAX.
—PI. FE. *Pius Felix;* as in Valerianus senior.

P. I. *Pius Imperator;* as on coins of the
Cæcilia family.—Q. C. M. P. I. *Quintus Cæcilius
Metellus Pius Imperator.*

P. I. or PRIN. IVVEN. *Principi* or *Princeps
Juventutis.* Prince of the youth.

PIA.—Why this name was given to colonies,
see Vaillant, *Col.* i., p. 189.

PIA. The surname of a Roman legion.—
LEG. XXX. VLPIA. PIA. F. *Legio Tricessima
Ulpia Pia Fidelis.*

PI. A. *Pius Augustus.*

PIA FELIX.—These denominations, applied
to some of the *Augustæ,* appear to have reference to their fellowship in the imperial
government.—Spanheim and Liebe concur in
the opinion that the above appellation of *Pia*
and *Felix,* like that of the *Pius* and *Felix* of
the Emperors, was not a title of virtue and of
praise, but is simply to be regarded as the
hereditary surname of the Empress's family,
Thus in *Julia Domna,* wife of Severus; in
Severina, wife of Aurelian; in *Aelia Eudoxia,*
wife of Arcadius; in *Galla Placidia,* mother of
Valentinian, and in other Empresses, we find
Pia *Felix* preceding the title of AVG*usta.*

PIET. AVG. *Pietas Augusta.*—August
piety.

PIETAS.—On many coins of Roman
families, and on a vast variety of Imperial
medals from Augustus, in almost uninterrupted
succession down to Constantine the Great, we
see the personification of *Piety,* a virtue which,
elevated by the Romans to the rank of a
divinity, had a temple erected to its honour in
the ninth and in the eleventh region of Rome.
They expressed by this word not only the
worship and reverence due towards the gods,
but also in a more extended sense applied it to
love and charity borne towards parents, children,
friends, and neighbours, to their country, prince,
and soldiers.

Piety has her head ornamented with a veil or
with a fillet, and in this form, with the title
PIETAS, is found on denarii of the *Herennia*
family, and also on some coins of the Emperor
Tiberius: although in the latter instance the
effigy is by some considered to be that of an
imperial lady; for at that period they had not
the boldness and confidence to place female
portraits publicly on coins, or as it were to deify
them. It is generally supposed that the image
in question (beneath which is inscribed PIETAS)
is that of *Livia* Drusilla, mother of Tiberius.

Piety is for the most part represented under
the figure of a devout woman, with veiled head,
near a lighted altar, before which, as in Hadrian
and Antonine, she sometimes stands with both
hands lifted up, which is peculiarly the attitude
of praying (as in Antonine and Verus); at
others she is seen with a patera in the right and
the *acerra* (or censer) in the left hand; or with
the right hand extended she is dropping grains
of frankincense into the fire, as we observe in
the silver coins of L. Aelius, and of Faustina,
all with the title PIETAS, by which representation is clearly shewn the pious feeling, and
religious worship, implied by both the legend
and the type.—To these are to be conjoined
many Imperial medals bearing the circumscription PIETAS AVGVSTI, or AVG*ustorum,*
and which, having the same professed object of
reverence for the gods, exhibit on their reverses
the façades of splendid temples, as in Antoninus
Pius and Faustina senior; others represent
pontificial and augural vases, pateras, altars;
also sacrifices and sacrificial instruments (such
as the lituus, the urceolus, the aspergillum, the
simpulum, and on the larger coins the secespita
(or axe)—as in Commodus, Maximus Cæsar,
Gordianus Pius, &c.

Pietas, when intended by the Romans to
signify the love and affection of parents towards
their children, or of children towards their
parents, and in like manner those of Emperors
and Empresses towards subjects, is found
symbolized under the figure of a stork, an
example of which we have on a denarius of
Q. Metellus Pius.—The same attribute of filial
love is displayed under the figure of Æneas, in
the act of carrying on his shoulders his aged
father Anchises, after having been taken captive,
and expelled from the city of Troy, as may be
seen not only on denarii of the Herennia
family, but also on coins of Pompey the Great

and of Julius Cæsar's moneyers.—The story of the pious brothers (*Pii Fratres*) of Catania, in Sicily, who, during a destructive eruption of Etna, were content to lose all their property in order to secure the safety of their father and mother, is also made the subject of a type on silver of the Herennia family, and on a denarius of Sextus Pompey. See *Amphinomous* and *Anapius*.—Another coin of the Pompeia family, with the legend of PIETAS, has a female figure, in the stola, holding a hasta transversely in her left hand, and a laurel branch in her right. And as it was a frequent custom of the Romans to include in the use of the words *Pius* and *Pietas*, love towards parents, children, country, &c., so on Imperial coins *Piety* frequently shadows forth the same mutual affection, not only under the symbol of a mother cherishing her children in her bosom, or extending her hand protectively over them; but also, as in a gold coin of Antoninus Pius, designates it by a female figure standing with three children, one in her arms, the other two by her side; whilst below is the inscription PIETATI AVG. COS. IIII. Nor ought mention to be omitted of a third brass struck in honour of Fl. Maximiana Theodora, second wife of Constantius Chlorus, which represents a woman standing, with an infant (and in rarer coins two infants) at her breast, with the inscription PIETAS ROMANA.

On coins of the Imperial series we also see represented the submission and the veneration of the Senate towards the Prince, as towards a common parent, or even as a kind of tutelary deity. This is finely illustrated on a rare first brass of Galba, where the Emperor stands, in a military dress, crowned by a Senator, accompanied with the significant legend SENATVS PIETATI AVGVSTI. (See the words).—An utterly prostituted instance of similar honours was afterwards wrung from the senatorial body during the reign of terror established under Commodus, who (on gold and large brass) complimented them on their affection for *him*— PIETATI SENATVS—whilst he was at the same period thinning their affrighted ranks by daily murders.—Could we find this legend and its accompanying type (two men clothed in the toga, joining hands) amongst the genuine coins of Antoninus Pius, they would indeed be pronounced worthily appropriated; but none such receive authentication from Eckhel, Mionnet, or Akerman.

The concord (more matter of boast than of reality) subsisting between the two Augusti, Balbinus and Pupienus, is symbolized by their favourite device of two hands joined, and round it is read PIETAS MVTVA AVGG.

There is something very peculiar in the mode of representing PIETAS AVGG. The piety of the Emperors, by the mint of Trajanus Decius, on one *large brass* specimen of which we see Mercury, with the *crumena* or purse in his right hand, and his caduceus in the left, with the above circumscription.—The same legend and type is continued on coins of Herennius

and Hostillianus, sons and successors of the above-named emperor.—Similar to this is a medal of M. Aurelius, on which also Mercury appears, holding in his right hand the *crumena* (or purse), if indeed it be not a patera. But the legend round the type is, not *Pietas*, but RELIG*io* AVG*usti*, under which expression the Emperor perhaps wished to teach the Roman people, that in paying all honour and service to the gods, was the way to proceed in the path of national improvement, to preserve peace with their neighbours, and to increase the fertility of their country.—See RELIG. AVG.

With reference to the PIETAS AVGVSTA, or Imperial Piety, a word or two may here be said, respecting coins of Matidia, on which "August Piety" appears as a female standing between two children; also respecting a rare medal of Faustina, wife of Antoninus Pius, on the reverse of which that princess is seen seated in an elevated place, in the act of receiving from Roman matrons their infant daughters, for the benevolent purpose of educating and providing for them, as is further illustrated by the legend of PVELLAE FAVSTINIANAE.

On a coin belonging to the Antonia family, *Piety* is represented standing with a lighted altar in her right hand, and with a cornucopiæ in her left. On a coin of Trajan, she appears with a caduceus in one hand and cornucopiæ in the other; and on coins of Constantine the Great, Piety is represented under the image of a soldier, who holds in his right hand a globe, with the usual monogram of Christ, and in the left a hasta, with the circumscription PIETAS AETERNA.

PIETAS.—A first brass of Caligula, a very beautiful though not a very rare coin, has on one side the Goddess Piety seated, with patera in her right hand, and on the other side are three figures sacrificing a bull before a temple of six columns, richly ornamented: thus representing divine honours paid to Augustus, and indicating the pious affection professed by Caligula for the memory of his deified progenitor.—At the bottom of the obverse is the PIETAS, and round the figure is this legend, C. CAESAR DIVI AVGVS*ti* PRON*epos* AVGV*stus* Pontifex Maximus TR*ibunicia* P*otestate* IIII. Pater Patriæ.—The inscription of the reverse explains to whom the sacrifice was offered, namely, DIVO AVG. S. C. To the divine Augustus by decree of the Senate.

PIETAS, a surname of L. Antonius *the consul*, brother of Mark Antony the triumvir. According to Dion, he assumed this addition to his name during his consulate in the year of Rome 713, out of fraternal piety towards Marcus, then absent in the Perusinian war. This accounts for the legend of PIETAS COS., with the type of a woman standing with rudder and cornucopiæ, and stork at her feet, appearing on a denarius of M. Antonius, who caused it to be struck in memory of the act. Storks were chosen as symbols of Piety, because it was believed of them that they supported on their wings their parents when enfeebled by old age.

PIETAS AVGVST.—This legend accompanying the type of a female figure seated, with a boy at her feet, appears on a silver coin of Domitilla, which the filial piety of Titus caused him to have struck in honour of his mother's memory, who had educated and taken care of him in early youth. Thus we find the virtuous wife of Vespasian represented as Piety seated and veiled, whilst a boy stands before her clothed in the *toga pretexta*, which noble youths were accustomed to wear until their 17th year.

PIETAS AVGVST*a*. S. C.—Titus and Domitian joining hands; between them is a female veiled. On first brass of Titus.

This beautifully designed type exhibits an interesting symbol of fraternal union. The Goddess Concord herself here joins the hands of the two sons of Vespasian, Titus and Domitian. The sincerity, however, of the reconciliation to which this fine medal alludes, was exclusively on the side of the former.—Titus, according to Suetonius, often adjured his brother, in private and with tears, *ut tandem mutuo erga se animo vellet esse*, but in vain. Domitian never ceased to aim at the possession of the empire, unscrupulous as to the means.—PIETAS AVGVSTA, therefore, as expressive of natural affection, is an inscription congenial to the character of Titus, but the very reverse of applicable to such a prince as Domitian.

PIETAS AVG.—This legend appears on an extremely rare silver coin of Alexander Severus, having for its type certain pontificial and sacrificial instruments) which indicate that with the title of Cæsar all the sacerdotal offices were conferred upon Alexander, as on the destined successor to an imperial throne.—For on the death of Macrinus, Elagabalus being proclaimed Augustus, Alexander, the cousin-german of Elagabalus, was forthwith honoured with the appellation of Cæsar by the Roman Senate. Soon after this, by the persuasion of Julia Mæsa, who advised it as a means of removing from him the general hatred, Elagabalus adopted him and again declared him Cæsar.— Coins of Hostilianus (gold and silver) exhibit the same inscription and type, as indicating the piety of that young prince towards the gods, on account of the priesthood conferred upon him as a candidate for the throne, after the custom first established by Augustus.

PIETAS AVGG.—On a remarkably elegant and rare silver coin of Philip senior there appear on the reverse the heads of *Otacilia* and of *Philip junior*, fronting each other. The Emperor there denotes his *piety*, or love, towards his wife and son, the latter of whom under the auspices of the empire he had nominated Cæsar, whilst he takes care to inscribe the name round the image of both.—[Vaillant.]

PIETAS AVG. N.—A woman in a robe standing, holds out a globe in her right hand: a boy at her feet. On silver of Otacilia Severa.— The boy who stands before the figure, evidently intended to represent the Empress, is her son Philip, and the coin was designed to proclaim her maternal piety in educating him for the empire. Otacilia here holds out to him a globe, the symbol of imperial power, for the infant prince had already been declared Cæsar by his father, and young Philip uplifts his own little right hand as if to clutch the proffered gift— splendid delusion ; for soon after the Tribunitian power and title of Imperator were conferred upon him and stamped on his coins, at the premature age of 12, he was slain by the Prætorians, whose hands were reeking with his father's blood.

PIETAS AVGG. *(Pietas Augustorum.)*— A robust female seated, with the *hasta pura* in her left hand, and extending her right towards a couple of children before her, whilst a third child stands by the side of the throne. In this group Pedrusi sees the offspring of Gallienus and Salonina—or as he (in more high flown language) expresses it, "the three precious pledges, with which the Cæsarean lady had enriched the marriage bed of her august Consort." This is perhaps the case, though it may be merely a symbol of Charity towards the *Puellæ Alimentariæ*, subsisted by her bounty. The female is not veiled, for the reason which Beger gives in his Selection from the *Thesaurus Palatinus:*—"Piety towards God was customarily depicted in a veiled dress. But Piety towards men without veil."—Smyth, p. 303.

[There is a similar reverse on a silver coin of the same empress, except that the female figure holds a patera in her extended right hand over the heads of the two children before her.]

PIETAS FALERI.—A goat under a tree, with two children, one of which is sucking the udder of the animal, the other sits on the ground ; near it is an eagle ; at the bottom a thunderbolt.

In his appendix to Vaillant, Khell has given a plate of this singular silver medallion of Gallienus, and also written copiously in illustration of its meaning.—" His exposition of this type, however (says Eckhel), is far-fetched ; as will be shewn by a comparison of it with the following reverse on a silver coin of the same Emperor, viz. :—

PIETAS SAECVLI.—A goat giving suck to a child.—Silver of Gallienus.

" It is easy to perceive (adds the author of *Doct. Num. Vet.*) that allusion in these coins is made to the infant Jove nourished by a goat, to which myth certain well-known coins of the same age also allude, bearing the inscription IOVI CRESCENTI, and the type of the *boy Jove seated on a goat.*—[On a brass medallion of Antoninus Pius, without legend, the *infant Jupiter appears riding on a goat* before an altar, on which is the figure of an eagle.]—But to what do the infant twins of the preceding coin, inscribed *Pietas Faleri*, allude ? Khell's opinion is that one boy relates to Jupiter, the other to Saloninus (son of Gallienus) as likened to Jupiter, an opinion which, I fear, will not be approved by all learned numismatists. That by this '*piety of the age*' was intended to shew the care bestowed on infants by Gallienus, after the example of Trajan and Antoninus, was an opinion founded on extreme probability; for the word *pietas* often appears used in conjunction with a woman taking care of children, in place of which σνμβολικως now comes the self-same goat which nurtured Jove of old. Nevertheless there was one erudite writer who dissented from this interpretation.—In the next place it is to be observed, respecting the word FALERI, that it is perhaps inadvertently written for VALERI, seeing that there are coins inscribed VIRTVS VALERI, written short for VALERI*ana*. And the name of Valerianus, according to the Alexandrina coins, was applied to Gallienus, though it more properly belonged to his father, brother, and son."

PIETAS DDD. NNN. AVGVSTORVM.— Three figures standing, each clothed in the paludamentum, and each holding a spear and shield; the middle figure, which is the tallest, has the nimbus over its head. The figure on the left is somewhat shorter, and that on the right shorter still; both are without the nimbus; in the exergue, TESOB.—There are two gold coins of Valens of unusual weight, and similar to each other, in the Imperial cabinet at Vienna, bearing this singular legend and type.—Eckhel, in describing them, observes as follows:—" That the three upright figures are all of them men of the Imperial house the triplicate D. and N. leave no doubt. During the reign of Valens, there were on two occasions three *Augusti* in colleagueship with each other. First the two brothers *Valentinianus* and *Valens*, and *Gratianus* the son of Valentinian. At a later period (Valentinianus the first being dead), there were *Valens* and his two nephews (sons of the first Valentinianus) *Gratianus* and *Valentinianus II.*

The first trio cannot be intended to be represented on the coins now in question, for the honour of the *nimbus* (or circlet of glory) would not have been denied to Valens, who reigned in the East with equal power to that with which Valentinianus governed the West; after which fashion, on another coin of Valens, inscribed GLORIA ROMANORVM, we see each brother seated on a common throne, and each adorned with the refulgent *nimbus*. It is, therefore, to be held that these coins were struck after the death of Valentinianus I., and that he who stands in the midst is Valens (uncle to Gratian and to Valentinian the Second), to whom the honour of the nimbus is exclusively given from the greater reverence due to more advanced age."

PIETATI AVGVSTAE S.C. To the piety of the Empress.—On a first brass (bearing on its obverse the head of Julia Domna, with the inscription IVLIA AVGVSTA) the above legend appears round its obverse, the type of which represents a military figure crowned with laurel, and giving his hand to another figure clothed in the toga. In the midst of these two stands a third, also in the toga, and wearing a beard.

Havercamp (in his notes on the Queen of Sweden's Cabinet) refers this fine medal to Caracalla and Geta, the sons of Severus and of his Empress. " The Senate (he observes) in

causing it to be struck, evidently intended to record thereby the vows which they had put up for the establishment of union and good understanding between the two brothers—an union which might have subsisted had one of them devoted his attention to warlike affairs, and the other applied himself to those connected with the civil government. But, in questions of sovereign power and rule, *Fratrum quoque gratia rara est.*"

PII AVG. F. *Pii Augusti Filia.*—On coins of Faustina junior, who was the daughter of Antoninus Pius.

PII F. *Pii Filius.*—This is read on coins of M. Aurelius, Sept. Severus, Geta, and Caracalla.

Pii Fratres.—See *Amphinomus* and *Anapias*; also *Pietas.*

PII IMPERATORIS.—See BONO GENIO PII IMPERATORIS, on coins of *Maximinus Daza.*

Pileus, a bonnet, or cap, composed by the ancients usually of woven wool. The form of the Roman *pilei* was varied; some were round, others resembled the helmet, others were shaped almost like a pyramid, others again were of a more depressed form. The Romans for the most part went with the head naked, and dispensed altogether with the use of caps, except on religious occasions, and the *saturnalia*, or when on journies and on military service. There are, moreover, examples of the sick, the aged men, and the newly affranchised (the latter in token of liberty), wearing the *pileus.*

Pileati fratres; that is to say the *brothers who have bonnets or caps.*—Castor and Pollux, or the Dioscuri, are so called, because they are represented with caps on their heads.

Pileatum caput, the bonneted head of Liberty, appears on a coin of the *Plancia* family.

Pilei duo.—Two caps surmounted by stars indicate the *Dioscuri.* Castor and Pollux were marked by stars, because those stars themselves were believed to serve as a guide to mariners.— The starred caps of the *Dioscuri* are found on coins of the *Cordia, Fonteia,* and *Vibia* family.

The *Pileus* covers the head of certain provinces on Roman coins; of the Dioscuri on consular coins; and it also appears on several of the imperial series, usually as a provincial or foreign head-dress.

The *Pileus*, or cap of Liberty, appears between two daggers on a celebrated denarius of the *Junia* family.—See EID. MAR. and LIBERTAS P.R. RESTITVTA.—Also on coins of the *Plætoria* and *Sestia* families.—The *Pileus* was in fact the common symbol of liberty amongst the Romans, and it was given to whomsoever emancipation from a state of servitude was granted, in token of freedom conferred; as such it occurs on numerous coins both in the Consular and in the Imperial series.—The Phrygian *Pileus* was curved at the extremity. This is observed on coins where the god *Lunus*, also *Atys*, the companion of Cybele, and *Iulus*, the son of Aeneas, are adorned with it.

PI. MAX. *Pius Maximus.*—On a first brass of Commodus.

PINARIA, a most ancient Roman family, of the patrician order.—It was already a race of great renown in the times of the monarchy. According to Livy, the Pinarii, together with the Potitii, had been appointed by Evander to the ministration of sacred rights paid to Hercules. The surnames of this family are *Natta* and *Scarpus*.—Its coins consist of ten varieties. Some of the brass pieces are the *As*, or parts of the *As*. And there are others which were struck in honour of Mark Antony.

The following is in silver, and very rare, viz :—

M. ANTO. COS. III. IMP. IIII.—Head of Jupiter Ammon.

Rev.—Victory walking.

On another, and the rarest, denarius of this family, given in the Pembroke collection, the obverse exhibits M. ANTO. COS. III. IMP. IIII. *Marcus Antonius Consul Tertium Imperator Quartum.* Head of Jupiter Ammon.—*Rev.* SCARPVS IMP. A legionary eagle between two ensigns, inscribed LEG. VIII.

The following are also amongst the rare denarii of Pinarius Scarpus :—

CAESAR DIVI F. AVG. PONT.—Victory standing with crown in right hand, and palm branch in left.

Rev.—IMP. CAESARI SCARPVS IMP. An open hand in the middle of the field.

AVGVSTVS DIVI F.—Victory standing on a globe, holds out a crown in her right hand.

Rev.—IMP. CAESARI SCARPVS IMP. A human hand in the field of the coin.

A first brass medal, with the conjoined portraits of Antony and Cleopatra, has L. PINAR. SCARPVS IMP. AF., and a ship with sail spread on its reverse, given in Angeloni. The coins which have the type of Jupiter Ammon indicate that they were struck in Egypt, between the years 719 and 726.

The date of the first denarius, inscribed COS. III. (signifying that the honour of the Consulate was then for the third time enjoyed by M. Antony), is thereby ascertained to be the year V.C. 723. The account given by Dion is eminently serviceable in explaining this medal, viz. : That Antony, after his defeat at Actium, directed his course into Africa, to join Pinarius Scarpus, who was stationed there with an army to defend Egypt, but that, not being received by Scarpus, he was obliged to proceed in another direction, without attaining his object. There is no doubt that the Scarpus whose name appears on this denarius was that individual; for it was first struck just about the time of Antony's downfall. Moreover, the type of Jupiter Ammon points to the African Præfecture held by Pinarius. It may be concluded, therefore, that the present coin was struck in that province. The denarius of the Pembroke Museum, also above quoted, shews by the military standards (and inscription LEG. VIII.) on it, that the command of the army had devolved on Scarpus. And the opinion which, on this point, I have just stated, is fully borne out by a brass coin published in Angeloni's work, the legend of which, if rightly given, furnishes us with LVCIVS as the prenomen of

Pinarius,.and the letters AF. denoting his African governorship.—(Eckhel vol. v. p. 272.)

PINCENSIA (AELIANA). Within a crown. —These words appear on a second brass, having on its obverse the head of Hadrian, and on the reverse AELIANA PINCENSIA. Harduin, and even Froelich and Morell, have thought it related to contests or feats of wrestling, &c., celebrated in honour of *Ælius* Hadrianus, at *Pincus* in Mœsia. But Eckhel differs entirely from this opinion—observing "that it is not credible that games which required great expense and vast preparations should have been instituted in an inconsiderable and scarcely known town of Mœsia, especially as there is not a single example of games inscribed on coins of cities in that tract of country. But (he adds) we have many coins struck in that region which commemorate *metalla*, or mines—such as the Dalmatian, Pannonian, and Dardanian, with which the above coin coincides in workmanship, magnitude, and also in age; for only with the head of Trajan and of Hadrian have we coins of the mines *(numi metallorum)*, at least that are certain. Nor does the type of this coin differ from the fashion of those, for the epigraph within a crown of laurel appears also in the *Metallum Noricum* and the *Metallum Aurelianum*. If, therefore, we supply the omitted word *metallum*, which also we see suppressed in the instances of two coins of Trajan, inscribed DARDANICI, we shall have the most suitable interpretation of the meaning : METALLA AELIANA PINCENSIA ; doubtless called *Aeliana* from their author, *Aelius Hadrianus*, as we see the word *Ulpiana* used to designate the *Metalla* struck by order of *Ulpius* Trajanus, and *Pincensia*, from Pincus, at which city they were fabricated."

PIO.—See DIVO PIO, on coins of Antoninus Pius.

PIO IMP. OMNIA FELICIA. P. M. TR. P. XV. IMP. VIII. COS VI. P. P.—Neptune standing, his left foot placed on the prow of a vessel; a dolphin in his right hand.—Opposite is the figure of the Emperor, clothed in the toga, and veiled, with a patera in his right hand, sacrificing at an altar.—Brass medallion of Commodus.

The singular form of words inscribed on this reverse Eckhel would consider to relate to the *vota* XX, discharged in the year when the coin was struck (about A.D. 190). "Did not the type of Neptune militate against such an interpretation. Perhaps, therefore, this type has a retrospective allusion to some sea voyage, such as, Lampridius tells us, was often announced to be in contemplation by Commodus, either for true or for fictitious reasons."

Pirene, a nymph transformed into a fountain. Her effigy appears on a colonial coin of Corinth, struck under Septimius Severus, and also on one of the same colony, dedicated to Plautila. (Vaillant's Col. ii., pp. 9 and 51). The type represents her sitting on a rock, with a cup in her right hand. Pirene is seated on a rocky hill, to indicate the city of Corinth, where she was worshipped, and her spring of water flowed into the town; hence she holds the *urceus* or water pot, just as her symbol is represented in the citadel of Corinth.—See *Corinthus*.

PISO, a noble surname peculiar to the *Calpurnia* family.

PISO CAEPIO Q. *Piso and Cæpio Quæstores.*—This appears on the obverse of a denarius of the Calpurnia family, with the type of a bearded head crowned with laurel: behind a sickle, and below a trident.—On the reverse, AD. FRV. EMV. EX. S. C. *Ad fruges emundas or emendas*, or *ad frumentum emundum.* Two figures in the toga, sitting between two ears of corn.—See AD. FRV. EMV.—Also see *Calpurnia*.

PIVS.—*Metellus*, son of Numidicus, was thus surnamed, because through his tears and prayers he obtained the revocation of his father's sentence of banishment from Rome. Hence the common surname which appears on coins of the Cæcilia family Q. METEL. PIVS.—See *Cæcilia*.

PIVS is a surname which, after Sextus Pompey, was borne by the *Pompeia* family.

PIVS.—Nearly all the Roman Emperors, from Antoninus to Julian the Apostate, appear by their respective coins to have assumed this venerable, but in most instances unmerited, epithet.

P. IVVENT. *Princeps* or *Principi Juventutis*.

P. K. *Percussa* moneta *Karthagine.*—Money struck at Carthage.

P. L. *Percussa Moneta Lugduni.*—Money struck at Lyon (France.)

PL. *Plebis.*—AED. PL. *Aediles Plebis.*—Edile of the people.

P. L. *Publius Licinius.*—P. L. VALERIANVS CAESAR. *Valerianus jun.*

PLA. or PLAC. *Placidius.*—D. N. PLA. VALENTINIANVS AVG.

PLACIDIA *(Galla)*, daughter of Theodosius the Great and of Galla, second wife of that prince. Being detained at Rome as a hostage by Alaric, she afterwards was married to that Visigothic King's successor, Ataulphus, A.D. 414.—Ataulphus being slain, Placidia was restored to her brother Honorius, and her first widowhood terminated by Constantius III. *(Patricius)* taking her to wife A.D. 417. He also dying, she retired into private life, which extended till 450, when she expired at Rome.—All her coins, especially *gold*, and second and third *brass*, are of extreme rarity. On these she is styled GALLA PLACIDIA. P.F. AVG.

PLACIDIA, daughter of Valentinian III., and wife of Olybrius, to which Emperor she was married in A.D. 462.

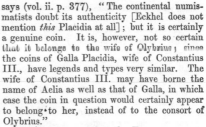

—On a gold coin of the greatest rarity she is styled AEL. PLACIDIA AVG.—The reverse bears the inscription VOT. XX. MVLT. XXXI. Victory holding a long cross: above it is a star. In the exergue CONOB.

This aureus is in the collection of the British Museum. Mr. Akerman, who has given an engraving of it in his *Descriptive Catalogue*,

says (vol. ii. p. 377), "The continental numismatists doubt its authenticity [Eckhel does not mention *this* Placidia at all]; but it is certainly a genuine coin. It is, however, not so certain that it belongs to the wife of Olybrius; since the coins of Galla Placidia, wife of Constantius III., have legends and types very similar. The wife of Constantius III. may have borne the name of Aelia as well as that of Galla, in which case the coin in question would certainly appear to belong to her, instead of to the consort of Olybrius."

M. Hennin says that the Empress appears only on a *leaden* coin of Olybrius.

PLAE. TRAN. *Plaetorius Tranquillus*.

PLAET. sometimes in separate letters; at others with the AET joined in a knot; also PLAETOR. *Plaetorinus*; the family name of the house of *Plætoria*.

PLAETORIA, a plebeian family, of Sabine origin. They had the surname of *Cestianus*. Fifty-seven varieties of the coins of this family are engraved by Morell, all silver; amongst which there are pieces struck in honour of Brutus, including the celebrated one that bears the subjoined legend and type:—BRVT. IMP. L. PLAET. CEST. *Brutus Imperator: Lucius Plætorius Cestianus.* Bare head of Marcus Brutus, the stabber of Cæsar.—*Rev.* EID. MAR. *Eidus Martiæ.* A cap of liberty between two daggers.—This very rare denarius was struck by Lucius Plætorius, who took part with Brutus in the civil war.—See BRVTVS IMP.

A female head; a globe or some other symbol behind. No legend.—*Rev.* M. PLAETOR (or PLAETORI) CEST. S. C. Youthful bust placed on a plinth, on which is inscribed SORS.—For an explanation of this denarius see the word SORS.

I.—The first denarius has the effigy of Sors, or chance.—And according to Cicero, Sors, *idem propemodum, quod micare, quod talos jacere, quod tesseras, quibus in rebus temeritas et casus, non ratio nec consilium valet.*—*De Divin.* lib. ii.

II.—A female head, with hair gathered up in a kind of net work.—*Rev.* M. PLAETORI CEST. S. C. The pediment or triangular summit of the portico of a temple.—Eckhel thinks it probable the reverse type is intended to represent the temple of Dea SORS.

III.—CESTIANVS S. C. Female bust, winged, and helmeted; before it a cornucopiæ, behind it a quiver.—*Rev.* M. PLAETORIVS M. F. AED. CVR. An eagle with wings displayed, standing on a thunderbolt. The type on each side is within an ornamented circle.

IV.—CESTIANVS. The head of a woman, turret-crowned, before which is a globe.—*Rev.* M. PLAETORIVS. AED. CVR. A curule chair.

V.—A juvenile head, with long hair.—*Rev.* M. PLAETORI CEST. EX. S. C. A caduceus.

VI.—A female head, with reticulated coiffure. On others MONETA, with head of Moneta.—*Rev.* M. PLAETORI CEST. EX. S. C. The *guttus* (or cruet) and a lighted torch.

VII.—MONETA. S. C. Head of the Goddess Moneta.—*Rev.* L. PLAETORI. L. F. Q. S. C. A naked man running, holding something in each hand.

"It were wearisome (says Eckhel) to detail in what manner both Vaillant and Havercamp have attempted to explain the doubtful type, which appears on the above coin (No. VII.) I think it better that the point should be left in a state of uncertainty."

The coins numbered III. and IV. of the above bear record to the curule edileship (AED. CVR.) of Plætorius. Cicero himself notices Plætorius as having conducted himself memorably in that magistracy, and the types of the coins seem to allude to the same fact. The *sella curulis* places this beyond dispute. The eagle and the turreted head of Cybele indicate that the public games sacred to Jupiter and Mater Magna were, as usual, caused to be performed by the curule ediles. But the bust of the female winged and helmeted on coin No. III., unless it be a pantheon, which the union of attributes would seem to shew, is of the enigmatical kind. Nor are the coins V. and VI. sufficiently open to a rational interpretation, to make it worth while to dwell upon the investigation of their respective meanings.

PLANC. *Plancus*, the surname of the *Munatia* family.

PLANCVS COS.—The bare head of Munatius Plancus.

Rev. S. P. Q. R. OB. CIV. SER.—*Within an oaken crown.* A medal, in large and middle brass, bearing the above legend and type, formerly belonged to the cabinet of M. D'Ennery. A similar one was published by Goltzius, and, at a much later period, was given in the Pembroke collection; but in both these instances the word cos is wanting.

The author of the *Catalogue d'Ennery* professes to regard each of these coins as genuinely antique, and supposes them to have been struck by the *Lugdunenses* (people of Lyon, in France), in gratitude to L. Munatius Plancus, who planted that colony of the Romans. (Eckhel v., 258.) This extremely rare medal could not, in the opinion of M. Visconti, have been issued as money. "It is known," says this learned numismatist, that "on the occasion of feasts and of funeral games, medals were struck, which served as *tesseræ*, or admission tickets to the public shows, and were distributed among the people.— The one before us exhibits on one side the head of *Plancus*, at a very advanced age. The legend records his name and dignity, PLANCVS COS. (Plancus Consul). The type of the reverse is a representation of the civic crown, which that consul had caused to be offered by the Senate to Octavian, with the title of *Augustus*, and which was to be suspended before the gate of his palace. The inscription, engraved within the centre of this crown, announces it to have been decreed by the Senate and by the Roman people to the saviour of the citizens: S.P.Q.R. OB CIVES SERVATOS."—(See *Iconographie Romaine*, Part i, p. 158.)

There are, as is well known, three more medals, which recall to mind the dignities with which the Consul Plancus was invested. The first is a denarius, bearing on one side the head of *Julius Cæsar*, with the legend DIVVS IVLVS, and on the reverse L. MVNATI PLANCVS PRAEF*ectus* VRB*is*.—The second is a gold coin of the consular class, having on its obverse C. CAESAR DICT. TER., with a head of Victory, winged on the shoulders, and on the reverse the sacrificial vase named *Præfericulum*, used to contain the wine with which the victim was sprinkled at the altar.—The legend, L. PLANCVS PRAEF. or PR. VRB., is the same as the preceding one.

The third is a denarius, inscribed on its reverse L. MVNATIVS PRO COS.—See *Munatia* family.

Plancus, after Cæsar's death, leaned sometimes towards one side, sometimes towards another, always, however, declaring himself in favour of the dominant party. An able and profound politician, from the moment that he saw civil war approaching, he decided for Octavian, to whom every probability augured success. A refined and highly cultivated intellect, an exquisite literary taste, a prudent though timid conduct, a character whose suppleness could accommodate itself to times and circumstances—these were the qualities which, added to great skill in the management of public affairs, both civil and military, together with the favours of fortune, carried *Munatius Plancus* to the pinnacle of honours and dignities under Julius Cæsar, under Mark Antony, and under Octavian. During his lifetime he had caused a magnificent mausoleum to be built near Gaeta, on an eminence which commanded a view of the sea, where he doubtless had a villa. This monument, which has been preserved to the present time, is described as a model of purity in its design and of elegance in its ornaments, thus proving the good taste of the individual who had destined it to contain his ashes.—There is yet to be seen, in the court of the Hotel de Ville, at Basle, in Switzerland, the statue which that city raised in 1528 to the memory of *Plancus*, founder of the Roman colony of *Augst. (Augusta Rauracorum.)*

The inscription on the above-mentioned monument at Gaeta, of which Gruter furnishes the following copy, clearly explains those on the denarii and other coins of the *Munatia* family:— L. Munatius L. F. L. N. L. Pron. Plancus Cos. Cens. Imp. iter. VIIvir epul. triump. ex Raetis, aedem Saturni fecit, de manubiis agros divisit in Italia Beneventi, in Gallia colonias deduxit Lugdunum et Rauricam. "Lucius Munatius Plancus, son of Lucius, grandson of Lucius, great grandson of Lucius: Consul, Censor, declared general of the army for the second time; one of the seven superintendents of the banquet of the gods; triumphed over the Rhæti; built, out of the spoils of the enemy, the temple of Saturn; divided amongst the soldiers the lands of Beneventum in Italy; established two colonies in Gaul (namely), Lugdunum and Raurica.

Plancia was a plebeian family, for some of its members bore office as tribunes of the people. It has no Latin cognomen, but on its

Greek coins the surname of *Verus* is read. Of eight varieties, one rare denarius is noted, viz., C. PLANCIVS. AED*ilis* CVR*ulis* S. C. A female head covered with the *pileus*, ornamented with ear-rings, and a collar of pendent gems.— *Rev.* without inscription : a goat, a bow, and a quiver.—Beger, remarking on this coin, says : " this mountain or forest goat, probably of Lybia, is, together with the bow and quiver, a sign of hunting, which connects itself with the edileship. For Cicero hath testified that the business of superintending the public sports, amongst which the chase of wild beasts was customary, belonged specially to the Ediles."— According to Visconti, quoted by Eckhel (v., 275), the woman's head was intended to represent Diana, as mention is made of an ancient marble of DIANA PLANCIANA, who is supposed to have been worshipped by the Plancii, and to have received this appellation from them. The attributes on the reverse are also evidently those of Diana, as goddess of hunting.—M. Plancius Varus appears as pro-consul, on coins of cities, in Bithynia, during Vespasian's reign.

PLAVTIA was a plebeian family, as is indicated by the tribunes of the people elected therefrom, but some of its members enjoyed the highest, viz., the consular and triumphal honours of the republic (Ant. Augustino). Its surnames on coins, of which there are nine varieties (in silver), are *Hypsæus* and *Plancus*.—Under the former cognomen there are two denarii of historical interest, viz. :—

P. YPSAE. S. C. A female head encircled with a broad fillet : behind it a dolphin. In others, the head of Neptune: behind it is a trident.

Rev.—C. YPSAE. COS. PRIV. CEPIT. (or PRIEVER CAPT.) Jupiter, the fulminator, in a quadriga at full speed.

In the year of Rome 413, C. Plautius, being consul, took Privernum, a town of the Volsci, and triumphed on the occasion of that conquest.

P. HYPSAEVS. AED. CVR. C. HYPSAE COS. PREIVER*num* CAPTV*m*.—Jupiter in a quadriga at full speed, brandishing the thunderbolt.

Rev.—M. SCAVR. AED. CVR. EX. S. C. REX ARETAS.—Aretas kneeling beside a camel offers a branch of olive.—This denarius is explained, in reference to Scaurus, in noticing the *Aemilia* family—also see *Rex Aretas.*

P. Hypsæus and M. Scaurus served the edileship together in the year V.C. 696 (B.C. 58), and the coin commemorates on one side the submission of Aretas, King of Arabia, to the Roman arms under M. Scaurus; and on the other the capture of Privernum, mentioned in the foregoing.

Connected with the surname of *Plancus*, we have the following interesting medal of the Plautia family.

L. PLAVTIVS.—A masque representing a woman's head, of which the hair is formed of serpents, like that of Medusa.

Rev.—PLANCVS. Aurora winged, conducting the four coursers of the sun.

Various interpretations have been put on the types of this denarius; Vaillant refers it to the Appollinarian games, and Havercamp supposes it to have been struck in the East from the effigy of Aurora. But Eckhel refers to Ovid for a lucid explanation. It seems that the minstrels or flute-players *(tibicines)*, who were accustomed to be employed in public festivals, having taken offence at the behaviour of the Censor Appius Claudius towards them, quitted Rome and retired to Tibur (Tivoli).—The Romans, however, not being able to dispense with their services, which were so much in request at theatricals, sacrifices, and funeral dirges, the second Censor Plautius undertook to calm the popular irritation excited by his colleague. But in order to bring these *mimes* back to Rome he employed the following stratagem ;—He went to Tibur, ingratiated himself with the voluntary exiles, gave them a banquet; and having plied them liberally with wine, had no difficulty, in prolonging conviviality, to steep their senses in the *lethe* of intoxication. In this state he caused a mask to be placed over the face of each, in order that they might not be recognised by the magistracy, and conveyed them in a carriage to Rome, where he deposited them in the middle of one of the public places. At break of day (the *Aurora*) all the people ran to the spot and welcomed the *tibicines* with an universal shout of laughter. They were at length induced to be again on good terms with the public. And in memory of the event which had thus taken place, *L. Plautius Plancus,* one of the Censor *Plautius'* descendants, stamped on one side of his medal the masque which we see, and on the other the figure of Aurora, which shews that the consummation of the scheme in question occurred at sun-rise.— Leaving out the rest of Ovid's verses *(Fast.* vi. 651), Eckhel concludes with giving the following extract :—

Jamque per Esquilias Romanam intraverat urbem,
   El MANE *in medio plaustra fuere foro.*
PLAVTIVS, *ut posset specie numeroque senatum*
   Fallere, personis imperat ora tegi.

If a narrative like this affords us but a low idea of Roman civilization in the earlier days of the republic, it should be recollected that the festivals of Europe in the middle ages were many of them indebted to as rustical and strange an origin.

There is another coin of the *Plautia* family, on the obverse of which is the head of a woman, crowned with towers, and the inscription A. PLAVTIVS AED. CVR. S. C. ; and on the reverse the inscription BACCHIVS IVDAEVS. Bacchius kneeling, holds a camel by the bridle with his left hand ; in his right a branch of olive. Since of the Plautii it is only the Silvani that are found with the prænomen of Aulus, Havercamp justly conjectures that the present denarius must be referred to some one of these. The head on the obverse alludes to the games of the *Mater Magna,* which used to be celebrated by the Curule Ædiles, as we have stated respecting a similar head on coins of the

Plætoria family.—But the reverse offers a subject not recorded by historians, viz., Bacchius Judæus in the same suppliant posture, in which we find King Aretas on coins of Æmilius Scaurus.—It cannot, therefore, be questioned, that at the same time that Cn. Pompey, through the agency of Scaurus, brought Aretas to terms, he imposed conditions, through A. Plautius, on Bacchius, then as it would appear the Governor of Arabia, and by religion a Jew; and that he afterwards recorded this success on the denarii struck during his ædileship.

PLAVTILLA (*Justa Fulvia*), daughter of the enormously rich Plautianus, and the unhappy wife of the cruel Caracalla, to whom she was married A.D. 202, her arrogant and conceited father having, it is said, given with her a dowry which would have sufficed to portion off fifty queens. This young Empress had a fine figure, regular features, and might have been esteemed a beauty, but for the imperious manner in which she behaved to everybody, not excepting even her husband, who soon returned her haughtiness with deadly hatred. At the instigation of Caracalla, she was banished by Sept. Severus to the isle of Lipari, where, after languishing miserably amidst constant alarms and total privations till the commencement of her husband's reign, she was assassinated by his order A.D. 212 (after seven years suffering), along with a daughter whom she had by this union, and whom the same execrable tyrant caused to be slain as the companion of her exile.—The coins of Plautilla are extremely rare in gold, but common in silver, with exception of some reverses. First brass are the rarest, second and third brass not so scarce.—Some silver pieces of this Empress represent her with Caracalla.—Her name and title on *Latin* coins is thus inscribed— PLAVTILLA AVG., or PLAVTILLAE AVGVSTAE.

PLEB. *Plebis.*—Of the common people.— C. VAL.—C. SEXT. AED. PLEB,—*Caius Valerius* and *Caius Sextus Ædiles Plebis.*

PLEBEI VRBANAE FRVMENTO CONSTITVTO. S.C.—A modius, or measure, out of which issue corn-ears and a poppy.—On a rare large brass of Nerva.

Plebs Urbana, as used in the above inscription, means only the lowest and most indigent class of the population of Rome, who had from the earliest period been accustomed to receive gratuitous distributions of corn for food. Under the imperial government, these donations became regular in their periods of delivery, and fixed in their proportions to each citizen.—They are to be regarded as totally distinct from the largesses made to the whole body of the Roman people, under the names of *Liberalitas* or of *Congiarium.* —The poppy is associated with the ears of corn, as being also a plant dedicated to *Ceres.*—See *Frumentariæ Largitiones.*

Plebeii, those who belonged to the commonalty (*qui ex plebe erant*).—Romulus divided the entire people into two ranks or orders.—To such as in the general state were conspicuous for wisdom and wealth, and were qualified to furnish him with good counsel in government, he gave the appellation of *Patres.* All the rest were called *Plebs,* or the common people. Those, therefore, who were *ex plebe* went under the denomination of *Plebeii,* or Plebeians; whilst those *ex patribus* were called *Patricii,* or Patricians.—Each class had its peculiar rights. And in the earlier ages the principal power was vested in the patricians, who exclusively bore office in the government and magistracy of Rome. In process of time, however, almost all the privileges, at first solely enjoyed by the patricians, whether in relation to the senate, the priesthood, the magistracy, or the judgment-seat, were extended to the common people. Hence the *plebeius ordo* embraced within its extensive scope not only artizans and other persons of low estate, but also the greatest and most illustrious members of the republic.

Plebis scita, as Pomponius Festus explains it, were those laws, statutes, or ordinances, which were made by the aggregate vote and consent of the common people, without the senate, on the petition of the plebeian magistracy.

Plebs is sometimes used in contradistinction to *Populus,* as designating the vilest class of the city's inhabitants.—On the other hand, it is a word by which is understood the whole state, so far as it consisted of patricians and plebeians.

Plectrum.— An instrument which was employed to strike the chords of the Grecian lyre, or *cithara.*—The *plectrum* and lyre are found on coins of the *Junia* family, and in the right hand of Apollo on gold and silver coins of Augustus, also of Nero, M. Aurelius, and the Pomponia family.

P. LIC. or LICI. *Publius Licinius.*—It is thus read on a coin of Valerian, sen., IMP. P. LICI. VALERIANVS AVG.

PLON. *Pecunia Londinensis.*—Money coined at Londinium, now London.—See coins of Constantine the Great and of his family, in Mr. Akerman's "Coins of the Romans relating to Britain."

Plotia, the same (says Eckhel) as *Plautia.*— In like manner also Claudius and Clodius; Cauponius and Coponius; Faustulus and Fostulus; &c.

C. PLOTIVS. RVFVS. IIIVIR A.A.A.F.F. appears on brass coins of Augustus. This perhaps is the Plotius Rufus whom Suetonius states to have conspired against Augustus.

PLOTINA (*Pompeia*), the Empress of Trajan, had been married to that prince whilst as yet he himself was in a private station. On his accession to the empire, she accompanied him at his entry into Rome, amidst the universal acclamations of the people, whose admiration she had won, not less by her humility and modesty than by her noble-mindedness and her exalted fortune. This princess, amiable in disposition, dignified in manners, rich in intellectual endowments, and truly benevolent in all her actions, conferred honour by her virtues on the throne itself; and greatly added to the glory of her husband's reign by the wisdom of her councils, and the fidelity

with which she repaid his unbounded confidence. She lived in perfect union with Marciana, the sister of Trajan; and these two ladies received each from the Senate the title of AVGVSTA, at the moment when that great Emperor accepted the appellation of PATER PATRIAE.—It was through her influence that Trajan consented to give his grand niece Sabina in marriage to Hadrian; and it is even asserted that at her earnest entreaty, her husband on his death bed adopted the above-named prince as his successor. —Plotina, who had followed Trajan in his eastern expedition, returned after his death to Rome, with the urn of gold, containing the ashes of her imperial spouse.—The death of this celebrated woman took place A.D. 129, and the deifying honours of consecration were bestowed upon her by the Emperor Hadrian.—Her coins are very rare in gold; rarer in silver and first brass, and unknown in second and third. She is styled PLOTINA AVG. IMP. TRAIANI. Some represent her with Trajan, Matidia, and Hadrian.

The *colonial* coins of Plotina are, according to Vaillant, of the highest degree of rarity. Amongst the *Latin* are Cassendreia in Macedonia, and Corinth in Achaia.

Plumbei Numi. Leaden Coins.—" Roman coins in lead (says Pinkerton) are all extremely rare. Most of them are pieces struck or cast on occasions of the Saturnalia. Others are for tickets to the guests at festivals and private exhibitions, some for public. The common tickets for the theatres seem to have been lead, as well as . bone." Ficoroni, in his *Piombi Antichi*, has published a numerous and curious collection of leaden coins from his own cabinet. He observes that " in Rome leaden coins must have been pretty ancient, for Plautus mentions them in one or two passages of his plays; and a few imperial ones have been found, but they are chiefly trial pieces, in order to enable the artist to judge of the progress of the die. Others are those which have been plated by forgers, but the covering worn off." Many of these leaden pieces have been found of late years in the Thames at London Bridge.—See Eckhel, *Numi Plumbei*, vol. viii., 317-318. See also Rasche, *Plumbei Numi.*

PLVR. NATAL. FEL.—This epigraph, which appears within an oaken garland, on the reverse

of one of Constantine the Great's third brass, and is the only instance of the kind extant, appears to have originated in the fancy of some pious mint-master, who prays for *Plurimi Natales Felices* to Constantine. The Kalendars assign three natal days to that Emperor; one the natural time, or, as it was called, *genuinus;* the second, on which he was created Cæsar; the third, when he was proclaimed Augustus.— [Eckhel, D.N.V., viii., 72.]

P.M. *Pontifex Maximus.*—Grand or Sovereign Pontiff. This appellation is, after the reign of Gallienus, more rarely expressed on the coins of succeeding princes, on which at length we find P.F. AVG., or *Pius Felix Augustus*, inscribed, other titles being almost entirely omitted.

P. MAX., or PON MAX., or PONT., or PONTIF MAX., and sometimes with the words at full length, PONTIFEX MAXIMVS., is very frequently read on imperial coins from Augustus to the time of Gallienus, and, indeed, is found almost always to take priority before the other imperial titles. And this we may readily suppose to have been done, in order that by such a union of the priestly and imperial functions in their own single persons, the Emperors might make it known to the world that the Senate and people of Rome invested them with the supreme administration as well of sacred and religious affairs, as of the civil and military business of the state.

P.M.S. COL. VIM. *Provinciæ Moesiæ Superioris Colonia Viminiacum; vel Viminacium.* —Colony of Viminiacum, in the province of Upper Moesia (now Widin, in Servia).

P.M. T.R. P. VII. COS P.P. *Pontifex Maximus, Tribunitia Potestate Septimum, Consul, Pater Patriæ.*—On a gold coin of Gallienus.

P. MAX. *Parthicus Maximus.*—Caracalla is thus denominated.

P. MET. SID. *Pia Metropolis Sidon.*—See *Sidon.*

P.N. *Publii Nepos.*—A frequent abbreviation on *denarii* of Roman families.

PNR.—These letters are found on a third brass coin of Claudius. The reverse type of it is a right hand holding a balance, between the scales of which are these initials.—Havercamp and others interpret them *Pondus Numi Romani.* Eckhel agrees with Bellori in thinking it better explained by *Pondus Numi Restitutum.*—[D.N.V., vi., 238.]

PO. *Pontifex.*—PO. MAX. *Pontifex Maximus.*—On a first brass of Galba.

PO. *Populi.*—FELICITATEM PO. R. *Populi Romani.*—On a first brass of Gordian III.

PO. *Potestate.*—TR. PO., &c. *Tribunitia Potestate.*—On a first brass of Hadrian.

POBLICIA, a plebeian family, but of consular rank. Its cognomen on coins is Malleolus. There are fifteen varieties, all of silver, on some of which a small hammer or mallett is engraved, evidently alluding to the surname Malleolus, but none of these are scarce or of historical interest, except a *denarius* of Cneius Pompey, the son (without his portrait), which bears the name of the family.

M. POBLICI. LEG. PRO. PR.—Head of Minerva. *Rev.*—CN. MAGNVS IMP.—Pompey the Great, in a military habit, with his right foot on the prow of a ship, is receiving a palm branch, which a female figure (with two javelins and a small shield) is offering to his acceptance.

According to the received opinion, this silver coin was struck by M. Poblicius, proprætor, under Pompeius Magnus, and the type signifies the benignant reception of that Roman *Imperator* by the Genius of Spain, at the period when he landed in that country to assist in carrying on the war against Sertorius. (See Pompeia family.) An almost similar subject appears on the reverse of a denarius of Minatius Sabinus.—See *Minatia.*

Poenæ militares. Military punishments.— Well aware of the advantages to be derived in their armies by a prompt and liberal attention to the reward of valour, the Romans were no less convinced of the bad consequences resulting from too great indulgence; and accordingly, they manifested the same strictness in chastising cowardice and relaxation of discipline. Amongst the military punishments of this truly warlike people were decimation (or death inflicted on one in ten) in cases of mutiny against the general. Deserters were publicly whipped, and sold as slaves. Cowardice in an individual soldier, if not with death, was punished with degradation and prohibition to wear arms again. For sedition a legion or a corps would be broken with infamy. For exhibiting want of courage in face of an enemy, a whole body of troops would be deprived of their rations of wheat, and obliged to live on barley; they were also made to take up their quarters out of the enclosure of the camp, exposed to the enemy. Nor were either generals or consuls exempt from condign punishment and disgrace, if found guilty of gross misconduct, treachery, or peculation.

A military punishment is thought to be represented on a denarius of the *Didia* family, inscribed T. DEIDI., *Titi Didii,* wherein a centurion is seen beating a soldier, who is supposed to be stopped in the act of deserting from the camp.—See *Didia.*

POL. *Pollio,* a surname found on Corinthian colonials.

Pollux, the son of Jupiter, brother of *Castor.* —See *Dioscuri.*

POM. signifies the *Pompeia* family.

POMP. *Pompilius.*—POMP. *Pomponius.*

Pompeia.—This was a plebeian, but at the same time a consular family, which derived its name, it is said, from Pompeii, a town of Campania. Certain it is that it furnished the Republic of Rome with several illustrious citizens. The surnames of this family, as they appear on coins, are *Faustulus, Magnus, Pius, Rufus.*—There are thirty-three varieties, amongst which we find some rare types in gold and silver. Of the latter metal, some pieces are extant, struck by Sextus Pompey, with MAGNVS, one of the surnames of this family, borne by Cn. Pompeius. —The brass coins of the Pompeii are the *As,* or its parts.

Of this *Pompeia* family, one of the *Faustulus*

branch, treating the fable of Romulus and Remus being suckled by a wolf as *true history,* and assuming himself to be a descendant of the shepherd *Faustulus,* who, according to that ancient figment, adopted and brought up the twin brothers, caused a silver coin to be struck, on the reverse of which the subject in question is represented as follows:—

SEX. POM. FOSTLVS.—Romulus and Remus taking nourishment from their four-footed nurse

of the forest, beneath the shade of a fig tree. A woodpecker or magpie is perched on a branch of this tree, and the shepherd Faustulus, in the attitude of admiration, appears contemplating this extraordinary group.

In this case *Fostlus* is read instead of *Faustulus,* the same as *Clodius* was written for *Claudius,* and *vinclum* for *vinculum.*

POMPEIVS *Magnus Cnæius* (commonly called Pompey the Great) was born in the year of Rome 648, one hundred and odd years before the Christian era. His father, Pompeius Strabo, was of a distinguished Roman family, through whose care he received the highest advantages of education. Of a lofty genius, vaunting ambition, and heroic courage, he early embraced a military life, and at nineteen years of age gained a famous victory over the Marsi, in Gaul. At twenty-three, he received the title of IMP*erator* from Sylla, the Dictator. Was honoured with a triumph for his conquests in Sicily and Africa. Three times he served the office of Consul, and the last time (in the year of Rome 702) had the unique distinction conferred on him of being named Sole Consul. The senate having, with the title of PRO*consul,* given him unlimited power as a naval commander, he destroyed with his fleets the piratical marauders who had long ravaged the coasts of Italy. Supremely skilled in the art of war, his valour and success, in a numerous series of brilliant actions, established him in the opinion of his contemporaries as one of the first captains that ever commanded an army. Besides terminating the revolt of Sertorius in Spain, he vanquished Tigranes, King of Armenia, routed the great Mithridates, sovereign of the Medes and Parthians, took the temple of Jerusalem, and reduced a part of Judæa; and for all these victories enjoyed triumphal honours of the most magnificent kind at Rome. Hence on some coins Pompey is seen in a triumphal quadriga, crowned by a figure of Victory. It was for these splendid exploits that the title of *Magnus,* or Great, was awarded to him. But blinded by false ambition, and aiming at the mastership of the Republic, he formed with Julius Cæsar and Crassus the first *Triumvirate.*

Soon after quarrelling with his more artful rival, a civil war ensued, and Pompey was defeated at Pharsalia. At this adverse turn of his affairs he shewed himself as deficient in fortitude as his friends in fidelity. Seeking the protection of Ptolemy in Egypt, he was basely assassinated within sight of Alexandria by Achillas, the præfect of that perfidious king, in the year of Rome 706; before the birth of Christ 48 years.—His style on coins (which in each metal are of great, and some of excessive, rarity) is MAGNVS.—MAGN. (or MAGNVS) PRO. COS.—CN. MAGN. IMPERATOR.

Some pieces represent him with his sons, *Cnæius Pompeius* and *Sextus Pompeius.*—There is a fine portrait of this celebrated man on a silver coin, inscribed MAG*nus* PIVS IM*Perator* ITER*um.* The bare head of Pompey is between the *lituus* and the *præfericulum,* as denoting his augural dignity. On the reverse the legend is PRAEF. ORAE. MARIT. ET CLAS., allusive to his supreme naval command against the corsairs of the Mediterranean. The accompanying type exhibits Neptune standing between Anapius and Amphinomus.—See PRAEF., &c.—Also see *Anapius,* &c.

MAGN. The two-faced and beardless head of Janus.—*Rev.* PIVS IMP. A ship's prow.

Sextus Pompey was in the habit of placing the head of his father *Magnus* on the coins which he caused to be struck whilst carrying on (as Lucan intimates) "the trade of pirate on the coasts of Sicily, and thus inconsistently tarnishing the laurels which his great sire had won in those very seas."—Havercamp, in giving an engraving of this coin, remarks that the two faces of Janus are thereon represented under the lineaments of the Great Pompey, and in this opinion he is decisively supported by Eckhel.

Pompeius Cnæius, son of Pompey the Great, fell at the battle of Munda, in Spain, in the year of Rome 709 (B.C. 45). Silver coins without his head are not very scarce, but those *with* his head are of a high degree of rarity.— Some pieces represent him with his father and his brother, *Cnæius Pompeius Magnus* and *Sextus Pompeius.* He bore by hereditary right from his father both the title of IMP. (meaning in consular times simply a military chief) and the surname of MAGNVS.—There are curious reverses on certain very rare denarii, the coinage of which is ascribed by all numismatic antiquaries to *Cnæius Pompeius jun.*—See *Minatia* in this Dictionary: see also Mr. Akerman's Catalogue, wherein there is an engraving of a coin (pl. 5, No. 9) from Mr. Brumell's cabinet, with that distinguished collector's observations upon it.—(Vol. i. p.p. 109, 110.)

Pompeius Sextus, second son of the Great Pompey, was born in the year of Rome 689 (B.C. 65). Under his father's instructions, he soon became an able general.—His elder brother Cnæius and himself uniting together in the great and perilous enterprise of avenging their father's death, these two young men formed powerful alliances, and bravely sustained their own cause, with that of the free Roman Republic, against Julius Cæsar, who at length defeated them at the battle of Munda, in Spain (709).—Cnæius Pompey was slain in his flight from that disastrous field. But Sextus, though alone, continued to lead the army of the Republic, and carried on the war with so much resolution that Octavius and Antony came to terms with him, and the senate conferred upon him the title of PRAEF. CLAS. (Admiral of the Fleet) in 710.— But with characteristic inconstancy he soon quarrelled with Octavius, who sent Agrippa against him with a powerful navy. The result was the total defeat of Sextus, who lost the greater part of his vessels, and was compelled, for his own immediate safety, to join Mark Antony against Octavius. This alliance was short-lived; disagreeing with Anthony, he fled into Phrygia, and being abandoned by all his soldiers, fell into the hands of one of Antony's officers, who caused him to be beheaded on the banks of the river Sargaris in 719 (B.C. 35).— On his coins (gold and silver) he is styled S. POMP. MAGN.—SEX. MAG. PIVS IMP.—also NEPTVNI (by implication *filius*).—*Sextus* not only assumed the surname of *Magnus,* as of hereditary right, but was also distinguished by that of *Pius,* on account of his filial piety in devoting himself with such extraordinary zeal and perseverance to *appease the manes* of his illustrious parent, by waging war against the parties who had caused his death.—On some silver coins his head and name both appear; on others his head only, without his name. There are some pieces which represent him with his father and brother; these are in gold and of great rarity.

Pomponia.—This family, although it aspired to derive its origin from Numa, or from Pompo, the son of that king, was nevertheless of the plebeian order, as is shewn by the tribunes of the people, who belonged to it.—Its surnames on Roman denarii are *Molo, Musa, Rufus.*— Morell gives three varieties. Amongst the rarest types of which are the following in silver:—

Molo.—L. POMPON. (or POMPONI.) MOLO. Laureated head of Apollo.

Rev.—NVM. POMPIL. A figure clothed in the toga, holding the *lituus,* and sacrificing at an altar, to which another male figure is leading a goat.

The *Molones* are unknown in Roman history. We have the testimony of Plutarch that the *Pomponia* family referred their origin to Numa. For after recording that there were four sons of Numa, viz., Pompo, Pinus, Calpus, and Manercus, he adds—"for the Pomponii are descended from

Pompo."—For this reason, Numa is represented on the reverse of the above denarius engaged in performing a sacred rite, of which he was himself the principal originator.—On the same ground of pretension, the *Calpurnii* also, the descendants of Calpas, and the *Marcii Censorini* have introduced *Numa* on their coins.

Musa.—Q. POMPONI. MVSA. A youthful head, with the hair arranged in curls.—*Rev.* HERCVLES MVSARVM. Hercules, clad in the lion's skin, stands playing on the lyre.

On the reverse of another denarius is the same epigraph of Q. POMPONI. MVSA ; and *Urania*, one of the Nine Muses, with her attributes.

Apparently governed in his choice by the analogy of appellation, this *Pomponius Musa*, has adopted the Muses for types to enrich his family coins. The first of the above two denarii offer to us *Hercules Musarum ;* the second, and eight other medals, present the full chorus of those personifications of the arts and sciences, in the order mythologically assigned to them.—See *Muses.*

Hercules Musagetes, or conductor of the Muses, was known in Greece under that name, and his worship was often associated with that paid to the nine virgin goddesses of poetry and civilisation. It is difficult to account for this seeming abandonment of his maiden companions by the God of Song himself to the protection of another and an inferior divinity. But such were the contradictions and inconsistencies of the superstitious patchwork which formed the Græco Roman system of deification. The subject before us has been reasonably supposed to indicate, by an allegory, that the cultivation of intellectual pursuits rests secure under the guardianship of strength and courage, and that the heroic genius of Hercules can be worthily proclaimed only through the magic organ of the Muses.

On different denarii of the *Pomponia* family, given in Morell, we see each of the Muses respectively distinguished by their peculiar attributes. Thus we easily recognise *Urania*, whose Greek denomination signifies *heaven*, by her holding a globe and a compass, as the Muse of Astronomy. Millin observes "that the comparison of these medals with the Muses represented in the paintings of Herculaneum, in the apotheosis of Homer, the marble of the Capitol, and the nine Muses, antique copies of those by Philiscus in the Museum Pio-Clementine, serves to ascertain those true attributes of each muse, which artists sometimes depicture too arbitrarily."

The following are rare denarii, viz. :—

I.—C. N. PISO. PRO Q*uæstor*. Head of Numa, bearded, and encircled with a diadem ; the inscription NVMA.—*Rev.* MAGN*us* PRO CO*n*S*ul*. The prow of a galley.

II.—VARRO PROQ. A bearded and diademed head and bust like a terminus.—*Rev.* MAGN. PRO COS. An eagle and a dolphin, and between them a sceptre is erected.

III.—MAGNVS. A female head covered with the skin of an elephant's head, between the *lituus* and the *urceus*, all within a garland.—*Rev.* PRO COS. Pompey in a quadriga, Victory standing near him. On a gold coin of the *highest degree of rarity*, [catalogued in the *Collection d'Ennery*, p. 195.]

It is universally agreed that the above-described coins were struck, at the time when Pompey was engaged in the war with the pirates, during the proquæstorship of Cnæius, Piso and Varro, respecting whom, as also concerning the obverses of these medals, notice is taken under the head of the *Calpurnia* and *Terentia* families. This may safely be inferred from the maritime types of the reverses. Pompey is in these called Pro-consul ; no doubt by a decree, that he should, during the war, have pro-consular authority over the whole sea, and to the distance of fifty miles inland from the coast. The addition of the title *magnus* throws some light on the date when this honour was conferred. Appian, in two passages, but doubtingly, intimates, that, after the Mithridatic war, or at least after the subjugation of the pirates, this title was given him.—Lampridius makes Alexander Severus assert, that Pompey received the appellation of MAGNUS after great victories. Since, therefore, in the present denarii, which were undoubtedly coined during the war with the pirates, Pompey is already invested with the name of Magnus, greater credit is to be given to the account of Plutarch and Pliny, who affirm that it was conferred on him by Sulla.

For other coins of *Pompeia* family, see *Cnæius Pompeius.*

Pontifex.—Pontif or Priest of the Gods, amongst the people of heathen Rome. Many were the persons dedicated to the service of those false deities, and in their corporate capacity they formed a college. It is, however, to be observed, that the individuals thus employed (and whose principal function was to offer sacrifices, not to any particular divinity, but to all the gods of their mythology), did not constitute any separate order set apart like that of the Christian clergy from civil employments, but were eligible, with other citizens, to exercise, at the same time, the office of magistrate, and also to act in a military capacity.— The number of Pontifs instituted by Numa was four ; they were taken from the body of the Patricians. In the year 454, under the consulate of Apuleius Pansa and Valerius Corvus, four more were added from the plebeians. In Sylla's time the number was augmented to fifteen ; and from that period commenced the distinction of the greater and the inferior priests. The eight ancient ones were called *Pontifices majores*, and the other *Pontifices minores.*—The pontifs were regarded as sacred personages, and for distinction's sake took precedence before all the magistrates : they presided at all such games of the circus, of the amphitheatre, and of the theatre, as were celebrated in honour of any deity. The insignia of the sacerdotal dignity were the veil called *tutulus*, the *apex* (a pointed cap), and the *suffibulum.* The pontifs also wore the *pretexta,* and had all the equipage of great magistrates, as well as the same kind of retinue.—On coins with the inscription of PIETAS AVGVSTA we see, amongst the symbols of the priesthood, the instruments of sacrifice, such as the secespita, the lituus, the simpulum, the aspergillum, &c. (See those words.)—Morell's work furnishes representations of pontificial insignia *without* the augural, on coins of Julius Cæsar, and *with* the augural signs, united to the legend AVGVR. PONT. MAX.

Pontifex Maximus (the High Priest or Chief Pontif) was thus called, not only because he was president of the whole college of priests or pontiffs, but also because he was the judge and superintendent of whatever related to the religion and sacred ceremonies of the Romans, whether in public or in private. Accordingly it was the accustomed practice of the Senate to delegate its authority over all matters connected with the established worship of their gods to the *Pontifex Maximus,* and it was his duty to lay before the sacerdotal college, of which he was the head, all such questions as arose on the subject of their peculiar superstition, and to report their aggregate opinion thereon to the Senate.

The Sovereign *Pontificate* was a dignity of Numa's creation, and the privilege of conferring it on any one was vested at first in the elective choice of the Patricians; but in process of time this, as well as other offices, which had once belonged exclusively to the nobles, was occasionally conferred on plebeian candidates by the suffrages of the people. Cicero, as if to indicate the immense influence of this office over the whole commonwealth, remarks that temples, altars, penates, gods, houses, wealth, and fortune of the people were subject to its power.

The *Pontifex Maximus,* under the republic, was, indeed, one of the principal personages of the state, and his functions were held in profound veneration. Entrusted, as has been already observed with the direction of religious matters, of which he prescribed the ceremonies and explained the mysteries, it was the high priest who had the government of the Vestals, and the inspection of every order of the priesthood. He dictated the form in which the public statutes were to be couched; and professed the right of presiding at adoptions, was keeper of the public annals, regulated the calendar, and took cognizance of certain cases relating to marriages. To him it solely appertained to grant dispensations; nor was he, except in very extraordinary cases, required to answer for his conduct either to the Senate or to the people. Moreover, it was a dignity always held for life; he on whom it was once conferred continuing in it without even the form of a renewal, and without acknowledging an equal in his office. This fact is evidenced by the circumstance of Lepidus having been allowed to hold it alone to the day of his death, although the people were desirous that Augustus should accept the office in his stead, or at least share its exercise with the retired triumvir. Manifold,

however, as were the prerogatives, and decided as was the superiority of power enjoyed by the Chief Pontif, there still were bounds to his authority. The consent of the sacerdotal college was indispensable on several points to give validity to his proceedings; and appeals might be made, on questions of peculiar importance, as well from his decisions as from those of the college, to the people at large.—Crassus, according to Livy, was the first *Pontifex Maximus* who contravened the ancient law which prohibited that high dignitary of religion from proceeding beyond the boundaries of Italy. Others afterwards availed themselves of the same relaxation, and a law (that of Vatinia) was passed which permitted the Grand Pontiff to draw lots for the provinces he was to govern. The consecration of this highly privileged and exalted officer was attended with ceremonies of a very extraordinary description.— There is a great distinction to be observed between the Pontifex Maximus of the republic and the same high functionary under the imperial form of government.—Julius Cæsar united this office with the perpetual dictatorship in his own person. And from the period when (prudently declining the latter distinction) he was invested with the honours of Sovereign Pontificate, and had increased the measure of its authority, the first emperors, knowing the importance of such an office, from the hold which it had on the feelings of the people, did not fail to attach it to their own persons, conjunctively with their other attributes, and in conformity with a regulation made by Tiberius, to whom the senate had yielded the privilege, the example of using the title of PONT. MAX. was followed through an extended portion of the imperial series.

Until the reign of Balbinus and Pupienus, who were chosen as joint Emperors at one and the same time, the *Pontificatus Maximus* was held by the principal sovereign alone, and not by his colleague or colleagues, in those instances wherein he had deemed it fit to associate one or more with him in the government. But the others might be simply *Pontifices,* and they often assumed the title.

After the time of Balbinus and Pupienus it would seem that the dignity in question was divided amongst all the colleagues of the senior prince, and that regardless of the (gradually fading) prerogatives of the senate, they all assumed to call themselves Grand Pontiffs, and to stamp the designation on their respective medals almost as a matter of course.

The sacerdotal dignities of Paganism were retained for some time by even Christian emperors, as their coins serve to shew. Doubtless this was done from motives of policy and expediency (the governing rule of most princes) on account of the state influence and the wealthy endowments still attached to the Pontificate of Rome. But though, after the complete establishment of Christianity, the title of *Pontifex Maximus* ought naturally and consistently to have been abandoned by the emperors long before it was, it does appear to have finally and entirely ceased in the reign of *Gratianus.*

PONTIFEX.—On a middle brass of Tiberius, struck in the year of Rome 763, during the life time of Augustus (who had twelve years before granted his adopted son the Tribunitian power), the former prince is called simply Pontiff and son of the emperor, without being honoured himself with the name of Augustus. But after his accession to the throne, Tiberius took the DIVI AVG. F. AUGUST. *(August son of the divine Augustus)*, and also that of P. M. *(Pontifex Maximus)*, as many of his coins testify.

Pondus et Pretium.—Both weight and value are inscribed on some Roman coins.

Pontes. Bridges.—Public structures of this most useful description are referred to as amongst the works of illustrious Romans.—In proportion as Rome itself increased in size, comprising within its enclosure more and more space on each bank of the Tiber, bridges were obliged to be built to facilitate access from one quarter of the city to the other, as well as to avoid the accidents so liable to occur from the passage of the river in boats. On account of the rapid current of the Tiber, bridges were kept up at very considerable expense, and their inspection and repair were at first entrusted to the Pontiffs, afterwards to the censors and to certain commissioners charged with the care of the highways. Nor, lastly, did the Emperors themselves deem it beneath them to undertake personally to superintend the repair of old bridges and the erection of new ones.—In Rome there were eight, and many more in Italy and the different provinces of the empire.

Pons Ælius, or the bridge of Hadrian, was thus called from the family name of the emperor who caused it to be built on the Tiber, so it is now called the bridge of St. Angelo. It was constructed for the purpose of uniting with Rome the superb mausoleum which he had raised, and which, under the name of the Castle of St. Angelo, still constitutes one of the finest monuments of the ancient city.

Oiselius, and some other early numismatic writers, have given as genuine, a brass medallion, bearing the portrait of Hadrian on its obverse, whilst the reverse, without epigraph, presents a bridge with eight columns, on which stand as many statues. The bridge thrown over the Tiber by Hadrian, and called *Ælius,* is obviously intended to be referred to in this instance. But Eckhel, in remarking that the Museum at Vienna contains a specimen of the coin, adds that it is without question a spurious medal. And neither Mionnet nor Akerman deign to notice it further than by saying that "the *Pons Ælius* is a fabrication."

Pons Aemilius.—This bridge, the most ancient in Rome, at first built of wood, and called *Sublicius,* was re-constructed of stone many ages after by Aemilius Lepidus, and thence called Aemilius. It was the same which Horatius Cocles defended against the Tuscans. Its remains are still to be seen in the channel of the Tiber. The Emperor Antoninus re-built it entirely of marble.—There is a rare denarius of the *Aemilia*

family, which with the epigraph of M. AEMILIO, has for its type a bridge, on which is an equestrian statue, holding a spear in the right hand, and within the three arches is written LEP*idus.*—If Plutarch be right in ascribing the architectural merit of this work to Man. Æmilius Lepidus, who was quæstor in the year 675, then this coin may be regarded as a memorial of the act, offered by one of his posterity. Who the equestrian statue was meant for is doubtful. Havercamp supposes it to be that of King Ancus Martius, who first joined the Mons Janiculum to the city by means of the old Sublician bridge. This silver coin is amongst the most ancient of the middle age of the Roman mint (between the early republic and the commencement of the Cæsars).

Pons fractus.—A broken bridge and a man in armour swimming across a river is represented on a medallion of Antoninus Pius.—See COCLES.

Pons Milvius, now the Ponte Mole, is about a thousand paces from Rome. It was constructed by the Censor Ælius Scaurus; and it was near that bridge that Constantine the Great defeated the horrible tyrant Maxentius, A.D. 313. See VICTORIA CONSTANTINI AVG.—Vaillant, in his remarks on a coin of Maximinus II., bearing the above legend, and having for the type of its reverse Victory walking, with laurel in one hand and a palm branch in the other, says that Constantine gained this signal and decisive battle, " *Signo Crucis protectus,*" and then proceeds as follows :—" *Christianorum hostis acerrimus Maximinus, quamvis invitus, et fremens, celebrare illam in nummis coactus fuit metu, ne ob societatem cum Maxentio initam ad pœnam postularetur.*

Pons navalis.—The bridge of boats, constructed for the immediate passage of troops, is seen on more medals than one in the Imperial series.—On a brass medallion of Caracalla, the Emperor · is seen passing a river, with his

soldiers, by one of these pontoons. See TRAIECTVS.—A similar epigraph and type present themselves on coins of M. Aurelius, Severus, Gordianus Pius, Valerianus, &c.—The engraving is from a large brass of M. Aurelius.

Pons Danubii.—The bridge of stone which Trajan caused to be constructed over the Danube, was the most glorious feature of his

Dacian campaign. It was a work which, if the description that Dion has given of it may be relied on, far exceeded all the other works of Trajan, and showed that nothing of the kind, however difficult, is beyond the reach of human ingenuity and labour. It is said to have been 4,600 feet in length. The form of this magnificent pile, some remains of which are yet to be seen, is depictured on the arch of Trajan, and has been copied and placed by Morell in his *Thesaurus*, at the finish of his coins of the twelve Emperors.—An arch of this bridge is considered, by Eckhel *(Doct. Num Vet.*, vol. vi. p. 427), to be represented on a large brass coin of Trajan. [See S. P. Q. R. OPTIMO PRINCIPI.]—But the large bronze medal, edited by Mediobarbus, on which a type of this famous edifice is represented, with the epigraph of PONS TRAIANI DANVVIVS, is rejected by Eckhel and other modern judges as a fabrication.

On a gold and a brass coin of Constantinus, bearing the epigraph of SALVS REIP. DANVVIVS, and having for its type a stone bridge of three arches, on which are three figures (the Emperor, a Victory, and a barbarian in the act of supplication.)—The bridge over the Danube here delineated alludes, not to the work of Trajan, but, according to the opinion of Eckhel, to that of Constantine, who often and often crossed the Danube in his military expeditions, and built a stone bridge over that magnificent river.

Pons (Severi.)—On a second brass of Sept. Severus, inscribed on its reverse P.M. TR. P. XVI. (sometimes XII., at others XIII. or XIV.), there is a bridge of a single arch, fortified with a tower at each extremity. On the top of these towers stand sentinels or guards, unless the figures in question be intended to represent statues placed there for ornament. Below, in the water, beneath the arch, is a small bark.—The entire legend (viz., as well that of the head as of the reverse) reads as follows:—SEVERVS PIVS. AVG. P.M. TR. XVI.; viz., *Severus, Pious, August, Sovereign Pontiff, exerising the Tribunitian power for the sixteenth time.* COS. III. P. P.—A somewhat similar type has already been noticed as exhibited on a well-known medal of Trajan, in which some think they discern a sea-port; others, the arch of a bridge.—With respect to the present coin of Severus, opinions differ both as to the occasion when it was struck and the definition of the type. Eckhel contents himself with referring his readers to his observations on Trajan's first brass.—The remarks of Havercamp (in *Num. Reg. Christinæ*, p. 461) have at least the merit of historical research and good sense to recommend them. "Many antiquaries (says he) believe that this type relates to Severus's expedition into Britain, where he was often obliged to construct bridges over marshes, in order to enable his soldiers to fight with firm foot-hold and with greater security (as Herodian eulogistically affirms of that warlike prince.) But the bridge delineated on the above medal seems to be a different kind of thing to the pontoons employed

in a military campaign, for it is vaulted or arched over the water, so that vessels may pass under it. Whereas on the contrary, bridges constructed across marshy lands are made flat, and it is only by joining many of these together that the troops can conveniently stand upon them and combat with an enemy, as upon solid ground. I think, therefore (adds the learned antiquary), that the type in question refers rather to some other work of a more durable and magnificent description, executed by order of Severus—that is to say, some handsome bridge built over a large river, or considerable stream, and flanked with strong turrets at each end, as is shewn in this medal."

Ponticus, one of the titles, says Eckhel, assumed by Sept. Severus in honour of his conquests, as appears from a marble published by Muratori; but which no coin, hitherto found, of that emperor commemorates.

Pontificalia signa.—The pontificial symbols consisted of vases, instruments, and habits.— A baton or staff turned up, called the *lituus,* was a mark of the augurs.—A cap, pointed at the top and with two pendants on each side, which the Romans called *apex,* designated the priestly and pontifical dignity. The instruments which were used at the sacrifices were the *urceus,* or water urn, a *simpulum,* the *præfericulum,* or wine vase, a *patera,* or round shallow dish, an *aspergillum,* or sprinkler, a *securis,* or hatchet, and a *secespita,* or knife; to these are to be added the *ara,* or altar, and the *tripos,* or tripod.

The head represents the victim, sometimes ornamented with the *infula,* or garland; the hatchet serves to slaughter him, the basin to receive the entrails and the meats which were to be offered, the vase for containing the lustral water, and the sprinkler to throw it over the assistants to purify them.—The simpulum, a ladle or cup with a long handle, to make libations with, and to take the liquors which were to be poured out on the head of the victim, from the *crater,* or other deep vessel.

These pontifical signs (a further explanation of which will be found under their respective heads) are exhibited on coins of Julius Cæsar, Antony, Lepidus, Augustus, &c., to denote that each was invested in succession with the office of *Pontifex Maximus.*—See PIETAS—PIETAS AVG., &c.

POP. *Populo.*—See CONG. DAT. POP. *Congiarium Datum Populo.*

POP. ROM. *Populus Romanus,* on a third brass, struck under Constantine or his family.

Popa, was the sacerdotal minister, who, crowned with laurel, and naked to the waist, conducted the victims to the altar, provided the knives, mallets, water, and other necessaries, for the sacrifices, felled the victims, and cut their throats.—Vaillant, in his brass medallions, gives a fine group of this kind, in which the Emperor Commodus stands as Pontifex at a lighted altar, and opposite him is the *Popa,* answering to the above description, standing by a bull with his slaughtering hammer. [See VOTA PUBLICA.]— A gold coin of Caracalla also exhibits the *Popa,* with the victim, near the altar, before which the veiled high priest, in the person of the emperor, stands in the act of sacrificing, whilst a flute-player performs on his double instrument.—The *Popa* appears with a pig as the victim on a bronze medal of Domitian.—See *Porca.*

POPPAEA *(Sabina)*, daughter of Titus Ollius, was married to Nero, as his second wife, A.D. 63. This woman, equally celebrated for her beauty and voluptuous extravagance, was three years afterwards the victim of that execrable tyrant's murderous brutality. She died in consequence of the injuries she received from a kick, which Nero, in a fit of anger, gave her on the abdomen, when she was in a state of pregnancy.—With the exception of two small brass, no Latin coins referring to this princess are known. Upon these her name is inscribed as DIVI POPPAEA, on the reverse of that of her daughter Claudia. These medals, says Mionnet, seem to have been struck in some colony.—See CLAVDIA, *the daughter of Nero.*

P. OPTIMO. *Pio Optimo.*—On a coin of Val. Maximianus.

POPVL. *Populi.*—POPVL. IVSSV. (by order of the Roman people).—An equestrian figure in a military garb, lifting up the right hand. On a silver coin of Augustus.

The learned are of opinion that this represents the equestrian statue which was erected in the year of Rome 710, in honour of Augustus Cæsar, by a decree of the Senate, pursuant to the command of the people, when he went forth against M. Antony to the Mutinian war, of which Velleius Paterculus speaks.

POPVLI.—See FELICITAS POPVLI ROMANI. and GENIO POPVLI ROMANI.

POR. *Portus.*—A port or harbour.

Porca, a sow.—This animal was sacrificed to Ceres, and, says Gellius, was called *præcidanea ;* a silver coin of the Vibia family in Oiselius represents Ceres walking, holding before her a torch in each hand, and a pig is at her feet. Those also, who formed a treaty of alliance with each other, ratified it by the immolation of a sow or a hog. It is depicted in connection with federal rites on several Roman denarii. The animal on these occasions was killed by the blow of a stone struck by the *Fecial* priests.—See *Scrofa.*

Amongst the *incerta* of the Roman family coins is one on which is a man squatting down with a pig, or sow, on his knees; behind him is an obelisk ; on each side of him are four men pointing with their daggers towards the pig.

On a denarius of the *Veturia* family (C. SVLPICI. C.F.) engraved in Morell's *Thesaurus*, is the type of a sow crouching down between two men standing, in military garb, each with spear in his left hand, and pointing to her with his right.—See *Veturia.*

Amongst the series of Domitian's coins that serve to illustrate the ceremonies of the *Ludi Sæculares*, there is a fine first brass, on which the Emperor is represented sacrificing at an altar, to the accompanying music of the lyre

and the flute. Mother Earth *(Tellus Mater)* personified by a woman, who holds a cornucopiæ, sits on one side on the ground : on the other a sow is brought forward by the *popa*, as if about to be sacrificed to *Tellus ;* it being prescribed by the Sibylline verses, among other solemnities, due to that fruitful goddess, that there should be sacrificed to her honour the hog and the black sow.—See *Ludi Sæculares.*

PORCIA, a plebeian family, whose surnames on its coins are *Cato, Læca, Licinus.*—Out of twenty-six varieties of types, the following two are the only rare and (historically speaking) interesting for their legends or reverses.

Cato.—M. CATo PRO. PR. A female head, behind which is ROMA.—*Rev.* VICTRIX. Victory seated, holds out a patera in her right hand, and a palm branch in her left.

There is a quinarius similar to the above denarius, but without the word ROMA; and doubtless struck by the same person, that

is to say, by Marcus Porcius Cato Uticensis as is generally supposed, although there is a difference of opinion on this point ; inasmuch as some imagine them to have been coined, when Cato was sent to Cyprus, as Proprætor, to receive the treasure of Ptolemy, while others think they were struck when the war was carried on by Scipio against Cæsar in Africa. The question remains doubtful.—Havercamp unites the legend of the obverse with that of the reverse, so as to read ROMA VICTRIX.—The more ancient view seems to be taken by Ursin, viz., that the ancient glory of the *Porcia* family was restored by Cato. According to the account of Livy, A.V.C. 561; "at the same time Marcus Porcius Cato dedicated a small temple to *Victoria Virgo*, near the temple of Victory." The illustration is from a quinarius.

P. LAECA.—The winged head of Pallas; in the field of the coin X and above the head, ROMA. On the reverse a man, in military dress, standing, places his right hand on the head of a togated citizen ; near him stands a lictor with rods ; below PROVOCO.

This remarkable silver medal recals the memory of the *Porcian Law* carried by Porcius Læca in the year of Rome 454, in favour of Roman citizens, to whom it gave, on appeal *(provocatio)*, exemption from the ignominious punishment of scourging. *Porcia Lex*, says Cicero, *virgas ab omnium civium Romanorum corpore amovit ; hic misericors flagella retulit. —Orat. pro C. Rabirio.* This exemption, however, was confined in its operation to towns and cities. Soldiers on duty were still left entirely dependent on the will of their commander-in-chief.—See PROVOCO.

The brass pieces of the *Porcia* family were struck in *Cyrenaica* (now *Barca*) in Africa.

Porcia Lex.—It was the Porcian law, according to Cicero, which rescued the liberty of the citizens from the rod of the lictors, and, as Livy records, *sola pro tergo civium videtur lata*, "The only law which seems to have been carried to save the backs of the citizens." Hence the Apostle *Paul*, when scourged by a centurion, asked the question : is it just or lawful to scourge a Roman citizen?—The law is expressed by the word PROVOCO, on a coin of the *Porcia* family above quoted.

Porphyrogenitus.—This title is frequently found on those medals of the Byzantine Emperors, who were of the family of the *Comnenæ* and their successors. This word ΠΟΡΦΥΡΟΓΕΝΗΤΟC, (says Jobert) derives its origin and adoption from an apartment of his imperial palace, which Constantine the Great had caused to be built, paved and lined with a precious kind of marble, having a red ground spotted with white, and which was destined for the *lyings-in* of Empresses, whose children were in consequence said to be (*nati in purpura*) born in the purple.

PORT. *Portus.* PORT. AVGVSTI.—A port with ships in the midst of it, and the river Tiber recumbent at its mouth.—See OST*ia*.

Porta.—A gate or entrance to a camp or walled town.—The Romans, when they built a city, traced the line of its enclosure with a plough, and the person entrusted with this office, according to the plan drawn out, lifted up the plough at the place where a gate was intended. It was also the custom to place images of the gods at the gates of towns ; and subsequently those of the emperors were placed there instead. They were plated with iron, so that the enemy might neither break nor burn them.—On a denarius of Augustus is the gate of a walled city, before which is placed an equestrian statue on a pedestal, with SPQR. IMP. CAES.

The gates of *cities* are often to be found on Roman coins, especially those of the colonies.

Portæ Castrorum.—The gates of (Prætorian) *camps* appear, with two or more towers, sometimes with a star above them, on coins of the Constantine family, Gratian, Magnus Maximus, and Victor.

On silver coins of Diocletian, Maximian, and Constantine Chlorus, with the legend of VIRTVS MILITVM, is the gate of the Prætorian camp, with four soldiers sacrificing before it.

Gates of Temples were sometimes surmounted with the round arch, but more frequently square in form.—See the Temple of Janus, on coins of Nero.

POR. (in some PORT.) OST. AVGVSTI.—The *Portus Ostiensis*, or Port of Ostia, represented on first and second brass of Nero, who in this instance appropriates to himself the honour of those immense works, which, according to Suetonius, were caused to be commenced, and in a great measure executed, if not entirely completed, by the Emperor Claudius, at the mouth of the Tiber.

The medal exhibits a sea port, with several vessels in it, and a recumbent figure of Neptune at the entrance.—See *Ostiensis Portus.*

PORTVM TRAIANI. S. C.—A port adorned

with various edifices, and in the middle of which are three gallies. On a first brass of Trajan.

"There are three Italian sea-ports, which seem (says Eckhel) to have claimed each for itself this title of the *port of Trajan.*" Our great numismatist then enumerates them as follows :—I. *Centum Cellæ*, now called *Civita Vecchia;* II. *Ostia*, at the mouth of the Tiber: III. *Ancona*, in the Adriatic; and (after apposite quotations from Roman writers) concludes with expressing an opinion in which his readers can hardly fail to concur—that "all things duly considered it appears most probable that this *portus Trajani* is the port of *Centum Cellæ*, which was wholly the work of that Emperor, according to the testimony of Pliny. And although Ostia was also called the port of Trajan, it is not likely that the Senate would make boast, on its coinage, of a port which Trajan had only restored and augmented, and yet neglect the *other* port of Centum Cellæ, raised as it was by that prince, at an immense expense, from the very foundations. Much less is to be regarded as the port of Ancona, which it appears by certain inscriptions was indeed enlarged, and rendered more secure, at Trajan's own cost, but which did not bear the honour of his name."

The form of this port of Trajan, on the medal engraved in Oiselius (p. 533), and also in Havercamp's Cabinet of the Queen of Sweden, is hexagonal. That on Nero's coin, with the inscription of PORT. OST. is nearly round.—As, however, the Roman moneyers were not distinguished for their skill in perspective, so neither, perhaps, is much reliance to be placed on the geometrical accuracy of their designs.

Portus Anconitanus.—The type of a seaport, or the arch of a bridge, underneath which a boat or vessel is seen, on a first brass of Trajan (with the inscription S. P. Q. R. OPTIMO PRINCIPI. S. C.) is by some thought to be the *port of Ancona;* but by others, an arch of that celebrated bridge of stone which the Emperor caused to be built over the Danube.—See *Pons Danubii.*

Portus Frugifer.—See *Patræ Colonia.*

Portraits.—The coins of the ancients have been the means of handing down to us the features of numerous sovereigns and celebrated personages.

Under the Greeks and other nations who followed their policy in this particular, the right of engraving portraits or money was vested solely in the government. And the types which the magistrates adopted to attest their superintendence over that most useful and important sign of commerce, and to secure the standard and weight of the coins, were the images of their tutelary and national deities, the emblems of those divinities, or the symbols of peoples and cities.

It is desirable, however, in order to put on their guard those who are but little versed in numismatic science, that a remark should be made with reference to those ancient coins which exhibit the effigies of persons who existed long before the invention of coinage, as Homer, Pythagoras, Numa Pompilius, Ancus Martius, and others. These pieces are not coeval with the times in which the individuals they represent flourished, but are purely commemorative, and only serve to prove how high must have been the character and fame of men who were thus honoured so long after their death, by traditional portraits, which were believed to resemble them.

The Romans were late in allowing the images of living men to be placed on their money. But as the Republic hastened to its fall it was a prominent object with those ambitious men who possessed themselves of ascendancy in power to cause medals to be fabricated with their effigies.—This became an invariable custom and peculiar privilege of the Emperors ; and we find that even those usurping adventurers who, in different provinces of the empire raised the standard of revolt against the reigning prince, lost no time in circulating coins bearing their portraits whenever they had the means of striking them.

In the earlier times of the Republic no one was allowed the privilege of coining money ; still less was it permitted to stamp the portrait of any living person on a medal.—In particular instances the senate, by an express ordinance, conceded this honourable distinction to some illustrious characters *after their death*. And we know that the Monetary Triumvirs occasionally obtained the official privilege of placing on the coinage with which they were entrusted the head of some ancestor or other of theirs renowned in Roman story. Even Sylla, all powerful as he was, both over the lives and legislation of his countrymen, had not the hardihood to perpetuate the traits of his physiognomy by that *moneta* over which he, for a time, held dictatorial and unlimited power. It was Julius Cæsar on whom this mark of supremacy *first* was bestowed by the Senate of Rome. His example was imitated by Pompey and his sons ; and, strange to say, that stern tyrannicide Marcus Junius Brutus, after assisting to slay Cæsar, for the love of freedom and to restore the republic, was likewise the man to adopt this *regal* practice of numismatic portraiture, as witness the celebrated denarius, on the reverse of which is the EID. MAR., with the

cap of liberty and two daggers, clearly allusive to the assassination of the Great Julius. The example thus set never ceased to have followers in those who attained sovereign authority in the state. Octavius and his colleagus, Mark Antony and Lepidus, no sooner began their triumvirate than they placed their likenesses on the products of the Roman mint. Afterwards as sole master of the Roman world, Augustus conferred this peculiar privilege on the members of his family ; as we see from the coins of Tiberius, Marcus Agrippa, and Caius and Lucius his adopted grandsons, which respectively bear their portraits. In like manner Tiberius placed the effigies of his son Drusus, and afterwards of Germanicus, son of Nero Claudius Drusus, his adopted son, on the early medals of his reign.

The Roman government having become "a monarchy," though still preserving some outward shew of respect for "republican institutions," a series of coins commences, which, besides its other numerous claims to attention, possesses the merit of presenting to us, in uninterrupted succession, the portraits of Princes, who, during a period of fifteen centuries, reigned over the greatest empire in the world. The portraits of the Emperors, Cæsars, and other personages of their families, together with most of the generals who assumed the purple emblem of imperial authority in divers provinces of that vast dominion, form indeed a suite not only precious and instructive in themselves, but rendered still more valuable as affording almost the only means of ascertaining the personal identity of various statues, busts, and relievos, which without comparison with medals on which names are united to effigies, would remain totally void of historical interest.

Postica pars, or *aversa pars*. The *reverse* side of a coin.—See the word *Reverse*.

POSTVMIA, a patrician family, and as such always remained unadopted by any plebeian family. It was divided into several branches, the noblest of which, as recorded by name on Roman denarii, was the *Albini*. With the exception of a few rare reverses, its coins, all in silver, are common.

The following is rare and of historical interest :—

I.—A. POSTVMIVS. COS. The bare head of Postumius the consul.—*Rev.* ALBINVS. BRVTI. F. inscribed within a crown of corn-ears.

This denarius was struck by Junius Brutus, who, after being adopted by Postumius Albinus, was called *Albinus Bruti F.*, and who, to indicate the conspicuous rank of the family into which he was admitted, inscribed on these coins the name of A. Postumius Albus, who, in the year of Rome 258, whilst as yet the republic was in its infancy, gained a signal victory over the Latins near the lake Regillus, whence he received the appellation of Regillensis. Titus and Sextus Tarquinius, sons of King Tarquin the Proud, the chief authors of the war, having both been slain in that battle, according to the copious narratives of the Roman historians.

The following serves to illustrate a fabulous passage built on the above-named fact of Postumius's victory, as related by Dionysius of Halicarnassus :—

II.—On the obverse is the head of Apollo, crowned with laurel, before which is the sign X ; behind, there is a star ; at the bottom is inscribed ROMA.

On the reverse we see the Dioscuri (Castor and Pollux) wearing the distinctive caps of *conical* shape ; they stand resting on their lances by the side of their horses, which are

drinking at a *fountain ;* above their heads are stars, and before them is a crescent. Below we read the most illustrious *cognomen* of the family : A. ALBINVS. S. F. (Aulus Albinus, son of Spurius.)

After the Regillensian victory achieved by Postumius Albinus over the Latins and the sons of Tarquinius Superbus, it is said the Dioscuri appeared, as they are represented on this medal, in the *forum* of Rome, and brought the intelligence of this battle, at a moment, when, on account of the distance, no one could as yet have known of its occurrence. The story goes on to say, that, during the action, two young men were seen fighting valiantly on two white horses for the Romans ; and this figment gave rise to the worship of the twin brothers at Rome.—This silver coin was struck by a monetal triumvir of the Postumia family, in memory of his consular ancestor's great exploit.

III.—There is another denarius of this family, which doubtless refers to the same subject. It exhibits on one side the head of Diana with the inscription ROMA, and on the reverse the epigraph A. ALBINVS. S. F., with the type of three horsemen armed with bucklers and lances, riding at full speed, whilst a foot-soldier is running before, as if endeavouring to escape them.

Roman historians relate that, as at the fight near lake Regillus, victory at one time was doubtful, the Master of the Horse ordered his men to give the reigns to their horses, that they might the more powerfully charge the enemy, and it was by this means that they broke the ranks of the Latins, and took their camp.

The following denarii of this family are *serrated* and rare :—

IV.—Head of Diana, over which is placed the head of a stag, and behind her shoulders are bow and quiver.—*Rev.* A. POST. A. F. S. N. ALBIN. The top of a rock or hill, on which stands a togated man, who extends his right hand over a victim bull ; in the middle between each is a lighted altar.

V.—HISPAN*ia*. A female head, wearing a veil and with dishevelled hair.—*Rev.* A. POST.

A. F. S. N. ALBIN. A man clothed in the toga, stretches forth his right hand towards a legionary eagle planted near him ; behind are the fasces with their axes.

In commenting on the former of these two denarii (IV. and V), Eckhel cites Livy to shew that A. Postumius Albinus was created a *Decemvir sacris faciundis* in the room of L. Cornelius Lentulus. Antiquaries (he goes on to observe) are of opinion that as it belonged to these *Decemviri* to superintend the secular games, those public shews were celebrated by him, or by his son appointed to the same office, and that this honour was long afterwards recorded on these silver coins of Aulus. For the games above-mentioned were performed in honour of Apollo and of Diana, accordingly the the image of the latter deity is placed on the obverse. Moreover, the temple and altar of that goddess stood on Mount Aventine, and that at these games of Diana oxen were immolated we have the testimony of Horace in his *Carmen sæculare :*—

> Quæque vos bobus veneratur albis.

> — — — —

> Quæque Aventinum tenet, Algidumque,
> Quindecim Diana preces virorum
> Curet.

The type of the denarius (No. V.) is thought by Ursin to allude to the triumph which L. Postumius Albinus obtained in the year V.C. 576, for his victories over the Lusitani and Vaccæi in Hispania ulterior, as Livy and the *Fasti triumphales* record.

POSTVMVS (*Marcus Cassianus Latinius*), born in an obscure village of Gaul, was, on account of his remarkable valour and other good qualities, appointed by Valerianus to be Præfect of Gaul, and guardian of its frontier against the

Germans, whose incursions he also effectively repressed during the first years of Gallienus's reign. That prince had already entrusted to him the care of his son, Saloninus, a mark of confidence which he faithfully repaid, until the year 258, when he assumed the title of *Augustus*, and all the accustomed honours connected therewith. The commencement of his usurpation was sullied by an act as cruel as it was traitorous. He caused Saloninus, who had taken refuge in Cologne, to be delivered up to him, and he put him to death with Sylvanus, the youth's preceptor, who had become his enemy. He then established his reign over

Gaul, Spain, and Britain, in each of which three provinces the people acknowledged him with joy as their Emperor, whilst he, by his courage and wisdom, defended them from every foe, and, though an usurper, saved the empire from threatened destruction. At the head of the Roman armies in the west, he drove the barbarians beyond the Rhine, and built forts to restrain them. This *Restitutor Galliarum*, as he is styled on his medals, having established public tranquillity, not less by the influence of his character for justice, moderation, and sagacity, than by the power of his victorious sword, took the dignity of consul three times, and associated his son Postumus with him in the government, under the title of Cæsar and Augustus.— Gallienus having made war upon him with fluctuating success, Postumus took Victorinus, a brave and able general, into colleagueship; and by their united efforts, in spite of the hostility of the legitimate Emperor, and the numerous *tyranni* who were tearing the empire to pieces, the provinces were nobly rescued from the attacks of the barbarous tribes that swarmed on the frontiers. Crowned with success in arms, Postumus reigned with glory and honour over the western provinces, until the period when Lælianus assumed the purple in the city of Mayence. It was, after vanquishing this adventurer about A.D. 268, that he and his son were assassinated by his own soldiers, instigated by an officer named Lollianus. Thus perished Postumus after a reign, which, rendered alike brilliant by his personal merit and his military talents, caused him justly to be regarded not only as by far the most illustrious of "the thirty tyrants," but also as one whom nature had formed to be a hero, and qualified at once to govern and defend a state.

On the coins of Postumus, which are numerous, especially in *base silver*, and *first* and *third* brass, he is styled IMP. POSTVMVS. AVG.—IMP. CAES. POSTVMVS. P. F. AVG.—Also IMP. C. M. CASS. LAT. POSTVMVS. P. F. AVG., with sometimes P. P. or GERMANICVS MAXIMVS, or RESTI-TVTOR GALLIARVM on the reverse.

Some pieces of Postumus likewise bear another head, which was for a long time supposed to represent that of his son. (See Postumus junior). All his coins, though of Roman die, were struck in the provinces of Gaul, where he reigned as Emperor. His gold coins are of the highest rarity, and one is *unique.*—See Akerman's *Catalogue.*

Junia Donata is conjectured to have been the wife of Postumus; but nothing is known of a princess so named, nor is even her existence proved.—The piece published by Chifflet from a MS. of Goltzius is suspected by Beauvais, and pronounced by Eckhel, Mionnet, and Akerman, to be false.

As the authority of Postumus did not extend over Italy, he was never acknowledged by the Senate of Rome. This circumstance did not, however, deter him from investing himself with the usual titles of legitimate Emperors. He even caused the senatorial mark of S. C. on many of his brass monies, but not on the greater portion. His coins generally exhibit the portrait *radiated*; sometimes, however, crowned with *laurel*, but more rarely is the head covered with a *helmet.*—A great number of his medals seem to have been, not struck, but *cast.* Others, evidently re-struck, still retain remains of the impression of preceding emperors and empresses: a circumstance which shews that he hastily re-stamped with his own "image and super-scription" a part of the current coin of the empire.

POSTVMVS junior, was the son of Postumus, and (according to conjecture) of Junia Donata. He is described by Trebellius Pollio as ə most eloquent youth, and so skilful in his harangues and declamations, that they were sometimes taken for those of the celebrated Quinctilian. Associated by his father in the government, under the title of Cæsar, and soon afterwards with the supreme dignity of Augustus (A.D. 258), the younger Postumus is affirmed, by the author above-named, to have partaken with his father both in civil government and in military command. Thus united, they bade defiance to all the efforts of Gallienus to conquer them, and held possession of the three great provinces of Gaul, Spain, and Britain for seven years, that is to say until A.D. 267, when they both perished by the hands of the soldiers under their command.

It is by no means certain that there are any pieces of Postumus the son extant, and those which were formerly ascribed to him have been re-appropriated to his father, with the exception of a very small number, and even those cannot with positive certainty be attributed to him.

Mionnet gives an engraving as of Postumus junior, of the ordinary size in base silver *(billon)*, which on the obverse is inscribed IMP. C. POSTVMVS. P. F. AVG., with the laureated head of Postumus senior; and on the reverse bears the legend INVICTO AVG., with the radiated bust of Postumus the son, holding a sceptre on his shoulder.—See Mionnet's note on Eckhel's opinion relative to the alleged medals of the younger Postumus, and Akerman's animad-versions on both.

The heads represented on the reverse of some coins of Postumus senior may be with great probability regarded as those of Mars or of Hercules.

POT. *Potestate.*—AED. POT. *Aedilitia Potestate.*—CENS. POT. *Censoria Potestate.*—TR. POT. *Tribunitia Potestate.*

Potin.—This is *one* of the names given by French numismatists to base *silver.* The writers of that nation have adopted both this denomina-tion and that of *billon*, either indiscriminately, or in their endeavour to discover the differences between the nature of the alloys which form the materials thus qualified. *Potin* is a composition of copper, tin, and lead, of which some of the money of the ancients was fabricated. "Its name (says Millin) is derived from the mixture of metals employed in the manufacture of pots."—Savot denies that there is any silver in *potin;*

an opinion not coincided in by Rinckens, who agrees in sentiment with Savot.—Bimard asserts, that, "besides copper, lead, and a little tin, there enters into the components of that potin, of which medals were coined, about one-fifth of silver." In which case there is but little distinction between *potin* and *billon*, the latter containing a slight portion of silver.

"These discussions respecting the real meaning of two modern appellations (as M. Hennin justly observes), lead to no result of any importance. It is sufficient to know that *silver* was subjected to various degrees of adulteration, in different countries and at different epochas; and this species of ancient coinage is designated by the names of *potin* or of *billon*, always bearing in mind that the denomination of *potin* is more generally applied to Imperial Greek; and that of *billon* to Roman money."

P. P. *Pater Patriæ.*—Father of the Country. (See the words.)—It was by this title that *Augustus* was most desirous of being called on his coins, as indicating the clemency of his government, and the security of the people under it;—a name of honour which, after his example, the successors of that prince seldom, if ever, omitted to couple with their own.— Augustus began to assume the name of P. P. in the year of Rome 752.—It is found on medals of *Tiberius* and of *Caligula*. *Nero* at the commencement of his reign refused the title, but subsequently P. P. is read on his money. *Otho, Vespasian, Domitian, Nerva, Trajan,* exhibit on their respective mints the same initials. *Hadrian* adopted it in the twelfth year of his reign. *Antoninus* began to use the title A.D. 130. Capitolinus relates that the name was proffered by the Senate to this good Emperor, who at first declined, but afterwards accepted it. Hence on ·his coins we read ANTONINVS AVG. PIVS. P. P. M. Aurelius first took this denomination A.D. 139. *Commodus,* amongst his other profanations, must also pass for the *Father* of his Country! Sept. Severus appears first as P. P. in the year 190; Geta A.D. 211, and Caracalla about the same time. Postumus and Tetricus also assumed it; and the same title appears on coins of Æmilianus, Valerianus, and other Emperors, down to Theodosius Magnus; bestowed, as in the preceding instances, sometimes on princes who possessed claims on the public gratitude, but much more frequently awarded to unworthy and even odious men in a spirit of servile flattery by a frightened and a degraded senate.

P. P. *Penates,* or *Penates Patrii.*—Two joined heads laureated and youthful, with stars over them. On coins of the *Fonteia* and *Sulpitia* families.

P. P. A. *Perpetuus Augustus.*—These initials appear on Imperial medals of the lower age.

P. Q. R. *Populique Romani.*—See CONSENSV SENATus ET. EQVestris ORDINis P. Q. R. On coins of Augustus.—Also *Populusque Romanus.*—See S. P. Q. R.

PR. or PRAE. *Prætor,* and sometimes *Præfectus.* Prefect.

PR. *Prætextatus.*—PR. H. O. C. S. *Prætextatus Hostem Occidit, Civem Servavit.* On a coin of the *Æmilia* family.—See *Aemilia.*

PR. *Prætoria.*—COH. PR. *Cohors Prætoria.* On a coin of Gallienus.

PR. *Primum.*—CONG. PR. *Congiarium Primum.*

PR. *Principi.*

PR. The preposition *Pro.*—PR. S. IMP. CAE. &c. *Pro Salute Imperatoris Cæsaris.*

P. R. *Percussa Romæ.* Struck at Rome.

P. R. *Populus Romanus.*

PRAEF. CLAS. ET ORAE MARIT. EX. S. C. *Præfectus Classis et Oræ Maritimæ.* Prefect (or Commander-in-Chief) of the Fleet and of the Sea Coasts.

This legend appears on denarii of Sextus Pompeius. (See the name.)—The type which accompanies one of these very rare silver coins represents the fabulous Scylla, with dogs issuing from her waist, and striking around her with her rudder. This subject shadows forth a naval victory. Sextus had gained some advantage over Octavianus (afterwards Augustus) at the entrance of the straits of Sicily; and this event the former designed to commemorate, by placing on his medals the personification of that whirlpool-environed rock which the terror of ancient mariners and the imagination of Greek poets had converted into a monster, depicted with the body of a sea-nymph, but the tail of a fish, and a belt of dogs' heads ready to devour the unfortunates whom the fatal stroke of her massive weapon had dashed into the foaming billows.

As the zealous and brave, but unsuccessful champion of the republic, after the death of Julius Cæsar, against the Triumvirate, Sextus Pompey received from the Senate a high naval appointment, under the same title as that which had been previously conferred on his father, when the latter went out to destroy the Mediterranean pirates. And hence we find him inscribing it on his medals. To this empire of the seas, he alludes with no little portion of insane presumption, on another of his coins bearing the dedicatory inscription of NEPTVNI, with a type of the God whose *son* he pretended to be.

Præfecturæ.—Those cities of Italy were called Prefectures which were governed by Roman magistrates, according to the laws which these magistrates thought proper to impose on them.— The condition of these towns Festus describes as having been worse than that of the colonies and *municipia.*—It was the lot of those nations who had resisted to the last extremity the yoke of Rome, or who had revolted from her domination after having been subjected to it. This hard and unjust distinction was removed by the operation of the *Lex Julia,* by which all the Italian cities received the rights of Roman citizenship, and all the privileges of colonies, municipalities, and prefectures were amalgamated.

Præfectus.—The name of Prefect, so long as Rome retained even a shadow of a republican government, was confined to certain magistrates of the city and to the governors of provincial towns in Italy. But under the emperors, such changes took place both in the authority and influence which had formerly belonged to the first officers of state, that some were reduced to mere ciphers, and others were called by new appellations. Julius Cæsar appointed *Prefects* instead of Prætors.—Augustus was the first to confer the title of Prefect on governors of provinces.—The title of Prefect is frequently found on leaden coins.—Præfecti Classium and Præfecti Fabrum are found on silver coins of the republican mint, and of the triumvirate of Octavius Lepidus and Antony.—Prefects are also enumerated among the magistrates of colonies.

Præfectus Classis.—The commander of a naval armament was thus called. It answers to our term *Admiral of the Fleet*, which under the republic was usually entrusted by the senate to men of consular or prætorian rank. Those who in M. Antony's time enjoyed the maritime prefecture had his permission to place their names on his coins, as for example, L. ATRATINVS, L. BIBVLVS, M. OPPIVS CAPITO, who as PRAEF. CLAS., or *Præfecti Classis*, are, with the prætorian galley (the symbol of their prefecture), thus inscribed. For as to this day in maritime states, so amongst the Romans, in the fleet of the prefect, which consisted of a vast number of vessels, there was one which took precedence of all others, as the "Admiral's ship."—That both the Pompeys, father and son, claimed the empire of the sea as a charge delegated to them by the senate is shown, under different titles, on well-known denarii of that family, which designate the parent as MAGN. PRO. COS., with the prow of a galley; and Sextus, the son, as PRAEF. CLASS. ET. ORAE MARIT.

A prefect of the British fleet is recorded in an inscription found at Lymne, in Kent.—"Report on Excavations made on the site of the Roman Castrum at Lymne," pl. vii., by C. Roach Smith.

Præfectus Prætorii.—Prefect of the Pretorium. He was the chief commander of the Prætorian bands, and, as a high military officer in a monarchy, may be termed Colonel of the Imperial Guard. The office, established, as we learn from Dion, by Augustus, was, at first, of little importance, being purely military, and given only to one of the Equestrian Order. But afterwards these prefects, by the concentration of their cohorts within the prætorian camp on the outskirts of Rome, rendered themselves equal in real power to the emperors themselves, whose constant companions they were. For as, after Augustus, most of the Cæsars were tyrants, their security was solely placed in the fidelity of the prætorian soldiers, with whom their commander was an object of greater attachment than the sovereign himself. Hence it was the custom for the Prætorian Prefects to be constantly near the emperors for the protection of their persons, and fatal indeed was *such* protection to some of those who trusted in it.—During the reign of Constantine the Great, four Præfecti Prætorii were appointed, to whom that

Emperor gave supreme civil and judicial power in the provinces, but deprived them of the command of the army, which originally belonged to them.—On medals which commemorate *Liberalities*, the military figure which stands behind the Emperor, seated on an *estrade*, and distributing the *congiarium*, is considered to be that of the Prætorian prefect, who always stood near his prince on public occasions.—See *Liberalitas* and *Congiarium*.

Prefectus Annonæ.—The prefect of provisions was appointed only at periods of scarcity and of pressing necessity with regard to the supply of food for the people. It was then their especial duty to take measures for the promptest possible conveyance of corn from the provinces and neighbouring states to Rome. Afterwards this dignity was conferred with greater extent of power on Pompey, as Cicero *(L. iv. ep. i. ad Atticum)* writes.—Subsequently Augustus took upon himself the care of the *Annona*, and to avoid the personal trouble of this prefecture, appointed two persons to whom he committed the task of distributing wheat and other victuals to the people (according to Dion Cass. L. iv. p. 521).

Prefectus Urbis. Prefect or Warden of the City (of Rome).—Under the free republic there was no such magistrate, except for a short space of time, when the consuls were absent on account of the peculiar ceremonies called *Feriæ Latinæ*, celebrated on Mount Albanus at the breaking out of a war, in order that Rome should not be left without a government and a magistrate *(Tacit. Annal. L. vi.).* But Augustus re-created this Urban Prefecture, and his counsellor Mæcenas was the first to fill it.—The jurisdiction of this officer extended entirely over Rome, and to the hundredth stadium beyond its walls, and his authority became at length so considerable as to equal that of the Pretorian Prefect.

On the reverse of a denarius of the *Livineia* family we see a curule chair between two fasces, and the inscription REGVLVS F. PRAEF. VR. *Regulus Filius Prefectus Urbis.*—There are also extant coins of M. Lepidus and L. Plancus, of the *Munatia* family, on which is inscribed the same dignity of PRAEF*ectus* VRB*is*, but without the insignia of the fasces. In after times, however, the Prefects of the City had the privilege of the fasces.—See *Livineia fam.*

Præfericulum, a metal vase, used by the Roman augurs and priesthood at their sacrifices for holding wine used in the libations. It had a prominent mouth, and an ear or handle like our modern ewers; and in it was put the wine or other liquors dedicated to libations.—Du Choul (p. 283) observes that it was generally carried in religious processions by one of the sacrificial ministers.

Like the *lituus*, these *præfericula* were amongst the sacerdotal insignia, and although the former was the principal symbol of the augur, yet on coins of pontiffs both are promiscuously exhibited.—See *Pontificalia.*

PRAE. ITER. *(Præfectus Iterum).*—The

pretorian galley with sails set.—On the reverse of a first brass coin, having on its obverse three heads assigned to M. Antony, Octavia, and Augustus.—*See Seguin's Selecta Numismata*, p. 106, where the medal is engraved and explained. Havercamp in *Morell's Thesaur.* gives a similar type with this legend; but neither Eckhel, Mionnet, or Akerman, makes any allusion to it.

Præmia.—The rewards or prizes of gladiators and wrestlers (athletæ) were palms, money, and wands. They were placed before the eyes of the contending parties in the midst of the course or the arena. (Vaillant on *Colonial Coins*, p. 218.)—The prizes distributed to the victors in the various public games of the Greeks and Romans were distinguished by numerical marks, from one to three and even four.

Præneste, a celebrated city of *Latium*, about ten miles from Rome, where the Dictator Sylla planted a Roman colony, now called Palestrina.

Prænestinæ Sortes, as if of some sibyl or prophetess.—See *Plætoria* family.—*Sors.*

Praenomen.—The first name of the three, by which each Roman citizen was called, took its place before the *nomen gentilicium*, or family name, for the sake of distinction, that they might be known from others who were of the same high and honourable race. Of these prenomina some are derived from the Roman people, others more frequently from neighbouring nations.

Praenomina, for the sake of brevity, were accustomed to be written, some with a single letter only, others with two, others with three letters.—Thus the following are designated on coins by one letter only:—A. *Aulus*; C. *Caius*; D. *Decimus*; K. *Caso*; L. *Lucius*; M. *Manius*, or *Marcus*; N. *Numerius*; P. *Publius*; Q. *Quintus*; T. *Titus.* In like manner, with two letters, AP. *Appius*; CN. *Cnæus*; OP. *Opiter* (according to Sigonius); SP. *Spurius*; TI. *Tiberius.* Lastly with three letters, as MAM. *Mamercus*; MAN. *Manius*; SER. *Servius*; SEX *Sextus*; TVL. *Tullus.*

That in the earliest times of Rome, *prænomina* occupied the place of a *proper name*, there are sufficient examples to be found, as well on coins as in ancient authors. This is abundantly shewn in the instances of the Kings *Numa, Tullus, Ancus, Servius.*—In like manner the same usage prevails among the Roman families, which for the most part want the *cognomen*.—[Spanheim, *Pr.* ii., p. 23, *sq.*]

Prænomina are sometimes *peculiar* to one family or race. There are extant *denarii* of the Domitia family which show this. And particularly in those of the Ahenobarbi, on which no other than CN. or the *prænomen* Cnæus is read; otherwise the common name of *Caius*, as belonging to the Octavia family. The *prænomen* of *Numerius* is peculiar to the *Fabia* family. *Manius* is the first name of the *Aquillia* family, and the name is likewise given on coins of the *Acilia* family.

Prænomina of fathers and grandfathers are ordinarily retained, as M. ANTONIVS M.F.M.N. the son of which triumvir by Fulvia, *Marcus*, is in like manner named on a coin of *Seguin's*, M. ANTONIVS M. F. On other denarii the same prænomina of parents and ancestors occur, e.g. M. AIMILI M. F. M. N., and so likewise M. AQVILIVS M. F. M. N.—AP. CLAVDIVS. AP. F. AP. AN.—C. PANSA. C. F. C. N.—C. VIBIVS. C. F. C. N.—CN. FVLVI. CN. F. CN. N.—L. CAECIL. L. F. L. N., and others similar to these.—In fact, we learn from coins that the prænomen of a great grandfather passes down to a great grandchild, as in the case of C. OCTAVIVS. C. F. C. N. C. P. *Caii Pronepos.* In like manner, L. MVNATIVS. L. F. L. N. L. PRON*epos.*

The *Prænomina* belonging to some families, the *nomen gentile* being omitted, are used *instead of the names*, as APPIVS on medals of the Claudia family, and SERVIVS on those of the Sulpicia family.—See *Sigonius* and *Nomina Romanorum.*

PRAE. ORB. or ORBIS.—See IOVI PRAE., &c.

PRAES. *Præsidi.* To the Patron or President.—IOVI PRAES. ORBIS.—*Presidents* or Governors of the Provinces of the Roman people were called *Proconsuls*, but Presidents of the Provinces of Augustus were distinguished by the appellation of *Legati Augusti* (Lieutenants of the Emperor); or *Legati Pro Prætore*, or both those titles conjoined, *Legati Augusti Pro Prætore.*—In process of time the name of *Præses*, or President, was given indeed to those who administered public affairs even in the minor provinces of the empire; thence it came to pass that provinces were divided into proconsular, and prætorian, and even into præsidial.

PRAESIDIA REIPVBLIC.—Two soldiers armed with spears, stand with hands joined, supporting a figure of Victory; between them is a captive on his knees.—On the reverse of a third brass of Constantius Chlorus.

Eckhel, from whose catalogue of the Vienna cabinet the above is quoted, says—"This epigraph has hitherto been unknown. It indicates [in conjunction with the type] clearly enough that the defence of the commonwealth was confided to the valour of the soldiers."

Præstantia numorum.—The excellence of numismatics.

PRAET. *Prætor—Prætore.*—HERENNIO PRAET*ore.* On a coin of M. Agrippa.—PRO PRAET. AFRIC*ae.*—See *Clodius Macer.*

PRAET. *Prætoriæ*, or *Prætorianæ.*—COHH. PRAET. VI. P. VI. and COOHH. PRAET. VII, P. VII. F. (*Cohortes Prætorianæ septimam pia septimam fidelis.*)

Prætexta.—A long white robe bordered with purple, and much resembling the toga. It was worn by noblemen's children; that is to say by boys, from the time of their entering the age of adolescence to their assumption of the manly gown: and by girls till they were married. It was also used by ædiles, censors, tribunes of the people, and even by consuls and dictators on certain occasions of ceremony, when it was likewise worn by the priests and augurs.

Prætor.—This was a title which the Romans, immediately after the expulsion of the kings, conferred on the consul and other great magistrates, who in the law, the army, and amongst the people *(præirent)* took the lead, or who were appointed to any office of dignity, whether for things sacred or profane. But in the year of Rome 387, a magistrate was created to whom this name was thenceforward exclusively appropriated. Two causes led to his institution. The first was to abate the discontent of the Patricians with the law which had rendered the Plebeians eligible to the consulship. The second was to provide some competent person as president at the tribunals, during the too frequent absences of the consuls, on warlike expeditions. At first only one *Prætor* was elected, but on account of the numerous strangers whom business of every kind drew to Rome, a second was appointed, whose functions were solely confined to the administration of justice, and this officer was called *Prætor Peregrinus*, to distinguish him from the former, who was called *Prætor Urbanus*. In or about the year 526, two prætors were chosen to govern the recently conquered provinces of Sicily and Sardinia, in the name of the republic. And the same year, six prætors were created to govern subjugated Spain. It was thus that as Rome extended her conquests beyond Italy she augmented the number of her magistrates to rule over her territorial aggrandisements, and these were called *Prætores Provinciales.*—Cæsar constituted ten Prætors instead of the eight who had continued to preside from the time of Sylla.

The Prætors were denominated "Colleagues of the Consuls;" and the honour of the fasces was extended to them also, but with a less number of lictors than attended the consuls. These magistrates wore the *pretexta;* and each took his seat on a curule chair placed on an elevated tribunal. All the prætors, after having exercised their functions at Rome for a whole year, were sent to govern their respective provinces. (Spanheim, 107.) The duties of these magistrates were principally to administer justice to the citizens and to strangers, to preside at the public games, and to superintend the sacrifices. Jurisdiction appertained as well to the provincial as to the urban prætors. The governmental powers of the prætorship in the provinces embraced the right of punishing criminals. Neither during the republic, nor even under the emperors, were the prætors invested with the *jus gladii* in Rome itself.— Under Augustus the prætors discharged the duties of prefects of the city; afterwards the official employments of the prætors were transferred to the urban præfects.

Prætor Urbanus.—The government of the city, as above observed, was in the first instance entrusted to a single magistrate, called simply *Prætor;* but the immense increase of public business in Rome subsequently led to the appointment of a colleague for him, under the name of *Prætor Peregrinus.*—The authority of the *Prætor Urbanus* was great in Rome compared with that of all the other prætors, who were of later creation. Besides sustaining the consular functions during the absence of the consuls themselves, a privilege which they sometimes were allowed to exercise under the emperors, the *Prætores Urbani* performed the office of introducing ambassadors from the allies of Rome to the senate, and of replying to those ambassadors in the name of that illustrious assembly; they heard and determined on matters of petition, when the consuls were not present, and under like circumstances, this prætor, *honoratus et maximus*, put his name to epistles and edicts. This dignity was expressed on the public money.—The *Prætor Urbanus* had the care of the games celebrated in honour of Apollo, on which occasion, clothed in the triumphal robe, he was carried round the circus *(per circum)* in a quadriga—a mark of distinction which was afterwards denied by Augustus to the tribunes of the people, although they had offered to exhibit these shews to the public at their own expense. He also had the management of the *venationes*, or wild beast hunting, and the spectacles in which rare foreign animals were displayed. The *ludi votivi*, or extraordinary games, likewise devolved on the Prætor Urbanus to conduct, and at length the whole of the various festal celebrations fell under the superintendence of that magistrate. The name and office remained in use down to a later period of the empire, and even in Constantinople there were several prætors, whose functions were especially connected with the public games. Spanheim, *Pr.* ii. p. 120 *et seq.*—The Urban Prætors did not strike money.

Prætor Peregrinus, so called, because he administered the law to foreigners at Rome; for as the state increased, many natives of foreign countries, subject to the power of the Romans, came to reside at, or to visit, the "eternal city."

Prætor.—A figure representing this high officer of the republic appears on coins of the *Postumia* family, standing, in the toga, with right hand uplifted, between the legionary eagle and the fasces with axe.

PRAETOR. RECEPT. *Prætorianis Receptis.*—The Emperor in the toga, and upstanding, gives his right hand to one of the Prætorian soldiers (or imperial body-guard), who holds in his left hand the eagle of the Roman legions. On silver of Claudius.

This is the second of two medals, both of them illustrious as confirmatory of historical facts; the first inscribed IMPER*atore* RECEPTo, (see p. 477 of this Dictionary), shewing the manner in which Claudius was presented to the guard, who acknowledged him for Emperor, and placed him under their protection. The present denarius has for its subject the patronage and favour which the same Emperor granted in his turn to the Prætorians, on the occasion of their taking the oath of fidelity to him.—The "Prætorians received;" (that is to say, received into allegiance), is the appropriate inscription of this coin, for it is an allusion to the military oath as "on that same day (according to Suetonius, c. 10, quoted by Eckhel,) he (Claudius) suffered the Prætorian guards to swear in his name."

Prætorium Castrum or *Castra Prætoriana.*— The camp of the Prætorian soldiers.—The Emperor Tiberius built for the cohorts, who were under the command of the Prætorian Prefect in the immediate vicinity of Rome, a permanent camp enclosed within walls, and, moreover, defended by a rampart and ditch, in the form of a fortress, where they were generally stationed.—The earliest instance in which the Prætorian camp is represented on Roman coins is that of the *Imperatore Recepto* of Claudius above alluded to. [See IMP. RECEP.]— On coins of the later empire we see the *Prætoria Castra* with towers and gates, sometimes without figures; at others, with two or four soldiers performing sacrifice at a tripod, or otherwise.

The *Prætorian camp*, with or without figures, is represented on reverses of the following Imperial coins, chiefly silver and third brass, viz:—On GLORIA ROMANORVM of Gratian; on PROVIDENT*ia* CAES*arum* of Licinius jun., Crispus, and Constantinus jun.; on PROVI-DENTIA AVG. or AVGG. of Diocletian, Maximian Hercules, Constantius Chlorus, Gal. Maximianus, Licinius senior, Constantinus Magnus, and Constantinus jun.; on SPES ROMANORVM of Magnus Maximus and Fl. Victor; on VICTORIA AVGG. of Diocletian, Val. Maximian, Constantius Chlorus, Gal. Maximian, &c.; on VICTORIA SARMAT. or VICTORIA SARMATICA of Diocletian, Maximianus Hercules, and Constantius Chlorus; on VIRTVS MILITVM of Diocletian, of Val. Maximianus, of Constantius Chlorus, of Gal. Maximianus, Maxentius, Maximinus Daza, Licinius jun., and Constantinus M.

"The prætorian camp (says Millin), which is believed to have been situated to the east of Rome, behind the Baths of Diocletian, was constructed of bricks, of reticulated work, faced with stucco, finished with great nicety, and enriched with superb porticos, supported by columns. It was surrounded by an enclosure, sometimes double, more or less extended, in which were wrought, on a quadrangular plan of two stories in height, the *barracks* of the guards, between which an easy communication was effected by means of covered galleries. Towers placed on the outside gave to this camp the aspect of a formidable castle, or fortified town; whilst the vast space included within its walls conduced to its salubrity, and afforded every facility for exercising the troops."

Prætoria Navis, the galley on board of which was the commander-in-chief of the naval armament—or as we should call a modern vessel of war, the admiral's flag ship.—The *navis prætoria* is seen on various coins from Augustus to Hadrian and thence to Commodus, Sept. Severus, Caracalla, and other Emperors, some with sails and others with rowers; a figure seated at the helm,

and others standing in other parts of the galley. —See FELICITAS AVG.

Prætorium.—This word in its original acceptation meant the prætor's or general's tent, which was placed in the situation best suited to render it conspicuously visible to the whole camp. It was afterwards used to signify the palace or other place where the prætor of a province resided, and where he administered justice to the people. There was a prætorium in all the cities of the Roman empire.

PREIVER. CAPTVM.*(Preivernum Captum).* —P. HYPSAEVS. AED. CVR. C. HYPSAE. COS. This inscription appears on a denarius of the *Plautia* family, which bears on its reverse *Jupiter fulminator in a quadriga.* This coin was, it seems, struck to commemorate the event of C. Plautius, who was consul in the year of Rome 425, having taken the city of Preivernum, or rather Privernum, and received triumphal honours on that account.—See *Plautia*, p. 220.

Pretium numorum antiquiorum.—The relative value of coins was indicated in the early times of the Roman mintage, either by single letters or by points, thus—

X. or ✳ the denarius.

V. the Quinarius or Victoriatus.

S. Semis.

L. Libra, or as.

LLS. Sestertius, or two asses and a half.

O. one globule or point, the uncia.

OO. two points, the sextans.

OOO. three points, the quadrans.

OOOO. lastly, four points or globules signify the triens.

PRI. FL. *Primus Flavit.*—This appears on a coin of the *Flaminia* family, bearing the inscription L. FLAMINI. CHILO. IIIIVIR. PRI. FL., that is to say, L. Flaminius Chilo, one of the *four* magistrates appointed by Julius Cæsar to superintend the coinage of denarii, *(primus flavit)*, was the *first* præfect of that department of the *moneta* at Rome.

PRIMI DECEN. *Primi Decennales.*—The first period of ten years. This epigraph (with COS. IIII. in a crown of laurel) appears for the first time, either abridged or at full length, on coins, in all three metals, of Antoninus Pius, and afterwards on those of his immediate successors, M. Aurelius and Commodus.—These *decennales* (says Eckhel) like the *vota*, whether *suscepta* or *soluta*, were doubtless celebrated for the health and safety of the reigning prince. Recorded in the first instance during the reign of the Antonines, they afterwards became a constantly recurring subject of numismatic inscription, and especially in the age of the Constantines. The *primi decennales* of Antoninus ended on the tenth of July, A.D. 148, and then the second term of ten years began.

PRIMIGENIA.—A name given to the 22nd Legion, on a silver coin of Mark Antony, as given by Morell, in the *Antonia* family, exhibiting also a legionary eagle between two military standards. With a capricorn it occurs on a small brass coin of Carausius.—*Num. Chron.* vol. ii. p. 121.

PRIMIS X MVLTIS XX.—*Primis Decennalibus Multis Vicennalibus.*—Two figures of Victory attach a shield to a palm, on which is inscribed VOT. X. FEL. *(Vota Decennalia Felicia.)* On the reverse of a gold coin of Diocletian.—On a medal of Val. Maximianus the same legend appears, but a single figure of Victory inscribes VO. XX. on the shield.

In the Lower Empire, as has been already observed under the head of PRIMI DECENNALES, these votive legends are continually recurring; the vows themselves being carried forward even beyond the term. This is expressed by the word *multis;* for instance, votis X., multis XX., or by the word *sic;* for example, sic X., sic. XX.

On epigraphs of this kind, Bimard, in his *Notes on Jobert,* remarks that "among those medals, on which allusion is made to *Vota Decennalia* and *Vicennalia,* there are scarcely any more curious than those of Diocletian and of Maximian his colleague, which have for their legend PRIMIS X. MVLTIS XX.—Banduri has quoted two of these medals, but there were more than thirty varieties in the cabinet of the Abbé de Rothelin. Some bear the type of Jupiter standing; others of Hercules also standing. A Victory seated is seen on several, holding with the left hand a buckler resting on her knee, and with her right hand inscribing on this buckler, VOTIS X. or VOT X. Others, lastly, represent two Victories, who sustain a buckler, on which we read VOT. X. FEL., and sometimes VOT. X. ET XX. These medals are so much the more remarkable, as the vows form the legend and not the inscription; and as they are repeated on those where we again read them in the buckler.

PRIMI XX. IOVI AVGVSTI,—Jupiter sitting, with thunderbolt and *hasta.* This legend and type appear on a very rare gold coin of Diocletian, who celebrated the *vota vicennalia,* the twentieth year of his reign being been completed A.D. 303.—Banduri and Vaillant.

PRIMO AVSP.—The infant Hercules strangling two serpents. On a fourth brass of Gal. Maximianus. This fine and remarkable little coin, in the Imperial Cabinet at Vienna, was first noticed by Eckhel in his *Syllog.* i. *Num. Vet.* And the same great numismatist in his *Doct. Num. Vet.* thus explains the epigraph: "Two modes (he observes) suggest themselves. It is called PRIMO AVSP*ice,* as on coins of S. Severus we read DIS AVSPICIBVS, or it is PRIMO. AVSPI*cio;* for on coins of that very age, viz., that of Diocletian and Maximinian Hercules, we find it written AVSPIC. FEL., which may be held certainly to mean AVSPIC*io* FEL*ici.*

PRIMVS.—Those who were the first *(primi)* to do any particular thing of public importance, or who bore any office first, were noted, by writers accordingly, and the memory of the event struck on coins, as L. BRVTVS PRIM*us* CONSUL. A similar instance is read on a denarius of the *Flaminia* family see PRI. FL. or *Quatuor Vir Monetalis Primus flavit).*—On other coins the word *primus* occurs: SEX.

NONI. PR. LVD. V. P. F. *Sextus Nonius Prætor Ludos Votivos Primus fecit.* The Prætor Sextus Nonius was the *first* who celebrated the Votive Games; and C. SERVEIL. M. F. FLORA. PRIMVS. *Caius Serveillius, Marci Filius, Floralia Primus;* that is to say, he *first* instituted the *Floral Games.*

PRIN. *Princeps.*—PRIN. IVVENTVTIS. S. C. On a third brass of Maximus Cæsar.

PRIN. *Principes.*—TITVS ET DOMITIANVS PRIN. IVVEN*tutis.*—C. L. CAESARES AVGVSTI F. COS. DES. PRIN. IVVENT. *Caius Lucius Caesares, Augusti Filii, Consules Designati, Principes Juventutis.*

PRIN. *Principi.*—OPTIMO PRIN. On coins of Trajan.—DIVO CONSTANTIO PIO PRIN. On a coin of Constantius Chlorus.

PRINC. *Princeps, Principis, Principi, Principes.*—PRINC. IVV., or IVVEN., or IVVENT., or IVVENTVT., or at full length IVVENTVTIS. *Princeps Juventutis.*

Princeps Juventutis was a name of dignity even in the most flourishing days of the republic. It was an honorary appellation given to him who took the lead of the greater and lesser boys appointed to perform a part in the game of Troy *(ad ludum Trojæ). The prince of the youth* was, in the earlier times, the chief of the Equestrian Order. Under the empire, and from the very commencement of that monarchical form of government, this title, although simply honorary, appears to have been given, as an apanage, to such young princes of the imperial family as were destined to reign, and was sometimes conferred on them at a very early age. The dignity in certain instances accompanied that of *Cæsar.* It is a mark of distinction of which the memorial is found perpetuated, either directly or indirectly on the medals dedicated to these youthful heirs of the throne. Sometimes, as in the case of *Caius* and *Lucius,* sons of M. Agrippa, adopted by Augustus, two princes were honoured together with this title. The types which bear reference to it present to us usually, under the first reigns, horsemen, with spears, as in Nero and Drusus, Titus, Domitian,

[First brass of Geta.]

and Geta. But after Geta, the *Princeps Juventutis* was no longer represented by an equestrian figure, but appeared on foot, in a military habit, either by the side of two ensigns, and holding the hasta pura and a short wand, as in Alex. Severus and Maximus; or holding a globe in left hand and a javelin in the right, as in Gordianus Pius and Philippus jun.; or the prince standing, in a military habit, holding a sceptre, with three standards, as on first brass of Diadumenianus, of which an example is here

given. There are several slight varieties of this coin, in which Diadumenianus holds also a javelin; or the hasta pura in the right hand, a globe in the left, as in the younger Philip and Numerianus, and with a captive at his feet, as on a rare medallion of Saloninus; or holding a military standard in the right and a spear reversed in the left hand; or with *bacillum* and javelin, or hasta pura, as in Herennius and Numerianus; or holding a military ensign in the right and the hasta in the left hand, near to which a sacred standard is sometimes planted, as in Hostilianus; lastly, the frequently recurring legend of PRINC. IVVENT. accompanies the unusual and scarcely appropriate type of a *woman* seated, holding an olive branch in her right hand, and resting her left arm on the back of the chair, as is seen on the coins of Herennius and Hostilianus alone.

On a silver coin of Saloninus, son of Gallienus, we find the legend of PRINC. IVVENTVTIS, accompanying the type of a military figure (evidently intended for that of the young prince), standing, not, however (as is commonly the case on coins of the Lower Empire), holding a military standard, but with spear and buckler in his left hand, and crowning a trophy with his right.— A coin of *Tetricus, junior*, shows the *prince of the youth*, holding an olive branch, and the *hasta pura*.

PRINC. IVVENTVT. *Principes Juventutis.* —On a very rare silver coin, bearing on its obverse the naked head of Augustus, and on the reverse two horsemen galloping, this legend appears, with the letters C. L. *(Caius* and *Lucius)* at the bottom. The former received the honours when he was 14 (v. c. 749); the latter when he was 15 years old (v.c. 750). For the emperor above-named having destined these sons of Agrippa (whom he had adopted) to be his successors in the empire, it became the delight of the Equestrian Order to call them *Principes Juventutis (Tacit. Annal.)* The spear and buckler *(hasta et clypeum)* were the insignia of the Princes of the Youth: see a denarius of Augustus, on the reverse of which the two Cæsars, *Caius* and *Lucius*, are standing, veiled and togated, each holding the above-named description of arms.

PRINCIPI IVVENTVTIS. S. C.—Two right hands joined, hold a military ensign, fixed into a ship's prow.—Second brass of Commodus. This coin on its obverse bears the young head of Commodus, and the inscription CAES. AVG. FIL. GERM. SARM. Its date is assigned to the year 930 (A.D. 177), when the title of IMP*erator*, and the dignity of the Tribunition Power (TR. P.) began to be added to that of CAESAR AVG. FIL., &c., which had previous to that period appeared on the coins of that emperor. It was about the same time that he took Crispina to wife.—The meaning of a type so unusual as an accompaniment to the legend is not explained by Eckhel, through he quotes the coin from the Vienna cabinet.

The title of Princeps Juventutis, which at the beginning was accustomed to be bestowed only on the young princes who were as yet only Cæsars, and on actually appointed successors, was at a later period accepted even by the Augusti themselves. "Volusian," says Bimard, "is, I believe, the first on whose medals *Princeps Juventutis* appears, on the reverse of a head which has in the legend the title of *Imperator;* but in the lower empire a thousand examples of it are found."

PRINCIPI IMPERII ROMANI.—Mars helmeted, walking, with spear in right hand and trophy on his left shoulder.—On a *gold* coin of Maxentius.

A dedication to *Mars*, as the *Prince* of the Roman Empire, was a new title for their God of War, created by the ingenuity of Maxentius, who had already inscribed one of his silver coins to *Mars Propagator Imperii*.

PRINCIPIA IVVENTVTIS.—Crispus Cæsar in a military habit, standing with spear and shield. On a third brass. So many coins of Crispus with this inscription are extant, that it would exceed the bounds of reasonable belief to suppose PRINCIPIA written by mistake for PRINCIPI, especially as there are medals with this epigraph which yet differ in type from those which exhibit the word PRINCIPI. This epigraph seems to occur only in the mint of Crispus; for Bandurius, who produces one similarly inscribed among the gold coins of Constantine the younger, draws his authority from Harduin only, and it was seen by no one else. Lastly, there are the coins of Gratian inscribed PRINCIPIVM IVVENTVTIS. "I shall not (says Eckhel), perhaps, seem to go wide of the mark, if I express my opinion that by the *principia juventutis* here in question are to be understood those principles or that description of youth, required in camps by Crispus, whose image is represented by the military figure on the reverse of this coin." How greatly distinguished by warlike deeds was the youth of this truly noble but ill-fated Cæsar, the pen of history has with sufficient clearness proved.

PRISCVS.—He was called Priscus, who was the eldest born. It is the cognomen of the Bæbia, Mussidia, and Tarquitia families.

PRISCVS ATTALVS, an Ionian by birth, and of no ignoble family, was appointed Prefect

of Rome by Honorius the same year (A.D. 509(
that Alaric took possession of that city. The
Gothic King, having a friendship for Attalus,
compelled the conquered Romans to recognise
him as Emperor; but disgusted with the indolence, imprudence, and presumption of his
protégé, Alaric deposed him the following year
(A.D. 410); and this feeble puppet of the
northern conqueror remained in a state of
obscurity and humiliation until the death of
Alaric, which happened shortly afterwards.
Attalus then re-assumed the purple in Gaul, but
meeting with no support either from the soldiers
or the inhabitants, and being destitute of resources, he continued to dwell with the Goths
till A.D. 416, when he was delivered into the
hands of Constantius, general of the armies of
Honorius, who sent him to Ravenna, where that
Emperor then resided. After experiencing again
the most extraordinary vicissitudes of fortune,
sometimes being suddenly re-elevated to a
semblance of dignity, and at others as speedily
plunged into the lowest depths of degradation,
he was condemned, after the amputation of his
right hand, to a perpetual banishment in the
Isle of Lipari, where, supplied with decent
necessaries, he ended his eventful but unhappy
life.

The coins of this Emperor are, in all metals,
classed by numismatists among the rarest of the
imperial series.—His style on them is PRISC.
(or PRISCVS) ATTALVS. P.F. AVG.—IMP. PRISCVS
ATTALVS P.F. AVG.

The engraving of a silver medallion of very
large size (weight 2oz. 10dwt. 4gr.) bearing on
its obverse the portrait and imperial superscription of Priscus Attalus, and on its reverse
INVICTA ROMA AETERNA, with type of Rome
seated, holding a globe surmounted by Victory,
and the hasta, is given by Mr. Akerman (see
Descriptive Cat., vol. ii. p. 353) who observes
that "it is in the collection of the British
Museum, and is probably unique."—The dete-
rioration of the arts, betrayed in the bad design
and coarse workmanship of this coin (supposing
the engraving to be from a faithful copy) renders
it alike *congenial* to the degeneracy of the
Lower Empire, and *worthy* of being issued from
the *gothic* mint of Rome.

PR. IV. *Princeps Juventutis*.—On a coin
of Tetricus the younger, published by Bandurius
(i. p, 411).

PRIV. CEPIT. *Privernum Cepit*.—On coins
of the *Aemilia* and *Plautia* families.

PR. L. V. P. F. *Prætor Ludos Votivos
Publicos Fecit*.—See *Nonia* family (Spanheim).

PR. N. *Pronepos*.—See *Caligula*.

PRO. *Preposition*.—PRO. R. CAES. *Pro
Reditu Caesaris*.—PRO. S. CAES. *Pro Salute
Caesaris*.

PRO. VALETVDINE CAESARIS. S.P.Q.R.
On a very rare gold coin of the *Antestia*
family this legend appears, accompanying the
type of a veiled priest standing before a lighted
altar, holding a patera in his right hand; whilst
on the other side is the *victimarius* bringing up
a bull for sacrifice.

This, and the coins inscribed PRO S*alute*
ET RED*itu* AV*Gusti*, or CAES*aris* S. P. Q. R.,
struck respectively by the Monetal Triumvirs
Antistius Vetus and *Mescinius Rufus*, are all
referred by Eckhel to the year V.C. 738 (before
Christ 16), when, in consequence of war being
threatened by the Germans, Augustus made a
journey towards Gaul, and when (as Dion
records), vows were made at Rome for his health
and safe return.—*Doct. Num. Vet.* vol. v. p.
137, vol. vi. p. 103.

Alluding to these votive medals, Dr. Clarke
says—"Although the Emperor, who had removed
to Ariminium (Rimini) for the greater convenience of giving his orders and receiving
intelligence, did not purpose to go farther, yet
it appears that public vows were made for his
safety and return with as much solemnity as if
he had been personally engaged in foreign
war;" and indeed "the apprehensions of the
public were great, the enemy being numerous,
bold, well disciplined, and near at hand."—
Medal. Hist. vol. i. p. 294.

PRO. *Providentia*.—PRO. AVG. *Providentia
Augusti.* The providence of the Emperor.

PROB. *Probi*.—*See* ADVENTVS PROBI. AVG.

Proboscis.—An elephant's proboscis is a
symbol of Africa.—[Vail. *Pr.* ii., p. 75.]

PROBVS *(Marcus Aurelius)*.—This illustrious Emperor was born at Sirmium (Sermiel),
in Pannonia, A.D. 232. His father's name was
Maximus, of an obscure family; that of his
mother is not known. Eminently favoured by
nature, from the dawn of manhood, his look was
noble, his carriage majestic, and his inclinations
heroic. Valerian, discovering his rising merit,
made him a military tribune, at an unusually
early age. In the reigns of Claudius II., of
Aurelian, of Tacitus, he displayed his valour
and skill; as rendering himself formidable in
Africa, Egypt, and the Gallic provinces; the
Rhine, the Danube, the Euphrates, also bore
witness to his warlike triumphs over the foes ot
the empire. Prefect of the East, at the period
of the death of Tacitus, he was about 44 years
of age when he ascended the imperial throne;
"in the full possession of his fame, of the love
of the army, and of mature mental and bodily
vigour" (A.D. 276). After having vanquished
Florianus, he was confirmed in his title by the
Senate, who in homage to his exploits and to
his virtues conferred upon him at once the
names of Cæsar, Augustus, Pontifex Maximus,
the Tribunitian power, and the Proconsular
command. Thus honoured by "the Conscript
Fathers,", he was no less acknowledged by the
whole empire, and his reign was a succession of
victories and useful labours. He strengthened
the Rhætian frontier; made the Goths feel the
keen edge of the sword, and induced them to
seek his alliance; broke the power of the
Sarmatians in the north and of the Isaurians in
the east; defeated the Blemmyes, and constrained the King of Persia to sue for peace.
Then retracing his steps westward, Probus delivered Gaul from an invasion of the barbarous
tribes of Germany—drove back the Franks into

their morasses; and carrying his arms into the German fastnesses, built a wall from the Rhine to the Danube. Victor in all these expeditions and encounters both with foreign and domestic enemies, he enjoyed triumphal honours at Rome A.D. 279; on which occasion, as is shewn by his coins, he distributed the congiarium, and treated the people with magnificent shows. In quelling the subsequent revolt of Saturninus, Proculus, and Bonosus, who had severally usurped the purple under his reign, he used his good fortune with remarkable moderation and humanity. Many and stupendous were the works which this ever active Prince caused to be effected by the labour of his soldiers, after having restored peace to the world. But the treaty between Rome and Persia having been broken by "the Great King," Probus prepared for war again on a grand and decisive scale; but his rigid and exact discipline, and certain expressions which had unguardedly escaped him respecting the military, provoked his own troops to mutiny, and they assassinated him on the march, in the month of August, A.D. 282. Probus had reigned six years and four months; and his death was deplored, not only by the Senate and people, but also by the very soldiers, whose discontent at his severity, and jealousy of his preference for civil over military government, had prompted this murderous attack on the life of their Emperor. His superior genius, both in the council and in the field, had indeed placed him on a level at least with the best and ablest princes of the Roman Empire; and the eulogium inscribed on his tomb at his native town of Sirmium, where he died, fell far short of justice to his memory, in designating him merely as the vanquisher of the barbarous nations: for his wisdom, probity, good morals, and disinterestedness, had established for him a more valid claim to be called "the Father of his Country," than could ever be truly advanced for an Augustus, or even for a Trajan.

Probus is styled on his coins—IMP. C. PROBVS PIVS AVG.—IMP. CAES. M. AVR. PROBVS P. F. AVG.—PERPETVVS IMP. PROBVS.—PROBVS INVICTVS.—BONVS IMP. PROBVS INVICT. AVG.

The gold and silver of this Emperor are rare; his brass money of the third form is extremely common. Beauvais states that the Abbé de Rothelin had formed a set of them, amounting to no less than two thousand in number, with differences. One of the most interesting with the reverse of VIRTVS PROBI AVG., Probus on horseback spearing an enemy, is here given.

Vopiscus, in his life of Probus (c. ii.), relates that this Emperor was called *Gothicus*, and also

by the other cognomina of *Parthicus, Sarmaticus,* and *Francicus*, by the senate. None of these honorary appellations, however, are to be found on his coins. But we do read on some of his medals VICTORIA GERMANICA, and also VICTORIA GOTHICA. Moreover, in the room of his other more usual titles, we see on some coins of this prince VIRTVS PROBI INVICTI AVG., with his head radiated, javelin in his right, and a shield in his left hand. Another piece of Probus's money is inscribed VICTORIOSO SEMPER.

The *wife* of this Emperor appears on coins, but her name is unknown. Mionnet describes a very rare bronze medallion, on the obverse of which are the heads side by side *(accolées)* of *Probus et Uxor*. By *Strada* she is called *Julia Procla; but Tristan*, from whom Strada quotes, does not profess to have discovered the name.— *Beauvais* says "By his wife PROCLA, Probus had several children, whose names are not known. All that is ascertained is that they established themselves in the city of Rome."

PROC. *Proconsul.*—L. BIBVLVS M. F. PROC. SIC. *Proconsul Siciliæ.*—See *Calpurnia* family.

PROCE. *Processus.*—FELIX PROCES. CONSVL. AVG. *Felix Processus Consulis Augusti*, and a quadriga of elephants, on a coin of Maxentius.

Processus Consularis.—This term was used by the Romans in express reference to a solemn progress or procession.—See *Consularis Processus.*

Procilia.—This family, said to be of Lanuvian origin, was of the plebeian order, as appears from its name being associated with the tribunate of the people. Its coins, which are rare, offer but two varieties, both silver. The first and

rarest has on the obverse the laureated head of Jupiter, with the mark of the senate's authority, S. C.; on the reverse is L. PROCILI. F., and *Juno Sospita,* or *Sispita,* is typified walking with lance and buckler raised, a serpent before her, rising from the ground.—See *Roscia* family; also see *Juno Sispita.*

There is a serrated denarius of this family, bearing the same legend on its reverse, but with the type of Juno Sispita in a biga at full speed, and exhibiting on its obverse the head of Juno Sispita, as recognisable by the *goat-skin* head-dress.—The letter F. in the legend of the reverse claims a word or two of observation. Havercamp has expressed his opinion that it indicates *Flamen,* the priest or arch-priest of Juno Sispita. But, says Eckhel, "when that learned antiquary wrote to the above effect, it could not have occurred to him that on certain other (consular) coins the names of a man is in like manner followed by the letter F., as REGVLVS F.—MESSAL*ius* F.—C.

CVR*iatius* F.—Therefore in the same way L. PROCILI. F. is also to be explained, and the F. is in all probability to be read *Filius.*" It is doubtful who this L. Procilius was.

PROCONS. *Proconsul.*—IMP. CAESAR TRAIANVS AVG. P.M. TR. P.P. PROCONS., a legend round the head of Trajan on a contorniate medal catalogued by Eckhel. The words *Consul* and *Proconsul* are to be read at full length on coins of Licinius senior and of Constantine the Great.

Proconsul, one who under the Republic was sent by the consuls to govern a province; for which purpose he was invested with powers almost as extraordinary as those which appertained to the consulship itself.—Names of proconsuls and propraetors were *stamped* on coins of Roman families under the authority of the senate. Thus we see on denarii of the *Annia, Appuleia, Coecilia, Junia, Manlia,* and *Scribonia* families, the EX S.C. added to the title of PROCOS., together sometimes with the names of the provinces whose affairs those magisterial delegates administered, as in the case of Sicily. The *Proconsul* governed the province to which he was appointed, according to the Roman laws. The year of the proconsulate dated its commencement from the time that this magistrate made his official entry upon his provincial government. At the expiration of the year, he resigned his charge, which included the command of the soldiers, into the hands of his successor, if arrived, and in thirty days quitted the province. If the successor was not yet arrived, the proconsul left his lieutenant to act during the interval, and on his return to Rome rendered an account of his administration to the senate.—These magistrates enjoyed in their respective provinces the same honours as the consuls did at Rome. All proconsuls of provinces were called rectors or presidents of the Roman people; they were attended on state occasions by twelve lictors, armed with fasces and axes, if they had served the consulate; otherwise by six only. The heads of proconsuls were not, as a matter of custom, engraven on coins; but their titles were recorded on the products of the mint, and they are represented, in quadrigæ, bearing the ivory sceptre, as the symbol of proconsular government, on coins of the Servilia, Sextia, and Sosia families.

Under the empire the *proconsulate* was preserved: and with the stronger reason for its continuance that as the dominion of Rome increased in extent, it became requisite to multiply the number of officers, invested with sounding titles and armed with the fullest authority, for the government of territories at a distance, more or less remote, from the great centre of supreme power. From the period when Augustus divided the administration of the empire between himself and the senate, the latter sent to those provinces which had been conceded by the Emperor to their care, governors, who under the names of proconsuls or propraetors, administered justice there; but these senatorial representatives held no military command, nor any control over the revenue, both which were exclusively confined to the sovereign's officers.—" Under the Emperors (says Eckhel) the proconsular dignity soon became perpetual in their persons, or in those of their destined successors. By authority of the senate, Claudius decreed that Nero Cæsar should possess proconsular power *(extra urbem)* out of the jurisdiction of the city. Antoninus Pius was made by Hadrian, at one and the same time, his colleague in proconsular government and in the tribunitian power. And a similar privilege was conferred, in his turn, by Antoninus Pius on his adopted son M. Aurelius."

"There were, therefore, (adds the same writer), three kinds of proconsulates among the Romans; of these the first were the ordinary ones, who went out to govern provinces, having acquired the office either by lot, or by agreement, or subsequently by the mission of the prince himself. The second was an extraordinary proconsulship, to which, for a certain period of time, greater power, than usually belonged to proconsuls, and extending over more provinces, was entrusted. The third was perpetual, and its authority prevailed throughout all the provinces; and this, therefore, was decreed by Augustus to all Emperors, and by them frequently to the Cæsars, and to the destined successors to the throne."—Vol vii.. 340.

The proconsulate of the *Augusti* and *Cæsars* is seldom read on the monumental inscriptions of antiquity, either on marble or brass. Of such coins, still fewer in number, as add the title of proconsul to that of emperor, the following list is furnished by Eckhel:—

CONSVL. IIII. P. P. PROCOS. in others CONSVL. VII. P. P. PROCOS. On coins of Diocletian.

COS. III. P. P. PROCOS.; on others CONSVL. IIII.—VI.—VII.—VIII.—P. P. PROCOS. On coins of Maximian Hercules.

CONSVL. V. P. P. PROCOS. On coins of Constantius Chlorus.

CONSVL. P. P. PROCONSVL. On coins of Licinius, senior.

CONSVL. P. P. PROCONSVL.—P. M. TRIB. P. COS. IIII. P. P. PRO. COS.—P. M. TRIB. P. COS. VI. P. P. PROCOS. On coins of Constantine the Great.

PROCOPIVS, born A.D. 334, in Cilicia, related to Julian the Apostate, who honoured him with various dignities; he was charged by Jovian to conduct the dead body of that emperor to Tarsus, for interment. But as the rumour prevailed that Julian had made choice of him as his successor to the throne, Procopius retired first into Chersonesus Taurica, afterwards to Chalcedon; at length, having proceeded to Constantinople, he took advantage of the known unpopularity of Valens to assume the title of Augustus in that city, A. D. 365. But although at first successful in this assumption, his pride, extortion, and cruelty plunged him into ruin, by rendering his own government insupportable. Valens, having been joined by the legions of the east, who had remained faithful to his cause, encountered Procopius at Nacolia, in Phrygia, vanquished him in a hard fought battle, and caused him to be put to death A.D. 366, in his 32nd year, and after he had borne the vainly ambitious title of Augustus for the space of eight months.

The coins of Procopius are extremely rare in gold, silver, and middle brass, and almost equally so in third brass. On these he is styled D. N. PROCOPIVS. P. F. AVG. The example

here given is in brass, from the cabinet of Mr. Roach Smith.

Proculeia, a plebeian family, first known under Augustus. Its coins are of third brass, and exhibit only two varieties; one having a head of Neptune, and the reverse a bipennis, with C. PROCVLEIus L. F.; on another, a skate fish.

Proculus, a usurper in Gaul, born among the Albigauni, a people of the maritime Alps (now Albenga, on the coast of Genoa), a powerful man, of outrageous lustfulness. At Lyons he was named Emperor, at first in jest, but being afterwards proclaimed as such in good earnest, his revolt was speedily suppressed by Probus, and he himself was put to death near Cologne, about the time that Bonosus and Saturninus met the same fate.—Goltzius gives a coin as belonging to this *Proculus*, and Mediobarbus publishes another, equally unauthenticated.

Procuratores Monetæ.—Officers holding the management of the various mints of the empire under the appointment of and for the Emperor or Cæsar. In the *Notitia Dignitatum* appear the *Procurator Monetæ Aquileiensis;* the *Procurator Monetæ Arelatensis*, &c.——See *Monetæ et seq.*

PROF. AVG. *Profectio Augusti.*—The departure of the emperor.

Profectiones Imperatorum.—The journies or marches of an emperor were undertaken with great pomp, as had also in the times of the republic been the expeditionary departure of the consuls.—Spanheim *(Pr.* ii., p. 619) assigns various causes for these imperial *profectiones*, which are designated by different symbols on coins; chiefly by a representation of the prince himself on horseback, preceded by a soldier or a figure of victory, and by two or three soldiers following him.—Thus on a gold and on a first brass coin of Trajan, we see the inscription of PROFECTIO AVGVSTI; and the type, an equestrian figure of that emperor, with a spear in his right hand, a military personage going before, and three others following—a medal struck in commemoration of his proceeding on a campaign against the Parthians.—Of all the Roman *Augusti*, none performed these *profectiones ab urbe* more frequently or more extendedly than Hadrian, who, according to Spartianus, made

journies into the Gallic provinces, afterwards into Germany, Britain, &c. Then after having returned to Rome, he made a voyage to Africa, and from thence, coming back again to the capital of his empire, he made a visit to the East—yet not a single medal has hitherto been found that records any of his numerous wanderings from the Roman metropolis, under the term of *Profectio.*—On the brass coinage, however, of M. Aurelius and of Verus, we read PROFECTIO AVG., and find that inscription invariably accompanied, in the mintages of both these princes, with the figure of an emperor on

horseback, preceded and followed by soldiery, as doubtless allusive to the many warlike expeditions of the two imperial brothers and colleagues against the Germans, the Marcomanni, the Sarmatians, the Parthians, &c. On a rare silver coin of Sept. Severus, we see the image of that warlike emperor on horseback, and the inscription of PROFECTIO AVG., marking the period (A.D. 196) of his expedition into Gaul against Albinus, whom, early the next year, he vanquished at the sanguinary battle of Lyons.—Another denarius, bearing on its reverse the same inscription and type, shows the same prince in the same year, going forth on his contemplated war with the Parthians.—There is a third coin of Severus, incribed PROFECT. AVGG. FELIX, with the prince on a horse at full speed, which Mediobarbus believed to indicate the expedition undertaken by Severus into Britain; but which Eckhel, on apparently better grounds, understands to mean the march that indefatigable warrior prosecuted from Syria towards the confines of Parthia.—Medals of Caracalla exhibit the effigy of that prince, sometimes on horseback, as in the above-quoted examples of his father. On a large brass, inscribed PROF. AVGG. PONTIF. TR. P. XI. COS. III., Caracalla is depicted, galloping his horse over a prostrate barbarian, at whom he is darting a javelin. This medal was struck (A.D. 209) during his Britannic campaigns.—On other coins, the same emperor appears marching on foot, in a military habit, and holding a spear, with two legionary standards behind him, or another figure carrying an ensign. This *profectio* is referred by Eckhel to Caracalla's Gallic expedition, A.D. 213, the year after he commenced his imperial atrocities by the murder of his brother Geta.—In the monetal relics of Alexander Severus, there are three coins of this description : the first represents the Emperor on horseback, preceded by a Victory, recording the fact of his having set out from Rome on his successful expedition against the Persians (A.D. 231). Of the two others, one is a medallion, bearing on its obverse the portraits, face to face, of Alexander and Mamaea his mother, with a corresponding legend, and on the reverse PROFECTIO AVGVSTI.; the type, an equestrian figure of the Emperor, his right hand raised, and a spear in his left, a Victory going before him holding out a laurel crown, and (on some reverses) soldiers following or preceding. Both these are shewn by Eckhel to be memorials of Alexander's having marched an army against the Germans who, crossing the Rhine (A.D. 234), had made devastating incursions upon the Gallic borders of that river.—Besides the term *Profectio*, we find that of EXPEDITIO and of TRAIECTVS used for a similar purpose of indication; and when the emperor returned to the capital after a war or a victory, his entry was denoted by the inscriptive distinction of ADVENTVS.—See the words.

P. ROMANI. *Populi Romani.*—SOL. DOMIN. P. ROMANI. On a coin of Aurelian.

Prometheus forming man.—The ancient story of man being formed by Prometheus, and animated by Minerva, is made the reverse type of a bronze medallion of Antoninus Pius. On this beautiful specimen of the ornamental mint of Rome, in her best days of numismatic art, Prometheus appears seated on a rock, contemplating the recent work of his hands, a naked human figure, placed before him like a statue. Behind this image, distinguishable by her helmet and the ægis, is seen Minerva giving life to it by placing a butterfly (emblem of the soul) upon its head. Near the goddess is a tree, round which a serpent has entwined itself—symbol of that prudence which regulates all the actions of the wise daughter of Jove.

According to the well-known interpretation of the myth, Psyché and Love signify the union of the soul with the body: hence Psyche is frequently depicted with a butterfly above her head.—The above medallion is quoted by Eckhel, as from the Museum Albani, and as bearing on its obverse the laureated head of the emperor, with inscription ANTONINVS AVG. PIVS. P.P.—Millin also assigns a medallion of brass, representing the same subject, and without legend, to Antoninus Pius, as preserved in the Museum of the Vatican.

¶ However disguised in the fabulous mask of heathen mythology and of ancient poetry, Prometheus's real character appears to have been properly recognised by the Greeks, amongst whom his name passed proverbially for that of a skilful and ingenious man. The name of Prometheus also signifies a potter, because he was said to excel in works made of white clay. An engraved stone represents him modelling statues. The name likewise means foresight; and the individual who bore it was evidently famous in his time for the number, utility, and ingenuity of his inventions.—Beger derives from writings less figurative and extravagant than the dramas of ancient Greece, that Prometheus was the first to instruct the Assyrians in astronomy, that he comprehended the nature of thunder, and that it was from his knowledge of causes with regard to atmospheric phenomena that he gained the dangerous reputation of having stolen Jupiter's own lightning.—Bocchart also gleans from the writings of the ancients that Prometheus was the author of medicine, divination, music, and other arts of man in a civilized state.

PRON. *Pronepos.*—A great grandson.— C. OCTAVIVS C. F. C. N. C. *PRON.* C. ABN. *Caius Octavius, Caii Filius, Caii Nepos, Caii Pronepos, Caii Abnepos* (a grandchild's grandson). So on a coin of Caligula C. CAESAR DIVI AVG. PRON. *Pronepos Augusti.*

PROPAGO IMPERI*i.*—This legend accompanies the type of a man and a woman standing face to face, and joining hands, on gold and silver of Caracalla and Plautilla.

Struck during the life-time of Severus in honour of his eldest son's marriage (A.D. 202) this coin shews the hope entertained by that Emperor of male descendants from this union, to perpetuate the empire in his family, as the denarius with *Aeternitas Imperii* also serves to demonstrate—a hope blighted by the event—a marriage rendered fatally miserable to the wife by the atrocious brutality of the husband.—See AETERNITAT. IMPERI.

PROPR. or PROPRAE. AFRICAE. Propraetor of Africa.—See *Clodius Macer.*

PRO. SIC.—*Propraetor Siciliæ.*

Propraetores.—Among the magisterial personages employed in the government of the different provinces of the Roman empire, and of whom mention is made on coins, are the Propraetors, to whom full Praetorian power and dignity was extended within the sphere of their administration. As the territories of the republic increased, so was the necessity forced upon her of increasing in proportion the number of provincial officers, and consequently magistrates were sent by the senate with the titles of proconsul and propraetor, according to the estimated importance, either for extent or for situation, of the particular position of country subjected to Roman domination. The only difference between the relative position of the proconsular and the propraetorian governors consisted in the former having an attendance of twelve lictors, and the latter but six; and that the retinue and soldiery of the proconsul were generally the more numerous. The *propraetores*, as well as the proconsuls, by whom the larger provinces were ruled, are found recorded on many coins of families given by Morell and Vaillant.

PROPVGNAT. *Propugnator.* Defender.— MARS PROPVGNAT. on coins of Gordian III.

PROPVGNATORI (understand IOVI.) IMP. VIIII. COS. III. P.P.—Jupiter shaking his thunderbolt over a barbarian lying prostrate on the ground.

This silver coin of M. Aurelius, inscribed (as by associating the legend with the type will appear) to *Jupiter the Defender*, was struck in the year of Christ 178, when the Germans having again revolted against Rome, the Emperor set out in August on a military expedition to Germany, with his son Commodus. This is the first time the inscription of PROPVGNATOR appears in the Imperial series. Afterwards we find it joined sometimes to the word IOVI, at others to the word MARTI, and even to APOLLINI, according to the choice made by the reigning prince of a particular champion from amongst the various gods of his Pantheon.— Examples of this kind are to be found on coins of Alex. Severus, Sept. Severus, Caracalla, Gordianus Pius, Volusianus, Aemilianus, Valerianus, Gallienus, Postumus, Tetricus, Diocletianus, Val. Maximianus, Gal. Maximianus, Constantinus Magn.

PROQ: *Proquæstor.*—PROQ. P.—As on a denarius of the *Cocceia* family with the epigraph M. NERVA PROQ. P., which Vaillant reads *Proquæstor Provincialis*, or *Provinciæ;* but which Eckhel says is most likely to mean *Proquæstore Proprætore.*—The title of Proquæstor, expressed as above, not unfrequently appears on coins of Roman families.

Proquæstores.—The quæstors and proquæstors were the paymasters-general of the Roman legions: nay even the business of the coinage came also under their care. And, in the event of a quæstor dying, or leaving his province, the proquæstor acted in his room.

Prora, the prow or fore part of a ship.—This figure on colonial coins indicates a city situated on the sea-coast.—It is a symbol of maritime power, as on coins of M. Antony and of the Pompeys.

Prows are seen on brass coins of many Roman families, which are thence denominated *ratiti.*—They are also found on medals of Julius Cæsar, Augustus, Vespasian, (with a star above, and COS. VIII.) and Hadrian.—Also with the goddess *Annona* standing on or near, as in Titus, Domitian, Nerva, Trajan, Hadrian, Antoninus Pius, M. Aurelius, Severus, Gallienus. On a second brass of Commodus (PRINCIPI IVVENTVTIS) a legionary eagle, supported by two right hands joined, is seen planted on the *prow* of a galley.

The *prow* of a galley, with the figure of Felicity, of Fortune, of Lætitia, of Neptune, of Minerva, and of Rome, is seen on coins of Vespasian, Hadrian, Commodus, Antoninus Pius, Severus, Postumus, Philip, and Gallienus. —The same object, on which stands a *Victoria Navalis,* appears on medals of Augustus, Vespasian, and Titus.—See VICTORIA AVGVSTI.— VICTORIA NAVALIS.

PRO. R. CAES.   *Pro Reditu Cæsaris.*—For the return of the Emperor.

PRO. S.   *Pro Salute.*—PRO. S. ET RED. AVG. *Pro Salute et Reditu Augusti.*—See S. P. Q. R. v. s., &c.

Proserpina, daughter of Jupiter and Ceres, and the wife of Pluto, by whom, according to the fable, she was forcibly borne away from Enna, or Mount Aetna, and conveyed to his infernal kingdom [see *Ceres*].—Vaillant, in a

selection of brass medallions from the Abbé De Camp's cabinet, gives from a coin of Cyzicus, with Greek inscription, a portrait of Faustina sen. under the type of Proserpine, with Ceres, on the reverse, in search of her lost daughter. Millin (in his *Gal. Myth.* t. i. pl. xlix., 340) gives the reverse of a coin of Antoninus Pius, with legend of LAETITIA COS. IIII. and type of two women standing, one holding corn-ears, the other a globular figure ; and he interprets the device as follows :—"Proserpine has been found again by Ceres, who is characterised by the ears of corn which she holds in her right hand. The daughter holds in her left hand the pomegranate of which she had eaten, and which was the cause of her not being permitted always to remain in heaven."—With the foregoing exception, the figure of Proserpine does not appear on any coin of Roman die. But the medals of Syracuse present her image, the Sicilians worshiping her as a goddess, and swearing fidelity to their promises by her name.

PROV. AVG.   *Providentiæ Augusti.*—To the foresight of the Emperor.—PROV. DEOR. *Providentia,* or *Providentiæ, Deorum.*—The providence, or to the providence, of the gods.

Providentia. (Providence).—With all their vices, follies, and gross superstitions (indeed, in spite of them), the Romans still appear to have cherished a belief in the perpetual and direct interposition of the gods with respect to human affairs.—Among the various monuments which attest this religious feeling, or at least this profession of religion, on the part of both princes and people, none are more conspicuous than those to be found on their *imperial* coins, for it is to be observed that previous to the substitution of the monarchical for the republican form of government, that allegorical divinity whose name is derived from *providere* (to foresee) is not seen either on metal or on marble.—The first coin on which the name of *Providence* appears is a unique one of small brass, having on one side a radiated head surrounded with the inscription DIVOS IVLIVS CAESAR, and on the other an altar lighted, with PROVID. S. C.— From the commencement of the reign of Augustus and afterwards, the words *Providence* and *Providence of the Gods* came very frequently into use, and the accompanying symbols were greatly multiplied, insomuch that *Ant. Augustino* in his second Dialogue exhibits twelve varieties of types, taken from reverses of different emperors' coins, for adulation soon proceeded to lavish upon princes all the attributes of divinity.—Providence (PROVIDENTIA DEORVM) however, is oftenest depicted under the form of a female, clothed in a matron's gown, holding in her left hand a cornucopiæ, or the hasta pura, and in her right a short wand, with which she either touches or points to a globe. Sometimes she holds this globe in her right hand, at others it lies at her feet. This type is intended to mark the power and wisdom of the emperor, who ruled the Roman world.—On a first brass of Alexander Severus, inscribed PROVIDENTIA AVG., is a woman resting her right hand on an anchor, and holding two corn-ears over an altar.—On a second brass of Numerianus the *Providence of the Emperor* holds a cornucopiæ in her right hand.—Other types, peculiar to certain emperors and events, will be found described below.

PROVID. S. C.   A lighted altar.—This is the legend and type alluded to above as forming the reverse of a middle brass of Julius Cæsar.— Pellerin was the first to publish it, in his *Mélange de Médailles* (vol. i. p. 196), and Eckhel quotes the coin from the work of that great French numismatist as an evidence that *Providence* was an attribute almost exclusively assigned to the gods. But, at the same time, he denies the correctness of Pellerin's assertion that the word *Providentia* coupled with the figure of an altar was, in the age of Julius, a mark of consecration, "for (says the German medallist) we also see both of them conjoined on coins of Galba and Vitellius." This is the earliest Roman coin hitherto found which exhibits such a reverse, but it is common on those of *Divus Augustus.*

PROVIDENT. S. C.   An altar.—On a second brass coin restored by Vespasian.

By the old masters of the numismatic science it was thought that this and other coins having on the obverse a radiated head of Augustus, with the inscription DIVVS AVGVSTVS PATER, were struck in the life-time of Augustus, and that by the type of the reverse the temple of Janus was represented—that temple being closed in consequence of Cæsar having, by his PROVI- DENCE, restored peace to the world. These coins, therefore, as *Pighius* expresses his opinion, were struck in the year of Rome 725. But the radiated head and legend DIVVS AVGVSTVS on the obverse fully prove that they were struck after that emperor's death; and that the type of the reverse is not the temple of Janus, is sufficiently shewn, by that remarkable and unique coin of Julius Cæsar above described from Pellerin—a coin very like the one now in question, except that on the obverse is read DIVOS. IVLIVS. CÆSAR. It is known, however, that this Dictator never shut the temple of Janus.—The type, therefore, represents an altar, as not only its form suggests, but as we moreover perceive it must be from the circum- stance, of that, on the above-mentioned coin of Julius, being lighted. There are likewise coins of the Lusitanian colony of Emerita (Merida), which by their great similitude corroborate this opinion.—See EMERITA.

It appears that the Romans not only inscribed coins, but erected statues to the Providence of the Gods. In his *Thesaurus*, entitled *Inscriptiones Antiquæ totius orbis Romani, &c.* (1, ii., p. 1075), Gruter, after Boissard, has published a bas-relief, which represents a Goddess crowned with laurel. She holds in her right hand a kind of baton; the left hand is wanting : at her feet are seen, on one side, a horn of plenty, and on the other a basket of flowers : on the base we read PROVIDENTIAE DEORVM.

PROVIDENTIA.—Seguin in his *Selecta Numismata Impp.* (p. 148) has given us the engraving of a beautiful gold coin, on the obverse of which is the head of Septim. Severus, with the epigraph SEVERVS PIVS AVG., and on the reverse a head similar to that of Medusa, with the word PROVIDENTIA.— In reference to this remarkable medal, both Seguin and Vaillant consider it to mean, in an allegorical sense, that Minerva is the Goddess of Prudence or of *Providence*, which is indicated by the head of Medusa, sacred to her, and which she bore affixed to her ægis.—Eckhel appears to be of the same opinion, and refers to other medals of Severus in confirmation thereof.

PROVIDENT. AVG*usti* IMP. VI. COS. III.—On a first brass of M. Aurelius. This medal, eulogising the Emperor for his foresight *(Providentia)*, is rare, and its type very re- markable. The Emperor stands on an estrade, addressing his soldiers. The Prætorian prefect stands close behind him, The troops are com- posed of cavalry as well as infantry, as is shewn by four military figures, and by a horse whose head appears amidst them.—Havercamp *(Museum Reg. Suevorum)* gleans the explana- tion of this fine medal from one of the same emperor's (see p. 640 of this Dictionary), which, with the legend IMP. VI. COS. III. re- presents in the type of its reverse the *trajectus*, or passage of the Emperor with his troops over a bridge of boats. As the ordering of bridges to be constructed whenever they were needful, belonged peculiarly to the *provident* care of the reigning prince, so Marcus Aurelius is depicted in the act of haranguing his soldiers, on the present coin, in which he would seem to be exhorting them gallantly to brave the dangers of war, since on his part no means were neglected that human prudence could suggest, to ensure success to the Roman arms.

PROVID. AVG, *(Providentia Augusti.)*— This legend appears on a first brass of Com- modus, with the type of a ship, whose two sails are expanded.—Vaillant.

Even that monster of cruelty, and of bru- talized voluptuousness, is not without the his- torical honour of having, amidst a reign of atrocities and indecencies, been the author of an establishment advantageously useful for the supply of provisions to Rome and to Italy.— "The fleet of Alexandria (says Crevier, quoting Lampridius as his authority,) was the accustomed vehicle for conveying thither the corn of Egypt. Commodus employed a similar one at Carthage for the transport of grain from Africa, in order that in case of need, the one might supply what the other failed to bring. But here again he spoiled this really laudable institution, by the ridiculous vanity which he mingled with it, in changing the name of Carthage into that of *Alexandria Commodiana*, and in causing the fleet to be called *fleet of Commodus Hercules.*" Eckhel considers this coin to refer to the African fleet destined for the purpose above described, and which was established by Com- modus in the year of Rome 944 (A.D. 191).

PROVIDENTIA AVG.—A woman standing with the proboscis of an elephant on her head, and at her feet a lion, displays a sistrum in her

left hand. Opposite is a naked figure of Hercules, whose foot is placed on the prow of a vessel, and whose left hand holds a club; both figures, symbolical of Hercules and Africa, join right hands with each other.

This legend and type, on a large brass of Commodus, is regarded by the learned as referring to the African fleet of corn transports, alluded to in the preceding coin, and which is also believed to be referred to in a medallion of the same emperor. (See VOTIS FELICIBVS.)—The elephant's head, the sistrum, the lion, are attributes peculiar to Egypt and to Africa proper, which were the granaries of Rome. But Commodus having sent his ships for freights of corn is on this coin represented paying worship to Hercules, and he himself plants his foot on the prow of one of the vessels, as if shewing care for his new colony.

PROVIDENTIA AVGVSTI. S. C.—Two figures in the toga standing; one presenting a globe to the other; between them is a rudder. On a first brass of Titus.

As the coin on which this fine historical reverse appears is recognised as genuine by Mionnet and Akerman, although unnoticed by Eckhel, we shall here append an explanation of the type from Havercamp's Commentaries on the Cabinet of Queen Christina:—"This medal was struck in praise of the Providence, or foresight of the Emperor, that is to say of Titus, who to annihilate factions, and to prevent the occurrence of every thing calculated to disturb the public tranquillity, had associated his brother Domitian with himself in the government of the empire. For, according to Suetonius (in his *Life of Titus*, chap. ix.), *à primo Imperii die consortem successoremque testari perseveravit.* And this he did doubtless to gratify the haughty and ambitious disposition of Domitian, who, as the same writer (in *vita Domit.* c. ii.) says, *nunquam jactare dubitavit, relictum se participem Imperii, sed fraudem testamento adhibitam.* To disprove this foul charge of having falsified his father's will was, therefore, the provident policy of the Emperor, by sharing the imperial inheritance with his unworthy brother. And accordingly on this medal Titus and Domitian are represented as taking each other by the hand, and together supporting a globe *(orbem terrarum* of the Roman world), under which is placed a rudder, to mark (that *one-sided* reciprocity) their *mutual concord in the government of the state.* On this coin we see one of the two figures wearing a *radiated crown* (corona radiata).—By some antiquaries this type is described as representing Vespasian delivering over a globe to his son Titus, as a symbol of entrusting him with the management of state affairs. But this supposition is not borne out either by the countenances of the two figures, which are both those of young men, or by the assignment of the medal to the reign of Titus.

PROVIDENTIA DEORVM. S. C.—*Imperator togatus stans d. extenta, s. volumen respicit aquilam superne advolantem, et scipionem unquibus deferentem,* AE. I. and II. (*Mus. Cæs.)*

It is in the above terms that Eckhel (*Doct. Num. Vet.* vol. vi. p. 507), describes a coin of Hadrian, in first and second brass, as from the Imperial Cabinet at Vienna. viz., the magnificent collection over the safe keeping and arrangement of which that most able and judicious numismatic antiquary presided.—The same remarkable type of the Roman PROVIDENTIA is given in, and commented on, first by Tristan (*Comment. Hist.* tom. i. p. 462), and afterwards by Pedrusi (vol. vi. p. 336, *Museum Farnese).* But it is not included in Mionnet's *Recueil,* nor in Akerman's Catalogue.

In the descriptions respectively made by Trajan, Pedrusi, and Eckhel, there are some minor points of difference; but all agree about the togated figure standing, with right hand extended towards an eagle, which appears flying down with something in his talons, either a branch, or a wand, or sceptre.—Tristan (after observing that Antonio Augustino is wrong in ascribing this medal to Trajan, and in speaking of the bird not as an eagle but as a dove,) says, " *Pour le certain, ce revers regarde la piété d'Hadrian, qui refere à la providence des Dieux, et non au Destin, sa promotion a l'Empire, cet Aigle lui en presentant le sceptre de la part de Jupiter."* He then quotes Eustatius on the subject, to the effect of shewing it to be that Greek writer's opinion, that "the Eagle is the sign of the Providence and the Love of Jupiter towards mankind." This seems a felicitous explanation of an otherwise obscure subject; and, supposing the great German medallist not to have been deceived by the specimens immediately under his own eye, the coin is an interesting and curious adjunct to the legend of PROVIDENTIA DEORVM.—It may be as well, however, to add that Pedrusi considers the figure to be, not that of Hadrian, but of an Augur, who stands in the act of taking the auspices, for some purposes of superstitious inquiry into future events, to which that emperor was greatly addicted.—Dion says that Hadrian was much addicted to divination and the use of magic in sacred ceremonies.

PROVIDENTIAE DEORVM. COS. II.—
A woman stands holding out both hands towards

a globe suspended in the air and radiated. On
a first brass of Pertinax.

It has already been remarked that, from the
time of Augustus, frequent mention is made of
Providence by the mint of Rome. The first
types were the altar, the thunderbolt, the
eagle. At a later period a globe is generally
employed to designate it, as being the image of
the *orbis terrarum*, or the whole world.—
"This globe, therefore, serves to symbolise that
orb of earth whose government is entrusted to
princes by the providence of the gods; and
those princes themselves often bear it in one of
their hands with that signification. A small
figure of Victory is frequently placed on this
globe; but afterwards, under Christian Emperors and Cæsars, a cross was substituted for
the Victory. And lest it should be taken for a
common globular figure, it was sometimes encircled with zones, which correspond with the
celestial zones, as may be seen on the denarii
of Mussidius Longus. A female genius either
points to this globe, with a rod or short
stick, or, what is almost solely observed on this
coin of Pertinax, she seems to accept it as
descending from above, occasionally adorned
with rays, as if it was to be regarded as a
heavenly gift. A similar type appears on the
second brass as well as on the gold and silver of
Pertinax.

PROVIDENTIA DEORVM QVIES. AVGG.
(Quies Augustorum.)—A woman standing with
a branch in right hand and a hasta in the left,
opposite another female figure, who has no
attribute. [This type, therefore, presents the
respective images of *Providence* and *Repose*.]

This legend is common on the coins of
Diocletian and of Maximian Hercules, as associated with the well-known fact of those two
partners in empire having (A.D. 305) abdicated
their high positions, and retired from the administration of public affairs to lead, as private
individuals, a more tranquil, if not a happier
life. That Diocletian's abdication was performed with a sincerity, and persevered in with
a temper of mind, which justified the appellation of *Quies*, in its calmest and most peaceful
sense, we have the concurrent authorities of
both ecclesiastical and profane historians for
believing. Not so with respect to Maximian,
who, during the whole period of his reluctant
privacy, appears to have been the very *imago*

inquietudinis, and whose perturbed spirit was
ever at variance with anything like resignation.

In illustration of the above reverse, as well
as in explanation of the term SEN*ior* AVG*ustus*,
which forms part of the inscription on the
obverse of this coin, Baron Bimard makes the
following instructive remarks :—" Although
(says he) Diocletian and his colleague had quitted
the throne, and had divested themselves of all
their authority in favour of the two Cæsars,
Constantius Chlorus and Galerius Maximianus ;
yet they nevertheless retained the ·title of
Augusti, because the character which that title
imparted to those who bore it legitimately, was
regarded as ineffaceable. The only point about
which care was taken, being to join the name of
Senior to that of *Augustus* (thus designating
Diocletian and Maximinian as the *elder emperors*) in the laws wherein Diocletian and
Maximinian were spoken of ; in the medals which
were continued to be struck in their die, and
even in the inscriptions, in order to distinguish
them from the reigning emperors. It is so well
authenticated a truth, that the honours appertaining to their rank were preserved to these
princes, after they had voluntarily laid them
down, that in the year of Christ 307, Maximian Hercules was consul with Constantine,
and the following year with Galerius Maximianus. The Chronicler of Alexandria, Cassiodorus, the Greek *Fasti* at Florence, and Prosper,
also place in the year of our Lord 308 a tenth
consulate of Diocletian, who had abdicated the
empire three years before."

PROVIDENTISSIMI.—See SAPIENTIA
PRINCIPIS PROVIDENTISSIMI.—On coins of
Constantinus M.

Providentia.—Besides the instances which
have been already noticed, shewing the various
modes of typifying *Providence*, whether in
praise of an emperor's care and foresight, or in
acknowledgment of a divine superintendence,
the following, *among many others*, appear in
the Roman series :—A thunderbolt as in Antoninus Pius—the Emperor addressing his soldiers
on large bronze of M. Aurelius—on coins of
Gallienus, Mercury with his usual attributes
appears, accompanied by the legend of PRO-
VIDENTIA AVG.—the *Providence of the Gods* is
symbolised by a thunderbolt, on gold and silver
coins of Antoninus Pius—on a second brass of
Aurelian, the same legend is accompanied by
the figure of a woman holding two military
ensigns, opposite whom stands the Sun, with
radiated head, uplifted right hand, and globe
in his left—on coins of Postumus the same
legend has for its type a woman leaning on
a column. The type of Providence, as applied
to an Emperor's acts, assumes the form of
some edifice, such as a temple, an altar, or the
castra prætoria, frequently with a *star* above,
on medals of Constantius Chlorus, the two
Licinii, and Constantine the Great and his
family.

PROVIDENTIA SENATVS. S. C.—Two
men clothed in the toga, one of whom gives a
globe to the other.—On a first brass of Nerva.

These two figures (says Havercamp) are designed to represent the Senate and Nerva.—The republic (or, more properly speaking, the imperial monarchy) began to breathe again, and to recover from the effects of past calamities, after the death of Domitian, under Nerva, the excellent prince who succeeded that cruel tyrant. In fact Nerva not only in his own person rendered great services to the state, but also by his choice of a successor as the public interest required. Having no child of his own, he adopted Ulpius Trajan, who from his virtues and great qualities was most worthy of being selected for so glorious a destiny. Nerva, whilst living, transmitted to Trajan all the rights of empire, which he had himself received from the senate, for Nerva had been chosen by the senate, who had placed the supreme power in his hands as the worthiest to which they could be confided. Accordingly the present medal is made to bear the inscription of PROVIDENTIA SENATVS.

PROVINCIA DACIA. AN. I.—The province of Dacia, on brass of Philip the elder.

Havercamp, in his commentary on the Queen of Sweden's cabinet, says in reference to this coin :—"Dacia was the second province (Moesia was the first) that struck a medal in honour of Philip. It is dated of the year 1. The type consists of a figure standing, clothed after the manner of the Dacians, and representing the genius of that province. She holds a Dacian sword in the right and a standard in the left hand, on which is marked the number xiii." Vaillant, in his colonies, gives a medal of Æmilianus, with *Provincia Dacia*, A.N. vii., and a female figure holding an ensign marked xiii., and a number v. being in the field of the coin. "The numbers (says Havercamp) signify that the veterans of the fifth legion, called Macedonian, and of the thirteenth, called *Gemina*, had been placed in the province of Dacia by the Emperor Philip. These legions, from the time of Trajan, were almost always stationed in that province."

On a medal of Trajanus Decius, given by Spanheim in his notes on Julian's "Cæsars," the *Dacian Province* assumes an upright posture, standing, with right hand elevated, between an eagle and a lion.

Provincia Dacia Romana.—This vast and very noted province, as has already been observed (p. 334), comprehended within its limits, not only the modern Transylvania, Wallachia, and Moldavia, but also part of Hungary. How much too, after its dearly purchased acquisition by the victorious arms of Trajan, it was the care of Imperial Rome to civilize and adorn it, is shewn by various remains of its acknowledged importance, in sculptured marbles, and inscribed stones, in public roads and edifices, in the ruins of Trajan's bridge and other monuments. But although the name of Dacia, and the memory of its conquest, are recorded on many coins of Roman die, struck in all the three metals, yet it does not appear that any of its cities or districts were admitted to partake of colonial or municipal privileges, nor that any pieces of money were struck within the provinces itself, until the reign of Philip senior, who was the first emperor that changed its political condition from subjugation to free-citizenship, and gave it immunities which placed its inhabitants on an equality, as to rights, with the Romans themselves.—The Imperial Greek pieces which bear the name of this country in Greek, were fabricated elsewhere, in memory of the advantages which the Romans had gained over the Dacians. "It has not been possible," says M. Hennin (*Manuel* vol. ii. p. 107), "to ascertain positively the places where those pieces were coined. M. Sestini ascribes them to the Isle of Crete, and believes them to have been struck in the city of Thalassa." Be this, however, as it may, it was under Philip senior that it began to use Latin legends. And from notations of years which appear on the exergue of these coins, such as AN. I., AN. II., AN. III., &c., the inference seems warranted that, having been rendered free under Philip, and admitted by him to share in the immunities of the *Jus Italicum*, and thus to be placed on the footing of Roman citizens, the entire province, out of grateful remembrance of benefits thereby conferred upon it, adopted the plan of computing dates from that period, as being the æra of its liberation. The marks of years appear on coins of the two Philips and Otacilia, also on coins of Decius, Etruscilla, Herennius, Hostilianus, Gallus, Volusianus, Æmilianus, Valerianus sen., and Gallienus; and they begin in the year of Rome 1,000, A.D. 247, being the fourth year of Philip senior's reign, in which, as may be gathered from Zosimus, that emperor rescued Dacia from the incursions of the Carpi.—On the coins of Philip only I. II. and III. are engraved. Under Trajanus Decius, this province struck coins with the years IIII. and V., answering to the years of Rome 1003 and 1004, in which last Decius perished.—There is a medallion of extreme rarity, struck under Volusianus (as given by Froëlich, *Tert.* p. 137), which bears for legend PROVINCIA DACIA AN. V. as the *Fifth year* of this Dacian æra.—The next which are noted are the years VI. and VII. under Treb. Gallus, agreeing with the years of the City 1005 and 1006, in which last Gallus was slain.—But, as Dacia in the same year, VII. of its æra, inscribed coins to Hostilianus, Gallus, Æmilianus, and Gallienus, the fact shews that all these princes reigned in the course of that year : viz., that Hostilianus died at the beginning of the year of this æra, that Gallus was put to death some months afterwards, that Æmilianus was killed after three months more, lastly that Valerianus and Gallienus were proclaimed emperors at the close of the same year. The *Annus* VIIII., or Ninth year of *Free* Dacian, engraved on a coin of Valerian, falls within the third year of Valerian and Gallienus. The *Tenth* year of the Dacian æra, which is the fourth of Gallienus, is revealed on a coin of his by Froëlich *(ibid,* p. 140), with the assistance of chronology.— So long as Dacia was treated as a conquest, the personification of the province was, on coins of Roman die, almost invariably in a sitting posture, before some trophy, as if weeping for the loss of her barbaric independence ; but from the period when Philip senior bestowed upon her, less perhaps from choice than from necessity, the too tardily conceded boon of liberty, *Dacia Provincia* is seldom found seated. —Neumann *(Pop. Num.* i. ᵗb. 3, 4, 2) has edited a second brass of Philip, on the reverse of which the genius of the province is seated, her head covered with the *mitra*, or bonnet, of her country.—But on the colonial imperial coins of Dacia in general, from Philip to Gallienus, the province is represented as follows :—

A woman, adorned with the *pileus,* and wearing a sort of tunic and long cloak, *stands* holding in each hand a military ensign. On the *velum*, or small flag, of the right hand is the numeral v. ; on that of the left, the numeral XIII.—On others the woman bears in her right hand a curved sword, peculiar to the inhabitants of the country ; and a military ensign is planted near her to the right. At her feet is on one side an eagle with a crown in its beak, and on on the other side a lion.—On another coin the *velum* of the military standard contains the letters D. F.—The above types belong to coins dedicated to Philip senior and junior, and to Otacilia Severa.—On a very rare second brass inscribed to Trebonianus Gallus, the female figure holds in her right hand a branch ; and in her left a staff, on the top of which is an ass's head. [According to the explanations of these types given by Vaillant, Froëlich, and others, the woman represents the *Genius Provinciæ :* her head is covered with the *pileus* held to be the symbol of liberty, and allusion in this instance to the freedom conceded to Dacia by Philip.— D. F. is *Dacia Felix.* Dacia, as is well known, was added to the empire by Trajan, yet in an ancient inscription the merit of this annexation and of giving this province the appellation of *Felix* is (strangely enough) awarded to Hadrian, in the following terms :—IMP. CAES. DIVO NERVAE TRAIANO HADRIANO PONT. MAX. COS. III. P. P. CVIVS VIRTVTE DACIA IMPERIO ADDITA FELIX EST.—Under Philip it resumed the name of *Felix,* having been declared free by that emperor, and on coins of Trajanus Decius, Philip's successor, it is also called *Dacia Felix.* —In reference to the figures v. and XIII. on the military ensigns, Vaillant observes that as Trajan had placed the *fifth* Macedouian and the *thirteenth Gemina* Legions in Dacia, so Philip, having transmitted their veteran soldiers into all the colonies of the province, proclaimed them Roman citizens, a fact shadowed forth in the military ensigns borne in each hand by the

Genius of the Province.—Dion states that, under Alex. Severus, both legions (viz., v. Macedonica and XIII. Gemina) were stationed in Dacia. And Philip having sent the veterans of these legions into the colonies of the province, made a new levy of soldiers to guard Dacia from the inroads of the barbarians. The sword in the hand of the female figure, is called by Clemens Alexand. [Strom. lib. 1] ἄρπη, and, according to that writer, was borrowed from the Thracians.—On some of these Dacian coins it more resembles the *lituus* than a sword.—The eagle, which is the ensign of the Roman empire, is here adopted by Dacia because she has been made Roman. The lion is the accustomed symbol of the province.—The female figure representing Dacia, which on coins of the Philips and of Trajanus Decius holds (as already described) a military ensign in each hand, is exhibited on a very rare second brass of Treb. Gallus, in a different manner. Instead of those legionary standards allusive to the Roman soldiers appointed to guard her confines, the genius of the province now presents the olive branch, indicating (says Vaillant ii., p. 213) that peace had been entered into by Gallus with the barbarian invaders—a peace which that emperor had ignominiously purchased by the payment of an annual tribute, of 200 gold drachmas." The figure in question bears in her left hand a tall staff, on which is placed the head of an ass, seemingly as though it were a national ensign, as may be observed on coins of Trajanus Decius struck by the Senate : likewise on the silver mint of that emperor.

We shall here append the series of annual notations on coins of DACIA PROVINCIA, making the æra of her freedom, as exhibited by Eckhel [*Cat . Mus. Cæs.* i. p. 48, 49, 50] ; not like Vaillant and others, taking them in the chronological order of the imperial reigns, from Philip to Gallienus; but according to the order of years, commencing under the first named emperor.

Annus I.; as in Philip senior, Otacilia Severa, and Philip junior.

Annus II.; as in Philip junior and Otacilia Severa.

Annus III.; as in Philip sen., Otacilia, Philip jun,, Trajanus Decius, and Volusianus.

Annus IV.; as in Trajanus Decius, and Herennius Etruscus.

[In honour of Decius, who dethroned and succeeded to the founder of her freedom, Dacia nevertheless deemed it policy, no doubt, to strike coins. But as the Illyrian army acknowledged the inactive Philip, it first proclaimed Marinus, and afterwards Decius, Emperors against the Barbarians then pouring into the Roman territories, the neighbouring provinces followed the same movement, especially as Decius was born in Pannonia, on the borders of Dacia, whilst Philip being a native of Arabia, was less popular with the provinces. It was for this reason that the senate struck coins of Decius with the epigraph of GENIVS EXERCITVS ILLYRICIANI, and recorded the names of those provinces which had proclaimed him emperor, viz., Pannonia and Dacia. In fact they inscribed DACIA FELIX, on the coins of the latter, as if she had recovered her pristine felicity under such a prince as Decius, she having become, to the most privileged extent, a Roman province, to which allusion is made on a marble edited by Zamosius.—See Vaillant, ii. p. 196.—With regard to the AN. IV. appearing on a coin inscribed to Herennius, Vaillant remarks—" Dacia, on receiving intelligence that Trajanus Decius, at the entreaty of the senate, had proclaimed his son Herennius Etruscus, Cæsar, struck coins of congratulation as well to the son as to the father, and placed the marks of the year IV. (*annus quartus*) on those of the former, as a monument of liberty derived from Philip."—ii. p. 206.]

Annus V. ; as in Trajanus Decius, Herennia Etruscilla, Hostilianus, Treb. Gallus, and Volusianus.

[The fifth year of the Dacian æra is the second of Decius's reign.—Vaillant, ii. 206.]

Annus VI.; as in Treb. Gallus, Valerianus, and Gallienus.

Annus VII. ; as in Hostilianus, Æmilianus, and Gallienus.

Annus VIII. ; as in Æmilianus and Valerianus.

Annus IX. ; as in Valerianus.

Annus X.; as in Gallienus.

Provinciæ. Provinces.—These were territories which the Romans had either conquered in war or obtained possession of by other means. They formed a third part of the empire, and for the purposes of government were divided into consular, proconsular, prætorian, and præsidial, according to the respective rank and dignity of the magistrates appointed to rule over them ; the maxim of the republic being to form the countries which it subdued into so many distinct governments. As soon as it acquired them, their laws were annulled, their own magistrates removed, and themselves subjected to the Roman laws, for the administration of which, according to the extent and importance of the provinces, a *proconsul*, or a *prætor*, or a *præses* (see these words) was sent from Rome—each with a *quæstor*, whose business it was to enforce payment of the tributes imposed by the conquerors. In return for the loss of its independence, in being reduced to a provincial state (*redacta in formam Provinciæ*), its *generous* masters granted to such country the *Jus Provinciæ*, a privilege very inferior to the *Jus Italicum* and to the *Jus Latium*, inasmuch as it not only fell short of exempting its inhabitants from tribute, but compelled them to receive their laws and governors from Rome.—Thus during the republic, the provinces, as well those of Italy as those at a greater distance from the capital, were altogether under the control of the senate and people. But when Augustus became master, that subtle personage, to serve his own ambitious policy, made a division of the provinces, which, whilst it apparently abolished a monopoly of administrative power on his part, had the effect of placing the whole military force of the state at his sole disposal.

To the senate he yielded those provinces which were situated in the centre of the empire, reserving for himself and successors the frontier lines of country, under pretence of defending them from the attacks of barbarian and other hostile nations. The *provinciæ suburbanæ*, as those of Italy were called, from their comparative proximity to Rome, were placed under the authority of annually appointed magistrates, sent to them by the *Senatus Populusque Romanus*, whether proconsuls or prætors. On the other hand, the provinces reserved for imperial government were presided over by the *Legati Augusti*, or lieutenants chosen by the prince himself.

After the partition above referred to, conquered territories, moulded into provinces, fell to the sway, not of the people, but of the emperor, as Dion informs us. Thus Thrace, at length made a province of, in the reign of Vespasian, likewise Dacia and Arabia under Trajan, increased the number of Cæsarean provinces. Hence it is that on the coins of those provinces so acquired, we read the name not of the proconsul or of any other popular magistrate, but of the legates of the emperor.—On this point Spanheim, in his notes on the *Cæsars of Julian*, makes the following remarks on those medals of Trajan, which display *Dacia*, under various types, as a *subjugated nation* :—" We see these coins (says this erudite and observant author) with inscriptions not only of VICT. DAC. and of DACIA CAPTA, but even of DACIA AVGVSTI PROVINCIA.; that is to say, according to the custom alluded to by Dion that *nations* or *conquered provinces*, subsequently to the division made by Augustus, fell no longer within the jurisdiction of the Roman people, but devolved to that of the Emperor, and became *his* provinces, and were therefore governed by his Lieutenants, and by Prætors or Proconsuls, except in those changes which the Emperors themselves made on the subject from time to time."—Spanheim then cites the well-known medal of Trajan, commemorative of his capture of Dacia; and also the less common, but not less interesting coin of the same emperor, which bears the legend of *Dacia Augusti Provincia*—that province being represented by a Dacian seated on a rock, with

two children near him, and with a Roman ensign in his left hand. [See *Dacia*.]—The same numismatist refers to other medals of Trajan, as marking the fact that this emperor, after having conquered ARABIA, had made a

Roman province of it, particularly that inscribed ARABIA AVGVST. PROVINCIA ; also ARABIA ADQVIS. *Arabia Adquisita*, or ARABIA CAPTA.—See those inscriptions.

PROVOCO, title of the Porcian Law *(Lex Porcia)*, on the denarius of that family, in which the prætor is represented standing with his hand extended towards a citizen clothed in the toga: behind the prætor stands a lictor, holding in his right hand a rod.—See *Porcia* family.

PR. P.   *Pro Prætore.*—PRO PR. PR. A. *Pro Prætore Provinciæ Achaiæ*.

PR. Q.   *Pro Quæstore.*—M. MINAT. SABIN. PR. Q.   On a denarius of the *Minatia* family.

PR. S. P. or PAL.   *Provinciæ Syriæ Palestinæ*. Of the province of Syria in Palestine.

PRVDENTIA AVG.——Banduri, citing Mediobarbus, gives this epigraph as inscribed on the reverse of a gold coin of *Aureolus*, in which a female figure stands holding a short wand in her right hand, and resting her left arm on a column.

The word *Prudentia* is in this instance obviously used instead of *Providentia*, one of whose well-known types is here represented.—Millin indeed says that "Prudence is the same allegorical divinity as Providence, and that there are medals on which she is figured." But as Eckhel, Mionnet, and Akerman are all silent on the subject, it is probable they consider the word misread or blundered for *Providentia*.

P. R. VOT.   *Populi Romani Vota.*—In a shield, held by two victories, round which VICTORIAE LAETAE. PRIN. PERP. on a gold medal of Constantine the Great.

PR. VRB.   *Præfectus Urbi*, or *Prætor Urbanus.*—Præfect of the city, or rather Prætor of the city.

P. S.   *Percussa* moneta *Sisciæ.*—Money struck at Sicia (a town of Croatia now Sisseg) on the exergue of a coin of Licinius sen.

Pseudomoneta.—This term is applied to such numismatic irregularities as the *Contorniati*, the *Spintriæ, Tesseræ*, &c.

P. T.   *Percussa Treveris.*—Money struck at Treves.

Ptolomæus IV. Philopator.—One of the many Egyptian kings who rejoiced in the regal patronymic of Ptolomæus, died in the year of Rome 550, having appointed by his will that the Roman people should be tutor to his infant son. This remarkable fact, which history, by the pens of Valerius Maximus, and Justinus, affirms and explains, forms the subject of typical allusion, on a rare denarius of the *Æmilia* family, described by Eckhel as follows, from one in the Imperial cabinet at Vienna:—

ALEXANDREA.—The turreted head of a female Genius.

M. LEPIDVS. PONT. MAX. TVTOR. REG. S. C.— Two figures, in the Roman toga, standing ; one placing a crown on the head of another. Here then we have Lepidus in the consular robe, crowning with the regal diadem the young Ptolemy (V. Epiphanes), whom the king, his father, had left under the tutelage of the Roman

people. And on the other side is seen, under the image of a woman crowned with towers, the city of Alexandria, capital of the kingdom, where the ceremony took place.(See *Aemilia* family in this Dictionary.)—The year in which an event so strikingly illustrative of the power and influence of republican Rome occurred is not exactly known. But it appears that the Marcus Æmilius Lepidus, to whom the office of *Tutor Regis* was entrusted by the senate, commenced his *first* consulate A.V.C. 567, was elevated to the supreme pontificate V.C. 574, and served his *second* consulate V.C. 578.

Ptolemais Galilaeæ, a town on the Phœnicean coast, originally called Ace, from Hercules, now St. John of *Acre*. It took its Greek name from one of the Ptolemies, Kings of Egypt, and was the only city of that name converted by the Romans into a colony—an event which occurred under Claudius. Except, however, the bare title of colony, it does not appear that any right or privilege was conferred upon the place. For example, if Ulpian is to be relied upon, Ptolemais was never admitted to a participation in the *Jus Italicum*, and was invested with nothing but the name of a colony *(nihil præter nomen coloniæ habet)*. Yet it does not seem probable, that an emperor would send citizens and veterans to colonize a distant territory, without investing them with some special liberties and immunities, to enjoy in their establishment there. At any rate we know that Ptolemais had its series of colonial-imperial coins, from Claudius to Saloninus, including also those of Nero, Trajan, Hadrian, Severus, Caracalla, Alexander Severus, Philip senior, Valerianus, and Otacilia Severa.

The following are the chief *types* found on coins of this colony :—

Altar and Serpents.—On a fine and rare first brass of Valerianus, bearing the legend COLONIA PTOLEMAIDENS*is*, the type is a lighted altar, from underneath the base of which, on each side, rises a serpent. On the left is a caduceus.

[This appears to be the memorial of a sacrifice offered by the people of Ptolemais for a happy issue to the war with Persia, commenced by Valerian about the time when the medal was struck. We see in it the altar on which sacred rites, according to the usages of paganism, were performed to the gods on this account. The serpents are an augury of victories, as the *caduceus* is a symbol of felicity. But the auspices, which thus promised triumphs over the barbarians, proved fatally deceitful ; for the emperor was defeated, made prisoner and, after the most ignominiously cruel treatment, put to death by Sapor, King of the Persians.]

Bust of a Bearded Man.—On a second brass of Sept. Severus, struck at Ptolemais, is the head of a man with long beard flowing in thick curls, and as if adorned with several horns ; before whom is a cornucopiæ.

[Vaillant regards this as intended to personify the Nile. He observes that the people of Ptolemais had borrowed the worship of that celebrated stream as well as the worship of Serapis, from Egypt—the Nile being, according to Parmenides, the Jupiter of the Egyptians. The images of rivers were exhibited on ancient coins, with beards unshorn and with dishevelled hair, as in the instance of the Nile itself on Egyptian medals. Horns were appended to the heads of these effigies, as denoting the different mouths through which a river debouched into the sea: accordingly Virgil calls the Rhine *bicornis*. But the Nile has several horns assigned to it, because it was said to branch into seven arms, as Virgil himself sings:—

Et septem gemini turbant trepida ostia Nili.
[*Æn.* vi., l. 800.]

The cornucopiæ shadows forth the fertility, and the abundance of all fruits, of the earth.]

Colonist and Military Ensigns.—On second and third brass of this colony, dedicated, in the first instance, to Claudius its founder, and afterwards in succession to Nero and to Hadrian, the type of *colonus boves agens*, is accompanied with four or five military standards placed behind the oxen.—The legend is COL. PTOL. or PTOLEM. *Colonia Ptolemais.*—On a very rare and fine large brass of Philip senior, with the legend COL. PTOL*emais*, there are the colonist and oxen, but not the military ensigns.

[The colonist, or more properly the pontiff guiding a plough team of oxen, refers to the origin and antiquity of the settlement. The military ensigns are introduced because not only citizens from Rome, but veterans from a legion, were sent to Ptolemais by Claudius.]

It is doubtful whether this medal of Ptolemais has been correctly copied as having *five* military ensigns. Pellerin has given two coins of this colony, one with the head of Claudius, and the other with the head of Nero.—On the reverse of each of these, behind the colonist at plough, appear *four* military standards. And on the square of each of these standards are seen certain numbers, not visible on the medals published by Vaillant. These numerals shew the Legions whence were drafted the veteran soldiers who were sent to *Ptolemais* to form that colony. It seems that it is the vIth, IXth, xIth, and xIIth Legions which are marked thereon. Nevertheless, adds Pellerin, it is very possible that the last two numbers were only x. and xI., the unit which apparently terminates both those numbers being, perhaps, only the lateral line of the squares in which they are enclosed.—[*Recueil*, tom. ii. p. xi. and 2, which see for an explanation of the *legends* of these coins.]

Cybele.—On a first brass of Valerianus, struck at Ptolemais, the type of the reverse is Cybele, who, seated between two lions which are at her feet, holds in her right hand something which resembles an infant in swaddling clothes. Behind the chair of the goddess is a caduceus winged.—See Pellerin, *Mélange*, i. pl. xxii. No. 8, p. 329.

Diana Venatrix.—On a rare second brass dedicated to Valerian, the people of this colony have stamped the image of the hunter-goddess within a temple of two columns, round which are the signs of the Zodiac.

[This is one of the coins struck by the city of Ptolemais under Valerian, whilst he was engaged in the Persian war.—By the temple and its idol, it shews that Diana was adored in quality of *Venatrix* by the people of this colony.—The twelve signs of the Zodiac, referring to astronomy, seems to have been introduced into this type in memory of a science in which their (Phœnician) ancestors were, according to Strabo and Pliny, pre-eminently skilled.]

Emperor on Horseback, with right hand elevated, and holding the reins in his left, on a second brass of Caracalla, with legend COLONIA PTOLEMAIS.

[This appears intended to record the arrival of the above named Emperor at Ptolemais; for he is represented as an equestrian, and in the garb of a pacificator, just as coins of Roman die exhibit the entry of Emperors into Rome itself. This also agrees with what Herodianus relates of Caracalla's advent and sojourn in Syria: when on his military expedition against Armenia and Parthia, he visited Antioch, and most probably Ptolemais, which is situated between the former place and Syria.]

Emperor on Horseback.—An exactly similar type and legend (to that of Caracalla's) appears on a second brass, bearing on its obverse the portrait and titles of Alexander Severus.

[Struck in congratulation to that Emperor on his having defeated and dispersed the invading armies of Persia, and (as Lampridius testifies) vanquished their powerful King, Artaxerxes. The equestrian figure is viewed by Vaillant as relating, not to Alexander Severus, but rather to a statue raised at Ptolemais to Caracalla's honour (and represented on the preceding coin). For Alexander, according to Herodianus, took the name of Severus from reverence for his ancestor Septimius Severus, and called himself the son of Caracalla, professing to have won his many trophies of success over the barbarians, under the auspices and tutelage of those two Emperors].

Fortune, standing, clothed in the stola, with, as usual, the rudder and cornucopiæ, on a small brass of Hadrian.

[The many coins of this colony, dedicated to Hadrian, afford an indication that some singular benefit had been conferred by that munificent Emperor on Ptolemais. Fortune forms the type of the reverse, as a goddess worshipped by the inhabitants of the city, and also as a favourite object of Hadrian's veneration.]

On an elegant second brass, inscribed to Caracalla, stands Fortune as designated by her accustomed attributes, and with the *calathus* on her head. Behind, is a small figure of Victory, placed on a cippus or column, extending a crown over the head of the Goddess.—There is a similar type of Fortune crowned by Victory, placed on a cippus, on a second brass of Valerianus, with the sole addition of a winged caduceus in the field of the coin.—See Pellerin, *Mélange*, i. pl. xxii., No. 8, p. 332.

[Vaillant says that the *Victoriola* standing on a short column frequently appears on colonial coins of Phœnicia, in allusion to the victories gained by the ancient and enterprising people of that country, and to the colonies which they established far and wide]

Human Foot.—Pellerin furnishes us with the engraving of a singular coin dedicated by the city of Ptolemais to Salonina, wife of Gallienus (to whom Vaillant assigns no medals of this colony). It bears on its reverse a human foot with part of the leg [most probably an *ex voto* on account of some cure supposed to be miraculously effected]. Above it is a thunderbolt, and by its left side a caduceus.—[See also *Recueil—Lettres Addition.* t. ix. p. 36.]

Hercules and the Emperor.—On a first brass of this colony inscribed to Otacilia, wife of Philip senior, given in Pellerin (*Mélange* i. pl. xxi. No. 5, p. 317), Hercules joins his right hand to that of the Emperor, both standing opposite each other. Between them is an altar, and above them a caduceus. Legend, COL. PTOL.

Neptune and Proserpine.—Pellerin, in supplying an omission of Vaillant, who has given no medals of Otacilia, as struck by this colony, has noted one which exhibits on one side the head of that Empress, and on the other Neptune [contrary to the well-known myth which makes Pluto the ravisher of Ceres' daughter] driving a quadriga, in which he is carrying away Proserpine. Above are horses, and Mercury flying with a caduceus in his right hand.

Serapis.—A second and third brass of Sept. Severus and of Caracalla, bearing the legend of COL*onia* PTOL*emais*, the head of Serapis appears with the *Modius*.

[The image of this divinity occurs on a great many coins of Phœnicia and Palestine, those countries having respectively adopted his worship from Egypt, where he was held in the highest adoration.—See *Serapis.*

Thunderbolt.—This type presents itself on second brass of Ptolemais, inscribed to S. Severus.

[The thunderbolt (see the word *Fulmen*) is the mark of Providence and the symbol of empire; but on this coin its appearance seemingly refers to some passage in the history of the city. Perhaps (says Vaillant) as the *Ptolemaidenses* were in the habit of admitting the deities of their Egyptian neighbours among their own objects of worship, so also is there room for conjecture that the Ceraunian Jove of the Seleucensians was adored at Ptolemais under the symbol of a *fulmen*, or thunderbolt. They afterwards called Jupiter by the surname of *Fulminator*, and dedicated a temple to him under that title.]

Woman and River God.—On second brass of this colony, dedicated to Trajan and to Hadrian, a woman, turret crowned, is seated on a rock, with corn-ears in her right hand. At her feet a male figure appears, emerging from water with outspread hands.

[The seated female is the *Genius urbis*, crowned with towers, as Ptolemais was surrounded with strong walls; she sits on rocks, as the city was on every side encompassed by lofty mountains; she carries corn-ears, as the colony was situated in a fertile and well cultivated plain; the foot treads on the shoulder of a river god, being the personification of the Pagida or Beleus, which flowed past Ptolemais, as Josephus states, at the distance of two stadia.]

On second and small brass of Julia Domna, there is a similar figure of a woman, sometimes with, sometimes without, the male figure.

Woman with Turreted Head, clothed in the stola, holding a rudder in the right hand, and a cornucopia in the left hand. She stands beside a column, on which are placed the infants Romulus and Remus, suckled by the wolf.

[The colony of Ptolemais, deriving its foundation from Claudius, has, to indicate that origin, placed on its coinage the graphic illustration of Rome's *pet* legend, in like manner as all Roman colonies were accustomed to adorn their marketplaces with the same group in statuary.]

PVB.—PUBL. *Publica.*

PUBLICA.—See AEQVITAS PUBLICA.—FIDES PVBLICA, &c.

Pudicitia.—Modesty was worshipped at Rome as a goddess, especially by females. She bore the surnames of *Patricia* and *Plebeia*. The temple of the latter was erected by Virginia, the daughter of Aulus, who had married a plebeian, and to whom the Patricians, in consequence, had refused entry into the temple of *Pudicitia patricia*. The image of this divinity is rarely found on coins of emperors, but it is frequently seen figured (not *always* appropriately) on those of the *Augustæ*, viz., Plotina, Sabina, Lucilla, Faustina junior, Crispina, Julia Mæsa, Mamæa, Otacilia, Etruscilla, Salonina, &c., under the traits of a woman, in a matronly gown and veiled; or, on the point of veiling herself, holding in one hand the *hasta pura;* she is sometimes standing, as in Lucilla; but oftener seated, as in Julia Mæsa and Herennia Etruscilla.

PVDIC. P. M. TR. P. COS. III.—A woman, veiled, stands with her hands concealed within her robe.

This dedicatory legend appears on a silver coin of Hadrian, who, as Eckhel observes, was by turns both "*pudicus et impudicus.*"—With this special point for our remembrance, that although his modesty (*pudicitia*) could on certain occasions be grievously offended at the vices and indecencies of others, yet it nevertheless easily reconciled itself to his own more numerous and infinitely more odious criminalities. But as coins of contemporaneous date record the virtues only of princes, it remains for history, after their death, to make mention of their vices. Thus also the medals of Hadrian boast of his clemency; but history, not to be corrupted, calls to mind the violent deaths of illustrious men whom he caused to be sacrificed to his hatred and revenge.

PVDICITIA.—This legend appears, with a variety of types, in every metal and form, on coins of Faustina the younger, wife of M. Aurelius, and of Lucilla, wife of L. Verus.—Whether the *modesty* of these two princesses is boasted of on these medals according to the custom of court flattery? or whether, after the manner in which we hold up princes, as wishing to be what they ought to be? is a question we presume not to decide.—We have seen that even the coins of Hadrian make a vaunt of his *pudicitia*, a claim to commendation which no one less than he had established for himself.

PVDICITIA AVG*ustæ.*—This form of legend by which the attributes of deified modesty are more closely identified with the person of the Empress than they are in the previously cited instances, appears with the usual type of a veiled woman, on coins of Orbiana, Tranquillina, Magnia Urbica. And also, by an inappropriate ostentation, if not by a mistake of the moneyers, the same reverse is found on medals of Gordianus III., Trajanus Decius, Hostilianus, Volusianus.

Puellæ, or *Pueruli.*—Infants of both sexes in the arms of females, or standing by the side of women, appear on many coins of the Imperial series, especially of the Trajan and Antonine families.—See *Children* or *Infants.*

Puellæ Alimentariæ.—This term will be, perhaps, most significantly rendered by the English phrase "Charity Girls," the objects of an institution by Antoninus Pius, in honour of his wife Faustina senior, and called *Faustinianæ,* after that Empress. Two of these *Puellæ Alimentariæ* are seen standing before the Emperor on a gold medal of Trajan, which thus commemorates the signal liberality of that great prince in constituting and assigning throughout Italy permanent funds for the maintainance and education of destitute children, both girls and boys.

PVELLAE FAVSTINIANAE.——Reference has already been made to these benevolent institutions, founded by the Emperor Trajan, who took under his protection and support such children as were orphans, or had been deserted. Antoninus Pius followed this excellent example, and in honour of his wife, Faustina senior, caused a great number of poor girls and young women to be brought up, at the expense of the state. The memory of this institution, which reflects equal honour on the Emperor and on the Empress, is preserved on medals in gold and silver.—The obverse is inscribed DIVA AVG FAVSTINA, accompanying the head of Faustina. On the reverse, Antoninus is represented sitting on an estrade, in the attitude of extending his arms to a child whom one of the people presents to him. Faustina had promised to many distressed persons that she would take care of their children's education and future interests: she had even given these unfortunate infants her own name, as a further assurance of her generous intentions in their behalf, as we perceive by the legend of *Puellæ* Faustinianæ. It seems evident, however, that this institution was not carried into effect until after her death, as well from the word DIVA, which announces that Faustina had already received the honours of the Apotheosis—as from that passage in Julius Capitolinus, which says " Antoninus appropriated a fund for the nurture of a number of girls whom he called *Faustinianæ*, in honour of Faustina."—It is also said that Marcus Aurelius formed a similar establishment in compliment to his wife, the younger Faustina.

To a similar institution for the children of citizens, who (according to Pliny the younger) were nourished and provided for, at the public cost, under Antoninus Pius, a bronze medallion is considered to refer, on which stands a female figure, holding a child and a globe, and having at her feet two children, with the inscription PIETATI. AVG. COS. IIII.—See PIETATI.

Puer or *Puella,* (see *Infant).*—Children at the breast, or in the arms, or at the feet of their mother are seen on various coins of the Imperial series—such as of Lucilla, Julia Domna, Faustina, Otacilia, Urbica; with epigraphs of FECVNDITAS AVG. and IVNONI LVCINAE. A naked boy sits on a globe, between seven stars (the *Triones)* on a denarius of Domitia, wife of Domitian, .in memory of a son they had lost. See DIVVS CAES. IMP. DOMITIAN. A boy sitting on a goat, with the epigraph AETERNITAS; and another seated on the same animal, with legend of IOVI CRESCENTI, appear on coins of Gallienus, Saloninus, and Valerianus jun.—See *Fecunditas, Juno Lucina, Æternitas Imperii.*

Puer alatus.—A winged boy (see Cupido) appears in the area of a coin of the *Julia* family; and is seated on a goat in a denarius of the same family.—See *Julia.*

Puer.—A boy as the sign of *Felicitas,* or of Succession, appears on medals of the Faustinas, Lucilla, Crispina, Domna, Mæsa, Aquilia, Mamæa, Orbiana, Etruscilla, and other *Augustæ.*—The same figure is an index of Hilaritas, on coins of Hadrian, Caracalla, Elagabalus, Tetricus.

Pueri quatuor.—Four boys, with the attributes of the seasons of the year, on first brass of Commodus, Caracalla, and other Emperors; and on a small brass of Carausius.——See FELICIA TEMPORVM.

Pugiones.—The figure of two daggers, or poignards, with the *pileus* or cap of liberty, appear on coins of Brutus.—See EID. MAR.

Pugna.—The combat of a lion with a stag, on a silver coin of the *Durmia* family, is regarded as allusive to some celebration of the secular games *(ludi sæculares).*

Pulcheria (Aelia), daughter of the Emperor Arcadius, sister of Theodosius the second, and the wife of Marcianus, was born at Constantinople (A.D. 399). .This princess was associated in the imperial government by her brother, from whom she received the rank and title of *Augusta* (A.D. 414). Pulcheria's historical character is that of a woman, as virtuous as she was beautiful; no less distinguished for charity and beneficence than for sweetness of temper and affability of manners. That her piety, however, partook of the ascetic taint of the age in which she lived, is strongly indicated by the unconjugal condition on·which, after the death of Theodosius (A.D. 450), she gave her hand in marriage and a seat on the throne of empire to Marcianus—viz., that he should not claim his rights as a husband, but leave her to live chaste. Accordingly she re- mained in a state of perpetual virginity, and died in "the odour of sanctity" (A.D. 453). There are silver and gold coins of Pulcheria extant, but they are of extreme rarity. Bimard and Beauvais both assert the non-existence of any brass medals of this empress, but Tanini gives two examples of third brass coinage to her reign, which Mionnet recognises as genuine, and values at twenty francs each.—Her style is ALE. PVLCHERIA. AVG.

Pulli.—Two chickens are seen in the act of feeding, at the bottom of a tripod, on a silver coin of Lepidus. A cockerel appears among the insignia of the augural office on a denarius of Mark Antony.—See AVGVR.

Punic (or Carthaginian) characters.—We find these on the reverse of a silver coin of Juba the younger, King of Mauretania, whose por- trait, and title in *Latin*, is engraved on the obverse.—See IVBA REX.

Puncta.—For points on Roman Coins, espe- cially Consular, see *Globulus.*

PUPIENUS *(Marcus Clodius),* with the sur- name of *Maximus,* born about the year of Christ 164, of humble parentage, attained, through the various grades of military rank and civil service, to the highest honours and powers of the state. For his exploits in the field the senate received him into their body; made prætor and twice elected consul, he afterwards governed in succes- sion the provinces of Bithynia and Gaul with great credit. Victorious over the Sarmatians and the Germans, he was rewarded with the Prefecture of Rome, and discharged that respon- sible office with great talent and prudence. At length he was elected Emperor, in association with Balbinus, about the year 237, and con- tributed by his courage, activity, and generalship mainly to the deliverance of the empire from the insupportable tyranny of Maximinus. On the death of that ferocious Thracian and his son, the· army acknowledged Pupienus as *Augustus,* con- jointly with Balbinus, who had remained at Rome. This virtuous prince was lofty in statue, grave in demeanour, and venerable in aspect. Of a melancholy turn of character, he was strict, yet humane; firm and decisive, without rudeness or irascibility. Irreproachable in morals, the friend of his country and obedient to her laws, he rendered impartial justice to all, and main- tained discipline amongst the soldiery. After enjoying for a brief space, with his colleague, the state of peace which he had procured for the empire, Pupienus was preparing to carry the Roman arms into Persia, when he and Balbinus were suddenly dragged from the imperial palace by the Prætorian guards, and massacred in the streets of Rome, on the 15th day of July, A.D. 238, in his 74th year, after having reigned three months and a few days.

On his coins, which are rare in silver and brass, and of great rarity in gold, Pupienus is

styled IMP. CLOD. PVPIENVS AVG.—IMP

CAES. M. CLOD. PVPIENVS. AVG.—IMP. CAES. PVPIEN. MAXIMVS. AVG. On reverses sometimes *Pater Patriæ* and PATRES SENATVS. The silver is of two sizes, the larger of which exhibits the head of this emperor with the radiated crown. The second brass are very rare, and so are such of the first brass as have the title of *Maximus* after Pupienus.

Puppis.—The poop or hinder part of a ship; the image of which does not appear on Roman coins so frequently as the *prora,* or prow. It was on the *puppis* or stern of ancient vessels, as in those of our own day, that the pilot or helms- man *(Gubernator)* took his station, and where the commander had his post. This part of the ship was held inviolably sacred; it was also in the larger gallies formed into a kind of temple, ornamented with crowns, fillets, and other religious decorations in honour of the gods.—On a medal of Hadrian, the Emperor is seated on the poop of the prætorian galley, and Pallas on the prow.

PUTEAL.—In the *comitium,* or place of popular assembly, at Rome, there is said to have been a spot, on which a statue of Accius Nævius (of Tarquinius Priscus's time) was placed, because there the celebrated augur was said to have severed, or caused the above-named king to sever, the whetstone with a razor. Under this statue there was (according to Dionysius Halicarnassus) a subterranean cavity, called *puteus* (a well or pit), in which beneath an altar, the whetstone of Accius was deposited; over the well a cover was placed, whence it derived its name of *Puteal.* But when the place fell into decay, *Scribonius Libo,* by order of the senate, caused it to be.restored, which led to its being called PUTEAL SCRIBONII, as certain denarii show.—According to Beger's opinion, this covering to the well was called LIBO, because that person (see *Scribonia* family) lived in the vicinity, or because it was erected or repaired at his expense. Thus Horace would seem to infer (lib. 1. ep. xix. l. 8.)

Forum Putealque Libonis.

It was, however, not the tribunal itself, but only in the neighbourhood of the tribunal.— One of the numerous opinions subsisting, as well among ancient authors as among modern commentators, respecting this place, so often alluded to in Roman history, is this, that on some occasion or other, lightning had fallen upon it, and that in consequence a covered well was con- structed there, under authority, by the functionary whose name it bears. Be this as it may, it seems agreed on all hands that the *Puteal of Libo* was much frequented, as a sort of exchange, by the commercial and banking classes of Rome. —See *Scribonia.*

Spanheim (*Pr.* ii., p. 189) contends that the *Puteal Libonis* or *Scribonii* ought not to be confounded with the one constructed in the *comitium*, to which Cicero refers.

The object represented on medals of the *Aemilia* and *Scribonia* families looks more like an altar adorned with sculptured flowers than the tribunal or seat of a prætor. But the whole matter remains involved in obscurity, and is too much associated with fabulous history, and too little with events of any importance, to repay or to deserve the learned researches and conjectures which have been bestowed on it.

Q.

This letter (the sixteenth of the Latin alphabet) by itself signifies *Quæstor,* or *Quinarius,* or *Quintus,* or *Quinquennalis,* or *Quod,* because Q. is sometimes put for C. on early denarii, as QVM. for CVM. in the *Antestia* family.

Q. or QV.　*Quinquennalis.*—Duumvir or Quatuorvir Quinquennalis, a magistrate peculiar to some Roman colonies, so called because the term of his government was limited to five years. Two or four of these magistrates were elected according to the size of the colonial city.—*Quinquennalis* was also the name of the Roman censors, who exercised their office for five years.

Q. C.　*Quintus Cassius.*—Name of a man.

Q. C. M. P. I.　*Quintus Cæcilius Metellus Pius Imperator.*—See his initials among the denarii of the Cæcilia family.—These are the prenomen, surname, and qualities of *Quintus Metellus Scipio,* who served as Consul v.c. 702, and was a contemporary of Pompey the Great. He was the natural son of P. Cornelius Scipio Nasica, but adopted by Q. Metellus Pius Pontifex Maximus.

Q. DES.　*Quæstor Designatus.*—The Quæstor Elect.

Q. HER. ETR. MES. DEC. NOB. C. *Quintus Herennius Etruscus Messius Decius Nobilis Cæsar.*

Q. M.　*Quintus Marcius.*—Prænomen and name.

Q. O. C. F. or FAB.　*Quinto Ogulnio* (et) *Caio Fabio.*—Prenomen and name respectively of two men.

Q. P.　*Quæstor Prætoris,* or *Prætorius,* or *Prætorianorum.*—Quæstor of the Prætor, or of the Prætorians.

Q. PAPIR. CAR. Q. TER. MON.　*Quinto Papirio Carbone* (et) *Quinto Terentio Montano.*

Q. PR.　*Quæstor Provincialis.*—The Quæstor of the Province.

Q. PRO. C. or COS.　*Quæstor Proconsulis.*— The Proconsul's Quæstor.

QQ.　*Quinquennales.*—QQ. II.　*Quinquennales Iterum.*—Quinquenals for the second time.

QVAD.　*Quadrans.*—The fourth part of a Roman *As,* that is to say three *unciæ.*—See *As.*

QVAD.　*Quadratus.*—Name of a man.

Quadi —A nation or tribe formerly inhabiting that part of Europe now called Bohemia ; as the *Marcomanni* occupied the modern Moravia, and the country bordering upon Austria. The *Quadi* accepted kings at the hands of the Roman Emperors, and frequent mention is made of them in the annals of the reign of Marcus Aurelius.

QVADIS.—See REX QVADIS DATVS.

QVADORVM TRIVMPHVS.—See *Triumphus.*

QVADRAGENSVM *(sic)* REMISSA. S. C. On second brass of Galba, or on others.

QVADRAGENS. REMISSAE. S. C. (first and second brass), or QVADRAGENSVMA REMISSA., or XXXX REMISSAE., with types of a triumphal arch.—These legends refer to the remission made by the Emperor above named, either of a tax called the fortieth, or of the fortieth part of certain imposts.

Eckhel's remarks on this subject are in substance as follows :—That Galba was unseasonably parsimonious is the concurrent affirmation of all historians—that there was, however an occasion in which he showed some little liberality of disposition, and doubtless immediately on his accession to the empire for the sake of conciliating public favour, is proved by these medals, which proclaim a benefit conceded on his part to the people, amounting to the remission, or at least the reduction of a tax *(quadragesimæ remissæ).* To this may be added the testimony given by implication in that passage of Suetonius, stating that Vespasian reinforced the fiscal burthen remitted under Galba *(omissa sub Galba vectigalia revocasse).*"—What was the nature of the *quadragesima,* and whether the abolition of this tax was the act of Galba—for there are some who, from what Tacitus has written, assign this boon to Nero—are points which the learned do not seem to have ascertained, although it would appear that the law alluded to as having been repealed in this instance was one by which the fortieth part of the property of individuals was required to be brought into the public treasury.

Quadrans.—Three globules are the certain token of the *Quadrans,* or of the *as* divided into four parts, and the head of Hercules is the equally sure type.

Quadrans—The brass coin so called had its name from a mark of three globules, originally denoting three *uncia,* whilst the *as* weighed a pound *(libra),* but in the second Punic war it was reduced to one *uncia.*

Quadrantis nota.—The mark of the *quadrans,* namely, three globules struck on each side of the coin, and indicating its price, is to be seen on coins of many Roman families. On the obverse of this money appears either the head of Hercules, covered with the spoils of the lion, as in Aburia and Acilia, &c. ; or the head of Mercury, as in Fabrinia, or the head of Rome helmeted, as in the Apuleia and other families ; on the reverse of these early brass coins of Rome, the representation of a ship is to be observed, whence their appellation of *numi ratiti.*—See *As.*

Quadriga.—A chariot drawn by four horses, by four elephants, or indeed by four animals of any other kind. The quadriga on coins does not always signify a triumph, for it was also employed in the consular procession, and in the conveyance of him who was victor at the public games. In like manner it was used at the funeral ceremony of an Emperor's consecration. (Froëlich, *Num. Reg.* p. 79, 80.)—The right of using *quadrigæ* in the *processus consularis*, or at the assuming of the tribunitian power, was bestowed by the senate.—See *Car.*

Quadriga.—On a medal of M. Aurelius, in memory of Faustina jun., is a quadriga of elephants drawing a thensa, with a statue of the deceased empress; and on a coin of Constantine the Great, who, veiled, is carried upwards in a quadriga, a hand from above being extended to receive him. We see a *quadriga* placed on the summit of the funeral pile *(rogus)* on the CONSECRATION medals of M. Aurelius, Sept. Severus, and Constantius Chlorus.—See CONSECRATIO.

The *Quadrigæ* (and the same remark applies to the *Bigæ* and *Trigæ)*, which so frequently occur on coins of Roman families, do not relate to the honours of the triumph, as we learn from an historical dissertation published by the French Academy of Inscriptions.—On some coins, both consular and imperial, we see a quadriga, without a driver, and without any figure standing or sitting in it, but only a flower, or some ornamental object, as in Aquilia, and coins of Augustus, and in Titus. On others a legionary eagle appears in the quadriga, as on a coin of Augustus.

Quadrigæ of horses and elephants are seen placed on the summit of triumphal arches in coins of Julius, Augustus, Tiberius, Nero, Galba, Domitian, Trajan.—A car with four horses, on which is a species of *cone*, or stone, with four small *vexillæ*, or standards, appears on gold and silver of Elagabalus, with the epigraph of SANCT. DEO SOLI ELAGABAL. *(See the Inscription)*—A quadriga of centaurs, carrying Hercules, appears on a medallion of M. Aurelius.—See TEMPORVM FELICITAS.

Quadrigæ, in which the Emperor himself is the charioteer, is a type of very frequent occurrence, and extends through the Imperial series from Julius Cæsar, Augustus, Tiberius, Caligula, Vespasian, Domitian, and so on down to Placidius Valentinianus.—Some Roman Emperors are represented on coins standing in quadrigæ, who took no triumphal honours; and in these cases we must suppose the medals to refer to their having participated in the pompous solemnity of the consular procession, as those coins indicate, on which the imperial functionary *waggons his own team of four*, with the inscription FEL. PROCES.

Quadrigæ, in which the Emperor is crowned by Victory, whilst a prætorian soldier leads the horses, and another or more prætorians follow the car, appears on coins of Gordianus Pius, Alex. Severus, Probus.

Quadrigæ, in which are the figures of *two* Emperors, occur on coins of Titus, M. Aurelius and L. Verus; of M. Aurelius and Commodus; the two Philips, Treb. Gallus and Volusianus; Carus and Numerianus; Diocletian and Val. Maximian. In all these the Emperors are crowned by standing or flying Victories, and preceded and followed by soldiers bearing trophies. On a medal of Valerianus senior, with legend of FELICITAS TEMPORVM, the Emperor and his two sons appear in a quadriga—and there is a medallion selected by Vaillant from the collection of *De Camps* (p. 109), wherein Victory crowns Valerian, standing between his two sons—all in the same quadriga, the four horses of which are led by two soldiers, one on each side.

Jupiter standing in a *quadriga* is the distinguishing mark of those quinarii and *denarii* called *quadrigati* (that is to say having the stamp of a chariot on them), which belong to the class of family coins.—In Vaillant's selection from the *De Camps* cabinet (p. 31), we see a bronze medallion of M. Aurelius, in which Jupiter, driving furiously in a quadriga, shakes his thunderbolt at the King of the Quadi, who is falling prostrate on the ground at the horses' feet.

Mars, Neptune, Pallas, Pluto, Sol, and other deities of pagan worship appear on a variety of coins, and the favourite Genius of *Victory* guides the four horses of the Roman car, on numerous *denarii* both consular and imperial.

Quadrigæ Consulares.—These in memory of the pomp and circumstance attendant on the consular procession, appear on coins of M. Aurelius and of Alexander Severus, and also on denarii of the *Cæcilia* family; in these the consul holds the ivory sceptre in his right and reins of the horses in his left hand, and in some instances is crowned by a Victory behind. Similar memorials of *proconsular* and of *proprætorian* honours were recorded by the mint of Republican Rome.

Quadrigæ Triumphales.—Amongst the chariots with four horses represented on consular medals, are those which are regarded as *triumphal,* and in which the triumpher stands crowned with laurel, and holding the *scipio eburneus.* In these they appear going at a slow pace as if in a state procession. A figure of Victory, moreover, standing in a quadriga with a palm branch, and a crown above, also designates the occasion of a triumph, whilst the head and name of Rome, on the obverse of the medal serves as a fit symbol of the subject.—Triumphal *quadrigæ* were drawn not only by horses, but also by elephants, and indeed sometimes their drivers or conductors were boys, an example of which was for the first time given in the case of L. Metellus, who triumphed over the Carthaginians in the first Punic war. [Baudelot, quoted by Rasche.]—On a silver coin of Augustus (CAES. IMP.) a figure stands in a triumphal quadriga, holding a laurel crown in the right hand.—Vaillant (ii. p. 29) states it to have been struck, on the occasion of the triple triumph, which

Augustus enjoyed in the year 725, for the victory gained, in the preceding year, over Mark Antony; from which circumstance he wore a crown of laurel as the conqueror of all his foes.

Quadrigæ Elephantorum.—These are rarely represented on the coins of Roman families; but on coins of the Imperial series their occurrence is not unfrequent. The honour of this species of quadriga is found bestowed on Augustus, Tiberius, Caligula, Vespasian, Titus, Antoninus Pius, M. Aurelius, L. Verus, after their deaths, as the words DIVO and CONSECRATIO inscribed on such coins of those emperors shew.—Nero and his mother Agrippina, are represented sitting in a car drawn by four elephants. Diocletian and Val. Maximian appear on a medallion in Banduri, standing in a magnificent triumphal chariot drawn by four elephants, on whose shoulders sit as many drivers. One of the Emperors carries a trophy, and behind them hovers a Victory.

Quadrigatus, an early Roman coin, so called from *quadrigæ.*—"The marks of silver money were *bigæ* and *quadrigæ*, and hence their appellations (says Pliny) of *bigati* and *quadrigati.* That piece of money which is now (he adds) called *Victoriatus*, was struck under the *Lex Clodia.* It was also stamped with the figure of Victory, and thence derived its name.—In the course of time, however, the types of *denarii* varied. For each individual magistrate, at his own will and pleasure, placed on the coin which he was officially privileged to have struck, that particular god or goddess, who was the favourite object of his worship, or whom for any other reason he might choose in that manner to honour. Thus for example C. Licinius Macer represented Pallas wearing a helmet, in a car drawn by four horses at full speed. In like manner C. Aburius stamped his denarii with the figure of Mars, as his brother M. Aburius did that of the Sun.

Quadrussis, a coin of the Romans, of the weight and value of four *asses*, with the figure of an ox on each side.

Quæstores.—The quæstors were magistrates, thus named, amongst the Romans, from the duties attached to their office, which was the first and the lowest in public honours. Their origin seems to have been very ancient, but whether it was coeval or not with the regal institutions of Rome old writers and modern commentators are not agreed. Be this as it may, the quæstor was a public treasurer, a kind of receiver general of taxes and tributes, whose function was to watch over the sources of revenue, and to detect and bring to justice the perpetrators of peculations and frauds in that department. At first, there were only two quæstors appointed, but afterwards their number was increased to four. Two of these were assigned to the city, and the other two were appointed to accompany the consuls, in time of war, as paymasters in the armies.—Towards the close of the republic, the number of these magistrates was still further augmented. Sylla created as

many as twenty of them; Julius Cæsar appointed forty; and under the empire there were no limits to their number. One portion of them was named by the prince, the other by the senate and people. It was customary for the booty taken in war to be sold by the quæstors. As the boundaries of the empire extended themselves, the discretionary power of these officers was great.

As the quæstorship was the first, so it was frequently an effectual, step towards the attainment of the highest honours among the Romans. "The fidelity of the quæstorship, the magnificence of the edileship, the punctuality and integrity of the prætorship, opened a sure path to the consulate."

Quæstura.—The quæstorship was of a twofold kind. There were the *quæstores urbani*, who presided over the treasury, and were for that reason called *quæstores ærarii.* There were also the *quæstores provinciales*, who were usually sent with the governors *(rectores)* into the provinces, and who sometimes presided in the absence of those governors. No one was eligible to the quæstorship who had not completed his twenty-sixth or twenty-seventh year. When a person had served this office, he might go into the senate, although he might not yet be a senator. The quæstorship was abolished and re-established several times under the emperors.

Quæstores Urbani.—The quæstors of the city exercised their functions within the walls of Rome. Besides being entrusted, as has been already stated, with the custody of the public money, with the receipt of tributes and imposts, and with the expenditure of the state revenue, they had in their keeping the laws and *senatus consulta;* and when the consuls went forth in their capacity at the head of the troops against an enemy, the quæstors brought to them the military ensigns from the treasury. It was also the duty of the same class of functionaries to give the first reception to the ambassadors or envoys of foreign nations, to shew them hospitality, provide for their accommodation, and conduct them to an audience with the supreme authorities of the republic. Frequent mention is made of quæstors on the coins of Roman families, the name of the consul or consuls being also thereon recorded.

On a denarius of the *Neria* family, the head of Saturn (as designated by the *harpa* or sickle behind it) is accompanied by the inscription NERI Q. VRB. *(Quæstor Urbanus).*—On the other side of the coin is a legionary eagle between two standards, with the epigraph of L. LENT. C. MARC. COS. (See *Neria*).—Here then, as Eckhel remarks, is not only the image of Saturn, but the title of *Quæstor* added to the name of Nerius, whilst military ensigns present themselves on the reverse. Thus it plainly appears not only that the Quæstors were prefects of the treasury *(præfecti ærarii)*, but also, what Plutarch teaches and inscriptions confirm, that the treasury itself was the temple of Saturn. "But (adds the German numismatist) what have the *signa mili-*

taria to do with the quæstorship? Rightly this, that those things were preserved in the temple of Saturn, assigned to the care of the quæstors. This is expressly stated by Livy. And thus we have a clear explanation of the cause why the Quæstor Nerius placed the head of Saturn and the military standards on his denarius. One more fact of interest may be gathered in reference to time. From the names of the consuls, L. Lentulus and C. Marcellus, being inscribed on this denarius it is manifest that it was struck in the year of Rome 705—that year in which Julius Cæsar, eager to possess himself of the public money, broke open and plundered the treasury; L. Metellus, tribune of the people, who endeavoured to defend the sacred wealth of the republic, by opposing his person to the violence of Cæsar, being driven from his post through fear of death. It therefore pleased the Quæstor Nerius, who, together with the consuls had left the city from dread of Cæsar's power and vengeance, to insert on this medal (for the purpose of increasing popular hatred against the perpetrator of such sacrilege) the head of Saturn, whose very divinity had by force been violated."

Quæstores Provinciales.—The quæstors of provinces accompanied the proconsuls and propraetors to the appointed seats of provincial government, as superintendents over that department through which provisions and money were supplied to the soldiers—or (in modern phraseology to express it) as heads of the *commissariat.* If it happened that a governor left his province before the arrival of his successor, the quæstor performed his functions during the interval. Under such circumstances the quæstor was called *Quæstor Propraetore* (as inscribed marbles show) or *Quæstor Proconsule,* as is read on a denarius (quoted by Spanheim) M. SILANVS. AVG. Q. PROCOS.— Quæstors went out from Rome to the provinces, by authority of a senatus consultum; and when money was struck in those provinces, "there is no doubt (says Eckhel) but that the care and mastership of the provincial mint devolved on the quæstors. The words of Cicero *(in epistola ad Plancum)* expressly confirms this fact that the same kind of services were performed by the *quæstores provinciales,* that constituted the duties of the monetal triumvirs at Rome. For either they inscribed their names alone, or those of the proconsul or the propraetor, with whom they were sent to the province, or the name of the quæstor was joined to that of the proconsul. Of this an example is offered on coins of the *Annia* family, on one side of which appears C. ANNIVS PROCOS., on the other Q. TARQVITI. *Quæstor.*"

The curule chair was not included amongst the privileged distinctions of the quæstor, unless the individual himself had been proconsul.—They had the fasces and indeed the lictors in the provinces, but without the axes. Vaillant, in his *Colonies,* shews the *quæstor provincialis* on coins of the Antonia family—also an example of two quæstors under one and the same proconsul. Part of the quæstor's office was the importation

of wheat from the corn-growing provinces to Rome and other parts of Italy.

QVAR. *Quartum.*—As COS. QVAR. Consul for the fourth time.

QUARTINUS *(Titus).*—Proclaimed Emperor in Germany during the reign of Maximinus; and slain shortly after his assumption of the purple. To this personage has been attributed a denarius of base silver, bearing on one side DIVO TITO, and on its reverse CONSECRATIO. It is, however, says Eckhel, sufficiently evident that the coin in question is one referring to Titus Vespasian, and is of the number of those which about the time of Trebonianus Gallus were struck in honour of the memory of *consecrated* Cæsars. Herodianus calls the usurper *Quartinus.* Mediobarbus, who has engraved the coin, names him *Quarcinus,* and makes the strange mistake of ascribing it to an ephemeral tyrant whose *name* is not mentioned in the inscription, and whose *prænomen* is scarcely ascertained, some writers calling him Tyrus, others Titus.

Quartuorviri monetales.—Four joint masters of the Roman mint, appointed by Julius Cæsar, who (according to Suetonius) had increased the number of the inferior magistrates, and added one to that of the monetary triumvirs. Accordingly, under the supreme triumvirate of Lepidus, Antony, and Octavianus, we find IIII. VIR*i.* inscribed on the denarii of Æmilius Buca, P. Clodius, L. Flaminius, Livineius Regulus, Maridianus, and others.—See *Triumviri.*

Quercea Corona, commonly called the civic crown. Such a crown of oak leaves was granted to him who saved a citizen, as one of laurel was awarded to the victor in battle.—The *corona quercea* was offered by the curule ediles to Jupiter, as to the supreme preserver of the citizens, previous to the celebration of the games, and whilst sacred rites were paid to him in the capitol. Before the doors of Augustus's house on the Palatine hill, crowns of oak were renewed yearly in the kalends of March, because he was, in the language of Roman flattery, "*perpetuus hostium victor ac civium servator.*" —See *Corona.*

Quercus.—The oak tree was, with the ancients, held sacred to *Jupiter.* It was also consecrated to *Juno.*

QVIES AVGG. or AVGVSTORVM. The rest or repose of the Emperors.—This legend either abbreviated or at full length (with the accompanying type of a woman, in the stola, with a laurel branch in one hand, and the *hasta pura* in the other) appears on coins of Diocletian and Val. Maximianus struck after their abdication of the Empire. "After having prosperously governed the empire for the period of twenty long years (says Harduin) the *Quies Augustorum* (by the voluntary resignation of their imperial power and retirement into private life) is here recorded as a subject of commendation."

QVI LVDIT ARRAM DET QVOD SATIS SIT.—On the reverse of a third brass coin, or tessera, published by Peter Seguin

(Selecta Numismata Antiqua) appears this remarkable legend, accompanied by the type of four *astragali*, or *tali lusorii* (bones of four sides to play with—in other words gamesters' dice.)—On the obverse of this piece is the head of a woman, with the letter c. on one side and s. on the other.

Seguin calls this the medal of *Sors*. He supposes the female head to be that of the ancient goddess of chance, or destiny, and that the letters c. and s. placed near it are to be explained *Casus, Sors,* influences which certainly govern most games, and especially that of the dice. The reverse of this tessera contains a saying of the gaming table—namely, let him who plays put down *arram*, or his *stake* of money, as agreed upon by the rule of the game. The subject itself therefore shows (says Eckhel) to what uses small coins of a similar description were applied. *Det, quod satis sit,* is a known form of legal expression, employed in testamentary documents.

Baudelot de Dairval thinks that this medal may be interpreted by referring the c. and the s. on the side of the head to the feast of the *Saturnalia* at Rome, and reads it *Comi Saturnalia* or *Consulto · Saturni,* or *Consuetudine Saturnaliorum,* or *Convivio Soluto,* in joining it with this legend of the reverse, *Qui ludit arram det quod satis sit,* which is in the midst of the four little pieces of bone, as above described.—Indeed it is certainly (adds the ingenious author of *L'Utilité des Voyages*) that the ancients made few festivities which did not terminate in play, as among other expressions of Plautus, this *jeu de mots* demonstrates :

Accuratote ut sine talis, domi agitent convivium.

Be careful that they have not the liberty at mine to make feasts; which means, *drive them away from my house.* The poet avails himself of a quirk or pun on the common people, which plays upon the *Tali,* or small bones, because that word in the plural expresses the same thing. *Lucian* makes Saturn order that folks should play particularly at that game; and *Macrobius,* saying that the *Saturnalia* did not anciently begin till the 14th of the January kalends, adds—*Quo solo die apud ædem Saturni convivio dissoluto,* SATVRNALIA. *clamitabantur. Sat.* c. x.—On which day only, at the end of the banquet given in the temple of Saturn, they made the cry, or exclamation of *Saturnalia.* Thus the medal should be a symbol of those festivals, and for the feast of some quarter, and for the gaming which is about to take place. For there are marks which were so called at that time—*Symbolum dedit, cœnavit :* "he has given his sign and has supped," says an actor in the Andria. Baudelot goes on to adduce another passage from Macrobius, which seems to him capable of throwing light on the medal of Monsieur Seguin; but, at the same time, he confesses himself (as well he may) to be not yet entirely satisfied. For instance, he admits that he is totally at a loss to conceive whose was the female head on the obverse; but a learned friend of his, he adds, had no hesitation in pronouncing it to be that of *Copa Syrisca,* a famous woman of Rome, who kept an academy for gambling, feasting, and lascivious dancing; and was the subject of an epigram written by Virgil, in which her Greek head-dress *(caput Graiâ redimita mitellâ),* and her accommodations for drinking and gaming *(merum et talos)* are alluded to in a lively manner. This rich and luxurious courtezan, it is remarked by the friend of Baudelot, could well afford to have her portrait engraved on the symbol (the tessera) which she was accustomed to bestow on those who frequented her abode; and also to have inscribed thereon the first letters of her name—c. s. *Copa Syrisca.* Be this as it may, comparing the *Pone merum et talos* of the epigram with the bones delineated on the reverse of the medal in question, Baudelot de Dairval thinks they do not ill serve to confirm the conjecture which he has endeavoured to explain—namely, that the legend and type of this singular medalet bear reference to the *Saturnalian* celebrations at Rome. This piece is engraved in Pinkerton's *Essay on Medals.*

QVIETVS *(Caius Fulvius),* second son of Macrianus (one of the numerous usurpers that assumed the imperial title and authority in most of the Roman provinces under the reigns of  Valerianus and of Gallienus), was first named Cæsar, and afterwards also Augustus, about the beginning of A.D. 261. His father and brother, however, having been overcome and slain by Aureolus, who afterwards himself assumed the purple, Quietus fled into Asia, and for a short time occupied Emesa, where he was besieged by Odenatus, Prince of Palmyra, and being taken prisoner was put to death A.D. 262.—Born with heroic qualities, he early distinguished himself in arms, and shewed great talents for government both civil and military. But the *Quies Augustorum* was not enjoyed by *Quietus.*—On his coins he is styled IMP. C. FVL*vius* QVIETVS P.F. AVG. All the medals of this prince are of *billon* or in small brass, and very rare.

QVIN. *Quinquennalis.*—The censors in Roman colonies were called *Duumviri Quinquennales,* because they were elected every five years.—P. POSTV*mius* ALBINVS II. VIR. QVIN. ITER. *Duumvir Quinquennalis Iterum.* —See Q.

Quinarius.—This word sufficiently indicates that the piece of money so called was the half of the *denarius.* The mark of this coin was v., as being worth five asses, or five lbs. in brass money. On some, as on those of the *Egnatuleia* family, the mark is Q., namely, the initial letter of *Quinarius.* In the most ancient quinarii, as also in the sestertii, the types were the same as in the denarii, namely, *the head of Pallas with a winged helmet.*—*Rev.* ROMA and the *Dioscuri* (Castor and Pollux) *on horseback*.—At a later period, however, a figure of Victory became its perpetual type—now occupying the obverse, now transferred to the reverse side of the coin. It also appears in various postures, sometimes standing, at others sitting; now *erecting* a trophy, now in the act of doing something else. "Out of so large a number of *quinarii* as are extant, I see (says Eckhel) extremely few that have any other type than *Victoria*, viz., those which were struck by Cordius, Mettius, Pappius, and Cestius. The quinarii coined in the times of the emperors conform to the same rule, having rarely any other type than a Victory. So that it may be considered as peculiarly designating that class of silver money"—and thence they were called *Victoriali*.—For an illustration of the *Quinarius*, see *Porcia*.

Quinctia was originally a patrician, afterwards a plebeian family. Its surname is *Crispinus*, with the *agnomen* of *Sulpicianus* added by adoption.—The brass are parts of the *As*, and pieces coined by the mint-masters of Augustus. Morell gives twelve varieties.—There is a gold coin struck in Macedonia (valued by Mionnet at 800 francs) which exhibits on its obverse the bare head of a man, but without legend; on the reverse is T. QVINCTI. with the type of Victory holding a palm branch and a garland.— The portrait on the obverse is ascribed to *Quinctius Flaminius*, who gained a victory over Philip of Macedon. And a Macedonian shield, which appears below the *Dioscuri* on a denarius of the same family, is supposed to have reference to the same event.

Quincunx, five *uncia*, or parts of the *as*, with the distinctive mark of five globules.— Eckhel describes one of these most rare of Roman coins, contained in the Imperial cabinet at Vienna, as having on one side the head of Apollo laureated, with Γ behind it, and on the reverse ROMA. The Dioscuri on galloping horses, and below five circles or globules.

Quindecimviri.—The sacerdotal functionaries thus named were, according to Livy, the specially appointed keepers of the Sybilline books, which were first entrusted to the care of two officials *(duumviri)*, by King Tarquin the Proud; afterwards (A.V.C. 387) their number was increased to ten, under the name of *Decemviri sacris faciundis*, that part should be of the plebeian and part of the patrician order. —Lastly, Sylla (at the same time that he augmented the numbers of the priesthoods) increased the Decemviri to fifteen (Quindecimviri), who were instituted in the same manner as the Pontiffs; and their chief was called *Magister Collegii*. The dignity was for life, and it exempted its possessors from military service and from every other civil office. Besides guarding with mysterious care the oracles of heaven, which the superstitious Romans believed to be contained in the volumes of the Sybils, and which were consulted, by order of the senate, in times of great actual calamity or of impending danger to the state, these magistrates were, moreover, charged with

the celebration of the secular games and also the Apollinarian games.

The memory of the Quindecimviral order of Priests is preserved on a silver coin of Vitellius, the reverse of which presents a tripod, upon which is a dolphin, and below, a crow, with the the inscription XV. VIR. SAC. FAC. *Quindecimvir Sacris Faciundis* (one of fifteen appointed to superintend sacred things).—"The whole type of this coin (says Eckhel) belongs to Apollo— the tripod symbolising the oracles of the Pythoness, and the dolphin and crow being (as everyone knows) sacred to Apollo.—Augustus, when he was himself *Quindecimvir*, was honoured with that title, on a silver coin of *Mescinius Rufus*, in the field of which on the one hand is x̄v.; on the other side SF. and on a *cippus* is inscribed IMP. CAES. AVG. LVD. SAEC., that is to say *Imperator Cæsar Augustus Ludos Sæculares (fecit* being understood) *Quindecimvir Sacris Feciundis:* because the Quindecimvirate had the care of the greater public sports, and at the secular games distributed the *lustralia* (or perfumes for purification) to the people.—Eckhel, in corroboration of this fact, happily quotes the authority of Tacitus—"*Collegio XVvirorum antiquitus ea cura:* and as happily that of Horace, who has immortalised the secular games and the Quindecimviri in his ode—" *Quindecim Diana preces virorum curet.—Doct. Num. Vet.* vol. vi. p. 102.

Quinquennales Ludi.——Games celebrated by the Romans every five years under such Emperors as had reigned during that period. They were instituted in the reign of Augustus, in whose honour many of the provincial cities, especially Nicopolis, near Actium, which (according to Suetonius) he built—established the quinquennial shows, which had some resemblance to the olympic games of the Greeks.

Quinquennalis, a magistrate in the colonies, so called because his term of government lasted five years. It was also the name of the Roman Censors, who exercised their functions for the same period.

QVINQVENNALES POSTVMI. AVG.— This legend appears on the reverse of a gold coin of Postumus, with the type of Victory inscribing on a shield the words VOT*is* X.

This emperor, as he deserves to be, although *legally* he cannot be, called, celebrated the quinquennalian games A.D. 262. The VOT. X. refers to his having, in his tenth tribunate, performed the vows registered for five years, engaged himself in fresh vows for ten years. The *quinquennalia* of the *Augusti* had not hitherto been recorded on their coins.

Quinquessis, or *Quincussis*, according to Spanheim, was of an oblong form, and of all the Roman coins the largest, earliest, and most rare, its weight equal to five of the *as libralis*.— Akerman, however, in his *Descriptive Cat.* (vol. i. p. i.) says, "the *quincussis* (five asses, equivalent to a quinarius) is only a nominal sum."

QVINTILLVS *(Marcus Aurelius Claudius)*, resolved to be the successor, although Aurelian was the choice of his brother Claudius the Second, took the title of Augustus, which the legions of Italy by acclamation had bestowed upon him, and which the senate, from a high opinion of his virtues, readily confirmed to him (A.D. 279). In the meantime, however, Aurelian was proclaimed Emperor by the army that was at Sirmium (Pannonia). And Quintillus, finding himself abandoned by the soldiery who had just elected him, but to whom the rigor of his military discipline was unwelcome, caused his veins to be opened, and thus terminated his life, in the city of Aquileia. Possessed of the moderation and integrity which distinguished Claudius Gothicus, he was deficient in that firmness and enterprise which also characterised that great prince, otherwise he would have been well worthy to occupy the imperial throne. "Most of the ancient writers (says Eckhel) agree in limiting the duration of his reign to the short period of seventeen days. But from the abundance of his coins and the remarkable variety of their types, the workmanship of which would require more time, the opinion expressed by Zozimus seems the most probable, that at least some months must have elapsed between his accession and his death. —He is numismatically styled IMP. C. M. AVR. CL. QVINTILLVS. P. F. AVG.—His gold coins are of the highest degree of rarity. There are no silver. One brass medallion is known. Third brass are common.—There are *Consecration* medals of this Emperor, indicating the honours of the apotheosis, which were in all probability rendered to his memory, through the intervention of Aurelian.

QVIRIN.—On a denarius of the Fabia family we find this written on a shield to the left of a sitting figure, helmeted, representing Rome, and holding in her right hand the pontificial *apex*, with the following inscription, N. FABI. PICTOR, *Numerius Fabias Pictor.*—Ursin, Vaillant, and Spanheim have all three interpreted the inscription QVIRIN on the shield by reading it QVIRIN*us*, and have expressed their belief that Quirinus (or the deified Romulus) himself is exhibited by the type of the seated figure. "But (says Eckhel) the coins when accurately inspected clearly represent the form of a woman. Besides which, it appears that *Quirinus* was usually represented with a flowing beard, as may be seen on a denarius of the Memmia family. For which reason, as Havercamp rightly observes, the figure on the coin of Fabius is rather to be regarded as the image of Rome, and to be read QVIRIN*alis*, namely *Flamen*, as is more fully inscribed on medals of the Cornelia family, L. LENTVLVS FLAMEN MARTIALIS.—Of the Fabii, who were Quirinalian Flamens (an order of priests attendant in the temple of Quirinus at Rome), frequent mention is made in Livy and by Valerius Maximus. To which Fabius Pictor, however, this denarius relates, there are not sufficient reasons for determining."

QVIRINVS.—Memmius, whose family coin is above alluded to, lived in the time of Julius Cæsar, and was one of the Curule Ediles named *Ceriales*, established by that dictator. The legend on the reverse of this medal—MEMMIVS AED. CERIALIA PREIMVS FECIT—simply shews that a certain person named Memmius was the first who presided at games, which it had been the custom to celebrate in honour of Ceres—a fact not noticed by any of the old writers, and which has led to a variety of conjectures among numismatists as to the age of this coin. But our present concern is with its obverse, on which appears the laureated head of a man, with a long and luxuriant beard, accompanied with this inscription, C. MEMMI. C. F. QVIRINVS.—Respecting the word *Quirinus*, Eckhel says, "It is still a question whether it refers to the surname of Memmius, or to the portrait as being that of Quirinus or Romulus. Those who regard it as a surname, adduce the instance of Calpurnius Quirinus, and of Sulpicius Quirinus, whence they, with seeming probability infer, that the same cognomen also belonged to some individual of the *Memmia* family. As these opinions do not amount to more than conjecture, so it is certain that the god Quirinus is indicated by this bearded head, and that the word QVIRINVS was added, in the same way, in which that of NVMA or of ANCVS is placed near each of their heads, although it still may be that the word, moreover, serves to denote the surname of the family, as in *gens Pomponia*, the word MVSA stands both for the surname of Pomponius, and the Muse; but which Memmius is not known, for none of the old writers bring forward a Memmius Quirinus. Of as little value are the examples of Calpurnius and Sulpicius, cited by Havercamp. For the name of Calpurnius Quirinus is found solely on a Spanish lapidary inscription quoted by Gruter; whilst in Tacitus, Sulpicius is not called Quirinus, but Quirinius. It still, therefore, (concludes Eckhel), remains uncertain why the head of Quirinus was engraved on this denarius."—See *Fabia*.

Quirinus, a surname of Mars, allusive to potency in war. The name is said to be derived from the spear, which the Sabines called Curis.—*Quirinus* was also the name given to *Romulus* (as the fabled son of Mars by Rhéa Sylvia) after his death. It was thence that the Romans took the name of *Quirites*, and it was under the appellation of the god *Quirinus*, that the first King of Rome had, in the city which he founded, many magnificent temples erected to his honour and worship, among others one on the Quirinal hill,

QVIRITIVM.—See VESTA P. R. QVIRITIVM.

Q. V. or QVOD V. M. S. *Quod Viæ munitæ sint,* or *sunt.*—On account of the public roads having been made safe and convenient.

QVOD VIAE MUNI*TA*E SVNT.—A figure, with Victory, in a biga of elephants, on the top of a triumphal arch, built on a bridge of several arches. This legend and type appear on a gold coin of Augustus; and there are other coins in silver as well as in gold, bearing the same legend, with the type somewhat varied from the first, such as a quadriga on a triumphal arch, or two triumphal arches, with an equestrian statue and a trophy on each. There is also a denarius, struck by the monetal triumvir Vinicius in honour of Augustus, which displays on its reverse a cippus (or the milliary column) on which is inscribed S.P.Q.R. IMP. CAESari QVOD Viæ Munitæ Sunt EX EA Pecunia, Quam IS AD Aerarium DEtulit. [The Senate and the Roman people to the Emperor (Augustus) for having caused the highways (or great public roads) to be repaired with the money which he had procured from the treasury of the state.] All these medals, therefore, it is evident, refer to that systematic reparation of the different roads of the Roman empire, on which Augustus bestowed the utmost care and attention, dedicating to those works of public utility and grandeur a portion of the contributions which he had levied on the foreign enemy. The simplicity of the last quoted inscription is remarkable. Yet nothing can be more clear, nothing more free from affectation or pomposity, than the manner in which the sense is conveyed (the meaning of the initial letters being once interpreted). It would be difficult indeed, if not impossible, to find a like subject for admiration and praise in the inscriptive memorials of modern times.

There are passages in Dion which point with singular and luminous exactitude to the facts commemorated and typified on the above-mentioned coins. "Augustus himself took the management of the formation of the Flaminian way; because he intended to lead forth an army in that direction, and so it was immediately renewed. On this account statues on arches were raised to Augustus as well as on the bridge over the Tiber as at Ariminum."—This work of repairing the principal highways (or military roads), which diverged from Rome to the most remote territories of the republic, appears to have been begun in the year v.c, 727. "But the labour was great, demanding both time and expense, and frequently it was obliged to be suspended. At length, in the year of Rome 738 (says Eckhel) it was finished, and then and for that reason were the statues placed and dedicated, which Dion notices and these medals represent. The same historian also adds that other roads were subsequently repaired.—There are, moreover, testimonies even more specific, which are related by Suetonius, who says, "In order, however, that the city might be more easy of access from all quarters, he took upon himself the task of constructing the Flaminian way as far as Ariminum, and distributed the others among individuals who had gained triumphs, to be laid down, and the expenses defrayed out of the money that the spoils of war were sold for."—And what Suetonius here states, without marking the time, is related by Dion to have taken place in the above year: "To those who had gained a triumph, he enjoined that they should erect some monument in memory of

their exploits, out of the money raised by the sale of the spoils."

QVOD. INSTINCTV. DIVINITATIS. MENTIS.MAGNITVDINE CVM.EXERCITV. SVO. TAM. DE TVRANNO. QVAM DE OMNI. EIVS FACTIONE. VNO. TEMP. IVSTIS. REMP. VLTVS. EST. ARMIS. ARC. TRIVMPHIS INSIGNEM. DICAVIT. S. P. Q. R.—Within a laurel crown. On a brass medallion of Constantine, having his head, on the obverse, within the signs of the zodiac.—See Mus. Pembrok. iii. tab. 89, fig. 2.

Banduri places the above in the class of Contorniate medals (see the word).—"But whatever it should be called (says Eckhel) it does not appear to me to be of antique workmanship. Be it however what it may, this inscription is altogether the same as that which is read at the present day on the arch of Constantine at Rome (near the Flavian amphitheatre), erected in honour of his victory over Maxentius, which freed the state from the reign of terror that had been established by that tyrant. The words instinctu Divinitatis, according to the opinion of many of our later writers, are to be referred to the Divine or Holy Cross, which is said to have appeared in the heavens to the above-named emperor.—(vol. viii. p. 87.)—Eckhel condemned this remarkable Contorniate medal without having seen it. In Messrs. Sotheby and Co.'s "Catalogue" for the sale of the Pembroke Collection, p. 297, are some very sensible remarks on this singular piece, from which it may be concluded that this Contorniate is genuine; but that the use of a graving tool to remove oxidation has been the chief cause of exciting suspicions of its antiquity.

R.

R. The seventeenth letter of the Latin alphabet.—Pomponius hands down a traditionary notice that the letter R. was invented by Appius Claudius, but the far more ancient appellations of Roma, Romulus, Remus, together with the brass and silver coinage of the earliest ages, refute this assertion, as Spanheim, commenting on the Dialogues of Augustino, justly observes.

R. This letter serves as a mint-mark on the denarii of several Roman families, and also on some coins of the Lower Empire.

R. Remissa, vel Restituit, vel Roma, vel Romanus, &c.—Remitted, or he re-established; or Rome, or Roman, &c.

R. Reditu.—PRO R. CAES. Pro Reditu Cæsaris.—R. AVG. Reditus Augusti.

R. placed before P. Rei Publicæ.

R. in the monetal subsignations shews the coin to have been struck at Rome.—M. R. Moneta Romæ (percussa vel signata).—P. R. Percussa Romæ, i.e. Moneta.

R. Romani.—IN PROTESTATEM P. R. Populi Romani, on a coin of Trajan.

R. Romano.—CONGIAR. DAT. POP. R. Congiarium Datum Populo Romano, as in Nero.

R. Romanorum.—GL. R. Gloria Romanorum.

R. *Romanus.*—P. R. *Populus Romanus,* on a coin of Constantinus Magn.—S. P. Q. R. *Senatus Populusque Romanus,* of frequent occurrence.

R. or RA. *Ravennæ.*

Radiata Corona. A crown composed of rays.—It first appears on coins encircling the head of Augustus, denoting his consecration, or as the Greeks called it *apotheosis.* But on the medals of succeeding Emperors, both during their life-time and after their death, it is displayed indiscriminately, as if thereby to claim openly some kind of divinity.—See *Corona.*

Ramus, a branch, or more properly *Ramusculus,* a little branch, is seen in the hands of many different personifications, figured on Roman as well as Greek coins.—A branch either of laurel or of olive (for the ancients used both the one and the other in performing the lustrations) is an attribute or sign of *Apollo Salutaris,* as may be seen on a coin of Trebonianus. It is also a symbol of Hilaritas and of Lætitia.—*Hercules, Mars,* and *Minerva,* in their respective qualities of *Pacifer,* or Peace-bearing, are distinguished by a branch held in the right hand.—The olive branch of Peace is held in the right hand of that goddess, on numerous coins of the Imperial series—PAX AVGVSTI.—The types of Concord, Hope, Fortune, Providence, Piety, Rest *(Quies),* Security, Victory, and Valour *(Virtus),* likewise bear palm or other branches among their other attributes on Roman coins.—On contorniate medals we see the *Quadrigarii,* or charioteers of the circus, holding palm branches.

Raptus Sabinarum.—The memorable rape of the Sabine women is graphically referred to on a coin of the Tituria family. A first brass of Antoninus Pius is quoted by Vaillant, on which are many figures representing the rape of the Sabines. The same numismatist speaks of a bronze medallion of Constantine jun., without epigraph, exhibiting traits of the same celebrated event.

Ratis, or the ship stamped on the Roman *triens* and *quadrans.*

Ratiti.—Certain brass consular coins were called *asses ratiti, quadrans ratitus,* because those *asses* and quarter *asses* were marked on the reverse with the figure of a ship. And this kind of money was in use among the Romans long before they had begun to coin silver money, whether *denarii,* or *quinarii,* or sesterces.—See *As* and *its parts.*

RAV. and RAVEN. *Ravennæ.*—Subsignations on coins of Justinian I. and of Mauricius, signifying that they were minted at Ravenna, an ancient city of Italy, situate on the shores of the Adriatic.

R. C. *Romana Civitas,* or *Romani Cives.*

R. CC. *Remissa Ducentesima.*—Initial letters inscribed on the reverse of a third brass coin of Caligula, commemorative of a tax having been abolished by that Emperor.—The treasury of the state having been exhausted by the civil wars, Augustus, to assist in replenishing the public revenues, had established an impost of the

hundredth denarius on all sales. But this burthen, in the year V.C. 770, Tiberius, yielding to the petitions of the people, had reduced one-half, that is to say to one denarius for 200. At length, in the year V.C. 792 (A.D. 39), the whole tax was taken off by Caligula, as the inscription, on this small brass coin, of *Remissa* CC. plainly tells; and Suetonius confirms the fact, in saying *ducentesimum auctionum Italiæ remisit,* although he does not specify the time. And that this act of liberality was permanent is proved by medals struck in subsequent years of Caligula's reign, on which the memory of this benefit is gratefully renewed by the senate.—The obverse is inscribed C. CAESAR. DIVI. AVG. PRON*epos* AVG. S. C. (Caius Cæsar Augustus, great grandson of the Divine Augustus), and the type is the *pileus,* or cap of liberty, an allusion made to the right of suffrage granted to the people in the year 791.

RE. *Receptis, Reditu, Redux.*

Rechiarius, king of the Suevi—his name inscribed on a coin of Honorius.—See IVSSV RICHIARI REGIS.

REC. *Recepto.*—IMP. REC. *Imperatore Recepto,* as in Claudius.

RECE. *Receptis.*—See SIGN*is* RECE*ptis,* as in Augustus.

RECEP. *Recepta.*—See ARMEN*ia* RECEP*ta,* as in Augustus.

Rector, a governor or ruler.—The proconsuls were *rectores provinciarum,* whether sent by the people or by the Emperor.—Spanheim observes that governors *(rectores)* were sent into the provinces, invested with consular authority.

RECTOR ORBIS.—This legend, with a togated figure holding a globe in his right hand for its accompanying type, appears on gold, silver, and first brass of Didius Julianus. The flattery was as gross as the times were venal which could give this ephemeral sovereign—this contemptible dealer and chapman in state affairs —the appellation of *Master of the World.*—The title occurs in this instance for the first time, and is found repeated in very few subsequent instances. A silver coin of Septimius Severus exhibits the same words; but, from the type of a naked man standing with a globe in his right hand and a spear in his left, it would seem that the sun, as a deity, and not the reigning prince, was referred to as *Rector Orbis;* and that, peace being restored in the East, Severus by this medal, paid religious homage to Sol, as the arbitrator of the world's destinies. Caracalla is perhaps the only other emperor (besides Julianus) on whose medals this legend presents itself.

RECVP. *Recuperatio.* Recovered—regained.—See *Civibus et Signis Militaribus a Parthis* RECVP*eratis,* as in Augustus.

RECVPERATOR VRBIS SVAE. The rescuer of his city.—The Emperor seated : a soldier presenting to him a figure of Victory. In the exergue SARL.—Mionnet gives this from the reverse of a third brass of Constantinus Magnus in the *Catalogue d'Ennery.*—Bimard, in his annotations on *Jobert* (vol. i. p. 27), gives the following minute description of a medal in small bronze of the same prince, which at the time he wrote was in the cabinet of the Abbé de Rothelin, and not then published, and which, considering its diminutive size, must be a wonder for design and workmanship.

RECVPERATORI VRB. SVAE. (in the exergue PARL.)—The Emperor seated on a kind of trophy, composed of cuirasses and bucklers, receives with his right hand a small image of Victory placed on a globe, and which is presented to him by a figure clothed in a military garb, having a helmet on, and standing before him. On the obverse is the head of Constantine crowned with laurels; the bust of the Emperor is visible to the middle of the chest, adorned with the Imperial habiliments; the right hand is also to be seen, and holds, resting on the right shoulder a javelin, or a sort of staff rounded at the two ends. The left hand, which is not in sight, holds a buckler, on which is engraved a man on horseback, who treads under-foot a captive thrown down.

These legends, together with that of ROMA RESTITVTA on another small brass coin of Constantine the Great, certainly refer to him as the *rescuer* of Rome by the defeat and destruction of the tyrant Maxentius, than whom no one ever more afflicted the inhabitants of that city.

RED. *Redacta.* Reduced, brought under.— *Armenia et Mesopotamia in Potestatem Populi Romani* REDactae, on a coin of Trajan.

RED. *Redux*, or *Reduci.*—See *Fortuna.*

REDDIT. *Redditam.*—See OB REDDITam LIBERTatem, as in Gallienus.

REDITVS AVGusti.—The return of the Emperor.—Rome seated, presents a globe to the Emperor as he approaches her. On a third brass of Florianus. It is common to read on the reverses of coins the words ADVENTVS AVG., or when the Emperor has returned to Rome, FORTVNAE REDVCI; but REDITVS AVG. is a legend that appears only on this coin, which Tanini has published. It is evident from this inscription that the return of Florianus is to be understood as an event desired; but his death prevented its being realised.

REF. *Refecta.* Re-built, or repaired.— AIMILIA REF. The Basilica *Æmilia Refecta* on a denarius of the Æmilia family.—*Reficere*, was a word peculiarly applied to such public edifices as were re-constructed afresh, or restored to a perfect state.

REG. *Regis.*—See TVTOR REGis, on a silver coin of the *Aemilia* family.

REGALIANVS, one of the usurpers in the reign of Gallienus.—Trebellius and Victor call him *Regillianus*, " and from this name (says Eckhel), Goltzius, on his own authority, has fabricated *Q. Nonnius Regillianus.* But there are genuine coins which call him P. C. Regalianus. He was a Dacian by birth, and was believed to be a lineal descendant of Decebalus, whom Trajan with difficulty subdued. Regalianus is said to have possessed the heroic courage and great qualities of that king. He served under Valerian, and commanded the Illyrian

army when Ingenuus assumed the title of Augustus, about the end of the year 260. The cruelties inflicted by Gallienus on the troops and inhabitants in Mœsia, who had declared in favour of Ingenuus, induced them, after the defeat of that usurper, to elect Regalianus, who had already distinguished himself by his victories over the Sarmatians, against whom, even after his election, he continued to signalise his valour and augment his military renown. Some say that he was defeated and slain in battle by Gallienus; others that he was killed by his own soldiers, in concert with the people of Illyria, who dreaded becoming victims again to the inhuman vengeance of Gallienus.—Beauvais calculates his death to have occurred about the end of August, A.D. 263, and Eckhel, on the authority of Trebellius, assigns the same date to the event. Instead, however, of agreeing with Beauvais that the medals of Regalianus are to be found only in the collection of Goltzius, Eckhel publishes two coins from the Cabinet of Vienna with the style IMP. C. P. C. REGALIANVS, and his head radiated; the legends of the reverses being respectively LIBERALITAS AVGGG. and ORIENS AVG. The great German numismatist also ascribes another coin to Regalianus, which is preserved in that Imperial collection.— The coins of Regalianus are in small brass or in billon, and of extreme rarity.

REGI ARTIS.—*To the King of Arts.*— Spanheim, in his *Cæsars of Julian* (107), mentions a rare coin of Claudius Gothicus in

third brass, contained in the French King's cabinet, with this unique inscription, and with the effigy of Vulcan, holding a hammer and pincers,—and observes that it alludes to a Greek word, *Cheironax*, or *Rex manuum*, that is to say, the chief of handicraftsmen, or *manufac*turers, the true epithet of Vulcan.—In reference to the same coin, Eckhel calls to mind those coins of Valerianus and Gallienus inscribed DEO. VOLKANO, with a similar type of Vulcan standing. At the same time he expresses an opinion that this *rex artis* is probably the god *Cabirus* commemorated on another coin of Claudius II., who (see DEO CABIRO) was believed to have been beneficent to that emperor, and who might likewise be called *rex artis*, as the type of that coin and the doctrine respecting the Cabiri lead one to suppose.

REGINAE REGVM. FILIORVM REGVM. —See *Cleopatra*, on a coin of M. Antony.

REGN. *Regna.*

Regina.—See *Juno.*

REGNA ADSIGNATA. Kingdoms assigned. —The legend of a coin of Trajan, in gold, silver, and large brass, (from the last of which an example is here given,) on which is the Emperor sitting on an estrade, and attended by two figures standing; before and below him are five other figures, the foremost of whom touches the hand of the Emperor with his own.

The subject of this coin, analogous with that of the first brass inscribed REX PARTHIS DATVS, (see the words) is alike glorious to the Roman name and to Trajan himself: for that this illustrious prince, when he was in the east, gave kings not only to the Parthians but also to other nations; that he received some foreign states into alliance; confirmed treaties with others; and settled differences existing between people and people, are facts vouched for by Dion, by Eutropius, and other writers.

REI.—REIP.—REIPV.—REIPVB.   *Reipublicæ.*— See FELICITAS—GLORIA—REPARATIO —RESTITVTOR—SALVS—SECVRITAS——SPES— *Reipublicæ.*

RELIG*io* AVG.—The Religion of the Emperor.—On the reverse of a first brass of M. Aurelius is a temple, supported by four *termini*, and in the centre of which stands the statue of Mercury on a pedestal; in the pediment appear

a *tortoise*, a *cock*, a *ram*, and other attributes of the messenger of the gods.—The first-named animal recalls the fable that Mercury was the inventor of the lyre, called in Latin *testudo.* The second is the symbol of watchfulness, a quality needful to his employment; and the shepherds having adopted him as their patron, he is sometimes seen accompanied by a ram.

The legend of this reverse presents itself for the first time on any medal—*Religio Augusti.* That Marcus Aurelius, *malgré* his love of philosophy, was zealous for all that related to Polytheistic worship, even to the utmost extent of its manifold superstitions, is proved by his oppressive and cruel rigor towards the Christians. But it would have been difficult to account for his having selected Mercury from so great a crowd of deities, in order to display his piety, had not Diodorus Siculus thrown a light on this point by stating that, in Egypt the bearer of the *caduceus* and wearer of the winged cap was reputed to be the author of sacred rites and sacrificial ceremonies connected with *religion.*—On coins of

Valerianus, we read RELIGIO AVGG*ustorum;* but as it was a privilege, freely exercised by princes, to choose the divinity whom they most delighted to honour, so the *religion* of Valerian and his imperial colleague is found associated *not* with *Mercurius* but with *Diana Venatrix.*

Religio Christiana.—We see the series of imperial medals consecrated to the Christian religion, from the time of Constantine the Great, with the sole exception of Julian the Apostate. The celebrated monogram composed of the Greek letters X and P, indicating the name of *Christ*, displays itself on a coin of Placidia, encircled with laurel; on the helmet of Constantine; and most frequently on military standards, with various inscriptions; such as GLORIA EXERCITVS —GLORIA ROMANORVM—IN HOC SIGNO VICTOR ERIS.—A brass medallion of the usurper Magnentius offers on his reverse the monogram between the *Alpha* and *Omega*, and SALVS DD. NN. AVG ET CAES. The monogram also occurs on the reverse of a coin of Procopius in the line of the legend.—See p. 657.

RELIQVA. VETERA. HS. NOVIES. MILL*ies*. ABOLITA.—The coin of Hadrian (in first brass), on the reverse of which this legend appears, is certainly one of the most remarkable monuments of imperial munificence that can be found within the recording province of numismatic art. They tell us that the emperor voluntarily remitted to his subjects all the arrears owing to his treasury, on account of tributes, revenues, or other debts, amounting to an immense sum of money, and that he caused the notes and bonds relating to arrears to be burnt in the *Forum Trajani*—an act of liberality unexampled in its extent, and every way worthy of a great and mighty prince. The inscription states the abolition or cancelling of old fiscal dues to the value of nine thousand *sestertia*, or (according to Eckhel, equal to 60 millions of Austrian florins, or 30 millions of Roman scudi— and by the calculation of the author of *Leçons de Numismatique Romaine*, to about 157 million French francs; and according to Pinkerton 7,500,000 pounds sterling).

The emperor is here represented standing, clothed in the chlamys, and with a lighted torch in the act of setting fire to a heap of scrolls.— There is another and a rarer medal of Hadrian

bearing the same legend; but in which the type exhibits the emperor standing in the attitude and act above-described, before three citizens of

Rome, who lift up their right hand as if in acclamations to their sovereign. The inscription of the obverse marks his third consulate.

There is a passage in Spartian's *Life of Hadrian* (c. vii.) with which these two medals perfectly correspond. He says that this prince, omitting nothing that was calculated to gain the favour and good opinion of the people, remitted his claims to immense sums, which were due to the imperial exchequer *(infinitam pecuniam quæ fisco debebatur)* by many private individuals, as well in Rome as in the rest of Italy, and even exempted the provinces from paying residues amounting to very large sums, and that he caused to be burnt *in foro Divi Trajani* all the *syngrapha* or documentary proofs of these pecuniary obligations, in order to remove thereby every subject of disquietude to the debtors for the future. The term *reliqua vetera* is used on coins to denote arrears of the last sixteen years; and the liberality of Hadrian in this memorable instance was also limited to that space of time, according to the testimony of Dion. Yet, the *reliqua* thus abolished were, it seems, not arrears of every kind of debt, but only of money. Hence, as Spanheim remarks, this act of generosity, however extraordinary, has not remained free from the shafts of detractors. And looking to so vast a sum of outstanding debts as are stated to have been remitted by Hadrian, the same author shrewdly asks, "whence could they have accumulated to such an amount within the space of sixteen years?" Nevertheless, making all proper allowances for uncertainty as to the exact value, and for exaggeration as to the scope of the benefit conceded, it was an illustrious boon worthy of a Roman Emperor to grant, and of the Roman Senate and people to applaud with heart and hand.

Reliqua were remitted by other Emperors also. Thus there is an act of vast liberality recorded of M. Antoninus, by whom, as Dion relates (l. lxxi.), arrears of six and forty years due to the Emperor's treasury and to the public exchequer were freely forgiven to the people.

Remus, the brother of Romulus, and reputed son of Mars by Rhea Sylvia.—See *Lupa;* also see *Romulus* and *Remus*.

According to fable, miscalled history, he appeared after his death to his foster father and mother, Acca Laurentia and Faustulus, to demand that divine honours should be rendered him. And certain it is that in the most remote times, a temple was consecrated to him in the fourth region, at Rome.

REN. This abbreviation, about the meaning of which there are various opinions, appears on the reverse of a silver medallion of great rarity, which, having the bare head of Augustus on its obverse, exhibits as the legend of its reverse an upright figure, holding out two ears of corn in his right hand, his left hand wrapped up in the toga which he wears, and inscribed HADRIANVS AVG. P. P. REN.

Baldini would explain this REN by reading it RENovavit, that is to say, as though Hadrian

had wished to renew the memory of Augustus, after a hundred years had elapsed since his decease. Others approve of the same reading, but think that the word *renovavit* was put for the more usual word *restituit*, and that it signifies that the original coin was restored by Hadrian, in like manner as was done by Titus and others. But this opinion is overturned by the subjoined observations of Eckhel, who, in opposing himself to Baldini, begins by remarking that this coin does not belong to the class of *numi restitutionum*. For, in the first place (says he) even if it were granted that the abbreviation meant RENovavit, yet it still would remain uncertain what Hadrian was to be understood to have renovated. Then, it is evident enough that this silver coin, because it is of the largest module not used in the mint of Rome, must have been struck at a distance from the city, respecting which rule a frequent lesson is read on Roman imperial coins. And, indeed, not a few silver medals of this size are extant with the names of Trajan and Hadrian, which were almost all of them struck in the eastern provinces of the empire. But, says Eckhel, I have sufficiently proved that this coin offers every indication of its having been struck abroad. It is, therefore, very likely that some such temple of Augustus (and there were many then existing in the provinces, especially in Asia), together with its image, as is exhibited on the reverse of this medallion, had been *renovated* by Hadrian. Nor (he adds) do I rashly imagine this; for it was not the only benefit bestowed by Hadrian on the temple of Augustus. Spartianus alluding to the journies of that emperor relates, *Post hæc Hispanias petit, et Tarracone hyemavit, ubi sumptu suo aedem Augusti restituit.* Cap. 12. Similar acts of bounty and liberality performed not only by princes, but also by private individuals, are sometimes boasted of on coins (abundant mention is made of such deeds on marbles), and on this point we are taught by the denarius of Aemilius Lepidus with the epigraph AIMILIA REF*ecta.* And that the word *renovare* is rightly applied to substructures, or buildings, may be learnt from Cicero—*vides Honoris templum a M. Marcello renovatum.* Let the reader judge (says Eckhel in conclusion) whose explanation may appear most entitled to the preference."

Renia, a family of whom historians make no mention. Its denarii have but one type, namely, the winged head of Pallas, on one side, and on the other, C. RENI. with a female driving a biga of goats, and ROMA in the exergue. Morell remarks: *Renius ille, triumvir monetalis, apte bigis imposuit: pro equis renos posuit ad nomen suum adludens.*

RENOBATIO. VRBIS. ROM*E.* For Renovatio Urbis Romæ.—This legend with its peculiar orthography appears on a second brass of Magnentius, forming one of four medals struck by that usurper, and which boast of the liberty of the republic, as vindicated, of victory and freedom as restored to the Roman world; of the renovation of the city itself as accomplished; and all this to be understood as the result of his having conquered and slain his rival in usurpation and tyranny. Nepotianus. Yet these vainglorious pretensions to the character of a liberator and a restorer are not confined to the coins only of Magnentius, but are assumed in an inscription on a marble quoted by Gruter, dedicated to his honour as LIBERATORI VRBIS ET ORBIS ROMANI RESTITUTORI LIBERTATIS, etc.

REP.—REPARA.—Reparatio.

REPARATIO. MVNERIS. FELICITER.— A man receiving on the point of his spear a bear which is rushing upon him.

This is one of those *Venationes*, or hunting subjects, which appear on the reverses of Contorniate medals, having on their obverses the head of *Nero*, included in Havercamp's Catalogue and represented in Morell's plates.—See Eckhel, who under the name of *Pseudomoneta*, has classified these peculiar productions of the Roman mint, not in the order of the Emperors' reigns, but according to their respective subjects, and these latter are so various as to embrace, among others, mythology, history, illustrious personages, public spectacles and sports, &c.

REP. *Reparatio.*—See FEL. TEM. REP. *Felix Temporum Reparatio.*—A legend which first appears on coins of Constans I. (from A.D. 337 to 350), with various types; and afterwards occurs frequently in succeeding reigns. See p. 378.

Repetitions of types and of inscriptions on the reverse as on the obverse, are among those errors of the mint, more or less gross, which occasionally betray themselves on Roman coins of the Imperial series; even in the earlier reigns such as Vespasian, Trajan, Hadrian not omitting Augustus himself. [See Rasche.]

REQVIES. OPTIMOR. MERIT. *(Optimorum Meritorum.)*—A figure veiled, wearing the toga, sits in a curule chair, the right hand extended, the left holding a sceptre.

This epigraph and the accompanying type present themselves, for the first time of their occurrence in the Imperial series, on a silver and on small brass coins of Claudius Gothicus. It appears, says Banduri, as well from the deified title on the obverse—(DIVO CLAVDIO OPTIMO IMP.)—as from the veil (likewise a symbol of divinity) with which the head of Claudius is covered, that these medals were struck after his death.—The *rest* or *repose of the highest merits*, was, as applied to him, the language, not of adulation or of exaggerated praise, (as, when similarly used in subsequent reigns on coins of Maximianus and Constantius Chlorus,) but of truth and justice, to the memory of a prince so universally beloved and lamented that all writers of Augustan history unite in making him the theme of the most glowing, and apparently as sincere as glowing, panegyric. Trebellius Pollio, in relating the various honours awarded to Claudius after his decease, says a golden shield was, by the unanimous vote of the whole senate, placed as a tribute to his virtues *in Romana curia*. And the people (a thing never before done) placed, at the public cost, a statue of him in gold, ten feet high, in the capitol before the temple of Jupiter; nor were similar demonstrations of respect confined to the authorities and population of Rome, but (we are told by the same writer) that in every city throughout all the provinces statues, standards, crowns, altars, temples, and arches, were dedicated and erected to his honour. Trebellius, indeed, in his life of this good, great, and victorious Emperor, finishes with saying—*Illum et Senatus et populus ante imperium et in imperio et post imperium sic dilexit, ut satis constet, neque Trajanum, neque Antoninos, neque quemquam alium principem sic amatum.*

RES. REST. RESTIT. *Restitutis* or *Restituit.*—Restored, or he has restored.

RESTIO.—The cognomen of *Antia gens*, on a denarius of which the obverse type is the head of a man, remarkable for its muscular, large featured, and hard favoured countenance. This is supposed, with much probability, to be the portrait of the C. Antius Restio who was the author of a sumptuary law, which not only placed the expenses of convivial banquets under restriction, but also prohibited any magistrate, or magistrate elect, from dining abroad, except at certain people's houses.—It is not worth while to inquire when this unsocial and fruitless limitation was enacted, for a law so absurd met its fate of remaining unobserved, and even its proposer is said to have never afterwards dined out, for fear of witnessing (and perhaps assisting in) the violation of his own legislative inhospitality.—See *Antia gens.*

Restitutions, or restored coins, is (from the verb *restituo)*, a name given to pieces of money copied from other pieces struck at an anterior period of time, with the adjunction of legends which prove the reproduction of these particular coins.—The motives which led to the fabrication of such medals do not appear susceptible of a satisfactory explanation, notwithstanding the pains bestowed and the ingenuity exercised by the most learned numismatists, with a view to throw light upon the subject. Certain it is, that many of the Roman Emperors caused the coins of several of their predecessors, and also coins of the consular or republican æra, to be *restored*—that is to say, they commanded pieces to be struck which reproduced the types and legends of those more ancient coins, with the addition of the name of the reigning emperor, together with the word REST*ituit*—a word which has been subjected to very different interpretations.

The learned and judicious *Bimard de la Bastie*, in his annotations on Jobert's work, thus defines the kind of money now in question : "We call (says he) those restored medals *(Médailles Restituées)*, be they consular or be they imperial, upon which, besides the type and the legend which they had at their first coinage, we see, moreover, the name of the emperor who caused them to be struck a second time, followed by the word REST.—Of such a sort is the second brass coin on which, round the radiated head of Augustus, we read DIVVS AVGVSTVS PATER, and of which the reverse type is a globe with a rudder, and the legend IMP. T. VESP. AVG. REST.—Of the same kind is that silver medal of the *Rubria* family, which represents on one side the head of Concord veiled, with the abbreviated word DOS., that is to say DOS*sennus*; and on the reverse a quadriga, on which is a Victory holding a crown, below it L. RUBRI., and round it IMP. CAES. TRAIAN. AVG. GER. DAC. P.P. REST.—There are other medals to which the epithet of *restored* has improperly been given, although they do not bear the word REST., which seems to be the distinctive mark of these restitutions. Such are the medals struck under Gallienus, to renew the remembrance of the consecration of many of his predecessors. Nor can the appellation of *restored* medals be in any sense given to those which Augustus, Tiberius, Caligula, Claudius, and Nero caused to be struck with the name and the head of Julius Cæsar, of Augustus, of Livia, of Agrippa, of Agrippina, of Drusus, and of Germanicus, because these are not instances of ancient types employed afresh, but absolutely new coinages, as well with respect to the type as to the matrix or die."—After correcting the error which (misled by *false* coins quoted by Oiselius and Hardouin) Jobert had made in stating the restorations to have commenced with the reigns of Claudius and Nero, Bimard proceeds: —"It is under *Titus* that we begin to see restored coins, and we know them to have been struck in memory of Augustus, of Livia, of Agrippa, of Drusus, of Tiberius, of Drusus son of Tiberius, of Germanicus, of Agrippina mother of Caligula, of Claudius, of Galba, and of Otho.—After Titus's example, *Domitian* restored certain medals of Augustus, of Agrippa, of Drusus, of Tiberius, of Drusus, son of Tiberius, and of Claudius.—*Nerva* restored none of his predecessors' coins except those of Augustus; but *Trajan* renewed by *restoration* the medals of almost all the emperors who had reigned before him." Besides which, he restored numerous coins of Roman families.—*Marcus Aurelius* and *L. Verus* jointly restored a denarius of M. Antony.

The majority of the earlier writers on Roman numismatics, and Bimard seems nearly to coincide with them in opinion, contend that the word REST., that is to say, *Restituit*, signifies merely that Titus, Domitian, Nerva, and Trajan caused the dies of their predecessors' coins to be re-made; that by their command medals were struck with these same dies; and that they allowed such medals to be circulated in commerce, like their own money. These antiquaries also believed that Trajan did not confine himself to this practice of coining medals from the dies of the princes who had preceded him; but took the further step of re-establishing all the *matrices* which had been used for the consular medals, at the period when they were the current coin of the state.

After combating at considerable length the objections of Pere Hardouin, who has ridiculed the above ideas on the subject, and who has

given *(Oper. Select.* p. 507), a counter explanation fraught with great ingenuity but equally fraught with greater difficulties, Bimard declares his preference for the opinion of Vaillant, as having much more of probability in it; namely, that Trajan, in order to conciliate in his own favour the sentiments of the senate and people, wished to shew marks of his veneration (generally) for the memory of his predecessors, and of his good-will towards the first houses of the republic. With this view he restored the money of emperors who had reigned before him, and those coins also upon which were inscribed the names of Roman families. A proof (adds Bimard) that Trajan had restored all the consular medals is that in the small number of such restorations extant at the present day, many are found of the same family, with different types, and sometimes of a family but little celebrated, as amongst others the *Rubria* family, of which we have three different coins restored by Trajan. According to this opinion, the meaning ascribed to the legend IMP. CAES. TRAIAN. AVG. GER. DAC. P.P. REST. is perfectly conformable to the rules of grammar and to the genius of the Latin tongue. When the inscription was engraved on the very monument itself which an emperor caused to be re-built, the name of the restored monument was frequently omitted, because it was impossible to make any mistake as to the case governed by the word *restituit*, and because everybody supplied it with ease. Thus when on the Nîmes road a military column is seen, with this inscription TI. CAESAR DIVI F. AVG. PONT. MAX. TR. POT. XXXII. REFECIT. ET RESTITVIT. V., we clearly understand that this column, which served to mark the fifth mile from Nîmes, had been re-erected by order of Tiberius. Amongst an infinity of examples exhibiting this elliptical mode of expression, there is in an ancient inscription on the Pons Fabricius at Rome the following: L. FABRICIVS C.F. CVR. VIARVM. FACIVNDVM COERAVIT; and that was sufficient to convey the meaning that Fabricius had caused this bridge to be built, because the inscription was engraven on the bridge itself. Nothing is more common than to find on *Cippi*, whether votive or sepulchral, POSVIT.—FECIT.—FACIENDVM CVRAVIT, without those verbs being followed by any governing noun, because the *Cippi* (or altars) themselves are supposed to supply the place of it. For the same reason, when we find on medals IMP. TITVS—IMP. DOMITI*anus* —IMP. TRAIAN*us* REST*ituit*, if it is, as I believe, of the re-fabrication of the coin itself that it is designed to make mention, it was not necessary to add *hunc nummum*, for we hold in our hand, and have under our eye the very thing which was re-established. But it would not be thus if it had been intended to record that these Emperors caused in some sort the revival of their predecessors, and of the great men whose names were engraved on these pieces of money, for it often happens that there is nothing in the type which bears relation to the virtues, or to the actions, by which the Emperors are supposed to represent them."

But, before he approaches the task of elucidating, so far as erudition, research, and numismatic skill can elucidate, the obscure and difficult, yet curious and engaging, subject of Restored Coins—Eckhel has applied himself to draw up a descriptive catalogue of these peculiar monuments, in composing which,—I. He has, in the order of the three metals, enumerated them, with the addition of the restorer's name.—II. He has noted such coins of this kind as are known to have archetypes; also such as have none yet known; and such as in any degree differ from, or fall short of, the archetype.—III. He has likewise inserted those coins of the *Augusti* and *Cæsares*, without which no decision could be arrived at in this examination.—IV. And, lastly, he mentions none but coins of perfectly authenticated genuineness, and which credible witnesses have seen and approved.—The catalogue is divided into the following heads :—

Silver Coins of Restitution.—These are all the work of Trajan (except the medal of Divus Trajanus, on which is read the name of Hadrian as the restorer; and the coin of Mark Antony the Triumvir, restored by M. Aurelius and L. Verus).—On the reverses of all the coins restored by Trajan we find the legend, inscribed circularly, IMP. TRAIAN. AVG. GER. DAC. P. P. REST.—Of this class we have the archetypes (with the exception of the above cited one of Hadrian) manifestly agreeing with the restored coins.—Of consular medals there are two, one with the head of Janus, the other with the head of Pallas—the reverse of the former has Jupiter in a quadriga, and the word ROMA; the reverse of the latter is the Genius of Rome seated, with ROMA and the wolf and twins before her.—Of family coins there are thirty-five—viz., of Aemilia, Cæcilia, Carisia, Cassia, Claudia, Cornelia, Cornuficia, Didia, Horatia, Junia, Livineia, Lucretia, Mamilia, Marcia, Maria, Memmia, Minucia, Norbana, Numonia, Pompeia, Rubria, Scribonia, Sulpicia, Titia, Tullia, Valeria.—The denarius restored by Hadrian bears on its obverse the head of Trajan, with the epigraph DIVVS TRAIANVS PATER AVGVSTVS; and on its reverse Hadrian sacrificing; it is inscribed IMP. HADRIAN. DIVI. NER. TRAIAN. OPT. FIL. REST.—The silver coin of M. Antony, restored jointly by M. Aurelius and L. Verus, is inscribed ANTONINVS AVGVR. III.VIR. R. P. C., the type a *Triremis*. On the reverse is the legionary eagle between two other military ensigns, and these words LEG*io* VI. ANTONINVS ET VERVS. AVGG. *REST.*

[The intelligent author of *Leçons de Numismatique Romaine*, in a passing observation on the silver coins of families restored by Trajan, says "*tout en conservant soigneusement les anciens types ces deniers n'ont que le poids ordinaire des autres deniers du même prince : ce qui prouve qu'ils étaient assimilées à la monnaie courante de son regne.*"]

Gold Coins of Restitution.—These also have Trajan for their restorer, with the exception of

six which, if genuine, were restored by Titus.— Of all these no archetype is known to exist, or if anything like their original be extant, there is some material difference between them. They consist of Julius Cæsar, Augustus, Tiberius, Claudius, Galba, Vespasian, Titus, Nerva.

Brass Coins of Restitution.—Coins of this metal have Titus, Domitian, and Nerva for their restorers. The epigraph of the restorers vary, as it also varies in other coins of theirs. In these medals Domitian often indicates his name by the single letter D.—At the end is added REST., or at full length RESTITVIT. These brass are of Augustus, Agrippa, Drusus senior, Tiberius, Drusus jun., Germanicus, Agrippina senior, Claudius, Galba, Otho, Julia Titi.

Le Beau, in his "Lucubrations on restored coins," rejects the views of the matter in question entertained by Bimard and others, and brings forward what he thinks a sounder opinion. He asserts that the word *restituit* signifies that the emperor whom the coin denominates as the restorer, had restored some public monument of him (whether emperor or other illustrious man) whose name the coin publishes. A compendium of the prolix arguments urged by this learned writer in support of this opinion is furnished by Eckhel, who characterises them as being all so specious as to be worthy of the genius of Hardouin alone.

II.—Brass coins, on which the portraits of Emperors are restored, belong chiefly to that class whose reverses exhibit nothing but the letters S. C.; a mark from which we cannot glean any other information than that it was the pleasure of Titus, of Domitian, and of Nerva, from what cause soever, to recall the images of those princes.

III.—To this class, in which the types only are restored, or the memory of some singular facts are recalled, belong all the gold and most of the brass coins of this kind. They cannot be called restored coins, because between these and the originals a striking difference presents itself, whether seen in the epigraph or in the types, and sometimes even another metal. The same coins may be seen in the first gold of Tiberius, and in others. In many the archetypes are manifestly wanting, as in the greater portion of the gold; and it is probable that they never did exist; but that the types of those medals were devised by Trajan, whatever might be the motives which actuated him. In the same manner Trebonianus also (others suppose it to have been Gallienus) restored the *consecrations* of preceding emperors; but after a new fashion, or certainly one but little in conformity with the size of the archetypes. But no one may persuade himself that the first models of the gold coins have perished, and (what follows) that in like manner the gold and the silver can be reckoned among the number of restored coins; for who would believe that the gold had suffered such a fate, as that their primeval forms should have been annihilated, when the originals of all the silver, so far as we have hitherto met with them, are still extant?

These are the things, adds Eckhel, which either ascertained, or probable, or uncertain, or wholly unknown, I find on the subject of restored medals *(de restitutionum numis)*. I shall conclude with but a few animadversions.— I. As Trajan restored the coins of obscure families, for instance three of *Rubria*, it is very likely that most of them (the Consular and Family coins), and perhaps all, were restored by that emperor, but they have hitherto not been seen. For we perceive that their numbers, although slowly, yet by degrees increase, and without doubt a great many lie in various museums hidden, and unknown to us.—II. We have no gold piece, either consular or of a family, restored by Trajan, who nevertheless ordered the restored imperial medals to be struck generally in gold. This deficiency serves greatly to confirm me in the conjecture which I have formed (and stated in section i. cap. iv.), that during the republic there were no gold coins struck. For what was the reason why Trajan should abstain from restoring the gold consulars? The cause of his omitting to restore the brass coinage of the republic, I think, was that these had common types, peculiar to the weight of each, and which therefore it did not seem worth while to restore.—III. As hitherto no restored coin of any family has been discovered, of which the archetype is not also extant, a ray of hope may now be indulged, that hereafter the series of family medals may be more amply enriched with the desired accessions.—IV. Out of the whole crowd of family medals, which the fertility of Goltzius has brought to light, though known to himself alone, we are cognizant of no restored coin; nor has any restored coin hitherto appeared, whose original the Thesaurus Goltzianus supplies. This may seem wonderful, but we can nevertheless divine the true cause. To forge restored coins will not have exercised much reflection, but he will never be able to furnish the archetypes, because the coins hitherto seen by him (Goltzius) alone are almost all esteemed fictitious.

Such is the substance as well of the various opinions hazarded, as of the different facts stated, by antiquaries, both of the new and of the elder school respecting *restored* coins. And, although some of the speculations on this subject are freer from objections as being more reconcileable to probabilities than others, yet when we look to these instances confined to a few reigns of emperors re-coining the money of the republic precisely after the designs of the original types, and also of renewing the medals of their predecessors on a less accurate principle of imitation, it must be confessed that the *restorations* in question are still left amongst the unsolved riddles of ancient numismatism.

RESTIT. GALLIAR. *Restitutor Galliarum.* —On the reverse of a silver coin of Gallienus that effeminate voluptuary, who by his heartless misconduct brought the Roman empire to the very verge of ruin, is here represented lifting the personified Genius of the Gauls from a kneeling posture. This piece of inscriptive adulation was fabricated after a victory which Gallienus obtained over the barbarous invaders of Gaul, by the assistance of Postumus; but that great commander, nevertheless, retained the government and improved the security of those important provinces, and therefore might with greater right have assumed that title on his own coins. That Gaul was spoken of by the Romans in the plural we have seen in the coin of Galba, inscribed TRES GALLIAE.

REST. ITAL. *Restituta Italia*, or *Restitutor Italiæ.*—The Emperor raising a woman that kneels before him; opposite are two children standing with uplifted hands.—This legend and type, on gold, silver, and first brass of Trajan, doubtless refer to the large funds appropriated by this beneficent prince to the maintenance and education of youth in various cities of Italy, which by this well-timed and paternal liberality of his may rightly be said to have been *restored.*

RESTITVTOR LIBERTATIS.—The Emperor holding in his right hand a figure of Victory, and in his left hand a banner with the monogram of Christ.—This medal, in gold and in silver (engraved in Khell's *Supplement. ad Vaillant*, p. 259), is one of several struck under Magnentius, in which that ferocious traitor and most cruel tyrant, who profaned the Christianity he professed, has impudently designated himself as the restorer, the renovator, the conqueror of liberty and of republican independence for Rome, whose lawful prince (Constans) he had caused to be assassinated, and whose Illyrian provinces he had deluged with Roman blood.

RESTITVTOR MON. *Restitutor Monetæ.* —The Emperor (Alexander Severus) standing with his right hand extended, and a spear in the left. Second brass. Of all the emperors, Alexander is the only one who boasts of himself as the *Restorer of the* (Roman) *Mint.* But this he has done, with the sanction of the senate (s. c.), both on the present coin and on another middle bronze, inscribed MON*eta* RESTITVTA. There is a long passage of Lampridius, in which that historian assigns to the prince in question the merit of having caused the silver coinage of Rome to be restored to greater purity.—Eckhel, however, who has quoted Lampridius at full length, denies that the silver medals of Alexander are such as to bear out this ancient writer's assertion, and concludes his remarks by saying—that "this emperor only in one respect deviated from the practice of his immediate predecessors, viz., by discontinuing the mintage of that larger-sized silver which Caracalla instituted. Nor, indeed, is the silver of Alexander's money of a better quality, but rather more impure, insomuch that, but for the testimony of Lampridius and of these legends on his coins, we should not know that Alexander had made any change whatever in the monetary affairs of his empire."

REST. *NVM* (as read by mistake) on a silver coin of Galba, having for the type of its reverse a female head with an ornament round the neck.—This medal, which is now in the French Imperial Cabinet, has given rise to various conflicting opinions among the learned. But M. Barthélemy, having again minutely inspected it, and also compared it with a similar one in the D'Ennery Collection, proved that the controversy on this abbreviation was a foolish one, and that it is to be read LIBERTAS RESTITVTA.

RESTITVTOR ORBIS.—This legend appears on a third brass of Aurelian, on which is typified the Emperor standing, and to whom Victory presents a laurel crown.—Another third brass of the same emperor exhibits the figure of a woman, clothed in the stola, offering a crown to him : a star in the field of the coin. In the exergue K, A. Γ.—And on another medal of the same metal, size, and reign, are the same legend and the same type, except that a captive kneeling before the emperor is substituted for the star in the field.—From these coins Spanheim takes occasion to animadvert upon the cruel, sanguinary, and ferocious disposition which characterised this celebrated prince. In fact, historians agree in speaking of him, as one who had no less·stained the empire by his cruelty, than he had restored it by his victories gained over the Sarmatians, the Goths, the Palmyrians, the Francs ;—victories which, amongst others, had given rise to that medal of Aurelian, on which he is crowned by Victory, and honoured with the glorious inscription above quoted.—*Césars de Julien,* p. 97.

Same legend, with the type of a woman offering a laurel crown to the Emperor, appears on the reverse of a small brass, bearing on its obverse the portrait of Carus (the successor of Probus), and the impious dedication DEO ET DOMINO CARO.

RESTITVTOR ORBIS.—A nearly naked figure, with the pallium on the right shoulder, and the hasta in the right hand, offers with his left a globe to another figure, in military habiliments, and laureated, holding a spear in left hand, and extending his right hand towards the proffered orb.

This appears to symbolize Jupiter placing the government of the world in the hands of an emperor.—Spanheim, in a note to his translation of the *Cæsars of Julian,* gives (p. 102) an engraving of this legend and type, as from the reverse of a coin of Probus. [The obverse type being the radiated head of that emperor, with the legend PERPETVO IMP. C. PROBO INVICT. AVG.]—And then, quoting Vopiscus, to shew how many provinces and allies of the empire were, by the warlike exploits of Probus, delivered from the oppression of the Goths, Germans, and other barbarians, as well as from various usurpers of the Imperial purple, thereby reestablishing peace throughout the Roman world, he concludes by saying—" *On voit des Médailles de Probus avec les Inscriptions et les Figures de* MARS PACIFER *et d'* HERCVLES PACIFER, *et d'ailleurs par un titre bien plus glorieux, et qui lui convenoit mieux encore qu'à Aurelian, viz.,* RESTITVTOR ORBIS."—But this reverse is

common to the coins of Valerian, Gallienus, Postumus, Aurelian, Tacitus, Probus, and Carus, from a third brass of the last of whom an engraving is taken.

RESTIT. ORIENTIS. A turreted female crowning the Emperor.—RESTITVTOR ORBIS. The Emperor raising a female, whose head is turreted ; also the Emperor, with spear and military ensigns.—RESTITVT. GENER. HVMANI. The Sun standing, holding a globe. —The appellations of " Restorer of the East," " of the World," " of the Human Race," as applied to Valerianus, on whose silver coins they appear, are indeed " more glorious than true."— All three medals were struck in anticipation of Valerian's success against the Persians. It was a fallacious augury. The event of this expedition proved signally disastrous ; he was taken prisoner by Sapor, and after suffering every species of indignity, miserably perished, to the disgrace of his son and successor Gallienus, and to the dishonour of the Roman race.

RESTITVTOR ORIENTIS.—*Aurelianus* is thus called, on a rare gold coin, which has the figure of the sun radiated for the type of its reverse, and which was struck after his victory over and capture of Zenobia, who had assumed the title of Queen of the East, the Persians and Armenians having also yielded to the power of his arms.—" *Pacato igitur Oriente,*" says Vopiscus, " *in Europam Aurelianus rediit victor.*"

RESTITVTOR REIPVBLICAE.—On a brass medallion (and also on a gold coin) of Valens, the Emperor is represented standing, with the labarum in his right hand and a *victoriola* in his left.

Valens, brother of Valentinian the First, is here, in the pompous inanity of imperial decadence, called the Restorer of the *Republic* of Rome.—Havercamp gives a similar reverse of a brass medallion of Gratian, but it is not recognised either in Mionnet or in Akerman.

RESTITVTOR SEC. or SAEC*uli.*—The Emperor (Probus) standing, holds a globe and the hasta ; a Victory behind him, with palm branch in left hand, holds with her right hand a crown above his head.—Third brass.

There is another and a rarer third brass coin of the same great and warlike prince, on which the legend is given RESTITVTOR SECV. in Akerman's Catalogue, and of which the type is there described to be the Emperor standing, holding the globe and spear ; his right foot on a captive; the Sun standing : in the exergue XXIQ.

Appearing, as this legend does, on coins of *Probus,* it serves as an instance to show that numismatic eulogies are sometimes based on truth and justice. This illustrious ruler of the Roman empire was indeed, by his wisdom, energy, and valour, the instrument of its restoration to peace and security, during the period in which he only too briefly flourished.

RESTITVTOR, or RESTITVTORI, VRBIS. —The Emperor standing at a sacrifice : another with the same epigraph, has the type of Rome seated.—This appears on *silver* of Sept. Severus, to whom this flattering appellation was given doubtless on account, not of his having either rebuilt or embellished Rome, but of his having restored the honour of the "Eternal City" by avenging the death of Pertinax, secured domestic tranquillity to the empire by the destruction of his competitors Albinus and Niger, and made the Roman name again respected abroad by his victories over the Parthians.—In a similar manner, but without the same pretence, coins were struck by order of his cut-throat son, Caracalla, in dedication to *himself* as to "*the Restorer of the City.*"

RESTITVTORI ACHAIAE,—AFRICAE, —ARABIAE,—ASIAE,—BITHYNIAE,— GALLIAE,—HISPANIAE,—ITALIAE,— LIBYAE,—MACEDONIAE,—MAVRETA- NIAE,—NICOMEDIAE,—PHRYGIAE,— SICILIAE.

These legends are all on coins of Hadrian, who travelled frequently over and surveyed with attention the different provinces of the Roman Empire, inspecting the armies, embellishing the cities, and everywhere leaving marks of his liberality and munificence.

These manifold proofs of solicitude for the interests and prosperity of his subjects were typified on medals with a carefulness that seems to have anticipated the records of history, and in a variety of modes most suitable to the circumstances of his visits.—Sometimes the provinces are represented simply by a figure and some attributes as on a first brass inscribed AEGVPTOS, where a woman is seen seated on the ground, having at her feet the bird Ibis ; sometimes the coins of this most magnificent of emperors present themselves as so many monuments of his arrival at and residence in these provinces, explained by the words ADVENTVI AUG*usti* ; as for example MOESIAE, with an analogous type, such as the Emperor and the Genius of the province, standing opposite each other at an altar, sacrificing : the Genius holding a patera in her right hand, and in her left a cornucopia or a sceptre.—At other times we see the armies which he inspected designated by the

names of their respective provinces in which they were stationed ; and distinguished further by some type of allocution, as on the large brass EXERCITVS MAVRETANICVS, with the Emperor on horseback, and four soldiers on foot bearing military ensigns.—Next, we observe, as in the present case, that the Emperor is termed *the Restorer* of a particular province, as in the large bronze medal dedicated by the Senate's decree, RESTITVTORI ACHAIAE, whereon Hadrian is represented extending his right hand to lift up a kneeling woman, an urn with a palm branch in it, standing in the midst—or in that of RESTITVTORI HISPANIAE, where the

kneeling genius has a rabbit at her foot. And lastly, to crown the climax of distinction, not unjustly due to the benefactor and re-establisher of so many component portions of a vast empire, we find a medal of the same size and metal, whose type exhibits Hadrian, in the imperial robe, raising from her posture of genuflexion a female figure, wearing a crown of towers on her head, and holding a globe in her left hand ; whilst the legend, in one emphatic title, designates him *Restitutor orbis terrarum*, the Restorer of the (Roman) world.

By *terrarum* here, of course, is meant every land inhabited by citizens in towns, and cultivated by a civilized rural population. Spartianus, in his Life of Hadrian, observes, "*Nec quisquam fere principum tantum terrarum tam celeriter peragravit.*"

The suite of these *geographical medals (numi geographici)*, as Eckhel calls them, is considerable in point of number, and deservedly sought after by all collectors of taste and intelligence. Some of them are very rare ; others are sufficiently common.

RESTITVTORI ITALIAE IMP. V. COS. III. S. C.—Marcus Aurelius, whose great and good qualities, as a prince, shone no less in peace than in war, had certainly a just title to the honour here bestowed upon him, *senatus consulto*, of being the acknowledged *Restorer of Italy* ; for, besides paying particular attention to that province, as the first in importance and the nearest to the capital, he may truly be said to have restored Italy, by averting the danger which at one time impended over her from the sanguinary revolt and threatened invasion of the Germans.—This transcendent merit, as Havercamp (in *Num. Reg. Christinæ)* observes, "it appears to have been the object to mark in the type of this (large brass) medal. The Emperor standing, holding a lance, and clothed in armour, offers his right hand to a female figure, who has one knee on the ground, and whom he assists to rise. This figure not only has a radiated crown on her head, but moreover a globe in the left hand, because she represents Italy, a country which then possessed the empire of the world."—The legend of the reverse tells us that the coin was struck when Marcus Aurelius was *Imperator* for the sixth and *Consul* for the third time : the inscription of the obverse shews that it was under his twenty-seventh renewal of the tribunitian power.— A.D. 159.

Reverse of a coin, in Latin called *aversa* and *postica*, is the side opposite to that of the head.

REX *v.* IVBA REX.—King of Numidia and Mauretania.

REX ARETAS.—This title and name appear on an elegant historical medal of the *Æmilia* family. Dion briefly alludes to the subject of the type by relating that Syria and Phœnicia having been assigned to the government of Aretas, King of Arabia Petræa, who had often disturbed Syria with his incursions, Pompey the Great waged war against, and delivered him as a conquered prince into captivity.—Josephus, however, imparts a clearer explanation concerning this denarius. He says that, affairs in Syria having been settled, Pompey made his preparations for returning to Rome, and committed all Syria, from the Euphrates as far as Egypt, to M. Æmilius Scaurus, who immediately attacked Aretas ; but the latter, mistrusting his own power to make a successful resistance, sued for peace and obtained it, at the expense of three hundred talents. These transactions took place v.c. 672.—Accordingly the denarius above alluded to (see *Aemilia* and *Aretas*) shews the Arabian king as if dismounted from the camel, (on which, after the Arabian fashion, he had been riding,) and kneeling, as in the act of supplication, holding up an olive branch (symbol of pacification), hanging from which are to be seen (as Havercamp has already observed) fillets or ribbands, according to that which Virgil (*Æneid*, viii. 127) mentions :

Optime Grajugenum, cui me Fortuna precari,
Et vitta comptos voluit prætendere ramos.

REX ARMENIIS DATVS.—There is a magnificence in this legend (on a large bronze medal of Antoninus Pius) which is by no means expatiated upon with corresponding precision in the annals of that prince's reign. The event which it commemorates is one illustrious for Rome :

A King given to the Armenians.—In the

type the Emperor stands clothed in the *toga*, and is in the act of placing a diadem on the head of the new monarch. The latter is covered with a royal mantle, and lifts his right hand to his head.—Notwithstanding the many fierce and bitter contests of the Romans with the Parthians, Armenia, situate between both those empires, was accustomed to receive its sovereigns sometimes from the one, sometimes from the other.— Eckhel observes that there is nothing to be gathered from the *res gesta* of Antoninus which bears upon this event, except what Capitolinus hands down : *Parthorum regem ab Armeniorum expugnatione solis literis repulit.*—Vaillant has been led to conjecture, from a passage of Jamblicus, quoted by Photius, that the king of Armenia, appointed by Antoninus, was named *Achaemenes.*

But, although the old writers have scarcely anything to say on the subject, yet the legend and type of this reverse unite in proving the occurrence of such an event, and form an addition to the many instances in which medals are not a little serviceable to history, and, if only on that account, are well entitled to be deposited in cabinets and studied as amongst the most useful, as well as the most curious, monuments of antiquity.—This point, amongst others, Ezekiel Spanheim has admirably demonstrated in his great work *De Præst. Num.*

REX ARMENIIS DATVS. IMP. II. TR. P. IIII. COS II. S.C.—The emperor, surrounded by three figures, is seated on an *estrade*, at the foot of which stands the king of Armenia.— First brass of Lucius Verus.

As in the case of the coin of Antoninus just described, so with respect to this of Verus, struck twenty-four years afterwards ; but little light has been thrown by historians on the fact of *another* " king given to the Armenians," though recorded and typified on this interesting reverse.— Capitolinus, as cited by Tristan, in allusion to Verus's campaign, says, " when the war was terminated, he gave kingdoms to kings, and the government of provinces to his officers."— For (adds the old French numismatist) " Armenia was a kingdom, and nevertheless sometimes made a province of by the emperors. But Capitolinus does not distinctly say that Verus had created a king in Armenia. Now, this medal supplies what the historian has neglected. It says in the inscription that the emperor established a king, a fact which in truth is not elsewhere mentioned. But Photius, on the authority of Jamblicus, states that the king in question was named *Soæmus*, and that he was living in his time ; that this prince was son of Achæmenes, and grandson of Arsaces, and descended from great kings ; that, nevertheless, he was only a Roman senator, and honoured with the consular dignity." Tristan goes on to say that this *Soæmus* was at length appointed king of the greater Armenia by the Romans ; that he was afterwards driven from his throne by *Vologeses*, king of the Parthians, and that he re-ascended it under the protection of the Emperor Verus.

REX ARTAXIAS.—On reverse of a denarius of Germanicus.—*Obv.* GERMANICVS, with other letters indistinct, round a naked head of Germanicus.—*Rev.* Two male figures standing; by

the side of one is inscribed ARTAXIAS; behind the other, GERMANICVS. This coin, introduced by Mr. Borrell, who procured it from Kaisar, the ancient Cæsarea of Cappadocia, records the crowning of Zeno, son of Polemon, king of Pontus, by Germanicus, the name *Artaxias* being received by him from Artaxata, the capital of Armenia. The coin is of the highest historical interest, and is fully explained by a passage in Tacitus *Ann.* lib. ii. cap. 206.—See also the *Numismatic Chronicle*, vol. ii. p. 4.

REX PARTHIS DATVS.—This superb legend, of which those of Antoninus and of Verus, as to the *Armenian* kings, are to be regarded in the light of *imitations*, appears on the reverse of a first brass of Trajan; and together with the REGNA ADSIGNATA of the same reign, already noticed in its alphabetical order, refers to events that must have been in the highest degree flattering to Roman pride and ambition. Towards the close of his reign this illustrious Prince, having conquered the Parthians and dethroned *Chosroes*, their king, imposed a new sovereign upon them, and the scene of this important transaction is represented with consummate *tact* on the present medal. We see here the personification of Parthia,

kneeling before the emperor, as if *soliciting* a king at his hands. Trajan, who is seated on a *suggestum*, attended by the commander of the Prætorian guards, complies with the request, by giving her one, whom he points to with his hand. The fact is attested by the words of the inscription—*A king given to the Parthians.*

REX PARTHVS.—This is also a very rare gold coin, allusive to the same transaction, having for the epigraph of its reverse REX PARTHVS; and for its type, the king of the Parthians bending the knee before Trajan, who is surrounded by soldiers and military ensigns.

—According to Dion (quoted by Vaillant) the *Rex Parthus* of this and the preceding coin, was *Parthamaspates*, son of Artabanes.

REX QVADIS DATVS.—The emperor Antoninus, clothed in the toga, with his right hand joined to that of the king of the Quadi.— Large brass.

This is another of those imperial medals which, like those described above, serve to show the superiority acquired by the Romans over foreign nations. History, however, is silent with regard to the fact of Antoninus having given a new king to the Quadi, who were a people inhabiting the left bank of the Danube, occupying that tract of country which now forms part of Lower Austria, and extends as far as Moravia. The history of this barbarous tribe was more fully known in the subsequent reign of Marcus Aurelius, to whom they became formidable.—Perhaps (says Eckhel) the king here given to the Quadi by Antoninus is the same as he, of whom Capitolinus speaks (in his life of Marcus): *Quadi autem amisso rege suo, non prius se confirmaturos eum qui erat creatus, dicebant, quam id nostris placuisset imperatoribus.*

Rhea Silvia, the daughter of Numitor, king of the Albans, whom, after she had been consecrated by her uncle Amulius as a virgin to the service of Vesta, became pregnant by Mars, and brought forth Romulus and Remus.—On a second coin of Antoninus Pius, she is represented half naked in a sleeping posture, and Mars descending towards her; to this remarkable coin there is no other legend than COS. III. S.C.

Rhenus, that celebrated river now called the *Rhine*, which, rising in the chain of the Rhætian Alps (amidst the terrific rocks and glaciers of the Grisons), flows through the lake of Constance *(Brigantinus Lacus)* past Basilia or *Basle;* then taking its true direction to the north-west, divided ancient *Germania* from *Gallia*, and empties itself into the sea through the country of the *Batavi*, of which *Lugdunum Batavorum*, now *Leyden*, was the capital.—The three Gallic provinces, on the western bank of the Rhine, contained several German nations—namely, the Vangiones, whose capital was Borbetomagus, now *Worms*, north of which were Moguntiacum, now *Mainz*, and Confluentes, now *Coblentz*— the Nemetes, whose capital was Noviomagus, now *Spires;* and the Triboci, whose chief town was Argentoratum, now *Strasburg.* Lower down, on the same bank of the river, were also the Ubii, whose capital was Colonia Agrippina (now *Cologne*), so called after Agrippina Claudii; and the Eburones, whose country, afterwards occupied by the Tungri, had for its principal city Aduataca, now called *Tongres.*—On the eastern bank of *Rhenus*, were the Frisii, occupying the country which now forms part of *Holland, Friesland,* and *Groningen.* It was across this tract that Drusus, in his campaigns against the Germans, caused a canal or dyke to be dug, called Flevo Lacus, as a fortification against the incursions of the barbarians. On the same bank were the Chauci Minores and Majores, of the race of the Suevi, praised by Tacitus as the best of the German tribes. On the east bank also were the Catti, a great and powerful nation, whose capital was Mattium, now *Marburg;* and to the south of them were the Mattiaci, occupying the present electorate of *Hesse Darmstadt.*

RHENVS.—There are two medals in large bronze, the types of which represent Germania vanquished—alluding to a victory to which Domitian falsely laid claim.—In the former a German, on his knee, surrenders a long shield, that is, his arms, to the emperor. In the latter the vain-glorious Domitian treads underfoot the Rhine, which serves here as the symbol of Germany.

That the river personified on the last-mentioned medal signifies the Rhine (which Domitian, as Zonaras writes, passed over in his expedition of A.D. 84), is indicated by other coins similar to this, except that, as Patin and Morell have delineated them, they exhibit RHENVS written in the exergue.—As coins of the former kind are common, so those with the word RHENVS are of the greatest rarity, unless perhaps it be safer to suspect them of being counterfeits; for it is exceedingly strange that the name in question was unknown to Vaillant, and that they are also unknown in the finest collections. Nor does Morell add to his engraving of the coin any reference to the museum which contains it; whence it would appear that he had followed only the authority of others. It was from the Rhine that Martial took a subject matter for adulation, when addressing the prince; he says: *Tibi summe Rheni domitor, &c.—Epig.* ix. vii.

Rhenus fluvius.—There is another image of the Rhine on a coin of Postumus (in gold and silver), in which the recumbent Genius of the mighty stream is represented with two horns *(bicornis),* as indicating the belief of ancient geographers that this river made its outlet to the sea by two mouths.—See SALVS PROVINCIARVM.

Rhesaena, or rather *Rhesaïna,* a city of Mesopotamia, situate on the declivity of Mount Masius, near the river Chabora, at its point of confluence with the Euphrates, not very far from Carrhae, and close upon the eastern frontier of the Roman empire. This place, which was in a later age called *Theodosiopolis,* has for its present name Ras-al-ain (Asiatic Turkey, province of Diarbekir). It was made a *colony* by Sept. Severus, as indicated by its assumed surname of *Septimias,* adopted from that of Severus's family.—Near Rhesaina, the Persian king was signally defeated and his army put to flight by Gordianus III.—Old writers furnish no particulars respecting this Mesopotamian town; but its coins, which take their date from the reign of Hadrian, form in this respect a supplemental monument to history.—They consist of *(Greek)* Imperial of Caracalla; and of Colonial Imperial successively dedicated to Alexander Severus, to Trajan Decius, to Herennia Etruscilla, and to Herennius. These latter have *Greek* legends with some few words in *Latin.* For example, there is, on a very rare second brass, struck in honour of Alex. Severus, the legend ΡΗϹΑΙΝΗϹΙΩΝ, *Rhesainesiorum,* accompanied by the type of a colonist at plough with oxen, together with a *vexillum,* on which is inscribed LEG. III. GAL. *Legio Tertia Gallica.*

The type of the *Colonus boves agens* here used shows that Rhesaina was a colony; and it is to be observed that although the word COL*onia* does not appear on the coin, yet it does appear (in Greek characters) on another of the same emperor, and also on one of Trajan Decius—*see below.* The present medal also denotes that the veterans of the Third Gallic Legion were settled in Rhesaina, which city dedicated coins to Alexander, as in gratitude bound, because that good emperor had freed them from the devastating presence of the Persians, as Eutropius states, by his waging war against that people, and gloriously vanquishing their king Artaxerxes.—The second brass of Alexander Severus and of Trajan Decius alluded to above exhibit the colonist and oxen, but without the *vexillum.* In that of Decius there is an *eagle,* typical of Roman government. Thus we have the *colonus* as representing the citizens, and the *vexillum* as symbolizing the legionary veterans.—" *Quanta igitur* (exclaims Vaillant) *Historiæ lux è nummis!*"

There is another type of this colony, which (like the Ptolemais of Trajan already quoted,) presents the figure of a turreted woman, sitting on a rock with corn-ears, and a river-god at her feet. This is meant for the Genius of the City, whose mountainous site is also here denoted, whilst the corn-ears serve to indicate the abundance of wheat produced on its fertile soil. The man emerging from the water represents the river Chabora, which, rising from Mount Masius, flowed past the walls of Rhesaina.

Rhinoceros.—This animal (according to Spanheim) indicates both games and wars: it is also the sign of imperial munificence and eternity.— The rhinoceros, as certain coins of Domitian shew, was seen at Rome in the times of the Flavian emperors, it being exhibited in the secular games.—Eckhel mentions three small brass coins, well preserved, in the Imperial cabinet, bearing on their obverses IMP. DOMIT. AVG. GERM., and on their reverses the figure of a Rhinoceros, from whose snout rise two horns: of these the one nearest the mouth is the longer, the other a little higher up and less prominent. The *rhinoceros bicornis* is the rarer species; the old writers, however, recall it to remembrance. Thus Martial, *Spectac.* xxii. :

Namque gravem GEMINO CORNV *sic extulit ursum.*

Pausanias's narrative corresponds clearly with these coins of Domitian, when he affirms himself to have seen *rhinocerotes* (which he calls *Æthiopian bulls*) from the extremity of whose nose a horn juts out, and a little higher up another, but not a large one.—These particulars (adds Eckhel) have demanded notice, because Hardouin teaches that from these identical coins of Domitian it is manifest that this wild beast is furnished with only one horn on its snout ; and the same error, derived perhaps from Hardouin, about only one horn being observable on the coins of Domitian, has since been propagated by James Bruce, an Englishman, who, in his travels in Abyssinia, relates many things respecting this animal, at one time as *unicornis*, at another as *bicornis*, when describing the natural history of quadrupeds in that region.

Right hands joined, are symbols of Concord and indications of mutual confidence, *real* or *assumed.*—See *Manus.*

Rogus funebris, or funeral pile of the Romans, was a quadrangular kind of scaffold, or compact structure of timber-work, on which the dead bodies of princes and princesses were burnt to ashes.—Vaillant says it was called *Rogus* because the *dii manes*, or deities of the shades below, *in eo rogantur*, were supplicated, and believed to be propitiated by the ceremonies performed at them.—The *rogus*, from the reign of Antoninus Pius, is the common type of consecration on coins of Imperial personages of both sexes.— Dion briefly speaks of this pile as in form like a tower of three stories, adorned with ivory, gold, and a few statues.—Herodianus gives a fuller description of it, observing that the ground-floor of this square building was filled with dry fuel ; that on this substructure stood another tier, similar in form and ornament, but narrower, and furnished with open doors ; that on these were erected a third and a fourth, still narrower in dimensions, so that the whole work presented the appearance of a *pharos ;* that the corpse being then deposited in the second story, and the accustomed ceremonies being performed, the lighted torch was applied, and the entire mass consumed by fire.—After making these citations from the old writers, Eckhel alludes to the abundance of coins, which place before our eyes the form of the *rogus*, exactly corresponding with their description ; and he particularly mentions a medal of Julia Mæsa, not long ago found at Rome ; the possessor of which, Viscount Ennius, an antiquary of great repute, wrote to the Papal Nuncio at Vienna, saying that it was in so beautiful and entire a state of preservation, that, what had never before been observed in these representations of funeral piles, the body of the *Augusta* appeared placed on a bier in the *second* story.

As symbols of consecration, these *Rogi* are seen on coins of Aelius Cæsar, Antoninus Pius, Faustina senior, M. Aurelius, Faustina jun., L.

Verus, Pertinax, Sept. Severus, Caracalla, Julia Mæsa, Saloninus, Valerianus jun., Claudius Gothicus, Tetricus jun., Nigrinianus, Constantius Chlorus.—See CONSECRATIO.

On the *Rogus* (says Vaillant, *Pr.* ii. 293), an eagle was placed at the consecration of emperors, and a peacock at that of empresses ; and when the cord by which it was tied became consumed in the flames, the bird thus freed, and flying through the air, was popularly believed to carry the spirit of the deified personage up to heaven. This image of consecration was afterwards struck on the Imperial medals.

RO. or ROM. *Romæ.* At Rome.—ROM. *Romani*, or *Romano*, or *Romanorum.*

Roma, formerly queen of almost the whole earth.—Horace (L. iv. od. 3) calls her the prince of cities ; and according to Martial (L. xii. epig. 8) she is *terrarum dea gentiumque :*— Rome, a city of Latium in Italy, situated on the Tiber, founded by the Alban youth, under the leadership of Romulus and Remus, the grandsons of Numitor. At least the most generally received opinion is that Rome was so called from Romulus, who was first named Romus, according to the authority of Servius. For when Romulus and Remus undertook jointly the building of the city, the latter wished that its name should be *Remuria*, from his own name. Romulus, on the other hand, preferred to have it named *Roma.* The auspices were given in favour of Romulus ; nevertheless, the city was not styled *Romula*, lest such a diminutive of the name should derogate in any degree from the majesty of the city.

Rome took for its sign the wolf suckling the twin brothers, in recognition of the well-known story. When, indeed, the power of the city became so great that the descendants of its founder began to be ashamed of their origin, its history was adorned with fables.—Hence the sagacious Livy, in his preface to his *Libr. Histor.*, says—"*Quæ ante conditam condendamve urbem, poeticis magis decora fabulis, quam incorruptis rerum gestarum monumentis traduntur, ea nec adfirmare, nec refellere, in animo est.*"—But although it is the common belief that Rome was built by Romulus, because he founded a monarchy there, yet there are many authors who assert that, before him, Evander, from Arcadia, reigned over that part of the city, afterwards called Mons Palatinus ; nay, there are others, especially the Greeks, who pretend that, before the time of Romulus, there existed in the same place a city named Rome which had been built by a certain noble lady, Greek or Trojan, named Roma, who was with Eneas, it is not known in what quality, whether slave or wife.

Leaving these, however, and other opinions which have been advanced respecting the origin of Rome, and which are founded only on conjectures altogether arbitrary, we may regard it thus far as certain, that she sprang from the smallest beginnings ; that her first foundations were on the Palatine mount ; and that her boundaries were then from time to time enlarged round that spot to a vast extent. For Pliny

(L. iii. c. 6) writes that, in the reign of Vespasian, the circuit of the city was 13,000 paces. And Vopiscus relates that the Emperor Aurelian increased the compass of · its walls to thirty thousand paces —So great and famous did this city in the end become, as the capital of the most powerful and extensive empire ever known, though it owed its origin to a troop of herdsmen, fugitive slaves, and robbers, conducted by a man of ability and resolution.— If writers have varied in their sentiments on the origin of Rome, they have equally differed with regard to the year of its foundation. The most general opinion assigns for that event the year from the creation of the world 3231, viz., 753 years before the birth of Jesus Christ, the third year of the sixth Olympiad, 431 years after the ruin of Troy, and during the reign of Jothan, King of Judah.

Rome was called *Septicollis*, because she inclosed within her mural boundaries seven hills,— viz., Palatinus, Quirinalis, Aventinus, Cœlius, Viminalius, Esquilinus, and Tarpeius, or Capitolinus. Such was "the eternal city" under King Romulus and his successors. And if, after the substitution of the consular for the monarchical form of government, she gained in point of extent, she was but a rude and unsightly mass of cabins and cottages, until the period of her being burnt by the Gauls. Subsequently to that event she assumed a better architectural character, having been re-built in a more commodious and durable manner. But it is stated by her historians, that even so far down as the arrival of Pyrrhus in Italy, the houses were covered with only shingle and planks. Nor was it till the year 622, that the embellishments of Rome commenced, thence proceeding to that pitch of splendour to which Augustus carried them. A splendour which Nero, after playing himself the part of an incendiary with the old city, still further improved upon in restoring it from its ashes. This high and palmy state was under Trajan not only maintained, but rendered still more noble; and long after that great emperor's time it exhibited almost undiminished magnificence, in spite of the ravages of the Goths, the Vandals, the Ostrogoths, and other barbarians, whose assaults were scarcely more ruinous than the degeneracy of the people themselves.—Rome still contains relics which serve to indicate what she must have been in the days of her imperial power and grandeur.

Romanum imperium.—The Roman dominion or territorial jurisdiction, which began under *kings* (viz., Romulus and his six successors, Numa Pompilius, Tullus Hostillius, Ancus Martius, Tarquinius Priscus, Servius Tullius, and Tarquinius Superbus), whose united reigns occupied a space of 243 years,—did not extend further than within 18 (Roman) miles each way from the city. But under the *Consuls*, amongst whom were sometimes Dictators, &c., the advance of Roman power, and the extent of Roman conquests, during a period of 447 years, were in effect nearly as follows :—Italy captured as far as beyond the Po; Africa and Spain subdued;

Gallia and Britannia rendered tributary; the Illyrians, the Istrians, the Liburni, the Dalmatians, vanquished; Achaia invaded; the Macedonians overcome; war waged with the Dardanians, the Mœsians, and the Thracians, the legionary eagle was planted on the banks of the Danube. Having defeated Antiochus, the Romans set foot for the first time in Asia; victorious over Mithridates, they take possession of the kingdom of Pontus, together with Armenia Minor, which that monarch had held; they march into Mesopotamia, and enter into a treaty with the Parthians; they fight against the Arabians; Judæa is conquered; Cilicia and Syria brought into subjection; at length Egypt is reached by the victorious arms of Rome, and her republic is no more.—Under the *Emperors*, from Augustus to the times of Theodosius and his sons, a period of 440 years—the Cantabri, the Astures, and all Spain were placed under the yoke; the Alps, Rhætia, Noricum, Pannonia, and Mœsia, were added to the empire; the whole tract of the Danube was reduced to the state of provinces; all Pontus and the Greater Armenia, Mesopotamia, Assyria, Arabia, and Egypt yielded obedience to the laws of Rome, And thus, by the successive efforts of these "foremost men of all the world," and by the valour and perseverance of the Roman people, this most august empire was elevated to the supremost height of human glory having for its limits the ocean on the west, the Rhine and the Danube on the north, the Tigris on the east, and Mount Atlas on the south.

ROMA.—This word is often found inscribed on nearly all the coins of families, in addition to their names, especially on the most ancient denarii, and even on coins anterior to them. They are generally wanting on such as were struck in the decline of the republic.—Vaillant says, and so does Havercamp, in very many places, that when the word ROMA is added it indicates that the medal was struck in the city; the omission of it signifies that the piece was coined in some province. " In the first place, this rule is fallible, because on coins of a later age the word is wanting; in the next place, I know not why coins, although struck in a province yet by a Roman magistrate, could not have been recognised as Roman, when they were doubtless Roman currency, especially as on even foreign coins the word ROMA is not unfrequently read, by which indeed the conquered people sought to prove their connexion with the governing city."—Eckhel, vol. viii. 70.

ROMA.—This word also appears in monogram on denarii of the *Didia* and *Marcia* families, and on a denarius of Calpurnius Piso Frugi.—ROMA likewise is inscribed on the Consular coinage, in silver, both denarii and quinarii. On family denarii it is generally accompanied by types of *Victory* in a *biga* or in a *quadriga*, or by the *Dioscuri*.

Rome was personified and worshipped as a deity by the Latins as by the Greeks, and the appellation of Θεά, or of *Dea Roma*, is found applied to that renowned but presumptuously proud city both amongst writers and on coins. Thus it was said of her: "*Terrarum dea gentiumque Roma.*"—Cassiodorus narrates that under Hadrian, Pompeianus and Alettius being consuls, a temple was raised to the worship of Rome ; and a representation of this temple appears on coins of Antoninus Pius, with the legend of ROMAE AETERNAE.—There are also several coins of Augustus and Tiberius, with an altar and the inscription ROM. ET AVG.—See the *words*.

Designed after statues of the best age of art, (which are, however, extremely rare,) we see her on medals of Nero, in the dress of an Amazon, seated on a mass of body-armour or spoils of war, holding in one hand a short sword and in the other a spear. On coins of Galba, Titus, Domitian, Nerva, Hadrian, Antoninus Pius, M. Aurelius, Commodus, L. Verus, Pertinax, Severus, and many other emperors, *Dea Roma* appears either standing or sitting, with her amazonian habit tucked up, and the right breast uncovered. On a first brass of Vespasian, she presents herself seated on seven

hills, at the foot of which are Romulus and Remus suckled by the wolf: in the front, the Tiber personified. The mint of ancient Rome invariably represents "the goddess" wearing a helmet, and frequently, besides the *hasta*, or the lance, holding a small image of Victory, and sometimes a globe. It is a remark of Eckhel's that, under the lower empire, Rome was represented with the head surmounted by a crown of towers, and resting the right foot on a ship's prow.

On *Greek* coins of the Imperial series, the effigy of *Dea Roma* is not always represented with a helmet, but is also ornamented with a turreted crown.—The people of Smyrna, according to Tacitus, built a temple to her, and she was worshipped as a goddess by most of the cities of Asia, as coins to this day testify. Nor did the adulation of the Greek cities stop at paying divine honours to Rome ; but many of them, with the view of conciliating favour from their conquerors, stamped on one side of their coins ΘΕΑΝ ΡΩΜΗΝ, *Deam Romam ;* and on the other side ΘΕΟΝ ϹΥΝΚΛΗΤΟΝ, *Deum Senatum ;* thus including the senate with the city of Rome within the "ample room and verge" of their impious flattery.

ROMA RENASC. vel RENASCES, vel RENASCENS.—Rome rising again—or Rome reborn.—A helmeted figure standing, with a Victoriola in right hand.—This epigraph, on gold and silver coins of Galba, was a vain augury of the Romans indulging in hopes of happier days, after the reigns of those impure and tyrannical men Tiberius, Caligula, Claudius, and Nero. Rome is here called *renascens*, as if appearing to be again free ; for after the death of Caligula the senate, though the government still continued in the family of the Cæsars, had it in contemplation to assert the cause of liberty, so it seemed that, the Cæsarian stock being, by the death of Nero, now extinct, Roman freedom came to a second birth through the election of Galba to the empire.

On the word RENASCES, Eckhel makes the following remark in reference to Havercamp, who interprets it in the *future* tense :—"An opinion this, truly, which imports a gross solecism in the Roman mint, since even tyros knew that it was (in that case) to be written RENASCERIS. But its true sense, the word placed on other coins being RENASCENS, is sufficiently clear. Thus on medals of Vespasian also is read ROMA RESVRGES. The Latins were often in the habit of leaving out the N, especially when it preceded the letter S. Thus also on marbles of the best age you may read INFAS for INFANS, and other instances similar to it have been searched out from lapidary inscriptions by Marinius. The same fancy prevails in the words *quotiens, quadragensima,* &c., the N. is omitted."

ROMA RENASCENS. S.C.—Rome seated, a helmet on her head, a victoriola in her right hand, and the *hasta pura* in her left. First brass of Nerva.

Eckhel does not notice this legend and type under the reign of Nerva ; but Mionnet and Akerman recognize its genuineness ; and Havercamp, from whose work this engraving is taken, makes the following comment :—"Medals were struck during the above reign with the type and inscription of ROMA RENASCENS. (Rome reviving, or springing up, rising, or being born again), in like manner as had already been done under Galba, but with more justice and truth in regard to the latter than to the former emperor. For under Galba the Roman people had cherished only a vain hope of better times—whereas their condition soon changed for the worse through the gross negligence and the shameful debaucheries of Vitellius. Under Nerva, on the contrary, the Roman commonwealth began really to revive, and was perfectly re-established under his successors."—*Cabinet de la Reine Christine*, p. 49.

ROMA R. XL.—See R. XL. ROMA.

ROMA RESTIT. S.C.—There is a first brass of Galba with this legend of *Roma Restituta* (Rome restored), which—accompanied by the type of the emperor raising up by the right hand a helmeted female figure having in her left hand a trophy, or in some coins a child—was obviously designed to shadow forth the same state of popular feelings of joy and confidence at the death of Nero and the accession of the veteran Galba, which is referred to under ROMA RENASCENS.

ROMA RESVRGENS.—S. C.—Vespasian, velled and clothed in the toga, and a female holding a shield, standing by a kneeling female, whom the Emperor is raising up. *First brass.*— Under Vitellius the Roman empire fell into decay and confusion. Assigning, therefore, to that glutton the merit of restoring Rome was an act of wretched flattery on the part of the senate. To Vespasian, on the contrary, it was an honour rightfully awarded. And the large bronze medal, which thus ascribes to him the re-establishment of the Eternal City, first by his military virtues and afterwards by his attention to her architectural embellishment, represents that fine old emperor standing, clothed in the toga, lifting up a kneeling woman; another female figure, helmeted, and with a buckler, stands at the back of the kneeling figure, as if supporting her.—Rubenius and Oiselius understand by the woman on her knees *Liberty* oppressed under Vitellius. This fallen goddess Vespasian raises up, and restores her to Rome, who is present in a military form.

ROMA RESVRGES.—Similar type.—The *Roma Renasces*, in Galba, has been noticed above.—Here we have *Resurges* doubtless for

Resurgens, as already stated.—" And truly (says Eckhel) Vespasian could speak of *Rome rising again* in his reign ; for he signally adorned her with new edifices, whilst he as effectively repaired the old buildings, which, either through neglect in antecedent times or from the ravages of incendiary fires under Nero and Vitellius, had sustained great injury. And it is this golden period of Vespasian of which a retrospect is taken by Tacitus, in that passage of his Annals (xv. 41) where, in dwelling on the splendid monuments of the city which were ruined by the Neronian conflagration, he goes on to say :—*quamvis in tanta RESVRGENTIS VRBIS pulchitudine multa seniores meminerant, quæ reparari nequibant.*"

Roma Aeterna.—Vaillant observes that the Genius of Rome bears a Victory in her hand, as conqueror of the world, and that the peculiar epithet of *Eternal* as applied to *Rome* is one which Livy, Ammianus, Dionysius of Halicarnassus, and Symmachus severally employ, either in prediction of her perpetual domination, or for the purpose of distinguishing her from other cities.

ROMA AETERNA.—This legend, with the type of Rome seated, supporting the heads of the sun and the moon, appears for the first time on a rare gold coin of Hadrian, " under whom (says Vaillant) Rome was called *Eternal*, on account of the many things restored, and the various edifices constructed by him, so as thereby to have been ensured a perpetual duration. A temple was constructed to the honour of *Rome*, as a goddess, on Mount Palatine, by Hadrian himself. It was in memory of these benefits that she holds in one hand the head of the sun, in the other that of the moon, as symbols of eternity, the Romans, from the religion of the Egyptians, regarding those planets as eternal."

Romæ Aeternæ.—From the earliest age it was the presentiment of the Romans that their city would be *Eternal ;* and to such a pitch of madness did this opinion of theirs proceed, that they paid divine honours to Rome, erected temples and altars to her honour, and instituted priests to perform sacrifices to this deity of their own creation.

ROMAE AETERNAE.—This legend, struck in each metal, with various types (but chiefly that of Roma Victrix seated, a shield by her side, a spear in her left hand, and a figure of Victory in her right,) appears on coins of Antoninus Pius, of Pescennius Niger, of Sept. Severus, of Gordianus I. and II., Alex. Severus (first brass), Philip son., Trcb. Gallus, Hostilianus, and others.—A silver medal of S. Severus bears on its reverse ROMAE AETERNAE, with a temple of six columns, adorned with many statues, in the midst of which Rome is seated.

ROMAE RESTITVTAE.—On the reverse of a third brass of Constantine the Great, are this legend, and the image of Rome seated, holding in her right hand a flower, and in her left a globe, divided into zones.

This doubtless was meant to describe the happy change in the state of the city which ensued on the death of the tyrant Maxentius, than whom no one had more cruelly afflicted the inhabitants of Rome ; and in contrast to whose atrocious government the lawful and comparatively merciful sway of Constantine was, therefore, in the eyes of the Romans a renovation of Rome.

Romans.—The following heads of illustrious Romans occur on coins of families, viz., of *Agrippa, M. Antony,* and *M. Antony the Younger, Lucius Antony,* gens Antonia; *L. Brutus* and also *M. Brutus,* g. Junia; *Coelius* Caldus, g. Coelia; *Dolabella,* g. Trebonia; *Domitius* Ahenobarbus, g. Domitia; *L. Libo,* g. Livia; *Livineius* Regulus, g. Livineia; *Munatius* Plancus, g. Munatia; *Norbanus* Flaccus, g. Norbana; *Pompeius Magnus,* as also *Cn. Pompeius F.* and *Sextus Pompeius,* and *Pompeius Rufus,* g. Pompeia; *Numonius* Vaala, g. Numonia; *A. Postumius,* g. Postumia; *Servius* Rufus, g. Servia: *Servilius* Ahala, g. Junia; *M. Silanus,* g. Junia; *Sulla,* g. Cornelia.

Roman Emperors—Portraits of on coins.— See *Imperatores.*

Romanus I. Lecapenus, born in Armenia, of a family in private life, became distinguished in arms, and was made *præfectus classis*, or admiral, under Constantine X., by whom he was afterwards declared Augustus, and associated in the empire at the same time he married Helena, daughter of that prince, A.D. 919.—He soon usurped priority of rank, and gave the second station with title of emperor to his son Christopher, compelling his benefactor Constantine to content himself with the lowest place.—Driven from the throne and banished to the isle of Prota, by his son Stephen, whom, after Christopher's birth, he had taken as his imperial colleague, A.D. 944, he died in a monastery, A.D. 946.—Romanus and his son Christopher united on coins are called ROMAN. ET. XRISTOFO. AVGG. His medals are most rare, both in gold and silver.

Romanus II. surnamed *Junior*, the son of Constantinus X. Porphyrogenitus, and of Helena, daughter of Romanus Lecapenus, born at Constantinople, A.D. 938. Succeeded his father in the eastern empire A.D. 959—a bad prince, and suspected to have been a parricide.—Died A.D. 963, aged twenty-one.—The inscriptions on his coins are in Greek.

Romanus III. surnamed *Argyrus*, the son of Leo, born about A.D. 973, married Zoe (another Messalina), daughter of Constantinus XI., a few days before the death of that Emperor, and through that union arrived at the throne, A.D. 1028.—Poisoned and stifled in a bath by his lascivious and wicked wife, who then bestowed her hand and the empire on Michael of Paphlagonia, A.D. 1034.—Mionnet says there are no coins of this prince.

Romanus IV. surnamed *Diogenes*, of eminent Cappadocian family, and himself a great commander, was the son of Constantinus Diogenes; raised to the throne by Eudocia, widow of Constantine Ducas, whom he married A.D. 1068; he was made prisoner by the Turks A.D. 1071. Restored to freedom the same year he was deprived of sight by Michael Ducas, who, during his captivity, had usurped the throne, and he died in a convent a short time afterwards. There are no Latin inscriptions on this emperor's medals, which are all extremely rare.

Roma Latii.—From certain coins of Commodus, we find "the Eternal City" itself treated as a *colony* by that mad-brained emperor—thus confirming the assertion of Dion, in which, speaking of the unworthy son of Aurelius, he states that he wished his City to seem to be a colony; and to this refers his golden statue with a bull and a cow. It is on large and middle brass, struck *senatus consulto*, that the insane idea of changing the very name of Rome to that of COL*onia* L*ucia* ANT*oniniana* COMM*odiana*, is proved to have been entertained by Commodus—and not only entertained but recorded as a work actually wrought with the usual ceremonial observed in founding a *new* colony, by a veiled priest (in this case the Imperial *Pontifex Maximus* himself), tracing its circuit with a plough, to which are harnessed a bull and a cow. See COL. L. AN. COM.

ROM. COND.—See HERC. ROM. COND. *Herculi Romano Conditori.*—On a coin of Commodus.

ROM. ET AVG. (*Romæ et Augusto.* To Rome and Augustus.) COM. ASIAE.—*Communitas Asiæ.*—A silver medallion in the Imperial cabinet at Vienna, exhibits on one side the naked head of Augustus, with IMP. IX. TR. PO. V., and bears this inscription on its reverse. The type is a temple of six columns, on the epistyle of which the words ROM. ET AVG. are engraved. See COM. ASIAE.

The most learned and skilful numismatists unite in opinion that coins of this type (and there is a variety of them as well in brass as in silver) were struck out of Rome with the character and workmanship of whose *mint* they have indeed nothing in common.

Suetonius, in his life of Augustus, says— "*Templa quamvis sciret etiam proconsulibus decerni solere*, (namely Titus Flaminius, by the people of Calchedon), *in nulla tamen provincia, nisi communi SVO ROMAEQVE nomine recepit: nam in urbe quidem pertinacissime abstinuit hoc honore.*—Eckhel, after making the above citation, alludes to the supposition hazarded by Schlegel, that the temple represented on this medallion was that of the Olympic Jove, at Athens, the construction of which was finished at the common cost of the kings of Asia. This Eckhel treats as an unfortunate conjecture, and proceeds to observe on the contrary—"We have other and most decisive evidences that the temple in question was that of Pergamus (now *Bergamo*), the capital of a province of Asia (Minor). This in the first place is proved by Tacitus—*cum divus Augustus SIBI atque urbi ROMAE templum apud Pergamum sisti non prohibuisset.* To corroborate the fact there are also Greek coins of Pergamus, struck not only after Augustus's death but during his lifetime, on which he is represented standing with a spear in his hand, within a temple inscribed ΘΕΟΝ ΣΕΒΑΣΤΟΝ (Deum Augustum).—Moreover, on other coins struck also in the age of Augustus, at the same city of Pergamus, is seen the head of Rome turreted, with the epigraph ΘΕΑΝ ΡΩΜΗΝ (Deam Romam).—And likewise on a Pergamanean coin, in the Imperial Museum, struck under Trajan, is read: ΡΩΜΗ. ΚΑΙ. ΣΕΒΑΣΤΩ. accompanied with the type of a temple, within which Augustus stands, and, holding a spear, is crowned by Rome, who supports a cornucopiæ in her left arm. If therewith be compared those silver medallions which severally. bearing the heads of Claudius, Nerva, and Trajan, are inscribed COM. ASI. (*Communitas Asiæ); ROM. ET. AVG.*, accompanied with a similar type; and also the beautiful silver medallion of Hadrian, bearing on its reverse the words COM. BIT. (*Communitas Bithyniæ)*, and for its type a temple of four columns with the statue of the emperor in the portico, and the legend ROM. S. P. AVG. on the entablature above, it will be apparent enough that the coins which both in inscription and in type thus agree, although they may differ in language, yet were struck in one and the same city, namely in Pergamus. Still more applicable to the present medal are the words of Dion, who after having stated that Cæsar had permitted a temple to be erected at Ephesus and at Nicæa, in honour of Rome and father Julius, adds: *extraneis autem hominibus quos Græcos ipse appellabat, concessit, ut SIBI quoque templa facerent, ASIANIS quidem Pergami, Bithynis vero Nicomediæ.* Therefore those also are Asiatics, who, on this coin, call themselves COM*munitas* ASIAE, and who show that it was purposed to raise at their own expense the temple ROM*ae* ET. AVGVST*i.* —See the word COM*mune* or COM*munitas.*

ROM. ET. AVG.—An altar richly ornamented between two columns surmounted by Victories, who themselves bear other *images of Victory* and palms. On the face of the altar, two *Genii* support a crown placed between two pines. On a brass medallion of Augustus, also on first and second brass of the same emperor, and of his successor Tiberius. There is a splendid bronze medallion of Tiberius with his portrait and TIB. CAESAR AVGVST. F. IMPERAT. VII. on the obverse—and this same type of an altar and two Victories with ROM. ET. AVG. on the reverse—in the Imperial Cabinet at Vienna.

Antiquaries, in treating of these coins, which are to be found in all large collections, have adopted various opinions concerning them. Amongst the more modern writers, reference may be made to Schlegel and Havercamp, both of whom regard it as beyond a doubt that all of them were struck at Rome, but differ from each other in assigning reasons for their having been publicly stamped.—Eckhel on the contrary asserts, and in the most masterly way makes good his opinion, that they are all of foreign workmanship.—Schlegel thinks it sufficiently proved from these coins that even whilst Augustus lived, an altar was dedicated in the city, and a temple built to his honour, and that this was done about the year V.C. 741, as on the cóin itself Augustus is called PONT. MAX.; and, moreover, he names from Sex. Rufus the region (of Rome) in which these sacred structures stood. But that, so long as Augustus lived, no divine honours were paid to him in the city, is placed beyond a doubt by the arguments of Eckhel on the medals of DIVVS Augustus. The coins in question, therefore, could not have been struck in Rome itself during the life-time of that prince. As, however, from Suetonius and others it is clear that altars and temples were everywhere established in the provinces, to the joint worship of *Rome* and *Augustus,* Havercamp strangely reconciles himself to the notion that these medals are of Roman die, by supposing that the senate wished, by this type, to evince the respect of the conquered people towards the emperor, but that divine worship had not been decreed to the living prince in the city itself.— On these two opinions Eckhel passes judgment to the following effect:—"Even though we may arrive at the conclusion that all these coins were struck beyond the walls of the city, in some one or other of the provinces, it will not be needful either that with Schlegel, against the authority of historians the most worthy of belief, we should rashly assert that Augustus, whilst still

living, received the honours of consecration *at Rome;* or that with Havercamp we should devise the evasion above-mentioned. But I have proofs, not a few, and these of the most valid kind, to shew that this money was coined abroad. I. Augustus, though he forbade divine worship to be paid to him in the city, allowed it freely out of Rome. From a mass of testimonies too numerous to cite at length, I shall adduce some which spontaneously occur to me. Suetonius says: *Provinciarum pleræque super templa et aras, ludos quoque quinquennales paene oppidatim constituerunt.* Aug. c. lxi. The testimonies of Tacitus and of Appianus may be added, from which it partly appears that divine honours were paid to Augustus, on the defeat of Sextus Pompey, and therefore early enough. We have already noticed the altar erected to Augustus at Tarracona. Concerning that at Lugdunum, Strabo states it was erected to Augustus, with a temple, at the confluence of the rivers (the Saone and Rhone), in the name of the Gaulish nations, or peoples, sixty in number. Suetonius hands it down to us that this altar was dedicated V.C. 744; but Dion informs us that the festal day of Augustus had already been celebrated two years before at the altar of Lyons. Livy moreover notices the dedication of an altar to Cæsar (Augustus) at the confluence of *Arar* and *Rhodanus* (Saone and Rhone), and the appointment of C. Julius Vercundaridubius of the Ædui as priest of the same. An epigraph in Gruter makes mention of the altar erected at Narbo *(Narbonne),* by Martius; and the priest of the altar of Rome and Augustus is mentioned in inscriptions found at Lyons. But, what still more closely applies to the present coins, I have brought forward several testimonies under the year V.C. 735 [see ROM. ET. AVG. COM. ASIAE above], that everywhere throughout the provinces temples were dedicated to *Rome, and* at the same time to *Augustus.* I add to these the inscription, which (as mentioned by Pocock) to this very day is read at Pola in Istria, inscribed on the fronts of the temples: ROMAE. ET. AVGVSTO. CAESARI. DIVI. F. PATRI. PATRIAE."— After having quoted Josephus's History for Cæsarea in Palestine, Chishull's *Ant. Asiat.* for Mylæ in Caria, and ancient marbles for Pergamus and other cities in Asia, to shew that in the Greek provinces of the empire, temples were consecrated and inscribed to Augustus, and that the worship paid to him, in his life-time, was associated with that to Rome, the learned and acute author of *Doctrina Numorum Veterum,* proceeds, II. To observe, that "the (religious) veneration jointly paid to each of the divinities (Roma et Augustus) is also marked by the coins themselves, which were doubtless struck *extra urbem.*"—With regard to the medal above described, which exhibits the temple erected by COM*munitas* ASIAE ROM*ae* ET AVGVST*o,* Eckhel expresses his belief that "no one would wish to deny that as a temple established in Asia itself is thereby indicated, so also the medallion itself was struck in Asia; and, therefore, for the coins now in question, a country foreign to

Rome must be sought. III. If these coins had been struck in "the city," there would not have been wanting the mark s. c. *(Senatus Consulto)*, which, on brass money of assuredly Roman die, struck under Augustus, it was never the practice to omit. IV. Many proofs of this are derived from medals of the largest size, but of this age there are none of such volume coined at Rome ; not a few, however, appear which were struck in Spain and in other colonies. V. We have extremely few coins, in large brass, of Roman die, on the obverse of which the head of Augustus, he still living, was engraved. It is therefore in no way probable that the mint-masters, in stamping coins of this kind, should have wished to infringe upon the custom of his age. Lastly, VI. If their fabric be examined, the eye accustomed to inspect coins will easily perceive that it differs exceedingly from that which is found peculiarly to distinguish Roman workmanship. Indeed there is in the Imperial Museum (at Vienna) a coin of this kind extant, with Nero's head upon it, of a fabric so barbarous, and with the letters of the reverse so gaping, that there is evidently no likelihood whatever of its having seen the light in Rome.

No one, therefore (says Eckhel in conclusion), will now, I think, question the fact that all these coins were executed at a distance from Rome. But it is less safe to hazard an opinion as to the particular city which brought forth this commodity ; for the worship of Augustus, as may thus far be seen, was prevalent in all the provinces of the Roman world. All things duly weighed, the supposition may at length be allowed that those divine honours paid to Augustus at Lyons *(Lugdunum Galliæ)* must have been on the days of his nativity. This opinion is the more strongly countenanced by the high celebrity, at that period, of the above-named town, in which Augustus himself resided many years, that he might keep a watch, from its neighbourhood, over the turbulent Germans : Tiberius and Drusus also often took up their abode in that city, not to say anything of its being the birthplace of the Emperor Claudius. The chief reason, however, for ascribing these coins to *Lugdunum Galliæ* is the altar itself of Augustus, the image of which is so conspicuous on their reverse—an altar consecrated with particular devotion, and, according to Strabo, in the name of all *Gallia ;* insomuch that the day on which those religious solemnities were performed, was made a festival in perpetuity, and this custom obtained up to the age of Dion. The same writer also relates that the chief men of Gaul, during the life-time of Augustus, assembled together every year on the anniversary day of the festival to renew their vows. Nor was the city [of Lyons] without a mint *(officina monetalis) ;* for Strabo expressly states that both gold and silver money was struck there. It is, therefore, extremely probable that on the occasion of Augustus's festal day, these coins were then struck and distributed amongst the common people. To the same city of Lyons, in all likelihood, belongs an inscription (cited by

Muratori) in which C. Julius is called SACERDOS ROMAE ET AVGVSTO. AD. ARAM. QVAE. EST. AD. CONFLVENTEM, namely of the Rhone and the Saone *(Rhodani et Araris)*, near which, we see from Strabo, this altar stood.—*Doct. Num. Vet.* vol. vi., pp. 135, 136, 137.

The author of *La Gallerie Mythologique* informs us (t. ii. p. 120) that the columns of this altar have been sawn in two, and form at the present day the pillars which support *la voûte*, or the arched roof, of the Church of Dismay, at Lyon.

ROM. ET. AVG.—Under the head of " *Monnaies frappées hors de Rome,"* the intelligent author of " *Leçons de Numismatique Romaine"* (p. 72-3) has given as an unedited coin a second brass of Augustus, having on its obverse the laureated head of that Emperor, with legend of CAESAR PONT. MAX. ; and on the reverse the words ꓛVA. TENO, and the type, already noticed, of an altar between two Victories placed on pedestals, or columns.

The following are the remarks of this judicious writer on the above singular variety of a well-known coin :—" The ablest antiquaries agree in regarding the medals of this type as not being of Roman die, of which indeed they exhibit neither the workmanship nor the distinctive mark s.c.— It is supposed that they must have been struck at Lyons, where a temple and an altar had been erected, by sixty Gaulish tribes, to *Rome* and to *Augustus*."—He then goes on to say : " This same type is found again on the above described medal ; but with a legend calculated to excite the curiosity of the learned. The word (or words) below the altar (ꓛVA. TENO) : does it present the name of one of the sixty peoples, or of some magistrate ? or, rather, is it anything more than a defective (or blundered) inscription ? Be this as it may, the coin in question was found in *Vivarais* (south of France)." In the engraving the first letter seems more like s than ꓛ.

ROMANO RENOVA. Wolf and Twins.— ROMANO RENOV. Same type.—On coins of *Carausius.*—The epigraph is to be read *Romanorum Renovatio.*—That is to say, Carausius wrests a part of the Roman empire from the hands of Diocletian and Maximian ; and excuses the robbery under an honourable term—*the renewal of the Romans.*

Romulea, or *Romula,* a colony founded by Julius Cæsar in Hispania Baetica, now *Seville* in Andalusia.—It is, according to both Pliny and Strabo, the same place as *Hispalis Colonia;* and it was situate on the banks of the River Baetis (Guadalquiver).—Of this city there are colonial imperial coins, bearing the heads of Augustus and of Tiberius, and their families.

A first brass of this colony, inscribed COL. ROM. *Colonia Romulea,* or *Romulensis,* and struck in honour of the former emperor, after his death (as indicated by the title of *Divus,* the radiated crown and the thunderbolt, symbols of apotheosis), exhibits on its reverse the head of Julia placed on a globe and adorned with a crescent. The legend : IVLIA AVG*usta* GENETRIX ORBIS.—To flatter Tiberius, the colo-

nists of Romula caused a similar coin to be
struck in honour of his mother Julia, with the
preposterous appellation of *Mother of the
World*. For this reason her portrait is placed
on a globe, and adorned with a half moon, as
though she were Lucina, presiding over women
in child-bed, or, to adopt Tristan's suggestion,
as though she were *Venus Genetrix*.

A small brass of the greatest rarity, struck
by the *Romulenses* of Hispania Baetica; the
head of Germanicus is engraven on the obverse,
and the reverse presents a votive shield within a
laurel crown, and COL*onia* ROM*ulea* PERM*issu*
AVGVS*ti*.

[Vaillant is of opinion that this type of a
shield was struck by the colonists in honour of
Germanicus, for having compelled the Germans
to restore the military standards and legionary
eagles captured by the Germans when the legions
under Varus were destroyed.]

On a very rare second brass, bearing the legend
COL. ROM., appears the head of Tiberius on
one side, and on the other the head of Nero
and Drusus Cæsars.—See Akerman's Coins of
Hispania, p. 51, pl. vi. No. 5.

ROMVLO AVGVSTO.—This dedicatory
legend is inscribed on a large brass of Antoninus
Pius. The type depictures the warlike founder
of Rome, in a military habit, marching with a

spear in his right hand, and a trophy on his
left shoulder.—The same type is also found on
coins of Hadrian.—Nevertheless, as Havercamp
(in *Num. Regin. Christin.)* observes, this comparison, whether of Hadrian or of Antonine
with Romulus is by no means too suitable either
to the one or the other; for neither had followed
the example of Romulus by enriching himself
with booty personally won from an enemy in
the field.—By senatorial adulation, however, it
would seem, that allusion is made on the medals
of both emperors to victories gained by their
generals abroad. We learn, indeed, from Capitolinus, that Antonine's love of peace and tranquillity did not prevent him from employing the
Roman arms in repressing such wars as occasionally broke out in the provinces and other
more distant countries. *Per legatos suos plurima
bella gessit*, are the first words of that historian
in the passage of this Emperor's life, where he
states the defeat of the Britons by Lollius
Urbicus, and the construction of another wall,
of turf, to restrain their incursions. By means
of presidents and lieutenants, Antonine also
compelled the Moors to sue for peace; kept

down the insurrectionary spirit of the Germans,
Dacians, and Jews; put an end to rebellions in
Achaia and Egypt; and stopped the hostile
progress of the Alani and other barbarous tribes.

Eckhel observes that this type of Romulus
appears to have been chosen on account of the
singularly fond attachment of Antoninus for the
religious antiquities and customs of the city, a
fondness which embraced even the prodigies recorded in its early history. It seemed good,
therefore, to the moneyers, that this emperor,
who endeavoured to revive, by every means in
his power, a love for the country which had been
carried to the height of greatness by so many
wonders, should be held up as another Romulus;
that is, as a ROMVLVS AVGVSTVS; although by
reason of his pacific policy and pious character
he should rather have been assimilated to Numa.

ROMVLO CONDITORI.—Hadrian, on one
of whose *silver*, as well as *first brass* coins, this
legend is engraved, with a type similar to the preceding, is said to have held Romulus, as founder
of the city, in great honour. The truth of this
assertion is manifested by his having caused the
day of Rome's foundation to be celebrated with
more than usually grand ceremonies, as may be
seen by the memorable coin inscribed ANN.
DCCCLXXIIII. NAT. VRB. P. CIR. CON. (See the
description of it in its place.)—Nor is the claim
of this emperor to be regarded himself as
another *Romulus the founder*, otherwise than
fairly to be allowed, so many were the edifices
at Rome which he built and repaired.—Spartianus
thus enumerates some of the renovations and
enrichments of the capital accomplished under
this magnificent prince: *Romæ instauravit
Pantheum, Septa, basilicam Neptuni, sacras ædes
plurimas, forum Augusti, lavacrum Agrippæ.
Fecit et sui nominis pontem, et sepulchrum, et
ædem Bonæ Deæ transtulit.*

Romulus et Remus.—See *Lupa*.

ROMVLVS *(Marcus Aurelius)*, eldest son of
Maxentius and of the daughter of Galerius
Maximianus, born, as it appears, A.D. 306. Of
this youth, who is said to have been very handsome, nothing more is known for a certainty
than that he was declared Cæsar by his father
when he had completed only his first year, and
Augustus a short time after—that he twice proceeded as the colleague of Maxentius in the
consulship, whilst as yet a mere boy, as his
countenance on the coins shews, and that dying
A.D. 309, his father placed him in the rank
of the gods—all the medals which are extant
of him being struck in memory of his consecration.—Mionnet has given (in his work, *De
la rareté des Médailles Romaines)* a highly
finished engraving from an unique gold medallion,
in the most perfect state of preservation; on the
obverse of this with his bust clothed in the toga,
the young prince is styled DIVO ROMVLO NVBIS
CONS. On the reverse is a temple round in form
and having on its domed top an eagle with wings
spread: the legend surrounding it is AETERNAE
MEMORIAE, and in the exergue POST. or other
letters.—The great French numismatist values
this superb coin at 1,200 francs, but professes,

with Eckhel, his entire ignorance of the meaning of the words NVBIS. CONS. (see p. 578), which have given rise to so many conjectures amongst the older schools of medallists.—There is a fine silver coin of Romulus, cited by Beauvais, as unique.—The second and third brass are not very rare.—One brass medallion, of great rarity, represents him on one side, and *Maxentius*, his father, on the other.—See NVBISCONS.

ROMVLVS AVGVSTVS, son of Orestes, who was one of Julius Nepos's favourite generals, but who, devoured by ambition, ungratefully returned the confidence of his imperial master by driving him from the throne, and proclaiming in his place this young prince, Augustus and Emperor of the West, A.D. 475. But Odoacer, the Herulian, having captured Rome, assumed the title of King of Italy in 476, stripped Romulus of the purple; but compassionating his youth, spared his life; and this last emperor of Rome, being sent away into Campania, finished his days as a private individual near Naples, enjoying a considerable yearly income assigned to him by Odoacer.

This Romulus, on his coins, is styled D. N. ROMVLVS AVGVSTVS P. F. AVG.

The head of Romulus Augustus, as on the gold quinarius here given, is diademed with pearls: usually it is helmeted; and he holds a spear in his right hand, and in his left a buckler, on which is the figure of a horse.—The reverses are, on third brass, SALVS REIPVBLICAE. : a Victory marching with trophy on right shoulder, and dragging a captive.—VICTORIA AVG.: Victory marching. On one gold,—VICTORIA AVGGG.: Victory holding a long cross.—Without legend: a cross within a laurel garland; in the exergue CONOB. : a *quinarius* (see cut.)—Without legend: a soldier standing. All are extremely rare.

ROSCIA, a plebeian family, having for its surname *Fabatus*, of Lanuvinian origin. It was at Lavinia, the ancient *Lanuvium*, and also at Rome, that I. S. M. R.—*Juno Sispita Magna Regina* (Juno the Preserver, the Great Queen), was worshipped with particular devotion; and accordingly we find on the coins of this family (which are all silver, serrated, and common), L. ROSCI, with the head of the above-mentioned goddess covered with a goat skin, and behind it some small figure. On the other side FABATI, with the figure of one of her priestesses performing her allotted task of feeding the sacred serpent of the Lanuvian grove. Propertius gives an interesting description of this ceremony.—*Lucius Roscius Fabatus* was a very great admirer of Julius Cæsar, and was his quæstor in the year V.C. 698, in Gallia Transalpina. He is mentioned by Cæsar himself in his Commentaries, amongst the Legati of the XIIIth Legion.—Morell enumerates forty-three varieties

of the *Roscia* coins, but the variety lies almost exclusively in the *sigilla*, or mint-marks, and none are of historical interest.—See *Juno Sispita*.

Rostra, from *Rostrum.*—This name was given to a public place in Rome, where a species of *estrade* or scaffold stood, surmounted by a tribune, whence the magistrates or other orators harangued the people. It was square in form, supported on columns, ornamented at its base with beaks of ships, and ascended by a staircase. There were two *Rostra, vetera* and *nova.* The former were placed in the Forum, or great square, near the spot called *curia hostilia.* The naval beaks with which they were originally enriched were from the ships taken from the Antiati by the Romans, commanded by the Consul Mænius, who, in the year V.C. 416, destroyed the port of Antium, took their fleet of twenty-two gallies, six of which were armed with spurs or beaks. The figure of these *rostra* is to be seen on a medal of the *Lollia* family in the *Thesaurus Morellianus*, on the obverse of which is a female head, with the name of LIBERTAS, to whom the *rostra* were sacred; also on a denarius of C. Junius Silanus, published by Gessner, and upon other coins both consular and imperial.—The *rostra nova* were called *rostra Julia,* either in consequence of their being situated near the temple of Augustus, or because they were the work of Julius Cæsar, or from Augustus having ordered them to be restored.— Two medals (given in Ursinus) refer to the *rostra nova* or *Julia.* On one is the bare head of Augustus, as is testified by the inscription, CAESAR AVGVSTVS. The reverse of this medal exhibits two persons (whom some have supposed to be Augustus and Agrippa) seated in curule chairs, on a suggestum ornamented with three rostrated prows of ships. Above it is inscribed Caius SVLPICIVS PLATORINus.—The other coin, illustrative of the *rostra nova,* is thus briefly described and explained by Spanheim (*Pr.* ii. p. 193): There exists (says he) a coin of the *Mussidia* family, which shews the *comitium* (or place of legislative assembly) situated near the *rostra vetera,* or elsewhere, in the Roman forum, or by its side, with the *cancelli (lattice),* and with two personages clothed in the toga, who cast the voting balls into urns. At the bottom of the medal is inscribed the surname CLOACIN*ae* Veneris (the Cloacinian Venus), whose image stood in the same place. Thus *Plautus* (in *Curcul.* iv. l. 10) is illustrated, whilst in his turn he throws light on the medal—

Qui perjurum convenire volt hominem, mitto in Comitium ;
Qui mendacem et gloriosum, apud CLOACINAE sacrum.　　See *Mussidia.*

Rostrata Columna.—See *Columna Rostrata.*
Rostrata Corona.—See *Corona Rostrata.*
Rostrum, the beck or spur of an ancient galley, placed on a level with the water. It protruded in front of the prow, and was armed with a sharp point of copper or of iron. It was

almost exclusively used in ships of war (thence denominated *Rostratæ naves*), to render them more formidable against an enemy's vessel, which, when near enough to strike, they frequently sank, by piercing a hole through the side, and letting in the water.—The figure of these *rostrated* vessels occurs frequently on Roman coins, both consular and imperial.— There is a denarius of Pompey the Great, bearing on its reverse a galley with a legionary eagle on its rostrated prow, and with oars and rudder; its stern ornamented with the *aplustrum*, and on the deck a tower stands, surmounted by the figure of Neptune, who holds the trident in his right hand, and plants his left foot on a *rostrum*. Round this type are the words MAG. PIVS. IMP. ITER.

That, in the earliest times of the Romans, *coins* were struck with the prow and beak of a ship appears from Pliny (l. xxxiii. c. 3), *Nota aeris fuit ex altera parte Janus geminus; ex altera rostrum navis; in triente vero et quadrante rates.*—See *Prora navis;* also the *As* and its parts.

On the *rostrum* of a ship Minerva Jaculatrix stands, in gold and silver coins of Domitian.— A silver medal of Augustus also exhibits the prow of a *rostrated* galley, on which a naval trophy is fixed, together with a rudder and anchor placed transversely; the inscription is CAESAR. DIVI. F.

RO. P. S. *Romæ Pecunia Signata.*—Money struck at Rome.

Rota, the figure of a wheel, is the symbol of public roads repaired by order of the reigning prince, for the convenience of carriages, as in VIA TRAIANA.—At the feet of Fortune, it signifies the mutability and inconstancy of that goddess.—We see the wheel, beneath the chair of Fortune sitting, on coins of Sept. Severus, Caracalla, Gordianus Pius, Aurelianus, Gallienus, and other emperors, with the epigraph of FORTVNA REDVX.

R. P. *Romæ Percussa.*—Money struck at Rome.

R. P. *Rei Publicæ.*—See IIIVIR. R. P. C. *Triumvir Rei Publicæ Constituendæ* (for establishing the Republic), on coins of Antony, Lepidus, and Octavianus (Augustus).

R. S. *Romæ Signata.*—Money struck at Rome.

RUBELLIA, a family of the equestrian order, according to Tacitus, originally from Tibur. Its cognomen *Blandus.*—The only coins are small brass, struck under Augustus, inscribed C. RVBELLIVS. BLANDVS. IIIVIR. A. A. A. F. F.

RUBRIA, a plebeian family. Surnamed *Dossenus.* Its plebeian rank is inferred from Rubrius, a tribune of the people, having carried a law, named after him *Lex Rubria.*—There are ten varieties in its coins, of which the silver are common; some of them were restored by Trajan. The bronze pieces of this family are the *as*, or parts of the *as.*—Some denarii present reverses which have given rise to various unsatisfactory conjectures amongst the learned—Havercamp in particular; and even Eckhel himself, though he bestowed two erudite notes on the types in question, acknowledges his ignorance of their exact meaning.

The following quinarius is rare:—DOSSEN. Head of Neptune, with trident.—*Rev.* L. RVBRI. Victory walking, holds a long palm branch above her shoulders; before her feet is an altar, upon which is a serpent.

R. V. *Roma Victrix.*—Rome the victorious.

RVLLI. *Rullus*, surname of the *Servilia* family.

Ruminalis ficus.—The tree under which the wolf (it is said) gave suck to Romulus and Remus. —It is represented, together with the shepherd Faustulus, the wolf, and the twins, on several Roman coins.—A brass medallion of Antoninus Pius exhibits the *ficus Ruminalis*, with Rome in her helmet sitting under it, before whom are the emperor and other figures.

The same fig tree of traditionary fame appears, with a bird *(picus)*, on a denarius of the *Pompeia* family. See *Pompeia.*—And, with the twins, on the shield which Val. Maximianus bears.

Rocks.—These figured on medals indicate a city built on, or situate near, a hill or small mounts. The personified genius of a Roman province is sometimes seen seated or reclining upon rocks or hills. (See *Roma.*)—Thus *Africa*, on a coin of Antoninus Pius; *Britannia* in Antoninus and Commodus; *Dacia*, in Trajan and Hadrian; *Hispania*, in Hadrian; &c.—Rome herself, on the coin which represents the *ficus Ruminalis*, above alluded to, is seated on rocks, allusive to the seven hills on which the city was built.

RVS. *Rusticus*, the surname of the *Aufidia* family.

RVS.—The names of several Roman colonies begin with the letters RVS. Amongst others *Ruscino*, a city in Gallia Narbonensis, which Pliny calls *oppidum Latinorum Ruscinorum*, and to which Mela assigns the title of colony; but by whom founded, whether by Augustus or by Julius Cæsar, is a matter of question.—Its modern name is Tour de Rousillon, in the county of that name, province of Languedoc, not far from Perpignan.—To this place, situate on the Telis (Tela), near where that river empties itself into the Mediterranean, the following small brass coin is referred, alike by Vaillant, Morell, and the editor of the *Mus. Theup*:—IMP. CAES. AVGVSTVS. Head of Augustus, without laurel. —*Rev.* COL. RVS. LEG. VI. *(Colonia Ruscino. Legiones Sextæ).* Two legionary eagles.

[The above military type denotes, says Vaillant (i. 43), the planting of veterans from two legions in this colony. For the *Sixth* Legion was a double one *(Gemina)*, namely, *Victrix*, which Augustus sent to Syria, and *Ferrata*, which he established in Spain. But before he stationed them in the provinces, that emperor drafted off the discharged and worthy soldiers *(Emeriti)* of each, partly to colonise *Cæsaraugusta* and *Acci* (as we know from their coins) and partly to occupy Ruscino. Hence on the reverse in question, two legionary eagles are engraved, with the inscription of LEG. VI. *Legio Sexta.*— Vaillant describes this medal as one of singular elegance and rarity; and further observes that it had been found in the district of Ruscino, given to him, and held a place in his cabinet whilst he was composing his work on the colonial coins.]

Ruso, a surname of various Roman families.

Rustia, a family scarcely known in the time of the republic. Its coins (which in silver are not very rare, but in gold *rarissimi)* exhibit but two varieties, one of which offers on one side two female busts (one of them wearing a helmet), placed on a flattened *cippus*, ornamented on each side with a ram's head, with the epigraph Q. RVSTIVS. FORTVNAE. ANTIAT.—The obverse of the denarius has CAESARI. AVGVSTO. EX. S. C., and an altar, inscribed FOR. RE.—See FORTVNAE ANTIAT.—An almost similar type accompanies SORS, on a coin of the *Plætoria* family The reverse applies to Augustus, and shows that this denarius was struck V. C. 735."

Rutilia, a plebeian family; surnamed *Flaccus*. The following is the only medal (in silver, and not very rare) extant of this family, viz. :—FLAC. Head of Pallas.—*Rev.* L. RVTILI. Victory in a biga at full speed. This denarius refers to L. Rutilius Flaccus, who was an *edilis plebis* in the year V.C. 597, and prætor of a province in 600. This coin seems, however, to have been struck before, viz., in his provincial quæstorship.

R. XL. LIBERTAS. AVG*usti*. S. C.—Liberty standing. On first and second brass of Galba.

R. XL. *(Remissa Quadragesima.* The fortieth abolished or remitted to the people.) ROMA.— On a first brass of Galba we see Rome, helmeted and paludated, standing, with right hand extended, on which stands a female figure, holding a branch or garland in right hand and cornucopiæ in left. The left arm of the Genius of Rome rests on a coat of mail, and holds a caduceus, or in some a legionary eagle; she sets her left foot on a helmet, and before her right foot is a shield.

All writers agree in characterising Galba as unseasonably penurious. Nevertheless, that there was an interval in which he indulged in some liberal acts, and doubtless at his accession to the empire, for the sake of winning favour from the public, is proved by those medals, which predicate a benefit to the public in the no small sum of *quadragesima remissa;* to which is to be added the testimony of Suetonius, who states that Vespasian renewed the taxes remitted under Galba—*(omissa sub Galba vectigalia revocasse.)* —See QVADRAGENSVMA REMISSAE.

S.

S. *Sacra.*—As in the subsigning of Roman coins.—S. M. *Sacra Moneta;* thus SMA *Sacra Moneta Alexandriæ, &c.*

S. M. VRB.—*Sacra Moneta Urbis, &c.,* at the bottom of a coin of Constantius Chlorus.

S. *Sacris.*—AED. S. *Aedibus Sacris.*— S. F. *Sacris Faciundis.*

S. *Sacratissimi.*—ADVENTVS. S. D. N. AVG; the emperor crowned with the nimbus, and on horseback in the habit of peace.—On the reverse of a gold medallion of Marcianus, published by Pellerin, who reads the inscription thus, ADVENTVS *Secundus Domini Nostri*

AVG*usti.* But Eckhel, with better ground of probability for his opinion, thinks that the single letter S constitutes part of the titles of Marcianus, and that it should be read *Sacratissimi.* This name, he adds, is by no means in the present case a newly invented attribute of the emperors. Frontinus had said of Trajan, *clara sacratissimi imperatoris nostri expeditio.* But in the age of Marcianus—namely, the fifth century, nothing is more hackuied than this title of *sacratissimus* as applied to a Roman emperor, especially amongst lawyers.

S. *Salute.*—PRO. S. CAES. *Pro Salute Cæsaris.*

S. *Senatus.*—S. R. *Senatus Romanus.*

S. *Seni or Seniori.*—D. N. DIOCLETIANO. P. F. S. AVG. *Domino Nostro Diocletiano Pio Felici Seni Augusto.*

S. *Servatos.*—O. C. S. *Ob Cives Servatos.*

S. *Servavit.*—H. O. C. S. *Hostem Occidit Civem Servavit.*

S. *Sextus.*—S. ATIL. *Sextus 'Atilius.*— S. POMP. *Sextus Pompeius.*

S. *Signata Moneta.*—P. S. *Pecunia Signata.*

S. *Sint.*—QVOD. V. M. S. *Quod Viæ Munitæ Sint,* or *Sunt.*—See *Vinicia* family.

S. Money struck at *Siscia.*—S. C. *Sisciæ Cusus,* at bottom of a gold coin of Diocletian.

S. *Sispita.*—I. S. M. R. *Juno Sispita,* or *Sospita.*

S. *Solvit.*—V. S. *Votum Solvit,* on a coin of Augustus.

S. *Soluta.*—VOT. XX. S. *Vota Vicennalia Soluta,* on coin of *Val. Maximinianus.*

S. *Solutum.*—V. and S.—*Votum Solutum,* on coin of Augustus.

S. *Spes.*—S. A. *Spes Augusta.*—S. R. *Spes Reipublicæ.*

S. *Spurius,* a surname.—S. N. *Spurii Nepos, &c.*—See *Postumia* family.

S. *Sumptibus.*—D. S. S. *Dedit Suis Sumptibus.*

S. *Suo.*—CONS. S. *Conservatori Suo.*

S. *Suscepto.*—V. S. *Voto Suscepto.*

S. A. in the field of some coins. *Salus Augusti,* or *Securitas Augusti,* or *Spes Augusti,* or *Signata Antiochiæ* (money struck at Antioch).

SABIN. *Sabina.*—SABIN. AVG.—See *Sabina,* wife of Hadrian.

SABIN. *Sabinus,* surname of the *Minatia* and *Tituria* families; the heads of which produced their origin from the Sabines.

SABINA *(Julia),* the consort of Hadrian,

daughter of Mitidia, and great niece of Trajan,

by his sister Marciana. History has not recorded the name of her father. She was given in marriage A.D. 100, to Hadrian, who, through this alliance and the influence of Plotina, was enabled to become the successor of Trajan But although coins in plenty boast of *Concordia Augusta*, and some even exhibit Hadrian and Sabina together, yet mutual disagreements in domestic life, which resulted fatally to Sabina, abundantly prove that these nuptials were uncongenial to Hymen. The infamous passion of the emperor for his minion Antinous was partly the cause, and a just one too, of that irreconcileable hatred which Sabina entertained towards her husband. And, he no sooner saw himself in possession of the throne, than, throwing off the mask of pretended courtesy and of conjugal regard, he became the morose and persecuting tyrant of his wife. On her arrival at Rome, this princess received the title of *Augusta* (SABINA. AVGVSTA. IMP. HADRIANI. AVG.); and the senate flattered her with the name of *Nova Ceres.* But treated by Hadrian rather as his slave than as his empress, her life was one continual course of vexation and unhappiness. Nor on her side was there any display of resignation or forbearance under the insults and indignities to which she was exposed by the brutality of him who ought to have been her protector. She openly declared that the sterility of their marriage was owing to a determination on her part never to bear children to him, lest she should give birth to one who should be more wicked than his father, and become the scourge of mankind. Enraged at her alienation and reproaches, Hadrian, though feeling himself sinking under a mortal disease, had the barbarity to compel her to commit suicide, or, as Roman writers singularly express it, *ad mortem voluntariam compulsa est.* It has been said he poisoned her himself (A.D. 137), a short time before his own death,—and, according to the sarcastic remark of Beauvais, *satisfait de l'avoir ravie à la terre, il la fit placer dans le ciel!*—That she was *canonised* into the number of the goddesses we indisputably learn from the coins of *diva Sabina ;* but that this honour was conferred on her by Hadrian, is scarcely credible under all the circumstances of the case. Eckhel argues this point with his usual intelligence, and refers to the two following silver coins, as confirmatory of his opinion, that Sabina was consecrated not by her husband, but by his successor Antoninus, whose mother she was by the law of adoption.

DIVA. AVG. SABINA.—Head of Sabina, veiled. *Rev.* CONSECRATIO.—An eagle standing; on others, Sabina with hasta in right hand, carried upwards by an eagle.

The second medal has the same obverse. *Rev.* PIETATI. AVG.—An altar.

According to the opinion of some ancient writers, Antoninus was called *Pius* because he wrought upon the senate by the earnestness of his entreaties to decree celestial honours to his father Hadrian. He would seem to have obtained the same requested object in favour of Sabina, from the coinage of this medal with the type of an *Altar*, which he dedicated to her with the epigraph of *Pietas Augusta.*

This empress is described by historians as particularly handsome and well formed, of noble manners and gracious demeanour, of great rectitude and even elevation of mind, in short a truly virtuous woman, whose temper, naturally amiable, had been soured only by the ill-treatment of her husband. That her countenance beamed with an air of majestic dignity will readily be believed by those who have contemplated the lineaments of her profile and the symmetry of her bust handed down on coins of the Imperial and Senatorial mints of Rome. The head dress of Sabina, like those of Marciana, Matidia, and Plotina, is arranged in different styles, sometimes with the hair flowing straight and terminating in a long braid behind, with or without a veil; at other times bound upwards tightly from the back of the neck in a circular knot, and ornamented with a tiara or diadem in front, but almost always with great elegance, proving the diversity and inconstancy of female fashions, whilst the medal fixes the epocha of their change.

The Roman coins of Sabina are common in silver and brass, except medallions ; but the gold are somewhat rare.

Sabina called *Tranquillina*, wife of Gordianus Pius.—See *Tranquillina.*

SABINAE.—The rape of the Sabine women is represented on Contorniate medals, one of which has the image and superscription of Nero ; another those of Agrippina senior ; and a third those of Constantius II.—On these the soldiers of Romulus are seen engaged in their violent breach of hospitality and good faith ; behind the group of men and women are seen three obelisks, constituting one of the Circensian *metæ*, at Rome.

Eckhel, in his no less instructive than copious observations on what he terms " Pseudomoneta," states that, amongst the various subjects to which the types of this peculiar class of medals refer, only one example is to be found drawn from the history of Rome's earliest age—viz., that flagrant injury inflicted on the whole Sabine nation, which the denarii of the *Tituria* family also typify, but upon which it would have been more honourable to have remained silent, instead of restoring its characteristic incidents as the fabricators of these *contorniati* have done. The *meta* is introduced as indicating the place in which the affront was given, namely the Circus.

Sabini.—The Sabines, a people of ancient Italy *(Italia Propria)*, whose country lay between Latium and Etruria. Pliny writes that it was enclosed on both sides by the chain of the Appennines.—Strabo says the Sabines inhabit a narrow field.—*Feronia* was their goddess. See *Petronia* family in Morell.—Butler, in his Ancient and Modern Geography, describes the territory of the Sabini as south-east of the Umbria, separated from Latium by the river Anio, now the *Teverone.*

SABVLA.—See *Cossutia* family.

SAC. *Sacra.* Thus SAC. MON. VRB., &c. *Sacra Moneta Urbis*, as in Diocletian.

SACR. F. *Sacris Faciundis*, vel *Sacra Faciens*. Appointed to take care of sacred things.

C. SACR. FAC. *Censor Sacris Faciundis.* XV. VIR. SACR. FAC. *Quindecimvir Sacris Faciundis.* A tripod, with a dolphin upon and a crow below it, on a silver and gold coin of Vitellius.

SACER. *Sacerdos, Sacerdotes.* Priests, ministers, who, under the Pagan system, were entrusted with all the affairs, interests, and ceremonies of religion. Amongst the Romans the sacerdotal institution commenced with their worship of the gods. Romulus appointed two persons in each curia, to the priesthood. Numa, in adding to the number of the deities, increased also the number of those who were dedicated to the service of their temples. This important function was for some ages exclusively confined to the Patricians and the most illustrious families, but after a time the Plebeians were allowed to share every branch of the priesthood with the nobles. At first, these priests were chosen by the college in which they entered; but in the sequel, after a hard struggle, the privilege of electing them was transferred to the people, and the colleges retained only the right of admitting the candidate into their body. Under Sylla's dictatorship, things resumed their former state, and the people were deprived of the privilege they had usurped. But the alteration was short-lived. Atius Labrinus, a tribune of the people, carried the revival of the *Lex Domitia*, which Marc Antony caused to be again abrogated. At length a monarchical form of government rose on the ruins of republican liberty; and the emperors seized upon the rights which had so long been the subject of mutual contention between the priests and the people. [See the word *Pontifex*.] Augustus augmented the number of priests. The emperors who followed him made a great point of having those destined to succeed them in the empire, even boys, admitted into the College of Priests, which was called *cooptari*, and *cooptari supra numerum*. The case of Nero presents a flagrant instance of many different *sacerdotia* being heaped upon one individual, and he a youth. [See SACERD. COOPT. IN OMN. CONL., &c.]—The emperors went under the assumed name of *Pontifex Maximus.*—The members of the pontifical order possessed several privileges; they could not be deprived of their dignity; they were, moreover, exempt from serving in the army, and from the obligation to discharge the duties of any civic office. The heathen priesthood continued to exist some time under the Christian emperors, and was not wholly suppressed until the reign of Theodosius, who expelled from Rome the whole sacerdotal body, of both sexes, as Zozimus states—*Expellebantur utriusque sexus Sacerdotes, et fana destituta sacrificiis omnibus jacebant.*—The Roman priests may be divided into two classes, viz., those who were attached to the service of no duty in particular, but whose duty was to offer sacrifices to all the gods. Of this class were the Pontiffs, the Augurs, the Decemvirs, the Aruspices, the

Curiones, the Septemvirs, named *Epulones*, the *Feciales*, the *Rex Sacrificulus.*—The other priests had each their peculiar divinity, such as the Flamens, the Salians, the Lupercals, the *Potitii*, the *Pinarii*, the priests (of Cybele) called *Galli*, the Vestals. These priests had assistant ministers to serve them at the sacrifices, such as the *Camilli* and *Camillæ*, the *Flamines* and *Flaminicæ*, the *Cultrarii*, the *Popæ*, the *Victimarii*, the *Fictores*, the *Præclamitatores*, the Lictors, the Scribes, the attendants on the Aruspices, the *Pullarii*, the *Calatores*, &c.

Sacerdos.—The figure of a priest appears at the altar, holding a patera, and behind him is the *victimariis*, or slaughterer of the victim, with the ox for sacrifice, appears on a gold coin of Augustus, with legend of VOTA. PVBLICA.—On a coin of the *Postumia* family, a priest stands on a bullock, with his right hand extended above an ox, the altar being between them.

SACERD. COOPT. IN. OMN. CONL. SVPRA. NVMR. *Sacerdos Cooptatus In Omnia Collegia Supra Numerum.*—This legend, having for its accompanying type four instruments of sacrifice (namely, *simpulum, tripus, lituus, patera*) appears on a gold and silver coin of Nero, with the addition of EX. S. C.

By the manœuvres of Agrippina, unscrupulously ambitious to procure from the senate fresh accessions of honours for her son Nero, at the age of fourteen, he, already designated for emperor, and made *Princeps Juventutis*, was (as this medal tells us) adopted priest in all the colleges, and admitted as supernumerary. The various sacerdotal companies into which this boy was *co-optatus*, or elected a member, are thus enumerated in a lapidary inscription, copied by Pighius.—PONTIF. AVGVR. XVFIR. EPVLON.—And a Gruterian marble marks the time with singular preciseness. ADLECTVS. AD. NVMERVM. EX. S. C. *Nero Claudius* CAES. AVG*usti filius* GERMANICVS. &c. ANN. DCCCIIII. (v.c. 804). These four colleges are also indicated by the type itself. For the *simpulum* is the sign of the pontificate, as coins of Caius Agrippæ F. manifestly show; the *lituus* denotes the office of augur, or soothsayer; the *tripus*, or tripod, is the mark of the quindecimvirate (or commission of fifteen magistrates for ordering religious affairs); the *patera* is that of septemdecimvirate, officers called *Epulones*, whose number had been increased from three (or seven) to seventeen, and whose duty it was, according to the testimony of Cicero, *ludorum epulare sacrificium facere*, to furnish banquets on feast days for Jupiter and the rest of the Gods.

SARERD*os.* DEI SOLIS ELAGAB*alus.*—A figure, clothed in the stola, stands holding in the right hand a patera over an altar, as in the act of sacrificing.—On silver and bronze of Elagabalus.

At the period of his being elected emperor, the son of Soæmias, whose real name was *not* Antoninus, but *Varius Avitus Bassianus*, held at Emesa, in Syria, the office of the Phoenician

Deity called Elagabalus, or Heliogabalus (which his coins lead us to believe was the sun.)—The present is one of a set consisting of six or seven coins (all struck A.D. 219), which bear witness to the insane devotion of this wretched youth for his favourite divinity; of which he brought to Rome both the worship and the idol (the latter being a large black coloured stone of a conical form); and built a temple, where he himself exercised the priestly office. Herodianus, speaking of him and his cousin Alexander, says, they were both high priests of the Sun, which the people of the country chiefly worshipped under the Phœnician name of *Elagabalus*. So when he had brought his oriental tutelary to Rome, and adored him in preference to others, he himself always adopted the title of the God, of whom he was called *Summus et Invictus Sacerdos*.—See *Elagabalus*.

The medals convey but a faint idea of the extravagant veneration which this half madman, half monster, paid to the symbol of the Deity, whose barbaric appellative has remained a nick-name to the execrable pontiff.—The star placed above in the field of the coin, in this and most others of the emperor in question, signifies *Deus Sol*—the Sun, as an object of Divine worship, according to the religion of the Phœnicians and other Asiatic nations. On a marble, in Muratori, is read Junius Maternus SACER. D. S. HALAGAB.

SACERDOS DIVI AVGVSTI.—Two torches with garlands attached. The legend and type appear on gold and silver of Antonia, whose head on the obverse is crowned with corn-ears, as if she had been another Ceres.—Caligula, who was grandson to this princess, conferred upon her the title of *Augusta*, made her *Priestess* of (the temple of) *Augustus*, and appropriated to her all the honours of a Vestal.—Vaillant considers the torches on the reverse as referring to the mysteries of Ceres. But Eckhel is of opinion that this type bears simply on the rites of her Augustan priesthood. He adds that "as it is certain from the very titles themselves that the present coin could not have been struck before the government of Caligula, so is it most probable that it saw light in the reign of Claudius."

Similar reverses to this and to another coin (CONSTANTIAE AVGVSTI) is found also amongst the money of her son Claudius, who frequently restored the memory of ancestors.—See *Antonia Augusta*.

It was this circumstance which induced Havercamp to suspect that the dies had been changed through the carelessness of the mint-master.— Eckhel sees no reason for supposing any such thing. For, he remarks, "Claudius, as well as his mother Antonia, had been appointed a *Sacerdos D. Augusti*, and he indeed by Tiberius, as Tacitus affirms. And there seems to have been another cause for Claudius's choice of this. reverse. For, besides his professing to reverence Augustus so much as to hold no oath-taking more sacred than that of swearing *per Augustum*, he appears to have employed this type for the purpose of removing the disgrace

of another priesthood, the office of which he was himself forced by Caligula to accept, when the latter called himself *Jupiter Latialis*, &c.— *Doct. Num. Vet.* vol. vi. p. 236.

SACERDOS VRBIS.—The emperor stands before an altar; his right hand, hanging down holds a branch; in his left is a spear.—On a third brass of Alexander Severus, the obverse of which bears his laureated head, with the epigraph of IMP. MARCO. AVR. SE. AL. AV.—In the imperial cabinet at Vienna.

Eckhel, in his Sylloge (i., p. 103), has edited and copiously illustrated this remarkable and genuine antique coin. It will have been seen, from the description of some of his medals, that Elagabalus, treating with contempt the sacred rites of the Romans, had the stupid folly to introduce the religion of his Syrian god into the city, and attempt to spread through the empire the worship of the *Dea Coelestis* of the Carthaginians. But it also appears, on the positive authority of Herodianus, that, immediately on his accession to the throne, Alexander, having abolished those barbaric ceremonies, restored in all their former splendor the forms of the ancestral worship. "To this fact, therefore (adds the great German numismatist), both the inscription and the type of the present coin allude. For the reason above mentioned, Alexander called himself *Sacerdos Urbis*—the priest of the city—namely of Rome, which was itself regarded as a goddess, by whose influence Roman affairs were governed, and not by the power of that deity, from whom either Emesa or Carthage sought protection. In the same manner, on an inscriptive marble (*Rosci Memoriæ Breasc.*), a certain Sex. Valerius boasts of being SACERDos VRBIS ROMAE AETERNAE. —On account of the metal, the bad workmanship, and the epigraphs on the obverse, the like of which does not occur in the Roman mint, there is no doubt but that this coin was struck out of the city.—[Eckhel, vol. viii, p. 270.]

Sacerdotalia Instrumenta.—Instruments, or insignia of sacrifices—such as the *apex, securis, culter, capeduncula, adspergillum*, &c., are represented on coins of the pontiffs and priests.— Spanheim (*Pr.* ii. p. 370), with his usual display of learning and ability, treats of those coins which, exhibiting the sacerdotal instruments and the names of the sons of emperors, refer to the offices of priesthood borne by those Cæsars. Thus that class of coins which bears the inscription SEVERI. PII. AVG. FIL. is to be explained as relating to the adoption of, and admission of the children of Severus (Caracalla and Geta), into the sacerdotal colleges.—See *Pontificali* and *Sacrificia*.

Sacerdotal Crowns.—The priests, to denote their sacred office, took for their model the skulls of oxen, and the dishes into which they put the entrails of victims, strung together with the ribands that served to decorate them when led to the altar, and wrought the representation of these objects into the form of a crown.—Such an one is found on a medal of Augustus.

SACR. PER. *Sacra Periodica.*—Sacrificers, periodical or perpetual vows.

SACR. MON. VRB. AVGG. ET. CAESS. NOSTR. *Sacra Moneta Urbis Augustorum Et Cæsarum Nostrorum.*—This legend, more ' or less abbreviated, and with the type of a woman holding a balance in one hand and a cornucopiæ in the other, appears frequently on second brass coins of Diocletian, Maximianus, Maximinus Daza, and other emperors of the same age.

Sacra Moneta Urbis, an inscription which, from the period of its adoption by Diocletian, appears more and more frequently on the coins of the empire, is also engraved on a marble (in Muratori), at the end of which, according to the amended reading of Marini, is CVRANTE. VAL. PELAGIO. V*iro Egregio* PROC*uratore Sacræ Monetæ* V*rbis* VNA. CVM. P. P. *(præpositis)* ET OFFICINATORIBVS.—The inscription of MON*eta* VRB*is* occurs also on medals of Antioch.

SACRA MONETA VRBIS, and MONETA VRBIS VESTRAE, with the type of the three *Monetæ* standing, appear on fine bronze medallions of Constantine junior.

Sacrificia. Sacrifices.—To make these constituted a principal part of the worship which the heathens paid to their fabled deities. In this act the ceremonies performed had relation to the individuals who sacrificed, the animals to be immolated, and the sacrifices themselves. With reference to the sacrificers, they were, in the first place, required to be pure and chaste, and without spot or blemish; secondly, to wash themselves, especially their hands, for which purpose near the temples there were vases, called *Fanissæ*, or *Futilia.* The sacrificer was clothed in white, and wore a crown formed of the leaves of the tree sacred to the god to whom he made the sacrifice. When the sacrifice was votive, or promised by a vow, the priest performed it with dishevelled hair, with robe unloosed, with naked feet, and the ceremony always began with pledges and prayers. The animals intended to be offered up were called *Victimæ* or *Hostiæ.*—At the commencement of the sacrificial rites a herald proclaimed silence, the profane were driven away, and the priests threw upon the victim a sort of paste made of wheaten flour and ' of salt; this was termed *immolatio,* or the offering. He afterwards lightly tasted of wine, and gave it to others present, for them in like manner to taste, pouring the remainder between the horns of the victim. This was called *Libatio,* or the drink offering. After the libations, the fire was lighted, and, as soon as incense had been burnt, certain menial attendants, named *Popæ*, naked to the middle, led up the victim before the altar; another of the priest's servants, named *Cultrarius*, struck it with an axe, and instantly cut its throat. The blood was received into goblets, or broad circular plates, called *pateræ*, and poured over the altar. The slain victim was then laid on the sacred table, *Anclabris*, and there it was skinned and cut into pieces. Sometimes it was burnt whole, but more frequently the sacrificers and their friends shared it with the gods, whence it often happened that many

persons performed this religious solemnity solely from gluttony. The ceremony being finished, the sacrificers washed their hands, said some prayers, and, having made fresh libations, were dismissed in the customary form. If the sacrifice was in the name of the public, it was succeeded by a public feast, called *Epulæ sacrificales,* but if it was a private act of worship the feasting was also in private, and the parties eat of that portion of the victims shared with the gods.—Allusion having just been made to public, in contradistinction to private, sacrifices, it should be mentioned that the Romans had, in effect, three sorts of sacrifices—viz., public, private or domestic, and foreign. The first of these was conducted at the expense of the state; the second was performed by each family, and at the expense of the particular family on whose account the sacrifice was undertaken, and they were called *Gentilitia;* the third class was celebrated on occasions when the tutelary gods of conquered cities and provinces, together with their mysteries or ceremonies, were transported to Rome.—The sacrifices themselves differed from each other according to the diversity of gods adored by the ancients. There were sacrificial rites peculiar to the celestial deities, others for the infernal gods, others again for the marine deities, for those of the air, and for those of the earth. So there was, moreover, as already observed, a difference both in the victim and in the manner of sacrificing it. In the public sacrifices, there were some called *Stata,* fixed and solemn ones, which were reckoned as feast days, marked in the Roman calendar; others extraordinary, named *Indicta,* because they were ordered for some extraordinary and important reason; others again depended on chance; such were those of the *Expiationes,* or atonement; the *Denicales* and *Novendiales feriæ,* viz., ten or nine days together kept holy, for the expiation of some awful prodigy or calamitous event.

Sacrificial preparations are minutely set forth on Roman coins, revealing the clearest representations of sacred vestments and instruments. Thus we see the pontifical mitre, or *albogalerus,* with its *infulæ* or labels hanging on each side. The peculiar form of the *apex* or top of this cap, said to be the sign of the *flamen martialis,* is also learnt from medals. Then there is the whole apparatus of sacrificial weapons spread before us through the same ancient medium— viz., *secespita,* a species of knife; *securis,* the axe; *præfericulum,* the vase; *urceolus,* the small water pitcher; *patera,* the broad dish; *simpulum,* a ladle, or cup with long handle; and *capeduncula,* a little pitcher; all suited to hold wine or blood; *acerra,* or *turibulum,* the censer; also altars and tripods in great variety. On coins of M. Antony the *lituus,* or augural staff, is frequently seen with the *præfericulum.*—The *adspergillum,* or sprinkler, as well in its ordinary form (see the word) as in that of the lustral branch, which the censors used in their office of purification may also be seen on coins of Augustus.—Nor are the instruments solely, but all the "pomp and circumstance" of the sacrifice are offered to our view, on coins of the Imperial series, as in the PIETAS of Caligula, the VOTA PVBLICA of Commodus, &c. The sacrificer dressed in the toga and veiled; the doomed and decorated ox held bound by the *victimarius*, and standing under the uplifted axe of the *popa*; the *sacerdos*, with head veiled, pouring from a patera libations on the altar; lastly, the augural crows, together with the *tibicen*, or flute player, the *citharoedus*, the harper, and other assistants at a pagan sacrifice, are clearly and graphically displayed on these medallic monuments of Roman antiquity.

Sacrificans Imperator.—The emperor sacrificing before an altar appears on *Latin* coins of Domitian.—Also of Nerva, Trajan, Hadrian, Antonine, M. Aurelius, L. Verus, Commodus, Severus, Caracalla, Geta, Elagabalus, Alex. Severus, Gordianus Pius, Trebonianus Gallus, and their successors down to Licinius senior.

The emperors, as soon as elected, performed solemn sacrifices, in quality of their pontificate. After Tiberius, they were admitted to all the orders of priesthood.—On a first brass of Severus are three figures clothed in the toga, veiled, and in the act of sacrificing, two joining hands across a lighted altar, and one in the centre behind the altar.——In the *Cabinet Farnèse* a similar type is given as from a first brass of Caracalla. And as the former medal bears the 18th Tribunitian power of the Father (COS. III.), and the latter medal records the 13th Tribunitian power (COS. III.) of his eldest son and successor, the supposition of Havercamp (in *Mus. Christin.* 164) appears extremely probable, that the type in question of an offered sacrifice refers to the subject of the Britannic victory, achieved by the emperor and his sons, A.D. 210, and that Severus, Caracalla, and Geta here are represented redeeming the vows which they had made to the gods at the commencement of that memorable, but to the emperor himself fatal, expedition.—On a coin of Caracalla and Geta, two emperors are seen sacrificing (see SAECVLARIA SACRA); the same type occurs in the Philips, father and son; in Valerianus and Gallienus; and on a medal of Aurelian the Emperor and a woman standing opposite each other perform sacrifice at an altar. On some imperial coins, *three, four, five*, and even *six* figures—for example, the SAECVLVM NOVVM of Philip sen.

SAE. *Sæculares.*——See LVD. SAE. FEC. *Ludos Saeculares Fecit.*—On coins of Domitian, Severus, Caracalla, referring to the celebration of the secular games.

SAEC. *Sæculi.*—SAECVLI FELICITAS.

 SAECVLARES AVGG.—This legend, with the type of a *cippus*, or of Romulus and Remus suckled by a wolf, or of some wild beast (such as a hippopotamus, an ibex, a stag, a lion, &c.), appears on coins, in each

metal, of Philip, father and son, and of *Otacilia*, empress of the former. They bear reference to the *secular games* celebrated in the thousandth year from the foundation of Rome. The animals represented on the reverses of some of these medals are amongst those which were exhibited in the amphitheatre on that and similar occasions. The *cippus* is a column with an inscription, which it was customary to erect for the purpose of preserving the memory of some particular public event; as may be seen on coins of Augustus, struck *ob vias munitas;* and as in former cases of secular celebrations may be observed to have been before done, in the respective reigns of Domitian and Severus.—See *Ludi Sæculares*.

SAECVLARES AVG.—A stag standing, beneath it a palm branch. This appears on a silver coin of Gallienus in the Vienna Museum. On others it is engraved SAECVLARHS.

As, not very long before the reign of Gallienus, the secular games were performed, viz., under Philip and his son, it has been supposed by some that the above reverse was rashly counterfeited by Gallienus from the mint of those two predecessors of his.—But, says Eckhel, they certainly are mistaken; for on the coins of the Philips AVGG. is always read, and at the bottom of them, instead of the palm-branch, there is invariably a numeral mark; nor on any medals of the last-named princes do we ever find that barbarous SAECVLARHS which is common on the coins of Gallienus. It must be acknowledged, therefore, on numismatic testimony, that among other proofs of madness by which Gallienus signalised his reign, was his having at an irregular period ordered the secular games—an instance by no means without precedent—the time for these particular celebrations having been anticipated by Claudius also.—We learn from Trebellius, that on receiving intelligence of Macrinus's death, Gallienus began to indulge in pleasures, and to give to the public sports of every description, amongst which it is probable were also the *ludi sæculares.*--But, respecting the apparently improper times in which these games were suffered to take place, our illustrious numismatist has more copiously discussed the question in his annotation on a third brass of Maximianus Hercules (in the Imperial Cabinet at Vienna), bearing on its reverse the following inscription:—

SAECVLARES AVGG. A *cippus;* below it IAXX.—This remarkable coin, however, from which all suspicion of fraud is to the remotest degree removed, openly attests the celebration of those games, which were secular, as is manifestly shewn, not only by the epigraph (SAECVLARES AVGG.) but also by the type (a *cippus*), which is also the symbol of the *Ludi Sæculares* on the coins of the Philips.

Eckhel in an elaborate dissertation observes that this is not the only coin bearing witness to the fact of secular games performed at an irregular period of time, yet on which historians are silent. He then refers to the two silver coins of Gallienus, which have just been noticed, as the subject of his own elucidations; and remarks that Banduri is one of those who, aware of the existence of both the above medals, charges Gallienus with having recklessly applied to his own coin a reverse which belongs to the Philips.—*Doct. Num. Vet.* vol. viii. pp. 20 *et seq.*

SAECVLARIA SACRA. S. C.—Sacrifice, with victim, flute-players, *popa*, and some other assistants. On a first brass of Sept. Severus.

This is one of three medals which commemorate the secular games performed by Severus,—a fact corroborated by Caracalla's coins of the same year, and still further authenticated by Herodian and Zosimus.

SAEC. AVR. *Sæculum Aureum.*—This legend appears on a silver and a gold coin (both of them transcendently rare) of Hadrian. The accompanying type is a half naked man, standing in the middle of a circle, which he touches with his right hand; his left hand holds a globe, on which rests a phœnix.

The Genius of the Senate seems to be in this circle, as if to denote that Hadrian's reign deserved to be called the *Golden Age*. For this reason the circle is introduced, as likewise a phœnix placed on a globe, both these constituting symbols of eternity.

SAECVLI FELICITAS.—On a third brass of Julia Domna, this legend appears with the type of a female figure, standing with a child on her arm, and her left foot on a galley.—Akerman.

SAEC. FEL. *Sæculi Felicitas.*—On a silver coin of Commodus, which has for its type a figure of Victory inscribing on the trunk of a palm-tree VO. DE. *Vota Decennalia.*

SAECVLI FELICIT*as. The happiness of the age.*—On silver and brass of Faustina junior this legend appears, with the type of two boys in a *lectisternium.*—See *Lectisternium.*

Commodus and Antoninus, whom Faustina brought forth at one birth, are here dedicated in worship to the Dioscuri (Castor and Pollux). As to any degree of *felicity* imparted to the age by that event, it is certain that the subsequent æra utterly failed to prove the reality of the anticipated blessing.

SAECVLI FELICITAS.—Accompanying this legend there is a rare and curious type, from the mint of Severus, given among the second brass of the *Mus. Christinæ*, and also from a gold coin in the Imperial *Greek Cabinet*, pub-

lished by Andrew Morell, in his *Specimen Rei Numariæ*. The inscription of the obverse round the laureated head of the emperor is—SEVERVS PIVS AVG.; and on the reverse is read CO*n*Sul III. P*ater* P*atriæ*. SAECVLI FELICITAS. In the field of the coin stands a female figure, clothed in the *stola*, holding on her left arm a cornucopiæ filled with grain and fruit, and in her left a dish or patera, which she extends before her over the heads of two smaller figures (apparently children), as if in the act of showering its contents over them : there are three other little figures close behind her, lifting their faces and hands up towards this personification of the *Felicity of the Age*. The particular occasion on which this singular medal was struck is but matter of conjecture.—Havercamp quotes the commentary of Morell, who regards the medal as referring to the great and munificent care taken by Severus in furnishing an abundance of provisions to the Roman people. On this subject he cites the authority of Spanheim *(Biography of Severus*, c. xxiii.) to the effect, that this emperor " bequeathed for public distribution so great a number of measures of corn, as would supply every day, for seven years, 75,000 bushels; and that he likewise left by his dying will for the same purpose a quantity of oil sufficient for the consumption, during five years, not only of the city of Rome, but even of all Italy !"—Mionnet and Akerman both include this among the rare reverses. It is not noticed in Eckhel.

Sæculi Felicitas.—This flattering legend also appears on bronze medals and medallions of Trebonianus, Marius, Probus, and Carus, with the elegant type, copied from the well-known coin of four boys, representing the four seasons and their attributes.

SAECVLI GLORIA.—See GLORIA SAECVLI.

SAECVLO FECVNDO.—On a first and second brass of Clodius Albinus, exhibiting the type of a man with radiated head, holding in one hand a caduceus and in the other a rake, or some instrument resembling a trident.

The age of Albinus and his successful rival Severus, was indeed fruitful, but its fecundity chiefly consisted in human misery and in social desolation, produced by the wars of ambitious chieftains and their military adherents fighting for supremacy at the expense of a mighty empire in its period of decline.

SAECVLO FRUGIFERO.—A caduceus between corn-ears. On silver of Pertinax.—To the honour of this good but ill-fated emperor, it is recorded by Dion, that scarcely had he ascended the throne when he himself undertook a sea-voyage for the sake of procuring a supply of corn for the people. *Annonæ consultissimè providisse* is a merit on the part of Pertinax expressly ascribed to him by Capitolinus.—It was therefore to signify the abundance of all articles of subsistence which prevailed under his government that this epigraph of the fruit-bearing or plentiful age *(Sæculum Frugiferum)* was adopted, with the appropriate type of ears of corn and the caduceus, as a symbol of peace.

SAECVLO FRVGIFERO. COS. II.—On first and second brass of Clodius Albinus. The type, which is given here, from a large brass coin, resembles that described above. In the gold series, however, occurs a remarkable variety. The *Saeculum Frugifer* is represented as a seated, bearded, figure, wearing an eastern head-dress; his right hand is raised; and in his left he holds a flower. On each side of the chair is a winged sphinx, wearing the Phrygian cap. A similar type is found on two medallions in brass in the French cabinet.—See M. Lenormant's remarks in *Revue Num.*, 1842, p. 20.

The same legend (SAECVLO FRVGIFERO) is found on a first brass of S. Severus, who certainly appears to have been almost unprecedentedly provident for the wants of his subjects, *in re frumentariâ.*—Immediately on his arrival at Rome, he evinced his policy as well as his providence by sending legions into Africa, lest Pescennius Niger should, through Libya and Egypt, occupy the former province, and cause the Romans to suffer under a scarcity of corn. And (as Spartian affirms) he extended his care in this respect during all the remaining years of his reign, *ut moriens septem annonum canonem reliquit;* so that 75,000 measures of oil alone might be expended daily, which should suffice for five year's consumption not only of the city but of all Italy. "The type of this coin represents a man with a radiated head, holding a caduceus with corn ears and a trident, and (observes Eckhel) is composite; for the rays indicate the sun, by whose ripening influence the fruits of the earth come to maturity; the caduceus and the corn ears apply to Mercury, the presiding deity of trading people; the trident symbolises Neptune, across whose waves the corn-laden fleet was borne."

SAECVLVM. An altar with fire on it.—Banduri gives this as on a third brass of *Tetricus filius.*

Eckhel briefly says of this coin, that the epigraph of its reverse is new, and that its type has a recondite meaning, which he does not attempt to explain.

SAECVLVM NOVVM.—A temple of six, in other coins, of eight columns, in which is an idol seated.—Silver and first and second brass of Philip sen.—There is also a middle brass, in which Philip and his son, veiled, are sacrificing at an altar, with flute players and four other figures standing near, in front of a temple.

This *New Age*, like the *Thousandth Year*, (MILLIARIVM SAECVLVM, which see,) commemorated on a coin of the same emperor, bears reference to the secular games so munificently celebrated by him in the 10th century from the foundation of the city, the charge and management of which was entrusted to the Quindecimvirs. The temple is that of Jupiter Capitolinus.

The same reverse occurs on coins of Herennius Etruscus, Hostilianus, Trebonianus, and Volusianus, from which it appears that *Novum Sæculum* does not necessarily signify the first year of a new century or age; for we read this epigraph on the coins of the above-mentioned princes, although the *sæculum* was not renewed during their reigns.

Sagitta, an arrow.—This missile is seen in the hand of *Diana Venatrix,* on coins of Titus, Domitian, Hadrian, Trebonianus, Aemilianus, Gallienus, and other emperors.—Also with quiver and bow, between two serpents, on a medal of M. Antony.—An arrow, bow, and tiara appear on a coin of Augustus.—Three arrows appear in the hand of the figure of Asia, on a coin of Hadrian.—On a denarius of the *Cornelia* family, Bacchus (standing between two females) holds in his right hand the thyrsus, and in his left a bundle of arrows, *both* of which Eckhel shows to have been attributes of the god of wine.

Saguntum, a city of Hispania Tarraconensis, founded by the Zacynthians, "and situate beyond the river Iberus, or *Ebro,* at the foot of a chain of mountains (says Pliny) which divides the Hispani from the Celtiberi, about a thousand paces distant from the sea. It was once a flourishing and faithful ally of the Romans.—During the second Punic war (A.V.C. 535, B.C. 216,) Saguntum was rendered famous by the siege which it endured for four months, at the expiration of which time Hannibal took it, and the inhabitants, rather than that their persons and property should fall into his hands, committed *both* to the flames.—*Saguntum* is stated by Pliny to have been neither a colony nor a municipium, but simply a town of Roman citizens, for that writer makes a distinction between the *colonia,* and the *urbs* or *oppidum civium Romanorum.*—It is still a place of some consequence in Valencia, under the modern Spanish name of *Murviedro,* at the mouth of the river of that name (the ancient *Turia*).—The coins of the Saguntines (brass) are autonomous and imperial, the latter with the head and name of Tiberius only.—*Rev.* SAG. *Saguntum,* and the names of the Duumvir, with the type of a trireme and military standard. The galley either refers to its site, or implies its maritime importance.—See Akerman's *Coins of Cities and Princes*, p. 102-3.

Salacia, the reflux or ebb of the sea personified.—*Venilia* was the flow of the tide.—Millin—*Diction. de la Fable.*

SAL.—These three letters are engraved on a silver coin of Sextus Pompey, immediately beneath the head of Cn. Pompey his father.—On the subject of this singular abbreviation, which has given rise to some conflicting conjectures, Jobert, among others, reads it SAL*duba*, which was the old name of *Cæsaraugusta* (Sarragossa.) Bimard, on the other hand, shews the fallacy of this opinion; but, in its place (for reasons with which, however, he seems himself not sufficiently satisfied), proposes that it should be read SAL*us*.—There is ingenuity in the explanation offered by Vaillant, citing Appian, who reads it SAL*acia*, a marine goddess regarded as the spouse of Neptune. Vaillant thinks, therefore, that as Sextus Pompey had, on other denarii, caused himself to be called the son of Neptune, so, on the coin in question, he openly professes to be the son of Salacia.—Against Vaillant's ingenious interpretation is the question as to what the word in the Greek text of Appian may have been, for it reads Θαλασση and not Σαλατια, and thus would mean merely *mare*, the sea. Still Eckhel thinks the latter may have been the word, as in H. Stevens' edition, quoted by Vaillant, and that it may have been altered by some transcriber who was ignorant of the goddess Salacia.—See *Doct. Num. Vet.* vol. vi. pp. 27 and 28.

SAL. AVG. *Salus 'Augusta*, or *Saluti Augustæ;* on a silver coin of Hadrian.

Salduba, a city of Hispania Tarraconensis, situate on the river Iberus *(Ebro)*.—Its name was changed by Augustus to *Cæsarea Augusta;* afterwards it was called in one word *Cæsaraugusta* (now *Saragossa)*.—Cæsaraugusta was made a free colony, and its imperial coins extend from Augustus to Caligula.—COL. CAESAREA. AVG. SALDVBA.—See *Cæsar-Augusta.*

SAL. GEN. HVM. *Salus Generis Humani;* on a coin of Commodus.

Salii Sacerdotes.—The origin of the Salian priesthood is uncertain. Its usages and ceremonies do not appear to have ever been practised by the Greeks, though it is probable that the Romans modelled their institution in imitation of the Pyrrhic system of religious dances. Numa Pompilius was the first to establish a college of them as priests of Mars, on the occasion of an alleged prodigy, related by Dionysius of Halicarnassus. A buckler having fallen from heaven, the Aruspices oracularly pronounced the event to signify that the city, in which it should be preserved, was destined to possess the empire of the world. The politic monarch affecting to be apprehensive lest this precious monument should be stolen, caused eleven others to be made like it, in order that the recognition of the true one might be rendered impossible, and by his com-

mand also they were all deposited in the temple of Mars, where twelve young patricians, who had father and mother, were appointed to guard them. Tullus Hostilius doubled the number of these priests, and also of the *Ancilia*, as the sacred bucklers were called. And every year, on the feast of the god, the Salians carried these shields in procession through the city, dancing and leaping, whence came their name of *Salii*. At these festivities, which lasted three days, they also sang verses which bore reference to the solemnity.—This priesthood was held in great veneration at Rome, and the noblest families of the city regarded it as a high honour to have any of their members admitted into the college of the Salians. These priests, when performing their functions, wore a gold embroidered tunic, a sword in a belt of brass, and on their heads either the cap called *apex*, or brazen helmets; in their right hand they held a lance, or a wand; and on the left arm each bore an *ancilium*.—It was thus dressed, accoutred, and armed that they executed their leaping dances to the sound of flutes, and between the dancing chanted obsolete hymns of praise to all the dieties, and in honour of the great men of the republic.

Saliorum Apex.—This head dress of the Salian priesthood appears between two ancilia, on a very rare gold coin of Augustus, struck by his moneyer, P. Licinius *Stolo.*—See *Ancilia.*

Saliorum Capita.—Gesner and Morell in their family and consular coins respectively give the heads of Salians, with an *ancilium*, as from a denarius of C. Aufidius Orestis Aurelianus, struck on the occasion of some successful war. For it was the custom for him, who had the charge and command of any war, before he went out on his expedition, to enter the *sacrarium* of Mars with the Salian priests, and there to move or raise up *(commovere)* first the *ancilia*, and afterwards the spear of the God's idol, saying—*Mars, vigila.*

A *Salian* priest is represented on a coin of *Sanquinia* family. And one of this sacerdotal order is on account of the military dance which the Salians performed at the secular games, represented on a silver medal of Domitian, standing before a *cippus*, holding in one hand a winged caduceus, and in the other a shield.—See LVD. SAEC. FEC. COS. XIIII.—Also see *Sanquinia.*

SALONINA *(Cornelia)* wife of Gallienus.—

Of her family nothing is known, but all historians agree in characterising this lady as one whose beauty and wisdom were equalled only by her prudence, courage, and conjugal virtue. Married to Gallienus about ten years before his accession to the throne, she was named Augusta, when her husband became associated with his father Valerian, in the sovereign power A.D. 254. Without pride, without luxury or ostentation, and, though flagrantly outraged by the infidelities of her imperial consort, superior to the provocation of jealousy ; ever zealous for the public good, and distinguished by her true benevolence and amiable condescension, this accomplished princess patronised learning and encouraged meritorious talent throughout the empire, which her voluptuous consort would have left without a struggle on his part to be torn to pieces, but that she more than once stimulated his dormant valour by her remonstrances, and conciliated the wavering loyalty of his legions by her companionship in the dangers and privations of war. The vicious misconduct of her husband had, however, brought state affairs into inextricable difficulties ; and at the siege of Milan, where the usurper Aureolus had shut himself up, she fell a victim to the fatal conspiracy formed against Gallienus, and perished with him A.D. 268.   She was the mother of two princes, Saloninus and Julius Gallienus ; and of one daughter Licinia Galliena.

Her small brass coins and the silver ones of of the ordinary size are common ; first and second brass rare ; the gold very rare.   On these she is styled SALONINA AVG.— CORnelia SALONINA AVGusta.—Some pieces represent her with Gallienus.

M. de Witte, with good reason, considers the coins of Salonina, bearing on the reverse AVGusta IN PACE, to have been struck by Christian moneyers after her death.—*Revue de la Numismatique Belge*, 1852, p. 321.   An example, in small brass, from Mr. R. Smith's collection, is here given.

SALONINVS *(Cornelius)*, eldest son of Gallienus and Salonina, born A.D. 242, was declared Cæsar by Valerian, his grandfather, at the same time that his father was associated to the imperial government, A.D. 253.—About the year 258 (according to Beauvais) he received from his father the titles of *Imperator* and *Augustus*.   Sent by Gallienus into Gaul, under a preceptor, named Sylvanus, his residence in those provinces contributed to maintain them in obedience to the Romans till 260.—Gallienus, after the captivity of his father, being compelled to go into Pannonia, then disturbed by the revolt of the usurper Ingenuus, continued to entrust his son to the care of Sylvanus, who,

jealous of the warlike exploits and increasing glory of Postumus, prefect of the Gauls, embroiled his young master with the soldiers of that experienced general, in the paltry matter

of some booty taken from barbarians who had been repulsed in an attempt to pillage the borders of the Rhine.   The consequence was their revolt from Saloninus, and their election of Postumus as emperor—immediately followed by his laying siege to Colonia Agrippina (Cologne), where the youthful Augustus and his preceptor resided, and where on their being delivered up by the cowardly garrison, both were put to death by order of Postumus, A.D. 259.—Saloninus was placed amongst the number of the gods by his sorrowing father, who, however, did not fulfil his oath to avenge his death on the head of Postumus.

The coins of this young prince are in ordinary sized silver, and in small brass, common ; rare in first and second brass, and very rare in gold, as also are his bronze medallions.—On these he is styled P. LIC. COR. VALERIANVS CAES.—SALON. VALERIANVS NOB. CAES.—IMP. C. L. VALERI-ANVS. NOB. CAESAR.   VALERIANVS NOBIL CAES. —IMP. C. P. LIC. VALERIANVS. P. F. AVG.— DIVVS CORN. SAL. VALERIANVS.—Some of the pieces represent him with Gallienus.

The medals which numismatists were formerly accustomed to divide between Saloninus and Valerianus junior, are now assigned solely to Saloninus.   The researches and opinions of Eckhel have led to this decision amongst antiquaries on a once perplexed and unsettled question.   The learned and acute author of *Doct. Num. Vet.* has, in two copious and elaborate *diatribes* (see tom. vii. p. 427 *et seq.*), clearly shewn that Valerianus the younger, brother of Gallienus, never took the title either of Cæsar or of Augustus, and consequently that no medals were ever struck in honour of that prince.

"The medals of Saloninus (says Mionnet— *Med. Rom.* tom. ii. p. 54) have this peculiarity, that great numbers of those struck during the life-time of this young prince give him the title of Augustus, whilst on the greater part of the medals struck after his death he bears only the title of Cæsar.   From this latter circumstance, it seems to follow that Saloninus had no legal claim to be called Augustus ; that is to say, if this title was conferred on him by his father, it was not confirmed to him by the senate.   But, in that case, how does it happen that this title is found on medals which were struck before the death of that prince ?   We must believe, with Eckhel, who seems to have given the most satisfactory solution to this difficulty, that Gallienus, in departing from Gaul on his expedition to

pacify Pannonia, and in leaving there his son
(Saloninus) under the care of Sylvanus, had
previously taken the step of conferring upon him
the title of *Imperator*, in order to give him
more authority, and that many mint-masters,
deceived by this title, which was usually accompanied by that of Augustus, were induced to
add that title also on their medals, believing
that it really belonged to the prince. The
supposition respecting the title of *Imperator*
given to Saloninus is warranted by several
monuments in which this honour is united to
that of CAESAR, or of NOBILISSIMVS CÆSAR."—
See *Doct. Num. Vet.* tom. vii. p. 426.

SALVATOR REIPVBLICAE.—This legend
occurs on a most rare gold coin of Vetranio (an
usurper in the reign of Constantius, about
A.D. 350), the type being a common one of that
age—viz., the Emperor holding a labarum with
the monogram of Christ, and a Victory crowning
him.

Eckhel, who gives it from the *Mus. Cæs.*,
says—"This inscription is new, but it is also
barbarous. For by Seidelius, and other learned
commentators, it has already been remarked
that, instead of *salvatore* and *salvare*, words
taken from the discipline of the Christians, and
inverted by the Holy Fathers (of the Church),
it would be in better latinity to say *servator* and
servare."

SALVIA, a plebeian family; surname *Otho*.
Its coins present four varieties. There are pieces
in silver and in brass bearing the name of this
family, struck by the moneyers of Augustus;
and among others the following:—M. SALVIVS.
OTHO IIIVIR A. A. F. F., in first and second
brass, with the head of Augustus, behind which
is a victory, as if crowning the emperor with
laurel.—This monetal triumvir was the grandfather of the Emperor Otho, and had himself
served the prætorship.

SALVIS AVGG. ET CAESS. AVCTA. (vel
FELIX) KART.—A woman standing, holds in
outstretched hand a branch or some fruits.

This reverse frequently occurs on second brass
coins of Diocletian, and of his imperial colleague
Maximian. Victor thus explains it:—*Ac mirum
in modum novis adhuc, cultisque moenibus
Romana culmina, et ceteræ urbes ornatæ; maxime
Carthago, Mediolanum, Nicomedia.*—It is certain,
therefore, that Carthage was enriched and improved (AVCTA) by the senior *Augusti*, with
similar bounties to what the same city experienced
under Severus, some examples of which are
referred to by the mint masters of that emperor,
in the year V.C. 956, on the coin inscribed
INDVLGENTIA AVGG. IN CARTH.—Accordingly
we find the medals of Diocletian and Maximian
predicting the happiness of Carthage, FELIX
KART.—Indeed, Herodianus, speaking of that
city as it existed in his time, highly extols its
prosperous condition, in point of population,
extent, and resources. And it appears to have
continued a most flourishing place under subsequent emperors, until a rival sprung up in the
Byzantine capital of Constantine the Great.—It
is not sufficiently clear what the woman holds in

her hand, whether a chaplet or a branch, corn
ears or grapes, nor what connection there is
between the type and the inscription. The
epigraph of the reverse is some form of acclamation.

SALVIS. AVGG. ET. CAESS. FEL*ix* ORBIS
TER*Rarum*.—One of the *monetæ* standing
between a woman, and Mars who bears a Victory.

—On the other side is a bust of Maximian,
armed with a buckler, and holding his horse by
the bridle, with this legend, VIRTVS MAXIMIANI
AVG.

Here not merely a single city like Carthage,
or Nicomedia, or Milan, but the *whole world* is
made *happy* in the health and safety of the
Augusti and *Caesares* of Rome!—Medallion in
bronze, of great rarity.

Salus (Health), a Goddess of the Romans,
the same that was worshipped under the name
of Hygièa by the Greeks, who feigned her to be
the daughter of Æsculapius and of Minerva.
On a denarius of the Acilia family appears the
head of the goddess, and on the reverse a
female standing with a serpent in her hand.
The types of this divinity on imperial coins most
frequently present to view a woman clothed in
the stola; sometimes she is sitting, at others
standing; in others in a recumbent posture,
with a serpent either on her right or her left
arm in a quiescent state, rising in folds, or
entwined round an altar before her, and receiving food from a patera, which she holds in
her extended hand. It is in this form (which
was doubtless that of her statues and with
these symbols) that she is exhibited on most
of the coins of the imperial series from
Galba to Maximianus She had a celebrated
temple at Rome, painted, it is said, by Q.
Fabius, who thence was surnamed *Pictor* (the
painter).—There appears to be some affinity
between this personification of *Salus*, when
offering food in a *patella* to a serpent, and the
Lanuvian virgin represented in the same act on
coins bearing the head of *Juno Sospita*.—The
opinion also has probability on the face of it,
which refers the *serpent* on coins, where mention
is made of *Salus Augusti*, or *Augustorum*, to
Æsculapius and his daughter *Hygæia* (or *Salus)*
as deities of Health.—Certain it is that when
those sanitary divinities, and especially when
Dea *Salus*, occur on coins of Emperors, they
indicate that those princes were labouring at the
time under some diseases; on which account, it
would seem, sacred rites had been performed for

them, and the memorial of the event recorded on public monuments.—See VOTA PVBLICA PRO. SAL*uti* PR., as in Commodus; SALVS AVG*usti*, as in Tetricus Filius and Claudius Gothicus; and SALVTI AVG*usii*, or AVGVG-TOR*um*, as in M. Aurelius.

Salus and *Aesculapius* standing, with their customary attributes, viz., the former carrying the serpent, the latter bearing a staff, round which a serpent is coiled, appear on coins of L. Aelius, Antoninus Pius, Faustina sen., M. Aurelius, Faustina jun., L. Verus, Commodus, and other emperors.—On a bronze medallion of Antonine, quoted by Vaillant, *Salus* stands pouring wine into a patera, which *Aesculapius* sitting holds out in his right hand; a small altar is between both figures, and a tree behind. Vaillant also gives a first brass of Hadrian, in which the Goddess of Health is holding a wand with serpent entwined on it; a naked figure of *Hercules* stands opposite, and behind him is Trajan's pillar.—On a brass medallion of Aurelius, without legend, the type of the reverse is a female with her legs crossed, standing under a tree, feeding a serpent entwined around Hygeia, who is standing on a table, on one side of which is a vase.

SALVS.—Head of the Goddess of Health within a collar or chain *(torques)*.—On a denarius of the *Junia* family, the obverse of which is Victory in a biga, around which D. SILANVS L. F., who was, perhaps, one of the descendants of C. Junius Bubulcus, consul v.c. 443, by whom the temple of *Salus* was built at Rome, and who designed by this coin to restore the memory of the piety of his ancestors. —See *Torques*.

SALVS.—The goddess sitting, holds a patera in her right hand.—On common gold and silver of Nero. This tyrant made frequent vows for his own health, and also instituted *certamina* on that account. Indeed, Tacitus records that, for his escape from a plot laid against him in the year of Rome 818, he erected a temple to *Salus*. But so little did he care about the health of others, that he made the same conspiracy against his life a pretext for sacrificing hundreds to his revenge.

SALVS. P.M. TR. P. X. IMP. VI. COS. III. P.P.—On a bronze medallion of Commodus the foregoing legend accompanies the type of *Salus* seated on a chair ornamented with the figure of a griffin. The goddess is in the act of giving food to a serpent, which raises itself on its tail before a column, behind which is a tree. On the top of this column there is a small statue, which Havercamp believes to be that of Mars, but which Mionnet describes as that of Bacchus. —This medal, of which the design is very elegant, appears to have been struck on the occasion of some vows pledged, or prayer put up flatteringly for the health of the Emperor, or secretly, and with greater propriety, for the safety of the commonwealth, which the imperial gladiator was so ruinously misgoverning.

SALVS AVGVSTA.—A female head; on second brass.—This is one of the medals struck under Tiberius (about twenty-two years after the birth of Christ), and which represent Livia (or Julia), the wife of Augustus, under the figure, or under the symbol, of several different deities. On one she is called IVSTITIA; on a second PIETAS; on a third, as in the present instance, SALVS AVGVSTA.

SALVS AVG*usta*.—This legend is used on several third brass coins of Claudius Gothicus, the type of one being *Hygeia* standing; of another, *Apollo* holding a branch and his lyre; of another, *Isis* holding the sistrum.

"An agreeable variety of divinities (says Eckhel) for Claudius to entrust with the charge of his health."

SALVS AVGVSTA PERM. AVGVSTI.—A first brass, assigned to Livia, bears on its obverse this legend, together with the type of a female head.—The reverse bears IVLIA AVGVSTA —a female seated with *hasta* and *patera*.

That *Salus Augusta* was worshipped as one of the greatest deities by the Romans is well known; but why Livia should have been identified with, and even delineated as that goddess, it would be difficult to imagine, except that, as on coins struck to her in the altered name of Julia (as she was called after the death of Augustus), she was personified not only as *Pietas* and *Justitia*, but also as Vesta, Juno, and Ceres; so, in the same spirit of senatorial flattery, to please her son Tiberius, this poor helpless mortal might have been honoured as the dispenser of that greatest of earthly blessings— health; or, as Havercamp renders it, SALVS AVGVSTA—August Prosperity.—The above coin is quoted by Eckhel, from *Florez*, on the coins of Emerita *(Merida)*, in Spain, a Roman colony.—The intelligent author of *Leçons de Numismatique Romaine* describes a large brass (from his own cabinet) of the same empress, struck in the colony of *Romula*, now *Seville*, which presents openly both the image and the name of (Livia as) *Julia*, followed by the preposterous title of *(Genetrix Orbis)* Mother of the World. And he calls attention to the fact, that "excessive flatteries and divine honours had their beginning in the *provinces*."—The word PERM*(issu)* AVGVSTI mark the privilege of coining money, granted by Augustus to Emerita, Romula, and other cities of Spain.

SALVS AVG*usti*. (The health of the Emperor.)—The type of a first brass of Commodus with this legend.

SALVS. AVG. NOSTRI. (The health of our Emperor.)—This legend appears for the first time on a second brass of Constantius II, (son of Constantine the Great), though the type which accompanies it (the monogram of Christ) had been abundantly used in prior reigns of Christian princes, as well as the A and Ω in the field of the coin.

SALVS DD. NN. AVG. ET CAES., with monogram of Christ and A and Ω in the field. —See *Decentius*.

SALVS EXERCITI.—Æsculapius standing. On gold coin of Postumus.

Salus Generis Humani.—This eulogistic testimonial was bestowed on emperors of very different characters. It is, for example, applied on coins in common to Galba, Trajan, Commodus, and Caracalla; and if the truth of history depended on these monuments alone, they would seem all to have equally merited the widely embracing expression of praise.—Eckhel describes, and comments on, three reputed medals of Augustus, also bearing the above legend (with types of Victory standing on a globe, and writing on a shield); but as he quotes them not from his own (the Vienna) cabinet; on the authority of others; and as neither Mionnet nor Akerman recognises any coin of Augustus with such an inscription, their genuineness may be regarded as doubtful. Passing on then to Galba, we find amongst the rare reverses of that reign, in gold and silver, as follows:

SALVS GEN. HVMANI.—A woman standing with patera in her right hand sacrifices at an altar; in her left she holds a rudder reversed, and plants her right foot on a globe.—This coin alludes to what Suetonius relates, viz., that Galba was induced to take charge of the government by Julius Vindex, who (having already raised the Gauls against Nero) wrote to the noble veteran (then governor of the Tarraconensian province in Spain), telling him that his high birth and established reputation warranted him to aspire to the first place, if it became vacant, and concluding with these words—*ut humano generi adsertorem, ducemque se adcommodaret.*

SALVS GENERIS HVMANI.—This legend, with similar type to the above, appears on a rare silver coin of Trajan.—By the figure of a woman sacrificing, and holding a rudder whilst placing her foot on a globe, is signified (says Vaillant) that health and stability were derived to the human race from the piety and the government of Trajan, so that the emperor himself is called *Salus generis humani,* as we read it on Galba's coin; and as Nerva, in Pliny's panegyric, is termed *Imperator, et parens generis humani.*

SAL. GEN. HVM.—The Emperor raising up a figure.—Mionnet and Akerman both assign this legend and type to a silver coin of Commodus. But they take no notice of a medal which Havercamp includes amongst the *large brass* of Queen Christina of Sweden's Cabinet, which to the abbreviated words SAL. GEN. HVM. adds COS. VI. P.P. S.C., &c., and which has for its alleged type the Goddess of Health with staff, round which a serpent is entwined, and lifting up a kneeling male figure.—Laurent Beger, in *Thesaurus Brandenburgicus* (tom. ii. 680), has given this last-named coin, but without any explanation.— Tristan, on the other hand, who (tom. i. p. 729), has engraved nearly the same type as that in Bartolo's plate, supposes "*que la Déesse Hygée, ou Salus, ayant rendu la santé à Commode en une maladie fort perilleuse, elle devoit, par flatterie envers ce monstre, être reconnue pour le salut de tout le reste des hommes.*—Whilst Havercamp, and apparently with great probability, thinks that the type of Health raising up a man from his knees, "refers to the *vota* which were made in the year of the sixth con-

sulate of Commodus, for the health or preservation of the Roman people; seeing that during the year preceding, viz., A.V.C. 942, the city of Rome and all Italy were afflicted with a cruel pestilence."—But whether the standing figure in the group be meant for Hygeia or for the Emperor himself, there never was a more shameless prostitution than this nobly eulogistic dedication to a monster, who was in the most odious and destructive sense of the phrase— *gravissima pestis humani generis*—the execrable plague and desolating ruin of the world.

SALVS. MVNDI.—A cross in the middle of the coin.—On *gold* of Olybrius (A.D. 472).

SALVS PROVINCIARVM.—The Rhine personified, under the recumbent figure of a

bearded man, having two horns on his forehead, his right hand placed on a prow, his left holding a reed, and resting on an urn.—On gold and silver of Postumus—a type of elegant design for the age in which it was struck.—Having in the strongest manner fortified the Rhine on both its banks with camps and citadels, Postumus watched over the welfare (salus) of the Gallic *provinces.* It is thus that Trebellius speaks of him: *Si quidem nimius amor erga Postumum omnium erat in Gallica gente populorum, quod submotis omnibus Germanicis gentibus, Romanum in pristinam securitatem revocasset imperium.*

The title bestowed jn the above legend on the Rhine, as being the health or safety of the Provinces, was doubtless appropriate to that mighty stream, which either hindered altogether, or rendered extremely difficult, the incursions of barbarians into a most important portion of the Roman empire. The river god is represented furnished with two horns, exactly according to Virgil, *Rhenusque bicornis*—an epithet which is repeated also by Ausonius; and Eumenius likewise calls the Rhine *bicornis.* The attribute of horns, which the ancients usually assigned to rivers, is in this case with more than ordinary suitableness applied, because the Rhine emptied itself into the sea by two horns, or channels. Hence the above-named Eumenius observes :— *alvei unius impatiens in sua cornua gestit excedere.*—*Paneg. Cons. Aug.* vii. 13.

SALVS PVBLICA.—A woman seated, holding corn-ears in her right hand. On gold of Nerva. As the scarcity of wheat at Rome, during the reign of Domitian, had occasioned the greatest inconvenience and distress to the people, Nerva had no sooner been elevated to the imperial sovereignty, than he commanded corn to be imported to the great capital of his dominions. Hence the public safety *(Salus Publica)* secured by an abundant supply of corn, *(annona,)* is signified by this type.

Salus Reipublicæ.—The health or safety of the Roman commonwealth is represented in various ways on coins of the lower empire. It is, for example, seen typified by the monogram of Christ's name, with Alpha and Omega, on medals of Constantius II., Valentinianus, Lib. Severus, and Anthemius; also of the Empresses Eudoxia, Galla Placidia, and Grata Honoria. Four military standards, in Valentinian I. and Valens. A military figure standing with a captive at his feet, in Honorius. The emperor standing with globe and spear, in Constantius jun. The Emperor holding a globe surmounted by a *victoriola*, and treading on a captive, in Valentinian I. and Valens. Two emperors sitting on a throne, holding a *volumen* in the right, and a cross in the left hand, on coins of Theodosius jun. A woman veiled, holding two children to her breast, on coins of Fausta, wife of Constantine the Great (see *Spes Reipublicæ*). A female figure (Victory) walking, carries a trophy on her left shoulder, and with her left hand drags along a captive by the hair of the head, on medals of Theodosius Magnus, Arcadius, and Honorius. Victory sitting, inscribes on a shield fixed to the trunk of a tree the monogram of Christ, on coins of Flaccilla (see Flaccilla, wife of Arcadius), Galla Placidia, Aelia Eudoxia (wife of Theodosius jun.), and Pulcheria.—See the words.

SALVS REIP.—A stone bridge of three arches, on which a Victory is marching with a trophy on her shoulder, followed by the Emperor, armed with cuirass, javelin, and buckler; at the feet of Victory is a suppliant captive, and below the bridge the figure of a river god.—Pellerin, in his *Mélange* (i. p. 215), gives this, with the word DANVBIVS, as the reverse of a bronze medallion of Constantine the Great.

SALVS REIP.—A stone bridge of three arches, on which a soldier with his spear either pursues a woman or is following her, who points the way; near her are two suppliants on bended knees. On one side is the god of the river sitting with his urn, whence water is flowing. On the other side is a tower; at the bottom, the word DANVBIVS.—This is described by Eckhel, from the Imperial collection at Vienna, as a brass medallion of Constantinus M., and as having two ships with rowers in the river itself.—See DANVVIVS.

SALVS ET GLORIA ROMANORVM.— This magniloquent legend appears on a gold medallion of Justinian, described by Akerman, after Eckhel and Mionnet, as *unique*.—The type of the reverse represents the Emperor on horseback, his helmet adorned with the *nimbus*, and holding a spear in the right hand. Before him goes Victory, bearing a trophy on her left shoulder, and pointing the way with her right hand. In the exergue, CONOB.—On the obverse is the bust of the Emperor, helmeted and nimbed: he holds a spear before him in his right hand, and bears a shield cast behind his shoulder.

Distinguished not only by its *unique* character, but also by its unusual volume and weight (for, according to Eckhel), it equals five ounces and nearly three drachms, and Mionnet gives its diameter as 38 *lines* (French measure), this splendid coin was found in the year 1751, near

Caesarea ad Argœum (Mazaca), formerly the capital of Cappadocia, amongst some rubbish in the foundations of an old building, cast out from the depth of twenty feet underground, and having been presented to Louis XV., is now an illustrious ornament of the Royal collection at Paris.

"With respect (says Eckhel) to this and other coins of Justinian inscribed GLORIA ROMANORVM, Cedrenus affirms that that Emperor delighted so much in the warlike virtues of Belisarius, that he caused a medal to be engraved with his own effigy on one side, and that of Belisarius armed on the other, and near it to be written BELI-SARIVS GLORIA ROMANORVM. No similar coin, with the name of Belisarius expressed thereon, has yet been found, if you pass by that which Ducange quotes from the cabinet of Peter Gyllius, but which I suspect to be counterfeit.— It was possible, however, to happen that money of one kind or other, such as we have just described, had met Cedrenus's observation, with the epigraph GLORIA ROMANORVM, and that he thought Belisarius appeared on their reverse. And, so many enemies of the empire being vanquished, Justinianus no doubt thought that this *Glory of the Romans* constituted his own also, for he is found assigning to himself a crowd of surnames taken from conquered nations— *Alemanici, Gotthici, Francici, Germanici, Antici, Alanici, Vandalici, Africani*, as they are read in various laws made by himself, and indeed written in the preface to his Institutes; and they appear also in the same order on a Greek marble edited by Muratori, although he evidently used some of them too much by anticipation."

Salutaris is a title of praise dedicated to the gods by the Romans on their coins. It is an epithet assigned to *Apollo*, as the god of medicine, on medals of Trebon. Gallus, Volusianus, Valerian, Gallienus, Postumus; and indeed, was one of the modes dictated by the blind spirit of heathen superstition for averting the plague which, during the reigns of the above-mentioned princes, raged with more or less violence throughout the empire.—See *Apollo; Moneta;* and also *Cybele*, Salutaris being likewise an attribute of MATER DEVM.

SALVTI. AVGVSTORum.—A woman stands feeding, from a patera, a serpent rising from an altar; in her left hand she holds the *hasta*. From a passage in the 8th chaper of Capitolinus's *Life of Marcus Aurelius*, it would appear that this legend, which occurs on gold and brass coins struck COS. III. of that emperor, has reference to the circumstance of his colleague Verus having, on his expedition against the Parthians, fallen sick near Canusium, a fact of which Aurelius was no sooner apprised than he set off in great haste to see him, after pledging vows (for the health of Verus) in the senate, which, on his return to Rome, the news of Verus's safe passage being reported, he immediately fulfilled.

SALVTIS.—This word occurs on the obverse of a denarius of the *Acilia* family, having for its type the laureated head of a woman.—The reverse is inscribed M. ACILIVS III.VIR. VALETV., and represents the figure of a female standing, who holds in her right hand a serpent, and rests her left arm on a little pillar.—Eckhel observes, on this silver coin (vol. v. 119) the obverse exhibits the head of *Salus*, to whom, as Livy relates, a temple was vowed, raised, and dedicated by C. Junius Bubulcus, and which Victor states to have stood in the sixth region of Rome. But the word VALETV has induced learned men to hazard various opinions upon it. Onuphrius lengthens out the whole epigraph by conjoining III.VIR*i* VALE*tudinis* TV*endæ*, functionaries hitherto unknown in Roman institutions. The same objection applies to the IIIVIR VALETV*dinarius* of Patin.

SALVSTIVS AVTOR.—On a contorniate medal (given in Morell's *Thesaurus)* appears the bare head and bearded chin of a man, which are allowed to be intended for those of *C. Sallustius Crispus*, the celebrated writer on Roman affairs. In others of this pseudo-monetary class, the beard is wanting, a circumstance which goes to invalidate the hypothesis of Gesner *(Num. Viror. Illustr.),* who thinks that this medal was struck in the reign of Julian, because that Emperor was also addicted to the nourishment of his own beard.

SANCT*o* DEO SOLI ELAGABAL*o*.—Four horses drawing a chariot, upon which is a species of cone, surmounted by an eagle, and round it four poles *(perticæ).—Gold* and *silver* of Elagabalus.

On this very rare and singular coin Elagabalus, whom the frenzied emperor of that assumed name worshipped as his favourite deity, is represented under the form of a black conical stone, drawn in state. The subject is with surprising clearness illustrated by Herodianus.— Vaillant interprets the word SANCTVS as used in the legend, to meaning in this instance *propitius,* or favourable.

Respecting this public exhibition of the Syrian God Elagabalus (or the Sun) at Rome, we learn from the copious narrative of the historian above quoted that the vehicle which bore it, glittering with gold and gems, proceeded out of the city into the suburb, where its temple stood, the emperor going before the car, and holding the reins.—As to the four *perticæ* or poles, which encompass the body of the carriage, and sustain as many cones, Eckhel acknowledges himself unable to discover what they denote, "nor (he sensibly adds) is it worth while to inquire more fully into all the mysteries of a foolish superstition." The god Heliopolitanus, under which name also the sun was worshipped, was conveyed in the same manner at Heliopolis, for it is thus that Macrobius writes : *Vehitur enim simulacrum dei Heliopolitani ferculo, uti vehuntur in pompa ludorum Circensium deorum simulacra.* Sat. l. i. —Lampridius affirms that the son of Soaemias was the priest of Heliogabalus, or of Jupiter, or of the Sun, as if it were doubtful which, unless they were all considered as identical.

Mr. Akerman, in alluding to the conical shaped stone represented on Latin coins of Elagabalus,

observes that "they appear on many Imperial Greek coins." The same able numismatist remarks that "the gods of the ancient Greeks were originally worshipped under such forms ; so that the veneration of Elagabalus for his block of stone is not deserving of the ridicule it has met with. In a superstitious age, the feeling was natural enough."—For an apposite passage from *Winkelman* on the subject of stone worship, see Akerman's "Descriptive Catalogue," vol. i. p. 414 ; and SACER. DEI. SOLIS. ELAGAB.

Sanquinia.—With the exception of its coins (which have four varieties, and are not very rare), there are no memorials of this family, although Tacitus and Dion have recorded the consulate of Sanquinius Maximus under Tiberius and Caligula.—There are pieces in silver and brass bearing the name of this family, which were struck by the moneyers of Augustus ; on a denarius of M. SANQVINIVS is inscribed AVGVST. DIVI. F. LVDOS SAE., and it commemorates the secular games celebrated by that emperor in the year V.C. 737. Therefore this Sanquinius was in that year a monetal triumvir. The type of the reverse represents a man, clothed in the toga, standing with a helmet on his head, a caduceus in his right hand, and bearing in his left a round shield. Eckhel holds opinion with those who think that this is the *præco,* or herald, in his sacred dress, announcing and inviting the people to the solemnities of the *ludi sæculares.*

Sapientia.—The propensity of the Romans to imitate the Greeks, among and above other things in selecting objects of religious worship, is well known to the classic reader, and to none more than the numismatic antiquary. It will appear, therefore, the more remarkable that, although they built temples and paid their adorations to Honour and Valour, to Hope, Health, and Security, and rendered peculiar devotion to the fickle divinity of Fortune, yet to that concentration and result of pre-eminent virtues SAPIENTIA, no altar was raised, no acknowledgment of tutelary influence offered ; and that, until a late period of the empire (viz., the times of Licinius and Constantine), *Wisdom,* that sovereign mistress as she is of human existence and advancement, should have obtained no place, and that but an insulated one, in the mintage of Rome.

SAPIENTIA PRINCIPIS.—An owl placed on a pedestal, between a shield, a spear, and a helmet.—This new sort of reverse is given by Banduri, as from a third brass of Licinius Pater. —The same legend, and a type of an owl sitting on the top of a column, against which rest a helmet, spear, and shield, appears on a medal of Constantine the Great, with legend of SAPIENTIA on the column and PRINCIPIS PROVIDENTISSIMI round the coin. Also on a contorniate medal of Honorius SAPIENTIA is read, with the type of Pallas, who stands holding a branch of laurel or of olive in her right hand.

Sarmatia.—That part of Europe which lay east of Germania and north of the immediate vicinity of the Danube was known by the Romans, and inscribed on their coins, under the generic name of Sarmatia, and the inhabitants were called Sarmatæ and Sauromatæ. These barbarous and almost unknown tribes also occupied the vast tracts of territory now called *Russia*.

SARM. *Sarmatico*, on a coin of Commodus.

SARM. (DE). This appears, with the type of a heap of armour, on gold, silver, and brass coins of M. Aurelius, who in his thirty-first tribunitian power and third consulship (viz., A.D. 930) triumphed over the Germans and *Sarmatæ*, and in the following year these coins, with a representation of the arms of those warlike tribes engraved for a trophy on their reverse, were struck in remembrance of the event.—In the year V.C. 932 (A.D. 178), another revolt having taken place on the part of these trans-Danubian nations against the Roman power, Aurelius, who had gone forth on this second northern expedition a year before, conquered the Marcomanni, the Hermunduri, the Quadi, and the *Sarmatæ* in a bloody battle, and for that victory was called *Imperator X*.—The next year, engaged in an almost internecine contest against the same obstinate enemies of the empire, he died of disease, at Vindobona, in Pannonia (Vienna) at the age of 50.

SARMATIA. DEVICTA.—Victory standing, treads with one foot on a captive, while she holds a palm branch in her right and a trophy in her left hand.

This coin (in silver and third brass) alludes to the Sarmatian war and the victories of Constantine in the year of Christ 322. According to Zosimus (lib. 2) that great emperor drove back the routed *Sarmatæ* beyond the Danube, and pursued them to a place where they had rallied for the purpose of renewing the fight. He there again defeated and put them to flight, taking a great number of them prisoners, whom he doomed to captivity, and their King, Rausimodus, being left among the slain.

SARMATIA.—This word appears at the bottom of a coin (gold and silver) of Constantinus II., which bears on its reverse the legend GAVDIVM ROMANORVM, with the type of a trophy, near which a woman sits in a sorrowful attitude.

Similar medals are extant both of the father of the above emperor and of his brother Crispus, but those are inscribed ALAMANNIA or FRANCIA, and never SARMATIA.—See GAVDIVM ROMANORVM.

SARMATICVS.—M. Aurelius received this surname (A.D. 175), and his medals also ascribe it to him on account of his success in subduing the *Sarmatæ*; a general appellation designating not only the Sarmatians but also the neighbouring tribes, such as the Marcomanni, the Quadi, &c. See SARM.—His unworthy son Commodus *assumed* the same title, but without having performed the same services to the empire, and he is styled also in his coins GERMANICVS and SARMATICVS.

SASERN. *Saserna*, a surname of the *Hostilia* family.—See HOSTILIA.

SAT. *Saturninus*, surname of the *Sentia* family.

SATRIE. *Satrienus*, the Roman *nomen gentile* of a family known only by the denarii on which it is inscribed. Yet of these silver coins (which are common) Morell enumerates twenty-two varieties, none of them, however, offering any other legend and type than the following:—A juvenile head, helmeted.—*Rev.* P. SATRIENVS. A she wolf: above, ROMA.

Some take the head on the obverse of this denarius for that of Mars, others think it is that of Minerva. But supposing it to be Mars, it will easily accord with the wolf on the reverse. Albricus *(Deorum Imag*., p. 3) affirms that "the wolf is depictured bringing a sheep before Mars, because that animal was by the ancients specially consecrated to that deity."—On this point, still more properly belongs what is related in *Origo Gentis Romanæ*, ascribed to Aurelius Victor, that the wolf was under the protection of Mars, Mars bestowing on her this signal favour, because she suckled *his* twin children (Romulus and Remus) by Rhea. "I think (adds Eckhel) this was the reason why the wolf is called *Martius* by Virgil, and also why Livy (l. x. c. 27) thus expresses himself—*hinc victor Martius lupus gentis nos Martiæ, et conditoris nostri admonuit*.—Therefore, Laurentius Lydus *(De Mensibus)* rightly says—"the eagle is the symbol of Jupiter, Lions of the Sun, the wolf of Mars, serpents of Mercury."—*Doct. Num. Vet*. vol. v. p. 300.

SATVRNINVS I., an excellent general under Valerian, and an unwilling usurper of the purple in the time of Gallienus; he perished by the murderous hands of the soldiers who forcibly elected him.—It is uncertain in what region he performed for a little while the part of emperor.

Two tyrants of the name of Saturninus are handed down to us, one the above-mentioned under Gallienus in the writings of Trebellius, another in Egypt under Probus, according to Vopiscus, equally the reluctant instrument of a licentious and cruel soldiery. The former of these is *Publius Sempronius*, the second *Sextus Julius*.—The medals ascribed to the *first* Saturninus were copied from Goltzius by Mediobarbus and Banduri, but are considered false by Eckhel. Those of the *second* Saturninus are given by Goltzius and Ursinus, but are as yet unknown.—But if a third brass coin described by Banduri is to be regarded as genuine, there was a *third* Saturninus, who in some necessarily remote province was recognised as emperor. The medal in question bears on its obverse a radiated head, with the inscription IMP. CAE. SATVRNINVS. AV.—The type of its reverse is a soldier, who pierces with his lance an enemy fallen from his horse: the legend is FEL. TEMP. REPARATIO., and at the bottom BSIS.

Eckhel, in quoting the above, says this coin can belong neither to the Saturninus of Gallienus's reign, nor to the other tyrant of that name who revolted under Probus, because it offers a reverse which was not in use in the age of either of those emperors. "However (adds our authority) as this coin is justly entitled to be ascribed to the age in which we live, in other words, is a forgery; so by all the historians who have written concerning the transactions of this age (viz., that of Constans and Constantius II.), Saturninus tyrannus III. is manifestly an unknown personage."—"There are also those," he adds, "who raise doubts as to the authenticity of this coin, as Banduri bears witness." [Vol. vii. p. 113.]—Mionnet evidently suspects the genuineness of the coin.

Saturnus.—Saturn, under whose fabled reign —the "golden age"—the happiest times were enjoyed by all, was nevertheless affirmed by the ancients to have been himself expelled from his kingdom of felicity by his son Jupiter, and to have sought refuge in Italy at the court of king Janus.—There is a passage in Macrobius (quoted by Bimard) which attributes, *not* to Saturn (as Jobert makes Eutropius do), but to Janus, the first use of money, adding, however, that out of respect for Saturn *(in Saturni reverentiam)* Janus caused to be engraved, on these first specimens of coinage, the ship which had brought Saturn to Italy.—Saturn was regarded as the God of Time, and is represented on ancient monuments as a decrepit old man, holding a sickle or reaping-hook, called *falx.* Sometimes also he is represented with his infant son in his arms, and lifting the child up to his mouth, as if intending to devour it, as the old myth relates on that point.

Spanheim (in his *Notes on the Cæsars of Julian,* p. 10) refers to this god a figure on an ancient marble published by Spon, in which Saturn is represented in the form of an old man veiled, and with his falx. The same writer also mentions to have seen a small silver medal bearing a similar bust, which he likewise refers to Saturn, on account of the attribute of the curved knife, also engraved upon it. Besides which (he adds) there is a medal in the French King's Cabinet, struck under Elagabalus, by the city of *Heraclea,* and published in the collection of Patin, which represents Saturn, or Time, with a scythe in his hands, and moreover with wings on his shoulders.—According to Plutarch, he was believed by the Romans to have presided over agriculture and fruits— to have been, in short, the guardian of rural affairs, as well as the Father of the year and of the months.—For this reason a laureated and bearded head, with a sickle behind it, on a denarius of the *Calpurnia* family, commemorative of the mission of Piso and Caepio as *Quæstores AD FRVmentum EMVndum,* to buy *corn,* and distribute it among the people, is considered by Eckhel as most probably the head of Saturn.— Another head of the same deity, as designated by the *falx asperis dentibus,* or reaping hook, with serrated edge—an instrument allusive to him as the reputed inventor of agriculture, and whence he is called *falcifer* by Ovid, is to be found on coins of the *Memmia, Servilia,* and *Sentia* families.

Saturn is most certainly represented on a silver coin of the *Neria* family—his symbol the *harpa,* or *falx,* is prominent behind the head. "But this (says Eckhel) is not the only proof that it is Saturn. The title given to NERI*us*

of *Quæstor* VRB*anus,* and the military standards which are on the reverse additionally testify it. It is well known that the Quæstors were the Præfects or principal officers of the Roman treasury *(Præfecti aerarii),* but it is also known that the *ærarium* was in the temple of Saturn.

Saturn is considered to be typified, in a quadriga, on a denarius of Saturninus.—See *Sentia* family.

Saturni navis.—The ship of Saturn, which appears on the reverse of the Roman as, was in the most ancient times the peculiar symbol of Saturn, it being, according to the story, with a fleet that he came to Janus, in Italy.

Saturn, under the form of a man with a beard, veiled, and wearing the toga, who standing holds the *harpa* in his left hand, appears on coins of Valerianus and of Gallienus, as a symbol of Eternity. See AETERNITATI AVGG.

It is thus that Eckhel decidedly considers the above described effigy should be understood, and and not as an image of Pluto, which Tanini supposes it. In proof of its being Saturn, he refers *inter alia* to the *harpa* (reaping hook), the beard, the veil covering the head, all sure indications of that pagan deity, the two former attributes being never omitted in his typification. The Romans gave him the *falx* or *harpa* on account of agriculture, over which they commonly believed him to preside. Macrobius says : *Simulacrum ejus indicio est, cui falcem insigne messis adjecit.* Cyprian observes : *Rusticitatis hic cultor fuit; inde falcem ferens pingitur.*

SAT.—In Morell's *Thesaurus (Fam. Incert.* tab. 4) a silver piece of the form of a denarius is published, which, with the foregoing abbreviation, has for its type the bearded head of a man, whose hair is bound with a fillet, and below it the falx, to which is affixed a longer handle than usually is seen on this attribute of Saturn, and more like our modern scythe.— Eckhel is of opinion that this coin (which he classes under the head of *Pseudomoneta)* is one of those which refer to the *Saturnalia,* and that SAT and the type allude to Saturn, in whose honour those extraordinary *outbreaks* of society were professedly originated among the Romans. But the form of the *falx* he regards as of doubtful antiquity, observing that the true shape of Saturn's scythe is typified on the denarii of the *Neria* family, and especially on the silver coins of the Emperor *Valerian,* inscribed AETER-NITATI AVGG.

Saucées.—The French distinguish by this epithet medals, which were struck simply on copper, and then covered with a leaf of pewter, or a wash of silver.—Jobert says "such coins are found from Postumus to Diocletian."

SAUFEIA, a plebeian family ; there are five varieties of its coins ; one denarius bears the head of Pallas ; and Victory in a biga, galloping, inscribed L. SAVF. and, below, the type ROMA. "This Lucius Saufeius (says Vaillant) *may* be he who was the familiar friend of Cicero and of Atticus, and who was Quæstor Urbanus in the year V.C. 696, when the above described medal was struck."—The brass pieces belonging to this family are the *as* or parts of the *as*.

S. AVG. *Seculi Augusti.*—RESTITVT S. AVG. *Restitutor Sœculi Augusti.*

S. AVG. *Seniori Augusto.* (To the Senior Emperor.)—On coins of Diocletian and Val. Maximianus.

S. C.—The letters placed in the reverse (generally on each side of the type, but sometimes below it) intimate that the coins were struck by *the public authority of the Senate*, according to the constitution of the republic, and the laws of the Roman mint.

Found constantly on the brass coins of the Roman emperors, from Augustus to Gallienus, and but very rarely on their gold and silver: that these are initials of the words *Senatus Consulto* has scarcely been at any time disputed or doubted. But there have been differences of opinion amongst the learned as to the way in which these words ought to be understood, with reference to the precise meaning involved in this memorandum (as it were) of a decree of the Senate, which exhibits itself on almost all brass money of Roman die, struck after the commencement of the empire. The justly celebrated Bimard de la Bastie is the author who first advanced, against the doctrines of a fanciful school, what is now held to be the true opinion on this subject; and the views of that acute and judicious antiquary, have since had a full tribute paid to their accuracy and shrewdness by the congenial sagacity of the learned Eckhel. That great luminary of numismatics and most trustworthy guide in all difficult points of discussion connected with the science, has, in the *Prolegomena Generalia* of his immortal work *(Doct. Num. Vet.*, vol. i., p. 73, et seq.), given so clear and conclusive an exposition of all that is materially important, to guide the judgment and to fix the decision in this matter, that we cannot do better than subjoin the substance of his remarks.

After a slight passing allusion to the various but obsolete notions which Jobert has collected together in his *Science des Mèdailles*, he commences by observing that the common and almost universally received opinion is that Augustus, became possessed of the whole power of the republic, appropriated to himself the rights of the gold and silver mint, and permitted the Senate to preside over the coinage of brass money. There are two principal and most decisive grounds on which this division of the fabrication of money between the emperors and the senate, without being textually recorded by historians, appears fully established. First, it is certain that the letters S. C. are not to be found on imperial gold and silver medals, or, if there be any instance of the coin, those initials refer to the type of the piece and not to the piece itself. Secondly, it is also certain that the letters S. C. are to be seen on almost all the brass coins, from Augustus to Gallienus, with the exception of a very small number, and these admit of a clear and satisfactory explanation. From so constant a rule, therefore, we may

rightly infer the monetary partition of the three metals between the emperors and the senate, in the manner above mentioned. In support of this opinion, as founded on metals, he then brings forward evidence from monuments of another kind. A marble, published by Gruter, bears these words:—OFFICINATORES MONETAE AVRARIAE ARGENTARIAE CAESARIS. If the brass mint had belonged to the emperor, a notice of it would doubtless have been included in this inscription.

Some historical facts handed down by ancient writers corroborate the truth of this opinion. We learn from Dion, that after the death of Caligula, the senate, out of hatred to his very name, ordered the whole of his brass coinage to be melted down. Why, since the object was to abolish the memorials of this imperial tyrant, did the ordinance confine itself to the brass money alone? Assuredly we shall find no other suitable reason than that the senate had no authority over the gold and silver mints, but solely over the brass.—Lastly, what is indeed one amongst the most weighty reasons, but hitherto untouched by those who have entered into the disputation on this subject, it can be proved by the most certain testimonies that the emperors had entirely relinquished all claims to the right of coining brass money. In the first place, there are extant a great quantity of Otho's gold and silver coins, but not one genuine brass coin of that prince of Roman die, struck at Rome. Those who think that the whole monetal department of the public business was entrusted to the senate, are bound to furnish some substantially good reason, why that body should have dedicated to Otho coins of the more precious metals, and to have withheld that of less value; notwithstanding the greater portion of the money usually struck at Rome was from brass? The division of the right of coinage between the emperor and the senate constitutes an explanatory answer to this otherwise insurmountably difficult question. In causing money to be struck in gold and silver, Otho exercised his right as emperor; he did not interfere with the brass, because that coinage came under another jurisdiction. The causes which induced the senate not to strike brass money for this emperor, like many other things connected with matters of antiquity, are unknown.—Tacitus relates that at Vespasian's accession to the throne, one of that emperor's first cares *(apud Antiochenses aurum argentumque signatur)* was to have gold and silver money struck at Antioch. Then why not brass also? Certainly because, though the right of the former belonged to him, that of the latter was exclusively senatorial. The coins of Pescennius Niger are likewise a support to this opinion. There are of this personage not a few silver ones extant, as published by numismatists worthy of credit, and probably, one in gold; but no brass coin of his with *latin* inscription, uncondemned as counterfeit, has hitherto been found. This was not without cause. For Pescennius, after he had once assumed the imperial title, struck silver and gold as belonging to him, but not brass also, the senate in the meantime being occupied at Rome in the coinage of brass money with the effigy of Severus, in whose power it then was.—An examination of Clodius Albinus's coins will be found still more decisively to bear on the present point. Of this general, to whom Severus had given the title of Cæsar, we have not only gold and silver money, but also brass. From the moment, however, that he had separated himself from Severus, and proclaimed himself Augustus, of his own accord, brass money evidently ceased to be coined in his name. For no brass coin of Albinus has hitherto been discovered, which call him Augustus, although there is an abundance in silver on which he is so styled. The cause of this fact is clearly developed. It appears, from the express testimony of Herodianus, that Severus ordered money to be struck at Rome in the name of Albinus, then absent in Gaul. The senate, therefore, minted brass coins, as well in the name of Severus Augustus as in that of Albinus Cæsar, after the manner in which the same body, at one and the same time, struck coins in the name of Antoninus Pius Augustus and of M. Aurelius Cæsar. But as soon as Albinus, having taken the title of Augustus, was denounced by Severus as an enemy of the country, his brass coinage must have ceased, Albinus not arrogating to himself a right which belonged to another power, viz., to the senate; and the senate, under the control of Severus, not daring to continue the honours of its mint to Albinus. We find, therefore, those coins of Albinus with the title of Augustus are all of the nobler metals (viz., *silver* and a few gold), having been struck by his orders in Gaul or in Britain, of which provinces he held the government.

Having by these proofs, drawn as they are from the very sources of numismatic knowledge, the medals themselves, manifestly shown that the business and control of the Roman mint was divided between the reigning princes and the senate; having, moreover, shown that these proofs chiefly arise from affinities, which indicate an identity of workmanship and regulation between the gold and silver medals, in respect to types and legends—affinities which fail to exemplify themselves on the brass coinage—the same learned and eminent writer proceeds to deduce fresh arguments in favour of all that he has just advanced, from the legends which appear on gold and silver coins of the imperial series, and which do not appear on the brass; as also from those legends which are found on the brass, but neither on the gold nor on the silver medals of the empire, the types themselves likewise corroborate the accuracy of this opinion.

The details into which our illustrious "teacher" enters in his further observations on this subject are more copious than would be compatible with the plan of the present compilation to give at length. But referring to the *Doctrina Numorum Veterum* (vol. 1. p. lxxiv) itself, it shall suffice with us to say that those particulars, and the remarks which accompany them, are of a nature fully to establish the exactness of his ex-

planation, as well as the accuracy of his research, in adopting as he has done the views, and in strengthening the arguments of Baron Bimard, respecting the letters S. C. which appear on the brass coins of the Roman die.—To the grounds and inferences, however, on which this explanation is based, certain objections have been opposed, one of which has been drawn from the excessive flatteries which were lavished on the emperors in the inscriptions and legends of their medals. It has been argued that it was not possible that the emperors should have decreed to themselves such adulations, and that, therefore, it was to be believed that the senate had the management of what related to the fabrication of money of the three metals. But it may be supposed that the emperors took cognizance of what concerned the due weight and purity of the coinage, leaving to the monetary triumvirs to determine upon the legends and the types. Add to which princes, who had deified their parents, and who had allowed almost divine honours to be rendered to themselves, might well be supposed capable of ordering themselves the flattering legends, which were placed on so great a number of their monies. To complete these ideas it will be right to add the following observations :—

1st.—The letters S.C. are found, as we have seen, on all the brass money of Roman die struck from Augustus's reign. Nevertheless, some pieces unquestionably of Roman die, and undoubted money, are without that indication. These are coins of the second size, on middle brass, struck under Tiberius; and also under Vespasian and Domitian, which represent, on the reverse, a caduceus between two horns of plenty. But this type (as Eckhel has shown on coins of Tiberius, struck in the year v.c. 775), is the symbol of the senate and the people of Rome, and it is probable that on this account the usual sign S.C. was not placed on those pieces.

2nd.—The greatest number of medallions of Roman die in brass, struck after the time of Hadrian, do not bear the mark S.C.; some few, however, are to be found. This omission of the indication, so far as regards the greater part of the brass medallions, added to the consideration of their large volume and extreme rarity, has led to the very probable supposition that these pieces were not money, or at least that they had not the character of actual money like all the rest. This point has already been animadverted upon (see Medallion). But the absence of the letters S.C. from most of the medallions alters in no respect whatever the principle on which the right of coining money was divided between the emperor and the senate, even admitting that the medallions which do not bear S.C. were not money; an opinion which may be applied even to the greater part of those which exhibit that mark.

3rd.—After the reign of Gallienus, the S.C. does not appear on the brass coins of Roman die. Two causes probably led to this change. First, the successive diminution of the rights and of the authority of the senate, which retained no more, so to speak, than a shadow of power; secondly, the establishment of monetary workshops in different provinces of the empire, and the habit which those provincial establishments contracted, as a consequence of their distance from the capital, viz., of withdrawing themselves from the central authority on points connected with the coining of monies.

4th.—The notation s. c. sometimes occurs on Roman imperial coins of gold and silver. It does not follow, however, that this money was struck under the authority of the senate. The mark of a *Senatus Consultum*, in that case, indicates that what the type of the piece alludes to was done by order of the senate, and it does not apply to the piece itself. Thus for example, the gold and silver coins of Vespasian relative to his consecration bear EX S.C. This signifies that the above-mentioned emperor had been consecrated by a *Senatus Consultum*, and not that these coins had been struck by order of the senate. The money fabricated under the republic, had before offered similar examples, at an epocha when the senate regulated the coinage of all the three metals. Accordingly we read on denarii of M. Lepidus, S.C.; on denarii of M. Scaurus, EX S.C., viz., that Lepidus, as this consular coin declares, was made TVTOR REGIS *(Ptolemæi V.,* King of Egypt), *Senatus Consulto,* by a decree of the senate; and that Scaurus, as the other consular medal records, was made AED*ilis* CVR*ulis* (Curule Ædile) EX S.C.—Other denarii, such as those of Manlius Torquatus, Sex. Pompeius, and Lentulus, present additional examples. In like manner, the epigraph of POPVL*i* IVSSV on a silver coin of Octavianus (afterwards Augustus), indicates that the equestrian statue, which this denarius exhibits, not the coin itself, was executed *populi jussu.*—Some gold coins of Diocletian and Maximian bear the two letters S.C. It would be difficult to find a satisfactory explanation of this singularity, as well as of many others which occur on Roman money, at that æra of political confusion and decay of art.

5th.—We also see the mark S.C. on the imperial coins of some cities: these are chiefly pieces struck at Antioch in Syria, and money of certain Roman colonies; the cause of which has not been sufficiently unravelled.—[M. Hennin, in reference to this passage from Eckhel, observes that—" *L'explication la plus naturelle de ce fait serait que ces villes avaient recu la faveur de voir leur monnaie de cuivre assimilée à cette de l'Empire, et placée sous la jurisdiction de la Senate; mais ce fait n'a pas été convenablement expliqué.*" [The most natural explanation would be that these cities had received the favour of seeing their brass money assimilated with that of the empire, and placed under the jurisdiction of the senate; this fact, however, has not been suitably explained.]—But what is much more surprising, and equally unaccountable, the same mark, *senatus consulto,* appears on some coins of Agrippa II., king of Judæa.

6th.—Eckhel, in conclusion, remarks that " the Emperors of the East *(Imperatores Orientis)* were so desirous of appropriating the gold coinage wholly to themselves, that they were unwilling that gold should be coined by foreign kings, unless with their assent and authority; and if it happened that any of those foreign sovereigns dared to do in this respect what the Romans were not able to prevent, such money was prohibited from having currency at any value within the confines of the Roman empire."

S.C.—It has already been stated that this mark is omitted on some of the brass coins of the first emperors. In describing those of Tiberius, under the year 774, Eckhel notices, as a fact worthy of observation, that from such as have for their type the double cornucopiæ and caduceus, the letters S.C., contrary to the custom of the brass mint, are absent, and that there is the same omission on coins of the same metal, exhibiting the same type, struck under Vespasian in the year v.c. 827, as well as on coins of Domitian (Cæsar) in 826.—As, therefore, it is solely the brass coins with this type which want the mark in question, there must necessarily be some particular reason for the circumstance. "I am of opinion (says our authority) that it is to be sought in the type itself; namely, that the cornucopiæ and the caduceus, inasmuch as they were symbols of the senate and people, supplied the mention of the senate. That those insignia were appropriate to each of the two orders is shewn by an ancient gem, on which is engraved a cornucopiæ and a caduceus, with this inscription SEN. POP. QVE. ROM. For a similar cause, on common coins of Caligula, with the epigraph S. P. Q. R. P. P. OB. CIVES SERVATOS, the S.C. is suppressed, because the authority of the senate is already indicated in the inscription."—[Vol. vi. p. 192.]

SCANTILLA.—See *Manlia Scantilla.*

SCAVR. *Scaurus,* surname of the *Aemilia* family.—M. Aemilius Scaurus, one of the lieutenants of Pompey the Great, in the year v.c. 692, being appointed to the governorship of Syria, repelled the incursions of Aretas, king of Arabia Petræa, and compelled him to sue for peace.—See *Aemilia,* a denarius of which family elegantly alludes to this historical fact.—The ædileship of the same Scaurus was distinguished by the excessive magnificence of the public shews which he and his colleague, P. Hypsæus, gave during their year of office.—See *Rex Aretas.*

S. C. D. T.—These letters, added to the type of a serpent twined round a tripod, and to the name of VOLTEIVS, on a silver coin of the *Volteia* family, are by some explained to be *Senatus Consulto Die Tertio ;* by others, *Dedicato Tripode.*—Eckhel calls them both " *inanes conjecturæ.*"

Sceptrum, sceptre, an ancient ornament held by kings in their right hand when they performed any of the important functions attached to royalty, especially when they administered justice.—The sceptre is, on coins, the sign of divinity, and particularly an attribute of Jupiter. Tarquin is said to have been the first who carried a golden sceptre surmounted by an eagle; and the Romans, who invested their consul with regal power and authority, added to other marks of dignity enjoyed by those chief magistrates of the republic a kind of sceptre called *scipio* (see the word).—It served afterwards to designate imperial power.—Jobert observes that on medallions, and even on the smaller coins of the lower empire, the *Augusti*, when represented in the consular habit, hold the *sceptre*; and it is thus that almost all the Constantinopolitan emperors appear. The *sceptre* is surmounted by a globe, on which an eagle is placed, to shew by these tokens of sovereignty that the prince governs by himself. From the time of Augustus this *consular sceptre* of which we speak is seen on medals of the Imperial series.—" Phocas (adds the same author) was the first who caused the cross [which sacred symbol of Christianity, by the way, he insulted by his murderous ingratitude to an earthly benefactor] to be added to his sceptre; his successors relinquished the sceptre altogether, in order to hold in their hands nothing but crosses of different forms and sizes."

The *Sceptre* appears in the hands respectively of Cybele, Jupiter, Juno, Mars, Pallas, The Sun, Venus, Vesta, Aeternitas, Pax, Pietas, Pudicitia, Salus, Securitas, Arabia, Asia, Italia, and Macedonia, with other deities and personifications, on numerous coins of emperors and also on several coins of Roman families.

The *Sceptre* is seen in the hand of the emperor, on medals throughout nearly the whole series from Augustus to Johannis Comnenis. It also appears in the hand of other figures on various family coins and many imperial medals from Julius Cæsar to Honorius.

A *Sceptre*, on whose point a globe and an eagle appear, being the sign of empire acquired by arms, is often observed in the hand of emperors whose effigies are adorned with a breastplate.

A *Sceptre*, to which a *laurel crown*, a globe, and a rudder are added, on a denarius of the *Cornelia* family, indicates the sovereign power of the Romans, since kings for the sake of majesty used the sceptre. The *globe* is displayed to signify the earth, as the *rudder* does the sea, over both which the Roman empire extended itself. Moreover, the *Corona laurea* is united to the *Sceptre* to denote that the power of Rome was strengthened by victories.

A *Sceptre* and a *peacock* on a lectisternium form the type of the reverse on a coin of Faustina senior, allusive to her consecration.

SCIP. *Scipio*, surname of the *Cæcilia*, and likewise of the *Cornelia* family.

Scipio Eburneus, a wand or stick, made of ivory, which it was the custom of those who were allowed triumphal honours to bear in their hand.—Many representations of this are seen on coins of ancient Roman families, such as those of *Acilia, Aemilia, Curiatia,* and others, on which we see figures, carried in triumphal *quadrigæ*, holding the *scipio* in their right hand.

—This ivory staff was a prominent mark of the higher magistracies, viz., of the consuls, the prætors, and in like manner of the proconsuls. In the time of the republic, the *scipio eburneus* had no sort of ornament; and the senate alone had the right of giving it to the consuls elect.— Under the emperors it was surmounted by the image of *an eagle*, or as Juvenal (Satyr x., v. 43) expresses it:—*volucrem sceptro quæ surgit eburno.* During the republic the consuls bore this distinctive symbol of their great office only on the day of their triumph; but under the emperors they carried it every day, and entered the senate with it in their hands.—Millin says "the emperor never carried the scipio." True, *not as emperor*—the *sceptrum* being the mark of imperial distinction—but probably an emperor carried the *scipio* when he made *procession* as one of the consuls, for Morell has given us the *scipio eburneus*, with an eagle on the top of it, as in the hand of Vespasian and of Titus, on a brass coin of the former emperor.—The same ensign of consular dignity appears in the hand of Trebonianus Gallus, of Probus, of Numerianus, of Val. Maximianus, on the respective coins of those *Augusti*.

SCIPIO, surname of the *Cornelia*, likewise of the *Cæcilia* family, derived, according to *Macrobius*, from a certain Roman citizen, named Cornelius, who, in filial piety, made himself, as it were, a walking-staff to his blind father, by conducting him through the streets. *Qui cognominem patrem luminibus carentem, pro baculo regebat, Scipio cognominatus, nomen ex cognomine posteris dedit.* Sat. l. i., c. vi.— The race of the Cornelii, divided into many branches, took for distinction sake various *cognomina.*—The first was Cornelius *Scipio,* without any other surname.—2. *Scipio Africanus,* the celebrated son of P. Cornelius Scipio. —3. *Scipio Aemilianus,* also called *Africanus minor,* adopted out of the *Æmilia* family into that of *Cornelia Scipionum.*—4, *Scipio Asiageta,* elder brother of *Scipio Africanus major.*— 5. *Scipio Asina.*—6. *Scipio Calvus.*—7. *Scipio Hispalus.*—8. *Scipio Nasica,* son of the Scipio who, together with his brother, fell in Spain; a man held in the highest reverence by the senate.

SCIPIO, a surname of adoption; for the natural son of P. Cornelius Scipio Nasica being adopted in the will of Quintus Metellus Pius, pontifex maximus, was on that account called Q. Cæcilius Metellus Pius, but retained the surname *Scipio,* in order to show, as Spanheim says, that he had passed over from the *Cornelia* into the *Cæcilia* family.

SCIPIO IMP.—Hence on one of his coins is read SCIPIO IMP*erator*. On another appear the letters Q. C. M. P. I., which are explained to be the *siglæ* of all his names, as collected from his denarii—namely, *Q. Cæcilius Metellus Pius Imperator.* This man (according to Suetonius) was, in the year v.c. 702, associated for the remaining five months of the consulship with Pompey the Great, whose father-in-law he was, and to whose party he adhered during the civil war. The Pompeians being conquered at Pharsalia, and the war being renewed in Africa, he was appointed *summus Imperator*, or general of the whole army of that province, from superstitious regard for the name of Scipio, which in Africa was held to be invincible. But Cæsar, to whom he was opposed, proved the omen to be fallacious, by defeating his forces in the field, and compelling him to embark on board ship; when finding himself on the point of falling into the enemy's hands, he drove his sword through his own body, and at the same moment plunged into the sea.—See *Cæcilia*.

SCON. *Signata (moneta) Constantinopoli.* —Money struck at Constantinople, in the exergue of coins of Constantius jun., Constantius Gallus, Julian II., and others subsequent.

Scorpio, a symbol of Africa, is seen in the right hand or at the feet of the figure personifying that country on Roman coins.

SCR. *Scribonia*, or *Scribonius*.—Name of a Roman family or of a man.

Scribonia, a plebeian family; surname *Libo*. —Six varieties of coins, some of which, in silver, were restored by Trajan.—The brass pieces belonging to this family are *Asses*, or parts of the *As*.—The only medal of historical interest is a denarius, on the obverse of which we read PAVLLVS LEPIDVS CONCORD., with the veiled head of Concordia; on others appears a woman's head, encircled with a fascia, and the

epigraph LIBO. BON. EVENT.; on the reverse of both is PUTEAL SCRIBON., and a structure, to which are attached two lyres and a garland of flowers. The *Puteal* of *Libo*, a celebrated place in Rome, was the round parapet of a wall with a cover to it, which *Scribonius Libo* had caused to be raised, by order of the senate, over a place where thunder had fallen, in the field of the *Comitia*, and near the statues of Marsyas and Janus. It contained within its enclosure an altar and a chapel. It seems, moreover, that it was a kind of tribunal or seat of justice, like our Court of Common Pleas.—On some medals, with the same type of *puteal*, the inscription is PUTEAL LIBO*nis*.—See the word *Puteal*.

The *Bonus Eventus*, which occurs on one of the above denarii, has reference to the custom of the Romans in holding sacred whatever was capable of bringing good or evil, as fortune, hope, genius, &c. So also *Eventus*, according to the list enumerated by Lucretius in his "Eventa," brought slavery, liberty, riches, poverty, war, and concord. But Cicero's definition of *Eventus* is *alicujus exitus negotii, in quo quæri solet, quid ex quaque re evenerit, eveniat, eventurumque sit*. Therefore, if any-

thing happened well, it was received as the gift of *Bonus Eventus*. That this was esteemed to be a Genius of the same nature as *Felicitas* is shown by a denarius which Morell gives.

SCROFA, a surname used by the Romans.

Scrofa.—The figure of a sow, with or without a litter of pigs, appears on several Roman coins, as well imperial as consular. Among other instances, on a denarius of the *Veturia* family, there is a sow, which a man on his knees holds between two soldiers, one of whom carries a spear upright, the other a spear reversed, and each touches the sow with a stick or with their daggers. (See *Veturia*.)—This is considered by some allusive to the treaty of peace between Romulus and Tatius.—Another silver family coin (amongst the *Incerta* of Morell) represents eight men standing, four on one side and four on the other of the kneeling figure, and each touches the sow with his short stick or dagger. On a coin of the *Sulpicia* family are seen standing two military figures, armed with spears, who point with the right hand to a sow lying on the ground between them. (See *Sulpicia*.)—This curious reverse, and others similar to it, have given rise to various opinions amongst the learned. Eckhel, after stating all, gives his in favour of the view taken by Ericius, namely, that the figures personify the *Dei Penates* of Lavinium, and that the animal represents the sow, with its thirty pigs, which was the cause, according to the Roman legend, of Æneas building in a certain spot the city of Lavinium. (See *Æneas*.) —On a silver coin of Vespasian, accompanying the abbreviated inscription IMP. XIX. is the figure of a sow and pigs, doubtless referring to the same portentous mother and brood of thirty which were seen by Æneas, and to which Virgil adverts at the beginning of the eighth book of his immortal poem, in the words addressed in a dream by "Father Tiber" to the Trojan chief.

This favourite incident of Roman tradition, in the way of marvellous augury, is graphically shadowed forth on two finely designed and boldly relieved medallions in bronze of Antoninus Pius, both without epigraph. The former of these represents Æneas disembarking by a plank from a ship on the shore of Latium, where, holding his son Ascanius by the hand, he contemplates a sow suckling its little ones under an oak tree, above which appear the walls of a city. The latter exhibits the fortified gate of a city, above which stands a sow with her young: behind is Æneas carrying Anchises, an altar lighted, and a round temple. The town, which is depicted on the last-mentioned coin, is Lavinium, according to Eckhel, who has more fully explained the subject in his annotations on the denarii of Sulpicius Rufus.—See *Sulpicius*.

Kolb, in his *Traité de Numismatique Ancienne*, gives (pl. vii. fig. 13) a second brass of Antoninus, with a sow and litter under a tree, evidently in allusion to the same fable.

Scutum, a shield.—Spanheim observes that the ancient shields, as figured on coins, were of an oblong or circular form. The *oblongum scutum* formed part of the defensive armour appropriated to the cavalry of the Romans, as the *clipeus* was the buckler of the foot-soldier.

The *scutum* appears on the left arm of *Juno Sospita*, on coins of the *Procilia* family ; and on the arm, or by the side, or at the feet, of *Pallas*, and of *Dea Roma.*—See *Clipeus*, and *Victoria.*

Scutum Macedonicum.—See *Pelta.*

Scylla, a fabulous monster of the sea, described by the poets and mythologists to have borne the form of a woman downwards to the waist, and thence divided into two tails of a fish, with the heads of three dogs, open mouthed, at her waist. It is in this shape she is seen on an ancient Sicilian medal and on some other monuments. In her hands she is usually made to hold a rudder in the act of striking some one ; thus is she figured on a denarius of Sextus Pompey (PRAEF. ORAE MARIT. ET CLAS. S.C.), to indicate that spot in the gulf of Sicily, where (after the death of his greater father) he gained some successes by sea over Julius Cæsar. Scylla, in fact, was a lofty and dangerous rock, overlooking the narrow straits that divide Sicily from Italy, and opposite the whirlpool of Carybdis ; the two together were regarded by the ancients as presenting the very *acme* of perilous navigation ; and the extreme difficulty of steering safely between them gave rise to the proverb—*Incidit in Scyllam qui vult vitare Charybdin.*

Scylla.—See *Contorniate Medals.*

Scythæ, Scythians, a people, who in the time of the earlier emperors, inhabited the borders of the Euxine, on the confines of the two Mœsias (now Servia and Bulgaria).—The Scythians, a very ancient as well as warlike nation, possessed themselves by conquest not only of a large portion of Northern Europe, but also of Northeastern Asia. Hence the terms *Scythia intra Imaum* and *Scythia extra Imaum*, as applied by the Romans to the vast tracts of country, on either side of Mount Imaus, part of a chain supposed to be that which extends to Thibet.— In the progress of their southern incursions the *Scythæ* penetrated as far as Cappadocia, during the reign of Gallienus, and afterwards devastated Italy.

SCYTHIA, S. C.—This legend appears on first and second brass of Antoninus Pius, with the figure of a woman (personifying the country) standing with a crown in her right hand, and a staff in the left.

This coin is classed by Eckhel, under the head of those *numi geographici*, on which, as in the money of Hadrian, so in that of his adopted son and successor Antoninus, are exhibited images of various provinces and peoples. In doing so the author above-named has thrown a clearer light on the subject of the types, which present themselves in this *batch* (so to speak) of medals struck, by a decree of the senate (s.c.), in the first year of the reign, or in the second consulate, of Antoninus Pius: For this purpose he has entered into a most learned dissertation on the subject of presenting crowns of gold *(coronæ aureæ)* to princes and other great men—a custom, originating with the Greeks, but afterwards readily sanctioned by the Romans, and not a little abused by them as well in the time of the republic as in the subsequent period of the empire, for it led at last to the gift called *aurum coronarium*, that is to say of *gold itself.*—Referring to those erudite and luminous observations as much too diffuse to quote at length, it must here suffice to note the confidence and respect in which (by the concurrent testimony of historians) Antoninus was held by the neighbours and by the subjects of his vast empire ; a fact which Eckhel considers to have caused not only all the Roman dominions, whether more or less distant from the capital, (such as Africa, Alexandria, Asia, Britannia, Cappadocia, Italia, Dacia, Hispania, Mauretania, Sicilia, Syria,) but also certain foreign regions and independent kingdoms and states bordering on some of the remoter pro- vinces, to be brought within the scope of commemoration by the senatorial mint, as evidencing at once the *flourishing state of all the provinces*, during this happy reign, and the amicable terms on which the prince's conciliatory yet firm policy enabled him to continue even with the hitherto hostile and aggressive powers of PARTHIA and SCYTHIA.—It is related of Antoninus, by Capitolinus, that of that expensive, and to the donors frequently over burthensome, present—the *aurum coronarium*—offered to him on the occasion of his adoption, he restored the whole to the Italians, and half of it to the provinces. The manifestation of grateful feelings which this considerate remission of a *quasi* tax naturally produced towards him throughout the empire at large, serves strongly to countenance the opinion, that the type of the coins above alluded to, bearing the names of so many provinces, directly points to this liberal conduct of the emperor. On most of them we see standing the Genius of the province, who holds out, with extended arm, what she carries in her hand, in an attitude which indicates the offering of something. This is on some of the medals in question either a crown, or a little chest *(canistrum vel capsa)*, which might be supposed to contain either the *aurea corona*, or a quantity of gold itself, instead of the coronal ornament.

To this view of the subject, Eckhel anticipates the objection, that besides the provinces of the Roman empire, commemoration is also made of *Parthia* and *Scythia*, from which, being foreign states, such a gift could not be exacted. For indeed the provinces from custom which becomes law, were wont to pay it, and foreign nations spontaneously to offer it ; whether because they were allies and friends, or because from hope or fear they curried favour. If that be true, which Photius relates from Memnon, author of the Heraclean history of Pontus, the Romans sent to Alexander the Great, at that time preparing for war with the Persians, a golden crown of high price, as a gift for the sake of esteem. Dion affirms that Julius Cæsar received many crowns from kings and princes after his achievement of so many victories. And Josephus states what particularly belongs to this point, that Vologeses, king of Parthia, sent a gold crown to Titus, on account of his conquest of Judæa; nor was this custom extinct at a later age, as is attested by Eusebius, who narrates that *aureæ coronæ* were presented to Constantine by distant nations, whereby they signified, as he proceeds to add, the offer on their part of obedience and alliance to the emperor, if he was willing to accept it. When Julianus, having engaged in war with the Persians, had crossed the Euphrates, the petty kings of the Saracens (according to Ammianus) *genibus supplices nixi oblata ex auro corona tanquam mundi nationumque suarum dominum adorarunt.* L. xxiii. c. iii.—Influenced by the same notions, therefore, the Parthians and the *Scythians,* that they might ingratiate themselves with the recently adopted Antoninus immediately on his entrance upon imperial dignities, sent to the destined successor those accustomed gifts which render both men and gods propitious. Nor was this done without hope by the Parthians, for it appears from Spartianus, that Hadrian had promised that nation that he would restore to them the chair of their kings *(sella regia)* which Trajan had taken away; but that he did not make good his promise, we learn from Capitolinus, who states Antoninus to have stoutly refused the same chair to the renewed entreaty of the Parthian monarch. Concerning the *Scythians* nothing certain appears, except, perhaps, that they endeavoured to win the favour of Antonine, lest he should assist certain bordering states, with whom they were at war. Indeed, it is affirmed by Capitolinus that the *Tauroscythæ* of Olbiopolis were molested by an army from *Pontus* (on the shore of the Euxine), but that an auxiliary force having been sent by Antoninus to that city, the invaders were expelled, and had to give hostages for maintenance of peace."—See *Aurum coronarium.*

S. D. *Senatus Decreto.*

S. DEN. *Sicinius Dentatus.*—On a coin of the *Sicinia* family.

SE. *Severus,* or *Severo.*—IMP. C. SE. ALEXANDer AVG*ustus.*

Seasons (the four of the year) are designated on coins of the imperial series by four little boys, or girls; these types are found on medals and medallions of Hadrian, Antoninus Pius, Faustina sen., L. Verus, Commodus, Julia Domna, Caracalla, Alexander Severus, Trebon. Gallus, Probus, Diocletian, Licinius jun., Constantine the Great, &c.—See TELLVS STABIL.— TEMPORVM FELICITAS.—FELICIA TEMPORA.

SEBAST. *Sebaste.*—COL. SEBAST. *Colonia Sebaste.*—An Augustan colony, distinguished from others of the same name by the title of *Sebaste Pontica,* formerly called *Cabira.*

Sebaste, Samaria, in *Syria Palæstina* (now Chiemrum).—A city of very great antiquity, situate on the mountain Samaria. After becoming subject in succession to kings of Israel, to the Assyrians, to Alexander the Great, to

the Ptolemies, and to the Jews, it was augmented by Herod the Great, and called by him *Sebaste* in honour of Augustus (about the year V.C. 728). Its imperial coins do not, however, commence before the reign of Nero, and afterwards appear only under Domitian, Commodus, and Caracalla. It was not until the reign of Sept. Severus that *Sebaste,* (or Samaria) was made a Roman colony; on which occasion it took from that Emperor the names of *Lucia Septimia;* and the colonists, out of gratitude to the founder of their privileges, struck on their coins the heads of Severus's family—namely, Julia Domna, Caracalla, and Geta, with the inscription COL. CEBACTE, and on some others COL*onia* Lucia SEP*timia.* No later medals of this colony than these are extant.— The imperials of Domitian and of Commodus are *bilingual* Greek and Latin.—The colonial imperial have also *Latin* inscriptions on the obverse, and Greek on the reverse.

Vaillant gives the two following *types* of this colony from coins of the greatest rarity, viz. :—

1.—On a second and third brass of Julia the empress of Severus, three figures standing within a temple of four columns, accompanied by the legend of COL. CEBACTE, *Colonia Sebaste.*

[The middle figure of this group is that of Jupiter, whose temple it appears to be.]

2.—On second brass of the same empress, a figure in military garments standing, is crowned by Victory; on the other side stands a woman, clothed in the stola, wearing towers on her head, her right hand extended towards the centre figure, and her left hand holding a cornucopiæ.

[The colonists of Sebaste here dedicate to Julia Domna, the wife of their founder, a medal on which his effigy, taken perhaps from a statue erected in their forum, is exhibited, crowned by Victory in presence of the Genius of their city, in memory of Severus's splendid exploits against the Parthians, Adiabenians, and Arabians.]

Sebastianus, brother of Jovinus, was associated in sovereignty with that usurper of the purple, during the reign of Honorius, A.D. 412, and proclaimed Augustus in Gaul, of which country Jovinus had been the most powerful nobleman. But Ataulphus, King of the Goths, who had just abandoned Italy to enter Gaul as the ally and colleague of Jovinus against the rightful emperor, offended at the elevation of Sebastian put him to death at Narbonne as the condition of his own peace with Honorius, A.D. 413. Thus perished, after a few months of false glory, a gay-hearted, thoughtless, unwarlike young man, premature victim to the ambition of a brother, who himself was also captured and beheaded by the unscrupulous and vindictive Ataulphus, a short time afterwards.— The coin of Sebastian, in silver, published by Mionnet and Akerman, it is to be feared is not authenticated as genuine.

SEC. or SECVRIT. ORB. *Securitas Orbis.*— On silver of Commodus (the safety, security, or tranquillity of the world.)

Secespita, a long knife with a round ivory

handle, ornamented with gold or silver, which the priests at sacrifices used to slaughter the victims or to extract the entrails.

Securis, axe, or hatchet.—The *fasces* which the Lictors carried before the Roman consuls and other very high magistrates, consisted originally of axes, the long handles of which were bound up in a surrounding case of rods. The custom dated itself so far back as the age of Romulus, who, it is said, borrowed it from the kings of Etruria. But soon after the establishment of a republican government at Rome, the *fasces* (as we learn from Dionysius of Halicarnassus) were allowed to be armed with the *secures* only when the consuls left the city to join the army. These awful instruments, as denoting the power of life and death, were, however, permitted to be joined to the *fasces* of the dictator, whether in the city or at a distance from it, to the number of twenty-four. The same number was also granted to *both consuls* if they happened both to march forth together.

Havercamp observes that the *Secures in fascibus* have, by way of ornament, the head sometimes of a horse, sometimes of a ram, placed on the middle of them. An example of this kind is given in Morell, on coins of the *Licinia* family; and also of the *gens Norbana*, so far as relates to the *fasces*, but the *securis* does not appear on them. [The types in question may, therefore, perhaps be considered to represent the *fasces* in the state in which they were borne before the consuls *within* the city.]

Securis victimaria, the sacred axe, used in dividing the bones and the flesh of the victim into many parts, and the same sacrificial instrument was also employed to slay the victim.—The figure of it appears, as a mark of the chief pontificate, on coins of *Julius Cæsar* and others. It is likewise seen on coins of the *Aemilia, Antonia, Domitia,* and *Junia* families, accompanied with the *capeduncula* and other sacerdotal insignia.

Securitas.—Security, as a goddess worshipped by the Romans, is delineated in a great variety of ways on their imperial coins. She appears for the most part under the form of a woman in matronly costume; though in some few instances she is but half clothed, having a veil thrown over the lower extremities. Sometimes she is quietly seated, as if perfectly at her ease and having nothing to fear. That is to say, her right or her left elbow rests on her chair, and the hand supports her head, as in Nero. Or else one of her arms is placed above the head; an attitude which ancient artists regarded as characteristic of repose. She holds in one or other of her hands either a sceptre, or a *scipio*, or the *hasta pura*, or a cornucopiæ, or a patera, or a globe. On some medals there is near her a lighted altar; on others she stands leaning against, or with her arm upon, a column or *cippus*, having sometimes the legs crossed in a tranquil, easy posture, carrying one of the above-mentioned symbols, or otherwise holding before her a branch or a crown of olive, or a palm branch. The meaning of these various attitudes

and attributes is on the whole too evident to require explanation. There are medals of nearly all the emperors (with flagrant inappropriateness to most of the reigns) from Otho and Vitellius to Constans and Constantius jun., which have for the type of their reverses this figure of *Security*, and present for their legend the word SECVRITAS, with the addition of the words, AVGVSTI, or AVGVSTORVM (security of the emperor or of the emperors); ORBIS (security of the world); PVBLICA (public security); PERPETVA (perpetual security); POPVLI ROMANI (security of the Roman people); TEMPORVM (of the Times); IMPERII (of the empire); SAECVLI (of the age); REPVBLICAE (of the republic), &c.

SECVRITAS. AVGG.—The emperor in a triumphal quadriga, with an olive branch in his right hand.—On a gold coin of *Licinius Pater*.

The *security* boasted of by the base-born and brutal prince, who caused this medal to be struck, is considered by Eckhel as indicated to have been obtained in the first place by the defeat of Maxentius, and afterwards by that of Maximinus Daza, [after whose death Licinius and Constantinus (the *Augg* alluded to in the legend) remained masters of the empire, the former receiving for his allotted portion the eastern provinces.] And the present coin proves beyond a doubt that the unruly Licinius, having overthrown his rival, assumed the honours of the triumph in some city of the east for a victory gained over his own countrymen. The more modest Constantine had indeed used the same sort of inscription (*Securitas reipublicæ*), but with a very different type, namely, the usual figure of Security, leaning on a column.

SECVRIT. PERPET. DD. NN.—The usual type and attributes of Security.

The above legend appears on a middle brass of Galerius Maximus (in which, by the way, the mintmaster has blundered the word *Perpet.* into *Pepret*).—Eckhel is of opinion that this coin was struck not long after the period when Diocletian and Maximianus abdicated the imperial throne which they had filled together as associated emperors; and that to those two princes alone belongs the inscription of its reverse, by which *securitas perpetua* is promised to them, under the care and management of new *Augusti* and Cæsars; for in that age (beginning of the fourth century) the title of *Dominus Noster* was customarily given on money to the *Augusti* only as private individuals, but it was soon afterwards greedily caught at both by *Augusti* and *Caesares.*

SECVRITAS PERPETVA.—Minerva standing, holding in her left hand a spear reversed, and resting her right hand on a shield.—Silver of Caracalla.

SECVRITAS P. R. *Security of the Roman People.*—Gold and silver of Otho bear this legend on their reverse, with the type of *Securitas* in a matron's habit, who, lifting the left hand to her head, and resting her elbow on a chair, sits at her ease, holding the *hasta pura* in her right hand.

Eckhel gives the above as a genuine coin from the Imperial Cabinet of Vienna, and alludes to another published in Morell, which is more fully inscribed POP. ROM. as "seeming to be suspected."—Rasche quotes from the Arschot collection a silver medal of Titus (to whom indeed, but *not* to ephemeral Otho, the legend might have been dedicated without either falsehood or flattery); but Eckhel, Mionnet, and Akerman are alike ignorant of its existence, or more than doubtful of its authenticity, for they take no notice of such a coin under Titus. On the other hand, Eckhel describes from the illustrious museum of which he was himself the *conservator*, a silver coin of Vitellius (rather a *gluttonous guarantee* for the security of a people), inscribed SECVRITAS P. R., with a woman seated before an altar.—Mionnet, who does not give this with P. R., quotes one as reading SECVRITAS P. ROMANI, and affixes thereto the words *Médaille Suspecte*.—Mr. Akerman's Catalogue contains neither of the above under Vitellius, but ascribes to that Emperor's mint a gold medal, bearing on its reverse SECVRITAS IMP. GERMAN. and the figure of a female seated, which is not in either Eckhel or Mionnet.

SECVRITAS PVBLICA.—This legend (which for *once*, and only once, in the whole imperial series of coins, was well applied in the case of M. Aurelius) appears on a third brass of Hanniballianus (brother of Delmatius, and nephew of Constantine, who was murdered A.D. 337). It claims remark only on account of the unusual type, namely, a river god reclining on the ground, his right hand resting on a staff, near him is an urn whence water issues forth, and also a reed.—On the exergue, CONS.—There is another coin of the same unfortunate young prince, inscribed SECVRITAS REIPVBLICAE, with a similar type to the above, published by Banduri.—It is the conjecture of Tristan that the river here meant is the Euphrates, which divides Cappadocia from Syria and Armenia, and which afforded some sort of security (a very poor one it must be confessed) to the former province, of which, together with Pontus and Armenia, the government, with the title of king, had been assigned to Hanniballianus by his uncle Constantine.

SECVRITAS REIPVB*licæ*.—A bull standing: above its head are two stars; on some there is a crown near the bull, on which an eagle stands. In the exergue are the names of various cities.—Second brass of Julianus II.

Of this type on medals of Julian, Socrates and Sozomenus (says Eckhel) have made mention. Namely, that the townsmen of Antioch falling short of provisions, and the emperor being present, as they were of their own peculiar inclination given to banter and jest, said that a bull should be engraved on coins, and the whole world (*orbis terrarum*) be perverted by its example. For, as Socrates explains the point (of this joke), Julian, when continually immolating bulls on the altars of the gods, commanded an altar and a bull to be engraved on coins.—As to what relates to the altar, Socrates is certainly in error, for among the many coins

that are extant with this type, not one has hitherto been found with the aforesaid altar. Nor has Sozomenus alluded to it.—Neither does Banduri agree with Socrates respecting the reason why such like coins were struck. For, judging from Julian's pertinacious adherence to the superstition of the Egyptians, he is of opinion that by the bull standing with two stars are to be understood *Mnevis* [one of the oxen worshipped as the living symbol of the Nile, and] consecrated to the sun [Osiris], and Apis [another "sacred" bull also adored by the people of Egypt] consecrated to the moon [Isis]. In good earnest, Ammianus relates that, at the time he (Julian) tarried at Antioch, the new Apis, having been diligently sought for in Egypt, was at last found.—Coins of the kind in question (adds Eckhel), besides being collected in astonishing numbers, also serve this purpose—that, on the lower part, they shew the cities from whose respective mints they were issued, and that more distinctly than other monies exhibit them. Accordingly, there may be read on them—ANT., AQVIL., CONS., CYZIC., HERACL., LVGD., NIC., SIRM., SIS., TES., with the addition of various arithmetical signs, either in Latin or in Greek characters, thus serving very clearly to explain the mint-marks of that age. On other medals of the same emperor, especially those of the *Vota*, there is a careful notation of the cities [wherein they were struck], amongst which is also found VRB. ROM. (the city of Rome).

The same legend of SECVRITAS REIPVBLICAE, but with a type more worthy of a Roman coin than the above favourite of Julian (the beast worshipper), appears on a gold and third brass of Flavia Helena. On these the Security of the Commonwealth is personified by a woman in the stola, standing with a branch in her right hand.—In the exergue SMT.

Mr. Akerman, in noticing this type in *gold*, observes that it brought £23 at the sale of the Trattle collection. It is valued at 1000 francs by Mionnet, who says a coin of modern fabric is known, bearing on the exergue SMR.

SECVRITAS REIPVBLICAE.—This legend, but with types of a very different kind to those on Julian's, and likewise varying from each other, also appear on coins of that philosophical pantheist's *nominally* Christian successor, *Jovian*. —One of these (in gold) exhibits two women sitting, the right hand one of whom wears a helmet, she to the left having her head turreted, a spear in her left hand, and her left foot on the prow of a ship. They together hold a buckler, inscribed VOT. V. MVLT. X., on the exergue SIRM. or the like.—A similar type, but with Gloria instead of SECVRITAS, appears on gold of Constantinus II. in *Mus. Cæs.*—On others (in gold and silver), the emperor standing in a military habit holds in his right hand a *labarum*, with the monogram of Christ, and in his left a globe, a captive sitting at his feet.—The *silver* of this epigraph, with the last described type, are in the highest degree of rarity, one of which Eckhel records as being in the Imperial Museum at

Vienna.—A female figure draped, standing, and holding a branch. See HELENA.

SECVRITAS TEMPORVM.—Security resting her elbow on a column, and holding the hasta.—Silver and gold, and second brass coins of Macrinus bear this legend, with the usual type of Security. And, perhaps, so far as reasonable hopes seemed to be warranted by the appearance and prospect of things at the outset of this emperor's accession to the throne of the Cæsars, it may be remarked in reference to the epigraph of the present medal (what Vaillant says, Pr. ii. vol. 2 p. 264, of another of the same reign, inscribed FELICITAS TEMPORVM), that it was not to be wondered at if Macrinus became an object of eulogy on the ground of having restored Security to the Times in which he was elevated by the acclamation of the whole senate to the supreme rank and honours of the *Augusti ;* for Herodianus says—*Neque vero tantopere gaudebant omnes Macrini successione, quantopere exultabant festamque lætitiam universi agitabant, quod Antonino* (Caracalla) *liberati essent.* Indeed, the fratricidal, and *would have been* parricidal, son of Severus had long been looked upon as the most cruel tyrant of Rome, beloved only by a venal soldiery, whom his largesses had enriched, and whom his ruffianism encouraged in their profligacy.

Segetia, or *Segesta,* so called from *segetes ;* was supposed to preside over wheat and other corn when they appeared above ground.—*Cum verò jam super terram essent,* says St. Augustin *(De Civit. Dei), et segetem facerent Deam Segitiam præposuerunt.* We are informed by Millin (in his *Dictionnaire de la Fable)* that this *female* deity was invoked for the fields at seed time, under the name of *Seia,* and that she was not called *Segetia* until the plant had grown up.

The virtuous and beneficent, though in a religious sense benighted and ignorant, Salonina, wife of Gallienus, paid peculiar worship to this goddess, as is attested by those coins of hers inscribed DEAE SEGETIAE. It was that exemplary princess who took upon herself, in a time of great public calamity, the care of procuring a plentiful supply of provisions for the population of Rome, and it was her real sentiment of piety, however mistaken and ill-directed, which caused her to build in that city a temple to the rural divinity, who, under the above name, was supposed to yield her special protection to the crops of corn and other grain at the time of harvest.—See *Deae Segetiæ.*

Segobriga (now Segorbe), a city of the *Celtiberi,* in Hispania Tarraconensis (part of modern Arragon and Valencia), respecting which and *Bilbilis* Sertorius and Metellus waged a bloody war. It was a Roman *municipium,* possessing the privileges of the *jus Italicum,* and its imperial coins bear successively the heads of Augustus, Tiberius, and Caligula,

with SEGOBRIGA within an oaken crown, on their reverse.—There are no others of this Roman station.

Sella Curulis.—The curule chair was a seat of dignity, of which the Romans, it is believed, first adopted the use under king Tarquinius Priscus, having borrowed it from the Etruscans, from whom they copied many other customs besides this, and on whose monuments a chair of similar form often presents itself. Numa had already-granted it to the *Flamen* of Jupiter as a mark of his pontificial office. It was made of, or at least covered with, ivory, high and ornamented with engraved signs and figures, supported on four carved feet, in form almost like two pair of horse shoes, each pair placed inversely one above the other, as is shown on several family coins.—After the change from monarchical to republican government at Rome, the *sella curulis* was appropriated, as a peculiar mark of their high office, to dictators, consuls, prætors, censors, ediles, and also to the prefect of the city *(prefectus urbis),* who for that reason were called *curule magistrates.* The pontiffs and the vestals likewise had the right of the curule chair. But neither the questores nor the tribunes were honoured with a similar distinction. The high magistrates endowed with the *jus sellæ curulis* were at liberty to have it carried with them wherever they went, not only at home, but also *extra urbem,* if sent on any military expedition, or appointed to administer the government of any province.

Sella Curulis.—On a denarius of the *Cornelia* family appears a curule chair, between the lituus and a garland; with legend of SVLLA. COS. Q. POMPEI. RVF.—*Rev.* RVFVS. COS. Q. POMPEI. Q. F.—A curule chair, between an arrow and a branch of laurel.

This silver coin records the colleagueship of the celebrated L. Cornelius Sulla and Q. Pompeius Rufus, who made the *processus consularis* together in the year of Rome 666.—In these types the curule chair indicates the supreme honour of the consulate enjoyed by Sulla ; the lituus shows the augural dignity with which he was also invested. The other attributes are of doubtful signification.—See *Cornelia.*

On one denarius of the *Lollia* family we see a laurel crown, and on one of the *Norbana* family a helmet, placed on a curule chair. On another the *sella curulis* is placed between two corn ears.

The *Sella Curulis* appears on coins of the *Furia* and other families, between two *fasces,* with the *secures.* This is considered to indicate the provincial prætorship of the individual, or of the ancestor of the individual, BROCCHVS, who, as monetal iiivir, struck the coin. On a coin of the *Livineia* family, the curule chair stands between six fasces *without* the *secures,* viz., three on each side.—This denarius, which bears on its obverse the bare head of a man, was struck by L. LIVINEIVS REGVLVS, who, as the words PRAEF. VRB. intimates, was (according to the opinion of Havercamp) one of the præfects of the city, whom Julius Cæsar, on going into Spain, left at Rome, as Dion states, and who assumed to himself the *jus lictorum et sella curulis*. And the circumstance of the *fasces*, wanting, in this instance, the *secures* (or axes), serves to support the doctrine of Spanheim that those *edged tools* were additions not tolerated during the consular government as part of the insignia of the Urban Præfects.

The *Sella Curulis* appears on a denarius of M. PLAETORIVS, whose office is also verbally expressed by AED. CVR. Cicero himself has commemorated *(Pro A. Cluentio)* the curule edileship of that eminent magistrate.

Sella aurea et corona.—A curule chair of gold and a crown were decreed by the senate to honour the memory of Julius Cæsar.

In reference to this fact, a *sella curulis*, upon which is a *laurel crown*, presents itself on a silver coin, struck in honour of Julius after his death by order of Octavianus, his adopted son and heir, whose head (CAESAR IIIVIR. R. P. C.) is on the obverse. (See Morell's Fam. *Julia*, tab. 7). In this instance the curule chair itself bears the inscription CAESAR DIC. PER.; in others there is EX. S. C. in the field. It was doubtless the *sella* decreed among other honours by the senate as related by Dion.

(Duæ) *Sellæ Curules.*—Rasche says that to the above-mentioned ceremony of placing magisterial mementos of illustrious personages, even when absent or dead, in the theatres at Rome, is to be referred the circumstance of two curule chairs appearing on silver coins dedicated to Vespasian and Titus after their death and consecration. But with this remark of the learned lexicographer, I do not find any coin in Morell or elsewhere to correspond. A gold coin bearing a type of the same character, having a curule chair with a laurel crown upon it, ·occurs in the case of Titus, but struck during his lifetime, as its inscription (TR. P. IX. IMP. XV. COS. VIII. P. P.) manifestly shows.—This custom, however, seems to have been revived amongst the Romans from the usages of the old republic, during which, at funerals of illustrious men, the effigies of their ancestors were placed in ivory chairs, such as were the *sellæ curules.*—Seats of this kind were placed in the theatres in honour not only of deceased or absent emperors, but also of their wives, as in the instance of Faustina, empress of Antoninus Pius, or of their relations and progeny, as in the case of Marcellus and Germanicus.—By degrees also it was so ordered, that not merely one chair of this sort was assigned to one emperor, but, out of greater reverence for the defunct Augustus, several of them were in this manner publicly dedicated, as in the case of Pertinax, at whose death three *sellæ curules* were so appropriated. Spanheim, *Pr.* ii. p. 210.— The same honours of the *sella* were sometimes exhibited in temples to the Cæsars.

Sella curulis, supra quam fulmen.—A curule seat, with a thunderbolt upon it, appears on gold and silver of *Vespasian,* inscribed IMP. CAES. TRAIAN, &c., REST.—It is well known (says Vaillant) that the *fulmen* is a symbol of imperial power, and we see it on this coin deposited on the *sella curulis* in memory of the consecrated Vespasian.· This was also placed in a temple as a sign of the highest respect for the new *deity,* the remembrance of which honour paid to so great a prince Trajan has here restored —A similar restitution by the same emperor is also extant, of which *Titus's* consecration is in like manner the object of reverence.

Sella Imperatoria, called also *Castrensis,* was the curule chair which the generals of a Roman army, in the time of the republic, used when in camp with their troops, and which afterwards became the throne of the emperors.

Sella Principis Juventutis,—A chair was given, as a token of honour, to such sons of emperors as were graced with the title of *Prince of the* (Roman) *Youth.* A seat with an *anaclinterium,* or back, richly ornamented, and with a *stragulum,* or embroidered cover, spread over it, is elaborately figured on the reverse of a silver coin of Domitian, with the inscription PRINCEPS IVVENTVT*is;* on the obverse appear CAES. DIVI. F. DOMITIANVS. COS. VII., and the laureated head of that emperor, who, in his seventh consulate, on the death of his father, was declared by his brother Titus partner with and successor to him in the empire *(imperii consors et successor),* and to whom a chair of this ornamental and honorary description was assigned.—In Morell is an engraving of the above coin, and the commentary of Gorias thereupon, who says: that "the *sella* was classed amongst those decorations with which the *sons of emperors* were endowed, as soon as they were called *Cæsars,* may be gathered from Tacitus *(Hist.* l. iv. c. i.), who says respecting Domitian: *Nomen SEDEMQVE CAESARIS Domitianus acceperat;* it is therefore not surprising if on his medals the *sella* is so often assigned to him."

Sella Junonis, or *Matronalis.*—This was a seat on which matrons at Rome performed sacred rites to the goddess Juno. Hence on Roman coins (as in Faustina sen.), a curule chair, traversed by a hasta, or a sceptre, is used as a symbol of Juno, to designate the consecration of *Augustæ.*

Semis, or *Semissis,* or *Semi as,* the half *as,* indicating half a pound, weighed at first six ounces. But when the Roman commonwealth found itself unequal to meet the expenses incurred from the Punic wars, it began to diminish the weight of this early piece of brass money. Besides the face of Jupiter, there were struck on the *semisses* the heads of Apollo, Hercules, Mars, Pallas, Rome, &c. But the ship of Saturn (represented by the prow of a galley) was impressed on the reverse side of most of them. And for the most part, on each field of the coin, is the mark S, (or the same reversed S, or lying ∽,) or six globules • • • • • • Many of these coins bear the names of Roman families.—See *As Romanus,* and its parts illustrated.

SEMP. *Semper.*—SEMP. AVG. *Semper Augustus.*—This title (according to Banduri) is seen first on coins as given to the Emperor Julian II.—[It seems but another mode of expressing the permanent possession of the imperial dignity by the reigning prince, as implied, is the PERP*etuus* IMP*erator,* and the PERP. AVG. of an earlier period, as in Probus, and in Constantius II.]

Sempronia.—The surnames of this Roman family as they appear on coins are *Atratinus, Graccus,* and *Pitio.* Of these (as Livy shews) the Atratini were patricians, the Gracchi plebeians; of what order were the Pitiones is uncertain.—Although Morell gives twenty-two varieties, in silver and first brass, yet the types are, as Mr. Akerman observes, "for the most part uninteresting; consisting of the winged head of Minerva, with the reverse of the Dioscuri."—A very rare gold coin, bearing on its obverse the moderately bearded face of Octavian, with DIVI IVLI. F., and on its reverse a female figure holding rudder and cornucopiæ, together with the imposing inscription of TI. SEMPRONIVS GRACCVS IIII.VIR. Q. DESIG. has given rise to a dissertation of Havercamp's, in which Eckhel finds him to have twice shewn symptoms of somnolence *(bis dormitat)* ; and about which nothing of consequence seems probable than what the coin itself indicates, viz., that this Graccus (of plebeian parentage, to say nothing "*de seditione*" of his famous agitating ancestors,) officiated as *Quatuor vir monetalis* to Augustus, and at the time when he struck the coin was Quæstor elect.—There are silver pieces of this family coined by the mintmasters of Julius Cæsar and Augustus. The brass are either the *as,* or parts of the *as.*

SEN. *Senatus.*—See MAT. SEN. MAT. PAT. *Mater Senatus, Mater Patriæ* of Julia Domna.

SEN. *Senior or Seniori.*—This title is frequently read on coins of the Emperors Diocletian and Maximian, to indicate (Spanheim observes), or to explain the cause of their both abdicating the government at the time when the strength of Maximian was still unimpaired.

SENAT. *Senatus.*—See CONSENSV SENAT., &c. *Consensu Senatus, &c.,* as in Augustus.

SENAT.—See PATER SENAT. of Commodus, and PATRES SENAT. of Balbinus.

SENATVS.—The emperor in imperial or senatorial habit, richly ornamented with the *clavus latus,* holding in his right hand a globe,

and in his left a sceptre. In the exergue SMTS. This beautiful gold medallion of Constantine the Great forms the *vignette* to the second volume of Mr. Akerman's "Rare and Unedited Roman Coins." He observes it is most probably unique. The obverse shews the bust of Constantine arrayed in robes covered with ornament, holding a globe in his left hand ; and a sceptre, surmounted by an eagle, in the right. It was struck at Treves, in compliment to the emperor and the senate.

SENATVS - - - NVS.—Victory walking, holds a shield in her right hand, on which is inscribed VI. AV.

Eckhel gives the above from a silver coin of Vitellius, in the imperial cabinet, and, filling up the letters which are wanting in the legend thus : SENATVS *Roma*NVS, he remarks that the inscription appears in this case for the first time on the coinage of the Romans. "By its type (he adds) the senate rejoices at the August Victory (VI*ctoria* AV*gusta*) gained by Vitellius over Otho."—Vol. vi. p. 317.

SENATVS.—See EX SENATVS CONSVLTO.—GENIO SENATVS P. Q. R., in Gallienus.—MAT*er* SEN*atus,* a title given to Julia Domna.—PATER SENATVS, in Commodus.—PATRES SENATVS, in Balbinus. PIETATI SENATVS, in Commodus.

Senatus, Senate, or assembly of senators, the name given (from *senes,* because, at first, *elders* alone, on account of their experience and supposed prudence, were alone selected for members) to that council of state, which Romulus instituted to assist him in the government of his infant kingdom, and to regulate its public affairs, during his absence on any warlike expedition. The original number appointed by the founder of Rome was one hundred, and these being chosen from the oldest, as well as the wealthiest and wisest of the citizens, were called patricians, from the word *pater.*—Tarquinius Priscus (himself a *novus homo* and of foreign descent) was the first who, from among the most eminent of the commonalty *(plebes),* took another hundred men of advanced age, and conferred upon them the senatorial title and dignity. It was the object of Romulus, in creating the senate, to establish a body who should perform a leading part in the administration of government, and occasionally to command in his place. His successors supported it in the exercise of this great authority until Tarquin the Proud began to reign ; and he, according to Livy, abolished their former prerogatives ; had a council of his own, consulting neither senate nor people, but made peace and war, treaties and alliances, with whom he pleased. After the expulsion of that tyrant, and the abolition of the Roman monarchy, the first *consuls,* in order to supply the places of those whom Tarquin had slain, and at the same time to augment the order, made it to consist of three hundred. It was at this epocha that the senate possessed its highest degree of political power. It then became absolute master of the commonwealth, and a *senatus consultum* was the sole channel of information about public matters to "the masses." The people, in fact, appeared to have enjoyed infinitely less liberty under the consular government than had been granted by Romulus, and continued to them by the majority of their kings. For the insupportable weight of the Patrician yoke the people revolted in the year v.c. 259, and their retreat to Mons Sacer proved the means of obtaining for them the right of electing *Tribunes* as the peculiar magistracy of the Plebeians; and the subsequent law by which, on the occasion of the affair of Coriolanus, every Roman citizen, without respect for order or dignity, should be compelled to answer, when duly summoned to appear, before the people assembled in *comitia* by tribes; the patricians having previously acknowledged themselves amenable to no other judges than the senate itself. But, although thus materially shorn of its over predominating power, this aristocratic and justly influential body still remained the sole guardian of the public treasure; it took cognizance of all political affairs committed in Italy, retained the right of sending ambassadors to, and of receiving envoys from, foreign princes and states; it continued to exercise the prerogative of decreeing triumphs, of receiving the despatches transmitted by those who commanded the Roman armies; and in great emergencies of ordering the consuls to raise forces for the preservation of the state. The senate was moreover entrusted with the superintendence of all that concerned the festival rites and the functionaries of religion. In a word, so long as the free republic lasted, it was regarded by all as the sacred head, the perpetual council, the support, defender, and preserver of the commonwealth. Three hundred remained the number of the senate up to the age of Sylla. And, although the amount to which he increased it cannot be precisely ascertained, yet probably it then exceeded four hundred, which was the number in Cicero's time, as may be gathered from his letters to Atticus.—When the empire supplanted the republic a corresponding change took place in the constitution of the senate, which had already been enormously increased by Julius Cæsar. (Dion says to nine hundred, and Suetonius carries it to one thousand). But as a great many of these new members were totally unworthy of the honour (for strangers from Gaul and elsewhere had been introduced into association with the *patres conscripti* of Rome) Augustus signalised his accession to supreme power, amongst other things, by bringing the senate back again to the numbers, and restoring it to the outward splendour which it had before the civil war; or, perhaps, he permitted it to be numerically greater, as, according to Dion, it then consisted barely of six hundred senators; and, although succeeding emperors sometimes made augmentations, its average number was never afterwards much more. The revolution, still rejecting the name of King, gave a monarchical form to the government, and soon influenced the position of the senate. Augustus's appointment of a distinct council of state was the first blow struck at the pristine authority of that celebrated assembly. Tiberius managed step by step to deprive it of executive power in matters of any leading importance. There was, indeed, a show

of re-establishing the senate in its old rights under Nero; but Tacitus, who alludes to the circumstance, observes that it was a mere disguise of that prince, who, under some such a fair outside, sought to mask his real intentions, which soon betrayed themselves in the most atrocious encroachments. Succeeding Cæsars, equally arbitrary, and some of them still more artful, proceeded in the gradual but effectual task of robbing this powerful and once majestic body of all its state privileges, and of erecting imperial despotism on the ruin, humiliation, and disgrace of the senatorial order.

Senatus Consultum.—See s. c.

SENATVS. PIETATI. AVGVSTI. S. C.— On an elegant first brass of Galba, with the foregoing legend, a senator is represented in the act of crowning the emperor. Havercamp, in his commentary on Morell's engraving of this coin, says he has no doubt but that this remarkable type refers to two similar statues, which were erected at Rome by a decree of the senate in honour of Galba. For he is here seen crowned by the senate, or by the Genius of the senate, a rite originally performed among the Greeks at the ceremony of raising statues, and which seems to have been adopted from them by the Romans. As to the Piety celebrated on this medal, the same numismatist regards it as an allusion to that display of modesty which distinguished the conduct of Galba, who shunned the appearance of assuming the empire without the consent of the senate, and who, after he had revolted from Nero and been saluted as emperor by the army, had the prudent shrewdness (as Suetonius relates) to call himself only *Legatum Senatus ac Populi Romani.*—See GENIO SENATVS.

SENATVS. POPVLVSQVE. ROMANVS. S. C.—A column, on which is an owl. This legend and type present themselves on a first brass of Trajan. And in reference to the column, Ficorini, in his dissertation on leaden coins, has expressed an opinion that it was intended to represent the one which is to this day seen lying on the ground within the palace called *Curia Innocenziana* on *Monte Citorio* at Rome.

SEN. AVG.—*Senior Augustus,* additions to the title of the Emperor *Val. Maximianus.* The word *Senior* appears on coins of Diocletian and his colleague Maximian, who reserved to themselves this honour, in their abdication of the empire.

SEN. ET. P. R.—See VOTA ORBIS, &c., of Constantine the Great.

Senex, an old man, bearded, with a staff, which a serpent entwines with his folds.—See *Æsculapius.*

An old man borne on the shoulders of a younger.—See *Herennia* family.

SEN. FORT. IMP.—Senior Fortissimus Imperator, on a consecration medal of Val. Maximianus, given by Banduri.

Sentia, a plebian family, from which sprang C. SENTIVS, who served as tribune of the people A.V.C. 651.—It had the surname of *Saturninus.*—On the obverse of one of the many denarii of this family, bearing the winged head of Pallas, is inscribed ARG. PVB.—on the reverse is the name L. SENTI*us* C. F.

L. SENTI*us Caii Filius*, and the type Jupiter in a quadriga.—On the reverse of another denarius we read L. SATVRN*inus*; the type being a naked man driving a four-horsed car at full speed, and holding up in his right hand a *curved knife*.—It is not clearly known who was the L. Sentius who had the charge of coining these earlier denarii *(prioris denariis)* out of the public silver—ARG*entum* PVB*licum*. As to what the naked man on the latter coin holds in his right hand, Eckhel agrees with Havercamp in pronouncing it to be the *falx* (or curved reaping hook), and, from that symbol recognizing Saturn, the more likely to be figured by Sentius on his coins, because the name of that deity bore allusion to his own cognomen of *Saturninus*. (See *Saturn.)*—There are thirty-one varieties, but differing only in minute particulars. The silver common.

SENTIAM.—Fortune standing, with her rudder and cornucopiæ.—*Rev.* FELICITER, without type.—These appear on a *leaden* coin, or *tessera*, of the third magnitude; and Seguin in his *Selecta Num. Antiq.* has honoured it with an attempt at explanation, more copious and much more serious than merited by, or elucidative of, the subject; on which Baudelot, in his *Utilité des Voyages*, is judiciously briefer, but scarcely more luminous.—These counters, in the heaviest and dullest of metals, if they have any meaning, have most probably reference to the *feelings* and *fortunes* of the private individual who caused them to be struck,

SEP., or SEPT.—*Septima*, an appellation adopted by the several colonies of Laodicæa in Syria, Sebaste in Palestine, and Tyrus in Phœnicia, from the prænomen of their founder, or benefactor, Septimius Severus.

Septa, places in the Campus Martius at Rome enclosed with rails, in which the people were accustomed to assemble for the purpose of giving their votes. From the resemblance which they originally bore to sheep-folds, these *septa* were also called *oviles*. They were thirty-five in number, one for each *tribus* or ward. Built at first of wood, they were afterwards more solidly constructed, and, under the emperors, shews of gladiators and other spectacles were occasionally given in them to the people.—The *septa*, as used for the purpose of collecting the popular suffrages, are seen depicted on denarii of the *Cocceia*, *Hostilia*, *Licinia*, and *Mussidia* families.—v. *suis locis.*

Septem. Septima, Septimum.—This number, seven, we find written on Roman coins VII.— Thus, VII. VIR. *Septemvir.*—LEG. VII. *Legio Septima.*—IMP. VII. *Imperator Septimum.*

SEPVL.—*Sepullius.*—Family name of a Roman.—P. SEPVL. MACER. *Publius Sepullius Macer.*—See *Sepullia.*

SEPVLLIA, a family surnamed *Macer*, known only from its coins, struck in silver by the moneyers of Julius Cæsar and Mark Antony.— It has thus been the instrument, however, of

handing down to us portraits of Julius Cæsar in various attire, and with different inscriptions. And, on the reverse accompanying the names of P. SEPVLLIVS MACER, we see in one instance the favourite tutelary of the Dictator, *Venus Victrix;* and in another the dedicatory epigraph CLEMEN-TIAE CAESARIS, also of frequent occurrence on the coins of Julius.—The following is one of the rarer types of this family:—

No legend.—A veiled head, *bearded*, before it the lituus, behind it the præfericulum.

Rev.—P. SEPVLLIVS MACER. An equestrian *(Desultor)* guiding two horses, which he urges on with raised whip; behind is a palm branch and a garland.

The veiled head on this denarius is considered to be that of Mark Antony. And from the circumstance of its exhibiting *a beard* (the fact being recorded that Antony suffered his beard to grow for some time in token of his grief for Cæsar's murder), it would appear that these silver coins of Sepullius were struck not long after the death of the Dictator, the head of Julius being placed on some of them, in grateful remembrance of such a man, by the then governing triumvirate.

The male figure on the reverse, riding on one horse and leading another, is regarded by numismatic antiquaries as one of the *desultores*, or equestrian vaulters [the Ducrows and Battys of their day], whose part it was, at the Apollinarian and other public games, to spur on two horses together at their fullest speed, so that, being mounted on one, they presently jumped upon the other, and back again alternately, with wonderful quickness.—Hence, by a metaphor, the light and fickle character, he who courted many mistresses, or who often changed political sides, was called *desultor*. Thus Ovid—

Non mihi mille placent, non sum desultor amoris.

But Manilius (*Astron.* l. v. 85), whom Eckhel happily quotes, affords the clearest illustration to the type in question:

Nec non alterno desultor sidere dorso Quadrupedum, et stabiles poterit defigere plantas, Perque volebat equos, ludens per terga volantum.

These bold and skilful horseriders are likewise typified on coins of the *Marcia* and *Calpurnia* families.

SER. *Sergius.*—On coins of Galba, whose prænomen it was.

SER. *Servatos.*—See OB CIVES SER*vatos.*

Serapis.—The mythology of the Egyptians is more than usually obscure and difficult in explaining the powers and attributes of this divinity, whose name and worship, however, though not known to them in the earliest age, was at a later period held above all others in the highest reverence and distinction by that superstitious people. —That the ancients themselves were at variance with each other respecting Serapis is shown by that passage in Tacitus wherein it is affirmed that many recognised in this god, *Æsculapius*, imputing the healing of sickness to his intervention; some thought him identical with *Osiris*, the oldest deity of the Egyptians; others again regarded him as Jupiter, possessing universal power; but by most he was believed to be the same as Pluto, the "gloomy" *Dis Pater* of the infernal regions. Be this as it may, the general impression of the ancients obviously seemed to have been, that by Serapis, was to be understood the beginning and foundation of things; and accordingly we find him adored in process of time not only at Alexandria, but at Athens, and in other Greek cities, some of which charged their coins with the figure of this deity. At length the Romans, whose fondness for new gods increased with the corrupting influence of their foreign conquests, introduced the worship of Serapis within the walls of their city; not, however, without opposition and resistance for a season on the part of the senate to the popular thirst after such novelties. Through the influence of P. Victor an altar was erected to Serapis in the *Circus Flaminii*, and it quickly assumed the form of a superb temple, which, after its Alexandrine prototype, was called the *Serapéon*. The principal Italian cities, never far behind Rome in the race of idolatry, soon imitated her example in this instance; and it was not long before the worship of Serapis was extended from Italy by the different colonies sent from that country into Asia Minor.—It has already been noticed that amongst the motives for invoking this fabled deity, was his healing attribute, especially in cases of acute diseases. Marcus Aurelius, tortured with the malady which afterwards proved fatal to him, made a visit to the temple of Serapis, at Perintheus, in Thrace; and thence, according to his historian, he returned in health. The circumstance is recorded on a medal (struck by the Perinthians), on which is seen the head of the emperor, and on the reverse that of Serapis.—At a much later æra, and with not the same excuse of educational prejudices, the Emperor Julian II., another philosopher, but bigotedly preferring Paganism to Christianity, and especially delighting to honour Egyptian Polytheism, under Grecian and Roman names, consulted the oracle of Apollo, for the purpose of learning whether Pluto and Serapis were different gods; and he received for answer that *Jupiter-Serapis and Pluto were one and the same divinity.*—We see the use of this made by that able, brave, accomplished, but wretchedly inconsistent man and most eccentric prince, in his coins inscribed DEO SERAPIDI; VOTA PVBLICA, &c.

Serapis is represented with thick hair and rough beard; he is also furnished on his head with the measure *(modius)* or basket *(calathus)* seen in Greek coins on the head of Jupiter.—In the Roman imperial series, he usually stands with right hand elevated and holding a staff transversely, and the skirts of his garment in his left, always with the *modius in capite.* It is thus that he is delineated on coins of Commodus, Caracalla, Trebonianus Gallus, Gallienus, Postumus, Claudius Gothicus, and Helena.

Serapis, on a first brass of Hadrian, given by Vaillant, appears with *Isis*, and they both join hands with that emperor and Sabina, across an altar placed between them.—See ADVENTVI AVG. ALEXANDRIAE.

On a coin of the colony of Cæsarea (COL. PRIMA FL. AVG. CAESAR.), struck under M. Aurelius, the head of Serapis is depicted, covered with the *calathus*, or bushel measure. This serves as one of numerous proofs that the worship of Serapis was greatly spread at this time among the different nations of the pagan world; and corroborates the observation made by Vaillant (tom. i. p. 167), that the ancients understood, by the name of Serapis, the universe itself, or rather the soul of the world, that is to say, that ancient principle which gives life and motion to all created beings.

On a coin of Commodus, in Eckhel's *Cat.* (ii. p. 264), Serapis is depicted with *Isis* behind holding the *sistrum*. Opposite to them is Commodus wearing the toga, Victory standing at his back and crowning him. Serapis and the Emperor join right hands together.

Jobert *(Science des Médailles*, vol. ii. p. 369) in animadverting on the word *Pantheon*, which signifies an assemblage of the symbols of several different deities in one personification, illustrates his meaning by reference to a bronze medal (coined in Egypt) of Antoninus Pius. This presents on its reverse the head of a man in which (says he), all in one, is to be recognised "Serapis by the *boisseau* or measure which it carries; the Sun by its crown of rays; Jupiter Ammon by the two rams' horns; Neptune by the trident; and Æsculapius by the serpent entwined round the handle of the trident. See *Pantheon*. —[This coin is given not only in Jobert but also by Seguin.]

On a large brass, struck by the colony of Sinope in honour of Geta, is a majestic figure of Serapis standing.—See Pellerin, *Mélange*, i. xviii. No. 10.

The Emperor Julian, in his "Cæsars," makes Jupiter address himself to his "brother" *Serapis* (the imperial author taking him here for *Pluto),* because (says his translator Spanheim) it was in his celebrated temple at Alexandria *(the grandest and most beautiful in the world,* as we learn from Theodoret,) that Vespasian received intelligence of the death of Vitellius, and even other auguries of his own accession to the throne. This perhaps led his son Domitian to raise a temple to that god of Rome, or at least to re-build the one which was burnt during the reign of Titus."

M. Dumersan, in his *Descriptive Selection of Ancient Medals* from the *Allier de Hauteroche* Cabinet, has given an engraving of an unedited first brass, struck at Sinope, and dedicated to Marcus Aurelius.—The reverse of this beautiful coin bears for its legend C. I. F. SINOPE ANN. CCVII., and for type the busts of Serapis and Isis.—See pl. x. No. 17, pl. 67.

SERAPIDI CONSER. AVG.—Serapis standing with the modius on his head, his right hand extended, and a spear or wand in his left. On a rare silver coin of Commodus.

Lampridius bears witness to the fact that Commodus was mightily addicted to the superstition of the Egyptians, that he sacrificed to Isis, shaved his head, and officiated as a priest in the procession of Anubis. As, therefore, Serapis was thought by many to be Æsculapius, Vaillant supposes that the medal was struck on the occasion of Commodus being cured of some disease, after paying his vows to Serapis, who is for that reason here called the Emperor's preserver *(Conservator Augusti.)*

SERAPIDI COMITI AV*Gusti.*—This legend, with the type of the god, and an ibis at his feet, appears on a first brass of Gallienus, who, having selected a multitude of deities as his preservers, here condescends to acknowledge the great Serapis for his " *companion.*"

SERGIA, a family of high patrician rank, which, according to Virgil *(Aeneid.* v. 121), referred its origin to Sergestus, the companion of Æneas:

Sergestusque, domus tenet a quo Sergia nomen.

From this stock sprang Catilina, the mortal enemy of Cicero, and the profligately daring conspirator against the very existence of Rome itself. Its coins are silver, and exhibit the word *Silus* as the surname of the *Sergia* family. There is only one type, but that claims notice as being of historical interest, as follows :—

On the *obverse* is the winged head of Minerva: behind which is ROMA, and before it EX. S. C.— On the *reverse* M. SERGI. SILYS. A horseman helmeted and in military habit, riding at speed, holding in his left hand a human head and a sword.

This denarius represents a Roman veteran, named M. Sergius, a prodigy of courage and fortitude, as evinced by his exploits in the Gallic and Hannibalic wars. Respecting this extraordinary man there is a remarkable passage in Pliny (l. vii. § 29), who describes Sergius as having lost his right hand in one battle, and in two campaigns receiving three and twenty wounds—yet fighting four times with his left hand only—and afterwards having made for himself an *iron* right hand, fastening it on (the stump) and again skirmishing in mortal combat with the foe! To this Sergius, Eckhel considers the coin relates.

Serpent—Serpents appear to have been the symbol of Asia. Pomponius Mela says " the figure of Asia Minor holds in its hands a serpent, because perhaps serpents abound in that region."—Serpents may have become the symbol of Asia after that country had adopted them on its coinage, for the purpose of calling to mind the worship of Bacchus, which they carried to a great extent.—The Bacchantes in the mysteries were crowned with serpents. The serpent was one of the symbols of initiation into the Bacchanalian orgies.

Serpent.—This reptile, as an image of divinity and of nature, is figured both in its natural shape, and under a variety of monstrous and imaginary forms, on a great multitude of coins of Greek cities, and also on Greek Imperial medals. It is less frequently found on coins with Latin inscriptions; but still there are not

a few instances in which it is represented both on the Consular and on the Imperial medals of Rome.—The inventor of medicine, Æsculapius, son of Apollo, was worshipped by the Romans under the form of a *serpent.* That animal was the sign of the health-restoring faculty, because, as the serpent, in casting off its skin, was supposed to become young again, so the sick, through the tutelary aid of the healing deity, were believed by the ancients to renew life and to put off old age. It was in consequence of this animal being thus regarded as the symbol of renovation, that the name *Serpentarius* took its rise in reference to the constant attribute of Æsculapius.

The *Serpent,* with the head of Serapis, on medals struck under Antonine, is thought, by Millin, to signify a beneficent genius and the master of nature. This serpent is also seen on a medal of Nero, with a legend which indicates that this emperor was a new benefactor for Egypt.—On a medal of Memphis, and in the hand of Isis, it symbolises fecundity and fertility. And as the serpent was said to renew its youth by the annual casting of its skin, the above-mentioned writer thinks it may be taken for the symbol of the Sun, on a medal of the Emperor Verus, on which a *serpent,* with the head of Serapis, is mounted on the back of a horse, whose march symbolises the year passing away : the head of Serapis representing the Sun as the sovereign of the universe.

The *Serpent* was a symbol of Apollo, and as *salutifer* accompanies the image of that deity whom the ancients regarded as the guardian of health, on coins both of the Greeks and of the Romans.

The *Serpent* was assigned to Bacchus under various titles, and for various reasons founded like the object symbolised on fable and superstition. Clement of Alexandria affirms " *Signum Bacchicorum Orgiorum esse initiatum serpentem.*" The same author describes Bacchantes as crowned with serpents. Hence a serpent creeping out of a half opened chest (cista) betokens the orgies of Bacchus. A *serpent* appears on coins of M. Antony, who called himself a second Bacchus.

Twin *Serpents,* rising in tortuous folds, attached by the tails to each other, but with a *cista* between them, appear on silver medallions, bearing the heads of Antony and Cleopatra, as given in Morell.

Two *Serpents* are seen on a medal of Hadrian, a male and a female; one has by its side a sistrum and a poppy, the attributes of Isis ; the other is represented with a caduceus and cornears, attributes of Anubis.—" This type, (says Millin) incontestably refers to the mysteries of Isis, and the fecundity of nature."

It is sacred to and attendant on *Juno Lanuvina,* or *Sospita,* in whose temple or grove, according to ancient custom, it was required that a virgin, in proof of her chastity, should offer food to the sacred serpent (" *corruptis virginibus periculosus,*" says Woltereck). Coins of the *Popilia* and *Procilia* families, and of Antoninus Pius and Commodus, have types allusive to this legendary subject. The same animal was also held sacred to Jupiter, Neptune, Minerva, Pluto, Ceres, Proserpine, Mercury, Isis, and Serapis.—And that its image was used by the ancients to denote Felicity, Vigilance, Concord, Prudence, Power, Victory, and, above all, Health (Salus), is shewn on Roman as well as Greek coins.

A dead Serpent twined round a tree appears on a fine brass medallion of Antoninus Pius. Hercules, who has slain this Hydra, stands on one side of the tree gathering its fruit: on the other side are the three Hesperides.

A Serpent is the sign of Asia (see Asia Recepta); also of Africa; we see a serpent trampled upon by the fore feet of an elephant on a well-known denarius of Julius Cæsar.—Likewise a serpent before the figure of Africa, on one of Diocletian's medals.—It is seen entwined in folds, erecting itself above an altar, on coins of the Claudia, Nonia, Rubria, and Tullia families; and on imperial medals of Augustus, Tiberius, Nero, Hadrian, Antonine, Aurelius, Alexander Severus, and Maximian.

A Serpent coiled round a tripod is, according to Jobert (p. 415), referable to Apollo, or indicates the Delphic oracles. This type is seen on Greek coins of Nero and Domitian.—[But it is seldom seen on imperial medals of Roman die, except as an attribute of Æsculapius and Salus.]

A Serpent issuing forth from a ship, occurs on a fine medallion of Antoninus Pius.—See AESCVLAPIVS.—There is one that crawls before Victory on a gold coin of Julius Cæsar, restored by Trajan.—Another is seen erecting itself before the face of a woman, in Faustina sen.

A Serpent invariably appears either in the hand or near the figure of Salus, goddess of health, on numerous coins of emperors and empresses. On a contorniate medal of Nero a serpent appears as if lapping food from a patera offered to it by a woman [Olympias?] lying on a couch; on another a huge snake, raising itself in a spiral form, directs its head towards some apples deposited on an altar; behind the serpent is a tree.

A Serpent is placed on the back of a horse on coins of Vespasian struck in Egypt, and the same reptile creeps with head uplifted on the prow of a ship on a Greek medal of Domitian.

A Serpent occupies the reverse of a coin of the Fabricia family, which Eckhel calls "the serpent of Esculapius." L. Fabricius is recorded to have caused the stone bridge to be built at Rome which communicated with the island in the Tiber, in the year v.c. 692.—To this fact the epigraph of L. FABRICIus on a tablet with Populus Romanus above it, which appears on this second brass medal, most probably alludes. And this opinion is the more strongly corroborated by the type of the serpent, inasmuch as Æsculapius being brought under the form of that creature [as the story goes] from Epidaurus to Rome had a temple in that very insula Tiberina, which the bridge of Fabricius served to unite with the city.

A Serpent folded round an egg placed on an altar appears on a first brass of the Djppiu family. The signification of which type Havercamp has attempted to explain with various conjectures, no ways satisfactory to the judgment of Eckhel, who, in his turn, displays as usual his learning and research, but perhaps not with his accustomed success in solving the enigma of the snake and the egg.

A Serpent wound (tortuosus) into many circles, or rising in spiral folds, occurs on denarii of the Aemilia, Papia, Pompeia, and Pomponia families, and on Greek coins of Trajan, Hadrian, and Faustina sen.—A sinuous snake glides before the biga of Juno Sospita, in Procilia.

A Serpent with a lion's head is given by Banduri, from a coin of Diocletian.

A Serpent creeps before Minerva on a brass coin of the Clovia family.

Two Serpents twined round a winged wand constitute the caduceus of Mercury.

A Serpent is placed at the bottom of the labarum on medals of Constantine the Great (see SPES. PVB.); and on coins of some of the later Christian emperors (such as Petronius Maximus) a serpent prostrate is seen with the foot of. the emperor placed upon it.

Serpentina cista.—See Cista Mystica.

Serrati Numi.—Coins are thus called which have their edges regularly notched round like the teeth of a saw. These serrated, or denticulated, medals are common amongst products of the consular mint as far as the time of Augustus, after which scarcely one is to be found.—Thus specimens of this ancient practice are seen on coins of the Antonia, Aquilia, Claudia, Cornelia, Domitia, Mamilia, Maria, Memmia, Papia, Porcia, Postumia, Procilia, Roscia, Sulpicia, and other families. It was a precaution adopted, as Pinkerton observes, by incision, to prevent forgery, by shewing the inside of the metal. "But," adds this scientific numismatist, though churlish writer, "the old forgers also imitated this; and I have a serrated consular coin, of which the incisions, like the rest, are plated with silver over copper."—From a brief passage in Tacitus (l. v. De Mor. Germ.), it would seem that the Germans had a partiality for this class of Roman money—"Pecuniam probant veterem et diu notam, serratos, bigatosque."—The brass coins of the Syrian kings (such as the Seleucidæ) also exhibit the same peculiarity; but this probably was done to them as an ornamental feature, and the metal was cast in that shape before they were struck.

Sertum, a garland or wreath, of leaves or flowers, a chaplet.—See Corolla and Corona.—Seen in the talons or the beak of an eagle (see Aquila); and in the hands of Victory (see Victoria).

SERVATOS.—See OB CIVES SERVATOS, on coins of Augustus; to be found amongst those of many Roman families ; also on medals of Caligula, Claudius, Galba, Vespasian.

SERVILIA, an Alban family, transferred to Rome, after the destruction of Alba, by king Tullus, and elected into the patrician order, according to Livy and Dionysius of Halicarnassus. It became divided into many branches, none of whose names, however, are recorded on coins except *Ahala, Caepio, Casca,* and *Rullus.* The two last were plebeian.

Ahala.—A coin of the *Servilia* family (most rare in gold, though common in silver,) exhibits on one side the head and name of AHALA, and on the other the head and name of BRVTVS, remarks on which denarius will be found under the head of *Junia.*—See *Ahala.*

Caepio.—For denarii inscribed PISO CAEPIO Q.—See *Calpurnia.*

The following silver coin, belonging to the *Servilia* family, is of historical interest:—A laureated female head. No legend.—*Rev.* Q. CAEPIO BRVTVS. IMP. (on some others PRO COS.) Two captives at the foot of a trophy.

The above are the names and titles of that M. Junius Brutus, who stabbed Cæsar. It is thus that he is designated on denarii, and the fact is confirmed by writers of his time; among others by Cicero, who, at the end of the Tenth Philipic, repeatedly calls him *Q. Cæpio Brutus, proconsul.* Whence (adds Eckhel) it becomes certain that he was adopted by Q. Servilius Cæpio, who was his uncle on the side of his mother Servilia. But he did not, after the usual custom of using the family name, call himself *Junianus;* perhaps because at that period there was already a Crassus Junianus; but he turns the surname of his adoption *Cæpio* into the name, retaining his cognomen of Brutus.

With respect to the inscription of IMP*erator* on the above denarius and others of Brutus, Dion assigns the time and the reason of Brutus's accepting this title, namely, that he went on an expedition against the *Bessi* of Thrace, as well with a view to punish the hostilities of that savage tribe, as in order to gain for himself the name and dignity of *Imperator* (see the word), wherewith he might the more easily carry on war against Cæsar, and against Antony, and make an end of both. According to Plutarch, Brutus, together with Cassius, was proclaimed *Imperator* by the army, at Sandis.

On a denarius of Brutus, bearing on its obverse a female head and the word LIBERTAS, the reverse is charged with the inscription CAEPIO BRVTVS PRO. COS., and the type is a lyre between a laurel branch and a *stylus.*

The word PROCOS is affixed (instead of *Imp.*) on this coin and others of M. Brutus, because he governed the province of Macedonia with proconsular authority.

Casca.—Connected with this surname there are two coins, one most rare in gold, the other very rare in silver, both inscribed CASCA LONGVS; the gold has on the obverse a trophy between two prows, the silver bears the laureated head of Neptune. On the reverse of the former is BRVTVS IMP. and the bare head of Marcus Brutus. The reverse of the latter exhibits Victory marching, with a garland and palm branch, and the same inscription BRVTVS. IMP.

Plutarch states that the two brothers *Servilii Cascæ* were amongst the assassins of Cæsar. Of these P. Casca, whom Dion asserts to have been a tribune of the people, struck the first blow at the Dictator. Afterwards, when war was declared against the murderers, he associated himself with Brutus, amongst whose friends in that war P. Casca is classed, by Plutarch, and we see their names united on the above described coins. Appin states that Caius was the prenomen of the other Casca. But there is a prolix and tedious examination in Havercamp, as to whether Casca and Longus be surnames *(cognomina)* of different families, and whether Longus be the *agnomen* of Casca, or otherwise. —The types of these two denarii allude to some maritime victory; which it was is uncertain.— *Doct. Num. Vet.* vol. v. p. 308.

Rullus.—A common silver coin exhibits the cognomen of the *Servilia* family, viz., RVLLI, with the bust of Minerva. On the reverse side is P. SERVILI. M. F. and Victory galloping in a biga.

P. Servilius Rullus is known as that plebeian tribune whose agrarian law Cicero, when consul, stoutly opposed in an oration which is still extant. The father of the tribune, also named P. Servilius Rullus, was the man of whom Pliny says, that he first at feasts served up a wild boar whole to table. It is uncertain to which of the two this denarius belongs.

Amongst other uncertain coins of the *Servilii,* Eckhel takes a copiously intelligent notice of a denarius of no rarity, but nevertheless of some historical interest, from the legend and type of its obverse, allusive to the public shews celebrated at Rome under the name of *Floralia.* —See FLORAL. PRIMVS.

To which M. Servilius, lieutenant (LEG*atus)* of Brutus and Cassius the following coins belong, has been matter of much controversy, hitherto with no benefit resulting. He seems to have been the same individual whom Cicero calls a tribune of the people, and to have arrayed himself on the side of liberty; but the surname does not appear. The former of the two denarii (very rare in gold) presents types that agree with the times of Brutus and of Cassius; viz., C. CASSEI. IMP. A young female head laureated.— *Rev.* SERVILIVS. LEG. The aplustrum.

The latter denarius bears the same head on its obverse, and on the reverse appears the inscription SERVILIVS (M.) LEG., with a crab fish griping an *acrostolium* in its claws; below it is the flower of the pomegranate *(balaustium)* and a diadem unbound.—On this enigmatical reverse both Vaillant and Havercamp have offered comments, abounding more in the wondrous, but partaking much less of the probable, than the following remarks of Eckhel:—

" As the above type is plainly allegorical, the very *manes* of the ancients will pardon us, if we sometimes decline attempting to explain the riddles under which they often veil the truth.

The following conjecture alone perhaps carries probability with it, viz., that the *balaustium* or flower of the pomegranate (since this obviously was the symbol of the Rhodians), alludes to the victory gained by Cassius over these islanders, recorded by Dion and Appian. It may be added, that there appears in the lower part of the coin, a diadem unbound; and that it is a diadem, I confidently assert, from an inspection of the best preserved specimens of this denarius in the Imperial Museum (at Vienna); although in engravings it is always represented as if it were a shoot springing from the stem of the pomegranate flower. It is difficult to imagine what is the meaning of this diadem; unless it may perhaps allude to the fall of the regal power which Julius Cæsar aimed at."

For a description of the acrostolium see the word *in loco.*

Twenty-five varieties of the *Servilia* coins are given in Morell.—The gold are extremely rare, the silver common. The brass pieces of this family are parts of the *As,* and are very rare.

Servius Tullius, king of the Romans, who died about the 218th year of the city, and who, (passing by as fabulous the asserted claims for Saturn and Janus), there appears something like historical ground for believing to have been the founder of a money coinage in brass at Rome.— On this point the words of Pliny are *Servius rex primus signavit æs. Antea rudi usos Romæ Timæus tradit.* In this opinion Cassiodorus also concurs—*Servius rex monetam in aere primum impressisse perhibetur.*—See *Moneta.*

Goltzius has published a medal as belonging to the *Tullia* family, exhibiting in the legend the names of *Servius Decula,* and in the type the head of King Servius Tullius. And Morell has copied the same into his *Thesaurus Familiarum,* under the head of *Numi incertæ fidei* (pl. xxxiii. No. 2). But, as Visconti observes, this numismatic monument has never been seen by antiquaries whose fidelity and judgment are above suspicion; and, therefore, it is very properly consigned to the class of apocryphal monuments.

Servus Christi.—Justinian the Second is thus called on his coins; the reverse of which exhibit a figure of that Byzantine *Augustus* (who died A.D. 711), standing with his right hand taking hold of a cross placed on steps, and inscribed D. JVSTINIANVS. SERV. CHRISTI.

That for the first time in three hundred and seventy years *after* the cross had been numismatically acknowledged as the sign and surety of imperial success, (see HOC SIGNO VICTOR ERIS of Constantius II.), the title of *Christi Servus* should have been assumed by a Roman Emperor, and he the most avaricious, the most debauched, and the most barbarously cruel of princes, is remarkable in a two-fold point of view. The fact, however, constitutes only one, though a flagrant, example amongst many which history furnishes, that the wickedness of the very worst men is found equalled by their hypocrisy.—The *Servus Servorum Dei* of the papal style too often marked the ecclesiastical 'pride that apes humility;" and the title of

Fidei Defensor was in as bad keeping with the character of the lustful tyrant on whom pretended infallibility, for his own worldly purposes, bestowed it.

Sestertius (quasi semitertius), the sesterce, a coin in value two asses and a half. It was, therefore, one fourth part of the *denarius,* and the half of the *quinarius,* and, when the value of the Roman coinage underwent a change, it shared with them a common fate. It was the smallest coin of the Roman *silver* mint (exclusive of the "pretended *libella,*" which was the tenth part of a denarius, about three farthings of our money).—The sestertius is marked IIS., shewing it to be worth two *as* and a *semis,* which multiplied by four make the denarius.— On the well-known medal of Hadrian inscribed RELIQVA VETERA &c. (see the words), as well as on other ancient monuments and in published books, it is written HS., namely, with a small line joining together each mark of the *as,* thus resembling the letter H.

Hoffman, quoted by Rasche, says—"Four sesterces make a denarius, that is ten asses, which, if it is silver, is equal in weight to a drachm."

The sesterce has for its types, on one side a *female head helmeted* and winged, behind it IIS., on the reverse are the *Dioscuri* on horseback, and below ROMA.—This little coin is by no means common. Eckhel had seen but two; one belonging to the *Cordia* family, ascertained to be a sesterce solely by its weight; the other to the *Sepullia* family, which, besides the right weight, had the mark HS.

The simple sesterce, or little sesterce, says Kolb, was worth about four *sous* French money (2d. English).

At the epocha when, according to the generally received opinion, silver money was introduced at Rome, viz., in the year 269 before Christ (485th of the city), the monetal unit (*l'unité monétaire*) was changed; the *As,* which had become successively of a less important value, ceased to be used in numbering sums. The *sesterce* was adopted as the monetal unit, probably because this real money (*monnaie effective*) was the intermedial coin of three established forms of specie.

Sestertium.—Under this word, as contradistinguished in its terminal letters from *sestertius,* it is here expedient to explain the Roman mode of reckoning and designating sums in sesterces, an object which has been accomplished with no less accuracy than conciseness by M. Hennin, as follows :—

1st.—*Sestertius,* in the masculine singular, signified a single sesterce; and, in order to describe any number whatever of these pieces, the Romans put, with the number, the plural masculine *sestertii;* thus, *centum sestertii,* one hundred sesterce pieces.

2nd.—*Sestertium,* in the neuter singular, signified *mille sestertii,* one thousand sesterces; its plural *sestertia,* with a number, denoted as many thousand sesterce-pieces as that number contained units. Thus, *decem sestertia* was equivalent to *decem millia sestertiorum*, ten thousand of the pieces called sesterces.

3rd.—If the word *sestertium* was used with the adverbs *decies, vicies, centies, millies,* &c., *centies millies,* a hundred thousand, was understood; thus *decies sestertium* signified *decies centies millies sestertiorum,* ten times a hundred thousand, or a million of sesterces; *centies sestertium* was *centies centies millies sestertiorum,* one hundred times a hundred thousand, or ten millions of sesterces.—Of this mode of reckoning in sesterces there is an example in the coins of the imperial series: HS NOVIES MILL. ABOLITA.—See RELIQVA.

According to some authors, *sestertium* would here be an adjective referring to *mille* understood, and would signify *a sestertiary thousand;* as *sestertia* would be the adjective of *millia,* sestertiary thousands; but with the adverbs *decies, centies, sestertium* would be a contraction of the genitive plural *sestertiorum.*

When Claudius was elected emperor he gave to each Prætorian soldier *sestertia quindena,* which (means not fifteen sesterces but) is equivalent to *quindena millia sestertiorum,* fifteen thousand sesterces.

SESTIA, originally a patrician, at a later period a plebeian family.—Four varieties in its coins; all of silver and rare.—There are two quinarii of this family, the former of which bears on one side L. SESTI. PRO. Q. *Lucius Sestius Pro-Quæstore,* with a chair and the hasta. The latter has on its obverse the same name of the Proquæstor Sestius, and for its type the veiled head of a woman. The reverse of both is inscribed Q. CAEPIO BRVTVS PRO. COS. *Quintus Cœpio Brutus Pro Consule.*—On the reverse of the former is a tripod between the apex and the simpulum; on the reverse of the latter is a tripod, on either side of which is the securis and the simpulum.

The *Lucius Sestius* mentioned above not only was a zealous personal friend and most intrepid adherent to the cause of Brutus, but what exhibits a rarer virtue, he shewed unequivocal proofs of his affection for him *after* his death. On the authority of Dion, quoted by Ursin, and adopted by Eckhel, it appears that Augustus, in the year v.c. 731, appointed to the consular dignity, L. Sestius, who had always favoured Brutus, had taken part with him in his wars, and reverenced his memory in possessing his statue and extolling his merits, Augustus regarding the friendship and fidelity of Sestius as honourable to him.—This anecdote, so creditable to both parties, deserves to be adduced, as it has been, in illustration of these two seemingly uninteresting coins, on the former of which the *sedile* and the *hasta* indicate the rights of the Quæstorship.

SEV. *Severa.*——See IVL*ia* AQVILIA SEV*era* AVG*usta.*

SEV. SEVER. *Severus.*

SEVERA *(Julia Aquilia),* second wife of Elagabalus.—See AQVILIA SEVERA.

SEVERINA *(Ulpia),* wife of the Emperor Aurelian, as she is certainly proved to have been

as well from coins as from the dedicatory inscription of a marble copied by Muratori, which names her as ULPIA SEVERINA AVG. CO*n*IVX INVICTI AVRELIANI AVG. But scarcely anything is historically or personally known of this princess. Her medals, as Beauvais observes, do not represent her as handsome, and give great severity to her countenance. She is said to have been warlike in disposition, and even as Empress to have followed Aurelian on his military expeditions, on which occasion she gained the affection of the soldiers by her kindness and her liberalities. The eyes of her cruelly rigid husband were watchful over her conduct, but she never gave the least pretence for slander.—Greek medals of Severina, struck at Alexandria, acquaint us that she survived her husband. These same medals give her the name of the *Ulpia* family: a circumstance which induces Eckhel to believe (what indeed Beauvais had already stated) that she was the daughter of Ulpius Crinitus, a celebrated general in Valerian's time, who, descended from the family of Trajan, resembled him in valour and talents for war. This great captain adopted Aurelian (A.D. 258), named him for his heir, and gave him his daughter in marriage.—Her coins are of the highest rarity in gold; second brass scarce; base silver and small brass common. Some pieces represent her with Aurelian.—Style: SEVERINA AVG.—SEVERINA P.F. AVG. —The portrait given above is from an *aureus* in the British Museum.

SEVERVS *(Septimius),* whose talents, judgment, prudence, and courage qualified him, before all other men of his age, for the arduous

task of restoring the empire to that stability which it had lost under the baneful sway of Commodus—was born at Leptis, in Africa, year of Rome, 899 (A.D. 146.) His father, Septimius Geta, was of a senatorial family; his mother's name was Fulvia Pia. Before his attainment of sovereignty, he held a command in Gallia Lugdunensis; administered affairs in Sicily with proconsular authority; was honoured with the consulship in the year v.c. 938; became governor of Pannonia and Illyria under Commodus, after whose death he was equally faithful to Pertinax. That virtuous prince having been basely slain, the legions of the above-named provinces revolted against the venal election of Didius Julianus, and proclaimed Severus Emperor at Carnuntum (now Altenburg on the Danube), he effecting a rapid march upon Rome, caused himself to be acknowledged by the senate, who put Julianus to death, in the year of the city 946 (A.D. 193.) Having first disgraced the Præ-torian guards for their baseness in selling the empire, he entered Rome with a magnificent retinue, amidst the favouring acclamations of the people; on which occasion he added to his other names that of Pertinax. Then proceeding with-out delay to the East, he defeated Pescennius Niger; returning with equal celerity to the West, he vanquished Albinus at Lyons; and thus by the successive fall and death of his rivals he remained sole and undisputed master of millions (A.D. 197). No less victorious over foreign foes than successful against domestic enemies, Severus, as emperor, subdued the Parthians, the Adiabenians, and the Britons, adding the several names of those regions to his own titles, in memory of his conquests. He formed three new legions; celebrated (A.D. 204) the secular games with a magnificence that astonished the Romans; adorned Rome itself with many edifices, to which architectural em-bellishments he added the restoration of the pantheon; above all he made a constant and liberal distribution of corn and provisions to the people. He founded several colonies in the Asiatic theatre of his military glory, among others Helvia Ricina in Picenum, Laodicea in Syria, Nisibis in Mesopotamia, Tyre in Phœnicia. Moreover, Heliopolis in Phœnicia, Carthage, Leptis Magna, and Utica in Africa were in-cluded by him in the privileges of the *jus Italicum*. In the year of our Lord 209, he set out from Rome with his wife and his two sons, for the purpose of conquering Caledonia; that expedition is recorded to have cost the Romans above fifty thousand men. The next year, under his orders, commenced the con-struction or reparation of the fortified wall which, crossing from sea to sea, separated the bar-barians of the North from that part of the island forming the Roman province of Britain, and of which the vestiges still remain. It was after fighting with his usual success in many battles, and whilst preparing a war of extermination to punish the renewed invasion of the Caledonians that this emperor terminated his mortal career. He died of a disease (it is said) in the joints, on the 4th of February, 211, aged 65, at the city of York *(Eboracum)*, not without suspicion of having been poisoned by his execrable son Caracalla, who, impatient to reign, had already tried, though in vain, to seduce the troops from their allegiance, and was even on the point of making an attempt on his father's life, whilst the latter was at the head of his army.

Severus had great qualities, but their glory was tarnished and their utility impaired by atrocious crimes. In his character there was no mediocrity; his vices were enormous, whilst even his virtues carried to excess, approximated to the most odious faults. Simple in his habits, patient under laborious exertion, content with the coarsest fare, and temperate amidst luxu-rious abundance, persevering, intrepid, self-possessed in danger, and unsubdued by adverse circumstances; skilful in war, indefatigable in state affairs, he had early cultivated eloquence, philosophy, and other liberal acts congenial to peace; an able statesman, a victorious com-mander, a prosperous ruler; on the other hand his sanguinary disposition and vindictive temper revelled in the destruction of Roman competitors and their families, whilst his cruelty no less frightfully displayed itself in the brutal fury with which he persecuted the Christians. Wise and just in his general policy, a friend to order and the public good, he oppressed a defenceless senate whom he hated, and relaxed the discipline of soldiers whom he both loved and feared. Craft and dissimulation equally with force and bloodshed ministered to his remorseless ambition and to his insatiate avarice. "He promised, only to betray; he flattered, only to ruin," as in the instances of Niger and Albinus. And though he left the empire in a state of glory, peace, and plenty, yet the consequence of his system and conduct, especially as regarded his licentious children, was destructive to the permanence of its power; and of this sovereign of the Roman world, as of Augustus, it was said, "that he ought never to have been born, or that he should have lived for ever"—so bloodstained was the path of his ascent to supremacy—with so firm a hand did he hold the reins—with so sagacious a mind did he direct the course of government—so ruinous an example of military despotism, and so fatal a legacy of calamities in his immediate successor did he bequeath to his subjects and their posterity.— He had two wives, namely *Martia*, who died before he became emperor, and *Julia Domna*, by whom he had Caracalla and Geta.—His coins are very numerous; those of Roman die are rare in gold, common in silver, first and second brass; his bronze medallions are very rare. There are no third brass of his.

Severus is styled IMP. CAES. L. SEP-TIMIVS PERTINAX AVG.; also SEVERVS PIVS AVG. BRIT*annicus*.—On reverses his ad-ditional titles are often ARAB*icus*, ADIAB*enicus*, PART*hicus*, PART*hicus* MAX*imus*, DIVI M*arci* PII F*ilius*, P*ater* P*atriæ*.—[This last reverse, observes M. Mionnet, confirms the statement of historians who have recorded that in the year V.C. 948 (A.D. 195), Septimius Severus declared himself the adopted son of Marcus Aurelius, although that prince had then been dead fifteen years.]—On other reverses we see him further distinguished by the appellation of FVNDATOR PACIS, or of PACATOR ORBIS, or of RECTOR ORBIS, or of RESTITVTOR VRBIS.—His style in association with his son Caracalla is IMP. INVICTI. PII. AVG.—Some pieces of this Emperor represent him with *Julia Domna, Caracalla,* and *Geta.*

It was during the reign of Septimius Severus that the silver money of Roman die began to be adulterated. Coins of that metal are mentioned in the following reigns, as far as that of Gallienus inclusive, as being of silver, although the standard of them was successively debased, insomuch as to render them no longer anything but *billon* of the lowest alloy.

The coins of this Emperor are exceedingly numerous, and present a great variety of reverses, many of which are historically interesting. The denarii are particularly common, but include many rare reverses, and a legionary series of at least fourteen legions. The gold coins are somewhat rare, with several rare reverses, from which that of the Circus Maximus (see the word) is here given. Quinarii in gold are still rarer. Silver and brass medallions are rare. The large brass and the second also may be termed scarce ; the third brass rare.—For a list of the rarer coins of Severus, see Akerman's "Descriptive Catalogue."

SEVERI INVICTI. AVG. PII. FIL.—A youthful bust with radiated head and right hand uplifted.—The obverse exhibits the legend of P. SEPT. GETA. CAES. PONT., and the portrait of Geta as Cæsar.—Eckhel gives this from a gold medal in the imperial cabinet at Vienna, with the following remarks on the singularity of the reverse type :—

Geta is here exhibited in the guise of the Sun, as appears from the radiated head and elevated right hand, which, coins commonly teach us, are peculiar to the God of Day, or, what is the same thing, to the East *(Oriens)*, which is delineated with those attributes as well as the Sun. It was about this period, V.C. 957 (A.D. 204), that Severus effected his Oriental conquests, whence he derived the title of *Invictus*, or Invincible, engraved on this medal. This was the reason why Geta is here depictured under the figure and usual attitude of *Sol*, for, indeed, from that son, Severus received aid throughout his campaigns in the East.

SEVERI PII AVG. FIL. *Son of the August Severus Pius.*—This legend appears on the reverse of coins (in all three metals) of Antoninus (Caracalla), the type of which presents the figure of that Emperor standing in the dress of war, holding in his right hand a figure of Victory placed on a globe, a spear in his left hand, and a captive at his feet.

This medal, which is rare in gold and silver, was struck in the year V.C. 951 (A.D. 198), when Caracalla was called *Augustus* by his father, and soon after his brother Geta had been declared Cæsar. It was in that year when Severus, at the expostulations of friends, having relinquished the assumed name of Pertinax, took the surname of *Pius*.

SEVERVS *(Flavius Valerius)*, second of the name, Cæsar, and afterwards Augustus. Born of an humble family in Illyria, he was distinguished chiefly if not solely for his vices.

But the very perverseness of the man was the

cause of his advancement. For, in the year V.C. 1058 (A D. 305), Galerius, whom his profligacy and subservience alike suited, raised him to the dignity of Cæsar ; and soon after, on the the death of Constantius Chlorus, refused to recognise Constantine, son of that emperor (whose superior merit he dreaded), in any other quality than that of Cæsar, whilst he persuaded Maximianus Herculius to invest the debauched Severus with the title of Augustus, and in the partition of provinces, Italy, Africa, and Upper Pannonia, were allotted to his share. But when, by Galerius's orders, Severus marched at the head of a numerous army from Milan upon Rome, for the purpose of dethroning Maxentius, who had there assumed the purple, Maximianus, resuming his recently abdicated titles, came to the assistance of his intrusive son, and besieged Severus in Ravenna. There, having surrendered himself to Maximian, on the promise of being allowed the unmolested enjoyment of his imperial dignity, this unhappy prince was perfidiously sent captive to Rome, in the neighbourhood of which he was put to death, April, 307, after having borne, without glory and without desert, the name of Cæsar for fifteen months, and the supreme title of Emperor about nine months. He left a son named Severianus, whom Licinius caused to be slain six months afterwards. His *gold* coins and small *silver* medallions are extremely rare. Eckhel doubts whether any silver of the ordinary size exist. His *brass* medallions and small brass are very rare, and his second brass are scarce. On these he is styled SEVERVS. NOB. CAESAR; or IMP. FL. VAL. SEVERVS. P. F. AVG.

SEVERVS *(Libius)*, the third emperor who bore that name, successor of Majorianus, was a native of Lucania. This phantom of a sovereign, enslaved to the will of Ricimer, who induced the soldiers to give him the title of Augustus, in the city of Ravenna (A.D. 461), passed his days carelessly and iniquitously at Rome, and died there in the palace of the Cæsars, A.D. 465, after about three years and eight months' occupation of a degraded throne, during which the barbarians under Genseric invaded the empire on all sides, scarcely leaving a single province except Gaul in the possession of the Romans. He

is styled on his coins, which (of each metal) are more or less rare, D. N. LIB. SEVERVS AVG., and IMP. SEVERVS P. F. AVG., with the monogram of Christ, or the emperor holding a long cross, and planting his foot on the head of a dragon; or Victory standing; or Rome seated. In the exergue COMOB. or other letters.—The portrait here given is from a gold coin in the British Museum. *Rev.* VICTORIA AVGGG.

Six globules, or circular marks, indicate a *semiss.*

SEX. *Sextus,* a Roman prænomen.—SEX. F. *Sexti Filius,* son of Sextus.

SEX. NONI. PR. L. V. P. F.—See *Nonia* family.

Sexdecim, marked thus XVI. denotes the increased value of denaria.—[Havercamp and Morell, tom. p. 202, 419.]

Sextans, a Roman coin, which is marked sometimes on the obverse, sometimes on the reverse, or on both sides with *two globules* or [. .], denoting it to be the sixth part of the *as,* or two ounces *(uncia),* because the *as* was divided into twelve. It has for its types the head of Mercury and the prow of a ship.—Some of these pieces bear the names of Roman families. The sextans was also a measure for liquids, which contained two *cyathi,* or twelfth part of a *sextarius.*

Sextarius, a Roman measure for liquids, which, like the *as,* was divided in twelve ounces, that was also called *cyathi.* This measure held two *cotylæ,* or *heminæ,* being about an English pint and a half.—"Hence (says Eckhel) the phrases *duo cyathi sextans, tres cyathi, quadrans,* &c., by which is easily explained that passage of Martial: Ep. xi. 37.

Quincunces et sex cyathos bessemque bibamus,
  Caius ut fiat Julius, et Proculus.

Namely, nineteen *cyathi* for the number of letters, which are in *Caius, Julius, Proculus.*"—The *sextarius* was also the sixth part of a *congius,* a liquid measure of ten *libra* in weight (about one gallon). It was the moderate quantity of wine which persons of sober habits drank at their meals, as Vopiscus remarks of the Emperor Tacitus:—*Ipse fuit vitæ parcissimæ, ita ut sextarium vini totâ die nunquam potaverit.* On the other hand, the *congius* was the scale and criterion of "deep drinking;" some topers being celebrated under the names of *bicongii,* whilst those more daring were called *tricongii;* three or rather six bottle men!

S. F. *Sacris Faciundis.*——See *Mescinia* family.—s. F. *Sæculi Felicitas.* On coins of Diocletian and his colleagues.

Shield.—See *Buckler;* also CL. V. *(Clipeus Votivus.)*

SIBYLLAE, the Sibylls, women who, pretending to be divinely inspired, predicted future events. Authors agree neither as to who the Sibyls were, nor respecting their numbers, nor the times and places where they prophesied. Some reckon fourteen, others ten, others only four, and even three. The principal were the Erythrean and the Cumæan. It is the

Sibyll of Cumæa in Italy, whom Virgil makes Æneas consult, at a time when, according to the fable of Apollo's gift of longevity to her, she had lived some hundred out of the thousand years allotted to her. The same attribute of supernaturally prolonged existence has been given to another of these prophetesses; so that to signify an extremely old woman, she is termed a Sibyl. Nothing is known of the way in which, what are called, the *Sibylline verses* were composed.—Among the records of antiquity no information is to be found as to how this alleged mass of predictions, put into hexameters, happened to be discovered, nor at what period it appeared, nor who was the author of it. The early Romans boasted of being the preservers of the Cumæan Sibylls' verses. But all that their historians state which can be construed to bear on the subject, is the well-known story they tell in connection with the reign of Tarquinius Superbus, of a woman who offered to that prince nine books of this prophetic poetry, for three hundred pieces of gold, and obtained her price after burning six and leaving Tarquin only three for his money. So profoundly secret was the custody of this precious deposit, that fifteen officers formed specially into a college alone were allowed to see and examine it. They were called the Sibylline Quindecimvirs; and so implicit was the popular belief in the truth of the things foretold in this collection, that the Romans, whenever they had a war to undertake, or whenever pestilence, famine, or any extraordinary calamity afflicted the city or the country, invariably had recourse to it. The senate itself set the example of consulting these mysterious volumes on occasions of seditious insurrections or of any serious defeat sustained by the armies of the republic, or when the appearance of prodigies seemed to threaten some great misfortune. Many examples are furnished in the annals of Rome, which shew the solemnity with which the Sibylls' books were referred to in similar conjunctures. The Sibylline verses continued to be held in respect even under the emperors, but a large portion of the senate having become professed Christians about the time of Theodosius, the sentiment of veneration for these supposed revelations began to decline, and at length Stilicho, the general of Honorius, caused them to be burnt. Such, however, was the degree of superstitious regard which the different Sibyls and their oracles had at one time obtained, that some of them received divine honours; the *Sibylla Tiburtina* was worshipped at Tibur as a goddess; and the *Sibylla Cumæa* had her temple at Cuma.

On a denarius of the *Manlia* family, the obverse bears a female head, beneath which is the word SIBVLLA; on the reverse of the coin is a tripod, with two stars above it; the whole within an ornamented circle, including the name of L. TORQVAT*us* III.VIR.

The learned have hitherto adduced nothing either probable or consistent on the subject of these types. Havercamp, in Morell, inclines to regard the female head as that of the Erythræan Sibyl, and, in confirmation, points to the *tripos*, as the sure and constant sign of the quindecemvirs specially entrusted with the guardianship and inspection of the Sibylline books. Eckhel offers no explanation of his own; nevertheless, in describing the medal, he speaks of the *caput Sibyllæ*, and shews the accompanying word, SIBVLLA, to have been written for SIBYLLA (the V. being on ancient monuments not unfrequently substituted for Y.) If the same *Lucius Manlius Torquatus* who struck the coin had been called *XV.VIR*, instead of *III.*VIR, the direct allusion of these types to the Sibyll and her sacred books would have been indubitably clear. It is, however, not unlikely that he who, as Monetal Triumvir to Cæsar, has encircled the reverse with his ancestral collar *(torques)*, should have decreed the word SIBYLLA on one side, and the tripos figured on the other, to be sufficient designations of the Sibylline Oracles *entrusted* to the authorities of Rome. And, considering the importance in which they were ostensibly held, and the care bestowed on their preservation, as well as the many occasions on which they were consulted, the matter of surprise is that these denarii should be the only known memorials, at least of a numismatic kind, pointing to so favourite and long prevailing a superstition.—See *Manlia*.

SIC. *Sic.—Sicut.*

SIC. V. SIC. X. *Sic Quinquennalia, sic Decennalia (decurrant feliciter)!*—These monosyllabic words and numerals appear on a gold coin (given by Banduri) of Licinius junior, inscribed on the pedestal of a sitting statue of Jupiter, who holds in one hand the hasta pura, and in the other a small victory; an eagle at his feet; and encircled with the legend of IOVI CONSERVATORI CAES*aris.*

This most rare and remarkable medal represents on its obverse the full face of *Licinius Filius*, under the features of a child scarcely two years old, bare-headed, and clothed up to the bosom in the paludamentum. It was struck on the occasion of his being called Cæsar, when he was placed, with festal celebrations, under the protection of Jupiter, the tutelary god of his father. To this infant a happy five years are wished, and that ten years more may roll on with equal felicity to him. Alas, for the uncertain fate of imperial princes in the fourth century; he perished in his twelfth year, a victim to the same barbarous policy which subjected his ambitious father to a violent death, but which, carried out against the life of this meritorious and innocent youth, disgraces the memory, as it belies the pretensions, of the Emperor Constantine, his uncle.

SIC. X. SIC. XX.—By these marks of votive augmentation, it was the custom of the Roman mints of the Lower Empire, to wish that (xx.) *Vicennalia*, or a score of years, might be enjoyed in health and prosperity, after the completion of the first (x.) *Decennalia*, by the prince in whose honour the coin was struck.—This is extended from xx. to xxx., viz, *sicut*

Vicennalia sic Tricennalia (vota solvantur,) on medals of Diocletian and Maximian.

Sicilia, Sicily, the most celebrated island of that part of the Mediterranean, called *Tyrrhenum mare*, or the Tuscan sea. It was anciently denominated *Sicania*, from the *Sicani*, a Spanish tribe, who held possession of it until driven to its western extremity by the *Siculi*, a nation of Italy, the original inhabitants of Latium.—The soil of Sicily, favoured by its fine climate, was so luxuriantly fertile, especially in corn, as to have obtained for it the not undeserved appellation of the granary of the Roman empire; it was regarded as the *cella panaria*, or bread store-houses of the Romans—*plebisque Romanæ nutrix*. It is believed, at a very remote period of antiquity, to have been joined to Italy, from which it afterwards was divided by some great natural convulsion. Thence it is supposed to have derived its name *quasi*.

Sicilita, i.e. *Resecta*.—The very narrow sea which separated it from the main land, presented two well-known objects of terror to ancient mariners, in Chrybdis and Scylla, the former rock being on the Sicilian, the latter on the Italian shore. On the general principle of assimilating countries to the form of some familiar object, Sicily was called *Triquetra*, from the figure of a triangle. It was also called *Trinacria*, from its three promontories Peloram, Pachynum, and Lilybæum.

Sicily, (observes M. Hennin,) from the remarkable events which have taken place in it, offers, in a numismatic point of view, the greatest degree of interest. The principal cities of the island issued a very considerable number of coins, in all the metals, which do not yield to those of any other country in historical importance and in beauty of workmanship. Some of them are perhaps even superior to all that can be mentioned as belonging to other countries—particularly those pieces of unusual size, commonly named *large silver medallions of Syracuse*. These are in the highest degree to be admired for the style and grand character which they display in their fabric. It is doubtful whether they were current money. There seems better ground for believing that they were used as prizes at the games, or on other occasions.

[In this class, holding a chief place in the foremost rank for excellence of design and execution, is that with the head of Proserpine on one side, and on the other a *quadriga*, and a Victory flying to meet and crown the successful charioteer, who seems to be cheering on his fleet coursers to the goal.—The *Arethusa*, with a similar reverse, is also a splendid specimen of the Greco-Sicilian mint.—Syracuse indeed, as Kolb says, is a veritable Peru for the antiquary, for no city produces so many gold and silver pieces, nor of such heavy weight, and, what is most remarkable, they surpass in perfection everthing that presents itself on other medals.]

Money appears to have been coined in Sicily from almost the original period of the art.

Passing the autonoms and the coins of kings and tyrants, it may be remarked that the Carthaginians, who conquered and occupied a portion of Sicily, struck money there which is conspicuous for its elegance. These pieces, with Punic characters, are considered to have been coined at *Panormus* (Palermo), the central seat of Carthaginian power in the island.

The neighbourhood of Magna-Græcia, and the relations existing between the monetary systems of those two countries, warrant the belief that Sicily was subjected by the Romans to the same regulations as those they imposed upon Italy, and that the independent rights of coinage ceased to be exercised in both those countries towards the same epocha. Some cities of Sicily, however, issued Imperial-Greek pieces, which was not the case in Italy; but those pieces were struck only under Augustus and Tiberius. Subsequently, there is reason to believe, offices were established in that island for minting coins of Roman die.

In the partition of territory, which took place after the death of Sextus Pompey, who at one time held despotic sway over the island, whilst Corinth and Achaia were ceded to M. Antony, *Sicily*, with Sardinia, was assigned to Octavianus (afterwards Augustus). By that emperor the Sicilians were included in the number of Roman citizens; and Panormus (Palermo) made a Roman colony, with the power of coining money, which privileges were continued to that city under Tiberius. The whole island became a prætorian or proconsular province. Hence it is that so many coins, both denarii and brass money, are extant, on which the remembrance of those Roman proconsuls and prætors, who were sent into Sicily, are preserved. From family medals we also learn that Sicily received two Quæstors from Rome.

Sicily is represented, as well on Latin as on Greek coins by the *Triquetra*, composed of three human legs, spread out from one another in a triangular form, in allusion to the three-sided shape of the island, or to its three promontories. On some also of these medals, in the centre between the three uniting thighs, a female head (namely, of Medusa) is seen. See *Panormus.*—The *tria crura*, and a Medusa's head in the centre, and sometimes with corn-ears joined thereto, as upon the above denarius of the Cornelia family; also a maritime trophy in a temple, whose pediment exhibits the same symbol of Sicily, appear on certain medals of Augustus, and refer, says Spanheim, to the defeat of Sextus Pompeius (shortly after that of Brutus and Cassius,) in the straights of Sicily, where this son of the Great Pompey had become a captain of pirates, as Florus states: not to say that Augustus oppressed this young man under the appearance of Peace, as some wise men view it in Tacitus, and moreover that Agrippa had the better share in all the successes of that war of which Sicily was the theatre.—On a denarius of L. AQVILIVS FLORVS,

monetal III.VIR. to Augustus, we see the three legs with the head of Medusa, which symbolise Sicily, which coin he caused to be struck in memory of his ancestors, the Caii and Manii who were proconsuls of that province.

SICIL. *Sicilia.*—This abbreviated word appears on the exergue of a denarius struck by the above-mentioned mint-master, to revive the memory of his ancestor Manius Aquilius Florus, who, as proconsul of Sicily in the year V.C. 654, put an end to the servile war. Round the reverse of this historically interesting coin is the inscription MAN*ius* AQVIL*ius* MAN*ii* Filius. MAN*ii* Nepos. The type is a soldier holding a shield on his right arm, and looking back, he lifts up with his right a female figure, who, with a shield on her left arm, is sunk down on her knees. It is thus elegantly that Sicily, which had been despoiled and insulted by the fugitive Italian slaves, is figured under the traits of a helpless and almost prostrate woman, raised from degradation and misery by the rescuing hand of a brave warrior, who, on his return to Rome after this service performed, enjoyed the honours of an ovation.—See *Aquilia* gens.

SICIL. IMP. VIII. IX. X. &c.—The word *Sicilia*, thus abbreviated, is exhibited on other gold and silver coins of Augustus, after he had recovered possession of that island, on the expulsion therefrom of Sextus Pompey. On the obverses of these medals are AVGVSTVS DIVI F. and his head; on the reverse is Diana, who, walking, with a dog at her feet, holds a bow and arrow.

Vaillant, and other learned antiquaries, have referred the coinage of this denarius to the year of Rome 733 (before Christ 21), because during that year Augustus tarried in Sicily, and arranged his affairs there. On many similar coins the numbers IX. X. XI. and XII. are added to IMP*erator*, in the same manner as other denarii of Augustus are inscribed ACT. IMP., with various numbers and with the type of Apollo of Actium.—On these circumstances, Eckhel comments with his usual sagacity and intelligence. These types of the Sicilian Diana and of the Actian Apollo (says he) are not without motive repeated through many consecutive years; for (according to the popular superstition of the Romans) Augustus owed his good fortune to both those divinities, namely, at Artemisium or *Dianium Siciliæ*, near Mylas, when Sextus Pompey was vanquished, and at Actium, sacred to Apollo, where M. Antony sustained his decisive defeat.—The same pre-eminent teacher of the numismatic science, refers to the priesthood *(sacerdotium)* DIAN*æ* VICTR*icis* ET APOLLINIS PALAT*ini*, recorded on a marble by Muratori, and which priesthood was unquestionably instituted by Augustus, when, by the assistance, as was believed, of the divine brother and sister (Apollo and Diana) he achieved the victory over his enemies..

SICILIA. S. C.—On a first brass of Hadrian, with this legend of the reverse is a juvenile head which presents a full face without neck: it has the hair dishevelled, and the chin without beard.

Beneath it is some sea monster, having the figure of a woman from the head to the waist, and having serpents for the legs and arms. Vaillant thinks that this head represents that of Medusa. Havercamp regards it as more likely to be intended for the Sun, such as it is represented on medals of Rhodes, which often sent colonists to Syracuse.—Eckhel believes that, if the head be really that of the sun, of which, however, he thinks, there is strong ground for doubt, it alludes to the sun as seen at the rising by Hadrian at Mount Etna (as related by Spartian) rather than to the Rhodian strangers, especially as the inhabitants of his Mount Ætna engraved the head of the sun on their money. But (he adds) the head is more probably that of Medusa, which often appears on Sicilian medals, placed (as above described) in the centre of the *triquetra*. —There can be no doubt but that the marine monster, placed below, is Scylla, which, in the Sicilian straights *(fretum Siculum)*, appears to have exercised a grievous tyranny, and which in a form not greatly dissimilar is typified on coins of Sextus Pompey.

SICILIAE (ADVENTVI AVG.)—An altar, by which on one side stands the emperor, and and on the other a woman whose hand is adorned with ears of corn, and who also holds corn ears in her left hand.—On *first* and *second* brass of Hadrian.

SICILIAE (RESTITVTORI).—The emperor raising up a kneeling woman, whose left hand holds, and whose head is bound round with ears of corn.—On *first* and *second* brass of Hadrian.

The types of the above described, forming as they do part of the series of geographical medals, furnished by the rich and varied mint of Hadrian, are susceptible of easy explanation; since the ears of corn clearly denote fertility; one of the well-known qualities of Sicily. It was to that island, on his returning from Achaia (to which event Tillemont assigns the date of v. c. 879), that Hadrian made a voyage, on which occasion, according to Spartianus, *Aetnam montem conscendit, ut solis ortum videret arcus specie, ut dicetur, varium.* On first and second brass of Antoninus Pius, bearing the word SICILIA, was the same figure of a woman holding corn ears, thus associating with the name of Sicily the symbol of abundance in agricultural products, which served long to distinguish her as the granary of Rome.

SICINIA.—A plebeian, but formerly also a pratrician family.—Its coins consist of three varieties, in silver, rare.—On a denarius of Q. SICINIVS IIIVIR *monetalis*, are FORT. P.R., and the type of a female head. The type of the reverse is a palm branch, caduceus, and laurel crown.

Ursinus explains the word FORT. as meaning *Fortitudo.* Eckhel and others as *Fortuna.* His observation is that Fortitude does not appear to have been worshipped by the Romans, though *Virtus,* which is almost equivalent, was placed among the qualities deified by that people. But the Romans on the other hand paid vast honour to Fortune, to whom splendid temples, under a

multiplicity of epithets, were raised, as Plutarch says, who besides unhesitatingly affirms that more to fortune than to their virtue the Romans owed their aggrandisements, which gradually extended their empire from the banks of the Tiber over the greatest nations of the known world.

Fortuna Populi Romani appears also on coins of the *Arria* family.—Another denarius of the above Q. Sicinius is classed with the *Coponia* family.

SIDERIBVS RECEPTA.—On a first brass of Faustina junior (Empress of M. Aurelius), bearing this legend, is the type of Diana Lucifera walking. On another bronze medal, we see her conducting a car, after the fashion of Diana. Other medals struck in honour of her apotheosis, represent her seated on a peacock that wings its flight heavenward. But the present type was evidently intended to announce to the subjects of an emperor who loved this wife of his "not wisely, but too well," that she was already *received* into the firmament, and had become a new *star.*—On the obverse, round the head, we read DIVA FAVSTINA PIA. The Divine Faustina Pia.—See *Consecration.*

Sidon, or Zidon (now Seyde), a maritime city, in that part of Syria called Phœnicia, renowned for its great antiquity, being celebrated in history both sacred and profane.—Sidon has its name from the son of Canaan, mentioned in Genesis (c. x. v. 15). The equally famous city of Tyre long contended with it for primacy. But, as Isaiah (c. xxiii. v. 12) calls Tyre the "daughter of Zidon," thus confirming what Strabo says, that Sidon only, and not Tyre, was celebrated by Homer, the palm of antiquity must necessarily be yielded to Sidon. Its inhabitants were early famous for their naval power, insomuch that, according to Diodorus, they could send out a hundred gallies of the largest class. At length the opulence of this grand emporium of commerce became a prey to Persian cupidity.—Falling afterwards under the sway of the Romans, Sidon was deprived of her long enjoyed dignity of a metropolis by Augustus.—But Trajan, mindful of its ancient glory, reconstituted its pre-eminence in the Syrian province; and at length this most ancient city was restored to its metropolitan rank, and made a Roman colony, by one utterly unworthy to hold the sceptre of imperial Rome, viz., by Elagabalus, himself a Syrian by birth.—These metropolitical rights, however, seem to have been soon abolished, for beyond the reign of Alexander Severus no coins assign that title to her.—That Sidon was constituted a colony, with the distinctive appellation of *Aurelia Pia,* by Elagabalus is shown by the numerous coins struck in honour of himself and wives, of his mother and aunts.—The autonomous coins of this place, many of which have Phœnician legends, bear the heads of Syrian kings from Antiochus IV. to Demetrius III. Its imperial medals, with Greek legends, are from Augustus to Hadrian. The *colonial* are inscribed to Elagabalus, Julia Paula, Annia Faustina, and Julia Mæsa, and also to Alexander Severus. These all have *Latin* legends, such as COL. MET. AVR. PIA. SIDON. *Colonia Metropolis Aurelia Pia Sidon;* and on their reverses the features of the Greek and Roman are singularly mingled with those of the Syrian and oriental superstition.

The following are the types found on coins of this colony, as given by Vaillant, whose work is rich in *Latin* medals of Sidon, and no less so in explanatory animadversions on the subjects to which the different types refer :—

Astarte.—Among the numerous numismatic dedications made by the Sidonians to the Syrian Elagabalus and to members of his house, are first and second brass, bearing the legend of COL. AVR. PIA. METR. SID. *(Colonia Aurelia Pia Metropolis Sidon),* and exhibiting the effigy of their favourite goddess, standing with her right hand placed on a trophy, and with her left holding a wand. A figure of Victory, placed on a column, extends to her a crown, and at the feet of Astarte is the figure of Silenus.—On another first brass, inscribed to the same emperor, the same deity appears, and the same *Victoriola,* within a temple supported by four columns, but without the trophy. This type also appears on coins of Julia Paula.

[The Sidonians, like their Tyrian neighbours and rivals, paid supreme adoration to Astarte *(see the word);* and their city contained a temple erected to her honour. The goddess lays her hand on a trophy, in the same way as will be seen on the Tyrian money, and seemingly for the same purpose—namely, to point at the various colonies established far and wide from Phœnicia, and in which trophies had been placed as tokens of conquest; for which reason, perhaps, the small figure of Victory is made to offer a crown to Astarte, who holds the *scipio,* or a sceptre, her appropriate symbol, as queen of the place, *loci regina.*]

[Sidon, after having experienced many changes of fortune, was at length made a colony, and the metropolis of Phœnicia, by Elagabalus. And he, having invested Alexander Severus with the title and rank of Cæsar, had this medal dedicated to him, in congratulation of the event, and especially in remembrance of Alexander's victory over the Persian invaders of Syria. The Sidonians, therefore, adopted the deified hero as a type on their coins, perhaps in flattery to Alexander himself, as if he were another conqueror of the eastern world.]

Colonus agens boves.—On the first brass of Elagabalus, the colonial priest drives his plough-team of oxen, by whose side stands a *vexillum,* on which is inscribed LEG. III. PAR.—*Legio Tertia Parthica.*—On a similar reverse of Annia Faustina, the colonist extends his right hand, which holds a staff over the oxen.

[The *third* legion had its appellation of *Parthian* conferred upon it by Sept. Severus; and the military standard here inscribed with its name denotes that old soldiers from that legion were sent as a reinforcement to the Roman population of this colony.—It appears that in order to supply the place of the many veterans who had fallen in the civil con-

tests between him and Pescennius and Albinus, and also to fulfil his determination of waging war against the Parthians, Severus established *three new legions,* which, that he might give them a character for valour, as it they had already gained victories over the enemy, he called *Parthicæ.* But having brought the war to a successful conclusion, he ordered the first and third of these newly formed legions to winter in Mesopotamia for the protection of that province. Subsequently, as many of the soldiers had completed their term of service, they were ordered by Elagabalus to be stationed in this colony of his own founding, not far remote from the place of their winter quarters.

Europa, riding on the back of a bull, holds with both hands a veil, which floats above her

head; on a second brass of Elagabalus and of Annia Faustina, his third wife, the legend of this coin is C. A. PI. MET. SID., *Colonia Aurelia Pia Metropolis Sidon.*

[Vaillant observes that this elegant type, representing the rape of Europa by Jupiter under the form of a bull, refers to the antiquity of Sidon. Bimard *(ad Jobert.* ii. 261) views it in the same light, in opposition to the conjecture of some writers, who contend that the young woman and the bull simply designate the united beauty and strength of the Sidonians, qualities for which they were by no means remarkable.—The same learned annotator judiciously adds that " Sidon, at the period when its Roman authorities caused these medals to be struck, was inhabited not only by Phœnicians, but also by Greeks, the latter of whom had established themselves there from Alexander the Great's time. And the Greeks, adopting on their part the worship of Astarte (the most ancient divinity of the Sidonians), imparted in their turn to the Sidonians, the worship of Europa." Thus, the figure of Astarte and of Europa, with their respective attributes and indications, were alternately engraven on the colonial-imperial coins of Sidon, whose inhabitants, like the rest of Phœnicia, had eventually become composed of people who paid adoration equally to each of these deifications.]

Emperor Sacrificing.—On a coin of Sidon, struck under Elagabalus.—The emperor, in the garb of a pontiff, stands before an altar with patera in right hand; star in field.—Pl. xix. 10, p. 203.

Modius.—On a first brass of Elagabalus, struck at Sidon, appears the *modius,* or bushel measure, filled with ears of corn, and at the bottom of the coin is AETERNV. BENEFI. *Aeternum Beneficium.*

[Allusive to the donations of corn which, after the custom of Rome (see *Annona*), were made by Elagabalus to the Sidonians. This type seems to have been borrowed from a celebrated coin of Nerva, struck by order of the senate, with the epigraph *Plebei Urbanæ Frumento Constituto*.]

The epigraph is singular, but still in keeping with the monstrous exaggerations and fulsome flatteries of a hideous reign.

Signa Militaria.—There is a first brass of Sidon, struck under the same Emperor, which exhibits three military ensigns, whose tops are surmounted by small eagles. These refer to the veterans of the *Third Parthian* legion sent by Elagabalus as colonists to Sidon, and on which remarks have already been made in describing the type of *Colonus boves agens;* see above.

On small brass, dedicated by this colony respectively to Julia Soæmias, the mother, and to Julia Mæsa, the grandmother of Elagabalus, are three military standards, but without the eagles.

Tables and Urns.—A coin of Sidon, inscribed to Elagabalus, has a table with two urns upon

it, each urn having a palm branch. Around is inscribed COL. METRO. AVR. PIA. SID.; or COL. AVR. PIA., etc., as in the example here given. Below are a vase, apples, and the epigraph CER. or CERT. PER. ISEL. OECVM. *(Periodonica, Iselastica, Œcumenica)*. In the coin engraved above it must read, CE. PE. OEC. IS.

[Vaillant considers CER. or CERT. PER. to signify *Certamina Periodonica*. But Bimard, who rejects *Periodonicum* as an unknown and even barbarous word, and who equally rejects the explanation offered by Hardouin of *Certamen Perpetuum*, adopts the opinion of Iselin, that by CER. PER. is to be understood *Certamen Periodicum*, that is to say, public games, in which all the different kinds of combats and contests were united, as was the custom at the four great games of Greece. Compare with Vaillant "Num. Imp. in Coloniis Percussa," vol. ii. p. 90.

On a very rare first brass coin of this colony, struck under the same emperor, and on a second brass of Annia Faustina, his wife, appears a *laurel crown*, within which is read CERT. SAC. PER. OECVME. ISELA., the whole surrounded by COL*onia* AVR*elia* PIA. METR*opolis* SIDON.—alluding to the celebration by the Sidonians of the same *certamen periodicum*.

Triremis, or Galley.—On a rare second brass of Elagabalus, bearing the usual legend of this colony, are two gallies, in the right hand one of

which a male figure stands with hands extended towards two figures (one of them a female), in the other galley. At the top of the coin is the car of Astarte, and in the lower part is a dolphin.

[This naval group is supposed to refer to the story of Dido's flight from Sidon.]

On another Sidonian medal of Elagabalus a half naked woman is seen standing on the prow of a galley, with right hand extended, and left hand holding a wand transversely.

[Some regard this type as alluding to the flight of Dido; others, as merely representing Astarte.]

Woman, with turreted head, standing, clothed in the *stola*, holds her right hand over an altar, opposite to which is a legionary eagle placed on the prow of a ship.—On a first brass of Elagabalus.

[This figure represents the genius of Sidon. She wears a crown of towers, as a Metropolis; she is dressed in the garb of a Roman matron, as a colony; she holds a patera over the altar, as in the act of sacrificing for the emperor. The legionary eagle refers to the veterans with which the colony was peopled; it is placed on a ship's prow, either to shew the site of the place (Sidon, till its capture by the Persians, being, according to Mela, the greatest and most opulent of maritime cities), or to demonstrate the naval power of the place.]

Sidonia dea, or goddess of the Sidonians, is believed to have been the same object of worship as that called *Europa* by the Greeks, *Astaroth*, or *Astarte* by the Hebrews, and *Venus Caelestis* by the African colonists of the Sidonians. Nor is she otherwise considered by Froëlich, who shews her *(Ann. Syr.* p. 113) on many Greek Imperial coins to be denominated *Dea Syria*.

Sidus.—A star or sign in the heavens.—See *Astra—Stella*.

Sidus Julium, a star with hairy train, like a comet, is near the head of Julius Cæsar, sometimes opposite his face, at others behind his neck, on coins of his struck after his death.

SIG.   *Signis*.—SIG. REC.—*Signis Receptis*.

Sigillum, a little image of something, imprinted on a medal as a mark.

Siglæ, abbreviations in writing on coins and on marbles.

Signa militaria.   Military ensigns.——The Romans entrusted these to the custody of the Quæstors, who preserved them with the *ærarium* or public treasury, in the temple of Saturn.—See *Saturnus*.

The *ensigns* of the legions are common on Roman coins, especially the imperial, not with the bundle of hay *(manipulus foeni)*, but with small bucklers on the top, in which were painted images of the Gods and of the Cæsars, and even of illustrious men. On a colonial medal (of *Cæsaraugusta*) the simpler and more ancient form of the *signum manipulare* is exhibited, viz., *fasciculi* of corn-ears, straw, or hay. As symbols of the soldiery they were held by the Romans in the highest veneration; auspices were taken upon, and divine worship paid to, them.

The *signa militaria*, captured by the Parthians from M. Crassus and M. Antony, but restored by that nation to Augustus, in consequence of a renewed treaty between the Parthians and the Romans, are found alluded to on several family denarii, such as those of *Aquillia*, *Caninia*, *Durmia*, *Petronia*, which have perpetuated the remembrance of this event by a diversity of types and symbols; that is to say, by the kneeling figure of a Parthian holding an ensign; or by a triumphal arch with a quadriga on the top of it; or by the naked image of Mars standing with an eagle in his right hand, and the standard of the legion in his left; or by a similar figure holding a trophy and standing in the temple of Mars. The same fact is also typified by an eagle in a *thensa*, or sacred chariot, drawn by four horses; or by votive shields placed between the eagle and the ensign of the legion; likewise by oaken garlands and civic crowns; or by a *capricorn*, the astrological sign of Augustus's birth, with the addition of various inscriptions.—Augustus always treated his recovery of these last standards as holding the place of a great triumph to himself.—The *signa militaria*, taken by the Germans in the slaughter of the legions under Varus, and recovered by Germanicus, are also commemorated on coins of Tiberius.—Domitian's pretended re-capture of Roman standards from the Sarmatians occasioned coins to be struck, like Augustus's, *mutato nomine*, Sarmati for Parthi.

Signa militaria form a frequent type on colonial coins, and they were engraved thereupon in memory of the colony having in its origin been formed of legionary veterans. "For (as Rubenius says in his notes on the Arschot collection) Augustus, who had partly associated the legions of Lepidus and Mark Antony with his own, after the division of the provinces with the people, disbanded a great many soldiers, and sent them into such of the colonies as needed a supply of men." This fact is proved from a multitude of coins, the most rare of which exhibit the names of the legions. Thus, as Vaillant teaches us, the *signa veteranorum* are found on medals of *Antioch* in Pisidia, under Caracalla, Elagabalus, Gordianus Pius, Philip, and Decius; on those of *Apamea*, under Caracalla; on those of *Cremna* and of *Sidon*, under Elagabalus and his family.; of *Dacia*, under Philip; of *Deultum*, in honour of Tranquillina; of *Heliopolis*, under Macrinus; of *Viminacium*, under Gordian.

On the reverse of a fine brass medal of Tiberius, struck at Cæsaraugusta (Sarragoza) in the thirty-seventh year of that emperor's tribunitian power, appears a standard (or *labarum*) between two military ensigns, with the initial letters of the colony, and with the names of the duumvirs and of the legions who had been sent to settle there. Nor are any types more common on Imperial coins of Roman die than the legionary eagle, the *vexillum*, and other ensigns

of the army, in the hands either of the emperor himself or of his cohorts, or in the grasp of some personification, or placed before an Emperor, Empress, or Cæsar, throughout the series from Tiberius down to Constantine, accompanied by legends declaratory of the concord, the fidelity, the glory of soldiers, who were continually quarrelling amongst themselves, murdering their sovereigns, oppressing their fellow-subjects, and betraying the empire they were entrusted to defend.

The eagle-standard, as distinguished from the ordinary ensigns of the Roman legions, is well pourtrayed on a silver coin of Nero, and still better on a second brass of Galba, where these peculiar objects of the soldiers' idolatry are planted on prows of ships.—See *Legionum Insignia*.

SIGNA P. R. *Signa Populi Romani.*—On gold and silver of Augustus; this legend accompanies a legionary eagle placed on an altar between two military ensigns, thus typifying and designating the conquering *standards of the Roman people*.

SIGNIS RECEPTIS. *Capricornus.*—An elegant gold medal of Augustus bears this legend and type. It was under the Zodiacal sign of Capricorn that this emperor was born, to use the jargon of superstitious astrology (*"O faustum et felicem diem"*) ; and to which sidereal influence he was wont to ascribe all fortunate and happy events of his life. Even the very surrendering to him of the military ensigns, which the Parthians took from Crassus, and which Augustus most evidently wished for, seems here to be attributed to this genethliacal constellation, or star on which "his nativity was cast."

SIGNIS PARTHICIS RECEPTIS.—Still more specifically allusive to the same event is a denarius bearing on its obverse the youthful head of Augustus, and on the reverse side the legend annexed within the field of the coin, and without type.

SIGN. RECE. CAESAR AVGVSTVS.—A Parthian kneeling on one knee, and holding out in his right hand a military ensign, as if in the act of presenting it to some one.

This appears on a denarius minted by Aquilius Florus, one of the moneyers of Augustus, the obverse of which bears the radiated head of a man, and which, like several others, was struck in memory of the standards captured from, and sent back to the Romans by Phraates, King of the Parthians, to Cæsar Augustus whilst remaining in Syria (in the year v. c. 734), and which, says Dion, "he (the emperor) received as though he had been victorious in some battle with the Parthians."—See AVGVSTVS, p. 105; and FERONIA.

Another silver coin of Augustus, bearing the same legend, and allusive to the same event, exhibits the standing figure of Mars, who holds in his right hand a Roman eagle, and in his left a military ensign.— The god of war is here introduced, in immediate reference to the temple which Augustus, on the restitution of the military ensigns by the Parthians, caused to be built in the capitol, and which he dedicated to Mars the Avenger. (See *Mars Ultor*.) In grateful memory of an event so acceptable to heal their wounded national pride, the senate and people of Rome voted a buckler of honour to the emperor, which is represented with the above legend.

SIGNIS RECEPTIS. S. C.—The emperor standing on a pedestal, with a spear in his left hand, accepts with his right a legionary eagle, which Victory presents to him.—On a first brass of Vespasian.

Pellerin in giving this, from the treasures of his own cabinet, as a coin considered to be unique, observes that "there is no doubt but that it was struck after the model of those which Augustus caused to be struck at Rome, in each metal, to record the fact of his having obtained from the Parthians a restoration of those military ensigns, which they had kept as a glorious monument of victories they had gained over the Roman armies commanded by Crassus and Mark Antony; but history is not found to have made mention of a like event under the reign of Vespasian. It is only seen in Josephus and Tacitus, that, whilst in Italy he was contending for the empire with Vitellius, the Dacians attacked all the troops of his party, who were on the banks of the Danube, in Moesia; and it may be inferred (adds Pellerin) that having afterwards reduced these barbarous tribes to obedience, he compelled them to give up the military ensigns of which they had possessed themselves; a particular circumstance which probably was forgotten or neglected by the historians."—*Mélange*, vol i. p. 200.

Agreeing with the illustrious Frenchman above quoted, so far as relates to the motive of Vespasian being similar to that of Augustus in causing medals to be coined as a record of military honours recovered after being lost, the equally illustrious German, whose *Doctrina* is the text book of all Greek and Latin numismatists of the present day, goes on to express his opinion that this singular coin refers, not to transactions with the Dacians or any other barbarians inhabiting the borders of the Danube; but rather with barbarians occupying the regions washed by the Lower Rhine, and which followed that sanguinary and desolating revolt raised (v.c. 823, A.D. 70) by Civilis the Batavian, in which the Germans made common cause with his countrymen, and which would have been still more injurious to the Roman empire, if either there had been greater concord amongst the barbarians, or if a general, less discreet in policy and less self-possessed amidst surrounding dangers than Petilius Cerealis, had chanced in the end to command the Romans. That during that war military ensigns were lost by them in various unfortunate battles, Tacitus the eloquent historian of that rebellion distinctly declares. He states that Civilis went forth to the assault

environed with the *signa* of captured cohorts; again, after that disgrace the legions lost their standards also; and these were carried about in reproachful insult to the Romans *(in Romanorum opprobrium circumlata)*. And as, indeed, the coin in question distinctly exhibits the *aquila legionaria*, so we find the same author, Tacitus, not disguising the shame incurred by his own nation, in the cutting off of two legions by Civilis, but acknowledging that they were compelled to surrender.—Eckhel, under the circumstances, thinks it very likely that these ensigns were restored when the good fortune of Civilis had fallen way, and he was himself compelled to sue for peace, the beginning of which we have from Tacitus; but what afterwards happened between those things which have been narrated and that restitution of ensigns which this coin proclaims, together with the fact of the restitution itself, has had the misfortune to be omitted in Roman history. These medals, therefore, teach us what we are not allowed to learn from written history."

A similar case of *signa recepta* occurred, or was pretended to have occurred, under Domitian, whose duplicity and treachery sufficiently betrayed themselves in the war with Civilis. The imperial braggart caused medals in gold and silver to be struck with the type of a Dacian, who, kneeling in the attitude of a suppliant, presents a military ensign.—Pellerin on this point quotes Dion, who relates that the degenerate son of Vespasian, and unworthy successor of Titus, "received back arms and captives from Decebalus, king of the Dacians, of whom he had purchased peace at the price of great sums of money; and that he was so vain of it as to cause himself to be decreed a triumph by the senate, as if he had gained some signal victory; the same ancient writer also states that Domitian had required all the Roman prisoners and arms in the possession of the Dacians to be delivered up to him; but, Dion adds, that they kept many of them in their castles, where Trajan subsequently found them."

SIGNIS RECEPTIS.—This inscription, with the addition of *Senatus Populus Que Romanus*, appears on gold and silver coins of Augustus, some with the type of a votive shield and CL. V. (Clipeus Votivus) engraved on it, between a military ensign and a legionary eagle; others with a triumphal arch: all serving to accumulate evidences of the joy with which Augustus received the blood-stained ensigns of slaughtered legions from the Parthians, and for which he took an ovation, entering the city on horseback, and being honoured with a triumphal arch in the year v.c. 734. But why the memory of the event should have been renewed after his death it is certainly difficult to imagine. And yet, in the Museum Farnese, there is a second brass with Divus Augustus s. c. and his radiated head, having on its reverse the above inscription of SIGNIS RECEPTIS S. P. Q. R. and CL. V. between military standards, as in the gold and silver medals struck during his life time, and at the period of the transaction.

SIGNIS. RECEPT. DEVICTIS. GERM*anis*, S. C.—Germanicus, in military habiliments, stands with the right hand extended, and holding a legionary eagle in his left.—On the obverse is GERMANICVS CAESAR, who stands in a triumphal quadriga, holding a wand surmounted by an eagle in his left hand.—See p. 416.

This elegant and most interesting, although common coin, in second brass, was struck in the year of Rome 770, under Tiberius, to commemorate the celebrated triumph of Germanicus, on the occasion of having subdued several nations of Germany (such as the Cherusci, the Catti, the Angrivarii, &c.)—The obverse attests that triumph. The reverse by its inscription DEVICTIS GERM*anis* bespeaks the complete defeat of those tribes, and also marks the subject of the triumph: the other part of the epigraph, SIGNIS RECEPT*is* comprises an allusion to that renowned exploit of Germanicus, in which, after his victory, having instituted a search for the eagles lost in the overthrow and destruction of Varus and his legions (by the Cherusci, under Arminius, A.D. 10), and having found them in a grove, where they had been buried by the barbarians, he brought them back to Rome, as Tacitus most circumstantially relates.—P. Gabinius, one of Claudius's lieutenants, having in the year V.C. 794 (A.D. 41) conquered the Chauci (according to Dion) recovered the eagle which alone had remained with that noble and warlike nation as a relic of the Varian slaughter.

SIGNIS A SARMATIS RESTITVTIS.—A barbarian on his knee presents a military standard. On a gold coin of Domitian, published by Morell. —See CIVIB. ET SIGN. &c., and CLIPEVS.

Silenus, the Phrygian, to whom fable has assigned the distinction of being the foster-father, tutor, and companion of Bacchus, as one of the first that held the son of Jupiter and Semele in his arms, and who followed him in his travels and excited him in virtue and glory.—Indeed some ancient traditions have exalted the character of Silenus into that of a great captain, a great physician, and a sage counseller. But (as Spanheim in Julianus Cæsar sarcastically remarks) "he was evidently better versed in the knowledge of nature than in that of reasoning." In other words, he would seem to have been more the friend of wine and raillery than that of science and research—a sort of philosophic voluptuary. And as to the representations of this personage on antique monuments, the ridiculous considerably predominates over the dignified. He is ordinarily figured as an old man with a bald head and a thick beard, a snub turned-up nose, in a state of more than half nudity and of entire drunkenness, holding a staff, or the *cantharus* into which he was wont to press out the *juice of the grape;* sometimes standing, but seldom without support, sometimes lying along carelessly on the back of an ass.—The images of Silenus are found on medals of Macedonia, and of Ancyra in Galatia. It is a type seen on some family coins, and is of sufficiently frequent occurrence on Roman colonial medals. On a

denarius of Marcius L. Censorinus, Silenus stands with one hand raised, and the wine skin at his back; behind is a small pillar, on which stands an image.—Eckhel, in his commentary on the coins of the Marcia family, acknowledges himself ignorant of the reason why the figure of Silenus appears on the medals of Censorinus.— Among the colonial are those of *Troas*, in Phrygia, struck under Marcus Aurelius and Commodus, in which he is accurately recognised by Vaillant as an elderly male figure, naked, holding up his right hand towards the stars, and bearing his goat skin bottle on his left shoulder. The people of Troas, his reputed birth place, honoured his memory as the author and master of the best of studies, and worshipped him as a god.—A coin of *Bostra*, under Alexander Severus, exhibits Silenus in the same posture, and with the same attribute of the wine skin, but as a younger man.—The colonies of *Coillu*, in Numidia, under Caracalla, Elagabalus, and Gordianus Pius; of *Damascus*, under Philip senior; of *Deultum*, in Thrace, under Macrinus; and others, likewise bear the effigy of Silenus; on some of these his extended hand is pointing to a cypress tree.

SILIA, a plebeian family. Its surnames *Nerva* and *Italicus*.—A silver coin bearing the former cognomen, exhibits on one side ROMA, with the bust of Minerva holding spear and buckler—on the other side P. NERVA, with the *septa* or enclosure of the Comitia, within which a citizen standing puts a voting tablet into an urn, whilst another stands by in the act of receiving the tablet from the officer *(diribitor)* appointed for that purpose.

Morell inserts the denarius amongst those of the *Licinia* family, to which the same surname of Nerva belongs. Vaillant assigns it to the Silia family; and Eckhel thinks this the more accurate reference, " because (says he) we know of no Licinius with the prænomen of Nerva, whereas there are many Silii who bear the addition of Nerva."—A similar type of the Comitia appears on coins of the *Mussidia* family, under the head of which an explanation of the above described is given.—With respect to the surname of *Italicus*, Eckhel adds that C. Silius Italicus, the consular poet, is commemorated on medals of Smyrna.

Silvanus, the god of cattle, of fields, and of woods, at whose altar a hog was sacrificed.

Simpulum, or *Simpuvium*, a small vessel or ladle with a long handle, used at sacrifices to make libations, and to taste the wines and other liquors which were poured on the head of the victims. It is the sign of priesthood, and one of the insignia of the college of pontiffs. It appears on a coin of Patræ, struck under Augustus. It is also placed before the head of Vesta, as a mark of that goddess, on a coin of the *Domitia* family, and is seen in the hand of a vestal on coins of the *Claudia* family.—A togated and stolated man holds a simpulum in his hand on a coin of Antonio Drusi, sen.—This vase is united with the aspergillum, securis, apex, patera, secespita, præfericulum, lituus, that is to say, with one or other of these sacrificial and augural instruments, on coins of Julius Cæsar, M. Antony, Lepidus, Augustus, Caligula, Vespasian, Nerva, Antoninus, M. Aurelius, Caracalla, Geta, Philip jun., Volusianus, Salonicus, Valerianus jun., as well as on many consular and colonial medals.

Singara (now *Sengiar*), a city of Mesopotamia, appears to have been a Roman colony, from coins inscribed to Alexander Severus, and also to Gordianus Pius, with *Greek* legends, in which it is called *Aurelia Septimia Colonia Singara.*—Vaillant, who gives a specimen of her colonial mint under each of the above-named emperors, inclines however to the opinion, that Singara owed its first foundation as a colony to M. Aurelius and L. Verus rather than to Alexander Severus.—Its sole type is a female head, turreted and veiled, representing the Genius of a fortified town (the common symbol of the Mesopotamian cities); above the head is placed a centaur (Sagittarius), with bow in his right hand; allusive either to the surpassing skill of the Singarenes in archery, or more probably to the computation of their year commencing under that zodiacal sign.

Sinope, a very ancient city (now called *Sinub*), situate on the shore of Paphlagonia, in Asia Minor—the birth-place of Diogenes, the cynic philosopher. Originally founded by the Milesians (Greeks), it subsequently became the residence of the kings of Asiatic Pontus, and especially that of the great Mithridates, after whose death it was brought into subjection to the Romans, and reduced to the state of a province. But Pharnaces, having driven out Domitius Calvinius, one of Julius Cæsar's lieutenants, occupied for a time this kingdom of his ancestors. Cæsar, however, at the entreaty, as was said, of the Sinopians themselves, compelled Pharnaces to quit the province, and formed it into a *colony*, to which he gave the name of *Julia.* Its colonial-imperial coins extend from Julius Cæsar to Gallienus, including in that series those of Augustus, Tiberius, Caligula, Agrippina Claudii, Octavia Neronis, Nerva, Hadrian, L. Verus, Faustina Aurelii, Caracalla, Geta, Diadumenianus, Alex. Severus, and Maximus Cæsar. All these pieces have *Latin* legends, and are very numerous.—The first medal of Sinope given by Vaillant (who calls that city the oldest of Roman colonies) is dedicated to Hadrian. But Pellerin and the Abbé Belley agree in assigning one to Julius Cæsar. Its legend, however, shows it to have been coined after his death, viz., DIVOS IVLIVS. C . . . . . SIVS. IIVIR. C.R.F.S. Laureated head of Julius. *Rev.* AUGUSTUS DIVI F. Naked head of Augustus. (*Mélange*, i. p. 245.)

Those struck in this colony under Augustus bear the initial letters C. I. F. S. *Colonia Julia Felix Sinope.*—Pellerin gives a remarkable one of this reign, bearing his portrait on one side, and the united heads of M. Antony and Octavia on the other.—The legend of the obverse is C. I. F. S. A. XXXVI.

Respecting the date of the year 36 marked

on this coin, Pellerin observes that " it is reckoned from the æra of the year of Rome 684, which was established at Sinope in memory of the freedom which Lucullus that year granted to this city. This date of the year 36 falls in the year of Rome 719, in which M. Antony openly divorced himself from Octavia his wife, sending her from Greece into Italy. The city of Sinope (he adds) was doubtless unacquainted with that fact, when it caused that medal to be struck. The Abbé Belley has edited a similar medal, dated the year xxxi, accompanied with remarks on the two æras which Sinope followed at different times."—(*Mélange* i. p. 245.)

Sinope—Caligula—C. I. F. S. ANN. LXXXIII.— A colonist and oxen. (*Mélange* i. xvi. No. 8 p. 262.)

Sinope.—Agrippina Claudii, (xvi. No. 10.)

With respect to the types found on coins of this colony, as given in Vaillant, there is one struck under Hadrian, which bears the head of Serapis; another coined in honour of Geta exhibits a fish, and is inscribed C. I. F. SINOPES.— One of the most elegant as well as most remarkable types presented on the Latin coins of this Roman settlement was struck under Caracalla, who gave it the name of *Aurelia.*—C. I. AVR. SINOPE. ANN. CCLII. *Colonia, Julia, Augusta,* or *Aurelia Sinope, anno* 252. Jupiter recumbent on a *lectisternium*, his head adorned with the *calathus*, an eagle on his right hand, in his left the *hasta* of divinity.—The years 252 are the æra of the Sinopian colony, reckoning from the time (v. c. 706) when Julius Cæsar drove Pharnaces out of Pontus, and which, joined together (as Vaillant observes), make V.C. 958, in which year Caracalla was associated in the imperial government with his father.

Among many other reigns, to which Pellerin has supplied medals of this colony not to be found in Vaillant's work, are the following, viz. :—

1.—A very fine brass inscribed to Geta, on the obverse of which is the laureated head of that prince; on the reverse, C. I. F. SINOPE. ANN. CCLV. The type is a majestic figure of Serapis, having the *modius* on his head, with his right hand extended, and holding a *hasta pura* crosswise in his left hand. (*Mélange* i. pl. 18.) A similar figure of this great divinity of the Egyptians appears on a coin of Alexander Severus, pl. xix. 14; and of Maximus, xx. 3.

2.—On a small brass of Sinope, struck in honour of Diadumenianus, the youthful son of Macrinus (C. I. F. SINOPE. CCLXI.J; the type of the reverse is Mercury standing, holding a purse in his right hand, and a caduceus in the left. (*Mélange* i. pl. xix. No. 3.)

3.—On a large brass of Gallienus, struck at Sinope; the reverse exhibits a woman, crowned with towers, standing with the right hand pointing downwards, and resting her left hand on a *hasta.*

4.—Another large brass of this colony (C. I. F. S. AN. CCCXXX.), dedicated to the same emperor, represents Bacchus, clothed in a long dress, holding a cartharus or pitcher in the right haud, and supporting himself with the left hand on a thyrsus. At his feet is a panther.

Sirenes, Syrens.—The poets represent these fictitious monsters as persons, who, with the handsome countenance and voice of women and the thighs and legs of a bird, inhabiting steep rocks on the sea-coast, allured voyagers by the sweetness of their singing, and caused them to perish. On some ancient monuments the Syrens are figured as women, with the lower extremity of the body terminating in shape like a fish, but this is the form ascribed to Nereids.—On others, they have the head and breast of a woman, with the wings, thighs, and feet of a bird, which better agrees with the description given of them by the poets of antiquity. An instance of the former kind occurs on a coin of the *Valeria* family; an example of the latter is also given by Morell, in coins of the *Petronia* family. The Syren Parthenope, as depictured on the medals of Cuma, has the head and upper part of a young woman, with wings on her shoulders, and the lower part of the figure terminates in the form of a fish.—See *Parthenope.*

The medal struck by P. PETRON*ius* TURPILIANVS. IIIVIR (Monetal) of Augustus, has for the type of its reverse a figure presenting the head, body, and arms of a young woman; and the wings, legs, talons, and even tail of a bird; this monster stands holding a trumpet, or tibia, in each hand.

On this type, Eckhel makes the following observations:—"Here we see a single Syren; and, according to ancient fables, the true appearances of those beings, who sprung from Achelous, and as some say the muse Terpsichore, others Calliope, have been represented by the voice of antiquity as at once delightful from the allurements of their singing, and dangerous from the snares laid by them for the unwary. She appears with the face of a virgin, her shoulders have wings attached to them, her form ends below like a bird, and she holds in each hand a trumpet, or a flute, as if about to sing; that is to say, as Servius remarks—there were three Syrens; one of these sang with the voice, the other performed on the pipes *(tibiæ)* the third played the lyre; and they inhabited first the neighbourhood of Pelorus, afterwards the island of Capræa. The fact is (he adds) they were harlots, who, because they reduced passengers to extremities, were feigned to have occasioned shipwreck to them. The three Syrens standing together, and with their respective musical instruments, are represented on ancient anaglyphs, and especially on the sarcophagi of the Etruscans; and in the same design Ulysses is generally to be seen on board his ship with his hands tied to the mast." Why the type of a Syren is placed on a coin of Petronius does not appear to be known.

SIRM.—Letters engraved at the bottom of certain coins, doubtless designating *Sirmium* Pannoniæ, at present Sirmich in Sclavonia.—This mint mark is seen on the exergue of medals, struck under Constantius Chlorus, Licinius jun., Constantine the Great, Crispus, Fausta, Con- stantine jun., Julian II., Jovian, Valentinian I., and other Augusti and Cæsars of the Lower Empire.

Sirmium, situated in a pleasant and fertile spot, held a conspicuous and important rank amongst the ancient cities of Pannonia. Pliny (l. iii. cap. 25) mentions "*Sirmium oppidum*" and "*Civitas Sirmiensium.*" It is also mentioned by Herodian, Ammianus, Zosimus, and others; and was the birth-place of the Emperor Probus. It is now named *Sirmich*, in that part of Sclavonia which belongs to the Turks, between the Drave and the Save rivers.

SIS.—This abbreviation frequently occurs on coins of the lower empire, and denotes that they were struck at *Siscia.*

Siscia, a chief town and a colony of Pannonia, which was a Roman province, divided into upper and lower, comprising Styria, Austria, and Croatia of the present day.—It was situate at the confluence of the Colapis and Savus, and is now called *Sissech.* There were offices for coining imperial money at Siscia, and a mint master called *procurator monetæ Siscianæ.*

SISCIA. AVG*usti.*—On a silver coin of Gallienus this legend appears, accompanied by the type of a woman sitting, who holds a hasta in the right and a cornucopiæ in her left hand, below her is the recumbent personification of a river (the Save).—On another silver coin of Gallienus the female figure sits with outstretched hands, and the river deity is emerging below.—On a third brass of Probus is the inscription SISCIA PROBI AVG., with XXI Q in the exergue; but, in the type of this last-named coin, the seated female holds a sort of scarf in her extended hands, and there are the demi figures of *two* river gods, one on each side below her.

With regard to the former coin, Vaillant thinks that it was struck after Gallienus had conquered Ingenuus, the usurper of Pannonia. But as Siscia may be seen named on the mint of Probus, Eckhel conjectures that this city was considered as a sort of barrier to the empire, as well on account of its convenient situation (on the frontiers of Sarmatia) as because it was fortified by nature, and had, therefore, been constituted a place of arms amidst the wars which were perpetually breaking out in that tract of country.—On a marble found near Sabaria, in Pannonia, is read COLONIA. SEPTIMA. SISCIA. AVGVSTA.

SISC. P. *Sisciæ Percussa* (moneta).—Money struck at *Siscia* (Sissech.)

SISC. P. S. *Sisciæ percussa officina Septima.*—Money struck at Siscia, in the seventh office of the mint.

SISEN.—Sisenna, surname of the *Cornelia* family, on a coin of which it is written at length, but with only one N.—thus SISENA.

SISPITA, surname of the queen of the gods, as is shown on some rare coins of Antoninus Pius, with the inscription IVNONI SISPITAE; such as are in the Medicean and Barberini cabinets. Capitolinus refers to the *templa Lanuvina* as restored by that emperor; for this *Sispita* was the goddess of Lanuvium. The word SISPES with the ancients was the same as *Sospes;* whence

Festus remarks—"*Sispitam Junonem quam vulgo Sospitam appellant, antique usurpabant.*"—For thus it is to be read, not *Sospitam* and *Sospitem.* —Spanheim (Pr. i. p. 120) confirms this by an old inscription, in which mention is made not only of *Juno Sispes*, but also of *Jupiter Sispes.*— *Rasche's Lexicon.*

Sisters of Emperors were sometimes distinguished by the Roman moneyers by the surname of *Augustæ*, as is shown on coins of Drusilla, of Domitilla, of Julia Titi, and of Marciana, sister of Trajan. On the other hand, the names of Agrippina, Drusilla, and Julia, the three sisters of Caligula, are found inscribed together on a large brass medal of that Emperor, without the title of *Augusta* being affixed to either of them.

Sistrum.—This was a species of timbrel, or rattle, made of brass or some other sonorous metal. It was oval, and its circumference perforated with several holes opposite each other, through which were inserted horizontally several small metallic rods. This "tinkling cymbal or sounding brass," shaken in cadence, emitted a harsh sound, and was carried by the priests of Isis when sacrificing to that Egyptian idol. It is an instrument which is seen figured on a great many monuments of antiquity. It is described by Apuleius (*Metamorph.* lib. xi.)

The Sistrum, as one of the insignia of Isis is seen in the hands of that deity, on coins of the Cæcilia family; and on coins of Hadrian, the two Faustinas, Commodus, Claudius Gothicus, Julian the Apostate, and other emperors. The same instrument is generally seen in the right hand of *Egypt* and of *Alexandria* personified. "Isis (says Vaillant) was believed to be the genius of Egypt, who, by the shaking of the *sistrum*, signified the increase of the Nile." It also appears in the hand of Anubis, another of the monster-divinities of Egypt, on coins of Julian and of Helena.

Sitella (diminutive of *Situla*), a little vessel into which voting tablets were put : one of them is seen on a denarius of the *Cassia* family.

S. M. *Signata Moneta.*

S. M. A. *Signata Moneta Antiochiæ.* (Money struck at Antioch).—On the exergue of coins of Diocletian, Licinius jun., Constantinus, and several of their successors.

S. M. AQR. *Sacra Moneta Aquileiæ Percussa.*—On coins of Valentinian, Valens, and Gratian.

S. M. HER. *Signata Moneta Heracleiæ.* (Money struck at Heracleia).—At the bottom of coins of Constantine, Gratian, &c.

S. M. KA. *Signata Moneta Carthaginæ officina prima.* (Money struck at Carthage, in the first office of the mint)—On coins of Licinius and of the Constantines and their successors down to Theodosius the Great.

S. M. N. *Signata Moneta Narbonæ, or Nicomedeiæ.*—On coins of Val. Maximianus, Gal. Maximianus, Maximinus Daza, the two Licinii, and Constantine and his family.

S. M. R. *Signata Moneta Romæ.*—On coins of Diocletian, Theodosius M., Aelia Eudoxia, Gratian, Valentinian jun., and Valens.

S. M. SISC. *Signata Moneta Sisciæ*, on the exergue of coins of Valentinian I. and of Valens.

S. M. T. and S. M. TR. *Signata Moneta Treveris.*—(Money struck at Treves). On coins of Constans, Constantius jun., Valens, Magnus Maximus, &c.

S. M. T. SB. *Sacra Moneta Treveris Signata Secundo in Officina.*—(Sacred money struck at Treves in the second office of the mint). On coins of Constantine M. and Constantine jun.

Socrates.—There are two contorniate medals which bear, what are said to be, portraits of this great philosopher. One of these is taken from Ursinus by Havercamp. His name is given in Greek characters, and his head is naked and bearded. What was the reverse of this medal is not stated. The other is published by Pedrusi from the Farnese Museum, and on the obverse of which is a bearded head, but with no epigraph added. "I cannot (says Eckhel) discover on what grounds he should have ventured to pronounce this a head of Socrates."

SOAEMIAS *(Julia)*, mother of Elagabalus.— This princess was the daughter of Julius Avitus, a Syrian by birth, who was consul under Caracalla,

and of Julia Mæsa, sister of Julia Domna, wife of Sept. Severus. Married to a senator named Varius Marcellus, also a Syrian, she became the mother of Elagabalus in the year of our Lord 204. Becoming a widow she retired, after the death of her nephew Caracalla, to Emesa, in her native country, where she and her mother Mæsa caused Elagabalus to be declared emperor. By the influence of her beauty, and by her courageous example, she won the hearts and secured the aid of the legions in the east, by whose means she succeeded in defeating Macrinus and seating her son on the imperial throne. On her return to Rome she was declared Augusta and admitted into the senate, when she assumed so far as to give her vote like the rest of the senators. Vain, proud, and profligately ambitious, her whole conduct was that of a shameless, insolent, and cruel woman, who by the encouragement which she gave to the abominable crimes of her son, had made herself in a great degree answerable for the horrors of that monster's reign.—She fell a victim to the fury of the soldiers, who put her to death at the same time and in the same ignominious way that they killed her detestable son, A.D. 222.—She is styled on her coins IVL. (or IVLIA) SOAEMIAS AVG. (or AVGVSTA). The gold are extremely rare; silver of usual size common; large brass rare; and middle brass common.

Sol, the Sun.—This glorious luminary was originally regarded and worshipped by the Pagans as being the most brilliant and the most useful object in the universe—as constituting by his light and heat the natural source of life and health both to the animal and vegetable kingdoms, and as imparting his splendour to the other heavenly bodies, and his glory to the whole firmament. The more deeply investigations are carried into heathen mythology, the more clearly it is to be seen that almost all its principal divinities resolve themselves into an identity with the Sun, to whose predominating influence over the moon and stars the government and preservation of all things both in heaven and earth were ascribed. Ancient monuments represent the Sun under the form of a man, with a youthful face, the head encircled with rays: sometimes he is mounted on a chariot drawn by winged horses. A horse was sacrificed to him, on account of the great swiftness of that animal, a usage especially practised by the Lacedemonians.

The Sun was called *Mithras* by the Persians; *Osiris* by the Egyptians. He was considered by some to be the same deity with *Apollo ;* by others the same with *Æsculapius. Sol* and *Bacchus* were also one and the same according to the superstition of the Syrians; and in illustration of some Roman colonial medals, Vaillant quotes Macrobius to show that Hercules and even Jupiter were only other names under which the Sun was worshipped in the East.—The Romans, following in this and almost all other instances the polytheism of the Greeks, paid divine honours to the Sun, and on the silver coins of the republic his figure is represented.—A medal of the *Manlia* family exhibits him in a quadriga, which he is driving at full speed; on each side of him is a star. Amongst the coins of foreign die inscribed ROMANO, Eckhel notices one with the head of Apollo on one side and a horse leaping on the other ; a star above him, which he regards as confirming what is asserted by old writers, that the horse was consecrated to Apollo or the Sun ; and that the same animal was in many countries publicly dedicated and afterwards immolated to the honour of that deity. Thus by the Rhodians, who were especially noted for being Sun-worshippers, a quadriga of consecrated horses was cast into the sea, because, as Festus relates, the God of Day was believed to be carried round the world in such a chariot.

On a denarius of Cœlius Caldus, appears the radiated head of the Sun, evidently in allusion to the name of Caldus, for *Calidus*. (See Morell's *" Famil. Roman.")*

Sol is represented in various ways on coins of the Imperial series. A second brass of Aurelian presents the naked head of the god, with the inscription SOL DOMINVS IMPERII ROMANI (see the words); thus shewing how peculiarly he was the favourite deity of that emperor, who caused a magnificent temple to be built at Rome to his honour.—On another coin of Aurelian, with the same remarkable inscription, the head of *Sol* is radiated. Sometimes he appears in his

perfect stature, either standing, or in a walking attitude, or even as if running with great swiftness, and almost always with a circlet of rays diverging from the head ; the right hand is open and extended upwards, the left holds a globe or a whip *(flagellum)*, the symbol of his velocity. —On coins of Elagabalus, a huge *stone*, in the form of a cone, drawn in a chariot, represents the *Sun*, of whose temple at Emesa, in Syria, Elagabalus was a priest, before he was raised to disgrace the throne of the Cæsars.—Different types of the Sun are more frequently seen on the coins of Roman emperors without any other inscription than that of the letters P.M. TR. P. and so forth, as in Alexander Severus ; or in conjunction with the words CONSERVAT. AVG. as in Probus: also with the following legends: ORIENS AVG. or AVGVST.— SOLI INVICTO.— SOLI INVICTO COMITI.—INVICTVS. These are found on many Imperial coins from the time of Hadrian to Constantine, shortly after which there is no longer a recurrence of these signs of paganism. The personification of the *Sun* is accompanied with the inscription INVICTVS, on coins of Victorinus, Tetricus, and Carausius.

Sol was, with the Egyptians, the symbol of *eternity*, because, said they, he never grows old, but flourishes in perpetual youth. Hence it is that he is represented on some Roman coins under the figure of a naked young man, with radiated head and uplifted right hand, as an everlasting sign in the heavens. So we find *Sol* and Luna placed on other coins (see p. 23) in the hands of the female figure personifying eternity. Nor was the Sun adopted only as the symbol of eternity ; but he was held to denote *invincible fortitude* ; since diversity of times and seasons withdraws nothing from him, and he pursues unweariedly his ceaseless course.—The first of the emperors who dedicated coins to the *Sun*, under the name of *Invictus*, was *Elagabalus*, and he called himself *Solis Sacerdos.*

On a gold coin of Vespasian, given by Morell, is a rostrated column, surmounted by the image of a naked man, with radiated head, holding the *hasta* in his right hand, and in his left something like a *parazonium*.—This is considered to represent an image dedicated by Vespasian to the *Sun*, and which, on account of its vast height (respecting the exact number of feet, however, historians greatly differ), and of its wondrous perfection as a work of sculpture (on which latter point all coincide), the testimonies of the old historians designate as having ennobled the government of the above-mentioned emperor. This colossus is recorded to have had its head crowned with rays. —On the subject of this prodigy of art Eckhel quotes Martial :—*Epig.* i. 71.

> *Nec te detineat miri radiata Colossi,*
>   *Quæ Rhodium moles vincere gaudet opus.*

Now (says he) the image presented on this coin has also its head radiated. The time likewise corresponds accurately : for in the year V.C. 829, not before, this type was exhibited on medals. But it appears from Dion, that this famous colossus was in the year V.C. 828 placed in the

Via Sacra; and, therefore, as a work of such immense bulk, it was thought fit to bestow upon it the celebrity of coins.

The gold medal of Geta, whose bust is radiated in the likeness of that under which the *Sun* is generally represented on coins, has already been described and explained.—See SEVERI INVICTI AVG. PII. FIL.

SOL. AVG.—This epigraph, accompanying the type of *Sol* standing with right hand elevated, and with the *flagellum* in his left, appears on a third brass of Claudius Gothicus, in the Vienna Collection.—There is another with a similar type, but inscribed SOLVS AVG., given in Pellerin.—*(Suppl.* ii. p. 99.)

This allusion to the *Sun* recurs not unfrequently on the coins of the above-named emperor.—Pellerin supposes that the inscription SOLVS AVG. intimates that Claudius, to the exclusion of Tetricus and Zenobia, was to be acknowledged as the *sole* head and sovereign of the empire.—"This is a shrewd guess (says Eckhel); but as all the others agree with the first quoted coin (SOL. AVG.), the word SOLVS goes, doubtless, to augment the catalogue of those errors which careless moneyers have so very often committed."

SOL. DOM. IMP. ROMANI.—The radiated head of the Sun, before whom are his four horses. On second brass in the Vienna Cabinet and in the British Museum.

SOL. DOMINVS. IMPERI ROMANI.—The naked head of the sun, without rays. On a brass medallion in the Museum Pisani, and on second brass given by Banduri.

These very rare and curious medals bear reference to the worship which, according to historical as well as numismatic testimony, was in a peculiar manner and beyond the example of all preceding emperors, paid by Aurelian to the Sun. This avowed disposition to regard the Solar Orb, not only as a divinity, but also as supreme Lord of the Roman world, is said to have been hereditary in Aurelian, whose mother was priestess of the Sun, in the village which his family inhabited.—Eckhel, who quotes the authority of Callicrates, as adduced by Vopiscus on this point, proceeds to remark that this prince's religious reverence for the Sun displayed itself with increased ardour, when he took upon himself to wage war against Zenobia in the East—a region of the earth anciently believed to be peculiarly subject to the deified power of that luminary. This is the reason why the head of the Sun appears on coins of Trajan, and likewise on those of Mark Antony the triumvir, both of them having been much occupied with their Oriental expeditions and conquests. Nor were the Romans the first to acknowledge the government of the Sun in the East. The Greeks at an earlier age set the example of this devotion; and, according to Pausanias, erected an altar at Troezene (now *Dhamalá,* in the Morea), to *Sol* the liberator, because, as they thought, they were freed from the dread of Xerxes and of the Medes, by his assistance: and therefore influenced by the same

superstition, Aurelian, ascribing his military success in the East to the same celestial aid, performed his vows and founded temples. He also ordained the same honours to the Sun at Palmyra, a city greatly addicted to that kind of worship. But the chief proof of this emperor's devotion to the Sun was the temple which he caused to be built at Rome in honour of his favourite *Dominus Imperii Romani,* the magnificence and enormous cost of which edifice is a subject of record with almost all the old writers. Hence the fact, that the greater part of Aurelian's coins relate to the worship of the Sun, who either alone constitutes the type of the reverse, or at least his head is placed on the field of the coin. Of this kind there are ORIENS AVG. *The Sun standing,* of which the abundance is incredible.—PACATOR ORBIS. *The Sun standing.*—PROVIDEN*tia* DEOR*um. The Sun, and a woman carrying two military ensigns.*—RESTITVTOR ORIENTIS. *The Sun standing.*—SOLI INVICTO. *The Sun treading a captive underfoot.*—MARS IN-VICTVS. *The Sun delivering a globe to a military man standing opposite.*—On the two coins to which we are now directing our attention, there seems to be a concentration of the honours paid to the Sun, for they salute him as the *Lord of the Roman Empire.*—After quoting an expression of Julian the Apostate, in which he calls himself the serving attendant upon *Rex Sol,* Eckhel concludes by observing that the manifestation in Aurelian's time of so much obsequious reverence for the Sun as went to ascribe to it the absolute sovereignty of the universe, is not to be wondered at, since Pliny himself appears to have regarded the same King of Stars as almost the only deity.—The first type is the most illustrative, on account of the four horses of the Sun being added; on the other coin, the head could not have been understood to mean that of the Sun but by the help of the inscription.

SOLI COMITI AVG. N.—The Sun and the Emperor standing: a captive kneeling at the feet of the latter. On gold of Constantine the Great.

SOLI CONSER*vatori.* A centaur holding a bow.—On a third brass of Tetricus Filius, given by Banduri.

SOLI CON*Servatori* AVG*usti.*—Pegasus, or an ox standing.

SOLI INVICTO.—The Sun standing, with right hand raised, and a globe in the left.

These inscriptions and types occur on silver and third brass of Gallienus. They are founded on the very ancient and long-continued belief of paganism that Apollo, or the Sun, was both the author and dispeller of pestilence.—That the Sun was worshipped with the epithet of *Invictus* is attested by numerous marbles; so also the Emperor Julian, in one of his orations, says—"*Ultimo mense, qui Saturni est, splendidissimos ludos Soli facimus, festum illud SOLI INVICTO nuncupantes.*"

Pegasus, as the companion of the Muses readily applies to Apollo, "unless indeed (says

Eckhel) it may be more correctly considered as one of the horses of the Sun, to which wings are added for the purpose of signifying velocity. —What appertains to the figure of an ox, Homer (in the *Odyssey*) commemorates *the oxen of the Sun grazing*. Strabo alludes to the bull *Mnevis* consecrated to the Sun at Heliopolis in Egypt. Inscriptions on marbles are addressed DEO SOLI INVICTO MITHRAE.

SOLI. INVICTO.—The Sun personified, stands with his right foot pressing upon a captive, with his right hand he offers a globe to a military figure, helmeted and armed with a spear : below, XXII.—Small brass of Aurelian, in the Vienna cabinet, not noticed by Mionnet or by Akerman.

SOLI INVICTO.—The Sun in a quadriga: his right hand raised. On a small brass of Carausius.

SOLI INVICTO COMITI.—This legend, with the usual type of the Sun standing with right hand uplifted, and a globe in the left, occurs on brass coins of Constantine the Great— one of the relics of the old solar worship, which, like other symbols of paganism, appears on the mint of this professed convert to Christianity. The words SOLI INVICTO COMITI are found on two other medals of the same Emperor ; one (third brass) with the *radiated head of the Sun ;* and the other (gold and silver) wherein this god is represented standing with his crown of rays, a globe which he holds in his left hand ; whilst with his right he places a crown on the head of Constantine, who holds the *labarum*, or Imperial standard. Both these coins have the name and portrait of Constantine on their obverse. In noticing them, in his remarks on the Cæsars of Julian, Spanheim says they may be supposed to have been struck by the moneyers of some Roman cities still addicted to idolatry, or before they had solemnly renounced the worship of false gods. The fact is, however, that, with the exception of the *In hoc sig. vic.* legend of a doubtful medallion, all the epigraphs and types of the artful, cautious, and anything but pious or humane Constantine are drawn from *heathen* mythology, *not* from *Christian* theology. And, accordingly, we see on his medals the Sun represented as the *Guide*, *Protector*, and even *Colleague* of this emperor, with the inscription SOLI INVICTO and SOLI INVICTO COMITI.—See *Comes*.

The same inscription of *Soli invicto Comiti* occurs on coins of Probus, Maximinus Daza, Crispus, and others.

SOLI INVICTO COMITI.—The Sun placing a garland on the head of the Emperor, who

stands, in military costume, holding a globe

and spear : in the exergue SIRM. In gold and silver of Constantine. In the exergue of some, AQ. or other letters.

SOL. DOM. IMP. ROM. *Soli Domino Imperii Romani.*—Full-faced radiated head of

the Sun surmounting the horses of a quadriga. Obverse of second brass of Aurelian. The reverse reads AVRELIANVS AVG. CONS. The Emperor sacrificing. In the exergue s.

Solidus.—See GOLD COINAGE.—See *Exagium Solidi*.

SORS. Chance, or Fortune.—A denarius of the *Plætoria* family (given in Morell) presents on one side a female head, and on the other the half-length figure of a young woman (whose neck is adorned with a collar) ;. and the pedestal which this female bust rests upon is inscribed with the word *Sors ;* round the type is M. PLAETOR. CEST. *(Marcus Plætorius Cestius)* S.C.

The Romans (as M. Millin observes), not content with receiving Gods from the Greeks, from the Egyptians, and even from the Persians, undertook the imaginative task of deifying the *virtues*, the *qualities*, the *affections* of the mind. And these they have represented by various attributes on monuments, principally medals. Among such *allegorical* divinities was this personification of *Sors* (chance or hazard), which has been sometimes confounded with Destiny or Fate.—At Antium and Præneste were two most celebrated temples of fortune. The *Fortunæ Antiates* are already noticed in their place, as appearing on a silver coin of the *Rustia* family. The present denarius makes allusion to a similar piece of superstition called the *Sortes Prænestiæ*, which, it seems, were *tesseræ*, or tablets of oak inscribed with sentences of antique writing, and shut up in a casket of olive wood. It was believed that, under the secret guidance of the goddess Fortune, *Sors* drew these lots by the hand of a child, and it was supposed to learn its fate by the reading of what was written on the tablets by one of the ministers called *sortilegi*, or fortune-tellers.

SOSIA, a plebeian family.—The coins, which are of second and third brass, exhibit three varieties. Amongst them are pieces bearing the head of Mark Antony.—The following offers a reverse of historical interest :—C. SOSIVS IMP. A male and female captive sitting at the foot of a trophy.

This small medal, in bronze, commemorates the victory gained by Antony, in the year V.C. 716, over Antigonus, King of Judæa, the last of the race of the Asmoneans, who had retained the kingdom 120 years.—The C. SOSIVS whose name appears on this coin as IMP*erator* was M. Antony's Lieutenant in Syria, and sent by him (as Josephus informs us, l. xiv. c. 16) to assist Herod in taking the government from Antigonus, according to the decree of the senate. These two generals having, by their united forces, gained possession of Jerusalem, Antigonus surrendered himself to Sosius, who sent him to Antony at Antioch, where he was put to death, being the first king whom the Romans had ever beheaded. And thus was the cruel, corrupt, and low-born Herod confirmed in the sovereignty of Judæa, and an end put to the illustrious Asmonean family.

Sospita.—See *Sispita.*

SOVSTI.—A brass coin of Faustina senior bearing these six letters, followed by the senatorial authentication, s.c., and having for its reverse type Ceres standing on a globe, and holding a torch in each hand, is given in the *Mémoires de Trevoux,* as from the collection of P. Chamillart. It is accompanied by various attempts at interpretation—the productions of as many learned writers, whose conflicting opinions Rasche has, without comment, recapitulated; but respecting which, on account of their far-fetched extravagance or their ludicrous absurdity, sovsti is evidently, Eckhel says, an unhappy blunder of some careless mint-master, similar instances of which are not unfrequent on the reverses of Roman coins.

SP. A Roman prenomen.—SP. F. *Spurii Filius.*—On coins of the *Postumia* family.

SPE. AVG. *Spes Augusta.*

Speculator, derived from *Specula,* a prospect, that is to say a view from the summit of a place, whence anything may be seen advantageously at a distance.—Thus a cohort of this description *(Speculatorum Cohors)* was established by M. Antony, that they, from an elevated part of his ships, might explore and act as sentries or watchmen. There were other acceptations of the word, such as spies, and even executioners.

Speculatores under the early emperors were public attendants on the person of the prince; in effect, his body guard. Otho was attended by an escort of this kind; whence it is that Tacitus conjoins the *prætorian cohorts* with the *speculatores.* And, for the same reason, also in inscriptions on marbles the latter may frequently be seen commingled with the former, as SPEC. COH. IIII. PR.—On a denarius of M. Antony, the *cohors speculatorum* evidently relates to maritime affairs, as the military standard fixed on the prow of a ship serves to indicate, together with the prætorian galley and the triumvir's name on the obverse of the coin. —See CHORTIS SPECVLATORVM.

Spes.—The ancients worshipped *Hope* as a divinity. She had her temples and her altars, but nothing is said by old writers as to what victims were sacrificed to her. Livy speaks of the herb market *(forum olitorium)* at Rome as one of the places where this goddess had a temple; and he also makes mention of that which Publius Victor built in the seventh region of the city. The censor M. Fullius also dedi-

cated a temple to her honour near the Tibur. The personification of Hope appears on some ancient sculptures; but it is much more frequently seen figured on medals of the Imperial series, struck at the beginning of a prince's reign, indicating either the favourable anticipations which the people entertained of him, or the expectations which he wished to raise respecting himself. She is often exhibited on medals of the *Cæsars,* or adopted heirs to the Imperial throne, because her influence is peculiarly strong over youthful minds.—*Spes* is ordinarily represented in the shape of a young woman, standing, or walking, holding in her right hand a tender flower: for where a flower appears there is *hope* of *fruit* to come. Her left hand is usually employed in lifting up the skirt of her semi-transparent robe. Sometimes she holds in her left hand a cornucopiæ with other symbols, marking the benefits anticipated from her. On a brass coin of Drusus senior, the word SPES stands alone; it was with Claudius that the practice began of adding the words AVG. or AVGG. or AVGVSTA, or P.R. or PVB. PVBLIC. PVBLICA, &c., all serving respectively to designate the occasion for which she had been chosen as an appropriate type.— Vaillant gives a silver coin of Pescennius Niger, bearing on its reverse the legend BONAE SPEI, with the type of the goddess walking—Cicero opposes the feeling of *good hope (bona spes)* to that of despair in all human affairs.—And Plutarch remembers an altar at Rome inscribed *Fortunæ Bonæ Spei.*—Gruter quotes a marble inscribed BONAE SPEI AVG.—It is observable that on coins of the lower empire, the early image of Hope no longer appears. The legend *Spes Reipublicæ* of the Empress Fausta has for its accompanying type a woman suckling two children; and the *Spes Romanorum* of Magnus Maximus, the gate of the Prætorian camp.

Spes appears, in the form and with the attributes above described, on coins of Claudius, Vespasian, Hadrian, M. Aurelius, Commodus, Pescennius Niger, Albinus, S. Severus, Caracalla, Geta, Diadumenianus, Elagabalus, Alex. Severus, Philip senior and junior, Herennius, Hostillianus, Æmilianus, Gallienus, Postumus, Tetricus senior, Quietus, Claudius Gothicus, Tacitus, Probus, Carausius, Allectus, Julianus II., Valens, &c.—The following are the most rare of this legend and its types :—

SPES AVGVSTA. S.C.—Hope walking, with flower in right hand, and left raising her tunic behind, as if to disengage her tripping footsteps from impediment.

This type of Spes, which became afterwards so common on coins of the Imperial mint, appears for the first time on a large brass of Claudius. From other bronze medals, having the same legend, but with dissimilar types, as well as from an inscribed marble, it would seem that Claudius worshipped Hope as a favourite divinity, and on his natal day made vows to her honour.

SPES AVGVSTA. S.C.—Hope and three soldiers standing. On first brass of Vespasian.

[Mionnet and Akerman both recognise the genuineness of this fine coin, of which Haver-camp has given an engraving from the Mus. Christinæ. The last-named antiquary thus comments on the type—" Vespasian had very much greater pretensions to the empire, and a better founded hope for success in his enterprise, than many of those who had preceded him. In fact, before his accession to the throne, he had unequivocally displayed the virtuous qualities essential to the character of a great prince. Nor did he disappoint the high expectations entertained of him. For this reason SPES AVGVSTA—August Hope, was adopted as the type of this medal; and the goddess is represented under the form of a female, clothed in light drapery, who presents her right hand to the foremost of three soldiers, because Vespasian had assisted the republic with his victorious legions, and there was the strongest ground of hope that this warlike emperor would re-establish it on a firm foundation."]

SPES AVG. COS. II. and SPE. COS. II.— Hope with its accustomed attributes.—Silver of Albinus.—In reference to the former of these inscriptions, Vaillant remarks that on coins of the *Cæsars* (as contradistinguished from those of the *Augusti*), Hope was exhibited, chiefly to indicate those amongst the former who were actually designated as successors to the reigning prince; but as the harvest of empire was still in embryo, the goddess is pictured with a flower, portending fruit to the plant in its maturity.

SPES FELICITATIS ORBIS.—Hope standing in her usual attitude.

The elder Philip, one of whose silver coins bears this reverse, after having done everything in his power to conciliate the Roman senate and people in favour of his usurpation, and wheedled himself into the soldiers' good graces by his profuse largesses, here indicates his hope that the world, under his sway, would enjoy happiness. The commencement of his reign is therefore called *Spes felicitatis orbis*.

SPEI FIRMAE.—Hope walking.—This unusual legend appears for the first time on silver of Pescennius Niger, published by Gessner, from the Pfau cabinet; it is afterwards found repeated by the mint of Severus.

SPES PVBLICA.—Hope standing.—Silver of Diadumenianus.—Hope, as goddess of youth (says Vaillant), is represented on the coins of Cæsars, as if for the purpose of exciting the feeling of Good Hope (*Bonæ Spei*) in the

breasts of these young princes; each heir of an emperor being regarded, like Marcellus by Virgil, *Magna Spes altera Romæ*. So Diadumenianus is made, by Lampridius, to say to the soldiery of his father, Macrinus, *Ego autem elaborabo, ne desim nomini Antoninorum*.

SPES PVBLICA.—Hope advancing towards three military figures, extends in her right

hand towards the foremost and principal, who may be considered as the emperor himself, a figure of Victory. The obverse exhibits the laureated head and bust of Alexander Severus in armour; in his left hand he holds a baton; in his right, a figure of Victory bearing a trophy. Brass medallion in the cabinet of Mr. Roach Smith.

SPES PVBLICA. S. C.—Hope walking.— A coin of Aemilianus, in third brass (published by Banduri), bearing this legend and type, is remarkable on account of the s. c. being annexed thereto, after having for a long interval been almost wholly disused.

The same also appears on a rare and elegant quinarius of Gallienus. This coin was struck when that emperor was proclaimed *Imperator Augustus* by his father.—Vaillant (Pr. ii. 369) says of the type and legend that they unite in suggesting to the people to place their firm faith, not in the old age of Valerian, but in the youth of Gallienus, to whom *Spes* gives promise of a long life and a happy reign.—" Hope told a flattering tale" in this case.

SPES PVBLICA.—A serpent, on which stands the labarum, inscribed with the monogram of Christ. Small brass of Constantine.

SPES PUBLICA.—A figure in military garb, stands with right hand raised, opposite to which stands a female with flower in right hand, &c.; a star between them. On a rare and elegant silver coin of Saloninus. There we see Hope, the usual companion of the Cæsars, presenting herself to Saloninus, who is clothed as a soldier to denote his having just embarked in a war with the incursive barbarians. The goddess holds out a flower to the young prince, as if to assure him of victory.

SPEI PERPETVAE.—Hope with her usual attributes.—On a silver coin of Elagabalus, who is here, by a wretched piece of flattery, made to appear, whilst growing up, to be under Hope's good and perpetual influence.

Spei Perpetuae is first found on silver and bronze of Caracalla, whose conduct and disposition from his boyhood upwards also gave the lie perpetual, to such a compliment.

SPES REIPUBLICAE.—A woman suckling two infants.—See *Fausta.*

SPES R.P. *(Romani Populi)*.—The Hope of the Roman people.—On a gold coin of Valens given by Banduri, two imperial personages are seated, each with the *nimbus* encircling his head, and holding the hasta and a globe. A smaller figure stands between them, but without the *nimbus*, above whose head is a buckler inscribed VOT. V. MVL. X.

The two principal figures of this type were doubtless intended to represent the two emperors Valentinian and Valens, whilst the lesser figure is evidently designed for the boy Gratian, already destined to the throne, but who, not being yet proclaimed *Augustus*, remains undistinguished by the *nimbus.*

Sphinx.—This fabled monster, according to the myth of the Greeks, born of Typhon and Echidna, had the head and face of a young woman, with the wings of a bird; the rest of the body resembling that of a dog. This fictitious animal, whose mysterious origin is associated with the most remote antiquity, is said to have had its haunts in Mount Sphincius, near Thebes, and to have been accustomed thence to assail and destroy wayfarers. Apollo having been consulted in this matter, the oracle assumed that there was no other way to rescue the country from its fury than some one's solving the enigma of the Sphinx (allusive to man in his infancy, youth, and old age). Oedipus guessed this riddle, and the monster flung itself from its rocky seat and perished.—On numismatic and other ancient monuments, the Sphinx is represented in two ways, that of the Greeks and that of the Egyptians. The former has wings and breasts, the latter has neither. The early mint of Rome adopted, as usual, the Greek model. On denarii of the *Carisia* and *Rabinia* families (says Morell) is a figure of the Sphinx, sitting on its hind legs; it has wings, and a virgin's head, displaying the paps of a woman in front and the dugs of an animal of the canine species beneath the belly.

On coins of Augustus the Sphinx occurs often; in one instance it is accompanied by the legend ARMENIA CAPTA.—According to Suetonius, that emperor was accustomed to seal his diplomatic papers and private letters with a figure of this ænigmatical nondescript. Vaillant *(Pr.* i. 176), and Banduri, describe a first brass of Volusianus as having a Sphinx for the type of its reverse. But neither those writers, nor Eckhel, who quotes their authority, attempt to give any explanation on the subject of its appearance, so little to be looked for on a medal of that Emperor.

Spica.—An ear of corn, on ancient medals, sometimes signified the fertility of a particular country, and the abundance of grain produced in it; at others it denotes the care of the *Annona* (see the word), or import of corn into Rome as well as its distribution to the people by the Ædiles, to whom that important duty was especially committed in the time of the republic. Many denarii struck under the consular government exhibit (see AED. CVR. and AD. FRV. EMV.)

this symbol of the ædileship. In the Aemilia, Cornelia, Norbana, and other families, the *Spica* accompanies the *papaver*, or poppy, the *caduceus,* and the *fasces.* Sometimes a corn-ear is placed on each side of a curule chair; at others, on each side of the *modius,* as on a denarius of the Livineia family. On many imperial medals from Augustus to Val. Severus, *Spicæ* appear either in the *modius,* or bushel measure, or in the hand of Ceres, or combined, as before observed, with the caduceus and the poppy, or placed between a double cornucopiæ.—See TEMP. FELICITAS.— SAECVLO FRVGIFERO.—On a brass coin of the *Servilia* family two corn ears are engraved, which intimate certain shipments of wheat and other grain from the corn-growing provinces to Rome.—Ears of corn are the insignia of fertility in the hands of those figures which personify Egypt, Africa, Spain, Sicily, &c,

SPINT.—Spinther, a surname of the *Cornelia* family.

Spintria, in Italian *Spindria,* from " σπινθηρ, scintilla, *quod velut scintillæ et fomes libidinis sit,*" as Rasche, quoting Sabellicus, says:—It is a word used to denote the inventor or inventress of obscene monstrosities, such as were patronised and employed by Tiberius, according to a passage in the work of that depraved emperor's biographer —" *Secessu* (says Suetonius, *Tib. Nero Caes.* cap. xliii.) *vero Capreensi sellariam excogitavit, sedem arcanarum libidinum: in quam undique conquisiti puellarum et exoletorum greges, monstrosique concubitus repertores, quos SPINTRIAS appellabat.* – – – *Cubicula plurifariam disposita tabellis ac sigillis lascivissimarum picturarum et figurarum adornavit,* &c."—To the honour of the MONETA ROMA*na,* be it observed, however, that no numismatic monuments, even under the most profligate of her princes, have ever been found to fix the stain of such pollutions on any medallions or coins, either sanctioned by the senatorial mark of authentication, or in any way issued under the public guarantee of imperial authority. The only medals struck within the pale of Roman domination, on which shamelessly indecent figures appear, are a few *Greek* colonial, dedicated to the Lampsacan god—and that suite of brass *tesseræ,* or counters, known under the name of *Spintriæ,* which exhibit on one side, in designs of coarse workmanship, immodest representations; and on the other the numeral letters I. or II. or IV. or X. to XVI. and upwards.

Numismatic antiquaries, as well as other learned writers, are much divided in opinion respecting this "*ignobile vulgus*" of medallic relics; a vile class of remains, which, to use the sensible expressions of Eckhel (viii. 315) "thrown into the rear, like the suttlers, soldiers' boys, wine sellers, and strumpets of a great army, are to be recorded more to avoid the slightest deficiency in anything that could throw light upon the subject of Roman coins, than from the profit to be derived from them to learning and to a useful knowledge of antiquity." Some think that the *Spintriæ* were struck to ridicule and expose that perfidious tyrant and worn-out voluptuary, Tiberius, who made the sea-girt rocks of Capræa the scene of his brutal pleasures, and, to issue them with greater facility, numerous letters were imprinted on them as on those which served as admission tickets to the theatre, others consider them to have been stamped by "the rank old emperor's" express orders. Some, again, believe that they were used at the festivals of Venus; others, for the Saturnalia, and others that they were coined for the purpose of being flung, in showers, among the crowds of a corrupt metropolis, who flocked to the public exhibition of licentious spectacles, and which were of the kind alluded to in the epigram of Martial. (lib. viii. 78.)

Nunc veniunt subitis lasciva numismata nimbis: Nunc dant spectatas tessera larga feras.

Addison, who visited the island of Capræa, in 1701, observes (in his "Remarks on several parts of Italy") that these medals were never current money, but rather of the nature of medallions to perpetuate the monstrous inventions of an infamous society; and he adds—"What, I think, puts it beyond all doubt that these coins were rather made by the emperor's order than as a satire on him, is because they are now found in the very place that was the scene of his unnatural lusts." This is certainly a fact strongly calculated to support the opinion which ascribes to Tiberius himself the coinage of these Spintriæ and their circulation amongst the companions and victims of his infamies.—Yet it is to be remembered that such a belief is not borne out by the authority of any historian. Even Suetonius, whose language we have above quoted, and who touches more fully than any other ancient writer on these revolting traits in the biography of Tiberius, says indeed that the emperor had made a collection *lascivissimarum picturarum*, at Capræa, but does not speak of his distributing *medals* of that sort, unless by the word *sigillum* in the passage in question be meant a *medal*, as Patin interprets it. But as M. Kolb, in his *Traité de Numismatique*, observes, "*si Tibère eut fait frapper de pareilles médailles, elles se fussent répandues dans Rome, et ce trait d'infamie eût été rendu par Suétone avec plus de force et d'énergie.*" Execrable, therefore, as was the personal character and individual conduct of that emperor; disgusting as is the portraiture which historians have drawn of his vices and excesses, it appears to be not without sufficient reason that Spanheim acquits him of being the originator, or (by an express command of his) the author, so to speak, of these *numi obscœni*, or lewd counters; first, because they are not identified by any indication with his name; and next, because Tiberius was evidently disposed rather to conceal his base enjoyments within the recesses of Capræa than to reveal them by public representations and disclosures. Nor does that profoundly erudite man, whose opinion is above referred to, associate these coins with the *lascivi numismata* of Martial; but rather seems to be of opinion that what are called *Spintriæ* are to be added to the rest of those tesseræ, or species of marks

which, under impure and dissolute rules, served to admit persons to *Floralia*, and other public spectacles, where the grossest indecency was practised.—It is, however, a curiosity of no creditable kind that leads to minuteness of inquiry into so filthy and profitless a subject; and it shall here suffice, therefore, to add, from Spanheim, that in the cabinets of Roman antiquaries, medalets similar to the above, are found up to number XXIX. inscribed on them, whilst Beauvais greatly increases this estimate of their number and variety, by affirming that "more than sixty of them, with different attitudes, are known. Their module is uncertain, between middle and small brass."

Spolia bellica—spoils of war—are exhibited on coins of the Cornelia, Claudia, Furia, and many other Roman families; also on the imperial series commemorating victories over the Parthians, Sarmatians, &c. It is sitting on, or standing near, warlike spoils of armour that Rome is personified on coins, because she enriched and loaded herself with booty taken from the foes whom she had conquered. On a denarius of Lepidus we see a figure on horseback carrying on his shoulder a trophy composed of the *spolia bellica.—See Æmilia* fam.

Spolia opima.—These, "the most honourable" of military acquisitions, consisted of the armour which one general of an army took from another general whom he had encountered in single combat. In their origin they formed nothing more than a trophy of arms raised on a simple cross of wood, or the stem of a young oak tree. During the republic, they were carried by the Romans in a triumphal chariot, and afterwards dedicated in the temple of Jupiter Feretrius. This ceremony is shadowed forth on a denarius of Lentulus Marcellinus, whose ancestor Claudius Marcellus, v.c. 532, slew in single combat Viridomarus, chief of the Insubrian Gauls. Allusion to the consecration of the *Opima Spolia* is also regarded as made on a coin of Cossus Lentulus, struck in memory of his progenitor, Cornelius Cossus, who, v.c. 326, killed in battle Lartis Tolumnius, king of the Veientes.—See *Claudia* and *Cornelia* families.

SPONSIANVS.—Who this person was cannot be correctly ascertained, as historians are totally silent respecting him. It is supposed that he usurped the title of Augustus in Dacia, or some adjoining region of the empire, about the same time as the equally unknown *Iotapianus*, and the no less obscure *Pacatianus*, assumed the purple—viz., probably during the reign of Philip senior and junior; certainly after Gordianus Pius; because the following gold medallion is of the same workmanship, and seems to have had the same origin as the barbaric medallions, described by Mionnet (vol. i. 394 and 404). Eckhel enumerates two medallions in the Vienna Museum, and two in other Austrian cabinets.

IMP. SPONSIANI. Radiated head to the right.
Rev.—CAVG. A column surmounted by a statue, which has a spear in his right hand; on one side of the column is a man clothed in the

toga, holding something which cannot be defined; on the other side of the column is an augur bearing the *lituus;* and at the foot of the column are two ears of corn.—See Akerman, vol. i. p. 493, pl. viii. No. 7.

S. P. Q. R. Letters which were used by the Romans on their coins, standards, and public monuments, to signify *Senatus Populusque Romanus.* (The Senate and the Roman People).— These initials appear on several coins of uncertain families. They stand as an inscription by themselves, with some type or other, on coins of Augustus, Galba, Faustina jun., Gallienus, &c.

S. P. Q. R.—A lion, on which stands an eagle, both within a laurel crown.—On gold of Gallienus, in the Imperial cabinet at Vienna.

" It is for the reader to judge (says Eckhel in reference to this coin) whether it is because the senate, with its inveterate habit of adulation, had compared Gallienus to Jupiter and to Hercules, that the creature sacred to each of those deities is here brought forward: or, whether it is because the eagle and the lion are supposed, after a manner, to bear sway, each over its respective genus of animals, and to give place to no master—that Gallienus is here feigned to possess supreme power over the whole race of mankind, and even over the very usurpers themselves, who were at that identical period invading every part of the empire."— *Doct. Num. Vet.* vol. vii. p. 411.

S. P. Q. R.—These initials likewise exhibit themselves on numerous medals of the imperial series in each metal, from Augustus down to Constantine the Great: they are found placed either round the circumference of the coin, along with some other legend, or in the field of the coin on a shield, preceding the abbreviated word CL. V. (Clypeum vovit); or with some other legend, as in the following examples :—

S. P. Q. R. ADSERTORI LIBERTATIS PVBLICAE. (The Senate and the Roman People, to the Defender of Public Liberty.)— On first brass of Vespasian.—See p. 8. of this Dictionary.

S. P. Q. R. DIVO TRAIANO PARTHICO. —See *Aurora.*

S. P. Q. B. EX. S. C. *(Ex Senatus Consulto.)* —Hadrian.

S. P. Q. R. IMP. CAES. QVOD V. M. S. EX. EA. P. Q. IS. AD. A. DE. *(Senatus Populusque Romanus Imperatori Cæsari quod viæ munitæ sint ex ea pecunia quam is ærarium detulit.)* —This is inscribed on a coin of Augustus, struck by L. VINICIVS, monetal triumvir, as a monument of the gratitude of the Senate and Roman people towards the Emperor Cæsar Augustus, for having established high roads, and contributed to the public safety, at his own expense ; in causing to be conveyed to the public treasury the money which is the fruit of his victories, and of the advantages which he has gained over the enemies of the state.—See p. 19 of this Dictionary.

S. P. Q. R. IVLIAE AVGVST.—The Senate and Roman people to Julia Augusta.—On coins of Livia and Domna.

S. P. Q. R. MEMORIAE AGRIPPINAE.— See p. 552 of this Dictionary.

S. P. Q. R. OB. C. S. *(Ob Cives Servatos.)*— Caligula and Albinus.—See p. 166 of this Dictionary.

S. P. Q. R. A. N. F. F. OPTIMO PRINCIPI The Senate, &c., (pray for) a prosperous and happy new year *(annum novum, faustum, felicem)* to the best of Princes.—On coins of Hadrian, Antoninus Pius, and Alexander.—See p. 44 of this Dictionary.

S. P. Q. R. OPTIMO PRINCIPI.—On coins of Trajan, Hadrian, Antoninus Pius, Sept. Severus, Gallienus, Maximinus Daza, Alexand. Tyran. Licinius pater, and Constantinus Magnus. —See pp. 236–397 of this Dictionary.

S. P. Q. R. PARENT. CONS. SVO. *Senatus Populusque Romanus Parenti Conservatori Suo.* —This is engraved on a denarius of Augustus, as a memorial that the Senate and Roman people presented to that emperor the sceptre with an eagle, the toga picta, or embroidered robe, and the laurel crown, as to their parent and preserver.

S. P. Q. R. V. S. PRO. S. ET. RED. AVG. *Senatus Populusque Romanus Vota Solvunt pro Salute et Reditu Cæsaris.*—The Senate and Roman people acquit themselves of their vows for the health and happy return of Cæsar.—On a coin of Augustus.

S. P. Q. R. QVOD INSTINCTV DIVINI-TATIS, &c.—On a coin of Constantine the Great.—See p. 678 of this Dictionary.

S. P. Q. R. V. P. RED. CAES, *Senatus Populusque Romanus Vota pro Reditu Cæsaris.*— The Senate and Roman people offer vows for the safe return of Cæsar.—On a coin of Augustus.

S. P. Q. R. SVF. P. D. *Senatus Populusque Romanus suffimenta Populo data.*—On a first brass of Caligula this inscription is considered to signify that the emperor, in concurrence with the Senate and the Roman people, had made the usual distribution, that is to say, *of things necessary for the Secular Games.*—See *Suffimenta.*

SPVRILIA *gens.*—There is no authentic or precise information to be gleaned from the old writers respecting the *ordo* of this family. Its coins present but one type—namely, in silver; a winged head of Pallas on one side, and on the reverse A. SPVR*ilius,* and Diana in a biga of horses at full speed ; at the bottom, ROMA.

S. R. appears on the field of certain coins, about the time of Constantine, signifying *Salus Romanorum* or *Spes Reipublicæ.*

S. R. *Senatus Romanus.*—On coins of Antioch in Pisidia, instead of S. C. *Senatus Consulto.*

S. T. *Signata Treveris.*—A mint mark of coins struck at Treves.

STA. BOV.—These letters, accompanying the type of a bull walking, appear on the reverse of a second brass of Geta, in the Vienna Museum.—Gessner gives it as a third brass.

Patin and Hardouin have both commented on this coin of a foreign mint. The former *(Impp.* p. 367) reads STABOV as one word, and proceeds to ascribe the coin to *Stabiæ*, a town in Campania, at the bottom of the bay between Naples and Sorrento, now *Monte de la Torre.*— Hardouin (*Oper. Selec.* p. 161) divides STA. from BOV., professing to believe that the one means Stabiæ and the other Bovilla. He goes on to call them *oppidum geminum*, twin towns in Campania; adding that *Stabiæ* is now *Castell' a mare di Stabia*, between the mouth of the river Sarno and Sorrento; and that *Bovilla* was amongst the cities of Campania, on the shores of the Mediterranean. Eckhel, who, as well as Vaillant (*Col.* ii. 6.) places this coin in the list of *incerta numismata*, says, after quoting the above opinion of Hardouin, "I have my doubts whether this explanation of the enigma will be deemed satisfactory at the present day; for the prevailing impression now is that from the time when the supreme power of Rome was vested in the emperors, the cities of Italy at large abstained from striking money. And then, again, how can Hardouin say that Bovilla is a town of Campania, when in point of fact it stood in Latium and near Rome?"—Eckhel (vii. p. 234) concludes his note on the legend in question by referring his readers to a coin struck under Trebonianus Gallus, which bears the words ARN. ASI. as throwing light on the subject. In that particular case (see the words,) the enigma seems fairly solved by the reasonable conjecture of Pellerin; but the riddle STA. BOV. remains as dark as ever, and seems hardly worth the pains of being rightly guessed.

Star.—On many coins the figure of a star has reference to astrology. It was also among the Pagan Romans a symbol allusive to eternity or to consecration (see those words). It was likewise a sign of glory. It frequently is used as a mint-mark. Besides appearing on numerous medals of cities and kings, it is found on several coins of Roman families, such as Ælia, Aquillia, Manlia, Papiria, Portia, Rustia, &c.

A *Star* appears before the head of Mars, on a coin of the *Rustia* family, because the year was believed to begin with the month *Martius*, which took its name from the God of War.

Stars are seen on some one coin or other of nearly all the emperors, from Julius Cæsar to Justinian, and even still further down the series.

Long-haired *Star* (Stella Crinita), or comet, appears on denarii of Augustus, referring to an extraordinary meteor seen immediately after the death of Julius Cæsar. This cometary sign is placed on some medals behind the portrait of the murdered dictator, or occupies the reverse side of the medal.

A *Star*, under the heads of Mercury and Hercules, on coins of Vespasian (Khell 33–34).
— within a crescent moon, as in Domitian, Trajan, S. Severus, and Caracalla.
— by the side of an emperor sacrificing, as in Elagabalus.

Its frequent occurrence on the coins of this Emperor was associated with his Syrian birth and office as priest of the sun at Emesa.—See Bimard i. p. 399–426.

A *Star* appears opposite the personification of the Sun (SOLI INVICTO), as in S. Severus, Elagabalus, Gallienus, Maximinus Daza, Licinius senior, and Constantinus M. between two military figures, with GALVS REIPVB., as in Theodosius M.
— by the side of Fortune, as in Constantius Chlorus.
— before the figure of *Genius Augusti*, as in Licinius senior.
— above two emperors, standing with joined hands, as in Theodosius jun.
— is seen over the *spirit* (anima) of Constantine the Great, drawn in a quadriga.
— in a crown of laurel, on coins of Constantine and Constantius II.

A *Star* and *Cross* appear on coins of Constantinus Magnus; also of Flaccilla, wife of Theodosius, and Ælia Eudoxia. Also on Justinianus II. and other medals of the Byzantine series.

A *Star* at the back of Venus, as in a coin of Sœmias.—See *Venus Cœlestis.*
— under Vesta, seated.—(Khell, *Sup.* 74–75.)
— near the figure of Victory, as in Aurelian, Valentinian I., and Gratian.

Two *Stars* over the bonneted heads of the Dioscuri, who are distinguished thus as often as they are represented on coins or other ancient monuments.—See *Castor* and *Pollux.*
— over the head of a bull, as in Julian the Apostate.—See *Securitas Reipub.*
— under which Cupid sits on a dolphin, as in silver of Augustus, inscribed S.P.Q.R.
— above the wolf, with Romulus and Remus, and the epigraph VRBS ROMA, on coins of Constantine the Great.

Six *Stars* on a globe, on which Faustina is seated, with epigraph *Aeternitas.*
— surrounding the figure of Jupiter.—See IOVI DEFENS*ori* SALVTIS AVG.
— amidst which a naked child sits on a globe, appear on a silver coin of Domitilla, wife of Domitian.

Seven *Stars* encompassing Augustus, in a chariot drawn by elephants, as on coins of Caligula and Claudius.
— around the figure of Faustina senior, on a consecration coin of that empress.

Six *Stars*, surrounding a crescent moon, appear on coins of several families; and on some of Augustus, Hadrian, Faustina senior, Faustina junior, Sept. Severus, and Julia Domna.

Stars on Roman imperial coins sometimes serve to distinguish figures, as those representing the children of reigning princes; and, in other instances, their deceased offspring received into the ranks of the gods, and placed amongst the stars.

A *Stary* sphere, on which stands a phœnix, appears on a coin of Constans.—See FEL. TEMP. REPARATIO.
— on which stands an eagle, on a consecration medal of L. Verus.
— on which the emperor is seated, forms the type of a bronze medallion of Alex. Severus. —See TEMP. FELICITAS.

STABIL.—See TELLVS STABIL*ita*, on coins of Hadrian, Sabina, Faustina sen., and Commodus.

Stannei numi, pewter money, respecting which see Spanheim, *Pr.* i. p. 9.

STATIA, name of a Roman family; it was of the plebeian order, for T. Statius belonging to that *gens* is enumerated among the *tribuni plebis*: its surname *Murcus*. There are two varieties in its coins. One of them bears on one side the head of Neptune, on the other MVRCVS IMP. and a trophy, before which stands a male figure in the toga, who extends his hand to a kneeling woman. Lucius Statius Murcus was one of Julius Cæsar's lieutenants during the civil war. On the death of Julius, he first of all gave his aid to Octavianus (afterwards Augustus) in Syria. Subsequently he sided with the republican party; and Cassius not only gave him the rank he had before held, but also committed the fleet to his charge. This circumstance is alluded to by the head of Neptune on the above denarius. Cassius himself, in an epistle addressed to Cicero, calls L. Statius Murcus, *imperator ;* and he is termed *vir prætorius* and *imperator* by Valleius. It is not known why the honour was conferred upon him which led to the title IMP. being placed after his name on this coin. Cicero calls him publicly, proconsul. After distinguishing himself by his skill and courage in naval warfare, he fled, after the defeat of Brutus and Cassius, to Sicily, where he was at first kindly received by Sextus Pompey, but afterwards, out of either jealousy or distrust, he was put to death. On the reverse of this very rare silver medal, it is Asia which seems to be represented in a suppliant posture, soliciting the help of Cassius.—[Eckhel, vol. v. p. 316.]

STATILIA, a family of uncertain rank. It was first known under the Cæsars. Its surnames are Taurus and Libo. There are four varieties in its coins, all in brass, either Spanish money, or struck by the mint-masters of Augustus.

Stator, a surname of Jupiter, from *sisto* (to make or cause to be made to stand or continue.) See IOVI STATORI.

Statuaria ars.—See quotation from Baronius, in Rasche, vol. v. pt. i. p. 30.

Statues abounded in ancient Rome. It was the custom of the Romans to pourtray in images of brass and of marble, their various deities and illustrious men, whom the common people believed to be thereby rendered present to them. Hence it is that so many statues of gods and goddesses, demigods, emperors and heroes, remain to this day.—Spanheim *(Pr.* i. p. 26) animadverts on the multitude as well as the excellence of antique statues still extant. On family and on imperial medals we see representations of statues, both equestrian and pedestrian, of Consuls and Ediles, Emperors, Empresses, and Cæsars. Statues also appear in the interior and on the pediments, and on the steps of temples and triumphal arches, which form the types of numerous Roman coins. Amongst other denarii of the *Cornelia* family, relating to Sulla (the Dictator), is one, which, bearing for legend L. SVLLA. IMP,, and for type, a military figure on horseback, seems to derive illustration from a passage in Cicero, wherein he mentions a gilt statue of Sulla on horseback, erected to his honour in Rome. (Eckhel, v. 191).—An equestrian statue was customarily erected in a city on the occasion of the reigning prince's arrival within its walls. Vaillant enumerates seven different equestrian statues of Augustus, as represented on rare coins, chiefly silver. The statue of an Emperor on horseback *(Imperator eques)* is to be seen frequently on Imperial medals, sometimes in a military dress *(paludatus)*, at other times in the garb of peace *(habitu pacificatoris.)*—See *Cornelia.*

Statue of Trajan, on horseback.—There is on silver and first brass coins of this emperor, accompanying the legend S. P. Q. R. OPTIMO PRINCIPI, an equestrian figure of this "best of princes," holding a spear in his right hand.—Doubtless (says Eckhel) this was intended to represent what Ammianus (*L.* xvi. c. 10) speaks of in terms of the highest praise as a wonderful work of art. That writer relates that Constantius the Second, having come to Rome, viewed with admiration, among other objects of magnificence, the Forum of Trajan, and expressed his conviction he could himself construct nothing equal to it, but added that he was both willing and able to imitate the horse of Trajan, placed in the centre of the court-yard *(atrium)*, and which bore on its back the prince himself. One of the distinguished personages near the emperor at the time, Hormisda by name, replied by saying,—"*Ante stabulum tale condi jubeto, si vales: equus quem fabricare disponis, ita late succedat, ut iste quem videmus.*" "First build such a stable as this (Trajan's forum), and then let your horse be made of as ample dimensions as that which we now see."

Stephanus Quadrigarius.——A Contorniate medal, given by Pedrusi in the *Mus. Farnes.* bears on its obverse the head of Trajan, and on its reverse the word STEFANVS, accompanied with the type of a *Hieronices*, or conqueror at the public games, who, holding in his right hand a whip, and in his left a palm branch, stands in a chariot drawn by four palm-bearing horses.—Havercamp (in *Morelli Impp.)* also gives a contorniate which has a similar type on its reverse, and with the words STEFAN. NIKA.— On the obverse is the head of a man, which Eckhel, as well as other antiquaries, states to be that of *Apollonius Tyanensis.*

The reason which the portrait of *Apollonius Tyanensis* is here found on the same medal, with a representation of *Stephanus*, the charioteer, is affirmed to be, that the former happening to be in the act of public disputation at Ephesus, the very moment when Stephanus, the freedman, slew Domitian at Rome, suddenly became speechless, and seemingly like one thunderstruck; but presently, as if regaining his senses, he began to exclaim—" Well done Stephanus— bravo Stephanus—strike the homicide—you have struck—you have wounded—you have slain him." This story, fabulous as indeed it is, was, according to Dion and Philostratus, universally credited at the time.—Eckhel, vol. viii. 297.

Stobi, or *Stobas* was, according to Livy, one of the most ancient cities of Macedonia. Situate in Pelagonia, a central region of that kingdom, to the north-east of Pella, it is called by Pliny *oppidum civium Romanorum*, and its coins prove it to have been a *municipium;* but by whom it was invested with that character, whether by Augustus or by Vespasian, is uncertain.—Paulus includes this place amongst those of Macedonia, which enjoyed the privileges of the *Jus Italicum.*—The money, struck by the Stobenses, comprised but one Autonome; the rest are Imperial, with *Latin* legends, beginning with Vespasian, and continuing under Titus, Titus and Domitian, Domitian, Trajan, S. Severus, Domna, Caracalla, and Geta, finishing with Elagabalus.—The following are the principal types on the coins of MVNIC., MVNICI., or MVNICIP. STOBENS. *Municipium Stobensium*, as given in Vaillant's work on the *Roman Colonies:*—

Temple.—A second brass of Vespasian, Titus, and Domitian, has a temple of four columns, in which a military figure stands with right hand extended, and holding a spear in his left.

[The people of Stobi seem to have been much attached to the Flavian family, for we see coins of this *municipium* dedicated in succession to Vespasian and to his two sons and successors in the empire.—The temple on the above reverse is regarded by Vaillant as representing one which was erected in honour of Augustus, rather than of Vespasian. There is a similar type on a coin of the Stobenses bearing the head of Trajan.

Woman Turreted.—A second brass of Vespasian exhibits a female figure standing, clothed in a short dress, and wearing towers on her head. In her right hand is a Victory; in her left a cornucopiæ; at her feet on each side are spoils of armour.

[The woman thus depicted seems to be the Genius of Stobi. The crown of towers symbolises the *municipium*, whilst the horn of plenty is an especial attribute of an urban Genius. She holds a victory, in reference to the conquest of Judæa, the warlike spoils being indications of that recent event. It was by striking this medal that the people of Stobi congratulated the emperor on his decisive and appalling triumphs over the Jewish nation.—*Col.* i. p. 133.]

Victory.—A second brass of S. Severus has for legend on its reverse MVNIC. STOBENS., and for type Victory walking, with crown and palm branch.

[Vaillant supposes the *Stobenses* to have placed this type on the coins of Severus, in memory of the victory which that emperor had gained over the generals of Pescennius Niger, at Cyzicus.]

Victory.—There is a medal of the Stobenses dedicated to Julia Domna, on which a female figure, turret-crowned, and with wings, stands holding a cornucopiæ in her left hand, and in her right a *hasta pura*, round which a serpent coils itself.

[The people of Stobi, in consecrating a coin to the wife of Severus, as they had already done to himself, have flatteringly conjoined the Goddess of Victory with the Genius of their city. Respecting Victory with wings, Ovid writes *(Trist. Eleg.* i. lib. i.)

Victoria Dea te solitis circumvolat alis.

The serpent is added, as a companion of Victory, because, as Valerius Maximus observes, the former foretold the latter: in other words the serpent predicted military successes. The head of the woman is turreted, and bears a cornucopiæ, as the Genius of a city. Thus, in their self-exalting adulation, the Stobenses represent *Victoria* under the form of *Genius*, on the coins of Domna, as though that empress was herself at once the Guardian Deity of their town, and the companion of Severus in his victorious career.—*Col.* ii. 22.]

A similar type appears on coins struck by the same municipium in honour of Caracalla, whose successes over the Parthians had afforded security to the whole province of Macedonia.—The same type is also appropriated to a coin of Geta; and to Elagabalus (the last in the list of emperors whose portraits appear on Stobensian medals) a second brass is dedicated, with the same reverse, struck on the occasion of Macrinus's defeat and death.

River Deities.—On an extremely rare and rather singular coin, dedicated to Geta by the *Municipium Stobensium*, two Rivers are personified in a recumbent posture, resting each an elbow on an urn whence water flows, and between and above them is a military figure.

[The site of Stobi is pointed out by this type, as being at the confluence of two streams, one of which was called Erigon, the other Rhœdias. The figure, in warlike attire, would seem to be that of Geta, to whom the province dedicates itself.—*Col.* ii. 59.]

Observe—In the text of Vaillant one of the river deities is described as bearded, and the other as without a beard; but in the engraving inserted to illustrate the letter-press, both those recumbent figures are drawn as *females*, clothed in the stola, and of course *without* beards. Most probably the engraver has made a mistake.

Stola.—This was the long gown or robe worn by every honourable matron among the Romans. It was a dress with sleeves, and descended to the feet; usually of purple cloth, having quite round it at the bottom a plaited welt or border of fringe, sometimes of gold stuff; for which reason the words *stola et instita* are used by some authors to signify the chasteness and modesty which best become women of respectability, to whom alone it was allowed to wear the *stola*, as according to Festus, the *toga* had been abandoned to the lower classes of women and to courtesans. Hence the phrase *mulier stolata* designated a woman of quality. Over the stola Roman ladies put a sort of mantle, called palla, which was also an article of dress peculiar to the sex, inasmuch as men could not with any degree of propriety wear it.—The female colonists of Antioch used the *stola*, on which account the Genius of that Roman city appears on its coins *stolata* (Vaillant *Col.* ii. p. 4).—The Genius of the colony of Sidon is also personified as *mulier stolata*, after the Roman manner.

STOLO.—Surname of the Licinia family.—On first and second brass coins of Augustus we read P. LICINIVS STOLO IIIVIR A A A F F.—Also on denarii of the same emperor is the legend P. STOLO IIIVIR.—The apex between two ancilia. [According to Varro, one of this family, who as tribune, caused a law to be passed prohibiting any Roman citizen from having more than five acres of land, was called *Stolo*, on account of the extreme care which he took to have all such suckers and other useless offshoots rooted out from his land as might inconvenience his farming labourers.]

S. T. R. *Signata Treveris.*—M. S. TR., or MO. S. TR. *Moneta Signata Treveris.*—The mint mark of money coined at Treves.

STRAB. *Strabo.*—Surname of the Volteia and Pompeia families.

Strobilus (artichoke) or *nux pinea* (apple of the pine tree). Something that bore resemblance to each of these plants was an ensign of the *Vindelici.*—On a gold coin of Claudius appears a triumphal quadriga, in which is either the *strobilus* or the *nux pinea*, in the room of a human figure.

Strues Armorum.—A pile of arms; the sign of victory gained.—See DE GER, as in Domitian; DE GERM, as in Drusus senior, M. Aurelius, and Commodus; DE GERMANIS, as in Augustus; DE SARM*atis*, as in M. Aurelius.

Struthocamelus.—An ostrich appears on a coin of the Fabia family, as a symbol of Africa. —On a denarius of the Cornelia family this bird stands between a palm and a branch of laurel.

SVB.—SVBAC. *Subacta*, subdued.—See ALEMANNIA SVBACTA, as in M. Aurelius.

Subauratus numus. Plated money.——This species of false coin consisted of brass or copper covered over with a thin coating of silver leaf, both materials being so dexterously united together as frequently to baffle detection, except by the coin itself being cut in two. This description of counterfeiting commenced among the Romans (says Jobert i. 42) during the times of the early consuls, and was revived at the period of Augustus's triumvirate. It is at the same time an infallible proof of the antiquity of the medal, and even of its rarity; for, as Morell observes, as soon as this spurious coinage was discovered, the dies were broken and the fabrication denounced, under the heaviest penalties, by the state. —See *Pelliculati numi* and *Médailles Fourrées*.

Sublician Bridge.—See *Aemilia* family.

Subscriptiones (literæ).—Letters or characters, under-written, with which coins of a late age in the Imperial series are furnished, first present themselves in the reign of Gallienus.—Some, however, are observed on silver of Philip sen., and Otacilia Severa, his wife. But it is under Gallienus that this usage is more clearly found to have commenced: for on his coins are engraved

certain numeral letters, either Greek or Latin, placed sometimes in the field of the medal, viz., I. or II. or III. or IV. or V., as in small brass of Tacitus; at other times on the lower part of the coin, viz., B. C. Δ., &c., as in small brass of Probus. These under-struck characters are also found on small brass of Saloninus, Postumus, Victorinus, Claudius Gothicus, Quintillus, Aurelianus, Florianus, Carus, Numerianus, Carinus, Magnia Urbica, Maxentius, &c.

Suffibulum, the name, which according to Festus, was given to a long, white, bordered veil, or covering for the head, worn by the Vestals whenever they officiated at sacrifices. Its name derived itself from the word *Fibula*, because this vestment was fastened with a buckle, or broche, lest it should happen to fall off.— Oiselius *(Sel. Num.*, tb. 46, fig. 8) gives a coin of an uncertain family, inscribed *Vesta P. R. Quiritium*, and on which the *fibula* as well as the *suffibulum*, is very conspicuous. In the same work are several figures of Vesta, whence it is easy to perceive the form and length of the *suffibulum*, and also the mode in which it was put on by the priestess of Vesta.

Subsellia.—This word was originally applied to the public benches or seats in the amphitheatre. But it was afterwards used to denote a low sort of seat *(humilis mensa)*, of which Asconius describes the use by saying that they were appropriated to the plebeian tribunes and ediles, the triumvirs, the quæstors, pro quæstors, and other persons who, exercising judicial functions of a minor kind, sat, *not* in curule chairs nor on tribunals, but on *subsellia.*—Eckhel (vol. v. p. 317) refers to a silver coin of the *Sulpicia* family, on which two men clothed in the toga, sit together on a simple sort of low form, and comparing this common looking seat with certain ornamental and more elevated chairs, which are represented on denarii of Cornelius Sulla, Cestius, Norbanus, Lollius, and other consular dignitaries, he leaves his reader to judge whether the humble bench figured on a coin of Sulpicius Platorinus must not be one of the *subsellia* mentioned by Asconius.—See *Sulpicia* family.

Suffimenta, donatives of sulphur, bitumen, and other inflammable and combustible substances for the composition of torches, which were distributed among the people a few days before the celebration of the secular games, and with which they performed their part in the expiatory and lustral ceremonies peculiar to those occasions. Pitiscus takes notice of these *suffimenta*, which he observes were wont to be given in the way of atonement and purification, either by the emperors themselves, or by the consuls and decemvirs when sacrificing at Rome before the temples of Apollo Pallatinus and Jupiter Capitolinus. Bellori states that the *suffimenta* included frankincense and other kinds of perfume used by the Romans in their public lustrations.

SVF. P.D. *Suffimenta Populo Data*—Inscribed on a first brass of Domitian.—See LVD. SAEC. FEC., p. 527 of this Dictionary.

Suffragia, suffrages; the vote given to some one in elections for magistrates, and other public offices. The right of suffrage was the distinctive attribute of Roman citizens; and for a long time they exercised it *vivâ voce,* the votes being received by the seniors of tribes *(Rogatores),* who, each for his respective tribe, reported to the President of the Assembly the result of the polling. But this custom was annulled by the *Lex Cassia Tabellaria,* which enacted that in order to leave the suffrages of the citizens in a state of greater freedom they should thenceforward tender them by means of a ticket or tablet, called *Tabella,* which gave its name to the law.—This important change from open voting to the vote by ballot, was extremely popular at the time, inasmuch as it appeared favourable to the cause of republican liberty, but it was fraught with consequences destructive to the purity of election and fatal to the real freedom of the state. These *tabellæ* were very narrow bits of wood, or other materials, on which were written the names of candidates at the elections for magistrates, and were distributed among the voters according to the number of competitors.—If, however, the business before the assembly was that of passing some law or decree, which had already been proposed to the people, there was then given to each citizen two *tabellæ,* or billets; the one for approving, the other for rejecting. On the former was inscribed a V. and an R., which signified *Uti rogas,* "as you request;" and on the latter, which was for the negative, an A. meaning *Antiquo,* "I annul," or "I vote for the old law." If the matter in question was to pass a verdict in judgment, either to condemn or to acquit any one, three *tabellæ* were given to each elector; one of these had the letter A. *absolvo,* the other C. for *condemno;* and the third N. and L., meaning *non liquet,* "it does not appear," as expressing inability to decide, or a desire to put off the business in hand to another hearing. This last was used when the accused had not appeared to have fully cleared himself, and yet did not seem to be absolutely guilty.

It was L. Cassius Longinus, who, during his tribunate in the year v. c. 617, carried the *lex tabellaria,* whereby in all judgments, cases of murder excepted, the people were required to give their votes on inscribed tablets; and in effecting this great alteration in the law respecting suffrages, he was regarded, as it would appear, even by Cicero himself, to have eminently consulted the interests of public liberty.

There is a denarius of the *Cassia* family, which bears on its obverse Q. CASSIVS and the veiled head of a woman, with the word VEST. near it.—*Rev.* A round temple, within which is a curule chair. In the field of the coin is on one side an urn, and on the other a tablet inscribed A. C. The letters, as above explained, signify *Absolvo; Condemno;* and the urn, or little pot (often by Cicero called *sitella),* into which the *tabellæ* of the voters were thrown, is here seen standing near them.—Another denarius of the same family has on its obverse Q. CASSIVS, a female head, and the word LIBERT.; and on the reverse side the same type and letters as the preceding. The urn, the tablet marked A. C., and the head of Liberty, all evidently refer to the above-mentioned passage in the history of Cassius Longinus, as the author of the system of voting *per tabellas.* And it was in memory of this ancestor of his that Q. CASSIVS LONGINVS, a monetal triumvir, caused the coins to be struck.—See *Doct. Num. Vet.,* vol. v. 166.—See also *Cassia* family in this dictionary.

Suggestu, de suggestu, pro suggestu, &c.— A term used with respect to the emperor, when standing on his tribunal or *estrade* (suggestum); and about to make a speech to the soldiers (Spanheim, *Pr.* ii. p. 628).—See ADLOCVTIO.

SVL. *Sulpicius.*—See *Galba Imp.*

SVLL. *Sulla.*—Surname of the *Cornelia* family.

Sulla (or *Sylla).*—Lucius, descended from a high patrician family, was the son of L. Sulla, prætor of Sicily. In the thirty-ninth year of his age, he was appointed quæstor to Marius, who was then in his first consulship, and whom he accompanied into Africa. It is to Sulla that his biographer, Plutarch, ascribes, in an especial degree, the glory of those victories which crowned the Roman arms in the Jugurthine war. But in that war were at the same time laid the seeds of mutual hatred between the consul and his quæstor, which produced the most furious factions, and involved the republic in all the sanguinary horrors of domestic strife. Bocchus, the Numidian king's perfidious betrayal of Jugurtha into the hands of Sulla; and the ostentatious use which the aspiring Roman was prompted to make of praises bestowed by his countrymen on that early instance of his enterprise and courage, excited the ferocious jealousy of Marius, and led to results the most disastrous to the peace and prosperity of their common country. Ascending in the scale of public offices, he obtained his election for prætor, and was sent as general into Cappadocia. In the year v.c. 665 he obtained the consulship. And after Marius and himself by their antagonistic system of proscription had filled the families of Rome with terror, and her streets with blood, he succeeded in wresting from his defeated rival that favourite object of his ambition, the management of the war against Mithridates. Having taken and plundered Athens and vanquished Achelaus, the general of that monarch, near Mount Thurina in Bœotia, he erected two trophies, and was styled *Imperator.* Afterwards, having defeated Dorylaus, another of the Mithridatic commanders, he raised another trophy in Thessaly, and was called *Imperator Iterum.* Hence, we find *three* trophies on his coins, corresponding with the number of those which, it is to be inferred from Dion, were engraved on the signet ring of Sulla. The flattering surname of *Felix* (*i. e.* Fortunate) was added to his own. Indeed, according to Plutarch, he gave himself that appellation, making it his boast that he enjoyed perpetual felicity, or good success, in all his affairs. "For this reason," says Appianus, "he was designated as the happiest of men." Pliny also testifies: "*unus hominum ad hoc ævi Felicis sibi cognomen asseruit L. Sulla*." That this name of "Felix," at first bestowed upon him in private was afterwards publicly appended to his other titles, we further learn on the authority of Appianus, who writes that a gilt equestrian statue was placed in the *rostra* at Rome, with this inscription—"*Cornelio Sullæ Imperatori Felici*. Moreover, Cicero, whilst Sulla was still living, called him *Felix*. Certain it is also that Sulla, whether sincerely or affectedly, ascribed all the glory of his exploits, not to himself nor to human wisdom, but to Fortune, and what others imputed as a disgrace he professed to honour as proceeding from this leading tutelary of his choice and worship. In order still more closely to identify the source of his extraordinary prosperity with the favours of *Fortuna et Felicitas*, not only did he take the surname of *Faustus* (*i. e.* auspicious and happy), but he also conferred it upon each of the two children whom he had by his wife Metella, naming his son *Faustus*, and his daughter *Fausta*. There was, however, apparently much art and tact in the way in which Sulla made his subservience to the superstitions of the priesthood work together for advantage to his bold and unscrupulous plans of aggrandisement. Not only Fortune and Felicity, but Apollo and Venus, and Diana came in for a share of his grateful devotion. The character of this remarkable personage was one of strikingly contrasted qualities, in which, however, the vicious predominated frightfully over the better attributes of his nature. A gross voluptuary, and a licentious wit, yet strict and punctual even to austerity as a man of business; infamous for his libidinous excesses, and most disorderly in his convivial pleasures; he was a sage in council, and a hero on the field of battle. In the obscurity of his early life the associate of jesters, mimics, and profligate revellers of both sexes; he changed his exterior behaviour on the attainment of supreme power, displaying the highest talents for civil government, combined with consummate genius and capacity as a military commander. Yet, in these and in all other things, ever rushing to extremes and glorying in eccentricities, he exhibited himself as a monster of lust and of cruelty, checkering a life of the most splendid and important actions with flagrant inconsistencies, blackened by enormous crimes, and paying the forfeit of intemperance and debauchery by a horrible death from the most loathsome of diseases.—See the words FEELIX, FAVSTVS, and BOCCHVS.

As connected with the numismatic illustrations of Sulla's history, it may here be noted that on a denarius of the *Æmilia* family, bearing the name of L. BVCA., the figure of a man is represented as if sleeping in the presence of a female figure, who, distinguished by the crescent moon on her forehead, and by a veil floating above her, seems as if sitting in the clouds. In the midst stands Victory bearing a palm branch.—See *Æmilia* family.

[This type corresponds in its group of figures with the main incidents of Sulla's dream, in which he pretended to have been forewarned by some goddess of his future victorious fortunes, and on account of which he regarded his celestial monitress with "a grateful mind."—The relation by Plutarch of this incident is as follows :— "There appeared to him (Sulla) in a dream a goddess, whose worship the Romans borrowed from the Cappadocians, whether she be Luna (Diana), Minerva, or Bellona, who seemed to stand by him; and to put thunder into his hand; and who, having summoned each of his enemies by name, bade him strike them. They fell under his stroke, and were consumed. Inflamed by this vision, he related it to his colleague the next morning, and bent his way towards Rome." —This dream of Sulla's refers, in point of time, to v.c. 671, when he was threatening the city from Campania.—L. Æmilius Buca was quæstor in Sulla's time.]

The following are the only denarii of Sulla that were struck during his life-time :—

(L) SVLLA IMP*erator*.—A military figure, standing in a triumphal quadriga, holding a caduceus and crowned by a victory flying over his head.—On a coin, rare in silver, and most rare in gold, of the *Cornelia* family.—See also the *Manlia* family.

SVLLA IMP.—Sulla in military habiliments, standing with parazonium in his left hand, joins his right hand with that of a soldier standing opposite him, and holding a spear in his left; behind is the forepart of a galley, from which Sulla seems to have disembarked.—This type appears on the reverse of a very rare silver coin of the Cornelia family, the obverse of which has a bust of Minerva, with Victory behind placing a garland on her head.—See *Cornelia* family.

(L) SVLLA.—Head of Venus, before which a little figure of Cupid stands, holding a long branch of palm.

Rev.—IMPER. ITERVM.—The lituus and the præfericulum between two trophies.—On a denarius of the Cornelia family, common in silver, but most rare in gold.

[The *first* of the above three seems to record some signal triumph won by the Dictator over Mithridates.—Of the type on the second coin, Eckhel says, "I am in doubt what opinion to adopt. The conjectures which antiquaries have hitherto hazarded are not satisfactory."—The *third* denarius is more open to animadversion. The head of Venus is placed on the obverse, because, on the authority of Plutarch, it appears that Sulla caused the names of Mars, Fortune, and Venus to be inscribed on a trophy.—Cupid with palm branch readily points out Venus Victrix. We further learn from Plutarch that Sulla was singularly devoted to the worship of *Venus the Conqueror*, and that, in honour of that goddess, he adopted the Greek surname of *Epaphroditus*, or (as translated into Latin) *Venustus*.—Plutarch adds that, in writing to the

Greeks (in answer to their applications), he took this additional name, and that the inscription on the Roman trophies left at Cheronæa was *Lucius Cornelia Sulla Epaphroditus*—Appianus records this last adopted surname, and also says that *Sulla Imperator* dedicated certain gifts to Venus, because, as he pretended, he beheld in a dream that goddess meeting his soldiers, and mixing with them in martial attire.—The two trophies on the reverse denote the two victories, which, in the year V.C. 667, Sulla gained over Archelaus near Mount Thurium, and in the field of Cheronæa ; in memory of which events, as we learn from Plutarch, two trophies were erected. That on account of those two brilliant and decisive victories he was called IMP*erator* ITERVM, is shewn with sufficient clearness by the epigraph itself of this denarius—a coin which, by universal acknowledgment, was struck in Sulla's life-time ; and which, in its type of the *lituus* and *præfericulum*, or *guttus*, unquestionable insignia of the augurs, demonstrates that Sulla was one of that fraternity, as was also at a later period *Faustus* his son.—Appianus affirms that Sulla was admitted to the sacerdotal order. (*Num. Vet.* vol. v. p. 191.)—See *Cornelia* fam.

SVLLA. COS. Bare head with beardless face.—*Rev.* RVFVS COS. Q. POMP. RVFI. A bare head and beardless face. AR.

SVLLA COS. Q. POMPEI. RVF.— Curule chair, between the lituus and a garland.—*Rev.* RVFVS. COS. Q. POMPEI. Q. F. A curule chair, between an arrow and a branch of laurel. AR.

See Eckhel's observations on the above two denarii, vol. v. pp. 191, 192.—See also *Sella Curulis*.

SVLLA COS.—Head of a man, bare and beardless.

Rev.—RVFVS COS.—Q. POM. RVFI,—Another beardless and uncovered head.

This denarius of the Cornelia family presents the portraitures of two Romans, L. Cornelius Sulla, and Q. Pompeius Rufus, who were Consuls in the year V.C. 666.—"It is an acceptable thing to see, as we do on this coin, the effigy of Sylla, in contemplating whose countenance, a certain Chalcedon, versed in physiognomy (as Plutarch relates), exclaimed that such a man could not be otherwise than destined to future greatness, and that he even wondered how it could be that he did not already occupy the highest place in the Republic. Those traits of personal appearance, which of course are not perceivable on a medal or in a statue, are also mentioned by the same writer, who observes that " his eyes were of a lively blue, fierce and menacing ; and this ferocity of aspect was heightened by his complexion, which was of a strong red, interspersed with spots of white."—His shining hair of a golden colour is likewise mentioned.

SULP. *Sulpicia*.—See HISPANIA CLVNIA. SVLP., on a coin of Sulpicius Galba, on which Hispania is called Sulpicia after that emperor's family name.

SULPI. *Sulpicianus*, surname of the *Quinctia* family.

SVLPICIA.—This house, which possessed an illustrious name amongst the most ancient families of Rome, came originally from the city of Camera. —According to some writers, the Sulpitia were so called *sue specta*. And this is done by a sufficiently far-fetched process of derivation, founded on the legendary figment about one of Æneas's companions being the first to behold, beneath an oak, the sow lying with her litter of thirty, on the spot pointed out by the oracle, and on which the city of Lavinium was afterwards built. Hence, we are told, this fortunate sowfinder was by his immediate descendants, called *Suispicius*, which word was changed by their posterity into *Sulpicius !*—This family did not, however, make its appearance in history, it seems, until about the year V.C. 254, at which period Sulpicius, surnamed Camerinus, was consul with M. Tullius Longinus—although the Emperor Galba, who belonged to it, pretended to trace his descent from Jupiter. Its surnames, as recorded on coins, are *Galba, Rufus, Platorinus*, and *Proculus ;* of these the Galba branch was patrician, that of Rufus plebeian ; the others are of uncertain rank.—There are thirty-two varieties in the medals of this family. Its gold are of the highest rarity ; its silver common, except those restored by Trajan, which are very scarce. The second and third brass are also rare. The following are specimens of the Sulpician denarii, arranged according to surnames :—

Galba.—On the obverse, head of a woman, veiled, behind it S. C.

Rev.—P. GALB. (Publius Galba) AE. CVR., or AED. CVR. (Ædilis Curulis).—The simpulum and secespita.

[It is uncertain by what P. Galba this coin was struck during his year of office as curule edile ; but, as already stated, it was from this *gens* that the Emperor Galba sprang.]

Platorinus.—On the obverse of a very rare silver coin of this family we find the epigraph CAESAR AVGVSTVS, with the naked head of Augustus.

Rev.—PLATORINVS IIIVIR. M. AGRIPPA.— Naked head of Agrippa.

Another denarius of the Sulpicia family, with the same obverse, has on its *Rev.* C. SVLPICIVS PLATORIN.; and for type, two men clothed in the toga, sitting on a low table, or form, at the bottom of which are three *rostra*, or beaks of gallies.—[No mention is made of Platorinus, in ancient history. The reverse of the second denarius remains of doubtful interpretation. Ursinus sees in it the *rostra nova*, or *Julia*, which Cæsar caused to be erected at Rome. In this opinion, Spanheim, Vaillant, and Havercamp appear readily to coincide, and they even go so far as to recognise Augustus and Agrippa, as consuls, in the two figures sitting here with the *rostra* beneath their feet. " But (says Eckhel) on what a lowly and unbecoming *subsellium* would this supposition place two men of such high rank, who in their quality of consular dignitaries ought to be represented seated on curule chairs." The same sagacious commentator then refers to the form of seats assigned to inferior magistrates, to whom the *jus sellæ curulis* did not belong, many examples of which are furnished on consular medals; such for instance as those on which Piso and Cæpio, quæstors *ad frumendum emundum* (officers appointed for purchasing and importing corn to Rome), and also such as M. Fannius and L. Critonius are seated. (See *Fannia* family). Moreover, the *hasta* leaning against the seat, as in the denarius in question, is also seen on coins of Papius Rufus, quæstor, and L. Caninius Gallus. "We may consider ourselves, therefore, (concludes Eckhel,) to have before us in the type of this reverse the identical kind of benches or seats appropriated to the use of those less exalted functionaries of the Roman commonwealth, whom Asconius alludes to in these terms:—*Subsellia sunt tribunorum, triumvirorum, quæstorum, et hujus modi minora judicia exercentium, qui non in sellis curulibus, nec tribunalibus, sed in subselliis, considebant.*"]—See the word *Subsellia*.

Rufus.—1. The obverse of a rare denarius of the *Sulpicia gens* bears for legend L. SERVIVS RVFVS., and for type a bare head with short beard.

Rev.—No legend; but the type exhibits two naked men standing with spears; a star over the head of each. This, restored by Trajan, is very rare.

2. A gold coin of the highest rarity, with same legend on the obverse, has two heads of young men, jugated, each wearing the pileus and laureated; two stars over head.

Rev.—The walls of a town, over the gate of which is inscribed TVSCVL.—See below.

3. Another denarius of this family has on one side D. P.P.; two jugated heads of young men, laureated.—See *Penates*.

Rev.—C. SVLPICI. C. F. Two military figures, with spears, stand pointing with their right hands to a sow, which is lying on the ground between them.

Who the L. Servius Rufus of the first two coins was is a matter of uncertainty. Some erudite antiquaries believe him to have been the son of Ser. Sulpicius Rufus, a celebrated jurisconsult, the friend of Cicero, and who was consul v.c. 703; after that, having embraced the side of Cæsar, he was sent on a mission to M. Antony, at the time of the Mutinensian war. Whom the head on this denarius was meant for has likewise been made the subject of a controversy still undecided, and never worth the pains bestowed upon it. That the two standing

figures were meant for the *Dioscuri* (see the word) is plainly indicated by their caps and other attributes. The reason why the type of the second denarius was adopted, appears to have been that Servius Sulpicius, a military tribune, invested with consular authority, hastened from Rome with an army, and rescued Tusculum, when pressed with a close seige by the Latins.— But it seems from Cicero, that in his time there was a temple dedicated to Castor and Pollux, at Tusculum.—Festus also states that Castor was worshipped in that town. On account of this hereditary honour, not only the most venerated divinities of the Tusculans, but the very town of Tusculum itself, are exhibited on the pre-eminently rare gold coin.

Eckhel refers to the *Dioscuri* also, the two heads on the obverse of the third coin, although the letters D. P.P. *(Dii Penates)* are inscribed near them. Heads similarly conjoined, laureated, and surmounted with stars, are likewise found on denarii of the Fonteia family, with the addition of P.P. (i.e. *Penates.)* But still more explicitly on coins of the *Antia* family we read *Dii Penates*, at full length, near heads similarly yoked together. Deities in appearance different (because they are differently delineated on other coins) are in reality identical with these Dioscuri. The *Dii Penates* were so called, according to Cicero, because their name was derived from *Penus*, the name given to everything eaten by man, or from the fact of their having their situation within the house; whence also they are called by the poets *Penetrales*.—See PENATES.

The reverse type of the third coin has given rise to a difference of opinion among learned numismatists. Some have professed to regard it as exhibiting two of the companions of Æneas, who first beheld the white sow under the oak *(ilex)* with her litter of thirty, to which Varro and Virgil both allude.—Others suppose that it relates to the treaty ratified between Tullus Hostillianus and Metius Fuffetius, by the sacrifice of a pig.—Ericius, on the contrary, thinks that the *Dii Penates* (whom it was not unusual to depict armed with spears and in warlike costume) are exhibited in this instance also.—Eckhel (vol. v. p. 320–21) himself considers this last-mentioned opinion to correspond the most closely with the truth, and he goes on to quote old writers in support of it—amongst others Dionysius Halicarnassus, who adds that "the sow and the whole litter were offered by Æneas in sacrifice to the *Dii Penates.*" It was held as a great point of religion amongst the Romans that the public solemnities or rites connected with the worship of the Penates should always be celebrated at Lavinium. Insomuch that when it was alleged against M. Æmilius Scaurus, *princeps Senatus*, as a criminal charge, that the public solemnities, in honour of the Dii Penates were, through his neglect, omitted to be performed at Lavinium with the solemnity due to those sacred observances, he very narrowly escaped a sentence of condemnation from the people. (See Asconius on Cicero pro Scauro.) These testimonies being so closely in accordance with the type of the coin in question, and the *Dii Penates* being so distinctly named on the Sulpician medals, there can, adds Eckhel, be no doubt but that in this denarius allusion is made by the type of its reverse to those household deities.

SVLPICIVS URANIVS ANTONINVS.— Zosimus makes mention of two usurpers, who, with the support of a disaffected mutinous soldiery, assumed the purple in the reign of Alexander Severus. He adds that one of those was called *Antoninus;* the other *Uranius*— that the former, unable to sustain the weight of government, took to flight, and appeared no more; that the latter, a man of servile origin, was proclaimed in his room, but he being soon taken prisoner, was brought before Alexander with the purple robe on, in which he had arrayed himself.—It is to Sulpicius Uranius, (unless, as Eckhel observes, Zosimus, whose knowledge of the history of that period is deficient in accuracy, may perchance have made *two* out of *one* usurper,) that the unique gold coin, described below, is to be assigned :—

ʟ. IVL. AVR. SVLP. VRA. ANTONINVS.—Laureated head ; moderately bearded ; shoulders clothed with the paludamentum.

Rev.—FECVNDITAS AVG.—A woman standing, clothed in the stola, holding in one hand a cornucopiæ, in the other a rudder.

Meffei hesitates to allow the antiquity of this medal. His doubts are based on these grounds—first, that medals of gold, with Latin legends, and of such fine workmanship as this is, would not have been struck for a tyrant who was acknowledged only in the East, and whose reign lasted but a few days ; second, that the head of this usurper is accompanied by the type of Fecundity, and that *that* Fecundity is represented with the attributes of Fortune.— But Bimard, who (in *Jobert*, tom. ii. p. 348) has given an engraving of this coin, and written a long and, as usual with him, an ably critical commentary on it, contends that these difficulties are not such as to be in any degree calculated to overturn the strong intrinsic evidence of its genuineness offered by the medal itself. To the opinion of this eminent man, and of those equally experienced numismatists who coincided with him, " I (says Eckhel), who have not seen the medal, and have nothing to urge in opposition, most freely subscribe." *(Doct. Num. Vet.* vii. 288.)—Mr. Akerman, in his *Descriptive Catalogue*, states that this aureus of Sulpicius Uranius Antoninus "formed part of the plunder of the French Cabinet in November, 1834." The genuineness of the gold coin is confirmed by those in brass struck in the East, in Greek characters : like the gold they are extremely rare.

SVL*picia.*—See HISPANIA CLVNIA SVL.

SVMMVS SACERDOS AVG.—The emperor clothed in the toga, and holding a palm-branch, stands before a lighted altar : a bull, as a victim, on the ground ; a star in the field. The foregoing legend and type appear on a silver coin of Elagabalus.—There is another coin of the same

emperor, which has for legend of reverse P.M. TR. P. III. COS. III. P.P., and of which the type is similar, with the exception of there being in in the area of the medal, behind the figure, two darts, one of which is sharp-pointed, the other has a conical head.

[These coins, together with those bearing the legends of *Invictus Sacerdos ; Sancto Deo Soli Elagabal.,* etc., indicate the worship paid by the Syrian Bassianus at the time of his accession as emperor, to the Phœnician god, called Elagabalus, or Heliogabalus, believed to be the *Sun*, after whose name he has since been called, and of whom he here proclaims himself the High or Chief Priest, having the audacity to prefix it to the Imperial title. We here indeed see him officiating at those rites, for which functions, as his hateful biography informs us, that loathsome young maniac "circumcised himself and abstained from swine's flesh." These coins also exhibit the sort of dress which he used in these sacerdotal ministrations—viz., a something between the Phœnician sacred robe and the cloak of the Medes, according to Herodianus's description of it ; and as the author says in another passage, "he (Elagabalus) walked in barbarian costume, with purple tunic interwoven with gold, long-sleeved and down to the feet." The palm-branch which he holds in his hand, and which on most of his coins more resembles a club, perhaps points to the Phœnician origin of the worship. But the darts placed near the before-mentioned attributes no doubt constitute part of this absurd idolatry. The star placed above, in the field of the coin, as in many others of Elagabalus, denotes the god *Sol.*—On a marble published by Muratori is read IVNIVS MATERNVS SACER. D. S. HELAGAB.]

The able author of *Leçons de Numismatique Romaine,* in reference to the monstrous freaks of Elagabalus, as faintly shadowed forth on some of his coins, makes the following pertinent and comprehensive remarks :—*Conservent pour sa divinité favorite une extravagante vénération, il en apporta à Rome le culte et l'idole (qui etait une grosse pierre noirâtre de forme conique) et lui fit batir un temple, où il remplissait lui même les fonctions sacerdotales. Enfin de toutes ces démences, dont ces médailles offre un faible monument, il restu à l'infame pontife le nom de son dieu pour sobriquet.*"

SVPERA (CAIA CORNELIA.)—This lady is known only through the medium of the coins which bear her name as *Augusta.* Some antiquaries have regarded her as the consort of Trebonianus Gallus.—Tristan, who was the first to publish a medal of this princess, supposes her to have been the wife of Valerian the younger.—Vaillant, and as it would seem even Pellerin *(Mél.* i. p. 239) adopted the same opinion.—Beauvais also expresses himself in favour of this latter conjecture ; but candidly admits that he had been confidently assured by others of the existence of a *Greek* medal, bearing the name, with imperial title, of Cornelia Supera, the date of which led to the inference that she was the wife of the Emperor *Æmilianus.*

This opinion, Eckhel, by reference as well to numismatic monuments of indubitable authenticity, as to the chronology of the period, has proved to be correct. Adducing two medals of Cornelia Supera, one Greek of Ægea, in Cilicia; the other of the colony of Parium, in Mysia, the epochs and reverses on both which are to be retraced with exactness on the medals of Æmilianus; Eckhel, after a full investigation of dates and historical facts, comes unhesitatingly to the conclusion, that the emperor last named must have been the husband of the *unknown Augusta*. (See *Doct. Num, Vet.* vol. vii. p. 374 *et seq.)*

"In this decision (says the judicious author of *Leçons de Numismatique Romaine)* we are furnished with another, amongst many instances, to show us how the different departments of medallic science afford mutual aid and illustration to each other; teaching us at the same time how disadvantageous it is to confine ourselves to the study of a single branch of it exclusively." The style of this princess, on coins of Roman die, in silver, are :—

C. COR. or CORN. or CORNEL. SVPERA. AVG.— The head placed on a crescent moon.

The reverses are CONCORDIA. AVG.—IVNO REGINA.—VENVS VICTRIX.—VESTA; with the usual types accompanying each respectively.— These are in silver and at the highest degree of rarity. If small brass really exist, they are equally rare.

Sus.—The figure of a *sow* appears on the earliest of Roman coins. Thus, on the *semis*, a sow stands with s. above its back.—A sow, or bristly boar, accompanies the three globules which are the mark of the *quadrans*.—The head of a sow or boar is placed between the four globules that designate the *triens*.—The *sow*, with her litter, was represented on the coinage of Rome to indicate its primary origin.—The same animal is figured on medals of Vespasian and of Antoninus Pius.—The sow was consecrated and sacrificed to Ceres.—On a coin of M. Aurelius, given by Vaillant *(Pr.* iii. 138), the *popa*, or slaughterer of victims, is dragging by the ear a sow to the altar of immolation. It was employed in connection with oaths taken on the ratification of treaties.—(See *Feciales, Scrofa, Sulpicia.)*

SVSC. *Suscepta.*—See VOTA. SVSC. *(Vota Suscepta),* an epigraph of frequent recurrence on medals of the imperial series.

Sylvanus.—The name of an usurper, in the reign of Constantius II., the son of a Gaulish captain; proclaimed emperor at Cologne A.D. 355; slain within thirty days after his assumption of the purple. The coins, which have been ascribed by Goltzius and others to Sylvanus, are pronounced to be false.

Symbols, or signs, on Roman coins.—Some of these allude to the names of families; as *Acisculus*, on denarii of the *Valeria* family. *Flos*, an open round flower, the surname of Aquilius Florus. *The Muses*, as in the Pomponia family, on account of the surname MUSA. *Vitulus*, a calf walking, in a symbol of

the Voconia family, from the surname VITULUS, &c.—Other *symbols* are ænigmatical or fabulous, such as Pegasus, griffin, sphinx, chimæra, centaur, capricorn, &c.—The following symbols have their peculiar and appropriate signification on Roman coins, viz. :—

Aplustre, a ship's ornament, imports maritime power.

Apollo's head refers to the Apollinarian games.

Bow, symbolises Apollo.

Bow and club, Hercules.

Bow and quiver, Diana.

Buckler, round, Macedonia.

Caduceus, or winged rod with serpents, is an attribute of Mercury, Felicity, and Peace.

Caduceus, between two cornucopiæ, signifies Abundance and Peace.

Caduceus, between corn-ears, Fertility as well as Peace.

Camel, symbol of Arabia.

Capricorn, or sea goat, the astrological sign of Augustus's nativity.

Capricorn, or sea goat, also symbol of Plenty and Happiness.

Ceres, the goddess, denotes Fertility, and distribution of corn.

Cornucopiæ, or horn of plenty, Fecundity; also abundance of all things.

Corn ears *(spicæ tritici)* symbolise Egypt, Africa, Spain, and also Annona and Fertility.

Crowns, of various kinds, relate to public games.

Crocodile, symbol of Egypt.

Crabfish *(pagurus)* indicates a maritime city.

Chimæra belongs to Corinth.

Crane *(ciconia)*; this bird symbolises Piety, meaning affection to parents.

Club *(clava)* attribute of Hercules.

Colonist driving two oxen to plough, sign of a Roman colony.

Column, or pillar, denotes security.

Dog, attribute of Diana Venatrix; also of the Lares.

Dolphin, attribute of the Cyprian Venus; it also marks a maritime town.

Eagle, the wings of, Jupiter, whose attribute it is; also a type of Eternity.

Eagle, legionary, refers to the army of the commander-in-chief.

Elephant, symbol of Africa; also of Eternity.

Frankinscence, branch of *(thuris ramus)* attribute of Arabia.

Fasces with the axe, imports sovereign authority.

Fish, denotes a maritime state.

Grain of wheat, marks Fertility.

Grapes, bunch of, indicates a place celebrated for its produce in wine.

Horned head, Jupiter Ammon; also regal power.

Hasta pura, or spear with blunt point, mark of Divinity.

Laurel, attribute of Apollo and of Victory; also refers to public games.

Lion, symbol of Africa.

Lion's skin, attribute of Hercules.

Lituus, or staff with curved head, sign of the Augurship, or Soothsayers' office.

Lotus flower, Isis; the Egyptian people.

Lyre, attribute and symbol of Apollo.

Modius, or bushel measure, symbol of the Edileship.

Modius, or bushel measure, filled with corn ears, signifies provision, chiefly corn.

Owl, attribute of Pallas.

Olive branch, of Peace.

Prætorian galley, represents the fleet of the Republic.

Prow of a ship, refers to Rome, or some maritime city.

Palm tree, emblem of Alexandria, Damascus, Judæa, Sidon, Tyre, Phoenicia.

Panther, attribute of Bacchus.

Peacock, of Juno.

Pedum pastorale, shepherd's crook, emblem of Pan and Faunus.

Pegasus, a winged horse so called, symbol of Apollo ; also of Corinth.

Pegasus and Bellerophon, type of Colonial Corinth.

Pileus, cap so called, symbolises Liberty.

Rabbit, attribute of Spain.

Right hand raised, signifies Security, Peace, Health.

Right hands joined, denote concord.

Right hand holding a caduceus, concord; and at the same time Peace.

Rocks, or stones, indicate places on lofty sites.

Rudder, or helm of a ship, attribute of Fortune; also shows a maritime city.

Serpent signifies Prudence and Wisdom; it is also the attribute of Æsculapius ; and of Hygieia, or Salus.

Star, the numismatic mark of Elagabalus.

Stella crinita, or comet, alludes to Julius Cæsar.

Stars, over the heads of two young men, mark the Dioscuri.

Sow, with litter, symbolises the Romans.

Staff, round which a serpent is coiled, attribute of Æsculapius.

Thyrsus, or spear wrapped round with ivy, attribute of Bacchus.

Triquetra, three human legs triangularly joined, is an emblem of Sicily.

Tropæum, trophy with captives at foot, betokens a province captured or a people vanquished.

Table, with urns upon it, refers to the prizes at public games.

Urns, with palm branches issuing therefrom, allude to the same thing.

Vases, augural, pontificial, and sacerdotal, insignia of the Augurship, Pontificate, and Priesthood.

Veil on the head of a female, sign of Vesta or a Vestal virgin ; also of a consecrated empress.

Symbols.—On the subject of those, by which the superintendence and control of the Curule Ediles over the celebration of public games *(Ludi)* is designated on Roman medals, Spanheim should be consulted *(Pr.* i. p. 149), where he refers to such coins as bear the effigy either of the *dea spicifera,* Ceres ; or of the *mater magna,* Cybele, drawn in a biga of lions ; also where the same great writer treats of coins on which

appears a curule chair, with a crown upon it, the latter being the reward of victors at the public games, accompanied frequently, on the same medals, with the inscription itself of AED. or AEDIL. CVR. *(Ædilis Curulis),* viz., those same Curule Ediles, under whose management and direction these games were conducted with due dignity and order. Objects allusive to these matters, always of intense interest and predilection to the people of Rome and of her colonies, are to be found on coins of the Norbana, Papinia, and Vibia families.—Moreover, as to this class of ediles was committed the *curatio annonæ:* the important charge of securing a constant supply of provision to the Roman capital and circumjacent territories : so we see the exercise of these functions recorded on coins by the curule chair, and a corn ear on each side of it, together with, sometimes, a cornucopiæ added, as on denarii of the Lollia, Plautia, Quintia, and Rutilia families. Indeed, the title AED. CVR. is inscribed on the last three, whilst the *modius,* or bushel measure, placed between two corn ears, appears with obviously the same signification on medals of the Livineia family.—Spanheim, *Pr.* ii. p. 151, *et seq.*

Syria, a maritime region of Asia, the most interesting as well in a religious as in an historical sense, of any in the world. It anciently included Phœnicia and below it Palæstina, (the latter afterwards called the Holy Land, as having been the country of our Blessed Saviour's nativity, the theatre of his miracles and labours of love, the scene of his passion, death, burial, glorious resurrection and ascension.) Syria was bounded by Cilicia on the north, by Arabia and the river Euphrates on the east, by Arabia and Egypt on the south, and by the Mediterranean on the west. This magnificent region had, for ages before its subjugation by republican Rome, been governed by a succession of independent kings, conspicuous among whom were the Seleucidæ. The epocha when Syria became a Roman province is not precisely known; probably it was Pompey the Great who reduced it to that condition, as he appears to have invested its municipal authorities with the privilege of coining money (autonomes). It stands afterwards recorded amongst the provinces of the empire, under Julius Cæsar and Augustus ; and its famous city Antioch, (where *Christians* were first distinguished by that appellation,) situate on the Orontes, was by succeeding emperors made not only its metropolis, but also the metropolis of the whole East.—The Syrians were especially devoted to the worship of the Sun ; at the same time acknowledging Jupiter and Apollo as the chief, if not only, divinities.— The *Genius Urbis* is represented on Imperial colonial coins of cities in this province, particularly those of the first rank, under the form of a woman with turreted head.—See Vaillant's *Num. Imp. in Col. ;* also the words *Antioch* and *Astarte.*

SYRIA. S. C.—Eckhel gives from the Imperial cabinet, a large brass of Antoninus Pius, having on its reverse this legend, and for type a

woman with turreted head, holding in her right
hand, apparently, a triple crown, or perhaps a
basket *(canistrum)* ; in her left hand is a cornucopiæ. This female figure has her right foot
placed on an emerging river deity.—Mionnet
recognises this coin amongst the *grand* bronze
of Antonine.—In the catalogue of the Museum
Theupoli is a similar medal, with the addition
of COS. II. to the inscription.—The sagacious
author of *Doct. Num. Vet.* (vol. vii.) couples
this coin with the SCYTHIA, &c., of the same
emperor, as furnishing in the type of its reverse,
an instance of the *aurum coronarium*, presented by a Roman province to the reigning
prince.—See the word, p. 115 of this Dictionary.

T

T. This letter of the Roman alphabet is
seen as a mint-mark in the field of many family
coins, and also on medals of the lower empire.

T. double is a mark of the plural number.—
See GENTT. *Gentium*, as in Constantine the
Great.

T. *Tarraco* Hispaniæ.—C. V. T. T. *Colonia
Victrix Togata Tarraco.*—Bimard, and Vaillant.

T. *Tatius.*—TA SABIN. *Tatius Sabinus.*

T. *Temporum.*—T. F. *Temporum Felicitas.*—
Bimard ad Jobert, and Vaillant.

T. *Tertia.*—T. ARL. *Tertia Arelatensis
(officina monetaria signavit nummum.)*—Money
struck at Arles in the *third* mint. So T. CON.
Tertia Constantinopolis officina, &c.

T. *Tertio.*—D. T. *Die tertio,* as on coin of
Volteia.—Vaill. *Fam.*

T. *Tiberius.*—T. GRACCHVS. *Tiberius Gracchus.*—Eckhel *Cat.*

T. *Titus.*—T. DIVI. VESP. F. Titus son of
the Divine Vespasian.—On a large brass of
Titus, the legend of the head reads as follows :
—IMP*erator* T*itus* CAES*ar* VESP*asianus*
AVG*ustus* P*ontifix* M*aximus* TR*ibunicia*
P*otestate* P*ater* P*atriæ* CO*n*S*ul* VIII.—The
Emperor Titus Cæsar Vespasianus, the August
Sovereign Pontiff, enjoying the Tribunitian
Power, Father of the Country, Consul for the
8th time.

T. *Traducta.*—COL. I. T. *Colonia Julia
Traducta.*

T. *Tranquillitas.*—B. T., in the field of coins
of the lower empire : *Beata tranquillitas.*

T. *Tribunicia.*—T. P. *Tribunicia Potestate.*

T. P. *Treveris percussa.*—Coin struck at
Treves.

T. *Tutelaris,* or *Tutator,* on denarii of
the Fabia, Licinia, and Octavia families, this
letter being placed before the head of a Genius,
of whom Censorinus says,—"Genius, that guardian under whom every mortal was born and
lives."

Tabellæ—Tablets or Billets.—These are made
the subject of more than one type, on coins of
the *Cassia* family, on account of the *lex tabellaria* carried by L. Cassius in the year V.C. 653,
for the purpose of securing to the Roman people
the right of voting by billet (or ballot) in all
judgment cases, for all alleged crimes and mis-

demeanors, excepting murder.—See *Suffragia ;*
also *Cassia* gens.—The letters L.D. were inscribed
on *Tabellæ* to signify *Libero, Damno,* used in
voting on questions of guilty or not guilty, at
judicial assemblies. One of the tablets marked
L.D. is seen at the back of a man's head, C.
CALDVS. COS. on a denarius of the *Coelia*
family.

The *Tabella* or *Tessera* in the hand of the
statue of *Liberalitas* was a square brass tablet,
on which the quantity of bread and the name of
the recipient were engraved, according to what
the liberality of the emperors had ordained to
be distributed to each citizen.—See *Tessera.*

TACITVS (Marcus Claudius), a noble Roman
of consular rank, who was not ashamed to

reckon the historian Tacitus among his ancestors;
and who, after an interregnum of eight months,
during which the empire remained wholly without a head, was, by the united assent of the
senate and the army, elected and declared
Augustus, A.D. 275, as the successor of the
illustrious Aurelian. The elevation of this
prince, whose merit and virtues placed him on
the throne of the Cæsars, at the age, it is said,
of 65, was hailed with universal joy by the
people of Rome and of the provinces. He was
a man of strict integrity, correct in morals,
benign and affable, and so addicted to the pursuit of literature, that he never suffered a day
to pass without reading or writing something.
Temperate in his habits, he appeared, when
emperor, in the same unostentatious dress to
which he had been accustomed in individual life,
nor would he permit his wife to wear either
diamonds or pearls. Yet he expended his own
immense fortune in contributing to the popular
gratification and comfort, causing public baths
to be built at his own cost, but commanding them to be shut before night.—Although
an involuntary and unwilling occupant of the
imperial seat, Tacitus, after having established
several laws for the maintenance of good order
and the preservation of internal peace, proceeded
quickly from Rome to join the army in Thrace.
The Scythians, who, having crossed the *palus
Mæotis,* had penetrated into the provinces of
Pontus, Cappadocia, and Cilicia, were arrested
in their career of devastation and cruelty by the
arrival of this brave sovereign, who, in conjunction with his brother Florianus, vanquished
those barbarians of the north, and compelled
them to take refuge within their own native
forests. But, as he was returning from this
successful expedition into Europe, he died,
according to some writers, at Tarsus, according
to others, at Tyana, in March, A.D. 276, either

of fever, or through the treachery of certain military conspirators concerned in the assassination of Aurelian, whose death he had avenged by the capital punishment of most of his murderers.—His coins, which are very rare in gold, are still rarer in brass medallions and second brass; but common in small brass, from one of which the engraving above was made : his style is IMP. CL. TACITVS AVG.—IMP. C. M. CL. TACITVS P. F. AVG., or INVICTVS AVG.

Tæda.—See *Torch.*

T. AEL. Titus Aelius.—Prenomen and surname of Antoninus Pius.

Tænia, fillet or wreath.—An ornament for the head, which the figure of Victory on coins often holds in her hand. This head band, the attribute of heroes, in the Homeric age, and called by the Greeks στεφανὴ, became the coronal and diadem of a later period.

TAMPIL. *Tampilus.*—Surname of the Baebia family.

Tarpeia virgo.—On denarii of the *Petronia* and *Tituria* families two soldiers are seen, apparently in the act of casting their bucklers upon a young woman, who, with arms uplifted, seems already sinking amidst an overwhelming heap of shields. This type recalls to mind a well known incident of early Roman story, in which, with no small inconsistency of narration, a virgin, at the period of Romulus's war with Tatius and the Sabines, is made to earn immortality by a deed of perfidious treason to her country; and to give her name to the highest rock of the Capitoline Hill at the price of sacrificing her life to her sordid love for "gold bracelets."—" It is pretended (observes Visconti) that this woman was the daughter of a warrior to whom Romulus had confided the defence of the capitol, and it is added that the price of the treason was to have been the bracelets of gold which the Sabines wore round the left arm.—Propertius (*L.* iv. *el.* iv.) supposes that the female named Tarpeia was a priestess, and that she had fallen in love with the enemy's general or prince."—See *Petronia.*

Tarquinius Priscus, king of the Romans, having subdued the Tuscans, is said to have assumed the *paludamentum* from that conquered nation. His figure is represented, with that of the Augur Navius, on a brass medallion of Antoninus Pius.—See NAVIVS.—Eckhel quotes Macrobius to show that a son of this Tarquin distinguished himself whilst yet a boy by an act of valour against an enemy in battle, similar in description and in the honour of its reward to that which is alluded to in the remarkable inscription on a coin of the *Æmilia* family, as achieved by the stripling M. Lepidus, and which Val. Maximus explains to the very letter.—See *Aemilia.*

TARQVITIA.—a family embracing members both of the patrician and the plebeian order. Its surname, on a coin of foreign die, is *Priscus.* One in silver, out of but two numismatic varieties, has for legend and type of obverse C. ANNI*us* T. F. T. N. PRO COS. EX S. C. *Titi Filius, Titi Nepos, Proconsule Ex Senatus Consulto.* The head of a woman; and of the reverse Q.

TARQVITI. P. F. Q. *Quintus Tarquitius Publii Filius Quæstor.* Victory in a biga.—Tarquitius Priscus appears as proconsul on medals of Nicæa in Bithynia.—See *Annia gens.*

Tarraco, a city, and *colony* of Hispania citerior, or the nearer Spain—of which it was the capital, and thence the province itself was also called Hispania Tarraconensis. Situate at the mouths of the Tulcis (now Franconi) river, its foundation is ascribed to Scipio Africanus. The Romans of Tarraco took part with Cæsar against Pompey's lieutenants; and afterwards professed on all occasions to be influenced by the greatest attachment and devotion to the person and government of Augustus—a fact which the legends and types on some of its numismatic monuments serve to place in a very servile and superstitious point of view.—The modern name of this celebrated old city is *Tarragona,* on the coast of what is now *Catalonia.* Some of the coins of this colony are inscribed with the initial letters C. V. T., which are interpreted *Colonia Victrix Tarraco.* The surname of *Victrix* was generally given as a reward of good desert to cities and colonies founded or re-established by Julius Cæsar.—On others of its coins, we read C. V. T. T., which Vaillant considers to mean *Colonia Victrix Togata Tarraco,* founding as he does the epithet *Togata* on a passage in the 3rd book of Strabo, from which it would appear that the Tarraconensians distinguished themselves from the inhabitants of other colonies in Spain, by their use of the *toga* after the manner of the Romans. The judicious Bimard agrees in regarding this as a reasonable inference.—All the medals of Tarraco are of brass, and are rare—consisting of Colonial Autonomes and of Colonial Imperials, with Latin legends, from Augustus to Drusus.— On a first brass of this colony DIVVS. AVGVSTVS. PATER. is read on the obverse, accompanied by the head of Augustus.—The reverse has for legend only the letters C. V. T. T., the type being a handsome altar, with a palm tree on the top of it.

[This elegant coin forms an historical monument. When Augustus had set out on his warlike expedition against the Cantabri (a people occupying that region of Spain, now the Biscayan and Asturian provinces), in the year of Rome 728, the effects of anxiety and fatigue threw him into a bed of sickness. On this occasion the people of Tarraco, where he had halted, offered up public vows for his health, and afterwards raised an altar in memory of his restoration. It was on this altar that, according to the current story of that period, a palm tree was seen growing. Deputies from the colony made a journey to Rome, and congratulated the emperor on the remarkable circumstance, as being an auspicious presage of victory. To these he replied by saying—*Apparet quam sæpe accendatis*—"it is a sign that you do not very often light it." In quoting this shrewd and sarcastic *bon mot* from Quinctillian, Vaillant *(Col.* i. 45) adds that the Tarraconensians continued, nevertheless, to regard this event as an augury and symbol of their imperial founder's immortal glory; and we see that even after his death they studiously adorned their medals with a representation of this palm-surmounted altar.]

There is another first brass with similar obverse; but the reverse exhibits the initials c. v. t. t. within an oaken crown.

[The *corona quercea*, or wreath of oak leaves, being the civic crown, was struck on most coins of colonies, under Augustus, in honour of that emperor as the liberator of Roman citizens.

Both the altar and the oak crown appear on medals of this colony, dedicated to Tiberius—a fact which proves the continuance of the worship rendered to Augustus by the inhabitants of Tarraco, and their disposition to cherish and perpetuate the remembrance of the palm tree growing on his altar, as a marvellous event.]

On another first brass, struck at Tarraco, is seen on one side c. v. t. t. aeternitatis avgvstae, and a splendid temple of eight (in some ten) columns; on the other deo avgvsto, and the statue of Augustus, with radiated head, seated after the fashion and attitude of Jupiter, holding in the left hand the hasta, and in the right a *victoriola* (in other coins a patera).— See deo avgvsto, p. 318 of this Dictionary.

[The Tarraconensians, whilst as yet Augustus was living, and even suffering as a sick man within their walls, paid divine honours to him, as one in reality immortal. With Greek adulation (as Vaillant observes), pretending to recognise him, not merely as *Divus* (obtaining deification through the ceremonial of the apotheosis), but, as *Deus*, these colonists raised a statue to him, which they placed in a magnificent temple, consecrated, as this medal shews, *to his Eternity!*

Havercamp (in *Num. Reginæ Christinæ*) refers to Bartolo's engraving of this coin, which places a patera, instead of a figure of victory, in the right hand of the emperor.—Pellerin *(Mélange,* i. 255) edits two coins of Tarraco, one dedicated to Augustus, the other to Caius and Lucius Cæsares; the reverses of both which have for legend c. v. t. tar., thus marking the name of this colony by its three first letters, instead of the single initial t., as it is on all those coins of Tarraco, published by Vaillant.

Other medals of this colony bear the portraits of Tiberius, Julia, Drusus, and Germanicus.

TATIVS, king or general of the Sabines, who inhabited the city of Cures, with whom the Romans waged the first war. This brave chieftain proved a formidable enemy to the then infant colony of Rome, within whose walls he and his soldiers succeeded in penetrating, and they would perhaps have destroyed it, if the Sabine women, whom the Romans some time before carried off, had not made themselves the medium of consummating peace between their husbands and their own parents. The two people became united as one, at the expense of the power of Romulus, for he shared the functions of royalty with Tatius, and admitted into the senate one hundred of the principal Sabines. Tatius was soon after assassinated, and had no successor.— On a denarius of the *Tituria* family there is a

naked and bearded head, which accompanied by TA. in monogram, and the legend SABIN*us* [the Titurii, thus referring to their Sabine origin,] is generally considered by numismatists to be meant for that of Tatius, the Sabine.

Visconti, in his *Iconographie Romaine*, remarks that certain denarii of the *Tituria* and *Vettia* families present two very forcible instances of the eagerness with which those Roman magistrates, who presided over the mint of the republic, availed themselves of every opportunity to unite family pretensions with historical facts, in the legends and types of their coins. It is thus that Titurius Sabinus and Vettius Sabinus Judex, magistrates who prided themselves on their descent from the ancient Sabines, and probably from Tatius himself, have caused the head of this chieftain to be engraved on the coinage of their respective families. On both the medals in question we accordingly see the head of Tatius without ornament. And on the reverse of the Titurian denarius, the Sabines are represented as in the act of overwhelming, with their bucklers, the virgin Tarpeia, who had just betrayed the capital into their hands. The posterity of Tatius, doubtless, wished to do honour to the founder of their race by manifesting his hatred of traitors, even whilst profiting from the treason.—On the denarius of the Vettia family, we see, behind the head, the word SABIN*us*, being the surname of a branch of that family. The monogram, composed of a T. and an A., gives the two initial letters of the name *Tatius*. The two letters S. C.—*Senatus Consulto*—mark the fact that *Titus Vettius Sabinus Judex* caused this piece of money to be struck by the authority of the senate. "The bearded man, who stands in a car drawn by two horses (adds Visconti), is probably Tatius himself. The palm branch, which on the first described medal is at the side of the portrait, is on the second coin seen behind the figure of a Sabine prince, and bears allusion to his victories." [Part i., pp. 23-24.]

Taurus—A bull was immolated at the altars of several of the pagan deities.—Virgil points to two in particular—

Taurum Neptuno, taurum tibi pulcher Apollo.

It was also sacred to Jupiter, and to the Egyptian god *Apis*.—Represented on Roman coins, this animal is the symbol of a *colonia deducta*, or transplanted colony.—The figure of a bull appears on many family coins, and also on numerous imperial medals from Julian and Augustus down to Julianus II., either as a sacrificial victim, or at large, standing, walking, running, or butting with its horns.

Taurus et Elephas.—A brass medallion of Alexander Severus presents a bird's-eye view of the Flavian Amphitheatre at Rome, in which is seen an elephant, with driver on its neck, facing a bull.—See *Amphitheatre*.

Taurus et Leo.—The bull and the lion at the feet of a recumbent female are attributes of *Africa*, as on a coin of Sept. Severus.—The same two animals, with a human figure standing between them, appear on coins of *Viminacium* in

Mœsia Superior.—A bull torn in pieces by a lion appears on a coin of Probus; a bull, a lion, and a tiger, encountered by two men armed with spears, allusive to certain public shows and combats with wild beasts at Rome, are exhibited on a silver medal inscribed REGVLVS in the *Livineia* family.

Taurus et Mulier.—A bull on which a young woman is sitting, or rather, Jupiter under the form of a bull carrying away Europa on his back, is seen on a denarius of the *Valeria* family; also on a third brass colonial of Sidon, dedicated to Elagabalus.

Taurus irruens.—A bull rushing furiously along, delineated on a rare silver coin of the *Thoria* family is regarded by Eckhel as bearing allusion to the name of Thorius; "for Ͽ8ρıos or Ͽoρıos," says he, "signifies impetuous, and the bull on this medal carries himself with an air of great impetuosity, for which reason it seems probable that the Thurii, or Thorii, of Italy, caused the figure of a bull charging at full speed to be engraved on their coins."

Taurus Neptuni victima.—On a brass medallion of Commodus, inscribed VOTIS FELICIBVS, the reverse exhibits five ships, and a tower on a promontory, from which a bull is thrown down into the sea; before the tower are two men standing.—Haym (in his *Thesaur. Britan.* vol. ii.) explains this singular type as allusive to the African fleet sent out by the above-named emperor to fetch corn. "And here (says he) you see the sacrifice offered to Neptune, when the fleet set sail, it being the custom of the Romans on such an occasion to sacrifice a bull, and throw it into the sea; the two figures are priests who offered the sacrifice at the sea-side."
—Eckhel, who approves of this interpretation, goes on to explain an enigmatical type on a gold coin of Augustus, in the cabinet of Vienna, which represents Victory plunging a knife into the throat of a prostrate bull; and this he does at some length, by shewing it to be an ingenious mode of symbolizing Mount Taurus.

Taurus et Stellæ.—On coins of Julian II., with inscription SECVRITAS REIPVB*licæ,* a bull is frequently seen with two stars above its horns, or over its back. It is a well-known historical fact that this apostate from the Christian faith, with all his enlightened genius and philosophic learning, was superstitiously addicted to a system of polytheistic worship, chiefly borrowed from the Egyptians; and that he was in the habit of sacrificing whole hecatombs of bulls at the various altars of his favourite deities. Oiselius, commenting on this type, and referring to this leading feature in Julian's character, considers that by the bull that emperor meant to designate the god *Apis.*—Both Banduri and Eckhel favour this opinion.—See the words *Securitas Reipub.* for the substance of Eckhel's remarks on the question why a bull appears on so many of Julian the IInd's medals.

Telegonus, son of Ulysses, and the reputed founder of Tusculum. It is from him that the most noble family of the Mamilii, who came early to Rome from the former city, were accus-tomed to claim their origin.—See the word *Mamilia,* describing the elegant denarius of C. Mamilius Limetanus, on which the anecdote of Ulysses recognised by his faithful dog Argus is interestingly illustrated.

Telephus, the fabled son of Hercules, by Auge, daughter of Aleus, King of Tegea, in Arcadia.—On a brass medallion of Antoninus Pius, in the *Mus. Albano,* the reverse (without epigraph) exhibits Hercules standing near a tree, looking at a little boy suckled, on a mountain, by a doe. On the top of the mountain is an eagle.—Vaillant and Venuti both regard this type as referring to the twin brothers and wolf of the Roman story. But Eckhel, after comparing it with that on the coin of Pergamus in Mysia, clearly shows that it relates to the infancy of Telephus, who being, according to the Greek myth, the offspring of 'a furtive amour, was abandoned at his birth by his unhappy mother, on Mount Parthenius, where, left exposed to die, he was miraculously suckled and fostered with maternal fondness by a doe. The presence of the eagle above is explained as an interposition of Jupiter himself, who sends his watchful bird to guard the helpless child—ordaining that the deserted progeny of his own son by Alcmena should not miserably perish, but be preserved for a high destiny.—See copious reasons for this interpretation given in *Doct. Num. Vet.* vol. ii. 468, and vol. vii. 34.

Telesphorus, the son, or at least the companion, of Æsculapius—symbol of success attendant on the exercise of the healing art, and allusive to that state of a person with whom disease has ended, and to whom perfect health is restored. Telesphorus is figured as a little boy in a hooded cloak, standing by Æsculapius.—In an antique painting he is introduced at the side of Atropos (one of the Fates), whose arm he holds back at the moment when she is going to sever the thread of life.—Amongst those coins of Caracalla which bear express reference to the alleged recovery of that ferocious tyrant from a horrible complication of diseases, mental as well as bodily, and to the various deities (such as Apollo, Serapis, Hercules, Sol, Luna, &c.) who, during the paroxysms of his painful illness, were invoked for his relief, there is one on which are a bearded man, naked to the waist, with staff and serpent, and a dwarfish figure, wrapped in a mantle, standing near him.—Here then we see Æsculapius and *Telesphorus* jointly recognised as deities who were supposed to bestow their care and power on the reparation of health. Dion records the fact of Caracalla's having implored the aid of Æsculapius; and to the same period of Caracalla's history belongs what Herodianus relates of him—viz., that passing from Thrace into Asia, he went to Pergamus, in order that in the city where the god of medicine was adored with peculiar veneration, he might place himself under this salutary influence, as was the custom. This is clearly confirmed by the Greek coins of the Pergamenses, on not a few of which Caracalla is represented offering sacrifices and *vota* to Æsculapius. It is to this subject that allusion is made on that remarkable gold medal edited by Vaillant (*Pr.* ii. p. 249), the reverse of which has for epigraph PM. TR. P. XVII. COS. IIII. P. P.; and for type, the emperor dressed in the paludamentum, sacrificing at the altar of Æsculapius, which stands before the doors of a temple. (Pergamus contained a magnificent temple dedicated to that divinity.)—Buonarotti also gives a fine bronze medallion of Caracalla, with Æsculapius and Telesphorus, struck on the same occasion of that emperor's going to Pergamus (about A.D. 215), to be cured of his corporeal ailment, and (hopeless case for a fratricide!) of his *mind's disease.*—See *Æsculapius.*

Tellus (the earth), considered to be the same pagan deity as *Cybele, Mater Magna,* and *Rhea.* —At the celebration of the secular games at Rome, a sow pig was, as a customary victim, slain in sacrifice to *Tellus,* personifying the fertile mother of all things terrestrial.—See LVD. SAEC. FEC.

TELLVS STABIL.—A man in a short rustic vestment stands holding in his right hand an implement which appears to be a weed-hook; and in his left a rake. Gold and silver of Hadrian.

TELLVS STABIL.—A woman, seated on the ground, leaning upon a basket of fruit, and touching with her right hand a large globe. Silver and brass of Hadrian.

[These types, and the epigraph which accompanies each—*Tellus Stabilita*—(the earth firmly established) are evidently allegorical; but numismatists seem more inclined to reject each other's explanations on the subject than to impart any that shall be satisfactory either to themselves or to their readers.—Tristan gives us, in one of his neat engravings, a medal, having this legend on its reverse, with the male figure holding in one hand a plough share, in the other an *anchor,* and at his feet are two corn-ears. The commentary of this fine old French writer is to the following effect, viz., that the device of "the earth rendered firm" (*La Terre Affermie*), does not allude solely to the re-establishment of agriculture, by the country being relieved from all fears of war as well external as domestic, and a permanent state of peace being secured for "the whole world" by the prudent and wise policy of Hadrian; but it also seems to praise that emperor for his "piety," as evinced by the zealous attention he manifested to the ceremonies of religious worship in every part of the empire—conduct which had so propitiated the favour of the gods, that the Roman provinces, it was believed, would thenceforth be no more desolated by earthquakes, such as at the commencement of his reign had frequently occurred, to the ruin of many cities, but which, according to Spartian, Hadrian had caused to be effectually and in some instances splendidly rebuilt. Thus restoring confidence where terror before prevailed, and plenty where

famine had annihilated everything.—The anchor (adds Tristan, *Com. Hist.* i. 479) is the mark of the one, and the plough-share and corn-ears indicate the other.—Vaillant entertains an unhesitatingly expressed opinion that the drainage of the lake *Fucinus* is the subject alluded to— an opinion certainly untenable.—Eckhel, whilst throwing a doubt on Tristan's ingenious attempt at interpretation, and utterly rejecting Vaillant's as "preposterous," offers on his own part no other clue to the occult meaning of this reverse, *than one* which rests on a brass medallion of Hadrian, of whose genuineness he confesses a strong suspicion. It is quoted from the *Mus. Theupoli,* as having for legend TELLVS STA-BILITA (at full length), and for type a woman seated on the ground, who places her right hand on a globe, round which are seen several boys, or girls.—A similar type appears on a coin of Julia Domna, inscribed FELICITAS TEM-PORVM. But neither Mionnet nor Akerman recognises the medallion described by the editor of the *Museum Theupoli,* as bearing the epigraph of *Tellus Stabilita.*—Hadrian, however, as Eckhel himself observes, might truly be said (in a political sense) to have given stability to the earth, when, having suppressed all internal seditions, and banished all apprehension of foreign wars, he took measures for restraining the avarice of governors, and diffused throughout his vast dominions the blessings of peace, liberty, and public safety.]

TELLVS STABIL. P.M. TR. P. XII. IMP. VIII. COS. V. P.P.—On a very fine and rare brass medallion, the obverse of which (see Akerman's Catalogue) presents the head of Janus with the features of *Commodus,* we see (on the reverse) the above quoted legend, whilst the type is a woman seated on the ground,

touching with her right hand a large globe, which has stars on it, and over which four young boys, or girls, personifications of the seasons, seem to be passing. The woman's left arm rests on a basket: (in some specimens she holds a cornucopiæ on the same arm): close behind her is a vine tree.

[Vaillant, in his illustrations and interpretations of brass medallions, selected from the *De Camps* Cabinet, has given an engraving of this coin, remarking that, by its design and title, Commodus wished to make it appear that the husbandman, throughout the Roman world, was enabled in this year of peace to devote himself, with feelings of perfect security, to agricultural pursuits. Hence, *tellus stabilita est*—the earth is made fast—is established—society is restored to a settled and safe condition. The four young figures represent the four seasons of the year (typified also on another coin of this prince)—the celestial globe necessarily revolves to the increase of the earth's produce, at the will of *Tellus*, or Providence, who, personified in a sitting posture, lays her hand on it, as betokening that the abundance of all things is in her gift, as denoted by the cornucopiæ.—Although to Hadrian the exaggerated praise *telluris stabilitæ* might have been with some degree of political justice attributed, yet the same eulogy conferred, as by this coin it is, on so profligate, so degraded, and so ruinous a government as that of Commodus, wears too grossly the impress of adulatory prostitution to be viewed otherwise than with unmixed disgust.]—See FELICITAS TEMPORVM.

Temo.—The helm or rudder of a ship, which directs and holds it on its course. It was represented on coins to designate the sea, as a globe was to symbolise the land, over both which the power of Imperial Rome had so far and widely spread itself. The rudder is the sign of a maritime city, and also of excellence in nautical science and skill: it is also the emblem of naval strength. Thus we find maritimo sovereignty denoted by it on denarii of the *Carisia*, *Egnatia*, and *Mussidia* families. The *gubernaculum* or rudder appears as an invariable attribute in the right hand of *Fortune*, who was believed to hold sway over human affairs. It is held, or placed, sometimes in an inverted, at other times in a transverse position; and again, planted upright on the ground: occasionally we see it crosswise with the prow of a ship. On coins of the *Egnatia* family, it stands with a ship's prow, between Honos and Virtus. The rudder of a galley, under the guidance of the steersman, is a type on a coin of Hadrian. It is in the hand of Victory, on a medallion of Constantine jun. (Buonarotti, p. 398); in the right hand of *Annona*, as in Antoninus Pius and Caracalla; and is frequently held by the Genius of a colonial city. It is seen in the left hand of *Æternitas*, as in Faustina senior; and of *Asia*, as in Hadrian; of a *centaur*, as in Gallienus; of *Concord*, as in Postumus; of *Felicitas*, as in Tetricus; upon a *globe*, as in Tiberius and Elagabalus; in the left hand of *Salus Augusti*, as in Antoninus Pius. The rudder also is combined with an *anchor* on the prow of a ship, on a coin of the *Cæcilia* family; on a *naval trophy*, as in Augustus; at the feet of *Pietas*, on a denarius of M. Antony; on a *chariot* within a temple, as in Augustus; near a globe in the left hand of the emperor, as in Antoninus Pius; grouped with a globe, the apex, the caduceus, and the cornucopiæ, on a denarius of Julius Cæsar, struck by Mussidius. See FORTVNA.—There are medals on which the ancients have given to Nemesis the rudder which usually accompanies Fortune. Buonarotti furnishes an instance of this in his *Osservazioni.*

Tempestates Anni quatuor.—See *Seasons.*

Tempestas, the weather.—In his observations on a medallion of Commodus, bearing the legend of TOTIS FELICIBVS, and exhibiting a curious type, described by Haym (see *Taurus*), Eckhel, after successively quoting Plutarch and Valerius Flaccus, Cicero and Virgil, to shew that it was a custom of the ancients to sacrifice bulls and other victims, in imploring the gods, either to avert storms, or to send auspicious gales, or to appease the fury of the sea, goes on to prove that *Tempestas*, as a deity presiding over the weather, was worshipped at Rome. And this he does (*Doct. Num. Vet.* vol. vii. p. 129) through the medium of a very ancient inscription, a dedication by Scipio Barbatus (see *Reinesius Inscr.* vi. 34, p. 410); and also by the two following lines of Ovid (*Fast.* vi. 193) :—

Te quoque, Tempestas, meritam delubra fatemur;
Quum pœne est Corsis obruta classis aquis.

Templum, Temple; a building appropriated to the public exercise of a religious worship. In the earliest times, nations paid adoration to their divinities, simply at altars of coarse materials and of the rudest construction, raised in the open air on elevated ground, or in solitary woods. To these soon succeeded buildings little differing from the usual dwellings of the people, but consecrated to the service of their gods. The introduction of temple-building, properly so called, was gradual amongst the various nations of antiquity. The Egyptians, Phœnicians, and Syrians, taking the lead in civilization, taught, through the instrumentality of their colonies, the method of constructing temples to the Greeks, who in their turn, having in process of time surpassed all other communities in civilization, devoted their superior knowledge in the arts to the object of erecting temples in the most beautiful style as well as on the most majestic scale. It was solely from Grecian models, and under Grecian designs, that the Romans were subsequently enabled to render any of their own sacred edifices worthy of being numbered amongst the *chefs d'œuvre* of architecture. The first temples, neither of the Greeks nor of the Romans, were otherwise than inconsiderable in size. According to Vitruvius they were round in form, but afterwards built square. This fact is confirmed by coins struck in successive ages. Even in later times, when increased riches were employed in rearing temples, they were not distinguished by any extraordinary extent or magnitude, except in the case of those dedicated to the tutelary deities of a city or a colony, or to those principal divinities which were the common objects of worship among entire nations. The most usual form of Greek and Roman temples was that of an oblong square; sometimes it was circular; and then they were covered with a cupola, of which the Pantheon at Rome still offers a striking example.

As the statue of its presiding deity was the most sacred object in the temple and the most conspicuous ornament of the *adytum* or *cella*, so the utmost care was bestowed on the work-

manship of images, and the most eminently
gifted artists were employed to execute such
pieces of sculpture.—In the earliest periods
citron and cedar-wood were the materials used;
afterwards, these statues were cast in brass, but
more frequently chiseled in marble, especially
in the Parian and Pentelic marbles. Among
the bronze idols at Rome was that of *Jupiter
Tonans*. Gold and ivory, and even precious
stones, were conjoined with marble to increase
the magnificence of these images. The names
of Alcamenes, of Polyclitus, of Naucydes, of
Thrasymedes, and above all of Phidias, are recorded by Greek writers as those of the chief
statuaries whose talents were devoted to these
exquisite works. Nor was the sister art of
painting less in requisition to decorate the interior walls: on the contrary, the most celebrated pencils, such as those of Polygnotus,
Micon, Zeuxis, and others were dedicated to
honour gods and goddesses, demigods and heroes,
by producing vivid representations of their
fabled personifications, attributes, and exploits.
Besides the statue of the divinity to whom the
temple was consecrated, there were occasionally
other images placed either in the *cella*, or in the
portico. Some of these bore reference to the
principal deity; others served merely for ornament, or were preserved there as sacred gifts.
This was the case in most of the metropolitan
cities in Greece and Asia; whilst at Rome many
temples were adorned with various statues.
In the temple of Apollo Palatinus was an image
of Latona, by Cephisodotus, son of Praxiteles;
and one of Diana, by Timotheus.—The steps
by which the temples were surrounded appear
to have been amongst the most important features of their general design, constituting at
once their bases and distinguishing them from
all other edifices.

Besides what may be gleaned from the remains of many different kinds of temples both
in Greece and Italy, there is much that is well
calculated to throw light on the subject, which
medals exhibit relative to the various forms of
structures so clearly identified with the religious
rites and customs of the heathen world. "The
ancients (says M. Millin) often adopted these
buildings for the types of their coins; according
to which we find not only that the form of some
temples was square, and others circular; but
also that some were raised on steps that encompassed the buildings on all sides—whilst others
were elevated on an artificial foundation, to
which the ascent was by a flight of stairs. There
are to be seen on medals delineations of temples,
whose *façades* display from four to six, eight,
and even ten columns.—A coin of Verus, struck
at Corinth, shews a tetrastyle (temple with
four pillars in front); and a medal of Trajan,
struck in Galatia, presents to us a prostyle
(row of columns in front of a temple), in which
have been suppressed the two pillars that should
have appeared between those at the angles, in
order to give the needful room for the image
of *Mensis*, chief deity of the pagan Galatians.
Many medals of Corinth have on their reverses

different figures of circular temples, which are
also found on some Imperial coins, struck in
that city. On these latter the temples of Vesta,
of Mars, and of Juno Martialis, are favourite
types.—The temples of those gods, who were
the objects of a city's especial worship, are seen
on different medals, struck under the empire, in
Greece, Proconsular Asia, and other provinces and
colonies.—The temple of Jupiter Capitolinus at
Rome is represented not only on a medal of the
Petillia family, struck under the republic, but
afterwards on the coins of many emperors, such
as Vespasian and Domitian, who restored that
sacred edifice which had often become a prey to
the flames.—On medals of Augustus we also see
the temple of *Jupiter Tonans*, which that prince
caused to be built in a style of great magnificence."—For an able and copious article
on the temples of the ancients, see Millin's
Dictionnaire des Beaux Arts.

Temples of various forms, and situate in
divers places, are represented on medals of the
Imperial series, with scarcely a break, from
Julius Cæsar to Maxentius.—See also those
struck in the colonies.—The catalogue of the
Vienna Cabinet *(Cimel. Vindob.* i. p. 94),
Vaillant's *Præstant.* i. p. 67, and Buonarotti's
Num. Carpeg. (tb. f. 5, p. 16 and 19) respectively exhibit most beautiful specimens of
templa decastyla—temples with ten columns
in front.

Templa, or *Ædes deorum.*—The temples of
deities represented on Roman coins were those
which, to shew their "piety," were erected, at
first by the senate and people; and which, after
the extinction of the consular government,
were either built or restored by different emperors. They were also founded in honour, and
for the worship, of those emperors themselves,
as well at Rome as in the provinces. [See
Spanheim, *Pr.* ii. 643 seq.]—At Rome, when a
temple was about to be constructed, strict regard was had to certain rules of *inauguration*
and of *dedication*. It was under the forms
prescribed by the Augurs, as interpreters of the
will of the gods, that the spot where the temple
was to be placed, and the space it was to
occupy, were determined upon. The site was
then purified and the foundation stone laid by
the magistracy, amidst the solemn rites of the
priesthood, in the presence of the people. The
temple having thus been founded, the ceremony
of dedication was performed by the consuls, or
by the emperors, or sometimes by *duumvirs*
specially chosen with the people's consent, and
under the authority of the senate. On these
occasions the presiding pontiff announced, in a
set form of words, the appropriation of the
edifice to sacred purposes: he then proceeded to
consecrate it by laying his hand on the door-
posts, at the entrance of the temple; and then
followed sacrifices and public games.

Buildings called *Ædes Sacræ* differed, according to Varro, from *Templa*, inasmuch as the
former, though consecrated like the latter, were
never inaugurated, nor were they dedicated by
the authority of the senate. The *ædes* would

indeed seem to have been nearly of the same form as the *templum*, but less sumptuous. There were in Rome a great number of *ædes*, the smallest of which were called *ædicula*,— Structures called *delubra* were also distinct from *templa*, although the two are often confounded together in the works of ancient writers. The *delubrum* appears to have been the shrine; or the place where the statue of the deity or the altar stood. The *sacellum* (or chapel) differed entirely from a temple, being only enclosed within a wall, and without a roof.— It is evident, from Livy [L. x. c. 40], that *fana* were different from temples, although this word was in ordinary acceptation used by the old writers to designate whatever edifice was set apart for the worship of any deity or deities. Some contend that the *sacellum* was a small place, consecrated to some particular god or goddess, and furnished with an altar.— Sacred places, belonging to private individuals, were called *lararia*, or *sacraria*, the one from the *lares*, the other from being dedicated by each person to his household god.

Temples were erected not only to the celestial divinities but also to Rome itself as a deified city; not only to Clementia, Concordia, Pax, and other qualities, but to the healths of emperors whilst living, and to their memory after death. —It was also a custom with the Romans to dedicate temples, erect altars, and sacrifice victims to the angry or displeased gods : witness those coins which bear the images, or heads, of *Ve-Jupiter*, of *Pallor* and of *Pavor*. Nay, they erected altars and temples to Fever *(Febris)*, whom they worshipped through fear of that disorder, and that it might prove less hurtful.

Temples at Rome.—In that city nothing was more sacred, nor more· celebrated than the temple of *Jupiter Capitolinus* (see the words.)— A temple was also dedicated by Augustus to *Jupiter Tonans*, which appears, amongst the coins of that prince, represented with a front of six columns. Other medals of Augustus exhibit a four-columned temple, IOVI DEO; likewise one of six columns, inscribed IOV. OLY. *(Jovi Olympio)* to Jupiter Olympius.—Other temples, consecrated to this monarch of the heathen deities, display themselves on imperial coins, such as that of *Jupiter Custos*, which Domitian consecrated to that divinity, whose guardian image he also placed there.—Caracalla dedicated a temple, in the city, to Jupiter the Preserver *(Jovi Sospitatori)*, and Alexander Severus another to Jupiter the Avenger *(Jovi Ultori)*. These three edifices, their porticos adorned with statues, appear on coins of the said princes as edited by Tristan, Gessner, Spanheim, Vaillant, and others.—The image of *Jupiter Conservator*, within a temple of six columns, appears on the larger medals of Diocletian. The temples of Mars were numerous (see the word *Mars*.)—On a very rare gold coin of Augustus (CAESARI AVGVSTO S. P. Q. R.), the reverse type is a circular temple of four columns, in which a legionary eagle is placed in a triumphal chariot.— Vaillant referring to it *(Impp. Rom.* ii. 35)

says, "This round temple I imagine to be the one which Augustus built in honour of Mars the Avenger. That that edifice was of such a form is established by the type of a silver coin of the same emperor, bearing the epigraph of MARTI VLTO*ri.* For we find from Suetonius *(Oct. Aug.* c. 32), that Augustus had no temples erected to his honour even in the provinces, except in the name of Rome as well as of himself [ROM. ET AVG.] But within the walls of Rome he most strictly abstained from that honour."—It has already been said that temples were consecrated not only to gods and goddesses, and to others regarded in the light of divinities, but also to the emperors themselves in Rome. Thus, in pursuance of a *senatus consultum*, a temple was erected by Augustus, inscribed DIVO IVL. or DIVO IVLIO EX S.C., in the *adytum* or sanctuary of which was seen the image of Julius Cæsar holding the inaugural *insigne* of the *lituus*.—Vitruvius alludes to this temple and image, which also appear on a gold coin struck under Augustus, as edited by Spanheim and others, and confirmed as genuine and rare by Mionnet. This temple of "Cæsar deified" was afterwards held by the Romans so inviolably sacred that, according to Dion, no one who took refuge in that sanctuary could be withdrawn therefrom against his will—a privilege which, according to the same writer, had not been granted to the temple of any god, not even to the asylum of Romulus.—It is further related by Dion, that a *sacrarium*, or place set apart for divine worship was, by order of Tiberius, built in honour of Augustus ; and the house at Nola, where he died, was converted into a temple.—Pliny mentions the Palatine temple ; his words are—*in Palatii templo, quod fecerat D. Augusto conjux Augusta.* (N. H. L. xx. c. 19). This fact of a temple raised on Mount Palatinus to the honour of Augustus after his death by his widow is confirmed, through the medium of a first brass of Caligula, inscribed DIVO AVG, S.C., with three figures sacrificing before a temple ; and that this or some other temple of Augustus at Rome was restored by Antoninus Pius, we learn from coins of the last-named emperor, inscribed AEDES DIVI AVG. REST*ituta ;* and TEMPL*um* DIVI AVG. REST. COS. IIII., with a figure seated in an octostyle temple *(see the words).*—That there was a temple built and dedicated at Rome to Faustina senior, the wife of Antoninus Pius, is proved by the very beautiful one represented, with six columns in front, on a silver coin of that empress, struck after her death and consecration. The legend of the obverse gives her the title of DIVA, and that of the reverse reads AED*es* DIV*æ* FAVSTINAE.

Other temples at Rome, dedicated to the honour of different emperors, form the types of some of their coins, as in the MEMORIAE AETERNAE of Val. Maximinianus, Constantius Chlorus, Romulus, and others. And indeed not at Rome only, but in the provinces also, temples were consecrated to emperors, as ancient writers affirm, and as may be seen on medals.

An example of this kind is offered in the fine silver medallion of Augustus, which presents a temple of six columns, with ROMa ET AVGVSTus on the pediment, and COM. ASIA. *(Commune Asiæ)* on each side of the edifice, commemorative, as Tacitus and Dion both shew, of such a structure being raised, with the assent of Augustus, by "the commonwealth of Asia." Two remarkable coins of Hadrian bear witness to a similar honour paid to that prince during his life time, by the Bithynians—the one inscribed COM. BIT. *(Commune Bithyniæ)*, and with ROM. S. P. AVG. (on another it is S. P. R. AVG.) on the front of a temple with eight columns.—A brass medallion of Hadrian exhibits a temple with two columns; and the inscription S. P. Q. R. EX S. C. would seem to indicate that this architectural object had reference to some sacred fane dedicated to the same emperor's honour at Rome. There are likewise many Greek imperial medals of Pergamus, Smyrna, and Nicomedia, struck under Augustus, Tiberius, Trajan, Antoninus Pius, M. Aurelius, Commodus, Caracalla, &c., being representations of temples, some of the most magnificent of which were raised and consecrated to those princes respectively. Subjoined is a further notice of temples formerly existing *in Rome*, and which, as well as the divinities worshipped there, are typified on coins of the imperial mint, viz:—

Templum Apollinis Palatini.—Octavian (before he was called Augustus) built a temple to Apollo on the Palatine Hill. Indeed, according to Dion, in the year V.C. 718 he himself bore witness to its dedication, as is recorded on the marble of Ancyra:—TEMPLVMQVE APOLLINIS IN PALATIO FECI.—After the overthrow of Antony, at Actium, fresh honours were paid by Augustus to this Palatine Apollo, to whom we also find a dedicatory type and inscription on a brass medallion of Commodus, as edited by Vaillant from the De Camps cabinet.—See APOL. PALATINO.

Templum Bacchi et Herculis.—That Septimius Severus raised a magnificent temple to these two deities is proved by first and second brass coins, as well as by a bronze medallion of that emperor. —See DIS. AVSPICIBus.

Templum Clementiæ.—On the reverse of a silver coin, struck by one of the monetal triumvirs of Julius Cæsar, we see a temple with four columns in front, and the legend CLEMENTIAE CAESARIS. (See the words.) Eckhel places this medal under the date V.C. 710 B.C. 44; and quotes Dion as his authority for stating that, in the above-named year, it was decreed that a temple should be dedicated to Cæsar and to *Clementia;* and that M. Antony as *Flamen Dialis* (Priest of Jupiter) should be appointed to officiate in it as priest. There is a passage in Appian connected with this fact; and Plutarch also touches upon it, adding that the decree in question bestowed not pardon only, but honours, on Cæsar's enemies. Pliny likewise says that Julius was accounted *merciful* both by contemporaneous flattery and by the voice of posterity—*Cæsarei proprium et peculiare sit clementiæ insigne, qua usque ad pænitentiam omnes superavit.* (N. H. L. vii.

c. 25). And M. Aurelius, in a letter to his wife Faustina, which Valentius Gallicanus has preserved, says, "*Hæc* (Clementia) *Cæsarem deum fecit.*—See CLEMENTIA.

TEMPLVM DIVi AVGusti RESTitutum COS. IIII.—A temple with eight columns in front, within which are two figures; also two figures appear in the inter-columniation, and two more on the steps of the building.—This legend and type are found on gold, silver, and first brass of Antoninus Pius. There is likewise a silver coin of the same Emperor, bearing the same type, but having for legend AEDes DIVI AVG. REST. COS. IIII.

Representations of the temple of Augustus first appear on medals of Tiberius, struck about the year V.C. 787; also on coins of Caligula in various years of his reign.—The medals of Pius here quoted were struck in the year of Rome 912 (A.D. 159), and inform us, what history has omitted to mention, viz.: that the temple of Augustus, whether fallen into decay from time, or injured from other causes, was restored by the reverential piety of Antoninus Pius. There is every probability that, of the two images which appear within the temple, one is that of Livia *(Julia Augusta* as she is called on Latin coins), wife of Augustus, for Dion states that divine honours were conferred upon her by her grandson Claudius, who dedicated a statue to her in the temple of Augustus. Eckhel notices, as a circumstance worthy of observation, that this temple offers itself in the present instance under architectural features different from those which distinguish the same temple as exhibited on coins of Tiberius and of Caligula, above alluded to.—Whether this discrepancy arose from Antoninus having altered the form, in restoring the structure of the temple? or whether it was because the edifice represented on the medal above described was not the same as that typified on the coins of Tiberius and Caligula (for Sex. Rufus, besides the temple of Augustus in the eighth region, mentions another dedicated to the same Emperor in the fourth region, at Rome)? or whether the mint masters in depicturing the fronts of temples were always faithful to the originals? are questions which our illustrious German numismatist asks without offering any solution of his own.—But it has already been shewn that engravers of imperial medals, both Greek and Roman, were in the habit of taking liberties with architectural details to suit purposes connected with the introduction of figures. And the truth of the fact, respecting which, in the absence of all historical record, this medal furnishes the clearest proof, remains established in the legend which assigns to Antoninus Pius the honour of having *restored*, in his fourth consulate, *the temple of the deified Augustus.*— [See *Doct. Num. Vet.* vol. vii. p. 25.—See also a passing reference to this coin in p. 12 of this Dictionary; and the word DEDICATIO.]

Templum Jani.—See *Janus* and IAN. CLV. See also PACE., &c., IANVM CLVSIT.

Templum Jovis Capitolinis.—A first brass of Vespasian has for the type of its reverse (finely delineated in the *Thesaurus Morellianus* tab. 56, fig. 23) a most elegant temple of six columns, adorned with statues on the pediment and on each side. In the centre of this edifice is the image of Jupiter, on whose right stands the statue of Pallas, and on whose left appears that of Juno. This beautiful coin (another engraving of which is given by Pedrusi in his *Mus. Farnese)* exhibits a front view of the temple of Jupiter Capitolinus, which, after it had been destroyed by fire during the Vitellian disturbances, was magnificently restored by Vespasian; or, to use a more correct mode of expression, was raised anew from its foundations by order of that Emperor.—On the coin above described, besides the idol of Jupiter appear those of Minerva and Juno. We learn, indeed, from Tacitus, that Helvidius the Prætor, at the outset of the undertaking, invoked with prayers the united tutelage of those three principal divinities of the Greek and Roman superstition. Varro speaks of *Capitolinum vetus, quod ibi sacellum Jovis, Junonis, Minervæ.* And Martial, endeavouring to wheedle the Emperor Domitian into a resolution to repair the Capitol (for it had again been burnt during the reign of Titus) thus makes the flattering appeal :—

Quid pro culminibas geminis matrona Tonanti?
　　Pallada prætereo ; res agit illa tuas.
　　　　　　　　　　　　　　　Lib. ix. 4.

It is to be observed, that on the first brass medal in question Pallas stands on Jove's right hand, viz., in the place of greater dignity, and that to Juno is assigned the *second* place. Nor does this numismatic monument afford the only proof that, in the most superb and most venerated of all the temples in Rome, Pallas was placed on the right hand of Jupiter. As early after the foundation of the city as the year 391, Pallas occupied the same place in the same temple, according to Livy.—The mint of Antoninus Pius also furnishes confirmation to the fact, some of that Emperor's coins exhibiting the three deities above mentioned, sitting in the same order of personal distinction. From these and other evidences it clearly appears that the Romans assigned a higher degree of honour to Minerva than to Juno herself; the reason of which is doubtless to be traced to the fabled origin of their commonwealth, the Trojan Palladium having been transferred to Rome, as Horace sings :

Unde nil majus generatur ipso (Jove),
Nec viget quicquam simile, aut secundum:
Proximos illi tamen occupavit
　　Pallas honores.
　　　　　　　　　　　Lib. i. Carm. xii.

A similar type of the Capitoline temple, and the same order of the *cellæ* are to be seen on coins of Titus and Domitian.—*Doct. Num. Vet.* vi. 327-8.

Templum Mentis.—That *mens*—the mind— meaning that part of the rational soul which is the seat of understanding, thought, judgment—had a temple at Rome, and that vows were dedicated to it as to a deity, when the Romans were hard pressed by Hannibal, is affirmed by Livy. Plutarch also mentions a votive offering to *Dea Mens*, by Æmilius Scaurus, who lived in the time of the Cimbrian war. Cicero, and likewise S. Augustine *(de Civitate Dei)* allude to the same deification. *Mens quoque numen habet* is the expression of Ovid, who adds that *vota* were publicly made to "*mens*" as to a goddess, every year.—Propertius, too, makes this apostrophe :

Mens bona, si qua dea es, tua me in sacrario dono;

Indeed, as the philosophic Cicero in many passages of his writings truly affirms, the chief and noblest part of a living soul is "the mind," than which nothing that nature or that God has given to man is more excellent—more divine.

Templum Opis.—It is recorded by Victor, that there was a temple at Rome, situate in the eighth region, dedicated to Ops, the wife of Saturn— *Ædis Opis et Saturni in vico Jugario ;* to this edifice Cicero frequently alludes when he is complaining of seven million sesterces *(septies millies* HS) having been taken away from that temple by Mark Antony, which large sum had been deposited there by Julius Cæsar, as a provision towards meeting the expenses of a war then contemplated with the Parthians.—A marble, in Gruter, likewise confirms the fact of such a temple having existed at Rome, by the following inscription—LOCVS ADSIGNATVS AEDI OPIS ET SATVRNI. But, says Eckhel (vii. p. 143), it is to be observed that by the name *Ops* may be understood that abundance of all things, which makes life happy and comfortable *(commodum)* —a lot certainly not enjoyed by one who is *inops (i.e.* poor and destitute). And that *Ops*, in this sense, had a temple at Rome we have Cicero's authority for affirming.—Victor, moreover, describes an altar placed in the eighth region of that city, as that of *Ops et Ceres cum signo Vertumni.*—Macrobius says Saturn and Ops were believed to be the producers or inventors *(repertores)* as well of fruit as of corn. The same writer adds, *et terram Opem, cujus ope humanæ vitæ alimenta quæruntur ; vel ab opere, per quod fructus frugesque nascuntur.—Sat.* lib. i. (And the earth was called *Ops ;* by whose aid food for human sustenance was obtained ; or from *opus*, as being the work through which both fruit and corn are grown.) In another place Macrobius gives to *Ops* the name of *Consivia*, as from *conserendus*—to be sown or planted.— Plautus calls *Ops, opulenta*—rich and mighty Ops—the mother of Jupiter. The above passages, quoted by Eckhel from the old writers, combine to offer an easy explanation of the type on these coins, as well of Antoninus Pius as of Pertinax, which bear the unusual epigraph of OPI AVGustæ and OPI DIVINæ.—See these inscriptions.

Templum Pacis.—There is no *genuine* coin of Vespasian extant, bearing the representation of the Temple of Peace raised and dedicated by that emperor at Rome, in the year of the city 828 (A.D. 75). "This," says Eckhel, "is surprising, for the temple in question constituted a stupendous monument of Vespasian's munificence.

There have been those, indeed, and amongst them Spanheim himself, who thought that they had seen it so represented, but the coin which they have adduced in support of their opinion has for its type the temple, not of Peace, but of Jove in the Capitol. (For some description of which see IVPITER CAPITOLINVS.)—Herodianus calls Vespasian's temple of Peace the grandest and most beautiful in the world.—Pliny classes it *inter pulcherrima operum, quæ unquam;* and according to Josephus *(Bell. Jud.* l. vii., c. 5, 6, 7), there were collected together within its walls everything for the purpose of seeing which men had employed themselves in wandering over the face of the earth. Pliny enumerates the various master-pieces of art deposited there; and Josephus states that it contained the golden vases, and other sacred utensils of the Jews, brought from the temple at Jerusalem. But although, so far as is hitherto ascertained, Vespasian omitted to typify this celebrated temple of Peace on his coins, yet no deity or genius was more frequently exhibited on the products of his mint than Peace, as is shown by medals of every metal, struck in each successive year, from the commencement of his reign.—See PAX.

Templum Romæ et Veneris.—That Hadrian built a temple to Venus and Rome appears from the statement of Dion, who adds that the Emperor himself was his own architect in the erection of that edifice, and that by his orders Appollodorus, the most celebrated of the age, and whose works adorned Rome in the reign of Trajan, was put to death because he had freely found fault with those parts of the structure in which Hadrian had violated architectural rules. According to Spartian, this temple was of vast proportions—his expression is *"ita ut operi etiam elephantes XXIV adhiberet."* There is a brass medallion of Hadrian which bears on its reverse a beautiful temple with ten columns in front, adorned with various statues, inscribed with the initial letters S. P. Q. R. EX S. C.— Buonarotti, who gives an engraving of it in his *Osservazioni Istoriche* (pl.i. fig.5, p.16), thinks it highly probable that the fane represented on this medallion was intended for the very temple in question.—Eckhel dissents from this opinion, observing that the coin itself plainly records that the temple delineated on it, was raised in pursuance of a senatorial edict—EX. S. C.; whereas, according to Dion, as already cited, Hadrian himself was the architect of the temple erected to the honour of ROMA ET VENVS. It is, therefore, altogether uncertain to whom this sumptuous building was raised by order of the senate and the Roman people. But there is another brass medallion of Hadrian, described by the Editor of the *Museum Theupoli,* which has for legend VRBS ROMA AETERNA, and for type, Rome holding in her right hand a globe and in her left the *hasta,* and sitting within a a temple of six columns. To this medallion Eckhel joins a gold coin of the same Emperor, in the Vienna cabinet, on which Venus appears seated, holding a victory and spear, accompanied by the epigraph VENERIS FELICIS; and, in

explanation of this last-mentioned coin, he quotes Cassiodorus, from whose words it would appear that what was originally built for the temple of Rome and of Venus, was afterwards called the Temple of the City *(Templum Romæ et Veneris factum est, quod nunc Urbis appellatur).*—That the joint worship of those two deities continued to a late period in *templum Urbis* is amply attested by Prudentius *(Contra Symmach.* l. i. v. 219) in the following verses:—

Delubrum Romæ (colitur nam sanguine et ipsa
More deæ, nomenque loci ceu numen habetur
Atque Urbis: Venerisque pati se culmine tollunt
Templa, simul geminis adolentur thura deabus.)

TEMPORVM FELICITAS COS. IĪĪ.—A double cornucopiæ, on each of which is placed the head of an infant.

The type of this reverse, which is found on a first brass of Antoninus Pius, resembles that on a well known coin of Drusus junior. There seems no reason to doubt but that, in the present instance, it serves to represent two (twin) children born to M. Aurelius, probably about the year V.C. 902 (A.D. 149): their names, however, remain unascertained.

TEMPORVM FELICITAS.—A brass medallion of M. Aurelius, bearing on its obverse the bare head of that emperor, with legend of AVRELIVS CAESAR AVG. PII. F. TR. P. II. COS. II.; and on the other side, Hercules bearing a trophy in his left hand, and resting the right hand on his club, as he stands in a car drawn by four centaurs, each having different attributes.

In the second edition of his work *De la Rareté et du prix des Médailles Romaines,* Mionnet has given an exquisitely finished engraving of this splendid medallion. It is also engraved in Akerman's *Descriptive Catalogue,* vol. i. pl. c.

TEMPORVM FELICITAS,—Four children, designating the seasons of the year; on a brass medallion, the obverse of which exhibits the infant portrait of Annius Verus (son of Aurelius and of Faustina jun.) facing that of his brother Commodus—[in the French national cabinet]— with inscription of COMMODVS CAESar; VERVS CAESar.

It was during the childhood of these two princes (the former of whom died at a very early age), that this elegant type was produced for the first time on the coinage of Rome, though afterwards revived under Commodus, Caracalla, Diocletian, and others. It personifies, in suc-

cession, Spring, Summer, Autumn, and Winter, each season bearing some symbol of its respective gifts. The first holds a basket filled with flowers; the second a sickle ; the third a basket of apples and a bunch of grapes, which an animal (a panther) is leaping at ; the fourth a hare, and a bird suspended from a stick upon his shoulder ; all the figures are naked, except the one which represents winter, which is wrapped in vestments—as in the octagon tower of Andronicus, at Athens, Boreas is sculptured, enshrouding his face in a cloak. On the exergue we read an announcement of that public *happiness* which, in flattery to the reigning emperor, was boasted of as the characteristic *of the times* when the medallion was struck.—See FELICITAS TEMP. and FELICIA TEMPORA.

TEMPORVM FELICITAS—COS. IIII. P.P. —A woman, seated, holds forth corn-ears in her right hand ; before her four naked children are plucking fruit from a tree, and putting them into a vase.

Eckhel gives this as the reverse type of a brass medallion of Commodus, from the collection of Count De Vitzai, and after observing that the worn state of the coin prevents its date from being sufficiently ascertained, goes on to mention a similar . medallion in the Royal Museum at Paris, and in which specimen also the chronological marks are wholly wanting, apparently from the destructive effects of time. The four boys shew that the type was meant to symbolise the seasons, as clearly appears from a coin, with similar legend, struck under the same prince A.V.C. 944 (A.D. 191.)—See FELICITAS TEMP.

Same legend.—The emperor sitting on a globe, which is adorned with stars, holds in his extended right hand a large circle, on which four naked children are walking. He is himself crowned by Victory, who stands behind him. Jupiter, holding the *hasta*, is also present at the right hand of the prince.

The preceding is given by Eckhel, as from a brass medallion of Alexander Severus, from the Museum Albani.—The starry globe, the circle, the children—all indicate the Times *(Tempora)* and their eventful changes (under the form of the Seasons) as we learn from that rare coin of Hadrian, which bears for legend SAEC*ulum* AVR*eum*, and also from various medals of Commodus.—The obverse of the coin in question exhibits the head of the Emperor above-named opposite that of his mother, accompanied with the following inscription :—IMP. SEVERVS ALEXANDER AVG*ustus*, IVLIA MAMAEA AVG*usta* MATER AVG*usti* (The Empress Julia Mamæa, Mother of the Emperor).

TEMPORVM FELICITAS.—A woman lying on the ground, holds in her right hand an olive branch, and near her left hand is figured a rabbit.

Banduri gives this from the Vienna cabinet, as the legend and type on the reverse of a gold coin of Laelianus (one of those military chieftains who assumed the purple in the troubled reign of Gallienus).—From this monetary revival of the rabbit, as the old symbol of *Hispania*, it would appear that that country, or at least a portion of it, was subject at the period in question to these usurpers in Gaul.

TEMP. FEL. Buonarotti (in his *Osservazioni Istoriche*) gives the engraving of a fine and very rare brass medallion of Otacilia Severa (wife of Philip, sen.), on the reverse of which a matron of dignified appearance is seated in a chair of state, between two other female figures likewise clothed in the stola, who stand, the one holding a caduceus, the other the *hasta pura* and a small vase. At the knees of the seated woman are two children.

The learned and judicious Italian above cited describes this type as representing Otacilia in the form of Piety with her two children, one of which became the Philippus Cæsar and Augustus, whom his father associated with him in the empire, and the other a daughter whose name is not mentioned. In support of this interpretation, Buonarotti refers to the beautiful first brass of Domitia, in which that lady, wife of Domitian, is represented under the form of Piety, veiled and seated, and holding her right hand extended, as if pointing towards a child who stands before her. That child was meant for the infant Cæsar, her son by Domitian, as is shewn by the dedicatory legend, DIVI CAESAR*is* MATRI, and the epithet DIVVS as applied to the word CAESAR also shews that the imperial heir was already dead and consecrated. "And so likewise in the medallion before us (our author proceeds to say) the two figures of children were really meant for those of Otacilia, as is proved by the inscription FELICITAS TEMPORVM—as if the Roman empire had redoubled its happiness in the hope of that happiness being continued by the assurance of a succession to the throne, through the health and domestic felicity of the imperial family—hence it is that these two deities, *Hygeia* and *Felicitas*, are represented on the above-described coin, standing on each side of the Empress."—p. 297.

TEMPORVM FEL. or FELIC. or FELICIT. —A woman standing, holding a long caduceus and a cornucopiæ. On coins of Carausius and Allectus.

TER. or TERR. *Terrarum.*—ORB. TER. *Orbis Terrarum.*—PACI. ORB. TERR.

TER. *Tertium.*—CONG. TER. P. R. DAT. *Congiarium Tertium Populo Romano Datum.*— COS. DESIG. ITER. ET. TER. *Consul Designatus Iterum et Tertium.* Consul for the third time, was the highest honour in the republic of Rome.

TER. PAVLLVS.—The very rare gold coin, though common as a denarius, of the Aemilia family, on which this legend is found, has for its reverse type a subject of high historical interest ; for it serves to remind us of the defeat of Perseus, king of Macedonia, at the battle of Pydna, by the consul L. Aemilius Paullus, to whom he was compelled to surrender himself and his family. It also recalls to memory the important consequences of that victory ; namely, the reduction of the Macedonian kingdom to the state of a Roman province; and likewise refers to the magnificence of the triumph with which, in the year of Rome 587, Paullus was honoured for that signal achievement—a triumph than which, for wealth of spoils and gorgeousness of warlike pomp, nothing (according to the old writers) had till then been exhibited more splendid or on a grander scale. The type of this medal represents the consul, clothed in the toga, standing on one side of a trophy, with his right hand stretched forth as if he were in the act of delivering some command to Perseus, who himself stands on the opposite side, with his hands tied behind him, and accompanied by two children, his sons, with whom, as history informs us, this unhappy prince followed in chains the triumphal chariot of the victor. Respecting this remarkable coin there is much in Spanheim *(Pr.* ii. 220), but it is preferred to take advantage of the briefer and more useful observations of Eckhel, who regards the epigraph TER. PAVLLVS as ambiguous; for either, says he, it signifies the duration of the triumphal honours to have been extended over a space of three days, from the fourth kalends of December, of the year above-mentioned, of which Florus (L. ii. c. 12) thus speaks—*quippe cujus spectaculo triduum impleverit. Primus dies signa, tabulasque; sequens, arma, pecuniasque transvexit; tertius captivos, ipsumque regem attonitum adhuc, tanquam subito malo stupentem:* (alas, poor fallen monarch!) Or it means the three triumphs of Paullus, one of which was for his victories over the Ligurians; the second over Perseus; the third remains uncertain, (notwithstanding what the indefatigable Pighius could glean from Velleius.) But that there *were* three distinct triumphs, is a fact which, however controverted by some antiquaries, receives confirmation from a marble still existing at Rome, and which is quoted by Pighius as follows:—L. AEMILIVS. L. F. PAVLVS. COS. II. CENS. AVGVR. TRIVMPHAVIT. TER.—The obverse of the medal in question bears for legend PAVLLVS LEPIDVS CONCOR*Dia*, and for type the veiled head of Concord.—See *Aemilia* family.

TERENTIA, a plebeian family, whose surnames on its Roman coins were *Lucanus* and *Varro.* There are fourteen numismatic varieties belonging to this *gens*, the brass pieces of which are the *As*, or some of its parts, or struck by the moneyers of Augustus. The following is amongst the more rare in silver:—

VARRO PRO Q*uæstore*.—Bearded head with diadem, finishing in the form of a Terminus.

Rev.—MAG. PRO. COS. An eagle and dolphin with sceptre erect between them.

M. Terentius Varro, who on account of his singular ability and extensive acquirements was honoured with having, whilst still living, his statue placed by Asinius Pollio in the Bibliotheca, at Rome, had a high command under Pompey the Great in the war against the Pirates, and for his distinguished exploits in that war, as commander of the fleet in the Ionian sea, was rewarded with a naval crown, at the hands of his illustrious chief. The above denarius shews that Varro, in that arduous contest, was Pompey's *proquæstor.* And that it was struck during the *bellum prædonum* is rendered clear by the name *Magnus*, which had already been assumed by Pompey.—For similar obverses and reverses see *Pompeia* family.—In the civil war, he was compelled at length to surrender himself to Cæsar. The head of the obverse is by some thought to be intended for that of Quirinus; others make it a *Jupiter Terminalis;* both, however, are mere conjectures.

TERENTIVS.—Terence, so celebrated for his dramatic writings, was a native of Carthage, and the slave of *Terentius Lucanus*, who, in consideration of his genius and merit generously gave him his liberty. This *facile princeps comicorum* lived on terms of intimacy with many noble personages, and especially with Scipio Africanus and C. Lælius.—But though Rome was the scene of his fame, his ashes were not destined to repose there. He is said to have died at Stymphalus in Arcadia, from disease brought on by grief for the loss of many of his comedies.—Amongst the contorniates is one on which appears the name of TERENTIVS and the naked and beardless head of a man; on the other side is a wrestler, or a young man leading a horse by the bridle. Of the name inscribed on the reverse only the last letters are discernible . . . . IVS.

Terminus.—A divinity to whom the ancients generally, and the Romans in particular, paid worship, as presiding over the boundaries of fields. He is represented with a human face and a body terminating in the form of an inverted pyramid. On the feast days of these tutelary gods of landmarks (February 21), the inhabitants of the neighbouring villages crowned their images with flowers.—On the obverse of a denarius belonging to the *Calpurnia* family appears the statue of a man, the upper part of whose body is clothed in the toga; but it has neither arms nor feet, on one side of which is a laurel crown, and on the other a vase—without legend; but on the reverse M. PISO M.F. FRVGI.—Ursinus sees in this the symbol of Terminus; and supposes that Piso (whoever he might be) adopted it as a type for his coin, for the purpose of indicating the origin of certain religious rites performed in honour of that rural deity, as introduced by *Numa*, who (according to old writers whom Ursinus quotes) first erected a little temple *(sacellum)* to Terminus, on the Tarpeian hill, at Rome. A similar figure of the same guardian of *property* limits, having on its head a radiated crown, and with a thunderbolt lying beneath, exhibits itself on a silver coin of Augustus, inscribed IMP. CAESAR.

Terpsichore, one of the Muses, who was said to have taught men the art of playing on the musical reeds—or "Pan's pipes." Her head, covered with laurel, is delineated on a denarius of Q. Pomponius, and on the reverse she is herself represented standing (with the word MVSA before her), holding the above-mentioned instrument with both hands.—See *Pomponia* family.

Terra.—See *Cybele—Ops—Rhea—Tellus.*—The earth, which, according to the doctrine of the Pythagoreans, and now of all philosophers, moves round the sun.—Oiselius, *Selec. Num.* p. 253.

TERT. *Tertium.*—C. CAESAR. COS. TERT. *Consul Tertio* or *Tertium.*—C. Cæsar (Caligula), consul for the third time.

Teruncius, a silver coin of the Roman mint, so called from *ter* for tres, and *uncia.*—See AS *et partes ejus.*

Tessera, a square, marked with a certain number of points, to serve as a ticket or voucher.—*Tesseræ* were also small pieces of wood, of bone, or of ivory, or of bronze; which received various names, according to the different purposes to which they were applied. Accordingly there were theatrical, gladiatorial, liberal *(frumentariæ),* convivial, military, and hospitable *tesseræ.* Many of these are a species of coin, or counter, and are found in most large numismatic cabinets. From the times of the emperors they were chiefly employed for distribution amongst the people, to enable each individual to go with one or more of them, and receive the gifts which had been assigned to him, in corn, in oil, in money, and in every other article of greater or less value. For this reason they were called *tesseræ liberalitatis.*—Medals, struck when public distributions were made, present numerous examples of this kind, and the *tessera,* or tablet, appears in the right hand of the figure, which respectively personify *Annona,* and *Liberalitas.*—See the words.

TETRICVS *(Caius Pesuvius,* commonly called *Tetricus pater* or *senior),* one of those who took the name of *Augustus* during the

troubled state of the empire, under Gallienus. This prince belonged to a family of high distinction in the senate, and had been honoured with the consulship. Being governor of Aquitania at the time when the usurper Marius died, Tetricus was induced by the persuasions of that extraordinary heroine, *Victorina* (mother of Victorinus senior), to accept the title of emperor from the legionaries in Gaul, A.D. 268. Already in great repute for valour, prudence, and good principles, he disarmed envy by his unpretending simplicity, and conciliated general good opinion by the equity of his administration. His first act of sovereignty was to give the rank of Cæsar to his son Tetricus. He next undertook to reduce the revolted city of Autun, and succeeded after a six months' siege. But,

although he maintained himself in his government for more than five years, including the period of Claudius the Second's reign, yet frequent mutinies amongst his soldiers, who were continually threatening to depose him, rendered his crown insecure and his existence wretched and unsafe. Disgusted with the slavery of his situation, and anxious to regain the tranquillity of private life, he applied for succour to Aurelian, who, on his return from the East, advanced with his victorious army as far as Catalaunum (now Châlons-sur-Marne), delivered Tetricus from the power of his rebellious troops, and resumed for the Roman empire, the possession of those Gallic provinces, which the revolt of Postumus had detached from it. In thus surrendering himself, his son, his army, and his imperial authority into the hands of Aurelian, he did not escape the deep humiliation of having to follow the triumphal chariot of that proud conqueror; by whom, however, according to Treb. Pollio, he was afterwards treated with the utmost benevolence, friendship, and confidence. Among the honours heaped on him by the emperor, who called him his colleague, was his nomination as governor of the important Italian province of Lucania.—Tetricus died in retirement, at a very advanced age, in what year is not known, and, as his coins of consecration shew, he was placed in the rank of divinities—"a remarkable circumstance," observes Beauvais, "in the instance of a man who for many years before had renounced the title and sceptre of supreme power."

His style, on coins, is, by himself, IMP. TETRICVS AVG.—IMP. C. C. PESV. TETRICVS P. F. AVG.—in association with his son, IMPP. TETRICI. AVGG.—IMPP. TETRICI. PII. AVGG.—IMP. INVICTI PII. AVGG.

There is a gold medallion of this prince, said to be *unique,* on the obverse of which, with the inscription IMP. TETRICVS., is seen the bust of Tetricus as emperor; in his right hand is an olive branch, in his left a sceptre surmounted by an eagle. This medallion, according to a memoir of De Boze, is composed of two thin leaves of gold stamped together, and mounted in an ornamented circle of gold with two loops.

His gold of the ordinary size are of the highest rarity; base silver or billon very rare: third brass extremely common. The money of Tetricus senior, of Roman die, was fabricated in Gaul.—Among the third brass, of which the number extant is very considerable, there are not a few of which the workmanship is most barbarous, and the legends undecypherable.

TETRICVS filius, or junior, as he is commonly called.—Caius Pesuvius Pivesus Tetricus,

son of the preceding, was very young when his father became emperor in Gaul (A.D. 267). He was soon after named Cæsar; and associated with his father in sovereign power. Possessed of a good figure, of an agreeable countenance, and of high intellectual endowments, this young man reigned as his parent's colleague, under circumstances of great promise, until A.D. 272 or 273, when the elder Tetricus thought fit to abdicate, and voluntarily submit himself to Aurelian. Then it was that the son shared the degradation of the sire—walking through the streets of Rome, behind the triumphal car of "Restitutor Orbis," as Aurelian had the oriental presumptuousness to term himself; but who respected neither his own good fame nor the dignity of the senate in thus treating two such distinguished members of that body. However, after this indulgence of his pride as a triumpher, the emperor is said to have behaved towards both those princes as though they had not "fallen from their high estate." The younger Tetricus was re-established in the possessions of his family, and admitted to a seat in the senate. Such, indeed, was his conduct, says Beauvais, "that he obtained the friendship of the Romans by making himself useful to every one; and no man of senatorial rank was more honoured than himself by Aurelian and his successors."—His style on coins is PIVESVS TETRICVS CAES.—C. PIVESV. TETRICVS. CAES.—IMP. TETRICVS P. F. AVG.— and CAESAR TETRICVS AVG., as on the small brass (from the cabinet of Mr. Roach Smith) given above. Whether Tetricus the younger remained Cæsar only, or whether he also received the title of *Augustus*, is a question which historians appear to have left in doubt, and on which numismatists are not agreed. Referring the reader, who may desire further acquaintance with the *pros* and *cons* of the case, to what Banduri has advanced on this point and Eckhel stated in opposition, together with Mionnet's comments on both, in his notes on the medals of this young prince (vol. i. p. 83-4), it shall suffice for us here to observe that, with the fact, both historical and numismatical before us, that *Tetricus junior* was conjoined as IMPERATOR with his father, there is the greatest probability of his having also been proclaimed AVGVSTVS.— And as moreover a gold coin of the younger Tetricus, with the title AVG. has, since Eckhel's death, been published as genuine by Mionnet, we should hardly deem it premature to regard the question as already decided; in other words we are of opinion that there exists sufficient proof of *Tetricus filius* having been styled Augustus as well as Cæsar, especially as we find such a conclusion supported by those undoubtedly authentic medals whereon his portrait joined to that of his father is accompanied by IMPP. TETRICII PII. *AVGG*. for legend of obverse, and by AETERNITAS *AVGG*. (Augustorum) for legend of reverse.

The coins of *Tetricus* jun. are extremely rare in gold—very rare in base silver, or billon; but very common in small brass.

The pieces of this prince, of Roman die, were coined in Gaul, as were those of his father.— "A great many medals of the two *Tetrici* are found (says Beauvais) with their legends and types disfigured by the coarseness of their fabric, and the ignorance of the workmen.

T. FL. *Titi Filius.*—T. FL. *Titus Flavius.*

Theatra, places specially appropriated, amongst the Greeks and Romans, to the representations of dramatic spectacles.—The theatre differèd greatly as to form from the amphitheatre, the latter being of a circular, or, more properly speaking, of an oval figure: whilst the former was that of a half circle, at the extremity of which a structure was transversely erected. The *theatrum* consisted of three principal parts: the seats of the spectators occupied the semi-circular space, the stage was in the edifice transversely built, and between the two was the orchestra.—[For an accurate description of the construction, arrangement, and decoration of ancient theatres, see Dictionnaire des Beaux Arts par Millin, Dictionary of Greek and Roman Antiquities by Dr. Taylor, and Museum of Classical Antiquities.]—The reverse of a first brass coin, struck under Gordianus Pius, at Heraclea, in Bithynia, and engraved by Buonarotti from the Carpegna cabinet, presents a theatre with a portico behind the stage, which exhibits the scene of a temple; the semi-circular portion of the building is filled with spectators. —See *Amphitheatre*.

Thensa, a sacred car in which the images of the gods and godesses were carried to the games of the circus. Vehicles of this kind served with the Romans to symbolize that solemn consecration, or apotheosis, of defunct personages, which, confined to the imperial rank, was decreed by the senate alone.—The *thensa* was usually made of the wood of such tree as was consecrated to the deity whose statue was thus publicly displayed in procession, and which appeared with all his or her attributes.—This peculiar sort of carriage was also used to convey either the image of some emperor or empress already placed amongst the divinities, to some public scene of pompous celebration, or the dead body of a prince or princess round the *campus martius*, where the corpse was afterwards burnt on a funeral pile amidst very imposing rites and ceremonies.—On some of these occasions, elephants were employed to draw the *thensa*, those vast animals, on account of their longevity, being selected as the symbol of eternity.—Accordingly we find a first brass coin, struck under Tiberius, which exhibits the statue of Augustus, with radiated head and other marks of deification, seated on a thensa, drawn by four elephants, on the neck of each of which sits a driver.—See DIVO AVGVSTO.—There is also a large bronze medal, struck under Titus, with similar types of the thensa.—See DIVO AVG. VESPASiano.

From the above and several other numismatic monuments, the form of the *thensa* appears to have been that of a platform, richly ornamented, and mounted upon four wheels, by which mode of construction the idols or statues placed upon it were rendered conspicuously visible. In this respect it differed, as well from the *carpentum* which was covered with an arched roof, its front alone being open, as from the triumphal chariot which was an open vehicle sometimes of cylindrical, at others of semi-circular shape and entered at the back, both of them being two-wheeled vehicles.—See *Carpentum* and *Currus*.

THEODORA, second wife of the Emperor Constantius Chlorus, whom she married A.D. 292. She was the daughter of Galeria Valeria 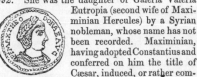 Eutropia (second wife of Maximinian Hercules) by a Syrian nobleman, whose name has not been recorded. Maximinian, having adopted Constantius and conferred on him the title of Cæsar, induced, or rather compelled him to divorce his wife Helena, and to marry this princess, who received the name of Augusta, but who is known only by her rank as empress, and by the numerous family she left. History is, indeed, equally silent respecting the incidents of her life, the qualities of her character, and the time of her death. "*Ses médailles* (says Beauvais) *la reprèsentent avec des traits assez fins, et un air spirituel.*" It speaks well of her merit as a wife, that so excellent a man as Constantius, was greatly attached to her, and made her the mother of three sons and three daughters. The former were—1. Delmatius Censor, father of Delmatius Cæsar, and of the younger Hannibalianus. 2. Julius Constantius, Consul, who had by Galla, his first wife, Constantius Gallus, Cæsar; and by Basilina, his second wife, the Emperor Julian the Apostate. 3. Constantinus Hannibalianus. The princesses were—1. Constantia, wife of the Emperor Licinius. 2. Anastatia, wife of Bassienus, Cæsar; and 3. Eutropia, mother of Nepotianus, who assumed the name of Augustus. The medals of this lady style her FL. MAX. THEODORA. AVG.—There are two (of very great rarity) catalogued in the *Cabinet d'Ennery*, and which Beauvais regarded as of pure silver and genuine: one has for its legend of reverse PIETAS ROMANA, the type is a woman who holds an infant in her bosom, as if suckling it, and in the exergue T. R. P. This legend and type also appear on her small brass coins, which are rather scarce. The coins of Theodora are considered to have been struck by Constantine the Great.

Theodoricus, first of the Gothic Kings in Italy, was the son of Theodemirus, king of the Ostrogoths, a tribe of people from northern Europe, who, about the middle of the fifth century, were in occupation of Pannonia and Illyria.—Sent at eight years of age to Constantinople, he lived there ten years as a hostage at the court of the emperor Zeno, who, with his able assistance, vanquished and deposed Basiliscus, and who rewarded his bravery and services with wealth, preferment, and the highest honours. But, in A.D. 478, having quarrelled with his imperial benefactor, Theodoricus marched the armies of which he had been appointed general into Thrace and Macedonia, where he rendered himself so formidable that Zeno was necessitated to negociate peace with him. In 483 he was elected consul. Four years afterwards he again broke with the emperor, whom he besieged in Constantinople. Zeno having once more come to terms with his

rebellious subject, surrendered to him his own rights over Italy, which he permitted him to invade A.D. 489, for the ostensible purpose of expelling Odoacer (who had already proclaimed himself king of that country), but in reality to rid himself of so dreaded a foe as Theodoricus.—At the head of a powerful army, the gothic chieftain arrived at Aquileia, on the 28th of August of the above-mentioned year; and, having defeated Odoacer, in three different battles, compelled that prince to yield, after sustaining a three years' siege at Ravenna. Theodoricus engaged to spare his life, and even entered into a treaty of friendship with him; but at the expiration of a few days, Odoacer and his son, together with the nobles of his court, were, by Theodoricus' orders, basely assassinated at a banquet to which their perfidious conqueror had invited them.—Proclaimed king of Italy at Ravenna A.D. 493, this barbarous successor to the Ausonian domains of the Cæsars, confirmed his power by an alliance with the emperor Anastatius, and by other political advantages.—After governing Italy and the Gaulish provinces with great wisdom and justice, preserving tranquillity between the Visigoths and the Italians, as well by the equity as by the vigour of his administration, the natural cruelty and mistrustfulness of his disposition regained its baneful influence over him, at the close of his reign, and led him to pollute with the blood of many distinguished and innocent persons the glory of its commencement. Theodoricus, full of remorse and terror at the remembrance of his murderous enormities, expired on the 30th of August, 526, at the age of seventy-two, having survived Odoacer thirty-three years and a half. He had married Anaflede, sister of king Clovis. On his medals, which are rare, he is styled *Dominus Noster* THEODORICVS REX. Some pieces represent him with *Anastatius* and with *Justinus I.*

There is a third brass given in the Pembroke collection, on the obverse of which his name and titles appear within a garland; the reverse exhibiting the helmed head of Rome, with the inscription INVICTA ROMA. The money of this prince was doubtless struck in Italy.

THEODOSIVS *(Flavius)*, customarily surnamed by historians (but not so on his coins) *Magnus*, was born of an illustriously noble family, at Italica (now Seville), in Spain, A.D. 346.—Son of Theodosius, one of the ablest generals of

his time, Flavius early showed his hereditary courage and his good soldiership in campaigns against the Sarmatians, and in 374 was created

Count of Moesia. Endangered by the jealousies and unjust suspicion which led to his father's decapitation at Carthage in 376, he retired into Spain, where, by order of Gratian himself who caused that father to perish, he headed an army against the Goths, whom he defeated in a great battle. On the death of Valens, he was chosen by Gratian for his colleague, and with the title of Augustus, declared Emperor of the East early in 379. This event took place at a time when that portion of the Roman empire was ravaged in every direction by the Goths. Assembling his forces with the utmost expedition, he attacked those barbarian hordes; overthrowing them in several successive engagements, and finally compelling them to sue for peace; and to take refuge within their own wild fortresses. From admiration of his valour and great qualities, Sapor III., king of Persia renounced his enmity to and entered into a treaty of alliance with the Romans, which lasted a considerable period. In the year 383, Theodosius conferred the title of Augustus on his eldest son Arcadius, an object of domestic policy, which he had no sooner accomplished than the conquest of Italy and the deposition of Valentinian, junior, by Magnus Maximus, called the imperial hero once more away from his own capital and dominions. Having vanquished and put to death the invading usurper (387), he re-established Valentinian on the throne of the west, and hastened back to quell an insurrection at Thessalonica, where one of his provincial lieutenants had been slain by the inhabitants of that city. On this occasion he sullied his hitherto irreproachable fame, by an act of the most inhuman cruelty, in permitting his victorious troops to massacre more than seven thousand persons, the greater portion of whom were guiltless of the sedition which had so violently irritated him. It was some time after this frightful atrocity that Theodosius, having presented himself at the portal of Milan cathedral, was denied permission to enter by St. Ambrose. It is further related that the emperor, under the impression of religious awe and compunction, humbly submitted to the sentence of the venerable arch-prelate, and abstained from again offering himself for admission into the church, until for a term of eight months he had exhibited signs of sincere penitence. Returned at length to the seat of his own government, he found the Gothic tribes pillaging Macedonia and Thessaly; and he chastised and expelled these barbarians from the confines of his empire. After the decease of the younger Valentinian, he returned again to the west, and achieved his last military exploit by gaining a decisive victory (though not till after some desperate struggles), near Aquileia, on the 5th of September, 394, over the usurper Eugenius, whom Arbogastes, the traitorous general of Valentinian and instigator of his murder, had caused to be proclaimed emperor. On the 17th of January in the following year, having just before obtained the senatorial recognition of his second son Honorius, as emperor of the east, this extraordinary man

fell ill of a dropsy and died (395), at Milan (Mediolanum), in the 50th year of his age, after an eventful reign of nearly sixteen years. He is recorded to have expired in the arms of St. Ambrose, regretted as one of the greatest and best of princes. For fortitude, sagacity, lion-heartedness, and consummate skill in all the acts of government, he might indeed justly be regarded as "the model for sovereigns;" but as to his piety, so much lauded by Roman historians, there is more than a doubt of its purity and genuineness, and to speak of his moderation and clemency of character would be an insult alike to humanity and common sense after the horrible proof of his savage vindictiveness at Thessalonica. Theodosius the Great had two wives—the first was Ælia Flacilla, mother of Arcadius and Honorius; the second was Galla, daughter of Valentinian I. and of Justinia, by whom he had Placidia, who was the mother of Valentinian III.

On the medals of this emperor he is constantly styled D. N. THEODOSIVS P. F. AU. (or AVG.), the head diademed with pearls. They are common in silver and gold, except gold quinarii and silver medallions, The middle and small brass of this prince are very common; but his bronze medallions are rare.—On the reverse of a silver medallion he is styled, and with historical truth, TRIVMFATOR GENT. BARB. Before Eckhel's time, there existed an almost insuperable difficulty to distinguish the medals which belong to Theodosius I. from those which were struck under Theodosius II. A note of Mionnet, of which Mr. Akerman has given in his *Descriptive Catalogue* (vol. ii. 330) a translation, furnishes in a condensed form the information on this subject so usefully afforded by the learned and sagacious author of *Doctrina Num. Vet.*, in vol. viii. (pp. 181 *et seq.*), of that invaluable work, to both of which the reader is referred.

THEODOSIVS *(Flavius)*, junior, or II., grandson of the above, being the son of Arcadius and Eudoxia, was born at Constantinople, A.D. 401; declared Augustus the following year;

and in A.D. 408, became Emperor of the East.— During his minority the administration of affairs devolved, first to the prefect Anthemius and afterwards to Pulcheria, sister of Theodosius, under whose influence he, in 421, married the celebrated Athenais. The same year he gained by his generals a victory over the Persians; and the peace which they concluded with the Romans after that defeat, lasted twenty-four years. On the decease of Honorius, becoming sovereign of the west, he conferred that division of the empire on his cousin-german Valentinian

III., and sent him at the head of an army, in 423, to expel the usurper Johannes who had possessed himself of Italy, Gaul, and Spain. Theodosius engaged Attila to renew the treaty subsisting between the Huns and the Romans by conditioning to pay an annual tribute of seven hundred pounds weight of gold to that barbaric chieftain, and by other humiliating concessions. In 438 he caused the publication of that code of laws which has come down to us under his name. After failing in an attempt to effect the assassination of Attila, who had broken the peace made between them; and who devasted many provinces of the empire, Theodosius the Second ended his days at Constantinople, dying either from disease, or in consequence of a fall from his horse, A.D. 450, in the 49th or 50th year of his age. He was a prince whose personal qualities and intellectual attainments are described to have been such as would have rendered him most estimable as an individual; but his monastic turn of piety and pusilanimity of disposition totally disqualified him for the position he occupied and for the times in which he lived; whilst his timid, temporising policy was ruinous to the empire, which he governed only to sacrifice its independence and dishonour its renown.

His gold coins of the usual size, are common: but the quinarii are rare; the silver extremely rare; but silver medallions less so; and small brass very uncommon. His style is D. N. THEODOSIVS P.F. AVG. But, as has already been observed, it is difficult to recognise the difference between the medals of the *Second* and those of the *First* Theodosius.—On this subject Eckhel expresses himself to the following effect:—Of the coins of *both the Theodosii* it should be remarked, that, even in the majority of instances no safe decision can be come to, whether they are to be refered to the *elder* or the *younger*, the same legend on the obverse above quoted appearing on the coins of each, and there being no clue afforded in that age by the lineaments of the countenance. This circumstance presented such difficulties to Banduri (ii., p. 558) that he preferred to give the point up, and in the classification of the respective coins, to rest on the opinion of others rather than on his own. For myself, adds Eckhel, having noticed that on *certain coins of the younger Theodosius* there usually occurs *a full-faced bust helmeted*, with spear and buckler (a type which does not appear on coins of Theodosius the grandfather), I have ascribed these without exception to the younger; and the rest, with the *diademed head*, to the *elder;* except where obvious reasons induced me to think that some even of these should be assigned to the junior.—See *Mus. Cæs. Vind.* ii., p. 523.

Thermæ Romanorum. Baths of the Romans.— During the republic the sole object of the Romans in building baths was to consult natural inclination, and attend to considerations of cleanliness as promotive of health. Accordingly they were content to render such places subservient to the purposes simply of ablution, and producing perspiration. And although even in the earlier ages, there were structures of this kind which far exceeded in extent what was actually needful, yet it was not until a much later period that the public *thermæ* at Rome arrived at that pitch of grandeur and magnificence to which they were brought with the increase of wealth and luxury, chiefly through the unbounded munificence, or more properly speaking, extravagance of princes, who, in the greatness of their works, sought to glorify their names in the eyes of posterity. The very ruins of these baths, indeed, exhibit at the present day evidences of their by-gone grandeur so stupendous as to excite the astonishment of every intelligent and observant person who has had the opportunity of contemplating them. Nero appears to have been the first who contrived a gymnasium for robust and athletic exercises with the *thermæ* for cold bathing and for sudatory purposes. Titus followed the example of Nero, and caused baths to be built by the side of his amphitheatre. Domitian and Trajan successively added to the number of these public establishments; and, like their predecessors, built them on a vast scale. Hadrian restored those which Agrippa (in Augustus's time) had erected. Commodus and Sept. Severus also built baths at Rome. And those with which Caracalla adorned the city were remarkable for their extraordinary extensiveness of plan and splendour of construction and embellishment; but it would appear that they were not completed until the reign of Elagabalus. Alexander Severus added porticoes to the baths of Caracalla; and it is the general opinion that he either conjoined new *thermæ* to those of Nero, or that he restored, enlarged, and improved them. The edifices thus combined, and provided through the liberality of that emperor with everything that could administer to public convenience and gratification, received the appellation of *Thermæ Alexandrinæ.* Diocletian was the last emperor who built baths, and those which still bear his name were the grandest of any in Rome. When, therefore, certain silver and brass medals of Alexander are found exhibiting an edifice profusely adorned with statues, columns, and other decorations, we may regard it as in the highest degree probable that such types were intended to depicture the baths which that prince dedicated to the use of the inhabitants of Rome. Nor is this probability at all lessened, when we note the exterior enrichments that mark the character of the buildings represented on these numismatic monuments. For as luxury increased so the *thermæ* of imperial Rome became more and more prodigally augmented and beautifully adorned, both inside and outside, with the most precious marbles, the most exquisite sculptures, and the most splendid works as well of pictorial as of architectural art. The Laocoon found in the ruins of Titus's baths, and the Farnesian Hercules in those of Caracalla, together with the fine paintings with which modern discoveries show the walls and ceilings of the bath of Titus to have been covered, are amongst the most convincing proofs of the fact above stated. And in the instance before us, although there is not, as in the *Basilica Ulpia,* or the *Forum* and *Aqua Trajani,* that conclusive aid which inscriptive precision affords, yet, with the s. c. conspicuous on the bronze medal, we may reasonably infer from such a type, that the senate caused it to be struck as a record of gratitude to Alexander for having undertaken and achieved so great a public work.

For a general description of the various apartments comprised in the interior of the Roman baths, such as the *spoliarium,* for undressing; the *frigidarium,* for bathing in cold water; the *tepidarium,* or warm bath room; the *sudatorium,* or vapour bath; the *balneum,* or *caldarium,* in which hot water bathing took place; and the *unctuarium,* where the oils and perfumes were applied to the persons of the bathers, together with the various utensils employed and arrangements made in each; see *Discours sur Bains Antiques, par Du Choul;* and *Dictionnaire des Beaux Arts, par Millin.*

Captain Smyth's remarks on the subject are so appropriate in themselves, as well as so characteristic in their tenour, of the manly views and correct feelings of the gallant author, that we are proud at once to grace our pages and express our concurrent statements with them:—
"The temples of idleness, called *thermæ,* were imitations of the Greek *gymnasia,* and consisted of vast buildings replete with splendid and fascinating luxuries, calculated to relax the mind, and afford voluptuous exercise for the body. But it may be questioned whether the health of the citizens was not substantially better, when they only bathed in the Tiber, than when hot baths became necessary to the very *fæx civitatis.*"

Furnos et balnia laudat
Ut fortunatam plene præstantia vitam.

"The hardy warriors of the republic lost but little time at their toilet, despised the *matutino amomo,* and made no difference between winter and summer rings; but even before the age of Cæsar, a "pretty gentleman" was unable to get under weigh until he had been shaved, scraped, shampooed, perfumed, and what not, as the father of the "Carmina Morum" says—

Scabor, suppelor, desquamor, pumicor, ornor,
Expilor, pingor.

There is no doubt (adds Capt. Smyth) that the enervating effects of the warm baths, engendered both vice and effeminacy; but though it is too clear that there were bagnios where the sexes bathed indiscriminately, the promiscuous intercourse was not general, and such could only have been frequented by the dregs of the females. Varro tells us—" *Ubi bina essent conjuncta ædificia lavandi causâ; unum ubi viri, alterum ubi mulieres lavarentur;*" and Lampridius, speaking of Alexander Severus, says, " *Balnea mixta, Romæ exhiberi, prohibuit.*" *Descriptive Catalogue,* p. 230.

Thermæ Alexandrinæ.—Alexander Severus is recorded to have adorned Rome with many noble structures—a fact which Lampridius, in his Life of that emperor (c. 25), at once confirms and elucidates by saying that he not only restored the

works of the earlier princes but also himself raised many new ones, amongst others the baths which bear his name. (*Thermas nominis sui, juxta eas quæ Neronianæ fuerunt, aqua inducta, quæ Alexandrina nunc dicitur.)* The remains of these baths of Alexander are still to be seen in the *Palazzo di Medici.* A representation of them also is, according to the generally received opinion, handed down to us on silver and bronze coins of his, bearing on their reverse the legend P. M. TR. P. V. COS II. P. P. (his second consulship corresponding with A.D. 226). That in silver is edited by Vaillant (*Pr.* ii. 285)—a brass medallion is given in Angeloni (p. 226); also one by Havercamp, from the Museum Christina; and another by Eckhel, from the Imperial cabinet at Vienna. The types of all these, though differing in some features of design from each other, yet agree in delineating an elegant and lofty edifice, adorned with statues and enclosed in front with a portico. Angeloni's specimen is profusely charged with imagery, and surmounted by a quadriga, with the emperor himself in the act of enjoying triumphal honours. The same writer goes on to point out in his engraving of what he describes as " *bellissimo medaglione,*" a fountain in front of the *Thermæ,* representing that which in Alexander's time poured forth the waters, called after him *Alexandrinæ,* and which were conveyed to it at immense cost and trouble by two grand canals (or aquaducts). This coin was struck A.D. 226, "and either commemorates the erection of the baths or the lighting them up at night, at Alexander's expense;" *addidit et oleum luminibus thermarum, quum antea non ante auroram paterent, et antea solis occasum clauderentur.*—Lampridius, c. 24.

Theseus, son and successor of Ægeus, king of the Athenians. The history of this Grecian hero is so much mixed up with the fables of antiquity that it is scarcely possible to disentangle his real exploits from the marvellous adventures which poets and tragedians have ascribed to him. But Plutarch, in his life, has collected many things worthy of commemoration, and there are some passages in Apollodorus which also serve to justify his title to celebrity. The only circumstance by which a name, familiar enough to mythological associations, can with any shew of probability be brought within the range of *Roman numismatics*, is that of a contorniate medal given in *Morell's Thesaurus*. This pseudo monetal relic bears Nero's portrait on its obverse; it has for legend of reverse AGIT SPE TESEVS; and for type a naked warrior, with helmet on his head, and spear and buckler in his left hand. He stands, with his right hand pressing on the neck of a Centaur, who holds a lyre, and whom he seems in the act of forcibly compelling to go down on his knees.—Ovid (in *Metamorph.* lib. xii.) in recounting the incidents of a bloody skirmish between the Centaurs and the Lapithæ, assembled together at the nuptial feast of Pirithous, sings the praises of Theseus, who slew Eurytus and others of the double-limbed race, "half men, half beasts," for committing a brutal outrage on fair *Hippodame*, the bride of his faithful friend.—Of the meaning to be attached to the inscription above-quoted, no satisfactory explanation has been offered; and whether the group pourtrayed on the contorniate was intended to shadow forth the triumphant prowess of Theseus, as the ally of "the horse-tamers," and the avenger of outraged hospitality and the insulted honour of marriage, is a question still left to be determined by those who may deem it worthy of further inquiry. But the type shews at least that the family or tribe of the Centaurs continued to cultivate the science of music after the example of their great progenitor Chiron.—See *Centaur*.

Thorax, the breastplate or corslet of a Roman warrior's suit of defensive armour. This is shewn on numerous coins of the imperial series, from Domitian, Trajan, Hadrian, and Antoninus Pius, down to the lower ages of the empire. The breastplate is placed on a trophy, or by the side of the emperor. It serves also as a seat for *Pallas*, *Roma*, *Virtus*, and *Victoria*.

Thoria, a plebeian family, surname *Balbus*. Its coins consist but of two varieties, both in silver, one of which is rare, viz., I. S. M. R. Head of Juno Sispita.

Rev.—L. THORIVS BALBVS. A bull running furiously.

The reason why I*uno* S*ispita* M*agna* R*egina* (for thus are the letters on the obverse to be explained by copious authorities deduced from ancient marbles) is represented on this denarius, is supplied by Cicero, in a memorable passage of his works, in which he describes the character of L. Thorius Balbus, as that of a wealthy and systematic voluptuary, yet at the same time as a man of rare and wonderful genius. He was born at Lanuvium: hence the adoption of *Juno Lanuvina's* image on his coin.—See *Roscia* family for what relates to that superstition, and the words *Taurus irruens*, for what is alluded to by the type of the bull on the reverse.

Thracia, one of the most extensive, and, with the exception of a few Greek colonies on its maritime confines, one of the most uncivilised countries of ancient Europe, now forming that part of Turkey called *Roumelia*. Thrace bordered westward on Macedonia, from which it was divided by the river Nessus, according to

Ptolemy, or by the river Strymon as Pliny gives it. It touched Moesia on the north; the Pontus Euxinus (Black Sea) was its boundary eastward; and the Egean sea on the south.—Spanheim (*P*. ii. 600) includes it amongst the provinces of Julius; but from an observation of Suetonius it would appear not to have been reduced to that form of subjection to the Roman government until the reign of Vespasian. There is a rare medal of Hadrian, in large brass, which records his visit to this distant part of the empire, by the legend ADVENTVI AVG*usti* THRACIAE, and by the type of the Emperor, and the Genius of Thrace, sacrificing together before an altar.

Thyrsus, one of the peculiar attributes of Bacchus. It was a spear or lance, the iron head of which was wrapped round, sometimes with ivy leaves, at other times with vine leaves and branches of the vine. The ancients feigned that Bacchus used this weapon against the Indians, with whom he was said to have waged successful war. In memory of this event, it was the custom of his votaries at their sacrificial feasts to have the thyrsus borne in triumphant procession by the Bacchantes, who employed it in the frenzied ceremonies of their wild and licentious worship. The *thyrsus* is seen almost always in the left hand of Bacchus, as may have been observed on coins of the Cosconia and Trebonia families, and on many imperial and colonial, imperial medals, such as those of Trajan, Hadrian, Antonine, Commodus, Sept. Severus, Caracalla, &c.

Tiara.—The cap or turban worn by the ancient Kings of Persia and of Armenia. This differs from the *cidaris*, inasmuch as it was larger at the top than at the bottom, whilst the cidaris was of a conical form and terminated in a point, as may be seen on various medals of the Parthian King's. The cidaris, with bow and quiver, on a denarius of Marc Antony (with legend of IMP. TERTIO IIIVIR. R.P.C.), is a monument of the conquest of Armenia by that triumvir. For Tigranes, the father of Artavasdes, who was taken captive by Antony, laid this symbol of royalty at Pompey's feet.—That the cidaris was also the mark as well of *Armenian* as of *Parthian* royalty, is shewn from the medals of Augustus, where the same kind of tiara, with bow and quiver, accompanies the inscription DE PARTHIS, and ARMENIA CAPTA.

TI. *Tiberii.*—TI. AVG. F.—*Tiberii Augusti Filii.*

TI. F.—TI. N. *Tiberii Filius, or Tiberii Nepos.* Son or nephew of Tiberius.

TI. *Titus.*—TI. CAES. DIVI. VESP. F.—*Titus Cæsar Divi Vespasiani Filius.*

Tiber and Tiberis.—Though not the largest, yet the most noted river in Italy, on whose banks, according to the well-known legend, a wolf suckled the twin brothers, Romulus and Remus. Taking its source in the mountains of Etruria, the Tiber flows into the Mediterranean at Ostia, on the Latian shore, about twenty miles from where Rome stands, on its southern bank, just below its junction with the Anio. The Tiber was at first called *Albula;* but Tiberinus or Tiberis, son of one of the Alban kings, having been drowned in that river, his name was given to it, and he was regarded as god of the stream.

TIBERIS. S. C.—A river god seated on the ground—his right hand placed on a boat, and his left hand, reposing on an urn, holds a reed. The Tiber, thus distinctly named, is finely personified on a brass medallion of Antoninus Pius. There is also another brass medallion of the same emperor, the type of which alludes to one of the fabulous legends of early Rome; such as he delighted to restore in public memory, viz., the arrival of Æsculapius in Italy from Epidaurus, under the form of a serpent. On this beautiful reverse, *Tiber* is seated amidst the waters, as a venerably bearded old man, with a bulrush in his left hand, and his elbow resting on a vase pouring forth a billowy stream that completely covers his lower extremities. [See AESCVLAPIVS.]—On a first and second brass of Domitian, forming one of the series of medals, struck under that prince to commemorate his celebration of the secular games, a river god, in a recumbent position, occupies a prominent place in the group of figures, and is shown by Eckhel to be unquestionably a personification of the *Tiber.* [See LVD. SAEC. FEC.]—In the *Catalogue D'Ennery* a gold medal is ascribed to Galba, with TIBERIS. P. M. TR. P. COS. II. and an aquatic divinity seated. Eckhel quotes and comments upon this coin, without intimating any doubt of its genuineness. Mionnet and Akerman, however, do not include such a piece in their respective catalogues of Roman money.—Vaillant *(Pr.* iii. 115) gives a bronze medallion of Hadrian, the type of which he describes, as exhibiting the emperor on horseback, to whom the genius of Rome offers a branch; and below, the recumbent figure of a river god, resting his arm on an urn whence water is flowing, with the word TIBERIS. But no notice is taken of this remarkable reverse by either Eckhel, Mionnet, or Akerman.

TIBERIVS *(Claudius Nero),* born on the 16th of November, in the 712th year of Rome, forty-two years before the birth of Christ, was

the son of the Pontiff Tiberius Claudius Nero and of Livia, afterwards the wife of Augustus. Descended from the high patrician family of *Claudia,* this prince united a penetrating comprehensive mind to the qualities of a suspicious, cruel, and perfidious disposition. Having become early conversant with the literature of Greece and Rome, and having devoted particular attention to his political and military studies, Tiberius shewed so great a capacity for public life, that Augustus caused him to be passed through all the civil offices of the republic, and conferred upon him frequent appointments to important commands in the wars which he had to carry on with external foes. In all these charges he acquitted himself with superior talent, energy, and courage. When but 22 years of age (V.C. 734), he entered Armenia with an army, and restored Tigranes to the throne of that kingdom. The same year he received back for Augustus from the Parthians, the legionary eagles which M. Crassus had lost. In 738 he served the Prætorship, and at the same time accompanied Augustus into Gaul. With his brother Drusus, in 739, he subdued the Rhæti. In 742 reduced the Pannonians to submission, and though denied a triumph was invested with triumphal honours. Divorced from his wife, Vipsania Agrippina, he, in 743, married Julia, daughter of Augustus, and widow of Marcus Agrippa. He made the same year a successful campaign against the Dalmatians and Pannonians. In 745 he entered Rome with the honours of an ovation for fresh victories gained over the Dalmatians. In 746 he marched into Germany, and having restored the power and influence of Rome in that quarter, he received the title of *Imperator ;* was decreed a triumph ; and elected Consul for the second time. In 748 (A.D. 6) the tribunitian power was extended to him for the unusual term of five years. In 750, he retired to Rhodes, ostensibly as the lieutenant of Augustus, but in reality, as it is said, to avoid being a witness of the abandoned conduct of his wife Julia; and in this sort of exile he passed several years in a manner that rendered him generally despised. On his return to Rome he was adopted by Augustus, V.C. 757, on which occasion, being received into the Julia family, he took the appellative of TIBERIVS CAESAR, and as he had himself sprung from the Claudia family, he was also, according to the custom, called CLAVDIVS. From that period till the death of Augustus, an interval of ten years, Tiberius was continually engaged in military expeditions against the Germans, Dalmatians, Pannonians, and Illyrians, sustaining several severe checks but gaining many victories, and obtaining the highest honours from both emperor and senate. In the year of Rome 767, he succeeded to the empire (18th August, A.D. 14.) The first ten years of his reign his behaviour appears to have been on the whole that of a prince, studious of promoting, by the maintenance of civil order and an adherence to good policy, the interests and happiness of his subjects. Amongst the good actions of his early government, the munificent liberality with which he extended aid, and supplied the means of restoration to twelve cities in Asia destroyed by an earthquake in one night, deserves the record which has eternised it, if only as a vivid contrast to the gloomy despotism of his subsequent career. [See CIVITATIBVS ASIAE RESTITVTIS.]— The sequel of his biography is one continued series of barbarity and oppression—he overwhelmed with taxation the provinces which his tyranny had depopulated—most of the greatest families of Rome were ruined by his confiscatory decrees—he put Archélaus, King of Cappadocia, to death in prison : Germanicus, who had saved him and his troops from destruction in Germany, was sacrificed to his jealousy; Agrippina, the wife of that hero, and her son, also fell victims to his cruelty and ingratitude—even Sejanus, his minister and favourite, he had the pusillanimity to give up to the clamorous demands of a bloodthirsty rabble—and many of the best and most patriotic senators were delivered into the hands of the public executioner, he being himself their accuser as well as judge. In the midst of these atrocities, and sinking into a dishonoured old age, Tiberius quitted Rome in which, during nearly twelve years, he had lived only to desolate and oppress it, and took up his abode in the isle of Capræ, whither his enslavement to horrible debaucheries had led him, for the purpose of concealing his enormities from the public eye. *Multarum virtutum capax, omnium vitiorum compos, pessimum egit Principem.* This wicked prince, who became in old age an object of mortal dread from his murderous crimes, and of detestation and contempt for his hideous vices, expired on the 16th March, in the year v.c. 790 (A.D. 37), at Myseum, in Campania, where he was suffocated, as is believed, by order of Caligula, whom he had named for his successor.—It was in the seventeenth year of Tiberius's reign that Our Blessed Lord and Saviour, Jesus Christ, underwent the cruel death of the cross, on the 3rd of April, in the 31st year of the Christian æra.

Names and Titles.—Tiberius was called *Claudianus* and *Germanicus*, but not on his coins.—The name of *Augustus* appertained to him by hereditary right; it appears invariably on his mintages, and was used by him in his state letters and public documents, but he did not otherwise adopt it.—That the honourable addition of *Pater Patriæ* was the one which he uniformly refused, and abstained from, appears to be the unanimous assertion of the Roman historians ; the words do not appear, either in the full or the abbreviated form, on any of his genuine coins.—There is a second brass of this prince which has for legend of the head TI. CAESAR AVGVST. F. IMPERAT. V., and for that of the reverse PONTIF. TRIBVN. POTESTATE XII. s.c.—The author of "*Leçons de Numismatique Romaine*" gives this medal, from his collection, not on account of its rarity, but because it is the first which is known of Tiberius. This medal was struck in the year of Rome 763, during the life-time of Augustus, who for twelve years had granted to his adopted son the tribunitian power.—On this he is simply styled *Pontiff* and *Son of Augustus*, without being honoured himself with that name. But after his accession to the throne, he took the appella-

tion of *Augustus, son of the Divine Augustus* (AVG. DIVI F. AVG*usti*), and also the title of *Grand Pontiff* (PONT. MAX.)

With regard to the title of *Imperator*, Tiberius is said to have also abstained from applying it to himself as a prenomen. This is borne out both by coins and inscriptive marbles, on which he is styled, not IMP. TI. CAESAR, but simply TI. CAESAR.—Nevertheless, he allowed himself to be called IMPERATOR in a military sense, and on account of his victories. Accordingly we find by his coins that Tiberius in his 12th investiture with the Tribunitian Power, was *Imperator V.*, and at his accession to the empire Imperator VII. On the authority of Dion and Velleius it appears that this prince was called Imperator seven times, and decreed to have deserved triumphal honours for a like number, though content with enjoying them thrice ; but what these particular victories and triumphs were which caused the title to be so often renewed, it is difficult to decide.—See Eckhel *Doct. Num. Vet.* vol vi. p. 201.

The coins of Tiberius are—*Gold* C. (worth double with head of Augustus on reverse) ; ditto restored by Titus, RRR ; ditto quinarii, RR.— *Silver* C., with the head of Augustus, R ; ditto medallions, RRR.—Brass medallions of Roman die, RRRR ; first brass (with his head), RR, without it, R ; first brass of the colonies, RR ; second brass, C ; ditto restored by Titus or Domitian, RR ; third brass, S ; *Spintriati* (see the word), RR.

Tiberius, son of Drusus junior.—In the year of Rome, 772, male twins were born to the younger Drusus by his wife Livilla, an event greatly rejoiced at and boasted of at the time by the emperor Tiberius, who is said to have bestowed his own name on one of these children. The other, whose appellation remains unknown, died at the age of four years. The less fortunate survivor was appointed in the grandfather's will to be associated in the empire with Caligula, on whose accession to the supreme power in the year v.c. 790 the youthful Tiberius was put to death. The infant heads of his brother and himself, placed on two horns of plenty, with a caduceus between them, but without inscription, appear on 1st brass coins of Drusus their father. It is a type which elegantly symbolises the fertility and happiness of the imperial family.— See *Cornucopiæ.*

Tiberius Constantinus, emperor of the East, a native of Thrace, adopted by Justin II., was named Augustus, A.D. 578, and succeeded to the empire by the death of Justin the same year. He is reported to have been a prudent, mild, yet energetic prince, under whom the Persians were twice defeated. He died at Constantinople, A.D. 582. His gold coins are R., his silver RRR.; his brass common. On them he is styled D.N. or TIB. CONSTANT. or CONSTANTINVS P.P. AVG.—The reverse of a quinarius bears the legend LVX MVNDI, and the type of a cross, the whole in a crown of myrtle.

Tiberius Mauricius, successor of the above.— See *Mauricius.*

Tibia, pipe or flute.—Passing over the myth in which the invention of this instrument of music is ascribed to Minerva, and the praise of celebrity as performers thereon awarded to Marsyas, Pan, and Olympus, it may suffice for our present purpose to observe that the flutes of the Greeks and Romans were made either of a peculiar sort of reed, or of some light kind of wood; and were of two descriptions—*single* and *double.* Of the latter, which is by far the more frequently delineated on coins, sculptures, and in pictures: one was called *sinistra,* from its being held in the left hand, and serving for the treble; the other was called *dextra,* because held in the right hand, and employed as a second to accompany the first.

There is, however, one particular which Visconti in describing this musical instrument has omitted to mention, but which the sight of his graphic illustration suggests as a subject of remark —namely, that *above* as well as below the cross mouth-piece of the instrument in question, the fingers of the performer seem employed as if in covering stops—a peculiarity in the conformation of the *tibia simplex* which we have never before seen in ancient representations.

Tibicines, players on the pipe or flute.—This class of musicians amongst the Romans formed a corporate body under the name of a college, and possessed the privilege of attending to play at feasts, and on all occasions of a ceremonial kind. This privilege was at one time taken from, but afterwards restored to them. There is a denarius of the *Plautia* family, the type of which alludes to the banishment of these *Tibicines* from Rome, and their return to that city.—See *Plautia.*

Tibicines are represented, generally blowing the doubled flute, at sacrifices, on coins of Augustus, Domitianus, Hadrian, Antoninus Pius, Commodus, Sept. Severus, Caracalla, Geta, Philip sen. and jun., Trebonianus, Gallus, Volusianus, &c.

Tigris. Tiger.—This animal, observes Spanheim *(Pr.* i. 207), is not to be confounded with the leopard or the panther. His skin is marked, not with round spots like theirs, but with long stripes.—The tiger is the symbol of Bacchus. On denarii of the Vibia family one is present at a sacrifice to *Liber Pater.*—He is often seen at the feet of Bacchus on coins of Roman colonies. Havercamp gives a contorniate medal of Nero, on which the god of wine is figured, seated in a car drawn by Tigers.

Tigris—a celebrated river in Asia, which, rising in the greater Armenia, and flowing thence in a southerly direction, formed the eastern boundary of Mesopotamia (a tract of country lying, as its name signifies, between two rivers), the equally renowned Euphrates washing it on the western side. Below the site of the ancient Babylon, the Tigris forms a confluence with the Euphrates, and their streams, thus united, enter the *Sinus Persicus,* or Persian Gulf.—The extension of the Roman empire to the right bank of the Tigris, by the intervening regions, is at once recorded by the legend and symbolised by the type of a fine first brass medal of Trajan, which represents this river with the Euphrates. The emperor is standing between the personifications of these two mighty streams, with the figure of an Armenian at his feet.—See ARMENIA ET MESOPOTAMIA IN POTESTATEM P. R. REDACTAE.

TIT. *Titus.*—TIT. CAESAR, &c.—TIT. ET DOMIT. *Titus et Domitianus.*

Timor.—Fear, amongst various other affections, passions, and qualities of the mind, was, according to Plutarch, held sacred as a deity by the Lacedæmonians. And from such types as those of *Pallor* and *Pavor,* on coins of the Hostilia family, it would seem that the Romans, ever fond of intimating Greek examples, adopted this absurd system of worshipping the *mali,* as well as the *boni genii.*

Titia, a plebian family. Its coins present six varieties. One of its silver pieces, restored by Trajan, has on the obverse a winged and diademed head with long beard; and on others there is the head of Bacchus, crowned with ivy; the reverse exhibiting a flying pegasus, with Q. TITI.—The opinions of the learned on these types amount to nothing satisfactory or useful. And who the Q. Titus of the above cited denarius was is involved in conjectures neither interesting nor probable enough to claim further notice.

Titinia, a patrician as well as a plebeian family. Its denarii, which are common, have the winged head of Minerva, and the numeral letters XVI. behind it.—On the reverse, C. TITINI; and a victory in a biga. Its bronze money are the *As* or some of its divisions.

Tituria.—The order to which this family belonged (whether patrician or plebeian) is uncertain. Its surname was *Sabinus.*—Morell gives thirty-three varieties of its coins, which are all silver, and common. Nor, with the exception of two, do they offer any features of the least interest.—The former of these has on the obverse a bearded head, and is inscribed SABIN. A. P.V. On the reverse, a female with dishevelled hair and uplifted arms, sitting amidst a heap of bucklers, and on each side of her is a soldier, with shield in hand, as if about to cast it on her. Above is a crescent and a star. In the exergue L. TITVRI.

The surname SABIN*us* on the obverse of this medal was borne by Lucius Titurius, who caused it to be struck. "It may," says Visconti, "also refer to the portrait of Tatius, who was a Sabine." The legend of the reverse presents the prenomen and the name of this magistrate: L. TITVRI. *Lucius Titurius:* the crescent and the star, emblems of night, serve to point out the time when the act of treachery was perpetrated, according to this traditionary incident of Rome's earliest days.

The second denarius of the Tituria family, to which allusion has been made, as exhibiting an interesting connection with early Roman history, has on one side SABIN. and a bearded head, near which is TA in monogram; or, in others, A. P.V. —On the reverse, L. TITVRI. Two soldiers, each carrying a female figure.

The name of *Sabinus*, and the types on both the above described coins, associating themselves, as they do, with well-known narratives of the old writers, sufficiently prove that the *gens Tituria* was of Sabine origin. On the first medal (as in one of the Petronia family), we see Tarpeia sinking beneath the weight of shields successively flung upon her by the avengers of her perfidy, themselves not less perfidious, and adding brutal cruelty to the evasion of their mutually understood pledge to give their gold armlets, *not* their *brazen* bucklers, to the betrayer of her countrymen's stronghold.—But the type of the other denarius obviously alludes to the Sabine rape. And on this point, Eckhel reminds his classical readers that the manner in which the women are represented as carried off by their Roman ravishers, agrees with the graphic expressions of Ovid (*Art. Amator.* l. i. v. 127).

Si qua repugnarat nimium, comitemque negarat;
Sublatam cupido vir tulit ipse sinu.

That the head of the obverse was designed to pourtray the lineaments of Tatius, at that time king of the Sabines, is rendered the more highly probable from the letters TA in monogram, appearing on most of the denarii. This supposition is further strengthened by the circumstance of the same monogram occurring on a silver coin of Vettius Sabinus [see *Vettia* family].—As to the letters A.P. they have, says Eckhel, undoubtedly the same meaning as the ARG. PVB. (*Argento Publico*) on denarii of the Sextia family.—See *Tatius.*

TITVS (*Flavius Vespasianus*), eldest son of the emperor Vespasian by Domitilla, was born at Rome in the year v.c. 794 (Dec. 30th, A.D. 41).—Although brought up along with Britannicus, in the same licentious court where Nero's vicious propensities were nurtured, and not uncontaminated with its seductions, his docility in education saved him from utter ruin. Assisted in his devoted application to study by an extraordinary memory he was eloquent in speech, and felicitous in poetical composition. Skilful and adroit in gymnastic and equestrian exercises,

his warlike courage and his moral firmness were early displayed. Possessing the ability to execute, as well as the judgment to form great designs, he proved himself, often amidst the severest trials and under the most disastrous

circumstances, one of the first commanders of his time. To the loftiest qualities of genius there were, in his character conjoined a sweetness of temper and an affability of manners, that might truly be said to have won for him "golden opinions" from people of every sort and condition. Whilst yet a mere youth Titus began his military career in Germany; he afterwards served in Britain: in both those countries he was the companion and pupil of his father; and in the latter theatre of sanguinary warfare he gave a signal proof at once of his intrepidity and his filial affection, by rescuing Vespasian from a situation of the most imminent peril. On his return to Rome he was promoted by Nero from the rank of tribune to that of prefect, and to the command of a legion. Following his father to the Jewish war he successively planted the Roman eagles on the walls of Tarichæa and Gamala, two strong cities of Judæa.—At the end of the year v.c. 821 (A.D. 69) he went on a mission from Vespasian to salute Galba, when, hearing of the murder of that emperor, and of the aspiring movements of Vitellius, he opportunely halted, and returned to his father. Then taking advantage of the public hatred to Vitellius, he entered into negotiations with Mucius, governor of Syria, for transferring the sovereignty to Vespasian; and so successful was he in conciliating the favour of the legions, stationed in that and the neighbouring provinces, that they quickly proclaimed his father emperor in the room of Vitellius. Left by himself in the year v.c. 822 (A.D. 69), to complete the conquest of Judæa he was proclaimed by the senate, Cæsar, and Princeps Juventutis, and elected for the consulate of the following year as colleague of his father. And now, being specially entrusted by his imperial sire with the awful charge of carrying on the siege of Jerusalem, he directed his whole strength against the place, which he at length took by assault on the 8th of September, v.c. 823 (A.D. 70). "This celebrated city (as Beauvais says) was then destroyed, as had been predicted by the Son of God, after having flourished two thousand one hundred years, and its defence cost the life and the liberty of twelve hundred thousand Jews. It was not without shedding tears that Titus saw, in spite of all his efforts to save it, the destruction by fire of that famous temple of the Hebrews, a monument the most superb which the piety of men had ever raised to the honour of the Almighty." For this splendid achievement he was proclaimed *Imperator* by the soldiers. The following year (A.D. 71) quitting Palestine he went to Egypt, and thence returned to Rome, where, as his coins shew, he was designated *Imperator II.* by his father with whom he also shared triumphal honours, and was soon afterwards associated in the government of the empire, as Vespasian's sole colleague and appointed successor. His first exercise of the supreme power was marked by pride, and tainted by injustice, not unmixed with despotic violence and even with excesses of an odious kind. But on his accession to an undivided throne, at his father's death (year of Rome 832, 79th of our æra), these blots on his fair fame were effaced by a reformation so complete as to render him the model of good princes and of virtuous men. Humanely anxious for the welfare of his subjects, his liberality and munificence knew no bounds when either public calamities required to be assuaged through his ample funds, or when, in happier periods, the Roman taste for amphitheatric and circensean spectacles could be gratified, as they were always sure to be at his own enormous cost. The conquest of Britain, by his lieutenant Agricola (v.c. 832, A.D. 79), is recorded amongst the most interesting successes of his arms abroad. At home his course of policy bore the true impress of magnanimity and beneficence. The year above-mentioned was marked by a dreadful eruption of Mount Vesuvius, which laid waste the beautiful shores of Campania, and buried Herculaneum and Pompeii in lava and in ashes. In the following year (A.D. 80), by a most destructive fire at Rome, the temple of Jupiter Capitolinus and other edifices, both sacred and secular, were destroyed. On the other hand, whilst these structures were put in progress of restoration, Titus dedicated the stupendous ampitheatre, now commonly called the *Coliseum;* opened public baths; and gave the most magnificent shews to the people. Benignant and glorious indeed, yet eventful was the reign of this great prince; but too short for that generation of mankind in which he lived, and of which, for his active benevolence, he was justly named *(amor deliciæque)* the admiration and the delight. From the effects of poison, administered, as is believed, by his own ungrateful and wicked brother Domitian, this renowned emperor expired on the 13th of September, year of Rome 834, A.D. 81, in about the fortieth year of his age, having swayed the sceptre of the empire two years and nearly three months.

The coins of Titus are numerous. Some represent him with Vespasian, others with Domitian and with his daughter Julia.—On these, *as associated with his brother*, he is styled TIT. ET DOMIT. VESP. AVG. F.—Also CAESARES VESP. F.—LIBERI. IMP. AVG. VESP.

Alone, he is called, T. CAESar AUGusti *Filius:* on the reverse sometimes IMP.

After his father's death, IMP. TITVS CAES. VESP. or VESPASIAN. AVG. P. M., &c.

On coins struck after his death and consecration (which latter event took place by a *senatus consultum*), DIVVS TITVS AVGVSTVS, or DIVO AVG. T. DIVI. VESP. F. VESPASIANO.

In animadverting on the mint of Titus, for some singular points in the order of which it is difficult to assign any precise reason, Eckhel refers, with an expression of astonishment, to the fact, that there is no coin of this emperor, bearing the date of v. c. 824 (A.D. 71), which attests the conquest of Judæa; whereas it was Titus alone who brought the Jewish war to a decisive close, and in consequence of which he enjoyed a triumph with his father. "Beyond

all doubt (says the author of *Doct. Num. Vet.* vol. vi. p. 352), the medals which commemorate the conquest of Judæa, were without exception struck in subsequent years, although many coins are extant, with the head of Vespasian, up to the year in question. And, therefore, judging from the absence of this record on other undisputed coins of the same date, we may conclude it to be altogether probable that during this whole year (824) there were no coins of Titus struck, except those on which he appears in fellowship with Domitian. For had such been the case, it would seem strange that there should not be found, as a matter of course, on the coins of Titus, some memorial of a victory so signal, and so mainly attributable to his prowess and generalship."

The title of *Imperator* is variously placed on the coins of Titus, and in a manner differing from the general usage of all others of the Cæsars. On those struck v.c. 822–823, that title is omitted to be given him.—In 824, on his medals of the first half year, he is called CAES. DESIG. IMP., or *designatus imperator* (imperator elect): whilst on coins struck later in the same year he is styled T. IMP. CAESAR. And thenceforward, until he became *Augustus*, he is constantly termed T. CAES. IMP., the other titles following. From that time also he continuously presents the laureated head (with however the radiated crown on many second brass), but never the bare head.—It was in v.c. 832 that Titus received the dignity of Augustus; and then we find that the IMP., which was invariably put *last* on the coins of Titus, as *Cæsar*, was thenceforth put *first* on his coins as *Augustus*, and the inscription, by a perpetual rule, became IMP. TITVS CAES. VESP. AVG. &c.—On his coins struck in v.c. 824, he is called DESIGnatus IMPerator. "To this title," observes Eckhel, "it being the fruit of victory, no one was designated, or pre-ordained; but it was conferred *after* a victory by military acclamation. Moreover, Titus had been in the preceding year (823) already styled Imperator for the capture of Jerusalem.—The title of *Imperator*, therefore, given him in v.c. 824, is certainly to be understood of Titus as the *designatus consors*, or elect associate (with his father) in the imperial government."

Nor is it less certain, that on the medals of Titus, the word IMP. sometimes serves to denote colleagueship in government as well as the military title of *Imperator*, as conferred on account of victories. And from a chronological series of inscriptions on Titus's coins, Eckhel shews that he was *Imperator* for the first time in the year of Rome 823, and that the same title was renewed to him every successive year, and in some instances twice, and even four times, in one year, successively till 833–834, when he was IMP. XVI. (Imperator for the sixteenth and last time.)

Of this emperor's coins, the gold and silver, and the first and second brass, are common. The third brass rare. Brass medallions rare. Silver medallions (foreign die) RRR.

Titus had two wives. The first *Arricidia*, daughter of Tertullus, a Roman knight, whom he married when a young man, but who is not named on any medals. The other, *Marcia Furnilla*, born of an illustrious family, to whom a Greek medal has been, but in Eckhel's opinion erroneously, ascribed.

Toga.—A species of garment so peculiarly in use amongst the Romans, that *romanus* and *togatus* became synonymous terms. It was made of woollen stuff, generally white, without sleeves, circular, or as some say, semi-circular in form, and of such dimensions that when thrown over the body it entirely covered it down to the feet, as appears from coins and statues.—*Togæ* were of course different in colour and ornament, as well as in quality of material, according to the diversities of rank and age. It was large and fine and with ample folds for the rich man's wear, whilst for the frugal and the poor it was scanty and coarse. Only Roman citizens were allowed to clothe themselves in the toga. It is said that King Tullus Hostillius invented that called *prætexta*, a robe bordered with purple, as a distinction for men of rank.—(See *Prætexta*.)—In the first age of Rome the toga was a dress common to both sexes, but subsequently the women exchanged it for the *palla* or the *stola*.—Towards the decline of the republic, persons of high quality wore the toga lined with purple, and so adjusted on them that the front part fell a little below the knee. Statues, bas reliefs, and some medals serve to elucidate better than any verbal attempt at explanation what was the disposition and effect of the toga on the person. It was essentially the garb of peace, as contradistinguished from the *paludamentum* or military cloak. Hence to indicate a peaceful condition of public affairs, emperors were represented on their coins clothed in the toga prætexta. The expression *cedunt arma togæ* clearly points to the difference between the warlike and the pacific habiliment. Nevertheless, it appears that there was what bore the name of *Toga militaris*, which was expressly for the use of the soldiery, and so made as to be easily girded round the waist and shoulders so as to leave the legs free and unencumbered. When on coins emperors are figured with a portion of the toga thrown over the head, such an appearance is meant to signify that the personage himself was of sacerdotal dignity.

Toga picta, properly called the *vestis triumphalis*, being part of the usual costume of the triumphers—although also worn by the Consuls, at their inaugural *processus*. It was covered with embroidery, and with figures of divers

colours—and so far resembling the *toga purpurea*, which latter derived its name either from its being ornamented with large flowers of purple, or from its being dyed purple: it was the robe of the senators.—The *toga picta*, accompanying a legionary eagle, and a laurel crown, is exhibited on a denarius of Augustus.— See PARENS CONS. SVO. S. P. Q. R.

Togati, and *togata gens*—appellations given to those colonies and municipia whose inhabitants dressed themselves after the Roman fashion, and wore the *toga*.

Togatus—a male figure clothed in the toga, ascending a biga, appears on a silver coin of the *Farsuleia* family.—On a medal of the Postumia family we find a togated man, raising his right hand towards a legionary eagle.—On a denarius of the Cassia family, a male figure in the toga holds a voting tablet in his hand.

TON. *Tonans*—thundering—an epithet of Jupiter.—See IOV. TON. *Jovi Tonanti*.

TORQ. *Torquatus*; a surname of honour borne by the *Manlii*, derived from *torques*, a collar, which one of that high patrician race took from an enemy in battle.—Livy (*L.* vii. c. 10) says that (in the year V.C. 394, B.C. 357) T. Manlius, son of Lucius, one of the noblest of the Roman senators, having slain in single combat a Gaulish chieftain of remarkably large stature (who had challenged the Roman army to send for a chieftain against him), snatched a golden collar or torque from the body of his slaughtered foe, and without offering it any other indignity threw the gold spoil round his own neck. The historian concludes his animated description of the combat, by saying that in the soldiers' congratulatory effusions—*Torquati cognomen auditum, celebratum deinde posteris etiam, familiæque honori fuit*. "The appellation Torquatus was heard joined with his name; which, being generally adopted, has since done honour to the descendants of that whole line." Nor is the military exploit, with its consequences, recorded by Livy alone. Suetonius also makes it incidentally a subject of allusion that the posterity of Manlius wore the *torques* in memory of the event: *vetera familiarum insignia nobolissimo cuique ademit* (says he, speaking of the tyrant Caligula), *Torquato torquem, Cincinnato crinem, C. Pompeio stirpis antiquæ, Magni cognomen*. And it was for the same reason that the Manlii caused this honourable decoration of the golden collar to be engraved on their coins; nor was it the distinctive mark of those only who continued to be the members of the Manlia family. It is likewise seen, together with the surname TORQVATVS, on denarii of the *Junia* family, in consequence, as Ursinus explains, of T. Manlius Torquatus having, about the year of Rome 600 and odd, been adopted by D. Junius Silanus, and become therefore transferred into that family.—See *Manlia*.

TOXXOTES.—A horse walking, on whose thigh a mark is impressed; before the horse is a palm-branch. To this may be added AMOR: a horse standing, a palm-branch before it, and a similar mark on its thigh. Each figure of a horse is scooped out of the brass of the medal, and filled up with silver *(Morelli Specim.* p. 43.)

These several legends and types appear on two contorniates, each bearing on their obverse the head of Honorius. They unite in presenting examples of a practice, common amongst the ancients, and which prevails to this day— namely, that of giving names to horses.—From Homer we learn that Achilles had his Xanthus: Virgil sings of the Aethon of Pallas, and the Phoebus of Mezentius. Suetonius informs us that Incitatus was the name of the horse which the demented Caligula caused to be elected Consul. Dion names Borysthenes as the favourite steed of Hadrian ; and Capitolinus records that Volucris was the appellation which L. Verus bestowed on a "winning one" of his imperial stud. Names appear to have been selected for these noble quadrupeds, on account either of some corporeal quality, such as colour, swiftness, &c., or of disposition, as courage, good temper, &c. Frequently the name of the country, to the breed of which the animal belonged, such as *Seracusus,* for *Syracusius,* was adopted for it.—The horse *Toxotes,* on the first of these medals (wrong spelt with a *double* x.), was doubtless so denominated, from his speed, τοξότης being Greek for *Sagittarius* (an archer). The other was called *Amor,* most probably as indicating his master's affection for him. Each horse, therefore, may be considered to have been introduced on the coin where he is represented, on account of a race won (as shewn by that symbol of victory a palm-branch), an honour which ought not to be thought greater than the ancients would readily bestow on the merits of horses, since it is well-known that sumptuous monuments were erected to the memory of those noble creatures, and that even a city was built by Alexander the Great in honour of his Bucephalus.—See *Doct. Num. Vet.* vol. viii. p. 299 ; and *Contorniate Coins.*

TR. P. *Tribunitia Potestas.*—The Tribunitian power.—See the word.

TR. *Treveris.*—A mint-mark of money struck at Treves.

TROB. *Treveris in Officina Secunda.*—Coin struck in the second office of the mint at Treves.

TRA or TRAI. *Trajanus.*—IMP, CAES. TRAIANus.

Trabea—a vestment which differed from the common *toga* and likewise from the *prætexta* in being shorter and less ample. Its colour was white like the *sagum* of the soldiers, but ornamented with bands of purple called *trabes,* or *virgæ,* according as they were more or less broad. Liebe *(Goth. Numaria,* p. 254) says that the paludamentum and the chlamys are not to be confounded with the trabea ; but other writers assert that there was at least much analogy between them. What appears certain is that the trabea was placed over the tunic like the toga, and was particularly in vogue amongst the younger Romans of the equestrian order.

Traducta (Julia).—A city of this name was founded on the southern shore of Hispania Bætica, and on its site now stands Algesiras

in Andalusia, to the west of Carteia (now Rocadillo), and consequently near Gibraltar. The coins of the Roman colony, or municipium, are all Imperial, some having on their obverse the head of Augustus, with the legend PERM*issu* CAES*aris* AV*Gusti ;* the inscription of the reverse is IVL. TRAD., and the type presents either the heads of his two grandsons Caius Lucius Cæsars (looking opposite ways), or objects symbolical of those honours and functions which belonged to Augustus, such as the *oaken crown,* and *pontifical instruments,* allusive to the sovereign priesthood.—Other coins of this *Julia Traducta* bear on their obverses the head of Caius Cæsar, or that of Lucius Cæsar, singly and separately, and have for the respective types of their reverses either *an ear of bearded corn,* placed horizontally, or a *bunch of grapes,* serving, Vaillant says, (and he supports his interpretation on Strabo's authority) to denote that the *Traductani* of Spain possessed both corn and wine in abundance.—For a description of these rare medals, and for *fac simile* engravings, see Akerman's learned and valuable work on *Ancient Coins of Cities and Princes.*

A medal ascribed by Goltzius to the Emperor Claudius, and which that writer publishes as exhibiting the epigraph of COL. IVL. TRADVCTA, has given rise to much disputation amongst the learned. Whether the Goltzian coin be genuine, or whether it be spurious, thus much is certain, that there was *another* town of the same name, and it appears to have been situate on the coast of Mauritania Tingitana (now Fez, in Northern Africa.) According to a passage in the elder Pliny, its original appellation was Tingis (now Tangier), and it was made a colony by Claudius under the title of *Julia Traducta.*

TRAJANVS *(M. Ulpius)* was born at Italica (now *Sevilla la vieja,* or Old Seville*),* in Spain, in the year of Rome 806, 18th of September, A.D. 52. His family was more distinguished for

its antiquity than its rank ; his father being a soldier of high reputation (whose portrait was afterwards placed on his son's coinage), was the first of his race who enjoyed the honour of the consulate. Whilst yet a boy in age, Trajan commenced his practical study of the art of war, under the paternal auspices, in campaigns against the Parthians, and with so much success that he became one of the most celebrated generals, whose victories are enrolled in the annals of Rome. He was made prætor v.c. 839

(A.D. 86), and consul 844 (A.D. 91). After which he was sent by Domitian into Spain, whence by command of the same emperor he proceed to quell an insurrection in Germany. It was in the autumn of the year v.c. 850 (A.D. 97). whilst residing at Colonia Agrippina (now Cologne), as prefect of the Lower Germany, and, entertaining no views of such elevation, that he was adopted by Nerva, being, as Pliny the consul expresses it—*Simul FILIVS, simul CAESAR, mox IMPERATOR, et censors TRIB. POTESTATIS, et omnia pariter, et statim, factus es.* Nerva also shared with him the title of *Germanicus.*—Those two princes, indeed, seemed as men destined by their union to secure the prosperity and happiness of the empire. The reign of Nerva was too brief; but that of Trajan was extended long enough to exhibit him as the approved friend of the Roman people, and the firm protector of all the Roman families.—At the death of Nerva (v.c. 851, A.D. 98), Trajan took the title of Augustus, being still at Cologne employed in suppressing the outbreaks of certain barbarous tribes in that vicinity.—The following year he returned to Rome, entering the city on foot, amidst the applauses of the citizens. Not only the panegyric of Pliny who spoils the praise of truth itself by the extravagance of flattery; but also the more calm and sober evidences of coins, unite in attesting that his largesses *(congiaria)* were distributed to the people on a scale of most munificent liberality. This year (v.c.832, A.D.99) not only the title of *Pater Patriæ* was assigned to him, but also the novel and to him peculiarly acceptable appellation of *Optimus* was conferred on him by the senate, although it does not appear so early on his medals. Having refused to pay the annual tribute which Decebalus, king of the Dacians, had exacted from the pusillanimous Domitian, Trajan followed up his determination to wipe away this ignominy from the Roman name, by entering Dacia at the head of his armies, v.c. 854, A.D. 101. The war continued till v.c. 856, A.D. 103, when having lost his capital Sarmizegethusa, and the greater part of his kingdom, Decebalus sought an audience of Trajan and humbly sued for peace, which he obtained on very hard conditions. Returning shortly after these successes to Rome, Trajan enjoyed *ex invicta gente primum trumphum,* and received from the senate his surname of *Dacicus.*—In the year v. c. 847 A. D. 104, Decebalus, being openly charged with having violated the terms of his treaty with the empire, and with having been guilty of renewed acts of aggression, was again denounced by the senate as the enemy of the Roman people.— Accordingly, the following year, Trajan having completed his stupendous work of constructing a stone bridge over the Danube, entered Dacia, for the second time, and again totally defeated its brave but rash and unfortunate monarch, who killed himself in despair. The royal treasures of Decebalus were found either sunk in the river Sargetia, or buried in caves. The emperor made a province of this kingdom, and returning to

Rome (v. c. 859 A. D. 106), received the fullest honours of a triumph for his conquest. Meanwhile, an expedition was undertaken by one of Trajan's generals against that part of Arabia which borders on Judæa. It was crowned with success, and is recorded to the emperor's honour, on coins by the legend ARAB*ia* ADQVIS*ita,* struck in the name and by authority of S.P.Q.R. —In the same year he began to construct a road through the Pontine Marshes, besides repairing the old paved road from Beneventum to Brundusium, which great works he finished v.c. 863 A.D. 110, at his own expense. [See VIA TRAIANA.]—From the last-mentioned period he employed an interval of nearly five years in embellishing Rome and Italy with numbers of useful as well as magnificent works, and in return (v. c. 866 A.D. 113) had the sculptured pillar of the Forum dedicated to his name and honour—a monument still existing to perpetuate the memory of his Dacian victories. In v. c. 867 A.D. 114, hearing that Chosroes, king of Parthia, had disposed of the crown of Armenia, Trajan, from a professed regard for the rights of the Roman empire which he deemed violated by this procedure, but in reality from a too great love of conquest and military glory, carried the terror of his arms into the east, when he placed a Roman governor over the Parthians, whom he had conquered, and afterwards (v. c. 868 A.D. 115) compelled Armenia and Mesopotamia to acknowledge his government.—For these brilliant achievements he was called *Parthicus* by the soldiers, a title soon afterwards confirmed by the senate and inscribed on his coins : nor was it an empty name; for Dion narrates the admission of the Parthian king to the presence of Trajan as a suppliant for the Parthian throne. In v. c. 869 A.D. 116, he entered Assyria, and having first made a treaty of occupation with the city of Ctesiphon, on the Tigris, he penetrated to the shores of the Persian Gulf. On his return to Ctesiphon he appointed Parthamaspates, king of Parthia, in the room of Chosroes, whom he had deposed.—[See REX PARTHIS DATVS.]—And he explored that part of Arabia, situate between the rivers Tigris and Euphrates (called from that circumstance Mesopotamia).—Nor was it to the Parthians only that this great emperor assigned a sovereign ; but, according to Dion, Eutropius, and other writers, he also appointed rulers to other nations, and bestowed sceptres on other princes—[See REGNA ADSIGNATA.]—at the same time receiving some into alliance with him ; forming treaties of peace and amity with others; and adjusting quarrels which had subsisted between different states that owned his influence or felt his power. But the days of this great prince were numbered, and his career of existence, as well as of glory, was fast verging to its close. In returning from his oriental expedition, Trajan became a prey to disease. He hastened to embark for Rome, but the disorder, which was dropsical, made such rapid progress that he was obliged to halt at Selinuntum, in Cilicia, where, having adopted Hadrian, he expired, on the 10th August, v.c. 870, A.D. 117, at the age of 61, according to some, of 65 as others assert. He had reigned nineteen years and a half. His body was burnt at Selinuntum; and his ashes, enclosed in a golden urn, were carried to Rome by Plotina and Matidia (his wife and sister), and there deposited within, or upon, the celebrated column which the senate and people had raised to his imperishable renown.—Of portly stature, robust in frame, and hardy in constitution yet exhibiting in his countenance an air of grandeur that commanded reverence, Trajan was a man not less intellectually than physically qualified by nature to govern such an empire as that of Rome. After all the atrocities which had characterised most of his predecessors, he was regarded as a blessing specially sent by Providence to comfort and restore an afflicted world. His great and beneficent actions, emanated from a noble mind and an amiable disposition—simple and modest in his manners, benevolent, sincere, indulgent, generous, patient, yet just, firm, and decisive, he comported himself towards the senate with that respect, and towards the people with that benign affability, which made all feel that under him the ancient freedom was restored, and that the surname of *Optimus*, bestowed on him by universal concurrence, was a title well deserved. A hero in valour, Trajan re-established the discipline of the armies, by being himself an example equally of the civil and the military virtues. As in private life moderate and unostentatious, so whenever state policy or the majesty of the Roman name, whether in peace or in war, required it, he was most liberal in expenditure, and conspicuous for the highest display of imperial magnificence. His coins bear inscriptive testimony to the realization of many of his great projects for the benefit of his subjects and advantage of his vast territories, in the founding of cities, the formation of roads, the construction of ports and bridges, and the building of edifices at once superb and useful. Great and good in general character and conduct, he was not without vices. A proneness to excess in wine is mentioned as one, and that not the worst of two degrading propensities laid to his charge. But the fault which comes most prominently into view, as affecting his character for princely wisdom and prudence, was his extreme fondness for military glory—a passion which led him into continual warfare, thus endangering the safety of his empire by too great an extension of its boundaries, and consequently absenting himself too often and too long from the proper seat of administrative power—the metropolitan centre of his dominions. Nevertheless so dearly, and indeed so justly upon the whole, was the memory of this illustrious emperor prized by the Romans, that for ages afterwards in congratulating each succeeding prince on his accession to the throne of the Cæsars, the senate expressed its wish that he might be "happier than Augustus, and better than Trajan:" *felicior Augusto—Trajano melior.*— We have the evidence of coins, as well as of numerous inscriptions, together with not a few passages from historians to show that

Trajan was placed after his death, according to the superstitious system of the Greek apotheosis, in the number of the celestial divinities. Spartianus affirms that even a temple was dedicated to the worship of DIVVS TRAIANVS.

TITLES OF TRAJAN.

Optimus.—Pliny, in whose Panegyric the titles conferred by the senate on Trajan are enumerated, attests the fact that that of *Optimus* was given to him soon after his arrival at Rome from Germany—namely, about the year v.c. 853 (A.D. 100); but neither on coins, marbles, nor public monuments, does this title appear to have been used in conjunction with his own name, before the year 858, A.D. 105; and then, as regards his medals, it never appears on the obverse, but always on the reverse, and almost always this, S. P. Q. R. OPTIMO PRINCIPI.—It is also to be observed, that at the same period in which this form begins to obtain, the custom also began of inscribing the names and titles of Trajan always in the dative; in other words, in the dedicatory style. Hence, it is sufficiently evident, that about the same time, by a new *senatus consultum*, it was decreed that the title *Optimus Princeps* should be inscribed on public monuments. At length, however, in the year v.c. 867, A.D. 114, it became the practice to omit *Optimus Princeps* on the reverse of his coins, and to transfer the word *Optimus* by itself to the obverse, in such a way, as that it always is found to occupy the intermediate space between TRAIANO and AVG.—From this date, therefore, it appears that the title in question began to be applied to Trajan as a real cognomen, and its use as such extended to the coins of his successor Hadrian, to whom, because it was become a true surname, it passed by adoption.—See Eckhel's observations on the titles of Trajan, vol. vi., p. 458.

Germanicus.—The title of *Germanicus* was not assigned to Trajan on account of any victory gained by him in Germany, but devolved to him as the adopted son of Nerva—the law of adoption causing the son to succeed to all the titles of the father. An instance of the operation of this same legal right was exhibited in the case of Hadrian, who when first recognised by the Roman Senate and people as Trajan's adopted son, was called *Optimus, Dacicus, Parthicus*—the cognomina of his predecessor. Pliny, therefore, asserts what is quite in accordance with truth, when he says of Trajan—*cum Germaniæ præsideret, GERMANICI nomen hinc* (Roma) *missum.* Indeed the title was communicated to him by adoption. In like manner, and on the same principle, the titles *Filius, Cæsar,* and *Imperator* were also sent to him from Rome. Accordingly, the first coins of Trajan exhibit the title of *Ger-manicus*, as belonging to him by adoption, nor are they omitted even in the latest products of his mint.

Dacicus.—This title was conferred on Trajan, for his glorious victories over the Dacians, and began to be used on coins and other public monuments in the year v.c. 356-57, A.D. 104.

Parthicus.—It has been observed, in the biographical notice of this emperor, that the epithet *Parthicus* (the Parthian) began to be included amongst the titles of Trajan, v.c. 869 (A.D. 116), in which year the tribunitian power is numbered XIX. and XX. In a copious note of explanation on this point, the learned Eckhel shews on the authority of Dion that, v.c. 868 (A.D. 115), after or on the taking of Nisibis (now Nisbin), an important town in Mesopotamia (and for nearly two centuries and a half afterwards a frontier of the empire), Trajan was called *Parthicus* by his soldiers. But, not choosing to rest his pretensions to that honour on their acclaims alone, he waited for the confirmatory act of the senate before he assumed it. That confirmation appears to have been awarded on the occasion of his taking Ctesiphon, which happened about the year v.c. 369 (A.D. 116), from which time the title began to be ascribed to him on public monuments. There is extant an extremely rare consecration medal of Trajan, struck in gold, which proves that, on account of his great successes against the Parthians, not only was the name of *Parthicus* decreed to him, but permanent games *(ludi)* or spectacles of triumph *(spectacula triumphalia)* called "Parthian" were instituted to the honour of his name and memory by the senate and people of Rome.—See TRIVMPHVS PARTHICVS.

The coins of Trajan are very numerous.—On these, amongst other inscriptions, he is styled —IMP. CAES. NERVA TRAIAN. AVG.—IMP. CAES. TRAIAN. AVG. GERM. DACICVS. P. P.— IMP. CAES. NER. TRAIANVS. OPTIMVS. AVG. GER. DAC. PARTHICVS. P. P.—After his death and consecration, DIVVS TRAIANVS PARTHICVS.—DIVVS TRAIANVS PARTH. AVG. PATER.

Of Roman die.—Gold ᶜ. Some reverses RR.; that with the head of Trajan's father RRR.— Silver C. There are a few rare reverses in this metal.—Silver medallions RR. First, second, and third brass C. Some reverses RR. and RRR.—Brass medallions RRR.

Of Foreign fabric.—Silver medallions RR.— Brass Latin Colonial RR. RRR.

Several pieces represent Trajan with Nerva, with his father, with his Empress Plotina, and with Hadrian. These are of great rarity. Trajan restored many coins of Roman families, and several of his imperial predecessors. For a list of these see Akerman's *Descript. Cat.* Amongst the coinage of this emperor have been found some very remarkable pieces, to which Eckhel and other erudite medallists give the appellation of *numi metallorum*, as having been struck in the metal of different provinces of the empire, such as Dalmatia, Pannonia, Noricum, &c.— See METAL. DELM, &c.

TRAJANVS (*M. Ulpius*), the father of Trajanus Augustus, born in Spain, appears to have been a distinguished soldier during the reign of Nero. For it is recorded by Josephus (*Bell. Jud.* l. iii. c. 7, s. 31) that Vespasian, then in chief command of the Roman army employed in the Jewish war, sent out Trajan, commander of the tenth legion, with one thousand horsemen

and two thousand foot, against a city called *Japha*, near Iotapata, in which expedition he showed great courage, skill, and prudence; but, at the moment when the besieged were reduced to the last extremity, he solicited Vespasian to send Titus with a small reinforcement, that to the son of his general might devolve the honour of taking the place.—The same historian records another instance during the same memorable contest, in which Trajan again served ably and successfully as Titus's companion in arms. For the qualities of a brave and good officer, therefore, he stood high in the confidence of Vespasian, who soon after his own accession to the imperial throne, caused him to be elected consul. Pliny the younger calls the elder Trajan *consularis* (of consular dignity) and has thus preserved the remembrance of this event.—the Calendars *(Fasti)* making no mention of his name (yet there is no doubt, says Eckhel, of his having been *consul suffectus*—i.e., chosen to fill the consulate). He also seems to have been at that time enrolled amongst the patricians; for, Pliny (in the same passage of his Panegyric on the emperor, his son), also designates him as *patricius.* After the period of his consulship, he was sent as propraetor into Syria. This fact is ascertained from a remarkable brass medal published in the Pembroke Museum (part 3, tab. 87), and the existence of which was previously unknown to Vaillant and to Spanheim. The coin in question bears on its obverse the laureated head of Titus, with the letters IMP. PON., the rest of the legend being effaced.— For legend of reverse it has ΕΠΙ ΤΡΑΙΑΝΟΥ ΑΝΤΙΟΧΕΩΝ ΕΤ ΕΚΡ *(Sub Traiano, Antiochensium, Anno* 125).—Eckhel shews from the epocha, ΕΚΡ, marked on this coin of Antioch in Syria, that it was struck in the year of Rome 829 (A.D. 76); and, moreover, that it proves, what is not to be gleaned from any writer, the fact of Syria being then governed by *Trajanus Pater* as propraetor.—There is a fine passage in the Panegyric of Pliny above alluded to, which expressly bears testimony to the fact that Trajan the father boldly grappled in the field of battle with Parthian ferocity and haughtiness *(ferociam, superbiamque Parthicam)*, and won well deserved laurels in victory over that formidable enemy of the Romans. But the time and other circumstances are not known. "It appears, however (says Eckhel), from what I have observed in the annals of Vespasian up to the year v.c. 828 (A.D. 75), and Belley has carried his remarks still further, that it was about the period when Vespasian was embroiled with Vologeses the Parthian."—Since, therefore, according to the coin above quoted, *Trajanus Pater* was governor of Syria, and since he is mentioned by Pliny as decorated with the Parthian laurel, the probability is that the conduct of that war had been entrusted to the Propraetor Trajan by Vespasian, and that he, in consequence, obtained the ornaments of a triumph, for Pliny in another place also calls him *triumphalis.* That he was promoted from the propraetorship of Syria to the proconsular government of Asia, is a fact discovered in a celebrated Greek inscription found at Laodicea in Phrygia. It is a marble dedicated to Titus Cæsar in his seventh consulship by *Marcus Ulpius Trajanus Proconsul,* thus demonstrating that the Trajanus named on this monumental stone was of the *Ulpia* family ; whilst from the circumstance of Titus's seventh consulate being recorded thereon, it is rendered no less certain that the marble was dedicated in the year V.C. 832, A.D. 79. And as it belongs without doubt to Trajan the father, so it shews that he was at that time Proconsul of Asia. What afterwards were the incidents of his life, and in what year he died, is not known. But it is clear from the tenour of a passage in Pliny's Panegyric, that at the time when that composition was delivered to the emperor in the name of the senate, viz., in the year V.C. 853, A.D. 100, Trajan the elder was no longer living. It has been seen from Pliny's account that he was *patricius, consularis,* and *triumphalis ;* and, from both coin and marble, that he had been governor first of Syria, next of Asia. That after his death he was deified is equally certain, although all the ancient historians are silent upon it. This fact is attested by Latin coins, struck in gold and silver by order of Trajan the son, and which bearing on one side the name, titles, and portraiture of that emperor, exhibit for legend on the other side DIVVS PATER TRAIANVS. The type of one of these very rare reverses is the bare head of *Trajanus Pater,* and that of the other represents him seated, holding in his right hand a patera, and in his left the *hasta pura,* attributes of divinity. There are also gold and silver medals, with the head of Trajan the Emperor on their obverse, and the head of Nerva laureated, and that of Trajan's father without laurel, on the reverse, of which the legend is DIVI NERVA ET TRAIANVS PATER.—Respecting these three coins, Eckhel remarks that they furnish a second example (that of Domitilla, wife of Vespasian, being the first) of a private individual being numbered with the deities.—It also deserves attention that Trajan's father is depicted without the laurel crown, whilst a similar consecration medal, dedicated by the same emperor to his father by adoption, presents Nerva with laureated head ; thus making the distinction between a private person and an emperor.— The year in which *Trajanus Augustus,* in filial piety, caused divine honours to be paid to his father, is uncertain.—Eckhel assigns good reasons for thinking that, as these medals bear the same date, and also exhibit the same form of inscription on their respective obverses, which appear on the coin of the *Forum Trajani* and on that of the *Basilica Ulpia* (V.C. 867, A.D. 114), it is probable that Trajan the emperor, when he dedicated his forum, added some new testimonies of his veneration for the memory of the already consecrated Nerva, and willingly took the same opportunity to offer similar honours of deification to his natural parent.—See *Doct. Num. Vet.* vol. vi. p. 433 *et. seq.*

Trajanus.—See *Decius Trajanus.*

TRAIECTVS.—This epigraph, signifying the passage over a river, or a short transit by sea, appears on brass medallions of Caracalla, of Gordianus III., and of Carinus.—On the coin of the first named Emperor, the accompanying type represents him in the act of passing over a river, at the head of his guards, on a bridge of boats. In the second and third instance of the word *Trajectus* being used, we see the prætorian galley, with the emperor at the helm, soldiers bearing military ensigns, and rowers at their oars.—The TRAIECTVS of Caracalla is shown by the remainder of the inscription (PONTIF. TR. P. XII. COS. III.) to have been struck A.V.C. 962, A.D. 209, whilst that prince was engaged with Severus, his father, in war with the Britons. The TRAIECTVS AVG. *(Trajectus Augusti)* of Gordianus III., marked with the record of his fifth tribunate and second consulate (TR. P. V. COS. III.), corresponds in the date of its coinage with A.V.C. 995 A.D. 242—the year in which that emperor, according to Capitolinus, passed over from Thrace into Asia, namely by the traject of the Hellespont, at the head of an army. The TRAIECTVS AVGG. *(Trajectus Augustorum)* of Carinus is assigned by Eckhel to the first year of that prince's association in the imperial government, viz., V.C. 1035, A.D. 282.— Banduri thinks that the legend refers to the passage of the river Euphrates or of the Tigris. But Eckhel, looking to the *ship* and its military freight, which form the type, with greater probability, regards the coin as having been struck by Carinus in honour of his father Carus and his brother Numerianus, to perpetuate the remembrance of their joint traject across the Hellespontian straight, preparatory to an expedition against the Persians, undertaken the following year.

TRANQUILLINA *(Furia Sabinia),* daughter of Misitheus, Præfect of the Prætorians and Prime Minister of Gordianus III.—That promising  young prince's friendship for and confidence in so wise, eloquent, and able a statesman, and so eminently good a man, rendered him the more capable of appreciating the merits of Tranquillina; and, preferring her to any of the daughters of the most illustrious Roman families, he gave her his hand in marriage, V.C. 994, A.D. 241. Young, beautiful, and intelligent, she graced, by the sweetness of her disposition and the purity of her morals, the illustrious elevation to which Gordian had raised her, and secured to her from the virtuous of all ranks of both sexes throughout the empire, congenial tributes and public testimonies of love, respect, and admiration. She survived her murdered husband ; but her subsequent lot in life and the period of her death remain equally without record.—Of this empress's coins there are but few of Roman die— none *genuine* in gold. The silver and first and second brass in the highest degree of rarity. She is styled on these SABINIA TRANQVILLINA AVG*usta*. Her prenomen *Furia* is omitted on her Latin coins; but it frequently appears on the more numerous Greek medals struck in honour of this excellent princess, from one of which the portrait above is engraved.

Tranquillitas.—Tranquillity. The companion of peace *(Comes Pacis)* as Froëlich terms her.— Security and tranquillity, or quiet, are usually found united, and on some coins are typified under a similar figure and with similar attributes—namely, those of a woman resting her left elbow on a pilaster, and holding the *hasta* in her right hand. The effigy of *Tranquillitas* is seen on a silver coin of Antoninus Pius, as a female standing with a rudder and ears of corn, and with the circumscription TRANQ*uillitas* TR. POT. XIII. (or XIIII.) COS. III. (A.D. 153). Also on a gold coin of the same emperor, with legend of reverse TRANQVILLITAS AVG. It is truly appropriate to the reign of this wise and good emperor. Not so the following.

TRANQVILLITAS AVGG. — This legend appears on the reverse of a first brass and of

a denarius of Phillip senior, from the latter of which the annexed cut is taken. The type is that of a woman standing. She holds in her right hand some animal; and the *hasta pura* in her left.—Mediobarbus calls what the female figure on this coin holds in her right hand a dolphin in one instance, and in another describes it as a capricorn: on some it is not unlike a rabbit, but which is not confirmed by a close inspection. Eckhel, who quotes the type from finely preserved specimens in the imperial cabinet of Vienna, pronounces it to be a dragon; and of the same form which the Romans were accustomed to place on their military ensigns— with this difference, that the *draco* of the coin has two feet outspread, which the dragons on the military ensigns have not.—An enigma is presented in this numismatic image of the dragon, or great serpent, which the erudite and acute author of *Doctrina Num. Vet.* (vol. vii., p. 328) thus undertakes the task of solving:— That dragons were the ensigns of the Roman cohorts, is expressly stated by Vegetius—"The chief standard (says he) of the whole legion is the eagle, which is carried by an officer styled the *Aquilifer*. Dragons *(dracones)* are also borne in battle, in each cohort, by officers called *draconarii*." That they were interwoven on the standards we learn from Ammianus, in his description of Constantius's solemn entry into Rome. "Others (says that writer) were surrounded by dragons woven in purple threads fixed on spears, with gold and jewelled heads; blown about with their gaping mouths, and so appearing to hiss with indignation, lashing the long folds of their tails in the wind." Ammianus elsewhere mentions dragons fixed to spears. And Trebellius alludes to the appearance of

dragons, among the military ensigns at the vain pompous processions of Gallienus. The learned Frenchman Le Beau has collected further testimony on this subject even from the poets. It moreover appears, as well from the Trajan column as from Lucian's account, that long prior to the period of Philip senior, dragons fixed on the tops of spears, were used as standards by the Dacians and the Parthians. We may, therefore conclude that the dragon on the coin in question, borne by a woman, alludes to the *tranquillity* (which this murderous traitor to his own sovereign *wished to be thought*) ensured to the empire, by the fidelity and valour of the cohorts. The same reverse is likewise found on a very rare coin of Tacitus, with doubtless a similar meaning.—See *Draco*.

In the mintage of Constantine the Great are some coins, circumscribed on their reverses BEATA TRANQVILLITAS—the types of these are a globe or an altar, on which we read the words VOTIS XX.

TRB. *Treveris in Officina Secunda*.—Mintmark of coins struck at Treves in the second monetal office of that city.

TRB. *Tribunitia*.—TRB. P. CONS. IIII. *Tribunitia Potestate, Consul, Quartum*, on third brass of Constantinus Magnus.

Trebania, a family of uncertain order. Its coins exhibit four varieties, none of which are of any interest. The name of *Lucius* TREBAN*ius*, an urban quæstor, or monetal triumvir appears on a denarius of this family, with the head of Minerva on one side, and with Jupiter Fulminator in a quadriga on the other.

Trebellianus—one of the usurpers of imperial power—proclaimed Augustus in Isauria, towards A.D. 264; killed some months afterwards. The coins ascribed to Trebellianus are false.

TREBONIANVS GALLVS *(Caius Vibius)*.
—This emperor's family, native country, and time of birth are not known with any degree of

certainty. As general of the Mœsian army, he was at the battle which Trajanus Decius fought with the Goths, and is said to have most perfidiously betrayed his trust, causing that brave prince and his son to perish in the morasses near Abricium (A.V.C. 1004) A.D. 251.—Being immediately afterwards proclaimed Augustus, he began his reign by conferring the title of Cæsar on his son Volusianus, and by making Hostillianus, son of Trajanus Decius, his colleague in the supreme government.—In the same year he advanced Volusianus to the sovereign rank of Augustus; and precipitately concluded an ignominious treaty of peace with the Gothic invaders of the empire, whom he not only permitted to return to their own country with their booty, and even with their Roman prisoners, but also engaged to pay them an annual tribute in gold. Having in this base and impolitic manner pacified for a time the foreign enemies of the state, he arrived at Rome, into which he made as pompous an entry as if the peace he had just concluded with the barbarians had been the fruit of his victories over them. The pestilence, which was then ravaging the world, had attained its most frightful mortality. Hostilianus is said to have been one of its numberless victims A.D. 252.—Trebonianus, ascribing to the Christians this wide-spread and desolating plague, subjected them to a cruel persecution. Meanwhile, he and his son remained in the city, endeavouring to gain popular favour by their courtesies and liberalities; nor with all such as were as indolent, voluptuous, and corrupt as themselves did they fail of success. But famine accompanied pestilence.—The Goths, in another invasion, on one side, and the Persians, rushing across the eastern frontier on the other, over-ran the finest provinces, and the reign of Trebonianus became a succession of miseries, devastations, and horrors. In 253, Aemilianus, commander of the legions in Thrace and Mœsia, who had just vanquished the Gothic invaders, was proclaimed emperor by his soldiers. On hearing this, Trebonianus at length abandoned the course of effeminate luxury, which had brought his affairs to the verge of ruin, and began to take measures for the defence of his throne. He entrusted the first operations of the war to Valerianus, who had for that purpose drawn forces from Gaul and Germany. But Æmilian was beforehand with him, and ere the close of the year had entered Italy at the head of a great army.—In the beginning of 254, Trebonianus set out from Rome to encounter Æmilian, by whom he was totally defeated in a pitched battle; his own soldiers, despising his cowardice, slew him in his flight, together with his son Volusianus, near Interamna (now Terni), in Umbria. He died in the 49th year of his age. During the eighteen months of his holding the government, he had done nothing worthy of praise, nor had he been favoured with a single incident of good fortune; on the contrary, his reign was one of the most calamitous, as well as the most disgraceful, recorded in the annals of the empire. For the consequences which immediately followed the deaths of Trebonianus and Volusianus, see *Æmilianus* and *Valerianus*.

The coins of Trebonianus Gallus are—in gold, RRR.; in silver C. (with very few exceptions); first and second brass C.; Latin colonial R.—On them he is styled IMP. C. GALLVS. AVG. IMP. CAES. VIB. TREB. GALLVS. AVG.—IMP. CAE. C. VIB. TREB. GALLVS. AUG.

TRES GALLIAE.—This epigraph, on the reverse of a very rare silver coin of Galba, accompanies the type of three female heads upon globes; before each of which is (sometimes) an ear of corn.—The obverse exhibits an equestrian figure of Galba, with the circumscription of SERV. GALBA IMP.

This coin would seem to make *Gallia* consist of three divisions only as described by Julius

Cæsar; whereas later historians inform us that it was portioned off by Augustus (A.V.C. 727, B.C. 27) into four great provinces—namely, Narbonensis, Aquitania, Lugdunensis, and Belgica.—On the testimony of Tacitus, however, it may be believed that Belgica was afterwards excluded from this arrangement, because those Gaulish cities which lay nearest to the Germanic legions obtained from Galba neither the *jus civitatis*, nor any relief from taxation, as the others had done; nay, some of those cities were subjected to a diminution of territory, probably on account of their having too tardily given in their adhesion to him even after Vindex had been slain.—But this omission of Belgic Gaul is observable on marble also. Thus on one, in Gruter, we read TRIVM. PROV. GALL. LVGDVNENS. NARBONENS. ET AQVITANENS. The same three provinces are doubtless alluded to on other marbles inscribed TRES. PROVINC. GALL. It is likely then that Belgica was separated from the other three Galliæ, the whole tract of Gaul situated on the banks of the Rhine having been reduced to subjection and divided by Augustus into *Germania Superior* and *Inferior*. This fact is gathered from Tacitus, who, in his *Annals* (i. 31), speaks of two armies formed on the Rhine, one in the Upper, the other in the Lower Germany, and both subordinate to Germanicus, the commander-in-chief, then in the interior of Gaul, holding the assembly of states and collecting the revenues of that nation. The same writer mentions, under the reign of Tiberius, "Germania superior" and "Germania inferior." But it is to be remembered that both these districts lay on the left bank of the Rhine, and formed no part of Germany properly so called. From that time the *provincia Belgica* and *Germania superior* and *inferior* seem to have constituted one and the same territorial body. Hence they are often united together in inscriptions, as in Gruter, T. Varius Clemens is called PROC. PROVINC. BELGICAE. ET. VTRIVSQ. GERMANIAE. And in Spon, C. Furius Sabinus is styled PROC. PROV. BELGIC. ET DVARVM. GERMANIAR.—Hardouin excludes Narbonensis (instead of Belgica) from the Tres Galliæ of this singular coin, on the ground that Pliny divides *Gallia Comata* into three distinct tribes—viz., Aquitani, Lugdunenses, or Celtæ, and Belgæ.— Baron Bimard also unites these provinces to the exclusion of Narbonensis. Vaillant, in noticing the denarius in question, affirms that under Galba the three provincial divisions of Gaul were respectively denominated Belgica, Celtica, and Aquitanica.—Amidst these uncertainties, the opinion of Eckhel, which has been first referred to, appears in every respect to be the best supported, and consequently the most entitled to adoption.

Treveri—a numerous and important tribe of people in *Gallia Belgica*. The Romans gave the name of *Augusta* to their chief city, which still reveals its antiquity under its modern name of Treves, situated on the Moselle, or *Mosella*, a tributary of the Rhine.—It was one of six cities in Gaul to which the privilege of coining money was granted, during the lower empire. The appellation of the *Treveri* abbreviated, is of very frequent occurrence as a monetal subsignation such as TR. P. *Treveris percussa*, or *Treverensis Pecunia*. (Money struck at Treves.) TR. OBS. *Treveris Obsignata*, or *Treveris Officina Secunda Signata*. (Money struck at Treves : or, money struck at Treves in the second office of the mint of that city.)

TRIB. P. ; or TRIB. POT. ; or TRIBV. POTEST.—See *Tribunitia Potestas*.

Tribunitia Potestas. The tribunitian power.— It is well known that the Tribunes of the People *(tribuni plebis)* were magistrates created at Rome, sixteen years (as it is said) after the abolition of Royalty (v.c. 262), to protect the rights and advocate the claims of the plebeians against the over-bearing and tyrannical conduct of the patricians. It is equally well known, that by means, and under circumstances, which historians have fully explained, but which it comes not within the province of this work to do more than incidentally allude to, the strength and power of this popular magistracy, gradually increasing, arrived at such a pitch as rendered it not only a perpetual source of vexation and annoyance to the aristocracy ; but also enabled it to make inroads on the privileges, and to compete with the functions, of the highest magistrates. After being thus elevated in the scale of political and judicial importance, the tribunate became in its turn an object of jealousy and hatred to those ambitious factionaries, who, like Sylla and Marius, either by their corrupt proceedings undermined, or by their open violence overthrew, the liberties of the republic, and paved the way for the usurpations of Julius Cæsar, and for the proscriptive tyranny of that triumvirate on which the artful Augustus subsequently built a superstructure of imperial power.—There is a denarius of the *Lollia* family (see p. 521 of this Dictionary), the type of which, according to Morell, alludes to the restoration, A.V.C. 684, of that authority *(potestas)*, which the constitution had assigned to the *Tribuni Plebis*, but which, under Sylla's dictatorship, had dwindled into a mere name. As one of the attributes of sovereignty it eventually fell, with other dignities, into the hands of the emperors, who, reserving it to themselves, assumed the tribunitian title, not because it was the first in rank, but because it would have given too much authority to any individual citizen. Hence Roman monuments, under the emperors, instead of bearing the first, second, or third years of their reigns, exhibit an enumeration of their tribunate, which was renewed to them from year to year ; and, accordingly, the legends *Tribunitia Potestas*, or *Potestate*, which are found on most coins of the imperial series, mark the years when their tribunitian power was re-assigned to them. For example, when TR. POT. X̄X̄. appears on a medal, it signifies that the emperor had just entered into the twentieth year of his tribunate, or that the tribunitian power had devolved to him for the twentieth time.—It is in the 731st

year from the foundation of Rome (before Christ 23), that the most accurate numismatists place the first medals on which appeared the date of the *tribunitian power*. But although that legend serves as a means for calculating the years of an emperor's reign, yet it is not to be relied on as the basis of an invariable rule ; for some princes, sons of emperors, or adopted by them, were invested with this dignity (so formidable under the commonwealth), more than once *before* their accession to the imperial throne. The *tribunitia potestas* (says the author of *Leçons de Numismatique Romaine)* was in some sort the foundation of the inviolability and unlimited powers of the emperors (who were supposed to have succeeded to the rights of the ancient tribunes of the people, and who certainly augmented those rights). This power or dignity was the title which of all others they generally least neglected to mention ; but as it was considered to be removed each year, it was by that renewal they almost always reckoned the years of their reigns, thereby offering the greatest help to chronological researches. Unfortunately, however, for those researches, *le quantième* of the tribunitian power is not always expressed on medals.

The above may suffice to convey a general idea of what is meant by the *Tribunitia Potestas ;* and to explain some of the reasons why those words, either in full length or in a more or less abbreviated form, so frequently occupy a place on Roman coins and marbles. As, however, it is a point of considerable importance to be correctly understood by those who are willing to devote themselves to " the *science* of Latin medals ;" and is, morever, one on which the talents and researches of several very learned antiquaries have been employed, we shall proceed to add the subjoined passages, translated from Eckhel, including the purport of his sagacious remarks on the subject in question, after his having critically examined the lucubrations of others :

Whence the Emperors derived the Tribunitia Potestas.—So important were the rights, and so extensive the powers, which had been conceded to the old Tribunes, that nothing was more likely than that the princes, who overturned the republic, and who afterwards endeavoured to appropriate to themselves all the magisterial functions, should also canvass for the tribunitian authority, or at least be desirous to have it spontaneously offered to them. Nor was it indeed a slight addition either to their supreme power or to their permanent welfare to be personally inviolate *(sacrosanctum) ;* and that, as Cicero says, not only against force of arms *(contra vim et ferrum)*, but also, under the protection of sacred laws, against words also, to be enabled to negative any order of the senate, to convoke and to dismiss at pleasure both the senate and the people, and to compel obedience from even opposing magistrates.—Julius Cæsar was the first to whom, according to Dion, the tribunitian power was decreed out of regular course. Indeed amongst other honours which, on hearing of the victory of Pharsalia, the people conferred upon him, was that of his being privileged to retain, after a manner, the tribunitan power for life. The same honour was bestowed on Octavian (after his victory over Sextus Pompey and Lepidus in Sicily, according to Orosius, or over Antony at Actium, as Dion asserts); but he seems at that time to have declined accepting it, or at least to have treated it with indifference. Because, seven years after these events (v.c. 731), as Dion affirms, it was decreed by the senate that Augustus should be perpetual tribune of the people *(tribunus plebis perpetuus)*; and he immediately adds, hence it arose that Augustus and the emperors who succeeded him, under some such law, assumed, with the other honours, that of the tribunitian power. Augustus, therefore, was the first who received and retained it under the authority of that law, of which his successors availed themselves, as we learn from ancient monuments.

Why Augustus coveted this dignity.—In doing this, Augustus was actuated by more than one motive. For besides the reason above adverted to, he increased thereby his own power and security, whilst he avoided, in appearance, an invidious assumption of the power of the people.—Tacitus *(Ann.* L. iii. s. 56), in treating of the Tribunitian power, intimates that this policy of Augustus did not in fact escape the discernment of the quick-sighted.—"That specious title *(id summi fastigii vocabulum)*—that term of the proudest assumption, importing nothing less than sovereign power, was invented (says he) by Augustus at a time when the names of *rex* and *dictator* were not only unconstitutional, but universally detested. And yet a new name was wanted to overstep the magistrates, and the forms of the constitution. The same historian *(Ann.* L. i. s. 2) had said of the same emperor, that he laid aside the invidious title of Triumvir, content with the more popular name of Consul, and with the Tribunitian power, which he professed to assume for the protection of the people." Augustus indeed pretended by that course, which seemed most agreeable to the people, to be in the highest degree regardful of the public welfare; and, in strict conformity to the institutions of the state, to protect the lives and property of the citizens. This sort of affected decorum was the more needful at that time, when the recollections of liberty were still cherished in the minds of men. Yet, it is to be observed, that Tiberius—a man in other respects of violent character but of keen craftiness—adopted the same line of policy.—"He (says Tacitus, *Ann.* L. i. s. 7) began all his movements through the consuls, affecting the appearance of republican principles, as if the constitution still existed, and he himself had formed no design for destroying it. The proclamation itself, indeed, by which he convened the senate, professed no other authority than that of the *Tribunitian power* conferred upon him by Augustus."—Hence, it is clear, how available was that power for the strengthening of the sovereignty, and how much more surely by those treacherous dealings, disguised, however, under a popular mask, than by more open assaults, the commonwealth might be overthrown.—Well and truly was it called by Tacitus—*summi fastigii vocabulum*—not that it signified, but that it was the means of procuring the supreme authority; insomuch as to warrant Velleius in affirming of Tiberius that "by his being associated in the tribunitian power he became equal to Augustus." And Vopiscus also calls that power "the most important part of regal government."—There are writers who have not sufficiently appreciated it, whilst others have ascribed to it too much. Amongst the former, Noris, too sparing, is of opinion that the tribunitian power of the emperors had no reference to the actual administration of public affairs, but only meant the right of putting in a *veto*, and of enjoying perfect immunity from harm or violence. Amongst the latter, Henry Dodwell, too liberal, asserts that in the power of the tribunate was included that of the proconsulate. But both these extreme opinions have been accurately refuted by Schwartz, in his learned work, *Exercitatio Academica de Augustorum, Cæsarumque Trib. Potestate;* and also by Mazzoleni in his dissertation on the same subject.

Difference between the republican and the imperial tribunate.—Between the old tribunes of the people and the emperors endued with the tribunitian power, there was a great difference, the nature of which Dion explains in certain passages of his work:—First, he says that neither Augustus nor any other emperor bore the name of *Tribunus Plebis,* but simply the title of the tribunitian power. This, indeed he affirms in another place, as follows:—"The emperors esteem it inauspicious to hold the plebeian tribunate, they being themselves patricians; but they accept the whole tribunitian power at the highest pitch of greatness to which it ever attained." From this we learn that the emperors, although they might have been of the plebeian order, were immediately elected into the order of patricians, of which Spartianus also has given an example, in Didius Julianus. In the next place, during the freedom of the republic, a tribune of the people could not be at the same time consul, nor fill any other magisterial office, but the emperors were permitted to do so. Moreover, the ancient tribunate, according to the usual course of law, was only an annual office, entered upon the fourth ides of December in each year; whereas the tribunitian power of the emperors was perpetual, and decreed to them at any period whatsoever of the year. Lastly, the old tribunes were not allowed to be absent from the city, nor even to pass a single night out of its walls, except during certain holidays called *feriæ Latinæ;* besides which their authority did not extend beyond the city; but it was lawful for the emperors to absent themselves from Rome, and the tribunitian power lost none of its force during their absence. Of this Tiberius furnished an example when, being at Rhodes, he ordered some one who had been cited before the judgment seat as a slanderer *(convitiator)* to be dragged to prison (Suetonius in Tib. c. 11). But although the emperors possessed themselves of the tribunitian power, yet the ancient custom of appointing tribunes was not discontinued; and there are frequent examples of the tribunitian prerogative of the *veto*, being exercised against decrees of the senate, as may be seen in Pighius. But it may readily be supposed, that, as to the rest of the magistracies so also of the tribuneship, the authority gradually decayed, and at length nothing but the mere name was left.—Panvinius is of opinion that the tribunes lasted till the reign of Constantine the Great, by whom, in establishing as he did, a new form of state government, many old institutions were abolished.

The tribunitian power conferred by the senate. —The right of investing the emperors with the power of the tribunate belonged to the senatorial body, by whom, as already observed, it was granted to Julius Cæsar and to Augustus. But afterwards, even when the imperial government became fully established, and when such princes as had the inclination, were not deficient in the strength of means, to usurp the privileges entrusted to the senate, yet those honours do not appear to have been wrested from it by force. Thus, according to Tacitus *(Ann.* iii. c. 56), Tiberius himself requested the senate to confer the tribunitian power on his son Drusus. It is for pursuing an opposite course, in this respect, that Dion, among other things, reprobates the conduct of Elagabalus, who, without waiting for the sanction of a *senatus consultum*, seized, with the rest of the honours usually paid to princes, on the name of the tribunitian power. On the other hand, respecting the immediate successor of Elagabalus, viz., Alexander Severus, we learn from Lampridius, that on one and the same day the senate proclaimed him, by the respective titles of Augustus, Tribunitia Potestas, and Pater Patriæ.—Nor can I (adds Eckhel) discover the reason why a coin of Pescennius, struck after he had openly declared himself Augustus, should make no mention of the tribunitian power, unless, since it could not be decreed to him by the senate, who were under the control first of Didius Julianus and next of Sept. Severus, he had the moderation to abstain from taking it unopposed. But certainly, on no coin of Pescennius hitherto discovered, is this power found inscribed. Moreover, as the people of Antioch from the time of Trajan, and subsequently, were accustomed constantly to stamp on their tetradrachms the words ΔΗΜΑΡΧΙΚΗϹ ΕΞΟΥϹΙΑϹ, *Tribunitia Potestate*, so for the reason alone stated, they have on a Pescennius omitted that epigraph, substituting in its stead that of ΠΡΟΝΟΙΑ ΘΕΩΝ, *Providentia Deorum.*

Emperors had their colleagues in the tribunate.—Instances are frequent of the reigning prince associating with himself a colleague in the tribunitian power.—According to Dion, Augustus himself supplies three examples. In the year v.c. 736, he conferred it upon M. Agrippa, for the space of five years; after that, in v.c. 741, it was continued to him for another five years. In v.c. 748, with a view to repress the insolence of Caius and Lucius, Cæsars, he gave it for the same quinquennial period to his son-in-law, Tiberius, who, being banished from Rome, was again reduced to a private station. But Caius and Lucius both dying, Augustus, to prevent uncertainty respecting his choice of a successor, and to curb the perverse hopes of others, as Tacitus remarks *(Ann.* iii. c. 56), adopted Tiberius in the year v.c. 757, and gave him the tribunitian power for ten years; at the expiration of which term he extended it to him beyond that period, as is shewn on the coins of Tiberius. It was Augustus, therefore, who set the example of an emperor treating him whom he had invested with a share of the tribunitian power as his colleague in the empire, and as his destined successor; which measure of his became a precedent. For succeeding emperors took especial care that the tribunitian power should be immediately decreed to those, whom by adoption they had selected for the government, provided only they were, in point of age, competent to administer public affairs. Examples of this pre-arrangement were given by Augustus as regarded Tiberius, by Nerva towards Trajan, by Hadrian towards Ælius, and afterwards towards Antoninus. It has been advisedly said, provided such adopted heirs to the imperial throne had attained an age to qualify them for the public service; for neither did Augustus allow the tribunitian power to be bestowed upon Caius and Lucius (his grandsons), although by adoption his appointed successors, and although the former had already served the consulship; nor did Claudius permit it in the case of Nero; nor Antoninus give it directly to Aurelius. The same rule also prevailed with respect to the natural sons *(filii naturales)*, as contradistinguished from the adopted sons, of emperors, and consequently to the Cæsars. Of this a conspicuous example was afforded by Tiberius, who, when he asked the senate to bestow the tribunitian power on his son Drusus, amongst other reasons, mentioned the circumstance of that young prince being then of age, which he himself had attained when raised by "the Divine Augustus," to the same honourable office. Nor could the favour which he now sought be regarded as premature (he added); for Drusus had gone through eight years of probation. It was by seditions quelled, by wars successfully terminated, by triumphal honours earned, and by two consulships served, that his merits had been proved, and his qualifications for duly discharging the duties of public office established. (Tacitus, *Ann.* iii. s. 56).—Vespasian made his son Titus, already of mature age and of well-known virtue, partaker with himself in the same dignity.—The worst examples were—that in which Marcus Aurelius bestowed the tribunitian power on his son Commodus, then aged only 16, besides adding to it in the same year the title of Augustus—and the more insane folly of Severus, who signalised the tenth year of his son Antoninus (*vulgo* Caracalla), by giving him the tribunate together with the Augustan title.—Afterwards, all rules and proprieties were set at naught, as in the instances of Philip the younger, and of Volusianus, whose respective fathers heaped the honours of the consulate and the tribunitian power, with the titles of Cæsar, Imperator, Augustus, and Pontifex Maximus, on these beardless boys of theirs, in disordered haste and in " much admired confusion."

The tribunitian power customarily renewed year after year.—As the *potestas tribunitia*, conjoined to the title of emperor, was something like a foundation or basis of government; and as he who bore it was either a reigning prince, or an appointed successor to the sovereignty—so each of those princes, in his turn was pleased, from the day of this power being bestowed upon him, to take that (if such an expression be allowable) as an epocha, from which to date his admission into the supreme government. For what, says Dion, on this point ? "They (the emperors) assume the whole tribunitian power, in the most enlarged degree in which it was ever exercised; and they reckon according to that the succeeding years of their reign, as though they had accepted it yearly with the tribunes of the people."—Nothing, however, is more common than to see, on coins and on marbles, the tribunitian power of each prince so numbered as to increase a unit every year. For we see the tribunitian power, and its number, inscribed on the public monuments of Augustus; yet the same Augustus, on the celebrated monument at Ancyra (a town of Galatia, now Ancyre), which sets forth a train of achievements performed by himself, has marked out their dates, not only from the consulships, but also from the tribunitian power. For instance, in recounting the different *congiaria* (or gifts either in corn or in money) which he had caused to be distributed, the time is noted to have been TRIBVNITIA POTESTATE DVODECIMVM; and presently after TRIBVNITIAE POTESTATIS DVODEVICESIMVM CONSVL XII. Thus, when Augustus departed this life, his last tribunitian power was XXXVII.—From this one may easily perceive how much the numbers of the tribunitian power, if correctly described and known, contribute as well to fix the chronology of the emperors, as to reconcile certain acts and events with their dates in each reign.

Tribunitian power—opinions as to the mode of its renewal to the emperors.—Eckhel then adverts to the different opinions which, in the application of their great erudition and intellectual acuteness to this point of research, have been advanced by various eminent antiquaries— from amongst these he selects two opinions as appearing to him the most probable, namely,—1st, that of Onuphrius Panvinius (*De Civit. Rom.* c. 60), who contends that *the tribunitian power was renewed yearly, on the day on which it was first received;* and 2ndly, that of Nicholas Toinard, who thinks that *it was repeated yearly, on the IVth ides of*

December in each year.—The author of *Doct. Num. Vet.* then enters (vol. viii. p. 397) into a critical examination of these respective opinions, shewing, with his usual clearness and candour, to what extent, as he conceives, each may safely be adopted, or should prudently be rejected. And having fully and impartially delivered his judgment on the sentiments of other learned men, he next proceeds to state his own, which are in substance as follows:—That *the tribunitian power of the emperors, from Augustus to Antoninus Pius, was renewed yearly, on the same day of the year on which it was first conferred ;* and that *from Antoninus Pius down to Gallienus, it was renewed on the kalends of January, in each year.*

Rules for illustrating the mode of renewal.— In exhibiting the grounds of proof on which his doctrine rests, Eckhel lays down the following seven *regulæ*, viz. :—1. That coins are the surest testimony to rely upon in the attempt to investigate the method of renewing the tribunitian power.—2. That no coins, however, are to be admitted as evidence, in the course of research on this branch of the subject, but such as are of clear and acknowledged genuineness.—3. That the testimony of marbles, in the case of the tribunitian power, is uncertain.—4. That it is not the adverse tenour of some few monumental inscriptions, although of unquestionable antiquity, and supported by the best authority, which can overturn an opinion confirmed by sure and abundant numismatic proofs.—5. That wherever the emperors are found to have renewed the tribunitian power on any day within the same Julian year after the kalends of January, it is most certainly shown that the tribunates were conjoined with the consulates.—6. That if emperors have renewed the tribunitian power with the Julian year, it was doubtless renewed on the very day on which it had been first received.— 7. That on coins of those emperors the tribunitian power never alters, within one and the same Julian year; thence it is certain it was renewed in the January kalends.

Having with copious citations and apposite examples supported the above rules for ascertaining the mode of renewing the tribunitian power, and for avoiding those errors into which an incautious handling of the matter in question has led some even of the most learned men, Eckhel goes on to adduce a perfect series of evidences from such numismatic monuments as are themselves of undoubted authenticity to corroborate his opinion, as already stated—namely, that from the reign of Augustus (A.V.C. 727) to that of Antoninus (A.V.C. 891, A.D. 138) this fictitious renewal of the tribunitian power was accustomed to be made to each emperor on the anniversary of the day on which he first received it ; and that from the eighth year of Antoninus Pius as far as Gallienus (A.D. 253), both inclusive, it was renewed each year in the January kalends, whatever might have been the day on which the prince was first invested with it. This opinion, however, he does not give as incontestible : on the contrary, he acknowledges that it does not serve to explain all the various combinations of dates, without exception, that present themselves on Roman medals; but he regards it, and with apparent reasonableness and justice, as more probable than any other.

Discontinuance of the Tribunitian Power.— Referring the reader to vol. viii. of our great author's work above quoted, for a masterly accumulation of monetal evidences, which occupy more than forty consecutive pages, we must content ourselves with subjoining a short extract from the remarks with which he concludes his own faithful, accurate, and judicious treatment of a subject peculiarly beset with conflicting difficulties:—" As we have traced (says he) this custom of mentioning, on Roman coins and other monuments, the tribunitian power, and of enumerating its renewal, from its rise and through its progress, it remains for us to mark that period of the lower empire when, having previously become less and less frequent, the practice at length entirely ceased.—We find that Constantine the Great was the last emperor who inscribed it on his coinage. But on marbles it continued in use some time after the reign of Constantine; for there are lapidary inscriptions extant, which exhibit this dignity as still added to the imperial titles of Julian, Valentinian, and Gratian. In the lowest age of the Augustan history (including Justinus I.) instead of TRIBVNITIA POTESTATE I. II. III., &c., we see ANNO I. II. III., &c., inscribed for a time on coins of the imperial series, to mark the year of each prince's reign."

A different way was adopted by the Greeks, in marking the year of an emperor's reign, on medals—viz., by A, B, Γ, &c., up to Θ, for 1, 2, 9, &c., to Ϙ, I for 10; K for 20, &c.; sometimes by ΕΤΟΥΣ or contracted ET. or ETO., preceding the numerals. In this class of imperial medals, there is a fine and numerous suite, which were struck at Alexandria, in Egypt, from Augustus to Diocletian, and which all bear the year of the reign of the different Roman emperors. For example, on the reverse of a medal of Trajan, the Nile appears under the figure of an old man, and on the exergue of the same coin is inscribed **L. Δ.** or the fourth year of that prince's reign. [See the word NILE.]

TR. P.—TR. PO.—TR. POT.—TRI.POT.— TRIB. P.—TRIB. POT.—TRIBVNIC. P. or POT or POTEST.—TRIBVNICIA, or TRIBVNITIA POTESTATE.—We see this record of the Tribunitian power, generally more or less abbreviated, though on some few medallions at full length, either with or without the addition of a number, and either followed or not by a similar record of the Consulate (cos.) and of the Imperatorship (IMP.), on coins of the imperial series from Augustus to Gallienus, and from Gallienus to Constantine the Great.—The following list of the renewals of the Tribunitian power, by each emperor respectively, is drawn from Eckhel's catalogue of the Cæsarean cabinet at Vienna, collated with and completed from the same author's later and greater work, his *Doctrina Numorum Veterum :—*

Augustus .... TR. P. I.* II. (year of Rome 731-32; before Christ 24-23) to XXXVI. and XXXVII. (V.C. 767; after Christ 14.)

Tiberius .... TR. P.* (for the first time, V.C. 748.)—TR. P. VI. (V.C. 757; after Christ 4) to XXXVIII. (V.C. 790, A.D. 37.)

Caligula .... TR. P. I. II. (V.C. 791-92, A.D. 38-39)—TR. P. III. IIII. (793-94, A.D. 40-41.)

Claudius .... TR. P. II. (V.C. 794-5, A.D. 41-42) to XIII. and XIV. (V.C. 806-807, A.D. 53-54.)

Nero .... —— I. II. (807-808, A.D. 54-55) to XIII. XIIII. (820-821, A.D. 67-68.)

Galba .... TR. P. simply—(821, A.D. 68.)

Otho .... TR. P. simply—(821, A.D. 68-69.)

Vitellius .... Ibid. (822, A.D. 69.)

Vespasian .... TR. P. I. II. (822-823, A.D. 69-70) to IX. X. (831-832.)

Titus .... —— I. II. (824,825, A.D. 71-72) to X. XI. (834, A.D. 81.)

Domitianus .... —— I. II. (year of Rome 824-825, A.D. 71-72) to XV. XVI. (849, A.D. 96.)

Nerva .... —— I. II. (849-850,851, A.D. 96-97-98.)—Some chronologers have assigned, on numismatic authority, a third tribunate to the emperor; but Eckhel vouches for only *two.*

Trajanus .... —— I. II. (850-851, A.D. 97-98) to XIX. XX. (869-870, A.D. 116-117).

Hadrianus .... —— I. II. (870-871, A.D. 117-118) to XXI. (891, A.D. 138.)

Antoninus Pius .... —— I. II. (891-892, A.D. 138-139) to XXIII. XXIV. (913-914, A.D. 160-161.)

M. Aurelius .... —— I. II. (900-901, A.D. 147-148) to XXXIII. XXXIIII. (932-933, A.D. 170-180.)

L. Verus .... —— I. II. (914-915, A.D. 161-162) to VIII. IX. (921-922, A.D. 168-169.)

Commodus .... —— I. II. (930, A.D. 177) to XVII. XVIII. (945, A.D. 192.)—This emperor appears to have had the Tribunitian power conferred upon him as early as the year V.C. 924 (A.D. 171), although not recorded on his coins of that date.

---

* *Obs.*—In order to distinguish the *first* holding of the Tribunitian power by such emperors as reigned sufficiently long to enjoy the renewal of that dignity, the Roman numeral I. is in the above list added, in all these instances, to the letters TR. P. But on the coins themselves throughout the whole series (*Æmilianus* alone excepted) the first Tribunate is noted simply with a TR. P.

Pertinax, and *Didius Julianus.*—No Tribunitian power inscribed on their coins (945, A.D192; 946, A.D. 193.)

Sept. Severus............ TR. P. I. II. III. (946, A.D. 193-194-5) to XVII. XVIII. XVIIII. (962, A.D. 209-210-211.)

Caracalla .... —— I. II. III. (951, A.D. 198-199-200) to XIX. XX. (969, A.D. 216-217.)
Geta .... —— I. II. III. IV. (962, A.D. 209-210-211-212.)
Macrinus .... —— I. II. (970, A.D. 217-218.)
Elagabalus .... —— I. II. III. IV. V. (971, A.D. 218-219.220-221-222.)
Sev. Alexander ...... —— I. II. III. (975, A.D. 222-223-224) to XII. XIII. XIV. (986, A.D. 233-234-235.)
Maximinus .... —— I. II. III. IV. (988, A.D. 235-236-237-238.)
Gordianus I. .... TR. P. simply—(991, A.D. 238.)
Gordianus II. .... (Ibid.)—No coin with mark of Tribunate.

Balbinus .... (Ibid.) ⎰ Like the African Gordians, each too short a reign
Pupienus .... (Ibid.) ⎱ for the Tribunitian power to be renewed to, if indeed it was ever conferred on, them.

Gordianus III. ...... TR. P. I. II. III. (991, A.D. 238-239-240) to IV. V. VI. VII. (994, A.D. 241-242-243-244.)
Philippus Pater ...... —— I. II. III. IV. V. VI. (997, A.D. 244-245-246-247-248-249.)
Philippus Fil. .... —— I. II. III. (1000, A.D. 247-248-249.)
Trajanus Decius ...... —— I. II. III. (1002, A.D. 249-250-251.)
Herennius .... —— II. (Ibid.)
Hostilianus .... No mark of the Tribunitian power on this young prince's coins (1002 A.D. 249-250.)
Trebonianus Gallus ... TR. P. I. II. III. IV. (1004, A.D. 251-252-253-254.)
Volusianus .... No mention made of his first Tribunate, but the II. III. and IVth renewal correspond in date with those of his father whose fate he shared.
Æmilianus .... TR. P. I. II. (1006, A.D. 253-254.)—This emperor is the only one on whose coins the *first* Tribunate is numbered, (viz., TR. P. I.) and that only on the silver—the brass are all without.
Valerianus .... TR. P. I. II. III. IV. V. VI. VII. (1006, A.D. 253-254 to 259.—Some writers quote coins which carry the Trib. Pot. to an eighth renewal (A.D. 260), the year he was taken prisoner by the Persians.
Gallienus .... TR. P. I. II. III. (1006, A.D. 253-254-255) to XV. XVI. (A.D. 267-268.)
Postumus .... —— I. II. III. (1011, A.D. 258-259-260) to VIII. IX. X. (A.D. 265-266-267.)
Tetricus Pater .... TR. P. (A.D. 267), TR. P. II. (268.)
Claudius Gothicus ... TR. P. (A.D. 268), II. (269), III. (270.)
Quintillus .... TR. P. (A.D. 270.)
Aurelianus .... TR. P. (A.D. 270), II. III. IV. V. VI. (A.D. 271-272-273-274-275.)
Tacitus.................. Only on one coin of this prince are the chronological marks placed, viz., P.M. TR. P. CONSVL. (A.D. 276.)
Florianus............... No mark of Tribunitian power on his coins, (A.D. 276, a three months' reign.)
Probus.................. TR. P. (A.D. 276) II. III. IV. V. VI. VII. (A.D. 277 to 282.)
Carus .... No mention of the Tribunate on his coins (A.D. 282-283.)
Numerianus............ The simple TR. P. appears on a third brass of this prince (A.D. 284), given by Tanini.
Carinus .... The Tribunitian power of this emperor is recorded on a single gold coin which Eckhel quotes from *Beger. Thes. Brand.* and assigns to the year 284.
Diocletianus .... TR. P. (A.V.C. 1037, A.D. 284, when he was proclaimed emperor.)— From II. III. (A.D. 285-286) to XVII. (A.D. 300), sixteen yearly *renewals* of the Tribunitian power are consecutively recorded on the coins of this prince. The eighteenth (A.D. 301) is not mentioned, being the only *hiatus* in the series; XIX. XX. XXI. and XXII. appearing regularly from A.D. 302 to 305, in which last year Diocletian abdicated the imperial government.
Maximianus Herculeus TR. P. (A.V.C. 1039, A.D. 286, when he commenced his joint reign with Diocletian,) II. III. (A.D. 287-288). Of the fourth renewal there is no notice. The remainder are enumerated in Eckhel as follows:—TR. P. V. (290), VIII. (293), IX. (294), XIV. (299), XVIII. XIX. (303-304), and XX. (A.D. 305), when he reluctantly followed the example of his imperial colleague, and abdicated the empire; to resume it, however, only too readily at the persuasion of his son Maxentius, in 306; but no renewal of the Tribunitian power is noted on the few medals struck under Maximianus Herculeus after his resumption of the government.

Constantius I. (vulgo Chlorus)—Father of Constantine the Great).—From A.V.C. 1058, A.D. 292, when he was created Cæsar by Maximianus Herculeus to 305, when he was proclaimed Augustus, and to 306, when he died at York. No *Tribunitian power* is marked on his coins. *Galerius Maximianus.* From the year V.C. 1045, A.D. 292, to 1064, A.D. 311, *no* TR. P. . The same observation applies to the following Augusti, VIZ.:—*Val. Severus*, 305 to 307; *Maximinus Daza*, 305 to 313; *Maxentius*, 306 to 312; *Licinius* pater, 307 to 324; *Licinius* filius, 317 to 323.

Constantinus Magnus.—The only mention of the Tribunitian power on the numerous coins of this celebrated emperor, from V.C. 1059, A.D. 306 to 337, is on a single third brass, which Eckhel places under date of 312, viz.:—P.M. TR. P. (without a numeral) COS. II. And it is at this period that all notice of the dignity and authority of the Tribunate appears to have ceased on Roman monuments of every kind. For, with respect to the epigraphs TR. P. XXXVII. and XXXXII., both of which are stated by Banduri, quoting from Mezzobarbi, to be extant on gold coins of Theodosius II. (A.D. 408 to 450).—Eckhel declares the assertion to be erroneous, as he had never seen such a medal, nor ever read of it in any authentic catalogue; neither does it agree with the ascertained chronology of that emperor's reign.— We are, indeed, disposed to think that the mistake arose from reading TR. P. instead of IM*Perator;* for there are gold of Theodosius II. with IMP. XXXXII. COS. XVII.

It will be seen from the foregoing list, that in some instances more years of the Tribunitian power are to be found ascribed to certain Roman emperors than there were years of those emperors' reigns. The fact is, the renewal of this power to each was accustomed to be dated, *not* from the beginning of their highest, that is to say of their Augustal rank, but from their first reception of the Tribunitian authority; and thus more years of TR. P. than of imperial government were assigned to them on their respective coins. Hence we find struck on the medals of Tiberius—TRIB. POT. XXXVII., though his reign as the successor of Augustus did not last longer than twenty-three years. In like manner there are coins of Titus which bear the mark of TR. P. X. and XI., whereas he died in little more than a year after his accession to the empire.— So of Antoninus Pius, whose medals record XXIIII. receptions of the Tribunitian power, his reign as emperor being twenty-three years.—And the medals of M. Aurelius note XXXIIII. TR. P., though, as the successor of Antoninus, he reigned only nineteen years.—On the other hand, the coins of Augustus exhibit no more than XXXVII. renewals of the Tribunitian Potestas, although Suetonius, Dion, Victor, Eutropius, and others, assign to that prince the supreme government of the Roman empire during the space of from forty-two to forty-four years, reckoning from the victory at Actium, which took place A.V.C. 723 (before Christ 31), or from 725, when the title of Imperator was conferred upon him by the Senate.

Tridens—Trident—a fork with three tines, which the ancients have represented as the sceptre and peculiar symbol of Neptune. The poets make it the gift of the Cyclops to that deity. And thus the harpoon or fishing-spear was converted by one of the ingenious myths of paganism into an attribute inseparable from the God of the Sea. Such an instrument is still in use amongst the fishermen of the Mediterranean archipelago.—The *trident* appears behind the head of Neptune on many family coins of the Romans.—On a coin of Pompey the Great it is stamped before the face of Neptune. It is most frequently carried in the left hand of that marine divinity, whence he is called by Ovid *(Metam.* ii.) *Tridentiger,* and by the Greeks τριαινοφερος. It is in this manner that Neptune is pourtrayed on a coin of the *Postumia* family; and on medals of Augustus, Agrippa, Caligula, Vespasian, Hadrian, M. Aurelius, S. Severus. Gallienus, Postumus, Claudius Gothicus, Aurelian.—The trident is seen beneath a dolphin on coins of the *Valeria* family, and surmounting a trophy on a denarius of the gens *Pompeia.*

Triones—seven stars, called by the ancients the *Pleiades.* This constellation is thought to be alluded to in types which appear on coins of the Asinia, Claudia, Lucretia, Petronia, and Sempronia families; also on coins of Augustus, Nero, Domitian and Domitia, Hadrian, Faustina sen., Commodus, &c.

Tripus—Tripod—either a table, a seat, or any other instrument, standing on three feet. The ancients made frequent use of tripods, as well for domestic as for religious purposes. In the latter case these served sometimes to burn incense upon during sacrificial rites; at others to contain the lustral water in the temples; and most of them were so formed in the upper part as to be capable of holding a vase, or any other hollow utensil.—The *tripus* was at once sacred to and symbolical of Apollo. Indeed one of the most famous of these objects was that at Delphos, on which the *Pythia*, or priestess of Apollo, placed herself to inhale the intoxicating fumes of the Delphian cavern, and to give out the oracles.—The original appropriation of the tripod was merely to cover the opening of the cave at Delphos: but in course of time it became an ornamental piece of workmanship, with which superstitious mysteries were associated. As the tripod was one of the most peculiar attributes of Apollo, so it is most frequently seen on ancient monuments. The prophetic god *(Vates)*, as he was called, is often figured on medals, standing near his tripod, which is occasionally surmounted by the *cortina*, as the Romans denominated a concave vessel, or cauldron, generally made of some kind of metal. This *cortina* appears in a tripod typified on a denarius of Brutus. (See *Junia* family).—On a gold coin of the Cassia family we see the figure of a tripod, with its concave *cortina*, and its convex cover, presenting, when thus united, a spherical form.   Over the upper *cortina* is spread a covering as of net-work, with *lemnisci*, or lables hanging down, like ribbons, on each side of the tripod.—To this example may be added the well-known but curious silver coin of Vitellius, exhibiting a tripod with spherical *cortina*, on the top of which is a dolphin, and below it a crow.—See XV. VIR. SACR. FAC.

The *tripod* was occasionally used in sacrifices instead of the *ara*, or altar.   Hence, as Spanheim *(Pr.* ii. 135) observes, it became *sacerdotii insigne*, and on Roman coins serves to designate an individual holding the pontifical office.— Eckhel, in commenting on a coin of Sextus Pompey, shews, on the authority of old writers, that the *tripus*, as well as the *lituus*, was a sign of the augurship.—On consular medals, the tripod appears in conjunction with the capeduncula or simplum, the apex, the lituus, culter, securis, and other sacerdotal and sacrificial instruments.   It is placed between two fasces armed with the axes, on coins of the Sepullia family.—On a medal of Lepidus, in the *gens Aemilia*, a serpent winds its folds around, and lifts its head above the tripod, on one side of which is the lituus and the simplum.   This clearly indicates its connection with the worship of the Pythian Apollo ; whilst on medals of Caracalla, and of Trebonianus Gallus, we see the figure itself of that deity represented, with one of his elbows resting on a tripod.   The same symbol, with or without the image of the oracular god, appears with two, three, and four figures sacrificing at it, on coins of the Emperors Hadrian, Antoninus Pius, Aurelius, Commodus, Severus, Caracalla, Gordianus Pius, Valerianus, &c.—The tripod is, however, not exclusively confined to Apollo.—We also see it placed between the figures of Jupiter and the Emperor on coins of Diocletian, and between Hercules and the Emperor on coins of Val. Maximianus.—See CONSERV. AVGG.

Triens—a coin of the value of one-third of the *as*.   Four globules, designating four unciæ, or ounces, are the sure mark of this coin.   The head of Minerva forms the constant type of its obverse ; and it has generally the prow of a ship for the type of its reverse.—See *As* and its parts of this Dictionary.

Tripondius—a multiple of the *as*.   It is one of the earliest and rarest pieces of Roman copper money—equal in weight and value to three *ases*.   It exhibits on one side the head of Minerva with the numeral III. behind ; on the other side a ship's prow with III. below it.— Augini assigns to it the weight of 12 unc.— Zalada estimates it at unc. 10, drachm. 5½.— See *As*.

Triquetra.—Three human thighs and legs, so conjoined together by their tops as in a centre that they form every way a triangular figure, whence its name is derived.   It frequently appears on coins of Sicily, and is generally considered as bearing reference to the three prin-

cipal promontories of that island.—Eckhel, however, in animadverting upon a disputed coin, classed amongst those of Mark Antony, controverts the opinion of Mazzolenus (who has Vaillant's and Spanheim's authority to support him), that the *triquetra* on ancient coins is a sure symbol of Sicily ; and he adduces examples from medals of Suessa in Campania, of Metapatus and Velia in Lucania, of Aspendus in Pamphilia, of Selge in Pisidia, of Lalassis in Isauria, of Argos and Olba in Cilicia, and of other cities, all which have the *triquetra* upon them, like those struck in Sicily, or which were coined at Rome with reference to Roman transactions in that island.   From these it appears that this *three-legged* device is by no means a conclusive evidence of the Sicilian mint.   On certain Roman medals differences are observable in the form of the limbs which compose the triquetra.—Placed behind the beardless head of a man, the *triquetra* alludes, on a denarius of the Claudia family, to the conquest of Sicily, by the celebrated Claudius Marcellus. —It appears, with the winged head of Medusa in the centre, on silver coins of the Aquileia family and Cornelia family ; in the latter instance, corn-ears (allusive to Sicilian fertility) are added.   The same three-cornered figure offers itself on a gold coin of Augustus.—See *Sicilia*—also see *Claudia*.

Triremis—a galley, or long ship, furnished, as its name is considered to import, with three ranks, or tiers of oars.   It was this kind of vessel which the Greeks and Romans, but more particularly the latter, were accustomed to use for the purposes of war.—M. Millin, in his *Dictionnaire des Beaux Arts*, has given a most intelligent *resumé*, first of the difficulties which embarrass the question of these triremes ; and next of the various attempts at explanation made by a succession of authors with a view to surmount those difficulties.   But, notwithstanding all the pains that have been taken as well practically as theoretically, by learned antiquaries, by military and naval officers, and by other ingenious and indefatigable investigators of the subject, in Italy, France, Germany, and England, it is not easy to comprehend how even three tiers or stages of oars could all be plunged into, and raised out of, the water, at the same moment of time, without collision or impediment.   Still less easy it is to be understood by what practicable mode rowing vessels could be manœuvred, whose number of tiers for oars, according to the concurrent testimony of several ancient writers, not only exceeded three, but amounted, some to ten, and even to fourteen ! The most plausible but still far from satisfactory supposition is, that the different ranges of oars were indeed placed one above another, but in chequered or zig-zag fashion, to enable each to be worked freely, effectively, and without clashing with, or being restricted in its action by, the movement of any of the others.—On different bas reliefs at Rome, as also among the paintings discovered in the excavations of Herculaneum are seen figures of ships, wherein the oars, protruding from their sides, are placed in an oblique direction.—M. Millin quotes a medallion of Gordianus III., as from the collection of the *Capo di Monte,* in which there is a trireme, with fourteen or fifteen rowers, whose oars range from the side obliquely. It is remarkable, however, that, with scarcely more than one exception, there are no Roman coins, either consular or imperial (even in the most elaborately executed types,), that exibit an example either of the *prætorian,* or any other *galley,* with more than a *single* tier of oars.—The Tyrians boasted of being the inventors of the *triremis;* but its representation on coins, struck at the colonial city of Tyre, under the emperors, forms no exception to the above remark.

The *triremis,* with rowers, and with or without sail spread, indicates generally maritime power, or sometimes the site of a city (Vaillant, *Col.* i. 80, 120.)—It appears on many coins of Roman families, especially on those of *Pompeia.* This type on a great variety of imperial medals serves to commemorate a prosperous voyage or a happy arrival, or to symbolise the felicity of the emperor, of the age, &c.—Among other objects associated on Roman coins, with the representation of the *triremis* are the following, viz. :—1. The *aplustre* on the stern (as in the Lutatia fam.)　2. A legionary eagle and a column (on a coin of Pompeius Magnus).　3. A labarum (as in Elagabalus).　4. A figure seated at the stern, and two military ensigns (as in Hadrian and Caracalla).　5. Neptune standing at the helm, and the emperor at the prow (as in M. Aurelius).　6. The emperor, as steersman, seated on the poop (as in Hadrian).　7. The emperor seated at the stern, Pallas and marine deities, or cupids, at the prow (as on a medallion of Hadrian in Mus. Alban.)　8. The emperor standing at the prow, Victory seated steering the vessel (as in Constantinus Magnus, Constans, &c.)　9. Soldiers and military ensigns (as in Gordianus Pius—see TRAIECTVS AVG.)　10. Victory seated, her hand on the rudder (as in Gratian—see GLORIA ROM.), &c., &c.

Triton, a sea god, (son of Neptune and of Salacia, a marine nymph), whom the poets feigned to be the trumpeter *(tubicen)* of Neptune, (Vaillant, *Col.*) The effigy of a Triton, a human form above, a fish below the waist, frequently appears on ancient coins, both Roman and Greek, where it serves occasionally as a symbol of the sea. He is seen under a quadriga drawn by Jupiter, on a coin of the Cornelia family.—The same figure on one side of Venus, whilst Cupid stands on the other, occurs on a brass medallion of Faustina jun.—A Triton, with a Nereid, is drawing the car of Venus, on a colonial medal of Corinth.—On a medal of Maximinus and Maximus, two Tritons support a plateau on which Neptune sits.

Triumphus—triumph—an honour conferred on the general-in-chief of an army, who had gained some signal victory over an enemy not before conquered. It was a solemn and imposing show, constituting the highest military reward which a Roman could receive from his country—

the crowning distinction which the senate and people decreed on his return to a commander gloriously and decisively successful in foreign war. It is a recorded expression of Augustus himself—*Neque magnificentius quidquam triumpho apud Romanos.* A day having been appointed for the ceremony, the *Imperator triumphans* employed the interval in making the most magnificent preparations in his power for the occasion. At sun-rise, he was clothed in the *toga palmata,* and crowned with laurel. Holding a palm-branch in his right hand, he ascended an ivory car, of circular form, the exterior of which exhibited relievos enriched with, and sometimes even formed of, gold ; at others the entire chariot was of sculptured silver, and of the most exquisite workmanship. In this splendid vehicle, drawn by four white horses, or occasionally by as many elephants, he was conducted at a slow and stately pace through the city to the capitol, where the solemnity terminated. In the proud pomp and circumstance of so glorious a procession, the hero of the triumph was preceded by the magistrates, headed by their lictors—the members of the senate and a vast assemblage of the citizens, all in white apparel, before whom went the *tibicines,* and others playing on musical instruments. Then came vehicles filled with the treasures and arms of the vanquished—helmets, breast-plates, bucklers, spears, and other defensive and offensive weapons, so disposed that in moving along they clashed against each other, making a warlike noise congenial to the martial character of the celebration. Other cars followed, on which were placed the plans, or symbols, of captured cities and fortresses, modelled in gilt wood, wax, or silver, with inscriptions in large letters : to these were added pictures of battles, sieges, and assaults. There were also representations of mountains, rivers, extraordinary plants, and even of the different deities peculiar to the conquered countries. Next to these were the treasure—spoils, consisting of gold, silver, brazen, and ivory ensigns, precious gems, coined money, silver and gold vases, rich robes of various kinds, together with horses, elephants, and equipages in select and brilliant array. Then appeared a melancholy group—the captive kings and chiefs—"fallen from their high estate"—their heads shaved in token of their servitude, and themselves loaded with chains, either of iron, silver, or gold, according to circumstances, and the quantity of rich booty taken : these unfortunates with their whole families, and the rest of the prisoners, having arrived before the capitol were led to a dungeon, and not unfrequently, with the ungenerous cruelty of Roman exultation at the moment of victory, were put to death. In the suite of these human victims, were the brute animals destined for immolation, which, garlanded with flowers, and their horns gilt, were led by the *victimarii,* naked to the waist and axe in hand, succeeded by the priests who presided at the sacrificial ceremony. Then advanced the chief officers of the army, serving as the immediate harbingers of the victor on whom these triumphal honours were conferred. Preceded by trumpeters, flute-players, and bearers of costly perfumes, and escorted by lictors, whose fasces were adorned with laurel, the Imperator stood in his magnificent car, in which sometimes were his children also, always followed by his other relations, by his friends, by the most illustrious members of the commonwealth, and by a host of public functionaries, shield-bearers, general officers and military tribunes. The line of march was closed by the soldiers of the Roman army, divided into legions, cohorts, centuries, and maniples, all in their warrior habits, decorated with laurels, and many wearing crowns and other marks of honourable distinction, which in recompense of their valour, they had received at the hands of their chief commander. They advanced with the joyous air of conquerors, some gaily repeating the usual acclaim of *Io triumphe*, others singing military ditties, either in praise of, or in satirical raillery upon, the hero of the day ; for this was a privileged time, and the legionaries failed not to exercise the freedom of speech in which it permitted them to indulge. Arrived at the capitol, the triumpher, whether consul, dictator, or emperor, sacrificed white bulls to Jupiter, and addressing an invocation at the altar, took from his own head the crown of laurel and placed it on that of the idol. He then made presents to the temple of the God, and gave largesses to the people. A feast was afterwards given at the public expense, to which all persons of rank and consequence were invited ; nor did the glory of the triumpher end with the actual proceedings of the day ; but a decree of the senate granted him a house, under the appellation of *domus triumphalis*, and statues were also raised to his honour.—For the ceremonies of a lesser triumph, see OVATIO.

Triumphal quadrigæ, with the *Imperator* as charioteer, appear on coins of the Cornelia family (Scipio Africanus), and on coins of the imperial series from Augustus to Constantine the Great, with few exceptions. On these medals the emperor holds sometimes the ivory sceptre, at others the laurel crown, and occasionally both the one and the other.

Triumphales quadrigæ vacuæ.—Triumphal cars, drawn by four horses, without any person in them, appear on coins of the Æmilia, Aquillia, and Pompeia families ; and in the imperial series on coins of Julius Cæsar, Augustus (Lepidus), Tiberius, Vespasian, Titus, Domitian, Sept. Severus, Macrinus, Gordianus Pius, and Maximianus.—On a first brass of Tiberius we see a triumphal car without a charioteer. Schlegel supposes that by this type was denoted a triumph voted indeed to Tiberius, but not celebrated by him, about the year v.c. 763. On gold and silver of Titus, we see a quadriga of horses drawing a chariot, on which, instead of a triumpher guiding it, are merely some flowers.—These coins, Eckhel observes, were struck at the very beginning of that emperor's reign, and before he accepted the name of *pater patriæ*, which was never afterwards omitted on similar

medals of his.—Vaillant (*Pr.* ii., 97) in reference to this reverse expresses his opinion that the car with four horses moving slowly, represents a triumphal quadriga in honour of Titus; and that a flower, or plant, like what is borne by the goddess *Spes*, is placed on the chariot to denote that the hope of the commonwealth relied on the victorious arms of Titus, which had achieved the capture of Jerusalem, and obtained for him a triumph as the conqueror of the Jews.

Triumphal quadrigæ with figures, standing in them, appear on coins of the Plautia and Vargunteia families; also, in the imperial series, on coins of Julius Cæsar, Claudius, Nero, Trajan, Severus, Caracalla, Elagabalus, Valerianus, senior, &c.

Triumphal ensigns and honours.—The monetal triumvirs took care, among other things, to strike on the reverses of consular coins triumphal cars, *fercula* (see below), corollæ (or chaplets), the laurel, military ensigns, and vexillæ, also spoils of war. Typifications of signal triumphs appear on coins of Roman families, as for example of Manius Acilius Glabrio for his victory over King Antiochus; of L. Scipio for his defeat of the same king, and his conquest of certain regions in Asia, whence he received the name of Asiagenis or Asiaticus; of P. Scipio, brother of Africanus, for his victories over the Carthaginians, Hannibal, and the Numidians ; of L. Sulla, over King Mithridates ; of L. Lucullus over the same king, and over Tigranes ; of Pompey, for his victories over the same two monarchs, and his conquest of many provinces in the East, and for his having, moreover, subdued the pirates.

Triumphalia ornamenta.—A silver coin of Augustus presents in the type of its reverse some of the personal decorations by which the victorious general was distinguished on the day of his triumph ; namely, the sceptre with the figure of an eagle at the top, the upper part of the *toga picta*, and the laurel wreath. Livy (lxxx. c. 15) states that Augustus, after having conferred on Masinissa the title of king, presented to him a golden crown, a golden patera, a curule chair, an ivory sceptre, the *toga picta* (or embroidered robe), and the *palmata tunica* (or vest striped with purple). And he added to these honours by saying, that "among the Romans there was nothing more magnificent than a triumph, and that those who were so distinguished had not a more splendid dress than that of which Masinissa, of all foreigners, was esteemed worthy by the Roman people."—Eckhel shows the presentation of these triumphal ornaments to have undoubtedly been derived from an Etrurian origin. He quotes Dionysius of Halicarnassus as relating that Tarquinius Priscus, in token of regard for the Etruscans, accepted from them those insignia of sovereignty with which they were accustomed to invest their kings—viz., a crown of gold and an ivory chair, a sceptre surmounted by an eagle, a purple tunic embellished with gold, and a *toga picta* of purple. Florus gives a similar account. And the same Dionysius also states that Tarquin continued to use these ornaments as symbols of regal power, as did the kings his successors; and after the extinction of royalty at Rome, the annual consuls adopted the same ornaments, except the crown and the *toga picta*, and they assumed even those whenever a triumph was decreed to them. In the times, however, of the emperors, under whom no private individual was allowed a triumph, although triumphal ornaments were decreed to some persons in reward of valour, yet all these insignia seem to have been permitted to be used by the consuls.—There are passages in Juvenal, in Ausonius, and in Prudentius, which corroborate the fact that the privilege of using ensigns and ornaments, originally granted to triumphers, was afterwards extended to the consuls.—Appian, in describing the triumph of Africanus senior, says, that the person triumphing usually bore an ivory sceptre and a laurel branch, which the Romans viewed as the symbol of victory. Nevertheless, we learn from coins, that when the emperors made the *processus consularis* they were accustomed to bear both these insignia. And on this account, unless other and more pointed indications offer themselves, it is difficult, when such imperial medals exhibit the *imperator* carried in a quadriga, holding in his right hand the *scipio cum aquilâ*, to determine whether the type be that of a triumph or of a consular prosession.—The *scipio aquilifera*, the *toga picta*, and the laurel crown, which appear on the denarius in question, are beyond all doubt representations of the *ornamenta triumphalia*, and were placed on its reverse in honour of a triumph enjoyed by Augustus, somewhere about v.c. 729.—See PARENT*i* CON*servatori* SVO. S.P.Q.R.

Triumphal honours were, according to Dion, conferred by the senate on Drusus senior (brother of the Emperor Tiberius), consisting of statues and triumphal arches, on account of his successful campaigns against the Germans. And Suetonius mentions a marble arch surmounted with trophies, in the Via Appia, decreed to the same prince.—See (DE) GERMANIS.

Triumphers sometimes took children into their cars.—On a brass medallion of L. Verus and M. Aurelius (edited in the *Mus. Descamps)*, we see two personages standing in a triumphal car, and a little boy behind them in the same vehicle, whilst soldiers precede, and a *ferculum*, or stage, conveying a trophy and captives, accompanies them.—This coin commemorates the Parthian triumph, which both the emperors above mentioned enjoyed. On that occasion, as Capitolinus states, children of both sexes were admitted into the chariot of M. Aurelius. This, however, was not a new practice; but it was a custom as old as the republic, for children to be carried in the same car with the triumpher. Zonaras narrates, from Dion, that " it was usual for him, who entered the city in triumph, to have with him in the chariot his children or other young relations, provided they were only *prætextati—i. e.* of so early an age as still to wear the long white purple-bordered gown (which noblemen's children were wont to do). But if they were

older, he placed them on horses harnessed together *(jugalibus funalibus ve).*—And if there were more, they followed the car, each mounted on a single horse."—Appian, in alluding to a triumph on Africanus senior, describes this peculiar feature of a Roman triumph in these general terms—"the sons and daughters (of the *Imperator)* are admitted into the same car, and the rest of the young blood relations are carried on horses bridled together."—Cicero *(Pro Muræna,* c. 5) also speaks of this custom : *An cum sedere in equis triumphantium prætextati potissimum filii soleant, &c.*—Suetonius, in his life of Tiberius, relates of him that, having just entered his prime of youth, after the battle of Actium, he appeared on horseback beside the triumphal car of Augustus, along with Marcellus, son of Octavia *(sinisteriore funali equo, quum Marcellus, Octaviæ filius, dexteriore veheretur).* Domitian, in like manner, attended the *triumphus Judaicus* of his father and brother (v.c. 824), riding conspicuously on a white horse.

Triumphal processions—represented on imperial medals.—There are, in the first place, silver and gold coins of Augustus, in which he is seen in a quadriga, holding in his right hand the reins of the horses, and in his left sometimes a branch of laurel, at others a sceptre surmounted by an eagle—and again holding the sceptre in his right and a branch in his left hand—the reins of the four horses being attached to the front of the car.—On the well known second brass, coined under Tiberius to commemorate the triumph of Germanicus (see SIGNIS RECEPTIS, &c.), we see the figure of that victorious but ill-requited hero, standing in a triumphal quadriga, holding the eagle-bearing sceptre in his left hand. —On gold and silver of Tiberius, that emperor appears in a car of triumph with sceptre and laurel branch.—From that period we find no more types of emperors triumphing until the reign of Vespasian, amongst whose gold coins are two quadrigæ with their imperial charioteer guiding the horses and holding the sceptre. There is also a beautiful aureus of Vespasian, with legend TRIVMP. AVG. (see below), referring to his triumph for *Judæa capta,* a subject which also furnishes similar types for the coins of Titus, especially a very fine large brass.— Domitian, having had the effrontery to assume the title of GERMANICUS, for a pretended victory over the German tribes, his gold and brass coins exhibit him in triumphal quadrigæ, with sceptre and laurel.—Trajan's *Triumphus* Parthicus will be found noticed below; the triumphal processions of L. Verus and M. Aurelius are already referred to.—Buonarotti, in his *Osservazioni sopra Medaglioni* (ii. No. 1), has published an imperial medallion of Caracalla, in which that emperor is seen in a quadriga, having the sceptre or ivory *baton* in his left and the laurel branch in his right hand; Victory behind crowning him. In triumphal ceremonies, the car was preceded by towers on wheels, called by the Latins *fercula,* on the top of which were placed prisoners of war, and spoils of the vanquished; and the medallion above described presents a *ferculum* of this kind.—The same accurate author has also in the same work given an engraving (tb. 22, No. 6), of a Latin silver medallion of Probus, with GLORIA ORBIS COS. V. for legend of reverse; and of which the type represents that warlike prince, crowned by Victory as a *triumphator*, holding a laurel branch, and drawn in a circular car, to which the unusual number of six horses are harnessed, led by two armed figures: on each side of the car and above the horses appear figures carrying palms.—Probus held his fifth consulate with Victorinus in the year v.c. 1035, A.D. 282; and this medallion was probably struck not only in honour of his triumph over the Germans and the Persians, but also in allusion to victories gained throughout the whole extent of the Roman world. This is Buonarotti's opinion; and Khell, who, in his Supplement to Vaillant, has also given an engraving of the coin, seems to view it in the same light.

The following inscriptions appear on Roman medals, relative to triumphs :—

TRIVMPVS.—Accompanying this legend, a youthful laureated head, with a trophy behind it, appears on a denarius of the *Papia* family— in apparent conformity to the invariable custom of the Romans, who delighted in representing by images whatever was subsidiary to the fortunate events and honours of life.—TRIVMPE, observes Eckhel, "is five times repeated in the very ancient lay or ballad of the Arvalian brothers, inscribed on a stone which was dug up at Rome in the year 1778." He adds, however, "no old writer mentions the worship of Triumpus (or Triumphus) as a deity," which shows that the practice of some numismatists of calling the youthful head above mentioned *caput Dei Triumphi* is not warranted. The same head and inscription are found on no other coins of Roman families. Allusion has already been made to the magnificence of the triumph decreed by the consul Paullus for his victories over the Macedonian king Perseus.— See TER. PAVLLVS.—See also *Papia* for an explanation of the curious type, exhibited on the *reverse* of the silver coin above quoted.

TRIVMP. AVG.—The emperor in a triumphal quadriga, holding a branch, is crowned by a Victory; a military figure and a naked captive with hands tied behind him, precede the car; in the group is a *tubicen* blowing his trumpet.— On a gold coin of Vespasian, in the imperial cabinet of Vienna.

This is one of the rarest and most elegant of those coins which attest the victories of Vespasian and Titus over the Jews, and which commemorate the triumph decreed to them on that account.—The events themselves, forming as they do so awfully important a subject of record on the pages of ancient history, and the honours conferred by the senate on the conquering generals, both father and son, who enjoyed their triumph on the same day, but apart from each other, are narrated by Suetonius and by Dion, and still more copiously described by Josephus. Appian mentions the employment of *tubicines* (trumpeters or horn-players), in a vivid account

which he gives of Scipio's triumph. Vaillant and Morell each give an engraving of this medal, which differs from the type of that quoted by Eckhel from the Vienna museum, inasmuch as both the two figures that precede the car of triumph appear as captives, having their hands bound behind them. The editor of the *Catalogue d'Ennery*, in alluding to the same type, says—"*Deux chefs des Juifs (Simon et Jean) precèdent le char de triomphe de Vespasian.*"

TRIVMPHVS PARTHICVS.—The emperor in a triumphal quadriga, holding a sceptre, surmounted by an eagle, in one hand, and in the

other a branch. On *gold* of Trajan, in the *Mus. Farnese.*—Eckhel quotes, as illustrative of this remarkable and very rare coin, a passage in Spartian, to the effect that, as the senate had conferred on Hadrian the triumph which was Trajan's due, he declined the honour, and carried the image of that deceased emperor with him in the triumphal car, in order that so admirable a military commander (*optimus imperator*) might not even after his death be deprived of the dignity of a triumph.—On this point of fact Victor also concurs.—It moreover appears, from Dion, that, after the death of Trajan, public shews were decreed by the senate in honour of his memory and deification, which were called *Parthica*, and were celebrated for many years, but at length ceased to be repeated.—What Dion denominates *Parthica* were doubtless, says Eckhel, the same as, in an old kalendarium (or book of accounts), published by Lambecius from the Imperial library, are termed TRIVMPHALES, and which were annexed to the xiv. kalends of October; in fact, the natal day of Trajan.—It seems certain, therefore, that these *certamina* PARTHICA, or TRIVMPHALIA, instituted in commemoration of the Parthian triumph (Triumphus Parthicus) were fixed by the senate, to be held on Trajan's birth-day, and that for a series of consecutive years they were accustomed to be renewed.—To this circumstance Eckhel considers the cause is to be traced, why there are so many contorniate medals, with the portrait of Trajan on them—namely, that they might be distributed amongst those who assisted at those *spectacula triumphalia*. It may therefore be further supposed, that the celebration of such triumphal solemnities, not discontinued, as Dion affirms, but only neglected in his time, were at a later period restored to indulge the Romans in their known fondness for public games and exhibitions.

TRIVMPHVS QVADORVM.—Two emperors in a car of triumph, drawn by four horses, preceded by a Victory. There are also two figures at the top of the reverse, and two others below, with spoils.—Banduri gives this from Vaillant, who has placed it amongst the brass medallions of Numerianus.—Tanini, in his Supplement to Banduri, says the legend reads TRIVNFV. QVADOR.

The tract of country occupied by the *Quadi*

is shewn under that word in p. 671 of this Dictionary, and also in remarks on the REX QVADIS DATVS of Antoninus Pius.—But what Numerianus had to do with the *Quadi*, or when, if he ever fought with them, he established his claim to a triumph by conquering them, are questions to which no satisfactory answers appear to have yet been given. Indeed, according to Vopiscus, this young prince, immediately after his victory over the Sarmatians, went with his father (Carus) to the East, and was slain before he could accomplish his return to the West. Even supposing that the historian above-named had given the name of Sarmatæ to the people who are the *Quadi* of this medal; still comes the inquiry, where was there a triumph celebrated by two emperors? Eckhel regards the subject as involved in the thickest Cimmerian darkness; and Banduri himself, in his commentary on this coin, despairs of being able to throw light upon it.

TRIVMFATOR GENTIVM BARBA-RARVM.—The emperor clothed in the toga, stands holding in his right hand the *labarum*, on which is inscribed the monogram of Christ.

This legend appears for the first time on gold and silver medallions of Constans I.—It is a title, which, if not in the instance of Constans, certainly in the case of *most* of his successors who adopted the pompous designation, is more specious than true. The same legend, sometimes with similar, sometimes with different types, occurs on coins of Constantinus II., of Valentinianus I., of Valens, of Theodosius the Great (who alone deserved it), of Arcadius, and Honorius. It also appears on a fine silver medallion of Magnentius, struck at Aquileia. *Rev. Num.*, 1850, p. 108.

TRIVMFVS CAESARVM, with type of Victory, is given by Tanini, as from a second brass of Constans I.

Triumviri Monetales. Monetal Triumvirs.— These were officers specially appointed by the Romans to direct or superintend the coinage of their money. From the time of the republic, the management of the mint was entrusted to three magistrates, who were called *Triumviri Auro, Argento, Aeri, Flando, Feriundo*—that is to say, a commission of three, under whom coins in gold, silver, and brass were struck. Julius Cæsar, who increased the magistracies that he might confer the more favours, was the first to add one to their original number.—This, says Eckhel (v. 62), took place doubtless in the year of Rome 709, for it is on the coins of that year, pertaining to the dictator, that we first find mention of *Quatuorviri* instead of *Triumviri.*— Suetonius relates of the first Cæsar that "he moreover appointed special slaves over the mint and the public revenues."—In order to reconcile this statement with certain testimonies from coins, which indicate rather that the number of the triumvirs was increased than that the super-intendence of the mint was taken out of their hands and entrusted to slaves—it will be necessary to say that Cæsar committed to slaves, *not* the business of coining the public money,

but its custody when coined. And this is the very fact alluded to (*i.e.* by Suetonius) as a proof of Cæsar's disregard of the custom observed by his predecessors, that he should have transferred to slaves property belonging to the quæstors.

Under Augustus the changes made in the monetal magistracy by his predecessor were abolished; the number of these officers was restored to three, as Dion states. In what year this reformation took place appears to be uncertain; but we know that they continued throughout that emperor's reign to engrave their names on the coins which they caused to be struck.— Aquillius, Caninius, Durmius, and Petronius, whose coins were struck in the year v.c. 734, or near that time, call themselves III*VIRI.* Whether this alteration took place in any year anterior to this date is unknown. "With respect to the rank or station (says Eckhel) which these monetary prefects held at Rome, Dion affords us information (v.c. 741). For, after saying that Augustus selected from out of the *Equites*, xx. men, who having filled the inferior offices, might have liberty to aspire to the senatorial dignity, he enumerates among them, besides the *Triumviri Capitales* (or judges appointed to try criminal cases), "*the* THREE *who had the office of striking the coinage.*"— Now, therefore (proceeds Eckhel), looking to the fact recorded by Tacitus, that Tiberius had requested from the senate that Nero, son of Germanicus, should be exempted from serving on the Vigintivirate and be allowed to be candidate for the Quæstorship five years earlier than the legal period; and considering nevertheless, what Lipsius, in his commentary on this passage of Tacitus, assuredly proves, that it was not lawful to assume the quæstorship before the age of at least 25 years (the very *five* years, be it observed, which Tiberius desired Nero to be exempted from), we gather, that it was legal to assume the *Vigintiviratus Monetalis,* at the age of 20 years.—Hence Ovid speaks correctly in the description of his life—

Cepimus et teneræ primos ætatis honores,
Eque VIRIS quondam pars TRIBVS una fui.
　　　　　　　　　　Trist. L. iv. el. x. v. 33.

After filling which office, as he says, they were eligible to the senate *(Curia restabat, &c.)*; but to this dignity he preferred a literary leisure. From this it appears that the monetal triumvir could be also styled a Vigintivir, as is really the case, on an engraved marble edited by Spon, viz., XXVIRO MONETALI. The Vigintivirate, therefore, was a magistracy, which, though of an inferior order, was nevertheless of such a kind, that through it the higher honours of the state could be arrived at. This fact is shewn, not merely by the above-mentioned passage of Tacitus, but on the authority of Dion, when he says that Claudius ordered L. Junius Silanus, and Cn. Pompeius Magnus, his sons-in-law, to hold office among the XXviri; and that it was after a considerable interval that they were allowed to assume the other magistracies, five years earlier than the usual period. To these testimonies may be added two inscriptions on marbles, published by Marini and Gruter, which, after the enumeration of other and more illustrious offices, give to Julius Proculus, and to Q. Hedius, the title of IIIvir A.A.A. F.F.—It is well-known, however, that marbles, in enumerating the magistracies, for the most part preserve such an arrangement of time, that the offices which an individual last served are recorded first, and the first placed last in order. It is not, therefore, to be wondered at, that the names of the most distinguished families should be found among the *Triumviri Monetales*, who were also, as we have seen, in the list of the XXviri. And doubtless, on this principle, are to be explained the following denarii:—

The head of *Octavianus* (afterwards *Augustus*).
—TI. SEMPRONIVS. GRACCVS. IIIIVIR. Q. DESIG.
The head of *Julius Cæsar.*—Q. VOCONIVS. VITVLVS. Q. DESIGN.

That is to say, Sempronius and Voconius were *Quatuorviri Monetales*, and having been fully established in this office, and already Quæstors Elect *(Quæstores Designati)*, they caused these silver coins to be struck.

Triumviri Monetales how marked on coins.—After refuting the theory of Vaillant and Havercamp, who have constantly asserted that the monetal triumvirate was an annual office, Eckhel proceeds to observe that these magistrates are numismatically indicated by the addition of IIIVIR. to their names, or from the time of Julius Cæsar, by that of IIIIVIR. On a denarius of Cossutius we read C. COSSVTIVS MARIDIANVS. A. A. A. F. F., viz., *Auro, Argento, Aeri, Flando, Feriundo.* Frequently on coins of Augustus IIIVIR. A. A. A. F. F., although it is highly probable that the triumvirs of the mint did not always make mention of their office. The most remarkable formulæ hitherto discovered are—IIIVIR. PRI. FL. on a denarius of the Flaminia family. This has been interpreted *Primus Flavit.* But in treating of the coins of this family, our author does not undertake to vouch for the accuracy of that explanation.—There is also IIIVIR. A. P. F. on gold of the Livineia and Musidia families, viz., *Auro, Publice, Feriundo,* or as Khell (in Supplement to Vaillant, p. 8) will have it *Ad Pecuniam Feriundum.* To which may be also added the A. PV. *(Aere Publico),* or ARG. PVB. *(Argento Publico),* or P. A., or EX. A. P., or EX. A. PV. *(Ex Aerario Publico,* or *Ex Aere Publico)* marked on the field of certain silver coins of the Lucilia, Tituria, Sentia, Critonia, Fabia, and Fonteia families, by which is denoted that the metal of the money to be struck was furnished by the state. Contrary to the usual custom is the inscription LEN. CVR. X. FL. EX. S. C. *(Lentulus Curator Denariorum Flandorum Ex Senatus Consulto),* by which we are taught that those, to whom the care of the mint was entrusted, were also called CVR*atores.*

An inspection of the coins of the emperors will sufficiently shew that Augustus assumed to himself the right of striking the gold and silver coinage (the brass being conceded to the senate), in which circumstance he went beyond his predecessors. Moreover from brass coins on which to the names of the Triumvirs are constantly added A. A. A. F. F., it appears that to one and the same Triumvir belonged the right of striking gold and silver coins in the name of Augustus, and brass coins in the name of the senate; and this point is accurately established in the example of M. Sanguinius, who equally caused silver coins to be struck with the head of Augustus, and brass with the mark s. c.

At the command of Augustus, the names of Triumvirs and of all other magistrates ceased to be inscribed on Roman coins, somewhere about the year v.c. 740, as would appear on reference to the medals of that emperor.—This is Eckhel's opinion, who concludes his observations on the subject in question, by giving the following list of the *Monetal Triumvirs* under the republic, and the *Quatuorviri* under Julius Cæsar:—

TRIUMVIRI MONETALES.

NV. ACILIVS IIIVIR.
T. CARISIVS. IIIVIR.
CALDVS. IIIVIR.   *Cælia family.*
RVFVS IIIVIR.   *Cordia family.*
P. FONTEIVS P. F. CAPITO IIIVIR.
GETA IIIVIR.   *Hosidia family.*
L. PAPIVS. CELSVS. IIIVIR.
Q. SICILIVS IIIVIR.

QUATUORVIRI MONETALES.

L. AEMILIVS. BVCA. IIIIVIR.
C. COSSVTIVS MARIDIANVS. A. A. F. F.
L. FLAMIN. CHILO. IIIIVIR. PRI. FL.
L. REGVLVS. IIIIVIR. A. P. F. *Livineia fam.*
L. MVSSIDIVS. T. F. LONGVS. IIIIVIR. A. P. F.
TI. SEMPRONIVS. GRACCVS. IIIIVIR. Q. DESIG.

Under the lower empire, not only did these officers cease to be any longer mentioned, but even the old-established s. c. was discontinued on the brass coinage. Hence it is inferred that the emperors, claiming as part of their prerogative, the exclusive right of striking money, abolished the triple office of those who presided over the operations of the Roman mint.—"According to appearances (says Millin) this change took place under Aurelian, against whom the moneyers revolted. The workmen employed under the orders of the triumvirs, and who were either freedmen or slaves, were divided into several classes. Those called *signatores* engraved the coins: those denominated *suppostores* were charged with the placing of the piece of metal between the dies; others named *malleatores* struck the dies, so supplied, with the hammer. Besides these there were other workmen engaged in the melting and preparation of the metals. Some were entrusted with the important duty of verifying the standard and weight of the respective coinages, in the three metals—an office similar to that of the modern assayers of the mint, who make especial trial of the gold and silver money. They were called *exactores auri, argenti, æris,* and hence proceeds the term *exagium solidi* (see the words), which is read on certain square formed medals of Honorius and Valentinian.—See *Moneta—Moneta Romana—Monetal Triumvirs—Monetarii.*

Troas—a Roman colony.—See *Alexandria Troas.*

Trojæ lusus or *ludus.*—The Trojan games, said to have been instituted by Æneas, in Sicily, to exercise his son Ascanius and the young Trojans of his suite. It appears certain that sports bearing this appellation were practised at Rome in the circus by youths of the noblest patrician families, who raced on horseback; formed themselves into opposing squadrons; and represented a sort of combat.—*Troja et Regia Priami* (says Festus) *et lusus puerorum equestris dicetur.*—Julius Cæsar restored it to its pristine vigour, and the Romans, after his death, long continued to practice it with enthusiastic fondness.—On a gold coin of Caius (one of the two sons of Agrippa), styled C. CAES. AVGVST*i Filius,* the young prince appears on horseback, riding at full speed, holding spear and shield: behind him is a legionary eagle between two military standards.—Havercamp, on account of the military ensigns, believes this type to exhibit the *profectio* of Caius on an expedition against the Parthians. But Eckhel thinks it much more likely that the type was intended to commemorate the *Troja*—or riding at tilt, an exercise which, according to Dion, was performed by Caius in the year v.c. 741, he being then only in the seventh year of his age. *Augustus theatrum Marcelli dedicavit, ludisque ejus rei gratia factis Trojam inter alios patricios pueros nepos Augusti Caius lusit.* The *signa militaria,* adds Eckhel, are to be accounted for, from the fact that this *game of Troy* was a military one; and Virgil, doubtless alluding to Caius under the image of Ascanius thus describes it —

Vade age, et Ascanio, si jam puerile paratum
Agmen habet secum, cursusque instruxit equorum,
Ducat avo turmas, et sese ostendat in armis.
　　　　　　　Æneid. L. v. l. 548.

Tropæum.—Trophy, formed of the spoils taken from the enemy, and set up as a public monument. Trophies, equally by the Romans and the Greeks, were esteemed as the rewards and insignia of victories. In the earlier ages they consisted simply of a trunk of a tree, to which a little below the top another piece of wood was fastened crosswise, and set up on the field of battle immediately after a victory; this was adorned with spoils, or the armour of the vanquished, customarily a cuirass, a helmet, and a buckler.—The first trophy of which the Roman history makes mention is the one erected by C. Flaminius, in the year v.c. 530, it is affirmed to have been of gold, and was placed in the Capitol.—Florus, in recording this fact, also speaks of two other trophies, raised a hundred years after, in their war with the Allobroges by Domitius Aenobarbus and Fabius Maximus, at

the confluence of the Isere with the Rhone. To this day there are to be seen at Rome two trophies in marble, believed to have been erected by Marius, in commemoration of his double victory over Jugurtha and over the Cimbri, of which Suetonius speaks. In the latter period of the republic, the Romans were in the habit of carrying trophies before the car of the triumpher. And when it was the object to render these symbols of victory more durable, they were constructed of stone, marble, brass, and any other solid material, dedicated to some divinity, and inscribed with the details of the victory gained.—From the time of Augustus, who caused a trophy to the glory of the Roman arms to be raised on the Alps, monuments of this description multiplied greatly. The Trajan and Antonine columns are, in fact, trophies on a grand scale.—Spanheim, in his notes on the Cæsars of Julian, has given a representation (finely engraved by Picard) of one of those magnificent trophies which still exist at Rome, and which are ascribed to Trajan. It is in this example that we see the rough trunk of a tree, surmounted with a helmet, enriched with sculpture, and covered with a chlamys; it is furthermore decorated with quivers, arrows, and bucklers, held by winged figures of sphinxes, tritons, centaurs, &c.

Trophies are frequently represented on denarii of Roman families. Sometimes these objects are exhibited with other military insignia—namely, darts, shields, and *litui,* as may be seen on coins of the *Julia* family; at other times they are accompanied with figures of kneeling captives, bound to the same trophies, as in medals of the Cornelia, Fundania, Junia, and Servilia families. Again we see trophies crowned by Victory, as in Fundania, and Memmia, or by the Genius of Rome, as in Furia. (Spanheim, *Pr.* ii. 220).—For an historical explanation of the trophies engraved on certain denarii of the Cornelia family, see the word *Sulla.*

Trophies are typified on Roman coins, in vast numbers, both of the early and lower empire, from Julius to Gallienus. If the object were to commemorate a victory over the barbarians, it is signified by the figure of Victory herself adorning the oaken trunk with the arms of the conquered tribes.

A *trophy* formed of a suit of body armour, to which are suspended a buckler and a military lituus, one on the right, the other on the left arm of its cross-piece—there is an axe and the word CAESAR on the field of a gold coin of Julius Cæsar.—A splendid trophy within a temple of two columns appears on a gold medal of Augustus.—That trophies were used for ornaments to triumphal arches is shewn on a large brass of Nero Claudius Drusus, brother of the Emperor Tiberius.—On medals of Trajan, we see *Mars Gradivus* carrying a trophy on his shoulder, composed sometimes of a cuirass and buckler, at others simply of a cuirass.—Two trophies finely decorated with armour of the enemy are seen on coins of

Trajan; in one of these types the emperor stands between them.

For an explanation of the trophy and accompanying figures on the reverse of a denarius of the *Æmilia* family, struck in honour of the Consul Æmilius Paullus: see TER PAVLLVS.

TR. P. *Treveris Percussa*, or *Treverensis Pecunia.*

Tullia, a family partly patrician, partly plebeian. Three varieties in its coins: one of these is described to be a denarius, having on its obverse a winged head of Minerva; behind which is the word ROMA; and on the reverse M. TVLLI. Victory in a quadriga, holding a palm-branch in the left hand; in the field of the coin a crown and the mark X.—The same restored by Trajan is RRR.—By many numismatists this silver medal has been ascribed to Cicero the Orator, and it has thus become a subject of naturally great interest, as supposed to be identified with the name and times of that famous man who is justly reckoned amongst the most illustrious characters of antiquity. Eckhel, however, far from countenancing this supposition, contents himself with remarking that it is a matter of uncertainty to which *Tullius* this denarius is to be assigned, or by what surname it is to be distinguished, for the *Tullia gens* spreads widely through many and various *cognomina*. The form itself of the coin, he adds, reveals a higher antiquity than can possibly be compatible with the opinion which refers it to Cicero.

A denarius of the *Tullia* family, having on its obverse the winged head of Minerva, with the word ROMA; exhibits on the reverse side M. TVLLI. The type is Victory in a quadriga, holding a palm-branch; above is a laurel garland; below X. It would seem by this singular coin, in which his prenomen and name are associated with Victory in a car, that the triumph of Cicero was meant to be designated. But the most remarkable and personally interesting numismatic memorial of this illustrious Roman, is a second brass colonial of Magnesia, in Lydia, with his portrait—a coin of the greatest rarity. —See Mionnet—*Tullia* fam.

There is also a silver medallion classed under the head of this family, on the obverse of which appears the mystic basket (see *Cistophori),* half opened, whence issues a serpent; the whole within a wreath composed of ivy leaves and its berries. For legend of reverse it has M. TVLL. IMP. ΛΑΒΑΣ. ΠΤΡΡΟΤ. ΛΑΟ. and two serpents, with tails interwined, form its accompanying type.

This most elegant and rare Cistophorus was first published by that eminent French antiquary Seguin, and illustrated by him in his learned commentary, as a relic unquestionably connected with the chief of Roman orators and philosophers. Eckhel moreover, who, as we have seen, denies that the preceding coin has any relation to Cicero, decidedly vindicates the genuine claim of this beautiful medallion to be acknowledged as having been struck at Laodicea in honour of that celebrated personage :—

"It is well established (says he) that Cistophori were coined in the province of Asia only. Cicero was, in the year of Rome 703, sent as proconsul into Cilicia, and to his jurisdiction at that time belonged also Pamphylia, Lycaonia, and part of Phrygia, that part indeed in which Laodicea was situated; the town which struck this coin, as the addition ΛΑΟ. shews us. That Cicero frequently held assemblies here we may infer from many passages of his letters; and in fact, from the ides of February to the calends of May, he held a court, including all the Asiatic districts. The word IMP*erator* is added, being an honour which he himself says he had obtained in a letter to Cælius Rufus :— 'So by a just victory I gained the title of Imperator at Issus, a spot at which, as I have often heard that Clitarchus told you, Darius was defeated by Alexander.'"

On the other hand, respecting a reputed second brass colonial of Magnesia, in Lydia, to which allusion is made in both Mionnet and Akerman, as bearing on its obverse the *head of Cicero*, the author of *Doctrina* makes the following observations :—

"As we have adduced a genuine coin of M. Tullius Cicero, it would appear a proper opportunity here to notice the counterfeit productions, to which the hope of gain has given birth; a hope which could not fail of its object, whilst there exists the universal desire of gazing on the likeness of such a man. Passing by those coins, however, which at the first glance are distinctly to be recognised as forgeries, we shall select out of their number, one which the opinion of many individuals have even to the present moment stamped with the character of genuineness, and this is it: ΜΑΡΚΟΣ ΤΟΥΛΑΙΟΣ. ΚΙΚΕΡΩΝ. A naked head of Cicero. *Rev.* ΜΑΓΝΗΤΩΝ. ΑΠΟ. ΣΙΠΤΛΟΤ. ΘΕΟΔΩΡΟΣ. A right hand holding a crown, a branch, and a palm (or vine) shoot. Second brass: see Eckhel; and a Paper by Mr. Birch, on a *Coin of Magnesia, with the head of Cicero*, published, with an engraving, in the *Numismatic Chronicle*, vol. ii. p. 107.

Tullius Hostilius, third king of Rome, the immediate successor of Numa. Sprung from the ancient and illustrious stock of the *gens* Hostilia, he was elected by the suffrages of the people: an evidence of this is considered to be shewn on that coin of the *Hostilia* family, on which there is a representation of the voting place in the Comitia at Rome. The treaty of the same king with the Albans is supposed to be shadowed forth in the type of a denarius of the *Veturia* family.

Tunica—the Tunic.—This was not a single garment, but was capable of being multiplied so as to be distinguished by the names of the *vestis interior* and the *vestis exterior*. It was of linen or woollen. That of the women had sleeves, was very wide, descended much lower than the men's, and was put on immediately under the robe. On ancient monuments, as well numismatic as lapidary, Diana is sometimes represented with her tunic tucked up and fastened with a girdle: hence she was called *Diana cincta*, or *succincta*. At other times the same goddess is depictured with the girdle loosened, and then it is called *discincta*.—The *tunica*, like the *toga*, received different epithets. Amongst the rest there were the

Tunica palmata.—This was of purple, and was bordered with a band of gold stuff. It was the dress of those who received triumphal honours, and of those who presided at the sports of the circus. And the *Tunica picta*, which like the *Toga picta* was enriched with embroidery, and interlaced with flowers. The large band which bordered the tunic from top to bottom was called *clavus*. The *angusticlavia* or narrow border was the distinction of the knights; the *laticlavia*, or broad band, that of the senators of Rome.—For other particulars relative to this article of dress, see Millin, *Des Beaux Arts;* and Pitiscus, *Dictionary of Greek and Roman Antiquities.*

Turiaso, a municipium of Hispania Tarraconensis, now *Tarazona*, situate on a small river that runs into the Ebro, to the south of Tudela.—For a description, and *fac simile* engravings of the imperial colonial coins, struck in this municipium, under Augustus and Tiberius, see the accurate work of Mr. Akerman, entitled *Ancient Coins of Cities and Princes.*—Hispania, No. 4, p. 110, pl. xi. No. 7, and pl. xii. No. 1 and No. 2.

Turrita mulier—a woman wearing a crown of towers. This figure is of very frequent occurrence on colonial coins. Almost all the cities of Syria, Phœnicia, and Mesopotamia, exhibit their respective *genii*, under the form of a female with *turres* on her head, as if denoting their exposure to, and state of mural defence against, the incursive attacks of neighbouring enemies.

Turritum caput muliebre.—The turreted head of a woman serves on Greek and Roman medals as a typification of goddesses, and of virtues.—See Astarte, Ceres, Cybele, Diana, Vesta; also Genius, Concordia, Fortuna, Indulgentia, Pax Orbis, Victoria.—The same type symbolises the various provinces and countries subject to the domination of Imperial Rome.—See Asia, Cappadocia, Gallia, Hispania, Italia, Pannonia, Syria, &c.—It is likewise a sign of some principal town, fortified with walls and towers.—According to Vaillant, all colonies were designated by the turreted head of a female stamped on their coin.

TVSCVL. Tusculum.—This legend appears on gold and silver coins of the highest rarity, belonging to the Sulpicia family. It is inscribed on the reverse over the gates of a walled and turreted city. (See *Sulpicia*).—On the obverse are the heads of the Dioscuri, whose attributes and worship are plainly bespoken, and the above described type of the reverse, connecting itself with the same deification, bears reference to Servius Sulpicius, a tribune of the people, who in the year v.c. 878, invested with consular power, went to Rome, at the head of an army, to the relief of Tusculum, which city he rescued from the power of the Latins, who had laid

seige to it.—It appears from Cicero, that the temple of Castor and Pollux stood at Tusculum; and, according also to Festus, Castor was worshipped in that town. Thus we find not only the chief divinities of the *Tusculanei*, but the city of Tusculum itself represented on this extremely rare gold coin.

Tusculum, a most ancient colony and municipium of Latium. Many noble and consular families derived their origin from Tusculum. Situate about 12 miles south-west of Rome, it was the locality of Cicero's celebrated villa, and the scene of his Tusculan disputations. *Frascati* is its modern name.—See *Manlia* family; also see the word *Telegonus*, which fabled son of Ulysses, by Circe, as some say, by Calypso as others have it, is the reputed founder of this Latian city.

Tutela—Defence or Protection; a name bearing affinity to Genius and to Fortune. That Genii, Fortunæ, and Tutelæ were not always regarded as identical by the ancients is shewn on the marble edited by Maffei—GENIO ET FORTVNAE TVTELAEQVE HVJVS LOCI. But it also appears that these deified guardians and tutelaries, although distinguished from each other by various old writers, yet on account of the similitude of the functions ascribed to them, were often interchanged and confounded with each other—a circumstance not surprising, adds Eckhel, when theories on matters, unconnected with human nature, depend on popular opinion and frequently on that of individuals.—See *Doct. Num. Vet.* vol. viii. p. 141.—Respecting this Tutela, as a deity, St. Jerome (on *Isaiah*, l. xvi., c. 58) says—there was no place (in the heathen world) which was not defiled by the abominations of idolatry, insomuch that they placed behind the doors of houses, idols which they called their household gods, or *Lares*. To this error and most pernicious custom, the cities of many provinces of the empire were addicted; Rome herself, the mistress of the world, *worshipping with wax lights and with lamps*, the image of *Tutela*, so called because they believed her to be their defence."—*Gusseme* vi. p. 464.

Tutela, as indicating the protection of Jupiter and of other gods, under which the emperors placed themselves, is attended to in the legends of some of their coins—such, for example, as DIS AVSPICIBVS of Sept. Severus; the DIS GENITALIBVS of Crispina; the DII NVTRITORES of Salonius. On other medals, it is read, not only in general terms, as DIS CVSTODIBVS, or IVPITER CVSTOS; but specially and by name as IOVI CONSERVATORI AV*Gusti*—IOVI DEFENS. SALVTIS AVG., or I. O. M. SPONSORI SEC. AVG. (Commodus and Postumus). See the words. In like manner, Jupiter Conservator with thunderbolt, spear, and pallium, in the attitude of encompassing, as it were, the person of the emperor, denotes that he fortifies and assists the ruler of the Roman world with his guardianship and power. (Rasche). The tutelage of other deities is similarly typified.—See *Apollini Cons. Aug.*—*Marti Patri Conservatori.* &c.

TUTELA AVGVSTI.—A woman seated, extending her right hand towards a boy, whilst another stands by her side.

Valliant thus describes the reverse of a second brass which he assigns to Vitellius, but of which the obverse is not exhibited.—Mionnet and Akerman both include a similarly described medal, amongst the rare *middle* brass of that emperor, notwithstanding that it is classed by Eckhel amongst the *numi suspecti* of that short and turbulent reign. He observes that "the entire reverse belongs to Vespasian," there being middle brass frequently met with which were struck in the year of Rome, with Vespasian's portrait, and the above-mentioned type on the reverse (see below).—"It is not possible," he

adds, "that the two boys could belong to Vitellius, because he, on his accession to the empire, had only a son and a daughter."—See LIBERI IMP. GERM. AVG.—The example here given is from a second brass of Vespasian.

TVTELA AVG. S. C.—A woman seated, extends her right hand over Titus and her left over Domitian, who are respectively standing by her side.

Eckhel, in describing this legend and type, from a second brass in the imperial cabinet at Vienna, says "This is allegorical. Vespasian, through paternal affection, hereby publicly avows himself the guardian and tutor of his sons. But he also assumed this title for the sake of his own security, as the life of a monarch is the safer the greater number of aids he relies upon. It was from this feeling that Titus exerted himself to produce a reconciliation between Domitian and his father, who had been justly incensed at his open profligacy; on which occasion Titus said, 'the bulwarks of empire consist greatly in legions and fleets; but the best resources of a sovereign are in his own family.'" (*Tacit* iv. 52.)

TVTELA ITALIAE.—The emperor seated on a curule chair, extends his right hand towards a boy and girl, near whom a woman is standing. First brass of Nerva.

Eckhel, in quoting the above from Tristan, makes the following observations:—"Victor relates of Nerva, that he commanded boys and girls, born of indigent parents, to be supported at the public expense throughout the cities of Italy. The guardianship (*Tutela*) commemorated on this coin refers to the above-mentioned fact; and we recognise in the mint of Trajan, how illustrious a successor Nerva had, in the carrying out of his benevolent design."—It is,

however, to be noticed that neither Mionnet nor Mr. Akerman include this coin in their catalogues; yet the animadversions of Eckhel, as well as the commentary of Tristan, must of course have recurred equally to each of those eminent numismatists; the inference to be drawn from its omission in both works is, we presume, that they did not regard it as genuine.

TVTELA AVG.—A woman, with turreted (?) head, stands holding in her right hand a patera over an altar, and a cornucopiæ in her left—at the bottom of the coin is LO.—This appears among the third brass of Carausius in Banduri's work, and in the *Cat.* D'Ennery.

With the same legend on the reverse, as on the coins of Vespasian, it presents quite a different type. The health and safety of Carausius would here seem to have been committed to the guardianship (*Tutela*) of some female genius.—Eckhel thinks it not improbable that the letters LO. mark the coin as having been struck at London (Londinum). Akerman gives a similar medal from the Hunter collection, but without describing the head ornament of the woman, and also without adding the letters LO.

TUTOR REGIS.—On the reverse of a denarius of the Æmilia family we read M. LEPIDVS. PONT. MAX. TVTOR. REG. S. C.—The type

represents Lepidus standing, clothed in the toga, places a crown on the head of the king (a youth), who stands by him, in a similar dress, and holding a spear in his right hand.—On the obverse of this very rare silver coin, is the word ALEXANDREA, with the turreted head of a woman.

The remarkable legend of the above described reverse receives illustration from Valerius Maximus (c. 6)—"King Ptolemy having left the guardianship of his son to the hands of the Roman people, the senate sent M. Aemilius Lepidus, who had twice been consul, to Alexandria for the purpose of undertaking the guardianship of the youth."—Justin (l. 30) is still more explanatory:—"At the death of the king, the inhabitants of Alexandria sent an embassy to the Romans, praying them to undertake the guardianship of the young king, and the charge of the affairs of Egypt. . . . . And M. Lepidus is sent to Egypt to administer the government of the minor, under the title of *Tutor*" (or guardian). The same event is incidentally adverted to by Tacitus (*Ann.* ii. c. 67): "Just as our ancestors sent M. Lepidus into Egypt, as guardian to the children of Ptolemy."

"It is indeed marvellous (says Eckhel, after citing the above authorities,) that so important an incident, confirmed by testimonies so numerous and so eminent, should be involved in such a dense obscurity, that we should not even now have clear information of the identity of this Ptolemy, with whose guardianship Lepidus was entrusted. The occasion of this uncertainty is indeed justly attributed to the negligence of the ancient writers, who in making no distinction between the host of Ptolemies, acted neglectfully towards posterity, for whose benefit they professed to write."

Having weighed all the arguments *pro* and *con* the particular Ptolemy implied, Eckhel gives it as his opinion, grounding it principally on Justin, that this remarkable event fully and satisfactorily admits of the following explanation :—"Ptolemy IV. Philopator dies A.V.C. 550, at which time the Romans sought occasion of war with Philip (V. king of Macedonia). The Alexandrians send ambassadors to petition the senate for a guardian for the infant king, Ptolemy V. Epiphanes. And on this account it is, that on the obverse of the denarius in question appears the genius of Alexandria, supplicating this favour. The war with Philip progresses, and he falls a victim, A.V.C. 557.—Lepidus having accomplished his duties as guardian (it is not known in what year), became Consul for the first time v.c. 567, obtained the honour of Pontifex Maximus v.c. 574, and was made Consul for the second time v.c. 578."—*Doct. Num. Vet.* vol. v. p. 123 *et seqq.*

Tutulata mulier.—A female figure engraved on ancient medals is said to be *tutulata*, when the head is ornamented with a *modius*, or measure, or with a basket *(calathus)*. The same term is also sometimes applied to the tower-like head-dress which distinguishes Astarte, goddess of the Syrians.

Tympanum ; timbrel, tabor, or drum.—A symbol of Cybele, which she holds in her right hand or sustains on her left knee. Vaillant *(Col.* ii. 139) says that by this attribute some of the ancients supposed the globe of the earth to be signified ; others regarded it as simply representing the *cymbalum*, or musical instrument of brass, which the priests of the above-named goddess used at her sacred rites.—See *Crotalum*, *Cybele*, MATRI DEVM.—The tympanum is seen in the hands of Cybele, on coins of Hadrian, Sabina, Faustina junior, Lucilla, Commodus, Albinus, Julia Domna, &c.

Typi permutati.—It frequently happens in the Roman mint that part of one coin is conjoined to part of another. Copious examples of this are found on medals of the imperial series ; nor are they rare in those of Roman families. Eckhel gives a few specimens of this latter class in his *Prelegomena ad numos familiarum,* vol v. p. 92.

Types on family coins, in attestation of ancestral virtues.—See remarks on this subject in *Doct. Num. Vet.* vol 5 p. 88.

Tyranni.—By this name certain commanders of armies in various Roman provinces were called, who, in the disordered and tumultuous reigns of Valerianus and Gallienus, usurped the augustal titles, and exercised "a little brief authority," as Cæsars and as Emperors. Trebellius Pollio professed to write the history of " The Thirty Tyrants," as they are commonly called, but who are scarcely known except from coins. And of these Odenathus, Macrianus, Quietus, Postumus, Victorinus, Tetricus father and son, Regalianus, Domitius Domitianus, and a few others, are the only ones of whom medals are extant, which

antiquaries agree in recognising as genuine.—See *Rasche.*

Tyrus, or *Tyros.*—Tyre, a maritime city of Phœnicia. It was an offspring of *Sidon* (see the word), but far excelled the mother state in enterprise, in achievements, in opulence, and power. Of her pre-eminent commercial character, Esaiah thus speaks (c. xxiii. v. 8), in his awful prophecy of her destruction—" Who hath taken counsel against Tyre, the *crowning* city, whose merchants are princes, whose traffickers are the honourable of the earth." This city, celebrated alike in sacred and in profane history, is said by Eusebius (in *Chron.)* to have been founded 242 years before the building of Solomon's temple. It consisted of two towns—one situate on the shore of the mainland, called *Palætyros* : the other, for the convenience of mercantile pursuits, was constructed on an adjacent island. The two together (connected as they were doubtless by bridges or other works of communication) were about nineteen miles in circumference, but the newer city did not exceed four miles in circuit. The great antiquity of Tyre, carrying it beyond the records of pagan history into the regions of mythology and fable, we find accordingly the foundation of the insular portion of Tyre ascribed to the advice of Hercules, to which deified hero, they in gratitude raised a temple and paid the honours due to a tutelary god.—Carthage and Cadiz were both of them amongst the colonies of the Tyrians.—Tyre had a succession of its own kings ; and it was during the reign of Azelmius that Alexander the Great gained possession of the place, after a siege of seven months, rendered alike remarkable by the obstinate bravery of its defenders, by the various and extraordinary difficulties opposed to the enormous efforts of the assailants, and by the vengeful desolation inflicted on the wretched inhabitants by the hand of the royal conqueror. —It then fell under the sway of Antigonus and Demetrius, two of Alexander's generals : afterwards it became subject to the Ptolemies ; and at length devolved to the rule of the *Seleucidæ.* So great were the naval strength and the nautical skill of the Tyrians that to them was ascribed the invention of the *Trireme* or galley, with three banks of oars. On the earliest coins of Tyre, she is called *Coronata* and *Coronaria.* [Compare this with the passage from Isaiah above quoted.] Strabo says that this famous city contested with Sidon the right to be styled a metropolis ; and for a time enjoyed that distinction, which, however, appears to have been afterwards omitted, or at least interrupted. Certain it is that both Tyre and Sidon were deprived of this dignity by Augustus, on account of some seditions fomented by their respective inhabitants against their Roman victors.—The name and privileges of Tyre, as a capital city, was restored to it by Hadrian. But it was not till the reign of Sept. Severus that it was made a Roman colony, invested with the *jus Italicum*, and surnamed Septimia, in honour of its imperial founder —its coins bearing the legend of COL. SEPT. TYROS. METROPOL., also COLONIA TYRVS METRO-

POLIS AVGVSTA, and the type (amongst others) of the colonist at plough, accompanied with a *vexillum*, or standard, on which is read LEG. III. GALL. *Legio Tertia Gallica*.—The colony of Tyre is called *Splendidissima* by Ulpian. It joined the party of Macrinus against Elagabalus: and the latter, on being elected emperor, deprived the city of its privileges in consequence; it nevertheless dedicated coins to that emperor.— The idols worshipped at Tyre were those of Astarte, Hercules, Angerona (as the Latins called the goddess of Silence) and Silenus.—The coins of this city are exceedingly numerous. They consist of autonomes, and of imperial colonial. On the former of these appear the heads of Antiochus IV., Demetrius I., Alexander I., Demetrius II., Antiochus VII.,. with Greek legends—many of the autonomous pieces are to be found with Phœnician letters and legends.— Not only coins but ancient records shew that the epocha whence the Tyrians dated their year was, *at least*, a duplicate one, viz.:—First, that of the Seleucidæ, which it preserved under the Roman emperors from the year v.c. 442 (this era is struck on coins of Elagabalus); and, secondly, that peculiar to the Tyrians, which Cardinal Noris *(Epoch Syn. Mac.*, p. 395) fixes in the year v.c. 628.—Pellerin adds a *third*, on the evidence of a coin dedicated by the colonists of Tyre to Caracalla.

Colonial Era of Tyre.—On a coin of Gallienus, COL. TYRO MET. (omitted in Vaillant's work but supplied by Pellerin), we see the figure of a man, naked to the waist, standing with his right arm stretched forth, and holding in his left a staff in form of the *hasta*. In the field of the reverse are, on the right the letter N. and on the left the letter Γ., and below is the Tyrian shell.

[This is a singular medal, says Pellerin, on account of the letters NΓ., which are stamped on the field, and which seem to form an epocha, that is to say, a date of the year 53. It is supposed that this date originates with an era, which Tyre instituted for itself, when it was made a colony by Sept. Severus. History clearly informs us that he was the emperor who restored this city, after it had been pillaged and even burnt by order of Pescennius Niger for not having sided with his party. But it is not reorded exactly in what year Severus sent a colony to Tyre. There is reason to believe that that event did not take place until after his return from the war which he had been carrying on in Mesopotamia, and against the Parthians, whence he returned to Syria, in the year 201 of the Christian era.—On this calculation, the above described medal of Gallienus must have been struck in the second year of his reign, reckoning from the year 253, when he began to govern with his father. It is not astonishing that the Tyrians should have coined the medals of these two princes, which are extant. They had caused money likewise to be struck under the reigns of Trebonianus Gallus and of Volusianus, because from those princes, father and son, they wer ɛ anxiously waiting for succour ot deliver them

from the incursions of the Parthians. What seems to confirm the supposition that it was *after* the expedition of S. Severus against the last-named people that Tyre was made a Roman colony, is the type seen on the first medals, which that city afterwards struck in honour of that emperor and of his wife and sons.—Each of these has on its reverse a standard, on which is inscribed LEG. III. GAL. Now, the Third Gallic Legion was stationed in Syria when S. Severus set out from that province to commence hostilities against the Parthians. There is no doubt but that, having then and there assembled all his forces, he took that legion with him; and the medals alluded to prove that it was the veteran soldiers, whom he drafted from his victorious army, who formed the colony of Tyre, after the rebuilding of that city.—Tyre had previously followed two other eras; that is to say, the epocha of the Seleucidæ, corresponding with the year 442 of Rome, 312 years before the Christian era; and the other, that of its autonomy (or period of its self-government), from the year 628 of Rome, 125 years before Jesus Christ. The third era, which the present medals records, may be added to the list of all the other eras known from medals, which have been published by different antiquaries.—See *Mélange* i. p. 337 *et seq.*

The colonial coins have Latin legends. They were struck under the following emperors and empresses, viz.:—Sept. Severus, Julia Domna, Caracalla, Plautilla, Geta, Macrinus, Diadumenianus, Elagabalus, Julia Mæsa, Alexander Severus, Gordianus Pius, Philip senior, Otacilia Severa, Trebonianus Gallus, Volusianus, Valerianus senior, Gallienus, and Salonina.—We subjoin a description of their reverse types from Vaillant, collated with completeness from Pellerin. Nearly all of them exhibit on some part of the field a representation of the *conchylium*, or *murex*, a purple shell fish, the invariable sign of the city of Tyre.

Astarte.—On a second brass of this colony, dedicated to Caracalla, and bearing on its reverse SEP. TYROS MET. COLONIA. *Septimia Tyrus Metropolis Colonia*—the Syrian goddess, (as Astarte was called, of whom the Syrians, like the Sidonians, were gross worshippers)—stands with her right hand placed on a trophy, whilst she carries a *hasta* crosswise in the other.—At her left hand, a figure of Victory placed on a column presents to her a crown. At her feet on one side is a shell, and on the other a small figure of Silenus: in other coins it is a palm tree.

A similar type of Astarte appears on a Tyrian first brass of Geta, and on a second brass of Elagabalus. Also on a second brass of Aquillia Severa [omitted by Vaillant, but given by Pellerin], and on a first brass of Alexander Severus, of Gordianus III., and of Otacilia Severa, Volusianus, and Valerianus.

On a second brass of Elagabalus, to whom the colony of Tyre, not out of love but in propitiatory obsequiousness, dedicated numerous medals, the legend is simply TYRIORVM, without mention of either *Colonia* or *Metropolis*; titles and privileges probably taken away from the Tyrians by Elagabalus, on account of their taking part with Macrinus.—The type exhibits Astarte, with the above described attributes, but within a temple of six columns. There is a small altar before the temple.—Josephus records the building of a superb temple by Hiran, king of the Tyrians, in honour of Astarte (or Astaroth.) The altar before the temple indicates sacrifices performed for the health of Elagabalus.—A similar type occurs on a second brass of this colony inscribed to Aquillia Severa, and on first brass of Philip senior, Trebonianus Gallus, and Gallienus.

Astarte and *Angerona.*—There is a medal of Plautilla, in large brass, struck at Tyre, not noticed by Vaillant, but which is given by Pellerin avowedly on account of the singularity of its reverse type. It represents a car drawn by four horses, two of which turn to the right, and the other two to the left. On the car is placed a large globe, and on the globe stand two small female figures, one of whom has upon her head a *modius*, or a tower, and holds in her right hand a sceptre, or short wand, inclined downwards, and in her left a cornucopiæ. The second figure also carries a cornucopiæ in her left hand ; and seems to raise the left hand to her mouth.—Pellerin considers the former of the above described figures to represent Astarte, and the latter the Goddess of Silence, *Angerona* (see the word), both being among the divinities worshipped by the idolatrous Tyrians.

Athletæ with urns.—A middle brass of Treb. Gallus exhibits two naked wrestlers, between whom stands an urn ; they each hold with both their hands a *discus* or a small vase, out of which a palm-branch rises.

[The coins of Tyre shew that many public games, or exercises, were celebrated in that city, under the Romans, and particularly those called *Actia* and *Heraclia*, as may be seen on medals of Caracalla (see below.) This type, in which two master wrestlers hold the prizes they have won, seems to indicate the commemoration of games under the Emperor above-named.—The palm, according to Plutarch, was usually awarded to those who excelled in all athletic trials of skill. The urn between the two figures is the grand *præmium victoris.*]—See *Athletæ.*

Bos cum Vexillo.—On a second brass of this colony, dedicated to Julia Domna, the wife of its founder, we see the type of a bull, and above its back appears a military banner inscribed LEG. III. GAL.—Before the bull is a shell.

[This coin with its legend of COLON. SEP. TYRO. METROP. confirms, says Vaillant, the statement of Suidas, that Hadrian conceded the dignity of a metropolis to Tyre ; but it was Elagabalus who made Sidon a colony and a metropolis.—The bull refers to the immigration of Roman citizens to Tyre. The vexillum, or labarum, on which is *Legio Tertia Gallica,* shews that the veterans of the Third Gallic Legion, being sent to Tyre, took up their winter quarters in Phœnicia. The *conchylium,* or shell-fish, is the peculiar symbol of the city, representing as it does the

murex, from whose blood was made that *purple* dye, once so celebrated throughout the ancient world, and of which Virgil speaks *(Georg.* lib. iii. l. 307)—

Vellera mutentur Tyrios incocta rubores.

There are a similar legend and type on coins of Macrinus, to whom the citizens of Tyre were well affected, as is proved by the numismatic honours which they dedicated to him during his short and inauspicious reign.]

Cadmus.—A coin of Gallienus, omitted in Vaillant, but supplied by Pellerin *(Mélange* i. p. 334), presents on its reverse COL. TYRO. METR., and the figure of a naked man, standing with a patera in his right, and the *hasta* in his left hand. Before this male figure, in the upper part of the medal, an edifice is seen, which represents a castle, or the gate of a city. In the field of the reverse are the Greek letters ΘHBE. Below are a bull lying down, and a shell fish.

" Ancient writers (says Pellerin) were for the most part accustomed to make graphic allusion on their coins to events which interested them, and which by their celebrity could impart to them some distinction. Such are the medals of Tyre, on which we see *Dido* in the act of directing and superintending the building of Carthage—the city itself being also attempted to be represented.—And in the present instance, according to appearances, it is Cadmus who stands in the middle of the coin, and before him is the castle, or fortress, called after his name *Cadmeia,* which he caused to be built in Bœotia, and which, with the other edifices that were afterwards added to it, formed the city of *Thebes,* whose name is written on the medal."

Cadmus and Serpent.—Coins of Gordianus Pius and of Gallienus, struck by Colonial Tyre, exhibit the figure of a man, striking at a serpent with a stone : COL. TYRO. METROP.

[Vaillant interprets this type as referring to Cadmus, son of Agenor, king of Tyre, in the act of killing a dragon or large serpent with a stone. The truth of which story appears to be that there was a king of the Thebans, named *Draco,* whom Cadmus slew, and of whose kingdom he took possession. The Tyrians, to shew the high antiquity of their city, commemorated the reputed fact by this allegorical type, just as the Syrians exhibited Europa and the Bull, on their coins; for Agenor, the father both of Cadmus and Europa, was the earliest king of Tyre.]—Vaillant, ii. 243.

Colonus agens Boves.—On a first brass of this colony, dedicated to Sept. Severus, appear the legend of COL. SEPT. TYRVS. METROP. *Colonia Septimia Tyrus Metropolis;* and the type of a colonist ploughing; behind whose oxen is the *vexillum*, inscribed LEG. III. GAL. *Legio Tertia Gallica*—Vaillant, ii. p. 16.

[Tyre, having been constituted a colony, with great munificence, by the above-named emperor, on account of the sacrifices she had made, and the services she had rendered to him during his sanguinary struggle for the government with Pescennius Niger, was additionally favoured by receiving Severus's family name of *Septimia*, together with the *jus italicum.*—A similar reverse appears on a coin of Geta, to whom, as the younger son of their founder, the Tyrians naturally sought to render themselves agreeable.]

Diana.—On a large brass of Elagabalus, "struck at the Septimian colony, metropolis of the Tyrians," this goddess of the chase, clothed in the stola, stands with a dart raised in her right hand; on her left arm a buckler, and at her feet a stag.

[On the obverse of this medal, the heads of Elagabalus and his grandmother Julia Mæsa are joined.—All historians agree (and Capitolinus expressly narrates) that to the activity, courage, and presence of mind of Mæsa, the effeminate wretch Elagabalus owed his accession to the empire. It is not to be wondered at, therefore, that the Tyrians, in flattery, should have united their portraits in one coin.—Diana, on the reverse, is represented in the manner in which her statue was worshipped at maritime Laodicæ, in Syria.]—Vaillant, *Col.* ii. p. 94.

Dido (1).—Vaillant *(Col.* ii.) notices a small brass, struck by the Tyrians in honour of Elagabalus, the reverse of which has for legend —TYRIORVM round the circuit, and ΔEIΔΩN at the bottom of the coin.—The type is remarkable, and may be thus described:—A woman attired in the stola, holding in her left hand a wand, or hasta, transversely. She seems to be given orders to a man, who is at work, digging the earth with a mattock. Above is seen another figure, on a building, representing the gate of a city. On the left is a palm tree. In the field of the coin is the usual figure of a shell.

[It is supposed that Dido, the celebrated daughter of Belus, king of Tyre, is here represented in the act of causing the city of Carthage to be built.—The Tyrians, proud of alluding to the great antiquity of their city, exhibit on their coins the celebrated personage of heroic history, who, fleeing from her brother Pygmalion, after various wanderings by sea, at length lands in Africa, and becomes the founder and queen of Carthage.—There is, in Vaillant (ii. p. 183), another coin of this colony, with similar type, dedicated to Otacilia Severa, wife of Philip senior; also another (in second brass) inscribed to Valerianus, with the same type, and the

legend COL. TYRO METR.—And Pellerin supplies a medal of the same legend and type, having on the obverse the head of Philip junior.]

Dido (2).—On a large brass of Philip senior, struck at Tyre, a woman stands with the *acrostolium* (see the word) in her right hand, and gathering up the skirts of her robe with the left hand. At her feet on one side is the prow of a galley; on the other a palm-tree and a shell.

[As the woman represented on this coin is clothed in a vestment similar to that of the female figure in the foregoing medal, Vaillant supposes it to typify Dido herself, who meditating to flee from her brother Pygmalion, seems, by the acrostolium and the trireme, to regard the sea as her only means of escape.— According to Justin (lib. 18, c. 6) the Tyrians were not only fond of referring back to the remote age of their city when Dido fled to Lybia and founded Carthage, but they likewise venerated her as a deity,—On a coin of this colony inscribed to Volusianus (as engraved in Vaillant), we see the same type, and Dido, with towers on her head as tutelary goddess of the city, whilst she bears the sceptre of royalty as a queen, and as the daughter of a king.]— ii. 175.

Dido (3).—A Tyrian first brass, inscribed to Philip senior, has for the reverse type a female figure, dressed in the stola, holding a wand or sceptre transversely in her left hand, and in her right a plan, as if of a city. She seems to be offering it to a man dressed in a long robe, or toga, behind whom are three men similarly attired.

Vaillant, ii. 174, considers the woman bearing the sceptre to be Dido, whose image the Tyrians (as above observed) were in the habit of engraving on their coins, to indicate the antiquity of their city.

In this type Dido hands the ichnography of her newly founded city to the foremost of four men attendant upon her.

Eagle.—A colonial medal of Caracalla, struck

at Tyre, COL. TYRO. METR., exhibits an eagle, with expanded wings and a crown in its beak, behind which is the vexillum of the third Gallic legion, inscribed LEG. III. GAL. in three lines. In the field the *Conchylium*.

[The eagle on this coin designates the Roman empire. For the city of Tyre having been made a colony, took the symbol of Rome herself. Tacitus *(Ann.* 2) calls the eagle the Roman bird, *Irent, sequerentur Romanas aves, propria legionum numina.*]

The vexillum or standard as already explained, refers to the veterans of a legion sent with a number of Roman citizens to colonize Tyre by the emperor Septimius Severus.—A similar reverse on first brass, consecrated by this colony to Valerianus.—The *Legio Tertia Gallica* was, amongst others, first levied by Julius Cæsar in Transalpine Gaul; and, distinguished by the numerical appellation of *Tertia*, it was stationed by Augustus in, for the defence of that province. Afterwards in Germany under Claudius; then sent to Syria by Nero; and, during subsequent reigns, occupied winter quarters in Phœnicia.—Septimius Severus having led it against the Parthians, in the war with whom it fought bravely, he placed his veterans in his newly established colony of Tyre.—See Vaillant *Col.* ii.

Genius Urbis.—An elegant middle brass of this colony, consecrated to Caracalla, represents a woman in a short dress, with the *calathus* on her head; she raises her left hand up to her mouth, and bears a cornucopiæ on her left arm; at her feet on one side is an altar and on the other side the *conchylium*.

[The female figure, standing before an altar, is the genius or tutelary deity of Tyre, and in raising her finger to her mouth would seem to be that goddess of silence, *Angerona*, to whom allusion has before been made.]—See Vaillant, *Coloniæ* ii.

Hercules.—On coins of Caracalla, Diadumenianus, Treb. Gallus, and Valerianus, this demi-god appears naked, standing with a patera in his right hand; in some reverses holding it over a lighted altar: his club and the lion's spoils are in his left hand. In others he is represented placing his right hand on a trophy.—Hercules is represented on coins of the Tyrians, a tutelary divinity who shared with *Astarte* the highest rites of their idolatry.

Mercury.—On a second brass of Valerian, bearing the metropolitan legend of colonial Tyre, we see the figure of Mercury, naked to the waist, holding a *baton*, or short staff, in his right and the caduceus in his left hand; on one side of him is an ibis, and on the other a palm tree.

[This type indicates that Mercury, here plainly designated by the caduceus, was worshipped at Tyre. He is represented holding the *baculum*, or *virga*, in his right hand, which the ancients called *radium*, and which was made use of for geometrical and astrological purposes, Mercury being the reputed master of those sciences. The ibis is placed before his feet, that bird (according to Plato) having been consecrated to him, because,

as the myth narrates, when he and the rest of the gods were in fear of the giant Typhon, in Egypt, he changed himself into an ibis.]

There is a first brass, struck in Tyre, to the honour of Salonina, wife of Gallienus, in which Mercury stands clothed in the *pallium*, holding the *baculum* and *caduceus*, the ibis being at his feet.

[Tyre, as the metropolis of Phœnicia and a Roman colony, struck coins not only in honour of Valerian, who had sojourned in that territory preparatory to departing on his fatal expedition against the Persians; but also in congratulation to his son Gallienus and the Empress Salonina. In the present instance Mercury is depicted, not naked or even half clothed, but attired in a cloak *(palliatus)*, as a philosopher; for the Phœnicians paid divine honours to him as to the wisest of philosophers; and Cicero *(De Natur. Deor.* lib. 3), alludes to Mercury as the instructor of the Egyptians in legislation and literature.]—See Vaillant *Col.* ii.

Man standing on a Galley.—On first brass coins of Philip senior, and of Gallienus, bearing the colonial and metropolitan legend of Tyre, a male figure stands naked in the middle of a galley, with both hands extended, but seeming to point with his right.

[Vaillant supposes this figure to be intended for the Tyrian Hercules, but whether as the reputed inventor of the Trireme, or as proceeding on his voyage from Tyros to Gades (now Cadiz) he leaves others to determine.]

Pellerin edites a coin of Tyre, which is not found in Vaillant; it is dedicated to Etruscilla, and exhibits on its reverse type the figure of a naked man, having his left foot placed on the prow of a galley, whilst his right hand rests on a trophy. In the field of the medal is the usual mark of the city of Tyre—the shell of the purple fish.

Pallas.—Pellerin gives the engraving of a coin, struck at Tyre, in honour of Valerianus, COL. TYRO. METR., which has for the type of its reverse Pallas, or Minerva, seated. She holds in the palm of her right hand two idols, and rests her left hand on a spear. A buckler is seen near her seat, and there is a shell in the field of the coin to the left.

Palm Tree.—This type appears on small brass of the Tyrian colony, bearing the portraiture of Diadumenianus.—Amongst the cities of the east that adhered to his father Macrinus, that of Tyre was foremost, and by that demonstration seems to have greatly incensed the vindictive Elagabalus. The palm indicates the abundance of that species of tree in Phœnicia, which country, indeed, is said to have derived its name from φοῖνιξ a palm.

Quadriga of Stags.—A first brass of Gordian III. exhibits a car, drawn by four stags, and in which a naked male figure stands, holding in his right arm a garment, and in his left hand a wand. There is a star in the field of the coin and the usual shell-form symbol of Tyre, beneath the fore-feet of the stags.

[Vaillant quotes several passages from Nonnus

in support of his opinion that the man in the car is meant for the Tyrian Hercules, who, it seems, was amongst other names called *Astrochiton*, as if the leader of the stars (*Dux Astrorum.*) The Tyrians furnish the chariot of this god of theirs with stags instead of horses, in allusion to the rapidity of his movements. A stag was the emblem of the sun's velocity; and Hercules and the sun, according to Macrobius, were the same.]

Rome.—A second brass of Trebonianus Gallus, struck in this colony, exhibits a helmeted female seated, holding in the right hand an eagle, between whose wings are placed two small images; her left hand rests on a spear, and in the field of the coin is the *conchylium*.

[Vaillant's opinion is that the helmeted woman, supporting on her hand the bird of Jove, typifies the city of Rome, and that the two little figures placed on the eagle, represent Trebonianus Gallus and his son Volusianus, who then conjointly ruled the empire (*Col.* ii., p. 216.)—Pellerin, who describes a Valerian struck at Tyre, with the same reverse, thinks on the other hand that the two little images in question, on these several medals, have now the appearance of being intended to represent Astarte and Angerona.]—[Tom. ii. p. iv.]

Serpent and Stone.—On a second brass of Elagabalus, having for legend of reverse TVRIORVM, we see a serpent coiled round a large oval stone.

[There is no doubt, says Vaillant, but that this type has reference to some passage in the more ancient history of Tyre; and from two coins of this colony (one a Gordian III., the other a Gallienus), in the former of which a serpent is twined round a tree, standing between two large pillars like stones; and in the latter a serpent is struck at with a stone by a man—the same learned numismatist infers that the stone encircled by the folds of a serpent was on this coin of the Tyrians, also struck in memory of Cadmus.]—See *Col.* ii. p. 93.

Silenus.—A second brass of this colony, inscribed to Elagabalus, has for the type of its reverse Silenus, who, carrying on his shoulders the usual attribute of the goat's skin bottle, lifts his right arm on high towards a palm tree before him. The accompanying legend is METR. TYRO. COLO. *Metropolis Tyro Colonia*.

[Here, says the author of the work on coins of Roman colonies, we at length see a medal of Tyre, struck in honour of Elagabalus, with the epigraph of *Metropolis*, and the title of *Colonia*. If then the opinion be founded on fact, that Elagabalus deprived the city of its dignities on account of its adherence to Macrinus, this medal would seem to shew, by its inscription, that under the conciliated indulgence of the same emperor, those metropolitan and colonial rights and privileges were restored to it.—Silenus often appears on medals struck at Tyre, where he was worshipped *summâ veneratione*.]—*Col.* ii. p. 94.

Stones between an Altar and a Tree.—On a first brass of Gordian III., and also of Valeri-

anus and Gallienus, struck in "the Colonial and Metropolitan City of Tyre," the type of the reverse consists of two carved stones, resting on one base, and placed between a lighted altar and a tree. At the bottom are the Greek words AMBPOCIE ΠETPE. In other types the tree stands between the stones, and a small altar appears at the bottom of the coin.—[The stones, says Vaillant, are *Ambrosiæ Petræ*, which (as Nonnus relates) the Tyrians, having offered sacrifice to the gods, made fast in the ground, and, taking them for a foundation, built Tyre upon them. The Tyrians were fond of striking on their coins types whose subjects related to the origin of their city, for which they professed to regard themselves as indebted to the advice of Hercules. But this was New Tyre, situate on an island; for the *Palætyrus* was built on the mainland by the Sidonians.

Tree and Serpent, Dog and Shell-fish.—Another coin of Gordian, with legend of *Colonia Tyrus Metropolis*, exhibits the remarkable type of a tree, round the trunk of which a serpent has coiled itself, on each side of the tree is a stone similar in form to the *Ambrosiæ Petræ* described as appearing on the preceding coin. In the exergue is a dog, with a shell fish before him.

[The tree, round which the serpent twines itself, is an olive, sacred to Minerva—The dog and shell-fish refer to the traditionary incident under which the secret of this purple dye was discovered by the Tyrians. According to their own story, whilst a girl was journeying with Hercules to Tyre, along the sea shore, a dog, which accompanied them, fed upon the flesh of the *Murex*, which happened to lie in its path; the girl seeing the dog's open mouth tinged with the most beautiful purple asked of Hercules a garment of a similar colour, and he, having first collected the blood from the shell-fish dyed some wool with it, which being afterwards made into cloth he gave to his mistress.]

Temple.—A coin of Macrinus, bearing the legend SEP*timia* TYRO. METRO*polis* COLON*ia*, has for type of reverse a temple of four columns (in others six) presenting itself in a two-sided view.

[Vaillant pronounces this to be meant for a representation of either a temple of Hercules or that of Astarte, those being the two principal deities of Tyre; but he thinks it more likely to be meant for the former, as the reputed founder and tutelary hero of the city.—*Col.* ii. 69-139.]

Trireme.—On a second brass of the above-named emperor, bearing the same legend, is a galley, with eight rowers; on other specimens of the same coin this galley has a sail as well as oars.

[The vessel called *triremis*, (see the word), forms an appropriate type on coins of the Tyrians, whether as allusive to their assumed merit of being the inventors of that class of galleys, or as indicating their maritime power and importance Nonnus (*Dionys.* 4) records that Hercules taught them the art of navigation by setting before them the example of "the little *nautilus*" making a sail of its bright and buoyant shell: hence Tibullus (lib. i. Eleg. 8.)]

Prima ratem ventis credere docta Tyrus.

The Tyrians, according to Diodorus, were the founders of many colonies in Africa, and of not a few in the western parts of Europe.—*Col.* ii. p. 68. *et seq.*

Tripod.—Second and third brass coins of Salonina (wife of Gallienus), struck by this colony, present on their reverses a tripos, which Vaillant regards as referring to Apollo, one of the several tutelary gods of the city.— Plutarch indeed relates, that when Alexander besieged Tyre, many of its inhabitants dreamt that they saw Apollo addressing himself to Alexander, and telling him to come over, as things were going on in the place, which were not to his mind. On this pretence they cast chains over an image of Apollo, as if it had been that of a convicted traitor or deserter, and attached them with nails to the base of his statue, calling him the partizan of Alexander; but when Tyre was captured, that monarch took away those chains, and commanded that Apollo should be termed "the friend of Alexander" *(Philalexander)*—The tripos is an attribute of Apollo, in his quality of *Vates*, it being an instrument placed on the ground wherever oracles were sought, taking its name from the three legs or feet which support it.—Diodorus Siculus describes a tripos as a machine with three bases.—*Col.* ii. p. 248.

Victory.—A coin of this colonial city, inscribed to Valeria, bears the type of Victory walking, with crown in right hand and palm in left.

[The figure of this peculiarly Roman goddess, struck on a Tyrian medal, seems to denote some military success gained by Valerian, or some of his generals; but what particular victory is uncertain, although inscriptions of VICTORIA AVGG. are of frequent occurrence on this emperor's medals.]

Urns or Vases.—On a coin dedicated to the Roman colony of Tyre, as metropolis of Phœnicia, to Caracalla, appears a table on which are two urns, or bowls. A branch of palm is also seen on each side of the table: above is the word ACTIA ; below ERACL*ea.*— On some specimens of this medal a star is seen between the two urns.

[*Two* urns, or large vases, and *two* palm branches indicate (says Vaillant) the same number of *certamina* or public trials of skill and strength, as indeed the two names of divinities, in whose honour they were celebrated would appear to confirm. Apollo (designated by the epithet ACTIA) and Hercules (Eraclea from Heraclides) were both of them tutelary deities of Tyre, whose citizens evidently conceived that they would not have too many of *such* "strings to their bow."—And every one knows that in memory of his naval victory over M. Antony, near Actium, Augustus built a temple to Apollo, and restored games in gratitude to that deity.

Public games were also instituted by the Tyrians out of respect for their guardian hero, which were denominated *Eraclios* or *Herculanos.* Palm branches were the rewards of the conquerors at those exercitations]

A similar reverse occurs on a medal of Otacilia.—Pellerin gives the engraving of the same reverse, struck at Tyre under Galhenus, not mentioned by Vaillant.

On a medal of Elagabalus, struck in this colony, as described and engraved by Vaillant, there is an olive branch in a vase, or urn, on which urn is written *Heraclia Olympia,* in Greek characters.

An urn with a branch is the well-known sign of public games or exercises. We have already seen, on a coin of Caracalla, an allusion made to such celebrations specifically in honour of Apollo and of Hercules. It is not surprising, says Vaillant, if the Tyrians instituted games in commemoration of *Jupiter Olympius,* for he was a very ancient tutelary of their city. The olive branch was appointed by the oracle to be the reward of the victors at the Olympic games; for, when king Iphatus sent to ask the question, the Pythia answered, with the fruit of the forest olive.]

Urns and a Club.—A second brass of Gordianus Pius exhibits two urns and a club set upright in the midst. On each side stands a palm branch.

[The Tyrians frequently placed on their money types allusive to the celebration of grand public spectacles held within their walls, as has been seen in the case of the Apollo and Hercules inscriptions on the medal of Caracalla, and also in the instance of an Olympic to the honour of Jupiter and Hercules, as apparently referred to on the medal of Elagabalus.—Vaillant considers two urns and as many palms to mean two *certamina,* and one urn to signify only one *certamen* or prize-match—therefore two urns and two palm branches, as on this coin, denote two occasions of public trials of strength and skill. But whether those *spectacula* were *Actian* and *Heraclian,* or whether they were *Olympian* and *Heraclian,* our learned commentator confesses the difficulty of pronouncing; but is induced, from the apperance of the club between the vases, to think it refers to Hercules, the favourite guardian of Tyre.]—See *Col.* ii 152.

On a Tyrian coin of Volusianus, there are two vases, with palms, which point to certain public games that took place at Tyre during the short reign of that prince, and the memory of which they wished to record on their medals. Although the names of these *certamina* are not affixed, Vaillant is yet of opinion that they were those *Actia* and *Heraclia,* instituted in honour of Apollo and Hercules, as tutelary deities of the city, as the already described medal of Caracalla explains, on which their respective names are inscribed, the two urns as indicating two contests confirming the supposition.—*Ibid,* p. 225.

[Besides the authors of Numismatic books known at the period when this Dictionary was commenced, such as Banduri, Tanini, Eckhel, Rasche, Akerman, etc., reference has been largely made to the works of Mommsen, Cohen, Sabatier, Lenormant, Froehner, and many others. The value in *francs* attached to the coins has been principally taken from Cohen and Sabatier, and it should be remembered (as Cohen has stated in his Preface) that the estimation is that of the actual market of Paris and London, supposing the coins of good preservation, but not of an exceptional fabric or patina, and certainly not *à fleur de coin.*—F. W. M.]

U.V.

U (Originally V from the Greek Υ) the twentieth letter of the Latin alphabet, a vowel. As an abbreviation, V, as the sign of the vowel U, stands for *Uti*—V. *uti* [*rogas*]—also U in U. C. *urbis conditæ*, A. U. C. *ab urbe conditá.*

V (from the Greek Υ) the twentieth letter of the Latin alphabet, a consonant. As a *vowel* as well as a *consonant* this letter occurs on the coins of L. Julius Bursio *(Julia gens)* B.C. 84— BA, BE, BI, BO, BV; CA, CE, CI, CO, CV, up to VA, VE, VI, VO, VV, and XA, &c. As an abbreviation V (the consonant) stands for *Vir, Vota, Votum, &c.*—V. C. *Vir Consularis, &c.*

V as a mark of value—5 *asses* on the *quinarii* of the Republic (B.C. 268—224) and on the Victoriates *(circ.* B.C. 229.)

V *(five)* is the half of the cross X *(ten.)*

V or U changed into Ͷ and Ꮞ. The first form occurs as early as A.D. 451 on a coin of Marcian, commemorating his marriage with Pulcheria, and bearing the legend FELICITER NͶBTIIS (Madden, *Num. Chron.*, N.S., 1878, vol. xviii. pp. 47, 199; pl. v., no. 14; Madden, art. *Money* in Smith and Cheetham, *Dict. of Christian Antiquities*, vol. ii., p. 1288; pl. iv., fig. 33); and on coins of Basiliscus (A.D. 476-477) and Anastasius (A.D. 491-518), but its use seems to have been limited. The second form was afterwards generally adopted on the Byzantine coinage from the time of Justinian I. (A.D. 527-566), both as a letter THЄꮞP. *(Theopolis)* and as a numeral ANNO Ꮞ (5), Ꮞl (6), XꮞII (17), XXꮞIII (28), &c.

V replaced by B, or *vice versá*, as BENERI GENETRICI on *billon* coins of Salonina— DANVBIVS on brass medallions of Constantine I.—IVBENTVS on *billon* coins of Gallienus— GLORIA ORVIS TERRAR. on gold coins of Theodosius I. and Marcianus.

V for I in MAXSVMVS *(Egnatia gens)*; and on a contorniate of Petronius Maxsumus with, on the obverse, the head of Placidius Valentinianus III. [See V. *Vir.*]; and in CRASSVPES *(Furia gens.)*

V replaced by O, as AEGYPTOS on gold, silver, and brass coins of Hadrian—DIVOS IVLIVS on large brass of Augustus—VOLKA-NUS VLTOR on autonomous silver coins struck between reigns of Nero and Vespasian—DEO

VOLKANO on *billon* coins of Gallienus and Saloninus.

V for VV as FLAVS for FLAVVS *(Decimia gens.)*

VV for V. MAKEΔONΩN-SVVRA LEG. PRO Q., *Suura legatus pro Quæstore* on tetradrachms struck by Bruttius *Sura*, proquæstor of the prætor Sentius Saturninus, governor of Macedonia, B.C. 89-87.

V for Y in HVPSAEVS or HVPSAE *(Plautia gens)*, ERVC. *(Considia gens)*, SIBVLLA *(Manlia gens.)*

V replaced by OV in FOVRI—FOVRIVS *(Furia gens.)*

V accentuated in FV̌R1 *(Furia gens)*, in MV̌SA *(Pomponia gens)*, and in BRV̌TI on coins of Decimus Brutus, struck in B.C 44-43, with the legend ALBINVS BRV̌TI F. *(Postumia gens.)*

V. Mint-mark (?) on early *semis* and *triens* B.C. 134-114 (Mommsen, *Histoire de la Monnaie Romaine*, ed. Blacas and de Witte, vol. ii., p. 345.)

V. *Valens.* C. V. HOS. MES. QUINTVS AVG. *Caius Valens Hostilianus Messius Quintus Augustus.*

V. *Valeria.* LEG. XX V.V. *Legio XX Valeria Victrix* on small brass coins of Carausius.

V. *Valerius.* C. V. C., perhaps *Caius Valerius Catullus*, on an early *quadrans* (Mommsen, *Mon. Rom.*, vol. ii., p. 344.) IMP. C. FL. V. CONSTANTIVS P. F. AVG. *Imperator Cæsar Flavius Valerius Constantius Pius Felix Augustus* (Constantius Chlorus —Musée de Turin.)—IMP. C. V. A. MAX-IMIANVS P. F. AVG. *Imperator Cæsar Valerius Aurelius Maximianus Pius Felix Augustus* (Maximian I. Hercules.)—G. V. MAXIMIANVS. NOB. C. *Galerius Valerius Maximianus Nobilis Cæsar* (Banduri); IMP. C. GAL. V. MAXIMIANVS P. F. AVG. *Imperator Cæsar Galerius Valerius Maximianus Pius Felix Augustus* (Galerius Maximian.)

V. *Valerius (?.)* P. I. SP. D. V. SP. IIVIR C. I. C.—*Publius Junius Spendo Decimus Valerius (?) Speratus* ~~Triumviri~~ *Coloniæ Juliæ Carthaginis*, on brass coins of Augustus and Tiberius struck at Carthago Zeugitanæ (Borghesi, Dec. x oss. iv; Müller, *Num de l'anc. Afrique*, vol. ii., p. 153; Cohen, *Méd. Imp.*, 2nd ed., vol. i., pp. 167, 208.) In the *field* P. P. D. D. *Permissu Proconsulis, Decreto Decurionum.*

V on the diadem of *Venus* according to Cavedoni *(Ann. de l'Inst. Arch.* 1854, p. 62) on a silver coin of the *Æmilia gens* (cf. Cohen, *Méd. Cons.* Pl. i. Æmilia, No. 11.)

V. *Vero.* V. Q. *Vero Quieto. Rev.* coss. *Consulibus.* Leaden piece of Verus Quietus, consul in A.D. 167 (Garrucci, *Rev. Num.*, 1862, p. 421.)

V. *Viæ.* QUOD V. M. S. *Quod viæ munitæ sunt.* See *Vinicia gens.*

V. *Vienna.* C. I. V. *Colonia Julia Vienna.*

V. *Vibio.* IM. C. V. AF. GAL. VEND.

VOLUSIANO AVG. *Imperatori Caio Vibio Afinio Gallo Vendumniano Volusiano Augusto.* [VOLVSIANVS.]—C. V. MARSO PROCOS, &c. *Caio Vibio Marco Proconsule* &c., on brass coins of Tiberius struck at Utica Zeugitanæ.

V. *Vibius.* IMP. C. V. AF. GAL. VEND. VOLVSIANVS AVG. *Imperator Caius Vibius Afinius Gallus Vendumnianus Volusianus Augustus.* [VOLVSIANVS.]

V**β**. *Vibo.*—the town *Vibo-Valentia* on silver coins (Victoriats and half-Victoriats) (Mommsen *Mon. Rom.*., vol. ii., p. 231; vol. iv., p. 30, pl. xxiii., No. 10.) [VALENTIA.]

V. *Victoriæ.* SEX NONI. PR. L. V. P. F. *Sex Nonius Prætor ludos Victoriæ primus fecit,* on a silver coin of the *Nonia gens* (Mommsen, *Mon. Rom.*, vol. ii., p. 487.)

V. *Victrix.* C. V. I. CEL. or CELS. or CELSA, *Colonia Victrix Julia Celsa.*—C. V. T. T. or TAR. or TARRA. *Colonia Victrix Togata Tarraco.*—V. I. N. K. or C. *Victrix Julia Nova Karthago* or *Carthago.*—V. V. OSCA *Urbs Victrix Osca.*—LEG. XIIII GEM. M. V. *Legio XIV Gemina Martia Victrix* on gold and silver coins of Septimius Severus.—LEG. XX V. V. *Legio XX Valeria Victrix* on small brass coins of Carausius.

V. *Vir.* IIV. (sometimes II**VR**) *Duumvir* on brass coins of Hispania Tarraconensis, of Juba II and Ptolemy struck at Carthago Nova, of Utica Zeugitanæ, Agrigentum Siciliæ, &c.—IIIV. *Triumvir,* LONGIN. IIIV. *Longinus triumvir* on a silver coin of the *Cassia gens;* IIIV. R. P. C. *Triumvir reipublicæ constituendæ* on gold and silver coins of Mark Antony and Mark Antony and his son *(Antonia gens.)*—VII**VR** EP. or EPV. or EP**V**. *Septemvir Epulonum* on silver coins of the *Coelia gens*—V. C. R. IM. D. R. *Vir Consularis Romanorum Imperator Dux Romanorum* on brass coins of Vabalathus [VABALATHVS.]—PETRONIVS MAXSVMVS V. C. CONS. *Petronius Maxsumus Vir Consularis Consul* on a contorniate bearing on the obverse the head and inscription of Placidius Valentinianus (Sabatier, *Contorniates,* pl. xvi., No. 4; Cohen, *Méd. Imp.,* vol. vi., p. 585.) [CONTORNIATE COINS.]

V. *Viro.* DIVO ROMVLO N. V. BIS CONS. *Divo Romulo Nobilissimo Viro bis Consuli* on coins of Romulus, the son of Maxentius, an interpretation placed beyond all doubt by the late A. de Longpérier *(Rev. Num.* N.S., vol. v., p. 36; cf. *Num. Chron.,* 1866, vol. vi., p. 169.)

V. *Virtutis.* C. V. *Clypeus Virtutis,* or CL. V. *Clypeus Virtutis,* according to the interpretation of the late Cavedoni, the former on a shield on silver coins of Augustus *(Cornelia gens),* the latter on gold and silver coins of Augustus. —See V. *Votivus.*

V. *Vota.* S. P. Q. R. V. P. RED. CAES. *Senatus Populusque Romanus vota pro reditu Cæsaris* on silver coins of Augustus *(Mescinia gens)*—V.S.PRO RED., &c. *Vota suscepta pro reditu,* &c., on a gold coin of Hadrian.

V. *Votivus (?)* C. V. or CL. V. *Clypeus Votivus.—See* V. *Virtutis.*

V. *Votum.* I. O. M. S. P. Q. R. V. S. PR. S. IMP. CAE. QVOD PER EV. RP. IN AMP. ATQ. TRAN. S.E. *Jovi optimo maximo Senatus Populusque Romanus Votum susceptum pro salute Imperatoris Cæsaris, quod per eum Respublica in ampliore atque tranquilliore statu est.*—S. P. Q. R. V. S. PRO S. ET RED. AVG. *Senatus Populusque Romanus Votum solvit pro salute et reditu Augusti* on silver coins of Augustus *(Mescinia gens.)*

V. *Urbs.* V. V. OSCA. *Urbs Victrix Osca.* [OSCA.]

V. *Uti* on a silver coin of Longinus triumvir *(Cassia gens),* identified with Lucius Cassius Longinus, the brother of C. Cassius, the murderer of Julius Cæsar, and struck in B.C. 54. The reverse represents a Roman citizen, placing in an urn a voting tablet marked V [ti rogas]— "I vote for the law," alluding to the Cassian law of B.C. 137 on votes. See *Tabellæ.*

V. *Uticensis.* M. M. I. V. *Municipes Municipii Julii Uticensis.*—M. V. D. D. P. P. (or P. P. D. D.) *Municipium Uticense Permissu Proconsulis Decurionum Decreto.* [VTICA.]

V. as a numeral, *quinque, quinquennales, quinta, quintus, &c.*

V. *Quinquennalia.* VOT. V. *Vota quinquennalia*—SIC V. *Sic quinquennalia.*

V. *Quinquennalibus.* VOT. V. MVL.X. *Votis quinquennalibus, Multis decennalibus.*

V. *Quinta.* LEG. V. *Legio quinta.*—LIB. (or LIBERAL. or LIBERALITAS) AVG. (or AVGG., or AVGVSTI) V. *Liberalitas Augusti quinta.*—P. S. T. Q. V. VIXXT. *Prima, Secunda, Tertia, Quarta, Quinta, Sexta XX Tarracone;* or XXIV, 21 *Quinta* on small brass coins of Aurelian (Madden, *Num. Chron.,* N.S., 1862, vol. ii., pp. 49, 243.)

V. *Quinto.* AN. V. *Anno Quinto.*

V. *Quintum.* CONSVL V. *Consul Quintum.*—C. V. or COS. V. *Consul Quintum*—IMP. V. *Imperator Quintum.*—GERMAN1CVS MAX. V. *Germanicus Maximus Quintum,* on billon coin of Gallienus.—OB. D. V. *Ob diem quintum* [natalem] on some rare gold coins of Licinius I., and interpreted by the late Count de Salis as meaning "struck on the fifth birthday of his son." Other interpretations have been given (Madden, *Num. Chron.,* N.S., 1862, vol. ii., p. 45.)

VA.—Q. **VA**. Name of a Roman magistrate on *triens* and *sextans* of Pæstum Lucaniæ, a Roman colony, founded *circ.* B.C. 273.

VAALA for VALA. Surname of the *Numonia gens* [NVMONIA.] Numonius Vaala was probably one of the monetary quatuorvirs in B.C. 42, with, as colleagues, Vibius Varus, Arrius Secundus, and Servius Rufus (Lenormant, *La Mon. dans l'Antiq,* vol. iii., p. 174.) It is thought by Cohen *(Méd. Imp.,* 2nd ed., vol. i., p. 51) that the winged head of Victory on the coins of Numonius Vaala may really be a portrait of Fulvia, the wife of M. Antony, comparing it with a bronze coin of *Fulvia* in Phrygia, on

which a similar head occurs, recognized by Waddington as that of Fulvia. The same head may
be seen on *quinarii* of Mark Antony, struck at
Lugdunum (Lyons.)

VABALATHVS or VHABALATHVS (Latin
coins), VABALLATHVS (Greek coins.) Vabalathus, son of Odenathus and Zenobia, called
by Vopiscus *(Aurel.* 38) *Balbatus,* governed
Palmyra with his mother after the murder of
his father in A.D. 267. He probably perished
in the war with Aurelian in A. D. 272.

[A gold coin has been attributed to Odenathus by Ch. Lenormant *(Rev. Num.,* 1846, p.
278, pl. xvi., No. 14), and by Victor Langlois
(Num. des Arabes avant l'Islamisme, pl. iii.,
No. 1), who fancies that he can read on it the
letters OΔHN, but the drawing given of the
piece is, as M. Cohen says *(Méd. Imp.,* vol. v.,
p. 156), *très flatté,* and as M. Lenormant adds,
(La Mon. dans l'Antiq, vol. ii., p. 386) *quelque
peu arrangée.* M. Lenormant, however, does
not consider that this coin can be classed among
the *plagia barbarorum,* and suggests that it was
issued by order of Sapor for Cyriades or Miri-
ades, whom he recognised as Emperor, and that
its style well corresponds with the bas-relief of
Sapor on which he is presenting Cyriades to the
Roman troops as their Emperor; and on another
where Valerian is doing homage to Cyriades
(Flandin, pl. xxxiii., xlix.; Rawlinson, *The
Seventh Oriental Monarchy,* pp. 82, 91.) M.
Lenormant further suggests *(op. cit.,* pp. 382,
383), that the rare silver medallion of Gallienus,
with the legend VIRTVS AVGVSTORVM, on
which Gallienus, seated, is receiving from an
armed warrior, standing, a branch of laurel
(Cohen, *Méd. Imp.,* vol. iv., p. 354, pl. xviii.,
No. 24), gives a representation of an association
between Gallienus and Odenathus.]

The coins of Vabalathus are of two classes;
those with his name and head without the titles
of Cæsar or Augustus, and on the reverse the
name and head of Aurelian; and those with his
name and head and the titles of Cæsar and Augustus, and on the reverse various types. They
were struck at Antioch with Latin inscriptions,
and at Alexandria with Greek. As they offer
some difficulty in their interpretation, it is advisable to give both series:—

I. ROMAN COINS.

A. *Without the title of Augustus.*

1. *Obv.* VABALATHVS VCRIMDR. Bust
of Vabalathus to r. laureated.
   Rev. IMP. C. AVRELIANVS AVG.
   Bust of Aurelian to r. radiated; below A
   or B or Γ or Є or Ϛ or Z or H. *Bil.*
   (12 frcs.)

B. *With the title of Augustus.*

2. *Obv.* IM. C. VHABALATHVS AVG.
Bust of Vabalathus, to r. radiated.
   Rev. IOVI STATORI. Jupiter, holding
   globe and leaning on spear; before him
   a star, at his feet an eagle. *Bil.* (2G0
   frcs.)

3. *Rev.* VENVS AVG. Venus standing l.
holding helmet and spear, and leaning on
a shield. *Bil.* (200 frcs.)

4. *Rev.* VICTORIA AVG. Victory walking l. holding a crown and a palm; in
the *field* a star. *Bil.* (200 frcs.)
   Other reverse types—AEQVITAS AVG.,
   AETERNITAS AVG., VIRTVS AVG.
   are given by Cohen *(Méd. Imp.,* vol. v.,
   p. 159) from various sources, but are not
   authenticated. Dr. Von Sallet *(Num.
   Zeits.,* 1871) describes a specimen with
   legend IVENVS AVG. (? IVVENTVS
   AVG.), and the type Hercules, with
   in the *field* a star and in the *exergue*
   two points (? privy mark of the mint.)

II.—GREEK COINS.

A. *Without the Title of Augustus.*

5. *Obv.* IAC. OΥABAΛΛAΘOC AΘHN. Υ.
ACP. Bust of Vaballathus to r.
laureated and below diademed; no date.
   Rev. A. K. Λ. ΔOM. AΥPHΛIANOC
   ΣЄB. Bust of Aurelian to r. laureated.
   Date L. A. (year 1.)

6. *Obv.* IAC. OΥABAΛΛAΘOC AΘHN. Υ.
ACPⱲ. As No. 5. Date L. Δ. (year 4.)
   Rev. As No. 5. Date L. A. (year 1.)

7. *Obv.* As No. 5. Date L. Є. (year 5.)
   Rev. As No. 5. Date L. B. (year 2.)

8. *Obv.* IAC. OΥABAΛΛAΘOC AΘHNO.
Υ. AΥΤ. ΣPⱲ. As No. 5. Dates L. Δ.
(year 4), or L. Є. (year 5.)
   Rev. AΥΤ. K. Λ. Δ. AΥPHΛIANOC CЄB.
   As No. 5. Dates L. A. (year 1), or
   L. B. (year 2.)

9. *Obv.* AΥPHΛIANOC AΘHNOΔΩPOC.
Busts of Aurelian and Athenodorus facing
each other, the former laureated, the
latter laureated and diademed (on a specimen in the B. M. the bust of Vaballathus
is radiated.)
   Rev. L. A. (year 1.) L. Δ. (year 4), within
   laurel wreath.

B. *With the title of Augustus.*

10. *Obv.* AΥΤ. K. OΥABAΛΛAΘOC AΘHNO.
ΣЄB. Bust of Vaballathus to r. laureated.
    Rev. L. Є. (year 5.) Providence standing
    l. raising r. hand and holding a double
    cornucopiæ.

11. *Obv.* Same legend and type.
    Rev. L. Є. (year 5.) Bust of the Sun to
    r. radiated.

From these coins it seems clear that in the fourth year of Vabalathus and the first of Aurelian, A.D. 269-270 (Nos. 1, 5, 6, 7, 8, 9), Aurelian recognised the government of Vabalathus, and in the following year (A.D. 271) associated him as Augustus (Nos. 2, 3), but very soon after Vabalathus and his mother, Zenobia, revolted, and struck independent coins, both at Antioch and Alexandria (Nos. 4, 10, 11), [ZENOBIA.]

[It is thought (Von Sallet, *Zeitschrift f. Num.*, vol. ii., pp. 252—257; Lenormant, *La Mon. dans l'Antiq.*, vol. ii., p. 381), that the coins of Aurelian, with the legends VIRTVS AVG. and VIRTVS MILITVM, representing two warriors standing, recall on the coins of the West the co-regency which Aurelian recognised with Vabalathus in the East.]

The curious letters VCRIMDR (No. 1) and Υ. A. CΡIAC or Υ. AΥT. CΡⲱIAC (Nos. 5, 6, 7, 8), which were so long a puzzle to numismatists, and of which the Υ had been interpreted as Υιος [AΘHNO. Υ. Ἀθηνοδώρου υἱος] have been satisfactorily explained by Dr. Von Sallet, who, proving from Palmyrene inscriptions that the names of *Julius*, *Aurelius*, and *Septimius* were common at the period of Odenathus and Zenobia, has arrived at the following interpretation of the legends :—

VABALATHVS *Vir Consularis Romanorum* IMperator Dux Romanorum.

Ἰούλιος Αὐρήλιος Σεπτίμιος ΟΤΑΒΑΛΛΑΘΟC AΘHNOδωρος [or AΘHNόδωρος] Ὑπατικὸς AΥTοκράτωρ [or Αὐτοκράτωρ] Στρατηγὸς Ῥωμαίων.

With respect to No. 9, bearing the name AΘHNOΔⲰΡΟC Dr. Von Sallet has shown that Athenodorus is the *second* name of Vabalathus, which is confirmed by the Palmyrene inscription AυτοΚΡΑΤΟΡΟΣ ΟΤΑΒΑΛΛΑθου AΘHNOΔⲰΡOΥ (C. I. G. 4503 b. p. 1174; Sir G. Wilkinson, *Num. Chron.*, O. S., vol. ix., p. 128), and that there is no reason for supposing that Athenodorus was another son of Odenathus.

On the whole question the following works should be consulted :—Ch. Lenormant, *Rev. Num.*, 1846, pp. 268, 280; Langlois, *Num. des Arabes avant l'Islamisme;* Cohen, *Méd. Imp.*, vol. v., p. 158; Madden, *Handbook of Rom. Num.*, 1861, pp. 124-128, 165, pl. ii., 3-7; in "*The Athenæum*," 6 Dec., 1862; Von Sallet, *Die Fürsten von Palmyra*, 1866 ; *Berliner Blätter f. Münz Siegel und Wappenkunde*, 1867, vol. iii.; *Num. Zeitschrift*, 1870, 1871 ; *Zeitschrift f. Num.*, 1875, vol. ii.; De Vogüé, *Syrie Centrale—Inscriptions Sémitiques;* Waddington, *Inscriptions Grecques et Latines d'Asie Mineure et de Syrie;* F. Lenormant, *La Monnaie dans l'Antiquité*, 1878, Vol. ii., pp. 378-387.

VAC *(sic)* **YSC** *(sic)* for AVG on coins of Postumus—EXERCITVS VAC or YSC.

Vacca. A cow is represented on gold and silver coins of Augustus, with reverse legend AVGVSTVS, which are generally of magnificent style ; on a brass medallion of Antoninus Pius,

representing Tellus reclining leaning on its back ; and on gold and silver coins of Carausius [VBERITA. AV., VBERITAS AVGG. and VBERTA. AVG].

VAL. *Valeant !* **VAL.** SATVRNALIA *Valeant Saturnalia* on a lead coin (Eckhel, vol. viii., p. 318).

VAL. *Valens* on coins of the Emperor Hostilian.

VAL. *Valentia.* [VALENTIA].

VAL. NOB. C. *(Valentinianus Nobilis Cæsar).* A *bestiarius* with a shield attacked by a panther and a bear; below, another *bestiarius* attacking a lion with his spear—on contorniates of Nero (common) and Valentinian III. *(peu rare).*

VAL. *Valerio* on brass coins of Hispania Tarraconensis—Bilbilis, Cæsar Augusta, Saguntum, Turiaso, etc.

VAL. *Valerius* on brass coins of Calagurris Nassica, C. VAL. C. SEX. AEDILES, *Caius Valerius Caius Sextius Ædiles*—and on coins of Diocletian, Maximian I. Hercules, Constantius I. Chlorus, Galerius Maximian II., Severus II., Maximinus II. Daza, Maxentius, Licinius I. and II., Valens (under Licinius, if genuine), Constantine I. and Constantius II.

VAL. *Valerius*, on brass coins of *Valeria gens* (Cohen, *Méd. Cons.*, pl. lxviii., Valeria, Nos. 1, 2) ;—c. VAL. c. F. *Caius Valerius Caii filius* on silver coins, and on *semis* (Riccio, pl. lxv., no. 1) and c. VAL. FLAC. IMPERAT. on silver coins all of the *Valeria gens* (Cohen, pl. xl., Nos. 1, 2, 4).

VALENS, one of the thirty tyrants, who had been nominated proconsul of Achaia by Gallienus. He assumed the purple to avoid the usurper Macrianus, who had sent Piso, another usurper, to put him to death. He was killed by his own soldiers about A.D. 260. No coins.

VALENS (Aurelius Valerius) an officer upon whom Licinius I. bestowed the title of Cæsar after the battle of Cibalis in A.D. 314, and who was soon after put to death when Licinius concluded a peace with Constantine, who stipulated positively for his abdication. The following coin is from the Ennery Catalogue—IMP. C. AVR. VAL. VALENS P. F. AVG. Head laureated. *Rev.* IOVI CONSERVATORI AVGG. Jupiter holding Victory and sceptre ; at his feet an eagle, in the *field* to l., A. ; to r. a crown and XA. ; in the *exergue* ALE. *(Alexandriæ).* It is not above suspicion, especially as it is not certain that Valens ever received any higher title than that of *Cæsar.*

VALENS (Flavius), the brother of Valentinian I., was born in A.D. 328, and made

Emperor of the East by his brother in A.D. 364. After the death of the usurper Procopius [PROCOPIVS] in A.D. 366, he was engaged in war for several years with the Goths, who eventually sued for peace, and with Sapor, king of Persia, who came to terms with Valens not very advantageous to the Romans. About A.D. 376-377 the Goths, to the number of 200,000, appeared on the banks of the Danube and asked for permission to enter Roman territory, which was granted on certain conditions. They soon spread over the country, and Valens met them at Hadrianople. Here the Roman army was defeated and Valens was wounded, either dying on the field, or, as some say, being burnt alive in the house of a peasant, where he had taken refuge, A.D. 378.

The money issued by Valens consisted of gold and silver medallions, gold and silver coins, and first, second, and third brass coins. It is during his reign, if we except the large medallion of Constantine II. [GAVDIVM ROMANORVM], that the enormous gold medallions now preserved in the *Musée de Vienne*, first appear (Cohen, *Méd. Imp.*, vol. vi., pp. 408-410, Nos. 1, 6, 7, 8-10). They seem to have been decorations or recompenses for services rather than money. The obverse legend of the coins of Valens is D. N. VALENS MAX. AVGVSTVS, or D. N. VALENS P. or PER. F. AVG.; the principal reverse legends on the *gold medallions* are D. N. VALENS VICTOR SEMPER AVG. Valens with *nimbus* in a car drawn by six horses; on either side Victory; in *exergue* RM=Romæ (2000 frcs.), FELIX ADVENTVS AVGG. (400 frcs.), GLORIA ROMANORVM (400 to 5000 frcs.), PIETAS DDD. NNN. AVGVSTORVM. Valentinianus I., with *nimbus* standing between Valens and Valentinian II., in *exergue* TESOB=Thessalonicæ 72 (1500 frcs.); on the *silver medallions* RESTITVTOR REIP., or REIPVBLICAE (40 to 1800 frcs.), SALVS REIPVBLICAE (50 frcs.), TRIVMFATOR GENT. BARB. (300 frcs.), VICTORIA AVGVSTORVM (40 frcs.), VICTORIA D. N. AVGVSTI (1200 frcs.), VIRTVS EXERCITVS (40 frcs.), VOTIS V MVLTIS X to VOTIS XV MVLTIS XX (40 frcs.); on the *gold coins*, GLORIA ROMANORVM. Rome and Constantinople seated holding a shield surmounted by ✳ and on which is VOT. X MVL. XX (30 frcs.); same legend, Valens standing holding *mappa* and sceptre; in *field* ✠ (100 frcs.); another type, Valens on horseback (100 frcs.), PAX PERPETVA *(tremissis* 50 frcs.), RESTITVTOR or SALVS or SECVRITAS REIP. or REIPVBLICAE (25 to 40 frcs.), SPES R. P. Valens and Valentinian with *nimbus* seated, between them a shield inscribed VOT. V. MVL X. placed on the head of a small figure (? Valentinian II.) in *toga* (80 frcs.), VICTORES AVGVSTI, VICTORIA AVGG. or AVGVSTI N. or D. N. AVG. or AVGVSTORVM (25 to 60 frs.), VIRTVS ROMANORVM (50 frcs.), VOTA PVBLICA (100 frcs.); on the *silver coins*, RESTITVTOR REIP. or REIPVBLICAE (8 to 10 frcs.); VOT. V. or VOT. V. MVL. X &c., (3 to 20 frcs.), VRBS ROMA (3 frcs.); on the *brass coins*, GLORIA ROMANORVM (c), MONETA AVGG. (60 to 80 frcs.),

RESTITVTOR or SECVRITAS REIPVBLICAE (c to 100 frcs.), VICTORIA DD. NN. AVG. (10 to 15 frcs.) VOTA PVBLICA, with types of Isis, Anubis, Harpocrates, and the Nile (40 to 60 frcs.) VOT. V. MVLT. X to VOT. XX. MVLT. XXX. (10 frcs.)

Valens. The giant Valens is represented on silver coins of the *Valeria gens* (De Witte, *Rev. Num.*, 1849, pp. 325-349) [VALERIA GENS.]

VALENTI or VALENTINI. *Valentinianus.* On coins of Placidius Valentinianus III.

VALENTIA (now *Valentia*) a town in Hispania Tarraconensis in which the consul Junius Brutus settled the soldiers of Viriathus *circ.* B.C. 138 (Livy, *Epit.*, lv.) It is called by Pliny (*Nat. Hist.*, iii., 3), a colony, but the extant coins do not support this statement. The following are the principal ones :—

1. *Obv.* TI. AHI. T. FL. TRINI. L. F. Q. or C. LVCIEN. Q. MVNI. Q. Winged helmeted head to r.
   Rev. VALENTIA. A cornucopiæ and a thunderbolt, placed crosswise within a myrtle garland.
2. *Obv.* Head as on No. 1; behind S *(Semis.)*
   Rev. VAL. Same type.
3. *Obv.* T. AT. L. T. Same head; s.
   Rev. VAL. Same type.

The Q signifies *Quinquennalis.* The reverse types appear to have been borrowed from the *denarii* of the *Fabia gens*, which probably allude to a victory near this town over Viriathus by Q. Fabius Maximus Æmilianus in B.C. 145; or by Q. Fabius Maximus Servilianus in B.C. 142. (Mommsen, *Mon. Rom.*, vol. ii., p. 338.)

VALENTIA or VALENTA. The names of the Spanish mint on coins of the Visigothic kings Suinthila (A.D. 621-631), Chintilla (VALENTIA—PIVS—Brit. Mus. A.D. 636-640), Egica (A.D. 687-696), and Leovigild (VALENTA ✠ REX—A.D. 573-586; C. Lenormant, *Rev. Num.*, 1854, p. 328, pl. xii., No. 10.)

VALENTIA, originally Hipponium, a city of the Bruttii, but eventually (*circ.* B.C. 189) made a Roman colony under the name of VIBO VALENTIA. Brass coins on the semi-uncial system were there issued. They are—

1. *As.—Obv.* Head of Jupiter to r. laureated, behind |.
   Rev. VALENTIA. Winged thunderbolt; in *field* to r. | and lyre.
2. *Semis—Obv.* Head of Juno to r.; behind s.
   Rev. VALENTIA. Double cornucopiæ, in *field* s.
3. *Triens—Obv.* Head of Minerva to r.; behind ⠆.
   Rev. VALENTIA. Owl to r.; in front ⠆.
4. *Quadrans—Obv.* Head of bearded Hercules to r.; behind ⠆.
   Rev. VALENTIA. Two clubs upwards, handles united; in *field* ⠆.
5. *Sextans—Obv.* Head of Apollo to r. laureated; behind ∴.

Rev. VALENTIA. Lyre; in *field* :.
6. *Uncia—Obv.* Head of Diana to r.; over shoulder quiver and
Rev. VALENTIA. Hound running to r.; above *.
7. *Semuncia—Obv.* Head of Mercury to r., wearing winged diadem; behind Σ.
Rev. VALENTIA. *Caduceus;* in *field* to l. Σ.

The emblems in the *field* of all these pieces vary.

Previous to the change of name to Valentia in B.C. 189, the town was called VIBO (the Bruttian or Oscan name of Hippo), and certain of the Victoriats and half Victoriats, bearing the monogram VB *(Vibo)*, formally attributed to the *Vibia gens* (Cohen, *Méd. Cons.*, Nos. 1 and 2), were there issued between B.C. 228-189 (Mommsen, *Mon. Rom.*, vol. ii., pp. 88, 102, 231; vol. iv., p. 30, pl. xxiii., No. 10.)

VALENTIA. A name supposed to be given to Rome from the most ancient silver coin of this city, inscribed OVALANE V. (type, a sow with four young), and assigned by the late Duc de Luynes to the time of Servius Tullius. The antiquity and attribution of this coin, and of another with the legends POMA and KVPI (type, sow suckling her young), is contested by Mommsen, but their genuineness is supported by Queipo and the late Duc de Blacas, whilst De Witte is not able to arrive at any satisfactory conclusion on the subject (Mommsen, *Mon. Rom.*, vol. i., pp. 250-252; vol. iv., pp. 19, 20, pl. xviii., Nos. 2, 3.)

VALENTINIANVS I. (Flavius), born at Cibalis in Pannonia in A.D. 321, was the son of

Gratianus. He was elected Emperor in A.D. 364 after the death of Jovian, and associated with him his brother Valens, assigning to him the Eastern provinces, and keeping for himself the Western, including Western Illyricum and Africa. In A.D. 367 he further associated his eldest son Gratianus, a lad of eight, as *Augustus.* The principal trouble of his reign was the insurrection of the Quadi, commencing in A.D. 374, and it was during an interview in A.D. 375 with deputies from this people that he from rage fell down in a fit and suddenly expired.

He was twice married, (1) to Valeria Severa, by whom he had Gratian; and (2) to Justina, by whom he had Valentinian II. and three daughters, Justa, Galla, and Grata, the second of whom was afterwards the wife of Theodosius I.

Remarks on the coins of the three Valentinians with the legend D. N. VALENTINIANVS P. F. AVG.

The question of the manner of distinguishing the coins of the three Valentinians has already occupied the attention of the present writer (*Num. Chron.*, N.S., 1861, vol. i., p. 112), and of M. Cohen (*Méd. Imp.*, vol. vi., p. 391), and with a few guiding rules and careful comparison of fabric the student may readily distinguish them.

Valentinian I., when he commenced to reign, was forty-three years of age, and he died when nearly fifty-five, whilst his son Valentinian II. succeeded to the throne at five or six years of age, and died when about twenty. The difficulty, therefore, of comparison between the coins of a *man* and a *boy* is consequently considerably lessened. Valentinian I., who, according to Ammianus Marcellinus (xxx., 9) had a *corpus lacertosum et validum*, is represented on his coins as a stout full-faced man, whilst his son is shown with a young and delicate face.

The brass coins with *helmeted bust*, and on the reverse the legend GLORIA ROMANORVM belong to Valentinian II.; the gold coins with *helmeted bust*, and with the legends IMP. XXXXII COS. XVII P. P., SALVS REIPVBLICAE VOT. XXX MVLT. XXXX, or VICTORIA AVGGG., and in the *exergue* CONOB. belong to Valentinian III.

The coins with *diademed head* and the legend D. N. VALENTINIANVS P. F. AVG., and which have on the reverse in the *exergue* COMOB or CONOB, belong either to Valentinian II. or Valentinian III., and can easily be distinguished by their fabric, which in the case of the coins of Valentinian III. is much coarser than that of those of Valentinian II.

All the coins with IVN. *(Junior)* belong to Valentinian II., and with PLA. *(Placidius)* to Valentinian III.

Remarks on the explanation of the letters OB, CONOB, COMOB, &c.

The letters OB first occur in the *field* on gold coins of Valentinian I. and Valens with the legend VICTORIA AVGVSTORVM. Victory seated on a cuirass writing on a shield VOT. V. MVL. X, and in the *exergue* CONS. (Constantinopoli), and a star. [*See* woodcut—VALENS.]

TROB *(Treveris* 72) and TESOB *(Thessalonicæ* 72) first occur in the *exergue* of the gold medallions of Valentinian I., as also on those of Valens with the addition of ANOB (Antiochiæ 72), and ANOB, TESOB or THCOB and TROB on their gold coins. MDOB *(Mediolani* 72) first occurs on the gold coins of Gratian.

CONOB occurs for the first time under Gratianus, Valentinianus II., and Theodosius I., and is a distinctive mark of the mint of *Constantinople.*

COMOB appears for the first time under Valentinian II. and Theodosius I., and is the especial mark of a *Western* mint. These letters may be interpreted *Constantinæ Moneta* 72. Constantina was the name given to Arelate (Arles) by Constantine I. the Great. Its earliest mintmarks, dating from the time of Constantius II., are KONSTN̄., KA., KONT., CON. or CONST., and the two last may be distinguished from CON. or CONS. *(Constantinople)* from the fact that they are always preceded by a *Latin* letter, whilst the Constantinople mint is always followed by a *Greek.* The letters COM *(Constantinæ Moneta)* seem to have been introduced late in the reign of Gratian, and are found *alone* also on the coins of his cotemporaries Valentinian II. and Theodosius I. It is the mint-mark of Gaul and the greater part of the West, and is sometimes accompanied by the letters TR. *(Treveris)*, LD. *(Lugduni)*, AQ. *(Aquileiæ)*, and MD. *(Mediolani)* in the *field*. Coins with COM. and COMOB alone belong to Rome. When COMOB became common to every Western mint, the letters RM. *(Romæ)*, SM. *(Sirmii)*, etc., appear in the *field*. On a gold coin of Magnus Maximus, who killed Gratian in A.D. 383, we find KONOB *(Constantinæ* 72), a form also occurring on a gold coin of Constantinus III., the usurper under Honorius, accompanied by AR. *(Arelatæ)* in the *field*, as well as the usual form AR. COMOB. After the death of Theodosius I. and the division of the Empire between his two sons Arcadius and Honorius, the forms COMOB for the *Western* and CONOB for the *Eastern* Empire became the adopted *exergual* mint-marks, the former almost always accompanied by letters in the *field*; the latter *never*. There is little doubt that the M in COMOB was substituted from the first for the N in CONOB to resemble the mint-mark of Constantinople, and yet to show a distinctive mark for all Western mints.

CORMOB on a gold coin of Anthemius. RM= *Roma,* and the CO is prefixed and the OB affixed to resemble as nearly as possible COMOB, and yet to designate the actual mint at which the coin was struck. The usual form is $\frac{R \mid M}{COMOB}$.—CORVOB on a gold coin of Anthemius. RV=*Ravennæ.* The usual form is $\frac{R \mid V}{COMOB}$.

CONOBRV on a gold coin of Zeno. RV=*Ravennæ.* The usual form is $\frac{R \mid V}{COMOB}$.

COB, abbreviated form of COMOB, on gold coins of Honorius and Theodosius II., struck at Ravenna (RV in the *field*.)

AVGOB *(Augustæ=Londinii* 72) on coins of Magnus Maximus, struck on his assuming the imperial power in Britain.

[Egressus tendensque ad *Lundinium*, vetus oppidum, quod *Augustam* posteritas appellavit— Amm. Marcell. xxvii, 8.]—Theodosius vero, dux nominis inclyti, animo vigore collecto ab *Augustá* profectus, quam veteres appellavere *Lundinium.* xxviii., 3.]

Other letters such as CORNOB, IOLOB, CONOS, etc., if existing on coins, are not genuine mint marks, but barbarous imitations.

Various interpretations have been offered of the letters OB. Senckler proposes *officina secunda,* San Quintino *obsignatus,* Petigny and de Salis *obryza,* supposed by Brambilla to be confirmed by the coin of Zeno reading CONOBRV (see above), Cohen, *Olbiopolis,* Pinder and Friedlaerder, Missong, and the present writer 72. It is unnecessary to enter into any lengthy account of these various theories as the subject has already been thoroughly sifted in the papers to which I shall presently refer. Suffice it to say that the figures **lxxii.** in the *field* are found

on coins of Constantine I., Constantius II., and Constans Cæsar, struck at Antioch *circ.*, A.D. 333-335, signifying that 72 *solidi* were coined to the pound, Constantine I. having reduced the *aureus* about A.D. 312; that Valentinian I. and Valens issued a law about A.D. 367, by which the gold pound was always to be reckoned at 72 solidi, thus accounting for the letters O—B on their coinage; and that from that time the letters OB were placed in the *exergue*, accompanied by the name of the town as TROB, ANOB, etc., or else CONOB or COMOB was placed in the *exergue,* the latter being frequently accompanied by the name of the town in the *field* as AR., MD., etc. The following table shows the different forms of marking the figures 72 and OB—

乊 LXXII	O ∣ B		
SMAN	CONS	CONOB or COMOB	TROB ANOB &c.

R ∣ M	A ∣ R	&c.	
COMOB	COMOB		

The following is the principal literature on the subject:—Senckler, *Rev. Num.* 1847: San Quintino, *Sur les méd. de Justinien Rhinotmetus,* 1845; Petigny, *Rev. Num.,* 1857; Pinder and Friedlaender, *Beiträge zür älteren Münzkunde,* 1851; Friedlaender, *Berl. Blätter f. Münz Siegel und Wappenkunde,* vol. i., 1863, cf. *Num. Chron.,* N.S. 1863, vol. iii., p. 143, *Rev. Num.,* 1866; *Num. Zeitschrift,* Vienna, 1872; *De la signification des lettres* OB., Berlin, 1873, cf. *Num. Chron.,* N.S., 1873, vol. xiii. p. 172; Cohen, *Méd. Imp.* vol. vi., p. 392; Madden, *Handbook to Rom. Num.* 1861; *Num. Chron.,* N.S., 1861, vol i., pp. 112, 175; 1862, Vol. ii., p. 240: Brambilla, *Altre Annotazioni Num.,* Paris, 1870, cf. Mommsen, *La Mon Rom.* ed. Blacas and De Witte, vol. iv., p. 96, with letter from M. Lavoix; A. Missong, *Die Vorläufer der Werthzahl* OB *auf Römischen Goldmünzen* in the *Zeits. f. Num.* 1880, p. 240, who shows that the letter O (=70 to the pound) was employed between A.D. 286 and 290, and ⋜ [ℨ] (= 60 to the pound) between A.D. 290 and 312, in which year the standard of the gold coin was fixed at 72 to the pound:—

A.D. 286—290.		A.D. 290—312.	
O ∣ SMA	∣ O SMA	℥ ∣ SMA	∣ ℥ SMSD
℥ ∣ SMSD		℥ TS	

(For OB see above.)

The principal reverse legends on the coins of Valentinian I. are:—On the gold *medallions,* FELIX ADVENTVS AVG. M. or FELIX ADVENTVS

AVGGG. (400 or 500 frcs); GLORIA ROMAN-
ORVM (600 frcs); VICTORIA D. N. AVGVSTI (400
frcs); on the *silver medallions* RESTITVTOR or
SALVS REIPVBLICAE (00 frcs.); VICTORIA
AVGVSTORVM (60 to 100 frcs.); VIRTVS
EXERCITVS, and VOTIS V MVLTIS X or X and XV or
XV and XX (60 frcs.); on the *gold coins*, GLORIA
ROMANORVM (60 to 150 frcs.); PAX PERPETVA or
PVBLICA (50 frcs.); RESTITVTOR or SALVS REIP.
or REIPVBLICAE (20 to 45 frcs.); TRIVMFATOR
GENT. BARB. (150 frcs.); VICTORES AVGVSTI
Valentinian I. and his son Valentinian II. seated
facing holding a globe; a Victory flying above
crowns them; in *ex.* TROB (150 frcs.); VICTORIA
AVG. or AVGG. or AVGVSTORVM (20 to 60 frcs.);
VICTORIA DD. NN. AVG. (80 frcs.); VIRTVS
ROMANORVM (50 frcs.); VOTA PVBLICA (50
frcs.); on the *silver coins* RESTITVTOR REIP. or
REIPVBLICAE (6 to 30 frcs.) VOT. V. or VOT. V.
MVLT. X. or VOTIS V MULTIS X or X and XX or XV
and XX (6 to 10 frcs.); VRBS ROMA (6 frcs.); on
the *brass coins*, GLORIA ROMANORVM (c),
MONETA AVGGG. (40 frcs.) RESTITVTOR or
SECVRITAS REIP. or REIPVBLICAE (c to 40
frcs.); VICTORIA AVGGG. or AVGVSTORVM (60
frcs.); VIRTVS EXERCITI (6 frcs.); VOTA PVBLICA
—types of Isis, Harpocrates and Anubis (40
frcs.), VOT. V MVLT. X (c), VRBS ROMA (40 frcs.)

VALENTINIANVS II. (Flavius), son of
Valentinianus I. and Justina, was proclaimed
 Augustus after his father's
death in A.D. 375, when
about five or six years of age.
Gratian, his elder brother,
was then about sixteen,
and the two brothers di-
vided the West between
them, Valentinian II. taking
Italy, Illyricum, and Africa, and Gratian Gaul,
Spain, and Britain, but as the former was
so young, the latter really was sovereign of
the West. The year after the death of
Valens, in A.D. 379, Gratian appointed Theodosius I. to succeed him, and in A.D. 383
was killed by Magnus Maximus. In A.D. 388
Theodosius I. defeated and killed Magnus Maximus, who had driven Valentinian II. out of
Italy, and reinstated the latter as sole Emperor
of the West. Valentinian II. leaving too much
power in the hands of Arbogastes, commander
of the Roman forces in Gaul, and attempting,
when too late, to deprive him of his command,
was strangled by order of Arbogastes in A.D.
392.

The principal reverse legends on the coins of
Valentinian II. are:—On the *gold medallions*,
FELIX ADVENTVS AVG. M. or N. (400 frcs.),
GLORIA ROMANORVM (600 frcs.), RESTITVTOR
REIPVBLICAE. Val. II., with *nimbus* standing
facing, raising with the hand a turreted female,
and holding the *labarum* on which ☧. In *ex.*
AQOB. or TROBT, or TROBS. (T and S = *tertia*
and *secunda)* (1200 frcs.); on the *silver
medallions*, GLORIA ROMANORVM (60 frcs.);
VIRTVS EXERCITVS (100 frcs.); on the *gold
coins*, CONCORDIA AVGGG. (20 to 30 frcs.),

VICTORIA AVGG. or AVGVSTORVM (4 to 50
frcs.); on the *silver coins*, VIRTVS EXERC.
or ROMANORVM (6 frcs.), VOT. V. MVLT. X
or VOT. X. or VOT. X. MVLT. XX (10 to 20
frcs.), VOTA PVBLICA (80 frcs.), VRBS ROMA (6
frcs.); on the *brass coins*, VICTORIA AVGGG.
(medallion, Tanini 200 frcs.), CONCORDIA AVGGG.
(c), GLORIA REIPVBLICAE or ROMANORVM (c to
100 frcs.), REPARATIO REIPVB. (c), SALVS or
SPES REIPVBLICAE (c to to 3 frcs.), VICTORIA
AVGG. or AVGGG. (c), VIRTVS AVGGG. or EXERCITI
or ROMANORVM (c to 5 frcs.), VOT V. MVLT. X or X
and XX or XV and XX or XX and XXX (c), VRBS
ROMA (c.)

VALENTINIANUS III. (Placidius), son of
Constantius III. and Placidia was declared
 Cæsar by Theodosius II in
A.D. 424, when about five
or six years of age, and
Augustus the following year,
under the regency of his
mother Placidia, who re-
ceived the title of *Augusta*.
In A.D. 437, Valentinian
III., then 18 years of age, went to Constanti-
nople to marry Licinia Eudoxia, the daughter of
Theodosius II. During his reign the Western
Empire was continually the scene of war.
Theodoric, King of the Goths, laid siege to
Arelate (Arles), Richila, King of the Suevi,
took Merida in Spain, Genseric, King of the
Vandals, seized Carthage, and Attila, King
of the Huns, gave great trouble in Italy.
Fortunately Valentinian III. possessed an accomplished commander in Aetius, but fearing
his power and influence he murdered him in
cold blood A.D. 354. Having violated the wife
of Petronius Maximus, he was, the following
year, killed by the injured husband. Valentinian III. left two daughters, Eudocia, married to
Hunneric, King of the Vandals, and Placidia,
married to Anicius Olybrius, of neither of whom
are there coins.

The principal reverse legends on the coins of
Valentinian III. are:—*Gold medallion*, VOT.
XXX MVLT. XXXX (Banduri, 500 frcs.); on the
gold coins, GLORIA ROMANORVM (40 to 100
frcs.), IMP. XXXXII. COS. XVII P.P. (100 frcs.),
SALVS REIPVBLICAE (60 frcs.), VICTORIA AVGGG.
or AVGVSTORVM (12 to 80 frcs.), VOT. X. MVLT.
XX or XXX or XXXX (50 to 100 frcs.), VRBS
ROMA (12 to 50 frcs.); on the *silver coins*,
VICTORIA AVGG. (25 frcs.), VIRTVS ROMANORVM
(40 frcs.); on the *brass coins*, SALVS REIPVB-
LICAE (40 frcs.), VICTORIA AVGG. (30 to 40
frcs.), VOT. PVB. (Tanini, 40 frcs.)

Valentinianus Solidus. In the laws of Gondo-
bald, king of the Burgundians (A.D. 500-516),
mention is made of certain *solidi* called *Valentiniani*, which being of base gold were to be withdrawn from circulation. These *solidi* have been
thought by Petigny *(Rev. Num.,* 1851, p. 127,
seq.), and F. Lenormant *(La Mon. dans l'Antiq.,*
vol. ii., p. 437) to be those of Valentinian III.,
but Keary *(Num. Chron.,* N.S., 1878, vol. xviii.,
p, 225) is disposed to believe, especially as the
reading *Valentiniani* is uncertain, the coins

spoken of to have been those of the *town of Valence* rather than imitations of the money of Valentinianus III.

VALENTINO IIVIR. *Valentino Duumviro* on brass coins of Augustus, struck at Cæsar Augusta and Calagurris in Hispania Tarraconensis. (Cohen, *Méd. Imp.* 2nd ed., Vol. I., p. 154, No. 672, p. 155, No. 683.)

VALER. *Valerio.*—L. CASSIO C. VALER. FEN. IIVIR. *Lucio Cassio Valerio Fenes-. tella Duumviris* on brass coins of Augustus struck at Cæsar Augusta in Hispania Tarraconensis. (Cohen *Méd. Imp.*, 2nd ed., vol. i., p. 154, No. 661.)

VALER. *Valerius.* VOLVSVS VALER. MESSAL. IIIVIR. A. A. F. F. S. C. *Volusus Valerius Messalla triumvir auro argento ære feriundo. Senatus consulto,* on brass coins of the *Valeria gens.* Also on second brass coins of Licinius I.

VALERI. *Valerii*—L. VALERI. FLACCI. *Lucii Valerii Flacci,* on silver coins of the *Valeria gens.*

VALERI—VIRTVS VALERI (?), on *billon* coins of Gallienus,—PIETAS FALERI, on silver medallions of Gallienus and Salonina, from *Khell*—written FALERI, on coins known to Cohen *(Méd. Imp.,* vol. iv., p. 436, 459); ? for *Valeriana* (Eckhel, vol. vii., p. 409.)

VALERIA GENS. A patrician and afterwards plebian family, one of the oldest and most celebrated at Rome. This *gens* was divided into various families under the Republic, the names of which are CORVVS or CORVINVS, FALTO, FLACCVS, LARVINVS, MAXIMVS, MESSALLA, POTITVS, PVBLICOLA, TAPPO, TRIARIVS, VOLVSVS. On the coins of the *gens* we find the *cognomina* —*Asisculus, Catullus,* and *Flaccus.*

The following are the principal coins of this *gens* :—

1st *Period.* B.C. 268—154.—*As, semis triens, quadrans, sextans,* and *uncia,* with marks of their value. Legend—VA *(Valerius.)* ROMA. (c to 25 frcs.; Cohen, *Méd. Cons.,* Valeria, Nos. 3, 5-9; Mommsen, *Mon. Rom.,* vol. ii., No. 84.)

2nd *Period,* B.C. 154—134.—1. *Obv.* Head of Minerva to r., with winged helmet; behind x or XVI. *Rev.* C. VA .C.F.FLACC. *(Caius Valerius Caii filius Flaccus.)* Victory on a biga to r.; in the *exergue* ROMA. Æ. (2 to 5 frcs.)

2. *Obv.* Head of Jupiter to r., laureated; behind S. *Rev.* C. VA . C. F. *(Caius Valerius Caii filius);* in *exergue* ROMA. Semis. (Cohen, Nos. 1, 2, 4; Mommsen, No. 99.)

3rd *and* 4th *Period,* B.C. 134—114; 114— 104.—*Obv.* Ordinary type. *Rev.* (?) C. V. C. *(Caius Valerius Catullus.)* ? ROMA. *Quadrans.* (Mommsen, No. 152.)

4th *Period,* B.C. 114—104.—*Obv.* Winged bust of Victory to r.; before ✳. *Rev.* L. VALERI. FLACCI *(Lucii Valerii Flacci).* Mars, helmeted, standing to l., holding sword and trophy; to left, *apex;* to right, ear of corn.

Æ. (3 frcs.). (Cohen, No. 10; Mommsen, No. 174.)

This piece was at one time attributed to the son of L. Valerius Flaccus, Consul in B.C. 131, and *Flamen Martialis,* or to L. Valerius Flaccus, Consul in B.C. 100, and *Interrex* in B.C. 82, or still better to L. Valerius Flaccus, who was Consul in B.C. 86. It is now thought probable that the moneyer of this coin was Lucius Valerius Flaccus, who was Consul in B.C. 86.

B.C. 82-81.—*Obv.* Winged bust of Victory to r.; in the *field* latin letters up to X; or symbols, or ✳. *Rev.* C. VA. FLA. IMPERAT. EX S.C. *(Caius Valerius Flaccus Imperator. Ex Senatus Consulto).* Eagle ensign between two other military ensigns; on one H. *(Hastati);* on the other P. *(Principes).* Æ. (2 frcs.). (Cohen, No. 11; Mommsen, No. 237).

Valerius Flaccus was governor of Gaul and *Imperator* in B.C. 83. He embraced the cause of Sulla, and obtained the honour of a triumph over the Celtiberians and Gauls in B.C. 81.

This coin was restored by the Emperor Trajan (Cohen, pl. xlv., No. 16; 350 frcs.) The same type occurs on the coins of the *Claudia, Cornelia,* and *Neria* families.

B.C. 53. *Obv.* MESSA. F. *(Messalla filius).* Bust of Mars, helmeted, to r., with spear. *Rev.* PA RE COS. *(Patre Consule).* Curule chair; beneath a sceptre and a diadem; in *field* S. C. *(Senatus Consulto).* Æ. (80 frcs). (Cohen, No. 12; Mommsen, No. 277).

This coin was probably struck during the consulship of M. Valerius Messalla in B.C. 53.

The sceptre and diadem under the curule chair are supposed to allude to the kings who obeyed the orders of the Consul of Rome.

B.C. 49-45.—1. *Obv.* ACISCVLVS. Head of Apollo, radiated to r.; behind, a hammer. *Rev.* L. VALERIVS *(Lucius Valerius).* Diana in a *biga* to r., holding a whip. Æ. (3 frcs).

2. *Obv.* ACISCVLVS. Head of Apollo, diademed, to r; above, a star; behind, a hammer; sometimes within a laurel wreath. *Rev.* L. VALERIVS (in *exergue).* Europa on a bull to r., holding a scarf. Æ. (5 frcs).

3. *Obv.* ACISCVLVS. Head of Apollo, diademed to r.; above a star, behind a hammer, all within a laurel wreath. *Rev.* L. VALERIVS (or sometimes without legend). Head of Sibylla to r., all within a laurel wreath. Æ. (50 to 80 frcs).

4. *Obv.* Same as No. 3. *Rev.* L. VALERIVS (in *exergue* or otherwise). Bird with female helmeted head, to r., armed with two lances and a shield; all within a laurel wreath. Æ. (10 frcs).

5. *Obv.* ACISCVLVS. Head of Jupiter, laureated, to r.; behind, a hammer; all within laurel wreath. *Rev.* L. VALERIVS (in *exergue*). Giant (the giant Valens) whose trunk terminates in two tails of fishes. Æ. (100 frcs.)

6. *Obv.* Bust of Victory to r. *Rev.* ACISCVLVS. A hammer, all within a laurel wreath. Æ. *Quin.* (60 frcs.)

7. *Obv.* Double cornucopiæ. *Rev.* ACISCVLVS. A hammer. Æ. *Sest.* (100 frcs.) (Cohen, Nos. 13—21; Mommsen, vol. ii., p. 545.)

These coins were struck by a moneyer, unknown, of the name of Lucius Valerius Acisculus. The word *Acisculus* signified a hammer or adze, and *Aciscularius* is translated in the old glossaries by λατόμος and thus the moneyer by representing this instrument on his coins, has wished to allude to his *cognomen.*

Nos. 1 and 2 were restored by Trajan. (300 to 350 frcs.)

For an explanation of the types on these coins of L. Valerius, see Ch. Lenormant, *Nouvelles Annales de l'Inst. Arch.*, vol. ii., p. 142, and *compte-rendu* of this paper in the *Rev. Num.* 1840 p. 299; J. de Witte, *Rev. Num.*, 1849, p. 325.

MONEYERS OF AUGUSTUS.

B.C. 15—5. 1. *Obv.* MESSALLA GALVS IIIVIR *(Triumviri.)* Anvil. *Rev.* APRONIVS SISENNA (or SISENNA APRONIVS) A.A.A.F.F. around S.C. *(Apronius Sisenna auro, argento, ære, flando, feriundo, Senatus consulto.)* Æ. III.

2. *Obv.* MESSALLA APRONIVS IIIVIR. Anvil. *Rev.* GALVS SISENNA (or SISENNA GALVS) A.A.A.F.F. around S.C. Æ. III.

3. *Obv.* MESSALLA SISENNA IIIVIR. Anvil. *Rev.* GALVS APRONIVS (or APRONIVS GALVS) A.A.A.F.F. around S.C. Æ. III.

4. *Obv.* L. VALERIVS CATVLLVS around S.C. *Rev.* IIIVIR A.A.A.F.F. Anvil. Æ. III.

5. *Obv.* VOLVSVS VALER. MESSAL. around S.C. *Rev.* IIIVIR. A.A.A.F.F. Anvil. Æ. II. and III.

6. *Obv.* CAESAR AVGVS. PONT. MAX. TRIBVNIC. POTEST. Head of Augustus, bare, to r. or to l. *Rev.* VOLVSVS VALER. MESSAL. IIIVIR A.A.A. F.F. around S.C. Æ. II.

(1 to 3 frcs.; Cohen, *Méd. Cons.* Nos. 22-30; *Méd. Imp.*, 2nd ed., vol. i., p. 141; Mommsen, vol. iii., p. 8).

The three first coins belong also to the families, *Apronia, Asinia,* and *Cornelia.*

Valeria Messalina [MESSALINA.]

VALERIA (Galeria) was daughter of Diocletian and Prisca and was married to Galerius Maximian in A.D. 292. Having no children she adopted her husband's illegitimate son Candidianus. On the death of Galerius in A.D. 311, his successor, Maximinus Daza, offered to divorce his own wife and marry Valeria, and on her rejecting his suit, confiscated all her estates and banished her, with her mother, to Syria, in spite of the protestations of her father Diocletian. Maximinus dying in A.D. 314, the exiles escaped and repaired to the Court of Licinius, to whose care Valeria had been committed by her dying husband. But Licinius murdered Candidianus, and Valeria and her mother wandered for many months through the provinces, till at last discovered at Thessalonica, they were beheaded and their bodies thrown into the sea in A.D. 315.

GOLD COINS.

1. *Obv.* GAL. VALERIA AVG. Bust of Valeria with diadem, to r., sometimes on a crescent. *Rev.* VENERI VICTRICI. Venus standing to l., holding an apple and lifting her veil. In the *field* ⊕. In the *exergue* SMAZ (*Signata Moneta Antiochiæ* Ƶ.) BRIT. MVS.; or in the *field* a crescent and Ƶ and in the *exergue* SM SD (*Signata Moneta Serdicæ*). BRIT. MVS.; or in the *exergue* SIS (*Siscia*). BRIT. MVS.; or in the *exergue* SMN (*Signata Moneta Nicomediæ*). PARIS and BRIT. MVS.

2. *Obv.* The same. *Rev.* VENERI VICTRICI NЖY XC. Same type. In the *exergue* SMN. (*Signata Moneta Nicomediæ*). BEGER and COLL. OF Dr. J. EVANS.

Brass Coins. Same legends and types.

The gold coins, of which it will be noticed that four are in the Museum collection, are very rare, and are valued at from 1000 to 1200 frcs.; the brass coins from eight to twelve francs.

The ⊕ in the *field* of the coin struck at Antioch, is probably borrowed from the earliest representation of the Sun and as both Prisca and Valeria are supposed to have embraced Christianity, may allude latently to the cross ✝ (De Witte, *Du Christianisme de quelques Imperatrices Romaines,* in *Mél. d'Arch.*, vol. III., 1853; Madden, *Christian Emblems on the coins of Constantine I. and his successors* in *Num. Chron.*, N.S. 1877, vol. xvii., p. 297.)

The Ƶ (Ξ or Ƨ or I) = 60 to the pound, introduced by Diocletian, and employed between A.D. 290-312. [VALENTINIANUS I.]

The letters NЖY XC also occur on the coins of Galerius Maximian (Cohen, *Méd. Imp.*, No. 68, but attributed to Maximian Hercules), Severus II. (barbarous fabric Welzl, *Cat.* No. 14464), Maximinus Daza Cæsar (Cohen, No. 19), struck at Nicomedia; and the letters NЖ on those of Constantius Chlorus (Cohen, No. 12), Galerius Maximian (Cohen, No. 67, but attributed to Maximian Hercules), Severus Cæsar (*Num. Zeits*, 1869), Severus Augustus (Cohen, No. 12), Maximinus Daza Cæsar (Cohen *Suppl.* No. 1), Constantine Cæsar (Cohen, No. 74), also issued at Nicomedia. The true explanation of these letters has not yet been discovered (Friedlaender, *Ueber einige räthsel-*

hafte Buchstaben auf Münzen aus der Zeit Diocletians in the *Zeits. f. Num.* 1875, vol. ii., and Missong, *Die Vorläufer der Werthzahl* OB *auf Romischen Goldmünzen*, in the *Zeits. f. Num.* 1880, vol vii, p. 240.)

Valeria (Flavia Valeria CONSTANTIA) was the daughter of Constantine Chlorus and his second wife Theodora, the daughter-in-law of Maximian Hercules. Her half-brother Constantine I., gave her in marriage to Licinius I. about A.D. 312—313. After the defeat of Licinius I. in A.D. 323, Constantia begged for her husband's life; but Constantine, though acceding at the moment, put him to death at Thessalonica, where he had been placed in confinement. Constantine I. in A.D. 326 also ordered the death of her son Licinius II., but Constantia still remained to the date of her death, about 328—330, friends with Constantine.

The following brass coin was found not many years ago, and is published by Cohen *(Méd. Imp. Suppl.* vol. vii., pl. vii.), as in the possession of M. Roman:—

Obv. CONSTANTIA N. F. *(Nobilissima femina).* Bust to r. *Rev.* SOROR CONSTANTINI AVG. around a wreath, within which PIETAS PVBLICA; in the *exergue* CONS. B. *(Constantinopoli* 2.) Æ. III.

Valerianæ legiones were legions probably levied by L. Valerius Flaccus, consul in B.C. 131, and *Flamen Martialis*, and named after him, and which are mentioned in the war of Lucullus against Mithridates (Liv., *Epit.* xcviii.; Dion. Cass. xxxv., 14, 15, 16; xxxvi. 29; Sall. *Hist.* v.) [See VALERIA GENS, 4th Period.]

VALERIANVS I. (Caius Publius Licinius), who had been voted worthy of the honour of the Censorship under the Emperor Decius, was unanimously elected Emperor in A.D. 253, solely on account of his merits, and associated with him his eldest son Gallienus. In A.D. 258 he started for the East to repel the attacks of Sapor, and in the following year was successful in re-capturing Antioch from the Persians, commemorated by coins with the legend VICT. PART., and VICTORIA PARTHICA. Valerian having entrusted the further conduct of the war against Sapor to Macrianus, his Prætorian prefect, the latter purposely betrayed the Roman army, and the Emperor was taken in A.D. 260, and died in captivity. Of his treatment during his captivity, there are conflicting statements, but the bas-reliefs do not give any representation of extreme degradation. On two it is thought that he is shown doing homage to Cyriades, the usurper set up by Sapor (Rawlinson, *Seventh Anc. Mon.* pp. 82, 91) [VABALATHVS], but generally Sapor seems to have treated his prisoner with consideration, and to have made use of his engineering talents. (Thomas, *Sassanian Inscriptions,* p. 64.)

Valerian was twice married (1) to an unknown and (2) to Mariniana, of whom coins are extant, and had two children, Gallienus by his first wife, and Valerian II by his second, and perhaps another, (cf. Eckhel, vol. vii., p. 379.)

The obverse legends of the medallions and coins of Valerian I. are IMP. C. P. LIC. VALERIANVS AVG. or P. F. AVG., IMP. P. LIC. VALERIANO AVG., IMP. VALERIANVS P. or PIVS AVG.,

IMP. VALERIANVS AVG., IMP. VALERIANVS P. F. AVG., VALERIANVS P. F. AVG. [see Valerian II.]

The principal reverse legends are: *Silver Medallions:* ADLOCVTIO AVGVSTORVM (400 frcs.), AEQVITAS AVGG. (300 frcs.), MONETA AVGG. (150 to 250 frcs.) *Gold Coins:* AETERNITAS AVGG. (350 frcs.), ANNONA AVGG. (350 frcs.), APOLINI CONSERVA. (400 frcs.), FELICITAS AVGG (350 frcs.), FIDES MILITVM (350 frcs.), IOVI CONSERVA. (350 frcs.), LAETITIA AVGG. (400 frcs.), LIBERALITAS AVGG. (350 frcs.), ORIENS AVGG., (350 frcs., *Quin.* 350 frcs.), RESTITVTOR ORBIS (*Quin.* 350 frcs.), ROMAE AETERNAE (350 frcs.), VICTORIA or VICTORIAE AVGG. (350 to 450 frcs.), VIRTVS AVGG. (400 frcs.) *Billon or small Brass Coins* (c to 12 or 30 frcs.): AEQVITAS AVGG., AETERNITAS AVGG., ANNONA AVGG., APOLINI CONSERVA, or PROPVG., APOLL. SALVTARI, CONCORDIA AVGG., CONCORDIA EXERCIT. or MILIT., CONSERVAT. AVGG., DIANA LVCIFERA, FELICITAS AVGG. or SAECVLI, FIDES MILITVM, FORTVNA REDVX, GALLIENVS CVM EXERC. SVO; Jupiter holding victory and sceptre standing on a *cippus,* which is inscribed IOVI VICTORI; IOVI CONSERVA., CONSERVAT., or CONSERVATORI, or STATORI, LAETITIA AVGG., LIBERALITAS AVGG., or AVGG. II., ORIENS AVGG., PACATORI ORBIS, PAX AVGG. or AVGVSTI, PIETAS or PIETATI AVGG., P.M. TR. P. II., COS. II. P.P. (A.D. 254), P.M. TR. P. III. COS. III. P.P. (A.D. 255), P.M. TR. P. IIII. COS. III. P.P. (A.D. 256), P.M. TR. P. V. COS. IIII. P.P. (A.D. 257)—one type, Valerian and Gallienus standing facing each other leaning on their shields, in the *field* two spears—an imitation of that of the coins of Caius and Lucius Cæsares on the reverse of coins of Augustus,—PROVID. or PROVIDENTIA AVGG., RELIGIO AVGG., RESTITVT. or RESTITVTI GENER. HVMANI., RESTITVTOR or RESTITVTORI ORBIS, RESTITVT. ORIENTIS, ROMAE AETERNAE, SAECVLI FELICITAS, SALVS AVGG., SECVRIT. PERPET., SPES PVBLICA, TEMPORVM FELICITAS, VENVS VICTRIX, VICTORIA or VICTORIAE AVGG., VICTORIA EXERCIT., or GERM. or GERMANICA, VICT. PART. or PARTHICA, VIRTVS AVGG., VOTA ORBIS, VOTIS DECENNALIBVS (? A.D. 250). *Brass Medallions*: ADLOCVTIO AVGVSTORVM (300 frcs.), FELICITAS TEMPORVM IIII. ET III. COS. (A.D. 257, 400 frcs.), MONETA AVGG. (200 frcs.), PONTIFF. MAX. TRI. P. P. (400 frcs.), VICTORIA AVGG. (200 frcs.), VICTORIA AVGVSTORVM (400 frcs.) *Large Brass* (200 to 400 frcs.) *Second Brass* (6 to 150 frcs) All the *Billon* or third brass coins of Valerian I. having the *bust laureated* are of smaller size and better fabric than the others, they seem to have been struck from gold dies. (Cohen, *Méd. Imp.*, 1st ed., vol. iv., p. 329, *note.)*

Coins of Valerian I. were struck in the following colonies: Aelia Capitolina, Berytus, Heliopolis, Ptolemais, Thessalonica, Macedonia, Troas, Tyrus, and Viminacium.

Valerianus [SALONINVS.] The obverse legends of the coins of Saloninus Valerian are: LIC. COR. SAL. VALERIANVS N. CAES., SAL. VALERIANVS CS. (*Cæsar*) or NOB. CAES., P. COR. SAL. VALERIANO CES. (*sic*), P. COR. SAL. VALERIANVS CAES., P. LIC. or P. LIC. COR. VALERIANVS CAES., P. C. L. VALERIANVS N. C. or NOB. CAES., COR. or COR. LIC. VALERIANVS CAES. (?), SALON. VALERIANVS CAES. or NOB. CAES., IMP. SALON. VALERIANVS AVG., DIVO CAES. or CAESARI VALERIANO, DIVO VALERIANO AVG.

VALERIANVS II. was son of Valerianus I., and half brother of Gallienus. He was killed at Milan in A.D. 268, together with Gallienus.

Eckhel, in a long dissertation (vol. vii. p. 427), overthrew the opinion of the early numismatists, who had attributed coins to Valerian II., but Cohen has attempted (*Méd. Imp.*, 1st ed., vol. iv., p. 492) to prove that this time Eckhel is wrong. He assigns all the coins bearing the legend VALERIANVS P. F. AVG. to Valerian the younger. M. Deville shortly after followed with an essay "on the coins of the family of Gallienus" (*Rev. Num.* 1861), in which he divided the coins usually attributed to Saloninus between Cornelius Valerianus, elder son of Gallienus, and Saloninus, second son of Gallienus, assigning one piece with obverse P. LIC. VALERIANVS CAES., and reverse IOVI CRESCENTI, to Valerian II., the brother of Gallienus, but as I have already pointed out (*Handbook to Rom. Num.*, 1861, p. 117; *Num. Chron.*, N.S., 1861, p. 196), the coins attributed by him to Saloninus and Valerian II. are of much too good a metal to be of the late period of Gallienus. Moreover the coin given by him to Valerian II. was

struck in the East, and belongs to Saloninus Valerian, the eldest son of Gallienus, and the legend IOVI CRESCENTI could hardly apply to a man of thirty. Besides, if any coins of Valerian II. existed they would probably bear the title of *Augustus*, and not that of *Cæsar*. The late M. de Salis also was opposed to the attribution on similar grounds, and maintained that if any were issued they would necessarily be of the *base metal* of the late years of Gallienus. The coins of the family of Gallienus are therefore only recognized by me as follows:

Valerianus I.	...	...	...	*Coins.*
Gallienus ...	...	...	...	*Coins.*
Cornelius Saloninus Valerianus		...	*Coins.*
(elder son of Gallienus)				
Saloninus Valerianus	...	...	*No Coins.*
(second son of Gallienus)				
Q. Julius Gallienus	...	...	*No Coins.*
(third son of Gallienus)				
Valerianus II.	...	...	...	*No Coins.*
(brother of Gallienus)				

There are, however, some medallions struck by Valerianus I., which may give a portrait of Valerianus II. Their description is as follows:

1. *Obv.* PIETAS AVGVSTORVM. Busts facing each other of Valerian I., laureated with cuirass, and of Valerian II., bare with *paludamentum* and cuirass. *Rev.* CONCORDIA AVGVSTORVM. Busts facing each other of Gallienus laureated with *paludamentum* and cuirass, and of Salonina with diadem. BRIT. MVS. Æ. Med. (1200 frcs.) (Cohen, *Méd. Imp.*, 1st ed., vol. iv., p. 343, pl. xx.; Grueber, *Rom. Med.*, p. 62, pl. xlvii., No. 4.)

2. *Obv.* IMP. C. P. LIC. VALERIANVS P. F. AVG. Bust of Valerian I. to l., laureated with the *paludamentum*, and armed with a sceptre surmounted by an eagle. *Rev.* CONC. . . . Busts facing each other of Gallienus, laureated, and of Valerian II., bare. CAB. OF HOFFMANN. Æ. Med. (500 frcs.). (Cohen, *Méd. Imp.*, p. 343.)

3. *Obv.* CONCORDIA AVGVSTORVM. Busts facing each other of Gallienus, laureated with cuirass, and Valerian II. bare with *paludamentum* and cuirass. *Rev.* ADVENTVS AVGG. Valerian I., Gallienus, and Valerian II. on horseback to left, preceded by Victory and accompanied by five soldiers; behind three ensigns, and on the ground two captives seated, their hands tied behind their backs. PARIS. Æ. Med. (600 frcs.) (Cohen, *Méd. Imp.*, 1st ed., vol. iv., p. 461, pl. xix.; cf. vol. v., *Errata* of vol. iv.)

Valerianus aureus mentioned in a letter of Gallienus (Treb. Poll. *Claud.* 17) as the name of one of the gold coins, probably the double *triens*, in circulation in the third century.

Valerius [VAL. *Valerius*.]

VALERIVS ACISCVLVS, moneyer towards the end of the Republic. [VALERIA *gens*.]

VALERIVS CATVLLVS, moneyer of Augustus. [VALERIA *gens*.]

VALET.—HOC VALET AD BIBERRIVM. Uncertain object. *Obv.* P. (? B.) M. Head of Tiberius to r. A curious lead published by

Garrucci after Millingen *(Rev. Num.*, 1862, p. 416, pl. xv., No. 7), illustrating the following passage of Suetonius *(Tib.* 42), "In castris, tiro etiam tum, propter nimiam vini aviditatem, pro Tiberio, *Biberius;* pro Claudio, *Caldius;* pro Nerone, *Mero* vocabatur," and, alluding to Tiberius' fondness of wine, Garrucci suggests that the P. M. is probably B. M., *Biberius Mero.*

VALE**V**. *(Valetudinis)* ou a silver coin of the *Acilia gens*, struck about B.C. 54, by the moneyer Manius Acilius. *Obv.* SALVTIS. Head of the goddess *Salus* to r, laureated, with neck-lace and earrings. *Rev.* **M**. ACILIVS IIIVIR VALE**V**. The goddess *Valetudo* standing to l., leaning on a column, and holding in her r. hand a serpent. (Cohen, *Méd. Cons.*, pl. i., *Acilia* No. 3; Mommsen, *Mon. Rom.*, vol. ii., p. 497; vol. iv., p. 65, pl. xxxi., No. 8.)

This type recalls the Greek word ἀκέομαι to *heal*, from which the *Acilia gens* might have borrowed their name, more especially as it is recorded (Plin., *Nat. Hist.*, xxix., cap. i.) that the first Greek doctor who came to Rome obtained leave to open a shop in the *cross-road Acilia* (primum é Medicis venisse Romam Peloponneso Archagathum Lysaniæ filium, L. Æmilio, M. Livio Coss. anno urbis DXXXV [B.C. 219], eique jus Quiritium datum et tabernam in *compito Acilio* emptam ob id publice). The head of *Salus* on the obverse is that of the goddess to whom C. Julius Bubulius dedicated a temple in B.C. 304 (Livy, ix., 43; x., 1; cf. Plin., *Nat. Hist.*, xxxv., 4), and it also occurs upon coins of the *Junia gens*, struck by Silanus about B.C. 89—88. It seems likely that the same goddess—*Salus* and *Valetudo*—is represented on the obverse and reverse of this *denarius [Valetudo.]*

VALETVDINE. On a gold coin of the *Antistia gens*, struck by C. Antistius Vetus, moneyer of Augustus, with L. Mescinius Rufus and L. Vinicius in B.C. 16-15. *Obv.* C. ANTISTI. VETVS IIIVIR. Winged bust of Victory to r. *Rev.* PRO VALETVDINE CAESARIS S. P. Q. R. Veiled priest, standing to l., sacrificing before an altar and holding a *patera*; an assistant at sacrifices *(victimarius)* is bringing to him a bull. (VIENNA, 1500 frcs. Cohen, *Méd. Cons.*, pl. ii., *Antistia*, No. 4; *Méd. Imp.*, 2nd ed., vol. i., p. 3.)

Augustus was in these years (B.C. 16-15) absent in Gaul, and the vows of the Senate and Roman people were offered for his health and safe return. [MESCINIA *gens*.]

Valetudo, (health), generally bears the same meaning as *Salus*, and from the coin described under VALE**V**, where the goddess is represented, it would seem that these two goddesses were considered the same by the Romans, further corroborated from the fact that on certain coins of Augustus, struck in the same years, (B.C. 16-15), vows were made *pro salute Cæsaris* and *pro valetudine Cæsaris.*

Vallum the rampart of a Roman encamp-ment, composed of earth with sharp stakes inserted in it, and derived from *vallus* a stake, is represented on the coins of the *Numonia gens* struck by Numonius Vaala in B.C. 43. The surname *Vaala* or *Vala* was given to him for successfully assaulting the entrenchment *(vallum)* of an enemy [NUMONIA; VAALA.] It is thought that the form of a *vallum* may be seen on the coins of Licinius I., Constantine I. and II., &c., bearing the legend VIRT. or VIRTVS EXERC., in any case this type seems to re-present a camp on the top of which is stand-ing the sun raising the r. hand and holding a globe.

Vandals. The following is the list of the Vandal kings in Africa:—

I. Genseric, A.D. 427, *no coins.* II. Huneric, A.D. 477, *no coins.* III. Gunthamund, A.D. 484, silver and copper? coins. IV. Thrasa-mund, A.D., 496, silver coins. V. Hilderic, A.D., 523, silver and copper coins. VI. Gelimir, A.D. 530, silver and copper coins. For a full description of the types and their explanation see Friedländer, *Münzen der Vandalen* and C. F. Keary, *Num. Chron.*, N.S., 1878, vol. xviii., pp. 137—149.

VANE. *[Vanesia.]*

Vanesia, a town of Gaul, close to the Ausci and the passage of the *Baise.* The following coin is attributed to it:—

Obv. Female head to l. *Rev.* VANE. An eagle with wings expanded; in the *field*, two pentagons and three circles with pellets in the centre. Æ. (Akerman, *Coins of Cities and Princes*, p. 132.)

VR. *(Varo)*, on *denarius, quinarius*, and *quadrans* [see **VRO**] struck perhaps by Caius Terentius Varro in B.C. 216 [TERENTIA *gens*]; and on coins of Tiberius struck at Turiaso—T. SVLP. Q. **VR**. Q. PONT. PILA. *(Pontio Pilato)* AED. MVN. TVRI. [VL, NT, PIL and MVN also joined.] (Cohen, *Méd. Imp.*, 2nd ed., vol. i., p. 204, No. 172.)

VAR. *(Vario)*, on a second brass coin of Augustus of an uncertain colony, C. VAR. RVF. SEX. IVL. POL. IIVIR. Q. *Caio Vario Rufo, Sexto Julio Pollione Duumviris Quin-quennalibus.* (Eckhel, vol. vi., p. 132.)

VRG. *(Vargunteius)*, on *denarius, semis, triens, quadrans*, and *sextans* of Marcus Vargunteius, [VARGVNTEIA *gens*.] The *as* attributed by Cohen *(Méd. Cons.* p. 325, No 2,) to this moneyer has been shown to have been misread **VR**G. instead of **VR**O *(Varo)*, and belongs to the *Terentia gens.* (Mommsen, *Mon. Rom.*, vol. ii., p. 325.)

VARGUNTEIA GENS, a family completely unknown. The coins of Vargunteius were probably issued about B.C. 134-114. *Obv.* M. VⱤG. *(Marcus Vargunteius.)* Head of Pallas to r. with winged helmet; before ✕. *Rev.* ROMA. Jupiter in a *quadriga* to r., holding laurel branch and thunderbolt. There are also existing specimens of the *semis, triens, quadrans* and *sextans* with M. VⱤG., and marks of their value. The *as* given by Cohen with M. VⱤG. should be read VⱤO. [see VⱤG.]

VARI, on brass coins of Augustus, struck at Achulla Byzacenæ, by the proconsul of Africa, P. Quinctilius Varus, in B.C. 7—P. QUINCTILI. VARI. ACHVLLA. The name of AGRIPPA, which has been read by some on these coins in the place of that of ACHVLLA, has been shown to be erroneous. (Müller, *Num. de l'Anc. Afrique,* vol. ii., pp. 44—46).

VARIO, on brass coins of Germanicus and Caligula, struck at Corinth—GERM. CAESAR PVLCHRO III. VARIO IIVIR. (Cohen, *Méd. Imp.,* 2nd ed., vol. i., p. 229, No. 8.)

Varius, a name of the Emperor Elagabalus, from his father, Sextus Varius Marcellus, but it does not occur upon his coins. [ELAGABALVS.]

VⱤO. *(Varo),* on the *as, semis, triens, sextans,* and *uncia,* struck perhaps by Caius Terentius Varo, in B.C. 216 [see VⱤ and TERENTIA *gens*], and on coins of Augustus struck at Bilbilis Tarraconensis—MVN. AVGVSTA BILBILIS M. SEMP. TIBERI. L. LICI. VⱤO IIVIR [MVN, AV, MP also joined.] (Cohen, *Méd. Imp.,* 2nd ed., vol. i., p. 152, No. 640.)

VARO, on brass coins of Augustus, struck at Cæsar Augusta Hispaniæ—CAESAR AVGVSTA C. SABINO P. VARO IIVIR, and on brass coins of Tiberius, struck at Clunia Hispaniæ—M. LVCR. TER. E. *(sic)* C. CALP. VARO AED. CLVNI [TE joined.] (Cohen, *Méd. Imp.,* 2nd ed., vol. i., p. 154, No. 670; p. 201, No. 132.)

VARRO PRO. Q. *(Varro pro Quæstore).* Bust of Jupiter Terminalis bearded with diadem to r. on a base. *Rev.* MAGN. PRO. COS. Sceptre between a dolphin and an eagle. Æ. (12 frcs.) [EAGLE.] A coin of Pompey the Great assigned by Cohen to the year B.C. 67, but it has been with more probability attributed to B.C. 49. (Mommsen, *Mon. Rom.,* vol. ii., p. 533; Lenormant, *La Mon. dans l' Antiq.,* vol. ii. p. 307.) [TERENTIA *gens.*] Cohen (*Méd. Cons.,* pl. xxxix., No. 5), publishes a specimen with the legend VARRO. PRO. Q., and the bust of Jupiter on both obverse and reverse.

VARVS. See VIBIA *gens.*

VATRANIO on coins of Augustus struck at Corinthus Achaiæ. A. VATRANIO LABEONE

IIVIR. (Cohen, *Méd. Imp.,* 2nd ed., vol. i., p. 161, Nos. 758-764.)

VBERITA. AV. Cow to r., milked by a female seated. *Obv.* IMP. CARAVSIVS P. F. A. Bust of Carausius to l., laureated, with imperial cloak, holding a sceptre surmounted by an eagle. Æ. (Brit. Mus., 300 frcs.) A variety in the Hunter Museum reads on the obverse IMP. CARAVSIVS AVG. Bust, holding a globe.

VBERITAS AVG. Same reverse type. *Obv.* IMP. CARAVSIVS P. F. AVG. Bust of Carausius to r., radiated with *paludamentum.* Æ. III. (30 frcs.)

VBERITAS AVG. Fertility standing to l., holding a purse and cornucopiæ on silver coins of Trajan Decius, Etruscilla, Herennius, Hostilian, Trebonianus, and Volusian.

VBERITAS AVG. Fertility standing to l., holding a bunch of grapes (?) and a cornucopiæ, on gold and billon coins of Gallienus and on copper coins of Claudius II., Quintillus, Tetricus II., and Tacitus.

VBERITAS AVG. Female figure standing to r., holding a standard and giving her hand to a soldier who holds a spear, on silver and copper coins of Carausius (300 frcs.—40 frcs.)

VBERITAS AVG. Fertility standing to l., holding bunch of grapes (?) and a cornucopiæ. *Obv.* IMP. TETRICVS P. F. AVG. Head of Tetricus I. to r., laureated. N. (300 frcs.)

VBERTA. AVG. Cow to r., milked by a female seated; in the *exergue* R. S. R. *Obv.* IMP. CARAVSIVS AVG. Bust of Carausius to r., laureated with *paludamentum.* Æ. (300 frcs.)

VBERTAS AVG. Fertility standing to l., holding bunch of grapes (?) and a cornucopiæ on billon or copper coins of Gallienus, Postumus, Victorinus I., Tetricus I., Tetricus II., Tacitus and Florian.

Ubertas (or on coins sometimes *Uberitas)* Fertility. This goddess, it will have been seen, is described sometimes as holding "a purse," sometimes "a bunch of grapes (?)." The late Abbé Cavedoni considered the object to be a "cow's udder" *(uber),* as also upon certain coins of Vespasian and Titus with the legend PAX AVG. (Cohen, *Méd. Imp.,* 2nd ed., vol. i., p. 390, Nos. 297-299, p. 440, Nos. 131-133). M. Cohen and M. De Witte both adopted this opinion, but M. Henri de Longperier has conclusively shown, from researches made into the different forms of purses, that the goddess Fertility holds a purse of money, and that the object on the tripod of the coins, with PAX. AVG., is also a purse. M. De Witte has consequently returned to the original explanation, which I have little, or any, doubt is the correct one (cf. De Witte, *Rev. Num.,* 1869, pp. 133-136.)

VBERTAS SAECVLI. Female figure standing holding a balance and cornucopiæ. *Obv.* CONSTANTINVS P. F. AVG. Bust of Constantine I. to r., with cuirass. Æ. III., from *Banduri* after *Hardouin* (20 frcs.) A variety is given by *Tanini,* having the obverse legend FL. VAL. CONSTANTINVS NOB. CAES.

VBERTAS SAECVLI. Three female figures standing each holding a balance and a cornucopiæ ; in the *exergue* s. TR. *Obv.* CONSTANTINVS NOB. c. Head of Constantîne II., laureated. Æ. III., from *Tanini* (20 frcs.)

VBI. [*Ubii.*]

Ubii. A people of Gaul, having for their capital *Colonia Agrippina* (Cologne.) The following coin is attributed to them. *Obv.* NIDI. Head to r. ; before a star. *Rev.* VBI. Horse galloping to r. ; in the *field*, a star and three circles. Æ. (Akerman, *Coins of Cities and Princes*, p. 168.)

VBIQ. *(Ubique)*, on second brass coins of Nero,—PACE P.R. VBIQ. PARTA IANVM CLVSIT. s. c.—Also on the Contorniates with the head of Nero (Sabatier, *Méd. Contorn.*, pl. xvii., 9 ; Cohen, *Méd. Imp.*, 1st ed., vol. vi., p. 562, No. 26.)

VBIQVE PAX. Victory in a *biga* galloping to r., holding a whip. *Obv.* GALLIENAE AVGVSTAE. Head of Gallienus to l., crowned with reeds. *N.* (300 frs.) *Bil.* (60 frcs.)

VBIQVE PAX. Same reverse type. *Obv.* GALLIENVS AVG. Head of Gallienus crowned with ears of corn (?). *N.* from *Banduri, du Musée du grand duc de Toscane* (250 frcs.)

VBIQVE PAX. Same reverse type. *Obv.* GALLIENVS P. F. AVG. Head of Gallienus crowned with grass (?). *N.* from *Tanini, du Musée du grand duc de Toscane* (250 frcs.), or crowned with ears of corn (?). *Bil. Musée de Vienne* (40 frcs).

The following remarks have been made on these curious coins by M. Cohen *(Méd. Imp.*, 1st ed. vol. iv., p. 416, *note)* :—

" There are few coins which have exercised and puzzled scholars more than these. The names of GALLIENAE AVGVSTAE accompanying a head which is without dispute that of Gallienus, the crown in a particular form which seems to be a crown of ears of corn, the extraordinary legend of the reverse, VBIQVE PAX, when the State was rent by dissensions, revolutions, and misfortunes of every kind, all has contributed to make one believe that this coin conveyed a satire against Gallienus, whose weakness and little anxiety about public misfortunes caused him to be regarded as a woman. Eckhel, in a very lengthy treatise, finished by ranking himself of the opinion of Barthelemy, who has declared that " these coins were the ornament of a cabinet and the despair of antiquaries." M. Ch. Lenormant in his *Trésor de Numismatique et de Glyptique*, has decided in favour of Vaillant, who maintained that this coin was ironical ; moreover, he has sought to prove, putting aside altogether the importance which might be attached to the

kind of crown which adorns the head of Gallienus, since it is seen upon others of his coins,—to prove, I say, that this coin, according to its weight, which is that of the gold coins of Postumus, must have been struck by this usurper to turn him into ridicule. Certainly, it is very probable that the coin in question is satirical ; it is necessary, however, to guard oneself against believing too easily in satire as a fact on money having a public circulation. Thus, I believe to have shewn, volume iii., page 663, in the note, that the coin of Faustina II., which has on the reverse VENERI VICTRICI, could not have a sense which impaired her honour ; in reality, Faustina, in spite of some errors of temperament, was far from deserving a public insult, which, besides, Marcus Aurelius would not have allowed, especially from the Senate, as the letters s. c. testify. But here the case is not the same. Gallienus only inspiring contempt because of his cowardice and weakness, the claimants to the empire, could very well strike and circulate money which, in default of other means of publicity, exposed to broad daylight all his wickedness, and it is for that that they would have made him ridiculous in naming him GALLIENA. As to the crown it is an error that it has been described by many authors as a crown of ears of corn ; it by no means resembles it. Hardouin has considered it as a crown of grass ; Tanini likewise ; Pellerin, whose manuscript catalogue exists in the *Cabinet des Médailles* has called it *Corona Arundinea* (crown of reeds), and, really, if one compares it with that which adorns the head of Arethusa upon the large medallion of Syracuse one will see that it is exactly similar. Now, could its satirical character be upheld in regarding it, either as being of grass, or as being of reeds ? There would be no doubt in my opinion of the crown of grass, since this was considered in the time of the Roman republic as the most honourable of all. Looked upon as a crown of reeds (as it is), besides that one could well in derision ornament the hair of Gallienus as that of a nymph, M. Chabouillet, keeper of the *Cabinet des Médailles*, puts forth the very plausible opinion that in the same manner as the Jews offered out of derision to Jesus Christ a reed by way of a sceptre, (a proof that the ancients gave sometimes an ironical meaning to the reed), those who wished to turn Gallienus into ridicule could well crown him with reeds in place of laurels. It is true that this same crown is met with upon three other coins of Gallienus, which have for the reverse : FIDES MILITVM, VICTORIA AVG., and P.M. TR. P. vii. (Gallienus standing between two rivers). But who knows if these were not satirical also, although less openly ? In short, will anyone tell me how to explain the coin of Gallienus with this reverse VBIQVE PAX, and combined with the proper legend and head ? To that I will answer that if the legend of the head is sometimes serious, the crown is never ; and that as one knows that satire is not begun by hurling at first its keenest shafts, one may perhaps conclude that these coins have followed the following order of issue, which would have been a gradation in their satirical signification: 1, P.M. TR. P. vii.; 2, VICTORIA AVG., where Gallienus is crowned by Victory; 3, FIDES MILITVM; 4, VBIQVE PAX (these four coins with the simple crown of reeds); 5, lastly, VICTORIA AVG. (*méd.* 596), and VBIQVE PAX (with the crown of reeds and the name of GALLIENAE AVGVSTAE.)"

VBIQVE VICTOR. Constantine I. in military dress, laureated, standing to r., holding a spear and a globe, between two captives seated on the ground; in the *exergue* P. TR. (*Prima Treveris.*) *Obv.* CONSTANTINVS P. F. AVG. Head of Constantine I., to r., laureated. *N.* (100 frs.)

VBIQVE VICTORES. The Emperor in military dress standing to r., holding a spear and a globe, at his feet on each side a captive seated; in the *exergue*, P. TR. (*Prima Treveris*); on gold coins of Maximinus II. Daza (200 frcs.); Licinius I. (200 frcs.); Constantine I. (in *exergue* P.R. or TR. 100 frcs.; *Quin.* 100 frcs.), Crispus (in *exergue* TR. *Tremissis* 500 frcs.); and Constantine II. (in *exergue* SMTS medallion 500 frcs.; in *exergue* TR. 200 frcs.)

V. C. *Vir Consularis* [VABALATHVS.]

V. C. R. IM. D. R. *Vir Consularis Romanorum Imperator Dux Romanorum* [VABALATHVS.]

VCCETIO. [*Ucetia.*]

Ucetia, a town of Gaul, known from Roman remains found there, and from the inscription VCETIAE, on a stone found at Nimes. Now *Uzes*. The following coin is attributed to it:—

Obv. VCCETIO. Head of Apollo to r. *Rev.* A lion walking to l., above a branch. *Æ.* (Akerman, *Coins of Cities and Princes*, p. 151.)

VCVC (?) within a crown. *Obv.* CONSTANTIVS CAESAR. Head of Constantius Chlorus to r. *Æ.* (Cohen, *Méd. Imp.* 1st ed., vol. v., p. 562, No. 68 from *Banduri, du musée Farnése*, 30 frcs.) [see xcvi.]

Ⅴ (*Venusia*), on certain early brass pieces struck at Venusia Apuliæ (Mommsen, *Mon. Rom.* vol i., pp. 349—354, vol. iv., p. 14, pl. xv.; *Cat. of Greek coins in the Brit. Mus. Italy*, pp. 148—153.) [*Venusia.*]

VE. VER or VERO. [*Veromandui.*]

Veromandui, a people of Gaul. The modern *Vermandois*. Coins are—

1. *Obv.* VER. Horse to r.; above, a wheel, in the field, a symbol. *Rev.* VE. A lion to r.; monogram and C. *Æ.*

2. *Obv.* VERO. Horse galloping to r.; above a wheel. *Rev.* VE. A lion to r.; behind 10. *Æ.* (Akerman, *Coins of Cities and Princes*, p. 169.)

VEGE. (*Vegeto*) or ⅤEGETO, on brass coins of Tiberius, struck at Turiaso—MARIO VEGE. LICI. CRES. MVN. TVRIASO AED. [MA joined]—M. PONT. MARSO C. MARI ⅤEGETO

IIVIR MVN. TVR. [NT, AR, MAR, MVN and TVR also joined.] (Cohen, *Méd. Imp.*, 2nd ed., vol. i., p. 204, Nos. 173, 171.)

Vehiculatio or munus *vehicularium* was the office of providing horses, mules and conveyances, along the roads of the Empire for persons travelling upon public business.

VEHICVLATIONE ITALIAE REMISSA. Two mules feeding liberated from their yokes, which appear in the background; in the *exergue* S. C. (*Senatús consulto.*) *Obv.* IMP. NERVA CAES. AVG. P.M. TR. P. [or TR. P. II.] COS. III. P.P. Head of Nerva to r., laureated. *Æ.* I. (20 frcs.) It is evident from this coin that Nerva, in A.D. 97, relieved the people of Italy from this oppression, though his biographers have made no mention of the fact, subsequent writers assigning the merit of establishing posts to Hadrian and Antoninus Pius, by whom the plan was only perfected and completed.

VEIBIVS VAARVS, see VIBIA *gens.*

Velatum caput, veiled head, [CONSECRATION.]

VELITER. *Veliternis.* SODALI VELITER. FEL. GERANO CURA. FEL. *Sodalibus Veliternis feliciter Gerano Curatori feliciter*, on a lead (Garrucci, *Rev. Num.*, 1862, p. 416):—FEL. MVNICIPI VELITER FEL. VENA. VELITER. *Feliciter Municipibus Veliternis feliciter Juvenalia Veliterna*, on a lead (Eckhel, vol. viii., p. 319.)

VEN. TVSC. *Venus Tusculana.* *Obv.* Venus, regarding in a mirror and arranging her hair. Lead. (Garrucci, *Rev. Num.*, 1862, p. 425.)

Venatio (hunting), the name given to an exhibition of wild beasts which fought with one another and with men, who were called *Bestiarii.* This was a favourite entertainment with the Romans (see Smith, *Dict. of Antiq.*, s. v. VENATIO), and is represented on family coins [*Livineia*], on Imperial coins of Severus and Caracalla (Madden, *Num. Chron.*, 1861, N.S., vol. i., p. 101) [LAETITIA AVG], and on some of the Contorniates (Sabatier *Méd. Contorn.*, pl. iv., No. 1; pl. ix. and x., No. 1) [CONTORNIATE COINS.]

VEN. (*Venerandæ*), on small brass coins of Constantine I., struck after his death—IVST. VEN. MEM. *Justa [soluta] venerandæ memoriæ.*

VEN. (*Ventidio*), on brass coins of Nero, struck at Corinth—P. VEN. FRONTONE IIVIR. COR. (Cohen, *Méd. Imp.*, 2nd ed., vol. i., p. 306, Nos. 398—400) [VENTIDIO.]

VEND. *(Vendumniano)* IM. C. V. AF. GAL. VEND. VOLVSIANO AVG. *Imperatori Caio Vibio Afinio Gallo Vendumniano Volusiano Augusto* [VOLVSIANVS].

VΞNE — L. VΞNE. Name of a Roman magistrate on *semis* of Pæstum Lucaniæ, a Roman colony founded *circ.* B.C. 273.

VENER. AVG. Health, standing to l., feeding a serpent, which glides out close to an altar, and holding a sceptre. *Obv.* IMP. CARAVSIVS P.F. AVG. Bust of Carausius to r., radiated, with the *paludamentum*. Æ. III. *(Hunter Mus.* 20 frcs.)

VENER. VICTOR. Venus, half naked, standing to r., holding an apple and a palm, and leaning against a column. *Obv.* IVLIA DOMNA AVG. Bust of Julia Domna to r. Æ. (3 frcs.)

VENER. VICTRIX *(sic.)* Venus, standing to l., holding a helmet and a spear, and leaning on a shield. In the *exergue* S. P. Q. R. *(Senatus Populusque Romanus.) Obv.* GALLIENVS AVG. Bust of Gallienus to r., radiated, with the *paludamentum* and cuirass. *Bil.* (3 frcs.)

VENERAB. or VENERAN. on a small brass coin of Constantine I., struck after his death— IVST. VENERAB... or VENERAN...[MEM.] *Justa [soluta] Venerandæ Memoriæ.*

VENEREM GENETRICEM. Venus standing to l., holding an apple and a sceptre. *Obv.* CORN. SALONINA AVG. Bust of Salonina to r., diademed with the crescent. *Bil.* (15 frs.)

VENERI AVGVSTAE S. C. *(Senatus Consulto).* Venus standing to r. or l., throwing her robe on her shoulders with her r. hand, and holding an apple. *Obv.* FAVSTINA AVGVSTA [or AVG.] ANTONINI AVG. PII P. P. Bust of Faustina I. to r. Æ. I. and II. (8 or 3 frs.)

VENERI AVGVSTAE. Venus standing to r., raising her veil, and holding an apple. *Obv.* FAVSTINA AVG. ANTONINI AVG. P. P. or FAVSTINA AVGVSTA. Bust of Faustina I. to r. Æ. (60 frs.)

VENERI AVGVSTAE. Venus seated to l., holding a victory and a spear. *Obv.* FAVSTINA AVGVSTA. Bust of Faustina II. to r. Æ. *(Mionnet,* 150 frcs.) Æ. *(Wiczay,* 20 frcs.)

VENERI FELICI S.C. A decastyle temple, in the middle (sometimes) a statue of Venus; on the pediment three figures standing between two seated; on the top of the pediment, a figure seated between two figures kneeling; at each corner of the pediment a Victory holding a diadem. *Obv.* ANTONINVS AVG. PIVS P.P. TR. P. COS. III. Head or bust of Antoninus Pius, laureated to r. Æ. I. (c to 12 frcs.) Struck in A.D. 140—143. A second brass coin of similar type has the head radiate. *(Wiczay,* 10 frcs.)

VENERI FELICI. Dove to r. *Obv.* FAVSTINA AVG. ANTONINI AVG. PII FIL. Bust of Faustina II. to r. Æ. *(Brit. Mus.,* 80 frcs.)

VENERI FELICI. Venus standing to r., holding a sceptre and an infant. *Obv.* IVLIA

MAMAEA AVG. Bust of Julia Mamæa to r. with diadem. Æ. *(Musée de Vienne,* 800 frcs.). Æ (c). Æ. Quin. *(Vaillant,* 30 frcs.)

VENERI GENETRICI. Venus standing facing, holding a Victory, who carries a trophy, and placing her l. hand on a large shield, resting on a helmet. The shield is adorned with the head of Medusa, and a sceptre rests on her l. arm. *Obv.* HADRIANVS AVG. COS. III P.P. Bust of Hadrian, bare, to r. [or head bare to l.] with *paludamentum* and cuirass. Æ. (60 frcs.)

VENERI GENETRICI. Same type; but on the shield Æneas carrying Anchises and holding his son by the hand. *Obv.* HADRIANVS AVG. COS III. P. P. Head of Hadrian to r., bare, Æ. Med. *(Coll. de M. le Comte Tyskiewich,* 600 frcs.)

VENERI GENETRICI (on some specimens GENTRICI). Venus standing to r. lifting her robe on to her shoulder with her l. hand and holding an apple. *Obv.* SABINA AVGVSTA, Bust of Sabina to r., diademed. Æ. (2 frcs.)

VENERI GENETRICI S.C. Same type. *Obv.* SABINA AVGVSTA HADRIANI AVG. P. P. Bust of Sabina to r. or to l. diademed. Æ. I. (8 frcs.) Second brass coins exist with the obverse legend SABINA AVGVSTA. (4 frcs.)

VENERI GENETRICI S.C. Venus standing to l., raising the r. hand and holding a shield. *Obv.* M. AVREL. ANTONINVS AVG. P.M. Head of Marcus Aurelius to r. Æ. I. (12 frcs.)

VENERI GENETRICI. Venus standing to l., holding an apple and a sceptre. *Obv.* FAVSTINA AVG. [or AVGVSTA] PII AVG. FIL. Bust of Faustina II. to r. Æ. *(Brit. Mus.* 50 frcs.)

VENERI GENETRICI. Venus standing to l., holding an apple and an infant in swaddling clothes. *Obv.* FAVSTINA AVG. [or AVGVSTA] ANTONINI AVG. PII FIL. Bust of Faustina II. to r., sometimes with diadem. Æ. *(Brit. Mus.,* 50 frs.)

VENERI GENETRICI S. C. Same type. *Obv.* FAVSTINAE AVG. PII AVG. FIL. Bust of Faustina to r., sometimes with diadem. Æ. I. (c) ; Æ. II. (c.)

The type of *Venus Genetrix,* as M. Cohen remarks *(Méd. Imp.,* 1st ed., vol. ii., page 602, *note* 3), holding an infant in swaddling clothes, occurs also with that of *Juno Lucina,* as may be seen on the coins of Lucilla and Julia Mamæa. On the coins of this latter the legend instead of being IVNONI LVCINAE is IVNO. AVGVSTAE.

VENERI GENETRICI S. C. Venus standing to l., holding a Victory, and leaning on a shield placed on a helmet (?) *Obv.* FAVSTINA AVGVSTA. Bust of Faustina II. to r. Æ. I. (c.)

VENERI GENETRICI S.C. Venus standing holding a Victory (?) and leaning on a shield. *Obv.* LVCILLAE AVG. ANTONINI AVG. F. Bust of Lucilla to r. Æ. I. *(Brit. Mus.,* 10 frcs.)

VENERI GENETRICI. Venus standing to l., holding a *patera* and a sceptre. *Obv.*

IVLIA AVGVSTA. Head of Julia Domna to r., N. (200 frcs.)

VENERI GENETRICI. Venus standing to l., holding a sceptre. Obv. IVLIA PIA FELIX AVG. [or IVLIA AVGVSTA.] Bust of Julia Domna to r. Æ. (c to 3 frcs). A similar type occurs in Æ. I. (8 frcs.)

VENERI GENETRICI. Venus standing to l., holding an apple on a sceptre. Obv. CORN. SALONINA AVG. Bust of Salonina to r., diademed, with or without crescent. N. (Brit. Mus., 600 frcs). Bil. (c.)

VENERI VICT. (Victrici.) Venus standing to l., holding an apple and a sceptre. Obv. IVLIA DOMNA AVG. Bust of Julia Domna to r. Æ. (5 frcs.)

VENERI VICTR. (Victrici.) Venus half naked standing to r., holding an apple and a palm, and leaning on a column. Obv. IVLIA AVGVSTA. Bust of Julia Domna to r. N. (200 frcs.)

VENERI VICTRI. (Victrici.) Venus standing to r., holding up her dress, and holding an apple. Obv. IMP. NVMERIANVS AVG. Bust of Numerian to r., laureated. Æ. III. Quin. from Banduri (20 frcs.)

VENERI VICTRICI. Venus, half-naked, standing to r., leaning on a column and holding a spear and a helmet. Obv. FAVSTINA AVGVSTA Bust of Faustina II. to r. Æ. (5 frcs.)

VENERI VICTRICI S. C. Venus, half-naked, with the features of Faustina II., standing to r., trying to hold Mars, naked, helmeted, standing to l., who holds a shield and sometimes a parazonium. Obv. FAVSTINA AVGVSTA. Bust of Faustina II. to r. Æ. II. (12 frcs.)

On this coin M. Cohen makes the following remarks (Méd. Imp., 1st ed., vol. ii., p. 603, note; 2nd ed., vol. iii., p. 156, note): "This type has much tried the ingenuity of antiquaries. The old Numismatists have thought that this was a satirical coin of which the reverse made allusion to the weakness that Faustina had for gladiators. The distinguished English author, Addison, a very enlightened amateur of coins, seems, in his Travels in Italy to participate in this opinion up to a certain point. Eckhel regards the interpretation as stupid (ineptam et jam nunc nemini creditam). Caroni, on the contrary, in his description of the coins of the Musée Hedervar, frankly describes this reverse 'Faustina holding back the gladiator Narcissus.' In my opinion Venus on this coin is undoubtedly represented with the features and with the head-dress of Faustina; but I regard as absurd the idea that a satirical coin respecting the Empress, and consequently offensive to the best of Emperors, could ever have been struck under the authority of the Senate. So, whilst recognising Faustina on this piece, I sooner believe that the moneyer wished to pay homage to this princess, who, by her charms, knew how to retain her valorous husband, by borrowing from mythology the names of Mars and Venus, and from sculpture the attitude in which the ancients were accustomed to represent these two divinities."

VENERI VICTRICI S. C. Venus standing to l., holding a Victory and leaning on a shield on which is represented Castor and Pollux (?), Obv. Same bust and legend as previous coin. Æ. I. (c); Æ. II. (Musée de Danemarc, 6 frcs.)

VENERI VICTRICI. Venus standing to l., holding a small Victory and a spear, and leaning on a shield placed on a helmet. Obv. ANTONINVS PIVS AVG. GERM. Bust of Caracalla to r., radiated, with paludamentum and cuirass. Æ. (3 frcs.)

VENERI VICTRICI. Venus standing to l., holding a helmet and a sceptre, and leaning on a shield. Obv. GALLIENVS AVG. Bust of Gallienus to r., radiated, with paludamentum and cuirass. Bil. (c.)

VENERI VICTRICI. Venus standing to l., holding a Victory and a globe. Obv. IMP. NVMERIANVS P. F. AVG. Bust of Numerian to r., laureated, with the cuirass. N. (200 frcs.)

VENERI VICTRICI. Venus, diademed, standing to r., raising her robe on her shoulder, and holding a globe. Obv. MAGNIA VRBICA AVG. Bust of Magnia Urbica, diademed, to r. N. (500 frcs.)

VENERI VICTRICI. On gold and brass coins of Galeria Valeria [VALERIA.]

VENERIS FELICIS. Venus, seated, to l., holding a small Cupid and a spear: in the exergue, sometimes a globe. Obv. HADRIANVS AVG. COS. III. P.P. Head of Hadrian to r., bare, or sometimes draped. N. (40 frcs.) Æ. (2 frcs.)

VENERIS KAR. (Veneris Karthago.) On a brass coin of Carthago Zeugitanæ, struck before the reign of Augustus—KAR. VENERIS. Tetrastyle temple of (?) Jupiter or of (?) Baal; on the pediment an eagle. Obv. ARISTO MVTVMBAL. RICOCE SVF. (? Sufes or Sufetes.) Two heads, jugate, bare (? J. Cæsar and Augustus.) Æ. Carthage probably took the name of Veneris after Astarte, the tutelary deity of ancient Carthage, and who was identified by the Romans with Venus (Müller, Num. de l'Anc. Afrique, vol. ii., pp. 149—152.) The names Mutumbal and Ricoce are Phœnician; Aristo appears to be Greek, though it occurs on inscriptions with other Punic names (Gesenius, Mon. Phoen., pp. 411, 413; 396 note, 401; plate 16.)

VENETO. On contorniates, with heads of Alexander and Trajan, and of the miscellaneous class—DOMNINVS IN VENETO. Victorious charioteer in quadriga facing. The legend DOMNINVS IN VENETO applies to the Victorious charioteer in the blue faction (Veneta), as the Dominus IN PRASINO was in the green. The colours of the other factions were white (alba) and red (russata.) (Sabatier, Mon. Contorn., pp. 35, 37, pl. iii., No. 10; iv., No. 2; Cohen, Méd. Imp., 1st ed., vol. vi., pp. 553, 575, 589.)

VENI. On gold (?), silver, and billon coins of Carausius—EXPECTATE VENI.

VE**N**IDI. *(Ventidius.)* On silver coins of
Marcus Antonius (500 frcs.) – P. VE**N**IDI.
PON. IMP. *(Publius Ventidius Pontifex
Imperator)*, struck in B.C. 39—38, when Ventidius
repulsed the Parthians and killed Labienus
[BARBA.]

VENTIDIA GENS, a family of low extraction.
Publius Ventidius Bassus was originally a
seller of mules, but afterwards became tribune,
pontiff, prætor, consul, and *imperator* as the
coin mentioned above under VE**N**IDI proves.

VENTIDIO. On brass coins of Nero, struck
at Corinthus Achaiæ—P. VENTIDIO FRONTONE
IIVIR COR. *(duumviro Corinthi.)* (Cohen,
Méd. Imp., 2nd ed., vol. i., p. 306, No. 401.)
[VEN.]

VENTIPO. Helmeted figure standing to l.,
holding a spear, terminating in a sort of trident
(?). *Obv.* Helmeted head (? Mars) to l. Æ.
A coin of Ventisponte, a town of Hispania
Bœticæ. Florez cites inscriptions with
EQVITIVS VENTIPONENSIS and EQVITIA VEN-
TIPONENSIA. (Eckhel, vol. i., p. 32.)

VENVS, the goddess of love, is frequently
represented both on family and Imperial coins.
[IVLIA *gens;* CORNELIA *gens;* VIBIA *gens.*]
Venus *Erycina* [ERVC. and CONSIDIA *gens*] is
represented on coins of Considius Nonianus,
struck between B.C. 74—50, and her temple
shown, the worship having been introduced
from Eryx in Sicily. The epithets upon Imperial
coins are *Cœlestis*, first occurring under
Elagabalus, *Felix* and *Genetrix* first under
Hadrian, and *Victrix* first under Faustina II.

VENVS [V**Ǝ**NVS *sic*.] S. C. Venus standing
to l., holding an arrow and a bow. *Obv.*
DIVA AVGVSTA FAVSTINA. Bust of Faustina I.,
veiled to r. Æ. I. (25 frcs.) Struck out of
Rome.

VENVS. Venus standing to l., holding an
apple and a rudder, sometimes placed on or entwined
by a dolphin, or on a dove, or holding
a dove and a sceptre, or an apple or a sceptre, or
an apple alone, or an apple and leaning on a
column. *Obv.* FAVSTINA [or FAVSTINAE]
AVG. PII AVG. F. [or FIL] or FAVSTINA AVGVSTA,
Bust of Faustina II. to r. N. (40 to 150 frcs.)
Æ. (3 frcs.) Similar types in Æ. I and II (c.)
with obverse legend sometimes FAVSTINA AVG.
ANTONINI AVG. PII. FIL.

VENVS. Venus, diademed, standing to r.,
with the face of Faustina II., holding a sceptre
and an apple between Cupid seated on a Triton
and a Triton. *Obv.* FAVSTINA AVG. PII.
AVG. FIL. Bust of Faustina II. to r. Æ.
Med. (250 frcs.) [VENERI VICTRICI S. C.]

VENVS. Venus standing to l., holding an
apple and a sceptre, or a Victory and leaning on
a shield. *Obv.* LVCILLAE AVG. ANTONINI
AVG. F. or LVCILLA AVGVSTA. Bust of Lucilla
to r. N. (130 frcs.) Æ. (c.) Same types
in Æ. I. and II. (10 frcs.—3 frcs.)

VENVS. Venus standing to l., holding a
sceptre, and placing her r. arm round the neck
of a naked Cupid without wings, standing to
r. who holds an arrow and a scarf (?) ; to the
r. a lighted altar. *Obv.* LVCILLAE AVG.

ANTONINI AVG. F. Bust of Lucilla to r. Æ.
Med. (300 frcs.)

VENV**Ṣ** C. I. C. APAM. D.D. *(Venus.
Colonia Julia Concordia Apameia Decreto Decurionum,)*
Venus on a dolphin, holding in
r. hand the helm of a rudder, and in the l. the
acrostolium. *Obv.* IMP. M. AVR. COMMODVS
ANTONINVS. Head of Commodus laureated. Æ.
II. Struck at Apameia Bithyniæ (Cohen, 2nd
ed., vol. iii., p. 369.)

VENVS C. I. C. A. AVG. D. D. *(Venus.
Colonia Julia Concordia Apameia Augusta
Decreto Decurionum).* Venus standing. *Obv.*
IVL. DOMNA AVG. Bust of Julia Domna to r.
Æ. II. Struck at Apameia Bithyniæ (Cohen,
2nd ed., vol. iv., p. 131.)

VENVS S. C. Venus seated to l., holding
a Victory, sometimes without wings, and a
sceptre ; Victory holds a diadem with both
hands. *Obv.* LVCILLAE AVG. M. [sometimes
omitted] ANTONINI AVG. F. or LVCILLA
AVGVSTA. Bust of Lucilla to r. Æ I. and II.
(5 frcs — 3 frcs.)

VENVS. Venus standing to l. holding an
apple and raising her robe, or an apple and a
sceptre. *Obv.* CRISPINA AVGVSTA. Bust of
Crispina to r. N. from *Caylus* (300 frcs.) ;
Æ. (3 frcs.) ; Æ. II. (3 frcs.)

VENVS AVG. Venus, half naked, standing
leaning on a column and holding a helmet and
a sceptre. *Obv.* IVLIA AVGVSTA T. [or TITI]
AVG. [or AVGVSTI] F. Bust of Julia, diademed,
to r. Æ. (30 frcs.)

A similar type, but Venus holds a spear,
occurs on a silver medallion of Domitia, struck
in Asia (120 frcs.)

VENVS AVG. Venus standing holding a
globe (? a helmet) and a spear, and leaning on a
shield. *Obv.* IMP. C.M. AVR. CLAVDIVS AVG.
Bust of Claudius II. to r., radiated. Æ. III.
from *Banduri* (10 frcs.)

VENVS AVGVST. On a silver coin of
Julia Titi, of same type as that described under
VENVS AVG.

VENVS CAEL. *(Cœlestis.)* Venus standing
—on a coin of Elagabalus from *Arneth, Synopsis*.
Æ.

VENVS CAELESTIS. Venus standing to l.,
or seated to l., holding an apple and a sceptre ;
in the *field* a star, or at her feet a child. *Obv.*
IVLIA SOAEMIAS AVG. Bust of Julia Sœmias
to r. or to l. N. (if existing 1000 frcs.) Æ.
(3 frcs.). Æ. Quin. (60 frcs.). Æ. II. (5 to
25 frcs.)

VENVS CELEST. *(Celestis.)* Venus
standing to l., holding an apple and a sceptre.
Obv. MAGNIA VRBICA AVG. Bust of Magnia
Urbica to r., diademed with crescent. Æ. III.
(20 frcs.)

VENVS FELIX. Venus, diademed, seated
to l., holding a small Victory, who holds a
sceptre or a diadem and a sceptre. *Obv.*
FAVSTINA AVGVSTA. Bust of Faustina II. to
r. Æ. (6 frcs.). Æ. Med. (300 frcs.) On Æ.
I. and II. (c.) Venus holds a child and a sceptre,
and the obverse legend is sometimes DIVA
FAVSTINA PIA.

Varieties of this type occur on coins of Crispina—under seat of Venus a dove. (*N*. 300 frcs.; *Æ*. without dove 3 frcs.; *Æ*. I. and II. 6 and 3 frcs.); of Aquillia Severa in the *field* a star. (*Æ*. I. 200 frcs.) ; of Julia Mamæa. (*Æ*. from *Wiczay* 3 frcs.; *Æ*. I. and II. c.) Venus holding a statuette and a sceptre; — and of Salonina. (*N*. 600 frcs.; *Bil*. c.)

VENVS FELIX. Venus standing to l., holding an apple, or an apple and a sceptre. *Obv.* IVLIA AVGVSTA. Bust of Julia Domna to r. *Æ*. (c.) *Æ*. Quin. (25 frcs.) *Æ*. I. and II. (8 and 3 frcs.)

Varieties of this type occur on coins of Plautilla, (*Æ*. Quin. 60 frcs.) ; of Gallienus (*Bil*. 3 frcs.); of Salonina—Venus holding sceptre and child (*Bil*. c.); and of Severina (*Æ*. III. 3 frcs.)

VENVS FELIX. Venus seated to l., holding a globe and a palm; in the *exergue* TR. (*Treveris*.) *Obv.* FAVSTAE NOBILISSIMAE FEMINAE. Bust of Fausta to l. *Æ*. Quin. (200 frcs.)

VENVS GENETRIX. Venus standing to l., holding a victory and leaning on a shield, at the foot of which are two javelins. *Obv.* FAVSTINA AVGVSTA. Bust of Faustina II. to r. *N*. (100 frcs.) *Æ*. (3 frcs.) On the shield Castor and Pollux (?) and beneath sometimes an infant.

VENVS GENETRIX. Venus seated to l., holding victory and sceptre. *Obv.* FAVSTINA AVGVSTA. Bust of Faustina II. to r. *Æ*. (6 frcs.).

VENVS GENETRIX. Venus seated to l., holding an apple and a sceptre; at her feet Cupid standing. *Obv.* LVCILLA AVGVSTA. Bust of Lucilla to r. *Æ*. I. (10 frcs.)

Varieties of this type occur on coins of Septimius Severus of Syrian fabric. (*Æ*. 10 frcs.);—of Julia Domna (*N*. 200 frcs.; *Æ*. c.), sometimes with observe legend IVLIA PIA FELIX AVG.

VENVS GENETRIX. Venus seated to l., offering an apple to a child and holding a spear. *Obv.* P. SEPT. GETA CAES. PONT. Bust of Geta, to r., bare, with *paludamentum*. *Æ*. plated from *Wiczay* and *Musée de Vienne*.

VENVS GENETRIX. Venus seated to l., holding globe and sceptre. *Obv.* IVLIA PAVLA AVG. Bust of Julia Paula to r. *Æ*. (10 frcs.)

VENVS GENETRIX. Venus seated to l., holding a *patera* and a sceptre. *Obv.* SALL. BARBIA ORBIANA AVG. Bust of Orbiana to r., diademed. *Æ*. (80 frcs.)

VENVS GENETRIX. Venus standing holding an apple and a spear. Orbiana. *Æ*. from *Wiczay* (80 frcs.)

VENVS GENETRIX. Venus standing to l., holding an apple and a sceptre; at her feet a child. *Obv.* IVLIA MAMAEA AVG. Bust of Julia Mamæa to r., sometimes with diadem. *N*. (800 frcs.) *Æ*. (c.)

Similar types occur on coins of Salonina (*N*. 600 frcs. *Bil*. c. *Bil*. Quin. 30 frcs. *Æ*. I. and II. 12 and 6 frcs.) ; and of Magnia Urbica. (*Æ*. III. 50 frcs.)

VENVS GENETRIX. Venus standing to l., holding an apple and a sceptre. *Obv.* MAGNIA VRBICA AVG. Bust of Magnia Urbica to r., with diadem. *N*. from *Wiczay* (500 frcs.) *Æ*. III. (20 frcs.)

VENVS VICT. (*Victrix*). Venus standing to l., holding helmet and sceptre (or a spear); at her feet Cupid standing; sometimes in the *field* P or in the *exergue* M. S. *Obv.* SALONINA AVG. Bust of Salonina to r. diademed with crescent. *Bil*. (c).

VENVS VICTRIX. Venus with the face of Faustina II. standing to l., holding a small Victory and a spear resting on a helmet; on the shield Romulus and Remus suckled by the wolf. *Obv.* FAVSTINA AVGVSTA. Bust of Faustina II. to r. *N*. (100 frcs.) There are also large brass coins of similar type, but representing *Venus* herself, and sometimes on the shield Castor and Pollux (c). [See VENERI VICTRICI S. C.]

VENVS VICTRIX. Venus standing to l., holding Victory and leaning on a shield. *Obv.* LVCILLA AVGVSTA. Bust of Lucilla to r. *Æ*. (6 frcs.) *Æ*. III. (10 frcs.)

VENVS VICTRIX. Venus standing to l., leaning against a column, and holding a helmet and a sceptre. *Obv.* CRISPINA AVGVSTA. Bust of Crispina to r. *N*. (300 frcs.)

VENVS VICTRIX. Venus seated to l., holding a statuette and a spear. *Obv.* CRISPINA AVGVSTA. Bust of Crispina to r. *Æ*. from *Wiczay*.

VENVS VICTRIX. Venus standing to l., holding a small Victory and a spear, and leaning on a shield placed on a helmet. *Obv.* ANTONINVS PIVS AVG. GERM. Bust of Caracalla to r., laureated or radiated with *paludamentum* and cuirass. *N*. from *Wiczay* (150 frcs.). *Æ*. (c). *Æ*. I. with obv. legend M. AVREL. ANTONINVS, etc. (10 frcs.) *Æ*. II. (4 frcs.)

VENVS VICTRIX. Venus standing to l., holding helmet and sceptre, and leaning on shield; at her feet on either side a seated captive. Caracalla. *Æ*. (3 frcs.)

VENVS VICTRIX. Venus standing to l., holding an apple and a palm, and leaning on a shield, before her Cupid standing holding a helmet. *Obv.* PLAVTILLA AVGVSTA. Bust of Plautilla to r. *N*. (600 frcs.). *Æ*. (4 frcs.). *Æ*. I. (800 frcs.). *Æ*. II. (12 frcs.)

VENVS VICTRIX. Venus seated to l., holding globe and sceptre. *Obv.* IVLIA PAVLA AVG. Bust of Julia Paula to r. *Æ*. (10 frcs.)

VENVS VICTRIX. Venus standing to l., holding a helmet and sceptre; at her feet a shield. *Obv.* IVLIA MAMAEA AVG. Bust of Julia Mamæa to r., with diadem. *N*. Quin. (700 frcs.) *Æ*. I. and II. (c.)

VENVS VICTRIX. Venus standing to l., holding a helmet and a sceptre, and leaning on a shield. *Obv.* IMP. GORDIANVS PIVS FEL. AVG. Bust of Gordianus III. to r.   *N.* Quin. from *Caylus* (300 frcs.) Æ. (c.)

A similar type may be found on the coins of Valerian I. (*Bil.* 3 frcs. Æ. II. from *Vaillant* 12 frcs.), of Gallienus, (*Bil.* c.), of Salonina (*Bil.* c.); and of Magnia Urbica, (Æ. III. 10 frcs.)

VENVS VICTRIX. Venus standing to r., holding palm and helmet, and leaning against a column. *Obv.* SALONINA AVG. Bust of Salonina to r., with diadem. *N.* from *Caylus*, (600 frcs.). *Bil.* bust with crescent (c.)

VENVS VICTRIX. Venus standing to l., holding an apple and a palm, and leaning on a shield. Salonina. *Bil* (c.)

VENVS VICTRIX. Venus standing to l., holding a helmet and a spear. Salonina. *N.* from *Banduri* (600 frcs.)

Venusia, a city of Apulia, captured by the Roman Consul L. Postumius in B.C. 262, and shortly afterwards made a Roman colony, a rank which it held under the Empire. Cicero had a villa there, and it was the birth-place of Horace. The following coins are attributed to Venusia (Mommsen, *Mon. Rom.*, vol. i., pp. 349-354, vol. iv., p. 14., pl. xv.; *Cat. of Greek coins in the British Museum. Italy*, pp., 148-153) : —*Æs grave.* Libral system; *As, Quincunx, Triens, Quadrans, Sextans, Uncia.* Uncertain system; *Sextans* without and with monogram Ⅴ., uncertain denominations with mon. Ⅴ. STRUCK COINS. Triental system; *Quadrans* without mon., *Sextans, uncia* and *Semuncia* with mon. Ⅴ. Sextantal and Uncial systems; *Nummus, Quincunx, Quadrans, Sextans* and *Sescuncia* with mon. Ⅴ.

VER. *(Verus)*, on coins of Maximus—C. IVL. VER. MAXIMVS CAES. *Caius Julius Verus Maximus Cæsar.*

VER. *(Vergilius?)*, GAR. *(Garvilius?)*, OC Ⅴ. *(Oculnius?)* or VER. OC Ⅴ . GAR. Moneyers on coins struck about B.C. 81, and usually attributed to the *Vergilia, Garvilia* and *Oculnia* families. The reading GAR. (instead of CAR.) has been definitely established by Borghesi (*Dec.* iii., 6; *Œuvres compl.*, vol. i., p. 206). Mommsen is of opinion *(Mon. Rom.*, vol. ii., p. 451, *note)* that the three names are three surnames *(cognomina)*, and that consequently one must erase from the list of monetary families the *Carvilia* or *Garvilia*, the *Gargonia*, the *Oculnia*, the *Vergilia*, or *Verginia*, but he allows that the legends are not any the less difficult to complete. The following varieties of the legends may be found :—

    (a) GAR. OCVL. VER.
    (b) GAR. VER. OCVL.
    (c) OCVL. GAR. VER.
    (d) OCVL. VER. GAR.
    (e) VER. GAR. OCVL.
    (f) VER. OCVL. GAR.
    (g) Without legend and without name of moneyer. *Denarii.*

The legends *a, b, c, d, e,* occur upon the *denarii*, and *a, b, c, d, e, f,* on the *asses.* Sometimes on the *as* the AR of CAR. is joined. The *denarii a, b, c,* and *d,* exist with the countermark of Vespasian [VES.] See CARVILIA *gens*, where a specimen of the ordinary type is engraved.

Ⅴ RGILIV. *(Vergilius)* on a brass coin of Pæstum.—A. Ⅴ RGILIV. A. Ⱶ. (for F) IIVIR. *Aulus Vergilius Auli filius duumvir.* (Eckhel, *Cat. Mus. Cæs.* I., p. 25, Nos. 14, 15, pl. i., fig. 9.)

VERINA *(Ælia)*, wife of Leo. I. (A.D. 457-474), by whom she had two daughters, one Ariadne, married to Zeno (of whom there are extant coins), the other Leontia, married to Marcian, son of Anthemius. After the death of her husband she assisted at the coronation of her grandson, Leo II., the son of Ariadne and Zeno, to whom Leo I. had bequeathed the kingdom, but who died the same year. Verina conspired against Zeno and was banished and confined in the Fort of Papurius in Cilicia, from which place she was released by the consul Illus about A.D. 484, who defeated the army of Zeno near Antioch, and was induced to crown Leontius, an officer of the army, at Tarsus. Illus, however, soon sent Verina back to Papurius, where she shortly afterwards died. The following coins of Ælia Verina are in existence :—

1. *Obv.* AEL. VERINA [or Ɔ ERINA] AVG. Bust of Verina to r., diademed, crowned by a hand. *Rev.* VICTORIA AVGGG. A or B or O or Θ. Victory standing to l., holding a long cross. In the *field* to r. a star ; in the *exergue* CONOB. *N.* (250 frcs.)

2. *Obv.* AEL. VERINA AVG. Bust of Verina to r. *Rev.* Cross in a laurel crown. In the *exergue* CONOB. *N.* *Tremissis*. (150 frcs.)

3. *Obv.* Same as No. 1. *Rev.* SALVS REIPVBLICAE. Victory seated to r., before a pillar, surmounted by a shield, on which she is drawing the monogram of Christ. In the *exergue* CON. Æ. (80 frcs.)

Verissimus, a title of affection bestowed upon Marcus Aurelius by Hadrian (Xiph. ex. Dio. L. lxix., § 21.) It does not occur on Latin coins, but on a piece struck at Tyra Sarmatiæ, on which is the head of Marcus Aurelius, may be read the legend BHPICCIMOC KAICAP. According to Herodian (I, 2.) Annius Verus was also called βηρισσιμος.

VERITAS *(sic.)* AVG. for VBERITAS AVG., on coins of Trajan Decius and Etruscilla.

VERO. On a brass coin of Lucius Verus, struck at Parlais Lycaoniæ—L. AVRELIO VERO. (Eckhel, *Sylloge* I., p. 53, pl. v., fig. 11.)

VERRIO. On brass coins of Augustus struck at Cæsar Augusta Hispaniæ—CAESAR AVGVSTA C. ALLIARIO [or C. ALLIAR. or ALLIÁR.] T. VERRIO IIVIR. (Cohen, *Méd Imp.*, 2nd ed., vol. i., p. 153, Nos. 654—656.)

Verus. A name of Ælius Cæsar (Lucius Aurelius *Verus*), of Marcus Aurelius (Annius *Verus*), of Maximinus I. (Caius Julius *Verus*), and of Maximus (Caius Julius *Verus.*)

VERVS (Annius), son of Marcus Aurelius and Faustina II. was born in A.D. 163, and was made *Cæsar* in A.D. 166, together with his brother Commodus. He died at Præneste in A.D. 170 at the age of seven years.

No Roman coins of Annius Verus with his head *alone* exist, though Cohen has suggested (*Méd. Imp.*, 1st ed., vol. i., p. 464) that some third brass coins (Nos. 17, 18), with the head of an infant may give a representation of him. There are, however, some accompanied by the head of Commodus; 1. *Obv.* COMMODVS CAES. VERVS CAES. Busts of Commodus and Verus facing, bare, with *paludamentum. Rev.* TEMPORVM FELICITAS. The four seasons represented by four children; the first (Spring), naked, bears on his shoulders a basket; the second (Summer), naked, holds a *falx* and ears of corn; the third (Autumn), naked, holds by its legs a fawn and a *patera* of fruit; the fourth (Winter), hooded and wearing tunic, holds a hare and a stick, from which hang a brace of birds (?). Æ. Med. (700 frcs.) 2. *Obv.* ANNIVS VERVS CAES. ANTONINI AVG. FIL. Bust of Annius Verus to l., bare, with *paludamentum. Rev.* COMMODVS CAES. ANTONINI AVG. FIL. Bust of Commodus to r., bare, with *paludamentum.* Æ. I. (1200 frcs.)—The head on the Latin coins, probably struck at Parium, with the legend VERVS ET FAVSTINA AVG., attributed by Cohen (*Méd. Imp.*, 2nd ed., vol. ii., p. 413) to Antoninus Pius, Annius Verus, and Faustina II., is considered by the editors to be more probably that of Marcus Aurelius. Greek coins of Marcus Aurelius, Lucius Verus, Annius Verus and Commodus, and of Marcus Aurelius, Annius Verus and Commodus are known (Cohen, *Méd. Imp.*, 1st ed., vol. ii., p. 576.)

VERUS (Lucius), whose original name was *Lucius Ceionius Commodus*, to which was added *Ælius Aurelius* and perhaps *Antoninus*, son of Ælius Verus, was born at Rome in A.D. 130. After the death of Antoninus Pius in A.D. 161, he received the titles of *Cæsar* and *Augustus*, and was raised to the joint sovereignty by Marcus Aurelius, his brother by adoption. After being betrothed to Lucilla, the daughter of Aurelius, he started in A.D. 161 for Syria to fight Vologeses III., King of

Parthia. Having succeeded by means of his generals in conquering Parthia, Mesopotamia, and Armenia (as recorded on his coins), and reinstating the King Soæmus on the throne (represented on coins), he returned home in A.D. 166 to celebrate a triumph with his brother, receiving the titles of *Armeniacus, Parthicus Maximus*, and *Medicus*, the first two of which occur frequently upon his coins, and the third only *once* on a large brass coin, with the reverse legend TR. POT. VI. IMP. III., &c. His marriage with Lucilla had taken place in A.D. 164. Later the two emperors started to prosecute the war in Germany, and in A.D. 168, returned to Rome. The following year, however, on again starting to join the army, Verus was seized with apoplexy and died at Altinum, a city of Venetia. Lucius Verus was three times *Consul*, received the *Tribunitia Potestas* nine times, and was five times *Imperator.*

The principal reverse legends are—*Silver medallions :*—SALVS (in *exergue)* TR. POT. V. IMP. II. COS. II. (400 frcs.) *Gold Coins :*—ARMEN (in *exergue)* TR. P. III. [or IIII.] IMP. II. COS. II. (45 frcs.) CONCORDIAE AVGVSTOR. TR. P. COS. II. Lucius Verus and Marcus Aurelius standing shaking hands (35 frcs.) ; CONG. AVG. IIII. TR. P. VII. IMP. IIII. COS. III. (40 frcs.) ; FORT. RED. TR. POT. COS. II. or TR. P. VIII. IMP. V. COS. III. (35 frcs.) ; HERC. PAC. TR. P. IIII. IMP. II. COS. II. (100 frcs.) ; LIB. AVGVSTOR. TR. P. COS. II. Lucius Verus and M. Aurelius, seated (100 frcs.) ; PAX (in *exergue)* TR. P. VI. IMP. IIII. COS. II. (35 frcs.) ; PROFECTIO AVG. TR. P. II. COS. II. Verus on horseback (60 frcs.) ; PROV. DEOR. TR. P. COS. II. (40 frcs.) ; REX. ARMEN. DAT. (in *exergue)* TR. P. IIII. IMP. II. COS. II. Verus seated on a stage, behind him a prætorian præfect ; in front a soldier ; at the foot of the stage, the King Soæmus standing (100 frcs.) ; SALVTI AVGVSTOR. TR. P. III. COS. II. (35 (frcs) ; TR. POT. COS. I. Verus and Aurelius seated (100 frcs.) ; TR. POT. COS. II. *(Quin.* 120 frcs.) ; a variety of types with TR. P. III. IMP. II. COS. II. to TR. P. VIII. IMP. V. COS. III. (35 to 60 frcs. ; *Quin.* 120 frcs.) ; VICT. AVG. TR. P. VI. COS. II. (45 frcs.)

Silver Coins :—ARMEN. (in *exergue)* TR. P. III. IMP. COS. II. (3 frcs.) ; CONCORD. AVG. COS. II. (c.) ; CONSECRATIO (12 frcs.) ; COS. II. (5 frcs.) ; FORT. RED. TR. P. VIII. IMP. V. COS. III. (c.) ; LIB. AVG. III. TR. P. VI. COS. II. (6 frcs.) ; PAX (in *exergue)* TR. P. VI. IMP. IIII. COS. II. (c.), PIETAS AVG. TR. P. VI. COS. II. (3 frcs.) ; PROV. DEOR. TR. P. COS. II. (c.) ; a variety of types with TR. P. III. IMP. II. COS. II. to TR. P. VIII. IMP. V. COS. III. (c.) ; VICT. AVG. TR. P. VI. COS. II. (3 frcs.)

Brass Medallions :—ADLOCVT. M. Aurelius and Verus standing on a stage, accompanied by a prætorian præfect haranguing five soldiers (400 frcs.) ; ARMENIA (in *exergue)* TR. P. VIII. IMP. IIII. COS. III.—sometimes ARMENIA alone —Lucius Verus galloping to r., and directing his spear against an Armenian ; two soldiers standing (600 frcs.) ; COS. III. Rome, helmeted, seated, and Victory standing crowning her; Lucius Verus standing presenting an olive wreath (200 frcs.); FELICITAS (?) SAECVLI (150 frcs.); various types with the legend TR. P. VI. IMP. IIII. COS. III. to TR. P. VIII. IMP. V. COS. III. (300 to 500 frcs.); various types without legend (250 to 300 frcs.) *Brass coins :* Legends and types similar to those of the gold and silver (2 to 200 frcs.), CONSECRA-TIO. Lucius Verus seated in a quadriga of elephants (30 frcs.)   Brass medallions and first and second brass coins of M. Aurelius and Verus (400 frcs.—100 frcs.) and Greek coins of Aurelius, Faustina II., and Lucius Verus, struck at Sagalassa, and of Aurelius, Lucius Verus, Annius Verus, and Commodus, struck at Syros, are in existence.

Coins of Lucius Verus were struck in the following colonies :—Coela Chersonesi; Cassandrea Macedoniæ; Corinthus and Patras Achaiæ; Parium Mysiæ; Parlais Lycaoniæ; Antiochia Pisidiæ; Cæsarea Samariæ; Ælia Capitolina Judææ, and Berytus Phoeniciæ, generally with head of M. Aurelius.

VES. *Vespasianus.*—IMP. VES. *Imperator Vespasianus* or sometimes VESPAS. (in monogram) *Vespasianus*, a counter-mark of frequent occurrence on family *denarii*, notably the *Sergia, Porcia, Servilia, Carvilia* and *Plancia* families. (Mommsen, *Mom. Rom.*, vol. ii., pp. 361, 397, 451, 496; cf. M. Bahrfeldt, *Contremarken Vespasians auf Römischen Familiendenaren* in the *Zeitschrift für Num.*, 1876, vol. iii., pp. 354—374) ; and on legionary *denarii* of M. Antony and coins of Augustus. The countermarks IMP. GAL. *(Imperator Galba)* and IMP. OTHO as well as IMP. VES. were stamped by the army of Syria, and VESPAS. by the army of Mœsia always on the portrait of Nero (Lenormant, *La Mon. dans l'Antiq.*, vol. ii., p. 390), but as a rule the countermarks were placed to avoid the head of the Emperor. Countermarks cease generally about the reign of Vespasian.

VES. *(Vespasianus)*, on coins of Vespasian, of Vespasian with Titus (VES.) and Domitian, of Domitilla I. struck after her death, and of Titus.

VES. or VE꜏. [*Vestini.*]

VESP. *Vespasiani.* CAESARES VESP. AVG. FILI. *Cæsares Augusti Vespasiani filii*, on coins of Vespasian;—AVG. VESP. LIBERI IMP. *Augusti Vespasiani Liberi Imperatoris* on coins of Vespasian with Titus and Domitian;—VESP. AVG. EIᴦL *(sic)* CAESERES *(sic)*. *Vespasiani Augusti Liberi* (?) *Cæsares* (Titus and Domitian standing) on coins of Vespasian; IMP. T. CAES. DIVI VESP. F. AVG., &c., *Imperator Titus Cæsar Divi Vespasiani filius Augustus*, &c., on coins of Domitilla I., struck to her memory by Titus; CAES. DIVI [AVG.] VESP. F. &c., *Cæsar Divi [Augusti] Vespasiani filius*, &c., on coins of Domitian.

VESP. *Vespasiano.*—DIVO AVG. VESP. S. P. Q. R. *Divo Augusto Vespasiano Senatus Populusque Romanus* on coins of Vespasian struck after his death by Titus in A.D. 80; DIVO

VESP. *Divo Vespasiano* on silver medallion of Domitian, struck in Asia in A.D. 80.

VESP. *(Vespasianus)*, on coins of Vespasian and Titus.

VESPA. *(Vespasianus)*, on coins of Vespasian and Vespasian with Titus and Domitian.

VESPAS. *Vespasiani.* CAE. DVM. *(sic)* ET TI. *(sic)* CAES. IMP. VESPAS. *(Imperatoris Vespasiani)* ; LIBERI IMP. VESPAS. *Liberi Imperatoris Vespasiani* on coins of Vespasian with Titus and Domitian.

VESPAS. *Vespasiano.* DIVO. AVG. VESPAS. S. P. Q. R. *Divo Augusto Vespasiano Senatus Populusque Romanus* on coins of Vespasian, struck after his death by Titus in A.D. 80.

VESPAS. *(Vespasianus)*, on coins of Vespasian (Rome) and of Titus struck at Sinope Paphlagoniæ (Cohen, *Méd. Imp.*, 2nd ed., vol. i., p. 463, No. 408.)

VESPASI. *Vespasiani.* IMP. T. CAESAR DIVI VESPASI. AVG. *Imperator Titus Cæsar Divi Vespasiani Augusti*, on coins of Titus.

VESPASIA. *Vespasianus.* IMP. CAES. VESPASIA. AVG. *Imperator Cæsar Vespasianus Augustus*, on brass coins of Vespasian, struck at Cassandrea Macedoniæ (Cohen, *Méd. Imp.*, 2nd ed., vol. i., p. 420, No. 653.)

Vespasia Polla, mother of Vespasian. No coins.

VESPASIAN. *(Vespasianus)*, on coins of Vespasian and Titus.

VESPASIANVS. Vespasian standing to l. in military dress, raising r. hand, and holding a spear. *Obv.* No legend. Head of the sun facing, radiated. Æ. (250 frcs.)

VESPASIANVS (Flavius), Roman Emperor from A.D. 70—79, was born in the country of the Sabines A.D. 9, his father being Flavius Sabinus, a man of low extraction, and his mother Vespasia Polla, the daughter of a *Præfectus Castrorum.* During the reign of Claudius he was employed in a military capacity in Germany and in the Isle of Wight, and under Nero he was made Proconsul of Africa; and when the Jewish war broke out in A.D. 66 he was sent by Nero to the East. He continued the Jewish war during the struggles between Galba, Otho and Vitellius, and towards the end of A.D. 69, on the death of Otho, he was proclaimed Emperor at Alexandria, in Judæa, and soon after (A.D. 70), on the death of Vitellius, at Rome. In A.D. 71 his son Titus, who had been left to prosecute the Jewish war, returned to Rome, taking with him the spoils from the Temple at Jerusalem, and celebrated with his father a triumph. The Temple of Janus was closed, and Vespasian rebuilt the Temple of Jupiter Capitolinus, which had been burnt during the troubles under Vitellius. The Temple is represented on coins. In A.D. 72, owing to information received by Vespasian that Antiochus king of Commagene and his son Epiphanes were in treaty with the Parthian king, Commagene was occupied by Pætus, Governor of Syria, and made a Roman province. The murder of Sabinus and his faithful wife Epponina leaves a stain upon the memory of Vespasian. He died in A.D. 79, at the age of 69, having reigned nearly 10 years. His wife Domitilla and her daughter Domitilla died before he came to the throne, but his two sons, Titus and Domitian succeeded him in turn.

Vespasian was nine times *Consul*, twenty times *Imperator*, and received the *Tribunitia Potestas* ten times.

The principal reverse legends are: *Gold Coins:*—AETERNITAS (45 frcs.); ANNONA AVG. (35 to 40 frcs.); CAESARES VESP. AVG. FILI. Titus and Domitian standing, from *Caylus* (200 frcs.); CERES AVGVST. (50 frcs.); CONCORDIA AVG. (40 frcs.); CONSEN. EXERCIT. from *Caylus* (70 frcs.); COS. DESIG. III. TR. POT. (50 frcs.); COS. ITER. TR. POT. (40 frcs.); COS III. FORT RED. (40 to 50 frcs.); COS. III. TR. POT. (50 frcs.); COS. V. or VI. or VII. or VIII. (45 to 100 frs.): DE IVDAEIS. Trophy (50 frcs.); EX S. C. struck after his death (50 to 100 frcs.); FORTVNA AVGVST. (40 frcs.); HISPANIA (80 frcs.); IMP. V. P. P. COS. II. DESIG. III. Rome standing, presenting a small Victory to Vespasian standing (150 frcs.); IMP. XIIII. Bull rushing (100 frcs.); IVDAEA (50 frs.); IVDAEA DEVICTA (50 frcs.); MARS VLTOR (40 frcs.); NEP. RED. (40 frcs.); PACI AVGVSTI (40 frcs.); PACI ORB. TERR. AVG. Turreted bust of Peace (350 frcs.); PAX or PAX AVG. or AVGVST. (40 to 300 frcs.); ROMA (200 frcs.); S. C. on a shield held by two capricorns—struck after his death (45 frcs.); S.P.Q.R. (45 frcs.); TITVS ET DOMITIAN. CAES. PRIN. IVVEN. Titus and Domitian seated; or on horseback (60 frcs.); TR. POT. COS. III. or VIIII. (40 frcs.); TR. POT. X COS. VIIII. (50 to 100 frcs.); TRIVMP. AVG. Vespasian in a quadriga crowned by Victory; in front a soldier and a captive, behind a flute player (300 frcs.); VESTA. Temple (50 frcs.); VIC. AVG. (40 frcs.); VICT. AVG., perhaps struck in Judæa (250 frcs.); VICTORIA AVGVST. (40 to 120 frcs.); No legend. Vespasian in a quadriga (60 frcs.); Judæa seated at foot of palm tree; behind, Vespasian standing (120 frcs.)

Silver Coins:—ANNONA AVG. (2 frcs.); AVG. in a laurel crown—sometimes ⊖, struck at Ephesus (10 frcs.); AVG. EPHE. in monogram (20 frcs.); AVGVR PON. MAX. or TRI. POT. (2 frcs.); CERES AVGVST. (2 frcs.); CONCORDIA AVG. sometimes in the *exergue* EPHE. in monogram or ⊖, struck at Ephesus (10 frcs.); CONCORDIA AVGVSTI or EXERCITVVM (10 frcs.);

CONSEN. or CONSENSVS EXERCIT. (20 frcs.); COS. ITER. FORT. RED or TR. POT. (2 frcs.); COS. III. Eagle (20 frcs.); COS. III. FORT. RED (2 frcs.); COS. V. or VI. or VII. or VIII. (2 frcs.); DE IVDAEIS (20 frcs.); EX S. C. struck after his death (6 to 10 frcs.); FIDES PVBL. (5 frcs.); FORTVNA AVGVST. (2 frcs.); GENIVM P. R. (30 frcs.); IMP. XIII. Sow and three young (20 frcs.); IMP. XIX. (2 frcs.); IMP. XIX. Herdsman seated milking a goat (50 frcs.); IMPER. Vespasian galloping to l. (20 frcs.); IOVIS CVSTOS (2 frcs.); IVDAEA (5 to 12 frcs.); IVDAEA DEVICTA (15 frcs.); LIBERI IMP. AVG. VESPAS. Titus and Domitian standing, on some in *exergue* EPE., struck at Ephesus (12 to 15 frcs.); LIBERTAS PVBLICA (6 frcs.); MARS CONSERV. (50 frcs.); MARS VLTOR (6 frcs.); NEP. RED. (20 frcs.): PACI AVGVSTAE, sometimes in the *field* a star or EPE., struck at Ephesus (12 to 20 frcs.); PACI AVGVSTI (2 frcs.); PACI ORB. TERR. AVG. Turreted bust of Peace; below ⊖, struck at Ephesus (20 frcs.); PACIS EVENT. (50 frcs.); PAX AVG. (6 to 40 frcs.); PON. MAX. (3 frcs.); PON. MAX. TR. P. COS. III. or COS. V. or COS. VI. or COS. VII. (2 frcs.); PONT. MAX. or PONTIF. MAXIM. (2 frcs.); PONTIF. TR. P. COS. III. or COS. IIII. (6 frcs.); PRINCEPS IVVENTVT. or PRINCIP. IVVENT. (10 frcs.); ROMA RESVRGENS. Vespasian standing, raising Rome kneeling (80 frcs.); SALVS. AVG. (2 frcs.); S. C. on a shield held by two capricorns—struck after his death (6 frcs.); S. P. Q. R. (2 to 6 frcs.); T. CAESAR. Titus in a *quadriga* (20 frcs.); TITVS ET DOMITIAN CAES. PRIN. IV. or CAESARES PRIN. IVVEN. Titus and Domitian seated (12 frcs.); TR. P. IX. IMP. C. . . (20 frcs.); TR. POT. X. COS. VIIII. (3 to 6 frcs.); TRI. POT. Vesta seated (2 frcs., *Quinarius?* 20 frcs.); TRI. POT. II. COS. III. P. P. (2 frcs.); VESPASIANVS. Vespasian standing (250 frcs.); VESTA. Vesta standing (2 frcs.); Temple (25 frcs.); VIC. AVG. or VICTORIA AVG. (2 frcs.); VICTORIA AVGVST. or AVGVSTI. *Quinarius* (20 frcs.); VICTORIA IMP. VESPASIANI (100 frcs.); VIRTVS AVGVST. (30 frcs.); *No legend.* Vespasian in a *quadriga* (6 frcs.); Judæa seated at the foot of palm tree; behind, Vespasian standing (6 frcs.); Two hands joined, holding the Roman eagle between two military standards (20 frcs.)

Brass Coins:—AEQVITAS AVGVST. or AVGVSTI S. C. (Æ. II. 2 to 6 frcs.); AETERNITAS AVGVSTI S. C. (Æ. II. 8 frcs.); AETERNITAS P.R.S.C. Victory presenting the *palladium* to Vespasian (Æ. I. 150 frcs., Æ. II. 30 frcs.); ANNONA AVGVST. S. C. (Æ. I. 6 frcs.); CAES. AVG. F. DES. [or DESIG.] IMP. AVG. F. COS DES. [or DESIG.] IT. [or ITE. or ITER.] [or COS. DES. II.] S. C. Titus and Domitian standing, holding spear and *parazonium* (Æ. I. 20 frcs.); CERES AVGVST. (Æ. II. 3 frcs.)—struck after his death (Æ. II. 20 frcs.); CONCOR. AVG. S. C. (Æ. I., 6 frcs.); CONCORD. AVGVST S. C. (Æ. II., 10 frcs.); CONCORDIA AVG. or AVGVST. or AVGVSTI (Æ. I. and II. 2 to 6 frcs.); CONCORDIA SENATVI (*sic*) S. C. Vespasian standing, holding Victory and branch, and crowned by a Senator (or the Genius of the Senate) who holds an olive branch (Æ. I. 200 frcs.); COS. ITER. FORT. RED. S. C. (Æ. II. 6 frcs.); DEVICTA IVDAEA S. C. Victory standing, fixing a shield to a palm tree, at the foot of which Judæa is seated; on the shield S.P.Q.R. (Æ. I. 40 frcs.); FELICITAS PVBLICA S. C. (Æ. II. 2 to 10 frcs.); FIDES EXERCI-TVVM S. C. (Æ. I. 10 frcs.); FIDES FORTVNA S. C. (Æ. II. 50 frcs.); FIDES PVBLICA S. C. (Æ. I. and II. 2 to 4 frcs.); FORTVNAE REDVCI S. C. (Æ. I. and II. 2 to 6 frcs.); HONOS ET VIRTVS S. C. (Æ. I. 15 frcs.); IMP. (T. CAES AVG. F. DES.?) IMP. DOMITIAN. AVG. F. COS. DESIG. II. S. C. Titus and Domitian standing (Æ. I. 30 frcs.); IVD. CAP. S. C. (Æ. III. 10 frcs.); IVDAEA CAPTA S. C.—variety of types (Æ. I. and II. 3 to 20 frcs.); LIBERTAS AVGVSTI S. C. (Æ. I. and II. 2 to 6 frcs.); LIBERTAS RESTITVTA S. C. Vespasian standing, raising Liberty, who kneels, and who is presented to him by Rome, in military dress (Æ. I. 150 frcs.); MARS VICTOR S. C. (Æ. I. 6 to 10 frcs.); PAX AVG. [or AVGVST. or AVGVSTI] S. C. (Æ. I. and II. 2 to 20 frcs.); P.M. [or PON. M.] TR. P. P.P. COS. III. [or V. or VI. or VIII.] S. C. (Æ. III. 2 frcs.); P. M. TRIB. POT. COS. IIII. (3 frcs); PON. MAX TR. POT. P. P. COS. V. CENS. (Æ. II. 10 frcs.); PONTIF. MAX.? TR. P. COS. VII. CENS. (Æ. III. 12 frcs.); (PON.? or PONTIF. MAX.) TR. POT. P.P. COS. VIIII. CENS. S. C. Victory standing striking a bull with a hammer (Æ. II. 100 frcs.); PONTIF. MAXIM. S. C. (Æ. II. 2 frcs.); PRINCIP. INVENT. S.C. Titus, or Domitian galloping to l. (Æ. II. 2 frcs.); PROVIDENT. S. C. (Æ. II., 2 frcs.); REDVCI FORTVNAE S. C. (Æ. II. 2 frcs.); REDVCIS FELICITA. S.C. (Æ. II. 8 frcs.); ROMA S. C. Rome seated leaning her back against seven hills, holding the para-zonium; at the foot of the hills, a wolf suck-ling Romulus and Remus; to the r. the Tiber seated (Æ. I. 150 frcs.); ROMA S. C. Rome seated or standing (Æ. I. and II. 2 to 15 frcs.); COS. ITERVM TRIBVN. POT. ROMA ET AVGVSTVS. Rome standing giving her hand to Vespasian (Æ. I. 100 frcs.); ROMA RESVRGES S. C. Ves-pasian standing raising Rome kneeling, who is presented to him by Minerva (Æ. I. 100 frcs.); ROMA VICTRIX S. C. (Æ. I. and II. 2 to 20 frcs); SALVS AVGVSTA [or AVGVSTI] S. C. Salus seated (Æ. I. 4 frcs.); SALVS AVGVSTI S. C. Salus standing (Æ. II. 10 frcs.); S. C. Various types, among them Vespasian in a quadriga to r.; Vespasian, radiated, his foot placed on a prow, holding a Victory, at his feet a Jew kneel-ing and a Jewess running, behind, a palm; Hexastyle Temple (of Jupiter Capitolinus), in the middle, Jupiter between Juno and Minerva, on either side a statue, on the pedi-ment a statue between two figures, two gronps of wrestlers, standards, warriors, and at each corner an eagle (Æ. I. and II. 2 to 100 frcs., Æ. III. 2 frcs.); SECVRITAS AVGVSTI S. C. (Æ. II. 3 frcs.); SIGNIS RECEPTIS S. C. Victory presenting a Roman eagle to Vespasian on a stage (Æ. I. 100 frcs.); SPES AVGVSTA S. C. (Æ. I. 150 frcs.); S. P. Q. R. ADSERTORI LIBERTA-

TIS PVBLIC. [or PVBLICAE] S.C. (Æ. I. 40 frcs.); S. P. Q. R. OB CIV. SER [or CIVES SERVATOS] S. C. (Æ. I. and II. 6 frcs.); T. ET DOM. C. EX S. C. Titus and Domitian seated (Æ. I. 60 frcs.); T. ET DOMITIAN. CAESARES PRIN. [or PRINC.] IVVEN. S C. Titus and Domitian on horseback (Æ. I. and II. 15 to 80 frcs.); IMP. . . . SAR DOMITIANVS AVG. F. COS. DESG. (sic) II. S. C. Titus and Domitian standing (Æ. I. 60 frcs.); VESTA S. C. (Æ. II. 3 to 6 frcs.); VICTORIA AVG. [or AVGVST. or AVGVSTI] S. C. (Æ. I. and II. 2 to 100 frcs.) :· VICTORIA NAVALIS S. C. (Æ. II. 2 frcs.) Gold coins of Vespasian restored by Trajan (400 to 1200 frcs.); Billon coins restored by Gallienus (4 frcs.)

Coins of Vespasian were struck in the fol-following colonies: Cassandrea, Stobi, Philippi Macedoniæ, Antiochia Syriæ, and Berytus Phoeniciæ.

VESPASIANVS (Flavius) [TITVS.]

VESPASIANVS IVNIOR was the son of Flavius Clemens, cousin-german of the Emperor Domitian and his colleague in the consulship A.D. 95, and of Domitilla, a relation of Domi-tian, perhaps the daughter of Domitilla II., the daughter of Vespasian. Domitian had destined the two sons of Clemens as his suc-cessors, and discarding their former names, ordered one to be called Vespasian and the other Domitian (Suet. in Dom. 15.) Flavius Clemens was however put to death during his consulship by order of Domitian, and history is silent as to the fate of his two sons.

The only coins existing of Vespasian Junior are Greek, struck at Smyrna. Obv. ΟΥΕCΠΑCΙΑΝΟC ΝΕΩΤΕΡΟC. Head to r., laureated. Rev. CΜΥΡΝΑΙΩΝ. Victory walking to r., holding crown and palm. Æ. III. (100 frcs.)

VEST. (Vesta), on a denarius of the Cassia gens, probably struck by L. Cassius, quæstor in B.C. 55, and Tribune of the people in B.C. 49. Obv. Q. CASSIVS. VEST. Veiled female head to r. Rev. A temple within which a curule chair; in the field to l. a voting urn, and to r., a voting tablet, on which are the letters A (Absolvo) and C (Condemno). R. (3 frcs., Cohen, Méd. Cons. Cassia, pl. xi., No. 8; Mommsen, Mon. Rom., vol. ii., p. 503.) This coin was restored by Trajan (300 frcs.)

Vesta, one of the great Roman Divinities, the goddess of the hearth and of fire, and identical with the Greek Ἑστία. She was supposed to personify the Earth, and conse-quently her temple was built round, in which a fire was continually kept burning by the Vestal Virgins. [VESTALES.] The type of Vesta as well as that of her temple, occurs frequently on Roman coins from the time of Caligula.

VESTA. Vesta veiled, seated to l., holding palladium and patera or sceptre, on coins of Caligula (Æ. II. 2 frcs.), of Claudius (Æ. II.), of Galba (Æ. II. 6 frcs.), of Vespasian and Titus (Æ. II. 3 frcs.). of Julia, daughter of Titus (Æ. Med. 150 frcs., R. 30 to 40 frcs., Æ. II. 8 frcs), of Trajan (R. 2 frcs.), of

Hadrian (Æ. I. 200 frcs.), of Sabina (N. 120 frcs., Æ. 2 frcs., Æ. I. and II. 4 to 8 frcs.), of Faustina I. (N. 35 frcs., Æ., c., Æ. II. 3 frcs.), and on her medallions without legend (Æ. Med., 300 to 400 frcs.), of Faustina II. (Æ. 3 frcs.), of J. Domna (N. 200 frcs. Æ. c., Æ. I. and II. 3 to 15 frcs.), of Cornelia Supera (Æ. 400 frcs.), and of Salonina (Bil. c.)

A brass medallion of Faustina II. (300 frcs.), represents Vesta veiled, seated to l., holding a sceptre; before her Faustina II., standing, presenting to her three small statues, representing the three Graces.

VESTA. Vesta standing to l., holding *simpulum* and sceptre—sometimes *palladium*—on coins of Vespasian and Titus (Æ. II., 3 frcs.), of Faustina I. (Æ. c. Æ. I. 10 frcs.),—also Vesta standing near an altar behind which a column, surmounted by a statue of Minerva, behind a temple—a type also on a medallion of Aurelius and L. Verus (Æ. Med., 300 to 400 frcs.), of Faustina II. (Æ. I. and II. c.), of Lucilla, (Æ. c. Æ. I. 5 frcs.), of Julia Domna (Æ. c.) of Aquillia Severa (Æ. 40 frcs.), of Soæmias (Æ. 10. frcs.), of Mæsa (Æ. 4 frcs.), of Cornelia Supera (Æ. 400 frcs.), of Valerian I. Æ. I. 15 frcs.), of Gallienus (Bil. 2 frcs., Æ. I. 30 frcs.), and of Salonina (N. 600 frcs.; Bil. c., Æ. I. 20 frcs.)

VESTA. Hexastyle round temple; in the centre, Vesta seated, holding a sceptre. Obv. NERO CAESAR AVGVSTVS. Head of Nero to r., laureated (N. 60 frs.; Æ. 10 frcs.)

VESTA. Tetrastyle round temple; in the centre, and on either side a statue; on coins of Vespasian and Titus (Vespasian N. 50 frcs., Æ. 25 frcs., Titus Æ. 25 frcs.)

VESTA S. C. Vesta standing in a tetrastyle temple, with or without a statue above; on coins of Vespasian and Titus (Æ. II. 6 to 12 frcs.)

VESTA S. C. Four or six vestals standing accompanied by two children, sacrificing at an adorned and lighted altar outside a tetrastyle round temple, in the centre of which a statue of Vesta is seated; above a statue. Obv. IVLIA PIA FELIX AVG. Bust of J. Domna to r. or to l. (N. 300 frcs.; Æ. I. 40 to 50 frcs.; Æ. II. 12 to 60 frcs.)

Brass medallions of Faustina I., and of Lucilla (300 frcs.) represent six Vestals sacrificing at an altar outside a tetrastyle round temple, within which a statue of Vesta. Other examples of Vesta or her temple doubtless occur.

VESTA AETERNA. Vesta standing to l. holding the *palladium* and a sceptre. Obv. CORN. SALONINA AVG. Bust of Salonina to r., diademed with the crescent. Bil. (3 frcs.)

VESTA FELIX. Vesta standing to l., holding *simpulum* and a sceptre on a coin of Gallienus from *Banduri* (Bil. 8 frcs.) and on coins of Salonina. (Bil. 2 frcs.; Æ. II. from *Wiczay*, 15 frcs.)

VESTA MATER. Tetrastyle temple with statues, before which one, two, or six Vestals sacrificing. (N. 60 to 300 frcs., Æ. 25 frcs.,

Æ. Med. 600 frcs., Æ. I. and II. 15 to 60 frcs.); or Vesta seated to l., holding *palladium* and sceptre (Æ. c.), on coins of Julia Domna.

VESTA P. R. [*Populi Romani*] QVIRITIVM. Vesta seated to l. holding a *patera* and a torch. Obv. A VITELLIVS IMP. GERMAN. Head of Vitellius to r., laureated. (N. 200 frcs.; Æ. 10 frcs.; a variety in silver has the obv. leg. A. VITELLIVS GER. IMP. AVG. P. MAX. TR. P.) The same reverse type occurs on a silver autonomous coin struck between the reigns of Nero and Vespasian. Obv. I. O. M. [*Jupiter Optimus Maximus*] CAPITOLINVS. Bust of Jupiter to l., laureated; in front a palm. (30 frcs.)

VESTA P. R. [*Populi Romani*] QVIRITIVM. Bust of Vesta to r. diademed and veiled; in front a lighted torch. Rev. FIDES EXERCITVVM (VVM in monogram.) Two hands joined; or I. O. M. [or MAX.] CAPITOLINVS. Jupiter seated to l., in a distyle temple, holding a thunderbolt and a sceptre. Æ. (40 to 60 frcs.), or SENATVS. P Q. [*Populusque*] . . . . NVS [ROMANVS.] Victory walking to l., and holding a shield on which VI. AV. [*Victoria Augusti.*] Æ. (80 frcs.) Autonomous coins struck between the reigns of Nero and Vespasian.

VESTAE S. C. Three Priests and three Vestals, accompanied by an infant, sacrificing at an altar before a round tetrastyle temple. Obv. FAVSTINA AVG. ANTONINI AVG. PII F. Bust of Faustina to r. Æ. Med. (250 frcs. Note by Cohen—"a true medallion in spite of the letters s. c.")

VESTAE SANCTAE. Vesta standing to l., holding a *patera* and a sceptre. Obv. IVLIA AVGVSTA. Bust of Julia Domna to r. Æ. (4 frcs.)

Vestales Virgines or *Virgines Vestæ* were the Virgin Priestesses of Vesta. Their existence at Alba Longa dated from soon after the foundation of Rome. At first there were two, then four, and finally six, a number never exceeded. Their chief duty was to keep the eternal fire burning in the temple, each Vestal taking her turn in watching. Breach of chastity incurred fearful punishment.

VESTALIS. Vestal seated holding a *simpulum*. Obv. C. CLODIVS C. F. (*Caius Clodius Caii Filius.*) Head of Flora to r., crowned with flowers; behind, a flower. N. (250 frcs.) Æ. (6 frcs.) This coin was struck by Caius Clodius, who fought under Brutus, monetary quatuorvir in B.C. 43. The head of Flora recalls the fêtes instituted by Clodius Certho in B.C. 240, which were probably made annual in B.C. 173 by C. Servilius, whose son struck coins in B.C. 74-50 with the legend C. SERVEIL. C. F. FLORAL. PRIMVS. (*Caius Servilius Caii filius Floralia primus.*) The type of the Vestal recalls either Quinta Claudia (*circ.* B.C. 212), who, when a ship laden with things sacred to Cybele struck in the shallows of the Tiber, called upon the goddess to vindicate her innocence, and drew the vessel safe to shore; or the Vestal Virgin Claudia (B.C. 143) who, when her father Appius Claudius Pulcher resolved to have a triumph contrary to the will of the people, walked by his chariot to the Capitol, so that it might not be lawful for any of the tribunes to interfere and forbid it.

Vestini, a people of central Italy. The first mention of them in history is when they concluded an alliance with the Samnites against Rome in B.C. 324, but were defeated. In B.C. 301 they concluded a treaty with the Romans and remained faithful to Rome till the Social War in B.C. 90. They were again reduced to submission and received the Roman Franchise. The following coins are attributed to them (Mommsen, *Mon. Rom.*, vol. ii., p. 354 ; *Cat. of Greek Coins in British Museum.* Italy, p. 43):—Æs grave. *Triens* with VE≤ ; *Sextans* with VE≤ ; *Uncia* with VES ; *Semuncia* with VES.

VESTRAE. MONETA VRBIS VESTRAE on brass medallions of Crispus and Constantine II.

VET. *Veteranorum* ?— COL. I. F. DIAN. VET. *Colonia Julia Felix Diana Veteranorum* on a large brass coin of Juba II., struck at Zama Numidiæ. (Boutkowski, *Dictionnaire Numismatique*, vol. i., pp. 215-218.)

VET. *Vettio.* CAES. AVGVS. [AE and AV joined] or CAESAR AVGVSTA CN. DOM. AMP. C. VET. LANC. [AMP. aud AN. joined] IIVIR on brass coins of Augustus, struck at Cæsar Augusta Hispaniæ. (Cohen, *Méd. Imp.*, 2nd ed., vol. i., pp. 153, 154, Nos. 657-660). Akerman *(Coins of Cities and Princes*, p. 73), gives a similar legend on brass coins of Caius and Lucius Cæsar.

VETE. *Vetere.* C. CARRI. [RI joined] AQVIL. L. IVNI. VETE. IIVIR C. C. A. on brass coins of Tiberius struck at Cæsar Augusta Hispaniæ. (Cohen, *Méd. Imp.*, 2nd ed., vol. i., p. 199, No. 109).

VETERA. RELIQVA VETERA HS NOVIES MILL. ABOLITA, on large brass coins of Hadrian.

VETRANIO, who commanded the legions iu Illyria and Pannonia at the murder of Constans by Magnentius in A.D. 350, followed the example of this usurper and assumed the purple at Sirmium. Constantius II. marched with his army to meet him, and on a plain near Serdica, Constantius II. appealing to the assembled armies that he was a son of the great Constantine, Vetrauio took off his diadem and abdicated. Constantius treated him with kindness and allowed him to retire to Prusa, in Bithynia, where he spent the remaining six years of his life.

The following coins were struck during his short reign of ten months :—

Gold Coins.

1. *Obv.* D. N. VETRANIO P. F. AVG. Bust of Vetranio to r., laureated, with *paludamentum* and cuirass. *Rev.* SALVATOR REIPVBLICAE. Vetranio walking to l., holding the *labarum* on which ⚹, and spear, and crowned by Victory, holding a palm, who is following him ; in the *exergue* SIS. *(Siscia.)* N. (1000 frcs.)

Silver Coins.

2. *Obv.* Same legend. Bust of Vetranio to r., diademed with *paludamentum.* *Rev.* RESTITVTOR REIP. Vetranio standing in military dress, holding the *labarum* and a small Victory on a globe; in the *field* FIII and a star; in the *exergue* CONS. *(Constantinopolis.)* Æ. from *Welzl.* (300 frcs.)

3. *Obv.* Same legend. Bust of Vetranio to r., laureated with *paludamentum* and cuirass. *Rev.* VICTORIA AVGVSTORVM. Victory walking to l., holding a palm and a trophy ; in the *exergue* SIS. *(Siscia)* sometimes followed by a crescent and a dot. Æ. (300 frcs.)

Brass Coins.

4. *Obv.* Same legend. Bust of Vetranio to r., laureated with *paludamentum* and cuirass ; sometimes behind the head A. and before a star. *Rev.* CONCORDIA MILITVM. Vetranio standing in military dress to l., holding two *labara* ; over his head a star ; in the *exergue* SIS. *(Siscia)* or TS. *(Thessalonicæ.)* Æ. II. (25 frcs.)

5. *Obv.* Same legend and type. *Rev.* GLORIA ROMANORVM. Vetranio standing in military dress to l., holding a *labarum* and a sceptre. Æ. III. (40 frcs.)

6. *Obv.* Same legend and type. *Rev.* HOC SIGNO VICTOR ERIS. Vetranio standing in military dress to l., holding the *labarum* and a spear, and crowned by a Victory, holding a palm, who follows him; in the *exergue* SIS. *(Siscia.)* Æ. II. (25 frcs.)

7. *Obv.* Same legend and type. *Rev.* VIRTVS AVGVSTORVM. Vetranio standing in military dress to r., holding a spear and a globe and placing his foot on a seated captive. Æ. III. (40 frcs.)

8. *Obv.* Same legend and type. *Rev.* VIRTVS EXERCITVM *(sic)* or EXERCITVS. Vetranio standing in military dress to l., holding a *labarum* and leaning on a shield ; in the *exergue* TS. or TES. *(Thessalonicæ.)* Æ. II. (25 frcs.) Æ. III. (40 frcs.)

The following coin is given by Banduri. *Obv.* VETRANIO NOB. CAES. Head of Vetranio bare and beardless. *Rev.* FEL. TEMP. REPARATIO. Vetranio holding a barbarian seated on the ground ; in the *exergue* ALE. *(Alexandriæ.)* Æ. III. (40 frcs.)

The legend SALVATOR REIPVBLICAE (No. 1) is new and only occurs on the coins of Vetranio. Eckhel writes *(Doct. Num. Vet.*, vol. viii., p. 120), " ab eruditis jam est observatum, vocabula *salvator, salvare* a Christianorum disciplina, et SS. Patribus inventa, pro quo melius Latine dices *servator, servare.*"

The legend HOC SIGNO VICTOR ERIS was first issued under Constantius II. and also occurs on the coins of Constantius Gallus.

VETTIA GENS. A plebeian family. The following coins are attributed to it :—

1. *Obv.* Head of Jupiter to r., laureated; behind, a letter of the alphabet. *Rev.* P SABIN, *(Publius Sabinus.)* Victory crowning a trophy; in the *exergue* Q. *(Quinarius)*; in the *field* a letter of the alphabet as on the obverse. *Æ. Quin.* (c.) (Cohen, *Méd. Cons.* No. 1., Mommsen, *Mon. Rom.*, vol. ii., No. 185.)

2. *Obv.* SABINUS. Head of Tatius to r., bare; in front Ā̄. *(Tatius)* and s. c. *(Senatus Consulto.)* *Rev.* T. *(Titus)* VETTIVS in *exergue;* above, IVDEX. Male figure in *biga* to l., holding the reins and a sceptre; behind, an ear of corn. *Æ.* (12 frcs.) (Cohen, No. 2; Mommsen, No. 303).

The Publius Sabinus mentioned on No. 1 is an unknown personage, but probably belonged to the *Vettia gens,* as the *prænomen Publius* and *cognomen Sabinus* were often borne about the time (B.C. 104-84) that this coin must have been issued. (Borghesi, *Dec.* xi. 7; *Œuvres compl.* vol. ii., p, 28.)

The Titus Vettius Sabinus on No. 2 is probably Titus Vettius, prætor in B.C. 59, mentioned by Cicero *(Orat. pro Flacco,* 34.) It seems as if the moneyer counted his descent from the Sabines, and thus took as a type a portrait of Tatius, king of the Sabines. As to IVDEX there is a difficulty. It is thought that the word is not part of the name of the moneyer, but refers to the type, and that perhaps there is here represented Tatius or Numa, as judge and king in his chariot (Mommsen, *Mon. Rom.,* vol. ii., p. 520) an opinion approved by the late Cavedoni *(Nuovi studi sopra le ant. mon. consolari, &c.,* p. 27, Modena, 1861.) Eckhel *(Doct. Num. Vet.,* vol. v., p. 337) mentions a Spurius Vettius, who was *Interrex,* and put it to the vote whether Numa should be King (Plut. *Numa.*)

" Some modern writers have maintained that, in all those passages where mention is made of the L. Vettius, who gave information concerning the conspiracy of Catiline, with the surname *Index,* that we ought to read *Judex ;* but this opinion hardly needs refutation, as it is clear that he was called *Index,* from giving information *(indicium)* respecting the conspiracy— comp. Cic. *ad Att.* II. 24, Vettius ille, ille noster *index.*" (Smith's *Dict. of Biog.,* vol. ii., p. 637.)

With respect to the letters s. c., Mommsen has shown *(Mon. Rom.,* vol. ii., p. 65) that the coins of the Roman Republic on which a name occurs without any title, but followed by the formulas D. s. s. *(De Senatus Sententia),* PE. s. c. *(Publice or Publice ex Senatus consulto),* or simply s. c. *(Senatus Consulto)* were not issued by one of the regular monetary triumvirs, but by some person charged with an extraordinary commission (cf. Lenormant, *La Mon. dans l'Antiq.,* vol. ii., p. 251.)

VETTIACVS. M. CATO L. VETTIACVS IIVIR c. c. A. On brass coins of Tiberius struck at Cæsar Augusta Hispaniæ. (Cohen, *Méd. Imp.,* 2nd ed., vol. i., pp. 198-199, Nos. 100-102.)

VETTIVS IVDEX [VETTIA GENS.]

Vetulonia or *Vetulonium,* one of the twelve principal cities of Etruria. The identification of its site is uncertain. (Smith, *Dict. of Geog. s. v.)* The following *struck* coin *(sextans)* is attributed to it (Mommsen, *Mon. Rom.,* vol. i., pp. 221, 227, 388):—*Obv.* Young head of Hercules; ● ●. *Rev.* Trident between two dolphins; ● ●; *Vatl . . . .* in Etruscan characters. *Æ.*

Ⅴ. or Ⅴ Ｅ Ⅴ. *Veturius* [VETVRIA GENS.]

VETVRIA GENS. An ancient and patrician family. According to tradition one of the family, Mamurius Veturius, lived at the time of Numa and was the armourer who made the eleven *ancilia* or sacred shields like the one sent from heaven [ANCILIA.] The following coins are attributed to it :—

1. *Obv.* TI. Ⅴ̲. *(Titus Veturius).* Bust of Mars to r., helmeted; behind, X *(denarius).* *Rev.* ROMA. Two soldiers holding a spear and a sword touching with their swords a pig, which is held by a man kneeling. *Æ.* (3 frcs.)

2. *Obv.* Head of Hercules to r., covered with the skin of a lion; behind ● ● ● *Rev.* TI. Ⅴ Ｅ. [or Ⅴ Ｅ Ⅴ.] B. *(Titus Veturius Barrus).* Strigil and vase containing perfumes. *Æ. Quadrans* (12 frcs.) (Cohen, *Méd. Cons.,*Nos. 1 and 2; Mommsen, *Mon. Rom.,* vol. ii., No. 111.)

The type of No. 1 is supposed by Mommsen *(Mon. Rom.,* vol. ii., p. 306) to recall either the humiliating treaty with the Samnites made by the consuls T. Veturius Calvinus and Sp. Postumius Albinus after the defeat of the Roman army at the Caudine Forks *(Furculæ Caudinæ)* in B.C. 321, or the treaty concluded by the same consuls in B.C. 334 with the Campanians and Samnites, but Lenormant *(La Mon. dans l'Antiq.,* vol. ii., p. 243) rejects the former suggestion as most unlikely [FOEDVS.] The same types of both obverse and reverse were reproduced on the coins of the Social War (B.C. 90-81), and a similar reverse type occurs on the *sextans* of Atella and Capua Campaniæ *(circ.* B.C. 268-211.)

The letter B on No. 2 reminds us of T. Beturius Barrus, a native cf Asculum in Picenum, who lived *circ.* B.C. 94 (Cic. *Brut.*, 46), and it may be that the moneyer who struck this coin *circ.* B.C. 154-134, belonged to the same family. (Mommsen, *Mon. Rom.*, vol. ii., p. 306.)

The strigil and vase of perfumes on the *quadrans* may refer to the *Quadrante lavari* (Juv. *Sat.* vi. 447; *quadrante lavatum* Hor. *Sat.* i., 3, 137; cf. Cic. *Pro Cælio*, 62), a *quadrans* being the ordinary fee paid by each visitor to the public baths.

VETVS. C. ANTISTIVS VETVS IIIVIR APOLLINI ACTIO. (Æ.)—C. ANTIST. VETVS FOED. P. R. *(Foedus Populi Romani)* CVM GABINIS (Æ.)—C. ANTIST. VETVS FOEDVS P. R. QVM [for CVM] GABINIS (Æ.)—C. ANTISTIVS VETVS IIIVIR. (Æ.)—C. ANTISTI. VETVS IIIVIR. (*N.*) On gold and silver coins of Antistius Vetus, monetary triumvir under Augustus, B.C. 16 [ANTESTIA.—FOEDVS.]

Vexillum. [LEGIONVM INSIGNIA.—SIGNA MILITARIA.]

VGIA. A town of Hispania Bæticæ now *Las Cabezas.* The following coin is attributed to it, but it is not authenticated:—*Obv.* Head of Vulcan to r.; behind, *forceps. Rev.* VGIA above a camel to r. Æ. (Akerman, *Anc. Coins of Cities and Princes*, p. 59.)

VI. *Sexta, Sexto, Sextum.*—LEG. VI. *Legio sexta.*—LEG. VI. F. *Legio sexta Ferrata.*—AN. or ANNO VI.—VI. F. *Sextum Fidelis* and VI. P. *Sextum Pia*, on legionary coins of Gallienus, &c.

VI. *Victrix.* LEG. XXX VLPIA VI. *Legio tricesima Ulpia Victrix* on brass coins of Carausius.

VI. *Viro.* EXAG. SOL. SVB VI. INL. IOHANNI COM. S. L. *Exagium solidi sub viro inlustri Johanni comite sacrarum largitionum*, on an *exagium solidi* (weight) of Arcadius, Theodosius II., and Honorius. [EXAGIVM SOLIDI.]

VI. AV. (?)—IL. S. VI. AV. (?) on a silver coin of Carausius.

VI. AVGGG. *(Virtus* or *Virtuti Augustorum.)* Soldier, helmeted, standing to r., hurling an enemy to his feet. *Obv.* IMP. C. CARAVSIVS P. F. AVG. Bust of Carausius to r., radiated with cuirass. Æ. III. (40 frcs.)

and a reed. On gold (80 frcs.), silver (6 frcs.), and brass (6 to 10 frcs.) coins of Trajan.

This coin commemorates the new road constructed by the Emperor Trajan at his own expense from Beneventum to Brundusium *(Viam a Benevento Brundusium pecunia sua fecit.* Gruter, *Inscr.*, p. 151.2), which came to be considered as the *Via Appia*, of which it took the place. (Smith, *Dict. of Geog.*, vol. ii., pp. 1289, 1293.) This coin was restored by Gordianus Pius in silver. (400 frcs.)

VIAE—QVOD VIAE MVN. SVNT. On gold and silver coins of Augustus [QVOD VIAE, &c. —VINICIA GENS.]

VIB. *Vibio.* C. VIB. MARSO PR. COS., &c. *Caio Vibio Marso Proconsule*, &c. On brass coins of Tiberius, struck at Utica Zeugitanæ. (Cohen, *Méd. Imp.*, 2nd ed., vol. i., p. 210, Nos. 241, 242)—IMP. CAE. C. VIB. VOLVSIANO AVG. On coins of Volusian [VOLVSIANVS.]

VIB. *Vibius*, on coins of Trebonianus Gallus and Volusian.—C. VIB. AID. CARTEIA. *Caius Vibius Ædilis. Carteia*—on brass coins of Carteia Hispaniæ.

VIBI. *Vibius*—C. VIBI ℞ S. *Caius Vibius Pansa* on *as* and *semis*,—C. VIBI. on *quadrans* and *sextans* of *Vibia gens.* [VIBIA GENS.]

VIBIA GENS. A plebeian family. The coins of this *gens* bear the *cognomina* Pansa and Varus. The *cognomen Marsus* occurs on coins of C. Vibius Marsus struck at Utica Zeugitanæ. [VTICA.] The following coins belong to this family:—

B.C. 82-81. *As* with legend ROMA. C. PANSA or ROMA. C. VIBI. ℞ S. *(Caius Vibius Pansa)*; or C. VIBIVS. *Semis* with legend C. VIBI. ℞ S.; *quadrans* and *sextans* with legend C. VIBI. (2 to 25 frcs.; Cohen, *Méd. Cons.*, Nos. 11-16; Mommsen, *Mon. Rom.*, vol. ii., No. 216.)

Denarii. 1. *Obv.* PANSA. Head of Apollo to r., in front a symbol or a letter. *Rev.* C. VIBIVS C. F. *(Caius Vibius Caii Filius).* Pallas in a *quadriga* to r. or l., holding a trophy and a shield. Æ. (c. to 2 frcs.)

2. The same legend and for type the *quadriga* on both obverse and reverse.

3. *Obv.* PANSA. Head of Apollo to r. *Rev.* C. VIBIVS C. F. Ceres walking, holding two torches and preceded by a pig; sometimes a crown of laurel surrounds the type. Æ. (10 frcs.)

VIA TRAIANA S. C. (in the *exergue)* S. P. Q. R. OPTIMO PRINCIPI. Female lying on the ground to l., holding a wheel on her knee

4. *Obv.* PANSA. Mask of Pan to r. *Rev.* C. VIBIVS C. F. Mask of Silenus to r., crowned with laurel. (Sometimes the types are transposed.) Æ. (15 frcs.) (Cohen, *Méd. Cons.*, Nos. 3-10; Mommsen, *Mon. Rom.*, vol. ii., No. 216.)

These coins are attributed to the father of C. Vibius Pansa, of whom it is only known that he was proscribed by Sulla in B.C. 82-81.

B.C. 43. 1. *Obv.* PANSA. Head of Bacchus or a bacchante to r., crowned with ivy and grapes. *Rev.* C. VIBIVS C. F. C. N. *(Caius Vibius Caii Filius Caii Nepos.)* Ceres, crowned with ear of corn, walking to r., holding two torches; in front a plough-share. Æ. (c.)

2. *Obv.* Same legend and type. *Rev.* Same legend. Ceres in a *biga* of serpents holding a torch. Æ. (3 frcs.)

3. *Obv.* PANSA. Bearded mask of Pan to r., sometimes with the *pedum* (shepherd's crook) behind. *Rev.* C. VIBIVS C. F. C. N. IOVIS AXVR. Jupiter Axur, radiated, seated to l., holding a *petera* and a spear. Æ. (2 frcs.)

4. *Obv.* Head of Mercury to r., with winged *petasus* (cap.) *Rev.* C. PANSA. *(Caius Pansa.)* Tortoise and *caduceus.* Æ. *Sestertius.* (100 frcs.)

5. *Obv.* LIBERTATIS. Head of Liberty to r., laureated. *Rev.* C. PANSA C. F. C. N. *(Caius Pansa Caii Filius Caii Nepos).* Rome, helmeted, seated on shields to r., holding a *parazonium*, and placing one of her feet on a globe; between her legs a piece of armour; to r., Victory crowning her. (Sometimes no legend on the reverse). Æ. (8 frcs.)

6. *Obv.* PANSA. Bearded mask of Pan to r. *Rev.* ALBINVS BRVTI F. *(filius.)* Two hands joined holding a winged *caduceus.* Æ. (6 frcs.) (Cohen, *Méd. Cons.*, Nos. 17-22; Mommsen, *Mon. Rom.*, vol. ii., p. 548.)

These six coins are attributed to Caius Vibius Pansa, consul with A. Histius in B.C. 43, and who, together with Histius, perished whilst engaged against M. Antony near Mutina in April of the same year.

For Jupiter Axur on No. 3 see AXVR. The bearded mask of Pan on Nos. 3 and 6 doubtless alludes to the surname of the moneyer, *Pansa.* (Eckhel, *Doct. Num. Vet.*, vol. v., p. 340.)

The legend LIBERTATIS on No 5, and the coin No. 6, struck conjointly with Decimus Brutus, bear allusion to the death of Julius Cæsar. Decimus Brutus was adopted by Aulus Postumius Albinus. It is worthy of notice that Brutus is called on his coins Albinus *son* of Brutus instead of Brutus *son* of Albinus.

B.C. 43-42. 1. *Obv.* Head of Hercules to r., laureated. *Rev.* C. *(Caius)* VIBIVS VARVS. Pallas standing holding a spear and a Victory; at her feet a shield. Æ. (3 frcs.)

2. *Obv.* Head of Bacchus to r., crowned with ivy and grapes. *Rev.* C. VIBIVS VARVS. Panther mounting up to an altar, on which a mask of Pan and a thyrsus. Æ. (2 frcs.)

3. *Obv.* Bust of Pallas to l., with shield and spear. *Rev.* C. VIBIVS VARVS. Nemesis, winged, standing to r. N. (400 frcs.)

4. *Obv.* Bust of Pallas to l., with *ægis.* *Rev.* C. VIBIVS VARVS. Hercules, naked, standing to l., holding a club and a lion's skin. Æ. (5 frcs.)

5. *Obv.* Head of Venus to r., laureated. *Rev.* C. VIBIVS VARVS. Venus, half-naked,

5 R 2

standing near a column and looking in a mirror, which she holds in her hand. N. (400 frcs.)

A silver coin of this type is given by Mionnet and Riccio, but Cohen has never seen it, and if it exists it is of the greatest rarity. (Cohen, *Méd. Cons.*, Nos. 23-27.)

6. *Obv.* Head of M. Antony, bearded, to r. *Rev.* C. VIBIVS VARVS. Female standing to l., holding a small Victory and a cornucopiæ. Æ. (10 frcs.) (Cohen, *Méd. Cons.*, No. 28; *Méd. Imp.*, 2nd ed., vol. i., p. 36, No. 4.)

7. *Obv.* Head of Octavian to r., bare. *Rev.* C. VIBIVS VARVS. Venus standing to l., holding a Victory and a cornucopiæ. Æ. (200 frcs.) (Cohen, *Méd. Imp.*, 2nd ed., Vol. i., p. 142, No. 539.)

8. *Obv.* Same as No. 7. *Rev.* C. VIBIVS VARVS. Pallas standing to r., holding a spear; at her feet a shield. Æ. *plated.* (Cohen, *Méd. Cons.*, No. 29; *Méd. Imp.*, 2nd ed., vol. i., p. 142).

9. *Obv.* C. CAESAR IIIVIR R. P. C. *(Caius Cæsar triumvir Reipublicæ constituendæ.)* Same type as No. 7. *Rev.* C. VEIBIVS VAARVS. Two hands joined. N. (800 frcs.) (Cohen, *Méd. Imp.*, 2nd ed., vol. i., p. 142, No. 540.)

10. *Obv.* M. LEPIDVS IIIVIR. R. P. C. Head of Lepidus to l., bare. *Rev.* C. VEIBIVS VAARVS. Same type as No. 9. N. (2,500 frcs.)

11. *Obv.* M. ANTONIVS IIIVIR. R. P. C. Head of Antony, to r., bare. *Rev.* C. VEIBIVS VAARVS. Same type as No. 9. N. (1200 frcs.) (Cohen, *Méd. Imp.*, 2nd ed., vol. i., p. 28, Nos. 1 and 2.)

Some interesting remarks on the monetary quatuorvirs of B.C. 43—42 will be found in Lenormant's *Hist. de la Mon. Dans l' Antiq.*, vol. ii., pp. 343-344; vol. iii., pp. 170-174.

Uncertain.—Obv. VIBIVS. Head of Apollo, laureated. *Rev.* NORBANVS. Hercules naked, seated, holding a club; at his feet a lion sleeping; in the *field*, a crescent. Æ.

This coin was at one time in the possession of Antonio Benedetti, and its authenticity has been vouched for by Odorico and Pietro Borghesi, it being described by Borghesi the son. *(Dec. x., 10; Œuvres Compl.*, vol. i., p. 514.) Since then it has disappeared. The coin cannot be attributed to a *Vibius Norbanus*, for Norbanus is a distinct family name. It is therefore probable that there is a portion of the legend missing on the reverse, and that the piece should be assigned to two moneyers Vibius and Norbanus. (Cohen, *Méd. Cons.*, p. 230; Mommsen, *Mon. Rom.*, vol. ii., p. 525, No. 310.)

The coins attributed by Cohen *(Méd. Cons.*, Nos. 1 and 2) to the *Vibia gens* with the monogram VB. (? *Vibius*) are now assigned to *Vibo Valentia.* [VB; VALENTIA].

Vibia—Colonia Vibia, a title given to Perusia Etruriæ, at which place the Emperor *Vibius* Trebonianus Gallus was born.

Vibia Aurelia Faustina, daughter of Marcus Aurelius and Faustina II. No coins.

VIBIO.—C. VIBIO MARSO PR. COS. *(Proconsule)*, or PR. COS. II. or III., &c., on brass coins of Tiberius, struck at Utica Zeugitanæ [VTICA]. (Cohen, *Méd Imp.*, 2nd ed., vol. ii., pp. 209-210, Nos. 232-233, 243-250)—P. VIBIO SAC, CAES. Q. or M. BARBA. PRAEF. PRO. IIVIR. *Publio Vibio sacerdote Cæsaris Q.* (?) or *M.* [*Murci*] (?) *Barbatii præfecto pro duumviro* on brass coin of Augustus, struck at Parium Mysiæ (Mionnet, vol. ii., p. 578, No. 426; Cohen, *Méd. Imp.*, 2nd ed., vol. i., p. 163, No. 782; Lenormant, *La Mon. dans l'Antiq.*, vol. iii., p. 226.) A variety given by Vaillant (Eckhel, *Doct. Num. Vet.*, vol. iv., p. 478), and attributed incorrectly to Corinth, gives the legend P. VIBIO M. BARBA. PRAEF. IIVIR. *Publio Vibio Marci Barbatii Præfecto duumviro.*—VIBIO VOLVSIANO on coins of Volusianus. [VOLVSIANVS.]

Vibius—name of Trebonianus Gallus, on whose coins VIBIVS occurs in full, and of Volusianus. [VOLVSIANVS.]

VIC.—IN HOC SIN. VIC. on a large brass coin of Constantine I.. published as existing in the Pisani Museum. Cohen has shown *(Méd. Imp.*, 1st ed., vol. vi., p. 119, *note* 2), that though the metal is antique the piece has been entirely remade, probably from a large brass coin in circulation between the times of Trajanus Decius and Gallienus. It is now in the *Cabinet des Médailles*, Paris.

VIC. *Victori.*—IOVI VIC., on gold coins of Caracalla—.OIV IVOI (IOVI VIC. retrograde), on brass coins of Caracusius.

VIC. AVG. *(Victoria Augusti).* Victory standing to r., on a globe, holding a crown and a palm. *Obv.* IMP. CAES. AVG. P. M. *(Imperator Cæsar Augustus Pontifex Maximus)* or IMP. CAES. VESP. AVG. P.M. COS. IIII. Head of Vespasian to r., laureated. *N.* (40 frcs.). *Æ.* with obv. leg. IMP. CAES. VESPAS. AVG. TR. P. COS. III. (2 frcs.) Same reverse type on gold coins of Titus (40 frcs.)

VIC. AVG. *(Victoria Augusti)*, within a crown of laurel. *Obv.* HADRIANVS AVG. COS. III. P. P. Bust of Hadrian to r., bare. *Æ. Quin.* (60 frcs.)

VIC. AVG. *Victoria Augusti* frequently occurs on the shield held by Victory.

VIC. DAC. *Victoria Dacica* on shield held by Victory—brass coin of Trajan.

VIC. GALL. AVG. III. *(Victoria Gallieni Augusti III.)* Victory walking to l., holding a crown and a palm; in the *field* T. *Obv.* GALLIENVS AVG. Bust of Gallienus to l., radiated, with *paludamentum* and cuirass. *Bil.* (2 frcs.) Same coin with IMP. GALLIENVS AVG., and no letter in *field* of reverse (2 frcs.)

VIC. GER. *Victoria Germanica*, on shield held by Victory—coins of M. Aurelius.

VIC. GERM. P.M. TR. P. V. COS. III. P. P. *(Victoria Germanica, Pontifex Maximus Tribunitiá Potestate V. Consul III. Pater Patriæ.)* Postumus in military dress standing to l., holding a globe and a spear, and crowned by Victory, standing, who holds a palm. *Obv.* POSTVMVS AVG. Bust of Postumus to l.,

helmeted, with cuirass; on the helmet a Victory in a *biga.* *N.* (300 frs.); *Bil.* (30 frcs.)

VIC. PAR. *Victoria Parthica*, on shield held by Victory—coins of M. Aurelius and L. Verus.

VIC. PART. *(Victoria Parthica.)* Victory standing to l., writing AVG. *(Augusti)* on a shield placed on a column and holding a palm. *Obv.* IMP. CAE. L. SEP. SEV. PERT. AVG. COS. II. *(Imperator Cæsar Lucius Septimius Severus Pertinax Augustus Consul II.)* Head of Septimius Severus to r., laureated. *Æ.* (3 frcs.)

VIC. PART. *(Victoria Parthica.)* P. M. TR. P. XX. COS. IIII. P. P. Victory seated to r., on a cuirass, holding a shield on which VO. or VOT. XX. *(vota xx.)*; before her a trophy, at the foot of which are two captives. *Obv.* ANTONINVS PIVS AVG. GERM. *(Augustus Germanicus.)* Bust of Caracalla to r., laureated or radiated with *paludamentum* and cuirass. *N.* (300 frcs.); *Æ.* (8 frcs.)

VIC. PART. *(Victoria Parthica)* P. M. TR. P. XX. COS. III. P. P. Caracalla in military dress standing to l., holding a globe and a sceptre, crowned by Victory, who holds a palm; at his feet a captive seated. *N.* (200 frcs.); *Æ.* (30 frs.)

VIC. *(Victoriæ)* PARTHICAE.—S. P. Q. R. VIC. PARTHICAE on shield held by two captives—brass medallion of M. Aurelius (350 frcs.)

VIC. *Victrix*—VRB. VIC. OSCA, on brass coins of Augustus struck at Osca Hispaniæ. (Cohen, *Méd. Imp.*, 2nd ed., vol. i., p. 157, No. 721.)—VRBS VIC. OSCA. Tiberius. (Cohen, *op. cit.*, p. 202, No. 148.)—COL. VIC. IVL. LEP., *Colonia Victrix Julia Lepida*, on brass coins struck at Celsa Hispaniæ, B.C. 45—41 (Lenormant, *La Mon. dans l'Antiq.*, vol. iii., p. 227.)

Vicennalia Vota. [*Vota.*]

VICENNALIA or VIGENNALIA. [VOTA VICENNALIA or VIGENNALIA.]

VICENNALIBVS. [VOTIS VIGENNALIBVS.]

VICENNALIOR. [VOTA VICENNALIOR.]

VIC. or VICT. *Victor.* VIC. or VICT. CONSTANTINVS AVG. on medallions and small brass coins of Constantine II. D. N. CONSTANTIVS VICT. P. F. AVG. *Dominus Noster Constantius Victor Pius Felix Augustus* on brass coins of Constantius II. The coins bearing the name of Constantine, with the surname of VICT. *(Victor)*, were previously assigned by all numismatists to Constantine I., but Cohen *(Méd. Imp.*, vol. vi., pp. 119, 211, 222) has attributed them to Constantine II., chiefly on the ground that the features on all these coins can only be those of a young man, and, moreover, that the portraits are exactly like those on a great number of pieces bearing the title IVN. *(Junior).* Cohen adds that the title *Victor* belonged or was given to the sons of Constantine I. There seem to be valid grounds for this attribution, at the same time Eusebius expressly states *(Vit. Const.* II., c. 19) that the title *Victor* (NIKHTHΣ) was adopted by Constantine I. as a fitting appellation to express the Victory which

God had granted him over all his enemies; and the laws of Constantine I. respecting piety towards God, &c., as given by Eusebius *(Vit. Const.* II., c. 24, 46, 48, &c.), commence ΝΙΚΗΤΗΣ Κωνσταντῖνος μέγιστος σεβαστός, *Victor* Constantinus Maximus Augustus (Madden, *Num. Chron.*, N. S., 1877, vol. xvii., p. 37.)

VICT. *Victori.* IOVI VICT. *Jovi Victori* and MART. VICT. *Marti Victori* on silver coins of Septimius Severus.

VICT. *Victoriæ.* I. O. M. ET VICT. CONSER. DD. NN. AVG. ET. CAES. *Jovi Optimo Maximo et Victoriæ Conservatoribus Dominorum Nostrorum Augusti et Cæsaris* on second brass coins of Licinius I. with Licinius II.

VICT. AETERN. *(Victoriæ Æternæ.)* Victory writing on a shield; or Victory flying to l., holding with both hands a diadem; before her a shield on a base—on silver coins of Septimius Severus. Æ. (c to 5 frcs.)

VICT. AETERN. or AETERNAE on silver coins of Sept. Severus, Caracalla, and Geta.

VICT. AVG. *Victoria Augusti*, with the usual types of Victory [*Victoria*], on coins of Nero (N. Quin 200 frcs.), Vespasian (N. struck in Judæa, 250 frcs.), Antoninus Pius (Æ. II. 6 frcs.), M. Aurelius (N. 60 frcs., Æ. c to 6 frcs., Æ. I. 10 to 12 frcs., Æ. II. 3 frcs.), L. Verus (N. 45 frcs. Æ. 3 frcs., Æ. I., 12 frcs., Æ. II. 3 frcs.) Albinus (Æ. 10 to 12 frcs.) Septimius Severus (N. 150 frcs., Æ. c. to 6 frcs.; Æ. I. 8 frcs.; Æ. II. 3 frcs.); and Constans I. (Æ. III. *Quin.*, 3 frcs.)

VIC. AVG. LIB. ROM. ORB. *(Victoria Augusti Libertas Romani Orbis.)* Victory and Liberty standing, holding together a trophy; Liberty holding also a sceptre; in the *exergue* N. (?) LVG. *(Lugduni)* or TR. P. *(Treveris Prima)* on gold (35 frcs), silver (50 frcs.), and second brass (15 frcs.) coins of Magnentius.

VICT. AVGG. *Victoria Augustorum*, with the usual type of Victory [*Victoria*], on coins of Septimius Severus (N. 150 frcs. Æ. c. to 12 frcs.), Caracalla (Æ. *Quin.* 25 frcs.), Geta (Æ., *Quin.*, 50 frcs.), and Saloninus *(Bil.* 6 frcs.)

VICT. ASꞭ. *(Victoria Augusti.)* Cross. *Obv.* D. N. COTINVS. *(sic)* AV. Bust of Constantine IV. Pogonatus to r., diademed. N. (100 frcs.)

VICT. AꞭSV. *(Victoria Augusti.)* Cross on three steps; in *field* to r. a star; in the *exergue*, CONOB. *Obv.* D. N. ANACT. *(sic)*— Bust facing of Artemius Anastasius II. holding a cross in r. hand and a signal cloth *(mappa)* in the l. N. *Tremissis.* (125 frcs.)

VICT. BRIT. *Victoriæ Britannicæ* on coins of Commodus (Æ. I. 10 frcs.), Septimius Severus (Æ. I. 25 frcs., Æ. II., 6 frcs.), and Geta (Æ. I., 20 to 25 frcs.); also on shield held by Victory on brass medallions of Commodus (300 frcs.)

VICT. CAES. LIB. ROM. ORB. *Victoria Cæsaris Libertas Romani Orbis.* Type as above under VICT. AVG. LIB., &c., on coins of

Magnentius (N. 100 frcs.), and Decentius (N. 300 frcs.)

VICT. . . . COL . . . A. AP. *(Victoriæ Colonia . . . Augusta Apameia.)* Victory walking to l., holding a branch and a shield; in the *field* D. D. *(Decreto Decurionum)*. DIVO IVLIO. Head of Julius Cæsar, radiated. Æ. II., from *Sestini*. Struck at Apameia Bithyniæ.

VICT. *(Victoria)* COMES AVG. *(Augusti).* Postumus helmeted, and in military dress, on horseback, holding a spear and preceded by Victory, who holds a palm—on second brass coin of Postumus from *Vaillant* (100 frcs.)

VICT. CONSTANT. AVG. *(Victoria Constantii Augusti)* Victory walking to l., holding wreath and palm; at her feet two captives seated; in the *exergue* S. M. T. *(Signata Moneta Tarraconis).* *Obv.* CONSTANTIVS P. F. AVG. Head of Constantius I. Chlorus, laureated. N. from *Banduri* (300 frcs).

VICT. D. N. COL. ANTIOCH. *(Victoriæ Domini Nostri. Colonia Antiochensis.)* Victory walking to l., holding laurel wreath and palm; in *field* S. R. *(Senatus Romanus)* *Obv.* IMP. CAE. M. AVR. ANTONINVS PIVS. AVG. Head of Caracalla to r., laureated. Æ. Med., struck at Antiochia Pisidiæ.

VICT. DD. NN. AVG. ET. CAES. *(Victoriæ Dominorum Nostrorum Augusti et Cæsaris.)* Two Victories holding a shield, on which VOT. XXX.; above, a star. *Obv.* D. N. CONSTANTIVS P. F. AVG. Bust of Constantius II. to r., diademed, with *paludamentum.* Æ. III. (6 frcs.) The same legend and similar type occur on second brass coins of Magnentius (c.) and Decentius (c.)

VICT. FEL. *(Victoriæ Felici.)* P. M. TR. P. XIIII., &c., on silver coins of Commodus (6 frcs.), or VICT. FELI. P. M. TR. P. XIIII, &c., on large brass coins of Commodus (20 frcs.)

VICT. GAL. AVG. *(Victoria Gallieni Augusti.)* Three Victories standing to l., each raising in the air a cornucopia and holding a palm, sometimes in the *exergue*, V. *Obv.* GALLIENVS AVG. Bust of Gallienus to r., radiated. *Bil.* (6 frcs.) Sometimes the reverse legend on the *billon* is VICT. GAL. AVG. III. [or in the *exergue* v.], as it is on the brass medallions—Victory in a *biga* (150 frcs.)—and sometimes the type on the *billon* Victory walking.

VIC. GER. II. or VICT. GERM. *Victoria Germanica*, on brass from *Wiczay*, and *billon* coins of Gallienus (c.)

VICT. GERM. *(Victoria Germanica)* IMP. VI. COS. III. Victory in a *quadriga* l., looking to r. *Obv.* M. ANTONINVS AVG. TR. P. XXVII. or XXVIII. Bust of M. Aurelius to r., laureated. Æ. Med. (250 to 350 frcs.)

VICT. GERM. [or GERMA.] *(Victoria Germanica.)* IMP. VI. COS. III. S. C., within a laurel crown. *Obv.* M. ANTONINVS AVG. TR. P. XXVII. Head or bust of M. Aurelius to r., Æ. I. (15 frcs.) Æ. II. (6 to 9 frcs.)

VICT. GERM. *(Victoria Germanica—in exergue)*, IMP. VI. COS. III. (around.) Victory in a *quadriga* to l., her hand placed on eagle before her. *Obv.* IMP. M. ANTONINVS AVG. COS. III. IMP. L. VERVS AVG. COS. II. Busts of Marcus Aurelius and Lucius Verus. Æ. Med. from *Borghesi* (Cohen, *Méd. Imp.*, 2nd ed., vol. iii., p. 129.) This medallion is hybrid. The dates on obverse and reverse do not coincide.

VICT. *(Victoria)* GERMANICA. Various types of Victory [*Victoria*] on coins of Gallienus. Nγ. (150 frcs.); *Bil.* (c.)

VICT. LAETAE PRINC. PERP. *(Victoriæ Lætæ Principum Perpetuæ).* Two Victories placing on a base or an altar a shield on which VOT. P. R. *(Vota Populi Romani)*; on the base s. or I. on third brass coins of Licinius I. (1 frc.), Licinius II., Constantine II., Crispus and Constantine II. (c.) [VICTORIAE LAETAE, &c.]

VICT. PART. or PARTH. MAX. *(Victoria Parthica Maxima),* Victory walking to l., holding wreath and palm, on coins of Septimius Severus (Nγ. 150 frcs.; Æ. c.), and Caracalla (Nγ. 150 frs., Æ. 5 frcs.)

VICT. *(Victoria)* PARTHICA. Victory seated to r. on a cuirass, holding a shield on which VO. XX.; behind her a shield; beneath her feet a helmet, in the *exergue* a javelin and a spear. *Obv.* ANTONINVS PIVS AVG. GERM. Head of Caracalla to r., laureated. Æ. (10 frcs.)

VICT. *(Victoria)* PARTHICA. Caracalla in military dress to r., holding a Victory and a spear; on each side a captive seated. Obverse, same as previous coin. Æ. (5 frcs.)

VICT. *(Victoria)* PARTHICA. Victory walking to l., holding a wreath and a trophy; at her feet a Parthian seated. *Obv.* L. SEPT. SEV. AVG. IMP. XI. PART. MAX. *(Parthicus Maximus.)* Head of Septimius Severus to l., laureated. Æ. (c.)

VICT. *(Victoria)* PARTICA. Victory walking to l., hurling at her feet an enemy, and holding a wreath and a palm. *Obv.* VALERIANVS P. F. AVG. Bust of Valerian I. to r., radiated, with *paludamentum* and cuirass. *Bil.* (6 frcs.)

VICT. *(Victoria.)* PROBI AVG. *(Augusti.)* Rome helmeted, seated to l., holding a sceptre; in front two soldiers, one holding a Victory, the other a standard; in the *field* another standard; in the *exergue* a wreath. *Obv.* IMP. PROBVS P. F. AVG. Bust of Probus to l., laureated with the *ægis* strapped on l. shoulder and holding a spear. Nγ. (400 frcs.)

VICT. *Victrici.* MIN. OR MINER. VICT. *Minervæ Victrici* on gold, silver, brass coins, and brass medallions of Commodus—VENERI VICT. *Veneri Victrici* on silver coins of Julia Domna.

VICT. *Victrix.* VENVS VICT. *Venus Victrix* on billon coins of Salonina.—LEG. VI. VICT. *Legio Sexta Victrix* on billon coins of Carausius —LEG. XXX VLP. VICT. P. F. *Legio* XXX *Ulpia Victrix Pia Fidelis* on gold coins of Victorinus —VRB. VICT. *Urbs Victrix* on second brass coins of Augustus, struck at Osca Hispaniæ

(Cohen *Méd. Imp.*, 2nd ed., vol. i., p. 157, No. 718.)—G. TARRACINA P. PRISCO II VIR VRBS VICT. *Gaio Tarracina Publio Prisco duumviris Urbs Victrix*, on second brass coins of Caligula of Osca Hispaniæ (Cohen, *op. cit.*, p. 243, No. 52.)

Victimarius, an assistant at sacrifices, is frequently represented on Roman coins and medallions.

VICTOR. *Victor.* IVPPITER VICTOR, on gold and silver coins of Vitellius.—MARS VICTOR on coins of Galba, Vitellius, Vespasian, Caracalla, Elagabalus, Gallienus, Postumus, Victorinus, Claudius II.. Tetricus I., Tetricus II., Tacitus, Probus, Carus, Numerianus, Carinus, Diocletian, Maximian Hercules, Carausius (sometimes VICTO) and Constantine I.—FIDES VICTOR on third brass coins of Probus.—VBIQVE VICTOR on gold coins of Constantine I.—HOC SIGNO VICTOR ERIS on second brass coins of Constantius II., Vetranio and Constantius Gallus, of the latter also in gold.—D.N. CONSTANTIVS VICTOR AVG. on brass medallions of Constantius II.—D.N. CONSTANTIVS VICTOR SEMPER AVG. on gold medallion of Constantius II [VIC. or VICT.]—D. N. VALENS VICTOR SEMPER AVG. on gold medallions of Valens.—D. N. TH ЄOD ЄB ЄRTVS VICTOR on gold coins of the Merovingian King Theodebert I. A.D. 534-548.

VICTOR *(Flavius)*, the son of Magnus Maximus, who ruled in Spain, Gaul, and Britain (A.D. 383), was associated by his father in the Empire with the title of *Augustus.* Maximus was defeated by Theodosius I. on the banks of the Save, and fled to Aquileia, but was given up by the people and killed by the soldiers. Arbogastes, the General of Theodosius, seized Victor, who had been left in Gaul, and put him to death in A.D. 388.

The obverse legend of the coins of Victor is D. N. FL. VICTOR P. F. AVG. The reverse legends are—*Gold coins:* BONO REIPVBLICAE NATI. Maximus and Victor seated facing holding a globe, between them a Victory facing; in the *exergue* TROB *Treveris* 72 (800 frcs.) [see woodcut]; VICTORIA AVGVSTORVM. Victory seated, in *exergue* MDOB. *Mediolano* 72 *(Quin.* 300 frcs.); VIRTVS ROMANORVM. Rome, seated; in the *exergue* M D. P. S. *Mediolano pecunia signata* (*D'Ennery*); *Silver coins:* SPES ROMANORVM Prætorian camp; in the *exergue* ANLOP? (*Mionnet*, 60 frcs.); VICTORIA AVGVSTORVM Victory walking, in the *exergue* AQ. P. S. *Aquileiæ pecunia signata* (15 frcs.); VIRTVS ROMANORVM, Rome seated; in the *exergue* AQ. P. S. or MD. P. S. or TR P. S. (15 frcs.)

Third brass coins: SPES ROMANORVM. Open gate of a camp, surmounted by two towers, between which a star; in the *exergue* LVG. P. *Lugduni prima*, P. CON. *Prima Constantinæ* (Arles), SM. *Sirmii*, SMAQP. *Signata Moneta Aquileiæ prima*, SMAQS. *Signata Moneta Aquileiæ secunda*, SMRP. *Signata Moneta Romæ prima*, SMRS. *Signata Moneta Romæ secunda*. (6 frcs.)

VICTOR. *Victori*. MARTI VICTOR. *Marti Victori* on silver coin of Pescennius Niger— MARTI VICTOR. (sometimes VICTO.) *Marti Victori* on silver coins of Septimius Severus.

VICTOR. AETER. (*Victoria Æterna*) Victory standing, leaning on, or holding shield and wreath or palm; below a captive, on coins of Gordianus III. (Æ. c.) and Valerian I. (Æ I. 30 frcs.)

VICTOR. (*Victoria*) ANTONINI AVG. (*Augusti*). Victory running to right, holding a crown and a palm on coins of Elagabalus *N*. (150 frcs.), Æ. (c. to 3 frcs., *Quin.* 40 frcs.)

VICTOR. AVG. *Victoria Augusti*. A trophy. *Obv.* IMP. DOMIT. AVG. GERM. Head of Domitian to r., laureated. Æ. III. (40 frcs.). Struck in Judæa. Similar coins exist with the legend VICTORIA AVG. [VICTORIA AVG.]

VICTOR. AVG. *Victoria Augusti*. Victory holding a trophy or a wreath and a palm, on silver coins of Septimius Severus. (c.)

VICTOR. (*Victoria*) AVGVSTI S.C. (*Senatus Consulto*.) Victory standing to l., placing a trophy on a captive seated on a globe. *Obv.* A. VITELLIVS GERM. [or GERMA. or GERMAN.] IMP. AVG. P.M. TR.P. Bust or head of Vitellius to r., laureated. Æ. II. (15 frcs.)

VICTOR. (*Victoria*) AVGVSTI. Victory standing to l., holding 'a wreath and a palm. *Obv.* IMP. MAXIMINVS PIVS. AVG. Bust of Maximinus to r., laureated. (Bad fabric.) Æ. I. (5 frcs.)

VICTOR. (*Victoria*.) CARO. Victory walking to r., holding a spear and a trophy (Carus) or a wreath and a palm (Carinus) on gold coins of Carus and Carinus (300 to 400 frcs.)

VICTOR. DD. NN. AVG. ET. C. (*Victoriæ Dominorum Nostrorum Augusti et Cæsaris.*) Two Victories standing, holding a crown in which OT. VLT. (*sic*.) *Obv.* D. N. MAG-NENNTVS (*sic*) P. F. AVG. Bust of Magnentius to r., bare. Æ. III. *Quin.* (6 frcs.) Another specimen, struck by Magnentius *Cæsar*, has the legend VICTOR [DD. NN. ET. C.] Æ. III. (3 frcs.)

VICTOR. GER. (*Victoria Germanica.*) Victory walking to r., holding wreath and trophy, between two captives seated on the ground. *Obv.* IMP. PROBVS P. F. AVG. Bust of Probus to r., laureated, with cuirass. Æ. III. *Quin.* (10 frcs.) A similar type on coin of Claudius II., with legend VICTOR. GERM. Æ. III. (20 frcs.)

VICTOR. GERMAN. (*Victoria Germanica.*) Trophy between two captives, seated on the ground. *Obv.* IMP. CLAVDIVS P. F. AVG.

Head of Claudius II. to r., radiated; below, three dots. Æ. III. (20 frcs.)

VICTOR. IVST. AV. (*Victoria Justa Augusti*). Victory seated to l., holding a wreath and a palm. *Obv.* IVLIA DOMNA AVG. Bust of Julia Domna to r. (*Médaille hybride.*) Æ.

VICTOR. IVST. AVG. (*Victoria Justi Augusti.*) Victory walking to left, holding a wreath and a palm. *Obv.* IMP. CAES. C. PESC. NIGER IVS. (*Justus*) COS. II. Head of Pescennius Niger to r., laureated. Æ. (200 frcs.) Coins with similar reverse legend and type, were issued by Septimius Severus, who defeated Pescennius Niger in A.D. 194, and Eckhel thinks (*Doct. Num. Vet.*, vol. vii., p. 156,) that the legend VICTOR. IVST. AVG. on his coins should be interpreted *Victoria Justa Augusti*, in contradistinction to *Victoria Justi Augusti* on the coins of Pescennius Niger. The latter took the surname of *Justus*.

VICTOR. OMNIVM GEN. (*Gentium—retrograde.*) Mars helmeted, naked, with flowing mantle, walking to r., holding a spear and a trophy; on either side at his feet a captive seated; in the *exergue* P T P ? (retrograde.) *Obv.* FL. IVL. CRISPVS NOB. C. (*Nobilis Cæsar.*) Bust of Crispus to l., laureated, holding a globe surmounted by a Victory. *N*. from *Khell* (300 frcs.)

VICTOR OMNIVM GENTIVM. The Emperor, laureated, in military dress standing to l., holding a military standard and leaning on a shield; before him at his feet two captives kneeling; behind him a captive seated weeping; in the *exergue* P. TR. (*Prima Treveris*), TR. (*Treveris*), SMT. (*Signata Moneta Thessalonicæ,*) SMTSA. (*Signata Moneta Thessalonicæ I.*) or SMA. (*Signata Moneta Antiochiæ*), on gold coins of Constantine I. (150 frcs.), Constantine II. (400 frcs.), Constans I. (100 frcs.), and Constantius II. (50 frcs.)

VICTOR OMNIVM GENTIVM. Constantine I., in military dress standing to l., holding globe and spear, and crowned by Victory behind him, who holds a palm. In the *exergue* SMT. (*Signata Moneta Thessalonicæ.*) *Obv.* CONSTANTINVS P. F. AVG. Head of Constantine I., to r. laureated. *N*. (200 frcs.)

The letter T on the coins that may be attributed to *Thessalonica* can be distinguished from those of *Tarraco* by their style and type. The other mint-letters of Thessalonica are TES. ӨES. or TS. The letters TR. are always the initials of *Treves*. The mint of *Tarraco* was the suggestion of the late M. de Salis, who gave to that town the coins whose fabric approaches most that of the mints of Italy. The first pieces that were certainly struck there are those of Aurelian bearing the letters PXXT, SXXT, TXXT, QXXT, VXXT, VIXXT, *Prima* XX *Tarraconis*, *Secunda* XX *Tarraconis*, *Tertia* XX *Tarraconis*, *Quarta* XX *Tarraconis*, *Quinta* XX *Tarraconis*, *Sexta* XX *Tarraconis*. The usual *exergual* letters are P. T., *Prima Tarraconis*, S. T. *Secunda Tarraconis*, T. T. *Tertia Tarraconis*, &c. This series ceases about the time that that of Arles commences, and it is probable that Constantine transferred the monetary establishment of Tarraco to his new capital. (Madden, *Handbook of Rom. Num.*, p. 160; *Num. Chron.*, N.S., 1862, vol. ii., pp. 49, 243.)

VICTOR OMNIVM GENTIVM AVG. N. *(Augustus noster.)* Maxentius in military dress standing to r., holding in l. hand a spear, and receiving a victory from Mars, helmeted, standing to l., holding a trophy; between them a figure, prostrate at the feet of the Emperor; in the *exergue* P. OST. *(Prima Ostiæ.)* Obv. MAXENTIVS P. F. AVG. Head of Maxentius to r, laureated. N̶. (500 frcs.), Æ II. (30 frcs.)

After the defeat of Alexander in A.D. 311, the mint of Carthage was transferred by Maxentius to *Ostia*, and soon after the defeat of Maxentius by Constantine the mint of *Ostia* was transferred to Rome. (Madden, *Num. Chron.*, N.S., 1862, vol. ii., pp. 46, 47; 1865, vol. v., p. 3.)

VICTOR. SEVER. AVG. [or C. AVG.] *(Victoria Severi Augusti)* [or *Cæsaris Augusti.*] Victory walking to l., holding wreath and palm. *Obv.* IMP. CAE. L. SEP. SEV. PERT. AVG. COS. I. or II. Head of Septimius Severus to r., laureated. Æ. (12 frcs.)

VICTOR. TIBЄRI. A⧖S. *(Victoria Tiberii Augusti).* Cross on four steps or on a globe, or alone—on *Solidi* (60 frcs.), *Semisses* (60 frcs.), and *Tremisses* (15 frcs.), of Tiberius II. Constantine—also the legend VICTOR MAVRI. AVG on *Semissis* of Mauricius Tiberius. (40 frcs.)

VICTORE AVG. N. *(Augusti Nostri)* VOTIS. Victory seated to r., on a cuirass and shield, holding on her knees a shield on which VOT. X MVL. XX [or XXX alone in two lines] : before her a trophy at the foot of which two captives weeping; in the *exergue* P. T. *(Prima Tarraconis)* or R. *(Romæ.)* N̶. from Caylus and Wiczay (150 frcs.) [*Vota.*]

VICTORES AVGVSTI. Valentinian I. and his son, seated facing, holding a globe; above, Victory flying crowning them both; between them sometimes a palm; in the *exergue* TROB. *(Treveris 72).* Obv. D.N. VALENTINIANVS P. F. AVG. Bust of Valentinian I. to l., with helmet ornamented with three stars and a cuirass, holding a spear and a shield, on which is represented the Emperor on horseback, throwing down an enemy. N̶. (150 frcs.) Similar reverse type representing Valentinian I. and Valens on gold coin of Valens. (60 frcs.)

VICTORES [VBIQVE VICTORES; VNDIQVE VICTORES.]
VICTORI. AVG. *(Victoria Augusti).* Victory walking to l., holding a crown and a spear.

Obv. IMP. C. POSTVMVS P. F. AVG. Bust of Postumus to r., radiated. Æ. II. (10 frcs.)

VICTORI. AVG. *(Victoria Augusti.)* Victory in a *biga* to l., holding a wreath and a palm on gold coins of Carus (200 frcs.) and Diocletian (150 frcs.)

VICTORI. AVG. *(Victoria Augusti.)* Carausius standing to l. in military dress, holding globe and spear, and crowned by Victory, who holds a palm. *Obv.* IMP. CARAVSIVS P. F. AVG. Bust of Carausius to r. Æ. (300 frcs.)

VICTORI. AVG. *(Victoria Augustorum.)* Maximus standing to l. in military dress, holding a globe surmounted by a Victory and a standard. *Obv.* D. N. MAGNTVS *(sic)* P. F. AVG. Bust of Magnus Maximus to r., diademed. Æ. (2 frcs.)

VICTORI. AVGGG. *(Victoria Augustorum.)* Severus III. standing facing, placing his right foot on a *human* headed serpent, and holding a cross and a globe surmounted by a Victory; in the *field* RV. *(Ravennæ);* in the *exergue* COMOB. *Obv.* D. N. IBVS [for LIBIS or LIBIVS] SEVERVS P. F. AVG. Bust of Libius Severus III. to r., diademed. N̶. (30 frcs.)

VICTORI. A⧖S⧖S. *(Victoria Augusti)* Cross; in the *exergue* CONOB. *Obv.* P. or D.N. TIBЄRI. A⧖. Bust of Tiberius II. Constantine to r., diademed. N̶. *Semi-solidus* (40 frcs.)

VICTORI. MAVRI. AVG. *(Victoria Mauricii Augusti.)* Cross; in *exergue* CONOB. on *tremissis* of Tiberius II. Constantine (20 frcs.), and on *semissis* of Mauricius Tiberius (40 frcs.).

VICTORI. AVGGGG. *(Victoria Augustorum).* Victory standing l., holding a cross; in the *exergue* CONOB. *Obv.* D.N. IB or LIB. SEVERVS P. F. AVG. Bust of Libius Severus III. to r., diademed. N̶. *Tremissis* (15 frcs.)

VICTORI. AVGVS. *(Victoria Augusti.)* The *Labarum* terminating in a cross, with the monogram of Christ ☧; and two captives, on a brass medallion of Jovian, given by *Mionnet.*

VICTORI GENTIVM BARBARR. *(Barbararum).* The Emperor galloping to r., hurling his spear at a kneeling foe, who defends himself with spear and buckler; under the feet of the horse, a dying enemy—on brass medallions of Constantine II., (250 frcs.) and Constans I. (150 frcs.)

VICTORI. *(Victori.)* ERCVL. VICTORI. *Erculi Victori*, on gold and silver coins of Æmilianus—HERCVLI VICTORI on coins of Maximian Hercules, Constantius Chlorus, Galerius Maximianus, Severus II., Maximinus II., Licinius I., and Constantine I.—IOVI VICTORI on coins of Domitianus, Hadrianus, Commodus, Albinus, Septimius Severus, Elagabalus, Gallienus, Postumus, Victorinus I., Claudius II., Aurelianus, Vabalathus, Tetricus I., Tetricus II., Tacitus, Florianus, Probus and Carausius—MARTI VICTORI on coins of M. Aurelius, Pescennius Niger, Septimius Severus, Geta, Alexander Severus, Claudius II., and Florianus—MARTI VICTORI AVG. *(Augusti)* on small brass coins of Probus—MARTI VICTORI AVG. N. *(Augusti Nostri)* on second brass

of Maxentius, or MARTI VICTORI COMITI AVG.
N. *(Nostri)* on gold coin of Maxentius (1000
frcs.)

VICTORIA or VICTORINA. Victoria or
Victorina (for both names are given to her by
Trebellius Pollio) was the mother of Victorinus
I., and it was due to her influence that he was
chosen as colleague by Postumus about the
year A.D. 265. After the death of her son and
of her grandson in A.D. 267 [VICTORINVS I. and
II.], she was hailed as *Mater Castrorum* by
the soldiers and conferred the government of the
empire first on Marius and then on Tetricus, by
whom some say she was killed, though others
affirm she died a natural death (Treb. Poll. xxx
Tyr. c. 5, 6, 24, 25, 31.) Trebellius Pollio
further states that coins were struck of Victoria
in brass, gold, and silver. *(Cusi sunt ejus nummi
ærei, aurei et argentei, quorum, hodieque forma
extat apud Treviros.* xxx *Tyr.* c. 31.) There
is no doubt that allusion is here made to certain
gold coins of Victorinus I. on which may be
seen the portrait of Victoria with the attributes
of Victory and of Rome, of which the following
is a description :—

1. *Obv.* IMP. VICTORINVS AVG. Half
length bust of Victorinus I. to r., laureated
with cuirass, on which is the *ægis*, and armed
with a spear and a shield. *Rev.* VICTORIA AVG.
Bust of Victoria to r., laureated, with wings,
holding wreath and palm. *N*. (800 frcs.)

2. *Obv.* IMP. VICTORINVS PIVS AVG. Bust
of Victorinus I. to r., laureated, yoked to that of
Mars, also laureated. *Rev.* VICTORIA AVG.
Same reverse as No. 1. *N*. (800 frcs.)

3. *Obv.* IMP. C. VICTORINVS P. F. AVG.

Bust of Victorinus I. to r.,
laureated. *Rev.* LEG. IIII.
FLAVIA P. F. *(Pia Fide-
lis.)* Helmeted bust of
Victoria to r. above two
lions standing facing each
other. *N*. (600 frcs.)

4. *Obv.* IMP. VICTORINVS P. F. AVG. Bust
of Victorinus I. to l., laureated with cuirass,

holding a sceptre and a
shield. *Rev.* ROMAE AETER-
NAE. Helmeted bust of
Rome to r. with the
features of Victoria. *N*.
(800 frcs.)

5. *Obv.* IMP. CAES.
VICTORINVS P. F. AVG. Bust of Victorinus I.
to r., laureated. *Rev.* VOTA AVGVSTI. Hel-
meted bust of Rome to r. (with the features of
Victoria) yoked to that of Diana; before, a bow.
N. (800 frcs.)

6. *Obv.* IMP. VICTORINVS P. F. AVG. Bust
of Victorinus I. to l., laureated with cuirass,
holding a sceptre and a shield on which two
figures. *Rev.* VOTA AVGVSTI. Same reverse as
No. 5. *N*. (800 frcs.)

The two brass coins published in the catalogue
of D'Ennery and Pembroke (p. 306) with the
legend IMP. VICTORIA AVG., and on the reverse
CONSECRATIO, an eagle—are false. The Pembroke
piece is re-made from the second brass anonymous Gothic coins, with the legend INVICTA
ROMA and type an eagle (Sabatier, *Mon. Byz.*,
vol. i., p. 210, pl. xix.)

Victoria. The personification of Victory
among the Romans as Νίκη was among the
Greeks. The type of Victory is one of frequent
occurrence on coins, and may be found on the
early pieces of Campania, on the Victoriates, on
those of the Republic, and on those of the
Imperial and Byzantine series. Among the
more usual types with the legend VICTORIA
AVG. *(Augusti)*, AVGG. or AVGGG. *(Augustorum)*
may be mentioned—Victory seated, Victory
standing foot on helmet, or leaning against a
column or on a shield, or standing on a globe,
Victory erecting a trophy, Victory in a *biga* or
quadriga, Victory flying, Victory writing on a
shield, Victory walking, holding wreath and
palm or trophy (a very common type), Victory
crowning Emperor, trophy, gate of a camp,
Emperor standing holding standard or *labarum*
and a globe surmounted by Victory, Victory
standing holding a cross, &c.

VICTORIA. Victory standing, facing, placing
upon an altar or a base a shield on which P. R.
(Populi Romani.) *Obv.* SER. *(Servius)* GALBA
IMP. Head of Galba to r., laureated. *N*. from
Caylus (250 frcs.), *Æ.* (50 frcs.)

VICTORIA. Victory writing AVG. *(Augusti)*
on a shield placed on a column, on silver coins
of Pescennius Niger from *Vaillant* (250 frcs.) and
of Septimius Severus from *Wiczay* (10 frcs.)

VICTORIA. Victory standing to l., near an
altar, holding wreath and palm. *Obv.* IMP.
TETRICVS P. F. AVG. Bust of Tetricus I. to r.,
radiated. *Æ.* III. (3 frcs.)

VICTORIA. Justin I. standing to l., holding a long cross—on small brass coins of Justin
I. (10 frcs.)

VICTORIA AET. *(Æterna.)* Victory standing to l., holding wreath and palm. *Obv.* GAL-
LIENVS AVG. Head or bust of Gallienus to r.,
laureated or radiated. *N*. *Quin.* (100 frcs.),
Bil. (c.)

VICTORIA AETERNA. Victory walking
to r., holding wreath and palm, on gold coins of
Diocletian (80 frcs.), and second brass coins of
Maxentius (3 frcs.)

VICTORIA AETERNA AVG. N. *(Augusti
Nostri.)* Victory standing to r., presenting a
globe to Maxentius, in military dress, seated to l.,
at his side a cuirass, helmet, or shield; in the ex-
ergue P. OST. *(Prima Ostiæ)* or PR. *(Prima Romæ.)*
Obv. MAXENTIVS P. F. INV. *(Invictus)* AVG.
Helmeted bust of Maxentius to l.; on the helmet
Victory in *biga*. *N*. (600 frcs.) The same

legend, with various types of Victory, also occurs on his second (2 to 60 frcs.), and third brass coins (c. to 5 frcs.)

VICTORIA AETERNA AVG. N. (*Augusti Nostri*.) Victory standing to r., holding shield, on which VOTIS X, on a pedestal and placing l. foot on prow ; behind, a captive seated on the ground. In the *exergue* P. OST. (*Prima Ostiæ*.) *Obv.* MAXENTIVS. P. F. AVG. Full-faced bust of Maxentius, bare. *N.* (600 frcs.)

Full-faced busts on Roman coins are comparatively rare (Madden, *Num. Chron.*, N.S., 1862, vol. ii., p. 46 ; 1865, vol. v., pp. 86, 110; Evans, *Num. Chron.*, N.S., 1863, p. 119.)

VICTORIA AETERNA AVGG. (*Augustorum*), on a gold coin of Maxentius, given by *Tanini* (500 frcs.), and on a silver given by *Banduri* (200 frcs.)

VICTORIA ALEXANDRI AVG. N. (*Augusti Nostri.*) Victory walking to l., holding wreath and palm. *Obv.* IMP. ALEXANDER P. F. AVG. Head of Alexander to r., laureated. In the *exergue* P.K. (*Prima Karthaginis.*) Æ. (300 frcs.) Alexander was a usurper in Africa under Maxentius A.D. 308–311.

VICTORIA ANTONINI AVG. (*Augusti*.) Æ. I. of Elagabalus (12 frcs.) [VICTOR. ANTONINI AVG.]

VICTORIA AVG. (*Augusti*), with various types [*Victoria*] on coins of Vitellius, Vespasian, Titus, Domitian, Hadrian, Antoninus Pius, Lucius Verus, Pescennius Niger, Septimius Severus, Elagabalus, Alexander Severus, Maximinus I., Gordianus III., Philip I., Jotapian, Trajan Decius, Hostilian, Trebonianus Gallus, Volusian, Æmilian, Valerian I., Gallienus, Postumus, Lælian, Victorinus, Marius, Claudius II., Quintillus, Aurelian, Tetricus I. and II., Tacitus, Florian, Probus, Carus, Carinus, Julian Tyrannus, Diocletian, Carausius, Allectus, Constantius I., Constantine I. (with CONSTANTINOPOLIS), Constantius II.. Magnentius, Valentinian I., Procopius, Severus III., Romulus Augustulus, and on a contorniate of Antinous. The same legend and types occur on the Byzantine series down to the time of Constantine V. (A.D. 751—775.)

VICTORIA AVG. (*Augusti.*) Gordianus in military dress seated to l., on a curule chair, holding a spear and crowned by Victory, standing, who holds a palm ; before him a soldier standing holding a spear, and a figure standing facing; at the feet of the soldier a captive kneeling; above, a standard, a military standard and a legionary eagle. *Obv.* IMP. GORDIANVS PIVS FELIX AVG. Bust of Gordianus Pius to r. laureated, with *paludamentum* and cuirass, or with cuirass on which *ægis*. Æ. *Med.* (250 frcs.)

VICTORIA AVG. (*Augusti.*) Round tetrastyle temple; within the *tympanum* is the inscription NEIKH, and on the frieze ΟΠΛΟΦΟΡΟC. Within, a standing statue of the Emperor as Mars; on r. of Temple, the Emperor wearing pontifical robes and holding *patera* sacrificing at a lighted altar; behind him two attendants holding palms ; on left of temple the sacerdotal minister

[*Popa*] with axe raised slaying an ox, behind which a *Victimarius*. Brass medallion of Gordianus Pius with various types of obverse (500 frcs.) Also on Æ. II. (80 frcs.) These coins and that with ΘΕΟΣ ΟΠΛΟΦΟΡΟΣ [VICTORIA AVGVSTI] are, as Cohen remarks, (*Méd. Imp.*, 2nd ed., vol. v., p. 62), the only examples in the Roman coinage of a mixed inscription of Greek and Latin. They are also the only examples of the titles of *Victoria armigera* and *Mars armiger*. Froehner (*Médaillons Romaines*, p. 188), does not believe that a Greek inscription can be suitable for a Roman Temple, and considers that the Temple on the coin must have been erected either on the field of battle or in some city of Mesopotamia. Another reverse with MART. VICTOR. (*Marti Victori*)—Sacrifice before a round temple, on which ΘΕΟΥ ΟΠΛΟΦΟΡΟΥ is given by Eckhel (*Doct. Num. Vet.*, vol. vii., p. 314) from *Vaillant*, but Cohen states (*Méd. Imp.*, 2nd ed., vol. v., p. 63 *note*) that he has never met with it.

VICTORIA AVG. (*Augusti.*) Victory, walking to l., holding wreath and palm. *Obv.* IMP. [or IMP. C.] M. F. R. [or RV.] IOTAPIANVS AVG. (*Imperator Cæsar Marcus Fulvius Rufus Iotapianus Augustus.*) Bust of Iotapian to r., radiated, with cuirass. Æ. (1000 frcs.) Iotapianus was tyrant in Syria, under Philip, A.D. 249.

VICTORIA AVG. (*Augusti.*) On coins of Victorinus and Victoria. [VICTORIA.]

VICTORIA AVG. (*Augusti.*) Vessel to r., commanded by the captain seated at the prow, with five rowers, at the poop the *acrostolium* [ACROSTOLIVM] and three military standards ; at the prow Victory standing, holding wreath and palm. *Obv.* CONSTANTINOPOLIS. Bust of Constantinopolis to l., with helmet, laureated, wearing the Imperial mantle and holding a sceptre. Æ. I. (120 frcs.) These pieces are supposed to have been issued under Constantine I. and his sons.

VICTORIA AVG. (*Augusti.*) Vessel to r., on the poop of which the Emperor, seated, five rowers and a Victory standing at the prow. The poop is ornamented with an *acrostolium*, and above are three military standards. *Obv.* CONSTANTINVS IVN. NOB. C. (*Junior Nobilis Cæsar.*) Bust of Constantine II. to r., laureated. Æ. Small med. (250 frcs.)

VICTORIA AVG. (*Augusti*) II. or III. or VI. or VII., or VIII. or VIIII., usual type, [*Victoria*] on gold (150 to 200 frcs.) coins (II., III., and VII.), and billon (c. to 6 frcs.) coins (II., III., VI., VII., VIII. VIIII.) of Gallienus. VICTORIA AVG. III. also occurs on third brass coins of Tetricus I. (10 frcs.)

VICTORIA AVG. (*Augusti*) inscribed by Victory on a shield, which she is placing on a pedestal, on gold coins of Constantine I. with the legend VOTIS V. MVLTIS X (80 frcs.)

VICTORIA AVG. ET CAES. (*Augusti et Cæsaris.*) The Emperor standing to r., in military dress, holding the *labarum* and a laurel branch, and placing his foot on a captive, on second brass coins of Magnentius from *Banduri* and *Welzl* (10 frcs.) and Decentius from *Wiczay* (10 frcs.)

VICTORIA AVG. [or AVGG.] FEL. *('Augusti Felicis or Augustorum Felicium.)* Victory holding a wreath ; on the ground a shield on a base. On a gold coin of Carus from *Mionnet* (200 frcs.)

VICTORIA AVG. LIB. ROMANOR. *(Augusti. Libertas Romanorum.)* Victory and Liberty standing, holding together a trophy; Victory also holds a palm and Liberty a sceptre; in the *exergue* PR. *(Prima Romæ)*, R. *(Romæ)*, RP. *(Romæ Prima)*, RQ. *(Romæ Quarta)*, TR. *(Treveris)*, SMAQ. *(Signata Moneta Aquileiæ)*, &c., on gold (35 frcs.), and second and third brass (8 frcs.) coins of Magnentius, and on gold (Med. 800 frcs.—*solidus* 300 frcs.) of Decentius.

VICTORIA AVG. LIB. ROMANOR. *(Augusti. Libertas Romanorum.)* Magnentius standing in military dress to r., holding the *labarum* and a branch of laurel; to r. captive seated on the ground, his hands bound behind his back—on silver coins from *Banduri* (80 frcs.) and first, second, and third brass (c. to 6 frcs.) coins of Magnentius.

VICTORIA AVG. N. *(Augusti Nostri.)* Various types of Victory [*Victoria*] on third brass coins of Probus (10 frcs.), second brass of Maxentius (3 to 20 frcs.), and brass medallions of Constantius II. (100 frcs.) Sometimes VICTORIA AVG. NN. (*sic*) on brass medallions of Constantius II. (50 frcs.)

VICTORIA AVG. *(Augusti)* NOSTRI. Victory walking to l., holding wreath and palm ; behind, Constantius II. standing, holding globe and spear—on gold coins (80 frcs.) and brass medallion from *D'Ennery* (60 frcs.) of Constantius II.

VICTORIA AVGG. *(Augustorum.)* With various types [*Victoria*] on coins of Macrinus, Gordianus I., Gordianus II., Balbinus, Pupienus, Philip I., Philip II. Trebonianus Gallus, Volusianus, Valerianus, Gallienus, Quietus, Tetricus I., Carus, Carus and Carinus, Carinus, Numerianus, Carinus and Numerianus, Diocletianus, Maximianus Hercules, Constantius I. Chlorus, Galerius Maximianus, Constantinus I., Constans I., Constantius II., Magnentius, Decentius, Constantius Gallus, Julianus II., Valentinianus I., Valens, Gratianus, Valentinianus II., Theodosius I., Magnus Maximus, Eugenius, Honorius, Jovinus, Sebastianus, Johannes, Valentinianus III., Avitus, and Glycerius. The same legend and types occur on the coins of the Byzantine series down to the time of Heraclius A.D. 641.

VICTORIA AVGG. *(Augustorum.)* Four soldiers sacrificing at a tripod before the gate of a camp; in the *exergue* SIS. *(Sisciæ)*, and a star, on gold (300 frcs.) and silver (20 frcs.) coins of Diocletian and silver coins (30 frcs.) of Constantius Chlorus.

VICTORIA AVGG. *(Augustorum.)* Diocletianus and Maximianus Hercules standing facing each other, shaking hands; between them

Victory, standing facing, placing her hands on their shoulders. *Obv.* IMP. C. C. VAL. DIOCLETIANVS P. AVG. *(Imperator Cæsar Caius Valerius Diocletianus Pius Augustus.)* Bust of Diocletianus to r., radiated with cuirass. *Æ* III., from *Wiczay* (30 frcs.)

VICTORIA AVGG. *(Augustorum.)* Maximianus Hercules standing to r., holding a spear and supporting, with another figure standing, a small Victory. *Obv.* IMP. C. M. A. VAL. MAXIMIANVS P. AVG. *(Imperator Cæsar Marcus Aurelius Valerius Maximianus Pius Augustus.)* Bust of Maximianus Hercules to r., radiated. Æ. III. (20 frcs.)

VICTORIA AVGG. *(Augustorum.)* Two Emperors seated facing, holding a globe ; between them generally a palm ; above a Victory facing ; in the *exergue* various mint marks, on gold coins of Valentinianus I. (20 frcs.), of Valens (25 frcs.), of Gratianus (20 frcs.), Valentinianus III. (20 frcs.) of Theodosius I. (25 frcs.) and of Magnus Maximus (35 frcs.) The mint mark on the coins of Magnus Maximus is sometimes AVGOB. *(Augusta 72)*, and these were struck in London, a name of which was *Augusta*— "Egressus tendensque ad *Lundinium*, vetus oppidum quod *Augustam* posteritas appellavit" (Amm. Marcell., xxvii., 8.) "Theodosius vero . . . ab *Augustâ* profectus, quam veteres appellavere *Lundinium*" (Amm. Marcell., xxviii., 3.) For OB= 72 *see* VALENTINIANVS I.

VICTORIA AVGG. *(Augustorum.)* Military figure standing, holding a Victory and a spear. *Obv.* D. N. *(Dominus Noster)* EVGENIVS P. F. AVG. Bust of Eugenius to r., diademed. Æ. III., from *Welzl* (40 frcs.)

VICTORIA AVGG. *(Augustorum.)* Rome seated, holding a Victory, or globe surmounted by a Victory and a spear ; in the *exergue* various mint marks on silver coins of Honorius from *D'Ennery* (10 frcs.), of Jovinus from *D'Ennery* (30 frcs.), and of Sebastianus (300 frcs.) In the *exergue* of the coin of Sebastian are the letters KONT.—*Constantinæ*—Arles.

VICTORIA AVGG. *(Augustorum.)* Honorius, in military dress, standing facing, holding a standard, on which VOT. X. and a shield, on which MVLT. XX., and placing his left foot on a captive: in the *field* MD. *(Mediolani*-Milan) ; in the *exergue* COMOB on gold coins of Honorius (60 frcs.), and very similar type on gold coins of Jovinus (200 frcs.)

VICTORIA AVGG. *(Augustorum.)* Glycerius standing facing, placing his right or left foot on a stool, and holding a cross and a globe surmounted by a Victory ; in the *field* RV. *(Ravennæ)* or MD. *(Mediolani)* ; in the *exergue* COMOB. *Obv.* D. N. GLYCERIVS P. F. AVG. Bust of Glycerius to r., diademed. *N*. (250 frcs.)

VICTORIA AVGG. *(Augustorum.)* Constans I. on horseback to l., preceded by Victory. *Obv.* CONSTANS P. F. AVG. Bust of Constans I. to l., diademed. Æ. Contorniate. (Rare.)

VICTORIA AVGG. ET CAESS. NN. *(Augustorum et Cæsarum Nostrorum.)* Victory seated on arms, holding a shield, on which VOT. XX.; near her a trophy, at the foot of which a captive; in the *exergue* SIRM. *(Sirmii)* or SMNK. *(Signata Moneta Nicomediæ.)* *Obv.* CONSTANTINVS P. F. AVG. Head of Constantine I. to r., laureated. *N.* (60 frcs.)

VICTORIA AVGG. NN. *(Augustorum Nostrorum.)* Victory walking to l., holding a wreath and a palm on small brass of Licinius I. (20 frcs.), on silver (100 frcs.) and small brass coins (10 to 12 frcs.) of Constantine I., on silver of Constans I. (30 frcs.), and on small brass from *Wiczay* of Constantius II. (4 frcs.)

VICTORIA AVGG. NN. *(Augustorum Nostrorum.)* Victory standing to r., placing her l. foot on a helmet, and attaching to a palm tree a shield on which VOT. X. *Obv.* CONSTANTINVS MAX. *(Maximus)* AVG. Bust of Constantine I. to l., with the helmet ornamented with a Victory and a cuirass, holding in the r. hand a spear and a horse by the bridle, and in the l. a shield, on which is represented the Emperor on horseback. Æ. III. (30 frcs.)

VICTORIA AVGG. NN. *(Augustorum Nostrorum.)* Victory seated to r. on a cuirass, writing VOT. X. on a shield which she holds on her knees; in the *exergue* sometimes CONST. *(Constantinæ-*Arles.) *Obv.* CONSTANS P. F. AVG. Bust of Constans I. to r., diademed. Æ. Med. (100 frcs.)

VICTORIA AVGGG. *(Augustorum),* with various types [*Victoria*] on coins of Gratian, Valentinian II., Theodosius I., Honorius, Placidia, Constantine III., Johannes, Valentinian III., Avitus, Majorian, Severus III., Eufemia, Glycerius, Julius Nepos, and Romulus Augustulus. The same legend and types occur on the coins of the Byzantine series down to the time of Mauricius Tiberius, A.D. 582-602.

VICTORIA AVGGG. *(Augustorum.)* Armed figure, standing, holding in the r. hand a spear surmounted by a cross, and in the left a small Victory, and placing the r. foot on a helmet; to the l. a shield. *Obv.* D. N. VALENTINIANVS P. F. AVG. Bust of Valentinian I. to r., diademed. Æ. I., from *Mionnet* (60 frcs.)

VICTORIA AVGGG. *(Augustorum.)* Two Victories, standing, facing each other, holding a wreath and a palm. *Obv.* D. N. THEODOSIVS. P. F. AVG. Bust of Theodosius I. to r., diademed. Æ. III. (4 frcs.) Similar type on Æ. III. of Magnus Maximus, from *Wiczay* (5 frcs.)

VICTORIA AVGGG. *(Augustorum.)* Rome, helmeted, seated to l., on a cuirass, holding a Victory on a globe, or a standard and a spear, on silver coins of Honorius (6 to 20 frcs.), and Jovinus (30 frcs.)

VICTORIA AVGGG. *(Augustorum.)* The Emperor standing, placing his foot on the head of a dragon, and holding a cross and a globe surmounted by a Victory, in the *field* various letters RM. *(Romæ),* RV. *(Ravennæ),* MD. *(Mediolani),* &c.; in the *exergue* COMOB, on gold coins of Valentinian III. (25 to 50 frcs.), Petronius Maximus (400 frcs.), Majorian (50

frcs.), Severus III. (30 to 40 frcs.), and Anthemius (150 frcs.)

VICTORIA AVGGG. *(Augustorum.)* Theodosius II. and Valentinian III., standing, facing, each holding a cross and a globe; a hand crowns Valentinian III.; in the *field* RM. *(Romæ)*; in the *exergue* COMOB. *Obv.* D. N. PLA. *(Placidius)* VALENTINIANVS P. F. AVG. Bust of Valentinian III. to r., diademed. *N.* (100 frcs.)

VICTORIA AVGVST. or AVGVSTI, with various types [*Victoria*] on coins of Claudius, Nero, Vitellius, Vespasian, Titus, Domitian, Nerva, Hadrian, Commodus, Septimius Severus, Alexander Severus, Maximinus I., Gordian III., Constantine I., Constans I., and Attalus. The coins of Vespasian and Titus with this legend and the type of Victory writing on a shield OB. CIV. SER. *(ob Cives Servatos)* or VIC. AVG. *(Victoria Augusti)* attached to a palm, beneath which Judæa seated weeping, commemorate the conquest of Judæa.

VICTORIA AVGVSTI S. C. Victory turreted flying to l., and holding a diadem with both hands on brass medallions (250 frcs.), and first brass coins (8 frcs.) of Antoninus Pius.

VICTORIA AVGVSTI. Same type as that described under VICTORIA AVG. (Gordian III.), but on the Temple ΘΕΟΣ ΟΠΛΟΦΟΡΟΣ. Æ. Med. (500 frcs.)

VICTORIA AVGVSTI. Gordian III. on horseback raising the r. hand and holding a spear. *Obv.* IMP. . . . GORDIANVS . . . Bust of Gordian III. to r., radiated. Æ. (30 frcs.)

VICTORIA AVGVSTI. Gallienus in military dress, standing, holding a globe and crowned by Victory behind him. *Obv.* GALLIENAE AVGVSTAE. Head of Gallienus crowned with ears of corn (?). *N.* (400 frcs.) [VBIQVE PAX.]

VICTORIA AVGVSTI. Turreted female (Constantinople), seated to l., placing her foot on a prow, holding olive branch and cornucopiæ, and crowned by Victory standing behind her and holding a palm. *Obv.* VICT. *(Victor)* CONSTANTINVS AVG. Bust of Constantine II. to r., diademed. Æ. Med. (250 frcs.) [VIC. or VICT.]

VICTORIA AVGVSTI N. *(Nostri.)* Usual types [*Victoria*], on coins of Constantius II. (*N.* *Quin.,* 35 frcs.; Æ. Med., from *Tanini* 10 frcs.), Julian II. (Æ. 25 frcs.), Jovian (Æ. Med., from *Wiczay,* 100 frcs.); and Valens (*N.* *Quin.,* from *Mionnet,* 50 frcs.)

VICTORIA AVGVSTI NOSTRI. Constans I., holding spear and shield, walking and dragging a male captive by the hair, to r. a female captive kneeling, in *exergue* AQ. *(Aquileiæ)* and trophies. *Obv.* FL. IVL. CONSTANS PIVS FELIX AVG. Bust of Constans I. to r., raising r. hand, and holding globe, on which a Victory; gold medallion of Constans I. of the weight of nine *solidi,* and struck at Aquileia *(Berliner Blätter für Munz-Siegel-und-Wappenkunde,* vol. iv., 1868; Frochner, *Médaillons Romaines,* p. 300.)

VICTORIA AVGVSTORVM. Usual types [*Victoria*] on coins of Hostilian, Carinus, Constantine I., Constans I., Constantius II., Vetranio, Magnentius, Decentius, Constantius Gallus, Julian II., Valentinian I., Valens, Gratian, Valentinian II., Theodosius I., Magnus Maximus, Victor, Eugenius, Honorius, Constantius III., Johannes and Valentinian III., and on coins of the Byzantine series down to the time of Heraclius, A.D. 641.

VICTORIA AVGVSTORVM S. C. Maximinus I. in military dress, and Maximus in *toga*, standing, facing each other holding a Victory; behind each of them a soldier; between them two captives seated on the ground. *Obv.* MAXIMINVS PIVS AVG. GERM. Bust of Maximinus I. to r., laureated. Æ. I. (50 frcs.)

VICTORIA AVGVSTORVM. Philip I. and Philip II., standing, in military dress, holding a globe on which is a Victory; behind each of them a soldier standing. *Obv.* CONCORDIA AVGVSTORVM. Busts jugate of Philip I. laureated and Otacilia diademed to r., facing the bust of Philip II. to l., bare. Æ. Med. from *Vaillant* (400 frcs.) A similar reverse type on brass medallions of Valerian I. (400 frcs.) and on brass coins of Gallienus and Saloninus from *Mionnet* (300 frcs.)

VICTORIA AVGVSTORVM. Victory half naked, seated on a cuirass, writing VOT. V. MVL. X. on a shield placed on a base; in the *field* to l. O; to r. B; in the *exergue* CONS. *(Constantinopolis)* on gold coins of Valentinian I. and Valens (30 frcs.) [*Remarks on letters* OB, &c., *under* VALENTINIANVS I.]

VICTORIA BAEATISSIMORVM *(sic)* CAESS. *(Cæsarum.)* Victory seated to r., on a cuirass, holding on her knee a shield, on which VOT. X.; behind her a shield. *Obv.* CONSTANTINVS IVN. NOB. CAES. Bust of Constantine II. to r., laureated. Æ. Med. (150 frcs.)

VICTORIA BEATISSIMORVM CAESS. *(Cæsarum.)* Similar type to previous piece, on brass medallions of Constantius Chlorus (400 frcs.) and Constantine I. (300 frcs.)

VICTORIA BRIT. *(Britannica.)* Victory standing to r. *Obv.* ANTONINVS PIVS. AVG. Head of Caracalla to r. Æ. from *Wiczay* (6 frcs.)

VICTORIA CAES. LIB. ROMANOR. *(Cæsarum. Libertas Romanorum.)* Victory standing to r. and Liberty to l., holding a trophy together; Victory holds a palm and Liberty a spear; in the *exergue* TR. *(Treveris.)* *Obv.* D. N. DECENTIVS FORT. *(Fortissimus)* CAES. Bust of Decentius to r. bare. N. (300 frcs.)

VICTORIA CAESAR. NN. *(Cæsarum Nostrorum.)* Victory walking to l., holding trophy and palm, in the *field* to r., LXXII; to l. a star with seven or eight rays; in the *exergue* SMAN. *(Signata Moneta Antiochiæ)*, on gold coins of Constantius II. (80 frcs.), and Constans I. (80 frcs.) The same legend and type, but said to be without the LXXII in the *field*, occur on a gold coin of Constantine II.

(200 frcs.) The figures LXXII signify that 72 *solidi* were coined to the pound, Constantine I. having reduced the *aureus* about the year A.D. 312. [*Remarks on the letters* OB &c., *under* VALENTINIANVS I.] The star on these coins occupying the same position in the *field* as the ☧ on the coin of Constantine I. [VICTORIA CONSTANTINI AVG.] probably has some Christian signification. It was at Antioch that the name Χριστιανός was first used about A.D. 44. (Acts xi., 26; Madden, *Christian Emblems on the Coins of Constantine I., &c.*, in the *Num. Chron.*, N.S., 1877, vol. xvii., pp. 279—281.)

VICTORIA CAESARIS. Victory in a *biga*, on gold coins of Numerian (300 frcs.), and Carinus (300 frcs.)

VICTORIA CAES. *(Cæsarum.)* Victory walking to l., holding wreath and palm. *Obv.* CONSTANTINVS IVN. NOB. C. *(Junior Nobilis Cæsar.)* Bust of Constantine II. to r., laureated N. *Tremissis* (200 frcs.)

VICTORIA CAESS. NN. *(Cæsarum Nostrorum.)* Victory walking to l., holding wreath and palm, on small brass coins of Licinius II. (10 frcs.), Crispus (5 frcs.), and Constantine II. (6 frcs.)

VICTORIA CARPICA. Victory running to r., holding wreath and palm. *Obv.* IMP. PHILIPPVS AVG. Bust of Philip I. to r., radiated, Æ. (12 frcs.) This coin commemorates the successful war against the Carpi, a Scythian or Gothic tribe, in A.D. 247, by which victory Philip I. gained for himself and his son the titles of *Germanicus Maximus* and *Carpicus Maximus*, as corroborated by a brass medallion of Philip I., Otacilia and Philip II., with the legend GERM. MAX. CARPICI. MAX III. ET II. COS. (500 frcs.)

VICTORIA CONSTANTI AVG. *(Augusti.)* Victory seated on shield and cuirass, writing on shield VOT. X MVLT. XX. or VOT. XV. or VOT. XXXX.; in the *exergue* SMAN. *(Signata Moneta Antiochiæ)* or CONS. *(Constantinopolis)* or SMN. *(Signata Moneta Nicomediæ)* on gold coins of Constantius II. (25 to 30 frcs.)

VICTORIA CONSTANTI CAES. *(Cæsaris.)* Same type, on the shield VOT. XV.; in the *exergue* CONS. *(Constantinopolis.)* *Obv.* FL. IVL. CONSTANTIVS NOB. C. Bust of Constantius II. to r., diademed. N. (25 frcs.)

VICTORIA CONSTANTINI AVG. *(Augusti.)* Various types *(Victoria)* on gold coins of Maximinus II. (300 frcs.), gold coins (50 to 150 frcs.) and second brass (40 frcs.) of Constantine I., gold coins (40 frcs.) and brass medallions (250 frcs.) of Constantine II., and on a contorniate of Constantine I. (Very rare.)

VICTORIA CONSTANTINI AVG. *(Augusti.)* Victory walking to l., holding trophy and palm; in the *field* to l. ☧; to r. LXXII.; in the *exergue* SMAN. *(Signata Moneta Antiochiæ.)* *Obv.* CONSTANTINVS P. F. AVG. Head of Constantine I. to r., laureated. N. (200 frcs.) [VICTORIA CAESAR. NN.; *Remarks on the letters* OB, &c., *under* VALENTINIANVS I.]

VICTORIA CONSTANTINI CAES. *(Cæsaris.)* Victory seated on cuirass and shield, writing on another shield VOT. X. or VOT. XX.; in the *exergue* SIRM. *(Sirmii)* on gold coins of Constantine II. (250 frcs.; *Quin.*, 200 frcs.)

VICTORIA CONSTANTIS *(sic)* AVG. *(Augusti.)* Victory seated to r. on a cuirass and shield, writing VOT. V. MVLT. X. on a shield: in the *exergue* SIS *(Sisciæ)* on gold coins of Constantine II. (250 frcs.); a similar legend (correct) and type (the vows varying) on gold coins of Constans I. (60 frcs., *Quin.* 40 frcs.) Victory walking to r., placing foot on captive, and holding shield on which VOT. V. MVLT. X. on gold coins of Constans I. (60 frcs.)

VICTORIA CONSVΛIIB. Cross on three steps; in the *exergue* CONOB. *(Constantinopolis* 72*).* *Obv.* DM. N. *(Domini Nostri)* HЄRACLI CONSVΛIIB. Busts of Heraclius I., bearded, and Heracleonas unbearded, facing, separated by a cross. *N.* (300 frcs.) Other gold coins have the legend VICTORIA CONSΛBIA. The letters IIB and BIA are unexplained. This is the last occurrence of the title of *Consul.* (A.D. 610-640.)

VICTORIA D. N. AVG. *(Domini Nostri Augusti.)* Victory walking to l., holding wreath and palm, in the *exergue* CONS. *(Constantinopolis.)* *Obv.* D. N. VALENS P. F. AVG. Bust of Valens r., diademed. *N. Tremissis* (40 frcs.)

VICTORIA D. N. *(Domini Nostri)* AV-GVSTI. Victory seated to l., writing VOT. V. MULT. X. on a shield, presented by a winged genius; in the *exergue* TESOB. *(Thessalonicæ,* 72*).* *Obv.* D. N. VALENTINIANVS P. F. AVG. Helmeted bust of Valentinian I. to l., holding a spear and a shield, on which is represented the Emperor on horseback. *N.* Med. (400 frcs.)

VICTORIA D. N. *(Domini Nostri)* ET PRINCIPVM. Two Victories standing, placing on an altar a shield, on which VOT. P.R. *(Vota Populi Romani)*; in the *exergue* two captives, seated between R. and P. *(Romæ prima.)* *Obv.* D.N. CONSTANTINO IVN. NOB. C. Bust of Constantine II. to r., laureated. Æ. III. from *Tanini* (15 frcs.)

VICTORIA DD. NN. *(Dominorum Nostrorum.)* Victory walking l., holding wreath and palm; in the *exergue* CON. A. *(Constantinopolis I.)* *Obv.* PL. CL. IVLIANVS NOB. CAES. Bust of JulianII. to r., bare. *N. Quin.* (50 frcs.)

VICTORIA DD. NN. AVG. *(sic)* *(Dominorum Nostrorum Augustorum.)* Victory walking; in the *exergue* LVG. *(Lugduni-*Lyons.) *Obv.* IMP. CE. VALENS P. F. AG. *(sic.)* Bust of Valens diademed. Æ. III. in the *Musée de Vienne* (10 frcs.) A similar legend and type occurs on gold *quinarius* of Valentinian I. (80 frcs.)

VICTORIA DD. NN. AVGG. *(Dominorum Nostrorum Augustorum)* on coins of Constantine II., Constans I., Constantius II., Magnentius, Decentius, and Julian II.

VICTORIA DDD. NNN. AVGGG. *(Dominorum Nostrorum Augustorum.)* Vic-

tory walking l., holding shield, on which VOT. V. MVLT. X., on gold coin of Constans I. (100 frcs.), and SIC. X SIC. XX on gold coin of Constantius II. (30 frcs.)

VICTORIA DOMINI ANTI. COLONI. *(sic)* S. R. *(Antiochia Colonia Senatus Romanus.)* Victory walking to r., holding trophy. *Obv.* IMP. CAES. M. ANT. GORDIANVS AVG. Bust of Gordianus Pius to r., radiated, Æ. I. (Cohen, *Méd. Imp.*, 2nd ed., vol. v., p. 77, Nos. 501—503.)

VICTORIA G. M. *(Germanici Maximi.)* Victory standing to l., holding wreath and palm; at her feet a captive or a trophy between two captives. *Obv.* IMP. GALLIENVS P. F. AVG. GERM or G.M. *(Germanicus Maximus.)* Bust of Gallienus to r., radiated. *Bil.* (c. to 3 frcs.); also same reverse type Æ I. (8 frcs.) The same legend and type on small brass coin of Claudius II. (30 frcs.)

VICTORIA GALBAE AVG. *(Augusti.)* Victory standing to r. or to l., on a globe, holding wreath and palm. *Obv.* SER. *(Servius)* GALBA IMP. CAESAR AVG. P.M. TR. P. Head of Galba to r., laureated. *R. Quin.* (30 frcs.)

VICTORIA GER. *(Germanica.)* Trophy between two captives seated, on gold (300 frcs.) and small brass coins (6 frcs.) of Probus and small brass of Carausius (15 frcs.)

VICTORIA GERM. *(Germanica.)* Various types [*Victoria*] on coins of Maximinus I. (*N.* 700 frcs.; *N.*, Quin, 600 frcs.; *R.* 4 frcs., *R. Quin*, 50 frcs.), Valerian I. (*Bil.* 2 frcs.; *R.* I., 20 frcs., Æ. II., 10 frcs.), Gallienus (*N.* 150 frcs., *Bil.* c.; *Bil. Quin*, 20 frcs; Æ. I., 15 frcs., Æ. II., 8 frcs.), Tetricus I. (*N.* 350 frcs.); and Probus (*N.* 200 frcs.; Æ. II., 50 frcs., Æ. III., c. to 10 frcs.)

VICTORIA GERMAN. *(Germanica.)* Victory standing to r., holding a palm and presenting a wreath to the Emperor, standing, who holds a globe and a spear on *billon* coins of Gallienus (4 frcs.) and Saloninus (20 frcs.)

VICTORIA GERMAN. *(Germanica.)* Trophy between two captives. *Obv.* IMP. CLAVDIVS AVG. or P. F. AVG. Bust of Claudius II. to r., radiated. Æ. III. (30 frcs.) The same type occurs with VICTORIA GERMANIC., and in the *exergue* S. P. Q. R. Æ. III. (30 frcs.)

VICTORIA GERMANICA. Various types [*Victoria*] on coins of Caracalla (*N.* 200 frcs., *R.* 6 frcs.), Maximinus I. (*R.* from *Vaillant* 60 frcs.; Æ. Med., 500 frcs., Æ. I., 8 to 15 frcs., Æ. II., 4 to 6 frcs.), Herennius (*R.* 20 frcs.), Hostilian (*R.* 40 frcs.), Valerian I. (*Bil.* 4 frcs.), Gallienus (*Bil.* 3 frcs., Æ. Med. 360 frcs., Æ. II. 20 frcs.), Postumus (*Bil.* 30 frcs., Æ. I. 60 frcs.), and Carinus (*N.* 300 frcs.)

VICTORIA GERMANICA. Maximinus I. galloping to l., overthrowing two Germans: he is preceded by Victory, who holds a wreath, and followed by a soldier armed with a shield. *Obv.* MAXIMINVS ET MAXIMVS AVGVSTI GERMANICI. Busts facing each other of Maximinus I. to r., laureated, and of Maximus to l., bare. Æ. Med. (600 frcs.)

VICTORIA GERMANICA. Trajan Decius, in military dress on horseback to l., raising his r. hand and holding a sceptre; he is preceded by Victory holding a palm. *Obv.* IMP. CAE. TRA. DECIVS AVG. Bust of Trajanus Decius to r., radiated. Æ. (12 frcs.)

VICTORIA GORDIANI AVG. *(Augusti.)* Victory walking to r., holding wreath and palm. *Obv.* IMP. GORDIANVS PIVS FEL. AVG. Bust of Gordianus Pius to r., radiated. Æ. (5 frcs.)

VICTORIA GOTHIC. *(Gothica.)* Victory walking to l., holding wreath and palm; at her feet a captive seated. *Obv.* IMP. C. M. *(Cæsar Marcus)* AVR. PROBVS AVG. Bust of Probus to r., laureated. N. (180 frcs.)

VICTORIA GOTHICA. Rome, helmeted, seated to r. on a shield, holding a sceptre; Victory approaching presents her a wreath and a Goth bowing. *Obv.* CONSTANTINVS MAX. AVG. *(Maximus Augustus.)* Bust of Constantine I. to r., diademed. Æ. Med. (300 frcs.)

VICTORIA GOTTHI. *(Gotthica.)* Victory standing to l., holding wreath and palm, on small brass coins of Tacitus (6 to 12 frcs.)— one obverse legend is IMP. C. M. CL. *(Cæsar Marcus Claudius)* TACITVS P. F. INVICTVS AVG.

VICTORIA GOTTHICA COS. II. Victory walking to l., holding wreath and palm; at her feet a captive seated. *Obv.* IMP. C. M. CL. *(Cæsar Marcus Claudius)* TACITVS AVG. Bust of Tacitus to r., laureated. N. (300 frcs.) The Victory over the Goths was the most memorable event of the short reign (six months) of Tacitus [VICTORIA PONTICA AVG.]

VICTORIA NAVALIS S. C. Victory holding a wreath, standing on the prow of a vessel, sometimes terminating in a serpent, on second brass coins of Vespasian (2 frcs.), of Titus (5 frcs.), and of Domitian (5 frcs.) These coins commemorate either the great naval loss by tempest sustained by the Jews who had fled from Joppa to their ships when the town was attacked by Cestius, or the naval victory gained by the vessels of Vespasian over the barks of the Jews on the lake of Gennesareth. There is a very rare second brass coin of Titus, bearing the legend, IVDAEA NAVALIS S.C., and having for type a palm tree; on the l. arms, and on the r. Judæa seated on the ground; and on some of the large brass coins of Vespasian and Titus, with the legend IVDAEA CAPTA, the Emperors are represented resting their r. foot on the prow of a vessel (Madden, *Coins of the Jews,* p. 222). In the account of the triumph of Vespasian and Titus it is recorded (Joseph. *Bell. Jud.,* vii., 5, 5) that at one part of the procession there "followed a *great number of ships.*" This naval victory was considered of such importance that it was commemorated at a later period. Coins of Marcus Aurelius exist struck at Gadara with the legend ΝΑΥΜΑ. ΓΑΔΑΡΕΩΝ and the type a trireme, from which it may be assumed that a *naumachia* was celebrated under this Emperor on the lake of Gennesareth.

VICTORIA OTHONIS. Victory to l. or r., holding wreath and palm, on gold (250 to 300 frcs.) and silver coins (30 frcs.) of Otho.

VICTORIA P. R. *(Populi Romani.)* Victory standing, sometimes on a globe, holding wreath and palm, on silver (plated) coin (12 frcs.) of Augustus, and on gold (200 frcs.) and silver coins (12 to 20 frcs.) of Galba. The coin of Augustus is hybrid, and the reverse legend belongs to Galba, by whom it was probably struck.

VICTORIA PART. *(Parthica).* Victory presenting wreath to Emperor, on *billon* coins of Gallienus from *Banduri* (20 frcs.), and of Saloninus (10 frcs.) On another *billon* coin of Gallienus from *Banduri* (20 frcs.), the type is Victory standing, holding wreath and palm.

VICTORIA PARTH. MAX. *(Parthica Maxima),* usual types [*Victoria*] on silver coins of Septimius Severus (c.), and Caracalla (10 frcs.)

VICTORIA PARTHICA, usual types [*Victoria*] on coins of Macrinus (Æ. 8 frcs., Æ. I. 50 frcs.), and Valerian I. from *Vaillant (Bil.,* 12 frcs.)

VICTORIA PARTHICA MAXIMA, usual types [*Victoria*] on coins of Septimius Severus, (N. 200 frcs.), Septimius and Caracalla with obverse legend IMPP. *(Imperatores)* INVICTI PII AVGG. *(Augusti)* and busts jugate of Severus and Caracalla (N. 250 frcs., Æ. 60 frcs.), and of Caracalla (N. 150 frcs.)

VICTORIA PERPET. *(Perpetua.)* Victory standing to r., placing l. foot on helmet, and writing XXX on a shield placed on the trunk of a tree. *Obv.* VIRTVS FLORIANI AVG. *(Augusti.)* Bust of Florian to l., laureated, holding sceptre and shield. N. (500 frcs.)

VICTORIA PERPETV. *(Perpetua.)* Victory walking to l., holding wreath and palm; in *exergue* TR. *(Treveris.) Obv.* FL. CL. *(Flavius Claudius)* IVLIANVS AVG. Bust of Julian II. to r., laureated. Æ. (30 frcs.)

VICTORIA PERPETVA. Victory in *biga* to l. *Obv.* IMP. C. M. AVR. *(Imperator Cæsar Marcus Aurelius)* PROBVS AVG. Bust of Probus to r., laureated. N. (200 frcs.)

VICTORIA PERSICA. Galerius Maximian on horseback to r., spearing several enemies and crowned by Victory. In the *exergue* SIS. *(Sisciæ.) Obv.* GAL. VAL. MAXIMIANVS NOB. C. *(Nobilis Cæsar.)* Bust of Galerius Maximian to r., laureated, in consular dress, holding a sceptre, surmounted by an eagle. Æ. Med. (Froehner, *Médaillons Romaines,* p. 266.)

VICTORIA PONTICA AVG. *(Augusti.)* Victory standing offering wreath to Tacitus; in the middle a star; in the *exergue* KAΔ (21·4. *Obv.* IMP. C. M. CL. *(Cæsar Marcus Claudius)* TACITVS AVG. Bust of Tacitus, radiated. Æ. III. (100 frcs.) [VICTORIA GOTTHI. and GOTTHICA COS. II.]

VICTORIA PRINCIPVM. Victory standing on prow of vessel to r., holding wreath and a long palm over l. shoulder; in the *field*

s. c. *(Senatus Consulto.)* *Obv.* D. N. THEO-
DAHADVS REX. Bust of Theodahatus to r.,
bearded and crowned. Æ. I. (10 frcs.) A
similar reverse type on silver coin of Justinian
I. is given by *Mionnet* (12 frcs.) The
letters s. c. generally disappeared from the
Roman coinage during the reign of Gallienus,
but may be found on the second brass coins of
Florian. Two centuries later they re-appeared
on the large brass pieces of Zeno and of Zeno and
Leo, struck at Rome with the legend INVICTA
ROMA, and then upon the coins of Theodahatus,
king of the Ostrogoths, A.D. 534. This piece is
" forty *nummi*," and the first coin ever issued
having the portrait of a king of the Teutonic
race (Lenormant, *La Mon. dans l'Antiq.*,
vol. ii., p. 418; Keary, *Num. Chron.*, N.S., 1878,
vol. xviii., p. 157.)

VICTORIA ROMANOR. *(Romanorum.)*
Rome helmeted, seated to l. on cuirass, holding
a globe, surmounted by a Victory and a spear;
in the *exergue* SM. *(Sirmii.)* *Obv.* D. N.
MAXIMVS P. F. AVG. Bust of Maximus
Tyrannus to r., diademed. Æ. from *Banduri*
(200 frcs.) Maximus was a usurper under
Constantine III. and Constans in A.D. 411.

VICTORIA ROMANORVM. Victory walk-
ing, holding wreath and palm; sometimes at her
feet a captive, on coins of Constantius II. (Æ.
Med., 100 frcs.), Constantius Gallus (Æ. Med.
from *Tanini*, 150 frcs.), Eugenius (Æ. III. 40
frcs.), Constantius III. (VICTORIA ROMANORVM
in *exergue* S. M. N. *Signata Moneta Nicomediæ*,
Æ. 200 frcs.), and Attalus (Æ. 100 frcs.)

VICTORIA ROMANORVM. An arch
supported by two columns, beneath which Julian,
in military attire, standing facing, holding sceptre
and globe and turning his face towards Victory,
who crowns him and holds a palm; in the
exergue SIRM. *(Sirmii.)* *Obv.* FL. CL. IVLIANVS
P. F. AVG. Bust of Julian II., bearded, to r.,
diademed. Æ. Med. (150 frcs.)

VICTORIA ROMANORVM. The Emperor,
in military dress, standing r., holding sceptre
or standard or *labarum*, and Victory sometimes
on globe, on large brass coins of Julian II. (30
frcs.) and Jovian (8 frcs.)

VICTORIA SARMAT. *(Sarmatica.)* Four
soldiers sacrificing on a tripod before the gate of
a camp; in the *exergue* nothing, or various
letters, on coins of Diocletian (Æ. 8 frcs.),
Maximian Hercules (Æ. 8 frcs.), Constantius
Chlorus (12 frcs.), and Galerius Maximian (Æ.
10 frcs.)

VICTORIA SARMATI. *(Sarmatica.)* Same
type. *Obv.* D. N. *(Domino Nostro)* CONSTANTIO
NOB. C. *(Nobili Cæsari.)* Head of Constantius
Chlorus, laureated. Æ. from *Banduri* (100
frcs.)

VICTORIA SARMATICA. Same type.
Obv. MAXIMIANVS AVG. Head of Maximian
Hercules to r., laureated. Æ. (8 frcs.)

VICTORIAE. Two Victories flying, holding
a shield, on which AVGG. *(Augustorum)*, and
each holding a palm; above, Caracalla standing,
laureated, in military dress, holding globe and
sceptre; below, two captives seated back to

back; behind, a shield. *Obv.* ANTONINVS PIVS
AVG. Bust of Caracalla to r., laureated. Æ.
(80 frcs.)

VICTORIAE AETERNAE AVGG. *(Augustorum.)* Caracalla and Geta in *toga*, shaking
hands; between them a Victory, on coins of
Caracalla, from *Vaillant* (Æ. I., 50 frcs.; Æ.
II., 30 frcs.)

VICTORIAE AVG. *(Augusti.)* Various
types [*Victoria*] on coins of Pescennius Niger
(Æ. 250 frcs.), Septimius Severus (Æ. Med.
50 frcs.), Caracalla (Æ. from *Khell*, 8 frcs.),
Postumus (Æ. I. 6 to 20 frcs., Æ. II. 4
frcs.), and Probus (N. 2C0 frcs., Æ. III. 6
to 20 frcs.)

VICTORIAE AVG. *(Augusti.)* Two Victories, standing, holding a globe, on which a
third Victory, facing, with outspread wings,
holding wreath and palm, on coins of Gallienus
(N. from *Mionnet* 250 frcs.; *Bil.* 30 frcs.)

VICTORIAE AVGG. *(Augustorum.)* Va-
rious types [*Victoria*] on coins of Septimius
Severus (N. 150 to 250 frcs., Æ. 5 frcs., Æ.
II., 6 frcs.), Caracalla (Æ. 10 frcs., Æ. I. 20
frcs., Æ. II. 8 frcs.), Valerian I. (N. 450 frcs.,
Bil. 30 frcs.), Gallienus (N. 200 frcs.), and
Maxentius (Æ. III. from *Banduri*, 3 frcs.)

VICTORIAE AVGG. *(Augustorum.)* Severus carrying a Victory crowned by a flying
Victory; to l. Atlas kneeling holding the world
with two hands. *Obv.* SEVERVS PIVS AVG.
Head of Septimius Severus to r., laureated. Æ.
(100 frcs.)

VICTORIAE AVGG. *(Augustorum.)* Soldier
helmeted standing to r., holding a spear and
leaning on a shield, on *billon* coins of Valerian
I. (10 frcs.), and Gallienus (6 frcs.)

VICTORIAE AVGG. FEL. *(Augustorum
Felici.)* Victory flying, holding diadem with
both hands; before her a shield on a *cippus*, on
coins of Septimius Severus (N. 250 frcs., Æ. c.,
Æ. I. 15 frcs.), and Julia Domna (hybrid coin.)

VICTORIAE AVGG. IT. GERM. *(Augustorum iterum Germanicæ.)* Victory standing,
holding wreath and palm; at her feet a captive,
on *billon* coins of Valerian I. (2 frcs.), and
Gallienus (2 frcs.)

VICTORIAE AVGVSTI. S. C. Victory
standing to l. holding palm and writing on a
German shield fixed to a trophy composed of
German arms, on second brass coins of Domitian (3 frcs.)

VICTORIAE AVGVSTI. Two Victories
standing holding a shield on which VOT. *(Votis)*
X. *Obv.* IMP. C. M. ANN. *(Imperator Cæsar
Marcus Annius)* FLORIANVS AVG. Bust of
Florian to r., radiated. Æ. III. (8 frcs.)

VICTORIAE AVGVSTI. Two Victories
standing fixing a shield, on which VOT. *(Votis)*
X., to a palm, near which two captives seated;
in the *exergue* SIS. *(Sisciæ.)* *Obv.* IMP. C. M.
AVR. *(Imperator Cæsar Marcus Aurelius)*
PROBVS AVG. Bust of Probus to r., radiated.
N. Med. (400 frcs.)

VICTORIAE AVGVSTI. Turreted female

seated to l., holding a branch of a tree and a cornucopiæ, and crowned by Victory standing beside her. *Obv.* CONSTANTINOPOLIS. Bust of Constantinople to r., with helmet, laureated, wearing the Imperial mantle, and holding a sceptre. Æ. I. (80 frcs.) These pieces are attributed to Constantine I. or to his sons.

VICTORIAE AVGVSTORVM. Victory walking to r., holding a wreath with both hands. *Obv.* IMP. ANTONINVS AVG. COS. III. IMP. VERVS AVG. COS II. Heads, bare, of Marcus Aurelius and Lucius Verus facing each other. Æ. Med. (400 frcs.)

VICTORIAE AVGVSTORVM. S. C. Caracalla and Geta standing facing each other, holding a globe; a Victory between them, standing facing, with outspread wings, on a trophy, at the foot of which a captive seated. *Obv.* P. SEPT. GETA CAES. PONT. *(Publius Septimius Geta Cæsar Pontifex.)* Young bust of Geta to r., bare. Æ. I. (100 frcs.); Æ. II. (40 frcs.)

VICTORIAE AVGVSTORVM. Two Victories standing holding a shield, on which VOTIS; or Philip I. and his son standing, holding a globe on which a Victory, behind each of them a soldier holding a spear *(Vaillant.)* *Obv.* CONCORDIA AVGVSTORVM. Busts jugate of Philip I. laureated, and Otacilia diademed to r., opposite the bust of Philip II. to l., bare. Æ. Med. (350 to 400 frcs.)

VICTORIAE AVGVSTORVM. Victory dragging a captive by the hair and carrying a trophy, in the *exergue* ROMA. *Obv.* D. N. VALENTINIANVS P. F. AVG. Bust of Valentinian I. to r., diademed. Æ. I. from *D'Ennery* (60 frcs.)

VICTORIAE AVGVSTT. *(Augustorum.)* Two Victories standing holding a shield on which VOTIS X; below SIS. *(Siscia.)* *Obv.* IMPP. *(Imperatores)* CARVS ET CARINVS AVGG. *(Augusti.)* Busts of Carus and Carinus facing. *N.* Med. (2000 frcs.)

VICTORIAE BEATISSIMORVM CAESS. *(Cæsarum.)* Victory seated to r. on a cuirass, writing VOT. *(Votis)* X. on a shield which she holds on her knees; behind her a shield. *Obv.* FL. VAL. *(Flavius Valerius)* CONSTANTIVS NOB. C. *(Nobilis Cæsar.)* Bust of Constantius II. to r., laureated. Æ. Med. (50 frcs.)

VICTORIAE BRIT. *(Britannicæ.)* Various types [*Victoria*] on coins of Septimius Severus (Æ. c. to 3 frcs.), Caracalla (*N.* 150 to 250 frcs., Æ. c.) and Geta (Æ. c. to 3 frcs.)

VICTORIAE BRITANNICAE S. C. Trophy between a Victory and a female figure; below, a captive. *Obv.* SEPT. SEVERVS PIVS AVG. Head of Septimius Severus, laureated. Æ. I. from *Musée Tiepolo* (25 frcs.)

VICTORIAE BRITANNICAE S.C. Various types [*Victoria*] on coins of Septimius Severus (Æ. I. 25 frcs., Æ. II. 6 frcs.), Caracalla (Æ. I. 30 frcs., Æ. II. 6 frcs.), and Geta (Æ. I. 15 to 50 frcs.) These coins commemorate the expedition of Severus and his sons to Britain in A.D. 210-211. All three Emperors took the title of *Britannicus*. Two examples

of the large brass coins of Severus with this legend in a magnificent state of preservation were sold at the sale of General Ramsay's cabinet in London in 1856, one for £20 (500 frcs.) and the other for £17 (425 frcs.)

VICTORIAE BRITANNICAE S. C. Victory standing to r., placing her foot on a helmet and erecting a trophy; opposite her, Britain, sometimes turreted, standing facing, her hands bound behind her back, and at her feet a captive seated, on large brass coins of Caracalla (30 frcs.) and Geta (50 frcs.)

VICTORIAE CAESS. AVGG. Q. NN. or VICTORIAE DD. AVGG. Q. NN. Two Victories walking towards each other, each holding a wreath and palm. The former legend occurs on the third brass coins of Constantine II. from *Banduri* (15 frcs.), the latter on the third brass of Constans I. and Constantius II. The legend might be interpreted *Victoriæ Cæsarum* [or *Dominorum*] *Augustorumque Nostrorum;* but Cohen *(Méd. Imp.,* 1st ed., vol. vi., p. 270, *note)* suggests *Augustorum quinque Nostrorum.* These five princes—*Augusti* or *Cæsares*—would be Constantine II., Constans I., Constantius II., Delmatius and Hanniballian, and all the coins on which this legend occurs must have been struck before the end of A.D. 337, between the death of Constantine I. and the murder of Delmatius and Hanniballian.

VICTORIAE D.N. AVG. *(Domini Nostri Augusti.)* Two Victories standing holding a wreath within which VOT. *(Votis)* V MVLT. *(Multis)* X or VOT. X MVLT. XV or VOT. X MVLT. XX on silver coins of Constans I. (30 frcs.), and VOT. XXV MVLT. XXX on gold coins of Constantius II. (25 frcs.)

VICTORIAE DD. AVGGG. NNN. *(Dominorum Augustorum Nostrorum.)* Two Victories walking facing each other, and holding each a wreath and a palm; in the middle, a wreath. *Obv.* D. N. VALENS P. F. AVG. Bust of Valens to r., laureated. Æ. III. from *Banduri* (15 frcs.)

VICTORIAE DD. NN. AVG. ET CAE. or CAES. *(Dominorum Nostrorum Augusti et Cæsaris.)* Two Victories holding wreath within which VOT. V MVLT. X., sometimes the wreath is surmounted by ⚹ or ☧ on silver (80 frcs.) and second and third brass coins (1 to 3 frcs.) of Magnentius and second and third brass (c. to 4 frcs.) of Decentius.

VICTORIAE DD. NN. AVGG. *(Dominorum Nostrorum Augustorum.)* Victory seated on cuirass and shield, writing certain vows on a shield, which is sometimes presented by a genius, on coins of Constans I. (Æ. Med. 50 frcs., *N.* 50 frcs., *Quin.* 40 frcs), Constantius II. (*N.* Med., 600 frcs., Æ. Med. 200 frcs., *N.* 35 to 40 frcs.), and Magnentius (Æ. Med. 200 frcs., Æ. Med., 60 frcs.)

VICTORIAE DD. NN. AVGG. *(Dominorum Nostrorum Augustorum.)* Two Victories holding a wreath, in which various vows, on coins of Constans I. (*N.* Med. 300 frcs., *N.* 40 frcs.), and Constantius II. (*N.* 25 frcs.)

VICTORIAE DD. NN. AVGG. *(Dominorum Nostrorum Augustorum.)* Victory seated to r. holding on her knees a shield on which VOT. X MVLT. XX; behind her a cuirass, in the *exergue* LXAQ. (60 *Aquileiæ.)* Obv. FL. IVL. CONSTANS P. F. AVG. Bust of Constans I. to r. diademed. (Æ. Med. 150 frcs.) These large silver pieces of $\frac{1}{60}$ of the pound were in all probability struck for particular occasions, such as distribution at fêtes. In A.D. 384 Theodosius I. and Valentinian II. forbad those who gave public games to distribute to the spectators pieces weighing more than $\frac{1}{60}$ of the pound *(Cod. Theod.* XV. 9, 1), and after this period none of these large silver pieces were struck (Mommsen, *Mon. Rom.,* vol. iii., p. 73.)

VICTORIAE DD. NN. AVGG. *(Dominorum Nostrorum Augustorum.)* Victory walking to l., holding laurel wreath and palm, on coins of Magnentius *(N. Tremissis from Schellersheim* 150 frcs.), and Julian II. (Æ. 3 frcs.)

VICTORIAE DD. NN. AVG. AV. ? *(Dominorum Nostrorum Augustorum— ?)* Two Victories standing holding a wreath, in which VOT. X MVLT. XX.; in the *exergue* TR. *(Treveris.)* Obv. CONSTANTIVS P. F., AVG. Bust of Constantius II. to r. diademed. *(N.* 30 frcs.)

VICTORIAE DD. NN. COL. ANT. *(Dominorum Nostrorum. Colonia Antiochiensis.)* Victory walking to l., holding laurel wreath and palm or a trophy; in *field* S. R. *(Senatus Romanus),* on brass medallions and large brass coins of Septimius Severus, and on large brass coins of Caracalla and Geta, struck at Antiochia Pisidiæ. On some large brass coins of Geta the letters S. C. *(Senatus Consulto)* occur instead of S. R. *(Senatus Romanus.)*

VICTORIAE FELICI. Victory standing to l., holding a diadem with both hands; on a *cippus* C. V. P. P. *(Consul V Pater Patriæ)* on coins of Commodus (Æ. 6 frcs., Æ. I. 20 frcs., Æ. II. 6 frcs.)

VICTORIAE GOTHIC. *(Gothicæ.)* Trophy, at the foot of which two captives seated back to back; sometimes in the *exergue* S. P. Q. R. *(Senatus Populusque Romanus.)* Obv. IMP. CLAVDIVS P. F. AVG. Bust of Claudius II. to r., radiated. Æ. III. (20 frcs.)

VICTORIAE LAET. P. P. *(Lætæ Principum Perpetuæ.)* Two Victories standing, placing on an altar a shield, on which VOT. P. R. *(Votis Populi Romani)* on third brass coins of Constantine I. (3 frcs.)

VICTORIAE LAET. PRINC. PERP. *(Lætæ Principum Perpetuæ.)* Same type, sometimes in the *exergue* two captives seated back to back, on third brass coins of Licinius II. (1 frc.), Constantine I. (1 frc.), Crispus (2 frcs.) and Constantine II. (c.)

VICTORIAE LAETAE PR. P. *(Principum Perpetuæ.)* Same type on third brass coins of Constantine II. (3 frcs.)

VICTORIAE LAETAE PRIN. P. *(Principum Perpetuæ.)* Same type on third brass coins of Constantine I. (3 frcs.)

VICTORIAE LAETAE PRINC. PERP. *(Principum Perpetuæ.)* Two Victories stand-

ing, placing on a pedestal a shield, on which VOT. X.; in the *exergue* TR. (Treveris) on gold coins of Licinius I. (300 frcs.) and Constantine I—sometimes on a shield P. R. *(Populi Romani)* and S. TR. *(Secunda Treveris),* or SMT. *(Signata Moneta Thessalonicæ)* in *exergue* (100 frcs.); also on *Billon* coins (3 frcs.)

VICTORIAE LAETAE PRINC. PERP. *(Principum Perpetuæ.)* Two Victories standing, placing on a pedestal a shield, on which VOT. P. R. *(Votis Populi Romani)* ; in the *exergue* two captives; on the pedestal X, or nothing on coins of Licinius I. (Æ. III. 1 frc.), Licinius II.—no captives, sometimes I or a globe on pedestal (Æ. III., c to 2 frcs.), Constantine I. sometimes a captive, letters on pedestal or a shield or a wreath (Æ. III. c. to 10 frcs.), Crispus—no captives, sometimes C. on pedestal (Æ. III. c. to 5 frcs.), and Constantine II., with or without captives, sometimes on pedestal X or a wreath (Æ. III. c.)

It is on the coins of Constantine I. and Licinius I., with the legend VICTORIAE LAETAE PRINC. PERP. that it is supposed the symbol of Christianity first occurs. On the coins of Constantine I. his bust is sometimes helmeted, and on the helmet among other ornaments, the monogram ☧ may be found between two stars. On other pieces of Constantine I., with which may be joined some of Crispus and Constantine II., there may be seen on the pedestal an equilateral cross ⊹. (Madden, *Christian emblems on the coins of Constantine I., his family and his successors,* in the *Num. Chron.* N.S., 1877, vol. xvii., pp., 11, 242; 1878, pp. 1, 169.) These coins were probably struck anterior to A.D. 319, and certainly precede A.D. 323. The words VICTORIAE LAETAE may be compared (Cavedoni, *Ricerche critiche intorno alle med. di Costantino Magno, &c.,* p. 16; Madden, *op. cit.),* to the scriptural expressions "*Lætabor* ego super eloquia tua: sicut qui invenit spolia multa" (Psalm cxviii., 162) or "*Lætabuntur* . . . sicut exultant *Victores* capta præda, quando dividunt spolia" (Isaiah ix., 3), and to the line of Horace (1 *Sat.,* i., 8) "Momento cita mors venit aut *Victoria læta.*" With respect to the interpretation of the letters P. P. or PRINC. PERP., or PR. P. or PRIN. P. by *Principum Perpetuæ* it may be mentioned that Cavedoni prefers *Principis Perpetui,* but I am not inclined to agree with him as the word *perpetua* on other coins is made to agree with *Victoria*—VICTORIAE PERPETVAE *(q. v.)* comp. FELICITAS PERPETVA SAECVLI and VIRT. PERP. CONSTANTINI AVG. On coins of Constantine I. and Licinius II. the legend is sometimes VICTORIAI LAITAI *(sic)* or LEITAI *(sic)* PRINC . .

VICTORIAE LAETAE DOM. NOSTR. *(Dominorum Nostrorum.)* Two Victories standing, placing on a pedestal a shield, on which P. R. VOT. *(Populi Romani Votis.)* Obv. IMP. CONSTANTVS *(sic)* MAX. AVG. *(Maximus Augustus.)* Bust of Constantine I. to r. with helmet, laureated. Æ. III. from *Banduri* (20 frcs.)

VICTORIAE LIBERAE. Victory walking to l., holding wreath and palm; before her a seated captive. *Obv.* CONSTANTINVS P. F AVG, Bust of Constantine I. to r. laureated. Æ. III. from *Wiczay* (15 frcs.)

VICTORIAE PERPETVAE. Victory seated to r. on a cuirass, writing VOT. *(Votis)* XX, on a shield presented by a genius; in the *exergue* SMT. *(Signata Moneta Thessalonicæ.)* *Obv.* CONSTANTINVS P. F. AVG. Head of Constantine I. to r. laureated. (*N̄*. 100 frcs.)

VICTORIAE PERPETVAE. Same type as on the coin of Constantine I. with VICTORIAE LIBERAE. Æ. III. Quin. (15 frcs.)

VICTORIAE SARMATICAE. Four soldiers sacrificing on a tripod before the gate of a camp; in the *exergue* A Є (?) or HA. (Heracleiæ I.) or SMN Γ *(Signata Moneta Nicomediæ* 3), or ANT. *(Antiochiæ)* on silver coins of Diocletian (8 frcs), Maximian Hercules (8 frcs.), and Galerius Maximian (10f rcs.)

VICTORIAE SARMATICAE. Gate of a camp, with the leaves of the door open, surmounted by four towers; in the *exergue* SMM. or SMNA or SMN Γ *(Signata Moneta Nicomediæ,* or *Signata Moneta Nicomediæ* 1 or 3), on silver coins of Diocletian (8 frcs.), and Maximian Hercules (8 frcs.)

VICTORIAE TVM. *(sic.)* Two Victories standing, fastening a shield to a palm, at foot of which two captives seated. *Obv.* IMP. C. POSTVMVS PIVS F. AVG. Bust of Postumus to r. laureated. Æ. I. (6 frcs.)

VICTORIAM. *Victoriam.* OB VICTORIAM TRIVMPALEM or TRIVMPHALEM on gold coins of Constans I. and Constantius II.

Victoriatus aureus. The proper denomination of the two ordinary gold coins issued by Julius Cæsar and Augustus was borrowed from the silver, and they should be called *denarius aureus* and *Victoriatus aureus*, but the *denarius aureus* is generally called *aureus* (Mommsen, *Mon. Rom.*, vol. iii., p. 19.)

Victoriatus Numus. These coins consist of the *double Victoriat*, the *Victoriat*, and the *half Victoriat*, and have for type on the obverse the head of Jupiter, and on the reverse Victory crowning a trophy. The first issue of the *Victoriat* may be assigned to B.C. 228. The *Victoriat* never bore any mark of its value, but later the *half Victoriat* alone was marked S on the reverse. It was originally struck at 9⁄6 of a pound, and after the reduction of the other silver pieces at 1⁄12 of a pound. It was never a division of the *Denarius*, as proved by passages where *Victoriats* are placed side by side with *Denarii* (Livy, xli., 13), and it appears to have had its origin in Illyria (Plin., *Nat. Hist.*, xxxiii., 3, 46). A complete history of the *Victoriat* has been given by Mommsen *(Mon. Rom.*, vol. ii., pp. 85-103), to which the late Duc de Blacas has added (pp. 104-107) some important observations. (Comp. Babelon, *Mon. Cons.*, vol. i., pp. xxiv., 41 *seq.*, 1885.)

The following is a description of the principal coins of this series. The *double Victoriat* is

unique at the present time, the *Victoriat* not very common, and the *half Victoriat* very rare.

Double Victoriat. 1. *Obv.* Head of Jupiter to r., bearded and laureated. *Rev.* Victory standing to r., crowning a trophy; in the *exergue* ROMA. Æ. (Mommsen, *Mon. Rom.*, pl. xxiii., No. 1.)

Victoriat (early.) 2. Same types. Æ. (Mommsen, pl. xxiii., No 2.)

3. Same types, but with the word ROMA incuse. Æ. (Mommsen, pl. xxiii., No. 3.)

Half Victoriat. 4. Same types, but without mark of value. Æ. (Mommsen, pl. xxiii., No. 4.)

Victoriat. 5. *Obv.* Head of Jupiter to r., laureated. *Rev.* Victory to r., crowning trophy. In the *field* V initial of the mint of Luceria; in the *exergue* ROMA. Æ. (Mommsen, pl. xxiii., No. 8.)

6. Same types; in the *field* of reverse CROT. *(Croto.)*; in the *exergue* ROMA. Æ. (Mommsen, pl. xxiii. No. 9, Cohen, *Méd. Cons.*, pl. xxvii., *Metilia* No. 1.)

This piece was attributed by Borghesi *(Dec.* vi. 4; *Œuvres Compl.* i., p. 304) to T. Metillius or rather T. Mæcilius *Croto*, lieutenant of Appius Claudius prætor in Sicily in B.C. 215, who is mentioned in Livy (xxiii. 31, cf. iv. 48); but Mommsen, *(Mon. Rom.*, vol. ii., p. 230, *note)* prefers to assign it to the mint established by the Romans at *Crotona.*

7. Same types; in the *field* of reverse КОР. Κορκυρα. (Mommsen, vol. ii., p. 230, No. 9.) Attributed to the mint of Corcyra.

8. Same types; in the *field* of reverse ꞂB *(Vibo)*, in the *exergue* ROMA. Æ. (Cohen, pl. xli., *Vibia*, No. 1.)

Half Victoriat. 9. Same types; in the *field* of reverse ꞂB *(Vibo)*, and mark of the value S; in the *exergue* ROMA. Æ. (Mommsen, pl. xxiii. No. 10; Cohen, pl. xli., *Vibia*, No. 2.)

The pieces, Nos. 8 and 9, are attributed to the town of *Vibo-Valentia* (Mommsen, *Mon. Rom.*, vol. ii., p. 231, *note.*) [ꞂB—VALENTIA.]

VICTORIB. AVGG. ET CAESS. NN. *(Victoribus Augustorum et Cæsarum Nostrorum.)* Victory seated to r. on a cuirass and shield holding a shield on which VOT. *(Votis)* XX.; before her a trophy, at foot of which a barbarian seated; in the *exergue* SIRM. *(Sirmii)* or SMKO. ? *(Signata Moneta Kyzici ?)* on gold coins of Constantine I. (80 to 100 frcs.)

VICTORIBVS AVGG. ET CAESS. NN. *(Augustorum et Cæsarum Nostrorum)* VOTIS X. ET XX. Victory facing in a *quadriga* holding wreath and palm; in the *exergue* PTR. *(Prima Treveris)* on gold medallions (500 frcs.) and gold coins (150 frcs.) of Constantine I.

VICTORIBVS AVGG. NN. *(Augustorum Nostrorum)* VOTIS. Victory standing facing, holding a shield on which XXX.; in the *exergue* PTR. (*N*. Med. 400 frcs.); or Victory seated on cuirass holding shield on which XXX, presented to her by a genius; in the *exergue* PTR. (*N*. 80 frcs.) on coins of Constantine I. There is a similar gold coin in the *Musée de Vienne*, with Victory seated and described as having XX on the shield, respecting which Eckhel *(Doct. Num. Vet.,* vol. viii., p. 91) writes, "Olim iu hoc numo legi XXX pro XX, ut videre est in Catalogo Musei Cæsarei. Verum cum Vota XXX cum AVGG. NN. componi non possint, attentius eum iterum inspexi, et patuit superiores clypei flexus τοῦ X speciem præbere." I should, however, be inclined to consider this coin to be identical with the one in the British Museum. A coin of Licinius also in the Museum with the legend VBIQVE VICTORES of identical fabric, which is especially noticeable in the bust, shows that this style of coin must have been issued before the war with Licinius in A.D. 323, and as the *Vicennalia* of Constantine were not celebrated till A.D. 325, it follows that Constantine continued this system of coinage for a short time after the defeat and death of Licinius, altering the legend to VICTORIBVS AVGG. NN. VOTIS XXX. The letters AVGG. NN. which were the cause of Eckhel's remark evidently refer to the whole Constantinian family. These pieces weigh 83 + grains, and were probably issued as memorial coins, the average weight of the *aureus* being 68 grains (Madden, *Gold Coins of the late Duc de Blacas* in the *Num. Chron.,* N.S., 1868, vol. viii., p. 36.)

Victorina. [VICTORIA.]

VICTORINVS I. (Piauvonius) was chosen by Postumus as colleague about A.D. 265, through the exertion of his mother Victoria [VICTORIA], and reigned a short time alone after the deaths of Postumus and Lælianus. Having however, insulted the wife of one of his clerks, he was with his son Victorinus II. Cæsar put to death by his soldiers in A.D. 267 (Treb. Poll. XXX *Tyr.,* c. 6.)

The following are the principal reverse legends: *Gold coins.* ADIVTRIX AVG. Bust of Diana (600 frcs., *Quin.,* 500 frcs.); ADVENTVS AVG. (500 frcs.); COMES AVG. Helmeted bust of Mars (600 frcs.), Victory standing (300 frcs.); COS. II. Victorinus I. standing presenting a globe to Rome seated (600 frcs.); FIDES MILITVM *(Schellerscheim,* 600 frcs.); INVICTVS. Bust of the Sun (600 frcs.) [see *woodcut*]; INVICTVS AVG. Victorinus on horseback (600 frcs.); LEG. PRIMA MINERVINA P. F. *(Pia Fidelis)* (600 frcs.); LEG. II. TRAIANA

P. F. (600 frcs.); LEG. IIII. FLAVIA P. F. (600 frcs.) [VICTORIA]; LEG. V. MACIDONICA P. F. (600 frcs.); LEG. X. FRETENSIS P. F. (600 frcs.); LEG. XIII. GEMINA P. F. (600 frcs.); LEG. XIIII. GEMINA P. F. (600 frcs.); LEG. XX VAL. *(Valeria)* VICTRIX (600 to 800 frcs.) [VICTORINVS II.]; LEG. XXII. P. F. (600 frcs.); LEG. XXX. VLP. VICT. P. F. (600 to 800 frcs.); PAX AVG. *(Caylus* 300 frcs.); P. M. TR. P. III. COS II. P. P. *(Caylus, Quin,* 500 frcs.); PROVIDENTIA AVG. Head of Medusa (600 frcs.); ROMAE AETERNAE (800 frcs.) [VICTORIA]; SAECVLI FELICITAS (300 frcs.); VICTORIA AVG. (800 frcs.) [VICTORIA and VICTORINVS II.,] Victory standing (400 frcs.); VOTA AVGVSTI (800 frcs.) [VICTORIA and VICTORINVS II.]—*Silver coins.* DEFENSOR ORBIS (200 frcs.); VICTORIA AVG. (200 frcs.)— *Billon coins.* ADVENTVS AVG. (20 frcs.); AEQVITAS AVG. (2 frcs.); COMES AVG. (c); CONSACRATIO or CONSECRATIO (15 frcs.); DEFENSOR ORBIS (250 frcs.); FIDES MILITVM (3 frcs.); INVICTVS. The Sun walking (3 frcs.); IOVI CONSERVATORI or STATORI (3 to 10 frcs.); LEG XXII PRIMIGENIE (100 frcs.); MARS VICTOR (10 frcs.); ORIENS AVG. (c); PAX AVG. (2 to 6 frcs.); PIETAS AVG. (c); P. M. TR. P. COS. II. P. P. (10 frcs.); PROVIDENTIA AVG. (3 to 6 frcs.); SAECVLI FELICITAS (10 frcs.); SALVS AVG. (1 to 6 frcs.); SECVRITAS AVGG. (30 frcs.); SPES PVBLICA (6 frcs.); VBERTAS AVG. (6 to 10 frcs.: VICTORIA AVG. (2 to 10 frcs.); VIRTVS AVG. (2 to 20 frcs.)—*Brass medallion. Restitutori* GALLIARVM and in the *exergue* VOTIS PVBLICIS (1200 frcs.);—*Third brass.* COMES AVG. (6 frcs.); FELIC ? T. C. V. P. *(sic.) Quin.* (6 frcs.); MARS . . . CT. (6 frcs.)

VICTORINVS II., son of Victorinus I., was made *Cæsar* by his grandmother Victoria and his father shortly before the latter's death, and was himself killed soon after. A tomb near Agrippina (Cologne) is said to have borne the following inscription:—HIC DVO VICTORINI TYRANNI SITI SVNT (Treb. Poll. xxx., *Tyr.* c. 7.) There are no coins existing struck in his own name but his portrait may probably be seen on the following pieces struck by his father :—

1. *Obv.* IMP. C. VICTORINVS P. F. AVG. Head of Victorinus I. to r. laureated and joined with the bust of Apollo under the traits of Victorinus II. *Rev.* LEG. XX. VAL. *(Valeria)* VICTRIX. Boar, in the *exergue* P. F. *(Pia Fidelis.) N*. (800 frcs.)

2. *Obv.* IMP. VICTORINVS P. F. AVG. Heads jugate of Victorinus I. and II. to left, the one laureate, the other bare. *Rev.* VICTORIA AVG. Victory standing holding wreath and palm. *N*. (800 frcs.)

3. *Obv.* IMP. VICTORINVS P. F. AVG. Bust of Victorinus I. laureated to l. with cuirass, armed with spear and shield, on which are represented two figures. *Rev.* VOTA AVGVSTI. Busts facing each other of Apollo (with the features of Victorinus II.) laureated and of

Diana with a bow over her shoulders. _N._ (800 frcs,)

It may be that Diana on this piece represents the _daughter_ of Victorinus I., especially as Diana was the _sister_ of Apollo, but of this daughter there is no record. (Madden, _Coins of the Wigan Collection_ in the _Num. Chron._, N.S., 1865, vol. v., p. 87).

VICTORIOSO SEMPER. Probus, in military dress, standing between four captives; below, a wreath. _Obv._ IMP. PROBVS P. F. AVG. Bust of Probus to l., laureated, sometimes with _Ægis._ _N._ (500 frcs.)

VICTORIOSO SEMPER. Turreted female to l., presenting a wreath to Constantine I., who is crowned by Victory; in the _exergue_ SMT. (_Signata Moneta Thessalonicæ._) _Obv._ CONSTANTINVS P. F. AVG. Bust of Constantine I., facing with _nimbus_, raising a hand and holding a globe. _N._ (_Autrefois, Cab. des médailles, Paris_, 400 frcs.) Several other medallions and coins of Constantine I., or his wife Fausta, and of his sons Crispus, Constantine II., and Constantius II. give representations of the _nimbus_. After Constantine's death his sons continued to strike coins representing him with this symbol, and they themselves very soon adopted it, a custom continued under their successors, and especially on the gold medallions of Valens preserved at Vienna (Madden, _Christian Emblems on the coins of Constantine I._, _&c._, in the _Num. Chon._, N.S., 1878, vol. xviii., pp. 9—15). The late Cavedoni thought that the _nimbus_ was assumed by Constantine I. in imitation of the "face of Moses which shone" (Ex. xxxiv., 29, cf. 2 Cor., iii., 7), to whom he is compared by Eusebius (_Vit. Const._ I., c. 12), but whether this be the case or not, some of the heads of the Roman Emperors earlier than the time of Constantine are decorated with this symbol, notably Claudius, Trajan, and Antoninus Pius (Æ. I. with leg. COS. IIII, see _Nimbus_), so that it would be difficult to affirm that the presence of the _nimbus_ gives direct proof of the Christianity of Constantine, though it was doubtless adopted in this sense (Madden, _op. cit._)

VICTR. _Victrici._ DIANAE VICTR. _Dianæ Victrici_ on third brass coins of Claudius II.—MINER. VICTR. _Minervæ Victrici_ on second brass coins of Commodus.

VICTRI. _Victrici._ DIANAE VICTRI. _Dianæ Victrici_ on gold and silver coins of Æmilian.

VICTRIC. _Victrici._—MINER. VICTRIC. _Minervæ Victrici_ on silver coins of Septimius Severus.

VICTRICI—MINERVAE VICTRICI on silver coins of Geta—VENERI VICTRICI [VENERI VICTRICI.]

VICTRICIBVS—FATIS VICTRICIBVS on gold coins of Diocletian.

VICTRIS (_sic._) _Victrix._ MINER. VICTRIS (_sic._) _Minerva Victrix_ on silver coins of Pescennius Niger.

VICTRIX (in _exergue._) Victory seated to r. holding a _patera_ and a palm; sometimes under the seat the letters ST. _Obv._ M. CATO ROMA.

Female head to r. diademed. Æ. (c.) On the _quinarius_ (c.) there is a young head crowned with laurel, and no letters ST. on the reverse. These coins of the _Porcia gens_ [PORCIA] are considered to have been struck by the father of Cato of Utica in B.C. 95. The explanation of the letters ST. by _stipendium_ (Borghesi) or _stata, stabilis_ (Cavedoni) is not thought to be satisfactory (Mommsen, _Mon. Rom._, vol. ii., pp. 396, 397.) The _denarius_ is found with the countermark IMP. VES., and was restored by Trajan. Similar types occur on the _denarii and quinarii_ with the legend M. CATO PRO. PR. (_Proprætor_) struck by Cato, of Utica, in B.C. 49.

VICTRIX—IVNO VICTRIX on _billon_ coins of Salonina—LEG. XX. VAL. VICTRIX P. F. _Legio XX. Valeria Victrix Pia Fidelis_, on gold coins of Victorinus I.—MINER. VICTRIX _Minerva Victrix_ on gold and silver coins of Caracalla and Geta—MINERVA VICTRIX on silver coin (hybrid) of Orbiana, and on gold coins of Uranius Antoninus [VRANIVS ANTONINVS]—ROMA VICTRIX on gold and silver coins of Galba, and on brass coins of Vespasian and Titus—VENVS VICTRIX [VENVS VICTRIX.]

Vienna, now _Vienne_, a city of the Allobroges in Gallia Narbonensis. It was a flourishing town under the empire, and a _Colonia_, and many remains attest its ancient splendour. The following coin belongs to this city. _Obv._ DIVI IVLI CAESAR DIVI F. IMP. Bare heads of Julius Cæsar and Augustus back to back. _Rev._ C. I. V. _Colonia Julia Vienna._ Prow of a vessel to r., adorned with buildings. Æ. I.

The coins given by Akerman (_Coins of Cities and Princes_, p. 152; Nos. 2-5), probably belong to Lyons (Cf. Cohen, _Méd. Imp._, 2nd ed., vol. i., pp. 159, 182.)

VIENNA DE OFFICINA LAVRENTI. +. Christian monogram (✶) on a globe; on either side A and _w_ (_Alpha_ and _Omega._) _Obv._ D. N. MAVRICIVS P. P. AV. Bust of Mauricius Tiberius to r. laureated. _N._ (Ch. Lenormant. _Rev. Num._ 1854, p. 316, pl. xiii., No. 11; C. F. Keary, _Num. Chron._, N.S., 1878, vol. xviii., p. 232, plate iii., No. 8.) This coin was struck in the name of the moneyer _Laurentius_ by the Emperor Mauricius Tiberius for the use of Gundovald Ballomer, a pretender to the Merovingian throne A.D. 585-586.

VII. _Septem, Septima, Septimo, Septimum._ —VIIVIR. _Septemvir_—LEG. VII. _Legio Septima_ LEG. VII. P. VII. F. _Legio Septimum Pia Septimum Fidelis_—LIB. VII. _Liberalitas Septima_ —AN. or ANNO. VII. _Anno Septimo_—COS. VII. _Consul Septimum_—IMP. VII. TR. P. VII., &c.

VIII. _Octo, Octava, Octavo, Octavum_—LEG. VIII. _Legio Octava_—AN. or ANNO VIII. _Anno Octavo_—COS. VIII. _Consul Octavum_—IMP. VIII., TR. P. VIII., &c.

VIIII. _Novem, Nona, Nono, Nonum._—LEG. VIIII. _Legio nona._—VICTORIA AVG. VIIII. _Victoria Augusta Nona_ (Gallienus)—LIBERAL. AVG. VIIII _Liberalitas Augusta Nona_ (Caracalla)—CONG. AVG. VIIII. _Congiarium Augusti_

Nonum (Antoninus Pius)—AN or ANNO VIIII. *Anno Nono*—IMP. VIIII. *Imperator nonum*—COS. VIIII., TR. P. VIIII., &c.

VIIV. or VIIVIR. EP. or EPV. or EPVL. or EPVLO. *Septemviri Epulones* or *Septemvir Epulonum.* [VII*viri Epulones, &c.*]

VII*viri Epulones* or VII*vir Epulonum.* Their origin dates from B.C. 196, when a college of *three* members was founded principally to perform the rites of the sacrificial meal (*Epulum Jovis*) taken in the Temple of the Capitoline Jupiter, in the presence of the whole Senate. Their number was afterwards increased to *seven.* Julius Cæsar added *three more,* but after his time the number was again reduced to *seven.* [EPVLONES]. The title is found on the following coins :—

1. *Obv.* C. FABIVS CATVLVS IIVIR (*Duumvir*). Head of Neptune to r., before a trident. *Rev.* P. SEXTILIVS PR. P. AF. VIIV. EP. (*Pro Prætore Africæ Septemvir Epulonum.)* Bust of the sun facing, the head surrounded with a radiating disc. Æ. III. (Müller, *Num. de l'anc. Afrique,* vol. ii., p. 51, No. 25.)

Struck at Hadrumetum. P. Sextilius was governor of the province of Africa in B.C. 94.

2. *Obv.* AFRIC. FABIVS MAX. COS. VII. EPVL. (*Africanus Fabius Maximus Consul Septemvir Epulonum.)* Head of Fabius to r., bare. *Rev.* HADRVM. (*Hadrumetum.)* The upper part of a bearded god to r., with tiara, raising r. hand and holding two ears of corn in left. Æ. II. (Müller, *op. cit.,* vol. ii., p. 52, No. 29.)

3. *Obv.* AFR. FA. MAX. COS. PRO. COS. VIIVIR EPVLO. (*Africanus Fabius Maximus Consul Proconsul Septemvir Epulonum.)* Head of Fabius to r., bare. *Rev.* C. LIVIN. GALLVS Q. PRO. PR. (*C. Livineius Gallus Quæstor Pro Prætore.)* Elephant walking to l. crushing a serpent. Æ. II. (Müller, *op. cit.,* vol. ii., p. 61, No. 37.)

Nos. 2 and 3 were struck at Hadrumetum. L. Fabius Maximus Africanus was Consul in B.C. 10, and five years after, in B.C. 5, proconsul of Africa.

4. *Obv.* C. CCEL. CALDVS COS. (*Caius Coelius Caldus Consul.)* Head of Coelius Caldus to r.; behind, a standard on which HIS. (Hispania); in front a bear. *Rev.* Figure seated on a throne, on which L. CALPVS VIIVIR EP. or EPV. or EPVL. (*Lucius Caldus Septemvir Epulonum);* on either side a trophy; to l. c. CALDVS, to r. IMP. A. X. (*Caius Caldus imperator augur decem* [*vir-sacris-faciendis*]; in the *exergue* CALDVS IIIVIR (*triumvir*). AR. (8 frcs.) (Cohen, *Méd. Cons.,* Coelia, Nos. 5—10, pl. xiii., Nos. 5—10).

The moneyer is C. Coelius Caldus *triumvir,* who was quæstor in B.C. 51. C. Coelius Caldus is grandfather of the moneyer, consul in B.C. 94. C. Caldus X*vir* is perhaps an uncle of the moneyer, who is unknown, but who was proclaimed *Imperator* in the East. C. Caldus *Septemvir* is probably his father. (Mommsen, *Mon. Rom.,* vol. ii., p. 505, No. 286). [COELIA.]

VIL. PVB. *Villam Publicam.*—T. DIDI. IMP. VIL. PVB. *Titus Didius Imperator Villam Publicam* [*referit*] on silver coins of the *Didia Gens* [DIDIA ; FONTEIA].

VIM. *Viminacium.*—P. M. S. COL. VIM. *Provinciæ Moesiæ Superioris Colonia Viminacium,* on brass coins of Gordianus Pius, Philip I., Otacilia, Philip II., Trajan Decius, Etruscilla, Herennius Etruscus, Hostilian, Trebonianus Gallus, Volusian, Æmilian, Valerian, Maximian, and Gallienus.

Viminacium a town of Moesia Superior and a Roman colony, supposed to have been founded by Gordianus Pius in A.D. 240. Coins of the Emperors from Gordianus Pius with dates AN. I *Anno primo* (A.D. 240) to Valerian and Gallienus AN.XVI *Anno Sexto Decimo* (A.D. 255) are in existence. [VIM.] The usual legend is P.M.S. COL. VIM. *Provinciæ Moesiæ Superioris Colonia Viminacium,* and the usual type a female standing between a lion and a bull; on a coin of Gordianus Pius the female holds two standards inscribed VII. and IIII. respectively, and on coins of Philip I., and Trebonianus Gallus and Volusian, the Emperor or Emperors take the place of the female.

VIN. *Vincas*—M. . . . VIN. *Margarita Vincas* on contorniates of Theodosius I. from *Tanini* (rare) ; Placidius Valentinian III. (rare.)

VINCAS. *Vincas*—On various contorniates —ARTEMIVS VINCAS IMPERATOR PLENA Honorius (rare)—BONIFATI VINCAS VRSI Trajan (common)—EVTIMI VINCAS Miscellaneous (net common)—EXVPERANTI VINCAS Nero (common)—IM. . DATOR PENNA VINCAS Honorius from *Tanini* (rare)—MARGARITA VINCAS Placidius Valentinian III. (not rare)—M. (*Margarita*) VINCAS Theodosius I. (rare) and Placidius Valentinian III. (rare)—VRSE VINCAS Miscellaneous (not common)— . . . . VINCAS with VRBS ROMA (rare). [CONTORNIATE COINS.]

VINDEX. *Vindex*—IMP. CAESAR DIVI F. COS. VI LIBERTATIS P. R. (*Populi Romani*) VINDEX on silver medallion of Augustus, struck in B.C 28. On reverse PAX.

VINICAS (*sic*) for VINCAS. *Vincas.*—EVTIMI VINICAS (*sic*) on contorniates of Theodosius I. and Honorius (rare.)

VINICI. *Vinicius*—L. VINICI. *Lucius Vinicius* [*Vinicia gens.*]

Vinicia gens, an equestrian family, but also plebeian. The following coins belong to it :—

1. *Obv.* CONCORDIAI or CONCORDIAE. Head of Concord to r., laureated. *Rev.* L. VINICI. (*Lucius Vinicius.)* Victory flying, holding a palm adorned with four crowns. AR. (20 frcs.) (Cohen, *Méd. Cons.,* Vinicia No. 1 ; pl. lxii., Vinicia, No. 1 ; Mommsen, *Mon. Rom.,* vol. ii., p. 521, No. 304.)

This moneyer is probably Lucius Vinicius tribune of the people B.C. 51, and Consul in B.C. 33. He was moneyer about B.C. 58.

2. *Obv.* AVGVSTVS TR. POT. VII. or VIII. Head of Augustus to r., bare. *Rev.* L. VINICIVS L. F. IIIVIR. (*Lucius Vinicius Lucii filius triumvir.*) *Cippus* on which S. P. Q. R. IMP. CAE. QVOD V. M. S. EX EA P. Q. IS AD A. DE. (*Senatus Populusque Romanus Imperatori Cæsari Quod Viæ Munitæ Sunt ex ea Pecunia Quam is ad Aerarium Detulit).* Æ. (30 frcs.)

3. *Obv.* S. P. Q. R. IMP. CAES. on the pedestal of an equestrian statue to r., placed before the walls of a city. *Rev.* Same legend and type as No. 2. Æ. (30 frcs.)

4. *Obv.* Head of Augustus to r. bare. *Rev.* L. (*Lucius*) VINICIVS. Triumphal arch, on which is Augustus in a *quadriga* facing, holding a branch of laurel; on the pediment S.P.Q.R. IMP. CAES.; on either side an archer standing on a pedestal placed on side arches. Æ. (30 frcs.) (Cohen, *Méd. Imp.*, 2nd ed., vol. i., Nos. 541-544.)

These coins were struck by the Triumvir Lucius Vinicius, who with L. Mescinius Rufus and C. Antestius Vetus formed a college, and who entered on their duties in the viith tribunitian year of Augustus B.C. 16, and continued to the viiith tribunitian year B.C. 15. These are the last names of moneyers found on the gold and silver coins. Nos. 1—3 refer to the re-establishment of the roads [QVOD VIAE MVN. SVNT] and No. 4 to ·the restoration of the Roman standards by the Parthians [CIVIB. ET SIGN. MILIT. A PART. RECVP. or RECVPER.]

VINICIVS. *Vinicius.* [*Vinicia gens.*]

VINIRIO. *Vinirio* on small brass coins of Nero struck at Corinth from *Vaillant.* P. VINIRIO IIVIR COR. *Publio Vinirio Duumviro Corinthi* (Cohen, *Méd. Imp.* 2nd ed., vol. i., p. 307, No. 402.)

Vipsania gens equestrian family and later plebian. [AGRIPPA; SVLPICIA.]

Vipsania Agrippina, daughter of Agrippa by first wife Pomponia. Married to Tiberius, but divorced in A.D. 11. Died in A.D. 20. No coins.

VIR. *Vir, Viro, Viri, Viris*—IIVIR., IIIIVIR., IIIIVIR., VIIVIR., XVVIR. [VIIVIR EP.; XVVIR SAC. FAC.]

Virgin Mary is frequently represented on the Byzantine coinage, and accompanied by the letters MP—ΘV (Μήτηρ Θεοῦ.) The type of the Virgin in various postures, generally seated, commences on the gold coins of Leo VI., in A.D. 886-912, with the name +MARIA+ as well as the MP—ΘV, and continues till the reign of John V. Palæologus A.D. 1341-1391 (Madden, *Christian Emblems on the Coins of Constantine I., &c.*, in the *Num. Chron.* N.S., 1878, vol. xviii., pp. 183-188.)

VIRODV. (*Virodunum.*) Beardless head to r. helmeted. *Rev.* TVROCA. Equestrian figure with spear galloping to r. Æ. struck at Virodunum (*Verdun*) Galliæ Belgicæ (Akerman, *Coins of Cities and Princes*, p. 160).

VIRT. *Virtus* on silver coin of the *Fufia gens* [FVFIA; MVCIA.]

VIRT. (*Virtus.*) Helmeted bust of Valour to r. *Rev.* IVPPITER CVSTOS. Jupiter seated to l., holding thunderbolt and sceptre. Æ. (40 frcs.) Probably struck by Nero (Cohen. *Méd. Imp.*. 2nd ed., vol. i., p. 344, No. 373.)

VIRT. AETER. (*Virtus Aeterna.*) AVG. P. M. TR. P. XVII. COS. VII. P. P. Mars, nearly naked, walking to l. on a cuirass, holding branch in r. hand and spear and shield in l. *Obv.* L. AEL. AVREL. COMM. AVG. P. FEL. Bust of Commodus to r., laureated. N. (300 frcs.)

VIRT. AVG. (*Virtus Augusti—in field.*) P. M. TR. P. COS. III. (around.) Valour standing to l., foot on helmet holding *parazonium* and spear—on large brass coins of Hadrian (4 frcs.)

VIRT. AVG. (*Virtus Augusti.*) P. M. TR. P. X. IMP. VII. COS. IIII. Commodus galloping to r., hurling javelin at a lion or a panther—on gold coins (250 frcs.) and large brass (50 frcs.) of Commodus.

VIRT. AVG. (*Virtus Augusti.*) TR. P. COS. or TR. P. II. or VI. COS. II. P. P. Rome in military dress helmeted standing to l. holding Victory and spear—on gold coins (150 frcs.) and silver (c.) of Septimius Severus.

VIRT. AVG. (*Virtus Augusti.*) Vulcan and Minerva standing, the former holding a hammer and pincers, the latter a spear and leaning on a shield. *Obv.* IMP. C. CLAVDIVS AVG. Bust of Claudius II. to r., radiated. Æ. III. (8 frcs.)

VIRT. VG. (*sic—Virtus Augusti.*) Sun walking to l., raising r. hand and holding a whip. *Obv.* . . . TRICVS P. F. AVG. Bust of Tetricus I. to r. radiated. Æ. III. (3 fres.)

VIRT. AVGG. (*Virtus Augustorum.*) Rome or Valour helmeted, in military dress, standing to l., holding Victory and spear and leaning on shield, or holding spear and shield—on gold coins from *Caylus* (150 frcs.) and silver coins (c.) of Septimius Severus and Caracalla.

VIRT. AVGG. COL. ANTIOCH. S. R. (*Virtus Augustorum Colonia Antiochiensis. Senatus Romanus.*) Geta on horseback, striking an enemy with his spear. *Obv.* IMP. CAES. P. SEPT. GETA AVG. Head of Geta, laureated. Æ. I., struck at Antiochia Pisidiæ. A similar type on Æ. I. coins of Gordianus Pius.

VIRT. AVGVT. (*sic*) NOSTRI. (*Virtus Augusti Nostri.*) Probus on horseback to r., holding a spear and following an enemy; behind, a barbarian with long beard following the Emperor, his hands fastened on his chest; in the *exergue* SIS. (*Siscia*)—on brass medallions of Probus (300 frcs.)

VIRT. EXERC. (*Virtus Exercitus.*) Plan of a camp; above it the Sun standing facing, raising r. hand and holding a globe, on small brass coins of Licinius I. and II. (20 frcs.), Constantine I.

(10 frcs.), Crispus (10 frs.) and Constantine II.
(10 frcs.)

VIRT. EXERC. ROM. *(Virtus Exercitus
Romani.)* Emperor in military dress walking
r., dragging a captive by the hair and holding
a trophy; in the *field* a star; in the *exergue*
CONOB. *(Constantinopolis* 72)—on gold coins
of Majorian (80 frcs.), and of Theodosius II.
(35 frcs.)

VIRT. EXERCIT. GALL. *(Virtus Exercitus
Gallicani.)* Soldier, helmeted, standing facing,
holding spear and *parazonium*. *Obv.* FL. VAL.
CONSTANTINVS AVG. Bust of Constantine I.
r., radiated. Æ. III. (20 frcs.)

VIRT. GALLIENI AVG. *(Virtus Gallieni
Augusti.)* Hercules, helmeted, standing facing,
holding branch and club and carrying lion's skin
—on gold coins of Gallienus. (600 frcs.)

VIRT. GALLIENI AVG. *(Virtus Gallieni
Augusti.)* Gallienus on horseback piercing an
enemy or Gallienus walking holding spear and
shield, and placing foot on captive—on *Billon*
coins of Gallienus. (c., *Quin* 20 frcs.)

VIRT. *(Virtus)* MILITVM. Aurelian standing to r. holding spear and globe facing a soldier,
who holds Victory and spear. *Obv.* IMP.
AVRELIANVS AVG. Bust of Aurelian to r., radiated. Æ. III. (c.)

VIRT. PERP. CONSTANTINI AVG. *(Virtus Perpetua Constantini Augusti.)* Valour,
helmeted, standing to l. holding globe surmounted by Victory and spear, and leaning on a
shield. *Obv.* IMP. C. CONSTANTINVS P. F.
AVG. Bust of Constantine I. to r. Æ. III. (20
frcs.).

Virtus. Valour. The Roman personification
of Valour was represented helmeted with spear
and sword and standing with right foot on
helmet. There was a golden statue of her at
Rome which was melted by Alaric, king of the
Goths. Valour is frequently represented on
coins—VIRTVS AVG. or AVGG.

VIRTVS.—IIIVIR. *(Virtus.—Triumvir.)*
Helmeted head of Valour to r. *Rev.* M.
AQVIL. W. F. W. N. *(Manius Aquillius,
Manii filius, Manii Nepos.)* Soldier standing
with shield, raising female; in the *exergue*
SICIL. *(Sicilia.)* Æ. (2 frcs.) The moneyer
who issued this coin about B.C. 54, was probably
a descendant of the Manius Aquillius, Consul in
B.C. 101, who repressed the revolt of the slaves
in Sicily (Mommsen, *Mon Rom.* vol. ii., p. 502,
No. 282.) This exploit was again commemorated by Aquillius Florus, moneyer of Augustus
in B.C. 20, who also placed on some of his coins
the head of Valour. [AQVILLIA *gens*.]

VIRTVS. Rome (?) standing to l., holding
Victory and *parazonium*, or Mars standing holding *parazonium* and spear, or sword and spear—
on gold coins (250 frcs.), and silver coins (25
frcs.) of Galba.

VIRTVS. Helmeted bust of Valour to r.
Obv. SER. *(Servius)* GALBA IMP, Galba on
horseback to r. or l. raising r. hand. Æ. (50
frcs.)

VIRTVS. Helmeted head of Valour. *Rev.*
IVPPITER CVSTOS. Jupiter standing. Æ. (40

frcs.) Not in Cohen (Boutkowski, *Dict. Num.*,
tome i., p. 343, No. 755, *bis*.) Probably
struck under Nero [VIRT.]

VIRTVS S. C. Valour standing or seated
to l. holding *parazonium* and spear—on silver
(with COS. II) and first and second brass coins
(c.) of Marcus Aurelius.

VIRTVS. *Virtus.* HONOS ET VIRTVS on
large brass coins of Galba—GLORIA SAECVLI
VIRTVS CAES. on gold and silver coins from
Mionnet of Constantine I., or CAESS. and
CAESARIS on brass medallions of Constantine I.
—INVICTA VIRTVS on silver coins of Septimius
Severus and Caracalla, also on gold of Caracalla
from Vaillant—PERPETVA VIRTVS on second
brass coins of Constantine I.—PERPETVA VIRTVS
AVG. *(Augusti)* on gold coins from *Banduri*
of Licinius I.

VIRTVS. Victory walking to l. holding
wreath and globe on which Victory. *Obv.* D. N.
ЄRACLI. PP. A. *(Dominus Noster Eraclius
Perpetuus Augustus.)* Bust of Heraclius facing,
diademed. Æ. (75 frcs.)

VIRTVS frequently found on the *obverse* of
the coins and medallions of the later Roman
Emperors, sometimes representing them hold-
ing a horse and a shield on which are various
figures—as VIRTVS POSTVMI AVG., VIRTVS
FLORIANI AVG., VIRTVS PROBI AVG., VIRTVS
PROBI INVICTI AVG., VIRTVS CARI AVG.,
VIRTVS DIOCLETIANI AVG., VIRTVS MAXIM-
IANI AVG. [*see* SALVIS AVGG. ET CAESS.,
&c.], VIRTVS CARAVSI AVG., VIRTVS CONSTANTI.
AVGT. *(Constantii Augusti)*, &c.

VIRTVS A. *(Augusti.)* Providence (?)
standing to l. holding a globe and a cornucopiæ.
Obv. IMP. CARAVSIVS P. F. AVG. Bust of
Carausius to r., radiated. Æ. III. (20 frcs.)

VIRTVS AEQVIT. *(sic.)* Soldier walking
to r. holding spear and trophy. *Obv.* IMP. C.
POSTVMVS AVG. Bust of Postumus to r. radiated. *Bil.* (6 frcs.)

VIRTVS AVG. *(Augusti.)* Various types.
Valour standing l. holding spear and *parazonium*, sometimes placing foot on helmet; Valour
standing r. holding spear and leaning on shield
or holding Victory and spear; Valour seated l.
holding Victory and spear or branch and sceptre;
Valour seated r. holding spear and *parazonium*;
Emperor in military dress standing, l. foot on
helmet, holding globe and spear—sometimes
suppliant female and captives; Emperor gallop-

ing to r. striking an enemy with spear; Mars, helmeted, standing or walking, holding olive branch and spear, or globe and spear, or spear and trophy, or spear and leaning on shield; Hercules standing leaning on club, holding lion's skin and bow, or trophy ; Soldier standing leaning on shield and holding spear; Pallas helmeted, standing holding spear and leaning on shield—on coins of Antoninus Pius, Marcus Aurelius, Commodus, Pescennius Niger, Septimius Severus, Julia Domna (hybrid coin), Alexander Severus, Gordianus Pius, Philip I. and II., Trajan Decius, Æmilian, Gallienus, Postumus, Victorinus I., Marius, Claudius II., Quintillus, Aurelian, Tetricus I. and II., Tacitus, Florian, Diocletian, Carausius, Allectus, Constantius Chlorus, Severus II., Constans I., Constantius II., and Constantius Gallus.

VIRTVS AVG. *(Augusti—in exergue.)* IMP. VI. COS. III. Marcus Aurelius crossing a bridge over the Danube followed by two soldiers on foot and a horseman (*N.*) or by four or five soldiers on foot and a horseman (*Æ. I.*) on gold coins (400 frcs.) and large brass (50 frcs.) of Marcus Aurelius.

VIRTVS AVG. *(Augusti—in exergue.)* P. M. TR. P. XI. IMP. VII. COS. V. P. P. Rome or Valour seated to r. near a trophy on cuirass and shield, holding a *parazonium ;* behind, Victory standing, holding a shield and on the ground a helmet. *Obv.* M. COMMODVS ANTONINVS PIVS FELIX AVG. BRIT. *(Britannicus.)* Bust of Commodus to r. laureated. Æ. Med. (300 frcs.)

VIRTVS AVG. *(Augusti—retrograde.)* Pallas standing to l. holding spear and leaning on a shield. *Obv.* OAI . . . ESC. NIGER IVS. *(Justus)* AVG. Head of Pescennius Niger to r. laureated. *R.* from *Wiczay.* (200 frcs.)

VIRTVS AVG. *(Augusti.)* Hercules standing r., resting head on club, and holding bow and lion's skin. *Obv.* IMP. GALLIENVS AVG. Bust of Gallienus to l., helmeted, with cuirass, and armed with spear and shield, on which the head of Medusa. *N.* Med. (600 frcs.)

VIRTVS AVG. *(Augusti.)* Helmeted bust of Mars to l., with the features of Gallienus or helmeted head of Valour to r., on gold (400 frcs.) and *billon* coins (60 frcs.) of Gallienus.

VIRTVS. AVG. *(Augusti.)* Gallienus standing to r., holding spear and receiving a Victory from the hands of Rome, helmeted standing, leaning against a shield and holding a spear, on *billon* coins (4 frcs.) of Gallienus.

VIRTVS AVG. *(Augusti.)* Gallienus standing to l., holding spear, crowning a trophy, and leaning on a shield ; he is being crowned by Victory, standing, holding a palm; at the foot of trophy a captive kneeling between two captives, seated. *Obv.* IMP. GALLIENVS P. F. AVG. Bust of Gallienus to l., laureated, armed with spear and shield, ornamented with the head of Medusa. Æ. Med. (300 frcs.)

VIRTVS AVG. *(Augusti.)* Helmeted head of Gallienus to l. *Obv.* SALONINA AVG. *(Augusta.)* Bust of Salonina to r., diademed. *Bil.* (60 frcs.)

VIRTVS AVG. *(Augusti.)* Mars standing in a tetrastyle temple. *Obv.* IMP. C. VICTORINVS P. F. AVG. Bust of Victorinus I. to r., radiated. *Bil.* (20 frcs.)

VIRTVS AVG. *(Augusti.)* Victory walking to l. or to r., holding wreath and palm on *billon* coins (20 frcs.) of Carausius and Allectus.

VIRTVS AVG. *(Augusti.)* Vessel with four or seven rowers, or without rowers; sometimes on the prow a female standing—on billon coins of Allectus (10 to 20 frcs.)

VIRTVS AVG. *(Augusti)* Lion standing to l., above in the field a club; in the *exergue* P. ARL. *(Prima Arelati.) Obv.* LICINIVS P. F. AVG. Head of Licinius I. to r. laureated. *N.* from *Schellersheim* (400 frcs.).

VIRTVS AVG. *(Augusti.)* Constantius II. in military dress, bare head, standing to r. leaning on shield and holding a globe surmounted by a Victory ; to r. a female or a province seated on the ground. *Obv.* D. N. CONSTANTIVS P. F. AVG. Bust of Constantius II. to r. diademed. *Æ.* Med. (50 frcs.)

VIRTVS AVG. ET CAESS. NN. *(Augusti et Cæsarum Nostrorum.)* Mars, helmeted, walking to r., holding a spear and trophy ; at his feet to r. a captive, seated ; in the *exergue* SIRM. *(Sirmii.) Obv.* D. N. CONSTANTINVS MAX. AVG. Head of Constantine I. to r. laureated. *N.* Med. (300 frcs.)

VIRTVS AVG. N. *(Augusti Nostri.)* Constantine I. laureated, and in military dress, galloping to r. after a kneeling enemy. *Obv.* CONSTANTINVS MAX. AVG. Bust of Constantine I. to r. diademed. *Æ.* Med. (150 frcs.)

VIRTVS AVG. N. *(Augusti Nostri.)* Constantius II. laureated and in military dress standing to r., holding spear and globe; at his feet to l. and to r. captives seated ; or Constantius II. in military dress standing to l. holding globe and spear—on large brass (50 frcs.) and brass medallions (80 frcs.) of Constantius II.

VIRTVS AVG. N. *(Augusti Nostri.)* Julian in military dress standing to l., holding branch and *vexillum,* and placing r. foot on captive seated on ground. *Obv.* D. N. CL. IVLIANVS N. C. *(Dominus Noster Claudius Julianus Nobilis Cæsar.)* Bust of Julian to r., bare, with cuirass on which head of Medusa. *Æ.* Med. (60 frcs.)

VIRTVS AVG. N. *(Augusti Nostri.)* Julian in military dress standing to l., holding laurel branch and standard, and placing r. foot on the back of a captive : in the *exergue* CONSZ. *(Constantinopolis* 7.) *Obv.* D. N. CL. IVLIANVS N. C. *(Dominus Noster Claudius Julianus Nobilis Cæsar.)* Head of Julian, bare. *Æ.* I. from *Wiczay* (30 frcs.) *Æ.* Med., with NOB. CAES. on *obverse* (60 frcs.) A similar brass medallion to the coin described is given by *Wiczay* with under the standard ⚓. If this medallion is authentic, which is doubtful, it is the only piece known of Julian bearing the monogram of

Christ. (Madden, *Christian Emblems on the coins of Constantine* I. etc., in the *Num. Chron.* N.S., 1878, vol. xviii., p. 38.)

VIRTVS AVG. *(Augusti)* NOSTRI. Constantius II., bareheaded and in military dress, standing facing, leaning on a spear and holding a laurel branch. *Obv.* D. N. CONSTANTIVS P. F. AVG. Bust of Constantius II. to r., diademed. Æ. Med. (50 frcs.)

VIRTVS AVG. *(Augusti)* NOSTRI. Magnentius standing to l., holding globe and sceptre; at his feet to l. a captive kneeling; in the *exergue* TR. *(Treveris.) Obv.* IM. CAE. MAGNENTIVS AVG. Bust of Magnentius to r. Æ. Med. (200 frcs.)

VIRTVS AVGG. *(Augustorum.)* Various types [see VIRTVS AVG.] on coins of Septimius Severus, Caracalla, Gordianus Africanus I. and II., Philip II., Trebonianus Gallus, Volusian, Valerian, Gallienus, Saloninus, Tetricus I., Carus, Numerian, Carinus, Diocletian, Maximian Hercules, Carausius, Constantius Chlorus and Galerius Maximian.

VIRTVS AVGG. *(Augustorum.)* Caracalla in military dress standing facing, holding spear and *parazonium;* to l. a river reclining, leaning on an urn; to r., two figures reclining. *Obv.* ANTONINVS PIVS AVG. Head of Caracalla to r., laureated. Æ. (10 frcs.) A similar type occurs upon other silver coins with the legend PONTIF. TR. P. X. COS. II. Eckhel (*Cat. Mus. Vindob.*, 2nd part., p. 302), explains the three figures as Arabia, Parthia, and Adiabene.

VIRTVS AVGG. *(Augustorum.)* PONT. TR. P. IIII. S.C. Caracalla standing to l. in military dress, crowning a trophy and holding a spear; at foot of trophy two captives seated. *Obv.* ANTONINVS AVGVSTVS. Young bust of Caracalla to r., laureated. Æ. I. (60 frcs.)

VIRTVS AVGG. *(Augustorum)* S. C. Caracalla and Valour standing to l., helmeted, and each holding a spear; Caracalla also holds a Victory. *Obv.* ANTON. PIVS AVG. PON. TR. P. VI. Young bust of Caracalla to r., laureated. Æ. II. (10 frcs.)

VIRTVS AVGG. *(Augustorum.)* Valour standing facing, holding two standards. *Obv.* IMP. C. P. LIC. VALERIANVS AVG. Bust of Valerian to r., radiated. *Bil.* (6 frcs.)

VIRTVS AVGG. *(Augustorum.)* Romulus walking, carrying spear and trophy—on *billon* coins of Valerian (8 frcs.) and Gallienus (3 frcs.)

VIRTVS AVGG. *(Augustorum.)* Valerian and Gallienus standing facing each other, one holding spear and globe, the other a Victory and spear—on *billon* coins of Valerian and Gallienus (3 to 4 frcs.)

VIRTVS AVGG. *(Augustorum.)* Carus and Carinus in military dress, standing, holding a globe, on which sometimes a Victory, one holding a sceptre and the other a spear—on small brass coins of Carus (1 frc.) Varieties of this type occur on small brass coins of Numerian and Carinus (c.)

VIRTVS AVGG. *(Augustorum.)*—Various types, with Hercules either strangling the Nemæan lion or standing near the tree of the

Hesperides, or seizing a stag by its antlers, &c.—on small brass coins (10 to 40 frcs.) of Diocletian, Maximian Hercules and Constantius Chlorus. A gold coin of Constantius Chlorus, from *Wiczay* (300 frcs.) also represents Hercules seizing a stag by its antlers.

VIRTVS AVGG. *(Augustorum.)* Trophy between two captives seated—on small brass coins of Constantius Chlorus (c. to 1 frc.)

VIRTVS AVGG. *(Augustorum.)* Lion, holding a sceptre in his paws; in the *exergue* XXIΓ. *Obv.* FL. VAL. CONSTANTIVS NOB. C. Bust of Constantius Chlorus, radiated. Æ. III., from *Banduri* after *Hardouin* (30 frcs.)

VIRTVS AVGG. *(Augustorum.)* Gate of a camp, open or shut—on small brass coins (c. to 10 frcs.) of Licinius I., Constantine I., Crispus and Constantine II.

VIRTVS AVGG. *(Augustorum)* Victory standing to r., holding palm and cornucopiæ, facing Constans I., bare-headed, seated in front of a trophy. *Obv.* CONSTANS P. F. AVG. Head of Constans to r., diademed. Æ. Med. (100 frcs.)

VIRTVS AVGG. *(Augustorum.)* Decentius, galloping to r., against a captive kneeling *Obv.* MAG. *(Magnus)* DECENTIVS NOB. CAES. Bust of Decentius to r., bare, holding spear and globe, on which a Victory. Æ. Med. (100 frcs.)

VIRTVS AVGG. ET CAESS. *(Augustorum et Cæsarum.)* Maximian Hercules galloping to r., hurling javelin at a captive, and holding a shield; under his feet an enemy who has lost his shield; in the *exergue* SIS. *(Siscia.) Obv.* MAXIMIANVS AVG. Head of Maximian to r. laureated. N. *Autrefois Cabinet de France* (200 frcs.)

VIRTVS AVGG. ET CAESS. *(Augustorum et Cæsarum.)* Maximinus II. Daza walking to r., dragging a barbarian after him and holding a trophy; to r. a barbarian seated; in the *exergue* SIS. *(Siscia.) Obv.* MAXIMINVS NOB. C. *(Nobilis Cæsar.)* Head of Maximinus II. Daza to r., laureated. N. (300 frcs.)

VIRTVS AVGG. ET CAESS. NN. *(Augustorum et Cæsarum Nostrorum.)* The Emperor galloping, holding shield and spearing a barbarian : under his horse another barbarian and a shield—on second brass coins of Maximian Hercules, Constantius Chlorus, Severus II., Maximinus II. Daza, and Constantine I. (4 to 6 frcs.)

VIRTVS AVGG. ET CAESS. NN. *(Augustorum et Cæsarum Nostrorum.)* Mars, helmeted, walking to r. or l., holding spear and trophy or Victory and spear, sometimes leaning on shield : at his feet sometimes a captive seated—on second brass coins of Galerius Maximian (10 frcs.), and of Maximinus II. Daza. (c. to 10 frcs.)

VIRTVS AVGGG. *(Augustorum.)* Two Emperors (Carus and Carinus or Carinus and Numerian) in military dress, holding between them a globe surmounted by a Victory; one

holding a sceptre, the other leaning on a spear
—on small brass coins of Carus and Carinus
(1 to 8 frcs.)

VIRTVS AVGGG. *(Augustorum.)* Mars,
helmeted, standing to r., holding a spear and
leaning on a shield; in the *field* s. p. ; in the
exergue MLXXI *(Moneta Londinii* 21.) *Obv.*
IMP. C. MAXIMIANVS P. F. AVG. Bust of
Maximian Hercules to r., radiated. Æ. III.
from *Banduri* (30 frcs.) Struck at London by
Carausius in A.D. 289 [XXI.]

VIRTVS AVGGG. *(Augustorum.)* The
Emperor in military dress, standing on a vessel,
holding a Victory, or on a globe surmounted by a
Phœnix and a standard, and placing foot on
captive; Victory seated holds the rudder—on
small brass coins of Valentinian II. and Theodosius I. (c. to 2 frcs.)

VIRTVS AVGVST. *(Augusti.)* Valour
standing to r., foot on cuirass. *Obv.* IMP. CAES.
VESPASIANVS AVG. Head of Vespasian to r.,
laureated. Æ. Foreign fabric (30 frcs.)

VIRTVS AVGVST. *(Augusti.)* Soldier
standing to r., holding spear and club (?). *Obv.*
L. SEPT. SEV. AVG. IMP. XI. PART. MAX.
Head of Septimius Severus to r., laureated. Æ.
(c.)

VIRTVS AVGVSTI. Alexander Severus,
bare headed, in military dress, holding a spear,
walking to r., with a soldier who carries a
trophy, and holding a shield; a Victory standing
behind the Emperor is crowning him. *Obv.*
IMP. ALEXANDER PIVS AVG. Bust of Alexander
Severus to r. Æ. Med. (300 frcs.)

VIRTVS AVGVSTI S. C. Valour, helmeted,
standing r., holding spear and leaning on a
shield, or Romulus, bareheaded, walking to r.,
and holding spear and trophy, or Alexander
Severus, in military dress, standing to l., placing
foot on helmet and holding a globe and spear
—on large brass coins of Alexander Severus (c.
to 6 frcs.)

VIRTVS AVGVSTI. Gordianus Pius in
military dress standing to l., receiving a globe
presented to him by the Sun, radiated, and holding a spear; he is crowned by Valour standing
behind him leaning on a spear; to l. a soldier
standing holding a spear and a standard; in the
middle a child standing facing and three military
standards; on the ground two captives seated.
Obv. IMP. GORDIANVS PIVS FELIX AVG. Bust
of Gordianus Pius to r., laureated, or bust to l.
laureated, holding a sceptre; on his chest the
Emperor is represented on horseback to l.
raising the r. hand and preceded by Victory.
Æ. Med. (400 frcs.)

VIRTVS AVGVSTI. Gordianus Pius seated
to l., crowned by Victory standing, who holds a
palm ; in front, two soldiers holding standards;
in the middle, a figure standing facing; at the
side of the Emperor, on the ground, a cuirass
and shield. *Obv.* IMP. GORDIANVS PIVS FELIX
AVG. Bust of Gordianus to r., laureated. Æ.
Med. (300 frcs.)

VIRTVS AVGVSTI S. C. Gordianus Pius in
military dress on horseback to l., raising the r.
hand and hurling a javelin against an enemy.

Obv. IMP. GORDIANVS PIVS FEL. AVG. Bust
of Gordianus Pius to r. laureated. Æ. I. (30
frcs.)

VIRTVS AVGVSTI S. C. Gordianus Pius
in military dress seated to l. on a cuirass, holding
a spear and crowned by Victory standing behind
him, holding a palm ; he is receiving a laurel
branch from Valour helmeted, standing before
him ; in the middle of them standards. *Obv.*
IMP. GORDIANVS PIVS FEL. AVG. Bust of Gordianus Pius to r., laureated. Æ. II. (25 frcs.)

VIRTVS AVGVSTI. Hercules, naked, stand-
to r. leaning on a club placed on a rock, and
covered with a lion's skin—on gold (200 frcs.)
and *billon* coins (2 frcs.) of Gallienus.

VIRTVS AVGVSTI. Mars, helmeted, standing to l. placing foot on helmet and holding
a branch and a sceptre; in the field X—on
billon coins (c.) of Gallienus and Æ. III. (3
frcs.) of Claudius II.

VIRTVS AVGVSTI. Helmeted head of
Gallienus. *Rev.* SALONINA AVG. Bust of
Salonina. Æ. II. from *Vaillant.*

VIRTVS AVGVSTI. Trophy, with javelins,
shield, and a clarion between a female and a
male captive. *Obv.* IMP. C. AVRELIANVS AVG.
Bust of Aurelian to r., laureated. N. (300 frcs.)

VIRTVS AVGVSTI. Hercules, naked, standing placing r. hand on a trophy and holding in
the l. a club and lion's skin. *Obv.* IMP. C. M.
CL. ? *(Caius Marcus Claudius)* TACITVS AVG.
Bust of Tacitus, laureated, holding an ivory
baton. Æ. Med., from *Vaillant* (300 frcs.)

VIRTVS AVGVSTI. Mars, helmeted, naked,
with flowing mantle, walking to r. holding spear
and trophy; at his feet a captive. *Obv.* VIRTVS
FLORIANI AVG. Bust of Florian to l., laureated,
holding sceptre and shield. N. (500 frcs.)

VIRTVS AVGVSTI. Mars walking to r.,
holding spear and trophy, or Florian standing
holding spear and globe, or Florian in military
dress walking to r., holding spear and shield
and placing foot on captive—on third brass
coins of Florian. (3 frcs.)

VIRTVS AVGVSTI. Mars, half naked,
walking to r. holding spear and trophy; on
either side a captive; in the *exergue* SIS.
(Sisciæ) ; or Probus standing to l. crowning a
trophy and holding a sceptre; at foot of trophy
two captives—on gold coins of Probus (150
frcs.)

VIRTVS AVGVSTI. Probus galloping to
l., hurling to his feet two enemies and piercing a
third with his spear. *Obv.* IMP. PROBVS P. F.
AVG. Bust of Probus to l., laureated, with the
cuirass ornamented with the head of Medusa,
holding a globe surmounted by Victory and a
parazonium. Æ. Med. from *Tanini* (350 frcs.)
A similar type occurs on his small medallions
(150 frcs.)

VIRTVS AVGVSTI. Mars, helmeted, standing to l., leaning on his shield and holding a
spear ; or Mars, helmeted, naked, with mantle
flowing, walking to r. and holding spear and
trophy, or Probus standing to l. crowning a
trophy, at foot of which a captive, or Probus
walking to r., holding spear and shield and

placing foot on captive, or Probus on horseback riding to l. against a captive *(Wiczay)*—on small brass coins of Probus (c. to 6 frcs.)

VIRTVS AVGVSTI. Lion walking to l.; in the *field*, a club; in the *exergue* T.ARL. *(Tertia Arelati)* or ARL. *(Arelati)*. *Obv.* CONSTANTINVS P. F. AVG. Head of Constantine I. to r., laureated. *N.* (120 frcs.)

VIRTVS AVGVSTI. The Emperor standing facing looking to r., holding a spear and leaning on a shield—on small brass coins of Constantine I. (6 frcs.), and Constantine II. (10 frcs.)

VIRTVS AVGVSTI. Standard between two captives seated; on the standard VOT. X.—on small brass coins of Constantine I. from *Banduri* (20 frcs.)

VIRTVS AVGVSTI. Constans I., laureated, standing to r., holding spear and globe. *Obv.* CONSTANS P. F. AVG. Head of Constans I. to l. with diadem. *Æ.* I. from *Havercamp* (80 frcs.)

VIRTVS AVGVSTI. Constantius II., standing, holding spear and *parazonium*, kicking a captive with l. foot and crowned by a Victory standing behind him. *Obv.* D. N. *(Dominus Noster)* CONSTANTIVS VICTOR AVG. Bust of Constantius II., diademed. *Æ.* Med. (100 frcs.)

VIRTVS AGVSTI, *(sic.)* Leo I. standing wearing *paludamentum*, holding a cross in r. hand and the *labarum* in l. In the *field*, M. D. *Mediolani*—Milan): in the *exergue* COMOB. *Obv.* D. N. LEO PERPET., or PERPETV., or PERPETVVS AVG. Bust of Leo I. to r., diademed. *N.* (25 frcs.) [See remarks on the explanation of the letters OB., etc., under VALENTINIANVS I.]

VIRTVS AVGVSTI N. *(Nostri.)* Mars, helmeted, naked, with mantle flowing, walking to r., and carrying a spear and a trophy, between two captives seated; or Constantine I. galloping to r., and hurling a javelin against a kneeling enemy; under his feet a dead enemy; in the *exergue* P. TR. *(Prima Treveris)*—on gold coins of Constantine I. (100 to 200 frcs.)

VIRTVS AVGVSTI N. *(Nostri.)* Constantius II. in military dress, standing to r., holding a spear and laurel branch, and placing his feet on the back of a captive. *Obv.* D. N. *(Dominus Noster)* CONSTANTIVS P. F. AVG. or D. N. CONSTANTIVS VICTOR AVG. *(Tanini.)* Bust of Constantius II. to r., diademed. *Æ.* I. and and *Æ.* Med. (50 to 100 frcs.)

VIRTVS AVGVSTI N. *(Nostri.)* Military figure walking, holding javelin in r. hand and globe in l.; on the ground two captives, or armed man standing, holding globe in r. hand and spear in l.—on *Æ.* Med. of Constantius II. from *Mionnet* (50 frcs.)

VIRTVS AVGVSTI NOSTRI. Magnentius standing to r., holding the *labarum* and placing his l. hand on the head of a captive; in the *exergue* SMAQ. *(Signata Moneta Aquileiæ.)* *N.* Med. (400 frcs.)

VIRTVS AVGVSTOR. *(Augustorum.)* Rome or Valour, helmeted, seated to l., holding Victory

and a *parazonium*; before or behind her, a shield—on silver coins (c.) and second brass (4 frcs.) of Septimius Severus, on silver coins (3 frcs.) and *Æ.* I. (8 frcs.), *Æ.* II. (6 frcs.) of Caracalla, on silver coins of Caracalla and Geta (300 frcs.), and on silver coins (5 frcs.) and second brass (10 frcs.) of Geta.

VIRTVS AVGVSTOR. *(Augustorum.)* Carinus and Numerian standing opposite each other. The latter is crowned by the Sun and the former by Hercules who holds a club and lion's skin. *Obv.* IMP. C. M. AVR. *(Cæsar Marcus Aurelius)* CARINVS P. F. AVG. Bust of Carinus to r., laureated. *Æ.* Med. (200 frcs.)

VIRTVS AVGVSTORVM. Severus, Caracalla, and Geta galloping to l.—on gold coins of Severus and Caracalla (300 frcs.)

VIRTVS AVGVSTORVM. Volusian standing to l., sacrificing at a lighted tripod, and crowned by a soldier standing behind him leaning on his shield; before him, a flute-player; at the foot of tripod a bull; behind two legionary eagles. *Obv.* IMP. CAE. C. VIB. *(Caio Vibio)* VOLVSIANO AVG. Bust of Volusian to l., laureated, holding sceptre surmounted by an eagle. *Æ.* Med. (400 frcs.)

VIRTVS AVGVSTORVM. Gallienus helmeted, seated to l. on a cuirass, crowned by Victory standing behind him holding a palm; before him an armed warrior, helmeted and holding shield, presents to him a branch; in the *field* two standards. *Obv.* IMP. GALLIENVS PIVS FEL. AVG. Bust of Gallienus to l., laureated, armed with spear and shield ornamented with the head of Medusa. *Æ.* Med. (400 frcs.) [*See* VABALATHVS.]

VIRTVS AVGVSTORVM. Two horsemen attacking six captives; above two Victories presenting them with wreaths. *Obv.* IMP. NVMERIANVS AVG. Bust of Numerian to l., laureated, holding a horse by the bridle and a spear. *Æ.* Med. from *Vaillant* (400 frcs.)

VIRTVS AVGVSTORVM. Hercules standing to r., leaning on his club and holding with his left hand a bow and lion's skin—on *Æ.* III. of Diocletian (6 frcs.) and Maximian Hercules (4 frcs.)

VIRTVS AVGVSTORVM. Emperor standing, holding spear and globe; at his feet a captive; or holding a spear and laurel branch or a standard, and leaning on a spear—on *Æ.* III. (6 frcs.) of Constantius II., on *Æ.* Med. of Magnentius (50 frcs.), and of Theodosius I. (100 frcs.)

VIRTVS CAES. *(Cæsaris.)* Constantine II. standing before a trophy; on either side a captive seated. *Obv.* CONSTANTINVS IVN. NOB. CAES. *(Junior Nobilis Cæsar.)* Bust of Constantine II. to r., laureated. *Æ.* Med. from *Vaillant* (200 frcs.)

VIRTVS CAESARIS. Julian II., bareheaded, standing to r., holding spear and globe; on either side a captive seated; in the *exergue* R. *(Romæ.)* *Obv.* D. N. CL. *(Dominus*

Noster Claudius) IVLIANVS N. C. *(Nobilis Cæsar.)* Bust of Julian II. to r., bare. Æ. Med. (80 frcs.)

VIRTVS CAESARVM. The Emperor, laureated, standing, erecting a trophy or fixing a shield to a trophy, at foot of which a captive—on brass medallions of Constans I. and Constantius II. (80 frcs.)

VIRTVS CAESS. *(Cæsarum.)* Gate of a camp surmounted by a star—on small brass coins of Constantine I. (?) from *Banduri* (5 frcs.), Crispus from *Wiczay* (3 frcs.), Constantine II. (c.) and Constantius II. (c.)

VIRTVS CAESS. *(Cæsarum.)* Constantine II., galloping to r. over two enemies. *Obv.* CONSTANTINVS. IVN. NOB. C. *(Junior Nobilis Cæsar.)* Bust to r., laureated. Æ. Med. (25 frcs.)

VIRTVS CAESS. *(Cæsarum.)* Constans I., laureated, standing facing looking to l., attaching a shield to a trophy, at the foot of which a female seated holding a sceptre. *Obv.* D. N. FL. *(Dominus Noster Flavius)* CONSTANS AVG. Bust of Constans I. diademed. Æ. Med. from *Banduri* (80 frcs.)

VIRTVS CAESS. *(Cæsarum.)* Constantius II. standing before a trophy. *Obv.* FL. IVL. CONSTANTIVS NOB. C. *(Cæsar.)* Bust of Constantius II. to r. Æ. II. from *Banduri* (6 frcs.)

VIRTVS CAESS. *(Cæsarum.)*—GLORIA SAECVLI VIRTVS CAESS. *(Cæsarum)*—on brass medallions of Constantine I. [GLORIA SAECVLI, &c.]. VIRTVS CAES. *(Cæsaris)* occurs on some of his gold and silver coins given by *Mionnet.*

VIRTVS CARI INVICTI AVG. *(Augusti.)* Hercules, naked, standing, to r., leaning on his club, which is covered with a lion's skin and placed on a rock. *Obv.* IMP. C. M. AVR. *(Cæsar Marcus Aurelius)* CARVS P. F. AVG. Bust of Carus to r., laureated. N. (250 frcs.)

VIRTVS CLAVDI A . . . *(Claudii Augusti.)* Claudius II. on horseback to r., hurling his spear at a prostrate enemy; under the horse two others and a shield. *Obv.* IMP. C. M. AVR. CLAVDIVS AVG. Bust of Claudius II. to r., laureated. N. (1200 frcs.)

VIRTVS CONSTANTI AVG. *(Constantii Augusti.)* Constantius II. standing to l. holding the *labarum* and a sceptre; at his feet a captive seated; in the *exergue* SMAQ. *(Signata Moneta Aquileiæ.) Obv.* CONSTANTIVS P. F. AVG. Bust of Constantius II. to r., diademed. N. Med. (500 frcs.)

VIRTVS CONSTANTI CAES. *(Constantii Cæsaris.)* Constantius II. walking to r., holding spear and trophy; at his feet two captives; in the *exergue* SMN. *(Signata Moneta Nicomediæ.) Obv.* FL. IVL. CONSTANTIVS AVG. Bust of Constantius II. to r., diademed. N. Med. (300 frcs.)

VIRTVS CONSTANTINI AVG. *(Augusti.)* The Emperor standing between two captives, holding spear and trophy; in the *exergue* SMTS. *(Signata Moneta Thessalonicæ)*—on gold coins of Constantine I. from *Banduri* (200 frcs.) and gold medallion of Constantius II. (400 frcs.)

VIRTVS CONSTANTINI CAES. *(Cæsaris.)* Constantine I., laureated, galloping to r., holding a shield and piercing with his spear an enemy kneeling; under the horse a dead enemy and a shield. *Obv.* CONSTANTINVS NOB. CAES. Head of Constantine I. to r., laureated. Æ. II. (20 frcs.)

VIRTVS CONSTANTINI CAES. *(Cæsaris.)* Mars, walking, holding a spear and trophy; on either side a captive; in the *exergue* SMN (*Signata Moneta Nicomediæ* 3.) *Obv.* CONSTANTINVS IVN. NOB. C. *(Junior Nobilis Cæsar.)* Bust of Constantine II. to r., laureated. N. Med. (400 frcs.)

VIRTVS CONSTANTIS AVG. *(Augusti.)* Constans I. standing holding the *labarum* and a spear, at his feet a captive; in the *exergue* SMAQ. *(Signata Moneta Aquileiæ.) Obv.* (?) N. Med. from *Mionnet* (400 frcs.)

VIRTVS COS. II. Valour, helmeted, standing to r., the l. foot placed on a helmet, holding spear and *parazonium*—on silver and first and second brass coins of Marcus Aurelius (c.)

VIRTVS DD. NN. AVGG. *(Dominorum Nostrorum Augustorum.)* The Emperor standing to l. holding the *labarum;* in the *exergue* TR. *(Treveris)*—on silver medallions of Constans I. (80 frcs.) and Constantius II. (50 frcs.)

VIRTVS EQVIT. *(Equitum.)* Soldier walking to r. holding spear and shield; sometimes in the *exergue* T. *Obv.* IMP. POSTVMVS AVG. Bust of Postumus to r., radiated. *Bil.* (c.)

VIRTVS EQVITVM. Hercules, naked, standing to r., leaning on his club enveloped in al on's skin and placed on a rock; sometimes in the *exergue* S or Z. *Obv.* IMP. C. *(Cæsar)* POSTVMVS P. F. AVG. Bust of Postumus to r., radiated. *Bil.* (c.)

VIRTVS EXERC. *(Exercitus.)* Valentinian II. standing to l. on a vessel holding a globe surmounted by a Victory and the *labarum,* and placing r. foot on the back of a captive; to r. a figure holding the rudder. *Obv.* D. N. *(Dominus Noster)* VALENTINIANVS P. F. AVG. Bust of Valentinian II. to r., diademed. Æ. from *Wiczay* (20 frcs.)

VIRTVS EXERC. GALL. *(Exercitus Gallicani.)* Julian II., helmeted, walking to r.; dragging by the hair a captive and holding a trophy; in the *field* a wreath or an eagle holding a wreath in its beak; in the *exergue* KONSTAN (TAN in monogram—*(Constantinæ-Arles.) Obv.* FL. CL. IVLIANVS P. P. *(Pius Perpetuus)* or P. F. AVG. Bust of Julian II., bearded, to r., diademed. N. (60 frcs.)

VIRTVS EXERCIT. *(Exercitus.)* Trophy at foot of which two captives, or standard, on which VOT. *(Votis)* X. or XX. between two captives—on small brass coins (c.) of Licinius I., Licinius II., Constantine I., Crispus, and Constantine II. It is upon the coins with the legend VIRTVS EXERCIT. and the type of the standard on which VOT. XX. that the monogram ☧ occurs in the *field.* There is little reason to doubt that this sign is intended for the Christian monogram, though at this period of the reign of

Constantine I. expressed in somewhat a latent manner. This series was probably introduced about the year A.D. 319. It is anterior to 323, coins of both the Licinii being common to it, while those of Constantius II. *Cæsar* are wanting. Coins with this monogram cannot be classed as "common." (Madden, *Christian Emblems on Coins of Constantine I., &c.*, in the *Num. Chron.* N. S., 1877, vol. xviii., p. 53.) The *top* of the standard on some of these coins, on which there is no monogram in the *field*, sometimes ends in a cross. (Madden, *op. cit.*, p. 257.)

VIRTVS EXERCIT. *(Exercitus.)* Square altar, on which a globe surmounted by three stars; on the front of the altar VOTIS XX. *Obv.* CONSTANTINVS NOB. CAES. Bust of Constantine I. to r., helmeted. Æ. III., from *Banduri* (20 frcs.)

VIRTVS EXERCIT. *(Exercitus.)* The design of a camp; in the midst, above, the Sun, radiated, standing to l., holding a globe. *Obv.* D. N. CONSTANTIVS P. F. AVG. Bust of Constantius II. to r. Æ. III., from *Ducange* (10 frcs.)

VIRTVS EXERCIT. *(Exercitus.)* Theodosius I., diademed, standing to r., holding a standard and placing foot on a seated captive; sometimes a cross in the *field*. *Obv.* D. N. THEODOSIVS P. F. AVG. Bust of Theodosius I. to r. Æ. II. (c.)

VIRTVS EXERCITI. Valour or a soldier standing to r., holding spear and leaning on shield, in the *exergue* TR. *(Treveris)*—on silver coins of Magnentius (30 frcs.), and of Decentius (200 frcs.)

VIRTVS EXERCITI. The Emperor standing holding the *labarum* and globe, and placing foot on or kicking a captive, sometimes in the *field* ☧ or a palm—on third brass coins of Valentinian I. from *Wiczay* (6 frcs.), and on second brass coins of Valentinian II. (c.), Theodosius I. (c.), and Magnus Maximus (10 frcs.)

VIRTVS EXERCITI. The Emperor standing, facing, diademed, holding a spear and leaning on a shield; a Victory, standing to l., holding a palm, is crowning him—on third brass coins of Honorius (c.), and on gold of Arcadius (50 frcs.)

VIRTVS EXERCITI. Arcadius standing to r., holding the *labarum* and a globe, placing r. foot on a captive; in the *field* sometimes ☧, sometimes a star; in the *exergue* CONS. Δ *(Constantinopolis* 4); SMNΔ. *(Signata Moneta Nicomediæ* 4); ALEA *(Alexandriæ* I); ANTS *(Antiochiæ)*, &c. *Obv.* D. N. ARCADIVS P. F. AVGVSTVS or AVG. Bust of Arcadius to r., diademed. Æ. (c. to 2 frcs.)

VIRTVS EXERCITVM *(sic—Exercituum.)* The Emperor standing between two captives, holding a trophy and leaning on a shield; in the *exergue* TES. *(Thessalonicæ)*—on gold medallions of Constans I. (400 frcs.) and Constantius II. (1000 frcs.) A similar type also on second brass coins of Vetranio (25 frcs.)

VIRTVS EXERCITVM. *(sic—Exercituum.)* Four military standards; on the second the letter A, and on the third Ѡ ; above ☧ ; in *exergue* R. *(Romæ)*. *Obv.* D. N. CONSTANS P. F. AVG. Bust of Constans, diademed. Æ. Med. (80 frcs). Though this is the earliest example of the A and Ѡ on *coins*, these letters were probably employed before this date, perhaps even before the Council of Nice in A.D. 325, as proved by the tomb of the martyr Heraclius, who suffered long before the reign of Constantine, found in the cemetery of Priscilla (Aringhi vol. I., p. 605. Roma, 1651-59), by an inscription given by Fabretti *(Inscr. Ant. Explic.*, p. 739, Roma. 1699), and by a cup given by Boldetti from the cemetery of Callixtus *(Oss. sopra i cim.*, &c., p. 194, pl. iii., No. 4, Roma, 1720). The Arians carefully avoided their use (Giorgi, *De Mon. Christi*, p. 10, Roma, 1738), and it was not till about A.D. 347 that these letters commenced to come into general use in any case on coins. The origin of these letters can of course be traced to the words of St. John, Ἐγὼ τὸ Α καὶ τὸ Ω, ὁ πρῶτος καὶ ὁ ἔσχατος, ἡ ἀρχὴ καὶ τὸ τέλος. (Rev. xxii. 13, and cf. I, 8, 11 ; xxi. 6—"I am *A/pha* and *Omega*, the first and the last, the beginning and the end"), and the poet Prudentius *(Cathemerinon*, IX. 10), who was born during the reign of Constantius II. and Constans (A.D. 348), mentions them as follows:—

"Corde natus ex parentis ante mundi exordium,
Alpha et Ѡ cognominatus; ipse fons et clausula
Omnium, quæ sunt, fuerunt, quæque post futura sunt."

As to the form Ѡ instead of Ω the Padre Garrucci *(Hagioglypta*, p. 168, *note)*, asserts that the Ω nowhere occurs on any authentic Christian monument, and condemns, as does de Rossi, a ring published by Costadoni on which is a dolphin between the letters A and Ω. The letters A and Ѡ may also be found on either side of ☧ on second brass coins of Constantius II. (3 frcs.), with the legend SALVS AVG. NOSTRI. On the whole question see Madden, *Christian Emblems on the Coins of Constantine I., &c.*, in the *Num. Chron.* N. S., 1878, vol. xviii., p. 32. *seq.*, and art. *Money* in Smith's and Cheetham's *Dict. of Christian Antiq.*

VIRTVS EXERCITVS. Valour, helmeted, standing to r. holding a spear, leaning on a shield and placing l. foot on a helmet—on silver coins of Philip I. (3 frcs.)

VIRTVS EXERCITVS. Heap of arms, similar to those on the coins of Marcus Aurelius with DE GERM. and DE SARM. *Obv.* POSTVMVS PIVS AVG. Head of Postumus to r., laureated. N. (500 frcs.)

VIRTVS EXERCITVS. Mars, helmeted, walking r., holding spear and trophy, and on l. arm a shield—on second brass coins of Galerius Maximian (c.) and of Maximinus II. (3 frcs.)

On some Æ. II. of Maximinus II. (30 frcs.) Mars holds a spear and shield, and in front there is an altar.

VIRTVS EXERCITVS. Soldier standing holding spear and leaning on shield—on silver medallion of Constantine I. (100 frcs.), and on silver coins of Constantius II. (60 frcs.)

VIRTVS EXERCITVS. The Emperor standing holding *labarum* or standard (or globe and spear) and leaning on shield—on coins of Vetranio (Æ. III. from *Banduri* 40 frcs.), Decentius (Æ. III. from *Banduri* 8 frcs.), Valentinian I. (Æ. 60 frcs.), Valens (Æ. 60 frcs.), Gratian (Æ. 60 frcs.), Valentinian II. (Æ. Med. 100 frcs.), Theodosius I. (Æ. Med. 100 frcs.), Magnus Maximus (N. Med. 500 frcs.; Æ. Med. 300 frcs.), and Arcadius (N. 48 frcs.)

VIRTVS EXERCITVS. Three standards; in the *exergue* SMKΔ *(Signata Moneta Kyzici* 4.) *Obv.* D. N. FL. CL. *(Dominus Noster Flavius Claudius)* CONSTANTIVS NOB. CAES. Head of Constantius Gallus, bare. Æ. from *Eckhel* (150 frcs.)

VIRTVS EXERCITVS. Julian II., helmeted, standing r., holding in r. hand a spear and in the l. an eagle, who has a wreath in its beak; on the ground a shield; in the *exergue* P. CONST. *(Prima Constantinæ—Arles.) Obv.* D. N. FL. CL. IVLIANVS P. F. AVG. Bust of Julian II. to r., diademed. Æ. Med. (120 frcs.)

VIRTVS EXERCITVS. GALL. *(Gallicani.)* Mars, helmeted, walking r., holding spear and trophy; in *field* sometimes a star, and generally at his feet two captives seated—on gold coins of Licinius I. (from *Wiczay*, 400 frcs.), and Constantine I. [see woodcut *without* captives] (150 frcs.), Constantine II. (from *Schellersheim* (250 frcs), Constans (60 frcs.), and Constantius II. (50 frcs.)

VIRTVS EXERCITVS ROMANI or ROMANORVM. Same type as previous coin described—on gold coins of Julian II. (50 to 60 frcs.)

VIRTVS FALERI *(? Valeriani.)* Quiver, lion's skin, club, vase, and bow—on *billon* coins of Gallienus (30 to 50 frcs.) [VALERI.]

VIRTVS GALLIA[RVM.] Gallienus on horseback, to r., riding over two enemies; he is preceded by a soldier and two others are following him. *Obv.* GALLIENVS PIVS FEL. AVG. GERM. Bust of Gallienus to l., laureated, holding in r. hand a spear, and in l. a shield, on which a figure seated at foot of trophy. *Bil.* Med., from Boutkowski, *Dictionnaire Numismatique*, 1884, p. 1226. Now in the *Cabinet des Médailles*, Paris, (2000 frcs.)

VIRTVS GALLIENI AVGVSTI. Gallienus, bareheaded, walking to l., carrying a standard with two hands. *Obv.* IMP. GALLIENVS PIVS FELIX AVG. Bust of Gallienus to r., laureated, holding a *caduceus*. N. Med., from *Tanini* (2500 frcs.)

VIRTVS HERCVLI CAESARIS. Constantius I. Chlorus on horseback to r., holding a spear; in the *exergue* TR. *(Treveris.) Obv.* CONSTANTIVS NOB. C. *(Nobilis Cæsar.)* Head of Constantius I. Chlorus to r., laureated. N (300 frcs.)

VIRTVS ILLYRICI. Mars, helmeted, naked, with mantle flowing, walking r., carrying spear and trophy; at his feet a captive—on coins of Aurelian (N. 200 frcs.; Æ. III., from *Tanini* 10 frcs.)

VIRTVS ILLYRICI. Emperor galloping to r., holding spear; below, a galley with four rowers; in the *exergue* TR. *(Treveris)*—on gold coins of Diocletian (300 frcs.), Maximian Hercules (300 frcs.), and Constantius I. Chlorus (300 frcs.)

VIRTVS IN. AVG. *(Invicti Augusti.)* Carausius standing to r., holding a spear and a globe; in the *exergue* L. *(Londini,) Obv.* IMP. CARAVSIVS P. F. IN. *(Invictus)* Bust of Carausius to r., laureated. Æ. (250 frcs.)

VIRTVS INVIC. *(Banduri)* or INVICTI AVG. Probus galloping to r., spearing a fallen enemy and holding a shield. Sometimes a Victory is flying before Probus crowning him—on small brass coins of Probus (3 to 10 frcs.)

VIRTVS INVICTI AVG. Probus standing, placing foot on seated captive and holding a spear and *parazonium;* he is crowned by the Sun, standing, holding a whip. *Obv.* VIRTVS PROBI AVG. Bust of Probus to l., with helmet radiated, holding spear and shield. Æ. III. (20 frcs.)

VIRTVS IOVI CAESARIS. Galerius Maximian on horseback; in the *exergue* TR. *(Treveris). Obv.* MAXIMIANVS NOB. C. *(Nobilis Cæsar).* Head of Galerius Maximian to r., laureated. N. (300 frcs.) The title of *Jovius* was taken by Diocletian and that of *Herculeus* by Maximian (Vict. *In Cæs.)* and is attested by their coins. Galerius Maximian having married Valeria, the daughter of Diocletian, was called *Cæsar Jovius*, as on this coin; Constantius Chlorus, who married Theodora, the daughter-in-law of Maximian, was called *Cæsar Hercules* [VIRTVS HERCVLI CEASARIS]. Maximin II. Daza, who had been created by Galerius, *Cæsar*, assumed by right of adoption the title of *Jovius* (IOVIVS MAXIMINVS NOB. CAES.) as Eusebius (*Hist. Eccles.* ix., c. 9.), has given him. Licinius I. and II. also adopted it (DD. NN. IOVII LICINII INVICT. AVG. ET CAES.)

VIRTVS MIL. *(Militum.)* The Emperor (?) helmeted, standing, holding a spear and leaning on a shield. *Obv.* IMP. GALLIENVS AVG. Head of Gallienus, radiated. *Bil.* (10 frcs.)

VIRTVS MILIT. *(Militum.)* Aurelian on horseback to l., holding a sceptre. *Obv.* IMP. AVRELIANVS AVG. Bust of Aurelian to r. radiated. Æ. III. (10 frcs.)

VIRTVS MILITVM. Valour standing to l., holding a standard on which XXX—on gold coins (1800 frcs.), and silver coins (300 frcs.) of Lælian.

VIRTVS MILITVM. Aurelian standing to r. or to l., holding globe and spear; a soldier holding a spear presents him with a Victory—on small brass coins of Aurelian (c.)

VIRTVS MILITVM. Four soldiers sacrificing on a tripod before the gate of a camp; in the *exergue* A, B, C, D, E or ϵ, Γ &c., a club, or nothing—on silver coins of Diocletian (8 frcs.), Maximian Hercules (8 frcs.), Constantius I. Chlorus (12 to 20 frcs.), and Galerius Maximian (10 frcs.)

VIRTVS MILITVM. Gate of a camp with or without doors, surmounted by three or four towers; in the *exergue* various letters—on coins of Diocletian (Æ. 10 frcs.), Maximian Hercules (Æ. 10 frcs.), Constantius I. Chlorus (Æ. 12 frcs.), Galerius Maximian (Æ. 10 frcs. ; Æ. *Quin*. 60 frcs.), Maximinus II. Daza. (Æ. *Quin*. 100 frcs., Æ. II. 30 frcs.) ; Maxentius [*Obv.* PRINC. INVICT. *Princeps Invictus*] (Æ. 250 frcs.), and Constantine I. (Æ. 40 frcs., Æ. *Quin*., 25 frcs.)

VIRTVS MILITVM. Gate of a camp without doors surmounted by three towers; above four (sometimes five) towers—on gold coins of Diocletian (200 frcs.), Maximian Hercules (150 frcs.); and Galerius Maximian from *Caylus* (200 frcs.)

VIRTVS MILITVM. Prætorian camp—on coins of Maximian Hercules (Æ. 30 frcs.), Constantius I. Chlorus (N. 200 frcs.), and Maximinus II. Daza. (Æ. 100 frcs.)

VIRTVS MILITVM DD. NN. (*Dominorum Nostrorum*.) Mars, walking, holding a trophy and a spear. *Obv.* LICINIVS IVN. NOB. (*Junior Nobilis*) CAESAR. Head of Licinius II., laureated. Æ. III., from *D'Ennery* (10 frcs.)

VIRTVS PERPETVA AVG. (*Augusti*.) Hercules or the Emperor strangling a lion ; behind, a club—on second brass coins of Constantius I. Chlorus (10 frcs.) and Constantine I. (8 frcs.)

VIRTVS POSTVMI S. C. Postumus standing to l., holding a globe and a spear, and crowned by Victory, who holds a palm ; between them a captive on the ground. *Obv.* IMP. C. M. CASS. LAT. POSTVMVS. P. F. AVG. (*Imperator Cæsar Marcus Cassianus Latinius Postumus Pius Felix Augustus*) Bust of Postumus to r., radiated. Æ. I. (20 frcs.)

VIRTVS POSTVMI AVG. (*Augusti*.) Bust of Postumus to r., with the helmet much ornamented, and a cuirass—on gold coins of Postumus (600 frcs.) [*See* VIRTVS.]

VIRTVS POSTVMI AVG. (*Augusti*.)—Hercules, naked, standing to r. felling the stag of Ceryneia—on second brass coins of Postumus (100 frcs.) [*See* p. 451.]

VIRTVS PROBI AVG. (*Augusti*.) Probus standing holding spear and *parazonium*, and placing foot on back of captive; behind, a captive kneeling. *Obv.* IMP. C. M. AVR. PROBVS. AVG. Bust of Probus to r., laureated. N. (150 frcs.) [*See* VIRTVS.]

VIRTVS PROBI AVG. (*Augusti*.) Probus galloping to r. or to l., hurling javelin at an enemy on the ground ; another enemy under the horse; an armed soldier precedes the Emperor. *Obv.* IMP. C. M. AVR. PROBVS P. F. AVG. Bust of Probus, helmeted, to l., with the cuirass, holding sword and shield. Æ. Med. (150 frcs.) A somewhat similar coin in gold is given by *Caylus* (200 frcs.), and there are varieties in small brass (5 frcs.) [*See* VIRTVS.]

VIRTVS PROBI AVG (*Augusti*.) Mars, helmeted, naked, walking to r., holding spear and trophy—sometimes to l. and r. captives—on Æ. Medallions (150 frcs.) and small brass coins of Probus (c. to 1 frc.) [*See* VIRTVS.]

VIRTVS PROBI AVG. (*Augusti*.) Trophy between two captives seated on the ground—on small brass coins of Probus (2 frcs.) [*See* VIRTVS.]

VIRTVS ROMANOR. (*Romanorum*.) Julian II., helmeted, holding a trophy and dragging a captive by the hair. *Obv.* FL. CL. IVLIANVS P. F. AVG. Bearded bust of Julian II. Æ. III. *Quin*. (10 frcs.)

VIRTVS ROMANORVM. Victory seated on spoils, holding with both hands a shield on which VOT. XX. *Obv.* D. N. FL. CONSTANTIVS AVG. Bust of Constantius II. to r., laureated. Æ. Med. (100 frcs.)

VIRTVS ROMANORVM. Julian II. standing, holding spear in r. hand, and carrying in the l. Victory on a globe ; in the *exergue* ANT. S? (*Antiochiæ*)—on Æ. Med. of Julian II. from *Mionnet* (80 frcs.)

VIRTVS ROMANORVM. Valentinian I. and Valens, standing, facing, holding a globe surmounted by a Victory who crowns them ; in the *exergue* CONS. (*Constantinopolis*)—on gold coins of Valentinian I. and Valens (50 frcs.)

VIRTVS ROMANORVM. Rome, helmeted, seated on a cuirass, holding globe and spear ; in the *exergue* various mint-marks—on gold (30 frcs.) and silver (8 frcs.), and third brass (c.) coins of Gratian, and on silver coins of Valentinian II. (6 frcs.), Theodosius I. (3 to 6 frcs.—Æ. III., c.), Magnus Maximus (10 frcs.) globe surmounted by cross—*Tanini*, (15 frcs.), Victor (15 frcs.—N. from *D'Ennery*), Eugenius (20 frcs.), Honorius (4 frcs.—N. 40 frcs.) Arcadius (8 frcs.), Theodosius II. (100 frcs.), Sebastian (from *Wiczay*, 300 frcs.), and Attalus (100 frcs.)

VIRTVS ROMANORVM. Valentinian III. standing to r., holding globe, surmounted by Victory and a standard; in the *exergue* TRP. (?). *Obv.* D. N. VALENTINIANVS P. F. AVG. Bust of Valentinian III. to r., diademed. Æ. From *Cab. de M. Charvet* (40 frcs.) The mint mark TR. P. is doubtful. Treves was burnt by the Franks, in A.D. 413 (Madden, *Num. Chron.*, N.S., vol. i., p. 125), and Valentinian III. was not nominated *Augustus* till A.D. 425. Probably the coin is barbarous.

VIRTVT. AVG. (*Virtuti Augusti*.) TR. P. VII. IMP. IIII. COS. III. P. P. (A.D. 182). Rome seated to l., holding Victory and spear. *Obv.* M. ANTONINVS COMMODVS AVG. Bust of Commodus to r., laureated. N. (130 frcs.)

VIRTVT. AVG. *(Virtuti Augusti.)* P. M. TR. P. XII. IMP. VIII. COS. V. P. P. (A.D. 187.) Valour, helmeted, standing to l., holding Victory and leaning on a shield, a spear resting on her l. arm. *Obv.* M. COMM. ANT. P. FEL. AVG. BRIT. *(Marcus Commodus Antoninus Pius Felix Augustus Britannicus.)* Head of Commodus to r., laureated. Æ. (c.) The same type occurs on his first and second brass coins (c.), the legend commencing VIRTVTI AVG., &c.

VIRTVTE AVG. *(Augusti.)* Valour standing to r., holding spear and *parazonium*. *Obv.* IMP. CAE. L. SEP. SEV. PERT. AVG. COS. II. Head of Septimius Severus to r., laureated. Æ. (5 frcs.)

VIRTVTI.—IOVIS VIRTVTI on Æ. I. of Domitian, perhaps altered from IOVI VICTORI (Cohen, *Méd. Imp.*, vol. vii., *Suppl.*, p. 90.)—I. O. M. ET VIRTVTI DD. NN. AVG. ET. CAES. *(Jovi Optimo Maximo et Virtuti Dominorum Nostrorum Augusti et Cæsaris)* on Æ. II. of Licinius I. and Licinius II.

VIRTVTI AVG. *(Augusti.)* Valour standing to r., foot on helmet, holding spear and *parazonium*, or Hadrian on horseback to r., hurling a javelin—on gold coins of Hadrian (45 frcs. and 100 frcs.)

VIRTVTI AVG. *(Augusti.)* P. M. TR. P. XII., &c. [*See* VIRTVT. AVG., &c.]

VIRTVTI AVG. *(Augusti—*in *exergue.)* TR. P. VIII. IMP. V. COS. IIII. P. P. (A.D. 183.) Rome or Valour, helmeted, seated to l., on a cuirass, holding spear and *parazonium*, leaning l. arm on a shield, ornamented with the wolf suckling Romulus and Remus; before her, a trophy. *Obv.* M. AVREL. COMMODVS ANTONINVS AVG. Bust of Commodus to r., laureated. Æ. Med. (300 frcs.)

VIRTVTI AVG. *(Augusti.)* Mars standing to r. or to l., holding a spear and leaning on a shield. *Obv.* IMP. CAES. PESC. NIGER IVST. AVG. *(Imperator Cæsar Pescennius Niger Justus Augustus).* Head of Pescennius Niger to r. Æ. (200 frcs.)

VIRTVTI AVG. *(Augusti).* Mars walking, carrying a spear and a trophy. *Obv.* L. SEPT. SEVER. PERT. AVG. IMP. VIII. (A.D. 197). Head of Septimius Severus, laureated. *N.* (150 frcs.)

VIRTVTI AVG. *(Augusti.)* S. C. Septimius Severus standing to l., holding Victory and spear, and crowned by Rome standing, who holds a *parazonium* upside down. *Obv.* L. SEPT. SEV. PERT. AVG. IMP. V. (A.D. 195.) Head of Septimius Severus to r., laureated. Æ. I. (15 frcs.)

VIRTVTI AVG. *(Augusti.)* Trophy, at foot of which two captives; in the *exergue* S. P. Q. R. *(Senatus Populusque Romanus.) Obv.* IMP. GALLIENVS AVG. Bust of Gallienus, radiated. *Bil.* from *Banduri* (30 frcs.)

VIRTVTI AVG. *(Augusti.)* Bust of Postumus to r., laureated, and bust of Mars, helmeted, jugate. *Obv.* POSTVMVS PIVS FELIX AVG. Bust of Postumus to r. laureated, and bust of Hercules, jugate. *N.* (800 frcs.)

VIRTVTI AVG. *(Augusti.)* Hercules, naked, standing to r., leaning on club and holding

a bow; or strangling a lion and behind, a club—on small brass coins of Carausius (30 frcs.)

VIRTVTI AVGG. *(Augustorum.)* Rome, helmeted, seated to l on a cuirass, holding Victory and *parazonium*; behind, a shield. *Obv.* L. SEPT. SEV. AVG. IMP. XI. PART. MAX. *(Parthicus Maximus).* Bust of Septimius Severus to l., with *ægis*, and armed with spear (A.D. 198-201). *N.* from *Caylus* (150 frcs.)

VIRTVTI AVGG. *(Augustorum.)* Hercules, naked, standing to r., leaning on his club and holding a bow; lion's skin on left arm. *Obv.* IMP. C. M. AVR. CARINVS P. F. AVG. Bust of Carinus to r. Æ. III. (3 frcs.)

VIRTVTI AVGG. *(Augustorum.)* Hercules, naked, standing to r., strangling the Nemæan lion; behind, a club—sometimes Victory flying crowns him—on third brass coins of Diocletian and Maximian Hercules (3 frcs.)

VIRTVTI AVGG. *(Augustorum.)* Hercules, naked, standing to r., leaning on a club placed on rock; lion's skin on arm; or Hercules standing r., strangling Antæus—on third brass coins of Maximian Hercules (3 frcs. and 40 frcs.)

VIRTVTI AVGG. *(Augustorum.)* Hercules, naked, walking to r., holding club and carrying on his shoulders the wild boar of Erymanthus; in the *exergue* P. T. *(Prima Tarraconis.) Obv.* MAXIMIANVS AVGVSTVS. Head of Maximian Hercules to r. *N.* from *Caylus* (150 frcs.)

VIRTVTI AVGG. *(Augustorum.)* Hercules, naked, standing to r., killing the hydra; in the *exergue* TR. *(Treveris). Obv.* CONSTANTIVS N. C. *(Nobilis Cæsar.)* Head of Constantius Chlorus to r. *N.* from *Caylus* (300 frcs.)

VIRTVTI AVGVSTI S. C. Valour standing to r. or to l., foot on helmet, holding *parazonium* and spear—on coins of Domitian (Æ. II., 2 frcs.) and Albinus (Æ. without s. c. 12 frcs.)

VIRTVTI AVGVSTI. The Emperor galloping to r., hurling javelin at lion—on coins of Hadrian (Æ. I. *without* s. c., 200 frcs.) and Commodus (Æ. Med., 300 frcs.)

VIRTVTI AVGVSTI. Hercules, naked standing to r., leaning on a club, which is sometimes resting on a rock or sometimes on the head of an ox—on coins of Gordianus Pius (*N.* 80 to 150 frcs.; Æ. c. to 3 frcs.; Æ. *Quin.* 15 frcs.; Æ. II. 15 frcs.), Postumus *(Bil.* c.) and Tetricus I. (*N.* 300 frcs.)

VIRTVTI ET FELICITATI. Valour standing to r., foot on helmet, holding spear and *parazonium*, and Felicity standing to l., holding *caduceus* and cornucopiæ. *Obv.* IMP. TRAIANVS AVG. GER. DAC. P. M. TR. P. COS. VI. P. P. Head of Trajan, laureated. *N.* from *Caylus* (200 frcs.)

VIRTVTI EXERCITI. Mars, helmeted, naked, with flowing mantle, walking r., and holding spear and trophy. *Obv.* IMP. C. GAL. VAL. MAXIMINVS P. F. INV. *(Invictus)* AVG. Head of Maximinus II. Daza to r., laureated. Æ. II. (10 frcs.)

VIRTVTI EXERCITVS (sometimes CMH? in monogram—on coins of Maximinus II. Daza.) Mars helmeted, with flowing mantle, or in military dress, holding spear and trophy, sometimes holding shield on l. arm or dragging a captive, on second brass coins of Galerius Maximian (c.), Maximinus II. Daza (1 to 10 frcs.; Æ. III. 25 frcs., with FIL. AVGG. *Filius Augustorum*, 30 frcs.), and Constantius I. (5 frcs., with FIL. AVGG., 20 frcs.)

VIRTVTI HERCVLIS. Hercules, naked, standing to r., leaning on his club, which is resting on a rock—on gold coins of Maximian Hercules (100 frcs.), and Galerius Maximian, from *Tanini* (300 frcs.)

VIRTVTI MILITVM. Gate of a camp, with open doors, surmounted by four towers; in the *exergue* SMNA or SMNⲦ (*Signata Moneta Nicomediæ* 1 or 3)—on coins of Galerius Maximian (Æ. 20 frcs.; Æ. II. 30 frcs.)

Visigoths.—The coinage of the Visigoths has been exhaustively treated by M. Heiss *(Monnaies des Rois Wisigoths)*, and the following list of the names of the Visigothic Kings is taken from that given by Mr. Keary (*Num. Chron.*, N.S., 1878, vol. xviii., pp. 246-251):— Leovigild (A.D. 573-586), Reccaredus I. (A.D. 586-601), Liuva II. (A.D. 601-603), Witteric (A.D. 603-610), Gondemar (A.D. 610-612), Sisebut (A.D. 612-621), Suinthila (A.D. 621-631), Sisenand (A.D. 631-636), Chinthila (A.D. 636-640), Tulga (A.D. 640-642), Chindasuinthe (A.D. 642-649), Chindasuinthe and Reccasuinthe (A.D. 649-653), Reccasuinthe (A.D. 653-672), Wamba (A.D. 672-680), Ervigius (A.D. 680-687), Egica (A.D. 687-696), Egica and Wittiza (A.D. 696-700), Wittiza (A.D. 700-710), Roderigo (A.D. 710-711), Achila (uncertain king, A.D. 711?) The types of the coins, which consist almost exclusively of *trientes*, are Victory, holding wreath and palm, cross haussée on three steps, bust facing, and cruciform monogram. A complete list of the mints at which the coins were struck is also given by Mr. Keary [VALENTIA.]

Visontium, a town of the Pelendones in Hispania Taraconensis, supposed to have been a *municipium* from coins of Augustus and Galba (?) with the legend MVN. VISONTIVM, published by Hardouin and Morell (Eckhel, vol. I., p. 60), but I doubt if they are genuine. It has been suggested that the coin of Augustus might be attributed to *Vesontio* (now *Besançon*) in Gallia, at which place there was a *municipalis schola* (Auson. *Ad Grat. Act.)*

VIT. (*sic*) AVGG. *Victoria Augustorum.* Victory standing holding a large cross; in the *exergue* two stars. *Obv.* D. N. MAIORIANVS AVG. Bust of Majorian, helmeted. Æ. from *D'Ennery* (100 frcs.)

VITA—placed in the *exergue of the obverse* on coins of Justinus I. and Justinian I. (Æ. 60 frcs.), Justinus II. and Sophia (Æ. 100 frcs.; Æ. 3 to 25 frcs.), and Mauricius Tiberius (Æ. 10 frcs.) The word VITA which appears for the first time on the coins of Justinus I. and Justinianus I. (A.D. 527) may perhaps signify *Sit longa* VITA! as suggested by Marchant and de Saulcy, or may refer, as Martigny *(Dict. des Antiq. Chrét.*, p. 464) thinks, to the cross sometimes placed between the two heads on the coin as the source of true life. (Cf. Madden, *Christian Emblems on Coins of Constantine I.*, &c., in *Num. Chron.*, N.S., 1878, vol. xviii., p. 170.)

Vitalianus, grandson of Aspar (a general of barbarous descent) and general of the barbarian mercenaries, assumed the title of Emperor in A.D. 514, and attempted to take Constantinople, but in this he was defeated by Anastasius, and resigned the Imperial title on receiving a large sum of money and the government of Thrace. On the death of Anastasius it is said that Vitalian was recalled by Justin I., and made *Consul* and *magister militum*, but shortly after was treacherously murdered at a banquet in the presence of Justin and Justinian.

No authentic coins of Vitalian are in existence. The gold pieces published by *D'Ennery* and *Tanini*, and quoted by Eckhel (vol. viii., p. 208), are most probably misread.

VITELL. *Vitellius—*L. VITELL. CENSOR II. S. C. *Lucius Vitellius Censor II. Senatus Consulto—*on large brass coins of A. Vitellius, with reverse of L. Vitellius.

VITELLI. *Vitellius.*—L. VITELLI. III. COS. CENS. *Lucius Vitellius III. Consul Censor—* on gold coins of L. Vitellius (father) and A. Vitellius (son).

VITELLIVS.—L. VITELLIVS COS. III. CENSOR. *Lucius Vitellius Consul III. Censor—*on gold and silver coins of L. Vitellius with reverse of A. Vitellius.

VITELLIVS (Aulus), the son of Lucius Vitellius [VITELLIVS (Lucius)] was born in A.D. 15, and passed his early life at Capri with Tiberius, and was a favourite with Caligula, Claudius, and Nero. He was elected Consul in A.D. 48, and was Proconsul of Africa for a year. In A.D. 68 he was sent by Galba to Germany, and soon after, revolting against him, was proclaimed Emperor by the soldiers. Otho had in the meantime been elected Emperor at Rome, but was defeated by Vitellius in A.D. 69 at Bedriacum. He did not, however, long enjoy the supreme power, for his gluttony and prodigality were so disgraceful that Vespasian, who was in command of the war against the Jews, was persuaded to allow himself to be elected Emperor. Thus, after a reign of about eight months, Vitellius was captured at Rome by the soldiers of Vespasian and ignominiously killed at the *Gemoniæ Scalæ*, where the corpse of Flavius Sabinus, the brother of Vespasian, had a few days previously been thrown. Vitellius is said to have accepted the *cognomen* of *Germanicus*, deferred assuming the title of *Augustus*, and refused for ever that of *Cæsar* (Suet. *Vitell.*, c. 8; Tac., *Hist.* ii., c. 62.) He was twice married—1. to Petronia, by whom he had a son named Petronianus, who was blind of one eye, and whom he put to death ; 2. to Galeria Fundana, by whom he had sons and daughters, amongst the former of whom was one who stammered so much that he was almost dumb (Suet. *Vitell.*, 6.) Of the wives there are no coins, but gold and silver pieces are extant, representing some of the children [LIBERI. IMP. GERMAN. or GERM. AVG. ; LIBE-RIS IMP. GERMANICI ; *Vitellius and his children*,] thus refuting the statement of Josephus, who says that Vitellius died childless (ἄπαιδα, *Bell. Jud.* iv., 10, 3.)

The following are the principal reverse legends of his coins :—*Gold coins*—CLEMENTIA IMP. GERMAN. or GERMANICI (120 frcs.) ; CON-CORDIA P. R. (*Populi Romani*, 120 frcs.) ; CONSENSVS EXERCITVVM (120 frcs.) ; FIDES EXERCITVVM (150 frcs.) ; IVPPITER VICTOR (120 frcs.) ; LIBERTAS RESTITVTA (120 frcs.) ; L. VITELLIVS COS. III. CENSOR (150 frcs.—see VITELLIVS [Lucius]) ; PONT. MAXIM. *(Pontifex Maximus,* 120 frcs.) ; SECVRITAS IMP. GERMAN. *(Imperatoris Germanici,* 150 frcs.) ; SENATVS P. Q. *(Populusque)* ROMANVS (150 frcs.) ; S.P. Q. R. OB. C. S. *(Senatus Populusque Romanus ob Cives Servatos,* within an oak wreath, 120 frcs.) ; VESTA P. R. *(Populi Romani)* QVIRI-TIVM (200 frcs.) ; VICTORIA AVGVSTI. Victory holding a shield (*Caylus*, 150 frcs., sometimes on shield S. P. Q. R., 120 frcs.) ; VICTORIA IMP. GERMANICI *(Wiczay,* 220 frcs.) ; XVVIR. SACR. FAC. *Quindecimviri Sacris Faciendis*—120 frcs.) [XVVIR. SACR. FAC.] No legend. Victory seated (200 frcs.) *Silver coins*—CLE-MENTIA IMP. GERMAN (10 frcs.) ; CONCORDIA P. R. (*Populi Romani*—3 frcs.) ; CONCORDIA PRAETORIANORVM (15 frcs.) ; CONSENSVS EX-ERCITVVM (15 frcs.) ; FIDES EXERCITVVM (25 to 40 frcs.) ; FIDES PRAETORIANORVM (150 frcs.) ; I. O. MAX. (Jupiter Optimus Maximus) CAPITOLINVS. Jupiter seated to l. in distyle temple (30 frcs.) ; IVPPITER VICTOR (6 frcs.) ; LIBERTAS RESTITVTA (6 to 10 frcs.) ; L. VITEL-LIVS COS. III. CENSOR (40 frcs., see VITELLIVS [Lucius]). PONT. MAXIM. *(Pontifex Maxi-mus*—3 frcs.) ; S. P. Q. R. OB. C. S. *(Senatus Populusque Romanus ob Cives Servatos*—within an oak wreath—3 frcs.) ; VESTA P. R. *(Populi Romani)* QVIRITIVM (10 frcs.) ; VICTORIA AV-GVSTI. Victory, holding shield on which S. P. Q. R. (12 to 15 frcs.) ; VICTORIA AVGVSTI. Victory, walking, holding crown and palm *(Quin.* 100 frcs.) ; XVVIR. SACR. FAC. *(Quin-decimviri Sacris Faciendis)*—3 frcs.) [XVVIR. SACR. FAC.] No legend. Victory seated (12 frcs.)—*Brass coins* :—AEQVITAS AVGVSTI S. C. (Æ. II., 15 frcs.) ; ANNONA AVG. Vitellius, standing, holding spear and *parazonium* ; facing him, Ceres, seated ; between them an altar ; in

the background, a vessel (Æ. I., 200 frcs.) ; ANNONA AVGVSTI S. C. (Æ. II., 100 frcs.) ; CERES AVG. S. C. (Æ. I., 120 frcs. ; Æ. II., 15 frcs.) ; CLEMENTIA IMP. GERMAN. S. C. (Æ. II., 50 frcs.) ; CONCORDIA AVG. S. C. (Æ. I., 120 frcs. ; Æ. II., 15 frcs.) ; CONSENSVS EX-ERCITVVM S. C. (15 frcs.) ; CONSENSVS HISPA-NIARVM S. C. (Æ. II., 100 frcs.) ; FIDES EX-ERCITVVM S. C. (Æ. II., 15 frcs.) ; HONOS. ET VIRTVS (Æ. I., 150 frcs.) ; LIBERTAS RESTI-TVTA S. C. (15 frcs.) ; L. VITELL. CENSOR II. S. C. (Æ. I., 200 frcs.) *See* VITELLIVS [*Lu-cius*]) ; MARS VICTOR S. C. (Æ. I., 80 frcs.) ; PAX. AVGVSTI S. C. (Æ. I., 80 frcs. ; Æ. II., 50 to 60 frcs.) ; PAX. GER. *(Germanica)* S. C. Rome, seated, presenting Victory to Vitellius, standing ; to r. Peace, standing (Æ. I., 250 frcs.) ; PAX. AVGVSTI S. C. (Æ. II., 20 frcs.) ; PROVI-DENT. S. C. Altar (Æ. II., 15 frcs.) ; RESTI-TVTA LIBERTAS S. C. (Æ. II. 20 frcs.) ; ROMA RENASCENS S. C. (Æ. II., 30 frcs.) ; S. C. *(Senatus Consulto.)* Mars, naked, walking to r., holding spear and trophy (Æ. I., 80 frcs.), or three military standards on prow of a ship (Æ. II., from *Wiczay,* 30 frcs.) ; SECVRITAS P. *(Populi)* ROMANI S. C. (Æ. II., 50 frcs.) ; S. P. Q. R. OB CIV. SER., within an oak wreath (Æ. I., 150 frcs.) ; TVTELA AVGVSTI S. C. Vitel-lius, seated r., holding by the hand a child ; in front another child (Æ. II., 60 frcs.) ; VICTOR. *(Victoria)* AVGVSTI S. C. (Æ. II., 15 frcs.) ; VICTORIA AVG. or AVGVSTI S. C. Victory, standing, writing OB CIVIS SERV. on a shield attached to a palm (Æ. I., 100 frcs.) ; VIC-TORIA AVGVSTI S. C. Victory, walking, hold-ing a shield on which S. P. Q. R. (Æ. II., 15 frcs.) ; VICTORIA AVGVSTI S. C. Victory writing VIC. AVG., on a shield attached to a palm (Æ. I., from *Wiczay,* 100 frcs.) ; VRBEM RESTITVTAM S. C. (between Æ. I. and Æ. II., 150 frcs.)

Vitellius and his children.—The following coins are in existence :—

1. *Obv.* A. VITELLIVS GERM. IMP. AVG. TR. P. Head of Vitellius to r., laureated. *Rev.* LIBERI IMP. GERMAN. *(Imperatoris Germanici.)* Busts facing each other, of his son and his daughter. N. *(Caylus*—200 frcs.) R. (100 frcs.)

2. *Obv.* Same as No. 1. *Rev.* LIBERI IMP. GERM. AVG. Same busts. N. (200 frcs.) R. (100 frcs.) A *lead* of this type is pub-lished by Garrucci (*Rev. Num.*, 1862, p. 406.)

3. *Obv.* A. VITELLIVS GERMAN. IMP. TR. P. Head of Vitellius to r., laureated. *Rev.* LIBERI IMP. GERMAN. Same busts. N. *(Brit. Mus.,* 200 frcs.) R. (100 frcs.)

4. *Obv.* A. VITELLIVS IMP. GERMAN. Head of Vitellius to r., laureated. *Rev.* LIBERI IMP. GERMAN. Same busts. R. (100 frcs.)

5. *Obv.* A. VITELLIVS IMP. GERMANICVS. Bust of Vitellius to l., laureated. *Rev.* LIBERIS IM. GERMANICI. Same busts. N. (400 frcs.)

VITELLIVS (Lucius), father of the Emperor Vitellius, was three times *Consul.* (1) in A.D. 34 with P. F. Persicus, (2) in A.D. 43 with the

Emperor Claudius, and (3) in A.D. 47 with the same Emperor. He was *Censor* in A.D. 48 (when his two sons, Lucius and Aulus Vitellius, afterwards Emperor, were *Consuls*), also with Claudius, and he is so styled on coins struck in his memory by his son, accompanied by his son's portrait. Upon other gold and silver pieces he is represented on the reverse seated in the dress of a *censor*, and upon a remarkable large brass coin he is designated CENSOR II. No mention is made in history of the second censorship, and Eckhel concludes a long argument (vol. iv., pp. 314, 315) by suggesting that Aulus Vitellius to honour even more the name of his father gave him the title of *Censor for the second time* on his coins. Lucius Vitellius was a great flatterer. At his death in A.D. 48 or 49 the Senate honoured him with a public funeral, and erected a statue in front of the *rostra* with the inscription PIETATIS IMMOBILIS ERGA PRINCIPEM (Suet. *Vitell.* 3.) The coins, with the seated figure above alluded to, doubtless give a representation of the statue. It may also be observed that the head of Lucius Vitellius on the gold and silver coins has a *laurel wreath*, although he was a private individual, and had been dead some years. Eckhel has shown (vol. viii., p. 361) that the laurel wreath was not necessarily one of the *insignia* of an Emperor, but was conferred in honour of a victory. In the case of Lucius Vitellius it would allude to his having insisted on Artabanus, the Parthian King, making obeisance to the Roman standards in A.D. 34 (Dion. Cass. lix., 27; Suet. *Vitell.* 2.) The eagle in front of his bust on the gold and silver coins is doubtless an emblem of his consular dignity. The following are the coins struck by Aulus Vitellius in memory of his father :—

1. *Obv.* L. VITELLI. III. COS. CENS. Bust of Lucius Vitellius to l., laureated ; in front a Roman eagle. *Rev.* A. VITELLIVS IMP. GERMANICVS. Head of Aulus Vitellius to l., laureated; below, a globe. *N*. (1500 frcs.)

2. *Obv.* L. VITELLIVS COS. III. CENSOR.

Bust of Lucius Vitellius to r., laureated ; in front, Roman eagle. *Rev.* A. VITELLIVS GERM. IMP. AVG. TR. P. Head of Aulus Vitellius to r., laureated. *Æ.* (300 frcs.)

3. *Obv.* Same legend and type as No. 2. *Rev.* Same legend and type as No. 2. *N*. (1500 frcs.) Formerly in the possession of Messrs. Rollin and Feuardent (Madden, *Num. Chron.*, N.S., 1868, vol. viii., p. 253.)

4. *Obv.* L. VITELLIVS COS. III. CENSOR. Same type as No. 2. *Rev.* A. VITELLIVS GERMAN. IMP. TR. P. Same type as No. 2. *N*. (1500 frcs.)

5. *Obv.* A. VITELLIVS GERMAN. IMP. AVG. P. M. TR. P. Bust of Aulus Vitellius to r., laureated. *Rev.* L. VITELL. CENSOR II. S. C. Lucius Vitellius seated on a stage placed to r. ; to l. a person in *toga* on another stage;

below three persons, one of whom is giving his hand to the Censor. *Æ.* I. (200 frcs.) [*See* remarks above.]

6. *Obv.* A. VITELLIVS GERM. IMP. AVG. TR. P. Head of Aulus Vitellius to r., laureated. *Rev.* L. VITELLIVS COS. III. CENSOR. Lucius Vitellius seated to l., holding branch and Roman eagle. *N*. (150 frcs.) ; *Æ.* (40 frcs.)

VITIGES or WITIGES. King of the Ostrogoths from A.D. 536 to A.D. 540. Silver and copper coins are extant :—

1. *Obv.* D. N. IVSTINIANVS (or IVSTINIANVS P. F. AVG.) Bust of Justinian I. to r., diademed. *Rev.* D. IV.—VVIT—IGES—REX in four lines within wreath. *Æ.* (25 frcs.)

2. *Obv.* INVICTA ROMA. Helmeted bust of Rome to r. *Rev.* Same as No. 1. *Æ.* (3 frcs.)

VITORIA *(sic.)* Female figure standing to l., holding wreath and diadem ? *Obv.* IMP. TETRICVS V. Bust of Tetricus I. to r., radiated. *Æ.* III. (3 frcs.)

VITVLVS. *Vitulus*—Q. *(Quintus)* VOCONIVS VITVLVS Q. DESIG. *(Quæstor Designatus)*, or Q. VOCONIVS VITVLVS on silver coins of J. Cæsar—Q. VOCONIVS VITVLVS Q. DESIG. S. C. or Q. VOCONIVS VITVLVS on gold coins of Augustus. [*Voconia gens.*]

VIXXT. *Sexta* XX *Terracone.*—VIXXI *Sexta* XXI on small brass coins of Aurelian and Probus (Madden *on the letters* CONOB, &c., in the *Num. Chron.* N. S. 1862, vol. II., p. 243.)

VLATOS. A lion ? standing to r.; below, a pentagon, above ∽, in the *exergue* a crescent. *Obv.* ATEVLA. Young bust to l.; with a collar *(torques)* and wings on the shoulders. *Æ.* The names on this coin are supposed to be those of Gaulish chiefs, and it is attributed to the tribe of the Senones (Akerman, *Anc. Coins of Cities and Princes*, p. 162.)

Ulia, a town in Hispania Bœticia. It was a Roman *municipium* with the surname of *Fidentia*. Its modern name is *Monte Mayor* near Cordova. The following coin is attributed to it (Akerman, *Coins of Cities and Princes*, p. 59) :—

Obv. Female head to r. placed above a crescent; in front a branch. *Rev.* VLIA in a compartment between two branches. *Æ.*

VLO. *Ulo.*—*Volonius ?* or *Volteius ?*—L. VOL. F. STRA. *Lucius Volonius ?* or *Volteius ? Lucii filius Strabo*, on a silver coin usually attributed to the *Volteia* family. [*Volteia gens.*]

VL. *Ulpia*—see VLP. *Ulpia*.

VLP. *Ulpia.*—LEG. XXX VLP. [or VL.] TR. P. COS. *Legio tricesima Ulpia*, on silver coins of Septimius Severus.—LEG. XXX. VLP. VI P. VI F. [or VII P. VII F.] *Legio tricesima Ulpia Sextum Pia Sextum Fidelis* [or *Septimum Pia Septimum Fidelis*] on billon coins of Gallienus. —LEG. XXX. VLP. VICT. P. F. *Legio tricesima Ulpia Victrix Pia Fidelis*, on gold coins of Victorinus I.

VLP. *Ulpius.*—IMP. C. VLP. COR. LAELIANVS AVG. *Imperator Cæsar Ulpius Cornelius*

Lælianus Augustus on *billon* coins of Lælian, one of the thirty tyrants. [*Lælianus.*]

VLPIA. *Ulpia.*—BASILICA VLPIA, on gold and large brass coins of Trajan.—LEG. XXX. VLPIA PIA. F. *Legio tricesima Ulpia Pia Fidelis* on a gold coin of Victorinus I. from *Banduri.*—LEG. XXX. VLPIA [or VLPIA VI.] *Legio tricesima Ulpia* [or *Ulpia Victrix*] on third brass coins of Carausius.

Ulpia.—Ulpia Severina, wife of Aurelian [SEVERINA.]

Ulpia—Colonia Ulpia Trajana Augusta, a name bestowed by Trajan on the colonies of Hadrumetum, Byzacenæ and Sarmizeguthusa Daciæ.

VLPIANI. *Ulpiani.*—METALL. VLPIANI PANN. *Metalli Ulpiani Pannoniæ.*—METALLI VLPIANI [or VLPIANI DELM.] *Metalli Ulpiani* [or *Ulpiani Delmatiæ*] on small brass coins of Trajan.

Ulpius—Ulpius Trajanus [TRAIANVS.]

VLT. *Ultor.*—MAR. VLT. *Mars Ultor*, on gold and silver coins of Augustus, and on silver coins of Albinus, from *Wiczay*.

VLT. *Ultori.*—MART. VLT. *Marti Ultori*, on gold and silver coins of Augustus.—MARTI VLT. *Marti Ultori*, on large brass coins of Antoninus Pius.

VLTO. *Ultori.*—MART. VLTO. *Marti Ultori*, on silver medallions and gold coins of Augustus.

VLTOR. *Ultor.*—MARS. VLTOR. *Mars Ultor*, on autonomous coins of Galba, and on coins of Vespasian, Caracalla, Alexander Severus, Gallienus, Claudius II., Tacitus, Probus and Carausius.—VOLKANVS VLTOR, *Volcanus Ultor*, on autonomous coins of Galba. [VOLKANVS VLTOR.]

VLTORA AVG. (Augusti.) Female figure standing to r., giving her hand to Carausius, standing, holding a standard; between them a lighted altar. *Obv.* IMP. CARAVSIVS P. F. AVG. Bust of Carausius to r., laureated. Æ. (300 frcs.)

VLTORI. *Ultori.*—MARTI VLTORI, *Marti Ultori*, on autonomous coins of Galba, and on coins of Antoninus Pius, Marcus Aurelius, and Diocletian.—MARTI VLTORI AVG. *Marti Ultori Augusti.*, on first and second brass coins of Commodus.

VLTORIS. *Ultoris.*—MARTIS VLTORIS. *Martis Ultoris*—on gold and silver coins of Augustus.

VLTVS. *Ultus.*—S. P. Q. R. (*Senatus Populusque Romanus*) QVOD INSTINCTV DIVINITATIS MENTIS MAGNITVDINE CVM EXERCITV SVO TAM DE TYRANNO QVAM DE OMNI EIVS FACTIONE VNO TEMP (*ore*) IVSTIS REMP (*ublicam*) VLTVS EST ARMIS ARC (*um*) TRIVMPHIS INSIGNEM DICAVIT. A large brass medal (size, 14½) of Constantine I., of the contorniate class, formerly in the Pembroke collection (*Sale Cat.*, p. 297) [CONTORNIATE COINS; QVOD INSTINCTV, &c.] See Madden, *Christian Emblems on the Coins of Constantine I.*, &c., in the *Num. Chron.*, N.S., 1878, vol. xviii., p. 17.

Ulysses is represented on the contorniates of Alexander, Nero, Trajan, Caracalla, and Roma

(Sabatier, *Méd. Contorn.*, pp. 86-88, pl. xiii., Nos. 11-13, 17.) [CONTORNIATE COINS.]

Umbrella, or parasol, on gold coins of Uranius Antoninus [VRANIVS ANTONINVS], and on copper coins of Herod Agrippa I. (Madden, *Coins of the Jews*, 4to, 1881, p. 131.)

VN. MR. (*Venerandæ Memoriæ.*) Female figure, standing, to r., veiled. *Obv.* DV. CONSTANTINVS PT. AVGG. (*Divus Constantinus Pater Augustorum.*) Bust of Constantine I. to r., veiled. Æ. Quin. (1 frc.) This coin was struck after the death of Constantine I. [*see* (IVST.) VEN. MEM. and (IVST.) VENERAB.] With respect to the letters DV., Eckhel (vol. viii., p. 92) threw out the suggestion that they might stand for *Divus Victor*, as we know from Eusebius that Constantine I. had this title, though the coins with *Victor* are now attributed by Cohen to Constantine II. [VIC. or VICT.]; but on the strength of an inscription which he quotes, commencing DIVO AC VENERABILI, he inclined to explain them *Divus Venerabilis*. As there are, however, other coins with the words DIV. or DIVO, it seems preferable to consider the letters to stand for DIvus. The letters PT. AVGG. are explained by Eckhel as certainly *Pater Trium AVGGustorum;* but as Cohen has observed (*Méd. Imp.*, vol. vi., p. 170), for this reading it would be necessary to have three GS. The system of consecration seems to have obtained even after the time of Constantine among his Christain successors. Constantius II., "meruit inter *divos* referri" (Eutrop., x., 15; cf. "*divus* Constantius," Mamertinus, *Grat. Act. Jul. Aug.*, c. 3); Jovian, "benignitate principum qui ei successerunt inter *divos* relatus est " (Eutrop., x., 18; cf. "*Div.* Fl. Joviano Triumfatori semper Aug.," Gruter, p. 285; Clinton, *Fasti Romani*, vol. ii., p. 113); Valentinian I. was consecrated by his son Gratian, " hujus vero laudis locupletissimum testimonium est pater *divinis honoribus* consecratus" (Ausonius, *Ad Grat. Act.*, c. 8); to which may be added the name of Valentinian III., as appears from a marble of Chiusi, in Tuscany, published by Cavedoni (*Cimit. Chius.*, p. 45, Modena, 1853.) No coins, however, bearing the title *divus* are known of any of these Emperors. (Madden, *Christian Emblems on the Coins of Constantine I.*, &c., in the *Num. Chron.*, N.S., 1877, vol. xvii., p. 285.)

UMBRIA. One of the principal divisions of Central Italy, situated to the east of Etruria. Coins principally of the *aes grave* class have been attributed to the following towns of Umbria—Ariminum, Iguvium, and Tuder. (*Cat. of Greek Coins in Brit. Mus., Italy*, pp. 25-39; cf. Mommsen, *Mon. Rom.*, vol. i., pp. 360-362; 389-400.)

Uncia (ounce), a brass coin, the twelfth part of a Roman pound, or *As* [AS.] The issue of an *As* of a Roman pound of 12 *unciæ*, or the *as libralis*, took place in the time of the Decemvirs, B.C. 451 (Mommsen, *Mon. Rom.*, vol. i., pp. 179, seq., 200), but the existing *asses* rarely weigh more than 10 *unciæ* (Mommsen, vol. i., p. 206; vol. iv., p. 3.) Later the *as* fell successively from 10 *unciæ* to four, or perhaps this reduction was suddenly accomplished about the time of the first Punic war, B.C. 268. (Mommsen, vol. ii., pp. 2, 10, 15; vol. iii., p. 468.) In B.C. 217 the *as* was reduced to *one uncia* by the *Lex Flaminia* (Mommsen, vol. ii., pp. 2, 13, 18, 67, 68.) At last in B.C. 89, or thereabouts, under the *Lex Papiria*, the *as* fell to a *semuncia* (half-ounce) (Mommsen, vol. ii., p. 73; vol. iii., pp. 220, 221.) The *uncia* was rarely struck after the reduction of the *as* (Mommsen, vol. ii., p. 75.) The expression *heres ex uncia* denoted the heir to a tenth or twelfth part of an estate. The mark of value of the *uncia* was •; of the *semuncia* Σ. [Among the pieces struck at Pæstum there occurs the *Sescuncia* (semisqueuncia •Σ) equal to the eighth of an *as* (Mommsen, vol. ii., p. 76.)]

Descriptions of the earliest *unciæ* and *semunciæ* of the *aes grave* of Central Italy, of the coinage of Luceria, of Venusia, of the *aes grave* of North-Eastern Italy (Vestini, Hatria, Asculum? Ariminum), of the Etruscan *aes grave*, and of the *aes grave* of Umbria (Tuder, Iguvium) will be found in Mommsen, *Mon. Rom.*, vol. i., pp. 182—234, 332—400.) The principal types are, a knuckle-bone, acorn, grain of barley, vase, club, frog, spear-head, ear of corn, crescent, head of Apollo or Diana, the Dioscuri, Hercules, lion, boar's head, owl, axe with two edges *(bipennis)*, shell, anchor, thunderbolt, Gaulish head, prow of a ship, two-handled vase, *amphora*, anchor, sacrificial knife and hatchet, etc. A description of the principal types of the *unciæ* of Southern Italy struck on the triental system (4 ounces) after B.C. 268, and of the *unciæ* of Capua, Atella and Calatia are given also by Mommsen *(Mon. Rom.*, vol. iii., pp. 362—371; 377—381.)

The ordinary type of the *uncia* is: *Obv.* Helmeted head to l.; behind •. *Rev.* Prow of a vessel to r.; below •. *Æ.*, but the following is a description of the *unciæ* bearing types other than the usual "prow of a ship," issued at Rome after the suppression of the *as libralis* in B.C. 268:—

1st Period, B.C. 268—224.

Obv. Female head, helmeted; behind •. *Rev.* A cornucopiæ (rare.) *Æ.* (Mommsen, vol. ii., p. 215.)

Obv. Female head with Phrygian helmet terminating in the beak of a bird. *Rev.* One of the Dioscuri galloping. *Æ.* (Mommsen, vol. ii., p. 229.)

The *semuncia* (Σ) has on the obverse the heads of the Dioscuri, and on the reverse two horses galloping; above two stars.

Obv. Female head to r.; behind •. *Rev.* SAR. *(Saranus.)* Elephant to l. *Æ.* (15 frcs.; if genuine.) (Mommsen, vol. ii., p. 265, Cohen, *Méd. Cons.*, pl. xlviii., *Atilia*, No. 7.)

The moneyer is perhaps M. Atilius Serranus, who, in B.C. 190, was, with two other prætors, L. Valerius P. F. Flaccus and L. Valerius C. F. Tappus, named IIIVIR *Col. Ded. (triumviri ad colonos deducendos*, Liv. xxxvii., 46, 57), or

perhaps another of the same family, who was prætor in B.C. 174 (Liv. xli., 21.)

Obv. Female head. *Rev.* A. CAE. *(Aulus Cæcilius)* within a wreath. *Æ.* (30 frcs.) (Mommsen, vol. ii., p. 282.)

No mark of value on this *uncia*. Coins with this legend are usually attributed to the *Cæcina gens*, but it has been shown (Borghesi in Riccio, p. 40) that this family was not nationalized in Rome at the time the coins were struck. It is thought that A. Cæcilius is the ædile of B.C. 189.

2nd Period—B.C. 154—134.

Obv. Female head to r., helmeted ; behind •. *Rev.* L. H. TVB. (in monogram ; *Lucius Hostilius Tubulus)* within a laurel wreath; in the *exergue* ROMA. *Æ.* (30 frcs.) (Mommsen, vol. ii., p. 308; Cohen, *Méd. Cons.*, pl., xvi., *Hostilia.)*

This personage is probably L. Hostilius Tubulus, who was prætor in B.C. 142, and exiled the following year.

3rd Period—B.C. 134—114.

Obv. Female head to r., helmeted; behind •. *Rev.* Q. METE. (in monogram ; *Quintus Metellus)* within a laurel wreath; in the *exergue* ROMA. *Æ.* (30 frcs.) (Mommsen, vol. ii., p. 324; Cohen, *Méd. Cons.*, pl. 1. *Cæcilia*, No. 5, from *Riccio.)*

This Metellus is probably one of the three personages of the *Cæcilia gens*, who was Consul in B.C. 123, 109, and 98.

4th Period—B.C. 114—104.

Obv. L. PHILIPPVS. Head of Saturn to laureated; behind, sometimes, a sickle. *Rev.* Dog walking to r.; above •; sometimes a prow of a vessel, above a dog and •. *Æ.* (12 frcs.) (Mommsen, vol. ii., p. 347; vol. iv., pl. xxviii., No. 4; Cohen, *Méd. Cons.*, p. 203, Nos. 21, 22; pl. lviii. *Marcia*, No. 11.)

This personage is probably the son of the Moneyer Q. PILIPVS (B.C. 109), and was monetary triumvir about B.C. 112.

Obv. Bust of Minerva (?) helmeted; behind •. *Rev.* Q. LVTATI. *(Quintus Lutatius)* within an oak wreath. *Æ.* (30 frcs.) (Mommsen, vol. ii., p. 354.)

Unknown personage. Date about B.C. 104.

Obv. Female head to r., helmeted; behind •. *Rev.* C. FON. *(Caius Fonteius.)* Mars in a *quadriga* to r.; in the *exergue* ROMA ; above •. *Æ.* (15 frcs.) (Mommsen, vol. ii., p. 357.)

This personage is perhaps the Fonteius who perished at Asculum in B.C. 91.

Obv. CN. DOMI. *(Cnæus Domitius.)* Head of Venus to r., diademed; behind •. *Rev.* Q. CVRTI. M. SILA. *(Quintus Curtius. Marcus Silanus.)* A lyre. *Æ.* (25 frcs.) (Mommsen, vol. ii., p. 360; Cohen, *Méd. Cons.*, pl. liv., *Curtia*, No. 4.)

Q. Curtius is unknown, but perhaps was the father of Q. Curtius, who was *judex quæstionis* in B.C. 70. M. Silanus was probably the son of M. Junius D. F. Silanus, who was Consul in B.C. 109.

5th Period—B.C. 104—84.

Obv. Female head to r., helmeted; behind •. Rev. M. HERENNI (*Marcus Herennius*) ROMA. Two cornuacopiæ. Æ. (15 frcs.) (Mommsen, vol. ii., p. 392; Cohen, *Méd. Cons.*, p. 149. No. 4, from *Riccio*. A similar coin but without the name M. HERENNI. is engraved by Cohen, pl. lxxi., No. 16.)

This personage is perhaps the son of the Consul of B.C. 93.

Obv. Female head to r., helmeted; behind •. *Rev.* MAN. (in monogram) FONT. (*Manius Fonteius*) ROMA. A *quadriga.* Æ. (15 frcs.) (Mommsen, vol. ii., p. 445; Cohen, *Méd. Cons.*, p. 140 *note* from *Riccio*.)

This person is perhaps the quæstor in B.C. 84.

[The following piece is published by Cohen (*Méd. Cons.*, page 174, No 18, pl. lvi., *Junia*, No. 4), from the cabinet of M. Fénelon-Farez. *Obv.* SCAEVA. Helmeted head of Pallas (?) to r. *Rev.* M. AVF. (in monogram; *Marcus Aufidius.)* Centaur to r. Æ. (30 frcs.) The attribution of this coin is uncertain, though Cohen thinks it is not impossible that it may belong to the town of Larinum.]

VNDIQVE VICTORES. The Emperor standing to l., holding a globe, sometimes surmounted by a Victory, and a sceptre; sometimes a captive seated on either side—on small brass coins of Numerian (5 to 8 frcs.), and of Constantius Chlorus (2 frcs.)

VNI. (*Unimanus*) in *field; Victory crowning a trophy; in the *exergue* ROMA. *Obv.* Head of Apollo to r., laureated. Æ. *Quin.* (40 frcs.) This coin of the *Claudia gens* has been attributed by Borghesi (*Dec.* xvii., 5; *Œuvr. Compl.*, vol. ii., p. 311) to Claudius Unimanus, prætor in B.C. 149, but Mommsen (*Mon. Rom.*, vol. ii., p. 417), assigns it to a period between B.C. 104 and B.C. 84; whilst Babelon (*Mon. de la Repub. Rom.*, vol. i., p. 347) considers it should be placed about B.C. 89.

VNO. *Uno.*—on large brass medal of Constantine I. of the Contorniate class [see VLTVS.]

VOC. *Voconius.* CN. VOC. ST. F. *Cnæus Voconius Statii Filius*, on a brass coin struck at Astapa Hispaniæ Bæticæ (Akerman, *Coins of Cities and Princes*, p. 23.)

VOCONIA GENS, a plebeian family. The following silver and gold coins are extant :—

1. *Obv.* Head of Julius Cæsar to r., laureated. *Rev.* Q. VOCONIVS VITVLVS Q. DESIGN. (*Quintus Voconius Vitulus Quæstor Designatus.)* Calf walking to l.; in the *field*, s. c. (*Senatus Consulto.)* Æ. (12 frcs.) [See engraving No. 1, head of article CAESAR CAIVS IVLIVS, p. 151.]

2. *Obv.* DIVI IVLI. Head of Julius Cæsar to r., laureated; behind, the augur's staff. *Rev.* Q. (*Quintus*) VOCONIVS VITVLVS. Calf walking to l.; in the *field* s. c. (*Senatus Consulto.)* Æ. (20 frcs.)

3. *Obv.* DIVI F. (*Filius.)* Bearded head of Octavian to r., bare; in front the augur's staff. *Rev.* Q. VOCONIVS VITVLVS Q. DESIG. (*Quintus Voconius Vitulus Quæstor Designatus.)* Calf

walking to l.; in the *field*, s. c. (*Senatus Consulto.)* N. (500 frcs.)

4. *Obv.* DIVI IVLI F. (*Filius.)* Bearded head of Octavian to r., bare. *Rev.* Q. (*Quintus)* VOCONIVS VITVLVS. Calf walking to l. N. (500 frcs.)

These pieces, assigned by some to B.C. 43-42, or B.C. 38-36 (Cohen, *Méd. Cons.*, p. 336; *Méd. Imp.*, 2nd ed., vol. i., pp. 16, 114; Mommsen, *Mom. Rom.*, vol. iii, p. 5), were probably struck about B.C. 41-40 by Quintus Voconius Vitulus, conjointly with those of Tiberius Sempronius Gracchus, who took the double titles of *quatuorviri* and *quæstores designati*, and who show on some of their coins (see Nos. 1, 2, and 3) the Senatorial origin of their powers by the letters s. c. (Lenormant, *La Mon. dans l'Antiq.*, vol. iii., p. 175.) As to the beard, Lenormant (*loc. cit.)* writes, "The beard, which ornaments the chin of Octavian on the coins of Sempronius Gracchus and Voconius Vitulus, appears to me to have the appearance of a light beard of a young man rather than that which grown-up men allowed to grow as a sign of mourning, as Octavian did during the war against Sextus Pompeius. Now, in the coin portraits, although some engravers have omitted the circumstance, the nephew and heir of Cæsar could always, up to B.C. 39 (715 of Rome), be represented with the chin ornamented with his first beard, and, indeed, the portraits which show it are assuredly the most exact, since Dion Cassius (xlviii., 34; Eckhel, vol. vi., p. 76), informs us that it was only in this year that he shaved his beard for the first time." [BARBA.] The calf on the coins alludes to the name VITVLVS.

VOCONIVS—Q. VOCONIVS VITVLVS. [*Voconia gens.*]

Vocontii, a people of Gallia Narbonensis. The following coins are attributed to them (Akerman, *Coins of Cities and Princes*, p. 152) :—

1. *Obv.* Head to r. *Rev.* VOOC. Horse galloping to l. Æ.

2. *Obv.* ROW (sic.) Head of Pallas to r., helmeted. *Rev.* VOCVNT. Horseman, holding spear, galloping to r. Æ.

3. *Obv.* VOCONTII. Beardless head to r. *Rev.* Hog standing to l. Æ.

VOCVNT. [*Vocontii.*]

VO. DE. *Vota Decennalia*, written on a shield on silver and large brass coins of Commodus, with the legend SAEC. FEL. P. M. TR. P. X. [or XI.] IMP. VII. COS. IV. [or V.] P. P. S. C. [*Vota.*]

VO. *Vol. Volonius?* or *Volteius?*—L. VO. L. F. S ⚹⚹⚹. *Lucius Volonius?* or *Volteius? Lucii Filius Strabo*, on silver coins usually attributed to the *Volteia* family [*Volteia gens.*, see VO. *Ulo.*]

VOL. *Volcæ.* [*Volcæ Tectosages.*]

VOL.—CN. VOL. On coins of Celtic chiefs (Mommsen, *Mon. Rom.*, vol. iii., p. 252.)

Volaterræ (now *Volterra*), one of the most important of the Etruscan cities. A small gold coin—*Obv.* Young head to r. or to l; in front

x. *Rev.* Plain surface—has been attributed to it (Mommsen, *Mon. Rom.*, vol. i., pp. 214, 372; vol. iv., pl. xviii., No. 4.) Its brass coins of the *aes grave* class are numerous, and the attribution is certain from their all bearing the legend *Velathri* in Etruscan characters. The coins are of three series. 1. Head of Janus, without type on reverse—*Dupondius, as, semis, triens, quadrans, sextans, uncia.* 2. With club on reverse—*dupondius, as, semis, triens, quadrans, sextans, uncia.* 3. Dolphin on reverse—*as, semis. (Cat. of Greek Coins in Brit. Mus., Italy,* p. 11.) It is not known if other fractions of this third series exist. (Mommsen, *Mon. Rom.*, vol. i., pp. 220, 384—387.)

VOLC. *Volcæ.* [*Volcæ Arecomici.*]
VOLCAE. *Volcæ.* [*Volcæ Arecomici.*]

Volcæ Arecomici, a people of South Gallia, having for their chief city Nemausus Colonia [*Nemausus.*] Their coins are (Akerman, *Coins of Cities and Princes,* p. 153):—

1. *Obv.* Bare head to r.; in front Æ. *Rev.* VOLC. Between the spokes of a wheel. Æ.

2. *Obv.* Head of Diana to r.; in front Æ. *Rev.* VOLC. An eagle with expanded wings holding a palm branch in one claw and a wreath in another; the whole within a laurel wreath. Æ.

3. *Obv.* VOLCAE. Head of Diana to r.; in front, a wreath. *Rev.* AREC. A figure in *toga* standing to l.; in front a branch of laurel. Æ.

Volcæ Tectosages, a people of South Gallia, having the cities Illiberis, Ruscino, Tolosa Colonia, Cessero, Carcaso, Bæterræ, and Narbo Colonia, of which Tolosa was the chief, and which was plundered by Q. Servilius Cæpio, Consul in B.C. 106. Their coins were at one time confounded with those of the *Volcæ Arecomici,* but their different style and the occurrence of VOL. only without Æ. or AREC. have led to their assignment to the *Volcæ Tectosages.* (Akerman, *Coins of Cities and Princes,* p. 153) :—

1. *Obv.* Head of Apollo to l., laureated. *Rev.* VOL. Horse galloping to l.; below, a wheel with four spokes. Æ.

2. *Obv.* Rude head of Apollo (?) to l. *Rev.* A cross, as on Mediæval coins, in the angles of which various symbols, and an axe. Æ.

VOLCANO or VOLKANO—DEO. VOLCANO or VOLKANO. On *billon* coins of Gallienus from *Banduri* and of Saloninus (VALERIANVS P. F. AVG.) [DEO VOLKANO.]

VOLCANOM. Head of Vulcan to l., wearing laureated *pilos;* behind, tongs. *Rev.* ΛISERN in *exergue.* Jupiter in *biga* to r., hurling thunderbolt; above Victory flying to r., holding wreath. Æ. of Aesernia Samnii (*Cat. of Greek Coins in Brit. Mus. Italy,* p. 67.)

VOLKANVS VLTOR. Head of Vulcan to r., with cap, laureated. *Rev.* GENIO P. R. *(Populi Romani.)* Pincers, hammer, anvil, and die. Æ. (40 frcs.), or SIGNA P. R. *(Populi Romani.)* Roman eagle with wreath of pearls in its beak, between two military standards and a lighted altar. Æ. (30 frcs.) These coins are attributed to the period between the reigns of Nero and Vespasian. [VVLCANVS.]

Volsinii., one of the twelve important cities of Etruria. The following gold coins are attributed to it (Mommsen, *Mon. Rom.*, vol. i., pp. 24, 215, 372, 373) :—

1. *Obv.* Young head (Apollo ?) to l., laureated, or with myrtle wreath, on either side xx (20.) *Rev.* Bull walking to l.; above dove flying, holding wreath; in front a star of eight rays; in the *exergue*—*Velzpapi* in Etruscan characters. N.

2. *Obv.* Female head; Λ (5.) *Rev.* Dog running; in the *exergue*—*Velsu* in Etruscan characters. N.

VOLTEI. *Volteius.* M. VOLTEI. M. F. *Marcus Volteius Marci Filius,* on silver coins of the *Volteia gens.* [*Volteia gens.*]

VOLTEIA GENS, uncertain family only known from coins :—

1. *Obv.* Head of Jupiter to r., laureated. *Rev.* M. VOLTEI. M. F. *(Marcus Volteius Marci Filius.)* Tetrastyle temple with three doors; on the pediment, a thunderbolt. Æ. (2 frcs.)

2. *Obv.* Head of young Hercules to r., covered with the lion's skin. *Rev.* M. VOLTEI. M. F. Boar running to r. Æ. (3 frcs.)

3. *Obv.* Head of young Bacchus to r., crowned with ivy. *Rev.* M. VOLTEI. M. F. Ceres in a car to r., drawn by two serpents, and holding a torch in each hand; in the *field* various symbols. Æ. (2 frcs.)

4. *Obv.* Head of Apollo to r., laureated. *Rev.* M. VOLTEI. M. F. Tripod around which a serpent is entwined; in the *field* to l., S. C. *(Senatus Consulto)* to r., D. T. *(De Thesauro ?)* Æ. (80 frcs.)

5. *Obv.* Young head to r., helmeted, without crest, and ornamented with laurel; behind, symbols. *Rev.* M. VOLTEI. M. F. Cybele, with turreted crown, in a car drawn by lions to r., and holding a *patera;* in the *field,* various Greek numerals. Æ. (2 frcs.) (Mommsen, *Mon. Rom.*, vol ii., pp. 467-469, No. 257; Cohen, *Méd. Cons.*, pl. xiii.; *Volteia,* Nos. 1, 4, 3, 5, 2.)

These coins were found in the deposit of Hewisz-Szamos, in Transylvania, buried about B.C. 74. Marcus Volteius is unknown, but Mommsen has established (*Mon. Rom.*, vol. ii., p. 65; cf. Lenormant, *La Mon. dans l'Antiq.*, vol. ii., p. 251) that in all cases on coins of the Republic bearing a name without an expressed title, but accompanied with the formulas D. S. S. *(De Senatus Sententia),* PE. S. C. *(Publice Senatus Consulto),* EX S. C. *(Ex Senatus Consulto),* or S. C. *(Senatus Consulto),* as on the coin (No. 4) above described, that the moneyer was not a regular triumvir, but a person charged with an extraordinary commission.

The types of these five coins have been explained by M. Mommsen (*Mon. Rom.*, vol. ii., p. 468), and refer to the five great *fêtes* celebrated at Rome at this period—namely, the Roman *fête,* the Plebeian *fête,* and those of Ceres, of Apollo, and of the Megalesian games. No. 1, with the head of Jupiter and the Temple of the Capitol, refers to the *ludi Romani*—"ludos antiquissimos qui primi Romani appellati sunt . . . Jovi Junoni, Minervæque esse faciendos" (Cic. *in Verrem,* v. 14, 36.)—No. 2, with the head of young Hercules, refers to the *ludi Plebeii* founded by C. Flaminius in B.C. 220.—No. 3, on which is the head of young Bacchus and Ceres in a car drawn by two serpents, refers to the *Cerialia* or *fêtes* in honour of Ceres, which, it is said (Cic. *in Verrem*, v. 14, 36), were celebrated in honour of the three divinities in the temple of Ceres—*Cereri, Libero, Liberæque*. The same *fête* is alluded to on a coin of the *Memmia gens* (Mommsen, *op. cit.*, p. 514.)—No. 4, with the head of Apollo and tripod, refers to the games founded in B.C. 212, in honour of Apollo (Livy, xxv., 12 : xxvi., 23; xxvii., 11), games which are also commemorated on coins of the *Calpurnia gens* and the *Marcia gens* (Mommsen, *op. cit.*, pp. 408, 438.) The letters D. T. have been generally interpreted *donum tulit*, but Mommsen thinks that the explanation *De Thesauro* is more suitable, and signifies that tho ox penses of this *fête* were partly covered by the public treasury and partly by collection (Varro, *De Ling. Lat.* v., 181; Livy, xxv., 12.)—No. 5, representing Cybele in a car drawn by lions, refers to the *Megalesian* games instituted in B.C. 204. The head on the obverse of this coin is considered by Mommsen to be that of Atys, and by Cavedoni that of one of the Corybantes, or, perhaps, that of Corybas, son of Jason and of Cybele (Diodor. Sicul., v., 49.) This coin offers the only example of *Greek* numeral letters on family coins.

The following coin has also been attributed to the *Volteia gens* (Cohen, *Méd. Cons.*, *Volteia*, pl. xlii., No. 6) :—

Obv. Head of Jupiter to r., laureated; behind, a letter. *Rev.* L. Vo. L. F. s ⴲ ⵂ. *(Lucius Voltēius? Lucius Filius Strabo.)* Europa on a bull to l., holding a veil; in the *field* to r., a thunderbolt; below, an ivy-leaf. *R.* (30 frcs.) Mommsen, however, thinks *(Mon. Rom.*, vol. ii., p. 522) that the monogram Vo. can only be interpreted by VLO. or VOL., which would, perhaps, be the abbreviation of *Volonius.* [Vo. *Ulo ;* Vo. *Vol.*] The family of the moneyer is therefore uncertain. The coin was issued between B.C. 74-50.

VOLVMNIO. *Volumnio*, on second brass coins of Octavia and Nero, struck at Corinthus Achaiæ —LVRINO VOLVMNIO IIV. *(duumviro)* or LVRINO VOLVMNIO. (Cohen, *Méd. Imp.*, 2nd ed., vol. i., p. 313, Nos. 1-3.)

VOLVNT—CN. VOLVNT.,. on coins of Celtic chiefs (Mommsen, *Mon. Rom.*, vol. iii., p. 252.)

VOLVSI. *Volusii*, on brass medallions of Augustus, struck by Volusius Saturninus, proconsul of Africa, B.C. 6, at Gergis Syrticæ or Cercina—PERM. L. VOLVSI. PROCOS. GERG. or CERC. *Permissu Lucii Volusii Proconsulis Gergis* or *Cercinæ* (Cohen, *Méd. Imp.*, 2nd. ed., vol. i., p. 166, No. 818; Müller, *Num. de l'Anc. Afrique*, vol. ii., p. 35.)

VOLVSIVS. *Volusius*, on large brass coins of Augustus, struck by Volusius Saturninus at Achulla and Hadrumetum Byzacenæ—L. VOLV-

SIVS SATVR. or SATVRN. or SATVRN. ACHVL. (Müller, *Num. de l'Anc. Afrique*, vol. ii., pp. 44, 52.) [VOLVSI.]

VOLVSIANO—C. VIBIO VOLVSIANO CAES. or IMP. CAE. C. VIB. VOLVSIANO AVG. or IM. C. V. AF. GAL. VEND. VOLVSIANO AVG. *Imperatori Caio Vibio Afinio Gallo Vendumniano Volusiano Augusto*, etc., on coins of the Emperor Volusian. [VOLVSIANVS.]

VOLVSIANVS (Caius Vibius), son of Trebonianus Gallus, who, on his accession, in A.D. 251, made his son *Cæsar* and *Princeps Juventutis*, and *Augustus* in the following year. He followed the fortunes of his father, and with him was killed at Interamna *(Terni)* Umbriæ in A.D. 254. [TREBONIANVS GALLVS.]

The obverse legends of his coins are—C. VIBIO VOLVSIANO CAES., IMP. C. C. VIB. VOLVSIANVS AVG., IMP. CAE. C. VIB. VOLVSIANO AVG., and IM. C. V. AF. GAL. VEND. VOLVSIANO AVG. *Imperatori Caio Vibio Afinio Gallo Vendumniano Volusiano Augusto.*

The principal reverse legends are—*Silver Medallions :* FELICITAS PVBLICA. ? Double *Antoninianus* (30 frcs.), MONETA AVGG. (300 frcs.), *Gold coins :* AEQVITAS AVGG. (450 frcs.), AETERNITAS AVGG. (400 frcs.), APOLL. SALVTARI (from *Banduri*, 400 frcs.), CONCORDIA AVGG. (450 frcs.), FELICITAS PVBLICA (from *Tanini*, 450 frcs.), IVNONI MARTIALI (500 frcs.), LIBERTAS AVGG. (450 frcs.), PIETAS AVGG. (400 to 450 frcs.; *Quin.* 500 frcs.), PIETAS AVGG. Augur's staff, knife, *simpulum*, sacrificial vase, *aspergillum* and *patera* (from *Tanini* 500 frcs.), P. M. TR. P. IIII. COS. II. (from *Tanini*, 450 frcs.), PRINCIPI IVVENTVTIS (450 frcs., *Quin.* 500 frcs.), SALVS AVGG. (500 frcs.), VICTORIA AVGG. (400 frcs.), VIRTVS AVGG. (400 frcs.). —*Silver Coins :* ADVENTVS AVG. (8 frcs.), AEQVITAS AVGG. (c. to 12 frcs.), ANNONA AVG. (6 frcs.), APOLL. SALVTARI (3 frcs.), CONCORDIA AVGG. (c.), FELICITAS PVBL. (2 frcs.), IVNO MARTIALIS (c.), IVNONI MARTIALI (c.), LIBERALITAS AVGG. (3 frcs.), LIBERTAS AVGG. (c.), LIBERTAS PVBLICA (c.), MARTEM PROPVGNATOREM (8 frcs.), MARTI PACIFERO (12 frcs.), PAX AETERNA (c.), PAX AVG. (from *Wiczay*, 12 frcs.), PAX AVGG. or AVGVS. (c.), PIETAS AVGG. (c.), P. M. TR. P. IIII. COS. II. Felicity or Emperor standing (2 to 8 frcs.), PRINCIPI IVVENTVTIS (c. to 3 frcs.), PROVID. or PROVIDENTIA AVGG. (3 to 6 frcs.), PVDICITIA AVGG. (20 frcs.), ROMAE AETERNAE (c. to 10 frcs.), SAECVLVM NOVVM (2 frcs.), SALVS AVGG.

(c., *Quin.* 80 frcs.), SECVRITAS AVG. (c.), VBERITAS AVG. (12 frcs.), VICTORIA AVG. (6 to 20 frcs.), VIRTVS AVGG. (c.)—*Brass Medallions:* ADVENTVS AVGG. (400 frcs.), FORTVNAE REDVCI (400 frcs.), MONETA AVGG. (250 frcs.), VIRTVS AVGVSTORVM (400 frcs.)—*Brass Coins:* AEQVITAS AVGG. S. C. (Æ. I., c.), APOLLO SALVTARI s. c. (Æ. I. and II., c.), ARNAZI *(without* s. c., Æ. I., 80 frcs.; Æ. II., from *Wiczay*, 60 frcs.), CONCORDIA AVGG. S. C. (Æ. I., 5 frcs.; Æ. II., c.), FELICITAS PVBLICA S. C. (Æ. I. and II., c.), IVNONI MARTIALI S. C. (Æ. I., 10 frcs.; Æ. II., 6 frcs.), LIBERALITAS AVGG. S. C. (Æ. I., 6 frcs.; Æ. II., c.), LIBERTAS AVG. S. C. (Æ. I. c.), PAX. AVGG. S. C. (Æ. I. and II. c.), PIETAS AVGG. (Æ. I. and II. c.), P. M. TR. P. IIII. COS. II. P. P. S. C. (Æ. I., 5 frcs.), PRINCIPI IVVENTVTIS S. C. (8 frcs.), SALVS AVGG. S. C. (Æ. I. and II., c.), SECVRITAS AVGG. S. C, (Æ. I., c.), VICTORIA AVGG. S. C. (Æ. I., c.), VIRTVS AVGG. S. C. (Æ. I. and II. c.), VOTIS DECENNALIBVS S. C. (Æ. I., 8 frcs.; Æ. II., 6 frcs.)

There are also medallions of Trebonianus Gallus and Volusianus. Æ. (200 frcs.), Æ. Med. (400 frcs.), Æ. II. (100 frcs.)

Coins of Volusian were struck in the following colonies—Alexandria (Troas), Antiochia Pisidiæ, Apameia Bithyniæ, Cæsarea Samariæ, Coela, Dacia, Damascus, Tyre, and Viminacium.

[The curious coins of Trebonianus Gallus (Æ. Med.) with legend ARNASI. and (Æ. II.) with ARNAZI., and of Volusian (Æ. I. and II.) with ARNAZI., with type of Apollo on a mountain, holding a laurel branch and bow, have caused much discussion [ARN. ASI.] Pellerin *(Rec. des Méd.,* vol. iii., p. lii.) considers that the legend signifies two towns of Umbria—*Arna* and *Asisium,* at which a statue of Apollo was erected, and this interpretation was approved by Eckhel (vol. vii., p. 358), and accepted by Cohen *(Méd. Imp.,* 2nd ed., vol. v., p. 239, *note)* with reserve. The interpretation of Pellerin as to two towns seems dubious, but the legend may apply to one—*Arna* —for it is now known that the Emperor Vibius Trebonianus Gallus was born at Perusia (St. Marin, *Iscriz. Perugina,* p. 15-20; Noël des Vergers, *L'Etrurie et les Etrusques,* vol. ii., p. 381), and it was there that an inscription was dedicated to his wife Afinia Gemina before he became Emperor (Noël des Vergers, *op. cit.,* vol. iii.; *Append. Epig.,* p. iii., No. 32; Orelli, No. 997.) The colony then acquired the name of *Vibia,* and many benefits were conferred on the place. The town of Arna was in Perusia (Orelli, Nos. 90, 91, 5005), and it is very likely that the Emperor Trebonianus Gallus would erect a statue to Apollo *Arnazius* or *Arnasius* in his native country (Madden, *Num. Chron.,* N.S., 1868, vol. viii., pp. 8-10.) The late M. Adrien de Longpérier, in a letter to the writer, 27th May, 1868, says—" J'ai remarqué votre explication de la légende ARNASI qui est tres intéressant et tres bien fondée."

VOOC. [*Vocontii.*]

VOLVSVS [VALERIA GENS.]

VOT. *Vota* or *Votis* [see *Vota.*]

VOT. *(Vota* in the *exergue.)* Legend effaced. Tetricus I. and II. facing each other sacrificing at a lighted altar; one holds a globe and is crowned by Victory; to r. a citizen standing. *Obv.* [IMPP. TETRICI AVGG.] Busts facing each other of Tetricus I. and II., the former laureate, the latter bare. Æ. II. (200 frcs.)

VOT. *(Vota.)* Δ. or Δ. or Є., etc., within a laurel wreath. *Obv.* IMP. C. MAXIMIANVS P. F. AVG. Bust of Maximian Hercules to r., radiated. Æ. III. (c.)

VOT. *(Vota)* with a ram and an eagle within a wreath; in the *exergue* CONST. *(Constantinæ* —Arles.) *Obv.* D. N. FL. CL. IVLIANVS P. F. AVG. Bust of Julian II. to l., helmeted, holding spear and shield. Æ. III., from *Banduri.*

VOT. *Vota.*—IOVI VOT. SVSC. PRO SAL. CAES. AVG. S. P. Q. R. *Jovi Vota Suscepta pro salute Cæsaris Augusti Senatus Populusque Romanus,* on silver coins of Augustus.

VOT. CAESS. *(Vota Cæsarum.)* Two Victories holding a shield- on which VOT. XV. *(Vota Quindecennalia.)* *Obv.* CONSTANTINVS IVN. NOB. CAES. Head of Constantine II. to r., laureated. Æ. Med., from *Vaillant* (200 frcs.)

VOT. DECEN. TR. P. COS. II. *(Vota Decennalia. Tribunitia Potestate Consul Secundum.)* Pertinax veiled, standing to l., sacrificing at a lighted tripod. *Obv.* IMP. CAES. P. HELV. *(Publius Helvius)* PERTIN. AVG. Bust or head of Pertinax to r., laureated. N. (300 frcs.) Æ. (50 frcs.) VOT. DECE., etc., and similar types on Æ. I. (150 frcs.) and Æ. II. (80 frcs.)

VOT. M. *(Votis Multis)* formed as a cross V.—O. or O.—V. within a wreath. *Obv.* T.—M. or T.—M. D. N. IVSTINIANVS PP. *(Perpetuus)* AVG. Bust of Justinian I. to r., diademed. Æ. (20 to 25 frcs.)

VOT. MVLT. HTI. *(Votis Multis — ?)* in three lines within a laurel wreath; in the *exergue* CONOB. *(Constantinopolis,* 72.) *Obv.* D. N. IVSTINIANVS PP. AVG. Bust of Justinian I. to r., diademed, Æ. (12 frcs.)

VOT. MVLT. XXXX. *(Votis Multis Quadragennalibus)* within a laurel wreath. *Obv.* D. N. THEODOSIVS P. F. AVG. Bust of Theodosius II. to r., diademed. Æ. (100 frcs.)

VOT. P. C. *(Vota Populi Constantinopolitani ?)* on the shield held by Victory and a genius, on a gold coin of Anastasius with the legend VICTORIA AVGVSTORVM *(q. v.),* from *Tanini* and *Mionnet,* but doubtful.

VOT. P. R. *(Vota Populi Romani)* on altar or on shield, on small brass coins of Licinius I., Constantine I., Crispus, etc., with legend VICT. [or VICTORIAE] LAETAE PRINC. PERP. or DOM. NOSTR.

VOT. P. SVSC. PR. SAL. ET RED. I. O. M. SACR. *(Vota Publice Suscepta pro salute et reditu Jovi Optimo Maximo Sacrata*—sometimes a circular legend, sometimes in four lines.) Mars standing, facing, naked, helmeted, mantle on arm, holding standard and *parazonium. Obv.* S. P. Q. R. *(Senatus Populusque Romanus)*

CAESARI AVGVSTO. Head of Augustus to r. or l., laureated. *N.* (60 frcs.); *Æ.* (5 to 50 or 60 frcs.)

VOT. PVB. *(Vota Publica.)* The genius of the Senate standing, holding a sceptre in the presence of the genius of the Roman people, who holds a *patera* and a cornucopiæ; between them a lighted altar. *Obv.* HADRIANVS AVG. COS. III. P. P. Head or bust of Hadrian, bare, to r., or head bare to l. *N.* (100 frcs.)

VOT. PVB. *(Vota Publica*—in the *field)* P. M. TR. P. COS. II., or COS. DES. III., or COS. III. Piety veiled, standing to r., raising both hands. *Obv.* IMP. CAESAR TRAIAN. HADRIANVS AVG. Bust of Hadrian to r., laureated. *Æ.* (3 frcs.)

VOT. PVB. S. C. *(Vota Publica. Senatus Consulto.)* Hadrian veiled, sacrificing at a tripod, accompanied by a priest, an assistant *(Victimarius)*, and a flute player—on *Æ.* I. of Hadrian, from *Vaillant.*

VOT. PVB. *(Vota Publica.)* Gate of a camp, surmounted by two turrets and a star. *Obv.* D. N. VALENTINIANVS P. F. AVG. Bust of Valentinian III. to r. *Æ.* III. *Quin.* (10 frcs.) A variety from *Tanini* has RM. *(Roma)* in the *exergue* of the reverse.

VOT. Q. Q. MVL. X., or MVL. X. FEL., or MVL. XX. *(Votis Quinquennalibus, Multis Decennalibus,* or *Multis Decennalibus Felicibus,* or *Multis Vicennalibus)* within a laurel wreath. *Obv.* MAXENTIVS P. F. AVG. Head of Maxentius to r., laureated. *Æ.* III. (1 frc.) A variety from *Banduri* reads VOT. V. Q. MVL. X. (2 frcs.)

VOT. SOL. DEC. P. M. TR. P. XI. [or TR. P. XII.] IMP. VIII. COS. V. P. P. *(Votis Solutis Decennalibus,* etc.) Commodus veiled, standing to l., sacrificing on a tripod, behind which a victim. *Obv.* M. COMM. ANT. P. FEL. AVG. BRIT. Head of Commodus to r., laureated. Struck in A.D. 186 and 187. *Æ.* (3 frcs.)

VOT. SOL. DEC. PONTIF. TR. P. XI. COS. III. S. C. *(Votis Solutis Decennalibus,* etc.) Caracalla standing to l., sacrificing at a tripod, behind which a flute player, standing facing; opposite Caracalla a *Victimarius* killing a bull. *Obv.* ANTONINVS PIVS AVG. Bust of Caracalla to r., laureated. Struck in A.D. 208. *Æ.* III. (15 frcs.)

VOT. SOLVTA X. *(Vota Soluta Decennalia.)* Victory in a *biga* galloping to r., holding a laurel branch. *Obv.* PROBVS P. F. AVG. Bust of Probus to l., laureated, holding a spear. *Æ.* Med. (small), or *Æ.* III., from *Tanini* (50 frcs.)

VOT. SVSC. DEC. P. M. TR. P., etc. *(Votis Susceptis Decennalibus,* etc.) The Emperor sacrificing—on coins of Commodus (*N.* 130 frcs.; *Æ.* 3 frcs.); Septimius Severus (*Æ.* 3 frcs.), and Caracalla (*Æ.* 6 frcs.)

VOT. SVSC. DEC. III. COS. IIII. *(Votis Susceptis Decennalibus III.,* etc.) Antoninus Pius standing to l., sacrificing at a tripod, near him a person standing; facing him a child, and a flute-player, behind whom another person and

a *Victimarius* killing a bull. *Obv.* ANTONINVS AVG. PIVS P. P. TR. P. XXII. Head of Antoninus Pius to r., bare. Struck in A.D. 159. *Æ.* Med. (300 frcs.)

VOT. V. *(Votis Quinquennalibus),* or VOT. V. MVLT. X. *(Multis Decennalibus),* or VOT. X., or VOT. X. MVLT. XV. *(Quindecennalibus)* or XX. *(Vicennalibus)* up to VOT. XXX. *(Tricennalibus),* or VOT. XXX. MVLT. XXXX. *(Quadragennalibus)* or VOT. XXXX. *(Quadragennalibus)* occur upon the coins from the period of Constantine, either within a laurel wreath or on an altar, or on a standard, or on a shield held by Victories, with various legends surrounding the main type, such as CAESARVM NOSTRORVM, or DOMINOR. NOSTROR. [or DOMINORVM NOSTRORVM] CAESS., GAVDIVM POPVLI ROMANI, and many others.

VOT. V. *(Votis Quinquennalibus)* within a laurel wreath, on coins of Constantius II., from *Banduri* (*Æ.* III. 5 frcs.), of Jovian (*Æ.* III. c.), of Valentinian I. (*Æ.* 6 frcs.), of Valens (*Æ.* 3 frcs.), of Procopius (*Æ.* 150 frcs.), of Gratian (*Æ.* III., *Quin.* 2 frcs.), of Theodosius I. (*Æ.* III., *Quin.* c.), and of Arcadius (*Æ.* III. 3 frcs.)

VOT. V. MVLT. X. *(Votis Quinquennalibus Multis Decennalibus.)* Within a laurel wreath, on coins of Crispus (*Æ.* III., *Quin.,* from *Welz,* 6 frcs.), of Constantius Gallus (*Æ.* III., *Quin.* 10 frcs.), of Julian II. (*Æ.* 6 frcs.), of Jovian (*Æ.* 6 frcs., *Æ.* III. 2 frcs.), of Valentinian I. (*Æ.* 6 frcs., *Æ.* III., *Quin.* 3 frcs.), of Valens (*Æ.,* from *D'Ennery,* 40 frcs., *Æ.* III., *Quin.,* from *Tanini* 10 frcs.), of Gratian (*Æ.,* from *Khell,* 15 frcs., *Æ.* III., *Quin.* 3 frcs.), Valentinian II., in *exergue* T ✱ E or T ✱ H from *Tanini* (*Musée de Vienne, Æ.* 20 frcs., *Æ.* III., *Quin.* from *Wiczay,* 1 frc.), of Theodosius I. (*Æ.,* from *Beger,* 8 frcs., *Æ.* III., *Quin.* c.), of Magnus Maximus (*Æ.* III., *Quin.* 1 frc.), of Honorius (*Æ.* Med. 100 frcs., *Æ.* 6 frcs.), of Arcadius (*Æ.* III. 3 frcs.), of Constantius III. (*Æ.,* from *D'Ennery,* 200 frcs.), of Attalus (*Æ.,* from *D'Ennery,* 100 frcs.), and of Zeno (TOVVIMY MTI-VOT. V. MVLT. X. *Æ.* 30 frcs.)

VOT. V. MVLT. X. CAESS. *(Votis Quinquennalibus Multis Decennalibus Cæsarum)* within a laurel wreath, on coins of Licinius II. (*Æ.* III. 6 frcs.), of Crispus (*Æ.* III. I frc.), and of Constantine II. (*Æ.* III. 5 frcs.) These pieces were all struck at Thessalonica, as the letters TS. A. or B. or Є. (Thessalonicæ, 1, 2, 5) testify.

VOT. X. *(Votis Decennalibus)* within a laurel wreath, on coins of Constantius Chlorus (*Æ.* III. 1 frc.), of Galerius Maximian (*Æ.* III. c.), of Maximinus II. (*Æ.* II. 30 frcs.), of Constantine II., from *Banduri* (5 frcs.), and of Valentinian II., from *Tanini* (*Æ.* 20 frcs.) On the pieces of Constantius Chlorus and Galerius Maximian there occur the letters F. K. *(Felix Carthago),* and T. *(Tarraconis)*; on that of Maximus II. T., and on that of Valentinian II. P. CONS. (?)

VOT. X. AVG. N. *(Votis Decennalibus Augusti Nostri)* within a laurel wreath. *Obv.*

IMP. CONSTANTINVS AVG. Bust of Constantine I. to r. Æ. *Quin.* (3 frcs.)

VOT. X. CAES. *(Votis Decennalibus Cæsaris)* within a wreath of oak. *Obv.* CONSTANTIVS CAES. Head of Constantius II. to r., laureated. *N.* (50 frcs.)

VOT. X. CAESS. *(Votis Decennalibus Cæsarum)* within a laurel wreath, on coins of Galerius Maximian (*N.*, from *Caylus*, 200 frcs.) and of Severus II. (Æ. III. *Quin.* 15 frcs.)

VOT. X. CAESS. NN. *(Votis Decennalibus Cæsarum Nostrorum)* within a wreath. *Obv.* MAXIMINVS AVG. Head of Maximinus II. Daza to r., laureated. Æ. III. *Quin.*, from *Tanini* (25 frcs.)

VOT. X. ET XV. F. *(Votis Decennalibus et Quindecennalibus Felicibus)* within a laurel wreath, on coins of Licinius II. (Æ. III. 20 frcs.) and Constantine II. (Æ. III. 2 frcs.), accompanied by the letters Ɵs. *(Thessalonicæ)* or R. S., R. T. *(Romæ Secunda, Romæ Tertia)*, etc.

VOT. X. ET XV. FEL. *(Votis Decennalibus et Quindecennalibus Felicibus)* within a wreath; also the letters REDCS (?) *Obv.* IMP. LICINIVS AVG. Head of Licinius I. to r., laureated. Æ. III. from *Wiczay* (20 frcs.)

VOT. X. ET XX. *(Votis Decennalibus et Vicennalibus)* within a laurel wreath. *Obv.* GALLIENVS AVG. or P. F. AVG. Head or bust of Gallienus to r., radiated. *N.* (200 frcs.)

VOT. X. F. *(Votis Decennalibus Felicibus)* within a laurel wreath, on coins of Constantius Chlorus (Æ. III. 1 frc.) and of Galerius Maximian (Æ. III. c.)—both with mintmarks K. *Karthaginis* and T. *Tarraconis.*

VOT. X. FEL. *(Votis Decennalibus Felicibus)* within a laurel wreath; sometimes with the letters AQ. S. *(Aquileiæ Secunda)* or R. T. or R. Q. *(Romæ Tertia* or *Quarta.) Obv.* MAXENTIVS P. F. AVG. Head of Maxentius to r., laureated, or with lion's skin. Æ. III. (2 to 6 frcs.)

VOT. X. M. XX. *(Votis Decennalibus Multis Vicennalibus)* Victory standing on a globe holding wreath and palm, on coins of Diocletian (Æ. III. 10 frcs.), and of Galerius Maximian (Æ. III. 12 frcs.)

VOT. X. M. XX. *(Votis Decennalibus Multis Vicennalibus)* within a wreath. *Obv.* MAXIMIANVS P. F. AVG. Bust of Maximian Hercules to r., radiated. Æ. III. from *Banduri* (20 frcs.)

VOT. X. MVL. XX. *(Votis Decennalibus Multis Vicennalibus)* within a laurel wreath. *Obv.* CONSTANTINVS AVG. Bust of Constantine I. to r., laureated. Æ. *Quin.* (1 frc.)

VOT. X. MVLT. XV. *(Votis Decennalibus Multis Quindecennalibus)* within a laurel wreath, on coins of Valens (Æ. from *D'Ennery*, in the *exergue* TR. *Treveris,* or TR. P. S. *Treveris Pecunia Signata*, 40 frcs.), of Gratian (Æ. from *Welzl*—in the *exergue* TR., 10 frcs.), of Theodosius I. (Æ. Med.—in *exergue* TR. P. S.— from *D'Ennery*, 100 frcs.), and of Honorius (Æ. —in *exergue* CONS., *Constantinopolis*—6 frcs.)

VOT. X. MVLT. XX. *(Votis Decennalibus Multis Vicennalibus)* within a laurel wreath,

on coins of Licinius I. (Æ. III. from *Tanini*, 20 frcs.), of Julian II. (Æ.—various mint-letters in *exergue*—3 frcs., Æ. III. c.), of Jovian (Æ. —in *exergue* T. CONST. *Tertia Constantinæ*— Arles—30 frcs.), of Valentinian I. (Æ.—various mint-letters in the *exergue*—10 frcs.), of Valens (Æ.—various mint-letters in the *exergue*—4 to 20 frcs., Æ. III. *Quin.* 10 frcs.), of Gratian (Æ. —various mint-letters in the *exergue*—6 frcs., Æ. III. *Quin.* 1 frc.), of Valentinian II. (Æ.— in *exergue* MD. P. S. *Mediolani Pecunia Signata*—10 frcs., *N.* from *Mionnet*, 40 frcs., Æ. III. *Quin.* c.), of Theodosius I. (Æ.—various mint-letters in the *exergue*—5 frcs., Æ. III. *Quin.* c.), of Honorius (Æ.—in the *exergue* CONS. *Constantinopolis*—4 frcs.), and of Arcadius (Æ.—in the *exergue* CONS. or MD. P. S.—8 frcs., Æ. III—in the *exergue* ANT. Δ. Antiochiæ, 4, 2 frcs.)

VOT. X. MVLT. XX. *(Votis Decennalibus Multis Vicennalibus.)* Valentinian III., seated, facing, holding a signal-cloth *(Mappa)* and a cross; in the *field* RM. *(Romæ)* or RV. *(Ravennæ)*; in the *exergue* COMOB. *(Constantinæ Moneta—72)* [see VALENTINIAN I.] *Obv.* D. N. PLA. VALENTINIANVS P. F. AVG. Bust of Valentinian III. to l., diademed, with the Imperial mantle, holding a signal-cloth *(Mappa)* and a cross. *N.* (100 frcs.)

VOT. X. SIC XX. *(Votis Decennalibus Sic Vicennalibus)* within a laurel wreath. *Obv.* CONSTANTIVS N. C. *(Nobilis Cæsar.)* Head of Constantius Chlorus to r., laureated. Æ. *Quin.* (60 frcs.)

VOT. XIII. *(Votis Tredecennalibus)* within a laurel wreath. *Obv.* D. N. IVSTINIANVS P. A. *(Perpetuus Augustus.)* Bust of Justinian I. to r., diademed. Æ. (15 frcs.)

VOT. XIII. *(Votis Tredecennalibus)* within a laurel wreath. *Obv.* D. N. IVSTINVS PP. *(Perpetuus)* AVG. Bust of Justinus I. to r., diademed. Æ. *Semi-Siliqua* (25 frcs.)

VOT. XV. FEL. XX *(Votis Quindecennalibus Felicibus Vicennalibus)* within a laurel wreath on small brass coins of Licinius II. (20 frcs.), of Constantine I. (6 frcs.), and of Crispus (2 frcs.), with the mint-letters R. P., R. S., R. T., R. Q. *Romæ Prima, Secunda, Tertia, Quarta.*

VOT. XV. MVLT. XX. *(Votis Quindecennalibus Multis Vicennalibus)* within laurel wreath, on coins of Constans I. (Æ. III. 2 frcs.), of Constantius II. (Æ. III. *Quin.* 4 frcs.), of Valentinian I. (Æ.—in the *exergue* SISC. P. S. *Sisciæ Pecunia Signata.*—10 frcs.), of Valens (Æ.—in the *exergue* SISC. P. S.—10 frcs.; also VOT. VX. *(sic)* MVLT. XX.—in the *exergue* T⚹E or C⚹S. *(Banduri)*—Æ. 20 frcs., Æ. III. *Quin.* from *Tanini*, 10 frcs.), of Gratian (Æ.—in the *exergue* SISC. P. S. or T⚹E.—6 to 15 frcs., Æ. III. *Quin.* 1 frc.), of Valentinian II. (Æ. III. *Quin.* c.), of Theodosius I. (Æ. from *D'Ennery* 10 frcs., Æ. III. *Quin.* c.), and of Honorius (Æ.—in the *exergue* CONS. *Constantinopolis*—6 frcs.)

VOT. XV. MVLT. XXXX. *(Votis Quindecennalibus Multis·Quadragennalibus)* within

a laurel wreath; in the *exergue* T ✱ Є. *Obv.*
D. N. GRATIANVS P. F. AVG. Bust of Gratian
to r., diademed. Æ. (20 frcs.)

VOT. XV. MVLTIƆ XX. *(Votis Quindecennalibus Multis Vicennalibus)* within a
wreath; in the *exergue* SISC. P. or SISC. P. S.
(Sisciæ Prima or *Pecunia Signata.)* Æ. Med.,
of Valentinian I. from *D'Ennery and Mionnet*
(60 frcs.)

VOT. XX. *(Votis Vicennalibus)* within a
laurel wreath on coins of Diocletian, with or
without mint-letters, on small brass coins of
Diocletian (2 frcs.), of Maximian Hercules (c.),
of Constantius Chlorus (1 frc.), and of Galerius
Maximian (c.)

VOT. XX. AVGG. *(Votis Vicennalibus Augustorum)* in three lines within a laurel wreath,
below which sometimes an eagle, on coins of
Diocletian (*N.* 120 frcs., Æ. from *Tanini* 20
frcs.), of Maximian Hercules (*N.* 120 frcs.), of
Constantius Chlorus (Æ. III. *Quin.* 10 frcs.),
and of Severus II. (Æ. III. from *Hardouin*
20 frcs.)

VOT. XX. AVG. NN. *(Votis Vicennalibus
Augustorum Nostrorum)* in four lines within a
laurel wreath, on gold coins of Maximian Hercules (120 frcs.), and of Constantius Chlorus
(from *Tanini* 200 frcs.)

VOT. XX. CAESS. *(Votis Vicennalibus
Cæsarum)* within a laurel wreath. *Obv.* CON-
STANTIVS N. C. *(Nobilis Cæsar.)* Head of Con-
stantius Chlorus to r., laureated. Æ. III.
Quin. (10 frcs.)

VOT. XX. FEL. *(Votis Vicennalibus Felicibus)* on a shield, on third brass coins (3 frcs.),
of Maxentius, with legend VICTORIA AETERNA
AVG. N. *(q. v.)*

VOT. XX. MVL. XXX. *(Votis Vicennalibus
Multis Tricennalibus)* within a wreath; in the
exergue CONCM (?). *Obv.* D. N. VALENS P. F.
AVG. Bust of Valens to r., diademed. Æ. from
D'Ennery and *Tanini* (12 frcs.)

VOT. XX. MVLT. XXX. *(Votis Vicennalibus Multis Tricennalibus)* within a laurel wreath,
with or without mint-letters, on small brass coins,
principally *Quinarii*, of Constantine I. (1 frc.),
of Constans I. (2 frcs.), of Constantius II. (3
frcs.), of Valens (10 frcs.), and of Valentinian
II. (c.)

VOT. XX. MVLT. XXX. *(Votis Vicennalibus
Multis Tricennalibus.)* Victory standing to l.,
holding a cross, on gold coins of Honorius (in
exergue CONOB. 40 frcs.), of Placidia (with RM.
Romæ or RV. *Ravennæ*, or AQ. *Aquileiæ* in the
field, and in the *exergue* COMOB., 150 to 300
frcs.), of Honoria (with RV. *Ravennæ* in the
field, and in the *exergue* COMOB., 400 frcs.), of
Theodosius II. (with sometimes a star in the
field, and in the *exergue* COMOB. or CONOB., 25
frcs.), of Eudocia his wife (150 frcs.), and of
Pulcheria his sister (150 frcs.)

VOT. XX. *(Votis Vicennalibus)* P. M. TR.
P. XV. IMP. VIII. COS. VI. S. C., in five
lines, within a laurel wreath. *Obv.* M. COMM.
ANT. P. FELIX AVG. BRIT. P. P. Head of Commodus to r., laureated. Æ. II. (10 frcs.)

VOT. XX. SIC XXX. *(Votis Vicennalibus
Sic Tricennalibus)* within a laurel wreath, on
coins of Diocletian. (*N.* from *Banduri*, 200
frcs., Æ. III. *Quin.* 10 frcs.)

VOT. XXX. AVGG. *(Votis Tricennalibus
Augustorum)* or AVGG. NN. *(Augustorum Nostrorum)*, on small brass coins of Maximian Hercules (20 to 25 frcs.)

VOT. XXX. MVLT. XXXX. *(Votis Tricennalibus Multis Quadragennalibus)* within a laurel
wreath; in the *exergue* P. CON. *Prima Constantinæ*—Arles) on silver coin of Julian II. from
D'Ennery (15 frcs.)

VOT. XXX. MVLT. XXXX. *(Votis Tricennalibus Multis Quadragennalibus.)* Honorius
in Imperial dress, seated, facing, holding a signal-
cloth *(Mappa)* and a sceptre surmounted by an
eagle; the seat is ornamented with two lion's
heads; in the *field* RV. *(Ravennæ)*; in the
exergue COMOB. *Obv.* D. N. HONORIVS P. F.
AVG. Bust of Honorius, helmeted, facing, wearing the Imperial mantle, and holding a signal-
cloth *(Mappa)* and a sceptre surmounted by an
eagle. *N.* (40 frcs.)

VOT. XXX. MVLT. XXXX. *(Votis Tricennalibus Multis Quadragennalibus.)* Valentinian
III. in Consular dress, standing with a diadem
ornamented with a cross, presenting his hand to a
kneeling figure, and holding a sceptre surmounted
by a cross; in the *field* RM. *(Romæ)*; in the
exergue COMOB. *Obv.* D. N. PLACIDIVS VAL-
ENTINIANVS P. F. AVG. Bust of Valentinian
III. to l., diademed, with the Imperial mantle
holding a book (? the signal-cloth—*Mappa)* and
a sceptre surmounted by a cross. *N.* Med.
(500 frcs.) A very similar type occurs on the
gold coins with obverse legend D. N. PLA. VALEN-
TINIANVS P. F. AVG. (50 frcs.)

VOT. XXX. MVLT. XXXX. *(Votis Tricennalibus Multis Quadragennalibus)* sometimes
followed by B or Θ. Rome, helmeted, seated to
l., placing right foot on the prow of a vessel and
holding a cross surmounted by a globe and a
sceptre; behind her a shield; in the *field* a star;
in the *exergue* CONOB. *(Constantinopolis* 72.)
Obv. D. N. VALENTINIANVS P. F. AVG. Bust
of Valentinian III. facing, helmeted, with the
cuirass, holding a spear and a shield on which is
represented the Emperor on horseback felling an
enemy. *N.* (100 frcs.) Similar types occur on
the gold coins of Theodosius II. (in the *exergue*
sometimes TESOB. *Thessalonicæ* 72. 30 frcs.)
and of his sister Pulcheria (200 frcs.)

VOT. XXX. MVLT. XXXX. *(Votis Tricennalibus Multis Quadragennalibus.)* Theodosius
II. and Valentinian III. seated facing, each holding a signal-cloth *(Mappa)* and a cross; in the
exergue CONOB. *Obv.* D. N. THEODOSIVS P. F.
AVG. Bust of Theodosius II. to r., diademed.
N. (25 frcs.)

VOT. XXX. MVLT. XXXX. *(Votis Tricennalibus Multis Quadragennalibus.)* Eudoxia
and her husband Valentinian III. standing
facing; Eudoxia holds a sceptre and Valentinian
III. a globe surmounted by a cross; in the *field*
RM. *(Romæ)*; in the *exergue* COMOB. *Obv.*

LICINIA EVDOXIA P. F. AVG. Bust of Eudoxia, facing, with two long strings of pearls ; on her head a cross. *N.* (800 frcs.)

VOT. XXXV. MVLT. XXXX. *(Votis Quinque-Tricennalibus Multis Quadragennalibus)* within a laurel wreath; in the *exergue* CONS. *(Constantinopolis)* and two stars. *Obv.* D. N. LEO PERPET. AVG. Bust of Leo I. to r., diademed. *Æ.* Med. (800 frcs.)

VT. (for VOT.) XXXV. *(Votis Quinque-Tricennalibus)* within a wreath; in the *exergue* CON. *(Constantinopolis.)* *Obv.* D. N. THEODOSIVS P. F. AVG. Bust of Theodosius II. to r., diademed. *Æ.* III. (5 frcs.)

VOT. XXXX. *(Votis Quadragennalibus)* within a laurel wreath; in the *exergue* C. Θ. *Obv.* D. N. CONSTANTIVS P. F. AVG. Bust of Constantius II. to r., diademed. *Æ.* 2. (15 frcs.) M. Cohen has remarked *(Méd. Imp.*, 1st ed., vol. vi., p. 285, *note)* with respect to the silver of Constantius II., that under this Emperor and his successor Julian II. there exist two sizes of silver, the smaller not being the *quinarius.* The coin described is of the smaller size.

Vota. Vows were both *private* and *public.* As an example of the former may be mentioned the case of Horace, who, on escaping death from the fall of a tree on his farm, vowed sacrifices to Faunus and to Bacchus *(Odes*, II., 13, 17 ; III., 8.)* The latter VOTA PVBLICA "Public vows" were made on the marriage of an Emperor and Empress (Antoninus Pius with Faustina I., Marcus Aurelius with Faustina II., Commodus with Crispina, etc.), and on many other occasions [VOTA PVBLICA]—comp. PIO IMP [*eratori*] OMNIA FELICIA, etc., on brass medallions of Commodus, S. P. Q. R. A. N. F. F. HADRIANO AVG. P. P. *Senatus Populusque Romanus annum novum faustum felicem Hadriano Augusto Patri Patriæ,* on large brass of Hadrian, S. P. Q. R. A. N. F. F. OPTIMO PRINCIPI on brass medallion of Antoninus Pius, or with PIO. S. C. added on second brass of Alexander Severus, PLVR. NATAL. FELIC. *Plures Natales Feliciter* on third brass coins of Maximian Hercules and Constantine I., VOTA ORBIS ET VRBIS SEN. ET. P. R. *Senatus et Populi Romani,* on silver medallions of Licinius I. and Constantine I., and FELICITER NꝨBTIIS on a gold coin commemorating the marriage of Marcian and Pulcheria. It was the custom at Rome to make "public vows" on the Kalends of January, when the consuls were elected, for the safety of the Empire, and two days before the Nones of the same month for the preservation of the Emperors. Other "vows" were made at special events, or at certain periodical times. To the first class belong those vows made for the safety of Augustus in B.C. 16. —VOT. P. SVSC. PR. [or PRO.] SAL. ET RED. I. O. M. SACR. *Vota publice suscepta pro salute et reditu Jovi Optimo Maximo Sacrata,* I. O. M. S. P. Q. R. V. S. PR. S. IMP. CAE. QVOD. PER. EV. R. P. IN AMP. ATQ. TRAN. S. E. *Jovi Optimo Maximo Senatus Populusque Romanus Votum Susceptum pro salute Imperatoris Cæsaris quod per eum Respublica in* ampliore atque tranquil-

liore statu est, or V. P. RED. CAES. *Vota pro reditu Cæsaris,* or V. S. PRO S. ET RED. AVG. *Votum Solvit pro salute et reditu Augusti.* To the second the *Vota decennalia, quinquennalia,* etc. The "decennial vows" date from the reign of Augustus, who in B.C. 27 accepted the government for ten years, then in B.C. 18 for two periods of five years, in B.C. 8 for another ten years, in A.D. 4 for a further ten (Dion. Cass., liii., 13, 16), and in A.D. 13 a fifth time for ten years (Dion. Cass., lvi., 28.) These decennial vows were kept very regularly by the successors of Augustus, and are first mentioned on the coins of Antoninus Pius—PRIMI DECEN. COS. IIII. [TR. P. XI. on obverse=A.D. 148], PRIMI DECENNALES COS. IIII. [TR. P. XI. on obverse=A.D. 148.] (Cohen *Méd. Imp.,* 2nd ed., vol. ii., pp. 337, 346, 347. For the question of date see Cohen *op. cit.,* and vol. iii., p. 353, and T. J. Arnold, *Num. Chron.,* N.S., 1873, vol. xiii., p. 130.) At a later period the *decennalia* were celebrated every 5, 10, 15, 20, 25, 30, 35, and 40 years. The principal legends on the coins are—VOT. V. MVLT. X., VOT. X. ET XX. or XX., VOT. X. SIC XX., VOT. XV. MVLT. XX. or XXX., VOT. XX. SIC or MVLT. XXX., VOT. XXX. MVLT. XXXX., VOT. XXXV. or VOT. XXXV. MVLT. XXXX., XXXX. (last used on gold coins of Justinian I., Sabatier, *Mon. Byz.,* vol. i., p. 177), VOTIS MVLTIS, VOTIS X. ET XX., VOTIS XX. MVLTIS XXX., etc., PRIMIS X. MVLTIS XX., SIC. X. SIC XX. In the *Upper Empire* we find the legends— VOTA SVSCEPTA DECENNALIA, when the vows were made for ten years, and VOTA SOLVTA DECENNALIA when the vows were accomplished (Cohen, *Méd. Imp.,* 2nd ed., vol. vi., p. 458.) Cohen is of opinion that when the vows were only made or undertaken (SVSCEPTA) the bull to be sacrificed was not slain, but when accomplished (SOLVTA) the sacrifice was complete—" c'est pour cela qu'on voit un taureau au pied du trépied avec la légende VOTA SOL. et qu'on n'en voit point avec la légende VOTA SVSCEPTA *(Méd. Imp.,* 2nd ed., vol. ii., p. 377)—a rule not observed on the coinage of Caracalla, and supposed by Cohen to be a proof, amongst other things, of the decadence of art *(Méd. Imp.,* 2nd ed., vol. iv., p. 214), a general interpretation with which Froehner does not agree *(Les Médaillons de l'Empire Romain,* p. 66.) The curious forms of the *Later Empire* may be explained by "Vows made for five or more years, and for many others besides (MVLTIS) up to twenty, thirty, or forty years," and by "As (SIC) the vows are for ten years so (SIC) are they for twenty, thirty, etc." Very often vows were anticipated for a much longer period than were ever fulfilled, for instance Valens only reigned for fourteen years, and we find on the coins vows for twenty and thirty years—VOT. XX. MVLT. XXX. (Cohen, *Méd. Imp.,* 2nd ed., vol. vi., p. 458.) For fuller information on the "*Nummi votorum,*" Eckhel *(Doct. Num. Vet.,* vol. viii., pp. 473-488) should be consulted.

VOTA—HAEC VOTA MVLT. ANN. *(Multis Annis)* on silver coin of Constantine I., from Banduri.—SAE. VOTA MVLT. DD. NN. *(Sæculi Vota Multis [Annis] Dominorum Nostrorum)* on brass *quinarius* of Constantine I. from *D'Ennery*.

VOTA (in the *field* on gold coins, in the *exergue* on brass) COS. IIII. Antoninus Pius veiled, standing to l., holding *patera* and roll sacrificing at a tripod, on gold coins (45 frcs.) and large and second brass (6 to 3 frcs.) of Antoninus Pius.

VOTA (in *exergue*) TR. P. XXI. IMP. IIII. COS. III. Marcus Aurelius standing to l., sacrificing at a tripod. *Obv.* M. ANTONINVS AVG. ARM. PARTH. MAX. *(Armeniacus Parthicus Maximus.)* Head of Aurelius to r., laureated. Æ. II. (3 frcs.)

VOTA (in the *exergue*) P. M. TR. P. COS. III. P. P. Tetricus I. and II. facing each other, sacrificing at a lighted altar; the figure holding a globe is crowned by Victory. *Obv.* IMPP. TETRICI AVGG. Busts facing of Tetricus I., laureated, and Tetricus II. bare. *N*. (800 frcs.) Æ. III. (100 frcs.)

VOTA AVGVSTI. Helmeted bust of Rome to r. (with the features of Victoria) yoked to that of Diana, or busts facing of Apollo (with the features of Victorinus II. ?) laureated, and of Diana, on gold coins of Victorinus I. (800 frcs.) [VICTORIA or VICTORINA; VICTORINVS I. and II.]

VOTA CAESS. *(Cæsarum.)* Two Victories holding a shield on which VOT. XXX. *Obv.* CONSTANTINVS IVN. NOB. CAES. *(Junior Nobilis Cæsar.)* Bust of Constantine II. to r., laureated. Æ. Med. from *Tanini* (200 frcs.)

VOTA DEC. ANN. SVSC. TR. P. XX. IMP. IIII. COS. III. S. C. (Antoninus Pius) or TR. P. VI. IMP. IIII. COS. III. P. P. S. C (Commodus.) The Emperor, veiled, standing, sacrificing at a tripod, on second brass coins of Antoninus Pius and Commodus (3 frcs.) The legend should probably be interpreted VOTA DECEM ANNALIA and *not* VOTA DECANNALIA *(sic)*, in accordance with another legend on large brass coins of Antoninus Pius, SECVND. DECEM ANNALES. (Cohen, *Méd. Imp.*, 1st ed., vol. ii., p. 391; vol. iii., p. 185; 2nd ed., vol. ii., p. 346 [where DECEN. seems to be a misprint for DECEM.]; vol. iii., p. 353.) [See *Vota*.]

VOTA DECENALIA *(sic)* or DECENNALIA. Victory standing to r., writing on a shield attached to a palm, on *billon* coins of Gallienus (2 frcs.)

VOTA ORBIS. Two Victories standing, attaching a shield on which is S. C. *(Senatus Consulto)* to a palm, on coins of Valerian I. *(Bil.* 6 frcs.), of Gallienus *(Bil.* 3 frcs.), and of Claudius II. (Æ. III. 20 frcs.)

VOTA ORBIS ET VRBIS SEN. ET. P. R. *(Senatus et Populi Romani.)* Column surmounted by a basket (? ?). On the column FEL. *(Felicia ?)*; in the *field* L.; in the *exergue* AQ. *(Aquileiæ.) Obv.* IMP. LICINIVS PIVS FELIX AVG. Bust of Licinius I., helmeted, to r., with cuirass, holding spear and shield. Æ. Med. (300 frcs.)—*Same legend.* Cippus on which XX. XXX. AVG. placed on a square base; in the *field* two stars; in the *exergue* AQ. S. *(Aquileiæ Secunda.) Obv.* IMP. CONSTANTINVS MAX.

AVG. Bust of Constantine I., helmeted, to l., holding a spear and a shield. Æ. Med. (200 frcs.)

VOTA PVBL. *(Publica)* P. M. TR. P. On coins of Macrinus. Jupiter, naked, standing, holding thunderbolt and sceptre; to r. Macrinus standing (Æ. 6 frcs.; Æ. I. 40 frcs.);—The goddess Fidelity standing to l., between two standards, holding a standard in each hand (Æ. 6 to 12 frcs.; Æ. II. 12 frcs.);—The goddess Felicity standing to l., holding a *caduceus* and a sceptre (Æ. 6 frcs.; Æ. II. 12 frcs.);—The goddess Health standing to l., feeding a serpent entwined round an altar, and holding a sceptre (Æ. 6 to 12 frcs.);—The goddess Security seated to l., holding a spear; at her feet a lighted altar. (*N*. 500 frcs.; Æ. 6 frcs.; Æ. I. 40 frcs.; Æ. II. 12 frcs.)

VOTA PVBLICA. Hadrian standing to l., sacrificing at an altar or tripod, and holding a roll, to l. a *Victimarius* leading a bull and holding a hammer, a soldier holding a spear, a player on the double flute, and an infant—on gold (200 frcs.) and silver coins (4 to 6 frcs.) of Hadrian.

VOTA PVBLICA. Antoninus I. and Faustina I., or M. Aurelius and Faustina II., or Commodus and Crispina joining hands; behind, *Juno Pronuba* standing—on gold coins of Faustina I. (150 frcs.), and Aurelius (100 frcs.), and on brass medallions (500 frcs.) of Crispina and Commodus.

VOTA PVBLICA S. C. M. Aurelius holding a roll and Faustina II., standing, joining hands; between them *Juno Pronuba* standing to r.—on large brass (15 frcs.) and second brass coins (8 frcs.) of Aurelius.

VOTA PVBLICA S. C., within a wreath. *Obv.* IMP. M. ANTONINVS AVG. TR. P. XX. . . . Head of M. Aurelius to r., laureated. Æ. I. (10 frcs.)

VOTA PVBLICA IMP. VIIII. COS. III. P. P. S. C. The Emperor veiled standing to l., sacrificing on a tripod or altar, and holding a book—on large brass (6 frcs.) and second brass coins (3 frcs.) of Aurelius. Varieties of this type (with or without *book* or *patera*, and sometimes a victim) occur on the coins of Commodus (Æ. I. 6 frcs., Æ. II. 3 frcs.), of Septimius Severus (*N*. 200 frcs., Æ. c., Æ. II. 4 frcs.), of Caracalla (Æ. 3 frcs., Æ. I. 12 frcs., Æ. II. 6 frcs.), of Geta (*N*. 400 frcs., Æ. c., Æ. I. 15 frcs., Æ. II. 5 frcs.), and of Elagabalus (Æ. 6 frcs.)

VOTA PVBLICA (in *exergue*), etc. The Emperor standing to l., sacrificing at a tripod; facing is a child, behind whom a *Victimarius* about to sacrifice a bull; behind two flute-players to r. and a man standing to l.; beyond, a hexastyle temple—several varieties of type on brass medallions of Aurelius and Commodus (400 to 450 frcs.) Cf. Froehner, *Les Médaillons de l'Empire Romain*, pp. 93, 114, 122.

VOTA PVBLICA, within a laurel wreath; in the centre a dot. *Obv.* LVCILLAE AVG. ANTONINI AVG. F. *(filia.)* Bust of Lucilla to r. *N*. (130 frcs.), Æ. (10 frcs.) On some coins the legend is *outside* the laurel wreath. (Æ. 30 frcs.)

VOTA PVBLICA IMP. II. COS. P. P. S. C. Commodus, veiled, standing to l. (or, according to the late Abbé Cavedoni, "The Genius of the Senate"), sacrificing at a lighted tripod, and holding a short sceptre; facing him a *Victimarius* about to sacrifice a bull; or Commodus, veiled, standing to l., sacrificing at a tripod—on large brass (20 frcs.) and large and second brass (6 and 3 frcs.) coins of Commodus.

VOTA PVBLICA S. C. Severus veiled, and Caracalla standing facing each other, sacrificing at an altar—on large brass coins of Septimius Severus (25 frcs.), and Julia Domna from *Vaillant*.

VOTA PVBLICA. Eight figures sacrificing before a temple—on second brass coins of Septimius Severus from *Vaillant*.

VOTA PVBLICA S. C. Piety, veiled, standing to l., placing a grain of incense on the flame of a lighted altar, and holding a box of perfumes —on large (8 frcs.) and second brass (3 frcs.) coins of Julia Domna.

VOTA PVBLICA. Geta, veiled, standing to l., sacrificing at a tripod, facing a figure holding a sacrificial vase; behind the tripod, a flute-player standing facing and a dead bull. *Obv.* P. *(Publius)* SEPT. GETA CAES. PONT. Bust of Geta, unbearded, bare, to r. *N*. (500 frcs.)

VOTA PVBLICA. Two figures in *toga*, veiled, sacrificing; a third in the centre; near are a *camillus* and a flute-player—on silver coins (60 frcs.) of Geta from *Vaillant*.

VOTA PVBLICA. Altar. *Obv.* IMP. C. TETRICVS. Bust of Tetricus, radiated, to r. *Æ*. III. from *Banduri* (6 frcs.)

VOTA PVBLICA. Carinus and Numerian, standing in military dress facing each other, sacrificing at a lighted altar or tripod; in the back-ground two or one military standard—on third brass coins (5-3 frcs.) of Carinus and Numerian.

VOTA PVBLICA. Vessel with two masts or sails; at the poop, Serapis seated; at the prow, Isis standing drawing the sails towards her—on second brass coins of Diocletian (from *Banduri*) and Maximian Hercules (100 frcs.) These pieces were issued in A.D. 305 after the abdication of the two Emperors, and the obverse legends are D. N. *(Domino Nostro)* DIOCLETIANO [or MAXIMIANO] FELICISSIMO SEN. AVG. *(Seniori Augusto.)*

VOTA PVBLICA. The Emperor standing between two females, one of whom carries a Victory; in the *exergue* P. TR. *(Prima Treveris.)* *Obv.* MAXIMIANVS AVG. Head of Maximian Hercules to r., laureated. *N*. (300 frcs.)

VOTA PVBLICA. Isis standing to l. holding a *sistrum* and a bucket or a disc—on small brass coins *(Quin.)* of Licinius I. (50 frcs.) of Crispus (20 frcs.), and of Constantine I. and Constantine II. (25 frcs.), and on second brass coins of Valens (60 frcs.)

VOTA PVBLICA. Isis standing on a vessel with sails closed up, sometimes holding sail with both hands, sometimes accompanied with rowers —on small brass coins *(Quin.)* of Constantine I.

(25 frcs.), Crispus (20 frcs.), Constantine II. (25 frcs.), Constans I. (20 frcs.), and of Magnentius and Constantius Gallus (25 frcs.)

VOTA PVBLICA. Isis seated, sometimes holding a *sistrum*, near the rudder of a galley to l., with closed sail and two sailors—on small brass coins *(Quin.)* of Constantine I. (25 frcs.), and Crispus (20 frcs.)

VOTA PVBLICA. Anubis, standing, holding a *sistrum* or a palm and a *caduceus*—on small brass coins *(Quin.)* of Constantine I. (25 frcs.), Crispus (20 frcs.), Constantine II. (25 frcs.), Constantius II. (20 frcs.), Julian II. (15 frcs.), Julian II. and Helena (20 frcs.), Helena (15 to 25 frcs.), Valentinian I. from *Wiczay* (40 frcs.), Valens (40 frcs.), and Gratian from *D'Ennery* (30 frcs.)

VOTA PVBLICA. Constantine I., standing, facing, between two females; the one to the left is turreted, and offers him a globe surmounted by a Victory; the other offers a crown; in the *exergue* P. TR. *(Prima Treveris.)* *Obv.* CONSTANTINVS P. F. AVG. Head of Constantine I. to r., laureated. *N*. (200 frcs.)

VOTA PVBLICA. The Emperor, standing, holding a globe and a sceptre—on small brass coins *(Quin.)* of Constantine II. from *D'Ennery* (25 frcs.)

VOTA PVBLICA. River-god, half naked, reclining to l., holding a boat, with the left elbow leaning on an urn. *Obv.* D. N. FL. CL. CONSTANTIVS NOB. CAES. Bust of Constantius Gallus to r., bare. *Æ*. III. *Quin.* (25 frcs.)

VOTA PVBLICA. Various types—Harpocrates, Isis seated or standing or kneeling, or in a car drawn by two mules—sometimes accompanied by Anubis, sometimes holding a baton at the end of which an hippopotamus; a female seated or standing, holding a cornucopiæ or a branch; Serapis; Anubis; the Nile, etc.—on small brass coins (sometimes *Quin.*) of Julian (with obv. leg. DEO SARAPIDI or SERAPIDI and VOTA PVBLICA), Julian and Helena, Helena (with ISIS FARIA and DEO SERAPIDI), Jovian, Valentinian I., Valens and Gratian (20 to 40 frcs.) The types of Isis occur on the second brass of some of these Emperors (60 frcs.)

VOTA PVBLICA. Isis and Osiris, their bodies ending in a serpent, facing each other, holding a vase out of which rises a serpent. *Obv.* DEO SERAPIDI. Bust of Julian II., bearded, to r., radiated with the *modius*. *Æ*. III. (40 frcs.) ; or his bust to l., diademed, with curly hair and long beard, and highly ornamented cuirass, holding a globe surmounted by a Victory and a buckler, on which is represented the wolf suckling Romulus and Remus. *Æ*. III. (50 frcs.)

VOTA PVBLICA. Two females (Furies ?) standing, facing each other, with serpents on their heads, each holding a dagger and perhaps a *sistrum*—on coins of Julian II. (*Æ*. II. 100 frcs., *Æ*. III. 60 frcs.) and of Julian II. and Helena. (*Æ*. III. 60 frcs.)

VOTA PVBLICA. Centaur walking to l. *Obv.* DEO SERAPIDI. Bust of Julian II., bearded, to l., with the *modius*. *Æ*. III. *Quin.* (40 frcs.)

VOTA PVBLICA. The two Emperors (Valentinian I. and Valens, or Valens and Valentinian I., or Gratian and Valentinian II., or Honorius and Arcadius) with *nimbus* seated facing, each holding a book and a globe; sometimes at their feet two captives, and sometimes a branch of laurel between their feet; various mint-marks in the *exergue*—on gold coins of Valentinian I., Valens, Gratian, and Honorius (50 to 100 frcs.)

VOTA PVBLICA. Hercules, naked, standing to l., holding club and lion's skin. *Obv.* D. N. GRATIANVS P. F. AVG. Bust of Gratian to r., diademed. Æ. (50 frcs.)

VOTA PVBLLC. *(sic).* Isis standing on a vessel to l., looking to r., and drawing the sail towards her. *Obv.* CONSTANTINVS AVG. Head of Constantine I. to r. Æ. III. *Quin.* (25 frcs.)

VOTA QVICAE. *(sic).* Carausius standing to r., to whom Rome, helmeted, holding a sceptre, seated to l. on a shield, presents a Victory. *Obv.* IMP. CARAVSIVS P. F. AVG. Bust of Carausius to r., radiated. Æ. III. *Bodleian Library, Oxford* (50 frcs.)

VOTA ROMANORVM. The Emperor standing holding the *labarum* and a shield; on the ground a captive; in the *exergue*, A. *Obv.* D. N. ARCADIVS P. F. AVG. Bust of Arcadius to r., diademed. Æ. Med. from *Tanini* and *Mionnet* (24 frcs.)

VOTA SOL. DEC. II. [or DECENN. II.] COS. IIII. *(Soluta Decennalia Secunda. Consul Quartum.)* Antoninus Pius standing to l., holding a *patera* over a lighted tripod, and a roll; at the foot of the tripod, a bull lying down —on gold (45 frcs.), silver (45 frcs.), large brass (6 frcs.) and second brass (3 frcs.) of Antoninus Pius. A similar type with legend VOT. SOL. DECENN. COS. III. occurs on gold (100 frcs.), silver (5 frcs.), large brass (6 frcs.), and second brass (3 frcs.) coins of Marcus Aurelius.

VOTA SOL. DEC. PONTIF. TR. P. XI. COS. III. S. C. *(Soluta Decennalia. Pontifex Tribunitiâ Potestate Undecimâ Consul Tertium.)* Caracalla standing to r., sacrificing on a tripod, behind which a flute-player standing facing; opposite Caracalla a *Victimarius* sacrificing a bull. *Obv.* ANTONINVS PIVS AVG. Bust of Caracalla to r., laureated. Æ. II. (15 frcs.)

VOTA SOLV. PRO. SAL. P. R. *(Soluta pro Salute Populi Romani.)* Commodus, veiled, standing to l., sacrificing on a tripod, behind which a victim—on silver coins (3 frcs.) of Commodus. A similar legend with, in addition, COS. VI. P. P. S. C., and with additions to the type— a *Victimarius* raising an axe against a bull held by the horns, and a flute-player, etc., occurs on the large brass (40 frcs.) of Commodus.

VOTA SOLVT. DEC. COS. III. *(Soluta Decennalia. Consul Tertium.)* Three figures standing, sacrificing at an altar; at the side a bull. *Obv.* SEVERVS PIVS AVG. Head of Septimius Severus to r., laureated. Æ. (plated) from *Welzl.* (3 frcs.)

VOTA SOLVT. DEC. COS. III. *(Soluta Decennalia. Consul Tertium.)* Caracalla, veiled, standing to r., sacrificing on a tripod; facing him a *Victimarius* raising his axe against a bull behind, a flute-player. *Obv.* ANTONINVS PIVS AVG. Head of Caracalla to r., unbearded and laureated. N from *Ancien Cataloque, Paris* (350 frcs.) [*Vota.*] A similar legend with Caracalla standing before a lighted tripod, holding a *patera* and a book, and behind a slain bull, occurs on his silver coins (6 frcs.)

VOTA SOLVTA DECENNALIVM COS. III. S. C. Marcus Aurelius standing to l., veiled, sacrificing at a tripod; at his feet a slain bull. *Obv.* IMP. M. ANTONINVS AVG. TR. P. XXV. Head of Marcus Aurelius to r., laureated. Æ. I. (6 frcs.)

VOTA SVSCEP. DEC. III. COS. IIII. *(Suscepta Decennalia Tertia. Consul Quartum.)* Antoninus Pius, veiled, standing to l., holding a *patera* above a lighted tripod and a roll, but *without* the bull at the foot of the tripod— on silver coins (3 to 6 frcs.) of Antoninus Pius.

VOTA SVSCEP. DECEN. *(Suscepta Decennalia)* P. M. TR. P., etc. Commodus, veiled, standing to l., sacrificing at a tripod—on large (6 frcs.) and second brass (3 frcs.) of Commodus.

VOTA SVSCEP. DECEN. *(Suscepta Decennalia)* S. C. Septimius Severus, veiled, standing to l., accompanied by three persons, and sacrificing at a lighted altar before a hexastyle Temple; facing are two persons standing and a *Victimarius* killing a bull; above, behind the altar, a flute-player standing facing—on large brass (100 frcs.) and second brass (100 frcs.) coins of Septimius Severus.

VOTA SVSCEP. DECENN. II. COS. III. *(Suscepta Decennalia Secunda. Consul Tertium.)* Marcus Aurelius, veiled, standing to l., sacrificing at a tripod; but *without* a slain bull—on gold (100 frcs.) and silver coins (5 frcs.) of Marcus Aurelius; or Marcus Aurelius standing, placing a grain of incense in the flame on a tripod—on large brass (5 frcs.) and second brass (3 frcs.) coins of Marcus Aurelius.

VOTA SVSCEP. DECENN. III. COS. IIII. *(Suscepta Decennalia Tertia. Consul Quartum.)* Antoninus Pius, veiled, standing to l., sacrificing at a tripod; but *without* a slain bull—on silver (3 frcs.) and large brass coins (6 frcs.) of Antoninus Pius.

VOTA SVSCEPTA (in *exergue*) P. M. TR. P. COS. VI. P. P. S. P. Q. R. (around). The Genius of the Senate standing to r., sacrificing at an altar in the presence of the Genius of the Roman people, also standing and holding a *patera* and a cornucopiæ—on gold (150 frcs.) and silver coins (50 frcs.) of Trajan. On the obverse there is sometimes a globe below the bust. A similar type occurs on the brass medallions of Hadrian (300 frcs.)

VOTA SVSCEPTA, within a wreath of oak— on gold (60 frcs.) and second brass coins (30 frcs.) of Hadrian.

VOTA SVSCEPTA DEC. III. COS. IIII. S. C. *(Decennalia Tertia. Consul Quartum.)* Antoninus Pius, veiled, standing to l., holding a *patera* above a lighted tripod and a roll; but *without* a victim—on large brass (6 frcs.) and second brass (3 to 8 frcs.) of Antoninus Pius. On a silver coin (6 frcs.) of same type the legend is VOTA SVSCEPTA DECENNAL. III., etc.

VOTA SVSCEPTA DECENNALIA S. C. Type similar to that on coins with legend VOTA SVSCEP. DECEN. S. C. *(q. v.)*—on second brass coins (100 frcs.) of Septimius Severus, from *Wiczay.*

VOTA SVSCEPTA FELICIA P. M. TR. P. XV. IMP. VII. (? VIII.)   Two figures sacrificing at an altar—on brass medallions (? 200 frcs.) of Commodus, from *Vaillant.*

VOTA SVSCEPTA X. [or XX.]   *(Decennalia [or Vicennalia]).* The Emperor standing to l., sacrificing at a lighted tripod—on silver coins of Septimius Severus (3 frcs.) and Caracalla (6 frcs.)

VOTA SVSCEPTA XX. *(Vicennalia.)* Severus standing to r., sacrificing at a lighted tripod, facing him a lictor (?) standing, holding a rod and *fasces* [FASCES—*Lictores*] ; above Concord, veiled, standing— on gold (300 frcs.) and silver coins (25 frcs.) of Septimius Severus. A somewhat similar type, but, instead of Concord, a flute-player, occurs on his large brass coins (60 frcs.)

VOTA SVSCEPTA XX. *(Vicennalia.)* Severus and Caracalla sacrificing at a tripod ; between them, behind the tripod, a flute-player. *Obv.* ANTONINVS PIVS AVG.   Head of Caracalla to r., laureated. Æ. (50 frcs.)

VOTA SVSCEPTA XX. *(Vicennalia.)* Priest sacrificing at a tripod. *Obv.* IVLIA AVGVSTA. Head of Julia Domna. Æ. from *Khell.* (Hybrid coin.)

VOTA VICENNALIOR *(sic).*   Constantine II., laureated, seated to l., on a throne, holding a human head and a sceptre. *Obv.* CONSTANTINVS IVN. NOB. C. *(Junior Nobilis Cæsar.)* Bust of Constantine II. to r., laureated. Æ. III. *Quin.* (25 frcs.)

VOTA VIGENNALIA COS. IIII. Antoninus Pius sacrificing at a tripod, but *without* a victim—on gold (200 frcs.) and large brass coins (50 frcs.) of Antoninus Pius.

VOTA X. DD. NN. AVG. ET CAES. *(Decennalia Dominorum Nostrorum Augusti et Cæsaris.)* Two Victories standing, holding a wreath within which VOT. X. *(Votis Decennalibus.)* *Obv.* D. N. *(Dominus Noster)* MAGNENTIVS P. F. AVG. Bust of Magnentius to r., bare. Æ. III. from *Banduri.* Cohen *(Méd. Imp.,* 1st ed., vol. vi., p. 337) remarks that the legend of the reverse appears to be defective.

VOTA XX. Є. (in *exergue.*)   The Amphitheatre of Constantinople ; two *quadrigæ,* wild animals, two gladiators fighting, etc. *Obv.* D. N. PLA. VALENTINIANVS P. F. AVG. Bust of Valentinian III. to r., diademed. Contorniate (peu rare). See Sabatier, *Mon. Contorn.,* p. 60., pl, viii., No. 9. Cohen *(Méd. Imp.,* 1st ed., vol. vi., p. 504) says the specimen of this piece in the *Cabinet des Médailles, Paris,* is cast from the antique, and he does not know where authentic specimens exist.

VOTIS DECENNALIB *(us),* within a wreath

of laurel—on gold (200 frcs.) and *billon* coins (2 frcs.) of Gallienus.

VOTIS DECENNALIBVS. Septimius Severus, veiled, standing to l., sacrificing at a lighted tripod. *Obv.* L. SEPT. SEV. AVG. IMP. XI. PART. MAX. Head of Septimius Severus to r., laureated. Æ. (3 frcs.)

VOTIS DECENNALIBVS, within a wreath of oak—on gold from *Caylus* (180 frcs.) and silver coins (6 frcs.) of Septimius Severus.

VOTIS DECENNALIBVS, within a wreath of laurel—on coins of Maximinus I. (Æ. 20 frcs., Æ. I. 15 frcs., Æ. II. 8 frcs.), Balbinus (N. from *Vaillant,* Æ. 30 frcs., Æ. I. 25 frcs., Æ. II. 70 frcs.), Pupienus (N. from *Vaillant,* Æ. 30 frcs., Æ. I. 25 frcs., Æ. II. 80 frcs.), Gordianus Pius (Æ. 50 frcs., Æ. I. 15 frcs., Æ. II. from *Vaillant* 20 frcs.), Philip I. (Æ. I. 12 frcs., Æ. II. 6 frcs.), Philip II. (Æ. I. from *Mionnet* 25 frcs., Æ. II. 12 frcs.), Trajan Decius (Æ. 25 frcs., Æ. I. 20 frcs., Æ. II. 6 frcs.), Herennius (Æ. 30 frcs.), Hostilian (Æ. I. 50 frcs.), Trebonianus Gallus (Æ. 20 frcs., Æ. I. 10 frcs., Æ. II. 8 frcs.), Volusian (Æ. from *Vaillant* 10 frcs., Æ. I. 8 frcs., Æ. II. 6 frcs.), Æmilian (Æ. 30 frcs., Æ. I. 100 frcs., Æ. II. 60 frcs.), Valerian I. *(Bil.* 10 frcs., Æ. I. 6 frcs., Æ. II. 3 frcs.), and Gallienus *(Bil.* 2 frcs., Æ. Med. 120 frcs., Æ. I. 8 frcs., Æ. II. 5 frcs.)

VOTIS DECENNALIBVS. Victory standing to r., placing foot on globe and writing X on a shield which she holds on her knee. *Obv.* IMP. C. *(Cæsar)* TETRICVS AVG. Three-quarter bust of Tetricus I. N. *Quin.* (800 frcs.)

VOTIS FELICIBVS. Commodus standing to l., wearing pontifical robes, and holding *patera* and scroll, sacrificing at a tripod placed at entrance of the harbour of Ostia, towards which three galleys and two small boats are approaching—first a galley with four soldiers, and having at the prow two military standards ; behind it a vessel in full sail, having a *vexillum* at prow and piloted by Jupiter Serapis or *Fortuna dux,* seated at the stern ; above, a similar vessel in full sail, preceded by small boat with single oarsman ; below, a small boat with single oarsman, and near it a buoy (?). The Emperor is accompanied by a priest who stands behind the tripod ; behind the Emperor a *pharos* (Ostia), and beneath on the sea-shore a slain bull. *Obv.* IMP. COMMODVS

AVG. PIVS FELIX. Bust of Commodus to r., laureated and draped (Æ. Med. 500 frcs.) or three-quarter bust, laureated, draped, and with cuirass (800 frcs.); or M. *(Marcus)* COMMODVS ANTONINVS PIVS FELIX AVG. BRIT. *(Augustus Britannicus).* Bust of Commodus to l., laureated, draped, and with cuirass, or to r. with the *ægis* (500 frcs.), or COMMODVS ANTONINVS PIVS FELIX AVG. BRIT. Bust of Commodus to r., laureated, and with cuirass in scales (500 frcs.)

The type of these large brass medallions, which were issued in A.D. 191, refers to the African fleet established by Commodus in A.D. 186, as testified by coins of that year with the legend PROVID. AVG. *(Providentia Augusti)* and the type a ship in full sail, to search for corn in Africa, in case the Egyptian harvest failed (Classem Africanam instituit : quæ subsidio esset si forte Alexandrina frumenta cessassent—Lamprid. *in Comm.,* 17.) The fleet has returned successful and the vows have been granted (Cf. A. Chabouillet, *Rev. Num.,* 1841, vol. iv., p. 349; H. A. Grueber, *Cat. of the Roman Medallions in the British Museum,* 1874, p. 31, Nos. 44-46; W. Froehner, *Les Médaillons de l'Empire Romain,* 1878, pp. 124, 125; Cohen, *Méd. Imp.,* 2nd ed., 1883, vol. iii., pp. 356, 357.)

VOTIS FELICIBVS. Similar type, the vessels varying in number of rowers and other details; in the *exergue* SIS. *(Sisciæ.) Obv.* IMP. C. C. VAL. *(Cæsar Caius Valerius)* DIOCLE- TIANVS P. F. AVG. Bust of Diocletian to l., laureated with Imperial mantle, holding a sceptre surmounted by an eagle. Æ. Med. (400 frcs.)

The reverse of this medallion is copied from those of Commodus above described. It is not certain on what occasion it was coined, but in all probability it commemorates a military action, perhaps the return of the expedition from Africa, in which Maximian I. in A.D. 297 defeated the *Quinquegentiani* or confederacy of five warlike clans of the mountain range Atlas, in Maurc- tania. (Cf. A. de Longpérier, *Rev. Num.,* 1865, p. 403, pl. xviii., 2; Cohen, *Méd. Imp.,* 1st ed., *Suppl.,* 1868, vol. vii.. p, 343, pl. vii., 2nd ed., vol. vi., p. 475; W. Froehner, *Les Médaillons de l'Empire Romain,* 1878, p. 261.)

VOTIS MVLTIS. Majorian standing facing, holding a spear and a shield, ornamented with a star; in the *field* an unknown symbol. *Obv.* D. N. *(Dominus Noster)* MAIORIANVS P. F. AVG. Helmeted bust of Majorian to r., holding a spear, or helmeted bust to r., having at the top of the left arm a *fibula,* ornamented with ✠ . (Banduri) Æ. (100 frcs.)

VOTIS MVLTIS. Majorian and Leo I. seated facing, each holding a *mappa* and a cross; between them, in the *field* RV. *(Ravennæ)* ; in the *exergue* COMOB. [see p. 835]. *Obv.* D. N. IVL. [or IVLIVS] MAIORIANVS P. F. AVG. Bust of Majorian facing, diademed, with the Imperial mantle, holding a *mappa* and a cross. N. (100 frcs.)

VOTIS PVBLICIS (in *exergue)* [*Restitu- tori*] GALLIARVM (around.) Victorinus I. standing to l., between Victory, who is crowning him, and who holds a palm, and Felicity, who holds a sceptre and a cornucopiæ, raising a turreted female (Gaul). *Obv.* IMP. CAES. VICTORINVS PIVS FELIX. AVG. Bust of Victorinus I. to r. Æ. Med. (1200 frcs.)

VOTIS ROMANORVM. Two Victories stand- ing, holding a panel on which SIC. XX. SIC. XXX. ; in the *exergue* AQ. *(Aquileiæ.) Obv.* DIOCLETIANVS P. F. AVG. Head of Diocletian to r., laureated. N. (200 frcs.)

VOTIS VIGENNALIBVS, within a wreath of laurel—on gold (150 frcs.) and silver coins (30 frcs.) of Alexander Severus.

VOTIS V. *(Quinquennalibus)* within a wreath of laurel; in the *exergue* P. CON. *(Prima Con- stantinæ*—Arles.) *Obv.* D. N. MAG. *(Dominus Noster Magnus)* MAXIMVS P. F. AVG. Bust of Maximus to r., diademed. Æ. III, from *Ban- duri* (1 frc.)

VOTIS V. *(Quinquennalibus)* MVLTIS X. *(Decennalibus.)* Victory standing, holding a shield on a *cippus ;* on the shield VICTORIA AVG. ; in the *exergue,* various mint-marks—on gold coins of Licinius I. (300 frcs.) and Constantine I. (80 frcs.)

VOTIS V. *(Quinquennalibus)* MVLTIS X. *(Decennalibus)* within a laurel wreath ; in the *ex- ergue,* various mint-marks— on silver coins of Con- stantius Gallus (40 frcs.), Julian II. (2 to 6 frcs.), Jovian (Med. 200 frcs.), Valentinian I. (Med. 60 frcs., Æ. 6 frcs.), Valens (Med. 40 frcs.), Gratian (Med. 60 frcs.), Magnus Maxi- mus (Med. 300 frcs.), Constantius III. (from *Mionnet* 200 frcs.), and Jovinus (30 frcs.)

VOTIS X. *(Decennalibus.)* Diocletian and Maximian Hercules sacrificing at an altar—on small brass coins of Diocletian, from *D'Ennery* (50 frcs.), and Maximian Hercules (6 frcs.) Also on gold medallion of Maximian Hercules, from *Mionnet* (800 frcs.)

VOTIS X. *(Decennalibus),* within a laurel wreath—on small brass coins *(Quin.)* of Con- stantius Chlorus, from *Tanini* (10 frcs.) and Con- stantine I. (3 frcs.)

VOTIS X. *(Decennalibus.)* Galerius Max- imian, laureated, standing to l., sacrificing on a lighted altar. *Obv.* MAXIMIANVS NOB. C. *(No- bilis Cæsar.)* Bust of Galerius Maximian to r., radiated. Æ. III. from *Banduri* (10 frcs.)

VOTIS X. CAESS. NN. MNΓ. *(Decen- nalibus Cæsarum Nostrorum. Moneta Nicomediæ* 3) in four lines within a wreath, on top of which an eagle. *Obv.* D. N. *(Dominus Noster)* CON- STANTINVS IVN. NOB. CAES. *(Junior Nobilis Cæsar.)* Bust of Constantine II. to r., diademed.

VOTIS X. ET XX. *(Decennalibus et Vicen- nalibus),* within a wreath of laurel—on gold (200 to 250 frcs.) and *billon* coins (10 frcs.) of Gal- lienus.

VOTIS X. ET XX. *(Decennalibus et Vicen- nalibus.)* Tacitus standing to l., holding a spear reversed, and crowned by Valour, helmeted, standing, leaning on a shield : facing him, Victory seated to r., on a cuirass, holding on her knees a shield on which VOTIS XX. *Obv.* IMP. C. M. CL. *(Imperator Cæsar Marcus Claudius)* TACITVS P. F. AVG. Bust of Tacitus to the waist to l., with *Ægis,* holding a spear. Æ. II. (100 frcs.)

VOTIS X. ET XX. FEL. *(Decennalibus et Vicennalibus Felicibus)*, within a wreath of laurel. *Obv.* VIRTVS PROBI AVG. Bust of Probus to l., radiated, holding a spear. Æ. III. (30 frcs.)

VOTIS X. MVLT. XV. *(Votis Decennalibus Multis Quindecennalibus)*, within a wreath of laurel, in the *exergue?*—on silver medallion of Valentinian I., from *D'Ennery* (60 frcs.) Same type with VOTIS MVLTIS XV. on silver medallion of Valens (40 frcs.)

VOTIS X. MVLTIS XX. *(Votis Decennalibus Multis Vicennalibus)*, within laurel wreath *;* in *exergue* various mint-marks—on silver coins of Valens from *Tanini* (10 frcs.) and silver medallions (60 frcs.) and silver coins (10 frcs.) of Gratian.

VOTIS X. PROBI ET XX. *(Votis Decennalibus Probi et Vicennalibus)*, within a laurel wreath—on small brass coins (30 frcs.) of Probus.

VOTIS X. SIC XX. *(Votis Decennalibus Sic Vicennalibus)*, within a laurel wreath. *Obv.* MAXIMIANVS N. C. *(Nobilis Cæsar.)* *N.* Quin. (200 frcs.)

VOTIS XV. MVLTIS XX. *(Votis Quindecennalibus Multis Vicennalibus)*, within a laurel wreath; in the *exergue* various mint-marks—on silver medallions of Valens (40 frcs.) and on silver medallions (80 frcs.), and silver coins of Gratian from *Beger* and *Mionnet* (15 frcs.).

VOTIS XX. *(Vicennalibus)*, within a wreath —on silver coins from *Welzl* (60 frcs.) and small brass from *Banduri* (3 frcs.) of Constantine I.

VOTIS XX. COS. VI. *(Vicennalibus. Consul Sextum)* within a laurel wreath. *Obv.* M. COMM. ANT. P. FEL. AVG. BRIT. P. P. Head of Commodus to r., laureated. Æ. (50 frcs.)

VOTIS XX. *(Vicennalibus)* MVLTIS XXX. *(Tricennalibus)*, within a laurel wreath ; in the *exergue* various mint-marks—on silver coins of Constantine I. (60 frcs.), Constantine II. (60 frcs.), and Constantius II. (6 frcs.)

VOTIS XXV. *(Quinque-Vicennalibus)* MVL. TIS XXX. *(Tricennalibus)*, within laurel wreath ; in the *exergue*, mint-marks—on silver coins of Constantius II. (6 frcs.)

VOTIS XXX. *(Tricennalibus)* within a laurel wreath—on small brass coins (10 frcs.) of Maximian Hercules and gold medallions, with *exergual* letters TS **Є** *Thessalonicæ* 5, (400 frcs.) of Constantine I.

VOTIS XXX. *(Tricennalibus)* MVLTIS XXXX. *(Quadragennalibus)* within a laurel wreath ; in the *exergue*, mint-marks—on silver coins of Constantius II. (3 to 6 frcs.) and Julian II. (15 frcs.)

Votivus Clypeus [see CL. V. *Clypeus Votivus*]. I have already pointed out [p. 831] that Cavedoni interprets the letters CL. V. as *Clypeus Virtutis.*

Votivi Ludi. [see p. 525.]

VOTO PVBLICO, around a laurel wreath, within which MVLTIS XX. IMP. *(Vicennalibus Imperatoris) ;* or around a lighted altar, on which MVLTIS XX. IMP. ; in the *exergue*, R. S. R. *Obv.* IMP. CARAVSIVS P. F. AVG. Bust of Carausius to r., laureated. Æ. (350 frcs.)

VOTVM PVBLIC *(um)* around a lighted altar, on which MVLTIS XX. IMP. ; in the *exergue* R. S. R. Same obverse as previous coin. Æ. (350 frcs.)

Vowels, double, occur on the coins of the Cornelia *gens*—FEELIX for FELIX [CORNELIA GENS; FEELIX] ; and of the Numonia *gens*— VAALA for VALA [NVMONIA; VAALA].

VR. *Urbani*—AP. CL. T. MAL. Q. **VR.** *Appius Claudius, Titus Mallius, Quæstores Urbani,* or T. MAL. AP. CL. Q. **VR.**—on silver coins of the Claudia and Mallia *gentes* (Mommsen, *Mon. Rom.*, vol. ii., p. 387, Lenormant, *La Mon. dans l'Antiq.*, vol. iii., p. 150 ; Babelon, *Mon. de la Répub. Rom.*, vol. i., p. 346 ; vol. ii., p. 169. [See VRBINIA GENS.]

VR. *Urbis*—REGVLVS F. PRAEF. VR. *Regulus Filius Præfectus Urbis*—on silver coins of Regulus (son of Regulus the Prætor), *Præfectus Urbis* in B.C. 45. [*Livineia.*]

VRANI NICA. In *exergue* MVNIO. Athlete and Cupid. *Obv.* . . . Head of Trajan. Contorniate (c.)

VRANIVS ANTONINVS (Lucius Julius Aurelius Sulpicius) a usurper in the East under Alexander Severus (A.D. 223—235). According to Zosimus (i., 12) two usurpers took up arms in the East against Alexander Severus, one named *Antoninus*, the other *Uranius ;* whilst Aurelius Victor states *(Epit.* xl.) that a certain *Taurinus*, having been proclaimed Augustus, was so horrified that he threw himself into the Euphrates. There is not much difficulty in identifying the *Uranius* of Zosimus with the *Taurinus* of Victor, and as the two names *Uranius* and *Antoninus* occur on the same coins it is evident that Zosimus has made two persons out of one usurper. Some Greek Imperial coins struck at Emesa, which have been attributed to a usurper at the time of Valerian, as well as a coin struck at Antioch, all bearing the legend AYTOK. COYΛΠ. ANTⱲNINOC CЄB., most probably belong to the *Sulpicius Uranius Antoninus*, whose Latin coins are described below, and that these should be assigned to the time of Alexander Severus is proved by their style which is that of the Syrian fabric of the coins of Elagabalus. A good account is given of Uranius Antoninus by the late M. Ch. Lenormant *(Rev. Num.*, 1843, p. 255 ; cf. Madden; *Num. Chron.*, N.S., vol. v., p. 48). The coins of this usurper are of great rarity.

I. *Obv.* L. IVL. AVR. SVLP. VRA. ANTONINVS. Bust to r., laureated, with *paludamentum* and cuirass. *Rev.* CONSERVATOR AVG. *(Augusti.)* A conical sacred stone, enveloped in a shawl, the ends of which are fastened in front with a brooch (?), on either side a parasol. *N*. (0000 frcs.)

Cohen *(Méd. Imp.*, 1st ed. and 2nd ed., vol. iv., p. 503), describes the brooch (?) as "un objet qui paraît être la représentation des parties sexuelles extérieures de la femme." The conical stone represents the God "Elagabal," or the Sun, to whom the Emperor Elagabalus was priest and high priest, as testified by his coins (INVICTVS SACERDOS AVG.; SANCT. DEO SOLI ELAGABAL; SACERD. DEI SOLIS ELAGABAL.; SVMMVS SACERDOS AVG.) [ELAGABALVS.]

2. *Obv.* L. IVL. AVR. SVL[P. A]NTONINVS. Same bust to l. *Rev.* CONSERVATOR AVG. *(Augusti).* *Quadriga* to l., on which the conical sacred stone of Elagabal, ornamented with an eagle; on either side a parasol. *N*. (3000 frcs.)

3. *Obv.* Same legend and type as No. 1. *Rev.* FECVNDITAS AVG. *(Augusti.)* Fecundity (with the attributes of Fortune) standing to l., holding a rudder and a cornucopiæ. *N*. (3000 frcs.)

Eckhel (vol. vii., p. 289) doubted this coin, but as M. Ch. Lenormant *(op. cit.)* has suggested, the value of Latin words could not have been understood in the town in which this piece was struck. (Cf. Madden, *Num. Chron.*, N.S., 1865, vol. v., p. 50.)

4. *Obv.* Same legend and type as No. 1. *Rev.* MINERVA VICTRIX. Minerva standing to l., holding spear and shield. *N*. (3000 frcs.)

The following Colonial coins of Uranius Antoninus were struck at Ælia Capitolina (De Saulcy, *Num. de la Terre Sainte*, p. 104; Madden, *Coins of the Jews*, p. 270) :—

1. *Obv.* IMP. ANTONIN. Bust to r., laureated, with *paludamentum* and cuirass. *Rev.* COL. A. C. C. P. F. *(Colonia Ælia Capitolina Commodiana Pia Felix.)* *Quadriga* facing, on which is placed the conical stone of the god "Elagabal"; in the *exergue*, uncertain object. Æ. II.

2. *Obv.* . . . . P. M. AVG. (?) ANT. Head to r., laureated. *Rev.* COL. A. C. C. P. F. Jupiter in a *quadriga*. Æ. II.

The existence of coins of Uranius Antoninus struck at Ælia Capitolina, will probably explain the great rarity of those of Severus Alexander struck in this colony. The name *Commodiana* was given to the colony by Commodus. (Madden, *Coins of the Jews*, p. 262.)

VRB. *Urbanus.*—NERI Q. VRB. *Nerius Quæstor Urbanus*, on silver coins of the Claudia, Cornelia, and Neria *gentes*, struck in B.C. 49.

VRB. *Urbica.*—MON. VRB. *Moneta Urbica*, on the provincial tetradrachms, struck by Philip I. at Antiochia Syriæ.

VRB. *Urbis*—L. PLANC. PR. [or PRAEF.] VRB. *Lucius Plancus Præfectus Urbis*, on gold coins *(Aurei* and *quinarii)* of Julius Cæsar, struck in B.C. 46.—ANN. DCCCLXXIIII NAT. VRB. P. CIR. CON. *Anno* 874 *Natali Urbis primum* [or *populo] Circenses constituti*, on gold and large brass coins and brass medallions of Hadrian. This is the first and only coin giving a date from the foundation of Rome. The year 874 =

A.D. 121. The explanation of the letter P. is difficult, and has been variously interpreted as *Plebeiis, Populi*, or *Primum*. The whole legend, however, is probably intended to record that Hadrian, in celebrating the eight hundred and seventy-fourth birthday of Rome by holding the *Palilia*, added for the *first time* (or gave *to the people* in addition) to their simple games the splendid exhibitions of the circus (cf. Athenæus, *Deipnosoph.* viii., 63). [See ANN. DCCCLXXIII NAT. VRB., etc.]—INT. VRB. *Introitus Urbis*, on large and second brass coins of Gallienus, with the obverse legend GENIVS P. R. *(Populi Romani.)* These coins are generally attributed to the reign of Gallienus, but it is not known on what occasion they were struck. It may be that they were issued in A.D. 263, after the siege of Byzantium (Mommsen, *Mon. Rom.*, vol. iv., p. 92.)—CONSER. VRB. SVAE. *Conservator Urbis suæ*, on silver coins of Maxentius from *Banduri*—CONSERV. VRB. SVAE, on silver and second brass coins of Maximian Hercules, and on second brass coins of Maxentius and Constantine I.—CONSERVATORES VRB. SVAE, on second brass coins of Maximian Hercules, Maxentius, and Constantine I.—CONSERVATORI VRB. SVAE, on a gold coin of Maxentius from *Tanini*.—S. M. VRB. AVGG. ET CAESS. NN. *Sacra Moneta Urbis Augustorum et Cæsarum Nostrorum*, on second brass coins of Maximian Hercules and Constantius Chlorus—SAC. MON. VRB. AVGG. ET CAESS. NN., on second brass coins of Diocletian, Maximian Hercules, Constantius Chlorus, Galerius Maximian, Severus II., Maximinus II. Daza, and Constantine I. (rare)—SACRA MON. VRB. AVGG. ET CAESS. NN., on second brass coins of Diocletian, Maximian Hercules, Constantius Chlorus, and Galerius Maximian.

VRB. *Urbs.*—VRB. VIC. OSCA. *Urbs Victrix Osca* on coins of Osca Hispaniæ. [VRB. VIC. OSCA.]

VRB. *Urbs.*—ROMA S. (?), in the *exergue*, VRB., *Urbs*, Rome, seated to l., before an altar, holding a *patera* and a spear. *Obv.* IMP. CAE. L. SEPT. SEV. PERT. AVG. COS. II. Head of Septimius Severus to r. Æ. Med. (60 frcs.)

VRBANAE.—PLEBEI [or PLENEI] VRBANAE FRVMENTO CONSTITVTO, on large brass coins of Nerva, struck in A.D. 97.

Urbani—Quæstores Urbani. [VR *Urbani.*]

VRBEM RESTITVTAM S. C. Vitellius standing to l., followed by two soldiers, raising Rome from her knees. *Obv.* A. *(Aulus)* VITELLIVS GERMANICVS IMP. TRI. P. *(Imperator Tribunitiâ Potestate).* Bust of Vitellius to r. Between Æ. I. and Æ. II. (150 frcs.)

Urbes monetariæ inferioris ævi.—At the time when the earlier portion of this Dictionary was written the study of *mint-marks* was comparatively in its infancy, though the late M. Sabatier in his work entitled *Production de l'or, de l'argent, et du cuivre chez les anciens et hôtels monetaires Romaines et Byzantines*, 1850, had to a certain extent attempted an account of them. It was reserved for the late Count de Salis, who gave his magnificent collection of Roman and Byzantine coins to the British Museum, to develop this interesting subject, which has also received much attention from the present writer. The following works may be consulted:—Madden, *Handbook to Rom. Num,* 1861, pp. 155—160; *Num. Chron.,* N.S., vol. i., 1861, pp. 112—127, 175—184; vol. ii., 1862, pp. 39—63, 240—258; de Salis, *Arch. Journal,* vol. xxiv., July, 1866, reprinted in *Num. Chron.,* N.S., 1867, pp. 321—328, 57—62. [See *Remarks on the explanation of the letters* OB, etc., under VALENTINIANVS I.]

Londinium (London) *Mint-marks:*—L., LN., LON. AVGOB., AVG. The mint of London was established by the usurper Carausius about A.D. 290—293, and was suppressed about the time of the dedication of Constantinople by Constantine I., in A.D. 330. It was revived under Magnus Maximus in A.D. 383, who issued gold coins with the mint-marks AVG. OB. *(Augustæ,* 72), and silver with AVG. P. S. *(Augustæ Pecunia Signata.)* Ammianus Marcellinus states (xxvii., 8; xxviii., 3) that in his time (*circ.,* A.D. 380) *Londinium* (or as he writes it *Lundinium)* was called *Augusta* [see *Remarks on the letters* OB., etc., under VALENTINIANVS I.], and in the Chorography of Ravenna (ed. Pinder and Parthey, p. 429, Berlin, 1860), the name is given as *Londinium Augusta.* A *solidus* of Theodosius I. with the same reverse ((VICTORIA AVGG.) and type, as on the coins of Magnus Maximus, has also the *exergual* letters AVGOB. It was probably not struck at London, but belongs to the numerous series of barbarous imitations of the time.

Camulodunum or *Colonia?* (Colchester or Maldon?). *Mint-marks:* C., CL. This mint was established by Carausius A.D. 290—293, and disappears after the reign of Allectus, A.D. 296. Only brass coins exist with this mint-mark.

Treveri (Treves). *Mint-marks:*—TR., TROB., TR. (in *field)* COM. (in *exergue.)* Treves was established as a mint at the time of the monetary reform under Diocletian, A.D. 296—301.—TR. OB *(Treveris,* 72) occurs for the first time on the gold coins of Valentinianus I., and may also be found on the coins of Valens, Gratian, Magnus Maximus, Victor, Valentinianus II., and Theodosius I., as well as on those of Constantine III., usurper in Britain and Gaul A.D. 407—411. —TR. COM. was introduced under Valentinianus II. and Theodosius I. Gaul seems never to have recovered from the effects of the usurpation of Eugenius A.D. 392, and although Theodosius I. reconquered it, he did not live long enough to establish complete power there. Late in A.D. 406 the Vandals invaded Gaul, and commenced the destruction of Treves, and in A.D. 413 the Franks, who had sided with Jovinus, and of whom there are coins with TR. in the *field,* and COMOB. in the *exergue,* in order to avenge his murder by Dardanus, prefect of Honorius, again sacked the town and reduced it to ashes.

Lugdunum (Lyons). *Mint-marks:*—L., LG., LVG., LD. (in *field)* COM. or COMOB. (in *exergue).* Lyons was established as a mint by Gallienus between A.D. 253—268, of whom there are *billon* coins of the same fabric as those of Pos-

tumus. It was suppressed after the death of Eugenius by order of Theodosius I. in A.D. 394, but was restored for a short time by the usurpers Constantine III. in A.D. 407—411 (S. M. LD. *Signata Moneta Lugduni,* Æ.; LD. in *field,* COMOB. in *exergue, N.),* and Jovinus in A.D. 411 —413 (S. M. LD., LVG., Æ.; LD. in *field,* COMOB. in *exergue, N.)*

Arelate or *Constantina* (Arles). *Mint-marks:* A., AR., ARL., CON., CONST., KA., KON., KONT., KONST., KONSN̄. *(Konstan.),* KONOB. The mint of Arles was established by Constantine I. after A.D. 306, and coins with the mint-marks A., AR., or ARL., were not coined after the time of Constantius Gallus, A.D. 354.—The new name of *Constantina* was given to *Arelate* by Constantine I., when he improved the town and built a new one on the opposite side of the Rhone, after the overthrow of Maxentius and Maximinus Daza, A.D. 312—313. Ausonius *(Urbes Claræ,* No. 8) calls "Arelate" *duplex,* and says that there was a bridge of boats on the river. The mint-marks of *Constantina* CON. and CONST. are likely to be confounded with the mint-marks of *Constantinople* CON. and CONS. [*Constantinopolis*]; but CON. or CONST. *(Constantina)* is always *preceded* by a *Latin* differential letter, or accompanied by OF. *(Officina)* I., II., III. in the *field* of the reverse, whilst CON. or CONS. *(Constantinopolis)* is always *followed* by a *Greek* numeral.—KONSTAN. *(Constantina)* may be found on the gold coins of Constantius II., Julian the Apostate, Valentinian I., and Valens. On some large silver coins of Valentinian I. and Valens the mint-mark KA. occurs, the *exergual* letters being S. M. KAP. This P. cannot be a *Greek* P being too low. in the alphabet to be used as a differential letter, and the mint-mark may be interpreted *Signata Moneta Konstantina Prima.* This is the only instance where the final letter is used in a mint-mark (if we may except SM. *Sirmium),* the object in this case being to show its difference from Constantinople (C. *never* K.), and Cyzicus (K.) These coins cannot be attributed to *Carthage* for the three following reasons:—1. If we give these coins to Carthage we must suppose that that mint was restored for a very short time *only* under Valentinianus I. and Gratianus, as no other coins attributable to it are found from the time of Maxentius and Alexander Tyrannus down to the Vandal period. 2. We must suppose that *silver* only were struck there. 3. We must take no notice whatever of the fabric which is decidedly Gallic.—Constantina (Arles) was suppressed after the death of Eugenius in A.D. 394, but was restored for a short time by the usurpers Constantine III. in A.D. 407—411; (KONT. *Constantinæ,* Æ., and KON. OB *Constantinæ* 72, *N.),* and Jovinus and Sebastianus A.D. 411—413; (KONT. *Constantinæ,* Æ.)

Constantina [*Arelate*].

Ambianum (Amiens). *Mint-marks:*—AMB. This mint was established by Magnentius, usurper in Gaul A.D. 350—353, and continued under Decentius, Constantius II., and Constantius Gallus. It was suppressed soon after the death of Magnentius by Constantius II. Only brass coins were issued.

Tarraco (Tarragona). *Mint-mark :*—T. The mint of Tarraco was established by Aurelian A.D. 270—275. The first pieces struck there bear the marks P. XXT., S. XXT., T. XXT., Q. XXT., V. XXT., VI. XXT. *Prima XX Tarracone, Secunda XX Tarracone, Tertia XX Tarracone, Quarta XX Tarracone, Quinta XX Tarracone, Sexta XX Tarracone.* [XX.] The usual *exergual* letters are P. T., S. T., T. T., etc., *Prima, Secunda, Tertia,* etc., *Tarracone.* This new mint was the suggestion of the late Count de Salis, who removed from Treves to Tarraco, the coins whose fabric approaches most that of the mints of Italy. The letter T. also stands for *Thessalonicæ (q. v.)* Tarraco was suppressed at the same time as London, A.D. 330.

Karthago (Carthage). *Mint-marks :*—K. and KART. (as part of legend). Carthage was established as a mint at the time of the monetary reform under Diocletian [SALVIS AVGG. ET CAESS. AVCTA (or FEL.) KART., CONSERVATOR or CONSERVATORES KART. SVAE, FELIX CARTHAGO or KARTHAGO]. It was transferred to Ostia by Maxentius in consequence of the revolt of Alexander, A.D. 311 [ALEXANDER] and was suppressed or transferred to Arles by Constantine I. The mint of Carthage reappears in the Byzantine coinage (CAR., KAR., CART., KART., CARTA., CT., CPTS., KPTS., KARTAGO) from the time of Justinian I., A.D. 534, to that of Justinian II. Rhinotmetus, A.D. 685—695. Carthage was taken by the Vandal king Genseric in A.D. 439, but no coins were struck by him. Hilderic coined pieces A.D. 523—530 with the legend FELIX KARTC. Vandal large brass coins without the name of any king exist with the legend KARTHAGO, and of Justinian II. with KARTAGO. The Vandal kingdom was overthrown, and Carthage taken by Belisarius, general of Justinian I., in A.D. 534. The letter K. preceded by P. *(Prima)* i.e. *Prima Karthagini* belongs to Carthage, and when alone to Cyzicus. KA. on coins before the time of Diocletian is not a mint-mark, but signifies 21, the number of base *denarii* equal to the silver *denarius.* [XXI].

Roma (Rome). *Mint-marks :*—R., RM., ROM., RM. (in *field*) COM. or OOMOB. (in *exergue*), CORMOB. Letters in the *exergue* commence about the time of Aurelian, A.D. 270—275.—ROM. occurs on the coins of Julian III. the Apostate, and Jovian, A.D. 361—364.—RM. COM. or CONOB. was introduced under Honorius A.D. 395—423. —CORMOB is found on a coin of Anthemius, A.D. 467—472. RM. signifies *Roma*, the CO. being affixed and the OB. prefixed to resemble as nearly as possible COMOB., and at the same time to designate a mint. The mint-marks of Rome on the Byzantine coinage from the time of Anastasius I., A.D. 491, to that of Constantine IV. Pogonatus, A.D. 668, are ROMA., R., ROM., ROM. [See *Remarks on the letters* OB. *etc. under* VALENTINIANVS I.]

Ostia (Ostia). *Mint-mark :*—OST. After the defeat of Alexander by Maxentius in A.D.

311, the mint of *Carthage* was transferred to Ostia by Maxentius; and after the defeat of Maxentius, A.D. 312, Constantine I., now sole Emperor of the West, transferred the mint of Ostia to Rome. The coins of Constantius Chlorus and Galerius Maximianus with M. OST. P., M. OST. S. or T. or Q. *(Moneta Ostiæ Prima* or *Secunda,* or *Tertia,* or *Quarta)* were struck after their deaths by Maxentius.

Aquileia (Aquileia). *Mint-marks :*—AQ., AQVIL., AQOB., AQ. (in *field*) COM. (in *exergue*). The mint of Aquileia was established at the time of the monetary reform under Diocletian, and was probably transferred by Honorius, A.D. 395 —423 to Ravenna. It was restored for a short time by Theodosius II. during the war with the usurper John A.D. 423—425. In A.D. 452 it was besieged by Attila, King of the Huns, and burnt to the ground.

Mediolanum (Milan). *Mint-marks :*—MD., MED., MDOB., MD. (in *field*) COM. (in *exergue*). This mint was established after the defeat of Magnentius, A.D. 353, by Constantius II., and was suppressed under the Ostrogoths *circ.* A.D. 539.

Ravenna (Ravenna). *Mint-marks :*—RV., RV. (in *field*) COM. or COMOB. or COB., contraction of COMOB. (in *exergue*), CORVOB. [See p. 836 and *Roma* on this page.] This mint was established by Honorius A.D 404, when he fixed his residence at Ravenna. After the fall of the Western Empire, Ravenna was the capital of the Gothic kings, but was captured by Belisarius, in A.D. 539. It then became the residence of the Exarchs, under the Byzantine Emperors. The mint-marks on the Byzantine coinage from the time of Justinian I., A.D. 539 to that of Leo the Isaurian, A.D. 741, are RA., RAV., RAVEN., RAVENNA. It was eventually subdued by force or treachery by Astolphus, king of the Lombards, about A.D. 752.

Siscia (Sissek). *Mint-marks :*—S., SIS., SISC. Siscia was established as a mint about the time of Probus, A.D. 276—282, and was probably suppressed or transferred to *Sirmium* at the death of Valentinian II., in A.D. 392. Small brass coins of Probus are extant with the legend SISCIA PROBI AVG. The legend SISCIA AVG. occurs a little earlier on the *billon* coins of Gallienus, which are supposed to have been struck on the defeat in Pannonia of Ingenuus, one of the thirty tyrants. SIS. is given by Cohen *(Méd. Imp.,* 1st ed., vol. vi,, p. 219) as occurring in the *field* on a rare gold coin of Constantine II., formerly in the *Cabinet des Médailles, Paris.*

Serdica (Triaditza?). *Mint-marks :*—SD., SER., SERD. This mint was established by Aurelian, A.D. 270—275. It was transferred by Constantine I. to *Sirmium* after the first war against Licinius A.D. 314, and after the second war and defeat and death of Licinius, in A.D. 323, to *Constantinople* which was dedicated in A.D. 330.

Sirmium (Mitrovitz). *Mint-marks :*—SIRM., SM. (in *field*) COMOB. (in *exergue*). *Sirmium* was established by Constantine I. about A.D. 314, was suppressed after the death of Valentinianus

I., A.D. 375, and was restored for a short time by Theodosius I., A.D. 392—394.

Thessalonica (Saloniki). *Mint-marks :*—T., ΘES., TES., TS., THCOB., TESOB. Thessalonica was established as a mint at the time of the monetary reform under Diocletian, A.D. 296—301. The coins attributed to *Thessalonica*, with the mint-mark T, can be distinguished from those of *Tarraco* by their style and type, which resemble those of *Constantinople* and other Eastern coins. The *mint-marks* on the Byzantine coinage, which may be found from the time of Arcadius, A.D. 390, to that of Heraclius, A.D. 641, are TES., ΘES., TESOB., THCOB.

Constantinopolis (Constantinople). *Mint-marks :*—C., CP., CON., CONS., CONOB. *Constantinople* was founded by Constantine I., in A.D. 324, and dedicated in A.D. 330. The *mint-marks* on the Byzantine coinage from the time of Arcadius, A.D. 395, to that of Leo III. the Isaurian, A.D. 716—741, are CON., CONS., CONOB. —CON. or CONS. *(Constantinopolis)* is always *followed* by a *Greek* numeral, and so can be distinguished from CON. or CONST. *(Constantina)* which is always *preceded* by a *Latin* differential letter [*Arelate* or *Constantina ; Remarks on the letters* OB., *etc., under* VALENTINIANVS I.]

Heracleia—originally *Perinthus Thraciæ* (Eski Eregli). *Mint-marks :*—H. HERAC., HERACL. This mint was established before the monetary reform of Diocletian, A.D. 296—301, and was suppressed about the time of Leo I., A.D. 457—474.

Nicomedeia (Ismid). *Mint-marks :*—N., NIK. This mint was established before the monetary reform of Diocletian, A.D. 296—301. The letters NK. Y. XC. occur on the gold coins of Galerius Maximian, Valeria, Severus II., and Maximinus Daza, and the letters NK. on those of Constantius Chlorus, Galerius, Maximian, Severus II., Maximinus Daza, and Constantine I. All these coins were issued at Nicomedeia, as the *exergual* letters (S. M. N. *Signata Moneta Nicomedeiæ)* show, but a satisfactory explanation of the curious letters given above has not been discovered [VALERIA.] Since the article VALERIA was written, some suggestions have been made. Dr. J. Evans *(Num. Chron.* 3rd ser., 1886., vol. vi., pp. 281-284) considers that NK. refers to Nicomedeia, and that Y and XC. may denote numerals—as thought by Dr. Missong—L + V. = 55, or L — V. = 45. He adds : "Assuming that from some cause or other the local pound at Nicomedia was one-tenth lighter than the Roman pound, or as XC. to C., it will then be evident that if sixty *aurei* were struck from the Roman pound, only fifty-four of the same weight would be struck from the Nicomedian pound. If the number were fixed at fifty-five this might be typified by LV. or Y. Whether we take the Roman pound of 5050 Troy grains, and divide it by 60; or whether we take a pound of 4545 grains and divide it by 55, we come to nearly the same result—in one case 84¼ grains, in the other 82¼ grains. Of the two perhaps the latter comes nearer the usual weight of such coins.

LV. would then represent the number of coins struck from the Nicomedian pound, and XC. the proportion this bore to the Roman pound. The theory here suggested requires much corroboration before it can be accepted as in any degree satisfactory. All that can be said in its favour is that the actual weight of the coins is about 10 per cent. less than ⅟₅₅th of the Roman pound." M. Schmidt *(Zeits. für Num.*, Band. xv., part iv., 1888) suggests *Nicomedensi lege Valente* XC = ₉₀/₁₀₀th of the Nicomedian gold pound, whilst Prof. Mommsen (p. 243, *note*) considers these letters as equivalent to Νικομηδεια *Lux C[ivitatum]*. The *mint-marks* on the Byzantine coinage from the time of Arcadius, A.D. 395, to that of Heraclius and his two sons, A.D. 638—640, are N., NI., NIC., NIK., NIKO., NICO., NIKM., NIKOM.

Cyzicus (Chizico). *Mint-marks :*—K., KY., CVZ., CVZIC., CYZ., CYZIC. This mint was established about the time of Claudius II., A.D. 268—270, and suppressed about the same time as *Heracleia.* The *mint-marks* on the Byzantine coinage from the time of Justin I., A.D. 518, to that of Heraclius and Heraclius Constantine, A.D. 641, are KV., KVZ., KYZ.

Antiocheia (Antakieh). *Mint-marks :*—A., AN., ANT. This mint was established previous to the time of Valerian I., A.D. 253—260. Letters and symbols of various kinds occur in the *field* of coins commencing under Diocletian, A.D. 284—313, struck at *Antioch* and *Alexandria* (Cohen, *Méd. Imp.*, 2nd ed., vol. vi., p. 414). It was suppressed about the time of Theodosius II., A.D. 408—450. The mint was continued under Anastasius I., Justin I., and Justinian I., A.D. 491—565. In A.D. 538 Antioch was destroyed by the Persians, and Justinian I. built a new city, giving it the name of *Theupolis.* The following *mint-marks* occur on Byzantine coins from the time of Justinian I. to that of Heraclius I. and his two sons, A.D. 638—640—THEV., THEVP., THЄVP., TH ЄVΠo., THEЧoP., ΘV., ΘVΠ., ΘVΠo., CH., CH ЄЧN., etc.

Alexandreia (Alexandria). *Mint-marks :*—AL., ALE. The mint of *Alexandreia* became Imperial under Domitius Domitian (Achilleus), usurper in Egypt under Diocletian, A.D. 297 (Madden, *Handbook of Rom. Num.*, p. 134). It was suppressed about the time of Theodosius II., A.D. 408—450. The *mint-marks* on the Byzantine coinage from the time of Justin I., A.D. 518 to that of Constans II. and his son Constantine IV. Pogonatus, A.D. 659 is ΑΛΕξ.

Tarsus (Tersoos). The attribution of coins to this mint was suggested by the late Count de Salis, who considers that coins were struck there during the reign of Gallienus, A.D. 253—268, and that it was suppressed or transferred to *Heracleia* in the early part of the reign of Diocletian, being closed before the opening of *Treves*, which adopted its *mint-mark* TR. [*Treveri*].

Besides the above-mentioned mints others were established under the Byzantine Emperors— *Ephesus* (SEPSЧS), *Nicæa (?)* (N.C.), *Kherson* (Χ Ꞓ P., Χ Ꞓ PCONOS, Χ Ꞓ PCⱲNOC), *Cyprus* (κvΠP., κY∩P.), *Isaurus* (ISAVR.), *Auasis* or *Oasis* (ABAZI), *Sicilia* (SCL., SECILIA, SICILIA), *Catana* (CAT.), Naples (NϾ).

The letters F., S., T., or Q., are sometimes used *before* the mint-mark, as P. CON., S. CON., T. CON., Q. CON. *(Prima, Secunda, Tertia, Quarta Constantinæ)*, and sometimes *after* as R. P., R. S., R. T., etc. *(Romæ Prima, Secunda, Tertia*, etc.) When there is a differential letter either in *Greek* or *Latin* besides the P., as SISC. P. Z., P. K. T. the P. stands for *Pecunia* or *Percussa*—*Sisciæ Pecunia* or *Percussa* 7; *Pecunia* or *Percussa Karthagini Tertia*. The letters P. S. signify *Pecunia Signata*, and are usually *after* the mint-marks, as TR. P. S. *(Treveris Pecunia Signata)*, MD. P. S. *(Mediolani Pecunia Signata)*; whereas the letters S. M., *Signata Moneta*, are usually *before*, as S. M. AQ. *(Signata Moneta Aquileiæ)*, S. M. ANT. A. *(Signata Moneta Antiochiæ* 1), S. M. N. B. *(Signata Moneta Nicomediæ* 2), etc.

VRBICA (Magnia), a princess unknown to history, by some supposed to have lived at the time of Maxentius, by others to have been the wife of Carus. A unique coin, now in the British Museum, proves that she was one of the wives of Carinus, A.D. 282—285 (Madden, *Handbook of Rom. Num.*, 1861, p. 166, plate iii., No. 2.)—

Obv. IMP. CARINVS AVG. Bust of Carinus to l., helmeted, holding with r. hand a horse by the reins and a sceptre, and with l. hand a shield. *Rev.* MAGNIA VRBICA AVG. Bust of Magnia Urbica to r. Æ. *Quin.* (300 frcs.) Other coins in gold and brass—some with obverse legend MAGNIAE VRBICAE AVG. are in existence. *Gold coins:* CONCORDIA AVG. (500 frcs.), PVDICITIA AVG. (500 frcs.), VENERI VICTRICI (500 frcs.), VENVS GENETRIX *(Wiczay*, 500 frcs.) *Brass Medallions:*—PVDICITIA AVG. (800 frcs.), *Small brass:*—FIDES MILITVM *(Tanini*, 30 frcs.), IVNO REGINA, Juno standing with or without peacock (40 frcs.), SALVS PVBLICA (30 frcs.), VENVS CELEST. (20 frcs.), VENVS GENETRIX (30 to 50 frcs.), VENVS VICTRIX (10 frcs.)

VRBINIA GENS. Coins have been attributed by Cohen *(Méd. Cons.*, pp. 319, 320) to this *gens* with the legend Q. ℞. *Quintus Urbinius?*, but it has been shown (Mommsen, *Mon. Rom.*, vol. ii., p. 387; Lenormant, *La Mon. dans l'Antiq.*, vol. iii., p. 150; Babelon, *Mon. de la Répub. Rom.*, vol. i., p. 346; vol. ii., p. 169) that these letters should be interpreted *Quæstores Urbani*. [See ℞. *Urbani*.]

VRBIS. *Urbis*. CONSERVAT. VRBIS SVAE, on third brass coins of Maxentius, from *Tanini*—CONSERVATOR VRBIS SVAE, on gold and silver coins of Maxentius—CONSERVATORI VRBIS SVAE, on third brass coins of Constantine I., from *Tanini* after *d'Ennery*—LIBERATORI VRBIS SVAE, on second brass coins of Constantine I.—MONETA VRBIS VESTRAE, on brass medallions of Crispus and Constantine II.—RECVPERATOR VRBIS SVAE, on third brass coins of Constantine I., from *d'Ennery*—RENOVATIO VRBIS ROM.,

on second brass coins of Decentius, from *Tanini*, after *Pembroke*—RESTITVTOR VRBIS, on gold, silver, second and third brass coins of Septimius Severus; on gold, silver, first and second brass coins of Caracalla; and on silver and second brass coins of Geta—RESTITVTORI VRBIS, on gold and silver coins of Septimius Severus and silver coins of Geta—RESTITVTORES VRBIS, on silver coins of Septimius Severus—SACERDOS VRBIS, on third brass coins of Alexander Severus—SACRA MONETA VRBIS, on brass medallions of Crispus—VOTA ORBIS ET VRBIS SEN. ET P. R. *(Senatus et Populi Romani)*, on silver medallions of Licinius I. and Constantine I.

VRBIS ROMA. Rome, helmeted, seated to l., holding a Victory, or a globe surmounted by Victory, and a reversed spear, on silver coins of Avitus *(Banduri* and *d'Ennery*, 250 frcs.), Severus III. (30 frcs.), and Eufemia (400 frcs.)

VRBS RESTITVTA. Rome standing to l., in military dress, holding Victory and spear. *Obv.* A. *(Aulus)* VITELLIVS GERMAN. IMP. AVG. P. M. TR. P. Bust of Vitellius to r., laureated. Æ. I. This piece is in the French cabinet, but Cohen says *(Méd. Imp.*, 2nd ed., vol. i., p. 265, No. 109) that the reverse is remade in such a manner as to make it impossible to affirm what is the true type and true legend.

VRBS ROMA. Rome, helmeted, seated to l., holding a globe surmounted by a Victory, and a sceptre or spear; at her side a shield—on coins of Constans I. (Æ. Med. 80 frcs.), Constantius II. (Æ. I. 50 frcs.), Magnentius (Æ. II. 10 frcs.), Valentinian I. (with *exergual* letters—Æ. 6 frcs.), Valens (with *exergual* letters—Æ. 3 frcs.), Nepos (in *exergue* RV. P. S. *Ravennæ Pecunia Signata.*—Æ. 200 frcs.), and Basiliscus (in *exergue* PS. Æ. 40 frcs.)

VRBS ROMA. Rome, helmeted, seated to l., holding Victory and sceptre or spear; at her side a shield—on coins of Nepotian (with *exergual* letters—Æ. 120 to 160 frcs.), and Jovian (Æ. Med. from *Tanini* 100 frcs.)

VRBS ROMA. Rome, seated on a shield, holding Victory and spear. *Obv.* D. N. FL. CL. *(Dominus Noster Flavius Claudius)* CONSTANTIVS NOB. CAES. *(Nobilis Cæsar)*. Bust of Constantius Gallus, bare. Æ. Med. from *d'Ennery* (120 frcs.)

VRBS ROMA. Rome, helmeted, seated to l., on a cuirass, holding globe surmounted by Victory and a sceptre or reversed spear; various *exergual* letters—on coins of Gratian (Æ. 4 frcs.), Valentinian II. (Æ. 6 frcs.; *N.* from *Mionnet*, 40 frcs.; Æ. III. c.), Theodosius I. (Æ. 3 frcs.), Eugenius (Æ. 20 frcs.), Honorius (Æ. 4 frcs.), Johannes (Æ. from *Banduri* and *d'Ennery*, 200 frcs.), Valentinian III. (Æ. 40 frcs.), and Arcadius (Æ. 8 frcs.)

VRBS ROMA. Rome, helmeted, seated to l., holding a globe and a spear; at her side a shield; in the *exergue* R. T. *(Romæ tertia.) Obv.* D. N. GRATIANVS P. F. AVG. Bust of Gratian to r., diademed. Æ. I. (80 frcs.)

VRBS ROMA. Rome, helmeted, seated to l., holding a globe surmounted by ☀ and a reversed spear ; at her side a shield ; in the *exergue* R. P. *(Romæ prima.) Obv.* D. N. IVL. NEPOTIANVS P. F. AVG. Bust of Nepotian to r., diademed. *N.* (2000 frcs.)

VRBS ROMA. Rome, helmeted, seated to r.

on a seat, holding globe surmounted by Victory and a reversed spear ; various *exergual* letters— on coins of Valentinian I. (Æ. I. 40 frcs.), Gratian (Æ. 4 frcs.), and Theodosius I. (Æ. 3 frcs.)

VRBS ROMA. Bust of Rome, helmeted, to l. or to r. *Rev.* No legend. Wolf to l., suckling Romulus and Remus ; above two stars. Æ. I. (60 frcs.)

VRBS ROMA. Bust of Rome, helmeted, to r. *Rev.* No legend. Wolf to r., in a cave suckling Romulus and Remus ; outside cave and on either side of it a shepherd holding a crook ; above two stars. Æ. I. (100 frcs.)

VRBS ROMA. Bust of Rome, helmeted, to l., with an aigrette on the helmet. *Rev.* No legend. Wolf to l., suckling Romulus and Remus ; above, two stars ; sometimes between the stars a wreath, palm, or three points. Æ. III. (c. to 2 frcs.) ; Æ. *Quin.* (6 frcs.)

VRBS ROMA. Bust of Rome, helmeted, to l. *Rev.* No legend. Wolf suckling Romulus and Remus ; above, the monogram ✗ between two stars with eight rays. In the *exergue* P. CONST. *(Prima Constantinæ* [Arles.]) Æ. III. (c.) Madden, *Christian Emblems on the Coins of Constantine I.*, etc., in *Num. Chron.*, N.S., 1877, vol. xvii., p. 270.

VRBS ROMA. Bust of Rome, helmeted, to r. *Rev.* SECVRITAS ROMAE. Constantine seated, facing, holding a sceptre, apparently carried by two females, one of whom holds a torch ; on either side an infant carrying a rod or a torch. Æ. I. (150 frcs.)

VRBS ROMA. Bust of Rome, helmeted, to l. *Rev.* VIRTVS AVG. Constantine standing to r., holding a reversed spear and a globe ; on the ground two captives seated. Æ. I. (150 frcs.)

VRBS ROMA. Bust of Rome, helmeted, to l., with an aigrette on the helmet. *Rev.* GLORIA EXERCITVS. Two soldiers helmeted, standing, each leaning on a spear and shield ; between them, a standard ; various *exergual* letters. Æ. III. (3 frcs.)

VRBS ROMA. Bust of Rome, helmeted, to r. *Rev.* VRBS ROMA. Bust of female (? Fausta) to r., diademed. Æ. *Quin.* (6 frcs.) ; or VOT. XX. MVLT. XXX., within a wreath. Æ. III. (6 frcs.)

VRBS ROMA. Bust of Rome, helmeted, to l., with an aigrette on the helmet. *Rev.* No legend. Victory standing to l., holding a palm ?

and leaning on a shield ; in the *exergue* PLC. ? Æ. (3 frcs.)

VRBS ROMA. Bust of Rome, helmeted, to r. *Rev.* ANNONA AVGVSTA CERES. Ceres and Abundance. Contorniate (rare).

[The coins with the bust of Rome, for the most part, belong to the reigns of Constantine II. and Constans I., though a few may be attributed to the time of Constantine I. The introduction of the Contorniates may be fixed to the reign of Constans I. (Cohen, *Méd. Imp.*, 2nd ed., vol. i., p. xxv.)

VRBS ROMA AETERNA. Jupiter seated in a Temple. *Obv.* HADRIANVS AVG. COS. III. P. P. Head of Hadrian to r., bare. Contorniate (very rare.)

VRBS ROMA BEATA. Rome, helmeted, seated to l., holding a globe surmounted by a Victory, and a sceptre or spear ; at her side, a shield—on coins of Constans I. (Æ. Med. 80 frcs.), and Constantius II. (Æ. I. from *Banduri*, 50 frcs.)

VRBS ROMA BEATA. Bust of Rome, helmeted, to l. *Rev.* No legend. Wolf suckling Romulus and Remus ; no stars ; in the *exergue* AQ. ? Æ. III. (10 frcs.)

VRBS ROMA FELIX. The Emperor standing in military dress, holding a standard and a Victory ; at his feet, a shield ; or holding a spear, to which is fastened a trophy and a globe surmounted by a Victory—on small brass coins of Theodosius I. (15 frcs.), and Honorius (c.)

VRBS ROMA FELIX. Rome, holding globe surmounted by Victory, standing to l. *Obv.* D. N. ARCADIVS P. F. AVG. Bust of Arcadius, helmeted, holding shield and spear over r. shoulder. Æ. (3 frcs.)

VRBS ROMA HETERNA. Sacrifice before a Temple—on Contorniates of Trajan (c.) and of Hadrian. (Very rare.)

VRSE VINCAS. Athlete, standing to r. *Obv.* No legend. Bust of a horseman to r., holding a whip, and leading his horse by the bridle ; behind, Ǝ or a monogram composed of the letters TRAVCS backwards. Contorniate (c.)

VRSI. *Ursi.*—BONIFATI VINCAS VRSI. Athlete, standing. *Obv.* . . . . Head of Trajan. Contorniate (c.)

VRSO. *Urso.*—C. MAR. CAP. Q. VRSO IIVIR. *(Caio Marelo Capitono, Quinto Urso Duumviris)* and M. PLAE. TRAN. Q. VRSO IIVIR. ITER. *(Marco Plætorio Tranquillo, Quinto Urso Duumviro Iterum)*—on brass coins of Augustus, struck at Calagurris in Hispania Tarraconensis. (Cohen, *Méd. Imp.*, 2nd ed., vol. i., p. 155, Nos. 675, 676.

Urso, a town in Hispania Bætica. It was the Οὐρσων of Strabo (Lib. III.), the 'Ορσῶνα of Appian *(Bell. Hisp.,* 16), and the Urso of Pliny (Lib. III.) and was a Roman colony with the name of Genua Urbanorum. Its modern name is *Osuna.* The following coins are attributed to it :—

1. *Obv.* VRSONE. Head of Augustus (?) to r., laureated. *Rev.* L. AP. DEC. Q. *(Lucius Appuleius Decimus Quæstor).* Winged sphinx, helmeted, walking, to r. Æ. I. (30 frcs.) ; Æ. II. (25 frcs.)

2. *Obv.* No legend. Head of Augustus (?) to r., laureated. *Rev.* VRSONE. L. AP. DEC. Q. Same Sphinx. Æ. I. and II. (100 frcs.)

3. *Obv.* Same as No. 2. *Rev.* VRSONE. Same Sphinx. Æ. II. (100 frcs.)

4. *Obv.* Q. REDECAL. Head of Augustus (?) to r., bare. *Rev.* VRSONE. Sphinx, walking to l. ; in the field, two stars. Æ. II.

5. *Obv.* VRSONE. Head of Augustus (?) to r., bare. *Rev.* No legend. Bear, standing holding a wreath and a palm (?). Æ. II. (100 frcs.)

These coins are assigned by Aloïs Heiss (*Mon. Ant. d'Espagne)* to the time of Augustus, which is not quite certain. No. 4 is most probably not genuine (Cf. Florez, *Medallas de España*, 1757 ; Akerman, *Coins of Cities and Princes*, pp. 60 and 23 [where there is a coin given of Urso in alliance with Astapa] ; Lenormant, *La Mon. dans l'Antiq.*, vol. ii., p. 277 ; Cohen, *Méd. Imp.*, 2nd ed., vol. i., p. 151 ; Boutkowski, *Dict. Num.*, p. 820.)

VRSONE. [See *Urso.*]

VSSESSON. A word occurring on the gold coins of Leo IV. (A.D., 775-780) representing his grandfather Leo III. (Πάππος), his father Constantine V. Copronymus (Πατήρ), himself, and his son Constantine VI. (ὁ νέος), and of which no quite satisfactory explanation has been given. (Cavedoni, *Congetture intorno alla voce* VSSESSON, etc., in the *Bull. Arch. Nap.*, N.S., 1857, No. 121, p. 180 ; cf. *Opusc. Relig. lett.*, Modena, vol. ii., pp. 355-372, 1857 ; Sabatier, *Mon. Byz.*, vol. ii., p. 64, pl. xli., Nos. 2, 3 ; Friedlaender in the *Zeitschrift für Numismatik*, Berlin, vol. iv., 1876—1877 ; Madden, *Christian Emblems on the Coins of Constantine I.*, etc., in the *Num. Chron.*, N.S., 1878, vol. xviii., p. 203.)

VSTOR (in monogram) in the *exergue* of a Contorniate of Placidius Valentinian (Sabatier, *Mon. Contorn.*, pl. iv., No. 6 ; Cohen, *Méd. Imp.*, 1st ed., vol. vi., 585.)

VTI., VTIC. or VTICEN. *Uticensis.* [*Utica.*]

Utica, the most ancient of the Phoenician colonies in Africa, was founded by the Tyrians before Carthage, in B.C. 1100, on the north coast

of Zeugitana. [*Zeugitana.*] After the destruction of Carthage it became " the residence of the Roman governor, the principal emporium for the Roman commerce, and the port of debarkation for the Roman armaments designed to act in the interior of Africa." (T. H. Dyer, art., VTICA, Smith's *Dict. of Geography.)* It was at Utica that the younger Cato killed himself. It was presented by Augustus with the Roman *civitas* and became a Roman colony under Hadrian. It probably fell into the hands of the Vandals under Genseric, A.D. 439, and was eventually destroyed by the Arabs during the reign of Abdalmalik, A.D. 685—705. (Gibbon, *Decline and Fall*, vol. vi., p. 350. *seq.* ed., Smith.) The following coins are attributed to it (Müller, *Num. de l'Anc. Afrique*, vol. ii., pp. 159—162 ; cf. Lenormant, *La Mon. dans l'Antiq.*, vol. iii., pp. 221, 236 ; Cohen, *Méd. Imp.*, 2nd ed., vol. i., pp. 174, 209) :—

1. *Obv.* No legend. Bust of Livia to r., veiled ; behind, a sceptre. *Rev.* M. M. IVL. VTI. D. D. *(Municipes Municipii Julii Uticensis Decurionum Decreto)*, around, the letters P. P. *(Permissu Proconsulis.)* Æ. III. (20 frcs.)

2. *Obv.* TI. CAESAR AVG. F. AVG. Head of Tiberius to l., bare. *Rev.* M. M. IVL. VTIC. P. P. D. D. Livia, veiled, seated to l., holding a *patera* and a sceptre. Æ. II. (10 frcs.)

3. *Obv.* TI. CAE. DIVI AVG. F. AVG. [or F. A.] IMP. VII. Head of Tiberius to l. or to r., bare. *Rev.* M. M. [or M. MVN.] IVL. VTIC. [or VTICEN.] D. D. P. P. [or P. P. D. D.] Same type as No. 2. Æ. II. (6 frcs.)

4. *Obv.* TI. . . . IMP. VII. Head of Tiberius to l. or to r., bare. *Rev.* M. V. D. D. P. P. *(Municipium Uticense Decurionum Decreto Permissu Proconsulis)*, within a laurel wreath. Æ. III. (6 frcs.)

5. *Obv.* TI. CAESAR AVG. Head of Tiberius to l., bare. *Rev.* C. APRON. IIVIR *(Caius Apronius Duumvir.)* D. D. [P. P.] in the *field.* Æ. III. (6 frcs.)

The following pieces were struck by the *duumvirs* during three successive years of the proconsulate of Caius Vibius Marsus, A.D. 27—30 :—

1st year, A.D. 27—28.

1. *Obv.* TI. CAESAR DIVI AVG. [or AVGVST. or AVGVSTVS] IMP. VIII. Head of Tiberius to l., bare. *Rev.* C. V. [or VIB.] MARSO PROCOS. [or PRCOS.] NER. CAES. [or NE. CAE.] Q. PR. A. M. GEMELLVS [on some F. C.] *(Caio Vibio Marso Proconsule Nerone Cæsare Quinquennali Præfectus Aulus M . . . Gemellus [Faciendum Curavit.])* Livia, veiled, seated to r., holding *patera* and a long sceptre ; in the *field*, D. D. P. P. Æ. II. (2 to 4 frcs.)

2. *Obv.* Same as No. 1. *Rev.* C. VIB. [or VIBIO] MARSO PRCOS. DR. [or DRV.] CAE. Q. PR. [on some A.] T. G. RVFVS F. C. *(Caio Vibio Marso Proconsule Druso Cæsare Quinquennali Præfectus [Augustalis ?] Titus G . . . . Rufus Faciendum Curavit.)* Same type as No. 1. Æ. II. (5 frcs.)

3. *Obv.* Same as No. 1. *Rev.* c. vibio marso prcos. c. cassivs felix a. iivir. *(Caio Vibio Marso Proconsule Caius Cassius Felix Augustalis duumvir.)* Same type as No. 1. Æ. II. (2 to 4 frcs.)

2nd year, A.D. 28—29.

4. *Obv.* Same as No. 1. *Rev.* c. vibio marso procos. [or prcos.] ii. l. caecilivs pivs iiv. [or iivr.] [on some f. c.] *(Caio Vibio Marso Proconsule Anno Secundo. Lucius Cæcilius Pius duumvir [Faciendum curavit.])* Livia, seated to r., holding a *patera* and a long sceptre; in the *field*, m. m. i. v. *(Municipes Municipii Julii Uticensis.)* Æ. II. (4 frcs.)

5. *Obv.* Same as No. 1. *Rev.* c. vibio marso prcos. ii. q. caecilivs iovin. iiv. f. c. *(Caio Vibio Marso Proconsule Anno Secundo. Quintus Cæcilius Jovivus duumvir Faciendum curavit.)* Same type as No. 4. Æ. (2 frcs.)

6. *Obv.* Same as No. 1. *Rev.* c. vibio marso prcos. ii. sex. tadivs favstvs iiv. *(Caio Vibio Marso Proconsule Anno Secundo. Sextus Tadius Faustus duumvir.)* Same type as No. 4. Æ. II. (4 frcs.)

3rd year, A.D. 29—30.

7. *Obv.* Same as No. 1. *Rev.* c. vibio marso prcos. iii. c. caelivs. pax avg. [or a. or av.] iivir. *(Caio Vibio Marso Proconsule anno tertio. Caius Cælius Pax Augustalis duumvir.)* Livia, veiled, seated to l, holding patera and a long sceptre. In the *field*, d. d. p. p. *(Decurionum Decreto Permissu Proconsulis.)* Æ. II. (4 frcs.)

8. *Obv.* Same as No. 1. *Rev.* c. vibio marso prcos. iii. c. cassivs felix a. iivir. *(Caio Vibio Marso Proconsule anno tertio. Caius Cassius Felix Augustalis duumvir.)* Same type as No. 7. Æ. II. (4 frcs.)

9. *Obv.* Same as No. 1. *Rev.* c. vibio marso prcos. iii. c. sallvstivs ivstvs ii. [or iiv.] *(Caio Vibio Marso Proconsule anno tertio. Caius Sallustius Justus duumvir.)* Livia, seated to l., holding a *patera* and a long sceptre; in the *field*, m. m. i. v. *(Municipes Municipii Julii Uticensis.)* Æ. II. (4 frcs.)

10. *Obv.* Same as No. 1. *Rev.* c. vibio marso prcos. iii. m. tvllivs ivdex iivir. *(Caio Vibio Marso Proconsule anno tertio. Marcus Tullius Judex duumvir.)* Same type as No. 9. Æ. II. (4 frcs.)

The following silver coins were struck in Utica by M. Porcius Cato (Cato of Utica, whose death is above referred to), B.C. 49—46, where he took the title of Proprætor, and renewed the types already adopted by his father M. Porcius Cato, when he was moneyer in B.C. 101 :—

Obv. m. cato. pro. pr. [on some roma.] *(Marcus Cato Proprætor. Roma.)* Head or bust of Liberty to r. *Rev.* victrix. Winged Victory, seated to r., holding a *patera* [or a wreath] and a palm. Æ. (2 frcs.); Æ. *Quin.* (2 frcs.)

The type of Victory recalls the Temple consecrated to *Victoria Virgo* by Cato the Censor after his successes in Spain. (Livy, Lib. xxxv., cap. 9.)

VTILITAS PVBLICA. Female figure standing to l.; in the *exergue* t.—on coins of Diocletian (Æ. III. *Quin.* 20 frcs.), Maximian Hercules (in the *exergue* r. Æ. III. *Quin.* 20 frcs.), and Constantius Chlorus (no letters in the exergue, Æ. 20 frcs.)

VTILITAS PVBLICA. Female figure standing to l., her hands wrapped in her robe—on coins of Galerius Maximian (Æ. III. *Quin.* from *Tanini*, 15 frcs.), Severus II. (Æ. III. *Quin.* (30 frcs.), and Maximinus II. Daza (Æ. III. 25 frcs.)

VTILITAS PVBLICA. Female figure, standing on a vessel, holding a balance and a cornucopiæ; to r., a helmeted soldier giving her his hand, and holding a globe surmounted by a Victory; at the side, a shield. *Obv.* imp. constantinvs p. f. avg. Bust of Constantine I. to l., laureated, with the Imperial mantle, holding a sceptre surmounted by an eagle. Æ. III. from *Banduri.* (30 frcs.)

Vulcanus, one of the twelve great celestial deities, the god of fire *(Ignipotens*, Virg. Æn. x., 243) and of smiths, son of Jupiter and Juno, and husband of Venus. He is the same as the Greek *Hephæstus.* A Temple is said to have been erected at Rome to him in the earliest times, and the principal festival to his honour—called *Vulcanalia*—was celebrated at Rome on the 23rd of August. The head of Vulcan may be found on several coins of the Republic (Babelon, *Mon. de la Répub. Rom.)*—on those of L. Aurelius Cotta, B.C. 90 *(Aurelia gens)*, Marcus Metellus, B.C. 122 *(Cæcilia gens)*, C. Cassius Longinus, B.C. 109 *(Cassia gens)*, and on a rare small brass coin attributed to the *gens Statia ;* also as a symbol on coins of L. Cæsius, B.C. 104 *(Cæsia gens).* His cap is figured on the coins of Paullus Aemilius Lepidus, B.C. 54 *(Æmilia gens)*, and together with various coining implements on the coins of Titus Carisius, B.C. 48 *(Carisia gens) ;* also as a symbol on early *denarii*, *Victoriati* and *semisses.* He is designated *Ultor*—avenger, as also is Mars *(q. v.)*—on coins attributed to the period between the reigns of Nero and Vespasian [volcanvs vltor ; see also volcano and volcanom.] Vulcan is frequently represented on the brass medallions of Antoninus Pius (1) forging a helmet, or, on other examples, the thunderbolt of Jupiter, by order of Minerva, who stands by ; (2) the forge itself, showing statue of Minerva carrying Victory shield, helmet, etc., objects already finished by Vulcan, whilst he, holding a hammer, is forging a greave on the anvil (Cohen, *Méd. Imp.*, 2nd ed., vol. ii., Antoninus Pius, Nos. 1144, 1155, 1156 ; Froehner, *Médaillons de l'Emp. Romain*, pp. 51, 63, 65.)

VVV. *Three v's* in the legend, ddd. nnn. aaavvvggg. *Domini Nostri Augusti*—on *exagia solidi* [exagivm solidi] of the *three* Emperors, Honorius, Arcadius, and Theodosius II. (Cohen, *Méd. Imp.*, 1st ed., vol. vi., pp. 484, 485 ; Sabatier, *Mon. Byz.*, vol. i., pp. 96, 97.)

VX. for XV., on small brass coins of Augustus, struck at Emerita Hispaniæ—c. [or co.] A. E. LE. VX. *Colonia Augusta Emerita. Legio decima quinta* (Cohen, *Méd. Imp.*, 2nd. ed., vol. i., p. 149, Nos. 594, 595.)
Uxores Cæsarum [see *Augustæ.*]
VXXT., VIXXT. *Quinta XX. Tarracone, Sexta XX. Tarracone;* VXXI., VIXXI. *Quinta XXI., Sexta XXI.*—on small brass coins of Aurelian and Probus.

W.

Wamba, Witteric, Wittiza—Visigothic kings [see *Visigoths.*]
Witiges, Ostrogothic king [see VITIGES.]

X.

X, the twenty-first letter of the Greek alphabet, probably derived from the Greek Ξ, which came from the Phoenician letter *samekh* (Isaac Taylor, *The Alphabet,* vol. ii., pp. 92, 139).

X., as a mark of value—10 *asses*—on the *denarii* of the Republic and on the *decussis* (Babelon, *Mon. de la Répub. Rom.*, vol. i., pp. 38, 67, 68, 71, and 42, 43.)

X., as a figure on coins of the Republic, included in figures from I. to CC., on the same *denarius;* exceptionally these figures are raised to CCIƆƆ (= 10,000) on the *denarii* of L. Calpurnius Piso, who coined by virtue of the law Plautia-Papiria (Babelon, *Mon. de la Répub. Rom.*, vol. i., p. li.)

X., XI., XII., XIII., etc., on *tesseræ* or tickets of admission to the theatre or other places of amusement. Cohen, *(Méd. Imp.*, 1st ed., vol. vi., p. 534) divides the *tesseræ* as follows :— 1, Imperial ; 2, Mythological ; 3, Games ; 4, Erotic ; 5, Commemorative ; and 6, Mystical. [*Tessera.*]

X. A Christian emblem on the pedestal, on coins of Constantine I. and Licinius I., with the legend VICTORIAE LAETAE PRINC. PERP., struck at Siscia, ? A.D. 312—317—on the *labarum* on coins of Constantine I. and II. and Delmatius, with the legend GLORIA EXERCITVS, struck at Constantina (Arles) A.D. 335—337 (Madden, *Christian Emblems on the Coins of Constantine I.*, etc., in the *Num. Chron.* N.S., 1877, vol. xvii., pp. 11, 242 ; 1878, vol. xviii., pp. 1, 169.)

X., within a garland ; in the *exergue* TR. *(Treveris.)* Obv. Helmeted bust of Rome or of Constantinople to r. Æ. *Quin.* (40 frcs.) Cohen, *(Méd. Imp.*, 1st ed., vol. vii., *Suppl.*, p. 383) considers that this piece could not have been struck earlier than the reign of Valentinian II.

X. *Decemvir.* C. CALDVS IMP. [or AV.] X. *Caius Caldus Imperator, Augur Decemvir* [*sacris faciendis*] on *denarii* of C. Coelius Caldus, moneyer, in B.C. 54. [See VIIviri *Epulonum* and xviiri *sacris faciundis.*]

X. *Decennalia.* [VOT. SOLVTA X. ; X. MAXIMINI AVG.]

X. *Decennalibus.* VOT. X. ET XV. or XX., VOT. X. MVLT. XX., VOT. X. SIC. XX., VOTIS X. ET XX., SIC. X. SIC. XX., etc.

X. *Decima.* LEG. X. *Legio Decima*—TR. P. X. *Tribunitiâ Potestate Decima.*
X. *Decimo.* AN. X. *Anno Decimo.*
X. *Decimum.* COS. X. *Consul Decimum.*—IMP. X. *Imperator Decimum.* [And similarly with the compounds of X.—XI., XII., XIII. up to XIX. or XVIIII.]

X. MAXIMINI AVG. S. M. A. *(Decennalia Maximini Augusti. Signata Moneta Antiochiæ)* in five lines, within a laurel wreath. Obv. MAXIMINVS P. F. AVG. Head of Maximinus II. Daza to r., laureated. Æ. (200 frcs.)

XA., XE., XI., etc., on coins of L. Julius Bursio, B.C. 84 [see p. 830.]

XC.—XPICTOC. On coins of the Byzantine Emperors from A.D. 969 to A.D. 1391 (Madden, *Christian Emblems on the Coins of Constantine I.*, etc., *Num. Chron.*, N.S., 1878, vol. xviii., pp. 179—188.)

XE. ҌOHΘEI ROMANO δECПOҶH. Romanus I., standing facing, with diadem surmounted by a cross, holding in r. hand a globe *cruciger ;* to r., Christ with head leaning against cross, standing, placing r. hand on the head of the Emperor. Obv. CoҌ̈sҶanҶ. ЄҶ XPISTOF. Ҍ. R. Busts of Constantine X. and Christophorus facing, with diadem, surmounted by cross, holding together and between them a long cross. Æ. (300 frcs.) The obverse legend is probably Κωνσταντῖνος et (for Καὶ) Χριστοφόρος βασιλεῖς 'Ρωμαίων, the reverse Χριστὲ βοήθει 'Ρωμανῶ δεσπότη. The formula χριστΕ ҌOHΘEI, instead of the usual ΚύριΕ ҌOHΘ ЄI, is of rare occurrence, and may be corroborated by a Byzantine lead seal, published by Herr Miller *(Rev. Num.*, 1861, p. 23), on the obverse of which is the inscription Χρι[Ҭὲ Βοήθει τῷ. Cῶ. ΔӟΛΙῶ., and on the reverse +ΑΝΔ—Р ЄΑΜ—ΑΔΔΑ—ТОРІ, and which from the fact that Andreas bears the title of Μανδάτωρ (one who gives or carries [orders]), an office in vogue under Constantine X. Porphyrogenitus, A.D. 912—959, has been attributed by Herr Miller to the reign of this Emperor. M. le Bas has published *(Voyage Archéol.*, No. 8913) a marble found in the island of Delos with the inscription Χ ЄBOHΘЄ ι (χριστΕ BOHΘЄ ι), which Herr Miller thinks is of the same age as the seal of Andreas (Madden, *Num. Chron.*, N.S., 1878, vol. xviii., p. 205.)

XE. A figure in *toga,* standing to l., reading a book. Obv. D. N. *(Dominus Noster)* ARCADIVS P. F. AVG. Bust of Arcadius to r., with diadem. Æ. (10 frcs.) Published by Sabatier *(Mon. Byz.*, vol. i., p. 107) who states that the piece was found at *Kherson.*

XII. As a mark of value on copper coins of the Vandals, without name of king (Sabatier, *Mon. Byz.*, vol. i., p. 221 ; Keary, *Num. Chron*, N.S., vol. xviii., 1878, pp. 142, 143.)

XIIX. CONOB., in the *exergue* of a gold *tremissis* of Valentinian III., published and engraved by *Wiczay.* This coin, according to Cohen *(Méd. Imp.*, 1st ed., vol. vi., p. 508, *note),* furnishes a new argument against the interpretation of the letters OB. by 72, but, as the present writer has already pointed out *(Num. Chron.,* N.S., 1862, vol. ii., p. 246, *note)* the coin is, in the first place, only described from *Wiczay,* and, in the second, is as late as the reign of Valentinian III. (A.D. 425—455), at which period no value can be placed upon the legends on coins. [*See* p. 835.]

X—N. *Xristus Nica,* on copper coins of Constantine V. and Leo. IV., Leo IV. and Constantine VI., Constantine VI. and Irene. Sometimes the letters are triplicated as on coins of X—N.

Irene X—N. (Sabatier, *Mon. Byz.,* and Madden, *Christian Emblems on Coins of Constantine I.,* etc., in *Num. Chron.,* N.S., 1878, vol. xviii., p. 175.)

XS. for X. On coins of the Republic—as AXSIVS for AXIVS *(Axia gens),* ALEXSANDREA for ALEXANDREA *(Æmilia gens),* PAXS for PAX *(Æmilia and Julia gentes),* MAXSVMVS for MAXVMVS *(Egnatia gens.)*

XV. *Quindecennalibus.* VOT. X. ET XV. F., VOT. X. MVLT. XV., VOT. XV. FEL. [or MVLT.] XX., VOT. XV. MVLT. XXXX., etc.

XV.—P. XV. in the *exergue* of certain *billon* coins of Gallienus (Cohen, *Méd. Imp.,* 2nd ed., vol. v., Nos. 44, 219, 362, 376, 599, 927, 989) interpreted by Cohen, *Tribunitiâ Potestate XV.* But this is very doubtful. M. Fenardent, the editor of the second edition of Cohen's work, has some remarks (vol. v., p. 352, *note)* on these pieces as well as on those with the *exergual* letters VIIC. (Nos. 277, 415, 425, 598, 634, 788, 848, 989, 1250.) He says, "All these coins are of the same fabric and same locality; they were struck at Antioch, where, probably at this time, was in operation, as in all the mints of Asia, that monetary revolution, which swept away from everyone their ancient customs of striking coins 'a leurs types avec des inscriptions grecques. L'atelier d'Antioche employait ce moyen très simple de dater ses nouvelles monnaies.'" Coins of Gallienus with the XVth Tribunitian power and the letters VIIC. (No. 848), and with P. XV. and VIIC. on varieties of the same type (No. 989) show that all these pieces are contemporary, and that they were issued in A.D. 267.

XV. *Quindecim.*—M. LEPIDVS AN. XV. PR. H. O. C. S. *Marcus Lepidus Annis quindecim Progressus* [not *Prætextatus,* cf. Val. Max. III., i. 1.] *Hostem Occidit Civem Servavit*—on *denarii* of M. Æmilius Lepidus, monetary magistrate about B.C. 60, and afterwards (B.C. 43—36) *Imperator* and *Triumvir Reipublicæ Constituendæ.* [AEMILIA *gens.*]

XV. S. F. or XVVIR. SAC. FAC. *Quindecimviri Sacris Faciundis.* [XVviri *Sacris Faciundis.*]

XVviri *sacris faciundis.* This body had especial charge of the Sibylline books, and in public danger or calamity were ordered by the Senate to inspect them. Under Tarquinius Superbus the number of these priests were two *(Duumviri),* men of illustrious birth. In B.C. 367, ten men *(Decemviri)*—five patrician and five plebeian—were appointed [see p. 878 and

x. *Decemvir*]; and later—possibly in the time of Sulla—their number was further increased to fifteen *(Quindecimviri.)* Julius Cæsar added one more, but fifteen was afterwards the usual number. The *Quindecimviri* were priests of Apollo, and each of them had in his house a brazen tripod *(cortina* or *tripus)* sacred to this god.

The title is found on the following coins :—

1. *Obv.* CAESAR AVGVSTVS TR. POT. Head of Augustus to r., laureated. *Rev.* L. MESCINIVS RVFVS IIIVIR *(triumvir.)* *Cippus,* on which is engraved IMP. CAES. AVG. LVD. SAEC. *(Imperator Cæsar Augustus ludos sæculares* [fecit]). In the *field,* XV. S. F. *(Quindecimviri sacris faciundis.)* Æ. (80 frcs.)

L. Mescinius Rufus was *triumvir* in B.C. 16. (Babelon, *Mon de la Répub. Rom.,* vol. ii., pp. 86, 221; Cohen, *Méd. Imp.,* 2nd ed., vol. i., p. 128. [See p. 526 of this Dictionary.]

2. *Obv.* A. VITELLIVS GERM. IMP. AVG. TR. P. [or IMP. GERMAN. TR. P. or GERMANICVS IMP. or IMP. GERMAN.] Head of Vitellius to r., laureated. *Rev.* XVVIR SAC. FAC. *(Quindecimviri sacris faciundis.)*

Tripod; above, a dolphin; within the tripod, a crow [CORVVS.] *N.* (120 frs.); Æ. (3 frcs.)

Eckhel (vol. vi., p. 316) has the following remarks on these coins :—"According to Suetonius *(in Vitell.* 5) Vitellius 'by the favour of three princes was not only advanced to the great offices of state, but to the highest dignities of the sacred order'; and Tacitus *(Hist.* iii., 86) says 'he rose to the Consulship, to pontifical dignities . . . . without any personal merit, but obtained all from the splendid reputation of his father.' . . . The whole of this type refers to Apollo. Servius *(ad Æn.,* lib. iii., 332) excellently explains the *dolphin*—'*Hinc ergo et delphinum aiunt inter sacrata Apollinis receptum, cujus rei vestigium est, quod hodieque XVvirorum cortinis delphinus in summo honore ponitur, et pridie cum sacrificium faciunt, velut symbolum delphinus circumfertur, ob hoc scilicet, quia XVviri librorum Sibyllinorum sunt antistites, Sibylla autem Apollinis vates, et delphinus Apollini sacer est.'* I will also quote a passage from Martianus Capella (lib. ix., *De Music.)* in which he introduces Apollo speaking thus—'*Æonistice* [divination by augury] *tertia est, per quam tripus illa ventura denunciat, atque omnis eminuit nostra cortina; denique in argumentum præscientiæ corvus mihi adludit,* etc.' That the crow was sacred to Apollo is well known. It appears also on *quinarii* of M. Antony and Lepidus, the triumvirs, near an augural *lituus,* and a *guttus* (jug), and consequently agreeably to the type of our coin, the crow is called by Statius *(Theb.,* lib. iii., ver. 506) *comes obscurus tripodum,* by Silius Italicus *(Punic.* v. 78) *Phoebea avis,* and by Ælian *(De Animal. Nat.,* lib. i., c. 48) Ἀπολλωνος ἀκόλουθος, the attendant of Apollo. These coins were struck either before Vitellius entered upon the office of *Pontifex Maximus,* or immediately afterwards, and he probably caused them to be struck to proclaim his elevation to the first office in the priesthood, just as Vespasian and Titus, though already *Pontifices Maximi*, declared themselves publicly as *augurs* on their coins."

The *tripod* which occurs on the coins of Cassius Longinus *Imperator* in B.C. 42 *(Cassia gens)* doubtless alludes to the dignity of *Quindecimvir sacris faciundis* conferred upon Cassius, whilst on those of L. Manlius Torquatus, monetary *triumvir* in B.C. 54 *(Manlia gens)*, and of M. Opeimius, moneyer in B.C. 134, there is a probable allusion to the same dignity having been conferred on one of their ancestors (Babelon, *Mon. de la Répub. Rom.*, vol. i., pp. 334, 335 ; vol. ii., pp. 180, 274, 275.) It has been suggested (Babelon, *op. cit.*, vol. i., p. 313) that the head of the Sibyl and the Sphinx on the *denarii* of Titus Carisius, moneyer about B.C. 48, refers to the fact of one of his ancestors having been one of the *quindecimviri* charged to guard the Sibylline books.

The *crow* may be found on coins, besides those previously mentioned, of Domitian *(Rev. s. c.—Æ. III.)* and on a brass medallion of Marcus Aurelius (TR. POT. III. COS. II.) struck in A.D. 149 (Grueber, *Rom. Medallions*, pl. xix., No. 1 ; Froehner, *Médaillons de l'Emp. Romain*, p. 82), wrongly attributed earlier in this Dictionary (p. 64) to Antoninus Pius.

XVI., as a mark of value—16 *asses*—but rarely on the *denarii* of the Republic ; sometimes replaced by the sign ✕, monogram of XVI. (Babelon, *Mon. de la Répub. Rom.*, vol. i., pp. xxiii., 67, 68, 232 ; vol. ii., pp. 190 *note*, 495, 509, 510.)

XX., 20 sesterces—on the first gold coins struck for the Roman Republic at Capua in B.C. 217. Other marks of value found on these coins are ↓X. 60 *sesterces* and XXXX. 40 *sesterces* (Mommsen, *Mon. Rom.*, vol. ii., pp. 57, 113, 236 ; vol. iv., p. 30 ; Babelon, *Mon. de la Répub. Rom.*, vol. i., pp. xxvii., xxx., 24, 26.)

XX., as a mark of value on the copper coins of the Ostrogoths without name of king (Sabatier, *Mon. Byz.*, vol. i., p. 211 ; Keary, *Num. Chron.*, N.S., 1878, vol. xviii., pp. 163, 165.)

XX. *Vicennales (?)*—PRIMI XX. IOVI [*sic* IOVII] AVGVSTI—on a rare gold coin of Diocletian described in the *Ancien Catalogue du Cabinet des Médailles*, Paris (Cohen, *Méd. Imp.*, 2nd ed., vol. vi., p. 458, and *note.)* [See *Vota.*]

XX. *(Vicennalia ?)* DIOCLETIANI AVG. or MAXIMIANI AVG., within a laurel wreath, on gold coins of Diocletian and Maximian Hercules.

XX. *Vicennalibus*—VOT. XV. FEL. or MVLT. XX., VOT. XX. SIC. or MVLT. XXX., etc. [See x. *Decennalibus.*]

XX. *Vicesima, Vicesimo, Vicesimum*, and similarly with the compounds of xx. up to XXIX. or XXVIIII. [See x. *Decimum.*]

XX., within a laurel wreath ; in the *exergue*, AQ. *(Aquileiæ)* or CONST. *(Constantinæ*—Arles), or LVG. *(Lugduno.)* Obv. CAESAR. Head of Constantius Gallus to r., bare. Æ. Med. (300 frcs.) Froehner *(Médaillons de l'Emp. Romain*, p. 319), suggests that the xx. on these medal-

lions indicates the value of the pieces of which the weight equalled ₂₄th of the silver pound.

XX.—PXXT., SXXT., TXXT., QXXT., VXXT., VIXXT.   *Prima, Secunda, Tertia, Quarta, Quinta, Sexta, ΔΔ. Tarracone*—on coins of Aurelian and Probus. " On the accession of Aurelian (A.D. 270—275) to the throne he attempted to remedy the disordered state of the coinage, and to restore it from its degraded state under Gallienus. His first object was to put an end to the continual fluctuations in the price of gold, caused by the quantity of base money which was issued from the Imperial mint. To effect this with as little injury as possible, he reduced the base *denarii* in circulation to the rate at which they then circulated, which appears to have been 500 or 525 to an *aureus*, and he consequently issued from the mint pieces equal to 20 or 21 of these copper *denarii* as equivalent to a *denarius* of account. The weight of the common copper and plated coins of Aurelian and his successors, which have xx. and xxi. in the *exergue*, varies from 56 to 66 grains, and consequently from twenty to twenty-one are equal to four of the large copper coins, or *sesterces*, of Alexander Severus and Gordianus III." (Finlay, *Greece under the Romans*, pp. 530, 531.) The numbers xx. and xxi. occur also on the coins of Probus, but the former was discontinued after his reign, whilst the latter occurs to the time of Constantine (Madden, *Num. Chron.*, N.S., 1862, vol. ii., pp. 242, 243, cf. p. 49 ; *Handbook of Rom. Num.*, p. 160.) [See VXXT., VXX. and *Tarraco, Karthago*, p. 911.]

XXI.—(1) with *Latin* letters—XXIP., XXIS., XXIT., XXIQ., XXIV., XXIVI., XXIVII.,—XXI, *Prima, Secunda, Tertia, Quarta, Quinta, Sexta, Septima*, or P., S., T., Q., V., VIXXI. *Prima. Secunda, Tertia, Quarta, Quinta, Sexta* xxi. (2) with *Greek* letters XXIA. B., Γ., Δ., ϵ., S., z., 1, 2, 3, 4, 5, 6, 7, or A., B., Γ., Δ., ϵ. sxxi., 1, 2, 3, 4, 5, 6 xxi—on coins of Aurelian and Probus [xx.]

XXI., as a mark of value on the copper coins of the Vandals, without name of king (Sabatier, *Mon. Byz.*, vol. i., p. 221 ; Keary, *Num. Chron.*, N.S., 1878, vol. xviii., p. 142.)

XXV., as a mark of value, on the silver coins of the Vandal kings, in Africa (Friedlaender, *Münzen der Vandalen ;* Sabatier, *Mon. Byz.*, vol. i., pp. 212—220 ; Keary, *Num. Chron.*, N.S., 1878, vol. xviii., pp. 137—149.)

XXX., as a mark of value, on a Romano-Campanian gold coin published by Riccio *(Le Mon. delle ant. fam. di Roma.* Supp., pl. lxvii., 7), Cohen (*Méd. Cons.*, p. 346, No. 10, pl. xliv., 10), Mommsen *(Mon. Rom.*, vol. i., p. 371), and Garrucci *(Sylloge*, p. 46, No. 5) ; but the piece is rejected as false by the Baron d'Ailly *(Recherches sur la Mon. Rom.*, vol. i., p. 194) an opinion upheld by M. Babelon *(Mon. de la Répub. Rom.*, vol. i., p. 24.)

XXX. *Tricennalibus*—VOT. XX. MVLT. XXX., VOT. XXX. MVLT. XXXX. [See x. *Decennalibus*, xx. *Vicennalibus.*]

XXX.   *Tricesima, Tricesimo, Tricesimum*, and

similarly with the compounds of XXX. up to XXXIX. or XXXVIIII. [See X. *Decimum.*]

XXXV. *Quinque Tricennalibus*—VOT. XXXV. or VT. (for VOT.) XXXV.

XXXX. 40 *sesterces*—on the first gold coins struck for the Roman Republic at Capua in B.C. 217 [See XX., 20 *sesterces.*]

XXXX.—LEX XXXX.—on *sextans* of Pæstum Lucaniæ *(Cat. of Greek Coins in the Brit. Mus., Italy,* p. 281.)

XXXX. *Quadragennalibus*—VOT. XXX. MVLT. XXXX., VOT. XXXX. [See X. *Decennalibus,* XX. *Vicennalibus,* XXX. *Tricennalibus.*]

XXXX. *Quadragesima, Quadragesimo, Quadragesimum,* and similarly with the compounds of XXXX. up to XXXXVIIII. [See X. *Decimum.*]

XXXX. *(Quadragensuma)* REMISSA S. C. Triumphal arch, on which may be seen Galba in a *quadriga* crowned by Victory. *Obv.* SER. *(Servius)* GALBA IMP. CAESAR AVG. P. M. TR. P. P. P. Head of Galba to r., laureated; beneath, a globe. Æ. I. (250 frcs.) A similar type, but with two equestrian figures on the arch, and sometimes prisoners below, and with the legend QVADRAGENS. REMISSAE S. C. or QVADRAGENSVMA REMISSA S. C., occurs on his second brass coins (60 frcs.) These coins refer to the repeal of the imposts by Galba, of which no mention is made in history, except that it is recorded (Suet., *Vesp.,* 16) that Vespasian "not satisfied with reviving the imposts *which had been repealed in the time of Galba,* imposed new and onerous taxes," etc. The following brass coins of Galba also refer to the same remission—LIB. [or LIBERT.] AVG. R. XL. *(Remissa Quadragensuma)* S. C. Liberty standing to l., holding cap and sceptre (Æ. I. 50 frcs.; Æ. II. 15 frcs.); ROMA. R. XL. S. C. Rome, standing to l., leaning on a trophy, holding a Victory [or a statuette of Fortune or a laurel branch] and a spear surmounted by an eagle; sometimes at her feet a shield. Æ. I. (40 frcs.) [See pp. 671, 702.]

XL., as a mark of value, on the large copper coins of Zeno (Sabatier, *Mon. Byz.,* vol. i., p. 140, pl. viii., No. 11), and on the copper coins of the Ostrogoths without the name of the king (Sabatier, *Mon. Byz.,* vol. i., p. 210; Keary, *Num. Chron.,* N.S., 1878, vol. xviii., p. 162.)

XL. *Quadragensuma.—* R. XL. *Remissa Quadragensuma*—on coins of Galba. [XXXX. *(Quadragensuma)* REMISSA.]

XL. *Quadragesimo.*—LVGVDVNI. A. XL. *Anno Quadragesimo*—on silver *quinarii* of Mark Antony, struck in B.C. 43—42. The figures XL. here represent the *age* of Mark Antony at the time these coins were struck. [XLI.] The figures LII., on gold and silver coins of Julius Cæsar, also probably denote his *age.* (Madden, *Num. Chron.,* N.S., 1865, vol. v., pp. 5—8; De Salis, *Rev. Arch.,* 1866, vol. xiv., p. 17.)

XLI. *Quadragesimo et uno*—ANTONI. IMP. A. XLI. *Anno Quadragesimo et uno*—on silver quinarii of Mark Antony representing *his age.* [XL. *Quadragesimo.*]

XLII., as a mark of value, on the copper coins of the Vandals, without the name of the king

(Sabatier, *Mon. Byz.,* vol. i., p. 221; Keary, *Num. Chron.,* N.S., 1878, vol. xviii., p. 142.)

XCVI., within a laurel wreath; sometimes with *exergual* letters AQ. *(Aquileiæ)* or T. *(Tarracone)*—on silver coins of Diocletian (20 frcs.), Constantius Chlorus Cæsar (20 frcs.), and Galerius Maximian Cæsar (30 frcs.), or VCVC *(sic)* on a silver coin of Constantius Chlorus Cæsar, from *Banduri, du Musée Farnese* (30 frcs.)—XCVI. in the *exergue* of a silver coin of Constantine I. Cæsar, with the legend CONSERVATOR KART. *(Karthaginis)* SVAE. (100 frcs.)—[See p. 911.] These coins were issued by Diocletian about A.D. 292 as "96 pieces to the pound of silver." This has been satisfactorily established by Marchant, Cavedoni, Pinder and Friedlaender, Mommsen, Blacas, and de Witte (Mommsen, *Mon. Rom.,* vol. iii., p. 74; vol. iv., p. 99.) In Cohen's 1st edition *(Méd. Imp.,* vol. v., p. 387) he argues against this interpretation because there are coins of Diocletian in the *Cabinet of Vienna,* and of Maximian, according to *Banduri,* with the figures XCVIIT., which have been explained by Cavedoni *(Ann. Arch.,* 1860, p. 442) as XCVI. ITalicam [*libram.*] The *errata* of Cohen, *(Suppl.,* vol. vi., p. 627) point out, however, that Eckhel and Banduri both misread these coins, a fact, as regards the Vienna one, confirmed by the late M. Arneth (Cavedoni, *Bull. dell 'Instit.,* 1863, p. 220; cf. Madden, *Num. Chron.,* N.S., 1865, vol. v., p. 76.) The editor of the 2nd edition of Cohen (vol. vi., p. 478) is not very clear in his remarks on the coins of Diocletian, and gives a coin of Maximian Hercules from *Banduri,* with XCVIIT., which should be omitted.

Y.

Y. The letter Y was borrowed from the Greek alphabet in the time of Cicero in order to express more precisely the sound of *Upsilon.* Its introduction into the Latin alphabet was prior to that of Z, as shown by the arrangement of the final letters V X Y Z (Isaac Taylor, *The Alphabet,* vol. ii., p. 142.) This letter may be found on *denarii* of the *Quinctia* (B.C. 104), *Vibia* (B.C. 90), and *Poblicia* (B.C. 79) *gentes* (Mommsen, *Mon. Rom.,* vol. ii., pp. 177, 378, 417, 466.)

YPSAE. *Ypsæus*—P. YPSAE. S. C. *Publius Ypsæus. Senatus Consulto,* or C. YPSAE. COS. PRIV. CEPIT. *Caius Ypsæus Consul Privernum Cepit,* on *denarii* of Publius Plautius Ypsæus, curule edile about B.C. 58, commemorating the military successes of his ancestor C. Plautius Ypsæus, consul, who took Privernum in B.C. 341 (Livy, vii., 27, viii., 1.) [PLAVTIA *gens.*] On other *denarii* his name is rendered *Hupsæus*— P. HVPSAE. AED. CVR. C. HVPSAE. [or HVPSAEV. or HVPSAEVS] COS. PREIV. [or PREIVE. or PREIVI. or PREIVER.] CAPT. [or CAPTV. or CAPTVM.] *Publius Hupsæus Ædilis Curulis. Caius Hupsæus Consul. Preivernum Captum.*

Z.

Z, the twenty-third and last letter of the Latin alphabet, being reintroduced from the Greek alphabet in the time of Cicero for the transliteration of Greek words. (Isaac Taylor, *The Alphabet*, vol. ii., pp. 142—144.) The letter Z may be found on the *denarii* of the *Quinctia* and *Pollicia gentes* (Mommsen, *Mon. Rom.*, vol. ii., p. 177; p. 378, No. 186; p. 466, No. 255.) [See Y.]

Z, as a differential letter—7—SISC. P. Z. *Siscia Pecunia* or *Percussa* 7 ; S. M. A. Z. *Signata Moneta Antiochiæ* 7, etc.

ZA. *Zacynthus.* [*Zacynthus.*]

Zacynthus (Zante), an island in the Sicilian sea. The history of Zacynthus, illustrated numismatically, is given by Professor Gardner in the *Numismatic Chronicle,* 3rd ser., 1885, vol. v., pp. 81—107. One portion of its history falls in the time of Mark Antony and his General Sosius, B.C. 44—31, of whom there are the following coins :—

1. *Obv.* IMP. *(Imperator.)* Head of Mark Antony to r., bare. *Rev.* C. SOSIVS Q. *(Caius Sosius Quæstor.)* Eagle standing to r. on thunderbolt; in front, ZA. *(Zacynthus)* and a caduceus. Æ. II. (100 frcs.)

2. *Obv.* Head of Mark Antony to r., bare; behind, ZA. *(Zacynthus.)* *Rev.* C. SOSIVS IMP. *(Caius Sosius Imperator.)* Trophy between two captives. Æ. III. (100 frcs.)

3. *Obv.* Head of Apollo to r., laureated; behind, ZA. *(Zacynthus.)* *Rev.* C. SOSIVS COS. DESIG. *(Caius Sosius Consul Designatus.)* Tripod. Æ. III. (100 frcs.)

4. *Obv.* Head of Neptune to r., with diadem; behind, ZA. *(Zacynthus.)* *Rev.* C. SOSIVS COS. *(Caius Sosius Consul.)* Dolphin twined round trident. Æ. III. (100 frcs.)

No. 1 shows Sosius as *Quæstor* to Antony, and was probably struck about B.C. 38.

No. 2, on which Sosius is styled *Imperator*, refers to the assistance given by him to Herod in his attack on Jerusalem in B.C. 37, when Antigonus, the last of the Asmonæan princes, was defeated and captured. It is possible that the captive figures on this coin represent Judæa and Antigonus (Madden, *Coins of the Jews*, p. 99 ; the remarks given by me as to the attribution of these pieces to *Zabulon* must be withdrawn in favour of *Zacynthus.)*

On No. 3 Sosius appears as *Consul Designatus,* a title which he bore from the year B.C. 39 to B.C. 32, when he became *Consul,* as No. 4 testifies.

These coins belong to the *Antonia* and *Sosia gentes* (Babelon, *Mon. de la Répub. Rom.,* vol. i., pp. 181, 194; vol. ii., pp. 463—465.)

Prof. Gardner *(op. cit.)* publishes an autonomous coin of Zacynthus, which, from its type, shows obvious allusion to the augurate of Antony, and that Antony accorded to the island a certain degree of autonomy in return for favours rendered to Sosius.—*Obv.* Lituus and Oenochoe. *Rev.* ZA. within wreath. Æ. III.

Zante | *Zacynthus.*]

ZENO, Emperor of the East, A.D. 474—491, who was descended from an illustrious Isaurian family, was originally named Trassalisseus, which he changed for Zeno on his marriage, in A.D. 468, with Ariadne, daughter of the Emperor Leo I. and Verina [VERINA.] On the death of Leo I., in A.D. 474, with whom had been associated in the Empire his grandson Leo II., son of Zeno and Ariadne, Zeno conducted the government, his son being only a child, though taking the precedence, as testified by coins. The boy lived only a short time, and Zeno became sole Emperor. His reign was oppressive, and many revolts occurred. Verina, widow of Leo I., claimed the Empire, Zeno fled to Isauria, and Basiliscus, brother of Verina, was proclaimed Emperor in A.D. 476, but was deposed the following year. Zeno, on his restoration, showed no better qualities, and again rebellions were frequent. After a turbulent reign of seventeen years he died in A.D. 491, and was succeeded by Anastasius, who married his widow Ariadne. The following coins of Zeno are extant :—

LEO II. AND ZENO.

1. *Obv.* DN. *(Domini)* LEO ET ZENO PP. AVG. *(Perpetui Augusti.)* Helmeted bust, facing, of Leo II., with shield on which a horseman, and holding spear over r. shoulder. *Rev.* SALVS REIPVBLICAE I. or Θ. Leo II., and to the l. his father Zeno, both with *nimbus*, seated, facing; between their heads a cross, and above a star; in the *exergue* CONOB. N. (150 frcs.)

2. *Obv.* Same legend and type. *Rev.* VICTORIA AVGGG. *(Augustorum.)* Victory standing to l., holding a long cross; in the *field* a star; in the *exergue* CONOB. N. (150 frcs.)

3. *Obv.* Same legend. Bust of Leo II. to r., with diadem. *Rev.* VICTORIA AVGVSTORVM. Victory walking, holding wreath and globe; in the *field* a star. N. *Tremissis* (80 frcs.)

4. *Obv.* Same legend and type. *Rev.* Cross within a wreath; in the *exergue* CONOB. N. *Tremissis* (100 frcs.)

ZENO AND LEO II.

1. *Obv.* DN. *(Domini)* ZENO ET LEO. NOV. CAES. Bust of Zeno to r., with diadem. *Rev.* VICTORIA AVGVSTORVM. Victory standing to l., holding wreath and globe, surmounted by cross; in the *exergue* CONOB. N. *Tremissis* (75 frcs.)

2. *Obv.* ZENO ET LEO NOV. CAES. Head of Zeno to r., with diadem; in the *exergue* IIII. *Rev.* INVICTA ROMA. Victory walking to r., holding wreath and a trophy on left shoulder; in the *field* S. C.; in the *exergue* XL. Æ. I. (60 frcs.)

With respect to the letters NOV. CAES., some have considered them to stand for *Novus Cæsar*, but it is far more probable that the NOV. equals NOB., and should be interpreted *Nobilissimus*. A similar interchange of V and B may be found on the gold coins of Theodosius II. and Marcian in the legend GLORIA ORVIS [ORBIS] TERRAR. Why, as Eckhel observes *(Doct. Num. Vet.*, vol. viii., p. 200) Zeno and Leo are called *Nobilissimi Cæsares*, when they were certainly *Augusti*, as testified by history and other coins, cannot be explained "*nisi constaret, de titulorum hac ætate confusione*." Eckhel further gives a coin of Zeno—D. N. ZENO PERP. N. C., adding "*verum in aureo integerrimo musei Cæsarei est manifestum N.C. Ad hæc si Zeno et Leo simul sumpti potuere dici Nobilissimi Cæsares, nescio, cur non et Zeno solus.*" This coin, however, is not published by Sabatier *(Mon. Byz.)*

ZENO ALONE.

Obverse legend for *gold* and *silver* D. N. *(Dominus Noster)* ZENO PERP. [or PERPE.] *(Perpetuus)* AV. [or AVG.] *(Augustus)*. Principal reverse legends VICTORIA AVGGG. (*N*. 20 frcs.; *N*. *Semissis*, 70 frcs; *N*. *Tremissis*, 10 frcs.); VICTORIA AVGVSTORVM (*N*. *Tremissis*, 10 frcs.); SALVS REIPVBLICE *(sic)*. Monogram of Christ within a wreath (*N*. from *Mionnet*, 24 frcs.); *No legend*. Cross within a wreath (*N*. 8 frcs.) GLORIA ROMANORVM. Zeno standing facing; in the *exergue*, THCOB. (*Æ*. 100 frcs.) ; TOV—VIMV—MTI. [for VOT. V. MVLT. X.] within a wreath (*Æ*. 30 frcs.); *No legend*. Military figure; in the *field*, MD. *(Mediolani.)* Barbarous fabric (*Æ*. 60 frcs.); Military figure on the prow of a ship; in the *field*, RV. *(Ravennæ)* (*Æ*. 35 frcs.); Eagle to r. or to l. (*Æ*. 35 frcs.); Victory walking to l. (*Æ*. 60 frcs.) *Brass coins*—Obverse legends—IMP. *(Imperator)* ZEN. [or ZENO] FEL. [or FELIX] PERP. AVG. *(Perpetuus Augustus)*, or IMP. ZENO SEMPER AVG. *Rev.* INVICTA ROMA. Type as No. 2 of Zeno and Leo II. (*Æ*. I. 40 frcs.); *Obv.* D. N. ZENO PERP. AVGG. *Rev.* VICTORIA AVGG. (*Æ*. III. 15 frcs.); *Obv.* DN. ZENO P. F. *(Pius Felix)* AVG. *Rev.* No legend. Emperor standing (*Æ*. III. 20 frcs.) ; Monogram of Zeno within a wreath (*Æ*. III. 5 frcs.)

ZENOBIA *(Septimia)*, Queen of Palmyra, wife of Odenathus, and mother of Timolaus, Herennianus, and Vabalathus. [ODENATHVS ; VABALATHVS.] Though claiming her descent from the Macedonian kings of Egypt, she is supposed by some Christian writers to have been a Jewess (Jost, *Geschichte des Israel*, vol. iv., p. 166 ; Milman Hist. of the Jews, vol. iii., p. 175 ; cf. Gibbon, *Rom. Emp.*, ed. Smith, vol. ii., p. 20, *note* a.) After the death of Odenathus (A.D. 266—267) Zenobia attempted to place under her sway Syria, Asia, and Egypt, and assumed the title of Queen of they East [BACIΛICCA on an inscription found in Palmyra, dated 582 of the Seleucidan era = A.D. 271, *Bull. de l'Athén. Franc.*, 1855, p. 36.] Aurelian made war with her, and defeated her at the battles of Daphne and Emesa. After the capture of this latter city, Zenobia fled to Palmyra, which was besieged by Aurelian. She attempted to escape, but was captured by the cavalry of Aurelian, and Palmyra

soon afterwards surrendered. Zenobia—together with the Emperor Tetricus, who had given himself up to Aurelian at the great battle of Chalons, A.D. 274 [TETRICVS]—had to take a captive's part in the triumph of Aurelian, but afterwards (as well as Tetricus) was treated with great clemency, being allowed to pass the remainder of her life with her sons in a handsome villa at Tibur or Tivoli, which had been presented to her by her conqueror.

A full historical and numismatic account of Zenobia and the Princes of Palmyra has been written by Dr. von Sallet *(Die Fürsten von Palmyra unter Gallienus, Claudius, und Aurelian*, 1866), who, from coin-dates, inscriptions and ancient authors, has drawn up the following chronological table :—

A.D. 264—Odenathus conquers the Persians, and is recognised by Gallienus as ruler of the East.

266—267.—Odenathus and his son and co-regent Herodes are murdered by Mæonius.

266—267. (August 29.)—First year of the reign of Vabalathus, son of Odenathus and Zenobia. Under the reign of Claudius, Zabdas and Timagenes, the generals of Vabalathus and Zenobia, conquer the insurgent Egyptians. Homage rendered by the Egyptians to Vabalathus *Imperator*, the Deputy of the Emperor Claudius.

270 (Spring).—Aurelian *Augustus*. Recognition of Vabalathus in Syria and Egypt as *vir consularis* ROMANORVM IMPERATOR DVX ROMANORVM ('Υπατικὸς ΑΥΤοκράτωρ Cτρατηγὸς 'Ρωμαίων.) Zenobia *Augusta*. Coins with heads of Aurelian and Vabalathus.

270 (August 29.)—Beginning of the fifth Egyptian year of the reign of Vabalathus; coins with his and Aurelian's head.

270—271 (August 29.)—Revolt of Vabalathus and Zenobia against Aurelian. Vabalathus assumes the title of *Augustus*. Alexandrian and Latin coins of Vabalathus with the title of *Augustus*. Alexandrian coins of Zenobia *Augusta*, who also assumes the title of Queen. Battles of Daphne and Emesa (Im"mæ ?)

271. (Beginning of the Autumn.) Conquest of Egypt.

271. (In the second half of the year.) Conquest of Palmyra. Zenobia and Vabalathus taken prisoners. End of the Palmyrian rule. Revolt and conquest of Firmus in Egypt and of Achilleus (?) in Palmyra. Aurelian recognised as sole Emperor in Syria and Egypt.

The only genuine coins of Zenobia are Alexandrian ones, bearing the date L. $\mathbf{\epsilon}$. (year 5) of Vabalathus, and issued at the same time as the coins of Vabalathus *Augustus* with the same date. Other coins, namely—a silver medallion with L. Δ. (year 4) given by *D'Ennery*, a brass piece of Zenobia and Aurelian with no date in the *Mus. Theupoli*, a brass piece with date L. Z. (year 7) and ΠΑΛ. published by *Vaillant*, and a brass piece with ΑΠΟΛΛ. Γ., or remains of the legend ΤΡΙΠΟΛ ΕΙΤWΝ and no date in the *Pembroke* collection—are false; and so is the *Latin* coin given by Cohen *(Méd. Imp.*, 2nd ed., vol. vi., p. 214) from *Tanini*. However, it is not impossible

that cotemporary with the *Latin* coins of Vabalathus *Augustus, Latin* coins of Zenobia *Augusta*
were struck, but no genuine specimen has ever
yet been seen.

The coins of Zenobia, as extant, are:—

1. *Obv.* CЄΠT. ZHNOBIA CЄB. ` Bust of
Zenobia to r., with diadem. *Rev.* L. Є. (year
5). Female figure standing before an altar. *Pot.*
(200 frcs.) (Mionnet, vol. vi., No. 3534.)

2 *Obv.* Same legend and type as No. 1.
Rev. L. Є.   Providence standing to l., raising
r. hand, and holding a cornu-copiæ in her left.
Pot. (200 frcs.)   *(Cab. des Méd.,* Paris.)

3. *Obv.* CЄΠTIM. ZHNOBIA CЄB.   Same
type.   *Rev.* L. Є. Same type as No. 2.   *Pot.*
(200 frcs.)   *(British Museum.)*

4. *Obv.* Same legend and type as No. 3. *Rev.*
L. Є. Spes walking to l., holding flowers in r.
hand and raising her dress with left. *Pot.* (200
frcs.)   *(Cab. des Méd.,* Paris ; *British Museum.)*

5. *Obv.* CЄΠTIMIA ZHNOBIA CЄB. Same
type as No. 1.   *Rev.* L. Є.   Same type as No.
4.   *Pot.* (200 frcs.)   *(Cab. des Méd.,* Paris.)

6. *Obv.* CЄΠTIM. ZHNOBIA CЄB.   Same
type as No. 1.   *Rev.* L., Female bust (? Diana)
to r.; before, a large crescent.   *Pot.* (200 frcs.)
(British Museum.)

This piece is described by von Sallet *(op. cit.)*
with the obverse legend CЄΠT. ZHNOBIA CЄB.
and so also by Cohen *(Méd. Imp.,* 1st ed., vol.
v., p. 155 ; 2nd ed., vol. vi., p. 215) but in both
editions of Cohen the coin is engraved with the
legend CЄΠTIM. ZHNOBIA CЄB. from the specimen in the British Museum. The letter (*s*)
after L. Є. in the description of this coin in the
second edition of Cohen should be omitted. Why
the year date does not appear on this piece is
curious, more especially as there is no mark of
erasure visible on the coin.

ZENONIS *(Ælia),* wife of Basiliscus, usurper
of the Eastern throne A.D. 476—477, and brother
of the Empress Verina, wife of Leo I. The title
of *Augusta* was conferred upon her by her husband. Zeno sent her into exile with her husband
and her son Marcus (of whom there are no coins),
and they all perished of hunger in A.D. 477.

The following coins are in existence:—

1. *Obv.* AEL. ZENONIS AVG. Bust of Ze-

nonis to r., with diadem,
crowned by a hand from
above. *Rev.* VICTORIA AVGGG.
Victory walking to l., and
holding a long cross; in
the *field* to r., a star; in
the *exergue,* CONOB.   *N.*
(400 frcs.)

2. *Obv.* Same legend and type. *Rev.* Monogram of Zenonis. Æ. III. (60 frcs.)

Zeugitana, a region forming the more northern
part of the Roman province of Africa. After the
fall of Carthage in B.C. 146, it was united with
Byzacium in one province; this province was
called *Africa,* and later *Africa vetus,* to distinguish it from other countries also annexed—
Emporia and *Numidia* called *Africa Nova.*
(Müller, *Num de l'Anc. Afrique,* vol. ii., pp.
38—63, 65). Under the reign of Augustus
Zeugitana formed the centre of a large province
called *Africa* or *Libya,* which extended from the
Cyrenaica to *Numidia occidentalis.* On the division of the provinces between Augustus and the
Senate, in B.C. 27, Zeugitana fell to the latter,
and was governed from this time by a Proconsul
resident at Carthage, which had been rebuilt. In
the 3rd century, when Africa was divided into
several provinces, Zeugitana was constituted a
separate province under the title of *Africa pro-
consularis.* (Müller, *op. cit.,* vol. ii., p. 65.)

Of the coast towns of this province the following issued coins:—*Carthago* (Roman colony),
Clypea, Hippo Diarrhytus, and *Utica.*

CARTHAGO (Roman colony).

In B.C. 122, only twenty-four years after the
destruction of Carthage, Caius Gracchus sent out
a colony of 6000 settlers to found on the site of
Carthage the new city of *Junonia,* but the project was annulled by the Senate. In B.C. 46
Julius Cæsar planned the restoration of Carthage
and Corinth, but the former did not prosper till
Augustus, in B.C. 27, sent 3000 colonists to found
the new city, and from this time the colony
grew so rapidly that when Strabo wrote
(towards the end of the reign of Augustus) it was
as flourishing and populous as any city in Africa.
The Proconsul of the province resided there.
After the death of Nero, in A.D. 68, Clodius
Macer, governor of Africa, revolted and laid
claim to the throne, but was very soon defeated
and put to death by the procurator Trebonius
Garucianus, acting under the orders of the Emperor Galba. Carthage continued to increase in
prosperity, rivalling Rome and Constantinople.
Ausonius *(Claræ Urbes,* II.) compares it with
these cities :

> " *Constantinopoli assurgit Carthago priori*
> *Non toto cessura gradu, quia tertia dici*
> *Fastidit.*"

In A.D. 308 Alexander, who had been appointed by Maxentius, governor of Africa, usurped
the purple, but was defeated in A.D. 311. [Rare
gold, silver, and brass coins, with legend INVICTA
ROMA FEL. [or FELIX] KARTHAGO, and in the
exergue P. K. *Prima Karthagini—see* pp. 34
and 911.]

Carthage was captured by Genseric in A.D.
439, and made the capital of the Vandal kings
[silver coins of Hilderic with legend FELIX
KARTC.; Vandal copper with KARTHAGO—see
Vandals] till retaken by Belisarius, general of Justinian, in A.D. 533, and was finally taken and
utterly destroyed by the Arabs in A.D. 647.

The following coins of Roman Carthage are in existence (Müller, *op. cit*, vol. ii., p. 149 ; Cohen, *Méd. Imp.*, 2nd ed., vol. i., pp. 23, 167, 208) :—

Before the reign of Augustus.

Obv. ARISTO MVTVMBAL. RICOCE SUF. *(? Sufes or Sufetes).* Two heads, jugate, bare (? J. Cæsar and Augustus.) *Rev.* KAR. *(Karthago)* VENERIS. Tetrastyle temple of (?) Jupiter or of (?) Baal; on the pediment, an eagle. Æ. [*See* VENERIS KAR.]

During the reign of Augustus.

1. *Obv.* AVG . . . o C . . . Head of Augustus (?) to l., bare. *Rev.* . . . CAE. M. T. F. M. M. A. II. VIR. Head of Julius Cæsar (?) to r., bare. Æ. II.

2. *Obv.* C. I. C. D. D. P. P. Head of Augustus (?) to r., bare. *Rev.* . . . ON. M. T. F. M. M. . . . Head of Julius Caesar (?) to l., bare. Æ. III.

* Owing to the bad preservation of these coins the legend and types are not clear. The letters M. T. F. and M. M. A. on both pieces evidently present the initials of the same *duumviri.* The obverse legend of No. 2 is *Colonia Julia Carthago. Decreto Decurionum, Permissu Proconsulis.*

3. *Obv.* IMP. C. D. F. A. P. M. P. P. *(Imperator Cæsar Divi Filius Augustus Pontifex Maximus Pater Patriæ.)* Head of Augustus to r. or to l., bare. *Rev.* P. I. SP. D. V. SP. IIVIR. C. I. C. *(Publius Junius Spendo Decimus Valerius* (?) *Speratus Duumviri Coloniæ Juliæ Carthaginis).* In the *field*, P. P. D. D. *(Permissu Proconsulis, Decreto Decurionum.)* Æ. II.

4. *Obv.* TI. CAE. [or TI. CAE. A. F.] IMP. V. *(Tiberius Cæsar* [or *Tiberius Cæsar Augusti Filius*] *Imperator V.)* Head of Tiberius to r. or to l., bare. *Rev.* Same as No. 3. Æ. II.

Tiberius was *Imperator V.* in A. D. 10, and the coins (No. 4) were issued near the end of the reign of Augustus, who died in A.D. 14.

During the reign of Tiberius.

1. *Obv.* TI. CAESAR IMP. P. P. *(Tiberius Cæsar Imperator Pater Patriæ).* Head of Tiberius to l. *Rev.* L. A. FAVSTVS D. C. BASSVS IIVIR. Livia seated to r., holding a *patera* and a sceptre; in the *field*, P. P. D. D. Æ. II.

2. Same legend as No. 1. *Rev.* Same legend as No. 1. Three ears of corn bound together; in the *field*, P. P. D. D. Æ. III.

It will be seen that the title P. P. *(Pater Patriæ)* is given to Tiberius on these coins, whilst the historians Suetonius (in *Tib.* 26), Dion Cassius (lvii., 8; lviii., 12), and Tacitus *(Ann.* i., 72 ; ii., 87) state that he persistently refused this title, and Eckhel *(Doct. Num. Vet.,* vol. vi., p. 200) remarks that all his coins confirm the statements of the historians. It appears, however, from these pieces that the title was conferred upon Tiberius in Africa without his permission.

CLYPEA.

Clypea or Clupea, originally *Aspis* ('Aσπίς), so called from its site on a hill of shield-like shape, was founded by Agathocles in B.C. 310, and after his departure was occupied by the Carthaginians. It was taken in the First Punic war by Manlius and Regulus B.C. 256, and in the Third Punic war was besieged by Calpurnius Piso, B.C. 148, who was repulsed. In Pliny's time *(Nat. Hist.,* v. 3) it was a free city. Ruins, including a Roman fort, are still in existence, and a small town bears at the present time the name of *Clybea* or *Kalibiah.*

The following coins are extant (Müller, *op. cit..,* vol. ii., p. 155; Cohen, *op. cit.,* vol. i., pp. 167, 208, 218) :—

During the reign of Augustus.

Obv. AVGVSTVS IMP. *(Imperator).* Head of Augustus to l., bare; behind, a *simpulum* or *? lituus;* all within a laurel wreath. *Rev.* C. I. P. IIII. VIR. Mercury wearing winged *petasus,* seated on a rock to l., holding a *caduceus.* Æ. I.

The letters C. I. P. may be interpreted *Clypea Julia Pia,* or *Pulchra* or *Pacensis* (?) as the C. P. I. on coins of Tiberius, but Müller thinks that it seems more probable that they represent the initials of the names of the IIIIVIR *(Quatuorviri)* than those of the name of the colony.

During the reign of Tiberius.

1. *Obv.* TI. CAE. DIVI AVG. F. AVG. IMP. VIII. COS. IIII. Head of Tiberius to l., bare. *Rev.* PERMISSV L. APRONI. PROCOS. III. C. *(Curante)* SEX. POM. *(Pomponio)* CELSO. Mercury wearing winged *petasus,* seated on a rock to l., holding a *caduceus;* in the *field,* C. P. I. *(Clypea Pia* or *Pulchra* or *Pacensis ?)* Æ. I.

2. *Obv.* Same legend and type as No. 1. *Rev.* Same legend as No. 1. Livia seated to r., holding ears of corn and a sceptre; in the *field,* C. P. I. Æ. II.

3. *Obv.* Same legend and type as No. 1. *Rev.* PERMIS. P. DOLABELLAE PROCOS C. *(Curante)* P. G. CAS. [or P. GAVIO CASCA.] Same type as No. 2. Æ. II.

4. *Obv.* Same legend and type as No. 1. *Rev.* PERMIS. P. DOLABELLAE PROCOS. C. *(Curante)* P. G. CAS. D. D. *(Gavio Casca. Decreto Decurionum).* Same type as No. 1. Æ. Med.

5. *Obv.* Same legend and type as No. 1. *Rev.* PERMIS. P. CORNELI. DOLABELLAE PROCOS. C. *(Curante)* P. CAS. D. D. Same type as No. 1. Æ. Med.

6. *Obv.* Same legend and type as No. 1. *Rev.* PERMIS. P. DOLABELLAE PROCOS. C. *(Curante)* P. GAVIO CAS. Same type as No. 1. Æ. Med.

7. *Obv.* DRVSO CAESARI. Head of Drusus to l., bare. *Rev.* PERMISSV L. APRONI. PROCOS III. Bust of Mercury to r. or to l., with winged *petasus;* behind, a *caduceus.* Æ. II.

8. *Obv.* Same legend and type as No. 7. *Rev.* PERM. DOLABELLAE PROCOS. C. *(Curante)* P. G. CAS. Same type as No. 7. Æ. II.

The coins of L. Apronius PROCOS III were issued in A.D. 19, and of P. Cornelius Dolabella PROCOS. in A.D. 23—24.

HIPPO DIARRHYTUS.

Hippo Diarrhytus ('Ιππὼν Διάῤῥυτος) a Phoenician colony, founded by the Sidonians, and situated at the entrance of a large lake ('Ιππωνῖτις λίμνη), consequently being subject to frequent inundations, and hence its name διάῤῥυτος—intersected by streams—transformed by different authors to *Dirutus*, *Diaritus*, and *Zaritus*. It was fortified and provided with a new harbour by Agathocles, and is called *Hipponensis Colonia* by the younger Pliny (*Epist.* ix., 33.) Its coins bear the name *Hippone libera*. A small town called *Benizert* or *Bizerta* occupies the site.

The following coins are in existence (Müller, *op. cit.*, p. 167, vol. iii., p. 193; Cohen, *op. cit.*, vol. i., pp. 185, 210, 220):—

1. *Obv.* LIBERA. Head of Astarte to l., with diadem and veiled. *Rev.* HIPPONE. Goddess (Thuro-Chusartis) standing, facing, with *modius* on head, holding in l. hand *caduceus* and two ears of corn. Æ.

2. *Obv.* HIPPONE. Head of Ceres to r., crowned with ears of corn. *Rev.* LIBERA. Head of Juno to r., with diadem. Æ.

3. *Obv.* HIPPONE. Warrior standing, leaning on his spear; at his feet a dog. *Rev.* LIBERA. Ceres, veiled, standing. Æ.

During the reign of Augustus.

Obv. CAESAR AVG. Head of Augustus to r., bare. *Rev.* HIPPONE LIBERA. Head of Caius and Lucius, facing each other, bare; to l., C.; to r., L. Æ. I.

During the reign of Tiberius.

1. *Obv.* TI. CAESAR DIVI AVGVSTI F. AVGVSTVS. Head of Tiberius to r., bare. *Rev.* HIPPONE LIBERA. Livia seated to r., holding *patera* and sceptre; in the *field*, IVL. AVG. Æ. I.

2. *Obv.* Same legend and type as No. 1. *Rev.* DRVSVS CAESAR. HIPPONE LIBERA. Head of Drusus to l., bare. Æ.

3. *Obv.* Same legend and type as No. 1; in front, *lituus;* behind, *simpulum. Rev.* L. APRONIVS. HIPPONE LIBERA. Head of Drusus to r., bare. Æ. II,

During the reign of Clodius Albinus.

Obv. IMP. CAES. D. CLO. SEP. ALB. AVG. *(Imperator Cæsar Decimus Clodius Septimius Albinus Augustus).* Head of Albinus to r., bare. *Rev.* HIPPONE LIBERA. Goddess seated to l.; holding *patera* and sceptre. Æ.

This coin, published by Müller after Mionnet *(Suppl.,* ix., p. 207, No. 9) is remarkable as no other coins were struck in the towns of the province of Africa after the reign of Tiberius. It is

true that Albinus was of African origin, having been born at Hadrumetum, and that consequently a new right of coinage may have been permitted to Hippo, but it is not certain that the coin is genuine, and it is *not* mentioned by Cohen *(Méd. Imp.,* 2nd ed., vol. iii., p. 424.)

Its authenticity is perhaps confirmed by a brass coin in the Dresden Cabinet. This piece has on the obverse two heads facing, representing either Septimius Severus with one of his sons, or Macrinus with his son Diadumenianus, but the legend is very indistinct, so that it is not possible to determine with certainty. The reverse type is a vessel in full sail, and the legend LIBERA, a surname exclusively belonging to Hippo. Septimius Severus was born at Leptis, and Macrinus was a native of Cæsareia Mauretaniæ (Müller, *op. cit.*, vol. ii., p. 170.)

UTICA.

[*See Utica.*]

LUCIUS CLODIUS MACER.

Lucius Clodius Macer, who was appointed by Nero governor of Africa, revolted on the death of the Emperor in A.D. 68, but was soon subdued and executed by order of Galba.

The following coins are extant :—

A. *Without his head.*

1. *Obv.* L. CLODI. MACRI S. C. Female figure (Liberty) standing to l., holding a cap and a wreath or patera. *Rev.* LEG. I. (in *field*), LIB. MACRIANA (around). Roman eagle between two standards. Æ. (200 frcs.)

2. *Obv.* L. CLODI. MACRI. LIBERATRIX S. C. Head of Africa to r. *Rev.* Same legend and type as No. 1. Æ. (300 frcs.)

3. *Obv.* Same legend and type as No. 2. Sometimes two javelins behind the head of Africa. *Rev.* LEG. III. LIB. AVG. Roman eagle between two standards. Æ. (300 frcs.)

4. *Obv.* L. CLODI. MACRI. LIBERA S. C. Same type as No. 2. *Rev.* Same legend and type as No. 3. Æ. (300 frcs.)

5. *Obv.* L. CLODI. [or L. C.] MACRI. S. C. Head of lion to r. *Rev.* Same legend and type as No. 3. Æ. (300 frcs.)

6. *Obv.* L. CLODI. MACRI. S. C. Bust of Victory to r. *Rev.* Same legend and type as No. 3. Æ.* (250 frcs.)

7. *Obv.* ROMA S. C. Head of Rome to r., helmeted. *Rev.* L. CLODI. MACRI. Trophy. Æ. (300 frcs.)

8. *Obv.* L. C. [or L. CLODI. ?] MACRI. CARTHAGO S. C. Bust of Carthage to r., helmeted; behind, a cornu-copiæ. *Rev.* SICILIA. Triquetra with head of Medusa; between the three legs three ears of corn. Æ. (300 frcs.)

B. *With his head.*

Obv. L. CLODIVS MACER [or L. CLODI. MACRI.] S. C. Head of Clodius Macer to r., bare. *Rev.*

PROPRAE. AFRICAE [or PROPR. AFRCAE *sic*]. *(Proprætor Africæ).* Galley. Æ. (1500 frcs].

The types of the coins of Clodius Macer show that he had the idea of again establishing the Republic, confirmed by the fact of his reviving the ancient title of *Proprætor*, for which Augustus had substituted that of *Proconsul*, and also by the letters s. c., *Senatus Consulto*, to mark that the supreme power rested with the Senate and not with one man alone. In spite, however, of his pretences in favour of a Republic, he did not object to place his portrait on some of his *denarii* (cf. Lenormant, *La Mon. dans l'Antiq.*, vol. ii., p. 339.)

ZIMISCES (Joannes I.), Emperor of Constantinople, A.D. 969—976, was descended from an ancient Armenian family. His surname Zimisces (Τσιμισκῆs) was given to him on account of his diminutive size. He attained the throne through the intrigues of the Empress Theophano by the murder of her husband Nicephorus; but he banished the Empress soon after his accession. He was a great general, and on returning from a war with the Arabs, he observed that the finest lands belonged to the eunuchs. Basilius, one of the principal officers of the household, was informed of this, and Zimisces, probably poisoned, expired shortly after his return in January A.D. 976.

The following coins are attributed to him:— (Sabatier, *Mon. Byz.*, vol. ii., pp. 141—144; Madden, *Christian Emblems on the Coins of Constantine I.*, etc., in the *Num. Chron.*, N.S., 1878, vol. xviii., pp. 169—215; Smith's and Cheetham's *Dict. of Christian Antiq.*, art. *Money)* :—

1. *Obv.* +Θ ϹΟΤΟϹ. ЬΟΗΘ." ΙѠ.Ι ୪ΕSP. Bust of John I. Zimisces facing, holding in the left hand a long cross, and crowned by the Virgin with *nimbus* (half-length), above whom the letters M̄Θ̄; a hand descends from heaven over the Emperor. *Rev.* +Iħs. ХРs. ('Iησοῦs Χριστόs) ʀᴇх ʀᴇ Ϛ̄ΝΑΝΤΙ૫ℳ. Bust of Christ with *nimbus* on cross facing, holding in one hand his robe, and in the other the Gospels. *N.* (35 frcs.) Obverse legend Θεοτόκε Βοήθει 'Ιωάννῃ δεσπότῃ, *Mother of God, help the despot John.*

2. *Obv.* ΘϹ Ε. Ьθ. ᴜΟιs ЬASILS. Bust of the Virgin with *nimbus* facing, holding on her chest a medallion of Christ on the cross; on either side M̄·P̄—Θ̄ν̄. *Rev.* +ℳ ᴇʀΘ૫— DᴇDΟΞAsℳ—ΟᴇIS Sᴇ ᴇL ΠΙΖѠħΘ૫—CAΠΟᴜ ·K· in five lines. Æ. (250 frcs.)

The obverse legend is Θεοτόκε βοήθει τοῖs βασιλεῦσι, *i.e.*, *Mother of God, help the Kings*, and probably refers to John Zimisces in association with the two sons of Romanus II.—Basil II., and Constantine XI. The reverse legend is more difficult, and has been variously interpreted. M. de Saulcy, who published this coin *(Essai de Class. des Suites Mon. Byz.*, p. 244, pl. xxii., No. 1) explained it as " Μῆτερ Θεοῦ δεδοξασμένη ὁ εἰs σε ἐλπίζων οὐκ ἀποτυγχάνει, ou bien encore οὐκ ἄποτμος χαίρεσται; *Mère de Dieu, pleine de gloire, celui qui met en toi son espérance n'échoue jamais dans ses projets*, ou bien *n'est

jamais malheureux, mais est comblé de biens," the latter reading being adopted by M. Sabatier *(Mon. Byz.*, vol. ii., p. 141.) Both authors transcribe the last line of the legend as CAΠΟΤ́Х́Ι, and both engrave a x as the final letter. Mr. Grueber, of the Coin Department, British Museum, who had the cast made for me from the impression, seemed to think there was little doubt of the last letter being a x, and in this case the only reading that suggested itself was ἀποτεύξεται Χριστοῦ. Not, however, feeling quite satisfied about it, I sent the cast to Dr. Babington, who, rejecting De Saulcy's reading as untenable, thinks that the last letter is a ᴋ and *not* a x, and that it should be interpreted Κυρίου, this being somewhat more in accordance with Biblical usage than Χριστοῦ would be. If this view be correct, the last line of the inscription is CAΠΟᴜ ·K·, and the whole legend may be read Μῆτερ Θεοῦ δεδοξασμένη ὁ εἰs σε ἐλπίζων οὐκ ἀποτεύξεται Κυρίου, *O glorified Mother of God, he that trusteth in thee shall not fail of the Lord.*

3. *Obv.* +ΙѠAħħ—ᴇħ XѠ. AνᴜΟ— CΡΑΤ. ᴇνsᴇЬ—ЬASILᴇνs—ʀѠMAIѠ, in five lines. *Rev.* + Iħs૫s ХРIsᴜ૫s ħΙCA +. Cross bearing the portrait of John Zimisces, with the letters ΙѠ—Aħ. Æ. (25 frcs.) Obverse legend 'Ιωάννηs ἐν Χριστῷ αὐτοκράτωρ εὐσεβὴs βασιλεὺs 'Ρωμαίων John in Christ, ruler, pious king of the Romans.

4. *Obv.* Monogram, forming the letters ΙѠAN୪. *Rev.* Monogram forming the letters ΔᴇCΠ୪Τ. Æ. (30 frcs.)

Letters IC—ХC ('Ιησοῦs Χριστόs) *in the field.* Bust of Christ facing on a cross with *nimbus.* This type first appears on the brass coins of John I. Zimisces, but in some cases with the addition of the words ᴇMMANΟνħΛ, and on the reverse the legend +Iħs૫s ХRIsT૫s ЬASILᴇ૫ ЬASILᴇ. The attribution of these anonymous pieces to John Zimisces is founded on a passage of Scylitzes and Cedrenus, where it is said that " the Emperor ordered to be placed upon the coins the image of the Saviour, which had not been done before; and on the other side *Latin* letters forming the sentence IESVS CHRISTVS REX REGVM " (Eckhel, *Doct Num. Vet.*, vol. viii., p. 250; Sabatier, *Mon. Byz.*, vol. ii., p. 143), but this account can only refer to these *copper* coins, as the bust of Christ occurs on coins of all three metals of an earlier date (Madden, *op. cit.*) Brass coins are also attributed to him representing Christ with *nimbus cruciger*, seated, facing, with the legend + IS ХC ЬASILᴇ ЬASILI, or bust of Virgin with *nimbus* facing and hands raised, and the letters MR. Θ૫. (Μήτηυ Θεοῦ.)

To the reign of John Zimisces is attributed by Eckhel *(Doct. Num. Vet.*, vol. viii., p. 251) a curious brass coin or medal which Tanini (p. 280) had given to Constantine I., of which the following is a description :—

Obv.—Protome adversa nimbata servatoris prominentibus pone crucis radiis. Rev. ANAC-TACIC. *Templum rotundum, hinc et illinc miles excubitor humi jacens.* Æ. II.

It at one time caused considerable discussion, (see *H. Valesii Epistola de Anastasi et Martyrio Hierosolymitano*, in Eusebius, *Vita Const.*, ed. Heinichen, p. 501, Lips. 1830), and the temple on it has been supposed to represent the church built by Constantine I. the Great over the Sepulchre at Jerusalem from which Christ arose (τῆς σωτηρίου ᾽ΑΝΑΣΤΑΣΕΩΣ μαρτύριον, Euseb. *Vit. Const.*, iii., c. 28, 29 *seq.; Orat. de laud. Const.,* c. 9.), and hence the name of *Anastasis, i.e.,* Resurrection, and the orthodox Greek Church commemorate the dedication of the Church of the *Anastasis* by Constantine the Great (᾽Εγκαίνια τοῦ Ναοῦ τῆς ἁγίας τοῦ Χριστοῦ καὶ Θεοῦ ἡμῶν ᾽ΑΝΑΣΤΑΣΕΩΣ), on September 13th. (Arch. Cheetham, Smith's and Cheetham's *"Dict. of Christ. Antiq.," s. v. "Anastasis."*) But, as Eckhel has remarked, why go to *Jerusalem* for this church, when Sozomen relates *(Hist. Eccles.,* vii., c. 5*)* that Gregory of Nazianzen preached at *Constantinople* in a dwelling which had been altered into a house of prayer, and which, subsequently, became one of the most remarkable in the city by the magnificence of its decorations and the special revelations which were there vouchsafed by the grace of God. Sozomen adds that "the name of *Anastasia* was given to this church (᾽ΑΝΑΣΤΑΣΙΑΝ δὲ ταύτην τὴν ἐκκλησίαν ὀνομάζουσιν), because (as he believed) the Nicene doctrines which were buried beneath the errors of heterodoxy at Constantinople, were here brought to light (ἀνέστη) and maintained by Gregory," whilst others, he says, "ascribe the origin of this name to a miracle, and relate that one day, when the people were met for prayer, a pregnant woman fell from the highest gallery and was found dead, but that at the prayer of the whole congregation she was restored to life, and she and her infant were saved."

Whatever may be the interpretation of the legend, I must add that no specimen of this piece is in the British Museum; that no mention is made of it either by De Saulcy or Sabatier, and that it does not seem to me to be above suspicion.

From a representation of this piece in Mamachi (*Orig. et Ant. Christ.*, vol. i., p. 287, ed. Matranga, Rom. 1841), with a drawing of which I have been favoured by Dr. Babington, it would seem that this is a *medal*, and certainly of much later date than the time of Constantine. It was formerly in the Vettori Museum. Another medal given by the same author (vol. i., p. 240) has a similar bust of Christ on the obverse, but on the reverse the legend REDEMTIO FILIIS HOMINVM — IORDA (in *exe gue*), and the type the baptism of Christ by John. De Rossi *(Bullett. di Arch. Crist.*, 1869, p. 58) thinks that the ANACTACIC medal was made to be bought by the pilgrims as souvenirs of their visit to the Church of the Holy Sepulchre at Jerusalem, and evidently considers it mediæval, but says that both it and the IORDA medal are "non meno incerte ed enigmatiche" than the Pasqualini medal (Madden, *op. cit.*) The "Jordan medal" is now in the Vatican, and De Rossi confesses that

he cannot form in his mind " un giudizio sull' età e sull' arti di questa medaglie "—in fact, he rather suspects its genuineness.

During the same reign some brass coins or tokens, which have been published by Dr. Friedlaender (*Numismatische Zeitschrift*, Vienna, vol. ii., 1870), were issued, (1) having on the obverse the bust of Christ, with *nimbus* and the letters ιc—xc, and on the reverse the legend ΘΙͶΔΑΝ—ΕΙΖϚΙΤΟΥ—cΠ ϚΝΗΤΑc—ΟΤΡΕΦΙͶΝ, and (2) on the obverse ΔΑ— ΝϚΙΖϚΙ— ΘϚΙͶ, and on the reverse οϚΛϚ— ͶΝΠΤͶ—ΧΟΝ, which may be interpreted, Θεῷ δανείζει τοὺς πένητας ὁ τρέφων and δανείζει Θεῷ ὁ ἐλέων πτωχὸν *(He that hath pity upon the poor lendeth unto the Lord.)* Both are translations of the same Hebrew verse (Prov. xix. 17), and the latter is the exact translation of the LXX. The first piece is in the collection of Prince Philip of Saxe-Coburg, the second in the Museum at Basle. Dr. Friedlaender remarks, "It is curious that the coins of the smallest value are always those which remind the possessor to give them to the poor."

Zodiac. "The *Ecliptic* (or great circle which the sun describes in virtue of his proper motion) has been divided by astronomers from time immemorial into twelve equal parts called *Signs*. The names are *Aries, Taurus, Gemini, Cancer, Leo, Virgo, Libra, Scorpio, Sagittarius, Capricornus, Aquarius, and Pisces.* In each of these signs the ancients formed groups of stars, which they denominated *Zodiacal constellations* (ζώδια, *animals),* not confined to the ecliptic, but included within an imaginary belt, extending 9° on each side of it to which they gave the name of *Zodiac* (ζωδιακὸς κύκλος, *circle or zone of the animals.) (Encyc. Brit.*, 9th ed., art., *Astronomy*, vol. ii., p. 771.)" The Roman inferiority to the Greeks in the science of Astronomy is fully recognised by the Latin writers (Virg. *Æn.* vi., 848; Seneca, *Nat. Quæst.*, vii., 25), and while the astronomical science of the Greeks was in its infancy, that of the Romans had no existence (Sir G. C. Lewis, *An historical survey of the Astronomy of the Ancients*, 1862.)

The Zodiac is represented on several Greek Imperial coins (Alexander Severus—*Perinthus; Julia Mæsa—Amastris*; Valerian—*Ægæ*; Eckhel, *Doct. Num. Vet.*, vol. ii., pp. 40, 386, vol. iii., p. 37); and on Alexandrian coins of Antoninus Pius (Eckhel, *op. cit.*, vol. iv., p. 70; Head, *Hist. Num.*, p. 721.) It may also be found on the following Roman coins:—

HADRIAN.

Obv. IMP. CAESAR TRAIAN. HADRIANVS AVG. Bust of Hadrian to r., laureated. *Rev.* SAEC. AVR. *(Sæculum aureum* in the *exergue)* P. M. TR. P. COS. III. *(around.)* Male figure (? Trajan deified or Hadrian with the attributes of Eternity) half naked, standing to r., within a circular or oval band or zone, on the outer side of which are the signs of the Zodiac; his r. hand rests on the zone and his l. holds a globe, on which is a phœnix. *N.* (100 frcs.)

Cohen *(Méd. Imp.,* 1st ed., vol. ii., p. 157; 2nd ed., vol. ii., p. 216) describes the zone as " *une auréole ovale,*" but this piece is described in the " Pembroke Sale Catalogue," p. 135, as bearing the signs of the Zodiac, and traces of it can be seen on the specimen in the British Museum (Madden, *Num. Chron.,* N.S., 1862, vol. ii., p. 49.)

ANTONINUS PIUS.

1.   *Obv.* ANTONINVS AVG. PIVS. P. P. Head of Antoninus Pius to r. or to l., laureated.   *Rev.* ITALIA (in the *exergue*) TR. POT. COS. III. [or IIII.] S. C. Italy, laureated, seated to l., on a globe, around which is the Zodiac. Æ. I. (12 frcs.)

2.   *Obv.* ANTONINVS AVG. PIVS P. P. TR. P. COS. IIII. Bust of Antoninus Pius to r., laureated. *Rev.* No legend.   The Earth *(Tellus)* seated to r., leaning against a bull lying down, and holding a cornu-copiæ.   Four infants (the Seasons) are grouped around her, one is seated on her knees, another (Summer) holds a sickle; behind her a plough; above, a half circle of the Zodiac. Æ. Med. (500 frcs.)

COMMODUS.

Obv. M. COMMODVS ANTONINVS PIVS FELIX AVG. Bust of Commodus to r., laureated. *Rev.* COS. VI. P. P.   The Sun radiated, standing, holding a whip and about to get into a *quadriga,* which is raising itself to r. on the waves of the sea; in front, the star of the morning *(Phosphorus) ;* above, a portion of the Zodiac; to the r. the Earth *(Tellus)* lying to l., holding ears of corn and cornu-copiæ. Æ. Med. (500 frcs.)

A similar type, but *without the Zodiac,* occurs on the brass medallions of Antoninus Pius (Cohen, *Méd. Imp.,* 2nd ed., vol. ii., p. 381 ; Froehner, *Médaillons de l' Empire Romain,* p. 72.)

ELAGABALUS.

Obv.   IMP. CAES. M. ANTONINVS. AVG.   Head of Elagabalus, laureated. *Rev.* COL. PTOL. *(Colonia Ptolemais).* Diana *Venatrix* standing to r., in a distyle temple; the whole surrounded by the signs of the Zodiac. Æ. II.

Struck at Ptolemais Galilææ.   The same type occurs on the second brass of Valerian I.

CONSTANTINE I.

Obv. CONSTANTINVS P. F. AVG.   Head of Constantine I. to r., laureated. *Rev.* RECTOR TOTIVS ORBIS. The Emperor seated to l. on arms, holding in r. hand the Zodiac and in l. a *parazonium ;* behind, a Victory standing, holding a palm branch, and crowning him ; in the *exergue,* S. M. T. *(Signata Moneta Thessalonicæ).* N. (800 frcs.) This unique coin is in the British Museum, and has been historically illustrated by the present

writer *(Num. Chron.,* N.S., 1862, vol. ii., pp. 48—60.)   It was struck in A.D. 323, thirty-seven years after Diocletian had first divided the Empire, and when Constantine I. was entitled to inscribe on his coins that he was " sole master of the whole [Roman] world."

CONTORNIATES.

1.   *Obv.* DIVO TRAIANO AVGVSTO.   Bust of Trajan to r., laureated.   *Rev.* No legend.   Shield on which the head of the Sun and Moon, surrounded by the Zodiac ; a male figure seated ; behind, a statue of Minerva. Æ. (Eckhel, *Doct. Num. Vet.,* vol. viii., p. 308.)

2.   *Obv.* IMP. CAES. FL. CONSTANTINO MAX. P. F. AVG.   Head of Constantine to the right, laureated, and with *paludamentum,* surrounded by the twelve signs of the zodiac.   *Rev.* S. P. Q. R. *(Senatus Populusque Romanus)* QVOD IN- STINCTV DIVINITATIS MENTIS MAGNITVDINE CVM EXERCITV SVO TAM DE TYRANNO QVAM DE OMNI EIVS FACTIONE VNO TEMP *(ore)* IVSTIS REMP *(ublicam)* VLTVS EST ARMIS ARC *(um)* TRIVMPHIS INSIGNEM DICAVIT, within a laurel wreath. Æ. 14¼.

The reverse of this remarkable piece of the contorniate style is taken from the famous inscription on the arch of Constantine, dedicated in A.D. 315, placed thereon to commemorate the defeat of Maxentius *(tyrannus)* in A.D. 312, and which reads as follows (Orelli, *Inscr.,* No. 1075) :—

	IMP. CAES. FL. CONSTANTINO MAXIMO	
	P. F. AVGVSTO S. P. Q. R.	
VOTIS X	QVOD INSTINCTV DIVINITATIS MENTIS	SIC X
	MAGNITVDINE CVM EXERCITV SVO	
	TAM DE TYRANNO QVAM DE OMNI EIVS	
VOTIS XX	FACTIONE VNO TEMPORE IVSTIS	SIC XX
	REMPVBLICAM VLTVS EST ARMIS	
	ARCVM TRIVMPHIS INSIGNEM DICAVIT	
LIBERATORI VRBIS		FVNDATORI QVIETIS

It appears to have been first published by Banduri (vol. ii., pp. 256, 279), but was condemned by Eckhel though he had not seen it. *(" Qualiscunque dicatur, mihi opus antiquum non videtur."* *Doct. Num. Vet.,* vol. viii., p. 88.)   It was at one time in the collection of Sir Andrew Fountaine, and from thence passed into that of the Earl of Pembroke.   The compiler of the " Pembroke Sale Catalogue" (p. 297) in a lengthy note vindicated its authenticity, supposing it to have been " a ticket of admission " issued on the occasion of the dedication of the arch of Constantine, but whether it *sold* as a genuine piece I am unable to say.   Cavedoni *(Ricerche,* p. 21), did not accept it as genuine ; and Cohen *(Méd. Imp.,* vol. vi., p. 582) has not admitted it *tant il paraît suspect.*

As regards the inscription on the arch, it has been by some stated (Guattini, *Monumenti Antichi di Roma,* p. xciv., 1789 ; *Roma Descritta,* p. 42, 1805 ; Henzeu, *Suppl. ad. Orell.,* vol. iii., p. 113) that the words INSTINCTV DIVINITATIS appear to have been written *over* the effaced words NVTV IOVIS O. M., or perhaps DIIS FAVENTIBVS ; but Garrucci quite sets this question at rest by stating *(Num. Cost.,* 2nd ed., p.

245; *Rev. Num.*, 1886, p. 96), from personal inspection, that the marble was not lower in the portion where these words occur than in other parts, nor are the letters themselves confused, nor are there indeed any traces of letters to be seen that could have been previously engraved. The Padre Mozzoni assured Cavedoni *(Ricerche,* p. 21, *note)* that the words INSTINCTV DIVINITATIS were the original. Cf. De Rossi, *Bullet. d'Arch. Crist.*, 1863, Nos. 7 and 8.

I may add that Constantine himself, in his " Oration to the Assembly of the Saints," speaks of his services as owing their origin to the *inspiration of God* ('Εξ ἐπιπνοίας θεοῦ τὴν ἀρχὴν ἔχουσαν ἀρ' οὐ τῆς ἐμῆς ἀνδραγαθίας τὸν θεὸν αἴτιον εἶναι διαβεβαιοῦνται. *Ap. Euseb.,* c. 26), whilst both Constantine and Licinius gave thanks to the Deity *(Divinitas)* and to God *(Deus)* for the victories that they had gained over Maxentius. Cavedoni *(Ricerche,* p. 21, *note)* notices that Constantine is called *Divino monitus instinctu* by his anonymous panegyrist (viii., c. 11), and by Nazarius *(Paneg.,* ix., c. 17 ; cf. 12, 13) as governing *Divino instinctu.* For further particulars see Madden, *Christian Emblems on the Coins of Constantine I.*, etc., in the *Num. Chron.*, N.S., 1877, vol. xvii., pp. 11—56, 242—307; 1878, vol. xviii., pp. 1—48, 169—215; Smith's and Cheetham's *Dict. of Christian Antiq.* art. *Money.*

ZOE, surnamed Carbonopsina, fourth wife of Leo VI., the Philosopher, Emperor of Constantinople A.D. 886—911. She survived her husband, and her portrait may be seen on coins struck by her son Constantine X. Porphyrogenitus, A.D. 913—919, of which the following is a description : —

1. *Obv.* COꜦSᴜAꜧᴜ ,CЄ ZⱲH ЄꜦ XⱲ B.' R. Busts facing and with diadem of Constantine X. and his mother Zoe, holding between them a long cross. *Rev.* +IꜦS. XPS. ('Ιησοῦς Χριστὸς) REX REϚNANTIVM. Christ with *nimbus* on cross, seated facing, giving the benediction with the r. hand raised, and holding in the left the Gospels. *N.* (200 frcs.)

Obverse legend Κωνσταντῖνος καὶ Ζωὴ ἐν Χριστῷ βασιλεῖς 'Ρωμαίων, *Constantine and Zoe in Christ, kings of the Romans.*

2. +COꜦSᴜAꜧᴜ CЄ ZOH ꜧ. Same type as No. 1. *Rev.* +COꜦS—ᴜAꜧTINO—CЄ ZOH ꜧA —SILIS ROⱮЄOꜦ in five lines. Æ. (3 frcs.)

Obverse legend Κωνσταντῖνος καὶ Ζωὴ βασιλεῖς. Reverse legend Κωνσταντῖνος καὶ Ζωὴ βασιλεῖς 'Ρωμαίων.

There were several other Empresses of Constantinople named Zoe, notably Zoe, daughter of Stylianus, and second wife of Leo IV.; and Zoe, daughter of Constantine XI. Porphyrogenitus, and wife of (1) Romanus III. Argyrus, A.D. 1028—1034, (2) Michael IV., the Paphlagonian, A.D. 1034—1041, and (3) Constantine XII. Monomachus, A.D. 1042—1055 ; but of these there are *no coins.*

CORRIGENDA.

Page 830, 2nd col., line 20 from bottom, for *Triumviri* read *Duumviri.*
Page 864, 1st col., line 21 from top, for vol. v., p. 3, *read* p. 111.